W9-BRZ-251

THE NEW BIBLE COMMENTARY

The New BIBLE Commentary

Edited by the late

PROFESSOR F. DAVIDSON M.A., D.D.

Assisted by

THE REV. A. M. STIBBS M.A.
THE REV. E. F. KEVAN M.TH.

WM. B. EERDMANS PUBLISHING COMPANY
GRAND RAPIDS   MICHIGAN

First Edition	. . .	December 1953
Reprinted	. . .	March 1954
Second Edition	. . .	November 1954
Reprinted	. . .	April 1956
Reprinted	. . .	March 1958
Reprinted	. . .	March 1960

PHOTOLITHOPRINTED BY CUSHING - MALLOY, INC.
ANN ARBOR, MICHIGAN, UNITED STATES OF AMERICA

PREFACE

THIS Commentary has been produced to meet a widespread demand among serious students of the Bible for a new and up-to-date treatment of the text which would combine unqualified belief in its divine inspiration, essential historical trustworthiness and positive Christian usefulness with sound and careful scholarship. Attention has been chiefly directed to the understanding of the text as it exists in our most commonly used English versions. Consequently, and by deliberate choice, it has been felt unnecessary to devote any considerable amount of space to the source analysis, arbitrary criticism and speculative theories which so dominate many publications. Nor has it been the Editors' aim to produce a volume containing extensive devotional or homiletical notes. Holy Scripture has a way of applying its own message to the hearts and consciences of men when it is properly understood.

The Editors and Publishers are greatly indebted to the many contributors to this volume who have so freely given their services. They represent some of the best evangelical scholarship of the present day and, as will be seen from the List of Contributors, come from a wide range of church affiliation. Their willing co-operation in meeting the rather exacting requirements of a one-volume commentary of this kind is acknowledged with deep gratitude. It is natural that they should differ among themselves in some minor matters of interpretation. It ought perhaps to be stressed, therefore, that each contributor is responsible only for the article or articles appearing over his own name and is not to be regarded as necessarily endorsing everything which is written elsewhere.

One name which does not appear in this list must be mentioned. In the early stages of production the Rev. H. W. Oldham rendered invaluable service both as Reader and as Assistant Editor. It is greatly to be regretted that he did not live to see the completion of a work which he had so much at heart and to which he devoted so much of his time during the last two or three years of his life. The Editors would also like to acknowledge the splendid assistance given by the Rev. G. T. Manley, the Rev. L. E. H. Stephens-Hodge, the Rev. J. Stafford Wright and others who have advised and assisted them in the work of editing the Commentary and in preparing the various sections for press. In this connection the Editors would also like to acknowledge the invaluable help received in all aspects of the Commentary's production from Mr. Ronald Inchley, the Publications Secretary of the Inter-Varsity Fellowship.

With the publication of this Commentary the Inter-Varsity Fellowship completes a plan, conceived before the war, to provide Bible students with three basic aids to study. The first of these, *Search the Scriptures* (edited by G. T. Manley and H. W. Oldham) is a systematic study course which covers the whole of the Bible in three years. The second, *The New Bible Handbook* (edited by G. T. Manley, G. C. Robinson and A. M. Stibbs) has been designed to provide background information in the form of general articles, and contains, in addition, short introductions to every biblical book. We believe that the many who have welcomed and used these earlier volumes will find in this Commentary more of the kind of help for which they have been waiting.

The prayer of all concerned is that God may set His seal upon this Commentary, the spirit of which is supreme loyalty to God's revealed truth. May its reading be used of the Spirit of God to help many to gain from God's written Word fresh and increasing understanding of the ways of God and of His will for men.

FRANCIS DAVIDSON
ALAN M. STIBBS
ERNEST F. KEVAN

PREFACE TO SECOND EDITION

THIS second edition of *The New Bible Commentary* is sent forth by the editors and publishers with grateful praise to God for His blessing on the first edition. The editors are taking this opportunity to avail themselves of some of the constructive criticisms that have been sent to them, and a number of minor modifications of statement have been incorporated. A new article has been prepared on 'Revelation and Inspiration'. This takes the place of the one written by the late Dr. Lamont.

Some of the reviews of the first edition seem to have been made without a clear understanding of the purpose of the Commentary, and it may be useful, therefore, to repeat that the aim of this work is to give help in the understanding of the contents of the Bible rather than to indulge in speculative discussions of an introductory and critical kind.

The Commentary goes forth again in the confidence that God will confirm His own Word in the hearts of those who read.

ALAN M. STIBBS
ERNEST F. KEVAN

CONTENTS

            PAGE

PREFACE v

LIST OF CONTRIBUTORS xi

PART ONE: GENERAL ARTICLES

THE AUTHORITY OF SCRIPTURE 15

REVELATION AND INSPIRATION 24

THE HISTORICAL LITERATURE OF THE OLD TESTAMENT . . 31

THE POETRY OF THE OLD TESTAMENT . . . 39

THE WISDOM LITERATURE OF THE OLD TESTAMENT . . 42

THE PROPHETICAL LITERATURE OF THE OLD TESTAMENT . 45

THE APOCRYPHAL AND APOCALYPTIC LITERATURE . . . 52

THE FOURFOLD GOSPEL 58

THE PRIMITIVE CHURCH 64

THE PAULINE EPISTLES 68

PART TWO: THE OLD TESTAMENT

GENESIS 75

EXODUS 106

LEVITICUS 134

NUMBERS 162

DEUTERONOMY 195

JOSHUA 223

JUDGES 236

RUTH 258

I AND II SAMUEL 262

    Appendix I: The Ark of the Covenant . . . 292

    Appendix II: The Critical View of Sources and Documents . . 293

I AND II KINGS 300

    Appendix I: The Religion of Israel Under the Monarchy . . 333

    Appendix II: The Implications of Political Alliances . . 335

    Appendix III: The Great Empires During the Period of the Monarchy . . 336

I AND II CHRONICLES 339

EZRA AND NEHEMIAH 365

CONTENTS

	PAGE
ESTHER	380
JOB	387
PSALMS	412
PROVERBS	515
ECCLESIASTES	538
THE SONG OF SOLOMON	547
ISAIAH	556
JEREMIAH	608
LAMENTATIONS	640
EZEKIEL	645
DANIEL	668
HOSEA	682
JOEL	690
AMOS	698
OBADIAH	710
JONAH	714
MICAH	720
NAHUM	727
HABAKKUK	732
ZEPHANIAH	736
HAGGAI	743
ZECHARIAH	748
MALACHI	764

PART THREE: THE NEW TESTAMENT

MATTHEW	771
MARK	806
LUKE	840
JOHN	865
ACTS	897
ROMANS	939
I AND II CORINTHIANS	967
GALATIANS	1001

CONTENTS

	PAGE
EPHESIANS	1015
PHILIPPIANS	1031
COLOSSIANS	1043
I AND II THESSALONIANS	1052
I AND II TIMOTHY AND TITUS	1063
PHILEMON	1084
HEBREWS	1088
Appendix I: The New Covenant	1114
Appendix II: The Priesthood of Christ	1114
Appendix III: The Warning Passages	1116
JAMES	1118
I AND II PETER	1129
I, II AND III JOHN	1151
JUDE	1161
REVELATION	1168

SKETCH MAPS AND TABLES

CHRONOLOGICAL TABLE: ABRAHAM TO SOLOMON	38
THE NEAR EAST IN THE AGE OF THE PATRIARCHS	88
THE EXODUS	117
PALESTINE DIVIDED AMONG THE TWELVE TRIBES	233
THE EMPIRE OF DAVID AND SOLOMON	285
CHRONOLOGICAL TABLE: DIVISION OF THE KINGDOM TO THE FALL OF JERUSALEM	300
THE ASSYRIAN EMPIRE IN 700 B.C.	337
THE BABYLONIAN AND PERSIAN EMPIRES	363
EZEKIEL'S TEMPLE	664, 665
PALESTINE IN THE TIME OF CHRIST	775
PAUL'S FIRST MISSIONARY JOURNEY	916
PAUL'S SECOND MISSIONARY JOURNEY	921
PAUL'S THIRD MISSIONARY JOURNEY	926
PAUL'S JOURNEY TO ROME	935

EXPLANATIONS

THE articles on the biblical books each contain an Introduction and Outline of Contents as well as the Commentary on the text. The notes are based on the sections and paragraphs into which the text naturally falls. This necessitates departing at times from the strict chapter divisions. The Outline of Contents consists of the main headings used in dividing the text into these sections, together with the secondary headings used wherever this has been felt to be necessary. These outlines will not only help the student to study each book as a whole, but will act as a useful index to the Commentary itself.

Words and phrases which are the subject of comment are set in italic type, followed by the verse number within brackets. The Authorized Version has been generally used as the basis for the Commentary, but where there are important differences in the Revised and other English versions these have been noted. Extracts from these other versions are printed in ordinary type within quotation marks.

The following abbreviations have been used:

Books of the Old Testament: Gn., Ex., Lv., Nu., Dt., Jos., Jdg., Ru., 1, 2 Sa., 1, 2 Ki., 1, 2 Ch., Ezr., Ne., Est., Jb., Ps. (Pss.), Pr., Ec., Ct., Is., Je., La., Ezk., Dn., Ho., Joel, Am., Ob., Jon., Mi., Na., Hab., Zp., Hg., Zc., Mal.

Books of the New Testament: Mt., Mk., Lk., Jn., Acts, Rom., 1, 2 Cor., Gal., Eph., Phil., Col., 1, 2 Thes., 1, 2 Tim., Tit., Phm., Heb., Jas., 1, 2 Pet., 1, 2, 3 Jn., Jude, Rev.

Aram.	Aramaic	J.B.L.	Journal of Biblical Literature
AV	Authorized Version (1611)		
c.	about (with dates)	LXX	Septuagint Version
cf.	compare	mg.	Margin
Cam. Bible	The Cambridge Bible	Moff.	Moffatt's translation of the Bible
Cent. Bible	The Century Bible		
Clar. Bible	The Clarendon Bible	Moff. Comm.	The Moffatt Commentary on the Bible
E.B.	Encyclopaedia Britannica		
Exp. Bible	The Expositor's Bible	MS(s)	Manuscript(s)
f., ff.	following verse(s) or page(s)	n.	note
Gk.	Greek	RSV	Revised Standard Version (1952)
H.A.C.	Hastings' Dictionary of the Apostolic Church		
		RV	Revised Version (1885)
H.D.B.	Hastings' Dictionary of the Bible	Syr.	Syriac Version
		Tàrg.	Targum
Heb.	Hebrew	viz.	namely
Her.	Herodotus	Vulg.	Vulgate (Latin) Version
I.C.C.	International Critical Commentary	Wey.	Weymouth's translation of the New Testament.
I.S.B.E.	International Standard Bible Encyclopaedia		

LIST OF CONTRIBUTORS

*An * placed against the title of an article indicates joint authorship.*

G. C. AALDERS, D.THEOL, Emeritus Professor of Old Testament in the Free University of Amsterdam. *The Historical Literature of the Old Testament.*

J. T. H. ADAMSON, M.A., B.D., Minister of Scotstoun East Church (Church of Scotland), Glasgow. *Malachi.*

O. T. ALLIS, D.D., PH.D., Formerly Professor of Old Testament, Westminster Theological Seminary, Philadelphia. *Leviticus.*

BASIL F. C. ATKINSON, M.A., PH.D., Under Librarian in the University Library, Cambridge. *The Gospel of Matthew.*

G. R. BEASLEY-MURRAY, M.A., M.TH., PH.D., Tutor in New Testament Language and Literature, Spurgeon's Theological College, London. *The Apocryphal and Apocalyptic Literature, Ezekiel, Revelation.*

HUGH J. BLAIR, B.A., Minister of Ballymoney Church (Reformed Presbyterian Church of Ireland), Co. Antrim. *Joshua.*

G. W. BROMILEY, M.A., PH.D., D.LITT., Rector of St. Thomas' English Episcopal Church, Edinburgh. *The Authority of Scripture.*

F. F. BRUCE, M.A., Head of the Department of Biblical History and Literature in the University of Sheffield. *The Poetry of the Old Testament, The Wisdom Literature of the Old Testament*, The Fourfold Gospel, Judges, The Acts of the Apostles, I and II Thessalonians.*

JOHN H. S. BURLEIGH, B.LITT., D.D., Professor of Ecclesiastical History in the University of Edinburgh. *The Primitive Church.*

O. BUSSEY, M.A., B.D., PH.D., Minister of Kent Road-St. Vincent Church (Church of Scotland), Glasgow. *Amos.*

W. J. CAMERON, M.A., B.D., Professor of New Testament Language and Literature in the Free Church College, Edinburgh. *The Prophetical Literature of the Old Testament, The Song of Solomon.*

J. T. CARSON, B.A., Minister of Trinity Church (Presbyterian Church of Ireland), Bangor, Co. Down. *Joel, Zephaniah.*

F. CAWLEY, B.A., B.D., PH.D., Principal of Spurgeon's Theological College, London. *Jeremiah.*

G. N. M. COLLINS, B.A., B.D., Minister of St. Columba's Church (Free Church of Scotland), Edinburgh. *Zechariah.*

J. CLEMENT CONNELL, M.A., Tutor in Biblical Theology and Church History, The London Bible College. *Exodus.*

The late FRANCIS DAVIDSON, M.A., D.D., formerly Professor of Old Testament and New Testament Language and Literature, United Original Secession Church of Scotland and Principal of the Bible Training Institute, Glasgow. *The Wisdom Literature of the Old Testament*, Romans*, Philippians.*

The late R. J. DRUMMOND, D.D., formerly Minister of Lothian Road Church (Church of Scotland), Edinburgh. *I, II and III John*.*

H. L. ELLISON, B.D., B.A., Tutor for Old Testament Studies, The London Bible College. *I and II Kings, I and II Chronicles.*

W. FITCH, M.A., B.D., PH.D., Minister of Springburn Hill Church (Church of Scotland), Glasgow. *Isaiah.*

A. FRASER, M.A., B.D., Minister of Tayvallich Church (Church of Scotland), Lochgilphead. *Micah*, Nahum.*

G. A. HADJIANTONIOU, LL.B., M.A., PH.D., Minister of the Second Greek Evangelical Church, Athens. *Hosea*.*

E. S. P. HEAVENOR, M.A., B.D., Minister of the Webster Memorial Church, Presbyterian Church of Jamaica. *Job.*

G. S. HENDRY, M.A., D.D., Charles Hodge Professor of Systematic Theology in Princeton Theological Seminary. *Ecclesiastes.*

J. ITHEL JONES, M.A., B.D., Minister of Haven Green Baptist Church, Ealing, London. *Colossians.*

W. A. REES JONES, M.A., B.Sc., Canon of Lincoln, Vicar of North Somercotes, Louth. *Proverbs*.*

E. F. KEVAN, M.TH., Principal of the London Bible College. *Genesis, Note on the Resurrection Appearances of our Lord.*

LESLIE S. M'CAW, M.A., Principal of All Nations Bible College, Taplow, Maidenhead. *Psalms.*

A. MACDONALD, M.A., Minister of Duke Street Church (Free Church of Scotland), Glasgow. *Ruth, Esther.*

J. MCILMOYLE, M.A., Minister of Dublin Road Church (Reformed Presbyterian Church of Ireland), Belfast. *Haggai.*

A. J. MACLEOD, M.A., B.D., Church of Scotland Chaplain to the Iraq Petroleum Co., Kirkuk. *The Gospel of John.*

A. MCNAB, M.A., Superintendent of the Shankill Road Mission, Belfast. *James, I and II Peter.*

J. MCNICOL, B.A., B.D., D.D., Principal Emeritus of the Toronto Bible College. *The Gospel of Luke.*

A. A. MACRAE, PH.D., President of the Faculty, Faith Theological Seminary, Philadelphia. *Numbers.*

G. T. MANLEY, M.A., Sometime Fellow of Christ's College, Cambridge. *Deuteronomy.*

W. G. M. MARTIN, B.A., Minister of the First Presbyterian Church (Presbyterian Church of Ireland), Carrickfergus. *Ephesians.*

LEON MORRIS, B.Sc., M.TH., PH.D., Vice-Principal of Ridley College, Melbourne. *I, II and III John*.*

J. I. PACKER, M.A., Lecturer at Tyndale Hall, Bristol. *Revelation and Inspiration.*

W. C. G. PROCTOR, B.A., B.D., Rector of Harold's Cross, Dublin; Assistant Lecturer in the Divinity School, Trinity College, Dublin. *I and II Corinthians.*

A. M. RENWICK, M.A., D.D., D.LITT., Professor of Church History in the Free Church College, Edinburgh. *I and II Samuel.*

R. ROBERTSON, M.A., Minister of Collace Church (Church of Scotland), Perthshire. *Jude.*

T. E. ROBERTSON, M.A., B.D., Principal, O.S. Mission High School, Seoni, M.P., India. *Philemon.*

D. W. B. ROBINSON, M.A., Lecturer, Moore Theological College, Sydney. *Obadiah, Jonah.*

ALEXANDER ROSS, M.A., D.D., Minister of Burghead Church (Free Church of Scotland); Formerly Professor of New Testament Exegesis in the Free Church College, Edinburgh. *The Pauline Epistles, Galatians.*

L. E. H. STEPHENS-HODGE, M.A., Vicar of Rosedale, Pickering, Yorkshire. *Lamentations, Hosea*, Micah*, Habakkuk.*

A. M. STIBBS, M.A., Vice-Principal of Oak Hill Theological College, London. *I and II Timothy, Titus, Hebrews.*

C. E. GRAHAM SWIFT, M.A., Minister of Durham Road Baptist Church, Gateshead-on-Tyne. *The Gospel of Mark.*

G. T. THOMSON, M.A., D.D., Emeritus Professor of Christian Dogmatics in the University of Edinburgh. *Romans*.*

J. STAFFORD WRIGHT, M.A., Principal of Tyndale Hall, Bristol. *Ezra and Nehemiah.*

ANDREW F. WALLS, M.A., Secretary of Tyndale House, Cambridge. *Proverbs*.*

E. J. YOUNG, PH.D., Professor of Old Testament in Westminster Theological Seminary, Philadelphia. *Daniel.*

PART ONE

GENERAL ARTICLES

THE AUTHORITY OF SCRIPTURE

I. THE BIBLICAL WITNESS

OUR thinking concerning the authority and inspiration of Holy Scripture must start always from the fact that the Bible itself assumes everywhere that it is a message directly given by God Himself. In this first section it must be our main task to substantiate that fact and to discuss its implications. But one preliminary question must first be answered. When we assert the unique authority of the Bible, is it legitimate to appeal to the Bible's own testimony in support of that assertion? Is it not a most outrageous form of question-begging to make the Bible itself the first and final arbiter in its own case? Are we not guilty of presupposing the very thing which we are asked to substantiate?

The answer to this question is, of course, that we do not turn to the Bible for proof, but for information. Rational arguments may be advanced in favour of the unique authority of Scripture, but in the last analysis we accept that authority by faith. And we accept it only in so far as the Bible itself requires it. In other words, it is only as the inspiration and authenticity of the record are a part (and a necessary part) of the revelation that we make the Bible a supreme rule of faith and life. If the Bible did not make that claim, we should have no call to believe it. And we could have no general confidence in the teaching of Scripture. But if the Bible stands before us as an authoritative Word of God, a Word which itself claims authority, then it is as such that we must reckon with it, receiving that Word and the authority of that Word, or resisting it.

But does the Bible make any such assertion of authority? And if it does, what does that assertion imply? With regard to the first question, the answer is so vast that our main difficulty is that of compression. In the Old Testament as in the New the claim to a more than human authority is everywhere implicit, and in many places it finds direct and open expression. It is claimed, for example, that Moses received from God both the moral law and also more detailed commandments even extending to arrangements for the tabernacle. The prophets maintained that they were not speaking their own words, but the message which God Himself had given to them. The Lord Jesus Christ spoke with authority because He was conscious of speaking not merely as the historical teacher but as the eternal Son. The apostles had no doubt as to the authoritativeness of their pronouncements, whether they were quoting our Lord or developing the Christian message under the guidance of the outpoured Spirit.

It may be objected that in the majority of these cases the claim to authority is made only on behalf of the message delivered and not on behalf of the written record in which that message has been handed down to us. Thus it may well be the case that the prophets or Jesus Christ spoke with divine authority, but sometimes we have their words only at second-hand. The fact that inspiration is claimed for them does not mean that inspiration is claimed for those who compiled the record of their activity and teaching. And if that is the case there is no guarantee that what is written in the Bible is a verbatim or accurate account of the message actually delivered.

Against this objection we may set the fact that in the New Testament especially, and with reference to the Old, a definite authority is claimed for the written word of the Bible. This point emerges clearly in many parts of the teaching of our Lord Himself. Thus He answers the tempter with the threefold 'It is written'. On the Mount of Transfiguration He tells His disciples that it is written of the Son of Man that He should suffer many things and be set at naught. To the Jews who searched the Scriptures He gave counsel that 'these are they which testify of me'. After the resurrection He interpreted to the disciples in all the Scriptures the things concerning Himself, showing them that all things must needs be fulfilled, which 'were written in the law of Moses, and the prophets, and the psalms, concerning me'. These and similar statements make it quite plain that Jesus Himself accepted the inspiration and authority of the written Word, especially in so far as it gave prophetic witness to His own death and resurrection. It is also clear from verses like Jn. xiv. 26 and Jn. xvi. 13 that He expected and promised a similar inspiration in the case of the apostolic testimony yet to be made.

When we come to the apostles we find that their testimony to the divine authority of the Bible is equally clear. In all the Gospels great emphasis is laid upon the inspired foretelling of the work and person of Christ. The apostle Paul quotes extensively from the Old Testament, and his preaching to his own people is very largely an attempt to prove the Messiahship of Jesus from Old Testament history and prophecy. The statement in 2 Tim. iii. 16 sums up the whole attitude of Paul. Whatever translation we adopt it is plain from verse 15 that the apostle has the Old Testament in mind and that he thinks of it as peculiarly inspired by God. The other apostolic writers quote just as frequently from the Old Testament, and in 2 Peter open testimony is borne to the inspiration of the Bible in a way very similar to that in 2 Timothy. In 2 Pet. i. 21 the word of prophecy is traced back to its final author in God the Holy Spirit: 'For no prophecy ever came by the will of man; but men spake from God, being moved by the Holy Ghost.' Again, in

2 Pet. iii. 16 there seems to be a further allusion to the written Bible as an authoritative word which must be approached with reverence and humility. This latter verse is particularly interesting in that it couples together the Epistles of Paul and the other Scriptures: a fairly plain hint that the apostolic authors were conscious of adding to and completing the authoritative canon of the Old Testament.

Surveying the evidence, we may allow that the passages which treat directly of the inspiration of Scripture are few in number, and that there is no particular assertion of the status or authority of each individual book. On the other hand, we may note that almost all the books of the Old Testament are directly quoted in the New, and when we take into account the attitude of the New Testament in such quotations there can be little doubt that the 'Thus saith the Lord' of the prophets was taken to apply to the records of prophetic activity as well as to oral words delivered on this or that specific occasion. The written word was itself treated as the inspired and authoritative form in which the content of divine revelation had been expressed and handed down.

When we ask concerning the implications of this witness, several important points emerge. First, it may be noted that no specific theory of inspiration is introduced. From the two texts, Jn. xiv. 26 and 2 Pet. i. 21, it seems that there is a twofold activity: that of the human author on the one hand, and that of the inspiring and controlling Spirit on the other. Certainly there is no doubt as to the final initiative and supremacy of the Spirit. But there is also no suggestion of the obliteration of the personality and individuality of the human author. Again, we may notice that inspiration is seen particularly in the insight of the Old Testament writers into the future activity of God. The prophet was a forth-teller, no doubt; but the ultimate test of his prophecy was the correctness of his insight into the divinely directed future, and that necessarily meant foretelling. Even in the Old Testament itself the prophet who foretold incorrectly was discredited, and in the New Testament the main value of the Old is the prophetic witness to Jesus Christ. If it is true that that witness supports the messianic claim of Jesus, it is also true that the messianic work of Jesus vindicates the prophetic claim of the Old Testament. A very large proportion of the Old Testament citations are concerned with various forms of that prophetic witness.

A third point is that the historical setting of the Old Testament is everywhere accepted as authentic. Our Lord, for instance, does not question the connection of Moses with the Law, or the Davidic authorship of Ps. cx. The apostles accept all the main events of Old Testament history from Adam and the fall (1 Tim. ii. 13, 14) to the crossing of the Red Sea (1 Cor. x. 1), the Balaam incidents (2 Pet. ii. 16), the fall of Jericho (Heb. xi. 30), the deliverances under the Judges (Heb. xi. 32) and the miracles of Elijah (Ja. v. 17).

In face of this clear testimony the suggestion has been made that our Lord and the apostles simply shared the common assumptions of their age and made use of the historical happenings only in illustration of their theology. It certainly cannot be denied, however, that, in the New Testament, belief in the authority of the Old does involve an acceptance of its historical as well as its religious or doctrinal truth. It is worth remembering, too, that if that acceptance means acceptance of the supernatural control and intervention of almighty God, nowhere do we have a clearer or more decisive instance of such intervention and control than in the central facts of the Christian gospel, the life and death and resurrection of Jesus Christ.

Attention is sometimes drawn to the apparent freedom, even arbitrariness, of the New Testament in its citation of the Old. On the one hand, a common use is made of the Septuagint Greek, and at times this involves quite extensive divergences from the Massoretic Hebrew. On the other, Old Testament verses are often referred prophetically to Christ when their original application seems to be entirely different. The deduction is that this freedom suggests a far looser conception of inspiration than that traditionally associated with the Bible and its authors.

But the following points have to be remembered. With regard to the Septuagint it is quite possible that in many cases the Greek translation gives a more faithful and coherent account of the original than the Massoretic text. Again, the main aim in a translation is to convey the true sense rather than to provide word-for-word equivalents. In view of the inevitable differences in linguistic structure and provenance, this means that a freer rendering is often more truly accurate than a literal. In the Septuagint the New Testament authors had a carefully-weighed and long-standing translation with which many of their readers were already familiar. A further point is that, in some cases, the Holy Spirit may have used the Septuagint to bring out new aspects of divine truth, or to make a more forceful application. Where necessary, of course, importance could be attached even to the minuter details of the original text (cf. Gal. iii. 16).

The problem of the prophetic testimonies is no less serious, for here the whole meaning and application seems to have changed. Indeed, it is suggested that the verses have either consciously or unconsciously been misapplied in the search for detailed proofs from prophecy of the Messiahship of Christ. At a first glance, the suggestion is reasonable enough, for in their original context many of the verses do not seem to have even the slightest messianic reference. But although it is a collection of writings the Bible is a single book, and that means that there is a larger as well as an immediate context. Ultimately, all the history of Israel is concentrated and fulfilled in that of the only true Israelite, and throughout that history the same patterns of divine activity may be observed. Behind the seemingly artificial reference to Rachel in Matthew ii, for example, there stands a constantly recurring movement of aggression, death and exile. Taken merely as proof texts, the citations might not be convincing, but in the wider context of the divine purpose and activity they introduce us to types and patterns of which the history of Jesus Christ is the true fulfilment.

We must be careful, of course, not to read into the self-attestation of Scripture more than is actually there. With regard to authorships and dates, for example, tradition has often been vocal where the Bible itself is silent. The extent of the biblical silence is sometimes rather surprising. We know little about the compilation of the historical books of the Old Testament. We are not told the exact date and circumstances of some prophetic writings (e.g. Malachi). We do not know who wrote many of the Psalms or the book of Job. We are not told that Hebrews was written by Paul. The text itself does not tell us that Luke wrote the third Gospel and Acts, or that the Apostle John wrote the fourth Gospel, although the case for Luke and John rests on sound and legitimate inference. It is as well sometimes to remember that there is this line between a direct biblical testimony and even the reliable evidence of tradition. Otherwise we may easily identify the authority of Scripture with that of historical statements which are outside the scope of Scripture itself.

Yet when we have said that we must say too that the Bible does lay serious claim to a divine origin, status and authority. It states clearly that its message is of God. It traces back its authorship through the human writings to the Holy Spirit. It accepts the supernatural both in prophetic utterances and historical events. It makes no artificial distinction between the inward content of the Word of God and its outward form. By its self-authentication as God's Word written the Bible challenges us directly either to faith or to unbelief. In our approach to the Bible other considerations may obtrude, but that basic challenge certainly cannot be ignored.

II. THE REFORMED DOCTRINE

It was upon the foundation of the self-witness of the Bible that the Reformers built up their doctrine of Holy Scripture. They adopted this procedure because first and foremost their theology was a theology of faith: a revealed theology. Their starting-point was, therefore, the response of faith to the challenge of the biblical message. They accepted that message on its own terms, and in loyalty to it they tried to understand the Bible as the Bible understood itself. As we have already seen, the Reformed method is regarded as both illegitimate and futile by those who think that theology should be constructed upon purely rational foundations. But the Reformers themselves were theologians of faith, making use of reason only in response and

obedience to the divine revelation. And that meant that they were theologians who were pledged in faith to receive the testimony of the Word of God written even in matters concerning its own nature and being.

The Reformers believed, then, that the Bible was given by God, and that it was inspired both in content and also in form. They did not take any radical step when they propounded this view. The mediaeval Church had held a similar view. But they did take the step; and everywhere in their writings we find evidence of a whole-hearted acceptance of the inspiration and authority of the Bible. This is so even in the case of Luther, who was often very free in his handling of the text and his strictures upon individual sections. Efforts have been made to show either that Luther was an early critic or at any rate that he treated the message as inspired but not the wording. It is argued that Luther's was the true Reformed insight which was lost by his more legalistic successors. But against that view it may be pointed out that Luther frequently extolled the letter of Scripture and that for the most part his freedom of censure was in respect of books about whose canonicity he had serious doubts. Generally speaking, Luther shared the strict view of the Bible common to all the Reformers.

The Bible was inspired and authoritative, but it was also sole-sufficient in matters of faith and conduct. It would be an exaggeration to say that the Reformers set up the Bible as the only authority in the Church. But it is no exaggeration to say that they regarded the Bible as the supreme authority from which all other authorities derived and to which they were subject. Because it was itself from God the Bible contained everything necessary both to salvation and to the Christian life. Nothing was to be believed or taught in the Church unless it had the sanction either of the plain text of Scripture or of clear inferences from it. The Calvinists extended the direct rule of Scripture even to the details of Church order and worship, and the Lutherans and Anglicans all owed a negative authority to the Bible in these spheres—i.e. they would not permit anything which was excluded by Scripture or repugnant to it.

The emphasis upon the supremacy and sole-sufficiency of the Bible was clearly designed to destroy the mediaeval assertion of an authority of tradition and of the Church side by side and on an equality with that of Holy Scripture. A further step in the same direction was the insistence that the Bible must be understood only in its plain and literal sense and not according to the fourfold scheme of mediaeval exegesis. This did not mean that a symbolical or metaphorical sense could not be accorded to what was plainly symbol or metaphor. What it did mean was that a more than literal sense must not be introduced into the ordinary statements of Scripture except in cases where the Bible itself expressly sanctions it—for example, in the understanding of the Red Sea crossing as a type of baptism, or the reference of the Old Testament priesthood to Christ. Parallel types might be drawn for the purpose of spiritual edification, but they were not to be regarded as authoritative for Christian belief or conduct. Should difficulties of interpretation arise they were to be resolved by the comparison of Scripture with Scripture, the more luminous and straightforward passages being used to illuminate the more difficult and obscure. These exegetical rules were important for two reasons: they cleared away much of the confusion inevitably caused by the mediaeval scheme, thus making possible the erection of a genuine biblical theology; and they destroyed the authority of the official interpreters of Scripture who alone could manipulate successfully the complicated fourfold technique.

The Reformers accepted all parts of canonical Scripture as inspired and authoritative, although they did not accord an equal degree of inspiration and authority to every part. The insistence that all canonical Scripture is inspired was directed against some of the Anabaptist groups who could not agree to the full inspiration of the Old Testament. The Reformers saw clearly that the Old Testament is a most important part of the divine witness to Jesus Christ and to saving truth. They argued that the moral teaching of the Old Testament is eternally valid as an expression of God's will for His people. The theological principles underlying God's dealings with Israel are also the same as those underlying His dealings with Christians and the Christian Church, thus providing further illustration and confirmation of divine truth. The Old Testament and the New belong together, the one as preparation, the other as fulfilment.

All parts of the Bible are inspired and authoritative, the Reformers taught, but not all parts are of equal importance. The Mosaic legislation in Leviticus had not the same spiritual or theological value as the Gospel of John, or even the Decalogue. In this respect the Bible is in some sense analogous to the Church as the body of Christ. All the members constitute the body and are necessary to it. But although all the members are necessary they are not all of equal importance. Some members are more used than others, and some may be regarded as vital: without them the body would perish altogether. So it is with the Bible. We cannot mutilate the Bible without loss, but some parts are more dispensable than others. If the evangelical message is given it is possible to be a Christian with only a fragment of Scripture; but to be a full-grown Christian it is necessary to have the whole counsel of God.

A certain difficulty arises when the attempt is made to discriminate between the more and less relevant and important passages, for purely subjective considerations threaten to control and perhaps distort our judgment in this matter. Zwingli and Luther both gave helpful rules which are not so very different: the importance and relevance of a passage depend upon the measure in which it serves to promote the glory of God and to reveal and exalt the Lord Jesus Christ. It is because some parts of the Bible do this more directly and plainly than others that they are to be regarded as the more important passages of Scripture. But in the last resort all Scripture is in some way directed towards this twofold end.

The Reformers emphasized the importance of the letter of the Bible, but not at the expense of the sovereignty of the Holy Spirit in His use and application of the Bible message. In the thought of the Reformers the Holy Spirit was not merely the Author of Scripture, but He also determined the application of Scripture to its twofold end, and gave to the believer an inward persuasion of the authority of its message as revealed truth. Of the first of these further points there is not much to add except this: while it is true that the meaning of the Bible is plain, for an inward apprehension something more is needed than the ordinary rational intelligence. For genuine understanding there is needed that illumination of the Holy Spirit which is the individual counterpart of God's outward revelation.

Some modern theologians have seized upon this illumination as true inspiration according to the Reformed conception: i.e. the Bible is inspired only in so far as the Holy Spirit uses this or that passage to accomplish an inward enlightenment in the individual Christian. In the Reformers themselves, however, there seem to be few traces of any equation of the individual enlightenment with inspiration as such. The Bible is an inspired record of the divine self-revelation whether this or that individual receives its witness or not. The revelation and the recording of it in written form are both objective acts. Illumination by the Holy Spirit is the subjective counterpart of these acts within the individual and for the salvation of the individual. And as it is God the Holy Spirit who gave the objective record, so it is God the Holy Spirit who effects the subjective illumination. The message and the application of the message are both of God.

The fact that there is that inward enlightenment is the final guarantee of the authenticity of the record, whether in its general teaching or in its self-attestation. Although the Reformers accepted the Bible in faith, they were not unaware of the rational problems involved. The problems were perhaps not so acute then as they are today, but they were sufficiently acute to call for some general answer. The Reformers could advance many reasons in favour of their acceptance of the Bible. They could point, as Calvin did, to those characteristics and qualities which mark it off as an inspired record: its dignity, its literary quality, its antiquity, its combination of depth and simplicity, its preservation and historical power, its accuracy in the foretelling of the future. But in the last analysis the real reason for belief is that inward knowledge of the truth of Scripture which is necessarily present when the Holy Spirit applies that truth to the soul. To the self-attestation of the Bible there is added the inward testimony of the Holy Spirit. But that argument is a rational argument only for the believer. In other words, the truth of the Bible's claim cannot be made a matter simply of intellectual and academic debate. It must be known in experience. It must be known from within. It must be known by faith. And that means that, like the Bible itself, it is given by the Holy Spirit.

With that emphasis upon the Lordship of the Holy Spirit the Reformers safeguarded themselves against dead literalism and scholastic rationalism in their understanding of Holy Scripture. They yielded to none in their loyalty to the given form of the Bible. They had a high view both of the Bible itself and also of its inspiration. They believed that the Bible itself is inspired truth. They believed that it is the Word written, a Word given and applied by the Holy Spirit. They taught that that Word must always be respected and received and obeyed. Yet they remembered always that God is the Lord of Scripture, and that it is His voice which must be heard if the Bible is to do its work. The Bible is not an academic textbook of divine truth, the Euclid of the Christian faith. The text is indeed given by God, but it is always in the hands of God and always applied by God. The Bible must be respected and received and obeyed not because it is a fixed and static letter, but because under the Holy Spirit that letter is the living Word of the living God both to the individual and to the Church.

III. MODERN TRENDS

a. The Roman Catholic View

There are three broad schools of thinking which today challenge what we believe to be the orthodox, scriptural, apostolic and Reformed position in relation to the authority and inspiration of Holy Scripture. First, and not least formidable, is the Roman Catholic teaching. In one sense this is not a modern view, since the Roman position was fixed at the Council of Trent (1545–63), and in essentials has not altered or developed from that time. But in another sense it is very modern, partly because it is held by living Roman theologians, partly because it is likely to prove more lasting than the liberal view which now claims so much attention, and which superficially appears to be the more dangerous.

In the first question, that of the Scripture as a rule of faith, the Roman Catholic seems to adopt a position very much like the orthodox one. For him, the Word of God is an absolute rule. It displaces all private interpretations. It is inspired immediately by God. It is completely trustworthy, not only from the point of view of history, but also from that of doctrine. The value of textual studies is not questioned, since original texts correct errors in copying, give right readings, light up obscurities, and give force to the expressions used. The Roman Catholic Church does not approve of destructive rational or historical criticism, and indeed regards it as an evil fruit of the Lutheran heresy, the final stage in the assertion of freedom of interpretation.

Up to this point there would not be any essential quarrel with the Romans; but three further questions arise, in which the erroneous thinking of Rome is fully exposed. The first is: 'What is Scripture?' The Roman answer is that Scripture consists of the Old and New Testaments, including the Old Testament Apocrypha. Thus writings which cannot be included in the list of inspired and authoritative books have with them the same weight in doctrinal discussion as the truly canonical books. More than that, on the plea that Jerome had access to old and purer texts, and that his work has the sanction of centuries of use, the Vulgate is accorded the rank of a fully authoritative text. This means that doctrines may be grounded upon the Latin text even where it obviously does not correctly render the original.

The second question is: 'Who is to interpret Scripture?' and the Roman answer is that Scripture is too obscure to be self-interpreting, and that there is need for a further authority to decide which is the right sense. In the Old Testament the law was interpreted by Moses and the priests. Today the interpretation of the Bible is in the hands of the Church, speaking through *ex cathedra* pronouncements of the Pope, and the decisions of general councils, together with the expositions of the early Fathers. Truly, the Bible is the basic authority, but side by side with that basic authority there is this interpretative authority, to which all Christians must bow. For the Roman Catholic there can be no appeal to the Scripture as privately read and understood, only to the official Scripture officially interpreted. Whatever the Church reads into or out of the Bible is the rule of faith, not the Bible itself.

There is a third question: 'Does the Bible as a rule of faith suffice, or is there a further and necessary rule side by side with and supplementing the Bible?' The Roman answer is that the Bible is not enough, nor in the strictest sense is it even necessary. Before the written Word there was an oral tradition, and side by side with the written Word there is today a tradition (both teaching and customs) derived directly from the apostles, and of equal rank with the Bible. Authoritative traditions consist of teachings universally accepted (e.g. the virginity of Mary), and customs universally practised (e.g. infant baptism), those manifestly ancient, although not demonstrably apostolic (e.g. the Lenten fast), those held by most doctors and not disputed by others (e.g. baptismal rites, or the cult of images), and those which are held by apostolic churches, of which Rome is the only one at the present time (e.g. the doctrine of the Immaculate Conception). In effect, this means that the appeal to Scripture is set aside, and the authority of the Bible is to all intents and purposes overthrown.

The devastating effects of Roman teaching upon the Bible's authority are clear enough, both in theory and even more so in experience; but it must not be forgotten that the task of meeting Roman doctrine still remains. Many questions require a more precise and exact handling if heresy of this kind is to be excluded.

First, the textual. Why must the canonical books be given one authority, the Apocrypha another? What is the pure text, and to what extent, if any, can renderings be said to be inspired, or even to what extent can we rely on any text as fully inspired?

Second, the doctrinal. How is the doctrine of the Holy Spirit in Scripture interpretation to be correctly stated, so as to avoid the dangers of ecclesiastical monopoly on the one side, and of fanatical individualism on the other? In what sense are the Scriptures of public interpretation? How far are the expositions of others, the Fathers, or the Reformers—men who manifestly worked with prayer—to be taken into account in our own reading of the Bible?

Third, the questions of order. To what extent is tradition permissible, if not in matters of faith, at any rate in those of order? Must Church life be modelled exclusively upon the detailed practice of Scripture, in such a way that what is not in the Bible is necessarily excluded, or has any Church the power to maintain ceremonies and traditions so long as they are in accordance with scriptural principles, and of value for Christian life?

All these are questions which demand some treatment and answer if a true doctrine of the authority of the Bible is to be maintained. In the answering of them it might be that something of value will be gained from the very manifest Roman errors, the danger of exalting one translation (Vulgate, or Authorized Version) into the infallible Word, the undoubted worth of previous expositions, not of course as infallible authorities, but as useful guides, the necessity of relating Christian principles to the historical development of the Church (right or wrong) as it came face to face with historical situations.

b. Liberal Protestantism

A second unorthodox teaching, which during the last two centuries has occupied the energies of defenders of the authority of the Bible almost exclusively—and with much justification in view of the radical nature of the attack—is that of modern historical and liberal Protestantism. This is a modern movement in every sense, since its development has been largely during the post-Reformation period, and it has provided a view of the Bible which is that of the majority, perhaps, of Protestant theological teachers and ministers, allowing, of course, for the many varieties of presentation. Rome attacks and destroys the authority of the Bible, not by denying its divine origin and unique position, but by adding to it other authorities which rob it of its power. Historical liberalism knows nothing of these subtle methods of peaceful penetration. It attacks the Bible frontally, denying the absoluteness or divine nature of its authority, willing to grant it authority—a limited and relative authority—only on the human level.

A full analysis of this complex liberal movement, in which so many different forms of thought coalesced, is unfortunately quite impossible in this context. All that can be done is to outline the various thought-forms, and to indicate the points at which they come into conflict with the orthodox doctrine. Five main movements combined—generally speaking—to produce this modern view of the Bible: (i) Rationalism, which at its best, as with the German theology, sought to reduce revealed Christianity to the level of a religion of reason, and at its worst, as with Voltaire, sought to laugh Christianity out of court as contrary to reason. (ii) Empiricism, or Historicism, which had as its main aim the study of Christianity and all its phenomena along the strict lines of historical observation. (iii) Poeticism, which, as with Herder and many of the early critics, approached the Bible as a primitive poetry-book, in which religious truths—partly emotional, partly rational—are set out in aesthetic forms. (iv) Emotional Pietism, the special and most important contribution of Schleiermacher, by which the doctrines of Christianity (including that of Holy Scripture) are re-interpreted in terms, not now of reason, or history, or poetry, but of the individual emotional experience. (v) Philosophical Idealism, which, in its final form in Hegel, gave a new rational interpretation upon a different philosophical basis: a basis which has as its starting-point the individual thinking ego.

It is not to be supposed, of course, that there were not opposing tendencies in these movements, or that all of them are necessarily present, or present in equal proportions, in every liberal theologian; but generally speaking—and making full allowance for the many points of divergence —these are the movements which together constitute the liberal and humanistic challenge to the orthodox doctrine of Bible authority.

In what does that challenge consist? It consists first in the rejection of a transcendent Deity and of supernatural acts of God. This means that the Bible has to be explained as reason, or history, or poetry, or religion, but not as the Word of God. The Bible is reduced to the level of a human book, outstanding perhaps of its kind, but not above all other books. The Bible has to be studied comparatively, with other books of religion, poetry, history, or rational truth. It is inspired, but only in the same way as all other books are inspired, by the God immanent in all things. It is liable to error, because it is human, and all things human are equally liable to error. Thus the Bible ceases to be studied as a divine message, a Word of salvation; instead it comes to be studied as a product of the human spirit. In the investigation of it, questions of authorship, date, circumstances, style and development of thought replace the first and fundamental question, the question as to the content of the revelation of the Creator-Lord and Saviour.

The challenge of liberal humanism to the orthodox view of the Bible consists also in the compiehension of the Bible within a world-scheme of human progress, although this scheme is in actual fact quite contrary to the teaching of the Bible itself. It is not our present concern to discuss the wider and deeper aspects of the doctrine of progress, important as these are, even considered as a challenge to the divinely revealed message of the Bible. But it is our concern to notice that, according to this doctrine, the thought of the Bible, and the history which it records, and the culture which it represents, are all approached from the human standpoint and forced into the universal humanistic scheme.

At two points this has serious consequences. First, it means that the sequence of Bible history, as the Bible gives it, has to be rejected, because unfortunately it does not fit the evolutionary interpretation. The facts have to be sifted from the so-called additions of religious fancy, and worked up into a new scheme. Second, it means that the message of the Bible has similarly to be treated and amended in order that a neat progression of religious thought may be observed. Even if it is granted, as many will grant, that in the teaching of Jesus Christ the highest point in all religious thinking is reached, that teaching is still part of this same development of the religious instincts and faculties of the race, and the Bible has no superior authority as the Bible, only the authority of the highest human achievement in religion thus far. It will be seen that this is of a piece with the primary rejection of a transcendent God and a transcendent Word of God.

The challenge of liberal humanism consists again in individualistic subjectivism which it opposes to the objectivism of the orthodox doctrine of the Word of God. Outward authority is cast off, and it is replaced by the inward authority of the individual thought or experience. Reason here, emotion there, usurps the place of God. The thought or experience is valid and valuable, not because it accords with an external standard of divine truth, but because it is individual, a single manifestation of the divine spirit immanent in and working through all things. The thoughts and feelings of Bible-men have of course the same validity and value, in the case of the greatest Bible-men perhaps the highest value, but only as similar manifestations of the same spirit. This means not only that the basic authority of the Bible is rejected, not only that all religion is approached comparatively and judged relatively, but that every individual becomes a law unto himself in religious matters. God is dethroned, and humanity reigns, and in practice humanity means little more than individual man, the thinking or feeling self.

This is the challenge; and in face of this most potent and deadly heresy in Protestant Christianity, it is evident that much serious thinking, much close defining and much careful restating needs to be done. The whole question of an absolute and authoritative revelation has to be considered; the question of that revelation in its relation to history, to Israel, to Jesus Christ, to the Bible itself as a literary product; the question of that revelation in its relation to the world-religions, or to so-called natural religion. Again, there is the question, subsidiary but by no means unimportant, of the inspiration of the Bible; the question of that inspiration in its relation to the ordinary poetic inspiration of which literature speaks; the question of the special working of the Spirit of God in its relation to the general working in those activities which can be considered as products of common grace.

These matters have been dealt with in the past, but the new challenge carries with it a call, not for the abandonment of the old doctrine, not for its amendment, but for a new and more careful and searching statement of it. And at one point, while the general presuppositions which underlie liberal writing upon the Bible are unhesitatingly rejected, the issue must be faced. Is there not something to be learned from a more thoroughgoing relating of the Bible message to the historical circumstances and even the literary form? The Bible is first of all God's book, as Jesus Christ is first of all Son of God; but it is a human book too, God's book in the world, as Jesus is the Son of Man, the Word made flesh. Naturally, no one who truly accepts the Bible's authority as the Word of God will wish to study the historical setting at the expense of the revealed message, but may he not wish to investigate the historical setting as the means to a better understanding of that message? Can there not be a true and reverent criticism—in the constructive and not the destructive sense—even when hostile and rationalistic criticism is uncompromisingly opposed?

c. The Theology of Crisis

A third unorthodox teaching, which has grown up in recent years, largely as a reaction against contemporary humanism, is that associated with the theology of Karl Barth, or at any rate with the development which that theology has undergone at the hands of many of his disciples. It is not easy to make definite pronouncements with regard to Barthian doctrine, partly because it is to some extent still in the making, partly because it is of too recent an origin to allow of dispassionate treatment. Again, at many vital points, the so-called Barthian school does not present a united front. In so far as this doctrine does, or can, harmonize with traditional teaching —the form of presentation differs of course—it need not perhaps detain us now; but in so far as it seems to be moving in a different direction, or to allow of non-orthodox views, it ought to be studied with the closest possible care.

Many real or possible points of divergence between Barthian teaching upon the authority of the Bible and that of the Reformers have been suggested, and perhaps it would be most useful to list these, with such comments as appear to be necessary. They fall into two distinct classes, and first come those which concern the form of scriptural revelation, the Bible as a book. The Barthian is at pains to stress the fact that the Bible is, outwardly considered, a human book with others. This means that he may if he chooses regard it as fallible. He is not tied to the view that God is the author in the sense that God determined the individual words, phrases, or expressions. He can with quite a good conscience agree that there are in it historical or scientific errors. He does not stress the fact that the Bible is truth in itself—that is to say, truth objectively considered. It does not convey truth to the human mind apart from the divine act of revealing which takes place in and through it. The Bible is indeed the only basis upon which, or rather the only form through which, God does work in revelation, but this is to be regarded as a paradox of grace. The Barthian does not discard an objective Word of God, but he does tend to disparage that Word, seeing in it not an instrument fashioned expressly for the purpose of revelation, the very nature of which proclaims its divine origin, but an imperfect, disproportionate human work, paradoxically and perhaps even arbitrarily chosen and used for that purpose.

It must be admitted that most recent work has been along lines such as these, partly because of the not wholly imaginary fear of a worship of the outward form of the Bible at the expense of the inward content, and partly because many liberals have found here the way back to an authoritative faith without the sacrifice of their 'assured' critical findings. Whether such a development is the necessary outcome of the real thought of Barth is quite another matter, and it is certainly possible to follow him at many points without this disparagement of the outward form of revelation.

To the second class of possible errors belong those which are concerned with the content of the Bible, the Bible as divine revelation. First of all is the view that the Bible is inspired only as the Holy Spirit applies it and lights it up to the individual soul. Inspiration is confused with illumination, and if this teaching is pressed it means that the Bible has no divine content except when the Holy Spirit speaks through it to the individual man. Revelation in the Bible becomes then an act of God, God's revealing of Himself, rather than the product of a divine act, a given revelation. It is along these lines that Barth himself sees and points to a distinction between revelation and revealedness, verbal inspiration and verbal inspiredness, the former phrases being accepted but the latter rejected as not part of true Reformed teaching.

Within the limits that there can be no objective Word of God without also the application to individual souls there is truth in this distinction, but beyond those limits it leads in a dangerous direction. Pressed too far it means that the Bible can be authoritative, not as an outward law, but only as the Bible in the individual ego, as an inward experience. Thus, with all the insistence upon the fact that Christianity rests upon unique historical events, with all the stress upon the transcendence of God, in the last analysis we may easily be left with a faith which depends upon a subjective experience, and with the substantial autonomy of the individual ego. A further danger is that lawful paradox can easily be replaced by sheer irrationalities, for while it is no doubt a paradox that eternal truth is revealed in temporal events and witnessed through a human book, it is sheer unreason to say that that truth is revealed in and through that which is erroneous.

The questions raised by this theology are, of course, the central questions of all thinking upon the authority of Holy Scripture. They bring us to the very heart of the problem. Barth has performed a useful service by showing that the categories of a dead (as opposed to a living) orthodoxy simply will not do. An abstract objectivism, or a mechanical conception of revelation, is as far from the truth on the one side as is a pure subjectivism or a naturalistic view of revelation on the other. Thus the ultimate problem is that of the relationship of revelation to history on the one side and to the individual believer on the other. Ought we to think that the Bible is trustworthy merely because we can demonstrate its historical accuracy? Ought we to think it authoritative merely because we have come to know the truth of its message through the Holy Spirit, and irrespective of the historical reliability or otherwise? Ought we not to seek the authority of the Bible in the balanced relationship of a perfect form (the objective Word), and a perfect content (the Word applied subjectively by the Holy Ghost)—the form holding the content, the content not applied except in and through the form?

IV A COMPARISON WITH THE INCARNATION

It may be suggested in closing that a true doctrine of history and revelation in the Bible will be formulated only when the problem is studied in the light of the similar problem of the incarnation. In Christ, the Word revealed, there are the two: the divine and the human; the revelation and the history; and these two are distinct and yet one. So too it is in the Word written, which is the witness to Christ. It is not enough to deny the divine, to see only a man here, a book there. But it is also not enough to ignore the human, to see only a God here, an oracle there. It is a true paradox (i.e. it is not irrational) that the man Jesus is the Son of God (and faith by the Holy Ghost knows Him to be so). So too it is a true paradox (i.e. it is not irrational) that the book, the Bible, can be and is the revelation of God (and faith by the Holy Ghost apprehends it as such). The two sides are paradoxically related, but they are congruous the one to the other, and must be. Of course, the parallel must not be pressed too far, for Jesus Christ is God, Himself Person and Creator, whereas the Bible, however highly we value it, is a creature, the witness to a Person. But if the whole question is approached from this angle, with the incarnation as our guide, it may well be that the way will open up to a truer and fuller understanding, one which is orthodox, and which safeguards the authority and integrity of the Scriptures, not in content only but also in historical form.

G. W. Bromiley.

REVELATION AND INSPIRATION

CHRISTIAN theology as taught in the Bible is an organic unit, and should be studied as such. No part of it is properly understood except in relation to the whole. No single doctrine is mastered till one knows its place in the system. Our aim in this article is to formulate the view of revelation and inspiration which the Bible teaches and which underlies this Commentary. Accordingly, our first task must be to indicate the relation in which these topics stand to the rest of Christian truth. The doctrine of biblical inspiration, as we shall see, is a part of the general doctrine of revelation, which in its turn derives from, and must be constructed in terms of, the fundamental doctrines of creation and redemption. In the following exposition we shall try to exhibit these connections, and so to gain a fully biblical understanding of the subjects in question.

I. REVELATION

The English word 'revelation' may be taken either actively or passively. In the former sense it means that activity of God whereby He makes Himself known to men; in the latter, the knowledge thus imparted. The biblical idea of revelation must be elicited by means of a broad induction of evidence, of which the briefest outline must here suffice.

a. The Old Testament

The Old Testament constantly affirms that Israel's existence and history as a nation, and her religion as a Church, were wholly the result of divine revelation. God had revealed Himself in covenant to Abraham, as *his* God, and had pledged Himself to continue in covenant with Abraham's seed (Gn. xvii). Accordingly, He had brought them out of captivity into the promised land, and made them a nation to serve Him (Ex. vi. 2–8, xix. 3–6; Ps. cv. 43–45). He had given them His 'law' (*torah*; lit. 'instruction'), and taught them how to worship Him. Throughout their history He raised up a succession of spokesmen to declare to them 'the word of the Lord'. Again and again at decisive moments He demonstrated His own complete control of circumstances by foretelling what He would do for them before the event (cf. Is. xlviii. 3–7).

Israel was very conscious of the uniqueness of her relationship to God (Ps. cxlvii. 19, 20). True religion was to her, precisely, the knowledge of Jehovah, and presupposed Jehovah's self-disclosure in covenant. Lacking this, the Gentile world had fallen into idolatry. The revealed religion of Israel threw into relief the essential blasphemy of all other religion whatsoever. Hence, when God revealed Himself to other nations, with whom He had not entered into covenant, it was exclusively in judgment upon them for their sins (Ex. vii. 5; Ezk. xxv. 11, 17, xxviii. 22–24).

The Old Testament verdict upon Old Testament revelation was that it was not a complete whole, but preparatory for something greater. The prophets looked forward to a day when God would reveal Himself by mightier works than ever yet: He would raise up the Messiah, gather His scattered people and establish His kingdom among them. Heaven and earth would be made new (Is. lxv. 17–25); Israelite religion would be transformed (Je. xxxi. 31–34); and all nations would see and acknowledge the glory of God in Israel as never before (Is. lx. 1–14; Ezk. xxxvi. 23). On this forward-looking note the Old Testament closes (Mal. iv).

b. The New Testament

The New Testament writers were convinced that the meaning of Jewish history and of the Old Testament was to be found in Christ: that, in other words, the course of events in Israel from the very beginning and the composition of the Old Testament over the centuries had been completely controlled by God with the incarnation in view. The implications of this claim led naturally to the fundamental theological idea in terms of which they expounded the subject of revelation. The idea is this: God, the sovereign Creator, who within His word 'worketh all things after the counsel of his own will' (Eph. i. 11), foresaw the ruin of the race through sin, determined to glorify Himself by saving a Church, and appointed His Son to effect its salvation by His mediatorial ministry. World history has been to date, and will be to the end, nothing more nor less than God's execution of the plan which He then formed in order to compass His goal. After the Son had been raised, exalted and enthroned in His messianic kingdom, He sent the Holy Spirit into the world in order both to complete the disclosure, which He had Himself commenced while on earth, of His Father's purposes for the Church and also to bring His people, through faith in Himself, into the possession and enjoyment of the salvation He won for them. The revelation of God's plan was duly completed by the Spirit, who made it known in full to the apostles; its performance will be completed by Christ at His 'appearing' (*parousia*), when the Church will be made perfect.

This, in barest outline, is the dogmatic framework which underlies the New Testament teaching about revelation. It is most fully stated in Paul's Epistles (cf. Rom. viii. 28–39; Eph. i. 3–14, etc.) and John's Gospel (cf. vi. 37–45, x. 14–18, 27–29, xvi. 7–15, xvii), but is more or less explicit everywhere. The main passages relating to revelation fall into three classes:

i. Passages concerning Christ's disclosure of God. The Son is the perfect image of the Father (2 Cor. iv. 4; Col. i. 15; Heb. i. 3) and so is in Himself a perfect revelation of the Father to those who have eyes to see (Jn. i. 18, xiv. 7–11). All God's 'fulness' dwelt in the incarnate Son (Col. i. 19, ii. 9). Those who understand the full significance of His life and death thereby understand the whole eternal purpose ('wisdom') of God for the Church's salvation (Col. ii. 2, 3; 1 Cor. i. 24 and ii. 7–10; see also next section). None can apprehend any part of Christ's revelation of His Father without supernatural spiritual enlightenment (Jn. iii. 3–12, vi. 44, 45; Mt. xvi. 17; Gal. i. 16).

ii. Passages concerning God's disclosure of His plan. God's comprehensive scheme for the salvation of His elect out of every nation, Jew and Gentile alike, was the 'mystery', the divine 'wisdom', which God conceived before creation but concealed until the apostolic age. Now it was revealed, and the full meaning of Israel's election and history and of the Old Testament revelation for the first time became clear. All the time God's goal had been, not the salvation of one of the world's many nations, but the creation of a new nation, the members of which were to be drawn from every nation and to receive their spiritual nationality, not by natural, but by spiritual birth (cf. 1 Pet. ii. 9, 10). The destiny of the regenerate was to be glorified, as their Head ('the firstfruits' of the new race, 1 Cor. xv. 20, 23) had been already; and His very presence in heaven, 'the *man* in the glory,' was a pledge to them that they would some day share that glory with Him. Paul deals with the revelation of this mystery in several important passages which should be carefully studied (Eph. i. 8–12, iii. 3–11; 1 Cor. ii. 7–10; Rom. xvi. 25, 26; cf. xi. 25–36 and 2 Tim. i. 9–11). The source of this revelation is God; the mediator of it is Christ (Gal. i. 12; cf. Rev. i. 1); the agent in its communication is the Spirit (1 Cor. ii. 10–12; 2 Cor. iii. 15–18, cf. iv. 6; Eph. iii. 5). In order that it might be conveyed to the Church intact, the Spirit inspired the words of apostolic testimony (1 Cor. ii. 13), as He had inspired the words of Christ (Jn. iii. 34, cf. xii. 48–50). He caused the apostles to embody the revelation given to them in a 'form of doctrine', the 'form of sound words' (*typos*; lit. 'pattern', 'standard'; see Rom. vi. 17; cf. 2 Tim. i. 13). This is 'the sound doctrine' (1 Tim. i. 10, cf. vi. 3; 2 Tim. iv. 3; Tit. i. 9, ii. 1, all RV), the apostolic 'tradition' (2 Thes. ii. 15, iii. 6), the test and norm for the faith and life of the churches.

iii. Passages concerning God's performance of His plan. As was said, God discloses His purposes by what He does as well as in what He says; and any action which marks a further stage in His plan of redemptive history may be called 'revelation'. The New Testament knows two such acts of revelation yet to come: the appearing of antichrist (2 Thes. ii. 3, 6, 8) and the *parousia* of Jesus (1 Cor. i. 7, RV; 2 Thes.

i. 7–10; 1 Pet. i. 7, RV, 13). The latter concludes history and ushers in the day of judgment. Christ will then reveal by executive action God's eternal intentions with respect to the impenitent and the saints, wrath for the one and glory for the other (Rom. ii. 5–10, viii. 18; cf. 1 Pet. i. 5).

Such, in brief, is the biblical material from which the theological doctrine of revelation must be constructed. To this task we now turn.

c. The original revelation

The doctrine of revelation is grounded upon the fact that God made man in His own image, to know, love, worship, serve and so glorify Him. We saw that man's religion, if it is to be true, must be grounded on God's revelation; and God accordingly revealed Himself to Adam as fully as was necessary for Adam to live in fellowship with Him. Adam knew God, then, first through His works of creation. The world on which he looked out bore eloquent testimony to the power and wisdom of its Maker. The created order, though since involved in Adam's ruin (Gn. iii. 18; Rom. viii. 19–22), still proclaims God's glory (Ps. xix. 1f.; Rom. i. 19, 20); much more must it have done so before. Adam knew God, too, by his knowledge of himself; as God's noblest creature, he was a part of God's revelation of His glory, as well as being its recipient. Again, God's works of providence brought him knowledge of his Maker's goodness. If, despite the chaos that has entered the world through sin, the course of events still bears this testimony (Acts xiv. 17), doubtless it did so far more clearly to Adam when he knew only the garden, the animals God had brought him to rule, and the wife He had made for him (Gn. ii. 18–24). Finally, the testimony of God's works was supplemented by verbal revelation (how conveyed we do not know) as and when necessary (Gn. ii. 16, 17).

Much of this is necessarily obscure to us. The knowledge of God that Adam enjoyed in Eden before the fall is as far beyond our comprehension as is the knowledge of God which the Church will enjoy in heaven after the resurrection. But the permanent characteristics of God's self-revealing activity are already here made plain, and it is worth our while to pause and note them.

i. The purpose of revelation. God makes Himself known to man so that man may attain the end of his creation, which is to know, love and worship Him. The transcendent Creator is inaccessible to His creatures until He discloses Himself, and man's knowledge of God, where it exists, is correlative to and consequent on God's prior self-revelation. Adam in Eden needed revelation if he was to live in fellowship with God.

ii. The means of revelation. Revelation is God's personal self-disclosure to His rational creatures. The relationship which it initiates is compared in Scripture to that of husband and wife, father and son, friend and friend (cf. Je. iii;

Ho. xi. 1; Is. xli. 8; Mt. vii. 11; Jn. xv. 15; Eph. v. 25–27). Such a relationship could not be created apart from personal address by God to man. God must open His mind; He must speak. Action out of the context of conversation, movement divorced from explanation, is a very limited medium for making oneself known to another. It was not enough for Adam to see God in His works; he needed to hear His word, to receive verbal or propositional revelation.

Of course there is more to self-revelation than merely communicating information about oneself, just as there is more to faith than a mere 'notional' acquaintance with truths. In human relationships, personal attitudes, by their very nature, cannot be expressed in propositional form. Their existence can be indicated, and their nature to some extent suggested, by speech, but they can be expressed, and so fully manifested, only by action. So, when God reveals His love to men, the depths of meaning contained in the words in which He avows it to them become clear only in the light of their experience of what He does for them. God's personal attitudes towards men, therefore, require works as well as words for their revelation. But this does not affect our present contention, which is, simply, that without words such revelation could scarcely take place at all.

iii. **The effectiveness of revelation.** An unfathomable mystery underlies the claim that the transcendent, infinite Creator makes His thoughts known to finite man. But we may not imagine that God is somehow hampered or thwarted in His self-revealing action by the limitations of man's mind. That man's knowledge of God on earth is now, and was before the fall, imperfect, dim and inadequate to its object in very many ways, is not to be denied. But God made man's mind; and He made it as He did in order that man might be able to apprehend Him in a manner perfectly adequate for the ends of His self-disclosure—i.e., for the development of the religious relationship which was man's destiny. He made Adam's mind such that Adam could not but apprehend as much of God as was disclosed to him. And when God reveals Himself to sinful man, He restores to him his lost ability to recognize God's Word for what it is and receive it as such. The activity of trust which results from the exercise of this faculty is in Scripture termed faith; and in Heb. xi. 3 the faculty itself is so denoted. It appears correct to say that, in this sense, Adam in Eden had faith, and that it is no more than a restoration to man of what he lost at the fall when the Spirit implants the faculty of faith in those to whom God intends to make Himself known.

When man fell, he jeopardized his status and corrupted his nature. God therefore adapted His self-disclosing activity to the new situation, integrating it into the redemptive process which He had at once initiated in order to remedy sin's effects. But the three features of revelation noted above remained, and remain, constant.

d. God revealed as Redeemer

Through sin, man lost his ability to apprehend creation's witness to its God. The meaning and message of the book remained the same, but he could no longer read it; the heavens proclaimed God's glory into deaf ears. 'They did not like ('did not see fit', RSV; 'disdained', Moff.) to retain God in their knowledge' (Rom. i. 28). Man had lost his natural inclination to love and serve his Creator; the idea of a life so spent was profoundly distasteful to him (Rom. viii. 7). There remained in his heart an indelible sense of God, i.e., an awareness that there was something or someone greater than himself whom he should worship and serve, but he refused to let it lead him back to his Maker; for he was now under the sway of unbelief, which the Bible depicts as a positive, devilish thing, a passionate energy of blind denial, a resolute repudiation of the true God (cf. Rom. i. 21–32; Eph. ii. 2, 3, iv. 17–19).

In this situation, the insufficiency of God's self-revelation in creation and providence is manifest. God still shows Himself in His works (Rom. i. 19, 20); but men shut their eyes, and 'hold down the truth in unrighteousness' (Rom. i. 18, RV). Thus the continuance of the original revelation leads none to the knowledge of God and serves only to leave the world without excuse for its ignorance of Him. And, even supposing that fallen man succeeded in reading 'the book of the creatures' aright, what he read could only drive him to despair. For this *general revelation* (as it is best called) brings knowledge of a God who hates and punishes man's disobedience and ingratitude (Rom. i. 18), and says not a word about redeeming love. The good news that the God who is merciless to sin is at the same time merciful to sinners is made known only by *special revelation*, which centres upon Jesus Christ; and to this we now turn.

Since the fall, the Creator has been making Himself known as Redeemer upon the stage of human history, working out the eternal purpose which, as we saw, constitutes the 'mystery' which the apostles declared. The whole plan hinged upon the earthly ministry of the incarnate Son. In the fact of Christ all the types, shadows and prophecies of the Old Testament found their meaning, so that by it Israel's Scriptures were fulfilled (cf. Mt. v. 17; Lk. xxiv. 27; Jn. v. 39; Acts xiii. 26–33; Heb. vii—x). Again, upon this ministry all subsequent redemptive activity is grounded. When He ascended, Christ entered upon the exercise of His heavenly ministry, whereby He conveys to His people by His Spirit the benefits which He secured for them while on earth, and this ministry will not be completed until He perfects His Church at His return. And only when the whole Church is made perfect, possessing and exhibiting in all its fulness the glory of God (Rev. xxi. 11), and appearing with its glorified Saviour in a new-created universe (Rev. xxi—xxii. 5), will God's resources and intentions in redemption be fully manifested, and His purpose of perfect self-display be finally accomplished. Meanwhile every act of grace brings it one stage nearer completion. The new creation, therefore, no less than the old, God's works of special grace as well as those of common providence, are works of revelation, every one of which declares the glory of God.

e. Verbal revelation

In the redemptive process by which the Church is saved, verbal revelation has an indispensable place. First of all, it was an integral element in the series of acts by which redemption was wrought out. Without verbal revelation, Abraham would never have entered Canaan, nor Moses led Israel from Egypt, nor Jesus' life been preserved in infancy (cf. Gn. xii. 1–5; Ex. iii—vi. 13; Mt. ii. 13–15). Secondly, verbal revelation has always been necessary as a ground for faith. Its importance from this point of view is seen when we consider the soteriological significance of faith. Not merely is faith, as an activity, the instrument whereby a sinner lays hold of Christ and so obtains all promised benefits, but also, as a faculty, faith is, as we saw, the organ of that knowledge of and fellowship with God from which man fell and to which redemption restores him.

Now, the object which brings this faculty into exercise is God's Word, as such (cf. 1 Thes. ii. 13). Faith 'hears His voice' and responds to His Word of promise in trust and obedience. Without a word from God, faith cannot be (Rom. x. 17). The reason for this is clear. Without an explanatory word, God's redemptive action could not even be recognized for what it was. The creature, as we saw, cannot know the Creator's mind till He speaks. The case of the incarnation shows that the clearest revelation of God is nevertheless the most opaque to man. Christ, the personal Word of God, expressed and effected His Father's redemptive purpose completely. In Him, God fully manifested Himself in redemptive action; and, for that very reason, the fact of Christ utterly transcended man's powers of interpretation. 'It may be doubted,' wrote B. B. Warfield, 'whether even the supreme revelation of God in Jesus Christ could have been known as such in the absence of preparatory, accompanying and succeeding explanatory revelations in words.' Even that is an understatement. How could man ever have learned the utterly paradoxical and eternally mysterious truth, that Jesus was God incarnate and put away the world's sins by dying on a cross, without being told? Accordingly, in order to make possible faith in Christ, God gave the world a verbal explanation of the fact of Christ. This was the gospel, the apostolic *kerygma*, which announces God's gift of the living Word and promises eternal life to those who receive Him. It thus appears that the giving of propositional revelations concerning God's redemptive action in history is no mere adjunct or appendage to that action, but is itself part of it, as essential a link

in the chain as the events with which those revelations are concerned. For God's redemptive programme includes the conveyance as well as the procuring of salvation, and is not complete until sinners have been restored to faith and knowledge of God through the gospel.

In form and substance, the gospel promise has been one and the same throughout redemptive history, from the time of Adam and Abraham to the present day, namely, a covenant on God's part to be the God of the one to whom He speaks and to safeguard and reward him, both in this life and the next, if he will trust and obey. Saving faith, therefore, has been the same thing from Abel's time onwards (Heb. xi. 4). In content, however, the promise grew richer as time went on; for, within the framework of His covenant pledge, God gradually disclosed both the particular blessings which it included and also the objective ground—His own redemptive action—upon which it was based. This revelatory process continued intermittently for centuries. It was thus progressive: not in the sense that each new revelation antiquated the last, but rather in the sense that from time to time God underlined and amplified what He had taught already and added to it further intimations of what He intended to do until He had completed the pattern of truth which was to be fulfilled in Christ. Then, at the appointed time, He sent His Son to achieve redemption and crowned the revelatory process with the unveiling of the gospel and the 'mystery'. From first to last, the progress of revelation had been closely interlocked with the unfolding of God's plan of redemptive history; and the interpretation of the fact of Christ, itself the complete disclosure in action of the Creator as Redeemer, completed it.

The means by which verbal revelation was given were many and varied. Sometimes an abnormal quality of experience was the vehicle of its reception. This was the case with visions, dreams, and prophetic inspiration, which seems to have ranged on occasion from the slow crystallizing of prolonged meditations at one extreme to the hurricane rapture of complete ecstasy at the other. Sometimes, again, God conveyed truth through His chosen organs of revelation merely by His divine *concursus*—by operating, that is, in and with them in the exercise of their own natural powers and so leading them to His truth through the normal processes of their own thought—historical research, exegesis of canonical Scripture, meditation and prayer, logical and theological reasoning. Much of the Wisdom literature, the Old Testament historical books and all the New Testament writings save the Apocalypse appear to have resulted from revelation of this sort. Limitations of space preclude any discussion of these modes of revelation. But it is important to notice before we pass on that there is in Scripture no indication of any difference in the purity and reliability of revelations mediated through these various kinds of experience. All organs of revelation, however limited they may appear in themselves, become in the hands of the sovereign God completely effective to the end for which He employs them.

f. Biblical revelation

In order to ensure the safe preservation of what He had revealed, God 'inscripturated' it. The book which He thereby produced contains, not all the verbal revelations ever given (cf. e.g., the reference in 2 Ch. ix. 29 to prophetic books which have not survived), but those which were relevant for the book's designed purpose; which was, not merely to provide a ground for personal faith and guidance for individual Christian living, but also to enable the world-wide Church in every age to understand itself, to interpret its history, to reform and purify its life continually, and to rebuff all assaults made upon it, whether from within, by sin and heresy, or from without, by persecution and rival ideologies. All the problems that ever faced or will face the Church are in principle covered and solved in this book. For the Christian Bible, though a very human book, recording much sin and error, reflecting in many places the weaknesses and limitations of its authors, is yet—and this is the fundamental truth about it—a divine product, whose *auctor primarius* is God.

The proof of this divine authorship of the Bible (i.e., the proper ground of faith in it) may here be indicated. It is twofold:

i. **The testimony of Christ** (the external proof). This proof comprises two propositions. First, Christ's authority demands the acceptance of the Old Testament as divinely inspired. His witness concerning its character is unambiguous and emphatic. To Him, it was not a miscellany but a unity, 'the Scripture' (singular: Jn. x. 35), whose authority was permanent and absolute because of its divine origin (cf. Mt. v. 17–20; Lk. xvi. 17; Mt. xix. 4–6). Arguments from Scripture, therefore, possessed for Him clinching force (Mt. xxii. 32, 41ff.; Jn. x. 34, 35, etc.). The emphatic 'it is written' was final, and settled matters. His whole ministry was one great testimony to His acceptance of the divine authority of the Old Testament; for He preached and healed and died in obedience to what He found written (cf. Mt. viii. 16, 17, xxvi. 24, 54; Lk. iv. 18–21, xviii. 31–33, xxii. 37). He, the teacher to whom the Christian Church professes subjection, was Himself in everything subject to His Father's word in the Old Testament Scriptures. The apostolic writers everywhere echo this witness (cf. 2 Tim. iii. 16; 2 Pet. i. 20, 21, the phrase 'oracles of God' in Rom. iii. 2, and the quotation of Old Testament passages, spoken in their context by men, as words of God, or of the Holy Ghost, e.g. Mt. xix. 4, 5; Acts iv. 25, 26, xiii. 34, 35; Heb. i. 6ff., iii. 7).

Second, Christ's authority demands the acceptance of the New Testament as possessing the same character as the Old. Jesus taught His disciples to read the Old Testament Christologically, as a prophetic revelation of the things concerning Himself (Lk. xxiv. 24, 25, 44, 45; Jn. v. 39, 46). The apostles did so (cf. Acts iii. 18, 24; 1 Pet. i. 10–12), claiming that it was written primarily for the guidance and benefit of Christian believers (cf. Rom. iv. 23, 24, xv. 4; 1 Cor. ix. 10, x. 11; 2 Tim. iii. 16), and that it could not be understood at all by those who would not read it in the light of Christ (2 Cor. iii. 14–16).

Now, seeing that God had inscripturated His earlier, prophetic revelations so that they might be permanently accessible in an uncorrupted form for the benefit, not merely of old Israel, but of the Church universal, it would have been an unaccountable departure from a way of working so well established, and so patently wise and desirable, had He done nothing similar when His crowning revelation was given to the world. A New Testament, therefore, was only to be expected. Against the background of this presumption, certain facts acquire unmistakable significance. (1) Christ promised the Spirit to the apostles so that they might remember and understand what He had taught them already (Jn. xiv. 25, 26) and receive the further revelations concerning Himself which they could not as yet 'bear' (Jn. xvi. 12–14). So equipped, they were to be His authoritative witnesses and interpreters to the whole Church, in all ages and all parts of the world (Jn. xvii. 20; cf. Mt. xxviii. 19). How, we may ask, could Christ have envisaged this, unless He intended them to write their testimony? (2) The apostles claim that, in virtue of their possession of the Spirit, they teach and write the pure truth of God. They are verbally inspired (1 Cor. ii. 13); and a genuinely 'spiritual' man recognizes this fact (1 Cor. xiv. 37; cf. Gal. i. 8; 2 Thes. iii. 6, 14). These are unqualified affirmations; and there is no question that by making them the apostles claimed, and intended to claim, an authority for their own sermons and letters no less absolute than that which they attributed to the Old Testament. (3) Paul quotes Deuteronomy and Luke together, and Peter refers to Paul's Epistles, as part of the canon of Scripture (1 Tim. v. 18; 2 Pet. iii. 16). (4) Centuries of Christian exegesis have demonstrated that, theologically, the two Testaments together form an organic unit, each complementing the other in a harmonious testimony to Christ, each bringing to light more and more of the contents and meaning of the other in an endlessly fruitful dialectic of foreshadowing and fulfilment.

We conclude that, in the light of Christ's evident intention that His apostles should write their testimony and His promise to equip them for the task, the claims they made for themselves and each other, and the quality of what they produced, lead us irresistibly to acknowledge the New Testament as the expected and needed completion of the Old.

ii. **The testimony of the Spirit** (the internal proof). We saw that it is by the use of the faculty of faith that we discern God's Word for what it is. Faith sees the real nature of that at which it looks. This has been the Church's experience down the ages. Since it is the Spirit who implants faith and works in believers their acts of faith, the presence of this conviction is termed the Spirit's witness. (See further pp. 18f.)

The Bible, then, is the revealed Word of God, in the sense that in its pages God speaks His mind—all His mind—concerning His purpose for His people. To call the Bible a record of, or a witness to, a revelation made in history is insufficient. The Bible is all this, and more. It is not merely a report of what God said; it is what He says, here and now. It is itself a link in the chain of God's redemptive action. Its contents, heard or read, are the means whereby, on the grounds of the historical ministry of Christ which it records and explains, and through the regenerating action of the Spirit who works in and with the Word, sinners come to know the Father and the Son. It is not the Word of God in the sense that every separate sentence, including the words of evil men, expresses His mind or reflects His will. 'God's Word written' is the Bible as a whole, or, more accurately, the theology of the Bible, that organic unity which our fathers so happily and suggestively termed 'the body of divinity'. Here is the image of God's mind, the transcript of His thoughts, the declaration of His grace, the verbal embodiment of all the treasures of wisdom and knowledge that are hid in His Son. And here faith rests.

II. INSPIRATION

a. The meaning of inspiration

Inspiration is not itself a biblical word. It is usually, and most conveniently, defined as a supernatural influence of God's Spirit upon the biblical authors which ensured that what they wrote was precisely what God intended them to write for the communication of His truth, and hence could be truly termed 'inspired', *theopneustos*, lit. 'breathed out by God' (2 Tim. iii. 16). We have already dealt with this subject in constructive statement, and confine ourselves here to the correction of some misconceptions.

The 'inspiration' which secured the infallible communication of revealed truth is something distinct from the 'inspiration' of the creative artist, which does not. The two things should not therefore be confused. Nor does inspiration always imply an abnormal state of mind in the writer, e.g. a trance-state, a vision, or the hearing of a voice; nor does it imply the obliteration of his personality. God in His providence prepared the human vehicles of inspiration for their task, and caused them in many, perhaps most, cases to perform it through the normal exercise of the powers He had given them. Many states of mind, as we saw, were compatible with inspiration. There is no reason to think that the authors were always aware that they were being inspired in the sense defined, i.e. that they were writing canonical Scripture. Nor is there any ground for asserting that an inspired document could not in God's providence have been compiled from sources by an ordinary process of historical composition, or passed through various editions and recensions before reaching its final form. All that is claimed is that the finished product is *theopneustos*, precisely what God intended for the communication of saving truth.

Since truth is communicated through words, and verbal inaccuracy misrepresents meaning, inspiration must be verbal in the nature of the case. And if the words of Scripture are 'God-breathed', it is almost blasphemy to deny that it is free from error in that which it is intended to teach and infallible in the guidance it gives. Inerrancy and infallibility cannot be proved (nor, let us note, disproved) by argument. Both are articles of faith: corollaries of the confession, which Christ's teaching demands and the Spirit's testimony evokes, that canonical Scripture was breathed out by the God who cannot lie. He who denies them thereby shows that he rejects the witness of Christ, the apostles and the historic Christian Church concerning the nature of 'God's Word written', and either does not possess or has not understood the *testimonium Spiritus Sancti internum*.

b. The problems of inspiration

No Christian doctrine is free from problems; and that for a very good reason. God has put forward His truth as an object for faith, and the proper ground of faith is God's own authoritative testimony. Now, acceptance on grounds of another's authority and acceptance on grounds of rational demonstration are two distinct things. Man's original sin was a lust after self-sufficient knowledge, a craving to shake off all external authority and work things out for himself (cf. Gn. iii. 5, 6); and God deliberately presents saving truth to sinners in such a way that their acceptance of it involves an act of intellectual repentance, whereby they humble themselves and submit once more to be taught by Him. Thus they renounce their calamitous search after a self-made wisdom (cf. Rom. i. 22; 1 Cor. i. 19–25) in order to regain the kind of knowledge for which they were made, that which comes from taking their Creator's word. So as to make this renunciation clear-cut, God has ensured that no single article of faith should be demonstrable as, say, a geometrical theorem is, nor free from unsolved mystery. Man must be content to know by faith, and to know, in this world at any rate, in part. We must not, therefore, expect to find the doctrine of biblical inspiration free from difficulties, any more than are the doctrines of the Trinity, incarnation, or atonement. Nor must we expect to be able to solve all its problems in this world. Nor must we wonder that Christians easily fall into heresy over this doctrine, as over others. It is worth while, however, briefly to indicate the right attitude for faith to adopt in face of some prevalent errors concerning it.

First, the doctrine is sometimes diluted by those who profess to be its friends. It is said that the Bible is the product of inspiration in some sense, but not of verbal inspiration. God revealed truth to the writers, but it was inevitable that, being sinful, fallible men, they should distort it in the course of reporting it. We must expect, therefore, to find error in Scripture. This, however, as we saw, was not the view of Christ and the apostles. It appears to be a mistaken inference from the admitted fact that not all the biblical books are on the same level of spiritual profundity and doctrinal finality; but it amounts to a flat denial that God in His sovereign providence could do what it was evidently desirable that He should do, and so prepare and control the human instruments through whom He caused Scripture to be written that they put down exactly what He intended, no more and no less. In other words, the Bible, on this view, is neither what God intended it should be, nor what Christ thought and taught that it was. Such a position is plainly intolerable.

Secondly, the doctrine is sometimes rejected on the grounds of the internal characteristics of the Bible. Such objections, however, invariably prove on examination to be grounded upon an *a priori*, man-made idea of what a verbally inspired Bible ought to be like, and the very act of bringing them forward as valid grounds for doubting what God says about His book is itself a sign of continued intellectual impenitence, unconscious, perhaps, but no less real for that. The believing method of approach is, rather, to start by accepting God's testimony that the Bible is verbally inspired and then to examine the internal characteristics of Scripture in order to find out what this verbally inspired Bible is in fact like. The most cursory inspection shows that inspiration has completely accommodated itself to the thought-forms, literary methods, stylistic conventions and characteristic vocabulary of the writers. These are the media through which the inspired truth-content is conveyed, and unless we take pains to acquire a sympathetic understanding of them we shall be in danger of misinterpreting what God has said in terms of them, and thus manufacturing errors where none exist. We must be guided in biblical study by the principle—which is a certainty of faith—that Scripture nowhere misrepresents the truths it was inspired to teach and that every biblical fact has been recorded in the way best adapted for the communication of what the Church is meant to learn from it. What that is, however, can be determined in each case only by examining the passage in the context of Scripture as a whole. This is a principle of fundamental importance for biblical interpretation. We must not lose sight of it through controversial preoccupations, nor allow our confidence in its truth to be shaken by difficulties which may confront us when we try to apply it.

One example of its application may be given here. It has sometimes been asserted that the occasional appearance in the Old Testament of sub-Christian attitudes, actions and theological reflections is itself a refutation of the doctrine of an inspired Scripture. But this objection reveals a misunderstanding of the nature of the Bible. We stressed earlier that the Bible is not an aggregate of isolated texts, but an organism, no part of which can be rightly interpreted except in terms of its place and function in the whole. Now, God has included in His Word much exemplary material; and some of the examples He has recorded are bad examples. All is for our learning; but we must learn from different parts of Scripture in different ways. We learn from records of theological and practical error, not by supposing that, because they are included in Scripture, the words and deeds in question must have met with divine approval, but by detecting the mistakes in the light of Bible doctrine and taking warning. Principles of biblical theology must interpret, as they are in their turn illustrated by, facts of biblical history and biography. Scripture must interpret Scripture. Once it is grasped that the Bible is an organic unity, that the Word of God is its doctrine as a whole, and that each passage must be understood in the light of, even as it throws light upon, the truth as it is in Jesus, the grounds for this kind of objection vanish.

Lack of space forbids any further development of these principles here. We would conclude by reiterating our fundamental contention, that faith's attitude to the doctrine of biblical inspiration, as to all other doctrines, is one of acceptance on God's testimony. Nothing, therefore, will shake faith's certainty here, for nothing can shake the testimony on which it rests. When faced by difficulties in and objections to the doctrine as he understands it, the believer will infer that the cause is his own failure to comprehend God's testimony rather than God's failure to make the truth plain, and will accordingly be driven back to a closer re-thinking of the matter in the light of a closer study of the biblical evidence. This is how all doctrinal advance has been made throughout the history of the Church. And this is how a truer and fuller understanding of the doctrine of Holy Scripture as the inspired, and therefore infallible and inerrant, Word of God, can be reached in our own day.

J. I. PACKER.

30

THE HISTORICAL LITERATURE OF THE OLD TESTAMENT

WHEN we speak of the historical literature of the Old Testament we generally have in mind all the books from Genesis to Esther. But this does not mean, of course, that there are no passages of an historical nature in the other biblical books. There are, for example, the prologue and the epilogue to the book of Job, the historical fragments in some prophetic books such as chapters xxxvi—xxxix of Isaiah, various chapters in the book of Jeremiah, and the first half of the book of Daniel. But in this general survey we shall limit ourselves to a consideration of the books from Genesis to Esther which are generally regarded as being historical in a particular sense.

I. THE PENTATEUCH

'Pentateuch' is a Greek word meaning 'the five-volume book' and is frequently used to describe the first five books of the Old Testament. In the Hebrew Bible these books form a separate unit, called 'the Law', for although they contain a considerable amount of historical narrative, they are mainly legal in character. We often find this term used in the New Testament to describe this part of the Old Testament (see e.g. Mt. xii. 5; Jn. i. 45; Acts xiii. 15, xxiv. 14; 1 Cor. xiv. 34). In view of its distinctive nature it seems preferable to deal with the Pentateuch separately from the other historical books.

a. The fundamental revelation

The Pentateuch provides us with the basic facts of the divine revelation. In the very first chapters we learn that God is the Creator of the world in which we live. Then follows the account of the fall of man, that rebellion of the creature against his Creator by which humanity, together with the entire world, has been brought under the divine curse. Immediately the Saviour is promised (the 'seed of the woman' of Gn. iii. 15) and then the revelation proceeds to an elaborate disclosure of the divine action by which this Saviour will be brought into the world. First there is the picture of the universal period, wherein sin rises to such a height that the Lord decides to destroy man whom He has created from the face of the earth by the deluge; only Noah and his family found grace in the eyes of the Lord (Gn. vi. 8). After the flood there is a renewed apostasy, culminating in the endeavour to build a tower whose top might reach unto heaven (Gn. xi. 4).

After this God proceeds to prepare a new people from which the Saviour is to come forth. Out of Ur of the Chaldees He calls Abram, one of the descendants of Shem (cf. Gn. xi. 26). In him, God promises, all families of the earth shall be blessed (Gn. xii. 3). The sons of his descendant Jacob emigrate to Egypt and in the quiet and peace of their long stay there grow into a powerful nation. Slavery and an attempt to restrict their development follow, but the Lord delivers His people from the house of bondage and makes a new covenant with them at mount Sinai. The foundation of this covenant is the Mosaic Law, which is expounded in detail. But the redemption from Egypt and the deliverance through Moses are a figurative prediction of the Saviour and His redemptive work (cf. Jn. i. 17; Col. ii. 17). These early records cannot be read, therefore, as mere accounts of historical events. They have a spiritual significance as well.

b. The documentary theory examined

Many scholars deny most emphatically the Mosaic origin of these early books and divide the entire Pentateuch up into different strata originating from various periods of Israel's history. These strata are called 'sources' or 'documents', and it is supposed that they were not linked up together into the present unit earlier than the time of Ezra the scribe. At the end of the 19th century this was the prevailing view among Old Testament students. Since the beginning of the present century, however, very serious doubts have arisen as to the validity of this so-called 'documentary theory', and a most remarkable change in scholarly opinion has manifested itself. Nevertheless the theory is still taught in many schools and colleges, and it may not be out of place to mention here the most customary arguments which are adduced in its favour, and to demonstrate briefly their inadequacy.

i. *The use of the divine names.* From the very beginning the outstanding argument has been based on the variety in the use of the divine names. As a result of this variety scholars are accustomed to speak of 'Yahwistic' and 'Elohistic' sources according as the names *Yahweh* or *'Elohim* are employed to denote God in different passages. But it has been pointed out that in the Koran, the holy book of the Mohammedans, a similar feature is to be observed. In some places the name 'Allah' (Heb. *'Elohim*) is used and in others we find the word *'Rab'*, which may be considered as an Arabic equivalent of the Hebrew *Yahweh* (the Lord). Furthermore, attention may be drawn to the fact that the use of the combination *Yahweh-Elohim*, which is found only in Gn. ii. 4—iii. 24 (and once in Ex. ix. 30), has never led any scholar to suppose that this section must be due to a different author still. This seems to show that advocates of the theory are not very certain of the infallibility of their argument derived from the variety in the use of the names for God.

ii. Language and style. In the second place attention has been drawn to certain differences in language, style, and theological outlook. But judgments of this kind are notoriously subjective and little importance can be attached to them. One of the defenders of the 'documentary theory', having instituted a thorough and accurate examination, comes to the conclusion that there are only very few linguistic characteristics of the various sources, and he feels bound to admit that such a small number of differences may be simply accidental.

iii. Duplicate narratives. Of more importance is the contention that in many cases the same event is doubly recorded. It is maintained, for example, that there are duplicate narratives of the creation, of the deluge, of Abram denying his wife, of the transportation of Joseph to Egypt, of the ten plagues, and of the rebellion of Korah, Dathan and Abiram. Sometimes these accounts are given separately (for example, the story of the creation); in other cases it is argued that the accounts have been combined rather crudely into one story by a redactor (for example the story of Joseph). But, as can easily be seen, in none of these cases is there really a double record of the same event.

In the creation story we have to discern between the revelation of the creative work of God in Gn. i and the history of the created world in Gn. ii. In the account of the deluge, which is always put forward as an outstanding example of a twofold tradition, it is pointed out that at first Noah is bidden to take one pair of every species of animals with him into the Ark, and then he is ordered to take seven of each 'clean' species and two of each 'unclean' species. But why should this be regarded as an example of self-contradiction? The instruction to take one pair of every species is the general rule. This is followed by additional instructions with respect to the 'clean' animals. In the case of Abram denying his wife, we are not dealing with a double record of the same event (or even a triple record if the action of Isaac in Gn. xxvi. 6–11 is taken into account), but with various events. Abram requested of Sarai 'at every place whither we shall come, say of me, He is my brother' (Gn. xx. 13). Probably this was a common ruse employed not only by Abram but also by Isaac.

It is often alleged that in the account of Joseph's transportation to Egypt two different traditions are amalgamated. According to the one, Joseph is sold by his brothers to a caravan of Ishmeelites; according to the other, Midianites take him to Egypt. But this is clearly a misinterpretation of the biblical text. If we read the passage in question without prejudice we shall notice what actually happened. Midianite merchantmen passing by drew Joseph from the pit wherein he was cast by his brothers. It was they who actually sold him to the Ishmeelites, who in their turn brought him into Egypt. So they did what the brothers had intended to do.

In the story of the ten plagues of Egypt, advocates of the 'documentary theory' assume duplicate accounts, marked by a series of systematic differences. But the various traits are so closely interwoven that one can regard them only as slight alternatives in expression. In the case of the rebellion of Korah, two different records are again supposed, the first bearing upon an opposition of laymen against the civil authority of Moses, headed by Dathan and Abiram; the second referring to a discord between the tribe of Levi and the other tribes, in which Korah takes the principal place. But this supposition is entirely contrary to the text. For not only are the three conspirators acting in company in Nu. xvi. 1–3, where it is said that they contested the entire authority of Moses and Aaron, but also in verses 24 and 27 the three are again mentioned together. Remarkably enough, too, since the critical analysis reserves the ordeal of being swallowed up by the earth for Dathan and Abiram, the text in describing this terrifying event mentions only Korah (see Nu. xvi. 32); Dathan and Abiram are not explicitly indicated as having met with the same fate.

iv. Legal discrepancies. It is argued in the fourth place that the legal portions reveal troublesome discrepancies. For example, according to Nu. xxxv. 13ff., the number of the cities of refuge is fixed at six, whereas Dt. xix. 2, 7 speak of three cities. But in the text of Numbers the cities are specified as three in the land of Canaan and three in Transjordan; and as Moses had already allotted three cities in Transjordan (Dt. iv. 41–43) it is only natural that he orders three cities to be set apart in the land of Canaan proper. Certainly Dt. xix. 8f. provides for the possibility of three more cities should there be a considerable enlargement of the borders of Canaan proper, but this does not affect the situation to which the alleged discrepancy relates.

Another discrepancy is discovered in the laws concerning the great feasts. According to Ex. xxiii. 14ff., xxxiv. 22f., and Dt. xvi. 16 Israel has to celebrate three great festivals—the feast of unleavened bread, the feast of weeks, and the feast of ingathering. Lv. xxiii. 27ff., however, adds to these the day of atonement, from which it is inferred that the Levitical code must originate from a considerably later date. But there is no real inconsistency here if we bear in mind that the laws of Exodus and Deuteronomy are concerned with the obligation of every male Israelite to appear before the Lord three times in the year. No such obligation, however, is mentioned regarding the day of atonement. This fully accounts for the difference.

v. Priests and Levites. Of much more importance is the claim that there is a marked difference between Deuteronomy and the so-called 'Priestly Code' with respect to priests and Levites. Those who support the documentary theory maintain that the Deuteronomic code does not know of any difference between the two categories, and that this difference is of a much later date. But from Dt. xviii it is manifest that this contention is wrong. Verses 3–5 describe 'the priest's due from the people' and verses 6–8 continue 'and if a Levite come from any of thy gates'.

c. The background of the Mosaic law

In 'documentary theory' circles it is regarded as certain that Deuteronomy was written in or about the days of king Josiah. This is the Archimedian point in the theory. But if we carefully peruse the book of Deuteronomy we are struck by the fact that the speaker always, without one single exception, sees the people of Israel as not yet living in Canaan. For example, in xi. 2–7 he deliberately states that he is speaking to those who have personally witnessed the Lord's miracles in Egypt, at the exodus and in the desert. There are also a great many indirect references to the Mosaic age: the historical occurrences mentioned all date from before Moses' death; the description of Canaan as 'a land whose stones are iron, and out of whose hills thou mayest dig brass' (Dt. viii. 9) is intelligible only before Israel entered the Holy Land, since the people never troubled about the mineral treasures hidden in its soil once they had settled in the country. In addition the Deuteronomic code contains provisions which make it absolutely impossible for it to have been drawn up under the conditions and circumstances of the Josianic age. Take, for example, the drastic provisions against idolatry and false prophecy (see Dt. xiii and xviii). How can we imagine that such directions could have been given at a time when the worship of idols had penetrated practically the entire public life of Israel and when false prophets were very numerous and highly influential?

Furthermore, if we examine the Pentateuchal body of laws we discover some unintentional and incidental indications of the real background. We observe, for example, that a rather prominent place is occupied by references to cattle. It is interesting to notice how the tenth commandment as recorded in Exodus explicitly mentions 'ox' and 'ass', whereas the 'field' and other possible references to agricultural life are entirely lacking. But in the Deuteronomic repetition of the Decalogue it is noticeable that the 'field' is added. This points to the moment when Israel was just about to enter Canaan.

Again we find among the materials used for the construction of the tabernacle and its accessories 'fine linen', which was a native Egyptian product, 'goats' hair', which was employed by the nomads to weave the black-coloured covers to their tents, 'badgers' skins,' probably the skins of the seacow, an animal found in the Red Sea, which were used by the inhabitants of the Sinai peninsula for the manufacture of sandals, and 'shittim wood' which, according to the common view of scholars, is the wood of the 'acacia tree' which grows in Egypt and in the Sinai peninsula. (Notice the difference in the case of Solomon's temple, where no shittim wood is used but only cedar and fir or olive wood.) Among the spices for sweet incense we notice 'onycha', a kind of seasnail common in the Red Sea, of which the shell, when burnt, produces a sharp and penetrating smell. There are numerous references to precious stones of which Palestine is entirely devoid, but several kinds of which are found in Egypt and its immediate neighbourhood (the Sinai peninsula and the littoral of the Red Sea). The 'twined linen' for the curtains of the tabernacle again reminds us of Egypt, for the Egyptians were particularly skilful in this art. Passing to the lists of 'clean' and 'unclean' animals we observe that, although most of them are found in Palestine as well as in Egypt and on the Sinai peninsula, some preferentially point to Egypt rather than anywhere else; the 'swine' occurs there in large quantities in humid regions; the 'kite' is exceedingly common in the Nile area and along the littoral of the Red Sea; the 'pelican' is very numerous on the Egyptian lakes; the 'lapwing' or 'hoopoe' is particularly African. Noteworthy is the mention of the 'chamois' in Dt. xiv. 5 (not appearing in the list of Lv. xi), which according to biological information must be the oriental 'moufflon'. This is not found in Egypt, but is a native of Asia Minor, Transcaucasia and Persia and was reported at least thirty years ago in the Arabah in Southern Palestine. The presence of this animal in the Deuteronomic code is in complete harmony with the statement that this code was issued in the land of Moab.

Finally we call attention to the fact that all idolatrous practices which are mentioned in the law belong to the realm of Phoenician and Canaanite religion. We read of molten gods, graven images, sacred pillars, high places, and the hideous custom of letting the children pass through the fire, a Canaanite practice of which the excavations have brought to light the gloomy evidence. The particular practice referred to in Lv. xvii. 7 of sacrificing unto devils may be considered as the result of very old superstition which regarded the desert especially as inhabited by numerous demons in the shape of he-goats.

d. Authorship and date

More could be said. But what has been brought forward may suffice to corroborate the thesis that the law is not the product of widely different epochs in the history of Israel, but does indeed originate from the Mosaic era. This is its own testimony. Time and again we read that the Lord said unto Moses 'Thus shalt thou say unto the children of Israel.' This has not to be taken figuratively, as in the opening words of various ancient Eastern legislations (e.g. the famous code of Hammurabi). The Lord did in fact give His law unto His people through the medium of Moses. This law Moses committed to writing (see Ex. xxiv. 4, xxxiv. 27, and Dt. xxxi. 9, 24) and this may be assumed to cover the entire collection of divine statutes, judgments and ordinances.

Of course it is only natural that a legislator would provide for the writing down of his laws. But Moses wrote more than the laws. In Ex. xvii. 14 the Lord says to him, 'Write this for a memorial in a book, and rehearse it in the ears of Joshua.' This is a command to record God's judgment upon Amalek, involving their total destruction, together with the historical event which gave occasion to the pronouncement, the wanton assault of Amalek on Israel. And as for the book, this may have been combined with the itinerary of which mention is made in Nu. xxxiii. 2. It is surely probable that Moses did not merely note down the various localities which the Israelites passed through, but also recorded the principal events during their journey. Having received his education at the Egyptian court he cannot have been unacquainted with the way in which the Egyptian annals were kept, recording from day to day all events worthy of mention. We hear likewise of a 'Song' of Moses, which he wrote and taught to the children of Israel (Dt. xxxi. 22). This song is preserved in Dt. xxxii. 1–43.

As regards the pre-Mosaic history in the book of Genesis, this was doubtless compiled from previously existing written documents. The various genealogies were almost certainly obtained from such sources. Note, for example, the superscription of the genealogy from Adam to Noah in Gn. v, which reads 'This is the book of the generations of Adam.' The use of the word 'book' shows that this genealogy must have been taken from a written document, and presumably the superscription was the original heading of the document which, with its heading, was incorporated into the book of Genesis. Gn. xiv also is probably based on an old document. The fact that Abram is spoken of as 'the Hebrew' suggests that originally it may even have been non-Israelitic. It certainly seems unlikely that up to the time of Moses the entire history of the antediluvian human race, of the patriarchs, and of Joseph had been handed down by oral tradition only. Much is to be said in favour of the opinion that records of these ancient times belonged to the precious things which the Israelites took with them when they left Egypt.

In one or two places small additions and perhaps slight emendations seem to have been made to the original documents. There is, for example, the account of Moses' own death in Dt. xxxiv and the possibility of the introduction of modern place names to help the reader identify old localities such as the use of the name 'Dan' in Gn. xiv. 14 and 'Raamses' in Ex. i. 11.

Taking all these facts into consideration we find that there are two possible views on this question of authorship, both of which are held among conservative scholars. Some attach great importance to the fact that history knows nothing of any author other than Moses for this section of our Bible. It is allowed that there may have been some slight modification in the copying or translation and perhaps one or two small additions, in particular the account of

Moses' death. But it is concluded that these five books were put into the form in which they have come down to us by Moses himself. This view is well put forward in Dr. O. T. Allis' work *The Five Books of Moses*. A slightly different view is that the book as we know it was compiled by an author at a somewhat later date (probably during the early days of the monarchy) who made use of the extensive Mosaic literature together with some pre-Mosaic material. This thesis is worked out in detail in my own work, *A Short Introduction to the Pentateuch*. It is important to note, however, that in both cases it is maintained that the work was completed under divine inspiration and, as part of the Bible, is God's message to us.

II. JOSHUA TO ESTHER

a. Joshua

The character of the historical literature is determined by its place in God's revelation of His purpose and plan of redemption for mankind. Its aim is to reveal what the Lord has done in His mercy to save sinful man. The Pentateuch, as we have seen, presents us with what we may call the basic revelation, from the creation of the world to the establishing of a divine covenant with Israel, expounding in full the Mosaic legislation on which the covenant is founded. The book of Joshua then shows how the Lord brings the chosen people into the promised land in accordance with that covenant. The history which follows, however, teaches that it was impossible for the law to bring real salvation. Its main lesson for the Christian is that the redemption of sinners can be effected only by the Son of God incarnate. The books of Judges, Samuel and Kings record the continued apostasy of Israel, to which reference is already made in the closing verses of the book of Joshua, where it is said that 'Israel served the Lord all the days of Joshua, and all the days of the elders that overlived Joshua, and which had known all the works of the Lord, that he had done for Israel' (Jos. xxiv. 31). This gives a hint of later days when Israel no longer served the Lord.

b. Judges

The background to the period covered by the book of Judges may be summarized thus: 'The children of Israel forsook the Lord God of their fathers and served the pagan deities of Canaan, Baal and the Ashtaroth. Then the anger of the Lord became hot against Israel and He delivered them into the hands of their enemies round about. Nevertheless the Lord raised them up judges by whom He delivered them out of the hand of their enemies. When, however, the judge was dead, they returned to idolatry and they were again chastised and oppressed' (see, for example, Jdg. ii. 11–23). So the book gives in chapters i—xvi shorter or longer accounts of the activity of twelve judges. In the concluding chapters two appendices present a realistic picture of the deplorable state of affairs during this period of Israelitish history.

c. Ruth

In our English Bible the continuous course of history is then interrupted by the short book of Ruth. In the Hebrew Bible it is not placed here, but forms part of the 'Writings', as the Jews call a separate section (the third and last) of the Old Testament. It describes the history of the Moabite woman Ruth, who becomes the wife of a rich landowner Boaz, one of the forefathers of David. This introduction of a Gentile woman into the holy line of David, from whom the Messiah is to come, demonstrates that the election of Israel does not exclude the heathen absolutely and for ever from the salvation of the Lord. It is impossible to escape the inference that the Saviour will be the Redeemer both of Israel and of the nations.

d. Samuel, Kings and Chronicles

The books of Samuel and Kings narrate the rise of the kingdom, describe its glory during the reigns of David and Solomon, and then recount its decline and fall after the latter's death. After the division of the kingdom under Rehoboam and Jeroboam the parallel history of the kings of Judah and of Israel is given, a record of renewed and almost continuous apostasy, which leads first to the overthrow of the northern kingdom and then to the final catastrophe of the exile in the year 586 B.C. The Chronicler resumes the history from Adam onward. The period up to the death of Saul is dealt with very briefly, little more than genealogy being given. But from this point onwards he gives an account which in many ways is parallel to that provided by the books of Samuel and Kings. But from the division of the kingdom onwards the description of events is limited to the kingdom of Judah. Where the books of Chronicles cover the same series of events as a part of the books of Samuel and Kings, they do not offer a mere literal repetition. In this connection one may compare the various accounts by the four evangelists of our Lord's life on earth. In 'critical' circles many seem to be of the opinion that the Chronicler is not too reliable. But the fact that he sometimes gives a more or less different account of certain occurrences, and that he mentions certain events which are not related in Samuel and Kings or passes over happenings which have been commemorated in these books, proves his unreliability no more than the differences between the evangelists impair their truth and credibility. In particular it has to be noted that the Chronicler is deeply interested in matters of worship, and in this respect provides us with a great many details which are omitted in the earlier books.

For further matters of interest connected with these books see the various Appendices to the Commentaries on Samuel and Kings; also the section on the historical background to the prophetical literature (pp. 46ff.).

e. Ezra and Nehemiah

The capture of Jerusalem and the abduction of the population into Babylonia does not frustrate the redemptive plan of God. The nation from which the Saviour is to proceed is not entirely abandoned and annihilated. There is a return from captivity, as the Chronicler points out in his closing verses, referring to the decree of Cyrus, king of Persia, allowing those of the captives who wished to do so to return to the land of their fathers and to rebuild the Lord's temple in Jerusalem. This restoration is pictured in the books of Ezra and Nehemiah, together with a detailed account of the difficulties encountered by the returned exiles. These books show clearly that even the most severe blow of Jerusalem's ruin and the experiences of the exile have not been able to produce in Israel a faithful surrender to the service of the Lord. So the waiting is for the 'fulness of the time' when God will send forth His Son (Gal. iv. 4, 5).

f. Esther

Finally we have the book of Esther. This brings us a beautifully written and skilfully pictured narrative of what seems to have been the most dangerous menace to Israel's future—her total extermination by the monstrous plan of Haman. But the Lord preserves His people and in so doing secures the fulfilment of the promise of a Messiah given to our first parents in the garden of Eden. Many Old Testament students have seriously disputed the historicity and even the religious character of the book; but there is no sufficient reason to doubt the reality of the facts narrated in it. In particular, as has been observed by competent experts, the author shows a perfect and accurate knowledge of Persian manners and customs. A heinous crime such as that planned by Haman does not seem so impossible after the appalling massacre of European Jews by the German Nazis. Moreover, although it is true that the name of God is not employed, it is utterly impossible to overlook the fact that the book most emphatically proclaims the sovereign rule and providential intervention of the Almighty. And as for the contention that the book is drenched with Jewish chauvinism and fanatical vindictiveness, nothing is further from the truth than this. The simple facts are related objectively, and the attitude of the Jews who did not lay their hands on the spoil of their enemies, although they were entitled to do so, speaks for itself. Who, however, would justly rebuke the author for expressing his satisfaction that exactly in the day that the enemies hoped to have power over the Jews, the contrary was the case and they in fact had rule over those that hated them?

III. THE PLACE OF MIRACLES

Because they relate the history of God's redemptive plan, it is not surprising that the Old

Testament historical books contain a number of miracles. These occur not only in the Pentateuch, but also in the later history. For example, there is the crossing of the river Jordan and the fall of the walls of Jericho related in Joshua, the deeds of Samson described in Judges, and the miracles of the prophets Elijah and Elisha which are recounted at some length in 1 and 2 Kings. Many Old Testament scholars have disputed the historicity of these passages, but their arguments seem to be based chiefly on subjective human judgment. The Lord is a God 'doing wonders' and is not to be thought of as being hemmed in by His own natural laws. Since the redemption of sinful mankind is His greatest wonder of all, may we not then expect to meet with miracles as His plan of redemption is unfolded? There is nothing inconsistent with what we know of the character of God that such signs and manifestations of divine power should occur especially in connection with the great crises in the history of His chosen people. In some cases it may be possible that the events were the result of natural causes; and, indeed, the Bible occasionally indicates that this was so. But even where satisfactory explanations of this kind can be offered, the miracle of the timing of the event has still to be taken into account.

IV. THE HUMAN ELEMENT

A distinctive feature of this historical literature is that it is far from indulging in hero-worship. The men and women belonging to the great cloud of witnesses (Heb. xii. 1) are pictured exactly as they were, with their virtues and faults, their faith and their doubts, their righteousness and their sins. Abraham is sketched not only as the man who believed in the Lord (Gn. xv. 6) but also as one who doubted (cf. Gn. xvii. 17). And although David is described as a 'man after God's own heart', yet his scandalous behaviour in the case of Bath-sheba and his wanton murder of her husband Uriah are fully related and the judgment recorded, 'but the thing that David had done displeased the Lord' (2 Sa. xi. 27). The purpose of this is doubtless to make us acknowledge that the faith of these 'witnesses' is not the fruit of their own excellence, but is indeed the gift of God. And just as the Lord made such weak and imperfect people champions of the faith then, so He can and will do the same with us now in spite of our weaknesses and failure. There is therefore no need for despair.

The human element is also evidenced by the writers' selection and use of existing material. The historical books generally cover a period much longer than the lifetime of one man. It may therefore be safely assumed that their narrative rests partly on earlier oral tradition and partly on the use of written sources. There are numerous references to these sources. In the books of Joshua and of Samuel reference is made to 'the book of Jasher' (Jos. x. 13; 2 Sa. i. 18). The

books of Kings refer once to a 'book of the acts of Solomon' (1 Ki. xi. 41), and continually to 'the book of the chronicles of the kings of Judah' or 'the kings of Israel'. This book is not to be identified with our biblical books of Chronicles, but must be regarded as probably a kind of royal annals. The Chronicler refers to quite a number of sources: 'the chronicles of king David' (1 Ch. xxvii. 24); 'the book of Samuel the seer' (1 Ch. xxix. 29), which doubtless is not the same as our biblical books of Samuel; 'the book of Nathan the prophet' and 'the book of Gad the seer' (1 Ch. xxix. 29); 'the prophecy of Ahijah the Shilonite' (2 Ch. ix. 29); 'the visions of Iddo the seer' (2 Ch. ix. 29, cf. also 2 Ch. xii. 15) or 'the story of the prophet Iddo' (2 Ch. xiii. 22); 'the book of Shemaiah the prophet' (2 Ch. xii. 15); a writing of Isaiah the prophet, the son of Amoz (2 Ch. xxvi. 22) which was almost certainly not the same as the biblical book of Isaiah. There are also frequent references to 'the book of the kings of Judah and Israel', which is not identical with our biblical book of Kings, but may be the same source to which the author of Kings refers repeatedly, i.e. the royal annals.

In a number of cases parts of the employed sources have been literally copied and inserted in the narrative. The following may be taken as samples of such documentary insertion. The distribution of the inheritances of the tribes of Israel in Canaan (Jos. xiv—xix); the lists of David's heroes (2 Sa. xxiii. 8ff.; 1 Ch. xi. 11ff.) and of those who returned from the Babylonian captivity (Ezr. ii; Ne. vii. 6ff.); letters of officials to the Persian king (Ezr. iv. 11ff., v. 6ff.) and of the Persian king to such officials (Ezr. vi. 6ff.). Sometimes the authors of the various books refer to their personal experiences. This occurs of course when they themselves are playing some part in the history which they are recording. As examples of this notice Jos. v. 1 'until we were passed over'; Jos. v. 6 'the land . . . that he would give us'; and in particular Ezr. vii, ix, and the greater part of the book of Nehemiah.

It has been pointed out that Semitic literature in general reveals a manifest tendency towards the formation of larger units. This same tendency can be clearly observed in the historical literature of the Old Testament. So the Lord has employed this natural predisposition of the people of Israel, who were of course a Semitic race, in order to achieve the large body of historical narrative which presents us with a survey of the entire divine redemptive movement from the very beginning of human life unto the restoration of Israel after the exile. In view of their special scope and character it is not at all surprising that these books do not present a full and detailed account of everything that happened at a particular time. Nevertheless we are provided with all the information the Lord deems necessary in order to disclose to us His redemptive purpose. (See also Appendix II to the Commentary on 1 and 2 Samuel, 'The Critical View of Sources and Documents'.)

V. STYLE AND TREATMENT

Some general characteristics of the historical literature may be mentioned here.

First of all we observe how graphic and vivid the method of description generally is. This is such a continuous and regular feature that it is hardly necessary to illustrate it by choosing particular examples. One which is particularly striking is the skilful description of the surprise night attack on the Midianites by Gideon and his three hundred men (Jdg. vii). We can picture the three companies, every man provided with a trumpet, an empty pitcher and a lamp within the pitcher, surrounding the camp of the enemies. Then, all of a sudden, there is a blast of the trumpets, the noise of the broken pitchers, the glare of the lamps, and the shout 'The sword of the Lord, and of Gideon'. A vivid description of the confusion and terror of the Midianite host follows. Other examples are the battle between David and Goliath (1 Sa. xvii), the judgment of Solomon (1 Ki. iii), the ordeal on Mount Carmel (1 Ki. xviii), and the exposure of Haman (Est. vii). The liveliness of the narrative is also marked by a frequent use of direct speech. The motive for action is often reproduced in the form of personal deliberation, e.g. 1 Sa. xxvii. 1. In several cases dialogues are recorded, sometimes rather circumstantially. Notice, for example, that between David and Saul (1 Sa. xxiv), and that between David and the woman of Tekoah (2 Sa. xiv). In this particular connection notice the frequent use of words like 'behold' or 'lo' (e.g. Jos. viii. 20; Jdg. iii. 24; 2 Ki. vii. 6, etc.). In this way the biblical narrator fixes our attention on the events he is placing before our eyes and we become, so to speak, eye-witnesses of these happenings.

We may notice next the remarkable fact that a strict chronological order is not always observed. For example, we are confronted with a rather complicated situation in the book of Judges. If we assume that all the judges enumerated in the book follow each other in chronological order, we reach by counting together the years of their activities a number which is considerably too high to tally with the statement in 1 Ki. vi. 1, that Solomon began to build the house of the Lord in the four hundred and eightieth year after the children of Israel were come out of the land of Egypt. It is therefore necessary to suppose that some periods of oppression and of the activity of certain judges must have been contemporaneous. That this is so is suggested by the way in which Jdg. x. 7 combines the oppression by Philistines and Ammonites, though in the following chapters first the war with the children of Ammon (Jdg. xi and xii), and later on the delivery into the hand of the Philistines (Jdg. xiii. 1) is mentioned.

A further distinctive feature of Old Testament historiography is that, whereas on the one hand we have a certain broadness of delineation, on the other hand there is a striking conciseness. As an example of the detailed approach notice the story of the siege of Samaria in 2 Ki. vii, especially the repetition which seems to serve the purpose of emphasizing that what was predicted actually did come true. An instance of conciseness is found in Jos. x. 18ff. The defeated Canaanite kings hide themselves in a cave at Makkedah. When Joshua is told of it he says 'Roll great stones upon the mouth of the cave, and set men by it for to keep them; and stay ye not, but pursue after your enemies' (Jos. x. 18, 19). Here not a single word is added to indicate that the people obeyed the command of Joshua. Later, after the return from battle, we are told how the cave is opened and the kings are put to death. It is left to the reader to assume that the instruction of Joshua had been carried out.

VI. HOMILETICAL VALUE

The purpose of the historical literature was not only to describe how God has fulfilled His redemptive purpose. The events described happened, as the apostle Paul says, 'for ensamples', and 'they are written for our admonition' (1 Cor. x. 11). The prayer of Elijah is placed before us to assure us that 'the effectual fervent prayer of a righteous man availeth much' (Jas. v. 16); and the trespassings of the people of Israel serve as a warning that we ourselves should not act sinfully (cf. 1 Cor. x. 7–10). So the record of the history must be accepted as the divine word unto us, encouraging us to follow shining examples, or offering serious cautions.

G. CH. AALDERS.

CHRONOLOGICAL TABLE SHOWING THE HISTORY OF ISRAEL FROM ABRAHAM TO SOLOMON

In this table the two widely accepted schemes of dating the early history of Israel are set out side by side together with relevant dates in the history of the surrounding nations. For the earlier chronology see the Introduction to Joshua; for the later see the Introduction to Judges.

Date B.C.	Israel according to the dating of the earlier chronology	The Nations	Israel according to the average dates of the later chronology	Date B.C.
c. 2000	Abraham in Canaan			
c. 1785	Jacob goes to Egypt			
		Hammurabi, king of Babylon		c.1700
		Hyksos' invasion of Egypt 'Era of Tanis' begins		
			Abraham in Canaan	c. 1600
c. 1580		Expulsion of Hyksos		c. 1580 .
		Kassite domination of Babylon		
1501	The oppression in Egypt	Thotmes III		
1447		Amenhotep II		
c. 1440	The exodus from Egypt			
c. 1400	The entry into Canaan		Jacob goes to Egypt	c. 1400
		The 'Amarna' Age		c. 1400–1360
		Hittite Empire at peak of power		1370
		Seti I. King of Egypt	The oppression in Egypt	1319
		Rameses II. King of Egypt		1300
		430th year of 'Era of Tanis'	The exodus from Egypt	c. 1270
			The entry into Canaan	c. 1230
		Fall of Hittite Empire: Trojan War		c. 1200
		Rameses III. King of Egypt		c. 1194
		Philistines arrive in Palestine		1190
		Battle of Kishon		c. 1150
1070	Samuel	Shiloh destroyed by Philistines		c. 1070
1010	David's accession		David's accession	1010
970	Solomon		Solomon	970

Note : *For a further table showing the comparative dates for the kings of Israel and Judah, from the death of Solomon to the fall of Jerusalem, see the Introduction to 1 and 2 Kings*

THE POETRY OF THE OLD TESTAMENT

THE poetry of the Bible is not restricted to those books which we usually distinguish as 'The Poetical Books'—Job, Psalms, the Song of Songs, and Lamentations, with the versified wisdom of Proverbs and Ecclesiastes. The greater part of the Books of the Prophets consists of prophetical oracles in poetic form; and here and there throughout the historical narrative we come upon longer or shorter passages of poetry. These are sometimes said to be derived from collections of poetry like the 'Book of the Wars of Jehovah' (Nu. xxi. 14) or the 'Book of Jashar' (Jos. x. 13; 2 Sa. i. 18; 1 Ki. viii. 12f., LXX). Some writers have gone further, like Eduard Sievers, who in his *Metrische Studien* (1904 and later) traced the elements of an earlier poetical form beneath the prose narratives of such books as Genesis and Samuel (in a manner comparable to the attempt of some classical scholars to detect the elements of Saturnian metre beneath the earlier books of Livy's *Roman History*). But the results of such a study are too disputable to be included in this brief survey.

The New Testament, too, has a greater poetical element than is often realized. The five canticles of Luke's nativity narrative are well known, but the prologue of John is probably also based on a Christian hymn. The researches in particular of John Jebb, Bishop of Limerick (*Sacred Literature*, 1820), and C. F. Burney (*The Poetry of our Lord*, 1925) have shown how many of the Sayings of Jesus were cast in the established forms of Hebrew poetry. Not only did this ensure their being easily memorized, but, as C. H. Dodd points out, 'since Jesus appeared to His contemporaries as a prophet, and prophets were accustomed to give oracles in verse, it is credible that we have here something approaching His *ipsissima verba*' (*History and the Gospel*, 1938, pp. 89f.).

The New Testament Epistles, too, seem to contain some fragments of poetry: early Christian canticles probably underlie the Christological passage in Phil. ii. 6ff., the quotation *Awake thou that sleepest . . .* in Eph. v. 14 (from a primitive baptismal hymn?) and the summary of the *mystery of godliness* in 1 Tim. iii. 16, to mention no more. Then the last book of the New Testament is full of canticles, but there is no space here to discuss 'the metrics of Revelation—a fascinating subject which must be left to future investigators' (C. C. Torrey, *Documents of the Primitive Church*, 1941, p. 212).

I. POETICAL FORMS

The two distinctive features of biblical poetry are rhythm of thought and rhythm of sound. Rhythm of sound we are familiar with in most European poetry, where it commonly appears in a regular pattern of accented and unaccented syllables in the line or group of lines, and also in the form of rhyme. In the poetry of biblical Hebrew, rhythm of sound depends almost entirely on the regular pattern of accented syllables. It is still undecided whether the number of unaccented syllables in the line played any significant part in early Hebrew poetry (as it did in some other early Semitic poetry), and if so, what. A. Bentzen says 'The crucial question of Hebrew metrics is the problem of the *number of permissible unstressed syllables*' (*Introduction to the Old Testament*, i, 1948, p. 121). The sense of satisfaction, however, which our poetry affords by means of rhyme is largely produced in Hebrew poetry by another kind of rhythm altogether—what we have called rhythm of thought or sense. This sense-rhythm is usually known as parallelism, and it appears in early Egyptian, Mesopotamian and Canaanite poetry as well as in Hebrew.

The credit for determining the characteristics of Hebrew poetry belongs largely to two Englishmen—Robert Lowth, Professor of Poetry at Oxford and later Bishop of London, whose epochal *Academic Lectures on the Sacred Poetry of the Hebrews* were published in Latin in 1753, and a later Oxford scholar, George Buchanan Gray, Professor of Hebrew in Mansfield College, whose work on *The Forms of Hebrew Poetry* appeared in 1905.

Hebrew parallelism takes various forms, which can best be explained by means of actual examples. We have, first, complete parallelism, where a line or distich consists of two 'stichoi', each of which exactly balances the other. Such a distich is

> *Israel doth-not know,*
> *My-people doth-not consider* (Is. i. 3),

where *Israel* balances *my people* and *doth not know* balances *doth not consider*. Because the two 'stichoi' are exactly synonymous with each other, each saying the same thing in different words, this form of parallelism is also known as identical parallelism. Another form of complete parallelism is known as antithetic parallelism, because the one 'stichos' gives the obverse of the other. A good example is found in Pr. xv. 20:

> *A-wise son gladdens a-father*
> *And-a-foolish man despises his-mother.*

Yet another kind of parallelism is that known as 'emblematic' parallelism, where one 'stichos' makes a statement in literal terms and the other repeats it in figurative terms. This can be done in various ways; a good example is Ps. ciii. 13:

> As-a-father pities his-children,
> So-Jehovah pities his-fearers.

(Here there are three accented syllables in each 'stichos'.) Or the parallelism may be more elaborate, and take an introverted or chiastic form. Ps. xxx. 8–10 is commonly cited as an example of this:

> To-thee, Jehovah, I-cry; and-to-the-Lord I-make-supplication.
> What-profit (is there) in-my-blood when-I-go-down to-the-pit?
> Shall-the-dust praise-thee? shall-it-declare thy-truth?
> Hear, Jehovah, and-show-me-grace; Jehovah, be-a-helper to-me.

Here 'stichos' 1 is paralleled by 'stichos' 4, and 'stichos' 2 by 'stichos' 3, the accentual pattern being 5 : 4 : 4 : 5. A similar but not identical chiasmus appears in the Sayings of Jesus, e.g. in Mt. vii. 6:

> Give not that which is holy unto the dogs,
> Neither cast ye your pearls before swine,
> Lest they [the swine] trample them under their feet,
> And they [the dogs] turn again and rend you.

Thus far we have quoted examples of complete parallelism, where each unit of thought in one 'stichos' has its counterpart in the other 'stichos', and the parallel 'stichoi' have the same number of accented syllables. But we have also to reckon with incomplete parallelism, where, for example, one of the units of thought in the former 'stichos' has no counterpart in the latter 'stichos'. Take, for example, Ps. i. 5:

> Therefore-the-ungodly shall-not-stand in-the-judgment,
> Nor-sinners in-the-congregation of-the-righteous.

The verb 'shall not stand' in the former 'stichos' has no counterpart in the second 'stichos'. But the number of accented syllables is kept even by the fact that 'judgment' (with one accented syllable) in 'stichos' 1 is balanced by 'congrega-tion of the righteous' (with two accented syllables) in 'stichos' 2. Similarly in Is. i. 3a—

> The-ox knoweth his-owner,
> And-the-ass his-master's crib—

there is nothing in 'stichos' 2 corresponding to 'knoweth' in 'stichos' 1, but compensation is made by having two accented syllables, 'his-master's crib', in the second as against one, 'his-owner', in the first. This phenomenon, called by Gray 'incomplete parallelism with compensa-tion', is quite common in biblical poetry. Occasionally the parallelism is so incomplete that we are left with nothing but compensation, and then we have what Lowth called 'synthetic parallelism', but Gray, less ineptly, 'formal parallelism'. It is, in fact, not parallelism at all; there is only sound-rhythm and no thought-rhythm. An example is Ps. xxvii. 6a:

> But-now my-head shall-be-lifted-up
> Above my-enemies round-about-me.

There we have three accented syllables in each 'stichos', but no parallelism of sense at all.

At other times when the parallelism is in-complete there is no compensation, and thus we get 'stichoi' of unequal length, which can be arranged in regular patterns. One such pattern corresponds roughly to our common metre, where we have alternating 'stichoi' of four and three beats. A good example of this 4 : 3 pattern in the Old Testament is Jeremiah's description of Chaos-come-again (iv. 23–26):

> I-saw the-earth, and-lo waste-and-void,
> And-the-heavens, and-not their-light;
> I-saw the-mountains, and-lo they-were-trembl-ing,
> And-all the-hills moved-lightly.
> I-saw and-lo there-was-no man,
> And-all-birds of-the-heavens had-fled;
> I-saw and-lo the-fruitful-place a-wilderness,
> And-all-its-cities broken-down before-Jehovah.

But a much commoner form of 'incomplete parallelism without compensation' is the 3 : 2 pattern. This pattern has been called the qin'ah or 'dirge' metre, ever since Karl Budde first identified it in the book of Lamentations. Com-pare La. iii. 1:

> I-am-the-man that-hath-seen affliction
> By-the-rod of-his-wrath.

It is by no means confined to this kind of poetry, however; it may serve as the vehicle of joyful trust, as in Ps. xxvii. 1:

> Jehovah is-my-light and-my-salvation;
> Whom shall-I-fear?
> Jehovah is-the-strength of-my-life;
> Of-whom shall-I-be-afraid?

And C. F. Burney (op. cit., pp. 137ff.) has traced it in several of the Sayings of Jesus in the Gospels.

One form of parallelism which we have not mentioned yet is what is called step-parallelism or climactic parallelism; it is found 'where one member (or part of a member) in one line is repeated in the second, and made the starting-point for a fresh step' (T. H. Robinson, The Poetry of the Old Testament, 1947, p. 23). A good example is found in the opening 'stichoi' of Ps. xxix, with the step-effect produced by the repeated 'Give to Jehovah'; another is provided by Ps. xcii. 9—

> For-lo thine-enemies, Jehovah,
> For-lo thine-enemies shall-perish;
> All-workers of-iniquity shall-be-scattered—

which is of special interest because it shows so close a similarity in form to a passage from the Baal epic discovered among the Ras Shamra tablets (C. H. Gordon, Ugaritic Handbook, Text 68, lines 8f.):

> Lo thine-enemies O-Baal,
> Lo thine-enemies thou-shalt-slay,
> Lo thou-shalt-destroy thy-foes.

(W. F. Albright refers to this parallel in The Archaeology of Palestine, 1949, p. 231. On the same page he quotes a tristich from the Aqhat or

Dan'el epic which in language rather than form reminds one of Ps. xxi. 4:

> *Ask-thou life Aqhat my-boy,*
> *Ask-thou life and-I'll-give-it-thee,*
> *Life-immortal and-I'll-grant-it-thee.*)

The passage from Ps. xcii. 9 is noteworthy not only as an example of step-parallelism but also because the pattern takes the form of a tristich and not a distich. The rhythmical scheme is 3 : 3 : 3. Another tristich pattern occurs in Ps. xxiv. 7–10:

> *Lift-up O-gates your-heads,*
> *And-lift-up O-doors of-eternity,*
> *And-shall-enter the-king of-glory . . .*

Here we have a set of four tristichs, forming two short strophes.

The presence of strophes in biblical poetry has been much discussed, and certainly a strophic arrangement can be detected here and there. A repeated refrain is good evidence for a strophic arrangement. Such a refrain we get in Pss. xlii and xliii (originally one psalm), showing that the strophes end respectively at verses 5 and 11 of Ps. xlii and verse 5 of Ps. xliii. Another example is the oracle in Is. ix. 8—x. 4 (with Is. v. 25ff.), with its refrain 'For all this his anger is not turned away, but his hand is stretched out still'. Further examples of strophic arrangement have been recognized in the Sayings of Jesus.

Strophic arrangement is also involved in the acrostic schemes sometimes found in biblical poetry; thus in a purely formal way Ps. cxix inevitably consists of twenty-two strophes of eight 'distichs' each.

II. NON-BIBLICAL PARALLELS

We have already quoted parallels between certain poetical passages from the Old Testament and passages from the Canaanite poems discovered at Ras Shamra. The decipherment and study of the Ras Shamra documents (which are dated c. 1400 B.C.) have thrown a great deal of light on the circumstances of early Semitic poetry. For one thing, these documents have completely falsified Gunkel's theory that the longer poetical passages in the Bible are relatively late, since (as he thought) a ballad period of considerable duration came first. The Baal epic discovered at Ras Shamra, for example, had not less than 5,000 lines. That the Song of Deborah (Jdg. v) is practically simultaneous with the incidents it celebrates (c. 1150 B.C.) has been generally agreed, but one can trace a tendency now, under the impact of the Ras Shamra evidence, to agree that other poems to which the Bible ascribes an early date do in fact belong to the period in which the Bible places them. Albright argues, for example, that in their original forms such poems as the Song of Moses in Ex. xv and the oracles of Balaam in Nu. xxiii—xxiv may well have been composed in the thirteenth century B.C.

Among other contacts between biblical and non-biblical poetry we should note in particular the numerous resemblances between the hundred-and-fourth psalm and the Egyptian king Akhnaton's *Hymn to Aton* (c. 1377–1360 B.C.). But alongside all these and other resemblances we must mark the divergences; the stamp of Israel's covenant-monotheism imparts a basic religious uniqueness to all the poetry (as to all the prose) of the Old Testament.

III. TEXT AND EXEGESIS

Attempts are commonly made to emend the text of poetical parts of the Old Testament to make them conform to some metrical scheme. In view of the wide variation of metrical arrangements which present themselves to us, however, this is a criterion for establishing the text which should be used with great caution. As it is, one scholar's emendations based on this principle rarely win the approval of other scholars. It may be conceded that where we have an almost complete alphabetic acrostic we can be reasonably sure that it was originally complete, but that in itself does not guarantee that any particular emendation aimed at restoring the complete acrostic is the right one. As for restoring the original text by regard to the number of accented syllables in the 'stichoi' of a poetical passage, we have given an example above of yielding to this temptation, in the citation from Je. iv. 23–26. The closing words of the passage as we have it in the received text ('and before the fierceness of his anger') were omitted from our citation, as they could not be accommodated to the 4 : 3 metre and were therefore regarded as a prose expansion. But there is no assurance that the passage did in fact originally conform entirely to the 4 : 3 pattern.

On the other hand, a recognition of the basic forms of biblical poetry, particularly the forms of parallelism, makes an important contribution to accurate interpretation, as it will prevent us, for example, from thinking that an author is making two separate statements when he is actually saying the same thing twice.

But what we should emphasize above everything else is that the study of these poetical forms, whatever its limitations may be, and into whatever other fields it may lead us, is primarily important because of such help as it can give us in understanding the text of Scripture better. 'After all', as T. H. Robinson reminds us in his study of this subject (*op. cit.*, p. 46), 'it is sound exegesis which should be the final aim of all other branches of Biblical study'—and therefore of this branch too.

F. F. BRUCE.

THE WISDOM LITERATURE OF THE OLD TESTAMENT

THE canonical Wisdom literature of the Old Testament consists of the books of Job, Proverbs and Ecclesiastes, together with a number of Psalms—e.g. Pss. i, x, xiv, xix, xxxvii, xlix, lxxiii, xc, cxii. In the Apocrypha, Wisdom literature is represented chiefly by the book of Ecclesiasticus (The Wisdom of Jesus the son of Sirach, written in Hebrew c. 200 B.C. and translated into Greek by the author's grandson in 132 B.C.) and the book of Wisdom (probably written by an Alexandrian Jew early in the first century A.D.). The book of Baruch and the Fourth Book of Maccabees have also their contribution to make to the Wisdom literature of the Apocrypha.

The practical wisdom of the ancients takes the form firstly of popular proverbs (Heb. *mashal*, plural *meshalim*) which express in pithy terms certain observed regularities, whether in the external world of nature or in human behaviour ('A red sky at night is the shepherd's delight'; 'There are none so deaf as those who will not hear', and the like). A more developed form is the riddle or parable. The riddle of Samson (Jdg. xiv. 12ff.) and the fables of Jotham (Jdg. ix. 7ff.) and Jehoash (2 Ki. xiv. 9) come to mind as well-known examples; the parable, of course, reaches its perfection in the Gospels.

A further stage is reached when men begin to reflect upon the phenomena of nature and life, and come to realize that the popular generalizations are very often inadequate to cover all the facts. Problems like the suffering of the righteous and the meaning of life engage men's thoughts and are grappled with in such works as Job and Ecclesiastes and the Problem Psalms.

True wisdom (Heb. *ḥokhmah*), to the Hebrew thinkers, was not simply intellectual speculation. It was practical in the best sense: it had a very real moral and religious content. 'The fear of Jehovah is the beginning of wisdom'; the truly wise man (Heb. *ḥakham*) is he who views all life in a spirit of reverence towards God. Contrariwise the fool (Heb. *nabal*) is the man devoid of moral and religious sensibilities; when he says in his heart 'There is no God', he is not being a 'free-thinker' but behaving as if there were no God.

I. THE WISDOM MOVEMENT

The first thing to notice is that the Wisdom literature of the Old Testament is not something by itself. It is rather the expression of a moral and intellectual movement dating very early in the history of Hebrew religion. The Wisdom Books tell the story of earnest seekers after truth, who wrestled with problems both old and new. In the quest after reality we are indebted to thinkers of all races. This direction of the human mind 'was not peculiar to the mind of Israel. In 1 Ki. iv. 30 it is said that "Solomon's wisdom excelled the wisdom of all the children of the east country, and all the wisdom of Egypt. For he was wiser than all men: than Ethan the Ezrahite, and Heman, and Chalcol, and Darda, the sons of Mahol"; and in Obadiah, verse 8, we read, "Shall I not in that day . . . destroy the wise out of Edom, and understanding out of the mount of Esau?" with which may be compared Je. xlix. 7: "Is wisdom no more in Teman? is counsel perished from the prudent? is their wisdom vanished?" This wisdom of the Hebrews and other oriental nations has been compared, by those who have examined its operations and results, to the philosophy of other nations' (A. B. Davidson, *Biblical and Literary Essays*, 1903, p. 24).

Of course there is nothing surprising in finding the observed generalizations of everyday experience repeated in the proverbial lore of many nations. 'Even a fool, when he holdeth his peace, is counted wise: when he shutteth his lips, he is esteemed as prudent' (Pr. xvii. 28)—that is something which most people have observed, and we do not think of borrowing in either direction when we find the same proverb in Sanskrit literature in this form: 'Even a fool, covered with fine clothes, is fair in the assembly up to a point; yea, a fool is fair so long as he utters no word'.

But it is not simply in these generalizations that we can trace similarities to biblical Wisdom; Egypt, Mesopotamia and (at a later period) Greece provide us with more far-reaching parallels. Just as most of the other literary forms of the Old Testament can be paralleled from other literature of antiquity, so too Wisdom literature was not restricted to Israel. In Egypt, for example, we have Imhotep—priest, physician and architect—famed as the author of proverbs as early as the opening years of the Third Dynasty (c. 2700 B.C.), while two or three centuries later the maxims of Ptah-hotep constitute, as Breasted put it, 'the earliest formulation of right conduct to be found in any literature' (*Dawn of Conscience*, p. 129). The downfall of the Old Kingdom (c. 2200 B.C.) inspired other sages with a more pessimistic view of life, as they reflected on the vanity of material fortune; but one of these, Ipuwer, looks beyond the present evils to the advent of a righteous king who will bring rest to men as a shepherd to his sheep and who is described in terms not unlike those of the seventy-second Psalm and some other messianic passages of the Old Testament (cf. E. J. Young, *My Servants the Prophets*, 1952, pp. 200ff.).

The closest approximation that Egypt shows to biblical Wisdom literature, however, is in the sayings of Amenemope, a wise man of the Twenty-First Dynasty (c. 1150–930 B.C.). Amenemope was more or less contemporary with Solomon, and his Wisdom presents some remarkable parallels to the book of Proverbs, especially to Pr. xxii. 17—xxiii. 12. In one place, indeed, Amenemope's Wisdom has been thought to illuminate the text of the biblical book: namely, in Pr. xxii. 20, where the Hebrew word *sh-l-sh-m* may be vocalized not *shalishim* ('excellent things') nor *shilshom* ('heretofore') but *sheloshim* ('thirty'). Amenemope's Wisdom consists of thirty sections, and in one place it refers to them in the words: 'Consider these thirty chapters.' The verse in Proverbs is therefore held to be a parallel (Have I not written for thee *thirty* things in counsels and knowledge?). (So *The Bible in Basic English* and RSV: 'Have I not written for you thirty sayings?') But the emendation is not certain, and in any case there are other ways of accounting for the undoubtedly striking parallels than by the supposition of direct borrowing either way.

To some of the other forms of Wisdom literature in the Bible we find parallels more readily offered by Mesopotamia. The problem of the righteous sufferer, which finds classic expression in the book of Job, was treated in several Mesopotamian works, but notably in the composition called *Ludlul bel nemeqi* ('I will praise the lord of wisdom'). It describes the case of a man whose fortunes were very similar to Job's, although the treatment is much inferior to that of the Hebrew book. The pessimistic strain in Ecclesiastes, again, seems to echo passages from the Gilgamesh epic and from the 'Dialogue of Pessimism' in which a Babylonian master and his slave conclude that no values exist—in short, that all is vanity.

Of course, such pessimism is not restricted to any one age or country; and some of the most striking parallels to Ecclesiastes are to be found in the writings of Greek thinkers like Theognis (c. 500 B.C.). Many of these parallels have been collected by H. Ranston in *Ecclesiastes and the Early Greek Wisdom Literature* (1925), but here again we should not be too hasty in assuming that the very considerable similarity in thought and expression implies direct literary dependence. Like causes produce like effects all over the world. 'The Wisdom Literature of both Egypt and Mesopotamia', wrote Sir Frederic Kenyon, 'goes back to much earlier periods than the corresponding Hebrew books. The Hebrew writers were engaging in a kind of literature common to Eastern countries, and were no doubt influenced by the productions current in the countries to east and west of them; but their writings are not direct copies. They are original compositions in the same vein, and in their best portions, such as the praise of Wisdom as the mouthpiece of God, they reach a higher plane of thought and of emotional expression than their neighbours and predecessors' (*The Reading of the Bible*, 1944, p. 52).

In spite of numerous similarities, the Hebrew Wisdom literature bears unmistakable features which distinguish it from the Wisdom literature of other nations. These distinctive features are the product of the unique revelatory character of Hebrew religion, with its emphasis on one living and true God. Wisdom in the biblical literature is divine wisdom; in the deepest things of human need the clearest and surest light comes from the nation to which God chose to make Himself known.

The Hebrew Wisdom movement was closely associated with the name of Solomon, who became the royal patron of the school. 'Historical probability combines with trustworthy tradition in ascribing to the period of Solomon's reign a remarkable development of the national character. This was manifested in the various departments of commerce, art and literature in all that we call civilization; and whatever the extent of Solomon's extant writings, over and above those Proverbs "which the men of Hezekiah, king of Judah, copied out", it is clear that it is from his time that the strain of teaching known by the specific name of "Wisdom" takes its rise and derives much of its character' (W. T. Davison, *The Wisdom Literature of the Old Testament*, 1894, p. 13). Thus Solomon may be called the father of Hebrew Wisdom literature, although here and there there may have been fragmentary examples before his time.

II. THE WISDOM TEACHERS

It appears that a class of wise men (Heb. *hakhamim*) arose among the Jews, who transmitted their wisdom (*hokhmah*) from generation to generation. These *hakhamim* had their schools, disciples, discipline, doctrines and collections of wisdom (Pr. i. 6, xxii. 17; cf. xxiv. 23; Ec. ix. 17; xii. 11). They were recognized as a definite group or guild in the prophetic age, as may be inferred from a direct reference in Je. xviii. 18: 'The law shall not perish from the priest, nor counsel from the wise, nor the word from the prophet'. Here priest, wise man and prophet are distinguished as three separate types. 'Each of the three classes had its appropriate function, the priest to interpret the Law, the prophet to declare God's will and nature, the sage to give practical advice on the problems of everyday life. Their respective spheres were worship and ritual, theology and ethics; at least that distinction, as between the prophet and the sage, is broadly true. For while the prophets were practical reformers and had brought their message about God down into the realm of individual and social conduct, they, in doing so, had always moved, to begin with, on the high levels; it was from the starting-point of great principles that they passed to the assertion of ideals of moral conduct. The sage was more detailed and commonplace; he moved on a lower level, and his message for the most part was concerned with the ordinary duties of everyday life. The prophet was the man for a crisis, and the divine message which it called for he uttered with passionate conviction. The sage was a moralist, watching with shrewdness the happenings of life about him and drawing lessons from them which, with worldly wisdom, he expressed in the polished aphorisms and prudential maxims of the calm and leisured thinker' (A. Lewis Humphries, *The Old Testament and its Message*, pp. 83f.).

The following points about these sages or teachers of *ḥokhmah* are specially to be noted:—

1. They transcended the limits of nationalism. They were in the best sense the humanists of the Hebrew race and embraced knowledge from whatever source. Unlike the priest and prophet they had in their prime no tendencies to racial particularism. Only in the post-canonical Wisdom literature does this spirit begin to appear, and Wisdom is identified more narrowly with the Torah.

2. They became authors. They developed literary ability and enshrined their wisdom in a number of remarkable works.

3. They were eminently practical. Theirs was not philosophy for philosophy's sake. All their thinking was harnessed to the naked facts of daily existence. They sought a way of life, not a mere solution of speculation.

4. They continued the function of revelation when the voice of the prophet was stilled and the significance of the priest had lost its inspiration in Israel.

III. THE WISDOM DOCTRINE

The teaching of the *ḥakhamim* is the product of agonizing thought as pressing problems were nobly faced. Revelation of the truth, or as much of the truth as the age was able to bear, came in this way. The wise men of Israel have a place in God's redemptive movement within human history which distinguishes them from the sages of other nations. (For the bearing of the Wisdom literature on theology and the history of religion see the Kerr Lectures for 1933–6 by Professor O. S. Rankin, *Israel's Wisdom Literature*.)

Among the earliest examples of the work of the Hebrew sages are the Problem Psalms. Two types are discernible in these poems and are quite characteristic of the whole school. There is the calmer philosophical type (Pss. xiv, xix, xc) which contemplates the godless world made by a good God, the glory of the cosmos and the conscience and the mystery of mortal yet immortal man. Here the soul of man stands naked in the presence of the great and grim realities of life. Again, there is the type where the sage wrestles with doubt, his pulse agitated by fear (Pss. x, xxxvii, xlix, lxxiii). As the psalmist considers the boastful wicked, he cries out in distress: 'Why standest thou afar off, O Lord? Why hidest thou thyself in times of trouble?' The prosperity of the evildoers and the adversity of the righteous are recurring themes in the *ḥokhmah* literature. Nor are the problems left suspended in mid-air. A good way is travelled toward solution. Ps. xxxvii answers 'the prosperity of the wicked does not last'. Ps. xlix declares 'death brings the evildoer to condign punishment'. Ps. lxxiii concludes more positively that 'true prosperity belongs alone to the godly'.

The burning question of the book of Job is 'Why do the innocent suffer?' The traditional answer is first given to the suffering patriarch that sin and suffering are invariably wedded together. The divine principle of the moral government of the universe is retribution. Sin and suffering are without exception cause and effect. To repudiate this hard truth, not in its essence but in its inflexible incidence, Elihu is introduced into the argument. He advances with the solution that suffering is not penal but disciplinary, not given to punish but sent to profit. The teaching goes a stage further when Job comes into the divine presence and contents himself that the answer rests with God and all is well.

That the Wisdom of the inspired writers of the Old Testament was not the mere plaything of the mind, not airy speculation but most practical, with a direct bearing upon daily life, is the special contribution of the book of Proverbs. Qoheleth (Ecclesiastes, or The Preacher) corrects in its doctrine the materialism, fatalism and pessimism of its age. The three ways essayed in its day and all down the generations are exposed in all their futility as answers to the problem of 'how to be happy in the world as it is'—the ways of knowledge, pleasure, and the power of money. The teaching of the book is that there is one way, the way of Wisdom.

In all their attempts to deal with the most persistent problems of life, the Wisdom books do not call in a new world to redress the balance of the old. The examination is restricted almost entirely within the limits of the present earthly life. Only when we come to the relatively late book of Wisdom do we find the doctrine of immortality freely invoked.

The concept of divine Wisdom played no small part in preparing the way for the coming of Christ. Behind the Logos doctrine of the Johannine prologue, for example, we can see the personalized Wisdom of Old Testament times, especially in the famous passage in Pr. viii. 22ff. where Wisdom sits as God's assessor at the creation of the world. In this and other ways the Wisdom movement led on to the advent of Him 'who of God is made unto us wisdom'. The *ḥokhmah* books, when illuminated by the incarnation of Jesus Christ and viewed accordingly in the light of their end, may be accepted as presenting the Personal Wisdom of God and thus setting the stage for Him who declared 'I am the way, the truth, and the life'—the final solution to the problems of man and the world.

F. F. BRUCE.
F. DAVIDSON.

THE PROPHETICAL LITERATURE OF THE OLD TESTAMENT

THE books of the later prophets make up together about a third of the Old Testament. They contain the teaching and, in certain cases, give glimpses of the personal history of prophets who appeared at intervals, singly or contemporaneously, from the eighth to the fourth century B.C. This period is distinguished by a widespread development in human thought and the rise of outstanding teachers in different parts of the world. When Zephaniah was foretelling the judgment which was soon to overtake a paganized Jerusalem, and Nahum was graphically depicting the ruin of Nineveh, Zoroaster, according to a probable reckoning, was diligently employed in reforming the old Iranian religion. The years of Jeremiah's and Ezekiel's insistence upon pure worship, righteous conduct and individual responsibility saw Confucius giving classical expression to the orthodox religion of China, and Siddartha, in India, laying the foundations of Buddhism. By the time of the post-exilic prophets, the ancient Greek religion was in the melting pot; the Ionian philosophers were putting forward new views of the universe, and Attic tragedy was powerfully portraying the mystery of human life, in relation to a force that makes for righteousness.

It was also an age of great political upheavals. Israel as a kingdom ceased to exist; Assyria fell; Babylon passed into Persian control; Jerusalem was destroyed and restored. Greece won her gallant struggle with the ruthless invader, only to be crippled by internal strife. In Italy, Roman influence was rapidly extending. Seldom, indeed, has an epoch been so rich in great soldiers, brilliant statesmen and penetrating thinkers. Yet none of its famous men had a more honourable rôle than the prophets of Israel and Judah, nor did any bequeath to future generations a legacy of higher worth.

I. THE PROPHETIC CALLING

The preachers of the eighth century were not the first to be called prophets. They stand in a long succession of witnesses beginning with Abram, and are not, in their teaching, innovators to the extent which is sometimes supposed. They were indebted to the revealed truth of preceding ages, and especially to the teaching of Moses, on whose foundation they all built. Like him, each of them was 'called' by God and supernaturally fitted for His service.

The different names given to the prophet in Scripture throw light upon his character and the nature of his work. He is described as a 'man of God', implying that he was more closely related to God than others and indicating also that he was a man of righteous character. A second designation is 'servant of Jehovah', denoting that the prophet was specially commissioned by God to discharge certain duties for Him. The type of service in which he was engaged is brought out in a third phrase: 'messenger of Jehovah'. His chief task was the conveying of messages from God to men. His words were authoritative because they were uttered in the name of the Lord. A fourth term, 'man of the Spirit', occurs in Ho. ix. 7 (mg.). It draws attention to the source of the prophet's equipment and power. Yet another aspect of his work, that of explaining the acts of God to men, is aptly brought to view by a fifth term, 'interpreter'.

In addition to all these, three names occur which show how the prophet received his message and how, in the first instance, he made it known. Two of them, *roeh* and *chozeh*, are translated 'seer'. The prophet saw things to which other men were blind. But this was not due merely to poetic insight, nor to the penetrative power of a strong and exercised intellect. Neither did it depend on the use of means similar to those employed in heathen divination, nor on any occult practices. It resulted entirely from a supernatural gift, not always at the prophet's command. What he saw was revealed to him by God. He was not, however, wholly passive. The use of his ordinary faculties was not suspended, and a word, associated with those rendered 'seer', meaning a 'watchman', is a reminder that there was effort on the prophet's part. Prayer was doubtless a frequent preparation for the 'prophetic state' (Dn. ix. 3).

The third of the words commonly translated prophet, *nabi*, appears to emphasize the fact that the prophet was a 'spokesman'. What he saw, when under the special influence of the Holy Spirit, he was moved to declare, and was later enabled to record accurately by the same gracious power, his own individuality meanwhile being allowed free play.

Unlike Elijah and Elisha, the later prophets were not miracle workers. They relied entirely on the spoken and written word, enforced now and then by a symbolical action (e.g. Je. xxviii. 10). While inseparably linked to the past, they were keenly alive to the circumstances and tasks of their own times. Their writings reflect the political, economic, social, moral and religious life of the age to which they ministered, and so supplement the brief accounts of successive reigns given in the books of Kings and Chronicles.

II. THE HISTORICAL BACKGROUND

During the centuries covered by the activities of the literary prophets, the history of Israel and Judah was largely affected by the ambitions and policies of three great foreign powers. Assyria, Babylon and Persia became, in turn, their overlords, so that the main events may be grouped according to the period of supremacy to which they belong. Dates are in some cases necessarily approximate. Cf. the chronology given in the Introduction to Kings.

a. The Assyrian Period

For the greater part of the reign of Jeroboam II (783–743 B.C.) Assyria was fully occupied with her own affairs. The smaller nations were thus left free to pursue their respective policies unhindered. Jeroboam again extended the territory of the northern kingdom to the limits of the kingdom of David, Judah being excepted. This success, which had been foretold by the prophet Jonah (2 Ki. xiv. 25), was followed by years of great material prosperity, as may be inferred from the language of Amos and Hosea. These prophets also make clear that the period was characterized by spiritual declension and moral corruption.

In 745 B.C. Tiglath Pileser III began to extend the influence of Assyria by a new series of military campaigns and soon made his pressure felt in Western Asia. Both Amos and Hosea predicted that, on account of her sins, Israel would fall a prey to Assyria. Amos prophesied the ruin of the royal house, and his words were fulfilled when Zachariah, Jeroboam's successor, was assassinated by the usurper Shallum, after a six months' reign. With the passing of Jehu's dynasty the position of Israel rapidly deteriorated. Five kings ascended the throne and vanished within a score of years. At the end of one month Shallum was slain by Menahem, who succeeded in retaining the crown for ten years, although for about half that time he paid tribute to Assyria. The accession of his son Pekahiah, however, was the occasion of a reaction. He was killed by Pekah, who, being opposed to Assyria, formed an alliance with Syria and attacked Judah, possibly because she would not join the alliance. It was at this time that Isaiah foretold the downfall of Samaria and Damascus. Contrary to the advice of the prophet, Ahaz, king of Judah, appealed to Assyria for aid and Tiglath Pileser III responded by overrunning a large part of the land of Israel, carrying away the population from the conquered territory and reducing the northern kingdom to narrow limits. Pekah was murdered by Hoshea, under whom Israel became once more a tributary of Assyria. In 732 B.C. Damascus was overthrown by Assyria and ten years later, in 722 B.C., a similar catastrophe overtook Samaria. Hoshea, encouraged by Egypt, rebelled against Assyria, but the attempt to regain liberty failed. The city was encircled by the army of Shalmaneser V, and, after

three years, capitulated to his successor Sargon II. The survivors were deported and the northern kingdom ceased to exist.

Like Israel, in Jeroboam's reign, Judah under Uzziah had taken advantage of respite from external interference to develop her military strength and expand her trade. Her efforts were highly successful, although, in her case also, material prosperity led to forgetfulness of God. Isaiah, whose call to service in the year of Uzziah's death is recorded in Is. vi, gives a vivid picture of the social and religious evils of his successor Jotham's reign. Because Ahaz, who followed him as king, did not accept the guidance of the prophet at the time of the Syro-Ephraimite war, Judah became a vassal state, with further detrimental effects to the religious life of the nation.

For a time, Hezekiah continued the submissive policy of Ahaz, his father, and when Egypt sought to foster a revolt among the smaller states, Isaiah successfully opposed alliance with her and foretold her downfall. He did associate, however, with Merodach-Baladan the Babylonian usurper, after which Isaiah prophesied the Babylonian captivity (see 2 Ki. xx. 12–21). Then, on the death of Sargon II in 705 B.C., Hezekiah rebelled against Assyria and attacked the Philistines, who were her tributaries. The resulting invasion of Sennacherib terminating in the miraculous deliverance of Jerusalem produced a profound feeling of confidence in the Lord's favour towards the Holy City. During the crisis Isaiah encouraged the king and people to trust in the Lord. But later he reproved the nation for not giving the glory to God who had overthrown their enemy. The reformation of Hezekiah, carried out in all likelihood under the influence of Isaiah and Micah, his provincial contemporary, rid the land of practices introduced by his father Ahaz (see 2 Ki. xvi. 2–4, 10–16). His son Manasseh, however, became a vassal of Assyria and sponsored a great return to heathenism, accompanied by persecution and acts of violence, which made his long reign most miserable in the experience of Judah.

Zephaniah, who prophesied in the reign of Manasseh's son Amon, gives us a cross-section of the society of the time. At the end of two years Amon was assassinated by what was, perhaps, a reforming party. Meanwhile, the power of Assyria was beginning to show signs of decline. Towards the end of Ashurbanipal's reign (668–630 B.C.) the king's attention was so taken up by events in the east and south, where Scythian invasions were becoming an increasing menace, that Egypt was able to strengthen her position as an independent kingdom. Then after the death of the Assyrian king, in 625 B.C., Nabopolassar founded the Neo-Babylonian Empire. One result of these events was that in Judah, Josiah, the son of Amon, was able to carry out unhindered the programme of reform to which he was prompted by the book found in the temple, and to extend his activities to

Samaria. As Nahum foretold, Nineveh was conquered by the Babylonians and the Medes in 612 B.C. Assyrian power was hopelessly broken and for the next century the dominating influence was that of Babylon.

b. The Neo-Babylonian Period

In 608 B.C. Pharaoh Necho made an expedition to the Euphrates and Josiah, fearing perhaps for the liberty of his kingdom, went against him and fell in battle at Megiddo. The subsequent history of Judah bears a strange resemblance to that of Israel in her last years. Only one of the four remaining kings of Judah died a natural death. As in the case of Israel, the prophets Hosea and Isaiah, one within and the other without the kingdom, had kept in touch with the closing scenes, so their counterparts in Judah's final struggle, Jeremiah and Ezekiel, brought God's message to the people.

After the death of Josiah, his son Jehoahaz was placed on the throne. His reign, however, was very short. At the end of three months he was deposed and taken captive by Pharaoh Necho who gave the throne to his brother Jehoiakim. Jeremiah contrasts this ruler's injustice and greed with his father's righteous conduct towards the poor and needy (Je. xxii. 13–19). From his words it appears that in this reign also there was a heathen reaction on a large scale. The great reformation had left the heart of the nation unchanged and Egypt, being supreme, may have influenced the worship of those anxious to stand well with her.

The year 605 B.C. saw the overthrow of Necho at Carchemish in battle with the Babylonians. The subjection of Judah followed and for three years Jehoiakim paid homage to Nebuchadnezzar, the son of Nabopolassar. Judah then rebelled, but before Nebuchadnezzar could arrive to deal with the situation Jehoiakim died and was succeeded by his son Jehoiachin. Three months later, in 597 B.C., he surrendered to Nebuchadnezzar and was carried captive to Babylon, along with the most influential of the people. He remained in prison for thirty-five years.

His surrender prolonged the life of Jerusalem by ten years. Mattaniah, the uncle of the captive king, was made king by Nebuchadnezzar, who altered his name to Zedekiah. In 594 B.C. envoys arrived from the surrounding small states to gain support for a common revolt. This gave occasion to the dispute between Jeremiah, who was opposed to joining the revolt, and Hananiah, who favoured it (Je. xxviii. 1–17). The movement came to nothing, but on the accession of Pharaoh Hophra a rebellion, with his support, led to another siege of Jerusalem. Pharaoh was defeated by Nebuchadnezzar's army; and in 586 B.C., after eighteen months' stubborn resistance, the city was taken and the majority of the survivors deported.

Among those left in the land was Jeremiah, who was liberated by the Babylonians because he had favoured surrender (see Je. xxxix. 1–14). The governor Gedaliah set up by Nebuchadnezzar failed, however, to maintain peace and order. He was assassinated by a band of conspirators led by Ishmael (Je. xli. 2), who fled to the king of Ammon. The rest of the people, led by Johanan, fled to Egypt, taking Jeremiah with them. There they settled in the frontier towns and speedily fell away from the worship of Jehovah. The destruction of Jerusalem led to much confusion of thought. When Jeremiah protested against the worship of the queen of heaven among the Jews in Egypt, the women replied that they could not cease to worship her because things had fared ill with them since their fathers had abandoned that practice.

Of the earlier captives who were carried to Babylon, Daniel and his companions rose to eminence at the court, while remaining loyal to Jehovah. Some infer from two passages in Ezekiel (xiv. 14, 20) that Daniel's history was familiar and his example an inspiration to others of the exiles. (But see notes *ad loc.*)

The book of Ezekiel provides an illuminating picture of a larger group of Jewish captives who had been carried away with Jehoiachin and were settled at a place called Tel-abib. The prophet was a member of this colony. It is evident from Jeremiah's letter to them (Je. xxix) that they enjoyed a large amount of freedom. They probably had special quarters or territory assigned to them and were not prisoners in the strict sense. Their own elders organized their social and religious life. They engaged freely in trade and, as the contributions made later towards the temple at Jerusalem show, prospered exceedingly in the land of 'traffic and merchants'. In addition, their gain on the religious side was vast. Remote from Canaan, they no longer felt the fatal fascination of its Baals. Nothing could now be gained by worshipping the conquered gods of Assyria and Egypt. Under the powerful teaching of Ezekiel they withstood the appeal of the gods of Babylon and turned more earnestly to the God of their fathers. Sacrifice could not be offered, but prayer might. The keeping of the sabbath became their badge. Regular reading of the Scripture was practised, and probably in these years the synagogue, which was to become such a powerful force in the dissemination of truth, had its origin.

Nebuchadnezzar died in 561 B.C. The next three kings of Babylon reigned only for a few years each. It is thought that the last of them, Nabonidus, may have quarrelled with the powerful priesthood and retired to Arabia. His son Belshazzar was made co-regent. Some years earlier, Cyrus, the ruler of Shushan, a small province in Elam, revolted from Astyages, king of Media, and embarked on a career of conquest. His meteoric rise to power was anxiously watched by Lydia, Babylonia and Egypt, who formed an alliance against him. Croesus, king of Lydia, however, foolishly encountered him alone, and in 546 B.C., Sardis his capital was captured and his kingdom conquered. Cyrus then turned to Babylon, which submitted without fighting in 539 B.C. The military skill, character, clemency and considerateness of Cyrus stirred the imagination of ancient writers. With his attaining to imperial power, the Babylonian period ends.

For additional information on the historical background to this period see Appendices I, II and III to the Commentary on Kings.

c. The Persian Period

The opening of this period is marked by the fulfilment of the prophecies of restoration. Cyrus sympathized with the religious aspirations of the peoples in the various parts of his dominions. Josephus relates that he was led to favour the Jews by the prophecies of Isaiah having been brought before him. In 538 B.C. he issued a decree authorizing them to return and rebuild their city. The first party of fifty thousand set out that year, led by Sheshbazzar.

In the seventh month after their arrival, the altar was set up and sacrifices resumed. In the second year, they laid the foundation of the temple. Owing, however, to opposition from the people of the land, the work was halted until 520 B.C., when it was again set forward under the stimulus of Haggai's and Zechariah's prophesying. Zerubbabel, a grandson of Jehoiachin, was now governor of Judah. The Persian Empire was in a state of upheaval through a series of revolts which confronted Darius at the beginning of his reign. Any unusual activities readily came under suspicion at such a time. Tatnai, the Persian governor of Syria, made enquiries about the work of rebuilding the temple, which resulted in the matter being referred to the Persian court for the confirmation of the decree of Cyrus, quoted by the Jews as their authority. On ascertaining the correctness of their claim, Darius made state contributions towards the rebuilding, and the temple was completed in 516 B.C.

Nothing further is known of the returned Jews until the arrival of Ezra in 458 B.C., with a new band from Babylon and considerable gifts for the temple service. It is, perhaps, better to place Malachi's ministry in the unknown period before the coming of Ezra, than in the time of Nehemiah's absence in Persia. If this be the correct view, then light is thrown upon the necessity for the mission of Ezra and the reforming work of Nehemiah additional to what appears in the books that bear their names.

Ezra was commissioned by Artaxerxes to organize the temple services and instruct the people, in accordance with the law of Moses. Fourteen years after his arrival, Nehemiah was appointed governor of the province and succeeded in restoring the wall of the city in fifty-two days. This was preparatory to a reforming campaign, in which he set himself to correct existing abuses and to engage the people in a solemn covenant. The main provisions of this covenant were that they should keep the law of Moses, abstain from foreign marriages, sabbath trade and oppression, and subscribe a regular sum for the support of the temple worship. The close connection between these reforms to which the people pledged themselves and those to which Malachi called them seems to indicate that this covenant may have been to a considerable extent the fruit of his words.

III. THE PROPHETIC TEACHING

a. The nature of God

Religion has been generally defined as the effective endeavour to be on right terms with the governing Power of the universe (Gifford Lectures, 1910). Its character and value depend largely on the conception that is held of the object of worship. At the time of Joshua's death, although Israel had entered into possession of Canaan, the inhabitants of the land were neither entirely exterminated nor wholly subdued. The larger tribes and several others continued the struggle for some time longer, with varying success. But gradually the invaders settled down side by side with the survivors of the older population and, forgetting the commands of Jehovah, intermarried with them and began to worship their gods. Even when they did not altogether forsake the worship of the one God, their thoughts of Him were influenced by the opinions which their heathen neighbours held regarding the deities of the land. Thus there are indications that some of them believed Him to be but one of many gods. They thought, for example, they could ensure His help by merely bringing the ark into battle (1 Sa. iv. 5) or by offering sacrifices even though the moral law was being outraged by their conduct (Ho. viii. 12, 13). Such being the fruits of early apostasy, the task of the prophets was to make known the true nature and character of God, or rather to direct attention to it afresh, and bring it more fully to view. Each of them had his own way of doing this. Their messages vary according to their personal experience and the particular circumstances and outlook of those whom they were addressing. But there are certain leading truths which either underlie, or are more or less explicit in, the teaching of the prophets as a whole.

i. God is the almighty ruler of the universe. He is frequently named the God or Lord of hosts (Am. v. 27, etc.). What the name originally meant, whether it referred to the leadership of Israel or the heavenly hosts, is uncertain. In later times, however, it is chiefly connected with the latter. The myriad stars symbolized the armies of heaven. The command of these armies implied omnipotence (Is. xl. 26). The LXX translation, *pantokrator*, gives the right equivalent. The power of God was not only displayed at the time of creation. It is constantly exercised in the realm of nature. He is the creator of the ends of the earth, possessing inexhaustible energy (Is. xl. 28). He formed the heavenly bodies and the mountain masses. He sets in motion the variable wind, and controls the precious light and indispensable rain. The bountiful harvest is His gift. Mildew, locusts and other subtle forces of destruction work havoc at His bidding (Am. iv). His power is also exhibited on an incomparable scale in the events of human history. He brought the Israelites from Egypt and caused them to go into captivity beyond Damascus (Am. v. 27). He took the Syrians from Kir and is to send them back again (Am. i. 5, ix. 7). Assyria is the rod of His anger (Is. x. 5). He raises up the Chaldeans to fulfil His purposes (Hab. i. 6), and girds Cyrus the Mede to perform His pleasure (Is. xliv. 28, xlv. 5).

ii. **God is the moral governor of the world.** He is holy, righteous, just and merciful. The word 'holy', as referred to God, acquires in the prophets an ethical content, in addition to denoting all that is distinct from man in his creaturely and transient existence. The intervention of Jehovah in the affairs of men and nations has none of the caprice frequently attributed to heathen gods. He always acts in loyalty to His own character and the one gracious purpose of which history is the development. All men are accountable to Him. He is everywhere present and notes the conduct of all. Not only is He aware of deeds done in secret, but He is also fully acquainted with man's inmost thoughts (Am. iv. 13). When He punishes a nation or individual the cause is never a petty one such as was often said to move Olympian deities to anger. It is always because of violation of the law of righteousness and humanity, which is common to God and man.

iii. **God is the covenant God of Israel.** While He has made and governs all, He has entered into a unique relationship with Israel. He has chosen them from among all the families of the earth (Am. iii. 2), called them out of Egypt, instructed them as a father trains his child (Ho. xi. 1–4). He has written unto them the great things of His law for their guidance (Ho. viii. 12), and has frequently exhorted them to obey its commandments (Je. xi. 7). But His people have rebelled against Him and by continued disloyalty exposed themselves to punishment. Yet He will not utterly abandon them, nor will their failure frustrate His gracious purpose (Is. vi. 13; Mi. v. 7, 8). God desires their good, and only after a long series of warnings and appeals have been unheeded does He give them up to their enemies (Je. xxv. 4, 11).

b. Sin and repentance

The prophets denounce sin in uncompromising terms, but they insist on the value of repentance. Amos, notwithstanding his emphasis on inexorable justice, summons Israel in God's name to seek Him and live (Am. v. 4). Hosea gives prominence to the loving-kindness of God and makes tender appeals for a return to Him, with promises of forgiveness and blessing (Ho. xiv, etc.). In this he is closely followed by Jeremiah who, amidst many warnings of impending doom, proclaims God's condescension and compassion (Je. iii. 12, etc.). Isaiah, whose conception of God

is the most sublime, declares that the high and lofty One, that inhabiteth eternity, whose name is Holy, dwells also with him that is of a contrite and humble spirit, to revive the spirit of the humble, and to revive the heart of the contrite ones (Is. lvii. 15). He further announces that abundant pardon awaits the penitent seeker (Is. lv. 7). Ezekiel too, who unveiled for the exiles so impressive a picture of the divine majesty and holiness, assures them that God has no pleasure in the death of the wicked but longs that he should turn from his way and live (Ezk. xviii. 23). Nor are these mercies reserved for Israel alone. Strangers like Ebedmelech may take hold of the covenant and share in its blessings (Je. xxxix. 15ff.; Is. lvi. 4–7) and the ends of the earth are invited to look unto God for salvation (Is. xlv. 22).

The Hebrew prophets had not, like some religious teachers, to choose between their God and goodness. Their doctrine of man is directly dependent on their beliefs about God. They are first of all theologians, and then moral teachers. Like Isaiah, they were all sinners who had obtained mercy and were upheld by the divine power. Their chief business, next to making God known, was to convince their fellows of sin, warn them of retribution, win them to repentance, and guide them in the way of righteousness. Their writings are, therefore, not systematic treatises like those of the ethical teachers of Greece. Their teaching was of an occasional character. Much of it was given negatively, in the description and denunciation of sin. There are, however, a number of positive statements, e.g. Mi. vi. 8, in which duty is summarized.

In dealing with the ethical aspect of a body of teaching, it is usual to consider what is its conception of the highest good, or the ideal; what is its view of virtue, or character; and in what light it regards duty. Treating the moral teaching of the prophets along these lines, it will be found that the highest good is variously described. Sometimes it is thought of as the knowledge of God; more frequently it is righteousness, or the divine favour bestowed upon the righteous. But these different descriptions are closely related. Without the knowledge of God, righteousness cannot be attained. For while righteousness includes the idea of man's behaviour to his fellows and is, in pagan teaching, a social virtue of varying standard, it has, in the prophets, a religious reference. It is rightness according to the divine standard. To be righteous is to obtain a favourable verdict at the ideal tribunal of God. In some passages the word is so used as to be almost equivalent to 'prosperity'. Thus it is linked with the view of the highest good as the divine favour, implying both spiritual and temporal blessing.

The great hindrance to seeking and attaining to the highest good is sin. It affects the worship and conduct of the people as a whole. It moves them to prefer the idols of the heathen to the one true God and to carve out ruinously their own way rather than choose the good way appointed by Jehovah. Among those representative persons, who are singled out for special reproof on account of sin, are kings, statesmen, priests, false prophets, merchants and heads of households. Of the sins mentioned from time to time the following are the most outstanding.

i. Sins of worship. These include idolatry and practices associated with it, the careless performance of ceremonial duties, or formal attention to them when the weightier matters of the law were neglected (Mal. i. 13; Ho. vi. 6), and sabbath desecration (Je. xvii. 19ff.).

ii. Sins of pride which inclined men to unbelief and indifference to God's commands, and led them in times of crisis to place reliance on the policy of statesmen and the might of foreign nations rather than on His aid (Je. xiii; Is. ix. 9).

iii. Sins of violence and oppression. The prophets champion the cause of the defenceless classes—the poor, the orphans, the widows, the slaves—against the unscrupulous greed of the rich and powerful.

iv. Sins of luxury and intemperance, issuing on the one hand in a neglect of duty, and on the other in unfitness for the discharge of it.

v. Sins of deceit and impurity. By the former political, commercial and social confidence was undermined; by the latter the ends of family life were frustrated.

Virtue of character, according to the prophets, is to be acquired by repentance, faith and obedience to God. The repentance, to which they unwearyingly invite men, means the acknowledgment of sin, sorrow for it, a wholehearted turning to God, a recognition and choice of the good way, accompanied by a departure from iniquity. Trust in God is the source of strength for duty, guidance in perplexity, comfort in trouble, prosperity of soul. The knowledge of God as One who executes loving-kindness, judgment and righteousness in the earth, and delights in these things, is commended as a possession to be prized above others (Je. ix. 24), and together with the command to do justly, love mercy and walk humbly with God (Mi. vi. 8), implies that man is also required to take pleasure in these things in obedience to the will of God.

With regard to duty, the teaching of the whole company of the prophets may be summed up in the words of the latest of their line, 'Remember ye the law of Moses my servant, which I commanded unto him in Horeb for all Israel, with the statutes and judgments' (Mal. iv. 4).

c. Prediction and messianic hope

There is a further important aspect of the prophets' work which must not be overlooked in any attempt to form an estimate of their contribution towards the preparation of Israel for her share in the redemption of mankind. In addition to pointing out the lessons of the past and the duties of the present they turned the attention of the people towards the future. The idea of a 'day

of the Lord' in which He would powerfully reveal Himself was not new in the eighth century. In the popular conception, however, it meant a time when Israel would triumph and her foes be utterly destroyed. The prophets, on the other hand, proclaimed that for a disobedient people it would be a day of darkness and not light. The character of God would be vindicated by the punishment of all transgressors, whether heathen or Israelites, and the possession of higher privileges, far from sheltering the guilty, would rather ensure severer treatment.

There was, however, a brighter side to the prophetic outlook. They pointed to the future not merely to overawe sinners with the sense of Jehovah's retributive justice. They unveiled, in addition, the fulfilment of His gracious purpose for His chosen people. Like other nations, Israel required some ideal to the attainment of which she might direct her enthusiasm and energies. It was essential that her moral life be stimulated by hope as well as memory. There were periods in her history when she was attracted to the pursuits of the surrounding nations. She set her heart upon growing powerful in imperial sway and wealthy by the revenues of a far-extended commerce. But a succession of disasters caused these dreams of worldly influence and affluence to fade. Yet hope was not extinguished. The teaching of the prophets focused attention on the nation's true vocation and rebuked despondency by the vision of a future glory which would far transcend the highest achievement of her celebrated past. Though on account of sin the nation was to experience a great suffering, losing land, temple and independence, yet the time would come when they would be restored, purified, enriched, increased, and enabled to instruct the peoples of the world in the knowledge of the Lord, and to guide them in the paths of righteousness and peace. The fulfilment of such promises, however, is frequently associated with a Person, who is variously described and to whom, in later times, the name Messiah was applied, although it occurs as a proper name only once in the prophets (Dn. ix. 25, 26). There had been a number of predictions regarding this coming Person, from the time of the *Protoevangelium* (Gn. iii. 15) onwards. But prophecy relating to the Messiah reaches its climax in the prophets of the eighth and following centuries. In their writings He appears as the ideal prophet, priest and king. The portrait of the first of these is developed mainly in the second part of Isaiah. There He is described as the Servant of Jehovah. He has been called from the womb (xlix. 1); His mouth is a sharp sword; and He Himself is a polished shaft in the Lord's quiver (xlix. 2); His ear is wakened every morning to hear as the learned; He knows how to speak a word in season to the weary (l. 4); His message is good tidings to the meek (lxi. 1); He is gentle in dealing with the afflicted and restoring the fallen. He is not only to raise up the tribes of Israel, but to be a light to the Gentiles and salvation to the ends of the earth (xlix. 6). Relying on the help of God, He resolutely and confidently pursues His task, in the face of contempt and persecution (xlix. 7, l. 5–7).

To be a prophet to the nations was, of course, Israel's vocation, and the ideal prophet represents all that, in this respect, Israel should be. There is, however, another side to the prophetic picture. The Servant is seen triumphing through suffering. His message is not believed; His person is despised; His sufferings are misunderstood; He is led, without protesting, to the slaughter and cut off; He makes His grave with the wicked. Yet He has done no violence nor spoken deceitfully. He is afflicted for the sins of God's people, which are laid upon Him; and when His soul is made an offering for them, He is raised from the dead, to divide the spoil with the strong and rejoice in the justification of many. Thus His success is achieved through death (Is. lii. 13—liii. 12). The New Testament understands this passage as having in view a single individual (see Acts viii. 35), the Lord Jesus Christ, and does not interpret it of the nation as a whole.

In post-exilic times Zechariah speaks of an ideal priest, who is also an enthroned king. It seems most natural to take the words as referring to two functions exercised by the same person. This ideal is not largely developed in the other prophets, but it had already appeared in Ps. cx, and in the New Testament it is the dominating conception of the Epistle to the Hebrews.

By far the most common representation of the Messiah is that of the Davidic king. Springing from David's line, in lowly circumstances (Is. xi. 1), He is endowed with the sevenfold Spirit, and consequently judges not by the sight of His eyes, nor reproves by the hearing of His ears, but by true moral insight. His administration is distinguished by righteousness, equity, faithfulness and justice. Under His beneficent rule brute force and moral evil disappear as the knowledge of the Lord overspreads the earth. He is the rallying centre of the nations and gives satisfying rest to Jew and Gentile (Is. xi). Unlike other potentates, He neither obtains nor defends His kingdom by physical force. He requires neither warhorse nor chariot but is lowly, riding upon an ass. Yet His dominion extends from sea to sea, and from the river to the ends of the earth (Zc. ix. 9, 10).

Another set of passages makes even higher claims for the coming ruler. Isaiah expressly calls Him the mighty God (ix. 6); Jeremiah gives Him the title 'the Lord our Righteousness' (xxiii. 6); Micah declares that His goings forth have been of old, from everlasting (v. 2); Daniel foretells that His dominion will be an everlasting dominion that shall not pass away (vii. 14). The same indication of the divine dignity of His person is seen in other passages where the idea of the kingship is not in evidence. In Zechariah, He is described as the One who is the fellow of the Lord of hosts (xiii. 7), and Malachi promises that the Lord, the messenger of the covenant, will come suddenly to His temple (iii. 1).

These are only a few selections from the large number of allusions to the Saviour in the later prophets. They suffice, however, to show the main lines along which messianic prophecy developed in these centuries, and to provide some indication of the ways in which the prophets spoke when on the far horizon they beheld His glory shine forth with celestial splendour.

W. J. CAMERON.

THE APOCRYPHAL AND APOCA-LYPTIC LITERATURE

I. THE TERM 'APOCRYPHA'

THE noun 'Apocrypha' normally designates those books which are contained in the Latin Vulgate but which are not in the Hebrew Old Testament. Their presence in the Vulgate is due to their inclusion, with the exception of 2 Esdras, in the Greek translation of the Old Testament, the Septuagint, which was the source of the Latin version of these books. It is commonly asserted that this fact shows that the Greek-speaking Jews of Alexandria gave them full canonicity, and that the primitive Church, which took over the Greek Bible, did likewise. The assumption is dubious. The books in question are largely of Palestinian origin and were mainly written in Hebrew or Aramaic; they were popular both in Palestine and in the dispersion but seem to have been put on a different plane from the canonical Scriptures in all places. Torrey, accordingly, considers that the best equivalent of the term 'Apocrypha' is the 'outside' books.

Though this is a good equivalent it is not the literal meaning of *apocryphos*. The Greek term means 'hidden' and was applied to books which were kept from the public eye and allowed to be read only by a privileged circle. Far from being an opprobrious term, therefore, it connotes the special value of the books so described. It seems to have been so applied to the works of the Jewish seers who were especially active between the second century B.C. and the first century A.D. These writings were issued under the name of ancient heroes and prophets of Israel and were kept hidden until those days; even so, they were not for the public but for those worthy to read them. 2 Esdras xiv relates how Ezra dictated to five scribes ninety-four books, twenty-four of which were the Old Testament writings (the Minor Prophets being considered as one book) and seventy being for 'such as be wise among thy people: for in them is the spring of understanding, the fountain of wisdom, and the stream of knowledge' (xiv. 46, 47). This shows not only that these books were valued 'above' the Old Testament, but that the apocrypha here included much more than those books comprising our collection; they were rather the apocalyptic books of the same order as 2 Esdras itself. Origen used the term 'apocrypha' to designate the apocalyptic works, while he regarded our collection of 'apocrypha' as canonical. The truth of the matter appears to be that the apocrypha, in the sense of the outside books, were at first regarded as constituting all sacred books not in the canon; some were more popular than others, and the more popular ones have come down to us in the Latin Vulgate; but the so-called 'pseudepigrapha' (i.e. the books issued under the name of an ancient writer) were also highly valued in many circles and ought not to be regarded as apart from the others. For this reason it would almost seem desirable to let the term apocrypha suffice to cover all the books which are included in the phrase 'Apocrypha and Pseudepigrapha'. Torrey has adopted this procedure in his book *The Apocryphal Literature*.

II. THE BOOKS UNDER REVIEW

The following is a brief characterization of the books of the Apocrypha and Pseudepigrapha.

a. The Apocrypha proper

1 Esdras is a fragmentary account of events recorded in the canonical Ezra, together with the story of the three courtiers, one of whom is said to be Zerubbabel, at the feast of Darius. *2 Esdras* is a first-century A.D. apocalypse put into the mouth of Ezra, in some respects the most tragic of all apocalypses. *Tobit* is a romantic story telling how his piety in burying the untended dead was rewarded in his latter days, and how his son Tobias gained a wife; it was probably written at the end of the third century B.C. *Judith* is another piece of elevating fiction, narrating how she delivered her city from the Assyrian army; it may have come from the Maccabaean age, about 150 B.C. *The Rest of Esther* is additions to the canonical book, such as prayers and decrees mentioned during the story; they were meant to make the religious element of the book more explicit. *The Wisdom of Solomon* is often felt to be the loftiest production of the inter-testamental period; it is a good example of Jewish wisdom-writing, and especially dwells on the theme of retribution; the date of composition has been put variously between 150 B.C. and A.D. 40. *Ecclesiasticus*, often called 'The Wisdom of Jesus the Son of Sirach', is a similar work to the foregoing, but is a Sadducean writing and despite the years of reflection and experience of the author is of more slender spirituality than the former work; it was issued about 180 B.C. *Baruch*, with *The Epistle of Jeremiah*, is a composite book, mainly directed against idolatry; the former may have been composed in the third century B.C., the latter in the second century B.C. Of the additions to Daniel there are three, all later than the original work: *The History of Susanna* tells how the youth Daniel displayed his wisdom in vindicating an innocent woman who had been condemned to death; *The Prayer of Azarias* and *The Song of the Three Holy Children* are represented as having been uttered in the fiery furnace; *Bel and the Dragon* are two separate stories, narrating how Daniel discredited the priests of Bel and exploded the idea that the dragon was a god—and the dragon also! *The Prayer of Manasses* is a prayer of repentance put into the mouth of the king of this name in the Bible, based on 2 Ch. xxxiii. 12f., 19, and may have been written in the second century B.C. *1 Maccabees* is an excellent account of the struggle of the Jews, led by the sons of Mattathias, against Antiochus Epiphanes and his successors; it is thought by some that the writer lived during the events he records. *2 Maccabees* deals with a section of the period covered by the former book, notably with the exploits of Judas Maccabaeus, and is much more highly coloured than the earlier work.

b. The Pseudepigrapha

The Book of Enoch (1 Enoch) is the most important apocalypse of this class of writings; it is certainly composite, though whether it comes from one period or is a gradual accumulation of traditions ascribed to Enoch from 200 B.C. to the mid-first century A.D. is still being debated; its most important contribution is its conception of the heavenly Messiah, the Son of Man. *The Book of Jubilees* is a rewriting of Genesis, purporting to show that the Law was observed from the earliest times and dividing history into periods of 'Jubilees', i.e. forty-nine years (seven weeks of years); it is often dated about 100 B.C. *The Testaments of the Twelve Patriarchs* perhaps was written about the same time, and represents the last counsels and prophecies of each of the twelve sons of Jacob as they are about to die. *The Sibylline Oracles* are Jewish books imitating the style of the pagan Sibylline oracles in order to propagate Jewish thought among Gentiles; they come from the second century B.C. and onwards. *The Assumption of Moses* may have appeared during the lifetime of our Lord; it sets out to give a history of the world, under the guise of prophecy, from Moses to the end, which is of course the writer's own time. *The Book of the Secrets of Enoch* (2 Enoch) presupposes the former book of Enoch and is thought to have appeared in the mid-first century A.D., although some date it later by several centuries; it gives elaborate descriptions of the seven heavens and anticipates a thousand-year kingdom of God on earth. *The Syriac Apocalypse of Baruch* (2 Baruch) is almost certainly dependent on 2 Esdras and is a composite work, purporting to have come from the scribe of Jeremiah; it was written in the latter part of the first century A.D. *The Greek Apocalypse of Baruch* (3 Baruch), while having affinities with the former work, is independent of it and is slightly later in date. *The Psalms of Solomon* are eighteen psalms written in the name of Solomon but come from a Pharisee's pen; they are in the style of the canonical psalms and were written in the latter half of the first century A.D. *3 Maccabees* tells of an attempt to massacre the Jews in the reign of Ptolemy Philopator 222–205 B.C. but which ends in the triumphant vindication of the holy people. *4 Maccabees* is a philosophical treatise which uses certain Maccabaean martyrs to illustrate the writer's thesis. *The Letter of Aristeas* describes the supposed circumstances of the translating of the Hebrew Scriptures into Greek. *The Martyrdom of Isaiah*, as the title indicates, tells of the sawing of Isaiah into two; Charles dates it in the first century of our era, but there is reason to think that the book from which it comes, *The Ascension of Isaiah*, is a wholly Christian product of later date. *The Books of Adam and Eve* give us a great deal of 'information' about the lives of the ancestors of the race and emanates from the first century A.D. *Pirke Aboth*, or 'The Sayings of the Fathers', is a collection of sayings of notable Rabbis, covering the period of the third century B.C. to the third century A.D. *The Story of Ahikar* is a legend written about the fifth century B.C. telling of the adventures and wisdom of this sage and was popular throughout this period we are considering. *The Zadokite Fragments* are the records of a party of Jews who separated from the Sadducees, yet were not Pharisees; they were written perhaps at the junction of the two eras B.C. and A.D. *The Apocalypse of Abraham* and *The Testament of Abraham* both come from the first century A.D. and are Jewish works with Christian interpolations. *The Lives of the Prophets* shows by its title what it contains; it comes from the same era as the former two books and has been similarly expanded by Christians. *The Testament of Job* has received little attention but is conjectured by some to have been written in the first century B.C.

III. THE TEACHING OF THE APOCRYPHAL LITERATURE

a. The doctrine of God

There is a tendency in all this literature, increasing as time goes by, to think of God in terms of His transcendence. There is a reluctance to mention the divine name, so that various circumlocutions are used instead. In 1 Maccabees God is not mentioned once directly, but is usually referred to as 'heaven'; e.g. 'Victory in battle standeth not in the multitude of a host, but strength is from heaven'. With this we may compare the way in which the Jewish writer Matthew in his Gospel constantly uses the phrase 'The kingdom of heaven' instead of 'kingdom of God' as in the other Gospels. The Rabbis often refer to God as 'the Holy One, blessed be He'; as in the following example. 'Thou art to give just account and reckoning before the King of the kings of the kings, the Holy One, blessed be He' (Pir. Ab. iv. 29). For the same reason, the doctrine of angels developed much in this period, to avoid the necessity for God to interfere directly in the affairs of the world. In the Old Testament the Lord is a 'man of war' who fights Israel's battles.

In 2 Maccabees it is angels who fight for Israel. In 1 Maccabees the process is still further accentuated in that neither God nor angels fight, but the good generalship of Judas gains the victory; the thought is that it is not fitting that God should actively intervene in matters of this order. Similarly the direct contact that God has with creation in the Old Testament is replaced by multitudinous angels, some of which are appointed to look after the lightnings, others after the snow, rain, clouds, darkness, cold, heat, frost, etc. On the other hand, the doctrine of demons naturally came into prominence, though here other causes were at work.

With such a view of God, the thought of His sovereignty was naturally prominent. The consummation has not only been foreseen, it has been ordained, even to the precise hour. Individuals share in this process of predestination, but not to the exclusion of their freedom. The author of the Psalms of Solomon believed in God's complete sovereignty over man but also said, 'Our works are subject to our own choice and power to do right or wrong in the works of our hands' (ix. 7). Similarly God's transcendence did not exclude altogether His relationship with men; increasingly His Fatherhood was recognized. The phrase 'Thy Father which is in heaven' occurs in Pir. Ab. v. 23. Cf. also, 'The Lord shall rejoice in His children, and be well pleased in His beloved ones for ever' (Test. Levi xviii. 13, iv. 2; Sib. Or. iii. 702; 3 Macc. vi. 28; Pir. Ab. iii. 19).

b. The Law

The Law is eternal and of supreme importance to man. In Jubilees it is said that all the righteous men of old observed the Law, as indeed the angels of heaven, so that the work of Moses at Sinai was not to make it known for the first time but to re-promulgate it. It is the sum of the revelation of God. For most Jews, the Law (*Torah*) included the oral tradition, which was claimed to have come down from Moses through the prophets and the men of the Great Synagogue. This tradition included multitudinous applications of the Law to all possible circumstances (the *Mishnah*), together with further explanations of these explications (the *Gemara*), and they both formed the *Talmud*, of which there were two collections, the Jerusalem and the Babylonian. Our Lord's attitude to this mass of tradition is well known, but its observance was the life-blood of most orthodox Jews. Both Rabbis and apocalyptists agreed in teaching that one's only hope of obtaining the life of the world to come lay in obeying its precepts.

c. Wisdom

The attributes of Wisdom as set forth in Pr. viii. 22–31 were much thought on in this era, particularly as Greek thought made itself felt in Judaism. There is a long and beautiful description of Wisdom in the Wisdom of Solomon (vii. 22—viii. 1), where she is said to be 'a breath of the power of God, and a clear effluence of the Almighty . . . For she is an effulgence from everlasting light, and an unspotted mirror of the working of God, and an image of his goodness'. Both in the books of Wisdom and Ecclesiasticus there are set forth proverbs of practical wisdom.

At the same time speculation increased on the conception of 'the Word of God'. Its activity is startlingly portrayed in Wisdom xviii. 15–16: 'Thine all powerful word leaped out of the royal throne, a stern warrior, into the midst of the doomed land, bearing as a sharp sword thine unfeigned commandment; and standing it filled all things with death; and while it touched the heaven it trode upon the earth'. The reference is to the slaughter of the first-born in Egypt. In this same book, ix. 1, 2, the Word is identified with Wisdom: 'O God of the fathers . . . who madest all things by thy word, and by thy wisdom thou formedst man . . .'

With this teaching should be compared the view that Wisdom and the Law are one and the same. This view constantly appears in these books, especially in Ecclesiasticus and Pirke Aboth. E.g., Ben Sira gives a lengthy description of Wisdom in chapter xxiv and then says, 'All these things are the book of the covenant of the Most High God, even the law which Moses commanded us . . .' (Ecclus. xxiv. 23). Likewise the Law and the Word are one, as in Pir. Ab. iii. 19, 'Beloved are Israel in that to them was given the instrument wherewith the world was created . . .'. The importance of these developments for the student of the New Testament is clear; they provide the background against which the Prologue to the fourth Gospel may be studied. What the Jew claimed for Wisdom, the Word, the Law, John claimed to be fulfilled in Jesus the Word incarnate.

d. Sin

The origin of sin was much discussed in these times. The answers given to the question varied, but they mostly tended to centre upon the fall. Sometimes it is Eve who is largely to blame (Ecclus. xxv. 24), sometimes Adam (2 Esdras vii. 118), sometimes the devil (Wisdom ii. 24) or even the fallen angels (1 Enoch x. 7, 8). On the other hand, the author of 2 Baruch would protest at the view that we may lay all the blame on our forebears: 'Though Adam first sinned and brought untimely death upon all, yet of those who were born from him, each one of them has prepared for his own soul torment to come, and again each one of them has chosen for himself glories to come . . . Adam is therefore not the cause, save only of his own soul, but each of us has been the Adam of his own soul' (2 Baruch liv. 15, 19). With regard to atonement for sin, the sacrifices are the main means, as in the Old Testament. But works are also efficacious to this end; cf. Ecclus. iii. 3, 'He that honoureth his father shall make atonement for sins', and Tobit xii. 9, 'Alms doth deliver from death, and it shall purge away all sin'. Against sentiments of this order Paul vehemently protested. The merits of saints were also pleaded (2 Esdras viii. 28, 29) and in one book at least the martyrdom of faithful confessors is also regarded as making satisfaction for sins (4 Macc. vi. 28, 29).

e. Ethics

The chief end of man is to understand and obey the Law. As one Rabbi put it, 'If thou hast practised much Torah, take not credit to thyself, for thereunto wast thou created' (Pir. Ab. ii. 9). In an age when the Law was considered to be the sum of the revelation of God, this view was inevitable. Unfortunately, it led to the teaching of salvation by works in a crude fashion, as when Akiba compared God to a shopkeeper who gives men credit when they keep the law and exacts payment for their debts when they fail (Pir. Ab. iii. 20). Nevertheless, on the whole there is an advance in ethical conceptions in this literature as compared with some phases of the Old Testament. Several times in the Testaments of the Twelve Patriarchs the exhortation is given, 'Love the Lord and your neighbour' (e.g. Test. Issachar v. 2), a remarkable anticipation of our Lord's teaching. The same book has lofty teaching concerning forgiveness, as Test. Gad vi. 3–7: 'Love ye another from the heart; and if a man sin against thee, speak peaceably to him, and in thy soul hold not guile; and if he repent and confess, forgive him. But if he deny it, do not get into a passion with him, lest catching the poison from thee he take to swearing and so thou sin doubly. And though he deny it and yet have a sense of shame when reproved, give over reproving him. For he who denieth may repent so as not again to wrong thee; yea, he may also honour thee, and be at peace with thee. And if he be shameless and persist in his wrongdoing, even so forgive him from the heart, and leave to God the avenging.' Such passages as this run so parallel to some of our Lord's instruction that Charles is inclined to consider He was acquainted with the Testaments and used them. It may be so, though we cannot be sure. Moral maxims tend to be no one's property in an atmosphere where preaching is the bread of life, as it was to the Jew of this time.

f. Eschatology

It is in this subject where development is most marked in the inter-testamental period. Advance is particularly noticeable in the conceptions of personal immortality, the kingdom of God, and the Messiah.

i. **Personal immortality.** As far as we can tell, even the earliest Israelites believed in man's survival of death. But it was to a colourless existence that they expected to go, wherein one could not hope for fellowship with God. Ps. lxxxviii is instructive in this respect; to the psalmist, the Beyond is 'the land of forgetfulness', 'the dark', the place where the dead have no fellowship with God, for 'they are cut off from thy hand'. With such a conception of the

after life as this, some considered it as all but non-existence; 'O spare me, that I may recover strength, before I go hence, and be no more' (Ps. xxxix. 13). Clearer understanding on this matter was gained as the saints of God reflected more on their fellowship with God and by relating that experience to the certainty of the coming of the kingdom of God. Job thus believes he will see God's vindication of his innocence after death (Jb. xix. 25–27), and the writer of Ps. cxxxix believed that even Sheol could not exclude God: 'If I make my bed in Sheol, behold, thou art there' (verse 8). So also the writer of Ps. lxxiii looked forward to God's continuing His fellowship with him by welcoming him to glory after death (verses 24, 25). Such teaching is the exception, however, and it was not received by all. Ben Sira, a Sadducee, wrote, 'Whether it be ten, or a hundred, or a thousand years (that you live), there is no inquisition of life in Sheol' (Ecclus. xli. 4), this statement being a plain denial of retribution by God after death. It was left to the Hasids, the forebears of the Pharisees, to develop the teaching of the more spiritual sons of Israel. There is a remarkable parallel to our Lord's teaching on this matter in 4 Macc. vii. 18, 19: 'As many as with their whole heart make righteousness their first thought, these alone are able to master the weakness of the flesh, believing that unto God they die not, as our patriarchs Abraham and Isaac and Jacob died not, but that they live unto God'. We have travelled to the opposite pole of Ben Sira's dictum in the words of the Rabbi who said, 'This world is like a porch before the world to come. Make thyself ready in the porch, that thou mayest enter into the banqueting hall' (Pir. Ab. iv. 21). Such is the constant viewpoint of the apocalyptists and it is they who made it so widespread in the Judaism of our Lord's day.

ii. **The kingdom of God.** We may trace three stages of thought as to this. In the Old Testament the kingdom is anticipated as earthly and eternally of the earth. The famous messianic prophecy of Is. xi. 1–9 is typical. The early apocalyptists dwelt much on such passages as these and produced some highly sensuous pictures of that time. I Enoch x. 17f. says that the righteous shall live to a good old age and beget thousands of children; their seed shall produce a thousand-fold, every measure of olives shall yield ten presses of oil, etc. This is the source of Papias's famous description of the millennium.

Is. lxv. 17–22 speaks of a renewed heaven and earth, but it is not clear to what extent this is meant to apply to the moral or physical realms. Certain apocalyptists, however, of the first century B.C. and first century A.D. put forward the view that the messianic kingdom, though to be established on earth, is of temporary duration and will give place to an eternal kingdom of the heavens. In 2 Enoch this is linked with the notion that the history of the world is to last for seven thousand years, the last thousand being the millennial kingdom, after which the eternal kingdom will begin in a new creation (2 Enoch xxxii. 2—xxxiii. 2). To this writer the temporary kingdom is clearly of great importance. But in 2 Esdras it has assumed a decreased significance, owing to the pessimism of the author as to this world; it is limited to 400 years in duration, at the end of which time the Messiah and all living will die (2 Esdras vii. 26f.).

In view of the latter development, it is not surprising that some apocalyptists abandoned altogether the idea of a temporary messianic kingdom and looked only for the eternal kingdom in the new heavens. Such is the expectation of one line of tradition on which the author of 2 Baruch drew. He evidently felt this earth to be unworthy of the kingdom of God: 'Whatever is now is nothing, but that which shall be is very great. For everything that is corruptible shall pass away, and everything that dies shall depart, and all the present time shall be forgotten, nor shall there be any remembrance of the present time, which is defiled with evils' (2 Baruch xliv. 8f.).

Whatever view is taken as to the nature of the kingdom, its coming is usually conceived to be 'catastrophic', as in the dream of Nebuchadnezzar in Dn. ii. In some books, however, we find the thought that the kingdom would come to its fulness only gradually, as in Jub. xxxiii and 2 Baruch lxxiii—lxxiv. In the former work, the kingdom is conceived to come in ever-increasing fulness as the law is more fully studied and obeyed.

Similarly, all the apocalyptists expected the king to appear *soon*; they stand in the end of the days. Yet in several works it is stated that the great day would be hastened still further by repentance. 'Upon the day on which Israel shall repent, the kingdom of the enemy shall be brought to an end' (Test. Daniel vi. 4). In the Assumption of Moses i. 18, therefore, the last day is called 'the day of repentance in the visitation wherewith the Lord will visit them in the consummation of the end of the days'.

These different aspects of the kingdom of God could not but affect their adherents' views on immortality. It had long been recognized that since the purpose of God was the establishment of the kingdom, that purpose embraced not merely the generation of the end time but all the godly. Hence the doctrine of resurrection came into clear focus. In the Old Testament, that doctrine appears in Is. xxvi. 19 and Dn. xii. 3. Now, however, modifications arose. If the resurrection anticipated is to a kingdom of earthly bliss, naturally the resurrection body is of the same nature as the present body; so we find in the Sib. Or. iii. 179–192: 'God shall fashion again the bones and the ashes of men and shall raise up mortals once more as they were before.' Such a resurrection, of course, takes place at the commencement of the kingdom. But when the temporary kingdom is expected, the resurrection is postponed till the end of that kingdom; such is the case in the

Book of the Secrets of Enoch, where God tells Adam He will take him from the earth 'at my second coming' (xxxii. 1), i.e. at the end of the 7,000 years of earth's history. This writer seemed to conceive of the resurrection as being spiritual and not purely material; thus we read, 'The Lord said to Michael, Go and take Enoch from out his earthly garments, and anoint him with my sweet ointment, and put him into the garments of my glory' (xxii. 8). Such writers as the author of the Wisdom of Solomon, who expected no earthly realization of the kingdom, occasionally looked for resurrection to occur immediately on death; but this thought does not appear to be native to Palestinian Judaism and it was not generally accepted.

iii. The Messiah. It is a curious fact that the Messiah is not mentioned in a number of Old Testament prophets (e.g. Amos, Zephaniah, Nahum, Habakkuk, Joel, ? Daniel). Similarly, He is absent from several of the apocryphal books (the four Maccabaean books, Judith, Tobit, 1 Baruch, Wisdom, Assumption of Moses, 2 Enoch). Charles accordingly infers: 'It follows that in Jewish prophecy and apocalyptic the Messiah was no organic factor of the kingdom' (*Between the Old and New Testaments*, pp. 75, 76). Although it is a doubtful assumption that, in all the cases mentioned, the silence of the writers necessarily implies their rejection of the expectation of a Messiah, the statement of Charles is generally valid. The great difference between the eschatology of the Old and New Testaments is the relative importance of the Messiah; in the New Testament, eschatology is wholly bound up with the Person and work of Christ.

In those passages of the Old Testament in which the Messiah takes a prominent position in the kingdom, it is to be noticed that normally He begins to play His part after the establishment of the kingdom; He Himself does not found it. Ps. cx. 1 sums up the position admirably: 'The Lord said unto my Lord, Sit thou at my right hand, until I make thine enemies thy footstool.' Similarly in most of the apocalypses, the Messiah does not commence His activity till the kingdom is founded. One of the most important exceptions is the Similitudes of Enoch, to which we shall return presently.

Again, in the apocalypses, the Messiah almost always comes from the seed of David, as in the Old Testament. A puzzling conception meets us, however, in the Testaments of the Twelve Patriarchs, where salvation is said to arise from Levi and Judah and not from Judah alone. Most commentators insist that the Messiah in this book is viewed as springing from Levi; that is certainly the case in Test. Reuben vi. 7–12. It is equally clear that in Test. Judah xxii and xxiv the Messiah is stated to arise from Judah. Moreover, the normal view of the Testaments is that salvation is to arise from Levi and Judah, and not from one tribe alone.

The only satisfactory interpretation seems to be that this writer expected two Messiahs and not one. The reason for such a startling view is not simply the heroic achievements of the Maccabaean leaders, who were of the tribe of Levi, but because of the importance attached by this writer to the priesthood. Judah is made to say, 'To me the Lord gave the kingdom and to him (Levi) the priesthood, and he set the kingdom beneath the priesthood . . . As the heaven is higher than the earth, so is the priesthood of God higher than the earthly dominion . . .' (Test. Judah xxi. 1f.). The importance of this development, taking place so close to the birth of our Lord, lies in the preparation it must have made among the Jews for the preaching of a Messiah whose great work was atonement.

The other great deviation from the traditional picture of the Messiah is that given in the Similitudes of Enoch (1 Enoch xxxvii—lxxi). No longer is the Messiah a merely human figure; He is a transcendental being, pre-existent and exalted above all creatures, and is to be manifested in the last times, not only to rule for God but to establish the kingdom. According to Charles, here for the first time are applied to the coming Deliverer the titles of the Christ, the Righteous One, the Elect One, and the Son of Man (see 1 Enoch lii. 4, xxxviii. 2, xlv. 3, 4, xlvi. 1–6 respectively), all of which appear in the New Testament. Many means were used by God to prepare the way of the Lord and to bring about that 'fulness of time' for the coming of His Son from heaven about which Scripture speaks. In this sense these writings, with their references to a coming Deliverer, were important, for they were part and parcel of the general historical situation which God overruled for His own divine purpose.

G. R. BEASLEY-MURRAY.

THE FOURFOLD GOSPEL

See also the Introductions to the Commentaries on the four Gospels

I. THE GOSPEL COLLECTION

We are accustomed to call the first books of the New Testament the Four Gospels. Before the fourth century, however, the whole fourfold collection was usually called 'the Gospel'—the one and only Gospel of Christ—and the four components of the collection were distinguished by the addition of the words 'according to Matthew', 'according to Mark', and so on. Behind the written gospel, recorded by the four Evangelists, was the spoken or oral gospel, the good news or *euangelion* proclaimed by Christ and His disciples. The Christian use of the word *euangelion* and its cognates goes back to the use of the verb *euangelizomai* in the LXX of such passages as Is. xl. 9, lii. 7, lxi. 1 (cf. Christ's application to Himself of the last scripture in Lk. iv. 18).

Irenaeus, bishop of Lyons in Gaul, writing about A.D. 180, regards the fourfold gospel as one of the axiomatic facts of the universe. There are four quarters of the world, he says, and four winds, and thus it is natural that the Church Universal should rest upon four pillars, and these pillars are the four Gospels.

For a writer to write thus confidently about the number of the Gospels, there must have been by his time general agreement in the Churches throughout the world that these four were uniquely authoritative. And such a measure of agreement must have taken some time to materialize. In fact, we can trace a recognition of the fourfold gospel back from the time of Irenaeus to the beginning of the second century. The 'Muratorian Canon' is evidence of its recognition by the Roman Church about the time of Irenaeus, as also is the composition of the anti-Marcionite Prologues to the Gospels a few years earlier. Tatian, an Assyrian Christian, about A.D. 170, turned the fourfold gospel into a continuous narrative or 'Harmony of the Gospels', known as the *Diatessaron*, which in a Syriac form remained for a long time the favourite, if not the official, version of the Gospels in the Assyrian Church.

Tatian was a pupil of Justin Martyr, in whose writings reference is made to 'the memoirs of the apostles'. Justin does not mention Matthew, Mark or Luke by name, nor does he refer to John as an evangelist, but he pretty certainly makes use of all four Gospels, referring to Mark as Peter's memoirs, and if there are traces of gospel material in his works which may come from the pseudonymous Gospels of Peter or Thomas, these traces are remarkably slight compared with the extent of his use of the Four.

About the same time as Justin was writing in Rome, there appeared in Asia Minor a work called *The Epistle of the Apostles*, which is also a witness to the fourfold gospel.

In 1935 some papyrus fragments were published by the British Museum trustees (*Fragments of an Unknown Gospel and other Early Christian Papyri*, ed. H. I. Bell and T. C. Skeat), which appear to be the remnant of a manual designed to teach people the gospel stories. Their importance for our present purpose is that they belong to the first half of the second century and were certainly written by someone who had the fourfold gospel before him and knew it well, for all four Gospels are drawn upon.

Also from the first half of the second century comes the Docetic *Gospel of Peter*, written, according to E. J. Goodspeed, in Asia in the first decade of the second century, which clearly indicates its author's acquaintance with the Synoptic Gospels and very probably also with the fourth Gospel.

In the early decades of the same century Papias, bishop of Phrygian Hierapolis, wrote his *Expositions of the Oracles of the Lord*, in which he referred by name to Mark's Gospel and Matthew's compilation of Logia, drew probably upon the writings of Luke, and, if we may believe the anti-Marcionite *Prologue to the Fourth Gospel*, told how John dictated his Gospel 'while still in the body' in order to give it to the Churches. Eusebius, to whose quotations we owe nearly all our knowledge of this lost work of Papias, says nothing of any reference by Papias to John's Gospel, but he does say that Papias used 'testimonies' (proof-texts?) from John's first Epistle; and in view of the close connection between that Epistle and the fourth Gospel, it is likely that Papias knew that Gospel. There is, indeed, some ground for thinking that he helped to make it known and to win recognition for it among the Asian Churches.

Since, then, we can trace the existence and recognition of the four Gospels back to the early years of the second century, it seems the more likely that the references in Ignatius (c. 110), or even in the *Didache*, to 'the Gospel' as an authoritative writing indicate not any one Gospel but the fourfold collection. (See A. Souter, *Text and Canon of the New Testament*, 1912, p. 161.) C. R. Gregory wrote in 1907 that the four Gospels 'probably were brought together very soon after, it may be immediately after, the writing of the Gospel according to John'; and thirty years later E. J. Goodspeed has gone so far as to argue that the four were gathered into one collection in Ephesus, fifteen or twenty years after the first appearance of John, in order to win a wider hearing for John, and that Jn. xxi was added at that time as an epilogue to the fourfold collection.

58

At any rate, we may be pretty certain that the fourfold gospel, as a single collection, dates from about A.D. 100; in fact, from about the same period as saw the formation of the other great collection in the New Testament Canon, the Pauline corpus.

II. THE ORAL GOSPEL

But what of the history of these four Gospels in the first century? To examine this we must go back to the days immediately succeeding the great events of A.D. 30—the passion, resurrection and ascension of our Lord and the following day of Pentecost. These days witnessed the beginnings of what has been called 'the gospel behind the Gospels'. True, the gospel had been proclaimed even earlier: Jesus and His apostles before His passion had announced 'the good news of the kingdom of God'; but the full significance of this good news could not be apparent until after the great salvation-bringing events had taken place. Jesus and the apostles announced that the kingdom of God had drawn near, as indeed it had in His own Person. But the manner and implications of its drawing near were fully unfolded only in His death and resurrection. 'The kingdom of God is conceived as coming in the events of the life, death, and resurrection of Jesus, and to proclaim these facts, in their proper setting, is to preach the gospel of the kingdom of God'. (C. H. Dodd, *The Apostolic Preaching and its Developments*, 1936, pp. 46f.) There still remained the future consummation of the kingdom, associated with the appearance of Jesus as the Son of Man 'in power and great glory' to exercise the universal authority and judgment received from His Father; this consummation (to be preceded by the world-wide proclamation of the good news) was but the last of a series of events of which the others were the saving facts just mentioned.

The God of the Bible is the God who reveals Himself in mighty acts; the God of the fathers, who had revealed Himself to Israel in the never-forgotten events of the Exodus and Eisodus, had now revealed Himself in mightier acts, by which a greater redemption had been wrought, in the Person of Christ. This was the burden of the earliest apostolic proclamation of the Christian message, and it is to the records of that proclamation that we must turn to learn what the gospel behind the Gospels was.

Some idea of the outline of this proclamation, commonly referred to nowadays by its Greek name *kerygma* can be gathered (a) from the Pauline and other New Testament Epistles and (b) from the reports of early Christian preaching in Acts.

a. The Pauline and other New Testament Epistles

The Pauline Epistles were written to people already familiar with the *kerygma;* any reference to it in them will therefore be incidental and reminiscent. There are two outstanding references in 1 Corinthians (A.D. 54). In 1 Cor. xv. 3ff. Paul reminds his readers of the message whose proclamation had brought them salvation: 'that Christ died for our sins according to the scriptures; and that he was buried, and that he rose again the third day according to the scriptures; and that he was seen of Cephas, then of the twelve: after that, he was seen of above five hundred brethren at once; of whom the greater part remain unto this present, but some are fallen asleep. After that, he was seen of James; then of all the apostles . . .' The message thus summarized Paul says that he himself received from others (*parelabon*) before he handed it on in turn (*paredoka*) to the Corinthians. It is a fair guess in this connection that Paul made good use of the fortnight which he spent with Peter when he went up to Jerusalem to make inquiries of him (*historesai*) about A.D. 35 (Gal. i. 18).

This summary, brief as it is, contains more than a recital of the 'bare events' of a certain person's death, burial, rising again and appearing to a number of people who knew him. These events are interpreted: the person in question was the expected Messiah of the Jews ('Christ'), His death was in some sense endured for the sins of others, and both His death and resurrection were in accordance with the purpose of God revealed in the sacred scriptures of the Jewish people.

The other reference in this Epistle (1 Cor. xi. 23ff.) is marked by the same two verbs— *parelabon*, 'I received by tradition' (a tradition going back to the Lord Himself), and *paredoka*, 'I handed on'. In it Paul reminds his readers of a single incident which occurred on the night of the betrayal of 'the Lord Jesus'—His institution of an act of breaking bread and drinking wine in memory of Himself, an act which, Paul says, was to be repeated by Christians, 'proclaiming the Lord's death till he come'. This last clause suggests that the story was not yet complete; at least one event remained to finish it off.

From incidental references in the same Epistle we learn that the Messiah's death took the form of crucifixion, a fact which proved a stumblingblock to many who heard the gospel story. From other Epistles of Paul we gather that Jesus was born a Jew and lived under the Jewish law, that He was not only a descendant of Abraham but also a member of the royal house of David, that while His death was the Roman death by crucifixion, yet the ultimate responsibility for it rested with leading Jews. From 1 Tim. vi. 13 we learn that He appeared before Pontius Pilate and 'witnessed a good confession', although, according to 2 Tim. iv. 1, He was Himself the divinely appointed judge of living and dead. At the time when Paul was writing, Christ was believed to be exalted at God's right hand (an expression going back to Ps. cx. 1). As for His being appointed judge, 'we must all appear before the judgment seat of Christ' (2 Cor. v. 10). This judgment appears to be linked with the future appearance of Christ, an event to be accompanied by the rising of the believing dead and the receiving of immortality by those then living, at the sound of the last trump (1 Cor. xv. 52f., cf. 1 Thes. iv. 16). That Paul's *kerygma* contained some account of this consummation of the divine redemption in the Parousia of Christ is evident, e.g. when he writes to his Thessalonian converts, reminding them of their conversion, as follows: 'Ye turned to God from idols to serve the living and true God, and to wait for his Son from heaven, whom he raised from the dead, even Jesus, which delivered us from the wrath to come' (1 Thes. i. 9f.). This eschatological element is as constant in the New Testament *kerygma* as it was dominant in the message of the Old Testament prophets.

Paul insisted (1 Cor. xv. 11) that his gospel was the same as that preached by the other apostles. It is not surprising, therefore, to find in 1 Peter (which we have good reason to believe authentic) the same facts presented as the foundation of the *kerygma:* the death and resurrection of Jesus the Messiah, His exaltation to God's right hand, His glory yet to be revealed—all presented as the fulfilment of Old Testament prophecy and as basic for the receiving of salvation. The writer claims to have been a witness of Messiah's sufferings, and elaborates the saving events, especially the demeanour of Christ in His undeserved suffering and death, in such a way, to quote C. H. Dodd again: 'That in general its thought follows the apostolic preaching is clear, and we could easily believe that in places its very language is echoed . . . We shall not be so ready as some critics have been to put all this down to "Pauline influence". It is a clear echo of the preaching which lies behind Paul and the whole New Testament' (*op. cit.*, pp. 97f.).

A third New Testament writer, the author of Hebrews, assumes that his readers have a similar knowledge of the same fundamental facts.

In the earliest preaching, then, as reflected in the Pauline and other New Testament epistles, we can distinguish the following elements: **1.** God has visited and redeemed His people by sending His Son the Messiah, at the time of the fulfilment of His purpose revealed in Old Testament scripture. **2.** Messiah came, as was prophesied, of Israel's race, of Judah's tribe, of David's royal seed, in the person of Jesus of Nazareth. **3.** As the prophets had foretold, He died for men's sins upon a cross, was buried, and (**4**) rose again the third day thereafter, as many eyewitnesses could testify (this note of personal ocular evidence is specially emphasized). **5.** He was exalted to God's right hand, whence (**6**) He sent forth His Spirit to those who believed in Him, while (**7**) He Himself was later to return to earth to complete the work of redemption, to judge the living and the dead, and inaugurate in its fulness the visible kingdom of God on earth. **8.** On the basis of these facts remission of sins and 'the life of the age to come' were offered to all who repented and believed in the good

news; and those who believed were baptized into Christ's name and formed into a new community, the Christian Church.

b. Early Christian preaching

An examination of the speeches ascribed to Peter and Paul in the first half of Acts leads to the conclusion that they are not the free invention of the historian, but reliable summaries of the earliest Christian preaching. Of these speeches the most important are those delivered by Peter in Jerusalem on the day of Pentecost (ii. 14–36) and in Caesarea in the house of Cornelius (x. 34–43) and that delivered by Paul in the synagogue of Pisidian Antioch (xiii. 16–41). Further fragments of the *kerygma* can be traced in iii. 13–26, iv. 10–12, v. 30–32, viii. 32–35. In all these we find the same message as is reflected in the Epistles. The message itself is called the good news; it is announced as the fulfilment of Old Testament prophecy; its subject is Jesus of Nazareth, a descendant of David, whose public life dated from the ministry of His forerunner John the Baptist and whose mission was divinely attested by His works of mercy and power, to which the early preachers bore personal witness. He was betrayed to His enemies, handed over to the Romans by the Jewish rulers, who despite Pilate's desire to release Him insisted on His death, preferring the release of a murderer. He was consequently crucified (a fact referred to more than once in language reminiscent of Dt. xxi. 23, 'A curse of God is he that is hanged on a tree'); taken down from the cross and buried, raised by God the third day, the apostles constantly emphasizing their personal witness of His resurrection. The resurrection, they claimed, declared Him to be Lord and Messiah. Thereafter He ascended into heaven and took His seat at God's right hand, whence He sent forth His Spirit upon His followers; He was to return thence to assume His divinely-given office as judge of the living and the dead; meanwhile the call to those who heard the gospel was to repent, believe, be baptized and receive the remission of sins and the gift of the Holy Spirit.

The Acts and the Epistles tell the same story. The message in its essential outline was the same message every time. Stereotyped religious teaching was the regular practice throughout the world in those days and the gospel formed no exception.

c. The Markan outline

A similar outline of the *kerygma* has been discerned as the skeleton on which the body of Mark has been constructed. See especially C. H. Dodd in *The Expository Times*, xliii (1931–2), pp. 396ff. It is noteworthy that Mark begins where the outlines of the *kerygma* begin, with the activity of John the Baptist, and ends with an account of the passion and resurrection of Christ which, as in the other Gospels, receives what might appear from a purely biographical viewpoint to be a disproportionately large amount of space. But this is one prominent feature of the *kerygma* in all the forms in which we can trace it. The passion narrative is generally recognized to have been told in considerable detail as a unity from the earliest days of apostolic preaching.

Mark consists chiefly of *kerygma*, of the message about Jesus. The primitive Christian preaching was concerned more with what Jesus did than with what He said. In fact, Mark gives us a wonderfully accurate idea of that early preaching. The outline which forms its skeleton connects a brief summary of the Baptist's ministry (i. 1–13) to the passion narrative (xiv. 1ff.) by links which may be represented by the following sections: i. 14f., 21f., 39; ii. 13; iii. 7*b*–19; iv. 33f.; vi. 7, 12f., 30f., 53–56; vii. 24, 31; viii. 27—ix. 13; ix. 30–33*a*; x. 1, 32–34; xi. 1–11, 19. These sections correspond pretty well to the outline reconstructed from other New Testament passages leading up to the passion narrative. In the actual preaching, the outline must have been expanded by means of illustrative matter, increasingly so as the gospel was proclaimed among people previously unacquainted with the story of Jesus. For example, such a statement as that Jesus was 'a man approved of God . . . by miracles and wonders and signs, which God did by him', or that He 'went about doing good, and healing all that were oppressed of the devil' (Acts ii. 22, x. 38), would be amplified in practice by instances of healings and other works performed by Him. The self-contained sections or *pericopae* which make up the bulk of Mark give us a good idea of the illustrations used in the primitive preaching. Some of these take the form of 'paradigms' (as M. Dibelius calls them), examples cited in the early preaching, incidents which lead up to some notable utterance of Jesus, for the sake of which the incidents were remembered and related. These paradigms very often involved a controversial element, and the notable utterance to which they lead up is Jesus' answer to the objections raised against something which He or His disciples did or said. In Mark there are two outstanding groups of these controversial incidents—one of five in ii. 1—iii. 6, and one of three in xii. 13–34. These two groups probably existed as such in the oral stage before their incorporation into Mark; indeed, from the mention of a combination of Pharisees and Herodians in both iii. 6 and xii. 13, B. S. Easton concludes that they at one time formed one group, which was divided into two in order to be inserted in two different contexts in the Markan outline.

III. THE WRITTEN GOSPELS

The four Gospels fall naturally into two groups, the first three on one side and John by itself on the other. The first three are commonly called the Synoptic Gospels, a name apparently given them first by J. J. Griesbach towards the end of the eighteenth century, because they have so much common material that they can be con-veniently arranged in three parallel columns as a 'synopsis', a form in which they may be studied together.

Since Mark seems largely to represent the pattern of the early *kerygma*, and Peter appears in Acts as the chief preacher of this *kerygma*, it is reasonable to accept as true the tradition received and recorded by Papias, that Mark, having acted as Peter's interpreter, later committed to writing the preaching of Peter. We see, too, how little practical difference there is between the view of Alford, Westcott, and others which attributed the matter common to all three Synoptists to a common dependence on the primitive oral preaching, and the view now generally held, first set on a firm basis by Lachmann in 1835, that Mark (or something very like it) is a major source of Matthew and Luke, since Mark is to a large extent that oral preaching committed to writing. We should expect that the oral preaching was delivered first in Aramaic and then in Greek, as the area of apostolic activity widened; considerable traces of the earlier stage are found in the Aramaisms' underlying the Greek of our Gospels.

Even Mark, however, contains some account of the teaching of Jesus as well as of His works, and the other Gospels contain a much higher proportion of His teaching than Mark does. While the doings of Jesus formed the basis of the *kerygma*, His teaching (*didache*) was not for-gotten, but served as the basis for the instruction in righteousness imparted to those who had believed the good news. The New Testament Epistles consist of teaching rather than preach-ing, and the ethical instruction which they convey is in strict harmony with the teaching of Jesus recorded in the Gospels. We may compare, e.g., the ethical teaching of Paul in Rom. xii. 1—xv. 6 with that of the Sermon on the Mount in Mt. v—vii.

Alongside the oral preaching or *kerygma*, then, there was the oral teaching or *didache*, and these two both underlie our Gospel records. We may compare Luke's description of his Gospel in Acts i. 1 as the story of 'all that Jesus began both to do (*kerygma*) and teach' (*didache*). One important corpus of the teaching has been discerned behind those passages common to Matthew and Luke which are not found in Mark. These passages (amounting to something over two hundred verses) are usually indicated by the letter Q, and when viewed in isolation, especially in the order in which they appear in Luke, they present a striking measure of homo-geneity and continuity, although to suppose that the source must be identical with such recon-structions as some scholars have made by isolat-ing these verses and setting them in order is going beyond what is warranted. The Q passages were probably drawn from a collection of the sayings of Jesus set in a brief narrative frame-work, first composed in Aramaic and later circulating in more than one Greek version— very probably the compilation of the Lord's oracles which Papias ascribes to Matthew. Part of this collection may have been preserved in Matthew only and part in Luke only, and there are signs that Mark too has drawn upon it in places, perhaps in Mk. iv.

The *kerygma* as recorded by Mark and the *didache* as recorded in the Q-source are the two chief sources of the Synoptic tradition, but there are others. Chief among these should be reckoned the very valuable source or sources from which Luke drew much of his special information, conveniently denoted by L. A good part of this may have been derived from the circle of Philip at Caesarea (Acts xxi. 8). Luke's nativity narratives of the Baptist and Jesus represent what W. Sanday called 'the oldest evangelical fragment, or document, of the New Testament, and in any case the most archaic thing in the whole volume'. They may have been based on the memory of some members of the Jerusalem church which Luke visited in A.D. 57 (Acts xxi. 15ff.). A probable view envisages Luke as having amplified his collection of the sayings of Jesus (his Q-source) by means of the oral information which he could acquire at Antioch and Jerusalem and especially Caesarea; to this he added at a later time the information obtainable from Mark, perhaps during the period which found them both together in Paul's entourage in Rome (Col. iv. 10, 14).

The eschatological discourse in Mk. xiii (reproduced in Mt. xxiv and Lk. xxi) perhaps circulated independently in written form—in part if not in whole—a considerable time before its incorporation in the Gospels, even as early as A.D. 40. Something like it formed the basis of the eschatological instruction which Paul gave at Thessalonica in A.D. 50 (cf. 2 Thes. ii. 1–11, and especially verse 5). Probably the first Evangelist also drew independently on part of it for one section (verses 17–23) of his Mission Charge in Mt. x.

Matthew also has a good deal of material peculiar to itself, including a nativity narrative independent of Luke's, some narrative (especially centring on Peter) which was apparently preserved in 'Nazarene' or Jewish-Christian circles, and a body of teaching (M) on similar lines to that of Q, but with a more pronounced Jewish flavour. B. H. Streeter and T. W. Manson may be right in seeing a separate teaching-corpus here, but some reference ought to be made to B. S. Easton's view that this teaching is simply that portion of the Q-source which was incorporated in Matthew but not in Luke. A further source on which Matthew draws was a collection of messianic 'testimonies' or proof-texts from the Old Testament, fulfilled in Jesus, which have a Greek form independent of the LXX, representing an independent translation from the Hebrew.

According to the generally accepted view of the methods followed by the first and third Evangelists, Luke arranges his sources in alternate blocks, especially inserting blocks of Markan material into his other material (Q+L)

which, as many scholars in this country hold, already existed in the form of 'Proto-Luke', while Matthew conflates his sources, i.e. selects portions from them which he shapes into new unities. A consideration of Matthew's arrangement of the sayings of Jesus suggests that he rearranged them according to their subject-matter into five great discourse-groups, each dealing with some aspect of the Kingdom of Heaven: Discourse I (Mt. v—vii), the Law of the Kingdom; Discourse II (Mt. x), the Proclamation of the Kingdom; Discourse III (Mt. xiii), the Growth of the Kingdom; Discourse IV (Mt. xviii), the Fellowship of the Kingdom; Discourse V (Mt. xxiv—xxv), the Consummation of the Kingdom. In the Great Sermon of Mt. v—vii, for example, we find not only the substance of the parallel Sermon in Lk. vi. 20–49, but also many other 'Q' sayings found in other contexts in Luke, as well as some peculiar to Matthew. To be sure, we must not always assume that two fairly similar passages in Matthew and Luke must come from a common source; much that is reckoned to Q may have come to Luke from one of his special sources, especially where there is no real verbal identity with the Matthaean parallel. Even so, the likelihood remains strong that in Matthew the material has been re-grouped in the manner indicated; and the narrative-sections (almost all Markan) which precede the various discourse-groups in Matthew have also had their matter rearranged to suit this topical order. Not that Luke also did not depart on occasion from the order of his sources; for instance, he puts our Lord's visit to Nazareth earlier than is chronologically warranted, probably so as to set the programme of His messianic mission proclaimed in His synagogue-sermon there in the forefront of his account of the Ministry. Luke's choice and arrangement of his material also indicate that he had a much greater 'biographical' interest in Christ than had the other Evangelists; this is what we might expect in the one Greek among the New Testament writers.

It should be added that some scholars, such as J. Chapman, J. H. Ropes, B. C. Butler and M. S. Enslin, see no need for another sayings-source, since they regard it as sufficient to suppose that Luke derived his Q-material from Matthew. This view raises greater difficulties than it removes; it would then, among other things, be very difficult to explain the principle of Luke's dispersal of this material throughout his work.

When, however, we have discovered (or think we have discovered) the oral or documentary sources of our Gospels, we must not think that we have sufficiently accounted for these Gospels. The questions treated in this article are mere *prolegomena* to the really important studies of the Gospels themselves which follow. Each of our Gospels is an individual work of literature, with an ethos and genius all its own; each emphasizes a particular aspect of the Person of Christ, and all three Synoptists together with the fourth Evangelist combine to present us with the portrait of the Christ whom we know. Only a small part of the sayings and doings of Jesus has been recorded by them, but these have been selected with such wisdom that we know Him— even as a character in history, to say nothing of His living and abiding presence with His people —better than we know many about whom more details have been handed down to us. This selection forms no small element in that inspiration of the Gospels which helped to fulfil our Lord's promise to His disciples that the coming Spirit would bring to their remembrance the things that He Himself had taught them, and would reveal their significance.

The study of the Gospels along the lines of Form Criticism has been pursued actively during the last thirty years. This line of research tries to penetrate behind such written sources as may underlie our Gospels to the 'forms', or patterns, or moulds, in which the various types of incidents and sayings were cast in the early oral stage. The value of this approach has been exaggerated, but it has done good service by reminding us of the inadequacy of documentary theories alone to account for the phenomena of the Gospels and of the importance of considering the forms of the early oral preaching and teaching in the infant Church, and by revealing that the portrayal of Jesus as the Son of God pervades all the strata of our Gospel-material, even the most primitive of them, no matter how it is classified and cross-divided. Even in the earliest forms of the gospel tradition Jesus is one who makes total claims on men, who asserts His authority in forgiveness and judgment, and makes obedience to His own teaching the criterion of men's bliss or woe. One famous Q-logion, preserved in Mt. xi. 27 and Lk. x. 22, has well been called 'the fourth Gospel in a nutshell': 'All things are delivered unto me of my Father: and no man knoweth the Son, but the Father; neither knoweth any man the Father, save the Son, and he to whomsoever the Son will reveal him'. This is the line of our Lord's teaching which is elaborated in the fourth Gospel—and not there only, for traces of it are found in the writings of Paul and in Hebrews, as well as in the early-second-century hymn-book called the *Odes of Solomon,* in the letters of Ignatius and in the *Sayings of Jesus* discovered among the Oxyrhynchus papyri. It has been argued with some probability that two of the great Christological passages in the New Testament (Phil. ii. 4ff. and part of the Prologue of John) were based on early Christian hymns; at any rate, the aspect of the Person of Christ which they present is no late development in Christian theology, but goes back to His own words. This is the aspect emphasized in the fourth Gospel, but not at the expense of our Lord's real manhood; indeed, John is at pains to insist on His manhood as against Docetic tendencies. But despite the many differences between this Gospel and the other three, it is as faithful to the basic outline of the primitive *kerygma* as they are; beginning with the baptism of John, all the cardinal facts are here—the anointing of Jesus with the Holy Spirit and power, His mighty works of grace and authority, His ministry both in Galilee and in Jerusalem, His betrayal, arrest, trials before the Sanhedrin and Pilate, His crucifixion, burial and resurrection, His ascension, exaltation, and return to raise the dead and judge the world.

Tradition from the second century onwards has associated the composition of the fourth Gospel with Ephesus, and recent attempts to find its origin in Alexandria or elsewhere have not been successful. It may be that each of the Gospels was at first associated with some single centre of Christian witness: Mark with Rome, Matthew with Antioch, Luke possibly with some part of Greece, John with Ephesus. Other Gospels had local and temporary vogue, but these four, because of their intrinsic worth and apostolic authority (direct or indirect), transcended local limitations and speedily became accepted as the fourfold Gospel by the Church Universal. For each of them coincided in its aim with the mission of the Church in the world; the explicit object of the fourth (Jn. xx. 31) is equally applicable to all four: 'These are written, that ye might believe that Jesus is the Christ, the Son of God; and that believing ye might have life through his name.'

F. F. BRUCE.

THE PRIMITIVE CHURCH

See also the Introduction to the Commentary on Acts

THE New Testament in its entirety may be called in one sense the literature of the primitive Church. It is also, of course, the authoritative revelation of God and normative for Christian faith and practice; but for our present purpose we are to regard it as a collection of historical documents from which to draw information about the beginnings of the Christian Church. The Gospels, it is true, hardly mention the Church. Nevertheless they explain how it came into existence through the preaching of Jesus Christ. Moreover they contain what His original disciples thought important to remember of their Lord and what they handed on, first orally and then in writing, to their followers. They are not merely biographies in the modern sense of the word. They are works of edification for Christians. Even St. Luke, who has more of the biographical interest and manner than the others, and may be writing for a wider public, is concerned to explain those matters which have been 'fully established among us' (Lk. i. 1, RV mg.), and have been handed down by those 'which from the beginning were eyewitnesses' (Lk. i. 2). What Jesus did and taught was obviously the most important part of Christian instruction, and the preservation and handing down of the record is one of the greatest legacies of the primitive Church, showing where its heart was fixed. The idea of discipleship was perpetuated.

St. Paul's Epistles were mostly written to churches and give vivid glimpses of the communities which he founded and lovingly supervised. We see the questions that arose both as to faith and practice, the temptations which had to be overcome, the faithfulness and occasional failure of his converts no less than the tender solicitude of the apostle. Of the Corinthian church especially we can get a clear picture. But it is to the Acts of the Apostles that we must go for a connected account of the history of the apostolic Church from the resurrection to the year A.D. 62. It was written by St. Luke the beloved physician, a convert and companion of St. Paul's, a cultivated Gentile Christian. Having already explained in his Gospel the origin of the movement with which he has thrown in his lot, his purpose is now to show how it had attained in so short a time its world-wide expansion. So far as the Gentile mission is concerned he leaves St. Paul's letters to speak for themselves, though he helps us to trace the apostle's missionary journeys. But he has carefully sought all the information he could find about the events antecedent to St. Paul's conversion—an important period which he has rescued from oblivion. In drawing our picture of the primitive Church we must begin with Acts and fill in detail and colour from the Epistles.

I. THE APOSTOLIC PREACHING

Jesus came proclaiming that the kingdom of God was at hand. He did not openly claim to be Messiah, but He accepted the title when it was bestowed by His disciples, and He was crucified on that ground. To the Jewish mind a crucified Messiah was unthinkable and the crucifixion in itself was deemed to dispose of all His claims. Even the disciples, who had confessed Him Christ, were shaken, and only the resurrection restored their faith. They knew that Jesus had accepted the cross as God's will and they found evidence in the Scriptures that the Messiah should suffer. The cross was, therefore, the determinate counsel of God. No man felt more keenly the offence of the cross than did St. Paul, perhaps even after his vision of the risen Lord: but just for that reason he gloried in the message of Christ crucified. Here was the act of God's incredible mercy reconciling sinful men to Himself. The crucifixion did not mean that the proclamation of the kingdom was vain. On the contrary it opened the kingdom to all believers.

For all the riches and individuality of St. Paul's thought, for all his insistence on the fact that he received the truth by direct divine revelation, the central core of his preaching corresponds exactly to that of the speeches in the early chapters of Acts. (See the General Articles *The Fourfold Gospel*, p. 60, and *The Pauline Epistles*, p. 68.) As the prophets foretold, Jesus of Nazareth, of the seed of David, was sent by God. He was crucified by the Jews under Pontius Pilate, and died for our sins according to the Scriptures. He rose again from the dead the third day, and is exalted to the right hand of God whence He will return to judge mankind and to inaugurate His kingdom. To all who repent and believe is promised remission of sins, the gift of the Spirit and eternal life. These are the evangelical facts, the gospel preached by all the apostles, soon to assume confessional form in the Apostles' Creed.

II. THE ECCLESIA

From the beginning the gospel won believers. Individually they are called 'disciples', 'brethren', 'saints', 'elect', 'those who are being saved'. Collectively they form the new Israel, the Church of God. The believer is *ipso facto* added to the Church. He becomes a member in virtue of his faith. In the New Testament it is a simple fact that outside the Church there is no salvation. Moreover the Church is one. It is true that the word is used in the plural to denote local groups of Christians, but the churches are not confederate parts of the Church, but rather local embodiments of it. St. Paul was willing to contemplate

64

two mutually exclusive mission fields, one to the Jews and one to the Gentiles, where different customs might be followed; but that did not imply two Churches. The Epistle to the Ephesians gives rapturous expression to the primitive conception of the Church.

The epithet 'holy' is not applied in the New Testament to the Church. It is always an epithet of Church members and denotes primarily that they are dedicated to God. But such dedication implies a high degree of moral purity. Inevitably there were failures, and there was need of much moral exhortation for people who had been recently won from heathenism and could not at once free themselves from its faults. In the last resort, where exhortation is ineffectual, there is no remedy but expulsion from the Church and from all hope of salvation. The Church is the communion of saints and can endure no gross sinner in its membership.

III. THE HOLY SPIRIT

The Church is also the communion of the Holy Spirit. The Acts opens with the account of the gift of the Spirit at Pentecost, and also at later points tells of His bestowal on individuals in unexpected ways. It is the Spirit who initiates new ventures and directs to new mission fields. Baptism is commonly associated with the gift of the Spirit as being the outward aspect of the inward experience. In Acts the manifestation of the gift of the Spirit normally immediately follows baptism. Once, in the case of Cornelius, it precedes. But Philip's converts in Samaria have to wait for apostles to come down from Jerusalem to lay hands upon them. 'For as yet he (the Holy Spirit) was fallen upon none of them: only they were baptized in the name of the Lord Jesus' (Acts viii. 16). Not to know 'whether there be any Holy Spirit' (Acts xix. 2) is the mark of a defective Christianity.

It is in the letters of St. Paul, however, that we see most clearly what is meant by the experience of the Spirit. The whole Christian life is a life in the Spirit. All the gifts by which the Church is edified—prophecy, teaching, healing— are operations of the Spirit. So also are the distinctive Christian virtues, graces and experiences. Even abnormal phenomena, such as speaking with tongues incoherently which might not seem very edifying, are not to be despised though they are not to be unduly valued and ought to be controlled in the interests of decency and order. The rule, however, stands: Quench not the Spirit. For the Holy Spirit is God's own gift, vitalizing His faithful people both in their individual lives and in the common life and worship.

IV. CHURCH LIFE

The internal life of the Church was accordingly intense and enthusiastic. This is apparent wherever we get a glimpse of it, whether at Jerusalem or Antioch or Corinth. At Corinth, for example, we can see that the meetings for worship were inclined to be disorderly. Prophets could hardly wait their turn to declare the burning message that had been given them. The phenomenon of speaking with tongues occurred, as it has done since in times of religious excitement. Even partisan feeling could break out. St. Paul has to plead for order, but he does so very gently. Order is not to be imposed at the expense of vitality. The Jerusalem community also was deeply stirred. Pentecost was the first but not the last of such experiences. But here perhaps the presence of the apostles and later of James, the Lord's brother, secured a greater orderliness. 'They continued stedfastly in the apostles' doctrine and fellowship, and in breaking of bread, and in prayers' (Acts ii. 42).

But Church life was not supposed to embrace only the occasions of public worship. The whole day-to-day life of the believer was included. Christians in Jerusalem would have separate homes, but they lived in closest fellowship with one another. They had common meals, and for a time, like the Lord and His disciples, they had a common purse. No man called anything his own. Some, like Barnabas, who had property in distant places, sold it for the support of the brotherhood. But such action was purely voluntary, and does not seem to have lasted long. The painful incident of Ananias and Sapphira indicated how it could be abused, and in any case the capital resources of the community must soon have been exhausted. A Christian society requires to look to production as well as to distribution. At all events St. Paul made no attempt to introduce this primitive system of communal sharing into his Gentile churches. He recognizes that Christians cannot wholly come out of the world. They will have to share to some extent in the political, social and economic life of their neighbours while avoiding their idolatries and the gross sins of the heathen. They are as yet but a tiny minority and cannot hope to alter the external circumstances of life. Nevertheless they may not go to law one with another before pagan tribunals on matters of property. They should be able to find adjudicators among their own number and settle their disputes in true brotherly fashion.

Hence, though the primitive Church did not proclaim any new Christian social and economic order, it actually instituted one within its own borders, the order of brotherly love. The slave was not freed but he was regarded as a true brother in Christ. The widow and the orphan, the poor and the distressed, the stranger and the persecuted, became the special care of the community. In a hard and cruel world the churches formed a network of charity and mutual succour so that even pagans remarked, 'See how the Christians love one another.'

V. THE CHRISTIAN MINISTRY

The earliest form of the Christian ministry is of course the subject of much debate and controversy, for which this is no place. Almost

65

inevitably one goes to 1 Cor. xii with its list of the operations and manifestations of the Spirit, the varied but complementary *charismata* given by the Spirit for the edification of the Church. Those who receive and exercise these gifts are not an official ministry: indeed, in the earlier letters of St. Paul there are but three possible references to such: 1 Cor. xvi. 15f.; 1 Thes. v. 12; and Phil. i. 1. In the last passage bishops and deacons are mentioned, whose ideal qualifications are laid down in the pastoral Epistles.

At the head of the list of Spirit-endowed ministries there stand three quite definite types —apostles, prophets, and teachers. Prophets are those who receive urgent messages of truth to deliver to the people. Teachers may be those who, like Apollos, expound the Old Testament and apply it to the needs of the Christian apologetic. The apostle is the most important. He is a missionary to the outside world, but he has also authority over the churches he has founded. St. Paul has to defend his claim to be an apostle against some who would deny it. He might not be worthy to be called an apostle but he had seen the risen Lord, and had received from Him his commission. All the signs of an apostle had been wrought in him, and he can appeal to his more abundant labours, sufferings and achievements.

In Acts also we hear of apostles, prophets and teachers, with the apostles naturally pre-eminent. They are spokesmen in the mission to unbelievers, and they have special honour and leadership within the Church. They supervise new communities, and in consultation with the brethren make decisions where new problems arise. In Acts i. 21–22 we have an interesting account of what is regarded as the necessary qualification of an apostle. He must have companied with Jesus during His entire ministry from the baptism of John to the ascension, so as to be a fit witness to the resurrection. Nevertheless the title of apostle is at least once accorded to Barnabas and Paul.

But what of Stephen, Philip and their companions? In Acts vi an account is given of their election by the community and their ordination by the apostles to serve tables so that the apostles might be free for the ministry of the word. But they are not called deacons. They are full of the Spirit, and Stephen and Philip preach with striking effect. Indeed Philip appears afterwards as the evangelist, and Stephen's preaching is the stepping-stone to St. Paul's.

The characteristic title of the local ministry in Acts is presbyter or elder. Paul and Barnabas appoint elders in their churches (Acts xiv. 23). There are elders from the beginning in the Jerusalem church, and when the apostles have gone that church is ruled by James the Lord's brother with a council of elders. This is no doubt a legacy from the synagogue organization. In view of the nature of the New Testament evidence it is somewhat surprising to find that by the beginning of the second century each church is organized with a ministry of bishop, presbyters and deacons.

VI. THE CHRISTIAN MISSION

During the apostolic age there was an amazingly rapid spread of the new faith from its original centre in Jerusalem to Samaria, Caesarea and Antioch, from Antioch through Asia Minor to the Aegean coast, and from there over to Macedonia and Achaia. By A.D. 57 Rome, too, had a Christian community important enough to receive St. Paul's greatest letter and containing many of his personal friends. Curiously there was as yet no mission to Alexandria.

This expansion was not due entirely to St. Paul, though we may justly claim that he was the greatest missionary of them all. Every Christian was a missionary, eager to spread the gospel, whether he were a preacher by vocation or not. Antioch was reached by unnamed Christians driven there by persecution, and we do not know at all who founded the church of Rome. St. Paul's method of hurrying on from one city to another, so unlike the methods of modern missions, was successful in planting the faith in the strategic centres of the Roman Empire, from which it subsequently radiated. One must remember that circumstances were rather different in the first century. In all the cities of the Empire there were Jewish synagogues with their fringe of proselytes and adherents, every one of them in close contact with Jerusalem. Within a few months of the crucifixion the news of the claims of Jesus Christ would be received and discussed, and an impression would be made. In the year 49 the Emperor Claudius expelled the Jews from Rome because of continual tumults caused by one Chrestus. So Suetonius wrote. Possibly he mistook the name and is in fact relating the origin of the Roman church. At all events every synagogue was an open invitation to the Christian preacher. As an opportunity no less than as a task, the field was the world.

This mission at once raised a serious problem. Some in the Jerusalem church maintained that the law of Moses remained obligatory, not only for Jews who became Christian, but also for Gentiles. St. Paul held that Christ had abrogated the law as such. St. Peter seems to represent a middle way. A sort of compromise was reached allowing of two missions, one to the Jews and one to the Gentiles; but it could hardly have succeeded. The success of the Gentile mission settled the question and the Epistle to the Ephesians glories in the breaking down of the wall of partition and the bringing of Jews and Gentiles alike on equal terms into Jesus' fold. It is true that some Jewish Christians remained apart, but the Church as a whole had found the right way.

VII. OPPOSITION

It was to be expected that a propagandist movement on this scale should encounter opposition, and St. Paul has to complain of a good deal of it, mostly at the hands of his fellow-countrymen who resented his apostasy from Judaism, for so it seemed to them. Wherever he went they stirred up trouble, sometimes organizing riots against him. 'Of the Jews five times received I forty stripes save one . . . Once was I stoned' (2 Cor. xi. 24f.). Nevertheless his mission was not seriously interfered with.

In Acts also we read of Jewish persecution, which drove from Jerusalem first the followers of Stephen and then the apostles. It was responsible as well for the heathen mobs which gathered against St. Paul at Corinth and at Ephesus. But St. Luke shows us that this was merely popular agitation, and that the official government attitude was rather protective. King Agrippa, a *rex socius*, was anxious to hear Paul. The asiarchs (chief officers of Asia; Acts xix. 31) were his friends, and the town clerk of Ephesus was more concerned to still the riot than to persecute the apostle. At Philippi, indeed, the municipal authorities had him beaten and imprisoned, but released him with apologies when they knew that he was a Roman citizen. Gallio, Senatorial Proconsul of Achaia, would not entertain a Jewish complaint against his preaching on the ground that it was not his business to interfere in such matters (Acts xviii. 12ff.). And Festus, the imperial Legate of Syria, declared that he had no fault to find with the Christian mission as such. It is clear that St. Paul is speaking from personal experience when he says 'Rulers are not a terror to the good work, but to the evil . . . He (the ruler) is a minister of God to thee for good' (Rom. xiii. 3, 4, RV). Nor did he alter his tone when he was a prisoner in Jerusalem, Caesarea and Rome.

But Acts closes somewhat abruptly in A.D. 62 and so we do not know exactly what was the result of St. Paul's appeal to Caesar. The unanimous voice of tradition asserts that he died a martyr in A.D. 67, in Nero's savage persecution of the Christians of Rome. By that time, perhaps, it was becoming apparent to those in authority that the Christians were to be distinguished from the Jews, and could not claim the protection of the law that recognized Judaism as a tolerated religion. At all events, from that point there begins a period when to be a Christian was to be in danger of persecution. But by then the gospel was so widely and so securely planted that no human power could uproot it. The new faith and the life it engendered was destined to turn the world upside down.

J. H. S. BURLEIGH.

THE PAULINE EPISTLES

See also the Introductions to the Commentaries on the separate Epistles

The intention of this brief article is to describe, in broad outline, first the character and personality of Paul, secondly to touch upon the question of how and when the Pauline Epistles were gathered together, thirdly to describe the salient features of Paul's style, fourthly to indicate the dates of his thirteen Epistles and lastly to say something on the subject of the relationship of his teaching to that of our Lord Jesus Christ.

I. THE CHARACTER AND PERSONALITY OF PAUL

Deissmann went so far as to say that the Pauline letters 'differ from the messages of the homely papyrus leaves from Egypt not as letters but only as the letters of Paul'. That, however, is a tremendous difference, as Paul was the penman of the Holy Ghost, and his Epistles enunciate eternal truths which can never be outmoded: his Epistles are part of the Word of God, which liveth and abideth for ever. As Dr. G. G. Findlay said, 'It was his work to open a pathway for the truth of Christ to the conscience and intellect of the Gentile world'.

But, while his Epistles were written for edification, and are sometimes not unlike theological treatises (as, for example, the Epistle to the Romans), they are also written with all the freedom of epistolary correspondence, and they reveal very clearly the personality of the writer, indicating how rich and many-sided it was. Howson gives the following very suggestive titles to his Hulsean Lectures on *The Character of St. Paul:* 'Tact and Presence of Mind'; 'Tenderness and Sympathy'; 'Conscientiousness and Integrity'; 'Thanksgiving and Prayer'; 'Courage and Perseverance'. With a wealth of illustration drawn from all the Epistles, he shows that all these traits of character were conspicuously present in this great apostle.

Perhaps the most patent fact about Paul, as his Epistles reveal him to us, is the wonderful mingling of sternness and tenderness which can be discerned in him. How stern he can be at times, as in Galatians and in some parts of 2 Corinthians! The latter Epistle also reveals to us a deeply emotional nature that could suffer profoundly through the base ingratitude and the sad backsliding of some of his less satisfactory converts. As Farrar said, that Epistle 'opens a window into the very emotions of Paul's heart, and is the agitated self-defence of a wounded and loving heart to ungrateful and erring yet not wholly lost souls'. Yet stern though Paul could sometimes be in his faithful dealing with mischief-makers and men of lax moral character in some

of his churches, he could also claim that he had been gentle with the Thessalonian believers, 'as when a nurse cherisheth her own children' (1 Thes. ii. 7, RV), and that he had dealt with each one of them 'as a father with his own children' (1 Thes. ii. 11, RV). 'In the soul of the apostle Paul,' says Findlay, 'logic and sentiment, passion and severe thought, were fused into a combination of unexampled pliancy, tenderness and strength.'

Paul is revealed to us in his Epistles as a Christ-centred soul. To him life meant Christ (Phil. i. 21); it meant resting by faith every moment on the Son of God (Gal. ii. 20). He soars high as he sets before us the supra-mundane glory of this Son of God. Of the title 'Lord', which occurs over twenty times in 1 Thessalonians, one of his earliest letters, it has been said that 'the plummet of dogma can drop no deeper; the wing of adoration can soar no higher'. In Colossians, one of his later Epistles, he presents to us the Christ 'who is the image of the invisible God, the firstborn of all creation', in whom all things were created and in whom all things cohere (see Col. i. 15–17), but that conception of Christ was Paul's in his early Epistles as well; it is, indeed, implicit in the first revelation of the Son of God in him (Gal. i. 16), when 'the Lord of glory' (1 Cor. ii. 8) spoke to him out of 'the excellent glory' which was His eternal home.

Another contrast in the mind and thought of Paul emerges here. Paul was the greatest of Christian theologians, but he was also the greatest of Christian ethical teachers. In close and indissoluble connection with his deepest theological teaching we have very plain and searching exhortations to holy living, and this fact proves that he was no unpractical dreamer, lost in what some misguided people might describe as a 'theological mist'. His feet were planted on the solid earth. The well-balanced character of his thinking comes out in this, that his consistent teaching is that sound doctrine is a worthless thing without a holy life, and that, on the other hand, morality is a withering and dying thing unless it has its roots deep down in sound doctrine.

Paul's was indeed a royal mind; in some of his most soaring passages, we pant after him in vain. Yet, how intensely human he was! He had a 'genius for friendship'; he had the power of compelling love. We think of the long list of salutations sent to his friends in Rome (Rom. xvi), not cold, formal greetings, but many of them expressed in terms of deep tenderness. We can discern in him a natural craving for personal sympathy. How he longed to see Titus, for the sake of meeting whom he left an opportunity of usefulness at Troas: 'I had no rest in my spirit, because I found not Titus my brother' (2 Cor. ii. 13). In his last letter, we can hear the sob of deep heart-sorrow in such words as 'all they which are in Asia be turned away from me' (2 Tim. i. 15), and 'Demas hath forsaken me' (2 Tim. iv. 10). Then, there is the final appeal: 'Do thy diligence to come shortly unto me' . . . 'do thy diligence to come before winter', with a request for his old cloak (2 Tim. iv. 9, 21, 13). Paul's tears (Acts xx. 19, 31; 2 Cor. ii. 4; Phil. iii. 18) are emphasized by Adolphe Monod, in his little book on Paul, and he points out that the feminine traits in Paul acquired their significance from the masculine ones. When a woman weeps, it arouses no surprise; but there is something profoundly moving in the tears of a strong man.

II. PAUL'S COLLECTED EPISTLES

How early the Epistles of Paul were gathered together we have no means of knowing with certainty. Justin Martyr, round about the middle of the second century, informs us that the Gospels were read in the Church services of his day, 'on the day of the sun', alongside the Old Testament Scriptures. But, before the Gospels were written, Paul's Epistles were read as they were received, in the churches to which they were written, and a collection of them may have been made at quite an early date.

In 2 Pet. iii. 16 the writer speaks of the Epistles of Paul in language that seems to suggest that they must have existed, at the time of writing, in some kind of collected form. Strong defences of the Petrine authorship of 2 Peter have been written by Bigg (I.C.C.), by Zahn, by Warfield, and others. There is more to be said for this position than some critics are prepared to admit; and, if Simon Peter wrote 2 Peter, we have in 2 Pet. iii. 16 an indication that, round about A.D. 67, there was in existence a collection of Pauline Epistles; but what its extent was we cannot say.

About A.D. 140 the heretic Marcion prepared his New Testament Canon, which contained ten Pauline Epistles, that is, the Pastoral Epistles were omitted; but Marcion's Canon was a mutilated one, containing only one Gospel, the Gospel of Luke, and that in a truncated form. Marcion cannot be regarded as reflecting the opinion of the orthodox Church of his day, but his Canon does seem to prove that, before the middle of the second century, ten Epistles of Paul were regarded as genuine by heretics as well as by the Church, and existed in collected form.

The Muratorian Canon, which should possibly be dated c. 180, mentions a collection of Pauline Epistles, which comprised the thirteen Epistles which we now have in the New Testament, as existing in the Roman church at that date, and, quite likely, in other churches as well.

III. PAUL'S LITERARY STYLE

If it be true that 'the style is the man', then we can regard Paul's literary style as being the frank and spontaneous expression of his temperament. For one thing, it manifests the intensity of his mind. There is what can be described as a kind of tempestuousness in his writing: over and over again, he hurries along from point to point, swept on by some mighty wave of thought and feeling. Dr. G. G. Findlay's striking description may be quoted. 'With broken outcries and halting, yet impetuous, utterance, he sweeps us breathless through his long periods, as he pursues far up the steep some lofty thought, while language threatens every moment to break down under the weight it is compelled to carry; until at last he reaches his magnificent climax, and the tangled path through which he has forced his way lies clear beneath our feet.'

Sometimes, as Paul makes his way through some 'tangled path', he pays scant attention to the rules and laws of grammar. The construction of his sentences is sometimes involved, and the exact connection of one idea with another may occasionally be uncertain. This is due to the tempestuous rush with which his thoughts come crowding into his mind, but the thoughts themselves shine with a splendour that can never be dimmed, through all the complexities and the not infrequent obscurities of his style. These obscurities often require for their elucidation the keenest exegetical skill, as well as the deepest spiritual insight and something, too, of Paul's own vision of eternal realities. If we persevere with our study of Paul, we shall soon discover that we are sitting at the feet of one who, more than any other human being, has got 'far ben' into the wonders and the glories of that 'open secret of God' which is 'Christ in you, the hope of glory' (Col. ii. 2 and i. 27).

IV. THE CHRONOLOGY OF PAUL'S THIRTEEN EPISTLES

We do not forget old Thomas Fuller's quaint saying: 'Chronology is a surly, churlish cur, and hath bit many a man's fingers.' There are undoubted difficulties in connection with the dating of Paul's Epistles, and yet, in spite of them, a fair degree of certainty can be attained. The Epistles may be arranged as follows:

a. The earliest Epistle: Galatians

The old view was that this Epistle was written about the same time as the Epistle to the Romans, that is, possibly, early in A.D. 57; or, as Lightfoot said in his introduction to his Commentary on Galatians, 'some place must be found for the Galatian Epistle in the group which comprises the Epistles to the Corinthians and Romans'. Lightfoot drew up a long list of coincidences of thought and language between Galatians and Romans, but such coincidences come far short of furnishing convincing proof that the two Epistles were written about the same time. This does not seem to be a very cogent line of argument. To write about justification and the other themes common to Galatians and Romans would have been appropriate at any time. It has been said that Galatians is the 'rough block' of what appeared in more finished form in Romans, and it is reasonable to argue that, quite possibly, some years elapsed between the appearance of the 'rough block' and the appearance of the 'finished form'. In a similar way it can be argued that some years most likely elapsed between the briefer statements about being crucified with Christ and being 'baptized into Christ' in Galatians, and the more detailed treatment of these themes in Rom. vi. 3–11.

A very strong case can be made out in support of the South Galatian destination of the Galatian Epistle, and, as a consequence, in support of a date for that Epistle earlier than A.D. 57. This case is outlined in the section of this Commentary which deals with Galatians. The Epistle was almost certainly written to the churches oₗ Pisidian Antioch, Iconium, Lystra and Derbe, which were evangelized by Paul during his first missionary journey: he returned from that journey to Jerusalem, possibly in the midsummer of the year 49. The letter was written to counteract the activities of certain Judaizing teachers among the Galatian converts, probably before the end of the year 49. The arguments in support of this early date are far stronger than any arguments that can be adduced in support of the later date.

b. Epistles of the second missionary journey: 1 and 2 Thessalonians

During his second missionary journey Paul sailed from Troas, in Asia Minor, to Europe, bringing the gospel to Philippi, Thessalonica, Berea, Athens and Corinth, where he arrived towards the end of A.D. 51. In Corinth Timothy and Silas brought to him a full report of how things were going with the Thessalonian converts (Acts xviii. 5), and to these converts Paul wrote 1 Thessalonians, probably some time in the year 52. The second Epistle was apparently written very soon after, also from Corinth.

c. Epistles of the third missionary journey: 1 and 2 Corinthians and Romans

In the course of his third missionary journey, Paul spent about three years in Ephesus (A.D. 53–56), from which city he wrote 1 Corinthians, probably in A.D. 55 (1 Cor. xvi. 8). Thereafter, he sailed again from Troas to Macedonia (Acts xx. 1; 2 Cor. ii. 12, 13). From somewhere in Macedonia he probably wrote 2 Corinthians—fairly late in A.D. 56 (2 Cor. vii. 5). He journeyed on through Greece, or Achaia, in which province he spent three months (Acts xx. 2, 3). Part of that period must have been spent in Corinth, where he was the guest of Gaius (Rom. xvi. 23; 1 Cor. i. 14), and where he wrote the Epistle to the Romans, early in A.D. 57.

d. Epistles of the first Roman imprisonment: Ephesians, Colossians, Philemon and Philippians

After his voyage and shipwreck, Paul reached Rome, possibly early in A.D. 60. From there he wrote, possibly in the year 61, Ephesians, Colossians and Philemon, with only a short interval between them. The first two of these contain several parallel passages and they were sent by the same messenger, Tychicus (Eph. vi. 21 and Col. iv. 7). The letter to Philemon was addressed to a prominent Christian of Colosse: Tychicus probably brought it also to Colosse, along with the runaway slave, Onesimus, of whom it speaks (Col. iv. 7–9). Philippians seems to be slightly later in date than the other prison Epistles and was probably written in A.D. 62. Paul seems to be expecting near release in Phil. i. 25 and ii. 23, 24.

e. The Pastoral Epistles: 1 Timothy, Titus and 2 Timothy

Paul was probably released from prison in Rome A.D. 62, and may have travelled west to Spain, as he had purposed some years previously (Rom. xv. 24) and east to Colosse (Phm. 22), to Philippi (Phil. ii. 24) and Ephesus (1 Tim. i. 3). It seems certain that he visited the island of Crete, along with Titus, whom he left there (Tit. i. 5). Probably in the year 64, from somewhere in Macedonia, Paul wrote his first Epistle to Timothy, whom he had left in Ephesus (1 Tim. i. 3). The Epistle to Titus was probably written about the same time. 2 Timothy was written from Rome, when Paul was again in prison there (i. 8, 16, ii. 9), with only Luke as his companion (iv. 11). This letter was written either in A.D. 66 or A.D. 67. Paul knows that his martyrdom is very near. 'The last drops of my own sacrifice are falling', he writes (iv. 6, Moff.), and he declares his serene confidence in view of death and the hereafter (i. 10–12 and iv. 8).

V. OUR LORD'S TEACHING AND PAUL'S

On the question of the relation of Paul to Jesus saner views now prevail than those which at one time obsessed the minds of certain students of the New Testament. Close study of all the relevant facts has shown conclusively that the idea that Paul was a corrupter of the original message of Jesus is a complete delusion. No one now seriously believes that Paul created a new theology out of nothing. The original and all-originating mind in the New Testament era, it is now realized, with more or less clearness, was that of the Lord Himself. Paul was a faithful interpreter of the deepest implications of the life and teaching of Jesus.

In the moment of his conversion Paul became at once and for ever a man whose will was dominated by the will of Christ. Christ grasped hold of him, he says in one of his incidental references to his conversion (Phil. iii. 12); and if that meant, as stated already, that Paul was ever after a Christ-centred man, it also meant that he was ever after a Christ-mastered man. His first question to Him who had so suddenly broken into his life in new-creating power was, 'Who art thou, Lord?', and his second was, 'What wilt thou have me to do?' That attitude of absolute submission to Christ was the attitude of his mind, from first to last, so that the idea of inventing dogmas with regard to his divine Lord and Master would have been abhorrent to him. Paul had no desire whatever to evolve and promulgate a theology of his own, but only to preach 'the unsearchable riches of Christ' (Eph. iii. 8), as the Spirit of truth enabled him to do so. He could at all times make with good conscience the claim: 'We preach not ourselves but Christ Jesus as Lord' (2 Cor. iv. 5, RV).

By way of illustration we might glance at Paul's teaching on two themes, the deity of Jesus and the death of Jesus as an atonement for sin.

Jesus claimed a unique relation to God (Mt. xi. 27, etc.). Paul's loftiest language on the person of Jesus, as in Phil. ii. 5–11 and Col. i. 15–19, is only an unfolding of the far-reaching implications of our Lord's claims regarding Himself. Philippians and Colossians are among Paul's later Epistles, but in an earlier letter (1 Cor. viii. 6) we have the lofty doctrine of Col. i. 15–19 in germ. Both passages state the doctrine of the double Lordship of Christ, basing His redemptional upon His creational Lordship, the Corinthian passage stating it more simply, the Colossian passage more fully. Indeed, the truth of the deity of Jesus was impressed on the mind of Paul in the moment of his conversion. It was from 'the excellent glory' that Jesus spoke to him, and in that moment Paul knew that the light of the knowledge of God's glory was radiant on the face of Christ (2 Cor. iv. 6, Wey.). 'As the experience of the apostle was enlarged',

Dr. D. M. McIntyre writes in his book, *Christ the Lord*, 'his conceptions reached out into a land of far distances. As he meditated on that holy One and ever entered into a closer fellowship with Him, new glories adorning that One who is altogether lovely came into view.' And the point is that these glories were not dreamed of, or invented, by the ingenious mind of Paul, but are glories which are Christ's by right, glories which justify every one of the stupendous claims, which, according to the synoptic Gospels as clearly as according to the fourth Gospel, Jesus made for Himself.

We sometimes hear it said still that Paul is the only begetter of the doctrine that the death of Jesus was an atonement for sin. Again, the sounder position is that Paul is a true expounder of the teaching of Jesus. The germ of everything that Paul has written about the death of Jesus in its relation to sin can be found in our Lord's two outstanding utterances concerning the meaning of His death, namely, His words about the 'ransom for many' (Mt. xx. 28; Mk. x. 45) and His words about the new covenant which is established in His blood, and which contains as its fundamental blessing the forgiveness of sins (Mt. xxvi. 28; Mk. xiv. 24). 'If', says Denney in his book *The Death of Christ*, with regard to the saying about the ransom, 'we find the same thought in St. Paul, we shall not say that the evangelist has Paulinized, but that St. Paul has sat at the feet of Jesus.'

There we have the relation of Paul to Jesus in a nutshell. Jesus is Master and Lord, Paul is a humble scholar sitting at His feet; and he was used of his divine Lord to give to us the richest revelation that we have of the treasures of wisdom and knowledge that are hidden in Christ (Col. ii. 3).

ALEXANDER ROSS.

PART TWO

THE OLD TESTAMENT

GENESIS

INTRODUCTION

An introduction to such a book as Genesis needs either to be very extensive, covering all the major questions of authorship and origin, or else to be exceedingly concise, leaving the discussion of important critical points to their appropriate place in the text. In the present work, the latter alternative is the only one possible.

I. TITLE

The name 'Genesis' was given to the book by the Greek translators of it, and it means 'origin' or 'beginning'. The Hebrews had no descriptive title for the book, but merely indicated it by its opening phrase, 'In the beginning'. This opening sentence is highly significant, and provides us with a word which quite truly characterizes the contents. The book describes the beginning of the universe, the beginning of man, the beginning of human sin, the beginning of salvation, the beginning of the Hebrew people, as well as the beginning of many other things.

II. AUTHORSHIP

The documentary theories of authorship with their analysis into such literary sources as J, E, and P, are discussed briefly in the general article *The Historical Literature of the Old Testament* (see p. 31). Running the obvious risk of being dogmatic, it is here taken for granted that Moses was the writer of the book. No reason has yet been produced which categorically requires that the belief in the Mosaic authorship should be abandoned. This is the considered judgment of the present writer. But this view that Moses was the writer does not by any means deny the fact that Moses employed sources of some kind. What were these sources? It is thought by some, and with considerable probability, that the recurring phrase *toledoth*, 'these are the generations of', may be an indication of the historical sources which were available to him. The places where this phrase occurs are as follows: ii. 4, v. 1, vi. 9, x. 1, xi. 10, 27, xxv. 12, 19, xxxvi. 1, 9, xxxvii. 2. Nobody can say for certain whether the phrase constitutes a subscription indicating the source from which the information was derived. There is the amazing likelihood, however, that Moses may have possessed original writings, possibly on clay tablets, and that these may have come from the hands of men like Noah, Shem, Terah and others. That this is anything more than a possibility it would be foolish to assert, but it is a theory that is not without some reasonable justification.

OUTLINE OF CONTENTS

I. THE BEGINNINGS OF HISTORY. i. 1—xi. 32

    a. The creation of the universe (i. 1—ii. 3)
    b. The place of man (ii. 4–25)
    c. The entry of sin into the world (iii. 1—iv. 26)
    d. The genealogy from Adam to Noah (v. 1–32)
    e. The iniquity and judgment of the old world (vi. 1—ix. 29)
    f. The ancient families of mankind (x. 1—xi. 32)

II. THE STORY OF ABRAHAM. xii. 1—xxv. 18

    a. Abram's faith and obedience (xii. 1—xiv. 24)
    b. God's covenant with Abram (xv. 1—xvii. 27)
    c. The deliverance of Lot from Sodom and Gomorrah (xviii. 1—xix. 38)
    d. Abraham and Abimelech (xx. 1–18)
    e. The promised child (xxi. 1—xxiv. 67)
    f. The family of Abraham (xxv. 1–18)

III. THE STORY OF ISAAC. xxv. 19—xxvi. 35

    a. Birth of Esau and Jacob (xxv. 19–28)
    b. Esau sells his birthright to Jacob (xxv. 29–34)
    c. Isaac and Abimelech (xxvi. 1–16)
    d. A dispute about wells (xxvi. 17–33)
    e. Esau's marriages (xxvi. 34, 35)

IV. THE STORIES OF JACOB AND ESAU. xxvii. 1—xxxvii. 1

    a. Jacob in his father's home (xxvii. 1–46)
    b. Jacob's journey (xxviii. 1–22)
    c. Jacob in Syria (xxix. 1—xxxiii. 15)
    d. Jacob in the promised land (xxxiii. 16—xxxv. 20)
    e. The family registers of Jacob and Esau (xxxv. 21—xxxvii. 1)

V. THE STORY OF JOSEPH. xxxvii. 2—l. 26

    a. The boyhood of Joseph (xxxvii. 2–36)
    b. Judah and Tamar (xxxviii. 1–30)
    c. Joseph's promotion in Egypt (xxxix. 1—xli. 57)
    d. Joseph and his brothers (xlii. 1—xlv. 15)
    e. Joseph receives his father into Egypt (xlv. 16—xlvii. 26)
    f. Last days of Jacob (xlvii. 27—l. 14)
    g. Joseph cares for his brothers (l. 15–26)

COMMENTARY

I. THE BEGINNINGS OF HISTORY.
i. 1—xi. 32

The majestic language of the opening sentence of the book of Genesis is indicative of the place which the Bible gives to God all the way through. Revelation places God in the centre, and its opening chapter yields not so much a doctrine of creation as the doctrine of the Creator. All things are shown in their relation to God and in their dependence upon Him.

a. The creation of the universe (i. 1—ii. 3)

Is this account to be regarded as science, as myth, or as revelation? If by science is meant the systematic arrangement of the contents of knowledge, and the expression of that knowledge in formal statements, then the creation account does not claim to be 'scientific'. There is every advantage in this, for had the record been written in the scientific terminology of the twentieth century it would have remained unintelligible to everybody until the present time, and even then would have been understood only by those with a scientific training. Further, if it had been written in accordance with the scientific ideas of the present day it would most certainly be outdated and inaccurate in a century's time. The Genesis account of creation is not cast into scientific form, and this is one of the chief marks of its divine inspiration. The question may be further pressed, however, as to whether, even though not scientific in its language, it is scientific in its substance. The complete answer to this is that no errors have yet been proved. Immature science has sometimes come to hasty conclusions about the truth of the biblical record, and has charged that record with inaccuracy. Further scientific research, however, and a deeper study of the inspired record have eventually compelled the withdrawal of such charges, and science has had to acknowledge that what it was only just beginning to discover had been all the time implicit in the biblical statements.

Before the enquiry regarding the supposed mythical character of the Genesis account be pursued, it is necessary to be clear as to the meaning of myth. Popularly, a myth is regarded as a purely imaginative and quite untrue story. Myth, however, has another and rather more respectable meaning than that. In its classical sense a myth is a story constructed with a view to enshrining certain abstract truths which otherwise would be incapable of being communicated. The biblical record of creation is not a myth in either of these senses. It is rather to be regarded as a picturesque narrative, affording a graphic representation of those things which could not be understood if described with the formal precision of science. It is in this pictorial style that the divine wisdom in the inspiration of the writing is so signally exhibited. Only a record presented in this way could have met the needs of all time. The facts are given in pregnant language which is capable of containing within it all the established results of scientific research.

The opening chapter of Genesis must be regarded as divine revelation. That this revelation must have been given long before the time of Moses is apparent from the many modified versions which were current among the heathen people of antiquity. The Mosaic account is not to be regarded as a purification of Phoenician, Babylonian, or other polytheistic traditions. At some time the story of God's creative acts must have been expressly communicated by Him. This revelation was divinely preserved and kept free from all polytheistic contamination and other superstitious corruptions. In the purpose of God and under divine inspiration it was brought into the five-fold book of Moses.

From the point of view of science, practically nothing is known about the origin of things. It is a fact of high significance, however, that geological opinion as to the sequence of fossil remains tends more and more to conform to those stages of God's work which are described in Gn. i. On rather speculative grounds some have proposed the view, to which also they believe that Scripture points, that a terrible catastrophe must be supposed to have overwhelmed God's original creation. Verse 1, it is said, refers to the original act of God in bringing the universe into existence; it is then affirmed that verse 2 describes the ruined condition of this universe as 'waste and empty', though no reference is explicitly made to the occurrence of the overwhelming disaster or the occasion of it; next, it is said that the subsequent portions of the chapter tell only of the way in which God set to work to re-make the universe that had been destroyed. This interpretation, very anciently taught, and still held by many, is a sincere attempt to overcome a difficulty; but, unhappily, the proposed solution creates further problems of its own. Moreover, there are strong linguistic arguments against it. The 'gap' theory, as it is sometimes called, rests on very slender foundations so far as Scripture is concerned, and there is no geological evidence that categorically requires it.

There are two words used in the Hebrew text to indicate the divine activity in the making of the world: *bara*, commonly rendered 'create', and *'asah*, usually translated 'make'. The important word in the narrative of the creation is *bara*, and its importance is increased in the obviously sparing use that is made of it. *Bara* is found in verses 1, 21 and 27; that is to say, at the beginning of all existence; at the beginning of all animate existence; and at the beginning of all spiritual existence, so far as this world is concerned. It is obvious that no language can adequately describe God's creative action, which lies beyond human experience. The exact meaning of *bara*, the term here used, is difficult to determine. In one of its forms the word seems originally to have signified 'to cut off': it came ultimately to stand in another of its grammatical forms exclusively for the act of divine production which brings into existence something entirely new. In verse 1 the idea of creation excludes the idea of any previously existing material, and this is the sense in which the word is explained as a making of the universe 'out of nothing'; but in verses 21 and 27 the idea of creation plainly does not exclude the use of such pre-existing material. The chief thought to bear in mind, therefore, with regard to the meaning of the word *bara*, is not that of the exclusion of existing material from the act, but the achievement of something completely new, and without any causal relation to preceding agencies.

What was the 'day' which marked the divine stages of the work of creation? It is contended by some that this is an ordinary day of twenty-four hours. In support of this it is pointed out that the periods of evening and morning are specifically mentioned, but there are serious difficulties in the way of accepting this interpretation. Others conceive of these days as days of dramatic vision, the story being presented to Moses in a series of revelations spread over six days. This is an intensely interesting suggestion, but can scarcely be regarded as more than a conjecture. A third view is held by many at the present time. This is that each 'day' represents, not a period of twenty-four hours, but a geological age. It is pointed out that the sun, the measurer of planetary time, did not exist during the first three days; further, that the term 'day' is used in ii. 4 for the whole sixfold period of creation; and that in other parts of Scripture the word 'day' is employed figuratively of a time of undefined length, as in Ps. xc. 4. The chief difficulty attaching to this last interpretation is the mention of 'evening' and 'morning', but this may perhaps be but a purely figurative way of saying that the creation was characterized by clearly defined epochs.

The account of creation is given with a spiritual and religious aim. An account of the origin of things is provided here without which the relation between God and man would be left undefined. The revelation is put forward for the faith of the true worshipper. 'Through faith we understand that the worlds were framed by the word of God, so that things which are seen were not made of things which do appear' (Heb. xi. 3). The reader of this chapter who has a personal experience of God in Christ can readily believe the record it contains; but the things it describes are so astounding, and so beyond the range of scientific verification, that it is not surprising that some find great difficulty here. A second purpose in this narrative is to place man at the climax of earthly creation. Stage by stage the work of God proceeds until man is reached as the crown of all.

God (1). Heb. *'elohim*. Many derivations are suggested for this word. The meaning seems to be 'he who is in the highest degree to be reverenced'. The plural word *'elohim* is a plural of intensity, sometimes called a plural of 'majesty'. *Without form, and void* (2). The Hebrew (*tohu wabhohu*) is akin to an onomatopœic phrase, and suggests its meaning to the ear: it stands for wasteness and emptiness. The statement of this verse is not contradicted by Is. xlv. 18 where *bohu* appears once again. The Isaianic passage means that God did not leave the earth in an unfinished or waste state. 'He created it not in vain (to remain without form and void), he formed it to be inhabited.' The chaos was a means, not an end. *God said* (3). 'By the word of the Lord were the heavens made' (Ps. xxxiii. 6). Cf. Jn. i. 1–3. *Light* (3). The primary character of light even before the sun is one of the postulates of modern science. *The evening and the morning* (5). So far as the poetic language is concerned here the 'morning' is not to be regarded as if it were the second half of the day. The day began in the morning, then came the evening, and the morning which follows the evening is that which begins the second day and therefore terminates the first. *Firmament* (6). An expanse. This is the formation of the atmosphere. *Bring forth* (11). Here is mediate creation: but it must be observed that it is by the divine word. *After his kind* (11). See also verses 12, 21, 24, 25. This phrase may be translated 'in all their varieties': the divine record thus seems to refer to variation within certain general groups. *For signs* (14). This is not astrological but astronomical. The heavenly bodies determine the seasons and mark the divisions of time.

Let us make man (26). The creation of man is the summit of the divine work. The deliberation here should be interpreted of the Holy Trinity, not of divine consultation with the angels. *In our image, after our likeness* (26). No difference is to be found between the two terms 'image' and 'likeness', as if one were constitutional and the other acquired. The phrase conforms to the Hebrew style of parallelism in poetry. This likeness is both natural and moral, in the possession of personality and character. *Dominion* (26). From man's likeness to God flows his dominion over all created things. *Male and female created he them* (27). The more detailed account of this is found in the next chapter. *Replenish* (28). Heb. *male*, which means simply 'to fill', as in verse 22, and conveys no idea of refilling a world that has at some time become emptied. *God blessed the seventh day, and sanctified it* (ii. 3). The sabbath appears from this passage to have been a pre-Mosaic institution: it must have been the subject of some early revelation by which God set it apart.

b. The place of man (ii. 4–25)

i. The account of man's beginnings (ii. 4–7). *These are the generations* (4). This is the first occurrence of the word *toledoth*. See note in Introduction. From this general account of the origin of all things in God the attention is now focused more particularly on man. Is this a second account of creation? Some have thought that it is, but this is true only in so far as chapter ii gives a more detailed and special account of what is given in a general form in chapter i. Even though it be supposed, for the sake of argument, that this is a second account of creation as such, the conclusions of certain schools of criticism by no means follow. It is not unreasonable to assume that Moses had before him more than one ancient record from which, under divine inspiration, he wrote his sacred history. Inspiration does not require that the writer shall not use sources. It is probably much better, however, to regard the second passage as the sequel of the first: in the first, God is seen in relation to the universe as a whole, and in the second He is seen more particularly in His relation to man. Compared with the grandeur of i. 1—ii. 3, which describes the creation of the heavens and the earth, the account of man's beginnings is given in a strongly anthropomorphic and intimate style. This does not mean that the actions are any the less divine, but simply that the pictorial element becomes enlarged with the enlargement of the picture.

Lord (4). The name *Yahveh* (see Art. *The Historical Literature of the Old Testament*, p. 31) is introduced here for the first time. It is strictly a proper name and is that by which God made Himself known in history and redemption. The use of the two words in conjunction seems to identify the Creator with the historic God of Israel, as also in the expression 'Jehovah thy God'. The various forms of the divine name in Scripture are used with discrimination. See notes on Ex. iii. 14 and vi. 2. *Every plant . . . before it grew* (5). It is best to render this 'no plant of the field was yet upon the earth, and no herb of the field had as yet sprung up'. *Formed* (7). Heb. *'asah* quite properly translated 'formed' or 'made'. Man's body is certainly continuous with the rest of the material creation, and God is described here as forming man's body out of pre-existing substance. The similarity between the physical structure of the animals and that of man is to be attributed, however, not to a kind of self-impelled development from one to the other, but to the employment and combination by the Creator of His own standard patterns of organic life. Those standard patterns were just as capable of being built up into the higher forms of physical existence as they were into the lower. The whole purpose of this more particular account, however, is to unfold the meaning of the divine act for which *bara* was employed in i. 27. The original or utterly new thing in man, as distinguished from all previous creation, is that God *breathed into his nostrils the breath of life* (7). In this unique impartation of the divine breath man is created 'in the image of God' (i. 27). *Dust of the ground* (7). Heb. *'adamah*. The mould or arable soil which was on the surface of the ground. From this word man receives his name. Except in i. 26 and ii. 5, where the article would be inadmissible, the Hebrew narrative always speaks of him as 'the Adam' up to ii. 20, where the term seems to become a proper name without the article. *A living soul* (7). Heb. *nephesh*. Cf. i. 20 'creature that hath life' and i. 24 'living creature'. This passage lends no support to the trichotomist view which makes man to consist of three parts, body, soul and spirit. Man differs, however, from other 'living creatures' in the character of the life which he received. His is the life that has come from the breath of God. Man must not be thought of as *having* a soul: he *is* a soul.

ii. The Garden of Eden (ii. 8–17). *Eastward* (8). The precise location of this garden cannot be stated, but the term 'eastward' is as from the position of the narrator. *Eden* (8). The word means 'delight'. Paradise is a Persian name for just such a place of delight, and hence has come into use for the garden of Eden. *Tree of life . . . tree of knowledge* (9). These trees need not be regarded as mysterious or as possessing any physical or material power of conveying life and knowledge. Their place here is as symbols of spiritual realities. *The tree of the knowledge of good and evil* (17). This tree provided a test of man's loyalty and obedience to the will of his Maker. The meaning may simply be that the presence of this prohibited tree made man aware of the distinction between good and evil. But there would seem to be something more in it than this, especially in the light of iii. 22. It may therefore be that, by the ethical test imposed through this forbidden tree, man was to grow into moral maturity: he would acquire an experiential knowledge of good or evil according as he was stedfast in obedience or fell away into disobedience. *Surely die* (17). Observe that 'natural' death was not the original destiny of man. God may have had other ways of translating him to a higher mode of existence—ways which would not have meant corruption, or destruction, or violence. The words 'in the day' must not be pressed into meaning that man would drop dead within a few hours: they meant that the moment of his fall would be the beginning of the reign of death in human experience (cf. Rom. v. 12–21). That man was not at once executed by divine judgment is to be regarded as due to divine mercy. These words do not speak only of physical death, however. Sin brings the awful death of the soul, such a death as requires the quickening of the Holy Spirit in order that a man might again be made 'alive unto God'.

iii. **The making of woman (ii. 18–25).** *Every beast of the field* (19). This is not another account of the creation, this time in a different order from that given in chapter i. The lower creatures are now being studied in their relation to man, to whom belonged the dominion over them. *Adam* (20). It is here that Adam becomes truly a proper name. 'The man' is now seen developing the latent personality which is himself. The narrative shows the personality of Adam in contrast with the non-personal animals, and the divine act in bringing these creatures so definitely before the mind of Adam was with the view to stirring within him the desire for human and personal companionship. In the words *but for Adam there was not found an help meet for him* (20), it seems legitimate to see a hint of the discovery by Adam of this lack in his existence. *One of his ribs* (21). The significance of this act is that male and female are originally one. In their present separated existence each needs the other for self-completion. Mankind was made in the first place in a personal unity, not as a pair. Personality is therefore something greater than mere individuality. *Therefore shall a man leave his father* (24). It is difficult to decide whether by a divine insight into the nature of human sexual relationships these are the words of Adam, or whether they belong to the narrator. But the original source is, of course, God Himself, as is shown by our Lord's words in Mt. xix. 4, 5. The headship of the husband over the wife has its sanction in the divine act of the building of woman out of man, and is due to the fact that 'man is not of the woman; but the woman of the man' (1 Cor. xi. 8).

c. **The entry of sin into the world (iii. 1—iv. 26)**

i. **The temptation and fall of man (iii. 1–7).** The Bible nowhere provides a philosophical or speculative account of the ultimate origin of evil. As the book of redemption, it describes the mode by which sin made its entry into the sphere of human experience. This is an historical account of the fall of man. Some expositors invoke the concept of myth to explain this passage: but myth, even in its technical and legitimate sense, is not required for the narration of historical events. The idea of forbidden fruit is familiar in ancient stories, and these stories may be regarded as memories of the way in which man's fall occurred. The important theological point in this record is that it teaches that temptation came from without and that sin was an intruder into the life of man. Sin cannot be regarded, therefore, as 'good in the making': rather did it spoil a world made 'good' (i. 31).

The serpent (1). Nowhere in the Genesis account is the tempter named as the Devil or Satan. It is impossible, however, not to see more than the serpent here, for the event is far more than could be brought about by an irrational creature alone. The identification with the Devil is made in Jn. viii. 44; 2 Cor. xi. 3, 14; Rev. xii. 9, xx. 2. The evil one employed the exceptional character of the serpent for his destructive purpose. *Subtil* (1). The word may mean either 'wily' or 'clever'. Cf. 'wise as serpents' (Mt. x. 16). This sagacity must already have been observed by the woman, for she showed no signs of alarm when it actually spoke to her. *Said* (1). Cf. Nu. xxii. 28. The speaking of Balaam's ass is a divine miracle; the speaking of the serpent is a diabolical one. *Hath God said . . . ?* (1). A doubt and an insinuation. *Ye shall be as gods* (5). RV has 'God' (Heb. *'elohim*), which is to be preferred to the AV. The Heb. word for 'God' is *'el* which, as a common noun, has an analogous form in all Semitic tongues. The plural *'elohim* may therefore mean either 'gods', as in xxxi. 30, or 'God' (i. 1).

The lie had an element of truth in it which made it all the more deceptive (see verse 22). It is true that partaking of the forbidden fruit would lead to moral fixity, in which state, of course, God exists; but likeness to God in this case was of an opposite kind from the divine intention for man. From the position of moral equipoise, although this word is a little insufficient, since man was made in uprightness and with a tendency towards God, man was to move into an advanced position of moral perfection and be confirmed in character, this character being a holy one. It was thus the divine intention that man should be as God in this respect. By sin, however, man reached a different kind of moral fixity: he became confirmed in character, but that character was evil in its quality.

When the woman saw that the tree was good (6). The tempter had now turned the woman's mind away from God's purpose in the prohibition. The divine word taught that the prohibition was to shield man from evil; the doubting thought in the woman's mind now was that the prohibited fruit was not harmful after all. The psychology of the woman's fall is significantly demonstrated in 1 Jn. ii. 16. *The eyes of them both were opened* (7). Up to this moment they had been but children, but now adulthood rushed upon them.

ii. God questions the wrongdoers (iii. 8–13). *God walking in the garden* (8). The description at this point must not be regarded as entirely anthropomorphic. There was some unique mode of intercourse between God and man which the garden of Eden presupposes and which the subsequent incarnation of our Lord to some extent confirms. *Where art thou?* (9). 'God seeks him, not because he is lost from His knowledge, but from His communion' (Delitzsch).

iii. The divine judgment on sin (iii. 14–24). Punishment is primarily retributive: it is only in a secondary sense that it is correct to speak of it as reformative or deterrent. Punishment is vindicative rectitude, not vindictive passion, and it is the reaction of the holiness of God against all violations of it. Sin and punishment are not arbitrarily connected but are conjoined by the spiritual laws according to which man has been divinely constituted. Punishment, however, is not simply the natural process that is set in motion by a sinful action; that is to say, it is more than a natural penalty, such as the hurt that a man receives if he puts his hand in the fire. Suffering for sin is a judicial penalty, a penalty inflicted by divine judgment, and belongs to the moral realm.

Unto the serpent (14). It is part of the divine order that even though an animal is not morally responsible for its actions, it shall suffer for any harm that it may do to man. See Gn. ix. 5; Ex. xxi. 28. Everything was made to contribute to man's moral perfection, and in so far as either animate or inanimate creation fails to reach this end it comes under the judgment of God. Note the curse on 'the ground' in verse 17, and see Rom. viii. 21, 22. *Upon thy belly shalt thou go* (14). The degradation of the serpent's form was part of its curse. *Enmity* (15). This accounts, in the natural realm, for the deep feud that there seems to be between serpents and man, but it must surely stand for the conflict that belongs to the spiritual realm also.

It shall bruise thy head, and thou shalt bruise his heel (15). There is a natural suggestiveness in the figure used here. The serpent kills by striking the heel of man, but man destroys the serpent by crushing its head. The divine sentence goes beyond the animal here and reaches to the Devil himself. The words proclaim that victory shall be with man: as it was man who was overcome, so it shall be man who effects the triumph. These words have a collective meaning first; it is the race that crushes the evil one. They contain within them also an individual meaning. Note the transition from the serpent's 'seed' to the 'serpent' himself, and also the fact that the

'seed' of the woman is in the singular. Only in Christ, 'the seed of the woman', could this victory be accomplished (see 1 Jn. iii. 8), and from this it was to become true for mankind in Him (Rom. xvi. 20; 1 Cor. xv. 57). It is noteworthy how precisely true was the promise in relation to its fulfilment. The word is spoken specifically of the woman, and when the Redeemer came He was 'made of a woman' (Gal. iv. 4) in a miraculously exclusive manner. It is not right to infer the virgin birth from the Protevangelion, but it is certainly quite legitimate to look back from the point of view of the virgin birth and see how marvellously close were the words of promise to the mode of the performance. The fact should not go by unnoticed that the Protevangelion, as these words are called, was not spoken to the sinners but to the tempter. The work of Christ is at basis the vindication and victory of God over the evil one.

Unto the woman (16). The particular punishment of woman is twofold. First, her sexual life was no longer to be a joy to her, but a source of suffering; and second, she was put in subjection to her husband. The true subordination that belongs to the origin of woman from man now becomes subjection. One of the blessings of the gospel to women in western lands is the mitigation of this subjection.

Unto Adam (17). In the judgment on Adam particular attention is drawn to the character of his sin as a transgression of the commandment of God. See 1 Jn. iii. 4. If it is the incident of sin which is dealt with in the person of the woman, it is the principle of sin that comes into consideration in the person of Adam as the head of the race. The judgment is 'because thou . . . hast eaten of the tree, of which I commanded thee, saying, Thou shalt not eat of it'. *Cursed is the ground* (17). This is on account of Adam's sin. It is not possible, therefore, to judge from the present state of the earth what things were like when they left the Creator's hand. *In sorrow* (17). The same Hebrew word as in verse 16. With the end of sin will come the end of sorrow. See Rev. xxi. 4. *Dust thou art, and unto dust shalt thou return* (19). In his creation man was made glorious, with a moral likeness to God. When sin entered into his life the glory departed, and he was to be regarded in terms of the material aspects of his constitution. This does not mean, of course, that man ceased to be a living spirit, or that he lost any 'part' of his nature, but that he was now living according to the material and earthly rather than according to what was to have been his high destiny.

Eve (20). The name means 'living' or 'life'. As Adam bowed beneath the sentence of death, the presence of the woman who was his wife was the pledge of life. It was through the woman that the conquering seed was to come and life was to be restored. *Coats of skins* (21). It may be that hidden behind this verse there lies some hint of the divine origin of sacrifice. Either by some direct but unrecorded command, or perhaps by divinely inspired convictions wrought within him, Adam may have been led to offer the life of an animal in sacrifice, the skins of which he and his wife were guided to use as coverings for their shame. It is impossible, however, to dogmatize either as to the manner in which the Lord 'made coats of skins' or as to whether this passage does in any way provide an account of the origin of the principle of sacrifice.

As one of us (22). This means that man had acquired a state of moral determination. *Lest he put forth . . .* (22). The sentence is rhetorically left unfinished. *And take also of the tree of life* (22). There are those who regard the tree as having been a kind of sacramental means of transferring man without death to a higher stage of physical life: but its reappearance in the book of Revelation does not encourage this interpretation. There is no hint anywhere in the narrative that Adam and Eve knew anything at all of the existence of this tree as one of the trees of the garden. Note carefully what Eve says in verses 2 and 3. Despite the fact that the argument from silence is notoriously dangerous, there seems to be some significance in the absence of allusion to this tree in the narrative of the actions and thoughts of Adam and Eve. The interpretation of the character of this tree constitutes one of the perplexities of Scripture. In Rev. xxii. 2 'the tree of life' reappears, but it is in a highly symbolical passage (cf. Rev. ii. 7). It may be that the tree was any tree, and that it was but symbolical of the 'life' which unsinning man might enjoy in the communion of God. *And eat, and live for ever* (22). The taking and eating is a symbolical way of referring to the enjoyment of eternal life. This he cannot now enjoy; hence, in a figure he is put beyond reach of 'the tree' which, in his innocence, had been the symbol of his blessedness.

Therefore the Lord God sent him forth (23). Whatever be the true explanation of the tree there is no doubt about the meaning of God's action in removing man from the garden. Man was now cut off from God, and therefore in the truest sense cut off from 'life': this is symbolized by separating him from 'the tree of life'. Not until redemption is effected does the tree of life once more appear as within man's reach. Note that the 'tree of life' was the symbol of man's blessedness: the 'tree of the knowledge of good and evil' was the symbol of man's probation. Failing in the probation he lost the blessedness. *Cherubims* (24). The subject of the cherubims is a whole study in itself, but it seems reasonably true to say that they are not angels. Elsewhere God is shown as riding upon them (see, e.g., Ps. xviii. 10). They are best regarded as symbolic figures, but not of a static nature, for they are always represented as active and mobile. They may be defined as 'the animated symbol of the purposeful activity of God'. *And a flaming sword* (24). Thus, on account of sin man is kept out of Paradise in accordance with the purpose of God and in execution of the wrath of God.

Note that the symbolical and pictorial character of the tree of life, the cherubims, and the sword is seen in the fact that we have no historical record of their removal from the earth.

iv. The murder of Abel (iv. 1–15). *I have gotten a man* (1). The birth of the first human babe must have been a wonderful experience, especially in the light of all the events connected with the sin of Adam and Eve. *From the Lord* (1). The Hebrew text in this phrase is capable of a variety of interpretations. It may be rendered: 'from Jehovah', as in AV; 'with the help of Jehovah', as in RV; 'even Jehovah', which would be the literal translation. The first of these is grammatically impossible. The second involves an exceptional use of the Hebrew *eth*, but is possible, and gives good sense. It is supported by the LXX. *In process of time* (3). Attention to this phrase solves some of the problems that are occasionally regarded as belonging to this story. A long time elapsed between verses 1 and 3. Cain and Abel were not boys nor were they with their father and mother the only four human beings on the earth. *An offering unto the Lord* (3). It is not said here that the offering of sacrifice was based upon divine institution. It may have been a spontaneous act of gratitude and the recognition of God. The origin of sacrifice is shrouded in the unknown. *Had respect . . . had not respect* (4, 5). No satisfactory answer can be given to the question as to how the favour or disfavour of God was indicated. Those who think that there is some hint of the divine institution of sacrifice in chapter iii. 21 would argue that the reason for the acceptance of one and the rejection of the other is to be found in the fact that Cain's offering was a bloodless one. It is impossible to be sure about this, however, but the one certain thing in the narrative is that the two brothers were aware that God had regarded their offerings differently. *Abel and his offering . . . Cain and his offering* (4, 5). The offerer is put before the offering. Even under the Levitical law it was the state of mind of the offerer which gave moral worth to his sacrifice. See Heb. xi. 4, and compare the protest against hypocritical sacrifices (Is. i. 10–20).

If thou doest well . . . (7). God warns Cain that a terrible act of sin is dangerously near: it is there like a wild beast waiting to spring upon him. *Unto thee shall be his desire, and thou shalt rule over him* (7). 'Subject unto thee . . .' (AV mg.). The Hebrew of this verse is exceedingly difficult. By their gender the Hebrew pronouns 'his' and 'him' cannot belong to the crouching sin, but must be taken as referring to Abel. The thought of the verse transfers itself to the concrete situation. Cain is vexed and envious on account of Abel, but he is reminded by God that if he would but do well his younger brother would remain in subordination to him. For a similar use of the idea of subordination see the phrase in Gn. iii. 16. *And Cain talked with Abel* (8). Lit. 'And Cain said to'. The sentence in the Hebrew seems to be broken off. What Cain said to

Abel may be seen by the action that followed. *Slew him* (8). Mankind divides in this act of enmity and murder. Cain allies himself with the seed of the serpent (1 Jn. iii. 12 and cf. Jn. viii. 44) and Abel becomes the symbol of the suffering righteous. *The voice of thy brother's blood* (10). Cf. Heb. xii. 24. *Cursed from the earth* (11). The curse is to proceed from the cultivated ground itself (*'adamah*), and Cain's toil as an agriculturist is to be frustrated: he must therefore go forth as a wanderer.

My punishment (13). It seems right to conclude here, despite the hints of some versions, that it is only the punishment that troubles Cain, not the sin. *Every one that findeth me shall slay me* (14). There is no need to suppose a pre-Adamite race here. Cain's words are sufficiently explained either through the avenging wrath of his younger brothers, of whom he might justifiably be afraid, or through his own terrified imagination. Cain's imagination probably ran wild, but that there was a possibility of his suffering at the hands of others seems to be rightly inferred from what follows in verse 15. The important truth that comes to light in this passage is that the fear in Cain's heart is a testimony to the law of retribution. It may even be that the judicial sentence 'a fugitive and a vagabond shalt thou be' (12) received its execution in that by this divinely inspired dread Cain became a self-made fugitive. *Set a mark upon Cain* (15). 'Appointed a sign for Cain' (RV). The RV rendering suggests that God appointed some kind of sign to Cain, much in the same way as He appointed the sign of the rainbow to Noah (Gn. ix. 12), the regular recurrence of which would assure Cain of the divine protection. The rendering of the RV seems preferable to that of the AV, which would seem to indicate some outward mark that would fill Cain's potential enemies with awe and would render them incapable of doing him harm.

v. The descendants of Cain (iv. 16–24). *Cain knew his wife* (17). His wife was one of the daughters of Adam. There is no reason to suppose that Cain was not married before his crime; nor yet, assuming him to have been unmarried, that he did not sometimes return to the old home in the course of his wanderings and choose a wife for himself on one such occasion. *Builded a city* (17). The building of this city was separated from the settlement of Cain in the land of Nod by a considerable amount of time. The narrative draws attention to the building of the city as marking a new stage in the advance of civilization. It was no doubt the increase of Cain's family and circle of dependants which occasioned the building of the city. The place itself was probably no more than a defended centre of organized social life.

Unto Enoch was born Irad (18). The order in which the different genealogies are presented is instructive. It is one of the principles of arrangement of the book that where there are several family lines to be described the main genealogical line of divine purpose is reserved until last, all other family branches being disposed of first. In this instance, the line of Cain is given, and then the page is free to be given up to the story of God's purpose with the chosen line of Seth. *Lamech* (19). In the family of Lamech the invention of arts and crafts has its rise. It is not justifiable, however, to argue that these arts are of evil origin because they arose in this quarter. *Adah and Zillah, Hear my voice* (23). The RV should be followed in the third and fourth lines of this poem:

'For I have slain a man for wounding me,
And a young man for bruising me.'

This is 'The Song of the Sword'. Lamech, it appears, has been attacked by a 'young man' who 'wounds' and 'bruises' him, both words referring to that which might be caused by a blow with the fist. Lamech exults before his wives that he has avenged himself by having slain the young man, the word 'slain' meaning to run through with a sharp weapon. It is a boast of security through the possession of superior weapons.

vi. A new beginning in the line of Seth (iv. 25, 26). *Seth* (25). The name means either 'appointed' (passive) or 'appointer' (active). In the former sense attention is drawn to the son as the seed whom God appointed: in the latter the attention is focused on God the 'Appointer' whose activity Eve can discern in the gift of her son. The first electing act of God's grace appears in the birth of Seth: from now on the purpose of God may be seen operating through a chosen line until all is consummated in Christ. *Then began men to call upon the name of the Lord* (26). This means that the term *Yahveh* came to be associated with the worship of God.

d. The genealogy from Adam to Noah (v. 1–32)

Adam . . . begat a son (3). The purpose of the biblical genealogies is to trace the line of primogeniture and has no connection at all with the provision of a complete chronology of their respective periods. There is a poetic shape about the genealogical tables of Scripture which forbids us to use them for chronological calculations. Note the two 'tens' in the generations of Adam (chapter v) and Shem (chapter xi); the omission of names in the genealogy of Moses (cf. 1 Ch. vi. 1–3), and the three 'fourteens' in Mt. i. 1–17, a scheme which requires the omission of the names of three kings (Ahaziah, Joash, and Amaziah) from verse 8. The student of Scripture should also be aware that it is not easy to be sure of what the actual figures originally were, as in the three main lines of Old Testament textual evidence (Hebrew text, the Samaritan Pentateuch, and the Septuagint) there is no small divergence.

All the days that Adam lived were nine hundred and thirty years (5). The longevity of the antediluvian patriarchs has been explained away by various devices. It has been suggested that the names represent not individuals but tribes; that the years were possibly shorter; that the figures were mystical; that the numbers are unhistorical and serve only to exemplify Semitic theories of chronology. All of these attempts to avoid the plain meaning of the passage are both unnecessary and unsatisfactory. There is a well-nigh universal tradition that the fathers of the human race were endowed with longevity, and this may have been according to the divine purpose in His providential government of the race. It appears also to be consistent with man's condition as a fallen being that he now no longer possesses the power to live for so long a time. *Enoch walked with God* (24). Cf. Heb. xi. 5.

e. The iniquity and judgment of the old world (vi. 1—ix. 29)

i. The deepening wickedness of man (vi. 1–8).

The sons of God (2). There is no difficulty in understanding this title as a designation of the higher order of supernatural spiritual beings which surround God's throne. Elsewhere 'sons of God' (*'elohim*) refers to angelic beings, good or bad (Jb. i. 6; Dn. iii. 25); and some think we have here the record of a mysterious union between evil angels and the daughters of men. Others take it as referring to the union of the Sethite (sons of God) and Cainite lines. *My spirit shall not always strive with man* (3). The meaning of the Heb. word translated 'strive' is much controverted. It can also mean to rule, to act, to abide, or preside. The sentence is therefore better rendered 'The spirit that I have imparted to him shall not always act in man'. The 'spirit' here is the animating breath spoken of in ii. 7; it is not the Holy Spirit, the third person of the Trinity, but, being related to the Spirit, represents a special presidency or rule within man. The God-given 'spirit' of a man acts in him so long as it animates and rules his corporeal nature. *For that he also is flesh* (3). 'Flesh' in this context may suggest the merely animal or sensuous aspect of man's being. The meaning of the verse is that God will withdraw the rule of 'spirit' from man since man, too, on his part has already made himself but 'flesh' that perishes. Man has made himself sub-human, therefore a spirit-dominated race shall no longer exist. There shall be no more human race. This word of God, therefore, was a threat of destruction. See Ps. civ. 29 and cf. Gn. vi. 17 and vii. 22. *Yet his days shall be an hundred and twenty years* (3). God is about to destroy the human race, but he gives a respite of 120 years. Some regard this expression as indicating a shortening of the span of human life to this length of time; but the allusions to the 'long-suffering' of God in 1 Pet. iii. 20 and to Noah as a 'preacher of righteousness' in 2 Pet. ii. 5, compared with the hint of a last seven days' warning in Gn. vii. 4, seem to favour the view which regards the 120 years as a period of respite. *Giants* (4). Heb. *nephilim* may mean 'giants' (cf. Nu. xiii. 33), or it may be derived from the verb to fall, and so signify 'fallen ones'. As the etymology is difficult to ascertain

it is probably better to take the word in the former sense. *Mighty men which were of old, men of renown* (4). In this phrase allusion is made to the well-known stories of tradition.

The wickedness of man (5). See Rom. i. 18–32. *It repented the Lord* (6). To speak of God as repenting and experiencing grief is admittedly to use anthropomorphic language, but such language stands none the less for a real experience in God. The discussion of the passibility of God tends to be rather abstract; but the God who is revealed in Scripture is capable of feeling sorrow and being grieved. He has real reactions to human conduct. Nevertheless, it is impossible to conceive of the omniscient God regretting some false move that He has made. The repentance of God is not a change in purpose, but a change in attitude. Such a change, when it occurs in man, usually implies a change of mind, hence the word repentance in human speech represents such a change. God, however, never changes His mind: His mind is constant, both in love and in holiness. When man changes in his behaviour then God changes in His attitude. The expression 'it repented the Lord' is simply an indication in human language that God's attitude to man sinning is necessarily different from God's attitude to man obeying. *Both man, and beast* (7). The phrase indicates not entire destruction but the range of it. The Hebrew is more accurately rendered, 'from man unto cattle . . .' *Noah found grace* (8). The grace extended to Noah became in turn the cause of his being just and perfect among his contemporaries. The choice of Noah is another step in the divine purpose of redemption, and reveals that purpose to be one of unmerited 'grace'.

ii. The building of the ark by Noah (vi. 9–22).

Just . . . and perfect (9). These words do not teach that Noah was sinless, but that he was a man of uprightness and integrity. *Corrupt before God . . . filled with violence* (11). There is nothing surprising in the close link between corruption and violence; the one quickly follows upon the other, and the reason why men are at variance with one another is that they are at variance with God. *An ark* (14). This is an archaic Hebrew word, but it most likely indicates no more than a box which is intended to float. Noah did not build a ship in the proper sense: it was a kind of a covered raft intended to drift steadily. It was constructed of cypress (gopher) wood and sealed with bitumen, one of the natural products of Assyria. Taking the cubit at eighteen inches, the vessel was 450 ft. long and 75 ft. wide. It was built with three floors and was constructed to a height of 45 ft. The *window* referred to in verse 16 is called a *ṣohar*, meaning a 'light', and is to be distinguished from the aperture mentioned in viii. 6. So far as it is possible to understand the construction, the *ṣohar* appears to have been an open space for a depth of 18 ins. which ran round the top of the ark to let in light and air. *My covenant* (18). This is the first occurrence of this important Bible term. Note that it is a covenant of grace (8), and observe the probable connection with Gn. iii. 15.

iii. The entry of Noah into the ark (vii. 1–10).
Of every clean beast (2). It is not certain to what the term 'clean' would be applied at this period. Perhaps the distinction was between edible and inedible, or tame and wild, or sacrificial and non-sacrificial. It probably does not refer to the laws in Lv. xi. *By sevens* (2). This might mean seven pairs, but more probably three pairs and an additional one for an offering. *Every living substance* (4). The term here employed occurs again only in vii. 23 and Dt. xi. 6. It does not denote 'life' so much as subsistence. God will eliminate, or 'rub out', the whole established order of things and will begin again.

iv. The deluge (vii. 11–24). *The fountains of the great deep* (11).
Some great convulsion of the earth released the waters that were beneath its crust and caused a great surging up of waters which eventually carried the ark to the mountains of Ararat. In addition to this uprushing of subterranean waters there was also a pouring out of the waters 'which were above the firmament' as the floodgates (AV mg.) of heaven were opened. The restraints imposed on the waters on the second and third days of the creation were relaxed for the destruction of the sinful world. If the flood began in the autumn the bursting clouds would coincide in time with the period of the early rains. *Every . . . all* (14). The ark could not possibly have taken in two of every species of creature as we understand the term species today. Either the basis of differentiation was a popular one, or the area within which the species were to be collected was that of only the immediate vicinity, or the selection was to be made from among the restricted types of creature which God caused to come under Noah's hand. The first of these suggestions seems the most natural, and the beasts were most probably those which man would require for his renewed life on the earth. It was a gracious provision for the sake of man. *The Lord shut him in* (16). It must have been a day of deep emotion for Noah and his family. Observe the marvellous tenderness in the fact that it was the Lord who shut the door of safety. In the Babylonian account the man is told to do this for himself. 'Salvation is of the Lord.'

The question of the universality of the flood may perhaps be discussed at this point. The answer is probably to be found through a careful distinction as to what is meant by 'universal' in this connection. That the words 'whole', 'all', 'every', have always to be understood in the light of their context is clear from a glance at such passages as Gn. xli. 57; Dt. ii. 25; 1 Ki. x. 24; Rom. i. 8, x. 18. Was the flood universal in the geographical sense of covering every square mile of the earth's surface? Or was it universal only in the sense of including everybody within it? In favour of this latter alternative it may be remarked that, viewing the subject from the standpoint of human sin and divine judgment, so long as the flood was universal in the sense of blotting out the race of man, its geographical universality was not essential. 'The object of the flood', writes Delitzsch, 'was the establishment of a new and better race of men by means of the extermination of the incorrigible old race. It was sufficient for the effecting of a radical cure that the district in which the race had then spread should be placed under water. This district of the dissemination of men was also their geographical horizon, it was for them "the whole earth"' (*Genesis*, Vol. 1, p. 248). Sir Leonard Woolley's work at Ur confirms the conclusion that the flood was the complete blotting out of a civilization. (See *Ur of the Chaldees*, Chapter I.) The well-nigh universal traditions of the 'flood' constitute a very strong testimony to its importance. Sir Charles Marston gives his verdict as follows: 'A really balanced judgment must confess that the legends of a great deluge that come from all parts of the world have their significance. It has been suggested that while they may not apply to a universal flood, they certainly presume a general dispersion by the descendants of those who experienced the Bible one' (*The Bible is True*, p. 69). *Under the whole heaven* (19). Agreeably to the view taken above concerning the geographical extent of the flood this is equivalent to the phrase 'within the whole horizon'. *Fifteen cubits upward* (20). That is, about 24 ft.

v. The subsiding of the waters (viii. 1–14).
The waters asswaged (1). Lit. 'became still'. The strong currents of water caused by the breaking up of 'the fountains of the great deep' (vii. 11) now ceased, and the waters were stilled. They seem to have gone back, possibly towards the sea: note *returned* in verse 3. *The mountains of Ararat* (4). Ararat is mentioned again in 2 Ki. xix. 37 (mg.); Is. xxxvii. 38 (mg.); and Je. li. 27. From these allusions Ararat may be located somewhere in Armenia, and the resting place of the ark was probably in some flat space up among these mountains. *Tops of the mountains seen* (5). The word means 'became distinctly visible'. They were not then just beginning to emerge, but had been hidden by the mists which such a downpour of rain must have created. As is remarked by the editor of Lange's commentary on this passage, this is 'another example of the remarkably optical style of the whole narrative'. The story seems to have been written by one who was there. *Seven days* (10). Do the periods of seven days that are prominent in this narrative suggest the early observance of the 'sabbath'?

The seven and twentieth day of the month (14). The chronology of the flood may be tabulated thus:

There were 40 days during which the
  the rain fell (vii. 12)   ..   ..   40 days
Throughout another 110 days the
  waters continued to rise, making
  150 days in all for their 'prevailing'
  (vii. 24)   ..   ..   110 days

The waters occupied 74 days in their 'going and decreasing' (AV mg.). This was from the 17th of the seventh month to the 1st of the tenth month (viii. 5). There being 30 days to a month, the figures in days are 13 plus 30 plus 30 plus 1 ... 74 days

Forty days elapsed before Noah sent out the raven (viii. 6, 7) .. .. 40 days

Seven days elapsed before Noah sent out the dove for the first time (viii. 8). This period is necessary for reaching the total and is given by implication from the phrase 'other seven days' in verse 10 .. 7 days

Seven days passed before sending out the dove for the second time (viii. 10) .. .. 7 days

Seven more days passed before the third sending of the dove (viii. 12) 7 days

Up to this point 285 days are accounted for, but the next episode is • dated the 1st of the first month in the 601st year. From the date in vii. 11 to this point in viii. 13 is a period of 314 days; therefore an interval of 29 days elapses .. 29 days

From the removal of the covering of the ark to the very end of the experience was a further 57 days (viii. 14) .. .. 57 days

_____

TOTAL .. .. 371 days

_____

The calendar month was one of 30 days; thus from the 17th of the second month in the 600th year to the 27th of the second month in the 601st year was one calendar year and 11 days, that is, 371 days. The whole of this is a purely calendar reckoning. If the trouble is taken to investigate the real days as measured by the sun a remarkable fact emerges. There were only 29½ real days to a lunar month; but for calendar purposes the first 24-hour day of the month was counted twice, half of it belonging to the preceding month and half to the following. Twelve real lunar months were actually only 354 days. If then the 11 days (from the 17th to the 27th of the second month) be added the figure 365 is reached. The fact then comes to light that the flood occupied exactly one solar year. It is an utterly gratuitous assumption of the theories of destructive criticism that there are two accounts of the flood here, one 'document' of which states the duration of the flood to be one year and 11 days, while the other 'document' regards it as lasting only 61 days. The alleged 'discrepancies' are the production of the critical hypotheses and have no existence outside of those theories. The 'full' style of the narrative is due to that parallelism of expression which is characteristic of Hebrew literature. For the Babylonian and other accounts of the flood reference should be made to a Bible Dictionary.

vi. The end of the flood (viii. 15–22). *Noah builded an altar* (20). The new life of man on the earth began with an act of worship. This is the first reference to an altar in the pages of Scripture, though it is probably not to be regarded as the first altar to be built. *The imagination of man's heart is evil* (21). This, which had been the reason for the judgment, is now viewed as providing an occasion for the exercise of the divine mercy.

vii. The human race begins again (ix. 1–7). *God blessed Noah* (1). Noah stands forth under God's blessing as the second head of the human race. Observe the parallels between the blessing on Noah and that upon Adam (Gn. i. 28, 29). There were divine stipulations also. First, regarding the eating of blood. From verse 3 it would seem that only after the flood was animal food permitted to man. This permission may have been granted in connection with Noah's sacrifice, and it may be that here is the origin of the sacrificial 'feast' of which the worshipper himself partook. The prohibition of eating blood with the feast may be set in an instructive contrast with the prohibition in the garden of Eden. The forbidden 'tree', abstention from which was the sign of obedience, established the sanctity of law; the forbidden 'blood', the shedding of which was the token of divine propitiation, established the sanctity of grace. The second stipulation concerned the shedding of blood. This solemn warning (verses 5, 6) preserved the sanctity of human life. 'Blood' is representative of that mystery which we call 'life'. It is God's gift alone and man is not free to take it. The highest possible reason is employed here, 'for in the image of God made he man' (6).

viii. The covenant of the rainbow (ix. 8–17). A *covenant* (9) is more than a promise: it is an agreement. God enters into a covenant rather than uttering a bare promise in order to give Noah a greater assurance, and to declare that He has pledged Himself irrevocably. A *token* (12) or sign is attached to this covenant. *I do set my bow* (13) means 'I appoint my bow'. Noah had seen the rainbow many times before, but from henceforth it was to stand as a reminder and pledge of the covenant. This passage is instructive concerning the true nature of the sacramental principle. A 'sacrament' is an outward 'sign' to which a 'word' is attached. Faith lays hold of the promise annexed to the sign, and the sign strengthens and confirms the belief that God will fulfil His word. Where there is no faith in the promise there can be no assurance in the sign. The word and the sign can never be separated. *I will look upon it* (16). This stands for an intentional looking: God pledges Himself in this manner.

ix. The blessing on Shem and Japheth (ix. 18–29). *Shem, and Ham, and Japheth* (18). Because of the allusion in verse 24 to Noah's 'younger' ('youngest' RV) son, many entirely speculative suggestions have been made in connection with these names and their order.

The phrase in verse 24 is literally 'his son, the little one'. In view of the fact that in Hebrew usage 'son' often means 'grandson', and observing that the curse uttered by Noah actually fell upon Ham's son Canaan, it is perfectly reasonable to conclude that the allusion in verse 24 is not to Ham, but to Noah's grandson Canaan, who had possibly taken some vulgar part in this sad affair. *Drunken* (21). Noah had always been a husbandman, but the cultivation of the grape was new to him. Unaware of the intoxicating effects of the wine, Noah drank to excess. In this incapable state he committed a breach of modesty and 'uncovered himself'. Ham saw this, and seems to have been guilty of the unclean attitude which is condemned in Hab. ii. 15.

Verses 25–27 are possibly a scrap of ancient poetry. *A servant of servants* (25). This curse may possibly have its fulfilment in the later subjection of the Canaanites by Israel (see verse 26), or it may perhaps be religious in its significance. The phrase stands for the most abject slavery, and compared with the spiritual blessings of Shem, with which Canaan's curse is here contrasted, what could be more abject than the idolatrous superstition by which the Canaanite peoples were enslaved? *Blessed be the Lord God of Shem* (26). Note that it is not 'Blessed be Shem' but *Blessed be the Lord God of Shem*. The blessing of Shem is here prophetically revealed to reside in the fact that to them would be entrusted the knowledge of Jehovah: this was a blessing indeed. *God shall enlarge Japheth* (27). The title here is *'elohim*, whereas Jehovah is reserved for the covenant line in Shem. The reference to dwelling *in the tents of Shem* (27) probably points to the prospect of participation in the spiritual blessings of the gospel.

f. The ancient families of mankind (x. 1—xi. 32)

i. **Genealogies of the ancient world (x. 1–32).** This chapter is more strictly a genealogy of peoples than of individuals. The arrangement is threefold: the sons of Japheth (2–5); the sons of Ham (6–20); the sons of Shem (21–31). The order here is dictated by the usual plan in Genesis, which is to deal with the chosen line last after having disposed of the collateral branches. The Hamitic genealogy is placed next to that of Shem because in the history it was these peoples who were more closely connected with Shem's descendants. Other ancient lists of nations have been found, belonging to Assyria and Babylonia and other early peoples, but none is so comprehensive as this. The table of nations is not complete, however, and appears to include only those that came within the investigations of the one who compiled it. Identification of many of the peoples named is not easy, but some of the once controverted facts are now receiving striking confirmation through archaeological research. The inhabitants of Canaan are named here in the line of Ham, but they have always been known in history as possessed of Semitic ways of life. This historical character seemed at one time

to be a denial of Hamitic descent, but archaeological investigation has shown that the Semitic characteristics were probably acquired by them through centuries of Hyksos or other Semitic domination. The detailed statement of the boundaries of the land of the Canaanites seems to have been given with a special reference to the later possession of that country by the Israelites. Observe the inclusion of Sodom and Gomorrah in verse 19, thus showing the early date of this list. *The beginning of his kingdom* (10). The geographical facts contained in this passage are confirmed by the ancient inscriptions. Little is known of Nimrod however. By reason of his prowess as a *mighty hunter* (9) Nimrod seems to have achieved some ascendancy over his fellow men and to have welded them into a larger type of organized community. The phrase *before the Lord* (9) is merely a strong superlative.

Shem . . . the brother of Japheth the elder (21). The arrangement of the words is awkward in this English rendering and leads to a false impression. The meaning of the sentence is 'Shem . . . the elder brother of Japheth'. *Shem . . . the father of all the children of Eber* (21). This remark is made in view of the fact that the descendants of Peleg, Eber's elder son, are omitted from this table and are reserved for enumeration elsewhere. *Peleg; for in his days was the earth divided* (25). With Peleg there came a division of what we may call the Abrahamic and the Arabian families of the Semitic line. The Joktanites, descendants of Peleg's brother, are enumerated immediately, and appear to be the ancestors of the Semitic tribes who occupied Arabia. It is more likely, however, that the 'division' to which Peleg's name alludes is that great division of mankind which occurred in connection with the building of the city and tower of Babel.

ii. **The Tower of Babel (xi. 1–9).** The events recorded in this section were earlier in their happening than the resulting divisions of mankind which were outlined in chapter x. *Of one language, and of one speech* (1). Lit. 'one lip and one word', meaning that everybody spoke in the same way both as to pronunciation and vocabulary. The original unity of human language, though still far from demonstrable, becomes increasingly probable. *From the east* (2). Shinar is the plain of the Tigris and Euphrates. The region of Ararat was to the north-west of Shinar, therefore the migration, unless it was by a circular route, must have been in an easterly direction. The Hebrew *miqqedhem* is a vague one, and in the AV of Gn. xiii. 11 it is translated 'east'. This, it would seem, should be its translation here: cf. the rendering in the RV and the RV mg., and AV mg. *Burn* (3). Bricks were usually sun-dried, but at Birs Nimrud there are such hard fire-burnt bricks still to be found. This not only shows to what an advanced stage the ancient building arts had reached, but also serves to bear out the truth of this narrative. The *slime* (3) mentioned here was bitumen (asphalt). *Whose top may reach unto heaven* (4). The city and tower were primarily for defensive security and political domination (see the whole verse). It is possible also that the tower had a religious and astrological significance. The Hebrew is literally, 'whose top the heavens', and this may mean that on it were depicted the signs of the Zodiac and other drawings of the heavens. In view, however, of the use of this phrase in Dt. i. 28, and also bearing in mind the ancient Babylonian boasts about the height of their temples, this expression may not necessarily contain any astrological reference.

Man's proposed scheme of centralization appears to have been regarded by God as undesirable: it may be that it was in its deepest motives an act of human self-sufficiency and rebellion against God. It is highly significant that 'Babel' (Babylon) in the Bible story stands forth right through to the book of the Revelation for this idea of materialistic and humanistic federation in opposition to God. The reasons for God's destruction of these human plans were possibly first to deal effectively with the evil motive of opposition, and secondly to accomplish His design that men should cover the whole earth and develop its resources. Note that God did not destroy the tower; He confounded the language and scattered the people. There is no assertion of a sudden miracle here. The confounding of the language may have been by a providential direction and hastening of the natural tendencies of men to form dialects, on the basis of which they would separate into various groups with differing sympathies and interests. *Babel* (9). The proud builders of the city had called it Babel (the gate or court of God), but God, taking up their word and derisively giving it another meaning from a similar sounding root, also called it Babel (confusion).

iii. **Descendants of Shem in the line of Terah** (xi. 10–26). This genealogy bears marks of artificial design in its numbers as do the other lists in Scripture. Cf. Gn. xi. 10 with Lk. iii. 36, and observe the omission of Cainan. Note that Terah appears as tenth from Shem as Noah was the tenth from Adam. The first part of this genealogy has been given more fully in x. 21–25. *Eber* (14). The name possibly means 'immigrant' or 'one from across the border'; and may have been given by Salah to his son to commemorate some movement of the family over the Tigris. This is possibly the origin of the name 'Hebrew', a name which was used of Abram by the original dwellers in Palestine (see xiv. 13n.). Abram was thus a 'Hebrew' by descent from Eber and also as having himself come over the Euphrates. The aim of this genealogy is to bring the story down to Terah and his three sons.

iv. **Terah and his family** (xi. 27–32). *Ur* (28) has been definitely identified as the place now known by the Arabs as Al-Muqayyar. In Abram's time it was most probably a seaport, but the river silt during the past four millenniums has encroached upon the sea to such an extent that the ruins are now 130 miles inland. Sir Leonard Woolley and others have brought much of the details of the ancient life of the city vividly to light. *To go into the land of Canaan* (31). It is the divine rather than the human purpose that is here expressed. Terah is not known to have had any interest in Canaan, and it is expressly stated in Heb. xi. 8 that Abram 'went out, not knowing whither he went'. Cf. Gn. xii. 1. *They came unto Haran* (31). Terah's migration from Ur may have been made under the pressure of a religious motive which took the worshippers of the moon-god from one centre of her worship to another, namely Haran in the far north-west of Assyria. *Terah died in Haran* (32). This is a notice of Terah's death in order that, so far as the historian is concerned, Terah may now be forgotten. When Stephen recounts these events (Acts vii. 4), he seems to imply that Abram did not leave Haran till his father's death. The facts are that Abram left Haran when his father was 145 years of age (cf. xi. 26 and xii. 4), and Terah lived on another sixty years after Abram left him (see xi. 32). Stephen's speech merely gives the facts in the order in which they were narrated in Genesis, not in the chronological order of events. Compare the similar style of reference which is provided by the allusion to Melchizedek in Heb. vii. 3.

II. THE STORY OF ABRAHAM.
xii. 1—xxv. 18

a. Abram's faith and obedience (xii. 1—xiv. 24)

i. **The call of Abram (xii. 1–9).** At this point a distinct departure in the history occurs, and it is henceforth concerned more particularly with the promised 'seed'. The line makes its prominent beginning with Abram, whose exact date is unknown but which was probably in the 20th century B.C. *Had said* (1). The Heb. does not demand the pluperfect here, but the general sense of the passage does. Gn. xv. 7 and Acts vii. 2–4 compared with this verse raise the question as to whether there were two calls, one at Ur and another at Haran. The Scripture seems to require that we must certainly regard the call as belonging to Ur; it is then quite likely that the command may have been repeated in Haran. It may possibly be that the call was more explicit at Haran. A divine call had bidden Abram join in a (possibly general) migration from Ur to Haran, which was going on at that time. Terah is shown to have been the leader in this movement of the Abram clan. Then at Haran, after some years, God again spoke to Abram, and this time more explicitly. When he came to Haran in Mesopotamia, he obeyed the call to forsake his *country and . . . kindred* (1). When he removed from Haran to go to Canaan, he forsook his *father's house* (1).

A land that I will shew thee (1). It would seem from here and Heb. xi. 8 that Abram did not know his destination. In Gn. xi. 31 it was stated that it was Canaan, but this could be written by the historian only in the light of the subsequent events, not as revealing the conscious mind of Terah or Abram. *In thee shall all families of the earth be blessed* (3). Abram's line henceforth was to be mediatorial, and blessing to men was to flow through his seed. This promise came to its complete realization in Christ. *The plain of Moreh* (6). 'Plain' should read 'the teacher's oak' and was probably a well-known spot under which a religious teacher had been accustomed to sit. *The Canaanite* (6). This means that at the time of Abram's arrival the Canaanites had already become the possessors of this land. The Canaanite occupation of the country is confirmed by Egyptian history. There is therefore no anachronism, as is sometimes alleged. All the alleged 'anachronisms' of the book of Genesis are capable of reasonable explanation in this and similar ways.

ii. Abram in Egypt (xii. 10–20). *A famine* (10). A famine in the land of promise. This was a very great test of faith for Abram. A 'famine' of a local character would be quickly caused by the failure of the Palestine rains, which in Egypt would not be felt. *Abram went down into Egypt* (10). Was Abram right in doing this? Since the Scripture makes no adverse comment, it would seem that Abram did a perfectly reasonable thing. *Say . . . thou art my sister* (13). Compared with the darker Hamites, the Semites were 'fair' (11) and this would make their womenfolk exceedingly attractive. It is clear from xx. 13 that this was a settled policy with Abram. To say that

Sarai was his sister was a half truth (xx. 12). It was correct so far as it went, but it was an intentional falsehood. Here are the doubts of the father of the faithful. He 'staggered not' at the big things, but feared regarding the smaller affairs. *Why didst thou not tell me . . . ?* (18). The natural uprightness and morality revealed by these words must not be overlooked.

iii. The parting of Abram and Lot (xiii. 1–18). *Even to Bethel* (3). Abram, on his return to Canaan, seems to have gone to Bethel to renew his vows to God. The phrases *at the beginning* (3) and *at the first* (4) remind us that we may always make a new start. *Their substance was great* (6). Riches are not an unmixed blessing, and here they were likely to spoil good relations between Abram and Lot. There is the suggestion in verses 8 and 9 that Lot may have sided with his herdmen. *The Perizzite* (7). The origin of this name is uncertain. *Is not the whole land before thee?* (9). What a great soul was Abram! Lot was as materialistic as Abram was magnanimous, and he chose the plain of Jordan (11). *The plain of Jordan* (10). Lit. 'circle of Jordan'. This refers to an almost oval territory around the Dead Sea. The precise location of *Sodom and Gomorrah* (10) is not certainly known, but the weight of opinion favours the view that they were at the southern end of the sea. God is never any man's debtor, and says to Abram, *All the land which thou seest, to thee will I give it* (15). *The plain* ('oaks' RV) *of Mamre* (18). Mamre was an Amorite,

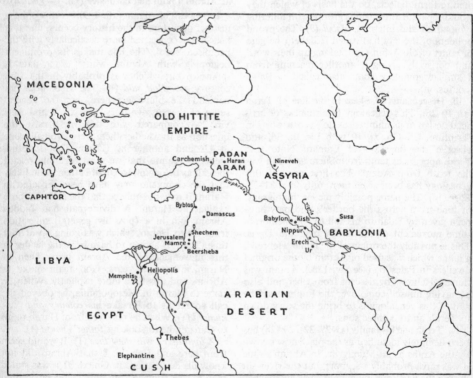

THE NEAR EAST IN THE AGE OF THE PATRIARCHS

then living, and he was later confederate with Abram (xiv. 13). Abram was but a 'guest' still.

iv. The battle of the kings (xiv. 1-12). From the unusual way of speaking of Abram as 'Abram the Hebrew' (13) it is thought by many that this narrative may have been originally of foreign origin. Seeing that Amraphel is given the prominence of being mentioned first, even though the expedition seems strictly to have been under the command of Chedorlaomer, the place of writing may have been Babylonia. Fourteen years previous to the time of the incident here narrated, Chedorlaomer had subjugated the plain of Jordan. Abram at this time was still in Haran (cf. the chronological data provided in Gn. xvi. 3). Five cities of the plain revolted and Chedorlaomer, with three allies, marched against them. *Amraphel* (1). Many historians have identified Amraphel with Hammurabi, whose laws for Babylon are now so famous, but this identification is now largely dropped as unproved. *Tidal* (1). Tidal might have been Tudhalia, king of the Hittites.

The course of the invasion seems to have been as follows. Approaching from the Damascus area, the kings swept through Bashan and the Amorite territories on the east of Jordan, and, reserving the rebels till last, pressed on to a point far south of the Dead Sea. At this point they *returned* (7), presumably moving northwards. They paused to make a raid into the southern desert (7), and then, moving round in a circular manner by way of Hazezon-tamar (possibly Engedi), the conquerors proceeded to deal with the leaders of the revolt. The battle was fought in the *vale of Siddim* (8), near to the cities of Sodom and Gomorrah. *Slimepits* (10). These were holes from which bitumen had been excavated. The kings of the plain, expecting to use this rough ground as a defence, were rushed into it to their own destruction. It is the capture of Lot (12) which brings this narrative into the inspired record.

v. The rescue of Lot (xiv. 13-16). *Abram the Hebrew* (13). The origin and meaning of this name is uncertain. There are two possibilities: either it comes from Eber (see Gn. xi. 14n.), or it is derived from the verb meaning to pass over (a river) and contains an allusion to the crossing of the river Euphrates by Abram and his great company. In this latter sense it might be translated 'immigrant', and it possibly reflects a Canaanite way of speaking of Abram. There is the further possibility that this is the term 'Habiru', which means a semi-nomad. *Trained servants* (14). These armed men were for the protection of flocks from marauding tribes, and the existence of 318 of them shows Abram to have been a powerful chieftain. Abram's own warriors were reinforced by bodies of Amorites under Aner, Eshcol and Mamre (24). Not being encumbered by booty, as were Chedorlaomer's troops, Abram and his allies overtook the victorious armies at Dan. Breaking upon them in the dark, he threw the numerically superior forces into confusion and pursued them almost as far as Damascus. He recovered Lot and his family and all the booty which had been lost. *Unto Dan* (14). This place was called Laish in Moses' time (Jdg. xviii. 29), but it is here referred to by its later name.

vi. Melchizedek blesses Abram (xiv. 17-20). Returning in victory, Abram received visits from two kings. The first was the king of Sodom, who came to express his gratitude, and the second was Melchizedek, king of Salem, who came to bestow a blessing. *The valley of Shaveh* (17) is 'the valley of the plain' and was situated just north of Salem (Jerusalem). It was called 'the king's dale' either as a memorial of this incident or from the fact that on this piece of level ground the kings of Judah assembled and exercised their forces. (If this latter be the case, and it probably is, we have here another example of a later scribal note to identify a place by using its modern name.) Who was Melchizedek? There is nothing mysterious about him in spite of the interpretation placed by some on Heb. vii. 3. He was king of some Semitic clan, which still occupied Salem, before the Jebusites captured it. There was never an utter extinction of the knowledge of God in the world, and here, too, God had preserved some knowledge of Himself. The typical significance of Melchizedek lies in his universal and unlimited priesthood, allegorically established in Heb. vii. 3; his dual office as 'king-priest'; and in his name (Heb. vii. 1-2). The appearance of Melchizedek provides us with the first occurrence of the word 'priest' in Scripture, and the biblical conception of priesthood cannot be properly grasped if this singular fact is ignored. *The most high God* (18). *El-'elyon* means 'the Supreme God'. Observe that Abram later identifies Jehovah and *El-'elyon* (22). *Tithes* (20). Abram's tithes ('tenths') to Melchizedek show the pre-Mosaic date of the custom. See Dt. xiv. 22-29n. In giving tithes Abram acknowledged Melchizedek's God as the true God and Melchizedek's priesthood as a true one. Cf. Heb. vii. 9.

vii. Abram and the king of Sodom (xiv. 21-24). This little episode reveals Abram's sagacity and piety. His sagacity was displayed in the division of the spoil. According to Arab law, and this may have obtained in Abram's time, if anyone recovers booty he gives up only the *persons* (21), but is entitled to keep the rest for himself. This is what the king of Sodom suggested. Abram's astuteness and practical wisdom led him to insist that his men receive only their food and that Aner, Eshcol and Mamre share the spoil. Abram thus made friends of these men, who otherwise might have first feared him and then have intrigued against him. Abram's piety shone forth in his loyalty to his vow to Jehovah. His action was both wise policy and good piety.

b. God's covenant with Abram (xv. 1—xvii. 27)

i. God promises Abram a son (xv. 1-6). The occasion of the promise is pointed out in the phrase *after these things* (1). Abram's natural reaction was met with a 'fear not'. *Great reward* (1). Abram had refused the spoil, but God would not allow him to be the loser. *Go childless* (2). This expression means 'go away' or 'depart' childless. Abram's sorrow was that Eliezer would, by the laws under which they lived, become the inheritor of his house. *Born in my house* (3). Lit. 'son of my house', and thus Abram's representative and heir. *He counted it to him for righteousness* (6). 'For' is translated in the LXX by the Greek preposition *eis*, and means 'to' or 'unto'. It does not mean that instead of righteousness Abram offered faith. Abram's faith was not here regarded as another form of righteousness ('works'), but in the divine plan it was to be the means whereby a man might attain 'unto' (*eis*) righteousness (cf. Rom. iv. 3).

ii. The solemn covenant concerning Canaan (xv. 7–21). *I am the Lord* (7). Heb. *Yahveh.* At the basis of any covenant which God makes is His character, and it is to this that God refers when He begins with this affirmation of His name. *Whereby shall I know . . . ?* (8). Abram is not here demanding a sign in order to believe, but after, and on account of, having believed. It was not doubt that asked this token, but faith. God gave Abram a sign related to faith, and this is the true nature of a sacrament. Ancient covenants were sometimes confirmed by the halving of sacrificial victims and the passing between them of the two parties to the covenant. Jehovah graciously condescended to confirm His promise to Abram by accommodating Himself to this custom. This paragraph therefore describes the 'cutting of a covenant' between Jehovah and Abram. Note that only one symbol is seen passing between the pieces, namely, 'the appearance as of a smoking furnace from which torch-like flames shot out' (17). This indicated that Jehovah alone was undertaking the fulfilment of all the conditions attaching to the covenant. The covenant of grace is thus not a pact, as between two, but a promise confirmed by covenantal forms. For the symbolism of fire for Jehovah, see Ex. xix. 18, xxiv. 17; Ps. xviii. 8. God makes a fourfold revelation: privation, deliverance, peace and triumph (13–16). *Four hundred years* (13). This is a round figure, the precise number being 430 (Ex. xii. 40, 41). *Iniquity of the Amorites* (16). It was this which justified their extirpation. *The river of Egypt* (18). This is either the Wady el Arish (brook of Egypt), the boundary between Egypt and the desert south of Palestine, or the River Nile itself.

iii. The birth of Ishmael (xvi. 1–16). *An Egyptian, whose name was Hagar* (1). Her name means 'run-away', and perhaps points to her having run away from a former mistress in Egypt. In the episode that follows it is important to observe that the initiative was taken, not by Abram, but by Sarai. Under the strict laws of monogamy (Gn. ii. 24), the conduct of Abram and Sarai was not permissible, but provision for this kind of arrangement found a place under the

laws of Abram's time. *Obtain children by her* (2). Lit. 'be builded by her', the children being the 'house'. *Her mistress was despised* (4). This must mean that in some way Hagar took wrong advantage of the position which Sarai had allowed her to occupy and disregarded the fact that she was still Sarai's maid. Rather unreasonably Sarai puts the blame for the domestic unhappiness on to Abram (5). *Thy maid is in thy hand* (6). In accordance with custom (see, e.g., the provisions of the Code of Hammurabi) Abram could do no other than leave Sarai to act as she wished. *Dealt hardly* (6). Sarai no doubt degraded her from being the 'wife' (3) of Abram, and reduced her to her former position (see verse 9). *She fled* (6). True to her name.

The angel of the Lord (7). This is the first occurrence in Scripture of the appearance of this mysterious messenger (angel). As in several places He is apparently identified with Jehovah a number of questions arise. Is He just one of the created angels? But the angel speaks in the first person interchangeably with Jehovah. Is He a direct theophany? But this does not do justice to the distinction which is made between Jehovah and the angel. Is He a self-distinction of Jehovah? This is to regard the revelation through the angel as pointing to a real distinction in the nature of God such as is found in the New Testament 'Logos' or 'Son'. So long as we avoid reading back the New Testament into the conceptions of the Old, we are justified in the light of the New Testament in seeing some hint and recognition of a richness within the unity of the Godhead. With the revelation of God in Christ before us, we may regard the angel as the Second Person of the Holy Trinity. For a further study of this remarkable Old Testament revelation, see Gn. xxxii. 30; Ex. iii. 2n., xiv. 19, xxiii. 20; Jos. v. 13–15; Jdg. xiii. 22; Is. lxiii. 9; and compare these also with the narrative in Gn. xviii.

Return . . . submit (9). These are the steps to restored peace and joy at all times. A blessing is given to Hagar (10) and a promise made concerning her son. Ishmael's name means 'God shall hear', and his character is to be that of 'a wild ass man' (12). The wild ass of the Arabian deserts was a noble creature (see Jb. xxxix. 5–8), and was thus a fine symbol of the free roving life of the Arab. *He shall dwell in the presence of all his brethren* (12). This means that he shall maintain his independence, continuing to exist as a free race in the very presence of the other Abrahamic peoples. *Thou God seest me* (13). This phrase represents the Hebrew 'Thou art El Roi', meaning 'A God of Seeing', or 'A God of Vision'. This means not so much a God who sees, but a God 'who permits Himself to be seen'. Hagar's comment is an equally difficult Hebrew phrase for us to translate, and possibly means 'Have I even seen God and survived?' *Beer-lahai-roi* (14). Word for word this name may be translated 'well/of the living/seeing', meaning more freely, 'Well of continuing to live after seeing God'. That a man should be allowed to see God and live was a mark of especial favour. Note Manoah's words 'We shall surely die, because we have seen God' (Jdg. xiii. 22), and cf. Gn. xxxii. 30 and Ex. iii. 6.

iv. Renewal of the covenant (xvii. 1–8). *The Almighty God* (1). The title is *El Shaddai*, and the AV translation of it still seems to be as good as any. It appears to have been something of a new title and therefore a new revelation to Abram. His corresponding conduct must be to walk before El Shaddai in uprightness. Allusion to this name is made in Ex. vi. 3 (see note there). This latter passage, however, does not mean that the name of Jehovah was completely unknown to the patriarchs, but that it was in His character of the Almighty God that Jehovah made His promises to the fathers. *A father of many nations* (4). The word suggests a 'din', and implies a thronging crowd of nations. The promise points on far beyond those who were to be his physical descendants and looks forward to the 'families of the earth' that were to be spiritually blessed in him. Cf. xii. 3n. *Abraham* (5). Abram had meant 'high father', but he is now to be called 'Abraham'. The longer form suggests by similarity of sound the Hebrew for 'father of a multitude'.

v. Circumcision the covenant sign (xvii. 9–14). *Circumcised* (10). The practice of circumcision was fairly extensive in the world of Abraham's time. In its original significance it may have been a kind of religious acknowledgment associated with the powers of human reproduction, but more commonly it seems to have served as a tribal mark, and it is likely that it was in this second meaning that God made use of it. For Abraham's family it was now to be regarded as *a token of the covenant* (11). This is one of the many instances of God's method of appropriating an already existing practice and dedicating it to His own purposes. Circumcision became a touch-stone of later Judaism. It is important not to overlook the difference between the old covenant and the new. Old covenant blessings came by physical descent, of which circumcision was the sign; new covenant blessings are spiritually conveyed and are expressed by a new sign. *Shall be cut off* (14). The Old Testament is full of foreshadowings of New Testament realities, and in the importance of membership within the covenant community there is an intimation of the necessity of membership in the body of Christ.

vi. God's promise to Sarai (xvii. 15–22). *Sarah* (15). The addition of the 'h', linked with the explanation about 'nations' in verse 16, serves to confirm this as the probable meaning of the change in Abraham's name (see on xvii. 4, 5 above). *Fell upon his face, and laughed* (17). Worship and incredulity seem intermixed here. We are under no necessity of making Abraham flawless as the Jewish commentators try to do. Abraham found the promise difficult to believe at first. This interpretation of Abraham's laughter is borne out by what he said *in his*

heart (17) and by his request to God that the promises might centre in Ishmael (18). The answer that God gives to Abraham's questioning is simply to repeat and amplify the promise. *Thou shalt call his name Isaac* (19). Isaac means 'he laughed', and was to serve as a reminder to Abraham of the 'ludicrously unlikely means by which this child was brought into the world' (Dods). *My covenant will I establish with Isaac* (21). All through the Scripture the importance of the settlement of the divine covenant on Isaac is to be heeded. Ishmael is to be blessed (20), but the covenant belongs to Isaac.

vii. Abraham and his house receive the sign of the covenant (xvii. 23–27). *In the selfsame day* (23). Abraham's promptitude is one of the characteristic features of his obedience. *All the men of his house . . . with him* (27). See verses 12 and 13 for the divine instruction covering this. At this early stage the blessing of Abraham was to extend to others even though they were not physically descended from him. The 'universal' purpose is always revealing itself even in the context of the particularism which necessarily had to belong to the old covenant.

c. The deliverance of Lot from Sodom and Gomorrah (xviii. 1—xix. 38)

i. Abraham entertains the heavenly visitors (xviii. 1–15). *The Lord appeared* (1). The phrase 'angel of Jehovah' is not used in this particular narrative, but there can be no doubt that one of the three who stood by Abraham was this 'angel'. His speech and manner are precisely those of the 'angel' who is named on other such occasions. The language of verses 10, 13, 14, 17–22, and the great intercession of 23–33, together with the employment of the word 'angels' in xix. 1, corroborate the suggestion that here we have to do with the 'angel of Jehovah'. The fact that the story opens with the categorical affirmation that it was 'the Lord' who appeared lends strong support to the suggestion that the 'angel' may be identified with the Second Person of the Trinity. Abraham at first regarded the 'three men' as ordinary travellers (cf. Heb. xiii. 2) and offered them the usual eastern courtesies in order that they might then 'pass on' (5). *The tent door* (1). The tent was usually divided into two halves, a closed and an open half. The open half, or 'sitting room', was called 'the tent door'. It was in or in front of this apartment that guests were entertained. The remark in verse 9 that Sarah was 'in the tent' has reference to the closed portion of the tent, divided from the 'tent door' only by the hangings. Sarah, however, was moving about in the whole of the tent, as verse 10 indicates. *Sarah laughed* (12). In defence of Sarah (though her laughter was no more sinful than Abraham's) it must be said that she had no reason to think that the 'men' were any more than three ordinary courteous visitors who were exchanging polite but extravagant salutations. Sarah's denial of her laughter was her wrong.

ii. Abraham's intercession for Sodom and Gomorrah (xviii. 16–33). *Shall I hide from Abraham . . . ?* (17). The reason for telling Abraham is not because he had a relative in the city of Sodom, but because 'all the nations of the earth shall be blessed in him' (18). The blessing that was to come to the one small family that was saved out of Sodom was to come through Abraham's intercession; Abraham therefore must be told of the threatened judgment. *For I know him* (19). The Hebrew of this sentence is better rendered, 'For I have known him in order that he may command . . .' God's confidences were going to be placed in Abraham not because of what he was (though his integrity was very high), but because of what God was intending to do through him. *I will go down . . . I will know* (21). The purpose of the going down is not strictly to 'discover', but to afford the Sodomites an opportunity of proving themselves. 'I will know' means that He will put the people to a trial. *Went toward Sodom* (22). These are described as 'two' in xix. 1, the One being detained by Abraham.

The righteous with the wicked (23). Abraham had a clear conception of the moral character of God. Cf. his exclamation *Shall not the Judge of all the earth do right?* (25), in which he revealed his knowledge of the universal sovereignty of God. Abraham was no tribal chieftain worshipping a tribal god. Great as was Abraham's faith and courage, his intercession was based on an insufficient principle. Abraham thought in terms of communities; God's salvation operates in terms of the individual. God was unable to save the city even on the lowest terms of Abraham's reasoning with Him, but He could be gracious to whom He would be gracious, and displayed this in the salvation of Lot and his family out of the city which, as a whole, was devoted to destruction.

iii. The vileness of Sodom (xix. 1–11). *The gate* (1). This was the public place of the city, where the business of the community was transacted. Cf. Ru. iv. 1. *We will abide in the street all night* (2). Cf. Jdg. xix. 15, 20. The 'street' was an open space within the city, and if a traveller were unsuccessful in finding hospitality, it would be quite the customary thing for him to settle down for the night within the protection of the city walls, but in the open air in this broad square. Knowing the custom, but knowing also the vileness of the Sodomites, Lot urged the visitors to come into his house, which they did (3). The filthy lust of the Sodomites could be neither restrained nor disguised, but led them to an attack on Lot's house in the early part of the night (5). Lot's crude sense of honour led him to a degraded gesture of cowardice (8). *Blindness* (11). This word occurs only here and in 2 Ki. vi. 18. It means not ordinary blindness, but a confusing of the vision in such a way that the eye deceived the brain.

iv. The escape of Lot (xix. 12–23). The abruptness of the narrative is in harmony with the tragic reality of the story. The guilt of the city is manifest; the angels therefore urge Lot to lose no time in hurrying away from it. *As one that mocked* (14). There can be no effective preaching where there is no significant living. *Consumed* (15). This verb, which appears again in verse 17, and which was translated 'destroyed' in Gn. vii. 23, means more exactly 'swept away'. Pitiful compulsion laid hold of Lot and brought him out of the doomed city (16). *Look not behind thee* (17). God required of them that they should forsake the city in heart, as well as in a local manner: they were to loathe the place as God loathed it. This was a moral demand as well as a physical one, hence the severity of the punishment on Lot's wife (26).

v. Destruction of Sodom and Gomorrah (xix. 24–29). *The Lord rained . . . brimstone and fire* (24). The use of natural agencies in the destruction of these cities makes that destruction no less the act of God. The true nature of the miracle lies in the fact that all that happened was according to the divine intention. The actual overthrow of the cities can be accounted for in the volcanic and sulphurous character of the country. Possibly by means of an earthquake (cf. 'overthrow', verse 21) compressed inflammable gases were set free; the gaseous matter became ignited, and then rained down in fiery showers. *His wife looked back* (26). See Lk. xvii. 32. Lot's wife is the type of those who look back with regretful longings upon things which are inconsistent with their salvation. *A pillar of salt* (26). Lingering, she became involved in the heaving up of the rock salt, and so perished, 'leaving the hill of salt, in which she was enclosed, as her memorial' (R. P. Smith).

vi. Lot and his family (xix. 30–38). This section gives the facts about the origin of the Moabites and Ammonites. What a miserable figure is Lot! Once so wealthy and so blessed, yet by a materialistic choice brought to live in a cave (30) and to suffer the indignity described in verse 36. This is the last we hear of Lot.

d. Abraham and Abimelech (xx. 1–18)

She is my sister (2). This passage is not a literary 'duplicate' of that in Gn. xii. 10–20. The details are strikingly different and, above all, the narrative itself tells us why such an incident occurred a second time. It was an agreed policy (xx. 13). *A dead man* (3). God had smitten Abimelech with a deadly disease. *Innocency* (5). Abimelech's words do not mean that he never practised this kind of thing, for the ancient records show it was frequent, but that in this case he did not know he was doing it. *I also withheld thee from sinning* (6). This was no doubt by means of the sickness referred to in verses 3, 17. *A prophet* (7). Although not strictly to be placed in the line of the Old Testament preacher-prophets, Abraham nevertheless stood in a special relation to Jehovah, and could thus mediate in a case of this kind (7). Abimelech's rebuke of Abraham puts the 'prophet' in a very bad light, and he speaks in stronger terms than those of Pharaoh (Gn. xii. 18ff.).

What sawest thou? (10). What danger did you foresee? *The fear of God* (11). Knowing the people generally to be morally debased, Abraham and Sarah had thought the same of Abimelech's court. Abraham is perfectly frank with Abimelech. *Daughter of my father, but not the daughter of my mother* (12). Sarah was apparently Terah's daughter by another wife. Marriages with a half-sister in this way were later on prohibited; see Lv. xviii. 9, xx. 17; Dt. xxvii. 22. *Every place* (13). By telling Abimelech that they had agreed to do this at 'every place' Abraham somewhat softened the reference that his comment about the fear of God bore in regard to Abimelech's court. *A covering of the eyes* (16). The 'he' here should be 'it'. The thought probably is that by making this gift he would make amends for the wrong which he had unwittingly committed. Cf. Gn. xxxii. 20, where the Hebrew phrase 'cover the face' is translated 'appease'. Abimelech hoped that his gift would blind the eyes of Abraham and his friends to any injury he may have done them. The phrase *thus she was reproved* (16), or better, 'thou art righted', seems to contain the suggestion that in Abimelech's mind there was also the hope that, by Abraham's acceptance of the gift, Sarah's chastity throughout the whole episode would be both acknowledged and vindicated.

e. The promised child (xxi. 1—xxiv. 67)

i. Birth of Isaac (xxi. 1–8). *An hundred years old* (5). Compare Gn. xii. 4 with xvi. 3 for evidence that Ishmael was about thirteen or fourteen years of age when Isaac was born. *God hath made me to laugh* (6). This is the third time that reference is made to the laughter that attached itself to the birth of Isaac. See xvii. 17 and xviii. 12. The former laughter of Abraham and Sarah had been incredulous. Everything was altered now, and the almost unbelievable had happened. As Sarah lies on her bed and thinks of the way all the women will laugh when they hear the news (6), she too laughs, but this time it is in overflowing delight. Sarah can see the humourous side of things, but also rejoices as only a woman with such longings as hers could rejoice. *Was weaned . . . a great feast* (8). Weaning normally occurred at about two or three years of age, and it was frequently the occasion of a family feast.

ii. Hagar and Ishmael leave the house of Abraham (xxi. 9–21). *The son of Hagar . . . mocking* (9). Observe how the very contempt that was in Sarah's mind for Ishmael is marvellously portrayed in the historical account—'the son of Hagar' (cf. 'this thy son' in Lk. xv. 30). 'Mocking' means 'making fun of'. Paul refers to this by the word 'persecuted' (Gal. iv. 29), which shows Ishmael's behaviour to have been provocative, to say the least. *Cast out this bondwoman and her son* (10). It would appear that Abraham would have no option but to do this, even though it

might be 'very grievous' to him (11). Sarah wanted Abraham to perform some kind of legal act, by which Ishmael might be excluded from all claim on the inheritance. The confirmation of this act would be to send Hagar and the boy away. For the position of Isaac compare verses 12, 13 with Gn. xvii. 19–21. Ishmael shall be truly blessed, but Abraham must not forget that the covenant is with Isaac.

She cast the child under one of the shrubs (15). There is no need to suppose any inconsistency here with the other parts of Genesis, or to imagine this boy of seventeen being carried by his mother like an infant in arms. The privations of the desert reduced both mother and son to exhaustion, but the growing youth would collapse under them sooner than the physique of the mother who had become accustomed to the desert life. Ishmael must have fainted with exhaustion. Hagar did her best to support him, but at last could hold him up no longer and 'cast' him under the shade of a bush. In his extreme weakness, the fainting of Ishmael could have but one end, but this the mother could not bear to witness. True to the name, Ishmael ('God hears'), it is twice recorded in verse 17 that God heard the voice of the lad. How great is God's care of the outcast and lonely! *The angel of God* (17). Cf. Gn. xvi. 7. The change of title is due to the change of Hagar's position. At the earlier time she was within the covenant as a member of Abraham's household; she is now outside of the covenant so far as her official standing is concerned. The discrimination in the use of God ('Elohim) and Lord (Jehovah) is too deep in the book to be ignored. *A wife out of the land of Egypt* (21). What more natural thing was there for Hagar to do? Hagar and Ishmael serve an allegorical purpose in Paul's discussion of the nature of the true people of God (Gal. iv. 21ff.); but their actual experiences of God provide us with great spiritual instruction.

iii. The agreement with Abimelech at Beersheba (xxi. 22–34). Some kind of trouble must have been brewing between Abraham's servants and those of Abimelech. In the customary oblique way of the ancient East Abimelech approaches Abraham for an assurance of continued friendship. Abraham interprets Abimelech's motive aright and comes directly to the point by raising the question of the well 'which Abimelech's servants had violently taken away' (25). Abimelech appears to have been unaware of the details of this, and the matter is amicably settled. In this narrative we discover yet another of the ancient ways of making a covenant, namely, by the giving and receiving of 'sevens'. From this custom the Hebrew term 'to seven oneself' (*shaba'*, from *sheba'*, 'seven') came into use. This 'sevening' could be effected by the use of seven objects of any kind. In commemoration of this covenant the place was called 'The well of seven' (31) because there both of them 'sevened' themselves. But see AV mg. and cf. Gn. xxvi. 32n. *Planted a grove* (33). 'A tamarisk tree' (RV). It was customary in Canaan to worship God under trees and to plant them in memory of some act of religious significance. *Philistines' land* (34). The power of the Philistines belongs to a later period: at this time they were something of a military colony.

iv. The offering of Isaac (xxii. 1–14). *God did tempt* (RV 'prove') *Abraham* (1). The sequel to this must be recognized in the words 'for now I know that thou fearest God' (12). *Thy son, thine only son Isaac, whom thou lovest* (2). Every word adds emotion to the story. *The land of Moriah* (2). There is nothing in ancient topography to certify the exact location of this place, nor yet the mountain itself, but 2 Ch. iii. 1 identifies the temple hill as 'mount Moriah'. *Offer him* (2). Child sacrifice was familiar in Abraham's time. Three purposes were served by this command: to prove Abraham, to express God's abhorrence of child-sacrifice, and to set forth Christ, 'the Lamb of God'. *Come again to you* (5). Abraham evidently believed that they would both return. From Heb. xi. 17–19 it is possible to infer that Abraham thought that Isaac could be raised from the dead. *They went both of them together* (6). The repetition of this phrase in verse 8 lets us into the pathos of the walk. The entire narrative is marked by a simple dignity.

God will provide himself a lamb (8). What did Abraham mean? It seems that he spoke better than he knew, both so far as the immediate circumstances were concerned, and also in relation to the ultimate provision which God made of 'himself' as the 'lamb'. In connection with the pilgrimage they were making to Moriah, some commentators think that Abraham had an inner conviction that in some way God would do something about the matter when they reached the place of sacrifice; but other commentators are of the opinion that Abraham fully expected to have to slay his son, but that God would in some way bring Isaac back from the dead. *The angel of the Lord* (11). If the 'angel' is He whom we have thought Him to be, how significant it is, in view of all the great things to which this scene pointed, that it was 'the angel' who should call out of heaven! *In the stead of his son* (13). Here is a perfect example of substitution. Cf. Jn. i. 29; Rom. v. 6. *Jehovah-jireh* (14). In verse 8 we read 'God will provide' (Heb. *'Elohim-jireh*) and here *Jehovah-jireh*. The latter name is evidence of the early use of the name Jehovah, and the connection here between *'Elohim-jireh* and *Jehovah-jireh* shows that the different divine names cannot here denote different authors. See p. 31.

v. God's blessing on Abraham (xxii. 15–19). *By myself have I sworn* (15). Observe the notice that is taken of this in Heb. vi. 17.

vi. Abraham's relatives (xxii. 20–24). The interest of the history now begins to transfer to Isaac, and the details of this paragraph are given to show the family from which Isaac's wife was to come. The names of *Huz* (Uz) and *Buz* (21) both appear again in the book of Job (see Jb. i. 1,

xxxii. 2). *Rebekah* (23) was granddaughter to Nahor and second cousin to Isaac.

vii. Death and burial of Sarah (xxiii. 1–20). *Kirjath-arba* (2). This place is identified here and in verse 19 with Hebron, Mamre and Machpelah. *Abraham came to mourn for Sarah* (2). This means either that Abraham was away from home when Sarah died, or that he now came into the tent where her body lay. *The sons of Heth* (3). The Hittites had scattered communities throughout Canaan for many centuries of Israel's history. At one time they were a people as powerful as the Egyptians or Assyrians. *Give me a possession* (4). Although Abraham was regarded as *a mighty prince* (6), he was nevertheless 'a stranger and a sojourner' in the country. It is pathetic that his first and only permanent possession in the land of promise was a grave. 'These all died in faith' (Heb. xi. 8–16). *None of us shall withhold from thee his sepulchre* (6). The sons of Heth make an unusual gesture to Abraham in offering to allow him to bury Sarah in one of their family graves. Or, since this would be so exceptional a thing, it may be that the Hittites are merely assuring Abraham that any one of them would be willing to sell him a burial place.

The field give I thee (11). The narrative is now one of the most entertaining in the Old Testament, giving us, as it does, an ancient account of buying and selling. The impression of the story is that they were not engaged in a business deal, but in friendly gestures of generosity. Ephron is not really making a gift of the field to Abraham, but is just beginning in true oriental style to drive a shrewd bargain. *The land is worth four hundred shekels of silver* (15). Ephron names a high price, to which Abraham promptly agrees. This silver was a kind of currency, but it was calculated by weight (16). *The field . . . the cave . . . all the trees . . . in the field . . . the borders . . .* (17). This reads very much like the deeds as drawn up by our lawyers today. *At the gate* (18). As at Sodom (Gn. xix. 1), this was the place of public business.

viii. The quest for a wife for Isaac (xxiv. 1–60). *Abraham was old* (1). He was about 140 years of age. Cf. xxi. 5 with xxv. 20. *His eldest servant* (2). This was most probably the Eliezer referred to in xv. 2. *Put . . . thy hand under my thigh* (2). Abraham brings Eliezer to make a particularly solemn form of oath, the symbolism of which was probably the calling of a man's descendants to see to it that any breach of the oath shall be avenged. It may be regarded perhaps as a 'swearing by posterity' and was particularly apt in the present oath, because it was in the interests of preserving a holy posterity. *The Lord, the God of heaven, and the God of the earth* (3). It is exhilarating, after reading some of the hypothetical accounts of the 'limited' views of God that Abraham was supposed to have held, to return again to Abraham's own words and hear him speak. Cf. xiv. 22. *Not take a wife* (3). There must have been a very great inducement to

94

Abraham to marry his son to one of the local chieftains, thus making an alliance with one of them, and also gaining a footing in the land; but his obedience and faith shine out with splendour. *Unto my country, and to my kindred* (4). The place to which Eliezer went was Haran (cf. xxvii. 43, xxix. 4). This does not mean, however, that Haran was Abraham's birthplace, as some would contend here. There are two quite straightforward ways of understanding this emphatic expression: either we may take it that the latter term defines the former, the main thing being that Isaac's bride shall come from his own people; or we may regard Abraham as meaning that if Eliezer failed in his mission at Haran he was to go on as far as Ur where Abraham probably had many relatives. The former is the better understanding of the phrase, and the latter is quite unlikely.

Took ten camels (10). Eliezer wished to appear as the representative of a wealthy master. *Mesopotamia* (10). This was the land between the two rivers, the Tigris and the Euphrates. *She that thou hast appointed* (14). Eliezer's prayer and his entire approach to the task show that he was conscious of a great spiritual responsibility. It would not have been difficult for Eliezer straight away to ask the first man he met where Abraham's relations might be found. He seems to have felt that the choice was to be God's, and so he proposed the sign to God. *I will draw water for thy camels also* (19). This was exceptional generosity, but it was 'of the Lord' to Eliezer. At once Eliezer began to realize he was near the object of his journey. The language of verse 21 shows that he suspected that there stood before him now the one who was to be Isaac's wife; and the answer to his question, given in verse 24, gave him the convincing proof. *Worshipped the Lord* (26). What else could Eliezer do?

Laban (29). It would seem that Bethuel, the father, was either too aged or infirm to take much responsibility; the weight of this fell upon the all too willing Laban. This appears also in verse 50. Eliezer's speech to the family (34–39) is most moving; it is possible almost to feel the breathless tension in the household of Bethuel as they listen to this long narration. *Bad or good* (50). There simply is not anything to be said. *Hinder me not* (56). In expressions like this the conscientious and expeditious character of Eliezer becomes conspicuous. *I will go* (58). This response shows something of the purposeful character of the woman who was to be the mother of Jacob and Esau.

ix. Rebekah is presented to Isaac (xxiv. 61–67). *She lighted off the camel* (64). This was a customary mark of respect, and was observed even while at some distance from a person of rank. *She took a vail* (65). According to eastern custom, a bride must not be seen unveiled by the bridegroom until the marriage rites are completed. Eliezer's mission has been taken as a remarkable picture of the work of the Holy Spirit in seeking a bride for Christ.

f. The family of Abraham (xxv. 1–18)

i. Abraham's other descendants (xxv. 1–4). *Keturah* (1). The best view of this passage is to regard this marriage as having taken place after Sarah's death. The fact that Abraham, whose body could have been regarded as 'dead' when he was 100 years old (xvii. 17; Rom. iv. 19), now had six sons by Keturah, is to be explained as due to the new generative strength which came to him with the gift of Isaac. *Midian* (2). Observe the origin of the Midianites from Abraham (cf. xxxvii. 28; Ex. ii. 15); and the activities of the Midianites recorded in the book of Judges. Observe a further link with the book of Job in the reference to Shuah (2; cf. Jb. ii. 11).

ii. Death and burial of Abraham (xxv. 5–11). *Unto Isaac* (5). This was a further indication that Isaac's line was to be regarded as the true family of Abraham. The giving of 'gifts' (6) to the sons of the concubines was accompanied by a significant sending of them away. *An hundred threescore and fifteen years* (7). Observe the triple way (8) of referring to the fulness of life which the patriarch attained. *These are the generations* (12). If this *toledoth* be a subscription, then it must probably be taken along with the one in verse 19, the two together marking the end of a series of tablets or records kept concerning their father by Ishmael and Isaac respectively. The significance of these occurrences of *toledoth*, however, is still an open question. (See note in Introduction, p. 75.)

iii. Ishmael's sons (xxv. 12–18). Note how the book disposes of the collateral line of Ishmael first.

III. THE STORY OF ISAAC.
xxv. 19—xxvi. 35

a. Birth of Esau and Jacob (xxv. 19–28)

The elder shall serve the younger (23). The whole message is poetic in form and the parallelisms are quite clear. The domination of Israel over Edom originates here. Edom ('the elder') was subjugated by David ('the younger'): see 2 Sa. viii. 14. *Like an hairy garment* (25). From xxvii. 16 we gain some idea of the extraordinary appearance of Esau's skin. Occasionally the birth has been reported, even in recent years, of children with the hide of a cow. Something like this must have been the case with Esau. *Jacob* (26). Lit. 'one who follows at another's heels'. 'One that takes by the heel, or supplants' (RV mg.). The idea is that of a determined and relentless pursuer who, on overtaking his foe, throws him down. See xxvii. 36; Je. ix. 4; Ho. xii. 3. *Isaac was threescore years old* (26). These two grandsons of Abraham knew their grandfather for fifteen years.

b. Esau sells his birthright to Jacob (xxv. 29–34)

Sod (29). This is the past tense of 'to seethe'. *Therefore was his name called Edom* (30). The historian does not mean that from this solitary incident Esau received the name 'the Red'. He must early have had this name attached to him because of his appearance (25). The further characteristic, however, of his uncontrolled passion for 'the Red' (AV mg.) provides an occasion for the narrator to comment that he was well-named 'the Red'. Esau's character should be studied in the light of the inspired estimate given in Heb. xii. 16. He is taken in this passage as the symbol of the materialistic mind. *Birthright* (31). This meant the better position and larger inheritance which usually belonged to the first-born.

c. Isaac and Abimelech (xxvi. 1–16)

Beside the first famine (1). In view of the opinion of some commentators that this is but a triplicate of the one incident belonging to the life of Abraham, it is significant to observe this phrase which definitely separates the time and place of this story from that recorded in chapter xii. So far as the incident in chapter xx is concerned, it is instructive to notice the totally different course of the narrative in that chapter and in the present one. *Abimelech* (1). Some uncertainty exists as to the use of this word: it is possibly not a proper name, but a title like 'Pharaoh'. It has the meaning 'the King my father'. *Philistines* (1). See Gn. xxi. 34n. *Go not down into Egypt* (2). When in 'the land of promise' there is no need to fear or move. Whether this reflects adversely on Abraham's conduct under similar circumstances it is hard to say. *I will be with thee* (3). This is the repetition of the Abrahamic covenant, but this time in the ears of Isaac, the seed of promise. This would seem to be the first occasion that God appeared to Isaac and spoke in such a direct manner to him. *She is my sister* (7). Compare this carefully with xii. 13 and xx. 2, 13. Isaac is following the precedent set by his father, but with less justification. *Sporting* (8). Delitzsch renders the word 'caressing'. *Guiltiness* (10). The first Abimelech (xx. 3) had been taught by Jehovah that to take another man's wife was sinful. This may or may not have been the view of himself and his people previously. The lesson was still remembered in the court, and the Abimelech of Isaac's time is conscious that for anyone to have taken Rebekah as a wife would have brought the people into a state of 'guiltiness'. *Put to death* (11). This stringent penalty shows the high moral code that existed in the kingdom of Abimelech. *An hundredfold* (12). This is remarkable fruitfulness in a time of famine (see verse 1), and was proof of Jehovah's blessing. *Stopped them* (15). The filling of wells was an act of hostility by which rights of property or residence were repudiated.

d. A dispute about wells (xxvi. 17–33)

The valley of Gerar (17). Isaac was expelled from the city, but he continued to live in the locality. *Strove for that also* (21). This foolish strife between the herdmen was more deeply a strife between Abimelech and Isaac as to where the latter might be permitted to settle. By this rough policy Isaac is being pushed farther and farther

away from Gerar. *The same day* (32). The naming of Beersheba on this occasion is not a literary and contradictory duplicate of xxi. 24–32. The giving of the name to the locality was especially associated with the fact that on the very day of the ratification of the oath between Isaac and Abimelech the water was found. Abraham called the place 'The well of seven' (*sheba*'), alluding to their 'sevening' of themselves by means of the seven lambs (xxi. 29–31). Isaac now gives the spot the same name as his father had given it (xxvi. 18), but for his own additional and strikingly confirmatory reason, namely, the discovery of the water on the day of the oath (*shaba*'). To Abraham it was 'The well of seven', but to Isaac it was 'The well of the oath', both of which ideas were expressed by the one phrase 'Beer-sheba'.

e. Esau's marriages (xxvi. 34, 35)

This marriage with those outside the family line was a breach of the purity of lineage to which Abraham had been called. See xxiv. 7, 47, 48.

IV. THE STORIES OF JACOB AND ESAU. xxvii. 1—xxxvii. 1

a. Jacob in his father's home (xxvii. 1–46)

i. Jacob secures his father's blessing by deceit (xxvii. 1–29). *Isaac was old* (1). Comparing xxv. 26 with xxvi. 34 it would seem that Isaac was over one hundred years old, but he lived to the age of 180 years (see xxxv. 28). Isaac must have thought he was about to die (4, 41) but seems to have recovered. *That my soul may bless thee* (4). In spite of the prophecy (xxv. 23) Isaac seems to have determined to give the blessing to Esau. *Before the Lord* (7). These words, spoken by Rebekah, were full of significance to the religiously minded Jacob, and their addition by the skilful mother was not undesigned. They brought an added solemnity into the whole event. *Goodly raiment* (15). This probably indicates an official garment such as would be worn by the firstborn in a family on festive or solemn occasions. *Because the Lord thy God brought it to me* (20). Jacob's deception was not clever enough. It was not Esau's way to drop into pious phrases of this kind, and Isaac, who knew Esau's general bearing, is left uncertain and uneasy in his mind (21, 22). *Let people serve thee* (29). It is in this dominion that the essence of the birthright blessing consists.

ii. Esau's interview with Isaac (xxvii. 30–40). *Yea, and he shall be blessed* (33). The patriarchal blessing is irrevocable. This is the meaning of Heb. xii. 17: 'for he found no place of repentance'. Try as he would, Esau could not secure a change of mind on his father's part. Isaac sees that, despite his own endeavour to thwart it, the will of Jehovah has been done, and the blessing must certainly remain on Jacob. *Supplanted* (36). More properly 'over-reached': see xxv. 26n. *When thou shalt have the dominion* (40). For this uncertain Hebrew phrase, it is better to follow the RV, 'when thou shalt break loose'. There were to be occasions when Edom would temporarily throw off the yoke of bondage to Israel.

iii. Rebekah secures Jacob's escape from Esau (xxvii. 41–46). *Deprived also of you both* (45). Observe Rebekah's self-interest. She infers that, if Esau were to kill Jacob, he would be banished from the house, and she would thus be the loser of both of them. *Because of the daughters of Heth* (46). Rebekah's plan was to remove Jacob out of Esau's reach. She could not send Jacob away without consulting Isaac. When she speaks to the father, however, she puts forward a very different reason for Jacob's departure than the real one.

b. Jacob's journey (xxviii. 1–22)

i. Jacob leaves home (xxviii. 1–9). *Go to Padan-aram* (2). The only motive for Jacob's departure shown in this portion of the story is that of marriage arrangements, and nothing whatever is said concerning the trouble between the brothers. There is no need to suppose the existence here of duplicate and divergent narratives. The psychology of the whole incident is sufficiently explained above. *Esau went unto Ishmael* (9). Esau endeavours to win his father's favour by conforming to the family regulations about marriage, for the Ishmaelites were true descendants of Abraham.

ii. Jacob's dream (xxviii. 10–15). *A ladder* (12) (or 'staircase'). This may have been suggested to Jacob's mind by the configuration of the locality. *Angels of God ascending and descending on it* (12). The wording here may perhaps signify no more than our own phrase 'going up and down'. But is there something of meaning in putting the word 'ascending' first? Perhaps God intended it to mean to Jacob that his need had truly come up before Him, and that in response He would send down His help. Whatever else this 'ladder' meant, it was intended to reveal that earth and heaven are truly linked and there is constant commerce between them. Note the allusion in Jn. i. 51 and cf. Jn. xiv. 6. *I am the Lord* (13). The covenant promise which had been given to Abraham and Isaac is now spoken to Jacob himself. This must have been an experience of incalculable value to Jacob at this time. He had known undoubtedly about the revelation concerning himself made at the time of his birth. It was this religious motive that led him to his most irreligious deed in the deception of his father. Many times, however, Jacob must have longed to have the assurance spoken directly to him from Jehovah as he knew had been the case with his father and grandfather. The sweet prize of the birthright blessing might already have been turning bitter in his mouth as the memory of the way he had forced the issue kept haunting him. But now, despite all his own sin and unworthiness, Jacob hears the gracious voice of Jehovah speaking the promise of the covenant into his own heart.

iii. The consecration of Bethel (xxviii. 16–22). *How dreadful* (17). A place of awe inspired by the sense of God's presence. *Set it up for a pillar, and poured oil* (18). The 'pillar' was intended to be a memorial of the fact that Jehovah had manifested Himself at this spot. Jacob's action was in harmony with ancient Semitic custom in this respect, though without the animistic motives that sometimes underlay such a custom. 'Pillars' of the latter kind were subsequently forbidden, because they lent themselves too readily to the debasing rites of the Canaanite shrines. See Lv. xxvi. 1; Dt. xvi. 22n. *Bethel* (19). Bethel was the place of the dream and Luz was the name of the neighbouring city. The name Bethel became later transferred to the city (Jdg. i. 23). *The tenth* (22). See xiv. 20n.; Lv. xxvii. 30–33n.; Dt. xiv. 22–29n.

c. Jacob in Syria (xxix. 1—xxxiii. 15)

i. Jacob meets Rachel (xxix. 1–14). *We cannot, until all the flocks be gathered* (8). It would appear that some kind of agreement existed among the shepherds to water all the flocks at the same time. *Rolled the stone* (10). Whether 'all the flocks' were gathered at this moment we have no means of knowing. The narrative reads like an impetuous act of Jacob. *Wept* (11). Jacob's emotional character constantly reveals itself, though all orientals were and still are expressive in this manner. Jacob is clearly overcome with joy at the happy termination of his journey.

ii. Jacob's marriage to Leah and Rachel (xxix. 15–30). *Tender eyed* (17). This probably indicates some eye-soreness which disfigured her. See RV. *I will serve thee seven years for Rachel* (18). Jacob offered service instead of the usual dowry given to the parents of the bride. *Wherefore then hast thou beguiled me?* (25). The deceiver deceived! Jacob, who had overreached his brother and deceived his old father, is now deceived himself. In this deception, Laban takes advantage of the fact that the bride was brought to her husband veiled. *To give the younger before the firstborn* (26). Laban's unscrupulous character displays itself here. The honourable thing would have been for Laban to have explained this before the bargain was made. *Fulfil her week* (27). This refers to the marriage festival of seven days (Jdg. xiv. 12), and Laban asks Jacob to go through with the present arrangements without making a disturbance, and promises that he will give Rachel to him quietly and without ceremony at the close of the festivities. Appeased by this promise, Jacob submits to the miserable, degrading situation into which Laban has forced him. *He gave him Rachel* (28). Jacob did not have to wait for her until he had completed another seven years of service (30), as xxxi. 41 might seem to suggest.

iii. The birth of Jacob's children (xxix. 31—xxx. 24). *Hated* (31). This word is used only in a relative sense. Cf. Mal. i. 3; Lk. xiv. 26. It would seem, however, that Jacob was positively unloving to her. *Now therefore my husband will love me* (32). These words and those in verses 33–35 reveal the heart of Leah. Who can read them without being moved by them? *Jacob's anger was*

97

D

kindled (xxx. 2). This bigamous marriage proves the folly of any human marriage arrangements which are contrary to the divine order of man and wife. *She shall bear upon my knees* (3). An old custom appears here by means of which a husband acknowledged his wife's children as his own. For Bilhah to bear on Rachel's knees meant that Bilhah's children would be legally regarded as Rachel's. *Have children by her* (3). Heb. 'be built by her'. See xvi. 2n. *A troop cometh* (11). There is reason to believe that this is not the best translation. Gad means 'Good fortune', and Zilpah really exclaimed: 'Fortunate am I', just as she was soon also to exclaim: 'Happy am I' (13). *Mandrakes* (14). 'Love apples' (RV mg.). Mandrakes were a soft pulpy fruit, round and yellow, about the size of a small plum. The ancients had a superstition that they were a remedy for barrenness. It was for this reason that Rachel wanted them, and Leah sold them at the price of a night with Jacob (15, 16). It is to depths of degradation of this kind that the purities of marriage are brought when men and women insist on any other basis for it than the óne which was laid down by their Creator. *Joseph* (24). Rachel at length bears a son of her own. The sons of Jacob are named in groupings around their respective mothers. There seems every reason to think that they are also named in the order of their birth and that Joseph was the eleventh son.

iv. Jacob outwits Laban (xxx. 25–43). *Send me away* (25). This appears to have been immediately after Joseph's birth. *He removed* (35). The person here is Laban, and he put these marked cattle into the hands of Jacob's sons. Laban then made his own settlement three days' journey away (36) and put the remainder of his flocks into Jacob's hands. *Pilled white strakes* (37). 'Pilled' is an old form of 'peeled' and 'strakes' is an old word for 'streaks'. *The flocks conceived before the rods, and brought forth cattle ringstraked, speckled, and spotted* (39). A physiological principle is here employed by Jacob. This kind of device is adopted for obtaining certain colours of horses and dogs. White lambs, even now, are secured by surrounding the troughs with white objects. *The feebler were Laban's, and the stronger Jacob's* (42). In this way Jacob 'overreached' Laban also.

v. Jacob decides to leave Laban (xxxi. 1–21). *Glory* (1). Heb. 'weight'. The idea is that of the weight of wealth. *Not toward him as before* (2). This is not surprising. *Changed my wages ten times* (7). We are not to look for ten occasions on which this occurred; the phrase corresponds to our way of speaking of having 'a hundred and one' things to do. Laban certainly had been unscrupulous; but here were two equally crafty men wrestling with each other. *In a dream* (10). It would seem from this that God had shown Jacob what to do in the matter of the breeding of the sheep, and that the parti-coloured cattle had been born through a special divine intervention. *Angel of God* (11). This was God Himself. See verse 13 and xvi. 7n. *Counted of him*

strangers (15). Leah and Rachel had become estranged from their father, and they give vent to their long-harboured resentment of his meanness. *The images* (19). 'Teraphim' (RV) were household gods such as were common to the religion of Mesopotamia; see Jdg. xviii. 17; 1 Sa. xix. 13. *The river* (21). This was the Euphrates.

vi. Laban overtakes Jacob (xxxi. 22–42). *They overtook him in the mount Gilead* (23). This was over 300 miles away from Haran. Jacob's strategy seems to have been to move the flocks gradually farther and farther away. In the beginning of things Laban had separated Jacob's flocks from his own by a distance of 'three days' journey' (xxx. 36). As the flocks were slow moving, Jacob steadily increased this distance, and at the zero hour of Jacob's own departure from Laban his flocks must have been some 200 miles away. This would have taken more than three weeks to accomplish, and reveals how carefully Jacob had planned his escape. With his wives and family Jacob remained in reasonably close proximity to Laban, but at last, placing them on swift camels (17), he silently fled. Three days elapsed before the news reached Laban (22) and it was not until a further four days after this that Laban succeeded in overtaking his son-in-law in Gilead. *Either good or bad* (24). Laban is told not to interfere at all.

With mirth . . . and with harp (27). Laban adds hypocrisy to his greed. The 'kiss' (28) of such a father would not be very welcome to his children. *The God of your father . . . my gods* (29, 30). Cf. xxx. 27. Laban was not himself a worshipper of Jehovah, though in accordance with the notions of his age he acknowledged that Jehovah was the God of Jacob and his fathers. *The camel's furniture* (34). The heavy saddle. *He searched, but found not the images* (35). Rachel was as good at deceiving as her father and her husband. *The fear of Isaac* (42). This means the God whom Isaac reverenced. See also verse 53.

vii. Jacob and Laban agree to keep apart (xxxi. 43–55). *Let us make a covenant* (44). The two men entered into a bond by means of a covenant sacrifice ('they did eat', 46). See also verse 54 and compare the similar incident in which Isaac and Abimelech were concerned (xxvi. 30). *Jegar-sahadutha . . . Galeed* (47). The first in Aramaic and the second in Hebrew mean 'heap of witnesses'. *Mizpah* (49). 'The watchtower' RV mg. Mizpah was not originally the pleasant term that uninstructed Christian sentiment has made it to become. It is a sinister word containing an implicit threat: see verses 50, 52.

viii. Jacob is afraid of Esau (xxxii. 1–8). *The angels of God met him* (1). Lit. 'drew near'. They had always been round about him, but at this moment they made their presence known. *Mahanaim* (2). The name means 'two hosts'. It referred either to Jacob's own company and that of the angels who were with him (cf. 2 Ki. vi. 14–17; Ps. xxxiv. 7), or to Jacob's 'two bands' (7). It is more likely that the word had reference to the former of these alternatives, particularly in view of the context. *The country of Edom* (3). This is the later name of the region of Seir. Esau's migration did not occur until some time afterwards (xxxvi. 7, 8). *Four hundred men* (6). Esau was probably engaged on some marauding expedition, when he heard of his brother's return to the country.

ix. Jacob's prayer and strategy (xxxii. 9–23). *O God . . . I am not worthy* (9, 10). A very different Jacob is here! *A present for Esau* (13). This, as verse 20 shows, was for the purpose of softening Esau and securing his goodwill. Cf. 2 Ki. viii. 9. The setting out of this great present, with the intervals between, shows the psychological insight of the master-mind of Jacob. *Sent them over the brook* (23). The valley was some four miles wide, with high ground to the south of it. Jacob seems to have conducted his family safely across this valley and on to the high ground beyond and then to have returned to the region of the ford to pray. (The appearance of repetition in verses 22 and 23 does not require that we should postulate two documents: the repetition belongs to the genius of the Hebrew language.)

x. Jacob wrestles with a man (xxxii. 24–32). *A man* (24). 'The angel of Jehovah' must be recognized here. See Ho. xii. 4. *Let me go* (26). Jacob had been weakened by the touch on his thigh, but appears to have clung tenaciously to his antagonist. So far as the physical aspect of the 'wrestling' goes, this request by the 'man' was an acknowledgment of Jacob's success (see verses 25, 28). *Except thou bless me* (26). Jacob claims the victor's privilege, but he recognizes the divine character of the 'man' with whom he wrestled. He no doubt discovered this in the miraculous power that had crippled him. The meaning of this strange experience of God is not easy to define in a few words. It may be that the first spiritual lesson for Jacob was to teach him his own helplessness. A second significance, however, and one more closely connected with the new title bestowed on him, may have been that as he had prevailed in this physical way (and the angel had clearly permitted him thus to prevail), so also would he prevail in spiritual things if he learned to submit and to pray. This last aspect of submission and prayer was demonstrated in the closing scene of the wrestling as Jacob still clung to his divine visitor. *My life is preserved* (30). See xvi. 13n.

xi. Esau and Jacob meet (xxxiii. 1–15). *Rachel and Joseph hindermost* (2). Observe the disposition of the family. *He* (RV 'himself') *passed over before them* (3). Jacob was never at any time a coward, but he is now strikingly courageous after having received the blessing of the previous night. *Seven times* (3). Eastern salutations begin at a great distance and take a long while to perform. There seems a hint here, however, of a rather excessive obeisance. Perhaps it was an acknowledgment of the wrong he had done, and a tacit though sincere way of honouring Esau with the respect due to an elder brother.

Esau ran . . . and they wept (4). The strong feelings of brotherhood surged up and swept aside the bitterness and estrangement of twenty long years. Esau's noble character must not be ignored in this incident: observe his large-heartedness and genuinely friendly interest (5–8). The Scripture does not hide the faults of the 'saints', neither does it conceal the virtues of the 'profane' person. 'Total depravity' means that every part (total) of man's nature is vitiated by sin; but it does not mean that every man is as bad as bad can be.

I have enough, my brother (9). This was unquestionably an affectionate gesture on Esau's part; though he knew perfectly well that not to accept the proffered gift would have been a mark of hostility against his brother. It was this consideration which finally compelled Esau to accept the gift (11). Not until the present was accepted could Jacob be sure, according to ancient custom, that all was well between Esau and himself. *The face of God* (10). Jacob spoke in hyperbolical, but truly oriental, language to say how deeply relieved he was that Esau was ready to act favourably towards him. There is probably this deeper and more religious element also that in the friendly countenance of Esau he recognized that God had been working for him, and learned once again that God's own face was truly turned towards him in blessing.

d. Jacob in the promised land (xxxiii. 16—xxxv. 20)

i. Jacob settles in Canaan (xxxiii. 16–20). *Jacob journeyed to Succoth* (17). In verse 14 Jacob had promised to come on to Seir, but the journey he takes to Succoth is not in the direction of Seir. This was no deception on Jacob's part; he needed to rest both his company and himself, and therefore proposed to *lead on softly* (14), that is, to take a slow journey, to halt at Succoth, and then to visit his brother later. *He bought a parcel of a field* (19). This is the second recorded purchase of ground made by Abraham's family. Cf. Jn. iv. 5. *El-elohe-Israel* (20). Jacob appropriates the name given to him at Peniel, and commemorates the first experience of its spiritual reality.

ii. Treachery and bloodshed over Dinah (xxxiv. 1–31). *Dinah* (1). She was the daughter of Leah, and her birth is recorded in xxx. 21. She appears to have been born some years before Joseph, and so must be regarded as round about fifteen years of age at the time of this unpleasant incident. Simeon and Levi may have been about ten years older. *Defiled* (2). 'Humbled' (RV). Dishonoured her by violence. *In Israel* (7). This phrase may be an indication that the story was not written down in its present form in patriarchal times, but received its shape in the time of Moses when the descendants of Jacob became known as 'Israel'. *Make ye marriages* (9). Hamor was proposing a kind of amalgamation of the two peoples. *Dowry* (12). This is the price paid to the parents of the bride; the 'gift' was the present made by the bridegroom to the bride herself. *Pleased Hamor* (18). The rite of circumcision, although not hitherto practised in this Hivite clan, was apparently nothing new to them. *Simeon and Levi, Dinah's brethren* (25). These two, being born of the same mother as Dinah, were especially under obligation to avenge their sister's honour. *Sons of Jacob* (27). The other brothers came in behind Levi and Simeon and flew upon the spoil. *Troubled me* (30). Jacob's only rebuke is to complain that the violent behaviour of his sons had exposed him to danger, and had brought him into ill odour with the other occupants of the country. *Should he deal . . . ?* (31). This was a sufficient answer to the weak reproof of mere expediency even though it did not justify the shameful massacre. See xlix. 5–7.

iii. A religious reformation in Jacob's household (xxxv. 1–15). *Go up* (1). From Shechem to Bethel was a climb of about 1,000 ft. There is a deep significance in the reference to *when thou fleddest*, for Jacob was fleeing again. His position at Shechem had become too dangerous for him to remain there. *Strange gods* (2). Jacob's household servants were all from Padan-aram and were idolaters. They had their own household gods, and there were also the teraphim which Rachel had carried with her from her father's house. *Let us arise* (3). Jacob initiates his wives and children, together with the multitude of his servants, into the ways and worship of Jehovah. Note that Jacob led his family to Jehovah by a testimony (3b). *Under the oak* (4). The fact that he did not destroy the images, but hid them under a tree, suggests that he regarded them with superstitious fear. *Terror of God* (5). A dread seized the neighbouring tribes, and Jacob made his escape before they recovered their sense of proportion.

El-bethel (7). The seeming redundancy in this phrase means that he dedicated the place to the glory of the God who had appeared to him at that critical moment of his life when he first gave it that name. *Deborah* (8). During his stay at Shechem Jacob may have visited his old father at Hebron and brought back Deborah with him. It is possible that verses 27–29, appearing as a detached note, and referring possibly to an earlier historical point, may provide information about the occasion when Jacob brought Deborah to his home. *God appeared* (9). In the going forth, and now in the coming back, God met Jacob at Bethel. The initial covenant promise is ratified, and the change of character is confirmed (10–12). *Bethel* (15). This does not mean that on this occasion Jacob named the place 'Bethel' for the first time. The name had remained unused (for who had known in that locality and at that earlier time that Jacob had given it the name?), but Jacob now teaches it to his family.

iv. Death of Rachel in the birth of Benjamin (xxxv. 16–20). This sad episode explains Jacob's particular affection for Benjamin. The sorrowful name 'Benoni' is not accepted by the father, but he prefers to call him 'Benjamin' (see RV mg.)— a son of hope and cheer.

e. The family registers of Jacob and Esau (xxxv. 21—xxxvii. 1)

i. Jacob's twelve sons (xxxv. 21–26). *Reuben* (22). For this sin Reuben forfeited the birthright (see xlix. 4). *The sons of Leah* (23). The sons are grouped according to their mothers. Study the account in xxx. 1–24.

ii. Death and burial of Isaac (xxxv. 27–29). *Isaac . . . died* (29). He lived longer than was anticipated (see xxvii. 2, 41). This note of Isaac's death may perhaps be just a formal one. In the actual history it may have occurred earlier, at a time previous to the death of Deborah (verse 8).

iii. Descendants of Esau (xxxvi. 1–19). *Esau took his wives* (2). Cf. xxvi. 34. The discrepancies are not real, but arise out of the fluid use of names in oriental custom. *Thus dwelt Esau in mount Seir* (8). This verse seems to indicate the formal separation of the families of Esau and Jacob after their father's death.

iv. Descendants of Seir (xxxvi. 20–30).

v. Kings and chiefs of Edom (xxxvi. 31–43). In these two sections we see adopted the usual method of disposing of the collateral lines first before going on with the history of the main line of God's purpose. See xvii. 6, xxxv. 11. In view of the archaeological evidence for the date when Edom first became a kingdom (c. 1300 B.C.) it is possible that the remark in verse 31 may be an editorial comment.

vi. Jacob in Canaan (xxxvii. 1).

V. THE STORY OF JOSEPH.
xxxvii. 2—l. 26

a. The boyhood of Joseph (xxxvii. 2–36)

i. Joseph's dreams (xxxvii. 2–11). *A coat of many colours* (3). Our AV translators were misguided through the use of the LXX in this passage. It is properly 'a coat of extremities', i.e. a coat which in length reached down to the feet and was made with long sleeves extending beyond the hands. The usual undergarment was sleeveless and came down only as far as the knees. The gift of the coat was a mark of distinction, but exactly what Jacob intended to signify by this gift it is hard to say. The honour could not have been the full rights of the firstborn, for these he gave to Judah (see xlix. 8–12). Some explanation may possibly be found in the fact that Joseph was the firstborn of his favourite wife Rachel. See also the significance of xlviii. 5, and see xlix. 8n. *Joseph dreamed a dream* (5). The two dreams recorded here both had their separate fulfilments in the subsequent events. Note the pivotal importance of dreams in Joseph's career.

ii. The plot against Joseph (xxxvii. 12–22). *See whether it be well* (14). Observe the reason for Jacob's anxiety: the brothers and the flocks were 'in Shechem' (12), a place where his name had been made 'to stink among the inhabitants of the land' (xxxiv. 30). *Some pit* (20). This would be an artificially prepared water cistern, usually consisting of a large hole in the ground with but a narrow opening. In many parts of the country the water was only just beneath the surface, and these scooped-out 'cisterns' would hold a good supply ready for watering the flocks. *Reuben* (21). There was a generous streak in Reuben and there is no reason to doubt the sincerity of his motives.

iii. Joseph sold as a slave (xxxvii. 23–36). *From Gilead . . . to Egypt* (25). An examination of the map will show what a highway of trade Canaan was. *Judah said* (26). The course of the narrative and the motives of Reuben and Judah are perfectly self-explanatory. The critical analysis, which divides this into two discordant accounts, so creating difficulties, is altogether improbable. *Midianites . . . Ishmeelites* (28). These traders are called Midianites, Ishmeelites, and *Medanites* (36. The word translated *Midianites* here differs from that used in verse 28). All three groups were descended from Abraham and appear to have had a common occupation. There were possibly men of all three families in this trading caravan. Some scholars interpret these verses as meaning that the brothers sold Joseph to the Ishmeelites who in their turn sold him to the Midianites, who then sold him to Potiphar. *Reuben returned* (29). Observe that Reuben was absent when Joseph was sold. *Twenty pieces of silver* (28). Cf. Lv. xxvii. 5; Ex. xxi. 32.

b. Judah and Tamar (xxxviii. 1–30)

This is an interlude in the main story. It serves two historical purposes: first, to show the origin of the three families of the tribe of Judah (Nu. xxvi. 20); and second, to establish the sanctity of the levirate law (Dt. xxv. 5–10). *Shuah* (2). This is the name of the father of the woman (see verse 12). Observe the entry of this foreign strain into the line of Judah, and so of our Lord, at this very early period. *Raise up seed to thy brother* (8). It is clear from this incident that the 'levirate law', as it is called, was considerably antecedent to the time of Moses. See Dt. xxv. 5n. *For he said* (11). This is what Judah said to himself. *Sat in an open place* (14). Tamar suspected that Judah, her father-in-law, was not being true to his word. She therefore took matters into her own hands and by this device she compelled Judah himself to perform the levirate duty. *Harlot* (15). For obvious reasons Tamar had veiled herself. The ordinary harlot was not veiled, and adopting this disguise she appeared to be a temple-prostitute. *Let her take it to her* (23). This is rather a rough way of saying, 'Let her come and fetch it'. *Let her be burnt* (24). Legally Tamar belonged to Shelah, but Judah had not made good the arrangement (14). As Shelah's legal wife she was held by Judah to have committed adultery. *Pharez* (29). Zarah strove to be firstborn, but Pharez 'broke forth' and was called 'breach'. It is important to observe that the Davidic line runs back through Pharez.

c. Joseph's promotion in Egypt (xxxix. 1—xli. 57)

i. The prosperity of Joseph in Potiphar's house (xxxix. 1–6). *Officer* (1). Lit. 'eunuch'. It may describe only an office, or it may properly indicate what Potiphar really was. It was not unknown for a eunuch to be married. *An Egyptian* (1). It is thought by some that this designation is inserted by way of distinction from the ruling Pharaohs, who, if they were the famous Hyksos kings, were not Egyptians. Much uncertainty shrouds the dates connected with the Hyksos' rule in Egypt, though it is quite possible that they were in power at this time. (See p. 38 for a table showing possible dates.) The courtiers of the Hyksos were for the most part Semitic, and so Potiphar 'an Egyptian' would be specially marked out. *Save the bread which he did eat* (6). Some have thought that the Egyptian Potiphar gave Joseph charge over everything except his food, which, as an Egyptian, he could not eat from the hand of a Semite. It is probably no more than a picturesque way of saying that Potiphar had placed his entire affairs into Joseph's hands (see verses 8, 9).

ii. Joseph falsely accused and imprisoned (xxxix. 7–23). *His master's wife* (7). Egyptian women did not live in seclusion like the Semites. *This great wickedness, and sin against God* (9). These words reveal a high moral conception of God in Joseph and are evidence against the view that such moral conceptions were but a later development. *Left his garment in her hand* (12). The reverse experience of Judah and Tamar. *To mock us* (14) . . . *to mock me* (17). In her outcry before 'the men of her house' this objectionable woman insinuates that other women had been similarly assaulted, but before the critical judgment of her husband she speaks more guardedly. *His wrath was kindled* (19). Did Potiphar believe his wife's story or was this only a kind of 'proper' wrath? If he had fully believed her tale he would have put Joseph to death. *The prison* (20). This was not the common gaol, as the following phrase makes clear. The early part of this period must have been hard to bear (Ps. cv. 18), but through the sympathetic discernment of the keeper he seems soon to have been entrusted with a fair measure of authority (see xl. 4).

iii. Joseph interprets the dreams of the butler and baker (xl. 1–23). *The chief of the butlers . . . the chief of the bakers* (2). These men were probably high-ranking officials of the Egyptian court. *Dreamed a dream* (5). The two dreams recorded at this point, together with those of Pharaoh later, seem to have been divinely given for the purpose of bringing Joseph before Pharaoh. It was for dreams that Joseph's brethren hated him: it was by the help of dreams that he was exalted in Egypt. *No interpreter* (8). By this the officials meant that they had no access to the professional 'wise men'. *Behold, a vine was before me* (9). Destructive criticism used to argue against the truth of this narrative on the ground that the vine was not cultivated in Egypt. Investigation has shown that the use of wine was quite commonly known. *Pharaoh's cup* (11). An interesting Hebrew idiom reveals itself in this narrative. True to Egyptian custom, the butler describes how he placed the cup 'upon (Heb.) Pharaoh's palm'. Joseph in his reply says, 'Thou wilt give Pharaoh's cup into (Heb.) his hand'. The Egyptian cups had no handles or stems, hence were placed on the palm. Such undesigned details speak in favour of the truth of the record. *Stolen away out of the land of the Hebrews* (15). This statement by no means contradicts the events that took place as described in chapter xxxvii. It was a chivalrous way of describing what happened. Notice, too, how little he exposes the crime of Potiphar's wife. 'The land of the Hebrews' means the land where the Hebrew settlements were known to be establishing themselves. *Baskets on my head* (16). Ancient Egyptian pictures show this to have been the way in which bakers carried their baskets. *Lift up thy head from off thee* (19). The last three words make all the difference between the prospects of the two courtiers (cf. verse 13). *Pharaoh's birthday* (20). The Pharaohs celebrated their birthdays with great assemblages and also by the release of prisoners.

iv. **Pharaoh's dreams (xli. 1–24).** *The river* (1). It was natural that the dream of a Pharaoh of Egypt should concern a river. The truly Egyptian character of this record provides one of the 'watermarks' of its authenticity. *Kine* (2). Kine were the familiar symbol of the earth and of agriculture. *In a meadow* (2). This is the word for the long marsh-grass. *Rank* (5), i.e. 'fat'. *The magicians of Egypt* (8). These men were the educated class among the ancient Egyptians: they also claimed a knowledge of things which belonged to the gods and to human destiny. *Shaved* (14). A beard was a mark of the degradation of a prisoner or of a slovenly person. It must therefore be removed in the royal presence. *In my dream* (17). Pharaoh describes his dreams at greater length and appears to indulge in a few extra touches at the same time.

v. **Joseph interprets the dreams (xli. 25–32).** *The thing is established by God* (32). Joseph's monotheism is prominent here and affords evidence against the supposed evolution of religion in Israel from cruder forms.

vi. **Joseph's advice (xli. 33–37).** *Take up the fifth part . . . and lay up corn* (34, 35). This was far more than a happy guess of Joseph's: it was an interpretation sufficiently strong to sustain a fourteen-year plan.

vii. **Joseph is made governor of Egypt (xli. 38–46).** *In whom the Spirit of God is* (38). Pharaoh acknowledged what Joseph said and recognized that this was a divine communication. *Took off his ring . . . and put it upon Joseph's hand* (42). The bestowal of legal authority. *Vestures of fine linen* (42). The Egyptian word *shesh* here used for fine linen is another indelible mark of the authenticity of this record. These robes of *shesh* were official garments associated with the nobility of the country. They probably signified his formal admission to the priesthood, and his marriage into the priestly family of Potipherah (45) would seem to confirm this view. *A gold chain* (42).

Egypt excelled in exquisitely wrought gold chains, and some of these have been discovered by modern excavation. The giving of a gold chain by the monarch was a custom familiar in Egyptian honours. *Bow the knee* (43). This represents an attempt to translate an Egyptian word, *abrech*, the meaning of which nobody knows! It may have been an acclamation of the crowd like our 'Long live the king'; or it may have been the shout of a forerunner or herald as the Hebraized form of the word has been imagined to suggest. *Zaphnath-paaneah* (45). This is a truly Egyptian word and any certainty as to its meaning still evades our grasp. It seems likely, however, that its best interpretation is 'Preserver of the Living'. *On* (45). This word means 'light'. The Greeks called it Heliopolis, 'the city of the Sun', and it served as a centre of sun-worship in Egypt. *Thirty years old* (46). This meant that Joseph had suffered thirteen years of humiliation in Egypt. See xxxvii. 2.

viii. **Pharaoh's dreams come true (xli. 47–57).** The dreams were clearly given by God, whose providential care of His people becomes thus evident. *Two sons . . . which Asenath . . . bare unto him* (50). Observe the Egyptian strain, therefore, in the blood of these two great tribes in Israel.

d. **Joseph and his brothers (xlii. 1—xlv. 15)**

i. **Jacob sends his sons to Egypt for food (xlii. 1–5).** *Why do ye look . . . ?* (1). The brothers seem to have been hesitant. A caravan was probably being formed and Jacob rebuked the apparent listlessness of his sons. Was there a disquieting memory at the slightest reference to Egypt? *But Benjamin . . . Jacob sent not* (4). Jacob would not trust Benjamin to the brothers. Had he some buried suspicion? See what he says in verse 36.

ii. **Joseph treats his brothers harshly (xlii. 6–24).** *He it was that sold* (6). This does not mean that he sold to every individual applicant. Special cases only would no doubt be submitted to him, and an imposing company of Semites, such as the brothers and their retinue of servants represented, would call for careful enquiry. *Bowed down themselves* (6). See xxxvii. 5–8. Here is the fulfilment of the first dream. *Spake roughly unto them* (7). 'Roughly' means roughly, and it is unrealistic to put Joseph in a stained-glass window! *They knew not him* (8). Twenty years had passed (thirteen of humiliation and the seven years of plenty) since they last saw him; he was dressed differently, and they were not expecting to meet him: all these factors served to make Joseph unrecognizable by his older brothers. *Nakedness* (9). By this Joseph meant its defenceless and impoverished condition. *By the life of Pharaoh* (15). An oath meaning, 'as truly as Pharaoh lives'. *We saw the anguish of his soul* (21). This sentence gives us an insight into Joseph's entreaties. *His blood is required* (22). The brothers had not killed Joseph, but they told their father that a beast had devoured him. The lie had become part of Reuben's thinking: he had told himself so many times that it was so, that now it had fastened itself on his mind.

iii. The return and dismay of the brothers (xlii. 25–38). *Restore every man's money* (25). This action, intended as a token of goodwill, became the cause of great fear. *Into his sack* (25). The AV 'sack' stands for three Hebrew words, but they all represent sacks of some kind. The money appears to have been in a kind of forage bag (the second word in verse 27) of which each brother would have several. Only one brother happened to open the particular bag which contained his money. Or it may have been that in one sack only the money was on the top ('mouth', 27) while it was at the bottom of the other sacks. *This that God hath done* (28). How strong were the workings of a convicting conscience! *Every man's bundle of money was in his sack* (35). Note that this discovery was made at home and occurred when the sacks were emptied. *My son shall not go down with you* (38). Jacob brushes aside the extravagant and theatrical gesture of the unstable Reuben.

iv. The second journey to Egypt for food (xliii. 1–15). *The man asked* (7). The narrative in chapter xlii was concise: this is an expansion of it, giving the old father the fullest possible account of what happened. In the repetitions there are extensions and abbreviations (cf. xliii. 21). These are perfectly natural features in such lively conversation as these chapters provide; they need occasion no difficulty. An historical perspective is all that is needed to resolve some of the 'difficulties'. *The lad* (8). Benjamin was probably over twenty years of age, but this expression was a general term of affectionate reference to a younger person. *Bear the blame* (9). This was no light thing; but was in a totally different category from Reuben's earlier offer. *The best fruits in the land* (11). Lit. 'the song of the land', i.e., the things for which the land was famed. *Double money* (12). More precisely this means 'second money' (see verse 22).

v. Joseph gives a banquet to the brothers (xliii. 16–34). *Came near to the steward* (19). How vivid is the narrative! *Every man's money was in the mouth of his sack* (21). In xlii. 27 it is stated that only one brother found his money. There is no discrepancy here, however. There are two alternative explanations. The first is that as the word 'every' does not belong to the Hebrew, the phrase is a general one only and means 'a man's money was'. This is not completely satisfactory, and a much simpler solution may be found. The verse is a telescoped narrative containing in one sentence what really happened in two stages (see xlii. 27, 35). Money was found first at the inn when they had gone too far to return, and was subsequently found by every one of them. This is stated in one movement in a very hurried and fearful whisper at the door. The reader has but to live again in the midst of the scene, and the story makes sense. *Eat bread* (25). The eating of food with the brothers was tantamount to giving them a pledge of safety. *Bowed themselves*

to him (26). A second fulfilment of the first dream. *By himself* (32). Joseph had been elevated to the Egyptian priesthood and hence had to sit apart. *Marvelled* (33). This was because they had been arranged in family order. *Messes* (34). These were merely token portions, not the main dishes constituting their meal, else how could Benjamin eat five times as much!

vi. Joseph's cup found in Benjamin's sack (xliv. 1–13). *Every man's money* (1). This is done a second time, for Joseph cannot make his father pay for bread. *The youngest* (2). There is a gentleness which operates with mighty strength in the whole of Joseph's demeanour. It would seem that Joseph's first motive was to have only Benjamin his own brother to live with him in Egypt (cf. verse 17); but when he learned from Judah's speech what grief this would occasion his father, he is compelled to go further and to have them all. This wider decision may have been helped by the new temper which he had discovered in the family. *He divineth* (5). Various methods of divination in a cup are described in the ancient histories. There is no reason to require that Joseph might not have 'divined' in his cup. To attempt to dissociate Joseph from this practice would be unhistorical.

vii. Judah's intercession for Benjamin (xliv. 14–34). *The iniquity of thy servants* (16). What did Judah mean? Was he referring to the alleged theft of the cup, and using the plural in the sense of corporate guilt through the ancient ideas of the solidarity of the family, or was he thinking about the pit, and the selling of Joseph, and the lies to their father? *Then Judah came near* (18). This is one of the most skilful speeches in literature. *Thou art even as Pharaoh* (18). Such was the pride of an oriental despot that it was almost a capital offence to speak in self-defence when accused by the ruler. *Thou saidst . . . Bring him down unto me* (21). Judah had possibly read something in Joseph's tones or looks in his earlier speeches which he now remembers, and he cleverly intimates that the governor had shown an almost friendly interest in their youngest brother. *My father said* (27). Here is another expansion of an earlier note as Judah fills in all the details in order to win the mind of the governor.

viii. Joseph makes himself known to his brothers (xlv. 1–15). The cumulative effect of his speech on Joseph was more than Judah, of course, could know. *Could not refrain* (1). This is an emphatic word meaning to force oneself. Joseph could no longer force himself to act a feigned part. All the 'brother' in him and all the 'son' in him rose up at once and overpowered his strongest resolutions. *Wept aloud* (2). This must mean in the usual demonstrative manner of the ancient East. *The house of Pharaoh heard* (2). They heard the loud weeping, or the passage may only mean that they heard the news that these men were Joseph's brothers. *Doth my father yet live?* (3). He had already learned this, but this is now the anxious question of an orphaned son.

Earing (6). An old English word for ploughing. *A father to Pharaoh* (8). This was either a figurative expression to indicate the way in which Joseph had cared for all Pharaoh's business, or, as many scholars think, it was a lofty title employed among the Egyptians. *The land of Goshen* (10). This was Joseph's choice for his family. It was east of the Nile and was probably an unsettled district, loosely attached to Egypt.

e. Joseph receives his father into Egypt (xlv. 16—xlvii. 26)

i. Pharaoh and Joseph send for Jacob (xlv. 16–24). *Take your father . . . and come unto me* (18). It was of great value that the household of Jacob should come into Egypt by the invitation of the ruler himself. *Wagons out of the land of Egypt* (19). Wagons were proper to a flat country like Egypt. *Regard not your stuff* (20). This meant that they were not to carry their heavy furniture with them. The detailed character of the narrative in xxxix—xlviii and its strong Egyptian colouring are evidence of its authentic and contemporary character.

ii. Jacob receives the news (xlv. 25–28). *Jacob's heart fainted* (26). Lit. 'went cold'. It seemed too good to be true. Jacob had come to live in a state of constant expectation of the worst, and 'he believed them not'. It is possible that this is the place where we must find room for a probable complete confession by the brothers of the whole miserable story of their treatment of Joseph.

iii. Jacob travels to Egypt (xlvi. 1–7). *Fear not* (3). Jacob would have a very natural hesitation (cf. xv. 13 and xxvi. 2); and so he stopped at Beersheba to consult God. *Joseph shall put his hand upon thine eyes* (4). These words meant that Jacob would die in peace, and that Joseph would do the respectful act of a son in closing his father's eyelids after death. *Their goods* (6). The more personal belongings of the family.

iv. The names of those who entered Egypt (xlvi. 8–27). *Hezron and Hamul* (12). It is calculated that Pharez their father could not himself have been more than four years old at the time of the descent into Egypt, and therefore that these two could not have come into Egypt with Jacob. The explanation of the inclusion of their names in this list belongs to the purely technical character of ancient genealogies, by which they were regarded as the legal representatives and substitutes of Er and Onan. *Threescore and six* (26). That is, without Jacob, Joseph, and Joseph's two sons. The entire family is summed up in verse 27 as 'threescore and ten', though this verse does not necessarily imply that they all 'came' with Jacob.

v. Joseph's welcome to his father (xlvi. 28–34). *Wept on his neck a good while* (29). This must have been a deeply moving scene. *Every shepherd is an abomination unto the Egyptians* (34). This is perhaps due to the Hyksos, shepherd-kings, who dominated Egypt for so long, and to which line the Pharaoh of this time possibly belonged. See the Chronological Table on p. 38.

vi. Joseph introduces Jacob to Pharaoh (xlvii. 1–12). *They are in the land of Goshen* (1). Joseph's aim had been to put his family there, both for its separation from Egypt generally, and also on account of its suitability for the flocks. Permission is formally applied for in verse 4. *Five men* (2). The figure five seems to appear rather often in this narrative: note its recurrence later. *Make them rulers over my cattle* (6). Not all of the cattle had been destroyed in the famine: cf. also verses 16, 17. *Jacob blessed Pharaoh* (7). The interview between Jacob and Pharaoh seems to have been later than the formal one with the five sons and to have taken place in a more free and friendly manner. As the Egyptians did not live to so great an age, Jacob would appear as a wonderful old man indeed, before whom even a Pharaoh would show respect. *Rameses* (11). This is possibly a reference to the region by the name that was subsequently given to it. For a discussion of the bearing of this verse on the possible dating of the exodus see the Introductions to Joshua and to Judges.

vii. Joseph's economic policy (xlvii. 13–26). *They came unto him the second year* (18). Not necessarily the second year of the famine, but possibly of the people's desperate situation. *Buy us and our land* (19). Joseph drove a hard bargain with the populace and greatly enhanced the power and wealth of the rulers of the country.

f. Last days of Jacob (xlvii. 27—l. 14)

i. Jacob's request about his burial (xlvii. 27–31). *Israel bowed himself upon the bed's head* (31). The Greek in Heb. xi. 21 follows a different vowel-pointing of the Hebrew phrase and so renders it 'staff'. This rendering is to be preferred, because it is much more likely to have been the case.

ii. The blessing of Ephraim and Manasseh (xlviii. 1–22). *At Luz* (3). Note how the old name still remained in use. *Ephraim and Manasseh* (5). Jacob names them in the order of the blessing which he intends to give them. Ephraim and Manasseh are made to correspond to Reuben and Simeon, the first and second born respectively. *Which were born unto thee . . . are mine* (5). Jacob means that he proposes to adopt them as of equal rank with his own sons, and their descendants were to enjoy full status as tribes. *Who are these?* (8). Jacob's eyesight must have weakened as his father's had done (see verse 10). These two sons of Joseph would probably be about twenty years of age at the time of this blessing. *From between his knees* (12). This has reference to their having stood between Jacob's knees: a ritual action which had symbolized Jacob's recognition of them as his own. *Guiding his hands wittingly* (14). Jacob's purpose is revealed in the subsequent discussion with Joseph. *His younger brother shall be greater than he* (19). This second son of Joseph became the strongest tribe of all the twelve, and 'Ephraim' became an alternative name used for the northern kingdom of Israel. *God shall . . . bring you again unto the land of your fathers* (21). This assurance became Joseph's own (see l. 24). *One portion* (22). This Hebrew phrase means 'one shoulder', or lit. 'Shechem'. See Jos. xxiv. 32. The taking of Shechem by sword and bow was a shameful deed at the time, and one which he had repudiated. He may mean only that by sword and bow he had defended himself afterwards against the avenging attacks of the neighbouring Amorites. ·

iii. Jacob's blessings on his sons (xlix. 1–27). *Thou shalt not excel* (4). The verb is an imperative and meant the displacement of Reuben from the privileges of the firstborn. *They slew a man* (6). This refers to the outrageous massacre at Shechem, as does also verse 7. *Digged down a wall* (7). 'Houghed an ox' (RV). A symbolic way of saying, they killed a man who was a prince. *I will divide them in Jacob* (7). Simeon became absorbed in Judah, and the tribe of Levi had no territory assigned to it. See note on Jos. xix. 1–9. *Thy father's children shall bow down before thee* (8). This is the firstborn's blessing; but from xxxvii. 3 and xlix. 22–26 some distinctive honour seems also to have been given to Joseph. Judah's blessing appears to have been that of spiritual leadership and that of Joseph to have consisted in material prosperity. *A lawgiver from between his feet* (10). This is a reference either to the ruler's staff which was customarily placed between his feet, or to the promise that a ruler should never be lacking from among Judah's descendants. *Until Shiloh come* (10). A difficult phrase, but the best interpretation seems to be the one that regards it as a way of speaking of the Messiah. If a different vowel-pointing is given to the Hebrew consonants, and this is a quite legitimate thing to do, the word may be translated 'whose it is', and this has a striking connection with Ezk. xxi. 27. *Unto him shall the gathering of the people be* (10). The word 'gathering' means 'obedience'. *Red with wine* (12). Bright with prosperity. *A fruitful bough* (22). This alludes to the greatness of the tribes of Ephraim and Manasseh, Joseph's

sons. *From thence is the shepherd* (24). Another cryptic phrase, which contains an allusion to the source of strength being found in God; from thence, that is, from the shepherd. *My progenitors* (26). The Samaritan Pentateuch and the LXX have the phrase 'mountains of eternity'. See RV mg. *Him that was separate from his brethren* (26). A 'prince' (RV mg.), and see Dt. xxxiii. 16. This contains an allusion to headship in the northern kingdom.

iv. Death of Jacob and his burial in Canaan (xlix. 28—l. 14). *The physicians embalmed Israel* (l. 2). This meant the complete mummification of Jacob's body. *Threescore and ten days* (3). These included the embalming period. *Beyond Jordan* (10). According to the position or mental viewpoint of the writer this phrase is capable of meaning either east or west of Jordan (see Dt. i. 1n.). The site of the floor of Atad cannot be identified in the present state of our knowledge. It may be that there were two 'mournings'; one east and one west of Jordan, one at the entry to Canaan and the other at Machpelah (see verse 13).

g. Joseph cares for his brothers (l. 15–26)

i. Joseph allays his brothers' fears (l. 15–21). *Thy father did command* (16). These words perhaps reveal an uncertainty that may have lingered in Jacob's mind as to what Joseph might do to his brothers after the father was gone. Is it too suspicious, however, to ask whether in saying this the brothers are lying and merely putting up a case? This crafty family seemed to be capable of anything. *Am I in the place of God?* (19). Joseph meant that he was no judge. *Ye thought evil against me* (20). He makes his brothers face a very ugly fact and then points out the overruling of the hand of God in the whole matter.

ii. Death of Joseph (l. 22–26). *Ye shall carry up my bones from hence* (25). See Ex. xiii. 19; Jos. xxiv. 32.

E. F. KEVAN.

EXODUS

INTRODUCTION

I. AUTHORSHIP

'The second book of Moses called Exodus' is the title which introduces this book to readers of the Authorized Version. We accept this as an accurate description. For a general study of this question of the authorship of the Pentateuch see article *The Historical Literature of the Old Testament* (p. 31). Here we would mention only that the tradition of the Mosaic authorship of Exodus was well established in the third century B.C., as evidenced by the reference to it in the book of Ecclesiasticus (xlv. 5). That the law was written by Moses was affirmed by Jesus Christ (Mk. i. 44; Jn. vii. 19–22), and by His disciples (Jn. i. 45; Acts xxvi. 23). The claim that certain parts of it were written by Moses is made in the book itself (xvii. 14, xxiv. 4).

Nothing within the book conflicts with this claim that Moses was the author. The frequent mention of Moses' name in the third person has its parallels in the books of Isaiah and Jeremiah, whilst the record of his call in chapter iii carries the same marks of authenticity as do the accounts of theirs.

II. SCOPE AND PURPOSE

The book of Exodus is the book of redemption. The Greek name 'Exodus' (lit. 'going out') here describes how God brought the children of Israel out of bondage in Egypt; but by redemption we understand that the Redeemer not only delivers His people out of bondage but also brings them into a special relationship with Himself, making them His own purchased possession, His 'peculiar treasure' (xix. 5).

The earlier part of the book describes, therefore, the great deliverance of God's people Israel, culminating in the Passover, and foreshadowing the still greater redemption worked out on Calvary. From this it passes to the covenant of Sinai, in which God declared Israel to be His people, giving them the ten commandments, whilst on their part they took Jehovah to be their God, pledging themselves to obedience. This covenant was the foundation of their national existence, to which the new covenant (1 Cor. xi. 25; Heb. viii. 6–13) forms the antitype in the calling of the Church. Finally, the story of the establishment of the tabernacle and its worship provides the basis on which the life of the redeemed people in their relationship to God must be maintained. In the new covenant the basis of fellowship with God is Christ. The tabernacle and its worship therefore provide many 'types' and foreshadowings of Christ (see e.g. Heb. viii. 5, ix. 1, 11, x. 1).

The references in the New Testament fully justify our seeing Christ in this book as its 'fulfilment'. In the miracles recorded we see 'signs' of the divine working (cf. Jn. ii. 11, RV), in the covenant of Sinai a forerunner of the new covenant, and in the tabernacle worship a 'shadow of good things to come' (Heb. x. 1).

III. ITS PLACE IN THE PENTATEUCH

The opening word 'Now' (Heb. 'And') marks Exodus as the sequel to Genesis. The first book is made up of patriarchal narratives, which read like autobiographies; here in the second we have a manifestation of God's power in the deliverance of His people and their birth as a nation. The tabernacle worship is then elaborated in Leviticus. Numbers sees the people as nomads in the wilderness and records the addition of further laws. Deuteronomy finds them looking across Jordan to the promised land and receiving from Moses his final exhortations and their national constitution. In this manner Exodus is seen as an integral part in the Pentateuchal scheme.

OUTLINE OF CONTENTS

I. THE OPPRESSION IN EGYPT. i. 1–22

II. THE BIRTH, TRAINING AND CALL OF MOSES. ii. 1—vii. 7

    a. The first eighty years of Moses' life (ii. 1–22)
    b. The call of Moses (ii. 23—iv. 17)
    c. Moses returns to Egypt (iv. 18–31)
    d. The first application to Pharaoh and its result (v. 1—vi. 1)
    e. The promises and the commission renewed (vi. 2–13)
    f. The genealogies of Moses and Aaron (vi. 14–27)
    g. The commission resumed (vi. 28—vii. 7)

III. THE PLAGUES, THE PASSOVER AND THE EXODUS. vii. 8—xv. 21

a. Pharaoh is given a sign (vii. 8–13)
b. The first nine plagues (vii. 14—x. 29)
c. Warning of the last plague (xi. 1–10)
d. The institution of the Passover (xii. 1–28)
e. The tenth plague and the departure from Egypt (xii. 29–51)
f. The sanctification and redemption of the firstborn (xiii. 1–16)
g. The crossing of the Red Sea (xiii. 17—xiv. 31)
h. The Song of Moses (xv. 1–21)

IV. THE JOURNEY TO HOREB. xv. 22—xviii. 27

a. Marah and Elim (xv. 22–27)
b. The provision of manna (xvi. 1–36)
c. The rebellion at Rephidim and the battle with Amalek (xvii. 1–16)
d. The visit of Jethro (xviii. 1–27)

V. THE GIVING OF THE LAW AT SINAI. xix. 1—xxiv. 18

a. Preparations for receiving the law of the covenant (xix. 1–25)
b. The Ten Commandments (xx. 1–17)
c. The fear of God falls on the people (xx. 18–21)
d. An altar to be erected (xx. 22–26)
e. Various judgments (xxi. 1—xxii. 20)
f. Various moral statutes (xxii. 21—xxiii. 19)
g. Rewards of obedience (xxiii. 20–33)
h. The ratification of the covenant (xxiv. 1–11)
i. Moses delegates his authority and again ascends Mount Sinai (xxiv. 12–18)

VI. THE DIVINE PLAN FOR THE TABERNACLE. xxv. 1—xxxi. 18

a. Gifts for the tabernacle (xxv. 1–9)
b. The tabernacle furniture (xxv. 10–40)
c. The tabernacle, altar and court (xxvi. 1—xxvii. 21)
d. The robes of the High Priest and his sons (xxviii. 1–43)
e. Ordinances for the consecration of the priests (xxix. 1–37)
f. The daily sacrifice and the promise of the Lord's presence (xxix. 38–46)
g. Further directions for the tabernacle (xxx. 1—xxxi. 11)
h. The sign of the sabbath (xxxi. 12–17)
i. The tables of testimony (xxxi. 18)

VII. THE IDOLATRY OF THE ISRAELITES AND MOSES' INTERCESSION. xxxii. 1—xxxiii. 23

a. The making of the golden calf (xxxii. 1–6)
b. Moses intercedes for the people (xxxii. 7–14)
c. The people are punished (xxxii. 15–29)
d. Moses again intercedes and is shown God's glory (xxxii. 30—xxxiii. 23)

VIII. THE RENEWAL OF THE COVENANT. xxxiv. 1–35

IX. THE CONSTRUCTION AND ERECTION OF THE TABERNACLE. xxxv. 1—xl. 38

a. The people offer willingly (xxxv. 1–29)
b. The craftsmen carry out the work according to pattern (xxxv. 30—xxxix. 43)
c. The tabernacle is set up (xl. 1–33)
d. The glory of the Lord (xl. 34–38)

COMMENTARY

I. THE OPPRESSION IN EGYPT. i. 1–22

Israel . . . Jacob (1). No significance seems to attach to the use of the two different names here and in subsequent verses. *Seventy souls* (5). Cf. Gn. xlvi. 8–27. Only two females are included in the list, Dinah and Sarah. To this number must be added the 'households' (verse 1), i.e. the wives and retainers of each son and grandson, totalling perhaps several hundreds.

Were fruitful (7). An abnormal multiplication is indicated, as promised in Gn. xxii. 17. *The land* (7), i.e. Goshen. See Gn. xlvi. 1–7. *A new king* (8). Possibly the first of a new dynasty. If the 'Hyksos', the Shepherd kings, were reigning at the time of Joseph and Jacob's entry into Egypt, they would be favourable to the newcomers, as they were also of Semitic stock. This assumes, of course, the adoption of the system of earlier dates for the oppression and the exodus. For details see the Chronological Table on p. 38 and the discussion of these questions of dating in the Introductions to Joshua and to Judges. *Knew not Joseph* (8). He may have heard of Joseph, but felt under no personal obligation to him. Moreover he may have been hostile toward the former dynasty whose rule had been resented by the true Egyptians and consequently towards all who had been favoured by them. *More and mightier than we* (9). Better as RV mg. 'too many and too mighty for us'. Numerically the Egyptian population was much greater. *Out of the land* (10). Although they hated the Israelites, the Egyptians were unwilling to lose the services of any of their subject peoples. *Taskmasters* (11). The Egyptians employed for their public works gangs of labourers, coerced and unpaid, controlled by two grades of overseers, who assigned the tasks and forced the work on with a lash. *Treasure cities* (11). 'Store cities' (RV). Cf. 1 Ki. ix. 19. Depots near the frontier for the store of military equipment as a provision for both defence and attack. *Raamses* (11). The same as Rameses (Gn. xlvii. 11, where see note). *The more they multiplied* (12). Due to the miraculous providence of their God. *With rigour* (13). We may realize how severe were the conditions of this forced labour from Herodotus' statement (ii. 158) that Pharaoh Necho lost 120,000 men (possibly an exaggerated figure) in the construction of a canal from the Red Sea to the Nile. *Midwives* (15). Probably Hebrew women. 'Shiphrah' is certainly and 'Puah' probably a Hebrew name; but whether Hebrew or Egyptian their saving quality was that they *feared God* (17). They respected His will and purpose for His people. *If it be a son* (16). In this way the Hebrew race would die out, the females being absorbed by marriage into the Egyptian families. *The Hebrew women are not as the Egyptian women* (19). This statement was probably true—but not the real reason why they saved the males alive. The

Scripture records but never commends the faults of God-fearing persons. (Cf. Rahab's lie, Jos. ii. 4, 5.) *Therefore God dealt well . . .* (20). Not because they deceived the king, but because they feared God and refused to obey his decree. Loyalty to God comes before the subjection to the king enjoined in Rom. xiii. Cf. 1 Pet. ii. 13, 17. *Made them houses* (21). Cf. 1 Ki. ii. 24. Gave families and descendants to those who had preserved alive the families of His people.

II. THE BIRTH, TRAINING AND CALL OF MOSES. ii. 1—vii. 7

a. The first eighty years of Moses' life (ii. 1–22)

Note the simplicity and tone of veracity in this account in contrast with the elaborate legends which record the birth of mythical heroes. *A man . . . a daughter* (1). The omission of their names does not indicate that the author did not know them. It is rather a mark of Moses' modesty. Compare John's references to himself in his Gospel. *Daughter of Levi* (1), i.e. a descendant of Levi. *Ark of bulrushes* (3). The word *tebah*, a 'box' or 'chest' (probably an Egyptian word), is used only here and for Noah's ark. The 'bulrushes' are papyrus reeds, a material put to many uses in Egypt, even for the construction of large boats. Cf. Is. xviii. 2. *In the flags* (3), where it would be less noticeable, and prevented from floating downstream. *His sister* (4). Miriam is the only sister of Moses mentioned in Scripture. See Nu. xxvi. 59. To judge by her action here recorded, she must have been twelve years or older at this time.

The babe wept (6). Naturally, under the circumstances! But the infant's cries were used in the providence of God to move the heart of the princess. *One of the Hebrews' children* (6). Egyptian children might also have been exposed, but this 'goodly child' so carefully cradled could be none other than one of the Hebrews. *Took the child, and nursed it* (9). Moses' mother was able to nurse her child in her own home until he was weaned, at the end of his first or possibly second or third year (cf. 2 Macc. vii. 27), when she brought him back to Pharaoh's daughter to be brought up in the royal house. We are not told whether she continued with him there, but we may well believe that she implanted in him the roots of faith in the true God, which directed his later conduct. *He became her son* (10). He enjoyed the privileges and education of an adopted son of the princess. The privileges he later renounced (Heb. xi. 24) but he never lost the benefits of the education (Acts vii. 22). *She called his name Moses* (10). The Hebrew word *Mosheh* is probably a form of the Egyptian *mesu*, meaning a child, a son, the noun being derived from a verb meaning 'to produce', 'to draw forth'. Hence the explanation given in this verse of the reason why she called him by this name. The Hebrew *mashah* also means 'to draw out', and the play upon words could therefore be shown in the Hebrew, although it cannot appear in the English version.

When Moses was grown (11). According to Stephen (Acts vii. 23), 'full forty years old'. *Unto his brethren* (11). He had not remained in ignorance of his true race. 'It is the first sign of that strong sympathy and tender affection for his people which characterizes him throughout the narrative, and which culminates in the pathetic cry, "Forgive them; and if not, blot me out of thy book" (xxxii. 32)' (Rawlinson). *He slew the Egyptian* (12). For this act he had no justification either by the law of the land or in the sight of God. He meant well, but even his best intentions were the product of a spirit not yet attuned to the will of God. Hence the need for a further forty years' discipline before his heart and mind were fully able to receive the revelation of God's purposes and laws. *In the sand* (12). Note the minute detail. Moses wrote what he himself had seen. The men of Israel attributed to Moses an officiousness which he did not really display (14). They could not understand his true motives (Acts vii. 25). His hasty action of the previous day rendered his actions liable to such misinterpretation. *Sought to slay Moses* (15). In the reasonable execution of justice. *Midian* (15). The Midian here referred to was probably the southeastern portion of the Sinai peninsula. *Priest of Midian* (16). See xviii. 12. For the relationship of the Midianites to the Israelites see Gn. xxv. 2. They worshipped the same true God. *Reuel* (18). Raguel in Nu. x. 29 is the Greek form of the same Hebrew word. Reuel means 'God is friend'. For the name Jethro see note on iii. 1. *An Egyptian* (19). Judging by his appearance and dress. *Gershom* (22). Derived from *ger*, 'a stranger', and *sham*, 'there'.

b. The call of Moses (ii. 23—iv. 17)

In process of time (23). Forty years after his flight from Egypt. See vii. 7. *Sighed by reason of the bondage* (23). The new Pharaoh did not relax the rigour of the oppression. According to the more probable dating the Pharaoh of the oppression was the mighty Thothmes III, but some think he was Rameses II. Many buildings of both kings can be seen today. *Had respect unto them* (25). 'Took knowledge of them' (RV). Cf. Ps. xxxi. 7; Ho. xiii. 5. God took notice of and sympathetically understood the sufferings and feelings of His people. Contrast Mt. vii. 23.

Jethro his father in law (iii. 1). The word may possibly mean 'brother-in-law' and Jethro would in that case be a son of Reuel (see ii. 18), but it is more probable that Jethro is another name of Reuel. *The backside of the desert* (1). Lit. 'behind the wilderness'. See Dt. i. 1n. *The mountain of God* (1), so called by Moses writing after his many experiences of God upon this mountain. *Horeb* (1), also called Sinai. Horeb usually denotes the region, Sinai the particular mountain. *The angel*

of the Lord (2), i.e. a special manifestation of Jehovah. In verse 4 he is called both Jehovah and Elohim. We may thereby infer that it was the second Person of the Trinity who appeared to Moses. (See note on Gn. xvi. 7.) No personal form appeared, but the flame and the voice were themselves evidence of the presence of the Lord. *Put off thy shoes* (5). A sign of respect before entering a holy place, or palace, used in the East from before the time of Moses to the present day. *Of thy father* (6). The name of Moses' mother Jochebed (see vi. 20) ('Jehovah gloried') shows that his parents were worshippers of Jehovah. See vi. 3n. *The God of Abraham* (6). See Gn. xv. 7, 8n. *To look upon God* (6). Cf. 1 Ki. xix. 13. God's presence was sufficiently manifest without any bodily form being seen.

I am come down (8). Cf. Gn. xi. 5, xviii. 21. The author did not intend this literally; see e.g. 1 Ki. viii. 27; Pr. xv. 3. The phrase is a way of expressing in human language the divine act of condescension and concern. *A good land and a large* (8) extending from the Mediterranean to the Euphrates, and as far as Taurus in the north. The expression *flowing with milk and honey* (8) was a proverbial expression used to denote plenty. See Dt. vi. 3n.

Certainly I will be with thee (12). A sufficient answer to any plea of unfitness for the work to which God calls. Cf. 2 Cor. xii. 9. A sign or token is also promised but, being itself yet in the future (contrast the immediate signs given in chapter iv), is a further stimulus to faith. Cf. 1 Sa. ii. 34. *What is his name?* (13). Moses implies that they will ask for his credentials, and will want to know the nature of this God whom he claims to be the God who has sent him and the God of their fathers. The name as often in Scripture stands for the description of the nature or character of the person who bears that name. See Dt. v. 11.

I AM THAT I AM (14). The word translated 'I am' is the Heb. *ehyeh*, first person imperfect of the verb *hayah*, 'to become'. The tense is indefinite, meaning equally 'I was', 'I am being', and 'I will be'. (The same word is used in verse 12 above, *Certainly I will be with thee*.) This fuller expression explains the shorter form of the name 'I AM' or 'Jehovah' (YHWH, verse 14) which is the third person of the same verb and has the same meaning. No other words could so perfectly express the revealed truth and infinite mystery of the nature of the true God. 'I AM THAT I AM' signifies that He is self-existent, the only real being and the source of all reality; that He is self-sufficient; that He is eternal and unchangeable in His promises; that He is what He will be, all choice being according to His own will and pleasure. In addition the name preserves much of His nature hidden from curious and presumptuous enquiry. We cannot by searching find Him out. See Pr. xxx. 4. Compare His announcement of Himself in Rev. i. 4, 8, etc.

The Lord God of your fathers (15). The word Lord used in each statement is really 'Jehovah.'

See the note on verse 14 and that on Gn. ii. 4. This is the name by which He will be remembered. *The elders of Israel* (16). The heads of families who exercised authority and judgment over them. *I have surely visited you* (16). Cf. Gn. 1. 24; Lk. i. 68. God has interposed on their behalf. *Three days' journey* (18). Since certain animals were sacred to the Egyptians it was necessary to get thus far to avoid giving offence to their neighbours by the slaughter of the sacrificial victims. See Dt. i. 1n. *That we may sacrifice* (18). No deception is implied here, as if under cover of this moderate request they intended leaving Egypt altogether. It served to test Pharaoh's attitude to their leaving his domain, and his abrupt refusal of this modest petition justified the display of God's power which followed—and their final and absolute removal from his borders.

I am sure . . . no, not by a mighty hand (19). Read with AV mg. and LXX 'but by strong hand', i.e. 'only after he has felt the power of My hand'. See verse 20. *Shall borrow* (22). RV 'ask' is the exact translation. After the terrors of these days the Egyptians would be glad to give them anything for which they asked, if only to be rid of them. *Shall spoil* (22). As spoil is lawfully taken from a conquered people. Cf. Gn. xv. 14. All that they received was no more than their just reward for their enforced labour.

The Lord hath not appeared (iv. 1). A natural objection considering that it was so long since the last special manifestation of the Lord to Israel. *A rod* (2). His shepherd's staff. *By the tail* (4). An act of faith; normally to avoid its bite one would take it by the neck. *That they may believe* (5). This verse continues the Lord's words above, *And he put . . . in his hand* being in parenthesis. God Himself here explains the true purpose of miracles. They are to serve as persuasive proofs or 'signs' of the presence of divine power and are therefore not to be expected at all times, but, as appears in the Scripture record, only when there is special need to establish God's authority in face of doubt, uncertainty or apostasy.

I am not eloquent (10). Heb. 'a man of words'. He may have found difficulty in expressing his thoughts and may even have suffered from some defect in his speech. On the other hand this may have merely been the excuse of one who was afraid to face the people. Many of God's spokesmen have thus at first sensed their own unreadiness and inability to speak. Cf. Is. vi. 5; Je. i. 6; Ezk. ii. 6. *Who hath made man's mouth?* (11). Human inability is no excuse for evading a commission from the divine Creator. *Send, I pray thee* (13). Moses almost, but not quite, declines to accept the task and reveals his unbelief in the promises just made by the Lord. *Aaron the Levite* (14). Moses' elder brother. Moses also was of the tribe of Levi, but the title 'Levite' is not without point, for, in Hebrew, affection for a person is expressed by giving the full name. Cf. Gn. xxii. 2. *Put words in his mouth* (15). Give him the subject matter for him to express in speech. *Instead of God* (16). This phrase perfectly describes the function of a prophet, one who mediates the mind of God to the people. *Do signs* (17). 'Do the signs' (RV), i.e. not only those of iv. 1–9 but also those intimated in iii. 20.

c. Moses returns to Egypt (iv. 18-31)

My brethren (18), i.e. kinsfolk. This was part, but not the whole, of Moses' purpose in returning to Egypt. *Go, return* (19). Moses was still delaying to carry out God's commission. *The rod of God* (20), i.e. his old staff, but now endowed with divine power.

I will harden his heart (21). It is said that Pharaoh hardened his own heart or that his heart was hardened in vii. 13 (see note), vii. 14, 22, viii. 15, 19, 32, ix. 7, 34, 35; and that God hardened Pharaoh's heart in ix. 12, x. 1, 20, 27, xiv. 4, 8. This action is foretold in iv. 21, vii. 3. Note that the action is at first mainly ascribed to Pharaoh himself and later more directly to God. God does not positively cause men to rebel against Himself, but He has so ordered man's heart that each time he refuses to do God's will he renders himself less responsive to the next call or command. The conscience thus becomes less sensitive and the heart grows harder. Man hardens his own heart, but in Bible idiom 'events, whether physical or moral, which are the inevitable result of the divine ordering of the universe, are spoken of as the direct work of God' (Hertz). In addition to this significance of the phrase we must note that, once Pharaoh had hardened his own heart, God directly smote him with a hardness from which it was impossible for him to be renewed unto repentance (cf. Heb. vi. 4–6), both as a penalty and in order to show His power in him (Rom. ix. 17, 18), as demonstrated both in Pharaoh's fall and in His people's deliverance.

Israel is my son, even my firstborn (22). This does not imply the universal fatherhood of God, as if the other nations were also His sons, but that Israel first was elected into spiritual sonship 'that the blessing of Abraham might come on the Gentiles through Jesus Christ' (Gal. iii. 14). See Rom. viii. 14–17.

The inn (24). Simply a resting-place. *Sought to kill him* (24). Perhaps by an illness. This seems to have been a punishment for neglecting the duty of circumcising his son. Before Moses could lay the commands of God before Pharaoh and the Israelites he must himself omit none of them. In this drastic way God brought Moses to the point of entire obedience, the necessary preparation for being used in His service. *A bloody husband* (25). Heb. ḥathan-damim, lit. 'cut with blood'. This expression was applied to a youthful bridegroom, circumcised before marriage. The words were either addressed to her son, denoting the fulfilment of the covenant rite, or to her husband as thus restored to her as a bridegroom. Whatever the exact meaning, her action averted the divine displeasure. *So he let him go* (26). God

110

spared Moses. It was probably at this time that Moses sent his wife and sons back to Jethro (see xviii. 2, 3). *The signs* (30) were the three miracles of verses 3–9.

d. The first application to Pharaoh and its result (v. 1—vi. 1)

A feast (1). See iii. 18n. *Who is the Lord?* (2). An expression of contempt, but Pharaoh, like many of the Israelites even, may have been ignorant of the name. *The God of the Hebrews* (3). This description was more likely to be understood by Pharaoh. *Let the people* (4), i.e. hinder them, distracting them by talk of a pilgrimage, etc. *The people of the land* (5). Heb. *'am ha-areṣ*. The word usually means the common people but probably here, as in Gn. xxiii. 7, 'the council of elders' who had come with Moses and Aaron. Pharaoh intimates that too many of them were doing no work. *Straw* (7). Either to reinforce the clay, or to keep the clay from sticking to the moulds. *They be idle . . . let them not regard vain words* (8, 9). Satan often represents the worship of God as vanity fit only for those who have nothing more constructive to do. *Stubble* (12). In Egypt only the heads of the corn were cut off, leaving long stalks of straw for the Israelites to cut, carry and chop before using it for the bricks. The word may also include all other kinds of field rubbish.

Stood in the way (20). *The officers* (19) were waiting to meet them as they came from the presence of Pharaoh, to learn the result of the interview. *Returned unto the Lord* (22). As one who constantly repeated his communion with God. *Wherefore* (22). Had Moses forgotten the warning of iii. 19? Yet there was a further problem in that instead of a straightforward refusal Pharaoh had increased the burdens beyond human endurance. *Now shalt thou see* (vi. 1). The greater the violence of Pharaoh, the greater the manifestation of God's power to deliver. *With a strong hand* (1), i.e. compelled by the strong hand of God. See iii. 19.

e. The promises and the commission renewed (vi. 2–13)

I am the Lord . . . (2, 3). Contrary to the statements of modern criticism, God is not here announcing to Moses a new name by which He is to be called. The succeeding verses show that God is declaring that the time has now come for Him to fulfil the covenant made with their fathers, and to do what He had then promised. He therefore strengthens the faith of Moses and the Israelites by reasserting His character, for the name indicates the character (see note on iii. 14). He is the covenant-keeping God, and it is this aspect of His character which He will now especially reveal to His people by fulfilling the promises of the covenant made with their fathers, so that the name 'Jehovah' was henceforth to be particularly associated with the covenant relationship between God and His people. Their fathers also used this name

'Jehovah', but the aspect of His character which He particularly revealed to them was that of His power with special reference to multiplying their seed (Gn. xvii. 1, 2, xxviii. 3, xxxv. 11). *God Almighty* (3) is not a name for God (the words 'the name of' are not in the Heb.) but the phrase is descriptive, 'the almighty God'. The Israelites in the days of Jeremiah and Ezekiel were well aware of the name 'Jehovah', but Je. xvi. 21, 'they shall know that my name is Jehovah'—a phrase often found in Ezekiel—proves that it was the character of God implied by that name which they did not know. Thus in Ex. vi. 7 the meaning is they would come to know that He was Jehovah their God, not by hearing that name announced, but by experiencing His acts of power and love. Another legitimate way of rendering verse 3, but one which gives a different meaning, is, 'I suffered myself to appear unto Abraham, unto Isaac, and unto Jacob as El Shaddai, and have I not even suffered myself to be known to them by my name Jehovah?' See also notes on Gn. ii. 4, xvii. 1, and Dt. v. 11.

My covenant (4). See notes on Gn. vi. 18, xv. 7–21; Dt. iv. 13. *Redeem* (6). This is the first instance in the Bible of the use of this word, expressing one of the fundamental elements in the divine act of salvation. The redemption of Israel from Egypt figures prominently in Scripture as a type of our redemption from sin. The Heb. *gaal* means to 'reclaim' or 'ransom', especially as the kinsman ransoms the property or person of a helpless relative. Thus God, the divine Kinsman, whose resources are inexhaustible, ransoms His helpless people at the cost of the exercise of His supernatural power and makes them His own peculiar property (verse 7). Cf. Is. xliii. 1. *Judgments* (6). The acts of power are a judgment on the oppressor. See Dt. iv. 1n. *I will take you to me for a people* (7). Cf. xix. 5, 6, etc. Israel was chosen to be the means through which God brought to the world His revelation of Himself and His salvation. *I will be to you a God* (7). He had a special relationship to Israel, yet ceased not to be the God of the whole earth. *I am the Lord* (8). The message closes with the same words with which it began. It is sealed at both ends with the authority of the living and the faithful God.

That he let . . . go (11). A greater demand than the first. See iii. 18n. *Uncircumcised lips* (12). This is not any admission of sinfulness, but a repetition of his complaint in iv. 10 that he is slow of speech. Similarly an 'uncircumcised ear' (Je. vi. 10) is one that 'cannot hearken'. Cf. Lv. xxvi. 41.

f. The genealogies of Moses and Aaron (vi. 14–27)

Fathers' houses (14). A technical term for 'clans' or 'families'. Reuben and Simeon are included here possibly to show the relative position of Levi in the family of Israel, and that in the dispensation of God it is not always the one who is born first who is the 'firstborn' in place of honour and leadership. *Jochebed his father's sister* (20). The name means 'Jehovah is my glory'. It is a further proof of the knowledge of the name Jehovah before the time of Moses. See iii. 14, 15n. The marriage of a man to his aunt was permitted until the law of Lv. xviii. 12. *Korah* (21). Cousin therefore to Moses. See Nu. xvi. 1 and xxvi. 11. His children did not perish with him, and their names are given in verse 24 as the heads of important priestly families. *Elisheba* (23). A name better known in its Greek form, Elizabeth. *Their armies* (26), i.e. marshalled in orderly array by tribes, families, etc.; no disorderly mob. There is no suggestion here of their being equipped with military weapons.

g. The commission resumed (vi. 28—vii. 7)

The narrative of verses 2–12, interrupted by the genealogies, is taken up again at this point. *A god to Pharaoh* (vii. 1). By the authority of his person and the power of his acts Moses would represent to Pharaoh the authority and power of the true God. *Thy prophet* (1). Cf. iv. 16. This is God's answer to Moses' objection in vi. 12. *Thou shalt speak* (2), i.e. to Aaron. For verse 3 see iv. 21n. *Know that I am the Lord* (5). God's acts on behalf of Israel throughout their history had one end in view, to demonstrate to a world which had gone after other gods the nature of Jehovah, the only true God. *Fourscore years* (7). God can prolong a man's life to any age, but it is noteworthy that Egyptian records show that service beyond 100 years was not uncommon.

III. THE PLAGUES, THE PASSOVER AND THE EXODUS. vii. 8—xv. 21

a. Pharaoh is given a sign (vii. 8–13)

Shew a miracle for you (9). Prove your claims by a supernatural act. *In like manner with their enchantments* (11). 'Secret arts' (RV mg.). By hypnotism and various tricks they could make a snake rigid like a stick. No supernatural power need be implied here. *He hardened Pharaoh's heart* (13). A mistranslation; 'heart' is the subject of the sentence. Read 'Pharaoh's heart was strong' or 'was hardened'. See iv. 21n.

b. The first nine plagues (vii. 14—x. 29)

The plagues not only caused great physical affliction; they were a judgment against the gods of Egypt. The Nile was a main object of worship; the frog was sacred as a symbol of fertility; of the cattle the ram, the goat and the bull were sacred; the sun-god Ra was eclipsed and proved impotent by the plague of darkness. 'Against all the gods of Egypt I will execute judgment: I am the Lord' (xii. 12).

i. The Nile turned to blood (vii. 14–25).

He goeth out unto the water (15). Either to bathe or for a religious festival. The miracle is announced beforehand (17) so that Pharaoh may realize that it is no disconnected wonder, but a proof that the Lord has power to fulfil His designs and decrees. *Turned to blood* (17). In Joel ii. 31 blood is used in a metaphorical sense, but here it is probably to be taken literally. The river was sometimes made red by the presence of certain vegetable matter, but this is not merely the intensification of a natural phenomenon; it is a miracle by which the very fish die and the water becomes loathsome. *The magicians . . . did so* (22). This may have been trickery; but see viii. 18n. The clear water was obtained probably as in verse 24. *Digged . . . for water* (24). Verse 19 indicates that all water derived from the Nile became blood. Water obtained from other sources was still pure. *Seven days* (25). After this God allowed the fresh water flowing down to cleanse the lower streams of the river.

ii. The plague of frogs (viii. 1–15). *Upon thy bed* (3).

Most distressing to the Egyptians, who were particular in their cleanliness. *The magicians did so* (7). They evidently had no power to remove the frogs sent by God. *Glory over me* (9). A form of polite address, 'have the honour of deciding'. *That thou mayest know* (10). The removal of the frogs at the exact time named by the king would be proof that no other power than that of the Lord had done so. Pharaoh said 'tomorrow', possibly in the hope that they would disappear of themselves in the night and that he would be relieved of the necessity of acknowledging the hand of God. *Moses cried unto the Lord* (12). Moses was convinced in his mind that God would do this, yet earnest entreaty was necessary. This is an illustration of the place of intercessory prayer. *Pharaoh . . . hardened his heart* (15). See iv. 21n. Temporary distress had forced Pharaoh to acknowledge the reality of God, the power of prayer, and the claims of His people (8), but the attitude of his heart towards God had remained unchanged and naturally his convictions and his promises vanished together with the frogs. We must look for a change of heart beneath the profession of the lips.

iii. The plague of lice (viii. 16–19). *The Lord said* (16).

This plague was sent without warning. Having hardened his heart, Pharaoh was given this time no opportunity to submit before the judgment was sent. *They could not* (18). This was outside the range of their experience or conjuring ability. If on the other hand we regard their previous imitations as real miracles and not illusions, we may learn from this verse that God allows the devil to go so far but no farther in reproducing signs and wonders. Cf. Mt. xxiv. 24. *The finger of God* (19). They acknowledge some divine power but not yet the name of Jehovah. Cf. Lk. xi. 20. *Pharaoh . . . hearkened not* (19). This plague probably did not inconvenience him personally so much as the others.

iv. The plague of flies (viii. 20–32). *Swarms of flies* (21).

Heb. *'arobh*. Many expositors consider that this was a species of beetle. This insect, the scarab, was an emblem of Ra the sun-god and therefore, as a sacred object like the frogs, its obnoxious presence could not be removed by killing it. *I will sever* (22). A new miracle demonstrating vividly the reality and providence of the

Lord. *The land was corrupted* (24). Better as mg., 'destroyed'. This plague is an advance on the others; it causes more than unpleasantness; the flies or beetles destroy personal property.

Pharaoh called (25). Being personally affected by this visitation he quickly appeals for relief, but offers a compromise, 'in the land', which is unacceptable to the man of God. *The abomination of the Egyptians* (26). Certain animals were sacred to the Egyptians and might not be killed. If the Israelites had sacrificed sheep, goats or bulls within the land of Egypt, it would have provoked a widespread riot among the Egyptian people. Similar riots have occurred in India in recent times when cows, sacred to the Hindus, have been killed, and in Egypt a Roman ambassador was once torn to pieces by the mob for accidentally killing a cat. *As he shall command us* (27). Cf. x. 26. The exact form of the sacrifice was not yet clear, but in any case there could be no compromise over the clearly defined commandments of God. *Not go very far away* (28). Evidence that Pharaoh's repentance was superficial. His sin was within as easy range of recall as he desired the Israelites to be. *I will intreat* (29). Moses accepted Pharaoh's 'not very far' as covering his demand for a 'three days' journey'. *Removed the swarms* (31). The dead bodies of the frogs had been left as an added affliction; the flies were miraculously removed as evidence of God's power to be merciful. *Pharaoh hardened his heart* (32). The partial repentance again served only to make his heart harder when relief came. See verse 15n.

v. The death of the cattle (ix. 1–7). *A set time* (5). Murrain in a general way was not uncommon in Egypt. Proof of the hand of God in this case was given by the fact that it came at the time appointed, that the Israelites were exempted, and that the plague affected only the cattle in the field. *Tomorrow* (5). Space was granted for any believing Egyptians to bring their cattle in from the field. *All* (6), i.e. literally all that were in the field. *Was hardened* (7). Pharaoh was little impressed, probably because less affected by this plague.

vi. The plague of boils (ix. 8–12). *The Lord said* (8). Like the third, this plague was sent without warning, as a judgment. *The magicians could not stand* (11). Now not only unable to imitate the miracle, but themselves the victims of the judgment; see 2 Tim. iii. 8, 9. *The Lord hardened* (12). Wilful hardness begins now to be punished with judicial hardness. See iv. 21n.

vii. The plague of hail (ix. 13–35). *All my plagues upon thine heart* (14). Here begins the last series of the strokes of God which will finally crush the resistance of Pharaoh's stubborn heart. The judgment is to come in such a way that Pharaoh shall release his captives, yet, while acknowledging the unique and sovereign power of ,the Lord, remain unreconciled to Him. Pharaoh's heart was smitten but still hardened. *I will stretch out* (15). See RV 'I had put forth my hand'. The last clause of verse 14 explains why

God did not destroy Pharaoh and his people before, and this reason is again given in verse 16, 'for this cause have I made thee to stand', i.e. 'kept thee alive'. His and their preservation was in order the more clearly to manifest by them the power and character of God: see Rom. ix. 16, 17. While they remained alive they served as the objects of God's activity and righteous judgments, otherwise He would have destroyed them sooner. Now the time was coming when not only their property but their persons would be smitten. *Gather thy cattle* (19). God is not ruthless. Opportunity was given even to the Egyptians to show by this outward action that they believed the Lord and respected His word. See verse 20. *Fire* (23, 24). Caused possibly by some form of electrical disturbance.

The earth is the Lord's (29). Cf. Jas. v. 17, 18. This extraordinary phenomenon in the physical world came in consequence of Moses' prediction and went in answer to his prayer. Both its infliction and its removal were therefore proof that the Lord the Creator can do what He chooses with the earth which He has made. *He sinned yet more* (34). The greater God's longsuffering towards Pharaoh, the greater his sin in repeatedly going back on his word. Moses' prayer could open the heavens but could not open the heart of a self-willed man. Yet even the opposition of God's enemies is made to subserve His plan of redemption.

viii. The plague of locusts (x. 1–20). *The heart of his servants* (1). They too had hardened their own hearts (ix. 34); therefore they suffered also the penal hardening. *That I might shew . . . signs* (1). God can utilize even the sin of men and the penalties He inflicts upon them as a means of instructing both the present and succeeding generations in His righteousness and His wrath. See 1 Cor. x. 11. *Locusts into thy coast* (4). Locusts always migrate into Egypt from some other country either on the south or the east. *They shall cover* (5). For a vivid biblical description of the ravages of locusts see Joel i. 6, 7, ii. 2–11. Modern eyewitnesses tell the same story. *The residue* (5). Left from the hail and the other plagues. *Pharaoh's servants* (7). Though hardened (1), they were not so hard as Pharaoh (ix. 20). They knew that the locusts would destroy the last remaining means of sustenance. Why should a nation be destroyed through the obduracy of its ruler? *Let the men go* (7). 'Men' here includes women and children. *With our young men . . .* (9). It was not unusual in Egypt for the whole population to observe great festivals, yet Moses' words here enforce the truth that those who would serve God must do so with all that they have. *Let the Lord be so* (10). 'So be the Lord with you' (RV); ironically 'May the Lord be with you as surely as I will let you go'. *Evil is before you* (10), i.e. evil is what you purpose. *Ye that are men* (11). The men would not remain away without their wives and children. Satan cares little for grown men, so long as he can hold the children. *That ye did desire* (11). But Moses had demanded before that all the people should go (vii. 16). *An east wind* (13). The long flight of locusts always depends on the auxiliary of a strong wind. *There remained not* (15). Egypt now depended entirely on the reserves in her granaries, instituted by Joseph, the Hebrew.

ix. The plague of darkness (x. 21–29). *The Lord said* (21). Like the third and the sixth, this plague comes unannounced. No space is here given for repentance. *Darkness which may be felt* (21). Its intensity and duration marks it as something more than a total eclipse of the sun. It penetrated even their dwellings (23). Their terror would be all the greater because Ra, the sun-god, was one of their chief deities. If he was defeated, all was lost. *From his place* (23), i.e. kept to their houses. Cf. xvi. 29. *Only let your flocks . . .* (24). This reserve in Pharaoh's consent nullified the whole. Cf. Jas. ii. 10. *Our cattle also* (26). When going to sacrifice nothing may be held back, because the extent of God's requirements is not known until the appointed time. All is devoted to Him to use as much of it as He chooses. *Get thee from me* (28). The exasperated temper of a man who rebels against his conscience and finds that God makes no concessions. In refusing to see Moses again Pharaoh refused his only means of deliverance. It was to plead for mercy that he had hitherto called Moses to stand before him. *I will see . . . no more* (29). Moses continues to speak to Pharaoh until he finally leaves him at xi. 8, xi. 1–3 being in parenthesis.

c. Warning of the last plague (xi. 1–10)

The Lord said (1). Read 'had said'. The tense is pluperfect, recording a word of God to Moses before this interview with Pharaoh. *Borrow* (2). See iii. 22n. *Moses was very great . . . in the sight of the people* (3). As a result of the wonders which he worked and his consideration for the people in giving them due warning. Moses writes thus of himself not without modesty, but to explain why the people were so willing to give their jewels, etc. *And Moses said* (4). The continuation of Moses' speech to Pharaoh. *About midnight* (4). The actual night was not specified. *All the firstborn* (5). The Hebrew word indicates the male line. *The firstborn of beasts* (5). Several of these were esteemed as objects of worship. *Not a dog move his tongue* (7). A proverbial expression. *That my wonders may be multiplied* (9). Cf. vii. 3. Pharaoh's wilfulness, now intensified by the judgment of God, served to call forth the exercise of God's power to impress both the Egyptians and the Israelites with His justice and His might.

d. The institution of the Passover (xii. 1–28)

The beginning of months (2). The Exodus was spiritually and nationally an epoch-making event. Cf. Nu. i. 1. Hitherto the Jewish year had begun with the month Tisri near the autumnal equinox. The month of the Exodus, Abib, came at the vernal equinox. The Jews now begin their civil year at Tisri and their sacred year at Abib. *A lamb* (3). The word may equally well mean the young of a sheep or a goat (see verse 5), but it appears that lambs were almost universally used. *The house of their fathers* (3), i.e. the family. The first and basic festival of Israel is a family one. The purity of family life is the foundation of spiritual as well as of national prosperity. *Too little* (4). Ten men, besides women and children, were considered the minimum to consume one lamb. *Without blemish* (5). Cf. 1 Pet. i. 19; Heb. vii. 26, ix. 14. Not only must all offerings to God be of the very best, but this lamb was to typify the spotless Lamb of God. *Of the first year* (5), i.e. not more than a year old, the age of innocence. *Keep it up* (6). To allow for thorough inspection. God's affairs must never be hurried. *In the evening* (6). Lit. 'between the evenings'. This means either 'between sunset and the end of the twilight' or 'between the cooling of the day, at about 3 o'clock, and sunset'. In any case, according to Josephus, the lamb was killed between the ninth and eleventh hour, i.e. three to five o'clock. Note that it was at the ninth hour that Jesus cried with a loud voice and gave up the ghost (Mt. xxvii. 45–50).

They shall take of the blood . . . (7). The explanation of the detailed requirements in verses 7–10 can appear only as we see in them a type of Christ. By the blood alone is there deliverance from destruction; the lamb is roast with fire to symbolize the fire of God's wrath which the Saviour endured; those who feed on Him must put away the leaven of malice and wickedness (1 Cor. v. 8), and eat with the bitter herbs of repentance; the whole is to be consumed: if it is physically impossible to do so by eating, then by fire, since the offering of Christ is whole and He is to be wholly received.

Thus shall ye eat it (11). This applies only to the Passover in Egypt, not to subsequent celebrations, yet the redeemed are always to be as those who have no settled dwelling in this world. See Lv. xxiii. 4, 5; Nu. xxviii. 16–25 for celebrations of the Passover in the wilderness, and Dt. xvi. 1–8, which restates the rules in view of its observance in the promised land. *Your loins girded* (11). Gathering up their long loose robes. *In haste* (11). As being ready at any moment for the summons to depart. *It is the Lord's passover* (11). The word 'passover', usually referring to the whole rite, is here applied only to the paschal lamb, as in 1 Cor. v. 7. It is derived from the verb *pasaḥ*, 'to pass over', including the idea 'to spare and protect'. See verse 13. *All the gods of Egypt* (12). Every Egyptian god was represented by some beast and would be powerless to protect its own representative. *I am the Lord* (12). Cf. vi. 2, 6, 8, 29, etc. *To you* (13). In your interest. *A token* (13). The appearance of the blood on the posts of the door would be evidence to God that the sacrifice had been offered, and that the inmates were exercising faith in His promises. These He would deliver. *A memorial . . . for ever* (14). In the same way that the ordinance of the Lord's Supper is a memorial and is observed for 'ever until He come'.

The instructions of verses 15–20 refer not to the immediate occasion but to the future observances of this festival. *Leaven* (15). Usually a symbol of corruption and sin, but not always. See Mt. xiii. 33; also verse 34n., Lv. ii. 11n. *Cut off* (15). Not killed, but banished from the congregation of Israel. See Gn. xvii. 14n. *The first day . . . an holy convocation* (16). This first of the seven days was the day after the killing of the Passover, i.e. 15th Abib. The term convocation is probably derived from the calling together of the people to assemble at the tabernacle, perhaps by the trumpets of Nu. x. 2. *No manner of work* (16), i.e. no servile work. Cf. Lv. xxiii. 7. *Stranger* (19). Heb. *ger*. Aliens who accepted the rite of circumcision and the law of the Lord were included in the congregation and accounted as Israelites. See Dt. i. 16n. *Born in the land* (19). Israelite by natural descent.

Draw out (21), i.e. out of the fold. *A bunch of hyssop* (22). The form of this plant made it particularly suitable for sprinkling the blood of expiation and from its frequent use for this purpose it came to be a symbol of spiritual purification. Cf. Ps. li. 7. *None of you shall go out* (22). Only under the cover of the blood is there protection. *The Lord will pass over* (23). Cf. verse 13. *The destroyer* (23). The destroying angel (2 Sa. xxiv. 16), called 'the plague' in verse 13. *This thing* (24). The sacrifice of the lamb (17, 27), not the sprinkling of the blood on the doorposts, which applied only to this occasion. *As he hath promised* (25). See Gn. xii. 7, etc. *When your children . . .* (26). Spiritual education in the home is the foundation of God's way of life for man. The observance of the rite provides opportunity to recount the history of God's mighty acts and promises. Thus the two Christian ordinances are the occasion of recalling to mind and heart the work and words of the Lord Jesus Christ.

e. The tenth plague and the departure from Egypt (xii. 29–51)

By night (31). So great was their distress that Pharaoh made an instantaneous appeal to Moses. Moses probably did not actually come to Pharaoh. See x. 29. *The firstborn of Pharaoh* (29). The culminating plague fulfilled God's first warning to Pharaoh (iv. 23). *Bless me also* (32). To avert further calamities. Note the extremity of Pharaoh's humiliation, but without heart contrition. See xiv. 5. *Dough before it was leavened* (34). The bread was on this occasion unleavened because of haste. Cf. verses 11, 39. The unleavened bread in subsequent celebrations was a reminder of this and also included the notion of freedom from corruption. See verse 15n. *Borrowed* (35). See iii. 22n. *Lent* (36). Better 'let them have' (RV). *Rameses* (37). See i. 11n. *Six hundred thousand* (37). A round figure representing the 603,550 of Nu. i. 46. *Men, beside children* (37). A note to indicate that adult

males only were included in this figure. It is of course assumed that females would not be counted. *A mixed multitude* (38). See Nu. xi. 4. Various foreigners came who were not included in the 'congregation of Israel'; contrast verse 19. *Flocks and herds* (38). They had not all been tied to slave labour.

Four hundred and thirty years (40). This corresponds to the round figure of 400 years in Gn. xv. 13, 14. It is natural to read the words here and in Genesis as referring to the length of time in Egypt, but the LXX, Paul (Gal. iii. 17), and Rabbinic tradition count the 430 from the time of the promise made to Abraham, and in this case we must understand the word 'sojourn' to include also the earlier period in the land of Canaan. *No stranger* (43). 'Alien' (RV). Not the *ger* of verse 19, but the uncircumcised foreigner, such as were the 'mixed multitude' (38, 45). Cf. Col. ii. 11. But all, whether servants or neighbours, who were willing to make Israel's God their God were welcomed and bidden to the feast (44, 48, 49). *Neither . . . break a bone thereof* (46). See Jn. xix. 33–36. Nothing can destroy the wholeness of Christ and of those who in Him are one with the Father. *One law . . .* (49). The people of Israel were the elect of God and the mediators to the world of His salvation, but He never intended them to be an exclusive race. Is. lvi. 3–8 shows how widely the door was opened to others even under the old covenant.

f. The sanctification and redemption of the first-born (xiii. 1–16)

Sanctify . . . the firstborn (2). 'Set apart as sacred.' It is reasonable that the life which God has spared should be devoted to Him (Rom. xii. 1). Just as the annual celebration of the Passover reminded the nation of their great redemption, so the dedication of the firstborn kept the memory of it fresh in every home. *Remember this day* (3). The sanctifying of the firstborn is associated with the day of deliverance; therefore Moses prefaces his instructions concerning the firstborn with a renewed exhortation concerning the keeping of the Passover, the memorial of that day. See Dt. v. 15n. *When the Lord shall bring thee into the land* (5). Cf. Dt. vi. 3–15. Prosperity tends to forgetfulness of past mercies, hence the need for vivid reminders.

A sign . . . upon thine hand (9). 'Tephillin' or 'phylacteries' were worn by male Jews when at prayer. Parchments on which were written three passages of the Law (Ex. xiii. 1–10; Dt. vi. 4–9, xi. 13–21) were folded small and placed in little boxes attached by bands to the left wrist and to the forehead. Cf. Mt. xxiii. 5. They thus had a perpetual reminder of the lessons of the Exodus. *This ordinance* (10), i.e. the Passover. *An ass* (13). Being an unclean animal, it could not be sacrificed and must therefore be redeemed, i.e. its place taken by a substitute. *Break his neck* (13). There can be no evasion of the law. If the owner was not willing to sacrifice a lamb, the ass was doomed; if not devoted to God, then to destruction. In practice this was an effective safeguard of the law, as an ass was so much more valuable commercially than a lamb. *Thy children shalt thou redeem* (13). Not with a lamb but with money (Nu. iii. 46, 47). No suggestion of child sacrifice ever taints the pages of the law. *A token* (16). See verse 9n.

g. The crossing of the Red Sea (xiii. 17—xiv. 31)

The way of . . . the Philistines (17). The direct route along the coast which would have taken about a fortnight. *Harnessed* (18). Lit. 'in battle array', i.e. probably not here equipped with armour or weapons, as RV, but 'organized'. *A pillar of a cloud* (21). As a signal and a guide for the direction of their march, but also as a visible token of God's presence. They would march part of the night as well as of the day, and rest in the hottest hours.

Pihahiroth (xiv. 2). The place names of this narrative cannot be identified with certainty, but this move was probably a right wheel towards the south, the Red Sea shutting them in on their left. The move which seemed to frustrate their escape was designed by God for a more miraculous deliverance and the greater destruction of the Egyptians. *From serving us* (5). The loss of so many thousand skilled labourers was a serious blow to the Egyptians. *With an high hand* (8), i.e. with proud confidence. Contrast their fear when they saw the pursuing army (10). *Hast thou taken us away?* (11). An ironical taunt such as the Israelites always employed against Moses when any setback occurred. *The word . . . in Egypt* (12). They had thus complained before the miracles were performed (v. 21, vi. 9). The new fear made them forget the mighty acts of God which had intervened since then. *Hold your peace* (14). The saving act of God will silence all faithless complaint. *Wherefore criest thou unto me?* (15). It was not wrong to cry, but prayer must be followed by action. *That they go forward* (15). This does not contradict the 'stand still' of verse 13. The move here commanded is in the same spirit of resting faith as is enjoined in the former verse.

The angel of God (19). See iii. 2n. The pillar of cloud was the instrument of the Lord (cf. xiii. 21) and moved exactly as He moved. *It was a cloud* (20). 'And there was a cloud and the darkness, yet gave it light by night' (RV) is exact, but the AV insertion of 'to them' and 'to these' expresses the sense. The bright light behind the Israelites at night would show them the way and at the same time hide them from the view of the Egyptians in their rear. *Moses stretched out* (21). The power was God's but it was exerted as Moses signified his obedience and faith by stretching out the rod. The Lord used a natural force, the wind, as His instrument in a supernatural act. The waters are called a *wall* (22) because literally they assumed this formation (see xv. 8; Ps. lxxviii. 13) and because they protected their flanks from Egyptian attack. *In the morning watch* (24). Between two and

six in the morning, some awful manifestation of God through the pillar of fire terrified the Egyptian host, and the ensuing confusion was aggravated by the disablement of their chariots, so that, turning to flee from the Lord (see verses 4, 18), they were reduced to a struggling mass in the middle of the passage. Thereby God gave the Israelites time to get clear while bringing even the rear of the Egyptian army into the place of destruction by daybreak. For the dramatic terror of this scene see Ps. lxxvii. 17–20. *The Lord saved Israel* (30). This deliverance not only laid the foundations of Israel's national unity, but also of their faith, for *the people feared . . . and believed the Lord* (31). It became for all time and all people the exemplar of God's purpose in redemption.

h. The Song of Moses (xv. 1–21)

The words *unto the Lord* (1) strike the keynote of this song. In verses 1-12 Moses ascribes to the Lord the glory displayed in the victory just won, in verses 13–18 he prophesies the vindication of the Lord's sovereignty in placing His people in the inheritance which He has prepared for them. *The Lord* (2) is the source of his strength, the theme of his song, the author of his deliverance and preservation; consequently He is the object of his worship and of his praise, the same God to him as to his ancestors. *Prepare him an habitation* (2). Better as RV 'I will praise him'. *The Lord is a man of war* (3). The poetic vividness of this description should not make us shy of the truth of the fact, so evidently proved by the events of the previous chapter and by the visions of the last book of the Bible (Rev. xix. 11). *Thy right hand* (6). At this point the singer turns and addresses his psalm direct to God. No abstract expression would be more fit than this anthropomorphic phrase to describe the active power of God. It is frequently used in Scripture both in this sense and also as the seat of divine authority. *The depths were congealed* (8). Not solid as ice, but in a wall-like formation contrary to nature. *Among the gods* (11). This rendering of AV and RV is preferable to AV mg. 'mighty ones'. The excellence of the living God over those which are no gods and which He has just defeated is declared in three respects: the spotless brilliance of His holiness, the awe He inspires in those who adore and praise Him, the marvel of His miraculous acts. See Dt. vi. 14n., xxxii. 21n.

Verse 13 marks the transition to the prophetic passage. The force of the Hebrew tense in this verse is present and would read better 'leadest . . . guidest'. *Thy holy habitation* (13) may refer to Mount Sinai, Canaan or Mount Zion. *The people* (14). 'The peoples' (RV), i.e. the nations round about, as instanced in verse 15. Hearing of the miraculous defeat of the Egyptians they would dread the coming of the Israelites. E.g. Jos. ii. 9–11. *Thou hast purchased* (16). The Heb. is lit. 'acquired', but the idea of cost is present in the verb. The sacrifice of the Passover is a token that the rescue of His people was not without cost to God. The Exodus was an act of redemption, and foreshadowed the cost to the Father of redeeming mankind through His Son. *The mountain of thine inheritance* (17). Probably refers to the whole of the promised land of Canaan, a mountainous country already in possession of Israel in the intention of God, just as in His irresistible purpose His sanctuary was in effect established on Mount Moriah. *The Lord shall reign* (18). The victory over Egypt, which forms the theme of the song, is but one example of the eternal reign of God.

The song ends at verse 18. Verse 19 is a summary of the events which occasioned the song. *Miriam the prophetess* (20). Miriam is the first of the women spoken of in Scripture as exercising a special ministry. Cf. Jdg. iv. 4; Lk. ii. 36, etc. *Dances* (20). Solemn dances as an expression of worship, although appropriate to the times of Moses and the psalmists, are liable to abuse and have never found a generally accepted place in the worship of the Christian Church. *Miriam answered* (21). The chorus with a refrain takes up the opening words of Moses' song (1).

IV. THE JOURNEY TO HOREB· xv. 22—xviii. 27

a. Marah and Elim (xv. 22–27)

The wilderness of Shur (22). The northern part of a strip of barren country along the gulf of Suez. The southern part is the wilderness of Sin. *Marah* (23). The Heb. word means 'bitterness'. The sweetening of the waters was by means of a divine miracle in which God made use of a natural element, as in many of the miracles of both the Old and New Testaments. *There he proved them* (25). The lack of sweet water was a test of their trust in God for the supply of material needs. This in its turn is the basis for the *statute* (25) that trustful obedience to God's will is the basic condition of the supply of physical and spiritual health. The patient must obey his physician if he is to be healed.

b. The provision of manna (xvi. 1–36)

Flesh pots (3). Their food in Egypt had probably not been so abundant as they said, but the murmuring spirit magnified the comparison between the present and past supplies and obliterated the memory of the burdens of slavery. *A certain rate every day* (4). 'A day's portion every day' (RV). *That I may prove them* (4). The supernatural means of providing their food and the precepts attached thereto were a test whether or not they would trust in the

power and obey the law of an unseen God. *Ye shall know* (6). The Lord would show that it was He (6) and not Moses and Aaron (3) who had brought them out of Egypt, by miraculously giving flesh in the evening (8; cf. 12, 13) and manna in the morning. Thereby, since the answer to their murmurings came from God, the people would be convicted that their complaints against Moses were in reality against the Lord, who alone was responsible for the situation in which they then were (7, 8). *The glory* (7). This was not that of verse 10, but the revelation of God seen in the giving of the manna; see Jn. vi. 32. *The cloud* (10), i.e. the pillar of cloud, the

THE EXODUS

The route shown is approximate only. Nu. xxxiii gives a list of the places which the Israelites passed through during the forty years' wanderings, but not many of them can be identified with any certainty. After being turned back from Kadesh-barnea they seem to have spent thirty-eight years in the neighbourhood of the Gulf of Aqaba. See Nu. xiv. 20–25 and xxxii. 8–13.

visible token of the Lord's presence, from which now shone some kind of divine light.

The quails (13). These would be migrating across the Red Sea in large numbers at this time of the year, and, exhausted by their long flight, they could easily be caught near the ground. In this case the miracle consisted not so much in the appearance of so great a number of birds in the desert, but in their coming at exactly the time predicted by God. *It is manna* (15). Heb. *man hu.* AV and RV mg. is better than RV 'What is it?' The latter is a possible translation, but the more probable rendering is 'It is a gift' or 'It is *man*', applying to this unknown substance the name of something they already knew in Egypt. All the circumstances of the giving and the using of the manna show that it was a unique substance, quite unknown as any natural product, provided by the Creator for a special purpose and a special time. *When they did mete it* (18). They gathered it according to rough estimation, but when each man measured it at home he found that it was, by a miracle, exactly an omer apiece, about three pints. The miraculous nature of the manna is further shown by its breeding worms on the second day (20), but never on the sabbath day (24). This was to teach entire dependence on God for the supply of each day, and obedience to His law regarding the sabbath. The sabbath was already an institution, so that when the ten commandments were given it was not proposed as a new law. *Coriander seed* (31). 'A small round seed of whitish grey.'

Although written by Moses, verses 32–35 refer to a time later, when the tabernacle had been raised, and the pot of manna was put with the tables of the Law (or testimony, see xxv. 22, xxxi. 18) in the ark. Moses writes of the continuance of the manna as far as the borders of Canaan, where he died. It did not cease until they had crossed Jordan (Jos. v. 10–12). *An omer* (36). A word not used outside this chapter. This note was therefore written either by Moses or a scribe to explain its meaning to a later generation for whom it was not in common use.

c. The rebellion at Rephidim and the battle with Amalek (xvii. 1–16)

Their journeys (1). See Nu. xxxiii. 12–14. *Give us water* (2). They did not expect that water would come, but this was said in a spirit of anger and unbelief. *Tempt the Lord* (2). Rather 'try the Lord'. To tempt means in modern English 'to incite to evil'. The word here has the sense of 'to test', to prove whether He will really do as He has said (see verse 7). It implies unbelief here, but not in Gn. xxii. 1. *Take . . . of the elders* (5). As representatives of the people to be witnesses of the divine miracle (6) and to pass on the lesson learnt by it to the people. *I will stand before thee* (6). 'I will be present with my omnipotence' (Dillmann). *The rock in Horeb* (6). One already known to Moses (see iii. 1). *Massah . . . Meribah* (7). These names, meaning the 'tempting' and the 'striving', like many other descriptive terms belong to the event even more than to the place where it occurred. If therefore the event was repeated, so may be the descriptive name. Thus there was more than one 'striving', so that Meribah was applied to more than one place and occasion. See Nu. xx. 13 and cf. Nu. xiv. 45, xxi. 3; Dt. i. 44.

Then came Amalek (8). Probably as a divine punishment upon their murmuring. The Amalekites were a branch of the Edomite race, descendants of Esau (Gn. xxxvi. 12, 16), a nomadic tribe living mainly in the desert south-west of Palestine and especially hostile to Israel. They first attacked the stragglers at the rear of the host (Dt. xxv. 17, 18). *Joshua* (9). His original name was Hoshea (salvation) and was called Jehoshua (Jehovah is salvation) by Moses (Nu. xiii. 16).

Choose us out men (9). Picked soldiers fought better than an unwieldy host. *Hur* (10). A descendant of Judah through Pharez and Hezron, and the grandfather of the craftsman Bezaleel (1 Ch. ii. 19, 20). He shared the government with Aaron when Moses went up to Sinai (xxiv. 14). *When Moses held up his hand . . .* (11). This scripture does not necessarily teach that the fighting men could see Moses' hands or that God's blessing on them varied with the physical position of the hands; but inasmuch as the uplifted hands were a symbol of the heart uplifted in intercessory prayer, they served to teach the value of prayer and man's entire dependence on God alone. *Stayed up his hands* (12). By upholding his body they also strengthened his mind and spirit for the exercise of prayer.

In a book (14). Perhaps we should read 'in the book'. It appears that the books of Moses are already being built up. See Dt. xvii. 18n. and cf. xxiv. 4, 7, xxxiv. 27. The severe doom upon Amalek (see Dt. xxv. 19; 1 Sa. xv. 3; 1 Ch. iv. 43) was a judgment for their refusal to recognize that it was the Lord who was the God who worked wonders for Israel, and that they provoked Him by their wanton attack upon the feeble rearguard of His people (Dt. xxv. 18) and by the abominations which they shared with the Canaanites. *Jehovah-nissi* (15). Probably there is no reference to the 'rod of God' as a banner in the hand of Moses. The Lord Himself, as their captain and deliverer, was their banner. *Because the Lord hath sworn* (16). See RV mg. ' Because there is a hand against the throne of the Lord'; Heb. 'A hand is lifted up upon the throne of Jah', i.e. because Amalek has lifted up his hand against the Lord, He will fight against him.

d. The visit of Jethro (xviii. 1–27)

When Jethro . . . heard (1). After the incident recorded in iv. 24–26 we must assume that Moses sent his wife and two sons back to her father Jethro. Impressed by the great deliverance which God has wrought through Moses, Jethro now comes out to him in the wilderness, bringing Moses' wife and sons with him (2, 3). Eliezer was probably the child whom Zipporah circumcised with the flint (iv. 25). If this is so, the deliverance referred to in verse 4 was probably that of ii. 15. *The mount of God* (5). Horeb, or Sinai, was near Rephidim, where Moses brought water out of the rock (xvii. 6). See xix. 2. *Did obeisance* (7). Lit. 'bowed himself down'. Cf. Gn. xxiii. 7, 12. This was the usual etiquette, but the fact that it was Moses who bowed may be a mark of the humility of this ruler of a nation. *The Lord is greater than all gods* (11). Jethro the Midianite, though a descendant of Abraham (Gn. xxv. 1–4), was not yet a monotheist. His declaration here may mean that he now recognized Jehovah as the one true God, or possibly that he merely viewed Him as the greatest among other gods. *Jethro . . . took a burnt offering* (12). His priestly office may have been due to his position as head of a tribe. Moses,

Aaron and the elders joined Jethro in the sacrificial meal associated with the sacrifice.

Moses sat to judge (13). Among the nomadic Semites the ruler was also the legislator and arbiter in disputes. Cf. 1 Sa. vii. 15–17. See Dt. i. 16n. *Why sittest thou . . . alone?* (14). Moses gives to Jethro two good reasons why he alone decides all the cases. First, the people require a decision which they can trust to be the answer of God Himself. Secondly, besides settling the immediate dispute, he can use it as a basis for imparting moral principles, *statutes* (see Dt. iv. 1n.), and specific *laws* to meet special circumstances. *Thou wilt surely wear away* (18). Not only is it too much for Moses' strength, but the people will be dissatisfied through not receiving all the attention they need. *Hearken now . . .* (19). Jethro offers his solution of the problem. In the first place Moses must clearly continue to act as God's representative to the people, teaching them the God-given principles by which the many detailed cases could be decided, and bringing all the specially difficult cases directly to God (cf. Nu. ix. 6–8). But the burden could be lightened by appointing legal officers who would severally hear the disputes according to the varying gravity of the cases. *Able men* (21). The qualifications for the under-judges were that they should be concerned only for God's approval, not man's (cf. i. 17), candid in their verdicts, and impervious to bribes. *If . . . God command thee* (23). Jethro submits his own advice to the ultimate direction of God. Not only would this plan relieve Moses, but the people would return contentedly to their tents whenever they had brought a case before their local officer. *Thousands . . . hundreds . . . tens* (25). Such a military numbering corresponded to their nomadic condition. Cf. Dt. xvi. 18.

V. THE GIVING OF THE LAW AT SINAI.
xix. 1—xxiv. 18

a. Preparations for receiving the law of the covenant (xix. 1–25)

Moses remembered the promise of Ex. iii. 12 and under the guidance of God brought the people to the mountain (2), which he himself ascended (3) in expectation of receiving a special revelation. *The wilderness of Sinai* (1) is the wide region in front of the mountain. Sinai has been identified as Jebel Musa. *Out of the mountain* (3). Probably out of the pillar of cloud now resting on the mountain; cf. verse 9. *On eagles' wings* (4). See Dt. xxxii. 11, 12. A phrase expressive of the tender care of God for His people in delivering them from their enemies. *Unto myself* (4). Away from the perverting influence of Egypt to the knowledge and worship of the true God.

A peculiar treasure (5). Heb. *segullah*, translated in 1 Ch. xxix. 3 as 'mine own proper good', that which one has made one's own special property by purchase or other effort. See Dt. vii. 6n. This became a frequent designation of Israel and hence of the Christian Church. Cf.

Tit. ii. 14; 1 Pet. ii. 9. In giving Israel a special place in His purposes God did not thereby disown the rest of the peoples, all of whom are His possession. *A kingdom of priests* (6). From 1 Pet. ii. 9 and Rev. i. 6 we understand that by 'kingdom' is meant that every person in Israel was to be endowed with royal prerogatives under one Sovereign, the Lord. Each had also equal access to God, as priests, but this did not preclude the appointment of official priests for the duties of the tabernacle. 'Priests' may also imply that Israel was to act as the mediary in bringing the other nations to God. *An holy nation* (6), i.e. separate from the other nations in being devoted to the Lord, who is holy. Cf. Lv. xi. 44; 1 Pet. i. 16.

Laid before their faces . . . (7). On the human side the covenant between the Lord and Israel was based on the willing assent of all the people. It was not imposed upon them. *That the people may hear* (9). The people were themselves both to see the manifestation of God's presence in the cloud and to hear His voice, so that they might receive a direct and lasting impression of the majesty of the Lord and also be assured that the law which Moses was about to give would come as the result of an immediate communication from God Himself.

Sanctify them (10). The infinite holiness of God was to be further impressed upon the people by two things. First, their own sanctification: the external ordinances of washing themselves and their clothes, and abstinence from sexual intercourse (cf. 1 Cor. vii. 5), symbolized the inner holiness without which no man can see God. Secondly, there was the fence which was to keep them, even sanctified as they were, from touching the mountain while it served as the 'holy of holies', the seat of God's immediate presence (12). *In the sight of all the people* (11). Yet all that they could bear to see was the thick cloud which shrouded God's unapproachable glory (9). *Touch it* (13). Read with RV, 'touch him', i.e. the man or beast who transgressed the bounds. By laying hands on him they would themselves have to touch the mountain. Therefore he was to be slain from a distance with stones or with arrows. *The trumpet* (13). This was the signal for Moses and Aaron to come into the mount (24). A call on the trumpet is the normal prelude to a special, particularly a royal, proclamation. This peculiarly terrible blast of the trumpet (16, 19), accompanied as it was by phenomena of supernatural awfulness, heralded a divine manifestation equalled in its cataclysmic effect only by the appearing of the Lord in the last day. Cf. 1 Thes. iv. 16; 1 Cor. xv. 52. *Altogether on a smoke* (18). Not merely clouds having the appearance of smoke, but the smoke of the fire with which the whole mountain burned. See Dt. iv. 12n.

Go down . . . (21). The Lord, having called Moses up to the top of the mountain, sends him down again to repeat even more emphatically the warning not to break through the barriers which had been erected in order to look more closely at the mountain. Moses urges that the repetition of the commandment is unnecessary (23), but God knows the intentions of the people, especially of the priests, who might think themselves holier than the rest; and Moses obeys (25). *Priests* (22). The Levitical priesthood has not yet been instituted, but certain individuals, probably the firstborn, were appointed for priestly duties; see xxiv. 5.

b. The Ten Commandments (xx. 1–17)

The first four comprise man's duty towards God, the second six his duty to his neighbour. The ten commandments are repeated, in a somewhat different form, in Dt. v, and the notes there should be compared with those below. It has been conjectured that the 'ten words' (xxxiv. 28 mg.), as originally announced and written on the tables, consisted each of one brief sentence, e.g. 'Honour thy father and thy mother', 'Thou shalt not covet'. Were this so, the expanded forms would represent Moses' inspired commentary as he declared them to the people on the two occasions (see Ex. xix. 9; Dt. v. 5). The translation 'commandments' for what the Scripture calls the 'ten words' imparts to them too severe a tone. They are given that the people may believe (Ex. xix. 9), walk in them and be blessed thereby (Dt. iv. 40, v. 1n.).

I am the Lord thy God (2). Jewish expositors take this as the first of the ten commandments, 'to believe in the existence of God' (Hertz), but it may be still better to take these words as declaring the authority upon which all the ten rest. The sovereignty of God over His people is the sanction for His claim to their obedience to the commandments which follow. He is a personal God who has already established an intimate relationship with His people by delivering them from Egypt.

i. The Lord is unique (xx. 3). His people were therefore not to add the worship of false gods to their worship of the Lord, as they tried to do later, e.g. in introducing the cult of Baal as an addition. The unity of God demands undivided devotion.

ii. The Lord is Spirit (xx. 4–6). Cf. Jn. iv. 24. He must not be worshipped under the form of any material representation, whether it be the product of plastic or pictorial art. Such not only divert the mind from the knowledge of the pure spirituality of God, but inevitably become themselves the object of veneration and also give rise to many sensual practices. The command of verse 4 does not prohibit all sculpture and painting. Cf. the brazen serpent of Nu. xxi. 8. *A jealous God* (5). Not in the sense that He begrudges success or happiness to others, but that He alone has a claim upon the love of His people. It is for their sakes, that they may hallow and reverence His name, that they must flee from idolatry. God's jealousy preserves the purity of His people's worship. *Visiting the iniquity* . . . (5). From Dt. xxiv. 16 (see note) it is clear that God does not punish the children for the offences of their fathers, but if the children commit the same sins as their fathers they will be punished in the same way ('of them that hate me'). Also the sins of parents influence their children towards evil and certain sins bring punishment which is inevitably shared by the offspring, e.g. diseases which are the direct result of immorality and poverty which results from extravagance. The fear of these latter consequences exercises a healthy check upon parents' conduct. Whereas evil conduct affects only three or four generations, the consequences of a good life benefit posterity to an almost limitless extent. God's wrath reaches only to the third or fourth, His mercy to the thousandth generation. See Dt. v. 9, 10n.

iii. The sanctity of God's name (xx. 7). The prohibition is against false swearing, i.e. using God's name to attest an untrue statement. It may also include flippant oaths. So serious was this offence that it could by no means be pardoned without punishment, 'The Lord will not hold him guiltless'. This commandment does not preclude the use of God's name in true and solemn oaths. See Dt. v. 11n.

iv. The sabbath (xx. 8–11). The sabbath (Heb. *shabbath* from the verb *shabath*, to 'cease' or 'rest') was to be principally a day of cessation from all except unavoidable labour, and was to include every member of the household and even the animals (the law of God is unique among the ancients for its regard for the dumb creatures). It was called 'a sabbath unto the Lord' (10, RV), because it is a holy day (8), one set apart for worship and attention to the things of God. Its observance is sanctioned by God's own example (11; see Gn. ii. 2, 3). We may infer that its institution is as ancient as creation, and it seems already to have been known before this time (see e.g. xvi. 23), but its specific details may have been set forth first on Sinai. The word *remember* (8) should then be taken to mean not 'bring to mind what you already know', but 'keep in perpetual remembrance'. The repeated disregard of the sabbath by later generations illustrates and confirms the need for this command to 'remember'. The blessing of the Lord upon the day (11) extends to those who observe His command to keep it as a holy day. See Dt. v. 12n.

v. The honouring of parents (xx. 12). The best commentary on this verse is the book of Proverbs and Eph. vi. 1–3. Respect for parents includes not only attention to their commands, wishes and advice, but also the care of them in their need (Mk. vii. 10–12) and the cloaking of their faults (Gn. ix. 23; Pr. xxx. 17). The promise *that thy days may be long* cannot be taken as a guarantee to every individual, but it asserts that the right order within the family is the foundation of both national and individual continuance and prosperity, and in general its literal fulfilment is to be expected. See Dt. v. 16n.

vi. The sanctity of human life (xx. 13). Read

with RV 'Thou shalt do no murder'. A general safeguard of the sanctity of human life is here first laid down. Later provision is made for excusable (xxi. 13), accidental (Nu. xxxv. 23), or justifiable homicide (xxii. 2). War for the Israelites, whether attack or defence, was always by the direct command or permission of God. See Dt. v. 17n.

vii. The sanctity of marriage (xx. 14). Another law emphasizing the inviolability of the bond of family life, the foundation of all human society and order. This law renders the man who breaks it no less guilty than the woman. For the Jews 'it involves the prohibition of immoral speech, immodest conduct, or association with persons who scoff at the sacredness of purity' (Hertz). See Dt. v. 18n.

viii. The sanctity of property (xx. 15). This law assumes the right to own personal property. To *steal* implies not only direct theft, but also the acquisition of property by taking advantage of another's ignorance or weakness. See Dt. v. 19n.

ix. The sanctity of our neighbour's good name (xx. 16). *Thy neighbour* includes all fellow men. Defamation of another's character is prohibited, not only formally in a court of law, but by any false statement whatever. See Dt. v. 20n.

x. Against covetousness (xx. 17). The last commandment lies at the root of the previous four. Man is responsible to God not only for his actions but also for his thoughts, and observance of this will save him from the breach of those others. Thus the word of Christ (Mt. v. 27, 28) was only, as He Himself said, a fulfilment of the ancient divine law. See Dt. v. 21n.

c. The fear of God falls on the people (xx. 18–21)

All the people saw . . . (18). The manifestations of God's majesty so terrified the people (even Moses feared, Heb. xii. 21) that they withdrew from the base of the mountain and requested that the rest of the law be given in the hearing of Moses alone, to be communicated to them by him (19). God granted this request and only Moses heard the rest of the divine communications (21). *Fear not* . . . *that his fear may be before your faces* (20). They were not to be afraid that they would be smitten by the lightning, etc., but they were to fear continually lest they offend God. Fear of grieving God both springs from and creates love for His person. *To prove you* (20). Cf. xvi. 4. 'To test whether you will respect His commandments.'

d. An altar to be erected (xx. 22–26)

Ye have seen . . . (22). The same God who appeared to give the ten commandments also gave the laws that follow. They are therefore to be observed with equal care. *Ye shall not make with me gods* (23). A warning against worshipping idols at the same time as Jehovah, or worshipping Jehovah under the form of an idol, as in xxxii. 5. The Israelites were particularly prone to the use of molten images of silver or gold. *An altar of earth* (24). Such simplicity suited the occasion,

in contrast to the worship of idols. Their offerings should be brought only to Jehovah's altar. See Dt. xii. 5, 6. *In all places* (24). 'Every place' (RV). The AV takes these words as referring to what follows, the RV to that which precedes. Some have taken them to refer to the land of promise; more probably they refer to every place of a special revelation. Cf. Gn. xxxv. 1. *An altar of stone* (25). See Dt. xxvii. 5n.

e. Various judgments (xxi. 1—xxii. 20)

The judgments (1). See Dt. iv. 1n. Those which follow embody ancient customary law, now divinely sanctioned for the recently appointed judges (xviii. 20). *Servant* (2). In the ancient world slavery was universally the basis of the labour system. The Mosaic law permitted to the Israelites also a form of bondservice, but it was unique in that the bondservant was not regarded as a mere chattel, but he preserved his rights as an individual personality and regained his freedom after six years (2) or at the year of jubilee, should that occur before the end of his six years (Lv. xxv. 10). If he entered upon his period of service as a married man, his wife and children were to be freed with him (3), but if he married one of the others of his master's servants, his wife and children remained the property of the master presumably until the end of their six years. He had also the right to choose whether he would remain in the service of his master, in which case his declaration was to be witnessed by the judicial officials and sealed by the mark of the aul in his ear (6). The ear was the symbol of willing obedience, and the door to which it was fastened represented the household to which he bound himself.

Maidservant (7). The rights of a girl sold by her father to be a bondservant were *not* . . . *as the menservants*, but even more carefully guarded. If unmarried, she could go free after six years, but if sold to become a wife of her master or her master's son, her rights were equal to those of a free wife, and were strictly safeguarded. *Dealt deceitfully* (8), i.e. not carried out his original intention. *These three* (11). This may refer to the three duties detailed in verse 10 or the three courses named above, i.e. marry her himself, marry her to his son, or transfer her to another Hebrew.

He that smiteth (12). Murder as a result of premeditation (14) is distinguished from unintentional manslaughter (13). For the latter, places of refuge were provided, where the slayer could be safe from the avenging relatives until the case was tried. For the former, even the altar of God could not save him from the just punishment of his crime. Cf. 1 Ki. ii. 28–34. *He that smiteth his father* (15). So sacred is parenthood that for one to strike his father or mother, even without doing serious injury, was a capital crime. *He that stealeth a man* (16). Kidnapping was equal to murder in that it robbed a man of his personal liberty. A similar rule is found in Hammurabi's code centuries earlier. *He that curseth his father* (17). This act would invoke the name of God in support of his rebellion against his parents. Hence the severity of the punishment.

If men strive together . . . (18). If a blow proved fatal, then the laws of murder or manslaughter applied, but otherwise the equivalent compensation was not that the guilty man should receive an equal blow, but that he should pay for the loss of work time and the cost of the doctor's bill. *If a man smite his servant* . . . (20). In all other nations masters have had the absolute right of life and death over their slaves. The divine law here preserves the slave's right to live. The degree of punishment for homicide in such cases is left to the discretion of the judges. If the slave survived a day or two after the beating and then died, no punishment was inflicted because this was evidence that the master did not intend to kill. It would not be to his own interest to lose a slave who was of pecuniary value to him. The case here is of foreign bondslaves, not Hebrew servants.

If men . . . *hurt a woman with child* . . . (22). If no further hurt was incurred than the loss of the child, then a fine was imposed, the amount being named by the husband but restricted by the judges, but if the woman lost her life then the law of homicide applied. The word for *judges* (22) here means 'arbitrators'. *Life for life, eye for eye* . . . (23–25). The general principle of taliation is here introduced from the special instance noted in verse 22. The requirement that the offender should suffer an equivalent injury was even in Mosaic times commuted to a money fine except in the case of murder (see Nu. xxxv. 31) and this later became the customary procedure. See Dt. xix. 21n. *The eye of his servant* (26). The old Semitic law regarded slaves as the absolute property of their owners. Here their persons are respected, and they are granted the right to claim their freedom as compensation for the injury.

If an ox . . . (28). Although a beast had no moral sense, this law was so ordered as to emphasize the extreme sanctity of human life. Even the ox which killed a man was to be put to death and its flesh so accursed that it might not be eaten; how much more should the man deserve death who knowingly allowed a dangerous beast to be at large. Yet the law was merciful in allowing a money compensation in place of the man's life. This is in contrast to the Code of Hammurabi which required like for like, and if a son or a daughter were killed so the owner of the ox should forfeit the life of his own son or daughter. *If a man shall open a pit* . . . (33). The pit would be a well or water storage tank, which should always be kept covered for safety. The owner is not to blame if a man falls in, for he should look where he is going. Having paid the full value of the live animal he may get what he can out of the carcase. *If one man's ox hurt* . . . (35). Blame attaches to the owner of the vicious ox only if he knows its habits. Otherwise the loss is to be equally shared by the two owners.

Breaking up (xxii. 2). 'Breaking in' (RV); i.e. into the house. The householder was justified in resisting by force even to death, if it was by night, but if in the daytime, when the burglar might be assumed to have no intention of violence and when help might easily be obtained, to kill him would amount to murder. *If the theft be* . . . *found* . . . *alive* (4). If the thief has not sold or killed the beast, then he restores it and one other besides. *If a man shall cause* . . . *to be eaten* (5). If cattle wandered accidentally into another's field, presumably the owner of the beasts was not liable. *If fire break out* (6). This would have been lit intentionally, e.g. to burn weeds, but insufficient care was taken to guard it from spreading. *For all manner of trespass* (9). This is in connection with deposits, as in the preceding verses. If a man claimed to identify an article in another's possession as his own, if the judges allowed his claim the accused was to restore it plus another equivalent article; if the judges refused his claim he was to give double as a penalty for false accusation. *If it be stolen* (12). The trustee could not prevent the animal being 'driven away' (10) by marauding bands, but he should take care to prevent its being stolen by an individual, and was therefore responsible to make it good.

If a man borrow (14). A man would borrow a thing for his own benefit, and was therefore responsible to return it whatever happened, unless the owner was in charge of it and able to guard it (15). *An hired thing* (15). The risk of losing this was included in the price of the hire. No restitution was therefore necessary. *Entice* (16), i.e. win her consent to the crime. Although she consented, it was still his responsibility to protect her from lifelong shame resulting from the sin of a moment by marrying her, not without payment of the regular dowry. If her father would not give her to this particular man, then he was to pay the equivalent of a dowry (fifty shekels of silver, Dt. xxii. 29), to give her more opportunity of marriage to another man. *A witch* (18). 'Sorceress' (RV). This law also applied to sorcerers (Lv. xx. 27). This verse does not prove the reality of the evil spirits, with which they professed to consort, but the very profession, real or false, was a denial of the supreme authority of God, and as grave a crime as rebellion or idolatry. The reality of demons we learn from the New Testament. *Utterly destroyed* (20). Lit. 'devoted', i.e. doomed to destruction. See Lv. xxvii. 29.

f. Various moral statutes (xxii. 21—xxiii. 19)

Here a new series of moral and religious ordinances begins, in which God and not man is the judge. Note how the people's sufferings in Egypt are made into a plea for mercy in xxii. 21, xxiii. 9. See Dt. x. 19n. *Vex a stranger* (21). What is stated here negatively concerning the 'stranger' (Heb. *ger*) receives positive emphasis in Deuteronomy. See Dt. i. 16n. The Israelites were a chosen race, but they did not thereby hold an exclusive right to God's protection. *Ye shall not afflict any widow* . . . (22). God Himself would vindicate those who were bereft of their human guardian, if men presumed to take advantage of their defenceless condition. Cf. Mt. xxiii. 14. *If thou lend money* . . . (25). *Usury* here means simply 'interest'. At this time only the poor would want to borrow, and it was strictly forbidden to exact interest on the loan from Israelites. It was allowed from foreigners (Dt. xxiii. 20). The borrowing of money for commercial ventures was a later development. No article of essential use to the borrower might be kept as a pledge. The thick cloak used as a blanket at night might be taken during the day, but never kept at night. The mercy of this law is in strong contrast to the debtor laws of other nations.

The gods (28). Heb. *'elohim*. Three translations are possible: 'the gods' (AV), 'God' (RV), or 'the mighty' or 'judges' (RV mg.). Of these the second is best. The ruler is associated with God as deriving his authority from Him. See Gn. i. 1n., Ex. xv. 11n. *The firstborn of thy sons* (29). See xiii. 2, 13, xxxiv. 19, 20. *Ye shall be holy men unto me* (31). Cf. xix. 6. In the Law the plural pronoun is always used in connection with the holiness of men. It is only in fulfilling his part in the body, the nation, that a man can realize God's purpose of holiness. This principle remains under the new covenant for members of the Church, the body of Christ. The holiness required is inward, but it could at this stage be approached only by attention to the outward obligations of the law, of which the requirement in this verse is one example. *Flesh that is torn of beasts* (31) is unclean both because it has not been killed in the prescribed manner, and because the beast which killed it was unclean.

Raise a false report (xxiii. 1). Better 'receive a false report'. This follows naturally on the principle of xx. 16. *An unrighteous witness* (1), i.e. one who takes sides with the guilty party on trial. *Follow a multitude* (2). In all circumstances a man must stand firm to what he believes to be right, not moved by the opinion of others just because they are a majority or the popular party. *A poor man* (3). Justice must be impartial, avoiding false sympathy on account of a man's poverty as much as fear of the rich man's power. *Thine enemy's ox* (4). The ill feeling which a man shows towards another, or even actual wrong done, does not absolve the injured party from the usual duties of kindness both to the man and his beast. The Lord Jesus fulfilled this law in His word 'Love your enemies . . . ' (Mt. v. 44; cf. Pr. xxv. 21, 22). *The judgment of thy poor* (6). This balances the injunction of verse 3. *A false matter* (7). Either a false accusation or the passing of an incorrect sentence of judgment, which might lead to the execution of an innocent person. It is better to err on the side of acquittal and leave it to God to punish the accused should he really be guilty. *Thou shalt take no gift* (8), i.e. bribe. This was a sin against which the

prophets often had to declaim, e.g. Mi. iii. 11. *A stranger* (9). See xxii. 21n.

Six years . . . *the seventh year* . . . (10, 11). The chief purpose of the sabbatical year, when the land was to be neither sown nor reaped, is here stated to be for the benefit of the poor who might take all that grew of itself. It also served to save the soil from exhaustion, and to give the people space for greater attention to the things of God. *The seventh day* (12). Similarly the emphasis here is on the value of the sabbath to servants, strangers and cattle. *Make no mention* (13). As the name of the true God was to be uttered only with the greatest reverence, so the names of the false gods were to be so abhorred that they were not even to be spoken, except, for example, by preachers or writers of history. See Dt. xii. 3.

Three times . . . *feast* (14). These three annual pilgrimage festivals are described in more detail in Lv. xxiii and Dt. xvi. *The feast of unleavened bread* (15). See xii. 14–20. *None shall appear* . . . *empty* (15). See Dt. xvi. 16, 17, where this practical expression of thanksgiving is enjoined for all three feasts. *The feast of harvest* (16). Pentecost, called in Dt. xvi. 10 the 'feast of weeks', being seven full weeks after the first day of the Passover. It celebrated the first reaping of the ripe wheat (much earlier there than in England), while the *feast of ingathering* (16) was a thanksgiving at the end of the agricultural year when all crops were in. *All thy males* (17), i.e. able-bodied adult men. The women often came also (cf. 1 Sa. i. 7), but were not obliged to do so, owing to home duties. *Not . . . with leavened bread* (18). This applied only to the Passover sacrifice. *The fat of my sacrifice* (18). Read with RV 'my feast'. See xii. 10. *Thou shalt not seethe* (19). Repeated in xxxiv. 26. See Dt. xiv. 21n.

g. Rewards of obedience (xxiii. 20–33)

An angel (20). The same word means either 'angel' or 'messenger'. This therefore might mean a human messenger divinely commissioned, such as Moses or Joshua; or the mysterious angel of Jehovah. See Gn. xvi. 7n. *My name is in him* (21), i.e. he is invested with divine authority. *Images* (24). 'Pillars' (RV). See Dt. xvi. 22n. *The number of thy days* (26). Cf. xx. 12. A full span of life. *My fear* (27). 'My terror' (RV). Cf. Nu. xxii. 2, 3. The nations, knowing in advance the power of Israel's God, would fear their approach.

Hornets (28). Swarms of such stinging insects would materially assist the Israelite soldiers in their attacks on the enemy, or the phrase may be metaphorical for some invading power such as bands of Egyptians, whose badge was a species of hornet. The dangers from having too much land to occupy all at once (29, 30) are exemplified by the large number of lions which appeared in Syria (see 2 Ki. xvii. 25). *Thy bounds* (31). This promise, made first to Abraham (Gn. xv. 18) and here renewed, was not completely fulfilled until the days of Solomon, not only for the reason given in verse 30, but also because of the unfaithfulness of the Israelites. *The river* (31) here refers to the Euphrates. *Thou shalt make no covenant . . .* (32). The Israelites failed to keep this condition, designed to preserve the purity of their worship and service of Jehovah. See, for example, Jos. ix. 15; Jdg. i. 27–36, with the result here foretold (33). See xxxiv. 12–16n.

h. The ratification of the covenant (xxiv. 1–11)

Come up (1). Moses was still on the mount, having received all the laws of the covenant. He then went down to the people, recounted the laws to them (3), sealed the covenant with the blood of the sacrifice, and returned to the mount with Aaron, Nadab and Abihu, Aaron's two sons, and the seventy elders, who were the heads of tribes and families. *The judgments* (3). See xxi. 1n.; Dt. iv. 1n.

The conditions upon which the covenant was ratified were as follows. The Lord promised to be their God (xx. 2) and consequently to visit them with His favour, if they on their part would adhere to His commandments and submit to His judgments. This they wholeheartedly promised to do (3, 7), and the covenant was thereupon sealed in blood. The altar (4) represented the presence of the Lord, and the blood, being half sprinkled on the altar (6) and half on the people (8), symbolized the union between the Lord and His people in this covenant. The blood was necessary because, willing as the people were to obey the commandments, their present sinful nature and their subsequent actual breaking of the laws debarred them from real union with the holy God except through the medium of an atoning sacrifice. Thus the first covenant, based as it was on the Law, nevertheless foreshadowed the new covenant based only on the grace of God through the atoning merits of His Son. See Je. xxxi. 31–34. *Twelve pillars* (4). These represented the presence of the twelve tribes. See Gn. xxviii. 18. The priesthood was not yet established, but even later the people themselves, as the *young men* of verse 5, could slay the sacrificial animals, while the priests alone presented the sacrifice on the altar. *Be obedient* (7). Lit. 'hear'. The word expresses the utmost attentiveness to the will of God. *Elders* (9). See Dt. xix. 12n. A sacrifice involved a sacrificial meal, and Moses, following the command of verse 1, took the elders up to the mount, there to eat the flesh of the sacrifice and so to commune with the God to whom it was offered. While they were eating God granted to them, as a token of His favour, a vision of Himself which revealed Him as the God who not only thunders in wrath at all iniquity, but whose glory is also manifested in surpassing loveliness (10). God has said, 'There shall no man see me, and live' (xxxiii. 20), and it must therefore have been only some reflection of His person which these men saw, but even so it was a marked favour that they were able to see Him thus and yet not die (11). Cf. Gn. xxxii. 30; Jdg. xiii. 22, 23.

i. Moses delegates his authority and again ascends Mount Sinai (xxiv. 12–18)

Come up (12). Moses and the elders probably returned to the plain after the vision of the preceding verses and subsequently God called Moses again to appear before Him on the summit of the mount. Joshua, his confidential servant, accompanied him, but probably only so far (13). Knowing that he would be a long time absent from the people, he delegated his authority to Aaron and Hur until his return (14). *A law* (12). Heb. *torah*. See Dt. i. 5n., iv. 44n. The divine revelation to Moses was only gradually made. *A cloud* (15). Read 'the cloud'. See xix. 9, 16. *Six days* (16). Spent by Moses in preparing himself for communion with God. *The glory of the Lord* (17). The manifestation of the divine presence as seen by the Israelites from the distance of the plain below. *Forty days* (18). During this time he ate and drank nothing (Dt. ix. 9).

VI. THE DIVINE PLAN FOR THE TABERNACLE. xxv. 1—xxxi. 18

a. Gifts for the tabernacle (xxv. 1–9)

That giveth it willingly with his heart (2). 'Whose heart maketh him willing' (RV). The treasures enumerated in the following verses had been accumulated from their ancestors, from the Egyptians (xii. 35, 36) and from the Amalekites (xvii). *Brass* (3). More exactly copper or bronze. *Blue, and purple, and scarlet* (4), i.e. yarn dyed these several colours. *Badgers' skins* (5). Heb. *taḥash*. The badger is not found in those lands, and the name is probably of some sea animal such as a seal or a porpoise. *Shittim wood* (5). The wood of the acacia tree, hard and close-grained.

A sanctuary (8). Heb. *miqdash*, 'a place set apart', from the same root as *qadosh*, 'holy'. *That I may dwell among them* (8). Note that He does not say, 'dwell in it'. The Lord never taught that He was confined to an earthly structure (see 1 Ki. viii. 27), but the tabernacle and later the temple served to focus the attention of His people on the fact that the Lord was among them, and particularly that His presence was infinitely holy, so that access to Him could only be through the atoning sacrifices and the mediation of the High Priest. *The pattern* (9). Given possibly through a vision. *The tabernacle* (9). See xxix. 42n. The Heb. here is *mishkan*, 'a dwelling', from the same root as the verb 'dwell' in the previous verse. The Eng. word 'tabernacle' is also used in the AV to translate the Heb. *'ohel*, 'a tent'. From Heb. ix. 1–5 we learn that the sacred objects described in these chapters had a real, although temporary, spiritual value.

b. The tabernacle furniture (xxv. 10–40)

i. The ark (xxv. 10–16). *An ark* (10). Heb. *'aron*, a different word from that used in Gn. vi.

14 and Ex. ii. 3. It was used to describe a chest or coffer. Such was the form of the ark, the main purpose of which was to hold the two tables of the Law. It measured 3 ft. 9 in. long, 2 ft. 3 in. wide and deep (10). The purest gold only was used and was laid over the wooden structure of the ark, probably in thin plates, both on the outside and also on the inside (11), although the latter could not be seen, thus teaching that the inward part of the life of God's people must be as pure and beautiful as that which is seen outwardly. *The crown* (11) was a rim along the four edges of the upper surface. *The four corners* (12). 'The four feet' (RV). The rings were to be at the base of the ark so that, when it was carried, it should be raised above the shoulders of the bearers and not touch their bodies. *The testimony* (16). The stone tablets containing the Law were called the 'testimony' as bearing continual witness to their divine institution and to the people's promise of obedience. See Dt. iv. 45n. The fact that their sacred shrine contained no image, but only the tables of the Law, reminded them that their God was both spiritual and holy.

ii. The mercy seat (xxv. 17–22). *A mercy seat* (17). Heb. *kapporeth*. The word is derived from the Heb. verb *kaphar*, the original meaning of which is 'to cover', but the tense from which this noun is derived is always used in the sense of 'to make atonement'. Hence the LXX *hilasterion* and the AV 'mercy seat' accurately give the sense of the original. Although it was exactly the same in area as the upper surface of the ark it is not correct to say that it was merely a covering. In 1 Ch. xxviii. 11 the holy of holies is called 'the place of the mercy seat', thus named after the most sacred object within it. *Of pure gold* (17). It was a single slab of solid gold, not wood plated with gold, its great value indicating the supreme place which this object held among all the furniture of the tabernacle. *Two cherubims* (18). Better 'cherubim', the singular being 'cherub'. The form of these figures is unknown, except that they had two wings. They may have been human figures. They were placed at the two ends of the mercy seat, not standing separately upon it, but of one piece with the mercy seat (19). Their wings were raised and bent forward to cover the mercy seat, and their faces bent downward gazing at the mercy seat (20). So holy is God that no human eye may look upon even that which represents His presence, but the wings of these angelic creatures protect it from the gaze even of the High Priest. *There I will meet with thee* (22). At the mercy seat, the place of propitiation, God accepted the people's representative, the High Priest, when he came by way of the atoning sacrifice, and there He answered their enquiries concerning His will for them. As this meeting of God with His people was the supreme object of the whole tabernacle, it was called the 'tent of meeting' (xxvii. 21, RV).

iii. The table and various utensils (xxv. 23–30). *A table* (23). The table of shewbread was made of material similar to that used for the ark. It measured 3 ft. by 1½ ft. and was 27 in. high. Like the ark (11) it had a *crown* (24) or rim along its upper edge. Judging by the representation of this table on the Arch of Titus, it had four legs held together about half-way up by a band about 3 in. wide, the *border* of verse 25. Like the ark, the rings for the carrying poles were placed at the feet of the table (26). *The dishes* (29). In these the loaves were brought to and from the table. The *spoons*, or rather cups, contained the frankincense (see Lv. xxiv. 7), the *covers* ('flagons' RV) held the wine for the libations and the *bowls* were chalices for pouring it out. *To cover* should be translated 'pour out' (RV). *Shewbread* (30). See Lv. xxiv. 5–9n.

iv. The candlestick (xxv. 31–40). *A candlestick* (31). For the whole of this intricate description see RV. The representation of it on the Arch of Titus shows that it was made with a central stem (called 'the candlestick' in verse 34) with three branches at each side of it all curving up to the same height, thus forming seven lamps in one line (32). The lamps themselves were in the form of an open lily holding a bowl. Each stem was embellished with ornaments consisting of an almond blossom, a knob (*knop*, like the chapiter of a column) and a lily flower, the side stems having three of these ornaments and the centre one four (33–35). The ornaments were not affixed externally but of one piece with the whole (36). The tongs were to trim the wick, and the snuffdishes to hold the pieces trimmed off (38). *Their pattern* (40). See verse 9. If Moses had a vision of these objects and of the tabernacle, he would know just how these measurements were to be fitted together.

c. The tabernacle, altar and court (xxvi. 1— xxvii. 21)

The tabernacle was to be a portable structure 45 ft. long, 15 ft. wide and 25 ft. high, formed by a framework of upright boards along three of its sides and pillars at the open front, roofed over with fabric and skin coverings.

i. The coverings (xxvi. 1–14). The first covering (1–6) was formed of two sets of fine linen curtains, each curtain being twenty-eight cubits long by four broad (a cubit is one and a half feet). Each set of five were permanently joined together forming two large curtains, which could be joined, when in position, by fifty loops along the edge of each and held together by gold clasps (6), taken apart when travelling. The curtains were probably stretched across the top of the framework of the tabernacle, thus making a flat roof. The twenty-eight cubits would then cover the ten across the width of the structure and hang over the boards for nine cubits each side, leaving one cubit of the boards bare near the ground. The ten curtains of four cubits' width would cover the length of the structure, thirty cubits, and the boards of the west end, ten cubits. They were made of fine linen woven with twisted threads in three colours, and interwoven by skilful craftsmen with a pattern of cherubim (1).

The second layer (7–13) consisted of curtains of woven goats' hair, one set of five and the other of six curtains (9) joined in the same way as the linen curtains, but with bronze instead of gold clasps (11). Being two cubits longer than the linen curtains, they would overlap them and protect the boards also right to the ground. They were each the same width as the linen curtains, but the extra curtain gave a total of four cubits more. Half of this hung over the front of the tabernacle and was doubled back, forming a sort of blind (9); the other two cubits made an extra covering at the back or western end (12). As a further protection these curtains were overlaid with two more coverings, one of dyed rams' skins, the other of seal skins (RV), probably the same size as the goats' hair curtains (14).

ii. **The walls (xxvi. 15–30).** The sides and back of the tabernacle were formed of upright boards each 15 ft. long by 2¼ ft. wide (16), made of shittim (acacia) wood and overlaid with gold (15, 29). Each board rested on two silver sockets (19, 21, 25) into which it was fastened by 'tenons', projecting pegs in the boards, the two being in some way linked to each other (17). Twenty boards each side made a total length of thirty cubits or 45 ft. The back was built up by six boards (22, see RV) making nine cubits, and the extra cubit was filled by two boards which overlapped the others and strengthened the corners (23, 24).

All the boards were held together laterally by long bars running through rings in each board (26–28). The two sides and the back (see RV for verse 27) each had five bars. The middle bar of the five ran the whole length of the side and had two shorter bars above and below it (28). *The fashion* (30). Moses would require some visual conception of the shape of the tabernacle in addition even to the minute instructions foregoing.

iii. **The vail and the placing of the furniture (xxvi. 31–35).** The inner sanctuary, *the most holy place* (34), in which was placed only the ark, was separated from the outer sanctuary by a curtain woven in one piece, similar to the inner covering of the tabernacle (31; cf. verse 1). It was supported on four pillars, which rested in golden sockets and held golden hooks at their top, upon which the vail was hung (32).

iv. **The hangings (xxvi. 36, 37).** The open end of the tabernacle was enclosed by a screen, made of similar material to the inner covering and the vail (36), and hung upon five pillars. These rested in sockets, not of silver, but of bronze (37). The vail had four pillars, but the five here were possibly needed for extra strength because of the frequent use of this entrance by the priests.

v. **The altar (xxvii. 1–8).** The altar for the burnt offering was in the form of a hollow box (8) of equal breadth and length but without base or top (1). Possibly it was filled with earth, upon which the offerings would be burnt. It was of acacia wood overlaid with bronze (1, 2). At each of the four corners an ornamental horn was set, made of one piece with the altar (2). It was in these horns that any symbolic virtue attaching to the altar was centred. See Ps. cxviii. 27; 1 Ki. i. 50; Ex. xxix. 12. The meaning of verses 4 and 5 is uncertain. The grating may have been fixed around the top of the altar to prevent pieces of the offerings from falling, or it may have been an ornamental grille fringing or supporting a ledge half-way up its sides. *The midst* (5) would then mean 'at half its height'.

vi. **The court of the tabernacle (xxvii. 9–19).** The tabernacle stood within an enclosed court, to which all ceremonially clean Israelites had access, and within which the altar and the laver were placed. The enclosure was formed by a wall of linen fabric 150 ft. long by 75 ft. wide, and 7½ ft. high (18). Bronze pillars resting in bronze sockets supported the hangings upon silver hooks, and further support was given by the silver tie-rods (the *fillets* of verses 10, 11, 17) which connected the pillars. At the eastern end a space 30 ft. wide was left for the entrance (13–15). Whereas the fabric for the sides of the court was a plain linen, the screen for this entrance was of embroidered material similar to that of the tabernacle itself (16; see xxvi. 36, 37). *The vessels* (19). All except those expressly stated to be of gold or silver. *The pins* (19), i.e. tent-pegs.

vii. **Oil for the light (xxvii. 20, 21).** The purest olive oil, procured by gently pounding the olives in a mortar, was to be brought for the lamp (20). This stood in the tent of meeting (*tabernacle of the congregation*) on the outer side of the vail concealing the ark of the testimony. It was to *burn always* (20), i.e. every night, not by day as well, as is clear from xxx. 8 and 1 Sa. iii. 3.

d. **The robes of the High Priest and his sons (xxviii. 1–43)**

The significance of the High Priest's robes cannot be understood without reference to the Lord Jesus Christ, whose perfections they typify. An explanation of such reference is not within the scope of this commentary, but this objective is surely implicit in the phrase *for glory and for beauty* (2); i.e. not to glorify Aaron but to display the glory and beauty of God, only fully revealed in the Person of His Son.

Wise hearted (3). Men endowed by God with the skill requisite for this specialized work. *To consecrate him* (3). Aaron's fitness for the priesthood lay not in himself but in those qualities which were represented and typified by the robes. *The ephod* (6). The outer garment, the chief purpose of which was to carry the stones of memorial and the breastplate, was of the same material as the inner covering and the vail of the tabernacle, with the addition of gold thread (6). The functions of the High Priest and of the tabernacle itself were thus intimately connected. The ephod seems to have been a short garment, perhaps no lower than the waist. It was joined only at the shoulders (7), leaving the two sides open, but held together by an embroidered girdle which was of one piece with the ephod (8).

Two onyx stones (9). By a twofold emblem Aaron brought the whole people before the Lord, by the stones on the shoulders of the ephod (12) and by the breastplate (21). In verse 12 read with RV 'for' instead of *unto the children of Israel*. The memorial was on their behalf. Aaron continually appeared before God as representing in his own person all the Lord's people. His presence in the tabernacle wearing the ephod was a continual act of intercession for them; cf. Heb. vii. 25. *The names . . . according to their birth* (9, 10). As there were twelve names on the stones, the tribes of Ephraim and Manasseh must have been represented by the one name of Joseph. They were arranged in order of seniority. *Ouches* (11). The same as in verses 13, 14, probably a kind of brooch of figured work to form settings for the stones and fastenings for the chains.

The breastplate (15). A square piece of cloth of the same material as the ephod (15), folded back at the bottom to give a double thickness about 9 in. square (16). It is in some cases uncertain what kind of stones the Hebrew words for these twelve jewels signify. Sufficient to say that they were all precious. *Chains* (22) are the same as in verse 14, and served to bind the upper part of the breastplate to the shoulders of the ephod, while the lower and inner or back part was held by golden rings bound by a lace of blue to similar rings on the body of the ephod just above the girdle (26–28). *Bear the names . . . upon his heart* (29). See verse 9n. The stones on his shoulders show that the true High Priest has strength to support his people, those on his heart that he holds them close in his affections. It is thus that they are brought before the Lord. *The Urim and the Thummim* (30). Lit. 'lights and perfections'. We might say 'Illumination and Truth'. The High Priest who wore this *breastplate of judgment* (29) containing the Urim and Thummim was endowed with power to pronounce the judgments or decisions of God upon all matters brought to him. Some think the words refer to the breastplate itself, but more probably they were stones set in the breastplate. See Dt. xxxiii. 8; 1 Sa. xxviii. 6n.; Ezr. ii. 63.

The robe of the ephod (31), i.e. that immediately under the ephod; a garment reaching probably a little below the knees, sleeveless and with an opening only at the top, probably woven without a seam (32). It was of plain blue throughout (31). Around the fringe of the skirt were pomegranates of richly coloured material alternating with golden bells (33, 34), the former signifying fruitfulness and the latter proclaiming that the High Priest was offering the prayers of the people at the altar of incense (not when he was in the Holiest of all, for there he wore only the linen garments; Lv. xvi. 4). As they heard the bells the people outside could join their prayers with those of their representative within the sanctuary. *That he die not* (35). So careful must

even the High Priest be to observe every detail of the divinely prescribed ordinances.

A plate . . . upon the mitre (36, 37). The mitre was a distinctive form of turban worn only by the High Priest. As the ephod served chiefly to bear the jewels, so the chief purpose of this head-dress was to carry the plate of gold on Aaron's forehead (37, 38). Crowning all the other garments, it proclaimed that holiness is of the essence of God's nature and is the end and objective of all the worship of priest and people. Even the best offerings were marred by some imperfection either in themselves or in the offerer. This imperfection or iniquity the priest himself bears (38), and secures the people's acceptance by the holy God. *Always* (38), i.e. whenever he officiates.

Embroider the coat (39). 'Weave' (RV) is preferable. It was all of white linen, perhaps woven like damask. The garment was a long robe with sleeves and reaching to the feet. It therefore was visible at the arms and below the skirt of the blue robe. *The girdle* (39). An inner girdle for this garment made of white linen, with coloured threads not woven into it like the ephod but embroidered upon it. *For Aaron's sons . . . coats* (40). The ordinary priests wore the simple white tunic and its girdle, probably without any embroidery. Although plain, its pure white simplicity was in itself *for glory and for beauty* (40). *The holy place* (43). This includes the court in which the altar of burnt offering was placed. *And die* (43). See verse 35n.

e. Ordinances for the consecration of the priests (xxix. 1–37)

See notes on Lv. viii. The consecration of Aaron and his sons to the priesthood was completed by five symbolic acts: washing (4) to purify; investiture (5–9) to clothe them with their priestly functions; anointing (7) to impart divine grace; sacrifice (10–21) for atonement and dedication; filling the hands (22–28) to invest them with authority to sacrifice. *The holy crown* (6), i.e. the gold plate of xxviii. 36, foreshadowing the royal dignity of our great High Priest.

The act of sacrifice was threefold: a bullock for a sin-offering (10–14), a ram for a burnt offering (15–18), another ram for consecration (19–22). For the form and significance of the sin and burnt offerings see notes on Lv. i and iv. *Their hands upon the head* (10). See also verses 15, 19. The offerer identified himself with the animal which was sacrificed, as being the bearer of his sin (10), or an offering dedicated to God (15), or the symbol of his consecration to his sacred charge (19). Substitution is clearly and repeatedly commanded in the Old Testament, so that there should be no doubt as to the way in which our Lord makes Himself an offering for us. *The other ram* (19), i.e. the ram of consecration (Lv. viii. 22). This ordinance constituted the unique climax of the whole act of consecration. When the priests had identified themselves with the ram, its blood, i.e. its life, as given up in death to atone for sin, was applied to their bodies and to their garments, thereby cleansing and wholly setting apart to the service of the holy God all that they were and did. Note especially in verse 20 the consecration of their attention to God's word, of the service of their hands and of their walk in the way of holiness. *The blood . . . the anointing oil* (21). Consecration is twofold, by the atoning blood which brings the man to God, and by the oil, symbol of the Holy Spirit, which brings the power of God into the man. Cf. Eph. i. 7, 14.

By the symbol of 'filling the hands' (22–28) the most sacred parts of the ram of consecration were placed in the hands of the priests by the consecrating minister (Moses in this instance) for them to make their first sacrificial offering and thus to be inducted into their charge as priests. Cf. xxviii. 41. The offering was 'waved', i.e. held out towards all quarters of the sky, to signify their presentation to the omnipresent God. *Sanctify* (27), i.e. set apart for the use of Aaron and his sons.

Verses 29 and 30 are a digression on the permanent rights of the priests. Verse 31 returns to the consecration service. *Aaron . . . shall eat . . .* (32). The meal of communion between God and the worshipper. *Seven days* (35). The rites of consecration (probably entire) were to be repeated on each of seven successive days. Each day also the altar had first to be cleansed by an atoning sacrifice (36). *Shall be holy* (37). The future tense has here, as often in Hebrew, the force of an imperative.

f. The daily sacrifice and the promise of the Lord's presence (xxix. 38–46)

Expiation, dedication, thanksgiving and prayer must be continually renewed. Hence the ordinance of the daily sacrifice and meat and drink offerings, with the incense (xxx. 8). *Where I will meet you* (42). The *tabernacle of the congregation* is therefore the 'tent of meeting' (RV), the place not where the people congregate together but where God meets with them, particularly through their representative, the High Priest. Note the change from 'you' to 'thee', the latter being the representative of the former. *I will dwell among* (45). Holy persons and holy things are sanctified not by outward ordinances (which merely symbolize inward grace), but by the indwelling presence of God Himself. The varied manifestations of God's presence impart knowledge of Himself, and it is those who accept and profit by such knowledge who may be assured of the continuation of His presence.

g. Further directions for the tabernacle (xxx. 1– xxxi. 11)

i. **The altar of incense (xxx. 1–10).** The altar of incense stood directly before the vail which concealed the ark within the holy of holies and was closely associated with the Holiest of all; for the ark, upon which was the mercy seat, was the place where God met with His people (6), and as incense represents prayer (Ps. cxli. 2) it was

appropriately placed near the ark, yet outside the vail, for the priest had to attend to it daily. Cf. Heb. ix. 4. *Strange incense* (9), i.e. not prepared in the prescribed manner, or offered improperly. For verses 1–10 cf. Rev. viii. 3–5, and see notes on Lv. x.

ii. **Money for the service of the tabernacle (xxx. 11–16).** No mention is made in this passage of military forces, and the plain meaning seems to be that all adult persons (14) of either sex were to be included in the census of the population. By the levy of half a shekel (about two shillings) not only was the service of the tabernacle supplied (16), but all the people were reminded that their great population was no glory to themselves, but that each was preserved alive by the mercy of God alone (12), and that their sinful souls were forfeit to Him. David forgot both these lessons (2 Sa. xxiv). The sum was so small as to make it clear that, while atonement is necessary, this was but a token of that fact, and that no sum of money could redeem the soul. The equal amount for rich and poor alike (15) saved the rich from pride and boasting and reminded them that in God's sight all souls are of equal value. See Ex. xxxviii. 25–28 for the use to which the first levy was put.

iii. **The laver (xxx. 17–21).** The twice repeated phrase *that they die not* (20, 21) shows that the washing had a ceremonial significance. For a New Testament application of this see Heb. x. 22.

iv. **The anointing oil (xxx. 22–33).** Throughout the Old Testament anointing fills a very important place in God's ordinances for His people, and signifies the enduement with the Holy Spirit for divinely appointed purposes. Prophets, priests and kings were anointed, and all these offices are found in Christ. ('Christ' is the Greek, as 'Messiah' is the Hebrew word for 'anointed'.) The ointment or oil was to be of the very best ingredients, to be compounded by those specially skilled, and to be unique, used for no other purpose than that specified in the sacred ordinances. *Shall be holy* (29), i.e. 'must be holy', as in xxix. 37. *Man's flesh* (32). Apart from the priests.

v. **The holy incense (xxx. 34–38).** Similar care was to be taken in the composition of the incense, and similar restrictions were laid upon its use as with the holy oil.

vi. **The craftsmen to be employed (xxxi. 1–11).** For this most sacred work not only were men of great skill required, such as Moses himself might have known and appointed, but men whose hearts were right for handling holy things. God alone could know and appoint such, and He marked out by name (2, 6) those whom He had chosen and fitted for this honour. These two men were both to use their own skill on a variety of tasks and also to supervise other unnamed craftsmen (6), who were equipped likewise by God, but whose appointment was left to Moses. *Filled . . . with the spirit of God* (3). Before Pentecost we read of the Holy Spirit being bestowed upon individuals for special services and in various manners; cf. Jdg. vi. 34, xiv. 6; 1 Sa. x. 10, xvi. 13; 1 Ch. xii. 18; Ps. li. 11. *The cloths of service* (10). These may be the coverings for the holy vessels when they were being transported (Nu. iv. 6–13), or a general description of the priests' robes, particularized in the next phrase.

h. The sign of the sabbath (xxxi. 12–17)

Over and above circumcision as the sign of the covenant between the Lord and Israel, the sabbath, an institution originating from the beginning of the world (Gn. ii. 2, 3), was used by God as the special token of His relationship to them. It marked them out from all other nations. The keeping of the sabbath was taken by the prophets as the crucial test of their obedience to their God, e.g. Je. xvii. 19–27; Ezk. xx. 12–24.

i. The tables of testimony (xxxi. 18)

Two tables . . . written (18). The culmination of the promise given in xxiv. 12. By *the finger of God* we are to understand not a literal hand, but some unseen divine power. See Lk. xi. 20. It is usually understood that the ten commandments only were inscribed on the tablets.

VII. THE IDOLATRY OF THE ISRAELITES AND MOSES' INTERCESSION. xxxii. 1—xxxiii. 23

a. The making of the golden calf (xxxii. 1–6)

During their stay in Egypt the Israelites had relapsed into idolatry (see Lv. xvii. 7; Jos. xxiv. 14; Ezk. xx. 8) and so deeply rooted in their hearts was their desire for a visible image to worship that scarcely six weeks passed, during which Moses' immediate influence was removed, before they were clamouring for an idol god. So closely was Moses in communion with God that it seems to them that without Moses they were without God, and they must have recourse to a created image. *Gods* (1). Should be translated in the singular, 'a god'. *Break off the . . . earrings* (2). Possibly Aaron hoped to restrain their frenzy by this order, expecting them to be reluctant to part with their ornaments, but their passion would stop at nothing. *Fashioned it with a graving tool* (4). Probably a better translation is 'bound it [i.e. the gold] in a bag, and made it a molten calf'. *These be thy gods* (4). Read 'this is thy god'. This representation was common in Egypt. It was renewed by Jeroboam (1 Ki. xii. 28–32) and became a grievous sin in Northern Israel. *Which brought thee up* (4). They did not replace Jehovah with the calf, but thought to worship Him under the form of the image; see also verse 5, where the feast to the Lord was a feast to the calf. *He built an altar* (5). Aaron aggravated the offence by adding the altar himself, surrounding the blasphemous object with an air of religious sanctity and opening the way for the people to offer worship to the work of their own hands. *To eat and to drink . . . to play* (6). Idolatry involves sensuality. It was vain for them to say

that they were in reality worshipping the Lord (a plea that is often made today by those who profess that they do not worship images, but that the images help them to visualize and worship the unseen God), for they were worshipping their own lusts. Eating and drinking were justified in the worship of Jehovah (Dt. xii. 18), but the rejoicing here was not spiritual but carnal. They gave full rein to their passions in the 'play', the orgiastic dance which followed and which almost invariably accompanied idolatrous rites. See also verse 25 and cf. 1 Cor. x. 6, 7.

b. Moses intercedes for the people (xxxii. 7–14)

Thy people (7). They had severed themselves from the Lord, but they still belonged to Moses. *Turned aside quickly* (8). In spite of the profession of their lips (xxiv. 3), how far from the Lord the heart of the people had been all this time! *Stiffnecked* (9). Like an ox or horse resisting the rein. *Let me alone* (10). By these words the Lord was testing Moses, as the Lord Jesus tested the two at Emmaus (Lk. xxiv. 28). It was not a final prohibition, that Moses should not intercede, but a trial of his character and of his reaction to God's suggestion to make him, instead of Abraham, the father of the chosen people. Moses' meekness and faithfulness stand the test and, denying himself, he persisted in prayer for them. *Moses besought the Lord . . .* (11). Cf. Moses' reminiscences in Dt. ix. 8–21. Moses' three arguments all plead for the honour of the Lord: The continued presence of these people here before Sinai was itself evidence of the great power of God (11). The Egyptians would falsely attribute to God evil intentions in His bringing them out of Egypt (12). God must surely stand by His promises to Abraham, Isaac and Jacob (13).

The Lord repented (14). An anthropomorphic expression adapting the infinite ways of God to the finite minds of men. God does not repent as men do, as though He had erred or was too weak-minded to carry out His purposes. When God 'repents' He changes, not His eternal purposes, but the course of events which He had previously stated, because the prayers or altered demeanour of His people alter the conditions under which He had originally made that statement.

c. The people are punished (xxxii. 15–29)

The work of God (16). Both the construction of the tablets and the writing were by direct divine agency. *Joshua* (17). He had been waiting lower down the mountain (xxiv. 13) and was now joined by Moses. *Shout . . . cry . . . sing* (18). In the Heb. the verb is the same in each case, not a cry of victory or of defeat, but just a cry undefined. *Anger* (19). Not of uncontrolled passion, but of righteous indignation. *He cast the tables out . . . and brake them* (19). The greatest punishment a people can suffer is to lose God's law. Cf. Am. viii. 11, 12.

What did this people unto thee? (21). Moses discerned that the sin originated from the people, but that Aaron, who was in charge of them, by his consenting was himself responsible for bringing the sin among them. Similarly Adam, the head of his wife, by consenting to Eve's suggestion was responsible for bringing sin upon the whole human race. Rom. v. 12 is right in saying 'by one man sin entered into the world', not 'by one woman'. *Thou knowest the people* (22). Like Adam, Aaron puts the blame on other shoulders and adds the absurd excuse that the calf made itself (24). Constraint and accident are frequently the excuses for sin.

Naked (25). RV translates 'let loose', but the AV is in keeping with the sense; see verse 6n. *Their enemies* (25). Possibly Amalekites, lurking in the recesses of the mountains, who would see all that transpired. *Slay every man his brother* (27). They were to slay instantly any whom they found still in the act of idolatry. In spite of Moses' action (20), many of the people persisted in their orgiastic ritual. Those who volunteered for this service were not to spare even brothers or sons (29). *Consecrate yourselves* (29). Heb. 'Fill your hands'; cf. xxviii. 41, xxix. 24. The use here of this technical term for installing a priest into his office indicates that by their zeal for the Lord on this occasion the tribe of Levi put themselves in the way of becoming the tribe of the priests. Cf. Nu. xxv. 11–13.

d. Moses again intercedes and is shown God's glory (xxxii. 30—xxxiii. 23)

Peradventure I shall make an atonement (30); i.e., by offering himself in their place (32). *If thou wilt forgive their sin* (32). Supply some such words as 'it is well'. These are the words not of formal petition, but of a heart burdened with a desire for the salvation of the people and for the honour of the Lord (cf. Rom. ix. 2, 3). The idea of vicarious punishment and atonement is found from the very beginning of the divine revelation. No mere man can atone for the sin of his brother (Ps. xlix. 7), but God was teaching the people to expect it from His Son. *Whosoever hath sinned* (33). God has mercy on the nation but reserves the right to punish the guilty individuals, whenever that day might come. But the nation as a whole is punished by God removing His own immediate presence and substituting an angel (34).

Depart, and go up hence (xxxiii. 1). The unfaithfulness of the people does not destroy the faithfulness of God. He must fulfil the promise made to their fathers, but He threatens to alter the manner of His doing so; an angel is now to lead them instead of God Himself (2). Verse 2 is similar to xxiii. 20, 23, but with this vital difference, that in chapter xxiii the angel was God Himself in the second Person of the Holy Trinity (see xxiii. 21, 'My name is in him'), whereas God's own person is now withdrawn (3, 'I will not go up in the midst of thee'). *Lest I consume thee* (3). Cf. Heb. xii. 29. For the unrepentant the presence of the infinitely holy God is like the white heat of a furnace. It was there-fore out of mercy that God said He would not Himself go in the midst. Cf. Rev. xxi. 27.

The people . . . mourned (4). The people still had sufficient love for God to be truly dismayed at this threat. They stripped off their ornaments as a mark of their godly sorrow and never replaced them (in verse 6 read with RV 'from mount Horeb onward'). *That I may know* (5). This was to be the test by which God could see how genuine was their sorrow. *Without the camp* (7). Moses could no longer meet with God inside the camp, which had been defiled by the gross idolatry. The tabernacle had not yet been made; so he took his own tent and pitched it outside the camp, to be a place where he, and others (7), could meet with God. *The tabernacle of the congregation* (7). This is better called 'the tent of meeting' here and wherever the phrase occurs. Cf. xxix. 42n. It was later to become the name of the great tabernacle. *Face to face* (11). This cannot mean that Moses saw God's face (cf. verse 20), but it expresses an immediate and direct communion with God to a degree granted to no other man; see Nu. xii. 8; Dt. xxxiv. 10n. To others the revelation came by visions and enigmas, but to Moses the mind of God was as plain as of a man speaking to his friend.

Shew me now thy way (13). Moses requires a fuller assurance of God's support in leading the people into the promised land. By saying *I know thee by name, and thou hast also found grace in my sight* (12), God had declared the supreme favour with which He regarded His chosen servant (cf. xxxi. 2), yet had given no explicit assurance of the way in which He would show that favour (13), for the nature of the angel was left uncertain (12). Moses reminds God that He has undertaken to be responsible for this people (13), and they are to be the reflection of His glory. In verse 14 the words *with thee* are not in the Heb. text. Moses seizes upon this first intimation of the continuance in some measure of God's presence, and presses his plea for the granting of this favour fully. He cannot bear the thought of moving one step with this great nation without God Himself in their midst (15). This presence was that which above all else witnessed to the world that they were the people of God (16); it was therefore to His honour in the eyes of the nations that He should go with them. The humble, reverent boldness with which Moses pleads with God, and the unique favour which he receives from the Lord (17), reveal something of the relationship in which Christ, our Intercessor, stands before His Father, and of the favours He wins for us because of the favour God has towards Him. The prayers of Moses in xxxii. 30–32 and xxxiii. 12–16 are the most beautiful precursors in the Old Testament to the prayers of our Saviour.

Shew me thy glory (18). Moses, encouraged by the gracious response to his prayer thus far, is bold to request that for which no other man has dared or aspired to ask, to see God's glory. *My goodness* (19). God's glory is manifested to mortal minds by the evidences of His goodness, yet this revelation to Moses was to be, in some way incomprehensible by us who have not seen it, a direct vision of His goodness undimmed by the limitations of its usual manifestation through earthly forms. *The name of the Lord* (19). See xxxiv. 5n. *I will be gracious* (19). Quoted in Rom. ix. 15 as an example of salvation by grace alone, apart from any merit or demerit in the saved. The late Rabbi Hertz allowed himself to say on this verse, 'God will show mercy to those who deserve it', a surprising comment. *My face* (20). Earthly eyes cannot behold the divine essence, nor can the mortal mind and spirit bear the unveiled light of the divine glory (cf. xxiv. 10n.; also Jn. i. 18). Jacob's words in Gn. xxxii. 30 must be a metaphorical expression; he saw the angel of God, but not the Father's unveiled face. Cf. Mt. xi. 27; 1 Jn. iii. 2. *Thou shalt stand upon a rock* (21). An ineffable spiritual experience is described in material terms adapted to our earthly state, yet the spiritual lessons of it are plain. If we regard the rock as Christ, we see how in Christ alone we are protected from the devouring fire of God's glory, and through Him alone we are enabled to behold that glory.

VIII. THE RENEWAL OF THE COVENANT. xxxiv. 1–35

The vision just promised is to be given when God renews the covenant, which the people have broken by their idolatry. Thus God turns even the rebellion of His people to His own praise, for it provided the occasion for Moses' requests in chapter xxxiii and for an answering revelation of the excellences of God's nature, which surpassed anything which had been granted before. *Hew thee* (1). Cf. xxxii. 16n. This time Moses prepares the tablets, but again God writes on them. The Law is as completely divine as before, yet sin lost something that it had been granted previously.

Passed by (6). As promised in xxxiii. 19–23. *Proclaimed the name of the Lord* . . . (5–7). Already God had made known to Moses His name, i.e. His nature, in iii. 14, vi. 3, and again at Sinai, xx. 5, 6 (see note), but here He reveals yet more of His character. In xx. 6 He had spoken of mercy, but now the infinite grace of God is revealed. Read with RV 'The Lord, the Lord, a God full of compassion and gracious, slow to anger, and plenteous in mercy and truth'. *Truth* (6). He is eternally true to Himself and His word. *Iniquity* (7). Heb. *'awon*. Sins committed from evil disposition. *Transgression* (7). Heb. *pesha'*. Rebellion against God. *Sin* (7). Heb. *hata'ah*, from *hata'*, to miss the mark; the most general word for sin in the Old Testament. Note that the order of xx. 5, 6 is here reversed. Here mercy and forgiveness are first declared and finally, as a corrective against presumption, they are reminded that God still maintains His justice. *Moses made haste . . . and worshipped* (8). Eager as he was to behold the divine glory, Moses'

heart was ever filled with reverent adoration. Contrast the spirit of the idolaters who make a god for their eyes to see, and play before it. *If now* (9). Rather 'since now . . .'

I make a covenant (10), i.e. God renews the covenant already made and already violated by the Israelites. In the following verses are laid down both the promises which God includes in His covenant and the conditions upon which the people may be in a position to accept the promises, i.e. *observe* . . . (11); after this a summary of the chief observances is given, representative of all the commandments issued before. *Marvels* (10). E.g. the passage through Jordan, the destruction of Jericho. *Take heed to thyself* (12). Cf. xxiii. 24, 25, 32, 33. Additional details are given here (12–17). *A snare* (12). Cf. xxiii. 33n. The snare is described in verses 15, 16. *Images* (13). See xxiii. 24n. *Groves* (13). Heb. *'Asherim*. Sacred trees or poles set up as symbols of the Canaanitish goddess Ashera. Grossly immoral rites were practised in connection with the pillars and groves, and these were a source of temptation to the Israelites continuously until the exile. *Jealous* (14). See xx. 5n. *Their daughters . . . thy sons* (16). Marriage of unbelievers to believers is to this day almost invariably a 'snare'. Solomon and Ahab are prominent examples (cf. 1 Ki. xi. 1–4, xvi. 31; Nu. xxv). *The feast of unleavened bread* (18). See xii. 14–20, xiii. 3–10, xxiii. 15. *Firstling* (19, 20). See xiii. 12, 13. *Empty* (20). See xxiii. 15. *Earing time* (21), i.e. ploughing time. *The feast of weeks* (22). See xxiii. 16. The same as the feast of harvest. *Thrice in the year* (23). See xxiii. 14. *Desire thy land* (24). God Himself would prevent their enemies from invading their lands when left unprotected at feast times. *Not . . . with leaven* (25). See xxiii. 18, 19. *The tenor of these words* (27), i.e. these words emphasized by way of repetition the most important terms of the covenant, the whole of which, as originally given, was to be observed. *Forty days and forty nights* (28). This second period of forty days spent on the mountain was mostly used in intercession for the rebellious people (Dt. ix. 18, 19; cf. Mt. iv. 1, 2). *Neither eat . . . nor drink* (28). He must therefore have been miraculously sustained. *He wrote upon the tables* (28). Verse 1 shows that the pronoun 'he' here refers to God.

The skin of his face shone (29). For the spiritual significance of this passage see 2 Cor. iii. 7–18. The glory of the Lord, which had surrounded Moses while he was receiving the Law, was now literally reflected from his face, impressing the people with the divine authority of the words which their human leader spoke to them. A like glory shone not only from the face but from the whole body and clothing of the Lord Jesus, when He was transfigured (Mt. xvii. 2), but He chose to keep that glory hidden from the multitudes. *Till Moses had done speaking* (33). The AV here reverses the meaning of the Heb., which is 'when Moses had done speaking'; so RV.

IX. THE CONSTRUCTION AND ERECTION OF THE TABERNACLE. xxxv. 1—xl. 38

a. The people offer willingly (xxxv. 1–29)

These are the words (1). Before calling the people to the work of constructing the tabernacle, Moses re-emphasizes the law of the sabbath, even as God had done when He concluded the giving of the pattern (xxxi. 12–17). Zeal for the Lord's work must not contravene His own holy laws. Moses probably said more than is given in these verses, as in xxxi. 12–17, and adds a warning against the special temptation to light a fire (3), an arduous task in the desert. See Nu. xv. 32. *Of a willing heart* (5). The value of any gift to the Lord lies solely in the heart of the offerer. He will not accept an offering made from any other motive than spontaneous love towards Him. Note the emphasis on the willingness of the people in verses 21, 22, 29, xxv. 2, xxxvi. 2 and cf. 1 Ch. xxix. 9; Ezr. i. 5, 6; 2 Cor. ix. 7. *Every wise hearted* (10). All could make a willing offering, but only those endowed with the requisite skill were to be entrusted with the actual making of the holy things. Cf. xxviii. 3n., verses 25, 26, 31, 35. For the details of the work and the workmen mentioned in these chapters see notes on the earlier chapters.

b. The craftsmen carry out the work according to pattern (xxxv. 30—xxxix. 43)

They brought yet unto him free offerings every morning (xxxvi. 3). The spirit of liberality was not a momentary outburst but continued so to prompt both the generosity of the givers and the industry of the spinners and weavers (verse 6, *make any more work*, refers to the latter), that soon they had more than enough. Cf. 2 Cor. viii. 3. *Their chapiters and their fillets* (xxxvi. 38). In xxvi. 37 the detail of the pillars having capitals and 'fillets' (connecting bars) was not stated, but Moses had seen details of the pattern, which were not stated verbally (xxv. 40). *Looking-glasses of the women* (xxxviii. 8). These mirrors were made not of glass but of polished bronze, and were used for the most sacred of the bronze objects of the tabernacle, both because their material was of the finest quality and because they came from the self-denial of the devout women who in large numbers ('troops', AV mg.) gathered to hear the words of the Lord at the door of the tent of meeting (see xxxiii. 7n.). Excavation has brought to light mirrors of this kind used by Egyptian women of the period. *This is the sum of the tabernacle* (21). The value of money changes so quickly that it is not possible to estimate accurately the present-day value of the materials stated here, but the gold alone would amount to nearly £200,000 sterling. The great wealth possessed by the Israelites in the wilderness was partly derived from their ancestors before they came into Egypt, and partly from the gifts of the Egyptians in the day when they sent them out of Egypt (see xii. 35, 36n.). *Them that were numbered* (25). See xxx. 11–16n.

Bekah means 'a half', but is used only of the half-shekel. It is significant that the tabernacle rested upon, and its curtains were hung upon, the representative contributions of every man of the congregation of Israel. No individual is insignificant in the spiritual house built up of the believers in Christ. *Beat the gold* (xxxix. 3). This explains how the gold thread was made which was used in so many of the fabrics for the tabernacle and the vestments. *The curious girdle* (5). Described in more detail here than before (cf. xxviii. 8). *Moses did look upon all the work* (43). Before it could be used for the tabernacle it was all inspected by him who had seen the pattern on the mount. Not only did he pass it but pronounced the blessing of God on those who had been so faithful to their charge. *As the Lord had commanded* (43). We may wonder why all the minute details of the tabernacle and its accessories were repeated so fully in these chapters. At least two reasons for this are as follows: the inspired record shows how careful were these men to follow faithfully every detail of the pattern which God had commanded them; and how God delights in and keeps exact account of the acts of obedience of His own people.

c. The tabernacle is set up (xl. 1–33)

The Lord spake unto Moses (1). The various parts and articles of the tabernacle were now completed but had yet to be put together and set in their appointed places. For this they had to wait for God's time and for His instructions, given through Moses, as to the order in which they were to place each portion of the tabernacle. *Cover the ark* (3). Read with RV 'screen the ark'. *Thou shalt . . . anoint the tabernacle* (9). This and the other ordinances for the consecration of the tabernacle and of the priests had already been given to Moses on the mount. See xxx. 26ff. All that concerns the worship of God must be touched by the sanctifying power of the Holy Spirit. *Anoint them, as . . . their father* (15). Comparing Lv. viii. 12 with Lv. viii. 30, it would seem that the oil was poured upon Aaron's head, but only sprinkled on his sons. See Ps. cxxxiii. 2. *An everlasting priesthood* (15). Not in the same sense as that the Lord Jesus Christ is a priest for ever (Heb. vii. 17, 23–25, 28). Aaron and his sons died, and when Christ appeared the Aaronic priesthood, which was a type, itself passed away. The meaning here is that so long as the priesthood remained it was reserved for Aaron's descendants. *In the first month* (17). On the fourteenth day of this month the Israelites left Egypt just two years before. On New Year's Day the tabernacle was erected, the whole task being completed in one day.

d. The glory of the Lord (xl. 34–38)

Then a cloud covered the tent (34). When all was completed according to His commandments, the Lord, by this visible token of His glory, declared that He accepted their obedience, and was fulfilling His promise to remain with them in person (xxxiii. 14–17). The same cloud and fire which had led them before (xiii. 20–22) was still their guide, but now it was the tabernacle, the symbol of God's rule over them and His dwelling among them, that was the centre of this manifestation. Cf. Ezk. xliii. 7. *Moses was not able to enter* (35). The light and fire of the *shekinah* ,the manifestation of the divine glory, were so awesome that even Moses, who had spoken with the Lord face to face, dare not approach. Cf. 1 Ki. viii. 11. But what Moses could not do Christ has done for us, entering into the holy place made without hands (Heb. ix. 24) so that by Him we may have boldness to enter into the holiest (Heb. x. 19–22).

J. C. CONNELL.

LEVITICUS

INTRODUCTION

I. TITLE AND CHARACTER

Leviticus is the third of the five books which compose the 'law' of Moses. It contains ten of the fifty-four pericopes or sections into which the Pentateuch was divided for the annual reading of the Law in the synagogue. The later Jews called it *Wayyiqra* ('and called'), using the initial phrase of the first verse. The name Leviticus is derived from the Greek (LXX) version. It is appropriate in a general way, since the priests were, of course, Levites in the sense of being members of the tribe of Levi. But it is inexact and to that extent misleading.

The book is especially intended for the priests. Aaron and his sons are mentioned many times in it. The Levites are mentioned only in one short passage (xxv. 32f.). But while the book is a manual for the priests, it is to be noted that many of the laws are introduced by the phrase, 'Speak unto the children of Israel'. Obviously this is because these laws, many of which required the services and mediation of the priests, concerned the people directly and vitally and formed an important part of that Law which it was to be the special responsibility of the priests to teach the people (Dt. xxxi. 9, xxxiii. 10; Ne. viii). Leviticus is in no sense an esoteric book. The people were entitled and expected to know exactly what was required of them, and of their priests, in that service of the sanctuary which so deeply concerned every true Israelite.

II. BACKGROUND

The place and time at which these laws were first given is carefully defined as during the sojourn at mount Sinai (vii. 38, xxv. 1, xxvi. 46, xxvii. 34), which lasted until 'the twentieth day of the second month of the second year' (Nu. x. 11). The statement of i. 1 presupposes the erection of the tabernacle which has just been described in Ex. xl. The mention of the eighth day (ix. 1) must refer to the day following the seven days of consecration of Aaron and his sons (viii. 33), which are apparently to be counted from the setting up of the tabernacle on the first day of the first month (Ex. xl. 2). The sin of Nadab and Abihu followed at once (x. 1, 2). The words 'and he did as the Lord commanded Moses' (xvi. 34), which are added to the ritual of the day of atonement, are important because they indicate that Aaron himself performed this ritual of atonement for all Israel, which means that there is added to the record of the law itself the record of its first observance, which took place nearly five months after Israel left Sinai. Note also xxiii. 44 which states that 'Moses declared the set feasts of the Lord unto the children of Israel'. Finally, it is to be noted that the deliverance from Egypt is represented as an actual personal experience (cf. xi. 45 and xviii. 3 with xxvi. 45) and that the possession of the land is represented as still future (xiv. 34, xix. 23, xxiii. 10, xxv. 2).

III. AUTHORSHIP

Nothing is said in this book as to the writing down of the laws which it contains. But the fact that these laws were given through Moses is stated again and again. The phrase, 'and the Lord spake unto Moses, saying,' occurs about thirty times. Twenty of the twenty-seven chapters begin in this way. Aaron's name is occasionally joined with that of Moses (xi. 1, xiv. 33, xv. 1); but he is directly addressed but once (x. 8). In view of the statements which occur in Exodus, Numbers and Deuteronomy regarding the writing down of the commandments given to Moses (e.g. Ex. xxiv. 4, 7), we are entitled to assume that these instructions, which so vitally concerned the welfare of God's people, and many of which are so precise and even minute in their requirements as clearly to require careful recording, were committed to writing either by Moses himself or at his command and under his supervision.

(For notes on the problems raised by the documentary theories of the compilation of the Pentateuch see the general article *The Historical Literature of the Old Testament*, p. 31.—ED.)

IV. PURPOSE AND APPLICATION

The immediate purpose of this book is to set forth those laws and principles by which Israel is to live as the people of God. Their God is a holy God; they are to be a holy people. 'Ye shall be holy, for I the Lord your God am holy' is its emphatic demand. His sanctuary is in their midst; and when they worship there they stand 'before the Lord', a phrase which occurs about sixty times in this book. This means separation from uncleanness and sin, and, since they are sinful and prone to sin, it necessitates atonement for sin and purification from it and from all uncleanness. Hence the law of sacrifice is placed impressively at the beginning. See the note on the significance of the sacrificial ritual at the end of Section I (p. 141).

The laws of Leviticus are very varied. They are both general and specific; they are both ceremonial and moral; they are severe and also merciful. They separate Israel from the nations and set her apart for the service of the God who has made this people His own by delivering them from Egyptian bondage. In so far as these laws are purely ceremonial, they are temporary and binding only during the Mosaic dispensation to which they belong. They had immediate reference to Israel as a nation which was to be governed in every aspect of its national and individual life by the Law of Moses. In this strictly historical sense this book still has great interest for the Christian reader. It tells him how God dealt with Israel as a people 'under age' and in need of training and preparation. Furthermore, in the case of many of these laws, e.g. the dietary, hygienic principles may be involved which have perpetual value and significance. To eat pork, for example, may be wholesome under certain conditions and unwholesome under others. For the New Testament application and interpretation see 1 Cor. x. 31; Rom. xiv. 20. In so far as these laws are moral, they are of perpetual obligation; and since the Christian is, like the Jew, prone to evil and constantly tempted to break the law of God as set forth in the Decalogue, they demand of him, as of the Israelite of old, perfect obedience to the moral law of God. See note on Dt. iv. 8. The insistent demand of Leviticus that Israel be holy because the God of Israel is holy is confirmed and strengthened in the New Testament (1 Pet. i. 15).

The book is particularly notable in that it brings together in blended harmony two elements which are regarded by many as quite distinct and even as incompatible. On the one hand, Leviticus is the most thoroughly legalistic of all the books of the Old Testament. It seeks to govern either by broad principle or specific precept the whole of the life of the people of God. Its demands may be summed up in the words of the apostle 'whether therefore ye eat, or drink, or whatsoever ye do, do all to the glory of God' (1 Cor. x. 31). Its insistent challenge and persistent demand is: 'Ye shall be holy, for I the Lord your God am holy.' On the other hand, there is no book in the Old Testament which more clearly sets forth the redemption which is in Christ than does Leviticus. It faces the question of Job, 'How should man be just with God?', and answers it in such words as the following: 'He shall bring his offering . . .' 'And he shall lay his hand on its head . . .' 'And he shall confess that he hath sinned . . .' 'And he shall slay it . . .' 'And the priest shall sprinkle the blood . . .' 'And he shall make an atonement for him, and it shall be forgiven him.'

This is the New Testament gospel for sinners stated in Old Testament terms and enshrined in the ritual of sacrifice; and it finds its fullest expression in the ritual of the day of atonement. 'For the like of the great day of atonement we look in vain in any other people. If every sacrifice pointed to Christ, this most luminously of all. What the fifty-third of Isaiah is to Messianic prophecy, that, we may truly say, is the sixteenth of Leviticus to the whole system of Mosaic types, the most consummate flower of the Messianic symbolism' (S. H. Kellogg). To understand Calvary, and to see it in its tragic glory, we must view it with all the light of sacred story centred upon it. With Isaiah, the 'evangelical' prophet of the old dispensation, and with the writer of the Epistle to the Hebrews, we must turn to Leviticus and read of the great day of atonement, and of the explanation which is given of it there: 'For the life of the flesh is in the blood: and I have given it to you upon the altar to make an atonement for your souls: for it is the blood that maketh an atonement for the soul' (Lv. xvii. 11). Thus we shall see the great drama of redemption unfolding before our eyes and, in the light of the type, begin to understand the Antitype.

OUTLINE OF CONTENTS

I. THE SACRIFICES. i. 1—vii. 38

    a. The Lord's portion of the sacrifices (i. 2—vi. 7)

    b. The portion of the priest and of the offerer (vi. 8—vii. 38)

    c. The significance of the ritual

II. THE CONSECRATION OF AARON AND HIS SONS. viii. 1—x. 20

    a. Aaron and his sons consecrated by Moses (viii. 1–36)

    b. Aaron takes up his office (ix. 1–24)

    c. Sacrilege and its consequences (x. 1–20)

III. LAWS REGARDING UNCLEANNESS. xi. 1—xv. 33

    a. Uncleanness due to animals (xi. 1–47)

    b. Uncleanness due to childbirth (xii. 1–8)

    c. Uncleanness due to leprosy (xiii. 1—xiv. 57)

    d. Uncleanness due to issues (xv. 1–33)

IV. THE DAY OF ATONEMENT. xvi. 1–34

    a. Aaron's preparation (xvi. 1–10)
    b. The sin offering for the priests (xvi. 11–14)
    c. The people's sin offering (xvi. 15–19)
    d. The scapegoat (xvi. 20–22)
    e. The offerings completed (xvi. 23–28)
    f. Some further instructions (xvi. 29–34)

V. THE PLACE OF SACRIFICE AND THE SANCTITY OF BLOOD. xvii. 1–16

VI. SINS AGAINST THE MORAL LAW. xviii. 1—xx. 27

    a. Prohibited degrees and sensuality (xviii. 1–30)
    b. A collection of sundry laws (xix. 1–37)
    c. Sundry laws regarding very heinous offences (xx. 1–27)

VII. INSTRUCTIONS FOR THE PRIESTS. xxi. 1—xxii. 33

    a. The priests must be holy (xxi. 1–9)
    b. Special rules for the High Priest (xxi. 10–15)
    c. The effect of physical deformity (xxi. 16–24)
    d. Defilement disqualifies the priest from touching holy things (xxii. 1–16)
    e. Rules for the offering of sacrifices (xxii. 17–33)

VIII. THE HOLY CONVOCATIONS. xxiii. 1–44

    a. The sabbath (xxiii. 3)
    b. The Passover and the feast of unleavened bread (xxiii. 4–8)
    c. The offering of firstfruits (xxiii. 9–14)
    d. The feast of weeks (xxiii. 15–22)
    e. The feasts of the seventh month (xxiii. 23–44)

IX. THE HOLY OIL, THE SHEWBREAD, THE SIN OF BLASPHEMY. xxiv. 1–23

    a. The oil for the candlestick (xxiv. 1–4)
    b. The shewbread (xxiv. 5–9)
    c. The sin of blasphemy and crimes of violence (xxiv. 10–23)

X. THE SABBATICAL YEAR AND THE YEAR OF JUBILE. xxv. 1–55

    a. The sabbatical year (xxv. 1–7)
    b. The jubile (xxv. 8–55)

XI. BLESSINGS AND CURSINGS. xxvi. 1–46

    a. Blessings as a reward of obedience (xxvi. 3–13)
    b. The chastisements for disobedience (xxvi. 14–45)

XII. VOWS AND TITHES. xxvii. 1–34

COMMENTARY

I. THE SACRIFICES. i. 1—vii. 38

It is significant of its great importance that this manual of sacrifice, as we may call it, is placed first, that the laws regarding the sacrifices precede even the ordination of the priests who are to perform them. Similarly in Numbers the census of the tribes is placed before the celebration of the Passover which is stated to have preceded it in time (Nu. i. 1, ix. 1). This code is introduced impressively. The opening word *and* connects it directly with Ex. xl. 34f. *Called* is a much stronger expression than *spake* (1). It suggests a peremptory summons (cf. Ex. xxiv. 16; Nu. xii. 5)

and an important communication (cf. Ex. iii. 4). It is used of the proclaiming of the feasts (xxiii. 2, 4, 21, 37) and of the announcing of the day of atonement (xxv. 10). *Called . . . and spake*, instead of the usual *spake*, increases the emphasis. 'Out of the tent of meeting' (RV) is a better rendering than *tabernacle of the congregation* (1). See Ex. xxv. 9n. RV uses 'tabernacle' for the *mishkan*, the structure formed of the gilded boards and covered by the linen covering embroidered with the cherubim (cf. Ex. xxvi. 7), and 'tent' (*'ohel*) for the tent composed of curtains which covered it or for the structure as a whole (cf. Ex. xl. 19, 34). AV, by rendering '*ohel* both as 'tent' and as 'tabernacle', occasions confusion. The statement indicates definitely that the tabernacle had already been erected and thus connects Leviticus with what immediately preceded in Exodus.

Before considering this section in detail, it will be well to note carefully several points with regard to it. First, the sacrifices are discussed twice and from different viewpoints: (a) the Lord's portion of the sacrifices (i. 2—vi. 7) and (b) the portion of the priest and of the offerer (vi. 8—vii. 36). Then, the five kinds of offering (burnt, meal, sin, trespass, peace) are discussed independently, without regard to any possible connection between them. In the third place, the description and inventory given here is not complete but is supplemented by other statements, both those previously made and others to follow (e.g., no mention is made of the drink offering or of the shewbread). Fourthly, the order of description varies here between (a) and (b) and is not the order of performance. (For a note on the significance of the sacrifices see p. 141.)

a. The Lord's portion of the sacrifices (i. 2—vi. 7)

Speak unto the children of Israel (2). These laws concern all of the people. It is as important for the layman to understand his duties as for the priest to perform his correctly. *Bring an offering* (2). 'Offereth an oblation' (RV). The Heb. word *qorban* (cf. Mk. vii. 11) is used of gifts as well as of sacrifices (e.g. Nu. vii. 11). These offerings are now more precisely defined. *Cattle* (2) would include such unclean animals as horses, asses and camels. Cf. Ex. ix. 3, where Pharaoh's 'live stock' is stated to consist of horses, asses, camels, herds and flocks. *Herd* (2) means the bovines, while *flock* includes sheep and goats. Only these domestic animals and certain birds could be offered in sacrifice.

i. The burnt offering (i. 3–17).

(See also under vi. 8–13.) So called because all of the flesh was consumed on the altar. Hence it is occasionally called the whole burnt offering (Dt. xxxiii. 10; Ps. li. 19). Cf. also Lv. vi. 22f. The Heb. word for burnt offering ('*olah*) means 'that which goes up', either because all of the offering ascended as a *sweet savour* unto God (17), or because the entire animal, and not simply part of it, was offered (went up) on the altar. This sacrifice is mentioned first, apparently, as being the most conspicuous, even if not the most important. Note that the great brasen (bronze) altar is called 'the altar of burnt offering' (Ex. xxx. 28, xxxi. 9; Lv. iv. 7, 10, 18). Cf. also the direction in iv. 24, 33 'where they kill the burnt offering'. It is also noteworthy that the 'continual offering' (*tamidh*) was a burnt offering (Ex. xxix. 42; Nu. xxviii—xxix).

That the burnt offering might be a voluntary offering is indicated by the contrast between i. 2, ii. 2 and iv. 2, v. 15. But this is not taught in i. 3 where 'for acceptance' (RV) is a better rendering than *of his own voluntary will*. The animal must be a *male without blemish* (3). This was also the case with the trespass offering (cf. v. 15). The ritual is carefully described (5–9). The offerer brings his animal to the door of the tent of meeting, places or presses his hand on its head, makes confession over it (xvi. 21; cf. Dt. xxvi. 13ff.), slays it *before the Lord*, flays it, divides it *into his pieces*, i.e. according to its joints (cf. Ex. xii. 46; Nu. ix. 12; Jn. xix. 36), and washes the inwards and the legs. The priest collects the blood and sprinkles it round about upon the altar, and burns all of the flesh on it. Note the emphatic phrase, *the priests, Aaron's sons* (i. 5, 8, 11, ii. 2, iii. 2). The rite of sacrifice is distinctly a priestly function. Neither priest nor offerer partakes of any part of the sacrifice. But the hide goes to the officiating priest (vii. 8). In this sacrifice, in contrast with the sin and trespass offerings, the stress seems to be on the complete consecration and dedication of the offerer. This is made especially clear in Rom. xii. 1, where the words 'your bodies' and 'a living sacrifice' indicate clearly that Paul had the burnt offering in mind. But the words *it shall be accepted for him to make atonement* (4) and the sprinkling of the blood around the altar make it quite clear that dedication must be preceded by confession and expiation (cf. xvii. 11). *To make atonement* (4) is literally 'to cover over'. It implies the covering over of sin as something upon which God of Israel who is holy cannot look (Hab. i. 13; cf. Ps. li. 1, 9, ciii. 12; Is. xliii. 25, xliv. 22; Mic. vii. 19; also Heb. x. 1–4). Sin must be covered over with atoning blood. It is used both with reference to persons (as here, cf. iv. 20) and to things (e.g. the altar, Ex. xxix. 36). It is a 'burnt offering, a fire offering, a sweet savour unto the Lord' (9). 'Fire offering' is a term which is applied to all those sacrifices, any part of which was burned on the altar. *Sweet savour* is used of most of them and probably applies to all. The words are an anthropomorphism which is not to be taken literally; it should be regarded as a human way of describing the satisfaction which the Lord takes in the offerings of His people. This applies also to the words 'bread of God' (food) which are used of the sacrifices as a whole (xxi. 6, 8, 17, 22f.), and also of the peace offerings (iii. 11, 16). Some take these statements literally and insist that they indicate a crude and primitive conception of the meaning of sacrifice. But such a view is forbidden by the larger context. The ignorant and carnal may have held this low view. But the fact that at this very time, when these laws were being given, Israel was being fed with manna at the hand of God, should have convinced them that the God who fed them did not need to be fed by them, but that it was His good pleasure to receive back from His children a portion of the good things which He had given them, as a sign of the recognition on their part that it was He who sustained their lives and gave them every blessing. Ps. 1 belongs to a much

137

later date, but it expresses clearly and emphatically the Mosaic conception of the meaning of sacrifice.

The requirements in the case of the sacrifice of a sheep or a goat are the same as in that of the bullock (10–13). The place of sacrifice is to be the north side of the altar (11). This is mentioned only here, but it applies to all of the sacrifices except the peace offering. When the offering consists of a bird, the ritual is much simpler, but follows the same general pattern (14–17). Birds were offered, either as the required and regular sacrifice (cf. xii. 6) or as a substitute for the normal sacrifice, permitted and accepted because of the poverty of the offerer (cf. v. 7–10).

ii. The meal offering (ii. 1–16). (See also under vi. 14–18.) Like the burnt offering this oblation is described as voluntary: *and when any* ('soul' or 'person', as often in Leviticus) *will offer* (1). It is here described independently but usually accompanied the animal sacrifices (cf. Nu. xv. 1–16). It was a cereal offering, the main ingredient being fine flour. Consequently 'meal offering' (RV) is preferable to *meat offering*. The flour is usually mixed with oil (vii. 10; cf. v. 11) and may have oil poured on it (6, 15); frankincense is placed on it (1). It may be either uncooked or cooked. The priest takes a handful to burn on the altar, which handful must contain all of the frankincense. This portion is called the *memorial* (2, Heb. *azkarah*), probably because the frankincense (*lebhonah*), being one of the four elements in the holy incense (Ex. xxx. 34) which was offered on the golden altar twice daily by the priest for all the people at the hour of prayer, was intended to serve the same purpose in the case of the individual worshipper and bring him into remembrance before God. Cf. the headings of Pss. xxxviii and lxx, which indicate that they were to be recited at the time of the offering of this memorial.

The smallest meal offering, one tenth of an ephah, was more than three quarts. Since a *handful* (2), which was the amount to be burnt on the altar as a fire offering, would be a relatively small part of it, it is stated here that the remainder is *most holy* (3) and is to be the portion of the priests. This means that the priest's portion was to be eaten only by male members of his family and in a holy place, i.e. within the court of the tabernacle (vi. 16; cf. x. 12f.). This was also the rule for the sin offering (vi. 25–29), and the trespass offering (vii. 16), and the shewbread (xxiv. 9). It did not apply to the burnt offering for the obvious reason that that offering was wholly consumed on the altar. On the other hand the peace offering was *holy*. The entire family of the priest might eat of this portion, and most of the sacrifice became the portion of the offerer and was to be eaten by him, his family, and his needy friends or dependents (Dt. xii. 11–18). It must be eaten in a *clean* place, but not necessarily within the court of the tabernacle.

Salt is to be used with all the sacrifices. Salt stands for permanence, for incorruption. Hence the expression, *the salt of the covenant of thy God* (13; cf. Nu. xviii. 19; 2 Ch. xiii. 5). *Leaven* and *honey* (11) may not be used with the fire offerings; they may not be placed on the altar. But both may be offered as firstfruits (12; cf. Ex. xxiii. 16f., xxxiv. 22f.; Lv. xxiii. 17f.). This seems intended to guard against the inference that leaven and honey were unclean in themselves. Ex. xii. 39 states definitely that the reason for eating unleavened bread when Israel went out of Egypt was that they went forth in haste and had no time to leaven it. The meal, and the oil, and the wine of the drink offerings (which is not mentioned here, but frequently or usually accompanied the meal offerings), were the three most important elements in the daily food of the people, frequently summarized in the phrase, 'corn, and wine, and oil' (e.g. Dt. xii. 17). Consequently the meal offering and the oil which went with it and the accompanying drink offering constituted an oblation of the daily food of the people. In offering it they recognized that they received their daily food from God. Oil, in view of its use in connection with the anointing of the priests and in the golden candlestick, symbolized also the gracious presence of the Holy Spirit in illumination and sanctification.

iii. The peace offering (iii. 1–17). (See also under vii. 11–34.) *And if his oblation be* (1). Like the burnt offering the peace offering may be voluntary. The animal may be a male or a female, and must be without blemish. Like all the other fire offerings, it differs from the burnt offering in this respect that only part is burnt on the altar. This portion is carefully described. It consists of the *fat* which is upon the internal organs, together with the *kidneys* and the *caul* (fatty appendage) which is upon the liver (3, 4). In the case of the sheep, the fat-tail is included (9). This was regarded as a luxury, and might weigh in the case of the adult animals 10–15 lbs., or even more. These details are repeated in the case of the sin offering (iv. 8f., 19, 26–35) and also apply to the trespass offering (vii. 3f.). The reason is that *it is the food of the offering made by fire for a sweet savour: all the fat is the Lord's* (16). The solemn injunction is added that the prohibition of eating the fat or the blood is to be perpetually observed. *A perpetual statute for your generations* (17) is an expression which occurs seventeen times in Leviticus. Dt. xii. 15f., 21–24, however, makes no mention of the fat but only of the blood. Nevertheless it is not to be regarded as modifying this perpetual statute. The cases are quite distinct. The killing and eating described in Deuteronomy is not a peace offering. It is not made at the altar, but within 'all thy gates' (Dt. xii. 15). The blood is poured out on the ground and covered with earth. Finally, the 'unclean' (Dt. xii. 15, 22) may eat of it as well as the 'clean', a permission which proves conclusively that Dt. xii is not dealing with the peace offering at all (cf. vii. 20f.). Since the term 'peace offering' apparently implies that the worshipper is in a state of reconciliation with

God (otherwise he would not be permitted to eat of the flesh of his offering), it is to be noted that the laying on of hands is stressed (2, 8, 13) as well as the manipulation of the blood. All of the fire offerings were expiatory. The failure to provide for the substitution of a bird in the case of a poor man is noticeable. The reason is probably that since this rite was a sacred meal which the offerer was expected to share with his family and friends, especially the poor and needy, a bird would not be adequate for the purpose; and the poor man, who could not afford a sheep or goat, might and should be invited to partake of the peace offerings presented by his well-to-do friends and neighbours.

iv. **The sin offering (iv. 1—v. 13).** (See also under vi. 24–30.) *If a soul shall sin . . . then let him bring* ('offer' RV) (2, 3; cf. v. 15). The sin and trespass offerings are obligatory as atonement for specific sins. The sins are sins of ignorance or error. The man has sinned 'unwittingly' and has done something which 'the Lord has commanded not to be done' (2, 13, 22, 27 RV). The list of such sins given in v. 1–4 indicates that more than mere ignorance is involved. Such uncleanness as is described, for example, in xi. 24–28 (cf. xvii. 15f.) is removed simply by washing and abstaining from acts of worship (which involve presence at the tabernacle) until sunset. But if a man has contracted such uncleanness without being aware of it (*and if it be hidden from him*, 2), and has consequently failed to comply with the law of purification (xi. 27f.), then he has sinned and is *guilty* (2, 3) and *when he knoweth of it* (4), then he must offer a sin offering. Here the sin is clearly one of ignorance. But on the other hand failure to come forward to testify to a crime when witnesses are publicly summoned may be due to any one of several reasons, as may also the case of the rash oath (1, 4). These may be sins of infirmity or weakness, without being sins of defiance (the 'high hand') for which there is no remission.

In chapter iv the sin offering is considered with special reference to the status of the one whose sin is to be expiated: the anointed priest (i.e. the High Priest, viii. 12) (3–12), the whole congregation (13–21), a ruler (22–26), one of the common people (27–35). Guilt varies according to rank. The anointed priest occupies a position of great importance. He is one of the people, but he represents all of them. Hence his sin brings guilt upon all of them (see verse 3, RV); and since he ministers in holy things and by virtue of his office is permitted to enter the holy place, his sin has profaned the holy place and atonement must be made in the holy place. Blood must be brought into the holy place and sprinkled toward the veil and placed on the horns of the golden altar (6, 7). The same ritual is to be performed when all the congregation sins (13–21), apparently because Israel, ideally considered, is a 'kingdom of priests' (Ex. xix. 6), and the Lord dwells in her midst. In this case the laying on of hands must be performed by the elders as representing the people. In the case of the lay individual, whether a ruler or one of the common people ('people of the land'), the blood is not brought into the holy place, but applied to the horns of the altar of burnt sacrifice and poured out beside it. The ruler offers a he-goat, the common man a she-goat or a ewe-lamb. In all cases the *fat* is burnt on the altar as in the case of the peace offerings (10, 31). But with regard to the rest of the sacrifice an important distinction is to be observed. In the case of the animals whose blood has been brought into the holy place, the rest of the flesh is to be burned *without the camp*, in a clean place where the ashes of the sacrifices are *poured out* (12). The principle involved is that the one for whom the sin offering is presented must not partake of any part of it (cf. vi. 24–30). The priest may not do this when making atonement for his own sin, nor when he makes atonement for the whole congregation of which he is a member. Cf. Heb. xiii. 10–13.

Verses 1–6 of chapter v specify, as we have seen, certain sins as requiring a sin offering: failure to come forward to testify when summoned, uncleanness through contact with the carcase of an unclean animal or with the uncleanness of a human being, or taking a rash oath. All of these being joined together by *or* (2, 3, 4) may be regarded as forming a protasis, the apodosis of which begins with verse 5. They are treated as sins of ignorance (see iv. 13, v. 2, 3, 4). So when he realizes his guilt, or it is brought to his attention, he is to *confess* it and *bring his trespass offering . . . for his sin . . . for a sin offering* (5, 6). This rendering seems to identify the sin and the trespass offerings; and AV in its chapter summary treats v. 1–13 as relating to the trespass offering. There is obviously a close connection between them. For the words 'and is guilty' ('*ashem*) comes from the same root as trespass offering ('*asham*), and are used in iv. 13, 22, 27 of sins which require a sin offering and in v. 17, vi. 4 of those which require a trespass offering. But since the difference seems to lie in the fact that the trespass offering requires and must be preceded by restitution, and since restitution is not mentioned until v. 14f., it seems best to regard the description of the trespass offering as beginning with v. 14. It is true, of course, that the mention of the trespass offering already in v. 6 is somewhat confusing, if this special form of sin offering is not discussed as such until v. 14f. But this may be intended to indicate the close connection between the two. The RV mg. rendering 'for his guilt' instead of *his trespass offering* (6) is doubtful, to say the least.

Since the sin offering is obligatory in such cases as have been stated, due allowance is made in the case of the poor who cannot afford a costly offering. Instead of the lamb the offerer may present *two turtledoves, or two young pigeons* (7). One is to be offered as a sin offering; the other as a burnt offering. Since in the case of the sin offering all of the flesh except the fat became the portion of the priest (vi. 26), the explanation is probably correct, that because of the difficulty or impossibility of removing the fat in the case of the bird, the flesh of the one bird was wholly consumed on the altar as representing the Lord's portion of the sin offering (but called a burnt offering, because it was wholly consumed on the altar) and the other given to the priest as representing his portion of the sin offering. This would account for the requirement that two birds be presented. In the case of the extremely poor a further concession is made: a meal offering may be substituted for the animal sacrifice (11). Being a sin offering it differed from the usual meal offering in an important respect: it was offered without oil and without frankincense. Furthermore the handful which was offered as a memorial was burnt on the altar 'upon the offerings of the Lord made by fire' (12, RV). This clearly gave it the value of a bloody sacrifice, by virtue of its being mingled with the fire offerings which were on the altar. Hence it could be called a sin offering, and in offering it the priest made atonement for sin. In this way what appears to be an exception to the principle that 'without shedding of blood is no remission' (Heb. ix. 22) really ceases to be an exception but rather serves to illustrate that principle of vicarious substitution which it is the main object of the ritual of sacrifice to illustrate and enforce.

v. **The trespass offering (v. 14—vi. 7).** (See also under vii. 1–10.) The distinctive feature of the trespass offering is, as we have seen, that it is made in the case of a sin which requires restitution, and restitution must precede the performing of the sacrifice. Two cases are specified. The first is the withholding of *the holy things of the Lord* (15), i.e. of such tithes, offerings, firstlings, etc., as belonged to God and must either be presented to the priest or redeemed. The second case has to do with acts *which are forbidden to be done by the commandments of the Lord* (17). Since the same phrase is used here as in iv. 2, 13, 22, 27, the difference must consist in the fact that the trespass requires restitution. The next section (vi. 1–7) deals with acts which involve injustice or injury to one's fellowmen. In all of these cases the property unjustly withheld is to be restored with the addition of one-fifth of its value, a fine which both served to reimburse the rightful owner and to punish the guilty party. Cf. Nu. v. 6–8. The offering in every case is a *ram* (cf. xix. 21f.), also called a 'he-lamb' (xiv. 12), a 'lamb of the first year' (Nu. vi. 12). The trespass offering formed part of the ritual for the cleansing of the leper (xiv. 12) and of the Nazirite (Nu. vi. 12).

b. The portion of the priest and of the offerer (vi. 8–vii. 38)

Up to this point, except in the case of the meal offering (ii. 10, cf. v. 13) attention has been focused on the Godward side of the sacrifices: the manipulation of the blood and the portions to be consumed upon the altar or burned without

the camp. A series of laws is now given which deal particularly with the portion of priest and offerer. This subject is introduced by the words *Command Aaron and his sons* (9), and each topic commences with the words, *This is the law of* (9, 14, 25, etc.). Each of the laws already discussed is now dealt with from this angle.

i. **The burnt offering (vi. 8–13).** (See also under i. 3–17.) Since the entire animal is consumed on the altar, there are only two matters of importance: the disposal of the ashes and the tending of the altar-fire. This fire is never to be allowed to go out. It is the sacred fire kindled on the altar by God Himself. Furthermore the burnt offering is to burn continually upon the altar as the token of Israel's consecration to God. The statement that the burnt offering shall burn during the night indicates that this law has the continual burnt offering (Ex. xxix. 38–42) primarily in view.

ii. **The meal offering (vi. 14–18).** (See also under ii. 1–16.) With the exception of the *memorial*, the entire offering goes to the officiating priest. Like the sin and trespass offerings, it is most holy and must be eaten in a *holy place* (16), i.e. within the courts of the tabernacle (26). *Every one that toucheth them shall be holy* (18). Cf. vi. 27; also Ex. xxix. 21, 37, xxx. 29. This apparently means that those who by virtue of their office are entitled to eat of the sacrifice are to remember that they may do so only if ceremonially clean. What applies to the laity (vii. 20) would be even more essential in the case of the priest and his sons. The eating of the priest's portion of the meal, sin and trespass offerings was restricted to males (vi. 18, 29, vii. 6; cf. Nu. xviii. 8–10).

To the law of the meal offering of the people there is added a brief statement (19–23) regarding the continual meal offering for the priests. It is to be offered by the anointed priest (Aaron or his successor in office) perpetually, morning and evening. It would seem to be a kind of priestly counterpart of the perpetual burnt offering. Since it is offered for the priests, no part of it can be eaten by them; it is to be wholly burnt.

iii. **The sin offering (vi. 24–30).** (See also under iv. 1—v. 13.) In the case of this sacrifice, all of the flesh except the fat became the portion of the officiating priest: *The priest that offereth it for sin shall eat it* (26). The holiness of this portion is particularly stressed. It is most holy and everything that touches it must be or becomes holy. This applies even to the vessel in which it is cooked. Here, where the reference is to things, *whatsoever* (27) is the preferable rendering, although RV mg. gives 'whosoever'. *Shall be holy* (27), i.e. be treated as holy and therefore withdrawn from common use. It must be thoroughly washed or, if made of earthenware, be broken. Every male of the priests may eat of the sin offering. But again it is pointed out (30) that this is not permissible when the offering is made for the priest himself.

iv. **The trespass offering (vii. 1–10).** (See also

under v. 14—vi. 7.) Since nothing has been said in the earlier passage about the Lord's portion in this sacrifice, the law as already stated for the peace offering (iii. 3f.) and for the sin offering (iv. 8–10), instead of simply being appealed to, as, e.g., in iv. 26, is repeated in detail (vii. 2–5). It is then stated that the portion of the priest is the same in this offering as in the case of the sin offering. Everything except the Lord's portion goes to the priest. The meal offerings referred to in this connection are the meal offerings which accompanied the animal sacrifices just mentioned.

v. The peace offering (vii. 11–34). (See also under iii. 1–17.) The peace offering is the only one of the sacrifices (burnt, sin, trespass, peace) of which the offerer is permitted to partake. Consequently, the Lord's portion, the priest's portion, and the offerer's portion are carefully distinguished. The Lord's portion is the fat, which is burned on the altar (22–25). The priest's portion (30–34) consists of the wave-breast and the heave-thigh (whether fore-leg or hind-leg is meant is not certain). The manipulation, waving and heaving, apparently signified that the offerer gave these portions to God through His priest, whose portion they thus became. All the rest of the flesh becomes the portion of the offerer, but with certain restrictions. If the offering is a vow or a free-will offering, any remainder may be eaten on the second day (16). But if it is *for thanksgiving*, it can be eaten only on the day of sacrifice (15). What is not eaten is to be burned. One object of this requirement was clearly to encourage a generous and hospitable spirit, the inviting of friends or neighbours, especially the poor and needy, to share in this joyful occasion (Dt. xii. 12).

With the sacrifice the offerer is to present cakes of several different kinds. Some are made with or mingled with oil and unleavened (12). But he is also to offer *leavened* 'cakes' (13, RV); and the words 'out of each oblation' (14, RV) indicate that the priest is to receive both leavened and unleavened cakes as his portion, together with the wave and heave offerings, which are his. Since the daily food of the people included leavened bread, this would indicate the hallowing and offering of a portion of their daily food to God in the person of His priest. But leavened bread could not of course be placed on the altar. It should be noted that these cakes are not a meal offering (*minḥah*). No incense is placed on them and no portion is burned on the altar. They simply accompany the peace offering and are partaken of by both priest and people. The priest's portion is called a *heave offering* (14). It is particularly stressed that the wave and heave portions of the priests are theirs by a perpetual statute. They are called the 'anointing-portion' (35, RV) of the priests because these portions were assigned to them on the day of their consecration to the priesthood. While the peace offering is holy, it is not 'most holy' (cf. vii. 6). This is indicated by the fact that it is to be slain in the court (iii. 2), and can be partaken of by the offerer and by any 'clean' person. The idea which is most prominent in connection with this sacrifice is that of joyous communion with God, and of fellowship with one another in this act of worship.

vi. The divine origin of the laws recalled (vii. 35–38). *This is the portion . . . This is the law* (35, 37). This elaborate treatment of the sacrifices is summed up in verses which draw attention to the fact that they are the divine perpetual provision for Aaron and his sons, and which stress the nature of their origin as being commanded by the Lord at Sinai.

c. The significance of the ritual

As we study these sacrifices we are impressed with the clearness with which they point forward to and have their fulfilment in the redemptive work of Christ. In the holy supper, the Christian remembers the death of Christ as his sin and trespass offering, a sacrifice made once for all at Calvary and in which he can neither participate nor share. He has communion with Christ as his Passover and peace offering, as he partakes of the sacred symbols of His broken body and shed blood, even drinking of the cup, because the wine of the sacrament symbolizes the blood which was shed to atone for sin and which has become the source and fountain of life for every believer (Jn. vi. 53). He dedicates himself anew to His service by presenting his own body a living sacrifice (the burnt offering) unto his Lord. And he looks forward to the coming forth of his great High Priest, from the heavenly temple into which He has entered, to complete and crown His glorious redemption by receiving unto Himself His redeemed ones who are keeping the feast 'until He come'. See also the note on the New Testament interpretation of the day of atonement (p. 150).

In view of the practical universality of some form of sacrifice among ancient peoples, the question has naturally been often discussed as to a possible connection between the Mosaic cultus and the practices of the neighbouring peoples. That there should be certain resemblances is only to be expected. But these should be estimated in the light of such considerations as the following. The Pentateuch represents the Mosaic ritual as a direct revelation from God: 'the Lord spake unto Moses, saying'. It repeatedly warns the people against adopting the customs and practices of the Egyptians or of the Canaanites. Its antecedents, where they exist, are to be found in the practices of the ancestors of Israel, going back to the earliest times. There are differences which are so thoroughgoing that they far outweigh any surface resemblances. These differences are both negative and positive. On the negative side we may note that there is no connection with divination or augury; no religious frenzy, self-mutilations, or sacred prostitution, sensual and orgiastic fertility rites being utterly forbidden; no human sacrifices; no sacrifices for the dead; no appeal to *quid pro quo* motive. On this last point we may note further that the amount of the offering was immaterial. The law 'prescribes for the whole year not quite 1,300 animals as public sacrifices, or on the average three or four daily'. Hecatombs were of no avail (Mic. vi. 7). On the positive side the most important differences are the emphasis on the ethical—the sinfulness of sin and the necessity of atonement; the necessity of a right attitude on the part of the offerer, with the stress on repentance and loyal obedience to the law of God; the unique sacredness of the blood as representing the life of the animal accepted in substitution for the offerer as the propitiation for his sins. All these considerations taken together show that, whatever the resemblances, the Mosaic ritual breathes a quite different spirit from that of the cults of other nations, and is essentially unique.

II. THE CONSECRATION OF AARON AND HIS SONS. viii. 1—x. 20

This narrative stands in close relation to that in Ex. xxviii—xxix. We have seen that in Exodus the construction of the tabernacle is dealt with three times. Chapters xxv—xxx deal mainly with its construction and furnishing but include instructions regarding the vestments of the priests and their consecration (xxviii—xxix); chapters xxxv—xxxix deal with the execution of the instructions regarding the tabernacle, and chapter xl with its erection and its acceptance by God. We might have expected that the account of the consecration of the priests would follow immediately, as the natural sequel of the dedication of the tabernacle, and form a part of Exodus. But since the chief function of the priests is to offer sacrifice and also because the offering of sacrifice on their behalf formed an indispensable part of their own consecration, the manual of sacrifice given in Lv. i—vii is very properly made to precede this important section.

a. Aaron and his sons consecrated by Moses (viii. 1–36)

The abruptness of the language, *Take Aaron and his sons with him, and the garments, and the anointing oil, and a bullock . . . and two rams, and a basket of unleavened bread* (2) carries us back directly to Ex. xxix. 1–3 where all these things are enumerated. Hence the use of the definite article which the rv of this verse brings out. That this rite is to be regarded as the conclusion of the consecration of the tabernacle and a continuation of Ex. xxix—xl is also indicated by the frequency of the phrase *as the Lord commanded Moses* or its equivalent (fifteen times) which runs like a refrain through those chapters. The unique position of Moses (cf. Ex. xxviii—xxix), who was over the whole 'house of God' as a servant (Nu. xii. 7; Heb. iii. 2, 5), is made clear. Thus Moses offers Aaron's sin offering (viii. 14–17); and the wave breast of the offering of consecration, which would normally have been the portion of

the officiating priest, becomes Moses' portion (28; Ex. xxix. 26).

The ritual of consecration to the priesthood and investiture with office was elaborate and impressive; and it was performed in the presence of 'all the congregation at the door of the tent of meeting' (3, rv). Note the solemn introduction: *This is the thing which the Lord commanded to be done* (5). Aaron and his sons were first washed with water, and Aaron was then arrayed in his holy garments (6–9; cf. Ex. xxviii). Then Moses anointed the tabernacle, the altar, and all its vessels, including the laver (10, 11). After that he poured oil on Aaron's head (12; cf. Ps. cxxxiii. 2). The purpose was sanctification and consecration. Having clothed Aaron's sons (13), he proceeded to offer a sin offering (14–17), a burnt offering (18–21) and a consecration offering (22–29). The latter is the only one not mentioned in the manual. The Heb. term is *millu'im*, lit. 'fillings', because 'to fill the hand(s)' is the technical term for invest with office. It resembled the peace offering in that the ones for whom it was offered were permitted to partake of the flesh (31). But in this case the special portion of the priest, the wave-breast and heave-thigh, could not be eaten by Aaron and his sons, because the offering was made on their behalf by Moses. So the former was assigned to Moses as his portion (29), since he acted as priest, and the latter was burned on the altar (25, 28, rv).

Aaron and his sons laid their hands upon the head of the sacrificial animal in the case of all of these offerings as a sign that they were offered on their behalf. But it is significant that the blood of the sin offering was used to cleanse and sanctify the altar at which the priests were to minister. The placing of the blood of consecration on ear, thumb and toe (23, 24), the sprinkling of oil mingled with sacrifical blood on Aaron and his sons (30) and the pouring of oil on Aaron's head (12), symbolized the consecration and sanctification in varying degree to holy office and use. Aaron and his sons were not to go out from the door of the tent of meeting during the seven days of their consecrating, and the same sacrifices were to be repeated on each of the seven days (33, 34, rv). Consequently an exception was made to the rule regarding the eating of the peace offerings which could be eaten on the day after they were offered (vii. 15–18). These were to be eaten the same day. During these seven days Moses performed the same sacrifices on each day (34), and Aaron and his sons remained in the court of the tabernacle.

b. Aaron takes up his office (ix. 1–24)

And it came to pass on the eighth day, i.e. the day which marked the end of their consecration, *Moses called Aaron and his sons* (1). 'Called' suggests the solemnity of the occasion. Every act performed by Aaron is commanded by Moses. The whole congregation is brought together to stand *before the Lord* (5) so that the Lord may appear unto them and manifest His glory

(4, 6, 23f.) as a sign of His approval and ratification of everything that has been done (cf. Ex. xl. 34f.).

The sacrifices which Aaron performed for himself and his sons and for the people (7)— Aaron and his sons were Israelites first of all— were a sin offering and a burnt offering (2, 8, 12). Those which he performed for the people were a sin, a burnt, a meal and a peace offering (3, 4). Since the ritual has already been described, detailed discussion is not needed. It is to be noted, however, that the order followed here is apparently the regular, and we may s̃ay the logical, order for the offerings—sin offering, burnt peace offering. Thus the three basic ideas are emphasized: first atonement for sin, then dedication and consecration of life, and finally communion with God in the eucharistic meal. In Lv. xiv. 10–20 the order of the offerings of the cleansed leper is trespass offering (12–18), sin offering (19), burnt offering and meal offering (20). Cf. xiv. 21–32 where the same order is prescribed. This would indicate that the trespass offering, which involved restitution, if offered came first of all, preceding even the sin offering.

After all the sacrifices had been offered Aaron blessed the people (22). He did this while still standing by the altar. The blessing was probably the formula of blessing given in Nu. vi. 22f. Then Moses and Aaron went into the tent of meeting. The reason for this is not stated. But it is proper to infer that at this time Moses placed Aaron in charge of the holy place, the candlestick, the table of shewbread, and the altar of incense, and instructed him as to his duties, all of which Moses had performed from the day of setting up the tabernacle (Ex. xl). Then they came forth and both blessed the people. And the glory of the Lord was manifested as on the day of the setting up of the tabernacle (23). The fire which burned up the sacrifices was the sacred fire which was not to be allowed to go out. The word *shouted* (24) implies joy and rejoicing. But the joy was mingled with awe, for they fell on their faces in worship before the Lord.

c. Sacrilege and its consequences (x. 1–20)

In this historical section the account of the consecration of Aaron and his four sons is followed at once by the record of the sacrilege which led to the tragic death of the two oldest who had beheld the glory of the Lord in the Mount (Ex. xxiv. 1). That this event followed immediately and is to be regarded as the sequel of the ceremony of consecration is indicated by the reference to the *goat of the sin offering* (16). This must be the offering referred to already in ix. 3, 15. Its blood had not been carried into the holy place as was done with Aaron's own sin offering (18). It was the sin offering for the people and the flesh was the priests' portion. Consequently its flesh should have been eaten by the priests in the holy place (17). The reason given is very significant: *God hath given it you to bear* (RV mg. 'take away') *the iniquity of the*

congregation, to make atonement for them before the Lord (17). Cf. Ex. xxviii. 12, 29, 30, 38. The function of the priests was one of mediation. This seems to mean that the priests by eating the sin offering exhibited God's gracious acceptance of the sacrifice just as, by permitting the offerer to partake of his peace offering, He indicated His acceptance of both gift and giver. Instead it had been burned (whether upon the altar or without the camp is not stated). This may mean either that the surviving sons of Aaron could not eat of their portion under such terrible circumstances, or that they did not dare to do so because they felt themselves to be involved in, or contaminated by, the sin of their brethren, since all four were priests. They had therefore burned the carcase of the goat which was the people's oblation, even as they had been required to burn the flesh of their own sin offering, outside the camp (ix. 11). That they erred in this is made clear by verse 17f. Verse 20 indicates that whether Aaron's scruples were primarily those of a father or those of a priest, the reason or excuse which he gave for the conduct of his surviving sons, and which apparently reflected his own attitude, was regarded by Moses as satisfactory. Mercy joined with judgment!

The exact nature of the sin of Nadab and Abihu is not fully explained. Note the words, *And Nadab and Abihu . . . took* (1). Nothing has been said in viii—ix about the offering of incense. They are represented as acting entirely on their own initiative and not at the command of Moses. *Offered strange fire* (cf. Ex. xxx. 9); apparently fire not taken from the brasen altar. Both of them did it. The offering of incense on the golden altar was the duty of the High Priest (Ex. xxx. 9) or of *one* of the priests (Lk. i. 9). For them to take precedence over their father in the first performance of this solemn function was an act of presumption. For the two of them to undertake it at the same time suggests rivalry and jealousy. Their act may also have been presumptuous because the time for offering incense (morning or evening) had not arrived. These and still other elements may have entered into this act of sacrilege. The occasion was so solemn and the ritual had been performed with such care, everything being done 'as the Lord commanded Moses', that such impulsive and arbitrary departure from it as Nadab and Abihu were guilty of must have been highly presumptuous and sacrilegious.

Significant in this connection is the special revelation and prohibition which is made directly to Aaron (8–11) and not through Moses. It is at least possible, though by no means certain, that we are to infer from the introduction at this point of this law prohibiting the use of wine or strong drink by the ministering priest (cf. Ezk. xliv. 21) that Nadab and Abihu acted as they did because they were under the influence of liquor. Whatever the explanation, the incident is a solemn warning against every sin of presumption, self-assertion and levity.

In view of the definite statements which are made in the manual regarding the portions of the animal and vegetable offerings which are to be given to the priest, it is rather remarkable that there is no corresponding statement about the drink offering. It would be natural to infer that a portion of the drink offering was poured out on or beside the altar and that the rest would be assigned to the priest as his portion, to be drunk with his meat and his bread *after* his service at the altar was completed. The analogy of the Passover (cf. Mt. xxvi. 29) would favour this. But according to Jewish tradition all of the drink offering was poured out; either on the altar of burnt sacrifice (Ex. xxx. 9 might imply this), or at the foot of the altar (Ecclus. l. 15), or perhaps part on the altar and the rest at its base.

The reason for this perpetual rule is that the priests may be able to *put a difference between holy and unholy* (RV 'common') *and between unclean and clean* (10), i.e., observe carefully all the ritual and ceremonial requirements of the law, and that they may *teach the children of Israel all the statutes* of that law. See Dt. xvii. 11, xxiv. 8, xxxiii. 10; cf. Mic. iii. 11.

This whole tragic incident may properly be regarded as intended to impress on Israel, both priests and people, the holiness of their God and to warn them against any presumption or laxity in the performance of the law of sacrifice which is so carefully stated in chapters i—vii. It also taught the important and needed lesson that no man is indispensable to God. Four priests were indeed very few to perform the service of a sanctuary which was to be the centre of worship for several million persons. Yet God put away half of their number at the very outset for disobedience. God is able of the 'stones to raise up children unto Abraham'.

This terribly impressive event concludes what has been called 'the law of the sanctuary' and we pass on now to consider 'the law of daily life'.

III. LAWS REGARDING UNCLEANNESS.
xi. 1—xv. 33

'Unclean' (defiled) is the conspicuous word in this group of chapters. It occurs more than 100 times. Almost equally noteworthy is the rare occurrence of the word 'sin' (evil, wickedness). This indicates that here the emphasis is on the ceremonial rather than on the ethical. Yet it does not follow that uncleanness is a matter of minor importance. Failure to do what God has commanded is sin, whether the act be ceremonial or moral. Unclean is the antithesis of holy. Everything which is inconsistent with the holiness of God may be described as uncleanness. It may be purely ceremonial, as the touching of a dead body, or it may be crimes which are so shocking to the moral sense that it is a shame even to speak of them (xviii. 20–25). In most cases the uncleanness is quite temporary, lasting only *until the even* (xi. 25), and in certain cases requires the washing of the garments or of

the person in water. But it may cover a considerable period of time and require the presenting of a sin offering. Ceremonial purity was indispensable for a holy people. The uncleannesses that are dealt with are of several kinds.

a. Uncleanness due to animals (xi. 1–47)

This subject is discussed under two aspects, living animals as food and contact with dead animals.

i. **The question considered from the standpoint of diet (xi. 1–23).** Cf. Dt. xiv. 1–21n. These verses prescribe the flesh which may or may not be eaten. Four classes are distinguished:

Quadrupeds (verses 2–8). Only those animals which divide the hoof completely and which chew the cud may be eaten. This rule is precisely stated and then four examples of animals which do not meet the requirements are given: camel, coney, hare and swine. The hare is not a ruminant, nor is the coney (generally identified with the rock-badger, *Hyrax Syriacus*). Both are rodents. But the fact that their jaws are constantly in motion gives the appearance of chewing the cud. This indicates clearly that the description is not intended to be strictly scientific, but simple and practical. The clean animals are not named here (cf. Gn. vii. 2), but Dt. xiv. 4, in listing them, adds to the three domestic animals (ox, sheep and goat) seven of the wild animals which are also members of the ruminant family (the *Pecora* according to present-day classification). For the average Israelite this restricted the meat diet largely to those domestic animals which were used in sacrifice.

Sea food (verses 9–12). Only fish which have both fins and scales may be eaten. This rules out eels, shell-fish, lobster, crab, oyster, frog, etc.

Birds (verses 13–19). Stated entirely from the negative side. *And these . . . ye shall have in abomination among the fowls* (13) introduces a list of twenty, including several species. Dt. xiv. 11 states positively, but briefly, 'all clean birds ye shall eat' without naming them, and then gives a list almost identical with the one given here. The clean birds would include doves, pigeons, quail, sparrows. No mention is made of the eating of eggs (cf. Dt. xxii. 6f.). Many of the prohibited birds are birds of prey. Birds which fed on carrion, like the kite and vulture, would be especially obnoxious.

Insects (verses 20–23). These are defined as *all fowls that creep, going upon all four* (20) or, as in RV, 'winged creeping things'. The phrase 'going upon all four' (lit. 'upon four legs') must mean 'those which walk or crawl like a quadruped', since six legs are characteristic of the great class of *Insecta*. All are banned with the notable exception of four classes of the locust family which are distinguished by their long jumping legs (21). If the RV rendering of verse 23 is followed then the phrase 'which have four feet' cannot mean the same as 'that go upon all four' (21), i.e. it must be taken as referring to insects which do not have the large jumping legs. By inserting the word *other* in verse 23 the AV assumes the two phrases to be more or less synonymous. This is probably the correct meaning. The fact that a sweeping statement is made after a definite exception to it has been already given should not confuse the careful reader.

ii. The question considered from the standpoint of physical contact (xi. 24–42). The words 'carcase' (eleven times) and 'when they are dead' (twice) indicate that the reference is to dead animals. The AV renders verse 26 by *the carcases of every beast*, taking the position that contact with a living animal, such as the camel or the ass, which were unlawful for eating, did not render one ceremonially unclean. This became an issue between Pharisees and Sadducees in later times, the latter holding that contact even with the living animal produced uncleanness. Verses 29–38 enlarge upon verses 20–23, which have merely stated the general prohibition and the important exceptions in the case of winged creeping things. Here eight kinds of *creeping things* are particularly specified as abominable (29, 30). Yet, as has been indicated, the emphasis seems to be on the contamination produced by their carcases. They are clearly unclean as food. But also their dead bodies render unclean; *whosoever doth touch them, when they be dead* (31) and the defilement extends to *any part of their carcase* (35, 37). The prohibition of the eating of the flesh of any creeping thing is sweeping and comprehensive (41). The law regarding uncleanness through contact with the carcases of any creeping thing may perhaps be regarded as singling out these eight animals for special mention because contact with their carcases was especially likely to take place. It is to be noted that in this chapter the rare word 'abomination' (*shiqquṣ*) is used of the eating of sea animals (10–12), birds (13), winged creeping things (20, 23), and creeping things (41, 43). This confirms the conclusion that 24–38 refer to uncleanness occasioned by contact with dead animals, and that verse 41 resumes the discussion of dietary laws.

It is worthy of note that the word *belly* (42, *gahon*) contains, according to the Massoretes, the middle letter of the Pentateuch. *Gahon* is written with a 'w' (*waw*), i.e. as *gaḥown*, because the 'o' is long. It is this 'w' which is the middle letter, and it is printed large with a marginal note: '*Waw* is large; and it is the middle of the law in letters'. Similarly viii. 8 is noted as the middle verse, and 'sought' in x. 16 as the middle word. The fact that the middle letter is 'w' is especially interesting, because there was no invariable rule as to whether such long vowels as the 'o' in *gahon* should be 'written fully', i.e. with the 'vowel letter', or 'defectively', i.e. without it. This shows the care with which for centuries the text of the Old Testament was safeguarded by the Jews.

iii. The people of God must be holy (xi. 43–47). This law regarding man's relation to the animal

kingdom over which he has been given dominion is followed by a most impressive sanction. *For I am the Lord your God: ye shall therefore sanctify yourselves, and ye shall be holy; for I am holy . . . For I am the Lord that bringeth you up out of the land of Egypt, to be your God: ye shall therefore be holy, for I am holy* (44, 45; cf. 1 Pet. i. 15–17). The necessity of holiness was first stressed in connection with the eating of those portions of the sacrifices which were for the priests and the people, and also in connection with the entire ritual of the consecration of Aaron and his sons. Now in this section the same command is most impressively applied to the daily life of the entire people. Cf. xix. 2, xx. 7, 8, 26, xxi. 6, 7, 8, 15, 23, xxii. 9, 16, 32 where the same or similar sanctions occur.

This section then concludes with a summary, the closing words of which are important; *to make a difference* ('distinction', RV) *between the unclean and the clean, and between the beast* ('living thing', RV) *that may be eaten and the beast* ('living thing', RV) *that may not be eaten* (47). Cf. xx. 25, 26. The first part of this summary seems to refer to uncleanness through contact with that which is unclean, especially that which is rendered unclean by the fact of death, and the second part to those living things which are proper for food and those which are prohibited.

b. Uncleanness due to childbirth (xii. 1–8)

The command to be fruitful is given in Gn. i. 28 and renewed to Noah after the flood (Gn. ix. 1). We are expressly told that it was obeyed by the post-diluvian ancestors of Abram (xi. 11, 13, etc.). The consistent attitude of the Old Testament may be summarized in the words of Pss. cxxvii. 3, cxxviii. 3f. Fruitfulness was a sign of divine favour; barrenness was regarded as a reproach (Gn. xxx. 24). Consequently, the laws given here and elsewhere regarding the marital relationship and parenthood are both impressive and significant. The only adequate explanation of the seeming anomaly presented by the command to be fruitful, the joy attending the realization of parenthood, and the uncleanness which is associated with it and which finds its most pronounced expression in the prolonged purification required of the mother after she has performed the high function of womanhood, must be found in the fact of the fall and the curse pronounced on woman immediately after it. Pain and suffering were to be the accompaniment of motherhood (Gn. iii. 16). Regarding Adam we read: 'And Adam lived an hundred and thirty years, and begat a son in his own likeness, after his image' (Gn. v. 3). When this took place Adam was a fallen and sinful being. He was under the curse pronounced by God 'in the day that thou eatest thereof thou shalt surely die' (Gn. ii. 17). So of Adam, and of all but one (Enoch) of his descendants mentioned in Gn. v, the last word spoken is 'and he died'.

From this it follows that, although the birth of a child is a joyous event, it is also a solemn one.

For the birth of the child will inevitably be followed ultimately by its death, and by eternal death unless the child is made an heir of life through the redemption which is in Christ. It is in this sense that we must understand David's words, 'Behold, I was shapen in iniquity; and in sin did my mother conceive me' (Ps. li. 5). David is not here reflecting upon the virtue of his own mother; she may have been a paragon among women. He is thinking of that inherited taint, that original sin, which she had transmitted to him and which was the root cause of the grievous sin against womanhood of which he is so painfully conscious at the time of composing the Psalm. Consequently, according to the law, everything connected with parenthood is treated as unclean, and especially as rendering the person unfit for the performance of religious duties. In fact the strictness with which anything which suggests the sexual and sensual is banned from the worship of God (Ex. xix. 15, xx. 26; Lv. xv. 16–18) is one of the most noteworthy characteristics of the religion of Israel and distinguishes it most sharply from the religions of the neighbouring peoples who worshipped gods who were male and female and even made orgiastic (fertility) rites a prominent feature in the worship of these gods.

In the case of the birth of a male child, the uncleanness of the mother as far as the home is concerned lasts until the eighth day, when the rite of circumcision is to be performed on her son (cf. Gn. xxi. 4). Then for thirty-three days she is still to be unclean as far as public religious duties are concerned. In the case of the birth of a female both periods are doubled. No reason is assigned. Since this is described as a period of uncleanness, the explanation is probably to be sought in connection with the considerations mentioned above. It does not seem probable that the reason is purely physical or biological. At the termination of this period of forty or eighty days she is to bring a yearling lamb for a burnt offering and a fowl for a sin offering, or two fowls, if she cannot afford a lamb. Cf. Lk. ii. 23. The specifying of the age of the lamb is exceptional (Ex. xii. 5, xxix. 38; Lv. ix. 3, xiv. 10, etc.) and is usually stated in the case of sacrifices for the feast days. The concluding words are impressive: *and the priest shall make an atonement for her, and she shall be clean* (8).

For the Christian of today this ancient law has special significance. Christians should realize that marriage ought not to be contracted lightly, that they should marry 'in the Lord' (1 Cor. vii. 39) in order that they may claim the promises and blessings of the covenant for their children (1 Cor. vii. 14). They may not like to be told that their children are sinful and unclean. But they need to remember that this is so. The view is widely held today that children are born *good*, that they should be allowed to develop naturally, that self-expression should be encouraged, and discipline and restraint reduced to the minimum. Christian parents who realize the truth set forth here will pray earnestly that the children who have been born in sin may be 'born again', may be regenerated by the Holy Spirit. They will pray that they as parents may be enabled to train up their children in the nurture and admonition of the Lord. Guidance, restraint, discipline and religious instruction are quite as essential as self-expression, in most cases far more essential.

c. Uncleanness due to leprosy (xiii. 1—xiv. 57)

As in the case of the two subjects last discussed, it is important to remember that leprosy is dealt with solely from the standpoint of the uncleanness which it occasions. It is most frequently called *the plague* (lit. 'stroke') or *the plague of leprosy* (e.g. xiii. 2, 3). The man who has it, or is suspected of having it, is *unclean*, so unclean that he must be *shut up* (mentioned eight times), apparently without the camp (xiv. 3), while his case is being decided. Then, if the verdict is unfavourable, he must be removed from the camp until he is healed (xiii. 45f.). The possibility of recovery is thus plainly included in the decree of banishment. But it is to be noted that, while elaborate rules are laid down for the recognition of leprosy and for distinguishing true leprosy from other diseases with which it might be easily confused, nothing is said about the treatment of the disease. This has led some to the conclusion that it was incurable, and even that it was not an ordinary disease, but a visitation from God. The cases of Miriam (Nu. xii. 10–15), Gehazi (2 Ki. v. 27) and Uzziah (2 Ch. xxvi. 19–23) are appealed to as proof of this. But were such the case it would seem as if the nature of the affliction and the cause of it would have been so plain that the elaborate rules for detecting it might have been dispensed with. Apparently we must distinguish between what we may call ordinary cases and such extraordinary cases as the ones just mentioned. It is interesting to note that leprosy is not included in the diseases which the Lord threatens as a punishment for apostasy, regarding which it is said 'whereof thou canst not be healed' (Dt. xxviii. 27, 35). The language of xiv. 2f., *This shall be the law of the leper in the day of his cleansing* and *if the plague of leprosy be healed in the leper*, seems to make it quite plain that leprosy was not incurable. Otherwise we would have to hold that *leper* here is to be understood to mean 'the man under suspicion of being a leper', or else that the elaborate ritual for the cleansing of the leper could be performed only in such a case as Miriam's when the hand of God was plainly manifested both in the smiting and the healing.

i. How leprosy is to be recognized (xiii. 1–46). Detailed discussion of the rules laid down for the detection of the disease cannot be entered into here. It is clear that it was hard to distinguish from a number of other diseases which were common among the Israelites. None of the more frightful symptoms of what we know as leprosy are mentioned here. It may be that the disease differed somewhat from the leprosy of New Testament times and from the leprosy which became such a scourge in Europe in the Middle Ages. But it is to be remembered that these laws have to do with the detection of the disease in its early stages and also that Aaron's words in pleading with Moses on behalf of Miriam describe with terrible clearness the real nature of the disease and its terrible results: 'Let her not be as one dead, of whom the flesh is half consumed when he cometh out of his mother's womb' (Nu. xii. 12). And Moses' prayer that God will heal does not necessarily mean that direct supernatural intervention was the only hope for the leper.

ii. **Leprosy in garments (xiii. 47–59).** A closely related subject is now dealt with in this section. Leprosy in a garment is discussed in connection with leprosy of the body, apparently because it was an immediate concern of the people. Significant is the regard which is shown for the property rights of the people. The destruction of an entire garment might work serious hardship, especially to the poor (Dt. xxiv. 10–13). So only the corrupted part is to be destroyed (56). *Fretting leprosy* (51f., xiv. 44). The word 'fret' seems to be used here in the sense of 'gnaw', i.e. make holes, to describe an infection that is not superficial but penetrating. The Hebrew word occurs only in these passages and in Ezk. xxviii. 24, where the reference to briars and thorns favours such a meaning. The LXX and Vulg. render by 'persistent'. Some have thought that the reference is to a form of mildew in the case of the garments, and to a form of dry rot in the case of the houses.

iii. **Cleansing and restoring the leper (xiv. 1–32).** The ritual for the cleansing of the leper is given in detail and is quite elaborate. In some respects it resembles the consecration of the priests (chapters vii—ix) and the ritual for the day of atonement. It covers a period of seven days, with special rites on the first and eighth. Cleansing is specially stressed (xiv. 8, 9) and this involves shaving of the hair (cf. Nu. viii. 7). Hyssop is used as at the Passover (xiv. 4ff.; cf. Ex. xii. 22), together with cedar wood and scarlet which are also used in making the water of purification (Nu. xix). The releasing of one of the birds *into the open field* (xiv. 7) suggests the sending away of the scapegoat (xvi. 21f.). But there may be no connection.

The ritual of the first day restores the leper to the camp but not to his home and the intimacies which were associated with it. Note that it was not sacrificial. The blood was not brought to the altar. The rite was one of purification. On the eighth day the cleansed man is to offer three lambs in sacrifice: a he-lamb for a trespass offering, a ewe for a sin offering, a he-lamb for a burnt offering. In the case of the poor, birds may be substituted for lambs as sin and burnt offerings. But apparently, as indicated by verse 21, the trespass offering must be a ram. The ritual of the oil is particularly detailed and

impressive. It is to be placed on the right ear, thumb and toe, of the leper, on which the blood of the trespass offering has already been placed, and to be sprinkled with the finger of the priest seven times before the Lord. Then the rest of the handful is to be poured out on his head (cf. viii. 23f.). This apparently represents the consecration of the restored leper to the service of his covenant God. It suggests an analogy between the admission (in this case, the readmission) of an unclean person (a Gentile) into the congregation of Israel, God's holy people, and the consecration of an Israelite to the special and peculiarly holy function of a priestly mediator between Israel and their God. Since the leper had for a time been debarred from the community and the service of the sanctuary, which involved the payment of tithes and offering of sacrifices, a trespass offering is required to atone for his failure in these respects.

The order of the offering of the sacrifices is trespass, sin, burnt offering. The fact that the meal offering for these three sacrifices is three tenth parts of fine flour justifies the conclusion that a meal offering was to be offered with each of the three sacrifices, since one-tenth was the regular meal offering with a lamb (Nu. xxix. 4; Ex. xxix. 40).

Although the leper is constantly described as 'unclean' and not as a sinner, despite the fact that the 'stroke' of leprosy may, as in the case of Miriam, be the punishment for grievous sin, it seems proper to see in the fact that leprosy is dealt with so elaborately, an indication that this particularly loathsome and intractable disease is to be regarded as a type of that indwelling sin in which all the afflictions and ills of mankind have their cause and origin. If death is the curse pronounced by God upon sin and contact with death is defiling, then disease which undermines health and is a stepping-stone to death carries with it a certain defilement whether it be infectious in the medical sense or not. We cannot affirm with certainty that the mention of hyssop in Ps. li ('purge me with hyssop, and I shall be clean') contains an allusion to the cleansing of the leper and justifies the inference that David is thinking of himself as a moral leper. But it seems not improbable.

iv. **Leprous houses in the land of Canaan (xiv. 33–57).** The leprosy of a house is dealt with separately because it concerns the future. *When ye be come into the land of Canaan* (xiv. 34). Cf. xix. 23, xxiii. 10, xxv. 2, which also refer to this future time. Israel was at the moment dwelling in tents; and the leprosy of stone houses was a matter which did not yet concern them. The words *and I put the plague of leprosy in a house* (xiv. 34) are decidedly arresting. They suggest, and have been taken to imply, a special supernatural plague visited upon a house because of the sin of its builder (like leprosy in an individual). But it is to be remembered that the Bible frequently ignores secondary causes and agencies. We note here the same regard for property as in the case of the garment. The destruction is to be restricted as much as possible. It is also to be noted that the ritual for the cleansing of the house is the same as that prescribed for the first stage in the cleansing of the leper, that which restored him to the congregation of Israel.

d. Uncleanness due to issues (xv. 1–33)

Since this chapter deals with matters of sex, it stands in close relation with chapter xii and must be interpreted on the same general principles. The conditions which are dealt with are both normal and abnormal. But in either case they are treated as defiling. In the case of the former, the uncleanness usually lasts only until sunset and is removed by washing with water. In the latter case, the uncleanness continues for seven days after normal health has been restored. Then the man or the woman shall bring to the priest an offering consisting of two birds, one of which shall be offered as a sin offering, the other as a burnt offering (14f., 29f., cf. v. 7–10). In both cases it is said that the priest shall *make an atonement* by means of the sacrifices. Whatever the nature of the uncleanness, every person who comes in contact with the unclean person or thing shall bathe, wash his clothes and be unclean until the evening.

The law of Moses refers elsewhere to a number of diseases besides those dealt with here (cf. xxvi. 16, 25; Dt. xxviii. 22, 27f., 35). It is perhaps significant that it does not refer to them here in dealing with the subject of uncleanness. Abnormalities and deformities are dealt with in xxi. 16ff.; Dt. xxiii. 1. *Thus shall ye separate* (31) refers primarily to the uncleannesses mentioned in chapter xv as is indicated by the summary which follows (32f.). But it is applicable to all the defilements mentioned in chapters xi—xv.

IV. THE DAY OF ATONEMENT. xvi. 1–34

The day of atonement (xxiii. 27f., xxv. 9) is the most important of all the holy ordinances with which the book of Leviticus is concerned, for it was the day on which atonement was made for *all* the sins of *all* the congregation of Israel (see verses 16f., 21f., 30, 33f.). In this respect it stands apart from all other private and public ordinances connected with the worship of Israel. It is also signalized by the fact that it is the only day in the year for which fasting is required: *ye shall afflict your souls* (29, 31, xxiii. 27, 32; Nu. xxix. 7). This phrase might also be rendered 'humble yourselves'. Arrogant self-sufficiency and self-will were characteristic of Israel from the beginning (cf. Dt. viii. 2, 3, 16 where the same verb is used), and it was met with constant reproof and chastening. Fasting would be the outward expression of their sorrow and repentance. In this regard the day of atonement stands in marked contrast to the annual feasts which were times of rejoicing, especially the feast of tabernacles (xxiii. 40; cf. Dt. xii. 7, 12). In view of this, its position in the book may

properly be regarded as significant. The fact that the full description of its ritual is given here instead of in Lv. xxiii which describes all the feasts, or in Nu. xxviii, xxix, which prescribe the special offerings for each of them, seems to be intended to emphasize both its importance and its uniqueness. It stands by itself among all the public ordinances prescribed for Israel. On the other hand, like many of the other ordinances, it is given a definite occasion or historical setting, the death of Nadab and Abihu for sacrilege (1). In fact some scholars regard the words *after the death of the two sons of Aaron* (1) as implying so close a connection between this chapter and chapter x that they are inclined to regard xi–xv as an insertion. Were this the case, it is difficult to understand why this insertion should consist only of these chapters and not include xvii–xxii, especially since it is in them that the moral element predominates over the ceremonial.

The chapter has both a backward and a forward reference. The one concerns especially Aaron and the priests (cf. Nu. iv. 17f.) and is to warn them against sacrilege and the frightful danger which attends it. The other is the application to the people. The grace of God in providing an all-sufficient atonement for sins of ignorance and frailty is set forth before the more heinous transgressions are described. The sins for which there is no forgiveness, which are to be punished by excision or death (see especially chapter xx), stand out in all their moral hideousness in the light of the seven times repeated 'all' of this chapter. The implication is clear that such sins as those for which there is no forgiveness (sins of presumption, of 'the high hand') prove the perpetrator to be no true Israelite at all, but a moral leper unworthy of the covenanted mercies of the God of Abraham and Moses. The tendency in Rabbinical Judaism has been to make this atonement all-inclusive. But such an interpretation is clearly excluded by the fact that the entire generation of wrath perished for disobedience in the wilderness (cf. Heb. x. 28). Whatever the explanation, the position of this chapter is certainly a significant one.

a. Aaron's preparation (xvi. 1–10)

Speak unto Aaron thy brother (2). Cf. Ex. xxviii. 1ff. It seems clear that the choice of Aaron for this high office was primarily due to his relationship to Moses (Ex. iv. 14) as was his choice to be Moses' 'prophet'. It was Moses' intercession which saved Aaron after the sin of the golden calf (Dt. ix. 20). The Bible both recognizes (Gn. xxi. 13) and ignores human relationships (Ex. xxxii. 27). Since Aaron and his sons have been mentioned already about sixty times in Leviticus, the words *Aaron thy brother* may suggest the loving care with which Moses is to impress this law upon him, *that he die not* (2). But cf. Ex. xxviii. 1–4. It is this fact which made the attitude of Aaron and Miriam described in Nu. xii. 1f. such a personal grief to Moses as well as so serious a challenge to the unique position assigned him by God Himself. *The holy place* (2) means the holy of holies as is indicated by the words *within the vail* (2; cf. verses 3, 16, 17, 20, 27). Every one of the sacrifices described or ordered in chapters i–xv is included in this prohibition. Most of the ritual of sacrifices was conducted in the court. Only exceptionally was the blood of the sacrifices brought into the holy place. Now the one occasion on which it may be brought 'within the vail' and into the holy of holies is dealt with in careful detail. When he does this, Aaron is to wash himself and then put on linen garments (the symbol of purity) instead of the usual ornate apparel distinctive of the High Priest. The sacrifices he is to offer are of two kinds: for himself and his sons, a young bullock for a sin offering and a ram for a burnt offering; for the people, two he-goats for a sin offering and a ram for a burnt offering.

Verses 6–10 give a brief and partial summary of the procedure as regards the sin offerings. The bullock and the goats are both presented before the Lord and the lot is cast over the two goats.

b. The sin offering for the priests (xvi. 11–14)

These verses describe the ritual for Aaron's bullock which is presented before the Lord. *And shall make an atonement for himself, and for his house* (11) apparently refers to the laying on of hands, either by himself alone as representing also his sons, or by his sons also. He is to fill the entire censer (lit. 'the fulness of the censer') with coals from the altar of burnt offering and to take two handfuls (lit. 'the fulness of his (two) hands') of incense. There is to be a great cloud of incense sufficient to cover the mercy seat *that he die not* (13). The blood is to be sprinkled with his finger upon the front of the mercy seat and before it, seven times.

c. The people's sin offering (xvi. 15–19)

The ritual for the goat which is the sin offering of the people is now described. Apparently the cloud of incense in the holy of holies suffices for both sin offerings; and the blood is to be similarly manipulated. The reason for this is stated with great care. Aaron is to 'make atonement for the holy place, because of the uncleannesses of the children of Israel, and because of their transgressions, even all their sins' (16, RV). For their sins have defiled it. Note that this cleansing is to include the entire tent of meeting and the altar of burnt offering (20).

d. The scapegoat (xvi. 20–22)

The live goat (20) has already been referred to in verses 8–10. The AV rendering *scapegoat* and the RV rendering 'Azazel' in verses 8 and 10 represent the principal interpretations of the meaning of this remarkable ritual. The former rendering is an ancient one, being supported by the LXX and the Vulg. It is based on the assumption that the word *azazel* comes from a root '*azal* meaning 'to remove' (such a reduplicated form would be

rare, but not without analogy). The chief argument in its favour is that it is scriptural and appropriate. The thought of removal of guilt is closely related to that of atonement for sin. Ps. ciii. 12, 'As far as the east is from the west, so far hath he removed our transgressions from us', perfectly expresses this idea. That this is the meaning is indicated by the emphasis which is placed on the words *send away* or *let go* (10, 21, 22), *wilderness* (10, 21, 22) and *not inhabited* (22; RV 'solitary land'). The rendering 'Azazel' takes the word as a proper name. In its favour is the fact that 'for Azazel' (10) seems to stand in contrast with 'for the Lord' (9). But if it is the name of a well-known demon of the desert or a name of Satan, it is strange that it should occur only here in the entire Bible. And if the reference is to a demon whom Israel feared, who exerted a powerful influence upon them and needed to be appeased, it is hard to understand why emphasis should be placed on the remoteness of the abode of this menacing being, a remoteness which might increase as Israel journeyed to Palestine. Sin is not a remote but an ever-present factor in the life of man (Gn. iv. 7). Furthermore the idea of atonement for sin as involving a ransom or sin offering to Satan, or to an unknown demon of the desert (and still more the idea of the goat bearing to the demon the tidings that atonement for sin has been made), seems improbable to say the least. Cf. xvii. 7 which forbids any such recognition of satyrs or of demon worship. It may be too much to say that this explanation is 'quite untenable'; but it seems to involve far more serious difficulties than does the other.

e. The offerings completed (xvi. 23–28)

After Aaron has performed those duties which require him to enter the holy of holies, he is to lay aside his linen garments, bathe, and then put on the regular garb of the High Priest, which is so fully described elsewhere, and which is stated to be 'for glory and for beauty' (Ex. xxviii. 2). Then he is to come forth from the holy place and complete the ritual in the outer court, the offering of his burnt offering and that for the people, also to burn the fat of the sin offering since it is only the manipulation of the blood which has thus far been described. This is to be done in the usual manner.

f. Some further instructions (xvi. 29–34)

This special day is to be *a statute for ever* (29). The rite is to be observed *once a year* (34) on the tenth day of the seventh month, and it is to be comprehensive, for the sanctuary and the priests who minister there and for the children of Israel, *for all their sins* (34). In verse 29, for the first time in Leviticus, the stranger (*ger*) is mentioned. (See Dt. i. 16n.) While he has no part in this national rite, he is to conform to its requirements (cf. Ex. xii. 19, 48f.). The Decalogue and the book of the covenant both recognize and provide for the presence of these 'strangers' in Israel. In view of the privileges which they enjoy they must conform to many of Israel's laws and customs (cf. xvii. 8, 10, 12, 13, 15).

Note that we are told that Aaron *did as the Lord commanded Moses* (34; cf. xxiv. 23). This must mean, as stated above, that the national apostasy at Kadesh did not take place until after the first observance of the day of atonement. That it could not have been observed subsequent to the apostasy and during the years of wandering is indicated by three facts. First, exclusion from the land was the punishment for refusal to take possession of it. This penalty was paid in full by the generation which transgressed: it was not remitted. Secondly, circumcision was not practised during the years of wandering (Jos. v. 1–9), although it was the indispensable sign and seal of the covenant (Gn. xvii. 9–14). Thirdly, Am. v. 25f. indicates that Israel fell away into idolatry during this period (cf. Acts vii. 42f.).

In view of the singular importance which attaches to this day—the later Jews have called it 'the Day' (*yoma*)—it is remarkable that no express reference to its observance is to be found anywhere in the Old Testament (Is. lviii. 3 is too general to appeal to). This is hard to account for, especially since mention of it would seem to be natural and appropriate in connection with the events described in 1 Ki. viii. 2, 65f.; Ezr. iii. 1–6; Ne. viii, all of which were important events which took place in the seventh month at about the time of the day of atonement. It is to be noted, however, that the Old Testament mentions only four Passovers (those of Joshua, Hezekiah, Josiah, Ezra) in treating of a period of about 1,000 years; also that from the time of the renewal of the covenant by Joshua no mention is made of the covenant rite of circumcision, except by implication (e.g., the Philistines are described as uncircumcised), or in a figurative sense (Je. vi. 10, ix. 26). The argument from silence, the inference that failure to mention a rite means that it had not yet been introduced, proves too much. It would place the date of the institution of this rite after the time of Ezra and Nehemiah. Furthermore it is to be noted that the sacrifices of this day are the only ones which are directly connected with the ark. The blood of the sin offerings for Aaron and the people was to be sprinkled on or toward the mercy seat. The Hebrew word for mercy seat is *kapporeth* (covering or expiation). It was pre-eminently the place of atonement. Hence the name, *yom kippur* (day of atonement). Yet Jeremiah definitely foretells the time when the ark will be forgotten (iii. 16); and we know that after the Babylonian captivity the ark was not brought back with the other sacred vessels. There was no ark in Zerubbabel's temple nor in that of Herod. Consequently this connection with the ark points to an early date for the introduction of this rite.

It is particularly to be stressed that while, as we have seen, the Old Testament is practically silent with regard to the post-Mosaic celebration of this all-important rite, the writer of the Epistle to the Hebrews represents it as that rite of the Mosaic covenant which most clearly sets forth the atoning work of Christ; both by way of resemblance and of contrast (Heb. ix, x). The High Priest alone could enter the holy of holies. He did this 'once every year' (ix. 7), and he offered sacrifices for himself and for the people, and then he came forth from the sanctuary. The Lord Jesus entered 'once' (ix. 12, 26, x. 12–14) into the heavenly sanctuary offering once for all His own blood, not for Himself, but only for the sins of others and, having purchased an eternal redemption by His blood, He will come again from the heavenly sanctuary to bless His saints whom He has redeemed. See also the notes on the significance of the sacrificial ritual at the end of Section I (p. 141) and the Introduction (p. 134f.).

Since the destruction of the temple (by Nebuchadnezzar and again by Titus) and the loss of the ark made it quite impossible to carry out fully the ritual of sacrifice, which is the aspect particularly stressed both in this chapter in Leviticus and also in Hebrews, later Jews have been forced to regard 'afflicting their souls' (Lv. xvi. 29, 31), understood to mean repentance, restitution, good works, and suffering, as the only 'atonement' which God requires of the Jew for all his sins. Thus the words, 'without shedding of blood is no remission' (Heb. ix. 22), which epitomize the meaning of the Old Testament ritual of sacrifice—a ritual which, according to the law, finds its supreme illustration in the day of atonement and, according to the gospel, finds its fulfilment in the cross—become a dead letter to the modern Jew, as they do to the Unitarian, because the cross, of which the mercy seat of the ark is the type, is a stumbling block and a mystery to him.

V. THE PLACE OF SACRIFICE AND THE SANCTITY OF BLOOD. xvii. 1–16

It has been customary in critical circles for many years to treat xvii—xxvi as a distinct section and to call it 'the Holiness Code'. To do this destroys the close connection which clearly exists between chapters xvi and xvii and also between chapter xvii and the manual of sacrifice in chapters i—vii. Whatever may be said of xviii—xxvi, chapter xvii clearly belongs to what precedes. It may properly be regarded as supplementary, but a climactic supplement or conclusion to the first part of Leviticus.

Since the day of atonement exhibits in a superlative degree the significance of sacrifice in the life of the covenant people, and points out the unique sacredness of the blood in that on this one day the sacrificial blood is brought into the holiest place and sprinkled on the ark of the covenant itself, to obtain the remission of all the sins of all the people, it is appropriate that in this next chapter the two aspects of sacrifice which specially concern all the people should be particularly emphasized.

The introductory formula is specially impressive. Notice that it is all-inclusive as well as being very emphatic. *This is the thing which the Lord hath commanded* (2; cf. viii. 5, ix. 6). *What man soever there be of the house of Israel* (3). The universal application of the law now to be declared is specially emphasized (cf. verses 8, 10, 13). *Killeth* (3), the same word as occurs in i. 5, where it is used of the slaughtering of the animal which has been brought for sacrifice. The reference here is to the domestic animals which were regularly used for that purpose. They are to be brought to the door of the tabernacle and offered as peace offerings. This served both to gratify the desire of the people to eat flesh and also established the proprietary right of God, more particularly in those animals which were so often offered to Him in sacrifice. It had two further aims: to prevent eating blood (10ff.) and also to prevent the sacrificing of these animals *in the open field* (5); which is at once defined as offering them to 'he-goats' (RV) or satyrs, an act which was not only idolatry (xix. 4, xxvi. 1, 30) but was accompanied by orgiastic rites (7). Cf. Ex. xxxiv. 15f.; Lv. xx. 5f. This indicates that such idolatrous practices were common among the Israelites at the time of the Exodus, having been learned by them in Egypt. The worship of Pan flourished, as we know, in ancient Greece and Rome. Consequently this law was not primarily a requirement that the Israelites sacrifice these animals to the Lord as peace offerings instead of simply devouring them anywhere they pleased, but rather that they offer them to the Lord instead of sacrificing them to the 'he-goats'. It is the substitution of an act of true worship for one of idolatry and licence. And it shows plainly how deeply the sojourn in Egypt had influenced the life of Israel. *This shall be a statute for ever* (7). In its negative aspect, the prohibition of eating with the blood and of idolatrous practices, this statute was irrevocable under the Mosaic dispensation. On its positive side it was later modified by Moses to accord with the changed conditions which would result from settlement in the land (Dt. xii. 20–24), changes which affected the letter without changing the spirit of the law. The difference between Leviticus and Deuteronomy here shows clearly that the former preceded the latter and not vice versa.

Verses 8, 9 refer more particularly to a 'killing' which is intended to be an act of worship. This is indicated by the specific reference to *burnt offering* in addition to *sacrifice* (i.e. of peace offerings; see verse 5), since no part of the burnt offering was used as food.

I . . . will cut him off (10). Usually the passive is used (see verses 4, 9, 14 and vii. 20, 21, 27). Here, as in xx. 3, 5, 6, the stronger form is used. This has been understood to mean that the cutting off is to be an act of God. The sacredness of the blood is taught very early. Although in

other respects unlimited, the permission given to Noah regarding the eating of flesh was qualified by the words 'But flesh with the life thereof, which is the blood thereof, shall ye not eat' (Gn. ix. 4). Here the fact is repeated three times that the life of the animal is in the blood (11, 14); and it is to be regarded as sacred because God has made it the means of expiation for sin by requiring that it be presented upon His altar. Consequently, even in the case of animals not suited for sacrifice, the blood must be treated reverently. It must be poured out upon the ground and covered with dust (13; cf. Dt. xii. 16n.). Verses 15, 16 make a further exception. If a man eats flesh with the blood ignorantly, not realizing the way in which the animal had died (this must be the meaning), he shall bathe himself and be unclean until the evening.

It is noteworthy that while for the modern Jews the ritual of sacrifice has lost all meaning, they still adhere strictly to the requirement concerning eating with the blood. Blood is still sacred for them as the symbol of life and the sacredness of life, but not for the reason so emphatically stated in the Old Testament—its connection with atonement for sin. A strict Jew will eat only *kosher* meat, i.e. meat 'rightly' and 'properly' prepared.

VI. SINS AGAINST THE MORAL LAW. xviii. 1—xx. 27

a. Prohibited degrees and sensuality (xviii. 1–30)
The introduction (1–5) is very impressive. The Lord's people are to keep His commandments. Their standards are not to be determined by the practices of Egypt where they were in bondage or of Canaan which they are to possess. The statutes and ordinances of their God are to be their sole standard of conduct; and the reward of obedience is life (cf. Dt. xxx. 15–20). The sanction is: *I am the Lord your God* (2). That the 'abominations' about to be described were practised in Egypt, and even among other cultured nations of antiquity, is a well-known fact. Modern marriage laws are largely based on the limitations stated in this chapter. But they have not seldom been made more strict than the law requires.

The general principle involved is stated in verse 6: *None of you shall approach to any that is near of kin to him* (lit. 'the flesh of his flesh'). Consanguinity or affinity is referred to repeatedly (12, 13, 14, 15, 16, 17; cf. xx. 19); and it is stressed by such expressions as *she is thy mother* (7), *it is thy father's nakedness* (8), *for their's is thine own nakedness* (10). That this phrase 'uncover the nakedness of' refers to actual marriage is made especially clear by the words *in her life time* (18). Illicit intercourse would come under the general heading of adultery or harlotry and be condemned as such (Dt. xxii. 13–30). On the other hand the use of such an expression, instead of the usual phrase 'to take a wife', is probably intended to stress the fact that such unions as are condemned here and in chapter xx cannot be true marriage, and that they are due to passion rather than natural and holy affection. No other reason is given for these prohibitions, however, except the fact of kinship. This may imply that the intimacies which result from near kinship or affinity are such as to render marriage unnatural or improper. But it also seems to be well established as a fact of experience that marriages between near relations are likely either to be barren or to result in unhealthy offspring. The prohibition which has occasioned the most discussion and controversy is marriage with the deceased wife's sister (18), and it is only comparatively recently that it has been made legal in England. Yet the meaning of the law šeems to be 'clear. The words to vex her (18), 'to be a rival' (RV), 'to be a secondary wife' (all three are possible renderings), taken in connection with the words in her life time (18), indicate that such a marriage is not barred on grounds of affinity; it is lawful, but only after the death of the wife. This is intended to prevent a man from divorcing his wife in order to marry her sister, a temptation which might easily result from the intimacies of family life. It is to be noted that only in one case is a moral judgment passed on these practices which are prohibited (17).

Verse 19 apparently refers to the contracting and consummating of marriage. Cf. xx. 18 and xv. 24.

Verses 20–23 deal with particularly heinous sins. Adultery violates the sanctity of the home. It involves the breaking of two of the ten commandments (Ex. xx. 14, 17). It undermines the foundations of human society. In verse 21 follow RV 'Thou shalt not give any of thy seed to make them pass through to Molech'. This rendering makes it plain that the prohibition refers to the abhorrent practice of infant sacrifice and that this awful sin is the sin of the parent (cf. xx. 2–5). For an Israelite to do this is to profane the name of his God. Other monstrous and unnatural sins are particularly denounced (22, 23). They are abomination and confusion. Yet most, if not all, of them were widely practised among the cultured peoples of antiquity.

Verses 24–30 form a concluding summary. These things are heathen practices which Israel is particularly to avoid. The promise to dispossess the Canaanites is coupled with the solemn warning to Israel of similar treatment in case of similar conduct. The sequence of tenses is difficult. Which I cast out (24) is a participle and would be better rendered, 'Which I am casting (or, going to cast) out'. It refers to the (imminent) future. AV and RV render most of the verbs in verses 25, 27 in the present tense. But the sequence of tenses would favour making them refer to the past, especially in view of their rendering of the last verb in verse 28, as it spued out (RV, 'vomited out') the nations (RV 'nation') that were before you. It is to be noted, therefore,

that this verb is ambiguous. If accented on the penult, it is the perfect tense (AV, RV, LXX, Vulg., Syr.). If accented on the ultima (the Massoretes), it is a participle, and may, like the participle in verse 24, refer to the future. The former rendering seems definitely preferable. Unless the use of the past tense is regarded as proleptic, which is unlikely, we must then face the fact that past and premonitory judgments are here referred to. We have very little information on this subject. The fact that ten nations occupied the land in the days of Abraham (Gn. xv. 19ff.) may mean that it had been a bone of contention for centuries; and that these nations lived peaceably together seems highly improbable. Situated at the bridgehead between Asia and Africa, the land was singularly exposed to the ravages of invading armies. The words 'the iniquity of the Amorites is not yet full' (Gn. xv. 16) suggest that there may have been severe visitations of judgment in the past. Famine, pestilence, the sword, and evil beasts (Lv. xxvi; cf. Ezk. xiv. 21) may have already taken a heavy toll. There may be more truth in the evil report of the spies than we might be inclined to suppose: 'a land that eateth up the inhabitants thereof' (Nu. xiii. 32). 'Eat up' and 'vomit out' suggest disorders that would decimate the inhabitants of the land and drive many of them into exile. But however severe these former judgments may have been, and they must have been sufficiently severe and also recent to be referred to here, they are only a foretaste, so to speak, of the judgment which is about to fall on the Canaanites, and which surely will be visited on Israel also if she follows their example. Those who regard the command to exterminate the Canaanites as 'cruel' should consider carefully the reason which is given for it. The impressive sanction, I am the Lord (your God) appears in 2, 4, 5, 21, 30.

b. A collection of sundry laws (xix. 1–37)

These laws are so various that it is difficult to classify them. They are introduced by the solemn exhortation Ye shall be holy : for I the Lord your God am holy (2), and fifteen times the words I am the Lord (your God) are repeated in its thirty-seven verses. They are both ceremonial and ethical, and the latter belong to both of the tables of the Decalogue. Thus verses 3 and 4 are covered by the fifth, fourth, and second commandments of the Decalogue. Honouring of parents, keeping of the sabbath, shunning of idolatry are placed first as particularly important. The phrasing of the first of these, 'a man (i.e., every one of you) his mother and his father ye shall fear', is striking and unusual (cf. xxi. 11). That 'fear' is sometimes used in the sense of 'revere or reverence' is made clear by verse 30 where 'fear my sanctuary' appears as reverence in AV and RV. Cf. Dt. vi where 'love the Lord' (5) is preceded (2) and followed (13) by 'fear the Lord' and see Dt. ix. 19n. 'Love' to God is not demanded in Leviticus and love to man only in

xix. 18, 34. But it is to be remembered that it is referred to in the Decalogue (Ex. xx. 6) and quite frequently in Deuteronomy.

Verses 5–8 concern the eating of the flesh of peace offerings (cf. vii. 15–18). The law regarding gleanings (9, 10) comes under the general summary of the second table of the Decalogue, which enjoins love of one's neighbour (cf. xxiii. 22; Dt. xxiv. 19–22). Verses 11 and 12 rest upon the eighth and third commandments. Verses 13 and 14 are closely related to the eighth commandment and the principle of humanity underlying it. Verses 15 and 16 are an exposition of the ninth commandment. Verses 17 and 18 stand in close relation to the tenth commandment and conclude with those words which represent the summary of the second table, *thou shalt love thy neighbour as thyself* (18). 'Neighbour' seems here to refer to the fellow-Israelite. Note the words *children of thy people* (18) which immediately precede. Its use in Ex. iii. 22 of the Egyptians does not prove a wider range for its ordinary use, since the conditions in Egypt were abnormal and Israel in Canaan was to be a separated people. But the broader meaning is indicated, or the meaning is broadened, by verse 34, where the law of love is extended to include the non-Israelite *sojourner* (*ger*). This fact is beautifully illustrated by Jesus' choice of the Samaritan to determine the meaning and scope of the word 'neighbour' (Lk. x. 33). See Dt. x. 18n. and cf. note on Lv. xxv. 35–55. In the case of verses 19–37 which begin and conclude with an exhortation to obedience, it almost seems as if an element of contrast had been intentionally introduced to emphasize the fact that every department and phase of life is covered by the ordinances of God. Thus the law of purity is to apply to the breeding of cattle, the sowing of seed and the texture of garments (19), and also to the planting of fruit trees (23–25). Cf. Dt. xxii. 9–11. But in between them is placed the law governing the trespass with a bondwoman (20–22). As regards the first of these prohibitions, since the word 'cattle' is broader than 'herd' and 'flock', and includes both clean and unclean animals, this law must be regarded as prohibiting the breeding of mules. Consequently, mules in the Old Testament, first mentioned in David's time, are properly to be regarded as a foreign importation (cf. 1 Ki. x. 25). Verses 26–28 may all be classed as heathen practices to be condemned as such. The same is true of verse 31. Similarly the sin of prostitution (29) is probably mentioned here for the same reason, as being a heathen practice. On the other hand, verse 30, enjoining reverence for the sabbath and the sanctuary, while referring back to verse 3 would seem to connect naturally with verse 32. The law of the stranger (33, 34) forms the counterpart of 17, 18, expanding the scope of the law already given. Verses 35 and 36 further apply the eighth commandment; and the chapter concludes with the oft-repeated reminder *I am the Lord your God, which brought you out of the land of Egypt* (36 ; cf. xi. 45, xxii. 33; Dt. v. 15, etc.).

c. Sundry laws regarding very heinous offences (xx. 1–27)

Again (2; RV 'moreover') is simply 'and' in Hebrew and joins this chapter closely with the preceding. Molech worship has already been briefly denounced (xviii. 21). But here, as in the rest of the chapter, severe penalties are pronounced on those who are guilty of some of the offences already described. Molech was the god of the Ammonites (1 Ki. xi. 7). The name contains the same consonants as the word 'king' (*melek*) apparently combined with the vowels of the word meaning 'shame' (*bosheth*), to change the word from an honourable title to one of dishonour. It is always written with the article 'the Molech', as if an appellative. This form of idolatry was particularly repulsive because it involved human sacrifice, the offering of children or infants, to the idol. The exact nature of this horrible rite is not certainly known. It has been interpreted as an act of purgation which did not involve death; as a sacrifice which resembled animal sacrifices in this respect, that the victim was first slain and its body then burned as an offering to the idol (Ezk. xvi. 20f. hardly justifies this interpretation); as a sacrifice in which the victims were actually burned alive. That human sacrifice is meant seems to be clearly taught in Ps. cvi. 38; Je. vii. 31, xix. 4f.; Ezk. xxiii. 37–39; Mic. vi. 7. And it is quite possible that the Phoenician practice of placing living infants in the arms of the idol to perish in the flames burning within it is what is meant, which would account for the severity with which it is denounced. Dt. xii. 31 implies that this awful practice was not confined to the worship of a single god, but was a prominent feature of Canaanite worship in general. This grievous sin is to be punished by stoning. Note the words *to defile my sanctuary, and to profane my holy name* (3) which indicate that this act was not merely horrible in itself but a gratuitous and intentional defiance of the exclusive right of Jehovah, as the covenant God of Israel, to the worship of His people, and one which the Lord would not permit to go unpunished. If the people ignore or condone it, He will not do so, but will cut off the man and those who participate with him (5).

The means by which Israel's neighbours sought to ascertain and if possible control the future are next condemned (cf. xix. 31) and the penalty of excision is pronounced (6). Cf. verse 27 which orders the death of the medium and see Ex. xxii. 18. The words *go a whoring* (6) apparently connect this sin closely with that of verses 2–5. In Dt. xviii. 9–14 both are included among the means of ascertaining the future.

Verses 7 and 8 contain a solemn exhortation to holiness (cf. xviii. 1–5, xix. 1, 2) and to the keeping of the commandments of God, which has both a backward and a forward reference. That 9–21 deal with some of the most heinous of the sins already mentioned in chapters xviii—xix is indicated by comparing verse 9 with xix. 3. Cursing of father or mother is a grievous violation of the fifth commandment. Adultery, incest, unnatural vice, bestiality are to be most severely punished. The fact that the phrase *uncover the nakedness*, which occurs frequently in chapter xviii, also appears seven times in this chapter and nowhere else in the Pentateuch, indicates the close connection between these two passages. The penalties are variously described: *shall surely be put to death* (10, 12, 13, 15), *stone him with stones* (2, 27, cf. xxiv. 14ff.), *burnt with fire* (14, cf. xxi. 9), *cut off* (5, 17, 18), *bear iniquity* (17, 19), *bear their sin; they shall die childless* (20), *they shall be childless* (21). Note also the words used to describe these crimes: *wrought confusion* (12), *committed an abomination* (13), *wickedness* (14, 17), *an unclean thing* (21; 'impurity' RV).

Verses 22–26 remind the Israelites that the enormities just described are those of the people whose land they are to possess. It has 'vomited out' (cf. xviii. 25) its inhabitants for their abominations, and Israel will suffer the same fate if she practises them (cf. xviii. 28). Yet the land is their inheritance and it is a goodly land (Ex. iii. 8, 17). The Lord has 'separated' them (24). Note the fourfold use of this word in verses 24–26 (see RV). This section indicates quite clearly that a principal aim of the dietary laws of chapter xi was to make and promote a definite separation between Israel and the Canaanites. Since eating and drinking was an important part of the daily life of the people, and since verses 22–26 serve as a kind of conclusion to this great body of laws, ceremonial and moral, which the people are to observe, a reference back to chapter xi with which it begins is entirely appropriate. *That ye should be mine* (26). Here the whole aim of the law is briefly summarized. The Lord's people must keep His law if they are to be truly His.

Verse 27 is simply the further application of verse 6. The mediums who lead the people astray are to be punished by stoning (2, cf. xxiv. 14f.). By returning again to this subject, the heinousness of this sin (cf. Dt. xviii. 9–14) is particularly stressed. It is a sin of idolatry, and Israel must shun idolatry in every form.

VII. INSTRUCTIONS FOR THE PRIESTS. xxi. 1—xxii. 33

a. The priests must be holy (xxi. 1–9)

If the people are to separate themselves from everything evil, how much more so the priests! They are not to defile themselves (xxi. 1, 3, 4), nor to profane the name of their God (6); they are to be holy to Him (6, 7) and must be treated as such (8). The reasons given are their high rank—a priest is *a chief man among his people* (4) —and *the offerings of the Lord made by fire, and the bread of their God, they do offer* (6), a statement which makes it clear that the offering of sacrifice was their chief function. *The bread*

(food) *of their God* is a phrase used frequently in this chapter (6, 8, 17, 21, 22; cf. xxii. 25, also iii. 11, 16).

The particular matter first dealt with is defilement by contact with the dead. This they must avoid, except in the case of their next of kin. Death being the penalty of sin, contact with it was defiling. The failure to mention the wife when mother, father, son, daughter, and sister are specified must mean that the wife's position is unique. She is not *his kin, that is near unto him* (2) but 'one flesh' with him (Gn. ii. 24); to mention her would be superfluous. The command to abstain from pagan practices is one which applies to priest and people alike (cf. xix. 27f.; Dt. xiv. 1). A priest must obviously be exemplary in all his conduct. He will of course marry. But he must marry a virtuous woman and one who has not been divorced. Again the reason is repeated: he ministers in holy things (7, 8). For the daughter of a priest to become a harlot is especially heinous and to be most severely punished.

b. Special rules for the High Priest (xxi. 10–15)

In view of the unique holiness of the High Priest, the rules against defilement are more rigid than in the case of the ordinary priest. This is because the consecration of his God is upon him. The holy oil has been poured on his head and he wears the holy garments. He may not exhibit the usual tokens of grief and may not defile himself with any dead body, the exceptions made for the ordinary priest being definitely withdrawn. The direction that he is not to leave the sanctuary (12) probably means not to leave it in order to do honour to the dead, not that he was always to stay in the courts of the tabernacle. A further restriction is that he must marry a virgin of his own people. His wife must be a daughter of Israel. *Neither shall he profane* (15); better as in RV 'and he shall not (by so doing) profane his seed', i.e. render them unfit for holy office, or to share in holy things by an unworthy marriage.

c. The effect of physical deformity (xxi. 16–24)

Just as the animals offered in sacrifice must be without blemish, so must the priests be who offer them. But those who are debarred from serving at the altar are to be permitted to eat of the holy things which are the priest's portion. Mention is made of abnormalities both of deficiency and of excess, e.g., six fingers instead of five. Castration came under this head, and eunuchs were barred from the congregation (Dt. xxiii. 1; cf. Is. lvi. 3ff.).

d. Defilement disqualifies the priest from touching holy things (xxii. 1–16)

While the priests are set apart to be holy ministers of the sanctuary, it is to be observed that they are liable to the same uncleannesses as are the laity. In addition to such abnormalities as have been mentioned above, a priest may become a leper, he may have an issue, or he may have come in contact with that which is unclean. This uncleanness makes him a source of pollution as long as it lasts and he must not touch any consecrated or holy thing lest he defile it. The principles laid down here have already been stated elsewhere. Cf. Heb. v. 2, vii. 28. A distinction is drawn between the family of the priest and his slaves on the one hand and a sojourner or hireling (10, 11). While the latter belong to the household of the priest, this does not entitle them to eat of the holy things. But a childless widow who returns to her father's house becomes once more a member of his family. A man who eats of the holy thing without being aware that he is doing so must replace it and as in the case of the trespass offering he is to add one fifth to it.

e. Rules for the offering of sacrifices (xxii. 17–33)

They must be *without blemish* (19), a law which concerns both priests and people even including the strangers (18). See Ex. xii. 5n. This is essential 'that ye may be accepted' (19, RV; cf. i. 3n.). The only exception is the freewill offering (23). Verse 24 refers to the gelding of animals. RV interprets this verse to mean that gelding was absolutely prohibited. 'Neither shall ye do this in your land.' This was the view of Josephus (*Antiq.* iv. 8, 40). AV understands it to apply only to animals intended for sacrifice (cf. RV mg.). The requirement that the animal be *seven days under the dam* (27) apparently means that not until then was it to be regarded as having an independent existence (cf. the law regarding circumcision, Gn. xvii. 12). The law forbidding the slaying of the mother and her young on the same day (28) suggests the thrice-repeated prohibition of the seething of a kid in its mother's milk (Ex. xxiii. 19, xxxiv. 26; Dt. xiv. 21). Apparently both were designed to impress upon the Israelite the fact that the strong tie which binds the members of the human family together has its counterpart in the affection which the lower animals show toward their young, protecting them even at the cost of life, and so to prohibit wanton cruelty. Such acts might be required by, and pleasing to, a Chemosh or Molech, but not to the God of Israel. See also note on Dt. xiv. 21. Verses 29, 30 stipulate that a sacrifice of thanksgiving must be eaten the same day. See vii. 15n. All of these commandments have the sanction, *I am the Lord.* To break them is to *profane* His holy name. By their very diversity they make it clear that the law of the Lord is to govern the life of Israel, priest and people, in all its aspects and in every detail.

VIII. THE HOLY CONVOCATIONS.
xxiii. 1–44

In this chapter we have a list of those meetings (Heb. *mo'edh*; the same word is used as in the phrase 'tent of meeting'), or 'appointed seasons', which were to be proclaimed as *holy convocations*

(2). This word *mo'edh* is rendered *feast* in AV, as is also another word, *hag*. RV renders the former by 'set feast' with margin 'appointed season', the other by 'feast', with a view to distinguishing them. The emphasis in the case of the former word is apparently on the time. Hence a literal rendering of verse 4 would be: 'These are the meetings (appointed seasons) of the Lord, even holy convocations, which ye shall proclaim in their appointed seasons.' The joyousness of most of these occasions is indicated by the fact that the word *feast* (*hag*) is also used of them. They are called *convocations* because the people were called together by the blowing of the silver trumpets (Nu. x. 1–10).

a. The sabbath (xxiii. 3)

God's resting on the seventh day is referred to in Gn. ii. 3 and there are various indications of the keeping of a seven-day week (Gn. xxix. 27) and of the sacredness of the number seven (e.g. Nu. xxiii. 1). But it is in connection with the giving of the manna that the sacredness of this day as a day of rest for Israel is first made clear (Ex. xvi. 5, 22–30). The giving of a double portion on the sixth day freed Israel from all necessity to work on that day; and God's resting on the seventh day from the providing of the manna was a reminder of His resting on that day from the work of creation. The same words, though not the same phrase, are used to describe it here as in Ex. xvi. It is a 'sabbath of solemn rest' (*shabbath shabbathon*). Here, as in Ex. xx. 9 and Dt. v. 13, the command to work on the six days is coupled with the command to rest on the seventh. A man who works on week-days is entitled to the rest of the Lord's day. The resting on this day is much more complete than in the case of the other set feasts which prohibit only *servile work*, or 'work of service' (RV mg.; see verses 7, 8, 21, 25, 35, 36), which apparently prohibits only the carrying on of one's ordinary business or the performance of manual labour, but not the preparation of food. Consequently, while the sabbath is a holy convocation, it differs from the other set feasts in this most important respect. It also differs in the fact that it is observed weekly while they are annual. In this we have also a definite indication that the regular, frequently occurring, weekly sabbath was intended to be a holier day than any of the set feasts. Yet in the history of the Church there has been a strong tendency, as there is today, to stress the importance of special occasions and to minimize that of the Lord's day, the first day of the week which is the only holy day expressly sanctioned in the New Testament. See note on Dt. v. 12ff.

b. The Passover and the feast of unleavened bread (xxiii. 4–8)

Since the sabbath differs from all the other set feasts in several important respects it is separated from them by verse 4 which serves the place of a heading to introduce the annual feasts. See Ex. xxiii. 14-17; Dt. xvi. First among the annual feasts is the Passover (5). No description is given since it has been fully described already in the account of its institution. See Ex. xii and notes there. The same is true of the feast of unleavened bread which is so closely connected with it (6-8). Nu. xxviii. 16-25 goes much more into detail with regard to the ritual for this feast.

c. The offering of firstfruits (xxiii. 9-14)

This is the third of four laws (cf. xiv. 34, xix. 23, xxv. 2) which apply to the future occupancy of the land. *A sheaf ('omer) of the firstfruits* (10; cf. Dt. xxiv. 19; Ru. ii. 7, 15) is to be presented as a 'wave offering' (ix. 21, xiv. 12, 24). Since the same word is used of a dry measure (Ex. xvi. 16ff.), defined as the tenth part of an ephah (Ex. xvi. 36), the view is held that the sheaf must contain enough grain (barley, since barley ripens two or three weeks before wheat) to produce an omer of fine flour for a meal offering. In the phrase *the morrow after the sabbath* (11) 'sabbath' has two possible meanings. It may refer to the regular weekly sabbath, which has just been mentioned, or to the Passover as the day of holy convocation, which was followed by the week of unleavened bread. The Pharisees took the one view, the Sadducees the other. This offering of the sheaf was to be accompanied by a burnt offering, with meal and drink offerings (12, 13). On this occasion the size of the meal offering is double the usual.

Here the drink offering is mentioned for the first time in Leviticus. It has been already referred to in Ex. xxix. 38-42 in the law regarding the continual burnt offering. Why there is no reference to it in Lv. i—vii which deals particularly with the sacrifices is not clear. The fact that it is mentioned so frequently in connection with the offerings for the set feasts might suggest that it was not, or need not be, offered on ordinary occasions or in the case of private offerings. But Nu. vi. 17 and xv. 1-12 indicate that such an inference is unwarranted. It was apparently never an independent offering under the law, but accompanied the meal offering. This may be the reason why it is not mentioned in chapters i—vii. A further reason may be that it was not to be offered until Israel entered the land (xxiii. 10). But this reason did not apply to the continual burnt offering, which is not mentioned in Leviticus but has been already described in Ex. xxix. 38-42.

The offering of the firstfruits symbolized the consecration of the entire harvest to God; and not until it was offered were the people permitted to partake of it (14). This law has a definitely typical significance and is referred to in the New Testament. It is used of the Gentile Christians (Rom. viii. 23), of the ancestors of the Jews (Rom. xi. 16), of individual Christians (Rom. xvi. 5) and of Christ as the firstfruits from the grave (1 Cor. xv. 20, 23). See also 1 Cor. xvi. 15; Jas. i. 18; Rev. xiv. 4.

d. The feast of weeks (xxiii. 15-22)

The fact that this feast is not introduced by the words 'And the Lord spake unto Moses, saying' has led to the inference that Pentecost (*shabhu'oth*) is a continuation or complement of the Passover. In the Talmud it is called '*aşarta* (cf. xxiii. 36 where this word is used of the eighth day of the feast of tabernacles and rendered 'an holy convocation'). Seven weeks are to be counted from the sabbath (see above) on which the wave offering of the firstfruits was made. Then a new meal offering in the form of two wave loaves is to be offered. They are to be of fine flour, baked *with leaven* and are described as *the firstfruits unto the Lord* (17). Since the daily bread of the Israelites was leavened, this naturally implies the consecration of the daily food of the people to God. The offerings consist of burnt, sin and peace offerings. Since this marked the end of the harvest of wheat, it is appropriate that the law regarding gleaning should be repeated here (see xix. 9). See Dt. xvi. 9-12n.

e. The feasts of the seventh month (xxiii. 23-44)

In view of the sacredness of the number seven, it is natural that the seventh month should be made distinctive. It has three special occasions: the feast of trumpets, the day of atonement, the feast of tabernacles.

i. The feast of trumpets (xxiii. 24, 25).

This is briefly described. The blowing of trumpets on the first day of the month directed especial attention to this important season of the year, the completion of the agricultural season. It was to be marked by two of the great events of the year. It is described as a *sabbath*, a *memorial* of blowing of trumpets, and as a *holy convocation* (24). According to Jewish tradition the trumpet used on this occasion was not the silver trumpet of Nu. x. 2-10, but the *shophar*, the ram's horn (*yobhel*) which was used on specially solemn occasions, notably to proclaim the year of jubile (cf. also Jos. vi and see note there). No servile work is to be done; and sacrifice is to be offered. This remembrance-blowing may be understood in two senses: God reminding the people of their duty to prepare themselves for the solemnities which this month has in store for them; and the people reminding God of His covenant and of His goodness to their fathers and to them. The word trumpet does not occur in the Hebrew. The word *teru'ah* may denote either 'shouting' of people, or trumpet-'blast'. Perhaps both were included. This day, the first of Tishri, is called by the Jews *rosh hashshanah*, the beginning of the year. It is the beginning of the civil year, new year's day.

ii. The day of atonement (xxiii. 26-32).

This festival, which has been so fully described in chapter xvi as regards the duties of Aaron, the sacrifices to be performed and the way in which they are to be performed, is described here entirely from the standpoint of the duties of the people (26-32). It is to be *a sabbath of rest* (32; Heb. *shabbath shabbathon*). No work of any kind is to be done and fasting is to be observed; they are to afflict their souls. Disobedience will be most severely punished. Cf. Nu. xxix. 7–11, which deals especially with the offerings.

iii. The feast of tabernacles (xxiii. 33–44). This resembles the Passover and the feast of unleavened bread in several important respects. Both are primarily historical feasts, the one recalling the Exodus, the deliverance from Egypt and the circumstances of their flight, the other recalling the long sojourn in the wilderness. Both are of considerable length, extending over eight days. Both are closely connected with the daily life and happiness of the people, the one standing at the beginning, the other at the close of the agricultural year. A marked difference is that in the latter feast there is no prohibition of the use of leaven. Nu. xxix. 12–38 describes this feast in greater detail, listing the special offerings for each day. The total is remarkable. The burnt offering consists of bullocks, rams and lambs. The number of rams (two) and of lambs (fourteen) remains the same for each of the seven days, while the number of bullocks begins with thirteen and is reduced gradually to seven, making a total of seventy bullocks, or an average of ten a day. On the eighth day the offering is one bullock, one ram and seven lambs. On each of the eight days there is a sin offering consisting of one goat. It is carefully pointed out that each separate burnt offering is to have its meal offering and its drink offering. It is rather remarkable that the number of the bullocks is decreased from day to day instead of increased.

The set feasts which have just been described are summed up in words very similar to verse 4. Then a further law is given with regard to the feast of tabernacles. The people are to live in booths for seven days that their generations may know that the Lord *made the children of Israel to dwell in booths* (43) when He brought them out of the land of Egypt. And the people are to *rejoice before the Lord* (40). Thus the fasting of the day of atonement as a sign of sorrow for sin is speedily followed by the joy of this festival. It is remarkable that it is called *the feast of tabernacles* (34; lit. 'booths', Heb. *sukkoth*; cf. verses 42, 43), since elsewhere in the Pentateuch, except for Gn. xxxiii. 17, the word 'booth' nowhere occurs, the Israelites being said to have dwelt in tents. The thought which is stressed is of course the frail and temporary character of the dwellings of the people during the wilderness sojourn. Thus Jerusalem is likened by Isaiah to a cottage (booth) in a vineyard (i. 8), so frail and poverty-stricken has the abode of the daughter of Zion become. It should hardly be necessary to point out that the word tabernacles has nothing at all in common with the word tabernacle as used of the sanctuary of the Lord. The words are entirely distinct. Cf. the references to this feast in 2 Ch. viii. 13; Ezr. iii. 4; Ne. viii. 13–18; Zc. xiv. 16–19. While these feasts were seasonal and suited to an agricultural people, the emphasis placed on historical events is clearly for the purpose of keeping alive in the minds of the people the great deliverance from Egypt in its most important aspects.

IX. THE HOLY OIL, THE SHEWBREAD, THE SIN OF BLASPHEMY. xxiv. 1–23

a. The oil for the candlestick (xxiv. 1–4)

Olive oil was used for illumination, for anointing, and in cooking as an article of food. All three were assigned a function in the service of the tabernacle. Here only the first is referred to. The oil for the lamps of the golden lampstand was to be pure, beaten oil (Ex. xxvii. 20). The oil for anointing was spiced (Ex. xxv. 6, xxxv. 8). Oil was one of the freewill offerings of the people at the time of the construction of the tabernacle and apparently was to continue to be so. The tending of the lamps is here assigned to Aaron, but in Ex. xxvii. 21 his sons are included with him as qualified to perform this important duty. *From the evening unto the morning . . . continually* (3) indicates that the lights burned throughout the night. 1 Sa. iii. 3 would seem to mean that the lamps were given only sufficient oil to last until the morning. Cf. the distinction made in Ex. xxx. 7f. between trimming (lit. 'making good') the lamps in the morning and lighting (lit. 'causing them to ascend') in the evening. If this is the correct view, we may assume that the lamps were lighted in the evening with fire from the altar of burnt sacrifice. According to others, continually means that the lamps burned both day and night.

b. The shewbread (xxiv. 5–9)

In Ex. xxv. 23–30 the description of the table of shewbread is given. But the bread itself is simply mentioned. Here the details of the service are described. Each loaf is to consist of two-tenths of an ephah of flour (about six quarts), probably prepared with oil like the meal offering, though this is not stated. They are to be placed in *two rows* (6), or 'arrangements' (hence the expression 'bread of arrangement' in Chronicles and Nehemiah), which probably means in two piles of six cakes each. Beside (probably better than *upon*) each pile, frankincense was placed, either in a bowl or a spoon. As in the case of the meal offering, it was not baked with the cakes; but according to later tradition it was burned on the altar of burnt sacrifice, together with the offerings of oil and wine, at the end of the seven days when the bread was taken from *before the Lord* and eaten by the priests. Cf. on Ex. xxv. 30, xxxv. 13, xxxix. 36. A possible reason for the placing of these two laws in between chapters xxiii and xxv, which seem to belong together, may be to direct attention to the important fact that permanent and unvarying rituals such as these are entirely independent of and not affected by the annual feasts and special days which have just been described.

c. The sin of blasphemy and crimes of violence (xxiv. 10–23)

The brief historical episode recorded in verses 10–16 may have occurred between the revelations which precede and follow it. Cf. Dt. iv. 41–49 and Nu. xv. 32–36 for similar examples. The half-Israelite referred to probably belonged to the 'mixed multitude' of Ex. xii. 38. *Went out* (or 'came out') *among the children of Israel* (10) hardly suggests that he was not living in the camp, but rather that he went abroad in the camp, engaged in a brawl with an Israelite, and became profane in his abuse of his opponent. When he is brought to trial, his mother's name and connections are briefly mentioned, probably because he owed his presence in the camp entirely to her. His father may have been dead; at any rate his name is not given. It is the principle, not the person, that concerns us. This was an obvious and flagrant breach of the third commandment. But that commandment did not assess the penalty, except that the guilty one would not be held 'guiltless' by God. The problem was further complicated by the irregular status of the culprit. Hence he was put 'in ward, that it might be declared unto them at the mouth of the Lord' (12, RV) what his punishment was to be.

The answer (cf. Nu. vii. 89) deals especially with the actual situation; but it also establishes the principle that no distinction is to be made between Israelite and non-Israelite in such matters (22). It is to be noted that blasphemy is here grouped with crimes of a violent nature such as murder, unlawful wounding, etc. This may indicate simply the enormity of this sin of the lips. It may also suggest that the strife of which the act of blasphemy formed the most serious part was a very violent one and threatened the life or limb of his opponent (cf. Ex. xxi. 22; Dt. xxv. 11). At least it is clear that these laws, which have already been given in Exodus (see xxi. 12, 23–36), are repeated here primarily for the purpose of making the law regarding blasphemy and other serious offences apply to the sojourner and stranger just as much as to the native-born Israelite.

With regard to this *lex talionis*, three things are to be noted. First, it was intended to be a law of exact justice, not of revenge. Secondly, it was not private vengeance, but public justice. Thirdly, by excluding murder from the crimes for which ransom is permissible (Nu. xxxv. 31f.) it makes it probable that compensation for injuries was often or usually allowed to take the form of a fine. The claim that 'there is in Jewish history no instance of the law of retaliation ever having been carried out literally—eye for an eye, tooth for a tooth' may or may not be justified, although such mutilating of the body was contrary to the spirit of the Mosaic law. Yet for centuries in Christian lands, torture and mutilation was the customary punishment for crime, and often, contrary to both the spirit and the letter of the Mosaic law, it was utterly out of proportion to the offence. This incident serves to remind us of the grievousness of the sin of profanity, which is one of the great evils of today.

X. THE SABBATICAL YEAR AND THE YEAR OF JUBILE. xxv. 1–55

a. The sabbatical year (xxv. 1–7)

The principle of a regularly recurring day of rest has been dealt with in chapter xxiii in connection with the annual feasts; and in a way which strongly emphasized the septadic principle. This principle is now carried still further, to the establishing of the sabbatical year of jubile. In the law of the sabbath rest, the principle is applied to all human beings, whether free or bond, and also to the cattle (Ex. xx. 10), to the ox, the ass, or any cattle, as beasts of burden (Dt. v. 14), as well as to the sojourner. Here it is extended to the land. Every seventh year the land is to have a *sabbath of rest* (4) (*shabbath shabbathon*) from sowing and reaping. The land is to be left untilled and that which grows of itself, called in verse 6 *the sabbath of the land* (i.e., what the sabbath of the land produces of itself), is to be food for all alike, for the owner and the servant, for the sojourner and the cattle. It is not the product of human industry and it is to be free to all. Furthermore, the promise is given that the yield of the sixth year, being ordered and blessed by God, will be sufficient (18–22) for this period of rest. It is the law of the manna on a larger scale (Ex. xvi. 22). This at least suggests that the sabbath increase (6, 7), unlike the gleanings of the ordinary year which were assigned to the widow and orphan, will suffice for the actual needs of everyone (cf. Ex. xvi. 17f.). According to Dt. xxxi. 10 this year is not to be spent in idleness, but to be used for the teaching and training of Israel in the law of God.

b. The jubile (xxv. 8–55)

i. Rules for its observance (xxv. 8–22). The fiftieth year is carefully defined as the one following seven sabbatical years (8). It is introduced by 'sending abroad' throughout the land the 'loud trumpet' on the day of atonement of the fiftieth year (9, RV). The trumpet (Heb. *shophar*) used was the horn (*qeren*) of the ram (cf. Jos. vi. 4f.) and consequently, by abbreviation, *yobhel* (ram), from which the term 'jubile' is derived, becomes synonymous with trumpet. Cf. Ex. xix. 13, 19, where both words are used. This trumpet blast, which introduces the jubile, is like the trumpet sound which prepared and summoned Israel to become the covenant people of their God. The same law regarding sowing and reaping applies to this year as to the sabbatical years which preceded it; and since it began in the autumn it seems clear that the sabbatical years did the same. It is a year of liberty, a year of return (10, 13) to possessions and to family. This return to normalcy, as we may call it, is to be on a strictly equitable basis (14–17). Buying and selling are to be carried on with due regard to the approaching year of jubile.

And if ye shall say, What shall we eat the seventh year? (20). This seems to imply that the hypothetical objectors have the sabbatical year only in mind. But the answer includes the larger problem as well, the case when the sabbatical year is followed by the jubile. This is indicated by the mention of *three years* (21) and of the *eighth* and *ninth* years (22). The answering of the greater difficulty includes, of course, the solution of the lesser.

ii. The law of redemption (xxv. 23–34). The principle involved in the law of redemption is that the land belongs not to any man but to God. They are not owners but *strangers and sojourners* (23), tenants by courtesy of the land which God has given to them. They are tenants at will, the will of God. See Ex. xxii. 21n. and Dt. x. 19n. The reclaiming of land (25–28) may be done by a kinsman (25), by the man himself (26f.), or it will take place automatically in the year of jubile. But this does not apply to *a dwelling house in a walled city* (29), which can be re-deemed only within a year of its sale, apparently because this has no direct connection with the land and its cultivation. On the other hand houses in villages are covered by the provision probably because farmers and shepherds dwell in them (31). The Levites and their possessions come within a special class (32–34).

iii. Treatment of the poor brother and of non-Israelites (xxv. 35–55). Verse 35 is difficult. 'As . . . a sojourner' (RV) and *though . . . a sojourner* (AV) are both possible renderings. RV seems better because the laws given here make a clear dis-tinction between Israelite and Gentile. Note the *if thy brother* (25, 35, 39, 47) and *your brethren the children of Israel* (46). Loving the stranger (see xix. 34 and Dt. x. 18) does not mean that no distinction is to be made between him and the brother Israelite. Rather the status of the Israelite is shown to be completely different. Loans made to him must be without interest. On this question of usury see Ex. xxii. 25n.; Dt. xxiii. 19n. If he sells himself, he is to be treated as a hired servant and not as a slave; he is to be treated with leniency and is to go free at the jubile, should this come before the termination of his six years of service (Ex. xxi. 2–4; Dt. xv. 12f.).

The law of release does not apply to the non-Israelites; they may be treated as slaves in-capable of redemption (44–46). The principles of redemption are then extended to the case of a man who sells himself to a sojourner or stranger, who, as indicated above, is required to obey the requirements of the law, or at least not to trans-gress them. The Israelite in such a position may be redeemed or simply go out at the jubile; and he must not be rigorously treated (47–54). The reason for this difference is that the Israelites are the Lord's servants and He has freed them from bondage to men, notably the bondage of Egypt (55).

XI. BLESSINGS AND CURSINGS. xxvi. 1–46

The immense importance which attaches to the keeping of the law, which has just been set before the people and the priests in such detail, is summed up by Moses in Dt. xxx. 15, in the words 'See, I have set before thee this day life and good, and death and evil'. Cf. Lv. xviii. 5. No reference is made to the solemn rite which is to be observed at Shechem (see Dt. xi. 26–29, xxvii. 4ff.; Jos. viii. 30–35). But here, as on that solemn occasion, the issue and the choice are placed before Israel with the utmost plainness, all the more impressive in this case because the Lord, while speaking of course through Moses, addresses the people in the first person (note the frequently recurring 'I') and without any introductory phrase. Cf. Dt. xxvii—xxviii where Moses speaks in the name of the Lord. Idolatry in any form is to be shunned, the sabbath is to be kept, and the sanctuary of the Lord is to be reverenced (1, 2). These three matters are first singled out for special emphasis because of their importance and also because of all that is involved and implied in their observance.

a. Blessings as a reward of obedience (xxvi. 3–13)

These blessings are only as it were an amplifica-tion of the promise given in Ex. xix. 5f. They give an idyllic picture, such as Isaiah delights to paint, of the prosperity and peace which is the reward of obedience to God. The Lord will give rain and the earth will yield its bounty. The harvest and the ingathering will be so abundant that it will require months instead of days to gather it. And with plenty there shall be peace. Neither man nor beast will be able to injure them or stand before them. The Lord *will have respect* (lit. 'turn') unto them (9), will set His tabernacle among them and will not abhor them (11). This last striking statement seems like an anticlimax, but is not. For Israel is a sinful people which deserves to be abhorred, and would be, were it not for the love and grace of their God. *And I will walk among you* (12). We are reminded of Gn. iii. 8. The land of Canaan will be like the garden of Eden, because the God of Eden will dwell there with His people. The Lord who will do all this is the One who delivered them from Egypt, the greatest proof of His love and almighty power. Again and again in the Old Testament it is referred to as evidence of this love and of the fact that Israel belongs to God and owes Him allegiance. See, e.g., Jos. xxiv. 17.

b. The chastisements for disobedience (xxvi. 14–45)

i. The evils described (xxvi. 14–33). It is signifi-cant that the evils which are threatened are described much more fully than the blessings that are promised. Man being what he is, sinful and prone to evil, fear is, in many if not most cases, a stronger stimulant to the will than love. *But if ye will not hearken unto me* (14). A sharp contrast is suggested by the one 'if' of obedience

(3) and the many 'ifs' or 'if nots' of disobedience (14, 15, 18, 21, 23, 27). The Hebrew verb translated 'hearken' has three main renderings in English: 'hear', 'hearken' and 'obey'. The old saying 'to hear is to obey' is especially applicable to Hebrew. Here obeying (hearing) is contrasted with despising, abhorring and disobeying which amount to breaking the covenant. Note especially the word *contrary* (used seven times), which suggests Am. iii. 3. The thought of reciprocity is stressed throughout. God will deal with Israel exactly as she deserves.

The evils which are threatened are in the main four: pestilence (16, 25), famine (19), wild beasts (22), and the sword as typifying war and the desolations which will result from it (25–39). The contrast with the rewards of obedience is made very glaring. Compare verses 7, 8 with 17, 36–38. Four times the word *seven* is used (18, 21, 24, 28). It might be well to render it 'sevenfold' rather than *seven times* since it is apparently the intensity rather than the duration that is referred to. It should not be connected with the prophetic 'times' of Daniel. But both Jeremiah and Ezekiel seem to have this chapter clearly in mind. Jeremiah speaks of four kinds of punishments (xv. 3f.). Cf. Ezk. xiv. 12–21. Both of these prophets refer especially to the sword. Dispersion is also definitely threatened here. Israel will be scattered *among the heathen* (33).

ii. The climax of desolation (xxvi. 34–39). *Then shall the land enjoy her sabbaths* (34), while Israel is in exile. Cf. 2 Ch. xxxvi. 21 where the same expression occurs with reference to the Babylonian captivity. This does not justify the inference that during the centuries between the conquest and the captivity exactly seventy sabbatic years (corresponding to the length of the captivity) had not been observed. But it does indicate that this Mosaic law requiring sabbath rest had been grievously abused and had been largely neglected. Isaiah, Jeremiah and Ezekiel reprove Israel for failure to keep the sabbath (cf. e.g., Je. xvii. 19–27). But they make no mention of the sabbatic year. Nor does Jeremiah represent the seventy years as a sabbath for the land (see Je. xxv. 8–11, xxvii. 6–8, xxix. 10). The *sword* (36, 37) is described in verse 25 as executing 'the vengeance of the covenant' (RV), a terrible phrase which suggests 'the wrath of the Lamb' (Rev. vi. 16).

iii. The result: confession and forgiveness· (xxvi. 40–45). In verse 40 follow the RV, 'And they shall confess'. The 'if' does not come till 41b, *if then their uncircumcised hearts be humbled*. When punishment has finally resulted in confession, if the people who have been scattered among the nations humble themselves, knowing that it is God who has brought them into their evil state, and *accept of the punishment of their iniquity* (41) then the Lord will remember His covenant with their fathers (42). The implication is that He will restore them to the land promised to their fathers, since its possession was an important element in the covenant promise. But it is noteworthy that this is here left to inference, quite different from Dt. xxx. 1–5, where return to the land is definitely promised on condition of repentance. Verse 46 concludes this group of laws with the emphatic declaration that they were delivered to Israel through Moses at mount Sinai (cf. vii. 38).

XII. VOWS AND TITHES. xxvii. 1–34

The subject of vows and freewill offerings has been mentioned several times in this book in dealing with the subject of sacrifices (see vii. 16, xxii. 18–23, xxiii. 38). Here 'devoted' or 'sanctified' oblations (*qorban*), which could not be offered in sacrifice, are discussed separately. The votive offerings here referred to consist of persons, animals, houses, fields. It is to be observed that in most cases no actual change in ownership takes place. The emphatic word is *estimation* which occurs about twenty times. We have already met it in connection with the trespass offering, which required the addition of one-fifth to the estimated value of the property which must be restored (v. 15f.). Here it is used of the value to be assigned to a person or to property.

In the case of persons (2–8), the estimation varies according to sex and age. It apparently contemplates the possibility of a man's vowing (to give) himself or some person of his household to the Lord. The valuation varies between fifty shekels and three shekels. That it is expected that the person will be *redeemed* in money is made clear by verse 8. Thus, if a man estimated at fifty shekels were not able to pay the full amount, the priest was to suit the estimate to the ability of the maker of the vow to make good his vow or pledge. In the case of animals (9–13) a distinction is made between clean beasts which could be used in sacrifice and unclean beasts. The former became the property of the Lord and could not be redeemed by the owner. The law was interpreted to mean that the priests might sell such animals to those who wished to offer a sacrifice, but not to the original owner. In the case of an unclean beast, the original owner might redeem it by paying a fifth more than the estimation. In the case of a house (14, 15) the same principle applied. If the owner wished to redeem it he must pay an additional one-fifth.

The case of the field (16–25) was much more complicated, since it involved the question of the jubile. But the owner could redeem it by adding one-fifth. The estimate was to be in terms of the sowing of the field, which was a relatively simple way of determining its value in an agricultural community. If he failed to redeem the field, which was his inheritance, or if he sold it (surreptitiously) after having devoted it, then he lost all claim to it when the year of jubile came round. The field became the property of the priests. The value of a field which a man had purchased was to be reckoned in terms of the nearness of the jubile, since it then returned to its original owner. Here (verse 25) and three times elsewhere in the Pentateuch (Ex. xxx. 13; Nu. iii. 47, xviii. 16) it is stated that the shekel of the sanctuary contains twenty gerahs.

Firstlings (26, 27) belonged to the Lord (cf. Ex. xiii. 2, 12; Dt. xv. 19–23), so could not be dedicated. But the firstlings of unclean animals could be redeemed by paying the extra one-fifth. If not redeemed they could be sold (see Ex. xiii. 13).

Devoted or 'banned' persons or things (28, 29) are an exception to the law regarding redemption. They cannot be redeemed and a banned person must be put to death. This must refer to the solemn and terrible ban (*ḥerem*) which was placed, for example, on Amalek, on Jericho, and on Achan, and not to the vows and acts of 'sanctifying' mentioned earlier in the chapter. See Dt. ii. 34n. The placing of such a ban upon nation or individual was certainly not within the right of any private person, but must have been of the nature of an official sentence pronounced by God through Moses, or through the duly constituted leaders. Cf. Jos. vi. 17–19.

Verses 30–33 deal with the question of tithes. One tenth of the increase of the fields, of the trees, of the herd or flock is holy unto the Lord. A man may redeem part of it by paying the usual one-fifth additional. But this exception does not apply to animals. On the tithes cf. Dt. xii and xiv. The apparent discrepancy between Leviticus and Deuteronomy was harmonized by the Rabbis by distinguishing three different tithes: the first, the second, and the third or 'poor' tithe.

The closing statement of 34 is briefer and less definite than that of xxvi. 46. It may be regarded, therefore, as referring primarily to chapter xxvii and not to the entire book. But however understood, this concluding statement is in accord with the total impression given by Leviticus, i.e. that it consists of laws given to Moses for Israel at Sinai.

OSWALD T. ALLIS.

NUMBERS

INTRODUCTION

The English name of this book is taken from the Greek translation, and may represent the hasty selection of someone only superficially familiar with the book. The names which the Greek translation gave to the other four books of the Pentateuch are good descriptions of their contents, while those appended to them in the Hebrew consist merely of the first word or the first two words of each book, and sometimes give no idea at all of what the book contains. Here the reverse is true. The Hebrew name, *bemidhbar*, 'in the wilderness' (which is the fifth word of the book), describes it excellently; but the Greek title fits only chapters i and xxvi. While it might loosely apply to one or two other chapters, it has no application to nine-tenths of the book. It is to be feared that the misleading title which the Latin and the English versions have taken over from the Greek translation has led many to neglect the book, and to miss the rich treasures which it contains.

As the Hebrew title suggests, the book contains a description of the wilderness journey of the Israelites. Exodus tells how they left Egypt, and traces their progress as far as Sinai. Joshua tells how they entered the Promised Land. Their long journey from Sinai to the borders of Canaan is described in Numbers.

Actually this book is of very great significance for the Christian. Like the Israelites, he has come out of Egypt, the region of slavery and oppression. He has been born again through the sacrifice of Christ on Calvary just as they were redeemed by the special power of God, as demonstrated in the Passover which marked their departure from Egypt. Like them he looks forward to entering into full possession of all the promises of God. But at present he is a pilgrim and a stranger, with a wilderness journey to pass through before he enters the Promised Land (cf. 1 Pet. ii. 11; Heb. xi. 8–16, xii. 1).

There are three reasons why the book is important for our study. First, it enables us to know the history of God's dealings with Israel at this vital stage of its progress. We learn from it many important facts of history, and we come to understand something of God's methods as we see what He did during the forty years described in the book. Secondly, it gives us background for understanding the many allusions to its history and its laws which occur in later sections of the Bible. Thirdly, it is particularly rich in spiritual lessons for the Christian, who is, as we have seen, in a stage of experience which corresponds exactly to that of the nation of Israel in the wilderness. The book is full of vital illustration and precept to guide the Christian in his journey. It presents the resources available to him, and shows the internal and external dangers which he must face.

Numbers contains three types of material: historical, describing events that occur; legal, presenting enactments that were intended to be observed by Israel throughout its history; and a third type, which stands between these two, consisting of regulations applying only to the wilderness journey, and statistical material of historical interest.

In the first part of the Old Testament, the tendency of the Christian student is to confine his attention to the narrative. Unfortunately, many readers fail to realize the great value of the narrative portion of Numbers because they become bogged down in the statistical section or in the detailed regulations for the progress of the march, a type of material which is preponderant in the first part of the book. These regulations were very important at the time, and are of much value for detailed study, but can easily give the student a false impression if they are studied before he has acquired familiarity with the later narrative material. It is therefore recommended that the student should first go through the book, skimming over the notes on the non-narrative sections, but carefully studying the narrative chapters themselves in the light of the notes. Going through the book a second time, he will find his interest in the non-narrative material enhanced, and will gain deeper understanding of the narrative material from it.

Lack of space prevents any attempt in the present commentary to deal exhaustively with the many problems of the book of Numbers. All that can be attempted here is to give the student an understanding of its framework, and to start him on the right path toward acquisition of the rich treasures which it contains.

Critical problems are touched upon where necessary, though the purpose of the commentary is mainly exegetical rather than apologetic. The viewpoint, like that of the commentary as a whole, is that the Scriptures give a true and factual account of God's dealings with His people, kept free from error in the original autographs by the inspiration of the Holy Spirit.

The text of Numbers has been well preserved. While there is the possibility of an occasional error in the transmission of a letter or two, even such small variations as this are quite rare in the text of this particular book.

It is the conviction of the writer that the entire Pentateuch was written by Moses, the man of

God. This seems to him to be plainly inferred in the references in the Pentateuch and in the New Testament, and not to be contrary to any proven fact. While it is possible that a sentence might in rare instances have been interpolated at a later time by someone who was himself inspired by the Holy Spirit in what he wrote, the writer knows of no passage in the Pentateuch where he considers such a conclusion to be necessary.

OUTLINE OF CONTENTS

The book divides naturally into four main sections: the preparation for the march through the wilderness (i. 1—x. 10), the journey from Sinai to the plains of Moab (x. 11—xxii. 1), the Balaam incident (xxii. 2—xxv. 18) and the preparations for entrance into Canaan (xxvi. 1—xxxvi. 13).

PREPARATION FOR THE WILDERNESS JOURNEY. i. 1—x. 10

I. THE MEN OF WAR NUMBERED AND POSITIONS ASSIGNED FOR THE MARCH. i. 1—ii. 34

II. THE LEVITES NUMBERED AND THEIR DUTIES DESCRIBED. iii. 1—iv. 49

III. REMOVAL OF UNCLEANNESS AND DEFILEMENT FROM THE CAMP. v. 1–31

IV. A SPECIAL TYPE OF SEPARATION—THE NAZARITE VOW. vi. 1–21

V. ARRANGEMENTS FOR THE RELIGIOUS LIFE OF THE CAMP. vi. 22—ix. 14

VI. THE DIVINE PROVISION FOR DIRECTION AND GUIDANCE. ix. 15—x. 10

FROM SINAI TO THE PLAINS OF MOAB. x. 11—xxii. 1

VII. THE FIRST STAGE OF THE JOURNEY. x. 11–36

VIII. REBELLION AND DISAFFECTION. xi. 1—xii. 16

IX. THE CRISIS AT KADESH-BARNEA. xiii. 1—xiv. 45

X. LAWS AFTER THE CRISIS. xv. 1–41

XI. THE GREAT REBELLION OF KORAH, DATHAN AND ABIRAM. xvi. 1–50

XII. THE AFTERMATH OF THE REBELLION. xvii. 1—xix. 22

XIII. INCIDENTS ON THE WAY TO THE PLAINS OF MOAB. xx. 1—xxii. 1

THE BALAAM INCIDENT. xxii. 2—xxv. 18

XIV. THE SUMMONING OF BALAAM. xxii. 2–40

XV. THE PROPHECIES OF BALAAM. xxii. 41—xxiv. 24

XVI. THE AFTERMATH OF THE BALAAM INCIDENT. xxiv. 25—xxv. 18

PREPARATIONS FOR ENTRANCE INTO CANAAN. xxvi. 1—xxxvi. 13

XVII. PREPARATIONS FOR THE CONQUEST AND APPORTIONMENT OF THE LAND. xxvi. 1—xxvii. 23

XVIII. LAWS REGARDING SACRIFICES AND VOWS. xxviii. 1—xxx. 16

XIX. VENGEANCE ON THE MIDIANITES. xxxi. 1–54

XX. THE APPORTIONMENT OF TRANSJORDAN. xxxii. 1–42

XXI. SUMMARY OF THE JOURNEYS FROM EGYPT TO THE PLAINS OF MOAB. xxxiii. 1–49

XXII. PLANS FOR THE DIVISION OF CANAAN. xxxiii. 50—xxxvi. 13

COMMENTARY

PREPARATION FOR THE WILDERNESS JOURNEY. i. 1—x. 10

I. THE MEN OF WAR NUMBERED AND POSITIONS ASSIGNED FOR THE MARCH. i. 1—ii. 34

a. The military census (i. 1–54)

This chapter gives the Greek (and English) name to the book. It describes the census of Israel at Sinai. This is a military census. It lists men, twenty years of age or older, *able to go forth to war* (3). It is taken at the beginning of the wilderness journey from Sinai in order to determine what human resources are available for defence.

The Christian is thus shown, at the beginning of the wilderness journey, the importance of carefully examining his resources, and knowing what he is prepared to do. This is a necessary counterbalance to the tendency to think that nothing but faith is needed. It is true, of course, that faith is absolutely vital, not only for salvation, but for every phase of Christian living. God may choose to accomplish great things through those who have faith, even when they are without adequate resources and when they fail in intelligence. Yet it is His will that such instances be the exception rather than the rule. Not only does He desire us at all times to look to Him for strength, and to know that results are entirely in His hands; it is also His will that we determine exactly what resources we have and use them carefully so as to accomplish the utmost for Him. The same truth was presented by Christ in the parables of the Pounds and of the Talents. See Mt. xxv. 14–30; Lk. xix. 12–27. Cf. also Lk. xiv. 28–33.

David was rebuked and severely punished for taking a census (2 Sa. xxiv and 1 Ch. xxi). At first sight this seems to contradict our present chapter, especially when we note that David's census, like the one described here, had a military purpose (cf. 2 Sa. xxiv. 9). However, the ultimate aims of the two numberings were quite different. In Nu. i God commanded the mustering of all the resources of the people for carrying out His orders; but in the later instance David wished to determine his resources for waging aggressive warfare after the divine purpose of freeing His people had already been accomplished. He desired to bolster his own pride by seeing how great his power was, and hence might be tempted to use it for further unjustified conquest. The line between the two situations is sometimes hard to draw exactly. God commands careful examination of resources and their effective use for His righteous purposes, but He forbids piling up possessions for our own selfish purposes and sinful pride.

i. God commands the census to be taken (i. 1–3). *The tabernacle of the congregation* (1), probably better rendered 'tent of meeting', as in RV. The Hebrew word *moedh* never denotes a group of people; it indicates the meeting together of God with Moses or of God with the people. *On the first day of the second month, in the second year* (1). Note that this date is just one month after the rearing up of the tabernacle (Ex. xl. 17), which occurred one year after the departure from Egypt. The departure from Sinai occurred exactly twenty days later (x. 11). The first ten chapters tell us many of the things which were done during this period. It hardly seems likely that Moses and Aaron, with twelve assistants, could have taken all this census in so short a time, and certainly not on a single day. About nine months earlier (Ex. xix. 1, xxx. 11ff., xxxviii. 26) God had commanded that the people be numbered and that a half shekel be collected from each. The total number was 603,550, exactly the number of our present census. It is most probable that our present chapter describes the tabulation by Moses of the full results of a census which actually began several months earlier.

ii. The census officials selected (i. 4–16). A leader was chosen from each tribe to take part in the numbering. These are men of special standing in their tribes. Note, however, that the word rendered *renowned* (16) simply means 'called'. It may indicate recognition of worth, but more likely means merely that these were men designated previously as leaders of the highest rank. It may be observed that the tribes are not named here in order of birth (cf. Gn. xxix. 32— xxx. 24, xxxv. 16–18). Leah's sons (omitting Levi) are all placed first, then Rachel's descendants, then the four sons of the two concubines. Nahshon, the son of Amminadab, the leader of Judah (7), was an ancestor of Christ (Mt. i. 4; Lk. iii. 32–33).

iii. The results of the census (i. 17–46). It is interesting to note the great difference in the sizes of the various tribes. The order of the tribes here is the same as in verses 4–16, except that Naphtali and Asher are interchanged, and Gad is placed third, perhaps because of its proximity to Reuben and Simeon in the camp position (ii. 10–16).

The large numbers in this census have created a difficulty for some readers, who find it hard to believe that the nation of Israel was so numerous during its march through the wilderness. Yet when we consider the large families that were customary and the length of time that was spent in Egypt before the beginning of the oppression, the amount of increase is seen to be not at all unreasonable. Passage of so large a group through the wilderness transcends ordinary history. Were it not for the constant divine provision it would have been impossible (cf. Dt. xxix. 5). Some have tried to escape the difficulty by assuming that the word thousand is to be taken as meaning family or clan rather than being an exact number. This interpretation overlooks the fact that most of the numbers include hundreds as well as thousands, that the tribe of Gad numbered 42,650 (25), and that the total number of fighting men is given as 603,550 (46).

It is difficult to preserve numbers accurately in ancient documents, which had to be copied and recopied. Various types of abbreviations may have occasionally been used and sometimes misunderstood. Actually, however, the number of figures in the Bible which occasion real difficulty is comparatively small. In only one instance among the many figures in Nu. i—iv is there reason to suspect an error of transmission, and in that case it is probably only a matter of the loss of one Hebrew letter. Cf. note on iii. 39 below.

iv. The omission of the Levites (i. 47–54). The tribe of Levi was not included in the military census (49), but was set apart for the care and transportation of the tabernacle (50–51). The Levites are not to have a place among the regular tribal encampments, but to pitch close to the tabernacle (53). Fuller explanation of these provisions is given in later chapters.

b. Positions assigned for the camp and for the march (ii. 1–34)

This chapter describes an orderly arrangement of the tribes, both for camping and for marching.

Each man is to camp according to his tribe and family group (2). Far off (2). Heb. minnegebh; better 'over against' as in AV mg. and RV. Doubtless the tribes would have to be some distance from the sanctuary, since the Levites were encamped around it (i. 53), but the emphasis here is on their position in relation to it, rather than on their distance from it.

The tribes were divided into four groups of three tribes each, which were called 'camps', and named after the first tribe in each group. Each camp was to encamp on a particular side of the tabernacle. The four camps are described in order, starting with the one on the east, and going clockwise around the compass. In connection with each camp its three tribes are taken up in order. A captain is designated for each tribe and the number of fighting men in the tribe is stated. The description of each camp ends with mention of the total number of its fighting men, and of its order in the march. This order of march is identical with that in which the tribes are listed in the chapter. It is interesting to note that the order of the tribes here is the same as in i. 21–43, except that the first three and the second three are interchanged, thus placing the three youngest sons of Leah before the two eldest.

i. The camp on the east side (ii. 3–9). This was the camp of Judah. It included the tribes of Judah, Issachar and Zebulun, and went first in the march.

ii. The camp on the south side (ii. 10–16). This was the camp of Reuben. It included the tribes of Reuben, Simeon and Gad, and had the second place in the march. The son of Reuel (14). This name occurs as Deuel in i. 14, vii. 42, 47 and x. 20. In ancient Hebrew writing D and R looked very much alike. Hence they were confused in transmission far oftener than any other two letters. Cf., for instance, Hadadezer in 2 Sa. viii. 3, 5, 7, 8, 9, 10, 12, with Hadarezer in 1 Ch. xviii. 3, 5, 7, 8, 9, 10.

iii. The place of the Levites (ii. 17). After the description of the camps of Judah and Reuben, mention is made of the Levites, since they would come next on the march. They camped in the centre, around the tabernacle (i. 53).

iv. The camp on the west side (ii. 18–25). This was the camp of Ephraim, which included the tribes of Ephraim, Manasseh and Benjamin. Thus the descendants of Joseph and Benjamin, Rachel's two sons, encamped together. On the march the camp of Ephraim followed the camp of the Levites.

v. The camp on the north side (ii. 26–31). This was the camp of Dan. It included the tribes of Dan, Asher and Naphtali, and came last in the march.

vi. A general summary (ii. 32–34). Verse 32 gives the grand total of fighting men (already given in i. 46). From this total the Levites, who did not fight, are excluded (33). Verse 34 states that the Israelites observed the prescribed order in camp and on the march. God desires His people to do things in orderly fashion. Cf. 1 Cor.

165

xii. 4-28. Each has his own task, which he should do as well as possible, without envying the task or the talent given another.

II. THE LEVITES NUMBERED AND THEIR DUTIES DESCRIBED. iii. 1—iv. 49

These two chapters describe the arrangements made for the care of the tabernacle, both in camp and on the march. Systematic arrangements are provided, and definite families assigned to specific tasks. God is a God of order. He desires the Christian Church, and the Christian individual, to apportion tasks and duties so that all may be performed without haste and without mistake.

Since the Israelites often marched through hostile territory, it might seem surprising that a whole tribe should be exempted from military service, not even being counted in the military census. This fact demonstrates the supreme importance of proper attention to God's requirements for worship. If a nation neglects these, it cannot expect any permanent success in other lines. God demands the first place in the life of His people. His requirements must be met, or all else is of no avail (Ps. cxxvii. 1).

The chapters contain several instances where two or three verses are repeated almost verbatim. This is because similar orders are given and carried out regarding various sections of the tribe of Levi. As a result, the modern reader is apt to lose himself in the legal phraseology of the repetitions, and to miss the significant variations.

a. The Levites to serve the tabernacle under priestly direction (iii. 1-13)

These verses state the duties of the Levites in a general way, preparatory to the more detailed description that follows. Since the Levites are to be under the direction of the priests (9) the first members of the priestly family are named (1–3). It is not the purpose of the chapter to tell how the priests were selected and set apart for their functions, since that has already been done in Ex. xxviii, xxix, and in Lv. viii, ix. The names are repeated here for the sole purpose of making absolutely clear the divine plan for leadership of the tribe of Levi. Verse 4 points out that only the two younger sons of Aaron were left to carry on the work, since the two older sons had lost their lives as a result of their sin (Lv. x). Verses 5–10 state the general function of the Levites, to serve the tabernacle (7–8) and to minister under the direction of the priests (6, 9). Verse 10 again lays emphasis on the fact that priesthood is to be limited to the family of Aaron. Verses 11–13 state the general principle, that God is taking the Levites for Himself as a substitute for the firstborn of Israel who were spared when He killed the firstborn of Egypt at the time of the original Passover (Ex. xi, xii).

Evolutionary criticism has sought to explain the origin of the Pentateuch by denying its Mosaic authorship and alleging that it represents a long development, with the Levites attaining a separate ecclesiastical status at a late period in Israel's history, and the restriction of the priesthood to the family of Aaron coming later yet. Such a theory requires the assumption that most of the history contained in the books of Exodus and Numbers is the product of the imagination of a later period and did not actually happen. It involves a degree of scepticism regarding ancient documents which is now scarcely found in other fields of study, and requires the division of the books of the Pentateuch into numerous tiny sections and the assumption of many changes and omissions in their contents. It is obvious that in this chapter the priests and the Levites each have their separate functions, and to eliminate either from the chapter leaves it incomplete. The principal reason advanced for the claim that the Aaronic priesthood developed later is the occurrence five times in Deuteronomy and twice in Joshua of the phrase 'the priests the Levites'. Actually, however, this lends no support to the critical theory. In Hebrew, directly contrary to English usage, the limiting word is always placed after the one which it limits. Thus the phrase could be correctly translated 'the Levitical priests'. This does not imply that all Levites are priests, but only that all priests belong to the tribe of Levi. Most modern or modernistic translations render the phrase in this way, but some of them, for example the RSV, insert in Dt. xviii. 1, between the phrases 'the Levitical priests' and 'all the tribe of Levi', the words 'that is'. These words do not occur in the Hebrew original and their insertion is utterly unwarranted apart from a doctrinaire assumption that Deuteronomy considers all the tribe of Levi to be priests. There was no reason why such a book as Deuteronomy, consisting of orations to the people as a whole, and not principally of detailed laws for study, should go into the details of the restriction of the priesthood to the descendants of Aaron. It was quite sufficient to refer to them as 'the Levitical priests'. In Deuteronomy xviii. 1 the restriction upon the priests applied equally to the rest of the tribe of Levi, and it is entirely justifiable to understand 'and' between the two phrases, as is done by the AV. Emphasis is placed first on the restriction as it applied to the priests so as to prevent the development in Israel of a situation such as Moses had observed in Egypt, where the priests gradually acquired the greater part of the land for themselves. It is unfortunate that the RV at this point inserted the word 'even' in the text, even though it gave the reading 'and' in the margin. Yet it should be noted that 'even' does not necessarily imply that all the members of the tribe of Levi were priests, as is done if the phrase 'that is' is inserted.

Throughout the book of Numbers the priests and the Levites are sharply distinguished and the position of the Levites is represented as one of great dignity. This does not accord with the critical view, according to which the distinction originated in post-exilic times, and the Levites actually were only degraded priests. Furthermore, the proportion of priests to Levites here is very different from that in Ezr. ii. 36–40.

b. The Levites numbered and the duties of their various families assigned (iii. 14–39)

The command is given that all Levite males over a month old be numbered according to their families (15). Levi's three sons are named (17), and the families descended from each son are listed (18–20). Next the three main divisions of the Levites, mentioned in verse 17, are taken up in turn, their numbers given, and their duties assigned. The sons of Gershon are treated first (21–26), next the sons of Kohath (27–32), then the sons of Merari (33–37).

In each case, the first verse (21, 27 and 33) repeats the names of the subdivisions, corresponding to the family names already listed (18–20). The next verse defines the age limit of the present census (one month and upward, already stated in the command in verse 15), and gives the number in each main division: Gershon 7,500 (22), Kohath 8,600 (28), Merari 6,200 (34); the third verse states where each is to encamp: Gershon to the west of the tabernacle (23), Kohath to the south (29), Merari to the north (35b). Then the chief of each division is named (24, 30 and 35a). Finally there is a general description of the duties of each division. Gershon has charge of the externals of the tabernacle (25–26), Kohath of the sacred vessels (31), and Merari of the boards, pillars, sockets, etc. (36–37). In connection with the Kohathites it is stated that one from this division, Eleazar, the son of Aaron the priest, is to be over all the chiefs of the Levites (32).

The area near the tabernacle on three sides having been allocated to the three great divisions of the Levites (23, 29, 35b), Moses and the Aaronic priests are directed to encamp east of the tabernacle (38), since they have charge of the sanctuary.

Verse 39 concludes this section by giving the total number of Levites as 22,000. At first sight this appears to be a round number, since the three divisions, 7,500, 8,600 and 6,200, give a total of 22,300. It is clear, however, that 22,000 is not a round number, but the exact number, since verse 46 states that the total number of firstborn, namely 22,273 (given in 43), is 273 more than the total number of the Levites. This presents a serious problem. Probably the best solution is that of Keil, who suggests that an error of one letter has occurred in the course of copying the manuscripts. He points out that the insertion of one letter in verse 28 of our text would change 8,600 to 8,300, since there is only a difference of one letter in the consonantal text between *shish*, 'six', and *shalosh*, 'three'.

c. The Levites taken by the Lord in place of the firstborn of Israel (iii. 40–51)

The Lord commands that the firstborn of the males of the children of Israel be numbered (40).

The result is given as 22,273 (43). This could hardly represent all living Israelite men who were firstborn in their families, since 22,273 out of 603,550 (cf. ii. 32) would be a ratio of about one out of twenty-seven, and the total number given is, after all, limited to males of twenty and upward, able to go to war. The full total would be far greater. Since the firstborn who were living at the departure from Egypt had been passed over by the destroying angel when he killed all the firstborn Egyptians (Ex. xiii. 13–15), the principle had been established that the firstborn belong to God (Nu. iii. 13). Our present numbering probably included only those firstborn males who were born subsequent to the departure from Egypt.

The Levites and their cattle were taken by the Lord in place of 22,000 of the Israelite firstborn (45) and the remaining 273 were redeemed with money (46–51). It is to be noted that the Lord took all the cattle of the Levites in place of the firstborn of the cattle of Israel (41 and 45; cf. Ex. xii. 29).

d. The mature Levites numbered and their service described in detail (iv. 1–33)

The numbering already described was for the purpose of setting the entire tribe of Levi apart for the service of the tabernacle. Now the Lord commands another numbering, this time limited to those individuals who are ready for actual service. Each of the three divisions of the tribe is taken in turn, but not in the same order as in chapter iii. Instead, the sons of Kohath, the division from which Moses and Aaron came, are placed first. This is logical, since the Kohathites are to have charge of the most important things in the tabernacle.

The three divisions are discussed in closely parallel fashion, with much repetition of phraseology. In each case a specific command to make a census is given first (2, 22, 29). Then the age limits of this particular census are stated (3, 23, 30). Next the service of each division is stated. The charge of Kohath describes in full the work of Aaron and his sons in packing up the sacred vessels (5–15a) and then states that the other sons of Kohath are to carry these vessels after they have been packed (15b). It ends with a statement that Eleazar, the son of Aaron, is to have charge over all the tabernacle, and over the most holy objects in particular (16), followed by an extensive warning against any intrusion among the uncovered holy things on the part of the Kohathites (17–20). The charge of the Gershonites (25–26) repeats with some further details the service described in iii. 36–37. The charge of Gershon and that of Merari end with a statement that immediate supervision over them is committed to Ithamar, the youngest son of Aaron (28 and 33). For fuller understanding of the work of each group it would be well to study the detailed account of the parts of the tabernacle in Ex. xxv–xxvii, xxx, xxxv–xxxviii.

Cut ye not off . . . the Kohathites (18). This

expression is used as a vivid way of showing the great responsibility of Moses and Aaron to impress on the Kohathites the danger of any intrusion upon the sacred things by individuals who are not priests. Failure to warn them adequately might lead to a transgression which would cause the entire family of Kohath to be killed, and thus to be entirely cut off from the tribe of Levi.

e. The results of the numbering (iv. 34–49)

Each division is taken up separately with Kohath first. The statements about the three sections agree almost word for word. A fourth parallel section gives the total. Each of these four sections begins by naming the division under consideration (34, 38, 42, 46). Next the age limit given above (3, 23, 30) is repeated (35, 39, 43, 47). The result is stated: Kohath, 2,750 (36); Gershon, 2,630 (40); Merari, 3,200 (44); total 8,580 (48). In conclusion, the name of each division is stated again (37, 41, 45, 49).

With this section we conclude the portion of the book which has led to the misleading title in Greek and in English. Only in these four chapters and in chapter xxvi do we find long lists of numbers. These numbers have sometimes been a cause of difficulty in accepting the narrative as true. It is asked how so many Levites could be occupied with the care of the tabernacle. While 8,580 men may seem a large number to be set aside for this task, we must remember that it was not only a matter of caring for the tabernacle, but also of setting apart a group to represent God in all the various sections of Palestine after the conquest. Moreover, although this section deals principally with the work of moving the tabernacle, there were doubtless many other duties to be performed while staying in one place and directing the religious life of a nation so large as to include 603,550 fighting men (i. 46). See also the remarks about the numbers under i. 17–46 above.

III. REMOVAL OF UNCLEANNESS AND DEFILEMENT FROM THE CAMP. v. 1–31

This section has three parts, each of which is concerned with a specific type of evil which must be eradicated from the camp, if God's blessing is to remain upon it. The first of these involves people who are hygienically or ceremonially defiled. The second deals with defilement which results from theft or injury to others. The third relates to matrimonial jealousy whether justified or not.

a. Removal of defiled persons (v. 1–4)

Commands are given for removal outside the camp of three classes of people: lepers, persons with certain other diseases, and persons who are temporarily unclean as a result of touching a dead body. This removal was vital to the Israelites in the wilderness both from a hygienic and from a ceremonial viewpoint.

Touching a dead body made one ritually

unclean. God wished to indicate that His people should be completely separate from sin and defilement. In addition there was a hygienic purpose, to hinder the spread of disease. It was also important to make a sharp break, in order that people should recognize that when a person has died the spirit has gone to be with the Lord, and the body is no longer something beautiful, but rather something that is laid aside. This would prevent wrong attitudes toward the dead.

b. Removal of the guilt of trespass (v. 5–10)

Trespass (6). Heb. *ma'al*. This word implies stealth or secrecy. Cf. its use in verses 12 and 27 below. The law given here presupposes the portion of the permanent priestly law contained in Lv. vi. 1–7. Full details are not now repeated, but the penalties of the law are restated in order to ensure removal of this type of defilement from the camp. A new feature is also added, providing for a special situation which might occasionally arise. Suppose that the man against whom the trespass has been committed can no longer be found and that there is no kinsman who would have the right to receive what is due him. In such a case the trespass and the accompanying penalties must be paid to the priest, as the Lord's representative. In order to avoid any misunderstanding verses 9–10 state plainly that the offerings and other things given become the property of the priest.

Here is a lesson for the Christian. He should have absolute probity in his dealings with all men. If he has defrauded and injured others before he was won to the Lord, it is his duty to make full restitution, as far as possible.

c. The law of jealousy (v. 11–31)

i. The cause of the jealousy. (v. 11–15). This interesting passage deals with a type of defilement that constitutes a special threat to the peace and progress of the camp. Two possible conditions are involved. Either a woman has been unfaithful but there are no witnesses, and her husband is jealous (12–14a); or the woman is innocent and the husband is jealous without cause (14b). It is a matter which cannot be determined by evidence. Yet it is necessary that the problem be settled. Regardless of whether the woman is guilty or innocent, harm is done by the jealousy itself, and the resulting suspicion and misunderstanding can easily become a source of grievous injury to the family and to the entire camp.

An offering (15). Since the sin is not only against the husband or wife, as the case may be, but also against the Lord, an offering is required. Similarly in every aspect of the life of the Christian it is important that he pay attention to the offering which Christ made of Himself on the cross. The atonement is the very foundation of the Christian life and must never be left out of account.

ii. The test of guilt (v. 16–31). These verses give detailed instructions for a test which the priest is to perform to determine whether the woman is guilty or not, and thus to put an end to the situation of jealousy and suspicion. This test seems strange to many today. In modern times it is usually found that physical causes have physical results regardless of the moral and spiritual situation back of them. It is not expected that the physical situation of a woman who has been unfaithful in her marital relations will necessarily be different from that of one who has been faithful to her husband.

It is sometimes said that this test was a primitive practice common to Israel's heathen neighbours and of animistic origin. Actually there is no evidence of any such practice among the nations contiguous to Israel. It is true that the idea that divinity would intervene to reveal the guilt or innocence of one accused of a crime is found among many peoples; yet in none of the nations neighbouring to Israel is there evidence of any custom with significant details similar to those of our present section. The nearest analogy would be the Babylonian ordeal described in the Code of Hammurabi, but this is very different from anything contained in the Bible.

It should be noted that it is nowhere stated that this test is intended to be used after the people settle in the Promised Land. Chapter v begins with specific references to the purity of 'the camp' (2–3), and there is no reference to such a practice in later parts of the Bible or in any other writing that has come down to us from the period prior to the destruction of the Jerusalem temple in A.D. 70. A century or more after that event the rabbis engaged in extensive speculations about every feature of the law and every aspect of the ancient life of Israel. In the Talmudic discussion of the law they add to this ordinance other features quite unknown to the book of Numbers, selecting a particular place in the temple where they say that the rite was administered, and say that it was abolished by a first-century rabbi for a very strange reason. Such evidence is of little value as far as actual events in first-century Jerusalem are concerned. Even assuming, however, that the practice might have been carried on at that time it would certainly not prove anything about the long period from Joshua to David, to Zedekiah, and during the centuries from Ezra to the Maccabees. It is most reasonable to consider the practice in the light of the context as a provision intended only for the wilderness journey. Our chapter teaches that God promised to perform a miracle during that brief period, and there is no other evidence of the existence of any type of 'ordeal' as a judicial procedure anywhere in the history of ancient Israel.

To understand the reason for such a unique procedure on the part of God at this time, we must remember the situation. Man had put God out of his thoughts and tried to forget Him (cf. Rom. i. 21, 28). God had selected one man, Abraham, and brought him out of Ur of the Chaldees in order that through him and his descendants He should keep alive His testimony and prepare the way for the coming of His Son through whom men should be saved. The witness of God was now confined in this one group of people coming up through the wilderness. If the testimony of this group were destroyed, the existing witness to God would be wiped out and it would be necessary to start to build one all over again. Naturally, therefore, this is one of the comparatively few periods in the Bible where there is an outpouring of divine miracles.

A similar situation existed in the early days of the Christian Church. There also God performed a great number of miracles in order that Satan should not stamp out the Christian witness while it was a very small thing. After it became so large that, if one portion was wiped out and destroyed, other portions would still keep going, miracles ceased.

Many people think that the Bible is filled with miracles. However, this is not the case. Large sections contain no miracle at all. It is interesting to compare the large number of miracles found in the period which includes the deliverance from Egypt, the wilderness journey, and the conquest of Canaan, with their infrequency in the lifetime of Abraham or in the reigns of David and Solomon.

The wilderness journey, then, was a crisis period in which God performed special miracles. Under these circumstances our present test is not strange at all, when we think of the serious results which might come from emotional and moral disturbances in the camp as a result of jealousy and suspicion, whether well or ill founded.

It is not impossible, however, that this test did not at that time require a supernatural divine act in every case. Only recently has medicine begun to give full attention to the influence of mental and emotional attitudes on the human body. Certain diseases are now recognized as primarily due to emotional stress or strain. Think of the situation of an Israelite woman at this time. She had seen the wonderful works of God in Egypt and in the wilderness. She had direct knowledge of the mighty power which He had displayed in so many ways. Brought before God's representative, and faced with this solemn exhortation, it would not be at all strange if the drinking of the water would be followed by the guilty woman experiencing all the physical pains described in the curse. On the other hand the innocent woman, trusting in the justice of the all-seeing God, might drink the water in utter peace and confidence. After noting this, however, it must be remembered that, in connection with this test, the divine provision necessarily carried with it the promise that God would miraculously intervene whenever it should be necessary.

IV. A SPECIAL TYPE OF SEPARATION —THE NAZARITE VOW. vi. 1–21

Nazarite (2; Heb. *nazir*) should be distinguished from *Nazarene* (from Heb. *neṣer*), the name applied to Christ in Mt. ii. 23. The middle consonants are quite different in Hebrew, although the words look so similar in English. The Nazarite was a man who desired for a period to set himself apart unto God in an unusual way. The vow represents special consecration for a limited time for unusual service to God. The Hebrew root means separation, or consecration. *Nazir* is used in this general sense in Dt. xxxiii. 16, to designate Joseph as one who was 'separated from' his brethren. The way the subject is introduced here suggests that it is regulating an institution already in existence, rather than instituting something new. Probably one reason for thus regulating it was to draw a sharp distinction between those who were Nazarites and those who were not, by fixing its requirements and making provisions for its termination. There is no reference after this to anyone taking upon himself a Nazarite vow which should last for the rest of his life. The case of Samson (Jdg. xiii–xvi) is quite different. He did not assume a vow; instead an obligation was laid upon him before his birth by the command that he should be a Nazarite (or separated one) all his life (Jdg. xiii. 5, 7, 13–14). Since the Nazariteship of Samson differs in these important features from the provisions of our present ordinance, there is no reason to think that it would agree with them in all other features, even though it is strikingly similar in a number of its characteristics. Cf. the case of Samuel, whose life was consecrated to God by his mother even before his conception (1 Sa. i. 11), and that of John the Baptist, where the angel made certain promises to Zacharias about his son's consecration, even before the child was conceived (Lk. i. 15).

These regulations are important for the Christian as he considers his relation to things which are not wrong in themselves, but which may prove to be hindrances to his Christian service (cf. Heb. xii. 1). The spiritual life of some people may be greatly advanced by giving up certain things which are not harmful in themselves. In the case of others such a course makes their lives unbalanced and produces tensions that retard their spiritual progress. Much harm has been done by forcing on people who desire to serve the Lord vows of abstention from normal life, the implications of which were not realized by those taking them. The widespread corruption of medieval monasticism was a natural result. God desires most of His people to live normal lives.

a. The requirements of the Nazarite vow (vi. 1–8)

Verse 2 points out the voluntary nature of the Nazarite oath and defines it. It means that one separates himself to the Lord for a specific length of time. It may be noted that either a man or a woman can become a Nazarite. The obligations of the Nazarite are three in number. First, he separates himself entirely from any use of wine or strong drink. He must not use anything which comes from the grape vine at all, whether it be fermented wine, or vinegar, or even ordinary grape juice (*mishrah*, translated *liquor* (3), means simply 'juice'), or fresh grapes, or raisins.

The second requirement is to *let the locks of the hair of his head grow* (5). This is contrary to ordinary usage and becomes a public indication of the fact that he is set apart.

The third requirement is to keep himself from any contact with a dead body. See note on Nu. v. 1–4 above. His standard here is above that of the priest, and equals that of the High Priest (Lv. xxi. 1–3, 10–11). Not even his love for members of his family can lead him to make a break in this. He must not voluntarily touch any dead body.

Touching a dead body was not sinful in itself. Ordinarily it was to be expected that the family of a dead person would touch his body. There were cases in which a Jew was considered as having done a very holy thing in defiling himself in order to give someone decent burial. Such an incident forms the beginning of the apocryphal book of Tobit. However, the Nazarite was specifically set apart to God and was forbidden voluntarily to enter upon any such uncleanness even in the case of his closest relative. All the days of his separation, he must be holy unto the Lord.

b. The penalty for involuntarily breaking the oath (vi. 9–12)

No remedy is given if the Nazarite uses a product of the vine, or if he cuts his hair. These are voluntary acts which he is obliged to avoid. The same is true if he voluntarily touches a dead body. However, there is the possibility that someone may suddenly die beside him so that he becomes ceremonially unclean, without any intentional breaking of the rule of the Nazarite. For this case, a special remedy is given. First, he must perform the same cleansing duties as anyone else who has become unclean through touching a dead body (cf. Nu. xix). Then he must shave his head on the seventh day, a procedure otherwise strictly forbidden during the period of Nazariteship. In addition to the turtle doves or pigeons which are the regular requirement for ending of uncleanness (cf. Lv. xv. 14), he must bring a lamb for a trespass offering. Worst of all, all the days of his separation previous to this time are lost. This requirement seems very severe for one who has become unclean through no fault of his own. It indicates the very strict standards of holiness which God requires of those who are set apart for special service to Himself. One who is consecrated to the Lord for special service must be particularly careful that he does not even unintentionally give an impression of wrong. When placed in a false light it is particularly important that he be cleansed in the fullest manner, in order that no taint or reproach shall come upon the work of the Lord.

c. Termination of the Nazariteship (vi. 13–21)

Verse 13 makes very clear the fact that Nazariteship normally is for a limited time. An extensive public ceremony is prescribed at its conclusion so that people can know very definitely whether one is a Nazarite or not. For this ceremony, the Nazarite must come to the door of the tent of meeting, bringing with him a number of special offerings, which are described in verses 14 and 15. The priest performs the ceremony (16–17); then the Nazarite shaves his head at the door of the tent of meeting and burns the long hair that has grown during his period of consecration in the fire under the sacrifice. Nothing can be kept to show as a trophy of the length of his consecration to the Lord. The priest performs additional ceremonies (19–20); after this the Nazarite vow has come to an end and the man or woman has become free from any restrictions which are not binding on ordinary people.

Verse 21 is a concluding title, with special reference to the offering of the Nazarite. *Beside that that his hand shall get* (21; Heb. *nasag*, lit. 'reach'): an idiomatic expression meaning 'beside whatever he otherwise is able to afford'; i.e., in addition to the prescribed offering.

V. ARRANGEMENTS FOR THE RELIGIOUS LIFE OF THE CAMP. vi. 22—ix. 14

In Exodus arrangements were made for the establishment of the tabernacle as the centre of the religious life of Israel. In Leviticus regulations were laid down for many different types of offerings and also for the special services of the priests and Levites. Our present section deals with particular aspects of the religious life of Israel during the long wilderness journey. It contains five sub-divisions. The first of these is a beautiful formula of blessing. Unfortunately, in our English Bible it is buried at the end of a long chapter of an entirely different nature. The second is an account of the offerings made by the leaders of the different tribes at the beginning of the journey. These included particular sacrifices for the tribes, and also materials which were needed for the service of the tabernacle. The third is an account of the lighting of the lamps in the candlestick in the tabernacle, showing the beginning of its use to bring light to the minds and hearts of the people. The fourth is an account of the specific preparation of the Levites for their work in the service of the tabernacle. The fifth is an account of the first great memorial Passover, one year after the event which the Passover memorializes, and a statement of new regulations in connection with it.

a. The formula for blessing the congregation (vi. 22–27)

This brief section presents a formula for the priests to use in blessing the congregation. Verses 22 and 23 introduce it, and verse 27 gives a concluding promise. The blessing itself consists of three verses, 24–26. It is one of the most beautiful and best-known sections of the book of Numbers.

Those who deny the Mosaic authorship of the Pentateuch generally divide these five books into documents, claiming that more primitive passages are found in the early documents, and that the later ones, which are supposed to be more spiritual and less anthropomorphic, were written at a much later time. They place this section in the latest document which they call 'P'. Therefore it is worth noticing that, with all its spirituality, the blessing contains statements which are markedly anthropomorphic, e.g., *the Lord make his face shine upon thee, the Lord lift up his countenance upon thee* (25, 26). This illustrates the fact that anthropomorphism is not inconsistent with spirituality. In fact, true spirituality must recognize the personality of God, and personality can hardly be described to a human being in terms other than those drawn from human life.

The blessing consists of three verses, and there is a noticeable progress in them. Verse 24 is rather general: *The Lord bless thee, and keep thee. Keep* (Heb. *shamar*) would be better rendered in modern English as 'guard' or 'protect'; it refers to physical well-being, and prevention of trouble from external sources. It is the first and lowest stage of our prayer for divine help. Many people never get beyond this stage. It is a vital stage, but the Christian must go past it into the next two.

The second verse of the blessing takes us a step higher: *The Lord make his face shine upon thee, and be gracious unto thee*. The expression is definitely in the spiritual realm, and involves a more personal relationship with God, but is still rather general in nature. The Lord causes the rain to fall upon the just and the unjust. The Lord shows His countenance to all the world. Here the prayer is that the Lord's face shall shine upon the one who is blessed, and that he shall be the recipient of favour from the Almighty. We might say that this verse is fulfilled most truly through the death of Christ on Calvary's cross, where God showed forth His love to a world lost in sin, where the shining of the face of our wonderful God was most clearly made manifest, and where He showed favour to all who believe in the name of Christ. This second verse, then, marks the step into distinctive Christianity.

The third verse goes yet a step higher: *The Lord lift up his countenance upon thee, and give thee peace.* The word that both AV and RV render here as *countenance* is exactly the same as the word which they translate *face* in the previous verse.

This third verse has a specific individual reference: 'The Lord lift up His face upon you.' Not merely that the face of the Lord shine out upon all the world and show it favour, and that you be included in that upon which it shines, but that He very specifically lift up His face toward you, and give particular attention to your individual welfare. If there be question as to this interpretation of the first part of the verse, there can be no question as to the meaning of its latter half, *and give thee peace*. The word here translated 'give' is not the ordinary Hebrew word for 'give'. Rather it means 'set', 'place', or 'establish'. 'May the Lord establish peace for you' would be a more exact rendering. The word translated 'peace' (Heb. *shalom*) does not mean simply 'cessation of hostility'. It indicates 'completeness', 'perfection', or 'well-being'. This, of course, includes cessation of war as one of its factors, but only one. 'The Lord give you that complete harmonious development, that perfection in every direction, that you need.' It is a wonderful blessing, one which can well be taken by every believer, and applied as his prayer to God for blessing upon himself, and upon those to whom he may have the opportunity of presenting God's message.

b. The offerings of the princes (vii. 1–89)

On the day that Moses had fully set up the tabernacle (1). This chapter does not chronologically follow the preceding ones, since the military census (Nu. i. 1) was taken at the beginning of the second month of the second year, and the tabernacle was set up at the beginning of the first month (Ex. xl. 17). Exodus gives the divine instructions for building the tabernacle, and describes its erection in accordance with these directions. Along with these directions, God also gave precise instructions for the priests, which are preserved in the book of Leviticus. Numbers continues the history, usually presenting it in chronological order, but sometimes arranging it logically instead of chronologically. Although the events of this chapter preceded those in the earlier chapters of the book, it is placed here because it includes the bringing of materials needed for transporting the tabernacle, and we are here concerned with preparations for journeying away from Sinai.

i. **The wagons and the oxen (vii. 1–9).** The twelve leaders of the tribes offered the six covered wagons and the twelve oxen needed for transporting the tabernacle. The cost was equally divided among them (3). Verses 4–9 tell how the wagons were divided among the Levites, not equally, but according to their service. The sons of Gershon, whose service was described in Nu. iv. 25–26, received one-third of the wagons and oxen (7). The sons of Merari, having the heaviest materials to carry (cf. iv. 31–32), received twice as many (8). The sons of Kohath received none at all (9), since it was their duty to carry the sacred vessels from the interior of the tabernacle upon their shoulders (iv. 1–15). At this point it is well to read the account in 2 Sa. vi. 3–7 of the death of Uzzah, a direct result of forgetting this requirement and carrying the ark on a wagon. God desires His work to be done in accordance with the directions of His Word.

ii. **Gifts for the dedicating of the altar (vii. 10–89).** It would seem that the altar was anointed on the first day of the month (10; cf. Ex. xl. 2,

10, 17), but that the actual dedication was spread over twelve days (11), with each prince bringing his gifts on a different day. The gifts of each are described in great detail, even though what was given was exactly identical on each separate day. There is great similarity in the things that God requires of each Christian, yet each of us is very important in His sight and He is interested in every detail of our life and service. It is interesting that the order of the tribes here is not that of the numbering in chapter i but of the description of the encampment in chapter ii. *Deuel* (42, 47). See note on ii. 14.

Verses 84–89 summarize the offerings given on the twelve days, which total exactly twelve times what was given by each prince. Full details are given in each case. God keeps record even of our smallest acts and deeds. He desires exactness. Careless and shoddy work is never acceptable to Him.

The account of the offerings ends in verse 88. In verse 89 we read that in the holy of holies Moses heard a voice speaking to him from above the altar. The next chapter gives us additional messages that God gave to Moses. It is impossible to say whether this verse is introducing viii. 1 or finishing the account of the dedication of the altar.

c. The lamps lit (viii. 1–4)

Now that the gifts have been received for the dedication of the altar, command is given that the lamps in the tabernacle be lit. These have already been described with more detail in Ex. xxv. It is necessary that they be lit before the journey can properly be commenced. We also must have our lamps burning if we are to serve God effectively.

d. Cleansing of the Levites for service (viii. 5–22)

At a formal meeting, with appropriate ceremonies, the Levites must be consecrated to God and inducted into His service. Details of their service have already been explained in chapter iv. It was necessary that the work of the altar be done by persons properly prepared for the task. Therefore, the Levites had to be cleansed both ceremonially and physically. Verses 5–19 contain God's command; verses 20–22 describe its performance.

There are many lessons for the Christian in this section. He sees here the importance of each member of God's family having his own particular task. Cf. 1 Cor. xii. It is necessary that special men be designated for particular duties, and the most important of these duties require ceremonies of installation, in order that the work of God's kingdom shall be done in orderly fashion. Those who do the work of God must be cleansed from all defilement of flesh and spirit. No one is fit in himself to serve God. It is only as we see ourselves as guilty sinners saved through the sacrifice of the Lord Jesus Christ at Calvary that we can do anything that is worth while in God's sight. All our righteousnesses apart from Him are but 'filthy rags' (Is. lxiv. 6).

e. The age of Levitical service (viii. 23–26)

This brief section states that the Levites are to carry on the service of the tabernacle from the age of twenty-five to the age of fifty. In chapter iv the age of beginning of service was given as thirty. It would seem that from twenty-five to thirty the Levites were in a sort of apprenticeship, unless the legislation in chapter iv be taken to apply only to the wilderness period. Verses 25, 26 describe a limited retirement after fifty. They no longer do the heavy tasks of waiting upon the service of the tabernacle, but they minister with their brethren in keeping charge, doing lighter tasks and exerting a certain amount of oversight. Our God sometimes works wonderful things through the very young, and sometimes gives people strength long after the normal age; yet there is a normal procedure which is found to work out in most cases.

f. The first Passover after leaving Egypt (ix. 1–14)

In the first month of the second year (1). Again a chapter begins with a date which precedes that of Nu. i. 1. Yet this chapter is both chronologically and logically in its proper place, since its principal event, the special Passover, occurred just six days before the beginning of the wilderness journey.

Shortly before the commencement of the events described in Nu. i, the first memorial Passover was observed (1–5), in accordance with all the regulations prescribed in Ex. xii. Then a new problem arose. Some of the people in the camp were faced with a question of conflicting laws. All Israelites must keep the Passover or be cut off from God's people. Yet men who had touched a dead body were defiled and could not keep the Passover. What should be done in such a case?

The problem of conflicting laws is often a difficult one. Among the modern Jews a very important law is sometimes disregarded in view of the application of a less important one. For instance there is a rule that every firstborn child must fast at certain times. Another rule says that whenever the reading of a portion of the Scripture is completed there shall be a time of celebration. As a result men who are interested in keeping the letter of the law rather than its spirit sometimes resort to the expedient of reading the last few chapters of a book at such a time that they will complete it just prior to the day when they are supposed to fast. Then they take their choice of the two conflicting laws and follow the one that allows them to ignore the fast. The situation described in our passage was not of this type. The men seem to have been sincerely anxious to follow God's will. So *they came before Moses* (6) with their problem and he laid it before the Lord (8).

In answer to Moses' request for information, the Lord declared that a second Passover could be held a month after the regular one for the sake of those who had been unable to participate for the reason given, or had been far off on a journey. This is an illustration of the principle stated by Christ in Mk. ii. 27 that 'the sabbath was made for man, and not man for the sabbath'. God's regulations are to be carried out exactly as far as possible; but when something interferes, the time may be changed to meet the emergency. It is interesting to note that while verse 10 makes special allowance for a man who is on a journey, no provision is made for permanent domicile abroad. This would be a strange omission if the critics were right in their claim that this section is post-exilic and was given to people whose centre of gravity was in Babylon.

Verses 11–12 contain a brief summary of the commands given in Ex. xii (see especially Ex. xii. 46), so that, even though the Passover is held a month late, it may be certain that its full meaning is clear to those who partake of it. They are to eat unleavened bread and bitter herbs and not a bone of the sacrificial lamb is to be broken. This represents in advance the bitter anguish of the death of Christ, the Lamb without blemish, slain for us and not a bone of Him broken (cf. Jn. xix. 36).

In this connection we may note the account in 2 Ch. xxx of a great Passover which was held after a period of neglect of God's ordinances. When it was decided to do this, there was not time enough to prepare to celebrate it at the regular time; therefore it was held on the fourteenth day of the second month. God seems to have wonderfully blessed that Passover, even though it was a month after the regular date.

Under normal conditions postponement of the Passover to the second month is strictly forbidden (13). Unless one really has a valid reason for missing the regular Passover, he must observe it at its proper time or be cut off from among God's people.

God always provided opportunity for Gentiles to enter into the family of Israel. To guard against any misunderstanding He stressed this fact by repeating the principle, already stated in Ex. xii. 45–49, that a stranger who sojourns among the Israelites can become an Israelite. In this case he is to observe the Passover in exactly the same way as if he had been born an Israelite (14). (See notes on the 'stranger' in Ex. xxii. 21 and Dt. i. 16.) Blessing before God was never simply a matter of birth. God promises to show His mercy to thousands of generations of those who love Him, but His mercy is always available to anyone who will join His people, taking upon himself the sign of faith in God's provision for cleansing from sin, which at that time was circumcision (Rom. iv. 11).

VI. THE DIVINE PROVISION FOR DIRECTION AND GUIDANCE. ix. 15—x. 10

a. The pillar of cloud and fire (ix. 15–23)

As the beginning of the new journey comes nearer, the divine leadership is re-emphasized. When the tabernacle was erected, a month before the events described in Nu. i. 1 (cf. Ex. xl. 1

with Nu. i. 1), the pillar of cloud had covered it (Ex. xl. 34). Our present passage adds nothing to the information given at that time, but lays increased stress upon it, since the journey is about to commence and it is vital that all the people have the divine guidance in mind. Accordingly, the information given there in five verses is repeated here in nine. The vital facts of our personal relation to God, who is the true leader of the wilderness journey of every Christian, need often to be brought into consciousness, and particularly at each turning point of our lives. If we keep our eyes fixed upon Him, many of our uncertainties and perplexities automatically disappear.

The facts stated in these two passages (Ex. xl and Nu. ix) were not new when the tabernacle was set up. God had led the people in this way ever since they left Egypt (Ex. xiii. 21–22).

These passages place such great emphasis upon the divine leadership that we might almost think that Moses and the people had no use for their own intelligence, but needed only blindly to follow a divine leading which would answer all questions. Such a conclusion would be contrary to the general teaching of the Bible and to the experience of every Christian. There are two sides of the matter, and neither can safely be left out of account. Our present passage stresses the faith aspect, and this aspect is extremely vital. Unless we see God's hand leading us and are ready to follow wherever He leads, we cannot expect success in our wilderness journey. Yet God has not made us automatons. He does not desire puppets, which jump whenever He pulls the cord, but have no mind of their own. He desires His people to learn to use their intelligence, and to follow Him because they love Him. Our earthly life is a period of training, in which He has many things to teach us.

The very next portion of this section shows that extreme conclusions must not be drawn. If it had been sufficient that all the people should see the guiding pillar, x. 1–10 would not have provided a method of signalling, so that the leaders could tell the people when to start and how to proceed.

Later, in chapter xi, we find Moses urging his brother-in-law, who was familiar with the wilderness, to stay with the people and give them the benefit of his experience in selecting their camping places. In chapter xiii we learn that God commanded that spies be sent to search out the land of Canaan. When Joshua planned to attack Jericho, he first sent spies into the city. It is God's will that His people should use ordinary foresight, and do their best to plan wisely. This side of the matter was stressed by the Lord Himself in Lk. xiv. 28–32. It is the Lord's will that all human means be utilized, but that His overruling control be constantly kept in mind.

b. The silver trumpets (x. 1–10)

After explaining the general rule for guidance, God provides a means by which the leaders can order united action by the entire host. Two trumpets of silver are to be made for use in calling an assembly and for the journeying of the camp. *Trumpet* (2). Heb. *ḥaṣoṣerah*, a tube about 18 inches long with a flared end; not a curved tube like the more extensively used *shophar*, or ram's horn (Ex. xix. 16, 19, xx. 18; Lv. xxv. 9). There are three ways in which the trumpets may be used. The blowing of both trumpets summons all of the assembly to come together at the door of the tent of meeting (3, 7). The blowing of but one trumpet calls the heads of the various sections of all the tribes to come to Moses (4). In both these cases there would probably be one loud note on the trumpet, perhaps repeated at intervals. The third way, designated in English by the words *blow an alarm*, means a long continued peal of the trumpets, and indicates that the tribes on the east side are to break camp and start forward. At a second peal the tribes on the south are to start (5–6). Use of the trumpets is to be continued after they reach the Promised Land, both in war and in peace (8–10).

God desires His people to work unitedly for carrying out His purposes. 'If the trumpet give an uncertain sound, who shall prepare himself to the battle?' (1 Cor. xiv. 8).

FROM SINAI TO THE PLAINS OF MOAB. x. 11—xxii. 1

VII. THE FIRST STAGE OF THE JOURNEY. x. 11–36

a. The departure from Sinai (x. 11–28)

We now begin a section of a book which runs to xxii. 1. It covers a period of nearly forty years, and includes the journey from Sinai to Kadesh, the crisis at Kadesh, and the journey to the Plains of Moab where the people made their last halt before the conquest of Canaan.

Verses 14–27 state the exact order in which the tribes marched. When the Israelites left Egypt their order was doubtless more or less haphazard. Now a definite system is to be used, as was announced in chapters i—iv. Here its details are put together, to show the orderly

march of the Israelites. Sometimes it is not nearly so important which order is used as that a definite order is followed, so that God's people may co-operate and accomplish the purposes that He desires.

In verses 14–27 the leaders of the various tribes are named again (cf. Nu. ii).

It is stated in x. 17 that two-thirds of the Levites *set forward, bearing the tabernacle* as soon as the first three tribes had gone. This seems at first sight to contradict ii. 17 which said, after the departure of six tribes: 'Then the tabernacle of the congregation shall set forward with the camp of the Levites in the midst of the camp.' The solution is found in x. 21, where we learn that after the departure of six tribes *the*

Kohathites set forward, bearing the sanctuary: and the other did set up the tabernacle against they came. This would seem to have been a further refinement of detail over the general plan announced in chapter ii. It was decided to send the bulk of the heavy materials of the tabernacle on ahead after the first three tribes, so that when the Kohathites arrived with the sanctuary everything would be ready for its installation.

b. Moses requests the help of Hobab (x. 29–32)

Hobab was the brother-in-law of Moses. Probably the Hebrew word *ḥothen*, which is generally rendered 'father-in-law', can also be applied to a brother-in-law, although it is not certain whether this would always be true, or only after he succeeded to the leadership of his family, after the death of the actual father-in-law. Cf. Jdg. iv. 11. *Raguel* (29). Although Hobab's father is usually called Jethro (in Ex. iii. 1 and thereafter in Exodus), he is called Reuel in Ex. ii. 18, where he is first mentioned, and the same name is found here. In Greek transliteration the middle consonant of Reuel, *ayin*, is frequently represented by a 'g' as in Gaza and in Gomorrah. In the case of Reuel, the English version has followed the Hebrew pronunciation in Ex. ii. 18, and the Greek pronunciation here. Evidently Hobab had stayed with Moses after Jethro's departure (Ex. xviii. 27). *Be to us instead of eyes* (31). Impressed with Hobab's knowledge of the desert, Moses asked him to perform a scouting service for the Israelites.

It might be asked why the incident is recorded here, after the march is actually under way. The explanation would seem to be that Hobab had intended going a certain distance with the people, before turning aside to his usual haunts. Consequently the request was made now, rather than earlier. Although it is not explicitly stated, it would seem quite certain that he accepted Moses' invitation, since we find his descendants in Canaan at a later time (Jdg. i. 16, iv. 11).

c. The ark and the blessing (x. 33–36)

The mount of the Lord (33). This is the only time this exact phrase is used, but the same place (Mt. Horeb) is called 'the mount of God' in Ex. iii. 1, iv. 27, xviii. 5, xxiv. 13; 1 Ki. xix. 8. The latter part of verse 33 has been much discussed, most critics insisting that it means that the ark of the covenant went a three days' journey ahead of the people in order to search out a resting place for them. Some critics say that this means that the ark moved of itself. Others say that it was probably carried in a wagon by oxen. An excessive literalness can reduce any book to nonsense. The phrase *the ark . . . went* need not mean that it moved of itself, but can perfectly well refer to its being carried on the shoulders of priests and Levites in the normal way. Moreover there is no grammatical necessity of interpreting the phrase 'three days' journey' as some critics take it. The AV renders it *in the three days'*

journey. While this involves a measure of interpretation, it is consistent with the context, and entirely possible grammatically. The critical interpretation involves the conclusion that the clause is a bit of mythology inconsistent with the rest of the book of Numbers. Such a conclusion is entirely unnecessary.

Yet there is an apparent contradiction between this statement and the previous instructions for transporting the tabernacle and its vessels in the midst of the host (ii. 17, iv. 15). There are two possible explanations. One is the result of close examination of the phrase *before them* (33), Heb. *lipheneihem*, which may simply mean 'in their presence', as in Dt. iii. 28, x. 11, and xxxi. 3. In these passages Joshua or Moses is said to go before the people under circumstances which clearly indicate that they were not physically in front of them, but before them in the sense of being visible to them and in authority over them. In line with this use of the phrase some interpreters consider that the verse simply means that the ark was carried in its normal place in the midst of the tribes, but that the priests who travelled near it observed the movements of the pillar of cloud and of fire, received reports from the scouts, and indicated by trumpet signals the proper times for the host to move and to encamp. Another and possibly better interpretation of the statement results in the conclusion that during the first three days the ark was carried ahead of all the tribes. There would be nothing strange in thus departing from the prescribed travel order for the first three days. We have already noticed (x. 17, 21) that the original directions for movement of the parts of the tabernacle were somewhat altered, for increased convenience. These first three days were through rough wilderness country, devoid of human enemies, but presenting unusual difficulty in finding suitable camping spots. At this time the ark may have been carried at the very head of the people to typify the divine leadership and the interest of God in providing suitable places for encampment. Afterwards it was carried at its normal place, where it would be protected against enemies. Similarly, at the beginning of the conquest of Canaan, when the Jordan was crossed, the priests were ordered to carry the ark at the head of the people, and when their feet touched the river its waters receded before them (Jos. iii. 6). At a later time people took the ark as a magical thing, rather than simply as a symbol of God's presence, and wicked men tried to use it to win a battle against the Philistines (1 Sa. iv). The effort proved disastrous. God is not to be compelled by the manipulation of physical things, but uses physical things as symbols of His presence to assure His people of His interest in them.

Verse 34 again stresses the divine leadership, as shown by the pillar of cloud. Verses 35 and 36 give the formula uttered by Moses at the beginning and end of the day's journey. The words of verse 35, uttered in the third instead of the second person, occur again in Ps. lxviii. 1. *Thousands* (36). Perhaps here and in i. 16 this word means families or divisions of the tribes, instead of literal thousands. However, this is obviously not applicable to the census, with its total of 603,550 (see i. 46n.).

VIII. REBELLION AND DISAFFECTION. xi. 1—xii. 16

a. Disaffection in the outskirts of the camp (xi. 1–3)

After the ideal picture in previous chapters of the divine arrangements for the care and progress of Israel, and the beautiful narrative of the beginning of the journey in chapter x, it is a shock to find rebellion and disaffection in the camp itself. The Israelites have been rescued from Egypt and constantly see the pillar of cloud and fire, visible proof of God's presence with them; yet we find disaffection and rebellion breaking out, first in the outskirts of the camp, next in its midst, and finally among the top leaders themselves.

Every Christian leader needs to be warned not to let his judgment be affected by the praise of those over whom God has placed him. Human nature is fickle, and a man's strongest supporters can suddenly become his worst enemies. Even the best of human beings may fall into rebellion against the Lord. The Christian leader should learn to place his trust in God alone; then he will not be too disappointed if those who should support him prove unfaithful. The two chapters are also of great interest for the man of lesser prominence. He should realize the burdens and responsibilities which weigh upon those whom God has placed in positions of leadership. He should not rebel against them, but should support them faithfully, unless, of course, they themselves rebel against the Lord.

b. Trouble in the midst of the camp (xi. 4–15)

It is easy to understand what happened when the people began to take their eyes away from God. In the journey through the wilderness, memory of deliverance from the harsh oppression of Egypt tended to become dim, while realization of the loss of the satisfaction of fleshly appetites enjoyed in Egypt became more vivid. The people began to be dissatisfied with the manna which God was providing and to long for the sensuous pleasures previously enjoyed. Verses 7–8 describe the appearance and use of the manna (cf. Ex. xvi. 31).

The weeping of the people throughout the camp greatly distressed Moses (10). He felt himself to be almost at the end of his endurance. These verses show how he poured out his prayer to God for help. There are two elements in Moses' prayer. One is that the load he is carrying and the responsibility for all the people seem to be more than he can bear. The other is that the people are demanding flesh to eat and there is no possible way in which he can satisfy this desire.

c. God's twofold answer to Moses' prayer (xi. 16–35)

God took up each element of the prayer in turn. First, He dealt with Moses' need of help, telling him to gather seventy leaders of Israel, and promising that He would put His spirit upon them so that they might take over part of Moses' responsibility.

Next, God dealt with the second element of Moses' request, promising that the desire of the people would be satisfied. In fact He declared it would be so fully satisfied that they would be utterly satiated with meat (18–20). Moses' faith was severely strained by this statement of God (21, 22). The nation contained 600,000 men. If God were to gather all the fish of the sea and to kill all the flocks and herds, how would even this suffice to fulfil such a promise? In verse 23 God answered this objection. He did not attempt to describe the means that He would use. He simply pointed to His own great power, and declared that Moses would see the promise fulfilled.

Moses went out and gathered the seventy men as God had directed (24). Evidently he was thoroughly familiar with the abilities of the various leaders of the people and had worked with them in many ways. This was not a sudden gathering of help, but a wonderful outpouring of God's power so as to enable these seventy elders to give Moses the assistance he needed. As they stood around the tabernacle, God's Spirit rested upon them. *They prophesied, and did not cease* (25).

In verses 26–29 we have an interesting parenthetical event. Two of these selected assistants were detained in the camp for some reason, yet when the Spirit of God rested upon the others He came upon them also, and they prophesied in the camp. When the news of this reached Joshua, the servant of Moses, he felt envy for his master's reputation. What would the people think if they found these two men assuming such leadership as had previously been restricted to Moses? In Moses' answer we see the greatness of the man. He did not envy those who might rise to positions of supremacy. His whole desire was that the work of God should go forward. He said, *Would God that all the Lord's people were prophets, and that the Lord would put his spirit upon them*! (29). What an example for each of us, if God puts us in a position of leadership in Christian service! It is so easy to become jealous as a new man advances.

Verses 31–32 describe the complete fulfilment of God's unbelievable promise to supply more meat than the people could possibly consume. The Lord sent a great wind which brought tremendous numbers of quails around the camp so that the people had only to go out and strike them down. This was very easy to do, as they flew about two cubits above the ground, almost blinded by the great wind that drove them inland. These quails are a type of partridge, about $7\frac{1}{2}$ inches long, generally brown in colour. They migrate twice a year, arriving in Palestine in great numbers in March, and coming southward again in the autumn. Occasionally, when the wind changes its course, or the birds become exhausted from the long flight, the entire flock will fall to the ground. Sometimes as a result they are captured in great quantities on the coasts or islands of the Mediterranean Sea. A similar event at an earlier time in the wilderness journey is described in Ex. xvi. The Israelites ate the birds uncooked. Those which they could not eat at once they spread around the camp, in order to dry them in the sun (32). Ps. lxxviii. 26–31 gives a poetic description of this event.

Soon God's wrath was poured out upon the people for their lust (33). He gave them their desire to the full, but it was not what they needed. The result was plague and sickness and misery. Sometimes, if we insist, God will give us our own way in life, but in the end we would be far better off if we sought God's will instead of our own. Cf. Ps. cvi. 13–15.

The place where this occurred was given the appropriate name, Kibroth-hattaavah, 'graves of lust', because many died there as a result of their fleshly appetites (34). With verse 35 cf. xii. 16, where another stage in the progress of the journey is noted.

d. Rebellion among the leaders (xii. 1–16)

Although it is bad for a leader to find disaffection in the rank and file of his followers, it is far worse when his leading subordinates begin to undermine his authority. In view of all that Moses had done for the Israelites he had every reason to expect his subordinates to respect and support him, and certainly he should have been able to count on those who had been elevated to high position on account of close relationship to himself. Yet here he finds his own brother and sister conspiring against him.

The whispering campaign against Moses centred around his marriage, which was used as an excuse to arouse opposition to him. In the succeeding divine intervention God never bothered to make any refutation of this attack. God's powerful intervention condemns all attempts to stir up hatred between races. In Christ there 'is neither Greek nor Jew . . . Barbarian, Scythian, bond nor free' (Col. iii. 11).

It seems strange to read of Moses marrying an *Ethiopian woman* (1) since there has been no mention of the death of Zipporah, whom Jethro had brought to the camp not long before (Ex. xviii. 2–6); however, there is no later mention of her death, either. *Kushi* (used twice in verse 1) is the regular Hebrew word for Ethiopian and is often used in that sense (cf. especially Is. xx. 3–5). It has been suggested that in Gn. ii. 13 and x. 6–8 the word might refer not to Ethiopia, but to the Cassites, a people north-east of Mesopotamia. This interpretation could hardly apply here. The attempt has been made to show that the *Kusi* mentioned in an inscription of Esarhaddon (about 750 B.C.) were a North Arabian tribe,

and hence could be equated with the Midianites. However, this evidence is extremely tenuous, and it is hardly likely that the wife referred to here can be Zipporah. The phrase *for he had married an Ethiopian woman* (1) does not sound like a reference to a marriage that had been in existence about forty years.

Verse 2 shows the real reason for the attack. Aaron and Miriam were not content with second place. They desired the top position for themselves. This is not the way to secure Christian leadership, although many attempt it by this method. God will elevate those who are worthy. He who cannot be faithful in a subordinate position proves himself unworthy of a higher one. *The Lord heard it* (2). Troublemakers often forget that the Lord hears everything they say. This passage should be a reminder that He is always present, and that when He thinks best He will take decisive action, as in this case.

Meek (3). Héb. *'anaw*, i.e. 'humble', not thinking of his own prestige nor looking out for his own interests. The word does not mean simply that Moses was willing to stand aside for God to judge, but rather that he endured the attacks patiently, not seeking vindication for himself or his family. He was so occupied with looking out for God's glory and seeking to forward God's purposes, that he paid no attention to the unfair attacks upon himself. Doubtless Moses himself marvelled in later days that he could have taken this attack on himself and his wife without showing indignation. His meekness surpassed that of all others, perhaps even of himself at other times. Engrossed in the superhuman task of leading the people from Sinai to Kadesh, supervising their lives, executing necessary judgment over them, resisting rebellion, interceding for the nation, doubtless hoping in the very near future to lead them into the Promised Land, the honour of God loomed so great before his eyes that he showed a meekness about his own honour that is almost beyond belief.

This verse has frequently been misunderstood, some writers even saying that it could not possibly have been written by Moses, and alleging that he would have to be extremely egotistic to make such a statement. Actually, one of the strong evidences of the divine inspiration of the Bible is its remarkable objectivity. It clearly shows the faults and weaknesses of Moses and other leaders, and even of the entire nation, in such a way as can be paralleled in no other literature. Faults are not hidden or glossed over, nor is there any false modesty about presenting good points exactly as they were. Writing under the inspiration of the Holy Spirit, Moses did not hesitate to record his own sins and weaknesses in the clearest of language. It would be contrary to the remarkable objectivity of the Bible if he did not also record his strongest point, his meekness. When Moses was standing for the honour of God, he was fearless and ready to overcome any opposition whatever. Attacks upon himself and his wife he took without a murmur, leaving it to God to vindicate him in His own time. While it cannot be proved that this verse is not an inspired insertion in the midst of Moses' writing, it is more likely that Moses wrote it himself, under the leading of the Holy Spirit. Its contents are necessary to a true understanding of the chapter.

In normal times God may allow one of His servants, for the man's own spiritual good, to remain under a cloud of unjust accusation for a long time before he is vindicated. The present situation was too vital for that. It was necessary that Moses' leadership be upheld and vindicated at once. Although Moses took no step in his own defence (a fact which could not possibly be understood without the statement in verse 3), God suddenly intervened (4). He called Moses and his two detractors to come before Him. Then He called Aaron and Miriam apart and rebuked them directly (5).

God pointed out the superiority of Moses to all other human leaders of His people (6–8). To others He might speak in a vision or in a dream; but to Moses He spoke face to face. God did not say that Aaron and Miriam had, or had not, received messages directly from Him. He simply pointed out the superiority of Moses to all other prophets, and then asked why they had ventured to speak against him.

When the cloud departed, Miriam was white with leprosy (10). There is no mention of Aaron's receiving any punishment. Perhaps this means that Miriam was the real instigator of the conspiracy, and Aaron only an accomplice; or perhaps it was a greater punishment to Aaron to see his beloved sister smitten with leprosy than anything that could have happened to himself. His fervent plea (12) argues strongly, though not conclusively, for the latter suggestion.

Aaron's forthright confession of sin (11, 12) gives evidence of true repentance. He addresses Moses as *my lord*. Never again do we have evidence of Aaron opposing Moses.

Aaron is particularly concerned about his sister's leprosy. He sees her *as one dead* (12), so great is his love for her. Fervently he pleads for her restoration. Having sinned against Moses, who is God's representative, he addresses his prayer not to God, but to the man against whom he has sinned.

Without a word of rebuke, Moses turns to God and pleads for his erring sister (13). This is Moses' only action in the entire chapter. Although reviled, he reviled not again, but rather prayed for his detractors. Who can deny the exact truth of the character given him in verse 3?

God shows reluctance to deny a request from Moses (14). It would seem that the leprosy was removed, in response to Moses' intercession, but the seven-day period of isolation which follows cleansing of leprosy must be observed. See Lv. xiv. 8. The offence is too serious for punishment to be remitted entirely. An example must be made to deter others. Also it is desirable to give Miriam time to realize fully the extent of her sin. Thus the Lord delivered the camp from this dangerous rebellion against Moses' authority. *And afterward the people removed* (16). See xi. 35n.

IX. THE CRISIS AT KADESH-BARNEA.
xiii. 1—xiv. 45

This section describes the great turning point of the entire wilderness journey. Here Israel proved its unreadiness to enter the Promised Land, and a whole generation was doomed to die in the wilderness. Moses' expectation of soon entering Canaan was rudely shattered, and the prospect of forty years of wilderness life was substituted. It is one of the most dramatic sections of the Scriptures, and one of the richest in spiritual lessons.

Before examining the section in detail, we must consider the critical view which claims that Nu. xiii and xiv can be broken up into two distinct accounts, each complete in itself, but contradicting the other at various points. It should be noted that in the narrative as it stands the progress of events is quite natural and easy to follow. It is true that a number of ideas are stated more than once. This, however, is frequently due to repetition for emphasis, which is common in most parts of the Bible, and in most other literature as well, particularly when, as here, the situation involves the presentation of the differing opinions of various people. In all such situations, vital ideas commonly find expression more than once. Thus stress is laid on the strength of the Canaanites in xiii. 28, 31, 32, 33, xiv. 3, 43 and 45. The goodness of the land is emphasized in xiii. 27, xiv. 7 and 8. The Lord's decision that all of that generation must die in the wilderness is stressed in xiv. 23, 29, 30, 33 and 35. It is easy to assign one occurrence of an idea to one alleged source, and another occurrence to the other; but after this is done it is frequently the case that there are still two or more repetitions of certain ideas in one or both of the alleged separate accounts. A second cause of repetition is the common Hebrew practice of summarizing an event before describing it in detail. This is very frequent in the Bible (as well as in modern newspapers).

Proof that there is actually a composite account requires evidence not only that repetitions occur, since they are found in almost every writing, but that the statements contradict one another. In this narrative, four contradictions are alleged. First, that one account says that the spies went from Kadesh and returned thither, while the other says that their point of departure and return was the wilderness of Paran. Second, that one account restricts the journey of the spies to the southern district around Hebron, while the other says that the whole land of Canaan was visited. Third, that in one account the unfaithful spies emphasize the strength of the inhabitants, while in the other they say that the land is unproductive and hence not worth trying to conquer. Fourth, that one account says that only Caleb was faithful, while the other mentions both Caleb and Joshua as being faithful. Let us briefly examine these points.

Regarding the first, it should be noted that the text nowhere mentions Kadesh as the starting point of the spies, but only *the wilderness of Paran* (3). The return is said to be *unto the wilderness of Paran, to Kadesh* (26). Clearly Kadesh is indicated as a place within the wilderness of Paran. Whether the spies started from Kadesh, or from some other place in the wilderness of Paran, is not stated. There is actually no contradiction.

Regarding the second alleged contradiction, see the discussion of xiii. 21-25 below.

The third alleged contradiction depends entirely upon the interpretation of one unusual phrase, *a land that eateth up the inhabitants thereof* (32), which occurs in a context that is emphasizing the strength of the inhabitants (xiii. 31-33). Even if the phrase meant that the land was unproductive, it would not prove two contradictory accounts, but would simply show a strange change of front on the part of the frightened spies. For the true meaning of the phrase, see the discussion of these verses below.

The fourth argument is an interesting one. It rests upon the fact that while both Caleb and Joshua are mentioned in xiv. 6, 30 and 38, only Caleb is mentioned in xiii. 30 and xiv. 24. However, it is not difficult to see why only Caleb is mentioned in these two instances. When the spies began to give undue prominence to the strength of the Canaanites, it was natural that one man should rise and try to quiet the people (xiii. 30), who were giving way to great fear as they heard of the number and strength of the Canaanites. It was more effective for Caleb to do this, since Joshua was so closely associated with Moses that he would not be so readily accepted as an independent witness. The next day, when the opposition had become widespread, both men exerted themselves to the utmost in the attempt to stem it (xiv. 6). When God first acceded to Moses' prayer of intercession, but said that that generation, except for Caleb, would die in the wilderness (xiv. 24), Moses hardly thought of himself or Aaron as being included in this condemnation; nor were they, for if they had been there would be no point in the special judgment upon them when they sinned at Meribah (xx. 12). Similarly it would not be necessary, in this preliminary statement, to mention Joshua, who had been Moses' faithful assistant for a long time. In the more formal statement of God's judgment which followed, both of the faithful spies were mentioned as exempted from the general judgment (xiv. 30). Similarly, when the death of the unfaithful spies is related (xiv. 36-37), it is naturally recorded that the two faithful spies survived (38).

This examination of the four alleged contradictions shows that there is no sufficient reason for holding that the narrative is a composite one. Moreover it should be observed that the attempt of the critics to reconstruct two such narratives along the line of the alleged contradictions results in this case in two accounts, neither of which is really complete. Each contains serious gaps and omissions, and neither reads smoothly, unless far-reaching changes and insertions in the text are made.

a. The sending of the spies (xiii. 1-25)

God commanded that spies be sent to search out the land (1-2). It was His will that His people should use their own intelligence as far as possible, even though He desired them to recognize His constant leading. Twelve outstanding men, one from each tribe, were selected to take part in the expedition (3-16). Verse 16 tells us that Moses changed the name of *Oshea the son of Nun* to *Jehoshua*. Joshua has already appeared several times in Exodus as one of Moses' right-hand men, and in Nu. xi. 28 he was called 'the servant of Moses'. The form *Oshea* never occurs except here (8, 16) and in Dt. xxxii. 44 (*Hoshea*). Perhaps this change of name was made by Moses even before the first appearance of Joshua in the Pentateuch (Ex. xvii. 9, where he is referred to as a man already recognized as a leader), and the change is mentioned here because of the desirability of listing him in the formal roster of spies under the original form of his name. On the other hand, it is not impossible that Moses made the change at this time, but chose, when he wrote the Pentateuch, to use the well-known form of the great leader's name in all other references to his activities, including those which occurred at an earlier time. For further discussion, cf. Ex. xvii. 9 and Dt. i. 38.

Verses 17-20 contain Moses' commission to the spies. Their expedition has a twofold purpose: to learn whether the inhabitants of Canaan are strong or weak (18) and to determine whether the land itself is fat or lean (19-20). Verse 17 directs them to go *up this way southward* and then *up into the mountain*. It seems strange to read that people encamped south of Canaan are ordered to go southward into Canaan. *Southward* (17). Heb. *bannegeb;* better 'into the south' as in RV mg. or 'into the Negeb'. The Negeb is the somewhat dry southernmost section of Palestine. Hence the word comes, quite naturally, to designate the southern direction. Frequently, however, it refers to the region of the Negeb, as here, in Nu. xiii. 22, and in Gn. xiii. 1 and xxiv. 62, and the word is used in modern Israel to designate this region. In Jos. xv. 19 the word simply means a dry region. The AV translation is not incorrect, if understood as similar to the description of a journey by a Scotsman into the North of England. *Into the mountain*. This is the regular designation of the hill country which forms the central backbone of Palestine, and in which most of the events of biblical history took place.

Verses 21–25 describe the journey of the spies. As is so often the case in Hebrew narration, the passage begins with a summary of the entire matter (21), and this is followed by a fuller description of some of its details (22–24). The twelve spies would hardly have travelled together, or in groups large enough to attract attention to themselves. The several groups searched the land from end to end, one group going as far as *Rehob, as men come to Hamath*, in the extreme north. Another group spent its time exploring the area around Hebron, where the sons of Anak lived (for discussion of the sons of Anak, see note on Dt. ii. 10). At the brook of Eshcol, near Hebron, they cut down a branch with a cluster of grapes, as an example of the fruit which the land produced. Even today the grapes of Hebron are famous throughout Palestine.

b. The report of the spies (xiii. 26–33)

After forty days (25) the spies returned to the congregation, which was now encamped at Kadesh in the wilderness of Paran, the region from which the spies had started out (3). Since Kadesh is not mentioned in verse 3 it is possible that the movement to this place had occurred during the absence of the spies. The large desert regions known as the wilderness of Paran and the wilderness of Zin are not precisely delimited, and may even have overlapped, since they are not political designations. The general report contains two elements: first, the excellence of the land (27), which must have appeared beautiful indeed after more than a year of life in the desert; and second, the great strength of its inhabitants (28–29). Verses 28–29 present in crescendo the difficulties of conquest, and one can almost feel the people's terror mounting as they listen. Then one of the spies interrupts the report of the others, in an attempt to slow down this reaction. *Caleb stilled the people* (30), asserting that they were well able to conquer the land. However, the other spies flatly contradicted him (31–33), declaring the conquest to be impossible, as indeed it was, apart from divine aid. In their terror they exaggerated the difficulties, giving the impression that all of its inhabitants were giants, and calling the country *a land that eateth up the inhabitants thereof* (32).

It is sometimes said that this contradicts verse 27, and proves that the account is really made up of a combination of two contradictory stories, one of which represents the unfaithful spies as opposing the attempt to conquer the land on the ground that its people are too powerful, while the other represents them as saying that it is not a good land at all. Such a claim rests upon an interpretation of this verse which makes it stand absolutely alone, since all other statements about the land in chapters xiii and xiv speak of it as fertile and desirable. Except for this one phrase, the entire stress in verses 31–33 is on the ferocity and strength of the inhabitants; this is true both of verse 31 which precedes this phrase, and of 32b and 33 which follow it. When the Israelites threaten to return to Egypt (xiv. 4) they do so, not on the ground that Canaan is not a good country, but that the attempt to conquer it will cause them to fall by the sword and their wives and little ones to become a prey (xiv. 3). Thus the whole content of the two chapters runs contrary to the idea that this one phrase means that the land is not a good land.

To determine the meaning of the phrase we must look at its use elsewhere. It occurs in two places: Lv. xxvi. 38 and Ezk. xxxvi. 13–14. In both passages, as in the passage before us, the phrase indicates that there is something about a land which leads to the early death of its inhabitants. In Ezk. xxxvi. 13–14 the factor in view is lack of sufficient crops, since the passage is a promise that the land of Canaan, which became a land of famine during the exile, would again yield its fruit (cf. xxxvi. 8, 11). In Lv. xxvi. 38, however, the situation is quite different. If the phrase specifically referred to death as a result of famine, it would have been used in Lv. xxvi. 20 or 26, where famine is in view, rather than twelve verses later, in 38. There, as in our present passage, death from the ferocity of an enemy is what is meant. When the spies said that the land eats up its inhabitants, perhaps they were referring to the constant wars between cities and between regions, which cursed Canaan at this time (as is evidenced by the El Amarna tablets). The inhabitants of the land were in constant danger from this source: what then would be the fate of a people, inexperienced in war, who would attempt to conquer a land of giants, battle-conditioned by constant strife? To make the phrase contain a denial of the fertility of the land is to contradict the entire stress of Nu. xiii and xiv, and also to go contrary to its use in Lv. xxvi.

c. The rebellion (xiv. 1–10)

Given the choice between faith in the judgment of the spies, who stood before them, and faith in the invisible God, the mass of the people put their faith in the words of the spies. All the memories of the great works that God had done through Moses were as nothing against the words of these men. Filled with despair, the people thought of selecting a new leader and going back to Egypt (4). Joshua and Caleb, the two spies who were faithful to God, urged them to trust God to give them victory, asserting that it would be as easy to conquer Canaan as to eat bread, if God delighted in them (6–9). But the people threatened to stone them (10).

d. God's judgment (xiv. 11–38)

God tells Moses that He contemplates destroying the unfaithful people, and starting a new nation from Moses' own descendants (11–12). Moses pleads for the people, urging the glory of God, and laying stress on God's wonderful grace (13–19). The Lord declares that He has pardoned, in accordance with Moses' request (20). However, the generation which had turned against Him will die in the wilderness (22–35). *By the way of the Red sea* (25). This does not mean that they would return in the direction of the body of water which was crossed soon after leaving Egypt (Ex. xiii. 18ff.). The northern end of the Red Sea is shaped like a 'Y'; its western branch is now called the Gulf of Suez; the eastern branch, which is on the eastern side of the Sinaitic Peninsula, is now called the Gulf of Akaba. It is to this latter that reference is made here. Only Caleb and Joshua will live to enter the Promised Land (30). The following generation will receive the victory from God's hand (31). The unfaithful spies died by the plague at once (36–37).

Ye shall know my breach of promise (34). RV 'alienation'. It is to be feared that the AV translation of the Hebrew word *tenuah* as 'breach of promise' might give the impression that God would go back on a promise which He had made. Actually *tenuah* simply means 'opposition' or 'hostility'. The ancient Greek LXX translated it 'purpose of wrath'; the Latin Vulgate as 'revenge'.

e. The unsuccessful repentance (xiv. 39–45)

This is one of the most tragic passages in the Bible. When the people heard the divine decision, they wept. They were greatly stirred by the death of the ten spies whose advice they had accepted. Now that the opportunity for immediate possession of the Promised Land was denied them, and they were told that they must wander forty years in the wilderness, the temper of the people completely changed. They confessed their sin (40), and declared that they would now go up to the place that the Lord had promised. Moses told them that the opportunity was gone. To attempt now to take the land would be only a further step of disobedience, and would accomplish nothing. However, the people took things in their own hands, and undertook in their own strength to do what they had previously feared to undertake with God helping them. The attempt failed at its beginning. Driven back by the Canaanites, frustrated and despondent, nothing remained but the forty years of wilderness wandering to which God had doomed them. *Hormah* (45). See notes on Dt. i. 44.

X. LAWS AFTER THE CRISIS. xv. 1–41

Chapters xv to xx encompass a period of about thirty-eight years, most of which is passed over in silence. There is no indication of the exact time of the events from xv. 1 to xx. 13. The condemnation at Kadesh-barnea was fulfilled. Nearly forty years were spent in the wilderness, and an entire generation passed away. It had been made clear that Israel was not yet ready for the Promised Land.

a. Rules of sacrifice for Canaan (xv. 1–21)

There is little in these rules that is not already contained in the laws given at Sinai for the priests. The purpose of the section is an indirect one. It focuses attention on the certainty that God will bring His people into the Promised Land. (Cf. verses 2 and 18.) Just when they have failed so miserably, and a whole generation has been doomed to die in the wilderness, specific stress is laid on God's plan for His people in Canaan, an indirect means of giving them assurance that His promises will be carried out in due time. It is to be noted that the various parts of this chapter are addressed to the nation as a whole (2, 8, 38) rather than to Aaron or to the Levites. Contrast xviii. 1.

b. Provision regarding sins of ignorance (xv. 22–31)

When a great crisis such as that at Kadesh is past, those who are truly repentant tend to give way to despair of ever satisfying God. From one extreme of carelessness they can easily pass to the other extreme of thinking that every slightest error may be fatal. To guard against such an attitude at this point God reminded the people of the special provisions regarding sins of ignorance, already explained more fully in Lv. iv and v. Every sin is wrong, even if committed in ignorance. It does injury to God's kingdom, is an affront to His holiness, and requires atonement. But it should not lead to worry or despair. It should be placed under the blood. Our present section first makes provision for remission of sins of ignorance by the entire congregation (22–26) and then provides atonement for individuals who fall into sin through ignorance (27–29). In order to guard this provision against being thought to cover wilful or presumptuous sin, the next two verses declare the utter condemnation of the man who continues in wilful sin (30–31). *Presumptuously* (30). Literally 'with a high hand', i.e. wilfully, in open rebellion.

c. An instance of presumptuous sin (xv. 32–36)

After the command, an instance of wilful sin is described, which occurred during the forty years in the wilderness. Despite the frequent reiteration of the sabbath law and the fact that thousands of people were observing this law around him, a man was caught flagrantly disobeying it. He was brought to Moses and Aaron, and they sought special wisdom as to what should be done. God ordered that he be killed as a warning to the people of the terrible nature of wilful sin.

d. The ribband of blue (xv. 37–41)

God knows how easy it is for a man living in Satan's world to forget His Creator. So He commanded the Israelites to make special borders on their clothes as a reminder. It is always a good thing to seek ever new ways of reminding ourselves of God and His desires for us. When one means has been used for a time its purpose tends to be forgotten, or it may become an end in itself instead of simply a reminder to do God's will. Hence all such means must be subject to frequent change, if they are to retain their effectiveness.

XI. THE GREAT REBELLION OF KORAH, DATHAN AND ABIRAM. xvi. 1–50

This chapter presents a complicated series of events with many involved details. Two distinct groups are joined in a temporary alliance against Moses and Aaron. One of these, headed by Korah, is composed principally of Levites, who are offended by the setting apart of the family of Aaron for the duties and privileges of the priesthood.

The other group, headed by Dathan and Abiram, feel that they, rather than Moses, should have the pre-eminence in the nation, since they are leaders of the tribe descended from the firstborn son of Jacob. Thus a rebellion against ecclesiastical authority and another against political authority are associated together, and the strength of each is greatly enhanced by co-operation with the other. Yet there is considerable difference in the attitude of the two groups, and to some extent they are dealt with separately and differently. In view of the complexity of these events the running summary below should be helpful in gaining an understanding of the chapter.

When events so complex as these are described, it is easy to attempt to put together the verses dealing with each of the two movements and to allege that the chapter is really a composite account formed by the interweaving of two distinct documents. This claim, however, lacks convincing proof. While there are two distinct movements there is one series of events, and the claim of some critics that there are two distinct sources has no foundation of solid evidence. Such alleged contradictions as have been discussed in connection with the story of the spies (cf. chapter xiii) are not found in this account.

The critical argument makes much of the fact that in Dt. xi. 6 Dathan and Abiram are mentioned but there is no mention of Korah, while in Nu. xxvii. 3 reference is made to the rebellion of Korah but no mention is made of Dathan and Abiram. In considering this argument certain factors should be noticed.

1. In Dt. xi. 6 Moses is calling the attention of the people to the fact that they themselves had seen the earth open up and swallow Dathan and Abiram. There was no reason to mention Korah, since he was not swallowed up by the earth, but died in a different way.

2. In Nu. xxvii. 3 the daughters of Zelophehad mention the fact that their father did not join the revolt headed by Korah. In any such brief mention it would seem quite normal merely to mention one leader without necessarily giving the whole roster of the heads of a revolt.

3. These two instances are not the only early allusions to this revolt. In Nu. xxvi. 9 Korah, Dathan and Abiram are all named together. In

Ecclus. xlv. 18 this is also the case. Cf. Ps. cvi. 16–18, where both the civil and ecclesiastical aspects of the rebellion are mentioned.

4. In writings as late as the beginning of the Christian era we sometimes find that the two sections of the revolt are mentioned separately, as in Jude 11 which refers only to Korah, and in 4 Macc. ii. 17 which refers only to Dathan and Abiram. Even if the critical theories were true, by this time the narrative would have been in its present form for many centuries and no one would retain any recollection of there having once been two distinct sources. Yet it seemed perfectly natural to Jude and to the writer of 4 Maccabees to mention only one of the two movements involved in this revolt. If this could be the case at so late a time, why not also at the time of Moses?

It should also be noticed that the attempt to divide the chapter into two different sources results in an account of the revolt of Dathan and Abiram which is extremely sketchy in its early part, and an account of that of Korah which has a large gap toward its end. The critics attempt partially to fill in this gap by sundering verses 24 and 27a from their context, deleting the names of Dathan and Abiram from each of them, and substituting the name of God for that of Korah in each of them, thus changing these verses into an attempt to clear the people away from around the tabernacle where the men were offering incense. Such a change in these two verses is quite unwarranted. They are perfectly natural as they stand, and are logically required on account of their relation to verse 26, which stands between them. Any suggestion that the word *tabernacle* here could refer only to God's tabernacle is not true to the meaning of the Hebrew word. (See discussion below under verse 24.) While it is true that some manuscripts of the LXX mention only Korah here, and not Dathan and Abiram, all Hebrew manuscripts mention all three leaders, as do most manuscripts of the LXX. It is also pointed out that in verse 24 the LXX reads 'company' instead of *tabernacle;* however, in verse 27 it reads 'tent' for *tabernacle.* Valid evidence for altering these verses is lacking. They present actually no support for the divisive theories. Moreover, since the Kohathites, the division of the tribe of Levi to which Korah belonged, camped on the southern side of the tabernacle and the tribe of Reuben was also at the southern side of the tabernacle, a command to get away from the dwelling place of Korah, Dathan and Abiram is not at all unnatural, for all three would be in one general area.

This rebellion probably occurred quite a long time after the crisis at Kadesh, for there seems to be no link between the two events. It is not indicated as a movement against the wilderness journey, nor against God's plan for progress to Canaan, nor yet against God's law in general. It seems to have been solely an insurrection against the authority of Moses and Aaron. There is no indication of its exact date, which was probably not near either end of the thirty-eight years of wandering.

The gravity of the revolt is seen in the character of its leaders. Korah was a member of the Kohathite branch of the tribe of Levi, the branch to which Moses and Aaron belonged. With him were three outstanding members of the tribe of Reuben, the firstborn of Israel, and 250 leaders of the congregation. They asserted that all members of the congregation were holy, and therefore that Moses and Aaron had no right to take supremacy over them.

It is true that all sincere believers are equal in God's sight. Yet man, born in sin, is very subject to error. It is necessary that there be a standard of authority. In our day this standard is found in the Word of God. At that time very little of the Bible was yet available. The people were in a crucial situation. The future of Israel's testimony depended on the safe passage of the nation through the wilderness and its establishment in Canaan. Although the insurgents claimed to be following the Lord, they were actually rebelling against Him, since they were opposing the leadership which He had raised up for this vital stage of the progress of His kingdom.

On (1). This man is not mentioned again. Whether he simply followed along with the others and was not considered important enough for further special mention, or whether he withdrew from participation in the opposition to Moses, is unknown.

A special point of contention seems to have been the restriction of the priesthood to Aaron's family. For the sake of good order it was necessary that this important work be restricted to those whom God had set apart for the purpose. At a later time when a good king of Judah attempted to take upon himself the priestly function, God smote him with leprosy (2 Ch. xxvi. 1–5, 16–21).

Often it is wise to meet disaffection head on and seek a settlement. Moses calls upon Korah and his followers to appear before the Lord, together with Aaron, in order that God Himself may decide who is in the right (4–11). Moses also summoned Dathan and Abiram (12), but, filled with bitter hatred, they reviled him and refused to appear (12–14). Moses declared to the Lord that he never had wronged them in any way (15).

Korah and his followers were summoned to appear at the tabernacle with incense in their censers (16–17). When they came (18) they brought the whole congregation with them as partisans (19). The Lord threatened to destroy the entire congregation, except for Moses and Aaron (20–21), who fell on their faces and besought Him not to do so (22). Then the Lord told Moses to order the congregation to go up *from about the tabernacle of Korah, Dathan, and Abiram* (23–24). Moses went to Dathan and Abiram, followed by the elders of Israel (25), and called on the people to depart *from the tents of these wicked men* (26). After they had gone up

from the tabernacle of Korah, Dathan and Abiram *on every side*, Dathan and Abiram and their entire families came out and stood in the door of their tents (27). Moses declared that it would be proof that God had really sent him if the earth were to open its mouth and swallow up the men and their possessions (28–30). This happened as he predicted (31–34); also fire came *from the Lord, and consumed the two hundred and fifty men that offered incense* (35).

This running summary will help in gaining a clear idea of the events described in this section. There is only one point needing further explanation, the references to the *tabernacle* of the offenders in verses 24 and 27. The word used here is *mishkan*, which is translated 'tabernacle' 119 times, and which in all but three of these refers to God's tabernacle. However, the literal meaning of the word is 'dwelling place', and it is translated 'dwelling' six times, 'dwelling place' six times, and 'tent' once (Ct. i. 8, 'beside the shepherds' tents'). In all thirteen of these instances it refers to ordinary dwellings, and has no reference to a place of worship. It would avoid confusion if it were translated 'dwelling place' instead of 'tabernacle' in Nu. xvi. 24, 27 and xxiv. 5.

After the destruction of Korah and his followers, God commanded that the censers of the dead men be taken out of the burning and used to make bronze plates for a covering of the altar, as a reminder that no one outside the family of Aaron should offer incense before the Lord (36–40).

The families of Dathan and Abiram perished with them. That of Korah did not (see Nu. xxvi. 9–11). Although excluded from the priesthood, his descendants came to hold an honoured place in the service of the sanctuary. One of them, Samuel, was one of the greatest of Hebrew prophets and judges (1 Ch. vi. 33–38). Samuel's grandson, Heman, was an outstanding singer in David's reign. A number of Psalms are designated as 'for the sons of Korah'. This is a remarkable instance of a situation where the lamentable failure of a man did not prevent his descendants from achieving outstanding success, and, indeed, in a way closely related to that in which the ancestor had so signally erred.

Although the leaders of the revolt were dead, the confusion continued for a time. Verses 41–50 show the people still in revolt, God threatening to destroy them all (44), and Moses and Aaron acting as intercessors on behalf of the people who were reviling them (46–48). At the end, 14,700 lay dead from God's wrath (49).

XII. THE AFTERMATH OF THE REBELLION. xvii. 1—xix. 22

a. The Lord vindicates Aaron's right to the priesthood (xvii. 1–11)

It was not enough to strike dead a multitude of those who opposed Moses and Aaron. Great issues are rarely decided by force alone. Reasonable proof is also requisite, if a decision is to be lasting. God commanded that the leader of each tribe present a rod to be placed in the tabernacle. The rod of Levi was to bear the name of Aaron. Then God caused the rod of Aaron to produce buds, blossoms and almonds (8). This gave proof of two facts, answering with one sign both portions of the rebellion. The fact that the rod of the tribe of Levi was singled out for such special treatment proved that Moses and Aaron were not wrong in asserting divine appointment to leadership over the nation, against the claims of Dathan and Abiram who belonged to the tribe of Reuben (xvi. 1). The budding of a rod which bore the name of Aaron gave added denial to the claims of Korah and his Levitical followers that they had as much right to the priesthood as the family of Aaron (xvi. 8–11), claims which already had been met by the death of Korah and his followers (xvi. 35). As permanent evidence of the divine decision, God commanded that Aaron's rod be preserved in the tabernacle (10; cf. Heb. ix. 4).

b. Reaffirmation of the privileges and responsibilities of Aaron and the Levites (xvii. 12— xviii. 32)

Instead of quieting the minds of the people, the miracle seems to have left them confused and uneasy. It was hard for them to forget the death of the 250 men who offered incense, and they began to think of the tabernacle of God as a place of terror and perplexity (12–13). In order to set their fears at rest, God proceeded next to give a comprehensive statement of the divine arrangements for the ministry of the tabernacle, *that there be no wrath any more upon the children of Israel* (xviii. 5). Priesthood is to be restricted to the family of Aaron (1–7). The other Levites are to serve the tabernacle under his direction, but never to do the actual task of the priesthood. Their position is one of great honour, but subordinate to the family of Aaron.

Verses 8–19 describe the offerings (8–11), firstfruits (12–13), devoted things (14), and firstlings (15–18), which are to become the property of the priests. *A covenant of salt* (19); i.e., an indissoluble covenant; cf. Je. xxxiii. 18–22. Salt was used with every sacrifice (Lv. ii. 13; Mk. ix. 49–50). Aaron is not, like the priests of other nations, to become a wealthy landholder (20), nor are the Levites to receive a section of Canaan, like the other tribes (23–24). The Levites are to be supported by the tithes of the nation (21, 24). Anyone who does not belong to this tribe risks his life if he tries to usurp their place in the service of the tabernacle (22). Thus God undertakes to remove the fears of the Israelites about the sanctuary by specifying the way in which His tabernacle may be served in safety by those whom He has selected for the particular tasks. The statement about the right of the Levites to the tithes (21, 24) has sometimes been thought to be contradicted by Dt. xiv. 22–29. However, there is no contradiction, but only an elaboration, caused by the fact that when

Moses gave the addresses recorded in Deuteronomy the people were about to enter the Promised Land, and soon the matter of distance from the sanctuary would become a problem. Also Deuteronomy brings in a new subject—the sacrificial meal, in which the people would eat a portion of the tithe before the Lord (Dt. xiv. 22–29; cf. xii. 7, 17–18). Exhortation to the people not to forget the Levites, after the nation is scattered over Canaan (Dt. xii. 12, 18–19, xiv. 27, 29), in no way contradicts the ideal arrangement of Nu. xviii. 21, 24, which might naturally be much harder to enforce after the people are scattered over the Promised Land than while they are camping together in the wilderness. Up to this point the various sections of this chapter have been addressed to Aaron (1, 8, 20). Now the Lord speaks to Moses (25), as representing the nation as a whole, telling him to order the Levites to give to the priests a tithe of the tithes which they themselves receive (26–32).

c. Removal of the uncleanness resulting from the rebellion (xix. 1–22)

Since so many people had died as a result of Korah's rebellion, ordinary means were insufficient to deal with the pollution. God commanded that Eleazar the priest should take a red heifer outside the camp, slay it, and then burn it with appropriate ceremonies, to remove the uncleanness from the people. This was to be a permanent statute (10). Everyone who touched a dead body should be unclean seven days. On the third day he should be sprinkled with water containing the ashes of the burnt heifer, and on the seventh day he should wash and be clean. All this would impress upon the people the nature of death (cf. note on Nu. v. 1), would provide hygienic protection, and would picture to their minds the future provision through the sacrifice of Christ as the only possible means of release from the guilt and power of sin (Heb. ix. 11–14).

XIII. INCIDENTS ON THE WAY TO THE PLAINS OF MOAB. xx. 1—xxii. 1

a. The death of Miriam (xx. 1)

The date of this event is uncertain. Some Bible students take *the first month* (1) as referring to the beginning of the fortieth year, at the end of the long period of wandering. Others insist that it means the first month of the third year, and that this and the following incident occurred prior to the crisis at Kadesh-barnea. There are interesting arguments on both sides, but the Bible does not give us data on which to decide with certainty. The importance of these events is not affected by our uncertainty as to the time when they occurred.

The people abode in Kadesh (1). Kadesh seems to designate an entire region, rather than a small area. During the thirty-eight years of wandering the people doubtless roamed through the desert, staying at one place until the forage gave out, and then moving to another section. Perhaps they passed through Kadesh several times. The long period of wandering began and ended in this neighbourhood.

b. The sin of Moses and Aaron (xx. 2–13)

Moses ranks as one of the godliest and most able men who ever lived. Therefore this passage is important, to keep us from elevating him too far. Despite his greatness, he was human, and he sinned. God punished him for sin, depriving him of the fulfilment of his great desire to enter the Promised Land. Great as Moses was, apart from the grace of Christ he was lost, deserving eternal punishment for his sin. God saved him, as He saves all who trust in Christ.

This passage illustrates the wonderful objectivity of the Bible. It shows the sins and weaknesses, as well as the strong points, of its heroes. Nu. xii. 3 contains a strong but factual statement of Moses' strongest point, his meekness; our present passage shows how he sinned at this very point. We need to be on guard, not only at our weak points, but also at our strong points, for that is where Satan may overcome us if we leave them unguarded.

It is easy to understand how lack of water would arouse severe dissatisfaction and complaint (2–5). Yet, after all that these people had seen of the wonderful care of God, they should have learned to trust Him fully. It would seem that Moses and Aaron felt that the murmuring of the people was now inexcusable and beyond endurance. Then *the glory of the Lord* appeared to them (6). Moses is told to *take the rod . . . and speak ye unto the rock* before all the congregation (8). He promised that it would give water before their eyes, as had occurred once before (Ex. xvii).

Next follows one of the saddest passages in the Bible (10,11). Moses failed at his strongest point. He let pride get the better of him. He called the people *rebels*, and put himself in the place of God, forgetting that 'the wrath of man worketh not the righteousness of God'. Perhaps he was becoming worn out after the long series of events which had tried his patience. At any rate he showed that he no longer had the endurance needed to lead the people into the Promised Land. Aaron and Moses stood together in this act, and were judged together; but it is primarily Moses with whom we are concerned, since Aaron was never in his class as a leader, and had fallen into serious error before (Nu. xii). God quickly announced His judgment upon Moses and Aaron (12). The place where this striving occurred is named Meribah (13). The same name had been given to Massah, where a similar event had previously occurred (Ex. xvii. 7). To distinguish the two places, which are a long way apart, this one is sometimes called Meribah-Kadesh (cf. Nu. xxvii. 14 and Dt. xxxii. 51).

c. Edom's refusal to allow passage through its land (xx. 14–21)

The Edomites were descended from Esau, the brother of Jacob. Moses expected that they would be friendly. He did not ask for unrequited assistance, but merely that the Israelites be allowed to pass through Edomite territory on the highway, promising to abstain from injuring any Edomite property or using anything, even water, without paying for it (19). However, the king of Edom was distrustful, and sent an army to guard his borders (20). This unbrotherly attitude cast a dark shadow over future relations between the two nations, and the prophetical books of the Old Testament contain many severe denunciations of the Edomites (e.g. Is. xxxiv. 1–17, note verses 5, 6; Je. xlix. 7–22; Ezk. xxv. 12–14, xxxv. 1–15; in some of these passages the AV uses *Idumea* to translate the same Hebrew word which is elsewhere rendered as *Edom*).

We learn from Jdg. xi. 17 that a similar request was sent from Kadesh to the king of Moab and that the same unfavourable answer was received from him as from the king of Edom. In his farewell address Moses does not mention either of these two requests but tells of God's command that, on account of the ancestral relationship, the Israelites should not injure the Edomites or the Moabites (Dt. ii. 5, 9), but that they should buy food and water from them for money. Later Moses tells of a similar request being sent to Sihon, king of Heshbon, and his words seem to imply that the Edomites and the Moabites had granted his request (Dt. ii. 29). At first sight this would appear to contradict Nu. xx. 14–21 and Jdg. xi. 17–18. However, Deuteronomy, like Numbers, describes a long march through the desert around the territory of both Edom and Moab. Moreover, Deuteronomy does not say that the Israelites passed through the actual territory of either nation, but merely along its 'coasts' (see note at xx. 23 below). The truth would seem to be that, though both Edom and Moab refused passage, and Edom sent a large army to prevent such passage, in both instances there were probably settlers on the edge of the wilderness who did not hesitate to sell food and water for money. The statements of Moses in Dt. ii. 4–9 show that he was extremely careful to avoid border incidents which might have led to a general conflict with the mass of the people of either nation.

d. The death of Aaron (xx. 22–29)

Aaron died near the border of Edom. The Hebrew word translated *coast* (23) means simply a border, whether of a body of water or of a section of land. The sin at Meribah is cited as the reason why Aaron could not enter the Promised Land, since he had not been a party to the rebellion at Kadesh. To prevent any interregnum, Eleazar, his son, was installed in his place even before his death. The death of Aaron occurred on the first day of the fifth month of the fortieth year (xxxiii. 38).

e. Victory over Arad (xxi. 1–3)

Verse 1 probably refers to the attack upon the Israelites which had occurred after the death of the spies nearly thirty-eight years earlier (xiv. 45). *Which dwelt in the south* (1). Heb. *negeb:* see note on xiii. 17. Before the start of the long march around Edom, the defeat was avenged and some of the Canaanite cities destroyed. *Hormah* (3). See Dt. i. 44n.

f. The incident of the brazen serpent (xxi. 4–9)

Since Edom had refused to allow Israel passage through its land, the congregation had already begun the long march which would take them south, east, and then north around the land of Edom (xx. 21–22).

By the way of the Red sea (4). See note on xiv. 25. In the course of the march, renewed murmuring against God and against Moses (4–5) led to divine punishment in the form of a scourge of serpents. Similar scourges occur in the same general region in modern times. For an account of one, cf. T. E. Lawrence, *The Seven Pillars of Wisdom*, pp. 269–270. When the people cried for help (7), God provided a means by which they could be healed (8). Moses made a serpent of brass and set it up on a pole (9). If a man who had been bitten looked at the brazen serpent on the pole, he would be healed. Christ used this as a symbol of the fact that He Himself would be lifted up on the cross, in order that the sins of His people might be laid upon Him (Jn. iii. 14). Our Lord's reference to this incident was particularly appropriate since He was stressing not only the objective fact that He would bear the sins of His people (cf. 2 Cor. v. 21), but also the vital point that a personal relationship of placing faith in Him is necessary for salvation (cf. esp. Jn. iii. 15, 16, 18 and 36). The Israelite in the wilderness was not benefited by the serpent on the pole unless he looked toward it (Nu. xxi. 8, 9). Later on the brazen serpent itself became an object of worship, just as any symbol of God's truth can become harmful if it assumes a primary place itself, instead of simply pointing us to God and the various aspects of the truth which He has revealed. It was therefore necessary for the good king Hezekiah to break it in pieces (2 Ki. xviii. 4) since it had become a snare and a cause of injury, instead of a useful symbol which would fulfil its purpose of pointing forward to the Saviour who was to come.

g. The march around Moab (xxi. 10–20)

After going south and east around Edom, the people marched further east and north around Moab (11), which was east of the southern part of the Dead Sea. This was a very dry region, in which the passing of even a small stream or brook was a memorable event (14–15). *The book of the wars of the Lord* (14). This was probably a poetical book glorifying the acts of God in protecting His people in the wilderness and in bringing them safely toward Canaan. Nothing is known about it apart from the allusion here. Perhaps it was written by Moses himself.

Verses 16–18 tell in rather condensed form of an incident which evidently made quite an impression upon the people. It would seem that, as the long trek was approaching its end, a region was entered where water flowed only a short distance below the surface. Here the Lord told Moses to gather the people together in order that He might give them water (16). Under Moses' direction the leaders of the tribes proceeded to dig into the dry earth with their staves and soon the water sprang up from its subterranean channel. This event was long celebrated in the song recorded in verses 17 and 18. *By the direction of the lawgiver* (18). The words 'the direction of' are not in the Hebrew text, yet they bring out the meaning of the Hebrew phrase. *Lawgiver* (Heb. *mehoqeq*) is sometimes translated 'sceptre' or 'chieftain's staff', but without sufficient philological justification. Even if so translated it hardly means that the sceptre was a tool used for digging, but that the bearer of the sceptre directed the work (so Dillmann). Another interpretation which has been suggested is that a well was found and its mouth covered with sand in order that there might be a formal opening of the well at which the leaders of the people would dig through the sand with their staves. It is said that such a practice is sometimes found among Bedouin of the desert. Verses 18–20 carry the journey to the northern part of Moab itself.

h. Victory over Sihon (xxi. 21–32)

The region north of Moab was occupied by Amorites, under a king named Sihon. The portion of his territory which lay east of the northern part of the Dead Sea had formerly belonged to Moab, but had been conquered by Sihon not long before (26). As in the case of Edom and Moab, he was asked to grant passage through his territory, but refused, and came with an army against Israel (21–23; cf. Dt. ii. 26–32). This time the Israelites attacked, utterly destroyed the forces of Sihon, and took possession of his territory (24–26, 31–32). This was the first part of the Promised Land to be conquered by the Israelites. Verses 27–30 contain a taunting song, directed against Moab, in which the Israelites gloated over their conquest of Heshbon, Sihon's capital city (26, 27, 29–30), and recalled that its people had been victors over Moab (28–29).

i. Victory over Og, king of Bashan (xxi. 33–35)

North of the river Jabbok was a region of fine pasture land with many strongly walled cities (Dt. iii. 5). Bulls of Bashan are famous throughout Old Testament times. Og led his army against the Israelites, but was utterly defeated. This left most of Palestine east of the Jordan and north of the river Arnon in the hands of Israel.

j. Arrival in the plains of Moab (xxii. 1)

The wilderness journey was now completed. Camp was established on the plains across from Jericho. It remained to prepare to cross the river and conquer Canaan itself. First, however, we must learn of an attempt on the part of the Moabites to destroy Israel by a new method.

THE BALAAM INCIDENT. xxii. 2—xxv. 18

XIV. THE SUMMONING OF BALAAM.
xxii. 2–40

In previous chapters the foe has directly attacked Israel and has been repulsed. Now a new method is attempted and it is one which every Christian individual and every Christian movement is bound to meet at some time or other. The adversary attempts to find someone who really belongs to the people of God and to use him against them. Those who have at one time seemed to be followers of the Lord, and sometimes even very effective witnesses for Him, are most sought after by Satan for this purpose. What a responsibility rests upon everyone who has been known as one of the Lord's people, not to allow his influence ever to be used against an uncompromising witness to the truth.

In this instance the attempt failed, but only on account of the supernatural intervention of God. Balaam proved rather weak and ready to succumb, but God stood by him and prevented it, thus making sure in a most marvellous way that nothing should prevent the children of Israel from entering the Promised Land.

a. Balak sends messengers to Balaam (xxii. 2–7)

Seeing what the Israelites had done to those who had attacked them directly, the king of Moab sought a more indirect method of destroying them. He began by calling *the elders of Midian* (4). Evidently Moab and Midian were co-operating at this time. Moab was a settled nation, east of the Dead Sea, just south of where the Israelites were encamped. Midian was a roving people in the Arabian desert. Perhaps Balak, who was king of the Moabites at the time, was himself a Midianite.

We have no previous mention of Balaam. It might seem strange that one who was not of Israel should be referred to as a worshipper of the Lord. However, as Peter mentioned to Cornelius in Acts x. 35, God's grace is not restricted to any one nation; wherever a man sincerely endeavours to follow the Lord, God is willing to listen to him. It should be noted that while Balaam sometimes refers to God by the term 'God', which could be applied to any divine being, he also frequently uses the specific proper name of the covenant God of Israel, which is rendered in the AV as LORD.

There has been much controversy as to whether Balaam was a true prophet or not, but it rests upon a false understanding of the meaning of the word 'prophet'. In the Bible this word does not indicate a permanent occupation or function, which, when it has once been given to a man, always belongs to him. A prophet is simply one through whom God gives a message. God may use one as such a spokesman for a time, and then lay him aside and use another one. The prophets were not inspired in everything they said. Thus, when David told Nathan, the prophet, that he would like to build a house for the name of the Lord, Nathan said at once: 'Go, do all that is in thine heart; for the Lord is with thee'. (2 Sa. vii. 1–3). The next day, however, Nathan corrected himself, for God gave him a message for David, declaring that David should not build a temple for the Lord, but should leave this for his son to do (2 Sa. vii. 4–16). Nathan was often used of God as a prophet, but when he used his own wisdom, as in telling David that the Lord would bless his plan to build a temple, he was mistaken, and God made him correct his false utterance. Since there can be no doubt that chapters xxiii–xxiv contain messages given by direct revelation of God through Balaam, it is evident that Balaam was God's mouthpiece, and it would be absurd to call him anything but a true prophet. This does not, of course, mean that he was a perfect man. He committed very serious sins (cf. notes on chapter xxiv), but so have other prophets.

Balak had a very high idea of Balaam's ability. He said he knew that whoever Balaam blessed would be blessed and whoever Balaam cursed would be cursed (6). It should be noted that the Bible does not say that Balaam had any magical power. It merely shows that Balak thought that Balaam had such a power. Balaam himself makes no such claim. He insists that he can bless only those whom the Lord blesses and can curse only those whom the Lord curses.

b. Balaam's first answer (xxii. 8–14)

Balaam at this point appears wiser than Nathan in the incident mentioned above. Even though he saw the rewards that were brought by the elders of Midian, he told them that he would have to inquire of the Lord before giving them any answer.

What men are these? (9). This does not imply that God did not already know who they were. God wants us, in praying to Him, not only to have wonderful communion with Him, but also to clarify our own ideas and spiritual understanding. Sometimes a problem almost solves itself, once it is expressed clearly.

c. The second embassy to Balaam (xxii. 15–21)

When Balak heard that Balaam refused to come, he immediately concluded, as a worldly man would, that what was needed was a more tempting offer. When Balaam did come he naturally concluded that this inference had been correct. The situation, when the new messengers reached Balaam, was quite changed. The first ones had come to him with a new proposal, and he did right to seek the Lord's will before replying. Now the Lord's will was already known to him. He should have immediately repeated his previous refusal, since there was no new fact which could possibly warrant a reopening of the question. However, instead of following the known will of God, Balaam declared that he would again seek to learn God's will in the matter. This was in itself an act of disloyalty to God. Once God's will is clear, it is not honouring to Him to seek further light: what He now desires is immediate and unquestioning obedience.

Balaam's new request for knowledge of God's will was due only to his greed for the rich gifts that the men had brought. How careful we need to be that we do not let our judgment as to God's will be swayed by ulterior considerations. 'He gave them their request; but sent leanness into their soul' (Ps. cvi. 15). Instead of repeating what Balaam already knew, God apparently granted Balaam's desire. He said: *If the men come to call thee, rise up, and go with them; but yet the word which I shall say unto thee, that shalt thou do* (20). This is the determination of many a Christian who allows himself to be inveigled into compromising associations. He does what he knows to be contrary to God's will, intending, in the course of it, to remain true to God. Such intentions usually fail. God is not satisfied with partial obedience. In this case, Balaam did carry out his intention, but only the supernatural power of God enabled him to do so. Since he said only what God desired, the expected profits did not materialize. He would have been better off if he had stayed at home.

d. The incident of the speaking donkey (xxii. 22-35)

We have noticed that the divine word which Balaam received at the second inquiry was not the whole story, but simply a response to Balaam's failure to obey what was already known to be God's will. If this inference seemed unwarranted before, verse 22 proves it to be true: *God's anger was kindled because he went: and the angel of the Lord stood in the way for an adversary against him.*

God wanted to drive home to Balaam's mind the necessity of standing by his determination to speak only the message that God desired. Since his going was contrary to God's clearly revealed will, such a result was hardly likely. Many a man has started with a similar intention, and ended by becoming a useful tool in Satan's hand. This time God miraculously intervened to strengthen his erring prophet, since it was necessary to God's plan of redemption that the Israelites should settle in Canaan, and the weakness of a prophet must not be allowed to injure this vital part of the divine programme. Therefore an incident followed which stands alone in the Bible.

There is no reason to think that these verses represent a mere dream, or parable, or vision. They are recorded in God's Word as having occurred in this way and there is no choice for the Bible believer but to understand that they actually did happen. The Bible is not a book like Aesop's Fables in which animals can talk like human beings. Such occurrences are extremely rare in Scripture. One instance is found in Gen. iii, where the serpent talked with Eve. It is clear that Satan spoke through the serpent on that occasion. If Satan could enable a serpent to speak, certainly God could make a donkey talk, if He chose to do so. It is not stated how God did this, but it is clear that Balaam heard an audible voice, coming from the animal.

The experience with the talking donkey and the strong words of the angel of the Lord must have established so powerful an impression on the mind of Balaam as to make it virtually impossible for him to depart from his determination to speak only what God would order, even though it meant losing all the rewards that Balak had promised. It was a divine interference in a situation of great importance for God's plan of redemption. Christians today have no right to expect similar miracles to keep them from lending themselves as agents to wickedness and unbelief. They should learn to live so constantly in the light of God's will, as revealed in His Word, that they are always conscious of His presence, without the necessity of seeing Him with physical eyes.

e. Balaam meets Balak (xxii. 36-40)

When Balak met Balaam he spoke like a man of the world: *Am I not able indeed to promote thee to honour?* (37). Balaam answered from an entirely different standpoint: *The word that God putteth in my mouth, that shall I speak* (38). Doubtless Balak considered Balaam's words as mere hypocrisy since they were sharply contradicted by the fact that he had come at all. *Balak offered oxen and sheep, and sent to Balaam, and to the princes that were with him* (40). In this context the Hebrew word *zabaḥ* (here translated 'offered') would be better rendered 'killed', as in Dt. xii. 15, 21; 1 Sa. xxviii. 24; 2 Ch. xviii. 2; and Ezk. xxxiv. 3; or 'slew' as in 1 Ki. i. 9, 19, 25, xix. 21; and 2 Ki. xxiii. 20. While the word most commonly indicates a sacrifice, it does not always do so. Balak simply gave a feast to celebrate Balaam's coming.

XV. THE PROPHECIES OF BALAAM.
xxii. 41—xxiv. 24

Four times Balaam declared the word of God, stating exactly the message that God gave him, even though it wrecked his opportunity to secure the rich rewards which Balak offered for cursing Israel. After each of the first two utterances, Balak took Balaam to a different place, thinking that this might change the spell and make it possible for Balaam to fulfil his desire. Each time Balaam insisted that he could say nothing but the word which the Lord would give him. After the third utterance Balak in disgust told him to desist, and neither bless nor curse Israel; yet Balaam proceeded to deliver a fourth message, this time not merely blessing Israel, but declaring the ultimate doom of Balak's people at Israel's hand. The outline of these eight sections follows, with occasional remarks on special points of interest or difficulty.

a. Introduction to the first utterance (xxii. 41— xxiii. 6)

This introduction sets the pattern for the next two. Balak takes Balaam to a certain place (xxii. 41, xxiii. 13–14a, xxiii. 27–28). Seven altars are built and appropriate sacrifices offered on them (xxiii. 1–2, 14b, 29–30). Balaam tells Balak to stand by his burnt offering while he goes a distance away (xxiii. 3, 15), Balaam receives a message from the Lord and returns to Balak (xxiii. 5, 16), and finds Balak and the princes of Moab standing by the burnt offering (xxiii. 6, 17). The departure and return are not repeated before the third utterance, as explained in xxiv. 1.

b. The first utterance (xxiii. 7–10)

These four verses are quite general in nature, merely stating Balaam's inability to curse a nation which God has not cursed, but has instead selected to occupy a unique place (9b) and to be an innumerable multitude (10a). Balaam knows that this defiance of Balak might cause his death, but declares his desire to *die the death of the righteous* (10b; but cf. xxxi. 8). *Yesharim* (righteous) is plural, and refers to the Israelites. See note on xxiii. 21 below. In verse 10b it is doubtful whether *aḥarith* should be translated *last end*. It is formed from the preposition *aḥar*, 'after', and probably really means 'that which comes after, or beyond'.

c. Introduction to the second utterance (xxiii. 11–17)

After each of the first three utterances, Balak rebukes Balaam for doing the opposite of what he was hired to do (xxiii. 11, 25, xxiv. 10–11), and Balaam replies that he can say only what God commands (xxiii. 12, 26, xxiv. 12–13). Then (after the first two utterances) Balak suggests that he move to another place in the hope that this will change the spell (xxiii. 13–14, 27–28). Balak evidently thinks of Balaam to some extent as a powerful magician, able to accomplish weird things by his incantations (xxii. 6, 17), and also as one subject to queer magical spells which a change of place may alter. Balaam never says anything to show agreement with these ideas, but always insists that he is merely a spokesman for the Lord (xxii. 18, 38, xxiii. 8, 12, 19–20, 26, xxiv. 3–4, 12–13, 16).

d. The second utterance (xxiii. 18–24)

Balak has brought Balaam to the top of Pisgah, in the hope that this will change the spell. Balaam declares that God cannot be forced in this way, but will stand by His word (19). He declares that Israel will overcome its enemies (24), since God has been working for Israel (22–23).

After noting the terrible accounts of murmurings and open rebellions among the Israelites, which occupy so large a part of chapters xi—xxi, it seems strange to read in verse 21: *He hath not beheld iniquity in Jacob, neither hath he seen perverseness in Israel.* God is clearly speaking of

Israel, not with reference to its actual state, but with reference to its standing before Him. How wonderful that everyone who belongs to the people of God, and trusts in the sacrifice of Christ, can answer Satan's onslaughts by appropriating this statement to himself! Our state is one of sin, and our sanctification is a long process, not completed until we actually see Christ as He is (1 Jn. iii. 2); but God sees us as justified in Christ, and as already perfect in Him.

e. Introduction to the third utterance (xxiii. 25— xxiv. 2)

The differences from the earlier introductions have already been noted.

f. The third utterance (xxiv. 3–9)

Still greater emphasis is placed upon the goodliness of Jacob (5) and his future victories (8). *Agag* (7) was probably a hereditary name for the kings of the Amalekites, like Pharaoh for the Egyptians.

g. Introduction to the fourth utterance (xxiv. 10–14)

Balak's patience is now exhausted. He declares that the Lord has kept Balaam back from receiving the honours he had planned to give him and tells Balaam to flee to his place (11). Balaam states that he will return to his people, but first will *advertise thee what this people shall do to thy people in the latter days* (14). The word translated *advertise*, Heb. *ya'aṣ*, means 'to counsel', and is usually so rendered in the AV. The phrase *latter days* has often been taken to prove that the events of the very end of the age, or at least of 'messianic times,' are in view. But the phrase has no such connotation. It is used by Moses to describe events fairly soon after his death (Dt. xxxi. 29). It simply means 'later on' or 'after a time'. We cannot tell from it whether the contents of Balaam's fourth utterance will describe events fairly soon or a long distance off. The same phrase is used (but translated 'last days' instead of 'latter days') in Gn. xlix. 1, introducing Jacob's blessing on his sons, most of which deals with predictions of the history of the tribes after the conquest of Canaan, and thus long before any period which could reasonably be designated as 'messianic times'.

h. The fourth utterance (xxiv. 15–24)

The prediction of coming Israelite victories now becomes specific. The certainty of what follows is stressed by a strong declaration of Balaam's claim to be the recipient of divine revelation (15–16; cf. xxiv. 3–4). Balaam sees one coming, but not immediately, who is to be a king (represented by *Star* and *Sceptre*), who will smite Balak's nation of Moab (17). Edom also is to be conquered (18). Verse 19 repeats the assertion that a king is to arise out of Jacob, who will destroy what remains of Balak's city. These three verses (17–19) form a unit. It is not difficult to determine what it predicts. A few centuries after the time of Balaam a king arose in Israel who was a great conqueror. His name was David, and he conquered both Moab and Edom (2 Sa. viii. 2 and 14). He exactly and completely fulfilled what Balaam predicted in these verses. Sometimes verse 17 is quoted as a prediction of Christ. It is true that He is a Star and a Sceptre, and that He arose out of Israel, but it is extremely unlikely that this verse has any direct reference to Him, save in the general sense that He alone fulfils the true ideal of kingship. As He is the climax of the line of kings of God's people, everything good ever said about any Israelite king has in a sense a certain reference to Him.

Verse 20 points out that the *first of the nations* to war against Israel was Amalek (Ex. xvii. 8), and declares that the later fate of Amalek is to be complete destruction. The Amalekites were almost annihilated in the time of Saul (1 Sa. xv. 1–9). Those who remained were so smitten by David that the nation seems never to have recovered (1 Sa. xxx). A small number escaped and fled to Mount Seir in the land of Edom, surviving there until the time of Hezekiah, when 500 men of the tribe of Simeon put a final end to their existence (1 Ch. iv. 41–43). Thus this verse, like those that precede or follow it, was fulfilled long before 'messianic times'.

Verses 21–22 predict the survival of the Kenites (Nu. x. 29–32; Jdg. iv. 11; 1 Sa. xv. 6, xxvii. 10, xxx. 29) until the time of the Assyrian captivity (721 B.C.). Here Balaam had a brief glimpse of the horrors of that catastrophe, so that he exclaimed, *Alas, who shall live when God doeth this!* (23). His look into the future then pierced still further, beyond the Assyrian empire, and the other eastern empires which succeeded it, to the time when these also would be overthrown by new forces from the west. *Chittim* (24) refers especially to Cyprus, but sums up all the regions to the west, and the verse predicts the coming of the forces of Alexander the Great which destroyed the eastern empires and opened up the whole area to the domination of Hellenism. Long after, when the apocryphal book of First Maccabees was written, its first verse spoke of Alexander the Great as having come out of the land of Chittim. Thus Balaam's vision in this utterance is strictly secular and political, looking forward to the victories of Israel over its enemies until the time of the Assyrian captivity, and even foretelling the ultimate destruction of the great eastern empires at about 300 B.C. Beyond this the vision of Balaam did not stretch.

XVI. THE AFTERMATH OF THE BALAAM INCIDENT. xxiv. 25–xxv. 18

a. The seduction (xxiv. 25—xxv. 5)

If it were not for Nu. xxxi. 16 and Rev. ii. 14, we would not realize the close connection between chapter xxv and the three preceding chapters. Balaam *returned to his place* (xxiv. 25), but this can hardly mean his home in distant Mesopotamia, since Nu. xxxi. 8 states that he died with the kings of Midian; evidently *his place* here means his tent among the Midianites. In xxxi. 16 we learn that the havoc wrought among the Israelites in chapter xxv was due to Balaam's evil counsel. He had spoken exactly what God wanted him to say and had performed the part of a true prophet, yet his heart was evidently far from right. Although bound by his determination not to prophesy anything which God did not command, he sought some other way to win the rich rewards that Balak had offered. Not fully realizing the great truth that salvation cannot be earned, but is a gift of God's free grace (Eph. ii. 8), he reasoned that the Moabites and Midianites might gain their end through seducing the Israelites into such immorality and idolatry that a holy God would have to wipe them out of existence. His logic was correct to this extent, that God did destroy great numbers of Israelites who fell into this trap. But the carrying out of God's plans is not dependent on the righteousness of man. God intervened to check the progress of the seduction, and accomplished the purposes which He had determined and which Balaam had himself predicted. *Baal-peor* (3,5) was a deity worshipped with immoral rites, particularly on Mount Peor. It is no wonder that the anger of the Lord was kindled, when the people committed such wickedness.

Verses 4 and 5 contain Moses' orders for cleansing the camp. To modern ears the commands in these two verses may seem barbarous. Yet we hang murderers, and the sin of these people, if not checked, would have brought misery and death to great numbers of Israelites. If a surgeon is justified in cutting off a limb to save a life, the action of destroying such wickedness to save the nation was even more justified. Certain facts, however, should be remembered, before making any general application to our own day. First, the destruction of these malefactors was specifically ordered by God. Human governments, being made up of sinful and fallible men, are apt to err, and we do well to give each man freedom of thought, since God alone is the lord of the conscience. Second, this was involved in a special act of God, in bringing His people into the Promised Land, as a centre where His Word might be given, and from which it might spread. The situation was more vital to His kingdom than anything in our day is apt to be. Third, while it is God's desire that each of us should be very strict in condemning sin in ourselves (Heb. xii. 4), He wants us to be charitable of others, and to try to help them, rather than to condemn them (see Jn. viii. 7; 1 Cor. vi. 9–11; Gal. vi. 1).

b. The zeal of Phinehas (xxv. 6–15)

When people of special prominence sanction evil, their influence is far greater than that of others. If not checked, it can ruin a nation. Hence God gave special praise to the man who took action in such an instance. Most men, however zealous in ordinary cases, might have been glad to look the other way when so outstanding a person was involved (14). Yet his influence would be especially great, if not stopped, since he did not sin in secret, but in the sight of all Israel (6). It is to be noted that Phinehas was not acting from any private jealousy or sense of personal wrong. His interest lay in the honour of God and the safety of God's people.

God promised to give to Phinehas *my covenant of peace: and he shall have it, and his seed after him, even the covenant of an everlasting priesthood* (12–13). Except for a short period in the times of the judges, Phinehas and his descendants held the office of High Priest throughout Jewish history. The Hebrew word, *shalom*, has a much fuller meaning than our English word, *peace*. It involves the total condition of prosperity and well-being. Cf. its use in Ex. xviii. 7 ('welfare'); 1 Ch. xviii. 10, etc.

c. The command to smite the Midianites (xxv. 16–18)

In this case the purpose of the Israelite campaign would not be to repel an armed attack, as on most previous occasions, but to remove a danger to their nation far worse than any military aggression. Probably the campaign was not undertaken immediately, since it is not described until chapter xxxi.

PREPARATIONS FOR ENTRANCE INTO CANAAN. xxvi. 1—xxxvi. 13

XVII. PREPARATIONS FOR THE CONQUEST AND APPORTIONMENT OF THE LAND. xxvi. 1—xxvii. 23

In comparison with the stirring events which have been described thus far, the remaining eleven chapters of the book of Numbers may seem dull and almost anticlimactic. Although forming a necessary preparation for the thrilling experience of entrance into the Promised Land, some of their parts are not particularly interesting in themselves.

a. The new census (xxvi. 1–65)

As a result of all that Israel has gone through in the wilderness, the size of the various tribes has been materially altered. A whole generation has died, and the new generation is actually a little smaller than the one that preceded it (51, cf. i. 46). Mortality in the desert has been high, and there have been frequent diminutions through rebellions and plagues. Now the long wilderness experience is over, and a firm basis can be established for determining the size of the tribes. So the command to number is given (1–5) *after the plague*.

The purpose of this census is partly military, to ascertain the number of fighting men available for taking Palestine. Even more, however, it is to establish a basis for division of the land after it is conquered (52–56). Therefore the names of the divisions of the tribes are listed now, which was not done in the previous census (chapter i). An interesting feature of this census is the mention in connection with various tribes of those members who figured prominently in events in the wilderness.

Secular tribes are taken in turn, their divisions named, and the total number of each tribe stated (5–51). Then general directions are prescribed for the division of the Promised Land among the various tribes (52–56). The tribe of Levi is taken separately (57–62). Its families are named (57–58), with special mention of the family of Aaron (59–61), and the total number of Levites is given (62). All male Levites over a month old were counted (62), not, as in the case of the secular tribes, only men of an age suitable for purposes of war, that is from twenty years old and upward (2). The chapter concludes by pointing out that, of all who had been numbered at Sinai, only two remained to be included in this number (63–65). This, of course, has special reference to fighting men and does not include the priests.

b. A special problem regarding inheritance of land (xxvii. 1–11)

The account makes entirely clear the problem raised by the daughters of Zelophehad (1–4), who have already been given special mention in the census (xxvi. 33). The Lord's answer to the problem (6–11) shows His desire that the land of Canaan be kept in small holdings and passed down along hereditary lines. See also xxxvi. 1–13.

c. The appointment of a new leader for the conquest of Canaan (xxvii. 12–23)

God commands Moses to climb a mountain where he can get a good view of the Promised Land (12), and informs him that afterwards he, like Aaron (xx. 23–29), will die, since the two of them had sinned at Kadesh (13–14; cf. xx. 7–13). *Abarim* (12) is a mountainous region; later the particular mountain is specified (Dt. xxxii. 49). Moses' response (15–17) reflects great credit on him. His immediate thought is for the welfare of the congregation; he spends no time bewailing his fate or pleading with God to remit the penalty, but thinks only of requesting that God appoint a suitable leader to take his place. There is no more crucial time in the history of a nation or of a church than when a change of leaders occurs. Many a man fails at this point, and the results of his work disappear. Moses knew that it required divine wisdom, and asked the Lord to determine the matter.

God answered Moses' request by directing him to lay his hand on Joshua, the son of Nun (18), and to consecrate him to be the new leader of Israel. *A man in whom is the spirit* (18). Joshua had long been associated with Moses (Ex. xvii.

9–14, xxiv. 13, xxxii. 17, xxxiii. 11; Nu. xi. 28). He was one of the two faithful spies (xiii. 16, xiv. 6, 30, 38). What a joy it must have been to Moses, when God appointed as his successor the one who had been his right-hand man so long! Moses did not seek this dignity for his own sons, but left the decision entirely in God's hand. Few men with the ability to be great leaders have the humility to occupy a second place as Joshua did for so many years, and to serve a long apprenticeship before themselves taking command. Few men comparable in power to Moses are able to work with a man of like calibre under them, without ruining the subordinate's individuality. The relationship does much honour both to Moses and to Joshua, as does the great record of accomplishment by Joshua after Moses' death. While Moses was still living, Joshua was installed as his successor (20–23), thus ensuring against any misunderstanding or uncertainty at Moses' death.

The command in verse 12 does not state how soon it is to be carried out. In this case several weeks intervened before the command was executed. Moses proceeded to do the work described in the remaining chapters of Numbers, and to give the great farewell addresses contained in the book of Deuteronomy. At their conclusion, God repeated the command, together with His judgment on Moses' sin (Dt. xxxii. 48–52). It is not unusual in the Bible for a command to be given some time before it is intended to be carried out (cf. 1 Ki. xix. 15–16 with 2 Ki. viii. 13 and ix. 5–6). Some critics claim that Dt. xxxii. 48–52 and Nu. xxvii. 12–14 are variant accounts of the same thing. However, there is nothing unreasonable in the Lord repeating the command in amplified form when the time came to carry it out. The material from here to the end of Deuteronomy reads continuously and there is no legitimate reason for breaking it up and parcelling it among various documents.

XVIII. LAWS REGARDING SACRIFICES AND VOWS. xxviii. 1—xxx. 16

a. Offerings required at prescribed intervals (xxviii. 1—xxix. 40)

As the wandering life of the wilderness was drawing to an end and the settled life in Canaan loomed on the horizon, stress was laid on the performance of sacrifice at regular intervals, thus showing the continuity of God's presence with His people, and stressing the importance of constantly remembering the necessity of cleansing from sin. This section contains provisions first for daily sacrifice (3–8), then weekly (9–10), then monthly (11–15), then at certain special festivals (xxviii. 16—xxix. 40). In connection with each of these, exact specifications for the offerings are given.

The special festivals come in two groups, in the first and seventh months. The festivals of the first month include the Passover (xxviii. 16), which has already been fully described (see reference at

Nu. ix. 1–14), the seven days of unleavened bread which immediately followed the Passover (17–25), and the day of the firstfruits (26–31). The festivals in the seventh month begin with celebration of the first day of the seventh month, when there was to be a great blowing of trumpets (xxix. 1–6). Then comes the day of atonement, which is the tenth day of the seventh month (7–11), and the feast of tabernacles, which begins on the fifteenth day of the seventh month (12–38). Further details about the day of atonement are given in Lv. xvi and xxiii. Additional details about the feast of tabernacles are found in Lv. xxiii. Here only the sacrifices are under consideration. On each of the first seven days two rams and fourteen lambs are offered; on the eighth day half as many. On the first day thirteen bullocks are sacrificed (13), on the second day twelve (17), on the third eleven (20), and so on down to the seventh day, when only seven bullocks are sacrificed (23, 26, 29, 32). On the eighth day one bullock is sacrificed (36).

Thus each half year would begin with a period of special festivals and sacrifices. Our present section has to do only with the prescribed services. Individuals would make thankofferings, or offerings with regard to their own special need of cleansing, in addition to these regular sacrifices (39).

b. Regulations about women's vows (xxx. 1–16)

An important aspect of family life is brought out in this chapter. The Bible never considers a woman as a mere chattel. Her individuality is stressed and respected. A mature woman who lives alone is answerable only to God (9). A woman who is a member of a family is subject to a definite but limited oversight by the head of that family.

The chapter begins by asserting that a man who makes a vow is bound by it, and cannot revoke it. A young woman who is living in her father's house, or a married woman, can make a vow, and must fulfil it unless her father or husband (as the case may be) cancels it. This he can do, if he chooses, on the day when he first hears of it, but not later on. If he interferes at a later time, he is as guilty before the Lord as if he had broken a vow which he had made himself (15).

XIX. VENGEANCE ON THE MIDIANITES. xxxi. 1–54

This chapter looks back to the terrible harm done to Israel by the Midianite seduction, but also looks ahead to the destruction of the Canaanites. The defilement and wickedness of the Midianites constituted a source of infection which was bound to destroy the testimony of Israel if allowed to continue. God might have wiped them out by pestilence, or by some natural calamity. Instead He chose to use the Israelites as His instrument for this purpose. Again we should note that their action was specifically commanded by the Lord (2) and should beware of taking it as warrant for any action on our part which does not have a similar divine revelation. While it is, of course, not inconceivable that a particular situation might be strikingly analogous to this one, we should remember that there is rarely, if ever, a particular group of God's people whose preservation is as vital to His programme as was that of the Israelites in Moses' time. It is all too easy to be influenced by selfish motives, and thus to be led to use God's glory as an excuse, when it is not the real reason at all. A mistake at this point can easily make an individual or a nation actually guilty of murder. Hence, although the Israelites were justified (in fact required) to destroy this branch of the Midianites, it is necessary to be extremely cautious in securing from it a warrant for any similar activity today.

Verses 1–12 describe the attack. Evidently the group of Midianites involved was not particularly large, for Moses sent only 12,000 men against them (4–5). After the list of slain kings of Midian, Balaam is mentioned (8; cf. Jos. xiii. 21–22). His wish to 'die the death of the righteous' (xxiii. 10) was not fulfilled. After speaking the word of God he must have remained in the neighbourhood to see if he could find another way to get the reward Balak had offered. The plague described in xxv had come as a result of his evil suggestion (16), but he received only death for his pains. When Moses met the returning warriors, he expressed anger that the Midianite women had been spared (13–16) and gave very severe instructions (17–18). The women were the cause of the evil done to Israel. They had willingly lent themselves as agents for Israel's destruction. It would have been absurd to punish the men and spare the women. The harsh directions were intended only for the present instance, where female wickedness had been the cause of such terrible harm to Israel. Cf. Dt. xxi. 10–14.

The soldiers had to remain outside the camp for seven days. Even though the slaying was done at God's direct command, those who had participated in it had to be cleansed, since a sharp line must always be drawn between the taking of human life and any normal activities (19–24; cf. notes on Nu. v. 1–4). It was also necessary to cleanse all the plunder, both for ceremonial and for sanitary reasons. Whatever was not inflammable must be cleansed by fire. All of it had to be thoroughly washed (22–24).

Verses 25–54 describe the apportionment of the plunder. The mathematical details of the system of division are interesting and fair to all (27–47). After the distribution had been made, the men who had taken part in the expedition, happy at finding that not one of them had perished in the attack on Midian, came to Moses and offered a further oblation, in addition to the portion of the spoil that had already been designated as belonging to God (48–54).

XX. THE APPORTIONMENT OF TRANSJORDAN. xxxii. 1–42

The two tribes of Reuben and Gad noticed that the land which had already been conquered was remarkably well suited for their large herds of cattle and began to desire that it might be given to them. Although God had brought them out of Egypt and promised them a share of the Promised Land they did not see the desirability of leaving the choice of their possession in His hand but hurriedly made request for what suited them (1–5). This brought their descendants into constant trouble in later times. The land they asked was one of the finest sections of Palestine, but it had a fatal defect—it lacked natural frontiers, and was somewhat isolated from the rest of the tribes. Time after time in later centuries the other tribes had to send armies to rescue them from foreign conquerors (e.g. 1 Sa. xi; 1 Ki. xxii. 3).

Moses was not at all pleased with the action of Reuben and Gad. The conquest of Canaan was a tremendous task. If these tribes remained behind it might jeopardize the entire conquest (6–7) and put Israel in a situation comparable to that which followed the return of the spies at Kadesh-barnea (8–13). In any great co-operative undertaking there is always a danger that those who reach their objectives first will desert the others. Moses rightly took measures to prevent this. He assured the petitioners that if they turned away from following God they would bring great misery on themselves and on all the people of Israel (14–15). Immediately the Reubenites and Gadites replied that they would be glad to go over and take part in conquering the rest of the land, leaving their families in the walled cities of Transjordan (16–19). Moses agreed to this (20–24) but made absolutely sure that the promise would be well remembered. He insisted that it be solemnly repeated twice (25–27; 31–32) and declared very serious penalties if it should be broken (23, 30). What startling evidence of the weakness and frailty of human promises, that Moses should insist on this triple repetition! Satan is ever active, to tempt people for their own advantage to forget their promises. Even in dealing with God's people, it is desirable that important agreements be made explicit and clear.

Moses gave the land of Gilead to the petitioners (22, 28–29, 33). Up to this point only Reuben and Gad were mentioned, but now half the tribe of Manasseh is also mentioned and verses 39–42 describe the territory which it received. Whether Manasseh had made a request, along with Gad and Reuben, but had not been mentioned in the record until this point, since only part of a tribe was involved, is not clear. Gad and Reuben received territory already conquered (34–38). Verses 39 and 41 describe a further conquest by members of the tribe of Manasseh. After the conquest of Canaan, Joshua thanked the men of the two and a half tribes for having kept their promise to Moses, and sent them home with his blessing (Jos. xxii. 1–6), but almost immediately their isolation led to misunderstanding and near war between them and the other Israelites (Jos. xxii. 10–34).

XXI. SUMMARY OF THE JOURNEYS FROM EGYPT TO THE PLAINS OF MOAB. xxxiii. 1–49

This tabulation summarizes the journeys described in Ex. xii—xvii and in Nu. x—xxi. It was written by Moses at the express command of God (2). Since Moses was trained in all the wisdom of the Egyptians, and the Egyptians had been adept in writing for more than a thousand years before this time, it is not at all strange that he should be able to keep careful records and to write all the books which are ascribed to him.

XXII. PLANS FOR THE DIVISION OF CANAAN. xxxiii. 50—xxxvi. 13

a. The general command (xxxiii. 50–56)

Division of the land is to be proportional to the size of the tribes (54). All the paraphernalia of idolatry are to be destroyed (52). Severe warning is given against leaving the conquest incomplete (55–56).

b. Delimitation of the land yet to be apportioned (xxxiv. 1–15)

The borders of the land to be divided among the remaining nine and a half tribes are described (1–13), since the other two and a half tribes have already received their inheritance, in Transjordan (14–15).

c. Designation of officials to conduct the apportionment (xxxiv. 16–29)

Even before the conquest of Canaan, the officials to divide the land were designated. It must have been a real test of faith to these men, to receive this appointment while the land was still in the hands of the powerful race which had so terrified the spies (Nu. xiii. 31–33). In addition to Eleazar the priest and Joshua the successor of Moses, ten men are listed, one from each of the tribes which had not yet received their full territory. It is interesting to observe, not only that none of the tribal princes listed in Nu. i is included (all of these having died in the wilderness), but also that no one of these is the son of a member of that list.

d. The order to assign cities to the Levites (xxxv. 1–8)

The tribe of Levi is not to receive a separate area, but its members are to be assigned forty-eight cities, scattered through the territory of all the other tribes. The carrying out of this provision is described in Jos. xxi.

e. The order to set aside cities of refuge (xxxv. 9–34)

This is the fullest description of the regulations concerning the cities of refuge—regulations designed to prevent the starting of blood feuds, but so guarded that they would not in any way protect a real murderer. Briefer descriptions of their purpose are contained in Moses' farewell address in Dt. xix. 1–13, and also in connection with the designation of the three cities west of the Jordan (Jos. xx). The three cities east of the Jordan were set aside by Moses before his death (Dt. iv. 41–43).

f. A further order regarding inheritance by women (xxxvi. 1–13)

The death of Zelophehad without male heirs had led his daughters to request a special provision, so that they might receive his inheritance (xxvii. 1–11). This now led to a new problem. The men of the tribe, who had just received their territory, feared that this provision might lead to alienation of the territory to another tribe, in case the women married outside the tribe. In answer the Lord commanded that the provision permitting women to inherit should require that the marriage of such women be confined to men of their own tribe, so that the tribal areas would not become mixed.

These are the commandments (13). This verse forms a conclusion to the whole passage from xxvi to xxxvi, with its varied enactments in preparation for entrance to Canaan.

A. A. MacRae.

DEUTERONOMY

INTRODUCTION

I. TITLE AND CHARACTER

The book of Deuteronomy takes its name from the Greek of the LXX *deuteronomion*, the 'second law' or 'the law repeated'. It consists of discourses addressed by Moses to the people on the eve of their entry into the promised land. The title is justified by the words of Dt. xvii. 18 and by the inclusion of 'the law' in chapters v—xxvi, for the religious, social and civil life of the people.

In contrast with the detailed rules contained in Exodus, Leviticus and Numbers regarding the tabernacle, its worship, and other matters, which were particularly intended for the instruction of the priests and Levites, the words of Deuteronomy are addressed to every member of the whole congregation. In terms easy to understand, the common man is told what God requires of him. When priests and Levites are mentioned here and there, it is from the layman's point of view, pointing to them as his ministers and teachers in the law, and commending them to his support.

II. BACKGROUND

The place and the time of Moses' discourses are minutely specified (i. 1–5, iii. 29, iv. 46, xxix. 1) and should be carefully borne in mind if their purport is to be understood and difficulties avoided.

They were addressed to the assembled multitude in the uplands of Moab, amid its green and fertile fields and pastures, overlooking Jericho and the plain of Jordan. Although distant from Horeb by only eleven days' journey (i. 2), they had wandered forty years in the wilderness (i. 3), and had fought their way through the territory east of Jordan which was now being settled by the tribes of Reuben and Gad and the half tribe of Manasseh.

They stood at a crisis of their history, facing new and formidable foes, and about to meet fresh trials and temptations, under a new leadef. At this time, and being warned of his approaching death, Moses calls them together, reminds them of God's gracious and mighty deliverances, gives them encouragements to faith and obedience, warnings against idolatry and other sins, promises of blessing and threats of judgment.

He repeats the Ten Words, first given 'from the midst of the fire', and expounds their meaning (v—xi). He then recapitulates laws received at divers times, some probably dating from the days of the patriarchs, some revealed during the stay at Horeb, and others as God had taught him from time to time. These are now modified and adapted to fit the new age and to provide guidance for Israel in the promised land. The best summary of them is found in the words, 'Thou shalt love the Lord thy God with all they heart, and with all thy soul, and with all thy strength, and with all thy mind; and thy neighbour as thyself' (Lk. x. 27) with the addition of the words, 'This do, and thou shalt live' (28).

The New Testament contains over eighty citations of and references to Deuteronomy: these must be studied if the meaning of the book is to be understood and its message received.

III. AUTHORSHIP

The claim is distinctly made that Moses 'declared' the law (i. 5) and that he wrote it in a book, which was placed beside the ark and delivered to the Levites for safe keeping (xxxi. 9, 26). Jewish tradition and Samaritan tradition are unanimous in attributing the book to Moses as the author, and this is confirmed by Ne. viii. 1. The passages in Joshua which presuppose it are too many and too closely interwoven with the context to be assigned simply to later insertion. On the other hand, the documentary theory at the beginning of this century asserted with confidence that Deuteronomy was the composition of an unknown prophet shortly before 621 B.C., the date of Josiah's reform (2 Ki. xxii, xxiii). It was thought to have been written with the purpose of promoting such a reform, and in particular of centralizing worship in Jerusalem, whereas up to that time the worship of Jehovah at 'the high places' (*bamoth*) was considered perfectly legitimate. (See General Article, *The Historical Literature of the Old Testament*, p. 33.)

The complete absence of any mention of these *bamoth* in the legislation of chapters xii—xxvi or in the previous discourse (see xii. 2n.), and the command to erect an altar on Mount Ebal (xxvii. 5n.), were formidable obstacles in the way of this theory, and an increasing number of liberal scholars began to favour a post-exilic date. Others pushed the compilation of the book back to the later days of Hezekiah, and others to the Davidic period. The arguments adduced in favour of these different hypotheses go far to nullify one another. The present tendency is towards a greater acknowledgment of the Mosaic origin of much of the contents of the book.

The internal evidence in favour of Mosaic authorship is very strong. The Moabite background crops up in scores of incidental geographical details. The reader feels himself with Moses crossing the torrent of Zered (ii. 13), halting at the wilderness of Kedemoth (ii. 26), turning on the road to Bashan and abiding at last in the valley over against Beth-peor (iii. 29).

The reminiscences of Moses interject themselves with unexpected suddenness into his discourses (ix. 22) and even into the delivery of the laws (xxiv. 9). Thus we are frequently and vividly reminded of his own thoughts, emotions and prayers.

The character of Moses, as revealed in the earlier books, shows itself in various ways. His ardent spirit (Ex. ii. 12, 13) manifests itself in bursts of fiery indignation (ix. 21ff.) and emotional appeal (x. 12–22). The effect of his early education (Acts vii. 22) is shown in his skill as a leader and writer. He knows how to combine positive teaching with imaginative picturing; how to emphasize essentials whilst not neglecting detail; how to draw upon his wide experience and yet to speak to the heart; and both his prose and poetic style are justly admired. As the devoted 'servant of the Lord' (xxxiv. 5) the name of Jehovah is constantly on his lips. His skill as a leader and the power of appeal which are displayed in the histories of Exodus and Numbers are here reproduced.

IV. DATE

The occupation of Palestine by the Israelites under Joshua is now an established fact, the archæological evidence testifying to the destruction and burning of Jericho and other cities at that time. The exact date is a matter of controversy, whether c. 1400 B.C. (Garstang) or c. 1280 B.C. (Albright). It can be noted that the historical references are all to events prior to the conquest; the writer betrays no knowledge of the division of the kingdom, nor of the oppression by the Philistines nor of other events recorded in the book of Judges.

The legislation of chapters xiii and xx was applicable to the conquest period, and would have been an anachronism under the monarchy. The most characteristic phrases, such as 'all Israel' and 'the inheritance which the Lord your God giveth you', point to the same time. Chapters xxxiii and xxxiv were clearly added after Moses' death, but probably not long after. These are some of the reasons why the present writer concludes that 'the book of the law' (xxxi. 9) was written by Moses before the crossing of Jordan, and the whole book compiled in its present form during the generation which followed. See also General Article, *The Historical Literature of the Old Testament*, p. 33.

V. LEADING IDEAS

The content and message of Deuteronomy can most easily be grasped by a study of certain leading ideas, which are expressed in characteristic words and phrases, repeated in order to give them emphasis. These are grouped below under seven headings; the references being to further notes in the commentary, where a list of places where each phrase recurs will be found.

a. Bondage and redemption

Israel must 'not forget' (iv. 9) that he was a 'bondman in the land of Egypt' (v. 15), often called the 'house of bondage' (v. 6), and that from this the Lord had 'redeemed' him (vii. 8) 'through a mighty hand and by an outstretched arm' (iv. 34).

b. The goodly inheritance

God 'gives' the people a 'good land' (i. 25), 'flowing with milk and honey' (vi. 3), as He 'sware unto (their) fathers' that they might 'go in and possess' it (i. 8) for an 'inheritance' (iv. 21).

c. The love of God

They must 'love' the Lord their God (v. 10) with 'all (their) heart and soul' (iv. 29), because He has first loved them (iv. 37). They must 'fear' Him (iv. 10) and 'cleave' unto Him (x. 20). As for 'other gods' (v. 7) 'which they have not known' (xi. 28), they must 'blot out their name' entirely (vii. 24).

d. The people of the Lord

'All Israel' (i. 1) is to be one people hearing the words of the Lord (v. 1), His 'holy' nation and 'peculiar possession' (vii. 6). Because they are 'brothers' (i. 16) they must care for the less fortunate, 'the stranger, the fatherless and the widow' (x. 18).

e. The Lord's altar

All gifts and sacrifices shall be brought to 'the place' which He 'shall choose' to 'cause his name to dwell there' (xii. 5, 11), and there they shall 'rejoice' before Him (xii. 7).

f. Sin and cleansing

All 'sins' are condemned (xv. 9), especially idolatry which is 'abomination' (vii. 25). As regards punishment for grievous sin the rulers are told 'thine eye shall not pity' (xiii. 8), in order that the people may 'hear and fear' (xiii. 11) and 'put away evil from (their) midst' (xiii. 5).

g. Promises of blessing

There are promises of 'blessing' (vii. 13) when God shall have given them 'rest' from their enemies (iii. 20). If they will 'observe and do' His commandments (v. 1), their 'days shall be long' (iv. 26), it shall 'be well' with them (iv. 40), the 'work of their hand' shall prosper (ii. 7), they shall 'eat and be full' (vi. 11) after 'all the desire of (their) soul' (xii. 15).

OUTLINE OF CONTENTS

I. INTRODUCTION. i. 1–5

II. MOSES' FIRST DISCOURSE. i. 6—iv. 40

    a. Historical retrospect (i. 6—iii. 29)
    b. A call to obedience (iv. 1–40)

III. THREE CITIES OF REFUGE APPOINTED. iv. 41–43

IV. MOSES' SECOND DISCOURSE. iv. 44—xxvi. 19

    a. Introductory preface (iv. 44–49)
    b. Exhortations to fidelity and obedience based on the revelation in Horeb
    (v. 1—xi. 32)
    c. Religious, civil and domestic laws and precepts (xii. 1—xxvi. 15)
    d. Concluding exhortation (xxvi. 16–19)

V. INSCRIPTION OF THE LAW; BLESSINGS AND CURSINGS.
xxvii. 1—xxviii. 68

    a. Inscription of the law (xxvii. 1–8)
    b. Obedience commanded (xxvii. 9, 10)
    c. Solemn curses (xxvii. 11–26)
    d. Sanctions of the law (xxviii. 1–68)

VI. MOSES' THIRD DISCOURSE. xxix. 1—xxx. 20

    a. Renewal of the covenant (xxix. 1–29)
    b. The way open to repentance (xxx. 1–14)
    c. The choice between life and death (xxx. 15–20)

VII. THE WRITING OF THE LAW AND THE SONG. xxxi. 1–30

    a. The law written (xxxi. 1–13)
    b. Joshua commissioned (xxxi. 14, 15)
    c. The song written and the law completed (xxxi. 16–30)

VIII. THE SONG. xxxii. 1–43

IX. MOSES TAKES LEAVE OF THE PEOPLE. xxxii. 44—xxxiii. 29

    a. His last exhortation (xxxii. 44–47)
    b. He is warned of his approaching death (xxxii. 48–52)
    c. The final blessing (xxxiii. 1–29)

X. MOSES' DEATH. xxxiv. 1–8

XI. CONCLUSION. xxxiv. 9–12

COMMENTARY

I. INTRODUCTION. i. 1–5

The words which Moses spake (1). The name of Moses occurs ninety-nine times in the New Testament and every reference throws light on this book. This is the first of several notices that the words were originally *spoken* (iv. 45, xxix. 2, xxxi. 30, xxxii. 44); afterwards they came to be *written* (xvii. 18, xxxi. 9). The ten commandments provide a parallel (v. 22, ix. 10). *All Israel* (1). See p. 196. Here we have one of the characteristic phrases of Deuteronomy. Called to lead the people at the time when they are being welded into a nation, Moses envisages the nation as a whole. He speaks to 'all' Israel and calls on them to hear (see v. 1n.). The expression *all Israel* recurs in xi. 6, xviii. 6, xxi. 21, xxvii. 9, xxxi. 11, xxxiv. 12. *On this side* ('beyond', RV) *Jordan* (1). A phrase used eighteen times in Deuteronomy and Joshua to denote one side of Jordan or the other, or perhaps 'the region of Jordan'. It refers twelve times to the eastern, and six times to the western side, and the AV varies the translation accordingly. In many instances some determining words are added. Its use in Nu. xxxii. 19; Jos. xii. 1, 7; 1 Sa. xiv. 4 for each side alternatively proves that it affords no decisive evidence of the standpoint of the writer. *The wilderness* (1) (Heb. *midhbar*). Lit. 'a place of driving', i.e. an open pasture, but applied to any uninhabited region whether fertile or barren. *The plain* (1) 'Arabah' (RV). This is the term used for the deep depression from the Red Sea to the gulf of Akaba, and similar tracts of country. *Paran* (1). See Nu. x. 12. It denotes the region southwards from Jordan towards Mt. Sinai. *Tophel* (1). This and the places that follow correspond roughly with those named in Nu. xxxiii. 18–20 which are on the route from Horeb to Kadesh-barnea. Their mention here suggests that some of the 'words' may have been first spoken by the way.

Horeb (2). Lit. 'desolation' (cf. Je. xliv. 2), a name fitly applied to the region round about Mt. Sinai, where God first appeared to Moses (Ex. iii. 1). *Kadesh-barnea* (2). See verse 46. The place cannot be exactly identified. Kadesh means 'holy', and several places were so called. Kadesh-barnea, in the extreme south of Judaea, was the first terminus of the journey of Israel from Sinai, from which the spies were sent out and to which they returned (Nu. xii. 16, xiii. 26). It lies about 165 miles, 'eleven days' journey', from Jebel Musa, the traditional Mt. Sinai.

In the land of Moab (5). See p. 195. *Declare* (5). Lit. to 'engrave', and so to 'make clear' or 'expound'. It recurs only in xxvii. 8 and Hab. ii. 2, in reference to writing. *This law* (5). The word *torah*, uniformly translated 'law', is derived from a root *yara* meaning to 'teach' (e.g. 1 Ki. viii. 36), and might be rendered 'instruction'. Its scope is much wider than that of our English word 'law', for it not only embraces 'commandments, statutes and judgments' (iv. 1, 2), but the whole scope of divine revelation. Here it refers to the discourses which follow, and, in Deuteronomy generally, to the whole or part of Moses' teaching. In this book it is found only in the singular, evidence that we have here a complete whole, and not a mere collection. In time it came to be the Hebrew name for the Pentateuch (Ezr. vii. 6; Mt. xii. 5), or for the whole Old Testament (Jn. x. 34, xv. 25). Its use (twenty-five times) in Ps. cxix is well worth study.

In the New Testament the following uses of the corresponding Greek word *nomos* should be distinguished: the Old Testament (Jn. x. 34); the Pentateuch (Lk. xxiv. 44); the Old Testament dispensation as a preparation for Christ's coming (Mt. xi. 13); the moral law (Lk. x. 26); the Jewish administrative and ceremonial law, the 'law of ordinances' (not binding upon Christian people). See also iv. 5n., 8n., vi. 25n.

II. MOSES' FIRST DISCOURSE. i. 6—iv. 40

a. Historical retrospect (i. 6—iii. 29)

i. Appointment of captains (i. 6–18). Moses' first discourse (i. 6—iv. 40) commences with a long retrospect of the events narrated in Nu. x—xxxii. Such recitals for the sake of the lessons they teach are a common feature in Holy Scripture (e.g. Ps. cvi; Acts vii). This one proves Moses' solicitude for the people.

In the hills, and in the vale, and in the south (7). Palestine west of the Jordan divides itself naturally into 'the vale' (*shephelah*) towards the sea, 'the hills' which run from Hebron northwards rising to 2,000 ft. above sea level, and 'the south' (*negeb*) which stretches away towards Gaza and the border of Egypt. Lebanon and the great river (Euphrates) form the ideal boundary of the Holy Land, beyond which lay the great kingdoms of the East (cf. Rev. xvi. 12). On *the plain* see i. 1n: *Amorites . . . Canaanites* (7). From early times Palestine was known as the land of Canaan, and its inhabitants as Canaanites (Gn. x. 19, xii. 6). The Amorites, or *Amurru*, are mentioned in monuments dating back to the third millennium B.C. They penetrated into Canaan from the north, and settled in the hilly district on both sides of the Jordan. The term Canaanite is sometimes used for all the inhabitants of the land (Gn. xii. 6n.) and sometimes, as here, of those living in the plain. See also vii. 1n.

I have set (8). See i. 25n. *Go in and possess* (8). See i. 21n. *The Lord sware unto your fathers* (8). The promise to the fathers, confirmed by an oath (Gn. xxii. 16), is again referred to in i. 35, iv. 31, vi. 10, 18, 23, vii. 8, 12, viii. 1, 18, ix. 5, x. 11, xi. 9, 21, xiii. 17, xix. 8, xxvi. 3, 15, xxviii. 11, xxix. 12, xxx. 20, xxxi. 7, 20, 21, 23, xxxiv. 4). An inspired commentary can be read in Heb. vi. 13–20. Moses constantly reminds the people that God's love to them was shown not for any merit of their own (vii. 7, ix. 4) but proceeds from pure grace and God's original promise. The elements of that promise, the seed, the land and the widespread blessing, are all repeated here.

Not able to bear (9). The Lord undertook what was beyond Moses' power (xxxii. 11). *Rulers* (13). The word signifies any person holding a leading position. Their appointment was first counselled by Jethro (Ex. xviii. 19), but we may infer that it had the divine approval, and it finds a place in the permanent legislation (xvi. 18). *Officers* (15). (Heb. *shoṭerim*). In Egypt (Ex. v. 6) such officers, or 'writers', worked under the taskmasters to keep count of the tale of bricks: now they serve captains and others as subordinates, no longer for slavery but for victory and justice (xvi. 18, xx. 5, 8, 9, xxix. 10, xxxi. 28). See vi. 9n. *Judges* (16). See iv. 1n. Their appointment and duties are further defined in xvi. 18, xvii. 9, xix. 17, 18, xxi. 2, xxv. 1. *Stranger* (16). See x. 18n.; Ex. xii. 19n.; Lv. xvi. 29n. In the tribal organization of Israel four classes can be distinguished. The actual descendants of the patriarchs, including their 'elders' and 'princes'; 'strangers' (Heb. *ger*) who were members received by Israel from other nations as residents; 'sojourners' (Heb. *toshab*), usually from conquered peoples (see Lv. xxv. 35); 'servants', whether those bought for money, or born in the house. Besides these were 'foreigners' (Heb. *nokhri*, see xvii. 15, RV), dwelling temporarily among them for trading or other purposes. The stranger is to be treated as a brother. This solicitude for all whose position might render them subject to oppression is a marked characteristic of Deuteronomy. The codes of Egypt and Babylon were of a different spirit. See further x. 18n., 19n.

ii. Mission of the spies (i. 19–46). *Great and terrible wilderness* (19). See i. 1n. All travellers agree with this description of the dreary waste of sand and rock to the north of Sinai. The mountains look as if they had been burned with fire and the earth is covered with stones and black sharp flints. Yet a few oases are found with wells or springs; and in some of the valleys there is considerable vegetation after rain which doubtless supported the flocks of Israel during their wanderings. There are several other references in Deuteronomy to the 'wilderness'. *Which ye saw* (19). Moses thus appeals to the experience which they had in common. *Go up and possess* (21). See i. 8n. This is a characteristic phrase relating to their entry into the land of promise (see p. 196). Their enemies will not be able to resist them (vii. 2). It is ever necessary for God to encourage His people to 'possess' all that He has graciously promised. The word *yarash* means to enter into possession of a land or property by casting out or by replacing its previous occupier, whether by conquest or by process of inheritance. It recurs no less than fifty-two times in Deuteronomy even in the legal sections (e.g. xix. 2, 14, xxiii. 20). It is translated 'inherit' in ii. 31, xvi. 20; its significance is allied to that of inheritance (see i. 38n.) but distinct from it. The whole complex of thought behind these expressions belongs essentially to the period of the conquest. *Fear not, neither be discouraged* (21). 'Dismayed' (RV). The fear of the Lord should cast out the fear of man (iii. 2, 22, xx. 3, 4, xxxi. 6, 8; Jos. i. 9).

Ye came near (22). Although the younger portion of his hearers were born only after the spies were sent forth, Moses identifies them with their elders who were present in their youth. *Eshcol* (24). A valley in the south famed for its fruitfulness. (See Nu. xiii. 23.)

A good land which the Lord our God doth give us (25). That the land is 'good' is often repeated in Moses' discourse (iii. 25, iv. 21, 22, vi. 11, 18, viii. 7, 10, ix. 6, xi. 17); and that it is God's gift permeates the whole book and forms an essential part of its message. It affords a reason for the respect of ancient boundaries (xix. 14) and for the sanctity of the soil (xxi. 23); it is connected with promises of victory (xxvii. 2, 3) and blessing (xv. 4), and with warnings of judgment (xxviii. 52). The Hebrew word *nathan*, translated here and in some sixty other places as *give*, is translated 'deliver' thirteen times (i. 27, ii. 30, 33, 36, iii. 2, 3, vii. 2, 16, 23, 24, xix. 12, xx. 13, xxi. 10), and 'set' three times (i. 8, 21, iv. 8). *Walled up to heaven* (28). Many walled cities of the pre-Mosaic period in Palestine have been excavated. The typical fortification of the Hyksos rose higher than the city inside, and presented a smooth outer surface. A single sloping road afforded entrance to the city at one point. *Sons of the Anakims* (28). See ii. 11, 21n. The high walls and the Anakim have their counterparts in the Christian life (Eph. vi. 12).

Dread not (29). Discouragement led to the sin of unbelief (32) and so to inevitable judgment (34). Moses seeks to bring home to the rising generation the lessons of the past. *As a man doth bear his son* (31). A beautiful simile, probably referred to by Paul (see Acts xiii. 18, RV mg.). Cf. xxxii. 11, 12. *The Lord . . . was wroth* (34). The 'wrath of God' is referred to both in the Old Testament and in the New (see e.g. Rom. i. 18), and all attempts to explain it away do violence to the text. As exhibited here the punishment was God's way of dealing with the spirit of rebellion which would have brought speedy ruin to the nation; to avert this the task of conquest was relegated to the younger generation now addressed.

Caleb (36). Moses' thoughts now turn to the two men of his contemporaries who were faithful, Caleb and Joshua. The story of Caleb (Nu. xiii, xiv; Jos. xiv, xv. 13–18; Jdg. i. 12–15) is full of inspiration to all who are prepared 'wholly' to follow the Lord. He is mentioned first as being probably the elder and the chief spokesman. *The Lord was angry with me for your sakes* (37) (see iii. 26n.). God's judgments are impartial, and when Moses rebelled he too had incurred God's anger. The exact nature of his sin is not made clear (Nu. xx. 7–13; Dt. xxxii. 51; cf. Ps. cvi. 32, 33); but both in transgression and in punishment he was identified with the older generation. Verses 36, 37, 38 are bound together not by unity of time, but by connection of thought. As Moses begins to think of Caleb's entry (36) the bitterness of his own exclusion forces itself forward (37), mitigated by the thought of the transference of his charge to Joshua, his trusted minister (38). *Encourage him* (38). With noble unselfishness Moses does so (iii. 23–28, xxxi. 3, 23). *Inherit* (38). This word, *nahal* (see i. 21n.), is also applied to the land. Its common meaning is seen in xii. 12, xxi. 16, but its most frequent use is in connection with God's gift of the land. See iii. 28, iv. 21, 38, xii. 9, 10, xv. 4, xix. 3, 14, xx. 16, xxi. 23, xxiv. 4, xxv. 19, xxvi. 1, xxix. 8, xxxi. 7. See also iv. 20n. *Moreover your little ones* (39). Moses continues his train of thought as to those who shall enter in.

I am not among you (42). Cf. Jn. xv. 5. *Amorites* (44). In Nu. xiv. 43 they are called Canaanites (see i. 7n.). *Hormah* (44); a word meaning 'destruction', from Heb. *herem*. See ii. 34n. As there was more than one destruction, so more than one place was called Hormah. See Ex. xvii. 7n. *Many days* (46). See also ii. 1, 14n. A veil of mystery surrounds these barren years spent partly at Kadesh and partly in the neighbouring wilderness. See Nu. xx.

iii. On the borders of Edom (ii. 1–8). *Mount Seir* (1). The mountains of Edom, of which Seir is the typical summit, rise to the south and east of the Dead Sea. *Northward* (3). This would be along the S.E. border of Edom. *Your brethren* *the children of Esau* (4). The request from Kadesh seeking a passage through the heart of Edom (Nu. xx. 14–21) was refused. Then (Nu. xxi. 4) they were bidden to journey by the 'border' (see RV). From verses 28 and 29 of this chapter it seems that some of the people, kinder than their king, were willing to sell them food and water, the latter a precious commodity. *Meddle not with them* (5). 'Contend not' (RV). The friendliness shown to Edom, Moab (see verse 9) and Ammon (see verse 19) as 'brethren' is characteristic of the patriarchal and Mosaic ages, and a testimony to the contemporary character of the narrative. In the days of the kingdom it gave place to constant wars, and prophecies of bitter woes. See Am. i, ii; Je. xlix. *I have given* (9). See i. 25n. In His sovereignty Jehovah determines the bounds of all nations (cf. xxxii. 8).

iv. **The approach to Moab** (ii. 9–15). *Ar* (9). This was the border-town of the Moabites, the children of Lot (Gn. xix. 37). See Nu. xxi. 15. *Emims* (10). See RV. Verses 10–12 and 20–23 may have been added later, as explanatory notes. The Emim and *Horims* (12) are mentioned in Gn. xiv. 5, 6, as occupying these same regions. These latter have recently been identified with the Hurrians who at a very early time descended from Armenia and occupied the northern part of Mesopotamia, where they established a powerful kingdom and whence they penetrated farther south. *The brook Zered* (13). See Nu. xxi. 12. The word 'brook' (*nahal*) denotes the course of a mountain stream, which after rain may be a rushing torrent and at other times entirely dry. These *nahals* are a distinctive feature of Transjordan. *Thirty and eight years* (14). The 'forty years in the wilderness' (ii. 7, viii. 2, 4, xxix. 5) include also the first year from the crossing of the Red Sea to the departure from Sinai and the final year spent in the conquest of the eastern territories. *The hand of the Lord* (15). The judgments of God are strictly impartial.

v. **Victory over the Amorite kings** (ii. 16–37). *It came to pass* (16). The account in verses 16–25 is fuller than that of Numbers. *Moab . . . Ammon* (18, 19). Moabites and Ammonites, the descendants of Lot (Gn. xix. 37, 38), are treated as 'brethren', in contrast with the Amorites, an alien race, sunken in idolatry (see ii. 5n.). *Giants* (20). 'Rephaim' (RV). This word, like *nephilim* (Gn. vi. 4), was probably a general term for primitive peoples of great strength and stature. *Anakims* (21). The Anakim, or 'sons of Anak', evidently inspired terror by their size. See i. 28, ii. 10, ix. 2. They are met with chiefly in the highlands. Cf. Jos. xi. 21. *Avims . . . Caphtorims* (23). Azzah is the modern Gaza. Caphtor is supposed to be Crete, and the Caphtorim are the Philistines, who descended upon the southern coasts of Palestine about the time of the exodus. Cf. Jos. xiii. 3; Am. ix. 7. This primitive name for them marks the passage as being of early date.

This day will I begin (25). We learn from Nu. xxi. 4 that the people were much discouraged, so these words of encouragement were timely. A new step forward was to be taken, and the Lord prepares the way before them. See verse 31 and cf. xi. 25. *Wilderness of Kedemoth* (26). That is, the open country round Kedemoth. Cf. Jos. xiii. 18. *Words of peace* (26). Whether to Edomite or Amorite, the first message is one of peace. See xx. 10 and cf. Lk. x. 5. *The Moabites which dwell in Ar* (29). See ii. 4n. It would seem from xxiii. 4 that the friendliness shown by this city was an exception to the rule. *The Lord . . . hardened his spirit* (30). What in Nu. xxi. 23 is put down to Sihon's unfriendliness is here seen as part of the divine purpose. The Old Testament steadily refuses to see any inconsistency between human freedom and God's sovereignty. See Ex. iv. 21n. *Begun to give . . . begin to possess . . . inherit* (31). For the meaning of the words see notes on i. 21, 25, 38; the same Hebrew word *yarash* stands here both for 'possess' and 'inherit'. God has prepared the way; it is for them to enter in by faith.

Utterly destroyed (34). 'Devoted' (RV). See Lv. xxvii. 28n. It is important to grasp the full meaning of *herem* which is thus translated. It is used in Deuteronomy in connection with persons or objects consecrated to the worship of false gods. These are to be regarded with abhorrence (as sin should be), as corrupt and corrupting, like a plague-infected garment, fit for nothing but utter destruction lest the ban upon them fall on those who spare them. *Cities in the mountains* (37). 'Cities of the hill country' (RV). This is the district about the sources of the Jabbok inhabited by the Ammonites, lying to the east of the table-land of iii. 10. The description is such as a traveller would give who had seen it all for himself.

vi. **The conquest of Bashan** (iii. 1–17). *Bashan* (1). The word means 'fertile'. The pastures of Bashan were famous for their richness (xxxii. 14). *Argob* (4). The LXX translates this by 'Trachonitis' but the identification is doubtful. *Hermon . . . Sirion . . . Shenir* (9). Sirion ('glistening') is a Sidonian name and may have been used by the Sidonian colony (Jdg. xviii. 7) which had settled at the foot of this snow-capped range. It is found without explanation in Ps. xxix. 6. The name Shenir (RV 'Senir'; cf. Ezk. xxvii. 5) was known to the Assyrians, and was used for a part of the range. Again we have a traveller's note. *Cities of the plain* (10). 'Table-land' (RV mg.). The word *mizhor* is generally used for high table-lands, and should be distinguished from the low-lying plain ('Arabah'). See i. 1n. *Bedstead of iron* (11). The meaning of both words is doubtful. Capt. Condor identified it with a throne of stone of about these dimensions discovered by him on a hillside at Rabbah. *Jair the son of Manasseh* (14). 'Son' is used for any descendant; his descent is given in 1 Ch. ii. 22, 23. Cf. Nu. xxxii. 41. *Chinnereth* (17). This is Gennesareth, the sea of Galilee. *Under Ashdoth-pisgah* (17). 'Slopes of Pisgah' (RV). See xxxiv. 1n. The southern slopes of Jebel Osha overlook the Salt or Dead Sea. The word 'eastward' refers to the territory extending in that direction.

vii. Joshua appointed leader (iii. 18–29). *I commanded you* (18). The reference is particularly to the tribes of Reuben and Gad, and to the half-tribe of Manasseh. See Nu. xxxii. 20ff. *Until the Lord have given rest* (20). 'Rest' is primary among the blessings promised in the 'land'. The rest promised to Moses in Ex. xxxiii. 14 had been fulfilled, but rest from their enemies was still future (xii. 10, xxv. 19). The word 'rest' sheds its benediction throughout the Bible. That promised to Israel was given to them under Solomon (1 Ki. v. 4).; but a richer fulfilment of the promise is to be found in Christ (Mt. xi. 28; Heb. iv. 5–8). *I commanded Joshua* (21). The glimpses given us of the relationship between Moses and Joshua will repay study. Joshua is seen first as army commandant (Ex. xvii. 9), then as Moses' minister (Ex. xxiv. 13) and devoted adherent (Nu. xi. 28). Moses' love for Joshua shines out in Dt. i. 38, xxxi. 3; Nu. xxvii. 18–23.

I besought the Lord (23). The thought of his own exclusion arises in Moses' mind, and he recalls his prayer. He requested two things, that he might go over and that he might see. One was refused, the other granted. Other prayers of Moses are recalled in Dt. ix. 20 and 26. For Israel he sought and obtained pardon; for himself the Lord's own presence and a vision of His glory. He also. taught the people to pray (xxi. 8, xxvi. 5, 13). *Thy servant* (24). See xxxiv. 4n. *What God?* (24). Follow the RV reading 'What god?' This does not prove any belief in the real existence of the false gods. See Ex. xv. 11n.; Dt. vi. 14n. *For your sakes* (26). See i. 37n., iv. 21, xxxii. 51. *Charge* (28). See xxxi. 14n. *Beth-peor* (29). 'The house (temple) of Peor.' Here the people had fallen into grievous sin (see Nu. xxv; Ps. cvi. 28ff.), and near here Moses was buried (xxxiv. 6).

b. A call to obedience (iv. 1–40).

i. The purpose and value of the law (iv. 1–8). *Hearken, O Israel* (1). Moses now calls all the people to attention, as he prepares to expound to them the law of the Lord. Cf. v. 1. See also i. 1n. The call to 'hearken' and the need for obedience to God's voice are frequently repeated. See e.g. iv. 30, viii. 20, ix. 23, xiii. 4, 18, xv. 5, xxvi. 14, 17, xxvii. 10, xxviii. 1, 2, 15, 45, 62, xxx. 2, 8, 10, 20. See also i. 1n. *Statutes* (1). The word *ḥuqqim* comes from a root meaning to engrave, and hence denotes permanent and prescribed rules of conduct, as addressed to the individual or national conscience. *Judgments* (1). A judgment (*mishpaṭ*) represents a decision. The word is cognate with that for a judge (*shophēṭ*) who issues the judgment (see i. 16, 17). The 'case law' of Ex. xxi—xxii. 17, doubtless intended for judges, affords an example. The word is also used of the decisive acts of God, judging the wicked and vindicating the innocent. Hence 'statutes and

judgments' together cover all the laws and the precepts. Cf. xii. 1—xxvi. 19. The two words are again mentioned together, sometimes with 'commandments', in iv. 5, 8, 14, v. 1, 31, vi. 1. vii. 11, viii. 11, xi. 1, 32, xii. 1, xxvi. 16, 17. 'Statutes' occurs alone in iv. 6, vi. 24, xvi. 12, and with 'commandments' in vi. 17, x. 13, xxviii. 15, 45, xxx. 10. *That ye may live* (1). Every word of God is the 'bread of life' (viii. 3) and His words point the way to eternal life. Cf. Mt. xix. 17; Jn. vi. 63.

Ye shall not add (2). Cf. xii. 32. This peremptory command creates a sharp distinction between the word of God and the word of man. It is scarcely conceivable that the writer of these words should have been guilty of disobeying them. Christ Himself emphasized the same distinction (Mt. v. 17–19, xv. 6); and when the oracles of God were completed a further warning was added (Rev. xxii. 18, 19). *Commandments* (2). The English word here closely corresponds with the Hebrew *miṣwah*, and covers any command, whether temporary or permanent, general or particular. In iv. 13 and x. 4 the word used is *dabar* (word) not *miṣwah*. Hence the marginal reading 'the ten words'.

Your eyes have seen (3). Moses frequently appeals to the experience of his hearers, reminding them of what they had seen (i. 19, iii. 21, vii. 19, xi. 7, xxix. 2, 3), heard (iv. 12, v. 23) and known (vii. 15). See iv. 10n. *Baal-peor* (3). That is, the Baal worshipped at Beth-peor (see iii. 29n. and Nu. xxv. 3). Many Baals are mentioned in Scripture and their worship was attended with gross immorality. Cf. Ho. ix. 10.

That ye should do so in the land (5). It is important to understand that the law, whilst intended primarily for Israel, was also written for the Christian believer. For Israel, the Mosaic law was God's gift to guide their conduct, draw them to Himself, and weld them into a nation. Its ceremonial and judicial regulations were intended for their use, as a nation in the land, until the fuller revelation to be made at Christ's coming. These were therefore transitory in nature, binding upon the Jews, but not upon Christians afterwards. Cf. Mt. viii. 4; Lk. xi. 42; Gal. iv. 9, v. 1–6; Heb. ix. 9, 10. See Introduction to Leviticus (p. 134) and also note on verse 8 below. *This is your wisdom and your understanding* (6). Moses multiplies inducements to obedience. *God so nigh* (7). This was the greatest privilege of all. See xxx. 14n. *Statutes and judgments so righteous* (8). See xxv. 1n., and cf. Rom. vii. 12, 14. *All this law, which I set before you this day* (8). These words may be taken to include the greater part of Deuteronomy (i. 5n.).

What is the relevance of the Mosaic law to the Christian reader? The answer may be summed up thus. First, the law contains certain transitory elements not binding upon Christians. See iv. 5n. Second, it also contains eternal principles of holiness, justice and truth, enshrined in the Decalogue and underlying all the legislation. These are binding upon all generations, Jews and

Christians alike. Such laws are quoted as commands in the New Testament with the words 'for it is written'. See Mt. iv. 10, v. 17; Rom. xiii. 9; 1 Pet. i. 16. Third, as part of the inspired Scripture the whole book is written for our learning (Rom. xv. 4) and is 'profitable' (2 Tim. iii. 16). Fourth, it is plainly told us that Moses wrote of Christ (Jn. v. 46; see Dt. xviii. 15n.). Christ therefore must be sought in all in its pages, since the whole law is intended to lead to Him (Gal. iii. 24).

ii. The covenant of the Lord (iv. 9–24). *Take heed to thyself . . . teach* (9). Moses was addressing a nation of young men. Theirs was the responsibility of passing on the revelation to future generations; hence the repeated emphasis upon teaching (iv. 9, 10, vi. 7, xi. 19, xxiv. 8, xxxi. 19). The lesson was not forgotten in pious households (2 Tim. iii. 14, 15). *Lest thou forget* (9). The duty of remembrance is repeatedly emphasized both negatively (iv. 23, 31, vi. 12, viii. 11, 14, 19, ix. 7, xxv. 19), and positively (v. 15, vii. 18, viii. 2, 18, ix. 7, xv. 15, xvi. 3, 12, xxiv. 9, 18, 22, xxv. 17, xxxii. 7). This is supplemented by the command to teach (see above) and write (vi. 9n.); and so the foundation is laid for a body of holy Scripture. *In Horeb* (10). Deuteronomy is full of Moses' 'reminiscences'. These may be divided into four groups relating, first, to Egypt and the journey to Sinai (see iv. 34n.); secondly, to the giving of the law at Sinai (see below); thirdly, to the journey from Horeb to Kadesh (see viii. 1n.); and fourthly, to the events of the last two years (see xxiii. 4n.). Those of the second group occupy a considerable part of chapters iv, v, ix and xi. They refer to the covenant, the ten commandments, the thunders and the fire of Sinai, the apostasy of the golden calf, Moses' intercessions for the people, the giving of the second tables and the separation of the tribe of Levi. *Learn to fear* (10). The phrase is repeated xiv. 23, xvii. 19, xxxi. 13; cf. vi. 24, viii. 6, x. 12, xxviii. 58. A sense of reverent filial fear towards God, as well as the feeling of dutiful love, should be cultivated. They are both elements in the covenant relationship between God and His people. See Lv. xix. 3n. The element of dread (ix. 19n.) may pass, whilst that of reverence remains. *Darkness* (11). Cf. Ex. xix. 18, xx. 21; Ps. xcvii. 2. God dwells in light unapproachable (1 Tim. vi. 16), but darkness hides Him from the eyes of sinful man. *Out of the midst of the fire* (12). This pregnant expression occurs ten times (see iv. 12, 15, 33, 36, v. 4, 22, 24, 26, ix. 10, x. 4; cf. xxxii. 22), showing the deep impression made upon Moses, to whom God first revealed Himself thus at the burning bush, and then in the fires of Sinai. Wherever there is true revival God still speaks 'out of the midst of the fire'. Fire symbolizes the majesty of God and the mighty elemental forces under His control (Ps. civ. 4).

His covenant (13). (See xxix. 1n.) This is the first of twenty-seven recurrences in Deuteronomy of this important theme. Whilst the word *berith* may be used of a *contract* based upon conditions,

it can also be used, as here, of the establishment of a *relationship*, an abiding bond between two parties. This may be one of brotherhood, as with David and Jonathan (1 Sa. xviii. 3), or of overlordship, as between David and Israel, or of pure grace, as God's covenant with Noah (Gn. ix. 9). By the covenant in Horeb Jehovah, by pure grace also, took Israel to be His 'peculiar people', whilst they took Him to be their God (Ex. xix. 5, 8). He then gave them the 'ten words of the covenant' (Ex. xxxiv. 28; cf. Dt. ix. 9), together with 'statutes and judgments', which, in virtue of the covenant already made, they promised to obey. Thus the 'promise' came before the 'law' (Gal. iii. 15ff.). *He wrote them* (13). See vi. 9n. Could anything be more explicit than this statement, twice repeated (v. 22, x. 4), of their divine origin? What instrumentality He used we need not inquire. But He who can write on the human heart (2 Cor. iii. 3) could certainly devise a means to write upon stone.

Take . . . good heed (15). The warning against idolatry which follows was fully justified by the events. Israel's calling as a nation was to witness to the glory and majesty of Jehovah, in contrast to the degrading idolatry of the heathen. *No manner of similitude* (15). See v. 8n. There is no contradiction between this statement and the fact that God manifested Himself through theophanies, or in visions to the prophets. Cf. Jn. i. 18. *Corrupt yourselves . . . , male or female* (16). The moral purity of the Mosaic law was in striking contrast to the licentious rites connected with the worship of Baal and Astarte. *The likeness of any beast . . . of any winged fowl* (17). The Egyptian god *Anubis* had the head of a jackal; *Thoth* had the head of a hawk. *The sun, and the moon* (19). Great temples of the moon existed at Ur and Haran in Abraham's day and the sun was worshipped at On (Heliopolis) in Egypt (Gn. xli. 45).

People of inheritance (20). See ix. 26 and i. 38n. As the Israelites, by God's gift, enter into the inheritance of the land, so God takes His redeemed people as His inheritance. (Cf. 1 Pet. i. 4.) To them He will entrust His oracles and through them prepare for the coming of Messiah. *For your sakes* (21). See i. 37n. *A consuming fire* (24). See iv. 12n. The fire which purifies precious metals consumes that which is worthless or corrupt, and is therefore a symbol of God's holiness and righteous judgment. The teaching here given by Moses is applied to the Christian dispensation in Heb. xii. 29. *A jealous God* (24). See Ex. xx. 5n.; Dt. v. 9. The Hebrew word *qana* stands for 'jealous' or 'zealous', two ideas which are closely akin. The love of God is frequently compared to that of a husband, which gives itself unreservedly and expects an undivided love in return.

iii. An appeal for fidelity (iv. 25–40). *Heaven and earth* (26). The silent witnesses of all our vows and all our sins. (Cf. xxx. 19, xxxi. 28.) *Prolong your days* (26). Length of days is one of the blessings frequently associated with obedience

(v. 16, 33, vi. 2, xi. 9, xvii. 20, xxii. 7, xxv. 15, xxx. 18, 20, xxxii. 47. Cf. Ps. xxi. 4). *Scatter* (27). In God's promise to Abraham the seed and the land for their inheritance are bound together. But if the nation shall prove unfaithful, they shall be disinherited (Nu. xiv. 12) and scattered (Dt. xxviii. 64). Yet, in His mercy, if they repent He will gather them again, even from the utmost parts of heaven (xxx. 1–4; Mt. xxiv. 31). *Serve gods* (28). That is to say, they shall be in bondage to the heathen nations, represented by their gods. To save the people from thinking that he attributes reality to these deities, Moses adds with scorn that they are but the work of men's hands. See vi. 14n.

With all thy heart and with all thy soul (29). The words are repeated (vi. 5, x. 12, xi. 13, xiii. 3, xxvi. 16, xxx. 2, 6, 10) and cast a clear light upon the wholehearted consecration which God expects from His own. *And shalt be obedient unto his voice* (30). 'Hearken unto his voice' (RV). The phrase is repeated (viii. 20, ix. 23, xiii. 4, 18, xv. 5, xxvi. 14, 17, xxvii. 10, xxviii. 1, 2, 15, 45, 62, xxx. 2, 8, 10, 20). This is part of the covenant relationship. *A merciful God* (31). The word here denotes compassion and is so translated in xiii. 17, xxx. 3 (see vii. 9n.). God's justice and mercy may seem to human eyes to conflict, yet Moses and the prophets steadfastly proclaim both. At last they meet in the cross of Christ. *Covenant* (31). See verse 13n.

The days that are past (32). Moses appeals to the experience of all that God has wrought for them as a proof of the divine character of the revelation made through Him, and as a call upon them to love Him in return. He refers particularly to the signs which accompanied the exodus. The repeated references to Egypt, forty-seven in all, are an index to Moses' character and are explicable only if he was the real author of this book. (See i. 27, 30, iv. 20, 34, 37, 45, 46, v. 6, 15, vi. 12, 21, 22, vii. 8, 15, 18, viii. 14, ix. 7, 12, 26, xvii. 16, xx. 1, xxiii. 4, xxiv. 9, 18, 22, xxv. 17, xxvi. 5, 8, xxviii. 27, 60, 68, xxix. 2, 16, 25, xxxiv. 11.) He recalls the bondage and affliction, the signs and wonders for which he gives all the glory to the Lord, the Passover and passage of the Red Sea, with the words 'out of Egypt' as a triumphant refrain. See xx. 1n. To these are added memories of God's mercies on the way to Mount Sinai, the manna (viii. 3, 16) and the water from the rock (vi. 16, ix. 22, xxxiii. 8).

Temptations (34) (RV 'many trials'). This refers to the various ways in which God tried or proved Israel (viii. 2, vi. 16n.). *By a mighty hand, and by a stretched out arm* (34). Repeated in v. 15, vii. 19, xi. 2, xxvi. 8. This combination is peculiar to Deuteronomy. *His great fire* (36). See verse 12n. *Because he loved . . . he chose* (37). See viii. 1n. The Heb. '*ahabh*, used for the electing love of God, corresponds with the Gk. *agapē* of the New Testament. Such love is spontaneous, all of grace, bestowed apart from any merit in its object (ix. 6). This appeal, based on the love

which God showed to their fathers, is repeated in vii. 7, 8, 13, x. 15, xxiii. 5. Moses can find no other ground than this for God's sovereign choice of Israel. Thus early in the Bible are grace and election linked together (cf. Rom. viii. 28, xi. 28, 29). Through Israel and the elect remnant first, and finally in His only begotten Son, God worked out His great plan of salvation. Because of God's love to them, Moses calls upon them to love Him, another constant theme of this book. See v. 10, vi. 5, vii. 9, x. 12, xi. 1, 13, 22, xiii. 3, xix. 9, xxx. 6, 16, 20.

I command thee this day (40). As Moses' life draws to a close, this note of urgency falls frequently from his lips. See vi. 6, viii. 11, viii. 1, 11. *That it may go well with thee* (40). These words are repeated in v. 16, 33, vi. 3, 18, xii. 25, 28, xxii. 7. This is one of the various blessings upon obedience. Behind these promises of material blessing there is always the love (see 37n.) which unites God with His people.

III. THREE CITIES OF REFUGE APPOINTED. iv. 41–43

Then (41). This word marks an interval between the previous discourse and the declaration of the law. In Nu. xxxv. 11 the command was given to 'appoint' three cities on each side of the river as cities of refuge. Moses now 'separates' three in the conquered territory and later (xix. 1) gives instructions regarding three in Canaan. In Jos. xx. 2 they are definitely 'assigned' (RV) to their use.

IV. MOSES' SECOND DISCOURSE. iv. 44—xxvi. 19

a. Introductory preface (iv. 44–49)

The place and time of the second discourse are carefully defined. It was given in full view of *Beth-Peor* (46; see iii. 29n.), which adds piquancy to its warnings, and of *Pisgah* (49), which sheds light on its promises. *Sion* (48) as a name for Hermon is found only here. *Testimonies* (45). The word 'testimony' ('*edah*) denotes a solemn assertion or witness. God's testimonies are the declaration of His character, will and purpose, as contained in Holy Scripture. In Ex. xxv. 21, 22, the ten commandments are called the 'testimony', and in 2 Ki. xi. 12 we are told that Jehoiada delivered 'the testimony' to Jehoash, which may have been the whole or part of this book of Deuteronomy. *This is the law* (44). See i. 5n. In this context 'the law' probably refers to chapters v—xxvi, which are presented as one discourse.

b. Exhortations to fidelity and obedience based on the revelation in Horeb (v. 1—xi. 32)

i. The Ten Commandments (v. 1–21). The ten commandments are the kernel of the law and the basis of God's covenant with Israel. The whole of chapters xii—xxvi may be looked upon as an application in detail of the principles they contain to the life of the people in the land of Canaan. When Christ bade the young ruler keep them if he would 'enter into life' (Mt. xix. 17), He constituted them a rule of life for all His followers; and when He spoke of them as the 'commandment of God' in contrast with the traditions of men (Mt. xv. 3) He recognized their binding force. Only the grace of God can enable man to keep them; but it is exactly in order that man keep them that grace is given. Law and grace are thus bound together.

Hear, O Israel (1). These words, repeated in iv. 1, vi. 3, 4, ix. 1, xx. 3 and xxvii. 9, make the beginning of a new appeal. This call to listen is also a call to obedience. *Statutes and judgments* (1). See iv. 1n. These follow later in chapters xii— xxvi, after chapters v—xi dealing with the ten commandments and with the exhortation based upon them. *And keep, and do them* (1). 'Observe to do them' (RV). A characteristic phrase repeated in v. 32, vi. 3, 25, vii. 11, viii. 1, xi. 22, 32, xii. 1, xiii. 18, xv. 5, xvii. 10, xix. 9, xxiv. 8, xxviii. 1, 15, 58, xxxi. 12, xxxii. 46. *Made a covenant with us in Horeb* (2). See iv. 13n. Moses recalls the actual place to bring home to them their responsibility and privilege. *Not . . . with our fathers, but with us* (3). According to the Hebrew idiom this means 'not only' with our fathers, 'but also' with us. Moses emphasizes their individual responsibility as the pioneers of the new national existence. *Went not up* (5). We learn from Ex. xix that this was at the divine command. *Saying* (5). The difference in form between the commandments in Ex. xx and here has led to the suggestion that the original 'words' consisted only of one brief sentence each, e.g. 'Honour thy father and thy mother', and that what is additional is inspired comment. The notes here should be compared with those on Ex. xx.

I am the Lord thy God (6). The first commandment does not begin 'Thou shalt not', but 'I am'. See Ex. iii. 14 and cf. Jn. xiv. 6. God is Alpha and Omega, the Creator, and must begin with Himself. Cf. Gn. i. 1; Rev. xxii. 13. He adds the covenant name 'Jehovah thy God' and so brings Himself into communication with His chosen people. He gives Himself to be their portion; as in the fullness of time He gave His Son (Jn. iii. 16). This personal relationship between God and man in Jesus Christ is the very foundation of the Christian faith. The first commandment also proclaims God as the Saviour, *which brought thee out of the . . . house of bondage* (6). Since Jehovah alone is God, their God and Redeemer, it follows that they can have *none other gods* (7). See vi. 14n. The stringent rules against the worship of false gods in chapter xiii, the national feasts of chapter xvi, and the covenant of chapter xxix, all illumine this first and great commandment.

Thou shalt not make thee any graven image (8). The second commandment forbids all low or false ideas of God. The Creator must not be worshipped in the form of a creature, such as the 'golden calf', neither must He be thought of as one of ourselves (Ps. 1. 21). Man cannot by searching find Him out (Jb. xi. 7). God can be

truly known only as He has revealed Himself in His word and in His Son Jesus Christ (Jn. xvii. 3, 14). Those who keep this commandment should feel shame at the thought that millions still worship idols because of the failure of the Church's witness. God is *jealous* (9), not for His own reputation, which cannot suffer, but with the jealousy of love which seeks our wholehearted love in response to His own. See Ex. xx. 5n. That *the iniquity of the fathers* (9) is visited upon the children (as regards its consequences, but not its guilt) is a fact of experience; and so is the validity of God's promise of mercy to those who *love me and keep my commandments* (10).

To expound the full meaning of the third commandment (verse 11) would involve the study of the name of God throughout the Bible. In Hebrew thought the 'name' is closely identified with the person who bears it; it expresses his character (see Ex. iii. 13n.; cf. Mt. i. 21), and carries his authority (see Ex. xxiii. 21n.). That name is 'wonderful' and wrapped in mystery (Is. ix. 6), it is holy and reverend (Ps. cxi. 9; Lk. i. 49), glorious and fearful (Dt. xxviii. 58); its glory is revealed by Moses (Dt. xxxii. 3) and the prophets (Ps. xcix. 3; Is. lxiii. 12, 14), in Christ and through Him by His disciples (Jn. xvii. 6, 26). Wonders are wrought by faith in His name (Acts iii. 16). God's name is taken in vain by the heathen when they think to exploit divine power to their own ends by witchcraft or necromancy (xviii. 9–14); by statesmen when they bring in God's name merely to give force to their own utterances; and by Christians when they use vain repetitions as the heathen do (Mt. vi. 7). To keep this commandment we need divine grace, and therefore we pray, 'Hallowed be thy name'. We need also a desire to see the divine sovereignty exercised, and so we pray, 'Thy kingdom come'.

Keep the sabbath day (12). See Ex. xx. 8n., xxxi. 12–17n. This fourth commandment is firstly a gracious provision for *rest* from labour, by setting aside a definite time for waiting upon God as, in the beginning, the 'seventh day' was spent by the whole creation in silent adoration (Gn. ii. 3). Lest man should be feverishly busy in the race for wealth or wisdom, he needs to sanctify this day, to wait upon God and listen to His voice, that life may be full of meaning and purpose under the divine direction. It is a prophecy of the eternal sabbath rest. See Heb. iv. 9. To Israel, as they became a nation, it was also given as a *sign* of their redemption from bondage, and their entrance upon a new life of liberty. See Lv. xxiii. 3n. It was thus a prophecy of the day of resurrection (Rom. iv. 25), and so became 'the first day of the week' and the 'Lord's day' of vision (Rev. i. 10). Thus the Jewish sabbath was transmuted into the Christian Sunday. The sanctifying of the seventh day does not contradict, but gives practical effect to, the truth that all days are holy. Cf. xiv. 22n.

Remember (15). See iv. 9n. Up to *within thy gates* (14) the words here are nearly identical with those of the fourth commandment in Ex. xx.

What follows may be regarded as comment. The memory of God's mighty works should make them courageous. See also ix. 7. To remember their own sins should make them humble. *Thou wast a servant* (15). These words are repeated in xv. 15, xvi. 12, xxiv. 18, 22; and the parallel expression 'the house of bondage' is found in v. 6, vi. 12, vii. 8, viii. 14, xiii. 5, 10. The memory of their own servitude is emphasized both as a proof of God's redeeming love (verse 6) and as a reason for generosity to the oppressed (xv. 15). The fact of their redemption 'out of the house of bondage' was to be commemorated in the Passover service (Ex. xii. 14).

Honour thy father and thy mother (16). See Ex. xx. 12n. This fifth commandment deals with the most sacred of human relationships, that of parenthood. The name of Father applies first of all to God, and when He allows men to share it He ennobles them accordingly. Men choose their own friends, but parents are the gift of God, His instruments in bringing them to birth, a ministry which has no parallel. For this reason parents must be honoured. The promise of length of days in the land, which is equally God's gift, is an incentive to obedience. See iv. 26n. and Eph. vi. 2. Honour to parents is limited by the honour due to God who is supreme. By studying the life of Christ we can see how both allegiances can be perfectly combined (Mt. x. 37, xix. 29; Lk. ii. 49, 51; Jn. xix. 26, 27). The laws of Dt. xxi. 15–21 illuminate this commandment.

Thou shalt not kill (17). See Ex. xx. 13n. This sixth commandment declares the sacredness of human life. All life proceeds from God, and must be regarded as His gift and treated with reverence. This was the primitive law (Gn. ix. 4–6). The mere taking of life, even human life, may not be sin. In order to deliver Israel God overwhelmed the Egyptians in the Red Sea, and in order to preserve them as a pure and holy seed He commanded the destruction of the Canaanites (xii. 2). He put also the sword of justice into the hands of judges and magistrates. See xvii. 2–7, xix. 12; Rom. xiii. 4. The guilt of murder is incurred when man for his own wicked ends takes his brother's life, that life which the Creator had bestowed for His own glory. Then his brother's blood cries out from the ground (Gn. iv. 10). Cf. Dt. xxi. 1–9.

Neither shalt thou commit adultery (18). See Ex. xx. 14n. This seventh commandment establishes the rule of a holy married life, and accounts for the detailed regulations for moral purity, the number and stringency of which testify to its importance (xxi. 10–17, xxii, xxiii. 1–18, xxiv. 1–5, xxv. 11, 12). In the beginning God instituted marriage (Gn. i. 28, ii. 24; Mt. xix. 4–6), and used it to signify His love to His people Israel (Hos. ii. 14–20), and the union between Christ and His Church (Mt. ix. 15; Eph. v. 32). Adultery is used as a symbol of Israel's unfaithfulness (xxxi. 16) and of Christian apostasy (Jas. iv. 4).

Neither shalt thou steal (19). See Ex. xx. 15n.

The eighth commandment, like the three preceding, is derived from the fact that a man's possessions, as well as his parentage, his life and his powers, are a gift from God. See Dt. viii. 17, 18; 1 Cor. iv. 7. Man is therefore responsible to his Maker for the right use and distribution of wealth. Landmarks must therefore be respected (xix. 14), wages duly paid (xxiv. 15), just measure given (xxv. 13), and generosity shown to the poor (xv. 7, 8). The Christian standard must not be lower; both goods and gospel are a trust from God. See Mt. v. 42; Rom. i. 14.

Neither shalt thou bear false witness (20). See Ex. xx. 16n. The ninth commandment, though negative in form, may be given a positive content. It sets the false in contrast to the true; by forbidding the one, it enforces the other. All our witness, our testimony, must be true (xiii. 14, xvii. 4–6) and judgment just (xvii. 8–13, xix. 15–21). Cf. Mt. xviii. 16. The Christian, like his Master, must bear witness to the truth (Jn. xviii. 37); and how can he do this except by bearing witness to Him who is the truth?

Neither shalt thou covet (21). See Ex. xx. 17n. The tenth commandment stands apart from the others in that it does not relate to outward conduct, but only to the state of the heart. Therefore God alone can see when it is broken. In its negative form it precludes unlawful desire for what others have; on the positive side it teaches contentment and faith (Heb. xiii. 5, 6).

The small variations between the form the commandment takes here and the form given in Ex. xx. 17 suggest the period just prior to settling in the promised land. Moses includes the neighbour's 'field' which henceforth might become an object of desire.

The tenth commandment is not quoted in our Lord's first reply to the young ruler (Mk. x. 19), but His further words (21) supply a searching commentary upon it.

ii. The commandments delivered (v. 22–33). Moses now repeats the circumstances of the giving of the two tables of the law in an exhortation to obedience. *The fire . . . the cloud . . . darkness* (22). See iv. 11n., 12n. *He added no more . . . he wrote* (22). See iv. 13n, and cf. Rev. xxii. 18. *His glory* (24). See Ex. xxxiii. 18. *Go thou near, and hear* (27). The people heard the thunder, but Moses heard the words. Cf. Jn. xii. 29; Acts ix. 7. Moses is here seen as a mediator between God and the people (see Gal. iii. 19), and so as a type of Christ. Cf. xxxiv. 10n. *Fear* (29). See iv. 10n. *Always . . . for ever* (29). The commandments are binding for all time. See iv. 8n.

iii. Exhortation to remember (vi. 1–9). Moses proceeds to 'teach' the commandments (see iv. 9n.) to the people as they in turn are to teach their children. The teaching will be mainly oral; but see verse 9. *Thou, and thy son* (2). The frequent transitions from the plural to the singular, that is, from the nation to the individual, would be natural in a spoken address. *The land that floweth with milk and honey* (3). Repeated xi. 9, xxvi. 9, 15, xxvii. 3, xxxi. 20.

Verses 4 and 5, known by their first word as the *Shema*, are recited by pious Jews twice daily, together with Dt. xi. 13–21 and Nu. xv. 37–41. Our Lord added the phrase 'with all thy mind' and quoted them as 'the first and great commandment' (Mk. xii. 30). The word employed here for 'one' (*eḥadh*) does not preclude the Christian concept of a trinity of persons within that unity; another word (*yaḥidh*) is used for the atomic unity of a monad, the barren Islamic idea which does not admit of a divine partnership. Here faith in the unity of God is combined with love (see iv. 37n.) which no heathen religion requires. *With all thine heart* (5). See iv. 29n. *Bind them . . . upon thine hand* (8). The Jews of a later age carried out the command in this verse literally, by enclosing written portions of the law in small cases, called phylacteries, and binding them upon their hands and foreheads. Cf. Mt. xxiii. 5. See xi. 20n., xvii. 18n. *Thou shalt write* (9). Writing is also mentioned in iv. 13, v. 22, ix. 10, x. 2, 4, xi. 20, xvii. 18, xxiv. 1, xxvii. 3, 8, xxviii. 58, 61, xxix. 20, 21, 27, xxx. 10, xxxi. 9, 19, 22, 24. These references were once regarded as anachronisms, but archaeological research has proved that writing was not uncommon in Moses' time, both cuneiform and a primitive Hebrew alphabet being used. Moses probably learned to write when in Egypt (Acts vii. 22) and others, Joshua included, may have done the same. But writing was not general and 'scribes' or 'writers' were often employed.

iv. Lessons from the past (vi. 10–19). Out of this short passage our Lord chose two verses to vanquish Satan. In quoting verse 13 He replaced (according to the Greek text of Mt. iv. 10) the word 'fear' by 'worship', in response to Satan's challenge. *When thou shalt have eaten and be full* (11). Repeated viii. 10, 12, xi. 15, xiv. 29, xxvi. 12, xxxi. 20. *Beware* (12). Blessing when remembered should result in praise (viii. 10). *Other gods* (14). See iii. 24n., xi. 28n., xxxii. 16, 17n. The words are repeated vii. 4, xiii. 6, 13, xvii. 3, xxviii. 36, 64, xxix. 26, xxx. 17, xxxi. 20. The current phraseology concerning 'other gods' and their connection with other lands is used, but their reality is not endorsed. They are 'demons', or 'the work of men's hands' (iv. 28). Jehovah is the only true God (xxxii. 39) and the rest are 'no-gods' (xxxii. 17, RV).

Jealous (15). See iv. 24n. *Massah* (16) means 'testing' or 'proving'. See Ex. xvii. 7; Dt. viii. 15n., ix. 22. It is right for God to prove man (see viii. 3 and cf. Heb. iv. 12); but, on man's part, it is presumption, proceeding from unbelief, to put God to the test. For inspired comment see Ps. xcv. 8 and Heb. iii. 15. By the use of this scripture Christ repelled the temptation to vain presumption into which the children of Israel had fallen.

v. Future generations are to be taught (vi. 20–25). *He brought us out . . . that he might bring us in* (23). Moses links the grace of God in redemption with the way of life which is set before them. Cf. Rom. iv. 25. *For our good*

always (24). There is nothing arbitrary about the statutes and judgments: they all conduce to a clean, just and holy life. Cf. x. 13. *Preserve us alive* (24). See iv. 26n. *Our righteousness* (25). Righteousness (Heb. *ṣedheqh*) is one of the key words of the Old Testament, and should be studied there as the background of the teaching on righteousness or justification in such passages as Rom. iii. 21–26 and Phil. iii. 6–9. It means whatever is straight and upright, just and true, such as a right judgment (xvi. 18) or a correct measure (xxv. 15). Because God is righteous (xxxii. 4), His law is 'holy, righteous and good' (Rom. vii. 12, RV).

vi. Israel's call to separation (vii. 1–11). These verses are full of teaching concerning God's purposes of judgment and mercy. The hopelessly corrupt nations are devoted to destruction (see ii. 34n.); but Israel is to be *an holy people unto the Lord* (6), not touching the unclean thing (cf. 2 Cor. vi. 17), and a witness of God's redeeming grace (8, 9). All the seven nations of verse 1 are mentioned in the world survey of Gn. x. 15–18, except the Perizzites who may have been, like the Rephaim, a pre-Canaanite tribe (see Jos. xvii. 16). *Seven nations* (1). Earlier in i. 7 (see note) only Amorites and Canaanites are mentioned, as including the rest. The Hittites are now known to have been a great nation established to the north of Palestine, whose members have filtered into the country. Cf. Gn. xxiii. 3, 'the sons of Heth'.

Images . . . groves (5). See xvi. 21, 22n. *An holy people* (6). Repeated in xiv. 2, 21, xxvi. 19, xxviii. 9. The word 'holy' in the Old Testament has a double signification. It means both 'dedicated to the Lord's service' and 'pure and radiant'. Owing to their divine calling the people should partake of both these attributes. *A special people* (6). 'A peculiar people' (RV). The word *segulah* (peculiar) was applied to a possession which belonged particularly to an individual, as his very own, distinguished from the general family inheritance. See Ex. xix. 5n. The expression is repeated in xiv. 2, xxvi. 18. Cf. Tit. ii. 14; 1 Pet. ii. 9. *Because the Lord loved you* (8). See iv. 37n. *Redeemed* (8). The word is repeated in ix. 26, xiii. 5, xv. 15, xxi. 8, xxiv. 18. It strikes a truly evangelical note. See Lk. i. 68, xxiv. 21; 1 Pet. i. 18. Their redemption provides a plea for forgiveness (xxi. 8) and a reason for showing justice and mercy (xxiv. 18). *Out of the house of bondmen* (8). See v. 15n. *Covenant and mercy* (9). See iv. 13n. The word *ḥesedh* (mercy) is used for the 'lovingkindness' of God (e.g. Ps. ciii. 4) and graciousness or kindness between friends. It is often associated with the 'covenant' (vii. 12). The word for 'holy' in xxxiii. 8 is from the same root. (See RV).

vii. Blessings and encouragements (vii. 12–26). Having set forth God's purpose in choosing Israel, Moses now promises manifold blessings if they keep His laws, and exhorts them to faith and courage.

The covenant and the mercy (12). See iv. 13n.

and vii. 9n. Note the definite article. See verse 9n. *Love thee, and bless thee* (13). The love is unconditional (iv. 37n.), the blessing conditional. The word 'bless' recurs in xii. 7, xiv. 24, 29, xv. 4, 6, 10, 14, 18, xvi. 10, 15, xxiii. 20, xxiv. 19, xxviii. 8. *Corn . . . wine . . . oil* (13). Repeated in xi. 14, xii. 17, xiv. 23, xviii. 4, xxviii. 51. These are the chief products of Palestine, symbolical of plenty, joy and spiritual prosperity. See Gn. xxii. 17. *The evil diseases of Egypt, which thou knowest* (15). Note how readily an illustration from Egypt springs to Moses' mind. Cf. xxviii. 27, 60. *Remember* (18). See v. 15n. *The hornet* (20). See Ex. xxiii. 28n. *Destroy their name* (24). Repeated in ix. 14, xii. 3, xxv. 19. (Cf. Rev. iii. 5.) The name of false gods should be blotted out of remembrance, but the name of the Lord shall abide upon His sanctuary and His people.

An abomination to the Lord (25). The expression is repeated, mainly in connection with idolatry or impurity, in xii. 31, xiii. 14, xiv. 3, xvii. 1, 4, xviii. 12, xxii. 5, xxiii. 18, xxiv. 4, xxv. 16, xxvii. 15, xxxii. 16. See also vi. 14n.

A cursed thing (26). 'A devoted thing' (RV). See ii. 34n.

viii. Promises and exhortations (viii. 1–20). Moses, as befits his age, calls on them again to remember (see iv. 9n.) God's mercies, promises and character (cf. Ex. xxxiv. 6), as a reason for gratitude and obedience. *All the way . . . these forty years* (2). See ii. 14n. Moses' 'reminiscences' in Deuteronomy include the experiences in Egypt (see iv. 34n.), the journey thence to Horeb and 'all the way' from there to the banks of the Jordan. The great experiences at Horeb are recalled in ix. 7—x. 11, and the final journey from Kadesh in chapters i—iii. In addition there are incidental references to murmurings at Taberah and Kibroth-hattaavah (Nu. xi. 4, 34; Dt. ix. 22); Miriam's leprosy (Nu. xii. 10; Dt. xxiv. 9); the judgment upon Dathan and Abiram (Nu. xvi. 27; Dt. xi. 6); the striking of the rock at Meribah (Nu. xx. 13; Dt. i. 37, xxxii. 51); the death of Aaron and investment of Eleazar (Nu. xx. 28; Dt. x. 6); the plague of serpents (Nu. xxi. 6; Dt. viii. 15); and the journeyings round Benejaakan, Gudgodah and Jotbath (Nu. xxxiii. 32f.; Dt. x. 6f.). The details of time and place, the incidental way in which they are mentioned, and their correspondence with the events most likely to impress themselves on Moses' memory, afford a cumulative and striking evidence of authenticity.

He humbled thee (3). The wilderness wanderings were a punishment upon the older generation and a humbling experience for those now addressed. *Man doth not live by bread only . . .* (3). These words were quoted by Christ in His temptation. In the Hebrew, 'word' is absent (see RV), but our Lord supplies it (Mt. iv. 4). When Moses first uttered these words he must have meant by 'every thing that proceedeth out of the mouth of God' the revelation made through *him*. Christ can have meant no less, thus setting His imprimatur upon this book. True

life is not to be derived from material things, but from the word of God. See xxxii. 46f.

Thy raiment (4). Cf. xxix. 5. Some kind of special divine provision is implied. *As a man chasteneth his son* (5). That is, with a view to his reformation and instruction, to bring forth the fruit of righteousness. See Heb. xii. 5–11 and cf. Dt. i. 31, xxxii. 6. *To walk in his ways* (6). The phrase recurs in x. 12, xi. 22, xix. 9, xxvi. 17, xxviii. 9, xxx. 16. Former discipline and future prospect should bring this about.

A good land (7). See i. 25n. Travellers by the desert route from Egypt tell of the sense of relief on reaching Palestine with its flowery plains, green hills and homely beauty. The variations of altitude supply it with the products of both a temperate and a semi-tropical climate. The *valleys* are the broad vales found between parallel ranges of hills. *Whose stones are iron* (9). This may refer to the hard basaltic rocks, put to various uses. *Brass* (9). Rather, copper, which is found in the neighbouring hills (cf. 2 Sa. viii. 8). Traces of copper-works have been discovered near Hamath. *Beware that thou forget not* (11). Israel's subsequent history shows that this warning was very necessary. Cf. 2 Ch. xii. 1. Ingratitude and self-sufficiency were all too common, then as now.

The rock of flint (15). See vi. 16n. On two occasions water was brought out of the rock, once in Horeb (Ex. xvii. 6), and again at Kadesh (Nu. xx. 8), and the word used for 'rock' is different in each case. In the former, and in this passage, the word is *ṣur*, which denotes solidity and strength; it is used metaphorically of God as the believer's source of strength, so in xxxii. 4, 13 ('flinty rock'), 15, 18, 30, 31, 37. Cf. Ps. xxxi. 2. In the latter case, the word used is *sela'*, which indicates a crag or fortress, and denotes security. It also is applied to God as the believer's refuge. Cf. Ps. xxxi. 3. See also vi. 16n., xxxii. 51n.; and 1 Cor. x. 4.

My power . . . hath gotten me this wealth (17). Wealth comes from the land, which is God's gift, by the use of time, energy and brains, which are also His gift. See v. 19n.

ix. The people reminded of their sins and demerits (ix. 1–29). Moses afresh urges humility as they remember their past sins and failures. He recalls their fears (*thou knowest* (2) is emphatic), but renews God's promise (*shall destroy* (3) is also emphatic). He repeats the nature of their calling to 'possess' the land (see i. 21n.), and God's purpose in the destruction of the Canaanites and the abolition of idolatry. *My righteousness* (4). See vii. 7n., and cf. Eph. ii. 9. *The word which the Lord sware* (5). See i. 8n. Moses sets the promise in sharp contrast with their unworthiness which is emphasized by the recital of ix. 7—x. 11, and preaches the doctrine of the unmerited grace of God as clearly as St. Paul. The calling of Israel is unconditional, springs from the sovereign choice of God's love (vii. 7–9), and is irrevocable (Rom. xi. 29). The blessings, on the other hand, are conditional upon obedience. See chapter xxviii. As regards the former, the promise is to Abraham's 'seed', which is Christ (Gal. iii. 16), and to all who are 'in Christ'. As regards the latter, 'Christ is the end of the law' (Rom. x. 4), and has 'abolished the enmity' of the broken law (Eph. ii. 15; Col. ii. 14). The distinction is important for the understanding of the book of Deuteronomy and its bearing on the Christian life. *A stiffnecked people* (6). The metaphor (see verse 13, xxxi. 27) is drawn from the example of an intractable animal. Cf. Ps. xxxii. 9; Je. xxxi. 18. Moses proceeds to substantiate the charge.

The assembly (10). The word *qahal* used here and in x. 4, xviii. 16, is in the LXX translated *ekklesia* or 'church', and so Stephen speaks of 'the church in the wilderness' (Acts vii. 38). Both the Hebrew word and the Greek signify a gathering *out* and a gathering *together*, an election and a collection. As Israel was called out of Egypt, so the members of Christ's Church are called out of the world. *I fell down before the Lord* (18). See verse 25. The events recalled in verses 8–21 are recorded in Ex. xxxii—xxxiv. Moses seems to mingle recollections of his first and second ascents into the Mount, his thoughts being bound together by their subject, which is the rebelliousness of the people and his own intercessions on their behalf. As Moses interceded then, so Christ does now (Heb. vii. 25). See iii. 23n.

I was afraid (19). A rare word is used here for 'afraid' which recurs as 'fear' in xxviii. 66. It is different from that used when the need to 'fear God' is being set before the people (see iv. 10n. and Lv. xix. 3n.). The words in Heb. xii. 21 are identical with those used by the LXX here. Moses' deep sense of reverence and awe in the divine presence commenced with his call (Ex. iii. 6), and deepened with his experiences at Sinai—it is reflected in all his discourses. (See iv. 10, 24, v. 29, ix. 3, xxviii. 58.) Such godly fear can be combined with a simple, childlike trust. Far different is the fear which leads to bondage. See Rom. viii. 15, and cf. 1 Jn. iv. 18. *I prayed for Aaron* (20). Could anyone but Moses have uttered these words? See viii. 2n. *Your sin, the calf* (21). See v. 8n. Not even Aaron could keep the second commandment once the visible tokens of God's presence had ceased. *Massah* (22). See vi. 16n., viii. 15n. The provoking at Rephidim, where the name Massah was first affixed, was before reaching Mount Sinai, the other incidents occurred after leaving there. The three names are descriptive of the events. See Ex. xvii. 7n.; Nu. xi. 3, 34. In a manner, although in varying ways, all of them were the causes of proving (Massah) and strife (Meribah). *Ye believed him not* (23). Unbelief was the radical sin, in the old dispensation as well as the new (i. 32. Cf. Jn. xvi. 9). Heb. iii, iv supplies a commentary.

x. The ark and the Levites (x. 1–11). In verses 1–11 Moses concludes his retrospect of the events at Horeb. His thoughts travel from his repeated intercessions back to the ten commandments, and the tables laid up in the ark, still in their midst; to the death of Aaron, to Eleazar (6) and to the Levites still carrying on their work. They may have been standing near him as he spoke.

I made an ark (3). See Ex. xxv. 10n. This apparently refers to the ark subsequently made by Bezaleel under Moses' direction (Ex. xxxv), or perhaps to a temporary receptacle made with his own hands. *He wrote* (4). Cf. 2 Cor. iii. 3. *As the Lord commanded me* (5). A frequent phrase in Exodus (e.g. vii. 6). Moses' own obedience (see Heb. iii. 2) gives force to his counsels to others.

From Beeroth (6). The sudden change to the third person in verses 6 and 7, and the reference to events many years later, make these verses look like a later addition, perhaps by Moses himself. The death of Aaron and the continuation of his office follow naturally upon ix. 20 and are also connected with verse 8. In Nu. xxxiii. 31–33, Mosera and the three other places here mentioned are described as in proximity to each other, but in a different order. Since the presence of water (*Beeroth* means 'wells') is mentioned in connection with two of them, they may have been visited more than once. *Mosera* means 'chastisement', and the place was perhaps so named in reference to Aaron's death (see Nu. xx. 28; Dt. ix. 22n.). *Eleazar his son ministered . . . in his stead* (6). The office of the high priesthood was thus perpetuated. The choice of Eleazar suggests that Aaron's sin had been forgiven.

At that time (8). That is, before leaving Horeb. (See Nu. i. 47–54.) *The Lord separated the tribe of Levi* (8). As one day in seven and a tithe of the people's wealth were both sanctified to the Lord, so one tribe in twelve was set apart for the service of the sanctuary. Moses displays special interest in Levi, his own tribe. It was the special office of the Levites *to bear the ark* (8) and of the priests *to bless in his name;* yet priests sometimes did the former (Jos. iii. 6), and any Israelite could 'bless' (xxvii. 12). Priests and Levites alike stood before the Lord and ministered (see xviii. 1n., 5n.).

xi. What the Lord requires of His people (x. 12–22). Moses again sums up the requirements of God's law in terms similar to those already used in vi. 5. Cf. Mt. xxii. 37 and the answer given by Micah to the question asked in verse 12 (Mi. vi. 8). The necessity for loving God seems to be continually in Moses' mind. *Only the Lord* (15). The amazing grace of God is shown by the fact that, although He possessed heaven and earth (14), nevertheless He, and He alone, chose to bless the children of Israel *above all people* (15). Their response should be submission to His rule and a love from the heart which is described in terms which Paul echoes in Rom. ii. 29. (Cf. xxx. 6n.) Note the lofty monotheism of verse 17. It pervades the whole of this book and is the keystone of its teaching.

The fatherless and widow . . . the stranger (18).

Repeated xiv. 29, xvi. 11, 14, xxiv. 17, 19, 20, 21, xxvi. 12, 13, xxvii. 19. See i. 16n. Solicitude for the 'stranger' runs through the Mosaic institutions. The Israelite had the backing of his family and clan, but the 'stranger' had no such protection, nor inheritance in the land. Nevertheless he is bidden to keep the sabbath (v. 14) and the national feasts (xvi. 11, 14. Cf. Acts ii. 10), and is included in the covenant (xxix. 11, 12). He thus belongs to the brotherhood of Israel, and becomes, like the fatherless and the widow, an object of special solicitude (cf. Mt. xxv. 35; Acts xiv. 27; Eph. ii. 19). *Ye were strangers* (19). Cf. Lv. xix. 34. The children of Israel, when they first went down into Egypt and became a great nation (22), had known kindness at the hands of Joseph and the kings who knew him; they had also known the bitterness of persecution. Moses now urges them to *love . . . the stranger* (19), bearing in mind their own past experience. *To him shalt thou cleave* (20). Repeated xi. 22, xiii. 4, xxx. 20. An indication of how close the bond is to be between the Lord and His people. *Threescore and ten persons* (22). See Gn. xlvi. 3, 27. God always fulfils His promises.

xii. Motives to love and obedience (xi. 1–25). Moses now addresses particularly the older men (2). His threefold *therefore* (1, 8, 18) offers reasons for their obedience: first, God's own greatness (x. 17–22); secondly, His signs and wonders (xi. 1–7); and thirdly, because blessing depends on obedience (xi. 8–17).

His charge (1). The word implies watchful guardianship, as over a treasure. It is used only this once in Deuteronomy, but frequently in the previous books in reference to the charge of the tabernacle (e.g. Lv. viii. 35). *His stretched out arm* (2). See iv. 34; Ex. vi. 6. A picturesque description of God's protecting care. *His miracles, and his acts* (3). 'His signs, and his works' (RV). God reveals Himself through 'signs' and 'works' as well as by words. Cf. Mt. xi. 4; Jn. ii. 11. The miraculous deliverance from Egypt is confirmed in the New Testament (Acts vii. 36; Heb. xi. 27–29). *Dathan and Abiram* (6). God's miracles of judgment are also object lessons (Nu. xvi; Jude 5). Dathan and Abiram called Egypt a land of 'milk and honey' (Nu. xvi. 13, 14), which may have suggested to Moses the thoughts expressed in verses 9–12. *Not as the land of Egypt* (10). In Egypt irrigation is ever the dominant problem. The Nile water has to be made to flow through the prepared channels. In Canaan fertilization is accomplished without labour or anxiety by God's gracious gift of the autumn rains which fall at the time of sowing and promote the growth of the seed, and the spring rains which fructify the corn and barley which are gathered in May and June (14; cf. Jas. v. 7). Everything reminds of God's providential care, and affords a parable of the life of the Christian, to whom God gives that for which the world labours.

Lay up . . . in your heart (18). Moses again appeals to the heart. With the heart the Lord

must be sought (iv. 29), loved (vi. 5) and served (x. 12). The heart must be circumcised (x. 16), for there wicked thoughts arise (ix. 4, xv. 9. Cf. Mt. xv. 18), and there the Lord's word resides (xxx. 14). *Frontlets* (18). See vi. 8n. *Ye shall teach them your children* (19). Cf. iv. 9, vi. 7, xi. 2. Moses does not directly address the children, but always bears them in mind and the responsibility of the parents for teaching them the Word of God. *Door posts . . . gates* (20). In the houses of orthodox Jews today there may be seen in the porch the *mazuza* (lit. 'doorpost'), a small box containing a copy of Dt. vi. 4–9, in continuance of the ancient custom. *As the days of heaven upon the earth* (21). 'The heavens' (RV) are the symbol of exaltation and freedom from earthly care and sin. *The uttermost sea* (24). 'The hinder sea' (RV). The Hebrew thought of the points of the compass as seen by a man facing the rising sun, with the south on his right hand and the west behind him, so that 'the hinder sea' means the western or Mediterranean Sea.

xiii. A blessing and a curse (xi. 26–32). There is a strict impartiality in the justice of God (Ezk. xviii. 25–29, xxxiii. 17–20). The whole of Israel's subsequent history bears out the truth of the principle here enunciated by Moses. *Other gods, which ye have not known* (28). Repeated xiii. 2, 6, 13, xxviii. 64, xxix. 26. The thought behind this phrase is that they are altogether alien. (See vi. 14n.) *Gerizim . : . Ebal* (29). See xxvii. 12, 13. From the plains of Moab (xxxiv. 1) the traveller can see the twin mountains of Gerizim and Ebal to the west across the Jordan valley, and the sun setting behind them (30). They stand as a witness to the necessity of the choice between right and wrong. *Gilgal, beside the plains* (RV 'oaks') *of Moreh* (30). At Sichem in the plain of Moreh God had first promised the land to Abraham (Gn. xii. 6, 7). The name Gilgal is still attached to a spot in this area about one and a half miles east of Jacob's well. There are, however, a number of places which bear this name and some think the reference may be to the Gilgal near Jericho which is mentioned in Jos. iv. 19 as the first camping site after the crossing of Jordan.

c. Religious, civil and domestic laws and precepts (xii. 1—xxvi. 15)

i. Idolatry to be destroyed (xii. 1–14). Chapters xii—xxvi are sometimes separated from the rest of the book and spoken of as the Deuteronomic 'Code', but they are better considered as a continuation of the previous discourse. Moses here proceeds to lay down rules and ordinances for the religious, civil, social and domestic life in Canaan, with encouragements and warnings.

In the land (1). The immediate entry of the children of Israel into the land of promise governs all that follows. (Cf. xii. 10, xxvi. 1.) Where material considerations seem to predominate, this is the reason. *Ye shall utterly destroy* (2). 'Ye shall surely destroy' (RV). Their first and most important task will be to cleanse 'the land' of all traces of idolatry, that it may be 'holy unto the Lord' (cf. Lv. xi. 44, 45). This duty is implicit in the first and second of the ten commandments. *Places . . . upon the high mountains* (2). The word for 'places' is *maqomoth*, a purely general term, not *bamoth* or 'high places', which is used for local shrines. Cf. 1 Ki. xv. 14. The fact that the word *bamoth* never occurs in Dt. xii—xxvi is sufficient to dispose of the theory that the chief object of the legislation was to prohibit the use of the 'high places'. See verse 5n.

Altars . . . pillars . . . groves (3). See Ex. xxxiv. 13; Dt. xvi. 21n. *Destroy the names of them* (3); 'their name' (RV). See v. 11n., xxviii. 10n.

The place which the Lord your God shall choose . . . to put his name there (5). The same word for 'place' is used as in verse 2. The contrast lies between the false and the true, rather than between the many and the one; between those places which are connected with the name of the false gods (3) and that on which Jehovah has put His name. (See v. 11n.) At first the tabernacle would remain the central place of worship (see Lv. xvii. 3–7n.), but later on any place chosen by Jehovah (Ex. xx. 24n.), such as the altar on Mount Ebal (xxvii. 5, 6), was His sanctuary and a gathering place for His people (Ex. xxiii. 19; Dt. xvi. 6). These words in verse 5 point forward to the temple (verse 11; 1 Ki. v. 5, viii. 16) and to the Lord Jesus Christ (Mt. i. 23; Jn. ii. 19–21). The form in which this command is cast is an evidence of its antiquity: there is no hint concerning Jerusalem or Shiloh, or the vicissitudes through which the ark and the tabernacle were to pass before 'rest' (9) was attained. The words 'the place which the Lord shall choose' are repeated xii. 11, 14, 18, 21, 26, xiv. 25, xv. 20, xvi. 7, 15, 16, xvii. 8, 10, xviii. 6, xxxi. 11.

Your burnt offerings, and your sacrifices (6). Regulations concerning these had already been given in Lv. i—vii. *Your tithes* (6). See xiv. 22ff.; Lv. xxvii. 30–33. The offering of tithes and firstlings was obligatory, the others voluntary. *Heave offerings* (6). The word *terumah* (lifted off) probably signifies a portion taken off and separated for sacred use. It might have been part of an animal sacrifice (Lv. vii. 14, 32) or of bread (Nu. xv. 17ff.). They are again referred to in verse 17. *The firstlings of your herds and of your flocks* (6). See Ex. xiii. 2n.; Dt. xv. 19n.

There ye shall eat (7). Chapters xii, xiv, xv deal mainly with the food of the people partaken in various ways. See verse 15n. The sanctuary, where the offerings and sacrifices were brought and the feasts held, was also a centre for the trial of hard cases (xvii. 8, 10). Thus the tabernacle had already become a unifying centre of the national worship. *Ye shall rejoice* (7). Repeated xii. 12, 18, xiv. 26, xvi. 11, 14, xxvi. 11, xxvii. 7. Cf. Jn. xv. 11; Phil. iii. 1, iv. 4. Joy is an essential element of the Christian religion. *All that ye put your hand unto* (7). The blessing of God is promised on the daily labour of His servants. Repeated ii. 7, xiv. 29, xv. 10, xvi. 15,

xxiii. 20, xxiv. 19, xxviii. 8, 12, xxx. 9. *Whatsoever is right in his own eyes* (8). The months of warfare in Moab had rendered orderly worship difficult or impossible. The same thing happened again in the troubled days of the judges (Jdg. xvii. 6). *When he giveth you rest* (10). See iii. 20n. Moses' prophetic soul anticipates this supreme blessing (xxv. 19), realized under Solomon (1 Ki. viii. 56).

To cause his name to dwell there (11). See verse 5n. The same thought is repeated in xii. 21, xiv. 23, 24, xvi. 2, 6, 11, xxvi. 2. The Lord caused the tabernacle to be erected that He might 'dwell' among His people (Ex. xxv. 8. Cf. Acts vii. 44–49). *The Levite that is within your gates* (12). The 'gates' might be those of either a household or a city. As a tribe the Levites had no territorial portion, but certain cities with their suburbs were about to be assigned to them (Nu. xxxv. 1–8). Meantime the Levite was a sojourner, and was to be the object of their special care (see xii. 18, xiv. 27, xvi. 11n.).

ii. The killing of animals for food and sacrifice (xii. 15–32). *Whatsoever thy soul lusteth after* (15). 'After all the desire of thy soul' (RV). See xviii. 6. Meat was not commonly an element in the daily food of the people, but was eaten when there were sacrifices or occasions for feasting. Some revision of the former rules (see Lv. xvii. 3–7n.) was required by the new conditions. The principle underlying those now issued is the sacredness of all life, as the direct gift of God (see v. 17n.). A distinction is made between 'holy things' (26), which are offered in sacrifice or dedicated to a religious purpose, and that which is killed simply for food (15, 20, 21). *The roebuck . . . the hart* (15). The hart and roebuck (RV 'gazelle') are species of game belonging to mountainous districts and noted for elegance and lightness of foot. At the time these words were spoken, they were evidently plentiful; at a later period, and in the city, they were counted a delicacy (1 Ki. iv. 23). *Ye shall not eat the blood* (16). See Lv. xvii. 11n. Blood, as the vital element and symbol of life, is treated with great reverence in the Old Testament (cf. Gn. ix. 4–6) and most particularly in connection with covenant and sacrifice, a noteworthy foreshadowing of Christ's atonement. (See Lv. xvi; Heb. ix. 12–14; 1 Pet. i. 18, 19.)

When the Lord . . . shall enlarge thy border (20). Verses 20–25 expand the permission in verses 15, 16. Moses' faith anticipates a large territory. (See xix. 8, 9.) *Right in the sight of the Lord* (25). Repeated xiii. 18, xxi. 9; see also vi. 18, xii. 28, and for the contrast see iv. 25, ix. 18, xvii. 2, xxxi. 29. The Lord watches over all His people (2 Ch. xvi. 9). *Upon the altar* (27). See xvi. 21n. *The blood of thy sacrifices* (27). See xii. 6n. *How did these nations serve their gods?* (30). See vi. 14n. Among the heathen a close connection is conceived to exist between a land and the gods which its people served. (See 2 Ki. xvii. 26, 27.) The Israelites would be tempted to think the same, and to fear the gods of Canaan. *Thou shalt not add thereto* (32). See iv. 2n.

iii. Enticement to idolatry (xiii. 1–18). Moses now deals with the negative side of the first commandment. If the laws seem severe, it should be remembered that if the land was to be purged of idolatry by the extermination of the Canaanites, those Israelites who partook of their sins must also share in their punishment. The New Testament is equally severe. See 2 Thes. ii. 8; Rev. xiv. 9–11. The false *prophet* (1) is an all too familiar figure in the Old Testament, and reappears in the New, as a minister of Satan, seducing to evil (Mt. xxiv. 24; Rev. xix. 20). *So shalt thou put the evil away from the midst of thee* (5). These stringent measures were necessary at that time; they belong essentially to the Mosaic period, and it is hardly conceivable that they should have been promulgated later when prophets had so much power and influence. The phrase is repeated in connection with other heinous sins in xvii. 7, 12, xix. 13, 19, xxi. 9, 21, xxii. 22, 24, xxiv. 7.

If thy brother (6). 'Brother' in Hebrew may include any relation. Modern missionary experience illustrates how heathen priests and family entanglements drag many back into apostasy. Temptation may assail us even in the family circle. *Neither shall thine eye pity* (8). Repeated xix. 13, 21, xxv. 12. *All Israel shall hear, and fear* (11). Repeated in xvii. 13, xix. 20, xxi. 21, xxxi. 12, 13. These words express the important principle that punishment should be publicly administered, so as to act as a deterrent; and they help to account for its severity at the commencement of a new dispensation. Cf. Acts v. 11. *Children of Belial* (13). 'Base fellows' (RV). Lit. 'sons of unprofitableness', 'good-for-nothings'. The word recurs in Jdg. xix. 22, xx. 13, where the story of Gibeah supplies a case in point. *Then shalt thou inquire, and make search* (14). A further principle of justice is here enunciated, namely that the fullest investigation should precede punitive action. Much of our British common law can be traced back to the Mosaic legislation. *The cursed thing* (17). 'Devoted' (RV). See ii. 34n., verse 5n. above. The story of Achan in Jos. vii illustrates the application of this law resulting in the Lord's turning from *the fierceness of his anger* (17; cf. Jos. vii. 26). *Right in the eyes of the Lord thy God* (18). See xii. 8n.

iv. Clean and unclean meats (xiv. 1–21). Moses repeats (see Lv. xi) rules of bodily health suitable for *the children of the Lord* (1). In the Christian dispensation they are no longer obligatory, but remain as indicating the need for discretion and self-restraint in regard to food. They anticipate in a notable way the advice which might be given by a modern medical officer. *Ye shall not cut yourselves* (1). As sons of God they must not deface His image (1 Cor. iii. 17) after the manner of the heathen (1 Ki. xviii. 28). *An holy people* (2). See vii. 6n.

These are the beasts (4). See notes on Lv. xi. 2–8. The various categories of animal life are the same as those in Gn. i, probably derived from Egyptian usage. The domestic animals come first, and then the products of the chase. Some of the latter are still to be found in the Sinai Peninsula and the borders of Palestine, but the endeavour to identify them has been only partially successful. *The hare, and the coney* (7). See Lv. xi. 2–8n. These appear to chew the cud, but do not do so in reality; however, as a guide to the people it was the appearance that mattered. In Palestine they feed on poisonous herbs and are often infested with vermin. *Fins and scales* (9). See Lv. xi. 9–12. There is an implied prohibition against the eating of shell-fish which feed upon garbage. The birds mentioned in verses 12–18 feed on carrion and are also prohibited. *Clean fowls* (20). The word for 'fowls' means 'winged things' in general. The meaning therefore is the same as in Lv. xi. 21, 22 where the reference is to edible locusts. *That dieth of itself* (21). Cf. Ex. xxii. 31; Lv. xvii. 15. A butcher exposing such meat today would be liable for prosecution, owing to risk of poisoning or infection. *Thou shalt not seethe* (21). Cf. Ex. xxiii. 19, xxxiv. 26. This unnatural custom was practised by the Canaanites, as a charm to promote fertility.

v. Tithes (xiv. 22–29). See xxvi. 12n.; Lv. xxvii. 30–33n.; Nu. xviii. 21n. When Moses spoke these words the custom of tithing was already ancient. Tithes were first given as a token of gratitude (Gn. xiv. 20) or devotion (Gn. xxviii. 22). The basic principle underlying the offering of tithes is the same as that of the sabbath law (see v. 12n.). All man's wealth, as all his time, is God's gift, and held in trust for Him (Dt. viii. 18; Mt. xxv. 14). To mark the sacredness of the whole, a definite proportion is to be set apart and dedicated at the sanctuary (23, 25). In Nu. xviii. 20–27 the people were bidden, when settled in the land, to set aside a tenth of its produce for the Levites, in lieu of an inheritance, and they in turn were to give a tenth part of their portion to the house of Aaron. The Talmud and Jewish writers generally refer all that is said in Dt. xii, xiv and xxvi, to a 'second' or 'sacred' tithe, and this accorded with Jewish practice. When allowance is made for the changing conditions, first in the wilderness, then during the conquest, and finally when the land was given rest, there is no need to see any contradiction between the various regulations, although their interpretation in detail is obscure. *Thou shalt rejoice* (26). See xii. 7n. The offering of tithes and firstfruits afforded an opportunity for feasting and generous kindness to all 'within thy gates' (27). Moses looks forward to times of peace and prosperity.

vi. The Lord's release (xv. 1–18). In this ordinance we get near to the heart of God, full of compassion and mercy (cf. Ex. xxxiv. 6). Every seventh year there was to be a release or 'letting go' for the debtor (2) and for the bondservant (12), probably the same year in which rest was ordained for the land. See Ex. xxiii. 10, 11 and Lv. xxv. 47–54n. Jewish commentators agree that the remission of the loan was not temporary, but absolute, so that it became a gift. *A foreigner* (3).

See i. 16n. These, mainly Egyptian or other traders, would be well able to pay. The release was to apply both to kinsman and 'neighbour' (2; cf. Lk. x. 27ff.). *Save when there shall be no poor* (4). Note AV marginal reading. *Thou shalt lend* (6). The fulfilment of these words in the latter days should not be overlooked. Despite his warnings, Moses is optimistic about the future of the nation.

Thou shalt not harden thine heart (7). Charity should proceed from the heart, as it does from the heart of God. *Thy poor brother* (7). To this day orthodox Jews are extraordinarily good in helping their own poor. *Sin* (9). The word recurs in xxiii. 21, xxiv. 15; in each case it describes the neglect of a duty. *Sold* (12). The release is to extend to the bondservant and bondmaid. Both sexes are included, but on different terms. A man sells himself into bondage, and so is 'empty' of resources (13); whereas a maid may be sold by another for money, and the price paid might have to be returned. See Ex. xxi. 2–11. *Liberally* (14). There is a generosity in the law of God which cannot be found in any human code. *Redeemed* (15). This evangelical word (see vii. 8n.) is specially appropriate in this place. John Newton, who, before his conversion, had been a slave in Africa, had this verse hanging in his study as a reminder of what he owed. Verses 16, 17 inform us that although slavery was not prohibited in Israel the conditions of service were frequently happy, and these laws contributed to this end. (Cf. Phm. 15, 16.) *Maidservant* (17). This would apply to those who, like the men referred to, had voluntarily undertaken bonded service, not to those sold into concubinage (Ex. xxi. 7).

vii. Firstlings (xv. 19–23). See Ex. xiii. 2n.; Lv. xxvii. 26n. In Exodus the principle is stated that all firstborn creatures should be dedicated to Jehovah, since all life is His gift. The causative form of the verb in verse 20 seems to imply the use of some ceremony of dedication (see xii. 6). *As the roebuck* (22). See xii. 15n.

viii. The three pilgrimage feasts (xvi. 1–17). See Lv. xxiii. In the wilderness the Passover had been eaten by the Israelites in their tents (7), which were pitched around the tabernacle; in the land, together with the two other feasts, it is to be the occasion for a gathering of the tribes, thus emphasizing their unity as the people of God. *The month of Abib* (1) was the time when the 'fresh ears' of corn appeared, as its name signifies. *Of the flock and the herd* (2). The Passover feast was closely associated with that of unleavened bread (3). For the former, a lamb was prescribed (Ex. xii. 21) to be sacrificed in the evening; for the latter, a ram and bullocks from 'the herd' (Nu. xxviii. 19) were offered on the following day. *That thou mayest remember* (3). 'Remember' is one of the keynotes of Deuteronomy. See iv. 9n. The New Testament antitype of the Passover is also a feast of remembrance (Lk. xxii. 19), to be celebrated with a putting away of the leaven of malice and wickedness

(1 Cor. v. 7, 8). *At the going down of the sun* (6). Cf. Mt. xxvi. 20. *A solemn assembly* (8). The Hebrew word for 'solemn' implies restraint, and in this context probably refers to refraining from work, or perhaps to a gathering within a restricted space.

Seven weeks (9). The time of the feast of weeks was to be counted from 'the day after the sabbath' (Ex. xxiii. 16; Lv. xxiii. 15–22n.). So we pass from Easter to Pentecost, the day which witnessed the firstfruits of the gift of the Spirit. See Acts ii. 14–18. The Passover celebrates the deliverance out of Egypt; Pentecost marks the entry into the land of promise. *A tribute* (10). 'Sufficiency' (AV mg.). The Hebrew word *missah* occurs only here. The meaning is thought to be that the free-will offering should be proportionate, as in 1 Cor. xvi. 2. *The Levite . . . and the stranger* (11). At Pentecost 'strangers' and proselytes rejoiced in company with Jews (Acts ii. 10).

After that thou hast gathered in (13). See Lv. xxiii. 33–44n.; 2 Ch. viii. 13. The feast of tabernacles marked the end of the agricultural year after the harvesting of barley (9), and wheat (13), and after the vintage (13). It becomes a symbol of the ingathering of God's elect and the outpouring of His wrath in judgment (Mt. xiii. 39, 41; Rev. xiv. 14–20) at the end of the age. *Seven days* (15). In Nu. xxix. 35 an eighth day is mentioned, a 'great day' of rejoicing (cf. Jn. vii. 37), added on to the feast as the days of unleavened bread followed the Passover. *Thou shalt surely rejoice* (15). 'Thou shalt be altogether joyful' (RV). Cf. Jn. xvi. 22.

ix. Administration of justice (xvi. 18–20). *Judges and officers* (18). See i. 16n., xvii. 9n. Moses had recalled (i. 15, 16) the appointment of judges and officers in the wilderness: he now provides for the civil jurisdiction by enjoining the appointment of these throughout the tribes. In patriarchal times village and tribal 'elders' had settled disputes; these still retained a certain authority (see xix. 12n.). *Thou shalt not respect persons* (19). Cf. i. 17, x. 17; Acts x. 34; Jas. ii. 9. *That which is altogether just . . .* (20). Lit. 'Justice, justice shalt thou follow'.

x. Heathen symbols forbidden (xvi. 21, 22). It is an evidence of authenticity that it is always the Canaanite forms of worship which supply the background of these prohibitions and not those which were introduced from surrounding countries at a later period. It should be noted that the erection of altars other than at the central sanctuary is not prohibited. *Grove* (21). The *asherah* (see RV) was a sacred tree or pole of wood, perhaps shaped in the image of a goddess and supposed to be invested with magical powers. *Image* (22). 'Pillar' (RV). The *mazzebah* or pillar was a stone with sacred significance. It might be a memorial (Gn. xxviii. 18n.), or a witness (Gn. xxxi. 52) to an agreement, or an obelisk (Is. xix. 19); or it might be, as is evidently meant here, an idolatrous stone carved with some symbol or representation.

xi. The perfect offering (xvii. 1). *Blemish.* See Ex. xii. 5n.; Lv. xxii. 17–33n. That which is offered to God must be without blemish. Cf. Heb. ix. 14.

xii. Civil ordinances (xvii. 2–13). *Man or woman* (2). There is an echo of this in 2 Ch. xv. 13. The rooting out of idolatry was the duty of all to whom the matter was reported. *At the mouth of two witnesses* (6). As the penalty was severe the proof must be beyond doubt. Cf. Mt. xviii. 16; Jn. viii. 17; 2 Cor. xiii. 1; Heb. x. 28. *Thou shalt put the evil away* (7). See xiii. 5n. The LXX translates 'the evil man' (cf. Mt. vi. 13, RV). Hebrew thought tends to the concrete, and identifies the sin with the sinner. *Between blood and blood* (8). That is, charges of murder or wounding. *The judge that shall be* (9). See xvi. 18n. In the first instance when judges were appointed, Moses himself acted as the supreme tribunal (Ex. xviii. 26), and afterwards gave Joshua a charge, together with Eleazar, regarding judgment (Nu. xxvii. 18–23). This system is now carried on into the future. (See 2 Ch. xix. 8–10.) *In those days* (9). Cf. xix. 17, xxvi. 3. *The sentence of judgment* (9). Moses anticipates his action (xxxi. 9–13) of handing the written law into the charge of the priests, who are to teach the law, whilst 'the judge' is to see it executed. In the theocratic system the priest and judge are to be respected, as acting on God's behalf. Cf. Rom. xiii. 1.

xiii. The law of the kingdom (xvii. 14–20). Instead of the supreme judge (9), the people may seek to emulate their neighbours and desire a king. Moses limits their choice and ensures the king's instruction in the law of God. *When thou art come unto the land* (14). See xii. 1n. There is a pathos in the constantly repeated reference by Moses to 'the land' which he might see but not enter. *A king* (14). The LXX has *archon*, 'ruler'. *One from among thy brethren* (15). Cf. Gn. xlix. 10. This limitation, necessary when the nation was weak, and might easily have looked to a foreign prince as leader, could not have originated after the establishment of David's line. Saul fulfilled the conditions here imposed, and David also, but most signally David's greater Son. (See Ps. lxxxix. 19; Acts xiii. 22, 23; Heb. ii. 11.) *He shall not multiply horses . . . nor . . . return to Egypt* (16). This warning was necessary at the time when the lure of Egypt was still strong. The military might, wealth and sensuality of the Egyptian rulers had proved powerless to save them from God's judgments; and at a later stage these things resulted in declension and humiliation for Israel (Is. ii. 7–11).

A copy of this law in a book (18). See Ex. xvii. 14n. 'This law' may mean part or the whole of Deuteronomy or possibly the Pentateuch. The 'law of the kingdom' in 1 Sa. x. 25 was presumably additional; but the 'book' of 2 Ch. xvii. 9 and the 'testimony' of 2 Ch. xxiii. 11 seem to be the same as this. The Hebrew word *sepher* (book), from a root meaning to inscribe, denotes a record of any kind. That of Gn. v. 1

may have been on a tablet of clay; in Nu. v. 23, some washable material, such as skin, is implied. The word recurs xxiv. 1, 3 (AV 'bill'), xxviii. 58, 61, xxix. 20, 21, 27, xxx. 10, xxxi. 24, 26. The word for 'copy', meaning a duplicate, is rendered in the LXX by *deuteronomion*. It has been conjectured that Jesus as a boy read the law from a copy which had come down to Joseph, who was of the 'house and lineage of David'. *His children, in the midst of Israel* (20). A hereditary monarchy is contemplated, but no hint of any division in the kingdom.

xiv. Revenues of priests and Levites (xviii. 1–8). *The priests the Levites, and all the tribe of Levi* (1). The word for 'and' is absent from the Hebrew, but the AV (and RV mg.) is here to be preferred to the RV, for the 'whole tribe' would include women and children. It is a mode of expression, where a special class is first named and then a larger group. The distinction is important because of the contention by some critics that Deuteronomy treats *all* Levites as priests, in contradiction to the book of Leviticus. This, however, is not the case (see General Article, *The Historical Literature*, p. 32). Note also the distinction in chapter xxxi between the priests who teach the law (9, 10) and the Levites who have the custody of the actual book (25, 26). See also x. 6, xxvi. 3 and xxxiii. 8. *To stand to minister* (5). See x. 8n. Whilst this is the special function of the priest, yet all the people 'stand before the Lord' (xxix. 10), and ministry is not confined to any class. *His patrimony* (8). Although Levi had no tribal inheritance, this did not prevent individuals from possessing property. Cf. Je. xxxii. 6–15.

xv. Witchcraft (xviii. 9–14). The practices described, still common in heathen lands, are a mixture of fraud and guesswork, of cruelty and dealing with evil spirits; in all points the opposite of the divine law. God has His agents, and so has Satan. Isaiah (viii. 19) truly interprets the spirit of this passage. *Through the fire* (10). The cruel ordeal by fire (cf. xii. 31), which is here prohibited, was allowed in Hammurabi's code. *Thou shalt be perfect* (13). The command to be perfect is given (Gn. xvii. 1; Mt. v. 48) because God can ask for nothing less. Absolute perfection is unattainable by sinful man, but it is possible to have a perfect heart (1 Ki. xi. 4; Col. ii. 10).

xvi. The coming Prophet (xviii. 15–22). Moses, in words of plainly messianic import, now announces a successor in his office as prophet. Peter (Acts iii. 22) and Stephen (Acts vii. 37) afterwards recognized the fulfilment of his words. Our Lord was doubtless acquainted with them (Jn. v. 46), and they are expounded in Heb. iii. 2–6. These New Testament references demonstrate the importance of this prediction. *A Prophet* (15). Its immediate meaning is not far to seek. In contrast with heathen necromancy and divination, Moses declares the rôle of the true prophet, one like himself, a brother and a mediator, a true messenger and revealer of God's word. When Dt. xxxiv. 10 was written, the promise

213

still remained unfulfilled. The long line of prophets from Samuel to Malachi possessed these characteristics in some degree, but only in Christ was the prediction truly fulfilled.

Like unto me (15). Moses was a type of Christ, both in his life and in his office. Like Jesus, his life was spared in infancy, he renounced a royal court to share the condition of his brethren, and he became a captain of salvation to Israel. He was faithful (Heb. iii. 2) and meek (Nu. xii. 3; Mt. xi. 29), full of compassion and love (Nu. xxvii. 17; Mt. ix. 36), a mighty intercessor on behalf of his people (Dt. ix. 18; Heb. vii. 25), speaking with God face to face, and reflecting the divine glory (2 Cor. iii. 7). Like our Lord, he was a prophet mighty in deed and word (cf. Lk. xxiv. 19), a revealer of God's will and purpose (Dt. vi. 1; Rev. i. 1), a mediator of the covenant (Dt. xxix. 1; Heb. viii. 6, 7), and a leader and commander of the people (cf. Is. lv. 3, 4).

How shall we know? (21). There are various tests to distinguish true prophets from false. They must be prophets of the Lord (xiii. 1–3), their word must come to pass (1 Ki. xxii. 28; Je. xxviii. 9), and they will honour the written law (Is. viii. 20). False prophets will continue to the end of the age (Mt. xxiv. 11; 1 Jn. iv. 1–3; Rev. xix. 20).

xvii. Cities of refuge (xix. 1–13). See iv. 41n. Having already separated three cities in Transjordan, Moses now provides for three more on the western side, as he had been commanded (Nu. xxxv. 14), and gives instructions concerning them. The rules concerning homicide, like some other laws in Deuteronomy, deal with customs still more ancient, confirming some and amending others. When compared with the code of Hammurabi and ancient Semitic customs, they are seen to have common elements, but the Mosaic law places a higher value on human life (v. 17n.), and sets a higher standard of love to God and to one's neighbour. *Thou shalt prepare thee a way* (3). The Talmud says that the way was prepared by the erection of signposts bearing the words 'Refuge, Refuge'. *The avenger of the blood* (6). The *goel*, or 'avenger of blood', is the same as the 'kinsman' who had the right to 'redeem' (Ru. iv; Je. xxxii), the 'redeemer' of Jb. xix. 25. Such retributive justice is far removed from murder and is, in fact, calculated to prevent it. It is therefore no violation of the sixth commandment (v. 17n.).

Then shalt thou add three cities more (9). The ancient promise of Gn. xv. 18 is not forgotten, but the actual conquest fell short of the promise, and there is no record of these additional cities ever having been required. We have here another undesigned evidence of authenticity: no late writer would have invented this provision. *Blood be upon thee* (10). See Gn. iv. 11n.; Dt. xxi. 6–8. Jehovah's land is 'holy', and the stain of blood must therefore be put away from it. *The elders of his city* (12). See xvi. 18n. The 'elders' were those who, by common consent, were granted a superior position because of their descent, age or ability. They formed a local authority for the transaction of judicial or other business. See xxi. 20, xxvii. 1, xxix. 10, xxxi. 28.

xviii. The landmark (xix. 14). The landmarks might be those set by the Israelites themselves or those they found. (See v. 21n., xxvii. 17.) In either case their removal would be fraudulent.

xix. The law of witness (xix. 15–21). See v. 20n., xvii. 6n. The law is careful for the sifting of evidence and for even-handed justice. In Jn. v. 32–46 the Lord cites three witnesses to His own claims, and two witnesses bear testimony to Him in Rev. xi. Cf. 2 Cor. xiii. 1. *The priests* (17). It was the priests, whose duty was to search out the truth, who suborned false witnesses against Christ (Mt. xxvi. 59–68). *Eye for eye* (21). The *lex talionis*, or law of a punishment equal to the offence, is very ancient, being found in Hammurabi's code. The rule is employed here to define the punishment of a false witness. The Lord's words in Mt. v. 38–42 apply to personal conduct.

xx. Laws of warfare (xx. 1–20). Every part of the life of Israel was to be hallowed by the consciousness of God's presence. The instructions given here are timely as they enter upon their further campaign, and remind them that 'the battle is the Lord's' (1 Sa. xvii. 47). *Be not afraid* (1). God's children constantly need this word of encouragement (i. 29). The deliverance from Egypt, ever in Moses' mind (iv. 32n.), is used here as a motive for courage; elsewhere for wholehearted devotion (iv. 20), for sabbath remembrance (v. 15), for reverential fear (vi. 12), humility (viii. 14), penitence (ix. 7), kindness to strangers (x. 19), obedience (xi. 3), constancy (xiii. 5), the emancipation of servants (xv. 15), mercy to the poor (xxiv. 18, 22), and thanksgiving (xxvi. 5, 8). *The priest* (2). The priests had their share in the capture of Jericho.

Gideon acted on the instructions given in verses 5–8 (Jdg. vii), and our Lord may also have thought of them (Lk. ix. 57–62). The exemptions were compassionate, but that which justified release from warfare was no excuse for declining an invitation to a feast (Lk. xiv. 18–20). *Hath not yet eaten of it* (6). 'Hath not used the fruit thereof' (RV). Lit. 'profaned, or put to common use' (Lv. xix. 23–25). *Captains of the armies* (9). The army was well ordered with priest, officers and captains. See i. 15n.

Proclaim peace (10). In this and the following verses we see two contrary principles at work: Jehovah's proclamation of peace and goodwill on the one hand, and the inevitable judgment of wickedness on the other. If the people will turn to the Lord they are to be spared, and ultimately received among His people; but where sin is ineradicable they are to be destroyed. Cf. Mt. x. 12, 13. *Thou shalt utterly destroy them* (17). See ii. 34n. and cf. Jos. xi. 12–15. The command in this extreme form is found only here. Cf. Rev. xxi. 27. *Trees for meat* (20). Fruit-bearing trees were to be spared because of the life-principle within them, and for future use. Elisha's command to the contrary (2 Ki. iii. 19) seems to imply a knowledge of this rule, but that the occasion demanded severer measures. Cf. Mk. xi. 13.

xxi. Undetected homicide (xxi. 1–9). The sixth commandment taught that human life is sacred, and now Moses rules that murder must be atoned for. See v. 17n. *The elders . . . shall take an heifer* (3). Rashi comments: 'A yearling heifer which has borne no fruit, shall come and be beheaded in a place which yieldeth no fruit, to atone for the murder of the man whom they did not suffer to bear fruit.' The ideas of atonement and cleansing are combined, and both point to Calvary (Heb. ix. 13). *Every controversy* (5). See xvii. 9n. *Wash their hands* (6). Cf. Ps. xxvi. 6; Mt. xxvii. 24. The RV should be read in verse 8. See how the people are taught to pray.

xxii. Domestic ordinances (xxi. 10–21). *When thou goest forth to war* (10). The law for marriage with a captive woman displayed consideration and respect of human personality. *She shall shave her head* (12). A common symbol of mourning in Eastern countries. *She shall be thy wife* (13). The prohibition in vii. 3 seems to be limited to the nations there enumerated, which were 'devoted' (xx. 17n.).

Hated (15). See Gn. xxix. 31n. This word is used comparatively, not absolutely. *The right of the firstborn* (17) was already ancient (Gn. xxvii), and is here protected from favouritism. *A double portion* (17). That is, twice as much as his brothers received. Cf. Gn. xlviii. 22; 2 Ki. ii. 9. *A stubborn and rebellious son* (18). Seeing that parents stand towards their children as God's representatives (see v. 16n.), obstinate rebellion is regarded as akin to blasphemy, and is condemned to the same punishment. It is assumed that the parents have tried in vain to reform him. *The elders of his city* (19). The father is not despotic; both parents must bring the charge before the appointed judges (see xvi. 18n.). The *gate* (19) is the traditional place of judgment.

xxiii. The curse of the tree (xxi. 22, 23). Hanging was not the means of execution, but was imposed as an additional disgrace after execution. It carried with it a recognition of the curse of God resting upon the sin, and upon the land in consequence (Gn. iv. 11; Jos. viii. 29). Our Saviour Christ in His humiliation could descend no lower than this (Gal. iii. 13). Vainly the rulers of the Jews thought to remove the curse by keeping the letter of this law (Jn. xix. 31).

xxiv. Various rules of charity and purity (xxii. 1–30). The miscellaneous character of the precepts in verses 1–12 has puzzled those critics who regard these chapters as a legal code, but it is natural enough in a spoken discourse. Verses 1–4 breathe the spirit of the Sermon on the Mount. *Thou shalt not see . . . and hide thyself* (4). Cf. the story of the good Samaritan in Lk. x.

A bird's nest (6). In Palestine bird life is important in keeping down the numerous insect pests: this rule therefore was wise as well as humane (cf. Mt. x. 29). Like the fifth commandment, it is coupled with a promise (see iv. 26n.,

iv. 40n.). *A battlement* (8). The flat roof of an Eastern house is where the host entertains his guests in the evening; therefore a parapet is a necessary precaution. *Divers seeds* (9). 'Two kinds of seed' (RV). These rules have a practical value with a spiritual background. See Lv. xix. 19n. Cf. Mt. ix. 17; 2 Cor. vi. 14. Unnatural combinations lead to confusion and discord; so does compromise with the world. *A garment of divers sorts* (11). 'A mingled stuff' (RV). The Hebrew word is of foreign, probably Egyptian, origin. Garments of this kind would not wash readily. The purpose of *fringes* (12) was to be a distinctive sign to themselves and others that they were the Lord's people. (Cf. Nu. xv. 37–41.) It was the 'fringe' of Christ's garment which the woman touched and was healed (Lk. viii. 44). *Occasions of speech* (14). Rather, 'wanton charges'. Much importance is still attached to these matters among Arabs and Moors, and slanderous charges are the cause of serious feuds.

The latter part of this chapter carries out the principle of the seventh commandment, moral purity and conjugal fidelity, in a manner suited to that age, when stern measures were necessary to keep unruly passions under control. The Jews were, and still are, notably more moral than their heathen neighbours. *She hath wrought folly* (21). The Hebrew word connotes serious moral obliquity. (Cf. Gn. xxxiv. 7.) *Betrothed* (23). In the East betrothal is considered equally binding with marriage, so that a betrothed maiden was called a 'wife' (Mt. i. 20). For verse 30 see notes on Lv. xviii.

xxv. Membership in the congregation (xxiii. 1–8). See ix. 10n. The circle of ideas which gathers round the Church of Christ in the Epistles is here foreshadowed; its holiness and its catholicity, its exclusiveness and inclusiveness, its nature as the representative on earth and the peculiar possession of Jehovah. *He that is wounded* (1). The exclusion of emasculated persons was a protest against heathen practice and helped to prevent its introduction into Israel. Cf. Lv. xxi. 16–23n. *An Ammonite or Moabite* (3). See Ne. xiii. 1–3. Although Egypt and Edom fought against the men of Israel, Moab and Ammon sought the ruin of their souls (Nu. xxii). The outlook on these four nations is that of the Mosaic age, and quite different from that under the later monarchy.

They hired against thee Balaam (4). This is a convenient place to summarize the reminiscences of Moses belonging to the recent past (see iv. 10n.). These include the unfriendly action of Edom and Ammon (ii. 1–14), the victories over Sihon and Og (ii. 30—iii. 11, xxix. 7, 8, xxxi. 4), the settlement of the two and a half tribes (iii. 12–22), the many references to his own sin at Meribah-Kadesh (i. 37, iv. 21, xxxi. 2, xxxii. 51, xxxiv. 4), the people's sin at Beth-peor (iv. 3), the plague of fiery serpents (viii. 15), and Balaam's curse turned into a blessing (xxiii. 3–6).

xxvi. Various social rules (xxiii. 9–25). *Without the camp* (12). Cleanliness in the camp is ordered

215

both for health and personal purity. The presence of Jehovah in their midst is a constant plea for holiness. *The servant which is escaped* (15). We see here a prophecy of the liberation of the slave once he sets foot on the holy land of freedom. (Cf. Phm. 16.) *The daughters of Israel . . . the sons of Israel* (17). The degrading temple prostitution common at heathen shrines is forbidden to the children of Israel. *Thou shalt not lend upon usury* (19). Loans to foreigners (i. 16n.) were usually of a commercial character, and therefore a charge of interest was unobjectionable; but it was forbidden, as contrary to the law of love, when the loan was from a rich man to his poor neighbour. Cf. Ex. xxii. 25; Lv. xxv. 36. *When thou shalt vow a vow* (21). See Nu. xxx. 3; Dt. xii. 6, 26. *The standing corn* (25). The vineyards and cornfields in Palestine were open to the passer-by, and the yields were so plentiful that he might take what he would. When the Pharisees complained (Mk. ii. 23, 24) of the disciples plucking the ears of corn, it was not in reference to this ordinance, which expressly allowed this action, but because they held that to rub the ears was a species of threshing, and therefore a violation of the sabbath rest.

xxvii. The bill of divorcement (xxiv. 1–4). Cf. Mt. v. 31, xix. 7. This rule does not create, but places a double limit upon, the ancient right of a husband to divorce his wife; for some substantial grievance must be urged, and a formal document must be issued. The Hebrew word for 'bill' (1) is *sepher* (see xvii. 18n.). Our Lord's teaching concerning this law gives it the true interpretation and puts it in right relationship to the primitive law.

xxviii. Humane regulations (xxiv. 5–22). *A new wife* (5). See xx. 5–8n. *Pledge* (6, 10–13). These rules are illustrations of that 'gentleness' which is the fruit of the Spirit, for they inculcate respect for the feelings as well as for the needs of the borrower. Willingness to pledge a millstone or a garment would betoken poverty under primitive conditions. *Stealing* (7). In Semitic custom manstealing was the occasion for a blood feud; Hammurabi's law punished it by death.

Leprosy (8). The laws concerning this dread disease had already been given (Lv. xiii, xiv). *Remember . . . Miriam* (9). Every wilderness experience was to be regarded as a lesson illustrating God's will and purpose for His people. Cf. xxv. 17. Who but Moses could have written this?

Thy strangers (14). See i. 16n., x. 18, 19n. God's care for the stranger, the fatherless and the widow is beautifully revealed in these exhortations, which were surely known and obeyed by Boaz (Ru. ii. 15). James, in his Epistle (v. 4), refers to the labourer's *hire* (15). The most advanced legislation of modern times cannot exceed the care shown for the poor in these chapters. *Shall not be put to death* (16). This limits the power of the judge. (Cf. 2 Ki. xiv. 6.) God visits the consequences of the fathers' sins upon their children, but then His judgments never err.

xxix. Rules of justice, mercy and purity (xxv. 1–19). *Justify the righteous* (1). Lit. 'declare righteous the righteous'. (Cf. vi. 25n.) This is the function of a judge (see xvi. 18–20). Righteousness is an essential attribute of God (xxxii. 4) and of His law. Human justice must condemn the wicked, but God has found a way to justify the ungodly (Rom. iii. 25). *Forty stripes* (3). Justice is to be tempered with mercy and punishment distinguished from humiliation. The Jews kept the letter (2 Cor. xi. 24) but not the spirit of this law. *Thou shalt not muzzle the ox* (4). St. Paul cites this precept in 1 Cor. ix. 9, which might be paraphrased thus: 'Does God care for oxen? He cares more for you.' The Hebrew expression exaggerates a difference into a seeming contradiction (cf. xxi. 15n.).

Her husband's brother (5). This custom, known as levirate marriage, goes back to patriarchal times (Gn. xxxviii. 8). Our Lord's answer to the Sadducees (Mk. xii. 24–27) shows that it is not inconsistent with the doctrine of the resurrection of the dead. *Loose his shoe* (9). The loosing of the shoe symbolizes the rejection of responsibility, or its transfer to another (see Ru. iv. 7, 8). *Divers weights* (13). Lit. 'a stone and a stone'; in the days when stones were used for weights, fraud would be easy. The principles of justice are carried into commercial relations. (Cf. Lk. vi. 38.) *A perfect and just weight* (15). See vi. 25n. *Remember . . . Amalek* (17). See Ex. xvii. 8–14. Justice is two-sided, and includes the punishment of the wicked. After the laws of humanity comes again the injunction to obliterate the most savage and inhuman of the Canaanite tribes (see ii. 34n., xiii. 1n., 1 Sa. xv. 3).

xxx. Firstfruits and tithes (xxvi. 1–15). See xiv. 22, 26n. The forms for the presentation of firstfruits and tithes are a beautiful model of praise and prayer. *Go unto the place* (2). See xii. 5n. Only those who are in communion with the Giver can rightly present the gift. *The priest* (3). The High Priest or his deputy; he is clearly different from 'the Levite' of verse 11. (See xviii. 1n.) The directions for the priest are found in Lv. xxiii; these are for the worshipper. *I profess* (3). The first act is to be a profession that God has fulfilled His ancient promise (Gn. xxviii. 13). The firstfruits contain the promise of the harvest, which God will provide in due time. *A Syrian* (5). 'Aramaean' (RV mg.). Jacob's mother and kindred came from Syria or 'Aram' (Gn. xxiv. 10, xxv. 20). The formula of verses 5–10 is Mosaic in style, with references to the hard bondage (6), the cry for deliverance (7), and the mighty arm that redeemed them (8).

An end of tithing (12). See xiv. 22n., Lv. xxvii. 30–33n. The festal character and generous mode of distribution indicate that the 'second tithe' is intended here. *I have brought away* (13). 'I have put away' (RV). Lit. 'burned' (from the same root as *taberah*, ix. 22). The meaning is that all that is due to Jehovah has been duly paid, and nothing left in the house. (Cf. Mal. iii. 10.)

d. Concluding exhortation (xxvi. 16–19)

A closing exhortation follows the commandments which gave to Israel a wonderful constitution, suited for a liberated people. *This day* (16). This note of time bounds the law at its commencement and its close (xi. 26, 32, xxvi. 16, 17). 'This day' God speaks to us through His Word (2 Cor. vi. 2). *Avouched* (17). A rare word, possibly a technical term relating to a covenant. There may have been some unrecorded token of assent by the people. *His peculiar people* (18). See vii. 6n.; 1 Pet. ii. 9. *As he hath promised* (18). Grace turns the law into promise. *To make thee* (19). Cf. Phil. ii. 13.

V. INSCRIPTION OF THE LAW; BLESSINGS AND CURSINGS. xxvii. 1—xxviii. 68

a. Inscription of the law (xxvii. 1–8)

The narrative form is resumed, the discourse of chapters v—xxvi being completed. Moses now gives a threefold direction about 'this law' just delivered, that it may be more deeply impressed upon the people. *Moses with the elders* (1). See xix. 12n. After Moses' death the elders would be responsible for carrying out these injunctions (Jos. viii. 33). *The day* (2). The word is used (cf. Gn. ii. 17) of a future time and not of a particular day. *Great stones* (2). Many such *stelae* have been found in Egypt and the East, some inscribed on the stone itself, and some on a surface of cement or lime. (Cf. Am. ii. 1.) *Thou shalt write* (3). Ancient inscriptions vary greatly in length; one upon the rocks at Behistun is about three· times as long as the book of Deuteronomy. *All the words of this law* (3). The wording of this command suggests that a written document existed, or was about to be prepared, from which a copy could be made on these stones. 'This law' might mean, as it seems to do in iv. 44 (see note), the contents of chapters v—xxvi, but this cannot be taken for granted. The inscription might have contained more than this, or might have been only a summary. *Mount Ebal* (4). The vale, flanked by the twin slopes of Ebal and Gerizim, forms a natural amphitheatre, admirably suited for this occasion. The mountains were visible from the place where these words were spoken (see xi. 29n.). *An altar of stones* (5). The altar is to be built of natural stones, untouched by any human implement. (Cf. Ex. xx. 25.) *Burnt offerings* (6) symbolize complete consecration and *peace offerings* (7) communion with God. *Thou shalt write* (8). See verse 3. *Very plainly* (8). Cf. Hab. ii. 2 where the same word is used (see i. 5n.). This may mean large and clear lettering, or it may refer (cf. Is. viii. 1) to the use of the alphabetic script of that period, of which many specimens have been recently discovered.

b. Obedience commanded (xxvii. 9, 10)

Moses and the priests (9). Not now the 'elders' (1) but the priests, who were the responsible teachers

of the law. *This day* (9). See verse 2n. *Thou art become the people of the Lord thy God* (9). The people of God always belong to Him in virtue of His election and calling; but they 'become' so in fact when they receive His Word and obey His law (Jn. i. 12).

c. Solemn curses (xxvii. 11–26)

Moses charged the people (11). Nothing could be more solemn than the cursings of xxvii. 11–26 and the promises and warnings of chapter xxviii. *These shall stand* (12). Jewish commentators say that the priests and Levites first addressed the tribes on Mount Gerizim with the words: 'Blessed is the man . . . that maketh *not* . . .', and then those on Mount Ebal with the same words, but omitting the negative, and commencing: 'Cursed is the man . . .', and that all in turn responded with 'Amen'. The tribes chosen for blessing (12) were all descended from Leah or Rachel. *Cursed be the man* (15). The curses are twelve in number, corresponding to the twelve tribes. The second, fifth and sixth commandments are quoted; the remainder represent grave breaches of honesty or purity. *Secretly* (24). 'In secret' (RV). Cf. verse 15. The sins are all such as might be perpetrated in secret. The appeal is therefore addressed to the individual conscience. *All the people* are called upon to condemn such practices openly. *All the words of this law* (26). Here the people bind themselves, in Eastern fashion, under a curse (cf. Acts xxiii. 12) to keep the whole law, an action repeated under Nehemiah (Ne. x. 29) and cited by Paul (Gal. iii. 10). This curse Christ took upon Himself (Gal. iii. 13), so setting His people free.

d. Sanctions of the law (xxviii. 1–68)

Here is a great challenge to the human will. Moses pronounces beatitudes upon those who obey, and woes to the disobedient. (Cf. Lk. vi. 20–26, xi. 42ff.) Lv. xxvi also contains blessings and warnings, but there declension is expected, and after each falling away new punishments are added, and at the end a word of promise (Lv. xxvi. 44, 45; see notes). If the reader wonders at the extent and severity of the threatened curses, let him remember that some of our Lord's expressions were no less severe. On the lips of Moses they were warnings given in mercy, which, if they had been taken to heart, would have saved Israel from endless misery. Jewish history up to the present day is a bitter commentary upon them.

Blessed shalt thou be (3). The blessings are pronounced upon the nation, the family and the individual, and they find their counterpart in the curses of verses 15–20. *The Lord shall establish thee* (9). The word 'establish' is the same as was used by Christ in the raising of Jairus' daughter (*cumi*, Mk. v. 41), and is translated 'raise up' in Dt. xviii. 15, 18; it denotes the setting up of something new and abiding. *Called by the name of the Lord* (10). See v. 11n., xii. 5n.; cf. Nu. vi. 27. To be called by His name means that they are His people and under His protection (Pr. xviii. 10). The name of Jehovah was placed upon the sanctuary (xii. 5), and in that name they were to swear (vi. 13), to bless (x. 8) or to prophesy (xviii. 19). See also verse 58n.

Ezekiel spoke of God's four sore judgments, pestilence, the sword, famine and noisome beasts (xiv. 21), and of these the three first are elaborated here (verses 21ff.). Intended as a warning, they cannot be pressed too literally, although many of the details have been fulfilled to the letter. See also notes on Lv. xxvi. 14–33. *The botch of Egypt* (27). 'The boil of Egypt' (RV). See Ex. ix. 9–11. The Egyptian colouring of this verse should not be overlooked (see also verses 35, 60 and 68). *Oppressed and crushed* (33). See Ho. v. 11, RV. *The sole of thy foot* (35). Cf. Ex. ix. 11. *Thou shalt not enjoy them* (41). 'They shall not be thine' (RV). See Ho. ix. 12. *As the eagle* (49). See Ho. viii. 1. *A nation of fierce countenance* (50). Lit. 'strong of face', i.e. pitiless (cf. Dn. viii. 23). From such enemies no human arm can save them. *He shall besiege thee* (52). The gruesome scenes here foretold (verses 52–57) were accomplished in the sieges of Samaria (2 Ki. vi. 28) and Jerusalem (La. ii. 20, 22).

This glorious and fearful name (58). The names of God in Deuteronomy will repay study. He is the 'living God' (v. 26); 'the Lord God of thy fathers' (vi. 3); the 'God of gods, and Lord of lords' (x. 17; Rev. xix. 16); 'the Rock . . . a God of truth' (xxxii. 4); 'the Most High' (xxxii. 8); 'the eternal God' (xxxiii. 27). But most commonly He is called 'the Lord thy God'. *Written in the book of this law* (61). See xxix. 21n., xxxi. 24n.; and Rev. xxii. 18. 'The seven last plagues' (Rev. xv, xvi) contain many features in common with this chapter. *The Lord shall scatter thee* (64). These prophetic words were fulfilled at the fall of Samaria and Jerusalem; again when Titus transported many Jews to the Egyptian mines, and even more terribly in the present era. *The Lord shall bring thee into Egypt again* (68). At the beginning of the Christian era, the Jews formed a substantial portion of the population of the Nile Delta. See Ho. viii. 13.

VI. MOSES' THIRD DISCOURSE.
xxix. 1—xxx. 20

a. Renewal of the covenant (xxix. 1–29)

A new discourse opens with this chapter and continues through the next. Moses calls on the people to renew the covenant made at Horeb, and predicts the declension and punishment of the whole nation. The blessing and the curse must both be experienced, but in the end divine grace will open a way for repentance and the remission of sins. *These are the words of the covenant* (1). See i. 1n., xxxi. 9n. The phrase denotes the commencement of a new section. *The land of Moab* (1). Cf. i. 5. It was so called because it had formerly belonged to Moab, although taken by the Amorite king. *Beside the*

covenant (1). See iv. 13n. The original covenant was made in Horeb but was quickly broken. Now at the end of his life, in the true spirit of the gospel, Moses calls on them to make a new beginning. The curses of the law are not the last word, for the land of promise lies ahead. In a later age, Jeremiah develops the thought of the 'new covenant' (Je. xxxi. 31–33; cf. Lk. xxii. 20). *Yet the Lord hath not given you* (4). In attributing their dullness of heart to Jehovah, Moses only adopts the mode of thought, which runs through the Old Testament, of attributing all things to Jehovah as their ultimate source. See Ex. iv. 21n. Paul reproduces these words (Rom. xi. 8; cf. Mt. xiii. 14). *I have led you* (5). Cf. viii. 2–4. These words are repeated by Amos (ii. 10). The desert discipline was the pathway to the knowledge of the Lord (6), which is the supreme good. *All of you* (10). The covenant of grace is all-embracing, from heads and elders (xix. 12n.) to little children and the menial slaves. Cf. Acts ii. 21. *Enter into covenant* (12). See Gn. xvii. 7, 8. *Also with him that is not here . . . this day* (15). That is, their posterity. *Their abominations, and their idols* (17). See vii. 25n. Lit. 'detestable things (see Je. xvi. 18) and idol-blocks'. Moses speaks of the idols with contempt and derision. In Heb. xii. 15 the writer may refer to verse 18, quoting from the Alexandrine version of the LXX. *I shall have peace* (19). The idolater knows the curse, but thinks he can sin with impunity. *To add drunkenness to thirst* (19). 'To destroy the moist with the dry' (RV). This appears to be a proverbial expression, meaning that none shall escape. It should then be read with what follows as Moses' comment upon their folly. *Written in this book of the law* (21). See xxviii. 61n. The curses are not only a warning, but recorded as a testimony to the sure judgment of God upon those who despise His Word. (Cf. Heb. x. 29.)

Admah, and Zeboim (23). The destruction of the cities of the plain became a standing illustration of divine judgment. This verse is alluded to by Hosea (xi. 8), whose prophecy shows acquaintance with Deuteronomy. *Gods whom they knew not* (26). See vi. 14n., xi. 28n. Moses sometimes treats the heathen gods as quasi-realities, and at other times with scorn as vanities. According to heathen ideas each race had its gods, which they looked upon as almost a tribal possession. Hence even the heathen would judge it wrong for Israel to forsake Jehovah to worship gods of another nation, 'whom they knew not'. *The secret things belong unto the Lord* (29). The chapter closes with a call to lay to heart the things plainly revealed, the covenant and its blessings, and to leave the rest to God; a wise and practical counsel.

b. The way open to repentance (xxx. 1–14)

Moses, knowing the sinfulness of human nature and its inevitable consequence, issues a call to repentance which is closely bound up with the covenant, for the title 'the Lord thy God' is used no less than twelve times in verses 1–10. He emphasizes the nearness of God's word, and the simplicity of faith. *Return* (2). See 'return' in verse 3. Verses 2, 3 are quoted by Nehemiah (i. 9). The return from Babylon began under Zerubbabel, and Zechariah prophesied a further fulfilment (ii. 6, 7). *With all thine heart* (2). A threefold appeal (2, 6, 10). *Gather thee from all the nations* (3). See iv. 27n. Christ, in announcing His second advent, united this with other prophecies and promises of the old covenant (Mk. xiii. 26, 27). *The Lord thy God will circumcise thy heart* (6). Jehovah will do for His repentant people what before they were bidden to do themselves (x. 16). The evangelical note grows clearer as he proceeds. (Cf. Rom. ii. 24–29.) *Written in this book of the law* (10). These are not the 'secret things' (xxix. 29), but those that are 'revealed'. Moses calls them the 'voice of the Lord' (8), as clear a claim to divine inspiration as could be made. We need not therefore hesitate to speak of this book as the Word of God. (Cf. Mk. vii. 13.)

This day (11). See iv. 40n., xxvi. 16n. This note of immediacy occurs more than sixty times in Deuteronomy. Cf. Heb. iii, iv. *It is not hidden from thee* (11). 'It is not too hard for thee' (RV). Verses 11–14 should be carefully compared with Rom. x. 5–8, where Paul expounds them of Christ, the incarnate Word. Moses states that the word did not remain in heaven where men could not reach (12), but that God had come down (cf. Ex. iii. 8) to their level in simple speech. *Beyond the sea* (13). As the word was not above them, so it was not beyond their horizon over the western sea. Paul slightly varies the metaphor to suit his purpose; but the meaning of inaccessibility is the same. *But the word is very nigh unto thee . . . in thy heart* (14). The appeal to the 'heart' (i.e. man's inmost nature) is a marked characteristic of Deuteronomy (the word occurs forty-four times). It is the heart that matters (Mt. xv. 18), and when that is right with God, obedience follows. See iv. 29n.

c. **The choice between life and death (xxx. 15–20)**

Over Jordan (18). As the end approaches, Moses' references to the crossing of the river grow more frequent. (Cf. xxxi. 2, 13, xxxii. 47.) *I call heaven and earth* (19). Cf. iv. 26 and Is. i. 2. *Therefore choose life* (19). The door is still open. *To Abraham, to Isaac, and to Jacob* (20). See i. 8n.

VII. **THE WRITING OF THE LAW AND THE SONG. xxxi. 1–30**

a. **The law written (xxxi. 1–13)**

Moses now resigns his leadership of the people into the hands of Joshua (verse 3) and his teaching office to the priests (verse 9), and hands the precious book containing the written law to the Levites for safe keeping. *Joshua* (3). See i. 38n., iii. 21n. Having been long since made leader of the army (Ex. xvii), and recently charged by the laying on of Moses' hands (Nu. xxvii. 18–23), Joshua is now to receive his commission directly from Jehovah (verse 14). *Be strong and of a good*

courage (6). Moses thus exhorts first the people and then Joshua (7). See Jos. i. 6, 9 and cf. Eph. vi. 10. *The Lord . . . doth go before thee* (8). The heathen thought of their divinities as confined to special localities (see xxix. 26n.), but the Lord delights to go before and with His people. *He will not fail thee* (8). Cf. Heb. xiii. 5. *Fear not, neither be dismayed* (8). Fear comes so naturally to fallen man that this word of encouragement is often repeated from Genesis (xv. 1) to Revelation (i. 17).

Moses wrote this law (9). These words, and those in verse 22, 'Moses wrote this song', are the only explicit statements in this book of what Moses himself wrote (cf. Nu. xxxiii. 2). The introductory phrases, 'these be the words' (i. 1), 'this is the law (iv. 44), 'these are the words' (xxix. 1), 'this is the blessing' (xxxiii. 1), read like the words of a compiler, probably the same as the inspired writer of chapter xxxiv. It may not be possible to draw the exact line between what Moses did, or did not, write with his own hand, but the contemporary character of the record is abundantly evident, and its inspired character can be safely trusted. (See General Article, *The Historical Literature*, p. 33.) *This law* (9) must refer at least to the greater part of the book of Deuteronomy, and everything points to Moses' purpose of making a record that should be permanent. Emphasis on their permanence is seen in the contrast between 'his writings' and 'my words' in Jn. v. 47.

The priests . . . which bare the ark (9). See xviii. 1n. The distinction is clearly made between priests who, together with the elders, are charged with teaching the law and the Levites who were charged with the care of the book. *Thou shalt read this law* (11). The reading of the law by Joshua is recorded in Jos. viii. 34; cf. 2 Ki. xxiii. 2. According to the Jewish *Mishna* the reading at the feasts included the first five chapters and other portions of Deuteronomy.

b. **Joshua commissioned (xxxi. 14, 15)**

The tabernacle of the congregation (14). 'The tent of meeting' (RV). See Ex. xxv. 9n. *The Lord appeared* (15). The cloudy pillar which had accompanied them through their wanderings (Ex. xxxiii. 9) now appears once more as Jehovah speaks 'face to face' with Moses for the last time

.c. **The song written and the law completed (xxxi. 16–30).**

From this point to the end of the next chapter attention is centred upon the future, and 'the song', which was given to Moses and Joshua both to write and to put into the mouth of the people for a continuing witness. *Break my covenant* (16). See iv. 13n. The ideas that lie behind the ark, the covenant, the law and the witness or testimony, are all closely linked together. *Write ye* (19). The plural should be noted, as including Joshua (cf. xxxii. 44). *A witness for me* (19). God has two witnesses, the song and the written law (26). *I know their imagination* (21). God's foreknowledge is due to His insight into the heart of man whose 'imagination' is continually towards evil (Gn. vi. 5). *The same day* (22). Another explicit claim to Mosaic authorship.

An end of writing (24). The first command to Moses to write occurs in Ex. xvii. 14 and this is the last reference to his so doing (see verse 9n.). *In a book* (24). Since Jewish custom from early times included the whole Pentateuch in the 'book of the law' (26), Jewish commentators think that this is the meaning here. See xvii. 18n., xxxi. 9n. *In the side of the ark* (26). 'By the side of the ark' (RV). It may be noted that there is no mention of the law among the contents of the ark in Heb. ix. 4. A better place for the law is within the heart (Ps. xl. 8). *In the latter days* (29). Cf. Gn. xlix. 1; Nu. xxiv. 14. The expression represents the horizon of prophetic vision, and is found in connection with messianic predictions (see Dn. ii. 28, 44). *Until they were ended* (30). The commencement and the ending of the writing, first of the book, and then of the song, are carefully noted.

VIII. THE SONG. xxxii. 1–43

At the crossing of the Red Sea Moses sang a song unto the Lord (Ex. xv. 1; cf. Rev. xv. 3), and now at the end he teaches the people the Lord's song. It has been called 'the key to all prophecy', for it recounts the birth and childhood of the nation, their ingratitude and apostasy, their punishment and restoration. Seen otherwise, its theme is the name of the Lord, His loving care for His people, His righteousness and His mercy. It carries us from the creation to the final judgment, and begins and ends with praise. *As the rain* (2). The doctrine is like the small rain and dew which fall gently to refresh and nourish the earth. *I will publish the name of the Lord* (3). See v. 11n., xxviii. 58n. The revelation of the name and attributes of God to Moses at the time of his call (Ex. iii. 13–15) fully accounts for his maintained enthusiasm for the 'name'. *The Rock* (4). Heb. *tsur*. See viii. 15n. The word is repeated in verses 13 ('flinty rock'), 15, 18, 30, 31, 37. Here it denotes God's eternal strength and unchangeableness. *A God of truth* (4). That is, true to His own word and promise. *Just and right is he* (4). See vi. 25n. *Their spot* (5). Note RV. The text is difficult, but the general purport is to contrast the 'blemish' of Israel with the perfection of God. *Thy father that hath bought thee* (6). All men are God's creatures, but the redeemed are the true children of God (Jn. i. 12).

The nations (8). The song recalls the teaching of Gn. x, xi. In Gn. x all nations are included in the covenant of grace and their bounds assigned to them, but in chapter xi they were 'separated' as a result of pride. This antithesis was resolved when Israel was chosen to be the channel of God's blessing to the world. Cf. Rom. xi. 25; Eph. ii. 11–18. *He found him* (10). Cf. Lk. xv. 5. Simile is heaped upon simile to bring home the

tenderness of God's love. *Wilderness* (10). Not the same word as elsewhere. Here it means 'desert'. *As the apple of his eye* (10). That is, the pupil, the tenderest and essential part. *As an eagle* (11). Cf. Ex. xix. 4. The parent eagle in teaching her young to fly spreads her wings to prevent them from falling. The calling, education and protection of Israel are all pictured. *Honey out of the rock* (13). The honey is from the lofty crag (*sela*) where the bees live in the crevices, and the oil is from the hard rocks (*tsur*) near which the olives flourish. (See viii. 15n.)

Jeshurun (15). A poetical title of affection for Israel, translated in the LXX by 'beloved'. *With strange gods, with abominations* (16). See vi. 14n. In view of Israel's calling to be a witness to Jehovah and His holy ways, their separation from idolatry was of vital importance. *They sacrificed unto devils* (17). Cf. Ps. cvi. 37; 1 Cor. x. 20. *Not to God* (17). Lit. 'no-god'. See verse 21. *They have moved me to jealousy* (21). See Ex. xx. 5n. and 1 Cor. x. 22. This verse is quoted in Rom. x. 19, and the thought is repeated in Ho. i. 9. The divine 'jealousy', like the divine 'provocation', always has as its aim to draw back the heart of God's people to Himself. *That which is not God* (21). Lit. 'with a no-god . . . with a no-people'.

Our Rock . . . our enemies (31). In verses 28–33 Moses speaks in his own person. He longs that Israel should consider and understand God's dealing with them. Their enemies are instruments which He uses to accomplish His purposes. It is only as He permits that defeat can come, for that in which their enemies trust is not to be compared with Jehovah. Constant victory is God's will for His people; though He sells them into the hands of their enemies, He can also deliver them. *Judges* (31). Rather 'umpires' (cf. Ex. xxi. 22). *The vine of Sodom* (32). Sodom and Gomorrah were notorious for their wickedness. *To me belongeth vengeance* (35). 'Vengeance is mine' (RV). Cited Rom. xii. 19; Heb. x. 30. *There is none shut up, or left* (36). That is, either captive or free. *I, even I, am he* (39). The song reaches a climax in the assertion of the absolute sovereignty of God. *I lift up my hand* (40). The lifting up of the hand betokens a solemn declaration (cf. Rev. x. 5). *Rejoice, O ye nations, with his people* (43). This verse is quoted verbatim from the LXX in Rom. xv. 10. The song, like the Apocalypse, uses the imagery of the battlefield to picture the awesomeness of God's judgment, but having done this it calls the Gentiles to rejoice with His restored and pardoned people (see Rev. xxi. 24).

IX. MOSES TAKES LEAVE OF THE PEOPLE. xxxii. 44—xxxiii. 29

a. His last exhortation (xxxii. 44–47)

Hoshea (44). Joshua's original name was Hoshea ('salvation'), but he was renamed Joshua ('Jehovah is salvation') by Moses (Nu. xiii. 8, 16). The occurrence of his original name here suggests that Joshua himself may have been responsible for its use (cf. the use of 'Symeon' in 2 Pet. i. 1, RV mg.). *Set your hearts* (46). The parting appeal to the heart of the people (see xxx. 14n.) is eminently characteristic. Moses' day is over, and their length of days depends upon their obedience. Only Jesus can say 'Lo, I am with you alway' (Mt. xxviii. 20).

b. He is warned of his approaching death (xxxii. 48–52)

The special marks of time and place in verses 49–51 suggest a contemporary narrative. *Abarim* (49) means the parts 'beyond' (cf. Nu. xxi. 11, xxvii. 12); *Nebo* (49) (modern 'Nebu') was apparently applied to the mountain (see xxxiv. 1n.). *Meribah-Kadesh* (51). See Nu. xx. 12, 13, xxvii. 14, xxxiii. 36. There is a play upon the word *Kadesh* which means 'holy' and is reproduced in the word for 'sanctify'. As Moses, the leader of the people, transgressed openly, so he must openly bear the punishment for his transgression (i. 37n., iv. 21).

c. The final blessing (xxxiii. 1–29)

The wording of verse 1 implies that it was written after the death of Moses, but what follows may have been written previously, by Moses himself, or by one who heard him. The 'blessing' is a prophetical utterance of prayer and praise (cf. Lk. ii. 28). Like Jacob's blessing (Gn. xlix), Moses declares in poetical form the favours of God bestowed upon each individual tribe. It contains marks of the Mosaic age both in the preface (verses 2–5) and in the theocratic character of the various references. The omission of Simeon may be deliberate (perhaps to keep the number twelve). See verse 6n. The tribe of Simeon was gradually absorbed into that of Judah. *Moses, the man of God* (1). This title suggests that the recorder is not Moses himself. See verse 4n. It was applied to Moses by Caleb (Jos. xiv. 6), and elsewhere only in the title of Ps. xc. *The Lord . . . rose up . . .; he shined forth* (2). The giving of the law is likened to the fiery glory of an eastern sunrise. *He came with ten thousands of saints* (2). Lit. 'from the myriads of holiness'. The LXX substitutes 'angels' for 'saints', and this is probably the true meaning. (Cf. Acts vii. 53.) *In thy hand* (3). The sudden introduction of the second person has led some to interpret this of the future messianic King. *Moses commanded us* (4). See verse 1n. This may be an insertion by the writer of verse 1; or possibly the whole of verses 1–5 were cast in this form by him. These words would fall naturally from one who had heard the law proclaimed. *He was king in Jeshurun* (5). The subject may be Jehovah (cf. 1 Sa. xii. 12), or the messianic King of verse 3, or Moses. *Reuben* (6). In the order of the tribes the children of Leah and Rachel come first, then those of their handmaidens. There is a reference to the diminished number of this tribe through the rebellion of Dathan and Abiram (Nu. xvi. 1, 30). Codex A of the LXX makes this verse read,

'Let Reuben live and not die, and Simeon, may he be many in number'.

Judah (7). It has been conjectured that this verse may have originally followed on verse 10 and have been displaced. If that were the case, verse 11 would also belong to the blessing of Judah.

Levi (8) was Moses' own tribe, and the blessing is full and detailed. *Thy Thummim and thy Urim.* See Ex. xxviii. 30n. The LXX translates the two words as 'light' and 'truth'. (Cf. Ps. xliii. 3.) They seem to have been precious stones which were instrumental in revealing the will of God. (Cf. 1 Sa. xxviii. 6.) *Thy holy one.* Heb. *ḥasidh* from the root *ḥesedh.* See vii. 9n. *Massah . . . Meribah.* See vi. 16n., xxxii. 51n. Moses and Aaron were 'proved' at Massah and 'contended' with God at Meribah, and are here taken as representing their tribe. *Who said unto* (RV 'of') *his father* (9). Being called to a sacred office, Levites must be free from partiality in the discharge of their duties (cf. Ex. xxxii. 27–29). *They have observed thy word* (9). The priests and Levites were charged with the preservation of the law and the instruction of the people (xxxi. 9). *Bless, Lord, his substance . . .* (11). See verse 7n.

Benjamin (12). The meaning of this verse may be that Jehovah, like a shepherd, bare Benjamin on His shoulders (cf. Lk. xv. 5); or it may be a prophecy that the future temple should be on the borders of his tribal inheritance.

Joseph (13). The promise of 'precious fruits' (14) was fulfilled every spring in the fruit-laden valleys of Ephraim and Manasseh. *The good will of him that dwelt in the bush* (16). The reference is to the burning bush of Ex. iii. 2. *Separated from his brethren* (16). The Hebrew, like our word 'distinguished', suggests the idea of pre-eminence. *The horns of unicorns* (17). 'The horns of the wild-ox' (RV). An animal with powerful horns and enormous strength (Jb. xxxix. 9–11).

Zebulun (18) is promised success in his commerce ('going out'). Cf. 2 Ch. xxx. 11–19.

Issachar (18) is promised prosperity in agriculture at home ('tents').

Gad (20). Swiftness and strength are needed for this tribe of mountaineers. Cf. Gn. xlix. 19. *A portion of the lawgiver* (21). 'The ruler's portion' (RV mg.). That is, a chief share in the spoil of conquest. *He came* (21). Namely, to the help of the western tribes in their battle for Canaan.

Dan (22) is likened here to a lion's whelp, in Gn. xlix to an adder, and is omitted altogether in Rev. vii. Jewish tradition connects Dan with apostasy. *He shall leap* (22). 'That leapeth forth' (RV). This refers to the lion, not to Dan.

Naphtali (23). To this tribe was assigned the beautiful and fertile land west and south of the Sea of Galilee.

Asher (24). The territory of Asher was famous for its olives. *Thy shoes* (25). 'Thy bars' (RV). The reference is to Asher's protection from its northern enemies. *As thy days, so shall thy strength be* (25). This beautiful promise has brought comfort to every succeeding generation (cf. Mt. xxviii. 20).

The God of Jeshurun (26). The AV is to be preferred, for it is as the God of Israel that Jehovah is praised. He is above, beneath, before and around His people. Beyond all nature and behind every mystery is a Person, their own Saviour and Lord. *Thine enemies shall be found liars unto thee* (29). 'Thine enemies shall submit themselves unto thee' (RV). The final note is one of victory, through the protecting shield and conquering sword of the Lord. (Cf. Eph. vi. 16, 17.) *Their high places* (29). The Hebrew word (*bamoth*) is applied in the books of Kings and Chronicles to the places where idolatrous or irregular worship was practised (1 Ki. xii. 31). Here it bears its earlier and literal sense of 'lofty heights' (see xii. 2n.).

X. MOSES' DEATH. xxxiv. 1–8

Moses went up (1). The writer records Moses' last act of obedience, as he ascends to the appointed place. All but two of his own generation had passed away, and his mission was accomplished. Before he dies, his prayer to see the land is granted. He next appears, in the sacred history, on another mount, again speaking 'face to face' with his Lord (Mk. ix. 4). *Pisgah* (1). Lit. 'the pisgah'. The word (lit. 'broken') denotes any jagged ridge, and would describe the mountain's highest peak, Jebal Osha, as seen from below. See verse 2n. *All the land* (2). The view seen from Jebal Osha on a clear day agrees exactly with this description in every particular, from snow-capped Hermon, Galilee, the mount of Olives, Bethlehem, to the Dead Sea and beyond. *The servant of the Lord* (5). Cf. Heb. iii. 5. Moses was in many ways a model servant; 'as the Lord commanded' was his life's motto. *He buried him in a valley* (6). Moslem tradition today locates the place of his grave in a depression not far below the summit. The Targum of Jonathan says that Jehovah gave Michael the archangel charge over his grave. Cf. Jude 9. *Thirty days* (8). Moses had appointed thirty days' mourning for Aaron (Nu. xx. 29).

XI. CONCLUSION. xxxiv. 9–12

These concluding verses suggest a later hand than Joshua. Perhaps they were added after Joshua's death by Eleazar or by one of the elders (Jos. xxiv. 31). *Full of the spirit of wisdom* (9). Cf. Ex. xxviii. 3. The Holy Spirit, who spake by the prophets, was at work from the beginning. *Moses had laid his hands upon him* (9). Cf. Gn. xlviii. 14; Nu. xxvii. 18; Acts xiii. 3. Blessing, commission and the conferring of spiritual gifts were all symbolized by the laying on of hands. *There arose not a prophet since* (10). Whatever prophets may have arisen before these words were penned, none was equal to Moses in the ways specified, nor were there any afterwards until He came whom Moses foretold (xviii. 15). As a prophet Moses led the people (Ho. xii. 13), delivered to them the revelation committed to him (xxix. 29) and pointed to Christ (xviii. 15). *Face to face* (10). See Ex. xxxiii. 11. *In all that mighty hand* (12). Not only in word did God work through Moses, but in deeds which were never to be forgotten. The signs and wonders wrought in Egypt were the divine preparation for the greater redemption wrought on Calvary.

G. T. MANLEY.

JOSHUA

INTRODUCTION

It has been said that the history of the world is the history of its great men. To be applied to history as a whole, that statement would require considerable qualification, but it can be set down as an accurate description of the kind of history to be found in the book of Joshua which, quite literally, is the 'book of Joshua'. It begins with his divine call and commission, and it ends with the record of his death. It is his leadership that binds the story of Israel's conquest of Canaan into a coherent whole.

I. THE MAN AND HIS TASK

Many things marked Joshua out for leadership. He was of the house of Joseph, which commanded most authority at this stage in the history of Israel: his grandfather, Elishama, had led the tribe of Ephraim through the wilderness and possibly had had the care of the embalmed body of his great ancestor, carried up for interment in the Promised Land. His contact with Egyptian civilization and culture—for he had been born in Egypt and had taken part in the exodus (Nu. xxxii. 11f.)—also fitted him, as it had fitted Moses, for the task of forging his people into a nation. It is significant in this connection that one of his last appeals in his final message to the people reminded them how their fathers had served other gods in Egypt (Jos. xxiv. 14). As Moses' personal attendant and colleague, in closest contact with him in the leadership of the people, Joshua had been naturally marked out as his successor, and he must have learned much from his master and from his own experience during the years of wandering in the wilderness.

His faith and courage had been amply revealed in the minority report submitted by Caleb and himself in favour of an invasion of Canaan from Kadesh, in contrast to the timid report of the other ten spies: 'The Lord will bring us into this land, and give it us.'

He had also already shown his prowess as a military commander in leading the forces of Israel which repelled the attack of the Amalekites at Rephidim, when they fell upon the rear of the Hebrew host, which was encumbered with women, children and baggage (Dt. xxv. 18). He won a decisive victory, and his generalship was the human channel through which came the answer to the prayers of Moses on the mountain-top (Ex. xvii. 8ff.).

This was the man, so highly qualified by nature, by training and by experience, whom God raised up to lead the Hebrew tribes into Palestine. But his supreme qualification lay in the fact that all his gifts and training and experience were fused into a dynamic force by the touch of God. It was at the call of God that all his potentialities were called forth, and that call brought to the leadership of Israel a man assured of his divine commission; it summoned to the task a soldier who had put on the whole armour of God.

II. AUTHORSHIP AND AUTHENTICITY

The widely held documentary theory of the composition of the Pentateuch is discussed in the General Article on *The Historical Literature of the Old Testament*. In the present Introduction it may suffice to mention one or two points where the book of Joshua impinges on the question.

The place assigned to Joshua in the Hebrew Canon is of considerable significance. The book was placed first in the section called 'The Early Prophets' and including Joshua, Judges, Samuel and Kings. If, as postulated by modern criticism, Joshua and the Pentateuch were of late date, and compiled from many documents of varying dates at a late stage in Jewish history, it seems more than a little strange that the ancient Hebrew Canon places Joshua at the head of a new section. In other words, the documentary theory almost demands the substitution of the Hexateuch for the Pentateuch, an arrangement which earlier critics adopted, but of which the ancient Canon knows nothing. That seems difficult to understand if the same editors were responsible for a late compilation of both the Pentateuch and Joshua.

It is significant that more recent critics do not now speak of the Hexateuch; even if the same sources are distinguished in Joshua as in the Pentateuch, a distinction is made in that P does not form the framework in Joshua as it does in the Pentateuch, but D. This admission, however, does not account sufficiently for the break which the ancient Hebrew Canon makes, for recent no less than earlier criticism distinguishes the same sources in Joshua as in the Pentateuch.

Secondly, archaeology has necessarily more to say about Joshua and the conquest of Palestine than about the Pentateuch; and its findings in recent years have given most illuminating information regarding the authenticity of the history that we have in these books. Albright, for example, in his *Archaeology of Palestine*, p. 229, writes: 'Thanks to archaeological determination of the site of most biblical places, it is possible to establish the age and historical significance of many lists of towns in the Bible. A good case in point is the list of Levitic cities in Jos. xxi and 1 Ch. vi, which Wellhausen, followed by most subsequent critics, considered an artificial product of some post-exilic scribe's imagination. Careful examination of this list in the light of all known archaeological facts makes it quite certain that the list is much more ancient . . . A date between about 975 and about 950 B.C. may thus be fixed for the extant form of the list, which seems to have had a pre-history going back to the Conquest.' G. E. Wright confirms Albright's view, and is prepared to go further. 'In my opinion', he writes in an essay on 'Present State of Biblical Archaeology' in *The Study of the Bible Today and Tomorrow*, 'the same can be held for the lists of tribal cities and perhaps even for the boundaries in Jos. xv—xix . . . If this is the case, then there is no reason whatsoever to ascribe these lists in Joshua to the priestly writers of the post-Exilic period.'

There are in the third place many internal evidences of an early date. Principal Douglas, in *The Book of Joshua* in the series 'Handbooks for Bible Classes', notes the following: 'Such a name as "great Zidon" alongside of "the strong city Tyre" (xi. 8, xix. 28, 29) suggests a writer at the remote age in which Zidon was the foremost Phoenician city, even above Tyre, its successful rival in a later age. And the age is one in which a stone or a cairn of stones is the usual, almost the exclusive mark of a great transaction, like the stones commemorating the crossing of the Jordan; the cairns over Achan's body, and at the graves of the kings of Ai and other towns; the great stone at Shechem (xxiv. 26) with which compare the stones (viii. 32) and the "great altar to see to", called Ed (xxii. 10, 34). And the way in which the territory given to the tribes is recorded suits best the writing of a contemporary. The fullest account by far is given of Judah, the tribe which was earliest settled, and which probably did its work most effectively, strong in numbers, and led by that faithful and devoted man, Caleb; Judah is described in its first over-large extent, as is also Joseph; and then we are told how Simeon's share was taken out of Judah's, and Dan's (it is implied) out of the two powerful houses, Judah's and Joseph's.'

It seems, therefore, that while nothing really definite can be said about the authorship of the book, there is evidence that the sources from which it is derived were contemporary with the events described, and that the book took its present form at an early date.

III. THE DATE OF ISRAEL'S CONQUEST

The data for a discussion of the date of Israel's conquest of Canaan are the biblical records and the information which has been derived from archaeological research. There are two main theories. Each starts from a biblical statement, each can be made to fit most of the known facts, and yet, at the same time, each proposes certain difficulties.

Ex. i. 11 tells us that the Israelites in Egyptian bondage built for Pharaoh treasure cities, Pithom and Raamses. It is claimed that excavations have shown that these cities were founded by Rameses II (1300–1224 B.C.). It has been maintained, therefore, that Rameses II was the Pharaoh of the oppression, and his successor, Merenptah, the Pharaoh of the Exodus. This would date the entry into Canaan c. 1230 B.C. (The arguments for this late date are given more fully in the Introduction to the commentary on Judges. See p. 237. See also the chronological table on p. 38.)

This view is opposed by a stele of victory set up by Merenptah about 1200 B.C. (discovered in 1896), giving particulars of his conquests, and naming Israel in such a way as to show that the Israelites are certainly outside Egypt, and to suggest—though scholars are not agreed on this—that they are in Palestine as a settled community. Similar evidence is derived from an inscription of Rameses II which suggests that Asher is a Palestinian tribe. A further difficulty for this theory is that it does not seem to give enough time for all the events of the settlement of Canaan and the rule of the judges before the establishment of the monarchy.

It seems, therefore, that the identification of Pithom and Raamses with Rameses II can be maintained only with some difficulty.

An alternative theory is derived from the record in 1 Ki. vi. 1, where it is stated that the exodus occurred 480 years before Solomon began to build the temple: This latter date has been fixed about 967 B.C., which sets Israel's invasion of Canaan about 1407 B.C.

Garstang in *Joshua–Judges* claims that this date can be confirmed by reference to available Egyptian records. He lays considerable stress on the fact that Israel's invasion of Canaan could scarcely have taken place when Egypt's power and consequent control of Canaan were strong and secure. Without going into the details of his argument, which shows many striking parallels between the history of Israel as recorded in Judges and the waves of prosperity alternating with depression which marked Egypt's history at this time, it is perhaps sufficient to state that this suggested date falls within the period of the Tell-el-Amarna letters (c. 1400 B.C.). These tablets, discovered in 1887, consist of correspondence between Egyptian officials in Palestine and other countries and the home government in Egypt, and point to the waning of Egyptian influence in face of the advance of the Hittite Empire. This evidence of a period of Egyptian weakness, it is justifiably claimed, confirms that this was the probable date of Israel's entry into Canaan. An objection to the dating of the conquest c. 1400 B.C. is that it fails to account for the building of Pithom and Raamses in the thirteenth century in the time of Rameses II. That difficulty can perhaps be met by assuming that these cities were indeed built by the Israelites, but were afterwards rebuilt and renamed in honour of Rameses II after the Israelites had left Egypt.

IV. THE MORAL PROBLEM IN ISRAEL'S WARFARE

The indiscriminate extermination of the Canaanites recorded in the book of Joshua has proved a stumbling-block to many who accept the divine inspiration of the scriptural record. Can we believe that God really commanded the Israelites utterly to destroy the inhabitants of the land? If He did, is such a revelation of His character consistent with the revelation of the Father that Christ has given us?

Modern criticism has two ways of cutting the Gordian knot. Some maintain that the accounts of the extermination of the Canaanites were written long after the events which they profess to describe, and that they give an ideal picture of what later ages considered should have happened if the worship of Jehovah was to be kept pure. In other words, the atrocities described never really happened. Others assert that the revelation of God that we have in the early religious history of Israel is His revelation of Himself limited by the capacity of those who had to receive it, and that the conception of His commanding the destruction of the Canaanites represents a very primitive stage of religious development.

In our consideration of the authorship and authenticity of Joshua we have already given reasons for dismissing the former of these two explanations: the latter now demands some attention. The theory holds that the Israelites of this period mistakenly thought of Jehovah as their tribal God, who naturally commanded the destruction of His people's enemies. Later revelation (e.g. the book of Jonah) was to show that God has purposes of love and mercy for nations outside the commonwealth of Israel, and so the earlier revelation was transcended. But this theory, however inviting it may seem, does not really give a satisfying explanation of the problem. It is true that the knowledge of God had to grow from more to more as His people were able to bear it, and that the Old Testament at best could give but a partial revelation of Him; but we cannot believe that a later revelation should flatly contradict an earlier one. God may reveal Himself progressively; He must reveal Himself consistently, if we are to accept His revelation of Himself at all.

Can we then find an explanation which does honour both to the inspiration of the record and to the God whom it reveals? It is necessary at the outset to get a clear idea of what was involved in the devotion of the Canaanites to destruction. To take Jericho as an example, the city, its inhabitants and all that it contained were 'devoted' or 'put to the ban' (Heb. *herem*, AV 'accursed'). This meant, as G. A. Cooke describes it in *Joshua* in the Cambridge Bible, that 'anything which might endanger the religious life of the community was put out of harm's way by being prohibited to human use; to secure this effectively it must be utterly destroyed.' It seems therefore that the ban had a religious and a prophylactic function—it was a religious service, and it was a protection for the religious life of Israel. It is along these two lines that a solution of our problem must be sought.

First, then, the destruction of the Canaanites was, as the record again and again proclaims it to be, a religious service. The people of Israel were the instrument by which God exercised judgment on the wickedness of the people of the land. Just as He had destroyed Sodom and Gomorrah for the same kind of unspeakable corruption, without the instrumentality of human hands, so He used the Israelites to punish and root out the cancerous depravity of the Canaanites. And if there be a moral government of the world at all, such a dread possibility of judgment and divine surgery, however executed, cannot be excluded.

Incidentally, it is noteworthy that the ban, being a religious service, imposed a moral restraint against the looting and excesses which were the normal, more terrible accompaniments of the warfare of the times. This was no lust for booty or for blood; it was a divine duty which must be performed.

The second function of the ban was, as we have said, prophylactic. If the religion of the Hebrews was to be kept pure and untainted, all possibility of infection by the abominations of the heathen must be removed. The means of removing the dread infection was a drastic one, but, in view of the revelation that the Hebrews were to transmit to the world, who will say that it was unjustified? And where there was failure in Israel's high task, the reason is seen in their failure to carry out the divine command of extermination. And so, for the sake of God's moral government of the world, for the sake of Israel, and for the sake of the message that Israel was to bring to the world, it was necessary that an evil nation should be utterly destroyed.

V. THE RELIGIOUS TEACHING OF THE BOOK

The criterion of the religious value of any book is, What does it tell us about God? What truth of God does it reveal? The detailed consideration of this is the task of a devotional commentary, and is outside the scope of this present work, but any introduction to the book of Joshua would be incomplete without some indication of its religious teaching.

The book of Joshua throws light upon three aspects of God's relationship to man:

a. God's faithfulness

Long years before, the promise had been given that the people of Israel would possess the Promised Land. It had seemed that that divine purpose had been thwarted by man's sin and disobedience; but God's plan could not be finally defeated, and this book gives the story of fulfilment in the conquest of Canaan.

b. God's holiness

This is seen in His judgment upon the original inhabitants of the land. The iniquity of the Amorites at last was full, and Israel became the instrument of His punishment. But God's holiness is seen no less in His insistence that His instrument of judgment must be holy. Again and again it is insisted that this is a holy war, and that Israel will succeed in the task committed to her only as every evil thing is put away from her.

c. God's salvation

The name Joshua means 'Jehovah is salvation',

and is the Hebrew form of Jesus, the name that is above every name. Is it any wonder then that Christian people have seen in Joshua a 'type' of Christ, and in this book a picture of the life of victory that is ours in Him? Crossing the Jordan has often been thought of as symbolical of death, but it is much more helpful, and truer to the facts,. to think of it as the entrance into the life of fulness of blessing to which the Captain of the Lord's host brings us. 'Let us therefore fear, lest, a promise being left us of entering into his rest, any of you should seem to come short of it' (Heb. iv. 1).

OUTLINE OF CONTENTS

I. JOSHUA'S COMMISSION. i. 1–9

II. THE ENTRY INTO CANAAN. i. 10—v. 12

    a. Mobilization (i. 10–18)
    b. Mission of the spies (ii. 1–24)
    c. Preparations for a holy war (iii. 1–13)
    d. The crossing of the Jordan (iii. 14—iv. 18)
    e. Encampment at Gilgal (iv. 19—v. 12)

III. THE CONQUEST OF CANAAN. v. 13—xii. 24

    a. The divine commander (v. 13–15)
    b. The first stage: Jericho and Ai (vi. 1—viii. 35)
    c. The second stage: the campaign in the south (ix. 1—x. 43)
    d. The third stage: the campaign in the north (xi. 1–23)
    e. List of conquered Canaanite kings (xii. 1–24)

IV. THE DIVISION OF THE LAND. xiii. 1—xxii. 34

    a. Command to divide the land (xiii. 1–7)
    b. Territory of the two and a half tribes (xiii. 8–33)
    c. Territory of Caleb and Judah (xiv. 1—xv. 63)
    d. Territory of Ephraim and Manasseh (xvi. 1—xvii. 18)
    e. Territory of the seven tribes (xviii. 1—xix. 51)
    f. Cities of refuge appointed (xx. 1–9)
    g. Cities of the Levites appointed (xxi. 1–45)
    h. Return of the eastern tribes and setting up of the altar of witness (xxii. 1–34)

V. JOSHUA'S LAST DAYS. xxiii. 1—xxiv. 33

    a. First address (xxiii. 1–16)
    b. Second address (xxiv. 1–28)
    c. Joshua's death and burial (xxiv. 29–33)

COMMENTARY

I. JOSHUA'S COMMISSION. i. 1–9

The Lord spake unto Joshua . . . Moses' minister (1). Cf. Ex. xxiv. 13; Nu. xxvii. 18–23; Dt. i. 38, xxxi. 23. These opening verses (1–9) bring Joshua on to the stage, and are a necessary prologue to the story of the conquest. *Moses my servant is dead* (2). Nevertheless, the work must go on: the continuity of the nation, of its task and of God's promises to it, is not broken by the

change of leadership. Cf. Dt. xxxiv. 5–9. God's promise still stands. *All the land of the Hittites* (4). See Dt. vii. 1n.; Jdg. i. 26n. *I will not fail thee* (5). Lit. 'I will not drop thee'. Cf. x. 6, where it is translated 'Slack not thy hand . . .' *Turn not from it . . . that thou mayest prosper* (7). The condition of success is unswerving obedience to the *book of the law* (8). This is the book referred to in Dt. xxxi. 24, 26: Cf. also Dt. xxxi. 9, 11.

Have not I commanded thee? (9). The campaign upon which Joshua and the people are entering is unmistakably divine. Joshua is no bandit, no aggressor; he is simply a servant carrying out the commands of his superior. Cf. Dt. xxxi. 1–8.

II. THE ENTRY INTO CANAAN. i. 10—v. 12

a. Mobilization (i. 10–18)

Then Joshua commanded (10). The army which awaited the order to advance into Palestine was well organized and disciplined, a much more effective fighting force than the undisciplined mob which had come out of Egypt. *The officers of the people* (10). See Dt. i. 15n., xvi. 18, xx. 5, 9. These, a familiar feature of Israel's organization since the days of the oppression, were now commanded to mobilize the people for crossing *within three days* (11). It seems that the spies had already been sent out, though the account of their mission is not recorded until later; the account does not follow the chronological order of events.

Ye shall pass before your brethren . . . and help them (14). At this supremely critical moment, the tribes were happily a vital unity; and the Reubenites, the Gadites and the half tribe of Manasseh (12), whose inheritance had already been allotted to them on the east of the Jordan (Nu. xxxii), responded with alacrity to the reminder that they were committed to marching with their brethren against the western land. It was this unity with its definitely religious basis that made Israel a force to be reckoned with. *On this side Jordan* (14). 'Beyond Jordan' (RV). See Dt. i. 1n.

b. Mission of the spies (ii. 1–24)

Two men to spy secretly (1). The spies were sent to view the land and, in the first instance, to report on the strategically important city of Jericho which stood at the entrance of the mountain passes into the interior. Instead of attacking the southern frontier, which bristled with fortresses to defend the land against attack from Egypt, and from which the forces of Israel had been so disastrously thrown back forty years before, Joshua anticipated Napoleon's favourite manœuvre by outflanking the southern fortresses, breaking through the eastern frontier, poorly defended except for the Jordan, and then striking with his whole force right and left in rapid succession. The crossing of the Jordan, therefore, and the capture of Jericho, were the key to the whole campaign.

They . . . came into an harlot's house, named Rahab (1). Attempts have often been made since the time of Josephus to represent Rahab merely as an innkeeper, but there seem to be no grounds for doubting the accuracy of the ordinary translation. The spies learned from her that at the approach of Israel a panic had spread through the town—a statement which was confirmed by the uneasy suspicions of the king of Jericho, who sent immediately to make inquiries about their presence (3). The falsehood by which Rahab

sent the king's messengers on the wrong scent is recorded simply without comment (4, 5). We have here a very imperfect morality. The New Testament commends Rahab, not for her falsehoods, but for her faith (Heb. xi. 31; Jas. ii. 25). Into her dark and tragic life had come some faint glimmering of the truth that here in Israel there was a God above all the gods she had ever known. Stories of His great deeds and the success in war of His people had reached the city (10). To the power and mercy of this supreme God she would trust herself. This faith, immature though it may have been, was the saving of her and of her family (13), for she received from the spies the promise that when the city fell the house with the scarlet cord hanging from the window would be spared (19). Some identify the scarlet thread with the cord by which she let the spies down, but the words are different.

At Rahab's suggestion, the spies hid themselves for three days. The hills around Jericho are full of caves and so would have given them ample cover. They then returned to Joshua, probably by swimming the Jordan, with their report of the utter despondency and alarm of the Canaanites.

c. Preparations for a holy war (iii. 1–13)

The people were given two reminders that this was a holy war upon which they were entering. First, *Sanctify yourselves* (5), necessary because God was about to work miraculously among them, giving evidence of His presence with Joshua no less than with Moses (7). The whole situation created an atmosphere of supernatural power waiting to be exercised. Secondly, the people were to be led across the Jordan by the ark, borne by the priests of the tribe of Levi (6). See Ex. xxv. 10n. and Dt. xxxi. 9n. Verses 11 and 13, taken literally, suggest that the ark of the covenant is taken as representing *the Lord of all the earth*. Verse 11 may be translated, 'Behold, the ark of the covenant. The Lord of all the earth is passing over before you into Jordan.' The ark was the sign that God was going before His people, to lead them against their enemies. Thus by their own preparations and by the sight of the ark going before them the people were reminded that this was no enterprise of their own in which they were engaged.

d. The crossing of the Jordan (iii. 14—iv. 18)

Commentators have suggested that two differing accounts of the crossing have been combined in this passage. Certainly if we read iv. 5 as in the AV it gives the impression that the crossing had not yet been started, whereas we gather from iii. 16, 17 and iv. 1 that the people have already completed it. But iv. 5 can be translated, 'Pass over to where the ark of the Lord your God is in the midst of Jordan . . .' With this reading it is possible to reconstruct the history without finding any breaks or discrepancies in the narrative. The sequence of events is then seen to be as follows:

i. **The twelve tribes pass over Jordan (iii.**

14-17). The priests bearing the ark took up their stand on the brink of Jordan, which was brimful at this time of the year, swollen by melting snows (15). As they advanced to mid-channel the bed of the river was dried up before them; the stream was checked in its course *very far from* (RV, 'a great way off, at') *the city Adam* (16). This has been placed sixteen miles up the river from Jericho, and it seems probable that a stretch of twenty or thirty miles of the river bed was left dry. An interesting parallel to the event recorded in this chapter has been found in the pages of an Arabic historian, describing how in 1266 A.D. near Tell-Damieh, which many experts have identified with Adam, the bed of the river was left dry for ten hours in consequence of a landslip. Garstang cites other parallels in 1906 and 1927. These events may indicate a 'natural' explanation of what happened centuries earlier, but to accept that explanation does not detract in any way from the supernatural intervention which opened the way to Israel just at the moment when they needed to cross. The priests standing in the dry bed of the river as the whole nation passed over were the sign that this was the doing of the Lord.

ii. The crossing commemorated (iv. 1–9). When the people had crossed, Joshua took the twelve men whom he had already chosen (iii. 12), and commanded them to go back to where the priests were standing with the ark, and to take out of the river bed twelve stones which were afterwards set up as a memorial at Gilgal. Joshua then set up twelve other stones in the midst of the Jordan where the feet of the priests had stood.

iii. The crossing completed (iv. 10, 11, 15–18). The priests stood in their places until the memorial stones had been arranged for and all the people had hastened across. Then they crossed last of all and the river returned to its spate of full flood. (A fuller account of this is given in iv. 15–18.) A note is inserted in verses 12–14 to stress the fact that the eastern tribes marched with their brethren across the Jordan, and to draw attention to the event as a fulfilment of the promise given to Joshua in iii. 7.

e. Encampment at Gilgal (iv. 19—v. 12)
The first encampment of the people of Israel in the Promised Land was at Gilgal, where the stones taken out of Jordan were set up as a memorial, and where the camp of Israel was based for the campaign. The name Gilgal means 'circle' or 'rolling', and it seems that, rather than giving it a new name, a new significance was given to the old name. See v. 9. *Amorites . . . Canaanites* (v. 1). See Dt. i. 7n. This note of the effect of the miracle on the surrounding nations presupposes the passage of a length of time during which the news reached them. It is inserted here as an immediate fulfilment of the purpose of the miracle as given in iv. 24.

Circumcise again the children of Israel (2). For nearly forty years the rite of circumcision had been neglected, not because there had been lack of opportunity, but because the nation was under judgment. If the people had been circumcised during the years of wandering it would have seemed that all was well, and that the covenant had never been suspended. But now they are back to the old relationship again, and they can once more bear in their bodies the seal of the covenant. *The second time* (2) means not that they had been circumcised already, but that they were returning to their former condition as a circumcised nation in covenant with God. *The reproach of Egypt* (9) suggests that the years of wandering had given the Egyptians reason for taunting the Israelites with being forsaken by their God; the renewal of the miracle of the Red Sea at the Jordan (see iv. 23) made it clear that they were Jehovah's people once again.

Since the people were now back on covenant ground, the next step was to keep the Passover, after which the people took the first step of entering on their inheritance by eating the produce of the land which was theirs by covenant. The writer records the stopping of the divine provision of manna (see Ex. xvi. 15n.) now that it was no longer needed.

III. THE CONQUEST OF CANAAN.
v. 13—xii. 24

a. The divine commander (v. 13–15)
As a prologue to the advance we have this most significant account of Joshua's encounter with the angel of Jehovah. This must have been a time of special anxiety and suspense for Joshua. The Jordan was crossed; there could be no going back now. The burden of leadership lay heavily upon his shoulders. But at the very moment when he was *by Jericho* (13), anxiously reconnoitring the strong city which lay in Israel's path, there appeared to him the representative of Jehovah, who called Himself the *captain of the host of the Lord* (14). We believe that this was the Son of God Himself.

Art thou for us, or for our adversaries? (13). Joshua had been thinking of the conflict as being between two sets of opposing forces, Israelite and Canaanite, and he was anxious to know if this armed warrior was to be his ally in the struggle. The answer was to the effect that He was not an ally, but a leader to whose leadership and control Joshua himself must submit. Thus he is reminded again that this is a holy war in which his position is that of a *servant* (14). The ultimate responsibility is borne not on the shoulders of a human leader but by God Himself.

The story of the conquest which follows shows this divine guidance at work influencing and controlling human strategy. It may help to make the history more intelligible if we glance at the broad outline of that strategy. There were three stages in the conquest. The first consisted in the capture of Jericho and Ai, which opened up the

228

passes into the interior of the country. A wedge was then driven between the northern and southern sections of the country and the second and third stages in the campaign were the defeat of the southern confederacy and the northern confederacy in turn.

b. The first stage: Jericho and Ai (vi. 1—viii. 35)

i. The capture of Jericho (vi. 1–27). Jericho, though a comparatively small city by modern standards, was very strongly fortified, and was an essential objective for the Israelites if they were to advance into Palestine. The city was closely shut up against attack, *none went out, and none came in* (1). But the angel of Jehovah had given explicit instructions for its capture, and these were carried out to the letter. Seven priests, bearing seven trumpets, and followed by the ark of the covenant, marched in solemn procession around the city for seven days, preceded and followed by the silent army. Each night they returned to the camp at Gilgal. On the seventh day the city was compassed seven times, and then, amid the blast of the trumpets and the great shout of the people, *the wall fell down flat, so that the people went up into the city, every man straight before him* (20).

The whole proceeding was designed to test Israel's faith in the supernatural resources which were theirs. *Trumpets of rams' horns* (4, 6). Better, as in RV mg., 'jubile trumpets'. The Heb. word *yobhel* is found outside the references to the year of jubile (see Lv. xxv. 8ff.n.) only here and in Ex. xix. 13, where there is a similar religious significance. This suggests that the trumpets carried by the priests had a ceremonial rather than a martial reference. This was a religious, not a military undertaking.

Excavations have given evidence of the collapse of the wall, and of the destruction of the city by fire. But even if a secondary cause of the event, such as an earthquake, could be given, it cannot explain its miraculous occurrence just at this critical moment of Israel's advance. 'By faith the walls of Jericho fell down, after they were compassed about seven days' (Heb. xi. 30). The city, its inhabitants and all that it contained were treated as *accursed* (17) or 'devoted' (Heb. *herem*). See notes on Lv. xxvii. 28 and Dt. ii. 34. *Accursed thing* (18) and *utterly destroyed* (21) are translations of the same word. In view of this a stern warning was given against taking any spoil for personal use. Everything was 'devoted' to Jehovah: the inhabitants were slain, with the exception of Rahab and those in her house; the city was destroyed by fire, as was everything in it except the silver and gold and vessels of brass and iron which were *consecrated unto the Lord* (19). Rahab and all her kindred were *without the camp of Israel* (23) because they were Gentiles and ceremonially unclean. Verse 25 indicates that they were ultimately fully identified with the people of Israel.

The putting of Jericho to the ban included the pronouncing of a curse on anyone who should

afterwards rebuild it as a fortified city. In the time of Ahab, 500 years later, this anathema was disregarded by Hiel the Bethelite at the cost of the lives of his two sons (1 Ki. xvi. 34). Garstang's excavations show that the city was rebuilt at this time. But a more immediate violation of the ban had much more disastrous consequences, when the Israelites went up against Ai.

ii. Reverse at Ai and Achan's sin (vii. 1–26.) Ai stood on rising ground to the west of Jericho, near Bethel, and was the next obvious objective for the Israelites. But the high hopes of the invaders received an unexpected setback. The first verse of the chapter anticipates by giving the reason for this reverse, and then the history proceeds. *Committed a trespass* (1). Lit. 'acted faithlessly', for this was a breach of the covenant. On the advice of the spies which Joshua had sent forward to make a reconnaissance, only part of the army was sent to attack the city, though it is made clear later that this was not the cause of the repulse. The garrison sallied out, and the Hebrews were driven in retreat down the steep descent towards Shebarim, or 'the stone quarries', leaving thirty-six of their number dead. *The hearts of the people melted* (5)—the expression used of their enemies in ii. 11. The cause was not merely the defeat and the loss of fighting men, but a terrible misgiving that Jehovah's help had been withdrawn from them (7). The thought that the defeat would mean renewed hope for the Canaanites was the chief element in Joshua's dejection. Joshua soon learned the reason for defeat: the ban had been violated. Verse 11 advances from the general to the particular in framing the indictment, and the emphasis is heightened in the Hebrew by the repetition of the phrase 'yea, they have even' before each item of the charge. The sin of one member of the community was held to be that of the whole people. Israel was now a nation, and the sin of the individual was the sin of the nation until the nation repudiated it and expiation was made.

Achan was identified by the sacred lot and made confession that he had taken gold and silver and 'a mantle of Shinar' (21, RV mg.) and had hidden them beneath his tent, from which they were now fetched and poured out (rather than *laid*) as an offering to the Lord (23). The final scene in the valley of Achor (lit. 'troubling') saw the execution of the sentence when Achan was stoned to death and he and all that he had were burned with fire. Did Achan's family share in his destruction? It is difficult to be certain. The plural 'them' used in verse 25 may refer only to his possessions, and Jos. xxii. 20 is not conclusive on the question since it can refer just as naturally to the thirty-six who died because of his sin. The law of Dt. xxiv. 16 clearly prohibits the putting to death of an offender's relatives, unless, of course, their knowledge of his sin involved them in his guilt. By Achan's death the act of sacrilege was expiated, and the scene of the tragedy, the valley of Achor, became a door of hope as the people set their faces once more to the advance.

iii. Capture of Ai (viii. 1–29). The way was now open for a renewed attack on Ai, and Joshua made use of an ambush to take and destroy the city. The text gives us some difficulty here, for there seems to be a discrepancy between verses 3–9, which speak of 30,000 men being set in ambush on the west side of the city, and verse 12, which gives the number in the same position as 5,000. Numbers are notoriously subject to copyists' errors, and it may be that such a mistake has been made here. Another more attractive explanation, however, is that there were two ambuscades, one of 30,000 in the hills nearer to Bethel, and the other of 5,000 close to Ai. Verse 17 tells that the men of Bethel—a city two ·miles from Ai, but hidden by intervening heights —joined in the pursuit after Israel; and it seems reasonable to assume that Joshua would make preparations to guard against such an attack from Bethel. Though the men of Bethel were defeated at this time and their king slain (see Jos. xii. 16), it is uncertain whether the city was actually occupied or destroyed. Its capture is recorded in Jdg. i. 22–26. Chronologically this may have preceded the death of Joshua, in spite of the reference to this event in Jdg. i. 1, for these verses precede the second mention of Joshua's death in Jdg. ii. 8.

The ambush proved entirely successful: the city was occupied and set on fire; the inhabitants, attacked in front and from the rear, were put to the sword; their king was slain and his body hanged on a tree until sunset (cf. Dt. xxi. 23), and then buried under a great heap of stones at the gate of the city; and Ai (meaning 'stone-heap') became like its name. It is noteworthy that the cattle and the spoil were this time given to the Israelites (27). Achan might have waited for his booty. Archaeological investigation into the site of Ai presents a very real difficulty. 'The peculiar problem of the conquest of Ai is more difficult for the modern exegete than it was for the children of Israel' (Burrows, *What Mean These Stones?*, p. 272). The excavation of the site has shown that it was unoccupied between 2000 and 1200 B.C., and lay in ruins all that time (hence presumably its name Ha-ai, 'the ruin'). L. H. Vincent has suggested that the inhabitants of Bethel had merely an outpost at Ai of such modest proportions and temporary nature that it has left no remains to betray its existence to the excavator. Such a solution does not tally with the biblical description of it as an inhabited city. Albright's view is that the tradition represented by the account in Joshua viii referred originally to the capture of the neighbouring town of Bethel. This is an attractive theory, in view of the uncertainty of some of the text, but it is perhaps safest to accept the possibility that there actually was a city there, even though no trace of it has been found in the excavation.

iv. Renewal of the covenant at Shechem (viii. 30–35). In a religious act of the utmost significance Joshua now reminded the Israelites of the true nature of their conquest. Making a pilgrimage into the heart of enemy country, he led the people to Shechem, and there, in surroundings rendered sacred by association with the patriarchs, and in accordance with the express command of Moses, he called them to renew their allegiance to Jehovah and to hear the conditions on which they were to retain possession of the land. See Dt. xi. 29, 30, xxvii. 1–26, and notes there. An altar of undressed stones was erected on mount Ebal, and solemn sacrifices were offered; a copy of the Law of Moses was written upon plastered stones and read aloud to the vast multitude, and public proclamation was made of its blessings and curses. Six tribes on Gerizim said 'Amen' to the blessings, and six on Ebal said 'Amen' to the curses. 'History can furnish few scenes so impressive in moral grandeur as that of a nation thus solemnly embracing God's law as the rule of its life and the condition of its prosperity' (Fairweather, *From the Exodus to the Monarchy*).

c. The second stage: the campaign in the south (ix. 1—x. 43)

i. Compromise with the Gibeonites (ix. 1–27). Israel's successes against Jericho and Ai had two contrasting consequences. On the one hand, opposition hardened and became more highly organized (ix. 1, 2, x. 1–43); on the other, some of the inhabitants of the land were prepared to make terms with the invaders (ix. 3–27).

The central part of the country was thrown wide open to the invaders by the defection of the Gibeonite cities—Gibeon, Chephirah, Beeroth and Kirjath-jearim (17). They are called Hivites in verse 7 (cf. Jdg. iii. 3n.). By pretending that they were ambassadors from a far country and therefore constituted no threat to Israel's advance, their representatives induced the Israelites to form an alliance with them and to guarantee that their lives would be spared. Their worn clothes, patched (*clouted*) shoes, and obviously old provisions convinced the princes of Israel that they had indeed come from a far country, especially since they had apparently heard only of the exploits of Israel beyond Jordan and knew nothing of Jericho and Ai (9, 10). A treaty was concluded before the deception was discovered; the men of Israel *took of their victuals*, thereby pledging themselves to friendship, and *asked not counsel at the mouth of the Lord* (14). The discovery of the fraud was made when Israel came to the cities of the Gibeonites; but the agreement was sacred and could not be annulled, despite the protests of some of the people. Justice was done by reducing the Gibeonites to the position of slaves of the sanctuary. Cf. Dt. xxix. 11. *Now therefore ye are cursed* (23) are Joshua's words; not God's. For the curse that came upon them was a blessing. 'Blessed are they that dwell in thy house' (Ps. lxxxiv. 4). That was the curse that fell on the Gibeonites—to be attached for ever to the congregation and to the altar of the Lord, in the place that He should choose (27). Such is the grace of God. It was for the Gibeonites that He wrought the miracle of the battle of Beth-horon (x. 7-15); and it was among them afterwards that He pitched His tent (2 Ch. i. 3): and in still later days, when priests and Levites failed, He made them take their places (see Ezr. ii. 43n., viii. 20).

The defection of the Gibeonites at this stage helped Joshua to drive a wedge still further into Central Palestine.

ii. Conquest of the southern confederacy (x. 1-43). The news of the treaty between Israel and the Gibeonites was the signal for war. Five kings of the Amorites resolved not only to punish their former allies for their treachery, but to crush Joshua at a point where defeat would be fatal to his plans. The confederacy was led by Adoni-zedec, king of Jerusalem (cf. Melchi-zedek in Gn. xiv. 18), which had for long been a city of great influence; the other members were the kings of Hebron, Jarmuth, Lachish and Eglon. Their united forces laid siege to Gibeon, whose inhabitants urgently appealed for help.

Joshua, encouraged by a reminder of his original commission (8; cf. i. 5), made a forced march by night from Gilgal, and fell upon the allied force at Gibeon. The Lord discomfited (10), i.e. sent a panic among them, and they broke and fled, past Upper and Lower Beth-horon, which were linked by a pass, called at its upper end 'the ascent of Beth-horon' (10, RV), and at its lower end 'the going down (or descent) of Beth-horon' (11, RV), and leading down from the heights of Gibeon to the western plain, towards Makkedah and Azekah. But they were not destined to escape, for the Lord intervened once again to help His people, and a great storm of hailstones killed multitudes of them and completed the rout.

There follows a quotation taken from the book of Jasher (13) (more accurately 'Jashar'), which seems to have been a collection of songs in praise of the heroes of Israel. It records Joshua's prayer: Sun, stand thou still upon Gibeon; and thou, Moon, in the valley of Ajalon and asserts that in answer the sun stood still, and the moon stayed, until the people had avenged themselves upon their enemies (12, 13). Two questions are raised by the passage. Where does the quotation begin and end? and how are we to explain the episode here recorded?

The quotation evidently begins at verse 12, and since Joshua did not return to Gilgal until after the utter defeat of the enemy—his return is narrated in verse 43—we must take it that verse 13 is part of the record taken from the book of Jashar.

Secondly, did the sun stand still? One explanation of the episode that has been offered is that the narrator has taken what was merely a highly figurative poetical description of God's intervention on behalf of Israel as historical fact. But there is no reason to reject a more literal interpretation, though this passage has often been the butt of scientific scorn, much of which, it

seems possible, may be based on a misunderstanding of the record. It has usually been unquestioningly assumed that Joshua prayed for the day to be prolonged. But is it not possible that what Joshua needed even more, since, as is expressly stated in verse 9, he came upon the camp of the enemy by night, was that the darkness should continue and the night be prolonged for his surprise attack? That it was early morning when he made his request is evident from the position of the moon in the valley of Ajalon (to the west) and the position of the sun over Gibeon (to the east) (12). The answer to his prayer came in a hailstorm which had the effect of prolonging the darkness.

An investigation of the exact meaning of the Hebrew words used confirms this interpretation. The word translated stand still means literally 'be silent' and frequently has the sense 'cease' or 'leave off', as also has the word translated 'stayed' (see Lam. ii. 18; 2 Ki. iv. 6); and the natural meaning of the word translated go down in the phrase hasted not to go down is simply 'come' or 'go'. Only once, in Gn. xxviii. 11, has it the meaning 'set'. The phrase can therefore be translated, 'The sun made no haste to come, about a whole day . . .' And so in the darkness of the storm the defeat of the enemy was complete. A more spectacular miracle is demanded by the more usual translation of the passage. W. J. Phythian-Adams in a well-authenticated article in the Palestine Exploration Quarterly, July–Oct., 1946, associates the phenomenon of this chapter and other parts of the conquest with the fall of a meteorite. A similar view is put forward in Velikovski's Worlds in Collision, which has achieved wide popularity, though it has not found favour with scientists. A good discussion of the question from the point of view of the more usual interpretation of the passage is found in Rendle Short's Modern Discovery and the Bible. These are all interesting contributions to a discussion of the question, but on the interpretation suggested above are unnecessary. It should be noted, however, that one is not disparaging the miraculous nature of the occurrence by suggesting that there was a less spectacular divine intervention than is postulated by the more customary interpretation. It was still God who lengthened the night by a miraculous intervention on behalf of His people.

The five kings had taken refuge in a cave at Makkedah (16), but the pursuit did not halt to deal with them; afterwards they were brought out, and when the captains of the Israelites had put their feet upon the necks of their prisoners to symbolize complete subjection, they were slain, their bodies hanged on trees until the evening and then entombed in the cave where they had fled for shelter.

This victory at Beth-horon inaugurated a campaign, which may have lasted for a considerable time, and the whole of southern Palestine was finally brought under Israel's control. The chapter closes with a summary of the conquest of the south from Gibeon and Gaza to Kadesh-barnea and Goshen. The carefully recorded detail is most certainly a mark of genuineness. Archaeological investigation has confirmed that the cities of this area suffered violent and complete destruction about this time. Lachish, for example, has been identified with Tell-el-Duweir (Albright and Garstang), and Eglon with Tell-el-Hesy: and both places give evidence of being overthrown by violence and fire.

d. The third stage: the campaign in the north (xi. 1–23)

i. Conquest of the northern confederacy (xi. 1–15). Joshua's successful campaign in the south aroused the alarm of the northern Canaanitish kings. Led by Jabin, king of Hazor (lit. 'the fortress'), they formed a great confederacy against Israel. This included Jabin's nearest neighbours, but the call to arms was not confined to them, but included the kings in the hill country of the north and in *the plains* (RV, 'Arabah') *south of Chinneroth* (2), a city on the Lake of Galilee. Cf. Jos. xii. 3 RV. 'Arabah' was the name given to the lowlands of the Jordan valley. The remnants of the defeated armies of the south were also summoned to make a supreme effort to repel the invaders.

All these forces, equipped with chariots and cavalry, mustered at the waters of Merom, a stream flowing into the Sea of Galilee from the north-west. Joshua was encouraged for the battle by the assurance of God's presence and of victory and was commanded to burn the chariots and hamstring the horses of the enemy (6), so that they could not be used afterwards by the Canaanites or by the victorious Israelites, who might thus be tempted to put their trust in horses. A sudden attack once again struck panic into the hearts of the Canaanites, *and the Lord delivered them into the hand of Israel* (8), who smote them and pursued them in headlong flight. Hazor was burned to the ground and its inhabitants utterly destroyed, but the smaller cities that 'stood on their mounts' (13, RV, rather than AV *stood still in their strength*) were left. Perhaps now that the Israelites were established in the land these were no longer a danger, but rather an advantage to settlers. Cf. Dt. ii. 34n. and xx. 17n.

ii. Summary of conquest (xi. 16–23). The battles of Beth-horon and Merom were decisive, and the power of the Canaanites to resist the invaders was shattered. All organized resistance was broken down. *And the land rested from war* (23) in the sense that no more pitched battles were required. But the completion of the campaign took *a long time* (18), and even at the end of Joshua's life there remained *yet very much land to be possessed* (xiii. 1). To deal with the parts of the country still unsubdued was now to be the responsibility of the individual tribes. A special note is made of the defeat of the Anakim, perhaps because it had been they who had terrified the spies of Israel so disastrously forty years before.

e. List of conquered Canaanite kings (xii. 1–24) This list may be regarded as an appendix to the history of the wars of Joshua, concluding the story of the conquest before going on to the colonization of the country. Verses 1–6 deal with the conquests *on the other* (eastern) *side Jordan* (1) under Moses (6). See Nu. xxi and Dt. ii. 24—iii. 17. The remainder of the chapter lists Joshua's successes in Canaan, *this side Jordan* (7). It is remarkable that such a small country should contain so many kings, even though these had merely local authority; its divisions were one factor which made the task of the Israelites easier than it might otherwise have been, though it should be noted that in face of an external threat the kings tended to combine their forces, as at Beth-horon in the south and Merom in the north.

IV. THE DIVISION OF THE LAND. xiii. 1—xxii. 34

The remaining chapters of the book of Joshua have been described as 'the geographical manual of the Holy Land, the Domesday Book of the Conquest of Palestine'. The necessarily detailed account of the settlement of the tribes given in these chapters may make it difficult to see the wood for the trees; and so it may be helpful to indicate in advance the broad outline of the colonization.

Reuben, Gad and the half-tribe of Manasseh already had their territory allotted to them on the east of Jordan. See Nu. xxxii. 1–42. Their settlement is described in chapter xiii.

Of the territory which was already in possession on the west of Jordan the main division was between the tribes of Judah and Joseph; the allotment made to the other tribes depended on this fundamental division.

The tribe of Judah were given their possession in the south—the territory of the five kings (chapter xv); with them were associated Caleb (xiv. 1–15, xv. 13–19) and, in the later division of the land, the tribe of Simeon (xix. 1–9) because 'the part of the children of Judah was too much for them' (xix. 9).

The powerful house of Joseph—the tribes of Manasseh and Ephraim—received the rich inheritance of Central Palestine (chapters xvi, xvii). They were handicapped, however, by the row of fortresses, Bethshean, Ibleam, Dor, Taanach and Megiddo (xvii. 11, 12; cf. xvi. 10), which barred the road to the north, and complained of the inadequacy of their possession (xvii. 14). Joshua assured them that though their possession was like a forest they should hew down its powerful inhabitants and finally dispossess the Canaanites, 'though they have chariots of iron, and though they be strong' (xvii. 15–18). Joshua chose Timnath-serah for his own inheritance (xix. 49, 50).

Between these two powerful sections of the nation, Judah and Joseph, territory was later assigned to Benjamin (xviii. 11–28), and, nearer the sea coast, to Dan (xix. 40–48); but the tribe of Dan had difficulty in maintaining themselves against the inhabitants of the coastal plain (Jdg. i. 34, 35), and later migrated to the far north.

The remaining tribes, Zebulun, Issachar, Asher and Naphtali, which, like Simeon, Benjamin and Dan, had not had their portion allotted to them in the first division of the land, were later established in the northern part of the country. See xix. 10–39.

PALESTINE DIVIDED AMONG THE TWELVE TRIBES

a. Command to divide the land (xiii. 1–7)

Though there still remained much land to be possessed, Joshua's age and growing frailty demanded that an allotment of the land, by anticipation if not by complete conquest, should be made (1). The chief sections where the Canaanites were still strong were the country of the Philistines on the south-west coast and the territory in the north of the country; but the command was given for a division of the whole land between the nine and a half tribes to be made, since final victory was assured (6, 7).

b. Territory of the two and a half tribes (xiii. 8–33)

Reuben, Gad and the half tribe of Manasseh had already been allotted their portion in eastern Palestine, and the boundaries of each of these tribes were now fixed, Reuben being placed in the south, Gad in the centre and Manasseh in

the north. Cf. Nu. xxxii and Dt. iii. 12–17. *Unto the tribe of Levi he gave none inheritance* (14; cf. xiv. 3, 4). Moses had left instructions for the allocating of cities to the Levites (see Nu. xxxv. 1–8), but they were to have no tribal area. Cf. Nu. xviii. 20–24. The appointing of the cities is dealt with later in chapter xxi.

c. Territory of Caleb and Judah (xiv. 1—xv. 63)

Caleb now sought the fulfilment of the promise made to him in Dt. i. 36 (cf. Nu. xiv. 24, 30), and at his own request was given the strong city of Hebron for his inheritance out of the possession of Judah. Chapter xv. 15–19 describes how he claimed and enlarged this inheritance by conquest, aided by the valour of his kinsman Othniel who became his son-in-law. The boundaries of Judah are described, and their cities enumerated; and it is noted that the tribe was unable to take possession of the fortified city of Jerusalem (xv. 63). *Valley* (xv. 33). 'Lowland' (RV); i.e. the Shephelah or western plain bordering the sea. *Mountains* (xv. 48). 'Hill country' (RV); i.e. the central highlands. *Wilderness* (61), the slopes of the hills leading down into the Arabah or Jordan plain.

d. Territory of Ephraim and Manasseh (xvi. 1—xvii. 18)

The territory of Ephraim and the remaining half-tribe of Manasseh was, as we have seen, the central part of the country. Ephraim had the rich district north and south of Shechem—the southern portion—and Manasseh the northern part fringed by the Canaanite fortresses that guarded the fertile plain of Esdraelon. Their inability to penetrate beyond these was a cause of complaint (xvii. 14), but Joshua in effect told them that if they were the great people they claimed to be they could extend their territory by conquest. In xvi. 1–4 note the RV rendering. The importance of a good water supply is indicated here and in xv. 9, 19. In xvii. 3–6 the daughters of Zelophehad claim and receive the possession promised to them by Moses. See Nu. xxvii. 1–11 and xxxvi. 1–12.

e. Territory of the seven tribes (xviii. 1—xix. 51)

It seems that the previous division of the land was carried out at Gilgal; but now the whole congregation removed to Shiloh, the earliest of the Hebrew sanctuaries, and set up the tabernacle there. See 1 Sa. i. 3 and cf. Je. vii. 12. For the seven tribes who were still without defined inheritance a rough survey of the land was made by a commission of twenty-one members, three from each tribe; the whole territory was then divided up into seven portions for which lots were then cast in Shiloh (xviii. 2–10). Verse 5 stresses that the further allocation of the land must be made with due regard to the positions already occupied by Judah and Joseph. Benjamin's inheritance was allotted between that of Judah and Ephraim (xviii. 11–28), and Simeon's was taken out of the possession of Judah, which had proved too large for them (xix. 1–9). Simeon was ultimately absorbed into Judah in literal fulfilment of the curse pronounced on Simeon and Levi—'I will divide (or disperse) them in Jacob, and scatter them in Israel' (Gn. xlix. 7).

The northern part of the country was allotted to Zebulun, Issachar, Asher and Naphtali. Issachar was settled on the northern border of Manasseh, separated from it by the line of Canaanite fortresses already mentioned. Zebulun had the area immediately north of Issachar, comprising the inland plain which was traversed by the most useful trade route of antiquity, the 'Way of the Sea', and extending to the sea coast. Asher and Naphtali divided the territory still further north, Asher's possession lying along the coast and stretching to the great commercial city of Tyre, and Naphtali's to the east of it.

Dan's allotment was a small territory compressed into the narrow space between the north-western hills of Judah and the sea. Verse 47 indicates that this territory was too small for them; and this is supplemented by Jdg. i. 34, which tells that the Amorites (the Philistines) forced them into the hills. The majority of the tribe accordingly migrated later to the far north and settled in Leshem (Laish); a full account of the migration is given in Jdg. xviii. See notes there.

Joshua chose his own inheritance in Timnath-serah in the territory of Ephraim.

f. Cities of refuge appointed (xx. 1–9)

According to the directions given in the Law of Moses, the six cities of refuge were set apart and sanctified ('appointed') for the asylum of those who had committed unintentional homicide. See Dt. xix. 4–6. The fugitive had to justify his claim to protection by first convincing the elders of the city of refuge of his innocence of murderous intentions, and then standing his trial before the congregation. At the death of the High Priest he was free to return home without fear of the avenger of blood.

In Dt. iv. 41–43 Moses 'separated' three cities east of Jordan. In Dt. xix. 1–10 he orders three more to be separated when they dwell in the land and provides for a third triad if needed. See also Nu. xxxv. 9–34. Joshua and Eleazar now appointed (RV, 'set apart') three cities in the west, Kedesh, Shechem and Kirjath-arba, and 'assigned', or handed over for use, the three formerly designated by Moses in Transjordan.

g. Cities of the Levites appointed (xxi. 1–45)

When all the tribes had received their inheritance, the Levites claimed the cities which had been promised to them by Moses. See Nu. xxxv. 1–8. As the representatives of the Hebrew faith and the ministers of its worship, it was necessary that they should be dispersed throughout the whole nation, and also that they should maintain their distinct position. To achieve both these purposes, they were given forty-eight cities out of all the tribes, along with the circle of pasture land (*suburbs*) around each of them. It may be that this pasture land, as distinct from agricultural land, was to be a reminder of the simple life which Israel had lived in the wilderness, and a constant recall to the simple religion with which that life was linked. Certainly the Levites were to be the custodians of the nation's spiritual life.

Levi's three sons gave their names to the three great branches of the Levites, the Kohathites, the Gershonites and the Merarites. The Kohathites were subdivided into the priests (Aaron's sons) and those who did not fill the priestly office: and the Levitical cities were therefore divided among these four sections of the Levites. It must be noted that once again the cities were allocated by anticipation and it seems that some of them, e.g. Gezer, were not occupied at this time.

This concludes the allocation of territory and cities and the section ends with three verses extolling the faithfulness of God: *There failed not aught of any good thing which the Lord had spoken unto the house of Israel; all came to pass* (45).

h. Return of the eastern tribes and setting up of the altar of witness (xxii. 1–34)

The final incident of the colonization was the dismissal of the eastern tribes to their own inheritance on the other side of Jordan. Having commended them warmly for their loyalty, Joshua sent them off with a solemn warning not to let their isolation make them forget their allegiance to Jehovah (1–9).

To denote their unity with the main body of Israel, the eastern tribes built a massive altar on the bank of the Jordan. Verse 11 makes it clear that it was on the western side of the river that it was built; *over against the land of Canaan* should be translated literally 'facing the same way as Canaan', i.e. on the same side. *At the passage of the children of Israel* is better translated, as in RV, 'on the side that pertaineth to the children of Israel'.

This innocent act was misconstrued by the western tribes as an attempt to set up a second altar of sacrifice, contrary to the Mosaic law (see Lv. xvii. 8, 9), and a deputation was sent from Shiloh, the site of the tabernacle, to investigate the alleged treachery (AV *trespass*) of their brethren. They reminded them of the disasters to the whole community that had followed previous acts of apostasy at Baal-peor and Ai, and magnanimously suggested that if the land to the east of Jordan was 'unclean' in the sense of not being hallowed by the evident presence of Jehovah, the eastern tribes could take their possession in the west.

The eastern tribes made their defence in the most solemn terms, swearing by the three names of their God (El, Elohim, Jehovah), twice repeated (22, see RV mg.), that the altar they had built was nothing more than a permanent monument to their kinship with the tribes across the river. Their action was 'out of carefulness . . . and of purpose' (24, RV), i.e. it was done deliberately in their anxiety lest their children should fail to realize their connection with the commonwealth of Israel.

The explanation was promptly accepted and a happy reconciliation ensued: the altar itself became a perpetual witness of the episode.

V. JOSHUA'S LAST DAYS. xxiii. 1—xxiv. 33

a. First address (xxiii. 1–16)

The book of Joshua begins with his call to leadership; it ends with his farewell addresses and the account of his death. This first address, given to the leaders of the people, reminded them of their own experience of God's faithfulness under his leadership: not one good thing of all God's promises had failed. Verse 10 should be translated not as future but as a generalization of their experience—'One of you could put a thousand to flight, because it is the Lord your God who has fought for you'. In view of God's faithfulness in His dealings with Israel, Joshua called for their faithfulness to Him. Their experience of God demanded courage for the future, loyalty to the divine law and separation from every evil thing. He warned them that apostasy would mean the turning of all the good they had known to terrible evil.

b. Second address (xxiv. 1–28)

Joshua's second farewell address, given amid the sacred surroundings of Shechem, went further back in its reminders of God's faithfulness. The recapitulation is given in the words of Jehovah Himself: the call of Abraham and the deliverance from Egypt were evidences of His special relationship to His people; in their own experience the defeat of the Amorites and the frustration of Balaam's evil designs, the crossing of the Jordan and the capture of Jericho, and the defeat of the nations of Canaan reinforced what history could teach them of God's mercies.

I sent the hornet before you, which drave them out from before you (12). In this striking sentence Jehovah stresses the fact that none of Israel's victories was of their own winning. Many commentators have taken the hornet merely as an expressive figure for the terror which Israel's advance inspired in their enemies. But Garstang, who argues for the earlier of the two dates for the exodus (see Introduction, p. 223), gives convincing reasons in his book *Joshua–Judges* for identifying the hornet with the sacred symbol of the Pharaohs, and maintains that earlier spoliation of Canaan by the Egyptians had devastated the country. After the sack of Megiddo by Thutmose III in 1479 B.C. Egypt carried on what seems to have been 'a deliberate policy of devastation' for over sixty years, until the accession of Amenhotep III in 1411 B.C. 'Thereafter', says Garstang, 'for fifty years no army was led by the Pharaoh into Syria': internal weakness, it seems, was responsible for this interlude; and it was just at the beginning of it, about 1406 B.C.,

that Joshua and the Israelites appeared before the walls of Jericho. They advanced on a land which had been softened up for their attack by this strange instrument—Egypt—in Jehovah's hand. An objection to Garstang's view is based on the fact that in Ex. xxiii. 28 and in Dt. vii. 20 (forty years later) the sending of the hornet is still spoken of as future: in Jos. xxiv. 12 the promise has been fulfilled and the hornet has been sent. Therefore the hornet attack must have coincided exactly with the years of the invasion and conquest under Joshua, and could not have been the much earlier softening-up process suggested by Garstang. This objection might be met by considering the *consequences* of the sending of the hornet as future so far as the children of Israel were concerned in Ex. xxiii. 28 and Dt. vii. 20, even though the event which was to have such consequences had already happened. When the children of Israel entered the land they would find that 'the hornet' had been sent before them; but when it had been sent was of no consequence to them. They would see its effects only when they entered the land, and so the sending of it might be considered future so far as they were concerned. The alternative is to interpret the passage as a reference to a literal plague of hornets which helped to depopulate areas of the land by driving the inhabitants to other parts.

In view of Jehovah's actions in history and in their own experience, Joshua solemnly called the people to loyalty—*serve him in sincerity and in truth* (14). Then follows the great challenge of verse 15. *The other side of the flood* is a reference to Ur of the Chaldees, beyond the Euphrates. The people answered their leader in promises that were too glib and too easy, and he reminded them that it was no slight thing which they were binding themselves to do. *Ye cannot serve the Lord* (19). But the people protested, *Nay; but we will serve the Lord* (21), and Joshua then bound them in the most solemn way possible. The covenant was solemnly renewed, and a great stone was set up under the famous oak of Shechem as a witness of the nation's dedication of itself to God.

c. Joshua's death and burial (xxiv. 29–33)

So Joshua died at a good old age, and the greatest tribute to his life was paid when the sacred writer wrote, *And Israel served the Lord all the days of Joshua, and all the days of the elders that overlived Joshua* (31).

The book closes with the account of the burying of the body of Joseph, carried through all the wanderings of the wilderness and at last laid to rest in the Promised Land. It may be, as many commentators have maintained, that his burial took place long before the death of Joshua. But surely it was inspired editing which placed the account of it here, symbolizing at the close the message of the whole book of Joshua—the faithfulness of God.

HUGH J. BLAIR.

JUDGES

INTRODUCTION

I. TITLE

The book of Judges (Heb. *shopheṭim*) is so called from the successive figures who are depicted in it as raised up by Yahweh to deliver the tribes of Israel from their enemies and to 'judge' them— i.e. not necessarily to rule them, but to execute the judgment of God on their behalf. The word *shopheṭim* is cognate with the Phoenician word by which, according to Roman writers, the chief magistrates of Carthage were known 1,000 years later (*suffetes*). In the Samaritan records the judges are called 'kings'. In the Hebrew Bible Judges is the second book of the 'Former Prophets', following Joshua and preceding Samuel and Kings.

II. HISTORICAL BACKGROUND

Judges deals with the first two or three centuries following the entry of the tribes of Israel into Canaan under Joshua (*c.* 1250–1200 B.C.). This period coincides with the beginning of the Iron Age in the Middle East. The Iron Age was inaugurated when an effective and economic process for smelting iron was devised. Iron is much commoner than copper and tin, the constituents of the metal which gave its name to the preceding Bronze Age, but not so easy to work. To be sure, we have isolated examples of wrought-iron implements several centuries earlier, frequently of meteoric iron; but not until the metal could be produced in bulk did its use begin to affect the course of civilization. When such a process was devised, the consequences were radical and far-reaching, for agriculture and industry as well as for warfare. The first place where it was devised was apparently in the district of Kizzuwatna, in eastern Asia Minor, in the territory of the Hittite Empire, about 1400 B.C. The Hebrew word for iron, *barzel*, is borrowed from Hittite *barzillu*. The kings of the Hittites and of the neighbouring Mitanni Empire adopted a policy of secrecy over the production, and controlled the output and export of iron. The Mitanni kings sent presents of iron objects to the Pharaohs, until Mitanni was conquered by the Hittites *c.* 1370 B.C.; but when Rameses II wrote to ask the Hittite king Hattusilis III for a supply of iron about 1260 B.C., his royal 'brother' put him off on various pretexts and sent him only one dagger. Such a policy of secrecy, however, was no more successful in antiquity than today; and by about 1200 B.C. the Bronze Age in the Middle East, with its great civilizations, passes out in the crashing of

empires, and the Iron Age dawns amid barbaric invasions.

In the Old Testament the advent of the Iron Age is reflected in the iron bedstead (or was it a basalt sarcophagus?) of Og king of Bashan, a museum-piece for later ages (Dt. iii. 11); in the iron chariots of the Canaanites (Jos. xvii. 16), including Sisera's 900 chariots of iron (Jdg. iv. 3); and in the Philistine retention of the monopoly of iron-working to the disadvantage of the Israelites (1 Sa. xiii. 19–22).

The Israelite entry into Canaan and settlement in the land was contemporary with a great movement of peoples in the Middle East (probably itself the result of large-scale 'folk-wanderings' in the Eurasian steppe-lands), which involved the downfall of the Minoan, Hittite and Mycenean Empires. Canaan found itself the centre of a great movement of invading bands, both from the land and from the sea. Its connection with Egypt was close under the Asiatic Hyksos dynasties (*c.* 1720–1580 B.C.); and the kings of the eighteenth dynasty (1580–1319), who expelled the Hyksos rulers, added Canaan to the Egyptian Empire. But towards the end of that dynasty we find the cities of Eastern Canaan attacked by people called the Habiru, a name given to semi-nomadic groups whom we meet all over Western Asia from the eighteenth to the thirteenth century B.C. The word 'Habiru' may be identical with 'Hebrews', the name of the group to which the Israelites belonged, though these Habiru are probably not to be identified with the Israelites led by Joshua. The diplomatic correspondence of the reign of Akhnaton (1377–1360), recorded on the tablets uncovered at Tell el-Amarna in 1887, contains despairing pleas from provincial governors in Canaan for help against the Habiru—help which never came.

In the earlier years of the nineteenth dynasty (1319–1200) an attempt was made by the Egyptian kings to reconquer Canaan, in the course of which they came into conflict with the Hittite Empire north of Palestine. After the indecisive battle of Kadesh on the Upper Orontes in 1297, the two emperors struck a treaty (*c.* 1280) and agreed on the delimitation of their realms— wisely, because both had cause to look anxiously over their shoulders at menaces from fresh quarters. The Hittite king was threatened by the Assyrians on the east, while from the west the Ahhiyawa (Achaeans?) pressed him hard, themselves pushed by the force of folk-migrations farther inside Europe; as for Egypt, its coasts began to be attacked by raiders from the sea.

These were repulsed by Merenptah (*c.* 1230 B.C.), as was also a second raiding coalition in the reign of Rameses III (*c.* 1194); but, unable to gain a footing in Egypt, some of them settled on the Canaanite coast. Of these the most notable were the Philistines, who speedily established and maintained their hegemony over great areas of Canaan until the reign of David (1010–970). It was they who gave to the country its name of Palestine, abridged from Gk. *Syria Palaistinē*, i.e. 'Philistine Syria'.

III. ERA OF THE JUDGES

In this historical setting we must place the Israelites' entry into Canaan and the era of the judges. But the exact point in this period at which the conquest is to be dated is not easy to determine. Various dates between 1400 and 1200 B.C. have been suggested. The events of Judges may be dated between 1250 and 1050 B.C.

J. Garstang, who places the entry into Canaan about 1400 B.C., in conformity with his dating of the destruction of Jericho, has worked out in his book *Joshua-Judges* (1931) a system of coincidences of the chronology of Egypt and Israel in the period of the judges, by which he makes it appear that the successive periods of 'rest' in Judges corresponded with those periods in which the Egyptian influence was dominant in Palestine. The periods of oppression then coincide with the years in which the Egyptian power was weaker and the peoples in and around Canaan could act with greater freedom. There are, however, grave difficulties in the way of dating the invasion of Canaan so early as Garstang does. It was not, apparently, until the thirteenth century B.C. that the Transjordanian kingdoms were founded, and they existed as kingdoms towards the end of the wilderness wanderings. Again, Garstang's scheme assumes all the judges to have been consecutive, whereas some of them at least arose simultaneously in separate parts of the land.

Even from the archaeological evidence on the site of Jericho, Garstang's dating of the fall of Jericho is too early, probably by several decades, and possibly by over a century. According to W. F. Albright, 'the evidence points to a date . . . in the latter part of the fourteenth century or the early thirteenth for the fall of Jericho; it must, however, be frankly confessed that our evidence against a date somewhat later in the thirteenth century . . . is mainly negative' (*The Archaeology of Palestine* [1949], pp. 108f.). The veteran French archaeologist L. H. Vincent has never wavered from a dating in the second half of the thirteenth century for the fall of Jericho. On all the aspects of this and related questions see H. H. Rowley, *From Joseph to Joshua* (1950). (See also the Introduction to Joshua, p. 224, and the chronological table on p. 38.)

IV. AUTHOR'S APPROACH TO HISTORY

The title 'Father of History' is traditionally, and with reason, accorded to Herodotus, the Greek historian, who wrote in the second half of the fifth century B.C. His predecessors were mere annalists or chroniclers; but an historian must be something more. He must see the underlying operation of cause and effect; he will have a philosophy of history by which he can present the course of events as the expression of basic principles. In this respect Herodotus had predecessors in the historians of Israel. To them history was the story of God's dealing with His people and the other nations; they penetrated beneath the surface to find the root cause of events in the ways of God. The historians from Joshua to 2 Kings are frequently said to display the Deuteronomic philosophy of history, so called because it finds clearest expression in Deuteronomy. The cause of prosperity is found in obedience to the will of God, and especially in avoidance of the native Baalism of Canaan, with its demoralizing fertility cults; adversity is the sure sequel to departure from this strait path. This attitude is plain in the framework of Judges. The people's lapsing from the worship of Yahweh and their serving of other gods is regularly followed by foreign oppression; then they cry to Yahweh in their affliction and He raises up a deliverer for them.

This picture of the history of the period is no pious fiction. When the tribes maintained their loyalty to Yahweh and the Sinaitic covenant, symbolized by the ark, they were united and strong; when they lapsed into Baalism their bond of union was lost and they were divided and weak. The times of deliverance were therefore generally accompanied by a return to the faith which they had learned in the wilderness, in the strength of which, nomads as they were, they were able to overthrow the more highly civilized nations of Canaan.

V. DATE AND COMPOSITION

As for the date of the book in its present form, we have a few indications: the words 'all the time that the house of God was in Shiloh' (xviii. 31) imply a time later than the destruction of Shiloh in the days of Samuel; the repeated words 'In those days there was no king in Israel' (xvii. 6, xviii. 1, etc.) suggest a date under the monarchy; the reference in xviii. 30, 'until the day of the captivity of the land', probably indicates the Assyrian captivity in the eighth century B.C., i.e. the carrying away of the population of Galilee by Tiglath-pileser III in 732.

The author's 'philosophy of history' may suggest a date after Josiah's reformation (621 B.C.), which was based on the recovery of the Deuteronomic law-code. E. Robertson, in *The Old Testament Problem* (1950), pp. 159ff., finds internal evidence that Judges belongs to a time when the rivalry between Jews and Samaritans was keen. Jdg. i. 21, indeed, more naturally indicates a date earlier than David's capture of Jerusalem (*c.* 1003 B.C.), and Jdg. i. 29 must be earlier than the acquisition of Gezer by Solomon

(c. 950). But such evidences of earlier date simply show that the component parts of Judges are mostly older than the finished book as it has come down to us. For the author had at his disposal much ancient material, the oldest being the Song of Deborah (v. 1–31), contemporary with the event it celebrates. Most of his materials he has arranged so as to bring out his philosophy of history. The main part of the book—the tale of repeated falling into idolatry, foreign oppression, deliverance by a 'saviour'—is put in a framework built up on a recurring form of this nature: 'And the children of Israel did evil in the sight of the Lord, and the Lord sold them into the hand of A, king of B, who oppressed them x years. And they cried unto the Lord, and he raised up a saviour unto them, C the son of D, and he prevailed against A, king of B, and delivered Israel, and the land had rest y years (or: and he judged Israel y years)'.

Into such a framework as this are fitted the oppressions of Chushan-rishathaim, Eglon, Jabin, Midian, Ammon, and the Philistines, with the corresponding deliverances wrought respectively by Othniel, Ehud, Deborah and Barak, Gideon, Jephthah, and Samson. This main part of Judges (iii—xvi) contains also the incident of Shamgar (iii. 31), the story of Abimelech (ix. 1–57), and brief notes on the five minor judges, Tola and Jair, and Ibzan, Elon, and Abdon (x. 1–5, xii. 8–15). All this is preceded by an introductory summary of the conquest of the land (i. 1—ii. 10), drawn from an early source, some parts of which appear also in Joshua, and by a statement of the author's philosophy of history, explaining why so many of the heathen peoples were left in the land (ii. 11—iii. 4). The book is concluded by two unattached narratives, chronologically referring to the early part of the period of the judges, which have not been incorporated into the author's framework; the migration of the tribe of Dan (xvii—xviii), and the war against Benjamin (xix—xxi), both of which illustrate the unsettled conditions of those days when 'there was no king in Israel: every man did that which was right in his own eyes'.

It is unnecessary here to discuss the sources and composition of the individual narratives. These subjects are treated in critical detail in the standard commentaries. J. Garstang's *Joshua-Judges* (Constable, 1931) may be studied for the archaeological background, though it needs to be corrected and supplemented by reference to later findings.

OUTLINE OF CONTENTS

I. PARTIAL CONQUEST OF CANAAN BY ISRAEL. i. 1—ii. 5

II. WHY SOME GENTILE NATIONS WERE LEFT IN THE LAND. ii. 6—iii. 6

III. OPPRESSION UNDER CHUSHAN-RISHATHAIM AND DELIVERANCE BY OTHNIEL. iii. 7–11

IV. OPPRESSION UNDER EGLON KING OF MOAB AND DELIVERANCE BY EHUD. iii. 12–30

V. EXPLOITS OF SHAMGAR BEN ANATH. iii. 31

VI. OPPRESSION UNDER JABIN KING OF CANAAN AND DELIVERANCE BY DEBORAH AND BARAK. iv. 1–24, v. 31b

VII. THE SONG OF DEBORAH AND BARAK. v. 1–31a

VIII. OPPRESSION UNDER MIDIAN AND DELIVERANCE BY GIDEON. vi. 1—viii. 32

IX. THE STORY OF ABIMELECH. viii. 33—ix. 57

X. TOLA AND JAIR, MINOR JUDGES. x. 1–5

XI. OPPRESSION UNDER AMMON AND DELIVERANCE BY JEPHTHAH. x. 6—xii. 7

XII. IBZAN, ELON, ABDON, MINOR JUDGES. xii. 8–15

XIII. OPPRESSION UNDER THE PHILISTINES AND EXPLOITS OF SAMSON. xiii. 1—xvi. 31

XIV. MICAH'S PRIEST AND THE DANITE MIGRATION. xvii. 1—xviii. 31

XV. THE WAR AGAINST BENJAMIN. xix. 1—xxi. 25

COMMENTARY

I. PARTIAL CONQUEST OF CANAAN BY ISRAEL. i. 1—ii. 5

a. Conquest of South Canaan (i. 1-21)

Now after the death of Joshua it came to pass (1). This is commonly regarded as an editorial note; the death of Joshua appears in its chronological setting at ii. 8. Jdg. i is a collection of miscellaneous fragments: verses 2–21, the conquest of South Canaan by Judah and affiliated groups; verses 22–26, the capture of Bethel by the Joseph tribes; verses 27–36, a list of cities from which the central and northern tribes could not drive out their Canaanite inhabitants. On the relation between these fragments and the narrative of Joshua see G. E. Wright, 'The Literary and Historical Problem of Joshua x and Judges i', *Journal of Near Eastern Studies*, 5 (1946), pp. 105–114 (with critique by Rowley, *From Joseph to Joshua*, pp. 100f.). *Who shall go up for us . . . first?* (1). Nu. xxi. 1–3 records an Israelite invasion from the south earlier than that from the east; cf. Jdg. i. 16, 17. *And Judah said unto Şimeon his brother* (3). A tribe or nation is often spoken of in terms of its ancestor; this is obviously so here, but it is also found in places where it is not so obvious. Simeon ceased at an early date to be a separate tribe and was incorporated with Judah. *And Judah went up* (4). Part of this territory had been inhabited by Judah and his family before the descent into Egypt (Gn. xxxviii). *The Canaanites and the Perizzites* (4). The Perizzites are obscure, but may have been an aboriginal people of different race from the Canaanites. *They found Adonibezek in Bezek* (5). This Bezek was presumably in the south of Canaan, but is otherwise unknown. The name of its king means 'lord of Bezek'. *Cut off his thumbs and his great toes* (6). Probably to degrade him by mutilation, and not merely to disable him from the use of weapons. *They brought him to Jerusalem* (7). The earliest city, on the hill Ophel, south of the temple area, is shown by archaeological evidence to go back to c. 3000 B.C. Jerusalem is mentioned in Egyptian texts c. 1900 B.C., and is no doubt the Salem of Gn. xiv. 18. The Canaanite city was a mixed Hittite-Amorite foundation (Ezk. xvi. 3). It was one of the chief Canaanite city-states in the 'Amarna Age' (c. 1400–1360 B.C.). *Now the children of Judah had fought against Jerusalem, and had taken it* (8). 'And the children of Judah fought against Jerusalem, and took it' (RV). This has been connected, on doubtful grounds, with the Habiru threat to the city under its governor Puti-Hepa in the reign of Akhnaton (c. 1370 B.C.). In any case, this capture can have been only an isolated incident in the conquest, immediately followed by the city's recapture by the Jebusites (cf. i. 21).

Now the name of Hebron before was Kirjath-arba (10). Kiriath-arba (RV) means 'city of four', i.e. tetrapolis or fourfold city, pointing to an early 'confederacy', which is the meaning of the name Hebron. According to Nu. xiii. 22 Hebron was built seven years before Tanis (Zoan) in Egypt. This probably refers to the Hyksos fortification of Tanis (Avaris), which dates the foundation of Hebron c. 1725 B.C. Jdg. i. 10–15 is parallel to Jos. xv. 14–19, where the capture of Hebron as well as of Debir is ascribed to Caleb. *And they slew Sheshai, and Ahiman, and Talmai* (10). These are named as 'children of Anak' (meaning perhaps 'the long-necked people') in the narrative of the spies in Nu. xiii. 22. Cf. Jdg. i. 20. *And from thence he went against the inhabitants of Debir* (11). The capture of Debir was easy after Hebron was taken. Its former name *Kirjath-sepher* (or Kiriath-sopher) means 'city of books' (or 'city of scribes'). The site (mod. Tell Beit Mirsim) has been excavated; the city is found to have been burnt c. 1230 B.C., and thereupon rebuilt with thinner walls, a smaller population and a lower culture. *Othniel the son of Kenaz, Caleb's younger brother, took it* (13). The 'sons of Kenaz' (Kenizzites), along with such other nomads as the Kenites (16) and the Jerahmeelites, were fused with the tribe of Judah.

The children of the Kenite, Moses' father in law (16). RV renders 'Moses' brother in law', regarding the Kenite in question as Hobab (cf. iv. 11). Heb. *ḥothen* (lit. 'circumciser'?) means *father in law* (AV), but if vocalized *ḥathan* it might mean 'brother in law' (RV). But the normal meaning of *ḥathan* is 'son-in-law' or 'bridegroom' (cf. Ex. iv. 25, 26), because at one time he was apparently circumcised by the father-in-law on the eve of the marriage. The Kenites (from Heb. *qain*, 'smith') were a nomad people, evidently travelling tinkers, inhabiting the Negeb and Arabah, neighbours of the Amalekites. *The city of palm trees* (16), i.e. date-palms. This expression usually denotes Jericho (cf. iii. 13); but the reference here may be to Tamar ('palm') eighty-five miles south of Arad. *Which lieth in the south of Arad* (16). Cf. the defeat of the king of Arad in Nu. xxi. 1–3. *And the name of the city was called Hormah* (17), i.e. 'devotion', in the sense of complete destruction. See Nu. xxi. 3 for another account, and cf. also Nu. xiv. 45; Dt. i. 44. *Also Judah took Gaza . . . Askelon . . . and Ekron* (18). These cities, with Ashdod and Gath, were shortly afterwards (early in the twelfth century) occupied by the Philistines. *He drave out the inhabitants of the mountain* (19). The Canaanites continued to maintain their centres of civilization on the lower ground which their iron chariots enabled them to control. Their knowledge of the working of iron, which the Israelites did not acquire till two centuries later, was derived from the Hittites and Mitanni (see Introduction). *And they gave Hebron unto Caleb* (20). Cf. Jos. xv. 13. *And the children of Benjamin did not drive out the Jebusites that inhabited Jerusalem* (21). Cf. Jos. xv. 63 where Judah is named instead of Benjamin. Cf. also Jos. xviii. 28. Jerusalem lay on the tribal border of Judah and Benjamin. The Jebusites were probably an Amorite group who settled on an earlier Hittite foundation in Jerusalem. *The Jebusites dwell with the children of Benjamin in Jerusalem unto this day* (21). This suggests a date for this part of Judges earlier than *c*. 1003 B.C., when David took the city, although the mixed Hittite-Amorite population continued to live there after that time; cf. Araunah the Jebusite (2 Sa. xxiv. 16) whose name has been thought to be an Indo-European Hittite word for 'nobleman'.

b. Capture of Bethel (i. 22–26)

And the house of Joseph, they also went up against Beth-el (22). We turn now from southern to central Canaan. Beth-el means 'the house of God' (cf. Gn. xii. 8, xiii. 3, 4, xxviii. 19; xxxi. 13, etc.); the name suggests an ancient sanctuary. Excavations on the site (mod. Beitin) show that it was burnt in the thirteenth century B.C. Here its capture is the first and most notable exploit of the house of Joseph. *And the man went into the land of the Hittites* (26), i.e. into North Syria, beyond the upper Orontes, the boundary between the Hittite and Egyptian Empires. This may indicate that the man was himself a member of the immigrant Hittite population which had settled in the hill country of Judah. The new city of Luz which the man founded is unknown.

c. Cities which Israel could not take (i. 27–36)

Neither did Manasseh drive out . . . Beth-shean . . . Taanach . . . Dor . . . Ibleam . . . Megiddo (27). Verses 27 and 28 are parallel to Jos. xvii. 11, 12. The cities named formed a line of Canaanite strong points across the Plain of Esdraelon from east to west, separating the Joseph tribes in central Canaan from the northern tribes. *Beth-shean* was occupied by Egyptian garrisons until the reign of Rameses III (1198–1167 B.C.). Early in the twelfth century *Dor* was occupied by the Thekels, one of the wandering sea-peoples. *Megiddo* was under Egyptian control during the first half of that century; then it was 'completely and violently destroyed' (G. E. Wright). *Neither did Ephraim drive out the Canaanites that dwelt in Gezer* (29). This is parallel to Jos. xvi. 10. *Gezer*, in the south-west of the territory of Ephraim, did not pass under Israelite control until *c*. 950 B.C. (cf. 1 Ki. ix. 16). *Neither did Asher drive out . . . Accho* ('Acco', RV), *nor . . . Zidon* (31). It was only along the Phoenician coast that the Canaanites maintained their independence, which they did until the sixth century B.C. *Acco* (N.T. Ptolemais) was used as a port though it had no properly protected harbour. *Zidon* in the time of the judges was more prominent than its sister-city Tyre, which gained the ascendancy by the time of David. Cf. Jos. xix. 28f. *Neither did Naphtali drive out . . . Beth-shemesh, nor . . . Beth-anath* (33). These were two sanctuaries, the former dedicated to the worship of the sun-god, and identified by J. Garstang with Kedesh-naphtali of iv. 6; the latter dedicated to the worship of Anath, the Canaanite goddess of fertility who appears in Ras Shamra tablets as the consort of Baal. *And the Amorites forced the children of Dan into the mountain* (34). This pressure soon caused the Danites to migrate northwards (see xviii). The Amorites (i.e. 'westerners'—from the Akkadian viewpoint) were Semitic invaders from the Arabian desert who arrived in the Fertile Crescent *c*. 2000 B.C. By 1750 they ruled the main cities from Syria to Babylon. The Amorite cities of verse 35 formed a barrier between the Joseph tribes and Judah. Their eastern border is given in verse 36 as *the going up to* ('ascent of', RV) *Akrabbim* (i.e. 'scorpions') in south-east Judah near the south of the Dead Sea, the district in which lay the Amorite Hazezon-tamar of Gn. xiv. 7.

d. The angel of the Lord at Bochim (ii. 1–5)

And an (RV, 'the') *angel of the Lord came up from Gilgal to Bochim* (1). The angel of Yahweh is the expression widely used in the Old Testament to denote Yahweh Himself in His manifestation to men. Cf. Jdg. vi. 11–24, xiii. 3–21. *Gilgal* (the name implies the presence of a circle, probably of standing stones) lies between the Jordan and Jericho, possibly on the site of mod. Khirbet el-Etheleh, near the pool Birket Jiljuliyeh. For *Bochim* the original text seems to have had 'Bethel', a reading which is preserved in LXX. *Ye shall make no league* (RV, 'covenant') *with the inhabitants of this land* (2). The words quoted in verses 2, 3 are part of the terms of Yahweh's covenant with Israel (cf. Ex. xxiii. 33, xxxiv. 12–16; Nu. xxxiii. 55; Dt. vii. 2, 5, 16, xii. 3). *They called the name of the place Bochim* (5), i.e. 'weepers'. Some have seen a connection with the 'oak of weeping' below Bethel (Gn. xxxv. 8).

II. WHY SOME GENTILE NATIONS WERE LEFT IN THE LAND. ii. 6—iii. 6

a. The death of Joshua and the elders (ii. 6–10)

And when Joshua had let the people go (6). Follow RV, 'Now when Joshua had sent the people away'. Cf. Jos. xxiv. 28–31. *And there arose another generation after them, which knew not the Lord* (10). Here begins the actual sequel to Joshua. For the language of this verse cf. Ex. i. 8.

b. The idolatry of the Israelites (ii. 11–13)

And the children of Israel did evil in the sight of the Lord, and served Baalim (11), i.e. the local varieties of the chief vegetation-god of Canaan (see verse 13). *And they forsook the Lord, and served Baal and Ashtaroth* (13). *Baal* ('lord') was a familiar name for the storm-god Hadad, son of El in the Canaanite mythology. He personified the rain and fertility-forces of nature, and his cult was attended by wild and enervating forms of licence. *Ashtaroth* is the plural of Ashtoreth or Ashtart (Gk. *Astarte*), the deity of the planet Venus, and in Palestine the consort of Baal.

(In North Syria his consort was Anath: see i. 33n.) There was a tendency to turn to Baal-worship in peace-time, as it was thought to ensure good harvests, but the pressure of invasion and war made Israel mindful of the God of their fathers who had led them to victory against their foes.

c. Summary of the period of the Judges (ii. 14–19)

Verses 14–19 are a general summary of Judges. *They could not any longer stand before their enemies* (14). In those periods when they exchanged the invigorating worship of Yahweh for the softening Baal-worship, the sense of Israelite unity was also lost because of the weakening of the covenant-bond which, in binding them to Yahweh, bound them also to each other; they thus presented a divided front to their assailants. *They went a whoring after other gods* (17). Idolatry is regularly represented as spiritual adultery, as the covenant relation between Yahweh and Israel is conceived of in terms of a marriage.

d. The leaving of some nations to prove Israel (ii. 20—iii. 6)

I also will not henceforth drive out any from before them of the nations which Joshua left when he died (21). Three reasons are given for Yahweh's allowing the Canaanites to remain in the land alongside Israel: to punish Israel for religious apostasy (ii. 3, 20, 21); to test Israel's fidelity to Yahweh (ii. 22, iii. 4); to provide Israel with experience in warfare (iii. 2). Dt. vii. 20–24 adds a fourth reason: to prevent the land from becoming a wilderness. *That through them I may prove Israel* (22). What we should express by a clause of result is here (as commonly in Heb.) expressed by a clause of purpose. *Even as many . . . as had not known all the wars of Canaan* (iii. 1), i.e. the generations following that which took part in the invasion and conquest. Here and in verse 2 the slowness of the conquest is represented as providential, to teach succeeding generations the art of war. Cf. Ex. xxiii. 29, 30; Dt. vii. 22. *Five lords of the Philistines* (3), i.e. the rulers of the five chief city-states, Ashdod, Ashkelon, Ekron, Gaza and Gath. The word translated 'lord' (Heb. *seren*) is not Semitic, but apparently a native Philistine word, taken by them from their Anatolian home. It appears to be cognate with Gk. *koiranos* or *tyrannos*. The Philistines seem to have come from Caria in Asia Minor. The Philistine guards of the palace in Jerusalem are called 'Carites' (Heb. *Karim*) in 2 Sa. xx. 23, RV mg.; 2 Ki. xi. 4, 19, RV. The other name, Chere-thites, by which they are sometimes called (1 Sa. xxx. 14), indicates a connection with Crete in the course of their migration southwards (cf. Am. ix. 7, where God brings up the Philistines from Caphtor, i.e. Crete). About 1190 B.C. they settled in Palestine (see p. 237) in territory previously occupied by the Avvim (cf. Dt. ii. 23). They later expanded north and east, conquering most of Palestine (see Jdg. xiii. 1). They are depicted on the monuments wearing helmets crowned with feathers, a head-dress which the ancients considered typically Carian. Their armour, as described in 1 Sa. xvii. 5–7, is reminiscent of that of the Homeric warriors. *And all the Canaanites* (3). Those mentioned in i. 27–33. *And the Sidonians* (3), i.e. the Phoenicians, so called because at this time their chief town was Sidon (see i. 31n.). *And the Hivites that dwelt in mount Lebanon* (3). These have not been identified with absolute certainty. The attempt by A. E. Cowley and A. H. Sayce to equate them with the Achaeans (comparing Heb. *Ḥiwwi* with Hitt. *Aḥḥiyawa*) has not commended itself. They are generally identified with the Horites; either they were a branch of the Horites, or else 'Hivite' wherever it occurs should be amended to 'Horite'. LXX reads 'Hittites' here. The Horites (or Hurrians) invaded northern Mesopotamia from the eastern highlands between 1750 and 1600 B.C. About 1500 they established the kingdom of Mitanni in Upper Mesopotamia. Many of the patriarchal customs appear to be of Horite origin. In the fifteenth and fourteenth centuries they spread so rapidly in Canaan that one of the Egyptian words for Canaan is Huru. In Joshua's day they occupied four cities north-west of Jerusalem—the Gibeonite confederacy (Jos. ix. 7, 17). *From mount Baal-hermon unto the entering in of Hamath* (3). Mount Baal-hermon (later Mount Hermon) is the more easterly range parallel to Lebanon, running south-west from Damascus. For *the entering in of Hamath* read 'Labo of Hamath', identified with mod. Lebweh, fourteen miles north-north-east of Baalbek. *And they were to prove Israel by them* (4). See ii. 22n. *And they took their daughters to be their wives . . .* (6). This procedure was a breach of the early injunction laid down in the covenant of Ex. xxxiv. 10–16 (repeated in Dt. vii. 1–5).

III. OPPRESSION UNDER CHUSHAN-RISHATHAIM AND DELIVERANCE BY OTHNIEL. iii. 7–11

And the children of Israel did evil in the sight of the Lord (7). This section gives us the full formulation of the repeated pattern in which the main episodes of Judges are set, with the bare minimum of detail added: the name of the oppressor, the duration of the oppression, the name of the deliverer, and the length of the ensuing period of 'rest'. *And served Baalim and the groves* (7); better as in RV 'and served the Baalim and the Asheroth', the male and female vegetation-deities respectively. *Asheroth* is a rare plural of Asherah, a Canaanite goddess who is named in the Ras Shamra tablets as the consort of the supreme god El. Asherah is regularly mistranslated *grove* in AV, an error which goes back to LXX. Elsewhere the female counterparts of the Baalim are the Ashtaroth (cf. ii. 13), and Ashtaroth may be the original reading here too, the more so as the normal plural of Asherah is Asherim. Cf. vi. 25. *Chushan-rishathaim king of*

Mesopotamia (8). Heb. *Aram-naharaim*. Egyptian records mention a district called Kushan-rom ('high Cushan') in the land of Naharen, in North Syria. But it is strange that a monarch from the north should have been repelled by a hero of southern Judah. Possibly a southern invader is intended, *Cushan rosh Teman* ('Cushan chief of Teman'), in which case *Aram* should be emended to *Edom*, as so often elsewhere in the Old Testament. His name has been vocalized in Hebrew so as to give the sense 'Cushan of double-dyed wickedness'. *Othniel the son of Kenaz, Caleb's younger brother* (9), i.e. the conqueror of Kiriath-sepher and son-in-law of Caleb (cf. i. 13). *And the Spirit of the Lord came upon him* (10). Similar language is used in Judges of Gideon (vi. 34), Jephthah (xi. 29) and Samson (xiii. 25, xiv. 6, 19, xv. 14); and in 1 Samuel of Saul (x. 10, xi. 6) and David (xvi. 13). These leaders have therefore been called 'charismatic', since they owed their position to the special power which resulted from an outpouring of the divine grace.

IV. OPPRESSION UNDER EGLON KING OF MOAB AND DELIVERANCE BY EHUD. iii. 12–30

a. Oppression under Eglon (iii. 12–14)

And the Lord strengthened Eglon the king of Moab against Israel (12). The land of Moab lay east of the Dead Sea, having the Arnon as its northern boundary and the Zered as its southern. Eglon invaded Canaan by the same route as that which the Israelites had followed, crossing the Jordan and capturing Jericho. It was natural, therefore, that his chief opponent, Ehud, should have been a Benjamite. According to N. Glueck, the kingdom of Moab, like the other Trans-jordanian kingdoms (Bashan, Heshbon, Ammon, Edom), was founded in the thirteenth century B.C., their inhabitants having previously been nomadic. The Moabite capital was Kir-hareseth. *The children of Ammon and Amalek* (13). Ammon, the people most closely related to the Moabites, lived to the north-east of them. The Amalekites were nomads (kinsmen of the Edomites) who were centred for long to the south of Canaan. They harassed Israel considerably during the wilderness journey. *The city of palm trees* (13), i.e. Jericho (cf. i. 16). This has been related to the occupation of the 'Middle Building' of Jericho, overlooking the spring—an occupation dated some two generations later than the destruction of the late bronze age city.

b. Deliverance under Ehud the Benjamite (iii. 15–30)

The Lord raised them up a deliverer, Ehud the son of Gera, a Benjamite, a man lefthanded (15). The last word is in Heb. *'itter yad-yemino*, lit. 'bound of his right hand'. Cf. the same phrase in xx. 16, also with reference to Benjamites. LXX and Vulg. render 'ambidextrous'. *By him the children of Israel sent a present unto Eglon* (15). Probably to

Jericho, to judge by the reference to Gilgal in verse 19. *The quarries that were by Gilgal* (19). The word for 'quarries' (Heb. *pesilim*) means lit. 'graven images' or 'carvings'—perhaps figures carved on the standing stones from which Gilgal received its name (see ii. 1n.). *Keep silence* (19). Heb. *has*, an onomatopoetic word, like Eng. 'Hush'. *He was sitting in a summer parlour* (20). Lit. 'in his upper-chamber (or roof-chamber) of coolness', a room built on the flat roof, well aired by large windows (cf. the window through which Ahaziah fell in 2 Ki. i. 2). *And the dirt came out* (22); 'And it came out behind' (RV). Better 'and he went out into the porch'. This clause in the Hebrew is so like the following one, *Then Ehud went forth through the porch* (23), that some think they are two conflated variant readings of one and the same clause; but there is some doubt of the proper meaning of the two rare words translated 'porch'. *Surely he covereth his feet* (24); a euphemism for going to stool (cf. 1 Sa. xxiv. 3). *They took a key, and opened them* (25). The key was a flat piece of wood furnished with pins corresponding to holes in a hollow bolt. The bolt was on the inside, shot into a socket in the doorpost and fastened by pins which fell into the holes in the bolt from an upright piece of wood (the lock) attached to the inside of the door. To unlock the door one put one's hand in by a hole in the door (cf. Ct. v. 4) and raised the pins in the bolt by means of the corresponding pins in the key. *He blew a trumpet in the mountain of Ephraim* (27), which lay north of the territory of Benjamin, and had probably also been invaded by Eglon.

V. EXPLOITS OF SHAMGAR BEN ANATH. iii. 31

Shamgar (31) does not seem to have been an Israelite; Albright says his name is Hittite. The words *son of Anath* may mean that he was a native of Beth-anath in Galilee (see i. 33n.) or some other place where Anath had a sanctuary. But even if he was a Canaanite, his attack on the Philistines *delivered Israel*. J. Garstang has identified him with Ben Anath, a Syrian sea-captain allied with Rameses II towards the end of his reign. In that case, the Philistines whom he attacked must have been an earlier vanguard of the main body which settled on the Palestinian coast fifty years later. (As for the *ox goad*, Sir C. Marston suggested that that was the name of his ship!) But the identification is highly improbable for chronological and other reasons. That Shamgar was a man of considerable fame is evident from the way in which he is recalled in the Song of Deborah (Jdg. v. 6).

VI. OPPRESSION UNDER JABIN KING OF CANAAN AND DELIVERANCE BY DEBORAH AND BARAK. iv. 1–24, v. 31b

a. Oppression under Jabin and Sisera (iv. 1–3)

And the Lord sold them into the hand of Jabin king of Canaan, that reigned in Hazor (2). Hitherto the oppressors have come from the east and south-east and overrun parts of southern and central Canaan; now we have a northern menace. Hazor lies some four miles south-west of Lake Huleh and was the capital of a Canaanite kingdom. Its site was identified by Garstang in 1927. It occupied a key position—a large protected camp dating back to Hyksos times—and was connected with Zidon by a permanent road. As we read of Jabin king of Hazor in a previous generation (Jos. xi. 1), this name may have been a hereditary title. The Jabin of Jos. xi led a coalition which was defeated by Joshua at the Water of Merom, which flows into the Sea of Galilee from the north-west; the Canaanite army of Jdg. iv and v was defeated in the Kishon valley farther west. It is commonly held that Jdg. iv combines a victory over Jabin of Hazor by Zebulun and Naphtali with a victory over Sisera of Harosheth by a wider combination of tribes, celebrated in Jdg. v. The Canaanites here are those mentioned in i. 27, 33 as dwelling among the Manassites and Naphtalites. *The captain of whose host was Sisera* (2). Sisera is possibly a Hittite name, though some think he may have been an Egyptian official in the Megiddo district, which appears to have been under Egyptian influence until *c.* 1150 B.C. But Megiddo itself was probably derelict by the time of the battle of Kishon (cf. v. 19). *Harosheth of the Gentiles* (2)—perhaps El-Haritiyeh, south-east of Haifa. *For he had nine hundred chariots of iron* (3). This force of armed vehicles made Sisera invincible until a situation arose in which, instead of being a source of strength, they became a hindrance. The mustering of the united tribes of Israel against him under Barak coincided with a storm in which the Kishon, normally a dry river-bed, rapidly became a raging torrent in which the chariotry was engulfed.

b. The battle of Kishon (iv. 4–16)

She dwelt under the palm tree of Deborah (5). This should not be confused with the oak under which an earlier Deborah was buried 'below Beth-el' (Gn. xxxv. 8). The name Deborah means 'bee'. *And the children of Israel came up to her for judgment* (5). She was thus a *shopheteth* in the normal and non-military sense, but the charismatic element was present in her too, as she was a prophetess. *Barak* (6). The name means 'lightning'; cf. Carthaginian Barca. *Kedesh-naphtali* (6). A sanctuary identified by Garstang with Beth-shemesh of i. 33. *Mount Tabor* (6). At the meeting place of the tribal territories of Issachar, Zebulun and Naphtali. *The river Kishon* (7). A wadi which quickly becomes an impetuous torrent in time of rain; it runs north-west through the valley of Jezreel into the Mediterranean on the north side of Mount Carmel. *Heber the Kenite . . . had severed himself from the Kenites* (11). See note on i. 16. Here we have a Kenite family separating itself from the main body in the south and coming as far north as the valley of Jezreel to live. *And the Lord dis-*

comfited Sisera, and all his chariots (15). The manner of the discomfiture is made plain in the older, poetical version of v. 20–22. A sudden and terrific rainstorm filled the wadi, making it impassable and bogging the chariots. The situation was repeated when Napoleon defeated the Turkish army at the Battle of Mount Tabor on April 16, A.D. 1799.

c. The death of Sisera (iv. 17–24)

She covered him with a mantle (18), properly with a 'fly-net' (Heb. *semikhah*). *She opened a bottle of milk* (19), i.e. a skin of curds (cf. v. 25), the modern 'lebben', which has a markedly soporific effect. *Then Jael Heber's wife took a nail of the tent* (21). For a more vivid description of his death see v. 26f. The mallet and tent-peg, for pitching the tent, were ready to her hand, as pitching the tent was a woman's work. *For he was fast asleep and weary. So he died* (21). The AV is better than RV ('for he was in a deep sleep: so he swooned and died'); it depends, to be sure, on a change in the vocalization (*we-ya'eph* for *wayya'aph*), but 'he swooned' is not what we should naturally say of a man through whose temples a tent-peg had been driven. *Until they had destroyed Jabin king of Canaan* (24). The prose narrative is continued in v. 31b. The poetical version intervenes.

VII. THE SONG OF DEBORAH AND BARAK. v. 1–31a

Then sang Deborah and Barak (1). This song takes its place alongside other poetical records of episodes in the conquest of Canaan. It may have been preserved, like these, in some such collection as the book of Jashar (cf. Jos. x. 12f.) or the book of the Wars of Yahweh (cf. Nu. xxi. 14f.). These records are practically contemporary with the events they celebrate, and the Song of Deborah is the longest and most important of them. It is the oldest element in Judges, as is evident from its archaic language, some of which was unintelligible as early as the LXX translation of Judges. The RV translation is vastly superior to the AV. Attempts have been made by drastic emendation to restore the original form of the song, but few of these have been widely accepted. The song may be divided thus:—verses 2, 3: exordium of praise; verses 4, 5: invocation of Yahweh; verses 6–8: the desolation under the oppressors; verses 9–18: the mustering of the tribes; verses 19–23: the Battle of Kishon; verses 24–27: the death of Sisera; verses 28–30: the mother of Sisera awaits his coming; verse 31a: epilogue.

Lord, when thou wentest out of Seir (4). The picture in verses 4 and 5 is of Yahweh in the midst of the storm-cloud leading His people up from Sinai, where He had first revealed Himself to them, by *the field of Edom* into Canaan. Cf. Dt. xxxiii. 2; Ps. lxviii. 7ff.; Hab. iii. 3ff. *In the days of Shamgar the son of Anath, in the days of Jael* (6). See iii. 31n. We naturally think of Jael as the wife of Heber the Kenite, celebrated in v. 24, but it is strange to find her coupled with Shamgar in this way, and the allusion here may be to someone of an earlier generation, no longer known. *Until that I Deborah arose, that I arose a mother in Israel* (7). The old Heb. *qamti* may be second singular feminine as well as first singular, and possibly Deborah is here apostrophized as in verse 12, in which case render 'until thou, O Deborah, didst arise . . .' (cf. RSV). From the phrase *a mother in Israel*, which is used of a city in 2 Sa. xx. 19, it has been inferred that the town of Deborah at the foot of Tabor was originally meant, but this is quite improbable. *They chose new gods; then was war in the gates* (8); a significant sequence: see ii. 14n. *Was there a shield or spear seen among forty thousand in Israel?* (8). This reflects the unarmed state of the Israelites during their twenty years' oppression; cf. their disarmament under the Philistines in 1 Sa. xiii. 19ff. Notice the estimate of the contemporary Israelite manpower.

Ye that ride on white asses (10), a mark of nobility; cf. x. 4, xii. 14. *There shall they rehearse the righteous acts of the Lord* (11). His *righteous acts* or 'righteousnesses' are those by which He intervenes for His people to give them salvation and victory. The co-operation of the northern and central tribes was due not only to the pressure of a common foe but also to a common memory of the covenant with Yahweh, which revived at such a time. The song regards all the tribes as worshippers of Yahweh. The word *rehearse* or 'chant' (*yethannu*) is an Aramaism, the presence of which in Hebrew of so early a date is noteworthy (cf. xi. 40). The actual sense is 'sing responsively', and the reference is to the songs of victory sung by the maidens at the wells in the following times of peace.

Out of Ephraim was there a root of them against Amalek (14). Follow RV: 'Out of Ephraim came down they whose root is in Amalek'. Some of the Amalekite nomads from the south had, like Heber the Kenite (iv. 11), left their home and invaded central Canaan (cf. iii. 13, vi. 3f., 33, xii. 15). *After thee, Benjamin* (14). For the Benjamite war-cry cf. Ho. v. 8. *Out of Machir* (14). Usually eastern Manasseh; here, perhaps, eastern and western Manasseh combined. *They that handle the pen of the writer* (14). Read with RV mg. 'the staff of the writer' (Heb. *shebhet sopher*). The staff was probably the scribe's wand of office. Reference at this date (*c.* 1150 B.C.) to a writer is no more surprising than the mention of 'the city of books' in i. 11. Writing, and alphabetic writing at that, had been practised for some centuries along the Syrian coast, from the primitive alphabet of Serabit in the Sinai peninsula (an early form of the original North Semitic alphabet from which the Phoenician and other Semitic alphabets were derived), to the cuneiform alphabet of Ras Shamra (an adaptation of the same North Semitic alphabet). Quantities of papyrus were exported from Egypt to Phoenicia *c.* 1100 B.C. Cf. Jdg. viii. 14.

Gilead abode beyond Jordan (17). This refers to the tribesmen of Gad who, like their Reubenite neighbours (16), did not take part in the struggle. *And why did Dan remain in ships?* (17). Garstang suggests that the reference is to the later, northern home of the Danites and that the ships were on Lake Huleh; but it is more natural to think of their earlier home on the west coast of Canaan, and even if their northern migration had already taken place (cf. xviii. 1ff.), some of them certainly remained behind (cf. xiii. 2). *Asher continued on the sea shore* (17). 'Asher sat still at the haven of the sea' (RV). The territory of Asher was soon encroached upon by the Phoenicians. *In Taanach by the waters of Megiddo* (19), i.e. by the torrent of Kishon. The city of Megiddo probably lay waste at this time (cf. Albright, *Archaeology of Palestine*, pp. 117f.). *They fought from heaven; the stars in their courses fought against Sisera* (20). The reference is to the cloudburst which flooded Kishon and swept away Sisera's chariotry; for the language cf. that of the poetical fragment of Jos. x. 12ff. *Meroz* (23) has been identified with Khirbet Marus, about seven and a half miles south of Kedesh-naphtali. Meroz apparently played false to some special obligation resting upon it.

Blessed above women shall Jael . . . be (24). The feminine hand has been discerned in the space allotted in the song to Jael's exploit, as also in the vivid depicting of Sisera's mother (28ff.). *She brought forth butter* (25), i.e. curds (Heb. *hem'ah*); see iv. 19n. *She put her hand to the nail* (26). Better 'tent-pin' as in RV mg. This was her left hand, as LXX and other versions say. It is not necessary to conclude that in the parallelism of this verse *hand* must be synonymous with *right hand* and *nail* with *workmen's hammer*: Burney aptly compares Pr. iii. 16. *She smote off* (RV 'through') *his head* (26). The verb, Heb. *halaph* (lit. 'pass away'), is used of piercing in Jb. xx. 24.

The mother of Sisera . . . cried through the lattice (28). The closing scene of the song is unforgettably vivid and moving. The network of the crossed laths which covered the window-opening (the *lattice*) may have been decorated outside in the Egyptian manner. *Yea, she returned answer to herself* (29), as if to convince herself that all was well; but RV mg., 'Yet she repeateth her words unto herself', may be right; in spite of the ladies' reassuring confidence, her forebodings will not be stilled. *To every man a damsel or two* (30). The word for *damsel* (Heb. *raham*) is found on Mesha's Moabite stone (*c.* 850 B.C.) in the same rather contemptuous sense (like Eng. 'wench'). *Divers colours of needlework* (30). 'Embroidery' (RV). The Hebrews excelled in the art of dyeing, as is evident from the description of the wilderness tent of meeting and the priestly robes. They may have acquired the art from the Egyptians. Excavation reveals that wool dyeing was a leading industry in Debir and Benjamite Mizpah. *Meet for the necks of them that take the spoil* (30). 'On the necks of the spoil' (RV). The changing of one vowel-point gives the more probable reading, 'a spoil for my neck'. *So let all thine enemies perish* (31a). The epilogue of the song, invoking a malison on Yahweh's enemies and blessing on His friends, is markedly parallel to Ps. lxviii. 1–3.

VIII. OPPRESSION UNDER MIDIAN AND DELIVERANCE BY GIDEON.
vi. 1—viii. 32

a. The Midianite oppression (v. 31b—vi. 6)

And the land had rest forty years (31b). This is actually the conclusion of the prose narrative of Jabin's overthrow, following on from iv. 24. *And the hand of Midian prevailed against Israel* (vi. 2). The Midianites were nomads from the desert who for the first time were using domesticated camels on a large scale. This made long-distance raids easy. They probably came from their home round the head of the Gulf of Aqaba (cf. Ex. ii. 15ff.) north through Transjordan, by the same route as that previously taken by the Israelites, crossing the Jordan and invading central Canaan, penetrating as far west as Gaza (4). It was probably on their way through Transjordan, in the land of Moab, that they met the defeat at the hands of Hadad I, king of Edom, mentioned in Gn. xxxvi. 35 (*c.* 1100 B.C.). *The children of Israel made them the dens which are in the mountains* (2), an explanation of the rock-dwellings in the hill country of Ephraim and Judah. *The Amalekites, and the children of the east* (3). These had attached themselves to the Midianites. For the Amalekites see iii. 13n.; they seem to have made a habit of joining invasions of Canaan from Transjordan. *The children of the east* (Heb. *bene qedem*) is a general description of the nomads in the Syrian desert. Cf. Gn. xxix. 1, where, however, the expression is used of the pastoral people of Upper Mesopotamia. Cf. the Egyptian tale of Sinuhe who about 1900 B.C. found refuge with an Amorite chieftain who lived a semi-nomadic life in the country of Qedem. *As grasshoppers for multitude* (5). Better 'locusts' (RV); the simile is apt, for it suggests their destructiveness as well as their number.

b. The prophet (vi. 7–10)

The Lord sent a prophet unto the children of Israel (8). The message of the prophet is not unlike that of the angel at Bochim. The words in the latter half of verse 8 are reminiscent of the preamble to the ten commandments (Ex. xx. 2). *I delivered you out of the hand of the Egyptians* (9). Some have seen here a reference to encounters with the Egyptians in Canaan, but this is not necessarily implied; the exodus satisfies the reference. *I said unto you* (10). The following words summarize once more the injunctions of Ex. xxxiv. 10–16; Dt. vii. 1ff. Cf. Jdg. iii. 5f.

c. The angel of the Lord visits Gideon (vi. 11–24)

An (RV 'the') *angel of the Lord* (11). See ii. 1n. *Under an oak which was in Ophrah* (11). For this kind of oak or 'terebinth' (Heb. *'elah*), a sacred tree, cf. Gn. xiii. 18, xiv. 13, xviii. 1, xxxv. 8; Ho. iv. 13. Ophrah is not certainly known, but was probably near the boundary of western Manasseh and Ephraim. *Joash the Abi-ezrite* (11). Abiezer was a sub-tribe of Manasseh, belonging to the western division of that tribe (cf. v. 14). *His son Gideon threshed wheat by the winepress* (11); 'was beating out wheat in the winepress' (RV), probably with a staff or rod, a method sometimes used for small quantities of grain (cf. Ru. ii. 17). *Where be all his miracles which our fathers told us of?* (13). For the language as well as the general sentiment, cf. Ps. xliv. 1ff. *And the Lord looked upon him* (14). This alternation between Yahweh's angel and Yahweh Himself is common in such theophanic narratives. *My present* (18). Heb. *minhah* is an unusual term for a meal, but natural if an offering to a divine being is intended. *Lay them upon this rock, and pour out the broth* (20). The surface of the rock served as an improvised altar. The 'broth' may have been poured as a libation into one of the cup-shaped rock-hollows which are found in Palestine and England alike. *The angel of the Lord departed out of his sight* (21). For the whole theophany, as for its closing scene, cf. Jdg. xiii. 3–21. *Alas, O Lord God!* (22). For the fear of death and divine reassurance cf. Jdg. xiii. 22f. Cf. also Ex. xxxiii. 20, 'Man shall not see me and live'. *Jehovah-shalom* (24), i.e. 'Yahweh is peace', the name being here connected with the words *Peace be unto thee* (Heb. *shalom lekha*) of verse 23.

d. Gideon overthrows the altar of Baal (vi. 25–32)

Take thy father's young bullock, even the second bullock of seven years old (25). Lit. 'Take the bull of Shor which thy father has . . .' The text is difficult, but it is worth noting that Shor ('ox') occurs as a divine title in the Ras Shamra tablets, one of the manifestations of the supreme god El. Cf. Ps. cvi. 20. The animal was probably reserved for sacrifice. *Throw down the altar of Baal . . . and cut down the grove* (RV, 'Asherah') *that is by it* (25). For Baal and Asherah see ii. 13n., iii. 7n. We are here confronted by a situation in which Yahwism and Baalism have been syncretized, Yahweh being perhaps regarded as one of the Baalim. Joash has a name containing Yahweh ('Yahweh has given'), but he erects an altar to Baal and an image (or sacred pole) of Asherah, and calls his son Jerub-baal ('may Baal give increase') which, as a result of the present iconoclasm, is given the new significance 'Let Baal strive'. *Upon the top of this rock, in the ordered place* (26). 'In the orderly manner' (RV). The last phrase probably refers to the conventional arrangement of the altar stones. On the altar thus erected was piled the wood of the Asherah which Gideon cut down, and on that the bullock was laid and consumed. *He called him Jerubbaal* (32). The name acquires a new sense, as the equivalent of 'let Baal strive' (Heb. *yareb Ba'al*). In 2 Sa. xi. 21 it appears as

Jerubbesheth, in accordance with the convention of replacing Baal by *bosheth, besheth*, 'shame' (as in Ish-bosheth, Mephibosheth, etc.).

e. Gideon gathers an army (vi. 33–35)

Went over, and pitched in the valley of Jezreel (33). It was probably at this time that the Midianites killed Gideon's brothers at Tabor (viii. 18). *But the Spirit of the Lord came upon Gideon* (34). Lit. 'clothed itself with Gideon': an expression repeated in 1 Ch. xii. 18f.; 2 Ch. xxiv. 20. It denotes complete possession; Gideon becomes the garment of the Spirit and thus enters the succession of Israel's charismatic leaders. *And they came up to meet them* (35). Practically all northern Israel is indicated; the omission of Ephraim, the most powerful of the central tribes, is noteworthy in view of the sequel.

f. Gideon's fleece (vi. 36–40)

I will speak but this once (39). For the language cf. Gn. xviii. 32. Gideon may have reflected after the former sign that, as the rocky threshing-floor would in any case dry more quickly than the fleece, it was not really a 'sign'; the reverse result would be truly remarkable.

g. The reduction of Gideon's army (vii. 1–8)

The well of Harod (1), i.e. the spring of trembling, possibly referring to verse 3, *whosoever is fearful and afraid* (RV, 'trembling'). It may be identified with 'Ain Jalud, which springs from the foot of Mount Gilboa. *The hill of Moreh* (1) ('the oracle-giver') may be Jebel Nebi Dahi to the north of Gilboa, across the valley of Jezreel. *Let him return and depart early from mount Gilead* (3). The only Gilead known to us is in northern Transjordan. Was there another Gilead in Naphtali? C. F. Burney vocalizes 'Galud' ('coward'?) here; cf. mod. 'Ain Jalud. Another suggestion is to emend to 'Gilboa'. *I will try them for thee there* (4). The nature of the test is not quite clear in the Massoretic text; to lap with one's tongue like a dog (5) cannot be done by putting one's hand to one's mouth (6). Kneeling to drink and lapping might 'seem to amount to criminal carelessness in presence of the enemy' (Burney); those who conveyed water from the spring to their mouths in their cupped hands would be able to keep a wary eye open for sudden attack.

h. Gideon in the camp of Midian (vii. 9–14)

Like grasshoppers (RV, 'locusts') . . . *as the sand* (12). The numerical analogies are typical oriental hyperbole. *There was a man that told a dream unto his fellow* (13). Dreams were treated as of high importance; it is clear throughout the Old Testament that a dream has an interpretation, though that cannot always be discovered. *A cake of barley bread* (13), i.e. a 'scone' or 'bannock'. Barley was the commonest cereal in Palestine and barley bread was the staple food of the poorer people.

i. Gideon's victory (vii. 15–25)

He divided the three hundred men into three companies (16). The threefold division of forces appears elsewhere in the Old Testament; cf. 1 Sa. xi. 11; 2 Sa. xviii. 2. The surprise attack by night is also illustrated in 1 Sa. xi. 11. Here the sudden appearance of the lights at close quarters, the sound of the trumpets, and the war-cry from 300 throats, 'For the Lord and for Gideon' (RV), struck panic into the Midianites. The trumpets were horns of cattle or of rams (Heb. *shofaroth*). The pitchers served the double purpose of guarding the torches from the wind and hiding the light until the critical moment. *The beginning of the middle watch* (19), implying a division into three watches, of about four hours each. The time therefore was about 10 p.m. *To Beth-shittah* (22). The places mentioned cannot be certainly identified, but it is obvious that the Midianites fled towards Jordan, and crossed it (cf. verse 24) at points where their retreat could best be cut off by men of Ephraim. For the tribes named in verse 23 cf. γi. 35. *Oreb and Zeeb* (25), meaning 'raven' and 'wolf' respectively. 'The slaughter of Midian at the rock of Oreb' is remembered in Is. x. 26; cf. also the reference to 'the day of Midian' in Is. ix. 4, alluding to this same rout. The sites of the rock of Oreb and the winepress of Zeeb are unknown. *And they . . . brought the heads of Oreb and Zeeb to Gideon on the other side Jordan* (25), i.e. in Transjordan, where he had gone in pursuit of the Midianite kings Zebah and Zalmunna (viii. 4).

j. The Ephraimites' complaint (viii. 1–3)

Why hast thou served us thus . . . ? (1). The Ephraimites seem to have thought that the failure to enlist their aid at the outset was calculated to deprive them of the honour of a share in the victory; perhaps also they did not like the idea of a strong 'northern bloc' from which they were excluded. Gideon, however, speaks them fair and appeases their resentment. His treatment of them is in striking contrast to Jephthah's, later on (xii. 1ff.).

k. Pursuit and capture of Zebah and Zalmunna (viii. 4–21)

Faint, yet pursuing (4). Possibly we should read with some of the versions 'faint and famished'. *The men of Succoth* (5). This place (meaning 'booths') lay in Transjordan, north of the Jabbok. *Zebah and Zalmunna, kings of Midian* (5), vocalized so as to mean 'sacrifice' and 'shelter withheld'. *I will tear your flesh* (7). Lit. 'I will thresh your flesh', perhaps by laying them on a carpet of thorns and threshing them as corn is threshed. *Penuel* (8), some miles east of Succoth (cf. Gn. xxxii. 30f.). *I will break down this tower* (9). The tower of Penuel was an Amorite fortification of *c.* 1700 B.C. (the same period as the tower of Shechem, ix. 6, 46ff.); it was rebuilt by Jeroboam I (1 Ki. xii. 25). It probably occupied a height overlooking the city. The city was probably unwalled, the tower serving as a refuge for the population. J. G. Duncan suggests that this tower may be mod. Es-Salt in Transjordan.

Now Zebah and Zalmunna were in Karkor (10). The place is not known, but must have been near *Nobah and Jogbehah* (11). The name of Jogbehah is preserved in mod. Jubeihah, six miles north-west of Amman. The site of Nobah is identified with a 'tell' near Safut. *For the host was secure* (11), i.e. off its guard (cf. xviii. 7, 27). *Discomfited all the host* (12). Lit. 'terrified the host' (Heb. *heḥerid*). Burney emends to *heḥerim* ('devoted' or 'destroyed utterly'); so Josephus (*Ant*. 5. 6. 5) 'he destroyed all the enemy'. *Before the sun was up* (13). 'From the ascent of Heres' (RV). (Heres is a rare word for 'sun'.) The words may be a scribal doublet of the last clause of verse 12. *He described unto him the princes of Succoth* (14). The literal rendering is better: 'he wrote down for him . . .' The translation ' "described" has obscured to the English reader an important biblical item on the early diffusion of the alphabet' (J. A. Montgomery). It was the invention of alphabetic writing (see v. 14n.) that enabled ordinary people like this chance captive to read and write. The older ideographic and syllabic scripts were by their very nature the preserve of a specialized class. The youth possibly wrote down a list of the chief men of Succoth on a piece of pottery. *And with them he taught the men of Succoth* (16), as though the verb had its usual sense 'caused to know' (hiphil of *yada'*); but D. W. Thomas points out an alternative meaning of this root: 'made quiet or submissive' (cf. Jdg. xvi. 9; 1 Sa. xiv. 12). *What manner of men were they whom ye slew at Tabor?* (18). See vi. 33n. *As the Lord liveth* (19), or 'by the life of Yahweh'; the form of oath implies belief in Yahweh as 'the living God'. *For as the man is, so is his strength* (21). It would be an honour to die by the hand of a warrior like Gideon, who besides might be trusted to kill them at one blow, and not bungle the business as the boy might. *The ornaments that were on their camels' necks* (21). These 'crescents' (RV) or 'little moons' were probably threaded on necklaces and worn as amulets. They may indicate that these Bedouin were moon-worshippers.

l. Gideon's rule over Israel (viii. 22–32)

Both thou, and thy son, and thy son's son also (22). It is an hereditary monarchy that Gideon is invited to set up. In spite of his refusal, his son Abimelech attempted to perpetuate his father's ascendancy (ix. 1–6). *The Lord shall rule over you* (23). For the idea of God as Israel's sole king cf. 1 Sa. x. 19. *Because they were Ishmaelites* (24), possibly trading nomads. This is a striking parallel to the interchange of the terms 'Midianites' and 'Ishmaelites' in the story of the sale of Joseph (Gn. xxxvii. 25ff., xxxix. 1). Both Ishmael and Midian are recorded as sons of Abraham. *A thousand and seven hundred shekels of gold* (26), about forty-two pounds avoirdupois. *And Gideon*

made an ephod (27). Possibly here and in xvii. 5 'ephod' means something different from the priestly vestment called by that name, though Burney does not think so. Whatever it was, it was apparently used for divination. *His concubine that was in Shechem, she also bare him a son* (31). The chief difference between the *threescore and ten sons of his body begotten* (30) and Abimelech was probably that their descent was reckoned through the male line, and his through the female. They would belong to their father's clan of Abiezer, he to his mother's Shechemite family.

IX. THE STORY OF ABIMELECH.
viii. 33—ix. 57

And it came to pass, as soon as Gideon was dead (33). In verses 33–35 of chapter viii the author gives an ethical summary of the following narrative. *Baal-berith* (33). See ix. 4n., 46n. *And Abimelech the son of Jerubbaal went to Shechem unto his mother's brethren* (ix. 1). While Gideon himself refused an hereditary monarchy, some of his family seem to have had other ideas; cf. verse 2 where Abimelech appears to envisage the possibility of the sons who belonged to the Abiezer clan exercising a condominium over that part of the country. Abimelech, however, who retained his mother's Shechemite citizenship, forestalled any possible attempt by his Abi-ezrite brothers by killing them; and he established a kingdom with its centre at Shechem. Shechem had been seized by the sons of Jacob before the descent into Egypt (Gn. xxxiv. 25ff.; cf. Gn. xlviii. 22). In the Tell el-Amarna correspondence Shechem is allied with the Habiru. Although there is no record of its being captured by Joshua, it was chosen as a religious centre after the conquest. The Israelites under Joshua possibly found it occupied by their kinsmen. Shechem appears in Jos. xx. 7, xxi. 21 as a Levitical city and city of refuge; the blessings and cursings were recited on the hills Ebal and Gerizim which overlook it (Jos. viii. 30ff.), and there Joshua gathered all Israel before his death. The name of the place means 'shoulder', from its position on the saddle between Ebal and Gerizim. It is 'the natural capital of Canaan' (A. T. Olmstead). Its importance continued to be observed by the Samaritans, who made it their holy city; it is at the adjacent Greek foundation of Neapolis (mod. Nablus) that the Samaritan community survives to this day.

The house of Baal-berith (4). The divine name implies the existence of a confederacy associated with the city. A shrine belonging to this period has been uncovered at Shechem. *The house of Millo* (6), i.e. 'house of the fortress', probably the same as the tower of Shechem in verse 46. *And made Abimelech king, by the plain* (RV, 'oak') *of the pillar that was in Shechem* (6). The oak or terebinth was no doubt a sacred tree (that of Gn. xxxv. 4?) associated with a standing-stone (that of Jos. xxiv. 26?). The kingdom of Abimelech was not an extensive one; it hardly extended beyond western Manasseh. *In the top of mount Gerizim* (7). The sacred mountain of the Samaritans (cf. Jn. iv. 20f.) lay west of the city. By standing on one of the cliffs overhanging Shechem Jotham would make himself heard by the citizens. *The trees went forth on a time to anoint a king over them* (8). For this type of fable cf. that of King Joash in 2 Ki. xiv. 9. The fable reflects a poor opinion of the value of kingship. The *bramble* (15, 'briar'), which is good for nothing else, has the necessary leisure to become king of the trees, but it cannot afford them shelter, and is more likely to catch fire and involve them all in its ruin. Trees which perform some useful service (as Gideon had done) have no time to become king. This contempt for monarchy may well reflect an early date. The fable is cast in rhythmical form. *The fig tree* (10), the commonest fruit-tree of Palestine. *My wine, which cheereth God and man* (13), or rather 'gods and men'; it cheered gods by being offered to them in libations. *Abimelech, the son of his maidservant* (18). Jotham uses a word meaning 'slave-concubine', deliberately ascribing to her a status inferior to her real one, as implied in viii. 31. *Went to Beer, and dwelt there* (21). *Beer* simply means 'well' and the name is therefore widespread; this one may be El-Bireh between Shechem and Jerusalem.

And they robbed all that came along that way by them (25), thus depriving Abimelech of the dues which he exacted from merchants passing through his realm. *Gaal the son of Ebed* (26). He offers himself as leader to the native Shechemites against Abimelech and his governor Zebul. *And they went out into the fields* (27). The time of grape-harvest is meant, when the grapes were gathered and trodden in the wine-vats—a Canaanite counterpart to the Israelite feast of ingathering or tabernacles. The ensuing merry-making was chosen as an occasion for throwing off their allegiance to Abimelech. *Is not he the son of Jerubbaal?* (28). The meaning of the second part of verse 28, by a slight emendation, may be: 'Should not the son of Jerubbaal and Zebul his officer serve the men of Hamor, the father of Shechem?' (Cf. RSV.) In spite of the massacre of Gn. xxxiv. 25f., the Shechemites still maintain the connection with Hamor, the ancestor of their clan. Hamor means 'ass'; Albright points out that the sacrifice of an ass was an essential feature of a treaty among the Amorites in the eighteenth century B.C., and compares the evidence of a Shechemite federal treaty in the name Baal-berith. *And he sent messengers unto Abimelech privily* (31). For *privily* read 'at Arumah' with RSV. It appears that Abimelech did not live in Shechem, but in Arumah (41), and set Zebul over Shechem as his lieutenant-governor; this may partly account for the Shechemites' hostility to him. *They laid wait against Shechem in four companies* (34). So the contingent in the city under Zebul was literally a 'fifth column'. *See, there come people down* (37). Translate: 'See, men are descending from the

navel of the land and one body is advancing by way of the diviners' oak.' The 'navel of the land' must be equivalent to *the top of the mountains* (36), and probably indicates what was regarded as the central eminence of the hill country of central Canaan. The oak or terebinth of the diviners may be the sacred tree of verse 6 or a similar one. *And Abimelech dwelt at Arumah* (41), i.e. he returned there, leaving Zebul to complete the work of driving out Gaal. *Beat down the city, and sowed it with salt* (45). It was rebuilt by Jeroboam I as his first capital after the disruption of the monarchy (1 Ki. xii. 25).

The men of the tower of Shechem (46), which was probably the Beth-millo of verse 6. Shechem was a walled city with the additional defence of an outlying tower. *An hold of the house of the god Berith* (46), or 'the crypt of the temple of El-berith' (cf. verse 4), apparently part of Beth-millo. El as a divine title is found widely distributed over Palestine at an early date. The supreme god bears this name in the Ras Shamra tablets and in the Phoenician historian San-chuniathon. We gather that at Shechem it was El who was invoked as patron of the federal union, and who thus came to be called El-berith ('God of the covenant') or Baal-berith ('Lord of the covenant'). *Mount Zalmon* (48). Cf. Ps. lxviii. 14. Its name means 'shaded', perhaps because of the woods which covered its slopes.

Then went Abimelech to Thebez (50), usually identified, though on slender linguistic grounds, with mod. Tubas, about ten miles north-east of Nablus, on the road to Beth-shan. This town had no doubt joined in the revolt against Abimelech. *There was a strong tower within the city* (51), by contrast with Shechem and Penuel, where the tower was outside. *A certain woman cast a piece of a millstone* (53). '. . . an upper millstone' (RV), lit. 'a stone of riding' (Heb. *pelaḥ rekhebh*). Cf. 2 Sa. xi. 21, where an allusion is made to this incident as a warning against going too near the wall of a besieged fort or city. *Draw thy sword, and slay me* (54). Cf. Saul's request to his armour-bearer to prevent the Philistines from taking him alive (1 Sa. xxxi. 4). *The men of Israel* (55). The rebels were probably Canaanites; the Israelite population perhaps supported Abimelech because of his relation to Gideon. *Thus God rendered,* (RV, 'requited') *the wickedness of Abimelech* (56). The author of Judges draws a moral after his fashion.

X. TOLA AND JAIR, MINOR JUDGES.
x. 1–5

There arose to defend Israel Tola the son of Puah, the son of Dodo, a man of Issachar (1). Tola was a tribal name; a son of Issachar is named Tola in Gn. xlvi. 13, etc. Dodo ('beloved') is perhaps the same name as David. These minor judges (Tola and Jair in this chapter and Ibzan, Elon and Abdon in chapter xii) have no mighty deeds recorded of them, such as are told of the great judges. Their function may have been more purely judicial: Albright, describes them as 'intertribal arbitrators'. We may compare Samuel, who later in the eleventh century went in circuit from place to place judging Israel (1 Sa. vii. 15–17). E. Robertson, on the other hand, calls them 'military leaders holding office at a time when no military activity was called for', and hazards the suggestion that they were appointed by the High Priest of the time, a suggestion supported (for what it is worth) by Samaritan tradition. *Jair, a Gileadite* (3). Gilead in the tribal genealogies is the son of Machir, who was Manasseh's son by an Aramaean concubine. Jair is the same name as New Testament Jairus. *And he had thirty sons* (4). That these should ride on ass-colts is intended as a mark of distinction; cf. what is said of Abdon's sons and grandsons in xii. 14. *Which are called Havoth-jair* (4), i.e. the tent-villages of Jair. In Nu. xxxii. 41, Dt. iii. 14, and 1 Ch. ii. 23 Havoth-jair is associated with Jair the grandson of Judah's grandson Hezron who married a daughter of Machir. *And was buried in Camon* (5), probably Qamm in Gilead.

XI. OPPRESSION UNDER AMMON AND DELIVERANCE BY JEPHTHAH.
x. 6—xii. 7

a. The Ammonite oppression (x. 6–18)

He sold them into the hands of the Philistines, and into the hands of the children of Ammon (7). The Philistines invaded the Israelite territory west of Jordan from the coastal plain where they had settled over a century before, while the Ammonites overran the Israelite territory in Transjordan. The Ammonite menace is dealt with first, as that was quickly crushed—for the present, at any rate—but we find a recrudescence of the Ammonite threat some decades later, at the beginning of Saul's reign (1 Sa. xi. 1ff.). The Ammonites, like their Moabite kinsmen and other Transjordanian neighbours, appear to have organized themselves as a kingdom in the thirteenth century B.C. In their present invasion of Israelite territory they were apparently accompanied by the Moabites (see xi. 15n., 24n.), as Eglon had been by the Ammonites (iii. 13). *And the Lord said unto the children of Israel* (11), probably by the mouth of a prophet, as in vi. 8ff. *Did not I deliver you from the Egyptians, and from the Amorites, from the children of Ammon, and from the Philistines?* (11). References respectively to the exodus, the overthrow of Sihon (see xi. 13ff. n.), and the deliverances under Ehud (iii. 13) and Shamgar (iii. 31). *The Zidonians also, and the Amalekites, and the Maonites, did oppress you* (12). There is no other reference to a Zidonian oppression; for Amalek cf. iii. 13, vi. 3. For 'Maonites' LXX has 'Midianites'; the name may be associated with mod. Ma'an near Petra. *His soul was grieved* (16), lit. 'was short', i.e. impatient. *And the children of Israel assembled themselves together, and encamped in Mizpeh* (17). Mizpeh ('watchtower') may be identical with the Mizpah where Jacob and Laban piled the 'cairn of witness' (Gn. xxxi. 46ff.), and also with Ramath-Mizpeh or Ramoth-Gilead (Dt. iv. 43; Jos. xiii. 26; 1 Ki. iv. 13), about forty miles north of Amman.

b. Jephthah chosen as captain (xi. 1–11)

Jephthah (1). Heb. *Yiphtaḥ*, probably shortened from *yiphtaḥ-'El*, 'God opens (*sc.* the womb)', which is cited as a proper name in Sabean. *The son of an harlot* (1). Therefore, like Abimelech, he was half-Canaanite, and not acknowledged as a member of his father's clan. *The land of Tob* (3). Probably to the north of the kingdom of Ammon, on the east of Transjordanian Manasseh. *There were gathered vain men to Jephthah* (3). These 'empty men' were probably 'broken men' such as later gathered to David in the cave of Adullam. *And went out with him* (3), i.e. on forays; Jephthah, in other words, was a brigand chief. *Come, and be our captain* (6). Heb. *qaṣin*, cognate with Arab *qadi*, one who gives a legal decision; LXX renders *archegos*, applied to Christ four times in the New Testament. *And Jephthah uttered all his words before the Lord in Mizpeh* (11). A solemn compact was made at this sanctuary between Jephthah and the elders of Gilead, they confirming with an oath their undertaking to make him their ruler, and he similarly swearing a sort of 'coronation oath'.

c. Jephthah's protest to the king of Ammon (xi. 12–28)

Because Israel took away my land (13). The reference, as we gather from Jephthah's reply, is to the territory of Sihon, which (according to Nu. xxi. 26–30) Sihon had taken from the Moabites. From this and the mention of Chemosh in verse 24 it is commonly inferred that verses 12–28 originally concerned a dispute with the Moabites, in which case *nor the land of the children of Ammon* (15) would be an editorial addition. But if we take the text as it stands, it is plain that both Moab and Ammon were engaged in this dispute with Israel. *From Arnon even unto Jabbok, and unto Jordan* (13). The southern, northern and western boundaries respectively of Sihon's kingdom, which was bounded on the east by Ammon. Sihon may well have carved out his kingdom at the expense of Ammon as well as of Moab. *Israel took not away the land of Moab, nor the land of the children of Ammon* (15), indicating (as has been said) a Moabite-Ammonite association at this time. *Walked through the wilderness unto the Red Sea* (16), possibly the Gulf of Aqaba. No mention is made here of the events at Sinai, as they were irrelevant for Jephthah's purpose. *And came to Kadesh* (16), i.e. Kadesh-barnea, to the south of the Negeb, on the border of the kingdom of Edom. *Then Israel sent messengers unto the king of Edom* (17). Cf. Nu. xx. 14–21. *And in like manner they sent unto the king of Moab* (17). This is not recorded in the Pentateuch. The Israelites accepted the unfavourable answer given by their kinsfolk the Edomites and Moabites, but took violent action against the Amorite Sihon when he did the same. *The wilderness* (18), i.e. of Zin. *And compassed the land of Edom, and the land of Moab* (18), i.e. passing south and east of Edom and east of Moab, instead of following the 'king's high way' which ran from south to north through these kingdoms and the kingdoms of Sihon and Og. Cf. Nu. xxi. 4, 13. Strong fortresses barred the way on the frontiers of the kingdoms of Edom and of Moab. It must have been spring when Israel journeyed east of those territories, for only then could enough water and grazing have been found. *Arnon was the border of Moab* (18), on the north, dividing it from Sihon's kingdom, and later from the territory of Reuben.

And Israel sent messengers unto Sihon (19). Cf. Nu. xxi. 21ff. *Heshbon* (19), mod. Hesban, sixteen miles east of Jordan and twenty-four miles north of Arnon. *Jahaz* (20). This place (not yet identified) is mentioned on the Moabite Stone as an outpost of the king of Israel against Moab, and later taken by Mesha and added to Dibon, which was four miles north of Arnon. *From Arnon even unto Jabbok* (22). In the division of the land the northern part of this territory went to Gad and the southern to Reuben. *Wilt not thou possess that which Chemosh thy god giveth thee to possess?* (24). Chemosh was the god of the Moabites, the Ammonite deity being Milcom (1 Ki. xi. 5). Jephthah's sarcastic 'argumentum ad hominem' (as Albright holds) does not necessarily mean that he himself regarded Chemosh and Yahweh as national deities on an equal footing, though it would not be surprising if a half-Canaanite like Jephthah did take this attitude. Mesha, on the Moabite Stone, ascribes his defeats and victories to the anger and favour of Chemosh. Jephthah argues that the two deities had shown their will—Yahweh by giving Israel victory over Sihon, and Chemosh by not enabling Moab to resist Sihon's earlier encroachments. In either case the divine will must be accepted as a 'fait accompli'. The very fact that Yahweh had done more for Israel than Chemosh had been able to do for Moab proved the superior power of Yahweh. *Art thou any thing better than Balak . . . ?* (25). The fact that the king of Moab at the time of the overthrow of Sihon made no attempt to reclaim the land won by Israel from Sihon, even if it had previously been Moabite territory, is a strong argument against the present claim. *Aroer* (26), the southernmost 'city' of Sihon's kingdom, on the north bank of the Arnon. *Three hundred years* (26), an inclusive number indicating that they were now in the third century since the events referred to.

d. Jephthah's victory and vow (xi. 29–40)

Then the Spirit of the Lord came upon Jephthah (29), who thus enters the list of the charismatic leaders. *And he passed over Gilead, and Manasseh* (29), to raise his army. *And passed over Mizpeh of Gilead* (29). Read 'passed over to Mizpeh of Gilead' (Heb. '*el* for '*eth*; cf. RSV), where the Israelite camp was (x. 17), from which *he passed*

over unto (or 'against') *the children of Ammon. And Jephthah vowed a vow unto the Lord* (30). It is customary to cite the similar story told by Servius (Latin commentator on Virgil) about Idomeneus, king of Crete, who was caught in a storm while returning home from the Trojan War, and vowed to sacrifice to the gods in return for his safety whatever should first meet him on his arrival home. This proved to be his son. *And he smote them from Aroer, even till thou come to Minnith . . . and unto the plain of the vineyards* (RV, 'Abel-cheramim') (33). Aroer is on the north bank of the Arnon, four miles south-west of Dibon. The other two places, presumably in the same general area, are unidentified. *And, behold, his daughter came out to meet him* (34). The simple and moving narrative-style of this passage illustrates Hebrew story-telling at its best. It has sometimes been inferred from verses 38–40 that Jephthah commuted his daughter's fate from burnt-offering to perpetual virginity, but this is hardly warranted by the narrative. The plain and restrained statement that he *did with her according to his vow* (39) is best taken as implying her actual sacrifice. Although human sacrifice was strictly forbidden to Israelites, we need not be surprised at a man of Jephthah's half-Canaanite antecedents following Canaanite usage in this matter. The closest biblical parallel is Mesha's sacrifice of his eldest son (2 Ki. iii. 27). Cf. also the sacrifice of Iphigeneia and Polyxena in Greek legend. The nobility of character shown by Jephthah's daughter has made her one of the world's great heroines; cf. stanzas 45–62 of Tennyson's 'Dream of Fair Women'. *Bewail my virginity* (37). Dean Stanley has compared Sophocles' picture of the Theban maiden Antigone bewailing her virginity before going to her living death as the price of obeying the call of sisterly duty. *The daughters of Israel went yearly to lament the daughter of Jephthah* (40). The verb rendered 'lament', or rather 'celebrate' (RV) or 'chant', is the same as that rendered 'rehearse' in Jdg. v. 11. The custom seems to have been a diversion to this particular purpose of a vegetation festival after the fashion of the annual wailing for Tammuz. Epiphanius says that in his day (4th century A.D.) Jephthah's daughter was honoured at Shechem by the Greek name *Kore* ('Maiden')—the name by which Persephone was honoured at Eleusis.

e. Jephthah's strife with Ephraim (xii. 1–7)

And the men of Ephraim gathered themselves together (1). This tribe now expresses resentment against Jephthah, as previously against Gideon. Probably they aimed at establishing their hegemony among the tribes; otherwise, as the Ammonites had crossed Jordan and attacked some of the western tribes, including Ephraim (x. 9), it is strange that Ephraim did not accept Jephthah's invitation to join his forces against Ammon (2). *Then Jephthah gathered together all the men of Gilead, and fought with Ephraim* (4). Evidently Ephraim had crossed Jordan and invaded Gilead, to pursue their quarrel with Jephthah. The Ephraimite taunt, *Ye Gileadites are fugitives . . .* (4), implied that these Transjordanians were deserters from the Joseph tribes. *And the Gileadites took the passages* (RV, 'fords') *of Jordan against the Ephraimites* (5). The invaders of Transjordan, worsted, were making their way home again, when they found their retreat thus cut off by the Transjordanians. The linguistic test that followed shows that in the Ephraimite dialect, as in Amorite and Arabic, s took the place of sh. The word *Shibboleth* means 'ear of corn'. Similarly, in the border wars between Scotland and England, a Northumbrian intruder in Scotland was immediately detected by his speech and summarily dealt with. *Was buried in one of the cities of Gilead* (7) or 'in his city, Mizpeh of Gilead', a reading supported by some MSS of LXX.

XII. IBZAN, ELON, ABDON: MINOR JUDGES. xii. 8–15

On the rôle of these minor judges see x. 1n. *That rode on threescore and ten ass colts* (14). Cf. x. 4. *In the land of Ephraim, in the mount of the Amalekites* (15). Cf. v. 14 for Amalekites in central Canaan.

XIII. OPPRESSION UNDER THE PHILISTINES AND EXPLOITS OF SAMSON. xiii. 1—xvi. 31

a. Annunciation and birth of Samson (xiii. 1–25)

And the Lord delivered them into the hand of the Philistines forty years (1). Having dealt with the Ammonite invasion, the author now turns to the other invaders mentioned in x. 7. These forty years lasted at least until the second battle of Ebenezer (1 Sa. vii. 10ff.), if not until the reign of Saul. At the end of Saul's reign (*c.* 1010 B.C.) we find that the Philistines have penetrated as far inland as Beth-shan (1 Sa. xxxi. 10). *There was a certain man of Zorah, of the family of the Danites* (2). Zorah (mod. Sar'ah) lay on the boundary of the old Danite territory and that of Judah. The northward migration of the Danites (xviii. 1ff.) had probably taken place by now; if so, a remnant must have remained in the old territory. *And his wife was barren, and bare not* (2). The birth of the coming child was thus marked by such divine interposition as attended the births of Isaac, Samuel and John the Baptist; and was announced by an angel, as were the first and third of these. *The angel of the Lord appeared unto the woman* (3). Cf. ii. 1, vi. 11, 12. *The child shall be a Nazarite unto God from the womb* (5). Therefore his mother, too, must observe some at least of the Nazirite precautions for the time being, especially those pertaining to food and drink (4, 14). On the Nazirite vow see Nu. vi. 2ff. The word itself (Heb. *nazir*, whence 'Nazirite' is the preferable spelling) is a passive participle meaning 'consecrated' or 'dedicated'. The Nazirite abstention from strong drink is implied in

Am. ii. 12. *And he shall begin to deliver Israel out of the hand of the Philistines* (5). This may mean 'he will be the first to save . . .'; the work was continued by Samuel, Saul and Jonathan, and completed by David. *Let us detain thee, until we shall have made ready a kid for thee* (15). The narrative at this point becomes remarkably similar to vi. 18ff., though there are differences, e.g. in the angel's response to the offer of a meal. *What is thy name . . .?* (17). Cf. Gn. xxxii. 29. *Why askest thou thus after my name, seeing it is secret?* (18). For the angel's unwillingness to reveal his name cf. Gn. xxxii. 29. Heb. *pel'i*, rendered *secret* (RV, 'wonderful'), is found again in Ps. cxxxix. 6, in the feminine *pel'iyah*. Cf. the noun *pele'* (from which this adjective is derived), rendered 'wonderful' in Is. ix. 6. *So Manoah took a kid with a meat offering* (19). Heb. *minḥah* (see vi. 18n.) is here used of something additional to the burnt-offering, hence in the sense 'meal offering' (RV) as in the vegetable oblation of Lv. ii. 1ff. *And offered it upon a rock unto the Lord* (19). 'To this day, the rock-stepped altar, covered with cup holes, is sprinkled with the blood of animals sacrificed by it' (A. T. Olmstead). *And the angel did wondrously* (19). Lit. 'and doing wondrously' (Heb. *maphli*), a participial comment attached to the main verb, showing how the angel lived up to his 'wonderful' name. *The flame went up toward heaven from off the altar* (20). Cf. vi. 21. *We shall surely die* (22). Cf. vi. 22f., with note. *Because we have seen God* (22). Lit. 'for it is a god that we have seen'. *If the Lord were pleased to kill us* (23). The woman's common sense prevails over her husband's numinous terror.

And the woman bare a son, and called his name Samson (24). Heb. *Shimshon*, derived from *shemesh*, 'sun' (cf. the neighbouring place-name Beth-shemesh). This name has been thought to fit in well with the view that the story of Samson, like the 'labours' of Gilgamesh and Heracles, is in origin a sun-myth. The arguments for this view are very slender, although it has been elaborated by several scholars. There is much more to be said for Burney's statement that the Samson narratives 'possess unique value as illustrating the village-life of the time, and the relations between Israelites and Philistines living in the border-country'. Twelve 'labours of Samson' have been reckoned: **1.** slaying the lion; **2.** killing the Philistines at Ashkelon; **3.** sending the foxes among the corn; **4.** the slaughter near Etam; **5.** bursting the cords of the men of Judah; **6.** the massacre with the jawbone; **7.** carrying off the gates of Gaza; **8.** quenching his thirst in Lehi; **9.** breaking the seven bowstrings; **10.** bursting the new ropes; **11.** tearing away the loom and web; **12.** pulling down the pillars. This enumeration, however, does not lie on the surface, and other ways of counting the episodes are possible. It is unlikely that the quenching of his thirst in Lehi should be reckoned a 'labour'. In any case, we are not dealing with mythology here. *And the Spirit of the Lord began to move* *him* (25). Thus Samson too becomes a charismatic hero. His 'judging' does not seem to have had a judicial character, but to have consisted in the exploits by which he became his people's champion against the enemy. *The camp of Dan* (25). 'Mahaneh-dan' (RV). See xviii. 12 for the origin of the name and the location of the place. *Between Zorah and Eshtaol* (25). Eshtaol, in the lowlands of Judah, is frequently identified with Eshwa', one and a half miles north-east of Zorah. The name may indicate the site of an ancient oracle.

b. The wedding of Samson (xiv. 1–20)

And Samson went down to Timnath (1), which, like Zorah and Eshtaol, lay on the boundary between Judah and Dan (cf. Jos. xv. 10, xix. 43), but at this time seems to have been occupied by Philistines (mod. Tibnah, three miles south-west of Beth-shemesh). *Now therefore get her for me to wife* (2). The fathers of the prospective bridal pair arranged the details of an ordinary wedding, including the fixing of the bride-price. In the event, however, it seems that it was not the ordinary type of marriage that was concluded, in which case the bride would have come to live with Samson, but the other form (cf. viii. 31) in which the bride remained with her own family, being visited by her husband from time to time, and any children would belong to their mother's family. *The uncircumcised Philistines* (3). So the Philistines are distinctively called, as the other peoples whom the Israelites knew at this period, the Egyptians, Canaanites, etc., practised circumcision like the Israelites themselves. *Get her for me* (3). This time the pronoun *her* is emphatic; in answer to his parents' suggestion that he would do better to marry an Israelite wife, he says, 'Get her and no other'. *A young lion roared against him* (5). In Old Testament times the lion was common in Palestine, especially in the 'jungle' of Jordan, but also in other parts of the country. *He rent him as he would have rent a kid* (6). The rushing of the divine power upon Samson enables him to act with strength above the ordinary (cf. verse 19, xv. 14). The rending of the lion is paralleled in ancient art, where mighty figures (e.g. Enkidu, the comrade of Gilgamesh) are depicted rending a lion down the middle by tearing its hind legs apart. *And he had nothing in his hand* (6). So Heracles strangled the Nemean lion with his hands. Josephus, possibly under the influence of the Heracles story, says that Samson strangled the lion. *There was a swarm of bees and honey in the carcase of the lion* (8). The carcase was by now thoroughly dry. Herodotus has a comparable story of a swarm of bees and a honeycomb found in the skull of Onesilos. We should not see here an allusion to the ancient belief, attested by Virgil, that bees were generated in putrefying carcases; this belief may have arisen from observation of the drone-fly in such an environment, but would not explain the presence of the honey. *He took thereof in his hands* (9). Lit. 'He scraped

it out with his hands'; this was a violation of the Nazirite code, and may explain why he did not tell his parents that he had taken the honey out of the dead lion.

Samson made there a feast (10). The fact that the feast was held at the bride's home and that the bridegroom's companions were Philistines suggests that the marriage was of the second type referred to above (verse 1n.). The writer explains it as an ancient custom, implying that at the time of writing it had become obsolete. *When they saw him* (11). We may perhaps read 'because they feared him' (*ke-yir'atham* for *ki-r'otham*). *Thirty companions* (11). The 'sons of the bride-chamber' of Mk. ii. 19. They may originally have been intended as a bodyguard for the bridegroom, but on this occasion they seem to have served as bodyguard for the others present against the bridegroom. *Thirty sheets and thirty change of garments* (12). The sheets (RV, 'linen garments') were large rectangular sheets which might be worn by day and slept in at night; the 'changes of raiment' (RV) were suits for festive occasions. *Out of the eater . . .* (14). In Hebrew the riddle takes the form of a rhythmical couplet, the two lines having three beats each. *And it came to pass on the seventh day* (15). The LXX and Syriac versions have 'fourth day', which agrees with the *three days* of verse 14. But there is still a discrepancy with *the seven days* of verse 17; where exactly the corruption lies is not easy to determine now. *Before the sun went down* (18), or perhaps 'before he entered the bridal chamber'. *What is sweeter than honey . . .?* (18). Again a rhythmical couplet, this time with two beats to the line. Samson's retort, *If ye had not plowed with my heifer . . .* (18), is a couplet of three beats to the line with rhyme as well as rhythm. Burney translates it well: 'If ye had not plowed with this heifer of mine, Ye would not have found out this riddle of mine'. *And he went down to Ashkelon* (19). Twenty-three miles away, on the coast, one of the cities of the Philistine pentapolis (cf. i. 18). *And his anger was kindled, and he went up to his father's house* (19), without entering the bridal chamber. *His companion, whom he had used as his friend* (20). In mod. English parlance, his 'best man'. Cf. 'the friend of the bridegroom' in Jn. iii. 29.

c. Other exploits of Samson (xv. 1—xvi. 3)

In the time of wheat harvest (xv. 1). This varied in Palestine according to the locality and climate, but fell about May (cf. the festival of Pentecost). Wheat was sown in November or December. *Samson visited his wife with a kid* (1), to appease her for his insult in leaving her so abruptly at the time of the wedding. But to take away the disgrace in which she was involved by Samson's desertion, her father had already given her in marriage to Samson's 'best man'. He now offers Samson instead *her younger sister* (2). Cf. 1 Sa. xviii. 19ff., and for a less close parallel Gn. xxix. 23ff. *Now shall I be more blameless . . .* (3). Read with RV mg. 'This time shall I be quits with he Philistines'. *And Samson went and caught three hundred foxes* (4). This is the proper meaning of Heb. *shu'al*, but it is commonly supposed that 'jackals' are meant here, as jackals are gregarious and easily caught, whereas the fox is solitary and more elusive. But foxes may be intended all the same. The use to which Samson put them is very similar to the custom at the Roman feast of Ceres (the corn-goddess), when foxes with burning torches attached to their brushes were hunted in the circus. *Burnt her and her father with fire* (6). Several MSS and versions read 'burnt her and her father's house'. Cf. the threat in xiv. 15. *He smote them hip and thigh* (8). Lit. 'leg upon thigh', probably a wrestling term, like Eng. 'cross-buttock'. The action is illustrated in Babylonian cylinder-seals where Gilgamesh is represented as using this device in wrestling. *He went down and dwelt in the top* (RV, 'cleft') *of the rock Etam* (8). Of proposed identifications of this 'cleft', that above the Wady Isma'in, two and a half miles east-south-east of Zorah, is most probable.

Spread themselves in Lehi (9). The place (meaning 'cheek', 'jawbone') may have been so called from the appearance of its crags, and can be identified with mod. Khirbet es-Siyyaj ('the ruin of Siyyaj'), where Siyyaj seems to be a loanword from Gk. *siagon* ('jawbone'), which is the rendering of Lehi found in Josephus and some Gk. versions of the Old Testament. *Knowest thou not that the Philistines are rulers over us?* (11). The people of Judah are obviously well content with the Philistine domination, and resent the disturbance caused by Samson's feud with them. *His bands loosed from off his hands* (14). Lit. 'his bands melted . . .' *And he found a new jawbone of an ass* (15). Lit. 'a moist jawbone'; an old one would have been too brittle. J. G. Duncan mentions the possibility that jawbones fitted with three or four flint knives may have served as primitive weapons. *With the jawbone of an ass . . .* (16). Samson's exultant shout takes the form of a couplet with four beats to the line. For *heaps upon heaps* (16) read 'I have heaped them in heaps'. It is not easy to reproduce in English the play on words in Hebrew between 'ass' and 'heap' (both *ḥamor*). Moffatt partly substitutes rhyme for word-play: 'With the jawbone of an ass I have piled them in a mass! With the jawbone of an ass I have assailed assailants!' This however, loses sight of the *thousand men* (16). *He cast away the jawbone out of his hand, and called that place Ramath-lehi* (17), i.e. 'the height of Lehi'; but there is a word-play with *ramah* ('throw'), as if the name meant 'the throwing of the jawbone' (though *ramah* is not the word rendered 'he cast away'). *But God clave an hollow place that was in the jaw* (19). 'But God clave the hollow place that is in Lehi' (RV). Heb. *makhtesh*, rendered *hollow place*, is lit. 'mortar'; it was evidently a rock-depression containing a spring, the origin of which is thus accounted for. The misleading AV rendering is due to the fact that the Hebrew word for *jaw* (*leḥi*) is the same as

that of the place; but the rendering is the more absurd because the narrator refers to the spring as existing in Lehi in his day. *En-hakkore* (19). Lit. 'spring of the caller' (this is the name of the partridge in biblical Hebrew, because of its distinctive call-note). *And he judged Israel in the days of the Philistines twenty years* (20), c. 1070–1050 B.C. There is no indication that in his case the word implies a judicial or military office; and his exploits are confined to the south, especially the Philistine border.

Then went Samson to Gaza (xvi. 1). Gaza was the most southerly city of the Philistine pentapolis. It was much older than the Philistine settlement; it is mentioned in the Tell el-Amarna tablets (fourteenth century B.C.), and was captured by Judah (Jdg. i. 18) before its occupation by the Philistines. It is fanciful to see in this narrative support for the sun-myth interpretation of the Samson saga, as some do, by drawing an analogy with the sun coming forth as a bridegroom from his chamber and rejoicing as a giant to run his course (cf. Ps. xix. 5). *And laid wait for him all night in the gate of the city, and were quiet all the night* (2). Kittel emends the first *all night* to 'all day'; the sense being that the men of Gaza watched the gates by day, but relaxed their vigilance at night, because the gates were closed then. But thus they played into Samson's hands, for he rose by night and went out, lifting the barred gates with their posts and carrying them away on his shoulders, *to the top of an hill that is before Hebron* (3), i.e. on the east side of Hebron. Hebron (see i. 20) is some thirty-eight miles east of Gaza.

d. Last exploits of Samson (xvi. 4–31)

He loved a woman in the valley of Sorek, whose name was Delilah (4). This place seems to have been the Wadi es-Sarar. A ruin north of the wady, about two miles from Zorah, still bears the name Surik. It is not clear whether Delilah was an Israelite or a Philistine, though the narrative suggests the latter. Her name is Semitic (meaning 'devotee'; possibly her full name included the name of the deity whose devotee she was). It recurs in the Greek text of 1 Ch. iv. 19 in the genealogy of the tribe of Judah. But Semitic names are found among the Philistines not unnaturally, since the Philistine immigrants brought few women with them and must have intermarried with the people of Canaan. *The lords of the Philistines* (5). See iii. 3n. *Eleven hundred pieces of silver* (5), i.e. 1,100 shekels, about thirty pound weight. No convincing reason has been offered for the figure 1100 rather than, say, the round number 1000. Cf. xvii. 2. *If they bind me with seven green withs* (7). Render, with RV mg., 'seven new bowstrings', made of twisted gut. *The Philistines be upon thee, Samson* (9). We are to understand that they were in readiness in case Samson had told the truth; when his strength is proved they remain hid and he thinks that she is playing with him. *So his strength was not known* (9), or rather, 'was not brought low'. *If they bind me fast with new ropes* (11). Cf. his binding by the Judaeans in xv. 13. *If thou weavest the seven locks of my head with the web* (13). Delilah, we may understand, having the sleeping Samson's head in her lap (as in verse 19), weaves his hair into the warp and beats it up into the web *with the pin* (14), a flat piece of wood, so that his hair actually becomes part of the woven material. The loom would be the primitive type with two upright posts fixed in the ground, the one holding the yarn-beam and the other the cloth-beam. When Samson wakes up, he goes off, loom and all fixed to his hair, dragging the upright posts out of the ground. For *went away with the pin of the beam, and with the web* (14), read 'plucked away the loom and the web'. *And she caused him to shave off the seven locks of his head* (19). Read 'and he shaved off . . .' Cf. the Greek story of how Minos took Megara when the golden lock of Nisos its king was shorn. *And she began to afflict him* (19). Rather: 'and he began to be afflicted' or 'weakened'. *I will go out as at other times before, and shake myself* (20). This may imply that he was already bound as well as shaved.

And he did grind in the prison house (21). Lit. 'He was (continually) grinding', probably at a hand mill with saddle-quern. The large mill which was normally turned by an ass, such as is called a *mylos onikos* in Mt. xviii. 6, is not known to have been used before 500 B.C. *The hair of his head began to grow again* (22), implying a con-current return of his strength. *Dagon their god* (23). Dagon (cf. Heb. *dagan*, 'grain') was a Semitic corn-deity, a temple of whom has been found at the Amorite city of Mari on the Euphrates (eighteenth century B.C.). He was introduced by the Amorites into Syria, and his name appears on the tablets of Ras Shamra, where also he had a temple. The Philistines evidently took over his cult. *Our god hath delivered into our hands . . .* (24). Their chant of triumph is a rhymed quatrain with two beats to the line. *Call for Samson, that he may make us sport* (25). Presumably he was to perform 'strong man acts'. *They set him between the pillars* (25). The character of the building is illustrated by discoveries at Gezer and Gaza. The roof was supported by wooden pillars set on stone bases. It was flat, consisting of logs of wood stretching from one wall to beams supported by the pillars and from these beams to other beams or to the opposite wall. The temple at Gezer had a fore-court leading into a paved inner chamber, separated from it by four circular stones, on which the wooden pillars stood. Samson probably stood between the two central pillars, if there were more than two. The Philistine lords and ladies were in the inner chamber; the crowd watched from the roof. *Samson made sport* (27) in the forecourt, and then asked the boy to lead him to the central pillars to rest against them. Then, putting an arm round each, and bending forward so as to force them out of the perpendicular, he brought the roof down. The weight of people on the roof may have made the feat all the easier. *That I may be at once avenged of the Philistines for my two eyes* (28). The idea probably is 'one vengeance for both my eyes'. RV mg., 'for one of my two eyes', is a grim jest, but perhaps out of place in this scene. *His brethren and all the house of his father came down* (31). Manoah was evidently dead by this time, despite Milton's effective introduction of him in *Samson Agonistes*.

XIV. MICAH'S PRIEST AND THE DANITE MIGRATION. xvii. 1—xviii. 31

a. Micah's priest (xvii. 1–13)

The eleven hundred shekels of silver (2). See xvi. 5n. *About which thou cursedst* (2). Or simply 'didst take an oath' (i.e. to dedicate the sum to religious purposes), which would involve a curse upon anyone who violated it. When Micah acknowledged that he had taken the money and restored it to the purpose to which his mother had dedicated it, she annulled the curse by invoking a blessing on him. *Now therefore I will restore it unto thee* (3). This clause seems to have been displaced from verse 2, where it would naturally follow *I took it. His mother took two hundred shekels of silver* (4). Perhaps, like Ananias and Sapphira, keeping back part of the sum originally dedicated. *Gave them to the founder* (4). In this case a silversmith. *The graven image* (4) will have been one carved out of wood and overlaid with silver; the *molten image* (4) would be entirely of silver. There are, however, indications in the text that only one image is meant; note RV 'and it was' (not *they were*) *in the house of Micah* (4). We are not told what form the image(s) took, but that of a young bull is not unlikely. *And the man Micah had an house of gods* (5), i.e. a shrine attached to his dwelling, to which people would come to ascertain the divine will. *And made an ephod, and teraphim* (5). For the divining ephod cf. viii. 27. Teraphim were probably images of household gods (cf. Gn. xxxi. 19; 1 Sa. xix. 13). *Consecrated one of his sons, who became his priest* (5). The term *consecrated* (Heb. *mille yadh*) means lit. 'filled his hand', i.e. with portions of a sacrifice (cf. Ex. xxviii. 41, etc.). There were other priests than those of the family of Levi, who are distinguished as 'the Levitical priests' (as in Dt. xviii. 1). But it appears from this narrative that a member of the tribe of Levi was preferred when he was available. When the national worship was centralized at the temple in Jerusalem under the monarchy, only the Aaronic priest-hood was recognized. Hence the explanatory remark of a writer who lived under very different conditions and was recording events of an earlier age: *In those days there was no king in Israel, but every man did that which was right in his own eyes* (6).

There was a young man out of Beth-lehem-judah, of the family of Judah, who was a Levite (7). As he was Moses' grandson (xviii. 30, RV), he was a

Levite by birth. Yet he is reckoned a member of the clan of Judah. The Levites, having no tribal territory of their own, depended on other tribes' hospitality (cf. xix. 1), which explains why this one lived in Bethlehem and is reckoned in Judah. The Levites had a close connection with the southern tribes, especially with Judah. *And he sojourned there* (7). Heb. *ger sham*, which is identical with the name of the Levite's father (xviii. 30); the original text here may have been 'and he was Jonathan the son of Gershom'. *Be unto me a father and a priest* (10). For *father* used as a term of honour cf. Gn. xlv. 8; 2 Ki. vi. 21, xiii. 14. In verse 11 exactly the opposite relationship is figuratively employed: *The young man was unto him as one of his sons* (11). But there Micah's care of him is implied. *Ten shekels of silver by the year* (10). About four ounces avoirdupois. *Seeing I have a Levite to my priest* (13). Quite obviously a Levite was regarded as possessing special priestly qualifications. Among the Minaeans of Arabia the cognate words *lawi'u* and its feminine *lawi'atu* appear with the sense 'person pledged for a vow or debt' (cf. Samuel).

b. The Danite migration (xviii. 1–31)

The tribe of the Danites sought them an inheritance to dwell in (1). According to i. 34 it was the Amorites (themselves no doubt pressed by the Philistines) who exercised pressure on the Danites. The story of their migration is summarized in Jos. xix. 47, where Laish is called Leshem. *From Zorah, and from Eshtaol* (2). See xiii. 25n. *They knew the voice of the young man the Levite* (3). This suggests that they knew him before, when he lived in Bethlehem, the connection between the tribes of Judah and Dan being fairly close. Or they may simply have recognized by his voice that he came from their neighbourhood. *Ask counsel, we pray thee, of God* (5). This was the evident object of Micah's 'house of gods' (xvii. 5). *Came to Laish* (7). Mod. Tell el-Qadi (Arab. *qadi*, 'judge'; cf. Heb. *Dan*), at one of the sources of Jordan. It is called Lus(i) in Egyptian texts of *c.* 1850–1825 B.C. *Had no business with any man* (7). Perhaps we should read with some texts of the Greek and Syrian versions, 'had no dealings with Syria' (*'Aram* instead of *'adam*). The district was isolated from Phoenicia by the Lebanon range and from Syria by Hermon and the Anti-Lebanon range. The account of the Laishites shows that it was not enough in ancient, any more than in modern, times for a people to live in quietness and neutrality if they wished to be secure against aggression. In this case it gave the Danites all the more reason to expropriate them, especially as their land had *no want of any thing that is in the earth* (10).

Six hundred men (11). The fewness of the men of war is a measure of the weakness of this tribe. *Pitched in Kirjath-jearim* (12). A city of Judah, eight miles west of Jerusalem, on the Benjamite border. *Wherefore they called that place Mahaneh-dan* (12), i.e. 'the camp of Dan'; cf.

xiii. 25. *Stood by the entering of the gate* (16). Presumably leading into the courtyard of Micah's house. *Lay thine hand upon thy mouth* (19). For the idiom (denoting silence) cf. Jb. xxi. 5, xxix. 9, xl. 4; Pr. xxx. 32; Mi. vii. 16. *Be to us a father and a priest* (19). Cf. xvii. 10. *My gods which I made* (24). We may trace here some irony on the writer's part similar to that expressed at greater length in Is. xliv. 9ff. *It was in the valley that lieth by Beth-rehob* (28). The valley is El-Buqa', between Lebanon and Hermon. Beth-rehob, possibly the Rehob of i. 31, is unknown. *They called the name of the city Dan* (29). It became the northernmost point of the land of the twelve tribes: cf. the phrase 'from Dan to Beer-sheba'.

Jonathan, the son of Gershom, the son of Manasseh (RV, 'Moses'), *he and his sons were priests to the tribe of Dan* (30). For Gershom cf. Ex. ii. 22. The Massoretes, jealous for the reputation of Moses, inserted a suspended 'N' between the 'M' and the 'S', as though the name were Manasseh, not wishing to disguise the true sense, but implying that this idolatrous priest behaved in a way befitting a descendant of Manasseh rather than of Moses. But the rabbis knew and admitted that Moses was meant. If no generation is omitted in this man's genealogy, the Danite migration must have taken place at an early point in the period of the judges. Probably some Danites remained behind in the southern territory (cf. v. 17, xiii. 2). The presence at Dan of a priesthood descended from Moses would give the place high prestige, which explains why Jeroboam I chose it as one of the two national shrines for the northern kingdom. Jeroboam's bull-calf at Dan may well have been the 'descendant' of Micah's graven image, which probably enough had the same form. It served as the visible pedestal for the invisible presence of the deity. *Until the day of the captivity of the land* (30), i.e. probably the captivity of the Galilaean population under Tiglath-pileser III in 733–732 B.C. (2 Ki. xv. 29), which would put an effective end to the priesthood and cult at Dan. Houbigant, however, emended *the captivity of the land* (30) to 'the captivity of the ark' (reading *ha'aron* for *ha'ares*), taking the phrase as a duplicate of *all the time that the house of God was in Shiloh* (31). But the effect of the Philistine victory at Aphek was hardly felt so far north as Dan. The introduction of the note *all the time that the house of God was in Shiloh* (31) may have been intended to indicate that the Dan cult was of comparable antiquity to that of Shiloh. Shiloh is mod. Seilun, about nineteen miles north of Jerusalem and twelve miles south of Shechem. There the 'tent of meeting' was set up soon after the entry into Canaan, to serve as the central sanctuary for the 'amphictyonic league' of the tribes of Israel (Jos. xviii. 1; cf. also Jos. xxi. 2; Jdg. xxi. 12, 19ff.). But the house of God at Shiloh in the early chapters of 1 Samuel was apparently a more stable structure than simply a tent. The destruction of Shiloh is not mentioned in 1 Samuel, but we can infer that it was destroyed by the Philistines after the battle of Aphek (1 Sa. iv. 10), and this is borne out by Je. vii. 12ff., xxvi. 6, 9; Ps. lxxviii. 60ff. Danish excavations in 1926 and 1928 have shown that there was an extensive settlement at Shiloh in the twelfth and early eleventh centuries B.C. until its destruction c. 1050 B.C.

XV. THE WAR AGAINST BENJAMIN. xix. 1—xxi. 25

a. The outrage at Gibeah (xix. 1-30)

There was a certain Levite sojourning on the side of mount Ephraim (1). Either on the western or eastern flanks of the Ephraim highlands. *Who took to him a concubine out of Beth-lehem-judah* (1). Like the Levite of xvii and xviii, this Levite had connections both with the Ephraim highlands and with Bethlehem in Judah. *And his concubine played the whore against him* (2), or, as several of the versions have it, 'was angry with him' (cf. RSV). *To speak friendly unto her* (3). Lit. 'to speak to her heart' (as in Is. xl. 2). *And they tarried until afternoon* (8), though it depends on an emendation, is preferable to 'and tarry ye until the day declineth' (RV, following the Massoretic text and all versions); as the father-in-law in verse 9 gives the day's declining as a reason for their staying another night. *The day groweth to an end* (9). Lit. 'the encamping of day', i.e. the time to pitch camp for the night. Nomadic idioms survived even when the Israelites had become a settled population. Cf. 2 Sa. xx. 1; 1 Ki. xii. 16. *And came over against Jebus, which is Jerusalem* (10). The city was still in the hands of the Jebusites. For this reason (12) the Levite refused to spend the night there, though in fact it could not have treated him less hospitably than Gibeah, a *city . . . of the children of Israel* (12). Jebus appears as a name for Jerusalem only here and in 1 Ch. xi. 4, 5, and is probably derived from the name of the Amorite group (Jebusites) who settled there. See i. 21n. *In Gibeah* (13). Mod. Tell el-Ful, four miles north of Jerusalem. It was a town of Benjamin, later known as 'Gibeah of Saul', because it was the home and capital of Saul (1 Sa. xi. 4). Excavations at Tell el-Ful have shown that the first fortress of Gibeah was founded soon after the conquest and destroyed in the twelfth century B.C.; the second fortress, that of Saul, has also been uncovered. *Or in Ramah* (13). Farther north than Gibeah, on the way to Bethel. Cf. iv. 5. *An old man . . . which was also of mount Ephraim* (16). As the Levite himself was; but it adds point to the story that the one man in Gibeah to offer hospitality to the strangers was not a Benjamite. *I am now going to the house of the Lord* (18). Read 'my house' with LXX; the pronominal suffix meaning 'my' has been misread as an abbreviation for Yahweh. *Certain sons of Belial* (22). This word is vocalized so as to mean 'worthless' (Heb. *beli*, 'without', and *ya'al*, 'worth'). 'Sons of Belial' are then 'lewd fellows of the baser sort'. Other suggestions are

that Belial means either 'the world of the dead' (a natural sense in 2 Sa. xxii. 5; Ps. xviii. 4), lit. 'the place from which there is no coming up', or 'lord of night'. In post-biblical Jewish writings Belial (Gk. *Beliar*) is the name of a person, the antichrist or incarnation of wickedness (cf. 2 Cor. vi. 15). The unpleasant narrative of these verses (22-24) is strikingly similar to the tale of Sodom (Gn. xix. 4-8). *Do not this folly* (23). *Folly* is inadequate as a translation of Heb. *nebhalah;* 'wantonness' or 'villainy' is better. AV gives a better rendering of the word at the end of verse 24: *do not so vile a thing.* The laws of hospitality here, as in Gn. xix, obviously took precedence over considerations of chivalry towards the female sex. *He took a knife . . .* (29). This dismemberment and distribution of a body as a call to national action is paralleled in 1 Sa. xi. 7; there, however, a yoke of oxen is so used and the distribution is accompanied by a threat to do the same to the oxen of anyone who will not join against the enemy. The twelve pieces into which the woman's body was divided no doubt correspond to the number of the tribes of Israel. The practice plainly imposed a solemn obligation on those to whom the grisly tokens were sent, calling on all to act in the spirit of the national covenant. *From the day that the children of Israel came up out of the land of Egypt* (30). The exodus, marking the birth of the nation, provided a starting-point from which events might be reckoned (cf. 1 Ki. vi. 1). The outrage at Gibeah stood out as a monument of wickedness for centuries to come (cf. Ho. x. 9).

b. The destruction of Gibeah (xx. 1-48)

The congregation was gathered together as one man (1). The Levite's summons had been effective; here all the tribes are gathered together—from north, south, and Transjordan—and they meet *in Mizpeh* (1), five miles northwest of Jerusalem (not the Transjordanian Mizpeh of x. 17, although the meaning 'watchtower' is the same). *Four hundred thousand footmen that drew sword* (2). This figure is in keeping with the Pentateuchal censuses, but the word rendered 'thousand' here as there (Heb. *'eleph*) may denote a much smaller unit, 'practically, perhaps exactly, equivalent to the subdivision of the tribe which was technically known as a father's house; cf. Jdg. vi. 15' (Westminster Bible Dictionary). *They have committed . . . folly in Israel* (6), i.e. 'wantonness' (see xix. 23n.); and for the whole phrase cf. Gn. xxxiv. 7; Dt. xxii. 21; Jos. vii. 15; 2 Sa. xiii. 12f.

Put away evil from Israel (13). Cf. for the phrase Dt. xvii. 12. *Twenty and six thousand* (15). Most of the versions read '25,000 men', which accords better with the later statements in verses 35 and 47. Benjamin was small in proportion to the other tribes; it numbered one seventeenth of the whole. *Seven hundred chosen men* (16). If this figure has been repeated from verse 15 by dittography, as Vulg. suggests, then the men of Gibeah are the 700 skilful slingers. *Lefthanded*

(16). Or possibly 'ambidextrous'; see iii. 15n. and cf. 1 Ch. xii. 2. *And not miss* (16). The Heb. verb is *ḥaṭa*, commonly used in the moral sense of 'sin'. *Went up to the house of God* (18). 'Bethel' (RV). This ancient sanctuary continued to be used as a religious centre throughout the northern monarchy. Here AV, following Vulg., renders *the house of God*, meaning Shiloh, from the mention of Phinehas and the ark in verses 27, 28. But the ark did not always stay in the same place.

Burnt offerings and peace offerings (26), i.e. piacular sacrifices to expiate the cause of their defeat, followed by a communion sacrifice and feast. *Phinehas, the son of Eleazar, the son of Aaron, stood before it in those days* (28). This incident therefore belongs to the same generation as the migration of the Danites (cf. xviii. 30). Phinehas (Heb. *Pinḥas*) is a word of Egyptian origin, meaning 'the Nubian' or 'the child of dark complexion' (cf. Nu. xxv. 1–13). Israelites with Egyptian names (cf. Moses) are found only in the tribe of Levi. *And Israel set liers in wait round about Gibeah* (29). The tactics are similar to those used against Ai (Jos. viii. 12ff.). *Of which one goeth up to the house of God* (RV, 'Bethel'), *and the other to Gibeah* (31). For Gibeah here we probably ought to read Gibeon—mod. El-jib, *c.* six miles north-west of Jerusalem, and four miles from Gibeah. *Baal-tamar* (33). On the border of Judah and Benjamin. The name means 'lord of the palm' and the place may have been called after a Canaanite deity of that name. *The children of Israel destroyed of the Benjamites that day twenty and five thousand and an hundred men* (35). Leaving as survivors only the 600 of verse 47; the original total being 25,700 (see verse 15n.). See also note on *thousand* in verse 2. The statement here is an anticipatory summary of the narrative of verses 36–46. *An appointed sign* (38). The word for *sign*, found also in Je. vi. 1 and in the Lachish letters, means a torch-beacon. Cf. Jos. viii. 20f. *The flame of the city ascended up to heaven* (40). The destruction of Gibeah at this period is confirmed by excavations carried out by American archaeologists in 1922–23. *Trode them down with ease* (43). 'At their resting-place' (RV), or 'from Nohah' (cf. 1 Ch. viii. 2). *Over against Gibeah* (43). Or Geba, on the direct route from Gibeah to Rimmon. Geba is about six miles north-north-east of Jerusalem, and *the rock Rimmon* (47) is about as far again in the same direction. The name survives in the mod. village Rammun. It is a detached limestone eminence, cut off by ravines on north, west and south, and containing caverns in which the fugitives could live.

c. Reconciliation (xxi. 1–25)

And the people came to the house of God (2). Again, as in xx. 18, 26, translate with RV 'to Bethel'. *And built there an altar* (4). A strange action, as xx. 26 makes it clear that there was an altar there already. It has been suggested (e.g. by Burney) that the original reference here was to the building of an altar at Mizpeh. *They had made a great oath* (5). Lit. 'the great oath had been': the reference may be to some peculiarly solemn form of oath. *There came none to the camp from Jabesh-gilead* (8). This is believed to have stood on the site of mod. Ed-Deir, nine and a half miles south-east of Beth-shan on the east of Jordan, on the Wadi el-Yabis. *Twelve thousand men of the valiantest* (10). For *thousand* see xx. 2n. *And this is the thing that ye shall do* (11). Cf. the policy adopted at Moses' instance with regard to the Midianite women (Nu. xxxi. 15ff.). *And they found among the inhabitants of Jabesh-gilead four hundred young virgins* (12). To the marriage of these girls with the Benjamite survivors may be due the close relationship of later days between Jabesh-gilead and the tribe of Benjamin (especially in the time of King Saul, a Benjamite); cf. in particular Saul's action in defence of the Jabeshites against the Ammonites (1 Sa. xi), and the Jabeshites' rescue of Saul's body from the walls of Beth-shan (1 Sa. xxxi. 11ff.). And in view of Saul's connection with Gibeah, was there some early tie which deterred the Jabeshites from joining the war of vengeance against that town? By the time of the incident of 1 Sa. xi (*c.* 1025 B.C.), Jabesh was again quite populous. *They brought them unto the camp to Shiloh* (12), which served as an inter-tribal centre (cf. xviii. 31, xxi. 19ff.). *Then they said* (19). Presumably to the Benjamites, at least to the 200 who were still unprovided with wives. Hence the particularity with which the location of the feast is described. *Behold, there is a feast* (RV mg., 'the feast') *of the Lord in Shiloh yearly* (19). This feast (Heb. *ḥag*, lit. 'pilgrimage') was a local variety of the feast of tabernacles, here more particularly to celebrate the ingathering of the year's vintage (cf. ix. 27). This may have been the feast which Elkanah and his family attended annually at Shiloh (1 Sa. i. 6ff.). The dancing of the maidens formed part of the 'harvest home' celebrations. *Catch you every man his wife* (21). A reversion to the practice of marriage by capture. The rape of the Sabines in Roman legend is a well-known parallel. *Be favourable unto them for our sakes* (22). 'Grant them graciously unto us' (RV). They adduce two reasons for the acquiescence of the men of Shiloh: they had not seized the maidens as an act of war; and they had thus delivered the Shilonites from the guilt of voluntarily handing over their daughters, which would have been a breach of the oath sworn at Mizpeh (verse 1). *In those days . . .* (25). Quoted from xvii. 6; cf. also xviii. 1, xix. 1.

F. F. BRUCE.

RUTH

INTRODUCTION

I. ITS PLACE IN THE CANON

In the LXX, the Vulgate and the Lutheran Versions, the book of Ruth comes in between the book of Judges and that of Samuel, and belongs to the same historical period. It is in fact supplementary to the one and introductory to the other, but affords a striking contrast to both in its contents. Judges and Samuel abound in scenes of lawlessness and strife. Armies march and countermarch. Israel is defeated and oppressed; then she hears the call of freedom and does valiantly in the name of Jehovah. Great leaders come to power, and play their part and pass on. There are scenes of savagery and lust.

In the book of Ruth, however, the clash of arms and the tumult of men are strangely stilled. Here, one feels, is the life the people really lived. Great men and nations rose and fell; battles were fought and won and lost; there were intrigues and rivalries in high places. Yet all the time the life of the people went on as it had done for ages past, and as it would do for ages still to come. The labour of men on the land, old country customs, love and marriage, the rearing of children, and simple faith in God went on behind the dreadful façade of cruelty and bloodshed depicted in the book of Judges.

The fact that it describes these enduring things and especially that it contains the history of David's immediate ancestors is probably the main reason why the Hebrew Codex places the book of Ruth among the *Hagiographa*, and the Talmud puts it at the top of them, even before the Psalms. In the Hebrew MSS it is to be found among the five *Megilloth* or Rolls.

II. BACKGROUND AND DATE

The events narrated took place during the reign of the judges (i. 1); but this period covered 450 years (Acts xiii. 20). In iv. 21, 22, however, we are told that Boaz was the great-grandfather of David, which would place the events of the book somewhat before the middle of the twelfth century B.C., that is about the time when Samuel was young. In this connection it is interesting to note that Josephus indicates that Ruth lived in the days of Eli (Ant. v. 9, 1). On the other hand Salmon, who is given here as the father of Boaz, was the husband of Rahab (Mt. i. 5) and this points to a very much earlier date. Indeed it is difficult to reconcile these two pointers except by assuming that there is a gap in the genealogy such as in fact occurs in Mt. i. 9 and elsewhere. If this assumption is correct it is impossible to assign even an approximate date to such a gap, and the book furnishes no internal evidence that would throw any reliable light on the question. Nevertheless there is no real reason why the date given by Josephus should not be accepted; it is but reasonable to suppose that he had sources of information denied to us, despite his historical unreliability.

III. DATE OF COMPOSITION

It is equally difficult to come to any definite conclusion on the question of when the book was written. Here again we must rely upon internal evidence, and as it happens even this is not very helpful. It was written after the days of the judges (i. 1) and a considerable time after the events took place, as some of the customs recorded had by then fallen into desuetude (iv. 6–8). Furthermore the book could not have been written before the reign of David as he is mentioned in the genealogy (iv. 22). Beyond these deductions one enters the field of pure conjecture, but the general outlook of the book seems to point to the reign of David.

The book of Ruth tells of the fortunes of the family of Elimelech of Bethlehem, who migrated to Moab under stress of famine and died there with his two sons. Whereupon his widow Naomi returned to her homeland with Ruth her widowed daughter-in-law who devotedly insisted on accompanying her. There, in their distress, they discovered Boaz, a near kinsman, who willingly assumed the full responsibilities of a *goel*, or next of kin, by marrying Ruth, thus raising and preserving a family for the dead son of Naomi. Of this union was born Obed, the forefather of David.

OUTLINE OF CONTENTS

I. THE FAMINE AND ELIMELECH'S DISASTROUS MIGRATION. i. 1–5

II. NAOMI AND RUTH DECIDE TO GO TO JUDAH. i. 6–18

III. A SAD HOMECOMING. i. 19–22

IV. A FRIEND IN NEED. ii. 1–23

V. THE LAW IS INVOKED. iii. 1–18

VI. THE GOEL ACCEPTS HIS RESPONSIBILITIES. iv. 1–16

VII. THE PROMISE. iv. 17–22

COMMENTARY

I. THE FAMINE AND ELIMELECH'S DISASTROUS MIGRATION. i. 1–5

Now it came to pass (1). Heb. *wayehi*, attaches the account that is to follow to other well known events (cf. Jos. i. 1). *When the judges ruled* (1). RV more accurately translates 'judged'. See Introduction to commentary on Judges, p. 236. *A famine* (1). There is no specific mention of a famine in the book of Judges, but there must have been many occasions during that turbulent period when 'the staff of bread was broken' either through natural causes or enemy invasions (cf. Jdg. vi. 3–6). *Beth-lehem-judah* (1). Probably so called to distinguish it from Bethlehem of Zebulun (Jos. xix. 15). *The country of Moab* (1). Heb. *şadhe* properly means a field or level place, a term that is by no means descriptive of Moab as a whole and seems here to refer to a particular part of that country, probably the rolling plateau south of the Arnon, still a rich pastureland. See description of the 'plentiful field' of Moab in Is. xvi. 10; Je. xlviii. 33. *Elimelech* (2) means 'to whom God is king'; *Naomi*, 'the pleasant one'; *Mahlon*, 'the weakly'; *Chilion*, 'pining'. *Ephrathites* (2). Ephrath was the old name for Bethlehem (Gn. xxxv. 19). *And they took them wives . . . of Moab* (4). The Targum inserts 'And they transgressed the commandment of the Lord and took . . .' Actually marriage with Moabite women was not specifically forbidden, although receiving Moabites into the congregation of the Lord was (cf. Dt. xxiii. 3n.). *Orpah . . . Ruth* (4). These are Moabite names and may possibly mean 'kind' or, perhaps, 'turning the back', and 'rose', but the difference between the two languages, although not great (see note on ii. 8 below), nevertheless makes a reliable translation impossible. Ruth was the wife of Mahlon, probably the elder son (iv. 10). The Targum says she was the daughter of Eglon king of Moab (Jdg. iii. 12), which is unlikely. *And Mahlon and Chilion died* (5). There is no hint that their deaths were a judgment for leaving the land of promise for Moab. These names—'wasting' and 'consumption'—might have been echoes of the famine that consumed the land, or they might have been descriptive of the weakly constitutions of these two young men.

II. NAOMI AND RUTH DECIDE TO GO TO JUDAH. i. 6–18

She arose . . . that she might return (6). Lit. 'She rose . . . and she returned'. Naomi was now actually on her way to Bethlehem. *She had heard*

(6). She had been ten years in Moab and if, as seems likely, it was toward the end of that period she heard this, the famine must have lasted very long. On the other hand the turbulence of the times may have made contacts between the two places very difficult. *And they went . . . to return* (7). Orpah and Ruth both clearly intended to return with Naomi to Bethlehem. The speech of Naomi, 'the gracious one', makes it easy to understand how she inspired the love and devotion of her daughters-in-law. *Each to her mother's house* (8). Ruth's father was still alive (ii. 11), but their mothers are mentioned probably in order to emphasize that after all Naomi is only their mother-in-law.

The Lord deal kindly (8). Note that Jehovah is invoked as a name already familiar to them. *Rest* (9). Heb. *menuchah* means a place of rest and is often used to give the idea of the fulfilment of a purpose or the realization of a hope or, as here, the end of trials and vicissitudes (see Dt. xii. 9; Is. xi. 10, etc.). *Surely* (10). Heb. *ki*. Placed before a direct statement this expression serves to strengthen it, as in Gn. xxix. 32 and Ex. iii. 12. *Any more sons* (11). The first mention in this book of the Israelite law of the levirate marriage, requiring a man to marry the widow of a brother who dies without issue in order to raise a family for his brother (Dt. xxv. 5; Mt. xxii. 23–28). We do not know whether this law was recognized in Moab, but it is safe to assume that Orpah and Ruth were familiar with it. Indeed verses 11–13 are an argument showing the folly of seeking to invoke it in this case. *Tarry* (13). Lit. 'hope', and hence 'wait for'. *It grieveth me* (13). Heb. 'I have much bitterness'. Cf. verse 20. *Gone back . . . unto her gods* (15). There is not a vestige of reproach in these words, and it is difficult to read even a feeling of disappointment into them. For Orpah, to return to Moab simply meant to revert to the gods of Moab. Unlike Naaman (2 Ki. v. 17) the worship of Jehovah made no abiding impression on her and Naomi clearly knew it. *The Lord do so* (17). Jehovah is deliberately invoked by Ruth to indicate her choice of the God of Israel, but it would be wrong to assume that this choice was not made before now. Her love to Him as well as her love to Naomi inspires the noble words of verses 16, 17. Cf. Jn. vi. 68. *Stedfastly minded* (18). Heb. 'strengthened herself'. Ruth has sworn by Jehovah, and that itself makes further reasoning useless, if not impious. Moreover the vow she used was in itself a confession of her faith in Him.

III. A SAD HOMECOMING. i. 19-22

So they two went (19). The journey was only about fifty miles but the times were lawless (Jdg. xxi. 25) and it was a dangerous undertaking for two defenceless women. *All the city was moved* (19). This seems to indicate that the family of Elimelech had been well known in Bethlehem —a suggestion that is supported by the obvious standing and wealth of Boaz, his kinsman and friend. *They said* (19); i.e. the women (of the town) said, for the verb is feminine. *Call me* (20). This play upon words is common in the Old Testament and Naomi had already said that her lot was bitter (13). *I went out full* (21). She had a husband and two sons. It is also probable that Elimelech had left Bethlehem with his possessions before he suffered too heavily from the famine. *Barley harvest* (22). This began on the low grounds in April, a fortnight before the wheat harvest.

IV. A FRIEND IN NEED. ii. 1-23

A kinsman (1). The Hebrew word here, as in iii. 2 and Pr. vii. 4, is *moda*, meaning an acquaintance or friend, and is a totally different word from that translated 'kinsman' elsewhere in the book. Probably the friendship and not the relationship of Boaz is being emphasized. *A mighty man of wealth* (1). Heb. *hayil* means any kind of spiritual, mental or natural resources and may refer to the valour rather than the wealth of Boaz. This, in fact, is its usual meaning (see iii. 11n.; cf. Jdg. vi. 12). *Let me now go* (2). The law of Moses gave the poor and the stranger the right to glean after the harvesters (Lv. xix. 9). *Kindred* (3). Heb. *mishpachah*, a different word from that used in ii. 1 and iii. 2, and at the same time entirely different from the word used elsewhere in the book when the kinsman is regarded as subject to the law of Moses. *The Lord be with you . . . the Lord bless thee* (4). Evidently the conventional salutation and response. Cf. Ps. cxxix. 8. *Whose damsel is this?* (5). It is possible that something foreign in the appearance or dress of Ruth arrested his attention. *Hath continued . . . until now* (7). She has worked hard all day long until now, when she has just taken a short rest. *My daughter* (8). This gives the impression that Boaz was no longer a young man. Boaz could easily converse with a Moabite as there was very little difference between the two languages. This is proved by the Moabite inscription on Mesha's Stone (890 B.C.). Cf. 2 Ki. iii. 5ff. *Abide here fast* (8). Lit. 'cleave to', the same word as in i. 14. *My maidens* (8), i.e. the women who tied the sheaves. Boaz had evidently made full arrangements for the protection of Ruth before he spoke to her himself. By rights only the hired workers could claim the privilege Boaz offered.

A stranger (10). The fact that she was an alien, and a Moabitess at that, made it extremely doubtful whether Ruth would meet with real kindness in her adopted country. *Left thy father*

(11). The pious Boaz obviously compared Ruth's venture of love with Abraham's venture of faith (cf. Gn. xii. 1). *Under whose wings* (12). This shows how completely Ruth had adopted the religion of Naomi (see i. 17n.). *Thine handmaid . . . handmaidens* (13). The meaning seems to be 'thy handmaiden—but I have no claim to be thy handmaiden' i.e. 'I am only a gleaner and my only claim upon you is the claim of the poor and the stranger'. *Vinegar* (14). Heb. *homez*. This was 'a beverage of sour wine mixed with oil still common in the East' (Delitzsch). *Parched corn* (14). 'The grains of wheat not yet fully dry and hard are roasted in a pan and constitute a very palatable article of food' (Robinson). *And left* (14). 'Left thereof' (RV), i.e. some of the corn was left over and put by for Naomi (18). *Let fall also some . . . of purpose* (16), i.e. as if it had been overlooked. The forgotten sheaf was the portion of the stranger, the fatherless and the widow (Dt. xxiv. 19). *And beat out . . . an ephah of barley* (17). The implements for beating out the corn could be had, of course, on the farm of Boaz, but not in the house of Naomi. The ephah of barley, about three pecks, could be carried home in her veil (iii. 15). This was far more than the most expert gleaner would have gathered under ordinary conditions. *Brought forth* (18). The Chaldee adds: 'from her pocket'. *Who hath not left off his kindness* (20). This may refer to the Lord, but more likely refers to Boaz. Naomi elsewhere (i. 8) speaks of the kindness of Orpah and Ruth to the dead, and it is reasonable to suppose that she would use the same language about Boaz (see iii. 10n.). *Near of kin* (20). Heb. *garobh* means near in time (Ezk. vii. 7) or near in place (Ex. xiii. 17). Here it is taken to mean near in kinship. *Kinsmen* (20). Heb. *goel* is from *gaal*, 'to redeem', and really means redeemer or one who has the right to redeem; and as this person was usually the next of kin the word is often translated kinsman. The use of the word by Naomi shows that she is already thinking of Boaz as a possible redeemer of her family and her patrimony. He is no longer a *moda* (1) or one of the *mishpachah* of Elimelech (3) or even a *garobh* (20); he is a *goel*.

V. THE LAW IS INVOKED. iii. 1-18

Rest (1). See i. 9n. Naomi had the prior claim upon Boaz, but was willing to abandon this claim in favour of Ruth. Her choice of Boaz to raise up a family for Mahlon was due either to her ignorance of a nearer *goel* or to a deliberate preference for him as one who had already shown kindness to the living and the dead. Her plan would show Boaz that her choice fell upon him and that she had waived her own claim in favour of Ruth. *He winnoweth barley to night* (2). There was evidently a night breeze suitable for the purpose. *Wash . . . anoint . . . put thy raiment upon thee* (3). A sign that her period of mourning was ended. *Did . . . all that her mother in law bade her* (6). Ruth is clearly conscious of taking part in

260

a well-recognized ritual by which such a claim as hers was regularly made as a matter of course, and which was so venerable that her action was devoid of even a suggestion of immodesty. It must be emphasized that we are getting a glimpse of country customs and conventions of which we know nothing, and it would be fantastic to discuss them in terms of the urban—and occidental—customs and conventions of the twentieth century. *Spread . . . thy skirt* (9). Lit. 'wing'. The Targum recognizes this as itself a claim to espousal (cf. Ezk. xvi. 8; Dt. xxii. 30). *Thou hast shewed more kindness* (10). 'Kindness' (Heb. *ḥesedh*) has another form meaning 'holiness'. The sense seems to be that Ruth showed piety (cf. Lat. *pietas*) in her faithfulness to the God of Israel and to Naomi; now she was showing even greater piety in her attitude to the law of Jehovah and to Boaz as her *goel*. *City* (11). Lit. 'gate', where the men of the city congregated. *Virtuous* (11). Heb. *ḥayil*; see ii. 1n. The exact meaning varies according to what is appropriate. Used of a man it may mean valour (e.g. Jos. i. 14); of a country, wealth (Is. lxi. 6); and of a woman, virtue (Pr. xii. 4). *A kinsman nearer* (12). One who had therefore a prior claim to fulfil the duties of a *goel*. *Let it not be known* (14). Ruth invoked the law of the *goel* in private because Boaz was not as yet her legal *goel*, but it was to be publicly invoked that day according to custom. *Vail* (15). 'Sheet' or 'apron' (AV mg.). Translated 'mantle' in Is. iii. 22. *The man will not be in rest* (18). It has been suggested that the number of measures of barley (six) may have been meant to bear some significance to Naomi, and this would explain her assurance. It could be explained equally well by her knowledge of the character of Boaz.

VI. THE GOEL ACCEPTS HIS RESPONSIBILITIES. iv. 1-16

Went . . . up (1). Bethlehem stood on a hill. *The gate* (1). The walls of eastern cities were very thick and the gate was consequently a short tunnel which provided shade and cool breezes. Here the men of the city congregated. (Cf. the term 'Sublime Porte' (Gate) by which the government of Turkey used to be designated.) *Such a one* (1), i.e. 'So and so'. The name of Naomi's nearest *goel* is not given, possibly because it was unknown to the writer. *Naomi . . . selleth* (3). More correctly 'has sold'. Either Elimelech sold the land before he went to Moab and the year of jubile came in in the interval so that the land reverted to Naomi (see Lv. xxv. 8ff.) or the land was for the last ten years left in the care of a friend. In any case Naomi sold it on her return, probably under pressure of poverty. *I thought* (4). See AV mg. *The inhabitants* (4). Heb. *yashabh* also means to sit down and may refer to the witnesses of the transaction. *Buy it . . redeem it . . . raise up the name of the dead*

(4, 5). The law of the *goel* was designed to prevent the alienation of any land or the extinction of any family. *I cannot . . . lest I mar mine own inheritance* (6). Josephus and the Targum suggest that he was already married, but seemingly that would not have relieved him of his obligations. Apart from this, however, he could mar his own inheritance by spending money on land that would belong not to him but to any issue Ruth would have.

In former time (7). This gives the impression that the story was written at some period when Dt. xxv. 5–10 had fallen into oblivion. Even at the time of the story this law was only partially observed, as the *goel* was approached by deputy and not directly by the widow in open assembly, and he himself loosed his shoe without any of the public odium ordered by the law. Actually the transfer of the shoe seems to have indicated nothing more contumelious than the transfer of the land to Boaz. The shoe symbolized the right of the owner to set foot upon the land (Ps. lx. 8). (Perhaps the shoes were given to the prodigal son to indicate his reinstatement in the inheritance he left.) The ceremoniousness of this transaction (10) reminds one strongly of the buying of the cave of Machpelah by Abraham (Gn. xxiii. 16–18). *Rachel and . . . Leah* (11). Rachel, although the younger sister, comes naturally first because it was at Bethlehem that she died (Gn. xxxv. 19). *Did build* (11). Heb. *bana*, to 'build', is allied to 'bear a son'. Thus Rachel gave Bilhah to Jacob 'that I may have children (lit. 'be built') by her' (Gn. xxx. 3). *Worthily* (11). Heb. *ḥayil*. See iii. 11n. *Pharez, whom Tamar bare unto Judah* (12). See Gn. xxxviii. This incident is introduced as an appropriate example of the responsibilities of a *goel*. *Which loveth thee* (15). The law has been fulfilled, the inheritance and family of Mahlon are saved, but the story closes, as it opens, on the love of Naomi and Ruth.

VII. THE PROMISE. iv. 17-22

The reader is here constrained to face the vital matter that is behind the story, namely the genealogy of the Messiah, for every Israelite knew that the Messiah was to spring from David. Ruth the Moabitess is seen no longer as the courageous stranger who came to Bethlehem, but as the woman whose great love for Naomi and devotion to Naomi's God put her into direct line of the Messiah. Tamar the Canaanite is no longer one who invoked the law of *goel* in a dreadful way, but the ancestress of the Messiah. Rahab received the same honour by seeing that God was with Israel. And so the stage is set for that great event because three alien women fulfilled an obscure law and read a wonderful meaning into the vision they saw. The genealogy given here is inserted by Matthew into the genealogy of our Lord (Mt. i. 3–6).

A. MACDONALD.

I AND II SAMUEL

INTRODUCTION

In the Hebrew text the two books of Samuel formed one only. The present division is inconvenient for it breaks up the history of David and the story of Saul's disaster on Gilboa. The authors of the Septuagint took the books of Samuel and Kings as a complete history of the kingdom, and divided it into four sections called 'Books of the Kingdom'. The Vulgate altered this to 'Books of the Kings'. The books of Samuel were called the first and second 'Book of the Kings' respectively.

Since the days of Daniel Bomberg, in the sixteenth century, most Hebrew Bibles have followed the arrangement of dividing the book of Samuel in two, and have called the parts the first and second books of Samuel. In our English Bible, these books have, as sub-title, the first and second 'Book of the Kings', and 1 and 2 Kings have, as sub-title, third and fourth 'Book of the Kings', respectively.

I. AUTHORSHIP

Although the books bear the name of Samuel, that does not imply that he wrote them. A late Jewish tradition ascribes the books to him, but, even if this tradition could be accepted, it would refer only to the first twenty-four chapters of 1 Samuel.

The evidence clearly indicates that the books are a compilation. It may very well be that Samuel was the author of the greater part of the first book, for, as head of the schools of the prophets, he would probably keep trace of the history of God's chosen people. These schools formed the centre of the nation's culture for generations, and records must have been kept there of God's dealings with His people.

In 1 Ch. xxix. 29 we read in the Hebrew text 'And the Chronicles of David the king, behold they are written in the Chronicles of Samuel the Roeh, and in the Chronicles of Nathan the Nabi, and in the Chronicles of Gad the Chozeh'. This clearly implies that records were kept by Samuel, Nathan, and Gad, and that the compiler of 1 Chronicles drew upon these records, so far as the history of David was concerned. This is entirely in keeping with what we would conclude from other lines of evidence. We find that certain parts of Chronicles are almost word for word the same as the record in Samuel, with very slight variations; and the facts stated are generally similar, although the compiler of Chronicles had apparently records before him not drawn upon by the compiler of Samuel.

We know that records were preserved with the ark, from the days of Moses onwards, and Samuel was reared at Shiloh beside the ark. What more natural than that he should be interested in the history of Israel and should add to it? He himself was a great maker of history, and when Saul was elected king at Mizpeh, Samuel prepared a constitution for the kingdom 'and wrote it in the book, and laid it up before the Lord' (1 Sa. x. 25, Heb. text). This shows there was a definite book kept, with records, and that it was with the ark. In 2 Ch. ix. 29 Nathan is again referred to, this time as an authority for the reign of Solomon; and he, and other prophets, are quoted as sources for the history of that reign.

There are many more references in the Old Testament to prophets as authorities for the history of other kings. Thus we are warranted in taking Samuel, Nathan, and Gad, either as direct authors of the book of Samuel or, at least, as having left records from which the narrative was mostly compiled.

We thus have the witness of contemporaries, for Samuel lived till near the end of Saul's reign, and Nathan and Gad overlived David. It is notable that David had a close connection not only with Samuel himself but with the school of the prophets at Naioth (cf. 1 Sa. xix. 18); and both Nathan and Gad were intimately associated with David (cf. 1 Sa. xxii. 5; 2 Sa. xxiv. 11; 2 Ch. xxix. 25; 2 Sa. vii. 2–17, xii. 25; 1 Ki. i. 8–27). It is clear that there were official chronicles of king David as is seen from 1 Ch. xxvii. 24.

There was also a poetic literature of the nation, such as the book of Jasher (2 Sa. i. 18) which must have been a collection of songs and ballads on the national heroes. From such sources as these the compiler of the book of Samuel would draw some of his material (cf. 1 Sa. ii. 1–10, 2 Sa. iii. 33–34, xxii. 1–51). For a detailed study of some of the problems see Appendix II, p. 293, 'The Critical View of Sources and Documents'.

II. THE NAME

The fact that these books should bear the name of Samuel shows the high esteem in which he was held. Among the Jews he was regarded as a national leader, second only to Moses. As Moses delivered Israel from Egypt, gave them the law, and brought them to the very borders of the promised land, so Samuel was sent of God to deliver Israel when the nation's fortunes seemed almost hopeless. Spiritually and politically, the

262

nation appeared virtually lost at the end of Eli's judgeship (cf. 1 Sa. iv. 12–22; Ps. lxxviii. 59–64; Je. xxvi. 6). Under Samuel came a wonderful spiritual renovation and a new hope (1 Sa. vii).

Many believe that it was Samuel who founded the schools of the prophets which for centuries exercised so profound an influence upon the life of the nation. Round these schools gathered not only the spiritual life of Israel, but also its cultural and educational life. If Moses gave the law, Samuel assured that it should be propagated, together with further revelations from God.

At the same time, Samuel was used of God to lead Israel when the momentous change was made from the judges to the monarchy. It was a time which called supremely for wise leadership and, without this, sore calamities might have befallen the nation. God led Samuel, at this time, to set before them the ideal of a constitutional monarchy under God's guidance, for the king was to observe the law and be guided by God's revelations through His prophets. When Saul, through his crimes and despotism, failed, Samuel, under God, trained up David to be the king 'after God's own heart'. With all his failings, David never set himself above God's law and never failed to respect God's prophets. It is because of this that the greatest aim of the books of Samuel was to tell the history of David.

It was Samuel's great privilege, then, to give to the prophets their due place in Israel; and at the same time he was used of God to bring in the monarchy and lay down laws for its guidance and thus prepare the way for Him who is, at once, prophet, priest and king. No man so much as Samuel deserves the honour of having his name given to these books.

III. DATE OF THE COMPILATION

The language points to an early date. It is pure Hebrew free from Aramaisms and late forms, such as are found in later books.

It must have been written a considerable time after Saul's first introduction to Samuel. At that time the term *ro'eh* (seer) was applied to a prophet; by the time the book was compiled *nabhi'* was used and it was necessary to explain to a new generation the meaning of *ro'eh* (cf. 1 Sa. ix. 9). Should it be proved, however, that this comment is an addition, it may have been added long after the compilation.

It must have been after the death of David (cf. 2 Sa. v. 5) for the length of his reign is given. It cannot have been earlier than the reign of Rehoboam for already Judah is separated from Israel (cf. 1 Sa. xxvii. 6) as is seen by the reference to 'the kings of Judah'. The Septuagint version also distinctly points to a date not earlier than Rehoboam (cf. 2 Sa. viii. 7, xiv. 27 LXX).

The style would suggest that it is not later than this reign, and no event from any later period is referred to.

IV. CHRONOLOGY

Any chronology of this era can only be approximately correct, with our present knowledge.

We may adopt provisionally the following dates:—

Samuel born	1090
Samuel called of God	1080
Death of Eli and beginning of Samuel's judgeship	1070
Saul begins to reign	1040
Samuel dies	1015
Saul slain on Gilboa	1010
David king over Judah	1010
David king of all Israel	1003

It should be noted that a very large part of Saul's history is passed over in silence—probably twenty years at least. At the time of his election (1 Sa. ix. 2) he is a young man, apparently unmarried. The events of chapters x and xi seem to follow quickly on those of chapter ix. When next we see Saul, he has a son, Jonathan, already a brilliant soldier. Some twenty years must have passed. The aim of the historian was not to present Saul's history but to lead on to David's.

OUTLINE OF CONTENTS

(In this Analysis the two books are treated as a whole)

I. FROM THE BIRTH OF SAMUEL TO THE LIBERATION OF ISRAEL FROM THE PHILISTINES. i. 1—vii. 17

    a. The birth and early years of Samuel (i. 1—iii. 21)
    b. War with the Philistines (iv. 1—vii. 17)

II. SAUL AS KING. viii. 1—xv. 35

    a. The choosing of Saul as king (viii. 1—xii. 25)
    b. War with the Philistines (xiii. 1—xiv. 52)
    c. The destruction of Amalek (xv. 1–35)

III. SAUL DEGENERATES AND DAVID GROWS IN MORAL STATURE. xvi. 1—xxxi. 13

    a. The anointing of David and his victory over Goliath (xvi. 1—xvii. 58)
    b. David and Jonathan (xviii. 1—xx. 42)

    c. David's exile (xxi. 1—xxiv. 22)
    d. Death of Samuel (xxv. 1)
    e. David and Abigail (xxv. 2–44)
    f. Gradual eclipse of Saul (xxvi. 1—xxx. 31)
    g. Defeat and death of Saul and Jonathan (xxxi. 1–13)

IV. DAVID AS KING. 2 Sa. i. 1—xx. 26

    a. David's lament over Saul and Jonathan (i. 1–27)
    b. David proclaimed king at Hebron and his reign in Jerusalem (ii. 1—v. 25)
    c. The ark brought to Zion and David's victories (vi. 1—xi. 1)
    d. David's sin and Nathan's rebuke (xi. 2—xii. 25)
    e. Absalom's flight, revolt and death (xii. 26—xviii. 33)
    f. David's return and Sheba's revolt (xix. 1—xx. 26)

V. LAST YEARS OF DAVID'S REIGN. xxi. 1—xxiv. 25

    a. The famine and the victory over the Philistines (xxi. 1–22)
    b. David's song of thanksgiving (xxii. 1–51)
    c. David's last words (xxiii. 1–7)
    d. A catalogue of David's mighty men (xxiii. 8–39)
    e. The census and the plague (xxiv. 1–25)

COMMENTARY

I. FROM THE BIRTH OF SAMUEL TO THE LIBERATION OF ISRAEL FROM THE PHILISTINES. i. 1—vii. 17

a. The birth and early years of Samuel (i. 1—iii. 21)

i. Elkanah and his two wives (i. 1–8). The conjunction *and*, with which the Heb. text begins, shows the continuation with the book of Judges which precedes in that text. *Elkanah* (1), the father of Samuel, was a Levite, and a descendant of Kohath (1 Ch. vi. 22–28, 33–38). He was a man of position—head of the family of the Zophim after which his village *Ramathaim-zophim* (1) was named. (*Ramathaim*, dual form of *Ramah*, 'the height'. *Zophim* from *Zuph* or *Zophai*, ancestor of Elkanah.) *He had two wives* (2). Though polygamy was tolerated by the Mosaic law (Dt. xxi. 15–17) it was not the original divine arrangement (Mt. xix. 8) and caused much misery to Elkanah, like others. *Peninnah* (i.e. coral or pearl) greatly vexed the favourite wife *Hannah* (i.e. grace), who was childless (2–8) —the greatest calamity for a Hebrew woman. *Went up . . . yearly* (3). They were pious people and faithfully attended each year at the central sanctuary at Shiloh (ten miles north of Bethel) to keep a religious feast. In spite of the depraved condition of the priests, Hophni and Phinehas, this family came to the feast to worship *the Lord of hosts* (3). Heb. *Jehovah Ṣebaoth*, the Lord of all powers and resources, especially the heavenly bodies.

ii. Hannah's prayer and its answer (i. 9–20). In her bitterness of soul she sought relief in the tabernacle, called in verse 9 *temple* (Heb. *hekal*, i.e. palace or stately building), where she poured out her soul to God. The aged Eli, the High Priest, seeing her lips move, thought at first she was drunken (13), like many loose women then.

But she was no *daughter of Belial* (16. Lit. 'worthless woman'. Cf. ii. 12), and her pious soul was greatly comforted (18). Jehovah answered her prayer and gave her a son, and in gratitude she called him *Samuel* (20. Heb. *Shemuel*, i.e. heard of God).

iii. Samuel's infancy and dedication to God (i. 21–28). At the next yearly feast, Elkanah returned 'to pay his vows and all the tithes of his land' (LXX), but Hannah went not until the child should be weaned (two or three years later), when she would leave him in the Lord's house for ever (21, 22). *Three bullocks* (24). One would be for a burnt offering for the dedication of Samuel; the others would be for the yearly sacrifice (cf. verse 2). The *bottle of wine* would be a skin, and would contain a considerable quantity. *I have lent him to the Lord* (28). Lit. 'I have returned him to Jehovah, as long as he liveth, because he was obtained by petition for Jehovah'. Hannah's words are beautiful, even in English, but the skilful play on words in the Hebrew text is lost in our language.

iv. The song of Hannah (ii. 1–10). This song ranks with those of Miriam, Deborah, and the virgin Mary. It expresses Hannah's triumph and thanksgiving, and merges into a prophecy of Christ's kingdom, and the ways of providence. Many commentators forget this and regard the song as a late celebration of victory in war.

God is the sole author of her triumph (1, 2). In Him her heart *rejoiceth* (RV, 'exulteth'), and her *horn* is exalted like that of a strong animal with its head tossed in the air. Her *mouth*, formerly shut in presence of her enemy, is now opened wide to praise God. *The adversaries of the Lord* (10). Lit. 'Jehovah—whoever striveth with Him shall be broken in pieces; out of heaven He will thunder upon him'. Jehovah will overcome all

His enemies, and the instrument for achieving His victories will be the king to be anointed by Hannah's son, Samuel; but, above all, Christ, the eternal King, is meant. Critics have seen, in the reference to a king, signs of a later interpolation, but the Israelites were familiar with the thought of a king from the days of Gideon (cf. Jdg. viii. 22), and the idea was growing that Israel must have a king. *His anointed* (10). The kingly title of Christ, the Anointed One, is first used here (Heb. *Mashiah*, from which we get Heb. 'Messiah' and Gk. 'Christ'). The term is very common in Samuel and the Psalms. The resemblance of Hannah's song to the Magnificat (Lk. i. 46–55) and Ps. cxiii is obvious.

v. The iniquity of Eli's sons (ii. 11–17). *Sons of Belial* (12). Lit. 'Sons of worthlessness'. They were ungodly men, vicious in spite of their sacred office. *The priests' custom ... was* (13). The worshipper had to give the priest the fat, the breast, and the shoulder (Lv. vii. 29–34), the fat being burnt unto the Lord (Lv. iii. 3–5). Hophni and Phinehas took from the offerer, by force, what belonged to his own sacrificial feast; and they insulted God by demanding their portion before His was burnt on the altar. Cf. Lv. viii. 31; 2 Ch. xxxv. 13.

vi. Samuel's ministry in the tabernacle (ii. 18–21). The *linen ephod* (18), worn by Samuel, was a tunic secured at the waist by a girdle (cf. 2 Sa. vi. 14). The *little coat* (19), brought yearly by his mother, was the *me'il* (Heb.) worn by priests, kings, princes, and prophets—an undergarment of wool woven without seam and reaching almost to the ground (cf. 1 Ch. xv. 27; 1 Sa. xv. 27; Jb. ii. 12; 2 Sa. xiii. 18). On one of their visits, Eli blessed Elkanah and Hannah anew, and they had five more children 'in return for the petition she asked for Jehovah' (20, AV mg.).

vii. Eli's expostulations with his sons (ii. 22–26). Their immorality was aggravated in that the women served in the tabernacle service (cf. Ex. xxxviii. 8), and the holy place was desecrated (22). Eli was constantly hearing about their evil behaviour (22). But although their example was leading the people astray (24), his rebuke was very feeble. *Because the Lord would slay them* (25). Cf. the case of Pharaoh (Ex. x. 1, 2). These men were sin-hardened and had deliberately set themselves against God. They were now abandoned by Him.

viii. God's judgment on Eli's house (ii. 27–36). Even in that dark day the Lord found *a man of God* (i.e. a prophet) to send to Eli (27), to remind him of the high honour of his family, from Aaron onwards (Ex. iv. 14–16), and that they had had a bountiful remuneration in offerings (Lv. x. 12–15), yet his sons kicked at His sacrifices and enriched themselves with them (29). Hence God would cut off the *arm* of their strength (31), and there would not be an old man left. This was partly fulfilled at Nob (1 Sa. xxii. 18, 19). A rival from another house would stand in the high priesthood (32), yet God would be merciful. *The man of thine* (33). Lit. 'I will not cut off every

one of thine from mine altar, to consume thine eyes and grieve thy soul'. Eli's descendants were not to be utterly consumed. Verse 35 is fulfilled completely only in Christ but has a partial reference to Samuel. In their poverty Eli's descendants would turn to Samuel for help.

ix. The Lord appears to Samuel in a vision (iii. 1–10). Samuel, now about twelve years old, was honoured by being a personal attendant to Eli, and no doubt was being educated, with others, for the tabernacle was the centre of culture as well as of religion. *The word of the Lord was precious ...* (1). Lit. 'The word of the Lord was rare in those days; there was no vision published openly'. It was a sad time with no recognized prophet to whom God spoke. *The ark of God* (3). See Appendix I, p. 292, on 'The Ark of the Covenant'. Before the seven-branched golden candlestick (Ex. xxv. 31–37) was extinguished, just before dawn, God called to Samuel (3–6). That voice in the night is deeply impressive. Though so active and willing, Samuel did not yet know the Lord in the way of receiving a personal revelation from Him (7). When God called the fourth time, and Samuel was ready to receive the message, He 'came and presented Himself' (10). There was some kind of manifestation of the Lord.

x. Message of doom to Eli's house (iii. 11–18). *I will do* (11). Lit. 'I am doing'. The train was already in motion to work a destruction which would stun like a blow on both ears of a man at once. God had warned Eli before, by the prophet (cf. 1 Sa. ii. 27), but without result. No *sacrifice* by blood (Heb. *zebhah*) and no unbloody *offering* (Heb. *minhah*) could now make expiation (14). We see the intensity of Eli's feelings, and his humility and resignation before God (16–18). He was a good man, who had done a great work for many years in the difficult and disorderly period of the judges; but he was too weak to take appropriate action against his degenerate sons, whom he ought to have expelled from the priesthood.

xi. Samuel as prophet (iii. 19–21). As he grew up, it was clear *the Lord was with him* (19), as with other great saints before him, and the fulfilment of his words proved this. *From Dan* (in the far north) *even to Beer-sheba* (in the extreme south) (20) is a phrase frequently used to denote the whole country (cf. Jdg. xx. 1).

b. War with the Philistines (iv. 1—vii. 17)

In the Vulg., Syriac, and LXX, the part of iv. 1 referring to Samuel is placed at the end of chapter iii, which is the natural place. *The Philistines* (1) were last mentioned in Jdg. xiii—xvi. They oppressed Israel forty years (cf. Jdg. xiii. 1), their dominion receiving a check in the twentieth year of Samuel's judgeship (1 Sa. vii. 2, 13, 14). It began before Samson's birth (Jdg. xiii. 5), and he judged Israel twenty years (Jdg. xv. 20). Hence, the judgeship of Eli and Samson must have been partly contemporaneous—Eli, attending to the civil and religious, at Shiloh, and

Samson to the warlike operations on the frontier. Philistines means in Heb. 'immigrants'. The LXX translates as *allophuloi*, i.e. aliens. Am. ix. 7 says they came from Caphtor, i.e. Crete. They destroyed the Avim along the coast of Canaan (Dt. ii. 23; Jos. xiii. 3. See 2 Sa. viii. 18n.). Gn. x. 13, 14 associates the Philistines with Egypt (*Miṣraim*), but there was much coming and going between Crete and Egypt.

i. Israel is overwhelmed by the Philistines (iv. 1–11). At the place afterwards called *Ebenezer*, the Philistines slew 4,000 Israelites *in the field* (2. Lit. 'in battle array in the open country'). Failing to realize that their defeat was because they had dishonoured God, the Israelites decided to bring the ark, as a talisman, to secure victory—an exhibition of the danger of pinning faith to symbols instead of repenting. *Which dwelleth between the cherubims* (4. Lit. 'which is enthroned upon the cherubim'). The ark symbolized this presence of God, and reminded of the covenant. (See 2 Sa. vi. 6–11n., and Appendix I, p. 292.)

Even the Philistines were afraid, for they felt that *God* (Heb. *'Elohim*) was come into the camp (7). Though plural in form, the Hebrews used this word with a singular verb, while the Philistines used it with a plural verb, pronoun, and adjective—showing how Israel was monotheistic, and the Philistines polytheistic (7, 8). Even the latter knew of God's mighty acts in the wilderness (8). Nevertheless, the Israelites were sorely smitten, losing 30,000 slain. Hophni and Phinehas were killed, and the ark was captured—fulfilling the predictions against Eli's house (chapters ii and iii), and showing that God had departed from Israel (cf. Ps. lxxviii. 56–64).

ii. The overthrow of Eli's house (iv. 12–22). The aged Eli sits pathetically on his official seat, at the gate of the tabernacle, awaiting tidings, his eyes *dim* (15. RV 'set', i.e. totally blind), and his heart trembling. Soon the arrival of a swift runner from Ebenezer (twenty miles away), bearing on his person the symbols of disaster (12), causes a tumultuous noise in all Shiloh (13). Every successive statement of the messenger increases Eli's agony, until, on hearing that the ark was taken, the aged judge, of ninety-eight, falls backward and breaks his neck. God was indeed departed from them (16–18).

Equally touching is the death of the wife of Phinehas. The sad tidings brought on the travail of childbirth (19). As she expired, she called her son *Ichabod*, meaning 'no glory' or 'where is glory?', and added, *The glory is departed from Israel* (21). The narrative suggests that the loss of the ark was a greater tragedy to her than the loss of her father-in-law and husband.

iii. The ark brings disaster to Dagon (v. 1–5). Shiloh was completely destroyed, and the priests slain. (Cf. Ps. lxxviii. 60–64; Je. vii. 12, xxvi. 9.) Samuel must have saved the sacred vessels of the tabernacle, proceeded to reorganize the government, and taken steps to maintain the flame of religion.

The ark was taken to *Ashdod* (1. Called Azotus in Acts viii. 40), a strong and prosperous city—one of the five Philistinian capitals. Here was a temple and an image of *Dagon* (2), a god highly honoured by the Philistines. He had also a temple at Gaza (cf. 1 Sa. v. 5; Jdg. xvi. 23, 24). The Philistines after their arrival in Palestine seem to have adopted this god from the Canaanites. From the days of Jerome, Dagon was regarded as a fish god on the supposition that the name was derived from the Hebrew word *Dag*, a fish. The greatest scholars accepted this view until recently. Now most authorities identify *Dagon* with *Dagan* the corn god who was honoured from an early period, as a god of the earth and agriculture, from Babylonia to the Mediterranean. At Ashdod God vindicated His own glory by defending His ark and breaking Dagon in pieces (3, 4). There may be a reference to the custom mentioned in 1 Sa. v. 5 as late as Zp. i. 9.

iv. The plague of emerods (v. 6–12). Then Ashdod and its territories were smitten with a plague of *emerods* (6. Heb. *'ophelim*, 'boils'). It has been suggested that the disease was bubonic plague and that the 'emerods' were swollen lymph glands in the groin, the characteristic symptom of this disease. (See, e.g., A. Rendle Short, *Modern Discovery and the Bible*, p. 125.) *The lords of the Philistines* (8. Heb. *sarne Pelishtim*), a federal government (cf. Jdg. xvi. 5, 23), decided to send the ark to Gath to save Ashdod, but in Gath the same divine judgment fell on small and great (6–9). On being sent to Ekron, eleven miles north of Gath, the ark there caused a *deadly destruction* (11. Lit. 'deadly panic'), for the havoc became greater in each successive city.

v. The Philistines resolve to send back the ark (vi. 1–12). The lords consulted the priests and the *diviners* (2. Heb. *qosemim*), men who, in all ancient lands, professed to tell the future (cf. Ezk. xxi. 21–23; Dn. ii. 2). They stressed the need for a trespass offering to atone for the wrong done (3). Following the prevalent belief of ancient times to make offerings of like for like, they made five golden 'emerods' and five golden mice. The reference to mice (Heb. *'akhbar*) is most interesting. It is thought that the term probably included 'rats', and it is now known, of course, that bubonic plague is really a disease of these animals. *Mar the land* (5). Both by reason of their numbers and because so many of them would be lying about dead.

To bear the ark, the priests and diviners ordered the making of *a new cart* (7) to be pulled by two untrained and unyoked heifers—a sign of reverence (cf. 2 Sa. vi. 3; Nu. xix. 2; Dt. xxi. 3, 4). The similarity of Philistine ideas with those of the Israelites suggests they inherited these from a primitive monotheistic source. Untrained heifers would normally jump hither and thither and break the cart; and they would on no account leave their calves. The fact that, on this occasion, the kine went straight along the highway to *Beth-shemesh* (an Israelite priests' city), turning neither to right nor left, reveals the hand of God—for the Philistines followed them, and did not lead them (7–12).

vi. The men of Beth-shemesh keep happy festival but commit sacrilege (vi. 13–21). Reaping time was ever a time for joy, but the men of Beth-shemesh ('house of the sun', anciently a centre of sun worship) rejoiced greatly to see the ark of God returning to Israel (13). They joined in a sacrifice which the Levites of the village carried out according to the law (14, 15). Probably inflamed with wine, the men of Beth-shemesh looked into the ark (19. Lit. 'looked with profane curiosity'). This was strictly forbidden on pain of death (cf. Nu. iv. 19, 20). *He smote the men* (19). The number slain, 50,070, presents a problem. Beth-shemesh did not contain anything like so many people. Jerusalem had no more than 70,000. Many scholars, following certain Heb. MSS, read simply 'threescore and ten men' as the number slain, but we cannot be certain.

God showed the Israelites, as well as the Philistines, that He would vindicate His honour. His ark was sacred and not to be touched (cf. Nu. i. 50, 51, iv. 5, 16–20). In terror the men of Beth-shemesh get the men of *Kirjath-jearim* (i.e. 'the city of forests') to take it. Kirjath was some nine miles north-east of Beth-shemesh and nearer Shiloh. It seems to have been associated with Baal worship in earlier times (cf. its names, Jos. xv. 9, 60; 2 Sa. vi. 2).

vii. The Israelites led to repentance (vii. 1–6). The ark was twenty years in Kirjath-jearim before reformation began in Israel (2). It was a time of Philistine oppression, unjust exactions, and idolatry. This, together with the occupation of Shiloh by the Philistines, led to neglect of the ark, and it was left at Kirjath. During these years, Samuel was secretly preparing for reformation—probably travelling about and calling for repentance. He is now the leader of Israel, judge and prophet. At last the people, under his guidance, *lamented after the Lord* (2) and showed sorrow for their sin. Samuel demands public reformation and the abandonment of *the strange gods* (3. Lit. 'the gods of the stranger'), which had brought on them the Philistine yoke. They put away *Baalim and Ashtaroth* (4), i.e. the images of these heathen divinities. *Baal* ('lord': pl. *Baalim*) was supreme lord of the Philistines and the Canaanites, related to the Babylonian *Bel*. *Astarte* (pl. *Ashtaroth*) was his wife. Her symbol was the *asherah*, often translated 'grove', but probably representing the Assyrian sacred tree. Baal and Astarte stood for the principle of fertility. At *Mizpeh* ('the watchtower'—applicable to any elevated place), about five miles north-west of Jerusalem, the Israelites prayed, fasted, and confessed their sin, with pouring out of water, symbolical of what they regarded as the source of life (5, 6).

viii. Great defeat of the Philistines at Ebenezer (vii. 7–12). Immediately they were attacked by the Philistines, but Israel turned to earnest prayer as their hope (7, 8). Samuel offered a lamb, burnt wholly (Lv. xxii. 27) as a symbol of Israel's complete dedication to God; no part was reserved for the priest; all was for God. God answered swiftly. He *thundered with a great thunder* (10) on the advancing Philistines, who were seized with panic and fled, hotly pursued by Israel (10, 11). On the same battlefield where Israel was defeated twenty years before, Samuel now sets up a stone in commemoration of this deliverance. *Ebenezer* (12), i.e. the stone of help, recognizing God's help hitherto. This victory secured peace and independence for Israel for twenty years.

ix. Summary of Samuel's life work (vii. 13–17). Not till the days of Saul did the Philistines trouble Israel again (13). Cf. 1 Sa. ix. 16, xiii. 19–23. (See also Appendix II, p. 296 for note on 1 Sa. vii. 13.) Israel recaptured many places on the Philistine border, and made peace with the *Amorites* (14), the ancient inhabitants of the mountains of Israel, in contradistinction from the Canaanites, or lowlanders. Samuel went on circuit to Bethel, Gilgal and Mizpeh, administering justice, all these being famous places with well-known sanctuaries for worship and sacrifice (15, 16). With this chapter ends the epoch of the judges. The next leads on to the monarchy.

II. SAUL AS KING. viii. 1—xv. 35

a. The choosing of Saul as king (viii. 1—xii. 25)

See Section III of Appendix II for a study of the critical approach to this section. Hitherto, Israel had been a theocracy, following a great ideal—government by God. But human perversity and weakness produced disobedience and failure. Only in times of peril would the nation listen to God's messengers. Now, from national pride, they demand a king. The kingdom was, in the course of providence, to perfect the idea of the messianic kingdom; but had they faithfully followed God, an earthly king would have been unnecessary.

i. The people demand a king (viii. 1–22). See Appendix II, p. 295, for a detailed study of this passage.

ii. Saul comes to Samuel (ix. 1–14). Saul's pedigree (1) is typical of how many links are omitted in Bible genealogies. Some links omitted here can be supplied from other passages. His father, Kish, was *a mighty man of power* (1. Lit. 'a mighty man of wealth'), and Saul's physical attractions were remarkable (2). *He passed through . . .* (4). The route taken is hard to trace—perhaps Mount Ephraim, Baal-shalisha, Shaalabbin, West Benjamin, to Ramah (4–6). When about to abandon the fruitless search, his servant tells him of Samuel, *an honourable man* (6. Lit. 'an honoured man'), and they visit him, taking a present according to the etiquette of the period (7, 8).

The fact that Saul apparently knows little or

nothing about Samuel (6) has caused much perplexity. In the opinion of some critics, like Prof. A. R. S. Kennedy in his Commentary on 1 and 2 Samuel in the *Century Bible*, the picture here of Samuel as the comparatively unknown seer of a country village offers a striking contrast to that of Samuel the theocratic judge of all Israel, 'the all-powerful vicegerent of Yahweh, as he appears in chapters vii, viii, xii.' On this, and other grounds, it has been argued that we have in chapters vii to xii two mutually independent documents giving divergent, if not contradictory, accounts of the history of Samuel. The fact of Saul's ignorance concerning Samuel is not sufficient to substantiate such a conclusion. As Kirkpatrick points out in the *Cambridge Bible*, 'up to this point Saul had been only the shy and retiring youth of the family, employed in the common work of the farm'. There is no reason to believe that he was particularly interested in either the political or religious movements of the time. Public figures were not then kept before country people by press and radio as they are today. Many a farmer's son would have little interest in much that was happening. Even today not a few in Great Britain have no idea what the name of the Archbishop of Canterbury is or where he lives.

Twenty years ago, at a large public meeting in Edinburgh, the Moderator of the Church of Scotland was called upon to speak. He was one of the most famous missionary leaders of his generation. For months the Scottish Press had been full of his doings and his portrait had appeared constantly in the newspapers. When the chairman called his name and mentioned his mission field, the civic head of a Scottish city (a capable business man well known as an administrator) leaned forward and asked a friend 'Who is that?' He himself belonged to that church, and was one of the platform party, and yet the Moderator's name signified nothing to him. It is incredible but true. Similarly, the fact that Saul apparently knew little about Samuel only reveals his own lack of interest. It does not warrant the supposition that two contradictory versions of the story of Samuel are embraced in these chapters—one representing him as the all-powerful head of the theocracy, and the other as an insignificant *ro'eh* in a village community. On the other hand, it is significant that even the servant (who may be assumed to be less well educated than his master's son) knew that Samuel was there, and that he was *a man of God* (6). This term was applied only to prophets and other great servants of God like Moses (Dt. xxxiii. 1); Elijah (2 Ki. i. 9); Elisha (2 Ki. viii. 2); David (2 Ch. viii. 14). The servant also knew that Samuel was 'held in honour' (6, RV) and that his prophecies were fulfilled. Obviously, the fame of Samuel had reached this comparatively ignorant man at a distance from Ramah, though Saul knew so little about him.

Is the seer here? (11). The word they use is *ro'eh*. It is strange to find in verse 9 an explanatory note as to the use of this word before it is used in verses 11, 18, 19. According to this note, the term *ro'eh* was formerly used in Israel for 'prophet' (Heb. *nabhi'*). The LXX reads 'for the people in old time used to call the prophet a seer'. According to this it was a word formerly used chiefly by the common people. *Nabhi'* (prophet) is the older word and maintains its place throughout the Old Testament. It suggests bubbling over with ecstatic utterance. The word *ro'eh* seems to have gradually lost caste after Samuel's time, and was dropped in favour of *hozeh*, a respectful name for a seer. The writer of the note in verse 9 is clearly anxious to show that Samuel was a *nabhi'* (prophet), and that *ro'eh* in Samuel's time was equivalent to this. This explanatory note must have been inserted a considerable time after the death of Samuel. Kirkpatrick says on verse 9: 'Probably *nabhi'* designates the prophet as the inspired interpreter of the will of God.' He believes that *ro'eh* and *hozeh* 'refer to the method of communication by dream and vision'. Dean Payne Smith in the *Pulpit Commentary* maintains that *ro'eh* refers to one who sees by the ordinary sight and in waking vision; and that *hozeh* refers to one who sees in ecstatic vision. He draws a parallel between these words and *hazon* and *mar'eh* in 1 Sa. iii. 1, 15. Others maintain that there is no difference in meaning between *ro'eh* and *hozeh*. It is significant of the care with which sacred documents were treated that the writer of the explanation in 1 Sa. ix. 9, while he was anxious to show that Samuel was truly a *nabhi'*, yet did not alter the word *ro'eh* but wrote it as in the document which had come down to him, where its meaning was equivalent to *nabhi'*.

Following the direction of the maidens (12, 13) Saul and the servant hurried on and met Samuel in the gate of the city as he was about to ascend to the *high place* (Heb. *bamah*).

iii. Saul is entertained by the prophet (ix. 15–24). God had told Samuel, the previous day, of the arrival of Saul, and given instructions to anoint him as king to save Israel from the Philistines, who were once more afflicting the nation (15, 16). Cf. chapter vii and see the note on verse 16 in Appendix II, p. 296. When Saul asked Samuel *in the gate* (18. Lit. 'in the midst of the gate') where the seer's house was, he was astonished to find that this aged man knew all about him and his journey, for God had told him (19, 20). He was especially amazed when Samuel said, *On whom is all the desire of Israel . . .?* (20. Lit. 'Whose shall be all the delectable things of Israel? Are they not for thee and for all thy father's house?'). Saul modestly replied that his tribe, Benjamin, was the smallest in Israel (21).

Samuel took Saul and his servant into *the parlour* (22. Lit. 'the chamber'), a room used for sacrificial feasts, and gave them the chief seats among the thirty select guests who were there. The cook, according to instructions, brought the priests' *portion* (23), the *shoulder* (i.e. the right leg), which belonged to Samuel, and *took up* (lit. 'heaved') the leg before the Lord (24). This reserved portion was then set before Saul—a most signal honour.

iv. Samuel instructs Saul and sends him on his way (ix. 25—x. 16). What a wonderful quiet talk, on spiritual and national questions, they had on the flat roof in the cool of that evening (25). As the morning arose, Samuel called Saul *to the top of the house* (26. 'On the housetop' RV), where he had probably slept in a booth, and they went on together to the end of the city, where the prophet announced his election as king (27).

Taking the *vial of oil* (x. 1), used for anointing priests, Samuel poured it on Saul's head, and kissed him in token of homage. Kings were anointed when there was a new dynasty, or when there was doubt as to the succession, and there was often private anointing, as here (cf. 1 Sa. xvi. 3, 13; 2 Sa. ii. 4, v. 3, xix. 10; 1 Ki. i. 39). Samuel gave Saul three signs to prove the truth of his declarations. His final instruction to him was to go to Gilgal, when the time came, to strike the blow for freedom. Saul was to do nothing there till Samuel arrived to offer the sacrifices (8). Saul later failed in this test (xiii. 8–14).

All fell out as foretold by Samuel. God gave Saul *another heart* (9), turning the rustic farmer's son into a statesman and warrior. At Gibeah his prophetic exaltation caused great surprise to his neighbours (10,11); and the LXX, Vulg., Syr., and Arabic versions make them ask 'who is his father?' (12) as an enhancement of the wonder. (See also Appendix II, p. 298, for the relation of verse 11 to 1 Sam. xix. 24).

v. Saul is elected king (x. 17—xi. 15). The questions arising out of the election of Saul as king are discussed at some length in Appendix II. See pp. 295-7.

vi. Samuel pleads his integrity and God testifies His approval (xii. 1–25). See the notes on this passage in Appendix II, p. 297. Normally there is no rain from April to October. To have rain and thunder in wheat harvest (middle of May to middle of June) was a miracle. This was the proof given of the divine approval of Samuel's words (16–18). The impression was profound, and the people plead for Samuel's intercession with God (18, 19).

b. War with the Philistines (xiii. 1—xiv. 52)

i. Saul prepares his army and summons the people to Gilgal (xiii. 1-7). The Heb. of verse 1 reads 'Saul was — years old when he began to reign, and he reigned — and two years over Israel'. The numbers are omitted. The LXX omits the verse completely. Saul may have been about thirty at his accession and have reigned thirty-two years, because Mephibosheth was five years old at Saul's death. The thirty-two added to the seven and a half years between Saul's death and that of Ishbosheth gives forty years for Saul's dynasty (cf. Acts xiii. 21). In 1 Sa. ix. 2 Saul is called 'a young man'; now Jonathan is a fully fledged warrior (2, 3). Hence twenty or more

years must have been passed in silence since the events of chapter xii. Saul forms a small standing army (2), an important development. War was begun at Geba and formally declared throughout Israel, and the people came to Saul at Gilgal according to Samuel's appointment (1 Sa. x. 8)— a place suitable to deploy armies and at the entrance to the gorge leading to Michmash (4).

The number of the enemy was enormous. They occupied Michmash, and Saul withdrew down the gorge to Gilgal, while Jonathan still remained at Geba on the south of the gorge. Terror possessed many of the Israelites and they showed great cowardice (6, 7).

ii. Saul's disobedience and its consequences (xiii. 8–14). Saul had received his instructions from Samuel, but, weary of waiting, and feeling the deadly peril of the Philistine invasion, he proceeded himself to offer the burnt offering— perhaps through Ahiah the priest (8, 9). Just then, Samuel appeared, and Saul's excuses were very flimsy. Samuel upbraids the king and announces that God will give the kingdom to another. The prophetic language presents the divine will as already accomplished (13, 14).

iii. The Philistine movements (xiii. 15–23). Saul joins Jonathan at Geba and they face the Philistines at Michmash, across the deep gorge. *The spoilers* (17. Lit. 'the destroyer') sallied forth on raids north and west and east from Michmash, to devastate the land.

The Philistines had imposed a thorough disarmament on the Israelites. No smiths were allowed, for fear that weapons of war would be made, and an Israelite had to go down to the Philistines *to sharpen . . . his share* (i.e. sickle), *his coulter* (i.e. ploughshare), *. . . and his mattock* (i.e. heavy hoe) (19, 20). Join verse 21 to the preceding and read: 'whenever the edges of the heavy hoes and the ploughshares and the forks and the axes were blunt, and also to set the goads'. The Philistines no doubt expected an easy victory. They occupied a pass leading out into the main defile to keep the route open and to watch Saul (22, 23).

iv. Jonathan miraculously smites the Philistine garrison (xiv. 1–16). Unknown to others, and with only his armourbearer, Jonathan crossed the valley secretly to the Philistine side—about three miles—while Saul remained at *Migron* (2), in the Geba district, with *Ahiah* (3) the grandson of Phinehas, now High Priest—believed by many to be the same as Ahimelech, later slain by Saul (1 Sa. xxii. 9). The place where Jonathan crossed is still recognizable from the two conical hills on each side, *Bozez* (i.e. shining, because the sun shines on that side) and *Seneh* (i.e. acacia). The valley still has acacia trees (4, 5). Jonathan was confident God would give them a sign by making the enemy say *Come up unto us* (10), truly a remarkable thing to expect. The Philistines, on seeing them, thought they were deserters *come forth out of the holes* (11), and gave the sign looked for (12). Jonathan knew the Lord had delivered them into their hand and rapidly slew the garrison of twenty men in *an half acre of land* (13, 14). The reference to a half acre of land is very difficult textually. It may be read 'in about half a furrow of a yoke of land', i.e. the length of one side of the piece which a yoke of oxen could plough in one day. When Jonathan attacked, an earthquake caused *a very great trembling* (lit. 'a terror of God') among *the spoilers* (i.e. the Philistine marauders); everywhere there was trembling (15). Saul's men, across the gorge, saw the excitement and *behold, the multitude melted away . . . beating down one another* (16. Lit. 'melted away hither and thither in confusion', LXX and Vulg.).

v. The Philistine débâcle (xiv. 17–23). The absence of Jonathan was then discovered (17). *Bring hither the ark of God* (18). The LXX reads 'bring hither the ephod' (see RV mg.). Saul called Ahiah to consult the Urim and Thummim, but in his characteristic impatience would not wait the answer (18, 19). For an extended note on Urim and Thummim see on xxviii. 6. See also note on verse 41 below. They went in pursuit of the enemy, who fought one another, and soon cowards and deserters joined Saul in the hour of victory (20–22).

vi. Saul's rash order (xiv. 24–35). To avoid delay, Saul took an oath of his men not to eat anything, a demand which weakened them physically and hindered them (24). Jonathan, ignorant of the oath, took a sip of the abundant honey (cf. Dt. xxxii. 13). He unwittingly trespassed and brought sin on the people. *His eyes were enlightened* (29), i.e. made clear, while the eyes of the rest were dim with fatigue. When the period of the oath was expired, they flew madly on the spoil (32), breaking the Mosaic law both by eating with the blood (Lv. xvii. 10–14) and by killing calves with the dams (Lv. xxii. 28). To drain the blood of the victims, a great stone was set up for the slaughtering, and *the same was the first altar that he built* (35. Lit. 'the same he began to build as an altar to Jehovah').

vii. Consequences of Jonathan's error (xiv. 36–46). As a result of Jonathan's unconscious lapse, the Lord refused to answer Saul's enquiry (36, 37). Saul now rashly swears that whoever is responsible shall die—a foolish oath. By casting lots they found Jonathan was responsible, and Saul declared he must die (38–44). The people, however, saved Jonathan, insisting that God had wrought a great victory through him (45). *Give a perfect lot* (41). 'Shew the innocent' (AV mg.). 'Shew the right' (RV). None of these renderings of Heb. *habhah thamim* is very satisfactory. Driver suggests: 'Give one who is perfect', but he is not satisfied. The LXX reads: 'And Saul said, O Yahweh, God of Israel, why hast thou not answered thy servant this day? If the iniquity be in me or in my son Jonathan, Yahweh, God of Israel, give Urim; but if thou sayest thus, the iniquity is in thy people Israel, give Thummim. And Saul and Jonathan were taken . . .' Those who accept this reading account for the omission in Hebrew by *homoioteleuton*. If the LXX version

is correct, it indicates that the manifestation of God's will by Urim and Thummim could be obtained by a special method of casting lots. If the Heb. text is correct, God's will was made known on this occasion by ordinary lots with no reference to Urim. The question is important in considering the nature of Urim and Thummim. (See 1 Sa. xxviii. 6n.)

viii. Saul's wars and family affairs (xiv. 47–52). Saul was brave and a great military leader. Hence, in spite of his failings, his people clung to him; even Samuel and David, who suffered through him, had pity and sympathy for him. We have here a brief summary of Saul's conquests and family matters. His victories extended very far, even to *Zobah*, between Damascus and the Euphrates (47).

c. The destruction of Amalek (xv. 1–35)

i. Saul sent to destroy Amalek (xv. 1–6). This is Saul's final test, some time after the warnings of xiii. 13, which produced no repentance. He is now specially warned to obey (1), but without result. This chapter is the connecting link between Saul's history and David's. *Amalek* (2), inhabiting the deserts from Judea to Egypt, was sentenced, long ago, for his wickedness towards Israel (cf. Nu. xxiv. 20; Dt. xxv. 17–19), and now is to be utterly destroyed (lit. 'devoted to destruction'. Heb. *haram*), i.e. set apart for God and not to be taken for spoil (3). Cf. Lv. xxvii. 28, 29; Jos. vi. 17, 18. God's justice needed to be signally vindicated against them to emphasize the supreme place of the moral element in life. The fewness of the men from Judah reveals the division in the nation (4), and the remembrance of the ancient friendship of the Kenites attracts our attention (6. Cf. Jdg. i. 16, iv. 11, 17; 1 Sa. xxx. 29).

ii. Saul's disobedience and penalty (xv. 7–31). The Amalekites were routed from Southern Judea to the Egyptian border, but the victory was marred by disobedience in sparing Agag (perhaps to grace a triumph) and the best of the herds which had been 'devoted'. God *repented* (11) that He had made Saul king. But, unlike man's repentance (see verse 29), God's repentance is the change of His dispensation. He changes His administration when new instruments are required; and when man repents God withdraws the threatened punishment. Samuel was deeply grieved because of Saul's rejection (11).

When Samuel comes to Saul at Gilgal on the latter's return from the great victory in the south via Carmel (near Hebron), the king did not seem to realize the gravity of his fault, and tries to pass the matter off by bluff, alleging that it was religious fervour which prompted them to keep the sheep and oxen to sacrifice them to God (12–14, 20, 21). The prophet's reply from God was very stern. When he was modest (17) God exalted him to the throne. Now he arrogantly sets aside God's conditions (18, 19). To Saul's persistent argument that they did well in saving the animals for sacrifice (a mere subterfuge), Samuel declares *Behold, to obey is better than sacrifice, and to hearken than the fat of rams* (22) —the religion of the heart is better than outward, formal ceremonies (cf. Ho. vi. 6; Ps. l. 8–14, li. 16; Is. i. 11; Je. vi. 20). Rebellion against God is as bad as divination by evil spirits, and stubborn resistance to Him is as bad as worshipping idols (Heb. *'awen*) and teraphim (23). For a comparison of the reference to teraphim here with Michal's use of an image to aid David's escape (1 Sa. xix. 13), see Appendix II, p. 297.

Although Saul confesses his sin, his words do not appear sincere; he blames the people and is too eager to stand well with them (24, 25). In spite of his pleading, his rejection by God as king is confirmed (26), being symbolized in a remarkable way by the accidental rending of the mantle (27, 28). On verse 29 see note on verse 11.

iii. **Agag is slain and Samuel departs (xv. 32–35).** *Agag came unto him delicately* (32). The AV is very obscure. The Heb. word *ma'adhan* may mean cheerfully or daintily. The LXX translates it 'trembling'. Samuel declared that justice demanded death for Agag's atrocities, and he hewed him in pieces, or ordered his execution by other hands (33). The relationship of Samuel and Saul as prophet and king, in God's service, was now irretrievably broken, but Samuel lamented all his days the tragedy of this once great man (34, 35).

III. SAUL DEGENERATES AND DAVID GROWS IN MORAL STATURE. xvi. 1— xxxi. 13

a. **The anointing of David and his victory over Goliath (xvi. 1—xvii. 58)**

i. **Samuel visits Bethlehem and anoints David (xvi. 1–13).** God calls Samuel to cease lamenting for Saul's rejection, and proceed to Bethlehem to anoint his successor (1). Saul was vindictive and the prophet's mission was dangerous (cf. 1 Sa. xxii. 18, 19). It was necessary, therefore, to say he had come to sacrifice to the Lord (2). It has been said that 'concealment of a good purpose for a good purpose is clearly justifiable'. There was nothing wrong here in concealing the primary object and announcing the second. The anointing would give David a sense of his destiny, and he would receive careful training from Samuel as the coming sovereign.

The Lord, who looketh on the heart, not the outward appearance (7), did not choose Eliab in spite of his good looks, nor any of the other six who passed before the prophet (6–10). David, the youngest, who was tending the sheep, was sent for—a red-haired, clear-complexioned lad *and goodly to look to* (12. Heb. and LXX 'with beautiful eyes'). He was marked out by God and anointed, and the Spirit of the Lord took possession of him to train him for his great work (13).

ii. **An evil spirit from the Lord troubles Saul and David is sent for (xvi. 14–23).** As David developed into a man of God and a hero, Saul degenerated; and the Spirit of God departed from him (14). He is assaulted by evil powers and suffers from something not far removed from insanity—a punishment from God. They seek out a clever harpist to soothe him; and send for David, known for his music, valour, prudence and beauty (18). With the customary presents in token of respect (20), David came to Saul who *loved him greatly* (21). It is perfectly in keeping with the nature of Hebrew narrative that the historian pursues his main theme to its ultimate consequences, and then returns to fill up the details. It is probable that these verses refer to what happened after David killed Goliath. (See Section iii below.)

iii. **Introductory note to chapters xvii and xviii.** There are serious textual difficulties in these chapters. The LXX, as preserved in the Vatican Codex B, omits the following verses which are found in the Heb. text: xvii. 12–31, 41, 48 (partly), 50, 55–58; and xviii. 1–5 with most of 6, 9–11, 17–19 and 30. It has been suggested that the translators of the LXX omitted these verses to get rid of the difficulties of the Hebrew text, and it is claimed that because of these omissions the narrative in the LXX is consistent and straightforward. The objection to this is that we cannot imagine the writers of the LXX being guilty of deliberately mutilating the text in this way.

The difficulties which are supposed to have been solved by these omissions may be summarized thus:—**1.** 1 Sa. xvi. 19–23 relates how Saul sent for David to play before him, and Saul loved him greatly and he became his armour bearer. It was a position of honour and of trust. This seems contrary to chapter xvii where David is absent from the army in time of national danger. He comes to camp only to bring victuals to his brothers and take back a report to his father. His brothers consider it absurd he should bear arms. Neither the king nor Abner recognizes David, which is strange if he had been Saul's armourbearer and beloved by him. **2.** 1 Sa. xvii. 12ff. is a repetition of what is already written in chapter xvi. **3.** 1 Sa. xviii. 1–5 tells out of the natural order what is written in verses 13 and 14. **4.** 1 Sa. xviii. 8, 9 appears to be out of place. Saul could scarcely cherish such deadly designs against David at this early stage. Indeed verse 13 tells how Saul promoted him. **5.** 1 Sa. xviii. 19, which says that Merab was given to Adriel, seems to clash with 2 Sa. xxi. 8 which tells that Michal bore five sons to Adriel.

Such are the alleged discrepancies. It must be remembered, however, with regard to the Hebrew text, that the books of Samuel were compiled from various documents. These were not arranged in their present form until considerable time had elapsed. The schools of the prophets would gradually train up men capable of keeping an orderly record of the nation's history. We know there were many annals, e.g. the Book of Jasher, the Book of the Wars of Jehovah, records by Gad, and other narratives. No doubt much historical matter was preserved at the various schools of the prophets. From these materials the narrative was compiled. There was little attempt to write it in strict chronological order. As the story was pieced together from various documents it is not surprising to find certain information repeated, as in 1 Sa. xvii. 12.

Bearing these facts in mind, it is not very difficult to explain the apparent discrepancies in the Hebrew text. The following explanation has been essayed by various writers: 1. 1 Sa. xvi. 15-18 refers to a short, casual visit of David to the court as a minstrel boy in early youth. His description as *a valiant man* (18) refers to such exploits as those with the lion and the bear; and the term *a man of war* (18) is to be taken as describing his potentiality as a brave youth. Saul's mental disorder prevented him from taking much notice of the boy. 2. On Saul's recovery, David returned to Bethlehem, and this is referred to in 1 Sa. xvii. 15. He may have remained there a few years, and so was changed from a boy into a young man when Saul next saw him at the time of the slaughter of Goliath. 3. 1 Sa. xvi. 19-23 refers to what took place after the victory over the giant when Saul, full of admiration, took him permanently into his service in the court, as armourbearer and harpist. The writer here carries his narrative to a conclusion as if it followed immediately on what has just been recorded in the previous verses. This is not uncommon in Hebrew. 4. In 1 Sa. xvii. 31ff. David is brought to Saul as a warrior. He does not recognize in the stalwart young man the minstrel boy of a few years before. Abner, as commander in chief, could not be expected to have paid much attention to a boy musician. 5. On this view it was very natural the king should enquire whose son David, his future son-in-law, was (1 Sa. xvii. 55, 58).

There are other ways in which different writers have tried to harmonize the terms of the Hebrew text, but what has been said shows that that explanation is possible. If only we knew more of the circumstances, probably our difficulties would vanish. It ought to be added that some of the verses cited as absent from the LXX are also absent from a few other MSS. While I Sa. xvii. 12-31 is present in the Alexandrine A, it is clear that it was inserted. The majority of the MSS, however, are more consonant with the Hebrew text than with the LXX. There is today more hesitation in setting aside the Hebrew Massoretic text in favour of the LXX than a generation ago. See also Appendix II, p. 298.

iv. The Philistines' invasion and Goliath's challenge (xvii. 1–11). It must have been several years after their defeat at Michmash (chapter xiv). They met the Israelite army between Shochoh and Azekah, about sixteen miles south-west of Jerusalem, on the way to Gath, in the valley of Elah (1, 2). The armies were separated by a deep ravine (Heb. *gayeʼ*) at this part (3). In verse 2 the valley is termed *ʻemeq*, i.e. a broad sweep between hills. At *Ephes-dammim* (the field of bloods) where the armies confronted one

another there seems to have been a deeper gorge in the wider valley, i.e. a *gayeʼ* within the *ʻemeq*.

The Philistine champion, Goliath, was between nine and ten feet in height (4); his *coat of mail* (lit. 'corselet of scales') to protect the body weighed about 157 lb. (5); his *target* (javelin) was carried between the shoulders (6), and the *staff* (shaft) of his spear was like a weaver's beam, and its iron head weighed 19 lb. (7). He claimed to be *the* Philistine (8), i.e. their well-known champion; and the Targum of Jonathan represents him as the slayer of Hophni and Phinehas. Fights between a few chosen representatives of armies, to decide the issue, were common in ancient times. The challenge of Goliath caused surprising terror among the Israelites (11, 24).

v. David meets the challenge (xvii. 12–40). See introductory note above on chapters xvii and xviii as to omissions in the LXX.

vi. The triumph of faith (xvii. 41–58). David put to shame the bravest warriors of Israel. He was certain God would defend him against the uncircumcised, however strong they might appear. His sling, with God's blessing, was far more powerful than the proud Goliath with his sword, spear, and *shield* (45. Heb. *bekhidhon*, javelin). It shows what real, living faith can do.

b. David and Jonathan (xviii. 1—xx. 42)

i. Friendship of David and Jonathan (xviii. 1–4). These verses reveal the beginning of the purest and noblest friendship ever known among men, apart from Christ. The giving of Jonathan's outer *robe* (Heb. *meʻil*) and his *garments* (Heb. *mad*, 'military dress'), including his sword and bow, was a public mark of honour to David (4).

ii. David's popularity and Saul's jealousy (xviii. 5–30). David's heroism and prudence (5) naturally brought him recognition, even from the courtiers and officers and the women of Israel. Saul's jealousy and murderous intentions towards David (6–12) seem to refer to a later victory. He could scarcely see in David a rival immediately after the slaughter of Goliath. The bitterness of soul engendered later in the monarch led to his undoing and caused infinite suffering. *The evil spirit from God* (10) which afflicted Saul has much that is mysterious. The 'prophesying' of Saul here is like that in 1 Ki. xxii. 22, where a 'lying spirit' is in the mouth of the prophets. It is judicial punishment from God because of certain tendencies in the king's character. This is shown in that *the Lord . . . departed from Saul* (12). The king's malevolence is seen in his brandishing his javelin to smite David (11), in his failure to give Merab to David in accordance with his promise (xvii. 25), in his demand of great exploits against the Philistines to encompass David's death (17–19), and in his offering Michal to David on conditions *to make David fall by the hand of the Philistines* (25).

iii. Jonathan pleads with Saul for David (xix. 1–7). Saul now openly declares that he wants to kill David (1). Jonathan shows his fidelity both to his friend David and to his blood-thirsty father. The result is reconciliation between the king and David (6, 7). Saul seems possessed of a new spirit; but it is not for long, for his repentance is not deep.

iv. Michal saves David from another attempt on his life (xix. 8-17). David returns after great victories (8), and is at peace, playing the harp, when the *evil spirit* comes again on Saul and he tries to kill David with his javelin. The latter flees, first to his house, and then to Samuel at Ramah (12, 18).

Michal proves her love to David by telling him of the messengers Saul had sent to his house *to slay him in the morning* when he went out (11. Cf. verse 2); by letting him down from a window (12); and by deceiving Saul's messengers by means of an image in the bed (13-17). *Image* (13. Heb. *teraphim*). The teraphim were household gods brought of old from Mesopotamia and used as charms, in spite of the prohibition of idolatry (cf. Gn. xxxi. 19; Jdg. xvii. 5, xviii. 14; 2 Ki. xxiii. 24). In this case, the teraphim seem to have been in human form and life size. Cf. 1 Sa. xv. 23 and see Appendix II, p. 297, for a note on the alleged discrepancy between the two passages. The word translated *bolster* (13) seems to have been a quilt of goats' hair, and this was covered with a *cloth* (Heb. *beghedh*, which may have been a loose mantle from David's dress). It is a pity Michal's relations with David were not happier in after years, seeing she loved him so. Saul gave her to Phalti (1 Sa. xxv. 44) as a token of his complete break with David. While king at Hebron, David got her back with the help of Abner (2 Sa. iii. 13-16)—thus securing partial reparation for the wrong done him. Some believe that Eglah (2 Sa. iii. 5) was another name for Michal, but it is not probable. The permanent estrangement between Michal and David is related in 2 Sa. vi. 20-23. Her story is sad. Both she and David suffered wrong. Injured feelings may partly explain the estrangement.

v. David flees to Samuel at Ramah (xix. 18-24). He felt he would be safe with this strong man of God whom he revered and trusted. *Naioth*, to which David came (18, 19), simply means 'dwellings'. The Targum renders it 'house of learning' and it appears to be the name for the school of the prophets at Ramah. The power of the divine Spirit is shown in the prophesying of the three successive groups of messengers sent by Saul. *Is Saul also among the prophets?* (24). For a note on this phrase and its relation to 1 Sa. x. 11 see Appendix II, p. 298.

vi. David returns and consults Jonathan (xx. 1-10). In spite of danger, David was probably advised by Samuel to return to the court so as not to break with Saul while there was any hope of reconciliation. David comprehended better than Jonathan the malevolence of Saul. The latter thought the king would tell him his intentions, and he hesitated to believe evil of his father. David shows him the truth (3). *The new moon* (5) was celebrated with special sacrifices and rejoicings (cf. Nu. x. 10, xxviii. 11-15); hence the duty of being at court. The *yearly sacrifice* (6) in the family was apparently recognized as a family custom. It is hard to say whether David meant to go to Bethlehem, or whether he wished to deceive Saul. The complete confidence between Jonathan and David is revealed by their conversation.

vii. The covenant is renewed between Jonathan and David (xx. 11-23). Jonathan shows David his plan to reveal to him the attitude of Saul. He begins with a divine invocation (12). It is only completed in verse 13. He solemnly vows that 'about this time tomorrow or the day after' (12) he would show David the truth. Jonathan knows David will be king (14, 15), but there is not a shade of jealousy or rivalry. The Hebrew version of verse 16 reads, 'So Jonathan made a covenant with the house of David'. The LXX puts all the words as spoken by Jonathan. *The stone Ezel* (19) means the 'stone of departure', perhaps so named from the departure of David. The words *the Lord be between thee and me for ever* (23) show the very solemn nature of the covenant (cf. Gn. xxxi. 49, 53).

viii. Jonathan proves Saul's intentions (xx. 24-34). In the LXX and Josephus verse 25 is read, 'And Jonathan went first, and Abner sat by Saul's other side,' showing the order of precedence at the king's table. Saul thought that David had not come to the religious feast the first day because of ceremonial uncleanness (26). The next day, however, when told that David had asked permission to go to Bethlehem, the wrath of the king breaks out violently. To an oriental, no words could be more offensive than *thou son of the perverse rebellious woman* (30). There could be no dubiety about the king's attitude to David when he declares *he shall surely die* (31. Lit. 'he is a son of death'). Saul *cast a javelin* (33. Lit. 'brandished his spear') even against his own son, as he did against David in xviii. 11.

ix. Jonathan and David part at Ezel (xx. 35-42). The signal agreed on is duly given to show that David must flee for his life. Jonathan sends back the lad, giving him *his artillery* (40), i.e. his bow and arrows, in the old sense of the Latin *artillaria*, meaning machines or equipment for war. David *arose out of a place toward the south* (41) should probably be read with the LXX, 'from beside the heap of stones', where he had been hiding. In spite of their great affection, David *fell on his face to the ground* (41), respecting the king's son and heir. The noble Jonathan, having assured David once more that he could *go in peace*, because of the oath between them, before God, *went into the city* (42) to fulfil his very difficult filial duties, and serve the interests of his nation in the terrible crisis being precipitated by his father.

c. David's exile (xxi. 1—xxiv. 22)

i. David obtains hallowed bread and Goliath's sword at Nob (xxi. 1-9). The location of *Nob* is

273

unknown, but it was in sight of Jerusalem (cf. Is. x. 29–32). David came hither to the tabernacle, for he wanted help and guidance. *Ahimelech*, the High Priest, was a good man, great-grandson of Eli, the High Priest in Samuel's childhood, on whose house a sentence of doom was passed (cf. 1 Sa. iii. 13, 14). David deceived Ahimelech in pretending that he travelled on a commission from Saul (2), and this deception produced disastrous consequences (1 Sa. xxii. 18, 19). Although David was alone at the moment he probably had appointed his *servants* (RV, 'the young men'), his followers, to meet him at a rendezvous (2).

The only bread available was *hallowed bread* (4), but in all the circumstances the priest gave him the *shewbread*, or 'bread of the Presence' (6). Verses 5 and 6 are difficult textually, but the sense is clear. The young men had had no sexual relations in the preceding days, and so were ceremonially pure according to the Law (cf. Ex. xix. 14, 15). The vessels or utensils in which the bread would be put were also ceremonially clean. David further argues that though it was treating the bread as, in a way, common, 'yet surely today the bread in the vessel is holy' (5), i.e. fresh shewbread had that day been baked and placed on the table in place of what they would receive, for the day was Friday. *Doeg*, a brutal and wicked Edomite, was there *detained before the Lord* (7). He was chief of Saul's herdsmen, and apparently a proselyte, kept at the tabernacle for some religious purification or a vow, or as a punishment for some crime. This scoundrel observed how Ahimelech gave David the shewbread and the sword of Goliath. The incident has special importance because of Christ's reference to it (Mt. xii. 3, 4; Mk. ii. 25, 26; Lk. vi. 3–5).

ii. David feigns madness at Gath (xxi. 10–15). The fact of going to Achish, the Philistine lord of Gath, shows how desperate was David's peril (10). David feigned madness, making marks on the doors, or, as the LXX says, 'he drummed on the doors of the gate'. To *let his spittle fall down upon his beard* (13) would be regarded in the East as possible only to a madman, for an indignity to the beard was regarded as intolerable. The ruse was successful.

iii. David escapes first to Adullam and then to Mizpeh (xxii. 1–8). This cave has been thought to be the modern Aid-el-Ma, some twelve miles south-west of Bethlehem. It is in the valley of Elah and there are, still, rows of enormous caves which could hold all David's men (cf. Jos. xv. 35; Mi. i. 15; 2 Sa. xxiii. 13–17; 1 Ch. xi. 15–18). To this cave came a motley crowd of discontented and distressed men (2), poor material for an army. It is a tribute to David's genius and personality that he forged them into a potent force of 400 men, which later increased to 600 men (cf. 1 Sa. xxiii. 13; 2 Sa. xxiii. 13; 1 Ch. xi. 15, xii. 8–15). From Adullam, David went temporarily to another stronghold at Mizpeh of Moab (3, 5). He secured a refuge for his father and mother with the king of Moab, possibly because of his descent from Ruth, the Moabitess (4). Then the prophet Gad ordered him to get back to Judah (5). Gad afterwards plays an important part (cf. 2 Sa. xxiv. 11–19; 2 Ch. xxix. 25; 1 Ch. xxix. 29). David now goes to the *forest of Hareth*, the site of which is unknown —perhaps near Keilah. When it was discovered where David was, Saul held a council *under a tree* (6. Lit. 'under the tamarisk tree on the height'). He refers scornfully to the son of Jesse and lashes his servants for not telling him of the league between Jonathan and David. He appeals to their cupidity and their tribal jealousy (7, 8).

iv. The slaughter of the priests (xxii. 9–23). The occasion appealed to the vile-hearted Doeg. He accuses Ahimelech of inquiring of the Lord for David and giving him victuals and the sword of Goliath (9, 10). The High Priest, and his father's house, are summoned from Nob (11). Ahimelech nobly defends David against the charge of treason and conspiracy. He maintains that none is more faithful than David, who is, moreover, *the king's son in law, and goeth at thy bidding* (lit. 'has access to thy audience'), *and is honourable in thine house* (14). The sentence of death on all the priests at Nob is that of an irreligious and implacable man, abandoned of God.

The nefarious Doeg slew eighty-five who wore *a linen ephod* (18), when the *footmen* (lit. 'runners') refused to obey Saul's order. Not content with this, the demented king ordered the utter destruction of Nob with its men, women, children and livestock. Abiathar alone escapes. Henceforth, Abiathar was to be David's constant friend through many a great crisis (1 Sa. xxiii. 9ff., xxx. 7f.; 2 Sa. ii. 1). He remained High Priest till David's death.

v. David rescues Keilah (xxiii. 1–6). David, with God's commission (2, 4), goes to smite the Philistines and save *Keilah*, a town in the Shephelah near the Philistine border, south of Adullam. Receiving promises from God, they attacked the Philistines and saved Keilah (4, 5). *Abiathar . . . fled to David to Keilah* (6), but Abiathar was with David before going to Keilah (1 Sa. xxii. 20). To avoid confusion as to when Abiathar joined David, read with the LXX, 'And it came to pass when Abiathar, the son of Ahimelech, fled to David, that he went down with David to Keilah with the ephod in his hand' (6).

vi. Saul's advance and the treachery of the Keilites (xxiii. 7–13). Saul, thinking David would be shut up in the fortified town, foolishly exclaims 'God hath rejected and delivered him into mine hand' (Heb. of verse 7), not seeing that he himself was the rejected man. The king with a great army advances, but *David knew that Saul secretly practised mischief against him* (9). God's message through the ephod saved David from both Saul and the treacherous Keilites (10–12). For the use of the ephod see 1 Sa. xxx. 7, 8n. and cf. 1 Sa. xxviii. 6n.

vii. David is betrayed by the Ziphites (xxiii.

14–29). David flees to the wild rocky tract between the mountains of Judah and the Dead Sea. Tell Zif is about three miles south of Hebron. In this wild region David found refuge in the wilderness of Ziph, in a thick *wood* (15; Heb. *ḥoresh*, 'brushwood'). Here occurred the last meeting between Jonathan and David which must have brightened the lives of both in that dark time (16–18). To the end, Jonathan is full of faith, reconciled to the divine will that David should be king, and content to be second in the kingdom. They renewed their covenant and parted, never to meet again on earth.

The Ziphites then came to Saul to tell him that David was hiding in strongholds in the hill of Hachilah, *which is on the south of Jeshimon* (19), i.e. south of the waste. Saul has to call off the search, however, to deal with a Philistine raid and David escapes from a difficult situation to find refuge in the strongholds of *En-gedi* (29), the modern Ain-Djedy, about 200 yards from the Dead Sea. The approach to this rocky place is most perilous. The rocks are still inhabited by many Syrian chamois and goats. Hence the name *En-gedi*, the 'fountain of the kid', and the reference in 1 Sa. xxiv. 2 to the 'rocks of the wild goats'.

viii. David encounters Saul (xxiv. 1–22). Once the Philistine attack was disposed of, Saul resumes his bitter pursuit of David. With 3,000 chosen men he comes to the rocks of En-gedi, and enters a vast cave in the sides of which David and his men are hiding. *To cover his feet* (3). A euphemism for going to stool. David might well have listened to the arguments of his men who saw a God-given chance to take the kingdom by force. David's tender conscience prevents his taking the matter into his own hands in this way.

His courage in showing himself to the king is derived from his good conscience. His profound respect for authority is seen as he *stooped* ('bowed himself') *with his face to the earth, and bowed himself* ('did obeisance') when he called to the king from the mouth of the cave (8). David complains of the king's acceptance of the slanders of calumniators (9). Cf. Ps. vii, which pertains to this period, and deals with the same theme; also Pss. x, xi, xii. If David were wicked, as Saul thought, he would have shown it when the king was in his power, for *wickedness proceedeth from the wicked* (13). Why, says David, should the king arrange such an expedition against an insignificant creature like himself? (14). He fearlessly appeals to God for justice (15).

The king temporarily recovers his old generous spirit. He affectionately calls David *my son* (16) and confesses how righteous he was, for he had spared his life. The king even invokes God's blessing on David and acknowledges that he will be king, and exacts an oath that he will not then destroy Saul's descendants (19–21).

For a further note on this chapter and its relation to chapter xxvi, where David again encounters Saul and spares his life, see Appendix II, p. 298.

d. Death of Samuel (xxv. 1)

He merited the highest honours they could give him. No greater man had died since Moses, and the nation mourned equally for both (cf. Dt. xxxiv. 5, 6, 8). From his early childhood he had preserved complete integrity among them as prophet and judge, and now a grateful nation bury him *in his house at Ramah*, i.e. in a garden or court at the house.

e. David and Abigail (xxv. 2–44)

i. David and Nabal (xxv. 2–13). David goes down to the *wilderness of Paran* (1). The LXX reads *Maon* instead of *Paran*, which is in keeping with the context. Nabal lived in Maon. He pastured his flocks on *Carmel* nearby (2), not the Carmel near Esdraelon where Elijah slew the prophets of Baal. Shearing time was an occasion for hospitality and goodwill among owners of flocks. David's request was only what any Arab sheikh might have presented, even in modern times, for protecting another's flocks. But Nabal, true to his name ('fool'), insulted David's messengers. He heaped contempt on David as a nobody. No wonder the latter was angry and marched up with 400 men with swords girded (12,13).

ii. Abigail's tact pacifies David (xxv. 14–35). Abigail was as tactful and attractive as her husband was foolish and repulsive. When told by one of the servants how David's men were insulted by her husband she immediately took action. The servant warmly acknowledges the protection which they had received from David's men: *They were a wall unto us both by night and day* (15, 16). Son of Belial (17). See 1 Sa. ii. 12n.

The covert of the hill (20). A defile or glen where Abigail was concealed from view. David and his men ride down the opposite hill fuming with indignation and threatening wholesale slaughter. Following the usual formula in oaths, the LXX reads 'God do so to David' (22), not *to the enemies of*, as in Hebrew and AV. Abigail very sincerely and tactfully presents her apologies (24, 25) and proceeds, 'And now, my lord, as Jehovah liveth, and as thy soul liveth, it is Jehovah that hath withholden thee from coming into blood-guiltiness and from saving thyself with thine own hand . . .' (26). She asks that her *blessing* ('gifts') be accepted as proof of David's forgiveness (27). *Bound in the bundle of life* (29). A figure taken from the custom of binding up valuables in a bag and descriptive of the Lord's great care for David. He is deeply moved and blesses God that he was saved from his contemplated crime, and he blesses her who has saved him *from coming to shed blood* (33).

iii. Nabal's death and Abigail's marriage with David (xxv. 36–44). When Abigail returned to the revels in Carmel, she found Nabal hopelessly drunk. Next morning, when she told him of the danger he had run, his violent emotions brought on a stroke of paralysis (37). He lingered for ten days and died, for *the Lord smote Nabal* (38). It was God's judgment, though natural means were employed. David's action in marrying Abigail was in keeping with the custom of eastern rulers, who, when they fancied a certain lady, sent for her to the palace and she implicitly obeyed. *David also took* ('had taken') *Ahinoam of Jezreel* to be his wife (43)—i.e. from the Jezreel near Maon. David thus shows that the manners of eastern courts were already being imitated in Israel. When he reigned in Hebron, he had six wives (1 Ch. iii. 1–3).

f. Gradual eclipse of Saul (xxvi. 1—xxx. 31)

i. David again encounters Saul (xxvi. 1–25).

The events of this chapter are very similar to those in xxiii. 19—xxiv. 22, but the occasions and the circumstances are different. See Appendix II, p. 298 for a detailed discussion of this point. With great boldness David seeks out Saul's encampment. *The trench* (5). Better as in RV, 'the place of the wagons', i.e. a rampart made with wagons or a 'barricade' (RV mg.) made with the baggage. Abishai's desire to slay Saul, out of hand, was typical of a *son of Zeruiah* (6). Cf. 2 Sa. iii. 30. As formerly, at En-gedi (xxiv. 6), David refuses to smite *the Lord's anointed* (10, 11). Nevertheless, he took the *spear* (symbol of royalty) and the *cruse of water from Saul's bolster* (12. Heb. 'from his head'). There was a miraculous element in the *deep sleep from the Lord* that had fallen upon the king and his bodyguard (12). Mistrusting Saul, David placed *a great space* between himself and the king, across one of the deep gullies, before he addressed him (13). David argues that Saul's temptation to persecute him may come from God—that 'evil spirit from Jehovah' previously mentioned. In that case, let him go to God with an *offering* (Heb. *minḥah*, 'an offering of a sweet odour'), and in religion he would find his peace, for God would accept it. If, however, Saul were moved by the wicked calumnies of men, then let them be *cursed . . . before the Lord* (19), for they had driven David out from being associated with the people of God.

They have driven me out this day from abiding in the inheritance of the Lord . . . (19). Radical critics have long seen here proof that David believed that Yahweh could be worshipped only in the holy land. They have taken this as one of the stock passages to prove that in early days Yahweh was only a tribal god (e.g. Wellhausen, Robertson Smith, Kautzsch, etc.). Each god was believed to have his own land; his power and worship did not extend beyond its confines. This certainly did not apply to the religion of Israel, for Abraham was called by God in Chaldea, and he worshipped Him in Egypt; Jacob was protected by God in Padan-Aram, and he worshipped Him there and in Egypt; Joseph also served God in Egypt and was blessed by Him; Moses worked his mighty wonders in Egypt through his God; Elijah proved His power outside Palestine, in the territory of Zidon and afterwards in Horeb. Professor James Orr says: 'We have learned from Stade

himself, what all history teaches, that Jehovah accompanied His servants in their wanderings; how could David imagine it would be otherwise with him?' (*Problem of the Old Testament*, p. 132). Many of the Psalms most confidently ascribed to David show emphatically that he was far from regarding Yahweh as a tribal god (cf. Ps. viii. 9, xviii. 49, lxviii. 31, 32, cviii. 3, cx. 6). It is fantastic to suggest that when David entered Philistia he would no longer worship Yahweh, or would perhaps worship Dagon the god of the Philistines. All that David meant in verse 19 was that his enemies were banishing him from the land where was Yahweh's tabernacle with its orderly worship and sacrifices. In Israel there were holy places and priests dedicated to the service of Yahweh. In Old Testament times, worship depended more on such considerations than in New Testament times when worship became much more spiritual. David felt that to be driven away from the religious associations of his land would be an unspeakable spiritual loss. It was tantamount to bidding him 'serve strange gods'. Even today (notwithstanding the priesthood of all believers) a devout Christian feels it a dreadful loss to have to live among pagans and be deprived of the privileges of public Christian worship and association with fellow believers. It is, moreover, soul-deadening. David's words need not surprise us.

ii. David seeks refuge with Achish (xxvii. 1–4).

Convinced that he *will perish . . . by the hand of Saul* (cf. all the versions), he escapes into Gath, to Achish, one of the lords of the Philistines. This Achish, *son of Maoch*, is probably a successor of the Achish of xxi. 10. David then came as an individual—a known Israelitish hero—and was suspected. Now, because of his 600 warriors, he is welcomed as an ally, especially as everyone knew of the irreparable breach between him and Saul. The latter now leaves off the search for David (4).

iii. He gets Ziklag and attacks the surrounding tribes (xxvii. 5–12).

David with oriental subtlety gives reasons for not remaining at Gath. He really wanted freedom of movement, and wished to appear an enemy of Saul without attacking the Israelites. *Ziklag* was originally a city of Judah, then of Simeon (Jos. xv. 31, xix. 5), but was now for a long time in possession of the Philistines—somewhere in the far south of Palestine. The statement *wherefore Ziklag pertaineth unto the kings of Judah unto this day* (6) reveals that the book of Samuel was compiled after the separation from the ten tribes; and before the Babylonish captivity. (See *Introduction*, p. 263.) David *dwelt in the country of the Philistines . . . a full year and four months* (7). Literally the Hebrew is 'days (*yamim*) and four months', but this can be taken as a year of days and four months.

All the tribes mentioned must have been on the borderland of the desert south of Palestine. The *Geshurites* are mentioned in Jos. xiii. 2 as neighbours of the Philistines, and near the Amalekites. They are different from the Geshurites north-east of Bashan (2 Sa. xv. 8, iii. 3). The *Gezrites* are unknown. The RV reads 'Girzites'. They may have moved north to Mount Gerizim. The *Amalekites* were most bitter enemies of Israel in the wilderness (cf. Ex. xvii. 8–16; Nu. xxiv. 7, 20; Dt. xxv. 17–19). It is clear from these references that the conduct of Amalek must have been peculiarly abhorrent. Saul had been ordered to destroy them but many must have escaped (1 Sa. xv. 8). *Whither have ye made a road to day?* (10). The LXX and Vulgate make Achish ask 'Against whom made you invasion to-day?'. The *Jerahmeelites* were descendants of Jerahmeel, the son of Hezron of Judah (1 Ch. ii. 5–9, 25). They were, therefore, of the *south of Judah*, but in David's time appear to be independent. The *Kenites* were descendants of Jethro, Moses' father-in-law, and therefore a section of the Midianites. They were friendly to the Israelites and had been given a settlement in the south of Judah (Jdg. i. 16). It is certain that David was bluffing Achish when he told him he had attacked these tribes.

David *saved neither man nor woman alive, to bring tidings to Gath* (lit. 'brought neither man nor woman alive to Gath') of all he attacked and captured (11). This indiscriminate slaughter, and his facility in practising deceit at this time, give us an unfavourable view of David's history at this period. We cannot, however, judge him by the standards of New Testament morality. Achish completely believed that David had attacked his own people in Judah and that he would now be hated by the Israelites.

iv. **The Philistines prepare for the conflict** (xxviii. 1–6). David was in an awkward position. Achish expected him to accompany him. David could not deceive him and said cryptically, 'Therefore, now shalt thou know what thy servant can do' (2, LXX). Achish was satisfied and declared he would make David *keeper of mine head*, i.e. captain of his bodyguard. The Philistines assembled all their forces in the north on the plain of Esdraelon, at *Shunem* on the range of Little Hermon, opposite Jezreel. Saul was to the south across the valley on Mount *Gilboa*, facing the Philistines. The armies were several miles apart with the deep valley of Jezreel between them. The powerful Philistine army filled king Saul with dread. *He was afraid, and his heart greatly trembled* (5). What a contrast to the brave warrior of early days! The Lord had departed from him—the most awful of all experiences. He got no answer *by dreams, nor by Urim, nor by prophets* (6)—the usual means for learning the divine will.

v. **Special note on Urim and Thummim.** The reference to *Urim* in verse 6 is the only direct mention in the Hebrew text after the entry into Canaan. The text of 1 Sa. xiv. 41 in the LXX (dealing with Jonathan's inadvertent transgression) represents Urim and Thummim being used in a special method of casting lots. If the text of the LXX could be accepted as correct it would definitely settle that the answer of Urim and Thummim was obtained thus. We cannot be sure that the LXX is correct, and the Hebrew text of 1 Sa. xiv. 41, 42 suggests the use of ordinary lots with no Urim and Thummim. When Saul was chosen king (1 Sa. x. 20, 21) we are not told of the method of his selection, but many believe it was by Urim and Thummim with the special use of lots. There is nothing in the text to prove this.

What was the Urim and Thummim? A wise man will not be dogmatic on this question. It has been well said: 'Nothing in Scripture is more obscure than the nature of those things which were meant to make the obscure light and reveal the hidden will of God.' There are only five references in the Hebrew text to Urim and Thummim before the exile (see Ex. xxviii. 29, 30; Lv. viii. 8; Nu. xxvii. 21; Dt. xxxiii. 8 and 1 Sa. xxviii. 6). After the exile the only reference is that 'they should not eat of the most holy things, till there stood up a priest with Urim and with Thummim' (Ezr. ii. 63; Ne. vii. 65). This method of learning the divine will was not then in use. Ex. xxviii. 30 ordains: 'thou shalt put in the breastplate of judgment the Urim and the Thummim'. The Urim and Thummim was not the breastplate of the High Priest. It was something Moses put into it.

There is general agreement that Urim is from a Hebrew word meaning 'light' or 'fire'. The LXX uses the word *delosis* which indicates what is made clear or is revealed. Vulgate gives *doctrina* ('teaching', 'instruction') which is not correct. The words Urim and Thummim are 'plurals of excellence' and involve no numerical plurality. The Hebrew Thummim is almost universally taken to mean 'perfection' (from the word *tom*). Generally the LXX translates it *aletheia* ('truth'), and the Vulgate *veritas* ('truth'). 'Light and Perfection' seems to be the best translation of Urim and Thummim.

Among the theories as to Urim and Thummim are: **1.** That it was identical with the twelve stones, on which the names of the tribes were engraved, and that a message was given by the illumination of the letters which were to give the answer. This was a favourite view among Jewish writers. It is not in accordance with what the Bible says of the Urim. **2.** That there were two diamond dice to be used in casting lots. This is supported by Zullig, and has found much favour among those who accept the LXX text of 1 Sa. xiv. 36. Many believe that 'to ask of Jehovah' simply meant to use the Urim in this way. **3.** Some Rabbins held that inside the breastplate was the sacred name, and that this illuminated the names of the tribes—a variation of **1** above. **4.** Schultz held that there were probably two stones, the one called Urim for its transparency; the other Thummim for its opaqueness; their object being to give light and judgment. When Urim fell the answer was 'Yes'; when Thummim fell 'No'. **5.** That within the ephod was a shining stone with the name of Yahweh, and that the High Priest, fixing his eyes on this and standing before the mercy seat, or the veil of the tabernacle, was filled with the prophetic spirit and heard the voice. This view was supported by Lightfoot. 6. Smith, in his Bible Dictionary (which see for much information), urges that the High Priest fixed his eyes on the 'gems oracular' and concentrated his thoughts on the light and perfection they symbolized, and on the holy name, and passed into a half-ecstatic state. Then he received the insight he sought, because he was abstracted from the world, and in touch with the eternal Spirit. He suggests that the Urim and Thummim was an adaptation to high spiritual ends of what had been common among the Egyptians on a lower plane—the symbol of Truth worn by the priest-judges, and the symbol of Light worn by priests. It is clear that the purpose of the Urim and Thummim was to discover the will of God, but we can only conjecture what it really was.

vi. Saul visits the witch of Endor (xxviii. 7–25). Instead of seeking repentance when God refused to answer, Saul sought for a woman with *a familiar spirit* (7; Lit. 'a woman possessed of Ob'). This word *Ob* means a skin bottle and came to be applied to a man or woman possessed by a spirit of necromancy. Apparently the idea was that the magician, when possessed with the demon, became like a bottle or sheath to this spirit (cf. Lv. xx. 27; Is. xxix. 4). Saul's servants found such a woman at Endor, in spite of the campaign which he had waged against soothsayers at an earlier time (3, 9). It was no easy or pleasant journey which Saul and his two attendants made that night to Endor ('the fountain of the habitation'), which was across the shoulder of the hill occupied by the enemy, and at least ten miles distant. When Samuel appeared, the woman seemed terrified and cried out (11, 12). Her usual incantations may have been imposture, but now, to her terror, God sends Samuel to pronounce Saul's doom. When asked by Saul what she saw, she replied *I saw gods* (Heb. *'elohim*) *ascending out of the earth* (13); *'elohim* is plural in form, but here we should translate 'I saw a supernatural being ascending out of the earth'. Taking the narrative in its natural meaning, it certainly points to a real appearance of Samuel. The plain meaning is denied only because many refuse to believe in the possibility of anyone appearing from the dead, and others refuse to believe that God would have allowed the woman to call up one of the saints. God, however, sent Samuel to confound the necromancer and pronounce sentence on Saul, who had so long been obdurate to the prophet's warnings. The Jewish Church always believed that Samuel really appeared, and so did early Christians like Justin Martyr, Origen, and Augustine. Tertullian, Jerome, Luther, and Calvin believed that a demon appeared impersonating Samuel. With our present knowledge of psychic phenomena, it is an excess of scepticism

to deny that the dead can, in exceptional cases, appear to the living.

There is intense pathos in Saul, in his utter dejection, seeking a message from the prophet who was once his friend and so often counselled him in vain. When Samuel appeared, the king *stooped with his face to the ground*, in reverence (14)—a testimony from the king to Samuel's outstanding character. Saul's reason for calling up Samuel is awe-inspiring—the Lord had departed from him (15). Samuel's words are but the knell of doom: 'Why dost thou ask of me, seeing the Lord is departed from thee, and has turned to be with thy neighbour?' (16, LXX). Read verse 17 with the LXX and Vulgate: 'And the Lord hath done to thee as he spake by me.' So the kingdom was going to David, because of Saul's disobedience in the matter of Amalek (17, 18). Cf. 1 Sa. xv. 25, 26. Israel would be delivered into the hands of the Philistines and Saul and his sons would be tomorrow in Sheol (the place of the dead for good and evil alike) with Samuel (19). Cf. Jb. iii. 17; 2 Sa. xii. 23. The tidings were too much for Saul and he fell *all along* ('his full length') on the floor, completely overcome (20). There is a touching degree of kindness in the scene that follows (21–25).

vii. The Philistine lords object to David as an ally (xxix. 1–11). This chapter continues 1 Sa. xxviii. 1, 2. The Philistines gathered to *Aphek* (1. Lit. 'a fortress'), a common place name. This is identified by some as Feileh, two miles west of Shunem (cf. xxviii. 4). The objection of the Philistine lords to the presence of David (3) must have been made before they reached Esdraelon. It was most natural, and providential for David. The Philistine lords angrily ordered Achish to send his unwelcome ally back (3–5). On the third day, David and his men were back at Ziklag, which can give us an idea how far north they had accompanied the Philistines (1 Sa. xxx. 1).

viii. The Amalekites, after burning Ziklag, are pursued and destroyed (xxx. 1–31). Taking advantage of the absence of the Philistine forces and David's men in the north, the Amalekites ravaged and pillaged *the south* (i.e. the Negeb) and burnt Ziklag. When David returned, he found the town in ashes, and their women and children carried away to become slaves (1–3). As on many another occasion David *encouraged* (RV, 'strengthened') *himself in the Lord his God* (6). Cf. Ps. xviii. 2, xxvii. 14.

David gets Abiathar the priest, who has been long with him (cf. 1 Sa. xxii. 20, xxiii. 6), to consult the Urim, as on other occasions (e.g. 1 Sa. xxiii. 9–12). See note on 1 Sa. xxviii. 6. The reply is more pointed in Hebrew than in the AV and is virtually 'Pursue! for thou shalt overtake and set free' (8). *The Cherethites* (14). See 2 Sa. viii. 18n. The Amalekites, knowing that the Philistine army was far away, and believing David to be with them, abandoned themselves to debauchery (16). In spite of the weariness of the long march from Ziklag, David's men fell on them with devastating effect and pursued them from the evening twilight of that day till that of the next. Not a man of them escaped except 400 young men who fled on camels for which the Amalekites were renowned (17). David recovered everything the plunderers had taken and a great deal of booty besides. This appears from the Vulgate and LXX rendering of verse 20: 'And he took all the flocks and the herds, and drave them before him; and they said, This is David's spoil.' This was David's share as captain of the band, and he chose these flocks to make presents to his many friends in Judah (26–31). The rest of the vast spoil—arms, ornaments, jewels, money, clothes, etc.—was divided equally among his followers. David established the rule on this occasion *as his part is that goeth down to the battle, so shall his part be that tarrieth by the stuff,* i.e. the baggage (24). The same just rule was laid down in Nu. xxxi. 27 and Jos. xxii. 8. Polybius tells how the Romans observed the same law.

g. Defeat and death of Saul and Jonathan (xxxi. 1–13)

This chapter, which continues chapter xxix, is almost identical verbally with 1 Ch. x. 1–12. The battle was most disastrous for Israel. The fight may have begun in the plain of Jezreel. The arrows of the enemy wrought havoc among the Israelites. They attempted to rally on Mount Gilboa, but the day was hopelessly lost. The Vulgate says 'the whole weight of the battle was directed against Saul' (3). The Hebrew says 'And the battle went sore against Saul, and the shooters, men with the bow, found him, and he was sore wounded' (3). Cf. the account of Saul's death given in 2 Sa. i. 6–10 and see notes there. His armour was placed in *the house of Ashtaroth* (10), probably the temple of Venus at Askelon, described by Herodotus as the most ancient of the temples of Syrian Venus. His body and those of his sons were fastened to the wall in the public street at *Beth-shan,* the modern Beisan, formerly known as Scythopolis, four miles west of Jordan (10–12). The men of *Jabesh-gilead* had not forgotten how Saul had begun his military career by freeing their city from Nahash, the Ammonite (1 Sa. xi. 1–13). At great peril they went by night and carried the bodies of Saul and his sons the twenty miles to Jabesh (12, 13).

This chapter is a sad commentary on the fruits of Saul's disobedience to God, and, in the case of Jonathan, an example of the sins of the fathers being visited on the children.

IV. DAVID AS KING. 2 Sa. i. 1—xx. 26

a. David's lament over Saul and Jonathan (i. 1–27)

i. An Amalekite brings tidings of Saul's death and is slain (i. 1–16). The division of Samuel into two books is artificial and did not exist in the Hebrew text. The narrative of the last chapters of 1 Samuel is continued here. (See *Introduction,* p. 262.) Two days after David's return to Ziklag

after the great victory recorded in 1 Sa. xxx, there arrived a man *out of the camp from Saul* (2 Sa. i. 2) with sad tidings of the disaster of Gilboa (1 Sa. xxxi) and the death of Saul and his sons. Like the man who came to Eli to Shiloh, with similarly distressing news (1 Sa. iv. 12–17) of the Philistine victory, his clothes were *rent* and he had *earth upon his head* (2). This was conventional with those bearing heavy tidings and the similarity in the narratives is natural. The story is told in minute detail; e.g., David had abode *two days* in Ziklag; the man arrived *on the third day; he fell to the earth, and did obeisance,* because he knew David was to be king (1–3). This shows that the narrative is taken from exact, original sources. The man was *an Amalekite* (8, 13). He came *out of the camp from Saul,* according to verse 2, and in verse 3 he says, *Out of the camp of Israel am I escaped.* This looks as if he had claimed a connection with Saul's army. He may have been a camp follower. This would not be at variance with verse 6 where he tells how he found Saul *by chance* on Mount Gilboa. His moving about in this casual way suggests he was not in regular military service. In verse 13 he describes himself as *the son of a stranger.* The word *ger* (stranger) means a foreigner admitted to a modified civil status in Israel which conferred on him certain rights. He was clearly well acquainted with events in Israel, e.g. the relationship between Saul and David, and the expectation that David would become king. The Amalekite could easily cover the ninety or 100 miles from Gilboa to Ziklag in somewhat less than three days. The battle would thus have been fought about the time David returned home.

The story now brought to David differed materially from the account we have in 1 Sa. xxxi as to the manner of Saul's death. In 2 Sa. i. 6, *chariots and horsemen followed hard after* Saul, while in 1 Sa. xxxi. 3, archers overtook him (RV). Then in 1 Sa. xxxi. 3, 4, it may be inferred that Saul was wounded by the archers, although this is not certain; in 2 Sa. i. 6, Saul was leaning upon his spear. He may well have been wounded and leaning upon his spear for support, though some commentators say he is represented as unhurt. This is unreasonable. Both the narrative here and in 1 Sa. xxxi are quite reconcilable with 1 Ch. x. 3 in regard to Saul's being wounded. Critical commentators looking for discrepancies in the books of Samuel have made too much of such points. Again, Saul may have been sorely afflicted by *archers* (1 Sa. xxxi. 3), but these may easily have been followed by *horsemen and chariots* (2 Sa. i. 6). Though Gilboa was elevated, chariots have operated in equally difficult places. Then, again, the Amalekite tells how he slew Saul at his own request for he had seen how the *chariots and horsemen followed hard after him* (6), and *anguish* (Heb. *shabhas,* cramp, or giddiness) had seized upon him (9). In 1 Sa. xxxi. 4 Saul commits suicide, but in both cases his desire is to escape falling into the hands of his enemies alive with the prospect of torture and mockery. This is emphatically the case in 1 Ch. x. 4.

Ewald and those of his school make much of the discrepancies between the story of the Amalekite and that of 1 Sa. xxxi, and put it down to the work of different narrators whose statements contradict one another. Apparently the compiler had not the wit to see this and he put down the different versions unsuspectingly. The point where the story of the Amalekite really contradicts that of 1 Sa. xxxi and 1 Ch. x is where he claims to have slain Saul. It is easily seen why he makes this claim. He expected to ingratiate himself with David and stand high in the esteem of the new king. As proof of what he had done he brought the *crown* (lit. 'diadem') and the golden armlet (or *bracelet*) of Saul (10). Apparently he had found the body of the dead king while the tide of battle had passed farther on, and he took these ornaments and resolved to go straight to David in expectation of great gains and honour. There is no need to attempt to harmonize the narrative of the Amalekite with that of 1 Sa. xxxi. He was an unscrupulous man and told the story in the way which he believed would most appeal to David. This is not in opposition to 2 Sa. iv. 9–11, as some have averred. The meaning there obviously is, as Lange says, 'If I executed in Ziklag him who avowed having killed at his own request, on the battlefield, my adversary Saul, . . . how much more must I demand at your hands the blood of this righteous man whom ye murderously slew in his house on his bed?'

We may safely take the narratives in 1 Sa. xxxi and 1 Ch. x as giving us the real facts. At the same time the story of the Amalekite was not in every respect so contradictory as some commentators have maintained. The effect on David was very different from what the Amalekite had expected. David rent his clothes, *and likewise all the men that were with him* (11). They *mourned,* (Heb. 'beat their breasts'), *and wept, and fasted* (12). In verses 11, 12 we have a remarkable picture showing how David's attitude had influenced his followers. Although the way to the throne was now open, the defeat of Israel by the uncircumcised, and the slaughter of Saul, the Lord's anointed, and the death of his dearest friend, Jonathan, filled him with grief. To David, the person of *the Lord's anointed* was ever sacred (14. Cf. 1 Sa. xxiv. 6, xxvi. 9, 11, 16); and he ordered the man who professed himself guilty of slaying him to be put to death. Apparently this did not happen until their fast had terminated in the evening—giving time for consideration.

ii. **David's elegy on Saul and Jonathan (i. 17–27)**. This is one of the most beautiful and touching odes ever written, revealing marvellous generosity to Saul who had made David suffer so bitterly. The AV calls it a *lamentation* (17). The Heb. is *qinah*, i.e. a funeral dirge or mournful elegy. (Cf. 2 Sa. iii. 33, 34.) *He bade them teach . . . the use of the bow* (18). Rather, 'he gave

commandment to teach the children of Judah the bow.' The AV can scarcely be correct for they were already expert in the use of the bow. The AV inserted 'the use of', and the RV 'the song of' before 'bow'. Neither is in the Hebrew text. It is now generally accepted that the elegy was called 'the bow', and this was to be taught. *The book of Jasher* (18). Cf. Jos. x. 12–14; 1 Ki. viii. 12 (LXX). Here, and in Jos. x. 13, RV mg. renders 'the book of The Upright'. This book was apparently a collection of national ballads dealing with the exploits of heroes. Some connect the name *Jasher* with Jeshurun, a poetical name for Israel (cf. Dt. xxxii. 15).

The beauty of Israel is slain upon thy high places (19). The word translated *beauty* is Heb. *şebhi*. Ewald (and the Syriac Version) translates it 'gazelle' and argues that Jonathan was known by this name. There is no real evidence for this. The RV follows Vulgate in taking 'Israel' as a vocative and renders 'Thy glory (*şebhi*), O Israel, is slain upon thy high places'. Lange and others maintain that 'Israel' cannot be vocative, and renders 'The glory of Israel on thy heights slain, how are the heroes fallen'. The many suggestions of commentators on verse 19 improve little on the AV. The 'glory' or beauty of Israel refers to Saul and Jonathan. Verses 20 and 21 are poetical. Verse 20 in the LXX reads 'publish not the good news'. This is correct. David shrinks from the national humiliation being published among the Philistines where their women would celebrate the news with songs and dances according to custom. Gath and Askelon were principal cities. *Nor fields of offerings* (21). Heb. *terumoth*. These were heave offerings (cf. Lv. vii. 14, 32). Vulgate translates 'fields of first fruits', i.e. fields of corn such as was used for heave offerings. As Gilboa produces no corn the reading preserved by Theodoret, 'Ye forests and mountains of death', has been favoured by some like Thenius. There is no ground for such a change, and no need if we remember that the poetical aim is precisely to emphasize the desolation of Gilboa which cannot produce 'offerings'. *The shield of the mighty is vilely cast away, the shield of Saul, as though he had not been anointed with oil* (21). The AV follows the Vulgate here and makes the anointing apply to Saul. This is not according to the Hebrew which reads 'There the shield of the heroes was defiled: the shield of Saul not anointed with oil'. The anointing here refers to the shield, according to a Jewish custom to anoint the shields with oil before battle (Is. xxi. 5) and make them glisten. Now the shield is defiled with dust and blood. RV reads like AV 'vilely cast away', not realizing that the contrast with 'the shield not anointed with oil' requires 'defiled'. The shield of Saul is taken as a suitable emblem of the military chief. There is no justification for introducing 'as though . . .' into the text and referring the anointing to Saul.

Saul and Jonathan were lovely and pleasant in their lives (23). The adjectives here have the articles in Hebrew. Hence Thenius and Erdmann render 'Saul and Jonathan, the lovely and pleasant, in life and in death (they were) not divided'. The AV is supported by the ancient versions and most commentators. Camb. Bible has 'loving and kindly' for *lovely and pleasant*. *Ye daughters of Israel* (24). The women had been enriched by Saul and covered with ornaments. They once celebrated his victories with dances; now let them weep: an apposite appeal. *How are the mighty fallen* (25). Read 'How are the heroes fallen'—a moving refrain which gives tone to the whole elegy, repeated in verses 19, 25, and 27.

Some commentators have insisted that the Hebrew text of the elegy is hopelessly corrupt. Many of the emendations proposed by them have only landed us in fresh difficulties. If the text were so corrupt as they say, we could never have an elegy of such surpassing beauty and pathos. The statement has often been made that the poem is marked by an entire absence of religious feeling. Driver says the feeling expressed is purely human. This overlooks the wonderful love shown to Saul, an enemy, the lofty sentiment expressed all through, and the profound respect cherished for Saul just because he was God's anointed king. The love for Jonathan has rarely been excelled among men. All this reveals not only religious feeling but Christian feeling. There is little room for more religious sentiment in the circumstances of Saul's death.

b. David proclaimed king at Hebron and his reign in Jerusalem (ii. 1—v. 25)

i. God directs David to go to Hebron where he is made king of Judah (ii. 1–7). David seeks God's guidance before doing anything. God sends him to *Hebron* (1), a place easy to defend and with many sacred associations. It also contained many of David's friends (cf. 1 Sa. xxx. 26–31). He could not remain longer at Ziklag because of the turn of events. Soon the tribe of Judah anointed him as king of their own tribe (4). He had formerly been anointed by Samuel in secret (1 Sa. x. 1) and he was, afterwards, to be anointed by all Israel (2 Sa. v. 3). David's message to Jabesh-gilead was prompted by genuine admiration for their action (cf. 1 Sa. xxxi. 11–13), but it was also politic and was a tacit invitation to them to join him (5–7).

ii. Abner makes Ishbosheth king over Israel (ii. 8–11). *Abner* was Saul's cousin, and commander of the army, and so the natural defender of Saul's house. Though he knew that David was anointed by God to be king over Israel, he proclaimed Ishbosheth as successor to Saul. No doubt David's associations with Achish had roused many suspicions against him. According to verse 10, Ishbosheth must have been thirty-five years old when his father died. His elder brother Jonathan was, thus, older than we generally imagine. The two years' reign of Ishbosheth is no doubt dated from the time when he became master of all Israel.

iii. The fight at Gibeon and the pursuit of Abner (ii. 12–32). *Mahanaim* was still Ishbosheth's

capital, but they aimed at securing Gibeon, five miles north-west of Jerusalem, and closely associated with Saul. (Cf. Jos. x. 2, ix. 3, xxi. 17; 2 Sa. xx. 5–10; 2 Ch. i. 3, 5.) Here twelve men from the Ishbosheth side fought with twelve men from David's side, at the pool of Gibeon (13–15). The fact that both sides were entertained by the fight shows how callous they were to loss of life. The combat was fierce and ruthless and the twenty-four fighters all perished (16). This fight being indecisive, the two armies then fought, and Abner's men fled in disorder (17).

Asahel, the youngest of the three sons of Zeruiah, was determined to have the glory of slaying Abner. He was swift of foot as *a wild roe* (18. Lit. 'gazelle'), but was only a stripling. Abner magnanimously urged Asahel to be content with taking the *armour* (lit. 'the spoil') from a younger man (21). But he refused to desist, and was killed.

Abner skilfully marshalled his beaten army into a phalanx on the top of a hill (25), and appealed to Joab to desist: *Shall the sword devour for ever?* (26). Abner had begun this fratricidal war, but his argument was good that to continue the fight would only increase the bitterness. Joab signalled by trumpet the cessation of the pursuit. Abner and his men walked *all that night through the plain* (RV, 'Arabah'), the desert tract which extends along the valley of the Jordan, and went *through all Bithron*, seemingly a district full of ravines, and got back to Mahanaim (29). Abner had lost 360 men while Joab lost only twenty (30, 31).

iv. Six sons born to David (iii. 1–5). While at Hebron, David's cause *waxed stronger and stronger* (1), and six sons were born to him. At least three of these bitterly disappointed his hopes—Amnon (cf. 2 Sa. xiii); Absalom (cf. 2 Sa. xiii—xviii); and Adonijah (cf. 1 Ki. i. 5, ii. 25).

v. Quarrel of Abner and Ishbosheth (iii. 6–11). Abner took Rizpah, one of Saul's concubines. It was rightly regarded by Ishbosheth as tantamount to treason. Abner's reply to Ishbosheth's rebuke (8–10) is very obscure, and varies in the LXX, the Vulgate, and the Hebrew. It means that if he were as despicable as Ishbosheth thinks, he would not have supported him, and Saul's house, so long and faithfully. The breach between Abner and his tool, Ishbosheth, is complete. Abner belatedly recognizes that God had promised the throne to David and decides to fight for him (9, 10).

vi. Abner negotiates with David (iii. 12–21). Abner sent messengers to David virtually saying 'Is not the land thine by reason of God's promise?' and suggesting a league (12). David accepted the proposal on condition that Michal, his wife, be restored to him (13). (See 2 Sa. vi. 20–23n.) Ishbosheth was helpless without the support of Abner, and his compliance with David's demand for Michal shattered his prestige among the people (14, 15). Phaltiel weeping on the way to Bahurim is a sad commentary on the effects of Saul's wrongdoing which brought misery to both David and Phaltiel (16. Cf. 1 Sa. xxv. 44) and likewise to Michal.

vii. Joab treacherously kills Abner, and is cursed (iii. 22–39). Joab, finding he could not persuade David that Abner was a spy and a deceiver (22–25), sent, unknown to the king, a message after Abner to return for further conference. The latter came unsuspectingly, only to be slain treacherously by Joab 'by the side of the gate' (27, LXX reading), where he pretended to hold private conference with him. Joab had no ground for complaint against Abner for Asahel's death, for he slew the latter in honourable self-defence (2 Sa. ii. 23). In the strongest terms David pronounces the guilt of Joab, and the innocence of himself and his kingdom, and utters a terrible curse on Joab and his house (28, 29). Cf. Gn. iv. 11; Dt. xxi. 6–9; Mt. xxiii. 35. It appears from verses 30 and 39 that Abishai was a party to the plot.

David was profoundly moved by this wickedness, and gave his sincere feelings the widest publicity to dissociate himself from Joab's murderous action (31, 32). In the funeral dirge, David laments that this great and brave man should die an ignoble death befitting a fool (33, 34).

viii. Baanah and Rechab slay Ishbosheth and are condemned to death (iv. 1–12). Ishbosheth became despondent when he heard of Abner's death, and the Israelites were *troubled* (1. Lit. 'dismayed'). The only prop of Saul's house was gone. Baanah and Rechab were from *Beeroth* (2), of the seed of the Gibeonites (Jos. ix. 17), and hostile to Saul's house (2 Sa. xxi. 1, 2). Entering the dwelling of Ishbosheth under pretext of securing wheat for their troops, they slew him while taking his midday siesta, and took his head and journeyed from Mahanaim to David at Hebron (5–8). This dastardly murder of Ishbosheth left *Mephibosheth* (4), the lame twelve-year-old child of Jonathan, as the only claimant to Saul's throne.

The two conspirators expected a reward for their murder of Ishbosheth, but, with a solemn oath, David recalls how he slew the Amalekite who, for self-interest, pretended to have killed Saul (9, 10. Cf. 2 Sa. i. 15, 16). Much more did Baanah and Rechab deserve death, having slain, in dastardly fashion, *a righteous man in his own house upon his bed* (11). Hence they were taken *... away from the earth* (11)—an expression often used for putting away evil out of the land.

ix. David anointed king over all Israel (v. 1–5). The tribes of Israel in a national assembly at Hebron offered David the throne as the most suitable man in that time of danger (1–3). They recognized that God had appointed him to *feed* His people Israel (2. LXX, 'to shepherd'). They made a constitutional contract with David (cf. 1 Sa. x. 25). David had begun to reign in Hebron when thirty years old—which proves that the early history of Saul's reign, when Jonathan was growing up, is not recorded. From

1 Sa. xiii to the end of the book occupies only ten years or so. The history in 1 Ch. xi. 1–9 coincides exactly, even in the words, with 2 Sa. v. 1–10. We find, however, interesting details in 1 Ch. xii. 23–40 not given here.

x. Zion is captured from the Jebusites (v. 6–10). *Jerusalem* (6), although assigned to Benjamin (Jos. xviii. 28; Jdg. i. 8, 21), was held by the Jebusites till David's day. This great Canaanitish tribe lived hard by the Amorites and a section of the Hittites in the mountainous region of Judah (Nu. xiii. 29; Jos. xi. 3). Though beaten by Joshua in battle they retained possession of the strong fortress of Jebus on mount Zion, although the tribe of Judah got possession of the lower city (Jos. xv. 63; Jdg. i. 8, xix. 12; Josephus *Ant.* v. 2, 2). It was a strategic centre, ideal for a capital, and easily fortified. As long as it remained in hostile hands, central and southern Palestine were not safe. David ruled *in Jerusalem .... thirty and three years* (5), and so he must have captured the fortress soon after his anointing as king of all Israel. *Except thou take away ...* (6). Read 'and (the Jebusites) spake to David saying, Thou shalt not come hither, but the blind and the lame shall keep thee off' (cf. Coverdale's Bible, 1535), i.e. even the blind and lame are strong enough to keep off the Israelites. Such a strong fortress, they thought, needed no defence against David.

Verse 8 has been considered very obscure. Read (with RV) 'Whosoever smiteth the Jebusites, let him get up to the watercourse, and smite the lame and the blind, that are hated by David's soul.' The point which has always caused most difficulty has been the expression *ba-ṣinnor*, rendered 'to the gutter' (AV) and 'to the watercourse' (RV). *Ṣinnor* also occurs in Ps. xlii. 7 where AV translates it 'waterspouts' (pl.), and Cheyne and McFadyen, following the LXX, render it 'cataracts'. In 2 Sa. v. 8 Perowne renders it 'watercourse' and holds the word may mean the channel itself or the water in the channel. The LXX omits completely the reference to the watercourse in this verse. Modern archaeology has cast invaluable light on the term *ba-ṣinnor* since the Palestine Exploration Fund began its survey of mount Zion in 1922. Warren discovered a vertical shaft forty feet deep, and a horizontal tunnel over sixty feet long made by the Jebusites to secure water from the Virgin's Fountain, which was just outside the walls. It was the daring attack through this tunnel or watercourse which enabled Joab to overwhelm the overconfident Jebusites (2 Sa. v. 6–8; 1 Ch. xi. 4–7). (See Sir Frederic Kenyon's *The Bible and Archaeology*, pp. 176–181; and Garrow Duncan's *Digging up Biblical History*, pp. 201–206.) This explains a passage which long caused much perplexity. The rash hypotheses and emendations of the text put forward by able critics stand as a warning to the uncautious and overconfident.

Hated of David's soul (8). David was angered by the mocking taunts of the Jebusites as to *the blind and the lame.* He hated them and resolved to show them that they themselves were 'the lame and the blind' who could not circumvent his stratagem. Because of this, David's words became a kind of proverb in the form given in RV: 'There are the blind and the lame; he cannot come into the house'. It would be a mocking reference to over-confidence, for he entered 'the house' in spite of them. It may also have been a proverbial reference to disagreeable people. The capture of the fortress is also recorded in 1 Ch. xi. 4–9, but there is no reference to the watercourse. Here the writer of Chronicles differs from 2 Sa. v. 8, although verses 1–3 are almost identical. It remains to be said that other tunnels were made after the time of the Jebusites; e.g., Hezekiah made alterations in the watercourse (2 Ch. xxxii. 30).

xi. Hiram's friendship with David: the birth of eleven sons (v. 11–16). The building of the palace may have been last in David's life. Its mention here may not be in chronological order. Hiram continued his friendship to Solomon (cf. 1 Ki. v. 1; 1 Ch. xiv. 1). The introduction of carpenters and masons from Tyre shows how artisanship had declined in Israel because of the wars. The Phoenicians were closely akin to the Hebrews in race and language. The Hiram who was Solomon's friend more than fifty years afterwards (1 Ki. ix. 10–14) was perhaps a son of David's friend. The reference to the building of the palace leads naturally to the mention of the king's wives and the sons born to him.

xii. David defeats the Philistines twice (v. 17–25). The Philistines were alarmed at David's progress as king of a united people and resolved to crush him, so they came up from the Philistine plain. David *went down to the hold* (17; Heb. *meṣudhah*, a fortress—the same word translated 'strong hold' in verse 7). It was probably the hold at Adullam, so well known to David (cf. 2 Sa. xxiii. 13, 14; 1 Sa. xxii. 1). From here, he went up to *the valley of Rephaim* (18), called 'the valley of the giants' in Jos. xv. 8. It was west of Jerusalem. After their complete rout, again the Philistines dare to come up to the same place (23). God tells David to come against them from the rear, *over against the mulberry trees* (23. Heb. *bakha'*). A tear-like sap exudes from these trees, and the valley of Baca (Ps. lxxxiv. 6) may have got its name from this tree. *The sound of a going* (24) is better rendered 'the sound of marching'. This stately march was often ascribed to Jehovah (cf. Jdg. v. 4; Ps. lxviii. 7). David's victory was, thus, due to the presence of God. The Philistines were driven back as far as Gezer (25, RV; not *Gazer*, as in AV), a place between lower Bethhoron and the sea (Jos. xvi. 3).

c. The ark brought to Zion and David's victories (vi. 1—xi. 1)

i. David brings the ark from Kirjath-jearim (vi. 1–5). See Appendix I, p. 292, on 'The ark of the covenant'. After the national consolidation, David is anxious to attend to the demands of God's house and decides, with 30,000 men, to bring up the ark of God from *Baale of Judah* (i.e. Kirjath-jearim) where it has been nearly eighty years (cf. 1 Sa. vi. 21, vii. 1, 2). In 1 Ch. xiii. 1–5 we have an account of the elaborate national preparations made for bringing back the ark.

ii. Uzzah is smitten (vi. 6–11). *Nachon's threshingfloor* (6), where this terrible event occurred, is referred to as 'Chidon' in 1 Ch. xiii. 9. As often happens to this day, two names may have been in use for the same place. Böttcher and Erdmann suggest that Nachon is not a proper name but stands for a 'fixed threshingfloor' which did not change its place and probably had a roof. They derive this meaning from the passive participle (Niphal) of the verb *kun*. It seems best to take it as a proper name. Similarly it has been suggested that 'Chidon' (1 Ch. xiii. 9) means 'threshingfloor of destruction'. When the oxen 'stumbled' (6, RV) and the ark was in danger of being thrown off, *Uzzah put forth his hand to the ark of God, and took hold of it* (6). The anger of the Lord was kindled and He smote Uzzah *for his error* (7). 'For his rashness' RV mg., which is supported by other commentators; Ewald: 'unexpectedly'). 1 Ch. xiii. 10 reads simply: 'and he smote him, because he put his hand to the ark'. There is no contradiction between this and 2 Sa. vi. 7 as has been suggested by some. The one statement casts light on the other.

The punishment of Uzzah has often been objected to as excessive, especially as his intention was good. According to the law the ark had to be treated with very great reverence as a symbol of God's presence, e.g., not to be touched but carried on staves (Ex. xxv. 14, 15. Cf. Nu. iv. 15, 20). The majesty of the holy One was symbolized by the ark. It was necessary to teach the Israelites the infinite holiness of God even if by 'terrible acts'. The ark had been in the house of Abinadab for between seventy and eighty years. His son Eleazar had been consecrated to care for it (1 Sa. vii. 1). Uzzah and Ahio must have been sons of Abinadab in the wide sense of 'descendants'—in this case 'grandsons'. Having had the ark so long in their home they might have been expected to have learned the sacred regulations concerning it. The narrative shows, however, that neither they, nor David, nor his advisers, did so, although the priests and Levites were concerned in the arrangements (1 Ch. xiii. 1–8). The Levitical laws laid down that the ark must be carried by the Levites, but they could not come near it till it was covered by the priests, and they must not touch it except by staves on pain of death (cf. Nu. iv. 5, 15, 19, 20. See also 1 Ch. xv. 2).

What they did on this occasion was quite in keeping with the extraordinary neglect of the ark during very many years. It is suggested that this was because Kirjath-jearim was probably under Philistine suzerainty although outside their territory. Even if this were true (which is very uncertain) one would have expected Saul to have recovered the ark after his smashing victories over the Philistines. Instead, the ark, that sacred symbol of God's presence, was well-nigh forgotten in Israel. In the death of Uzzah there were probably factors which would alter the whole complexion of affairs if we knew them; e.g. his close association with the ark all his days, coupled with the general lack of interest in it in the community, may well have bred in him feelings of too great familiarity. This idea is strengthened from the fact that God blessed the house of Obed-edom (12) because of the ark, although it had been there only three months, but there is no mention that God blessed the house of Abinadab where the ark had been nearly eighty years. This is suggestive.

Perez-uzzah (8). T. K. Cheyne, in the *Encyclopaedia Biblica*, maintains that David and his men, having gained great victories over the Zarephathites and the Rehobothites (cf. 2 Sa. v, xxi, xxiii), originally named the place Zarephath-'azzah, and this got corrupted into Perez-uzzah. Then the corrupt word Perez suggested a divine judgment. The next step was to invent an imaginary person called Uzzah. Such an assumption is quite gratuitous and has nothing to support it. Wade, in his *Old Testament History*, regards the narrative as historical and accounts for the judgment on Uzzah as being due to failure to observe the ordinances of God.

And David was displeased (8). 'David was angry.' This was his first reaction, for he himself had had much to do with the faulty arrangements. Then his anger turned to fear of God (9) as he realized what was involved. He placed the ark in *the house of Obed-edom the Gittite* (10, 11). He was a Korahite, a branch of the family of Kohath (Ex. vi. 16, 18, 21; 1 Ch. xxvi. 1–4; Nu. xvi. 1). He was called a Gittite because he was of Gath-rimmon, a Levitical city (cf. Jos. xxi. 24, 25). The Korahites carried the ark through the wilderness, and it was appropriate that it should now be under the care of one of the tribe. The name Obed-edom (a servant of Edom) would suggest servitude of the family at some time to the Edomites.

iii. The ark is brought to Zion (vi. 12–19). After three months, David brings up the ark with songs and rejoicings (12). The law is observed this time (13). With God's favour, they offered a sacrifice of thanksgiving (cf. 1 Ch. xv. 25–29). They placed the ark in *the tabernacle* (17, RV, 'tent'), which David had prepared for it. The tabernacle proper was still at Gibeon (1 Ch. xvi. 39). It was a day of solemn rejoicing. *Burnt offerings* were offered as a solemn dedication to God; and *peace offerings* to provide a sacrificial meal for the people (17, 18; cf. Lv. vii. 15).

iv. Michal is solemnly rebuked (vi. 20–23). Michal, in her pride, thought the king's dancing before the Lord degrading to one of his station, and spoke sarcastically (16, 20). The reply is stinging: 'Before the Lord, who chose me

rather than thy father . . . yea, before the Lord have I danced' (21). David did not consider that anything done for the glory of God was a humiliation (22). The condemnation to childlessness (23) was the severest penalty for an oriental woman (cf. Gn. xxx. 1; 1 Sa. i. 5. See also 1 Sa. xix. 11–17n.).

v. David's plans for building a temple (vii. 1–17). The section 2 Sa. vii. 1 to 2 Sa. viii. 18 is found identically in 1 Ch. xvii and xviii with very slight variations. It appeared unseemly to David that he should dwell in a permanent house of cedar while the ark remained in a tent (1, 2). There now appears on the scene *Nathan the prophet* (2), destined to play an important part himself and to write much sacred history (cf. 2 Sa. xii. 1; 1 Ki. i. 10, 22, 34; 1 Ch. xxix. 29; 2 Ch. ix. 29). Nathan as a private individual approved David's purpose (3). Now he is sent from God with a direct prohibition (4)—a remarkable example of the difference made by divine inspiration. The great promises to David (12, 15, 16), though partly fulfilled in Solomon, find their complete fulfilment only in Christ, David's greater Son (1 Ki. viii. 15–20; Heb. i. 5; Lk. i. 31–33; Acts ii. 29–31, xiii. 22, 23).

vi. David's prayer and thanksgiving (vii. 18–29). This prayer is marked by great humility, thankfulness to God for His favours, submission to the divine will, and confidence in the Lord. David *sat before the Lord* (18), probably to meditate in the holy place. He would then stand to pray, standing or kneeling being the recognized posture in prayer (cf. 1 Ki. viii. 22, 54, 55). There are textual difficulties in verse 19, but the meaning is clear when we compare with 1 Ch. xvii. 17 (lit. 'but this is the law, or prerogative, of a great man'); i.e. David is amazed that God should choose one so humble as he to found a dynasty. David is confident that God will bless him and his house, and says 'The Lord of hosts is the God over Israel: and the house of thy servant David shall be established before thee' (26, RV).

vii. His victories over surrounding nations (viii. 1–14). Chapter viii reveals David's marvellous military successes against enemy nations. It is in the nature of a summary. *Metheg-ammah* (1) means 'the bridle of the metropolis' and probably means Gath, which was a key city of the Philistines. Cf. 1 Ch. xviii. 1. David also conquered *the Moabites* (2), his former friends (1 Sa. xxii. 3, 4), but now for some reason his enemies. He made them 'lie down on the ground' (2, RV) and had two-thirds of them measured by line for death. There must surely have been special treachery when they were so treated. In the north, David smote *Hadadezer*, king of Zobah, 'as he went to renew his attack at the river Euphrates' (Heb. of verse 3). This king is called Hadarezer in 1 Ch. xviii. 3, 5, 7, and 2 Sa. x. 16–19. *Hadad* was the sun god of Syria; *Zobah* was then a somewhat important kingdom north-east of Damascus between the Orontes and Euphrates. The circumstances of this war are described in 2 Sa. x. 15–19. *David houghed all the chariot horses* (4). The hamstringing of the horses was to deprive the enemy of their use. The great victory against the powerful kingdom of Damascus, an ally of Hadadezer, shows how strong David had become (5, 6. Cf. 1 Ki. xx; 2 Ki. xvi. 5–12; 1 Ki. xxii; 2 Ki. vi. 24). *The Syrians* (13). Read with the LXX and 1 Ch. xviii. 12, 'Edomites'. This was probably a prolonged war and 1 Ki. xi. 15, 16 and 1 Ch. xviii. 12 doubtless refer to different periods of it. David was now overlord of all the surrounding nations.

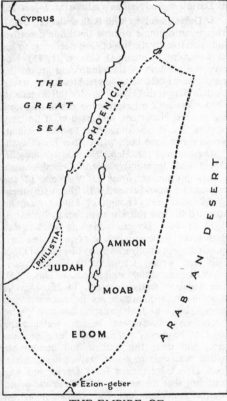

THE EMPIRE OF
DAVID AND SOLOMON

viii. His reign and his officers (viii. 15–18). Though so constantly engaged in war, David's administration was just and excellent (15). When Ahimelech and the priests at Nob were slain, Saul made Zadok High Priest (1 Ch. vi. 8), and he was continued under David, jointly with Abiathar, Ahimelech's son, who had been High Priest with David in exile. Cf. 1 Ch. xvi. 39. *And Ahimelech the son of Abiathar* (17). This AV reading is supported by the Hebrew text in 1 Ch. xviii. 16, except that the Chronicles passage reads 'Abimelech' for 'Ahimelech', an obvious copyist's error. See also 1 Ch. xxiv. 3, 6, 31. The LXX, Vulgate and Chaldee support the Hebrew, while the Syriac and Arabic invert the names and read 'Abiathar the son of Ahimelech'. This agrees with 2 Sa. xx. 25. The

history of the period amply supports this inversion. Cf. 1 Sa. xxi. 1–9, where Ahimelech the father is repeatedly mentioned, and 1 Sa. xxii. 20 which reads, 'and one of the sons of Ahimelech the son of Ahitub, named Abiathar, escaped, and fled after David'. Cf. also 1 Sa. xxiii. 6, 9. In David's time the only High Priests mentioned are Zadok and Abiathar. (Cf. 2 Sa. xvii. 15, xix. 11, xv. 24–36, xx. 25.) From 1 Ki. ii. 26, 27 we learn that Abiathar survived David.

Some authorities have suggested that in our present passage the reference is not to Abiathar the chief priest, but to a son of his, called Ahimelech after his grandfather, who was temporarily discharging his father's functions as did Hophni and Phinehas for Eli (1 Sa. iv. 4). See note on 1 Ch. xxiv. 6. The difficulty is that this verse is part of the list of David's *chief* officers. The simplest explanation is that an early copyist confused the names of Ahimelech and Abiathar and this found its way into 2 Sa. viii. 17 and 1 Ch. xviii. 16. See also the note on Mk. ii. 26.

The *recorder* (16) was a high officer of the king. He was king's remembrancer and a chronicler who kept a register of state events (cf. 2 Ki. xviii. 18, 37; 2 Ch. xxxiv. 8). *The Cherethites and the Pelethites* (18). These were afterwards David's bodyguard. The Cherethites were clearly a people in South Palestine bordering on Judah; 1 Sa. xxx. 14, 16 shows they were in 'the land of the Philistines'. In Ezk. xxv. 16 the Philistines and the Cherethites are associated and threatened with the same punishment. In Zp. ii. 5, the nation of the Cherethites is described as being 'of the sea coast', a description often applied to the Philistines; and it appears as if the Cherethites belonged to 'the land of the Philistines' according to this verse. The LXX in both Ezekiel and Zephaniah translates Cherethites as 'Cretans'. This is suggestive, as the Philistines are widely believed to have come originally from Crete. There can be no doubt that the Cherethites were a Philistine tribe. The Pelethites are mentioned with the Cherethites as David's bodyguard (cf. 2 Sa. xx. 23; 1 Ch. xviii. 17). Hastings, in his *Encyclopaedia of Religion and Ethics*, says 'the only reasonable explanation is that . . . it is a modification of the name of the Philistines used for the sake of the assonance'. In Hebrew the word 'Philistines' is *Pelishtim* and that for 'Pelethites' is *Pelethi*. In 2 Sa. xv. 18 the Gittites (from Gath) are mentioned along with the Cherethites and Pelethites—a further indication of Philistine connection. They were evidently mercenary troops from Philistia, not unnaturally, as David had defeated that vigorous people.

Gesenius renders *Cherethites and Pelethites* as 'executioners and runners'. The roots would equally well justify the rendering 'exiles and fugitives' which can be related to the word for Philistine as meaning 'wanderer' or 'stranger'. The Cherethites and Pelethites were no doubt valuable to David when rebellion was simmering in the Israelitish army.

ix. David's kindness to Mephibosheth (ix. 1–13).

This chapter shows the character of David in a beautiful light. The events of 2 Sa. xxi. 1–14 probably come before this chapter which treats of events about the middle of David's reign. *Mephibosheth* (6), Jonathan's son, was five years old when his father died, and was lame because of an accident in childhood (2 Sa. iv. 4). The king now remembers his oath to Jonathan (1 Sa. xx. 14–17, 42), and learns from Ziba, a steward of the house of Saul, that Mephibosheth is in the house of Machir (a rich landowner) in Lo-debar, near Mahanaim (cf. 2 Sa. xvii. 27–29). *Fear not* (7). Since it was a custom among eastern peoples to exterminate all the kindred of a previous dynasty, Mephibosheth had some reason to be afraid. Ziba was managing Saul's estate for David. Now he was ordered to manage it for Mephibosheth to give the latter a revenue befitting his position (9, 10). We should read verse 11 with the LXX, 'So Mephibosheth did eat at David's table, as one of the king's sons'. Thus David showed 'the kindness of the Lord' unto Jonathan's son (cf. 1 Sa. xx. 14, 15); i.e. such a gracious and unstinted mercy as God shows to men. The posterity of Jonathan was perpetuated through the descendants of *Micha*, Mephibosheth's son (12. Cf. 1 Ch. viii. 34). We have just seen David at his best in chapter ix. Now in chapter x the historian prepares the way to tell of the terrible sins which were to cloud his life to the end.

x. David's messengers disgracefully treated by Hanun (x. 1–5).

David was friendly disposed to Hanun because of some kindness received from his father, Nahash—perhaps when a refugee in the neighbouring country of Moab (1 Sa. xxii. 3, 4). David's ambassadors to Hanun, sent so courteously, were taken for spies and shamefully treated.

xi. The Ammonites and Syrians defeated and Rabbah besieged (x. 6—xi. 1).

As war was inevitable, the Ammonites hired the Syrians from the wide district north-east of mount Hermon, reaching the Euphrates to the east, and extending south to the Jabbok. This *Beth-rehob* (6) must be somewhere between Damascus and the Euphrates (cf. Gn. xxxvi. 37). The Syrians of Beth-rehob are called Mesopotamians in 1 Ch. xix. 6–19. *Maacah* (6) was a small Syrian kingdom near Geshur, north of Bashan. For *Zoba* (6) see 2 Sa. viii. 3n.

After their defeat near Medeba the Syrians, led by Hadadezer, king of Zobah (see 2 Sa. viii. 3n.), sought the help of other Syrian states beyond the Euphrates (15, 16. Cf. 1 Ch. xix. 16). They were *brought out* (16), i.e. led out to war, the causative form of the verb (cf. 1 Sa. viii. 20). Under Shobach, the Syrian allies had reached *Helam* (16), perhaps in eastern Manasseh. Here they met the Israelites, led by David in person, who gained an overwhelming victory. In verse 18 the Syrian losses are put at *seven hundred chariots . . . and forty thousand horsemen*. In 1 Ch. xix. 18 the losses are put at 'seven thousand . . . chariots, and forty thousand footmen'. The reading *seven hundred chariots* of 2 Sa. x. 18 is much more probable than that in 1 Ch. xix. 18; but, on the other hand, the reading 'footmen' of 1 Ch. xix. 18 is preferable to the *horsemen* of 2 Sa. x. 18. *After the year was expired . . .* (xi. 1). 'At the return of the year' (RV), i.e. in early spring, operations were resumed against the Ammonites. The Israelites besieged *Rabbah* (1) (lit. 'the great city'), the capital, and ravaged the country (cf. 1 Ch. xx. 1). David remained at Jerusalem in idleness and so was tempted.

d. David's sin and Nathan's rebuke (xi. 2—xii. 25)

i. David's adultery with Bath-sheba (xi. 2–13).

This is an example of how the Bible describes fully and frankly the sins of God's servants to act as a warning to others (1 Cor. x. 11, 12). Not even the position of the king could secure the suppression of the facts—a great testimony to the truth of Scripture. David's terrible fall is made to yield a lesson of priceless value as showing how the greatest sinner can find pardon, if he truly repents. Ps. li, so comforting to the penitent, would never have been written but for this sin. *And one said* (3). Heb. 'He said to himself'. David had apparently heard of Bath-sheba's beauty previously. *Uriah* (3) was one of the bravest of men and classed with 'the mighty men' (2 Sa. xxiii. 39). Though of Hittite race, he accepted the true religion as shown by his name, 'light of Jah'. David's action in sending for Bath-sheba, to lie with her, was typical of eastern monarchs, but totally unworthy of a man of God. This one wrong step led to dissimulation, hypocrisy, ingratitude, and murder (cf. Jas. i. 15).

ii. Uriah is foully slain (xi. 14–25).

David's treachery reached its climax in making Uriah carry a letter to Joab ordering his own death. According to instructions, as Joab watched the city (16), he chose for Uriah the most dangerous spot, and there this gallant and honourable soldier was slain to cover David's wickedness. Joab expected criticism from David, but was confident that the news of Uriah's death would completely mollify him. For *Abimelech the son of Jerubbesheth* (i.e. Gideon) see Jdg. ix. 53. The LXX ascribes verses 20, 21 to David in his reply. The words may have been misplaced by a copyist since it is strange that Joab should anticipate David's reply in such detail. The reference shows how well the history of the time of the Judges was known in David's day.

iii. Bath-sheba becomes David's wife (xi. 26, 27).

Her mourning was probably purely formal and would be for seven days according to custom. With indecent haste, David took her to be his wife. The whole episode, from first to last, has left an indelible stain on David's character, and was the beginning of life-long sorrow. Bath-sheba was a willing partner in his guilt. She was ambitious, and her ascendancy over David continued to the end (cf. 1 Ki. i. 11–31).

iv. Nathan's parable (xii. 1–6).

David's conscience remained dead for nearly a year until

Nathan, the prophet, came to him. The atrocious conduct of the rich man in taking the ewe lamb, so dearly beloved by the poor man's family, whilst sparing his own great flock, deeply moved David. He was ready to condemn severely another's fault while blind to the enormity of his own far greater crime. David's sentence was that this man was 'worthy to die' (5, RV. Lit. 'a son of death') and should restore fourfold according to the law (Ex. xxii. 1).

v. The prophet convicts David, who repents (xii. 7-14). The words of Nathan remind us of Samuel or Elijah in their stern denunciation of wrong on the part of kings. How directly his arrows go to the king's heart! *Thou art the man* (7). By committing first adultery and then murder he had doubly broken the Decalogue; and to use the accursed sword of the Ammonites as an added evil. David's punishments would suit the offence. The prophecy was fulfilled in the murder of Amnon (2 Sa. xiii. 28); Absalom's death (2 Sa. xviii. 14); and Adonijah's execution (1 Ki. ii. 25). His concubines were publicly taken by Absalom 'in the sight of all Israel' (2 Sa. xvi. 22). David's loss of character naturally affected his family so that evil was raised against him *out of his own house* (11). David frankly confessed his sin against God, and in spite of his own judgment of being worthy of death, God graciously pardoned his sin and spared his life (13). Psalms xxxii and li express David's contrition.

vi. The death of the child (xii. 15-23). The first chastisement was the death of the child born to him and Bath-sheba. David's tender nature comes out in his passionate intercession for the life of the child (16,17), unusual in an eastern monarch in regard to a child of the harem. When the child had died, David was prepared to leave all in God's hands (20-23). He clearly believed in immortality.

vii. Solomon is born (xii. 24, 25). Solomon (24) means 'peaceable'. In Heb. it is *Shelomoh*, in the LXX it is *Salomon*. God sent Nathan to give the child a second name, *Jedidiah* (25), i.e. 'beloved of Jah', which comes from the same root as *David* and was a guarantee of God's favour to the father and to the child.

e. Absalom's flight, revolt and death (xii. 26—xviii. 33)

i. Rabbah is taken (xii. 26-31). The narrative of chapter xi. 1 is now resumed. *He took their king's crown* (30). The word *malkam*, translated in AV 'their king', may just as easily be *Milcom*, their national idol known to us as *Moloch* (cf. Zp. i. 5; Je. xlix. 1, 3). It is, therefore, very debatable whether it was Hanun's crown or Moloch's crown which David took. Its weight of *a talent* was equal to 100 lb., and so too heavy to be worn by a king except for a few moments (30). *Put them under saws* (31). Read with 1 Ch. xx. 3, 'sawed them with saws' (cf. Heb. xi. 37)—a horrible cruelty in ancient days. The *harrows of iron* (31) were really 'threshing sledges of iron' armed with sharp spikes to bruise the corn and

break the straw in pieces. The Israelites made the Ammonites *pass through the brickkiln* (31) because they made their own children pass through the fire to Moloch.

ii. Amnon's crime against his sister Tamar (xiii. 1-22). This chapter traces the fulfilment of the judgment pronounced against David's house in Amnon's shameful outrage against Tamar and his murder by Absalom. Tamar, like other eastern women, was kept in seclusion in the dwelling of her mother. Her half-brother, Amnon, conceived an unholy passion towards her. It was against the law for him to marry her (Lv. xviii. 11), but he had Abraham's example (Gn. xx. 12), and marriage with half-sisters was common in other lands. *Amnon thought it hard for him* . . . (2). Heb. 'It seemed impossible for Amnon to do anything to her', because of her seclusion; but his wily friend, Jonadab, noticing his misery, demanded *Why art thou* . . . *lean from day to day?* (4). Lit. 'Why art thou so wasted . . . morning after morning?' He advised him to feign sickness and get the king to send Tamar from the women's apartments to prepare for him *a couple of cakes* (6. Heb. *lebhibhoth*—cakes of the shape of a heart, fancy cakes). The wickedness of Amnon is enhanced by his ruthlessly driving Tamar from his house once he had defiled her. Well may she have said 'Nay, my brother, for greater will be this latter wrong, in sending me away, than the former that thou didst unto me' (16, Old Latin Version of LXX). A *garment of divers colours* (18). Better, as in RV mg., 'a long garment with sleeves'. See Gn. xxxvii. 3n. David was *very wroth* (21) with Amnon, but weakly did nothing, which led to future calamities.

iii. Absalom slays Amnon and flees to Talmai (xiii. 23-39). Two years later, at the festive time of sheep-shearing at Baal-hazor, near Bethel, Absalom presses the king to honour them with his presence. It was a crafty device to secure the attendance of Amnon, the heir, in representation of his father who he knew would not go (23-27). At a preconcerted signal, Absalom's servants slew Amnon when he was under the influence of wine (28). Consternation reigned. The king's sons fled on their mules. Soon tidings reached David that all were slain, and he was prostrated in agonizing grief, but Jonadab assured the king that only Amnon was slain, 'for it has been set on Absalom's lips from the day that he forced his sister Tamar' (32, Heb.). He had actually noted the set purpose on Absalom's face. The king's sons soon arrived with loud lamentation (36), but Absalom fled to Geshur, to Talmai, his mother's father. As a murderer, he could not find sanctuary anywhere in Israel (cf. Nu. xxxv. 21). We may well read verse 39 with the Vulgate and LXX, 'David desisted from going forth against Absalom', which will explain David's attitude to Absalom on the return of the latter to Jerusalem.

iv. Joab sends a woman of Tekoah to David (xiv. 1-20). There is good ground for reading verse 1 'And Joab the son of Zeruiah knew that the king's heart was against Absalom'—the exact opposite of the AV. It better suits the facts, e.g. David's refusal to see Absalom for two years after his return. *Neither doth God respect any person* (14). This rendering cannot be supported. Kirkpatrick in the Cambridge Bible translates: 'and God doth not take away life, but deviseth devices (lit. thinketh thoughts) to the end that he may not (utterly) banish a banished one'. This is in line with AV mg. The RV has it: 'neither doth God take away life, but deviseth means, that he that is banished be not an outcast from him'— essentially the same as Cambridge Bible. The meaning here is that God does not take away the life (or soul) of one that is condemned and banished because of sin (so that he may be banished for ever), but deviseth devices so that the banished one may return. The wise woman pointedly calls on David to act in the same way towards Absalom. The words must have forcibly recalled to the king God's mercy to himself when he committed adultery and slew Uriah. In the first part of the verse David is reminded of the transitoriness of life. Hence it may be too late if he does not hasten to bring Absalom back. In the Heb. 'deviseth devices' is *ḥashabh maḥashaboth*, 'thinketh thoughts'. Ewald changed the verb into *ḥoshebh* and rendered 'but God will not take away the life of him who deviseth means whereby one that is banished may not remain banished from Him'. The effect of this is to make the 'devising' and the 'banishing' actions of the man, not of God. This altering of the thought to the idea that God will not slay a merciful man is not called for, and is inappropriate. There have been many attempts at emendation but none is satisfactory. Neither the LXX nor other ancient versions help us much. The Hebrew text is best.

v. Joab sent to bring Absalom to Jerusalem (xiv. 21–33). Joab carried out with alacrity the king's command to bring Absalom back, probably feeling that he had put father and son under lasting obligations (22). It seems David was bitterly conscious of the gravity of Absalom's crime and wanted to do nothing which would appear like favouritism. *Two hundred shekels* (26). About 6 lb., a surprising amount. But *after the king's weight* may mean that the lighter, royal shekel was the basis of the calculation, in which case the weight would be about 3½ lb.

Absalom resorts to the stratagem of burning Joab's field since all other efforts to persuade him to disobey the king's ban have failed. His plan works and, as a result of Joab's intercession, he receives a complete pardon.

vi. Absalom steals the hearts of the people (xv. 1–12). He knew how to use craft and flattery to win popular favour. With *chariots and horses* and fifty runners before them, he gave the impression of a grand prince (1). The king was overwhelmed with too much work and had no deputy; there was much discontent because of the arrogance of Joab, and because of David's fall with Bath-sheba. *After forty years* (7). Read with the LXX, Vulgate, Josephus, and certain versions,

'after four years.' Four years enabled him to *steal the hearts of the men of Israel* (6) and prepare his vile conspiracy.

vii. David flees from Jerusalem (xv. 13–37). The rebellion was strong (12, 13), and the king, with remarkable foresight, decided to leave Jerusalem—to save the city from destruction, and give time to organize his forces (14). He was readily supported by those around him in Jerusalem (15). He *tarried in a place that was far off* (17. 'At the far house,' RV mg.), in the suburbs, on the Jericho road, and reviewed his followers among whom the Cherethites and Pelethites, and the company of 600 men from Gath, are specially mentioned (see 2 Sa. viii. 18n.). *Ittai*, the leader of the Gittites, although a Philistine, is unflinchingly loyal to David (19–21). His noble reply is like Ruth's (cf. Ru. i. 16, 17). *The ark* (24), which accompanied them for a short distance, is now sent back under the High Priests Zadok and Abiathar. The priests could best serve David in Jerusalem, and send him information through the young men, Ahimaaz and Jonathan (27). They could safely go back because of their office (27, 35). David would wait information *in the plain of the wilderness* (28. Heb. *kthibh*, 'fords of Jordan').

At the top of Mount Olivet he meets a valuable ally in the aged counsellor *Hushai the Archite* (32), whom he persuades to return to Jerusalem and to feign loyalty to Absalom, in order to frustrate the counsel of Ahithophel. Such deceptions were practised from time to time and are related in Scripture without being specifically approved.

viii. Ziba by guile secures Mephibosheth's inheritance (xvi. 1–4). Ziba, with apparently great deference, comes to the king at the top of the ascent with a gift of the produce of the locality, and *a bottle of wine* (1. Lit. 'a skin of wine'). He wickedly maligns his master (3), and David rashly believed him and gave all Mephibosheth's property to this wretch. It was a grievous wrong to a good man.

ix. Shimei curses David (xvi. 5–14). At *Bahurim* (5), somewhere on the road from Olivet to Jordan, Shimei, a member of the house of Saul, bitterly curses David across a deep but narrow ravine which separated them, shouting *Come out, come out . . .* (7). Lit. 'Get out! Get out! thou man of blood, and thou wicked man'. David accepts it as part of God's judgment on himself, arguing that, when his own son turns against him, there is some excuse for a Benjamite to do the same. David's reaction to the whole situation suggests that he is content to leave the result of the rebellion in the Lord's hands.

x. Absalom enters Jerusalem (xvi. 15–23). When Absalom entered the capital with Ahithophel, Hushai, with great address, succeeded in ingratiating himself with him, though at first somewhat suspected (16–19). Ahithophel's first counsel to Absalom in Jerusalem was atrocious—to take possession of his father's harem, and so to make reconciliation impossible (21). This was an emphatic act of sovereignty

288

(cf. 1 Ki. ii. 22), and was the greatest insult that could be offered David.

xi. Hushai overthrows Ahithophel's counsel (xvii. 1–14). Ahithophel's plan to pursue David relentlessly before he could organize resistance would, no doubt, have given the victory to Absalom. Hushai ventured to suggest that *this time* (in contrast with xvi. 21) the counsel of Ahithophel was *not good* (7). He recalled David's vast military experience, and the bravery of himself and his warriors now infuriated by suffering. With great address, Hushai recommends a general levy to make sure of victory. The grandiose scheme appealed to the vanity of Absalom, and he accepted the counsel of Hushai, who thus gained time for David.

xii. Private intelligence sent to David (xvii. 15–22). For fear the fickle Absalom might change his mind, Hushai immediately sent intelligence to David to cross Jordan at once. Jonathan and Ahimaaz received the message from a *wench* (17), i.e. 'maidservant', at *En-rogel* ('the fuller's fountain'), where she probably pretended to draw water. It is now called the Virgin's Fountain, and is outside Jerusalem on the south-east near the village of Siloam. *A well in his court* (18). Perhaps a dry cistern in which they could easily take refuge, and the existence of which was cunningly hidden.

xiii. The death of Ahithophel and progress of the conflict (xvii. 23–29). The resemblance to Judas is noteworthy (cf. Mt. xxvii. 5). His vanity was wounded, and he knew Absalom would now be defeated and that retribution would fall on him as his chief instigator. His downfall was a result of David's prayer. See xv. 31 and cf. xvii. 14. David arrived at *Mahanaim*, in Gilead (24), a strong and distant city well provisioned and possessing a warrior race. It was formerly Ishbosheth's capital (2 Sa. ii. 8, 12). Soon, Absalom also arrived in Gilead, and made his cousin, Amasa, his general (25. Cf. 1 Ch. ii. 17).

At Mahanaim, David was entertained by three grand men: *Shobi*, a son of a former Ammonite king and brother, apparently, of the contemptible Hanun (see x. 1–4); *Machir*, who had befriended Jonathan's lame son Mephibosheth (ix. 4); and *Barzillai* of Gilead, old in years, independent in spirit, but generous and loyal (see xix. 31–39n.).

xiv. David prepares for battle (xviii. 1–5). At Mahanaim he *numbered* (1. Heb. *pakad*, 'mustered') the people that were with him, now a goodly number, and placed them under Joab, Abishai, and Ittai, in three divisions. The people insisted that David should not imperil his safety, and theirs, by taking a personal part in the fight (2, 3). His final charge to his captains was to deal gently with Absalom (5).

xv. The death of Absalom (xviii. 6–18). Although east of the Jordan, the wood where the battle was fought was called *the wood of Ephraim* (6), perhaps because of the slaughter of the Ephraimites by Jephthah (Jdg. xii. 6). The followers of Absalom, called here *the people of Israel* (7), were overwhelmed, losing 20,000 men, casualties being specially heavy in the wood (8). Absalom, fleeing from his enemies on muleback, was caught by the head in the tangled branches of *a great oak* (9); lit. 'the great terebinth'. He was suspended between earth and heaven, while his mule passed on—as can easily happen to anyone in a semi-tropical forest. Joab, on hearing of Absalom's position, was wroth that his informant had not killed him, but the latter, remembering David's command (12. Lit. 'Take care, whoever you be, of the young man Absalom'), declared he would not have done so for a thousand shekels. Joab, ever without scruple, *took three darts* (14. Heb. *shebhet*, 'pointed staves') and thrust them through Absalom's body, leaving ten soldiers to despatch him finally (15). With Absalom dead there was no purpose in continuing the battle and Joab stops the pursuit. The usurper is buried ignominiously in a wood under a great heap of stones. This was in marked contrast with the grand pillar he had *reared up for himself* (18). The three sons mentioned in xiv. 27 must have died.

xvi. David hears the news and mourns for Absalom (xviii. 19–33). Joab preferred to send *Cushi* (21. 'The Cushite,' RV), an Ethiopian slave, to tell David of his son's death, rather than Ahimaaz, for it would be a painful task. The story of the race to Mahanaim, their arrival, and the breaking of the tidings, is intensely dramatic —the king anxiously waiting *between the two gates* (24); the watchman; the first sight of the runners; David's premonition of good tidings (27); the tactful greeting and message of Ahimaaz; the king's tender anxiety for *the young man Absalom* (29); the blunt announcement by the Cushite of Absalom's death (32)—all is most vivid. David's lamentation is unspeakably pathetic. All Absalom's faults are forgotten in the welling up of parental love.

f. David's return and Sheba's revolt (xix. 1— xx. 26)

i. Joab upbraids the king for his mourning (xix. 1–8). The great *victory* (2. Lit. 'deliverance') that day was turned to mourning for the people because of the king's grief. They went stealthily into the city 'as people who have disgraced themselves by fleeing in battle' (Heb. of verse 3). The brusque and brutal Joab had much reason for his rebuke to David.

ii. The king is brought back (xix. 9–15). The nation was sadly divided by party faction. David wisely waited for a movement for restoration, knowing that a re-election would increase enormously his authority. Israel moved first (9, 10). Judah had taken a leading part in the rebellion and held back (11). David tactfully sent Zadok and Abiathar to secure the support of this powerful tribe—his own. Why should they be last in bringing the king back? (11, 12). Judah was completely won over by the king's words (14, 15) and so absorbed him that the other tribes became seriously offended (41–43). Clearly the

K

seeds of distrust and division were already present between Judah and the other tribes.

iii. Various personalities greet the returning king (xix. 16–43). Among the first to greet the king, as he was embarking to cross Jordan, were the contemptible creatures Shimei and Ziba, come to curry favour (16–18). Shimei professes humble penitence, the sincerity of which is doubtful (19, 20). Once more, Abishai would have slain him (cf. 2 Sa. xvi. 9), but David refused to put anyone to death in Israel on that joyful day (22), and swore to Shimei to spare him (cf. 1 Ki. ii. 8, 9). *Mephibosheth* (24) is somewhat roughly received by David, who still believed Ziba's slanders, but the explanations given satisfy the king at least partially. Nevertheless, the treatment of Mephibosheth was far from happy, and the award unsatisfactory (29). Mephibosheth comes well out of the interview, the king not so well. Everything predisposes us in favour of *Barzillai* (31–39)—his great age, rank, unfaltering loyalty and chivalry, his courteous convoy across Jordan, his declinature of a place at court, and his desire to be buried with his people amongst the hills of Gilead.

iv. Sheba rebels and is slain (xx. 1–22). Sheba, a Benjamite, and *a man of Belial* (1. Lit. 'worthless man'), took occasion of the dispute at Gilgal to raise an Israelite party against Judah. David commissioned Amasa to raise the men of Judah (4) but Abishai had later to be appointed to the command (6). The real commander was Joab (7), although David wanted to get rid of him. Meeting Amasa at Gibeon, Joab treacherously murdered him under guise of friendship (10, 12). In spite of this, and his constant aggressiveness, Joab remained the idol of the army, and is followed, in pursuit of Sheba, not only by his own men, but also by Amasa's men (11–13). *Abel* (14) means 'meadow' and *Beth-maachah* (14) is usually tacked on to distinguish it from other meadows. It is far up the Jordan, twelve miles north-west of Lake Huleh, the ancient Merom. Abel had been famous for the wisdom of its people, and there was still there *a wise woman* (16–19). She said they expected negotiation before the city was destroyed (cf. Dt. xx. 10ff.). The wise woman persuaded the citizens to behead Sheba, and throw his head over the wall to Joab. The latter shows a reasonable and patriotic spirit and at once raised the siege. Events seemed to show the army could not do without Joab.

v. David's chief officers (xx. 23–26). A similar list is given in 2 Sa. viii. 16–18 when David had established his kingdom. Here David makes a new beginning. The enumeration of the offices is, thus, appropriate.

V. LAST YEARS OF DAVID'S REIGN. xxi. 1—xxiv. 25

Chapters xxi—xxiv are made up of six appendices placed at the end of the second book of Samuel so as not to interrupt David's history.

a. The famine and the victory over the Philistines (xxi. 1–22)

i. Three years' famine (xxi. 1–10). To find the cause of the three years' famine, David *enquired of the Lord* (1. Lit. 'sought the face of the Lord') and found it was because Saul had massacred the Gibeonites. There is no indication of time or circumstances. Contrary to the oath given by Israel in Jos. ix. 3, 6, 15, Saul had attacked them, and the punishment is a terrible example of national responsibility for covenants. *Five sons of Michal* (8). From 1 Sa. xviii. 19 we know that it was because Merab, another of Saul's daughters, who was married to Adriel. Michal, as is suggested by the Targum, may have brought up the children for her brother-in-law. The action of Rizpah in erecting a tent and watching the bodies constantly to save them from the many birds of prey was a touching and beautiful one (10).

ii. Burial of the bones of Saul and Jonathan (xxi. 11–14). Apparently David was moved by the example of Rizpah to show respect to the bones of Saul and his sons which they brought from their obscure grave at Jabesh-gilead (cf. 1 Sa. xxxi. 11–13; 2 Sa. ii. 4) and buried them with public honours in the family sepulchre at *Zelah* (14), in Benjamin, together with the seven who were hanged at Gibeah. It looks as though David was anxious to demonstrate that the recent hangings had not been the result of any grudge of his against the house of Saul.

iii. Great exploits against the Philistines (xxi. 15–22). There is no indication when these events took place. They are probably copied from some official record of great deeds, and 2 Sa. xxiii. 8–39 is probably derived from a similar source. These mighty deeds were all done against *sons* or progeny (Heb. *yaldhe*) of *the giant* (Heb. *ha-Raphah*) (16, 18, 20, 22). The word *Raphah* (*Haraphah* with the article) may be a proper name for the father of a race of giants called the Rephaim (cf. Gn. xiv. 5, xv. 20; 2 Sa. v. 18). The sons mentioned here are different from the *nephilim* or 'giants' (Gn. vi. 4; Nu. xiii. 33), and from the 'sons of Anak' (Nu. xiii. 28, 33; Dt. ix. 2; Jos. xv. 13–14) who are described as *nephilim*.

Probably verse 17 should read 'and he (David) smote the Philistine and killed him', which is in line with verse 22. From then onwards, his people refused to allow David to run such peril, for his life was to them as *the light of Israel* (17).

Elhanan the son of Jaare-oregim . . . (19). The av inserts *the brother of* before *Goliath* to bring it into line with 1 Ch. xx. 5, but this insertion has no support from any of the ancient versions. In 1 Ch. xx. 5 the text is 'and Elhanan the son of Jair slew Lahmi the brother of Goliath the Gittite'. This raises the important question as to which is the correct reading, Samuel or Chronicles. Commentators with a liberal outlook have maintained that the story of David's slaying Goliath in 1 Sa. xvii is not historical. They claim support for their view in 2 Sa. xxi. 19, which ascribes the slaying of Goliath to Elhanan. In reply, some would say that there were two

Goliaths. This seems unlikely, and yet there were two Elhanans, both of Bethlehem, strange as it may appear (cf. 2 Sa. xxiii. 24). Similarly, there may have been two Goliaths of Gath, one killed by David and one by Elhanan. This explanation is scarcely satisfactory. There is, indeed, no doubt that 1 Ch. xx. 5 preserves the true reading, and that Elhanan slew Lahmi, the brother of Goliath. In 2 Sa. xxi. 19 there are two obvious copyists' errors. The verse ends with the word *'oregim*, i.e. 'weavers'. The Hebrew is 'weavers' beam' (pl.) not *weaver's beam* (AV). Now this word *'oregim* appears earlier in the verse in the name *Jaare-oregim*. The name Jair in 1 Ch. xx. 5 is certainly preferable to *Jaare* which occurs here. The copyist's eye had apparently fallen on *'oregim* at the end of the verse, and he got it in after Jair. Then the Hebrew letters of Jair were transposed to make it *Jaare* and make it obey the laws of Hebrew grammar. Again, in the Hebrew text of the Samuel passage the words 'Bethlehemite', 'Goliath' stand together (*beth ha-lachmi 'eth golyath ha-gitti*) and resemble very closely the Chronicles wording 'Lahmi the brother of Goliath' (*'eth lachmi 'achi golyath ha-gitti*). Textual scholars are agreed that the one reading is an accidental corruption of the other, but they hesitate in deciding as to which is the corruption. The fact that the copyist stumbled over Jaare-oregim shows that the corruption is in 2 Sa. xxi. 19, and that 1 Ch. xx. 5 is not an attempt to get rid of a supposed discrepancy between the statement of 2 Sa. xxi. 19 and 1 Sa. xvii which tells of the slaughter of Goliath by David.

Böttcher presents an elaborate plea for reading in 2 Sa. xxi. 19, 'Elhanan the son of Jesse the Bethlehemite slew Goliath . . .' This is based on the old Jewish tradition preserved in the Targum, and accepted by Jerome, that Elhanan was another name for David. Unfortunately there is no evidence of any kind for this view. The acceptance of the Hebrew text of 1 Ch. xx. 5 as the correct one goes a long way towards destroying the case of those commentators who find contradictory reports in 1 Sa. xvii as to the part played by David. (See comments on that chapter.)

b. David's song of thanksgiving (xxii. 1–51)

This song is the same as Ps. xviii, except for some very slight variations. It was written when David was newly established on the throne of Israel. It gives special thanks for the deliverance from Saul, his chief enemy, and for victories over the Philistines, Moabites, Syrians, Ammonites, and Edomites (44–46. Cf. 2 Sa. viii. 1–14). For a commentary on all the verses, see the book of Psalms. The slight variations between this chapter and Ps. xviii are explained by the fact that we have here the first copy. It was afterwards adapted by David for the music of the temple. Notice how David's long residence in the wilds as a fugitive has coloured the language of this song. God was his *rock* (2, 'cliffs'. Cf. 1

Sa. xxiii. 25, 28), his *fortress* (2, 'stronghold'. Cf. 1 Sa. xxiii. 14, 19, 29, xxiv. 2). His frequent refuges among the rocks reminded him that God was his *refuge* and *saviour* (3). The mountain torrents (5); the earthquake (8); the wind (11); the dark clouds (12); the lightning and thunder (13–15)—all are utilized to enhance the tremendous picture he paints—and so on to the end of the song.

c. David's last words (xxiii. 1–7)

These are his *last words* (1) in song, in distinction from Ps. xviii (in the previous chapter) written at an earlier date. Some think the words are his last as an inspired author (see verse 2). The Hebrew word *ne'um* in verse 1 (translated *said* in AV) is always used of a divinely inspired utterance (e.g. Nu. xxiv. 3, 4, 15, 16; Pr. xxx. 1). Hence the song is on the highest level. In brief and poetical words he describes the ideal ruler (3, 4); he is righteous, Godfearing and bringing blessing to his people. David himself has fallen short; yet God has made with him *an everlasting covenant* (5), the implication being that the righteous ruler will eventually spring from his house. Cf. Je. xxxiii. 15, 16. How different is the expectation of the wicked (6, 7).

d. A catalogue of David's mighty men (xxiii. 8–39)

This corresponds to 1 Ch. xi. 11–41 where it is given as the list of great men who helped David to win the throne and capture Zion. In verse 8 read for *Tachmonite* (following 1 Ch. xi. 11) 'Jashobeam, an Hachmonite'; and for *the same was Adino the Eznite* (8) read the words of 1 Ch. xi. 11, 'he lifted up his spear', omitting the reference to Adino (see 1 Ch. xii. 6, xxvii. 2 on Jashobeam). He was chief of the first three—the other two being *Eleazar* who, in a tight corner alone, smote the Philistines till his hand clave to the sword (9, 10), and *Shammah* who, alone, slew a troop of Philistines in defending a plot of lentil ground and wrought a great victory (11, 12). These were the first three. Now there appears a second group of three—Abishai, Benaiah, and one not named—perhaps Amasa (13. Cf. 1 Ch. xi. 15, 16). The thirty mighty men of verses 24–39 seem to have formed a sort of legion of honour. The list here is somewhat different from that in 1 Ch. xi. 26–41, possibly through being drawn up at different times. In 1 Ch. xi. 41–47 sixteen more names are given—perhaps those who were added on the death of original members. The total of all the mighty men is *thirty and seven* (39) —three in the first class, three in the second class, and thirty-one in the third. Joab, as supreme commander, is not included in these lists.

e. The census and the plague (xxiv. 1–25)

i. David numbers the people (xxiv. 1–9). There were, apparently, many national offences then (1), and David's sin in numbering the people became the occasion for nation-wide chastisement. God, to prove David's character, allowed him to be tempted. In 1 Ch. xxi. 1 it says 'Satan stood up against Israel, and provoked David to number Israel'. The taking of this census was from pride and a desire for aggrandisement. David insisted on counting the people in spite of the solemn warnings of Joab and the council of officers. The attitude of Joab did him much credit (3. Cf. 1 Ch. xxi. 3). It shows what excellent qualities he possessed, though his ambition, cruelty, and overbearing spirit so largely nullified these. Joab and his officers carried out faithfully the king's order, against their own better judgment (4). In nine months and twenty days (8) they returned to Jerusalem, reporting that Israel had 800,000 fit for military service, and Judah 500,000. These figures are different from those in 1 Ch. xxi. 5, where Israel is credited with 300,000 more and Judah with 30,000 fewer. Many commentators have followed the easy way of explaining this as being due to errors of text or of oral tradition. There are many ways in which the discrepancy can be explained, e.g., 1. that there were two countings, one according to the private lists in the various communities which appeared in Chronicles, and the other a digest made for the public registers; 2. that 2 Sa. xxiv. 9 does not contain the numbers for Benjamin and Levi, but that they are included in 1 Ch. xxi. 5; 3. that Chronicles includes the non-Israelitish men in the ten tribes; 4. that the regular army of 288,000 men (1 Ch. xxvii. 1–15) is included in Israel in 1 Chronicles, and excluded in 2 Samuel; and that the 30,000 men commanded by the thirty heroes (1 Ch. xi. 25) are included in Judah in Samuel but excluded in 1 Ch. xxi. 5. We cannot say with certainty that any of these explanations is correct, but they clearly prove that an explanation of the apparent discrepancy is possible without questioning the correctness of the figures. Objection has been taken to the numbers of men of military age mentioned because they imply a population of at least six million in the small country of Palestine. When the intense fertility of the land is considered, such a population is quite reasonable and this view is sustained by the innumerable ruins of cities and villages which still abound.

ii. David's punishment (xxiv. 10–17). Immediately the census ended, David's conscience smote him and he confessed his sin to God even before the arrival of the prophet Gad. This is clear from the Hebrew of verse 11. On being given choice of three punishments—famine, war, or pestilence (13, 14)—David resolved to leave himself in the hands of God, and the Lord sent the plague *from the morning even to the time appointed* (15), i.e. until the hour of the evening sacrifice, about 3 p.m., when 70,000 had perished.

iii. The threshing floor of Araunah (xxiv. 18–25). It was only after David had built his altar, and sacrificed on the threshingfloor of Araunah, where afterwards the temple was built, on Mount Moriah, that the plague was stayed (25). *Araunah* was one of the old Jebusite inhabitants of Jerusalem. He was a man of kingly spirit, apparently devout, though not an Israelite, and offered to give everything for the sacrifice as a free gift (21–23). David's reply was equally noble and worth writing in letters of gold for all generations—*Nay; but I will surely buy it of thee at a price: neither will I offer burnt offerings unto the Lord my God of that which doth cost me nothing* (24). David bought the threshingfloor and the oxen for fifty shekels of silver (24); but 1 Ch. xxi. 25 states that he paid Ornan (i.e. Araunah) six hundred shekels of gold 'for the place'. This would be a later transaction to purchase the whole place on which the temple was afterwards built (cf. 1 Ch. xxii. 1; 2 Ch. iii. 1).

A. M. RENWICK.

APPENDIX I: THE ARK OF THE COVENANT

In Hebrew the term is *'aron*, a chest or box. In the Latin Vulgate it is *arca*, and in the LXX *kibōtos*. It was made of acacia (or shittim) wood, 2½ cubits long, 1½ broad and 1½ deep. (Cf. Ex. xxv. 10; Dt. x. 3.) It was overlaid with gold, and the upper part supported the mercy seat which was overshadowed by the cherubim—one at either hand with wings extended. The ark had a gold ring at each corner. Through these were put staves covered with gold so that it could be carried by priests or Levites without being touched. (Cf. Ex. xxv. 10–20.) Inside the ark were placed the two tables of stone bearing the Decalogue (Ex. xxv. 16, xl. 20; Dt. x. 5). In Heb. ix. 3 we read that it contained also 'the golden pot that had manna, and Aaron's rod that budded'. According to 1 Ki. viii. 9, the ark contained nothing but the two tables of stone placed there by Moses. No doubt the other items had disappeared by the time that was written.

The Egyptians and other ancient peoples of the Middle East used arks with cherubim in their religious rites. We are familiar with representations of these. They appear to have been somewhat similar to the ark of the covenant. Clement of Alexandria calls them *kistai mustikai*.

The ark was very sacred, and was given its place in the 'holy of holies' after the temple was built. It was intended to be a symbol of the divine presence (Ex. xxx. 6; Jdg. ii. 1ff.; Nu. x. 33) and to conserve inviolate the two tables of the Law often called 'the testimony', as in Ex. xl. 20. It figures very prominently in 1 Samuel and 2 Samuel (see, e.g., 1 Sa. iii. 3, iv. 3–11, 17, 18, 21, vi. 1–21, vii. 1, 2; 2 Sa. vi. 1–17). For its later history read 1 Ki. viii. 3–8 and Je. iii. 16.

The name 'ark of the covenant' is in Heb. *'aron ha-berith*, lit. 'the chest of the covenant'. It is also known as the ark of God, the ark of the testimony, etc.

Critics of the advanced school have argued that the ark was an empty throne which was carried by the Israelites after they left Sinai and that they believed Yahweh occupied it—as they believed He had occupied a throne-like rock at Sinai. Hence, when they left, they carried an imitation of this throne. Writers like Reichel, Meinhold, Martin Dibelius, Gunkel, etc., have taken this view in one form or another. It must be noted, however, that it is never described as a throne in the Old Testament, but always as an ark, even by those writers recognized by critics as most ancient. Furthermore, the Semites never carried about empty thrones in religious processions as some Aryans did. Other critics, like Guthe, have maintained that the Israelites believed that God dwelt in the ark. Against this is the fact that a careful reading of the Old Testament shows that Yahweh dwelt 'above' the ark, between (or upon) the cherubim (cf. 1 Sa. iv. 4; 2 Sa. vi. 2).

Others, like Stade and Schwally, have believed the ark to be a fetish chest containing two stones, probably meteoric stones. Prof. H. P. Smith says this was natural as they considered the deity dwelt in a rock at Sinai. This does not square with any Old Testament writings. The special symbol of God's presence—the pillar of cloud or fire— is always represented as 'above' them or going before them, and not connected with the ark. Even the child Samuel, when addressing God, knew better than to imagine He was contained in the ark (1 Sa. iii. 10). There is not a shred of evidence that the ark was a fetish chest. Of course, the more radical schools of critics have denied that the two tables of the Law are historical and so deny that they were in the ark. The only extant tradition, however, tells that the tables of the Law were in the ark and it is admitted that even sections credited to J and E (the oldest sections of Old Testament on their theory) recognize this.

Much has been made of passagesl ike Nu. x. 35, 'when the ark set forward, . . . Moses said, Rise up, Lord, and let thine enemies be scattered', with a view to proving that the ark itself was Yahweh or that He dwelt in it. Such words simply mean that Moses called upon God to go forth before Israel as the ark did. It takes much misplaced ingenuity to give such words any other meaning.

The Israelites clearly believed that the ark had a special connection with Yahweh and that He often vouchsafed His presence with the ark. Like every other sacred symbol it could be debased to superstitious uses, as when the elders brought it as a talisman to the field of battle to secure victory over the Philistines, forgetting that their sins had deprived them of God's presence (1 Sa. iv. 3–7). Such references do not prove, as some commentators have said, that the ark was designed for military purposes. Nothing in its form or contents suggests this, but being associated in the popular mind with the divine presence it was easy to fall into the error of thinking that its mere presence would ensure success.

A. M. RENWICK

APPENDIX II : THE CRITICAL. VIEW OF SOURCES AND DOCUMENTS

I. INTRODUCTION

This is not the place to enter into a discussion of the principles on which liberal critics have built up their theory as to the division of the Old Testament among unknown writers like J, E, P, D, and a large number closely allied with these. We believe that Graf and Wellhausen and their school built their theory on false foundations. Many of their assumptions were erroneous and they were hostile to the admission of the supernatural element in revelation. In particular every effort was made to bring the sources down to a late date so as to explain the high moral and spiritual conceptions of the Old Testament on natural evolutionary principles and so eliminate the supernatural or, at least, minimize it radically. For this subject the student is referred to such works as James Orr's *Problem of the Old Testament; Old Testament Introduction* by John H. Raven (Revell & Co.); and G. T. Manley's *New Bible Handbook* (especially chapter IV).

Liberal critics have found even more distinct evidence of composite authórship in the books of Samuel than in the Pentateuch.

a. The 'two sources' theory

Much has been made of two supposed sources, one hostile to the monarchy and the other favourable. The former is found in 1 Sa. viii. 1–22, x. 17–24, xii. 1–25; the latter in 1 Sa. ix. 1 —x. 16 and xi. 1–11, 15.

Professor A. R. S. Kennedy (Cent. Bible) assigns the part of the book supposed to be hostile to the monarchy, as well as some other parts of Samuel, to D. This writer of the Deuteronomic school is said to have lived during the exile when the deficiencies of the monarchy were vividly realized. Imbued with the theocratic idea of his time, he drew an idealistic picture of the introduction of the monarchy, representing it as a breach of the divinely ordained theocracy.

In expressing this view Kennedy followed

Wellhausen, Kuenen, Stade, H. P. Smith (I.C.C.), and Nowack, who all ascribed these sections to D.

They are opposed by Budde and Cornill who regard these passages as from the same hand as E in the Hexateuch, with some revision from D later. Driver, too, regards most of Samuel as pre-Deuteronomic and so he, as well as Budde and Cornill, differ from the other eminent authorities mentioned as to the period and authorship of the passages referred to. This is worth noting. The claim is constantly made that critical experts can apportion even one half of a verse to one source and the other half to another; and yet the most eminent authorities are divided in opinion as to whether certain important sources are 'Deuteronomic' or 'pre-Deuteronomic'. They cannot decide whether large sections of Samuel were written as late as 450 B.C. (in the days of Ezra) or as early as 750 B.C.

b. Duplicate accounts

Some critics have laid great stress on what are known as 'duplicate accounts' of certain events in Samuel. These are often regarded as contradictory and as showing a different origin and different tradition. For a study of a few examples see section **IV** below.

c. The time and manner of David's first presentation to Saul

These, as well as the references to Saul's bitter jealousy towards David, have caused great difficulty. (Cf. 1 Sa. xvi. 14–23 and 1 Sa. xvii and xviii.) Prof. A. R. S. Kennedy (Cent. Bible) believes that extensive additions to the oldest text were made here by a post-Deuteronomic redactor later than 200 B.C. These additions, it is argued, were not present in the Hebrew text used by the translators of the LXX about 200 B.C. which explains why the LXX does not include certain sections found in the existing Hebrew text. The view expressed by A. R. S. Kennedy as to the text of chapters xvii and xviii is that of Robertson Smith, Stade, Cornill, H. P. Smith, Löhr, Nowack, and Kirkpatrick. On the other hand, the opposite view is taken by many great critics, like Wellhausen, Budde, Cheyne and Driver, that the LXX, instead of making additions to the original text, actually cut out 1 Sa. xvii. 12–31, 41, 50, 55–58 and xviii. 1–5 in an effort to harmonize the narrative.

The questions raised by 1 Sa. xvii and xviii are dealt with in a special note when dealing with these chapters (see p. 271).

d. The argument from style

As in other parts of the Old Testament differences of style are alleged to exist in different parts of Samuel and this is put forward as a proof of divergent origins. This argument from style may well be questioned. By common consent Samuel is characterized by remarkably pure Hebrew, which suggests the golden age of Hebrew literature. If it were a patchwork from many authors spread over many centuries there could not be this purity of diction.

Many commentators have commented on the unity of plan discernible in these two books of Samuel. This would not square with the numerous authors or compilers postulated by some authorities. It would not permit even two authors. Driver in his *Literature of the Old Testament* (p. 163) admits that the section 1 Sa. i—xiv (on the establishment of the monarchy) runs into and presupposes the section 1 Sa. xv—xxxi (on Saul and David). Then he adds: 'Some of the narratives contained in 1–2 Samuel point forwards, or backwards, to one another, and are in other ways so connected together as to show that they are the work of one and the same writer: this is not, however, the case in all . . .' This statement in spite of the qualification is significant.

Further, there are certain expressions which run right through Samuel, e.g. 'as thy soul liveth', 'sons of Belial', 'Jehovah of hosts', 'so may God do and more also', 'from Dan even to Beersheba', 'blessed be thou of Jehovah', etc. Such expressions occurring in different sections of the book point to common authorship.

It is not sufficient refutation to say with Driver that 'they appear to have formed part of the phraseology current at the time'. If the contention of the liberal critics is correct then the different sections of Samuel come from different times.

II. CRITICAL ATTEMPTS AT A SOLUTION

Because of the supposed differences in point of view and the supposed contradictions, as well as the alleged differences in style and the numerous 'doublets' which are believed to present themselves, critics have divided up Samuel into different sources and called in the help of several compilers and redactors by way of explaining the apparent discrepancies.

Budde and Cornill may be taken as a starting point. They find in Samuel two main strata— an older and a later. The earlier is assigned by Budde to J of the Pentateuch; and they both assign the later to E. Budde finds, however, that there are parts of the work of E where the Elohistic features are not so strongly marked and these parts he designates by E². These sections are supposed to have been influenced by the prophetic teaching of the eighth century, especially Hosea.

The older narrative (J) is assigned to the ninth century; E to the eighth century; and E² to the end of the eighth or beginning of the seventh century.

Budde calls in a redactor RᴶᴱE, who combines the two narratives. This is done before the 'Deuteronomic period' begins in 621. Then, a redactor D is postulated by Budde and Cornill for a later period.

Let it be noted that similar as Budde and Cornill are in their main positions they are of different opinions as to J and E².

Professor H. P. Smith (I.C.C.), unlike Budde and Cornill, finds the two chief sources Sl and Sm. The first of these was written soon after the death of Solomon and gave a short life of Saul, an account of David at the court of Saul and as a fugitive, and a history of David's reign. Sm, on the other hand, was theocratic and written from a different point of view, and gave narratives of the early life and actions of Samuel, and the early adventures of David and part of his reign. This work (Sm) was post-exilic. As to the date and viewpoint of Sm it is clear that Smith's view differs much from Budde and Cornill in so far as their opinions of E are concerned, for they place E in the eighth century B.C. In the main, Driver (in his Introduction) is with Budde and Cornill, and so is Stenning in H.D.B.

Yet H. P. Smith is nearer the position of Budde and Cornill than Wellhausen, Kuenen, Stade and Löhr, who ascribe the sections attributed to E and E² by Budde to a much later writer of the Deuteronomic period (i.e. some time between 621 and the end of the exile).

Prof. James Orr gives an example of the differences between Dr. Driver and H. P. Smith (Orr: *Problem of the Old Testament*). We quote it as a concrete illustration of the numerous differences which exist on matters of cardinal importance: 'Dr. Driver, who is not extreme here, divides 1 Sa. i—vii. 1 from what follows expressly on the ground that hitherto Samuel has appeared only as a "prophet"; here (1 Sa. vii. 2ff.) he is represented as a "judge". Yet all these chapters (i to vii), as shown above, Professor H. P. Smith gives to his "theocratic" narrator (Sm)—the same who represents Samuel as a "judge" ' (p. 387).

Another case showing how differently different critics can view a question is found in connection with the summaries found in 1 Sa. xiv. 47–51 and 2 Sa. viii. 1–18. Stenning in H.D.B. says: 'The present form of the Books of Samuel is largely due to an author of the Deuteronomic school whose hand may be clearly traced in the concluding summaries'.

Of the same summaries Dr. Driver writes (*Literature of the Old Testament*): 'Its contents (chapter xv) adapt it for the position which it now holds in the book, after the formal close of the history of Saul's reign, 1 Sa. xiv. 47–51, and before the introduction of David' (p. 169).

Again he writes (p. 172): 'Chapter viii (i.e. 2 Sa. viii) marks a break in the book, and closes the chief of David's public doings. It should be compared with the conclusion of the history of Saul's reign, 1 Sa. xiv. 46–51.' According to this the summaries are part of the original plan of the book. There is no suggestion that they were inserted long afterwards by a Deuteronomic writer as Stenning and others allege.

The literature on the sources of Samuel is very extensive and the whole question is intensely complicated. It is impossible here to give many extracts. We have given enough to show how unwise it is, when dealing with sources, to accept the conclusions of critical authorities without question. It would be well to lay to heart the wise words of Bleek (*Einl.*, p. 336): 'We may assume with tolerable certainty that the author of these books, beside the poetical passages which he has introduced, in some parts found and used written memorials of the times and events of which he treats; but it is impossible to determine throughout with any certainty or with particular probability (as several modern scholars have attempted to do) how many earlier writings the author uses, or precisely what he has taken from one or the other.'

III. PASSAGES HOSTILE AND FAVOURABLE TO THE MONARCHY

We have seen how the dissection of the narrative has been carried out on the supposition that these so-called discrepancies and doublets are real difficulties and cannot be harmonized. Some are dealt with in the notes. Let us examine briefly a few more to see whether they can be explained.

The most crucial is the supposed conflict in 1 Sa. viii—xii where viii. 1–22, x. 17–27, and xii. 1–25 are supposed to be from a source highly antagonistic to the monarchy and to be from D like chapter vii; or if not from D then some exilic or post-exilic source. The view favourable to monarchy is in ix. 1—x. 16, with xi. 1–11, 15, which are supposed to be from the oldest source of Samuel variously classed as from J, or Sl, or M, etc.

a. Passages hostile to monarchy

'Then all the elders of Israel gathered themselves together, and came to Samuel unto Ramah, and said unto him, Behold, thou art old, and thy sons walk not in thy ways: now make us a king to judge us like all the nations. But the thing displeased Samuel, when they said, Give us a king to judge us. And Samuel prayed unto the Lord' (1 Sa. viii. 4–6).

Is it surprising that Samuel was 'displeased'? After a lifetime of constant service in which the glory of God and their welfare had been his aim, he is now remorselessly cast off by the nation for which he had spent his strength. What the elders said about Samuel's sons was true, but this only increased his grief. He would have been more than human if he had not felt keenly his virtual dismissal.

Worse than the personal factor was their attitude to God who had delivered them so frequently under the theocracy. Clearly a generation had grown up which had forgotten the Lord's wonderful dealings with them. If only Israel would follow God and obey Him they would prosper and be safe. It was their departure from God which caused the failure of the theocracy as it would later cause the failure of the monarchy. Neither in the nations around nor in their despotic kings was there much to admire, yet Israel wanted to imitate them. All they wanted was a soldier to lead them, and deliver them from their foes 'like all the nations'. Matters had come to a sorry pass when Israel desired to imitate the surrounding nations and their methods, instead of turning in humility to God. Even under a king they could still have had a theocracy. It was not a question of monarchy versus theocracy. It was their low spiritual condition which vexed Samuel above all.

The prophet took the matter to God in prayer, and is told that the great sin of the people is against God. They had forsaken Him as their fathers had so often done (1 Sa. viii. 7–9). God instructed Samuel to 'hearken unto the voice of the people'. They had shown themselves unworthy of their high privileges; now they would receive what they wanted and their choice would bring its own chastisement. (Cf. Ps. cvi. 15 for a parallel.)

In 1 Sa. viii. 11–22, Samuel tells them of 'the manner of the king'. He would indeed have splendour, with bodyguard and chariots and horsemen, like the kings around them; but he would subject them to cruel exactions and forced labour. It would be a time of despotism and oppression.

It has been alleged that such words could not have been written until after the exile when the people had had plenty of experience of evil monarchs. There was no need to wait so long. The despotism, cruelty and vindictiveness of rulers in ancient times were only too well known. Their fathers had experienced it under Pharaoh in Egypt, and all the petty states around them were groaning under such rulers. The truth is that, without the fear of God, no rulers are ever good. The people of Israel, instead of seeking God, decided to have a king 'like all the nations'. To suggest that Samuel could not have spoken the words in 1 Sa. viii. 11–22 and that only someone after the exile could have written them is ludicrous. The ancient world from the remotest times was simply full of the evils which are spoken against in these verses. God's law alone showed how to avoid these evils, and Israel turned away from that law.

b. Passages in favour of monarchy

i. 1 Sa. ix. 1–1 Sa. x. 16. It is alleged that this passage is from the older document. Here Samuel is merely a simple *ro'eh* of a country village (ix. 6ff.) and not the 'all-powerful vicegerent' of Yahweh' of chapters vii, viii, and xii. This, it is said, is quite different from the idealized representation of Samuel in the 'Deuteronomic' and 'post-exilic' sections of the book. The point is sufficiently dealt with in the notes on 1 Sa. ix (q.v.).

More important is 1 Sa. ix. 16 where God announces to Samuel the arrival of Saul and says 'thou shalt anoint him to be prince over my people Israel, and he shall save my people out of the hand of the Philistines: for I have looked upon my people, because their cry is come unto me' (RV). This is supposed to be contrary to the spirit of chapter viii which we have already considered. In 1 Sa. viii there is alleged opposition to the monarchy; in 1 Sa. ix. 16 it is God's gracious gift. It is true that Samuel was deeply mortified when they asked for a king, but he had prayed to God about it (1 Sa. viii. 6). God told him to grant their request. 1 Sa. ix. 16 is quite in keeping with that. God would overrule the choice of the people to work out His own purposes, and would make the warrior, Saul, His instrument for overcoming the Philistines. It is common for God, in His economy, to overrule evil for good. We see the interplay of human and divine motives. God makes the purposes of man to work out for the accomplishment of His divine will. He would thus subdue the Philistines through Saul.

It is true that the reference to Philistine aggression in 1 Sa. ix. 16 seems to be in opposition to 1 Sa. vii. 13 which, after telling of the great victory under Samuel at Mizpeh, says 'So the Philistines were subdued, and they came no more into the coast (RV, 'within the border') of Israel: and the hand of the Lord was against the Philistines all the days of Samuel'.

This verse has often been misquoted. The statement that the Philistines 'came no more within the border of Israel' must be relative only. Far from this verse teaching that the Philistines were permanently subdued, the second part of it states emphatically that there were conflicts with them 'all the days of Samuel'. A regimental historian of the first World War might well record that after a crushing defeat the Germans made no more incursions on the trenches in that sector. That would not mean that they were subdued for all time. After the defeat at Mizpeh, the Philistines 'came no more' for a certain time.

ii. Saul's election at Mizpeh (1 Sa. x. 17–27). This is supposed to be part of the later (theocratic) version as to the election of Saul—written after 621 B.C., or in exilic or post-exilic times. The previous verses of the chapter (1–16) are taken as being from the older account favourable to the monarchy. In them Samuel could not be more gracious to Saul. This is easily accounted for because God had instructed him how to deal with Saul and to anoint him as king. That was done privately. Now in 1 Sa. x. 17–27 we are given the account of the national gathering where he is publicly selected. Samuel prefaces the proceedings with a terrible exposure of the low spiritual condition which had led them to ask for a king, and their forgetfulness of God's past deliverances. The Lord had always delivered them without a king when they followed Him. Now, however, God had granted their request, and He elected the king by lot in their presence. 'Then Samuel told the people the manner of the kingdom, and wrote it in a book, and laid it up before the Lord' (1 Sa. x. 25).

Although Yahweh was not King as He had been before, His covenant and His law were still binding and must be observed. Both king and people would find that there was no way of securing the prosperity and peace of the nation but by walking in God's ways. It is very hard to see how this conflicts with the sections of the book of Samuel already considered.

iii. Saul confirmed in the kingdom at Gilgal (1 Sa. xi. 1–12, 15). This is said to be from the older source and to be pro-monarchical, following up 1 Sa. x. 16.

After his selection at Mizpeh Saul had retired to the farm and went on with his usual pursuits. For some reason it was not considered opportune to take up his functions as king at once, perhaps because of the opposition of 'the sons of Belial' (1 Sa. x. 27).

He is brought into the forefront as leader when Nahash the Ammonite attacked Jabesh-gilead. The brutal terms of Nahash (xi. 2) were typical, and show how far astray Israel had gone in asking for a king 'like all the nations'. The attitude of the people of Jabesh, too, reveals their spiritual decline (xi. 1). At Gibeah, also, the degeneracy is apparent; a mass of people crying like babies but with no thought of seeking God (xi. 4). Such incidents, instead of confirming the theories of the liberal critics, prove that Samuel was right in censuring the people for their departure from God in the sections of the book which (unlike this section) are supposed to be theocentric. This *monarchic* section clearly brings out the spiritual destitution of the people, just as the so-called *theocentric* parts do.

Saul, under the influence of God's Spirit, rallies the people and gains an overwhelming victory over Nahash and his Ammonites. The enthusiasm for him became immense throughout the land. Samuel calls the people to Gilgal that the kingdom may be renewed to Saul (verses 12–14). The majority of modern critics have maintained that this report of the gathering at Gilgal (15) is the older version of Saul's appointment, and that the gathering at Mizpeh (1 Sa. x. 17–27) is the later (or Deuteronomic, or exilic) version. They allege that 1 Sa. xi. 12–14 was inserted by a late redactor in an attempt to harmonize the two accounts. It is, however, not necessary to regard the two accounts as incompatible. The great gathering at Gilgal was fully national. At Mizpeh there had been strong opposition; now Saul is confirmed as king by the unanimous voice of the nation. The difference between the election at Mizpeh and the confirmation at Gilgal was somewhat similar to the difference between the proclamation of a king and his coronation.

iv. Samuel's address at Gilgal (1 Sa. xii. 1–25). According to many critics this address comes from the same *theocentric* source as chapters vii and viii and should have followed 1 Sa. x. 20–24. If the views we have advanced are correct it is in its right place at Gilgal. Samuel had felt keenly the reflection on himself of their asking a king, but had waived that objection and gone on. God had indicated His will, and Samuel had dealt with the people for God as before. In all the circumstances the conduct of the prophet has been most magnanimous and worthy of the servant of the Lord.

It is not strictly a 'farewell address'. He does not withdraw into private life but promises to continue his intercession for them and his prophetic labours. He continued to intervene vigorously as prophet in the affairs of Israel until his death a few years before that of Saul.

As Saul takes over the political responsibilities of the judgeship, Samuel takes the opportunity of reviewing his own record as administrator. It is one of the noblest addresses ever delivered. Far from being an idealistic representation worked up centuries afterwards by the theocentric school of the exilic or post-exilic period, it produces the impression of historical truth and contains nothing which is not homogeneous with what goes before.

If it cannot be proved that the narratives of 1 Sa. viii—xii are from independent and contradictory sources, the one early and the other late, then it is impossible to show that such contradictory sources have contributed to any other part of the book; for such independent and contradictory sources could more easily be proved in chapters viii—xii than anywhere else. This is why we have given so much space to the matter.

IV. OTHER INCOMPATIBILITIES AND DUPLICATES

We shall discuss here a few sample cases. Others have been dealt with in the text.

a. Teraphim

These were images of private or household gods (*penates*), perhaps in human form. They were a remnant of the idolatry brought from the old Aramaean home. (Cf. Gn. xxxi. 19, 34.) They were prohibited by the laws against idolatry. Inasmuch as Michal used teraphim and is not condemned for it, 1 Sa. xix. 13 is assigned to an ancient document, while 1 Sa. xv. 23, where Samuel classifies teraphim with witchcraft and idolatry, is said to require a later date when prophetic teaching had borne effect.

We cannot assume, however, that teraphim were accepted by all as permissible in Michal's day. David probably knew nothing about the presence of teraphim in his house. (Cf. Jacob and Rachel, Gn. xxxi. 34.)

After so many centuries of Christian teaching, we can still find in the British Isles relics of paganism in our superstitions; e.g. the use of mascots, ceremonies at holy wells, the annual kindling of certain fires (going back to Druidism, etc.). Such customs are most persistent and we need not be surprised that Michal who, apparently, was not a very spiritually-minded woman, should have teraphim. The writer does not interrupt the thrilling story of David's escape to dwell upon the religious aspect of teraphim. Neither do we always denounce the superstitious practices which are common among us even when we mention them. It is taken for granted that deeply religious Christians condemn them, while others practise them.

Samuel's reference to teraphim in 1 Sa. xv. 23 as something evil came in naturally in the course of his rebuke to Saul. In the same way, today, an occasional sermon may condemn some of our common superstitious practices. There is no adequate ground for saying that 1 Sa. xv. 23 must belong to a later period than 1 Sa. xix. 13ff.

b. The origin of the proverb, Is Saul also among the prophets? (1 Sa. x. 11 and xix. 24)

The first of these incidents took place on the day Samuel anointed Saul as future king. On meeting a band of prophets the Spirit of God came on Saul and he prophesied. The second occasion was when he went in pursuit of David to Naioth where Samuel dwelt. Again Saul falls under the power of the spirit of prophecy and he prophesied and stripped off his clothes and lay down naked. 'Wherefore they say, Is Saul also among the prophets?' (1 Sa. xix. 24). The date of the insertion of this second incident has been put very late by some (post-redactional) and is alleged to be the outcome of tradition and legend.

On 1 Sa. xix. 18–24 Wellhausen wrote (*History of Israel*): 'We can scarcely avoid the suspicion that what we have before us here is a pious caricature; the point can be nothing but Samuel's and David's enjoyment of the disgrace of the naked king'. This is unfair comment. There are few things in the Bible more wonderful than the genuine kindliness shown by both Samuel and David to Saul. The caricature is in Wellhausen's representation of the case.

For a man of Saul's excitable temperament it would be easy to be impressed by the ecstatic utterances of the prophets, or by their chanting. Unless we are to accept such an unworthy suggestion as Wellhausen's there is no reason to believe that the narrative in 1 Sa. xix. 18–24 is the outcome of a distorted tradition, a misrepresentation of the first account.

On the first occasion there was surprise at the sudden change in Saul. He had never been pictured in the capacity of a prophet. He did not seem to have the qualities for such a position. Hence they asked, 'Is Saul also among the prophets?' (1 Sa. x. 11).

It is perfectly in keeping with the history of Saul that his excitement on the second occasion should be so much greater than on the first. His mental condition had by this time deteriorated sadly. Moreover, his coming into contact with Samuel would revive many memories and bring home to him his decline from the right way. It was in accordance with his nature, and the circumstances, that he should be cast down with a tempest of emotions. Even the presence of David would excite his emotions and exhaust him. We need not assume that he lay down stark naked; he probably had on a linen undergarment.

It was natural to remember the old question,

'Is Saul also among the prophets?' and to repeat it. In 1 Sa. x. 11 it is not suggested that it became a proverb. In 1 Sa. xix. 24 it is definitely stated that it had. This is not always remembered but ought to be. It was the second experience which made the question proverbial.

c. David's two encounters with Saul (1 Sa. xxiv and 1 Sa. xxvi)

Cornill says there is no more significant example of a doublet in the Old Testament than this. In essentials it is the same story. Most modern critics have taken this view. One version is assumed to be the outcome of tradition; the other to be from an older document and authentic. Strangely enough, authorities have had great difficulty in deciding which story is the outcome of tradition and which the original. With some hesitation, the majority decide that chapter xxvi is the original.

For supposed resemblances see Dr. Driver (*Literature of the Old Testament*, p. 171), and Löhr. Most of these resemblances are perfectly natural, e.g. the treachery of the Ziphites and David's position in the hill of Hachilah. David had found the region an ideal one for hiding from Saul. Conder and others have proved this from their descriptions of the area. The Ziphites, being hostile, would naturally report the presence of David and his men on both occasions. On the second occasion they would report for fear of vengeance. That Saul had 3,000 men on both occasions is explained by the fact that that was the number of his bodyguard.

There is nothing unnatural in the fact that David should refuse to lay hands on 'the Lord's anointed' on both occasions. This was a settled principle with him. Saul's recognition of David's voice on both occasions was also perfectly natural. Conder has shown how David could so easily and safely speak to Saul across one of those tremendous gullies. The other resemblances can be explained similarly.

On the other hand there are many differences which make it impossible that the two narratives refer to the same occasion. Thus, on the first occasion, David spared Saul's life in a cave in the daytime; on the second, in an entrenched camp at night. The first time David fled in haste; the second he awaits Saul's attack. On the second occasion David fled to the Philistines; on the first he did not. In the second case it is Saul who encamps on the hill of Hachilah, and David is safe to the south while his scouts watch Saul; on the first occasion David was nearly caught.

The fact that Saul should thus come out again to seek for David a second time in spite of the latter's magnanimity is perfectly in keeping with Saul's semi-madness and jealousy. It is alleged that it is remarkable that neither Saul nor David mentions the first occasion when Saul was spared a second time. The deep emotion of Saul and the whole tenor of his words suggest that he did remember David's goodness.

For such reasons, we may well take the

narratives in chapters xxiv and xxvi as describing separate occasions.

In the same way, an examination of the other so-called duplicates would lead us to a similar conclusion. We believe that Klostermann was right when he maintained that the discrepancies between the various duplicate accounts in Samuel were apparent and not real, and could be harmonized. The repetitions of occurrences are psychologically probable, and each story has its own characteristics.

A. M. RENWICK.

I AND II KINGS

INTRODUCTION

I. POSITION IN CANON

The Hebrew and all Versions agree in placing Kings after Samuel, to which it is an obvious sequel. Indeed, if Kings was a gradual growth (see below under Author), it is possible that 1 Ki. i and ii were originally the end of Samuel. In Hebrew it is one book (though the printed Hebrew Bibles have followed the Christian tradition), the division into two going back to the LXX.

II. TITLE AND DATE

The title *Kings* is a literal translation of the Hebrew, and is also found in the Vulgate. For the LXX name and the reason for the subtitle in AV see *Introduction* to Samuel.

The *terminus a quo* for the date is given by 2 Ki. xxv. 27, i.e. *c.* 560 B.C.; an almost equally certain *terminus ad quem* is given by the non-mention of the capture of Babylon in 538 B.C. and the permission for the exiles to return given by Cyrus in the following year. But so long as one author is not assumed, the probability is that much of the book is considerably earlier, and indeed there is much internal evidence for this.

III. THE AUTHOR

A not very early Jewish tradition ascribes Kings to Jeremiah (Josephus, in much more general terms, ascribes the historical books to the prophets); but while he may well have been concerned with its later portions and revision, he cannot well be the sole author.

Kings claims to be based in part on certain written authorities: 'the book of the acts of Solomon' (1 Ki. xi. 41), 'the book of the chronicles of the kings of Israel' (1 Ki. xiv. 19, etc.), 'the book of the chronicles of the kings of Judah' (1 Ki. xiv. 29, etc.), and indeed many portions bear an obvious annalistic stamp. But Chronicles used a number of prophetic sources; see, e.g., 2 Ch. ix. 29, xii. 15, xiii. 22, xxvi. 22, xxxiii. 19. Though these are not mentioned in Kings, they must have been known to its authors.

When we consider that Kings is reckoned in the Hebrew canon as belonging to the 'former prophets', the simplest explanation of these facts would seem to be that records were kept by many of the prophets, and that at a suitable time these were amalgamated with extracts from the royal records. The reign of Hezekiah, which was in any case a time of literary activity (Pr. xxv. 1), suggests itself as the most suitable time, for it can have been only then that escaping fugitives from Samaria will have brought the royal records with them. There are no grounds for assuming that the work must have been done by Isaiah, though the possibility cannot be excluded. The work will have been brought up to date and revised in the time of Josiah, and this may well have been done by Jeremiah. Finally, it was once more brought up to date and slightly revised by someone unknown in the Babylonian exile. Certain peculiarities of the LXX strongly suggest some such revision in the time of Josiah as suggested here.

IV. CHRONOLOGY

The only system of dating normally used in Israel was by the regnal years of the kings. Kings by a system of cross-reference between the kings of Judah and Israel would seem to offer the possibility of working out an outline chronology. But already by the second century A.D.

ISRAEL		JUDAH	
Jeroboam I	930–910	Rehoboam	930–914
Nadab	910–909	Abijam	913–911
Baasha	909–886	Asa	910–870
Elah	886–885		
Zimri	885		
Omri	885–874		
Ahab	874–853	Jehoshaphat	873–849
Ahaziah	853–852		
Jehoram	852–841	Jehoram	849–842
		Ahaziah	841
Jehu	841–814	Athaliah	841–836
		Joash	836–797
Jehoahaz	814–798		
Jehoash	798–782	Amaziah	797–768
Jeroboam II	793–753	Azariah	791–740
Zechariah	753–752	(Uzziah)	
Shallum	752		
Menahem	751–742	Jotham	751–736
Pekahiah	741–740		
Pekah	751–732	Ahaz	736–716
Hoshea	731–723	Hezekiah	729–687
		Manasseh	696–642
		Amon	641–640
		Josiah	639–609
		Jehoahaz	609
		Jehoiakim	608–598
		Jehoiachin	598
		Zedekiah	597–586

the rabbis were fully aware that there are a number of apparent discrepancies in the figures as they stand. For this there are a number of good reasons, the chief being the reckoning of part of a year as a complete year, the complications introduced by co-regencies, when a son reigned for a time with his father, which seem to have been fairly common, and in a few cases errors in copying numbers. A further complication is provided by the occasional mention of the Israelite kingdoms in Assyrian inscriptions, under conditions that permit the dating of the incident to within a year. The best discussion of the problem is probably that in Hastings, *Dictionary of the Bible*, Vol. I, p. 399. We give some approximate figures based mainly on van der Meer, *The Ancient Chronology of Western Asia and Egypt*. The figures given in the I.C.C. vary only a few years except for Azariah and the last kings of Israel. The uncertainties associated with the last troubled years of Israel make it almost certain that variant dates will be found elsewhere in this commentary. It cannot be too strongly insisted that no more than approximate accuracy is being claimed for most of these dates. Where reigns overlap co-regency is the reason, except perhaps in the case of Pekah, who may have been the power behind the throne

under Menahem and Pekahiah. A somewhat different calculation is offered by E. R. Thiele, *The Mysterious Numbers of the Hebrew Kings*.

V. PURPOSE

As already stated, in the Hebrew canon Kings is a prophetic book, and apart from this there are grounds for believing that its unnamed authors were prophets. God did not merely speak through His servants the prophets, but also through history, and it was part of the prophetic task to interpret the lessons of history. This is the explanation why certain of the kings who were most important for their contemporaries, e.g. Omri (1 Ki. xvi. 23–28), Azariah or Uzziah (2 Ki. xv. 1–7), Jeroboam II (2 Ki. xiv. 23–29), are passed over in virtual silence. It is spiritual, not political lessons, that we are to learn. That is why the two periods of crisis, the reigns of Ahab for the north and of Hezekiah for the south, are given at special length. We should not be surprised, then, that the archaeologist, with his different standards of judgment, often puts the kings and their actions in a rather different light. But their discoveries, while often confirming the accuracy of Kings, do not deepen our spiritual understanding of the period.

OUTLINE OF CONTENTS

THE UNDIVIDED KINGDOM. 1 Ki. i. 1—xi. 43

I. THE ACCESSION OF SOLOMON. i. 1—ii. 46

II. THE BEGINNING OF SOLOMON'S REIGN. iii. 1–28

III. EXTRACTS FROM THE ROYAL ANNALS. iv. 1–34

IV. SOLOMON AS BUILDER. v. 1—vii. 51

V. THE DEDICATION OF THE TEMPLE. viii. 1—ix. 9

VI. MISCELLANEOUS NOTICES. ix. 10—x. 29

VII. SOLOMON'S TROUBLES. xi. 1–43

THE DIVIDED KINGDOM. 1 Ki. xii. 1—2 Ki. xvii. 41

VIII. THE SCHISM. xii. 1–24

IX. JEROBOAM OF ISRAEL. xii. 25—xiv. 20

X. REHOBOAM, ABIJAM AND ASA OF JUDAH. xiv. 21—xv. 24

XI. NADAB TO OMRI OF ISRAEL. xv. 25—xvi. 28

XII. AHAB AND ELIJAH. xvi. 29—xxii. 40

XIII. JEHOSHAPHAT OF JUDAH. xxii. 41–50

XIV. AHAZIAH OF ISRAEL. xxii. 51—2 Ki. i. 18

XV. ELIJAH SUCCEEDED BY ELISHA. ii. 1–25

XVI. JEHORAM OF ISRAEL. iii. 1–27

XVII. ELISHA THE PROPHET. iv. 1—viii. 15

XVIII. JEHORAM AND AHAZIAH OF JUDAH. viii. 16–29

XIX. JEHU OF ISRAEL. ix. 1—x. 36

XX. ATHALIAH OF JUDAH. xi. 1–20

XXI. JEHOASH OF JUDAH. xi. 21—xii. 21

XXII. JEHOAHAZ AND JEHOASH OF ISRAEL. xiii. 1–25

XXIII. AMAZIAH OF JUDAH. xiv. 1–22

XXIV. JEROBOAM II OF ISRAEL. xiv. 23–29

XXV. AZARIAH (UZZIAH) OF JUDAH. xv. 1–7

XXVI. CHAOS IN ISRAEL. xv. 8–31

XXVII. JOTHAM AND AHAZ OF JUDAH. xv. 32—xvi. 20

XXVIII. THE END OF THE NORTHERN KINGDOM. xvii. 1–41

THE KINGDOM OF JUDAH ALONE. 2 Ki. xviii. 1—xxv. 30

XXIX. HEZEKIAH. xviii. 1—xx. 21

XXX. MANASSEH. xxi. 1–18

XXXI. AMON. xxi. 19–26

XXXII. JOSIAH. xxii. 1—xxiii. 30a

XXXIII. THE LAST DAYS OF JERUSALEM. xxiii. 30b—xxv. 7

XXXIV. DESTRUCTION AND EXILE. xxv. 8–30

COMMENTARY

THE UNDIVIDED KINGDOM. 1 Ki. i. 1—xi. 43

I. THE ACCESSION OF SOLOMON.
1 Ki. i. 1—ii. 46

There is no reasonable doubt that these chapters are the immediate continuation of 2 Sa. xx. 22. For their relationship to the story in 1 Chronicles see comments on 1 Ch. xxii. 2–5, xxviii, xxix. 24.

a. David's old age (i. 1–4)

David was only seventy when he died (2 Sa. v. 4). His premature collapse into senility was probably due to the shock of Absalom's rebellion and death. *Let her stand before . . .* (2); i.e. attend on; cf. x. 5 text and mg. *Abishag a Shunammite* (3); for Shunem cf. 2 Ki. iv. 8. It was a village in the plain of Esdraelon about five miles north of Jezreel.

b. Adonijah's attempt on the throne (i. 5–10)

There was no precedent in Israel to fix the succession to the throne. The people had elected Saul and David, and were later to express their wishes again (1 Ki. xii. 1; 2 Ki. xi. 17, xxiii. 30). On the other hand there was always the possible conflict between the Hebrew tradition of primogeniture and the royal father's choice. David's choice of Solomon to succeed him (13) could not have been unknown, but the fact that it had never been made public encouraged Adonijah to think that it had been a passing whim. He was evidently a simple-minded man (see note on ii.

13–25) and it is probable that he was urged on by Joab and Abiathar (7). There is here a clear cleavage between the older and younger of David's chief courtiers, and it is likely that the older did not approve of the policy they expected Solomon to follow. *And he also was a very goodly man; and his mother bare him after Absalom* (6); he was a very handsome man like Absalom, and was now David's eldest surviving son. Chileab (2 Sa. iii. 3) had presumably met an unmentioned death. *Shimei, and Rei* (8); otherwise unknown. LXX and Josephus had other readings. *The mighty men* (8); see 2 Sa. xxiii. 8–39. *And Adonijah slew sheep and oxen* (9). Better, as in RV mg., 'sacrificed'; cf. 2 Sa. xv. 12. *En-rogel* (9); though earlier identified by many (so H.D.B.) with the Virgin's Spring in the Kidron Valley, now almost universally taken as Bir-Eyyub, Job's Well, at the junction of the Kidron and Hinnom valleys.

c. Solomon anointed king (i. 11–40)

We are not to suppose that Adonijah's plottings were unknown to Solomon's supporters, or even to David. They were probably not taken seriously. There is no evidence that David was to be deposed. It was probably a sudden decision to face him with a *fait accompli*, which the old man was not expected to resist. *That thou mayest save thine own life, and the life of thy son Solomon*

(12); the failure to invite Solomon to the feast is invested with the most serious significance (cf. verse 19). His influential mother might be expected to share his fate. *Didst not thou . . . swear* (13); the incident is not previously recorded. *And Abishag the Shunammite ministered unto the king* (15). In the light of ii. 17 it is quite possible that she was in the plot, otherwise the mention seems irrelevant. Her rôle would have been to keep away anyone bearing the news, but she cannot keep out the favourite wife. *The captains of the host* (25). The LXX is almost certainly right in reading 'Joab, the captain of the host' (cf. verse 19). There is no evidence for extensive army support for Adonijah.

Call me Bath-sheba (28); according to oriental etiquette she had retired when Nathan was announced, just as Nathan left when she came in (cf. verse 32). David's vigorous and detailed instructions show that he was far from being as senile as he seemed. *Mine own mule* (33); cf. 2 Sa. xiii. 29, xviii. 9 for the use of the mule by the king and royal family. Lv. xix. 19 apparently forbids the breeding but not the use of the mule. *Gihon* (33); probably the Virgin's Spring in the Kidron Valley (see note on verse 9), nearer the city than En-rogel. *The Cherethites, and the Pelethites* (38); see note on 2 Sa. viii. 18. *The tabernacle* (39; RV 'tent'); see 2 Sa. vi. 17. *Piped with pipes* (40). Read with LXX and other versions 'danced in dances'.

d. The collapse of Adonijah's plot (i. 41–53)

The abject collapse of the plot shows clearly that no opposition had been expected. *A valiant* (RV 'worthy') *man* (42); more accurately 'a man of standing'. So far as possible the quality of the message was shown by the standing of the messenger; cf. 2 Sa. xviii. 21, where a negro (RV 'the Cushite') is chosen to announce Absalom's death. *The king bowed himself upon the bed* (47); i.e. in prayer (cf. Gn. xlvii. 31). *He hath caught hold on the horns of the altar* (51); though the right of sanctuary is not expressly mentioned in the law, it is implied by Ex. xxi. 14. *Let king Solomon swear unto me to day* (51); better, as in RV mg., 'first of all'. *He came and bowed himself* (53); RV 'did obeisance'; Adonijah's recognition of Solomon as king.

e. David's last charge to Solomon and death (ii. 1–11)

The days of David drew nigh that he should die (1). This does not suggest a very short period; it may well allow some years and is ample for 1 Ch. xxii. 6–xxix. 25. David's charge (2–4) is particularly reminiscent of God's charge to Joshua (Jos. i. 1–9) and of Deuteronomy generally, the book that the king had specially to study (Dt. xvii. 18f.).

David has been criticized for his instructions about Joab (5, 6), it being maintained that he should have acted himself. But the command that Solomon should find a pretext (*Do therefore according to thy wisdom . . .*) suggests that in the

murder of Abner (2 Sa. iii. 27) and Amasa (2 Sa. xx. 8–10) Joab had kept himself within the law. The former was avenging his brother's blood (2 Sa. ii. 23); in the latter he may have accused Amasa of treason. *Amasa the son of Jether* (5); and so 1 Ch. ii. 17; in 2 Sa. xvii. 25 'the son of Ithra', probably incorrectly, an easy scribal error. The fulfilment of the charge about the sons of Barzillai (7) is suggested by a comparison of 2 Sa. xix. 37 with Je. xli. 17; Chimham will have received a portion of the royal lands. No excuse can be made for the instructions about Shimei (8, 9; cf. 2 Sa. xvi. 5–14, xix. 16–23). The motive was probably David's sharing of the common opinion of the effectiveness of a curse, a thought that occurs frequently in the Psalms. *The city of David* (10); see 2 Sa. v. 9. He was probably buried within the city (cf. Ezk. xliii. 7–9, also 1 Ki. ii. 34n.).

f. The consolidation of Solomon's power (ii. 12–46)

Though this section covers at least three years (39), it stands here in accordance with the practice of Hebrew history of finishing off the subject under consideration, viz. dying David's commands, without attending to chronology.

i. Adonijah's fate (ii. 13–25). According to oriental custom the new king automatically inherited his predecessor's harem (cf. 2 Sa. xvi. 21f.). It is just possible that Adonijah hoped to strengthen his position by marrying Abishag, but it is far more likely that he was a simpleminded man genuinely in love with her. Nor need we take Bath-sheba's sympathy too literally. The very formality of the request (19) suggests that she inwardly rejoiced at the possibility of removing the last threat to her son, and that the publicity of her request and its refusal had been prearranged. *Comest thou peaceably?* (13). Peace (*shalom*) has a differing connotation in Hebrew (cf. note on 2 Ki. ix. 17); here it means no more than asking whether his visit had a pleasant purpose. *Even for him, and for . . .* (22); it is better to read with the versions, 'And on his side are Abiathar . . . and Joab . . .'; a deliberate implication of Abiathar and Joab to give an excuse for dealing with them.

ii. Abiathar's banishment (ii. 26, 27). It is likely that Abiathar's support of Adonijah was due to his dislike of the religious policy of Nathan and Zadok, which he expected Solomon to follow. His banishment was probably to prevent later religious controversy. *Anathoth* (26); cf. Jos. xxi. 18. Now Anata about three miles north-east of Jerusalem. Cf. also Je. i. 1. Jeremiah may well have been descended from him. *That he might fulfil the word of the Lord . . .* (27); see 1 Sa. ii. 36. This need not mean that his descendants were debarred from service, which in the light of 1 Ch. xxiv. 1–19 is improbable.

iii. Joab's execution (ii. 28–35). The phrase *for Joab had turned after Adonijah* (28) refers to the original plot, not to the alleged one for which Adonijah had lost his life. The reasons given in verses 31f. for Joab's execution suggest that verse 22 (see note above) was all along a pretext. *And caught hold on the horns of the altar* (28); see note on i. 51. Joab as a murderer had no claim to sanctuary (cf. Ex. xxi. 14). *He was buried in his own house in the wilderness* (34). The old general was not dishonoured. To be buried in one's own house was apparently an exceptional honour reserved for men like Samuel (1 Sa. xxv. 1) and kings (cf. Ezk. xliii. 7, RV mg.). Joab's home was just east of Bethlehem in the Wilderness of Judaea. Solomon's appointment of Zadok as High Priest (35) was a grave act, for it meant the subordination of the priestly to the royal power.

iv. **Shimei's fate (ii. 36–46).** It seems that Shimei was a most influential Benjamite (cf 2 Sa. xix. 16f.), and Solomon suspected him of trying to bring back the kingship to Benjamin (44). That is why the brook Kidron is specially mentioned (37), for he would have to cross it to reach his old home at Bahurim. *Two of the servants of Shimei* (39); here, as so often, the Hebrew *'ebhedh* should be rendered 'slave'. *Achish son of Maachah* (39); possibly, but not necessarily, Achish the son of Maoch (1 Sa. xxvii. 2). *Shimei . . . went to Gath* (40); the journey was not really necessary, but was a good excuse for a change. Shimei did not realize that Solomon did not only fear his plots in Benjamin, but was waiting for any excuse to deal with him. *King Solomon shall be blessed* (45); i.e. by the removal of Shimei's curse. *And the kingdom was established in the hand of Solomon* (46); remove the full stop and link with iii. 1.

II. THE BEGINNING OF SOLOMON'S REIGN. iii. 1–28

a. The keynote of Solomon's reign (iii. 1–3)

It should be obvious that this short section is out of chronological order, for there is no suggestion that David was in any way responsible for the marriage, and royal marriages are not arranged in a day. Just as in chapter ii the writer anticipated to round off the story, so here he does it (somewhat similarly to 2 Sa. v. 4–10) to give a keynote for the reign. By his marriage Solomon showed that his real confidence lay in political alliances. These, building ostentation (1) and religious compromise (2, 3), were the truest marks of his policy. *Made affinity with* (1); i.e. became the son-in-law of. His wife is otherwise unknown; she will have been the daughter of one of the weak Pharaohs of the XXI Dynasty, not of Shishak of the XXII (xiv. 25). Her dowry was Gezer (ix. 16). *The city of David* (1); the old Jebusite citadel on the ridge of Ophel (the true Zion), now, with the growth of the capital, differentiated from the city as a whole. She doubtless lived in David's old palace (2 Sa. v. 11). The mention here of *the house of the Lord, and the wall of Jerusalem* is not irrelevant; it stresses the scale of Solomon's building.

No blame rests on the people for their many sanctuaries (2, 3). They were an after-effect of the anarchy of the period of the judges, only partially reformed by Samuel. It is Solomon who is to be blamed. Though he had it in his power to abolish the high places, once he had built the central sanctuary, he deliberately compromised with the past. It is impossible to make verse 3b refer merely to the period before the building of the temple. *High places* (2). In Kings and Chronicles 'high place' (Heb. *bamah*) is the Canaanite name for 'an elevated platform on which cultic objects were placed' (Albright), and is used of any sanctuary on the Canaanite pattern, irrespective of the nature of the worship carried on, and especially of the sanctuaries where Jehovah was worshipped as though He were a Canaanite nature god (see Appendix I).

b. Solomon's initiatory sacrifices and vision at Gibeon (iii. 4–15)

Cf. 2 Ch. i. 1–13. Chronicles makes explicit (i. 1ff.) what is implicit in Kings; the sacrifice was an inaugural religious ceremony in lieu of the coronation already carried out (see 1 Ki. i. 39; 1 Ch. xxix. 22). It is not certain why semi-Canaanite Gibeon had become the principal sanctuary. Zadok was apparently priest of Gibeon (1 Ch. xvi. 39), and there may well have been an Aaronite priesthood there from the time of the treaty with Joshua (Jos. ix). This may explain why the tabernacle (or its remains) and the brazen altar (2 Ch. i. 3, 5) were brought there, presumably from Shiloh (there is no evidence for their having been at Nob), after the second defeat at Eben-ezer (1 Sa. iv. 4–11). This would account for the pre-eminence of the sanctuary even over Jerusalem, where the ark was (15). The impossibility of accounting for it in any other way is sufficient ground for ignoring the denials of the veracity of Chronicles in the matter.

A thousand burnt offerings (4); a thousand is used as a round figure for a very large number. *The Lord appeared . . . in a dream* (5); dreams were a recognized method of divine revelation (cf. 1 Sa. xxviii. 6; Jb. xxxiii. 14ff.). *I am but a little child* (7). The English goes beyond the Hebrew, which means no more than 'child'; in any case it is a typical example of oriental exaggeration for the sake of humility. 1 Ki. xiv. 21 shows that he already had a son. The traditions of the LXX (some MSS) and Josephus, making him twelve or fourteen years old, have no value. *To go out or come in* (7); i.e. the daily round of public life. See 2 Ch. i. 10 and cf. 1 Sa. xviii. 16. *That cannot be . . . counted for multitude* (8); cf. viii. 5. Because some perversely insist on taking such expressions literally, it does not follow that the Oriental did. Not so many years had passed since David's census (2 Sa. xxiv). *An understanding heart* (9); better, as in RV mg., 'a hearing heart'. He did not want to be swayed by haste, passion or prejudice. *A wise and an understanding heart* (12); the RV mg. is incorrect here. We would rather say 'a wise and discerning mind' (Cent. Bible). The wisdom Solomon asked for and received was secular rather than spiritual. The sequel and commentary (verses 16–28) show that it was largely intuitive shrewdness that was understood by wisdom; it had nothing philosophical in it. It is quite gratuitous to extend the comparison of verses 12f. beyond the borders of Israel. *All thy days* (13); omit with LXX (so I.C.C., Cent. Bible, Moffatt). The offering of sacrifices described in verse 15 was a court function; in verse 4 it was a national service.

c. Solomon's wisdom in judgment (iii. 16–28)

The fact that two such women had access to the king's court shows that it was really open to all, and explains why Solomon felt the prospect of his judicial functions to be such a burden. *The wisdom of God* (28); i.e. wisdom so great it could have come only from God.

III. EXTRACTS FROM THE ROYAL ANNALS. iv. 1–34

This chapter divides into two: the organization of the kingdom, verses 1–19 (the royal cabinet, verses 2–6, and the royal lieutenants, verses 7–19), and a miscellany describing Solomon's might, verses 20–34.

a. The royal cabinet (iv. 2–6)

Cf. 2 Sa. viii. 16ff., xx. 23–26; 1 Ch. xviii. 15–17. *Princes* (2; Heb. *sarim*); here, as elsewhere, the word does not mean members of the royal family, but the highest civil and military officials. *Azariah . . . Elihoreph and Ahiah, the sons of Shisha, scribes* (2, 3). In the light of verse 4 *the priest* refers to Zadok, and, following the punctuation of the AV, Azariah is a scribe. But since elsewhere there is only one scribe, i.e. 'secretary', the I.C.C. is probably correct in rendering on the basis of the Greek: 'Azariah the son of Zadok, Over-the-Year (i.e. calendar), and Ahijah the son of Shavsha (1 Ch. xviii. 16), Secretary.' *The recorder* (3); i.e. the king's remembrancer. *Abiathar* (4); the name has probably been introduced by a piece of mechanical scribal writing. However early in the reign we place this list, we cannot justify Abiathar's name, for he and Joab lost their office at the same time (ii. 35). *Officers* (5); see verses 7–19. 'Zabud . . . was priest, and the king's friend' (5, RV); render, 'Zabud . . . a priest was king's friend'; cf. 2 Sa. xv. 37; 1 Ch. xxvii. 33n.

Adoniram . . . was over the tribute (6). He could be the same as the Adoram of xii. 18 and also of 2 Sa. xx. 24, though the span of years makes it doubtful that one man held the office all these years. The hatred with which he was regarded suggests identification in the former case. For the *tribute* (RV 'levy') see v. 13n.

b. The royal lieutenants (iv. 7–19)

For general administrative purposes and particularly for the collection of revenue Solomon divided the Israelite kernel of his empire into twelve districts. In contradistinction to older works I.C.C., following Alt and Albright, considers rightly that only in special cases did the divisions depart widely from the old tribal boundaries. See plate VIIA, *Westminster Historical Atlas*, or, better, Jack, *Samaria in Ahab's Time*, p. 91. That we are dealing with officials of the highest rank is shown by two being sons-in-law of Solomon (11, 15), so Moffatt calls them 'prefects'. With six of them we have only their fathers' names. The I.C.C. explains this by suggesting that in the original in the royal archives the names were tabled one under another and the right-hand edge got damaged (Hebrew is written from right to left).

The areas were: 1. Ephraim (8). 2. South Dan (9). 3. Manasseh (10). 4. The Plain of Sharon down to Joppa (11); this had only recently become Israelite territory and so was treated as a special unit. 5. The Plain of Esdraelon (12); a district to itself because of its fertility and strategic importance. 6. Eastern Manasseh (13 and 19a); these two verses obviously refer to the same territory; Geber Ben-uri (19a) was evidently followed by his son (?) Ben-geber (13). 7. Reuben and Gad (14). 8. Naphtali (15). 9. Asher (16). 10. Issachar (17). 11. Benjamin (18). 12. Judah (19b); render with I.C.C. 'and one lieutenant, He-in-the-Land.' The land for a Judaean writer is Judah (see note on ix. 18); the official's name is not mentioned, for under the shadow of the court he will have been of less importance.

Baana the son of Ahilud (12); presumably the brother of Jehoshaphat (3). *Ramoth-gilead* (13). Modern identifications place it much further north than was the case; see *Westminster Historical Atlas*. *Ahimaaz* (15); on analogy with the others we should infer Ben-Ahimaaz, the damage to the list (see above) having taken off the 'Ben' (i.e. 'son of') as well as the personal name. *Aloth* (16); RV 'Bealoth'; unidentified; if the LXX (some MSS) 'Maaloth' is correct, it may be the coastal district north of Acre.

c. Solomon's greatness (iv. 20–34)

(N.B. iv. 21 is v. 1 in Heb.) This section is a miscellany in which no order can be discovered, possibly due to jottings from the archives. The commentary groups similar verses.

i. **The felicity of Israel (iv. 20, 25).** The rather optimistic note, when compared with xii. 4, is to be explained by their official source. *As the sand . . . in multitude* (20); see note on iii. 8. *Vine . . . fig tree* (25); a traditional picture of peace and prosperity (cf. 2 Ki. xviii. 31; Mi. iv. 4; Zc. iii. 10). *Dan to Beer-sheba* (25); the traditional limits of Israelite territory. It should be noted that Solomon seems to have made no attempt to enlarge true Israelite territory. The non-Israelite portions of his empire were merely tributary, and he exercised no direct rule over them. See note on viii. 65, and the outline sketch map on p. 285.

ii. **Solomon's empire (iv. 21, 24).** Cf. 2 Ch. ix.

26. 'The River' (21, RV); i.e. the Euphrates. *Presents* (21); i.e. tribute. *Unto the land of the Philistines* (21); cf. 2 Ch. ix. 26. *Even unto Azzah* (24; RV Gaza); it would seem that the Philistine country is excluded in both these verses. The Philistines probably put themselves under Egypt at David's death, and the recognition of this may have been part of the marriage terms (iii. 1). *This side the river* (24); RV mg. 'beyond the River' is correct. It is the technical term used later by the Assyrians (cf. Ne. ii. 7). *Tiphsah* (24); i.e. Thapsacus, commanding a most important crossing place on the Euphrates. It is not likely that Solomon's authority so far north meant more than a free and unhindered use of the great trade route as far as the river.

iii. **Solomon's expenses (iv. 22, 23, 26–28).** With verses 22f. Cam. Bible compares Nehemiah's 'one ox and six choice sheep' (Ne. v. 17f.) and estimates that Solomon provided for 4,000 to 5,000 persons. Other estimates range from 14,000 to 36,000. *Measures* (22); Heb. *kor*, i.e. about eleven bushels or ninety gallons (see H.D.B., IV, p. 912). *Those officers* (27); i.e. the lieutenants of verses 7–19. *They lacked nothing* (27); better, as in RV, 'they let nothing be lacking'. *Straw* (28); Heb. *tebhen*, i.e. the chopped or crushed straw from the threshing floors (see Neil, *Everyday Life in the Holy Land*, pp. 105f.). *Dromedaries* (28); render 'swift steeds' (RV).

iv. **Solomon's wisdom (iv. 29–34).** We can compare only the comparable, and in fact archaeology has demonstrated the wide existence of literature similar to Proverbs both in Egypt and Mesopotamia. This 'Wisdom Literature' depended on a drawing of general principles from an acute observation of life, and had almost invariably a moral purpose.

Largeness of heart (29); 'breadth of mind' (Cent. Bible). *The children of the east* (30); here perhaps the Babylonians, but more likely the Arabians. *Ethan . . . and Darda, the sons of Mahol* (31). These may very well have been Judaeans (see note on 1 Ch. ii. 6), though some would identify them as Edomites, the latter being famed for their wisdom. *Proverbs . . . songs* (32); the cream of his proverbs has been preserved in the book of Proverbs, but the vast bulk of his songs has perished, even if we count the various sections of the Song of Solomon as separate songs. Verse 33 does not imply a knowledge of natural history, but the use of nature to point a moral (e.g. the use of the ant in Proverbs). It is strange that it is just this portion of Solomon's wisdom that has been worst preserved for us.

IV. SOLOMON AS BUILDER. v. 1—vii. 51

With this section cf. 2 Ch. ii. 1—v. 1. The condensed description, the use of rare technical words and probable textual corruptions, make many parts of this section very difficult to understand. Owing to lack of space no general discussion of the difficulties is possible, and readers

are referred to the article on 'Temple' in H.D.B and I.S.B.E. and to the Cent. Bible *ad loc.*

a. Solomon and Hiram (v. 1–12)

Cf. 2 Ch. ii. 1–16. Chronicles has a longer version of the correspondence between the two kings. In certain portions in Chronicles (viz. ii. 7, 13f.) the stamp of authenticity is very evident; it is therefore likely that we have a contracted version in Kings.

With verse 1 cf. 2 Sa. x. 1f. *Hiram:* 'Hirom' in verses 10, 18, 'Huram' in Chronicles; it is a shortened form of Ahiram.. *A lover;* better, 'a friend'. *Occurrent* (4); i.e. 'occurrence', 'chance'. *Can skill to hew* (6); i.e. 'is able to hew'. *Sidonians* (6; RV 'Zidonians'); the usual Old Testament name for the Phoenicians. Tyre was at this time their chief city.

Fir (8). Opinions vary between this and RV mg. 'cypress'; but it is probably 'juniper'. Chronicles rightly inserts the request for 'fir' in Solomon's letter (2 Ch. ii. 8). *Floats* (9; RV 'rafts'); the traditional way of taking the wood of Lebanon by sea to Egypt or down the Euphrates to Babylonia. *Unto the place that thou shalt appoint me* (9). 2 Ch. ii. 16 rightly anticipates Solomon's answer by mentioning Joppa. Verse 11 indicates the price paid for the timber and labour. 2 Ch. ii. 10 probably gives the total annual amount, Kings mentioning the higher quality food reserved by Hiram for his court. The figures are very high (cf. iv. 22) but possible, though we must reject the 'twenty thousand baths of oil' (2 Ch. ii. 10), an easy scribal error in the circumstances. *Measures* (11); see iv. 22n. *They two made a league together* (12); lit. 'a covenant'. This was a solemn religious action involving Solomon in a recognition of Hiram's gods. This supports the estimate of Solomon suggested under iii. 1–3 (see Appendix II).

b. The preparation of materials (v. 13–18)

Cf. 2 Ch. ii. 2, 17f.; see also 1 Ki. ix. 15, 20ff. (2 Ch. viii. 7ff.). Forced labour was a recognized form of taxation in the ancient world (cf. 1 Sa. viii. 16), and this was particularly carried out by the levy or corvée, based presumably on a certain proportion of the population of each town or village. It had been begun already by David in the latter part of his reign (2 Sa. xx. 24). Solomon early in his reign vastly expanded the system. He enslaved all the descendants of the earlier inhabitants who had not accepted the religion of Jehovah (ix. 20f.). In addition there was a levy of Israelites—about one man in forty had to give three months a year of work (cf. v. 13f. with 2 Sa. xxiv. 9). There is no contradiction between ix. 22 and v. 13, for whereas the Canaanites became slaves, the Israelite was free once his turn of duty was finished. As 2 Ch. ii. 18 rightly interprets it, the labourers of v. 15 are the Canaanite slaves. If they had been sent to the Lebanon, they might have run away. *Hewers in the mountains* (15); cutters of limestone rock in the hills of Palestine. *Three thousand*

and three hundred (16). We cannot determine between this and the 3,600 of 2 Ch. ii. 2, 18; this is about one officer to fifty labourers, but see note on 2 Ch. viii. 10. *Costly stones* (17); i.e. by reason of their size. *The stonesquarers* (18); RV 'Gebalites'; i.e. stonemasons from Gebal or Byblos, rather more than sixty miles north of Tyre.

c. Description of the temple buildings (vi. 1–38)

i. The construction of the temple (vi. 1–10). Cf. 2 Ch. iii. 1–4. This is probably an account drawn up by a contemporary priest. *In the four hundred and eightieth year . . .* (1). This verse presents us with an at present insoluble chronological problem. Taking Solomon's fourth year as *c.* 967 B.C., we are brought back to *c.* 1447 B.C. for the exodus. Garstang (*Joshua–Judges*) presents a most attractive chronology on this basis, but all the weight of recent archaeology has been against it (see Introduction to Judges). The usual modern explanation of the 480 years as twelve generations of forty years hardly bears examination. *Zif* (1); i.e. 'flower month', the old name; changed to 'Iyyar' after the exile.

Threescore . . . twenty . . . thirty cubits (2). 2 Ch. iii. 3 specifies that they were 'cubits after the first (i.e. former) measure', i.e. of seven, not six, handbreadths, or *c.* 20½ in. compared to the *c.* 17½ in. of the later cubit (see H.D.B., 'Weights and Measures'). The length and breadth, but not the height, were exactly double those of the tabernacle. These are inside measurements (cf. verse 20). Conflicting opinions exist concerning the nature of *the porch* (3). On one's decision depends whether the height given in 2 Ch. iii. 4 (q.v.) can be accepted, at least in part. *Temple of the house* (3); 'hall of the house' (I.C.C.). *Windows* (4). These were above the external side-wings. *Narrow lights* (4); RV 'fixed lattice-work'; RSV 'recessed frames'. The meaning of the Hebrew is uncertain. *Chambers* (5); RV 'stories'; a 'side-wing' (I.C.C.). *Oracle* (5); see verse 16. Where in verse 5 AV repeats the word *chambers*, RV has 'side-chambers'. I.C.C. translates 'stories'. In verse 6 follow RV. The wall of the temple grew thinner higher up by steps; and it was on these 'rebatements' that the beams of the side-wing were laid, so that it was not structurally an integral part of the temple. *There was neither hammer . . . nor any tool of iron heard* (7). Cam. Bible and Moffatt suggest that it was built of merely 'rough dressed' stone, but it is doubtful whether this can be derived from the verse. *The door for the middle chamber* (8); an obvious scribal error; read with LXX, Targ., RSV, RV mg. 'lowest side-chambers'. There was only one doorway to the whole complex of chambers. *Winding stairs* (8); the possibility has been verified by archaeology; reject the rendering 'trapdoors' (Moffatt and others). *He . . . covered the house* (9); i.e. he roofed it. In verse 10 the RV, though translating freely, has correctly interpreted the meaning. Each story was five cubits high.

ii. Jehovah's encouraging promise (vi. 11–13). This section is not found in Chronicles. There is no indication how the promise came; probably it was to check despondency, when the task was proving greater than anticipated.

iii. The interior of the house (vi. 14–35). Cf. 2 Ch. iii. 5–14. The text is very difficult in parts. *Walls of the cieling* (15); read with change of one letter 'beams of the ceiling', and so also in verse 16 (I.C.C., Cent. Bible, Cam. Bible). *Fir* (15); see v. 8n. *And he built . . . on the sides* (RV 'hinder part') *of the house* (16); ambiguous; render with I.C.C. 'and he built off twenty cubits at the rear of the house'. *He even built them for it within, even for the oracle* (16); read, with change of one letter, 'and he built within for a shrine' (I.C.C.). The translation *oracle* (Heb. *debir*) goes back to a mistaken rendering of the Vulgate. *Debir* means 'the hinder part', and was evidently an early technical term for the 'holy of holies'. Verse 18 (which the LXX omits) and verse 19 are probably marginal comments later taken up in text. If we omit, we should probably read verses 17 and 20 with I.C.C. (mainly following LXX): 'And forty cubits long was the hall in front of the shrine; and the shrine twenty cubits in length. . . .' In verse 20 the RV reads 'He covered the altar with cedar': the AV is a desperate effort to rescue the sense. Read with LXX and add verse 21b: 'he made an altar of cedar before the shrine, and he overlaid it with gold.' *Chains of gold* (21). No satisfactory explanation has been given; it is not the same word as that for the ornamental chains in vii. 17; 2 Ch. iii. 5 (q.v.). They are not referred to elsewhere.

The two cherubim (23–28) must not be confused with the cherubim of the mercy seat (Ex. xxv. 18–20). They stood against the west wall of the Holiest facing the curtain (2 Ch. iii. 13, RV), as a symbolic protection for the ark, which will have stood between them under their outspread wings. The cherubim should not be pictured in the complex form we find in Ezekiel.

Open flowers (29). There is no contradiction with the chains of 2 Ch. iii. 5 (q.v.). In addition to the curtain (2 Ch. iii. 14) the Holiest was shut off by a door (31; cf. Ezk. xli. 3f.), which was not the case in the second temple. 'The lintel and doorposts formed a pentagon' (RSV) (for so we must render *the lintel and side posts were a fifth part*), the lintel being in two parts meeting at an angle. 'Out of a fourth part' (33, RV); render, 'rectangular'. The door of the Holy Place was rectangular, not pentagonal (cf. verse 31). From verse 34 it would seem not that the massive outer doors were folding, but that they had smaller two-leaved doors within them for ordinary use.

iv. The temple court (vi. 36). Cf. 2 Ch. iv. 9. See introductory note to vii. 1–12. On the basis of archaeological discovery (see I.C.C.) we are probably to understand the description to mean that there was a course of cedar as a kind of bonding to ensure alignment to every three courses of stone. If so, the height of the wall is not indicated.

v. The dating of the building (vi. 37, 38). Cf. verse 1. *Zif* and *Bul* are the older pre-exilic names, later replaced first by numerical names and then by 'Iyyar' and 'Marcheshvan'.

d. Solomon's Jerusalem palaces (vii. 1–12)

This section (not included in 2 Chronicles) is not out of place in the description of the temple. This was only one of a large complex of buildings. To the north stood the temple in its own court (vi. 36), then the royal palace and harem in their court (verse 8, q.v.), then southernmost, and nearest the city, certain public buildings. The whole complex was surrounded by the great court (12). Cf. Ezekiel's protest (Ezk. xliii. 8). (For an approximate plan see H.D.B., IV, p. 695; I.S.B.E., p. 2932; Cent. Bible, p. 442.) The description is very brief and hence difficult to follow.

The house of the forest of Lebanon (2), probably so called because of the effect of the rows of cedar pillars. It was probably a hall for public functions with the armoury and storehouse (x. 17; Is. xxii. 8); in front was an imposing pillared portico (6), and on the other side was the portico of justice (7). No details are given of the private buildings mentioned in verse 8. They lay in the second or middle (2 Ki. xx. 4) court. *An house for Pharaoh's daughter* (8) may have been the harem rather than a private palace for her alone. *And so . . . great court* (9); difficult to give any meaning. The Moffatt rendering is based on a dubious emendation, as also in verse 12b. The wall of *the great court* (12) was of the same type as that of the inner court (vi. 36). The second half of the verse seems to be corrupt.

e. Hiram, the bronze-worker (vii. 13, 14)

Cf. 2 Ch. ii. 13f. Hiram, or Huram, possibly Huramabi (see note on 2 Ch. ii. 13) had a Tyrian father, a mother from Naphtali (14) or Dan (2 Ch. ii. 14). The doubt may go back to a difference between residence and tribal origin. His mother's origin may have given Solomon a claim on him, suggested by the words *sent and fetched* (13). *Brass* (14); the Hebrew should be rendered 'copper' or 'bronze'; normally the latter.

f. The bronze pillars (vii. 15–22)

Cf. 2 Ch. iii. 15–17; Je. lii. 21–23. Archaeology has shown that such pillars were common, but has done little to explain their purpose. Analogy, supported by 2 Ch. iii. 17, suggests that they stood free of the porch, not supporting anything. They were probably merely ornamental. They were eighteen cubits high (the thirty-five of 2 Ch. iii. 15 is an error, due perhaps to the use of a defective text of Kings) with ornamental capitals (*chapiters*) of an additional five cubits. They were twelve cubits in circumference, hollow, the metal four finger-breadths thick (Je. lii. 21). The capitals, so far as we can interpret the very difficult text, were bowl-shaped (41), covered with a checker-work pattern, and ornamented with lily leaves. Each had two ornamental chains (2 Ch. iii. 16, q.v.), with ninety-six pomegranates hanging from each (Je. lii. 23), the remaining four being where the chains were fastened to the capital. *Jachin . . . Boaz* (21); see RV mg.; but the second may be an abbreviation of Baal-az, Baal is strength (for the use of Baal for Jehovah see note on 1 Ch. viii. 33). Scott (J.B.L., 1939) sees in the two names a cryptogram: 'In the name of Jehovah shall the king rejoice.'

g. The sea and the lavers (vii. 23–39)

Cf. 2 Ch. iv. 2–6. The shape of the sea is not given, but the estimate of its contents, 2,000 baths (26; the 3,000 baths of 2 Ch. iv. 5, though supported by Josephus, is probably an early textual error), probably over 16,000 gal. (the value of the bath is not certain), suggests that the conventional hemisphere would have been much too small. Whatever its shape, Josephus' interpretation of 2 Ch. iv. 6 must be correct; the priests drew the water for their ablutions from it, but did not wash in it. The measurements in verse 23 are approximate (see Cam. Bible). Apart from its practical use, the *sea* probably symbolized the sea as picturing, as so frequently in the Old Testament, the tamed power of chaos.

Our understanding of the lavers with their wheeled carriages (27–39) has been greatly helped by archaeological discovery, without which the Hebrew is almost unintelligible. For details see I.C.C. or Cent. Bible *ad loc*. Practical calculations by Kittel have made it questionable whether the dimensions as preserved are possible (see I.C.C.). Their use is given in 2 Ch. iv. 6.

h. A summary of Hiram's work (vii. 40–47)

Cf. 2 Ch. iv. 11–18. For the non-mention of the bronze altar (2 Ch. iv. 1) see additional note to chapter vii below. *Lavers* (40); Chronicles reads correctly 'pots'. *In the clay ground* (46); probably, 'in the earthen foundries'.

i. The golden vessels (vii. 48–51)

Cf. 2 Ch. iv. 19—v. 1. *The candlesticks* (49); better, 'lampstands'. For the number see additional note to chapter vii below. *The flowers . . . tongs of gold* (49) belong to the lampstands.

j. Additional note to chapter vii

The account of the temple furniture in 1 Kings and 2 Chronicles raises certain difficulties, all of which can most easily be met by assuming that certain furnishings of the tabernacle which were brought from Gibeon (2 Ch. i. 3; 1 Ki. viii. 4) were retained in use.

1. No mention is made of the making of the brazen altar in 1 Kings, though its existence is presupposed in 1 Ki. viii. 64. It has been suggested that the section accidentally disappeared from the text, but that would not explain its absence from the summary in vii. 40–47. 2 Ch. iv. 1 mentions the altar (note that 'he' refers to

Solomon, not Hiram), but it is omitted in the summary (2 Ch. iv. 11–18). The dimensions given in 2 Chronicles are greater than those of the altar in Ezekiel's temple and not much different from those of Herod's temple. It is probable that the old tabernacle altar (2 Ch. i. 5) was first used, but when it was found to be too small it was replaced by the much larger altar of 2 Ch. iv. 1.

2. Both 1 Ki. vii. 49 and 2 Ch. iv. 7, 20 speak of ten lampstands. Since 2 Ch. xiii. 11 implies only one, it is probable that the old tabernacle one was retained in use, but these were added because of the much greater building.

3. 1 Ki. vii. 48 tells of the making of a table for the shewbread; 2 Ch. iv. 8 tells of ten tables which in iv. 19 are explained to have been for the shewbread. There is nowhere else any mention of more than one table of shewbread, nor would ten be a suitable number in any case. Probably the tables of 2 Ch. iv. 8 were for the lampstands. Some scribe missing the point probably changed the singular of iv. 19 (cf. 1 Ki. vii. 48) to a plural.

V. THE DEDICATION OF THE TEMPLE.
viii. 1—ix. 9

Cf. 2 Ch. v. 2—vii. 22. This section consists of four main parts: the removal of the ark to its new abode (viii. 1–11); the actual dedication (viii. 12–61); the sacrifices and feast (viii. 62–66); God's answer to Solomon (ix. 1–9). The parallel narrative in 2 Ch. v. 2—vii. 22 is almost identical.

a. The moving of the ark (viii. 1–11)

Cf. 2 Ch. v. 2–14. The dedication feast coincided with the feast of tabernacles (2). The temple was not finished till the eighth month (vi. 38). The dedication may have taken place before all was finished, but more likely it was postponed nearly a year. Ethanim (2); the old name (cf. vi. 37f.); later called 'Tishri'. The ends of the staves were seen (8). The interpretation will depend on how we consider the ark was placed, either east and west in line with the axis of the temple, or north and south in the same line as the cherubim. The latter seems the more probable. In that case the veil was hung some distance within the Holiest, so that, for someone standing at the door, it effectively hid the ark itself, but the ends of the staves were just visible at either side. There was nothing in the ark save the two tables of stone (9). There is no point in speculating how the other items (Heb. ix. 4) had been lost. With verses 10, 11 cf. Ex. xl. 34f. Obviously the cloud rested on the temple only for the period of dedication, or even for a shorter time.

b. The actual dedication (viii. 12–61)

Cf. 2 Ch. vi. 1—vii. 3. There is a general agreement among modern scholars that the great dedication prayer (23–53) is a later invention. The only real argument is literary style, and this presupposes the usual critical date given for

Deuteronomy. Such a prayer cannot be extempore; it will have been written down before delivery and lodged in the royal archives.

i. A dedication ode (viii. 12, 13). We have here in all probability the beginning of a dedication ode which was preserved in the Book of Song (so LXX). On the basis of LXX (and so approximately I.C.C. and Cent. Bible) RSV renders:

> The Lord has set the sun in the heavens,
> but has said that he would dwell in thick
>   darkness.
> I have built thee an exalted house,
> a place for thee to dwell in for ever.

We have the contrast between Jehovah who hides Himself from the eyes of men and the glory of His creation; so too there was the contrast between the visible glory of the temple and the darkness of the inner shrine where Jehovah would sit invisible, enthroned among His people.

ii. An address to the people (viii. 14–21). The meaning is that by the choice of a royal house and the site for a temple the period of probation and preparation that began with the exodus had reached a happy end. Solomon was not spiritual enough to grasp the force of 2 Sa. vii. 5ff. When the 'tent' is lost to God's people, they have lost something of vital spiritual importance.

iii. Solomon's prayer (viii. 22–53). This is really for 'all sorts and conditions of men'. We may break it up as follows: for the royal family (23–26); that the temple may be truly God's house (27–32); in times of defeat (33, 34); in drought (35, 36); in all calamities (37–40); for the proselyte (41–43); in time of war (44, 45); in captivity (46–50); conclusion (51–53).

Mercy (23; Heb. ḥesedh): RSV 'steadfast love'. Ḥesedh is the quality of conduct expected in a covenant; between man and man, loyalty; from God to man (and from man to God, Ho. vi. 6), steadfast love. Dwell on the earth (27). LXX and Chronicles read, probably correctly, 'dwell with men on the earth'. In verse 31 note how justice is given primacy of place. The oath is in a case in which there is no conclusive evidence (cf. Lv. v. 1, RV; Nu. v. 19ff.). Blasting (37); cf. Gn. xli. 6. Caterpiller (37); a form of locust (see Joel i. 4). A stranger (41); the proselyte is intended. For verses 51–53 see note on 2 Ch. vi. 40–42.

iv. The benediction (viii. 54–61). For the probable motives that led to its omission in Chronicles see note on 2 Ch. vii. 1–3. He arose . . . from kneeling on his knees (54); cf. verse 22. Both standing and kneeling were recognized postures for prayer. Solomon probably knelt down for private prayer after his public prayer.

c. The sacrifices and feast (viii. 62–66)

Cf. 2 Ch. vii. 4–10. The numbers in verse 63 are by no means extravagant, if we remember that they are probably to be spread over the seven days of the dedication feast, or even over tabernacles as well (see verse 65), and that a high proportion were peace offerings, mainly eaten by the worshippers. The brasen altar (64); see additional note to chapter vii above. *A* (RV 'The') *feast* (65); i.e. the feast of the dedication and then the feast of tabernacles. *The entering in of Hamath* (65); RSV 'the entrance of Hamath'; in spite of the opinion of G. A. Smith (*Historical Geography*) this will not be the northern end of the great valley between Lebanon and Anti-Lebanon, but the southern, not far north of Dan (cf. iv. 25n). *On the eighth day* (66); see 2 Ch. vii. 9f.n.

d. God's answer to Solomon (ix. 1–9)

Cf. 2 Ch. vii. 11–22. In verse 8 AV and RV both pervert the Hebrew, which is correctly rendered in RV mg.; but the text is obviously impossible. Render with Versions: 'and this house will become a heap of ruins' (RSV). At a very early date a slight change was made in the text to prevent the reader speaking words of ill omen, though, as the Targum shows, the real reading was preserved. Already Chronicles has incorporated the alteration. *Hiss* (8); not a sound of disgust but of astonishment.

VI. MISCELLANEOUS NOTICES.
ix. 10—x. 29

Cf. 2 Ch. viii. 1—ix. 28. It is clear that this section is compiled from various notices in the royal chronicles.

a. Solomon's financial dealings with Hiram (ix. 10–14)

See also 2 Ch. viii. 1, 2. Failure to render the niceties of Hebrew idiom have led to a misunderstanding of this incident (RSV and Moff. are correct). Verse 11a explains how the transaction was possible, not its cause. Verse 14 is the cause; Solomon being short of ready money pawned the twenty towns. Difficulty is created by the very compressed narrative in 2 Ch. viii. 1f. If, as is generally suggested, it is trying to put the story in a better light, it is strange that it is not done more clearly. While it is fairly certain that the same towns are being referred to, it seems that we have only the end of the incident, when Solomon was able to redeem them by repaying the loan. *He called them the land of Cabul* (13). Cabul may mean 'good for nothing' (Moff.), this suggestion going back at least to Josephus. But the LXX translates 'boundary', and it is probably best to render with I.C.C., 'It was called March-land.'

b. Solomon's levy and city building (ix. 15–23)

Cf. 2 Ch. viii. 3–10. For the levy (15, 20–22) see note on v. 13–18. *Reason* (15); better, as in RV mg., 'account'. *Millo* (15); better, 'the Millo' (cf. xi. 27; 2 Sa. v. 9); presumably the fortification covering the breach (revealed by archaeology) which David had made in the old Jebusite wall of Zion. *Gezer* (16); cf. Jos. xvi. 10; Jdg. i. 29. It was evidently part of the dowry of Pharaoh's daughter. *Baalath* (18); cf. Jos. xix. 44. *Tadmor* (18); RV 'Tamar'; see note on 2 Ch. viii. 4; from

Ezk. xlvii. 19, xlviii. 28 we know that Tamar was the southernmost city of Judah. *In the land* (18), identical with iv. 19; i.e. Judah, the writer's home land. *Hazor* (15) covered the main ford of Jordan, near Lake Huleh, in the north; *Megiddo* (15) the main trade route as it crossed into Esdraelon; *Gezer, Beth-horon* and *Baalath* (17, 18) the approaches to Jerusalem; and Tamar (18) the southern frontier and the route to Ezion-geber. For verses 20–22 see note on v. 13–18. The AV of verse 21 is misleading; follow RV; they were totally enslaved. Ezr. ii. 58 may refer to their descendants. *Servants* (22), i.e. courtiers; *princes* (22), high officials of state. *Captains* (22); lit. 'thirdling'; i.e. originally the third in the royal chariot with the king and driver, and so a high court honour.

c. Incidental information (ix. 24, 25)

See notes on 2 Ch. viii. 11–16.

d. Solomon's Red Sea trade (ix. 26–28)

Cf. 2 Ch. viii. 17, 18. See also 1 Ki. x. 22. *Ezion-geber* (26). Excavations have shown that it was used for shipbuilding, copper-smelting and the making of copper tools. *Ophir* (28). Usually considered to be in Arabia, but on the basis of x. 22 (q.v.) perhaps in India.

e. The visit of the queen of Sheba (x. 1–13)

Cf. 2 Ch. ix. 1–12. Sheba was a north Arabian tribe (Gn. xxv. 3; Jb. i. 15). All the legends linking the queen with Ethiopia, etc., should be ignored. *Concerning the name of the Lord* (1); a difficult phrase omitted by Chronicles. *Told her all her questions* (3); better 'explained all her problems' (I.C.C.). *Had seen all Solomon's wisdom* (4); as the wisdom was his 'practical sagacity' (I.C.C.; see note on iii. 12) it could be seen in its fruits. *Servants* (5), i.e. 'courtiers'; *ministers* (5), i.e. 'servants'. The meaning of *his ascent* is doubtful; it may refer to the royal entrance to the temple, or the royal procession to the temple, or, with RV mg. and RSV, the royal burnt offering. The first is least likely. *Happy are thy men* (8); probably better rendered (with LXX, Syr., RSV, I.C.C.) by the addition of one letter, 'Happy are thy wives'. *To do judgment and justice* (9). Note that the doing of justice is the ideal of kingship (cf. iii. 9). The apparent generosity of the queen (verse 10) was in part at least mere exchange (cf. verse 13).

The navy also of Hiram (11); all the trained seamen will have been Phoenicians. *Almug trees* (11); in 2 Ch. ii. 8, ix. 10 'algum trees'; unidentified; the suggestion 'sandalwood', though plausible, is uncertain. *Pillars* (12); this is a technical word no longer understood by Chronicles, which has 'terraces'. From the use of the wood for musical instruments it is likely that some form of inlay or wainscoting is intended.

f. The trade and riches of Solomon (x. 14–29)

Cf. 2 Ch. ix. 13–28, i. 14–17). This section obviously consists of unconnected extracts from the royal annals. The gold of verse 14 should not be interpreted as Solomon's annual revenue, but is rather the figure for a specially prosperous year. In verse 15 render with LXX 'besides the taxes of the merchants and of the traffic of the traders'. This is the first extant mention of taxes on goods in transit. *Kings of Arabia* (15); the AV, in contrast to the RV, has rightly followed Chronicles here.

Targets . . . shields (16, 17); large oblong shields covering the body and smaller round shields; the former about twenty pounds in weight; the latter at sixty shekels to the *minah*, i.e. *pound*, were just over one-third the weight. 2 Ch. ix. 16 makes them half the bigger shields; the difference may be due to varying standards of weight (cf. H.D.B., IV, p. 903). They were of *beaten gold*, which suggests inlay and overlay (I.C.C.).

The throne was round behind (19). The correct reading is probably given by the versions: 'and at the back of the throne was a calf's head' (RSV); the difference between 'calf' and 'round' in Hebrew is only one of vowels. The rendering in 2 Ch. ix. 18 merely represents a corrupt version of the text of Kings.

A navy of Tharshish (22). Tarshish (RV) is generally identified with Tartessus in Spain, and hence a ship 'of Tarshish' was, perhaps, one capable of making such a long voyage. It seems more likely that they were ships intended to bring metal ore for smelting, Tarshish being a derivative of the root *rashash*, to smelt. In other words, the place (or places) got its name from the ore trade, not the ships from the place. *Peacocks* (22); possibly a species of ape; if peacocks is correct it would point to Ophir being in India.

Horsemen (26); probably 'horses' (I.C.C.). Render verse 28 with Moff., 'Solomon's horses were imported from Muzri and Kue; the royal dealers used to bring a troop of horses from Kue, paying cash for them.' (So also Cent. Bible, I.C.C.) 'Muzri' (see 2 Ki. vii. 6n.) is Cappadocia; 'Kue', Cilicia. Probably in verse 29 too, *Egypt* (*Mizraim*) should be replaced by Muzri. The end of the verse seems to mean that Solomon paid the same price as the Hittite and Syrian kings.

VII. SOLOMON'S TROUBLES. xi. 1–43

The usual impression is that the troubles here described arose late in Solomon's reign. But this is certainly not the case with Hadad (21), and probably not with Rezon. They probably did not become a serious menace till later in his reign. There is no parallel to this passage in Chronicles.

a. Solomon's polygamy and its results (xi. 1–13)

The fact that Solomon's wives outnumbered his concubines (3) shows that the size of his harem was not merely the result of unchecked lust. The marriages were mostly political unions. This meant that Solomon had to tolerate and provide for the religions of his foreign wives. At first this heathen worship will have been confined to the privacy of the palace, but as Solomon grew accustomed to it and the number of his heathen wives increased, he allowed it to find public expression. Note that it is not said to have had any public effect. For the moment it was a court concern. In spite of Asa's and Hezekiah's reformations Solomon's heathen sanctuaries remained until the time of Josiah (2 Ki. xxiii. 13). It was easier to destroy them than the memory of the worship carried on at them, and so they were repeatedly restored. (See also Appendix II.)

b. Hadad of Edom (xi. 14–22)

The reason for David's attempt to exterminate all males in Edom (in verse 15 read with LXX and Syr. 'when David smote Edom') is not clear. The slain whom Joab had to bury (15) were obviously Israelite. It is possible that the Israelite garrisons in Edom were treacherously massacred. Hadad probably carried on a guerilla struggle right through Solomon's reign (verse 25 may originally have been the end of the story of Hadad as well as of Rezon) until, towards its end, Israel could do little more than control the trade route to Ezion-geber.

c. Rezon of Damascus (xi. 23–25)

After David's defeat of Hadadezer of Zobah (2 Sa. viii. 3–8, 10) Rezon became a bandit leader. Shortly after David's death he captured (24, LXX) Damascus, probably by surprise, and Solomon was not able to eject him. Owing to the strategic position of Damascus on the main trade route to the east, it was a serious blow for Solomon.

d. Jeroboam the son of Nebat (xi. 26–40)

In the work on Millo (see note on ix. 15) Jeroboam attracted the attention of Solomon, who saw that he was *industrious* (28), 'very able' (RSV), 'active' (Moff.). He therefore put him over *the charge* (28) of Ephraim and Manasseh. This 'labour' (RV) may have been the levy of v. 13 (q.v.), but, since another word is used, it may have been labour in lieu of taxes. His position will have made Jeroboam well known to his tribesmen, and will have made him know their grievances better. The RV makes it clear that *the new garment* (29) was Ahijah's. The *twelve pieces* (30) were traditional, for counting Ephraim and the two halves of Manasseh there were really fourteen tribes. But Simeon had become so mixed with Judah that it could be ignored, and Levi, scattered through the land, would belong equally to both sides in the divided monarchy. So only Benjamin (the *one tribe* of verse 32) needed to be mentioned as remaining with Judah; it is taken for granted here and in verse 36 that Judah would remain loyal. RSV rightly follows the Versions in verse 33 and has singular throughout. In strict justice Solomon should have lost the throne at once, and so he is called *prince* (34; Heb. *nasi'*, not *sar*; for which see 1 Ch. xxii. 17n.). *That David . . . may have a light* (RV 'lamp') *alway* (36). If an Eastern house is dark at night it can only mean that it is empty or that the inhabitants are dead. Hence this means the continuance of the Davidic dynasty (cf. xv. 4; Jb. xviii. 5f.; Pr. xiii. 9).

Jeroboam was not content to wait God's time and plotted against Solomon—Solomon could not otherwise have known (40), for he did not know of the prophecy—and it is probable that the plot went on while he was in Egypt (see note on xii. 1–20). LXX has a striking variation in chapter xii, which affirms that Jeroboam actually raised a rebellion. But however we are to explain the variant story in LXX, authorities like Burney, Kittel and Montgomery (I.C.C.) all reject it, and Skinner (Cent. Bible) is hesitant to give it any authority, so it is wiser to regard verses 26 and 40 as a plot prematurely discovered by the king's spies.

e. Summary of Solomon's reign (xi. 41–43)

Cf. 2 Ch. ix. 29–31. Neither *the book of the acts of Solomon* (41) nor the authorities mentioned in 2 Chronicles are otherwise known. *The forty years* (42) probably include some years of co-regency with his father (see note on 1 Ch. xxii. 2–5). *He was buried in the city of David* (43); see note on ii. 10.

THE DIVIDED KINGDOM. 1 Ki. xii. 1—2 Ki. xvii. 41

VIII. THE SCHISM. xii. 1–24

a. The disruption (xii. 1–20)

Cf. 2 Ch. x. 1–19. It is generally thought that the disruption was caused by the impact of a young man's folly on an overtaxed people. Actually Rehoboam was forty-one (xiv. 21) and the lack of disorders under Solomon shows that the people's position was ñot so serious. Rehoboam was probably the victim of a very skilful plot. Jeroboam had already plotted against Solomon (xi. 26, 40) and will have continued his plotting from Egypt. He will have been quickly informed of Solomon's death. *When Jeroboam . . . heard of it* (2) must for reasons of distance and time refer to the news of the death. 'Then Jeroboam returned from Egypt', following LXX, Vulg. and 2 Ch. x. 2. In the interval his friends stirred up the tribes to demand an official recognition of the new king. There is no suggestion that Rehoboam was not already king, or that anyone else might have been chosen. The conspirators moved the people to make an apparently harmless request for lower taxes (4). Solomon's counsellors, with a true understanding of the position, advised a gentle answer (7). But Rehoboam's personal friends, who had been perturbed by the sight of Jeroboam (3), probably thought that the conspiracy was much further advanced, and that this was only a pretext to be followed by ever increasing demands. They therefore advised that the conspiracy should be boldly challenged (10, 11). The reaction of the people (16) showed that the bulk of them had not thought of rebellion. Even now a pause for reflection might have saved the day. But Rehoboam pursued his challenge by sending *Adoram* (18; probably the Adoniram of iv. 6, q.v.), the most hated man in the country, to bring them back to their allegiance and to show that he meant what he said. Probably at the instigation of the conspirators, Adoram was stoned (18). Only then was Jeroboam (20) brought forward to meet the crisis created by the unpremeditated rebellion. *For the cause was from the Lord* (15) is well rendered 'for it was a turn of affairs brought about . . .' (RSV). No stress should be laid on the non-mention of Benjamin in verse 20; cf. verse 21.

b. Civil war averted (xii. 21–24)

Cf. 2 Ch. xi. 1–4. Rehoboam, by his control of his father's wealth, chariots and mercenary troops, could have won a quick victory over the unorganized north. Not sufficient credit is given him for his obedience. He had not been so foolish at Shechem as most think, and he now bowed to the manifest overruling of God. The disruption was not merely a punishment on Solomon, but also on the north (Ho. viii. 4, x. 9, xiii. 11), which had never really accepted the ideals of Samuel or the divine choice of Judah.

IX. JEROBOAM OF ISRAEL. xii. 25—xiv. 20

a. Jeroboam's religious policy (xii. 25–33)

Jeroboam fortified *Shechem* (25), and made it his capital, a natural choice for its strategic position and importance as a sanctuary. Something, probably his religious policy, made the city uncongenial and he moved his capital to *Penuel* in Transjordan. This surprising choice may be connected with Shishak's invasion (xiv. 25–28). He later moved his capital to Tirzah; see xiv. 17. It is clear that the effect of Solomon's temple was already telling on the local sanctuaries (see note on iii. 2, 3), but verse 27 gives only the welcome excuse for Jeroboam's action. He was staking his claim as religious head of Israel, as 'divine king'. The *two calves* (or 'bulls') *of gold* (28) were to replace the cherubim of the mercy seat. Albright (*From the Stone Age to Christianity*, p. 229f.) insists strongly on archaeological grounds that the golden bulls were not images of Jehovah, but 'the visible pedestal on which the invisible Yahweh stood', even as the cherubim were His visible throne. But a God who stands on a bull (reminiscent of Canaanite fertility worship) is very different from one throned on the heavenly cherubim (see, further,

Appendix I). He also used his position to fill the gaps left in the Levitical priesthood (31; xiii. 33; see note on 2 Ch. xi. 14, 15) and to give the local sanctuaries (31) an official position. *An house of high places* (31) is wrong; it should be plural 'houses' (RV). He also moved the feast of tabernacles, which will have been his New Year feast (see Appendix I), a month later (32). Finally he took priestly functions on himself (32, 33, xiii. 1).

The choice of Bethel and Dan was probably not strategic (29), but because the priests were willing to accept the images; there was already an image in Dan (Jdg. xviii. 30, 31). A similar bull image was later put in Samaria (Ho. viii. 5, 6). *Behold thy gods* (28). As in Ex. xxxii. 4, the plural is deliberately used by the writer to stigmatize the whole proceeding as idolatry. Though we cannot reconstruct the text of verse 30 with certainty, it is clear it is corrupt; if anything the sanctuary of Bethel was the more popular. *Priests of the lowest of the people* (31) is wrong; render, as in RV, 'from among all the people'. Verse 33 is the transition to the next chapter.

b. The man of God from Judah (xiii. 1–32)

It was by his religious policy that Jeroboam 'made Israel to sin', so God did not leave him without warning. This story was obviously edited later (cf. verse 32; Samaria was not built for another half century), so it is quite probable that *Josiah by name* (2) is the editor's addition, the more so as no attention is drawn to the name in the story of the fulfilment (2 Ki. xxiii. 15–18). The prohibition against eating or drinking (9) was intended to show that the land was unclean. It is profitless to speculate why the Bethel prophet chose to deceive him (18).

c. Evil falls upon Jeroboam (xiii. 33—xiv. 20)

i. Jeroboam hardens his heart (xiii. 33, 34). The effect of the prophet's visit and signs wore off almost at once. Possibly the Bethel prophet by causing his death contributed largely to this.

ii. The beginning of the doom on Jeroboam's house (xiv. 1–18). At an unspecified time in Jeroboam's reign Abijah, the heir presumptive, a most promising lad (13, 18), on the verge of manhood, fell seriously ill. *Disguise thyself* (2); it is clear that Ahijah had broken with Jeroboam because of his religious policy. We get a striking picture of the crudeness of Jeroboam's religion. He thought that by tricking Jehovah's prophet he could trick Jehovah. *Child* (3); Heb. *na'ar*, is used of anyone who has no full place in society. It may be used of a slave of any age, or of someone too young to marry and set up his own home. In contexts like this it is much more likely to mean one in late adolescence than a child, for whom other words are available. *Thou . . . hast made thee other gods* (9). By calling his son Abijah Jeroboam claimed to worship Jehovah; for the prophet his religion was idolatry and worship of other gods (see Appendix I). In verse 10 render 'every man child' (RV), or 'every male' (RSV), for convention's sake. *Him that is shut up*

and left ('at large', RV): meaning uncertain. To be unburied (11) was considered the worst of all punishments. It goes back to primitive ideas about the dead. *But what? even now* (14); the meaning is doubtful; perhaps the RSV conjecture is right, 'Henceforth the Lord will smite. . .' *The river* (15); better with a capital (RV); here, as always, the Euphrates. *Groves* (15); the AV should on no account be followed; render Asherim (RV); for its meaning see verse 23.

iii. **Summary of Jeroboam's reign (xiv. 19, 20).** *How he warred* (19); see xiv. 30; 2 Ch. xiii. 2–20.

X. REHOBOAM, ABIJAM AND ASA OF JUDAH. xiv. 21—xv. 24

Cf. 2 Ch. xii. 1—xvi. 14. Chronicles has considerable additional information of importance in this section.

a. Rehoboam (xiv. 21–31)

i. His idolatry (xiv. 21–24). Cf. 2 Ch. xii. 1. *His mother's name was . . .* (21). The mention of the queen mother's name is mainly due to her importance at the court of Jerusalem (cf. Je. xiii. 18). *Images, and groves* (23); 'pillars (Heb. *maẓẓebhoth*), and Asherim' (RV); the *maẓẓebhah* (sing.) was a stone on end, representing the male side of deity, the Asherah (sing.) a pole, representing the female. They were regular features of the Canaanite sanctuaries, and were always introduced into Jehovah worship as soon as it was brought down to a naturalistic level. On this level it was natural to worship on hill tops and under age-old trees (see Appendix I). *Sodomites* (24); 'male cult prostitutes' (RSV); the sacred harlots are not mentioned, as they could be taken for granted or they are included in the masculine.

ii. Shishak's invasion (xiv. 25–28). See notes on 2 Ch. xii. 2–12.

iii. Summary of Rehoboam's reign (xiv. 29–31). Cf. 2 Ch. xii. 13–16.

b. Abijam (xv. 1–8)

A much fuller account is given in 2 Ch. xiii. 1–22 (q.v.). *Abijam* (1); see note on 2 Ch. xiii. 1. *Maachah, the daughter of Abishalom* (2); see note on 2 Ch. xi. 20; Abishalom is only a longer form of Absalom. Verse 6 is an accidental repetition of xiv. 30 (omitted by LXX).

c. Asa (xv. 9–24)

i. Asa's reformation (xv. 9–15). Cf. 2 Ch. xiv. 1–5, xv. 16–18. *His mother's name was Maachah, the daughter of Abishalom* (10). Unless we are to make the most improbable assumption, possible in itself, that Asa was Abijam's brother, we must interpret 'mother' as grandmother and assume that Maachah had inherited enough of her grandfather's spirit to make her position at court almost unassailable; hence the special mention of her deposition in verse 13 from being *queen*, i.e. 'queen mother' (RV mg.), for making *an idol in a grove*. This should be 'an abominable image for Asherah' (RV mg.). Asherah was not merely the name of the sanctuary pole (see note on xiv. 23) but also the mother goddess of the Canaanites (the pole may have represented her), who is here intended as 'wife' of Jehovah (see Appendix I). *But the high places were not removed* (14); whether these local sanctuaries were, under certain conditions, permitted depends on how we interpret Dt. xii. 5–14. At any rate they had not been suppressed by Solomon (see note on iii. 2, 3) and there were no cogent grounds for removing them now, though it became a spiritual necessity under Hezekiah and Josiah. But see note on 2 Ch. xiv. 3 and Appendix I. Verse 15 may be the beginning of a temple document now hardly understandable.

ii. **Asa's war with Baasha (xv. 16–22).** Cf. 2 Ch. xv. 19—xvi. 10 with its important addition. Under the conditions of the ancient world a sharply drawn frontier was almost impossible, and it was almost inevitable that much of Benjamin should be no man's land. Abijam had been able to force the frontier northwards (2 Ch. xiii. 19), but now Baasha, by making *Ramah* (17), just over four miles north of Jerusalem, a frontier fortress, virtually brought Jerusalem into the war area. *There is a league between me and thee, and between . . .* (19); the insertion of 'and' is obviously wrong; better 'as between . . .' (RSV). Evidently Syria had been changing sides to suit her own advantage. Ben-hadad now harried (20) the upper Jordan valley and the land round the Sea of Galilee (*Cinneroth*). Asa acted at once (22) and secured his frontier by fortifying *Geba* (Tell-el-Ful), three miles north of Jerusalem, and *Mizpah* (Tell-en-Nasbeh), eight miles north. Geba remained the effective northern frontier town of Judah till the time of Josiah (2 Ki. xxiii. 8). For the deeper implications of Asa's act see Appendix II.

iii. **Summary of Asa's reign (xv. 23, 24).** Cf. 2 Ch. xvi. 11–14. There is no indication of what the disease was from which he suffered (23).

XI. NADAB TO OMRI OF ISRAEL. xv. 25—xvi. 28

Two bloody changes of dynasty in twenty-five years seriously weakened Israel and gave Syria the upper hand.

a. Nadab (xv. 25–31)

We are told too little to know whether there was any justification for Baasha's act. He will have been either commander-in-chief or had the army officers behind him. *Gibbethon* (27), a Danite town (Jos. xix. 44), was in the hands of the Philistines, who had grown much stronger since the disruption; twenty-four years later it was still uncaptured (xvi. 15).

b. Baasha (xv. 32—xvi. 7)

His war with Asa having been already mentioned (xv. 16–22), there is nothing to tell but his doom and death. For xvi. 4 see note on xiv. 11. *Because*

he killed him (7); better 'smote it' (RV mg.), i.e. 'the house of Jeroboam'; either he is condemned because God had never commissioned him to be His executioner, or we should render 'despite that . . .' (I.C.C.).

c. Elah (xvi. 8–14)

Unlike Nadab, Elah was not with the army at Gibbethon (15). It seems likely he was given to dissipation, and *Arza* (9) may well have been in the plot against him. Zimri's rooting out of the house of Baasha (11) was more drastic than Baasha's of Jeroboam's house (xv. 29); Jehu was to go even further (2 Ki. x. 11).

d. Zimri (xvi. 15–20)

Zimri, though holding an important military command (9), does not have the name of his father mentioned; hence he was a nobody. This probably explains his unanimous rejection by the army at *Gibbethon* (15; see xv. 27); the sequel shows that, once Zimri was disposed of, the people were not as unanimous as verse 16 suggests. Many query verse 19, but in his formal service of accession Zimri will have shown that he had no intention of making religious changes.

e. Civil war (xvi. 21, 22)

We know nothing more of *Tibni the son of Ginath* (21) nor why he was supported. Comparing verses 15 and 23 we find that the civil war lasted four years. The LXX is probably correct in reading (22) 'And Tibni and Joram his brother died at that time . . .' (Cent. Bible, I.C.C., Moff.).

f. Omri (xvi. 23–28)

A most instructive section. Omri was politically one of Israel's greatest kings, but he is dismissed in a few sentences. For Shalmaneser III Jehu is 'son of Omri', and as late as 733 B.C. Tiglath-pileser III calls Israel 'the land of Omri'. But religiously *he walked in all the way of Jeroboam the son of Nebat* (26). In xx. 34 we find that he was unsuccessful in his wars with Syria. He was probably the initiator of the policy of peace with Judah that we find in operation under Ahab. Archaeology has confirmed the statement that *Samaria* (24) was built on a virgin site. The burning of the royal palace at Tirzah (18) and the stain of murder there (9, 10) will have decided Omri to build a new capital.

XII. AHAB AND ELIJAH. xvi. 29—xxii. 40

Though we are told far more about Ahab than about any other king of Israel, it is impossible to reconstruct the details of his reign. 1 Ki. xx, xxii. 1–40 belong to the last three years of his life. There is no means of dating xvii–xix, and there is no certainty that chapter xxi is in its chronological position (see note on xxi. 1). The real importance of his reign for Scripture is that in it Israel came to the moment of crisis, and failing (see note on xix. 14–18) there was nothing left for it but inevitable doom.

a. The religious evils of Ahab's reign (xvi. 29–34)
He took to wife Jezebel (31). The motives were doubtless political, to strengthen Israel against the pressure of Syria and the more distant danger of Assyria. But since, unlike the position in Solomon's time, Israel and Phoenicia stood on an equal footing, his wife's religion was not merely tolerated but given a special status. He *went and served Baal . . .* (31, 32). Here Baal is not a Canaanized Jehovah, but Melkarth, the chief god of Tyre. Though Ahab never officially ceased to be a Jehovah worshipper—all his known children's names are compounded with Jah, Ahaziah, Jehoram, Athaliah—and kept a band of 'prophets' of Jehovah at his court (xxii. 6, 11, 12), yet he seems to have given his wife a fairly free hand to propagate her faith, and to put to death those Jehovah worshippers who openly opposed her (xviii. 4). He *made a grove* (33); render 'the Asherah' (RV) and see note on xiv. 23; the sanctuaries at Bethel and Dan doubtless already had their Asherim; this was for the Baal temple.

The mention of how *Hiel* (34) defied Joshua's ban on the rebuilding of Jericho (Jos. vi. 26) is intended to show the religious deterioration of the time. *He laid the foundation thereof in Abiram . . . the gates thereof in . . . Segub* (34); render with RV 'with the loss of', or with Moff. 'at the cost of the life of'. It used to be widely believed that Hiel offered up his sons as foundation and completion sacrifices. This is now generally rejected; it was a divine visitation.

b. Elijah and the drought (xvii. 1–24)
We know nothing of the antecedents of *Elijah the Tishbite* (1) except that he was 'of Tishbe of Gilead' (so without change of consonants LXX, Josephus, RV mg., RSV, etc.). While we may infer that he was a prophet of long standing, this cannot be regarded as a certainty. *Before whom I stand* (1); a technical term for service of God or king (cf. x. 8). *Get thee hence* (3). Elijah will have prophesied just before the rainy season was due to start; Ahab will not have paid much attention until the rain failed to come. *The brook Cherith, that is before Jordan* (5); 'that is east of the Jordan' (RSV). The traditional identification with Wadi Kelt has only ready accessibility for pilgrims in its favour.

It would be hard to exaggerate the widow's faith; she probably knew Elijah as a prophet by his dress (see note on 2 Ki. i. 8), and she knew the name of the God of Israel (12), but she was a heathen. *Zarephath* (9) was a small port between Tyre and Sidon. It is useless to speculate how the miracle (16) happened. This sudden outburst of miracles, the first since the exodus and conquest, was intended as a sign that Israel once again stood at the crossroads of destiny. *Art thou come unto me to call my sin to remembrance, and to slay my son?* (18). No specific sin need be imagined. According to primitive ideas, the widow thinks that Elijah, a 'holy' man,

has brought divine 'holiness' into contact with her house, with disastrous results.

c. Elijah's meeting with Ahab (xviii. 1–19)
In the third year (1). The New Testament (Lk. iv. 25; Jas. v. 17) reckons three and a half years, because, if Elijah's message of xvii. 1 had been given just before the rains were due, there would have been half a year's rainless period before it. We do not know the circumstances in which Jezebel murdered the prophets (4). It is not likely to have been a result of the drought, for Obadiah takes for granted that Elijah knew of his action (13). It is more likely to have been the reason for the drought. The extent to which the awe of Elijah had fallen on Ahab is shown by his being able to summon him to his presence (8, 16). Elijah chose *mount Carmel* (19) because it was debatable ground between Israel and Phoenicia, and was held sacred to the Canaanite gods. *Gather . . . all Israel* (19); here, as so often, by its representatives. *The prophets of the groves* (19); 'the prophets of Asherah' (RSV), the goddess, not the symbol (see note on xv. 13); for some reason they drop out of the story.

d. The contest on mount Carmel (xviii. 20–46)
Heathen religions were always accommodating, and it would have been easy to accommodate Baal and Jehovah in one system; Jezebel almost certainly looked for no more than this. Elijah was uncompromising. Better the worship of Baal than of a watered-down Jehovah (21; cf. Jos. xxiv. 14, 15). *How long halt ye between two opinions?* (21); probably best rendered 'How long are ye hobbling at the two forks (of the road)?' (I.C.C.). *I only remain a prophet of the Lord* (22); probably here and xix. 14 an expression of great loneliness rather than a denial of the existence of others (xviii. 4, xx. 35, xxii. 8) or of their standing. The meaning of verse 24 is brought out by Moff., 'the God who answers by fire, he is the real God'. As the Baal prophets grew excited they danced a limping dance around, not *upon* (26), the altar, and *cut themselves . . . with knives and lancets* (28), i.e. lances (RV), which was the original meaning of the AV; in addition they *prophesied* (29), i.e. they worked themselves into a frenzy. All this is reminiscent of certain dervish practices to this day.

There is no evidence that Jehovah's altar had been recently *broken down* (30). The choice of *twelve stones* (31) was an implicit condemnation of the existence of the northern kingdom. The *water* (33) could have been brought from the sea. Elijah recognizes that the position is one of God's doing; in verse 37 we should render 'for thou didst turn their heart backward' (RV mg., I.C.C.). The slaughter of the prophets of Baal (40) may offend our sense of what is right. It was partly to avenge the murder of the prophets of Jehovah (4), partly because many will have been apostate Israelites, and so their lives were forfeit (Dt. xiii. 1–5).

The full vindication of the prophet was the coming of the rain. Completely victorious, Elijah humbled himself to act as Ahab's forerunner (46).

e. Elijah at Horeb (xix. 1–18)

Jezebel's message (2) was not just bluff intended to frighten Elijah (Cent. Bible); it was rather a proud confidence that she was really mistress of the situation. It was his realization that she was right that broke Elijah's nerve, 'and he was afraid' (3; so Versions and some MSS, RV mg.— the same consonants as he saw). It looks as though Elijah was conscious of his goal, i.e. Horeb, right along. The angel of the Lord (7) in the context of verse 5 is merely the angel already mentioned. We get the impression that and behold, the word (9b) to stand upon the mount before the Lord (11a) may be an accidental intrusion in the text (see verses 13, 14). Elijah did not leave the cave till he heard the still small voice (12) or, better, 'a sound of a light whisper' (Burney).

Elijah (14) then accused Israel (cf. Rom. xi. 2, RV). He had come to Sinai to tell Jehovah that the covenant had been a failure and, as once only Moses remained true (Ex. xxxii. 10), so again there was only one God-fearing man left. It is not indicated what led Elijah to the sudden realization that he had failed in his main purpose; fear of Jezebel would have evaporated long before. But the sequel shows he was essentially right. God accepted the charge and pronounced judgment (15–18). By the sword of a foreign enemy (Hazael) and of civil strife (Jehu) would doom come; but above all by the prophetic word (Elisha) which, when refused, hardens man for certain doom. 'Yet will I leave me' (the tense n AV is completely wrong and misleading) seven thousand in Israel (18); i.e. a remnant of hope for the future. This incident is for Israel what Is. vi. 9–13 is for Judah, though the implications are not so clearly drawn.

f. The call of Elisha (xix. 19–21)

No reason is given why Elijah, presumably, did not carry out his commission with Hazael and Jehu, but part of the story may not be recorded. The fact that no anointing of Elisha is mentioned does not mean it did not take place. Go back again: for what have I done to thee? (20); difficult. Presumably it means he has done nothing to rule out an expression of affection.

g. Ahab's victories over the Syrians (xx. 1–34)

There being virtually no doubt about the close connection between xx and xxii. 1–38, we need have no hesitation in dating the events of this chapter about 857/6 B.C., reckoning Ahab's death as late in 853 B.C. If so we are introduced to some of the events that preceded the battle of Qarqar (see Appendix III). Ben-hadad, having linked up all the Aramaean kings (1) in an alliance against the Assyrians, thought it well to eliminate the Israelite threat to his rear. As a result of his victories Ahab entered the league as a full member. It is not clear what was the exact difference between Ben-hadad's two demands (3, 5, 6). The LXX suggests possible textual corruption. The etiquette of the time forbad either attack (2 Ki. v. 7) or extreme measures (7) without some plausible pretext. Ben-hadad was so confident that he said (10) that his army was strong enough to carry away the city in handfuls (cf. 2 Sa. xvii. 13). The defeat was humanly due to the drunken pride that ordered the capture of the two hundred and thirty two (15) alive (18).

The Syrian attitude towards Jehovah (23) was typical of the time. Though the power of the gods was looked on as cosmic in extent, it was departmentalized (see Appendix I). The allied army was strengthened by putting professional soldiers in the place of the kings (24). No fewer than five places called Aphek (26) are known. Opinions vary as to whether this is a place near Mt. Gilboa, or east of the Lake of Galilee. An hundred thousand footmen (29), twenty and seven thousand (30); the former is equivalent to a great slaughter, the latter is to be taken literally. The (RV) wall fell (30) doubtless as a result of the Israelites' siege operations. The large number was due to the fact that the fugitive army had been trapped there. Sackcloth . . . ropes (31). The dress of the poorest, hence a sign of humiliation and mourning. The ropes were the akal, the twisted goat's-hair rope of the headdress. Ahab's lenient treatment of Ben-hadad (34) was not merely mercy but also policy. Threatened by the increasing power of Assyria, he did not want unduly to weaken Syria, which protected him to the north-east.

h. Ahab rebuked (xx. 35–43)

For the sons of the prophets (35) see note on 2 Ki. ii. 3. The prophet disguised himself as one wounded in the battle, with ashes upon his face (38); render 'with a bandage over his eyes', i.e. forehead. A talent of silver (39); an exorbitant figure; a silver talent had 3,000 shekels, and the price of a slave was thirty shekels. Evidently many of the prophets had marks on their foreheads, so that removal of the bandage (41) betrayed his identity. The condemnation (42) was partly due to the Syrian contempt for Jehovah (28), partly doubtless to Ahab's real motives for sparing Ben-hadad.

i. Naboth's vineyard (xxi. 1–29)

And it came to pass after these things (1). Owing to the way in which Kings was written (see Introduction under 'Author'), such phrases at the beginning of a new section may never be stressed, for we have no evidence (rather the contrary) that chapter xxi was in its original form connected with chapter xx. The words refer to the original context of the story. In its present position it is intended to confirm and justify the doom of xx. 42.

Ahab's whim (2) to join Naboth's vineyard to his own property and to turn it into 'a vegetable garden' (RSV)—normally a vineyard would be unsuited to such a purpose—was refused on religious grounds (3; cf. Lv. xxv. 23–28). Ahab would have acquiesced with bad grace (4), but when Jezebel taunted him (7) and promised him the vineyard, he asked no question. The story shows, not the greater democratic freedom in Israel, but the ruthlessness of one brought up in the ideas of 'divine kingship'. In her plot she wrote 'a letter' (8, RV mg.) sealed with the royal seal to *the elders* and 'freemen' (Moff.) of Jezreel commanding *a fast* (9) for some unspecified sacrilege; Naboth was to be *set on high*, i.e. be made chairman of the investigating tribunal; this, by stressing his social importance, would make his guilt the greater. *Two men, sons of Belial* (10), i.e. 'base fellows' (RSV), were to charge him: *Thou didst blaspheme* (RV 'curse') *God and the king* (God's representative), the penalty for which was death by stoning (Lv. xxiv. 10–16). Two witnesses were the minimum demanded by the law (Dt. xvii. 6). The recipients of the letter supinely obeyed (11–13), thus confirming Elijah's opinion of the people (xix. 14n.). Naboth's children shared his fate (2 Ki. ix. 26), and Ahab confiscated the heirless property (16).

The bitter language with which Ahab greeted Elijah (20)—*I have found thee* means just 'Yes!'—shows their paths had crossed on more occasions than those mentioned in Kings. For the general doom (21) see xiv. 10, 11n. Observe that the doom on Jezebel (23) was literally fulfilled (2 Ki. ix. 26). In verse 23, instead of *by the wall* (Heb. *ḥel*) read with nine MSS, LXX, etc. 'portion' (Heb. *ḥeleq*). That on Ahab was not fulfilled entirely (cf. verse 19 with xxii. 38, but also 2 Ki. ix. 25). The repentance of Ahab (27)—*and went softly* (RSV 'went about dejectedly')—and the postponement of the doom (29) show that his character was weak rather than vicious (cf. note on xvi. 29–33).

j. The death of Ahab (xxii. 1–38)

Cf. 2 Ch. xviii. 1–34, which is almost verbally identical. The serious check inflicted on Shalmaneser III at Qarqar left the confederates free to see to their own interests (see Appendix III), though Ben-hadad's attitude towards Ahab (31) may suggest that he considered Ahab's attack a breach of the treaty. What brought Jehoshaphat on a state visit to Ahab we are not told. It cannot have been the marriage of Jehoram with Athaliah, Ahab's daughter (2 Ki. viii. 18), for the age of their son Ahaziah at his accession (2 Ki. viii. 26) shows that it must have been at least ten years earlier. A common suggestion is that Jehoshaphat was tributary to Ahab, but there is no evidence for this, except his willingness (4) to join forces with Ahab. In those days much warfare was looked on as virtually a sport (cf. 2 Ki. xiv. 8n.).

For *Ramoth in Gilead* (3) see iv. 13n. *Inquire . . . at the word of the Lord* (5); a normal procedure before battle; cf. 1 Sa. xxviii. 6. That the *prophets* (6) claimed to be prophets of Jehovah

is clear from verses 11, 12. What made Jehoshaphat mistrustful is not said, for he did not challenge their status. *Is there not here a prophet of the Lord besides* (7) should be rendered 'is there not here another prophet of the Lord' (RSV). *In a void place* (10); 'at the threshingfloor' (RSV); the name may have remained after the original use of the open ground had disappeared; considerable space was needed for the ecstatic exercises of the 400 prophets.

Horns of iron (11); cf. 2 Ki. xiii. 14–19; Je. xxvii. 2, 3, xxviii. 10, 11; the doing of an action similar to that prophesied was popularly thought to have magic power. *That thou tell me nothing but that which is true* (16). Micaiah had by his tone of voice shown that his prophecy (15) was merely an act of courtesy. Challenged, he revealed that he had had two visions. The former (17) is a clear indication of disaster and Ahab's death; *in peace*, not suited to defeat, suggests that Ahab's death will be a gain. The latter (19–23) shows Jehovah deliberately leading Ahab to his doom. A *lying spirit* (22). To understand the vision we must remember that for the Old Testament it is clear that even evil spirits are under God's control (see note on 'Satan', 1 Ch. xxi. 1). Then, if even for the modern developed mind it is impossible to grasp how God works out His purposes of judgment by controlling evil men and evil spirits, obviously to Micaiah it had to be presented in an elementary way. *And smote Micaiah* (24); an insult. *In peace* (27); peace (Heb. *shalom*) means primarily completeness; hence here either 'victorious' (Moff.) or 'safe and sound' (cf. 2 Ki. ix. 17n.). The end of verse 28 'And he said, Hear, ye peoples, all of you' (RV) is unintelligible in its context, when rightly rendered. Since it is missing in the oldest LXX MSS and is in fact Mi. i. 2, it is probably the effort of an unintelligent scribe, at an early date, to identify Micaiah the son of Imlah with Micah (or Micaiah, Je. xxvi. 18 RV) the Morasthite (Mi. i. 1). *I will disguise myself* (30); neither cowardice nor treachery to Jehoshaphat, but an attempt to escape the doom spoken by Micaiah. *His thirty and two captains* (31). The orders are not for the army as a whole, but for his crack chariot force. *Jehoshaphat cried out* (32). It may well have been his battle cry; 2 Ch. xviii. 31 does not compel us to take it as a direct prayer. *Between the joints of the harness* (34); 'between the scale armour and the breastplate' (RSV); cf. RV mg. Ahab's first impulse was to leave the battle (34) but then he continued to take what part he could in it (35). *And died at even* (35); follow LXX and 2 Ch. xviii. 34, 'until the evening'. We should probably follow LXX at end of verse 36: 'Every man to his city, and every man to his own country, for the king is dead! And they came to Samaria.' *And they washed his armour* (38); an impossible rendering; it goes back to versions (Vulg., Syr., Targ.) made under rabbinic influence, which tried to avoid the objectionable 'harlots'. The lit. Hebrew is 'and the harlots washed'; probably, as RV, 'now the harlots washed themselves there', so Moff.; RSV is probably wrong.

k. Summary of Ahab's reign (xxii. 39, 40)

The ivory house (39); cf. Ps. xlv. 8; a palace with ivory inlay work and ornamentation, traces of which have been found by the archaeologist.

XIII. JEHOSHAPHAT OF JUDAH.
xxii. 41–50

Cf. 2 Ch. xx. 31–37. There is a great deal of additional material in 2 Ch. xvii, xix, xx. 1–30. *Nevertheless the high places were not taken away* (43); see xv. 14n. *Sodomites* (46); see xiv. 24n. *There was then no king in Edom* (47); i.e. Edom was under Judaean control. *But Jehoshaphat would not* (49); the destruction of the ships in a sudden squall showed the king his error. The part played by Ahaziah is made clearer in 2 Ch. xx. 35, 36. Probably when Ahaziah found Jehoshaphat discouraged, he offered to carry a heavier responsibility, which both for religious and political reasons was declined.

XIV. AHAZIAH OF ISRAEL.
1 Ki. xxii. 51—2 Ki. i. 18

If we compare xxii. 42, 51, 2 Ki. i. 17, iii. 1, it will be seen that 2 Ki. i. 17 is irreconcilable with the others, and in our present state of knowledge must be ignored in our chronological computations. For i. 1 see iii. 5n. *For he served Baal* (53). That he went further than Ahab is shown by his consultation of *Baal-zebub the god of Ekron* (i. 2). Zebub means 'flies', but this will be a scribal alteration from *Zebul*, meaning 'prince'. *The angel of the Lord* (3); 'Jehovah present in definite time and particular place' (A. B. Davidson); contrast note on 1 Ki. xix. 7. The outspoken apostasy led to a more powerful revelation than usual. *And Elijah departed* (4); to meet the messengers. There was no need to tell the sequel. *He was an hairy man* (8); 'he wore a garment of haircloth' (RSV). The prophets deliberately wore the outer garment and *girdle of leather* (8) of the poorest. This applied equally to the false (Zc. xiii. 4, RV) and the true prophet (Mk. i. 6). In the presence of apostasy there is no mercy for its agents (verses 9–12).

XV. ELIJAH SUCCEEDED BY ELISHA.
ii. 1–25

a. The translation of Elijah (ii. 1–18)

Into heaven by a whirlwind (1); it is never suggested that the *chariot of fire and horses of fire* (11) took Elijah into heaven. Note that Scripture never discusses what the translation involved. In Mk. ix. 4 (and parallels) Elijah appears on the same footing as Moses, who had indubitably died. *I will not leave thee* (2); Elisha had a prophetic premonition of what was to happen. *They went down to Beth-el* (2). This shows that Gilgal (1) cannot be the Gilgal of Jos. v. 9 in the Jordan valley. It was probably near Shechem.

The sons of the prophets (3). These are mentioned only in connection with the times of Elijah and Elisha and Am. vii. 14 (RV mg.); but there is no reason for doubting that the bands of prophets in the time of Samuel (1 Sa. x. 10, xix. 20) were of the same type. Most modern commentators seem inclined to equate them with the prophets; this would seem to be done in 1 Ki. xx. 35, 38, but Am. vii. 14 (RV mg.) seems to demand a distinction. In any case the metaphorical use of 'son' in Hebrew implies strong resemblance and connection, not identity. Pedersen is probably nearer the truth when he says, speaking of the ecstatic prophet: 'In order to be one of the prophets one must normally become a member of their societies. . . . It is possible that some few individuals might receive the spirit and see visions without associating themselves with others. . . . But everything . . . would seem to indicate that the prophet belonged to or had issued from a society in which he was taught the prophetic experience as an art . . .' (*Israel*, III–IV, p. 108). This is virtually what A. B. Davidson says more briefly (*Old Testament Prophecy*, p. 302): 'a Ben-Nabhi (a candidate for the office of prophet)'. There will have been good and bad groups among them, and from among the latter probably the bulk of the 'false prophets' were recruited. So far as they are mentioned in Scripture they seem to be under the control of Samuel, Elijah and Elisha. Doubtless their chief importance was spreading the message of their masters. In addition Elijah and Elisha probably looked on them as a possible nucleus for the future, when the judgments of God were passed (cf. 1 Ki. xix. 14–18n., 2 Ki. iv. 42–44n.). They clearly had limited prophetic power. *Will take away thy master from thy head* (3); 'from over you' (RSV). For the miracle see 1 Ki. xvii. 14n. *A double portion* (9); the firstborn's portion (Dt. xxi. 17). He was not asking to be greater than Elijah, but that he might be a worthy successor. *Chariot* (12); a collective; RV correctly 'chariots'. The prophet was of more value to Israel than all its chariots and horses (cf. xiii. 14). *Which were to view at Jericho* (15); clearer in RSV, 'who were at Jericho saw him over against them'; they had come out of Jericho (7) down nearer the Jordan. They had evidently been able to glimpse enough to have some inkling of what had happened (16).

b. The healing of the spring of Jericho (ii. 19–22)

Elisha's first miracle was symbolic. The water of Israel's religion had become corrupt and disease-bringing. If Elisha were listened to, he could heal it. The probable meaning of the Hebrew in verses 19, 21 is that the water caused miscarriage (RV).

c. Elisha and the boys of Beth-el (ii. 23–25)

Few stories in the Bible have been more misunderstood, thanks to the rendering *little children* (23). The Hebrew *ne'arim qetannim* can only legitimately be translated 'young lads' (RV mg.).

See note on 1 Ki. xiv. 3. Bethel was the home of Jeroboam's 'calf' and also of a group of sons of the prophets who had looked to Elijah as master. Hence there must have been a severe religious tension there. Elisha will have had his head covered, as is usual in the Near East, so *thou bald head* (23) is not mere childish rudeness, but a deliberate and deep insult, though its precise nuance is unknown. Addressed to the new head of the Bethel sons of the prophets, it was a deliberate insult to God. It can only have been the result of the teaching of the lads' parents, who in the conception of the time were the chief sufferers from the punishment.

XVI. JEHORAM OF ISRAEL. iii. 1–27

The story of Jehoram differs from most others in having its end separated from it (2 Ki. ix). This is because his death synchronized with that of Ahaziah of Judah. For practical reasons (see note at beginning of chapter iv) the stories of Elisha have been interposed as well.

a. Jehoram's religious policy (iii. 1–3)

He put away the image of Baal (2); 'the pillar' (RV); Heb. *maẓẓebhah*; see note on 1 Ki. xiv. 23, but possibly an image here. In the light of x. 18–21 it seems that he withdrew public support from the worship of Baal without proscribing it.

b. The war with Moab (iii. 4–27)

Mesha's (4) own version of his revolt (5) is given on the famous 'Moabite Stone'—for details see H.D.B., III, p. 406; I.S.B.E., p. 2071. The only apparent discrepancy is in Mesha's use of Omri's son to mean grandson. 2 Ch. xx will come from the earlier stages of the revolt. As a result of Jehoshaphat's victory Jehoram will have considered the reconquest of Moab easy. This is borne out by Jehoshaphat's presence, for he must have been nearly sixty. A walk-over was expected. The complete liberty of Moab probably followed on Jehu's wiping out of Omri's dynasty, which greatly weakened Israel (see 2 Ki. x. 1–11). *The king of Edom* (9); probably to be understood in the light of 1 Ki. xxii. 47, though possibly Jehoshaphat had now installed a vassal king; the fact that the Moabites had been joined in their earlier attack on Judah by many from Edom (2 Ch. xx. 1n.) may have showed him that the land was not sufficiently under control, and so he may have installed an Edomite as vassal king. *Which poured water on the hands of Elijah* (11); i.e. who was Elijah's servant (cf. Jn. xiii. 5). *And it came to pass, when the minstrel played* (15). This is not a fair translation of the Hebrew. Render 'for, whenever a minstrel played . . .' (Moff.). Elisha used music as a means for preparing himself for the prophetic message. *Make this valley full of ditches* (16). This is possible, but the RSV is more likely, 'I will make this dry stream-bed full of pools' (so Moff.). The reason for the very cruel way that Moab was to be treated (19), in contradiction to Dt. xx. 19, 20,

is explained by Mesha's killing of captured Israelites; he devoted them to Chemosh. *To break through even unto the king of Edom* (26). If the suggestion in the note to verse 9 is correct, it is just possible that Mesha looked on the king of Edom as a traitor; one would have expected him, however, to try to kill the king of Israel. The RSV 'opposite the king of Edom', as probably the weakest point, may be correct. Most likely seems the suggestion of I.C.C. 'to the king of Syria', his natural ally. Syria (*'rm*) and Edom (*'dm*) are frequently confused by scribes. Mesha's sacrifice of his eldest son to Chemosh (27) led to dread and panic falling on the semi-pagan Israelites; this seems to be the force of the RV mg. 'there came great wrath upon Israel'. The suggestion of the AV chapter heading, that it was the son of the king of Edom that was sacrificed, is certainly wrong.

XVII. ELISHA THE PROPHET.
iv. 1—viii. 15

Elisha had to find his place in Kings, for he had left no writings by which his work would be perpetuated. But he did not fit into the framework of the kings, as his work was rather the building up of the faith of the loyal Israelites in a time of God's judgment (note his attitude to Jehoram in iii. 14). See note on 1 Ki. xix. 14–18. So the stories to be preserved about him are mostly put together here without much attention to their chronological order or historic-setting; note how the names of the Israelite kings are deliberately omitted. We may tentatively arrange certain of the incidents in the following order: iv. 8–37, vi. 24—vii. 20, viii. 7–15, viii. 1–6, as regards its closing date, iv. 38–41 fitting into the famine period, vi. 8–23, v. 1–19, v. 20–27. The other incidents are timeless. For the sons of the prophets who appear frequently in this section see ii. 3n. For the miracles see 1 Ki. xvii. 14n.

a. The widow in debt (iv. 1–7)

The creditor is come (1); he would have had the right to enslave the man for the debt; now his right passes to the debtor's dependants. *A pot of oil* (2); a small ointment pot is implied, hence 'flask' (Moff.). *Shut the door* (4). Holy things are not for the public gaze.

b. The lady of Shunem (iv. 8–37)

See also viii. 1–6. *Shunem* (8); a few miles north of Jezreel in the plain of Esdraelon. *A great woman* (8); i.e. a wealthy woman. She seems to have been wealthy in her own right. *A little chamber . . . on the wall* (10); 'a small roof chamber with walls' (RSV). It was a permanent structure, not a booth. *Candlestick* (10); 'lamp' (RSV). *She stood before him* (12); better 'she presented herself' (I.C.C.). It was not etiquette for her to come into his room; she stood outside and Elisha talked to her through Gehazi (13) who stood in the doorway. Only later does she stand *in the door* (15) and Elisha speaks to her direct. *I dwell among mine own people* (13), showing the importance of the unity of the family group. *My head, my head* (19); obviously sunstroke. *A lad* (19), *one of the young men* (22). In both cases the Hebrew word is *na'ar* (see 1 Ki. xiv. 3n.); the RV correctly renders 'his servant . . . one of the servants'. *It shall be well* (23), *Is it well?* (26), etc.; Heb. *shalom*, lit. 'peace'; see ix. 17n. The servant ran behind the ass urging it on (24), so render 'Urge the beast on; do not slacken the pace for me unless I tell you' (RSV). The Shunammite felt that it would have been better to have had no child, than to have lost him (28). *Take my staff* (29); the symbol of Elisha's authority. *Salute him not* (29); cf. Lk. x. 4. The formal salutation, long in itself, would lead to even longer exchange of news about friends, etc.

c. The poisoned pottage (iv. 38–41)

There was a dearth in the land (38); cf. viii. 1. *Were sitting before him* (38); i.e. as his pupils. *Seethe pottage for the sons of the prophets* (38). We cannot argue from famine conditions that they always lived a communal life.

d. The miraculous feeding (iv. 42–44)

There is probably no link with the previous incident; there is no suggestion of famine conditions. *The firstfruits* (42) (Heb. *bikkurim*) were sacred to Jehovah (Ex. xxiii. 19, xxxiv. 26; Lv. ii. 12, xxiii. 10, 17, etc.). The action of the man showed that he looked on Elisha as the representative of Jehovah in contrast to the priests of the high places. Since the firstfruits were priestly food (Nu. xviii. 12, 13) Elisha's action in sharing them with *the people* (42), presumably sons of the prophets, shows that he looked on them as the holy remnant to whom the promise of Ex. xix. 6 ('a kingdom of priests') applied.

e. Naaman the leper (v. 1–19)

Internal evidence suggests that this is one of the last of the Elisha stories, coming after vi. 8–23 (note vi. 23), and hence during the reign of Jehu or one of his successors. *He brought the letter to the king of Israel* (6). The king of Syria doubtless took for granted that Elisha was attached to the court; in addition, the girl's statement that Elisha would cure Naaman did not rest on any actual cure of leprosy (cf. Lk. iv. 27), but on her faith in his powers. *See how he seeketh a quarrel* (RV mg. 'an occasion') *against me* (7). An example of such methods is when Apepi, the last great Hyksos Pharaoh, picked a quarrel with his Theban vassal by complaining that the roaring of the sacred hippopotami in Thebes was disturbing his sleep in Avaris more than 300 miles to the north! *And strike his hand over the place* (11); RV 'wave'. Naaman expected a proper exorcism. Elisha was concerned to show that the cure had nothing to do with magic, but was purely an act of the grace of Jehovah. *Take a blessing of thy servant* (15); the AV translates the Hebrew literally; the RV 'present' gives the sense.

Naaman's request for two mules' burden of earth did not imply that he thought that Jehovah's power was limited to Israelite soil, but that as God of Israel He would be more gracious to him if he worshipped on such holy soil. *Go in peace* (19). If the vast majority of Israelites indulged in a debased worship of Jehovah in which room for minor deities could be found (see Appendix I), no blame could be laid on a Syrian who did not rise to the heights of monotheism in a moment.

f. The curse on Gehazi (v. 20–27)

Oriental etiquette demanded apparent reluctance in accepting a gift. Naaman took for granted that Elisha was carrying the matter rather further than usual, and that Gehazi's story (22) was merely a polite invention. The evil of Gehazi was twofold; it was dishonesty, and it removed from Naaman's heart the picture of a God and His prophet who gave healing as an act of pure grace. So with Naaman's money he received also his leprosy.

g. The miracle of the axe (vi. 1–7)

This incident probably concerned the community of sons of the prophets at Jericho (ii. 5). No point would be served in enumerating various doubtful efforts to explain the miracle.

h. The Syrians trapped (vi. 8–23)

The relationship of Elisha to the king of Israel and the help given him (cf. iii. 14) suggest that we have a scene from the reign of Jehoahaz or Jehoash. The picture is one of guerilla bands and skirmishes (8–10). It is very true to human nature that the Syrian king should not realize that Elisha would be as aware of the plan to seize him as of his other plans. In verse 15 there are good reasons for thinking that with a small change of text (*shḥrth* for *mshrth*) we should render 'And at dawn the man of God rose early and went out' (I.C.C., Cent. Bible, Moff.); he went to meet the enemy he knew was there. *He led them to Samaria* (19); about nine and a half miles. *My father* (21); not language we should expect from Jehoram. *Wouldest thou smite those whom thou hast taken captive with thy sword and with thy bow?* (22). The answer being 'no', still less was he justified in killing these. *The bands of Syria came no more into the land of Israel* (23). This has no connection with verse 24. In any case, as often, 'no more' means for as long as the situation created endured, which was for quite a time.

i. The divine deliverance of Samaria (vi. 24— vii. 20)

It came to pass after this (24) refers to the original not the present setting of the story and so is no contradiction of verse 23. See note on 1 Ki. xxi. 1. *Ben-hadad* (24) was assassinated about 644 B.C. (viii. 15), so this incident probably falls in the reign of Jehoram (852–841 B.C.). The possibility cannot be excluded that Ben-hadad the son of Hazael (xiii. 3) is meant, but it does not seem to suit the setting. *An ass's head* (25). The ass was an unclean animal usually debarred from being eaten. *The fourth part of a cab* (25); about a pint. *Dove's dung* (25); possibly to be taken literally, but more likely some weed of which this was the popular name. The better rendering of verses 26, 27 is probably 'Save! my lord, O king. And he said, Not so! Jehovah save thee!' (I.C.C.). The king was humbling himself by wearing *sackcloth* (30); but since it had no effect, he blamed Elisha both for bringing the evil and for causing it to continue (31). *This son of a murderer* (32); no reference to Ahab is intended; it means one ready to commit murder, i.e. 'this murderous creature' (Moff.). *And he said* (33); this is the king himself. In the presence of Elisha his courage evaporated, and he gave himself up to despair. *A lord* (vii. 2); RV 'captain'; lit. 'thirdling'; see 1 Ki. ix. 22n. *The kings of the Egyptians* (6). This term is never used elsewhere. It is virtually certain we should read Muzri (Heb. *muzrim*) for Egypt (*mizraim*). Muzri was Cappadocia and so a neighbour to the Hittite lands (see 1 Ki. x. 28, 29n.).

j. Continuation of the story of the Shunammite (viii. 1–6)

See also iv. 8–37. The mention of *Gehazi* (4) puts the story before v. 1–27. The king's attitude towards Gehazi suggests Jehu rather than Jehoram. There seems little reason for the family's move (1), for with its wealth it could have continued living at home. It may well be that the deeper reason may have been Elisha's wish to save the family from becoming involved in the massacres that wiped out not merely the family but also the friends of Ahab (x. 11).

k. Elisha and Hazael (viii. 7–15)

We cannot argue that this must be later than the healing of Naaman, because Elisha is known in Damascus (7). *Go, say unto him, Thou mayest certainly* (RV 'shalt surely') *recover: howbeit . . .* (10). This is the way in which Hazael is 'anointed' king over Syria (1 Ki. xix. 15); so far as the illness was concerned, Ben-hadad would have lived. *And he settled his countenance stedfastly* (RV 'stedfastly upon him') (11); 'And he fixed his gaze and stared at him' (RSV). Elisha had just been given a vision of what Hazael would do (12) which caused him to break into tears. For Syrian cruelty, cf. Am. i. 3–5.

XVIII. JEHORAM AND AHAZIAH OF JUDAH. viii. 16–29

a. Jehoram (viii. 16–24)

See also 2 Ch. xxi. 1–20, which is much fuller. *Joram* (16); an abbreviation of Jehoram (iii. 1) in order to distinguish him from the Judaean king of the same name, but note same abbreviation in verses 21, 23. *In the fifth year of Joram* (16); there is an apparent contradiction between this and viii. 25 on the one side and 1 Ki. xxii. 42, 51, 2 Ki. iii. 1 on the other. The explanation is that Jehoshaphat had been co-regent with Asa (see Chronology, p. 300), and the reigns of Ahaziah and Jehoram of Israel are reckoned from the time when he was sole king. *Jehoshaphat being then king of Judah* (16); omitted by some Heb. MSS, LXX, Syr., Arabic, Vulg. (many MSS); if genuine it means that Jehoram was for a short time co-regent. *He did evil in the sight of the Lord* (18); not so much religiously (2 Ch. xxi. 11) which is implied by *he walked in the way of the kings of Israel* (18), but rather by killing his brothers (see 2 Ch. xxi. 2–4). *The daughter of Ahab* (18); Athaliah (viii. 26). *And to his children* (19). The AV rightly follows 2 Ch. xxi. 7, so sixty Heb. MSS of Kings, RV mg., RSV. The revolt of *Edom* (20) almost proved fatal to Jehoram. He was ambushed at *Zair* (21), south of the Dead Sea; he and the chariots were able to cut their way out, but the infantry was left to get home as it might. *Unto this day* (22); there was a control of Elath and the route to it from the time of Amaziah (xiv. 7, 22) to Ahaz (xvi. 6), but it probably did not involve the complete conquest of Edom. *Libnah* (22) in the Shephelah (Jos. x. 29); it probably had a strong Philistine admixture, and joined the Philistines. It is not clear whether it is Judaean or Philistine in xix. 8. For the closing disasters of the reign see 2 Ch. xxi. 12–20.

b. Ahaziah (viii. 25–29)

Cf. 2 Ch. xxii. 1–6. The account of Ahaziah's death is deferred to ix. 27–29. *Athaliah, the daughter of Omri* (26); i.e. grand-daughter (viii. 18). *In* (RV 'at') *Ramoth-gilead* (28); it is not stated whether they were defending the city or successfully attacking it (cf. ix. 1, 14, also 1 Ki. xxii. 3). *Ramah* (29); a variant spelling for Ramoth. *Ahaziah . . . went down* (29); i.e. from Jerusalem.

XIX. JEHU OF ISRAEL. ix. 1—x. 36

a. The anointing of Jehu (ix. 1–13)

Children of the prophets (1); RV 'sons of the prophets', see ii. 3n. *Box of oil* (1); 'flask of oil' (RSV). *Carry him* (2); 'lead him' (RSV). *So the young man* (4; Heb. *na'ar*; see 1 Ki. xiv. 3n.). Elisha chose one of the junior members of the prophetic guild as being least conspicuous; his haste (3) had the same intention. He evidently found the army leaders at a council of war in the citadel courtyard (5). For verses 7–10 cf. 1 Ki. xiv. 10, 11n. *Is all well?* (11); lit. 'peace?' (Heb. *shalom*); see note on verse 17. *This mad fellow* (11). Quite likely the young man had deliberately acted mad to prevent any guessing his real purpose. The question put Jehu in a quandary, for he did not know how his fellow-officers would take it. The meaning of his evasive answer is well represented by Moff. 'Oh you know how a fellow like that talks!' The anointing oil on his head will have given them a clue, and probably the tone of their reply, *It is false; tell us now* (12), encouraged him to tell the truth. *On the top of the stairs* (13). We know nothing of the detailed archaeology of Ramoth-gilead; the Hebrew uses a technical term and RV mg. and RSV may be correct in rendering 'on the bare steps'.

b. The killing of the kings (ix. 14–29)

Cf. 2 Ch. xxii. 7–9. *So Jehu rode in a chariot* (16); obviously accompanied (cf. verse 17 'I see a company'). *Is it peace?* (17). The Heb. *shalom* means fundamentally completeness; hence in a context like this render 'Is all well?' (Moff.), and so in verse 22. Jehu would not have abandoned his post in case of war. *For he driveth furiously* (20); 'he drives like a madman' (Moff.). The same root is used as in 'this mad fellow' (11). *And Joram said, Make ready* (21). He thought that the information must be so important that he must learn it at the first possible moment. *Whoredoms . . . witchcrafts* (22); i.e. idolatries. Jehu had evidently met the kings just where Naboth's vineyard had been (25).

Ahaziah (27). Elisha had probably deliberately chosen the right moment to involve him as well. *Fled by the way of the garden house* (27). The Hebrew should not be translated, but transliterated, 'in the direction of Beth-haggan' (RSV), i.e. En-gannim (Jos. xix. 21), the modern Jenin. Jehu left him to his men who caught him up near *Ibleam* (27), a little to the south of En-gannim, and left him mortally wounded. The road through the hills was too rough for a wounded man, so they turned north-west for *Megiddo* (27), where he died. Verse 29 is probably inserted to mean 'Here ends the story of Ahaziah'. The apparent story of his death in 2 Ch. xxii. 9 (q.v.), if correctly transmitted, is irreconcilable with the story in Kings.

c. The death of Jezebel (ix. 30–37)

Jezebel prepared for her death like a queen. *She painted her face* (30); i.e. as has been the custom in the Near East since time immemorial she blackened the edges of her eyelids, and perhaps her eyebrows, with a black paste (cf. Ezk. xxiii. 40; Je. iv. 30, RV). Her contemptuous greeting (31) is well rendered by Moff. 'How are you, you Zimri, murderer of your master?' *Throw her down* (33); such a window would be on the first floor.

d. The massacre of Ahab's family and friends (x. 1–11)

Seventy sons (1); i.e. male descendants; some, not all, were minors. *Letters* (1); i.e. 'a letter' (Moff.); cf. 1 Ki. xxi. 8n. *Jezreel* (1); follow the LXX 'of the city and to . . .' (Heb. *hyrw'l* for *yzr' 'l*); so RSV. *Them that brought up* (1); RSV 'the guardians of'. Jehu by his action gave the holders of office the opportunity of coming to terms, and effectively hindered any action by members of the royal family. *Ye be righteous* (9) is probably not meant as sarcasm; for the answer to *who slew all these?* is probably 'God'. Jehu's massacre (11) went far beyond anything

commanded by the prophets and is later condemned (Ho. i. 4); this is particularly true of the slaughter of the Baal worshippers (x. 25).

e. The massacre of Ahaziah's kindred (x. 12–14)

Cf. 2 Ch. xxii. 8. *At the shearing house* (12); RV inserts 'of the shepherds'; probably a proper name, 'at Beth-eked of the Shepherds' (RSV). *And the children of the queen* (13); 'of the queen mother' (RSV); i.e. of Jezebel.

f. The massacre of the Baal worshippers (x. 15–28)

No excuse can be found for Jehu. It is true that theoretically the lives of the Baal worshippers were forfeit (Dt. xiii. 12–18), but we cannot overlook the pressure that had been exercised for some thirty years in favour of Baal. In any case the method chosen was bound to involve many without strong views who wanted to stand well with the new régime. Israel never recovered from the blood bath.

Jehonadab the son of Rechab (15). The Rechabites were originally a Kenite clan incorporated into Judah (1 Ch. ii. 55n.). From Je. xxxv. 6 the natural inference is that Jehonadab (Jonadab is a shortened form), a descendant of Rechab, in his zeal for Jehovah, turned the Rechabites and those who would join them into an extremist group, opposed to everything linked with the fertility of the ground, for this was the main interest both of Canaanite religion and of those who copied it in their worship of Jehovah (see Appendix I). We do not know what brought him into Israel at this time. *Is thine heart right*, etc. (15). The I.C.C. gives the sense as 'Do we see straight together and alike?' When Jehonadab says *It is*, Jehu answers, *If it be, give me thine hand* (15). *Servants* (19); 'worshippers' (RV). The *house of Baal* (21); they were in the temple court. *Vestry* (22); 'wardrobe' (RSV). *The city of the house of Baal* (25); we no longer know what is meant; the conjecture in RSV and Moff. is doubtful. *Images* (26) . . . *image* (27); 'pillars . . . pillar' (RV); Heb. *maẓẓebhah*, see 1 Ki. xiv. 23n. Since a *maẓẓebhah* could not be burnt, it is probable that there is a textual error in verse 26.

g. Jehu's religious policy (x. 29–31)

Jehu saw no reason for leaving the traditional religion of the northern kingdom. The commendation of verse 30 must not be looked on as a contradiction to the condemnation in Ho. i. 4 of Jehu's large-scale massacres.

h. Summary of Jehu's reign (x. 32–36)

Jehu lost Transjordan (33) for Israel; it was Syrian till the time of Jeroboam II (xiv. 25, 28.) Jehu's submission to Shalmaneser III is not mentioned (see Appendix III).

XX. ATHALIAH OF JUDAH. xi. 1–20

Cf. 2 Ch. xxii. 10—xxiii. 21, where the rôle of the Levites in the plot against Athaliah is stressed.

a. Athaliah as queen (xi. 1–3)

Cf. 2 Ch. xxii. 10–12. In the story Athaliah's desperate action is not motivated; it is not clear what she hoped finally to accomplish. Her overlooking of *Joash* (2)—in chapter xii the fuller form Jehoash is used—is easily explained by the conditions of an oriental harem. His mother may have been a minor wife. *Jehosheba* ('Jehoshabeath' in 2 Chronicles) was the wife of *Jehoiada* (4) the priest; see 2 Ch. xxii. 11.

b. The plot against Athaliah (xi. 4–16)

Cf. 2 Ch. xxiii. 1–15. The plot was more complex and widespread than we gather at first sight. It started, as Chronicles stresses, in Levitical circles, then *the people of the land* (14 *et al.*; see additional note at end of chapter) were drawn in. Finally, when all was ready, Jehoiada won over 'the captains of the Carites and of the guards' (4, RSV). The Carites were foreign mercenaries serving as the royal bodyguard (see Jdg. iii. 3n.). The comment *the city was in quiet* (20) probably means that the influential men of Jerusalem acquiesced; they were in favour of Athaliah's policy, but were overawed by a popular revolt and reformation. The nonmention of the Levitical guards by Kings as against Chronicles is probably because the writer considered them ornamental rather than useful. It was the winning over of the royal guard that was decisive.

We have too little knowledge of the topography of Solomon's temple and palace and of the military arrangements to reconstruct Jehoiada's exact plan. It is plain that it was planned for a time when he could have a double force of Levites to hand (2 Ch. xxiii. 8) and similarly 'the two companies' (7, RV) of the guard that should have gone off duty remained as a guard to the temple. *Within the ranges* (8); 'whosoever approaches the ranks' (RSV). *King David's spears and shields* (10); these were doubtless mainly ornamental and were given to the Levites (2 Ch. xxiii. 9); the guard had their own arms. This mention shows that the editor of Kings had the Levites in his original authority, but eliminated them for the reason given above. *The testimony* (12); cf. Dt. xvii. 18–20; 1 Sa. x. 25. Wellhausen's emendation, adopted by Moff., 'the royal bracelets', has nothing to commend it. *Athaliah . . . came to the people* (13), an action as brave as Jezebel's when facing Jehu (ix. 30, 31). *By a pillar* (14); better, as in RV, 'the pillar', cf. xxiii. 3. *Without the ranges* (15); better, as in RV, 'between the ranks'.

c. The covenant (xi. 17–20)

Cf. 2 Ch. xxiii. 16–21. There was evidently a strong popular revulsion against the policy carried out by Jehoram, Ahaziah and Athaliah. This led to both a religious and a political covenant (17). Note that the destruction of *the house of Baal* (18) was a popular demonstration. *Mattan* (18) is a 'peculiarly Phoenician' name (I.C.C.).

d. Additional note: the people of the land

The people of the land (Heb. *'am ha-'areẓ*) is a term that shifted its meaning from time to time (cf. Hg. ii. 4; Ezr. iv. 4). In at least some Rabbinic writings it meant the simple, unlearned countryman uninterested in the law. Under the monarchy it meant 'the free, property-owning, full citizens of Judah' (Alt, *Studies in Deuteronomy*, p. 63). Their mention in 2 Ki. xi, xxi. 24, xxiii. 30 suggests not merely that they had considerable importance (cf. also 2 Ki. xxv. 19) but that they opposed a tendency both in religion and politics represented by court circles in Jerusalem (cf. also 2 Ki. xxiii. 35n.). Micah, Isaiah and Zephaniah seem on the whole to be more concerned with the sins of Jerusalem than with Judah generally, and a connection between the two facts may well exist. Special attention should be paid as well to the notes on xii. 20, 21 and xiv. 19–21.

XXI. JEHOASH OF JUDAH. xi. 21—xii. 21

a. The repair of the temple (xi. 21—xii. 16)

Cf. 2 Ch. xxiv. 1–14 (no important differences). *Jehoash* (21). In chapters xi and xii. 19–21, also in Chronicles, the shortened form Joash is used. *All his days wherein Jehoiada the priest instructed him* (xii. 2). The Hebrew would bear the translation 'because Jehoiada . . . instructed him' (RSV and similarly Moff.). It is claimed that Kings does not know of any later infidelity on Joash's part in contrast to Chronicles. But xii. 17, 18 and xii. 20, 21 tacitly assume something of the sort, so AV and RV should be retained. The addition in 2 Ch. xxiv. 3 that 'Jehoiada took for him two wives' suggests that the luxury of the court was considerably curbed. *The high places* (3); see 1 Ki. xv. 14n.

Kings tells us that Joash commanded the use of the temple dues and freewill offerings (4) for the repairs. The force of the Hebrew is disputed; perhaps as RSV, 'the money for which each man is assessed—the money from the assessment of persons—and the money which a man's heart prompts him to bring . . .' *Of his acquaintance* (5); the meaning of the word is doubtful; it is found with a cultic meaning in the Ras Shamra tablets; possibly here 'a class of temple-tellers' (I.C.C.). 2 Ch. xxiv. 5 speaks of a collection to be made through the country. There is no contradiction. When the order was given we do not know, but nothing had been done by *the three and twentieth year* of his reign (6). Chronicles is mild in saying 'the Levites hastened it not'. Owing to their failure Joash took over the responsibility for repairs and impounded the temple revenues (7, 8). In 2 Ch. xxiv. 6, 8 the chief source of revenue was 'the collection' (RV 'tax') that Moses laid upon Israel (see Ex. xxx. 14–16, xxxviii. 25, 26), i.e. the half-shekel (cf. Mt. xvii. 24). *When they saw* (10); better 'whenever they saw' (RSV); cf. 2 Ch. xxiv. 11. There is a contradiction between *and set it beside the altar* (9) and 'set it without at the gate'

(2 Ch. xxiv. 8). There is, however, general agreement that the text in Kings is doubtful here, while the statement in Chronicles is far more probable. There is another apparent contradiction between 2 Ki. xii. 13 and 2 Ch. xxiv. 14; the former means that during the work the money collected was applied exclusively to the repairs; the latter that when the repairs were finished there was money to spare for other purposes.

b. Summary of Jehoash's reign (xii. 17–21)

Cf. with important variants, 2 Ch. xxiv. 23–27. For *Hazael*'s (17) victories see x. 32–34, xiii. 3, 7. By his capture of *Gath* (17), which now lost its importance, he was extending his grip on the trade route to Egypt. It implies that he had cut off Galilee from the rest of Israel. Chronicles stresses the smallness of his army, due to the distance from his base, but it will have been his crack corps. It also makes explicit, what is implicit in verse 18, that Jerusalem was at his mercy. We see from Chronicles, too, that Joash was left with 'great diseases', probably seriously wounded. The reason for the *conspiracy* (20) is not clearly given—2 Ch. xxiv. 25 could refer to the divine purpose behind it—and the doubt about the identity of the conspirators (cf. verse 21 with verse 26 in Chronicles) makes judgment hazardous. It is, however, likely that since Joash left the policy of those who put him on the throne (see 2 Ch. xxiv. 17, 18n.), it was they that engineered his assassination. If the names are correct in Chronicles, they may have been the instruments rather than the chief conspirators.

XXII. JEHOAHAZ AND JEHOASH OF ISRAEL. xiii. 1–25

a. Jehoahaz of Israel (xiii. 1–9)

How completely Israel lay at the mercy of Hazael is suggested by xii. 17, which implies that Galilee had been lost to Jehoahaz. With the *ten chariots* (7) may be compared the two thousand which Shalmaneser III ascribes to Ahab in his account of the battle of Qarqar (see Appendix III). *And the Lord gave Israel a saviour* (5); either the Assyrian kings who about this time began to weaken Syria (see Appendix III) or Jeroboam II (xiv. 27). It is best to make the parenthesis include verse 4 instead of starting with verse 5. *There remained the grove* (6); 'the Asherah' (see 1 Ki. xiv. 23n. and Appendix I). The Jehovah worship left after Jehu had dealt with Baal was thoroughly naturalistic and Canaanized.

b. Jehoash of Israel (xiii. 10–13)

As in the case of Jehoash of Judah, *Jehoash* (10) and *Joash* (13, 14) are used interchangeably. His victories over Syria are mentioned later in the chapter (22–25).

c. Elisha's death (xiii. 14–21)

The chariot of Israel (14); a collective; render 'the chariots of Israel' (cf. ii. 12n.). Jehoash was not thinking only of the spiritual value of Elisha, most of whose teaching he will have ignored (11); see vi. 8–23. *My father* (14); cf. vi. 21. There seems to be an inversion of order, for verse 17 would be expected before verse 15; but since Jehoash was probably attended by an officer, no difficulty need be found. For the whole incident see note on 1 Ki. xxii. 11. *The man of God was wroth with him* (19). Jehoash knew very well what was being symbolized. He was probably unwilling to destroy Syria for the same reason as Ahab, i.e. fear of Assyria; see note on 1 Ki. xx. 31. *Aphek* (17); see 1 Ki. xx. 26n. *And the bands of the Moabites* (20); render 'used to invade the land in the spring of the year' (RSV); this was a frequent action. The time is not specified, but the period of anarchy between the death of Jeroboam II and the fall of Samaria is indicated. The purpose of the miracle was to show that even at the eleventh hour the power of the God of Elisha was available.

d. Victories over Syria (xiii. 22–25)

But Hazael . . . oppressed (22); render 'now Hazael . . . had oppressed'. *Ben-hadad* (24) had been weakened first by the successful resistance of Zakar of Hamath and then by the invasion of Adad-nirari III. Israel was probably tributary to Assyria at this time (see Appendix III).

XXIII. AMAZIAH OF JUDAH. xiv. 1–22

a. Amaziah's accession (xiv. 1–6)

Cf. 2 Ch. xxv. 1–4 (virtually identical). We here begin a period of very involved chronology in which absolute certainty will probably never be reached. The figures given by van der Meer (see p. 300), though differing considerably from most authorities, have the advantage of doing justice to the main statements of Scripture. The rather cryptic remarks in verse 3, *not like David his father . . . according to all things as Joash . . .*, suggest a knowledge of the facts mentioned in 2 Ch. xxiv. 15–22, xxv. 14, which, however, the author does not see fit to relate. *The high places* (4); see 1 Ki. xv. 14n. Verse 6, with its reference to Dt. xxiv. 16, is both a clear affirmation of the existence of Deuteronomy in the time of Amaziah, and a clear hint that this particular law had tended to be ignored.

b. The victory over Edom (xiv. 7)

See 2 Ch. xxv. 5–13 and cf. note on viii. 22.

c. Amaziah's encounter with Jehoash (xiv. 8–16)

Come, let us look one another in the face (8); cf. 1 Ki. xxii. 4n.; Amaziah challenged Jehoash practically as a sporting action. Jehoash, acutely conscious of the danger of Assyria, tried to avoid the challenge by a contemptuous parabolic answer (9). *Beth-shemesh* (11), to the west of Jerusalem in the Valley of Sorek. We get the impression that even the battle-field was carefully chosen. The result was disastrous for Amaziah (13, 14). Judah doubtless became tributary to Israel, and it was probably only a certain holy awe caused by the unbroken dynasty of David compared with the short-lived dynasties of Israel that prevented Jehoash from trying to amalgamate the kingdoms. Though it is not stated, Amaziah seems to have been so discredited that Azariah (Uzziah) became co-regent and perhaps rival ruler (see introductory note to chapter xv and xiv. 21n.). If so, Amaziah's sole rule will have lasted about seven years. This section probably originally belonged to the records of Israel, and so a summary note about *Jehoash* (15, 16) has remained attached to it (cf. xiii. 12, 13).

d. Summary of Amaziah's reign (xiv. 17–22)

Cf. 2 Ch. xxv. 25—xxvi. 2 (virtually identical). The unusual synchronistic statement in verse 17 may be due to Amaziah's equivocal position. If the argument based on chronology is sound (see above on verses 13, 14) then verse 21 refers to the action of *the people of Judah* after Amaziah's defeat; they are probably the same as 'the people of the land' (see xi. 14n. and additional note to chapter xi). If so, we probably have the following development. The people of the land made Jehoash king (xi. 14) against the wishes of court circles (xi. 20); they brought about his assassination (xii. 20, 21) when he abandoned their policy. When Amaziah went the same way as Jehoash (2 Ch. xxv. 14), they took advantage of his defeat virtually to depose him (21). When he tried increasingly to assert himself they had him assassinated (19, 20). It is to be noted that no mention is made of the execution of the conspirators. The mention of the conspiracy in 2 Ch. xxv. 27 is entirely consistent with this. The writer has joined the two conspiracies (as chronological grounds will show) to depose and to kill. *He built Elath* (22). 'He' refers to Amaziah, not Azariah. It is a detached quotation from the royal chronicles, possibly misplaced by scribal accident. See notes on viii. 22 and 2 Ch. xxv. 11, 12.

XXIV. JEROBOAM II OF ISRAEL. xiv. 23–29

Israel's Indian summer was made religiously important by the work of Amos and Hosea. The Assyrians had broken the power of Syria, but now several weak kings were probably happy to ally themselves with Jeroboam. As a result he was not only able to reconquer the whole of traditional Israelite territory *from the entering of Hamath* (25) (see 1 Ki. viii. 65n.), i.e. Galilee (cf. xii. 17n.), *unto the sea of the plain*, i.e. Transjordan, but also made *Damascus* and *Hamath* (28) tributary. *Which belonged to Judah* (28); this is taken from Israelite annals which looked on David and Solomon as Judaean kings. *Jonah, the son of Amittai* (25), the prophet whose book we have. It is not said whether he lived in or before the reign of Jeroboam. God gave Israel a last chance of repentance (26, 27), seeing

whether prosperity would accomplish what affliction had not. As Amos and Hosea show us, it only created social corruption.

XXV. AZARIAH (UZZIAH) OF JUDAH. xv. 1–7

See 2 Ch. xxvi. 3–23 where a much fuller account is given. It would almost seem that the editor of Kings would by his brevity stress that final failure can rob a valuable life of all its value.

Azariah (1); so normally in Kings and 1 Ch. iii. 12; Uzziah in verses 13, 30, 32, 34, 2 Chronicles and in Amos, Hosea and Isaiah. Evidently Azariah is his official name. If the note on xiv. 17–22 is correct, he may have changed his name when he became sole king. Azariah means Jehovah is help; Uzziah Jehovah is might. *The high places* (4); see 1 Ki. xv. 14n. For verses 5–7 see 2 Ch. xxvi. 16–23.

XXVI. CHAOS IN ISRAEL. xv. 8–31

The internal corruption denounced by Amos and Hosea would in itself have sufficed to destroy Israel, but in 744 B.C. the power of Assyria suddenly revived under Tiglath-pileser III, one of the greatest of her kings (see Appendix III), and it was only a matter of a few years until Assyrian attack and intrigue ended the history of the northern kingdom. There is a major chronological problem in this period. The known dates for the fall of Samaria and Menahem's payment of tribute to Tiglath-pileser III make it seemingly impossible to give Pekah the twenty years ascribed to him (xv. 27). Most modern scholars reduce his reign to two to five years, but there is much to be said for van der Meer's suggestion, adopted in our chronological table (p. 300), that he had been the power behind Menahem and Pekahiah, and so when he came to the throne counted his reign as beginning with Menahem's accession, as though he had been co-regent.

a. Zachariah (xv. 8–12)

His name should be written Zechariah (RV). *Smote him before the people* (10); the Hebrew cannot really bear this meaning; translate 'in Ibleam' (Lucian, RSV, Moff., I.C.C., etc.— *bybl'm* for *qbl'm*).

b. Shallum (xv. 13–16)

Menahem was probably military governor of *Tirzah* (14; cf. 1 Ki. xiv. 17). He marched against Shallum, and such was the barbarity of the age that when *Tiphsah* (not the town on the Euphrates (1 Ki. iv. 24); possibly Tappuah as in LXX, RSV, Moff., etc.) would not open its gates to him, he massacred its inhabitants with the utmost cruelty. Against such a man Shallum evidently put up only a feeble resistance.

c. Menahem (xv. 17–22)

Pul the king of Assyria (19). Pul or Pulu, an Assyrian general, usurped the throne on the death of Ashurnirari V. He adopted the name of Tiglath-pileser (III), see verse 29, but that his name of Pul remained in common use is shown by the fact that he used it as king of Babylon (729 B.C.). Cf. 1 Ch. v. 26, where one might get the impression that two separate men were intended. *To confirm the kingdom in his hand* (19). Menahem had probably been involved in an anti-Assyrian confederation (see Appendix III); so he had not merely to pay tribute, but a fine as well. *Menahem exacted the money . . . of all the mighty men of wealth* (20); neither the Hebrew nor the context justifies the rendering. Thirty shekels of silver was the accepted value of a slave (Ex. xxi. 32), and in the time of Cambyses we find an ass priced at fifty shekels. So render 'Menahem assessed all the wealthy men of Israel' (Moff.). The poll-tax is mentioned, not as an act of despotism, but as an indication of the state of the country. There were about 60,000 who could be classed as wealthy (I.C.C.).

d. Pekahiah (xv. 23–26)

Pekah . . . a captain of his (25); 'his captain' (RV); for 'captain' see 1 Ki. ix. 22n. The definite article suggests more than merely high court position, and if the chronological note at the head of this section is correct, Pekah was the real power in the kingdom. The sequel strongly suggests that his action was intended as anti-Assyrian. *With Argob and Arieh* (25); the former is a place name (1 Ki. iv. 13), and so RSV, Moff., I.C.C., etc., perhaps rightly, consider that they have been transferred by scribal error from verse 29.

e. Pekah (xv. 27–31)

Pekah's reign was important for its repercussions in Judah (xvi. 5n.; 2 Ch. xxviii. 5–15; Is. vii. 1, 2). He tried to build up an anti-Assyrian confederacy, but quickly collapsed before Tiglath-pileser III. As a result Israel lost all Transjordan and Galilee (29). *And carried them captive to Assyria* (29); see Appendix III and section XXVIII d below. As Tiglath-pileser claims to have deposed Pekah, *Hoshea* (30) was evidently acting with Assyrian support.

XXVII. JOTHAM AND AHAZ OF JUDAH. xv. 32—xvi. 20

a. Jotham (xv. 32–38)

See 2 Ch. xxvii. 1–9. *He reigned sixteen years in Jerusalem* (33); for the major part of this time he was co-regent with his father (xv. 5). *He did that which was right in the sight of the Lord* (34); 2 Ch. xxvii. 2 adds cogently 'and the people did yet corruptly', as is shown by Is. ii–v, which date predominantly from this reign. *The high places* (35); see 1 Ki. xv. 14n. *The higher gate* (35); probably the gate of Je. xx. 2. On the basis of Is. vii. 1, 2 it is clear that the invasion of *Rezin* and *Pekah* (37) must have begun only just before the death of the king.

b. Ahaz' apostasy (xvi. 1–4)

Cf. 2 Ch. xxviii. 1–4. *Ahaz* (1); from an Assyrian inscription we know his name was Jehoahaz. The abbreviation was in common use, for it is found on the seal ring of one of his courtiers, but it is probable that the consistent omission of the first part of his name (Jehovah) is deliberate on the part of the biblical writers to indicate their abhorrence of his apostasy. Ahaz reverted (3) to the religious policy of Jehoram (viii. 18), Ahaziah (viii. 27) and Joash (2 Ch. xxiv. 18). *He made his son to pass through the fire* (3); 'he even burned his son as an offering' (RSV). Cf. iii. 27, xxi. 6, xxiii. 10. From Je. vii. 31; Mi. vi. 7 it is clear that these sacrifices were offered to Jehovah (see Appendix I). It was probably made in the crisis of the siege (5).

c. The Syro-Ephraimite attack (xvi. 5, 6)

See 2 Ch. xxviii. 5–19; Is. vii. 1, 2. As we learn from Is. ii–v Judah, under Uzziah and Jotham, in spite of seeming prosperity, was as inwardly rotten as Israel had been under Jeroboam II. So in the moment of crisis Judah collapsed, and its smaller neighbours eagerly availed themselves of their opportunity (2 Ch. xxviii. 18). The motive of Rezin and Pekah was seemingly to force Judah into an anti-Assyrian confederacy. One result of the war for Judah was the final loss of *Elath* (6). Since Syrian power never reached down to the Red Sea, and indeed Syria ceased to exist nationally a few years later, we must assume the frequent confusion of *'rm* and *'dm* (cf. iii. 26n.; 2 Ch. xx. 2n.) and render as RSV 'At that time the king of Edom recovered Elath for Edom . . . and the Edomites came to Elath, where they dwell to this day'.

d. The appeal to Assyria and its results (xvi. 7–16)

Cf. 2 Ch. xxviii. 20–25. For the implications of Ahaz' appeal to Tiglath-pileser see Appendix II; see also Isaiah's appeal (Is. vii. 3—viii. 4). *Kir* (9); see Am. ix. 7, i. 5. *King Ahaz went to Damascus to meet Tiglath-pileser* (10) after the downfall of Syria. The price of Assyrian help was that Judah became its vassal state; with the exception of two or three rebellions it remained so until the time of Josiah (q.v.). *Ahaz . . . saw an* (RV 'the') *altar that was at Damascus* (10). This was an Assyrian, not a Syrian altar (2 Ch. xxviii. 23 does not refer to this). For the reasons explained in Appendix II Ahaz was doing honour to the gods of Assyria. In addition, as Olmstead says, 'As in all newly organized provinces, the cult of Ashur and the king had been established in Damascus, and the vassal rulers were ordered to follow this example' (*History of Palestine and Syria*, p. 452).

Since there is no suggestion of any alterations in ritual in verses 12–16, which would be involved in the worship of Assyrian gods, it seems clear that the sacrifices were still made officially to Jehovah, who was still God of Judah, but the power of the Assyrian gods was recognized by the use of an Assyrian altar. *And offered thereon* (12). We must understand this to mean that he was claiming to be 'divine king' and exercising priestly functions (see 1 Ki. xii. 27–33n.). *The brasen altar shall be for me to inquire by* (15); Ahaz was introducing the Babylonian omen-sacrifices (cf. Ezk. xxi. 21).

e. Summary of Ahaz' reign (xvi. 17–20)

Cf. 2 Ch. xxviii. 24, 26, 27. The cutting off of *the borders of the bases* (17), to which 2 Ch. xxviii. 24 adds the cutting in pieces of some of the vessels of the house of God, was doubtless for the sake of paying the tribute to Assyria. We can no longer understand the building references in verse 18.

XXVIII. THE END OF THE NORTHERN KINGDOM. xvii. 1–41

a. Hoshea, the last king of Israel (xvii. 1–6)

Although Hoshea had come to the throne with the help of Assyria (xv. 30n.) and began to reverse the religious policy of Israel when it was too late (*but not as the kings of Israel that were before him*, 2), yet he listened to the blandishments of Egypt (4; see Appendix III). *So*; better with the same Hebrew consonants 'Sewe'. The result was that his submission (3) was not accepted and he was *bound . . . in prison* (4). Samaria was left to fight on without its king. According as we attribute the capture of Samaria to Shalmaneser V or Sargon, his successor, Samaria fell in 723 or 722 B.C. The former seems more likely. The deportation was Sargon's work. *The king of Assyria . . . carried Israel away* (6). For the policy of deportation see Appendix III and section **d** below. Sargon's own account is: 'At the beginning of my royal rule . . . the town of the Samarians I besieged, conquered . . . I led away as prisoners 27,290 inhabitants of it (and) equipped from among them (soldiers to man) fifty chariots for my royal corps. . . . The town I rebuilt better than (it was) before and settled therein peoples from countries which I myself had conquered' (Pritchard, *Ancient Near Eastern Texts*, p. 284b). It should be clear in the light of xv. 20 that nothing like all the inhabitants were removed; see section **d** below on the Samaritans. The people deported were settled either in Mesopotamia, east of Haran, or in western Media, conquered by Sargon.

b. Review of the history of the northern kingdom (xvii. 7–23)

For the general religious picture drawn see Appendix I. *Images and groves* (10); 'pillars and Asherim' (RV); see 1 Ki. xiv. 23n. *A grove* (16); 'an Asherah' (RV). *Worshipped all the host of heaven* (16); the Assyrian planet and star worship, which was already entering in the time of Amos (Am. v. 26), but which did not seriously menace Judah till the reign of Manasseh (xxi. 3). *To pass through the fire* (17); see xvi. 3n.

c. The foreign settlers in Samaria (xvii. 24–41)

For the actual settlers see section **d** below. As in the case of the ark (1 Sa. v, vi) it was one matter for God to give up His people, another to let Himself be despised (25) in consequence. A similar plague of lions is reported from Babylonia less than a century later. The text of verse 27 is uncertain. With Lucian we should read 'whom I brought from thence'. *Let them go* should be singular (Syr., Vulg., RSV). The action of the colonists (29–33) was entirely consistent with the ideas of the time (see Appendix I). *Succoth-benoth* (30); probably Marduk and his wife Zer-banit (I.C.C.); *Nergal* (30), the god of the underworld; *Ashima* (30) and *Tartak* (31), Syrian goddesses; *Nibhaz* (31); the altar deified (I.C.C.). *Of the lowest of them* (32); RV 'from among themselves' (cf. 1 Ki. xii. 31n.). Verse 34a is continued by verse 41. *Unto this day* (34, 41); i.e. either till the time of Josiah when Kings was written, or possibly till the exilic date when it received its final revision. By the date of the return the position seems to have changed; see section **d** below. Verses 34b *they fear not the Lord . . .* to 40 are not merely in contradiction to the immediately preceding, but seem to have no reference to the Samaritans at all. They seem rather to be a detached portion of verses 7–23; the present tenses of verse 34 could as well be translated as past continuatives.

d. Additional note to chapter xvii: the Samaritans

In the society of the Near East the real control of a country was in the hands of a comparatively few families. The deportation policy of the Assyrian kings was therefore to remove this 'cream' (cf. 2 Ki. xxiv. 14, xxv. 12) and replace it by similar elements from other conquered areas. By making them a thorough mixture (xvii. 24) they could rely on a lack of common policy, while they were divided from the leaderless people by language and religion. In Galilee and Transjordan the Israelite elements had already been so watered down by Syrian conquest (x. 32, 33n., xii. 17n.) that after the deportations they gradually faded out. In Samaria, however, the deportation had been relatively small (xvii. 6n.; 2 Ch. xxx. 6n.) and the new arrivals began quickly to be assimilated, the more so because they had adopted the religion of the land, and presumably with it its language. It was delayed by there being several settlements (see note on Ezr. iv. 2), but by the return from exile it seems clear that, though they still remembered their foreign origin, they had given up their idolatry, for they are not taunted with it in Ezr. iv. 1–3. By the time of the New Testament they looked on themselves as the legitimate descendants of Ephraim and were in fact regarded by the rabbis as a heretical Jewish sect. Many of the changes in the Samaritan Pentateuch compared with the standard Hebrew support the suggestion that it was a version made for them by the priest who returned to bring them the religion of Jehovah.

THE KINGDOM OF JUDAH ALONE. 2 Ki. xviii. 1—xxv. 30

XXIX. HEZEKIAH. xviii. 1—xx. 21

The reign of Hezekiah faces us with major problems of chronology and historical interpretation. xviii. 10, which we must date 723/2 B.C., and xviii. 13, which was in 701 B.C., do not agree. The explanation is Hezekiah's co-regency with his father (see Chronology, p. 300), which may have been forced on Ahaz by reason of his disastrous foreign policy. In the former case the reckoning is from the beginning of his co-regency, in the latter from the beginning of his sole reign. We must date xx. 12 either before 710 B.C. or more likely about 705 B.C., in either case earlier than xviii. 13. The reason may be connected with the use of these chapters in Is. xxxvi–xxxix. Kings may well be borrowing directly from Isaiah, not vice versa as is usually assumed. The inversion of order in Isaiah has its own reason in the structure of that book. No effort is made in Kings to trace the relationship of Hezekiah to the Assyrians and there is therefore considerable controversy and no agreement whether xix. 9 follows immediately on verse 8, or whether there is a gap of at least fifteen years. The doubt arises from the inadequacies of the Assyrian records for Sennacherib's closing years.

a. Hezekiah's reformation (xviii. 1–8)

See also 2 Ch. xxix. 1—xxxi. 21, where the reformation is described in great detail. *Twenty and five years old* (2); the rabbis had already recognized the difficulty of reconciling this with xvi. 2. In view of 2 Ch. xxviii. 1 it is easiest to assume a scribal error in Ahaz' age. *He removed the high places* (4); see 1 Ki. xv. 14n. The religious corruption which had ruined Israel had now so attacked Judah that in Hezekiah's view the only way of dealing with it was to centralize worship at Jerusalem. The removal of illegitimate sanctuaries was not sufficient. *Images . . . groves* (4); RV 'pillars . . . Asherah'; see 1 Ki. xiv. 23n. *He called it Nehushtan* (4); i.e. a piece of brass; *nehushtan* is a pun both on *nahash*, serpent, and *nehosheth*, brass. Note that the serpent had been an object of worship for a long time, perhaps ever since the time of Moses; what could have been looked on as a concession to popular superstition in times of pure religion, now after Ahaz' apostasy became a source of danger. There is no mention or commendation of this reformation in either Isaiah or Micah. The reason is that, as these prophets show, it was purely external, and even at the court there was no real trust in Jehovah, as was shown by Judah's alliance with Egypt and lack of moral reformation (Is. xxviii. 7—xxxi. 9). *He rebelled against the king of Assyria* (7). The result was disastrous, and there is no indication that Isaiah approved.

b. The fall of Samaria (xviii. 9–12)

See xvii. 3–6. This was earlier than verse 7, and indeed fell in the period of Hezekiah's co-regency.

c. The bitter fruit of rebellion (xviii. 13–16)

2 Ch. xxxii. 1–8 gives the preparations for defence, but not the outcome; only verse 13 is reproduced in the parallel Is. xxxvi. 1. The most natural interpretation of this section is that Judah collapsed completely against Sennacherib (13). Hezekiah *in extremis* begged for terms, and had to accept what Sennacherib demanded (14). Then Sennacherib treacherously (cf. Is. xxxiii. 1, 7, 8) changed his mind and demanded the surrender of the city (17ff.). We have Sennacherib's own account, from which we quote the more important portions. (For the whole text see Pritchard, *Ancient Near Eastern Texts*, p. 287f. It is quoted in whole or in part in most works on biblical archaeology.) '. . . As to Hezekiah, the Jew, he did not submit to my yoke, I laid siege to forty-six of his strong cities, walled forts and to the countless small villages in their vicinity, and conquered them. . . . I drove out (of them) 200,150 people, young and old, male and female . . . and considered (them) booty. Himself I made a prisoner in Jerusalem, his royal residence, like a bird in a cage. . . . Hezekiah himself, whom the terror-inspiring splendour of my lordship had overwhelmed and whose irregular and élite troops . . . had deserted him, did send me later, to Nineveh . . . together with thirty talents of gold, 800 talents of silver, precious stones, antimony, large cuts of red stone, couches (inlaid) with ivory, *nimedu*-chairs (inlaid) with ivory, elephant hides, ebony wood, box wood (and) all kinds of valuable treasures, his (own) daughters, concubines, male and female musicians. . . .' How vivid Is. i. 7–9 becomes in the light of this!

I have offended (14); a technical expression meaning 'I have rebelled'. *Three hundred talents of silver* (14). The difference between this and the eight hundred of Sennacherib's inscription is probably due to the difference between the heavy and the light talent, though we must also allow for the possibility of Assyrian exaggeration.

d. The Rab-shakeh's call to surrender (xviii. 17–37)

This is found with only verbal variants in Is. xxxvi. 2–22; 2 Ch. xxxii. 9–19 gives a general summary. *Tartan . . . Rabsaris . . . Rab-shakeh* (17); these are all titles, so the definite article should be used as in RSV. The Tartan was commander-in-chief (Is. xx. 1), the Rabsaris also a high military official (Je. xxxix. 3), but the Rab-shakeh, literally the chief butler, was probably one of the heads of the civil service. *The conduit of the upper pool* (17); cf. Is. vii. 3, site uncertain. *Eliakim* (cf. Is. xxii. 20) . . . *Shebna the scribe* (cf. Is. xxii. 15), *and Joah the son of Asaph the recorder* (18; cf. 1 Ki. iv. 3n.). Verse 20 is best rendered 'You think that mere words are counsel and strength for war!' (RSV). Verse 22 bears tribute to the Assyrian intelligence service. In verse 23 render 'make a wager with my master

. . .' (RSV). The desertion of Hezekiah's crack soldiers left few able to handle horses. Verse 25 is an act of supreme arrogance. It is remarkable that the Rab-shakeh knew Hebrew; he was asked to speak *in the Syrian language* (26); i.e. Aramaic, the diplomatic language of the time. *Make an agreement with me by a present* (31); rather 'make your peace with me' (RV). The Rab-shakeh had a difficult task making deportation sound attractive (31, 32).

e. God's answer (xix. 1–8)

Cf. Is. xxxvii. 1–8. *Therefore lift up thy prayer for the remnant that are left* (4); the note on section c above gives some idea of the disaster. *I will send a blast upon him* (7); render, as in RV, 'I will put a spirit in him', i.e. of fear. *So Rab-shakeh returned* (8). It is clear that Sennacherib had not enough troops to spare for an attack on Jerusalem; the Rab-shakeh had tried a piece of enormous bluff.

f. Sennacherib's letter and Hezekiah's prayer (xix. 9–19)

Cf. Is. xxxvii. 9–20. *Tirhakah king of Ethiopia* (9) belonged to the XXV dynasty of Egypt, kings of Ethiopia who had conquered Egypt. He reigned 688–670 B.C. Either he was acting as general for his uncle Shabataka, and he is called king in anticipation, or this passage deals with a later invasion; see introduction to the section on Hezekiah. Because of Sennacherib's defiance of Jehovah (10) Hezekiah felt confidence in appealing to Him (15–19). *Which dwellest between the cherubims* (15); better 'who art enthroned above the cherubim' (RSV).

g. Isaiah's prophecy (xix. 20–34)

Cf. Is. xxxvii. 21–35. Note that Isaiah, without being asked, brings God's answer. Verses 21–28, like most prophecy, are in poetry (see RSV); it is a taunt-song. *The tall cedar trees* (23) regularly used as a picture of kings (cf. Is. x. 33, 34; Ezk. xxxi. 3, etc.). *Carmel* (23); 'fruitful field' (RV); cf. 2 Ch. xxvi. 10. Render verse 24 '. . . with the soles of my feet will I dry up all the rivers of Egypt'. *Thy tumult* (28); RV 'thine arrogancy'. *I will put my hook in thy nose* (28); as Assyrian inscriptions show, a treatment often meted out by them to captives (cf. 2 Ch. xxxiii. 11n.). The meaning of verse 29 is that they would lose two harvests, but no more, through the Assyrian's presence.

h. The destruction of the Assyrian army and Sennacherib's death (xix. 35–37)

Cf. Is. xxxvii. 36–38; 2 Ch. xxxii. 21–23. There is no basis for the popular view that the Assyrian army was outside the walls of Jerusalem. The note of time *that night* (35) is lacking in 2 Ch. xxxii. 21 and Is. xxxvii. 36; actually the Hebrew idiom is more indefinite than the English equivalent. Herodotus (ii. 141) preserves an Egyptian tradition which may point to the Assyrian army being plague-smitten on the frontiers of Egypt.

Sennacherib's assassination took place in 682 B.C. *Nisroch* (37) is probably Marduk, whom, though a Babylonian god, Sennacherib specially worshipped.

i. Hezekiah's illness (xx. 1–11)

Cf. Is. xxxviii. 1–8 (somewhat shorter); 2 Ch. xxxii. 24. Reasons have already been given in the general introduction to Hezekiah's reign for dating this incident before Sennacherib's invasion, probably about 705 B.C. Hezekiah was not quite so self-satisfied as *with a perfect heart* (3) suggests; 'with a whole heart' (RSV) is juster to the Hebrew; better perhaps 'a devoted heart' (I.C.C.). The suggestion that Hezekiah's grief (3) was caused by lack of an heir (Manasseh having been born later) is an artificial importation; the real reason is given in Is. xxxviii. 10–20. The then heir presumptive will have died before his father. *I will deliver thee . . .* (6). This may support the 705 B.C. date, since the revolt that was suppressed in 701 B.C. broke out then on Sargon's death. But Sargon also refers earlier to Hezekiah as revolting, though he seems to have escaped lightly.

No reason for *the sign* (8) is given, nor can we now explain how it occurred. There is no suggestion that the day was lengthened. It was probably due to some refraction of the sun's rays.

j. Merodach-baladan's embassy (xx. 12–19)

Cf. Is. xxxix. 1–8; 2 Ch. xxxii. 31. *Berodach-baladan* (12); Is. xxxix. 1 correctly 'Merodach-baladan'; he was a thorn in the Assyrian side, and ruled in Babylon 721–710 B.C. and again in 705–704 B.C. Verse 13 shows us both that this incident happened before Hezekiah had to pay tribute, and also that Hezekiah's illness (12) was only a pretext. He wanted to draw him into an alliance. Though it is not here stated, we know that Hezekiah did rebel as part of a widespread confederacy in 705 B.C. (xviii. 7); in fact Sennacherib looked on Hezekiah as the ringleader in the west. Merodach-baladan's purpose was to link up the rebellions east and west. The showing of his treasures (13) indicates Hezekiah's self-confidence, based perhaps partly on the divine promise of defence (6) and the divine grace showed him. *Hezekiah hearkened* (Heb. *wyshm*) *unto them* (13); better, as Is. xxxix. 2, 'was glad of' (Heb. *wyshmḥ*), i.e. welcomed them. Hezekiah's answer does not show that smug selfishness that some think. He acknowledged the justice of the sentence, and realized that if it were postponed to his descendants they could avert it by their loyalty to Jehovah.

k. Summary of Hezekiah's reign (xx. 20, 21)

Cf. 2 Ch. xxxii. 25–33. *How he made a* (RV 'the') *pool and a* (RV 'the') *conduit, and brought water into the city* (20). Further information is given in 2 Ch. xxxii. 2–4, 30. 2 Ch. xxxii. 4 may well imply a far-reaching programme to make water supplies hard of access to the invaders, but the chief work was the bringing of the water of the only spring near Jerusalem, the Virgin's Spring or Gihon Spring in the Kidron valley, to the pool of Siloam, at that time within the city walls. For full details see H.D.B., IV, p. 515; I.S.B.E., p. 2791.

XXX. MANASSEH. xxi. 1–18

Cf. with some variations and additions 2 Ch. xxxiii. 1–20. Manasseh inherited vassalage to Assyria from his father, and with Egypt an Assyrian province for much of his reign (see Appendix III) there was little temptation to rebel (but see 2 Ch. xxxiii. 11). On one occasion he had to accompany Ashurbanipal in a campaign against Egypt. He drew the same religious deductions from his vassalage as did his grandfather (see Appendix II), so he not only reintroduced the Canaanized Jehovah worship (3, *the high places*; 1 Ki. iii. 2n.), but made a special 'altar' (3, singular as in LXX) for this debased worship (*Baal*, as so often, standing for the debased conception of Jehovah) and made 'a graven image of Asherah' (7, RV; see 1 Ki. xv. 13n.) as Jehovah's 'wife'. With this came in all the polytheism of nature-worship (4), and especially the worship of the Assyrian gods (5; cf. xvii. 16n.). On at least one occasion he sacrificed his son (6; see 2 Ch. xxxiii. 6), cf. xvi. 3n., and from Babylonian religion introduced all the evil of divination and mediumship. A fuller picture of the corrupt religion introduced is given in xxiii. 4, 5, 10–14 (q.v.). For the underlying implications see Appendix I. The wholeheartedness of his policy and the length of his reign created a position that could not be reversed (11–15; cf. xxiii. 26, xxiv. 3, 4; Je. xv. 4). Corruption of religion brought injustice in its train (16) though the *innocent blood* was probably primarily of those who opposed his religious policy. It is likely that the black picture of Mi. vii. 1–6 comes from this period. *His sin that he sinned* (17); his religious policy was included in the chronicles of his reign.

XXXI. AMON. xxi. 19–26

Cf. in a slightly shortened form 2 Ch. xxxiii. 21–25. We do not know the reason for the plot against Amon. Since Assyria was showing the first real signs of weakening it may have been an Egyptian intrigue. For *the people of the land* (24) see additional note to chapter xii. Evidently it was a popular overthrow of the policy of the last two reigns, and it explains the education that Josiah will have received to make his later reforms possible.

XXXII. JOSIAH. xxii. 1—xxiii. 30a

The parallel in 2 Ch. xxxiv. 1—xxxv. 27 has considerable additions and omissions. This section was probably written by the main editor of Kings, who will have been an eye-witness of what is described. Certain of his omissions are very difficult to understand. It

may be that he was too heart-broken by the collapse of Josiah's kingdom to want to describe all his success and glory. For the correct understanding of much that happened, the international background must be known; see Appendix III. The course of the reformation can be fully understood only by referring to 2 Chronicles. 2 Ch. xxxiv. 3 (q.v.) describes the first stages and is an indication that the personal and political elements in the reformation cannot be separated. 'In the eighth year of his reign' (632 B.C.) Ashurbanipal was still alive, but it was getting clear that the Assyrian lion had lost his teeth, so Josiah dissociated himself personally from the worship of the Assyrian gods. Four years later, 'in the twelfth year' of his reign, the Scythian blow had probably fallen on Assyria and Josiah cautiously began his public reformation. By his *eighteenth year* (2 Ki. xxii. 3) he was a completely independent king.

a. Introduction (xxii. 1, 2)

Cf. 2 Ch. xxxiv. 1, 2.

b. The repair of the temple (xxii. 3–7)

Cf. 2 Ch. xxxiv. 8–14. It should be obvious that the repair of the temple presupposes a large-scale removal of idolatry, which in Kings for convenience of narration is put in its entirety later; it is put in its correct place in 2 Ch. xxxiv. 4–7, but there there are included certain reforms which were certainly later than the finding of the law-book (see note *ad loc.*). Verse 4 presupposes that the collection of money had been going on for some time—*which is brought into . . .*; RSV better, 'which has been brought'—cf. the story in xii. 7–10. The repair of the temple may have been necessary not merely because of neglect, but also of damage done when Manasseh was taken off to Babylon (2 Ch. xxxiii. 11).

c. The finding of the book of the law (xxii. 8–11)

Cf. 2 Ch. xxxiv. 15–19. *I have found the book of the law* (8). The translation 'a law-book' (Moff.) could be justified only if the context made it clearly necessary; here it is to support a theory. Practical reasons make it questionable whether the whole Pentateuch is meant, but though it is not unlikely that it was, as commonly assumed, Deuteronomy, this is unprovable, and is denied by modern scholars like Hölscher, Kennett and Schofield. Indeed, the chief argument for its being Deuteronomy is the nature of Josiah's reformation. But if we follow 2 Ch. xxxiv. 3–7, we see that the effect of the book was to create urgency and thoroughness, not to inaugurate the reformation or dictate its form, for which there was precedent from the time of Hezekiah. Note that Hilkiah and Shaphan showed no surprise. Where it had been we do not know; the frequently made suggestion that it had been part of the foundation cache made by Solomon has nothing to commend it. There is no suggestion that the temple was so damaged as to reveal the foundations. *He rent his clothes* (11); the full meaning· of the apostasy under Manasseh and Amon was brought home to Josiah.

d. Huldah's message (xxii. 12–20)

Cf. 2 Ch. xxxiv. 20–28 (virtually identical). *Asahiah a servant of the king's* (12); RV 'the king's servant'; i.e. minister, probably a special adviser. The commission was not sent to Huldah in particular (13), the choice was probably Hilkiah's (14). The king had his court prophets (xxiii. 2), but Hilkiah probably did not think much of them (cf. Jeremiah's opinion of the prophets of his time, Je. ii. 8, v. 30f. vi. 13, xiv. 14, xxiii. 9–40, etc.); Zephaniah and Jeremiah need not have been in Jerusalem at the time. *In the college* (14); 'in the second quarter' (RV). Note that Huldah showed no surprise about the book and she seemed to know its contents. Huldah gave no hope, because things had gone too far (cf. xxi. 11–15n.). In the glory of Josiah's reign her words were forgotten. Her promise to Josiah (20) was only partially fulfilled; see xxiii. 29, 30n. for the probable reason.

e. The covenant (xxiii. 1–3)

Cf. 2 Ch. xxxiv. 29–32 (virtually identical). *All the words of the book of the covenant* (2); no identification can be based on this, for it suits Ex. xxiv. 1–8, Lv. xxvi. 3–45 and Dt. xxvii, xxviii equally well. *By a* (RV 'the') *pillar* (3); cf. xi. 14.

f. The reformation (xxiii. 4–20)

Cf. 2 Ch. xxxiv. 3f., 7, 33. As stated in section **b** above, for convenience in narration Kings describes the whole of the reformation after the covenant, Chronicles before. There is no point in trying to space them out over the period. The frequent mention of defiling in this section (8, 10, 13, 16) and the defiling by certain acts (4, 6, 14, 16, 20) is explained by the fact that a sanctuary or high place did not lose its sanctity by the cult objects and buildings being destroyed. It needed more drastic action to make the spot 'profane' or ordinary. Unless this action was taken the sanctuaries would be restored at the next relapse. *The priests of the second order* (4); i.e. 'priests of the second rank' (I.C.C.), but on the basis of xxv. 18 and Je. lii. 24 possibly the singular should be read (so Moff.). *For Baal, and for the grove* (4); 'for Baal and for Asherah', see xxi. 3; 7n. *The host of heaven* (4); see xxi. 5n. All this must have taken place before the covenant. Kidron (4); cf. verses 6, 12; 1 Ki. xv. 13. *And carried the ashes . . . unto Beth-el* (4); this happened later, cf. verses 15–18. *Idolatrous priests* (5); Heb. *kemarim;* always used of priests of heathen religions. *Whom the kings of Judah had ordained* (5); misleading; better 'appointed' (Moff.). *Planets* (5); 'Zodiacal signs' (I.C.C.). *The grove* (6); 'the Asherah' (RV); see 1 Ki. xv. 13n., 2 Ki. xxi. 7n. *The graves of the children of the people* (6); 'of the common people' (RV). The Kidron valley had become, as it now is, a great cemetery. *Sodomites* (7); see 1 Ki. xiv. 24n.; the masculine may cover both sexes. *Which were*

by (RV 'in') *the house of the Lord* (7); i.e. in the temple area. *Hangings for the grove* (7); 'robes for the Asherah' (I.C.C.). See verse 6.

He brought all the priests (Heb. *kohanim;* contrast *kemarim* in verse 5) *out of the cities of Judah* (8). The context indicates that these were the Levitical priests of the high places (cf. Ezk. xliv. 10–14), who in contrast to those mentioned in verse 5 had maintained a relatively pure worship. They were probably brought to Jerusalem for surveillance. It is not clear (9) whether they carried out menial duties in the temple, but they were debarred from priestly duties; they were allowed to eat priestly food (this is the probable meaning of *unleavened bread,* 9, though it is not clear why this term should be used). It is argued that theirs is the position envisaged in Dt. xviii. 6–8, and it is adduced as an additional proof for a date of Deuteronomy not long before 621 B.C. But the alleged failure to carry out Dt. xviii. 7 rather bears out the objection that the background of Deuteronomy is not that of the time of Josiah. For *Geba* (8) see 1 Ki. xv. 22n.

The high places of the gates (8); probably 'the high places of the satyrs' (Moff., Cent. Bible, I.C.C.; the same consonants in Hebrew); see 2 Ch. xi. 15n. *Topheth* (10) probably means the burning place; cf. Je. vii. 31. *To pass through the fire to Molech* (10); see xvi. 3n. Molech (Heb. *molekh*) is the Heb. *melekh* (king) with the vowels of *bosheth* (shame); cf. 1 Ch. viii. 33n. In the light of Je. vii. 31 it seems indubitable that the 'king' to whom the sacrifices were made was Jehovah (see Appendix I). *Horses . . . chariots* (LXX, I.C.C., singular) *of the sun* (11); another trace of Assyrian worship. Star worship is indicated by the position of *the altars . . . on the top of the upper chamber* (12). For *the high places . . ., which Solomon had builded* (13) see 1 Ki. xi. 1–18. It must not be supposed that they had been allowed to remain undisturbed through all the reformations; the memories attached to the sites remained and they were quickly restored (see note at the beginning of this section). Verse 14 is a general summary; *images . . . groves: 'pillars . . . Asherim'* (RV); see 1 Ki. xiv. 23n.

Verses 15–20 (cf. 2 Ch. xxxiv. 4–7) must be later than Josiah's Passover (21–23). They have as background the extension of Josiah's power over the centre of the land as far as the plain of Esdraelon. For verses 15–18 cf. 1 Ki. xiii. 1–32. *He slew all the priests of the high places* (20); the contrast with Judah (5, 8) may be due to the fact that all, or most, in the south were Levites, while those in the north had no divine sanction at all for their priestly office (1 Ki. xii. 31n.).

g. Josiah's Passover (xxiii. 21–23)

See notes on 2 Ch. xxxv. 1–19.

h. Continued reformation (xxiii. 24)

The relics of heathenism mentioned in this verse are those that would not strike the eye at first sight. A strict control was kept up. *The images* ('teraphim', RV) were largely private property (cf. Gn. xxxi. 19, RV; 1 Sa. xix. 13, RV), and we need not doubt that it is household *idols* that are being referred to.

i. Summary of Josiah's reign (xxiii. 25–28)

Cf. 2 Ch. xxxv. 26, 27. The general reason for God's refusal to lift the destruction from Jerusalem has already been mentioned; see xxi. 11–15n. There was a deeper reason. Jeremiah's virtual ignoring of Josiah's reformation and his critical remarks about it, his picture of the lying, immorality and injustice of Jerusalem after the reformation (Je. v), the immediate relapse into idolatry under Jehoiakim, its brazen-faced justification (Je. xliv. 15–19), and Jeremiah's isolation all point to the fact that, however well-meaning Josiah and his collaborators had been, the reformation was never more than superficial. Note that in Je. xxii. 15, 16 the reformation is not even hinted at.

j. Josiah's death (xxiii. 29, 30a)

See also 2 Ch. xxxv. 20–24. Josiah had expanded his kingdom at least as far as the plain of Esdraelon (see note on xxiii. 15–20) during the last years of the Assyrian empire. Nineveh fell in 612 B.C., and the last vestiges of Assyria disappeared two or three years later (see Appendix III). When Necho marched north *against the king of Assyria* (29) in 609 B.C. it was no more than a pretext to grab what he could. Apparently he marched nominally in aid of Assyria, but the Bible does not deal with transparent excuses. The mention of Carchemish (2 Ch. xxxv. 20, RV) refers not so much to Necho's later defeat there in 605 B.C. (cf. Je. xlvi. 2) as to the fact that this was the furthest limit of what Necho might hope to seize. Josiah saw the danger of his newly gained independence disappearing. So he foolishly decided to resist Necho's passage, though the latter had more important things than the hills of Judaea to think about (2 Ch. xxxv. 21). Suggestions of loyalty to Assyria or a Babylonian alliance on Josiah's part have no foundation. The fact that Josiah disguised himself (2 Ch. xxxv. 22; cf. 1 Ki. xxii. 30n.) and the mysterious command of God to Necho suggest that the campaign had been opposed by some prophet like Jeremiah, but Josiah, like Ahab, had listened to the court prophets instead. The very brevity of the story in Kings suggests that the author could not bring himself to tell the story of the death of the good king, who had allowed himself to be led astray by self-confidence. That the battle was at *Megiddo* (29) shows that Necho had no wish to invade Judah, but was following the traditional route to the north.

XXXIII. THE LAST DAYS OF JERUSALEM. xxiii. 30b—xxv. 7

a. Jehoahaz (xxiii. 30b–33)

Cf. 2 Ch. xxxvi. 1–4. For *the people of the land* (30b) see additional note to chapter xii and xxi.

24n. Their action in passing over Josiah's second son Eliakim (Jehoiakim, 34) showed a shrewd estimate of his character. His eldest son (1 Ch. iii. 15) was presumably dead. In addition they probably thought that Jehoahaz was most likely to continue his father's policy. His real name was Shallum (1 Ch. iii. 15; Je. xxii. 11); Jehoahaz was adopted as his throne name. Necho treated the whole thing as null and void; cf. *in the room of Josiah his father* (34); not because of Jehoahaz' policy or possible contacts with Babylon, but simply to show Judah who was master.

b. Jehoiakim (xxiii. 34—xxiv. 7)

Cf. 2 Ch. xxxvi. 4–8. Necho's action in changing *Eliakim*'s name to *Jehoiakim* (34) had the same motive as his deposition of Jehoahaz, viz. to show that he was absolute lord over Judah. The size of the tribute (33) compared to that paid by Israel under Menahem (xv. 19) and Hezekiah (xviii. 14) shows how greatly the troubles in the reigns of Ahaz and Hezekiah had impoverished Judah. The special mention that the tribute was enacted of *the people of the land* (35) probably indicates that it was meant to cripple them. *He did that which was evil in the sight of the Lord* (37); no detailed picture is given us, but Je. vii. 16–18, Ezk. viii. 5–18 (in the time of Zedekiah), suggest not so much organized apostasy as in the reigns of Ahaz and Manasseh, as simply the unhindered flowing back of all the more popular superstitions. The assumption, on the basis of Ezk. viii. 10, that there was an inrush of Egyptian worship is improbable. Jehoiakim was in character one of Judah's worst kings; cf. Je. xxii. 13–15, 17–19, xxvi. 20–23, xxxvi. 21–26. *So Jehoiakim slept with his fathers* (6). Jeremiah (xxii. 19) had prophesied that he would have 'the burial of an ass', i.e. no burial; 2 Ch. xxxvi. 6 says that Nebuchadnezzar 'bound him in fetters, to carry him to Babylon'. Most probably he was wounded and captured in a skirmish; dying of wounds his body was flung away. Hence Kings does not mention his funeral. Je. xxxvii. 5–7 shows that verse 7 must be understood in a relative sense.

c. Jehoiachin (xxiv. 8–16)

Cf. 2 Ch. xxxvi. 9, 10. *Jehoiachin* (8) was the throne name; his real name was Jeconiah (1 Ch. iii. 16) or more briefly Coniah (Je. xxii. 24). *His mother* (12); cf. Je. xiii. 18, xxii. 26. *All the treasures of the house of the Lord . . . and cut in pieces all the vessels of gold* (13). We see from xxv. 15 that, as so often, 'all' must not be overstressed. Dn. v. 2; Ezr. i. 7–11 show us that only those vessels that were too large for convenient transport were cut up; the others were wanted as trophies for the temple of Marduk, as no image of Jehovah was available. *As the Lord had said* (13); Je. xx. 5. For the deportation figures (14, 16) see note on xxv. 12. *Craftsmen . . . smiths* (14, 16); the exact force of the words is uncertain. For the continuation of the story of Jehoiachin see xxv. 27–30. From ration documents discovered in the ruins of Babylon it seems that he continued to be regarded as the legal king of Judah, hence the reckoning of time in Ezekiel. Zedekiah was more regent than king.

d. Zedekiah (xxiv. 17—xxv. 7)

Cf. 2 Ch. xxxvi. 11–13; Je. lii. 1–11. For the change of *Mattaniah* (17) to *Zedekiah* see xxiii. 34n. *Zedekiah rebelled* (20). 2 Ch. xxxvi. 13; Ezk. xvii. 15, 16 stress that he broke his solemn oath of loyalty. It was the result of Egyptian intrigue, and the Egyptians did cause the siege to be raised for a short time (Je. xxxvii. 5–7, 11). But it was in vain. *The way toward the plain* (4); 'the way of Arabah' (RV); i.e. towards the Dead Sea. The punishment of Zedekiah (7; Je. lii. 10, 11) shows how seriously Nebuchadnezzar took his treachery. Je. xxxvii. 1—xxxix. 7 gives an interesting supplementary picture of this period.

XXXIV. DESTRUCTION AND EXILE.
xxv. 8–30

a. The fate of Jerusalem (xxv. 8–21)

Cf. 2 Ch. xxxvi. 14–21 (a general summary); Je. lii. 12–30 (considerable additions). Nebuchadnezzar's destruction of Jerusalem was a deliberate punishment (8–10). *The captain of the guard left of the poor of the land* (12). This statement has been denied by many on the basis of Je. lii. 28–30, where the total deported is given

as 4,600; Je. lii. 28 is in flat contradiction with xxiv. 14, 16, and Je. lii. 29 cannot be reconciled with xxv. 11; Je. xxxix. 9, lii. 15. It must be supposed that Je. lii. 28–30 refers to captives of rank designated by name. Archaeology has confirmed the virtual depopulation of Judaea; cf. Albright, *The Archaeology of Palestine*, p. 140ff. The matter is important, for on the denial of the truth of the picture in Kings has been based a denial of much in the earlier chapters of Ezra. A clean sweep was made of anything of value left in the temple (13–17, note the longer text in Je. lii. 17–23). The execution of certain leading citizens (18–21) is probably that referred to in Je. lii. 10 as taking place at the same time as the blinding of Zedekiah (xxv. 7).

b. The flight to Egypt (xxv. 22–26)

This is a very condensed version of the account in Je. xl. 7—xliii. 7 (q.v.). The effect of Ishmael's treachery (25) was to deprive Judaea of organized government.

c. Hope for the future (xxv. 27–30)

The parallel in Je. lii. 31–34 is virtually identical. The incident is recorded for the hope it gave of a favourable end to the exile. Chronicles, written after the return, therefore ignored it. For the importance of this section for dating Kings see Introduction, p. 300. *Evil-merodach* (561–560 B.C.) was the son of Nebuchadnezzar.

H. L. ELLISON.

APPENDIX I: THE RELIGION OF ISRAEL UNDER THE MONARCHY

I. NEAR-EASTERN RELIGION

In the 'Fertile Crescent', that comparatively narrow strip of fertile land running horseshoe-wise from the Persian Gulf to Palestine, and continuing on the other side of the desert in Egypt, the religious systems during the Old Testament period fit into a common pattern. They were very different in detail and emphasis, but they were all essentially a mythological expression of the regular annual cycle of nature. The deities were a personification of the forces of nature, or more exactly of the spirit side of nature that made it work. In such a system the deities must be part of nature and so subservient to nature as a whole; though much greater than puny man, they are still essentially natural, and their claims on man conform to what man conceives to be natural. As the phenomena of nature are interrelated, though sometimes in apparent strife, the gods were conceived of as being mainly in family relationship, though often hostile to one another.

In Babylonia, Assyria, Syria and Canaan the balance between security and disaster, prosperity and famine was so fine that the unpredictability

of nature and life, in spite of the regularity of their cycle, was explained by the continual effort of the defeated demonic and chaotic powers to bring in chaos once more. Religion was very largely man's putting himself on the side of the gods and so helping them to preserve the established order.

The great New Year feast (in Canaan held in the autumn) was of great importance in this. By the recitation of the myth of creation and the defeat of chaos and by various symbolic acts it was believed that the great circle of the ordered year was kept turning. In all more primitive religion it is believed that one can promote a desired result by the ritual performance of a similar action, and so much of the ritual was of this type.

In Canaan the mystery of fertility in man, beast and soil alike were mythologically explained in terms of divine marriage, and so sacred prostitution, both male and female, was looked on as a means of promoting this fertility, and became an integral part of religion. The bi-sexual nature of deity was proclaimed in every Canaanite sanctuary by the presence of the *mazzebhah* and the *'asherah* (see 1 Ki. xiv. 23n.), the former representing the male, the latter the female principle (the change of gender in Je. ii. 27 is probably irony). It is immaterial whether the latter represented Asherah, the mother goddess of the Canaanites (cf. 1 Ki. xv. 13n.), and the former some specific male god, or whether they were general recognitions of the universality of sex.

II. THE 'DIVINE KING'

If we may judge from Mesopotamian evidence, the most important man in the state was the king. He was not a god, as in Egypt, but he was in a special way the representative of the gods, and capable of achieving deity; so the title commonly used for him today, 'divine king', is not inappropriate. He was not merely the civil but also the religious head of the state. In the great festivals certain rites could be performed only by him or in his presence; though he did not normally claim prophetic powers, he was in the last analysis the one to whom the gods made their will known.

The many survivals of an older past, e.g. the appeasement of demons (cf. 2 Ch. xi. 15n.), the cult of the dead, etc., were secondary and need no special mention here.

III. THE UNIQUENESS OF ISRAEL'S RELIGION

Jehovah, who revealed Himself at Sinai, was not a nature god. He stood outside nature and was its Creator. The regularity of nature was not a necessity forced on Him, but depended on His decree (Gn. viii. 22). He was supernatural, and hence no human conceptions or images were adequate to express Him. His demands on men, though rational, were not such as natural man could ever have inferred by Himself. In particular He needed nothing from men, and the religion and cultus of Israel were rather His gifts to them than anything they did for Him or to help on His work.

Jehovah's supernatural power was shown by the exodus. In it He revealed that He was the Lord of history as well as of nature. Hence human experience is for the Bible not a meaningless and endless cycle, but a progression towards a goal of Jehovah's own fixing.

This new world-view was reinforced by the change of the New Year festival to the spring. Passover did not primarily mark any feature of the agricultural year, but commemorated the supreme proof that Jehovah was the Lord of history. The natural New Year festival for Canaan was in the autumn (the feast of tabernacles), when the whole harvest had been brought in, and when, with the first of the 'former rain', new life began to show itself. This explains why the Passover was specially kept at the great reformations under Hezekiah and Josiah.

IV. THE 'CANAANIZATION' OF JEHOVAH WORSHIP

Abram's father had shared the normal religion of his time (Jos. xxiv. 2), and there is no reason for thinking that in the Patriarchal circles the memory of the past had ever quite vanished. The golden calf (Ex. xxxii. 4) finds a better explanation in Semitic ideas, as shown in the Ras Shamra tablets, than it does in Egyptian bull worship. Then too the Israelite festivals were tied to the agricultural year as were the Canaanite. As the Ras Shamra tablets and the sacrificial inscriptions from Marseilles and Carthage show us, their sacrificial systems had striking similarities. It was therefore fatally easy for the ordinary Israelite to interpret Jehovah in Canaanite terms, to look on Him as the chief of the gods and not as the only God, to bring Him into nature, and therefore to look on Him as natural and to interpret His commands accordingly.

It is a matter of controversy to what extent Israel was influenced by Canaanite worship in the time of the judges, and also how far it was eradicated in the period Samuel to Solomon. Certainly the impression made by Ezk. xx, Je. ii. 1–13, Ho. ii, etc. is that the poison worked from the first and continuously. Solomon did much to create a favourable atmosphere for this Canaanized religion by the very glory of the temple, which became for the simpler the real residence of Jehovah, and still more by his provision of facilities for the worship of other gods (1 Ki. xi. 1–8). The elaboration of the temple ritual worked in the same direction, as may be seen by its frequent denunciation by the prophets. Jeroboam, by his assumption of 'divine kingship', by his making the autumn festival the most important not merely by popular estimation but also by right, and above all by his choice of a bull as Jehovah's pedestal and symbol of His presence (1 Ki. xii. 28n.), made the increasing Canaanization of Israel's religion a certainty, whatever may have been his purpose.

How far this Canaanization went, in both Israel and Judah, we cannot say with certainty. There can be no doubt that most of the time their religion was on a much higher level than that of their neighbours. There is no evidence that an image of Jehovah was ever made, and archaeological discovery supports this; the frequent discovery on probably all Israelite sites of small figures of the mother-goddess and the repeated mention of the Asherah, both as a symbol and as the goddess, make it reasonably certain that the popular mind gave Jehovah a wife, though there is no evidence that children were attributed to Him. The Elephantine papyri (see Clar. Bible, O.T., vol. IV, p. 212ff.) give definite evidence for such a corrupt worship, and since those who practised it were obviously ignorant that they were not good Israelites, it is clear that it must have been widespread.

In times of apostasy as under Jehoram, Ahaziah, Ahaz and Manasseh things went much further. Ritual prostitution was practised (Hosea seems to suggest that it had become a regular feature of religious life in the North), a whole range of other gods were brought in beside Jehovah, and abominations like human sacrifice were introduced. Since, whatever gods were worshipped, Jehovah remained God of Israel, even when, under Ahaz and Manasseh, the gods of Assyria were looked on as in measure more powerful than He, it meant that such abominations were practised in His name (see 2 Ki. xvi. 3n.).

The local sanctuaries, or high places (1 Ki. iii. 2, 3n., xv. 14n.), were of two classes. Some were the continuation or revival of old Canaanite sanctuaries, where the Canaanite traditions lived on. These were removed in Asa's reformation (2 Ch. xiv. 3n.), but doubtless revived under Jehoram. Others were Jehovah shrines, legitimate or illegitimate according to how the legislation of Deuteronomy is interpreted. But since for the most part they represented popular religious ideas they became increasingly a danger, and Hezekiah and Josiah found it necessary to destroy them.

V. THE PROPHETIC INTERPRETATION OF POPULAR RELIGION

The history of Israel was written either by prophets or their disciples. They refused to give any details of the heathen worship around them, lumping the gods under the name of Baal, the most popular of the Canaanite gods, and the goddesses under that of Ashtoreth (Ishtar, Astarte), though Asherah is also occasionally found.

What is far more important is that they regarded Jehovah reduced to the level of a nature god as a nature god, and not as the God who had brought them out of Egypt, and had made the covenant at Sinai. Hence they dismissed the popular Canaanized worship of Jehovah as being just Baal worship. That is one reason why they do not appear as reformers. They had not to do with the true religion, which in some points had lost its purity, but with a religion fundamentally false, however much it might use

the same language. It was their realization that kings like Hezekiah and Josiah had not really grasped this fact that made prophets like Isaiah and Jeremiah stand aside from the great reformations of their time.

VI. THE KING IN ISRAEL

Saul had not been anointed 'divine king' but captain (1 Sa. ix. 16, x. 1—Heb. *naghidh*), i.e. secular head of the state. By sacrificing (1 Sa. xiii. 9f.) and by claiming to know Jehovah's will better than Samuel (1 Sa. xv. 20f.), Saul laid claim to 'divine kingship', but it lost him his throne. There was always a strong temptation to follow his example. Solomon, by deposing Abiathar and placing Zadok in his place, established the primacy of the king over the priesthood which does not seem to have been challenged for as long as the monarchy lasted.

Solomon clearly took the initiative both in the building of the temple and its inauguration ceremonies. All later changes, both reforms and apostasy, are regularly attributed to the king. Not only Uzziah but also Ahaz (2 Ki. xvi. 12f.) are clearly depicted as acting as 'divine kings', and we need not doubt that this will have been true of the other kings that turned to the Canaanized religion; it will have been one of its attractions.

In the North what was only a tendency in Judah became a principle from the first, though it may not have been carried as far as in the surrounding lands. Jeroboam I by his religious policy (1 Ki. xii. 25–33n.) clearly claimed to be 'divine king', and there is no reason for thinking that his successors departed in any great measure from his position. It was part of the sin wherewith Jeroboam the son of Nebat caused Israel to sin.

One reason why God did not restore the monarchy after the exile may well be that only so could religion be freed from undue interference by the state. It must, however, be borne in mind that the independent attitude of the prophets will have prevented even the worst of the kings from going as far as their heathen contemporaries.

H. L. ELLISON.

APPENDIX II: THE IMPLICATIONS OF POLITICAL ALLIANCES

In the ancient world there was nothing purely secular, and in international affairs the gods of the countries were conceived to be as involved as the citizens of the countries themselves. This is clearly seen in the Rab-shakeh's speech (2 Ki. xviii. 33ff.), where the conquest of towns is equivalent to a conquest of their gods. In the extant Egyptian and Hittite treaties the gods of the countries are called as witnesses (cf. Pritchard, *Ancient Near Eastern Texts*, p. 199ff.).

It followed, then, that for Israel to enter into international alliances implied in the popular mind an understanding between Jehovah and the gods of the country concerned. In the type of alliance made between Solomon and Hiram of Tyre or Asa and Ben-hadad of Damascus Jehovah was being placed essentially on the same level as the gods of these countries. This in turn virtually involved the type of religion described in Appendix I.

When Israel entered into political alliance with Assyria or Egypt it was as very much the junior partner, and this implied a similar junior rôle for Jehovah in the divine sphere. In the former type of alliance the religious implications may well have been overlooked by all but the prophets, in the latter they were obvious to all. It was mere religious logic for Ahaz and Manasseh to look on Jehovah as a nature deity, and not the most important one at that, one of a vast family of gods, but inferior to the deities of Assyria. It

needed the vision of Isaiah (e.g. Is. x. 5-27) to reconcile the vassalage of Judah with the sole deity of Jehovah.

Other possible implications of political alliances are shown by the results of the political marriage of Ahab to Jezebel. It evidently gave the Tyrian Baal a legal standing in Israel. Such political marriages were particularly evil because of the influence exerted by the queen mother on her son.

H. L. ELLISON.

APPENDIX III: THE GREAT EMPIRES DURING THE PERIOD OF THE MONARCHY

I. THE BACKGROUND OF THE UNITED MONARCHY

Early in the twelfth century B.C. with the death of Rameses III Egyptian influence in Canaan rapidly vanished, and Egypt sank into a long period of internal weakness. Tiglath-pileser I (1112-1074) of Assyria broke the power of the Hittites and of Babylon and carried his arms to the Mediterranean, but soon after his death Assyria dropped into inanition. The result of this was that in the time of David and Solomon there was in the Near East no effective opponent to the rise of Israel. The one major power left in their vicinity was that of the Phoenician coastal cities which were mainly interested in developing their overseas interests.

II. THE BACKGROUND DOWN TO THE DEATH OF JEHU

The beginning of a new era was marked by the rise of the XXII dynasty in Egypt under Shishak, or Sheshenk (c. 946). The revival of Egyptian power was never sufficient to make lasting Egyptian conquests in Asia likely, but it was sufficient to break the strength of Rehoboam, and after that the Israelite kingdoms were constantly weakened by Egyptian intrigues and raids.

Assyria awoke from sleep under Adad-nirari II (909–889), and from then on, until its fall, was the major power in the Near East. The relatively slow advance of Assyria until the time of Tiglath-pileser III was mainly due to the lack of any thought-out system of holding down conquered territory. At any rate, from the time of Ashur-nasir-pal II (883–859) they relied on cruelty. 'His usual procedure after the capture of a hostile city was to burn it, and then to mutilate all the grown male prisoners by cutting off their hands and ears and putting out their eyes; after which they were piled up in a great heap to perish in torture from sun, flies, their wounds and suffocation; the children, both boys and girls, were all burnt alive at the stake; and the chief was carried off to Assyria to be flayed alive for the king's delectation' (Hall, *The Ancient History of the Near East*, p. 445).

Though his successors did not go to the same lengths they aroused such bitter hatred (cf. Na. iii) that the policy had only a short-term value. Every possibility of revolt was eagerly seized, and the Assyrian kings constantly found their vassal states in revolt when they ascended the throne.

Ashur-nasir-pal carried his arms to the Mediterranean and received the submission of Hamath and the Phoenician cities. Shalmaneser III (858–824) pressed further south and met a great Syrian confederation at Qarqar (853). According to the Assyrian account Ahab participated in it with 2,000 chariots (the largest contingent) and 10,000 infantry (a contingent exceeded only by that of Damascus). Though Shalmaneser claimed a victory, the sequel suggests a drawn battle or even defeat. Subsequent attacks on Damascus in 848 and 845 failed, but the Phoenician cities submitted again in 842. In 841 Damascus was seriously defeated and weakened, and among others Jehu paid tribute. Babylonia also became tributary.

III. TIGLATH-PILESER III

In Shalmaneser's old age civil war broke out in Assyria and so the West had breathing space. Under Adad-nirari III (810–783) Hamath, the Phoenician cities, Jehoahaz of Israel, the Philistines and Edom, as well as Damascus, paid tribute in 803.

In the middle of the ninth century B.C. there had arisen on the north-eastern frontier of Assyria a new power, Urartu. It was a threat to the heart of Assyria, and greatly weakened it. In the first half of the eighth century B.C. Assyria's power rapidly declined until little was left of its Empire except its home lands. This was the period of the revival of Israel's strength under Jeroboam II. Then in 745 the general Pulu seized the throne and under the name of Tiglath-pileser (III) reigned till 727.

He introduced the method of holding down conquered territory by deporting the cream of the population (cf. section XXVIII d of the commentary). Though this did not decrease the hatred of Assyria, but rather increased it, it was highly effective, and Assyria went from strength to strength until it bled itself white and collapsed.

After stabilizing his north-eastern and southern frontiers he advanced against the West, which by 742 submitted. It was at this time that Menahem paid tribute (2 Ki. xv. 19f.). There followed the breaking of the power of Urartu. Rezin of Damascus and Pekah of Israel, thinking that Tiglath-pileser's hands were full, formed a confederacy against him and attacked Ahaz of Judah, who would not join them (see sections **XXVII c, d** of the commentary). This brought the wrath of the Assyrian king on them. The Philistines and Israel collapsed in 734, Galilee and Transjordan being deported (2 Ki. xv. 29); in 732 Damascus was captured and its inhabitants deported. This was followed by the submission of all the lands round Israel. Ahaz had, of course, become tributary when he appealed to Assyria for help. Tiglath-pileser's work was rounded off when he became king of Babylon.

IV. ASSYRIA AT THE HEIGHT OF ITS POWER

Shalmaneser V (726–722) had to face a new situation. Egypt had come under the control of the XXV dynasty (Nubian or Ethiopian) who, alarmed by the presence of the Assyrians on the frontier, began to intrigue among the people of Palestine. This led to the revolt of Hoshea and the fall of Samaria (723/2) (see section **XXVIII a**

of the commentary). Sargon (721–705) had to face the revolt of Babylonia at the beginning of his reign and was seriously defeated by Elam, the ally of Merodach-baladan. This led to a general revolt in the West backed by Egypt. One sweeping campaign in 720 restored Assyrian power and led to a crushing defeat of the Egyptian army in south Palestine. Sargon had to be bought off from invading Egypt. There were further revolts in Palestine in 715 (cf. Is. xx. 1) and 711. It is not clear to what extent Hezekiah was involved and whether he was able to make his peace in time to avoid serious consequences. By the time of Sargon's death the Assyrian Empire stretched from the Persian Gulf to Cilicia and the Egyptian frontier; even Cyprus paid tribute.

Sennacherib's reign (704–681) was ushered in by a general revolt. The recently conquered portions of Media were lost for ever, but Babylon, in spite of Merodach-baladan's efforts, was soon recaptured. When Sennacherib turned to the West, he quickly beat down opposition in spite of Egyptian resistance (cf. section **XXIX c** of commentary). He avenged a later Babylonian revolt and a probable defeat by a supporting Elamite army by destroying Babylon in 689. In the years that followed (unless it was in 701; see sections **XXIX f, h** of commentary) he suffered a major disaster in southern Palestine or on the Egyptian frontier (2 Ki. xix. 35). Not long after he was assassinated by two of his sons. Already in his reign we see the beginning of that

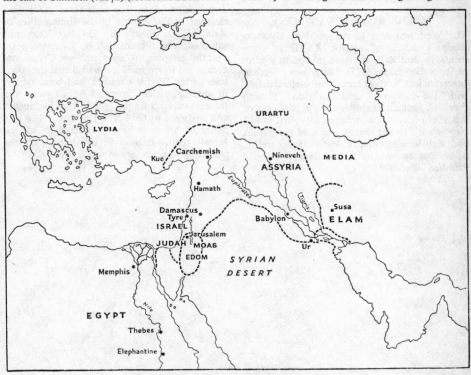

THE ASSYRIAN EMPIRE IN 700 B.C.

loss of Assyrian man-power that was to lead to the downfall of the Empire.

Esarhaddon (680–669) was one of the greatest of the Assyrian kings. One of his first acts was to rebuild Babylon, and his general policy seems to have created much more widespread quiet than usual. The movements of new peoples on the northern frontiers were troublesome but not yet seen as a real danger. The only trouble in the West seems to have been Phoenician revolts stirred up by Egypt; Manasseh of Judah appears as a loyal petty king. Esarhaddon conquered Egypt between 674 and 671, but no sooner had he left the country than Tirhakah, who had retreated into Ethiopia, returned and raised the standard of revolt.

It was left to Ashurbanipal (668–626) to reconquer Egypt, which he did easily. On an attempt of the Ethiopians to reconquer Egypt, which was at first successful, Thebes (No-amon, Na. iii. 8ff.) was sacked by the Assyrians in 663. Between 663 and 646 Elam was wantonly attacked and destroyed, and Assyria seemed to be at the height of its power. But the bitter fighting in Egypt and Elam had been too great a strain on the now slender reserves of Assyrian man-power. Already by 650 the Assyrian garrison will have been withdrawn from Egypt, and Psamatik, the viceroy of Egypt, was independent in all but name. Assyria had been bled white, and when the Scythians broke into the land shortly before Ashurbanipal's death there was little effective opposition to them.

V. THE RISE OF BABYLON

The West was lost to Assyria before Ashurbanipal's death (cf. section XXXII of commentary), and Babylon went immediately after under Nabopolassar (625). The growing Median power under Cyaxares came to an understanding with the Scythians and Babylon. Though Psamatik sent an Egyptian army to the help of Assyria in 616, it accomplished little, and in 612 Nineveh fell to the united attack of the Medes and Babylonians after a bitter siege, and it never rose again. The last vestiges of Assyria vanished about 609.

The Medes and Babylonians divided the Assyrian Empire between them, and they and the new state of Lydia in Asia Minor formed a triple alliance, loyally observed until they all in turn went down before Cyrus of Persia.

Necho, Psamatik's son, came to the throne of Egypt in 609 and promptly marched, nominally to help Assyria, now beyond help, if indeed she still existed, but really to grab what he could. On his way he defeated Josiah at Megiddo (see section XXXII j of commentary) and overran all Syria as far as the Euphrates. But when Nebuchadrezzar (the spelling Nebuchadnezzar is used in Kings), Nabopolassar's son and general, met him at Carchemish in 605 the issue was quickly decided and Babylon ruled as far as the Egyptian frontier. Egypt became an intriguer luring Judah to its doom, as it had Israel over a century earlier. The main supporters of Egypt were the Phoenician cities, and Tyre was able to resist Nebuchadrezzar for thirteen years before surrendering on terms (cf. Ezk. xxix. 17f.). It is doubtful whether the Babylonian king carried his arms across the Egyptian frontier.

Nebuchadrezzar (604–562) was mainly interested in peaceful pursuits, and he is most famous for his rebuilding of Babylon. His followers were weak and quite unable to deal with the new power that suddenly arose.

Cyrus, prince of Anshan in south Persia, attacked Astyages of Media and dethroned him in 550. In 547–6 the kingdom of Croesus of Lydia fell to him. The next three years were devoted to the capture of the Ionian cities of Asia Minor. Finally in 539 Babylonia was attacked, and the city fell in 538 after a six months' campaign. When Cambyses, Cyrus' son, conquered Egypt in 525, it meant that the countries of the 'Fertile Crescent' had been merged in an empire that stretched from Cyrene and the first cataract on the Nile to the Dardanelles and eastward to the borders of India. The new phase of spiritual history ushered in by the Jewish return from exile coincided with the beginning of a new era in world history.

H. L. ELLISON.

I AND II CHRONICLES

INTRODUCTION

I. ITS POSITION IN THE CANON

The English Versions follow the LXX and Vulg. in placing Chronicles immediately after Kings, but in the Hebrew Bible Chronicles is the last book of the Old Testament. It will have occupied that position as early as the time of Christ (see note on 2 Ch. xxiv. 20f.). In Hebrew it is one book (though the printed Hebrew Bibles have followed the Christian tradition); the division into two goes back to the LXX.

II. TITLE AND DATE

Our name, Chronicles, is derived from a suggestion by Jerome. It is a fair rendering of the Hebrew title *dibhre hayyamim*, i.e. 'The events of days' or 'Annals'; but it does not fairly express the nature or purpose of Chronicles. (See below under *Purpose*.)

An obvious *terminus a quo* for the date is given by 2 Ch. xxxvi. 22, i.e. 537 B.C. The evidence, however, seems conclusive that Chronicles and Ezra-Nehemiah were originally one book. This would bring the date down to after 430 B.C. The list of the descendants of Zerubbabel (1 Ch. iii. 19–24) to the sixth generation suggests a date not earlier than 400–340 B.C. (but see note on this passage). Ne. xii. 10f., 22f. brings the list of high priests down to Jaddua, who lived about 332 B.C. Rudolph (*Esra und Nehemia*, 1949) maintains, as is intrinsically quite possible, that these are later scribal additions, and dates the book shortly after 400 B.C. Albright (*J.B.L.*, 1921, pp. 104–124) from other premises reaches a similar date. In any case dates later than 300 B.C. may be ruled out as improbable.

III. AUTHOR

The facts just given make it very difficult to accept the Jewish ascription of authorship to Ezra, as does also the fragmentary description of Ezra's activity. But it seems that the tradition has been misunderstood, and that it is only the genealogies (1 Ch. i–ix) that are attributed to him (see *Jewish Enc.*, *ad loc.*). If so, Delitzsch's view that Ezra was the compiler of much of the material used by the Chronicler may well be right, or even Welch's (*Schweich Lectures*, 1939) that the bulk of the book is pre-exilic. In either case the Chronicler will remain unknown to us by name.

IV. PURPOSE

A chronicle differs from a history in that it is a record of passing events without any clear principle of selection in what is included and what omitted. The 'Chronicler' is obviously writing history, for there is a very clear principle both in his additions to Samuel and Kings and in his omissions. His additions concern mainly the temple and its services and such incidents as exalted the religious side of the state in contrast to the civil. Obviously he is concerned mainly with Israel as a religious community. His omissions show that he is concerned with the development of two divine institutions, the temple and the Davidic line of kings. Hence only the death of Saul is mentioned; his reign, David's sin, Absalom's rebellion, Adonijah's attempted usurpation are all omitted. The history of the northern kingdom, which was in rebellion against both of God's institutions, is mentioned only where it touches the fortunes of Judah.

That is why Chronicles is said to represent the priestly standpoint; it is concerned with the working out of what God has ordained and not, as Samuel and Kings, with the prophetic standpoint of how God dealt with His people and so revealed Himself.

The reasons for the writing of Chronicles are not far to seek. The post-exilic community had to understand how it had come into existence, that it was a true continuation of the pre-exilic kingdom (hence the genealogies), and what was the rôle of God's gift, the temple and its services, that had been entrusted to them. The omission of so many familiar scenes from Samuel and Kings underlined that, though those that had returned from exile were few in number, God had always been eliminating from the history of His people that which was in rebellion against Him.

In an age when there is an ever-growing tendency to abandon the old revelation of God in the Scriptures, Chronicles has its lesson of encouragement and warning for us.

V. SOURCES

It is clear that the main source of Chronicles is Samuel and Kings. In addition reference is made to a number of other sources, twenty in all, e.g. 1 Ch. v. 17, ix. 1, xxiii. 27, xxvii. 24, xxix. 29, 2 Ch. ix. 29, xii. 15, xiii. 22, xxiv. 27, xxvi. 22, xxvii. 7, xxxiii. 19, xxxv. 25, *et alia*. While there is no need to doubt that these sources existed (for their interpretation see I.C.C.), it does not follow that the Chronicler must have made direct use of them, for he may have been using one or more works based on them. He normally follows Samuel and Kings very closely, though he is prepared to make alterations at times;

there is no reason for supposing that he has not followed his other sources equally closely, though there is evidence that he felt free to recast their language.

VI. HISTORICAL VALUE

It is clear that Chronicles read by itself would give an unbalanced view of Israelite history; but it is equally clear that its author presupposed a knowledge of Samuel and Kings on the part of his readers so that criticism on this ground has no validity. More difficult is the large number of discrepancies between Chronicles and Samuel and Kings, some real, some imaginary. This is probably the reason why, in the Talmud, we find its historical accuracy queried, though not its canonicity.

In modern times the truth of all sections not found in Samuel and Kings has been queried (they have even been regarded as inventions of the Chronicler). But in the few cases where archaeology could pass an opinion it has tended to be favourable, and today the criticisms of scholars are normally much more cautious. There is no reason to doubt the essential accuracy of the Chronicler and his sources. Some of the

discrepancies may be due to textual corruption in his sources, and in places the text of Chronicles has been poorly transmitted.

One of the main problems in Chronicles is bound up with the numbers contained in it. Many are impossibly large, some disagree with Samuel and Kings, others are incompatible with the discoveries of archaeology. Yet there are other numbers that will not make sense of the usual suggestion that we are dealing with plain exaggeration, e.g. the 300 chariots in 2 Ch. xiv. 9 contrasted with the million footmen. The most obvious solution is that we are dealing with textual corruption either in the sources or in the transmission of Chronicles. A study of the variants in the genealogies will show how much of this there has been. There is, however, another aspect to be considered. Numbers from a thousand upwards were used not merely as round figures, but also hyperbolically (cf. H.D.B., III, p. 564; I.S.B.E., p. 2159). So in a number of cases mentioned in the commentary probably only a large, or very large, number is meant.

For the Chronology of the period covered by 1 and 2 Chronicles see *Introduction* to 1 and 2 Kings.

OUTLINE OF CONTENTS

I. GENEALOGIES. 1 Ch. i. 1—ix. 44

   a. Genealogies from Genesis (i. 1—ii. 2)
   b. Genealogies of Judah (ii. 3—iv. 23)
   c. Genealogies of Simeon, Reuben, Gad and Manasseh (iv. 24—v. 26)
   d. Genealogies of Levi (vi. 1–81)
   e. Genealogies of Issachar, Zebulun (?), Dan (?), Naphtali, Manasseh, Ephraim and Asher (vii. 1–40)
   f. Genealogies of Benjamin (viii. 1–40 and ix. 35–44)
   g. Post-exilic family heads resident in Jerusalem (ix. 1–34)

II. THE REIGN OF DAVID. 1 Ch. x. 1—xxix. 30

   a. The death of Saul (x. 1–14)
   b. David is made king (xi. 1—xii. 40)
   c. David and the ark (xiii. 1—xvii. 27)
   d. David's wars (xviii. 1—xx. 8)
   e. The preparations for the temple (xxi. 1—xxii. 19)
   f. Organization and duties of the Levites (xxiii. 1—xxvi. 32)
   g. The civil leaders of the nation (xxvii. 1–34)
   h. Solomon made king (xxviii. 1—xxix. 30)

III. THE REIGN OF SOLOMON. 2 Ch. i. 1—ix. 31

   a. Solomon confirmed in the kingdom by God (i. 1–17)
   b. The building of the temple (ii. 1—v. 1)
   c. The dedication of the temple (v. 2—vii. 22)
   d. Solomon's glory (viii. 1—ix. 31)

IV. THE KINGS OF JUDAH. 2 Ch. x. 1—xxxvi. 23

   a. Rehoboam (x. 1—xii. 16)
   b. Abijah (xiii. 1–22)
   c. Asa (xiv. 1—xvi. 14)
   d. Jehoshaphat (xvii. 1—xx. 37)

e. Jehoram and Ahaziah (xxi. 1—xxii. 9)
f. Joash (xxii. 10—xxiv. 27)
g. Amaziah (xxv. 1—xxvi. 2)
h. Uzziah (xxvi. 3–23)
i. Jotham (xxvii. 1–9)
j. Ahaz (xxviii. 1–27)
k. Hezekiah (xxix. 1—xxxii. 33)
l. Manasseh (xxxiii. 1–20)
m. Amon (xxxiii. 21–25)
n. Josiah (xxxiv. 1—xxxv. 27)
o. Downfall and restoration (xxxvi. 1–23)

COMMENTARY

I. GENEALOGIES. 1 Ch. i. 1—ix. 44

The purpose of the genealogies is one with the main purpose of Chronicles. It is plain that the Davidic line and the descendants of Levi are the chief interest (note the pointed omission of the house of Eli, which did not serve the Jerusalem temple). Next in importance are the two tribes especially connected with the monarchy, Judah and Benjamin. The passing mention of so many in the genealogies shows that their later omission s deliberate; they were not serving God's purposes. On the other hand the mention of many of no importance is the guarantee that none of God's people are forgotten.

Many of the names are taken from other canonical books; the sources of the others are generally not given, but the fragmentary nature of many of them is the best evidence that the Chronicler had portions of old records before him. In many cases, as elsewhere in Chronicles, there are variants in spelling compared with the same names in other canonical books. An * is placed against the form usually considered correct; where no * occurs we cannot be sure which is the original form. It will be seen that generally, but not always, it is the form in Chronicles that is inferior. For this the copiers of Chronicles are often responsible, not the author.

a. Genealogies from Genesis (i. 1—ii. 2)

The extremely condensed form of much of this section shows that a knowledge of Genesis was assumed.

i. The antediluvian patriarchs (i. 1–4). See Gn. v. 3–32. Note the omission of the line of Cain in full conformity with the principles of Chronicles.

ii. The genealogy of the nations (i. 5–23). See Gn. x. 2–29. *Riphath (6); RV 'Diphath'. Cf. Gn. x. 3. *Rodanim (7); 'Dodanim' (Gn. x. 4). Note that Uz, etc. (17) were the sons of Aram. Meshech (17); *'Mash' (Gn. x. 23). Ebal (22); 'Obal' (Gn. x. 28).

iii. The descent of Abraham (i. 24–27). See Gn. xi. 10–26.

iv. The descendants of Abraham through Ishmael and Keturah (i. 28–33). See Gn. xxv. 12–16 and 1–4.

v. The descendants of Esau (i. 34–54). See Gn. xxxvi. 10–14, 20–43. Zephi (36); *'Zepho' (Gn. xxxvi. 11). In Gn. xxxvi. 12 *Timna is the concubine of Eliphaz and the mother of Amalek. Homam (39); 'Hemam' (Gn. xxxvi. 22). Alian (40); 'Alvan' (Gn. xxxvi. 23). Shephi (40); 'Shepho' (Gn. xxxvi. 23). Amram (41); RV 'Hamran'; 'Hemdan' (Gn. xxxvi. 26). Jakan (42); RV *'Jaakan'; 'Akan' (Gn. xxxvi. 27). *Hadad (50); 'Hadar' (Gn. xxxvi. 39). Pai (50); 'Pau' (Gn. xxxvi. 39). Aliah (51); *'Alvah' (Gn. xxxvi. 40).

vi. The sons of Israel (ii. 1, 2). See Gn. xxxv. 22–26. There seems to be no explanation for the unusual position of Dan.

b. Genealogies of Judah (ii. 3—iv. 23)

It seems impossible now to unravel these genealogies with any certainty; the difficulties are due in part to the incomplete and sometimes even fragmentary nature of the genealogies and in part to the possible duplication of names. Textual corruptions and the fact that we are sometimes dealing with names of places rather than of persons further complicate matters.

i. Some descendants of Judah (ii. 3–9). Some descendants of Shelah (3) will be found in 1 Ch. iv. 21, ix. 5; Ne. xi. 5. They are not dealt with here because the Chronicler wishes to reach the royal house as soon as possible. The daughter of Shua (3). Cf. Gn. xxxviii. 2. Hezron, and Hamul (5). See Gn. xlvi. 12. The list of Hezron's descendants commences in verse 9. It must not be assumed that Hamul was childless. Cf. Nu. xxvi. 21. Zimri (6); *'Zabdi' (Jos. vii. 1). It is quite probable that Ethan, Heman, Calcol and Dara are to be identified with the Ethan the Ezrahite (i.e. descendant of Zerah), Heman, Chalcol and Darda of 1 Ki. iv. 31, in which case Mahol will be an intermediate link between them and Zerah. The fact that verse 8 speaks of the sons of Ethan but gives only one, suggests that the remainder of their genealogy has been omitted for the sake of brevity. Achar (7); 'Achan' (Jos. vii. 1). The form in Chronicles may be deliberate (cf. Jos. vii. 26). Achan was Carmi's grandson; this and the failure to mention the link between Carmi and Zimri presuppose a knowledge of Joshua in the reader.

341

The interpretation of the genealogies of Judah as a whole will depend in large measure on the interpretation of verse 9. *Chelubai*, i.e. *Caleb* (cf. verse 18; there is no justification for the spelling *ch*), is identified by most scholars with Caleb the Kenezite (see 1 Ch. iv. 15; Jos. xiv. 6), a non-Israelite incorporated into the tribe of Judah (Nu. xiii. 6). To do so is automatically to deny the authenticity of a considerable portion of these genealogies and to make a considerable part of Judah non-Israelite. It is much easier to assume two individuals, this Caleb antedating the hero of the conquest by several centuries. The mention of *Achsah* (49; cf. Jos. xv. 17; Jdg. i. 13) does not necessarily invalidate this view. The later Caleb's daughter must have been born after his incorporation into the tribe of Judah, and he may well have chosen the name deliberately. *Jerahmeel* (9). His descendants are mentioned in 1 Sa. xxvii. 10, xxx. 29. They are usually taken to be a non-Israelite clan that later coalesced with Judah. This would again destroy the historicity of the genealogy. It is much simpler to suppose that the descendants of Jerahmeel, who in any case were settled in the south of Judaea, retained their nomadic habits longer, and so in the days of David were reckoned separately from the rest of Judah.

ii. **The ancestry of David (ii. 10–17).** See Ru. iv. 18–22. *Salma* (11). So Ru. iv. 20 (Heb.); 'Salmon' in Ru. iv. 21; Mt. i. 5. Jesse had eight sons (1 Sa. xvi. 10, 11); only seven are mentioned here. 1 Ch. xxvii. 18 mentions a son Elihu, but this is almost certainly a variant of Eliab. The missing son probably died young. *Abigail* (16). According to 2 Sa. xvii. 25 she was the daughter of Nahash, in which case she was David's half-sister, or step-sister. *Jether the Ishmeelite* (17); 'Ithra the Israelite' (2 Sa. xvii. 25).

iii. **The descendants of Caleb (ii. 18–24).** See also notes on ii. 42–55. The context of verse 18 does not suggest that Caleb had two wives. Either Jerioth was another name of Azubah, or there is a textual corruption. (See Cam. Bible.) *Bezaleel* (20); see Ex. xxxi. 2. *And afterward Hezron* (21), i.e. after verse 9. *And he took . . .* (23). The time of the loss of these cities (see RV) is nowhere indicated, but it was probably before the reign of Ahab. In verse 24 the LXX suggests that there has been a textual corruption. Most read 'And after Hezron was dead Caleb went in to Ephrath, his father Hezron's wife, and bare him . . .' This was probably before the Mosaic lawgiving, which forbad such a marriage.

iv. **The descendants of Jerahmeel (ii. 25–41).** Nothing is known of any of those mentioned here. There is an apparent contradiction between verse 31 and verse 34. *Ahlai* may be a grandson by some daughter other than that mentioned in verse 34.

v. **Further descendants of Caleb (ii. 42–55).** See also notes on ii. 18–24. This is probably a supplementary genealogy to that in ii. 18–24. There are few points of contact between them. It should

be noticed that a number of names in these verses are names of towns. It is not always possible to interpret these remarks with certainty. Sometimes it means that a man had given his name to a town. For example, in a case like *Shobal the father of Kirjath-jearim* (50) it is clear that Shobal had founded or re-founded Kirjath-jearim, not that he had a son of that name. Verse 55 is a statement that the Rechabites were originally a Kenite family (cf. 2 Ki. x. 15n.; Je. xxxv) who were incorporated into Judah.

vi. **The sons of David (iii. 1–9).** With the list of David's sons in verses 1–9 cf. 2 Sa. iii. 2–5, v. 14–16. *Daniel* (1); 'Chileab' (2 Sa. iii. 3). *Shimea* (5); *'Shammua'* (1 Ch. xiv. 4; 2 Sa. v. 14). *Bath-shua* (5); *'Bath-sheba'* (in 2 Samuel and 1 Kings). Her father's name *Ammiel* is possibly only a variant of 'Eliam' (2 Sa. xi. 3). *Elishama, and Eliphelet* (6); *'Elishua, and Elpalet'* (1 Ch. xiv. 5; cf. 2 Sa. v. 15). In both these cases the second rendering is obviously the correct one, otherwise there would be two pairs of brothers with the same name. See verse 8. *Eliada* (8). So 2 Sa. v. 15; *'Beeliada'* in 1 Ch. xiv. 7. See note on 1 Ch. viii. 33.

vii. **From Solomon to the captivity (iii. 10–16).** *Abia* (10); RV 'Abijah'. So elsewhere in Chronicles; in 1 Kings 'Abijam'. *Azariah* (12). So generally in 2 Kings; but elsewhere in Chronicles, in 2 Ki. xv. 13, 32, 34, and the prophets, 'Uzziah'. *Johanan* (15), not otherwise known. *Zedekiah his son* (16). This seems to be a careless scribal error. He was Jeconiah's uncle, and has been mentioned already in verse 15.

viii. **The house of David from the captivity (iii. 17–24).** It should be noted that neither of the New Testament genealogies of our Lord makes any use of these names, except Shealtiel (AV *Salathiel*) and Zerubbabel. According to Ezr. iii. 2; Hg. i. 1; Mt. i. 12; Lk. iii. 27 Zerubbabel was the son, which may mean grandson, of Shealtiel. The natural inference of verses 17–19 is that he was his nephew. An old Jewish explanation interprets verse 18 as listing the sons of Shealtiel. Another explanation would be that he was grandson of both Shealtiel and Pedaiah. *Shenazar* (18), quite likely the Sheshbazzar of Ezr. i. 8, where see note.

This section, so important for the dating of Chronicles, cannot be interpreted with any certainty. The difficulty is the connection between the two halves of verse 21. The usual interpretation is that verses 21b–24 mention various other branches of the Davidic house, whose connection with Zerubbabel is unspecified, and of only one of which have we further details. On the basis of this Young (*Introduction to the Old Testament*) argues that we have only two generations from Zerubbabel given us, and therefore there is no obstacle to Ezra's authorship. There is weight in the argument, but it cannot be accepted as it stands, for, even if Shechaniah was not a contemporary of Hananiah, he can hardly be from an earlier generation than

that of Zerubbabel, and we have four generations reckoned from him. Also we cannot reject.
out of hand the reading of the LXX, Vulg. and
Syr.: 'And the son of Hananiah was Pelatiah
and Jeshiah his son, and Arnan his son, and
Obadiah his son, and Shechaniah his son.' If this
reading is correct, we have eleven generations
from Zerubbabel.

ix. Fragmentary genealogies of Judah (iv. 1–
23). This chapter is a collection of fragments
which have little or no connection one with
another or with the lists in chapter ii. *Carmi* (1).
A comparison with ii. 9, 19, 50 will show that it
should be Caleb. *Jabez* (9, 10; lit. 'He giveth
pain') has special attention given him because
his faith was triumphant over his name. *Othniel*
(13) and *Caleb* (15). These verses must be interpreted in the light of Jos. xv. 17. They confirm
the impression created by Jos. xiv. 6 that Caleb
was a non-Israelite adopted into the tribe of
Judah, for his genealogy does not link up
anywhere.

The sons of Shelah (21); see note on ii. 3. For
Jashubi-lehem (22) it is better to read with LXX
and Vulg. 'and returned to Bethlehem'. Though
unconnected with it, it is an interesting reminder
of Ruth. *Potters* (23). Archaeology has shown
that the potter's craft was hereditary.

c. Genealogies of Simeon, Reuben, Gad and
Manasseh (iv. 24—v. 26)

i. The descendants of Simeon (iv. 24–43). With
verse 24 cf. Gn. xlvi. 10; Ex. vi. 15; Nu. xxvi.
12–14. There are a number of minor variations
in the form of the names and it is difficult to
determine which are correct. With verses 28–33
cf. Jos. xix. 2–8. *Unto the reign of David* (31).
This points out that at this time one town
(Ziklag, 1 Sa. xxvii. 6), and possibly more,
became the possession of Judah.

Verses 39–43 describe some of the conquests
of Simeon and clearly show that the division
into ten tribes and one in the time of Rehoboam
(1 Ki. xi. 30n.) must not be interpreted too literally. Simeon neither separated from nor lost his
identity in - Judah. *Gedor* (39). Site unknown;
perhaps we should read 'Gerar'. *And they smote
the rest* (RV 'remnant') *of the Amalekites* (43). In
the light of 1 Sa. xiv. 48, xv. 3, 2 Sa. viii. 12
some time in the reign of David or Solomon is
probably meant. We know nothing further of
this Simeonite kingdom in Mount Seir, though
Is. xxi. 11, 12 may refer to it. *Unto this day* (43)
refers presumably to the time when this source
of Chronicles was written.

ii. The descendants of Reuben (v. 1–10). With
verse 3 cf. Gn. xlvi. 8, 9; Ex. vi. 14; Nu. xxvi.
5–9. Chronicles does not give all the names
mentioned in Numbers, nor does it indicate how
Joel (4) is to be linked with Reuben. *Tilgath-
pilneser* (6); *'Tiglath-pileser' (2 Ki. xv. 29).
Eastward he inhabited (9). Part of the reason for
this expansion into the steppe country east of
Gilead seems to have been Moabite pressure
on their original territory. *Hagarites* (10). RV

'Hagrites'. The AV rendering suggests a connection with Hagar which may not be justified.
It is quite likely that this war is the same as that
mentioned in verses 18–22.

iii. The descendants of Gad (v. 11–17). There
is no obvious reason why the details in Nu. xxvi.
15–18 have been omitted. *Jeroboam king of
Israel* (17). Obviously Jeroboam II; see 2 Ki.
xiv. 23.

iv. The war with the Hagarites (v. 18–22). See
note on verse 10. This section, together with
iv. 34–43, should warn us against assuming that
the Bible history is necessarily complete. There
may be many other gaps in Samuel and Kings
which Chronicles has not filled. This was a
major victory leading to an important addition
of territory.

v. The descendants of Manasseh (eastern half-
tribe) (v. 23–26). Earlier details are omitted to
avoid overlapping with vii. 14–19. With verses
25, 26 cf. 2 Ki. xv. 29 and note that this
captivity of the trans-Jordan tribes is not mentioned in 2 Chronicles. *Pul* and *Tilgath-pilneser*
(26; see note on verse 6) are the same man. See
2 Ki. xv. 19n.

d. Genealogies of Levi (vi. 1–81)

It should be borne in mind that the information
of this chapter is repeated and extended in 1 Ch.
xxiii–xxvi.

i. The high-priestly line (vi. 1–15). Cf. also
verses 49–53. The list is obviously incomplete;
not only does it deliberately omit the names of
the Shilonite high priests, the house of Eli, but
also Jehoiada (2 Ch. xxii. 11), Urijah (2 Ki.
xvi. 11) and Azariah (2 Ch. xxvi. 20).

ii. The Levitical genealogies (vi. 16–48). First
we have three genealogical trees beginning at
verses 20, 22 and 29 respectively. Then we have
the genealogies of *Heman* (33–38), *Asaph* (39–43)
and *Ethan* (44–47) in reverse. That of Heman
is the same as that beginning in verse 22, and
that of Asaph may perhaps be linked with that
in verse 20; no plausible connection can be made
between the other two. A comparison of verses
22–28 with verses 33–38 will reveal big variants.
Gershom (16, 20, 43). 'Gershon' in vi. 1 and
always in the Pentateuch. *Samuel* (28). Cf. verse
33, RV. This is the prophet Samuel. Cf. 1 Sa. i. 1,
viii. 2. It shows that the description 'Ephrathite'
in 1 Sa. i. 1 must be interpreted in the same way
as the phrase 'of the family of Judah' in Jdg.
xvii. 7 (where see note), and that he was a Levite,
though it could not be inferred from 1 Samuel.
Were this invention, we could confidently expect
him to have been linked with the Aaronic
priesthood.

Advocates of the Merenptah and Rameses II
dates of the exodus, *c.* 1225 or *c.* 1290 (see
Introduction to Judges, p. 236), point out that
from Aaron to Zadok (3–8, 50–53), Korah to
Heman (22–28, 33–35) and Mahli to Ethan
(44–47) are in each case eleven names, and from
Shimei to Asaph (39–42) are twelve. They argue
that this cannot be a coincidence and that this

number of generations comfortably spans two centuries, but could hardly span the four centuries demanded by the fifteenth-century date for the exodus. The argument should be treated with respect, for it shows that, if the genealogies have been shortened, there must have been some principle at work in the choice of the number to be mentioned. On the other hand it must not be overlooked that the argument demands a shortening of the list in verses 33–35, and ignores the lists beginning with verses 20 and 29, as well as the direct line of Korah to Shaul (24). These are all too short, and if they have had names omitted we can have no certainty that this has not been done with the others.

iii. The descendants of Aaron (vi. 49–53). Cf. verses 4–8 and see note on vi. 1–15.

iv. The Levitical cities (vi. 54–81). For this section see Jos. xxi. 1–42. Chronicles shows some rearrangement and abridgement. There are numerous variations in the names due mostly to copyists' carelessness. In verse 61 the text is corrupt. For the meaning see Jos. xxi. 5.

e. Genealogies of Issachar, Zebulun (?), Dan (?), Naphtali, Manasseh, Ephraim and Asher (vii. 1–40)

i. The descendants of Issachar (vii. 1–5). With verse 1 cf. Gn. xlvi. 13; Nu. xxvi. 23–25. *Puah* (1); 'Puvah' in Genesis and Numbers. **Jasub* (1). So in Nu. xxvi. 24, but 'Iob' in Gn. xlvi. 13.

ii. The descendants of Zebulun (?) (vii. 6–11). If verses 6–11 are taken as a genealogy of Benjamin, it seems impossible to reconcile them with chapter viii, nor is it possible to explain why two genealogies should be given. No genealogy of Zebulun is given, and since this is the place where it might be expected from the geographical point of view, it is very widely, and probably correctly, held that we have here a genealogy of Zebulun obscured by scribal errors. See I.C.C. or Cam. Bible for details.

iii. The descendants of Dan (?) (vii. 12). In precisely the same way as in the preceding verses a genealogy of Dan is generally found here; for details see above.

iv. The descendants of Naphtali (vii. 13). See Gn. xlvi. 24f.; Nu. xxvi. 48f.

v. The descendants of Manasseh (vii. 14–19). Cf. 1 Ch. v. 23f. The information is fragmentary and not easy to interpret. A number of the names in Nu. xxvi. 28–34 are not reproduced. *Zelophehad* (15). See Nu. xxvi. 33, xxvii. 1–11 *Maachah the wife of Machir* (16). In verse 15 she seems to be his sister (see RV mg.).

vi. The descendants of Ephraim (vii. 20–27). For the first four names in the list see Nu. xxvi. 35–37 although the spelling varies. Of the remainder it seems impossible to say whether they were sons or descendants of Ephraim—the non-mention in Nu. xxvi is inconclusive (cf. *Beriah* in verse 23). So we cannot say whether *Ezer* and *Elead* (21) are his sons. *Their father* (22) is inconclusive as the word is used loosely in Hebrew of any ancestor.

The cattle-lifting raid (21) must have been made from Egypt. Verse 24 presents problems that cannot be answered. Not only have we no other information about Uzzen-sherah, but its site has never been identified. The whole verse suggests connections of the Israelites with Canaan during their sojourn in Egypt (so also verse 21) which have left no trace in the Pentateuch, but which may point the way towards a solution of some of the problems connected with the conquest.

Joshua's genealogy is given in verses 25–27. Until Ammihud the names are unknown from the Pentateuch. It is worth noting that there are more names in it than in any comparable genealogy. The refusal to give more details about the Joseph tribes must be deliberate and links up with the consistent ignoring of the northern kingdom throughout the book as a rebel against the God-appointed Davidic kingship and Aaronic priesthood.

vii. The territory of the sons of Joseph (vii. 28, 29). Not a complete list of towns, but an indication of the borders by the mention of the main border towns. Such a mention, unique in the genealogical lists, for there is no real comparison with the mention of the Levitical cities (vi. 54–81), is probably intended to indicate that all later attempts of the Joseph tribes to obtain wider rule, e.g. Abimelech (Jdg. ix), the Ephraimite attack on Jephthah (Jdg. xii), and Jeroboam the son of Nebat (1 Ki. xi. 26) were usurpation.

viii. The descendants of Asher (vii. 30–40). With verses 30, 31 cf. Gn. xlvi. 17; Nu. xxvi. 44–46. The only new name is *Birzavith* (31), which is generally taken to be the name of a town. The names in verses 32–39 are all otherwise unknown. *Shamer* (34) and *Helem* (35) are almost certainly the same as *Shomer* and *Hotham* (32), though we have no guide to the correct forms. *Ulla* (39) is probably miswritten for one of the names in the previous verse. The figure given in verse 40 links neither with the census figures in Numbers nor yet with 1 Ch. xii. 36. With our fragmentary knowledge we cannot fix the period to which the number refers.

f. Genealogies of Benjamin (viii. 1–40, ix. 35–44)

The very full details about Benjamin as contrasted with most of the other tribes should not be put down to the availability of greater information, but should be regarded as a tribute to Benjamin's loyalty to the Davidic line. The parallel list in vii. 6–12 has been regarded as a corrupted genealogy of Zebulun and Dan; see comments *ad loc.* In any case it cannot be harmonized with this chapter.

i. The immediate descendants of Benjamin (viii. 1–5). Cf. Gn. xlvi. 21; Nu. xxvi. 38–40. The divergences between these three passages are very great, and no convincing harmonization has been offered.

*Bela his firstborn (1); 'Belah' and 'Becher' (Gn. xlvi. 21). Nu. xxvi. 38 omits 'Becher'. In

344

Hebrew 'Becher' and 'firstborn' have the same consonants. *Abihud* (3). Otherwise unmentioned; in the light of verse 6 it is probably to be read '(Gera) the father of Ehud'.

ii. **The descendants of Ehud (viii. 6–28).** This is probably the best way to treat these verses. For Ehud cf. Jdg. iii. 15, although the identification is not certain. Verses 6–8 are as obscure in Hebrew as in English and serious textual corruption probably exists. Various attempts at emendation have been made but they are probably of little serious value. All the names in this section are otherwise unknown to us. *Who* (i.e. Elpaal) *built Ono, and Lod* (12). We are unable to date the incident. *Who drove away . . .* (13). Again the incident cannot be dated.

These dwelt in Jerusalem (28). It is generally assumed that this is a reference to the post-exilic city and the inference is then drawn that the bulk of the names given are of post-exilic Benjamites. This must be considered a most hazardous assumption, the more so as none of the names are found in ix. 1–17 (cf. Ne. xi. 1–19), which specifically deals with the post-exilic community in Jerusalem. As virtually the whole of Jerusalem lay within the tribal area of Benjamin, we may expect there to have been a large Benjamite population in the period of the monarchy. Cf. verse 32.

iii. **The house of Saul (viii. 29–40).** Cf. ix. 35–44. These parallel passages are virtually identical, but where there are textual variations the latter is normally the better preserved. The RV has in one or two obvious cases corrected one from the other, and as this is indicated by italics attention is not here drawn to the fact. For other variations see AV mg., RV mg. *And Baal* (30). Read with ix. 36 and LXX, 'and Baal, and Ner'.

Zacher (31). In ix. 37 'Zechariah, and Mikloth'. *These also* (32). Probably refers to Mikloth and Shimeah (or Shimeam), in which case the verse as a whole would refer to a Benjamite settlement in Jerusalem after its capture by David (cf. verse 28).

Reference to 1 Sa. ix. 1 will show that in verse 33 Chronicles omits a large section of Saul's genealogy, once again showing that the gaps in Chronicles are often deliberate. A comparison of 1 Sa. ix. 1 with 1 Sa. xiv. 51 will show that Kish and Ner were brothers. Hence scholars are probably correct in proposing here: 'And Ner begat Abner; and Kish begat Saul,' though there is no support from MSS or Versions. The Hebrew seems incompatible with 1 Sa. ix. 1.

Abinadab (33). So 1 Sa. xxxi. 2, but omitted, probably by scribal accident, in 1 Sa. xiv. 49. AV mg., RV mg. are wrong in equating him with Ishvi. **Esh-baal* (33). In 1 Sa. xiv. 49 'Ishvi' (RV); everywhere else Ishbosheth. As Ishbosheth means Man of Shame, it needs no argument to show that this could not have been his name. Baal is not a proper name but a title—Master. In the period of the judges and under Canaanite in-

fluence it was applied by many to Jehovah. The custom seems to have been prevalent in the family of Saul. Cf. *Baal* (30) and *Merib-baal* (34). Late scribes found the custom so abhorrent that they put in the place of Baal *bosheth*, 'shame' (so Ishbosheth, Mephibosheth for Merib-baal, Jerubbesheth for **Jerubbaal*), or El, 'God' (so Eliada, 2 Sa. v. 16; 1 Ch. iii. 8, for Beeliada, 1 Ch. xiv. 7), or Jah (so Ishvi for Esh-baal). The various consonantal and especially vowel changes involved are only a matter of euphony.

*Merib-baal (34). Though the English versions hide the fact, the second occurrence in ix. 40 is spelt 'Meribaal'. Either spelling gives a good meaning in Hebrew. In 2 Samuel it is spelt 'Mephibosheth'; see note above on verse 33.

Verses 39, 40 do not occur in the parallel passage, as all that was necessary there was to show that Saul's line continued.

g. **Post-exilic family heads resident in Jerusalem (ix. 1–34)**

i. **The family heads (ix. 1–16).** See Ne. xi. 1–19 where a similar list is given. There are considerable variations, but only one outstanding case will be mentioned. Both Nehemiah and Chronicles show signs of copyists' carelessness.

It should be noted that no effort is made to link the names of this chapter with the detailed genealogies of the preceding chapters. The former give the framework in which the history of the divine ordinances unrolls; the latter stress that the post-exilic community was a legitimate sequel of what had gone before.

Verse 1 seems rather to be a summary of the preceding chapters than an introduction to the section which follows. *The book of the kings of Israel and Judah* (1). So LXX and Vulg. Cf. RV, RSV. AV is probably correct. Verse 2 is almost incomprehensible as it stands. It can be best understood as a compression of Ne. xi. 1, 3. *First* is probably to be taken in the sense of 'principal'. *Israelites* (RV 'Israel') has the meaning here of non-Levites. *Nethinims.* Cf. Ezr. ii. 43; Ne. xi. 3. Probably non-Israelite temple servants descended from the Gibeonites. Cf. Jos. ix. 27.

Of the children of Ephraim, and Manasseh (3). Though no details are given they are probably specially mentioned as an answer to the Samaritan claim to be the true representatives of these tribes. 2 Ch. xi. 16, xv. 9, xxx. 11, 18, xxxiv. 9 stress that a considerable number of northerners had joined Judah at various times.

Shilonites (5); i.e. Shelanites (Nu. xxvi. 20), descendants of Shelah. Cf. 1 Ch. ii. 3, iv. 21.

The ruler of the house of God (11). The meaning is not clear. It probably does not mean high priest. Cf. 2 Ch. xxxv. 8.

*Merari (14); 'Bunni' (Ne. xi. 15).

ii. **The gate-keepers and their duties (ix. 17–34).** There are a number of difficulties here, due probably to over-compression of the original record. The organization of the gate-keepers is dealt with also in 1 Ch. xxvi. 1–19. The reason for the section here is not so much any special importance of the names mentioned as a stress that the post-exilic community was primarily a religious community.

Porters (17); i.e. 'door-keepers'. The RV transation is inconsistent (cf. xvi. 38, xxvi. 1). It may be that a deliberate contrast with *keepers of the gates of the tabernacle* (19) was intended. Many think that a contrast with verse 14 is intended by the Chronicler and that the door-keepers were not Levites. This is improbable; cf. chapter xxvi and ix. 26n.

Hitherto (18); i.e. up to the time of the Chronicler; no change is implied. *The companies of* (18). Better as in RV 'the camp of the children of Levi', i.e. the temple (cf. 2 Ch. xxxi. 2). The phrase is derived from Nu. ii. 17, and has probably been used because of 'the camp of the Lord' (19, RV), probably meaning the tabernacle.

And the Lord was with him (20). Render 'May the Lord be with him!' Such phrases were very common in post-exilic Judaism when speaking of the illustrious dead. *Tabernacle of the congregation* (21). RV 'tent of meeting'. Not, as the context would suggest, the tabernacle, but the tent that housed the ark in David's time. *Zechariah* (21). Cf. xxvi. 2, 14.

David and Samuel the seer (22). The simple explanation would seem to be that, while the institution of gate-keeper went back to the time of Moses (19), the ornate temple to be built by Solomon demanded a great development of the service. The same was true of the Levitical singers. It is not clear what Samuel's rôle was; it is, however, reasonable to suppose that he may have prepared David from time to time for his coming responsibilities as king, or even have left written advice. Otherwise David's initiative in this sphere of organization is not easy to understand; but see Appendix I to Kings under section **vi** 'The king in Israel'.

For these Levites (26). Cf. RV and see comment on verse 17. The most natural interpretation is that the lower order of gate-keepers were not Levites, but the general tenor of the passage does not suggest this, nor was this the case in New Testament times. It seems safer to assume that compression has led to lack of clarity.

Certain of them (28). This could refer to the gate-keepers; but since the verses that follow cannot possibly do so, it is better to assume that here we have the beginning of a very compressed outline of some of the principal servile duties of the Levites and even priests (30). Verses 33 and 34 read like the heading or conclusion of lists that have been omitted.

iii. The genealogy of the house of Saul (ix. 35–44). For this section see viii. 29–40. From one point of view it might have been better to detach these verses from the genealogies and to have counted them as the beginning of the Book of David. They serve to link the story with the past as recorded in 1 Samuel.

II. THE REIGN OF DAVID
1 Ch. x. 1—xxix. 30

a. The death of Saul (x. 1–14)

See commentary on 1 Sa. xxxi. 1–13. Apart from verses 13 and 14, the two passages are virtually identical, the differences calling for no comment. In this, the sole longer reference to Saul's life, we learn something of the Chronicler's interpretation of history. As Saul had been appointed king by God, he could not be passed over in silence; but as he had later been rejected, an account of his death—the final proof of his rejection—was sufficient. David had been God's king from the time of his anointing by Samuel; the period of his rejection by men, however, is passed over in silence as being contrary to the will of God. But see comments on xii. 1–22. The Chronicler is silent regarding the short reign of Esh-baal (Ishbosheth) for the same reason.

b. David is made king (xi. 1—xii. 40)

The Chronicler normally follows the order of Samuel, but his omissions make the by no means clear chronology of the earlier book still more obscure. For information on these points see the relevant notes on 2 Samuel.

i. David, anointed king, captures Jerusalem (xi. 1–9). See 2 Sa. v. 1–10. *Which is Jebus* (4). Cf. Jdg. xix. 10. The name Jerusalem in the form 'Urusalim' is as old as the Amarna tablets, *c.* 1390 B.C. Cf. Gn. xiv. 18. But the Jebusites, whose centre the city was, may well have used the name Jebus. *Joab . . . was chief* (6). This information is peculiar to Chronicles and is in no contradiction with 2 Sa. ii. 13. The commander-in-chief of the king of Judah would not automatically have become commander-in-chief of the king of all Israel. *Joab repaired . . . the city* (8). Again the information is peculiar to Chronicles.

ii. David's mighty men (xi. 10–47). For verses 10–41a see 2 Sa. xxiii. 8–39. Owing to the natural link of this section with chapter xii, the list of David's mighty men has been put at the beginning of his reign; this must not be taken to imply that the incidents recounted took place before David became king. Verse 10 is peculiar to Chronicles. Its meaning must not be pressed too far. The majority, but probably not all, of the mighty men were with David in exile. Clearly as a result of a scribal error several lines have dropped out between verses 12 and 13. Cf. 2 Sa. xxiii. 9b, 10. Verses 41b–47 are a continuation of the list peculiar to Chronicles. The names do not occur elsewhere. *And thirty with him* (42); its setting obviously a scribal corruption. Moffatt may be correct in rendering 'captain of a Reubenite company of thirty'.

iii. David's adherents in exile (xii. 1–22). This section is peculiar to Chronicles. With one possible exception the names are otherwise unknown. This is sufficient to show that the list is no mere invention by the Chronicler, who would surely have introduced the names of great men of the time, if he had composed it himself.

Verses 1–7 give a list of Benjamites (2) who supported David. They are mentioned first because their action was the more remarkable, when we consider that Saul belonged to their tribe. A comparison of verse 1 with verses 8, 16 shows that they were not first to join David in point of time. *Ismaiah the Gibeonite* (4). His name is not in chapter xi. It may be that the list of mighty men is not complete, as the Chronicler's additions (xi. 41b–47) suggest; or simply that Ismaiah was worthy not merely to be a member of the thirty, but to be over them, or possibly a member of a third thirty.

The Korhites (6). RV 'Korahites'. Probably not Levites. Korah was a son of Kohath, and the Kohathite cities were not in Benjamin.

Of the Gadites (8). The Spirit moves as it pleases Him; no indication is given of the motives that drove these men from across the Jordan to join David while he was still a fugitive in the wilderness of Judaea (8). Their action was the more remarkable, as it exposed their relations to Saul's vengeance, which they would be powerless to hinder. The fact that they *separated themselves unto David* suggests that they could not even reckon on the sympathy of their fellow-tribesmen. *Into the hold* (8). Cf. verse 16. Probably the cave of Adullam is meant, but it cannot be affirmed with certainty. *Jeremiah* (10). Cf. verse 13. In Hebrew the names are spelt differently. With verse 15 cf. Jos. iii. 15. The Jordan flows through a flood plain as much as 150 feet below the level of the main Jordan valley and from 200 yards to a mile wide. It is the *ga'on ha-Yarden*, the jungle or pride of Jordan (mistranslated in AV 'the swelling'). In spring it is filled with rapidly flowing water from side to side. Not only did this handful of men cross this natural obstacle, but they routed those on both sides who, in the interests of Saul, tried to stop their march.

The children of Benjamin and Judah (16). Though those from Judah probably predominated, the Benjamites are mentioned first for the reason mentioned under verses 1–7. David's suspicion reflects exactly the conditions of 1 Sa. xxiii.

Then the spirit came upon Amasai (18). Lit. 'Then the spirit clothed himself with Amasai.' So Jdg. vi. 34; 2 Ch. xxiv. 20. Amasai, 'who was chief of the thirty' (RV), is unknown from the list of the mighty men. Some conjecture that Abishai is meant; others Amasa. See 2 Sa. xvii. 25, xix. 13.

Some of Manasseh (19). For the background see 1 Sa. xxix, xxx. David had to pass through the territory of Manasseh as he returned to Ziklag (20). The action of these Manassites was not as meritorious as that of the others already mentioned, for by this time Saul's fate was clear. *A great host* (22). There was evidently a continual increase of David's strength during the time he was king in Hebron. Cf. 2 Sa. iii. 1. *Like the host of God* (22) refers to size not quality; it is a common Hebrew idiom.

iv. The forces that came to Hebron to make David king (xii. 23–40). This account, which is peculiar to Chronicles, gives every impression of having been derived from the old official account of David's recognition and coronation, which may well have been hardly legible in parts. Note that we are not given the size of the contingent from Issachar, and there is a diversity in the size of the contingents which is hard to explain if we assume the correct transmission of the numbers. There is no reason to assume that *Jehoiada* (27) was the father of Benaiah (xi. 22 *et al.*, but see note on xxvii. 5); nor is it stated that he was High Priest. Presumably *Zadok* (28) is David's High Priest of the same name. *Men that had understanding of the times* (32). Cf. 2 Sa. xx. 14–22, especially verse 18. Abel of Beth-maachah was in Issachar.

c. David and the ark (xiii. 1—xvii. 27)

This section represents 2 Sa. vi. 11—vii. 29 with considerable additions of a religious nature. In order to enhance the importance of David's dealings with the ark, the Chronicler has put the first attempt to bring it to Jerusalem out of its proper chronological position as shown in 2 Samuel.

i. The first attempt to bring the ark to Jerusalem (xiii. 1–14). Except for verses 1–4 see 2 Sa. vi and notes there. *And David consulted* (1). The Chronicler is obviously making more of the occasion than the writer of Samuel, but the consultation described in verses 1–4 is clearly implied by 2 Sa. vi. 1.

So David gathered all Israel together (5). In spite of appearances there is no contradiction between this and 2 Sa. vi. 1. All Israel was present in its chosen representatives. Virtually all passages referring to the gathering of all Israel are to be interpreted thus. *Baalah* (6); i.e. the Kiriath-baal of Jos. xv. 60, a Gibeonite city. The name was evidently changed to Kiriath-jearim to avoid the hated name of Baal. *Chidon (9); 'Nachon' (2 Sa. vi. 6).

ii. Early events in David's reign (xiv. 1–17). See 2 Sa. v. 11–25 and notes there. For verses 4–7 see notes on 1 Ch. iii. 5–8. *And they were burned with fire* (12). Chronicles deliberately avoids the possible ambiguity of 2 Sa. v. 21. For the burning cf. Dt. vii. 5, 25. *Gibeon (16). 2 Sa. v. 25 has 'Geba' but LXX has 'Gibeon'.

iii. Preparations for the second attempt to bring up the ark (xv. 1–24). This section is peculiar to Chronicles. 2 Sa. vi. 12 (1 Ch. xiii. 14) tells how David hears of the blessing on the house of Obed-edom. This shows him that Jehovah had no objection to the removal of the ark, and this leads him to the true reason for the death of Uzza.

A tent (1). Not the tabernacle, which was in Gibeon (1 Ch. xvi. 39, 2 Ch. i. 3). We are not told how the tabernacle came to be moved there —but note that Gibeon was a neighbour of the less important Kiriath-jearim—nor why it was not moved to Jerusalem as well. It may be that

David already had the project of a temple in his mind, and so it suited him to respect the inevitable protests of the Gibeonites.

None ought to carry the ark of God but the Levites (2). The reason why a new cart was used in the first instance (1 Ch. xiii. 7) is quite clearly because God had tolerated that method for the return of the ark from the Philistine country (1 Sa. vi. 7). They had not learnt that God's exceptions do not put aside the express revelation of His will. David now recognized the mistake.

It is very striking that the names of the Levites (4ff.) do not link up with the Levitical lists in chapters xxiii–xxvi. Had these lists been a mere invention of the Chronicler, as is so often suggested, he would surely have tried to link them up for the sake of verisimilitude. *Sanctify yourselves* (12). This refers to outward, ritual holiness. It involved washing (Ex. xix. 10, 14), the avoidance of defilement (Lv. xi. 44) and refraining from sexual intercourse (Ex. xix. 15). It is not sufficient to be holy; there should be the outward appearance as well. *Their brethren of the second degree* (18). I.C.C. and Cam. Bible propose 'their brethren twelve'. *Ben* (18) means 'son' and therefore to regard it as a proper name is incorrect. *Azaziah* (21) is omitted in xvi. 5. *Obed-edom* (21). The name appears frequently in 1 Chronicles and it is not certain whether more than one individual is intended. It is simplest to assume that there was only one of this name. The ark was lodged in his house. It is usually assumed that 'Gittite' (1 Ch. xiii. 13) must mean from Gath; but it is incomprehensible that the ark should have been left with a Philistine, nor would he have been willing to take the risk on himself. In addition Gath (lit. winepress) appears in its dual form Gittaim as a place in the vicinity of Kiriath-jearim (2 Sa. iv. 3; Ne. xi. 33) as well as in a number of compound place-names. See 2 Sa. vi. 10, 11n. Quite naturally, as the result of the divine favour, he was appointed one of the special guardians of the ark (24). As he served well, he and his sons were appointed doorkeepers for the temple to be built by Solomon. Cf. 1 Ch. xxvi. 14, 15. On the day of the bringing up of the ark to Jerusalem Obed-edom and his companion Jeiel (18) acted exceptionally as singers (21), and so Berechiah and Elkanah were made temporary guardians of the ark (23). This seems the simplest interpretation. I.C.C. and Cam. Bible propose far-reaching textual reconstructions, which seem unnecessary. Obed-edom is a good example of the results of faithfully using unexpected opportunities of service. *Alamoth . . . Sheminith* (20, 21). Cf. the titles of Pss. xlvi (see note), vi, xii. *Jehiah* (24). Probably the Jeiel of verse 18.

iv. The ark brought to Jerusalem (xv. 25—xvi. 3). See 2 Sa. vi. 12–19. *Seven bullocks and seven rams* (26). This is the sacrifice of the elders and captains; David's sacrifice was an ox and a fatling (2 Sa. vi. 13, RV). *Playing* (29),

an old English synonym for dancing. Cf. Ex. xxxii. 6.

v. The ministry before the ark (xvi. 4–7). The smaller number of names compared with the lists given in chapter xv is accounted for by the ministry in the tabernacle at Gibeon. See verse 39. In verse 5 it is probable that the mention of Obed-edom and Jeiel, and the second mention of Asaph are to be referred to a scribal error. Cf. xv. 24n. and xvi. 38. See also note on xv. 21 above.

vi. The psalm of praise (xvi. 8–36). It should be noted that the RV does not state that David was responsible for this Psalm. It is actually composed from three Psalms. Ps. cv. 1–15 (verses 8–22); Ps. xcvi. 1–13 (verses 23–33); and Ps. cvi. 1, 47, 48 (verses 34–36). For a commentary the relevant passages should be referred to. There are a number of minor variants, some deliberate, some accidental. In the latter case the text of Psalms gives the better reading.

None of the three Psalms used is Davidic and all are later, possibly even post-exilic. Cf. verse 35; Ps. cvi. 47. The Chronicler evidently found no Psalm in his authority and so put together a suitable piece. By drawing from the Psalms and choosing anonymous ones he did not imply Davidic or contemporary authorship. Verse 36 is the doxology of Book IV of the Psalms and shows that the collection was in its present form by the time that Chronicles was written.

vii. The service in Jerusalem and Gibeon (xvi. 37–43). This section is really a continuation of verses 4–7, beginning with a summary of them. *Obed-edom with their brethren* (38); either read with LXX, Vulg., RSV 'and his brethren', or more probably 'Obed-edom and Hosah with their brethren.' *Zadok the priest* (39). We are obviously to infer that Abiathar, the senior in age, was in Jerusalem with the ark. *The sons of Jeduthun* (42). Cf. verse 38. This seems to refer to the sons of Obed-edom.

viii. David's wish to build a temple; God's answer; David's thanksgiving (xvii. 1–27). See notes on 2 Sa. vii. 1–29. The variations are minor. *But have gone from tent to tent . . .* (5). 2 Sa. vii. 6 gives the correct reading: 'but have walked in a tent and in a tabernacle.' **Judges* (6); 'tribes' (2 Sa. vii. 7). *And hast regarded me according to the estate of a man of high degree* (17). See 2 Sa. vii. 19n. It would seem that the text of both Samuel and Chronicles is faulty; there is no really satisfactory emendation.

d. David's wars (xviii. 1—xx. 8)

i. A summary of the wars (xviii. 1–13). See 2 Sa. viii. 1–14. *Gath and her towns* (1). This is probably the correct interpretation of 2 Sa. viii. 1. *Hadarezer* (3); **Hadadezer* (2 Sa. viii. 3). *A thousand chariots, and seven thousand horsemen* (4). The LXX of 2 Sa. viii. 4 agrees with Chronicles. **Tibhath* and *Chun* (8); 'Betah' and 'Berothai' (2 Sa. viii. 8). The sites of these towns are unknown. **Tou* (9). So also the LXX in 2 Sa. viii. 9. *Hadoram* (10); 'Joram' (2 Sa. viii. 10).

The victory of verse 12 evidently involved a number of contingents acting to some extent individually, for in 2 Sa. viii. 13 the credit is given to David, and in Ps. lx, title, to Joab.

ii. David's officers (xviii. 14–17). See 2 Sa. viii. 15–18. *Abimelech the son of Abiathar* (16). In the LXX, Vulg., and 2 Sa. viii. 17: 'Ahimelech the son of Abiathar.' See 1 Sa. xxii. 20; 1 Ch. xxiv. 3n. There is little doubt that we should read both here and 2 Sa. viii. 17 'Abiathar the son of Ahimelech'. *Shavsha* (16); 'Shisha' (1 Ki. iv. 3), 'Seraiah' (2 Sa. viii. 17), 'Sheva' (2 Sa. xx. 25). The variants in spelling are probably due to his having been a foreigner; cf. 'Uriah the Hittite', 'Ittai the Gittite'. *The sons of David were chief . . .* (17). A deliberate, but correct alteration of 2 Sa. viii. 18, 'were priests' (RV. Cf. RV mg.). By the time of the Chronicler the term 'priest' had become too technical to be used as it could be in Samuel. The original concept of a priest was that of an attendant on the god.

iii. War with the Ammonites (xix. 1—xx. 3). See 2 Sa. x. 1—xi. 1, xii. 26–31. *A thousand talents of silver* (6). An immense sum, for Amaziah could hire 100,000 men for a hundred talents (2 Ch. xxv. 6). As the mention of Mesopotamia is in anticipation of verse 16, it is probable that this is the total sum spent on foreign mercenaries during the war. *Mesopotamia* (6); Heb. *Aram-Naharaim*, the area immediately across the Euphrates and very much smaller than that included under the name Mesopotamia today, or perhaps rather the ancient Naharin, or North Syria. *Seven thousand . . . chariots* (18). 2 Sa. x. 18 has ' seven hundred chariots', the more possible reading. *Forty thousand footmen* (18). In 2 Sa. x. 18 'forty thousand horsemen'. There is no means of judging which is correct, or whether both are. *David tarried at Jerusalem* (xx. 1). At this point the account in 2 Samuel inserts the story of Bathsheba and the death of Uriah, etc. (2 Sa. xi. 2—xii. 25). The Chronicler's omission of the story is not to whitewash David; he wants to give the divine pattern, not the aberrations from it. *And cut them with* (3). The RV mg. of 2 Sa. xii. 31, reading *vyshm* for *vyshr*, translates 'put them to . . .' (cf. RSV). Extreme servitude rather than massacre is indicated.

iv. The death of Philistine champions (xx. 4–8). See 2 Sa. xxi. 18–22. *Gezer* (4); 'Gob' (2 Sa. xxi. 18). *Sippai* (4); 'Saph' (2 Sa. xxi. 18). *And Elhanan the son of Jair slew Lahmi the brother of Goliath the Gittite* (5). 2 Sa. xxi. 19, RV reads: 'And Elhanan the son of Jaare-oregim the Bethlehemite slew Goliath the Gittite.' It is axiomatic with the extreme critic that Samuel is correct and that as a result the story in 1 Sa. xvii is merely a worthless tradition. The reading of this verse is then dismissed as an attempt on the part of the Chronicler to get rid of a discrepancy. For a detailed discussion see the note on 2 Sa. xxi. 19. There is no adequate reason for not accepting the statement of Chronicles.

e. The preparations for the temple (xxi. 1—xxii. 19)
Except for chapter xxi this section is peculiar to Chronicles. Even chapter xxi has a different setting, for here it is not told as a story in itself but simply as an account of how the site of the future temple came to be bought. The question of where these chapters are to be placed in David's life is discussed in the note on xxii. 2.

i. The census and the plague (xxi. 1–27). See 2 Sa. xxiv. *Satan* (1). In 2 Samuel David's act is attributed to God's moving; here to Satan's. But the difference is only apparent. Popular Christian ideas of Satan, in so far as they are derived from the New Testament at all, are the result of that unsound exegesis which forgets that the foundations of all New Testament conceptions are in the Old. In the Old Testament Satan, however evil, is an angel of God, a minister of God, a being who has only as much power as God entrusts to him. Cf. Jb. i and ii; Zc. iii. 5. So Satan here is only the minister of God's purposes.

It does not look as though the divergence between the numbers given in verse 5 and those found in 2 Sa. xxiv. 9 is due to textual corruptions. No entirely satisfactory explanation has been given, but see the notes on the passage in 2 Samuel.

God was displeased (7). This verse is not represented in Samuel and must be looked on as anticipating the development of the story. There can be no question of the plague coming on Israel until after David's choice (13, 14). Moreover Samuel is quite clear that it was David's conscience, not the divine punishment, that made David recognize his sin. *Three years' famine* (12). In 2 Sa. xxiv. 13 the Hebrew has 'seven'. The Chronicles reading, with which the LXX of 2 Samuel agrees, is to be preferred. *Ornan the Jebusite* (15); 'Araunah the Jebusite' (2 Sa. xxiv. 16). The difference in the consonantal text is small, and the variations probably go back to its being a foreign name. Cf. note on xviii. 16. *His four sons . . . hid themselves* (20); i.e. to avoid seeing the angel. Cf. verses 15, 16. *Now Ornan was threshing wheat* (20). Obviously this was before the angel came; Ornan would then have hidden himself with his sons. Jewish tradition pictures him as hiding in the cave which undoubtedly existed under the rock on which the altar of burnt offering was later placed, and which can still be seen under the Dome of the Rock (the Mosque of Omar). With verse 25 cf. 2 Sa. xxiv. 24. It is generally recognized by all who are not out to discover discrepancies that there is no contradiction here. 2 Samuel gives the price of the rocky threshing-floor, Chronicles of the whole area (*the place*). The surroundings will have been bought somewhat later (and, since there was no plague to be stopped, at a much stiffer price); but it is characteristic of the Chronicler that he fuses the two events.

ii. The choice of the temple site (xxi. 28—

xxii. 1). The syntax of this section is difficult. Verses 29 and 30 should be printed in brackets; xxii. 1 follows straight on from xxi. 28. *Then he sacrificed there* (28) would be much better rendered 'when' or 'after he had sacrificed there'. This has been interpreted to mean that from this time on there were sacrifices on this site; but neither the Hebrew nor the context supports this.

iii. David's preparations for building the temple (xxii. 2–5). While this and the following sections are not dated, a consideration of the evidence in 1 Kings clarifies the position. The only rational interpretation of Adonijah's attempt to make himself king (1 Ki. i. 5) is that he hoped to face his father with a *fait accompli* made possible because David had never publicly designated his successor. Cf. 1 Ki. i. 5n., 11n. After xxii. 17 this could hardly be the case. So we are forced to look on chapters xxii—xxix as covering a limited period of time, from xxii. 6 onwards being after Solomon's anointing as king (1 Ki. i. 39).⁰

The apparent break at xxiii. 1 is due to the use of a new source, not any lapse of time (see note *ad loc.*).

It is often claimed that Chronicles is irreconcilable with 1 Kings. But 1 Ki. ii. 1 in itself implies an interval between Solomon's anointing and his father's death. It is no unusual thing for a crisis to call out unrealized reserves of vigour in an old man. Most chronological outlines find it hard to allow Solomon a full forty years' reign, and so strongly suggest a period of coregency with his father (see also note on xxii. 17). It is quite typical of Chronicles that while it ignores 1 Ki. i it reveals knowledge of it by xxix. 22.

Strangers (2). An inaccurate translation. The Hebrew *ger* is a tolerated sojourner. These remnants of the old inhabitants had not accepted the worship of Jehovah and therefore their presence in the land was not of right but of tolerance. David's treatment of them here is an anticipation of Solomon's policy (see 1 Ki. v. 13–18n.; 2 Ch. ii. 17f., viii. 7f.). At the time conditions in this type of work were so hard that it was not considered suited to freemen.

iv. David's charge to Solomon and the princes (xxii. 6–19). *Thou hast shed blood abundantly* (8). This is not mentioned in the prophetic message recorded in chapter xvii, nor does Solomon repeat it in 1 Ki. v. 3. The truth will have come to David as he pondered on God's refusal to allow him to build the temple. Very frequently God does not explain His refusals but allows them to be interpreted afterwards through prayer and the Word. *I will give him rest from all his enemies* (9). As so often, although no condition is expressed, one is implied. Cf. 1 Ki. xi. 14ff. There is no suggestion that Solomon stood higher morally than David, and still less that David's wars were not justified. Even then men felt that warfare was a contradiction of the divine order. David was paying for the

sins of his predecessors. Had Israel been faithful in the conquest of the land, they would not have experienced the dark period of the judges, and David would have ruled over a people too strong to be lightly attacked, as was Solomon's fortunate position.

Only the Lord give thee wisdom (12). Was it his father's prayer that prompted Solomon's request? See 2 Ch. i. 7ff. With verse 13 compare God's charge to Joshua in Jos. i. 7ff. *In my trouble* (14). This would refer to the many wars and troubles of his reign. Others render 'in my poverty', 'low estate' (RV mg.). 'By my hard labour' (I.C.C.) and 'with great pains' (RSV) are both attractive but doubtful. The numbers in this verse, if taken literally, would make David a much richer king than Solomon, which is contrary to the whole tenor of Scripture. It is better to treat them as equivalents of large, very large, enormous. *Of the gold . . . there is no number* (16). Remove the punctuation mark at the end of the preceding verse and read '. . . in any manner of work of gold, silver . . . without number'. It was the workmen that had not been numbered. So LXX and Syr.

The princes of Israel (17). 'Prince' is a very ambiguous and inadequate translation of *sar*. These were not principally or even primarily members of the royal family, but the tribal leaders and the civil and military officials (and so elsewhere in the Old Testament). In other words, this passage implies Solomon as coregent or at least king-designate. See note on verses 2–5 above.

f. Organization and duties of the Levites (xxiii. 1 —xxvi. 32)

i. The last acts of David (xxiii. 1, 2). No long interval need be read into the text between this section and the preceding one. The language implies merely a new section, probably based on a different source. These verses are a summary telling how David made Solomon king (cf. xxviii. 1—xxix. 25); gathered the princes of Israel (cf. xxvii. 1–34), with the priests (cf. xxiv. 1–19) and the Levites (xxiii. 3–32, xxiv. 20—xxvi. 32). As so often in Chronicles when it comes to detail the order is reversed, except for some supplementary details about the Levites.

ii. The twenty-four orders of Levites (xxiii. 3–23). *From the age of thirty years and upward* (3). See note on xxiii. 24. Though not expressly stated it may be inferred that they were under fifty (cf. Nu. iv. 3). Attempts to regard the figures in verse 4 as absurdly high overlook the fact that the Levites were divided into twenty-four courses. 1,000 overseers on duty at one time, considering the scale of the work, is not unreasonable; the same applies to the other groups. *Officers and judges* (4). Cf. Dt. xvii. 9; 2 Ch. xix. 8, 11. The number of Levitical orders (6) corresponded to the twenty-four orders of priests. This passage (6–23) is largely paralleled by the obviously fragmentary section xxiv. 20–31. The minor variants in names call for no mention.

What is more important is that only twenty-two orders can be counted, or twenty-three, if, as seems probable, *Eleazar* (22) is reckoned as the head of one through his daughters. We cannot say where the name may have dropped out. It may be in verse 9, where *Shimei* reveals some textual corruption (cf. verse 10), or in verse 16, where only one of Gershom's sons is mentioned. *Laadan* (7); 'Libni' (1 Ch. vi. 17). Many think that Laadan may have been a descendant of Libni.

iii. **The age of temple service (xxiii. 24–27).** It is impossible to interpret this section with certainty, but its general meaning is clear. David, as he considered the future, saw that the ornate ritual of the temple would need more Levites, but that their actual service would be easier. He therefore ordered that once the temple was completed the age at which service should begin should be lowered from thirty to twenty. It is not clear whether a second census was taken or not. See note on xxiv. 1–19.

The importance of this section is that it shows that a command in the law could be changed by lawful authority without any reference to an alleged Mosaic tradition. Why then, if modern criticism is right about the growth of the Pentateuch, should all the later laws have been attributed to Moses?

iv. **An outline of the duties of the Levites (xxiii. 28–32).** These regulations were necessary, as many of the Levites had been carrying out priestly duties at the smaller and less regular sanctuaries. Cf. 2 Ki. xxiii. 8n. and especially Jdg. xvii. 7–13, xviii. 30 (RV). *And to offer all burnt offerings* (31). A strange mistranslation. The verb 'stand' of verse 30 is understood; render 'and to stand (i.e. assist) at every offering of burnt offerings'.

v. **The priestly courses (xxiv. 1–19).** During the period of declension under the judges there was plenty of work for the descendants of Aaron at the many local sanctuaries; but now that Jerusalem was to become the central sanctuary, they were too many. They were divided up into twenty-four courses, which meant a fortnight's priestly duty a year, besides being on call at the great festivals, when in any case they should be in Jerusalem. As in the Jewish calendar the year has thirteen months on an average of about two years in five, the period of service would gradually move round the year. In New Testament times the service was for two separate weeks in the year (see Edersheim, *The Temple*, for this and other details of the New Testament period), and it may well have been so from the first. In verse 3 follow the RV rendering: 'And David with Zadok . . . and Ahimelech . . . divided them . . .' *Ahimelech of the sons of Ithamar* (3). Cf. verse 6, 'Ahimelech the son of Abiathar', and see note on xviii. 16. It would seem that the family tree was Ahitub, Ahimelech (1 Sa. xxii. 9), Abiathar (1 Sa. xxiii. 6), Ahimelech. It is easy to see how confusion could have arisen. Here the text will be correct. Abiathar was too old by

this time to be troubled with administrative details. The smaller number of descendants of Ithamar (4) can easily be explained by the misfortunes of the house of Eli, especially the massacre of the priests of Nob (see 1 Sa. xxii. 11ff.). In verse 5 read as in RV 'princes of the sanctuary, and princes of God'. The two phrases are probably synonymous. The whole verse probably means that except for the number of courses no distinction in honour was made between the two families. *Shemaiah . . . the scribe, one of the Levites* (6). The stress is not so much on his being a Levite, but that he was not the royal scribe. *One principal household* (RV 'father's house') *being taken for Eleazar, and one taken for Ithamar* (6). The order of service was decided by lot, the choice for the first sixteen courses being alternately from Eleazar and Ithamar. Some of the priestly names which follow seem to occur in Nehemiah. See note on Ne. xii. 1 in Cam. Bible. *Hakkoz* (10). Cf. the RV of Ezr. ii. 61 and Ne. iii. 4, 21.

vi. **Levitical families (xxiv. 20–31).** Cf. xxiii. 6–23. This section is obviously fragmentary, the Gershonites being omitted without obvious reason. In verses 26 and 27 there seems to be textual corruption. We have no other evidence for Jaaziah as a son of Merari; he was probably a later descendant. *Beno* (26) is not a proper name; it is lit. 'his son'. In verse 26 it has probably entered by dittography from verse 27, where it may well be an error for Bani.

vii. **The families and courses of the singers (xxv. 1–31).** *David and the captains of the host* (1). Seeing that no one has yet suggested a good reason why the captains of the host should be concerned here, it will be best to follow I.C.C. and render 'David and the chiefs of the serving host' (i.e. of the Levites). For the rest of the verse see RV. *Who should prophesy* (1). While there is probably a reference to 1 Sa. x. 5, it seems clear that these chosen singers are being given an honour higher than that of the ordinary Levite. It may be that many Christians do not rank music high enough in the service of God. Note that in verse 5 *Heman* is called a seer. These names listed in verses 2–4 are found again with certain minor variations in verses 9–31. *Hananiah, Hanani, Eliathah . . .* (4). These nine names are for the most part improbable, or impossible, as names. But if we take the consonantal text and occasionally divide the words otherwise we get:

> Be gracious unto me, O Jah, be gracious unto me!
> Thou art my God whom I magnify and exalt.
> O my help when in trouble, I say,
> Give an abundance of visions.

This cannot be accidental. The most reasonable explanation is that some early scribe saw the possibility of reading this petition in the names of Heman's sons and altered them slightly for his purpose. *And three daughters* (5). This may imply that they too took part in the temple worship. Cf. Ps. lxviii. 25. *The teacher* (8). Better rendered 'the skilful' as in verse 7, RV. The 288 were the skilful ones, the remainder (making a total of 4,000; see xxiii. 5) were the scholars. Both classes were divided into twenty-four courses to match those of the priests and Levites.

viii. The courses and stations of the door-keepers (xxvi. 1–19). Cf. ix. 17–27. It is not clear how the gate-keepers' duties were divided up. While twenty-four names seem to be mentioned in verses 1–11, there is no suggestion that there were twenty-four courses. Lots were cast (13) for the place, not time of service. Verses 8, 9, 11 may suggest that there were ninety-three chief door-keepers; but this may be an incorrect inference, as ix. 22 says 212. These would be the chiefs of the 4,000 (xxiii. 5). Verses 17, 18 give a total of twenty-four (chief?) door-keepers on duty at a time.

To Shuppim (16). Omit; it is a case of dittography from the previous verse. *Shallecheth* (16), *Parbar* (18). Neither can be identified with certainty.

ix. Various Levitical officers (xxvi. 20–32). *And of the Levites, Ahijah was over* (20). Read with LXX, 'And the Levites their brethren were over.' The alteration required is very small. Two treasures are here mentioned; that of *the house of God* under the descendants of Ladan, and that of *the dedicated things* under the descendants of Amram. *Jehieli* (21); *'Jehiel' (xxiii. 8). *The sons of Jehieli* (22). Probably to be deleted. *Zetham* and *Joel* were brothers of Jehiel (see xxiii. 8). *The house of the Lord* (27). This need not mean the temple. The earlier dedications were probably for the repair of the tabernacle. *The outward business* (29). Cf. Ne. xi. 16. It is quite probable that they were collectors of temple dues and royal taxes (cf. verse 30). There is no obvious reason why there should be *two thousand and seven hundred* (32) for Transjordan, while there were only *a thousand and seven hundred* (30) for western Palestine. This is one of the many indications that, while the numbers in Chronicles are often hard to understand, they are not inventions.

g. The civil leaders of the nation (xxvii. 1–34)

i. The army courses (xxvii. 1–15). I.C.C. and Cam. Bible assume that we have here the number of the royal bodyguard, which at 24,000 a month would be excessive. But this is not said. If we picture them as scattered over the kingdom, the number is reasonable. It should be noticed that verse 7, with its reference to Asahel, implies that this division was of long standing, though perhaps in a less developed form. Asahel was killed when David was still king in Hebron (2 Sa. ii. 19ff.). Though the forms of the names vary slightly in places all the twelve chiefs seem to come from the list of David's mighty men. *Benaiah the son of Jehoiada, a chief priest* (5); RV 'Jehoiada the priest.' This could be the Jehoiada of xii. 27. Since, however, there is no

other suggestion that Benaiah was a priest, we may well be dealing with a scribal error based on an association of ideas with 2 Sa. viii. 18. Benaiah acted as emergency executioner (1 Ki. ii. 25, 29, 34, 46), a post we can hardly associate with a priest.

ii. The tribal princes (xxvii. 16–24). These were appointed at the time of the census. See verses 23, 24. We have thirteen names. Zadok probably represents the whole people. The two halves of the tribe of Manasseh are reckoned separately. Gad and Asher are omitted, possibly by a defect of transmission. It is not likely to have been to preserve the number twelve, as that had already been broken by the introduction of Zadok. *Elihu* (18). Presumably 'Eliab' (1 Sa. xvi. 6; 1 Ch. ii. 13). *From twenty years old and under* (23). The omission of those under twenty conforms to the wilderness pattern (Nu. i. 3); it is implied by 2 Sa. xxiv. 9; 1 Ch. xxi. 5.

iii. Various royal officers (xxvii. 25–31). These are the chief stewards of David's landed property. Note that *Obil* (30) and *Jaziz* (31) are foreigners.

iv. The king's counsellors (xxvii. 32–34). This list is of a rather different nature from that of David's officers (see xviii. 14–17; cf. also a later list, 2 Sa. xx. 23–26), though some names are common to both; if so, they are found here in their capacity of counsellors. Like the previous list it has no particular connection with its setting at the end of David's reign. One at any rate had been dead for some time. *Jonathan David's uncle* (32). Not otherwise mentioned. On the basis of xx. 7 many would render David's nephew. While the Hebrew allows this, it seems unnecessary and on the grounds of age unlikely. *Jehiel* (32). Evidently the tutor of the king's sons. *Hushai . . . the king's companion* (33). RV the king's friend.' Cf. 2 Sa. xv. 32 *et al.* 'The king's friend' is an official title, probably borrowed from Egypt; hence the AV *companion* is to be rejected as misleading. *Ahithophel* (33). See 2 Sa. xv. 31 *et al.* *Jehoiada the son of Benaiah* (34); though otherwise unknown, there seems no reason for reversing it and reading 'Benaiah the son of Jehoiada'. For reasons of age it can hardly refer to the well-known Benaiah's son. *Abiathar* (34). Presumably the priest of that name.

h. Solomon made king (xxviii. 1—xxix. 30)

There is every probability that after a hurried anointing like that described in 1 Ki. i. 39 the new king would as soon as possible be introduced in a solemn assembly to the representative leaders of the people for their confirmation of what had been done. *Made Solomon . . . king the second time* (xxix. 22). This shows that the Chronicler knew of Adonijah's attempt and its result. The proper interpretation of xxiii. 1, 2 (see note *ad loc.*) rules out the possibility that the first time is the one mentioned in xxiii. 1. He is silent about Adonijah in conformity with his purpose of omitting, so far as possible, deviations from the divine pattern.

i. Solomon presented to the national assembly (xxviii. 1–10). *And of his sons* (1). Better as in AV mg. (following the LXX) 'and his sons'. *With the officers* (1). AV mg. and RV mg. correctly render 'with the eunuchs'. This is the first mention of this abomination at the Israelite court; but cf. 1 Sa. viii. 15, RV mg. The corruption of power had acted quickly.

Then David the king stood up upon his feet (2). In normal circumstances, as many archaeological discoveries suggest, David would have spoken seated, the more so because of his age. His standing emphasizes the religious nature of the occasion. David, the chosen of Jehovah (4), presents to the people the new chosen of Jehovah (5), who has been chosen for the special purpose of building the temple (6). Though there is no direct affirmation of God's choice of Solomon in Samuel and Kings, yet 2 Sa. xii. 24, 25 may hint at it. *To sit upon the throne of the kingdom of the Lord over Israel* (5). Cf. xxix. 23, 'the throne of the Lord'. The king was Jehovah's deputy. *Take heed now* (10). This charge is continued in verse 20.

ii. The plans of the temple (xxviii. 11–19). Our interpretation of the passage will depend on our interpretation of *pattern*. Ex. xxv. 40 clearly suggests an original seen by Moses, which he was later to describe to those carrying out the work. As Ex. xxv seems to lie behind this section, it is probable that David described to Solomon the vision that he had had by inspiration. (See verse 19, *by his hand upon me*.) If this is correct, then the writing in verse 19 is the account in Exodus of the tabernacle, the necessary modifications of which to suit the temple David was caused to understand by inspiration. This is the more likely, as there has never been any satisfactory typical interpretation given to those details of the temple where it varied from the tabernacle. The Bible never suggests a heavenly prototype of the temple as it does of the tabernacle. *The pattern of the chariot of the cherubims* (18). Read as in RV 'the chariot, even the cherubim'. The cherubim were thought of as forming God's chariot. Cf. Ps. xviii. 10 and especially Ezk. i.

iii. Concluding encouragement for Solomon (xxviii. 20, 21). The thought resumes from verse 10. The LXX shows us that a section has accidentally been dropped at the end of verse 20. It reads, 'Now behold the pattern of the porch (of the temple) and of the houses thereof, and of the treasuries thereof, and of the upper rooms thereof, and of the inner chambers thereof, and of the house of the mercy-seat, even the pattern of the house of the Lord.'

iv. David's appeal for liberality and the response (xxix. 1–9). David announced a huge gift from his own private fortune for the building of the temple over and above the sum mentioned in xxii. 14, and used this as the ground of an appeal to the generosity of the assembly. The motive is less likely to have been the need for further gifts than the wish to make as many as possible have a share in the building of the new temple. It seems impossible to accept the figures both of David's and the people's gifts as they stand. How enormous they cannot so easily be judged by turning them into modern currency as by comparing them with the tribute that Sennacherib was able to wring out of Hezekiah (2 Ki. xviii. 14) or Tiglath-pileser from Menahem (2 Ki. xv. 19). Some idea of the quantities can be obtained from the Moffatt translation.

The palace (1). Heb. *birah*; this late word is used only three times of the temple. But *hekhal*, the word normally translated temple, also has as its root meaning palace or great house.

To consecrate his service (5). Lit. 'to fill his hand.' This is a technical term of inducting a person into the priestly office (cf. Ex. xxviii. 41 *et al.*); but here it is used metaphorically with the approximate sense 'who will offer willingly like one consecrating himself to the priesthood?' (I.C.C.).

Ten thousand drams (7). Read as in RV 'ten thousand darics'. The daric was a Persian gold coin (an obvious anachronism indicating the date of Chronicles) worth about a guinea. The difference between the very large number of talents and the small amount in darics may be because the latter refers to minted coins (the talent is a weight). As, at present, we have no evidence for minted coins earlier than the seventh century B.C., we cannot disprove the suggestion that this may be a complete anachronism due to a misunderstanding of his source by the Chronicler.

v. David's closing prayer of thanksgiving (xxix. 10–19). One of the finest prayers in the Old Testament. *We thank thee, and praise thy glorious name* (13). The Hebrew expresses continual action. Moffatt renders well, 'Hence, O our God, we ever thank thee and praise thy glorious name.' *We are strangers before thee* (15). The thought is not that we are strangers to God. The picture is of the notoriously insecure position of the stranger; but as they dwell before, i.e. in the sight of, God, they are secure. *There is none abiding* (15). Better, as in RV mg., 'there is no hope', i.e. apart from God. Verse 17 shows that the merit of the gifts for the temple lay not in their amount but in that they had been given willingly. David trusts that God, who knows men's hearts, will see the same willingness in the others as has been already seen in him. *Keep this for ever in the imagination . . .* (18). Better, 'as the imagination'. David prays that they may always be kept in this generous spirit. *Prepare* (18). Better, as in AV mg., 'establish', or 'direct their hearts' (RSV).

vi. The close of the assembly: Solomon made king (xxix. 20–25). *And worshipped the Lord, and the king* (20). The word normally translated worship in the Old Testament means to prostrate oneself. Hence, as here, it can be used equally for God and the king. *King the second time* (22). See note at the beginning of this section. *And Zadok to be priest* (22). We do not know enough of the customs at the time to be dogmatic, but a literal interpretation seems to be hazardous. Zadok is always presented to us as joint High Priest, so any such consecration (or reconsecration) seems to be excluded. There is no evidence for the reconsecration of the High Priest at the accession of a new king. It is easiest to regard this as the Chronicler's hint at the deposition of Abiathar, known to his readers from 1 Ki. ii. 26. *The throne of the Lord* (23). See xxviii. 5n. *And all the sons likewise of king David, submitted themselves* (24). An indirect reference to Adonijah (1 Ki. i. 53). *Such royal majesty as had not been on any king before him in Israel* (25). Translated thus the comparison is limited to David and Saul. It is likely that we should take the Hebrew to mean, 'such royal majesty which was not on any king more than on him in Israel'. This would refer to Solomon's successors as well.

vii. A summary of David's reign (xxix. 26–30). On verse 27 see 1 Ki. ii. 11. *Samuel the seer (ro'eh) . . . Gad the seer (hozeh)* (29). See 1 Sa. ix. 11n. The former term, used of Samuel in 1 Sa. ix. 9, 11, suggests something akin to clairvoyance; the latter suggests the seeing of dreams or visions. *The times that went over him* (30); i.e., his vicissitudes.

III. THE REIGN OF SOLOMON.
2 Ch. i. 1—ix. 31

The Chronicler gives us very little information that is not in Kings, though a few of his additions are of importance. Some of his omissions, like Adonijah's attempt on the throne and Solomon's apostasy and its results, are in conformity with his general purpose; we get the impression that the majority of them are merely to save space. The most remarkable feature is the manner in which, instead of closely following Kings, he has repeatedly rewritten, expanded and contracted it.

a. Solomon confirmed in the kingdom by God (i. 1–17)

i. Solomon's initiatory sacrifice and vision at Gibeon (i. 1–13). The bulk of verses 1–6 is peculiar to Chronicles. Verses 7–13 are an abridgement of 1 Ki. iii. 5–15. For the main commentary see 1 Ki. iii. 4–15. *Came from his journey to the high place* (13). Read with LXX and RV mg. 'came from the high place'.

ii. Solomon's wealth (i. 14–17). See 1 Ki. x. 26–29, with which it is virtually verbally identical, and cf. 2 Ch. ix. 13–28.

b. The building of the temple (ii. 1—v. 1)
For this section see 1 Ki. v. 1—vii. 51. The Chronicler omits the details of Solomon's other buildings (1 Ki. vii. 1–12) and also some of the details of the temple itself.

i. Solomon and Hiram (ii. 1–16). See 1 Ki. v. 1–12. The Chronicler has a considerably expanded form of the correspondence. Since verses 7, 13f. bear the stamp of authenticity (cf. 1 Ki. vii. 1), it is likely that we have a condensed version in Kings. Verse 2 is a doublet of ii. 18 (q.v.). *Huram the king of Tyre* (3). Except in 1 Ch. xiv. 1, where it is found in the mg. of the Hebrew, Chronicles always uses this form instead of *Hiram, found in Samuel and Kings, which in turn is short for Ahiram. *Cunning . . . can skill to grave* (7); i.e. 'skilled . . . able to carve'. Archaeology has fully borne out Israel's backwardness in the arts at this time. *Fir trees, and algum trees* (8); for the former see 1 Ki. v. 8n.; for the latter 1 Ki. x. 11f.n., and the parallel of 2 Ch. ix. 10f. The latter have probably been accidentally introduced here. For the quantities of food listed in verse 10 see 1 Ki v. 11n.

The authenticity of Hiram's answer (11–16) has been objected to on the ground of the religious language he uses. In a polytheistic society politeness to a neighbour's god cost nothing. *Huram my father's* (13; Heb. *Huram-abi*); see note on 1 Ki. vii. 13f. There are no grounds on which we can choose between Huram and Hiram; the name of the king is no guide. The English rendering here and in iv. 16 is certainly wrong. Some claim his name was Huram-abi (or abiv), which is possible, but more likely it should be: 'Huram, my (his) trusted counsellor.'

ii. The preparation of materials (ii. 17, 18). See also verses 1, 2 and notes on 1 Ki. v. 13–18.

iii. The construction of the temple (iii. 1–4). See notes on 1 Ki. vi. 2–10. In Chronicles the account is strangely truncated. *Mount Moriah* (1); cf. Gn. xxii. 2; the only place where Mount Zion or the temple mount is so called. Follow LXX, Vulg., RV mg., and render '. . . David his father, in the place which David had prepared, in the threshingfloor . . .' *The height was an hundred and twenty* (4); if the porch was like an Egyptian pylon, the height is possible; if it was a portico, as seems more likely, we must omit the hundred as an accidental corruption.

iv. The interior of the house (iii. 5–14). See notes on 1 Ki. vi. 14–35. Again the description is greatly abbreviated, but a few details are added. *The greater house* (5); i.e. 'the larger house', meaning 'the holy place'. *Fir tree* (5); the material of the ceiling is not mentioned in Kings. *Chains* (5); a word used only of ornamental chains, the links here being of flowers; cf. 1 Ki. vi. 18, 29. I.C.C. renders 'garlands'. *Parvaim* (6); perhaps in Arabia, but not identified. *Six hundred talents* (8); on the most likely calculation nearly 65,000 lbs., a seemingly impossible figure (cf. note on 1 Ch. xxix. 1–9). This seems borne out by the weight of the nails (9). *Fifty shekels*, i.e. less than 2 lbs., impossibly low if the total weight of metal is correct. *Upper chambers* (9); cf. 1 Ch. xxviii. 11. It is not clear what is referred to. *The vail* (14); not mentioned in Kings, even as Chronicles does not mention the doors.

v. The bronze pillars (iii. 15–17). See notes on 1 Ki. vii. 15–22. *He made chains, as in the oracle*

(16; RV omits 'as'); the word used in verse 5, not that used in 1 Ki. vi. 21; render with a slight change of text: 'he made chains like a necklace.'

vi. The bronze altar (iv. 1). Not in 1 Kings. See additional note to 1 Ki. vii.

vii. The sea and the lavers (iv. 2–6, 10). See notes on 1 Ki. vii. 23–29. The difficult description of the stands for the lavers in 1 Kings is omitted. *The similitude of oxen . . . Two rows of oxen were cast* (3); an obvious scribal error; read 'knops' as in 1 Ki. vii. 24. *Three thousand baths* (5); 1 Ki. vii. 26 has 'two thousand'; see note *ad loc.*

viii. The lampstands (iv. 7). Cf. iv. 20f. and see additional note to 1 Ki. vii. Note that in Chronicles 'he' refers to Solomon, not to Hiram as in the parallel in 1 Kings. Hence there is no suggestion that the gold articles were made by Hiram.

ix. The tables (iv. 8). Cf. iv. 19 and 1 Ki. vii. 48; see additional note to 1 Ki. vii.

x. The courts (iv. 9). See note on 1 Ki. vii. 1–12.

xi. A summary of Hiram's work (iv. 11–18). Virtually identical with 1 Ki. vii. 40–47 (q.v.).

xii. The golden vessels (iv. 19—v. 1). Virtually identical with 1 Ki. vii. 48–51 (q.v.). *The tables whereon the shewbread was set* (19); 1 Ki. vii. 48 has, obviously correctly, only one table; see the additional note to 1 Ki. vii for an explanation.

c. The dedication of the temple (v. 2—vii. 22)

This section is virtually identical with the corresponding section in 1 Ki. viii. 1—ix. 9, the few additions giving mainly liturgical information.

i. The moving of the ark (v. 2–14). See notes on 1 Ki. viii. 1–11. *The Levites took up the ark . . . these did the priests and the Levites bring up* (4, 5). Chronicles alters 'priests' (1 Ki. viii. 3) to *Levites* in verse 4 and omits the 'and' between priests and Levites in verse 5 (there is no authority for its insertion in AV). It is clear that at this period the distinction between the descendants of Aaron and the other members of the tribe of Levi was not strictly enforced; see also note on Dt. xviii. 1–8.

Verses 11b–13a are an addition by Chronicles stressing the pomp of the occasion; all available priests and Levites were on duty, not merely the fortnightly course (cf. 1 Ch. xxiv). The blowing of the trumpets was specifically a priestly duty (Nu. x. 8).

ii. The actual dedication (vi. 1—vii. 3). See 1 Ki. viii. 12–61, from which this account differs only very slightly. *Scaffold* (13); better, as in RSV, 'platform'. This information is omitted by Kings. Verses 40–42 take the place of 1 Ki. viii. 50b–53. As they are in no way alternatives, it is likely that the concluding verses in Kings have dropped out by a scribal error in Chronicles. On the other hand Kings probably deliberately omitted the conclusion in Chronicles. The section vii. 1–3 is not in Kings. For *the fire . . . from heaven* (vii. 1) cf. Lv. ix. 24; 1 Ch. xxi. 26; 1 Ki. xviii. 24, 38. The remainder is an enlargement

of v. 13b, 14. Chronicles omits Solomon's blessing of the people (1 Ki. viii. 54–61) perhaps in disapproval of the king's taking priestly functions on himself. There was always a strong temptation to the king to arrogate priestly functions to himself in imitation of his heathen neighbours (cf. 1 Sa. xiii. 8–14; 2 Ch. xxvi. 16–20; see also note on 1 Ki. xii. 26–33 and Appendix I to Kings.)

iii. The sacrifices and feast (vii. 4–10). See 1 Ki. viii. 62–66. For *the brasen altar* (7) see additional note to 1 Ki. vii.

And in the eighth day . . . And on the three and twentieth day (9, 10). This is difficult to reconcile with 1 Ki. viii. 65f., where the picture seems to be of a seven days' dedication festival (8th to 14th Tishri), followed by the feast of tabernacles (15th to 21st Tishri), followed by the dismissal of the people next day. Chronicles, finding in its additional sources that the people had been dismissed on 23rd Tishri, rightly understood that there had been an extra day. Kings reckons a seven-day dedication feast with the day of atonement (10th Tishri) in the middle, i.e. 8th to 15th Tishri, followed by tabernacles a day late, i.e. 16th to 22nd Tishri. Chronicles reckons the dedication feast as including the day of atonement, i.e. 8th to 14th Tishri, followed by tabernacles (15th to 21st Tishri) plus the eighth day closing festival (Lv. xxiii. 36). So it is a question of how the festivities were broken up, and perhaps no clear line of demarcation was drawn, as there will have been little or no distinction between the two halves.

iv. God's answer to Solomon (vii. 11–22). See 1 Ki. ix. 1–9. There are only minor verbal differences except for verses 13–16, which are merely an expansion of what is implicit in 1 Ki. ix. 3.

d. Solomon's glory (viii. 1—ix. 31)

See 1 Ki. ix. 10—x. 29, xi. 41–43. The differences between Kings and Chronicles are for the most part insignificant. 1 Ki. ix. 11–16 are omitted, while 2 Ch. viii. 13–16 have no parallel in Kings.

i. Solomon's transactions with Hiram (viii. 1, 2). See 1 Ki. ix. 10–14. It is often alleged that Chronicles here contradicts Kings. It is more likely that the Chronicler disapproved of Solomon's transactions with Hiram, and therefore mentions only the final incident in them, which, however, is not mentioned in Kings (see notes *ad loc.*).

ii. Solomon's levy and city building (viii. 3–11). See 1 Ki. ix. 15–24. The campaign against *Hamath* (3) is peculiar to Chronicles. Hamath had voluntarily become tributary to David (2 Sa. viii. 9ff.) and probably took advantage of his death to try to regain independence. This, the only campaign waged by Solomon, was probably very brief. *Tadmor in the wilderness* (4) was interpreted by all the versions as Palmyra, about halfway between Damascus and the Euphrates. Tadmor existed already in the time of Tiglath-pileser I of Assyria, *c.* 1100 B.C., so it may have been in Solomon's possession. Since, however, in 1 Ki. ix. 18 the true reading is certainly Tamar (see note *ad loc.*), the mention of Hamath may have misled some scribe. *The store cities, which he built in Hamath* (4) may have been to cover the northern approaches of Israel (cf. note on 1 Ki. viii. 65). The discrepancy of *two hundred and fifty* (10) with the 550 of Kings hardly calls for comment; the number will not have remained constant throughout the reign. In fact if we add the figures in 1 Ki. v. 16 and ix. 23 we get the same total as when we add 2 Ch. ii. 18 and viii. 10. The statement about *the daughter of Pharaoh* (11) is hard to understand. *My wife shall not dwell* . . . is misleading for it suggests that the objection was that she was a foreigner; in fact we should render 'no wife of mine shall dwell . . .' (Cam. Bible, Moff.). It is no longer possible to reconstruct the circumstances.

iii. **Solomon's worship (viii. 12–16).** It would seem from verse 16 that this section originally wound up the description of the building of the temple. All modern commentators agree that the LXX should be followed, at least in part, in verse 16. RSV renders 'Thus was accomplished all the work of Solomon from the day the foundation of the house of the Lord was laid until it was finished. So the house of the Lord was completed.'

iv. **Solomon's Red Sea trade (viii. 17, 18).** See 1 Ki. ix. 26–28. *Then went Solomon* (17) need no more be taken literally than the parallel in Kings 'And king Solomon made a navy'. *Huram sent him* . . . *ships* (18). It is absurd to read into this that ships were transported overland. There is such shortage of timber round the Gulf of Aqaba that it would have to be brought from Phoenicia, and it was probably to a large degree shaped in advance.

v. **The visit of the queen of Sheba (ix. 1–12).** Almost verbally identical with 1 Ki. x. 1–13 (q.v.).

vi. **The trade and riches of Solomon (ix. 13–28).** See 1 Ki. x. 14–29. To 1 Ki. x. 26–29 we really have a doublet in 2 Chronicles, viz. i. 14–17 and ix. 25–28. For the weight of the *three hundred shields* (16) see note on 1 Ki. x. 17. *The footstool of gold* (18) is merely a corruption of the text of 1 Ki. x. 19 (see note *ad loc.*). *The king's ships went to Tarshish* (21). The Chronicler knew only of traffic based on Ezion-geber (viii. 17, ix. 10) and since verse 21 is obviously the same as 1 Ki. x. 22, we are dealing with a careless scribal error. The ships may have gone as far as India but they did not circumnavigate Africa to reach the Mediterranean where Tarshish was (Jon. i. 3). Nor are the products brought back Mediterranean products. The same error has slipped into xx. 36, 37.

vii. **Summary of Solomon's reign (ix. 29–31).** See 1 Ki. xi. 41–43. The Chronicler omits the story of Solomon's idolatry and troubles, even as he does that of David's sin and its results, and just for the same reason. He is concerned with the monarchy as an institution rather than with

the personal failings of those that sat on the throne; see *Introduction*, p. 339.

IV. THE KINGS OF JUDAH.
2 Ch. x. 1—xxxvi. 23

a. **Rehoboam (x. 1—xii. 16)**

Chronicles brings us a number of interesting points, some of importance, which are not mentioned by Kings.

i. **The disruption (x. 1–19).** See 1 Ki. xii. 1–20. Note the deliberate omission of 1 Ki. xii. 20. Not even the making of Jeroboam king is to be mentioned. For the Chronicler the northern kingdom is from the first apostate.

ii. **Civil war averted (xi. 1–4).** See 1 Ki. xii. 21–24. Note the insertion *and to all Israel in Judah and Benjamin* (3). The Chronicler constantly insists that there were always elements of the northern tribes that remained loyal to the Davidic king.

iii. **The organization of Judah (xi. 5–12).** Not in Kings. As soon as Jeroboam could organize the north it was bound to be stronger than Judah both in its population and natural resources. Jeroboam was an ambitious man not likely to be content with what God had given him, and so Rehoboam did his best to strengthen his diminished kingdom. *He built* (6); i.e. he refortified. This may have been after Shishak's invasion, for all the towns are in the south.

iv. **Immigration from Israel (xi. 13–17).** Cf. 1 Ki. xii. 31, xiii. 33. The mention not merely of *Jeroboam* but also of *his sons*, i.e. his successors (14), shows that while the major part of the immigration of priests and Levites took place at once, yet it continued over a period, the turn of phrase in Hebrew in verse 13 being consistent with this. *Had cast them off* (14). We may be sure Jeroboam would have been glad to keep them, but by his insistence on a Canaanized version of Jehovah worship (see Appendix I to Kings) he had made it impossible for those who were loyal to remain. We may be sure some will have put their pocket before their conscience and stayed. *Devils* (15; Heb. *se'irim*) are the demons or *jinn* believed to inhabit desert and waste places; they were looked on as hairy, or of animal shape; hence RV 'he-goats', RV mg. 'satyrs' (cf. Lv. xvii. 7 and Robertson Smith, *The Religion of the Semites*, p. 120). The return to nature worship meant a return to old superstitions. *The calves which he had made* (15); important as showing that Chronicles takes a knowledge of Kings for granted. The natural interpretation of verses 16, 17 is that some of those who disobeyed Jeroboam's ban then came to Jerusalem to worship and made their permanent home there; cf. xv. 9.

v. **The royal family (xi. 18–23).** Rehoboam's chief wife was *Mahalath* (18) whose parents were *Jerimoth*, an otherwise unnamed son of David, and *Abihail* (18; the RV is correct in inserting 'of'), a niece of David's. Buth is favourite wife was *Maachah* (20) or Michaiah (xiii. 2), the grand-daughter of *Absalom* (cf. 20 with xiii. 2).

He desired many wives (23); probably as RV 'he sought for them many wives'.

vi. Rehoboam's idolatry (xii. 1). See 1 Ki. xiv. 21, 22. It is not clear why we have no details, for they are clearly implied in xiv. 2, 3. *All Israel* means in Chronicles the southern kingdom.

vii. Shishak's invasion (xii. 2-12). Cf. 1 Ki. xiv. 25-28. We have Shishak's own account of the invasion recorded on the outside wall of the temple of Karnak. This and other archaeological evidence (see Petrie, *Palestine and Israel*, p. 82) shows that Israel was engulfed as well as Judah, even Ezion-geber being probably destroyed, and that Egyptian overlordship must have lasted some years. It is probable that no resistance was offered. *Lubims* (3); Libyans. *Sukkiims* (3); unidentified. *Some deliverance* (7); better 'deliverance within a little while' (RV mg.); the Egyptians could not keep up their effort for long. *That they may know my service* (8); that it is better than serving others. *And also in Judah things went well* (12); 'and moreover in Judah there were good things found' (RV). It is clear that while the north gladly accepted the Canaanized distortion of Jehovah worship patronized by Jeroboam, it did not really get a grip of Judah till the reigns of Ahaz and Manasseh.

viii. Summary of his reign (xii. 13-16). Cf. 1 Ki. xiv. 29-31. *Concerning genealogies* (15); an obscure expression perhaps arising from a textual corruption.

b. Abijah (xiii. 1-22)

Cf. 1 Ki. xv. 1-8. No satisfactory explanation of the difference between the forms *Abijah* (1) in Chronicles and Abijam in Kings has been given; so we cannot decide which was his real name. For his *mother* (2) see note on xi. 20. The size of the armies (3) should be compared with the census figures (2 Sa. xxiv. 9; 1 Ch. xxi. 5). This was an all-out effort at conquest. *Mount Zemaraim* (4); cf. Jos. xviii. 22. *A covenant of salt* (5) was unbreakable (Nu. xviii. 19). Abijah was far from practising what he preached (1 Ki. xv. 3); but what was settled religious policy in the north was still only an aberration in Judah. His picture of the disruption (6, 7) is rather fanciful. Abijah claims it is a holy war. *With sounding trumpets* (12). Render 'with the trumpets of alarm' (RV) and cf. Nu. x. 9. *God smote* (15). There would seem to have been some form of supernatural intervention. We must take the *five hundred thousand chosen men* (17) as no more than 'a very large number', for the only result of the victory was the capture of a few border towns which Asa soon lost (see note on 1 Ki. xv. 16-22).

c. Asa (xiv. 1—xvi. 14)

i. Asa's reformation (xiv. 1-5, xv. 16-18). See 1 Ki. xv. 9-15. There is no reason for thinking that Asa's reformation was really in two stages. The impression arises from the way the material from Kings has been joined to other sources. Maachah's *idol* (xv. 16) must have been disposed of right away.

If we put together 1 Ki. xv. 28 and 16, it becomes clear that the *ten years* (1) is only a round figure. Verses 3-5 only make explicit what is implicit in 1 Ki. xv. 12. *He took away the altars of the strange gods* (RV 'the strange altars'), *and the high places* (3). It is alleged that this is a deliberate contradiction of 1 Ki. xv. 14 (see note *ad loc.*). The self-consistency of Chronicles is then vindicated by suggesting that 2 Ch. xv. 17 is either a later addition from Kings or that *Israel* there means the northern kingdom. The more reasonable explanation is that *strange* should be construed with *high places* as well as *gods*; he removed these high places that could make no legitimate claim to existence (see Appendix I to Kings). *The images* (5); RSV correctly 'incense altars'. *The kingdom was quiet before him* (5); better 'the kingdom had rest under him' (RSV).

ii. Asa's defensive measures (xiv. 6-8). Not in Kings, but cf. 1 Ki. xv. 23.

iii. Asa's victory over Zerah (xiv. 9-15). Not in Kings. Zerah is generally identified with Pharaoh Osorkon I or II and there is a little archaeological evidence to favour an invasion by the latter. But he is called *ha-kushi*, 'the Cushite'. Cush is either Ethiopia, i.e. the Sudan, or part of Arabia (Gn. x. 7; 2 Ch. xxi. 16, q.v.). Since the XXII dynasty of Egypt was not Ethiopian, though they may have controlled part of the Sudan, it is quite possible that it was an Arabian invasion, but with Egyptian backing (cf. xvi. 8, 'Lubims', i.e. Libyans). Note the nature of the booty (15) which would suit an Arab invasion. The *three hundred chariots* (9) is proof enough that the numbers are not invented; therefore *a thousand thousand* probably means no more than an exceedingly large number. *Gerar* (13, 14) and the neighbouring cities were Philistine; they had probably aided Zerah. No satisfactory explanation of *tents of cattle* (15) is offered.

iv. Azariah's exhortation and its results (xv. 1-15). Not in Kings. The main thought of the passage is clear enough. *Azariah* (1) explained the victory by saying 'The Eternal was on your side, because you were on his side' (2, Moff.) and so encouraged them to carry through (7) the reformation which till that time had been carried on only at the official level. This was sealed at a great popular gathering at the feast of weeks (10). It is verses 3-6 that create a difficulty. They seem to describe the position under the judges, and are apparently a commentary on the last section of verse 2. But whether they are Azariah's words or a comment by the Chronicler is not clear.

The fifteenth year (10) compared with xiv. 1 shows that no complete chronology of Asa's reign is being attempted; see too note on xv. 19. *The strangers with them out of Ephraim and Manasseh, and . . . Simeon* (9). They may have migrated to Judah, especially in the troubled time when Baasha wiped out the house of Jeroboam (1 Ki. xv. 27-29); but why Simeon? There is no evidence for their living elsewhere than in the south, and they were always part of Judah (cf. note on 1 Ki. xi. 30). Either it implies that until now their hearts had been with the north, or more likely it is an unintelligent correction of an early scribal error.

v. Asa's war with Baasha (xv. 19—xvi. 6). (For xv. 16–18 see paragraph c i above.) See 1 Ki. xv. 16–22. The figures in xv. 19, xvi. 1 are impossible, for Baasha died in the twenty-sixth year of Asa. It has been suggested that the original reading was '. . . unto the five and thirtieth year (i.e. of the kingdom), that is, in the fifteenth year of the reign of Asa . . . in the six and thirtieth year, that is, in the sixteenth year of Asa', but this is more plausible than convincing.

vi. Hanani's rebuke of Asa (xvi. 7–10). Not in Kings. For the deeper reasons for this rebuke see Appendix II to Kings. Hanani tells Asa that if he had trusted he would have defeated the combined armies of Baasha and the Syrians (7). Asa's reply was not to *put him in a prison house* (10), but 'in the stocks' (RSV, Moff.). When he *oppressed* (better 'tortured', Moff.) *some of the people* (10), it may have been for showing sympathy with Hanani. This is the first recorded instance of the ill-treatment of a prophet.

vii. Summary of Asa's reign (xvi. 11–14). Cf. 1 Ki. xv. 23, 24. If, as is probable, *the physicians* (12) were foreigners, the condemnation is easily understandable, as their cures will have had more of magic than of medicine about them. *They made a very great burning for him* (14); they did not cremate him, but burned spices (cf. Je. xxxiv. 5); the worthy funeral for a worthy king is being stressed.

d. Jehoshaphat (xvii. 1—xx. 37)

i. The character of his reign (xvii. 1–6). *In the first ways of his father David* (3). The LXX is almost certainly correct in omitting David (cf. chapters xiv and xv with xvi). *He took away the high places* (6); cf. xx. 33 and the note on xiv. 3. The lack of detail about Jehoshaphat's reformation shows it was no more than the rectifying of slackness since Asa's reformation (cf. xix. 4n.).

ii. Regular teaching of the law (xvii. 7–9). The AV of verse 7 is strangely incorrect. Render with RV 'he sent his princes, even Benhail, and Obadiah . . .'.

iii. Jehoshaphat's greatness (xvii. 10–19). *The Arabians* (11). If Zerah was an Arabian (xiv. 9n.) this may have been a result of Asa's victory. The numbers of Jehoshaphat's army (14–18) are among those in Chronicles that we can no longer explain. See *Introduction*, p. 339. They are far too high when compared with those available to Ahab and with the probably inflated figures given by Shalmaneser III in his account of the battle of Qarqar (see Appendix III), and indeed with the evidence of archaeology generally. If we divide each figure by ten, we reach a total 112,000 of trained soldiers, not militia, which would have been within the powers of Judah at the height of its prosperity and comparable to the half-million militia in the time of David (2 Sa. xxiv. 9).

iv. Jehoshaphat's alliance with Ahab (xviii. 1–34). See 1 Ki. xxii. 1–38. Except for verses 1, 2 and the details following Ahab's death (1 Ki. xxii. 36–38), which have no bearing on Jehoshaphat, the parallels are almost identical. The main changes are intended to put Jehoshaphat more in the centre of the picture. *He joined affinity with Ahab* (1); 'he made a marriage alliance with Ahab' (RSV); see 2 Ki. viii. 18, 26; cf. 1 Ki. iii. 1n. *The son of Imla* (7); 1 Ki. xxii, probably correctly, Imlah.

v. Jehoshaphat's alliance rebuked (xix. 1–3). *In peace* (1); i.e. 'safe and sound'; see 1 Ki. xxii. 27n. *Jehu the son of Hanani* (2). In 1 Ki. xvi. 1 Jehu the son of Hanani pronounces the doom of Baasha; in 2 Ch. xvi. 7 Hanani the seer rebukes Asa. This Jehu is probably the grandson of the Jehu in 1 Ki. xvi. 1. It was not rare for names to alternate like this in some families. *Therefore is wrath upon thee* (2); fulfilled in the invasion of xx. 1.

vi. Administration of law (xix. 4–11). *Jehoshaphat dwelt at Jerusalem* (4); i.e. he paid no more visits to Israel. *And brought them back unto the Lord* (4); purity of religion could be bought only at the price of eternal vigilance.

A closer study of the Mosaic legislation will show that it is incomplete, though the Pharisees, by ingenious exposition, were able to make it cover all life; this becomes particularly obvious when it is compared with an ancient code like that of Hammurabi. In other words it did not entirely replace the existing tribal law, but showed how it had to be modified and developed. That meant that side by side there had been, from the first, civil (Ex. xviii. 25, 26) and religious (cf. Ex. xxi. 6, xxii. 8, 9, RV) judges. This is clearly legislated for in Dt. xvi. 18, xvii. 8–12. In his reform Jehoshaphat appointed civil judges throughout the land (5) probably because the old system, based on family headship, had broken down. In Jerusalem there was a mixed court of appeal (8); *for the judgment of the Lord*, i.e. cases covered by the law of Moses; *controversies*, i.e. civil cases. There were two chief judges (11), *Amariah the chief priest* (1 Ch. vi. 11), and *Zebadiah* representing the king. Increasingly the king was withdrawing from the actual administration of justice to a position where he could see that it was being administered.

vii. An invasion by Moabites and their allies (xx. 1–4). This invasion must have been earlier than the campaign in 2 Ki. iii, which may have been a sequel to it. (*Other*) *beside the Ammonites* (1); an unworthy attempt of the AV to dodge an obvious difficulty. Read with LXX 'and some of the Meunim' (Heb. read *mhm'wnym* for *mh-'mwnym*). The Meunim are mentioned in 1 Ch. iv. 41 (RV), 2 Ch. xxvi. 7. They were, if not Edomites, resident in Edom, and are in verses 10, 22 connected with Mount Seir. The reason why the name Edom is not mentioned is that Edom at this time was under Judah (1 Ki. xxii. 47n.; 2 Ki. iii. 9n.). These were some of the inhabitants who linked up with the invaders as they passed through their territory. *On this side Syria* (2). Read 'from Edom' (Heb. read as often *'dm* for *'rm*). To cross *the sea*, i.e. the Dead Sea, they had passed round its southern end through Edom. *And Jehoshaphat feared* (3) for he knew this was the expression of the divine wrath (xix. 2).

viii. Jehoshaphat's prayer and the divine answer (xx. 5–19). *The new court* (5); see note on 1 Ki. vii. 1–12. Evidently changes had been made since Solomon's time of which we are not told. *Cliff . . . brook* (16); in AV mg. and RV 'ascent . . . valley'. The reason for the particular form of victory promised is that Jehovah had brought the invaders as a punishment. Since they had achieved their purpose Jehovah would remove them Himself. This is the more striking because of Jehoshaphat's own strength.

ix. The deliverance (xx. 20–30). Jehoshaphat's trust is seen in the singing of praise before the fulfilment of the promise (21). *Praise the beauty of holiness* (21); here, as elsewhere (1 Ch. xvi. 29; Ps. xxix. 2, xcvi. 9, cx. 3), 'in holy attire' or 'in holy array' (RSV). *The Lord set ambushments* (22); 'liers in wait' (RV). Action by Jehoshaphat is excluded. It could refer to action by the inhabitants of the overrun area, but far more likely by supernatural agents, otherwise unspecified. *They were smitten* (22); explained by verse 23. *The watch tower* (24); better 'the outlook point' (Cam. Bible, I.C.C.). *With the dead bodies* (25); the RV is correct, but hardly possible. Follow seven Heb. MSS, LXX, RV mg. 'and garments'. *Berachah* (26); i.e. blessing; the name is preserved near Tekoa to this day.

x. Summary of Jehoshaphat's reign (xx. 31–37). See 1 Ki. xxii. 41–50. It is not clear why Chronicles should single out the section about Jehoshaphat's fleet (35–37) as it does. *The book of Jehu . . . who is mentioned* (34); 'which is inserted' (RV). *To Tarshish* (36, 37); they were ships of Tarshish to go to Ophir; see ix. 21n.

e. Jehoram and Ahaziah (xxi. 1—xxii. 9)

i. Jehoram's reign (xxi. 1–10). See 2 Ki. viii. 16–22. Except for verses 2–4 this is identical with the passage in Kings (q.v.). There is no reason suggested for Jehoram's act. The fact that it was not confined to his brothers but he *slew . . divers also of the princes of Israel* (4; Moff. renders correctly 'of the nobility in Israel'— Israel being, as usually in Chronicles, the southern kingdom) suggests that he was removing opponents to his intended religious policy.

ii. Jehoram's apostasy and its results (xxi. 11–20). Not in Kings. Since in xxiii. 17 (2 Ki. xi. 18) only one temple of Baal is mentioned, it is probable that Jehoram deliberately prepared for the introduction of Baal worship by fostering a debased form of Jehovah worship (11). Note that his son's name, Ahaziah, is compounded with Jah. *And compelled Judah thereto* (11); too strong; 'and led Judah astray'. The difficulty about Elijah's letter (12–15) is that Elijah was indubitably gone by this time (cf. 2 Ki. iii. 11, in

the reign of Jehoshaphat). We may only suppose that it was written before his translation so that, when Athaliah tried to carry out her mother's policy in Judah, she should be faced by the memory of her mother's great opponent. *The Arabians, that were near the Ethiopians* (16); see note on xiv. 9. *All the substance that was found in the king's house* (17); as they did not capture Jerusalem it is better to render 'that belonged to the king's house' (RSV, RV mg.) and cf. xxii. 1. *Save Jehoahaz, the youngest of his sons* (17). This is no contradiction with xxii. 1. Jehoahaz=Jah +ahaz, Ahaziah=ahaz+Jah; both mean 'Jehovah has grasped'. *His people made no burning for him* (19); see xvi. 14n.

iii. Ahaziah (xxii. 1–9). See 2 Ki. viii. 25–29. Verses 7–9 have no close parallel in Kings. For verse 1 cf. xxi. 16, 17. *The inhabitants of Jerusalem* (1); see additional note to 2 Ki. xi. It may be that the country people were so opposed to the policy of the court that they would have been willing to transfer the crown to some other branch of the Davidic family. *Forty and two years old* (2); an obvious scribal error; cf. xxi. 20; 2 Ki. viii. 26. For notes on verses 2–6 see the parallel passage in Kings. *He returned to be healed* (6); obviously Jehoram. *Azariah* (6); a scribal error; correct in versions and six Hebrew MSS.

Verse 7 presupposes a knowledge of 2 Ki. ix. 1–28, but verse 9 is irreconcilable with 2 Ki. ix. 27, 28 and verse 8 (read with LXX 'the brethren of Ahaziah', i.e. his kinsmen) with 2 Ki. x. 12–14, if we are to assume that Chronicles means to put their death before Ahaziah's. It is likely that we have to do here with a case of major textual disorder. What we may not do is to ascribe a deliberate contradiction to the Chronicler, for, as is his custom, he has already by verse 7 referred the interested reader to Kings for further details. *The house of Ahaziah had no power to keep still* (RV 'hold') *the kingdom* (9). The slaughter of xxi. 17, xxii. 8 had removed anyone able to stand up to Athaliah.

f. Joash (xxii. 10—xxiv. 27)

i. Athaliah as queen (xxii. 10–12). See 2 Ki. xi. 1–3.

ii. The plot against Athaliah (xxiii. 1–15). See 2 Ki. xi. 4–16.

iii. The covenant (xxiii. 16–21). See 2 Ki. xi. 17–20.

iv. The repair of the temple (xxiv. 1–14). See 2 Ki. xi. 21—xii. 16.

v. The apostasy of Joash (xxiv. 15–22). Not in Kings though hinted at. It is very strange that some scholars doubt the authenticity of this section. Why should the Chronicler so wantonly blacken the reputation of a king like Joash? The merciful silence of Kings is more easily understood in the light of this passage.

As explained in the comments on 2 Ki. xi. 21— xii. 16, especially in the additional note on chapter xi, the overthrow of Athaliah and the reforms that followed it were largely the work of the country people (the 'people of the land').

Now after the death of Jehoiada came the princes of Judah (17); better 'the nobles of Judah' (Moff.). The inheritors of the old court tradition came and won him back to the old ways (18). *The groves* (18); RV 'the Asherim' (see 1 Ki. xiv. 23n.). *Zechariah the son of Jehoiada* (20) . . . *they . . . stoned him . . . in the court of the house of the Lord* (21); cf. Mt. xxiii. 35; Lk. xi. 51. Our Lord's reference to Zechariah shows that in His time Chronicles stood in the Hebrew Canon, where it now does, as the last book. Zechariah is mentioned as the last-named martyr. *They conspired against him* (21); probably some trumped-up charge as in the case of Naboth (1 Ki. xxi. 8–13). *In the court of the house of the Lord* (21); 'between the temple and the altar' (Mt. xxiii. 35). Rabbinic tradition made this murder one of the chief reasons for the destruction of Solomon's temple. Certainly Judah never fully recovered spiritually from Joash's apostasy.

vi. Punishment for apostasy and death of Joash (xxiv. 23–27). See 2 Ki. xii. 17–21. *In the story* (RV 'commentary') *of the book of the kings* (27); cf. xiii. 22. It is not clear what authority is intended by this name.

g. Amaziah (xxv. 1—xxvi. 2)

i. Amaziah's accession (xxv. 1–4). See 2 Ki. xiv. 1–6.

ii. The victory over Edom (xxv. 5–13). Cf. 2 Ki. xiv. 7. The result of Amaziah's census (5) was to show a considerable fall since the days of Asa (xiv. 8). *He hired also an hundred thousand mighty men of valour out of Israel* (6). In the light of 2 Ki. xiii. 7 it is clear that once again we are dealing with round figures to express a large number. *Israel . . . to wit, with all the children of Ephraim* (7). This explanation of the term Israel is given because it is normally used of the southern kingdom in Chronicles. The LXX suggests that verse 8 is corrupt. As it stands, it tells Amaziah that, do what he may, he will be defeated. I.C.C. and Moff. may be correct in making a small insertion and rendering 'Go by yourself, strike your own blow, be brave in battle; God will not let you fall before the foe' (Moff.). RSV follows the LXX. *The valley of salt* (11); cf. 2 Sa. viii. 13; probably the extension of the rift valley south of the Dead Sea. The usual identification of Selah (2 Ki. xiv. 7) with Petra is far from certain, especially as there is no trace of Joktheel (2 Ki. xiv. 7), the later name of Selah, linked with Petra. Why *ten thousand* (12) captives were massacred is not said; but see Am. i. 11, which is not much later in time. It is probable that Amaziah's victory gave him the control only of the route down to Elath (2 Ki. viii. 22n., xiv. 22n.). The mercenaries had marched home in anger (10). When they reached *Samaria* (13) they heard that Amaziah was away in Edom, so they raided Judah. Though the *three thousand* seems to refer to the cities, both Hebrew grammar and the area of Judah prohibit this meaning; render 'killing three thousand men' (Moff.).

iii. Amaziah's idolatry (xxv. 14–16). Not in

Kings; but note the hint in 2 Ki. xiv. 3. The Bible is never concerned with a man's justification for his actions, but with his actions. Amaziah's rather contemptuous dismissal of the prophetic warning (16) shows that he regarded the whole incident otherwise. He held the debased view of Jehovah (see Appendix I to Kings) by which He was the supreme god, but yet one god among others. His victory over Edom was proof of Jehovah's victory over the gods of Edom (about whom we have no information). Yet they were gods in spite of their defeat, so he brought their images to Jerusalem (14) to deprive the Edomites of their help. Even captive gods deserve respect, so he *bowed down himself before them, and burned incense unto them* (14). But that did not mean for Amaziah a rejection of Jehovah. For the prophets Jehovah stood alone, and so the placing of other gods beside or even under Him meant rejecting Him.

iv. Amaziah's encounter with Joash (xxv. 17–24). See 2 Ki. xiv. 8–16 with which it is virtually identical. *Then Amaziah . . . took advice* (17); better 'let himself be counselled' (Moff.); this was the divine misleading (cf. 1 Ki. xxii. 19–23).

v. Summary of Amaziah's reign (xxv. 25—xxvi. 2). See 2 Ki. xiv. 17–22 with which it is virtually identical.

h. Uzziah (xxvi. 3–23)

i. Introduction to reign (xxvi. 3–5). See 2 Ki. xv. 1–4.

ii. The wars and greatness of Uzziah (xxvi. 6–15). For the *Mehunims* (7), i.e. 'Meunim' (RV), see xx. 1n. Not sufficient is known of pre-exilic Jerusalem to interpret verse 9 with certainty. The *towers* (10) were for the protection of the cattle. *The low country* (10); the Shephelah, the low hills between Judaea and the Philistine plain. *In the plains* (10); 'in the tableland' (RV mg.) probably of Transjordan (cf. verse 8). *In Carmel* (10); rather 'in the fruitful fields' (RV). *Habergeons* (14); i.e. 'coats of mail' (RV).

iii. Uzziah's sin and its punishment (xxvi. 16–23). Cf. 2 Ki. xv. 5–7. Uzziah's wish to perform priestly functions was, in fact, his giving way to the constant temptation of the kings to look on themselves as 'divine kings'; see 1 Ki. xii. 27n. and Appendix I to Kings. He was smitten with leprosy rather than another disease, because leprosy was considered a token of special divine judgment. *A several house* (21); RSV 'a separate house'.

i. Jotham (xxvii. 1–9)

See 2 Ki. xv. 32–38. *Ophel* (3); a spur of the temple hill at Jerusalem.

j. Ahaz (xxviii. 1–27)

i. Ahaz' apostasy (xxviii. 1–4). See 2 Ki. xv 1–4.

ii. The Syro-Ephraimite attack (xxviii. 5–19). See 2 Ki. xvi. 5, 6. We have here in addition the information about the Edomites and Philistines (17, 18) and about Israel's treatment of the prisoners they had taken (6–15). It would seem that there was a change of heart in some in the north, when it was already too late; cf. 2 Ki. xvii. 2n. *Which were expressed by name* (15); RSV 'who have been mentioned by name'. *The city of palm trees* (15); cf. Jdg. i. 16, iii. 13.

iii. **The appeal to Assyria and its result (xxviii. 16, 20–25).** See 2 Ki. xvi. 7–16. *Unto the kings of Assyria* (16); the versions are probably correct in reading the singular. *For he made Judah naked* (19); rather, as in RV, 'for he had dealt wantonly in Judah'. *Tilgath-pilneser* (20); i.e. Tiglath-pileser (cf. 1 Ch. v. 6, 26; 2 Ki. xv. 19n.). *And distressed him* (20); doubtless by the amount of tribute demanded. *He sacrificed unto the gods of Damascus, which smote him* (23). Verses 22, 23 are really parenthetic and refer to the time of the Syrian attack; this has no connection with 2 Ki. xvi. 10 (q.v.). *Ahaz . . . cut in pieces the vessels of the house of God* (24). This probably refers to the incident of 2 Ki. xvi. 17 with perhaps other items as well; xxix. 18, 19 shows that there had been no widespread destruction of the temple vessels. *Ahaz . . . shut up the doors of the house of the Lord* (24). As explained in the notes on Kings, Ahaz continued to worship Jehovah after his fashion, and 2 Ki. xvi. 12–16 clearly indicates the continued use of the temple courts. Ahaz may have considered the imageless sanctuary unsuited for his worship. This is supported by the continued use of the temple in the worse apostasy of Manasseh.

k. **Hezekiah (xxix. 1—xxxii. 33)**

Over half the information in Chronicles is peculiar to it, and where it is paralleled by 2 Kings and Is. xxxvi—xxxix the information has been largely abbreviated and rewritten. For certain general problems connected with the reign see introduction to section XXIX of Kings.

i. **Hezekiah's reign (xxix. 1, 2).** See 2 Ki. xviii. 1–3.

ii. **The cleansing of the temple (xxix. 3–19).** Not in 2 Kings. He *opened the doors of the house of the Lord* (3); see xxviii. 24n. *The east street* (4); RV 'the broad place on the east'; cf. Ezr. x. 9, RV. *The filthiness* (5); the accumulated dirt of years of neglect. *They have shut up the doors of the porch* (7); see note on xxviii. 24. *They . . . have not burned incense nor offered burnt offerings* (7); this is superficially in direct contradiction to 2 Ki. xvi. 15. Just as the prophets refused to regard the Canaanized worship of Jehovah as anything but Baal worship, so Hezekiah refused to look on the sacrifices offered on an Assyrian altar as offered to Jehovah; for him they were sacrifices to the Assyrian gods. *The wrath of the Lord* (8); see the disasters of chapter xxviii. *To make a covenant with the Lord* (10); cf. xv. 12, xxiii. 16, xxxiv. 31. The motive was good, but the power to keep the covenant lacking. The record of names of the Levites (12–14) confirms what we know from other sources (e.g. Pr. xxv. 1) that the time of Hezekiah was a time of literary activity leaving considerable records to the

future. *Into the brook Kidron* (16); cf. xv. 16, xxx. 14. *Which king Ahaz . . . did cast away* (19); see xxviii. 24n.; 'cast away' is much too strong a rendering for the Hebrew; 'discarded' (RSV) is correct.

iii. **The renewal of temple worship (xxix. 20–36).** Not in 2 Kings. The opening service was one of atonement in which seven he-goats (23) were brought as a sin offering, and seven bullocks, rams and lambs (22) as a burnt offering. A careful study will show that the sin offering was always accompanied by a burnt offering. The choice of seven animals may be due to the associations of the number, or because the people were divided into seven categories; three are mentioned in verse 21—*kingdom* means the royal house, *sanctuary* the priests and Levites. The mention of the music (25, 26) is probably due to Ahaz having changed the temple music along with his other ritual rearrangements. There will have been musical accompaniment to the burnt offering from at least the time of *David* (25, 26; cf. 1 Ch. xxiii. 5, xxv. 1), and probably earlier. *The song of the Lord* (27); it is now virtually universally recognized that the vast majority of the Psalms were written for use in the temple on various occasions; verse 30 makes it clear what was sung. *The princes* (30); here probably the chief priests (cf. 1 Ch. xxv. 1n.). The comparatively small number of offerings under the circumstances (32, 33) shows how greatly Judah had suffered under Ahaz. Normally (Lv. i. 5, 6) the killing and flaying of the burnt offering was the worshipper's duty; the exception here (34) may be due to their being congregational (32) rather than personal offerings. *The priests were too few* (34). Urijah, the High Priest (2 Ki. xvi. 10ff.), had done nothing to oppose Ahaz, but had co-operated. He probably drew in many of the other priests, while most of the Levites may have stood aloof.

iv. **The invitation to keep the Passover (xxx. 1–12).** Not in 2 Kings. The choice of the *passover* (1), even though it would have to be kept in the *second month* (2), cf. Nu. ix. 10, 11, was deliberate. The chief feast of the Canaanized Jehovah-worship was tabernacles (cf. 1 Ki. xii. 32), the great nature New Year feast, but Passover was the New Year feast of the supernatural Jehovah who ruled history (see Appendix I to Kings). As the discussion in the introduction to section XXIX of 2 Kings makes clear, the destruction of Samaria occurred when Hezekiah was co-regent with his father; so *Ephraim and Manasseh* (1) refer to those not carried into captivity (see 2 Ki. xvii. 6n., and additional note to 2 Ki. xvii). As Hezekiah was tributary to Assyria, the new settlers will have had no objection. That Hezekiah's messengers went only as far as *Zebulun* (10) suggests that in the far north of Galilee the Israelite elements had already disappeared. *The posts* (6); better 'couriers' (RSV).

v. **The celebration of the Passover (xxx. 13–27).** Not in 2 Kings. Even as the priests had cleansed the temple, so the people now cleansed the city (14). *Into the brook Kidron* (14); cf. xv. 16, xxix. 16. The zeal of the people shamed the backward priests and Levites (15) so that they sanctified themselves in time. The burden on them was heavier than usual, for the Levites had to kill the lambs instead of the worshippers doing it (17), for many of them were ritually unclean (18). In many cases the uncleanness needed seven days for removal, and the pilgrims had not reached Jerusalem in time to carry out the regulations. *The Lord . . . healed the people* (20); i.e. forgave them (cf. Ps. xli. 4; Je. iii. 22; Ho. xiv. 4). Render verse 22 'And Hezekiah spoke encouragingly to all the Levites who showed good skill in the service of the Lord. So the people ate the food of the festival for seven days, sacrificing peace offerings and giving thanks to the Lord . . .' (RSV). The feast of unleavened bread was doubled in length (23). The mention of the offerings in verse 24 is because they were mostly peace offerings, which were mainly eaten by the worshippers.

vi. Destruction of idolatrous shrines (xxxi. 1). Cf. 2 Ki. xviii. 4. *Images . . . groves* (1); 'pillars . . . Asherim' (RV); see 1 Ki. xiv. 23n. It being a purely popular demonstration, the representatives of Assyria in the province of Samaria had no grounds of objection.

vii. The organization of the priests and Levites and their support (xxxi. 2–21). Not in 2 Kings. Hezekiah regulated the priestly and Levitical courses (2), the official contribution to the sacrifices (3) and the tithes (4). These were brought in with great generosity (5–10). *The tithe of holy things* (6); it looks as though some scribe had simply written 'tithe' mechanically here; omit it. This long unpractised generosity made it necessary to organize, or reorganize, the control of the tithes. This involved the making of a register of those entitled to receive them. The RSV gives the sense of verses 17, 18 very well, 'The enrolment of the priests was according to their fathers' houses; that of the Levites from twenty years old. . . . The priests were enrolled with all their little children. . . .'

viii. Preparations for Sennacherib's invasion (xxxii. 1–8). There are only minor contacts with 2 Kings, but cf. section **XXIX c** in Kings. For verses 3, 4 see 2 Ki. xx. 20n. *And raised it up to the towers* (5); the Hebrew is corrupt and hardly translatable. Moffatt and RSV follow Vulg. 'and raised towers upon it'. *Millo* (5); cf. 1 Ki. ix. 15n. *Darts* (5); 'missiles' (Moff.). *With us . . .* (7, 8); perhaps a recollection of Isaiah's Immanuel ('God with us') prophecy (Is. vii. 14).

ix. Sennacherib's threats (xxxii. 9–23). This is a summary of 2 Ki. xviii. 17—xix. 37 (q.v.). Note that 2 Ki. xix. 9–13 is introduced parenthetically in verse 17; verse 18 continues verse 16. The prayer of *Hezekiah* (20) is given in 2 Ki. xix. 15–19; the prayer of *Isaiah* is not mentioned in 2 Kings. It is characteristic of the Chronicler that with the evil kings he goes into details with

their defeats, but he only hints at the extent of the troubles of the good kings.

x. Summary of Hezekiah's reign (xxxii. 24–33). For verse 24 see 2 Ki. xx. 1–11. For verses 25, 26, 31 see 2 Ki. xx. 12–19. For verse 30 see 2 Ki. xx. 20. With verse 27 may be compared 2 Ki. xx. 13. *In the chiefest of the sepulchres* (33); either 'in the ascent of the sepulchres' (RV) or 'in the upper part of the tombs' (Moff.).

l. Manasseh (xxxiii. 1–20) Cf. 2 Ki. xxi. 1–18. For verses 1–10 see 2 Ki. xxi. 1–15; Chronicles omits the details of God's message. We have plurals in verses 3, 6 (*children*), where Kings has singular. It may be that we should not stress the language, but look on it as general terms. *In the valley of the son of Hinnom* (6); cf. Je. vii. 31. Chronicles, which stresses the religious side, omits the murders (2 Ki. xxi. 16).

Late in his reign (648–647 B.C.) there was a rebellion against Ashurbanipal in favour of his brother, viceroy in Babylon. Whether Manasseh was involved or only suspected he was taken 'with hooks' (11, RV mg.; lit. 'with thorns') and bound *with fetters . . . to Babylon*. For the custom see 2 Ki. xix. 28n. Ashurbanipal was probably in Babylon because of the rebellion just suppressed. It was some time before he could turn to the west, so Manasseh was taken very late in his reign to Babylon and his reign after his return must have been very brief. This explains why his repentance and reformation (12, 13, 15–17) are not mentioned in Kings and why they left no lasting impression. It should be noted, too, that Chronicles does not mention the removal of the altars of the host of heaven. Having once accepted these signs of Assyrian rule, he would not have dared to reject them now. *His prayer unto his God* (18) . . . *his prayer also* (19). The Prayer of Manasses in the Apocrypha has no claim to be regarded as authentic. Verse 14 cannot be interpreted with certainty in our lack of closer knowledge of pre-exilic Jerusalem. *Among the sayings of the seers* (19); the AV rightly follows LXX.

m. Amon (xxxiii. 21–25) There are only minor variants from 2 Ki. xxi. 19–26 (q.v.).

n. Josiah (xxxiv. 1—xxxv. 27)

i. Introduction (xxxiv. 1, 2). Cf. 2 Ki. xxii. 1, 2.

ii. The reformation (xxxiv. 3–7, 33). See sections **XXXII f, h** in Kings. Whereas Chronicles places the whole reformation before the repair of the temple and the finding of the law-book, except by implication in verse 33, Kings puts it all after. In both cases convenience of narrative is being consulted. Most necessary notes will be found in the relevant sections on Kings. *Images* (4) . . . *idols* (7); RSV correctly 'incense altars' (cf. xiv. 5). *With their mattocks round about* (6). The Hebrew is doubtful: probably 'he laid waste their houses round about' (I.C.C., Moff.).

iii. The repair of the temple (xxxiv. 8–14). See notes on 2 Ki. xxii. 3–7. The mention of *Manasseh and Ephraim, and of all the remnant of Israel* (9) is probably to those from the northern tribes who had settled in the south (xi. 16, xv. 9), rather than to those left in the north, for, unlike Hezekiah's reign (xxx. 11), there is no special mention of people from the north at Josiah's Passover.

iv. The finding of the book of the law (xxxiv. 15–19). See notes on 2 Ki. xxii. 8–11.

v. Huldah's message (xxxiv. 20–28). See notes on 2 Ki. xxii. 12–20. *Abdon the son of Micah* (20); 2 Ki. xxii. 12 correctly 'Achbor the son of Michaiah'. *The son of Tikvah* (RV 'Tokhath'), *the son of Hasrah* (22); 2 Ki. xxii. 14 correctly 'the son of Tikvah, the son of Harhas'.

vi. The covenant (xxxiv. 29–32). See notes on 2 Ki. xxiii. 1–3. The omission of the prophets in verse 30 is deliberate; see 2 Ki. xxii. 14n.

vii. Josiah's Passover (xxxv. 1–19). Cf. 2 Ki. xxiii. 21–23. For the significance of the keeping of the Passover see xxx. 1, 2n. *Put the holy ark in the house . . .* (3); presumably it had been removed for the period of repairs. It is possibly figurative, meaning: Do not think about the past, but serve as described in verses 4–6. *According to the writing of David . . .* (4); see 1 Ch. xxiii–xxvi. *According to the writing of Solomon . . .* (4); cf. viii. 14. *Kill the passover* (6); cf. xxx. 17, but since the same reason did not hold good, it is likely we should not stress the

phrase. *Bullocks* (7) . . . *oxen* (8). These were for peace offerings during the feast of unleavened bread; cf. xxx. 24n. It would seem that in verses 11–13 the actual Passover sacrifices and the later sacrifices of the week have for brevity been amalgamated. *There was no passover like to that kept . . .* (18); cf. xxx. 26. Passover had been overshadowed by tabernacles celebrated as the New Year feast (see Appendix I to Kings).

viii. Josiah's death (xxxv. 20–25). See notes on 2 Ki. xxiii. 29, 30a. *Jeremiah lamented for Josiah* (25); this has not been preserved. Obviously it has no relation to the book of Lamentations.

ix. Summary of Josiah's reign (xxxv. 26, 27). See notes on 2 Ki. xxiii. 25–28.

o. Downfall and restoration (xxxvi. 1–23)

i. Jehoahaz (xxxvi. 1–4). See notes on 2 Ki. xxiii. 30b–34. *Put him down at Jerusalem* (3). On the basis of Esdras i. 35 we should read 'deposed him from reigning in Jerusalem'. *Condemned the land* (3); i.e. 'fined the country' (Moff.); the tribute was heavier than it would otherwise have been as a punishment.

ii. Jehoiakim (xxxvi. 5–8). See notes on 2 Ki. xxiii. 34—xxiv. 7. We should presumably look on verse 7 as anticipatory of verse 10, though it may refer to the incident of Dn. i. 2. It was due to Jehoiakim's sins and rebellion that Jerusalem was taken and the temple ransacked.

iii. Jehoiachin (xxxvi. 9, 10). See notes on 2 Ki. xxiv. 8–16.

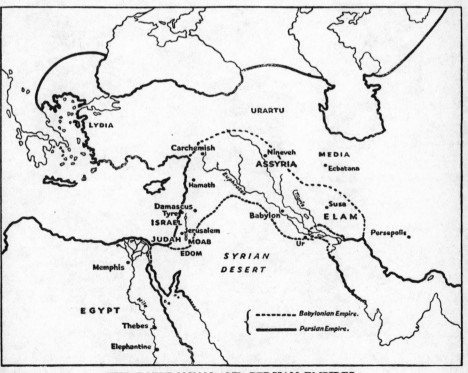

THE BABYLONIAN AND PERSIAN EMPIRES

iv. Zedekiah (xxxvi. 11–13). See notes on 2 Ki. xxiv. 17—xxv. 7. With the legitimate king in exile, and the temple ransacked, the Chronicler has no reason for describing the last agony of Jerusalem. The last generation in the city is well typified by its perjured king (13).

v. The destruction of Jerusalem (xxxvi. 14–21). Chronicles gives merely a general summary showing how the destruction of the city was the inevitable result of its sin. *To him and his sons* (20); i.e. his successors, Evil-merodach (2 Ki. xxv. 27), Neriglissar and Nabonidus, the last two being usurpers. *Until the land had enjoyed her sabbaths* (21). The implication is that the sabbatical year was not observed under the monarchy (cf. Lv. xxv. 1–7, xxvi. 34, 35). *Three-score and ten years* (21). Judah was subject to Babylon from the battle of Carchemish (605 B.C., Dn. i. 1) till the fall of Babylon (538 B.C.), i.e. sixty-seven years, seventy being a round number.

vi. Restoration (xxxvi. 22, 23). These verses are identical with the opening verses of Ezra; see notes *ad loc.*

H. L. ELLISON.

EZRA AND NEHEMIAH

INTRODUCTION

I. COMPILATION AND DATE

These two books were originally one, and the opening verses, which repeat the concluding verses of Chronicles, suggest that they were compiled by the chronicler as part of his history. The date of the compilation may be gathered from the list of High Priests in Ne. xii. 10–22. This list is carried down as far as Jaddua who, according to Josephus (*Ant.* xi. 8. 4), was High Priest in the time of Alexander the Great (*c.* 330). On the other hand it has been held that the Jaddua in Ne. xii is not the one mentioned by Josephus, but is to be dated earlier (R. Dick Wilson in the *International Standard Bible Encyclopedia*, Art. 'Ezra-Nehemiah'. A. C. Welch, *Post-Exilic Judaism*, p. 242).

II. SOURCES

The books appear to have been compiled from several sources. There are personal memoirs of Ezra and Nehemiah, written in the first person singular; incidents about Ezra, Nehemiah, and others, written in the third person; letters, decrees, genealogies, and other documents.

Two sections in Ezra (iv. 8—vi. 18 and vii. 12–26) are written in Aramaic. They consist almost entirely of letters and decrees. Aramaic, which was originally a language spoken to the east and north-east of Palestine (e.g. Gn. xxxi. 47), became the diplomatic language of the Near East. A conventional form of it was employed in written communications. There is every reason to think that the compiler of these books has given a transcript of the original letters.

The two books contain almost all that is known of the history of the Jews between 538 and about 430 B.C.

III. COMPARISON WITH I ESDRAS

A serious study of these books demands some comparison with 1 Esdras, which is printed in the Apocrypha. This is a Greek version of part of Chronicles, Ezra, and Nehemiah, running from 2 Ch. xxxv. 1 to the end of Ezra, adding Ne. viii. 1–12 at the end. In addition to minor variants from the account as it stands in the Hebrew text, there are certain substantial additions. There is a reconstruction of the course of events in the opening chapters. Thus Cyrus permits a return under Sheshbazzar, while Darius commissions Zerubbabel to go and build the temple and city. Zerubbabel's commission follows on the famous story of the three guardsmen, who in turn state before Darius and his court what they believe to be the strongest thing in the world. The first says that wine is the strongest, the second that the king is, while the third (Zerubbabel) maintains that women are stronger than either, but that truth is the strongest of all. But although 1 Esdras puts Zerubbabel's return under Darius, it also incorporates the Ezra statement that he was at work in Judah 'all the time that Cyrus lived' (1 Esdras v. 70–73). In view of this confusion, it is best to accept the Ezra order.

1 Esdras should not be confused with the other Greek version that follows the Hebrew text closely, and that is usually regarded as the LXX version of Ezra and Nehemiah, though C. C. Torrey regards this version as Theodotion's translation of the second century A.D., and 1 Esdras as the original LXX translation.

The way of referring to these different versions is confusing, but it may be set out as follows: 1 Esdras of our Apocrypha appears in the Greek Bible as Esdras, and in the Vulgate as 3 Esdras. In the Vulgate our Ezra is 1 Esdras and our Nehemiah is 2 Esdras. In the Greek Bible our Ezra-Nehemiah appears as Esdras.

IV. BACKGROUND

A secondary authority for the period is Josephus, whose book, *The Antiquities of the Jews*, was written at the end of the first century A.D. He was a Jewish writer, who may have had access to some sources of information other than those of the biblical records. But it is generally agreed that he must be used with discretion. (See, e.g., the note on Ne. xiii. 28.)

Contemporary documents include the Cyrus Cylinder, which describes, among other things, how Cyrus sent back the captive peoples to their own lands, together with their gods. There are also the Elephantine Papyri, which are copies of letters sent to and from a Jewish colony on the island of Yeb, in Upper Egypt, near Assouan. They are written in Aramaic, and belong to the end of the fifth century B.C. They refer to Sanballat and his sons, to Bigvai as governor of Jerusalem, and to Johanan as High Priest (see note on Ezr. x. 6). For a map showing the extent of the Persian Empire at the height of its power see p. 363.

V. CHRONOLOGY

For a proper understanding of the course of events, the dates of the kings of Persia should be noted:

538–529	Cyrus.
529–522	Cambyses.
522–521	Gaumata (Pseudo-Smerdis). A usurper.
521–486	Darius I. (Hystaspis).
486–465	Xerxes I. (Ahasuerus).
464–424	Artaxerxes I. (Longimanus).
424–423	Xerxes II.
423–404	Darius II. (Nothus).
404–359	Artaxerxes II. (Mnemon).
359–338	Artaxerxes III. (Ochus).
338–331	Darius III. (Codomannus).

At this date the Persian Empire was overthrown by Alexander the Great from Macedon.

EZRA
OUTLINE OF CONTENTS

I. THE RETURN OF EXILES TO JERUSALEM. i. 1—ii. 70

II. THE WORK OF RESTORATION BEGUN. iii. 1–13

III. THE WORK BROUGHT TO A STANDSTILL. iv. 1–24

IV. THE BUILDING OF THE TEMPLE RESUMED AND COMPLETED. v. 1—vi. 22

V. EZRA COMES TO JERUSALEM. vii. 1—viii. 36

VI. THE PROBLEM OF MIXED MARRIAGES. ix. 1—x. 44

EZRA
COMMENTARY

I. THE RETURN OF EXILES TO JERUSALEM. i. 1—ii. 70

a. The decree of Cyrus (i. 1–4)

In 538 B.C. Cyrus conquered Babylon. One of his first acts was to allow all the captive peoples, whom he found at Babylon, to return to their own countries. This is recorded on what is known as the 'Cyrus Cylinder'. The wording of this decree in Ezra might suggest that Cyrus was a believer in Jehovah. Yet we know from Cyrus's own inscriptions that he also attributed his victories to the Babylonian god, Marduk. It is probable that Cyrus had a general respect for a number of gods, and worded his decrees in terms that would appeal to each nation. He probably asked some Jewish leader (possibly Daniel) to word the decree in a form that would be acceptable to the Jews. See also note on vi. 3–5. Verses 1–3 are practically identical with 2 Ch. xxxvi. 22, 23, and serve to connect the two books.

The first year of Cyrus (1); i.e. the year in which he conquered Babylon. He was king of Persia before this. By the mouth of Jeremiah (1). See Je. xxv. 12, xxix. 10. It was almost seventy years since Jeremiah uttered his prophecy in the fourth year of Jehoiakim (Je. xxv. 1), i.e. 605 B.C. Hath charged me (2). Cf. Is. xliv. 28, xlv. 13. Whosoever remaineth (4); i.e. all who had survived the captivity. Cf. Hg. i. 14. In whatever part of the empire they were living, their neighbours were to help them if they wished to return.

b. The return from Babylon (i. 5–11)

Cyrus . . . brought forth the vessels of the house of the Lord (7). On the Cyrus Cylinder the king says that he returned all their idols to the captive peoples whom he allowed to go home after he had conquered Babylon. Since the Jews had no idols, this verse shows that they were allowed to take back their sacred vessels instead. Cf. 2 Ki. xxiv. 13; Je. xxvii. 19–22; Dn. v. 3. Sheshbazzar (8). In 1 Esdras ii he is called Sanabassar. Three views have been held about him. Some say that he is to be identified with Zerubbabel. This is unlikely in view of Ezr. v. 14 where, although Zerubbabel is alive, Sheshbazzar is referred to as though he is dead. Others identify him with Shenazar, a son of king Jehoiachin (1 Ch. iii. 18). Zerubbabel was of the royal line (1 Ch. iii. 18, 19; Mt. i. 12). If Sheshbazzar died soon after the return, Zerubbabel, the man of action, would be his natural successor. A third view is that he is a Persian official, appointed to superintend the resettlement of the Jews. See also introductory note to Ezr. v. The prince of Judah (8). This would naturally refer to one of the royal line of David. But the word 'prince' (nasi') has a wide use and, if the third view above is taken, it would indicate merely that Sheshbazzar was put in a position of authority over all Judah.

c. The register of those who returned (ii. 1–70)

This register is reproduced with slight variations in Ne. vii. 6–73 and 1 Esdras v. 4–46. It was evidently filed in the official records, and the historian includes it here in its natural place. Nehemiah also quotes it in his personal memoirs, which the historian again reproduces. Some, like C. C. Torrey, have dismissed it as a pure invention. L. W. Batten, in the International Critical Commentary, regards it as a comprehensive list of all who had come to Judah from the time of Zerubbabel to the time of Ezra. Galling treats it as the list given by the nationalists to Tatnai when he demanded the names of the builders in Ezr. v. A detailed discussion of the slight variations between some of the names and numbers in the three records is beyond the scope of this commentary. Lists of names and figures are particularly liable to small errors of transcription. But see note on verse 64.

i. **Zerubbabel and his companions (ii. 1, 2).** *Zerubbabel: Jeshua* (2). Follow RV and read a comma after Zerubbabel. The ten names are those of Zerubbabel's companions. In iii. 2 and elsewhere Zerubbabel is called 'the son of Shealtiel', but in 1 Ch. iii. 19 he is the son of Pedaiah. If Shealtiel was childless, Pedaiah was the brother who contracted a levirate marriage with the widow. Jeshua, or Joshua, is the High Priest who worked with Zerubbabel. *Nehemiah* (2). This is not the famous Nehemiah.

ii. **A classification of the people by families and clans (ii. 3–19).** *Pahath-moab* (6). Lit. 'Ruler of Moab'. Probably an ancestor had been a governor of Moab when Moab was under Israel.

iii. **A classification of the people according to the places to which they belonged (ii. 20–35).** *Bethel* (28). Mentioned again in Zc. vii. 2 (RV). *Ono* (33). See Ne. vi. 2.

iv. **A list of priests (ii. 36–39).** *Jeshua* (36). An earlier Joshua than the contemporary of Zerubbabel.

v. **The three divisions of Levites (ii. 40–42).** Only 341 Levites returned as compared with 4,289 priests. Ezra found a similar reluctance on the part of the Levites in viii. 15. Were they afraid that their position would be unimportant in the renewed community? We may contrast the relative numbers of priests and Levites in the 'Priestly Code' in the Pentateuch. Yet P is supposed to reflect post-exilic conditions. *Asaph* (41). See 2 Ch. xxix. 30. See also the headings of Pss. 1, lxxiii—lxxxiii.

vi. **The Nethinim (ii. 43–54).** Outside Ezra and Nehemiah these people are mentioned only in 1 Ch. ix. 2. It is not known who they were, but they may have been descendants of the Gibeonites of Jos. ix. 27. The name means 'given', and Ezr. viii. 20 says that David and the princes had appointed them for the service of the Levites. Cf. Nu. xxxi. 30.

vii. **The class known as Solomon's servants (ii. 55–58).** They are mentioned again in Ne. xi. 3. Some think that they were descendants of the Canaanites mentioned in 1 Ki. ix. 21.

viii. **Those of uncertain genealogy (ii. 59–63).** *Barzillai* (61). See 2 Sa. xvii. 27, xix. 32–39; 1 Ki.

ii. 7. *The Tirshatha* (63). Cf. Ne. vii. 65, 70, viii. 9, x. 1. A Persian title; probably a term of respect, equivalent to 'Excellency'. Here it refers to Sheshbazzar or Zerubbabel. *Eat of the most holy things* (63). The priests were allotted portions of the sacrifices. (See Lv. ii. 3, 10, vi. 26, etc.) There may also be a reference here to the sacrifice at the consecration of a priest. (See Ex. xxix. 31–37.) These men could not be consecrated as priests. *Till there stood up a priest with Urim and with Thummim* (63). The Urim and Thummim were part of the High Priest's vestments (Ex. xxviii. 30), and were used somehow to find out the will of the Lord (1 Sa. xxviii. 6). They had evidently been lost or destroyed at the destruction of Jerusalem. Since these people had no documentary proof of their claim to the priesthood, they must wait until the divinely-given means of finding out God's decisions was again in operation. See special note on Urim and Thummim under 1 Sa. xxviii. 6 (p. 277).

ix. **Various totals (ii. 64–70).** In spite of variations in the items in the list, the same total is given in Ezra, Nehemiah, and 1 Esdras. But in none of the lists do the items add up to 42,360. See the introductory note on this chapter. *Singing men and singing women* (65). These were for secular entertainment, as distinct from the Levitical singers of verse 41. Cf. 2 Sa. xix. 35; Ec. ii. 8. *Drams* (69). Better as in RV 'darics'. The daric was a Persian coin, worth just over £1.

There may be some confusion in the text of verse 70, since one would expect some reference to Jerusalem. The parallel in 1 Esdras v. 46 reads: 'So dwelt the priests and the Levites and some of the people in Jerusalem and in the country; the singers also and the porters; and all Israel in their villages.'

II. THE WORK OF RESTORATION BEGUN. iii. 1–13

a. The altar built: the feast of tabernacles observed (iii. 1–7)

It is possible that sacrifices had been offered at times on the temple site during the exile. See, e.g., Je. xli. 5. But the purpose now was to reinstate the divinely prescribed order of sacrifice. *The seventh month* (1), i.e. of 537 B.C. *As it is written* (2). See Nu. xxix. 1–6. *For fear was upon them* (3). They believed that by putting God first they would be delivered from the threats of the enemy round about.

The feast of tabernacles (4). See Lv. xxiii. 33–36; cf. Ne. viii. 14–17. 1 Esdras v. 53 connects the last clause of verse 5 with the following verse; 'All who had made a vow to God, from the new moon of the seventh month began to offer sacrifices to God', i.e. now that the altar was set up the people could pay any vows that they had made, such as for a safe journey to Jerusalem. *According to the grant* (7). This grant is mentioned in the more detailed decree of vi. 4.

b. The foundations of the temple laid (iii. 8–13)

Began Zerubbabel . . . (8, 9). The Hebrew here is not absolutely clear, but it appears that the returned exiles appointed the Levites in general to be responsible for the work of building (8), and four families of Levites, i.e. Jeshua, Kadmiel, Hodaviah (AV mg.) and Henadad, undertook the carrying out of the task. *After the ordinance of David* (10). See 1 Ch. xvi. 4, 5, xxv. 1, which mention cymbals. For trumpets see Nu. x. 8. *And they sang together by course* (11). Apparently there were two choirs singing antiphonally. See Ps. cxxxvi. 1 and the prophecy of Je. xxxiii. 11. *Wept* (12). Either for joy, or because the new temple was so small (cf. Hg. ii. 3).

III. THE WORK BROUGHT TO A STANDSTILL. iv. 1–24

The dates that the writer gives in this chapter must be noted carefully, and compared with the list of the Persian kings given in the *Introduction* (p. 366).

a. The work of building is opposed (iv. 1–5, 24)

The writer refers to the opponents as *the people of the land* (4). This was the accepted use of the term in his day, whereas in the time of Haggai (520 B.C.) the term was used of those Jews who had not gone into captivity (Hg. ii. 4). Those who wished to help in the rebuilding were the descendants of the races whom the Assyrian kings had imported into the northern kingdom (2 Ki. xvii. 24–41). It is likely that some of the Israelites who were not taken into captivity kept themselves from idolatry, since some took part in Josiah's celebration of the Passover (2 Ch. xxxv. 17, 18); but in the main the newcomers swamped the original inhabitants. This is clear from the evidence of 2 Ki. xvii, which refers to the situation in the writer's own day. Thus Zerubbabel and Joshua refused to allow them to take part in rebuilding Jehovah's temple. These people later became known as the Samaritans. *Esar-haddon* (2). An Assyrian king who reigned 680–668 B.C. The king is not named in 2 Ki. xvii. 24. But Ezr. iv. 10 speaks of Asnapper, whose name resembles that of Ashurbanipal (668–626 B.C.). Since Samaria fell in 721 B.C., there was either a considerable interval before the new colonists were brought in or, more probably, there were several importations. *All the days of Cyrus . . . until the reign of Darius* (5). The dates cover the period 536–520 B.C. The reference to Darius again in verse 24 shows that this story is picked up again at that point.

b. Examples of similar opposition at a later date (iv. 6–23)

The writer has chosen to introduce here two other examples of opposition, but has carefully dated them. They occurred in the reigns of *Ahasuerus* (6), or Xerxes, and his successor, *Artaxerxes I* (7); i.e. they came in the period 486–424 B.C. The contents of the letter show that the complaint is not about the temple, but about the rebuilding of the city walls (12, 16). The incident of verse 23 probably occurred shortly before the coming of Nehemiah. See also the notes on Ne. i. *Bishlam, Mithredath, Tabeel* (7). The first two are foreign colonists who are not mentioned again. Tabeel ('God is good') may be the same as Tobiah ('Jehovah is good') who opposed Nehemiah (see Ne. ii. 19, etc.). *In the Syrian tongue* (7); i.e. in Aramaic. Not only is the letter that follows in Aramaic, but the whole section as far as vi. 18 is in this dialect. Verse 8 indicates that the letter was dictated by Rehum, the chancellor, or perhaps the Master of the Decrees, to his secretary, Shimshai, and was sent in the name of the colonists introduced by the Assyrian kings. It is not possible to identify all the peoples mentioned here. Some translate the first four as 'judges, rulers, recorders, and secretaries'. *Archevites* (9). Perhaps the people of Erech in Babylonia. *Susanchites* (9). From Susa, the capital of Elam. *Dehavites* (9). A slight emendation gives 'that is'. The text then reads 'The Susians, that is, the Elamites'. *Asnapper* (10). See note on verse 2. *At such a time* (10). The phrase probably means 'and so forth' (RV), corresponding to our 'etc.' It occurs again in verses 11 and 17.

The king's reply (17–22) orders the work to cease, but leaves open in verse 21 a possible rescinding of the command. In fact Artaxerxes did rescind it in Ne. ii. *Plainly read* (18). RV mg. 'translated'. See note on Ne. viii. 8. *By force and power* (23). The Jews' opponents interpreted the letter as a command to use violence if necessary. If this took place shortly before the coming of Nehemiah, the report in Ne. i. 3 is an account of the damage done at this time.

IV. THE BUILDING OF THE TEMPLE RESUMED AND COMPLETED. v. 1—vi. 22

a. Haggai and Zechariah encourage a fresh beginning (v. 1–5)

The date is now 520 B.C. (Cf. iv. 24; Hg. i. 1.) For these events we have the contemporary records of Haggai and Zechariah who may have come only recently to Jerusalem. Haggai particularly shows how the people needed to be stirred up after the discouragement of the past sixteen years. So little work had been done on the new temple that a fresh foundation ceremony was now held (Hg. ii. 18). It is usually assumed that *Zerubbabel* (2) had now been appointed governor (*Peḥah*) in place of Sheshbazzar (v. 14), since this title is used of him in Hg. i. 1 and ii. 2. But Rudolph in his *Esra und Nehemia* argues that, if Zerubbabel had been governor, he, and not the leaders in general, would have been consulted by Tatnai on this occasion. Hence he believes that the title in Haggai is a courtesy one only. *Tatnai* (3). The Persian governor of the whole area west of the Euphrates. The word here clearly denotes the satrap. See note on viii. 36. *Shethar-boznai* (3). Probably his secretary. Cf. iv. 8.

EZRA V. 4—VII. 1

Then said we (4). Perhaps a direct quotation from a letter. LXX has 'They said'.

b. A letter from the Persian governor to Darius (v. 6–17)

Apharsachites (6). See iv. 9n. Possibly to be translated 'rulers'. This letter is concerned solely with the rebuilding of the temple. Contrast iv. 12. The governor is anxious to find out who is now in charge of the building, and whether, as is alleged, Cyrus ever gave permission to the returning Sheshbazzar to rebuild the temple. This opposition of the Persian governor and others is probably the 'great mountain' of Zc. iv. 7, which was evidently causing the people to feel that they might never complete the building. *Since that time . . . hath it been in building* (16). The Jews naturally did not wish to weaken their case by admitting that they had neglected the work altogether for sixteen years. *Let the king send his pleasure* (17); i.e. if the decree of Cyrus is found, Darius is asked to say whether he wishes to ratify it.

c. Darius orders the work to be encouraged (vi. 1–12)

The house of the rolls (1). The RV correctly shows that two different words are used here and in verse 2 for 'roll'. Search was made in 'the house of the archives', and the decree was found written on a roll. Most of the official records were kept on clay tablets, but for some reason this decree was written on papyrus or leather. *Achmetha* (2). This is Ecbatana, the capital of Media, and the summer residence of the Persian kings. One cannot say why the records had been transferred there, but the unexpected mention of Ecbatana is an indication of authenticity.

There is a natural difference between this decree (3–5), which was filed with the official records, and the public announcement to the Jews in chapter i. Here the name of Jehovah is not used, but since the king was giving grants towards the rebuilding, this official record states the precise amount of the grant. In reaffirming the decree and the grant, Darius makes additions of his own (9, 10). Some of the Persian kings were anxious to foster the religious cults of their subject peoples. The Elephantine Papyri of about 400 B.C. contain a letter of instructions from a Persian king to the Jews in Egypt about keeping the feast of unleavened bread. (See Clar. Bible, Old Testament, IV., p. 222f.) Someone corresponding to a Secretary of State for Jewish Affairs would give Darius the information that he needed in writing verses 9 and 10.

d. The completion and consecration of the temple (vi. 13–18)

I Esdras vii. 2 has the interesting addition to the information given in verse 13 that the governors who had written the letter of complaint 'did oversee the sacred works, very carefully working with the elders of the Jews and governors of the temple'. The reference to *Artaxerxes* (14) appears

to be a scribal error, based on a misunderstanding of iv. 7. There cannot really be an allusion to iv. 7–23, since there Artaxerxes hindered the building by his decree. But this verse might be anticipatory of vii. 21f. *The sixth year . . . of Darius* (15). This means that the temple was finished in 516 B.C. The offerings at the dedication (17) were far fewer than those made by Solomon in 1 Ki. viii. 5, 63. The bulk of the sacrifices on these occasions were eaten by the worshippers during the celebrations, and the community at this time was very small. *In the book of Moses* (18). Especially Nu. iii and viii. *The first month* (19). The ceremony follows naturally on the completion of the temple in the twelfth month, Adar (15).

e. The Passover is celebrated (vi. 19–22)

All such as had separated themselves (21). Possibly proselytes; but more likely those Jews and Israelites who had not been in captivity, and who were prepared to make a clean break with the idolatry and semi-Jehovah-worship of the Samaritans and surrounding peoples. *The king of Assyria* (22). The title is a strange one to use of the king of Persia, but it is probably used deliberately to remind the reader that the action of the king of Persia was the undoing of what had been begun by the king of Assyria. The Persian kings now ruled over the former Assyrian Empire.

V. EZRA COMES TO JERUSALEM. vii. 1—viii. 36

a. Artaxerxes sends Ezra with a letter of commission (vii. 1–28)

The date is now 458 B.C., and some sixty years divide chapters vi and vii. We have no certain information about what had happened in the interval, though it is possible that the book of Malachi is to be dated towards the end of the period. We do not know who succeeded Zerubbabel as governor, or leader, though Ne. v. 15 refers to a succession of governors. In these closing chapters of Ezra there is no reference to a governor.

Some suppose that Ezra's coming should really be dated after that of Nehemiah, and a common view is that the writer confused Artaxerxes I and II, so that Ezra really came to Jerusalem in 398 B.C. But it is almost incredible that the writer could have made such a mistake in the order. The latest reasonable date for the composition of this book is about 300 B.C. If Ezra had actually come to Jerusalem in 398 B.C., and had been active long enough to gain the reputation that he did, his death would have occurred within the living memory of a few people in Jerusalem, and very many would have heard their parents describe how they had known Ezra personally. But Nehemiah would have been a figure of the past. It would have been useless for the chronicler to reconstruct the history so as to make Ezra come before Nehemiah. We must assume that he wrote his record so that it might be read by his contemporaries, even though there could be no widespread publication, as with books today, and he could not hope to escape detection of his error. Moreover one cannot see any reason why the chronicler should wish to make the alteration.

A less drastic suggestion is that Ezra came between the two governorships of Nehemiah (Ne. xiii. 6); but any such rearrangement is unnecessary, and in this commentary the biblical order will be assumed to be correct. The statements that are felt to militate against the biblical order are dealt with where they occur. The matter is discussed in detail in *The Date of Ezra's Coming to Jerusalem*, by J. Stafford Wright (Tyndale Press).

i. Ezra's journey to Jerusalem (vii. 1–10). Ezra's genealogy (1–5) is clearly abbreviated, as is frequently the case in Scripture. *A ready scribe* (6). The term 'scribe' originally meant no more than 'secretary' or 'recorder' (e.g. 2 Sa. viii. 17). Before the exile there may have been a wider use of the title to denote those who were concerned with the interpretation, as well as the copying, of the law (Je. viii. 8). The application of the title to Ezra has this significance, which came more and more into prominence from this time onwards. *Nethinims* (7). See note on ii. 43.

ii. The letter of Artaxerxes (vii. 11–26). The contents of the letter are in Aramaic. Cf. iv. 7f. *At such a time* (12). See note on iv. 10. *His seven counsellors* (14). The king's Privy Council. Cf. Est. i. 14; Herodotus iii. 84. *To inquire* (14). It is likely that Ezra held a position at the Persian court corresponding to the head of the bureau that had charge of all Jewish affairs. He was now sent on an official mission to investigate the state of things in Judah. Artaxerxes showed his favour to the Jews and to Ezra by making considerable gifts of money and vessels (15–20). Eastern kings could be extremely generous or extremely cruel. With verse 22 cf. vi. 3, 4, 8–10. The maximum amounts fixed here are about £37,000, 800 bushels of wheat and 700 gallons of wine and oil. Note that in verse 24 the temple officials are granted immunity from tax.

Ezra was given permission where necessary to appoint magistrates over all Jews in the area west of the Euphrates (25). The purpose was to secure conformity to recognized Jewish practice. The interest of Persian kings in the religious conformity of their subjects has been referred to in the notes on vi. 6–12. But no doubt Ezra himself had some say in the drawing up of this decree, and indicated to Artaxerxes the importance that he believed to lie in the proper observance of the law. There is no indication that Artaxerxes was encouraging Ezra to introduce a new version of the law, such as the Priestly Code, and thus risk causing unrest amongst the people. In verse 26 the reference is to Jews only.

iii. An extract from the personal memoirs of Ezra (vii. 27, 28). The remainder of the book is again in Hebrew.

b. The register of those who returned with Ezra (viii. 1–14)

There are slight differences between the list here and that in 1 Esdras viii. 28–40. Here the total is 1,496, while in 1 Esdras it is 1,690. The names of the families in verses 3–14 are practically the same as in Ezr. ii. *Hattush* (2). Take with the next verse, and read, 'Hattush the son of Shechaniah'. In verse 5 read 'Of the sons of Zattu, Shechaniah the son of Jahaziel'. So 1 Esdras viii. 32 and LXX. Cf. Ezr. ii. 8. In verse 10 read 'Of the sons of Bani, Shelomith the son of Josiphiah'. So 1 Esdras viii. 36 and LXX. Cf. Ezr. ii. 10. *And of the last sons of Adonikam* (13). RV reads 'the sons . . . that were the last'. The meaning is obscure, but may be that the elder branch of the clan had already returned, and now the younger branch comes with Ezra.

c. The party assembles: a solemn fast is observed (viii. 15–23)

Ahava (15). The situation is unknown. Perhaps it is the name of a canal near Babylon. *The sons of Levi* (15). See note on ii. 40–42. But according to 1 Esdras viii. 42 Ezra found that priests were absent as well as Levites. *Casiphia* (17). The situation is unknown. Evidently there was a strong settlement of Levites and Nethinim there. Some have supposed that there was actually a Jewish temple and sacrifice there, as there was at Elephantine. *A man of understanding* (18). RV mg. transliterates as a proper name, 'Ishsechel'. *Expressed by name* (20). Lit. 'Pierced, or marked with a point'. As the roll was called, a mark was put opposite the name on the list. *Then I proclaimed a fast* (21). Its purpose was that they might humble themselves before God. With verse 22 contrast Ne. ii. 7, 9. God leads people in different ways.

d. Custodians appointed for the gifts (viii. 24–30)

The value of these gifts has been computed at a million pounds. But the amount is quite possible. There were vast reserve sums in the Persian treasuries. Alexander the Great took some £40 million from them. (*Cambridge Ancient History*, IV, 199.)

e. The journey and the arrival at Jerusalem (viii. 31–36)

The journey of some 900 miles took about four months (vii. 9). The party would follow the usual route to avoid the desert, and would enter Palestine from the north. The difference between the two departure dates in this verse and in vii. 9 is accounted for by the delay at the river Ahava. *Meremoth* (33). See Ne. iii. 4, 21. He received the money and the gifts. *Lieutenants* (36). RV 'satraps'. These were governors of provinces. It is not known how many there were at this date. Judah would be in the province that included the whole of Syria and Palestine, but the neighbouring satraps of Egypt and Cilicia would need to be informed of any decrees that applied to the adjoining province. *Governors* (36). These were the Persian or native administrators of districts within the satrapy. Since no governor of Judah is mentioned by name, it is likely that Judah and Jerusalem were included in a wider area, possibly under Sanballat.

VI. THE PROBLEM OF MIXED MARRIAGES. ix. 1—x. 44

a. Ezra's grief and dismay (ix. 1–5)

Although it is usually assumed that the guilty people were descendants of those who had returned with Zerubbabel, it is possible that they were members of Ezra's party. (See A. C. Welch, *Post-Exilic Judaism*, p. 247f.) But while 113 guilty people (see x. 18–43) may seem few after nearly one hundred years in the land, it is a large number for those who had recently returned with Ezra. *Princes* (1). Heads of families or clans. The nations named here are those with whom marriage and close association is forbidden in such places as Ex. xxxiv. 16; Dt. vii. 1–3, xxiii. 3. Even though all these peoples may not still have existed in an identifiable form, the leaders felt justified in quoting the rules of the law. *Rulers* (2). Perhaps no more than a synonym for 'princes'.

Ezra expresses his horror at the news by the customary signs of grief (3). Usually the hair was shaved (Jb. i. 20; Ezk. vii. 18), but Ezra pulls some of his hair out by the roots. *The evening sacrifice* (4). The word denotes the meal offering (Ex. xxix. 41). Cf. 1 Ki. xviii. 29, where the phrase denotes the time of day.

b. Ezra's prayer and confession (ix. 6–15)

Ezra's prayer should be compared with similar prayers in Dn. ix. 4–19 and Ne. ix. 6–38. Ezra rightly saw that the only hope for the returned Jewish community lay in exclusiveness of faith. Past and present experience had shown that true faith in Jehovah was ruined by intermarriage with the heathen peoples around. Exceptions such as Ruth did not warrant the breaking of the divine rule. Nehemiah is equally clear in this matter (Ne. xiii. 23–28), as is also Malachi (Mal. ii. 11, 14, 15). Similarly the New Testament warns against deliberate marriage with unbelievers (1 Cor. vii. 39), and modern psychologists point out that it is unwise for people with strong religious differences to marry one another. *A wall* (9). Since this is a different word from that used of the city wall in Nehemiah, many regard its use here as metaphorical of a protection. But it is used of the city walls in Mi. vii. 11, and there is an indication in Ezr. iv. 7–23 that work was proceeding on the walls at this time. The words that are quoted in verses 11

and 12 are a summary of the gist of teachings in the Law and the Prophets. The history of Israel is the story of a continual struggle between pure Jehovah worship and the degraded ideas of the Canaanites.

c. The people share in Ezra's grief (x. 1–5)

When Ezra had prayed (1). The RV is preferable, 'While Ezra prayed . . .' *Yet now there is hope* (2); i.e. if we repent. Cf. Dt. xxx. 1–10. *Be of good courage* (4). Cf. Jos. i. 6; 1 Ch. xxviii. 10, 20; 2 Ch. xix. 11. In verse 5 translate, 'The chiefs of the priests, of the Levites, and of all Israel'.

d. A great assembly is called to consider the matter (x. 6–15)

Johanan (6). Those who place Ezra after Nehemiah (see note on vii. 1–28) identify this Johanan with the Jonathan who was the grandson of Eliashib (Ne. xii. 10, 11) and who was High Priest in 408 B.C. according to the Elephantine Papyri. (See *Introduction*, p. 365.) But in this verse neither Johanan nor Eliashib is called High Priest, and according to Josephus (*Ant.* xi. 5. 5) Eliashib's father, Joiakim, was High Priest when Ezra arrived. The probability is that Joiakim was now an old man. Eliashib had at least two grown-up sons, Jaddua and Johanan. Both of them had rooms in the temple precincts. Jaddua, as the eldest son, ultimately succeeded Eliashib, and in turn was succeeded by his eldest son, who had been named Jonathan, or Johanan, after Jaddua's brother.

All the men of Judah and Benjamin (9). The people had been summoned from all the surrounding district as well as from Jerusalem. Their numbers were far too many for the limited accommodation of Jerusalem (Ne. vii. 4), and they were exposed to the heavy rains which fall during December. In verse 14 the proposal is that the guilty parties should be tried by the local judges in the places where they lived. *Were employed about* (15). The RV is likely to be correct in translating 'stood up against'.

e. A commission of inquiry appointed: a list of those found guilty (x. 16–44)

What is said in verse 19 about the *sons of the priests* (18) is probably intended to apply to each of the 113 guilty persons listed in verses 18–43. They took the judge's hand as a pledge of good faith (cf. 2 Ki. x. 15; Ezk. xvii. 18), and offered a ram as a guilt offering (Lv. v. 14–16). The sin could be regarded as done 'through ignorance' (Lv. v. 15), since there had been a general laxity over the application of the law. The Hebrew of verse 44 is difficult. 1 Esdras ix. 36 has 'They put them away with their children'.

J. STAFFORD WRIGHT.

NEHEMIAH
OUTLINE OF CONTENTS

I. NEHEMIAH HEARS OF THE DISTRESS OF JERUSALEM. i. 1–11

II. NEHEMIAH COMES TO JERUSALEM. ii. 1–20

III. A LIST OF THE BUILDERS. iii. 1–32

IV. THE WORK COMPLETED IN SPITE OF OPPOSITION. iv. 1—vii. 4

V. THE REGISTER OF THOSE WHO RETURNED WITH ZERUBBABEL. vii. 5–73

VI. THE LAW READ AND EXPOUNDED. viii. 1–18

VII. NATIONAL REPENTANCE AND A COVENANT OF OBEDIENCE. ix. 1—x. 39

VIII. LISTS OF INHABITANTS. xi. 1—xii. 26

IX. THE WALLS DEDICATED AND TEMPLE SERVICES ARRANGED. xii. 27–47

X. NEHEMIAH'S REFORMS. xiii. 1–31

NEHEMIAH
COMMENTARY

I. NEHEMIAH HEARS OF THE DISTRESS OF JERUSALEM. i. 1–11

a. The news reaches Nehemiah in Persia (i. 1–3)

The words of Nehemiah (1). The writer indicates that he is making an extract from Nehemiah's memoirs. *The month Chisleu* (1); i.e. the ninth month. *The twentieth year* (1); i.e. of Artaxerxes I; 445 B.C. But there must be a copyist's error either here or in ii. 1, for the month in ii. 1 is the first month. Hence perhaps the events of this chapter should be dated in the nineteenth year of Artaxerxes I. *Shushan* (1). Susa. *Hanani* (2). Cf. vii. 2. *Of the captivity* (2). Those who had returned from the captivity to Judah. The report summarized in verse 3 indicates that some fresh disaster had recently occurred. It could hardly refer to the original destruction of 586 B.C. Hence it is reasonable to refer it to the disaster described in Ezr. iv. 23. See notes on Ezr. iv. 6–23.

b. Nehemiah's confession and prayer (i. 4–11)

This confession and prayer should be compared with Ezr. ix and Dn. ix. Nehemiah knew the Scriptures, and called to mind such passages as Lv. xxvi. 33; Dt. xxx. 1–5. *The great and terrible God* (5). Cf. Dt. vii. 21. *Grant him mercy in the sight of this man* (11). The specific request follows the general confession. Nehemiah proposed to ask Artaxerxes to reverse a decree that he had made in Ezr. iv. 21. Yet the king had there left a

loophole for a change of mind (Ezr. iv. 21n.). Eastern monarchs could be fickle. *Cupbearer* (11). There is no definite article here. Nehemiah was not necessarily the only cupbearer, but he was evidently a favourite of the king, as the story shows. The cupbearer's duty was to serve and taste the wine in the presence of the king as a proof that it was not poisoned. In later times the cupbearer had to be a eunuch; and certainly there is no indication that Nehemiah was married.

II. NEHEMIAH COMES TO JERUSALEM. ii. 1–20

a. Artaxerxes commissions him to rebuild the city (ii. 1–8)

The month Nisan (7). For the date see note on i. 1. *Afraid* (2). Nehemiah knew that he might easily be put to death for his request. *I prayed* (4). Note this silent prayer in the crisis, although Nehemiah had been praying for several days about this very thing. The prayer life of Nehemiah may be studied in i. 4–11, ii. 4, iv. 4, 5, 9, v. 19, vi. 9, 14, xiii. 14, 22, 29, 31. The subsequent story shows that the king not only granted Nehemiah's request, but also made him governor of Jerusalem. The *time* (6) that is here mentioned is not specified. All that is known is that Nehemiah returned after twelve years (v. 14, xiii. 6), but it hardly seems likely that so long a period would have been fixed on this occasion. Thus we may suppose that either the period was extended, or Nehemiah returned for the first time after two or three years, and almost immediately went back to Jerusalem again. *The queen also sitting by him* (6). The suggestion is that Nehemiah could count on her co-operation. *Governors* (7). See note on Ezr. viii. 36. *Asaph* (8) is a Jewish name. *The king's forest* (8). Probably the so-called Garden of Solomon, some six miles south of Jerusalem. Lebanon would be too far away. 'Forest' here is the word from which 'paradise' comes.

b. Nehemiah secretly surveys the damaged walls (ii. 9–16)

The king had sent captains (9). Contrast Ezr. viii. 22. *Sanballat the Horonite* (10). Of Beth-horon, on the borders of Ephraim. The Elephantine Papyri show that later he was governor of Samaria. Doubtless he had hoped that he would have Judah also within his sphere of office. *San* is connected with *Sin*, the moon god. *Tobiah the servant* (10). See note on Ezr. iv. 7. He had probably once been an Ammonite slave.

One cannot speak dogmatically about the places mentioned in verses 13–15. It would seem that Nehemiah went out by the south-west gate that opened into the Valley of Hinnom, and turned east, going past a well on the south side of the city, and coming eventually to the Dung Gate at the south-east corner. Turning north-east he came almost immediately to the Fountain Gate by *the king's pool* (14) or pool of Siloam. Here he was forced to dismount and lead his donkey (or mule). He continued up the Kidron valley (*the brook*) to the north-east corner of the city. Here he *turned back* (15), or 'turned', either retracing his steps, or, more probably, turning westwards and completing his circuit of the walls until he once more reached the Valley Gate on the south-west corner.

The rest that did the work (16); i.e. those who had taken part in the building of the wall that had been destroyed.

c. The people agree to undertake the work (ii. 17–20)

Geshem (19). Mentioned again in vi. 1, 2, 6. In the last reference he is called *Gashmu*. He is an Arab leader, but it is not clear why he is in association with Sanballat, unless he belonged to an Arab tribe that had been transplanted into Samaria. *Memorial* (20). Either, a past memorial of having been associated with Jerusalem; or, a future memorial resulting from assisting Nehemiah now.

III. A LIST OF THE BUILDERS. iii. 1–32

Ezra is not mentioned as taking part in the building. It is possible that he had returned for a time to Babylon. Or his reputation may have been temporarily under a cloud owing to the recent failure of the building operations, and it

was not felt to be wise for him to be in charge of a party. If he had taken part in the previous attempt to rebuild the walls, he had exceeded the commission that had been given to him by the king.

Eliashib (1). First mentioned in Ezr. x. 6. See also Ne. xii. 10. *Sheep gate* (1). Cf. Jn. v. 2 (RV). North-east of the city. Perhaps a market for temple sacrifices was held nearby. *Sanctified it* (1). A special ceremony marked the completion of the work by the priests. Some by an emendation read, 'They laid its beams', as in verse 3. *The tower of Meah* (RV 'Hammeah') . . . *the tower of Hananeel* (1). Two towers to the west of the Sheep Gate. The latter is mentioned in Zc. xiv. 10.

Men of Jericho (2). Cf. Ezr. ii. 34. Contingents of the returned exiles occupied a fairly wide area round Jerusalem. *Fish gate* (3). This is the next prominent position on the walls as one moves west. It is north-west of the city, probably on the site of the modern Damascus Gate. Perhaps there was a fish market held nearby. It is mentioned again in 2 Ch. xxxiii. 14; Zp. i. 10. *Meremoth* (4). The priest who received the gifts that Ezra brought (Ezr. viii. 33). See also verse 21, where he builds another section. *Meshullam* (4). His daughter later married Tobiah's son (Ne. vi. 18).

Tekoites (5). The town from which Amos came. It was about ten miles south of Jerusalem. *Their Lord* (5). RV does not have the capital; in which case the reference is to Nehemiah as governor of the district. The leading men of Tekoa evidently sympathized with Sanballat.

The old gate (6). Perhaps the same as the corner gate of 2 Ki. xiv. 13; Je. xxxi. 38. It would be where the western wall turned north-east.

The throne of the governor on this side the river (7); i.e. the place where the Persian satrap had his official residence when he came to Jerusalem. The RV gives a different sense by translating: 'Mizpah, which appertained to the throne,' etc. The significance would then be that Gibeon and Mizpah were under the direct jurisdiction of the Persian satrap, yet their inhabitants came to help. Gibeon and Mizpah were in Benjamin, and close to Jerusalem. But since Mizpah is mentioned twice more in verses 15 and 19, it is possible that this one is further north. *Apothecaries* (8) were mixers of perfumes and spices. *Fortified* (8). The Hebrew normally means 'left'. The meaning may be that at this point the builders ceased to follow the original wall, and curved either inwards or outwards for a short space. The exact position of *the broad wall* (8) is unknown. See also xii. 38 for its general position. It was on the western side.

Ruler of the half part (9). Evidently Jerusalem and some other places were divided into two administrative districts. See also verses 12, 16, 17, 18. *Pahath-moab* (11). See note on Ezr. ii. 6. *The other piece* (11). RV 'another portion'. See also verses 19, 20, 21, 24, 27, 30. It is strange that some of the builders are recorded as building a second portion when nothing is said about a first.

(But compare verses 4 and 21, and verses 5 and 27.) This may indicate that they built their first portion under the direction of someone else, and since, together, they were a large party, the work on this section was finished sooner, and the subordinate group was given a section on its own. Others suppose that the list in this chapter is incomplete, and that a number of names and parts of the wall have been omitted, including the first mention of these people. Some support is lent to this second view by the obvious omission of the important Ephraim Gate (viii. 16, xii. 39). *The tower of the furnaces* (11). Perhaps the David Tower just south of the modern Jaffa Gate, on the west side. The bakers' ovens may have been in this area (Je. xxxvii. 21). *His daughters* (12). Some interpret this metaphorically, since 'daughters' is sometimes used of dependent villages or towns. See, e.g., Ne. xi. 25, 27, where it is translated 'the villages thereof'. Hence here the phrase could be translated 'ruler of the half part of Jerusalem, it and its villages'.

For the three gates mentioned in verses 13–15 see note on ii. 13–15. *Mizpah* (15). See verse 7n., and cf. verse 19. *Pool of Siloah* (15); i.e. Siloam, at the south-east corner. *The king's garden* (15). Cf. 2 Ki. xxv. 4. *The city of David* (15). This is now identified with the south part of the eastern hill of Jerusalem.

Beth-zur (16). Situated thirteen miles south of Jerusalem. *The sepulchres of David* (16). The royal tombs, the site of which are unknown. The phrase here indicates that they formed a rough landmark, and need not mean that they were very close to the wall. *The pool that was made* (16). Perhaps the pool referred to in Is. xxii. 11. *The house of the mighty* (16); RV, 'mighty men'; i.e. the barracks. Site unknown.

The Levites (17). Only one is mentioned, and some names may have fallen out. *Keilah* (17) was about fifteen miles south-west. See 1 Sa. xxiii. 1–13. *Bavai* (18). LXX, 'Binnui'. See verse 24. *Armoury* (19). The site is unknown. *The turning of the wall* (19). Cf. 2 Ch. xxvi. 9. The word denotes a corner that bends inward rather than outward. *Earnestly* (20). Some emend to 'toward the hill'. *The plain* (22). The Jordan area, where this group of priests was living.

The exact translation of verse 25 is difficult, but the reference seems to be to some tower projecting from the king's palace on the hill Ophel. *The court of the prison* (25). See Je. xxxii. 2. In verse 26 the text may be dislocated. The clause about the Nethinim (Ezr. ii. 43–54) would better follow the first mention of Ophel in verse 27, and the reference to *the water gate*, etc., seems to be to another stretch of the building. The gate was probably the one through which the water carriers entered on the east. There was an open area by it. See viii. 1, 3, 16. *Ophel* (27). Lit. 'a swelling'. The northern part of the south-east hill. *The horse gate* (28). Cf. Je. xxxi. 40. The description is still moving north. The gate was the one by which the king's horses were led to their stables. See 2 Ki. xi. 16; 2 Ch. xxiii. 15.

The keeper of the east gate (29). Perhaps the eastern approach to the temple. *Meshullam* (30). He also was repairing a second portion. See verse 4.

The place of the Nethinims (31). The description has moved beyond Ophel, where the Nethinim lived (26). The reference may therefore be to the residence where those Nethinim who were actually on duty stayed. According to this verse it was also associated with merchants, who perhaps sold things for use in the temple services. *The gate Miphkad* (31). RV, 'the gate of Hammiphkad'. The exact site is unknown, but clearly it is in the north-east. The name has been translated as 'place of mustering' (i.e. of the armies) or 'place of visitation' (i.e. of imprisonment or punishment). Some think that it is the gate through which the scapegoat was led on the day of atonement. (See note on xii. 31–39.) *The going up of the corner* (32). RV mg., 'the upper chamber of the corner'. Probably a reference to a look-out room on the corner of the wall. *The sheep gate* (32). This completes the circuit of the walls. See verse 1.

IV. THE WORK COMPLETED IN SPITE OF OPPOSITION. iv. 1—vii. 4

a. The mockery of Sanballat and Tobiah (iv. 1–6)

The army of Samaria (2). Probably a group of irregulars who accompanied Sanballat. *Fortify* (2). The same word as in iii. 8. See note. If the word is translated, as normally, 'leave', the word that follows may be emended to 'to God', thus giving the sense, 'will they leave the matter to God?' i.e. depend upon Him. This connects quite well with the reference to sacrifice that follows. *Before the builders* (5). Their taunts about the powerlessness of God had been made in the presence of the builders to discourage them. *Unto the half thereof* (6); i.e. half the height.

b. The workmen armed against a surprise attack (iv. 7–23)

Arabians . . . Ammonites . . . Ashdodites (7). Others besides the Samaritans were keen to stop the work. *Conspired . . . together* (8). Since Artaxerxes had authorized the building, any attack would have to be 'unofficial'. *Judah* (10); i.e. the people generally. Verse 11 describes the whispering report that was put around to discourage the builders.

The text of verse 12 is difficult. The Jews who lived outside the city amongst the enemy brought in a report on many occasions. 'From all the places where they live they will come up against us' (so RSV, emending text).

The arming of the builders (13) suggests that the previous verse indicates a possible attack. The Hebrew text of this verse is difficult, but the AV conveys what must be the general sense. *My servants* (16). Probably Nehemiah's bodyguard. *Habergeons* (16). Leather coats covered with thin plates of metal. *The rulers were behind all the house of Judah* (16). They were ready by each group. *With the other hand held a weapon* (17). This phrase must not be pressed too literally. Obviously the builders could not work quickly and well with only one hand in use. The point is that a weapon was always at hand. *By me* (18). A personal reminiscence of Nehemiah. The trumpeter stood ready to give the alarm. *A guard to us* (22). Those who came from the surrounding districts were asked to remain in the city at night, both for their own sake and also for an additional protection if an attack came. *My brethren . . . my servants* (23); i.e. Nehemiah's own clan and his Jewish bodyguard. *The men of the guard* (23); i.e. the Persian soldiers. *Saving that every one put them off for washing* (23). The Hebrew makes no sense. It reads literally, 'each man his weapon the water.' The RV translates, 'Every one went with his weapon to the water.'

c. Social injustices remedied (v. 1–19)

In spite of the position of this chapter, the contents indicate that it may belong to a later date in Nehemiah's administration. Note particularly verse 14, and the fact that Nehemiah calls an assembly of the people, whereas the previous chapter has spoken of the speed and urgency of the building. Those who think that the events of this chapter belong to the period of the wall-building say that the work caused a stoppage of trade, and that this caused economic difficulties. But all that is mentioned here could hardly have developed in under fifty-two days (see vi. 15).

We take up corn (2). Better as in RV, 'Let us get corn'. The ordinary labourers complain of shortage of food. In order to obtain it peasant farmers have mortgaged their property (3). According to the law all such property should return to the seller in the jubile year (see Lv. xxv. 25–34). Some had borrowed money to pay the royal taxes, and, being unable to repay it, had sold their children into slavery (4, 5). Slaves of this kind also were supposed to be returned to freedom in the seventh year (see Ex. xxi. 2–6). *Our children as their children* (5); i.e. as human beings we are no different from our richer brethren.

Usury (7). The lending of money, etc., at interest is not regarded in the Bible as wrong in itself (Dt. xxiii. 19, 20; Mt. xxv. 27), but it was forbidden as between one Israelite and another (Ex. xxii. 25), since the money was borrowed for the relief of distress and not for the development of trade. *We . . . have redeemed* (8). Nehemiah and others had redeemed Jews from slavery to the heathen round about. In verse 9 notice how Nehemiah sees the importance of a good moral witness by those who named the name of the true God.

Might exact (10). This is an interpretation rather than a translation. The RV gives the sense, 'I . . . do lend them money and corn on usury.' Perhaps Nehemiah and his associates had themselves also acted unthinkingly, yet not to the same drastic extent as others. But some omit 'on usury' and give the sense, 'We have lent them money and corn, and we have remitted the interest.' The moneylenders are to return the property that they held in pledge and refuse to accept any interest in future. This would make it possible for those who had borrowed to pay off the capital sum in due course. *The hundredth part* (11). If this is correct, the interest must have been paid monthly, thus making the rate 12% per annum. But a slight emendation makes the word mean 'interest'. *Then I called the priests* (12); i.e. to administer the oath. Cf. Nu. v. 19f. *I shook my lap* (13). The symbolism of the action is obvious.

Normally the people would have been taxed to supply the governor's salary, but Nehemiah had himself paid for his household and himself (14). The fact that he must have been a wealthy man shows the personal sacrifice that he made in coming to the struggling Jerusalem. In verse 15 follow the RV mg., reading 'bread and wine at the rate of forty shekels', i.e. supplies for his household up to £5 daily. *Neither bought we any land* (16). Nehemiah did not speculate. *From among the heathen* (17). Perhaps Jews who wanted to settle permanently in Jerusalem, and who had not yet got houses.

d. Further attempts to trap Nehemiah are defeated (vi. 1–14)

Ono (2). Associated with Lydda (Lod) in Ezr. ii. 33 and Ne. xi. 35. About twenty miles north of Jerusalem. Nehemiah could easily be murdered or kidnapped if he went so far from the city. The *open letter* (5), on a small piece of papyrus or leather or potsherd, would be read by others. *That thou mayest be their king* (6). To set up a king would be an act of rebellion. *Gashmu* (6). A variant of Geshem. *Prophets* (7). Malachi's prophecies may or may not have been uttered by this time. But it would be possible for the enemies to interpret any messianic prophecy in the wrong sense of this verse. Sanballat here pretends that he wishes to discuss how to prevent a false report being given to the king.

Shemaiah (10). Not mentioned elsewhere. He was evidently a prophet (see verse 12). *Shut up* (10). The meaning is unknown. It might stand for being ceremonially unclean, though, if so, he would hardly suggest going into the temple. Others think that it has some reference to being under a vow. More likely it has some reference to secrecy. Shemaiah invited Nehemiah to his house, since it was dangerous for him (Shemaiah) to go out knowing what he did. Once he had told Nehemiah the news, they would both seek sanctuary in the temple. *I will not go in* (11). Nehemiah, not being a priest, refuses to break the law of God to save his life. Verse 14 indicates that other prophets and prophetesses were hired in similar ways, so that Nehemiah might be trapped into an action out of which his enemies might make capital.

e. The completion of the walls (vi. 15, 16)

Elul (15). August-September. The sixth month. *Fifty and two days* (15). The wall did not have to be rebuilt from ground level. In many places it needed no more than extensive repairs.

f. Some Jewish nobles negotiate with the enemy (vi. 17–19)

Sworn unto him (18). Either as secret conspirators, or as kinsmen by the two marriages mentioned here. *Meshullam* (18). See iii. 4, 30.

g. Arrangements for the guarding of the city (vii. 1–4)

In verse 1 the suggestion seems to be that those temple officials who were not on duty in the temple were made guardians of the gates. They were more free than the ordinary manual workers. *Hanani* (2). See i. 2. *Hananiah* (2). The name is common at this time (e.g. iii. 8). This man was governor of the fortress to the north of the temple. *Appoint watches* (3). These are night watches. Presumably each street, or group of houses, would have one man on duty, standing in front of his own house. At a certain hour in the night he would be relieved by the next man. *The people were few therein* (4). Ezra and Nehemiah could gather large assemblies on special occasions from the district round about (see, e.g., Ezr. x. 7), but comparatively few had chosen to come and live in Jerusalem while it was unprotected by walls.

V. THE REGISTER OF THOSE WHO RETURNED WITH ZERUBBABEL. vii. 5–73

Nehemiah plans to obtain fresh inhabitants for Jerusalem, but wishes to make sure that only those come who are pure Jews. Hence he finds the register of those who returned with Sheshbazzar in 537 B.C., and makes this the basis of his plans (5). This register is virtually identical with the one in Ezr. ii, where see notes. *And when the seventh month came* . . . (73). Although this last clause is the same as Ezr. iii. 1, it probably introduces the incidents that follow. See vi. 15n.

VI. THE LAW READ AND EXPOUNDED. viii. 1–18

This chapter occurs as the closing chapter of 1 Esdras, where it follows on Ezra x. It is placed there to round off the story of Ezra, though the Hebrew text indicates that it belongs to the time of Nehemiah's governorship.

a. Ezra's public reading of the Law (viii. 1–8)

The water gate (1). See verse 16 and note on iii. 26. *Ezra* (1). See introductory note to Ne. iii. Whether or not Ezra had been in Babylon during the time of the rebuilding, he was now the obvious man to summon to read and expound the law. *The book of the law of Moses* (1). A common view is that this was the so-called Priestly Code, and that this story marks the introduction of this Code to Jerusalem. The chief objection to this view is that the Samaritans have a Pentateuch that is virtually identical with the Jewish Penta-

teuch. Since those who broke away to form the separate Samaritan religious group were perpetually at loggerheads with the religious leaders who came from Babylon, it is most unlikely that they would incorporate into their Pentateuch these new teachings that came from Babylon. It is more reasonable to believe that Ezra had the whole Pentateuch in front of him, though he need not have read every single law to the people. Deuteronomy was the most important for them to hear, since this was the book that was ordered to be read aloud (see Dt. xxxi. 9–13).

After the general statement, the details of the scene are described (4–8). There are general similarities with the form of the reading of the Law in the synagogue services today.

MSS and Versions differ over the numbers of the men named in verse 4. There may have been six on each side to represent the twelve tribes. It is usually thought that they were priests or Levites. Verses 7 and 8 indicate that, owing to the large crowds and, perhaps, to the fact that many of the people understood Aramaic better than Hebrew, the Levites helped to broadcast and expound the text. *Distinctly* (8). Some prefer to render this word 'with a translation'. Cf. Ezr. iv. 18, where the same word, there translated 'plainly', may have this meaning. The word is actually used as a technical term under the Persian Empire for the act of reading an Aramaic document aloud in the vernacular of the province concerned. (See F. F. Bruce, *The Books and the Parchments*, p. 52.) In Ne. xiii. 24 it is indicated that some people had difficulty in understanding Hebrew, though they were only a very small minority.

b. The effect on the people (viii. 9–12)

Tirshatha (9). See note. on Ezr. ii. 63. Here Nehemiah is clearly mentioned as the contemporary of Ezra. Those who believe that Ezra did not come until after 400 B.C. (see note on Ezr. vii. 1–28) regard Nehemiah's name here as an addition by the chronicler. It is pointed out that the corresponding passage in 1 Esdras ix. 49 has 'Then spake Attharates unto Esdras the chief priest and reader, and to the Levites that taught the multitude, even to all, saying, This day is holy . . .' But Attharates is the Greek misunderstanding of the title Tirshatha, as in 1 Esdras v. 40, where it appears as Attharias. Thus 1 Esdras mentions the governor as such, but does not give his name, as the writer has not yet come to the story of Nehemiah, and may not in fact be intending to relate the story of Nehemiah at all. Our text of 1 Esdras breaks off after this chapter and we do not know whether its history originally went further.

All the people wept (9). Cf. 2 Ki. xxii. 11. *This day is holy* (10). The day must be kept as a festival, being the first day of the month. The people must eat the best of the food, and share their good things with those who could not afford them for themselves. Cf. Est. ix. 19, 22. They would find their strength for the future in celebrating this day joyfully to the Lord.

c. The feast of tabernacles (viii. 13-18)

Verse 13 describes the leaders meeting on their own with Ezra for instruction in the Law. *The feast of the seventh month* (14). This was the feast of tabernacles which was kept from the fifteenth to the twenty-second of the seventh month (see Lv. xxiii. 33–44), so the people had plenty of time to prepare for it. No mention is here made of the day of atonement, which was prescribed for the tenth of the month (Lv. xxiii. 26–32). The writer, if he compiled this book about 300 B.C., obviously knew of this day, and could have included it here if he had wished. But the emphasis in this chapter is on rejoicing, and the inclusion of the fast would have seemed out of place, though there is no reason to suppose that the people did not observe it. There is also an emphasis upon the reading of the Law, and this was prescribed for the feast of tabernacles (Dt. xxxi. 9–13).

The gate of Ephraim (16). On the north-west of the city. See note on iii. 11. *Had not the children of Israel done so* (17). They had certainly kept the feast of tabernacles (Ezr. iii. 4). But they had not kept it so systematically and with such ceremony. Others think that the words *the son of Nun* have been included by a scribe in error, and that the reference is to Joshua the High Priest who returned with Zerubbabel, and who kept the feast in Ezr. iii. 4. *On the eighth day* (18). This eighth day is distinguished from the seven days of the feast. When the feast is mentioned in a general way, it is spoken of as consisting of the seven days (Dt. xvi. 13, 15), but when detailed ritual instructions are given, an eighth day of a final solemn assembly is prescribed (Lv. xxiii. 39; Nu. xxix. 35).

VII. NATIONAL REPENTANCE AND A COVENANT OF OBEDIENCE. ix. 1—x. 39

It had been appropriate to keep rejoicing in the forefront during the ceremonies that followed closely upon the completion of the wall. But now practically one month had elapsed since the wall was finished (vi. 15), and it was appropriate that a solemn review of the state of the nation should be made.

a. The people confess God's goodness and their own sin (ix. 1-38)

One fourth part of the day (3). Three hours of reading were followed by three of confession and prayer. *The stairs* (4). The platform of viii. 4, or some part of it. There is no reasonable way of accounting for the differences between the two lists of names in verses 4 and 5 unless, perhaps, the list in verse 4 is a list of families, and in verse 5 the actual individuals who represented the families.

This prayer (5–38) opens with a reminder of God's greatness, and then proceeds to a recital of important turning-points of history. Passing by the general creation of the world, the record singles out the call of Abraham (7, 8), one of the most important events in the whole history of mankind (Gal. iii. 8, 29). The next turning-point is the exodus (9–12) and the giving of the law to guide the people into the right way (13, 14). God's provision in the wilderness (15) was answered by secret and open rebellion (16–18), yet God continued to show one act of mercy after another (19–23). The next turning-point is the entry into Canaan, when again God showered blessings upon His people (24, 25). But the people continued to rebel, even in the light of fresh revelation through the prophets (26, 30). The hand of God was seen in history, using the forces of nature and of nations to bring His people to their senses (27–30). Although His people were crushed, they were preserved (31); and they now come in confession and prayer (32–35). They realize the difference between the promised ideal and what they were actually experiencing (36, 37), and they desire to renew their side of the covenant (38).

Note that in verse 14 God is said to have 'made known' His sabbath. The implication is that it was not arbitrarily invented at this time. *Appointed a captain* (17). See Nu. xiv. 4. *Thy good spirit* (20). See Nu. xi. 17; Is. lxiii. 10, 11. The instructions normally came through Moses when God spoke to him. With verse 21 cf. Dt. ii. 7, viii. 4, xxix. 5. *Divide them into corners* (22). Follow RV mg., 'didst distribute them into every corner'. *Withdrew the shoulder* (29); i.e. like an ox from the yoke. *We are in great distress* (37). They had to pay heavy tribute and taxes. *We make a sure covenant* (38). Probably the original covenant of Sinai was regarded as renewed by the leaders of the people. (Cf. Je. xi. 1–4.)

b. A list of the leaders who set their seal to the covenant (x. 1-27)

Zidkijah (1). RV 'Zedekiah'. Otherwise unknown. He may have been a member of the royal house and so comes high on the list. Most of the names listed in verses 2–8 occur again in the list of priests in xii. 1–3. The numbers of the priestly families had increased since Ezr. ii. 36–39. Verses 9–13 list the Levites and verses 14–27 the leaders of secular families. Twenty-one of them occur in Ezr. ii. Some others occur in Ne. iii.

c. The obligations of the covenant (x. 28-39)

Separated themselves (28). See note on Ezr. vi. 21. The marginal references in the Bible indicate where the ordinances mentioned in verses 30–39 are to be found in the law. *On the sabbath day* (31). There is nothing in the law that directly specifies not buying or selling on the sabbath, but Am. viii. 5 shows that this was understood from early times. Cf. Ne. xiii. 15–22. *The exaction of every debt* (31). See Dt. xv. 1–3. The debt was either completely remitted or its payment suspended during the jubile year. *The third part of a shekel* (32). The law in Ex. xxx. 13 prescribed half a shekel, and this was later the recognized amount (Mt. xvii. 24, RV). The preliminary phrase, *We made ordinances for us*, perhaps implies a variation from the law, and this may have been due to the comparative poverty of the people. *As it is written in the law* (34). There is no command for a wood offering in the law, but the reference is to the command in Lv. vi. 12 that the fire should be kept burning continually. *The tithes of our ground* (37). Note that the tithes of cattle are not mentioned here (Lv. xxvii. 32), though the firstborn are mentioned in verse 36 (see Nu. xviii. 15–18). There may well have been a shortage of cattle at this time, and God does not intend His commands to be arbitrarily burdensome.

VIII. LISTS OF INHABITANTS. xi. 1—xii. 26

This chapter links on in its theme to vii. 4.

a. The dwellers in Jerusalem (xi. 1–24)

The list of verses 3–19 is virtually identical with 1 Ch. ix. 2–17, though with some variations. See notes there. It appears to be the list of those who were already living in Jerusalem. It may be divided up as follows: leading laymen (3–9); priests (10–14); Levites (15–18); porters (19). Verses 20–24 give some general notes on the temple duties.

b. Towns and villages occupied by the Jews (xi. 25–36)

These verses list towns in the former territory of Judah (25–30) and towns in the former territory of Benjamin (31–36). *From Beer-sheba unto the valley of Hinnom* (30); i.e. from the extreme south of the territory allotted to the twelve tribes to the northern border of Judah. In verse 36 note the RV rendering, 'And of the Levites, certain courses in Judah were joined to Benjamin'; i.e. some who had formerly lived in Judah now lived in Benjamin. But the AV may be correct.

c. A list of priests and Levites connected with Zerubbabel's return (xii. 1–9)

The writer has taken the opportunity of grouping together several lists that he found preserved. The interpretation of these lists is most difficult. Thus we should expect 1–9 to tally with Ezr. ii. But since the names differ considerably, it is possible that the list here is the list of the names of descendants of those mentioned in Ezr. ii. *Over the thanksgiving* (8). RV mg. 'over the choirs'. *Over against them in the watches* (9); i.e. sang antiphonally with them when their turn came to be on duty.

d. Genealogy of the High Priests from Joshua to Jaddua (xii. 10, 11)

Jonathan (11). Probably the same as Johanan or Jehohanan (23). See note on Ezr. x. 6. *Jaddua* (11). See note in *Introduction* to Ezra and Nehemiah p. 365).

e. A list of priests in the days of Joiakim (xii. 12–21)

f. Heads of Levitical families in the days of Joiakim and afterwards (xii. 22–26)

Verse 22 means that a register of the heads of the priestly and Levitical families was kept during these periods. *Darius the Persian* (22). If Jaddua was the one who was High Priest in 333 B.C., this would be Darius III. But if he was High Priest earlier, it might be Darius II. See note in *Introduction* to Ezra and Nehemiah (p. 365). *The book of the chronicles* (23). Not our book of Chronicles, but official records. *The commandment of David* (24). See 1 Ch. xvi. 4–6, xxiii. 30. *Ward over against ward* (24); i.e. antiphonally. Cf. xii. 9 and see Ezr. iii. 11n.

IX. THE WALLS DEDICATED AND TEMPLE SERVICES ARRANGED. xii. 27–47

Note that Nehemiah's memoirs in the first person are here used again (27–43). The date of the dedication ceremony is not stated. Some infer from 2 Macc. i. 18 that the date was on the twenty-fifth of the ninth month, which would suitably be three months exactly after the completion (see Ne. vi. 15). *Psalteries . . . harps* (27), or 'Harps . . . lyres'. *Plain country* (28). In spite of the addition of *round about Jerusalem* the phrase may have its usual meaning of the low-lying area near Jordan, as in iii. 22. *Netophathi* (28). Situated fifteen miles south-west of Jerusalem. The places mentioned in verse 29 were probably north of Jerusalem. *Purified themselves* (30). The purification was presumably by the sprinkling of the blood of sacrifice.

Two great companies (31). It seems that the two processions started from the Valley Gate on the south-west. One, led by Ezra, proceeded via the south side of the city, while the other, led by Nehemiah, proceeded via the north. The landmarks here mentioned are those referred to in Ne. iii with the exception of the Ephraim Gate on the north-west (39) and the Prison Gate (39). The latter may be the same as the Gate of Hammiphkad in iii. 31 (see note). Note how verse 36 provides evidence from the memoirs of Nehemiah that Ezra was his contemporary. After *the fountain gate* (37) this party left the walls and kept within the city until they came out again by *the water gate*. Then one imagines that they kept along the wall until they met the other party by *the prison gate* (39).

The Levites that waited (44); i.e. that served in the temple. *The ward* (45); i.e. the appointed charge. For *the ward of the purification* see 1 Ch. xxiii. 28. *There were chief of the singers* (46). Probably a better translation of this verse is, 'For in the days of David, Asaph was of old the chief of the singers'. For Asaph see 1 Ch. xv. 16–19, etc. *They sanctified* (47); i.e. set apart. The people paid their tithes and dues to the Levites, and the Levites paid the tithe of the tithes to the priests. See x. 38 and Nu. xviii. 25–32.

X. NEHEMIAH'S REFORMS. xiii. 1–31

a. The heathen excluded from the congregation (xiii. 1–3)

On that day (1). Perhaps the same occasion as xii. 44, where the same words are used. Some think that this section may originally have followed verses 4–9. *Was found written* (1). See Dt. xxiii. 3–5. *Come into the congregation* (1). The phrase would seem to denote the possession of full rights and membership. *All the mixed multitude* (3). Did they go beyond the letter of the law here? Note that Dt. xxiii. 7, 8 allowed Edomites and Egyptians of the third generation to be members of the congregation. But popular enthusiasm may well have led to a drastic application of the law. Tobiah was an Ammonite (ii. 19).

b. Tobiah removed from a room in the temple (xiii. 4–9)

Before this (4). Nehemiah's memoirs are resumed from the time when he returned to Jerusalem after a period in Babylon or Susa (6). If *before this* refers to the incident of verses 1–3, it is obvious that *on that day* in verse 1 cannot refer to the occasion of chapter xii. But *before this* may refer to some portion of the memoirs that the compiler has not included here. *Eliashib* (4). Almost certainly the High Priest (iii. 1, xiii. 28). His alliance with Tobiah may have been through some connection with the parties mentioned in vi. 18, though the word has been interpreted as meaning an alliance of friendship apart from kinship. *A great chamber* (5). There were rooms for various purposes built on to the temple. Cf. 1 Ki. vi. 5; Ezk. xl. 6f.; Ezr. viii. 29, x. 6. *All this time* (6). For the date see note on ii. 6. *King of Babylon* (6). There was still a tendency to think of Babylon as the place of captivity, even though the empire was now Persian.

c. The temple officials provided for (xiii. 10–14)

Nehemiah's reproach of the people presupposes the oath in x. 35–39. *Levites* (10). Probably this includes some priests. *To his field* (10). In spite of the regulations of Dt. xviii. 1 the priests and Levites appear to have owned land; certainly they did so in post-exilic times (see Ezr. ii. 70). The relief that x. 35–39 had given them had not lasted. They had either had to return to their land, if they had not sold it, or had hired themselves out to landowners. For the men mentioned in verse 13 see also iii. 29, 30, viii. 4.

d. Sabbath reforms (xiii. 15–22)

It seems that verse 15 describes the preparation of commodities on the sabbath for sale during the week. Nehemiah noted the offenders, and denounced them on the day of sale. But others think that they did sell on the sabbath. *Men of Tyre* (16). Tyrian traders in dried fish and other goods had their headquarters in Jerusalem. *The nobles* (17) should have prevented this trading. With verse 18 cf. Je. xvii. 21–24.

The merchants . . . lodged without Jerusalem (20). They did not come into the city, but set up their stalls outside, so that the people could come out and buy. The smaller gates at the side of the main ones were probably not included in the ban of verse 19. *Keep the gates* (22). Now that the crisis was over, there was not the same need for what was evidently a band of soldiers at the gates (19). The Levites therefore took over the guard on the sabbath.

e. The scandal of mixed marriages (xiii. 23–31)

It was about twenty-five years since the marriage reforms of Ezra, and the evil of mixed marriages had broken out again. *Ashdod* (23). A Philistine city. *Half in the speech of Ashdod* (24); i.e. a corrupt form, which was half Ashdodite and half Hebrew. Nothing is said here about the Ammonite and Moabite dialect, and some omit the reference to Ammon and Moab in verse 23. *Made them swear by God* (25). Presumably they swore to put away their foreign wives, even though this is not actually stated. Anything less would hardly have satisfied the irate Nehemiah. *I chased him from me* (28); i.e. because he refused to put away his foreign wife.

Josephus (*Ant.* XI. vii, viii) has a story, which he places c. 335 B.C., of how a certain Manasseh, brother of the High Priest, had married a daughter of Sanballat, and was expelled from Jerusalem. Sanballat then built him a temple on Mount Gerizim, and this became the centre of the Samaritan worship. It is usually supposed that Josephus has confused his dates and names, and that he is either correct in his date, but wrong over Sanballat (who was long since dead), or correct about Manasseh and Sanballat, but approximately a century too late with his date. Most scholars accept the former supposition. W. F. Lofthouse (Clar. Bible, O.T., IV. 235f.), however, believes that there were two Sanballats, and that a similar incident happened twice, the rival temple being built on the second occasion.

The close of the book of Nehemiah shows mounting tension between the exclusive and the laxer parties in Jerusalem. Modern sympathies tend to be with the laxer party, but the warnings of the law and the experience of history had shown that the Jewish faith could not be preserved in its purity by those of laxer views and practice.

J. STAFFORD WRIGHT.

ESTHER

INTRODUCTION

I. BACKGROUND AND DATE

The scene of the book of Esther is laid in the palace of Shushan, or Susa, in Elam, one of the three capitals of the Persian Empire. Like the books of Daniel, Ezra and Nehemiah, it gives us a glimpse of the Jews in Babylon from the point of view of someone in authority at the royal court and familiar with its conventions and practices. But while Ezra and Nehemiah are passionately concerned with the spiritual and political aspirations of that section of Jewry which returned from the captivity, the book of Esther treats these matters with a studied and significant reserve. The whole book throbs with a fervent patriotism, and yet there is not a single reference to the God of Israel. It describes danger and distress and despair, but in the whole vivid picture there is no mention of any earnest prayers and supplications on the part of the people in their time of terrible trial. The Jews 'wept and wailed', and Mordecai 'cried with a loud and bitter cry', but the author carefully refrains from saying that they cried to God. They fasted, but no religious significance is given to this essentially religious practice.

Now it is quite clear that this careful avoidance of any explicit reference to religion is deliberate. It can best be explained by assuming that the book was written at some period when it was extremely dangerous to make any open profession of the worship of Jehovah (cf. Dn. vi. 7–17).

The period covered by the events described is discovered simply enough by identifying Ahasuerus. As it happens there is now no reasonable doubt as to his identity, the name being a close transliteration of the Persian name of the king known to the Greeks as Xerxes. His character shows a striking resemblance to that given to Xerxes by classical writers such as Herodotus. Moreover, Ahasuerus holds a great feast and assembly of all the leading men of the empire at Susa in the third year of his reign (Est. i. 3), and in the third year of Xerxes a great assembly of the 'principal Persians' was held at Susa to plan the expedition into Greece (Her. vii. 8). In the seventh year of Ahasuerus, fair young maidens were brought to him from which to choose his queen (Est. ii. 16), and in the seventh year of Xerxes, after his return from Europe, he consoled himself by adding to his seraglio (Her. ix. 108, 109). Ahasuerus ruled over Media (Est. i. 3); his empire extended from India to Ethiopia (i. 1) and included islands of the Mediterranean (x. 1), while his capital was at Susa. All this was true of Xerxes and of no other

Persian monarch. The identity of Ahasuerus as Xerxes may be accepted with some certainty, thus placing the opening of the book (the deposition of Vashti) in 483 B.C.

II. AUTHOR AND DATE OF COMPOSITION

There has been, especially in recent times, a very wide diversity of opinion on this question, and critics of a certain school have vied with each other in placing the compilation of Esther as late as possible in the Greek period, some even bringing the date as far forward as the middle of the first century B.C. There are, however, strong reasons for assigning the date of composition to a period very much nearer the events it records. The layout of the royal palace as described in the book of Esther agrees so well with the discoveries made by French excavators on the site that there is no reasonable doubt of the author's familiarity with the place; and yet the palace was destroyed by fire within thirty years of the death of Xerxes. This would place the composition any time within a century of the period of the story. The writer is manifestly familiar with Persian customs, and seems to have access to Persian documents (ix. 32). He uses purely Persian words such as Pur, bathshegen, 'ahashteranim and karpas and, as seen above, he is familiar with the dates of such events as the gathering of the Persian leaders at Susa. Furthermore the style closely resembles that of the books of Ezra, Nehemiah and Chronicles. All this argues an early date—a view that is held by practically all the early commentators. Josephus assigns it to the reign of Artaxerxes Longimanus (464–424 B.C.) whom he identifies with Ahasuerus. Augustine believed it was written by Ezra, and the Talmud assigns it to the Great Synagogue of which Ezra was president. Clement of Alexandria and many others believe that Mordecai was the author.

III. CANONICITY

Josephus, in the earliest statement we have about the Jewish canon (Contr. Ap. i. 8), places Esther among the books of the canon. In the Hebrew Bible it stands among the five Megilloth or Rolls. It is omitted from a number of the early Christian lists of the books of the Old Testament, possibly because it is there regarded as a part of Ezra, but it is found in the canon of the Alexandrian Jews, and has in fact always been accepted as canonical by the Jews. It is included in the LXX with considerable interpolations which do not appear in the Hebrew and were rejected by Jerome. These were clearly added at a later period to counterbalance the puzzling absence from the book of any reference to Jehovah or to the religion of Israel, and are themselves devotional to a degree.

OUTLINE OF CONTENTS

I. THE DIVORCE OF VASHTI. i. 1–22

II. THE CHOICE OF ESTHER AS QUEEN. ii. 1–23

III. HAMAN'S PLOT TO DESTROY THE JEWS. iii. 1—iv. 3

IV. MORDECAI PERSUADES ESTHER TO INTERVENE. iv. 4–17

V. ESTHER'S SUCCESSFUL PETITION. v. 1—viii. 2

VI. THE DELIVERANCE OF THE JEWS. viii. 3—ix. 16

VII. THE FEAST OF PURIM. ix. 17–32

VIII. CONCLUSION. x. 1–3

COMMENTARY

I. THE DIVORCE OF VASHTI. i. 1–22

a. The king's feast (i. 1–9)

Ahasuerus (1). Xerxes, king of Persia (486–465 B.C.), the son of Darius by Atossa, the daughter of Cyrus; he came to the throne five years after the battle of Marathon. After crushing a formidable revolt in Egypt he set out on his Grecian expedition in 481 B.C., and in the following year his vast fleet was destroyed in the battle of Salàmis, while his army suffered heavy defeats at Plataea and Mycale in 479 B.C. He returned to Persia in 478, and the rest of his reign is undistinguished except by debauchery and bloodshed. He was assassinated in 465 B.C. *This is Ahasuerus* (1). This note is inserted to distinguish him from two other monarchs of the same name. See Dn. ix. 1 (probably Cyaxares) and Ezr. iv. 6 (almost certainly Cambyses the son of Cyrus). *India* (1) here refers to that part of India conquered by Alexander the Great, viz. the Punjaub and perhaps Sind. *Ethiopia* (1). Heb. *Kush*, called Cash in the Egyptian inscriptions, Ka'si in the Tell el-Amarna tablets, Ka'su in the Assyrian inscriptions: mod. Nubia. Herodotus mentions that Ethiopia paid tribute to Xerxes (iii. 97). *An hundred and seven and twenty provinces* (1). In Dn. vi. 1 Darius appoints satraps over 120 provinces; thus the empire of Ahasuerus was greater. *Shushan* (2). Susa, the capital of Elam since the third millennium B.C., was the residence of Khudur Lagamar, the Chedorlaomer of Gn. xiv. 1. The Medo-Persian Empire had three capitals, Susa, Ecbatana and Babylon, but Persian kings generally resided in Susa.

In the third year (3); i.e. 483 B.C., when, according to Herodotus, he held a great assembly at Susa to plan the Grecian war. There can be no doubt that the feast mentioned here and the assembly of Herodotus refer to the same event. *Feast* (3). Heb. *mishteh*. Primarily a drinking feast. Herodotus (i. 133) mentions that the Persians discussed the most important affairs of state at such gatherings. *The riches of his glorious kingdom* (4). The amazing opulence of the Persian court is often mentioned by classical writers. This verse clearly refers to an assessment of the empire's resources which took half a year to compute rather than to a feast that lasted for that period. *A feast unto all the people* (5). Another feast is described here, different from that of verse 3 which was for courtiers and officials. This was for the people (cf. Her. i. 126), and was held for seven days in the palace grounds. Thus two feasts were held, one at the beginning of the assembly and one at the end, but the assumption of so many commentators that the book describes a feast that lasted half a year cannot be substantiated. *Where were white, green, and blue* (6). White and blue were the royal colours of Persia. Green (*karpas*) is found only here, and is the same word as the Sanskrit *karpasa*, cotton. This shows that the word is probably Persian, as Persian was an Aryan language and therefore related to Sanskrit. *Pillars* (6). Recent French excavations have laid bare the remains of these pillars on which the awnings hung. *Beds* (6). Herodotus (ix. 82) speaks of couches of gold and silver that the Greeks captured from the Persians. *Pavement of red . . . marble* (6). The meaning of most of these words is doubtful, but pavements of stones of various colours were common in the ancient

East. *Vessels of gold* (7). Herodotus (ix. 80 and 82) mentions drinking vessels of gold which the Greeks captured from the Persians. *None did compel* (8). The meaning is that each drank as he pleased. The Persian custom of making the drinking of a certain quantity obligatory was abandoned.

b. Vashti refuses the king's summons (i. 10-12)

Vashti (9). The name given by Greek writers to the chief queen of Xerxes was Amestris, a woman notorious for cruelty and profligacy, who married him before the third year of his reign and continued queen until his death. Rawlinson suggests that Vashti, a Persian word which means beautiful, is a title given to Amestris and that the deposition was only a temporary one. *The seven chamberlains* (10). Lit. 'eunuchs'. The number seven was sacred among the Persians as among the Hebrews. These names are probably not Persian. It must be remembered that many nationalities were represented among the royal slaves. *But . . . Vashti refused* (12). The summons was in reality a royal command sent in the recognized manner by the eunuchs—a fact that is emphasized in verses 10, 12, 15. The refusal of Vashti was therefore a public affront. As a matter of fact it was a Persian custom to have their wives present at their drinking feasts (cf. Her. v. 18). There is therefore no suggestion whatever of an affront to Vashti in the summons.

c. Vashti is deposed (i. 13-22)

Which knew the times (13). Perhaps the astrologers, but more probably the men who could quote precedents. *Manner* (13); i.e. 'practice'. *The seven princes* (14). Cf. Ezr. vii. 14. There were seven leading families in Persia whose heads were the king's chief advisers and from among whom the queen was chosen (Her. iii. 84). Note how the advice of the princes (16-20) is adapted to the mood of the king, and expressed so as to make the king's private vengeance appear a matter of public duty. *The ladies of Persia and Media* (18); i.e. 'princesses' in contrast to *all women* (17).

That it be not altered (19). Lit. 'that it pass not away'. The counsellors were taking steps to prevent the king from acting impulsively and therefore revocably. If Vashti returned to power she would punish them for their advice, therefore it was necessary that the king should depose her by royal decree, thus incorporating her deposition in the royal records that could not be altered. A previous struggle for power between Vashti and the nobles seems to be indicated. *He sent letters* (22). The Persian Empire had a very efficient and well organized postal system (cf. Xen. *Cyrop.* vii. 6). *Into every province . . .* (22). 'Unto every province in its own script and unto every single race in its own language' (Paton). Most of the inscriptions of this period are written in Old Persian, Babylonian and Susian in parallel columns; but this gives a very inadequate idea of the vast number of languages that were

spoken in the empire of Xerxes. *Be published* (22). Heb. 'speaking'. *That every man . . .* (22). Perhaps 'that every man should become ruler in his own house and should speak according to the tongue of his own people'. The meaning is obscure, but obviously the king's decree is made to carry some suggestion other than its main purpose, but sufficiently important to be included in it. The apparent suggestion that the language of the home should be the language of the father would simplify a situation complicated by the presence of numerous female captives from many lands.

II. THE CHOICE OF ESTHER AS QUEEN. ii. 1-23

a. A plot to prevent the restoration of Vashti (ii. 1-4)

He remembered Vashti (1). There seems to be a suggestion here that the king was beginning to be well disposed towards Vashti. *Said the king's servants* (2). The return of Vashti would spell terrible danger to them (cf. i. 19n.), and their realization of that danger is shown by their willingness to waive the custom of choosing the queen from among one of their own families, and even to take a foreign queen. *Chamberlain* (3). Lit. 'eunuch'. Only eunuchs had access to the women's apartments. *And let the maiden . . . be queen* (4). Josephus adds, 'for his longing for his former wife will be quenched in this way'.

b. Esther with other maidens is brought to the palace (ii. 5-11)

Esther is now introduced. *Mordecai* (5) was a Benjamite and therefore a Jew, because Benjamin adhered to the kingdom of Judah (1 Ki. xii. 21). In his genealogy given here appear the names of *Shimei* and *Kish* which Jewish tradition identifies with Shimei who cursed David (2 Sa. xvi. 5) and Kish the father of Saul (1 Sa. ix. 1. See however note on verse 6 below). Similarly it makes Haman the Agagite a descendant of king Agag the Amalekite whom Saul defeated (1 Sa. xv). A Mordecai returned to Jerusalem with Zerubbabel in 537 B.C. (Ezr. ii. 2; Ne. vii. 7), and it is not impossible that this is the same Mordecai fifty-four years afterwards living at Susa. *Who had been . . .* (6) obviously refers to Kish. It could hardly refer to Mordecai as the captivity in question took place 117 years before. *Hadassah . . . Esther* (7). Assuming that Hadassah is from *hadhas*, myrtle, and that Esther is *sitar*, the Persian for a star (sanskrit *sta'na*; Akk. *istar*), we have here an early example of the later Jewish practice of giving two names—a Hebrew and a Gentile name such as John Mark, Joses Justus, etc. *Fair* (7). Heb. *yephathto'ar*, fair of form; but *to'ar* itself conveys the idea of a fair form; so that Esther's beauty of figure is doubly emphasized. *Beautiful* (7). Heb. *tobhath mar'eh*, of beautiful appearance or possibly countenance (mg.), an expression also applied to Bath-sheba (2 Sa. xi. 2). Hebrew tradition places Esther among the three most beautiful women who ever lived. *Esther was brought* (8). In the apocryphal prayer of Esther she protests strongly her abhorrence of her high estate, but there is nothing in the text to indicate her reactions. *Esther had not shewed* . . . (10). It would seem therefore that Esther, unlike Daniel, conformed to Persian practices and ate forbidden food. It is possible, however, that the nobles, whose concern it was to secure a maiden most likely to make the king forget Vashti, whatever her nationality, took part in the deception. *Mordecai walked* (11). Some commentators have suggested that he was a doorkeeper; but Rawlinson points out that even this would not explain his access to the women's court unless he was also a eunuch.

c. Esther gains the king's approval (ii. 12–20)

The month Tebeth, in the seventh year (16). January–February 479 B.C., immediately after the return of Xerxes from Greece. Thus four years elapsed between the deposition of Vashti and the appointment of Esther.

d. Mordecai discovers a plot against the king's life (ii. 21–23)

Two of the king's chamberlains (21). Xerxes was in fact murdered fourteen years after this by a captain of the guard and a eunuch. *On a tree* (23), or 'pole'. Some commentators take this as meaning that they were impaled. Josephus and others say they were crucified. *The book of the chronicles* (23). Lit. 'the book of the acts of the days'. Seemingly a kind of log book of passing events (cf. 1 Ki. xiv. 19). Ktersias the Greek historian claims to have found materials for his Persian and Assyrian history in the Persian 'parchment' archives.

III. HAMAN'S PLOT TO DESTROY THE JEWS. iii. 1—iv. 3

a. Haman's anger with Mordecai (iii. 1–7)

Haman the Agagite (1). Jewish tradition makes him a descendant of Agag king of Amalek (1 Sa. xv. 32), and Josephus and the Chaldee Targum call him an Amalekite. On the other hand the apocryphal Esther says he is a Macedonian. There is nothing, however, to indicate either an Amalekite or Macedonian descent; indeed, his name, and the names of every member of his family given here, are Persian. *Bowed not* (2). It is very difficult to understand Mordecai's refusal. He himself explains it by saying he was a Jew (4), but nothing in the Jewish religion forbade the usual courtesy of bowing down before a superior. Josephus suggests that it was a refusal to give divine honours to Haman, but the studied avoidance of religious matters in the book makes it difficult to judge of the strength of this claim. It is interesting to note that the Spartan ambassadors refused to prostrate themselves before Xerxes (Her. vii. 136). *Why transgressest thou?* (3). Note that the servants ('slaves') showed Mordecai the courtesy of approaching him

before referring the matter to Haman, and their complaint was lack of loyalty to the king rather than lack of respect to Haman. *Whether Mordecai's matters* (lit. 'words') *would stand* (4); i.e. whether the fact of his being a Jew would absolve him from obeying the king's commandment.

In the first month . . . *Nisan* (7). March–April, known as Abib in the Pentateuch. During the exile the Jews learned to name and number their months in the Babylonian way. Abib was the month of the Passover and of the final and most terrible of the plagues of Egypt. *The twelfth year* (7). 474 B.C. Esther had now been queen for four years. *Pur* (7) refers to some form of divination by which auspicious days were discovered. It is manifestly a non-Hebrew word as the Hebrew translation is given. Most probably it is cognate with the Assyrian *buru* ('stone') which was used in a sense analogous to the Hebrew *goral* and the Greek *psephos*, meaning 'pebble', and hence 'lot'. *Adar* (7). February–March. Thus nearly a year intervened between Haman's decision and the date for carrying it out.

b. Haman persuades the king to order the destruction of the Jews (iii. 8–15)

A certain people (8). The overwhelming majority of the Jews were still in the Persian Empire, as only a comparatively small number (42,000) returned to Jerusalem under Zerubbabel in 537 B.C. *Neither keep they the king's laws* (8). This is the charge that has been made by anti-Jews throughout the ages. *Ten thousand talents of silver* (9). A talent weighed about 103 lb. The total yearly revenue of the Persian Empire was 17,000 talents (Her. iii. 95). Haman no doubt planned to enrich himself from the property of the proscribed Jews, and estimated that, as a result, he would be able to give the king this vast sum. Confiscation of property followed the death sentence as a matter of course (see viii. 1). *The silver is given to thee* (11). This refers to the wealth of the Jews who were to be destroyed. It was placed at Haman's disposal. *To do with them* . . . (11). One of the recurring objections to the historicity of the book is that no ruler could thus regard with indifference the destruction of such a large number of his subjects. Apart from the fact that the known character of the king makes such an objection invalid, we are unfortunately no longer in a position to question the likelihood of such a holocaust after the recent experiences of the Jews in Europe. The Empire, we must remember, was impoverished after the Greek war and Haman's offer of nearly two-thirds of the annual revenue was extremely attractive. *Lieutenants* (12). Heb. *'ahashdarpenim*. A Hebrew attempt to transliterate the Persian *khshatrapa* which the Greeks rendered *satrapes;* hence our 'satraps' (RV). *Posts* (13). See i. 22n.

c. The grief of the Jews (iv. 1–3)

Mordecai rent his clothes (1). The usual sign of sorrow among the Jews. His contemporaries Ezra, Nehemiah and Daniel cried to God in times of crisis (cf. Ezr. viii. 23; Ne. i. 4; Dn. vi. 10). *None might enter into the king's gate* (2). No sign of sorrow was tolerated in the presence of the king (cf. Ne. ii. 1, 2). *Fasting* (3). Although no direct reference is made to religion, fasting could only be a religious observance.

IV. MORDECAI PERSUADES ESTHER TO INTERVENE. iv. 4–17

Told it her (4). They apparently knew her connection with Mordecai and therefore her nationality. *He received it not* (4), as a sign that his grief was not assuaged. This had the desired effect of getting Esther to communicate with him. *Hatach* (6); manifestly a Jew, as the Second Targum gives her his other name as Daniel. The fact that Mordecai has discovered Haman's plans in detail (7) as well as the earlier plot to assassinate the king suggests that he was in a position to know a great deal of what was going on behind the scenes. *One law* (11); i.e. an invariable law. It was instituted by Deioces the first king of the Medes in order to increase his authority, and was adopted by the Persian kings (Her. i. 99). Esther might have legally requested an audience, but clearly feared that such a course might fail as she was not at that period in special favour, as she points out; and the failure of such a request would make its repetition or her own subsequent personal intervention extremely dangerous. A personal appeal was the only course left open to her. *Deliverance . . . from another place . . . and who knoweth . . . ?* (14). There can be no doubt that Mordecai is thinking of God's promises to Israel and His many deliverances in the past; yet he apparently goes out of his way to avoid mentioning Him by name. *Fast ye for me* (16). See note on verse 3. *If I perish, I perish* (16). Cf. Gn. xliii. 14.

V. ESTHER'S SUCCESSFUL PETITION. v. 1—viii. 2

a. She invites the king to a banquet (v. 1–8)

On the third day (1), i.e. of the feast. The Targum however adds 'of the Passover'. *The inner court* (1). Recent excavations have laid bare the royal palace and prove the writer's familiarity with the whole layout (see *Introduction*, p. 380). *Half of the kingdom* (3. Cf. v. 6, vii. 2). This is the usual formula for a promise of ready assistance (cf. Mk. vi. 23). Xerxes however was inclined to make princely promises (see Her. ix. 109). *Let the king . . . come* (4). It must be remembered that Esther was temporarily out of contact with the fickle king (iv. 11). It is therefore not surprising that she should postpone her petition till she was surer of her influence and had greater privacy for it. *I will do to morrow* (8). It is more difficult to account for this further delay, but one must always allow for elements in a situation unrecorded by the author. (The failure of Ehud to put his purpose into effect at his first interview with Eglon is perhaps a parallel case. See Jdg.

iii. 17–21.) Here for example it looks as if Esther began to voice her petition and then her courage failed her and she gave an invitation to a second banquet instead.

b. Haman plots the death of Mordecai (v. 9–14)

Haman . . . joyful and with a glad heart (9). Herodotus tells how Astyages king of the Medes, wishing to punish Harpagus one of his nobles, invited him to supper. Harpagus was highly delighted and told his wife of the honour he received, little dreaming what lay in store for him at the supper (i. 119). *Zeresh* (10). The Targum makes her the daughter of Tatnai (Ezr. v. 3). *The multitude of his children* (11). 'Next to bravery in battle it is considered among the Persians the greatest proof of manliness to exhibit many children' (Her. i. 136). *Mordecai the Jew* (13). Haman was apparently still ignorant of the connection of Esther with Mordecai, although Esther's personal attendants knew of it (iv. 4). *Gallows* (14). In view of its height (75–90 feet) this appears to be the right translation, although the Hebrew word means 'tree' or 'pole'. *He caused . . .* (14). This shows how sure Haman was of his influence over the king.

c. Haman forced to honour Mordecai (vi. 1–14)

Book of records (1). Such chronicles were commonly kept. In them were jotted down anything worth recording which took place or came to the notice of the king (Her. viii. 85, 90). *What honour . . . ?* (3). The Persians had an order called *Orosangae* or 'Benefactors of the king'—men who had rendered some signal service to the king and were duly and sometimes extravagantly rewarded (Her. viii. 85). *Now Haman was come* (4). The events covered by the previous three verses took place during the night, but there is no reason to conclude that Haman called then. Indeed the ancient versions add that he came in the morning. *In the court* (5). Haman could not enter without the express invitation of the king. *More than to myself* (6). Haman's assurance of the royal favour is very evident up to the moment of his fall. Each of Haman's suggestions (8, 9) was counted a very great honour among eastern peoples. *The king useth to wear* (8). Lit. 'that the king has worn' (cf. 1 Sa. xviii. 4). *The crown royal* (8). Grammatically it is the horse that is crowned, and in fact some eastern nations, notably Assyria, adorned their horses' heads with ornaments. It is more likely, however, that the person who is honoured wears the crown.

Mordecai the Jew (10). Some profess to find something very incongruous in the king thus honouring a member of a race he has just devoted to destruction. There is nothing in the incident at variance with the oriental outlook, much less with the character of Xerxes. *Thou shalt surely fall* (13). Anti-Semitism throughout the ages never denied the powers or resourcefulness of the Jews; on the contrary it was born of fear of these qualities.

d. Esther discloses Haman's plot to the king (vii. 1–6)

What is thy petition? (2). According to Herodotus, no petition offered up at a royal banquet could be refused. This, however, was a banquet given by the queen, and it is doubtful if the custom held good. *My people* (3). Esther at last avows her nationality. *To be destroyed . . . slain . . . . perish* (4). Lit. 'that they should destroy and kill and cause to perish'—the exact words of the king's decree (iii. 13). *Although the enemy . . .* (4). Lit. 'although the enemy is not equal to the king's hurt', probably meaning that Haman could never make up to the king what he would lose through the destruction of the queen and so many of his subjects. *The adversary* (6). Heb. *şar*, the most common word for adversary. It means one who binds or oppresses, as distinct from 'Satan', one who accuses or opposes.

e. Haman hanged and Mordecai honoured (vii. 7—viii. 2)

Haman was fallen upon the bed (8). RV 'upon the couch'. The Persians reclined at meals in the same way as the Greeks and Romans. It was a custom adopted by the Jews only during the Greek period and was current at the time of our Lord. This was the posture at the Last Supper. *As the word went out . . . they covered Haman's face* (8). The king's outburst showed that his anger against Haman was implacable, and the slaves well knew what this meant. Covering the face before execution was sometimes practised by the Greeks and Romans, but this is the only reference to it in Persian history. *Hang him* (9). LXX, 'Let him be crucified'. It is noteworthy how often the king falls in with the suggestions of those about him. *The house of Haman . . . to the queen* (viii. 1). See iii. 9n. *Esther had told . . .* (1). She had already disclosed her nationality (vii. 3). Neither the king nor Haman had known of her relationship to Mordecai till now. *Took off his ring* (2), thus appointing Mordecai grand vizier with powers to speak and write on behalf of the king. Pharaoh gave his ring to Joseph as a token of being invested with the same kind of authority (Gn. xli. 42).

VI. THE DELIVERANCE OF THE JEWS. viii. 3—ix. 16

a. The Jews permitted to defend themselves (viii. 3–17)

Esther's main task was not the destruction of Haman nor the advancement of Mordecai, but the salvation of the Jews. She now addresses herself to this task. *Devised by Haman* (5). Esther wisely ignores the king's responsibility for signing the decree, but emphasizes that the people doomed by it are in all the king's provinces; implying that the king himself would be harmed by carrying it out. Ahasuerus enumerates the benefits he has conferred upon Esther, not to discourage any expectations of further favours but as a proof of his good will (7). *May no man reverse* (8). A reminder that Esther's plan to reverse the decree (5) is unworkable. He throws the responsibility of saving the Jews on Mordecai, and reminds him that he has the king's ring, i.e. full authority to issue any decree as long as it does not reverse any former decree. Furthermore, the new decree itself cannot be cancelled.

Sivan (9). May–June. Over two months had elapsed since the decree had gone out for the destruction of the Jews and its execution was not due for nine months yet (iii. 13). *Mules* (10). Heb. *rekhesh*, more probably 'coursers'. Translated 'the swift beast' in Mi. i. 13. *Camels* (10). Heb. *'aḥashteranim*. The Jewish commentators confess that they do not know the meaning of this word, from which it can be inferred that it is probably Persian. It has been suggested that it means royal steeds. *Dromedaries* (10). Heb. *rammakhim*. Found only here, and of doubtful meaning. The speed with which these letters are sent out is contrasted with the method of posting Haman's decree (iii. 12, 15). In spite of the marvellous posting system of Persia, that decree had probably not yet reached some of the provinces, as it was only two months since it was promulgated and perhaps much less since it was despatched; so that there was a probability that Mordecai's messengers would in some cases overtake those of Haman. *To stand for their life* (11). This was the plan Mordecai adopted to circumvent the royal decree that could not be reversed; he issued a decree allowing the Jews to defend themselves and destroy their enemies. *Thirteenth day of the twelfth month* (12). The exact date on which the slaughter of the Jews was to take place (iii. 13). *Hastened and pressed* (14). See viii. 10n.

Blue and white (15). The royal colours of Persia. *Crown* (15). Heb. *'aṭarah*, as contrasted with *kether*, a royal diadem, in i. 11, ii. 17, vi. 8. As grand vizier and the king's favourite he no doubt had full right to wear these symbols of authority. *Became Jews* (17); i.e. embraced the Jewish religion.

b. The Jews destroy their enemies (ix. 1–16)

It was turned . . . (1). Another opportunity to acknowledge the intervention of God is given here, yet the author speaks indirectly and impersonally rather than embrace it. *The fear of them . . .* (2). The Jews were now in favour at the court, and it was probably fear of the king that inspired this fear. In addition to this Mordecai had now become a force to be reckoned with.

All the rulers . . . (3). The second edict had virtually superseded the first and plainly showed that the king favoured the Jews; hence the readiness of these officials to support them. The names listed in verses 7–9 are all Persian names, with the doubtful exception of *Adalia*. These names are written in a perpendicular column in the Hebrew Bible to show, according to the Rabbis, their position as they all hung upon the 75-foot gallows. *On the spoil . . .* (10). They do not avail themselves of the permission to possess their enemies' property, though on the other hand they seem to have exceeded the bounds permitted by the royal decree (cf. viii. 11) in avenging themselves on their enemies.

What have they done . . .? (12); i.e. if they have slain five hundred men in the palace how heavy must the slaughter be throughout the empire! The man who speaks so lightly about the slaughter of his subjects is the man who lost a million men in Greece a few years before. *Do to morrow also according unto this day's decree* (13). The Targum adds 'by keeping a holiday'; but it is difficult to give an interpretation other than that Esther demanded another day's slaughter. *Seventy and five thousand* (16). The Targum followed by the LXX makes it 15,000. According to the recension of Lucian of Nicomedia, the number was 10,107.

VII. THE FEAST OF PURIM. ix. 17–32

And Mordecai wrote these things (20), i.e. an account of the inauguration of the feast of Purim as given in verses 17–19. It is not impossible, however, that these words mean that Mordecai wrote the whole book up to that point (see *Introduction*, p. 380). *Purim* (26). Cf. iii. 7n. The feast of Purim (preceded by a fast) is still observed on the evening of the 14th Adar. In the morning the Roll of Esther is read through in the presence of women as well as men, in any language they understand; with the proviso that it can be read in Hebrew or Greek even when the audience does not know these languages. The feast has always been associated with merry-making and the giving of gifts (see verse 22) and has tended in modern times to develop along more secular lines than any other Jewish feast. Additional feasts of Purim have been instituted by Jews at various periods to commemorate other signal deliverances.

Second letter (29). The first letter may be the one referred to in viii. 8; and the second letter in ix. 20 is here confirmed by the added authority of the queen. *The matters of the fastings and their cry* (of distress?) (31). Cf. iv. 3. The LXX omits these words. *The book* (32). Rawlinson and others suggest that this is the book of the chronicles of ii. 23. The Vulgate, followed by a number of modern scholars, makes it refer to the book of Esther itself up to this point.

VIII. CONCLUSION. x. 1–3

Laid a tribute (1). The Grecian war continued in Asia Minor for years after the Battle of Salamis, and there was need of such a tribute to recoup the empire for its heavy expenses. *The isles of the sea* (1). An official phrase. Actually only Cyprus still belonged to the empire as all the other islands were lost after the retreat from Europe; but the old description was still current. *For Mordecai . . .* (3). He was mentioned in the book of the chronicles because he was so great. The *for* introduces verse 3 as an explanation of verse 2. *Next unto king Ahasuerus* (3). In 465 B.C. Artabanus, who murdered Xerxes in that year, was next the king. Mordecai must therefore have died or fallen from power some time in the interval between 470 B.C., to which date the book of Esther brings us, and 465 B.C. when Artabanus was the king's favourite. At the later date also Amestris, who is identified with Vashti by Rawlinson and others, was in full power as queen. One concludes, therefore, that Esther had also fallen from power or died during that interval and that Vashti (if she was Amestris) had been reinstated despite the efforts of the nobles to prevent this.

A. MACDONALD.

JOB

INTRODUCTION

I. AUTHORSHIP

The author is unknown. Various suggestions have been made: Job, Elihu, Moses, Solomon, Isaiah, Hezekiah, Baruch the friend of Jeremiah, etc. None can be established. All that can be said with certainty is that he was a loyal Jew who refused, however, to be shackled by every detail of the popular creed, in particular its remorseless bracketing of suffering and sin.

II. DATE AND BACKGROUND

Uncertainty also shrouds the question of date. There are no direct references to historical events which might assist in dating the book.

A distinction has to be drawn between the age of the historical background to the book which we find in the Prologue and Epilogue (i—ii, xlii. 7–16) and the rest of the book. The former is clearly pre-exilic. The atmosphere is patriarchal. Wealth is reckoned in cattle and Job appears as his own priest (i. 5). There is also a reference to Job in Ezekiel (xiv. 14). The historical basis would be preserved by tradition from generation to generation, until it was incorporated into the book of Job with the addition of the poetic form in which we find the dialogue. Some have maintained that the tradition was maintained orally; others have favoured Duhm's theory that Prologue and Epilogue are fragments of a popular book (*Volksbuch*) where the story of Job appeared. It cannot be said with any measure of certainty when the story of Job was incorporated into the book as we know it. A. B. Davidson argues cogently that its reflective atmosphere and the knowledge of distant lands in it exclude a date earlier than the age of Solomon. He maintains that probabilities favour the age of the captivity of Judah (597 B.C.). Others place it as late as the middle of the fourth century B.C. The question of date is not really important. Oesterley and Robinson say with truth: 'There are few poems in all literature whose date and historical background are of less importance than they are in the book of Job . . . It is a universal poem, and that is one of the features which give it its value and interest for us today.'

There are interesting points of contact with other books of Scripture. Compare Jb. iii with Je. xx. 14–18 and Jb. xv. 35 with Is. lix. 4. There are striking similarities between the figure of Job and the Servant of the Lord in Isaiah. Compare Is. l. 6, liii. 3 with Jb. xvi. 10, xxx. 9ff. See also Ps. viii. 4 (Jb. vii. 17); 1 Cor. iii. 19 (Jb. v. 13); Jas. v. 11.

III. CONTENTS AND VALUE

The setting of the story is 'the land of Uz', which probably is to be identified with Edom—a name with a stigma upon it in other Scriptures (e.g. Ps. cxxxvii. 7; Mal. i. 2ff.). The characters are all non-Israelites. We are reminded of the same breadth of view which made the hero of the 'Good Samaritan' a non-Jew.

Four friends of Job's, Eliphaz, Bildad, Zophar and Elihu, represent all that orthodox theology could say about the significance of the calamities which had devastated Job's happiness and stability. With the possible exception of Elihu, their contribution was seriously restricted by an inexorable interpretation of suffering in terms of personal sinfulness. If they had merely set out to establish human solidarity in sinfulness, they would have obtained Job's immediate assent, for nowhere does he claim to be a perfect man: but when they first hinted, and then directly affirmed, that Job's suffering was the inevitable harvest of seeds of sin sown when the eye of God alone was upon him, Job vehemently and consistently denied the accuracy of their judgment.

The book of Job is a universal book because it speaks to a universal need—the agony of the human heart when wracked by the 'heartache and the thousand natural shocks that flesh is heir to'. The testimony of a woman dying of cancer, that the book of Job spoke to her need as no other book in the Bible, is sufficient evidence. Great Christians and great poets have added their voices to the testimony of great sufferers, in appreciation and admiration of the truths the book conveys, sometimes through the medium of the most magnificent poetry. Luther held that Job is 'magnificent and sublime as no other book of Scripture'; Tennyson spoke of it as 'the greatest poem of ancient or modern times'.

What, then, has the book to say to the universal need?

It is a striking reminder of the inadequacy of human horizons for a proper understanding of the problem of suffering. All the human figures in the drama speak in total ignorance of Satan's allegations against Job's piety, reported in the Prologue, and of the resultant divine permission to prove his point, if he can. Against the background of the Prologue Job's sufferings appear, not as damning evidence of the divine judgment upon him, as the friends had sought to establish, but as evidence of the divine confidence in him. We must avoid the naïveté of using language which might seem to indicate that an omniscient God needed such a demonstration of His servant's integrity, to silence, as it were, some tiny doubt in His mind: but we are entitled to find here a suggestion of the truth that now we can only 'see through a glass darkly'. Job and the others were trying to fit together the pieces of a puzzle, without having all the pieces within their grasp. Consequently the book of Job is an eloquent commentary on the inadequacy of the human mind to reduce the complexity of the problem of suffering to some consistent pattern. It is a book where silent men accomplish more than speaking men. Cf. ii. 13, xiii. 5.

But while the author would certainly have recommended humility in any contemplation of the fact of suffering, he would not have advocated despair. He believes in a God who has the answer to human need. The appearance of men to counsel Job leads to controversy, disillusionment and despair; the appearance of God leads to submission, faith and courage. The word of man is unable to penetrate the darkness of Job's mind; the Word of God brings abiding light. The God of the theophany does not answer any of the burning questions that are debated so hotly in the course of the book; but He answers the need of Job's heart. He does not explain each phase of the battle; but He makes Job more than conqueror in it. (See detailed note at the beginning of chapter xl.)

Like the other books of the Old Testament Job is forward-looking to Christ. Questions are raised, great sobs of agony are heard, which Jesus alone can answer. The book takes its place in the testimony of the ages that there is a blank in the human heart which Jesus alone can fill.

OUTLINE OF CONTENTS

I. PROLOGUE. i. 1—ii. 13

II. FIRST CYCLE OF SPEECHES. iii. 1—xiv. 22

III. SECOND CYCLE OF SPEECHES. xv. 1—xxi. 34

IV. THIRD CYCLE OF SPEECHES. xxii. 1—xxxi. 40

V. THE ELIHU SECTION. xxxii. 1—xxxvii. 24

VI. THE LORD ANSWERS JOB. xxxviii. 1—xli. 34

VII. JOB'S RESPONSE TO THE DIVINE WORD. xlii. 1–6

VIII. EPILOGUE. xlii. 7–17

COMMENTARY

I. PROLOGUE. i. 1—ii. 13

a. A good man in a sinning universe (i. 1–5)

His character appears in a remarkable light as *perfect and upright* (1). Perfect does not imply sinless perfection, which is never claimed for Job. Rather it encourages us to think of Job as a moral all-rounder, a man of balanced, full-orbed character. (Cf. the use of *teleios* in the New Testament.) Spurgeon could have said of Job, as he said of Gladstone: 'We believe in no man's infallibility, but it is restful to be sure of one man's integrity.'

His moral maturity was explained by his profound reverence for God. The profundity of his spirituality is seen in the account of his domestic piety in verse 5. Spiritually ambitious for himself, he was no less so for his family. His regular sacrifices provided against even the bare possibility that his children had sinned against God. *In their hearts* (5) reveals impressively that Job's spirituality did not skim on the surface; it was aware of the necessity of praying 'Create in me a clean heart, O God'.

His moral and spiritual stability moved in the setting of a secure universe. The gift of children (2), extensive material possessions (3) and domestic unity and rejoicing (4) all contributed to his happiness. The words of Ps. i. 3 could be applied without qualification.

b. The sky begins to darken (i. 6–12)

We are introduced to a dramatic heavenly council attended by *the sons of God* (6), i.e. the angels, including Satan. We are not to look for any 'full-dress' doctrine of Satan as depicted in orthodox theology. He does not appear as a fallen angel but has regular access to heaven (i. 6, ii. 1). The name *Satan* (6) is preceded by the definite article and is rendered by 'the adversary' in Moffatt. Prof. N. H. Snaith summarizes his rôle by saying: 'He is God's Inspector-of-man on earth and man's adversary in heaven.' He is a divine agent whose duty is to give the closest attention to human virtue and vice. He appears as the supreme cynic of the heavenly court. God's affectionate praise of His servant (cf. Ps. cxlix. 4) calls forth the ugly question, *Doth Job fear God for nought?* (9). The material possessions hedging in his life, according to Satan, are a sufficient explanation of his piety. Remove the hedge, and the piety will disappear. The charge is that material prosperity is not an accretion to Job's faith but the root cause. The removal of the root would mean the withering of the bloom.

The challenge is accepted by God (12), but the theatre of investigation must not extend beyond Job's possessions to his person. The stage is set for the drama of which the book of Job is the discussion.

c. The storm breaks (i. 13–22)

Four staggering blows fill Job's world with pain. The Arabs (15), the lightning (16), the Chaldeans (17) and a whirlwind sweeping over the desert (19) deprive him of flocks and servants and, most agonizing of all, of his family. But with all the waters of affliction going over him he could still say in the words of Bunyan's Hopeful in the river of death: 'I feel the bottom and it is good.' So the lie was given to the adversary's insinuation. The loss of possessions had not entailed the loss of faith. Grief might change his appearance (20); it could not cheat him of the consolations of faith. He faced affliction in the attitude of the worshipper. In that attitude he found strength to give us one of the most beautiful expressions of submission to the will of God in the fragrant story of faith (21). In the darkest hour of his life he could bless God. In a similar spirit the Covenanter, Alexander Woodrow, in an hour of mourning was able to thank God 'for thretty-one years' loan of Sandie, my dear son'.

Naked came I out of my mother's womb (21). The general idea has a parallel in 1 Tim. vi. 7. The precise meaning is more difficult. Perhaps *mother's womb* is a reference to the womb of Mother Earth, an interpretation followed by Ewald and others. Cf. Gn. iii. 19. *Nor charged God foolishly* (22). Translate with RV 'with foolishness'. The word used conveys the idea of 'tastelessness, insipidity, and so, want of moral discernment' (Strahan). Cf. our colloquial condemnation of an action as 'in bad taste'.

d. The storm sweeps on (ii. 1–8)

A second heavenly council ushers in an extension in the adversary's theatre of investigation. He will not admit that he has been mistaken about Job's *integrity* (3) (Moff. 'loyalty'). The Lord claims that Job has come through the furnace of affliction as pure gold. The adversary complains that the trial has not been radical enough. He accuses Job of callousness. So far calamity has affected only the lives of others. His own skin has been untouched. Let his own person be involved and there will be no more 'holding fast his integrity'. *Skin for skin* (4) was probably a common proverb. Skins were in common use for business transactions. The charge is that Job was willing to give up the skins of others, cattle, servants and children, provided that his own skin was safe.

The adversary is given an opportunity to prove his point. Job's person is no longer shielded. Commentators are agreed that Job's affliction was a distressing and dangerous form of leprosy called elephantiasis, 'so named because the swollen limbs and the black and corrugated skin of those afflicted by it resemble those of the elephant' (A. B. Davidson). *The ashes* (8) is a reference to the local refuse heap outside the walls of the town. There the dung and other rubbish was burnt at regular intervals. It was the happy hunting-ground for dogs on the prowl for carcases which often were tossed there, and for the local urchins who were always eager to root about among things unwanted by others. There, in this place of discarded things, sat the man who once had been *the greatest of all the men of the east* (i. 3).

e. Reactions to the storm (ii. 9–13)

i. Job's wife (ii. 9, 10). The loss of family, of possessions, and now last of all, her husband's health, leaves her faith in ruins. She recommends that Job should curse God, even if death is the outcome of his blasphemy. Death is preferable to his present hapless lot. Job thus sees another support for his faith taken from him. He can no longer count on her spiritual support in the stern battle his faith is fighting. Resolutely he sets aside her suggestion. It is worthy only of impious folk. He bows before the sovereign hand of God whether it bestows or takes away, whether it caresses or strikes. He could have prayed 'Thy will be done' with a depth of meaning that it does not always possess in so-called Christian prayer.

ii. Job's friends (ii. 11–13). Job's friends have not always received the credit due to them. A 'Job's comforter' has come to be a very doubtful distinction. In fairness to these men let us remember that, when a multitude of fair-weather friends mysteriously disappeared, their friendship staunchly faced the storm. They had once rejoiced with a rejoicing Job; they were no less ready to weep with a weeping Job. The sight of Job's disfigured countenance filled them with profound anguish. For seven days they sat in silent sympathy with the sufferer—surely clear evidence of the sterling worth of their friendship. The ministry of silence helped Job much more than the ministry of words (cf. xiii. 5). There is a warning here for all who seek to comfort sorrowing hearts.

II. FIRST CYCLE OF SPEECHES.
iii. 1—xiv. 22

a. Wretched life! Blessed death! (iii. 1–26)

We hear a cry of anguish from a soul quivering with agony. In this and in other speeches we must not submit every statement to microscopic examination, assuming that every word has been thoroughly weighed before utterance and is an exact expression of Job's deepest thoughts. Job was soon to complain that his friends were training their verbal armoury upon the speeches of a desperate man, which he himself readily acknowledged were *as wind* (vi. 26). As this hurricane sweeps before us, we must marvel, not at every twist it takes, but at the agony of spirit behind it.

i. **Job curses his birthday (iii. 1–12).** *Let not God regard it from above* (4). Lit. 'seek after it'. God is thought of as summoning forth the successive days. Cf. Is. xl. 26, where He summons the stars. May the day which summoned Job to wretchedness never be called forth again! *Let darkness and the shadow of death stain it* (5). Better, 'claim it for their own' (rv). *Let the blackness of the day terrify it* (5). The reference is to eclipses. *Let it not be joined unto the days of the year . . .* (6). May it be blotted out from the calendar, from the joyful company of the days! See rv. A proud, joyful voice had once welcomed his coming into the world (cf. Jn. xvi. 21). May such a voice never be heard again on that night! *Let them curse it that curse the day* (8), i.e. the sorcerers, thought of as having the power to make a day unlucky. *Mourning* (8). rv reads 'leviathan', which in chapter xli refers to the crocodile. Some see here a reference to the dragon of popular mythology who, by twisting himself round the sun, could cause eclipses. *Dawning of the day* (9). Lit. 'the eyelids of the morning'. Dawn is thought of as a beautiful maiden. 'Oh that I had never been born, or had been born dead!' is the cry of verses 10–12. *Prevent* (12). Read 'receive' as in rv.

ii. **Life's fitful fever (iii. 13–26).** The troubles of life are contrasted with the placid sleep of death. The more Job dwells on the thought of death the more he finds himself fascinated by it. He thinks of his company in the dormitory of death: distinguished men (14, 15); stillborn children (16); the wicked (17) whose passions no longer shake themselves (cf. Is. lvii. 20) or other people; the weary who at last have found a place of rest (17); slaves who no longer hear the taskmaster's strident shout (18); the small and great, once severed by the world's standards, now lying side by side (19).

St. Francis of Assisi could address death as 'Thou, most kind and gentle death'. Job could have used exactly the same language but for different reasons. For St. Francis, death was a creature of his God and King whom he could summon to praise the Creator like other creatures; a signpost lit with the radiance of immortality pointing to the heavenly home where a Father's love had many glad surprises in store. For Job, it was an escape from life, an anaesthetic which would make his soul forget the 'slings and arrows of outrageous fortune'. The light of life appears as a doubtful privilege. It only shows up the hapless lot of the miserable

and the embittered (20). It can only mock the man who has lost the way in life, who has the feeling that God has hedged him in at every turn (23). Strahan comments pertinently: 'Light without liberty is a poor boon.' The most brilliant light can only mock a man in a dungeon, or a bird in a cage. In sharp contrast to the mood of verse 23, see Ps. cxviii. 5. In Job we have a man in whose eyes death is no longer the prince of terrors to be shunned, but a prize to be sought with the avidity of one digging for treasure. *For my sighing cometh before I eat* (24). See rv mg. Moffatt probably has the sense: 'Sighs are my daily bread.' Cf. Ps. xlii. 3. In verse 26 read the present tense throughout.

b. **Eliphaz speaks (iv. 1—v. 27)**

i. **He offers advice (iv. 1–11).** Job has broken the silence. Eliphaz now offers words of help, of healing, of warning. He hopes that by so doing he will not offend his friend. But he is in the grip of the inner constraint of truth. His duty to his friend, to his own convictions, and to his God forces him to speak (2).

His first appeal to Job is to one who has been a distinguished member of the 'ministry of encouragement' in the past. He had been quick to help all who were treading a *via dolorosa*. Now that he was on that way himself, let him apply the comfort he had offered to others (3–5). Let him turn to the consolations of his religion, and to the testimony of a clear conscience. Read verse 6 as in rv, 'Is not thy fear of God thy confidence, and thy hope the integrity of thy ways?'

The lesson of Job's fine record of service to those in need has been underlined. Eliphaz now gives expression to the thoughts set in motion by Job's cry of anguish still ringing in his ears. Job had revealed a passionate longing for death. Let him remember that sudden, unnatural death is the portion, not of the righteous, but of the wicked (7–11). Cf. v. 26.

ii. **Job's criticisms answered (iv. 12—v. 7).** Eliphaz replies to Job's implied criticism of God's treatment of him. How can frail, imperfect mortal man venture to raise critical eyes to his Maker? He bolsters his argument by impressively narrating a vision which he had once experienced (13). The authorities differ on the question whether Eliphaz was asleep or awake. The mysterious voice had clearly demonstrated the absurdity of mortal man expecting to be 'just before his God' (17, rv mg.). The av rendering *more just than God* is grammatically possible, but does not yield as good a meaning. Job never claims to be more righteous than God—an absurd claim for any man to make. His bearing had merely implied that his uprightness deserved better things at the hands of God. But when complete trustworthiness and service without error cannot be claimed by God's heavenly servants, how dare any man, with his fleeting life, with his only partially successful quest after wisdom, imply by his demeanour that he has a right to make that claim?

Before the moth (19) means 'sooner than the moth' or 'like the moth' (LXX). Read verse 21 as in RV: 'Is not their tent-cord plucked up within them?' Their death is compared to the pulling down of a tent.

Job's appeal against God can find no support among the angels (v. 1). The case of morally and spiritually senseless people who are fretful under God's chastening rod (cf. v. 17) ought to be a solemn warning against making any such appeal. *Wrath* (2). Better 'vexation' (RV). *Envy* (2). Better 'indignation' (RV mg.). Such impatience merely paves the way for further calamities, a truth Eliphaz deduces from his observations of life (3–5). *The gate* (4) refers to the gate of the town as the eastern place of justice. *Out of the thorns* (5) refers to the raids of nomads bursting through the thorn hedges about the fields. Trouble does not germinate itself, says Eliphaz; it springs from man's evil heart, as inevitably as sparks fly up from a fire (6, 7). For *although* (6) read 'for' and for *yet* (7) read 'but'.

iii. **Job urged to appeal to God** (v. 8–27). In verses 9–16 Eliphaz extols the power, kindness and justice of God. Accept, he says, the chastening of such a God, sent presumably to correct some flaw in the character (17), and all will yet be well. The Almighty hurts to heal (18). Bear the hurt, and the healing will extend to every conceivable trouble; it will ensure prosperity for field, flock and home alike, a prosperity for a ripe old age to enjoy. A man in harmony with God is in harmony with nature too. In verse 19 the numerals have the force of 'in every conceivable case'. *Thou shalt visit . . .* (24). The RV translates 'Thou shalt visit thy fold, and shalt miss nothing'. The verb translated 'sin' by the AV has usually such a force, but it sometimes means 'miss the mark' or 'miss the way'.

There is much to admire in Eliphaz. First, he is the most sympathetic of Job's friends. He does not probe Job's soul with clumsy fingers. His wounds are not the wounds of a foe, but the faithful wounds of a friend. Secondly, he comes, not as a man puffed up with human philosophy, but as a man with a real experience of God. He feels that God has spoken to him about suffering; that is why he must speak to Job. His words again and again have a ring about them which we find echoed in other Scriptures. With v. 13 cf. 1 Cor. iii. 19 (the only clear case of quotation of the book of Job in the New Testament). With v. 17 cf. Ps. xciv. 12; Pr. iii. 11; Heb. xii. 5, etc.

But while Eliphaz is the most sympathetic of Job's physicians, he is still a physician who fails. There is no acknowledgment of the extraordinary submission to God Job has already shown (e.g. in i. 21 and ii. 10). There is no clear word of sympathy in all his words. Strahan refers to him as 'a theologian chilled by his creed'. He resembles a commander urging a soldier who has been exhausted by struggling against fearful odds to still more resolute endeavour, without a word in praise of what has already been accomplished.

Again, his ready assumption that Job's suffering must be the reaping of his own sinfulness ill equipped him to be a true comforter. He was not wrong to claim that he had a divine explanation of the facts of human suffering. Experience abundantly testifies that in countless ways man brings trouble upon himself by his sinfulness. Eliphaz was a mouthpiece of divine revelation there; but when he went on to assume that he had a divine commentary upon all the facts of human suffering, and that he had correctly diagnosed Job's case, it was the word of man, not the Word of God. He has not stood where we have stood, witnessing the clash between God and the accuser in the heavenly places, where issues of which Job and Eliphaz are ignorant are being decided. He has not learned the salutary humility of Paul's confession of the limitations of human knowledge: 'now we see through a glass darkly.' How often a man must find a place for that confession in his religious thinking, and not least of all with regard to the problem of suffering!

c. **Job answers Eliphaz (vi. 1—vii. 21)**

i. **A cry for fair play (vi. 1–13).** Eliphaz obviously views with disapproval Job's impatience under suffering. Job accuses him of looking only at one side of the balance. He censures the weight of the impatience: but if only he were to look over to the affliction side, he would find the load there immeasurably heavier. *My words are swallowed up* (3). RV has 'Have my words been rash?' 'Don't condemn the cry of the afflicted before you consider his afflictions' is the plea. He feels like a man into whose body the almighty Archer is sending poisoned arrows. He cannot help their poison going right through him; he cannot help wild, delirious words. Is due allowance being made for that? Note the RV translation of verse 4: 'The poison whereof my spirit drinketh up.' There is reason for his cry of agony. His is not a case of 'much ado about nothing'. He has lost his taste for life (6, 7), which he compares to 'insipid food and saltless' (Moff.). A. B. Davidson translates verse 7: 'My soul refuseth to touch them! Such things are like loathsome food to me.' For death, on the other hand, he has an eager taste. The prospect of death is his only comfort (8–10). RV renders verse 10: 'Then should I yet have comfort; yea, I would exult in pain that spareth not: For I have not denied the words of the Holy One.'

The fearlessness of Job's attitude to death is emphasized. His mind runs to meet the thought of death, even death through a gateway of unsparing pain. He has nothing to fear from death, nor from the God whose commands he has never denied. Life has made too heavy demands upon his strength and patience. He can fight no further battles, for he is no superman, with the strength of stones and with flesh of brass. Natural resources are exhausted (11–13). Strahan translates verse 13: 'Is not my help within me gone, and resource driven away from me?'

ii. A rebuke to his friends (vi. 14–30). A man who is sinking under affliction ought to be able to count upon the sympathy of his friends. *But he forsaketh the fear of the Almighty* (14). Better as in RV, 'Even to him that forsaketh the fear of the Almighty'. Job has been denied this pity. In a striking figure he compares his friends to brooks. We have a picture of them, bound by snow and ice in the cold weather (16), and thawing with the return of warmer weather, until at length they dry up altogether. We are next given a glimpse of Arabian caravans, desperate for water, hurrying towards them, only to be disappointed. They swing away into the desert to their doom (18–20). In verse 18, RV has 'The caravans that travel by the way of them turn aside; they go up into the waste and perish'.

A reason for the friends becoming broken cisterns whose waters have failed is suggested (21). The fear roused by a contemplation of Job's calamities has chilled their sympathy. They are afraid that to take Job's side would mean standing on the opposite side from the God who has it within His power to bring similar trials upon them. To the end of this chapter there is a contrast between what Job expected of his friends and what he actually received from them. He had not requested considerable aid (22, 23), but he had hoped for genuine sympathy and for forthright dealing. Instead, there had been insinuations against his integrity. His friends had made the mistake of dealing with the wild, whirling speeches of a desperate man as if every word was cool and calculated (25, 26). He is ready to stand by his integrity, to look the whole world in the face with clear conscience and steady eye. *Return* (29) has the sense 'change your ground; look for some other interpretation of my suffering'. In verse 30, Job asks, 'Is my moral taste perverted? Cannot I differentiate between good and evil?'

iii. The hardness and brevity of human life (vii. 1–10). *Appointed time* (1). Better 'warfare' (RV). In a series of striking figures Job pictures life as a hard struggle. It is like a distasteful period of service laid upon a hired servant, whose only consolations are the cool shadows of the evening, in which the day's work is forgotten, and the wages which he receives at the end of the day. Job can think of no sweeter rest, and no more valuable wages, than death. Is it any wonder when life holds sleepless nights and loathsome disease? *Worms* (5) means that his sores breed maggots. He proceeds to dwell on the brevity of life (6–10). Life is a swiftly moving shuttle; wind; an insubstantial, fading cloud, moving towards the grave, the realm from which there is no return to familiar scenes.

iv. A remonstrance with God (vii. 11–21). Impelled by the weight of human misery, and by his own suffering, he utters a bitter complaint. The divine treatment of him might almost seem to imply that he was like the sea, to be kept under restraint, or a cruel monster endangering the order of the universe (12). What accounts for this

unremitting superintendence over him, which has scared the wits out of him and made him detest life? (13–19). *Strangling* (15) refers to the choking sensation which is one of the common characteristics of leprosy. In 15b RV follows the literal translation, 'death rather than these my bones'. The disease has reduced Job to a skeleton.

The atmosphere of verses 17, 18 is strikingly different from that of Ps. viii. 4, where the question arresting the attention is, 'How can a majestic, powerful God stoop so low that He notices and plans for insignificant man?' Here the question is rather, 'If God is so great why can't He leave man alone?' *Preserver of men* (20). 'Watcher of man' (RV), 'Spy upon mankind' (Moff.). Why must this great God be so restlessly on the prowl? Here Job seems to think of God as an irate inspector, whose visits are followed by unhappiness, for He is certain to find fault. *Till I swallow down my spittle* (19) is an expression still in use among the Arabs, meaning 'for a single moment'.

What can the little sin of a little man mean to the mighty God? Can He not find it in His heart to forgive? Soon a divine approach in forgiveness will be too late, for the sleep of death will have overtaken him (20, 21). In these verses we find a mistaken view of sin. It argues: 'I don't see that my sin can make very much difference to God. It is not asking much of a mighty God to forgive the little sins of little men.' There is a thoroughly modern ring about such words. Compare the puzzled question of a dying farmer following upon a Vicar's call to him to repent: 'What harm have I ever done Him?' He would have united with Job in wondering how his sin could disturb Almighty God. Gladstone was on safer ground when he held that the tiniest sin that settled on his soul gave God as much pain as the speck of grit blown into his own eye. Job could have listened to Calvary's commentary upon the 'exceeding sinfulness' of sin (Rom. vii. 13), his language would have been different. It is because God is so great, not in spite of it, that He has taken such drastically sacrificial action to deal with what people call so lightly the 'little sins of little men'.

d. Bildad speaks (viii. 1–22)

i. A rebuke (viii. 1–7). This friend calls upon Job to bow before traditional wisdom. First he rebukes Job for his 'wild and whirling words' (2, Moff.), which have involved a criticism of God's dealings with him, and with humanity as a whole. Bildad stands forth as the champion of the justice of God. Goodness and evil alike reap the harvest they have sown. Job's children had sown evil; God sent them an evil harvest. Let Job sow goodness; let him adopt the attitude of a humble suppliant; let him be *pure and upright* (6), and the harvest he will reap will defy comparison with anything in his past experience.

ii. Tradition (viii. 8–19). 'Listen to the voice of the past which has the last word to speak about the issues we are discussing' (8–10). Behind this section is the assumption that 'they are short-lived, ignorant moderns, not wise and happy antediluvians' (Strahan). Pearl after pearl of that ancient wisdom is offered for Job's examination and instruction. The perils of the ungodly man appear in striking figures. Bildad does not expressly state, 'Thou art the man'; but he is certainly keeping his mind open to the possibility of unrighteousness in Job. In verse 12, the picture is of the waters of the river receding from the papyrus and the reed-grass growing on the fringes. The healthy vegetation then withers and dies, sooner than any herb. The hope of the ungodly man does not save him (cf. Rom. viii. 24); it damns him, for his hope is not in God, but in himself. It is as insubstantial as a spider's web (14). The household which he has always looked upon as solid and lasting will suddenly crumble beneath him (15). He is a plant with the evidences of healthy life upon it, which suffers sudden destruction (16–18). The picture in verse 17 is of a plant with its roots snaking their way through the stones of the stone heap, going deep down into the earth. *Joy of his way* (19). The LXX reads 'This is the end of the godless'. If the AV text is followed, then Bildad must either be speaking ironically or is describing what has been a joyous way of life.

iii. **Destiny (viii. 20–22).** Is Job a man of integrity? If so, eventually he must find himself in a world of rejoicing. Calamity rounds off the life of the ungodly alone. We find two grave deficiencies in Bildad which made his words worse than useless from Job's standpoint. First, he was tragically lacking in the sympathy for which Job craved. His assumption that the sudden death of Job's family was the divine punishment for their sinfulness was a sword thrust into a heart already suffering agony. Job knew that it was untrue. In the second place he was totally hidebound by tradition. He was so busily engaged in looking into the past that he quite failed to realize that Job was feeling out for a richer and more intelligent experience of God than anything he had himself known. He assumed that the whole of the divine Word had been spoken; he would have been hostile to the thought that a clearer, more dynamic word was yet to be spoken through prophets, saints and apostles, and uniquely through One who was the Word come down from heaven.

e. **Job answers Bildad (ix. 1—x. 22)**

i. **How should a man be just with God? (ix. 1–16).** The theme of the whole of this chapter is the impossibility of obtaining justice from God. Job does not attempt a detailed answer to Bildad. He fastens rather on a general principle accepted by all the friends and expounded by Eliphaz in iv. 17, the impossibility of mortal man appearing just before God. Job accepts the truth of the principle (2), but goes on to deny that there can be a grain of comfort in it. What can be the use of man's attempting to establish his innocence before a God of infinite wisdom, who

might well ask him a thousand questions, not one of which he could answer (3)? He is a God of infinite power too; the shaker of heaven and earth, heaping up marvels beyond human ken. Plead one's case before such a God? How futile (4–10)! When God transfers His attention from nature to man, His power sweeps on just as arbitrarily. When He pounces on His prey who can challenge His action (11, 12)? When even the stoutest rebels at length have to capitulate before the naked power of God, how can he, Job, or anyone else, hope to stem its onward rush by mere words, no matter how carefully marshalled they may be (13, 14)? *The proud helpers* (13). 'The helpers of Rahab' (RV). The reference may be to a current myth which spoke of the overthrow of an assault on heaven made by the sea monster Rahab and her confederates. Even stainless innocence, Job goes on, would be struck dumb before Him, and would only break the menacing silence at length to blurt out a plea for pity (15). Even if God had answered Job's call that God and he should meet in some judgment court, he is sceptical about receiving a fair hearing (16).

ii. **A complaint against God (ix. 17–24).** A terrible picture of God follows in verses 17–24: a God storming and striking without cause; not giving him a moment's breathing space (18); relying, not on justice, but on might (19); destroying good and evil men indiscriminately (22); laughing at the tortures of the innocent (23); allowing the earth to be the happy hunting-ground of the wicked, covering the faces of judges so that they do not see aright (24). In verse 24 read as in RV, 'If it be not he, who then is it?'

A fair hearing from such a God? Job is tortured by the fear that he would be so upset and bewildered that he would confess a guilt that did not belong to him in reality (20, 21). Note the RV of verse 21: 'I am perfect; I regard not myself; I despise my life.' Squarely he takes his stand on his integrity. He cannot relinquish that, even if he dies for it. Connect this with *This is one thing* (22) ('It is all one', RV). Probably the sense is: 'It is all one whether I live or die. Life has become obnoxious.'

iii. **The brevity of life (ix. 25–35).** Job turns from the wounds of the world to consider his own sorrows and the fleeting nature of life. When more optimistic feelings struggle towards the surface (27) they are driven down again by the knowledge that God is determined to hold him guilty. He may as well give up the unequal struggle. *If I be wicked* (29). RV reads 'I shall be condemned'. Job is up against a God who is evidently determined to duck in filth a man genuinely craving for purity of soul (31, 32). 'Oh that I were dealing with man and not God!' cries Job, 'for then I would be on ground where I could feel at home. But it is not so, nor is there an umpire (RV mg. for *daysman*) to ensure fair play for God and me' (32, 33). The chapter closes with Job turning sadly from what might have been to the stern reality he knows—the terrifying, divine rod smiting him. If only God would take that away, he would be able to speak out fearlessly in affirmation of his innocence, for he has a 'conscience void of offence'.

In the remarkable yearning for the God of the mysterious, terrifying beyond to reveal Himself in the fabric of understandable human experience, one is reminded forcibly of the words in Browning's *Saul:* ' 'Tis my flesh that I seek in the Godhead'. In this cry for an umpire between God and man we see a prophetic reaching out for the 'one mediator between God and men, the man Christ Jesus' (1 Tim. ii. 5). There was no finally satisfactory answer to Job short of the incarnation. The passage is strongly forward-looking to Bethlehem.

iv. An appeal to God (x. 1–7). With no umpire to help him, Job is forced to appeal directly to God, in an attempt to solve the mystery of the divine antagonism to him. Note the RV reading in verse 1: 'I will give free course to my complaint.' Every suggestion his distraught imagination can concoct is now expressed, no matter how extraordinary. Is the divine oppression of him a paying concern (3)? Can it be explained by divine shortsightedness, which means that God cannot clearly see what He is doing in His dealings with men (4)? Or can it be that, like man, God knows that His span of life is limited? Therefore He must punish what He suspects to be sinfulness before there has been time to examine the case thoroughly (5, 6). Even while expressing these suggestions Job knows their emptiness. He cannot get past the conviction that God must know him to be a man of integrity (7).

v. The depths of despair (x. 8–22). There follows an appeal to the divine Potter who has lavished such painstaking care upon His handiwork. Both in the antenatal period and the years which followed (10–12) Job can see many signal evidences of divine preservation. What was the goal before the divine mind in such dealings with him? In the answer which follows (13–17), we see Job touching depths of doubt and despair blacker than anything found elsewhere in the book. 'All the while this was thy dark design', he says (13, Moff.). The potter has concentrated on making the vessel especially beautiful so that, in the hour when He decides to mar it, the contrast between past and present may be all the more striking. Job feels that he is dealing with a God who is swift to note down even trivial sins. His imagination quails at the prospect of what would happen if he were really guilty. Righteousness of his makes no difference. He still has to hang his head, cowed before a God who, like a fierce lion, delights in hunting him with marvellous assiduity (14–16). *For it increaseth* (16). Better as in RV 'And if my head exalt itself'. In verse 17 see RV mg. Host after host of the afflictions which are God's witnesses against his integrity lurk about him. Verses 18–22 form a most pathetic passage. There are two cries in it.

'Would that my one and only cradle had been the grave', and 'Cannot I have a brief breathing-space before the perpetual night of death?'

f. Zophar speaks (xi. 1–20)

i. Job is rebuked (xi. 1–6). Zophar bluntly reproves Job for his prodigality in empty words. He cannot expect men who know better to stand by in silence. Job's words have implied a claim to straight thinking and straight living. If only God would speak, he would find both claims utterly shattered. His puny human wisdom would wilt before the vast sweep of the divine wisdom; and he would discover that, in actual fact, God was recompensing his sinfulness very lightly.

ii. God's wisdom magnified (xi. 7–12). The meaning of this powerful and memorable passage is well brought out in the Moffatt translation: 'Can you discover the deep things of God? can you reach the Almighty's range of wisdom? Higher it is than heaven—how can you match it? deeper than death—how can you measure it? Its scope is vaster than the earth, and wider than the sea' (7–9). It is this wisdom which passes its verdict upon vain man, and such a verdict must be infallible. Let Job submit to the breaking-in process which the divine wisdom wants to carry through in his case, and there is hope that genuine understanding will be the final outcome, even though, like other men, he has the stubborn stupidity of a wild colt.

iii. A call to repentance (xi. 13–20). Zophar now calls on Job to put away all known sin and portrays the glittering rewards of repentance. One result will be the ability to look the world in the face fearless and unashamed. Compare verse 15 with x. 15. It will lead also to forgetfulness of the misery of the past, whose darkness will be swallowed up in the brilliant light of the present (16, 17); and to security and hope (18, 19; cf. vii. 6). But if there is no repentance, the only hope left for Job will be to breathe his last. Note the RV reading of verse 20.

Thou shalt dig about thee (18). The thought is of a sheikh carefully looking round about his tent before retiring to ensure that there are no lurking dangers.

Zophar is the narrow dogmatist *par excellence*. We find two flaws in him characteristic of his type. In the first place he is too confident in his religious standpoint. We find no traces of a reverent 'I do not know'. He is right in maintaining that he is in touch with truth (see, e.g., the lofty passage, xi. 7–11, which speaks of the peerless, transcendent wisdom of God). He is wrong in thinking that he has all the truth. He understands not a whit more than Job about the reason for Job's sufferings. Secondly, he is lacking in humility. He is swift to call Job to go down on his knees at the recollection of the limitations of human knowledge. Yet, as he talks down to Job, he forgets that the mind scrutinizing his sufferings is limited too. Unknown to himself his deductions from Job's misery have a far greater stamp of the *wild ass's colt* (12) on them than the most agonized cries of the sufferer.

g. Job answers his friends (xii. 1—xiv. 22)

i. He resents their assumed omniscience (xii. 1–12). Up to the present Job has given only scant attention to the sentiments of his friends. Now he brings to bear his powers of sarcasm and logic upon their facile assumption that they have a right to talk down to him. How easy for them to mouth their glib commonplaces in their still secure and comfortable world! 'In the thought of him that is at ease there is contempt for misfortune; it is ready for them whose foot slippeth' (5, RV). If he had been a successful robber, and not a religious man, his position perhaps would have commanded greater respect. *Into whose hand God bringeth abundantly* (6). The RV mg. alternative reading is interesting: 'That bring their god in their hand.' The only god these robbers worship is their own power, as symbolized by the sword in their strong hand.

Job now states his familiarity with everything that they have said about the wisdom and power of God. Even the beasts of the field are not ignorant of that. The voice of nature is one and undivided in that respect (7–9). He is also aware that all life is in the hand of God (10). The question perturbing his mind, which his friends will not face, concerns the use to which God puts His power. What kind of character controls the operation of the power? He is not prepared to swallow down, unexamined and undigested, the opinions of others, no matter how ancient, if they do not commend themselves to his moral and spiritual palate. Verse 12 may be an allusion to Bildad's deference to the wisdom of the ancients in viii. 8–10.

ii. A description of divine power (xii. 13–25). Job imagines God's power as sweeping on indiscriminately and irresistibly, devastating the earth in natural calamities, shattering the influence of the wise, the mighty, the respected, bringing them to power only in order to grind them down again, saddling the people with leaders whose idea of the direction they are taking is no clearer than that of one groping in the dark, or of an intoxicated man. We look in vain for any principle integrating the divine actions which he describes and feel that we are meant to conclude that for Job in this hour there was none. *The bond of kings* (18) is the bond by which they control the people. The exact force of verse 22 is elusive. Perhaps there is a reference to God's exact knowledge of the most deeply concealed secrets of the heart. Cf. Is. xxix. 15.

iii. He rejects their counsel (xiii. 1–12). Again Job turns upon his friends, scathingly and impatiently. They are *forgers of lies* (4), futile physicians of the soul, seeking to justify the ways of God by maxims of ashes and defences of clay (12, RV). He accuses them of being, not genuine allies of God, but cringing sycophants, using twisted arguments to bolster a cause they support out of a wholesome respect for their own

skin. We may compare them with a man supporting the cause of a bully, not because he is interested in the rights or wrongs involved in the cause, but because he is afraid of the man's strong right arm. The friends have made much of God's omniscient gaze upon Job. Are they remembering that the very same gaze is upon the motives for their championship of God? How will they fare when they stand at the bar of the majesty and the omniscience of God? A striking hint is given in verses 9–11 that sincere opposition to God may fare better than insincere support of Him.

iv. He appeals to God (xiii. 13–28). Conscious that further appeals to his friends are useless, Job turns to God. He is aware that such an appeal is a risky affair, but he cannot prevent himself defending his case. *Though he slay me, yet will I trust in him* (15). RV mg. reads 'Behold, he will slay me; I wait for him' (i.e. to strike). Another translation which adopts an alternative Hebrew reading *lo*' (not) for *lo* (for him) reads '. . . I will not wait' or 'I have no hope'. In the verses which follow, faith suddenly flares up in the assertion that the verdict will go favourably for him. It is only godless people who have reason to be afraid in God's presence. Recklessly he calls for a successful challenger of his innocence. If such a person could be found, he would not have one further word to say (19).

He proceeds to appeal for a fair hearing from God. This would mean the removal of the heavy hand now upon him, and of the numbing, frightening sense of the divine majesty (20, 21). If these conditions are granted, he will be equally happy in the rôle of plaintiff or defendant (22). As it is, he is ignorant of the charge against him. He asks for a clear statement of the reason for the divine hostility, which has issued in such a harsh sentence. Can it be that God is making him smart for the unthinking irresponsibilities of youth (23–26)? Whatever the reason, there is no denying the reality of the situation: the drastic restrictions God has imposed upon him. *Thou settest a print upon the heels of my feet* (27). Better as in RV, 'Thou drawest thee a line about the soles of my feet.' And yet, what is the target for the divine enmity? Just a humble creature, tossed about by life, with the mark of corruption upon him. In verse 28 follow the RV reading 'Though I am like a rotten thing that consumeth'.

v. The yearning for an after-life (xiv. 1–22). It is strange, says Job, that divine justice should fasten on a creature like man. His existence is fleeting, troublous, and involved in the universal sinfulness of humanity. Why then must a single individual, who is no heinous sinner, incur such a weight of divine displeasure? Cannot God grant the creature of a day a brief breathing-space from trouble?

In verses 7–12 the fate of things is contrasted with the fate of persons, to the advantage of the former. A felled tree may sprout again, but 'death writes an inexorable "nevermore" on man's life'. With this passage compare the case of

Brother Lawrence. One winter day, as he looked upon a gaunt, bare tree, he was powerfully moved by the recollection of the dramatic transformation which would be effected with the return of spring. Surely the God, so marvellously operative in nature, was no less ready to effect a miraculous change in man. The incident led to his conversion. Compare also our Lord's teaching in Mt. vi. 30.

The gloom of the picture penetrates Job's spirit so profoundly that there is a dramatic revulsion from it (13–15). His soul soars up in quest for the light of a worthwhile hereafter. At present he feels the rod of the God of wrath across his shoulders. Presumably he must bear it while the present life lasts. But after that? He gives expression to a lovely dream of the God of grace granting him asylum, first in Sheol, the abode of the dead, and then calling him back to an existence in which He, the Creator, would yearn over the work of His hands. If I could believe that, says Job, 'I could endure my weary post until relief arrived' (14b, Moff.). They are the words of a man who cannot let go his faith in the God whose present dealings are a blank mystery to him; a man raising questions which Jesus alone can answer. Cf. Jn. xi. 25; 2 Tim. i. 10, etc.

The glory of the dream fades in the recollection of the grim facts of the present. The God of grace retires to the background, and Job imagines a God who, miser-like, keeps constant check upon every sin (16, 17); a God who pulverizes the mightiest works of nature and dashes the hopes of man (18, 19). Death is the supreme trump card of man's divine Antagonist. It makes him unable to rejoice in the rejoicings of the children he leaves behind, or to weep with them in their perplexities (21). It does not even mean the cessation of his own pain (22). In this verse we have probably a reference to the terrible idea that the soul in Sheol had sympathy for the decomposing body, feeling the touch of corruption upon it.

III. SECOND CYCLE OF SPEECHES.
xv. 1—xxi. 34

a. Second speech of Eliphaz (xv. 1–35)

Eliphaz has been cut to the quick on finding Job treading under foot the pearls of wisdom let drop by the friends. It seems that their attempts to make Job bow in humble submission before the all-wise and all-powerful God have been unsuccessful. Perhaps he will be warned in time by a luminous commentary upon the divine judgment descending upon the wicked upon the earth. That is the spearhead of the friends' attack in the second cycle of speeches. It seems that the *consolations of God* (11) of which they have been the mouthpiece have been too small for Job. Perhaps the terrors of God will bring him to his senses.

As we listen to Eliphaz we feel that his pride has been wounded as well as his religious convictions.

i. Job's attitude criticized (xv. 1–16). Eliphaz accuses Job of being a windbag and irreligious at heart. *Restrainest prayer* (4). RV mg. reads 'diminishest devotion'. His assumption of integrity and his criticism of God have been a crafty defence mechanism (5). He accuses Job of being self-important. He talks like some primeval man, existing before the beginning of things, like a member of God's secret council, like a man with a monopoly of wisdom. How preposterous to reject the testimony of age and experience! His talk throughout has tragically ignored the uncleanness of man who greedily gulps down iniquity as a thirsty man drinks water (16). If only he would raise his eyes to the God before whom the very angels and the heavens are stained (15)! In verse 12 Strahan renders *wink at* by 'flash in wrath'.

ii. The fate of the wicked (xv. 17–35). Eliphaz takes up Job's statement in xii. 6. He calls to his aid the words of the wise, reaching back to the good old days when there were no foreign influences to corrupt morality and religion. Job had claimed that wicked men enjoy security. Monstrously untrue! Such security as they have is dogged by constant pain (20); it is haunted by the dread of coming calamity, the first threatening murmurs of which their ears are for ever catching (21). And when at last the dreaded darkness descends, all hope must be surrendered. For them, now, only violence, hunger, trouble and anguish (22–24). In their hour of fleeting security they may make their proud assaults upon the Almighty, as if their stout shields could keep them safe (25, 26); they may play the rôle of successful, bloated sensualists (27); they may be guilty of the impiety of building ruined cities which have borne the curse of God (28). But the final darkness of the day of doom is gathering, which will blot out their prosperity (29, 30). Their fate is the fate of a plant, withering and drying prematurely (31–35).

b. Job answers Eliphaz (xvi. 1—xvii. 16)

i. He spurns such empty comfort (xvi. 1–5). *Vain words* (3). Better as in RV mg. 'words of wind'. Eliphaz has accused Job of being a windbag rebel against God. Job hurls back the accusation that his friends are windbag comforters. If he were comforter instead of sufferer, there would be genuine substance in the comfort he would offer.

ii. His desperate condition described (xvi. 6–17). The woefulness of his impasse is drawn in poignant fashion. Speech and silence alike are powerless to ease his misery. His gaunt frame is proof positive that the grip of his divine Antagonist is upon him. Note the RV in verse 8: 'And thou hast laid fast hold on me, which is a witness against me: And my leanness riseth up against me, it testifieth to my face.' In his afflictions he feels that God is straddling him like a wild beast, looking down on its powerless prey with flashing eyes (9). The hostility of God is echoed in the hostility of men, 'the pack of petty foes that howl at the heels of his greater enemy' (A. B. Davidson). At the end of verse 12 the figure changes. God appears as an archer, sending a stream of arrows into his vitals. *His archers* (13). Better as in RV mg., 'his arrows'. In verse 14 there is yet another change of figure. God is now a warrior, repeatedly breaching the walls of the stronghold of his soul. These divine assaults have condemned him to habitual mourning and humiliation; and yet these assaults have taken as their target an innocent man.

iii. **His faith again triumphs (xvi. 18–21).** Once again Job rises from the profoundest depths to the greatest heights. He has been unable to let go his innocence in face of the insinuations of his friends. Now we find he cannot let go his God in face of his ugliest doubts and fears. When an unjust death lays in the dust his innocent life, the voice of his innocent blood will rise to highest heaven (18). Cf. Gn. iv. 10. And there in heaven he suddenly catches sight of a divine Champion, a divine Sympathizer, who will be prepared to vouch for his integrity. Verses 19–21 should be read as in the RV. Tearfully he appeals to the heavenly Witness to support his cause in the teeth of the insinuations of his friends, and of the shattering blows of the God who is responsible for his earthly afflictions. 'Mine eye poureth out tears unto God; that he would maintain the right of a man with God, and of a son of man with his neighbour!' This passionate longing for a heavenly Witness on his side strikingly points forward to the Christian thought of an 'advocate with the Father, Jesus Christ the righteous' (1 Jn. ii. 1). Here faith is reaching out for a 'God for us'. Again, Jesus alone can answer Job. Cf. Heb. ix. 24.

iv. **The brevity and sorrow of life (xvi. 22— xvii. 16).** The appeal gains force when he remembers that the years are rolling him forward inexorably towards the grave. Away with the mocking hopes of a bright tomorrow outlined by his friends, when the misery of today will be forgotten! Away with all hopes offered by men! Only God can undertake suretyship for him. *Strike hands* (3). Suretyship was commonly undertaken by the striking of hands. Note the RV rendering of verse 5: 'He that denounceth his friends for a prey, even the eyes of his children shall fail.' Perhaps the meaning is that the iniquity of those who callously surrender their friends to the unjustified criticisms of others will be visited on their children. The misery of Job's present lot is described in verses 6–16. He has become the butt of moralizing and insult. *And aforetime I was as a tabret* (6). Read as in RV mg. 'And I am become one in whose face they spit'. Righteous men may well be astonished at such suffering for such a man, though it cannot break their inflexible determination to pursue the way of righteousness whatever the price. Scholars have differed widely on verses 8, 9. Some have maintained that they have a foreign

ring on Job's lips, and have suggested that they have strayed to their present place from a speech of one of the friends. Delitzsch, on the other hand, leaving the passage in its position in the AV, speaks of it as 'a rocket which shoots above the tragic darkness of the book lighting it up suddenly although only for a short time'. In a similar strain A. B. Davidson describes it as 'perhaps the most surprising and lofty in the book'.

The gloom deepens as the chapter proceeds. Again the hopes of the friends that Job's night would be changed to day are swept aside (10–12). His only hope is in the grave for which he has almost a family affection. *If I wait* (13). Better as in RV mg. 'If I hope'.

c. Bildad's second speech (xviii. 1–21)

Bildad has nothing new to say, and certainly nothing that can have any significance for Job. A portrayal of the doom of the wicked can speak only to a man with a guilty conscience.

i. **Introduction (xviii. 1–4).** Verses 2–4 introduce his main theme and reveal how keenly he resents Job's attitude to the attempts of his friends to be helpful. *Ere ye make an end of words* (2). Lit. 'How long will ye set snares for words?' Bildad accuses Job of hunting for far-fetched arguments which are mere words without real content. Job is treating them like unintelligent beasts or unclean folk. He has accused an angry God of tearing him (xvi. 9), while in reality he is tearing himself. His attitude virtually demands that the whole earth, with its moral order, should be turned upside-down to substantiate his criticism of God and his championing of himself (4).

ii. **The fate of the wicked (xviii. 5–21).** In *the firstborn of death* (13) Strahan sees a reference to leprosy. The general sense is: 'Death's most loyal henchman will be his foe.' Note also the RV of verse 14: 'He shall be rooted out of his tent wherein he trusteth; and he shall be brought to the king of terrors', i.e. death. *Brimstone shall be scattered* (15). Strahan comments: 'It was the custom to spread salt over places which had come under a ban; and brimstone, suggestive of the cities of the plain, may have been used to symbolize a deeper curse.'

d. Job answers Bildad (xix. 1–29)

R. S. Franks speaks of this chapter as the 'watershed of the book'. From the most tragic sense of dereliction, Job rises to the most triumphant affirmation of faith.

i. **His humiliation at God's hand described (xix. 1–22).** Anger gives way to sorrow as he addresses the friends. Even if he has sinned, his sin cannot harm them. *Ten times* (3) means 'often' (cf. Gn. xxxi. 7). He complains that God is bent on humiliating him (6–12). *I cry out of wrong* (7). Moffatt translates expressively 'I cry out "Murder"'. Not content with prostrating him through this personal antagonism, God has enlisted a perfect host of co-operators (12).

Job's relatives, intimate friends, servants, and his very wife, all turn from him with loathing and he is thus robbed of the affection of all who mean most to him (13–19). Note the RV rendering of verse 17: 'My breath is strange to my wife, and my supplication to the children of my mother's womb.' This latter phrase is lit. 'children of my womb'. 'Womb' is occasionally used of the father (cf. Ps. cxxxii. 11). In view of the fact that the death of Job's family has already been recorded, some see here a reference to Job's grandchildren, others a reference to the children of concubines.

Quite broken down by the realization of his lonely state, Job pathetically appeals to his friends for pity. The tragic relationship between Job and his friends appears in a clear light in verse 21. Surely, says Job, the realization that the hand of God is afflicting him ought to move them to pity. Yet it was for that very reason, bearing in mind the background of their inflexible creed, that they could not pity him. They had to choose between their friend and their faith. Verse 22 demonstrates as strikingly as any verse in Scripture the extent of our debt to our Lord Jesus Christ as regards our view of God. In our Christian era, our complaint against men must often be that they are not Godlike enough. Cf. Lk. vi. 35, 36; Eph. iv. 32. But Job's complaint against his friends was that they were too Godlike. In their attitude to his suffering, which was gradually becoming more unsympathetic, he imagined he saw a reflection of the attitude of God who seemed to him so callous about the weight of sorrow with which He was crushing him down to despair.

ii. Faith again triumphs (xix. 23–29). He looks into the future to find the hope, denied him by the present, blazing forth again. If only his case could be recorded! Surely generations to come would react more favourably to it than does his own. But, dramatically and impressively, we see that this man cannot for long rest content with the thought of a future 'well done' from the lips of humanity. His sense of alienation from man is infinitely less serious than his sense of alienation from God. There we have the key to the agony of heart we see in the book. Suddenly we have a wonderful vision of a divine Vindicator appearing to champion his cause, to recall him from the shadows of Sheol to which he had retired in disgrace, to allow him to hear the 'not guilty' for which he craved and to gaze upon the countenance of his Champion (25–27). Redeemer (25), Heb. go'el, is rendered 'vindicator' by RV mg. Moffatt translates 'one to champion me'. Strahan summarizes the rôle of the go'el by saying, 'The go'el was the nearest blood-relation on whom civil law imposed the duty of redeeming the property or person of his kinsman, and criminal law that of avenging his kinsman's blood if it was unjustly shed.' At the latter day (25). Heb. 'aharon can mean 'last'. See, e.g., Is. xliv. 6. But it can also mean 'later'. The passage certainly does not tie down the vindication of Job's

innocence to some distant resurrection day. It merely points to a coming vindication. Various translations are possible for upon the earth (25); e.g., 'on the dust' or 'on my grave'. Cf. vii. 21, xvii. 16. Translate verse 26 as in RV: 'And after my skin hath been thus destroyed, yet from my flesh shall I see God.' There is nothing in the original to correspond with the worms and body of the AV. 'From my flesh' may mean that Job was expecting to be a spectator at his vindication from the vantage point of a body of flesh, or that he looked forward to being present at the scene as a disembodied spirit. The 'without my flesh' of RV mg. follows the latter interpretation. Dogmatism is futile as to whether 'from' means 'looking from' or 'away from'. In any case the spectator at the scene is of immeasurably less significance than the God who acts. The point of central importance with regard to the spectator is that he is there as a fully intelligent personality, although he has passed through the portals of the grave.

With I shall see for myself (27) cf. Luther's great remark that the whole of religion lies in the personal pronouns. No hearsay opinion of God for Job! RV mg., however, reminds us that for myself may not only have the force of 'I myself', but also of 'on my side'. And not another (27). RV mg. has the interesting alternative 'not as a stranger'. This suggests the beautiful thought that Job was eagerly anticipating the time when the God of the present, who so often appeared as a 'mystery God', as a Stranger with slumbering depths of puzzling hostility to him, would appear in His true character as a Friend who would be quick to reverse the adverse opinion the present life was writing across him. Note that the RV omits though before my reins (27). The thought of the coming vindication overwhelms him.

No Christian can read verses 25–27 without finding the passage a mirror of the One who 'ever liveth to make intercession' (Heb. vii. 25), who has 'brought life and immortality to light through the gospel' (2 Tim. i. 10). Of course Job was unaware of the most priceless jewels encased in his words. 'He was like an aeolian harp across which the wind sweeps making music', says G. C. Morgan.

The chapter closes with a note of warning. Job's Vindicator will punish those who have arrayed themselves against him, assuming that they have diagnosed the real cause of his affliction. LXX and RV mg. have the reading 'in him' for in me (28).

e. Zophar's second speech (xx. 1–29)

Zophar's text is the brevity of the wicked man's prosperity, and the inevitability of doom—a text equally cruel and irrelevant for Job's case. The text is expounded with power, heat and impetuosity. The whole of his speech must be interpreted in the light of the remark in verse 2, I make haste. Haste can be responsible for an incorrect view of man (cf. Ps. cxvi. 11); and no less for an incorrect or partial view of God. 'His haste explains his theology', says Strahan. 'Had he taken time to observe and reflect, he would have said, "Some sufferers are saints"; had he taken still more time, he might even have added, "And some are saviours".' Suffering Job appears in a false light as sinning Job. The false light on man results from a distorted vision of God. There is nothing in Zophar's words to suggest that God is anything more than an impatient judge, as impatient as Zophar himself. 'When the zealot makes his own opinions and sentiments the standard of divinity, there is a magnified Zophar on the throne of the universe' (Strahan).

Note the RV reading in verse 11, 'His bones are full of his youth'. Death strikes him down while he is still in the full flower of vigorous manhood. *He shall suck the poison of asps* (16). These words perhaps portray him stung by asps with his body sucking in the poison. *In his belly* (20). RV has 'in his greed'; i.e. his greed prompts him to unresting activity. In verse 22 LXX and Vulg. have the reading 'Every power of misery shall come upon him'. In verse 25 RV has 'He draweth it forth, and it cometh out of his body'. In a desperate attempt to save his life he draws out the arrow that has entered his body, only to find the terrors of death overwhelming him. *A fire not blown* (26) means that it is inexplicable by human agency. Cf. i. 16.

f. Job answers Zophar (xxi. 1–34)

i. Introduction (xxi. 1–6). Zophar's words sting Job into giving a more detailed answer to the theme of the friends than anything that has yet appeared in the second cycle of the dialogue. He appeals for a fair hearing. That is the only consolation he wants from them (2). His task is difficult enough without lack of co-operation from man, for his complaint is directed against the God of heaven (4). The very thought of pursuing it fills him with dread, but honesty compels him to face the tremendous facts his own observations are thrusting in upon him (6).

ii. The prosperity of the wicked (xxi. 7–22). Job flatly contradicts Zophar's dogmatic picture of the fleeting prosperity of the wicked (cf. xx. 4, 5, 11, etc.). In bold colours he paints their enduring prosperity in home, family, field and flock. At the end of the day they pass away without a struggle (7–13). All this is in spite of the flat defiance their manner of life has thrown in the face of God (14, 15). It is no reply to say, as the friends might be inclined to say in defence of their position, that the children of the wicked will feel the weight of the divine displeasure. That would imply that the wicked would get off scot-free. They cannot feel the weal or woe of their children after them. Suddenly Job accuses his friends of presumption in their cut-and-dried theories about divine government. They are virtually teaching God how He ought to govern, instead of facing the facts as they actually are (22). RV mg. inserts 'ye say' before verse 16, and so looks upon it as an objection raised by the friends. A similar insertion occurs before verse 19a. On this interpretation the force of *their good*

is not in their hand (16) is: 'it may vanish at any moment, plucked away by God's hand.' Throughout verses 17, 18 translate interrogatively with RV. Job is querying his friends' objection. Follow the RV also in 19b: 'Let him recompense it unto himself, that he may know it.'

iii. The facts as Job sees them (xxi. 23–34). One man dies in effortless prosperity; another in abject misery. Who has a right to assume that virtue explains the former and vice the latter? That is theory and not fact, theory that is wrecked on fact as can be borne out by the testimony of those who have a broad knowledge of men and affairs. They can point to specific cases where wickedness seems to pay. In view of that, what comfort can he expect to find in his friends' sweeping generalities, which are based on cases which suit their argument, and which conveniently ignore those which do not? (34).

Breasts (24). The Hebrew word can mean 'milk pails'. Translate verse 30 with RV mg., 'The evil man is spared in the day of calamity. They are led away in the day of wrath'. Verses 32, 33 describe how an honourable burial is given to the wicked man. His grave is carefully guarded; his success inspires widespread imitation. *And shall remain in the tomb* (32). Better as in RV mg., 'They shall keep watch over the tomb'.

IV. THIRD CYCLE OF SPEECHES.
xxii. 1—xxxi. 40

a. Third speech of Eliphaz (xxii. 1–30)

i. The reason for suffering (xxii. 1–5). Eliphaz proceeds to demonstrate that there must be some reason for human afflictions. The key cannot be found in God, since human morality cannot affect His almighty power. The explanation must be sought, therefore, in man. Is Job being punished for piety? Inconceivable! Then he must be paying for his wickedness (5). *For fear of thee* (4). Read with RV 'for thy fear of him', i.e. 'for thy religion'.

To Eliphaz the answer to the question he poses in verse 3 is as undoubtedly negative as it would be clearly positive to the writers of such passages as Je. xxxi. 20; Ho. xi. 8; Mt. xxiii. 37, etc. In his estimation, the aloof God, in the icy altitudes of His remote heaven, could not be concerned in His own person about human virtue or vice. Cf. vii. 20n. He could not have said, 'God so loved the world . . .'; he could only have said, 'God has so legislated for the world . . .' He had no cross on Calvary to inform him of the love and agony in God's heart as He surveys sinning men and women, and of His gladness when they allow themselves to be set in the right relationship to Him. He knew nothing of the miracles in which Christianity glories—'the election of man, from nonentity, to be the beloved of God, and therefore (in some sense) the needed and desired of God, who but for that act needs and desires nothing, since He eternally has, and is, all goodness' (C. S. Lewis).

ii. Job is openly accused (xxii. 6–20). Now that

Eliphaz has ventured out into the open with what has previously been only hinted by him, he proceeds with specific charges against Job. He fathers on him the typical outrages of an oriental tyrant. It is implied that he has been practising a 'Jekyll and Hyde' existence (6–9). This sinfulness has been responsible for Job's present calamities (10,11). Instead of giving to the exalted Lord of highest heaven the respect that is His due (12), he has wrongfully assumed that His remoteness guarantees the slackness of His supervision of human affairs (13, 14). As a result he has trodden the way of the godless (15). At the end of that way is doom (16). The moral conscience of the righteous man approves the judgment of God (19). Verse 15 is linked closely with verses 12–14. Moffatt renders: 'Is that the line you choose, the line that evil men took long ago?' Many scholars treat verses 17, 18 as an insertion. They strongly remind us of the words of Job in xxi. 7–16. See especially verses 14 and 16. Verse 18a sounds especially strange on the lips of Eliphaz and verse 19 certainly follows verse 16 much more smoothly than it does verse 18.

iii. **An invitation to return to God (xxii. 21–30).** The mild spirit of Eliphaz breaks through the fire and brimstone preaching, in a passage full of beauty and spiritual truth, when it is lifted out of its narrow application to Job and interpreted generally. Man finds authentic peace, not in his sins, but through the forgiveness of them (21, 23); through acceptance of the truth revealed by God (22); through a humble return to God (23) and through a new judgment of values whereby the preciousness of the divine treasure eclipses all else (24, 25). Such peace will bring with it joy (26), communion with God (27), triumph and usefulness to others (28–30).

The law (22). RV mg. has 'instruction'; there is no definite article in the Heb. The RV of verses 24, 25 brings out the beauty of the thought: 'And lay thou thy treasure in the dust, and the gold of Ophir among the stones of the brooks; and the Almighty shall be thy treasure, and precious silver unto thee.' Translate verse 30 as in the RV: 'He shall deliver even him that is not innocent: yea, he shall be delivered through the cleanness of thine hands.'

b. **Job answers Eliphaz (xxiii. 1—xxiv. 25)**

i. **Job's heart laid bare (xxiii. 1–17).** He is no rebel against God; he does not complain for the sheer joy of complaining. He has made a real effort to restrain his cries of protest, but his misery has wrung them out of him. *My stroke is heavier than my groaning* (2). Lit. 'My hand is heavy upon my groaning', i.e. 'I am attempting to control it'. If he does rebel, it is against what seems to be God's arbitrary wrath. Thus in verses 3–7 he expresses a passionate longing to find the God of grace. Such a God would deal intelligibly with him, meting out justice to his cause, and not numbing him by a parade of sheer power. The wistful cry of these verses from a man seeking to find God can again be answered

only by Jesus, in whom God takes the initiative to find man. Cf. Jn. xiv. 9. The frustration of his longing to find God is expressed in verses 8–12. The most untiring efforts to bring about the meeting for which he yearns are fruitless, although God has the means of knowing the integrity of his heart of hearts. *He knoweth the way that I take* (10). Lit., as in RV mg., 'the way that is in me'. Moffatt translates 'how I live'. In the words *When he hath tried me, I shall come forth as gold* (10) we are not to detect a reference to the gold which comes through the refining fires of suffering; nor is there an arrogant claim on the part of Job that his nature is gold all the way through. Rather he is contradicting the insinuations of his friends. They maintained that Job was being punished for secret dross in his nature, which he had successfully screened from men. In his sufferings, according to them, God was tearing the screen aside.

In verses 13–17 we see the longing to find God somewhat clouded over. Job finds himself wearily toiling up the hill of predestination 'with its icy altitudes' (W. M. Macgregor). His suffering has been determined by an iron divine decree. The exact force of verse 17 is elusive. A. B. Davidson translates: 'For I am not dismayed because of the darkness, nor because of myself whom thick darkness covereth.' If this translation is adopted, the verse means that Job's most baffling problem was not the external darkness of calamity about him, nor the darkness that had invaded his own person, but rather his sense of the arbitrariness of the divine action.

ii. **The providence of God (xxiv. 1–25).** This problem is considered in a world setting. Various classes of wrongdoers are mentioned. Why does not God intervene? Note the Moffatt rendering of verse 1: 'Why has not the Almighty sessions of set justice? Why do his followers never see him intervening?'

Verses 5–8 describe aboriginals, driven into the wilderness by the oppression of a stronger race. *Rising betimes for a prey* (5). Better as in RV, 'seeking diligently for meat'. *Corn* (6). Lit. 'fodder', coarse food more suitable for animals than for human beings. *They pluck* (9). Better as in RV, 'There are that pluck'.

Verses 10, 11 depict wretched labourers working for an inadequate wage, hungry and thirsty in the midst of plenty.

Verses 13–17 describe the nefarious doings of the murderer (14), the adulterer (15), and the robber (16). *With the light* (14). Many scholars read 'when there is no light'. Cf. verse 13. Note the RV rendering of verse 17: 'For they know the terrors of the shadow of death.' Apparently there is in the verse a contrast between the attitude of respectable people and that of the night-birds. The former dread the darkness with its unknown terrors; the latter 'love darkness rather than light, because their deeds are evil'. Their familiarity with the darkness had bred contempt. If they know fear, it is during the day, perhaps because of the knowledge that justice will then find it easier to catch up with them.

Verses 18–21 cannot express Job's own convictions. RV mg. inserts 'ye say' before verse 18. There is certainly the authentic accent of the friends in the passage. Strahan suggests that the doom of a notorious evil-doer is described. *He is swift as the waters* (18). Better as in RV, 'He is swift upon the face of the waters'. Perhaps the picture is of a twig, hurried along on the surface of a swiftly moving flood. Cf. Ho. x. 7.

In verse 22 note the RV mg. reading, 'Yet God by his power maketh the mighty to continue: they rise up when they believed not that they should live.' Follow the RV reading in verse 23: 'God giveth them to be in security, and they rest thereon.' In this passage Job again speaks his own mind. If verse 24 is a characteristic utterance of his, we are to look for the force of it, not in *for a little while*, but rather in *as all other*. In defiance of the sentiments of his friends Job maintained that there was nothing abnormal about the death of the wicked.

c. Bildad's third speech (xxv. 1–6)

Bildad passes over Job's arguments in silence, and strives rather to bring him to his knees before the might of God (2, 3). When the mightiest heavenly bodies must tremble before Him, subdued and convicted, how can insignificant and corrupt man hope to look up, unafraid of what the light may disclose (4–6)? Cf. iv. 17ff. and xv. 14ff. Bildad could have sung with feeling

'Eternal Light! Eternal Light!
  How pure the soul must be
When, placed within Thy searching sight,
It shrinks not, but with calm delight
  Can live, and look on Thee!'

There is point in the speech, but in the sense intended by Bildad it cannot help Job. The latter never claims that there is no darkness in him, but only that there is not the darkness suspected by his friends.

d. Job answers Bildad (xxvi. 1–14)

Job demonstrates that he understands full wel what Bildad has said about the might of God. His controversy with him and with the others cannot be explained by failure to stand where they have stood in appreciation of the omnipotence of God; it must rather be explained by his honesty in facing certain puzzling facts of experience which they have either overlooked or suppressed. A. B. Davidson has the chapter heading: 'Job rivals Bildad in magnifying the greatness of God.'

Verses 2–4 embody the most pointed sarcasm. Such words of wisdom as have been offered to Job bear the stamp of the inspiration of some great person! Verses 5, 6 speak of the divine power operative in the underworld. *Dead things are formed from under the waters* (5). Better as in RV, 'They that are deceased ('the shades', RV mg.) tremble beneath the waters'. The Hebrew word is *repha'im*. Two usages of it should be noted. It refers to pre-Israelitish people (e.g. Gn. xiv. 5, xv. 20). It can also refer to the dead (e.g. Ps. lxxxviii. 10). Schwally maintained that 'it was applied by the Israelites to people who were dead and gone, and of whom they knew little'. *Destruction* (6). Heb. *'abhaddon*. The word is a synonym for *Sheol*, translated *hell* in the same verse.

In verses 7–13 Job shows that heaven and earth and sea have the same testimony with regard to the power of God. How mighty must be the God of an ordered universe! Note the RV of verse 9: 'He closeth in the face of his throne', i.e. with clouds. *He smiteth through the proud* (12). RV reads 'He smiteth through Rahab'. See ix. 13n. *By his spirit he hath garnished the heavens* (13). The reference is to the wind of God blowing away the clouds and making the sky bright. *His hand hath formed the crooked serpent* (13). Better as in RV: 'His hand hath pierced the swift serpent.' See iii. 8n.

Verse 14 rounds off the chapter in a most impressive way. Moffatt translates: 'And all this is the mere fringe of his force ('the outskirts of his ways', RV), the faintest whisper we can hear of him! Who knows then the full thunder of his power?' The idea is that when you have fully described your most exact impressions of the power of God, there is always infinitely more that could be said.

e. Job replies to his friends (xxvii. 1—xxxi. 40)

Perhaps at this stage in the book we are to imagine a pause. Job waits in vain for Zophar to speak; but the friends have shot their bolt. There now follow two general replies to the friends, introduced by the same words, *Moreover Job continued his parable* (xxvii. 1, xxix. 1).

  i. Job reaffirms his innocence (xxvii. 1–6). Job again repudiates the charges insinuated or directly affirmed by his friends. His affirmation is introduced by what Strahan calls 'the most extraordinary form of oath to be found in the Scriptures'. He swears by a God who has taken away his 'right' (RV for *judgment* (2)). It is a remarkable picture of a man whose faith is abiding with him in the storm, who still can call 'my God' the God he is tempted to imagine is forsaking him. He cannot doubt the reality of an Almighty God, or the fact of His government of the world: it is the mode of His government, and in particular its application to himself, which puzzles him. The present vexations cannot be explained by his sinfulness.

  ii. The end of the wicked (xxvii. 7–23). This passage presents a number of difficulties. The connection between Job's affirmation of innocence and this picture of the end of the wicked is hard to fathom. The friends had maintained that sinfulness was the clue to adversity, and had accordingly denied Job's innocence. That denial was the logical outcome of their creed. And now, without a trace of warning, Job appears as a perfervid believer in that creed. In the second place the passage flatly contradicts what Job has already said about the prosperity of the wicked. Cf. xxi. 22ff., xxiv. 1ff. and note the contrast between xxvii. 14 and xxi. 11. We have no parallel to these verses in Job's speeches in any other part of the book. On the other hand, the passage would sound perfectly in place on the lips of the friends. There are two alternatives. We may argue that Job is modifying his previous sentiments. 'He strengthened all the arguments of his friends' is G. C. Morgan's comment on the passage. In chapter xxvi we found him rivalling Bildad in magnifying the greatness of God without renouncing a larger creed than his. Perhaps in the present passage the author meant us to think of Job as sympathetic with the general truth of his friends' sentiments, but unwilling to accept the arbitrariness and the narrowness of their application of them. On the other hand, many scholars hold that there has been a dislocation in the book at this point, and attribute this section to Zophar, which would mean that all the friends speak three times.

By the hand of God (11). RV has 'concerning the hand of God'. The words have a somewhat strange ring. He is undertaking to teach people whose past speeches have revealed that they are past masters in the lesson. *As a moth* (18). Read with Syriac and LXX 'as a spider'. *As a booth* (18) refers to the flimsy construction erected by the nightwatchman in a vineyard. Note the LXX reading of verse 19a: 'He lieth down rich, but he shall do so no more.' *He openeth his eyes, and he is not* (19b) means that his eyes have scarcely opened to glimpse the descent of destruction, when they are closed for ever. The clapping of hands (23) is a token of indignation. See, e.g., Nu. xxiv. 10.

iii. God's gift of wisdom (xxviii. 1–28). The chapter consists of a fine poem on wisdom which is meant to teach that wisdom is completely beyond the reach of man unless the quest is carried through in the setting of *the fear of the Lord* (28). Many scholars doubt whether the chapter can be attributed to the original drama and treat it as a later addition. In the first place the connection between chapters xxvii and xxviii is elusive. Secondly this placid acquiescence in the superior heights of the divine wisdom contrasts strangely with many of Job's statements before and after this stage in the book. Elsewhere Job appears as 'a chained eagle, who spreads his wings and dashes himself against the bars of his cage; he would soar unto God's place and pluck the mystery out of the darkness' (A. B. Davidson). See, e.g., xxiii. 3, xxxi. 35ff. One must, however, bear in mind that it is unreasonable to expect level-headed consistency in a sufferer. We have seen striking inconsistencies in Job's view of God. God has appeared sometimes as foe, sometimes as friend. The pendulum may also have swung in respect of Job's thoughts on human understanding of the ways of God.

In the first fourteen verses we have a remarkable picture of man's successful and unresting

activity in worrying out of the earth its treasures of precious ores and stones. The miner is seen groping his way through the darkness, carrying through complicated underground operations. In verse 4 note the RV which suggests a possible sense for a very obscure passage: 'He breaketh open a shaft away from where men sojourn; they are forgotten of the foot that passeth by; they hang afar from men, they swing to and fro.' Verses 9 and 10 describe the miner cutting through the rocks. *Rivers* (10). RV mg. has 'passages'. Verse 5 is meant as a contrast between the quiet growth of the corn above ground and the miner's forceful tactics underground.

The narrative speaks of a quest which must baffle the most careful ingenuity of man or beast: the quest for wisdom (7, 8, 12–14). Earth cannot work out an answer to the question, *Where shall wisdom be found?* (12). *Price* (13). LXX reads 'way'. Wisdom cannot be obtained in any human market (15–22). All living things and the dark forces of the underworld are alike impotent to answer the question asked in verse 12 and again in verse 20. The most they can do is allude to a vague rumour about wisdom which they have heard (22).

The only One who can answer the question is indicated in verse 23. The God who can restrain the mighty forces of the universe, the God of creation, has an exact mastery of all the hidden things of wisdom. If man would travel profitably towards an apprehension of that wisdom, of which God is, and can be, the only possessor, he must be God-fearing and moral.

iv. Job's memory of a golden past (xxix. 1–25). This is one of the most effective chapters in the book. The sources of Job's happiness are portrayed with consummate skill.

First, he was a God-preserved man (2–4). Note the RV in verse 2b, 'In the days when God watched over me'. Here we have the pathos of the whole book. At the heart of his past happiness was the conviction that God was watching over him. His present misery is explained by the feeling that God is no longer watching—or, if watching, with unreasonably critical eyes. *In the days of my youth* (4). Lit. 'in the days of autumn'. Read as in RV, 'in the ripeness of my days'. For *the secret of God* (4) cf. Ps. xxv. 14.

Secondly, Job was a domestically happy man. In the reference to his children (5) we hear the 'sob of a great agony' (G. C. Morgan).

Thirdly, he was a prosperous man. *The rock poured me out rivers of oil* (6) does not refer to a prosperity emerging even from unlikely quarters, as we might imagine. The olive tree thrives in a rocky soil, and oil presses are hewn out in the rock.

In the fourth place, he was a universally respected man (7–10, 21–25). When he took his seat as a city councillor it was noted with respect by all classes of the community (8–10). His opinion was waited upon with respect. When it had been expressed, there was nothing more to say (21, 22). His speech was like refreshing rain for drooping spirits. His very smile was a tonic for the irresolute. Note the RV mg. of verse 24, 'I smiled on them when they had no confidence'.

Verses 11–17 explain the 'well done' invariably written by men across Job's name. The man who was 'watched over' by God was scrupulous in watching over the interests of the needy. Even perfect stangers could depend on his thorough championing of their case (reading verse 16 as in RV, 'The cause of him that I knew not I searched out'). In all these social activities, righteousness was his garment, and justice his turban (14, RV mg.). The idea is almost that justice incarnated itself in Job. Cf. Jdg. vi. 34, which can be rendered 'But the spirit of the Lord clothed itself with Gideon'.

Job's anticipations for the future, so rudely shattered by the calamities of the first two chapters of the book, are portrayed in verses 12–20. He expected an unbroken prolongation of the 'golden' days. In verses 19, 20 use the present tense throughout with the RV. Moffatt translates 'I shall grow old among my brood' for *I shall die in my nest* (18). Verse 19 speaks of a prosperity in touch with unfailing springs; verse 20 of manly strength symbolized by the bow.

v. The contempt into which he has been brought (xxx. 1–31). The grey 'now' stands in bleak contrast to the golden 'then'. The misery of the present approaches from every quarter. First it comes from without. He is insulted by men (1–15), even by the 'underdog' class, which in the old days he had been quick to befriend (cf. xxix. 11–17). Bitterly he says: 'my juniors mock me, men whose sires I would have scorned to trust with a sheep-dog's task' (1, Moff.). The reason for his lack of confidence in them appears in the next verse. They are 'men in whom vigour is perished' (RV mg.). The miserable lot of the men who now revile Job is then depicted. Following the RV, use the present tense throughout. They are grateful to scrape a miserable livelihood from the roots of the ground (4) and to make their bed in rocky barren places, when respectable men harshly refuse them a place to lay their head (5–8). Such is the lot of people with an unknown and unloved name. Follow the RV in verse 6, 'clefts of the valleys', and RV mg. in verse 7, 'under the nettles they stretch themselves'. *Base men* (8). Lit. 'men of no name'.

Now Job himself is a target for the skits and the crude contempt of such people (9–15). 'Spit at the sight of me' (10, RV mg.) is probably better than *spit in my face*. Verse 11 speaks of unrestrained humiliation at the hands of God. RV mg. yields the good sense of God loosening Job's 'bowstring'. Cf. xxix. 20. The *youth* (12), or 'rabble' (RV), distressing Job appears as a host beleaguering a city, making escape impossible (13), and then pouring in when the wall has been breached (see 14, RV).

In the second place misery approaches from within (16–18, 30). Note the RV of verse 16, 'my soul is poured out within me'. He describes the

tormenting, burning pains of his disease. Verse 18 is difficult. 18a seems to refer to his garment hanging loosely on his shrunken frame (RV has 'disfigured' for *changed*). 18b, on the other hand, seems to imply a tight-fitting garment. Strahan translates 'it clings to me like my vest'. Peake suggests that the reference is to certain abnormally swollen parts of his otherwise emaciated body.

Thirdly, misery approaches from above (19–23). He is dealing with a God who has cast him into a miry pit (cf. Ps. xl. 2), and now is cruelly indifferent to his cry for help. God's tempest of trouble is inexorably sweeping him forward to the grey portals of the house of death. *Dissolvest my substance* (22). Better, 'dissolvest me in the storm' (RV).

Verse 24 has given much difficulty. RV mg. has 'Howbeit doth not one stretch out the hand in his fall? or in his calamity therefore cry for help?' Dillmann, reading *tobue'a* for *be'e*, translates the first phrase 'Howbeit, doth not a sinking man stretch forth his hand?' i.e. a drowning man will grasp at a straw. Job felt himself sinking in a storm he imagined a cruelly callous God had sent. Yet again and again the cry rose in his heart, 'Lord, save me'. It was the hand of faith reaching out for a Saviour he could not yet firmly trust. Underlying verses 25, 26 we hear the note: 'If only God had dealt with me as generously as I have dealt with others, how different my present position would be!' Verse 27 describes his feelings in ferment. Translate *prevented* (27b) by 'are come upon me' with RV. Verses 28 and 31 portray the sorrow that has taken the place of the gladness of old. Verse 29 speaks of him as fitter company for animals than for men.

vi. Job's final protestation of innocence (xxxi. 1–40). This chapter gives a very remarkable insight into the character of the man. His ideals are not easygoing and unambitious, but exacting and inward. 'He judges himself by an almost evangelical standard of excellence', says Strahan. Duhm speaks of the chapter as the high-water mark of the Old Testament ethic. We shall note several striking correspondences with New Testament teaching. Job makes six main claims for his former way of life.

1. He was untainted by immorality (1–12). His external conduct had been pure, but no purer than his secret thoughts (1, 7, 9; cf. Mt. v. 8, 28). Adultery appears in a terrible light. First, it deserves the punishment of God (2, 3). The purity of Job's action had emerged from a background of the 'fear of the Lord', that is wisdom' (xxviii. 28). Second, it deserves the punishment of man, for it is an offence, not only against God, but against society (11). *Grind unto another* (10) refers to the lowliest form of bondage, that of a slave-woman at the mill. Cf. Ex. xi. 5, Third, it is a fire that has in it the threat of indiscriminate destruction—of a man's health, home, happiness (12). Cf. Pr. vi. 27, 28.

Verses 5–8 paint on a canvas wider than that of sensualism. Here Job denies vanity and deceit of any kind. Strahan effectively speaks of vanity (5) (Heb. *shawe'*) as 'masked nothingness'. He is not afraid of the scales of God's justice, if only they are fair (6). If his claim to integrity is unsound, he will gladly forfeit the produce of his enterprise (translating 8b with RV, 'Let the produce of my field be rooted out').

2. He was untainted by thoughtlessness (13–22, 31, 32). His servants always received fair play from him, for he remembered that there was a God in heaven to whom he was answerable—the Creator of both master and servant (13–15. Cf. Eph. vi. 9). Verse 15 surely stands out as the gem, even in this passage, because of its remarkably sensitive social consciousness. Cf. Pr. xiv. 31, xxii. 2. Nor was it possible for his household to complain of frugal catering at his hands any more than they could complain of injustice. In verse 31 follow RV, 'If the men of my tent said not, who can find one that hath not been satisfied with his flesh?' But his kindness was not confined within the walls of his own household; it went out to seek and to save the needy; the poor, the widows, and the fatherless (16, 17). Exploitation and oppression of the weak were foreign to his nature, though he could easily have used his influence to twist the justice offered by the courts (21). Rather he had been a help of the helpless. Verse 17 is particularly striking. His full stomach had never made him indifferent to the empty stomachs of others. No Lazarus was allowed to lie at his gate, unnoticed and unhelped (cf. Lk. xvi. 20). He was 'given to hospitality' (Rom. xii. 13), when he could not have the faintest chance of return (16–20, 32; cf. Lk. xiv. 12–14).

3. He was untainted by what G. B. Shaw has called the 'Gospel of Getting on' (24, 25). He made friends by means of the 'mammon of unrighteousness' (cf. Lk. xvi. 9), but his attitude to his riches never ran the risk of the warning: 'You cannot serve God and mammon' (cf. Mt. vi. 19–21, 24).

4. He was untainted by any secret hankering after idols (26, 27). Verse 27 speaks of the throwing of the kiss of adoration to the heavenly bodies.

5. He was untainted by bitterness towards his enemies (29, 30). In a passage such as this Job is travelling in the direction of our Lord's words in Mt. v. 44.

6. He was untainted by insincerity (33, 34). As Adam (33) can be rendered 'after the manner of men'. 'His true eyes had never practised how to cloak offences with a cunning brow' because he dreaded popular disapproval, and more especially the disapproval of the great families. Translate verse 34 with RV: 'Because I feared the great multitude, and the contempt of families terrified me, so that I kept silence, and went not out of the door—' The sentence is unfinished.

The recollection of his past way of life causes Job to break into an almost reckless 'not guilty' cry, with which he challenges high heaven (35–37). Note especially the RV rendering of verse 35.

The appearance of the indictment would not confuse or humiliate him. He would carry it, triumphantly, joyfully and openly (36); and with princely, confident step enter the presence of the Adversary he had found so elusive, ready to give Him an exact account of his daily walk (37).

In this chapter Job has so far claimed that neither the voice of man nor the voice of God can convict and confuse him. He is guiltless of such charges as his friends have sought to fasten on him. In verses 38–40 he goes further and says in effect: 'Even if my land had a voice, no more could it condemn me.'

V. THE ELIHU SECTION.
xxxii. 1—xxxvii. 24

For the following reasons many scholars maintain that the Elihu section is an interpolation by another hand: there is no mention of Elihu in Prologue or Epilogue; the linguistic and stylistic differences from the rest of the book are regarded as favouring such a conclusion; the Elihu speeches, it is maintained, add nothing to what has gone before.

On the other hand, Budde, Cornill, Kamphausen, Wildeboer, Sellin, Bauer and Peters have argued for the originality of the speeches. It seems highly unlikely that a later interpolator, writing with a knowledge of the activities of the Satan mentioned in the Prologue, should ignore the Prologue altogether.

Characteristics of the Elihu speeches are a profound atmosphere of reverence for God; a view of sin deeper than that which appears elsewhere in the speeches of the other friends; the appearance of God as a Teacher (xxxv. 11 and xxxvi. 22), intent on leading man through the discipline of suffering to a wiser way of life. Budde maintains that the supreme function of the speeches is to expose Job's most potentially dangerous characteristic—spiritual pride (xxxiii. 17 and RV of xxxvi. 9). The curative value of suffering has no doubt appeared in other speeches but not with the same emphasis.

a. The reason for Elihu's intervention (xxxii. 1–22)

Throughout this chapter there is a clear ring of 'necessity is laid upon me'. The failure of the friends to answer Job's doubts and fears had forced him into the controversy. As he had listened, a twofold anger had burned in his breast—against Job, because of the confident eyes he was raising unflickeringly towards heaven, and against the friends for their failure to refute Job. We are surely meant to remember that it is an angry man who is speaking. There are four references to his anger in verses 2–5. Such a recollection will blunt the charge of boastfulness frequently made against Elihu. Hahn, e.g., dismisses him as 'a most conceited and arrogant young man'. (For his boastfulness see especially verses 14, 17, 18.) But anger may readily sweep a man beyond the strict frontiers of balanced humility. Also we must remember that it is an oriental man who is speaking and his words are meant for oriental ears. In such a setting the boastfulness, so clearly detected by Western ears, would assume almost a commonplace character. Cox looks upon his introduction as 'little more than a string of scholastic formulae, sentences which were the current form of debate'.

In verses 6–16 Elihu points out the reason for his silence up to the present stage in the debate: a young man's natural respect for grey hairs had sealed his lips. But a still more authoritative respect had broken the seal: his respect for the revelation of God which could come to young men as well as to old (8). Men who are 'great' in age are not always 'great' in their appreciation of spiritual wisdom. Silence now could only mean greater respect for the person of man than for his God. Elihu was not built on such lines (21, 22). Old men had failed to pierce Job's defence. Let them not conclude that it must be impregnable in the face of every human attack. Let them not say: 'We found him too clever for us! It must be God, not man, who puts him down!' (13, Moff.). Job has not yet had to reckon with Elihu's distinctive assault upon his positions.

Verses 17–21 graphically depict a man in the grip of the constraint of what he felt to be the truth of God. Cf. 1 Cor. ix. 16. He was bursting to speak. Only speech could relieve the inner tension (19, 20; see RV mg.).

b. Elihu denounces Job's attitude to his sufferings (xxxiii. 1–33)

In the opening verses of this chapter Elihu maintains first that he is utterly sincere, speaking directly from the heart (3), and secondly that he is on exactly the same plane as Job in creaturely dependence upon God (4, 6). In verse 6 translate with RV, 'I am toward God even as thou art'. Job had complained that the spectacle of the divine might numbed and terrified him (cf. ix. 34, xiii. 21), making it impossible for him to do himself justice before God, either in thought or in word. No such complaint could have relevance in the verbal warfare to which Elihu was challenging him (7). Job's present assailant was a man like himself.

In verses 8–13 Elihu rebukes Job for maintaining his integrity, and for charging God with hostility to him. Such a charge against the great God, whose greatness immeasurably transcends the power or wisdom of man, is totally unfounded. And yet Job seemed to assume that such a God would be prepared to assume the rôle of a disputant like some party in a petty human squabble! But while God will not speak as a disputant, He will speak (as the mighty God that He is) in ministries of mercy. Yet Job has denied that very fact. A. B. Davidson renders verse 13: 'Why dost thou contend against Him that He giveth not account of any of His matters?' In verses 14–30 Elihu refers to the various ways through which a patient God seeks to give an account of Himself in human affairs. First, He speaks through dreams and visions, through which He would leave the seal of His instruction upon human minds (16), and reclaim men from evil purposes (17) which must issue in death and destruction without His intervention (18). Secondly, He speaks through pain (19; cf. Heb. xii. 6). Suffering may deprive a man of his appetite (20), of his firm, healthy flesh (21); it may bring him to the very jaws of death, where destroying angels await him (22); but it may give God His chance with the soul. Verse 23 speaks of the intervention of an angel of mercy to cheat the destroying angels of their prey by interpreting to the sufferer the meaning of the chastening rod and the correct reaction to it. *One among a thousand* (23) has no idea of pre-eminence in it: the idea is rather that God has an indefinite number of ministers of mercy under His command.

Verses 24–30 speak of the results which follow a right response to the approach which a gracious God makes to the sufferer. First, his body regains its health (25). Secondly, health of soul is restored, with the joy which is its inevitable fruit (26). For *he will render* (26) read as in RV 'he restoreth'. Man is given back his righteous standing with God. Thirdly, joy of soul issues in joyful witness to others concerning God's dealings with the soul (27, 28). Translate verse 27 with RV and RV mg. 'He singeth before men, and saith, "I have sinned, and perverted that which was right, and it was not requited unto me"'. Cf. Ps. ciii. 10. *He will deliver his soul* (28). Better as in RV, 'He hath redeemed my soul'.

Elihu now challenges Job to speak, if he has anything worth saying (31–33). 'I fain would see you cleared' (32b, Moff.), he says. But if he cannot speak words of wisdom, let him listen to him.

c. Job's complaints summarized (xxxiv. 1–9)

Silence follows Elihu's challenge to Job, so his denunciation of Job's sentiments continues. He appeals first for the ear of all intelligent listeners. Let there be discrimination between words of truth and words of error. In which of these categories must Job's words be placed? Elihu condenses Job's speeches into two complaints: the first is that God has wronged an innocent man, inflicting a mortal wound on him quite capriciously (5, 6). Read verse 6 as in RV, 'Notwithstanding my right I am accounted a liar'. Such words, says Elihu, only go to show up Job as a man with a unique and insatiable thirst for scorning (7), a man of faulty opinions, which surely must be a significant commentary upon the faulty company he has been keeping (8). In the second place Job has complained that 'it is no use for man to be the friend of God' (9, Moff.).

d. Job's first complaint refuted (xxxiv. 10–33)

Job has complained of unrighteousness in God's dealings with him. With all the conviction of his pious nature Elihu affirms that God is just, and that He has placed man in a moral universe (10–12). Man reaps what he sows, whether the sowing is of evil or goodness. He supports his affirmation by various considerations.

First, absolute authority belongs to God and to God alone. The control of the universe has not been foisted on Him by some other power (13). That might entail indifferent or self-regarding government. Self-regard on the part of God would shatter the fabric of the universe in an instant (14, 15). In verse 14a follow AV mg., 'If he set his heart upon himself'. Human life is maintained by the breath of God. Where is there a motive for injustice in such a God?

He argues in the second place that the very continuance of the rule of God implies justice in that rule (17). The charge of injustice is a serious enough one to make against earthly monarchs (18), for justice wielded in an unjust way has the seeds of ruin in it (cf. Mt. xii. 25); but how can such a charge be made against the Creator of all men, whether princes or paupers, who shows partiality to neither prince nor pauper, but cares for all alike? (19). Again, where is there a motive for injustice?

Up to the present stage in the chapter Elihu has been moving on somewhat theoretical ground. He now moves on to more practical considerations. God's omniscience guarantees His justice (20–28). People and princes alike feel the weight of God's might. *Without hand* (20) means 'without human instrumentality'. Translate verse 23 with RV, 'For he needeth not further to consider a man, that he should go before God in judgment'. The verse is to be understood against the background of Job's appeal to God for 'sessions of set justice' (xxiv. 1, Moff.). Divine knowledge of human ways, and judgment upon them, are simultaneous. *Without number* (24). Better, 'without inquisition' (RV mg.), which links the thought with that of verse 23.

In verse 29 Elihu moves from a general contemplation of God's working in history towards Job's case. There is a ring of 'Thou art the man' about *or against a man only*. Translate verse 29a with RV, 'When he giveth quietness, who then can condemn?' The argument of the verse seems to be: whether nations or individuals are passing through days of quiet enjoyment of God's presence, or days when they lose sight of His face in the midst of trials, they must take the way of uncomplaining submission to His will. His justice is justly administered for the good of men (30). Elihu then asks Job 'if any man who uses the language of penitence (31, 32) will presume to dictate to God the chastisement he should receive' (Strahan). Translate 31a with RV, 'For hath any said unto God'. Note also the RV of verse 33. Elihu emphatically dissociates himself from Job.

Elihu then calls for the verdict of thinking men with regard to Job's rebellious words (34–37). For Elihu, Job's rebellion is more terrible than his trials. Until he surrenders that rebellion, for his own good the trials must continue. *He clappeth his hands* (37). See xxvii. 23n.

e. Job's second complaint refuted (xxxv. 1–16)

Job had argued that righteousness brings no advantage to the righteous man—no more than if he had been a flagrant sinner (cf. xxi. 15, xxxiv. 9). A. B. Davidson translates verses 2 and 3: 'Thinkest thou this to be thy right, and callest thou it, My just cause against God, that thou sayest, What advantage is it to thee? And, What am I profited more than if I had sinned?' Elihu replies that human virtue or vice cannot bring any advantage to the transcendent God (5–7). It is other men, and not God, who have reason to be concerned about human conduct (8). For the error in Elihu's argument, see vii. 20n., xxii. 3n.

Elihu proceeds to demolish certain considerations which might seem to support Job's contention that no advantage is attached to righteous conduct. There is the problem of unanswered prayer (9, 12). Note the RV of verse 9: 'By reason of the multitude of oppressions they cry out.' It is a case of 'Ye ask, and receive not, because ye ask amiss' (Jas. iv. 3). A deep religious note is missing from the prayer. It has the stamp of vanity upon it (13). It is a cry of pain, which does not raise man any higher than the level of the beasts (11). The divine Teacher has loftier altitudes of trust in store for man (10; cf. xxxvi. 22).

The thought of God as a Teacher, intent on steering man through a rough and thorny maze of pain to a deeper experience of Himself, gives us an important distinction between Elihu and the friends. For them, God appears more characteristically as a Sovereign or Judge. Verses 14–16 point out that there is not only a deep religious note lacking in Job's cry; there is a positively irreligious ring about it. The translation is problematical. A. B. Davidson makes good sense in the rendering, 'Yea when thou sayest, Thou seest Him not, the cause is before Him; therefore wait thou for Him' (14). In verse 15 follow RV mg., 'But now, because he hath not visited in his anger, thou sayest, he doth not greatly regard arrogance'. In thus questioning the reality of God's righteous rule, entailing profit for saint and punishment for sinner, Job is heaping up *words without knowledge* (16).

f. The mighty works of God (xxxvi. 1—xxxvii. 24)

Attention—to a man of 'unerring insight' (4, Moff.) into the ways of God with man in general, and with Job in particular. *From afar* (3) means that his argument is going to range widely through the realm of truth.

Behold a mighty and a gracious God! His providence is trustworthy, adamantly opposing the wicked, vigilantly superintending the righteous (5–7). Even when they are cramped and constrained by affliction, the divine Teacher is intent on leading them through to a large place (cf. verse 16) where they acknowledge and renounce the transgression that had involved them in affliction (8–10). *Their transgressions that they have exceeded* (9). Better as in RV, 'their transgressions, that they have behaved themselves proudly'. Obedience to the Teacher leads to happiness; disobedience to ruin (11–15). *Wrath* (13) refers to their smouldering resentment against God. *Cry not* (13) means 'pray not', with the content of trust in their prayers which is pleasing to God (cf. xxxv. 10). *In his affliction* (15) can mean 'through his affliction'.

The action of a mighty and gracious God, which has been generally enunciated, is not applied to Job's particular case. In verse 17 follow the RV, 'But thou art full of the judgment of the wicked'. In verse 18 combine RV mg. and RV: 'For beware lest wrath lead thee away into mockery, neither let the greatness of the ransom turn thee aside.' The greatness of the ransom is evidently a reference to the severity of the afflictions through which he is passing. Nothing else can win for him that larger trust in God to which God is calling him in his afflictions. Riches certainly cannot do it (19). The force of *night* (20) is elusive. Cox sees a reference to Job's loathing of life; Davidson, a synonym for judgment. Cf. Job's frequently expressed desire to meet God in judgment. Verse 21 expresses a warning against the way of rebellion, alias the way of iniquity, which, he says, Job has chosen in preference to walking the way of affliction with meekness. There will be a change if only he will behold the God of sovereign might (22; note RV, 'Behold, God doeth loftily in his power'), the mighty Teacher, who is answerable to no one (22, 23). Down on your knees before such a God! That is the place for man (24, 25).

In a passage full of literary beauty and spiritual significance Elihu takes up again his theme of the greatness of God (xxxvi. 26—xxxvii. 24). He calls the phenomena of nature to witness to the might of God.

i. The formation of the rain drops (xxxvi. 27, 28).
In verse 27 follow RV: 'For he draweth up the drops of water, which distil in rain from his vapour.'

ii. The thunderstorm (xxxvi. 29—xxxvii. 5).
Verse 30 is difficult. A. B. Davidson translates, 'Behold, He spreadeth His light around Him, and covereth Him over with the deeps of the sea'. He interprets *sea* as referring either to the 'masses of water in the thunder clouds which enshroud the Almighty', or to 'the sea on earth . . . as it were drawn up from its bottom in cloud and vapour to form the pavilion of the Lord'. Verse 31 speaks of the thunderstorm both as a minister of God's judgment and of His mercy (accompanied as it is by fructifying rain). In verse 32 translate with RV: 'He covereth his hands with the lightning; and giveth it a charge that it strike the mark.' Verse 33 is called by Gesenius *locus obscurissimus*. Many scholars adopt the reading 'The crash thereof announceth the fierceness of His wrath against iniquity'. *Them* (xxxvii. 4) refers to the lightnings.

iii. The snow and ice (xxxvii. 6–10).
He describes the paralysing effect of the rigours of winter upon human work and upon the animals (7, 8). Render 7b with RV, 'That all men whom he hath made may know it'. The helplessness of man before the severity of the weather is meant to serve as a timeless reminder that he is creature and not Creator. *Out of the south* (9). Lit. 'out of its chamber'. *Out of the north* (9) is properly 'out of the scatterers'—perhaps the north winds which scatter the clouds and bring frost.

iv. The clouds (xxxvii. 11–13).
These move in accordance with the divine command on ministries of discipline or mercy to man or land. Follow RV in verse 11: 'Yea, he ladeth the thick cloud with moisture; he spreadeth abroad the cloud of his lightning.' *They* (12) refers to the individual lightning flashes.

The weight of testimony of the 'wondrous works of God' to the God operative in them is applied to Job's case (14). It ought to pull him up in his tracks in the way of rebellion along which he had been hurrying; it ought to make him a reverent listener to the Word of the Lord spoken through such impressive testimony to the might of God. Only One is *perfect in knowledge* (16) of the ways of the Lord in nature. Man must confess the imperfection of his knowledge when confronted by the phenomena of nature (15–18).

Human understanding of the ways of the Lord with man is similarly conditioned by the limitations of the human mind. Such limitations make it impossible, in the first place, for man to address God aright (19); cf. Rom. viii. 26. By presumptuous speech a man is running the risk of destruction (20). Secondly, man cannot appear with confidence before a God whose majesty must completely blind him. The light shining in a cloudless sky dazzles man (21; see RV mg., 'And now men cannot look on the light when it is bright in the skies, when the wind hath passed and cleansed them', i.e. swept the clouds away). How much more must the light of God's majesty dazzle him! *Fair weather* (22). Lit. 'gold'. The RV has 'golden splendour'. The reference is evidently to the splendour of the light which results when the north wind sweeps away the clouds. For a striking commentary on these verses see T. Binney's hymn: 'Eternal Light! Eternal Light! How pure the soul must be.' Thirdly, these limitations mean that man cannot understand God aright. See Moffatt's moving translation of verse 23: 'The Almighty is beyond our minds. Supreme in power and rich in justice, he violates no right.'

In view of such human limitations, man's proper rôle is to lean, not on his own intelligence, which is the force of *wise of heart* (24), but on God in reverential fear.

VI. THE LORD ANSWERS JOB.
xxxviii. 1—xli. 34

a. Job is called to account (xxxviii. 1–3)
The silence of heaven in face of Job's challenging cries is broken. Verse 2 has been applied by some

commentators to Job; by others to Elihu. *Counsel* (2) implies that in His dealings with Job God was not acting in a haphazard fashion, but according to a consistent, intelligent design. All the speeches up to the present stage in the book, both by Job and the four friends, had sent shadows across that truth. In verse 3 an interesting word is used for man—*gebher*. 'It denotes man, not in frailty but in his strength, man as a combatant' (Strahan). Repeatedly Job had used language (e.g. xxxi. 35–37, xiii. 22) which seemed to suggest that in him God would find a worthy combatant. Ironically God takes him at his own valuation. But it is not long before the frail creature bows in abject confession of need before a fresh revelation of the mighty Creator (see xlii. 6). The combatant becomes a worshipper.

b. The marvels of the inanimate world (xxxviii. 4–38)

i. **Earth and sea (xxxviii. 4–11).** Was Job a partner with God in creation, initiated in all its mysteries? Verse 7 poetically speaks of stars and angels alike joining in the paean of praise on creation's morning: verses 8–11 magnificently depict the sea bursting forth from the womb, with clouds and darkness as its swaddling clothes, not as a rebel, but as a creature of God, called forth by God, controlled by God. In verse 10 follow RV mg., 'and brake for it my boundary'. The reference is to the rugged coastline bounding the sea.

ii. **The dawn (xxxviii. 12–15).** Understand 'began' after *since thy days* (12). Job is reminded of his fleeting life in contrast to the antiquity of the world and God's eternal being. The effect of the dawn on the wicked, who 'love darkness rather than light', is then described. The dawn shakes them out of their treasured refuge (13). Verse 14 portrays the effect of the dawn on the earth. It is 'changed as clay under the seal; and all things stand forth as a garment' (RV). Detail, beauty, colour appear. In verse 15 the light of the wicked is the darkness. Cf. xxiv. 17.

iii. **Job's ignorance of hidden things (xxxviii. 16–21).** Job is asked if he has roamed at large through the deep springs that supply the sea, and through the mysteries of the underworld. In verse 16 read with RV, 'Or hast thou walked in the recesses of the deep?' Does he know the extent of the earth's surface (18)? Is he versed in knowledge about the home of light and darkness? Can he conduct them to their proper spheres and then bring them home again (19, 20)? The irony of verse 21 is brought out in the RV: 'Doubtless, thou knowest, for thou wast then born, and the number of thy days is great.'

iv. **Natural phenomena (xxxviii. 22–30).** Even common things like snow and hail, the artillery of heaven, wind, rain, lightning, frost and ice, are mysteries too great for Job. Translate verse 24 with RV mg., 'Which is the way to the place where the light is parted, or the east wind scattered upon the earth?' The parting of the light may be a reference to the diffusion of light

over the earth. Verses 26, 27 are noteworthy. Let not proud man imagine that he is the sole object of the divine providence. God not only sends His rain 'on the just and on the unjust' (Mt. v. 45); He remembers also the dreary, uninhabited regions of the world. The inference is that Providence is a much more involved affair than Job had imagined it to be. *A father* (28) refers to a human father; i.e., is the rain Job's offspring? In verse 30 translate with RV mg., 'The waters are congealed like stone'.

v. **The universe (xxxviii. 31–38).** Does Job control the constellations and the heavens? *The sweet influences of Pleiades* (31). 'The cluster of the Pleiades' (RV), 'the chain of the Pleiades' (RV mg.) are both possible alternatives. The precise meaning of the verse is in any case elusive. Cox interprets it 'Canst thou bring back the gracious fruitful warmth of spring, and release the frozen earth from winter's sterile bands?' The *Mazzaroth* (32) refers, perhaps, to the Zodiac, *Arcturus* to the Bear. Verse 33b refers to the popular belief that the heavenly bodies exercised an influence over the affairs of men. In verse 36 it suits the context better to follow RV mg. by rendering *inward parts* and *heart* by 'dark clouds' and 'meteor'. It breaks the continuity of the portrayal of the marvels of the inanimate world to introduce a sudden reference to man. Moffatt translates 'Who taught the feathery clouds, or trained the meteors?' In verse 37b RV has 'pour out the bottles of heaven'. Verse 38 describes the soil caked by the sun after being fused together by the rain.

c. The marvels of the animal kingdom (xxxviii. 39 —xxxix. 30)

i. **Job's ignorance of their ways (xxxviii. 39— xxxix. 4).** A contrast between man and God is implied in these verses. Man is disposed to kill the lioness (RV for *lion*, 39), certainly not to assist her in finding food for her young. God, on the other hand, cares for her and her cubs. Let Job, who had accused God of savagery in dealing with him, remember God's attitude even to savage beasts. Lk. xii. 24 is the New Testament answer to the question in verse 41.

ii. **The wild ass and the wild ox (xxxix. 5–12).** The first reference is to an animal very different from the domestic ass, fleet of foot, graceful, wandering in herds over vast stretches of country. The emphasis is on its freedom. It is as high-spirited as if it had been suddenly released from captivity. This is not a work of man. *Unicorn* (9). Read as in RV, 'wild-ox'. Here the emphasis is on the animal's strength and unreliability. Can Job use this creature for agricultural purposes as men use the tame ox? Only One can control him, the God who created him.

iii. **The ostrich (xxxix. 13–18).** Translate verse 13 as in RV, 'The wing of the ostrich rejoiceth; but are her pinions and feathers kindly?' This latter phrase is a reference to the proverbial cruelty of the ostrich. Cf. La. iv. 3. This bird lays her eggs in the sand and will sometimes wander away from them during the day-time and lose her way back. This stupidity has no doubt given rise to the popular belief that she leaves the eggs to hatch in the sun. *Without fear* (16) means that she does not care if her labour in laying eggs goes all for nothing. Verse 17 is suggestive; her foolishness is ascribed to an act of God. Man does not know the reason for the act of God; he cannot, for he does not possess the universe-ranging wisdom of the Creator. Verse 18 is a reference to the great speed of the ostrich when running.

iv. **The horse (xxxix. 19–25).** *Thunder* (19). 'The quivering mane' (RV). Follow RV also in verse 20: 'Hast thou made him to leap as a locust?' (cf. Rev. ix. 7). *The quiver* in verse 23 is the quiver of his rider, exciting him by rattling against his side. *Neither believeth he* (24) may mean that he can scarcely believe his ears for joy. RV mg., however, has 'neither standeth he still at the sound of the trumpet'.

v. **The hawk and the eagle (xxxix. 26–30).** *Toward the south* (26) refers to the southward migration of the bird when the cold weather comes. The description of the eagle's powers and habits is particularly vivid. Job is further shown his human frailty by being reminded that he has no say in these matters.

d. **The mighty power of God (xl. 1—xli. 34)**

i. **Job's self-esteem shattered (xl. 1–5).** We are now moving towards the human response to the divine word. It is introduced by the question, 'Shall he that cavilleth contend with the Almighty? He that argueth with God, let him answer it' (2, RV). Ironically God had taken Job at his own evaluation as a combatant (see xxxviii. 3n.). Has Job, the combatant, any answer to offer after listening to the impressive commentary upon the wonders of nature, animate and inanimate, which the God of nature had graciously granted him? But the revelation of heaven has made the defiant combatant a humble worshipper. xl. 3–5 and xlii. 1–6 give us a classic illustration of the results which must always follow when the silence of heaven is broken, when the Almighty God appears with a fresh revelation of Himself, to which man listens in that posture of faith without which 'it is impossible to please him'. At such times the speech of earth is stilled (4, 5); Job could have bitten out his tongue for some of the hot words of complaint which he had poured out. At such times man sees himself in his true light (4, RV 'I am of small account'). It is not a confession of sin, although there is no doubt that Job would have immediately acknowledged the sinfulness of some of his words and attitudes. It is rather a confession of insignificance. As he looked away from himself to the God he was seeing in a more impressive way than ever before, he saw himself in a new perspective.

The above-mentioned passages are strikingly suggestive. The Word of God wrought a transformation which the word of man had been totally unable to achieve. From iii to xxxvii we have one long commentary on the inadequacy of the word of man, and the wisdom of man, to explain the mystery of suffering. Eliphaz, Bildad, Zophar and Elihu had all poured out words, without speaking a single word which brought conviction or comfort to Job. Job's replies had also failed to interpret the mystery; they had also darkened God's 'counsel by words without knowledge' (xxxviii. 2). The Word of God came, and the strife of words was over. It did not come through a carefully reasoned argument, dealing a deathblow to Job's intellectual difficulties by its inexorable logic; it did not come through a cut-and-dried explanation of the strands of suffering in Job's experience. There is silence on such issues; silence about the question of retribution, which had bulked so largely in speech after speech; silence about the disciplinary aspect of suffering. The Word came through a fresh vision of God—of the mighty, majestic God behind the marvels of animate and inanimate nature, painstakingly attentive to the unexpected and the insignificant (see especially xxxviii. 26, 27, 39, xxxix. 30), towering above human might and wisdom.

The Word in the vision convinced Job that he could trust such a God. It brought home to his heart the realization that Providence was a much more involved and painstaking affair than he had imagined it to be. He had been like a man living in a stuffy room, whose closed windows had been shutting out God's clean, sweet air, and whose drawn blinds had been shutting out God's sunshine. With the appearance of God, the windows had been thrown open and the blinds had gone up. God did not answer the problems in his mind, but He did answer Job; He healed the wounds of his heart, and brought quiet resignation flooding back into his heart. And yet Job had never heard that most impressive divine Word, which has given mankind the clearest vision of God, and the most irrefragable evidence that God can, and must, be trusted—the Word of the cross. The vision of the God of nature made Job a worshipper. How much more ought the vision of the God of Calvary bring the sufferer to his knees, 'lost in wonder, love, and praise'!

ii. **God's power and the moral order (xl. 6–14).** The irony that has been running through the divine speech is strongly reflected in verses 6–14. G. C. Morgan sees in the passage 'satire as gentle as the kiss of a mother when she laughs at a child'. Verse 8 asks if Job is prepared to hold on to his own innocence, at the price of rejecting the justice of God. The thought now swings from the natural order of the universe (xxxviii—xxxix) to the moral order. Has Job the mighty arm and the commanding voice of God (9)? If so, let him take God's glorious garments (10); let him mount the throne of the universe, to send the thunderbolts of his anger speeding against the proud and the wicked (11–13). Then, and only then, can he pass an intelligent judgment upon the divine ordering of things, and earn the divine 'well done'. Strahan renders verse 14: 'Then will I also praise thee, that thine own right hand getteth thee victory.' He points out that the Hebrew word *yadha*, used here for *confess* (RV 'praise'), is 'ordinarily used by a worshipper who is lauding or giving thanks to God'. Here the Creator lauds the creature!

iii. **Behemoth (xl. 15–24)**. In xl. 15—xli. 34 we have a description of two monsters, *behemoth*, usually identified as the hippopotamus, and *leviathan*, usually identified as the crocodile. The atmosphere of the passage is that of chapters xxxviii and xxxix rather than that of xl. 6–14. Its force in the argument proceeds on some such lines as: Can Job assume sway over the material order as represented by these formidable creatures? It is a much more formidable undertaking to stand forth as a combatant against their Creator (xli. 9–11). He is ill equipped for sway over the material order; he is less equipped for sway over the moral.

In verse 17b follow RV: 'The sinews of his thighs are knit together.' The description *He is the chief of the ways of God* (19) regards him as God's masterpiece. The remainder of the verse is obscure. RV mg. translates, 'He that made him hath furnished him with his sword'; a reference, perhaps, to the tusks of the creature. In verse 23 follow RV: 'Behold, if a river overflow, he trembleth not: he is confident, though Jordan swell even to his mouth.' Translate *Jordan* as 'a Jordan', i.e. any swollen stream. The hippopotamus is not found in Palestine. In verse 24 again follow RV: 'Shall any take him when he is on the watch, or pierce through his nose with a snare?'

iv. **Leviathan (xli. 1–34)**. The formidable qualities of the crocodile are emphasized in verses 1–9. Ironical questions run through the passage. Can Job look upon the crocodile as a suitable object on which to demonstrate his fishing ability? (1, 7); as a domestic servant? (4); as a plaything? (5). Verse 8 might be paraphrased to mean: 'Meddle with him in any of these ways, and you will rue the day.' *Companions* (6) refers to companies of fishermen. RV translates 'Shall the bands of fishermen make traffic of him?' *The hope of him* (9) must mean 'one's hope of him', i.e. of getting the better of him.

If a creature is too formidable to assail, what then must be said about the Creator of all things? (10, 11). Note the RV in verse 11: 'Who hath first given unto me, that I should repay him?' Cf. Rom. xi. 35. God is indebted to no man. Man has given Him nothing. He has given man everything. So it is preposterous for man to imagine that he can stand on an equal footing with God. Yet some of Job's reckless challenges to God had almost implied that he could.

A description of the crocodile is given in verses 12–34. Note the RV of verse 13: 'Who can strip off his outer garment? Who shall come within his double bridle?' i.e. his jaws. Verses 18–21 describe his steaming breath, luminous in the sunshine. *Sorrow is turned into joy before him* (22) describes the terrified movements of other creatures when the crocodile appears. The RV

translates 'terror danceth before him'. Follow RV also in verse 25b: 'By reason of consternation they are beside themselves': verse 30, as the RV makes clear, speaks of the impression left upon the mud in the place where he has been lying. 'His underparts are like sharp potsherds: he spreadeth as it were a threshing wain upon the mire.'

VII. JOB'S RESPONSE TO THE DIVINE WORD. xlii. 1–6

Cf. xl. 1–5 and see note there. The one who had been a combatant against God is again seen as a worshipper, humbly confessing his sinfulness, and entering into an experience of the divine forgiveness. The unveiling of God's glory led to an unprecedented realization of sinfulness. Cf. Rom. iii. 23. Associated with this new consciousness of sin is, first, an unprecedented confidence in God's providence. *Every thing* (2) certainly includes the fulfilment of a beneficent divine purpose in Job's suffering. Cf. Rom. viii. 28. In verse 2b follow RV: 'And that no purpose of thine can be restrained.' Job the rebel had no such confidence; Job the humble penitent possessed it in rich measure.

In the second place, Job now completely renunciates the force of human words and human reason. *Who is he that hideth counsel without knowledge?* (3) is an echo of the divine words in xxxviii. 2. His words, his wisdom, in which he had prided himself, had merely cast a clumsy screen across the consistent pattern running through God's dealings with him. We have a further echo of God's words in verse 4. Cf. xxxviii. 3 and xl. 7. Answer a challenge like that, with his puny human mind, unable to grapple with the range of the divine wisdom? Impossible! Job the rebel might have had a different answer to give.

Thirdly, Job now can rejoice in a fully personal religious experience (5). In comparison with the radiant personal faith the vision had brought to him, his earlier religious experience had been a matter of hearsay and not of experience.

VIII. EPILOGUE. xlii. 7–17

The text now passes from poetry to prose, the style of writing used for the Prologue. The conclusion opens with the condemnation of the three friends, Eliphaz, Bildad and Zophar. The omission of Elihu from public censure is significant and may have a bearing upon his repudiation of the traditional theology that suffering necessarily implies sin and is always in proportion to its gravity. The three friends are charged with not speaking *of me the thing that is right* (7, 8). Their view of the divine character was erroneous, especially in the case of God's rule upon earth and His dealing with men. Job, on the other hand, is commended. His theology was on the whole orthodox, although he was not consistently right. The narrative continues to portray the integrity of Job. The patriarch freely forgives the hurt that false words had given and even makes intercession for the three pseudo-comforters. God upholds Job publicly as a righteous man.

a. Job's spiritual blessings (xlii. 7–10)

The passage provides a beautiful picture of the spiritual and material tokens of this divine approval, of which the spiritual tokens are of supreme significance. Note first that God refers to Job as *my servant* four times in verses 7, 8. Cf. i. 8. Then God commends Job for his sincere quest for truth, and censures the friends for their opposition to that quest (7, 8). We remember, of course, and are meant to remember passages in the friends' speeches, redolent with beauty and spiritual truth, while, not infrequently, Job had gone perilously near error, rebellion and blasphemy: but, as McFadyen has pointedly said, 'Job was right in his intellectual temper, in the drift, the impulse, the sheer intrepid honesty of his thought . . . Out of all the welter of the discussion, Job stands forth as the champion of intellectual and religious freedom with the seal of the God of truth stamped upon his disfigured brow.' The passage is a striking warning that 'intrepid honesty' in facing the facts of existence —no matter how disturbing and unfamiliar—is much more pleasing to God than timid clinging to familiar and comfortable ideas in the teeth of the evidence. Finally, God honours Job's prayers for his friends (8–10).

b. Job's material blessings (xlii. 11–17)

In passing from the spiritual tokens of God's approval to the material (11–17), it is striking to note that it was when Job was praying for others that his material prosperity was restored (10). It was when his attention was focused on the spiritual interests of others that all other things were added to him. Cf. Mt. vi. 33. These verses speak of the restoration of friendship (11); of property (12); and of family (13–17). Many have taken strong exception to the portrayal of the material tokens of the divine approval. Cheyne, e.g., speaks of 'a sad concession to a low view of providential dealings'. The unfairness of such a criticism appears from various considerations. At a time when there was no clear picture of a life after death, how could the fact that righteousness is woven into the very texture of reality, and must ultimately bear the stamp of God's vindication, be demonstrated unless on the canvas of the present life? There is no inconsistency in this since the aim of the book has not been to deny that there is a connection between righteousness and material prosperity, but only that the connection is invariable. We should also remember that Job's material prosperity has been shattered as a test of the Satan's insinuations about the sincerity of Job's piety. The march of events has given the lie to the Satan. Justice now demands some restitution.

This Old Testament drama fittingly ends with the words *So Job died, being old and full of days* (17). Cf. Gn. xxv. 8, xxxv. 29. As a sort of commentary upon the great passage of resurrection hope in the book (xix. 25–27) the LXX adds 'and it is written that he will rise again with those whom the Lord raises up'.

E. S. P. HEAVENOR.

THE PSALMS

INTRODUCTION

The continual freshness and enduring quality of the Psalms is primarily due to their spiritual intensity. Whatever their mood, motive, or variety of circumstance, the psalmists are at one in worshipping God. Each of these hymns and prayers is a facet or echo of a vividly personal relationship with Him. In these poems a dynamic quality of life has been embodied. Behind the words lies a profound experience, and beyond the experience is found a manifestation of God. Thus every Psalm becomes a draught from the very fountain of life.

There are three main themes running through the Psalter. Firstly, one's personal encounter with God, involving the principle of His real existence. Secondly, the importance of the natural order of things, involving the principle of God's wise, universal and creative power. Thirdly, a consciousness of history, involving the principle of God's choice of Israel for a special and benevolent rôle among men (cf. xlviii, lxxiv, lxxviii, lxxxi, cv, cvi, cxiv).

The Hebrew name for the book is *Tehillim*, meaning 'Songs of Praise'. Although there is bewilderment at times because of temporal injustice (as in xxxvii and lxxiii), there is a dominant mood of hope, not only in the messianic concept of some unique future divine manifestation of God to man, but in the reality and efficacy of the divine forgiveness of sin. (See, e.g., xxv, li, lxx.) There is also a profound sense of the objective character of religion. The psalmists deal with God more than with men, and reach out to Him in abandonment of self. God is known as universal (as in lxv, lxvii), supreme in nature (xxix) and history (lxxviii), enduring (cii): and above all, faithful, personal, gracious, active and adored (cxxxix).

I. COMPILATION

Hymns for use in worship are known to have existed in Babylon and Egypt for many centuries before Abraham and Joseph. Although it would be remarkable if Hebrew psalmody showed no signs of having grown from such a soil, a similarity of literary structure such as, for example, the extensive use of parallelism (see General Article, *The Poetry of the Old Testament*, p. 39) is no index of equal spiritual wealth and vigour. In this latter respect the Psalms of Israel have no rival. Moreover, their common use by a congregation of worshippers, as well as by the officiating priests, was a practice unknown elsewhere.

When the children of Israel established the worship of Yahweh in Palestine they did so amidst a people who had a considerable store of religious poetry. This is indicated by the Ras Shamra tablets, and implied in the songs of jubilation and cursing sung by the Shechemites in the time of Abimelech (Jdg. ix. 27). It is to this period that we may assign such Israelite poetry as the Song of Moses (Ex. xv) and Deborah's Song (Jdg. v). These were precedents and incentives to later psalmists.

The basis of the Psalter appears to be a collection of Davidic hymns. David was traditionally associated with organized worship (cf. 1 Ch. xv, xvi; Ecclus. xlvii. 8–10) and his exceptional gifts matched his remarkable spiritual experiences. The main group would seem to be Pss. li—lxxii, but there are other Davidic groups, viz. ii—xli (omitting xxxiii), cviii—cx, and cxxxvii—cxlv. These are not all, it may be, attributable to David, but his compositions set the style and formed the nucleus (see introductory notes to Ps. cxxxviii). Presumably there was more than one centre where Hebraic hymns were collected, even as there was more than one 'school of the prophets'. During the centuries in which these groups were conflated some repetitions were accepted. These usually contained Elohistic variants of Yahwehistic hymns, but there were other slight differences (cf. 2 Sa. xxii and Ps. xviii). The chief duplicates are Pss. xiv and liii; xl. 13–17 and lxx.

Soon after the formation of the earlier Davidic groups (note the editorial comment at the end of Ps. lxxii) there came to be associated with them two collections of Levitical Psalms, the Korahite (xlii—xlix), and the Asaphite (l, lxxiii—lxxxiii). Some of these may have originated with the leading precentors of the schools of choristers (cf. 1 Ch. vi. 31 and 39); others received their titles as an indication of style or place of origin. The Asaphic Psalms are more didactic, give greater prominence to the tribes of Joseph, and make more use of the imagery of the shepherd and of direct speech on the part of God. To these combined groups a few anonymous Psalms were added (xxxiii, lxxxiv—lxxxix), also the introductory Ps. i.

The remaining Psalms, xc—cl, are far more liturgical in character and include several groups of hymns which have a strong traditional unity, e.g. the Egyptian Hallel (cxiii—cxviii), the fifteen Songs of Ascents (cxx—cxxxiv), and the final group (cxlv—cl). Others, such as xcv—c (the sabbatical anthems), are obviously related to one another, as are also Pss. xcii—xciv and ciii, civ.

Moses was traditionally associated with Pss. xc and xci, and there is a common historical background for such Psalms as cv, cvi, cvii, cxxxv and cxxxvi. Their emphasis upon the exodus is balanced by deep reverence for the Torah, such as finds an ingenious but devout expression in Ps. cxix. How these groups of Psalms came to be selected, arranged and finally combined in one great collection it is not possible to say. Few of them can be definitely dated: some are by David, some are plainly post-exilic. Many must have been revised and amended through centuries of liturgical use. (Note: some 'Psalms' survive elsewhere in the Old Testament, e.g. Ex. xv. 1–21; Dt. xxxii; Jon. ii; Hab. iii; and even the Balaam oracles in Nu. xxiii and xxiv.)

Another question on which there is much difference of opinion is to what extent the Psalms are in their origin private compositions, and to what extent they were composed for use in public worship. Some Psalms are as intimate and personal as love and death (e.g. xxii, cxxxix), but were later adapted for use in the temple services. An interesting example of this is found at the end of Ps. li (see notes *ad loc.*). But many Psalms were undoubtedly composed for use in corporate worship (e.g. lxvii, cxv), and some of the earliest Hebrew poems were of this character, such as the Songs of Miriam and Deborah (Ex. xv. 20f. and Jdg. v). Psalms, too, in which the pronoun 'I' occurs, may not have been originally individualistic. Hebrew society was knit together in such a way that the individual was capable of identifying himself with his group, and the people as a whole could be regarded as a corporate personality. Hence many Psalms which seem to be personal may be understood as expressions of a community, unified by some general experiences and speaking through some representative person.

II. CLASSIFICATION

These 150 songs of worship may be classified in a variety of ways. There are acrostic poems, Psalms of thanksgiving and lamentation (both individual and national), songs of trust, songs for pilgrims, hymns of penitence, prayers of the falsely accused, historical Psalms, Psalms concerning the king, prophetic Psalms; there are hymns for festivals and chants connected with the order of temple worship.

The traditional Jewish classification is apparent in the division of the Psalter into five books, each ending with a doxology (Pss. i—xli, xlii—lxxii, lxxiii—lxxxix, xc—cvi, cvii—cl). This five-fold scheme was regarded as the counterpart of the five books of Moses, and it may be assumed that each passage of the Pentateuch was read in turn with its corresponding Psalm.

The modern trend is towards a wholly different scheme of classification based upon the argument that the Psalms owe their main features to their use in the services of the temple in Jerusalem. That these were important and elaborate

appears in such passages as 2 Ch. xxix. 27–28, v. 11–14, 1 Ch. xvi. 4–7 and 36–42. The three great festivals of the Jewish year lasted several days and called for an increased use of chants in the sanctuary. This was especially the case with the festivities associated with the feast of tabernacles (cf. Nu. xxix) and some Psalms were almost certainly composed for such occasions (e.g. cxv, cxviii, cxxxiv). Moreover, many Psalms give special prominence to the theme of kingship, partly in celebration of royal enthronements and victories, but primarily to express the supreme sovereignty of Yahweh. This symbolical meaning is very evident in Pss. ii, xxiv, xcv—c and cx.

III. LITURGICAL USE

The close association of the Psalter and the Pentateuch and the continual reading of the Torah led in time to certain Psalms becoming attached to particular days and occasions. Ps. cxlv was used at each of the three annual festivals (it may be the hymn referred to in Mk. xiv. 26); Ps. cxxx, with its tense expectancy and desire for forgiveness, was used on the day of atonement; Ps. cxxxv was a customary Passover hymn. The old pilgrim songs (cxx—cxxxiv) were adopted for the feast of tabernacles and, in the time of Herod's temple, were usually sung by a choir of Levites standing on the fifteen steps which linked the two courts of the temple. Some were traditionally regarded as sabbatical (e.g. xcii—c), and each day of the week had its customary Psalm.

IV. TITLES

The titles affixed to about a hundred Psalms are known to antedate the LXX but are of uncertain value because they are unauthenticated and the Hebrew may signify either 'of' or 'for' or 'belonging to' (i.e. 'akin to'). These titles are of five types: those pointing to a source (e.g. xviii, li—lx, xc); those emphasizing a special purpose (e.g. xxxviii, lx, xcii, c, cii); titles indicating special melodies for the hymn (e.g. ix, xxii, xlv, lvi, lvii, lx, lxxx); titles referring to the kind of musical accompaniment (e.g. iv, v, vi, viii, xlv, liii; see Ps. cl for musical instruments). Finally, there are titles descriptive of the type of Psalm, e.g. Maschil—a wise or instructive Psalm; Michtam—for atonement (?). The meaning of some terms, e.g. Shiggaion, is obscure. The word 'Selah' which occurs in many Psalms (mostly Davidic) probably indicated a change in the accompanying melody, or a musical interval; or, if it be taken as marking a shorter version of the Psalm, it may itself be an abbreviated benediction (cf. the modern use of 'Gloria').

V. INTERPRETATION

The interpretation of the Psalms depends on our knowledge of the state of religious belief and revelation at the time of composition and our own experience of God in Christ. Some passages are often thought to refer to life after death (e.g. xvi. 10, xvii. 15, xlix. 16, lxxiii. 24, 36, cxviii. 17), and in so far as we know the power of Christ's resurrection we are apt to read such statements in the light of that truth. The psalmist knew no such certainty, although he shared with the prophet a partial discernment of greater things than he could express in words. Certainly these passages were not devoid of hope when first uttered, but the quality of that 'assurance' was variable. It was mainly an inference from the author's personal experience of God and his grasp of a divine purpose running through history. He had faith enough to glimpse the promise though it was from afar off. His words may often include a hope for deliverance from an immediate physical death, but we cannot limit his meaning to that.

The predictive element is even stronger in the more general prophetic mood of some Psalms. It is true that each prediction has to await the fulfilment before it can be fully perceived, but it exists in some form from its first expression. For example, Ps. xvi. 8–11 is interpreted in Acts ii. 25–32, and Ps. ii is understood in Acts iv. 26 and Heb. i. 5 and v. 5, in ways which clarify and fill out what could at the most have been only partial and in outline to the mind of the psalmist. Indeed the origin of the idea to him may bear only a secondary relationship to its ultimate interpretation. The revelation of God in Christ is the central point of world history (cf. Heb. ix. 26; Rom. viii. 19–22). It is not surprising, therefore, that, as the centuries ran out, such eternal truth should cause in godly men an increasing 'premonition' of imminent and related events. The Lord had chosen Israel for a certain purpose. From the divine viewpoint the attainment of that objective was already accomplished (cf. 1 Pet. i. 20; Eph. i. 10) and the stream of human experience, under God, included facilities for its disclosure. For a study of the various aspects of the messianic hope and the significance of the references in the Psalms, see Hebert, *The Throne of David* (pp. 39–69) and Manley, *The New Bible Handbook* (pp. 197, 265–275).

There remains the difficulty of reconciling divine goodness and mercy with some of the maledictions found in the Psalter (cf. Jas. iii. 9–11). Four points may be noted.

1. These imprecations are not in the spirit of the gospel, and yet there are stern words also in the New Testament (e.g. Mt. xiii. 50, xxiii. 13–33, xxv. 46; Lk. xviii. 7, 8, xix. 27; Acts xiii. 8–11; 2 Thes. i. 6–9; Rev. vi. 10, xviii. 4–6). The New Testament condemns human retaliation but plainly teaches that all reap the consequences of their choices (e.g. Mt. vii. 22, 23; 2 Cor. v. 10).

2. The psalmist may not have meant his bitter words to be predictive but in the wide providence of God they may become true (e.g. Acts i. 20 quotes Pss. lxix and cix; Rom. xi. 9, 10 quotes Ps. lxix). Moreover, it is not always grammatically possible to distinguish between the meanings 'Let this happen . . .' and 'This will happen . . .'

3. The psalmists lived under the law which taught the doctrine of retribution (cf. Lv. xxiv. 19; Pr. xvii. 13). Their imprecations are prayers that the righteous God may do as He has spoken. It is probable in some cases at least that the maledictions are quotations by the psalmist of what his enemies had (falsely) said about him (see notes on Ps. cix).

4. We have no authority to read back into the Psalter's imprecatory words any personal spite and cruelty. Good men desire the punishment of wrong: if we show sympathy toward those who, in the wisdom of God, are allowed to become fully that which they have chosen to be (against God), then we would be sharing their sin and godlessness.

In conclusion, let it be said once more that the inner life is always greater than its expression. We must regard the Psalter in much the same way as we do a cathedral; not merely as an aggregate of architectural styles and decorative schemes, bound by the course of history into one unit, but as a place whose purpose is to be an aid to the worship of our God. However interesting the architectural or literary elements may be, both would lose the essential cause of their existence if the spiritual significance and function is ignored or decried.

COMMENTARY

BOOK ONE. PSALMS i–xli.

PSALM I. LIFE'S ALTERNATIVES

This Psalm was probably composed as an Introduction to the Psalter. It crystallizes the belief which is so frequently elaborated in the following collection of poems, as also in the book of Proverbs (e.g. ii. 12, 20, iv. 14, 18) and in many sayings of Christ (e.g. Mt. vii. 13, 14, 24–27), that men consist of two types or classes—the godly and the ungodly. The behaviour of any man must therefore follow one of two directions and approximate to one of two patterns. Their difference in form and value is expressed in the pictures of the tree and the chaff: their divergence of character and destiny is stated in terms of ceaseless edification or complete ruin. It is partly for this reason that the second Psalm is often associated with the first, both being regarded as introductory because both deal with a basic motif in the Psalter, the behaviour and destiny of good and evil men. Ps. i presents the theme as an individual matter; Ps. ii deals with it as a national issue.

In this poem, the way of the godly man is dealt with first by an account of progressive distinction from the ungodly: he *walketh not* in their counsel, i.e. does not adopt their principles; nor *standeth* in their way, i.e. does not practise their wrongdoing; nor *sitteth* in their seat, i.e. does not of set purpose choose them as his associates. In its positive aspects the good life is characterized by concentration upon the *law* (2; Heb. *Torah*; see Dt. i. 5n.), denoting here the revealed will of God. The quality of this life is like that of a tree growing beside a perennial watercourse, duly bearing fruit because of that hidden sustenance, even when hot winds shrivel all else (cf. Je. xvii. 8).

That life which has no root, and which has not absorbed strength from the resources of God, is but chaff so light and worthless that the wind of the Spirit just hurries it hence. *Shall not stand* (5). Contrast this with the 'nor standeth' of verse 1. *The Lord knoweth* (6); i.e. takes interest in and watches over the righteous.

PSALM II. PLOT AND COUNTERPLOT

This is generally regarded as a messianic Psalm, but it was almost certainly based upon a historical occasion such as that recorded in 2 Sa. v. 17 or in 2 Sa. x. 6ff. A similar situation is commemorated in Ps. lxxxiii. 5–8, but the distinction of Ps. ii lies in its discernment of the cosmic crisis behind a national event.

The poem represents the whole world organized against the Lord in deliberate opposition to His rule. This suggests a fundamental difference between the outlook of earth and heaven; hence the contrast between the agitation and futility of rebellious peoples and the equanimity and immutable purposes of God.

a. The worldly conference (1–3)

The question in verse 1 is rhetorical not analytical; for any revolt against God is regarded as baseless. The *rage* of the nations is not the fury of concerted wrath but the uproar of noisy contention among people who *imagine a vain thing*, i.e. plot and scheme ineffectively. For *heathen* read 'nations' and for *people* 'peoples' as in RV. Historically the object of their attack was the anointed of the Lord, viz. David (cf. 1 Sa. xxiv. 6); essentially it was God Himself; prophetically it was the Messiah (cf. Acts iv. 25–27).

b. The heavenly confidence (4–6)

The situation can be truly assessed only by discerning the mind of God, who sits enthroned in heaven and views the whole tumult of insurrection with the utter confidence of truth's limitless power (cf. 2 Cor. xiii. 8). *Then* (5) has peculiar force: it signifies the termination of the age of man's apparent freedom and the establishment in the earth of the divine purpose. So sure is this appointed climax that God can afford to allow centuries to the rebellious nations so that all their plans may mature, all objections be utilized

and all resistance attempted (cf. Ezk. xxxiii. 11). Then, in the fulness of time, He intervenes with *wrath* (lit. 'blowing nostril') and *sore displeasure* (lit. 'burning anger') and utters His emphatic word (cf. Rom. i. 18; 2 Thes. ii. 8–13), *Yet have I set my king upon my holy hill* (6; cf. Heb. i. 2, 3). David's argument against his opponents was that God had appointed him to the throne; hence, any resistance to him meant disputing with God. Cf. Ps. iv. 3.

c. His royal authority (7–9)

It is imagined that the rebellious nations, gathered in tumultuous revolt upon the earth, have been momentarily quelled by the divine declaration which echoes from heaven. In the silence which is supposed to follow, David himself addresses the assembled kings and peoples. First of all he asserts his kingship to be authorized by the Lord on the grounds of relationship (7), endowment (8), and vocation, i.e. the power to overcome (9).

The phrase *Thou art my Son* (7) can be paralleled in Ps. lxxxix. 26, 27, and the words *this day have I begotten thee* may be understood historically as referring to the day of David's enthronement. But the New Testament interprets the saying as fulfilled only in Jesus Christ. Acts xiii. 33 and Rom. i. 4 declare that He was acclaimed 'Son' by the very fact of the resurrection. Heb. i. 5 and v. 5 quote the phrase as associated with the incarnation and priesthood of Christ. Some MSS, including Codex Bezæ, use it in connection with the baptism of Jesus (Lk. iii. 22). Similarly the promised gift of the peoples and realms of this world came to be a messianic expectation and has long been understood of Christ. Rev. ii. 27 quotes verse 9 in connection with 'the end', i.e. the coming of Christ in glory and power. Cf. also Rev. xix. 15.

d. Their reasonable action (10–12)

In the second part of David's address he reverts to the reality of the situation described in verses 1–3. That peril has not passed; the crisis is not yet resolved; the elasticity of the divine *Then* (5) has not yet snapped; the issue may still be moulded by men. Hence the appeal to the kings and rulers of the earth. *Be wise . . . serve the Lord . . . kiss* (i.e. pay homage to) *the Son*, for otherwise there can be no possible escape from disaster.

The Psalm does not describe the actual outcome, for it is an epitome of the whole of history, with time's strange power of renewable crisis.

PSALM III. PRAYER CHANGES THINGS

Pss. iii, iv and v are related as being prayers of the morning and evening. The title of this Psalm indicates that it was written when David fled from the usurping Absalom. The king's distress of heart (1) arose from the surprising magnitude of the rebellion (cf. 2 Sa. xv. 13) and also from the prevalent feeling among the people that David would no longer continue to receive help from God (2), so desperate did his position appear. The rest of the Psalm is distinguished from the preceding summary of the situation by the word *Selah*, which always appears to indicate a change in mood, a pause in the chant, or an alteration in the musical accompaniment. This word was inserted some time after the poem was composed in order to adapt it for use in the services of the temple. Verses 3–8, which express David's reaction to the overwhelming turn of events, are a sublime expression of unquenchable trust in God.

The poem can be regarded as falling into three parts.

a. Despondency at nightfall (1–4)

The sombre developments of the day (1–2) are summed up in an evening prayer and left with the Lord in confidence that He has heard and heeded. *Thou, O Lord, art a shield* (3). Cf. God's promise to Abraham (Gn. xv. 1). David's trust toward God is based upon His former faithfulness even though that has been associated with *his holy hill* (4), from which David is now driven out (cf. Ps. ii. 6). It was this knowledge of the Lord which enabled him to sleep.

b. Vigorous faith at morning (5, 6)

The Lord sustained me (5). The freshness of body and serenity of faith with which the writer awoke the next morning were due to an implicit assurance of divine mercy and preservation. This not only rid ominous circumstances of any power to intimidate but initiated a claim to actual triumph over them: i.e., as in the previous section, an account of personal feelings is followed by a prayer to the Lord. Contrast 2 Sa. xv. 30.

c. A call to God (7, 8)

This is prompted by the still existing peril but is worded as though the petition was already granted (cf. Mk. xi. 24). It concludes with an affirmation of divine sovereignty in the matter of salvation which evokes a final and intercessory benediction (see RV). This benediction is to be set over against the disappointment felt for the people in verses 1, 2.

PSALM IV. AN EVENING PRAYER

Verse 8 shows that this is an evening prayer, probably an expansion of the fourth verse in the previous psalm. It was later set to music for liturgical purposes: *Neginoth* in the title means 'accompanied by stringed instruments'.

a. The invocation (1)

Thou hast enlarged me (RV 'set me at large') *when I was in distress* implies that deliverance from an immediate peril has been granted. The narrow and restricted path of ii. 2 has broadened into a wide place. Nevertheless, all is not well. The peril is less obvious and personal than in Ps. iii; it has become a spiritual and communal danger, the nature of which is outlined in verses 2–6a.

Have mercy upon me. Lit. 'show favour'. Note AV and RV mg.

b. The rebuke to men (2, 3)

While David waits in prayer before God he makes a meditative appeal to the leaders of the people (*ye sons of men*) whom he imagines to be gathered before him. In the turmoil that followed the rebels' initial failure to organize promptly the capture of the fleeing king, through Absalom's mistake in not following Ahithophel's advice (see 2 Sa. xvii. 1ff.), there was opportunity for many to have second thoughts about supporting Absalom. David metaphorically appeals to them, charging them with dishonouring the royal dignity he has received from God and reminding them that such antagonism to God is utterly vain (cf. Ps. ii. 1) and a seeking after falsehood (2, RV). Let them consider afresh that he who loves God and whom the Lord chooses is guarded by Him (3a) and will be heard by Him in any emergency (3b).

c. The command to men (4, 5)

This is more direct and positive than the foregoing charge. Although these men may despise the king and rebel against him, let them consider that God is involved, let them tremble before the Lord and *sin not*, i.e. be kept from sinning against Him: let each heed his conscience and in the quiet reflective hours of the night decide to *be still*, i.e. to cease from further opposition to God's chosen king. *Stand in awe.* The LXX renders 'Be ye angry'. Cf. Eph. iv. 26. After a suitable pause (*Selah*) during which verse 3 may again be appreciated, David, in a spirit of royal graciousness, urges the rebel leaders to bring penitent and sacrificial offerings unto God, and to swear their loyalty to Him. *Sacrifices of righteousness.* Cf. Ps. li. 17, 19; Pr. xv. 8.

d. His prayer and praise (6–8)

In verse 6 David reconsiders that strange paralysis of communal godliness which had appalled him in Ps. iii. 2. It was a mark of that popular discontent which had been aggravated by Absalom's promises. David pleads with the Lord to fulfil upon the nation that age-old benediction of the Aaronic priesthood (Nu. vi. 26); he also confesses joyfully that in his own case a desperate plight had been transformed by an inward sense of divine grace, which far surpassed the material blessings of food brought by the aged Barzillai (cf. 2 Sa. xvii. 27–30). *Only* (8). The Hebrew word may mean either that God alone gives him protection or that God makes him to dwell in safety when alone (cf. RV mg.). Both meanings are applicable in this instance.

PSALM V. A MORNING PRAYER

This is a companion to the previous Psalm: the circumstances are similar but verse 3 marks it as a morning prayer.

a. The invocation (1–3)

The urgent and intense character of the poem is indicated by the first verse. The titles of *my King* and *my God* (2) imply a relationship between David and the Lord which enables him to claim the aid of supreme power and righteousness. *In the morning* (3). As the first act of the day he will *direct* (RV 'order') his prayer unto the Lord, and will then 'keep watch' (RV) in expectation of the Lord's response.

b. God's way with the wicked (4–8)

Meanwhile the psalmist meditates upon the character of God which is so unlike that of the men who oppose him, and is so highly esteemed in his own heart. In the sight of God the activities of wicked men are futile; in His presence the *foolish* (5; RV 'arrogant') or 'boastful' will be put down. All evil works and false words which God hates and abhors will be destroyed.

The speaker then emphasizes in two respects his own distinction from cruel, false and evil men. In reverential awe (*in thy fear*, 7) he worships in God's house (cf. Ps. xxvii. 4). He also petitions God to guide him. Not only does he need to know the right; he needs to have removed all those obstacles which would hinder him from walking in God's way. *Make thy way straight* (8); i.e. 'make thy pathway unimpeded' (cf. Is. xl. 4).

c. God's way with the righteous (9–12)

This part of the Psalm deals with the same elements as the previous section, i.e. the wicked and the godly, but the orientation and emphasis are quite different. Verses 4–6 consider the wicked as in the sight of God; verses 9, 10 describe them as they are in life. Verses 7, 8 form a humble confession of trust in God; verses 11, 12 speak of jubilant confidence in God's blessing. The prayer has become more precise and faith has become much more assured. *Their throat is an open sepulchre* (9); i.e. what they say will eventually bring about their destruction. This principle of sin bringing its own inevitable wages or results is frequently expressed in the Psalter. Cf. Ps. xxviii. 4 and see Gal. vi. 7, 8.

PSALM VI. A PRAYER OF ANGUISH

The first part of the title (cf. Ps. iv) refers to the leader of the stringed instruments: the other phrase *upon Sheminith*, meaning 'the eighth' (cf. 1 Ch. xv. 21, RV), probably refers to a setting which was an octave lower than usual. Moffatt translates 'harps set for bass voices'.

Anxiety and distress have reduced David to the paralysis of self-despair in which his only remedy is an implicit trust in the mercy of God. The period may have been coincident with 2 Sa. xv. 1–6. The poem divides into four parts.

a. The setting (1–3)

The repetition and parallelism of verse 1 creates a sense of tension and distress. Firstly, there is conflict between the ideal and the actual. The accentuation upon the *anger* of God's rebuke and the *hot displeasure* of His chastening implies a tension in David's mind arising from ignorance of the cause of such divine wrath.

Secondly, David's suffering is both psychological (*for I am weak*, RV 'withered away') and physical (*my bones are vexed*); i.e. his life is shrivelling up through the aridity and bleakness of his circumstances and also because of the apparent non-intervention of God. These give point to the taunts of his enemies and bring the uncertain shadows of doubt to his own mind. Nevertheless, he believes God can heal his disordered body which is tormented by sickness.

Thirdly, his anguish of *soul* (3) is greater than anything else. He is caught between the intensity of his trouble and the uncertainty of its cause and duration. *O Lord, how long?* (3). This is not a petulant questioning of God's ways but a poignant expression of his heartfelt agony. Cf. Jb. vii. 3–6, xvi. 9–16.

b. The petition (4, 5)

The basis of his pleading with God is now shifted from personal experience and human need to non-temporal issues and the divine character. *Return* (4) may have the meaning of 'repeat'; i.e. deliver me as Thou hast done in previous emergencies (of which verse 8 may be an echo). *For thy mercies' sake* (4). The appeal for salvation is grounded upon the essentially compassionate character of God. Cf. Ex. xxxiv. 6.

Verse 5 introduces a reason to strengthen the plea for salvation. If David lived, he would remember God in thanksgiving. But *in the grave* (RV 'Sheol', the place of the dead) he could not do this. Cf. xxx. 9, lxxxviii. 10; Is. xxxviii. 18. This use of a plea based upon what must lie outside earthly existence is the counterpart of the initial plea (1) based upon the belief that spiritual judgment was expressed in terms of personal welfare or distress. Both were mistaken assumptions, but they in no wise invalidated the fundamental appeal to God's mercy.

c. The distressing circumstances (6, 7)

There is a modified reversion here to the mood of the opening verses. The daily lamentation is expressed in the imagery of ceaseless tears and hollow-eyed weariness. On the one hand there is his own pain (6), and on the other are vexatious thoughts about those who hate him (7). These deprive him of sleep and make him to look prematurely old.

d. The vision of faith (8–10)

These verses are best interpreted as an anticipated experience of what is most desired. It may be coloured by memories of former occasions, but this is primarily an intuitive sense of a fulfilment which is yet in the future. Verse 10 (see RV) is a more sober but equally confident expectation of that fulfilment; his opponents will be disgraced by the obvious contradiction of their expectations. In place of his own vexation

417

o

of soul (3) they will be *sore vexed*. The inter-vention of God in response to his pleas (2–5) will invert all their values and utterly and un-expectedly throw them into confusion (cf. Pss. xxxv. 4–8, lxxxiii. 13–17; note such New Testa-ment passages as 2 Thes. ii. 4–10; 2 Pet. iii. 3–10).

PSALM VII. AN APPEAL FOR JUDGMENT

This is another prayer for divine protection against ruthlessness and calumny. *Cush* (see title) is not named in the chronicles of the time. The Talmud identifies him with Saul; he may have been one of Saul's fanatical fellow-tribesmen, like Shimei (2 Sa. xvi. 5). It is generally assumed that the poem belongs to the period of Saul's persecution of David. See *Introduction* to Ps. lii.

a. An appeal to God (1–10)

In the face of immediate danger David resorts to God. The situation is one of flight from cruel enemies, of which one is particularly to be feared because his malevolence is as irrational as the behaviour of an angry lion. Verses 3–5 reveal a conviction of personal innocence almost as vehement as that of Job when he closed the debate with his friends (Jb. xxxi). Evidently those who sought David's life accused him also of dishonour, i.e. of attempting to seek vengeance on the anointed Saul. The words of verse 4b recall the incident of 1 Sa. xxiv. 1–12.

Verses 6–7 are, in effect, a challenge to God's justice. Notice the RV rendering at the end of verse 6, as if David had suddenly become assured that his prayer was answered, and pleads for the judgment to begin. The appeal to divine judg-ment is necessarily absolute and final, and the psalmist links his own vindication with a vision of the trial of all humanity before the high court of heaven (cf. Is. xliii. 9). The last clause of verse 7 may be best taken as an appeal to God to return to His throne of judgment. Cf. ix. 11. In verse 8 follow RV. It is as though the court of heaven were already constituted and the uni-versal trial begun. The psalmist first appeals to God for a favourable judgment upon himself on the grounds of his own integrity (8b; Job's per-sistent attitude). He then asks for a true judg-ment on the wicked, i.e. those who seek his destruction, on the ground that, in such an ultimate and true assessment of life, all evil doing must be disclosed as engendering its own con-demnation. Verse 9a might be translated 'let the wickedness of the wicked be disclosed in its true calamity'. Confident that God assesses the inmost nature of man, the psalmist reiterates his own innocence and his unperturbed trust in such an exercise of divine power as would eliminate evil and establish righteousness. Cf. Ps. xxvi. 1–7 and contrast Rom. iii. 4; 1 Cor. iv. 4.

b. The divine judgment (11–17)

God judges the righteous (11). Better as in RV, 'God is a righteous judge, yea, a God that hath indignation every day.' The emphasis here is on the reality of God's continuous reaction to man's misdeeds (so correcting any inference of human impatience in 6–7). This reaction is depicted in the imagery of irresistible aggression—the sharpened sword, taut bow, deadly weapons and fiery darts—encountered by the sinner who obstinately advances to his doom because he will not turn (12) to the central fact of God's grace and mercy. The whole career of wicked-ness is then described in its beginning, its action, and its end (14–16; cf. Jas. i. 15). The evil man of his own nature gives birth to falsity and error (14); his work fails in its design and becomes a snare to himself (15; cf. Ps. ix. 16); his plans and methods ultimately cause his ruin (16; cf. 1 Sa. xxv. 39; also Mt. xxi. 33–41, xxv. 24–28).

All these thoughts evoke in the psalmist a profound conviction of God's worthiness of praise, not only for His innate righteousness but because of His sure response to this appeal for judgment, whose name is Yahweh most high (17).

PSALM VIII. MANKIND, A PARADOX

Unlike the supplicatory Psalms which im-mediately precede and follow, this poem is meditative and philosophical, and has the lyrical fragrance of David's earlier years. *Upon Gittith* (see title) may mean a tune associated with work in the winepress, or it may refer to an instru-ment or melody from Gath (cf. RV).

The first and last phrases are identical and form a frame for profound ideas concerning God's essential being and His works on earth.

a. The universal majesty of God (1, 2)

O Lord our Lord (1). Lit. 'O Yahweh, our Lord.' David speaks on behalf of the people of Yahweh, but also on behalf of all mankind. The excel-lency, or majesty, of His *name* (i.e. His wondrous nature) is expressed in and through His works *in all the earth. Above the heavens*. Better as in RV, 'upon the heavens', suggesting that the bril-liance and stability of the universe set forth God's power and splendour. The glory of God is also revealed to men even in such antithetical aspects as infancy and corrective judgment (cf. Mt. xxi. 16). *Ordained strength* (2); i.e. 'estab-lished strength'. *Avenger;* i.e. one who seeks to avenge himself, vindictive.

Moreover, the glory of God is disclosed in the phenomena of justice. When men seek of them-selves to rectify the wrong actions of their fellow-men because they doubt God's existence or deny His righteous concern, they are themselves testi-fying to the existence of justice, which, like language, is an evidence of God's glorious being (cf. Na. i. 2, 3).

b. The inscrutable ways of God (3–8)

A sense of paradox is being developed in the Psalm, and this is now elaborated with respect to man's existence. Meditation upon the varied work of creation in the skies (cf. Jb. xxxvi. 22—xxxvii. 12) and in the heavenly bodies (cf. Ps. xix. 1–6; Jb. ix. 7–10, xxxviii. 31–33) brings a conviction of man's frailty and insignificance. *Man . . . son of man* (4). The Hebrew words denote man's lowly origin and human frailty. *Visitest* (4); i.e. 'graciously seekest'. Why should God remember any man and, indeed, never leave him alone (cf. Ps. cxliv. 3; also xxxiii. 13–19 and Ex. iii. 15–16)? Reason and observation can offer no answer to this question. It can be met only by divine revelation, one which discloses a concept of man that seems wholly incompatible with man's own inferences. Cf. Jb. vii. 17. We know that what was revealed to the psalmist was authenticated in Christ.

Meditation upon the essential purpose of creation as revealed of old discloses a threefold peculiarity which lifts man from the negligible to a position of amazing eminence. He has been created by God as 'but little lower than God' Himself (5, RV). The Hebrew is *'elohim*. This image of God imparted to man is accompanied by certain attributes, *glory and honour*, which mark out man as superior to all other creatures. Moreover, the world and its forms of life have been placed under man's authority.

This consciousness of a high calling and destiny evokes in the psalmist the ultimate and exuberant praise of verse 9.

It must be noted that the New Testament amplifies this Psalm and also interprets it Christologically. Heb. ii. 5–9 first quotes the LXX version (where *'elohim* is translated *angelous*) and then bases its argument upon a full and literal exegesis of verse 6b. The statement *Thou hast put all things under his feet* is taken to be a prophetical allusion to Jesus. In a similar way 1 Cor. xv. 27 also interprets this same verse of Christ.

PSALM IX. THE BASIS OF PRAISE

The word *Muth-labben* in the title is usually translated 'death of the son', but this is incongruous with the note of praise in the song. It may have been the title of a chant, but a slight variation in the Hebrew would alter the meaning to 'death of the champion'. If, as Dr. Thirtle has suggested, the musical part of the Psalm titles belonged originally to the end of the preceding Psalm (as in Hab. iii. 19) then the musical title of Ps. ix belongs to Ps. viii, which might then be regarded as celebrating the death of the champion Goliath, slain by one whom he would despise as 'a babe and suckling' (Ps. viii. 2; cf. 1 Sa. xvii. 33, 42).

The Psalm has an imperfect acrostic structure and is the first of nine alphabetical poems in the Psalter. There are three main parts, and each sub-division expands the final thought in the previous section.

a. Personal exultation in God (1–10)

This is stated in verses 1–2 as being deep-rooted and called forth by an amazing intervention by

God. *Thy marvellous works*. Cf. Ps. xcviii. 1, cv. 5.

The historic cause of his elation and thanksgiving is, first, victory in battle (3, 4), whereby God has vindicated David's kingship. Truth and righteousness have been demonstrated as being with David's cause. Secondly, he rejoices in the destruction of his enemies (5, 6), who have ceased to exist as dangerous foes. *Destructions are come to a perpetual end* (6). Read as in RV. Cf. the end of the Amalekites (see notes on Nu. xxiv. 20).

The religious cause of his joy and praise is, first, the perpetuity of God's righteous rule (7, 8); the themes of God's inexhaustible being and essential justice are used to bind together the spheres of His celestial enthronement in power and His terrestrial administration of ceaseless vigilance. *People* (8); better 'peoples' as in RV. Secondly, he praises God for the infallibility of His gracious care (9, 10); all men who acknowledge and obey the Lord (*they that know thy name*) can fully rely upon His protective care even when they are harassed and oppressed.

b. Corporate exultation in God (11–16)

The historical basis of the psalmist's praise is particularly his own, but the religious basis can know no such restrictions, hence all men everywhere ('peoples', RV mg.) are called upon to praise God (11, 12; cf. Ps. xcvi. 3, 7–10). Such corporate recognition of God's sovereignty could not be evoked in the same way as the psalmist's, but it could be induced by the realization among men that the eye of God is inescapable (cf. Ps. xxxiii. 13–15). All bloodshed caused by human motives is repugnant to God (Gn. ix. 5; cf. Lk. xi. 50, 51; Rev. vi. 10) and His intervention is to be expected.

Verses 13 and 14 are a typical *cry of the humble* (12) to which God hearkens and upon which He acts. Peril has thrust him to *the gates of death*, i.e. to the very edge of life (cf. Ps. cvii. 18, 19); but his hope in God is that he will come again to the gates of Jerusalem where he will testify to divine deliverance. Verses 15 and 16 are a statement of the psalmist's own faith, the comment of a godly man upon disaster to the wicked, whether actual or anticipated, usually assumed to be the operation of 'natural retribution' (cf. Ps. vii. 15, 16). This is an aspect of divine irony wherein God's essential righteousness is inexorably displayed (cf. Gal. vi. 7, 8; 2 Cor. v. 10).

This is so solemn a thought that a pause is indicated (*Selah*) during which music of a meditative kind would be played such as *Higgaion*. This word is translated in Ps. xcii. 3 as 'with a solemn sound'.

c. Sober reflections (17–20)

Those men who wickedly ignore God or rebel against the principles of godliness must surely die. *Shall be turned into hell* (17); i.e. Sheol, the place of the dead. See RV and cf. Gn. iii. 19b. On the other hand *the needy* and *the poor* (18) are just as surely the objects of God's special care. Contrast verses 5b and 6. The frequent reference in the Psalter to 'poor and needy' does not necessarily imply material destitution; the phrase is applied to all who have been reduced to utter dependence upon God (cf. Mt. v. 3).

As though to compensate for the activity of evil-doers, there is always the possibility of the intervention of God. The confident trust in the Lord which marked the opening verse is now focused in a petition (19, 20) that He should assert His power, judge the peoples of the earth (cf. Ps. vii. 6–9), and so awe the arrogant by a demonstration of His majesty that every man shall have to confess his own human weakness and ephemeral nature (cf. Jas. iv. 14). *Man* (19). Heb. *enosh*; see Ps. viii. 4n. *Fear* (20). Used here in the sense of 'terror', as in Dt. xxvi. 8, xxxiv. 12.

PSALM X. THE URGENCY OF PETITION

Some Hebrew MSS as well as the LXX show this Psalm simply as a continuation of the ninth. In support of this there is a resumption of the alphabetical structure from verse 12 onwards, also the first eleven verses are an expansion of the concluding prayer of Ps. ix, so that there is a certain similarity of theme, viz. utter reliance upon God for deliverance from the pressure of evil men. Nevertheless, the differences between the two Psalms are such as to justify the traditional view that it is a separate and later composition, though written to correspond with the other. (Note such corresponding phrases as ix. 9a and x. 18, ix. 9b and x. 1b, ix. 12b and x. 12b, ix. 19a and x. 12a.) There are two main parts to the poem.

a. Why is God silent when wickedness abounds? (1–11)

Evil men and their deeds could never prosper if divine righteousness immediately checked their wickedness. But, on the other hand, wickedness could never bring its own condemnation unless wrongdoing found some expression. The psalmist's perplexity (1, 2) has arisen because God continues to seem indifferent long after injustice among His people has become flagrant, frequent and full-grown (cf. such Psalms as xxii, xxxv, xxxvii, xxxviii, lxxiii). *Let them be taken* (2). Follow RV mg. This phrase is best regarded as a case of inverted parallelism of thought. It is not the wicked that are 'taken', but the 'poor'.

Verses 3–11 give a detailed description of the ways of the wicked. They are characterized, first of all, by self-sufficiency based on worldly success. *The wicked boasteth* (3); i.e. sings praise to himself, thus making his own desire into his God (cf. Hab. i. 15, 16). The words which follow are difficult. See RV. RSV translates 'the man greedy for gain curses and renounces the Lord'. In verse 4 follow RV and note Ps. xiv. 1 and Jb. xxi. 14, 15. It is not that evil man denies the existence of God (atheism was virtually unknown among Jews at this time), but he ridicules

the notion that God is concerned how men behave (5, 6). The absence of immediate punishment upon wrongdoers is always a strong argument for a sinner whose values are located wholly within this world, so that even death has little menace for him (see Job's vehemence about this in Jb. xxi. 17). There is also an inner falsity which springs from his evil desires. Guiltiness is added to blindness, and this is incurred first through speech (7) and then in secret deeds against the innocent and helpless (8). These cruel practices are described again in verse 9, the deceitfulness is restated in verse 10, and the primary falsity of his speech is again expressed in verse 11.

b. An appeal to God to intervene (12–18)

Apart from verse 1 the theme of the first part of the Psalm has been the 'wicked', to whom there were a score of references; in the second part the theme is *The Lord is King* (16) and He is mentioned a dozen times. The direction of thought is changed from details of wicked practices to characteristics of God's rule. These are wholly at variance with the notions of evil men whose inward assurance about God's indifference is altogether untrue. The afflictions of His people are not only observed but become occasions of divine action (14). The Psalm thus becomes an appeal to God that He would intervene and eliminate wickedness (15). Moreover, because God is the eternal King, the establishment of truth and the restoration of burdened hearts is so sure as to be already virtually accomplished (17, 18). The incidence of divine judgment in human affairs was considered quite secondary to its inevitability; it was this latter conviction which impelled the psalmist to ask God to hasten His actions (12). This conclusion is parallel to that of the preceding Psalm, but the prayer in verses 17 and 18 is marked by serenity and trust, whereas ix. 19, 20 expresses vehemence and restlessness. *Man of the earth* (18). RV 'man which is of the earth'. See Gn. iii. 19. A reference to man's human frailty and final decay.

PSALM XI. A SONG OF STEADFASTNESS

The theme of serene Godward trust even in face of peril is the same as characterized Ps. vii and is a frequent topic in the Psalter (see, e.g., xxiii, xxvii, xxxiv). This poem reflects David's attitude at the time when friends advised him to flee from the brooding envy of Saul even before the third and most serious attempt on his life (see 1 Sa. xviii. 11, xix. 10). The body of the Psalm, i.e. verses 1b–6, sets out two differing points of view; the psalmist's conclusion is given in verse 7 and his personal affirmation of faith prefixed to the whole (1a).

a. The warning by prudence (1–3)

The advice *Flee as a bird . . . what can the righteous do?* may have been given to David by friends, or it may represent the voice of expediency in David's own heart. The warning was heeded eventually and David, with a few friends, took refuge in the remote places of the hills. Verse 2 is based upon the actual attempt to kill David by javelin, but the phrase *bend the bow* is often used with reference to a hostile attack by deed or word (cf. Pss. vii. 12, xxxvii. 14; Je. ix. 3). *Privily* (2); read 'in darkness' as in RV. In verse 3 the argument is strengthened by an appeal to general considerations: 'Wherever the foundations of society are undermined through kings and counsellors ignoring honour and justice, what have good and righteous men ever done to prevent its collapse?' (see RV mg.). Is David presuming to do what other great men have not achieved?

b. The watching by God (4–7)

Over against the danger of current events and the apparent ineffectiveness of innocency (2c) and goodness (3b) there is the supreme and vigilant holiness of God. He whose habitation is heaven, and whose authority is enthroned over all, is nevertheless ceaselessly scrutinizing the behaviour of all men (cf. Pss. xxxiii. 13–18, xciv. 9; fully elaborated in Ps. cxxxix) and submitting the godly to various tests (cf. Jas. i. 12). He responds in no uncertain manner to what He sees: to the godly He extends His protective presence; upon the wicked, whose deeds are repugnant to Him, He sends the disasters of natural calamity (cf. Gn. xix. 24; Ps. xviii. 7–14).

Faced with these two differing aspects of life (see a and b above), the psalmist has no hesitation in adopting the latter and committing himself to the ever-watchful Lord who loves those who seek His righteousness. In verse 7 follow RV. In utter contrast to the unsettled days of flight and the uncertainty of life amongst a deceitful court, the heart that steadfastly trusts the Lord shall have, after being tested (5), peace in His presence. Cf. Rev. xxii. 4.

PSALM XII. UNTRUTH VERSUS TRUTH

Although this Psalm belongs to the large group of laments over the success of evil-doers (e.g. Pss. vii, x, xvii, xxv, xxxvii), its theme is more specialized than some. The activity of the wicked is primarily felt by the innocent and godly as being in the realm of speech, i.e. the falsification and perversion of the divine gift of language. Hence the intervention of the Lord must be not only in deeds but in words. The poem sets the effective purity of God's word over against the specious claims of vain lips.

a. The social trend (1, 8)

The first and final verses outline the contemporary corruption of society, with worthless and base men in positions of influence and power, so that wickedness is openly approved and upright men of godly faith are being squeezed out of public life.

b. The specious tongue (2–4)

Communication amongst men is riddled with falsity, flattery, duplicity, and vanity of speech (cf. Jas. iii. 5–10). *The Lord shall cut off* (3). Better, 'May the Lord cut off . . .' The acme of human pride is when men forge language into such a powerful weapon that deceitful propaganda seems invincible (4).

c. The sublime truth (5, 6)

Although the vain and vile may disdain the poor man who cries to God, their contempt is as groundless as their pride. The truth is that God is quite aware of the oppression of the faithful and at the right moment He will intervene to bring them security. *From him that puffeth at him* (5). Read as in RV or RV mg. *As silver tried in a furnace* (6). This imagery of a crucible, from which the fully refined silver is poured down into moulds set in the earth, is an apt illustration of the purity, value, and applicability to worldly needs of the divine word, swiftly revealed and lastingly preserved. Elsewhere in the Old Testament the process of refining is almost always applied to the children of God, who are purged in the furnace of affliction. Cf. Ezk. xxii. 17–22; Mal. iii. 3.

d. The sure trust (7)

The word of God which has been acclaimed so fervently (6) is now appropriated by the trusting heart. Because God is kind (5) and His word true, He can be fully relied upon to safeguard the godly even in the midst of a crooked and perverse generation.

PSALM XIII. DESPONDENCY CHANGED TO CONFIDENCE

Whereas Ps. xii was a lament for the degeneration of society, Ps. xiii is a personal and poignant cry. Its initial mood is one of tedious frustration and strained patience; but the very act of appealing to God stimulates the psalmist's hope so that the final mood is one of joyous appreciation of God's work and purpose in his life. The Psalm falls into three parts.

a. A fourfold appeal (1, 2)

The words *How long . . . for ever?* are a question wherein hope and despair pursue each other in the closed circle of the pressing instant (cf. Pss. lxxiv. 10, lxxix. 5, lxxxix. 46). The four aspects of sorrow are: loneliness, because God is oblivious of him; shame, because God's seeming carelessness induces a sense of his insignificance; despair, because he is left to his own meagre resources in eluding the plans of his enemies; injustice, because his enemies have the upper hand and are elated, whereas he who seeks to live rightly as before the Lord is thrust down and powerless.

b. A fourfold fear (3, 4)

Lighten mine eyes (3); i.e. 'invigorate me' (cf. 1 Sa. xiv. 27). This one positive request is set amid negative expressions. *Consider* (3). The Hebrew word is usually translated 'look' or 'behold'. The direct address 'Look Thou and answer me, O Lord my God' covers the fear that God will not answer unless He is challenged to do so. The psalmist is constrained to cry to God, not only because it is painful to him to seem neglected by God, but also lest death come as inexorably as his next sleep, lest his enemies are finally triumphant over him, and lest they have cause to rejoice in his ultimate removal from human society. These fears are obviously parallel to the four aspects of sorrow in verses 1 and 2.

c. A fourfold assurance (5, 6)

To envisage that from which his soul is utterly averse is to rebound by faith into the experience of satisfaction. The impulsive appeals and sober reflections of verses 1–4 do not represent the fundamental attitude and disposition of his heart. *But I* (5); i.e. 'as for me I do trust in Thee'. *My heart shall rejoice . . . I will sing* (5, 6). His despondency is changed to confidence as his faith lays hold on four characteristics of the Lord: His mercy toward men, His delivering intervention, His readiness to give that which truly delights men, and His abounding goodness to the very man who had been restless. This irrepressible hope, always clarified and crystallized by prayer, is one of the constant features of the Psalter (cf. 1 Cor. xv. 19; Heb. vi. 18–19).

PSALM XIV. OUTLINE OF A CORRUPT SOCIETY

This description of degenerate and unrighteous men primarily refers to humanity as a whole and not merely to a period of extreme moral decay in Israel. This is endorsed by the use of the first three verses in Rom. iii. 10–12. The Psalm was rewritten in later years and reappears as Ps. liii, so the allusion to captivity in verse 7 can hardly refer to the exile. The Hebrew phrase translated *bringeth back the captivity of* (7) may also be rendered 'restoreth the fortunes of'. Cf. Jb. xlii. 10. It could apply to the period of Absalom's power or to a time of great misfortune. The poem adopts alternately the viewpoint of earth and heaven.

a. The iniquity of men (1)

Fool or 'vile person' (Is. xxxii. 5); i.e. a man wholly indifferent to the moral standards of the law, and who daily adopts as his own principle the belief that deity cares nothing about the differences between men's behaviour. Such persons cannot but live a dissolute life and be incapable of 'doing good'.

b. God's inquiry and verdict (2–4)

The question of ultimate standards of moral conduct is ceaselessly raised by the Lord. He is meticulously concerned about men's deeds, and is swift to note any who *understand;* i.e. any man who rejects the falsity of the fool's premiss. The diagnosis of verse 3 cannot be supplied by the godless man, for he has repudiated objective goodness, righteousness and truth. Indeed this is the first characteristic of such men; everyone has *gone aside* from right living and become tainted in his nature (cf. Jb. xv. 16). Hence, without exception, all are workers of evil; *there is none that doeth good* (3). *Have all the workers of iniquity no knowledge?* (4). This may be rendered 'Shall the workers of iniquity not know?'; i.e. these things will not remain hidden from those who pillage God's people as casually as they eat bread. Doubtless the standard example is Ex. v. 10–19.

c. Fear comes upon the wicked (5, 6)

There (5). Either 'in that place where judgment is exercised' (as e.g. at the Red Sea, Ex. xiv. 24, 25), or simply 'see there, how terrified they are'. Yet always God is with the few righteous men and their final preservation is their comfort and hope even when He is concealed from the eyes of fools (see 1a). In actual fact ungodly men may openly ridicule the warning given by the righteous (see RV) and scoff at their *counsel*, i.e. their reliance upon God (contrast 1a): nevertheless God is the secret refuge of the upright (cf. Heb. xi. 7). *Because* (6). Better, as in RV mg., 'but'.

d. A prayer for divine blessing (7)

This last verse may be a later addition to the Psalm to render it suitable for public use by devout worshippers in the temple. It voices the deep yearning of all godly people for the manifestation of the kingdom of God. (Cf. 2 Thes. i. 5–10; Rev. xxii. 20.)

PSALM XV. THE QUALIFICATION FOR FELLOWSHIP WITH GOD

This brief poem succinctly sets out the ideals which the psalmist believed God would expect in His guests. The blameless character thus portrayed is assessed by personal and social conduct only; i.e. the standard is purely ethical. Yet that the man described fears Yahweh is implied in verse 4b. A description in similar terms is found in Ps. xxiv. 3–5 and in Is. xxxiii. 14b–16. (Cf. Lk. i. 6, ii. 25; Acts x. 2, 35; Heb. xii. 14.)

Verses 1 and 5b set the theme of the poem, viz. the godly man's highest aspiration. On the one hand it is to have freedom of access to the presence of God—typified by His *tabernacle* or tent (the traditional emblem of His presence amid the exigencies of life's pilgrimage), and by His *holy hill* or Mount Zion (the historical symbol of His effective purpose amid the vicissitudes of national policies). On the other hand, it is to have enduring security amid the seeming haphazard of circumstances so that, as a righteous man, he *shall never be moved* by the scheming malice of evil-doers.

a. Personal conduct (2, 3)

On the positive side he is blameless in manner of life (cf. Gn. vi. 9, xvii. 1), actively upholding right dealing in all transactions, wholly free from duplicity because his heart is set upon truth. Negatively he is one *that backbiteth not* (3); the Hebrew verb means to go about as a tell-tale; i.e. unkind and discourteous in speech. He is careful to avoid mere gossip (cf. 1 Tim. iv. 2, 7, v. 13), never taking advantage of a fellow-man (3b), careful not to distress his friends by foolish and tactless talk about things they have done and since regretted (3c). *Neighbour.* Two different words are used in the Hebrew text. The RV distinguishes them by translating the first 'friend'.

b. Social conduct (4, 5)

Again the positive traits in the ideal character are first given. In that there are two paths in life, he is careful to estimate people by their moral standards rather than by other factors. He discounts a reprobate fellow for lack of humility before God (cf. Ps. cxxxi. 1) and respects any man who honours the Lord. *Vile person* (4). Better 'reprobate' as in RV. The Hebrew word is derived from a verb meaning 'to reject'. The negative side is next stressed. Should he have undertaken a duty, or sworn a bond, which later proves to be irksome and costly, he does not evade his responsibility, for the spoken word of a vow is a sacred thing (cf. Jos. ix. 19); he neither oppresses others nor complains when business turns against him (cf. Mt. xviii. 27–30), and he will have nothing to do with the corruption of justice by bribes, least of all if the inducement seems to injure an innocent party. *Usury*, i.e. lend on interest, and more particularly, high interest. Cf. Lv. xxv. 36, 37; Pr. xxviii. 8. *Reward* here means 'bribe'. *Shall never be moved* (5); i.e. he will enjoy safety, tranquillity and stability. Contrast Ps. x. 6.

PSALM XVI. THE WAY OF FAITH

The word *Michtam* in the title is of uncertain meaning. Some have connected it with Hebrew *kethem*, meaning 'gold', and take it to signify 'a golden poem'. This would be a very suitable description of Ps. xvi, which is one of the gems of the Psalter, but is less applicable to Pss. lvi–lx, which are also entitled Michtam. The Psalm is ascribed to David (cf. Acts ii. 25, xiii. 35, 36), and contains a number of expressions which would suit well the period of David's life when he was an outlaw. It falls into three divisions.

a. The marks of the believer (1–4)

These are four in number: God is the object of his trust (1); he acknowledges Yahweh as his all-sufficient Lord (2, RV); he takes pleasure in those that fear God (3, RV; cf. 1 Jn. iii. 14); he shuns false objects of worship (4; cf. Jos. xxiii. 7; 1 Jn. v. 21). *Preserve* (1). Better, 'keep'; the Hebrew word is translated 'preserve' nineteen times and 'keep' 284 times. *Trust* (1). Lit. 'take refuge'. *Saints* (3); i.e. 'holy ones', the people of God set apart to be His possession. *The excellent* (3). The true nobility. *Hasten after another god* (4). Better, as in RV, 'exchange (the Lord) for another'. Cf. Je. ii. 11.

b. The present blessings of the believer (5–8)

These are a satisfied heart (5, 6); counsel and correction (7); and security (8). *Inheritance* (5). The AV and RV are misleading here. The literal translation is 'Yahweh is the portion of my share and of my cup'. The mention of 'cup' suggests that the first word refers to a portion of food. The meaning then becomes 'Yahweh is all that I need to satisfy hunger and thirst'. *My lot* (5). My part of the inheritance. *The lines* (6). The portion of land measured out to him by line. Cf. Ps. lxxviii. 55; Am. vii. 17; Zc. ii. 1. In verses 5 and 6 the figures of a banquet and of an allotted inheritance are combined. *My reins* (7). Lit. 'kidneys'; used figuratively of the seat of the emotions and affections and here including the conscience (cf. Ps. lxxiii. 21, 22). *In the night seasons* (7). Cf. iv. 4, xvii. 3. Verse 8 presents a beautiful picture of the psalmist hidden behind God, who stands between him and his foe.

c. The prospects of the believer (9–11)

These are preservation from death (9, RV); the path of life made known to him (10, 11a); joy in God's presence (11b). David is thinking of his future prospects in this world; but his words in the light of the New Testament shine with deeper meaning. The Psalm is quoted by Peter and Paul in referring to Christ (Acts ii. 25–28, xiii. 35). It was perfectly fulfilled in Him, who is the leader of the faith-life (Heb. xii. 2), but it is true also of us who are His followers. *My glory* (9). The LXX renders 'my tongue'; cf. Acts ii. 26. *Rest in hope* (9). Better, as in RV, 'dwell in safety'. Cf. Dt. xxxiii. 12, 28; Je. xxiii. 6. *Thou wilt not leave my soul in hell . . .* (10). Lit. 'abandon my soul to Sheol, neither wilt thou suffer thy beloved one to see the pit'. *Shew* (11); i.e. cause me to know.

PSALM XVII. A RIGHTEOUS MAN'S PRAYER FOR VINDICATION

Three Psalms are entitled 'A Prayer of David' (xvii, lxxxvi and cxlii), but this is the most spontaneous of them. It may well express his fervent cry in the desperate situation at Maon (1 Sa. xxiii. 26), especially as David was very confident of his integrity at that time (1 Sa. xxiv. 11). The intensity and urgency of his prayer is not only conveyed in the general impression of anxiety and dogmatism but also in the three facets of his appeal.

a. His desire to be heard (1–5)

Such words as *hear, attend, give ear, let thine eyes behold* (1, 2) give shape and force both to the shrill *cry* (Heb. *rinna*, a loud cry) from his heart, and to the strong conviction of his own righteousness. These are thrown into greater prominence by an implicit comparison, first with the prayer of *feigned* (i.e. 'deceitful') *lips* (1b), and secondly with the unjust motives of his adversaries which would be unequal to his own when examined by divine justice (2, RV mg.).

The second element in his appeal, viz. his integrity, is more fully stated in verses 3–5. This conviction is supported and asserted first by reference to God's testing of his inmost soul as though by a personal and exhaustive examination, a search which has not disclosed anything false. *Shalt find nothing* (3). Better, as in RV, 'findest nothing'. See also RV mg. and cf. Jb. xxvii. 4–6. Secondly, he declares that in his dealings with men he has always watched and carefully heeded the word of the Lord (cf. cxix. 11), in consequence of which he has never strayed from nor stumbled in the path of honour and rectitude.

b. His prayer for protection (6–12)

The note of passionate appeal is reintroduced in such words as *I have called, thou wilt hear, incline, hear, shew,* and there is again an indirect allusion to his opponents (7c). The new note, as compared with the peremptoriness of verses 1, 2, is that of worship and trust. Note the phrase *thy marvellous lovingkindness* (7) and the concept of God as a refuge for the trusting heart reflected in such words as *thy right hand* (7; cf. Ex. xv. 6). The object of his prayer, i.e. his need of protection from his attackers, is specified more exactly in verses 8–12. First there is his own desire to be tenderly cared for, as though he were immensely precious to God, the centre of His attention (imaged in the pupil of the eye) and the object of His protection (sheltered under outspread wings, symbolical of love). Both the similes are in Dt. xxxii. 10, 11. This desire is quickened in him because he is surrounded by *deadly enemies* (9); i.e. men whose aim is his death.

Then his enemies' character is portrayed in various aspects. *They are inclosed in their own fat* (10). Follow RV mg., 'they have shut up their heart'. In their self-indulgence they are pitiless to others. They utter threats because they are confident of their power. And, because they have surrounded David and his friends, they already see the psalmist's company cast to the ground as captives. One (or each) of the attacking men is like an enraged lion (cf. 1 Pet. v. 8), and the thought of his stealthy power introduces the final phase of the prayer.

c. His plea to be vindicated (13–15)

This abrupt and repeated call to God is the natural reaction to the analogy of a lurking lion ready to spring upon him at any moment. The psalmist calls upon his protector to intervene and to *disappoint* his enemy (13; better, 'confront' as in RV or 'forestall' as in RV mg.), so making him

to cower down. The insistence upon an act of God is shown clearly in the RV: 'Deliver my soul . . . by thy sword; from men, by thy hand, O Lord.' This gives a further opportunity for antithesis to shape the final thoughts. The contrast is now developed with reference to the essential characters of the wicked and the godly.

The psalmist's foes are *men of the world* (14); i.e. men whose sphere of activity and range of thought is wholly in the physical realm (cf. 1 Jn. ii. 15–17). *Whose belly thou fillest with thy hid treasure* (14). As their ideals are wholly in this life, they are amply satisfied with the experience of material prosperity (cf. Phil. iii. 19), and are content to be rich in children to whom a large inheritance can be bequeathed. The godly psalmist is utterly different. His ambition is not to own earthly wealth, but to enjoy unbroken fellowship with God. *I will behold* (15) is to be understood in the sense of 'I yearn to behold' (cf. RV mg.). His supreme desire is to experience or share the *likeness* of God. The primary sense of this is not that of a transformation after death (cf. Phil. iii. 21; 1 Jn. iii. 2), for *when I awake* means either 'when this dark menace is passed and I can stir myself and be free' (cf. Ps. lvii. 8; Eph. v. 14), or 'when I awake each day let me be satisfied', etc. The psalmist craves for a present manifestation of the Lord as vividly real as that given to Moses. Cf. Nu. xii. 8.

PSALM XVIII. DAVID'S VICTORY SONG

This appears to be a version of 2 Sa. xxii slightly revised to make it suitable for general use. The title indicates the circumstances of this jubilant thanksgiving. His deliverance from *all his enemies* (see title) would suggest the period after 2 Sa. viii, when his life was crowned by almost unbroken successes. The words *the servant of the Lord* in the title are not found in the original. The phrase is a highly honourable one and, apart from two references to Joshua, it is almost always applied to Moses, or used prophetically of the Messiah.

a. Introduction (1–3)

The forceful and unusual first word is very striking: *raḥam* means to love very tenderly, and it has a root idea of mercy. God is called a *rock* (2) both by the precedent of Moses (Dt. xxxii. 4, 18, 30, 31, 37) and through David's own experience (1 Sa. xxiii. 25, 28). The seven graphic titles ascribed to God in the second verse are all expressive of impregnability and reflect the dominance of this thought during the years when he was hunted by Saul.

b. Dire peril and divine deliverance (4–19)

His feelings at this time are likened to those of a drowning man swirled round in strong floodwaters or of a wild beast in a net (4, 5). There was none who could help save the Lord, so to Him David cried out in his distress (6). The verb is in the present tense as if the event was still vividly before him. God came to his aid (7–15).

The divine coming is described in the most vigorous and awesome manner; the spiritual fact is translated into a disturbance of nature so profound that it might almost seem as though creation was being undone. The divine advent is seen as associated with smoke and blackness and the voice of words, as when the law was given at Sinai. It is also marked by brilliant radiance and lightning as in the swift illumination of the revelation of grace (cf. Heb. xii. 18–24). Both are the signs of judgment. Note that there is no similitude of God Himself in all this tumult (cf. Dt. iv. 11, 12). Abstract ideas are here expressed in most graphic imagery, a common feature of Scripture. The description of the divine coming is not to be pictorially constructed in the mind. The passage is to be translated back again into its original concepts. The contrast of God as intangible and yet mighty, as inscrutable yet inescapable, lies behind the imagery.

This act of God was intensely personal, and in this account of the psalmist's deliverance the background of the natural world fades away. Even his powerful foes are mentioned only indirectly, for the experience was so intimately his own. Hence the repetition of *He . . . me . . .* and the culminating marvel that the Lord delivered him out of all his troubles *because he delighted in me* (19). There is a suggestive parallel here with the rescue of the child Moses from forces which threatened to crush him. The verb *drew out* (16) is found only here and in Ex. ii. 10. The whole passage has many parallels also with the divine intervention described in the book of Job (cf. Jb. xxxvi. 29—xxxviii. 1).

c. The ground of God's intervention (20–27)

This section is an expansion of the thought that God delights in the psalmist. There are two aspects: David's character and work (20–23) and God's way (24–27). The phenomenal intervention of God on his behalf is claimed to be the reward of his godly living. This protective care is not claimed as of right, but the fact of it is asserted in the simplicity of a heart that feels unembarrassed even in the searching holiness of the court of heaven. David's righteousness is not limited to his relations with Saul; it has been upheld in every phase of his life which he claims to be upright, honourable, merciful, single-hearted and pure. *I kept myself from mine iniquity* (23); i.e. 'I have been so careful to be a man of God that I have not done anything which could be called "mine iniquity", i.e. something which had become, as it were, a part of me' (cf. 1 Ki. xiv. 8; Acts xxiii. 1). The principle underlying this section is that God reinforces the character which men choose to acquire, i.e. behaves toward them as they behave to Him (cf. 1 Sa. ii. 30; Rom. i. 28). *Froward* (26). God is stubborn against those who are stubborn. Cf. Pr. i. 24–33.

d. The high calling of God (28–45)

David's two declarations of personal righteousness, and of the divine principle whereby God deals with men in accordance with their character, are plainly endorsed by the preceding account of his deliverance. That is only one instance; but they can be supported also by the whole course of David's life. The Psalm now deals with these larger aspects of David's life.

The dynamic of David's life is *the Lord my God*, whose indwelling light and vigour both maintain the burning glow of personal existence and give incentive and power whereby difficulties are overcome (28, 29). Cf. 1 Sa. xxx. 8, where the word 'troop' is in Hebrew the same as that used here. *Leaped over a wall* (29). A reference, perhaps, to the incident of 2 Sa. v. 6–10. God is worthy of all honour and adoration, not merely because of the blessings He bestows but because of His essential qualities— absolutely true in all He says and perfect in all He does (30, 31). Therefore He cannot protect those who are antagonistic to Him, but to those who trust Him, He is utterly trustworthy. Beside Him there is none other (cf. Is. xlv. 5, 6). David has been carefully trained by God (32– 36). This preparation has been physical; health, strength and agility have been provided to bring David's way to completion. It has also been instructional—skill in the use of warlike methods and arms had been gained—and moral; the Lord had freely given His own equipment for resistance, His sustenance in danger, and His *gentleness* (35); i.e. His understanding patience or, more literally, meekness during all the long years since He so graciously raised a shepherd lad to a throne of power (cf. Ps. xxiii. 5, 6). David eagerly accepts the purpose of this training (37, 38). In fullest confidence that God has efficiently and adequately prepared him for this task, he undertakes the subjugation of his foes. It is God who worketh in him. The conquest of his foes is really the Lord's doing (39). God had made his enemies 'turn their backs' (40, RV) in retreat; thereupon he cut them off. It was inevitable therefore that any prayer by such rebellious foes would be unheeded by God, consequently David was able to crush their opposition (41, 42).

The climax of his supremacy is now described. Not only had all civil insurrection been put down (cf. 2 Sa. iii. 1), but God had made David the head of many nations (cf. 2 Sa. viii); and even those peoples with whom there had been no previous contact would immediately acknowledge his sovereignty as soon as they heard of him (43). There is some historical support for this in 2 Sa. x. 18, 19, but there is also a prophetical aspect. Cf. Is. lii. 15 and Ps. ii. 8.

e. Conclusion (46–50)

The pre-eminent inference from these reflections is the living reality of God to whom David is inexpressibly grateful. The phrase *avengeth me* (47; RV 'executeth vengeance for me') implies no vindictiveness; it is a declaration that God and not man had vindicated the rightness of a cause. The Psalm concludes with a promise by David that he will utilize his dominion over many peoples to spread abroad the praise of the Lord his God, a concept which Paul adjusts to the reign of David's Lord (Rom. xv. 9) in whom salvation and loving-kindness are fully exhibited. Finally David names himself in connection with the permanent alliance with God which was ultimately fulfilled in the eternal kingdom of the Son of David. Cf. 2 Sa. vii. 12–16; Lk. i. 32, 33.

PSALM XIX. THE TWO WITNESSES TO GOD

Apart from the concluding prayer (14), the Psalm obviously falls into two parts, verses 1–6 and 7–13, the change being quite abrupt. Each part deals with a source from or medium by which man may acquire or receive knowledge of God, first by inference from the visible cosmos, and secondly by instruction through the Torah or law. These are respectively the material and the moral realms, one infinite and impressive in grandeur, the other inward and direct in operation. Without the physical light of the sun and the spiritual light of the divine commandments, all life would fail (contrast 5) and become false (precipitated into concealed error through a darkened understanding, verses 12 and 13).

a. The universal glory overhead (1–6)

i. The glory of the firmament (1–4a). The wonder of the sky is a constant stimulus to praise in the book of Psalms (cf. xxix, xciii, civ, cxxxvi. 5–9, cxlviii). The emphasis here is upon objective testimony rather than subjective interpretations. The heavens ceaselessly declare and disclose the glory of God, and each day speaks to the following day, and each night makes Him known. (Cf. Pss. l. 1, cxiii. 3.) Whilst they themselves are silent and inarticulate, their testimony is heard everywhere, *their line* (4) of writing is blazoned abroad. Cf. Rom. i. 19, 20, x. 18.

ii. The special glory of the sun (4b–6). Far from worshipping the sun, the psalmist regards it as an agent of God who has set up a tent in the vast heavens for the sun's continual use. For the imagery of verse 5 cf. Is. lx. 20 and Jdg. v. 31. Certainly the wide range of the sun's light and heat is a reflection of God's universal power and knowledge. This thought leads to a meditation upon the inward light afforded by the law or Torah.

b. The perfect glory of the Torah (7–13)

i. The moral effect of the law (7–10). Whereas the visible creation bears witness to God's everlasting power and divinity, the revelation of Himself is given to the children of Israel in the Torah. This distinction is observed in the replacement of *God* (1–6) by *the Lord* (i.e. Yahweh) (7–14). Six aspects of the inward work of the Lord are described. The Torah is *perfect* (7) or inerrant (cf. Jas. i. 25), bringing strength and comfort to men (cf. Ps. xxiii. 3, 4). *The testimony* (7) or oft-repeated proclamation of the divine

will (particularly of the Decalogue) transforms the *simple*, i.e. the open-minded person who is liable to be swayed by whoever happens to be speaking (cf. 2 Tim. iii. 15). *The statutes* (RV 'precepts') *of the Lord* (8) are definite rules, the keeping of which gives a clear conscience. *The commandment* (8) is a divine imperative which shines as a guiding light to men who seek the way of life (cf. Acts xxvi. 18; Heb. xi. 13). *The fear of the Lord* (9), which it is the law's aim to inculcate, is a name for the law, based upon devout reverence for Him, wholly free from debasing practices (cf. Ps. cvi. 35–40). His *judgments* (9) are ordinances governing social life and practice, and are therefore absolutely true and righteous. All these qualities make the inward revelations of the Lord more desirable than wealth and more pleasurable than honey (10). The whole passage is elaborately extended in Ps. cxix.

ii. The personal desire for a life free from sin (11–13). Just as the first part of the poem focused thought upon the sun, so the second half concentrates on a man's life. Meditation upon the abstract concept of the revealed will of Yahweh turns into prayer for absolute cleansing from hidden defects in character and conduct. The law is esteemed as a major factor in living a true life, but it holds no guarantee of purity outside personal conviction. What of inadvertent and unwitting acts of sin and error? 'The Lord Himself must thoroughly cleanse my life and also prevent me from proud and impulsive sins which swiftly become habitual and turn me into an enemy of God.' This attitude of mind is labelled *the great transgression* (13; cf. 1 Jn. iii. 19–21).

The last verse echoes the dual themes of the poem: the outward word and inward meditation of the psalmist, and the objective reality and manward activity of the Lord.

PSALM XX. PRAYER FOR THE KING BEFORE BATTLE

This and the following Psalm form a pair, describing the people's intercession and thanksgiving before and after a battle in which they were led by the king. There is a possible occasion in the defeat of the Ammonites and Syrians by David (2 Sa. x. 14–19). In view of the public and liturgical form of the poems, they may not have been composed by David but written on his behalf and probably under his supervision. The use of the personal pronouns, 'thee', 'I', and 'we', indicate the three sections in the Psalm.

a. Intercession by the people (1–5)

It is uncertain whether the scene of the prayer is the sanctuary in Zion or the vicinity of the battlefield. *Accept thy burnt sacrifice* (3) suggests an actual service before the altar (cf. 1 Sa. vii. 9); but the comprehensive *all thy offerings, all thy counsel, all thy petitions* (3, 4, 5) may indicate a retrospective view inclusive of all previous acts of worship. The phrase would then be equivalent to 'receive the memorial of', i.e. remember. The primary emphasis of this section is on the initial word of *The Lord*: He is requested to 'answer', 'set up on high', 'send help', 'strengthen', 'receive', 'accept' (see RV). This petition is divided from what follows by *Selah*, indicative of a pause or of a change in the music after verse 3, but the prayer resumes with the same emphasis. The Lord *grant . . . and fulfil* all the king's plans for the battle so that his people may shout for joy and wave their banners in triumph.

b. Assurance for the king (6)

It is not clear whether the king or the High Priest is speaking; in either case the note of confidence is intended for the Lord's anointed one, whom the Lord will answer from heaven by mighty acts of salvation.

c. Final confession, anticipation and prayer of the people (7–9)

The allusion to enemies who trust in speedier and more powerful armies refers not only to the Syrians whom they would soon meet in battle (cf. 2 Sa. x. 18) but also to past victories over forces such as those of Jabin and Pharaoh. The vow to *remember* (RV 'make mention of') *the name of the Lord* (7) may echo David's words against Goliath (1 Sa. xvii. 45).

This trustful committal of their cause to the Lord fills them with such expectation of success as to warrant the use of the prophetic tense, as though the conflict was over. Finally, the reality and tension of the moment leads the assembled warriors to plead for victory. The prayer has a wider content if *king* (9) is understood as God. The implication would be that David was leading an army belonging to the true Monarch and engaged in His cause (see Prayer Book version).

PSALM XXI. THANKSGIVING FOR THE KING AFTER BATTLE

The connection with the previous Psalm is neatly summarized by comparing xx. 4 with xxi. 2. The language of 4b, 6a and 9a is perhaps indicative of the elation which followed victory, but there may be a reflection of actual events (cf. verses 8 and 9 with 2 Sa. xii. 30, 31). Nevertheless, the poem has been traditionally interpreted as messianic.

a. An acknowledgment of the Lord's goodness to the king (1–7)

The main thought of exuberant praise is focused upon the present moment. The verbs in verses 1–3 should be translated in the present tense. *A crown of pure gold* (3). There may be an echo here of the Ammonite crown (cf. 1 Ch. xx. 2) but there is also a metaphorical crowning as the following verses suggest. Divine *glory . . . honour and majesty* (5) are bestowed upon him (cf. Ps. viii. 5) and he is made to be blessed and to be a blessing for ever as he rejoices exceedingly in the presence of the Lord. These messianic ideas are

often incorporated in the New Testament (e.g. Eph. i. 3; Heb. i. 8, 9; Rev. v. 12–14). Finally, the reason why the king has been so divinely blessed is declared to be his attitude of trust in the Lord not merely for himself, but for his people. Cf. Mt. xxvii. 43; Heb. ii. 13.

b. The king's power extolled (8–13)

The change of theme is marked by the alteration from 'thou' (the Lord) and 'he' (the king) of the previous verses to 'thou' (the king) and 'the Lord' in this section. This is a forceful address to the king by his subjects who exalt his supremacy over all enemies. *In the time of thine anger* (9) means the occasion when the king appears in person, as at the fall of Rabbah, city of Ammon. But the destruction of enemies by the majesty of the king's presence is a messianic idea (cf. Mal. iii. 1, 2; Mt. xxi. 40, 41; 2 Thes. i. 7–9).

The last verse is spoken by king and people unto the Lord. They pray for the continued expression of the divine power and glory even as in the recent victory. So shall their boundless praise be sustained.

PSALM XXII. SALVATION IN EXTREMITY

To Christians this Psalm is inseparably associated with the crucifixion (as also Ps. lxix), not only because the opening words were quoted by the Lord, but because the first part of the poem seems to describe His bodily condition and emotional experience. Yet the first meaning of the poem must be sought in the days of its composition, although the Spirit of God undoubtedly constrained the psalmist so to frame his expression that it immediately acquired a significance beyond the range of his own life (see Acts ii. 30, 31a). In other words, the Christological intention of the poem has a basis of Davidic experience. What that experience was cannot be precisely stated: it is thought by some exegetes that the psalmist is speaking of the suffering of the community of Israel under the figure of a representative man (cf. 'the Servant' in Is. xlff.).

The Psalm falls into two distinct parts of contrasting mood and perspective: the turning point is verse 21, 'Save me from the lion's mouth—Yea, from the horns of the wild oxen Thou hast answered me'. The title probably alludes to the name of a melody used when the Psalm was chanted.

a. In extremis (1–21a)

i. Despair and two appeals to precedent (1–11). The poignant words of verses 1 and 2 indicate the profound perplexity of spirit which has been induced by the most severe affliction and the apparent heedlessness of his God. He still trusts in God, but finds intolerable the suspense of waiting for evidence that God has not turned from him. *My roaring* (1); i.e. my piercing cries of anguish. *Am not silent* (2); i.e. receive no relief to make my cries unnecessary. In the absence of any response from God the sufferer is cast back upon his former beliefs, foremost among them being the concept of God as just and righteous. This belief is strengthened by the long precedent of Israel's praises for deliverances in earlier years (3–5). *Inhabitest the praises* (3). Better, as in RV mg., 'enthroned upon the praises'. God had not failed to help those who trusted Him in previous generations. Why should the speaker be an exception and his trustfulness be turned into a reproach (8)? As soon as his thought touches upon himself he becomes engrossed with his affliction (6–8). He is despised as a worm, not recognized as one with human rights, or features (cf. Is. lii. 14, liii. 3). For the laughter of ridicule, the lips opened in the language of abuse, and the excited turning of heads in the animated conversation of a crowd. see Lk. xxiii. 35; Mt. xxvii. 39, 43. For the action of trustfulness cf. Pss. xxxvii. 5, lv. 22.

The thought of dependence upon one who delighted in him reminds the psalmist of the days when, as a baby, he was dependent upon his mother (9, 10). But the very fact of his birth is sure evidence of divine intervention in human life, and a habit of reliance upon God was implanted in him with his own life and his mother's milk (cf. Ps. cxxxix. 13–17; Is. xlix. 1–5). This section ends with a plea for the realization of God's presence even as He has been nigh in the years since his infancy, because now there is no one to help and trouble cometh (11; cf. Jb. iii. 24–26).

ii. **Intense anguish in the immediate distress (12–21a).** The mood changes here from the humiliation of misunderstood relationships (God does not heed his need, and men do not respect his person) to the pain of a tormented body. In the intensity of this anguish there is no reminiscence comparable with verses 4 and 9, and the awful loneliness of soul implied in verse 1 is replaced by the unforgettable impression of a multitude of savage faces which enclose him like a ring of snarling dogs. The telling of such an experience is sharpened by a series of graphic metaphors. He likens his tormentors to fierce animals ready to devour him (12, 13). His physical weakness and complete helplessness are vividly portrayed (14, 15). Then a note of evaluation enters. The crowd consists of evildoers, who are *dogs* (16), i.e. men beneath contempt (cf. 2 Sa. xvi. 9). But the personal anguish quickly reasserts its dominance, for the mass of howling beasts have begun to bite and gnaw at his feet and hands; whilst burning eyes already mark out the portions of his body which teeth will soon devour. *Tell* (17); i.e. 'number' or 'count'. *Stare* (17) means to gloat over.

This imaginative scene is abruptly replaced by another in which the scuffle of attacking beasts is replaced by the slow and impersonal allocation of his clothing amongst his enemies, a scene in which physical torment is suddenly swamped by a wave of bitterest humiliation arising from the casual sequestration of what was peculiarly his own. (Compare the alternation of moods in Job during the debate by his friends.)

Yet is his reliance upon God unblemished by disbelief: indeed, in the uttermost extremity of his soul, the bond with his Lord stands out the clearer in a strong cry for the aid of His presence. 'O Thou my Lord, O Thou my strength, hasten hither, deliver and save me. Rescue my soul from a violent death by the sword, yea deliver my only life from the power, action and weapons of these contemptible, acquisitive and ferocious men'—already described as dogs, lions and bulls in verses 12–16 (cf. 1 Pet. v. 8). *My darling* (20). Lit. 'my only one', as in RV mg. *Unicorns* (21). RV 'wild oxen'.

It is only at the very last breath that the crisis occurs and the incredible happens. What begins as a sentence of final appeal ends as a cry of immeasurable relief (see 21, RV). Nor is there the least hint of inadequacy on the part of God's answer. The whole outlook and experience is transformed through the unspecified intervention of the Lord. What had been an unbearable experience vanished almost in the twinkling of an eye. Cf. Heb. v. 7.

b. **Benedicite (21b–31)**

The remainder of the Psalm consists of praise and thanksgiving to God for His faithfulness and glory. The theme is *thy name* (22), which is amplified in verse 24 to mean the Lord's compassion, honour and gracious attentiveness. But the sphere wherein His praise is to be heard has two parts, one immediate and local, i.e. *the congregation* (22) or assembly of those who are his brethren by blood and by faith, the other more comprehensive in time and place.

i. **Praise among his brethren (22–26).** Those descendants of Israel who reverence God (cf. Ps. cxv. 13) are urged to bow before the Lord because of His greatness and magnanimity as disclosed in His actions (24) which are so unlike the deeds of the ungodly men who have attacked the psalmist. 'Of thee cometh my praise' (25, RV). Because all his praise is stimulated by God's salvation which has come to him, David invites other humble and godly men to join with him in the votive meal he has vowed to give to his Deliverer (cf. Lv. vii. 16), and in the imaginative anticipation of their presence he pronounces a benediction on his guests: 'Let your heart live (or rejoice) for ever' (26, RV). Cf. Jn. vi. 54–56.

ii. **Praise by all mankind (27–31).** The sense of having experienced the reality of God's essential goodwill toward the trustful heart prompts the psalmist to call upon all peoples. He can foresee no other outcome than that the nature of God should be known and revered throughout the earth (27). Is He not the supreme sovereign? (28; cf. Je. xvi. 19; Zc. xiv. 9; Rev. xi. 15). Even *they that be fat* (29), i.e. the prosperous and proud, will partake in His worship (cf. Is. xlix. 7; Rom. xiv. 11; Phil. ii. 10): indeed every mortal man shall render homage to the immortal Lord (cf. Is. xxv. 6; Rev. xix. 9, xxii. 17). An endless posterity shall serve Him and the story of His great deed of deliverance shall be the permanent heritage of every generation (30; see RV and cf. Lk. i. 48–50). Each shall come into being and shall declare the Lord's effective righteousness (cf. Is. lix. 21). The Hebrew text of verses 29–31 is obscure. Rotherham, following the LXX rendering of 29c and 30a, translates 'My soul shall live for Him, my seed shall serve Him. It shall be told of the Lord to the generation to come, and they shall show His righteousness to a people to be born—He hath done it'.

PSALM XXIII. SHEPHERD AND HOST

This poem owes much of its charm to the skilful blending of contrasted imagery which covers the major aspects of human life, viz. outdoors (1, 2) and indoors (6b); pastoral peace (2) and pilgrimage through peril (4b); the possibility of evil (4b) and the prospect of good (5); times of invigoration of soul (3a) and times of ominous gloom (4a); the experience of following (1, 2) and a life of stable security (6b). Nevertheless, all the literary facets of this lyrical gem are seen in the light of the Lord whose tender care, ceaseless vigilance and perpetual presence impart to life all its colour and satisfaction. Indeed the sevenfold activity of the Lord described in verses 2–5 (He maketh, He leadeth, He restoreth, He guideth, Thou art with me, Thou preparest a table, Thou anointest my head) is framed within the name of the Lord (the first and final words of the poem).

The dominant concept is that of God as guide and protector through the vicissitudes of life. The suggestive imagery of a shepherd as applied to the Lord goes back to the days of patriarchal pastoralism (cf. Jacob's statement in Gn. xlviii. 15) and it has been constantly enriched ever since (cf. Ps. lxxviii. 52–54; Is. xl. 11; Ezk. xxxiv. 1–23; Jn. x. 1–18). A second concept is introduced in verse 5—that of the Lord as a host of boundless benevolence. This imagery of man as a surprised guest at a sumptuous feast provided by God is likewise an integral part of the whole biblical panorama from the symbolism of Joseph the provider of food (Gn. xliii. 34) to the miracle of the feeding of five thousand (Mt. xiv. 19) and the parables of the great supper (Lk. xiv. 15–24) and the marriage feast of the Bridegroom (Mt. xxii. 1–14; Rev. xix. 9).

The Psalm may be analysed as follows:

a. Pilgrimage (1–4)

David is completely dependent on the Lord as a sheep on its shepherd. The two aspects are serenity, as of lying down in green pastures and by restful waters, with a suggestion of physical well-being; and safety, as of a protected journey along right paths, with a suggestion of personal calm and mental ease because anxiety is impossible when His strong care is evident. The theme is weighted in the direction of innocent carefreeness, a sense of the immediate (like that of a beast), and a bond with the shepherd of inexplicable affection.

b. Hospitality (5, 6)

These verses stress David's careful discernment of the Lord's munificence as the perfect host. The two aspects are fulness—the provision for his needs and enjoyment is complete in every sense, it is unhampered by any human antagonists; and finality—the rich relationship with the Lord is unlimited, and the privilege is fully personal. Contrast the use of Thou with the use of He in the earlier part.

The theme is weighted in the direction of surprised appreciation, an inspiration for the future (as of one who is attended), and the bond with the host is of unreserved allegiance.

PSALM XXIV. AN ANTHEM FOR THE INVESTITURE OF JERUSALEM

The great occasion in David's life when he brought the ark of the Lord from the house of Obed-edom to the recently captured city of the Jebusites was joyfully celebrated by several chants and Psalms (see 1 Ch. xv. 16–23). This was one of the first to be used, for it was sung while the procession approached the ancient city. The Psalm was greater than the occasion, and has generally been interpreted as a prophetic expression of Christ's ascension after victory over death and sin (see verse 8 and cf. Col. ii. 15; Heb. ii. 14, 15) and of His ultimate sovereignty over all (see verse 10 and cf. Jas. ii. 1; Rev. v. 11–14, xvii. 14). The Psalm is in two parts.

a. Approaching the hill of Yahweh (1–6)

This processional hymn has two themes. The first is the power and majesty of the Lord as maker and sovereign over all the earth (1–3). See Ps. cxxxvi. 6n. and cf. Je. v. 22. Such is the range of His knowledge, the perfection of His work and the purity and righteousness of His Person, that mere man must hesitate about his duty to worship Him, for to draw near unto the holy God is perilous to the sinner and awesome for all. Stand (3); i.e. maintain his ground. Cf. Ps. i. 5.

The second theme is the righteousness required of men if they are to be blessed of God (4–6). It was one thing to bring the ark of His covenant into Jerusalem, but another matter to approach the Lord in true worship. The incident of Uzzah three months before would still be fresh in mind (see 2 Sa. vi. 6–11). The necessity of a high standard of honesty, truthfulness and integrity on the part of the worshippers is also stated in Ps. xv (cf. Is. xxxiii. 14–17). Hath not lifted up his soul unto vanity (4); i.e. hath not directed affection and desires towards things that are empty and worthless instead of toward God. Cf. xxv. 1, lxxxvi. 4, cxliii. 8. Such men are strengthened by divine blessing in the impartation of God's own righteousness. O Jacob (6);

i.e. they only are the true Jacob (cf. Rom. ii. 28, 29). Many, however, prefer the RV rendering, 'O God of Jacob'.

b. Entering the gateway of Zion (7–10)

The contrast between the outer world of creation and the inner realm of the heart is reflected in the second part, which is heard as a double challenge and reply. The procession is halted awhile before the city's closed gates and the demand for entrance, i.e. submission, is formally made in the name of the King of glory (cf. Mt. xxi. 9, 10; 1 Cor. ii. 8). The command to *lift up* (7, 9), or extend, the gates and archways of the old citadel implies the superiority of the new King over all others who may have previously entered. In reply to the ceremonial challenge of the sentries (8) the name of the incoming king (cf. 2 Sa. vi. 2b) is declared to be the *Lord mighty in battle*. David had recently captured the Jebusite stronghold and won many other battles. This designation alone was insufficient to warrant the opening of the gates, and the call to provide access to the city is repeated (9). The Lord's presence and pre-eminence in Zion is based on grounds other than His intervention in Israel's historic battles. The Lord is king of all in His own right, possessing powers and qualities which transcend earth and time. The King of glory is *the Lord of hosts* (10; cf. 1 Ki. xxii. 19). This high concept of God has been foreshadowed in the Psalm's opening words, whose meaning extends far beyond the temporal and national outlook of Israel.

PSALM XXV. A PERSONAL PRAYER

Psalms xxv and xxxiv are a pair. Both have an acrostic arrangement with two identical irregularities, and, although one consists of extremely personal prayer and the other of public praise, both are liturgical and contain many similar thoughts.

The poem expresses the alternation of fervent petition and sober meditation which often characterizes the soul's waiting upon the Lord. There are three main moods in the prayer, but they are closely bound together.

a. A plea for guidance (1–7)

This is a prayer in itself, but its themes are dealt with more fully in the following verses; e.g. with the prayer for vindication from his enemies (2, 3), cf. verses 19–21; with the expression of his need for instruction and guidance by the Lord (4, 5), cf. verses 8–10 and 12; his penitence (6, 7) is brought out again in verse 11; and his avowal of trust in God (1) is repeated in verse 15.

The opening words set a tone of earnestness (cf. Ps. lxxxvi. 4). The tenacity of the psalmist's faith is indicated by the way in which the request that God by helping him should silence the taunts of his enemies (2) is immediately followed by the affirmation 'Yea, none that wait on thee shall be ashamed!' (3, RV). Nevertheless faith

seeks nourishment in a knowledge of God's will, so the chief expansion of thought occurs in verse 4, the plea for guidance in all the truth of God on the ground of a sincere and a full allegiance to Him (cf. Ex. xxxiii. 13; Ps. lxxxvi. 11; Jn. xiv. 6). Such a possibility needs safeguarding; the disclosure of the way of truth will throw into greater prominence the shadows of the past sins which would only add to his present burden. Hence the following entreaty that the light of divine goodness should illuminate more brilliantly his memories of the Lord's *tender mercies and . . . lovingkindnesses* (6). This is the basis of the heartfelt cry to God of verse 1; not the merit of man but the goodness of God as revealed in His former dealings with men (6, 7).

b. The goodness of the Lord (8–15)

In the expansion of the previous verses there is necessarily some shifting of emphasis, as well as a reversal of order. For example, the initial supplication (1–3) is accentuated in the final section (16–21), and in this central passage the note of penitence (11) is surpassed by praise (8–10) and vision (12–14).

In the usual manner of Old Testament meditation, the final thought of one passage is made the theme of the following section. The goodness of the Lord (7) becomes the dominant theme of this section. Because He is absolutely good and true, *therefore* He is sure to offer help to sinful men uncertain of the right way of life (8). Those who heed His instruction are *the meek* (9), i.e. those who, though sinful, are not arrogant and self-confident, but humble and obedient. See ix. 12n. Whichever way God may lead such men He acts toward them in a manner that is true and just but also tender and merciful. A God so kind may safely be trusted to deal with one's iniquities however heinous (cf. Ex. xxxiv. 6). Adoration of the Lord then becomes acknowledgment of His standards for human life. Whenever a man reverences God he learns to choose the way which is right. This brings lasting prosperity and a secret fellowship with the Lord Himself which results in a fuller revelation of His will (cf. Is. xlviii. 17–19). Just as praise led to penitence (11) so vision leads to a graphic statement of complete trust in the Lord who will surely disentangle him from the web of evil circumstance (15) and set him free to walk in the pathway of uprightness.

c. A prayer for deliverance (16–21)

The metaphor of being trapped in a net has reminded the psalmist of his present predicament, and this evokes a passionate supplication for deliverance. He is particularly oppressed, for his troubles have isolated him from all friends and his heart is swamped with anxieties, so he cries for deliverance, attentive care and forgiveness. *Have mercy upon me* (16); i.e. Be gracious unto me. Cf. Ps. iv. 1n. *Troubles* (17). Lit. 'strictnesses'. *Are enlarged* (17). Better, as in RV mg., 'relieve thou (or 'enlarge thou') and bring'. Nor are these fears and troubles subjective; his enemies are as implacable and violent as they are numerous, hence the appeal for protection and vindication on the ground both of his integrity toward God and uprightness before men, and of the purity (goodness) and uprightness of the Lord (see verse 8) who will guide him in the way of freedom.

Verse 22 is almost certainly a later addition to render the prayer more appropriate for corporate worship. It crystallizes the spirit of the Psalm and offers it to the Lord in the name of the community.

PSALM XXVI. THE WAY OF THE WORSHIPPER

This Psalm is not readily assigned to any particular period in David's life. It expresses the uneasiness of any devout soul when immersed in a godless society. If a good man seeks the strength which comes from the worship of the Lord, his moods and thoughts might well take the following form.

a. His approach to God (1, 2)

The outspoken request for the Lord to *judge, examine, prove* and *try* him implies an antecedent tension which is expressed in the contrasts of the following verses. He does not claim a sinless life but asserts a sincere and consistent endeavour to walk uprightly (cf. Ps. cxxxix. 23, 24). *Therefore I shall not slide* (1). Better, 'without wavering' as in RV.

b. His determination to avoid wicked men (3–11)

In verses 3–5 he describes on one hand the truth and loving-kindness of the Lord and, on the other, the vanity, duplicity and wickedness of certain men. The former he cherishes, the latter he shuns and hates (cf. Ps. i. 1). *Vain persons* (4); i.e. men devoid of real substance. *Dissemblers* (4); i.e. those who cover their real intentions.

His own choice is described in verses 6–8. He will take his place among those who surround God's altar, and in preparation for the act of dedication he will cleanse himself from defilement (cf. lxxiii. 13; Ex. xxx. 17–21). The metaphor of walking (3) is replaced by the more intimate one of entering the house of the Lord. His declaration that he will avoid ungodly men (4) is changed into a song of grateful testimony. The hatred of evil gatherings (5) is replaced by the love of the dwelling place where he meets the glory of God (8, RV).

In verses 9–11 he expresses his great desire to be strengthened in the choice he has made to avoid the company of sinful, violent, untrustworthy and corrupt men whom, as men of influence and wealth, he is bound to meet. The positive side of this prayer is his request for divine aid because his strong integrity is not a sufficient safeguard. *Gather not my soul with* (9); i.e. when evil men perish, let my life be spared.

c. His assurance (12)

The gracious consequence of worship is a confirmation of the goodness of God. Hence this affirmation of security, fellowship and blessedness. Cf. Ps. lxxiii, where a blurred view of the wicked is clarified by the act of worship (verse 16f.).

PSALM XXVII. AN ANTHEM OF DELIVERANCE

According to the LXX this Psalm originated before David's anointing; he was anointed on three occasions (1 Sa. xvi. 13; 2 Sa. ii. 4, v. 3). This song is most appropriate to the last of these.

The difference between the first and second halves of the Psalm is very obvious, and the change after verse 6 from exuberant praise to earnest petition may appear to be an inversion of mood. But verses 7–12 are retrospective and are inserted between passages which describe the encouragement derived from divine deliverance. This device of literary inversion can be seen clearly in Ex. xv, where the Song of Moses and Miriam describes the triumphant deliverance from Pharaoh (xv. 1–5) before describing the pursuit and the disaster (xv. 8–10).

There are four main themes.

a. Wholehearted trust (1–3)

A hymn of irrepressible gaiety wherein the threats and needs of life are abundantly met by the Lord. There is a triple parallelism. The Lord is my *light*, my *salvation* and my *strength*. Although I am faced with adversaries, multitudes, and the risk of war, my foes stumble in the darkness from which I am freed by His light; the massing of armies cannot affect my experience of heart-peace through His salvation, and the threat of widespread conflict has no power to disturb my faith which is in the Lord, the stronghold of my life (1, RV mg.).

b. A supreme desire (4–6)

A sublime expression of the constancy of a devout heart. The psalmist is determined to seek the abiding security and joy of God's presence. His desire is first to dwell with the Lord, to behold His *beauty* (Heb. 'loveliness') and to meditate upon Him (3; see RV mg.). Secondly, he longs to be hidden from trouble in His near presence (5), to see over and beyond others, and to worship with cries of joy (6, RV mg.).

c. A prayer for deliverance from danger (7–12)

This plea within a song of praise is a reminiscence of former moments of peril, a reversion to the exigencies of life when pursued by Saul. A description of his distress and his need for God's help (7–9a) is followed by an affirmation of the Lord's faithfulness (9b, 10). The section concludes with a prayer for guidance and preservation (11, 12).

d. The unfailing Lord (13, 14)

These words mark a return to the present moment. They are a testimony to the integration of experience through faith, and a strong exhortation to steadfast endurance. This conclusion of the anthem emphasizes human frailty, but stresses the fact of divine intervention, the utter certainty of the Lord's sufficiency, and the irrepressibility of a true faith (cf. Is. xxv. 9).

PSALM XXVIII. A PLEA FOR RETRIBUTION

This Psalm was first spoken in some time of peril at the hands of evil men. Although not so intensely subjective as Ps. xxii, it contains a similar abrupt transition from prayer to praise. See verse 6 and cf. xxii. 22. Its main themes are a plea for retribution to the wicked and thanksgiving for the intervention of the Lord. Both parts of the poem have a personal and a corporate section.

a. A cry for help (1–5)

The opening words originate in strong tension due to the speaker's implicit trust in the Lord, in spite of having received no aid nor evidence of sympathy from Him during a time of utmost danger. The silence of God is a terrible experience, a foretaste of the dumbness of the grave and suggestive of divine disfavour and therefore of threatened destruction (cf. Ps. lxxxviii. 4, 9). Hence the fervent lifting up of the hands towards God's holy sanctuary. Thy holy oracle (2); i.e. the most holy place. See RV mg. The burden of his prayer is separation of himself from the wicked and their ultimate reward. He beseeches his Lord not to drag him away with all the crowd of guilty men (3); but he pleads even more vehemently for a just recompense to be given to such evil-doers (4, 5), not vindictively but in demonstration of righteousness. The wicked are without excuse. They deliberately ignore or deny the power and superiority of God which is evident in nature (cf. Ps. viii; Rom. i. 18–21).

b. Thanksgiving for God's response (6–9)

This fulfilment of the prayer of verse 2 is not evoked by a sudden surge of remembered deliverances, but by the realization of an immediate response by the Lord. Greatly rejoiceth (7). Cf. 'exulteth' (1 Sa. ii. 1, RV). The quality of his reaction is an index of his former predicament. The experience of a divine blessing brings such relief and joy that the psalmist craves a like enrichment for all his people. Are not his subjects the Lord's people? Is He not their essential source of well-being, and are they not His inheritance? Oh, that He would constantly be their shepherd (feed them) and bear them up when wayward, weary and worried. Cf. Dt. i. 31; Is. lxiii. 9.

PSALM XXIX. THE THUNDER OF GOD

This song of a thunderstorm is heard within the auditorium of heaven, and the angels (see verse 1, RV mg.) are summoned to join in the praise and worship of Yahweh. In the beauty of holiness (2). 'In holy array' (RV mg.). Cf. Ex. xxviii. 2. Verses 3–9, the core of the poem, describe the passage of a storm from the waters of the western sea across the forested hills of northern Palestine, to the waste places of Kadesh in the uttermost borders of Edom (Nu. xx. 16). This event is depicted not as a demonstration of natural power, but as a symphony of praise to the Creator who indeed joins in with a voice of thunder (cf. Ps. xviii. 13).

The descriptive part of the poem falls into three equal stanzas which correspond with the formation, onset and passage of the storm, but the subordination of natural phenomena to spiritual forces is constantly emphasized.

a. The approach of the storm (3, 4)

This is presented by the suggestive repetitions as though of distant mutterings. Upon the waters (3); i.e. either the sea or the swollen floodwaters of the coastal hills where rain is already falling. The general impression is one of sultry foreboding, the activity is concealed, power is leashed, the God of glory (3) is not yet apparent, and His voice is muffled.

b. Its onset (5–7)

The word powerful (4) announces a new phase, a scene of increasing action as the branches of great trees are tossed about and then torn away by violent gusts which leave the trunks gaunt and shattered (5, 6). This climax of the storm is vividly described so as to convey the impression of reckless power—like the action of a bull-calf or a young wild-ox skipping about in mad exuberance (6, RV). This display of crude power is then modified. He whose voice produced the tempest causes fire to come out of hidden places which are cleft open by lightning (7).

c. The storm passes away (8, 9)

The activity abates, the shaking is of the distant wilderness. The frightened hinds have given birth to their young prematurely. With so many trees uprooted the remaining foliage of the forested hills is now insufficient to conceal the splintered limbs and fallen trunks. The impression that is left is one of breathlessness, as though the whole temple of nature echoed with a whispered 'Glory' to the Lord who had but to speak and it would be done, who uttered His voice and the earth melted (cf. Ps. xlvi. 6).

These three scenes, suggestive of boisterous energy, depicted in rain-fed torrents, dishevelled forests, and winds dancing into the distance, are set fast within a framework of wholly different quality. The glory and strength of the Lord are not fully disclosed in nature's wild power but in the impressive dignity of the high court of heaven, where the angelic 'sons of the mighty'

(1, RV) bow in holy adoration (2, RV mg.). Indeed the focus of all action and thought is the Lord Himself eternally enthroned, and unwaveringly bestowing upon His people not merely the gift of strength but the blessing of *peace* (verses 10, 11). The poem skilfully fuses the natural and the spiritual, but with clear emphasis on the latter aspect. The first word *give* is a call to worship and the last word *peace* implies His will to bless. Divine power prompts one and provides the other, but the created world cannot provide more than an elemental index to them. The psalmists were very conscious of nature providing an insight into divine power and glory. See, e.g., Pss. civ, cxlv, cxlviii; see also Jb. xxxviii, xxxix; Hab. iii.

PSALM XXX. MOURNING INTO DANCING

The allusion in the title to *the dedication of the house* might refer to the decision about Ornan's threshingfloor (1 Ch. xxi. 18–27), and the terrible experience of imminent death which is mentioned in the Psalm would be the pestilence which approached Jerusalem (1 Ch. xxi. 7, 13ff.). Alternatively it may refer to David's palace which he was prevented from occupying at first because of the great Philistine invasion which reached Bethlehem (2 Sa. v. 11, 18, 22; cf. xxiii. 13–17). A third possibility is that the phrase may have been added to the title when the Psalm was used at the dedication of the second temple, in which case the poem in its origin is a personal record of deliverance from some severe distress.

The background of experience is described in verses 6–10, and the consequent rejoicing because of deliverance is not limited to the final verse but comprises the preface as well (verses 1–5).

a. What God hath wrought (1–5)

A summary of past experience is presented in verses 1–3, the central theme being God's action in bringing David up from the dim depths of the well of the dead into which he had fallen and into which others had sunk beyond recall (3; see RV mg.). This deliverance had disappointed his enemies (1b), who had thought his plight to be beyond the power or likelihood of divine intervention. Cf. Ps. iii. 2. Verses 4 and 5 are a general expression of gratitude, a call to all godly men to offer thanksgivings, not merely for the psalmist's deliverance, but because their Lord was so ready to grant to men His gracious favour which is life indeed. In verse 5 see RV mg. Weeping and Joy are personified and thought of as guests. Cf. also Jn. xvi. 20–22; 2 Cor. iv. 17.

b. The psalmist's plight (6–10)

He now contrasts the apparent security afforded by prosperity with the appalling silence of death, and recalls a critical period of his past life. In verse 6 follow RV: 'As for me I (once) said.'

This is what the proud and wicked man declared in Ps. x. 6. It seemed as though the Lord had made him as strong and sure as the mountains. Then illness or sudden peril reminded him that his well-being was God's blessing. *Troubled* (7) is a strong word in Hebrew implying dismay and terror. Appalled by his previous boastfulness, he now called upon the Lord, asking what advantage God would gain by his death because once he has entered the grave he will no longer be able to praise Him (9; cf. Ps. vi. 5; Is. xxxviii. 17–18). He then pleads for divine aid because none other can help him.

c. A memorable resolve (11, 12)

The indisputable fact of God's response, whereby his grief was turned to joy (cf. Je. xxxi. 13), merits unceasing thanksgiving. *My glory* (12); i.e. my personality.

PSALM XXXI. TRIAL AND TRUST

This Psalm has the familiar motif of 'the distress of the innocent'. While it may have some basis in David's experience in fleeing from Saul (cf. 1 Sa. xxiii. 26), it has more interest for us in that subsequently it was so frequently in the mind of Jeremiah. The phrase *fear was on every side* (13) occurs in Je. vi. 25, xlvi. 5, xlix. 29, and is left untranslated as 'Magor-missabib' in xx. 3; indeed part of verse 13 is actually quoted in Je. xx. 10. The simile of *a broken vessel* (12) was a favourite phrase of Jeremiah (cf. xviii. 4, xix. 10, 11, xxii. 28), and he had thoroughly absorbed the whole spirit of this poem.

The second part of the Psalm (verses 9–24) is an expansion of the previous eight verses. The situation is first described as seen by faith, then secondly as it was actually experienced in its sequence of distress and deliverance.

a. Outline of an effective faith (1–8)

The Lord's honour, ability, holiness, graciousness and faithfulness, as known to the trusting soul, are the background to the psalmist's request to Him to demonstrate His nature in his immediate circumstances (1–3). There is tension due to the expectation of divine intervention; but there is also peace because of the unreserved confidence in the Lord so ardently expressed in the opening words. *Therefore for thy name's sake* (3). The thought is that, because of the Lord's character or name, He will lead, guide and deliver.

Faith toward God is the committal of life to Him (5a; cf. Lk. xxiii. 46). The act and confession of so doing strengthens trust and accentuates the difference between truth and falsity (cf. Jon. ii. 8). The cycle of adoration, expectation and committal is closed by thanksgiving for deliverance (7, 8). In this respect faith discounts time's delay and lays hold upon things not seen as yet.

b. Details of a profound experience (9–24)

First of all the psalmist deals with his plight. He makes an appeal to the Lord for mercy on the ground of extreme distress (9–13), and then seeks justification by an act of divine deliverance (14–18). His distress is poignantly described as affecting his body and his soul (cf. Ps. vi. 6, 7, lxxxviii. 3–7). His misery arises from anxiety and uncertainty; his life is withered by the misgivings and cold suspicion of his acquaintances; his enemies have shaken the loyalty even of his friends (11; cf. 1 Sa. xxii. 22). He feels like a useless broken vessel; his life has become so different from what it once was (cf. Jb. xxix and xxx) that his former self is like a man who is dead and forgotten. Nevertheless his trust is rooted in God and all his life is in His care (14, 15; cf. verse 5). He therefore pleads for the evident favour and approval of God, i.e. for the radiant joy and peace of His presence. This would also shame his adversaries and dispel all mists of suspicion about him. Indeed, those who are the source of such calumny and plottings should be imprisoned in the silence of Sheol (17b; see RV).

Secondly, the psalmist deals with the goodness of God. The past experiences of all godly men show that the Lord is especially concerned for their welfare (19, 20). The resources of His goodness are available for them, and the security of His presence ensures their immunity from the effects of slander and dissension. Cf. Ps. xxvii. 5, 6. But His own immediate experience also shows the Lord's goodness; for when he was beleaguered by evil and impulsively said he was beyond God's power to save, yet the Lord heard and answered (21, 22). An exhortation to all godly people to trust Him implicitly and fully through the future days naturally follows. With these words about divine faithfulness, righteousness and strength, the Psalm reminds us of the opening words of worship. The initial faith in God has furthered love toward Him (23) and fostered hope in Him (24).

PSALM XXXII. THE JOY OF FORGIVENESS

This Psalm may be associated with the fifty-first. The background of both is to be found in the story of 2 Sa. xi and xii. This Psalm deals with the blessedness which is known when sin is forgiven and gives insight into the psychological and religious implications of sin and its removal.

a. The joy of forgiveness (1–5)

These verses describe the great satisfaction and joyous freedom of the soul whose sin has been covered, cancelled and cleansed by the wholly righteous Lord (cf. Rom. iv. 6–8). The fact of sin and forgiveness is stated in four ways in verses 1 and 2, and repeated in verse 5 with an emphatic climax. Inserted in this comprehensive statement of a soul's transformation is an account of the deep conflict which accompanied the previous sense of guilt. Verses 3 and 4 narrate the sequences of a moral malady. The initial impulse to stifle guilt by silence simply

thrust it into the subconscious, but it seeped out in symptoms of physical distress—deep-seated pain and involuntary groans (3). Sleep brought no cessation from such profound disharmony, and its very persistence was an indication of the inescapable hand of God's righteousness. Obstinate endurance in such repression steadily reduced his vigour, like the withering of a tree in a prolonged drought (4).

The turning-point was when he decided to confess and openly acknowledge the corruption he had thought to banish by burial. So decisive was the act of penitence that the account of it in verse 5 is in the present tense. So effective was the act of forgiveness that from verse 6 the poem takes a new turn.

b. The basis of confident prayer (6–11)

David's personal experience of God's forgiveness (1, 2) is made the basis of a call for confident prayer by any godly person provided that the plea is offered whilst the Lord may yet be approached (6). The implication is of life's uncertainty demanding an immediate penitence for sin. Our deliverance by Him from the strong tides of passion and pride, like His forgiveness, will evoke songs of blessing (7).

Verses 8 and 9 are the counterpart of verses 3 and 4. David's guilty silence is replaced by the divine word of sympathetic guidance. The lonely isolation of the impenitent sinner is replaced by mutual understanding: 'I will counsel thee with mine eye upon thee' (8, RV) implies that ideal bond between teacher and pupil, between father and son. Verse 9 should also be read as in RV. In contrast to the sensitive response of the teachable heart is the stubborn will, which refuses to draw near to God and must be disciplined by judgment. These thoughts of instruction in godliness and of free confession should be compared with Ps. li. 13–15.

The last two verses speak first of the alternatives which were in mind in verse 5. Sin brings either punishment or mercy; the difference arises from confession to the Lord. His faithfulness and mercy are such that all who can claim to be righteous (through acceptance of His forgiveness) have a source of pure delight which springs from a guileless heart. Peace is inseparable from purity.

PSALM XXXIII. AN ANTHEM OF WORSHIP

This poem, which has no title, picks up part of the concluding sentence of the previous Psalm, but, unlike it, is not a personal record of experience. It is a corporate expression of praise and worship marked by balance of thought and symmetrical structure.

The introduction (1–3) and the conclusion (20–22) are clearly distinguished from the main body of the poem. The first three verses describe the enthusiastic singing of a choir which is being accompanied by the music of large and small harps (see RV). The last three verses describe the fervent faith of the worshippers who are surrounded by the protection and mercy of the Lord. The symmetry and sequence of these ideas are significant. The anthem of praise becomes the prayer of faith; the group of choristers (*O ye righteous*) is replaced by the inner consciousness (*we, our, us*); i.e. other people have receded and it is we ourselves who occupy the final scene. The change is also from the externals of music and song to the inward experiences of trust and hope, i.e. there is a movement from objective worship to personal relationship.

In the body of the Psalm are two sections, verses 4–11 and verses 12–19, each of which deals with the fundamental themes of the whole Psalter, viz. God, nature, man and history.

a. Let all creation fear the Lord (4–11)

These eight verses consist of four groups, each of four phrases, dealing with the major themes. First, the word, work and will of the Lord are described as true, righteous, holy and just; He is essentially truth-in-action and consequently the whole earth is full of the evidences of His kindness (4, 5). The allusion to a particular realm of divine action, *the earth* (5), introduces the next concept. In verses 6 and 7 the work and wisdom of the Lord are described, not in relation to His character, but as exhibited in His creative activity. This survey of the divine power to create and organize should evoke in men a sense of awe and worship, and the two following verses declare that the primary purpose of mankind is to *fear the Lord* (8). Every inhabitant of this world should revere His power and the immutability of His work (9). This concluding thought of permanence provides a link with the next concept, that of the course of history. The whole panorama of human existence is viewed, not as a haphazard wandering of men and nations, but as a sequence which inevitably leads to a climax rooted in the determinate counsel and foreknowledge of God. In so far as national and cultural developments deviate from this fundamental and approved end He *bringeth the counsel . . . to nought* of the one and makes *of none effect* the scheming of the other (10). Note the contrast in verses 10 and 11 between the vain thoughts of men and the eternal purposes of God.

b. The all-searching eye of the Lord (12–19)

This second portion of the poem has the same structure as the first—a fourfold grouping of phrases which deal with the same basic themes. But whereas the previous treatment of these had been objective, they are now dealt with in a subjective and personal way. (Cf. the difference between verses 1–3 and verses 20–22.) Verse 12 introduces the concept of a divine choosing which is inseparable from blessing, and which entails a peculiar destiny, viz. that of being *his own inheritance* (cf. Ps. xxviii. 9; Eph. i. 18; 1 Pet. ii. 9, 10). God's choice is not restricted:

it is made from *all the sons of men* (13). This thought leads to the next theme, that of divine comprehensiveness. God looks from heaven to earth and scans every living being. In verses 13 and 14 two Hebrew words for 'look' are used; see RV. Moreover, He looks not only upon the outward appearance; He discerns the thoughts and intentions of the hearts which He Himself has fashioned. Cf. Ps. cxxxix. 1–5; Heb. iv. 12, 13.

At this point a striking feature occurs. From verse 4 each new concept has been introduced by a remark in the preceding statement; but verse 16 brings forward a theme which has no precedent in the poem, that of human impotence. Whilst there has not been the slightest hint of imperfection or peril in all the wide survey of space and time, we are now to infer that the divine scrutiny ,of mankind has disclosed so prevalent a defect that the need for salvation is unquestionably accepted by all. Certainly there is no earthly power to deliver, neither rank, numbers, personal prowess, distance, nor natural forces (symbolized by the horse of great power) can effect redemption. If salvation is to be obtained, God must intervene. Hence, as a final theme the election of the godly is firmly declared (18, 19). This is not a repetition of the concept of divine sovereignty in verses 12 and 13, but a statement of the basis of true life. There is nothing arbitrary or capricious about it; it is a righteous principle available to all. The fundamental principle is simply that of the Lord's faithfulness; all who honour Him and rest or hope in His mercy and goodness, He will undertake to deliver from death and to sustain in every exigency of life. This inescapable law of faith is the personal counterpart of that immutable lot of the good and the true which was the closing thought of the first half of the poem.

PSALM XXXIV. TESTIMONY

This is an acrostic poem but, as in Ps. xxv, the alphabet is not quite complete. The title associates the hymn with David's escape from Gath to Adullam (1 Sa. xxi. 10—xxii. 1). See *Introduction* to Ps. lii. *Abimelech* (lit. 'my father the king') was very possibly the title of the king of Gath, in the same way as 'Pharaoh' was used in Egypt, and 'Agag' among the Amalekites (cf. Gn. xx. 2, xxvi. 1). In 1 Samuel his name is given as Achish.

The spirit of exuberant confidence in the Lord is of more importance than any logical structure in the poem. Many of its phrases have become an essential part of the vocabulary of devotional worship. Apart from the introduction and the conclusion, there are two main sections in the Psalm.

a. Introduction (1, 2)

Four thoughts are woven together. In the Lord shall my soul glory, He is pre-eminent (cf. Ps. xxix. 1, 2; Je. ix. 23f.). My speech will boldly proclaim His praise, my mouth shall boast in Him (cf. Ps. xliv. 8). This glad testimony will be maintained in all kinds of circumstances (cf. Jas. i. 2; Lk. vi. 23). Those who are oppressed and misjudged will be strengthened thereby.

b. Personal testimony (3–8)

The exhortations to *magnify the Lord* (3) and *taste and see that the Lord is good* (8) are a framework for an unforgettable experience. 'I enquired of the Lord, and He answered me.' Indeed, all who look unto Him become radiant-faced, and can never be abashed (5). The testimony is then repeated because of its endless inspiration, and because it is not limited to the psalmist. Such an amazing relationship between man and Deity can only be because of the invisible presence of spiritual agencies, viz. the angelic host (cf. Gn. xxviii. 12, xxxii. 2; 2 Ki. vi. 17; Heb. i. 14) under the authority of, or personified as, *the angel of the Lord* (7); i.e. the Captain of the Lord's host who so often appeared in the Old Testament theophanies (e.g. Ex. xiv. 19; Jos. v. 13–15; Jdg. vi. 12).

c. General exhortation (9–18)

In verse 9 the personal appeal of verse 3 is enlarged and generalized. Compare also verses 6 and 7 with verses 17 and 18. Two themes are then elaborated. First, the concept of deliverance from all fears is doubly illustrated by the imagery of young lions going hungry, because the Lord protected their intended prey (cf. Ps. xxii. 13), and also by the suggestion that even powerful beasts in their prime have less security of life than those who turn to God for sustenance and enjoy His abundant provision (10). Secondly, the simile in verse 5 of looking unto the Lord, with its suggestion of reflected radiance (cf. 2 Cor. iii. 18), is reversed in verse 15 where it is the eyes of the Lord which are upon the righteous (cf. Ps. xxxii. 8) and by His face the wicked shall be abashed (16).

Inserted within this general development of the Psalm is a sub-section (11–14) distinguished from the context by its didactic tone. David here teaches his followers what it means to *fear the Lord* (9, 11). He gives an instructive disclosure of the basic principles of noble action which is the more striking in view of the character of David's companions in the cave of Adullam (1 Sa. xxii. 2). The ideal life, the life which is marked by the joyfulness of the Lord's continual benevolence, has three characteristics: strict avoidance of all falsity of speech (cf. Mt. v. 37); an uncompromising activity in doing good; perseverance in the quest for peace with men (cf. Rom. xiv. 19; Heb. xii. 14). That David and his men acted thus is attested in 1 Sa. xxv. 14–16. These essential rules for godly living are quoted verbatim in 1 Pet. iii. 10–12, and are implicit in such synopses of Christian ethics as that given in Col. iii. 8–17.

d. Conclusion (19–22)

This is a summary statement of the two trends and issues of human life. On one hand there is the pursuit of righteousness and godliness which, for all its incidental affliction, is inseparably bound up with the goodness and power of the Lord who maintains the believer's inward strength. On the other hand there is the choice of wickedness and its inevitable doom; by its very antagonism to the good, the practice of evil will entail the ruin of its guilty adherents. Finally, there is an echo of the initial testimony in verses 1 and 2, and an emphatic assertion that it is impossible for those who trust in the Lord to share in the desolation (condemnation, RV) of the guilty. (Cf. Rom. viii. 1, 33, 34.) *He keepeth all his bones* (20). A vivid figure for complete preservation. It was literally fulfilled in the experience of Christ (Jn. xix. 36).

PSALM XXXV. A LITANY

This strong cry of distress dates from the period when David was being hunted by Saul, and it probably arose out of the experiences in the cave of En-gedi when David spared the life of the sleeping king. It may be regarded as an elaboration of 1 Sa. xxiv. 15. At such a time David's mind was extremely agitated because of his enemies at Saul's court, the king's instability of character, the awful scope of human ingratitude and hatred, and the elusive details of God's purposes which in themselves were plain and yet contradictory (cf. 1 Sa. xxiv. 6, 20). This prayer for judgment on his foes was no expression of secret malice against Saul, for had he not spared his life? It is a plea for the visible demonstration of essential righteousness.

The Psalm has three sections, each of which ends with the expectation of thanksgiving for deliverance: the last section (19–28) is considered by some to have been added by Hezekiah.

a. Prayer for a vigorous deliverance from violence (1–10)

The sequence is obvious. Verses 1–3 are a call to the Lord to help expressed in the terms of the battlefield. Verses 4–8 are an intimation of what should be done to those who are seeking his hurt (cf. Ps. i. 4; Je. xxiii. 12). Verses 9, 10 anticipate the time when fervent praise will be offered to God because of His gracious deliverance. *Plead my cause* (1). Better, as in RV, 'strive'. The Hebrew word is often used of disputes at law, but the AV translation is not really suitable here because the court of judgment is the field of battle. Cf. verses 11 and 23.

b. Argument for immediate deliverance from injustice (11–18)

The situation is one in which false witnesses bring fantastic charges against the psalmist. *They rewarded me evil for good* (12). His grief is the greater because those who accuse him are ones whom he has befriended. The contrast is presented in some detail. Verses 13 and 14 describe his solicitude for others; when they were ill or distressed he sympathized with them so deeply that he virtually identified himself with them (cf. Jb. ii. 12). He could not have done more even for his next of kin. *My prayer returned* (13). Better, as in RV mg., 'shall return'. The meaning is that his prayer, though seemingly fruitless, shall return in blessing to himself. When the situation is reversed how differently they act (15, 16). They do not wait for him to be in great need; he had but to stumble (RV 'when I halted') and they gloat over it and initiate a campaign of slander and calumny so that their words rend and stab. *With* (RV 'like') *hypocritical mockers in feasts* (16); a phrase of uncertain meaning, but usually understood as denoting worthless buffoons who would earn a meal by ribaldry upon any theme. This argument closes with an appeal similar to those in Pss. xiii. 1, 2, xxii. 19–21.

c. Appeal for a statement of acquittal (19–28)

The situation is now presented as a moral issue; i.e. the appeal to the Lord is made solely on the grounds of His righteousness (24). The conflict is not now one of weapons but of words; and the inwardness of the issue is seen in that the appeal is not for a stopping of mouths (21) but a silencing of their heart's intention (25). The wrongful imputation of evil against those who are law-abiding (20b) can do great mischief unless truth is made known. Hence the urgent appeal to the Lord who is addressed as *my God and my Lord* (23). Note the Hebrew names here, *'elohim* and *'adhon* (cf. Jn. xx. 28). This is possible only because the psalmist has a clear conscience and because his request that those who rejoice at his difficulties should be disgraced (cf. verse 4) springs from his deep aversion to the evil desires and practices of such men. His own desire is for the widest experience of God's goodness, hence the concluding intercession that the joyous testimonies of godly men may be incapable of denial by those who were formerly sceptical. *Wink with the eye* (19) and *opened their mouth wide* (21) are gestures of exultant malice and contempt.

PSALM XXXVI. THE GOODNESS OF GOD

The central theme of this Psalm is the lovingkindness of God (5, 7, 10). In sharp contrast is the picture of a wicked man (1–4). The Psalm ends with a prayer for deliverance, and the assurance through faith of the overthrow of the wicked (10–12).

a. The limitations of evil (1–4)

Transgression is imagined as speaking within the heart of a wicked man who regards it as an oracle (1; see RV mg.). In other words, sin leads the sinner to project his evil concepts on to the seat of moral authority, whence God has been dispossessed. This spirit of rebellion against God assures the sinner that he need have no *fear* (1b); i.e. he need not dread any consequences of

his conduct. This self-deception of the wicked is due to his deliberate blindness toward God: he shuts himself within himself and, by listening to the smooth words of his own oracle, persuades himself that he is immune from ultimate disgrace and dereliction. In verse 2 follow RV mg. and translate 'For it (transgression) flattereth him in his own eyes, that his iniquity shall not be found out and be hated'. This psychological diagnosis should be read in the light of Mk. vii. 21–23 (cf. Dt. xxix. 19). The rejection of the true God inevitably entails the erection of a false god endowed to the full with the deceitful and creaturely propensities of the rebellious heart.

After thus sketching the philosophy of the self-deceiving sinner, the actual process of his life is described (3, 4). His conversation is insincere, his words work wickedness, he ceases to exercise his senses to discern between good and evil, and he refrains from doing good (cf. Je. iv. 22 and contrast Is. i. 16, 17). When he lies resting he does not meditate upon God but is willing to be engrossed in base and wicked schemes. His whole life is shaped and set into the pattern of the 'not good' (cf. Is. xxviii. 15) and thus he neither recognizes nor rightly reacts to evil.

b. The greatness of God (5–9)

Language is not able adequately to express the attributes of God. Their greatness is of a quality other than size and surpasses any mental concept of it. But language is all we have to convey our apprehension of truth, so the psalmist uses material height and depth to illustrate spiritual infinities, and draws pictures of living needs such as parental protection and thirst's satisfaction to symbolize the rich realities of divine-human fellowship.

The *mercy* (RV 'lovingkindness') and *faithfulness* of God (5) are as limitless as the starry heavens and the endless perspectives of the clouds. His *righteousness* and *judgments* (6) are as immovable and unfathomable as the mountains and the ocean (cf. Rom. xi. 33). There is not a man or beast in all the earth that is uncared for by the Lord. His benevolent vigilance is unspeakably *excellent* (RV 'precious') to the psalmist (7; cf. Ps. cxxxix. 17). His love and His resources overshadow all people and, like the Garden of Eden, there is no dearth nor drought for the soul which commits itself to Him (8; the word *pleasures* is from the same root as Eden). Moreover the very opportunity and capacity to know both our existence (*life*) and His truth (*light*) is given by Him. The psalmist's whole outlook is the antithesis of the evil man's.

c. A prayer for continued blessing (10–12)

Whereas the wicked man is unaware of the glories of the divine nature, the godly man has been given some knowledge; hence the only consistent course for the psalmist is to ask the Lord for a continuance of His loving-kindness. He prays that godliness may always be the experience and characteristic of godly men; that he may neither be trodden down by insolent feet nor driven out by impious hands. In faith he foresees the ultimate downfall of the ungodly.

PSALM XXXVII. A MEDITATION UPON THE PROSPERITY OF THE WICKED

This poem is built upon an acrostic of the Hebrew alphabet and consists of a series of thoughts often expressed in a proverbial manner. For example, compare verse 1 with Pr. xxiv. 19; verse 5 with Pr. xvi. 3; verse 16 with Pr. xvi. 8; verse 23 with Pr. xvi. 9. There are some resemblances also to statements in the book of Job. Compare verse 6 with Jb. xi. 17; verse 10 with Jb. vii. 10; verse 13 with Jb. xviii. 20; verse 19 with Jb. v. 20. Taken as a whole, the psalmist's outlook is a modification of that which was so vehemently put forward by Job's friends (e.g. Zophar in Jb. xx. 5). The psalmist was certainly troubled by the prosperity and power of wicked men, but he believed this to be only a temporary reversal of true values. The poem should be read alongside Ps. lxxiii, where the issue is seen (17) from a spiritual and not a material standpoint.

The poem has no obvious structure apart from its main thread of confidence in God's future work; this links the various statements together and is particularly symbolized in the repeated words *shall inherit the earth* (or *land*) (9, 11, 22, 29, 34). The meditation may be studied in four sections.

a. Definition of the right attitude to life's problem (1-8)

The initial emphasis is negative (*fret not, neither be thou envious*), but the principal stress is on the positive actions of *trust, delight in, commit, rest, wait*, all in connection with the sufficiency and goodness of the Lord. Verses 7b, 8 repeat the exhortations of verse 1. On the negative side there is the use in verse 2 of a metaphor so apt that it is frequently used both in the Old Testament and in the New (e.g. Ps. xc. 6, ciii. 15; Is. xl. 6-8; Jas. i. 10, 11; note also verse 20 below). On the positive side there is the clear concept of a definite transaction between the Lord and the trusting soul. See, e.g., verse 5 (RV mg.), 'Roll thy way upon the Lord' (cf. Ps. lv. 22; 1 Pet. v. 7). This attitude must be maintained by the doing of good and the determination not to be distracted from, or weary in, well-doing (cf. Heb. x. 32-39). *So shalt thou dwell in the land* (3). Render with RV in the imperative tense, 'Dwell in the land'; i.e. in spite of trials, do not forsake the land of God's promise. On His part there will be the sure vindication of faith, as certain as the noonday sun, and also He will bestow upon the soul that delights in Him the fulfilment of his desires, i.e. Himself. The reminder to refrain from angry annoyance at injustice is repeated by James (Jas. i. 26, iii. 9); it is far better to be silent and to banish all fretfulness by an unswerving reliance upon God. Cf. Ps. lxii. 1, 5.

b. The psalmist's underlying belief analysed (9-21)

Verse 9, with its *for* and *but*, sets out the basis for the right attitude to the moral anomalies of life. After a little while the wicked shall disappear and the godly shall live undisturbed. Each aspect is expanded in verses 10 and 11 (cf. Mt. v. 5) and the theme thus introduced is further elaborated in verses 12-15. The wicked plot, gnash with the teeth, draw out the sword and bend their bow in order to cast down and slay the righteous who are 'upright in the way' (14, RV; cf. Ps. cxix. 1), as, for instance, in Ahab's plot against Naboth (1 Ki. xxi. 11-16). But their own weapons shall be their destruction (15). In contrast, righteous men are altogether different and their worth is measured by moral values, not by material well-being (16, 17). The meditation now turns to the upright who are further described in verses 18 and 19. Their outstanding characteristic is a conviction of security which is not rooted in the circumstances of everyday life, so that even when misfortune comes upon them they are not abashed. In contrast, the wicked have no enduring security, no more so than the finest pastures (verse 20, following RV) which disappear in smoke (cf. verse 2).

c. Belief and testimony (22-33)

The psalmist's thought now turns to the essential factor in life—the character of the Lord. He makes safe and sure the way that a righteous man takes, and even if that man should trip over he is not left prostrate (24; cf. Lk. x. 33-35; Jude 24). This is no fanciful notion but a fact of experience. Verse 25 does not mean that a good man is never destitute (cf. 1 Sa. xxi. 3, xxv. 8) but that he is never forsaken of the Lord and ultimately, in *his seed*, conditions become improved. At all times the only right principle is to keep on doing good (27; cf. Ps. xxxiv. 14) because equity in dealing with men and loyalty toward God are always approved by the Lord and fostered by His co-operation. The psalmist's meditation is now turning from the theme of the Lord's providential care to the actual experiences of *his saints* (28). Not only do they possess this enduring quality but their speech is marked by pleasant reflections upon the law and truth (30). His life is genuine for his heart is occupied with God's will. Even though evil men plot against the righteous and accuse him before corrupt judges, nevertheless the Lord will not fail to intervene sooner or later.

d. Concluding counsel (34-40)

Set your heart upon the Lord and keep your life on His path; then eventually the downfall of the wicked will be witnessed. This is not a matter for personal gratification; it is demanded by the moral bases of life. The psalmist here adds his second testimony to the effect that he himself had known a wicked man acting as a terrible tyrant and flourishing like a leafy tree in its own native soil; yet he was suddenly cut down and removed from the scene as though he had never existed. All transgressors are bound to be destroyed; there is no possible future for any wicked man. But let everyone take note of what happens to a man who is upright and godly; there is indeed a future for him, and for his posterity (37, RV mg.).

The two final verses are a confession of faith in the character, power and absolute trustworthiness of the Lord.

PSALM XXXVIII. CONTRITION WHEN HARASSED WITHIN AND WITHOUT

This prayer for divine aid was prompted by great physical and moral distress. The descriptive details in verses 1–8 may be metaphorical (cf. Is. i. 5, 6), but the pronounced element of personal experience in these verses suggests some serious disease. Probably moral perplexity and bodily affliction were concurrent as in the case of Job, who also experienced ostracism by friends (11) and humiliation through the success of the unworthy (19, 20). The phrase in the title, *to bring to remembrance*, or 'to make memorial' (RV mg.), represents a technical word which was probably associated with certain offerings of the Levites before the ark (cf. 1 Ch. xvi. 4, where the Hebrew word translated 'record' or 'celebrate' (RV) is the same as that used here). The Psalm can be analysed as follows.

a. The disquiet of sin (1–11)

His experience leads him to infer that the Lord's present attitude to him is one of wrath and displeasure. His agencies are as sharp piercing arrows and strong pressing hand. *Anger* (3); better, as in RV, 'indignation'. Ultimately sin is the cause of all his distress. These iniquities are described first as a suffocating flood (4a; cf. Jon. ii. 3–5; Ps. xlii. 7), then as a burden crushing the life out of him (4b; cf. Gn. iv. 13). The swift change of metaphor accentuates the restless and distraught spirit of a sinner convicted of guilt. Beginning with festering wounds, the consequences of his sinful folly are graphically described: a pain-racked body, bent and bowed like that of a mourner; his whole frame fevered and diseased. The description then gradually turns from outward symptoms of the flesh to evidences of an inner malady which is well known to God. There is a general sense of numbness and incapacity, the inarticulate groaning of an aching heart and a troubled conscience (8, 9). Such a moral malady finds expression in a throbbing heart (10, RV), a loss of zest in life, dullness of vision, and a suspicion on the part of friends and even of kinsmen which causes them to hold aloof from him, as if he were a leper (11). *My sore* (11); better, as in RV, 'plague'. The Hebrew word is used of leprosy in Lv. xiii. 3, etc.

b. The decision to turn to God (12–17)

This thought of other men provides a link for a theme of certainty. He knows that those who have sought his life are now, during his distress, actively plotting and scheming against him. Moreover, because of his sense of guilt, he must behave as though unaware of their slanders, for he cannot plead innocence in a matter of greater moment. *Reproofs* (14); better, as in RV mg., 'arguments'. The external pressure of his enemies clarifies the psalmist's real attitude of heart; his trust is rooted in the Lord. He who knows the sickness of his soul (9) will know how to answer the scornful (16). To this acknowledgment of the Lord's willingness to uphold a godly man is added that of his own helplessness, visibly hampered in body and inwardly burdened by sorrow (17). There is one step more to penitence.

c. The confession of sin (18–22)

He admits his sin, and recognizes that it is this which is the root cause of his sorrow and care. Nevertheless his enemies are still active and numerous and are apparently unaffected by his change of heart. Indeed they are quite ready to repay any graciousness on his part with ingratitude (20). *I follow the thing that good is* (20); i.e. in his behaviour towards them. The prayer concludes with an urgent call to the Lord not to forsake him nor to be slow to intervene. Faith has not yet risen to the triumphant certainty of Ps. vi. 8, 9, but the active committal of personal faith is seen in the final words, *O Lord my salvation*.

PSALM XXXIX. DEEP CONFLICT

The connection of this Psalm with the previous one is obvious; it may be taken as an expansion of xxxviii. 13, 14. But the lament has deeper roots than personal distress. See, e.g., verses 5, 6 and 11. The theme of repression and confession (verses 1 and 3) is similar to that in xxxii. 3–5. The circumstances of a righteous ideal for life, a powerful and humiliating experience, a period of intense reflection and introspection, and the absence of any hope of alleviation for his distress, are all parallel to those of Job, and it is not surprising that the poem has many points of similarity to that book.

The superscription *to Jeduthun* refers to a notable leader of the temple choir (cf. 1 Ch. xvi. 41, 42, xxv. 1–6). He is also named in the titles of Pss. lxii and lxxvii. The poem has four parts.

a. Suppression (1–3)

The decision to exercise a strict watch over all that he says may mean a determination either to say nothing about the prosperity enjoyed by the wicked or, more probably, to refrain from complaint about his own distress. *While the wicked is before me* (1); i.e. their presence is a warning to be cautious in speech. This suppression of his feelings, however, simply caused a psychological explosion; the emotions burst the restriction of the will; he could no longer restrain himself.

b. Outburst (4-6)

The outburst is not as Job's—an attack upon God for bringing him into so painful a situation. It is a request that the Lord should confirm him in his belief that man's life is so brief and tenuous as to be utterly vain. If he can be assured of this, then the vicissitudes of fortune can be largely written off. Man's life in its brevity cannot hold any great consequence compared with the unchangeableness of God. Even the most prosperous of men is only a shadow, a phantom, whose possessions, acquired by a lifetime of anxiety and effort, are soon left behind for others to misuse. Cf. Ec. i. 18, v. 16.

c. Reconsideration (7-11)

The mood wherein the psalmist is prepared dully to endure gives way to one that is more positive and active. The concept of his *end* (4) is changed from that of 'termination' to that of 'purpose', and in this respect his hope is wholly in the Lord to whom he now prays. The purpose and meaning of his life, as he sees it, cannot be attained without moral cleansing (8a), nor can it be possible if the taunts of base men are true, viz. that there is no God who would concern Himself about the matter. This inner need of forgiveness, and the outer need of vindication, show that his soul is conscious of dependence upon the Lord. It was the recognition of this submissive relationship which prompted his earlier but ineffective attempt to keep silent: it now provokes him to plead for relief (10) lest the affliction which is believed to come direct from God brings his life to a swift close. Verses 6 and 11 both refer to the vanity of life and the instability of its riches. But the former has no cognizance of God; the latter refers to Him thrice—He rebukes, He chastens, and He makes to perish. In one case the vanity of human life lay in its brevity; in the other the vanity of life lies in its poverty. Hence the strong necessity of a positive action by the Lord; He must do what no man can do.

d. Prayer (12, 13)

This is the counterpart of verses 1-3. The dominance of the subjective *I said, I will, I was*, etc. (1-3) disappears before the objective reference to the Lord whose ear, and word, and benevolence are desired because therein is true life. The initial desire—to know for certain that he had but a short time to live—is replaced by a passionate prayer for reprieve from anguish and for the experience of a period of strength and comfort before he dies. *Spare me* (13); i.e. 'turn away thy look of wrath' (cf. verse 10). The psalmist beseeches his Lord to attend to his need and yet asks to be spared any further scrutiny of God's critical eye. This conclusion to the Psalm is a composite echo from the book of Job. (Cf. phrases in Jb. vii. 19, x. 20, 21, vii. 21b.)

PSALM XL. A LITURGY OF A FULL HEART

It may quite well be that the contrasting moods reflected in this poem were occasioned by the circumstances related at the end of the first book of Samuel. The lament over the destruction of Ziklag (1 Sa. xxx. 4-6), the swift defeat of Amalek (1 Sa. xxx. 16-20), and the news of the Philistine victory at Gilboa and of the death of Saul with all its implications for David, occurred within three or four days (2 Sa. i. 1). The loss and recovery of his family, the elation of military success, the acquisition of great spoil, the death of Jonathan, the end of Saul's persecution, the prospect of a leaderless people, and of conflict with the Philistines among whom he had friends, all combined to stir the heart of David. This poem, therefore, may be the expression of his release from a perilous exile wherein had been great gain in Godward trust (1-3), of his readiness to undertake the expected call to be leader of the people (7) and of dedication to that work (8), of his recognition that not all his foes had fallen on Gilboa (14-16) and that many of his deeds in the period of Saul's animosity must now come home with painful consequences (12) if the exile became king. The poem certainly expresses his consciousness of utter dependence on the Lord (13, 17) as well as his delight in Him (1-5) and eager service of Him (6-10). The Psalm falls into three parts, each with two subsections.

a. Thanksgiving (1-5)

i. **The past experience (1-3).** David's patient waiting upon the Lord is in marked contrast to the tension and pleading of the two previous Psalms. The duration of this trustful waiting is of no consequence in view of what happened. The Lord's ear was alert to his prayer. *An horrible pit* (2). 'A pit of noise' (AV mg.); 'a pit of tumult or destruction' (RV mg.). A reference to the period of hiding, meagre in its amenities, tumultuous in its alarms. God has brought him out of the place of insecurity, and put him firmly on the rock of His sufficiency (cf. Ps. xviii. 31-33). He made plain the way of his going (cf. Ps. xxxvii. 23), and gave him a new song so that many others should hear and wonder and believe.

ii. **The new song (4, 5).** These verses might be paraphrased as follows: 'Blessed is that mature and vigorous man (the Hebrew word means 'a man of might') whose trust is not in himself but in the Lord. Blessed is he who has not compromised with the arrogant or resorted to such as trust in falsehoods. Marvellously hast Thou wrought Thine abundant works, O my Lord, and in Thy plans for us men there is none to be compared with Thee. Such works and wisdom are beyond my power to compute or my ability to comprehend' (see note on Ps. cxxxix. 17, 18).

b. Dedication (6-10)

i. **The supreme offering (6-8).** Supreme among the plans of God which have been disclosed to the ear of the psalmist is that whereby worship is consummated not in the ritual of the blood of beasts but in the willing surrender of the worshipper's life for continual obedience to the will of God. There are three parentheses in this section, and the direct speech runs: 'Sacrifice and meal offering thou hast no delight in; burnt offering and sin offering hast thou not required. Then said I, "Lo, I am come; I delight to do thy will, O my God".' The four offerings here mentioned are detailed in Lv. i–iv. But while they had a rightful place in divine worship centred in the altar, they were not the sole or primary requirement laid upon the worshipper (cf. Dt. x. 12f.). This passage is interpreted in Heb. x. 5–10 as being spoken by Jesus Christ and fulfilled in Him. In this quotation, which is dependent upon the LXX, the idea of *mine ears hast thou opened* (6) (i.e. a prepared avenue of divine revelation) is replaced by that of 'a body hast thou prepared me' (Heb. x. 5), and this enlarged concept is made the basis of the following exegesis (Heb. x. 10ff.). The incarnate Word heard perfectly (Jn. viii. 26).

ii. **The public testimony (9, 10).** The righteousness of God has been proclaimed before men; it has not been kept for his own secret delight. The faithfulness, mercy and truth of the Lord have been preached before crowds of men, His salvation has been advertised. The second part of verse 9 is a parenthesis, the main testimony being symmetrically announced: 'I have published abroad . . . I have not hidden within . . . I have declared . . . I have not concealed . . .'

c. **Supplication (11–17)**

i. **For salvation of soul (11–13).** The emphasis from the first word is on the Lord. 'Do thou, on thy part, not withhold thy compassions from me, even as I have not withheld (refrained) my life. Let thy lovingkindness and truth, which I have not concealed from men, continually be my protection, because a multitude of evils have coiled around me and the consequences of past sins have blurred my vision just when I need to see clearly.' Hence the petition of verse 13.

ii. **For deliverance from danger (14–17).** This request, as in the third portion of Ps. xxxv, seeks the overthrow of David's foes by a recoiling upon themselves of all their schemes and slanders against him. This appeal is linked with a desire for blessing upon all who can join from the heart in his song of praise (see verse 3). What if he is *poor and needy* (17); i.e. burdened and helpless? The Lord will certainly take thought for him (see verse 5) and free him from all difficulties however tenacious and troublesome (see verse 2). The poem's whole expression of praise, its reliance upon God's promise and its plea for help are caught up and crystallized in these words of verse 17, especially in the final cry, *Make no tarrying, O my God* (cf. Dn. ix. 19).

PSALM XLI. ABUSE AND ASSURANCE

The charge against *mine own familiar friend* (9) links this poem with Ps. lv (see verses 13, 14 and 20, 21). The usual inference is that Ahithophel was the faithless friend (2 Sa. xv. 12 and 31). There is no mention of David's being ill at that time, although it is reasonable to suppose that a long illness had contributed to the slackness of administration which Absalom exploited and helped to bring about the precipitate flight of a king formerly renowned for his courage and resourcefulness. Ps. xxxviii probably originated in the same period of bodily sickness. The poem obviously belongs to a time subsequent to the disclosure of Ahithophel's treachery and it reflects David's distress of mind as well as of body. He was able to see the motives behind some earlier activities of his unfriendly companions. The Psalm falls into three sections.

a. **A statement of principle (1–3).**

While the psalmist includes himself in the category of those who are *poor* (1), i.e. enfeebled in body, he is making a general statement valid in all similar cases. Happy is that man who considers how best he may aid the needy. *In time of trouble* (RV 'in the day of evil') the Lord will be his helper. The wicked hopes of his enemies will be confounded by actual events. Should such a man become seriously ill, the Lord will maintain him so that he does not change his bed for the grave. *Thou wilt make all his bed* (3). Lit. 'turn or change all his lying down', i.e. 'bring him back to health' (Moff.). See RV mg. and cf. Ps. xxx. 11.

b. **David's bitter experience (4–9)**

A specific case, his own, is now cited wherein the principle of benevolence has not been reciprocated. At a time when, because of illness, his enemies were openly desiring and forecasting his death, then those from whom he expected kindness and sympathy returned him deceitfulness and antagonism (5). Some of those who visited him in his sickness were obviously pleased to find him laid low, and lied when they expressed a desire for his speedy recovery (6). Their true thoughts were spread abroad outside the sick chamber so that his secret enemies were emboldened to plot against him (7) and circulated rumours of some incurable disease, brought on by evil doing, which would prevent his ever leaving his bed (8). Bitterest of all was the behaviour of that man with whom there was the peace of close agreement, the man whose counsel he implicitly trusted (cf. 2 Sa. xvi. 23) and who in turn was implicitly bound to loyalty because they had often dined together. He had magnified himself against the king, had tried to trip him even while David sought to rise by his aid, and would have spurned the prostrate ruler with his heel (cf. Jn. xiii. 18).

c. **A sure confidence in the Lord (10–12)**

In spite of the bitter disappointment caused by his trusted companion David's reliance upon

God is unimpaired. He not only prays for restoration to health so that wickedness might be refuted and thwarted, but affirms his unshakable confidence in the Lord's graciousness toward him on three grounds. First, his false friend has not triumphed; secondly, he is divinely sustained in his desire for the highest good;

thirdly, the Lord has established a permanent relationship of agreement with him (cf. 2 Sa. iii. 9; Acts xiii. 22).

The last verse is not part of the Psalm, though it is most appropriate. It is a doxology added by a compiler to mark the end of the first of the five books of Psalms.

BOOK TWO. PSALMS xlii–lxxii

PSALMS XLII AND XLIII. THE LONGING FOR GOD'S SANCTUARY

Whereas, in the first book of Psalms, no other author than David is mentioned (four are anonymous), in the second book only eighteen of the thirty-one poems are attributed to him; Pss. xlii to xlix being inscribed 'to (or for) the sons of Korah' (cf. Nu. xxvi. 11; 1 Ch. vi. 22, 31). Moreover the final verse (lxxii. 20) states that the songs of David have been completed.

Pss. xlii and xliii constitute one poem: in several Hebrew MSS they are joined together, and it may be observed that Ps. xliii is the only poem in the second book to lack a superscription. The theme in both is that of deep grief caused by exclusion from the crowded sanctuary of the Lord which is on His holy hill. Ps. xliii. 5 is virtually identical with Ps. xlii. 5 and 11. It is plain that these are a refrain and that the complete poem has three stanzas.

a. Yearning and regret (xlii. 1–5)

The imagery of a timid fallow deer audibly panting because of extreme thirst (cf. Joel i. 20) vividly expresses the intense and searing sense of want experienced by the psalmist (cf. Pss. lxiii. 1, lxxxiv. 2). His craving to draw near unto the living God who is the fountain of living water (Je. ii. 13) is inseparable from the remembered habit of going up to the sanctuary (cf. Ps. lxxxiv. 7; 1 Sa. i. 22). But the repetition of 'Elohim' (God) shows that the yearning is for communion with God Himself. This desire, the strength of which is evident in loss of appetite and frequent tears, has been intensified by the sceptical remarks of other men—either his enemies, or his companions in whom the tide of events has brought a loss of faith, or his new acquaintances in exile who sympathize with his loss but pity him trusting in a God who, if He exists, is obviously unable to help him (cf. Ps. iii. 2). This atmosphere of unbelief has enhanced his memories of how he used to lead the throng of pilgrims *that kept holyday* (4) in procession to the house of the Lord (cf. 2 Sa. vi. 15–19). This moody retrospect is suddenly challenged by an upwelling of irrepressible faith and the psalmist calls upon his mournful soul not only to trust in God but actively to hope for His deliverance. In verse 5 the LXX renders the last words as in verses 11 and xliii. 5. See RV mg.

b. Dejection and hope (xlii. 6–11)

The second stanza picks out of the refrain the words *cast down*, and the psalmist reaffirms the

depression of his soul because he is away from Jordan (cf. Mt. xxvi. 38). The scenery around him in the north-east of Gilead is such as to illustrate his despondency and thus strengthen it; the thunder of waterfalls fed by Hermon's snow and the ceaseless swirl of Jordan's flooded tributaries fill the air with the sound of ceaseless unrest which seems to parallel his spiritual turmoil (cf. Jon. ii. 3–6). Nevertheless the God who governs the physical world (cf. Ps. xxix. 3, 10) will overrule the distress of his soul (8) in his perplexity he will say unto Him who is his rock of security *Why . . . why . . .?* (9). 'Why am I left bereft of Thine aid so that I have no answer to the echoing taunts of my foes? I feel hurt in my very bones because there seems to be no immediate ground for me to say to them "See, God is my God now as always".'

The refrain takes up the query 'Why?' and throws it back at the doubting heart, challenging mistrust's right of place there in view of God's sure deliverance.

c. Confidence in God (xliii. 1–5)

In the third stanza of the complete poem the human elements of distress and despondency are replaced by a realization of God's faithfulness and power. The mood of plaintive regret in the first stanza and of fitful perplexity in the second is changed in the third to one of confidence and trust. The baffling circumstances of the soul, both without and within, are still present to the psalmist. Hence his plea for vindication against men who are unkind, deceitful and unjust, and his request for heartfelt assurance in the matter of divine care. God is his supreme resource, why then does He seem to have rejected him? Why must the psalmist go about by himself as solitary as a mourner? (2). Nevertheless, these needs are referred to God precisely because his desire and hope and faith are in Him. Whatever gloom may shade his soul, God Himself is unchangeable light; moreover, His trust must prevail over all misleading tendencies. Consequently God will surely remove the existing barriers both within and without which hinder him from going up to Mount Zion (3). He may therefore eagerly look forward to a renewal of communion with God before His altar through that method of worship which has been hallowed by precedent and custom (cf. 1 Ch. xxi. 26; 1 Sa. vii. 9, 12; Jdg. vi. 24; Gn. xii. 8). In so doing the psalmist will be gladdened not only by a resumption of his former habit (xlii. 4), but by the conviction of

God's blessing in that He will have brought him through his present experience (xliii. 4). This anticipation of unhindered fellowship with God who is the delight and source of all his joy introduces the final refrain, and although this is unchanged in words it is transformed in tone. Faith's rebuke to dejection (xlii. 5) and faith's exhortation in bewilderment (xlii. 11) become faith's triumphant declaration of certainty (xliii. 5).

PSALM XLIV. THE BEWILDERMENT OF A GODLY PEOPLE

This Psalm is the first of several national poems in the Psalter which are usually retrospective and often supplicatory. See, e.g., Pss. lxxxiii, cvi. In each case the underlying motive is an intense desire to know God's ways and specially to see how His actions in human history can be justified. The usual view regarded national distress or disaster as the direct result of the people's wrongdoing. God controlled their national life by the simple method of rewards and punishments, giving victory and prosperity at a time of godliness, and sending defeat and dearth when sinful practices dominated the nation. See, e.g., Jdg. ii. 16–23; Ps. cvi.

Ps. xliv is outstanding because it faces the problem of the sufferings of godly people. The same predicament is presented in the book of Job and it was a major theme in the teaching of the prophets (e.g. Hab. i. 13ff.; Je. xx. 7ff.; Is. liii. 4, 5). This treatment of a righteous people's ignomiy should be read in conjunction with Pss. xlvi and xlvii, which are poems expressive of national awe and rejoicing occasioned by some great deliverance. The poem falls into four sections.

a. Material blessings enjoyed in the days of old (1–8)

This review of the past first rehearses certain events (1–3) and then repeats the expression of faith (4–8) which accompanied and grew out of those events. Foremost in the nation's previous experience was the unique acquisition of the land of Canaan. In references to this event the emphasis was usually placed upon their deliverance from Egypt (e.g. Ps. lxxviii. 42–53); but here the settlement in Canaan is selected as a historical monument of divine activity not only because it was so amazingly accomplished (cf. Dt. iv. 35–38) but because it was so obviously the antithesis of their present experience (see 11b).

There could be no mistaking God's aid in the *times of old* (1): weapons alone were no guarantee of success (cf. Pss. xx. 7, xxxiii. 12, 16). Their Lord was a 'man of war' (Ex. xv. 3: note also Is. lix. 16, 17); that was why they had power to crush all opposition even as an ox will gore (*push down*, 5) his attacker. These memories of triumph are followed by a pause (*Selah*); a change of music would prepare for the introduction of another theme.

b. The profound dishonour of the present condition (9–16)

The word *But*, or 'Yet', introduces tremendous contradiction. Their King and God has cast off His people and repudiated His connection with them, or so it would appear (cf. Ps. xliii. 2, lxxxix. 38). Their armies have gone to battle and the Lord has held back (cf. Nu. xiv. 40–45; and contrast 2 Sa. v. 24). They are perplexed and at a loss, their enemies despoil them at their pleasure, and the people of the Lord are as helpless as sheep (11; cf. verse 22). It looks as though God has given them away, or sold them virtually for nothing (12; cf. Joel iii. 3). Certainly He has gained no prestige for Himself among the nations. The neighbouring Edomites and Moabites are elated at their misfortune (13; cf. Ps. lxxix. 4) and scoff derisively at the Jews' belief in a protecting God. Even the remoter nations regard the matter with levity (14, RV; cf. Dt. xxviii. 37; Ps. xxii. 7). In short, the people of God are humiliated and utterly crestfallen because of the inescapable mockery of men who blaspheme and say 'the promises of the Lord your God are obviously worthless'.

c. The unmerited nature of this experience (17–22)

The sting of all this arises from a lack of any sense of guilt on their part. If they had fallen away from God (cf. Ps. xvi) or been disobedient to the covenant (cf. Dt. xxviii. 15ff.) then their plight would be understandable. But the national conscience is clear, and yet their country is devastated so that it looks like the dreary haunts of jackals (19, RV, for *dragons*; cf. Is. xxxiv. 13). There is no claim here of individual blamelessness, but only a sincere conviction that the trend of national life and policy was without fault before God; and after all, He should know if this was falsely said. Indeed it would appear that the attack upon their national existence must be because they were God's people and other nations hated them for that (22; cf. Ps. lxxxiii).

This insight into the discipline of godliness was not understood or appropriated at the time, but it is taken as axiomatic in the New Testament (cf. Mt. v. 11; Jn. xv. 20, 25; Acts xiv. 22; Rom. viii. 36; 2 Tim. iii. 12).

d. The urgent need of divine aid (23–26)

The pressure of circumstances makes itself felt above any consolation afforded by the great truth just expressed (22). The bitterness of life is imaged in the outward gestures of physical prostration (cf. 2 Sa. xii. 16; Jb. i. 20); they mourn for the loss of personal fellowship with the Lord. For His sake they die daily (22) and for His loving-kindness' sake they plead for life (26).

PSALM XLV. A ROYAL WEDDING SONG

This song of a royal marriage was almost certainly prompted by the ceremony of a Hebrew king marrying a foreign princess. The identity of the king is uncertain, for his warlike activities (3, 5) hardly befit Solomon (cf. 1 Ki. iii. 1), and his devout character (6, 7) is not in keeping with Ahab—at least, after his marriage with Jezebel (1 Ki. xvi. 31).

The song was included in the Psalter because it illustrated an idea which is frequently used in Scripture, viz. that the human marriage relationship is an echo, or at least an allegory, of the covenant relationship between God and His people. This same basic idea is carried over into the New Testament where the Church is described as the Bride of Christ (see 2 Cor. xi. 2; and cf. Mt. xxii. 2ff., xxv. 1ff.; Rev. xix. 6–9).

a. Introduction (1)

The song is rightly entitled *A Song of loves*, i.e. of lovely things. Apart from this brief introduction of the first verse, it falls into two sections relating to the bridegroom and bride respectively. In the opening verse the author describes his irrepressible desire to speak of something particularly fine and good, his feelings of appreciative delight on behalf of the king are literally 'bubbling over' (RV 'overfloweth') and he hopes that the eloquence of his pen will be in keeping with so glorious a theme.

b. In praise of the royal bridegroom (2–9)

The king is so superior in face and in graciousness of speech to all other men that it is obvious that God has especially favoured him and will continue to bestow upon his descendants also His divine blessing. He is addressed as the 'mighty one' (3, RV) or warrior hero. He is bidden to gird on his sword, to gird on also his glory and majesty (RV; cf. Rev. xix. 14–16), and to ride on victoriously 'in behalf of truth' (4, RV mg.; cf. Is. xi. 4). On such occasions his prowess will demonstrate great and terrible things (cf. Ps. cxlv. 5, 6). His arrows are so sharp as to be fatal when they strike (cf. Ps. xviii. 14; Heb. iv. 12); he is able to ride over the fallen and sends his shafts into the hearts of his chief enemies (5, RV).

Thy throne, O God (6). Read as in RV mg., 'Thy throne is the throne of God'. This is why his dynasty will abide for ever (cf. 2 Sa. vii. 12–16). The token and emblem of his sovereignty is justice and equity, for he abhors wickedness. It is because of this effective zeal for righteousness that God has endowed him with a fuller joy than any other man can know (cf. Jn. iii. 29; Heb. xii. 2; 1 Pet. i. 8). The quotation of verses 6 and 7 in Heb. i. 8, 9 is a specific instance of the New Testament interpretation of the Old Testament by means of Christ's character and work.

The bridegroom is clothed with perfumed garments, and the rooms of his palace, tastefully decorated with ivory carvings, are filled with sweet music (see RV). Among the ladies of his court are kings' daughters—evidence of his prestige among neighbouring states—and im-

mediately beside him, adorned with fine gold, stands his queen. This introduces the next section of the poem. *Myrrh, and aloes* (8); cf. Ct. iv. 14. *Cassia* (the Hebrew word is found here only) may be a species of cinnamon.

c. In praise of the bride (10–17)

The change of subject is intimated by an appeal to the young bride, whose attention would probably have been partially diverted by the newness of her surroundings. She is exhorted to accept all that she sees as being part of her new life, and also to banish any regrets for the scenes and friends of her past girlhood. She is to identify her interests with those of her husband, who is also her king; he will repay her loyalty and co-operation with affection. *Worship thou him* (11); i.e. make submission to him. After describing the setting so as to give advice and assurance to the princess, the poem speaks of her waiting within the palace, resplendently dressed in her bridal array, whence she will be led to the king in 'raiment that is delicately embroidered' (14), accompanied by her bridesmaids and with joyful music.

The remaining words about the future are addressed to the king, as is implied in verse 17, RV. *I will make thy name* . . . The psalmist will do this by his poem. *For ever and ever.* Cf. verses 2, 6; 2 Sa. vii. 13, 16, 25, 29.

PSALM XLVI. A SAFE STRONGHOLD IS OUR GOD

This is the first of a group of three poems which have a common theme. God is extolled and adored because He has brought His people through a great military crisis which had threatened to become a national calamity. The actual occasion is uncertain. But compare the strange deliverance of Jerusalem from the menace of Moab and Ammon in the days of Jehoshaphat (2 Ch. xx. 1–28) and Sennacherib's sudden abandonment of the siege of Jerusalem (2 Ki. xviii, xix).

The word *Alamoth* in the title is a Hebrew word for 'maidens'; but the strong martial and civic theme of the poem is not in keeping with the idea of having a female choir to sing it. On the other hand such a chorus of maidens would have been most suitable for the chanting of the preceding marriage song, and this has been stated as one reason for supposing all titles to be footnotes to the Psalms which immediately precede them. (See the introductory note to Ps. ix.) Nevertheless, it is uncertain whether a choir of women's voices existed at the temple, and the term *Alamoth* is regarded by some as referring to musical instruments set to a high or treble pitch (cf. 1 Ch. xv. 20). The poem has three distinct stanzas, each terminating with *Selah*, and it is widely held that the refrain of verses 7 and 11 should also be inserted after verse 3.

a. Firm anchorage in God whilst all else is insecure (1–3)

The emphasis here is on external change. This may be regarded as a partial reversion to chaos of the physical creation (cf. Heb. xii. 26–28; 2 Pet. iii. 5–12) or, more probably, as a metaphor for the dissolution of kingdoms and empires. *Mountains* is often used as a symbolic term for 'the nations', and *the sea* is a general symbol for ungodly mankind. *A very present help in trouble* (1). Lit. 'a help in trouble to be found plentifully'; i.e. immediately accessible and able fully to meet the need.

b. Joyful assurance in the impregnable city of God (4–7)

The emphasis here is on internal resources, especially upon the security which ensures serenity even though outward powers rage and threaten. The source of this inward strength is pictured as a stream of quiet content (cf. Ps. xxiii. 2; Is. xxxiii. 21, lviii. 11), as the river of Paradise (Gn. ii. 10). This may be an allusion to Hezekiah's conduit by which the city was supplied with water (2 Ki. xx. 20), but the concept of an unfailing source of living water which brings health and freshness to all around is common to many Scriptures. See, e.g., Ezk. xlvii. 1–10; Rev. xxii. 1, 2; Jn. iv. 14; and 'All my fresh springs are in thee' (Ps. lxxxvii. 7). For the disintegrating effect of the voice of the Lord (6), hinted at in Ps. xxix, cf. Heb. xii. 26 and Rev. xx. 11. The allusion to the Lord's help becoming evident *right early* (5), i.e. at the approach of morning (see RV mg.), may be an echo of Is. xxxvii. 36.

c. A call to consider the works of the Lord (8–11)

The inference from the historical crisis must be plain to all peoples. Surely no nation could doubt that the Lord had done astonishing deeds. *Desolations* (8). Heb. *shammah*, which may be rendered 'astonishments', as in Je. xxv. 9, 11, 18. The rout of the enemy—whether Ammon or Assyria—was beyond dispute. Yet, greater than the event was the divine power which moulded it, and in the cessation of this campaign the psalmist catches a glimpse of the future inauguration of undisturbed peace when the weapons and baggage wagons (*chariot* (9) is probably better rendered 'wagon') will be transformed or burnt (cf. Is. ii. 4, ix. 5). *I will be exalted in the earth* (10). Because the Lord is God, let all men cease their efforts to usurp His sovereignty. Note that the refrain in verses 7 and 11 is threefold: *the Lord of hosts* is His title of divine power, *the God of Jacob* is His title of a covenant relationship, and God *is with us* is His name Immanuel (cf. Rom. viii. 31).

PSALM XLVII. OUR GOD IS THE EXALTED KING

This festive hymn elaborates the words 'I will be exalted in the earth' which occur at the end of the previous Psalm. The main concept is that God, having come down from heaven in power and great might to deliver His people, is now returning to His throne. Such an assumption of dignity and power calls for public acclamation (cf. 2 Ki. xi. 12) not only on the part of His people Israel, but also by all the nations (cf. Pss. lxvi. 1–7, cxvii. 1).

The poem, therefore, has two themes closely interwoven. The first is a call to the peoples of the earth, regarded as assembled to acclaim Jehovah as King, to clap hands and shout (1), to blow upon the horns and trumpets (5), to sing Psalms of praise, indeed to sing them incessantly (6), and with understanding, or with a skilful musical accompaniment (7; see RV mg.).

The second theme is a description of the majesty of God, who is the cause of their rejoicing (2). There are three phases. First, the Lord who controls the affairs of men is our king. The most High inspires us with awe and none in all the earth can withstand Him (2). He it is who chooses Canaan for our inheritance and we are proud of this token of His love toward us. (For the tense see RV mg.) *The excellency of Jacob* (4); better 'the pride of Jacob'. Secondly, the ascended Lord is our king. Indeed, in this aspect too He is the King of all the earth (cf. Je. x. 6–8; 1 Tim. i. 17, vi. 15, 16); and as He has demonstrated His rule in the nature of recent events, He now openly resumes His seat of supreme and holy power. Thirdly, the enthroned Lord is the supreme sovereign. Because He is thus exalted, there must ultimately be a gathering together of all peoples, represented by their princes, as His people (9; see RV). Abraham will be the father of a multitude of nations and the heir of the world (cf. Rom. iv. 16; Gal. iii. 7, 14, 29). To God belong all the shields of office; i.e. all rightful authority wielded by kings and governors. Thus He is exalted beyond all (cf. 1 Cor. xv. 24–28).

PSALM XLVIII. REJOICE, FOR THE LORD IS IN MOUNT ZION

The first poem in this group celebrated the nation's deliverance from peril; the second extolled the power and majesty of Him who wrought their salvation; this third poem describes the glory of the city which God has so marvellously preserved. The Hebrew word translated 'greatly' in verse 1 is found also in xlvii. 9 and in xlvi. 1 (where it is translated 'very'). It links the three Psalms together. God greatly helps, is greatly to be exalted, and is greatly to be praised.

a. The city of God extolled (1–3)

Just as the Lord is highly to be praised because He is King of all the earth (xlvii. 6, 7), so is His city worthy of all honour because by His presence He has made her great buildings to be towers of security. Jerusalem was regarded by the Jews as incomparable in situation (cf. Ps.

l. 2; La. ii. 15). The pre-exilic city was smaller than the present one and lay to the south-west of Mount Moriah (anciently known as Mount Zion) which could then be described as *on the sides* (or 'districts') *of the north* (2). The words translated *city* and *great* in the last clause of verse 2 are not the same as in verse 1, but are poetic and ceremonial terms.

b. Attackers dismayed and repulsed (4–8)

They passed by together (4). Better 'passed over together', i.e. joined forces. Even though a league of kings assembled together to besiege the city (cf. 2 Ch. xx. 1–7; Is. x. 8–11), yet when they saw its strength they lost heart, became confused, and turned away in panic. Their designs were wrecked as thoroughly as Jehoshaphat's ships at Ezion-geber (1 Ki. xxii. 48). Tarshish is commonly identified with Tartessus in S. Spain, but the term *ships of Tarshish* (7) was applied to any large vessel used in extensive trading voyages. *An east wind* (7). A frequent expression for destructive power (cf. Jb. xxvii. 21).

The people's praise is evoked by their witness of God's power (8). Even as they had heard of God's mighty acts in their fathers' days, so had they seen His hand in Jerusalem's recent history. This seemed to guarantee the city's preservation for ever. Such words, combined with Isaiah's teaching about Zion's perpetual glory, were in later years too readily stripped of their spiritual significance. They became the foundation of the fanaticism of the city's religious leaders when Nebuchadnezzar's army besieged it. The real citadel was the heart that trusted in God (cf. Je. i. 18f.).

c. A meditation of God's loving-kindness (9–14)

Since the threat of destruction was removed, the beloved city has been viewed with fresh delight and its walls and buildings have become objects of civic and regional tradition. *Daughters of Judah* (11). These are the surrounding towns and neighbouring settlements. But behind this affection for Jerusalem there is a deep love for the Lord of the city. When the inhabitants enter into the great temple (cf. 2 Ch. xx. 28) they know that the loving-kindness of the Lord is more to be contemplated than are the outward forms of civic pride, such as the number of the city's battlemented towers. Upon such a God, upon Him and none other, will they rely. *Even unto death* (14). It is generally agreed that this is not the correct rendering of the Hebrew. The LXX (see RV mg.) has 'for evermore'. God will be their eternal guide.

PSALM XLIX. DEATH DISCLOSES A MAN'S TRUE WORTH

a. Introduction (1–4)

This Psalm, like xlvii, is addressed to 'all ye peoples' (RV), and the comprehensiveness of this term is indicated by its threefold elaboration covering all who are living in this present world of human society, those who belong to all sections of the community, lowly as well as high born, and everyone, irrespective of their possessions (1, 2). The speaker makes this inclusive address because he is convinced that he has received by the inner ear of his heart an oracle or parable (cf. Jb. iv. 12ff.) which he is about to declare in words of profound wisdom. This message, or *dark saying* (4), concerns an age-old enigma, and will take the form of a song set to music.

The theme is that of human differences—variations in wealth, opportunity and social power. In that God is King of all the earth (see the previous three Psalms), He must be responsible for these unequal distributions (cf. 1 Cor. xii. 11b; Heb. ii. 4b). But how can such an arrangement be justified? This is one aspect of the larger problem presented by the existence and prosperity of evil men (cf. Pss. xxxvii and lxxiii and the book of Job). To the psalmist, the secret lies in the universal operation of death. The remainder of the poem has two parts, each ending with a similar refrain.

b. The power of death is altogether superior to the pride of wealth (5–12)

The speaker recalls a time when wealthy neighbours, arrogant in their riches, had treated him unfairly, dogged his heels, and taken advantage of his comparative poverty (5, see RV mg.). Now that the experience is past he asks himself why he should ever have been provoked by such behaviour. The major thing in one's existence is altogether beyond the power of riches. A wealthy man cannot *redeem his brother* (7; lit. 'a brother' in the sense of 'intimate friend') from the occurrence of death. No man can give to God that which will ransom his life or purchase his freedom from death and corruption. Verse 8 is a parenthesis; the meaning is: 'the redemption of a man's soul is costly beyond measure, and men must let it alone and realize that it is futile for them ever to attempt it.' Those who trust in material possessions and in the wealth of this world must surely see that the *wise* (the godly), the *fool* (the worldling), and the *brutish* (the coarse and sensual) are all subject to death, whereupon all material distinctions end. Cf. 1 Tim. vi. 7; Jas. i. 9, 10.

Men whose riches are confined to this world may reckon to evade this factor by establishing a strong hereditary house and name, and by endowing their families with landed estates. Nevertheless, no man himself abides, however impressive his property or person. Physically he dies *like the beasts* (11, 12).

c. God will deliver from death's power (13–20)

The foregoing description is the way of those who are foolishly confident about this world and it is also the way of those who, seeing the death of such men, yet follow their manner of life with obvious approval (13, RV mg.). In verse

446

14 the RV is important. Such people do not merely die as a wild beast dies; they die in droves like sheep who have death as a shepherd to tend them. But it is in death that the rich and proud shall be proved inferior to those upright souls whom they had formerly misused. Cf. Mal. iv. 1, 3. *In the morning* (14) may be a metaphor for any subsequent experience of freshness, light and opportunity (cf. Mt. iv. 16); but as the superiority of the upright is not seen in their outliving the rich, but through the experience of dying, the phrase must bear in some measure the expectation of a new day dawning after death. The last clause of verse 14 is of uncertain meaning; see RV. In Sheol all beauty is consumed; all prestige and wealth vanishes away. In fact they will not need a dwelling place for their shadowy wisp of a soul.

But God will redeem (or ransom) *my soul* (15) from any power of death that would keep me in Sheol (see RV; the same words occur in Ho. xiii. 14). This statement cannot be restricted to a belief on the psalmist's part that God would preserve him from a premature death. The whole force of the revelation (4) lies in the reversal after death of the distinctions between the man of God and the man of this world. There had been a foreshadowing of that in the passing of Enoch and Elijah (note Heb. ii. 14, 15). This positive note is also heard in the phrase *he shall receive me* (15; cf. Ps. lxxiii. 24), and the expression of that hope is followed by a meditative pause, *Selah*.

Verse 16 reverts to the thought of verse 5. The remainder of the Psalm restates the major thesis in an emphatic manner, viz. do not be cast down at the unequal distribution among men of moral and material worth.

PSALM L. MAN IMPEACHED AT HEAVEN'S COURT

This is the first of twelve Psalms entitled 'of, to, or for, Asaph'—a prominent leader of David's choir. His name is affixed to Pss. lxxiii–lxxxiii, but some of these cannot have been written by a man of David's time, e.g. Pss. lxxiv and lxxix are associated with the destruction of Jerusalem by the Babylonians. Hence the phrase 'to (of, or for) Asaph' is unlikely to refer to his authorship so much as to a certain style or school of psalmody. See *Introduction*, p. 412. The poem is in three distinct portions.

a. Introduction (1–6)

The impressive opening phrase, *The mighty God, even the Lord* ('*el 'elohim Yahweh*), is intended to evoke the solemnity and awe proper to the Psalm's theme of a Great Assize. The threefold name represents God as the Almighty One, God in the fulness of His Deity, and God as the eternal and gracious One who has made a covenant with men. (Cf. Jos. xxii. 22.) This God has uttered His voice and summoned all earth's inhabitants to attend His tribunal, to witness the judgment of His people. The summons emanates from Zion (cf. Ps. xlviii. 2 and Dt. xxxiii. 2) and is accompanied by the light of His truth which shines into all hearts and searches the deep things of every man (cf. Ps. lxxx. 3, 7, 19; 2 Cor. iv. 6; 1 Jn. i. 5). First His word is heard, then His light is seen, and now the poet sees as in a vision the coming of God Himself, whereupon he cries 'Let our God come and not keep silent' (3), i.e. let His summons be followed by His revelation. The approach of God is described in terms of lightning and tempest, whilst the scenery around Zion is correspondingly enlarged in perspective so as to include the crowds of witnesses in heaven and earth. *Gather my saints* (5). Unto these God now calls for the party to be arraigned, i.e. the people with whom He had a covenant, renewed on their part by each succeeding generation, and ratified from the first by sacrifice (Ex. xxiv. 3–8). In verse 6 follow RV mg. The psalmist hears the heavens declare God's righteousness as Judge.

b. God speaks to His people (7–15)

His word to Israel (and the Christian Church is spiritual Israel) is one of admonition. He speaks to them not merely as God the Creator, but as their own God and Redeemer. His accusation is not that they have been guilty of negligence in the ritual of sacrifices; that duty has been regularly performed. His charge concerns their motives. They have offered their beasts to Him as though He had immediate need of them and must therefore feel grateful for their generosity. It would be but a step from such an attitude to that described in Mal. i. 7, 8. God declares the absurdity of such a view of worship; all man's possessions, all nature in fact, belong to Him (cf. Jb. xxxviii–xxxix). He would be less likely to ask them for food than the ocean would be to ask its fishes for water. As if God needed meat like a man! Contrast Jn. vi. 53–57. True worship does not consist in the offering up of the dead flesh of beasts, but in the eager homage of men's hearts who are intent upon their utmost diligence for His most high praise (14). The mutual relationship He desires is based on His own answer of deliverance and His people's response in giving Him glory (cf. Is. i. 11–17; Mi. vi. 6–8; Je. vii. 21–23).

c. God speaks to the wicked (16–23)

This stern denunciation is directed against those who speak of God's laws but keep them not (cf. Mt. vii. 21–23), i.e. men who resent moral discipline and repudiate God's commandments; men who delight in the fellowship of thieves, condone sexual licence, connive at lies, and even betray those to whom they are bound in blood-brotherhood (16–20). God's patience they regard as weakness, and His forbearance, which would give them opportunity to repent, is construed as indifference or even acquiescence. Their casual assumption that God must be as lawless, fraudulent and faithless as themselves will be utterly demolished. Their every evil deed will be brought before them and its consequences upon their own selves will be demonstrated (21; cf. verse 3).

Ye that forget God (22). Cf. Is. xvii. 10; Je. xiii. 25; Ezk. xxii. 12. The poem concludes with a terrible warning to such godless people (cf. Jude 15) and also with the offer of reconciliation and salvation to those who alter their *conversation*, i.e. their 'way of life', and bring it into accord with the principles of humility, faith, obedience and steadfastness toward God. The whole of this section serves as a basis for Rom. i. 18–32; iii. 21–25.

PSALM LI. A PENITENT'S PRAYER

The explicit statement in the title associates this Psalm with Nathan's striking accusation of David (2 Sa. xii. 1–13). As an expression of a heart overwhelmed by shame, humbled and broken by guiltiness, and yet saved from despair through penitential faith in the mercy of God, this poem is unsurpassed. Verses 18 and 19 seem to have been added some centuries after David's time. They presuppose a time when the walls of the city were broken down, and sacrifices had ceased (cf. Neh. i. 3; Pss. cii. 16, 17, cxlvii. 2). Moreover they refer to the people as a whole rather than to an individual (cf. 'they' in verse 19). It is possible that after the return from exile the Psalm was adapted for use as a confession of the nation's sin, and these verses were added to make it more suitable for public worship.

a. Conviction of sin (1–8)

It is necessary to remember that, immediately David made confession of his sin, the prophet Nathan declared the forgiveness of the Lord. Consequently this Psalm, presumably composed in the hours that followed, commences with a consciousness of God's mercy—lavish, loving and unlimited. The psalmist is aware of a veritable multitude of divine compassions and, in particular, of an exceeding great and precious promise of pardon for a very great wrong (2 Sa. xii. 13); but he cannot rest in this until full and heartfelt confession has been made, and this is the function of the poem. David's conviction of sin is dominated by three themes.

i. **An inescapable sense of personal accountability.** Note the frequency of *my transgressions*, *mine iniquity*, *my sin*. There is no evasion of responsibility here on the grounds of chance circumstance or an instinctive urge; no blaming of ignorance, necessity or evil agency; no attempt to make Bath-sheba share the guilt of adultery and murder on the fictitious ground of her acquiescence or suggestion. The wrong which has been done is David's responsibility and this conviction is stressed in the words *my sin is ever before me* (3; cf. xxxii. 3, 4).

ii. **An indubitable conviction of having turned against God.** Irrespective of Bath-sheba and

Uriah, his action ultimately was against God. *Against thee,* *thee only, have I sinned* (4). All wrongdoing, in the final analysis, is against His holiness and therefore evil in His sight (cf. Gn. xxxix. 9). *This evil* (4); better, as RV, 'that which is evil'. The psalmist now makes unreserved confession of his guilt (3, 4) so that when God pronounces judgment upon the sinner He may be justified from any Satanic insinuation of divine caprice, harshness or bias (cf. Zc. iii. 2; Jb. ii. 3b).

iii. **An impassioned plea for complete cleansing from sin.** The phrases are massed together in vehemence and fervour. *Blot out* (1); i.e. obscure as by a thick cloud (Is. xliv. 22) or as a debt is eliminated through payment. Alternatively it may have the sense of 'wipe off', as writing is removed from a clay tablet (Ex. xxxii. 32), or as water from a dish (2 Ki. xxi. 13), or as a people from the earth (Gn. vii. 4, RV mg.). *Wash me throughly* (2); i.e. bleach away the stain; *cleanse me* (2) as a leper is declared pure by washing (Lv. xiv. 8, 9).

In sin did my mother conceive me (5). This does not imply that a sinful disposition was imparted to him because the physical act of conception was in itself sinful. The verse simply means that by the fact of being a member of the human race we are inextricably entangled in the reality of sin. The word *shapen* is better rendered 'brought forth' or 'born'. Cf. Ps. cxxxix. 13–16; and note the sinlessness of our Lord, born of a woman. The double *behold* (5, 6) indicates two facts which have come home forcibly to the psalmist and which he wants others to observe.

In verses 6–8 the intensity of David's conviction and desire is further strengthened by a recapitulation of the preceding ideas, with a stress upon the third one—that of the need for cleansing. First, God's mercy and compassion (see verse 1) are related to His desire for truth and wisdom to be within the hidden, inner being (6). Thereby the soul is kept from turning away from Him. Secondly, the need to be bathed and cleansed (2; cf. Jn. xiii. 8–10) is reflected in the need to be sprinkled with purging hyssop (cf. Nu. xix. 6) and made purer and whiter than snow (cf. Is. i. 18). Thirdly, the desire to know and partake of God's holiness and to submit to His righteous judgment (4b) is renewed and enlarged as a prayer. This asks for a sense of gladness through hearing God's word of forgiveness and for a healing of all inward anguish and distress.

b. Distress, and a longing for holiness (9–14)

The additional concept of sin as separation from God is now introduced with its twofold emphasis upon distress at the possibility of being severed from God for ever and deprived of His Holy Spirit (cf. 1 Sa. xvi. 14), and a craving for moral health, a cleansed record, a new heart and a steadfast spirit. Notice the abhorrence of loneliness (11) which was exceptionally feared by David because of his wide and sensitive sympathies with other people. He realizes that when any man sins it is not merely an action against God, but it leads the man himself away in the direction of outer darkness and disgrace. That is the selfish misery of hell.

Penitence implies the dispossession of sinful desires, and the psalmist now expands the positive aspect of his experience. He pleads for a restoration of joy toward God of which he had been robbed by sin, and for an unfettered spirit that shall be ever willing to do right (12, RV). If he is granted these things, he will be so relieved and transformed that other sinners can be convincingly urged likewise to turn in repentance unto such a gracious God (13). Moreover, if he can be released from bloodguiltiness concerning Uriah, his tongue shall never cease to proclaim God's faithfulness in granting true pardon to all penitents (14).

c. True worship (15-19)

As if in rehearsal of such public praise, the psalmist begins a song of expectant adoration. Of themselves his lips can make only confession of wrong and petition for mercy; but if God will speak through them, then shall they utter His praises. These shall set forth God's nature, viz. that He has little interest and no delight in outward forms of religious observance; the ritual of sacrificial offerings can too readily be interpreted by its sponsors as a process of appeasement (cf. Ps. l. 8ff.). *The sacrifices of God* (17), i.e. those which He accepts, are the service of a contrite heart free from all obstinacy and humbled by its very self-offering (cf. Rom. xii. 1, 2; Heb. ix. 14, xiii. 15).

PSALM LII. THE DOOM AWAITING A POWERFUL AND WICKED MAN

This is one of eight Psalms which are associated by their titles with David's experiences as an exile from Saul. The others are Pss. vii (concerning Cush); lix (Saul seeks to kill David); lvi (David goes to the Philistines at Gath); xxxiv (David at the court of Abimelech); lvii (he flees to the cave of Adullam); cxlii (a prayer in the cave); liv (David is almost betrayed by the people of Ziph). Ps. lii is one of the earlier poems. It relates to David's flight to the tabernacle at Nob which was on the northern slopes of the Mount of Olives. The help given him by Ahimelech the priest was reported to Saul. For the full story and the massacre of the priests which followed see 1 Sa. xxi. 1–9 and xxii. 9–23. This Psalm is an expression of David's righteous indignation at Doeg's betrayal of himself and Ahimelech. There are four phases of thought.

a. The mighty man of mischief and his words (1-3)

The opening words are vehement, sarcastic and contemptuous. Doeg is not worthy of being named. He is a boaster, one who not only does evil but takes pride in it. He spends his life in antagonism to the enduring mercy of God. He is deceitful, slanderous and false, using his tongue as his principal weapon (cf. Ps. vii. 14–16, x. 3–11). The psalmist is in no way admiring the efficiency of this means of warfare, he is referring to a manner and principle of life which is wholly repugnant to himself (cf. xxxiv. 13, 14), viz. the love of evil more than good, the high esteem given to words that work harmfulness.

b. His certain undoing (4, 5)

As surely as Doeg's speech had wrought the destruction of innocent lives, so *likewise* (5) would God utterly destroy him. This doom is vividly expressed: God shall take him up (see RV) as a burnt coal fallen from a fire and cast him out; God will pluck him out of his habitation and banish him from the fellowship of all men; God will root him up as a stricken tree in a tempest, so that his life will be bereft of nourishment and honour.

c. The comment of the righteous (6, 7)

The obvious retribution meted out to Doeg would fill all righteous men with awe (*fear*) and also with satisfaction at the evident vindication of righteousness. There is no need to read any personal vindictiveness, or mood of retaliation, into this; cf. Jb. xxxi. 29. Godly men will turn to each other and comment upon the flimsiness of all life which trusts in temporal power and evil purposes. There is a play here on the opening words as if to say 'Lo, this wreck is the mighty man who made not God his stronghold'.

d. The psalmist's enduring devotion (8, 9)

In contrast to the fate of the wicked, David sees himself as a flourishing leafy olive tree as enduring as those trees which still grew on the slopes of Nob after Doeg's outrage (cf. Ps. i. 3). This destruction of the wicked and permanence of the righteous arise from the character of God in whose mercy David trusted, in contrast to the 'mighty man' who defied it. Cf. xxxiv. 15, 16.

This characteristic of a godly life leads him to rest, silently, expectantly, confidently, in God's work and ways. All righteous men know that God is good.

PSALM LIII. OPPRESSION, PAST AND PRESENT

This is a revised version of Ps. xiv, where see notes. Its two chief differences are first the discarding of the tetragrammaton (i.e. the name Yahweh written in four letters in Hebrew) which occurred four times in the earlier poem, and the use of '*elohim* in each of the seven references to the Deity. Whatever the reasons behind this change it suggests a more universal scope for the poem than was implied in the former covenant-title of Yahweh, which was exclusively for Israel. Secondly, the fifth verse of Ps. xiv has been completely rewritten, a fact which suggests a phenomenal deliverance of the nation since the composition of the earlier poem. This may have been the collapse of the Ammonite league (2 Ch. xx. 22–24) or, more probably, the supernatural panic of the Syrian army (2 Ki. vii. 6, 7): *there were they in great fear, where no fear* (i.e. cause for fear) *was*.

PSALM LIV. GOD IS THE UPHOLDER OF MY SOUL

Soon after David had been joined at Keilah by Abiathar, who had escaped Doeg's massacre at Nob (Ps. lii), he heard that Saul was advancing upon the town to besiege it. Although David had rescued the town from the Philistines he was warned of the unreliability of the inhabitants, so he and his men fled eastwards before Saul arrived (see 1 Sa. xxiii. 5, 6 and 13). They took refuge in the wild and wooded hills south of Hebron, but their presence was betrayed to Saul by men of the adjoining township of Ziph (1 Sa. xxiii. 19). David moved into the wilderness of Maon and Saul was prevented from further pursuit only by urgent news of an invasion by the Philistines further north. According to the title this Psalm expresses David's reaction to the animosity of the Ziphites. It is in three parts.

a. A plea for help (1–3)

Deliverance is sought *by thy name*, i.e. on the grounds of the divine character as protector of the oppressed, and also by means of the manifestation of His might and mercy. These are reflected in the next phrase, 'demonstrate that I am right by virtue of Thy just power.' *Strangers* (3) does not necessarily mean non-Israelites. It appears to refer here to the Ziphites, who, though belonging to Judah, were as strangers in his eyes, because of their enmity against him. The word *oppressors* (3) (RV 'violent men') refers to the company of Saul. The enmity of both groups is attributed to their godlessness. *Seek after my soul* (3); i.e. seek my life. Cf. 1 Sa. xxiii. 15.

b. A profession of faith (4, 5)

Unlike his foes, David could point to God as his source of help. Indeed, he had none other. Verse 4b does not mean that the Lord was one of many supporters, but He was supremely the Helper and the Upholder (cf. RV; also Ps. iii. 5; Is. xli. 10; Jn. xiv. 16–18). Hence it is certain that He will take action to counter the wrong done to David. *Enemies* (5). Better, as in RV mg., 'them that lie in wait for me'.

c. A promise of gratitude (6, 7)

When David shall have been saved by the name of the Lord (1) he will gladly and freely express his gratitude to that good name. In the sincerity of his Godward trust he envisages his defeated enemies and tastes even now of that deliverance which 'He' (or *it*, i.e. the good name) will bring about (cf. Is. xxx. 27).

PSALM LV. BAFFLED AND BURDENED, BUT UPHELD

This is the expression of a heart, deeply wounded by the faithlessness of a friend, which turns to God in supplication and confidence. This Psalm has been traditionally associated with Absalom's rebellion, but, if so, it must have preceded David's flight from Jerusalem, and probably followed the defection of Ahithophel. See *Introduction* to Ps. xli. This poem should be regarded as an expression of David's heart and mind when the curtains of illusion and secrecy were being pulled apart to disclose an unexpected scene, in whose reality he found it hard to believe. The light of truth had not yet fully dawned; the worst was yet to come. The poem is in three parts.

a. Serious forebodings and the desire to escape (1–8)

The way this supplication is framed indicates the craving for certainty. *Hide not thyself* (1; cf. Ps. xxvii. 4). The psalmist desires an open vision and an immediate reply from God, because he is so distraught and 'restless' (2, RV). He cannot keep silent because of the suspense created by his suspicions, which have grown so rapidly as to be crushing and unbearable. Memories of a host of incidents, unheeded at the time, now suggest a network of evil schemes, and a barrage of malevolent plottings seems to be hurled at him (3). In such a mood he not only envisages the success of his enemies but has a presentiment of death by violent means.

The pressure of events has now become so intolerable that the heart makes a desperate move to escape in fantasy. He would change his conditions altogether and become a dove, dwelling in quiet places remote from men (6, 7). The pause (*Selah*) would prolong this idealized life woven from the finer threads of his former exile, but the colour fades and the craving remains. He pictures himself as a weary man who, struggling desperately to reach shelter and security, finds himself buffeted and breathless amid a sudden storm (8).

The urge to escape from reality is a perversion of a universal desire to be *at rest* (6; cf. Gn. ii. 2; Mt. xi. 28, 29; Heb. iv. 1–11; Rev. xiv. 13). The motif of 'fleeing away' (from duty, discipline, or from God) is very evident in Scripture, and is a basic factor in man's endless restlessness and discontent. The process is vain and futile (cf. Ps. cxxxix. 7ff.). No one yet found that an escape into the wilderness experience brought rest; rather is it found to be the realm of temptation.

b. A prayer for the destruction of the wicked (9–15)

David could not dwell long in fantasy, and his agitated thoughts were next canalized in anger against his fickle courtiers and especially against one man, formerly almost as close a friend as Jonathan had been, who was evidently one of the chief supporters of the coming rebellion. The psalmist pleads with God to send amongst these schemers such a confusion of tongues and division of counsel as will make their work as unsuccessful as Babel (cf. 2 Sa. xv. 34, xvii. 4). *Destroy* (9); rather, as many think, 'confound' (see Gn. xi. 7). Verses 10 and 11 imply that David had not been unaware of growing sedition and corruption in Jerusalem, both among the soldiers guarding the wall and among the shopkeepers in the streets. Some regard *violence* and *strife* (9) as personified, and the pronoun *they* as referring to these forces. So also with 'iniquity', 'mischief', etc. (9–11, RV). That kind of thing he could have borne; what incurs his wrath is the treachery of a trusted friend, one of like status as himself, a frequent companion, one with whom the rich exchanges of understanding had been a pleasure, a man with whom he had known unity of heart as they worshipped God. Let that intimacy be matched by the immediacy of divine judgment: let the ground swallow them all. *Quick into hell* (15); i.e. 'alive into Sheol' (RV mg.; cf. Nu. xvi. 30–33); for instead of living and moving in God (cf. Acts xvii. 28) they had made evil the outward atmosphere and inward breath of their life. *Among them* (15); i.e. in 'their inward part' (RV mg.).

c. Faith towards God (16–23)

Unlike his enemies, David can call on God with assurance. His incessant cries for help will be heard, his predicament resolved, his dire peril (as in battle) remedied notwithstanding the number of his foes (following RV in verse 18b). *Abideth* (19) means rather 'sitteth enthroned', as in xxix. 10; La. v. 19. God, who is eternally enthroned as Judge of righteousness, shall come to his aid and humiliate his foes by His answer— even those men whose career of self-interest has been hitherto successful (19b, RV) and who therefore reckon God's righteousness to be of no account. The psalmist's thoughts then revert to his false friend who moved in wickedness against those who were at peace with him and tore up the covenant of friendship between them (20). His heart was actuated by malice, for all the suavity of his speech. His former words, interpreted now by his subsequent action, are like sword thrusts in David's heart (21).

But neither escapism, regret, indignation or bitterness can provide a satisfactory avenue of life amid the profound psychological upheaval of which David, as friend and as king, is the centre. The right course of action is declared at last. It consists of unburdening the heart's sickness and care and placing all in the responsibility of the Lord. This David is resolved to do (23c), and thereby experiences the divine upholding of the heart itself (cf. 1 Pet. v. 7). The Lord watches over righteous persons and allows no fatal deflection to be evilly imposed upon their course. On the other hand wicked, false and murderous men shall never finish their days. Compare the experience of Paul in 2 Tim. iv. 10, 11 and 17.

PSALM LVI. 'IF GOD BE FOR ME, WHO CAN BE AGAINST ME?'

The title refers to David's first sojourn in Gath when he was evidently under some restraint (cf. 1 Sa. xxi. 13, xxii. 1). Ps. xxxiv was composed shortly after his escape from the Philistines, but Ps. lvi is expressive of his misgivings while actually in the hands of Achish. When David returned some time later, he had six hundred men with him and stayed for sixteen months (see 1 Sa. xxvii. 1–7).

The phrase *upon Jonath-elem-rechokim* in the title means 'the silent dove of those at a distance' or 'the dove of the distant terebinths' (RV mg.).

The Psalm's two parts are each followed by a refrain (4, 10 and 11). Verses 12 and 13 form a brief conclusion.

a. Contrast and tension (1–4)

This exists between *God* and frail *man* (the Hebrew word signifies man as mortal); between One who is gracious (*merciful*) and many who *daily* (RV 'all the day long') harass him and trample upon him (a variant reading for *swallow me up*) in their pride. *O thou most High* (2); follow RV and render 'proudly'. This dilemma of soul leads to the paradox *I am afraid* yet *I will trust* (3).

The tension is eased not simply by the decision to trust, but by the realization that God's word will not fail. *In God* praising, *in God* trusting, the psalmist will not be anxious or fearful: after all, what can mortal flesh do to him? (4, RV; cf. Heb. xiii. 6).

b. David's hunted life (5–11)

They wrest my words (5). Cf. 1 Sa. xxi. 11, 12. Distorted reports of what he had said daily reveal their deep antipathy. The situation can be remedied only by drastic measures; hence the psalmist's plea that God's righteous wrath should overturn the haughty assumptions and pernicious words of the suspicious Philistines in a general judgment upon all ungodly peoples (7; cf. vii. 6–9; Ezk. xxi. 25–27; Jude 14–16). *Tellest* (8); i.e. takest account of. *Bottle* (8); i.e. skin for holding precious liquid. God knows all about his life of insecurity, and his tears, registered in heaven, are precious in God's sight. Moreover his prayers are not merely appreciated by God but are efficacious: 'This I know, that God is for me' (9, RV; cf. Rom. viii. 31). Hence he is doubly sure of God's power and the Lord's faithfulness, and the refrain of verse 4 is amplified and strengthened (10, 11, RV).

c. Conclusion (12, 13)

Finally he foresees, as if already present, a state of deliverance wherein he shall be carrying out his present vows of praise to God for his complete salvation. Deliverance from death and preservation from falling will enable him always to walk before God in the 'light of life' (13, RV mg.).

PSALM LVII. NO DESPAIR IN SPITE OF PERIL

As indicated by the title this Psalm was composed soon after David's escape from Gath (see 1 Sa. xxii. 1) and it resembles the preceding Psalm both in theme and style. Both begin with identical words, are in two parts each followed by a refrain (see lvii. 5 and 11), speak of similar perils (lvi. 1 and 2, lvii. 3), and express the same deep trust in God. The whole Psalm may be compared with 2 Cor. iv. 7–11.

a. His plight and prayer (1–5)

The imagery of a young bird instinctively seeking protection under its mother's wings is used in Pss. xvii. 8, xxxvi. 7, xci. 1, 4. Note the RV repetition of 'take refuge' in the first verse. This is the same mood of escape from calamities as in lv. 6–8, but the movement is not away from God, but unto Him. His prayer is directed to *God most high* (2; Heb. *'elohim 'elyon*, used also in lxxviii. 5, 6). In this instance God will send forth mercy and truth (cf. verse 10) and rescue him from his pursuers who would trample him down. *Swallow me up* (3); see lvi. 1n. The imminence of his peril is seen in the fact that the psalmist has to sleep in hidden places while those whose hearts are aflame with enmity, and who speak words that are as sharp weapons, are searching in that vicinity. This seems to be the meaning of verse 4; see RV.

The refrain in verse 5 appeals to God to demonstrate the glory of His power and majesty by answering this prayer (cf. Jn. xii. 27, 28).

b. His preservation and praise (6–11)

The imagery of hot pursuit by wild beasts is replaced by that of men stealthily laying a trap for a hunted animal. The psalmist feels utterly despondent apart from trust in God, but his faith is so irrepressible and buoyant that he suddenly foresees the whole organization of evil recoiling upon his enemies. The wrong they do with the intention of harming the innocent is seen to encompass their own downfall (cf. Pss. vii. 14–16, ix. 15, 16).

This sense of deliverance is accentuated by the pause, *Selah* (6), even as the need for it was similarly emphasized in verse 3. Thereafter is full assurance of heart and a glad spirit of thanksgiving. The call, *awake up, my glory* (8), is an exhortation to the best and highest in himself (cf. xvi. 9, xxx. 12), and the familiar instruments of praise are likewise bidden to rouse themselves from the night of their inactivity so that the dawn of the day of deliverance may be heralded with eager anticipation. *I myself will awake early* (8). Better, as in RV mg., 'I will awake the dawn'. To balance these private devotions at daybreak there will be a later general thanksgiving among all the peoples. The theme of praise in both cases will be the heaven-sent *mercy* (compassion) and *truth* (righteousness) (10; cf. verse 3b) which bring the realm of God unto this earth. Finally and supremely is the pre-eminence of God Himself far above all (cf. Phil. ii. 9; 1 Cor. xv. 28).

PSALM LVIII. 'THERE IS A GOD WHO JUDGETH'

Al-taschith (see title) means 'Destroy not' and refers to the melody to which it should be set in the temple praise. The passionate denunciation here of corruption masquerading as justice is not readily associated with any period of David's reign, though it may echo the appearance of self-constituted judges as auxiliaries of the plausible Absalom (cf. 2 Sa. xv. 3–5). It should be noticed that the cause of the psalmist's vehemence did not lie in some personal grievance but in the general practice of false principles which were inimical to the spread of godliness. The poem is in two parts, and has a conclusion.

a. The indictment (1–5)

O congregation (1); RV 'in silence'. The Hebrew word is of uncertain meaning. By a change in the vowels it may be rendered 'Ye mighty ones' (RV mg.), and this is the most satisfactory reading for the question is plainly addressed to men of influence and authority, who occupied this position of judges. Translated thus, the answer is, of course, in the negative; for the actual state of affairs had nothing in common with righteousness. These men may claim office as judges but in their evil hearts justice is perverted. That is evident because their verdicts are biased, i.e. equity is violated: they weigh out not justice but violence (2). Such men were born with a moral twist away from righteousness and they have constantly exercised the inborn tendency to speak falsehood. In the judicial offices which they have managed to appropriate in their mature years, the evil of their words is as dangerous as snake's venom; indeed, their existence is as much a threat to good society as is the proximity of a deadly serpent which suddenly pays no heed at all to the shrill piping of the snake charmer who brought it with him (4, 5; cf. Jb. xx. 16; Je. viii. 17; Acts vii. 51, 57).

b. The petition (6–9)

The accuser now turns from those whom he arraigns and addresses God as the supreme Judge. He does not plead for a verdict of guilty so much as for a sentence which shall bring about the complete removal of these corrupt men from the kingdom; their power is to be broken so that they are as helpless as a fangless snake or a toothless lion, as ineffective as blunted arrows (7b, RV). The imagery used to convey this desire is extremely graphic. Let them vanish like the storm water in a gutter, and like a dried-up snail; let them be as still-born children (6), like the heap of dried thorns under a cauldron which are no sooner lighted than the whole pile (RV 'the green and the burning alike') is whisked away and scattered by a squall (9).

c. Conclusion (10, 11)

These verses express vehemently the profound satisfaction experienced by righteous people when evil is visibly crushed and removed. The language is figurative (cf. Rev. xix. 13–18), but the aspiration is praiseworthy, viz. that all other men should openly acknowledge the worth of righteousness and confess the inescapable judgment of God.

PSALM LIX. SAFEGUARDED AMIDST NIGHT'S LURKING TERROR

This Psalm affords us insight concerning the tension of David's life while at Saul's town of Gibeah (e.g. 1 Sa. xv. 34): although married to the king's daughter he knew he was dogged by men commissioned by Saul to murder him (1 Sa. xix. 1, 9–18). The prayer has two main movements, verses 1–10 and verses 11–14, which show a parallelism of thought. Each consists of two parts, the division being marked by *Selah* (5, 13).

a. Invocation of divine aid (1–5)

David pleads for divine protection from men who seek his blood. *Bloody* (2); RV 'bloodthirsty'. Having long lain in wait, they are become impudent and bold. Not only is he in peril but he is completely innocent; their malignity can find no cause in any blamable conduct on his part (3). Nevertheless, they act with alacrity against him (4a). Hence his cry to the Lord to awake and behold his peril. *Heathen* (5). The Hebrew word usually denotes foreign nations (RV mg.). Some commentators regard its introduction here as a later expansion of David's words, a change made when the Psalm was being used for public worship during a period of national insecurity. But the thought may be that these men are aliens in heart.

b. Description of a dangerous situation (6–10)

David's enemies are likened to scavenger-dogs in that they are most active at night-time. Such dogs prowl the city streets, intent on their own advantage and disturbing it with snarls and growls (cf. 2 Ki. ix. 36 and note the infamous tradition of night-life associated with this town of Gibeah in the story of Jdg. xix). The boldness of these men arises from their false belief that God will not hear the appeals of their intended victim .

The truth is that He already hears the psalmist's cry and He will yet ridicule their intentions and have all of them in derision (cf. Pss. ii. 4, xxxvii. 13). In verse 9 follow RV. The psalmist likens himself to a beleaguered outpost waiting for the fire signal of a distant beacon which would herald the approach of a relieving force. *The God of my mercy shall prevent me* (10); i.e. 'My God shall come to meet me with His mercy', or in other words, 'He shall go before me and meet me with reassurance at every turning of my way'. Consequently David will yet see his enemies helpless and utterly ashamed.

c. A plea for judgment (11–13)

In this second part of the Psalm David's appeal to God for a merciless visitation upon his would-be assassins (see verse 5b) is stated fully so as to show that this desire is neither vindictive nor harsh. *Slay them not* (11); i.e. at one blow. He does not ask for their swift destruction; the memory of his people would soon forget that. Rather he asks for these enemies to be made a lasting exhibition of the terrible consequences of falsity of speech and motive. Strangely, this was to be in later times the nature of Israel's own shame (cf. La. ii. 15ff.; Dt. xxviii. 65ff.). He wants them to be driven from home, deprived of office, and scattered abroad as vagrants like Cain (cf. La. iv. 14, 15), because they have misused speech (*cursing*) and perverted truth (*lying*) (12). The words *consume them in wrath* (13) signify a desire that when such men have been displayed as a warning to Israel they should be so treated that no recurrence of this peril could be possible (cf. Heb. xii. 29; 2 Thes. i. 8). Thereby men everywhere would acknowledge the sovereignty of God in the affairs of His chosen people. *Unto the ends of the earth* (13). Link this phrase with *let them know*, or better, 'let men know'.

d. Affirmation of confidence (14–17)

The psalmist views again the immediate situation (cf. verse 6), but now with a new assurance of security. *Grudge* (15). Translate as in RV 'tarry all night'. In spite of this relentless pursuit he is still able to sing to God's praise, who is his sure defence. God is a refuge, and doubly his 'high tower' (17, RV) and a high and impregnable fortress of power and mercy. *Thou hast been* (16). Faith sings with confidence as if coming mercies were already possessed.

PSALM LX. A LAMENT FOR DEFEAT

The title associates this Psalm with David's war with Aram-naharaim (the land of the two rivers, i.e. Mesopotamia) and Aram-zobah (the territory between Damascus and the upper Euphrates). Cf. 2 Sa. viii. 3–6. Apparently while David's armed forces were away in the north-east, the hereditary enemies of Israel, Edom and Moab, invaded southern Judah. A breach was made in the national boundary and the situation was viewed with sudden apprehension. David sent Joab back to deal with the emergency (cf. 1 Ch. xix. 6–9). This Psalm conveys the sense of national humiliation resulting from a wholly unforeseen military reverse. *Shushan-eduth* ('the lily of testimony') may have referred to the tune of a song (cf. titles of Pss. xlv and lxxx). The phrase *to teach* is peculiar to the title of this Psalm (cf. 2 Sa. i. 18; Dt. xxxi. 19). Note the incorporation of verses 5–12 in Ps. cviii. 6–13.

a. The people lament á national disaster (1–4)

It was typical of the psalmist's outlook (and of the book of Job) to regard God as responsible for every happening. Secondary causes, physical, strategical, cultural, etc., were not recognized. Hence this unexpected military reverse had struck a tremendous blow at the people's morale. It was like an earthquake which rends strong buildings (2). Divine action had led to defeat; both led to demoralization; the nation reeled as a man who has just drunk drugged wine (3; cf. Is. li. 17; Je. xxv. 15ff.): men were filled with fear and trembling. They believed themselves to be the people of the Lord, but the banner which He had given them (Ex. xvii. 15 mg.) in this instance had simply led the way to flight (4b; reading with RV mg. 'that they may flee from before the bow'). The AV reading makes these words a contrast to the previous despondency; but the pause indicated by *Selah* suggests the end of one train of thought.

b. The king seeks confirmation of a promise of victory (5–12)

A positive request for salvation replaces the preceding dejection (5). Before this plea is matured in faith's appropriation of God's sure response (12) the ground and basis for such a hope is examined.

There is first the promise of God about Israel's dominion: the words attributed to God (verses 6b–8, RV) are a composite echo of many promises over several centuries. David may have had in mind such promises as 2 Sa. vii. 9, 10 and Gn. xv. 18–21. *Shechem* and *Succoth* (6) were old centres of significance, west and east of Jordan (cf. Gn. xxxiii. 17ff.); *Gilead*, east of the river, was largely occupied by *Manasseh*; *Ephraim* and *Judah*, west of the river, were the two outstanding communities in Israel (7). The symbolism of a helmet and a 'sceptre' (7, RV) point to the privileges and differences between them, one noted for belligerency and stupidity (cf. Jdg. viii. 1ff., xii. 1ff.; Ps. lxxviii. 9ff.; Ho. vii. 8–11), the other for possessing the promise of God's rightful ruler (cf. Gn. xlix. 8–11; Ps. lxxviii. 67, 68). The traditional enemies of Israel would be reduced to servility. The imagery is that of the returning conqueror using Moab as a footbasin, throwing dusty sandals at Edom as a lackey, and calling to another slave, Philistia, to 'cry aloud', i.e. to acclaim the master of the house with a song of praise.

The second basis of the psalmist's hope is in the absolute incompetence of man to deal with the situation. The king asks, 'What general is there who would penetrate to the strong city of Petra, capital of Edom, if thou dost not go with the army? (9, 10). *Give us help*, O Lord, for it will be useless to rely upon human methods and powers' (11).

The final verse indicates the completion of the prayer in an affirmation of expectant triumph (cf. Ps. cxviii. 16).

PSALM LXI. A PRAYER OF AN EXILED KING

A poem of loneliness akin to Ps. xlii and probably associated with the same period of enforced absence from Jerusalem because of Absalom. The Psalm has two parts.

a. A cry for love and security (1–4)

This is an impassioned plea from a heart burdened by a sense of isolation and feebleness. *Overwhelmed* (2). RV 'fainteth'. He craves for a realization of security unattainable by his own efforts, i.e. to be led 'to a rock that is too high for me' (2, RV mg.), i.e. to which of himself he cannot attain. His desire for this arises out of his present need which is such a contrast to his former experiences of satisfaction and protection (3). *I will* (4) may be rendered 'Let me'. He longs to dwell for ever in God's tent, i.e. in the place of His abode; and to take refuge beneath the covering wings that overshadow the place where God would meet and commune with him (cf. Ex. xxv. 22, xxxvii. 9).

b. Confidence in God's goodness and care (5–8)

In the assurance that God hears his prayers and vows, David claims anew the heritage of the Promised Land, thus anticipating the end of Absalom's revolt. *Thou hast given me the heritage . . .* (5); better, as in RV mg., 'Thou hast given an inheritance unto those that fear thy name'; i.e. David's loyal followers shall regain possession of the kingdom. The LXX and Vulgate render 'Thou hast given (their) possession to them that fear thy name.' An alternative reading of the Hebrew text runs 'Thou hast granted the request . . .' David speaks of his office more than of his person; his thought is that his legal heirs shall occupy the throne for generations to come (cf. 2 Sa. vii. 16). May God ordain that loving-kindness and truth shall always characterize the rule of David's line! Many regard mercy and truth as here personified (cf. Pss. lvii. 3, lxxxv. 10), the psalmist conceiving them as angels perpetually watching over the throne, as the cherubim watch over the mercy-seat upon the ark (cf. 4). The prayer concludes with a vow to worship God daily with a glad heart.

PSALM LXII. GOD ALONE IS MY REFUGE

This is a song of trust wherein the psalmist cannot find words sufficiently strong and significant to describe the absolute security and unalterable strength of God who is accessible to him (cf. Pss. xviii. 1, 2, lix. 16, 17). The poem belongs probably to the time of Absalom's rebellion. Its two parts both deal with the action and reaction between godless and godly men; and are introduced by similar words (1, 2 and 5, 6).

a. The two forces at work in David's life (1–4)

On the one hand God is to David the sole basis and crown of life. God only is real, and in silence (see RV mg. of verse 1) his soul waits unreservedly upon Him (cf. Is. xliii. 10–13). It is not only that from God *cometh my salvation* (1) but that God is . . . *my salvation* (2). This relationship is the kingpost of his immediate existence, and though as mortal man he may be slightly displaced by external pressure (cf. 2 Cor. iv. 8, 9), he trusts that he will not be dislodged (2). On the other hand men are doing their utmost to wreck his life: he describes them as rushing upon him with menaces and blows; they think he is about to crumple like a collapsing wall or a rickety fence (3, RV). Their sole concern is *to cast him down from his excellency* (4) or throne (contrast verse 2), and to that end they have pleasure only in lies and untruths speciously disguised (cf. 2 Sa. xv. 2–6).

b. The ultimate resolution of the conflict (5–12)

Observe the contrast between the vision of sense and the vision of faith. To the vision of sense David appears as a wall already about to fall (3, RV), to the eye of faith he is secure in a high tower built upon a rock (2, 6, 7). To the soul whose trust is wholly in God, time can bring only confirmation of his faith. Hence, in this second portion of the Psalm, the fundamental principle of David's life (1, 2) is reaffirmed more strongly (5, 6). Cf. e.g. *not be greatly moved* (2) with *not be moved* (6).

The onslaught of his enemies (cf. verse 3) need not be a cause of anxiety, for his salvation and full regal dignity (*glory*) rest altogether upon God. Moreover David is confident that his loyal people also will be preserved if they commit their lives unto God (8).

On the other hand, men such as those who have usurped the royal powers will prove worthless and vain (cf. Ps. xxxix. 5, 11; Jas. i. 9–11, iv. 14). All reliance upon earthly possessions proves to be disappointing (cf. Pr. xi. 28).

The conclusion (11, 12) forcibly reiterates the sovereignty of God who is the sole origin of power, mercy and truth (cf. Pr. xxiv. 12; Rom. ii. 6). *Once . . . twice*, i.e. repeatedly (cf. Jb. xxxiii. 14, xl. 5).

PSALM LXIII. GOD IS MY JOY

According to the title this Psalm originated in David's experiences during his flight and exile. As *the wilderness* here mentioned was in Judah, i.e. west of Jordan, David's first passage through it must have been hurried and troubled (cf. 2 Sa. xv. 28, xvii. 16). The essential value of the poem lies in its expression of continual fellowship with God even though the psalmist is cut off from the outward and visible means of grace.

a. Introduction (1)

David's yearning for God was intensified by his keen sense of exclusion from the sanctuary in Jerusalem and his separation from the ark, the symbol of the divine presence (cf. 2 Sa. xv. 25, 26). His soul's desire, and his bodily habit of attending worship, were both thwarted by circumstances (cf. Ps. xlii. 1). The surrounding wilderness of Judah had become a spiritual desert (cf. 2 Sa. xvii. 29).

b. An immutable relationship (2–4)

The AV has transposed the clauses of verse 2. See RV. Some interpret the verse as meaning that in the wilderness David was granted a vision of God no less clear and distinct than that which he had seen in the sanctuary, and causing him in the midst of his despondency to break out in an ecstasy of wonder 'So have I seen thee in the sanctuary, beholding thy power and thy glory'. This would explain the sudden change from sadness to great joy. But the meaning may be that his longing for communion with God was as strong as in those former days when he had been able to behold God's power and glory in the sanctuary. *Thy lovingkindness is better than life* (3); i.e. better than all that life can give. David had lost his throne and kingdom, but in the vision that God gave him he saw that God's loving-kindness remained and was better than all else.

c. A satisfying experience (5–7)

The antithesis and independence of the national and spiritual realms of David's life are shown by the contrast of an arid waste land (1) with ample and sumptuous fare (5). The exigencies of his uprooted life will not prevent him in hours of wakefulness at night from dwelling upon the excellence of his upholding God (cf. Ps. xxxvi. 5–8). In the security of His presence there is cause for exultant joy (cf. Ps. xvi. 11, xxvii. 3–6).

d. A protected career (8–10)

In the closeness of his communion with God, David is conscious of amazing vigour and unalterable security. The words *followeth hard after* (8) signify 'an intent absorption in'; the same Hebrew word is used in Jb. xli. 15b to convey the sense of a bond which cannot be broken. On the other hand, David's enemies, who lack this union with God, must surely be destroyed, their souls going to the abode of the dead (cf. Ps. ix. 15) and their carcases, fallen in battle, will be the prey of jackals (10, RV mg.; cf. 2 Sa. xviii. 7f.).

e. Conclusion (11)

Not only David, but *everyone that sweareth by* God, i.e. acknowledges and obeys Him, shall rejoice because of God's care and goodness (cf. Dt. x. 20).

PSALM LXIV. PLOT AND PUNISHMENT

A prayer that the schemes and plots of unscrupulous men, who seek to overthrow those who are upright and godly, shall not only be in vain, but shall entail the condemnation of such evil-doers. The Psalm is in two parts.

a. Prayer for protection against plotters (1–6)

The plea is for a deliverance from threatened peril and from the fear or terror of that threat.

David prays to be hidden alike from the secret plottings of wicked men and from their open assaults. *Insurrection* (2); better 'tumult' (RV) or 'throng'. The gravity of the situation is shown by the forceful, skilful and open propaganda directed against him: their words are like sharp swords and swift arrows aimed from ambuscades (3, 4). *Perfect* (4); i.e. 'blameless'. These men strengthen each other in every possible method of working their wicked designs and believe that their intentions are effectually hidden (5). Verse 6 may be rendered 'They have devised iniquities: "We have wrought out," say they, "a perfect plan"; and the inner heart thought of each one is deep.' Every man concerned in the plot is deeply involved in its operation and consequences (6).

b. Assurance of divine retribution (7–10)

The psalmist's faith now overcomes his previous apprehension. That which wicked men desire against the blameless shall prove to be their own undoing. If they shoot arrows against him, God shall shower arrows upon them and wound them; because by words they seek to entrap him, so shall their own tongue trip them up. For *flee away* (8) read as in RV 'wag the head'. The meaning is that these men will become the object of popular contempt. In such judgment all men shall recognize the work of God and reverence Him (contrast the *fear not* of verse 4). Moreover every godly person shall be glad in the Lord's watchfulness and solicitude for those that are upright in heart, and shall take refuge in Him.

PSALM LXV. A SONG OF PRAISE FOR HARVEST

Although entitled *A Psalm and Song of David*, this poem is not readily associated with any suitable event in his lifetime; it may be modelled on his style but written later, possibly in Hezekiah's reign, after the retreat of the Assyrians. (Cf. the reference to the temple in verse 4.) In such circumstances the first good harvest for years would be specially welcome (cf. Is. xxxvii. 30). The allusion to some national preservation from the onslaught of foreign powers (symbolized by *seas*, 7) would then refer to Sennacherib's unsuccessful attempt to capture Jerusalem (cf. Ps. xlvi).

a. Waiting upon God (1–4)

The Psalm opens with an expression of praise and prayer. *Waiteth . . . in Sion* (1) implies a reverent stillness (cf. Ps. lxii. 1) as the vow, probably made during the nation's emergency, is performed. The assurance of prayer heard and answered arises from the experience of deliverance from danger, and so full is the psalmist's heart that he feels all humanity must ultimately recognize God's graciousness in this respect and likewise come to worship Him (2; cf. 1 Ki. viii. 43). Whenever *flesh* (2) comes before the

Lord, the question of iniquity has to be dealt with. Our transgressions are an intolerable element both to the worshipper and to God; the surprising thing is that He undertakes to forgive them freely (3). Thus the worshipper becomes a priest, chosen to draw near to God (cf. Nu. xvi. 5), to abide in His courts, and find his highest aspirations satisfied in the good life of His house (cf. Ex. xix. 6; 1 Pet. ii. 9; Rev. i. 6).

b. Adoration of God (5–8)

The worshipper's mood of prayer and penitence is now succeeded by awe because of the deeds of God in the history of nations. These terrible works—such as the discomfiture of the army of Sennacherib—demonstrate the righteousness of God; and His intervention in Israel's history is an example to all peoples, even those in the furthest isles (5; cf. Ps. lxxii. 10; Is. xli. 5). This introduction of the concept of distance leads the psalmist to consider God's creation. Earth's mountains and seas have been established by Him (6; cf. Ps. xciii. 2–4), but these words also symbolize the nations of the earth which stand out above the swirling tumult of mankind in general (7b). All communities, from the lands of dawn to the isles of the setting sun, have cause to rejoice in the divine vindication of the weak and upright.

c. Thanksgiving (9–13)

The supreme act of this worship is finally presented in a burst of spontaneous and vivid praise for the beauty, richness and comfort afforded by the harvest of fields and flocks. The natural increase is attributed directly to the divine presence and working. (Note the repetition of the word *Thou*.) It is He who gives the former rain (*the river of God*), which enriched the prepared ground, and the latter rain which swelled the grown crops. The language of verses 10 and 11 is exceedingly rich in imagery. The whole countryside—upland grazings (verse 12, *the wilderness*), hillside pastures encircling the cultivated land of the lower slopes, and even the meadows in the valley bottoms, all alike are rich, replete and rejoicing because of the goodness of God (cf. Ps. xcvi. 12).

PSALM LXVI. A SONG OF DELIVERANCE

This Psalm was obviously designed for public worship and to celebrate some national deliverance—probably the overthrow of the Assyrian forces under Sennacherib. There are two main divisions.

a. Corporate worship (1–12)

Note the world outlook of the Psalm. Such a call as this, addressed to *all ye lands* (1), implies that the nation's recent experience of deliverance is of world-wide significance (cf. Ps. xlvii. 1, 2). This arises not from the preservation of God's people so much as from the disclosure of God's glorious being—*the honour* (RV 'glory') *of his name* (2)—in and through the historic event. Hence all peoples are exhorted to proclaim and reflect the divine nature in their praises. A sample of such praise is then given (3, 4; cf. Is. xxxvii. 20; Rev. xv. 3, 4). As a cause and stimulant of such praise all the earth is invited to *come and see the works of God* (5). Foremost of these hitherto is the escape of the children of Israel from Egypt and their eventual entrance to Canaan, i.e. the dryshod crossing of *sea* and *flood* (6). The latter reference is to the flooded state of the Jordan at the time (see Jos. iii. 15). *There did we rejoice* (6; see Ex. xv; Jos. v). It is noteworthy that throughout the Psalter no other historical event is viewed with as much awe and wonder as the exodus (cf. Pss. xviii. 15–19, lxviii. 7, 8, lxxiv. 13–15, lxxvii. 16–20, lxxviii. 13, and 52, 53, lxxxix. 7–10, xciii. 3, 4, cv, cvi. 7–12, cxxxvi. 10–15). This song now affirms that God is ever the same; His rule is now as wide and His eye as watchful as always; therefore, *let not the rebellious exalt themselves* (7).

This last clause of verse 7 may contain an allusion to Sennacherib's retreat (cf. Is. xxxvii. 23); it certainly leads on to a heartfelt hymn of thankfulness for a recent national deliverance which is regarded as being of international importance. See verse 8 RV. This adoration is called forth by the evidence of a present security (9; cf. Ps. cxxi. 3; Jude 24, RV). Yet not long before this their condition was wellnigh hopeless. To test them God had caused them to lose their freedom like fish in a net (an alternative translation would suggest men imprisoned in a dungeon). Sore burdens had been laid upon them, and they had known defeat in battle. Nevertheless these trials and perils had been followed by a period of unhindered or abundant life (see 12, RV mg.).

b. Personal worship (13–20)

This final portion of the song appears to be the testimony of the king, for there is an unmistakable change to a singular pronoun and a personal emphasis. There are two phases. In verses 13–15 he speaks to God on behalf of himself, as representative of the nation. During the previous emergency of threatened calamity he had made certain vows to God which were to be fulfilled when deliverance came. These vows are now being fulfilled, not grudgingly, but in full measure (cf. Mal. i. 13, 14, and 8; Rom. xii. 1). Then in verses 16–20 the king speaks to all godly men on behalf of God to the effect that prayer (*I cried*) mingled with praise (*extolled*) which springs from a pure heart and a good conscience had been and always would be heard and heeded. *If I regard iniquity in my heart* (18); better, 'If I had regarded'. This basis of effectual prayer, i.e. a blameless heart, is a constant element in scriptural teaching (cf. Jb. xxvii. 2–9; Is. i. 15–17, lix. 1–3; Ezk. xiv. 2, 3;

Jn. ix. 31; 1 Jn. iii. 21). Blessed indeed be God for His faithfulness and graciousness in this respect (20).

PSALM LXVII. JUBILATE DEO

This festive song is considered by some commentators to be a harvest hymn of praise. This conclusion is based on verse 6a, but on the whole it seems improbable: less is said here of the gathered crops than was said in Ps. lxv. 9–13 of the growing corn. The Psalm is concerned with all nations, *the ends of the earth* (7), and the immeasurable benediction *God shall bless us* (6, 7). Moreover the placing of the Psalm between two great hymns of public praise, each with an exceptionally wide perspective of nations and history, suggests that its jubilation is rooted in some greater phenomenon than the occurrence of a good harvest.

The first verse is an echo of the priestly benediction in Nu. vi. 24–26, and it may well be that this blessing was spoken by the High Priest before the assembled people responded in the words of this Psalm. Verses 3 and 5 would then be refrains sung from the throats of the multitude with special emphasis, and the same words may have been repeated after verse 7 by the High Priest as he concluded this extended benediction (cf. the double blessing in Lv. ix. 22, 23). The Psalm would thus consist of three short motets. In verses 1 and 2 Israel is shown as the mirror of God wherein all nations may behold Him. In verse 4 all peoples are regarded as the Israel of God; they are radiantly happy because He judges them (in the sense of 'governs') and fully secure because He governs them (in the sense of 'guides'), even as He ruled and led the chosen people through the wilderness. Verse 6 is an acknowledgment of a bounteous harvest (see RV, 'hath yielded'). In verse 7 the psalmist looks into the future and sees God's blessing abiding upon Israel, and, through them, the whole earth united in the fear of God. Cf. Rom. xi. 15, 26. The Psalm thus becomes for the Church a very apt expression of its missionary aspirations.

PSALM LXVIII. A PROCESSIONAL HYMN

This is one of the most magnificent songs of triumph in the whole of the Old Testament. Its dramatic commentary upon a memorable event, its wide perspective of thought and speech, its spirit of invincible faith in God, and its presentation of the historic past and the envisaged future, combine to make it an outstanding portion of the Psalter.

While it is not explicitly associated with a Davidic episode, it was almost certainly written to celebrate the transference of the ark of the Lord from the house of Obed-edom to the new tabernacle which David had prepared for it on Mount Zion (cf. 2 Sa. vi. 2–18). But the Psalm was written not merely for this one occasion; it was constructed around the incident in such a manner as to convey a double teaching. First, the actual journey of the ark from its temporary resting-place near Nachon's threshingfloor to its final abode in Jerusalem is regarded as a dramatic reminiscence of the nation's journeyings from Egypt to Canaan. Indeed, that journey was the final phase of that great movement, for the temporary resting-places of the tabernacle at Gilgal, Bethel, and Shiloh had been necessary because of the long delay in capturing Jerusalem —traditional scene of the confirmed covenant (Gn. xxii. 16-18), and obvious choice for the nation's spiritual centre. Secondly, the actual completion of this great historical movement, which was to acquire such profound significance, provides a unique opportunity to present a fundamental theological truth concerning God. The whole action, historical and symbolical, was a tapestry whereon the divine name might be discerned with increasing clarity, e.g. *God* (1; *'Elohim*), *his name* (4; *JAH*), *the Almighty* (14; *El Shaddai*), *the Lord* (16; *Yahweh*), *the Lord God* (18; *Jah 'Elohim*), *the Lord* (19; *'Adonai*), *God the Lord* (20; *Yahweh 'Adonai*).

a. The procession (1-18)

i. The beginning (1-3). The ark is lifted from its resting-place and, because it was the pledge and symbol of God's presence with the people, its movement is a reflection of God's intervention. The scene is an echo of the wilderness experiences as recorded in Nu. x. 35 and Ex. xiv. 25. The brief and tenuous nature of human life is illustrated by the similes of *smoke* (cf. Ps. xxxvii. 20; Ho. xiii. 3) and *wax* (cf. Mi. i. 4). Yet that which is the undoing of the wicked (they *flee before him*) is actually the delight of the godly (they *rejoice before God*, 3; RV 'exult').

ii. The procession sets out (4-10). As the ark with the attendant priests, king, and singers moves off along the route, the cry is heard 'Cast up a highway for him that rideth through the deserts' (4, RV; cf. Is. xl. 3, lxii. 10). The name of this potentate, before whom all obstructions must be removed, is *JAH* (cf. Ex. xv. 2). The repetition of the phrase from verse 3, 'exult ye before him' (4, RV), suggests a further development of thought. The attention is turned from the route of the march to the personal character of God. He is enthroned in heaven, *his holy habitation* (5), yet He is intimately aware of human needs: He is a father to orphans and the protector of the weak and lonely (cf. Ex. xxii. 22, 23; Jn. xiv. 18); He cares for the solitary and He delivers the oppressed. He has especially blessed Israel in having brought them out of Egyptian bondage into comparative prosperity; on the other hand, the bodies of rebellious folk who could not enter in because of disbelief were left in a parched land (6, RV; cf. Heb. iii. 12, 19). This brief allusion to the exodus leads the psalmist to give a brief résumé of that inerasable memory which was now, in a very real sense, being relived (8-10).

iii. The approach to the city (11-18). The ark had been sent back from the Philistines in a manner comparable with the release of the children of Israel by the Egyptians; the incident of Uzzah's death had been an echo of the dread and death of Sinai. Now that the ark was approaching Jerusalem it was, in one sense, retraversing the route of the invasion and conquest of Canaan. This part of the chant consists at first of a series of disjointed sentences which seem to reproduce the shouts of the crowd. There are the hosts of women that proclaim the tidings (11, RV); contrast the reference to the official singers in 25. Some cried one thing, some another; snatches of old war songs (12, 17), fragments of unpreserved Psalms (18), and festive folk songs such as antedate Canticles (13), possibly symbolizing times of prosperity; phrases from traditional forms of tribal challenge and response (13a, 14, RV; cf. Jdg. v. 16a). All these are woven together so as to create a sense of pageantry enriched by memory, even as modern radio drama evokes a certain frame of mind by a series of recollections swiftly and successively faded in and out. The meaning of verse 14 seems to be that God dispersed the armies of invading kings, they fled like snowflakes driven by a storm against the dark wooded slopes of a hill called Zalmon, near Shechem (cf. Jdg. ix. 48).

The hill of Bashan (15); i.e. Mount Hermon. Even a mountain such as this is not to be compared with the holy hill in which *God desireth to dwell* (16). Honour lies not in physical majesty but in spiritual dignity. The procession and its attendant crowd is really a shadow of a greater concourse converging upon the house of God. His hosts are beyond numbers (17) and the divine glory of the sanctuary of Zion is as real as the awe-full theophany upon Sinai. Eventually, as the ark approaches the city gates (cf. Ps. xxiv), the recent capture of this strong and rebellious city is recalled (2 Sa. v. 6-10), and both events are seized upon as evidences of His irresistible purpose. *Yahweh*, the rightful King, has been exalted. All around Him bring their gifts. Even those who were rebellious are content that He, *Jah 'Elohim*, should dwell there (18, RV).

b. The arrival (19-35)

i. The procession ends (19-27). Verses 19-23 refer to the last public appearance of the ark until its transference to the temple of Solomon (1 Ki. viii. 1-8). But it is not described as an object; it is recognized as a token and symbol of the Lord, the God who is our salvation. Hence this fervent adoration of Him to whom *belong the issues* (or 'means of escape') *from death* (20), and wields unquestioned power over all men guilty of defiance no matter how far they may flee in the endeavour to escape Him (cf. Ps. cxxxix. 7-12). *The hairy scalp* (21). An allusion to the ancient practice of keeping the head unshorn until the enterprise embarked upon was completed. *I will bring my people again* (22); better, as in RV, 'them'; i.e. the enemies.

These thoughts concerning the invisible and irresistible God of righteousness are a fitting prelude to the disappearance of the ark within the curtained doorway of the tabernacle (see verse 24, RV). The priests, singers, minstrels, and the company of girls with timbrels have now passed out of sight, and the whole action of the procession from start to finish is seen to be symbolical of all God's glorious and inscrutable goings through Israel's history. In a sense, Israel has been the procession and the peoples of the earth have been the onlookers. Verses 26 and 27 introduce the hymn of praise sung by the concourse outside the tabernacle. This crowd is spoken of under four tribal names, though all who have sprung *from the fountain of Israel* (26b), i.e. Jacob, are included. *Benjamin* is named first as the specially beloved of his father and as the small tribe from whence came the first ruler, king Saul. *Judah* with its princes and council was the foremost southern tribe both as respects numbers and ability. *Zebulun* and *Naphtali* are chosen as representatives of the northern group probably because of their honourable mention in Deborah's Song, of which this Psalm is so strongly reminiscent.

ii. **The hymn of Israel (28–31).** This is local and historical, dealing with Jerusalem and Egypt. Because God has been the source of national strength and coherence the people beseech Him first to continue to be so, secondly to rebuke Egypt—'the wild beast of the reeds' (30, RV; i.e. the hippopotamus; cf. Jb. xl. 21)— and to constrain *the multitude of the bulls with the calves* (i.e. the rulers of other peoples around Israel) to offer tribute of silver coin. Thirdly they pray that God will scatter all potential enemies that *delight in war* and induce even the great and distant nations to turn to Israel's God. *Till every one submit . . .* (30). Note the alternative RV rendering, according to which God disdains to receive the presents brought to Him to avert His wrath.

iii. **The hymn of all the earth (32–35).** The finale of praise swells out to include all earth's kingdoms, for the Lord is high, strong, and mighty. He ruleth the heavens and His power is visible in the skies (33; cf. Ps. xix. 1–6): His works performed from His sanctuary in Israel arouse awe throughout the world. Let all men *ascribe* (i.e. 'testify') to His mighty power, and proclaim Him blessed because of His faithfulness.

PSALM LXIX. DESPAIR TRANSFORMED TO PRAISE

This Psalm is a companion to Ps. xxii; both deal with the theme of undeserved suffering which has been due in large part to a steadfast loyalty to God. The theme is encountered also in Pss. xxxv, xliv and cix. Although the title of this Psalm ascribes it to David it is not easily linked with any known episode in his life. The experience lying behind it recalls the suffering of Jeremiah (cf. Je. xxxviii. 6). Note also the similarities with the third chapter of Lamentations (e.g. cf. verse 2 with La. iii. 54; verse 12 with La. iii. 14; verse 21 with La. iii. 15). In verses 33–36 there are a number of phrases which could be interpreted as references to the exile and as expressing a longing for the restoration to Palestine.

The psalmist's thoughts move through four phases. His affliction is described, divine help is requested, retribution upon his enemies is desired, and the hope is expressed of deliverance for himself and all others like him. Note the many quotations of this Psalm in the New Testament, e.g. verse 4 (Jn. xv. 25); verse 9 (Jn. ii. 17 and Rom. xv. 3); verses 22, 23 (Rom. xi. 9, 10); verse 25 (Acts i. 20).

a. **Despair of himself (1–12)**

There are two parts in this section: the first is factual (1–6); the second is analytical (7–12). The psalmist begins with a cry for help, and then describes himself as a drowning man (1; cf. Jon. ii. 5), as one who is bogged in a morass and as one who, crossing a ford, is suddenly swept downstream to deep pools by an unexpected rush of flood-water (2). Moreover, he is beyond human help, for none has heard his cries, and now he steadily grows weaker (3). The occasion of this calamity is rooted in the antagonism of his fellows; it takes the form of an unjustifiable dislike of him even by friends and kindred (8), while those who actively hate him are pictured as an encircling crowd of cruel and unscrupulous men (4; cf. Ps. xxxviii. 19). These have used their power to press upon him claims which are quite unwarranted (cf. Mt. xii. 24ff.; Jn. viii. 48, 49); they have made him yield up things which he is wrongfully accused of having stolen (4; see RV mg.). This complaint carries no imputation of the psalmist's complete blamelessness: God knows the measure of his guiltiness, for no sins are hidden from Him (5). Nevertheless he has sought to live an upright life and he foresees despair as taking hold of other godly men who will become discouraged if his urgent need receives no recognition and response from God (6).

Having stated the facts of the situation, the psalmist proceeds to outline the conditions which preceded this perplexing development (7–12). Outstanding amongst these has been his personal allegiance to God. Reproach, separation, misunderstanding, tears, grief, ribaldry, and derision have been his lot simply because, in his zeal for the honour of the God of Israel, he has subordinated all personal interests to the welfare and glory of that name. People of all ranks of life, his brothers (8), the civic elders (12; *they that sit in the gate*), as well as the dissolute, have scoffed at God and at him. With verse 9 cf. Jn. ii. 17; Rom. xv. 3.

b. Dependence upon God (13–21)

Nevertheless, and in this lies the anomaly of true faith, the psalmist's trust in God is unshaken. Shame has no power to weaken constancy (cf. Heb. xii. 2, x. 32ff.) and all reproach would vanish if God so answered as to demonstrate the truth of His promised salvation (cf. Is. xlix. 8). The emphasis on *as for me* and *thy salvation* (13) is intended to echo the opening words of the Psalm, *Save me, O God*, and serves to direct attention to the deliberate parallel between this portion of the Psalm and the preceding one. Verse 14 reflects verse 2; the earlier statement of an experience is changed into a prayer for a transforming action. The whole imagery of flood, mire and deep pool (1–3) is altered from its original sense of extremity and finality to that of a temporary and remediable situation. Let God intervene and old values, meanings and possibilities, even *the pit* (15) or 'grave', will be done away; all will become new. In verse 16 there is an intentional contrast with verse 4. Both speak of that which is beyond counting, viz. *the hairs of mine head* and *the multitude of thy tender mercies*, but whereas the former is a metaphor for those *that hate me*, the latter is descriptive of Him whose *lovingkindness is good*. The antithesis is continued in the thought of a *servant* before the face of his righteous master (17), and the memory of *mighty enemies* who seek his dismissal from life (4b). Such men had wrongfully exacted from him that which was his own (4c, RV mg.), but God is now besought to *redeem* and *deliver* (RV 'ransom') him (18); i.e. let God reclaim His own possession (the psalmist's soul) and thus undo the work of unrighteousness. The shame and reproach of verse 7 also reappear in verse 19. The prayer ends at this point, but the parallel between the two portions of the Psalm continues. Verse 20 accentuates the existing plight out of which prayer has been offered and not yet answered. The agony becomes intensified: those who were expected to show compassion and comfort toward him (20, 21), because of a special bond of understanding with them, prove to be as disappointing and suspicious as his own kinsfolk (8; cf. Mt. xxvi. 37ff.). Formerly he had fasted (10) but now his enemies give him *gall for my meat* (21); i.e. it is as though they first poisoned his food and then served it in his name to any who mourned.

c. Denunciation of his foes (22–28)

Up to this point the rectification of wrong in the lives of other people has been implicit in any action of God for the deliverance of the psalmist. That major theme has been so urgent and individual that nothing has been said about the larger issue, viz. what is to be done with a community which engenders this kind of peril to a good man. But the sense of human injustice, cruelty and dishonour which has been expressed in the preceding verses releases the indignation which hitherto the psalmist has curbed. His denunciation of those who have maltreated him is not personally vindictive. He desires that these evil men shall come to know the truth: not that they shall merely see the truth of God's faithfulness in his own expected rescue, but that they shall learn the truth about themselves in their own experience. This could come about by God turning upon themselves the consequences which their conduct has effected upon others, such as himself. For example, as they had offered poisonous food (21), let their own feasts be a snare to them (22). In that they had brought darkness and weakness to him (2, 3), let them discover what it feels like to have no outlook and no power (shaking loins, 23). They had been zealous in their opposition to him (4); let them experience another's hot indignation pursuing them (24). They had caused him to be outcast by his family (8); let them become homeless vagrants (25). They had noticed God's chastening of the psalmist (10, 11), and had eagerly attacked him as well (26); let them find out what it is not only to have double sins (27), but double punishment too. They had sought to deprive him of God's blessing (20); so let them be debarred from the bliss of righteousness and let their name be erased from the register of godly men (28).

d. Dedication to the Lord (29–36)

Finally, the pressure of the present moment and the pre-eminence of his own plight (29) restores the central thread of the Psalm, viz. faith in God. Verse 29a should be translated 'But as for me (emphatic as in verse 13), who am afflicted . . .'. The psalmist's full reliance upon God brings about the prophetic realization of the Lord's transforming intervention. This stirs him to utmost praise and dedication, *I will praise the name of God with a song* (30), a form of worship which is more acceptable to God than any sacrifice of an ox *that hath horns* (i.e. mature) *and hoofs* (i.e. clean; cf. Lv. xi. 3). The psalmist feels that the most amazing phenomenon and fact of experience is not distress, frustration, conflict, misunderstanding, retribution, or even death; it is that 'the Lord heareth the needy' (33, RV) and responds. (The words *his prisoners* may allude to the exiles in Babylon.) That truth is cause enough for heaven and earth, the sea and all that therein is to praise the Lord. In this joyous assurance the future can be contemplated with hope; Zion shall yet be redeemed, the desolate cities of Judah rebuilt, and the heirs of the righteous shall dwell there and prosper.

PSALM LXX. AN URGENT PRAYER FOR DELIVERANCE

These five verses are the end portion of Ps. xl (verses 13 to 17) which has been detached for separate use in the temple services associated with the meat offering (see title, and cf. Ps. xxxviii title and Lv. ii. 2). A few words have been changed here and there, and the name for God, *Yahweh*, has sometimes been altered to *'Elohim*.

The fragment has been placed in the Psalter at this point probably as a kind of postscript to Ps. lxix, with which it has a number of points of agreement. Both open with a note of urgency, both invoke judgment on the opponents of righteousness (cf. lxx. 2, 3 with lxix. 23–27), and both appeal to God on the ground of personal necessity (lxx. 5a, lxix. 29a). Moreover, the Psalm of which this was formerly a part, Ps. xl, has also much in common with Ps. lxix; both begin with allusions to mire and darkness, and to the action of divine rescue. The difference is that in the former case the experience of deliverance has occurred so that the parched mouth (lxix. 3) has been filled with a new song (xl. 3; cf. lxix, 30). Compare also xl. 12 with lxix. 4; xl. 6 with lxix. 31; xl. 11 with lxix. 16; xl. 12a with lxix. 20. It was evidently thought that this congruity was sufficient to warrant the placing of the closing verses of Ps. xl as a postscript to Ps. lxix.

PSALM LXXI. THE CONFIDENCE OF A MATURE FAITH

This Psalm has no title, although the LXX ascribes it to 'David, the sons of Jonadab, and those who were first led captive', which seems to connect it with the first years of the exile (cf. Je. xxxv). It is the prayer of an old man (9, 18), and there is a mellowness and serenity about it which is characteristic of a long life spent in reliance upon God (cf. 5, 17). But there is no clue to authorship apart from the writer's acquaintance with many other Psalms, especially Pss. xxii (cf. verses 5, 6), xxxi (cf. verses 1–3) and xxxv (cf. verses 13, 14 and 19).

There is a marked parallel between verses 1–9 and verses 10–18. The rest of the Psalm has a different structure but also falls into two groups corresponding to the previous section.

a. Intimate communion with God (1–9)
The quiet dignity and confidence of these verses are unmistakable. The plea for divine aid is introduced in a gentle phrase (2) very different from the imperative and impetuous cries of Pss. xxii, xxxv, liv, lix, lxix, lxx, and is interwoven with an appreciation that God has always safeguarded him (3). The principal feature of this section is the spirit of adoration toward the Lord: each of the first eight verses speaks of Him with faith and gratitude. *In thee, O Lord* (1); *thy righteousness* (2); *thou art my rock* (3); *my God* (4); *thou art my hope* (5); *thou art he* (6); *thou art my strong refuge* (7); *thy praise and . . . honour* (8). The whole passage prepares the way for the personal petition of verse 9. *I am as a wonder unto many* (7). Either because his lifelong trust in God has not freed him from peril and oppression, or because of his remarkable experiences of previous deliverances from danger.

b. Resolution in spite of distress (10–18)
These verses are really another version of the previous prayer, but they have a wider and a more forward vision. The writer turns to consider his enemies (10) and those who form the next generation (18); judgment is desired (13), hope is an inspiration (14), praise is foreseen (15, 16) and work is anticipated (18). Contrast the backward view of verse 6. His enemies believe that the Lord has forsaken him and are about to attack him (11). That is why the prayer of verses 2 and 3 is urgently repeated in the words *O God, be not far from me* (12). The earlier confession of hope is reiterated in verse 14. The anticipation of ceaseless praise concerning the *honour* (i.e. 'glory') of God (8) is now reinforced by a lifetime of divine tutelage (17). Finally, the plaintive cry of verse 9 is transformed in verse 18; the former prospect of failing strength becomes indefinitely deferred until a full life's work has been accomplished.

The remaining verses of the Psalm are to be distinguished from the foregoing: there is in them no direct reference to youth or age, to persecution, or to a need of immediate rescue.

c. Hope in God (19–21)
The mood of these verses is comparable with that of verses 1–10. Not only is there a very real awareness of God's former acts of compassion (19, 20; note the repeated use of *again*), but there is a kinship of thought. For example, it was the loftiness of God's holiness (19) which prompted the prayer, *Incline* (RV 'Bow down') *thine ear* (2). Again, the notion of re-birth out of *the depths of the earth* (20), i.e. deliverance from the gates of death, is an extension of the thought of physical birth (6; cf. Ps. cxxxix. 15): both are regarded as works of God. Moreover, the psalmist's *greatness* which he prays to be increased (21) is primarily the rich quality of his mature years (cf. verse 9). In a secondary sense it may perhaps signify also the national prestige; for an alternative reading in verse 20 (see RV) uses the plural pronoun, viz. 'shewed us', 'quicken us', 'bring us up'. His plea, 'turn again and comfort me' (21, RV), may also be taken as a variant of verse 9, but may bear an additional interpretation as a national prayer (answered in Is. xl. 1).

d. Praise and adoration (22–24)
In this last portion the emphasis is placed upon the future, as in verses 14–18 (the pronoun 'I' is stressed in both verse 14 and verse 22). But in place of enemies and plots are the instruments of praise, the psaltery and harp. He is confident of the answer to the prayer expressed in verse 12 and therefore extols the *truth* (i.e. 'faithfulness') of his God (22). He had previously looked forward hopefully to declaring *thy salvation all the day* (15); now he grasps the certainty of so doing, for the redemption of his soul is cause enough for talking *all the day long* (24). Finally, the spirit of worship is enhanced by the title *thou Holy One of Israel* (22; found elsewhere in the Psalter only in lxxviii. 41 and lxxxix. 18), for

it is His holiness above all else which is the inspiration of joyful praise (cf. Jn. xv. 9–11).

PSALM LXXII. THE IDEAL FOUNDER OF A RIGHTEOUS DYNASTY

Whether this Psalm (i.e. verses 1–17) was written by or for Solomon is uncertain; but in view of the compiler's footnote in verse 20, it may well have been composed by David for the accession of Solomon (see 1 Ki. i. 30ff.). Many of the expressions which in the AV and RV bear a future or prophetic meaning (*shall* is used over thirty times) could equally be interpreted in a wishful or prayerful sense (i.e. 'let', or 'may'; see RV mg.). The kingly rule which is the theme of the poem is certainly described idealistically, though many approximations thereto could be put forward for the early part of Solomon's reign.

The king's life is treated from three aspects. The doxology in verses 18 and 19 does not belong to the Psalm but serves to mark the close of the second of the Psalter's five books (cf. those at the close of Pss. xli, lxxxix, cvi).

a. The king's administration of his own nation (1–7)

The primary characteristic of his rule is righteousness. This is rooted in the royal petition to God for an understanding heart so that the king (who is also *the king's son*) might discern between good and evil and govern the people in a manner comparable with God's own administration (1). His verdicts in all matters of dispute will embody justice to the poor (2) as well as to the wealthy. Hence the whole country shall be permeated with honour, integrity and peace. *Mountains* and *hills* (3) may represent the countryside generally, which would be immune from pillage and oppression; or the words may simply mean that the royal deputies and civil officers would be as just and upright as the king himself. The word *judge* (4) is different from that in verse 2; it means the general exercise of wise authority, as in the office of judge held by Deborah and Samuel. Because of his care for the needy and helpless, and his suppression of unjust but powerful men, all the people will come to esteem and honour him (5). Some, however, refer the pronoun *thee* to God. This harmonizes with 'thy' in verses 1 and 2, and gives an appropriate meaning. His benevolent rule will be as refreshing and productive of good as *rain upon the mown grass* (6); i.e. upon the meadows which have been mown (cf. 2 Sa. xxiii. 4). The word translated *mown grass* is rendered 'fleece' in

Jdg. vi. 37; it means 'that which is shorn'. This pastoral picture of the internal administration of the kingdom is rounded off in verse 7 with phrases similar to Pss. lxxxv. 10, 11 and xcii. 12ff.

b. The king's sovereignty in the eyes of all men (8–14)

So righteous a ruler will inevitably be acknowledged outside his own nation, and the extension of his power will include all the earth. The normal bounds of the promised land were the river Euphrates on the east, and the Mediterranean Sea on the west. These are surpassed in the words of verse 8 (cf. Zc. ix. 10). *They that dwell in the wilderness* (9); i.e. the nomadic tribes. Foreign states as far afield as *Tarshish* (S. Spain), the Mediterranean *isles*, *Sheba* (Southern Arabia), and *Seba* (Ethiopia), shall honour him with gifts (cf. 1 Ki. x. 25, 26). These wide dominions will not be acquired through personal ambition, or desire for imperial fame, but through the intrinsic merit of an ideally righteous administration. Verses 12–14 elaborate the thoughts of verses 2–4 (cf. Jb. xxix. 11–16). Not only has he sympathy with the helpless (*poor*) and destitute (*needy*), but he esteems each man's life (*blood*) precious and worthy of redemption from evil powers (cf. Ps. xlix. 7, 8).

c. The king's perpetual benevolence and glory (15–17)

It is best to take these words as a prayerful desire. Verse 15 should commence 'May he (the king) live, let there be given to him gold . . .' Let the ceaseless and unqualified praise of his subjects (15b) be due to the obvious improvement in the country's productivity; let cornfields extend up the hillsides and their heavy-eared stalks rustle in the wind as pleasantly as the boughs of Lebanon's cedars (16). In such prosperity the inhabitants will flourish and increase (cf. 1 Ki. iv. 20; Is. xxvii. 6), and they will wish this blissful condition to become permanent. 'May the king's dynasty go on for ever; let his name be self-propagated as long as the sun shall shine' (17). Thus shall come to pass the promised blessing of all nations which was first mentioned to Abraham (Gn. xii. 3 and subsequently).

The conditions of social righteousness, stability, prosperity and peace which the Psalm depicts are not merely ideals; their actual and ultimate fulfilment is fully implied because of the messianic hope (cf. Lk. ii. 14; Eph. i. 21; Heb. xi. 16).

For verses 18–20 see *Introduction* above.

BOOK THREE. PSALMS lxxiii–lxxxix

PSALM LXXIII. THE MYSTERY OF PROSPEROUS WICKEDNESS

The third book of the Psalter (Pss. lxxiii–lxxxix) consists largely of Psalms attributed to Asaph (Pss. lxxiii–lxxxiii: cf. title of Ps. 1), who was one

of the leading choristers of David's time. Not all the Psalms in this group of eleven can be attributed to the period of David's reign, and it is quite likely that Asaph founded a particular school of psalmody (cf. 2 Ch. xxix. 30).

Ps. lxxiii deals with the same theme as xxxvii (see also Pss. xlix and xciv). The problem is that of an apparent inversion of morality and success: in the life of this world evil men prosper whilst godly men are often in serious distress and need. The emphasis here, however, is not on the temporary nature of the prosperity of the wicked. It may, and often does, persist through life (see verse 4 and cf. Jb. xxi. 7–13), although ultimately there must be condemnation. The essential truth for a righteous man was that it is well with him really, i.e. the true test of one's well-being consists not in the power and riches of this world, but in personal relationship with God. The discovery of this truth is treated retrospectively. The Psalm is in five parts.

a. Previous doubting recalled (1–3)

Truly God is good (1). This positive statement indicates the absence of doubt in the psalmist's mind now. Nevertheless there had been a time when he had almost turned aside from the path of Godward trust, he had almost staggered through the sudden pull of unbelief (cf. Rom. iv. 20) and had gone so far as to feel envious at the success of those who spoke boastfully (3a, 8) and had *more than heart could wish* (3b, 7).

b. The facts stated objectively (4–12)

The characteristics of ungodly men are described first outwardly (conditions and conduct), and then inwardly (speech and motive). *There are no bands* (RV mg. 'pangs') *in their death* (4); i.e. they die peacefully. Their health is good; their life is untroubled by hardship (cf. Jb. v. 7); *neither are they plagued* (5; cf. verse 14), i.e. 'perplexed' or 'bewildered'. This state of affairs is reflected in their conduct. They behave insolently and unscrupulously as regularly as they wear their rich clothing (6). Their gaze is intent on self-gain and the thoughts and imaginations of their hearts are become utterly vain (see RV mg. of verse 7 and cf. Gn. vi. 5; contrast 2 Cor. x. 5). It is only to be expected that such behaviour should indicate an exaggerated self-opinion, and indeed these people *speak loftily* (8; RV mg. 'from on high'); i.e. they consider their pronouncements to have the authority of heaven.

These facts alone do not constitute a mystery; there are other elements in the situation. *His people* (the LXX reads 'my people', cf. Dt. vii. 6) *return hither* (10). Those who had been called out from the ungodly life of the nations and made into a people for God's own possession are being tempted to return to evil and corrupt practices, and the philosophy of the ungodly is being absorbed like the waters of a full cup drained by a thirsty man (see RV mg. and cf. Jb. xv. 16). It is the contradiction of facts and faith which creates perplexity in those who are not beguiled into scepticism, and which leads them to ask the questions of verses 11 and 12.

c. The problem described subjectively (13–17)

The psalmist himself was tempted to doubt the necessity of a strict integrity of heart and con-

science. His adherence to the high moral code of the law seemed vain so far as tangible advantage was concerned; indeed his endeavour to live a sober and godly life brought him no evidences of divine approval, but only a daily chastening (13, 14). Had he voiced his doubts in public, he would have misled many others whose faith was weak (15). The more he pondered over the meaning of this inversion of values the more elusive and wearisome (*painful*) it became (16). At last he *went into the sanctuary of God* (17) and meditated upon the ultimate state of the wicked. There he discovered a new outlook; he perceived that life had baffled him because he had not looked at it in the light of the final issue.

d. The nature of his readjustment is recalled (18–25)

The first phase of the psalmist's readjustment was the endorsement of the traditional belief in divine justice. The ungodly are surely brought at last to utter ruin (the word translated *destruction* (18) occurs elsewhere only in Ps. lxxiv. 3). It has to be so because the way they have chosen to take is slippery and insecure: let but judgment begin and immediately they are swept away by the consequences of their past actions which then fill them with dread (19). But it was the second phase of his experience which most stirred the psalmist. The fate of the wicked was really a subordinate issue; so far as God was concerned they were only phantoms, as unreal as dreams. (This does not imply that God has no concern for sinners; but the psalmist uses an exaggerated simile in order to emphasize the completely different point of view.) That which deeply troubled the godly was almost a minor matter with God. *Thus my heart was grieved* (21); better, 'when my heart was sour'; cf. RV mg. His former sour mood of brooding doubt had been as stupid and shortsighted as though he were a *beast* (the word is *behemoth*, as in Jb. xl. 15); i.e. without the capacity of fellowship with God. He had gone astray in viewing life as purely natural. The great reality of life was spiritual—God's continuous presence. He was always at hand to assure, to strengthen and advise, so that ultimately the psalmist would be brought to an experience of honour and glory. *Receive me* (24) has the sense of 'lead me', i.e. 'take me along with'; cf. Gn. xlviii. 1.

There is some uncertainty as to what insight the psalmist had about existence after death. To take verses 23 and 24 (AV and RV) at their face value would make them noteworthy in the Old Testament as a declaration of belief in a glorious life after death for those who have faithfully walked with God on earth. It is easy for us to interpret the words in this way because of our sure and certain hope as Christians through the resurrection of our Lord. But it is very doubtful whether the psalmist saw so far or so clearly. There are three points to note: *Glory* (24) has here no sense of spiritual glory hereafter; it stands for personal honour, for all that contributes to a man's personality in life whether it be abilities or possessions (cf. Pss. vii. 5, xvi. 9). *In heaven* (25), lit. 'in the heavens', means the physical realm of stars and sun (cf. Ps. xix. 1 and 6). Nothing is said here about dying, the word *afterward* (24) implies no more than 'after the present period of doubt and distress is over'. It is to be noted that in considering the 'latter end' of the wicked (17) there is nothing to show that the psalmist was looking beyond their death: the apparent discrepancy of verses 14 and 19 is due to difference of viewpoint. The mystery of prosperous wickedness had been satisfactorily dealt with by a realization of two things, viz. that the philosophy of the natural man, 'eat, drink and be merry', was false; that the whole problem had gained a false importance through an obscured vision of God's character and grace.

e. The relevance of his belief to the immediate circumstances (26–28)

My flesh and my heart faileth (26) seems to indicate a decline in physical and mental powers through increasing age. The readjustment of values, previously described, had to withstand the intensification of doubt arising from this and from the possible recurrences of material hardship. Nevertheless the knowledge he had gained of God's persistent and blessed fellowship had matured also (26b) and the psalmist was able confidently and fervently to state the ends of the whole matter, viz. those who withdraw from God's way would be inevitably destroyed, but, for himself, the proximity of God was the source and cause of all his well-being. The general statement of verse 1 has become a personal confession and a testimony. Note the contrast between *far from thee* (27) and *near to God* (28). The LXX rendering of verse 28b is the same as Ps. ix. 14a.

PSALM LXXIV. A LAMENT FOR THE DESTRUCTION OF THE SANCTUARY

This is one of several poignant lamentations which found utterance at the destruction of Jerusalem and the beginning of exile in Babylon (cf. Lamentations and Ps. lxxix). The tragedy was not merely that the centre of religious life, the temple, had been destroyed: that which cut the cord of hope and overwhelmed the nation with moral dismay was the inference that God had forsaken them. Where was God's faithfulness to the Abrahamic covenant concerning land and people; and what prospect had humanity if Israel perished? The Psalm is in two parts, one indignantly questioning and objective, the other humbly expectant and personal.

a. The appeal (1–11)

Disappointment is mingled with bewilderment as the psalmist voices the cry of the people in an insistent 'Why' to God (1 and 11). Into the midst of this challenging inquiry is inserted a less emotional statement of their distress (3–9).

The Psalm is too obviously related to the event of which it speaks for the phrase *cast us off for ever* (1; cf. verse 10) to imply the passage of a long interval of time (cf. Zc. i. 12). It expresses rather the sense of an irremediable and final catastrophe. The anomaly is that God's hot anger is directed against those who are His own flock (the 'Shepherd of Israel' is a metaphor much used in the Asaphic psalms), against His own purchase, and the tribe of His own inheritance (2, RV; cf. Ex. xv. 16, 17). His wrath is directed even against Mount Zion (2), His own habitation (cf. Ps. lxviii. 16). In other words, the people's distress and disgrace were a dilemma because God seemed to be ruining His own work and breaking His own word. The immediate inference was that somehow He did not know what had been done. Let Him come swiftly (*lift up thy feet*) and inspect the appalling ruins of His city and the defilement of His sanctuary (3, RV).

There follows (4) a more or less factual statement of what He would see, but details are given only of the sanctuary. *Thine enemies* (4), RV 'adversaries', have made tumult in the place of quiet. *Congregations* (4). The Hebrew word may mean either the people gathered in meeting or the meeting-place. Military ensigns have taken the place of divine symbols, and wanton damage has been caused to the beauty and form of the building (cf. 1 Ki. vi. 29) so that it looks like the derelict waste of splintered and futile stumps that mark a felled forest (4–6; in verse 5 follow the RV reading). Finally the place had been burnt (2 Ki. xxv. 9, 10; Is. lxiv. 11); and, furthermore, as the enemies' intention had been utter havoc, not only the temple but the religious life of the people had been destroyed (8). *Synagogues* (8) did not exist before the exile, but the word may mean 'meeting-places' (such as the traditional sites at Ramah and Bethel; cf. 1 Ki. xii. 32 ff.). Some ancient versions give the sense that 'they abolished the feasts in the land' (cf. La. ii. 6). The result was that not a vestige or outward sign of their religious life remained and there was not even a prophetic hint as to how long this would continue (cf. La. ii. 9). The allusion to *no more any prophet* (9) is not to be taken as a denial of such men as Obadiah, Ezekiel and Jeremiah. It indicates that such a serious blow had been struck at the nation's confidence in divine institutions on earth that the messages of such men were no longer believable. God Himself must intervene (cf. La. ii. 9; Joel ii. 28–32, iii. 17, 18; Acts ii).

The concluding phrase of this descriptive section, *how long* (10), is a resumption of the appeal to God in verses 1 and 2. Profound as the disaster was, the psalmist could not believe it to be permanent. It was unthinkable that the name of the Lord should be left permanently in disrepute. Judgment must surely fall upon their opponents, although for a mysterious interval God's chastening hand was withheld (11, RV; cf. Ex. xv. 6).

b. The hope (12–23)

That fervent appeal to God implied a hope which was not wishful merely but reasonable. They were appealing to a God whose character they knew of old; of His power there could be no doubt at all. This conviction is borne out by the emphatic *Thou* of verses 13–17. The indisputable facts of the exodus are recapitulated; the division of the Red Sea, the destruction of the Egyptian army (symbolized by the *dragons* of verse 13b; cf. Ezk. xxix. 3), the utter disgrace of the Egyptian power (symbolized by *leviathan*, verse 14, usually taken to mean the crocodile; cf. Jb. xli. 1ff.), the dishonour to the Egyptian carcases washed up as a prey to robbers and as food for the beasts of the desert. For *people* (14) or 'folk' applied to animals, cf. Pr. xxx. 25ff. God had wrought this: He also had brought water out of the cleft rock (Ps. lxxviii. 15ff.) and dried up the perennial Jordan (15). Indeed, day and night, the very light and sun, were His (16). All the physical features (*the borders*) of earth, all seasonal phenomena, were originated solely by Him (17).

The appeal and hope is now based, not on grounds of earthly circumstance, but on divine faithfulness. Let Him consider that His name has been blasphemed by a base or foolish people (18; cf. Dt. xxxii. 21). Where then is His honour? His poor family are harassed and defenceless as a dove among wild beasts (19). Where then is His compassion? The covenant whereby He pledged to them the land seems to be ignored, for His people are homeless and afflicted (20). Where then is His faithfulness? Let not the burdened souls which cry to Him turn back from Him in shame and confusion because of His apparent indifference (21). Where then would be His mercy and what source of divine praise would remain in earth? Oh that God would act in His own interests—so far as His name on earth is concerned! Let Him remember how vile persons abuse His name and continually cause their clamour to 'ascend' before Him (22, 23, RV). *The dark places of the earth* (20); i.e. where Israel was in exile, and which were full of the dwellings of violence.

PSALM LXXV. 'GOD IS THE JUDGE'

Unlike the preceding Psalm, this poem does not question the goodness of God but rather exults in His sovereignty and righteousness. There is a background of calamity (8) and a sense of recent relief from serious peril. In this respect the Psalm is akin to Pss. xlvi–xlviii and probably belongs to the same period (see Is. xxxvi and xxxvii). The LXX associates it with the Assyrian invasion. The word 'Al-Tashheth' (RV) in the title (cf. titles of Pss. lvii–lix) means 'destroy not'; its significance here is uncertain. It may be an allusion to Dt. ix. 26, in which case there would be an obvious link with the previous Psalm. See the note on the title of Ps. ix.

Verse 1 states the basis of corporate thanksgiving to God, viz. the unmistakable evidence that He (*thy name*) was close at hand. Verses 2–5 contain a statement by God concerning the immutability of the moral order. Verses 6–10 are the psalmist's development of that truth.

When I shall receive the congregation (2). Better, as in RV mg., 'When I shall take (i.e. select) the set time'; i.e. the right moment for strict and comprehensive judgment. Cf. Ps. cii. 13; Dn. viii. 19, xi. 35. The concept of absolute power in verse 3 is timeless and echoes the marvel of creation; as a metaphor it means that any dissolution of human society is followed by its divine re-establishment (as after the flood). See RV mg. The moral decay of a community cannot affect the foundations of divine righteousness and truth (Heb. xii. 26–28). The pause here, *Selah*, is to emphasize this statement. After the general principle has been declared, God speaks to the *fools* (4), i.e. arrogant, warning them not to behave as horned beasts that toss their heads in stubborn defiance. *Speak not with a stiff neck* (5); i.e. do not speak insolently and haughtily (cf. Is. xxxvii. 23).

Three observations are now made by the psalmist. First, the final authority and decisive factor in life and history do not lie in man, nor are they based upon this earth: *God is the judge* (6, 7; cf. Ps. cxlvii. 5, 6; Jb. xii. 13–24). Secondly, all human life is ultimately related to divine righteousness in an experience either of dismay or joy. The Hebrew prophets, in describing the eventual administration of divine justice, often used the imagery of God holding out to people and nations a cup of wine. Usually the contents are described as bitter and disappointing. *The wine is red* (8); 'the wine foameth' (RV). This wine is the wrath of God, but the wicked, either in haste, misapprehension, or necessity, are always described as draining the cup even to its last drops. Cf. Ps. lx. 3; Is. li. 17; Je. xxv. 15; Ezk. xxiii. 32–34. The same figure is used for the cup of joy and salvation which is proffered to the godly (cf. Pss. xvi. 5, xxiii. 5, cxvi. 13).

In the third place the psalmist stresses that divine sovereignty and righteousness, as exercised in human affairs, are compatible with and, indeed, productive of heartfelt praise by His people. The final verse identifies the psalmist, or rather, the nation for whom he speaks (cf. *we* in verse 1), with God, in so far as it is God's instrument sharing in the manifestation of His grace and judgment.

PSALM LXXVI. A SONG OF DELIVERANCE

The same circumstances which lay behind Ps. lxxv form the background of this poem also: it celebrates a victory over the nation's enemies. There are four parts.

a. The rejoicing (1–3)

Because of the victory which God is believed to have wrought, His name has become esteemed

465

and acknowledged among the people. *Israel* (1) should be understood as a synonym for *Judah*; since Israel as a kingdom had been overthrown, the tribe of Judah is now representative of the family of Jacob. *Tabernacle* (2); 'covert' (RV mg.). Jerusalem and Mount Zion are regarded as the lair of the Lion of Judah (cf. Je. xxv. 38). It was there, at the city, that He brake the swift arrows (see RV mg.) and brought to nought the enemy's equipment and plans of war (3; cf. Is. xxxvii. 33). *Battle* (3); i.e. weapons of war.

b. The victory (4–6)

The imagery of a lion is continued in the phrase 'Glorious art thou and excellent' (majestic), leaping down 'from the mountains of prey' (4, RV); i.e. upon the defeated Assyrians (cf. Is. xiv. 25). The invader's soldiers, confident of gaining much booty, were themselves bereft of what they had, and now sleep as the dead (cf. Ps. xiii. 3b). None of their hands which had threatened Jerusalem is now able to move (5; cf. 2 Ki. xix. 35). The battle had been decided by the *God of Jacob*; He had thrown the enemy into the profound sleep of death (6; cf. Is. xliii. 17).

c. Its effect (7–9)

Such a God must inspire all men with awe: who could stand before Him, especially when He is angry? He uttered *judgment* (8) in heaven, and forthwith all the inhabitants of earth were dumbfounded because so great an army met with such unexpected and complete disaster, and the humble men of Israel (*the meek of the earth*) were delivered.

d. Adoration of the Lord (10–12)

From the event the conclusion is drawn that the exercise of human violence and unscrupulous ambition can bring about an increased sense of thankfulness to God. The basic cause of this is not the manifestation of superior power, but the righteousness of its action. When evildoers are overthrown other people's observe it and honour Israel's God. The meaning of verse 10b is uncertain. *Restrain*; better, as in RV, 'gird upon thee'. Man's wrath is made to serve the greater glory of God. The only true response of the human heart is a careful fulfilment of all vows of homage made to Him.

The final verse summarizes the message of the Psalm, viz. God will severely prune the pride and life of all arrogant nations, taking away *the spirit* (i.e. courage) *of princes*, and afflicting kings with terror.

PSALM LXXVII. THE HISTORICAL BASIS OF HOPE

This cry of distress is couched in terms of personal experience but it obviously expresses a corporate sense of bewilderment and anguish. The Psalm says nothing of peril, pursuit, hardship, disease, or suchlike difficulties (contrast Ps. cxliii). The root cause of the distress which afflicts the psalmist is simply the continued absence of any sign of divine compassion (7–9). Whether the poem came from the gloomy years of the exile or from some previous period is uncertain. If Habakkuk incorporated some of its features into the poem at the end of his book (Hab. iii), then it antedates the period of Josiah's reform. On the other hand the psalmist may have developed a theme taken from this prophet.

a. His despondency (1–9)

The repetition of the first phrase is made more forceful by the omission of a verb in the Hebrew, 'My voice to God, and I would cry aloud; my voice to God . . .' The second phrase of verse 2 is better translated as in RV, 'my hand was stretched out in the night, and slacked not.' The extremity of soul is forcefully presented in this imagery of a sick and restless person calling in vain at night for someone to minister comfort. Actually the misery of soul arises from meditation about God (3, RV), nor is respite easily found in sleep, for God seems to keep His eyes wide open as if He were a guard on duty (4, RV). As he ponders over the ancient years of his people, *the days of old*, with its panorama of God's providential care, and recalls the times when he could even sing during the night, he is constrained to seek an answer to the present circumstances wherein it seems God's care and covenant have lapsed. The six questions of verses 7–9 probe the cause of Israel's neglect by God and voice his deep agitation of heart and mind. *For ever* (7a) is the same Hebrew word as *ancient times* (5b). A different word is used in verse 8. The implied question is whether the Lord's casting off will be as long as the past ages of His presence.

b. God's acts remembered (10–12)

The reiteration of doubt brought its own reaction of trust. *I said, This is my infirmity* (10); i.e. this supposition, that God is capable of changing His relationship with Israel, is the very cause of my despondency and distress: What a foolish thing I am assuming, that the right hand of the Most High doth change! (RV mg.). This decision transforms his outlook. He no longer remembers discontentedly, impatiently and enviously (5ff.), but he takes hold of these historic deeds as precious treasures from the past, and mentally rehearses God's work as constituting a sure testimony of His grace.

c. God's greatness extolled (13–20)

The initial reaction to the adoption of an attitude of faith is a surge of praise and adoration (verses 13–15). 'O God, Thy way is in holiness (RV mg.); what god could be as great as God is?' This reaction is very similar to the nation's feelings when, after being completely hemmed in at Pi-hahiroth, they found themselves safe and free on the other side of the Red Sea. Hence the echoes of Ex. xv. 11ff. in these three verses of the Psalm. *The sons of Jacob and Joseph* (15). Joseph is considered as being comparable with Jacob, firstly because he preserved the whole family from starvation, secondly because he was the father of Ephraim and Manasseh, the leading tribes of the northern kingdom. Cf. Ob. 18.

Finally the psalmist reviews the great miracle of the exodus, a theme developed in the following Psalm (cf. Pss. xviii. 7ff., lxxiv. 12ff.), and ends abruptly (cf. Nu. xxxiii. 1) so as to leave the most vivid impression of relief, freedom and power. The meaning of verse 19 is that, as the waters of the Red Sea returned, leaving no trace, so God covers His footsteps. The endurance of a Godward trust during long periods of desultory waiting is a major element in a mature faith (cf. Rom. xv. 4; Heb. x. 36, xii. 1ff.; Jas. i. 2–4). Five great periods of disciplined waiting in steadfast faith are Abraham's childlessness (Rom. iv. 17–21); the bondage in Egypt (Ex. ii. 23, 24); the exile in Babylon (Ps. lxxxix); the inter-Testamental period (Lk. ii. 25b; Acts xxvi. 7); the Church's waiting for His return (Heb. ix. 28b, vi. 19–20).

PSALM LXXVIII. GOD'S HAND IN HISTORY

This is one of the four great national hymns in the Psalter, the others being Pss. cv, cvi and cxxxvi. In each case the dominant theme is the experience of Israel's deliverance from Egypt. In Ps. lxxviii this subject appears to exclude all else, although it is obviously later than David's time (70). The purpose of the Psalm is so to rehearse the early story of the nation that future generations might be warned against a repetition of past failures (see verses 1–11, and cf. 1 Cor. x. 1–11; Heb. ii. 1–4, iii. 7, iv. 1, etc.).

The main section of the Psalm is in two parts (verses 12–42 and verses 43–66), the first of which is mainly concerned with the wilderness wanderings, and the second, after recalling a number of the plagues of Egypt, treats the entrance into Canaan up to the time of David. Each part is built up of alternate glimpses of the evil activity of man and the patience and power of God. Finally the conclusion (verses 67–72) emphasizes the rejection of unworthy Ephraim, the election of Judah, and the choice of the Davidic dynasty.

a. Introduction (1–11)

The word *law* (1), lit. *torah*, has the sense of 'teaching'. Note the way in which verse 2 is quoted in Mt. xiii. 35. The emphasis upon the *testimony in Jacob* (5), i.e. the traditional family teaching (see verses 3–6), is based on Ex. x. 2, xii. 26, xiii. 8. Two lines of thought are twined together in the poem to give alternate views of human frailty and divine energy. *The children of Ephraim . . . turned back* (9). There is no particular occasion of a military default in the psalmist's mind. Some have thought to see an allusion to the early departure of Ephraim from Egypt and their reverse at the hands of the men

of Gath (see 1 Ch. vii. 21); others relate these verses to the discontent of the Ephraimites on entering Canaan (see Jos. xvii. 14ff.). But the psalmist is simply stating a theme by means of verbal imagery; the children of Ephraim, i.e. northern Israel, were traitors to the covenant of God, just like soldiers who, although armed and equipped with weapons, turn back in the very midst of battle. The simile is used again in verse 57. Verse 67 declares that Ephraim has now been set aside as leader and another chosen.

b. Defection and deliverance. First phase (12–42)

Having set the stage, the two components of the drama, viz. God's faithfulness to His covenant and Israel's conduct, are described in turn (12–20). The process is then repeated and expanded (21–42).

i. **The wonderful deliverance from Egypt (12–16).** The district of *Zoan* (12) was the land of Goshen. For *the sea* and *the waters* (13) cf. Ex. xv. 8; *a cloud* and *a light of fire* (14), cf. Ex. xiii. 21; the cleft rocks (15), cf. Ex. xvii. 6; the water out of the storehouses of *the great depths* (15), cf. Ps. xxxiii. 7; the *streams . . . out of the rock* at Kadesh (16), cf. Nu. xx. 8.

ii. **Human frailty and distrust (17–20).** Their rebellion 'in a dry land' (17, RV mg.) consisted of doubts concerning God's care and ability, in spite of His previous miracles. The venom of their disbelief lay in the last phrase, *can he provide flesh for his people?* (20). Contrast verse 19 with Ps. xxiii. 5. The whole situation is regarded poetically rather than historically, for actually food was provided long before water was given from the rocks.

iii. **God's provision and punishment (21–31).** For the *fire* and *anger* of the Lord (21) cf. Nu. xi. 1 and Ps. xviii. 8ff. The food which *rained down* (24) through *the doors of heaven* (23) may carry an additional echo of 2 Ki. vii. 2. Manna was called *corn of heaven* (24) because it was like seeds; it was called 'bread of the mighty' (25, RV) because it was thought to be angels' food (cf. Ps. ciii. 20, RV). The plague which followed the consumption of flesh (30, 31) is described in Nu. xi. 33. Their craving was not satisfied even with God's gifts.

iv. **Apostasy and repentance, hypocrisy and forgetfulness (32–42).** This passage contains in itself an alternation of human perversity and divine mercy: *For all this they sinned still* (32); therefore their life was spent in aimless wandering (cf. Ps. xcv. 8–11) and their years in terror (cf. Lv. xxvi. 16). *Then they sought him* (34) and remembered that He was their rock and redeemer. The phrase 'Most High God' (35, RV) occurs elsewhere only in verse 56 and Gn. xiv. 18. *Nevertheless they did flatter* (beguile) *him* and lied and were unfaithful (36; cf. Is. xxix. 13). *But he . . . forgave* (38; cf. Nu. xiv. 18–20). From verse 38, as the finale of the first half of the poem is approached, the sequence is reversed and God's grace takes precedence over man's provocation: *Many a time turned he his anger away, and did not stir up . . . he remembered that they were but flesh* (38, 39) even though *they remembered not his hand* (42).

c. Deliverance and defection. Second phase (43–66)

The Psalm now proceeds to recount, more elaborately and with different purpose, the incidents of the exodus already assumed in verses 12ff. The major difference between this account of God's wonders in *the field of Zoan* and that in the earlier verses of the Psalm is not merely one of greater detail. There is a significant change of aspect and emphasis. Verses 12–16 dealt with the impersonal and physical realm of sea and waters, clouds and rocks, depths and rivers. Verses 44ff. speak of the human situation. For example, notice the constant repetition of 'their', 'they', 'them'. This change is not intended to illustrate the divine judgment upon the Egyptians so much as to show in a very graphic manner God's exceptional and distinctive treatment of *his own people* whom He led into the wilderness (i.e. caused to journey in stages) like a flock of sheep (52); whom He eventually brought *to the border of his sanctuary* (54); and whom He also established in the mountain-land of certain evicted nations (54, 55). In short, whereas the first phase dealt with the historical movements of the exodus and wanderings, the second phase deals with the personal experiences of the plagues and settlement.

Note that the plagues are treated poetically and not historically, i.e. only seven of the ten plagues are mentioned and these not in the original order (see notes on Ps. cv). *Caterpiller* (46); the larval stage of the locust. The word translated *frost* (47) does not occur elsewhere in Scripture; it probably means hailstones (cf RV mg.). The *hail* and *hot thunderbolts* (48) can be translated 'pestilence and disease' (cf. Hab. iii. 5), in which case the plague referred to is that of the murrain (Ex. ix. 3ff.). The *evil angels* or 'messengers of calamity' (49; see RV) were those sent to destroy the firstborn, *the chief of their strength* (51); i.e. the first-fruits of marriage.

So this sad story continues. One would have thought that, after all that God had done, Israel would have walked in His ways. But they went from bad to worse (56–58). Consequently God *greatly abhorred* (59), i.e. utterly rejected, Israel. He abandoned the tabernacle at Shiloh and allowed the ark of His strength to go into captivity (1 Sa. iv—vi). The priests, Hophni and Phinehas, were slain and such havoc was wrought in the land that many girls found no husbands (63b), and most widows were too full of anxiety and fear to carry out the usual lamentation for the dead. *Fire consumed* (63); i.e. the fire of war.

A most vivid and daring simile is now introduced to describe God's intervention in this interminable and apparently inevitable process of human depravity. God, the sovereign Lord, is pictured as waking out of sleep and, like a man made bellicose by wine, smashing the whole cycle of circumstances and conduct whereby His people had been enslaved to evil (65, 66). The primary reference is to the complete transformation of national policy and progress under the establishment of the kings, Saul and David, with the subsequent elimination of the Philistines as adversaries of Israel.

d. Conclusion (67–72)

The supreme intention of this dramatic presentation of a divine deed is to show the peculiar strength and responsibility of the southern kingdom. God has intervened, not merely to free the nation from their adversaries, Pharaoh (42) and the Philistines (66), but to select Judah to be His people, Zion to be His habitation, and David to be His servant who would feed (be shepherd of) His people (71; cf. 2 Sa. iii. 18 and v. 2). The final phrase which speaks of the skilful guidance of David's hands is obviously meant to gain force by the parallel with the redemptive hand of God in verse 42.

PSALM LXXIX. JERUSALEM MADE A HEAP OF RUINS

This is a companion Psalm to Ps. lxxiv (see introductory notes); but whereas that was a lament for the destruction of the temple, this poem is an elegy for a scattered people. Because they are *thy people and sheep of thy pasture* (13) the Psalm necessarily is in the form of a prayer. Its plea for divine redress and restoration is based on three grounds: first, the agony and distress of His *saints* (2); secondly, the compassionate nature and *tender mercies* of God (8); thirdly, the ignominy and dishonour which other nations will attach to God's name if He leaves desolate those who are His *servants* and representatives (10). These three aspects of the prayer are interwoven throughout the Psalm but are stressed in turn in its three sections.

a. Ruin and massacre (1–4)

With verse 1 compare Ps. lxxiv. 2, 7: also note the fulfilment of Micah's prophecy (iii. 12) quoted in Je. xxvi. 18. The corpse-strewn battle-field round about Jerusalem was so awful and ominous a memory that it became symbolic of the ultimate judgment of men (2, 3; cf. Ezk. xxxix. 1–20; Rev. xi. 8, 9, xix. 17, 18). The derision of surrounding peoples, like Edom, Moab and Philistia, was a continual source of irritation to the afflicted people of God (e.g. Ezk. xxv. 2, 12 and 15; Ob. 12).

b. Wrath and mercy (5–9)

The events of history were considered to be inseparable from the slow process of divine judgment. But would God never cease to be angry with His chosen ones? Should He not be more wrathful toward those who had no covenant

468

with Him (6; cf. Is. lxiii. 19)? Surely His compassion and the glorious salvation which was implicit in His name (cf. Ex. xxxiv. 6, 7) should not be hindered from 'coming speedily to meet us' (the meaning of *prevent*; cf. Ps. lix. 10) because of 'the iniquities of our forefathers' (8, RV). This thought evokes the urgent prayer of verse 9.

c. Revenge and majesty (10–13)

The final plea of the psalmist goes right outside all personal feelings of distress or vengeance. The intervention of God is sought for His own honour and glory. In the first place there should be no cause whatever for the heathen to scoff at God because of Israel's misery and dereliction (10). Compare the arguments of Moses about the Egyptian reactions to an exodus that failed (Ex. xxxii. 12; Nu. xiv. 13–17). 'Let the revenging of the blood of thy servants (cf. Rev. vi. 10) . . . be known among the heathen' (10, RV), and let us see it in our lifetime. Then, in the course of this demonstration of divine faithfulness, power and justice, let the derisive neighbouring states (12; cf. verse 4) experience the derision of the Lord (cf. Ps. ii. 4), for in reproaching Israel they have really scorned Him. Yet another result of God's action would be the perpetual praise offered by the contented *sheep of thy pasture* (13). These three thoughts reverse the order and invert the themes and situations of the three main sections of the whole poem.

PSALM LXXX. AN ELEGY FOR ISRAEL

The similarity between this and the preceding Psalm (cf. lxxx. 1 with lxxix. 13a; lxxx. 4 with lxxix. 5; lxxx. 6 with lxxix. 4) is offset by a different subject and imagery. Probably this is a prayer of the kingdom of Judah on behalf of the exiled northern tribes, although only the descendants of Rachel are actually mentioned (2). The LXX adds to the title the words 'concerning the Assyrian'.

The poem has three main parts (1–3, 4–7 and 17–19), each of which concludes with a similar refrain. Within these is an inset (8–16) giving an allegory or imagery of a vine. In verse 14 there is an echo of the principal refrain (see verses 3, 7 and 19).

a. The invocation (1–3)

The initial thought is rooted in the past. The Hebrew text begins with *O Shepherd of Israel*, and in view of the names which follow (sons and grandsons) the word 'Israel' here stands for Jacob (cf. Gn. xlviii. 15, xlix. 24) and in him for all the Israelites. That view of the exodus which saw in it a flock movement under a divine Shepherd is common to several Psalms (e.g. lxxviii. 52) and the concept is elaborated in Ezk. xxxiv. 1–31. The Shepherd is here regarded as enthroned between the cherubim of the ark. If the Shekinah glory again shines forth, the flock will be delivered from peril (3; cf. Is. lx. 1,

2; Ps. xciv. 1). This expectation of a divine self-manifestation, as public as the radiance of the dawn, was carried over to and clarified by the early Christian community (e.g. Tit. ii. 13; 2 Thes. i. 7, 8). The plea that God should stir or rouse Himself on behalf of His people is often heard in Scripture (cf. Is. li. 9; Ps. lxxviii. 65, 66, etc.). The phrase *turn us again* (3) is an echo of Ephraim's prayer in Je. xxxi. 18, and carries the meaning of 'cause us to repent' (cf. La. v. 21). It is also an expectation of God's promise in Je. xxx. 3, where it has the meaning of 'restore us from captivity'.

b. The basis of the prayer (4–7)

The initial emphasis is on the present situation. Israel's plight is obviously out of keeping with the original intention of the divine Shepherd (e.g. Ps. lxxviii. 52–55 and 69–71). His continued anger against them (4) is due to the stubbornness of their self-will (cf. Ps. lxxxi. 11, 12; contrast lxxxi. 16), and to their habitual apostasies (cf. Ps. lxxviii. 17, 32, 40, 56ff., xcv. 7–11). The consequences had been long foretold (e.g. Lv. xxvi, especially verses 26–41; Dt. xxviii, especially verses 64–67, and xxxii. 19–27) and so long as Israel is an irritant in the current world order, a persistent witness to and prophet of divine judgment, so long must words akin to these form their prayers amid the mockings of their enemies.

c. The allegory of the vine (8–16)

At this point, the psalmist breaks off in order to introduce the allegory of the vine which is often used as an emblem of Israel (cf. Hos. x. 1; Is. v. 1–7; Ezk. xv. 1–6; also Lk. xx. 9ff.; Jn. xv. 1ff.). The transplanting of a vine slip from Egypt (cf. Gn. xlix. 22) was possible only because of God's special intervention (8, 9; cf. Ps. xliv. 3). Once plante , the vine flourished so as to spread, during the empires of David and Solomon, over the mountains of Judaea as far as the cedar forests of Lebanon, the Mediterranean coast, and the Euphrates river (11, RV; cf. Dt. xi. 24). Now all the vineyard is derelict: the gardener has abandoned it and consequently it has been invaded by the Gentiles—symbolized by wild beasts and eagles as in Ps. l. 11; Ezk. xvii; Dn. vii. In short, the threat of Is. v. 5–7 has come true. This leads to the cry of penitence and need in verse 14. The whole anomaly of careful planting and utter rejection, the assiduous cultivation of the 'stock' (RV), or vineyard, and then the outcome of fire instead of fruit, is summed up in verses 15, 16.

d. The plea for divine action (17–19)

The main stress is on the outlook for the future. The theme of the refrain, i.e. their salvation and renewal, is expanded. Israel is personified not as Jacob (1) but as a weak and ordinary man whom God's right hand had formerly picked out from all mankind, and whose descendants had been strengthened by Him. (Note that 17b is virtually a repetition of 15b.) Let God replace His hand upon the direction of their affairs. Israel will thus become the 'ideal Israel'. This view was usually accompanied in thought by the messianic concept, an ultimate figure or archetype by whom the nation should be restored. Hence the Jewish Targums insert in verse 17 'King Messiah' for *son of man*. Cf. the frequent use of the phrase 'Son of man' in the Gospels, and the repeated allusion in the Epistles to Him who is seated 'at the right hand of the majesty on high'.

Note the changes in the divine name in the refrain: *O God* (3); Heb. *'Elohim*. *O God of hosts* (7); Heb. *'Elohim Seba'oth*. *O Lord God of hosts* (19), i.e. God everlasting and unchanging; Heb. *Yahweh 'Elohim Seba'oth*.

PSALM LXXXI. A HYMN AND HOMILY AT HARVEST-TIME

This Psalm is traditionally associated with the Jewish feast of tabernacles, though some commentators link it (with less probability) with the Passover, on the ground of the reference to Egypt in verse 5. *Gittith* (see title). See introductory note to Ps. viii. The song falls into two parts, the second of which is framed as a testimony of the Lord concerning His people.

a. The summons (1–5)

The whole congregation is called upon to *sing aloud* (cf. Ezr. iii. 11); the Levitical singers and musicians are given word to 'take up the psalm' (2, RV; the Hebrew word denotes a song in praise of God set to music), and to play upon their timbrels (small drums or tambourines), and their lyres and lutes. The feast of tabernacles began in the middle of the seventh month, i.e. at full moon (3b, RV). This festival was a *statute for Israel* (4), having been instituted *for a testimony* (5), i.e. to bear witness to the goodness of the God who redeemed Jacob and Joseph, as a people, from Egypt. That great event is perceived by the psalmist to have been an utterance of God in a speech that was previously unknown (5), i.e. the children of Israel then began to hear God as Him who redeemeth. It is the nature of this divine 'language' of grace and guidance which is the theme of the remainder of the Psalm. Verse 5 may be translated, 'He appointed it (i.e. the feast) in Joseph for a testimony when He (i.e. God) went out against the land of Egypt. The speech of one that I knew not did I (i.e. Israel) hear.' Alternatively the second phrase may mean 'when he (Israel) went out through the land of Egypt'. The event of the exodus is perceived by the psalmist to have been an utterance of God making Himself known in a new way.

b. The message (6–16)

That which God has to say falls into two parts because those who heard did not always heed.

i. His work of deliverance (6–10). Israel's burden of slave labour and tedious toil in Egypt was suddenly removed (6, RV). They had called upon God and He came down to deliver (Ex. vi. 5ff.). The thick darkness of the thunder cloud (Ex. x. 21ff., xiv. 20) was a sign of His presence (cf. Ps. xviii. 11ff.; Jb. xxxvii). The allusion to *the waters of Meribah* (7; meaning 'strife'; cf. Ex. xvii. 7; Ps. lxxviii. 20) may be typical of the testing of the people (cf. Ps. xcv. 8ff.; Heb. iii. 7ff.) as well as suggestive of the custom at the feast of tabernacles of fetching water from Siloam (cf. Jn. vii. 37; see also 1 Cor. x. 4) in remembrance of the miraculous provision of water in the wilderness.

This action of God was inseparable from His commandments to them. Only the first commandment is named here (9, 10; cf. Ex. xx. 2–7), for this embodied what in God's will for His chosen people was to be their essential and distinctive characteristic (cf. Dt. vi. 4, 5; see also Mk. xii. 28ff.). All He required of them was the eager reception of His gifts.

ii. Their waywardness of desire (11–16). The keen edge of this reproach lay in the rejection of God by those towards whom He had been especially kind, patient and active. Their wilfulness temporarily frustrated His purpose; in consequence they were left to 'go after the stubbornness of their heart', and allowed to 'walk in their own counsels' (12, RV; cf. Dt. xxix. 19; Pr. i. 30, 31) instead of in His ways (13).

Nevertheless, God did not utterly give them up. The repetition of the divine aside (8b and 13) suggests a willingness on His part to bless Israel even when their perversity is reminiscent of Sinai (e.g. Ex. xxxii. 9ff.). He is still prepared to lead them safely, to subdue their enemies, and to feed them with the choicest food even in seemingly barren surroundings. *Honey out of the rock* (16); cf. Dt. xxxii. 13, 14.

PSALM LXXXII. UNJUST JUDGES IMPEACHED BY GOD

The first verse is open to various interpretations: a literal translation is 'God (*'Elohim*) standeth in the congregation of God (*El*); in the midst of the judges (*'elohim*) He judgeth.' 'The congregation of God' (RV) may mean any assembly convened by the Almighty (cf. Mi. vi. 1ff.; Is. xli. 1) or, more particularly, Israel (e.g. Nu. xxvii. 17; Jos. xxii. 16). 'Among the judges' may mean 'in the midst of angels', i.e. a heavenly assize, before which earthly courts of justice are arraigned. But the rest of the Psalm points to another interpretation, viz. God as supreme judge in the midst of Israel's corrupt rulers and judges in order to rebuke and condemn them (cf. Ezk. xlv. 9; Am. v. 12; Mi. vii. 3). There is a close similarity with Is. iii. 13–15 and the Psalm may belong to Uzziah's reign. These earthly judges are called *'elohim* because the office they hold and the judgment they should give are really God's (see 2 Ch. xix. 6, 7; Dt. i. 17). The description of God as 'standing' for judgment is not opposed to the act of sitting (e.g. Pss. ii. 4, ix. 4, xxix. 10, xlvii. 8); the word means 'taking up a position for a solemn purpose'.

Verses 2–7 constitute the charge and condemnation of those who had exercised judicial authority in a false and unjust manner, i.e. having respect of persons (2, RV; see Lv. xix. 15; Pr. xviii. 5, xxiv. 23, xxviii. 21; Jas. ii. 1–9), and ignoring the necessitous cases of the afflicted, destitute and fatherless, so that the poor and needy are neither rescued nor vindicated. The cause is an inability to discern good and evil (5; contrast 1 Ki. iii. 9; Ps. lxviii. 1–5); hence the very foundations of a stable civil order are undermined. Therefore God (*I* is emphatic), who caused these men to be appointed to the office of judges (i.e. 'godlike persons', cf. verse 1) so that they became 'sons of the Most High' (RV), insists on behaviour and action in conformity with Himself. Their failure to do so entails a death like any descendant of Adam, and a disgrace comparable with the condemnation of many princes in former times. Note the quotation of verse 6 in Jn. x. 34–36.

In the final verse the psalmist calls upon God Himself to control all nations and administer true judgment. How else can His universal kingdom be established? Cf. Pss. cxviii. 8, 9, cxlvi. 3, 4.

PSALM LXXXIII. A CRY FOR HELP AGAINST A CONFEDERACY OF EVIL

Israel was often in peril because of armed and ambitious neighbours. No such widespread alliance of adjacent states as is described in verses 6–8 is mentioned in the Old Testament, however. The nearest approach to such a situation was the coalition against Jehoshaphat (see 2 Ch. xx. 1–12). It may be that, in presenting this urgent plea for help, the writer is reviewing attacks which were delivered at different times by different nations. Jahaziel (2 Ch. xx. 14) may have been the author of this poem. The Psalm may be considered in four parts.

a. The peril (1–4)

The serious nature of the threat, news of which must have been cumulative in effect as more and more enemies were known to be involved, is reflected in the impetuous words *Keep not thou silence, O God* (1); lit. 'O God, let there be no rest to thee.' This urgent plea is reinforced by the description of the aggressors as *thine enemies* and *they that hate thee* (2). Secret conferences have been held and plans prepared *against thy people* (3) whom God has promised to shield in time of danger (cf. Pss. xxvii. 5, xxxi. 20). Finally, the imperative need of immediate and drastic action by God is implicit in the disclosure of the plot utterly to wipe out Israel and remove from earth the memory of God's chosen people (4). Such a scheme was a direct attack upon God Himself (cf. Ps. ii. 2ff.).

b. The confederacy described (5–8)

The forces massed against Israel had two characteristics. They acted with complete unanimity; they had made an alliance against God Himself. Those concerned were mostly the semi-nomadic peoples whose petty kingdoms stretched along the east side of the Jordan valley, i.e. Edom, Moab, Ammon, with the Hagarites and Ishmaelites who lived still further east (cf. 1 Ch. v. 10) and also the people of Gebal (south of Edom). But, in addition, there were the forces of the western seaboard, Philistia and Phoenicia (cf. Am. i. 6, 9). And in the background was the might of Assyria which had already lent an arm of help to the children of Lot, i.e. to Moab and Ammon.

c. An appeal to history (9–12)

Ominous situations had occurred previously in Israel's history and astonishing deliverances had been experienced through the unmistakable intervention of God. Two of the most noteworthy had long been the themes of song and story, for they had threatened the immature nation in the early centuries of its settlement in Canaan. These were the attack by Sisera (Jdg. iv, v) and the invasion of the Midianites (Jdg. vi—viii). In both cases the Israelites were not merely outnumbered, but also outclassed in aggressive equipment. Sisera commanded nine hundred iron chariots, whilst Oreb and Zeeb (Jdg. vii. 25) led an immense horde of camel-riding Midianites. Nevertheless both perils were amazingly overcome; the menace was swiftly and entirely removed and at very little loss to the Israelites. Compare Isaiah's comment on the second event, Is. ix. 4, x. 26.

d. The plea for help (13–18)

The recollection of previous deliverances gives passion and eloquence to the cry for immediate help. Let God make the hosts of their present enemies to be 'like the whirling dust' (13, RV), as straw blown from the threshingfloor, like a brushwood fire upon a wooded hillside (cf. Is. x. 16–19), as litter in a gale (cf. Ps. xxxv. 5). This desire for a complete discomfiture of the confederacy is not so malevolent as to plead for their annihilation. The supreme aim of this prayer is the glory of God and the psalmist pleads for an unforgettable experience of humiliation by the opponents of God so that they and all men everywhere might acknowledge 'that thou alone, whose name is JEHOVAH (i.e. Yahweh, the Lord), art the Most High over all the earth' (18, RV).

PSALM LXXXIV. REJOICING IN THE SANCTUARY

Unlike the previous eleven Psalms, this has the superscription 'of (or 'for') the sons of Korah'. It is a companion to Ps. xlii (also a Korahite Psalm), and may be by the same author. But whereas that was a lament because of exile from the house of his God, this is a song of joy because the psalmist has been allowed to resume his worship in the dwelling-places of the Lord of hosts. See introductory note on Ps. viii for explanation of the title.

The opening words are an exclamation of wonder and gladness. *Amiable* (1). RV mg. 'lovely'. The use of the plurals *tabernacles* and *courts* (1, 2) is simply poetic diction (cf. Ps. xliii. 3). *Longeth . . . fainteth* (2). The recollection of a former experience is so vividly present in mind as to warrant the use of the present tense. But this echo of the past is immediately replaced by the joyfulness of the occasion. See RV mg. where the AV *crieth out* is rendered 'sing for joy'. *The living God* is found elsewhere in the Psalter only in Ps. xlii. 2. In verse 3 the illustration from nesting birds gives the sense, 'even so do I find my home and rest by thine altars'. Happy indeed are those whose life is spent in the service of the sanctuary; 'they are ever praising thee' (4). Happy also is that man who, on pilgrimage, has his mind set upon 'the high ways to Zion' (5, RV) and whose life is nourished by God. Though such a man may pass through the waterless valley of balsam trees (*Baca*; see RV mg.), yet, because he is on his way to Jerusalem, he finds it 'a place of springs' (6, RV; cf. Is. xxxv. 7, xlviii. 21) and the early (spring) showers cause it to be clothed 'with blessings' (RV), i.e. carpeted with grass and flowers. These pilgrims consequently are cheered and strengthened in their journey until they, like the psalmist, appear 'before God in Zion' (RV).

They have come to worship the Lord, and that thought leads the psalmist himself to offer prayer (verses 8-12). *O Lord God of hosts* (8); cf. verse 1. *Behold, O God our shield* (9); i.e. 'Thou who art our shield'. An alternative rendering is given in RV mg., 'Behold our shield, O God'. The word 'shield' would then denote the king. Cf. Ps. lxxxix. 18, RV. *Look upon the face of thine anointed* (9). For the Lord God is a sun to shine upon him (with the associated ideas of glory, growth and harvest; cf. Ps. lxxii. 16, 17), and a shield to protect him (11a). He bestows *grace and glory*, that is, the riches of His favour and the light of His presence, and gives munificently to all righteous men (11b). Truly and indeed blessed is he *that trusteth in thee* (12). These concluding words are far beyond the discipline of the pilgrimage and the jubilation of arrival at Zion; they express the permanent stability and deep resources of a godly life in any circumstances.

It will be seen that verse 10 has been treated as a parenthesis, an exuberant aside which expresses the essential mood of the poem. Note that the Korahites were the keepers of the gates of the sanctuary (cf. 1 Ch. ix. 19).

PSALM LXXXV. A PRAYER FOR REVIVAL

When the first exiles returned from Babylon to Judaea, their excitement and elation were chilled by the poverty and dereliction of the homeland (cf. Ne. i. 3a). This Psalm reflects the three dominant thoughts of the godly men who faced the labour and toil of reconstruction.

a. God's goodness recalled (1-3)

Although there is no word of praise here (contrast, e.g., Pss. lxvi. 1ff., lxxi. 19, lxxvii. 13ff., lxxxi. 1), the three actions of God which are described, viz. their territorial restoration, national forgiveness, and reconciliation to God, could not be named without a reaction of thankfulness. The period of exile had come to an end, the burden of sin had been lifted away (forgiven), the divine wrath had been withdrawn before it became fierce and irresistible.

b. Further blessing sought (4-8)

Nevertheless the psalmist expresses the attitude of his countrymen in beseeching their Lord for something further. Though He had ceased to be angry with them, their environment still bore abundant evidence of His former indignation. It was not enough that He should restore them to the land of their fathers; for such was its dearth and their weakness that merely to bring them back would condemn them to poverty and labour for years. Was His anger wholly gone or did He intend being displeased with them for ever? (5). They needed positive and continuous encouragement and blessing. *Thou* (6) is emphatic. Above all, they themselves needed restoring and reviving. They craved for unmistakable evidences of His mercy and salvation so that they might rejoice as His chosen people.

In the eighth verse the psalmist speaks to himself in tones of hopefulness. He is sure about God; He will *speak peace unto his people*. But that is conditional upon their continued godliness. In the Bible folly is moral, not mental. In this uncertainty he waits to hear the divine response to the people's prayer.

c. Promise (9-13)

The word of the Lord begins by reaffirming His blessing upon all who reverence Him; that kind of life would ensure that *glory* (i.e. God Himself) would *dwell in the land* (9; cf. Is. lx. 1ff.). His mercy would join with their righteous conduct as it sprang up or developed in the land. Their peace of heart, in the form of general well-being, would be inseparable from His righteousness, which already shone forth from heaven (10, 11). Every good thing, whether it be connected with the economic condition of the land, or the spiritual welfare of the people, would be made available through Him. Prosperity will accompany the improvement of national morality (cf. Is. xxxii. 16-18) and thus His righteousness will be the pioneer to clear the paths (13b; RV 'make his footsteps a way to walk in'), and facilitate the improvement of the land whose condition they now regard with dismay (cf. Is. lviii. 8-12).

PSALM LXXXVI. OH TURN UNTO ME!

Although entitled *A Prayer of David* (cf. Ps. lxxii. 20), it may be so called because it is largely compiled of fragments chosen from Davidic and other Psalms. To any worshippers in the temple who were familiar with the first two books of the Psalter, this compilation must have been extremely rich in associations of ideas. Primarily it is an expression of a devout soul seeking the assuring fellowship and strengthening grace of the Lord. The petition for aid against certain foes (14) does not necessarily root the poem in a particular historical situation. A striking feature of the Psalm is that each petition is accompanied by a reason why the prayer should be granted.

a. Supplication (1–7)

This is an expectant and humble cry for an experience of God's favour which shall re-invigorate the psalmist's soul and provide confidence respecting the future outlook. This plea is based on personal necessity (the 'godly' (*holy*) man who is *poor and needy*), on a relationship of faith (*thy servant that trusteth in thee*), and on the divine nature (*good, ready to forgive, plenteous in mercy*). For possible sources of these phrases see, e.g., Pss. lxx. 5a, lxxi. 2b, xxv. 20a; Is. xxvi. 3, xxv. 1; Ex. xxxiv. 6; Pss. lv. 1, l. 15.

b. Adoration (8–11)

This expression of the ground of the psalmist's faith in the Lord comprehends His creative power and ultimate purpose, His essential goodness and continuous activity, His sovereignty above all and His accessibility to man. This estimate of God leads to the desire to become like Him in mind and manner, i.e. to be integrated in a life inseparable from Him (cf. Je. xxxii. 39). Compare possible sources in, e.g., Ex. xv. 11; Dt. iii. 24; Pss. xxii. 27–29, lxxvii. 14, lxxxiii. 18, xxv. 4, xxvii. 11.

c. Thanksgiving (12, 13)

A climax of praise and worship is reached wherein the godly soul experiences a unity of being which is a partial participation in eternal glory: it is the affirmation of a God-centred life. The basis of this is a former experience of divine deliverance from uttermost desolation (*the lowest hell;* i.e. 'the lowest realms of the dead'; cf. Dt. xxxii. 22).

d. Petition (14–17)

Finally, mention is made of certain immediate circumstances of peril (see Ps. liv. 3). But the confession of faith toward God is repeated (see verses 5 and 15). The intensity of the whole prayer is then summarized in the passionate words *O turn unto me . . .* (16), *Shew me a token for good* (17). With verses 16 and 17a cf. Ps. xxv. 16, lxix. 16. The phrase *son of thine handmaid* (16) implies a relationship akin to that of a slave born into his master's household and therefore having a double claim upon his master's protection. The words *Thou, Lord* in the concluding phrase are emphatic. With verse 17b cf. Ps. xxxv. 4.

PSALM LXXXVII. ZION, THE MOTHER OF ALL MEN

This brief Psalm is an expansion of Ps. lxxxvi. 9. It may have sprung from the historical situation referred to in 2 Ch. xxxii. 23, but essentially it is prophetic (cf. Is. ii. 2, xliv. 5, lxvi. 23; Zc. ii. 11). The vision of Zion as the metropolis of the worldwide kingdom of God is not to be interpreted geographically, but spiritually (cf. Heb. xi. 10). The dominant thought is that of a universal and glad acceptance of God as Lord and King, in which allegiance all sources of international friction are removed. Note the New Testament development of this in Gal. iii. 8, iv. 26; Heb. xii. 22ff.; Rev. vii. 9, xv. 4. The prophetic and symbolic character of the Psalm is associated with a notable conciseness of language.

The city which God has founded is beloved by Him and its presence has hallowed the mountains around (cf. Ps. xlviii. 1, 2). The whole city, represented poetically by its *gates* (cf. Ps. cxxii. 2; Is. lx. 11) is pre-eminent above all other dwelling-places. This fact is illustrated by the exceptional statements which men make about Zion (3; cf., e.g., Is. ii. 3; Pss. xlvi. 4, 5, xlviii. 1–3).

Verses 4–6 contain the thrice repeated phrase *this man was born there*, or, *in her*. The words occur in three separate sentences attributed to God, and contain the basic concept of the whole poem. 'This one and that one' (5, RV) refers to the nations such as Rahab (Egypt; cf. Is. li. 9; Ps. lxxxix. 10), Babylon, from whose great power the children of Israel had been rescued, Philistia, Tyre (cf. Ps. lxxxiii. 7), both typical of Israel's age-long enemies, and Ethiopia (cf. Is. xviii. 7), representative of the remote peoples of the earth. The words *was born there* imply the identity of these Gentile nations with Israel; they receive similar privileges of citizenship (cf. Eph. ii. 19). Indeed in the spiritual Zion each and every nation, 'this man and that man', shall claim incorporation on the ground of a re-birth, and the most High Himself shall make it so. When He draws up the roll of the peoples in His city there will be no aliens (cf. Col. iii. 11; Phil. iii. 20, RV).

This reconstruction of the basis of society inaugurates a period of great jubilation. Whether folk sing or dance (or 'play on instruments'), whatever they may say or do, the theme and ground of their life is 'All my fresh springs are in Thee' (7). These words may be intended as the first line of a festive hymn, or they may summarize the thought that a full-orbed and divinely approved life finds its perpetual inspiration and vigour in the experience of dwelling in the city of God.

PSALM LXXXVIII. A CRY OF AFFLICTION

This lament is unique in the Psalter because of its gloom and unrelieved sense of misery devoid even of hope. Contrast the conclusions of Pss. xxii and xxxi with verses 15–18. Its authorship is uncertain. The chief Levitical musician in David's time was Heman, a grandson of Samuel, and a wise man in Solomon's time was known by the same name (see 1 Ki. iv. 31). While the poem may be expressive of the nation's grief during exile, it seems to be a personal elegy by someone who, like Job, was strained between an undeviating trust in God as the sole source of his salvation, and an intensely bewildering experience which appeared to negate the foundation of all such trust (cf. such experiences as related in 2 Ki. xx. 1–4; 2 Ch. xxvi. 21; Je. xxxviii. 6). The title suggests a melody, *Mahalath Leannoth*, conducive to 'the exercise of lamentation' (cf. Ps. liii). The Psalm falls into two halves.

a. The psalmist's anguished appeal (1–8)

I have cried day and night before thee (1); lit. 'I have cried through the day as in the night'. The Hebrew text is, however, broken. Some attribute this to the intensity of the speaker's feelings; but slight changes give a clearer reading. 'Yahweh, my God, I cry for help by day, and I cry by night before thee'. His despondency deepens as he descends the ladder of misery. *Counted with them that go down into the pit* (4); i.e. set apart and shunned as one already dead. *Free among the dead* (5); better, as in RV, 'Cast off among the dead.' The reference is to those slain in battle who are buried hurriedly in a common grave. *Cut off from thy hand* (5); i.e. deprived of His right hand of salvation. This idea that those who have entered the nether world of the dead are forgotten by God is common to the Psalter. See notes on Ps. vi. 4. Cf. Jb. xiv. 12; Ps. xxx. 9; Is. xxxviii. 18.

The psalmist now turns to consider the source of all his distress (6–8). His affliction is from God whose *wrath lieth hard upon* him (7). Notice the repetition of the words *thou hast*. Although still alive amidst men, he thinks he is already destined to *the lowest pit* (6); i.e. the lowest, darkest, deepest part of Sheol (cf. Jb. x. 21, 22, xvii. 13–16; Ps. lxxxvi. 13, cxliii. 3). In a sense this awful isolation has already commenced for, although he still breathes in this life, his intimate friends (*mine acquaintance*) shun him as unspeakably repugnant to them (*abomination* is emphatic). For a comparable experience see Jb. xix. 6–20 and cf. Ps. xxxi. 9–14.

b. Unanswered questions (9–18)

The fervent daily prayers and the swollen tearful eyes of verse 9 are an echo of verse 1. But the description of his sufferings gives way to questions (10–12). This pattern is then repeated; a statement of daily petition to the Lord (13) is followed by an inquiry which has no end and no answer (14–18).

The argument of verses 10–12 is akin to that in Ps. vi. 5. Since it was believed that no action or speech was possible in the grey, grim, dusty halls of Sheol, it was surely in God's own interests to keep alive as long as possible those whose earnest praises were always pleasing to Himself (cf. Ps. cxv. 17). Moreover His lovingkindness and faithfulness could not be exercised in that realm inhabited by mere shades (cf. Is. xxxviii. 18). *Destruction* (Heb. *Abaddon*) is simply another name for Sheol and conveys no sense of disintegration of being. Until the implications of Christ's resurrection were understood by the New Testament writers, it was thought that Sheol was occupied by all who died. Yet notions of a division therein, so that the good were separated from the wicked, had been developed in the centuries between the return from exile and the years of Jesus' ministry (cf. Lk. xvi. 22ff.).

The inquiry of verses 14–18, to which is added the appeal for deliverance from affliction, is more passionate than similar cries (see, e.g., Pss. xiii. 1, 2, lxxi. 9). *Ready to die from my youth up* (15) suggests that it has behind it the pressure of many years, probably because of some constitutional weakness, or through remorse for some wrong committed in early manhood. Moreover the afflictions which have come upon him continue to terrify and he seems to crave the anaesthesia of exhaustion or oblivion. *I am distracted* (15); the sense of the Hebrew word is uncertain. He feels his condition to be one of utter hopelessness. He is cut off without a hint of help (16). He is like a man carried away in a torrent (cf. Ps. lxix. 2), like one who is adrift and destitute on a raft in the lonely ocean (17). All his close friends have forsaken him and their place is now taken by darkness (18b, RV mg.). This final word leaves a strong impression of unrelieved gloom and despair. Whether the psalmist ever received a comforting revelation from God, as did Job, is not known; but his experience was caught up in that life which was made perfect by the things which He suffered (cf. Mt. xxvi. 38, xxvii. 46).

PSALM LXXXIX. GOD'S SURE COVENANT AND ISRAEL'S DISTRESS

The last Psalm in the third book of the Psalter may be regarded as a companion to the first one, Ps. lxxiii. Both deal with certain questions which confront a godly man in this earthly existence. On the one hand there is the problem of the prosperity of the wicked (lxxiii), and on the other there is the mystery of how God is faithful to His word when events seem to show His abhorrence of it (lxxxix). The themes are alike, viz. the reconciliation of faith in God with the facts of experience. One poem is concerned with human experiences, the other with divine government.

Note the background of gloom towards the end of the Psalm and the link with Ps. lxxxviii provided by the title. The double theme set out in the short introduction (verses 1–4) is considerably expanded in the next thirty-three verses. An antithetical attitude begins in verse 38 and is then elaborated from two aspects. The perplexity arising from the apparent reversal of divine purpose constitutes the burden of the Psalm. Note Acts xv. 16.

a. Introduction (1–4)

The speaker in the first two verses is the psalmist. He intends to sing first of *the mercies of the Lord*, i.e. of His loving-kindnesses to the children of Israel, and especially to the house of David (cf. Is. lv. 3). Secondly of His *faithfulness*, i.e. His consistent adherence to His promises and covenants. These two attributes of God are mentioned again in verse 2 together with the same qualities of perpetuity and permanence. They also form the foundation and scaffolding of the psalmist's subsequent worship (see verses 5, 8, 14, 24, 33, 49). This initial affirmation is an expression of faith, the greatness of which must be measured against the sombre conditions referred to at the close of the Psalm. This attitude of faith arises from God's own declaration in former times (cf. 2 Sa. vii. 8–16) which is quoted in verses 3, 4 as the origin of the psalmist's belief. Note the repetitions in verses 1, 2 of words in verses 3, 4 such as: *with my mouth (I have sworn); for ever; build up; establish; to all generations*. Thus the promises made by oath concerning David are transferred into the attributes of God Himself and become the main motif of the poem which follows.

b. God's majesty and covenant (5–37)

i. **The divine attributes extolled (5–18).** These verses are an expansion of verses 1 and 2. In place of the psalmist's voice (1), there is the angelic host (*the heavens, the saints*, or 'holy ones', as in RV; cf. Jb. xv. 15) which extols the ageless wonder of God's ways with men. 'Who in the skies can be compared' (6, RV); i.e. neither sun nor moon are worthy of adoration (cf. Ps. xix. 1ff.) and none of *the sons of the mighty*, or angels, are like Him (cf. Col. i. 16; Heb. i. 5ff.). He is held in terrible awe by the angelic council (7a, RV; cf. 1 Ki. xxii. 19; Je. xxiii. 18) of whom He is *Lord God of hosts*. None else has power like JAH who overthrew Pharaoh (Ex. xv. 11), and this supreme might is inseparable from His cloak of faithfulness (8, RV; cf. Is. lix. 17).

From verse 9 the emphasis is upon God's power in the earth rather than in the heavens. He rules the raging sea and stills the waves (cf. Ps. lxxvii. 17, 18); He crushed the power of Rahab (i.e. Egypt, as in Ps. lxxxvii. 4), and has scattered all other foes (9, 10; cf. Nu. x. 35). He is the Maker and Owner of heaven and earth (11; cf. Ps. xxiv. 1). Indeed the whole earth from one end to the other (*the north and the south*) is His and the most noticeable features of Palestine,

Mounts Tabor and Hermon, are testimonies and monuments to His greatness (12). Events have repeatedly shown His mighty arm and strong hand (13), and furthermore, in earth as in heaven, the divine power is inseparable from the divine righteousness. With verse 14 cf. Ps. xcvii. 2. *Mercy and truth* are always in attendance before Him, ready to run as His heralds.

As a consequence of this, Israel, chosen by God who is so great, must be exceptionally blessed (cf. Nu. vi. 25). *The joyful sound* (15); the Hebrew denotes both shouts of joy (cf. Ps. lxv. 13) and the sound of the trumpet (see Nu. x. 9). The people's joyful shouts have acclaimed Him as king. *In thy favour our horn shall be exalted* (17), i.e. all nations esteem Israel because the righteousness of God is made manifest among them. All His subjects glory in Him. In verse 18 follow RV. Their 'shield' or king (cf. Ps. lxxxiv. 9) is divinely appointed and acts for and on behalf of 'the Holy One of Israel'. This concept of sovereignty prepares the way for the next section of the Psalm.

ii. **The explicitness of the Davidic covenant (19–37).** These verses expand the theme outlined in verses 3 and 4, and are framed as direct speech by *the Holy One of Israel* (18). *Then* refers to the occasion of the oath to David declared in a vision to Nathan (2 Sa. vii. 4–17) and through him to the whole people, reading with RV 'thy saints' for AV *thy holy one* (19). *Laid help upon* (19), i.e. conferred (the power to give) help. *One chosen* (19) could be translated 'a youth'. *I have found David* (20), i.e. he was disclosed as the most suitable person to become the servant of the Lord (cf. Ps. lxxviii. 70) and was therefore anointed with the holy oil of the Spirit of God (cf. 1 Sa. xvi. 13). This divine strengthening meant that no enemy could seize him unawares and no foe prevail against him (cf. 2 Sa. xxii. 1). *Exact upon him* (22); 'do him violence' (RV mg.).

In addition to this definite promise of royal power and military strength, there was a further undertaking by the Lord to endow David with His mercy and faithfulness (24). Not only should his domain extend from the Mediterranean Sea to the rivers of the east (cf. Gn. xv. 18; Ps. lxxx. 11) but his relationship with God would be that of a firstborn son (26, 27; cf. 2 Sa. vii. 14; Heb. i. 5). The former promise to the whole community (Ex. iv. 22) is now focused in the king (note Rom. viii. 29; Rev. i. 5). As a result of this, the throne of Israel will be supreme above all (cf. Dt. xxviii. 1), and would be eternal *as the days of heaven* (29).

This aspect of the covenant, its infallibility and permanence, prepares the way for the major purpose of the Psalm, and in order to clear the ground for the subsequent protest the psalmist proceeds to dwell upon the inviolability of the oath (2 Sa. vii. 14–16). The faithlessness of David's descendants did not annul the covenant regarding the dynasty. If they should *forsake, walk not in, break* ('profane' RV mg.), *keep not* the ways of God, He would chastise them; but *My covenant will I not break* (profane), *nor alter . . .* (34). Once and for all time the Lord had sworn and He was not a man that He should lie (see Lk. i. 32, 33). That covenant was declared by God to be as steadfast 'as the faithful witness in the sky' (37, RV). This may mean 'as day or night' (Je. xxxiii. 20, 21), or literally 'as the witness in the sky, God Himself, is faithful' (cf. Jb. xvi. 19). This allusion to celestial faithfulness is reminiscent of verse 29; i.e. the psalmist reverts to the major concept of the immutability of the covenant.

c. The psalmist protests that God has now spurned the covenant (38–51)

The emphatic *But thou* initiates the forceful contrast which is provided by the following verses. The protest has two aspects which reflect the two themes of the preceding part of the Psalm. First, the honour and power of God and His goodness to Israel (5–18) are reversed in the evidences of the destruction He has wrought, the inversion of His promises, and the disgrace and shame brought to Israel (38–45). Secondly, the explicit and solemn covenant with David (20–37) is reversed in the inexplicable and seemingly capricious abandonment of the undertaking (46–51).

i. A deliberate parallel (38–45). The pattern of the words 'thou hast done so and so' is a deliberate parallel with the similar structure of verses 9–14. The raging sea is replaced by wrath toward the king (38), the humiliation of 'Rahab' is surpassed by the degradation of the throne (39; the crown cast down). The creation of the world, its bounds and its mountains (11, 12) is matched with the destruction of the kingdom, its frontiers (*hedges*) and citadels (40, 41). The might of the divine arm had exalted righteousness and judgment and made glad the people (13–15), whereas now it is *the right hand of his*

adversaries which is exalted and it is the enemies who rejoice (42). Once Israel had walked in the light of God's countenance (15), but now *Thou hast made his glory* (RV 'brightness') *to cease* (44): He who had been the glory of their strength (17) now fought only in pretence, for His weapons were reversed and harmless (43), and their throne was covered with shame (44). Verse 45 may refer to Jehoiachin who was only a lad who reigned for three and a half months (cf. 2 Ki. xxiv. 8).

ii. A deliberate contrast (46–51). The first thought, life's weakness and brevity, is the opposite of the strength and permanence of David in verses 22–29. Verse 46 is an echo of Ps. lxxix. 5. Verse 47 suggests the experience behind Ps. xxxix. 4, 5 and Jb. vii. 6–9, ix. 25–26. It seems that God has made men for a mere nothing; all must die and that comparatively quickly (48). Unless God reaffirms the covenant speedily the Davidic dynasty, the trusting psalmist and all men will come together to the grave and deliverance will be too late.

The second and final thought, Where are the Lord's faithfulness and mercies?, needs no repetition; but it is the counterpart of His perpetual presence and guidance which were implicit in verses 30–35. In conclusion the psalmist reverts to his opening words, first concerning the oath sworn to David (49; cf. verse 3), and secondly concerning the song of praise he intended to sing (1). In this matter he reminds the Lord of the burden of innumerable taunts and reproaches which are on his heart flung at him by surrounding peoples (50). The repetition of the words in verse 51 is probably intended to convey a sense of anguish long endured as the footsteps of the young king were dogged by scorn and derision on his journey to Babylon.

Verse 52 does not belong to the Psalm: it is the doxology marking the end of Book III of the Psalter.

BOOK FOUR. PSALMS xc–cvi

PSALM XC. REQUIEM FOR A DISOBEDIENT GENERATION

The title gives Moses as the author. This would make the Psalm the oldest in the Psalter. Note its complete independence of allusions to other Psalms and also the kinship of phrase and thought with Dt. xxxiii. The core of the poem, verses 7–12, appears to have as a definite historical background the later months of the thirty-eight years' wandering in the wilderness when the generation which was adult on leaving Egypt was rapidly dying off (see Nu. xiv. 21–23; Ps. xcv. 8–11; Heb. iii. 17). Moses would have felt increasingly isolated in spirit as these members of the community eventually all left their bones in the wilderness. And this sense of Israel's mortality, accentuated by the judgment of their stubborn unbelief, was added to his own peculiar childhood-link with a past generation

of Egyptian tutors who were saturated with a consciousness of ages past. He was in an excellent position to perceive the swift-moving panorama of the whole human race. Also he had the unique privilege of seeing it from the vantage point of Sinai. It was the timeless quality of a holy God which enhanced His anger, called forth Israel's penitence, and stirred Moses to pray that henceforth the eternal freshness, the very joy and beauty of the Lord, should characterize all His children.

The Psalm falls into three parts.

a. The eternal Creator and our ephemeral life (1–6)

The first verse is transcribed from Dt. xxxiii. 27. Since the days of Abraham the people of God had had no abiding place, but now their wanderings were coming to an end. It could be truly said that the Lord had always shown Himself to be the perpetual place of rest and refuge for His people (cf. Pss. xci. 9, lxxi. 3). Before He had given birth to the ancient mountains (for the metaphor cf. Dt. xxxii. 18; Jb. xxxviii. 8, 28), before the existence of the world, and even before that, 'Thou art to be found as God alone'. Thus shall it ever be. *The earth and the world* (2). The second of these two words means the cultivated parts of the earth.

In the greatest possible contrast to divine deathlessness is human frailty. Verse 3 is open to several interpretations: 1. God causes man 'to crumble to dust' (cf. RV mg.) even while He is calling forth another generation. 2. He brings living men back to the dust (Gn. iii. 19) by the word *Return, ye children of men*. 3. If the meaning of *dakka*, 'crumbling', is that of abasement and contrition, then the verse may be paraphrased 'Thou causest men to change and repent and then sayest "Come to me who am unchanging" '. The following verses, especially verse 6, favour 1. The three similes (4, 5) of a sleep or *watch in the night* (unheeded by the sleeper), the brief period of floodwaters after a storm, and the summer crop of hay, growing in the dew of dawn, but cut and dried by dusk (cf. Mt. vi. 30), are illustrations of the timelessness of God (4). To Him a thousand years pass by thus swiftly.

b. Life's sorrows related to God's holiness (7–12)
In contrast to the serenity of soul and security of life in God which is suggested in verse 1, the thought of verse 7 is man's experience of terrifying change, and of being hurried away. This reversal is due to human sin calling forth divine wrath. Not only obvious wrongs, but the inmost heart of each person is laid bare before the eyes of Him with whom we all have to do (cf. Heb. iv. 13). The promise of our sunny dawn swiftly wanes to the inevitable gloom of night (the Hebrew word translated *passed away* (9) means 'decline towards sunset', as in Je. vi. 4). *As a tale that is told* (9); better, as in RV mg., 'as a sigh'. In verse 10 see RV and cf. Jb. xx. 8.

Who knoweth . . . ? (11). The suggestion is that very few people realize that this is part of the operation of God's anger (cf. RV), and they seldom feel the urgent need of repentance. Oh that men would understand this and consequently prize each day rather than squander it in frivolous pursuits! (12; cf. Dt. v. 29, xxxii. 29).

c. A prayer that the survivors should partake of God's glory (13–17)
Whereas the two preceding portions of the poem were headed by the themes of God as the source of rest (1) and of wrath (7), the final section is introduced (13) by the concept of divine repentance (cf. Ex. xxxii. 12), not as an alteration of His purpose or His values, but as marking a change in the divine method of dealing with His servant Israel (cf. Dt. xxxii. 36). *Early* (14); RV 'in the morning'. The prayer asks for an end of trouble like unto the end of night (cf.

Ps. xxx. 5), i.e. for an immediate experience of mercy. Moreover, in that He is God for ever as well as from of old (2), let Him grant His blessing for as long as He has already imposed affliction (15; cf. Dt. viii. 2). Let the evident working of His grace and goodwill be seen by Israel; and, whereas they had seen God's judgment upon their parents who were buried in the wilderness, let the people now see His glorious salvation in the welfare of their children (16). So let nothing hinder them from taking part in the completion of His work, viz. the establishing of His people in Canaan (17). Thus would they experience the divine good pleasure (*beauty*) even amidst the daily work of their hands in conquest or occupation.

PSALM XCI. REFUGE FOR A DIVINELY GUIDED SOUL

This Psalm is generally regarded as a companion to the previous one, the title of which may be taken as applying to both. In support of this relationship it may be observed that they are both an elaboration of the same phrase in Dt. xxxiii. 27a, and that the message of security through intimate fellowship with the Lord in Ps. xci is the counterpart of the theme of human insignificance and desperate need in Ps. xc. The two Psalms also have a related structure.

Ps. xci opens with an assertion of human faith (1) and concludes with a declaration of divine faithfulness (14–16) in which the impersonal is replaced by God addressing His promises personally to the believer. The remaining verses (2–13) fall into two sections each introduced by a personal affirmation (see verses 2 and 9, RV). In the expansion of these confessions of faith there is in each case a change of the personal pronoun from *my* to *thee*; verses 3–8 and 9b–13 may have been intended to be spoken by another voice. Note how verse 9b (see RV) picks up the thought of the opening words, *dwelleth in . . . the most High*.

The imagery of verse 1, *the secret place* (or 'covert') and the *shadow* (of the wings), is often used elsewhere of God's solicitude for men. See verse 4 and cf. Pss. xvii. 8, lxi. 4; Dt. xxxii. 11. The *noisome pestilence* (3) means some form of destructive death. Note, however, the different reading of the LXX, 'the destroying word' (cf. Ps. xxxviii. 12). *His truth* (4) is His unquestionable faithfulness to His word.

The immunity from dangers described in verses 5–8 is almost certainly based upon the memory of Israel's experience during the plagues in Egypt; but it is intended to apply metaphorically, in the same way as God is referred to as a rock and a nesting eagle. Dt. xxxii. 24 suggests that *the destruction that wasteth at noonday* (6) was some form of sunstroke, but see Ps. lxxviii. 48. With verse 7 cf. Nu. xxi. 6. With verse 8 cf. Ex. xiv. 30b. Angelic guardianship (11, 12) is frequently mentioned in Scripture, e.g. Gn. xxiv. 40; Ex. xxiii. 20; Heb. i. 14.

But this protection is *in all thy ways*, i.e. of faith and godliness (cf. Ps. xxiii. 3; Pr. iii. 17); this qualification was understood by Satan when he omitted this phrase in quoting the Psalm to Jesus (Mt. iv. 6). *The dragon* (13); RV 'serpent'. The lion and serpent are representative of fierceness and persistence in outward and obvious attacks by foes, and inward and secret assaults by doubts and schemers. See Am. v. 19; Ps. lviii. 4, 6; and note Lk. x. 19. (Cf. also Pss. xxii. 13, lxiv. 2–6; Mt. xxiii. 33; 1 Pet. v. 8.)

The words attributed to the Lord in verses 14–16 may be taken as a fitting conclusion to both Psalms. Love is the foundation of all trust (Ps. xc. 14ff.) and triumph (Ps. xci. 11ff.). When a man 'cleaves affectionately' to the most High then he himself is set on high (cf. 2 Pet. i. 3, 4; Ps. ix. 9, 10) in closest companionship and security (cf. Jn. xiv. 23ff.; Ps. xxi. 4, 5).

PSALM XCII. A SABBATH HYMN

The title reminds us that this Psalm was chanted every sabbath in the temple worship after the return from Babylon. The Targum ascribes it to Adam on the morning of Creation's seventh day, but this is obviously a metaphorical allusion. The association of the song with the sabbath is probably due to its spirit of joyful praise and its outlook upon a world cleansed of sinners and evil-doers. In this latter sense, the Psalm may be anticipatory of the eternal sabbath rest for the children of God which in its fulness is yet to come (cf. Heb. iv. 9ff.). Note the similarity of verses 1–3 and Ps. xxxiii. 1–3 (another song of creative power and righteous rule) and the elaboration of the similes of grass (the wicked) and a green tree (the righteous) which were used in Ps. i.

After the introduction, the song falls into two symmetrical and contrasted parts each containing two themes.

a. Introduction (1–3)

The praise and worship of God is not merely approved by Him as good but is a most pleasant activity for men (cf. Ps. cxlvii. 1). The practice of having morning and evening periods of prayer and praise is often mentioned in the Psalter. See, e.g., Pss. v. 3, xlii. 8, lv. 17, lix. 16, lxiii. 6, lxxxviii. 13. The phrase *with a solemn sound* (3) occurs as *Higgaion* in Ps. ix. 16. In Ps. xix. 14 it denotes musing or meditation, and may here be a technical word for meditative music.

b. God's works and His judgment on the wicked (4–9)

God's activity is seen both in His works of creation and in His rule over the affairs of men. It is the latter which the psalmist has most in mind and is most evocative of his praise. *I will triumph* (4), or 'exult', because the designs and purposes of God are actually and continuously being disclosed in history (cf. Pss. xxxiii. 11, xl. 5, cxxxix. 17). We are thinking His thoughts

after Him but usually find them too deep for us to grasp (cf. Is. lv. 8ff.; Rom. xi. 33).

A brutish man . . . a fool (6); i.e. men who are dominated by sensuality or by moral perversity. Such cannot discern this providential government in the world nor understand why the wicked flourish as the spring grass. The psalmist not only declares the destruction of the wicked (see notes on Ps. xc. 6), but implies that their short-lived prosperity is an intentional lesson to the godly (cf. Ps. lxxiii. 17ff.). This is because the Lord ever sitteth on high in judgment (cf. Ps. xxix. 10) and all opposition to Him or His people shall be thoroughly disrupted.

c. Personal blessings and God's goodness to the righteous (10–15)

Adoration of God frequently arises from a realization that we are not merely observers of God's mercy and judgments, but are ourselves caught up into the pattern of His holy beneficence (cf. 2 Pet. i. 2–4; Eph. ii. 19ff.). This consciousness of being a partaker with God is often expressed by the psalmists in the metaphors of an upraised horn belonging to a source of great power (cf. Nu. xxiii. 22; Pss. xxix. 6, lxxxix. 17, cxlviii. 14) and of an inverted horn from whence flowed the anointing oil, symbol of identification and incorporation (cf. 1 Sa. xvi. 13; Ps. xlv. 7; Heb. i. 9). *Unicorn* (10); RV 'wild ox'. As he feels almost a partner with God, the psalmist knows that he will see and hear of the downfall of all those who oppose the servants of the Lord. He feels that he is inseparable from the triumphant activity of God.

The righteous shall flourish (12). The contrast now reaches its climax. It has been suggested in the antithesis of verses 11 and 6, and is expanded in the imagery of the tall, erect and ever-green palm tree which is so superior to the grass underfoot (7). The cedars of Lebanon were noted for their size and excellence (cf. Is. ii. 13; Ps. civ. 16). The imagery of such great trees growing luxuriantly in the house of the Lord has been found previously in Ps. lii. 8. The basic idea is that of permanence, dignity, ample resources of strength and nourishment, freedom from damage, an environment of honour and centuries of fruitfulness (cf. a similar concept in Ps. xxvii. 4–6). The final verse of the song is based on Dt. xxxii. 4.

PSALM XCIII. THE LORD'S ETERNAL SOVEREIGNTY

This Psalm, itself an expansion of Ps. xcii. 8, is a prologue to the great anthem of praise in Pss. xcv–c. The concept of God's throne, *established of old* (2), i.e. before time was, and surviving all attempts to shake it so that He remains king for ever (cf. Pss. xxix. 10, xxxiii. esp. 13, 14, xlvii), is not the same as that belief which envisages Him as ruling from Zion (cf. Pss. xxiv, xlvi, xlviii. 1, 2, lxviii. 16, 17). The two lines of thought were the necessary expression of a faith which believed that God would eventually disclose His true nature and glory in all earth and heaven, and also that He would also establish sovereignty over the peoples of this world by His personal rule and have an actual city (Zion) as His residence. The latter belief became part of the messianic hope. In the New Testament the two concepts are fused into one and thereby transformed (cf. Ps. cx).

The Psalm, together with xcv–c, is generally assumed to have been written after the return from Babylon when the apparent abdication of the throne of David by God (see Ps. lxxxix) was perceived to be temporary. *The Lord reigneth* (1), lit. 'The Lord hath become king', may allude to this resumption of His rule over Israel, or it may imply a world-wide acknowledgment of an eternal fact stated in the next verse. *Is clothed* (1). The thought is 'hath robed Himself in royal apparel'. With the recognition of His sovereignty the world-order becomes stable and firm (cf. Ps. xcvi. 10ff.). Previously there have been insidious, low and widespread elements of opposition, here described as floods (3) which have endeavoured to swamp and smash this divine purpose. Notice the development of the thought, from the first creep of these flood-waters, through the increasing swirl of their currents and the deepening roar of their destructive efforts, even to their final manifestation as broad waters whipped in tumult, thundering menaces ('voices') and crashing as breakers of a sea. Yet is the Lord on high unmoved and unperturbed, ever glorious in power (cf. Ps. xxix. 10). There may be some indirect allusion in verses 3 and 4 to the captivities of Israel when they were carried away and wellnigh immersed in the great river-states of Egypt, Assyria and Babylon.

The final verse is a comment by the psalmist upon the impregnable structure of God's kingdom. His unchangeableness is rooted in His own holiness and in His righteous administration of all creation (cf. Ps. xix. 7–9). *Thine house* refers particularly to the temple, or to Zion itself (cf. Ps. xlvii. 1–3), or to the place of His abiding (cf. Is. lxvi. 1 and Acts vii. 48, 49).

PSALM XCIV. AN APPEAL AGAINST THE DELAY OF GOD'S JUDGMENT

The theme of this Psalm is the age-old problem of reconciling what happens in the world with the goodness and power of God. Its relationship to the previous Psalm is shown in two ways: the triple protest (xciv. 3, 16 and 20) is made on the basis of God's eternal sovereignty (Ps. xciii), and a fondness for repetition of phrases is characteristic of both poems. Primarily this Psalm expresses the immediate reaction of the natural man to the affirmation of faith in Pss. xciii and xcv–c. It is the challenge of harsh realism to the confidence of heartfelt trust, a reminder of the anomaly of man's devilry within the moral order established by God. Apart from the invocation in the two opening verses the Psalm falls into three parts, each introduced by an inquiry or protest.

a. Introduction (1, 2)

The appeal is framed in forceful words, lit. 'O God of vengeances, Yahweh, God of vengeances, shine forth'. This has no sense of animosity or malice about it, but is simply a cry for recompense or retribution (cf. Je. li. 56c), that all false appearances may be terminated and all ungodly deeds recoil upon the perpetrators (cf. Jb. iv. 8; Ho. viii. 7a; Gal. vi. 7ff.). This process would inevitably accompany the manifestation of divine truth, hence the appeal *shew thyself* (RV 'shine forth'; cf. Pss. l. 2, lxxx. 1). He asks God to assert His sovereignty (cf. Gn. xviii. 25c; Ps. vii. 6ff.) and to bring home to the arrogant the consequences of their deeds (see RV).

b. How long shall the wicked triumph? (3–15)

The query concerns the present period of time; it does not imply any suspicion of divine impotence. The inquiry is elaborated in three respects:

i. **Facts (4–7).** The wicked are described as pouring forth a stream of arrogant and boastful words which spring from self-esteem. *Hard things* (4); better, as in RV, 'arrogantly'. They are not only pompous ranters but they also *break in pieces*, i.e. crush and harass, that remnant of devout souls who form the Lord's people and heritage (5). Their offences against their fellows (cf. Ex. xxii. 21, 22) and against JAH (RV mg.), the God of their fathers (who overthrew even an oppressor like Pharaoh), are sins of murder and pride which violate the essentials of law (see Dt. vi. 5; Mt. xxii. 37ff.; Lk. x. 27). For the common illusion that *the Lord shall not see* (7), or care, cf. Ps. x. 11; Jb. xxii. 13ff.; Ezk. viii. 12; Is. xxix. 15; Ps. cxxxix. 11, 12; Lk. viii. 17, xii. 2.

ii. **Principles (8–11).** The lack of discernment (7) is not on God's part but theirs (cf. Jn. ix. 39ff.). Such obtuseness is characteristic of men who live in the realm of animal experiences (*brutish*; see Ps. xcii. 6 and cf. lxxiii. 22). Three principles are declared.

1. The Creator must be greater than His creatures (9); i.e. He who made doors of access to the human mind must have the power and right of entry. Cf. the divine manifestation by ear (Ex. iii. 14) and eye (Jn. ix. 25).

2. The moral ruler of great historic movements must exercise His holy authority over every man (10), i.e. if the ordinary nations are trained and instructed in right and wrong (cf. Rom. i. 18ff.) and are held responsible for their misdeeds (Rom. i. 32), how much more shall He Himself, teacher of the knowledge of righteousness (RV), be righteous in His rebukes?

3. The Lord knows fully the number and nature of human thoughts (cf. Ps. cxxxix. 1–4; Jn. ii. 24, 25; 1 Cor. iii. 20) because *they*, i.e. men, are altogether vain (lit. 'a breath'; see Ps. xxxix. 6).

iii. Beliefs (12–15). After the historical and philosophical, there is the religious aspect. This is a development of the central thought in the previous paragraph (see verse 10). Blessed is he whom God teaches by imposing a discipline upon him (cf. Ps. cxix. 71; Heb. xii. 5–9) and instructing him in the law (Heb. *torah*) of the Lord, i.e. in the nature and meaning of the divine self-revelation (12). That man is given peace of heart and mind; he is at rest inwardly, even in times of adversity, which will continue until the full and final judgment of the wicked is effected (13). That ultimate action is inevitable, and equally sure is the faithfulness of the Lord to His chosen people (14). Judgment will become righteous (contrast verses 5, 6) and the upright shall follow the way of godliness without hindrance (15).

c. Who shall champion me against evil (16–19)

The belief in an ultimate vindication of the moral order provides a poor defence against immediate and unscrupulous injustice. The query of verse 16 is the natural response of the godly man who is oppressed. The answer is implied 'The Lord is my defender', and this is affirmed in detail in the following three verses which correspond to the three aspects previously outlined. The physical threat of being driven to an unjust death, the silence of the grave (see verses 5, 6), has been averted solely by the providence of the Lord (17). The psychological peril of slipping from the path of sober-minded trust in God because of the difficulties of going on (cf. verse 8 with *When I said*, i.e. to myself) has been prevented only by the effectual and sustaining mercy of the Lord (18; cf. Ps. cxlv. 14; Jude 24). The spiritual danger of lapsing into the intense solitariness of unbelief has never developed because, whenever anxious *thoughts* (RV mg. 'doubts') surged round his inmost soul, the *comforts* (i.e. consolations) of the Lord ensured real heart-peace (19; cf. verse 14; Ps. xxvii. 5).

d. But are the wicked to claim God as their ally? (20–23)

The satisfactory testimony of the godly soul, to the effect that the Lord fully sustains him in periods of adversity and oppression, did not touch the external situation which is the root of the whole problem. What, then, is God's relationship to the wicked? Is there any divine truth behind the fact that the wicked are in the places of authority (*throne*, i.e. 'seat of judgment') and administration? *Frameth mischief by a law* (20); i.e. use legal statutes to make wrong appear right. How are the upright to assess the phenomenon of wicked men occupying for long periods positions of power created by God for the necessary government of society? Contrast verse 2a.

The psalmist offers no solution to this point but simply reiterates the three major aspects of the matter. (See section **b** above.) He first declares the existence or fact of injustice (21) as in

verses 4–7. Secondly he testifies to the Lord's care and protection in his own case (22), replacing the abstract principles of verses 8–11 by personal experience. Thirdly he affirms his belief in the power and righteousness of God and in the ultimate retribution upon the wicked as in verses 12–15. *Condemn the innocent blood* (21) means to sentence to death men who are free from guilt.

GENERAL INTRODUCTION TO PSALMS XCV–C

These six liturgical Psalms have a common theme—the joyous adoration of Yahweh as the supreme ruler of His creation as well as the covenant God of Israel. Although written separately they have been fitted together into an elaborate choral work centred on the fact that 'the Lord reigneth'. The basic structure is the usual Hebraic alternation of parallel themes and it is almost certain that each of these Psalms was sung antiphonally. Similar groups of Psalms arranged for choral services of praise occur in cxiii–cxviii and cxlvi–cl. Throughout this group there is evidence of considerable borrowing of phrases from other Psalms and from the later part of the book of Isaiah. But the six poems have been skilfully combined into an impressive sequence which is particularly rich and extensive in thought.

The anthem begins (xcv) with an expression of Israel's worship in which the knowledge of God is shown to be inseparable from the imprint of His action upon them at the Red Sea and in the wilderness. A larger view develops in Ps. xcvi; Israel is unnamed and the call to worship is addressed to all nations and creatures. Israel's covenant of Ps. xcv, 'He is our God and we are His people', is replaced by the natural and general elements in which God is known as creator of the heavens and source of all righteousness and truth.

These two aspects of deity are amplified in Ps. xcvii, where He is described first as the supreme One before whom creation is ever on the verge of dissolution, and then as the faithful One whose goodness and holiness are always being disclosed to all people through Zion. This great privilege granted to Israel evokes a jubilant song of praise (Ps. xcviii), not so much on the grounds of Jewish monopoly, but because of the marvel that the divine revelation of salvation should be made known to the ends of the earth.

Nevertheless, although all creation is under an obligation to praise the Lord, He has chosen Zion as the centre and focus of His self-revelation. Consequently Ps. xcix is the most particular of the whole group—the cherubim in Zion's sanctuary, the divine purpose in the history of Jacob, God's personal response to such leaders as Moses, Aaron and Samuel, and His patient mercy in dealing with a wayward nation. Finally, in Ps. c, the appeal for universal adoration of the Lord is fused, both with Israel's position as

His peculiar people, and with the enduring quality of the Lord's mercy and goodness.

Observe the interweaving of many antitheses throughout the whole anthem. For example, human life and earth life (itself grouped into sheep and pasture, crops and woods, sea and land, darkness and light); past and future; Israel and other nations; the covenants of Sinai (Moses) and of Zion (David); God who is highly exalted in the heavens, and yet dwelleth between the cherubim in the temple; the severity and also the goodness of the Lord to Israel in the wilderness; the divine condemnation of all wicked men but the ultimate acceptance of the Gentiles.

PSALM XCV. PRAISE THE CREATOR'S POWER AND PATIENCE

See General Introduction above to Psalms xcv–c
This is a liturgical description of the approach to the temple of a body of worshippers. Note how the voice of a priest or prophet breaks in at the end of verse 7. For the Lord as *the rock* (1), see Pss. lxxxix. 26, lxxi. 3, lxii. 2, xviii. 1, 2. *Come before his presence with thanksgiving* (2); cf. Heb. xiii. 15. The reference to other gods (3) is to be interpreted in the light of xcvi. 5 (cf. Ex. xviii. 11). With 'In his hand are the deep places . . . the heights' (4, RV) cf. Ps. cxxxix. 7, 8.

Worship and bow down (6), i.e. prostrate ourselves and demonstrate our full allegiance. *Our maker* (6); cf. Dt. xxxii. 6, 15. This second call (cf. verse 1) infuses the initial joy with reverence and humility. *Pasture . . . sheep* (7); cf. lxxiv. 1, lxxix. 13, lxxx. 1 (see notes to these). 'Oh that ye would hear his voice' (7, RV) is a parenthesis. The voice says *To day . . . harden not your heart* (7, 8). Worship and warning go together in Israel's history; cf. Heb. iii. 7—iv. 11. Verse 8 is best translated as in RV 'as at Meribah, as in the day of Massah'. The core of the first place-name means strife, and the root of the second means 'test' or 'prove' (see Ex. xvii. 1–7). *Saw my work* (9); i.e. in the deliverance from Egypt, or generally as in Pss. lxiv. 9, xcii. 4. *Sware in my wrath* (11). See Nu. xiv. 21–23; there is another statement of the Lord's abhorrence in Dt. i. 34–39. *My rest* (11); see Dt. xii. 9 and Heb. iv. The abrupt ending of the Psalm accentuates the continual challenge presented by the action of God in our past experience.

PSALM XCVI. REJOICE, O EARTH, THY KING COMETH

See General Introduction above to Psalms xcv–c
The opening quotation is from Is. xlii. 10: the whole Psalm is virtually reproduced in the Davidic anthem for the installation of the ark in Zion (see 1 Ch. xvi. 23–33). *All the earth* (1); i.e. its inhabitants. *His name* (2); i.e. His self-disclosure in His great acts, especially toward Israel.

The second movement opens in verse 4 with a quotation from Ps. xlviii. 1. The unreality of all other 'gods' is a frequent theme in Isaiah.

See, e.g., Is. ii. 8, 18, 20, xl. 19ff., xli. 21–24, xliv. 12ff. On the other hand the glory and power of Yahweh are often said to be evident in the heavens. See, e.g., Pss. xix. 1–6, xxxiii. 6, civ. 1–3; cf. Rom. i. 18–20; 1 Cor. viii. 4. The attributes of God are represented in verse 6 as His regalia (cf. Pss. xciii. 1, civ. 1); His *strength and beauty* were symbolized in the ark of the covenant (cf. Ps. lxxviii. 61).

The third movement (verses 7–9) begins with a composite quotation from Pss. xxii. 27, xxix. 1, 2. Note the order of the service: homage, praise, offering, prayer. The invitation to all nations to enter the courts of the Lord was never put into practice; but see Is. lx. *The beauty of holiness* (9); i.e. in holy garments. Cf. Ps. xxix. 2.

The fourth movement (verse 10) repeats the theme of Ps. xciii. 1. Men must realize that the Lord is king and that only in Him does the world become stabilized. This cry of acclamation that the Lord is become king echoes against the background of His creation of the world out of chaos. Cf. Pss. ix. 8, xxii. 27, 28.

The two final stanzas of the Psalm seem to be messianic anticipations. The effect of His coming will be seen in the realm of creation (11, 12; cf. Is. xliv. 23ff., lv. 12; also Ps. xxiv. 1), and in the setting up of His righteous kingdom (cf. Is. xi. 1–9). The present tense of these words of faith is akin to such Gospel statements as Lk. xvii. 21; Jn. xii. 31.

PSALM XCVII. ASHAMED BE THOSE THAT SERVE HIM NOT

See General Introduction above to Psalms xcv–c
This majestic Psalm expands the concept of God as universal King already expressed in Ps. xcvi. 4 and 10. It is a mosaic of phrases from other Psalms prefaced (as is Ps. xcix) with the exultant cry of the Lord's enthronement. There are two parts.

The first portion (verses 1–6) deals imaginatively with the tremendous commotion in the natural realm consequent upon the coming or manifestation of God. (See Ps. xcvi. 13 and xviii. 7–15; see also Jdg. v. 5; Pss. xlvi. 6, l. 3, 4, lxxvii. 18, lxxxix. 14; Is. lxvi. 18; Mic. i. 3–5; 2 Pet. iii. 10–12; and cf. Rom. viii. 19–23.)

The second half (verses 7–12) speaks of the spiritual results of His advent. Paganism is revealed as utterly vain (cf. Is. xliv. 6–20, xlv. 16, xlvi. 1), whereas Zion and its 'daughter' villages are filled with rejoicing (an echo of Ex. xv; see also Pss. xxx. 4, xxxii. 11, lxxxiii. 18. *Light is sown for the righteous* (11); i.e. the source of future glory and knowledge is implanted in the godly soul and will later spring forth more fully (cf. Ps. cxxvi. 6; Pr. iv. 18; 2 Cor. iv. 6 and 16ff.).

PSALM XCVIII. INVOCATION TO GOD THE KING BY ALL THE WORLD

See General Introduction above to Psalms xcv–c
This Psalm opens and closes with the same

Q

phrases as Ps. xcvi, and shows considerable similarity to it throughout. In its description of Israel's deliverance from other nations and of the jubilation of a perfected creation the psalmist is really concerned with the interrelation of God and the world. *A new song* (1) is necessary because the sense of God's immediate presence has emptied all former expressions of praise. *His salvation* (2). For the means see Ps. xliv. 3; for the effect cf. Is. lii. 10. The manner of it has been by creating order out of confusion, by delivering Israel from Egypt, and by the renewal of those blessings to Israel promised aforetime to their fathers. The whole action of salvation is the outcome of His attribute of righteousness. The special experience of Israel was simply the fore-runner of a world-wide salvation (3b). Hence the call to all the inhabitants of earth to break forth into songs of joy (4; cf. Is. lii. 9) and to use all forms of music to augment their praise. Nor is salvation and praise limited to mankind. All creation is expected to join in, and even the sea, symbol hitherto of rebelliousness (cf. Ps. xciii. 3, 4), is heard in fullest acclamation (cf. Rom. viii. 19–21).

PSALM XCIX. SONG OF ISRAEL'S PRIESTLY PRIVILEGE

See General Introduction above to Psalms xcv–c
The nation's glad cry at the enthronement of their King forms the opening phrase of this Psalm as of Ps. xcvii. It closes also with a similar thought of the Lord's holiness. The body of the poem, however, follows the theme of Ps. xcv. The repetition of verse 5 in verse 9 clearly divides it into two parts.

In the first part there are two strands of thought. First, the psalmist considers the tran-scendent majesty of the Lord which, none the less, is focused in the temple in Zion *between the cherubims* (1). Cf. the paradox of Ps. xcv. 2 and 4, 'let us come before him who is above all and beneath all'. Secondly, the divine ordering of the system of law in Israel is recalled. Cf. the recognition in Ps. xcv. 6 of God as founder or 'maker' of Israel (see Dt. xxxii. 6 and 15). *His footstool* (5) may have several meanings; e.g. the sanctuary (Ps. cxxxii. 7), the ark of the covenant (1 Ch. xxviii. 2), the city of Zion (La. ii. 1), the whole earth (Is. lxvi. 1).

The second part (verses 6–9) also has two topics. The psalmist thinks first of the prayerful leadership of Moses, Aaron and Samuel, and prays for a display of divine power and faith-fulness similar to that given to these men (cf. 1 Sa. xii. 18–23; Je. xv. 1). The pillar of cloud and the allusion to divine statutes is reminiscent of Sinai. His object seems to be to draw atten-tion to the character of the priesthood when it was first inaugurated. Secondly, he considers the gracious forgiveness of the Lord. The reference to His vengeance, or chastisement, is an echo of Ps. xcv. 10, 11 (note Ps. lxxviii. 38 and 58) and, in view of the priestly emphasis of the Psalm,

the allusion may be to the judgment of Korah (Nu. xvi). The mood is that of Mal. ii. 1–9. The variation in the refrain (9 and 5) emphasizes the harmony between Yahweh and Israel; *the Lord our God* is a double affirmation.

PSALM C. PRAISE FOR GOD'S ENDURING FAITHFULNESS

See General Introduction above to Psalms xcv–c
This is the shortest Psalm in the group but the most comprehensive. Apart from the spirit of joyfulness in the service and worship of God the essential themes are: the sovereignty and one-ness of the Lord (cf. Dt. vi. 4; 1 Ki. xviii. 39); the recognition that He has both created us and made us what we are and also chosen us as His flock (cf. Is. xliii. 1; Eph. ii. 10; 1 Pet. ii. 25); the perpetual privilege of offering thanks to God for His essential goodness and eternal faith-fulness.

PSALM CI. THE DAVIDIC IDEAL

This Psalm of David sets out the principles upon which he intended to act during his reign in Zion, *the city of the Lord* (8). Purity of heart on his own part (cf. Pss. xvii. 1–5, xxvi) was not enough. He saw the desirability of a house that was perfect, of a court in which there was no evil thing, and of a people in whom envy, pride, deceit and falsity were ruthlessly destroyed. This ideal of a holy king and a perfect nation clearly belongs to the early part of David's reign when his experience at the courts of Saul and Achish, and his many perils because of evil men and corrupt practices, were still a major factor in shaping his outlook. The most notable feature of the Psalm is the king's desire for unanimity of heart amongst his companions. He expected no less from them than his own stan-dards of conduct and values, an ideal which becomes practicable only under the rule of David's Son and Lord (cf. Mt. v. 3; Rom. xii and xiii; 1 Jn. ii. 6, iii. 3).

There are various interpretations of the phrase *O when wilt thou come unto me?* (2). It may be an echo of 2 Sa. vi. 9, in which case the Psalm may express David's conviction, in view of Uzzah's death, that the city of Jerusalem needed to be thoroughly cleansed of any wickedness before the ark could be brought thither. On the other hand Jerusalem could hardly be described as *the city of the Lord* (8) if the visible ark and the invisible presence were not yet there. In this case the new urge toward the formation of a community of people with perfect hearts would naturally follow the disclosure, through Nathan, of the Lord's covenant with David. This phrase may therefore express his yearning for its fulfil-ment. See 2 Sa. vii. A similar reaction to a divine act of gracious revelation is seen in 1 Pet. iv. 17 and Col. iii. 1ff.

The two themes of the Psalm are dealt with consecutively.

a. A personal resolution toward holiness of life (1-4)

The psalmist's private life is to be marked by unswerving esteem for the character of God's rule (*mercy and judgment*). He desires to rule in a similar manner but realizes the need of the divine presence and power to enable him so to do. *Wicked thing* (3); RV 'base thing'; lit. 'thing of Belial'. In his home life he will choose integrity rather than indulgence, and uprightness rather than base or unworthy aims. Crooked or unfaithful things he will abhor and only straight and true purposes will be kept in his heart. Evil things (or 'persons', RV mg.) shall not claim acquaintance with him (4b; cf. Phil. iv. 8).

b. A personal resolution concerning holiness of society (5-8)

The court life of the king is to be purged of slander and arrogance (5). He intends being watchful for godly men whom he can appoint as his companions. He will seek for ministers and officials who walk in a way of integrity (or perfection) like himself (2c, 6b). Men of deceit (such as Doeg, 1 Sa. xxii. 22) should have no access to the king's affairs, and anyone found guilty of falsehood will be dismissed. Day by day (8, see RV) the king will sit to administer justice (cf. Je. xxi. 12; 2 Sa. xv. 2ff.) so that gradually the whole city will be made to reflect the righteousness of the Lord who has chosen to dwell there.

PSALM CII. A PRAYER OF THE AFFLICTED

The title affixed to this Psalm is peculiar in that it gives no musical instruction, nor indication of the author, but describes only the character of the poem and its applicability to any sufferer who wishes to pray. From the allusion to Zion's dust and the sighs of prisoners, the Psalm may with considerable confidence be assigned to the closing years of the exile. The writer speaks not only from his own experience of grief but as a partaker and representative of the sorrows of his people. The Psalm is in three parts.

a. A cry of suffering and despair (1-11)

The first two verses are a mosaic of phrases from other Psalms, e.g. xxxix. 12, xviii. 6, xxvii. 9, lix. 16, xxxi. 2, lxix. 17. After this invocation, which is expressive of the psalmist's sense of isolation from God (cf. verse 10), he proceeds to describe his brief and anguished life (3-5). His days drift and vanish into smoke because of the spiritual fever which burns upon the hearth of his physical existence. His heart has lost its freshness and vigour so that it is like grass scorched in the sun and unable to absorb nourishment. As a consequence of anxiety his body is wasting away and is nothing but skin and bone (cf. Ps. vi. 2, 3, xxii. 14, 15, xxxii. 3, 4, xxxviii. 6-10; Jb. xix. 20).

The third aspect of his misery is that of isolation from his fellows (6, 7). He is not merely gloomy as the pelican and melancholy as the owl, for they are accustomed to scenes of loneliness and ruin. But in his sleeplessness (*I watch*), he is also like the sociable sparrow that is made conscious of its timidity, insignificance and weakness as it hops in solitude upon a rooftop (cf. Is. xxxviii. 14).

The fourth aspect of his destitution (8-11) echoes the second (3-5). In place of inward worry there are outward taunts ('reproaches') and vehement curses (8b, RV). His groaning is accompanied by weeping (cf. Ps. lxxx. 5) and the metaphorical fire in his bones (3) has provided a constant flavour of ashes in his mouth (9). The days of his life, as devoid of the enduring quality of goodness as smoke is lacking in substance (3), lengthen out like shadows in a setting sun which point to the oncoming gloom of a long night (11). He is parched of joy and shrivelled by care like grass in the hot sun (11 and 4). The striking addition in the fourth phase of thought is in verse 10, which is an antithesis of verses 1 and 2. The psalmist's trouble is interpreted as evidence of divine anger against him. Indeed, the experience of the nation in exile suggests that God, having taken them up (cf. Is. xxxviii. 12) in past centuries as though to keep them and protect them, has actually done so simply to cast them away as a tempest would first lift a tent and then leave it tattered in a useless place (cf. Jb. xxvii. 21, xxx. 22; alternatively see Is. xxii. 17, 18).

b. The unchanging and compassionate Lord (12-22)

The contrast between man's nature and vicissitudes and God's nature and unchangeableness is introduced with an emphatic *But thou* (12; cf. Ps. lix. 8). This part of the Psalm is in three stanzas, each of which has Zion for its central thought.

i. **The time to restore Zion has come (12-14).** The perpetual abiding of the Lord is reflected in His enduring memorial among men (cf. Ex. iii. 15). Because of this He will eventually come in compassion to Zion and there could be no more needful time for His mercy than now. Surely the time of restoration foretold by the prophets (e.g. Je. xxv. 11, 12, xxix. 10; Is. xl. 2) has come, because the exiles do not mourn for themselves so much as for the ruins of Jerusalem.

ii. **The effect of the restoration on mankind (15-18).** When the time is fulfilled for the holy place to be restored all men will reverence the glory of the Lord because it would be revealed in Zion's re-creation. That will embody His faithfulness and compassion toward the prayers of the destitute, and it will be recorded and remembered in future generations of the re-created people of Zion.

iii. **The divine nature of the deliverance (19-22).** Their captivity in exile is likened to their former bondage in Egypt (cf. Ex. iii. 7; Ps.

lxxix. 11; see also Pss. xiv. 2, xxxiii. 13), and a similar deliverance from complete destruction is foreseen so that men in general may tell forth the name of the Lord in Jerusalem. That will initiate a gathering of all nations together in service to the Lord (cf. Pss. xxii. 27, lxviii. 32; Is. ii. 1–4 which quotes Mi. iv. 1–3; Ps. lx. 3, 4).

c. Man's weakness and God's strength contrasted (23–28)

The major themes of parts a and b, viz. human life, brief and anguished, and divine glory, stable and compassionate, are woven into the final prayer in which the dominant thought is that of God's ageless and unchangeable nature. After referring to the weakness which has abbreviated the days of his life and prevented him from reaching the expected end of his journey (23), the psalmist pleads for sympathy from one who knows no such experiences, 'whose years endure throughout all generations' (24). The inescapable being of God is related to the origin, extent and decay of the visible universe of earth and sky (cf. Col. i. 16). This panorama, from the beginning to the end of the physical order, leaves in splendid prominence the unalterable Lord. Time brings decay to all else; the entire universe shall become old, even as clothing, and shall in like fashion be discarded by Him who is ever the same. *Thou art the same* (27); lit. 'Thou art He', i.e. One who is eternally Himself; cf. Is. xli. 4, xliii. 10. It is not certain whether verse 26c goes beyond this thought of 'passing away' (cf. Is. li. 6; 1 Jn. ii. 17); but the concept of replacement or change cannot be excluded (cf. Is. lxv. 17, lxvi. 22). But even the prospect of a complete reconstitution of things, a wholly different order of creation, would entail no change in God. Cf. Rom. viii. 19–24; 2 Cor. v. 1, 17; and observe that Heb. i. 10–12 quotes these final verses of the Psalm as relating to Christ. The final verse is an anticipation grounded on the divine nature that the children of the exiles shall return to their homeland to dwell in safety (cf. Ps. lxix. 35).

PSALM CIII. IN PRAISE OF THE GOD OF ALL GRACE

This and the following Psalm form a double hymn of praise. Each begins and ends with the phrase *Bless the Lord, O my soul*, and together they cover the grounds which gave rise to this unrestrained adoration of the Lord. As the longer and more descriptive poem deals with the objective physical realm, it is placed second to that which deals with the subjective personal realm. Compare the similar arrangement of these basic themes in Ps. lxv, and contrast Pss. xix and xxxiii; see also notes on Ps. cxlvii.

The Psalm is an expression of praise evoked firstly by the psalmist's own experience (note the singular pronouns in verses 1–5). But it is tremendously strengthened by the evidences of the Lord's amazing compassion and mercy toward men in general: His re-creative forgiveness and boundless solicitude for such insignificant creatures as men must lead to endless and universal adoration. There are three parts to the hymn.

a. The nature and evidence of infinite grace (1–10)

After calling upon all the resources of his being to praise the name of the Lord (cf. Ps. xxxiii. 20, 21), the psalmist proceeds to describe the *benefits* of the Lord (2). These are described as the pardoning of sins and the healing of physical ailments, especially those caused by anxiety, remorse, fear, etc. (3); the deliverance from a premature death, the supreme experience of His love and tender care (4), the full satisfaction arising from all good things which leads to renewed vigour, like that of an eagle (5; cf. Is. xl. 31). *Satisfieth thy mouth* (5). See RV mg. The interpretation of this verse is uncertain.

The same divine goodness was evident in Israel's history; particularly in the deliverance from Egypt and the provision of food, water, health, guidance and power in the wilderness. More precisely, *He made known his ways unto Moses* (7; cf. Ex. xxxiii. 13). Verse 8 is a quotation of Ex. xxxiv. 6 (cf. Ps. lxxxvi. 15). *Chide* (9); i.e. 'contend', as in a court of law (cf. Is. lvii. 16). If He was to deal with men strictly in accordance with their sins we could not know Him truly, i.e. in His mercy (cf. Ezr. ix. 13).

b. The degree and quality of God's mercy (11–18)

The vast difference between heaven and earth is often used to illustrate the divine quality of mercy (cf. Ps. lvii. 10, xxxvi. 5). His compassion to men is as a parent's to a child (13; cf. Mi. vii. 18; Ps. lxxviii. 38ff.); He knows how we are formed (*our frame*) out of *dust* (14). Mortal man is like a tuft of grass (cf. Pss. xxxvii. 2, 20, RV, XC. 5, 6; Is. xl. 6–8) or a fragile flower (cf. Jb. xiv. 2); no sooner is it mature than it begins to fade and cannot be renewed. The mercy of the Lord is entirely different; it is ageless, ever fresh, and always extended to those who keep His words and carry out His commands.

c. A call to universal praise (19–22)

The Lord is not only good, faithful, compassionate and unchanging, He is also King of the universe. He is worthy of the adoration of all creatures, for all are His subjects. The call to praise Him is addressed to the higher orders of *angels* (cf. Ps. cxlviii. 2), who are 'mighty in strength' (20, RV; cf. Ps. xxix. 1; Joel iii. 11) and intent upon the carrying out of His every word; to *all ye his hosts* (21), either the multitude of angels (cf. 1 Ki. xxii. 19; Ps. xxiv. 10; Dn. vii. 10), or perhaps stars and winds, i.e. the forces of nature (cf. Pss. civ. 4, cxlviii. 3); to *all his works* (22), i.e. all creatures, men and things everywhere (cf. Ps. cxlviii. 6–12). Finally, *Bless the Lord, O my soul*. Amidst the praises of creation, let my voice also sing His praise!

PSALM CIV. IN PRAISE OF THE GOD OF ALL CREATION

This is one of the Scripture's outstanding descriptions of the glory of the natural world; it ranks with Jb. xxxviii and xxxix. See also Pss. viii and xxix; Hab. iii. The Psalm may be regarded as a poetical commentary upon the first chapter of Genesis. There are three parts.

a. Description (1–23)

This survey of the external realm of life covers five aspects, viz. the majesty and power of the Lord God (1–4); the creation of the major terrestrial features of sea and land (5–9); the inauguration of a comprehensive water-supply for the maintenance of life (10–13); the provision of food (especially for man) and of the natural means for secure habitation for men and beasts (14–18); finally, the institution of the daily and seasonal rhythm of life and work (19–23). Note the range of thought, from the immensity and versatility of the Lord (1ff.) to the tiring routine of a day in a man's life (23); from the vast labour and purpose of the earth's creation (5ff.) to the effortless song of a bird on a tree top (12). Similarly the thirst of wild asses (11) is matched by the hunger of young lions (21); the awesome expanse of the deep waters which clothe much of the earth (6ff.) is contrasted with the restful greenery of meadows and olive groves (14ff.); the timid and elusive goats of the high hills (18) are as well known as the beasts of the forest which creep stealthily in the shadows of evening (20).

Three principles lie behind the description. First there is the principle of wholeness or completion. For example, the earth is satisfied with the fruit of God's works in the same sense as the trees which the Lord has planted in Lebanon are full grown. The quenching of a creature's thirst (11), the enjoyment of food and drink by a healthy man (15), the sense of security possessed by conies amid the rocks (18), storks in the fir trees (17), and lions in their lairs (21), all are echoes of the divine wholeness expressed in the concept of the Lord clothed *with light as with a garment* (2), even as the deep waters once covered the whole earth. This latter thought (6–9) may include an allusion to the flood (cf. 2 Pet. iii. 5f.), as well as to Gn. i. 2. But since creation is often regarded as a cloak which both reveals the invisible Lord, and yet conceals some of His glory (cf. Rom. i. 20), so also the waters receding from the mountains may be regarded as figurative for the irreversible process of birth whereby new existences are brought to light (cf. Jn. iii. 4–9).

Secondly there is the principle of activity and sending forth. For example, the Lord is continually stretching out the heavens (until these are rolled up, Ps. cii. 26) (2), walking on the winds (3; cf. Ps. xviii. 10), and sending forth His angels as widely as the winds and as swiftly as *flaming fire* (4). He speaks His rebuke and the waters flee (7); He sends out springs so that streams run over the earth (10). The growing grass and agile beasts (14, 18), the nightly roving of animals (20) and the daily going out and coming in of labouring men (23), all reflect this principle of life, its movement, energy and rhythm.

The third principle is that man's life is knit together with that of other creatures and yet superior thereto. If the sea is placed in bounds it is for his welfare, but sunset and sunrise shape the period of his daily toil. If the soil brings forth herbage and food so that his heart may be cheered (cf. Jdg. xix. 5) and sustained, yet it is only through his service or labour in cultivation (Gn. iii. 19).

b. Meditation (24–30)

The psalmist turns from the realm of natural phenomena to that of philosophy. He exclaims first at the multiplicity and variety of God's works, then at the magnitude and richness of the divine wisdom that brought into being these creatures (called *thy riches* in verse 24) which crowd the earth.

He is particularly impressed by the greatness of the sea. (For *So is* (25) read with RV 'Yonder is'; i.e. he is viewing it from the mountains of Judaea and the Lebanon.) It extends so far and contains so much that moves; in it are countless living creatures, on it move ships and animals, all enhancing the sense of wonder we should have toward God's works. *Leviathan* (26). Perhaps 'dolphins' or possibly 'whales'.

All creatures are dependent on God for food, for their well-being, for their experiences of distress (29; cf. Ps. xxx. 7), for the duration of their lives (cf. Jb. xii. 9, 10, xxxiv. 14, 15) and for the renewal of their kind in the following generation. All have been created by the Spirit of God who continuously renews earth's natural life from year to year.

c. Adoration (31–35)

Finally the psalmist turns to the realm of spiritual experience. His environment (1–23) and his evaluation of it (24–30) are incomplete in themselves. He is not merely a creature, or a thinker, but one who can sing praise to the Lord his God (33), who finds such meditation to be acceptable (34a). So marvellous are His works in creation that their expression of God's glory ought to endure for ever (31; RV 'Let the glory . . . endure'), especially as God Himself has found them good and satisfying (Gn. i. 31). Yet, however glorious and wonderful, this realm of creation is not divine, nor has it any quality of self-existence or immutability. It is absolutely and constantly dependent upon the goodwill of Him who hateth iniquity. Should He frown, then the earth quakes; should He come hither, the most substantial monuments of His work might vanish in smoke (cf. Jb. xxvi. 7–14). Let sinners therefore be removed so that nothing displeases the Lord who is worthy of all homage and worship. The final word 'Hallelujah' has not previously occurred in the Psalter: it is the opening word of Pss. cvi, cxi, cxii, cxiii, cxvii, cxxxv, cxlvi–cl.

PSALM CV. PRAISE TO GOD FOR THE FULFILMENT OF HIS PROMISE

This is the second of four great songs of Israel's history (cf. also Pss. lxxviii, cvi, cxxxvi). It deals with Yahweh's covenant with Abraham concerning the land of Canaan and rehearses the events which led to its occupation by the children of Jacob. The emphasis throughout this survey is upon the mercy and faithfulness of the Lord as declared in *all his wondrous works* (2; cf. verse 5). Note the constant repetition of 'he' (e.g. 'he remembered', 'he made', 'he said', 'he suffered none', 'he called', etc.). The pronouns 'he' and 'his' referring to the Lord occur more than forty times in verses 5–45 (see RV).

This detailed rehearsal 'of what he hath done', especially in the deliverance from Egypt, concludes with a very generalized and brief statement about the invasion and possession of the Promised Land; but it should not be inferred from this that the Psalm dates from the early years of the settlement. It is obviously a companion Psalm to cvi, which interprets Israelite history from another viewpoint and for a much longer period, i.e. down to the early post-exilic years. In this poem the psalmist was solely concerned with the process whereby Israel grew from a weak and captive community into a people whom no nation could withstand in power, or excel in joyfulness, or match in righteous principles of life. In other words, the psalmist was pointing the exiles who had returned from Babylon to a precedent which was radiant with hope for themselves. Note that the first fifteen verses are also found in the anthem associated with the bringing of the ark to Jerusalem (1 Ch. xvi. 8–22).

a. The call to worship (1–4)

Call upon (1); the Hebrew word is used here, as often, in the sense of 'publicly proclaim' (cf. Ex. xxxiii. 19); i.e. set forth among all nations the facts about God's acts of remembrance and deliverance, with song and melody. *Sing psalms* (2); the Hebrew word may also mean 'make melody'. In verses 3 and 4 the thought turns from witness to worship. *Glory ye* (3); i.e. 'make your boasting' (cf. Ps. cvi. 5; Phil. iii. 3, RV).

b. God's covenant with the patriarchs (5–15)

Remember (5); cf. Dt. xxxii. 7; Ps. lxxviii. 7 and 42. The *works, wonders* and *judgments* (5) refer to the divine intervention in the plagues, exodus and the Red Sea calamity. *He is the Lord our God* (7). In a special sense He was Israel's God although in another sense He ruled over the whole earth. The strength of the exhortation to *remember* (5) lies in the action of God Himself: *He hath remembered his covenant for ever* (8). This He does because He abides faithful; His word is *commanded* ('established') without limit (cf. Dt. vii. 9). The supreme example of this is His covenant with Abraham (cf. Gn. xiii. 15, xv. 18: note Hg. ii. 5 for the expression 'a covenanted word'), which agreement by oath was also reaffirmed to Isaac and Israel (9; cf. Gn. xxviii. 13ff.). *The lot of your inheritance* (11). Lit. 'cord', hence a measuring line, and hence a share, a portion measured out. Evidence of the Lord's continual remembrance is seen in His ceaseless vigilance on behalf of the patriarchs, as they moved about between Egypt and Syria, when they were *very few* (12) and had no abiding place. *Kings* (14); cf. Gn. xii. 17, xxi. 25. *Mine anointed* (15); in the sense of 'set apart' (cf. Is. lxi. 1). Anointing with oil was a later custom associated with the ordinances of the tabernacle. *My prophets* (15); see Gn. xx. 7 and note Jacob's prediction in Gn. xlviii. 19.

c. Joseph and the settlement in Egypt (16–24)

Note that it was God who *called for a famine* (16) which led to Joseph's power and Israel's presence in Egypt. *Laid in iron* (18). See RV. Joseph was bound *until . . . his word came* (to pass) (19); i.e. either Joseph's word to his family (cf. Gn. xxxvii. 10), or more probably God's word spoken to Joseph in his early dreams about his pre-eminence. It was the knowledge of this utterance of God which was so powerful a factor in Joseph's time of testing and waiting. For the details in verses 20–22 see Gn. xli. Jacob's coming down to *the land of Ham* (23; cf. Ps. lxxviii. 51) was a notable point in the history of the chosen people (cf. Acts vii. 14, 15). Verse 24 is based on Ex. i. 7, but the psalmist emphasizes again that it was God (*He*) who brought these things to pass.

d. Moses and their deliverance from Egypt (25–38)

The supreme power and purpose of the Lord was shown not only in these things (16–24) but in that *He turned their heart* (25; i.e. of the Egyptians) to hate His people. This was not initiated by the Lord, but it occurred and was allowed within the major framework of His design for all men through Israel. The Egyptians' hatred was the natural response of envy and jealousy toward a privileged people. Their subtle or crafty dealing with the Israelites (25b; see Ex. i. 10) was evident in their plan to impoverish them by adult servitude and infant slaughter.

Moses and Aaron set forth among the Egyptians 'the words or facts of His signs' (the literal rendering of verse 27); i.e. they proclaimed the demands and warnings of God before and after each plague. The LXX, however, reads 'he' instead of 'they', and many accept this (cf. Ps. lxxviii. 43, RV). The sequence of the plagues as given in verses 28–36 differs from that in the book of Exodus because the psalmist was primarily concerned with showing the effectual working of God's will. He therefore skips over the first eight plagues and speaks immediately of that which caused the Egyptians to assent to Yahweh's claims (Ex. x. 24); note that the darkness was sent by the Lord even as Joseph (17) and Moses (26) had been. It may be remarked that the Book of Wisdom describes the plague of darkness more vividly and extensively than any of the other afflictions (Wisdom xvii). The psalmist now recapitulates the previous plagues but omits the fifth and sixth and puts the fourth (flies) before the third (lice). If there was any purpose in the choice and sequence that is given here it was probably to show the power of Yahweh operating in the whole realm of human existence. It was not so much that the order of nature was perverted, but that the withdrawal of the divine order was shown to be chaotic and ruinous, an echo in the physical world of the horror and rottenness of ungodliness. The six plagues inserted between darkness (28) and death (36) are grouped around three ideas: without God life turns corrupt on its own thresholds. First, the natural sources of life, water and blood, are not effective in themselves: the life-giving Nile brought death. Moreover the forms of social life, suggested by government chambers (30), become infested with the repulsive and grotesque. Secondly, the very stuff of human life is essentially trivial as the dust of the earth and short-lived as an insect: mere profusion cannot offset the vanity of it (cf. Jb. xiii. 28—xiv. 2). The physical realm emphasized this when hail drowned the hum of insect life and the flicker of lightning replaced the drifting swarms of gnats. Thirdly, the basic expression of human life centres around food production, but the original curse was doubled when a flaming sword (as of Eden) burnt the vines and figtrees and the creeping locusts (like the serpent) robbed man of his expected harvest. These aspects of physical dearth serve to introduce the final theme of death in verse 36 .

The immunity of the Israelites from these calamities is implied in their ability to leave Egypt without fatigue. *Not one feeble person among their tribes* (37); i.e. 'none that stumbled' (RV mg.).

e. God's care for the people (39–41)

This is a brief résumé of the years in the wilderness. The three miracles (cf. Ex. xiii. 21, xvi. 4–15, xvii. 6) are obviously chosen to offset the three main groups of plagues. The *cloud for a covering; and fire* . . . (39) protected and inspired Israel, even as the cloud of locusts and the flaming fire (32–34) damaged and discouraged Egypt. The quails and manna (40) were positive means of life, whereas the flies and lice (31) were emblems of frustration. The water gushing from the rock to form a river flowing in a dry place was a metaphorical Nile (cf. 1 Cor. x. 4; Jn. vii. 39).

f. The cause of this wondrous work (42–45)

The psalmist concludes with an echo of the spirit of worship in the opening verses, but blends with this a rich experience. The Lord has faithfully remembered His covenant. He has delivered Israel with singing (43, RV; cf. Ex. xv; but possibly there is here an allusion to Is. li. 11); He has installed them in a land already cultivated (cf. Jos. xxiv. 13). These things He has done solely in order that they might serve Him and keep His law (cf. Dt. iv. 40). Past blessings constitute an inescapable obligation upon those who have shared in them (cf. 2 Cor. vii. 1; Tit. ii. 14; Heb. iv. 6–11).

PSALM CVI. A SAGA OF SINS AND SALVATION

See also the Introductory Notes to Ps. cv

There is a resemblance to Ps. lxxviii in that this Psalm also describes the history of Israel after the exodus as a series of alternations between the goodness and power of Yahweh and the infidelity and weakness of the chosen people. National hymns which deal with national sins are exceptional, and the composition and preservation of these two Psalms can be attributed only to an unquenchable hope and an irrepressible faith in the covenanting God. The last two verses of the Psalm are repeated at the end of the anthem attributed to David when the ark was returned to Jerusalem (see 1 Ch. xvi. 35, 36). Of these verse 48 is an addition, for it is the doxology which marks the close of the fourth book of the Psalter. Cf. the final verses of Pss. xli, lxxii, and lxxxix.

a. Introduction (1–6)

The body of the poem (verses 7–46) contains four major movements. These are historical in character but they are not handled in strictly chronological order; the psalmist's main aim was to portray the process of spiritual degeneration in a privileged community. The incidents are grouped into the sequence: the exodus from Egypt (7–12); episodes in the wilderness wanderings (13–23); the defaults when twice they approached Canaan (24–31); and the corruption which followed their settlement (32–46). This section includes an echo of earlier obstinacy (32, 33) and an allusion to later instability (43). The introductory words of praise and prayer are expressive of the psalmist's point of view—delighting in God, declaring His works, doing His will, desiring His blessing both for himself and for the nation. The confession of sin in verse 6 summarizes and introduces the chronicle of failure which follows.

b. The exodus from Egypt (7–12)

Understood not (7); i.e. paid no heed to. *Provoked* (7); RV 'were rebellious'. But the emphasis is upon the divine action rather than upon the Israelites' sin. Although they were so stupid and provoking *nevertheless he saved them* (8), and this evoked in them a genuine response of trust and praise (12).

c. In the wilderness (13–23)

They soon forgat; they waited not; but lusted exceedingly (13, 14). Three instances are given of craving for things which would give immediate and personal pleasure. These were signs of so serious a moral degeneration that the Lord threatened to destroy them completely; but Moses interceded for them (23). The desperate craving for meat at Kibroth-hattaavah (14, 15) was a notable crisis in their journeyings. See Nu. xi. 4–34; Ps. lxxviii. 18–20, 25–31. The rebellion against Moses and Aaron (16–18) arose out of a claim of equality of holiness amongst all the congregation. See Nu. xvi. Note the writer's omission of Korah, perhaps out of respect for the Korahite priests and psalmists. The making of the bull calf (19, 20) was particularly offensive to the Lord because it was done at His holy mount of *Horeb* (see Dt. ix. 8) and because the Israelites ascribed to this image the wondrous works of the Lord (see Ex. xxxii. 4). Note the persistence of this heresy (1 Ki. xii. 28b). *Changed their glory* (20); i.e. chose another Lord (cf. Dt. x. 21; note Rom. i. 23). *Moses . . . stood . . . in the breach* (23). See Dt. ix. 18ff.

d. Further rebellion (24–31)

This third section of the main part of the Psalm links together the two blunders of the people when they were within sight of the promised land. On the first occasion, at Kadesh-barnea, *they despised the pleasant land, they believed not* ('hearkened not to') *his word* (24; cf. Nu. xiii. 32, xiv. 41). Some years later, when encamped by Jordan at Shittim (Jos. ii. 1; Nu. xxv. 1ff.), *they*

joined themselves also unto Baal-peor (28) and corrupted themselves with licentious idolatry. This was a serious default from the obligations of the covenant; for it arose not from their inexperienced bewilderment (7) or their concern for their welfare (15–20), but from an inward rottenness, the recurrent malady of unbelief. Hence the plague which was stayed only by the action of Phinehas.

e. Corruption in the Promised Land (32–46)

These verses describe how the people 'mingled themselves with the nations, and learned their works' (35, RV). This was a deliberate breaking of the covenant with Yahweh (see Ex. xx) and swiftly led to horrible idolatrous practices (36–39; cf. Lv. xx. 2–5; 1 Ki. xi. 7; 2 Ki. xvi. 3; Ezk. xvi. 20ff., xx. 23–30). In consequence of this *the wrath of the Lord* was aroused (40) and the people were oppressed, humiliated and eventually, when many opportunities for repentance had shown them to be intractable, He had exiled them from His land—but not without a continuance of His pity (41–46; cf. 1 Ki. viii. 46–53).

f. A concluding prayer (47)

The prayer, addressed to 'Yahweh our God', is based upon God's covenant relationship and arises out of the recollection of His unchanging loving-kindness (44–46). In some measure its four phrases are related to the preceding errors. *Save us* (cf. verses 41, 42), *gather us* (cf. verse 35), *to give thanks* (contrast verses 25 and 32), and *to triumph in thy praise* (cf. verse 12 and contrast 23a, 26).

BOOK FIVE. PSALMS cvii–cl

PSALM CVII. THE SONG OF THE REDEEMED

The fifth and final book within the Psalter opens with a poem belonging to the retrospective or historical group of which the previous Psalm also was an excellent example. The outstanding historical Psalms are lxxviii, cv, cvi, cvii, cxxxv and cxxxvi. See also parts of Pss. xliv, lxviii, lxxiv, lxxvii, lxxx, lxxxi, lxxxiii, lxxxix, xcv–c, cxiv. All these (with the exception of Pss. lxxxiii and lxxxix) look back to Israel's deliverance from Egypt.

Ps. cvii belongs to the early post-exilic period. This is implied by verses 2 and 3, especially as the phrase *the redeemed of the Lord* seems to be a quotation from Isaiah (e.g. lxii. 12). Moreover these introductory verses are obviously related to the prayer in Ps. cvi. 47; i.e. that prayer had been answered. The people have been saved from, and gathered out of, the nations; so they can now give thanks unto His holy name.

Verses 4–32 consist of a series of four pictures differing in scene, but similar in pattern. This

section can therefore be divided as follows: verses 4–9; verses 10–16; verses 17–21; and verses 22–32. Each of these stanzas opens with a description of a former period of human peril, followed in each case by a devotional account of an amazing deliverance by the Lord who guided them through the wilderness (7), released them from prison (14), healed their diseases (20) and brought them safely to the end of their voyage (30). Note the double refrain common to all the sections (verses 6, 13, 19, 28 and verses 8, 15, 21, 31) and the way in which each stanza concludes with a reasoned exhortation to 'praise the Lord'.

These four compositions incorporating life's tragedy and triumph as they picture the movement of a pilgrimage, the stagnation of a prison, the soul sickness that heralds death and the stormy sea that threatens drowning, have an elemental quality that is enduring. Some would see therein references to the experiences of the patriarchs, to Abraham's wanderings (4; cf. Acts vii. 5), to Isaac's bondage and blindness (10; see Gn. xxii. 9, xxvii. 1), to Jacob's grief

(18; cf. Gn. xxxvii. 34ff.), and to Joseph's journey to and vicissitudes in Egypt (23; cf. Gn. xl. 15, xlv. 7). Some would regard all four as representations of the exile. Others discern in the acts of the Lord (verses 7, 14, 20, 29, 30) an archetypal imprint of the way, the light, the word of life, and the peace of His presence whereof the fourth Gospel would have more to say. The adaptability of these four concepts to New Testament story and teaching cannot be overlooked. Indeed the psalmist has chosen four 'figures of the true' which reappear over and over again in the manifold facets of the long history of the people of God and the personal experiences of His children.

The fifth stanza (verses 33–43) stands apart. Its structure is quite different from that of the four pictures which have just been given, and its theme is not man's need but divine sovereignty. Note the repetition of the pronoun 'he'. Although there appears to be a return to the scenery of verses 4–9, the psalmist is really dealing with the phenomena of the exile. But he uses the word-image of the exodus because it was indelible and could not be hidden.

Note that in this last portion of the Psalm the activity of God is described in the four realms of nature, history, sorrow and surprise. But there is no precise reflection of the four previous pictures of the wilderness, a prison, disease and the sea. First there is the curse upon fruitful ground (33, 34); then there is a physical restoration (35–38). This is followed by confusion and grief (39, 40), and finally there is spiritual restoration, either typically as in Pss. xl and lxxi, or nationally as in Is. lxv. 9, 10. It is not clear whether any time-sequence must be rigidly assumed here. It would appear that the psalmist perceived in the exile and return a recapitulation of the nation's history, a blending of the fundamental motifs in the ways of God with men.

The final verse is an apostrophe of wisdom akin to the more lengthy exhortation which in Ps. lxxviii is placed at the beginning of the poem. It arises directly from the psalmist's attempt to interpret the purpose of God within the sphere of history. His own understanding of *the lovingkindness of the Lord* is expressed of course in the Psalm's opening sentences.

This Psalm is more comprehensive than Ps. lxviii and crowds the world scene of verse 3 with the most varied of lives: city dwellers and wanderers, prisoners and seamen, civic elders and herdsmen, princes and exiles. There is another difference too: the four scenes are plainly to be related to the nation's former experiences, but these stanzas are not ordinary memories. They may represent the aimless wanderings in the wilderness, the siege of Jerusalem by Sennacherib, the period of confusion and trembling described in the book of Jeremiah, or the Babylonian captivity. But the psalmist distilled from these experiences their essential elements and transformed them into symbols of much wider applicability. The children of Israel never sought a *city* through the wastes which lay between Egypt and the dawn (the concept of Zion as the city of God was Davidic rather than Mosaic in origin; cf. Heb. xi. 10, xii. 22); they were never actually immured in dungeons barred with iron, their bondage being that of the spirit (cf. Is. xlii. 7, xlv. 2; Jn. viii. 32); they had not been distressed in body as Job, but they had known despair in the sickness of a corrupt society (cf. Am. ii. 4–12; 2 Cor. iv. 8–18). Moreover, Judaeans were never sea-faring folk, although Jonah was certainly representative of a people commissioned to proclaim the message of the Lord but determined to pursue their own way, only to be engulfed in the sea of nations (cf. Ps. xlvi; Is. xvii. 12), miraculously preserved in captivity, and eventually cast back into the land of their destiny in a bewildered mood of penitence. Symbolical meanings can underlie actual events; the truth of God is greater than any colour it may give to individual experiences.

PSALM CVIII. ANTHEM OF VICTORY

This Psalm is composed of two earlier fragments, viz. Pss. lvii. 7–11 and lx. 5–12; hence the title 'A Psalm of David'. Evidently they were joined together for use in temple worship, presumably after the return from captivity. Both the original Psalms were associated with depressing experiences in the life of David, but whoever compiled this Psalm selected only those portions which expressed hope and confidence and faith in the Lord. There are sundry slight variations in the text but none of any significance: the reference to Edom in verses 9 and 10 was apposite in view of the Edomite aid to Nebuchadnezzar (cf. Ob. 8–12). For further details consult the notes on the original Psalms.

PSALM CIX. CURSING AND BLESSING

Two earlier Psalms (xxxv, lxix) have been outstanding in their treatment of the great theme of 'the suffering of righteous men' (cf. also Pss. xxii and xl), but Ps. cix is more outspoken than either. The title ascribes the poem to David and nothing is known of any powerful and unjust antagonist to him apart from Saul and Doeg.

The three major sections are a plea for divine help because of a wholly false and unjustified attack upon the psalmist (verses 1–5), a comprehensive curse invoked upon one man who has clothed himself with cursing (verses 6–20), and a prayer for divine protection and for judgment upon adversaries (verses 21–31). The discrepancy of attitude, theme and personal pronouns between the second portion and the rest of the Psalm has long constituted a problem (note Jas. iii. 9–12). Such vehement imprecations as are rehearsed in this section are not easily assigned to one who trusted in the Lord (21–31) and sought His blessing above all else (26 and 28).

There are two approaches to the difficulty. In view of the plain distinction that verses 6–19 speak only of *him*, *his* and *he*, whereas the Psalm elsewhere speaks of *they* and *them* who are opposed to *I* and *me*—it may be assumed that this passage is a quotation of curses directed against, not spoken by, a man of God, i.e. against the one who prays (7b). This view would remove the moral difficulty which is created by the presence of such malevolent words on the lips of a righteous man. Furthermore, this seems to be implied by the Psalm. Verses 1–3 declare that *they* have opened the deceitful mouths of wicked men (cf. 1 Ki. xxi. 8–10), spoken with lying tongues, and encompassed the psalmist with words of spite and hate. In short, as in Ps. xxxv, he has been subjected to an extensive campaign of evil, slander and calumny designed to injure and ruin him (20), and zealously pursued because of his weakness (22–25; cf. Pss. xxxviii. 2–14, 20, xli. 5–8). Yet there has been no just occasion for this attack (3b). The psalmist has given love and received hatred; he has encountered evil in return for good (5). Nor is there anything in the poem to suggest a sudden reversal of this righteous attitude, especially as, in seeking the strength and poise which comes through prayer (4b), the psalmist declares *Let them curse, but bless thou* (28).

Against this view there are three objections. First, let it be said that there exists a righteous indignation against evil (cf. Mt. xxiii. 13ff.) which is an echo of divine wrath. Secondly, the imprecatory words in verses 6–19 are in part a prayer that the Lord should remember His own word (Ex. xx. 5b) and visit the iniquities of the parents upon their children (14, 15). In part, also, they are an appeal, so often heard in the Psalter, to the universal law of retribution, i.e. the unveiling of reality (see verses 17–19 and cf. Gal. vi. 7). These motives scarcely fit an evil, lying and malicious enemy of the Lord's anointed. There is, in fact, no essential difference between verses 19 and 29; both expectations are attached to the working of the Lord as the following phrases imply. And since the latter is certainly David's prayer can the former be his enemy's?

A third objection to the other interpretation is that when Peter in Acts i. 20 quotes from the two chief imprecatory Psalms, he not only includes Pss. lxix and cix within the authorship of David, but attributes the two 'curses' he selects to the inspiration of the Holy Spirit, and asserts that they were prophetically uttered 'concerning Judas' (Acts i. 16). Peter obviously identifies the psalmist with Jesus and sees in Judas the enemy who has returned hatred for love. It is inevitable, therefore, that he should fall into condemnation, and verses 6–19 point to that. Nor should it be overlooked that it may be 'a righteous thing with God to recompense affliction to them that afflict you' (2 Thes. i. 6, RV; cf. also Jude 15).

a. A plea for God's help (1–5)

Hold not thy peace (1); i.e. 'be not silent' (cf. Ps. xxviii. 1). *God of my praise* (1); i.e. He whom I am accustomed to praise. *Compassed me about* (3; cf. Ho. xi. 12), i.e. whenever opportunity arose. *For my love they are my adversaries* (4); i.e. in return for my benevolence they accuse me (note verses 6, 20, 29), 'but I am always praying for them' (cf. Ps. xxxv. 12, 13).

b. An anathema upon the adversary (6–20)

Set thou . . . (6); i.e. let a wicked and unscrupulous man be placed in authority over him who is my enemy. *Satan* (6); lit. 'an adversary' (cf. 1 Sa. xxix. 4, 2 Sa. xix. 22), one who hinders, contends and prosecutes; contrast verse 31. Here, however, a human accuser is spoken of; see verses 20, 29. The psalmist had been falsely and publicly accused (2), so he desires his opponent to be tried and to come forth condemned. *Let his prayer become sin* (7); i.e. as the accused would plead for leniency from his judge, or even cry to God for vindication, so the verdict of guilty would emphasize his true nature (cf. Pr. xxviii. 9; Is. i. 15). *His office* (8) was evidently an important one; verses 16–19 suggest a position of authority, power and dignity akin to Job's (Jb. xxix. 11–17). The effects of this man's ruin are traced first in his family (9, 10), then in his prosperity (11), his reputation (12) and his descendants (13), even to the extinction of the family name (13–15). *The extortioner* (11); i.e. the creditor who claims the payment, but takes advantage of the situation to distrain on all he can involve. *The strangers* (11); i.e. foreigners who seize the produce of his toil. Verses 16–18 show the reason for this severity. There are no prayers in this section, only descriptions (see RV). His primary sin was complete absence of mercy even toward the most abject and needy (16; cf. Mt. xviii. 32ff.). This has become increasingly part of his nature; he loved cursing, he constantly clad himself in it as the habit of his mind, he took it into himself as water and oil until at last it was the very marrow of his bones (17, 18). *Let it be unto him* (19); i.e. let his cursings not reach others but cling to himself as his raiment and girdle.

c. A prayer for divine protection (21–31)

The foregoing anathema describes what God would do to the wicked if *they* (2–5) reaped what they had sown. But the psalmist pleads for his own treatment on another basis. *Do thou for me, O God* (Heb. *Yahweh*) *the Lord*, not as I deserve but *for thy name's sake* (21). This is necessary because in himself is no health or strength of heart; he is like a shadow that is rapidly lengthening (cf. Ps. cii. 11); like a locust driven helplessly in a wind (22, 23). His body has become feeble through loss of appetite (cf. Ps. cii. 4, xxxviii. 6ff.); and when he should be viewed with pity he is regarded only with *reproach*, or scorn (24, 25; cf. Ps. xxii. 7; Mt. xxvii. 39). Verse 26 introduces the final prayer for divine help. This is uttered in full confidence (as in Pss. xxii. 22ff., xxxv. 27ff., lxix. 30ff.) because, unlike his opponent (16), his Lord is characterized by mercy. *That they may know that this is thy hand* (27). This prayer seeks first the honour of God's name. Even though they contrive to curse, nevertheless Thou dost bless (28; cf. Mt. v. 44f.). When they stand up to act or speak against me, i.e. behave as *mine adversaries* (29; cf. verse 4, where, as here, the Hebrew word is *Satan*), they shall be put to shame in a way that shall be as apparent to all as is their *mantle* or outer garment (29; cf. Ps. xxxv. 26). The psalmist anticipates his action of public praise to the Lord because, unlike the circumstances of verses 1, 2, where the adversaries prosecuted him, the Lord is at his right hand as an advocate to protect him and deliver him from his antagonists. *Condemn his soul* (31); i.e. pronounce him guilty of death.

PSALM CX. KING AND PRIEST FOR EVER

The Davidic authorship and divine inspiration of this Psalm are maintained in the New Testament, where it is more often quoted than any other. It bore a messianic meaning in the time of the gospel (e.g. Mt. xxii. 43–45; Mk. xii. 36; Lk. xx. 42) and afterwards was given a Christological interpretation. See Acts ii. 34, 35; 1 Cor. xv. 25; Heb. i. 13, v. 6, vii. 17, 21, x. 12, 13. The exaltation of Christ to 'sit at the right hand of God' is frequently referred to elsewhere (e.g. Mt. xxvi. 64; Heb. i. 3, viii. 1, xii. 2; 1 Pet. iii. 22).

This brief poem obviously consists of two parts, each comprising a short explicit utterance of Yahweh (1, 4) which is expanded in a manner both surprising and enigmatical: surprising because the enthronement (1) is associated with an iron rule centred upon Zion (2), and because the priesthood (4) is linked with Melchizedek and not Aaron (5); enigmatical because the king's army (3) is described in terms of ecclesiastical beauty, whereas the priest's ministry involves widespread fatalities and martial conflict.

a. The King (1–3)

i. The source of His authority (1). 'The Lord saith' (RV). This is the only occurrence of this phrase in the Psalter, although it is often used in the writings of the prophets. It is a very forceful expression, suggesting 'the oracle of Yahweh', a solemn and authoritative word. *Unto my Lord;* Heb. *'Adonai,* generally an equivalent of *Yahweh* (e.g. Ps. lxviii. 19), but used also as a title of respect (e.g. Gn. xxiii. 6). *Sit thou at my right hand.* Even among men, this is a place of preference, privilege and power. It is not to be understood here literally of the heavenly session; but signifies rather exaltation to highest honour and sharing the divine rule. There was a certain historical basis for this both in David's own case, for his authority was exercised in the name of the Lord (see 2 Sa. viii. 14b, iii. 18, v. 2), and in David's elevation of Solomon to the place of his own sovereignty (cf. 1 Ch. xxviii. 5, xxix. 23). But the peculiar force of the introductory phrase

transcends both of these (cf. Mt. xxii. 43–45, etc.; also Lk. i. 32). *Until* (i.e. up to the time when) . . . *footstool;* a metaphor of complete power over an enemy (cf. Jos. x. 24; 1 Ki. v. 3).

ii. The character of His army (2, 3). 'The Lord (*Yahweh*) shall stretch forth (RV mg.; cf. Ex. xiv. 16) the rod of thy strength' (RV); i.e. 'the emblem of thy dominion'. *Rule thou* may be a further declaration by Yahweh as in verse 1; or it may be a spontaneous exclamation of the enthused psalmist who goes on to say that the king's subjects eagerly offer themselves for military service *in the day of thy power* (3); lit. 'thy army' (RV mg.), i.e. when the army is mustered for battle (cf. Jdg. v. 2–9). It is at this point that the concept of a priesthood is introduced, for these volunteers will be clad *in the beauties of holiness,* i.e. in garments of beauty and holiness (cf. Ex. xxviii. 2; Pss. xxix. 2, xcvi. 9). Those who offer themselves in the service of their king are young men (*thy youth* is equivalent to *thy people*), who are as fresh as the early morning and as widely, silently and surprisingly at hand as the dew at dawn (cf. 2 Sa. xvii. 12).

b. The Priest (4–7)

i. The irrevocable oath of His office (4). *The Lord* (*Yahweh*) *hath sworn,* i.e. unchangeably decreed, that he who sitteth at His right hand is priest as well as king. He is not of the Aaronic order (cf. Heb. vii. 13, 14), but altogether different. He is *after the order of Melchizedek* who in the tapestry of Genesis, appears without any previous mention of his family, and is left performing an endless act (Heb. vii. 1–3). This priesthood (as in this Psalm) is quite nonlevitical, because it is established by a divine oath, not by human act (Ex. xxviii. 1, xxix. 1ff.; cf. Heb. vii. 20, 21), it is indissoluble and cannot be altered (Heb. vii. 16), and it is inviolable and cannot be replaced as was Aaron's (Heb. vii. 24). In other words it is *for ever.*

ii. The irresistible operation of His sovereignty (5–7). *The Lord* (5). The word *'Adonai* and the reference to his position at the right hand of *Yahweh* (see verse 1) refer this and the following sentence to the subject 'thou' in all the previous verses. Hence, although as king he ruled by the authority of *Yahweh* (2), yet as priest he acts in his own power (5). He will *strike through* (shatter) *kings in the day of his wrath* (5; cf. Ps. lxxxix. 13–18; also Pss. ii. 10, 12, lxviii. 12, 14, 18; Rev. vi. 15); he will pass sentence upon antagonistic nations (cf. 1 Sa. ii. 10) and strew the place of conflict with corpses (6). Moreover he will shatter or crush the head (*wound,* i.e. 'wound severely') of the opposing forces (cf. Ps. lxviii. 21) that have been based upon an extensive territory (6, RV mg.), and in the pursuit of them the conqueror will refresh himself at a wayside stream (cf. the incident in David's life at the brook Besor, 1 Sa. xxx. 9, 10) and ultimately carry himself with triumph. *Lift up the head* (7); i.e. in consciousness of victory (cf. Ps. xxvii. 6; Col. ii. 15). It should be noted how inseparable the concepts of king and priest are not only here, but in such passages as Gn. xiv. 18; Is. liii. 12; Heb. x. 12, 13; Rev. i. 5, 6.

PSALM CXI. THE WORK OF THE LORD

This and the following Psalm are a pair: both consist of ten verses and each poem contains twenty-two phrases which are arranged as an acrostic, the phrases successively commencing with the letters of the Hebrew alphabet. Moreover, in their original form, almost every phrase consists of just three Hebrew words, and in both poems the last two verses contain three phrases and not two as is the case in the other verses. The two Psalms deal with twin themes. Ps. cxi is in praise of the Lord; Ps. cxii is a panegyric of the godly man. These characteristics point to a post-exilic origin (cf. Ps. cxix) and there can be little doubt that they are intended as a preface to the following group of liturgical Psalms (cxiii–cxviii), known as the 'Egyptian Hallel' (see Introduction to Pss. cxiii–cxviii), even as Ps. cxix may be regarded as a prologue to the pilgrims' 'Songs of Ascents' (Pss. cxx–cxxxiv).

The first word, 'Hallelujah', may be a rubric calling the congregation to join in the chanting of the Psalm. The assembly . . . the congregation (1). The first term refers to the inner council of the faithful, and is possibly a metaphor for private devotions (cf. Ps. xxv. 14a); the latter denotes corporate worship. The works of the Lord (2) are His acts of providence and mercy to all men (3–8), but especially to His people Israel (9, 10) which are sought out with delight by men who seek to gain understanding. His work (3), i.e. His activity toward men, shows Him as clothed with glory and honour (cf. Ps. civ. 1) and always doing righteousness. Verse 4 runs literally 'He hath made a memorial for his wonderful works'; e.g. the Passover has been instituted as a perpetual remembrance of His marvellous acts whereby Israel was brought out of Egypt (Ex. xii. 14). He hath given meat (5), i.e. 'food', probably referring to the manna of the wilderness. Read verse 6 as in RV. In that He brought His people into the land of Canaan, He showed His truth and justice, i.e. His faithfulness to earlier promises. Indeed all His precepts are established in truth and are therefore wholly reliable. Redemption (9) primarily refers to the exodus, but also includes the restoration from exile. Reverend (9); i.e. awe-inspiring. The fear of the Lord (10) means that attitude of reverence, and that obedience prompted by awe, which are developed in the following Psalm. It is the chief point in wisdom (cf. Pr. i. 7 mg., iv. 7), and they that fear the Lord acquire discernment of what is good.

PSALM CXII. THE WAY OF A GOOD MAN

See Introduction above to Ps. cxi

The theme of the concluding verse of Ps. cxi is developed, and a description is given of the life of a God-fearing man (cf. Jb. xxix and xxxi), who obeys because he delights to obey (cf. cxi. 2). The reference to a blessing on his descendants (2) is an echo of the Abrahamic blessing. With verse 3 cf. Ps. xxxvii. 25, 26; Pr. viii. 18; 1 Ki. iii. 13. His righteousness (3) abides because it is the Lord's (cf. Pss. cxi. 3b, xxiv. 5), and the light which shines upon him (cf. Ps. xxxiv. 5) imparts to him the very attributes of God (note 2 Cor. iii. 18, iv. 6; cf. Acts vii. 55ff.).

Verse 5 is a beatitude; 'Happy is the man that dealeth graciously and with compassion' (cf. RV) toward those in need, and exercises discretion and care in his business. He will guide his affairs with discretion (5). Another reading is 'he will maintain his affairs justly' (see RV). His prosperity continues and his name is held in honour even when he is dead (6). The idea of perpetuity here is the counterpart of Ps. cxi. 4. Though evil tidings may come to him he will not be disturbed overmuch (7; cf. Ps. lv. 22; Is. xxvi. 3). He will be strengthened and upheld (established) until he can look upon (see his desire upon) his adversaries with serenity and success (8; cf. Ps. xci. 8, xcii. 11).

He hath dispersed (9); i.e. 'scattered abroad'. This may be intended as a parallel to Ps. cxi. 9 for, though the primary meaning is the generosity of the godly man (cf. Pr. xi. 24; 2 Cor. ix. 9), the psalmist is careful to show that such a man is and does somewhat as God does, and He has scattered His people abroad among the nations (Ps. xliv. 11). Through all vicissitudes the good man bears the imprint of divine blessing. He sees his desire fulfilled (8), whereas the envious wicked shall see him enjoying honour and find their own desire shall perish (10); his generosity because of his compassion (9) will be matched by their loss through vexation (10).

GENERAL INTRODUCTION TO PSALMS CXIII–CXVIII: 'THE EGYPTIAN HALLEL'

These Psalms have always been associated with the great pilgrim festivals of the Jewish year, viz. Passover, Pentecost and the feast of tabernacles. They were also linked with the feast of dedication (originating in 165 B.C.; cf. Jn. x. 22), and were woven into the liturgies of the new moon (cf. Nu. x. 10). The Passover hymn which was sung after the Last Supper was probably one or more of the Psalms at the end of this group. The title 'Egyptian' was given because of the exceptionally fine poem of the exodus, Ps. cxiv, and also in contradistinction to the title 'The Great Hallel' variously applied to 'The Songs of Ascent' (Pss. cxx–cxxxiv) or simply to Ps. cxxxvi.

PSALM CXIII. PRAISE YE GOD

See General Introduction above to Psalms cxiii–cxviii

The structure of this Psalm is as follows: Let all men (always and everywhere) praise the Lord who is on high. Who is like the Lord on high, in every extremity of experience (beggary and royalty) bringing forth the generations of men?

a. A call to universal praise (1–4)

O ye servants of the Lord (1). Not merely priests and Levites, nor just the devout in Israel (cf. Ne. i. 10, 11), but all godly men in all nations. Note verse 3 and Ps. cxvii; cf. also Ps. lxix. 34, 36. *The name of the Lord* signifies His self-disclosure whereby He becomes known to men. The phrase is thrice used in verses 1–3 and also in Ps. cxvi (verses 4, 13 and 17) and in Ps. cxviii (verses 10b and 12b). *From this time forth* (2); probably from the period of the restoration from exile. *From the rising of the sun* . . . (3); not temporarily, i.e. during daylight, but comprehensively, i.e. wherever the sun shines (cf. Mal. i. 11). *High above all nations* (4); i.e. in a position of sovereignty regarding all peoples (cf. Ps. xlvii. 2, 3 and 8; also Pss. xcv. 3, xcvi. 4 and 10, xcvii. 1, xcix. 2, c. 1). *Above the heavens* (4); i.e. His glory is beyond our comprehension (cf. 1 Ki. viii. 27; Jb. xxvi. 11–14; Ps. cviii. 5).

b. Who is like unto the Lord? (5–9)

Who dwelleth on high (5); RV 'that hath his seat on high'; lit. 'who maketh high to dwell', a phrase which is balanced in the next verse by 'who cometh low to look'. His self-disclosure is of One whose transcendence is inseparable from His presence here, and whose glory is mingled with humility (cf. also Phil. ii. 5–9). Verses 7 and 8a are quoted from the Song of Hannah in 1 Sa. ii. 8 (cf. Lk. i. 52). *Poor* means 'unfortunate and distressed'. *Out of the dust . . . dunghill;* i.e. from insignificance (cf. 1 Ki. xvi. 2) and plight (cf. Jb. ii. 8c). This is a frequent topic in the Psalter. See Pss. xliv. 25, lxxv. 6, 7, cii. 15–20, cvii. 40f. Cf. the cases of David (Ps. lxxviii. 70–72) and Joseph (Ps. cv. 17–22). Verse 9 undoubtedly refers to Hannah, whose words have just been quoted, and to Sarah (Gn. xxi. 6, 7); but it includes the larger reference to faithful Israel. See Is. liv. 1–6 (cf. Gal. iv. 27ff.) and Is. lxvi. 7–13.

PSALM CXIV. SONG OF THE EXODUS

See General Introduction above to Psalms cxlii–cxviii

The antiphonal structure that was probable in the previous Psalm is unmistakable in this brief and beautiful poem of the exodus. No event known to mankind was more revered, treasured and appreciated in Israel than their deliverance from Egypt: it embodied their election and it expressed the mighty power of Yahweh. Even the return from captivity could be regarded as a secondary event, a repetition of the nation's earlier miraculous experience.

The structure of this poem is very logical. The house of Jacob is delivered from Egypt (1, 2); the realm of nature gladly prepares a way for them (3, 4); why was a way made in the realm

of nature? (5, 6); because the Lord came to bless the people of Jacob (7, 8).

a. The earth rejoices at Israel's deliverance (1–4)

A people of strange language (1); the speech of Egypt was foreign to the children of Israel (cf. Gn. xlii. 23). *Judah was* (RV 'became') *his sanctuary* (2); i.e. Judaea and especially Mount Zion (cf. Ps. lxxviii. 54; Ex. xv. 17). Note the absence here of the effective cause, 'the name of the Lord', which is so conspicuous a phrase in the previous and following Psalms. The omission makes the introduction of 'the Lord' in verse 7 more impressive. *The sea . . . fled* (3) before the wind (Ex. xiv. 21). The Jordan appeared to turn back because its floodwaters were temporarily held up by an obstruction at Adam (Jos. iii. 16). *The mountains skipped* (4). A poetic version (cf. Ps. xxix. 6) of the disturbances at Sinai (cf. Ex. xix. 18; Pss. lxviii. 8, xcvii. 5).

b. The coming of the Lord (5–8)

Nature is asked the reason for such abnormal phenomena and the reply is impressively given. The *presence of the Lord* (7) shall cause to tremble, not merely the hills, but the whole earth (cf. Heb. xii. 26). The word *tremble* is used in the sense of travail and be convulsed (cf. Mi. iv. 10). The final verse alludes to the incidents at the rock of Horeb (Ex. xvii. 6) and the flinty cliffs of Kadesh (Nu. xx. 11). The same two incidents are mentioned in Ps. lxxviii. 15–16 as outstanding evidences of the Lord's power and compassion.

PSALM CXV. NOT UNTO US, O GOD

See General Introduction above to Psalms cxiii–cxviii

The antiphonal structure and dual themes of this group of Psalms reach their climax in this central poem. As regards its structure it is most probable that the first and final portions of it (verses 1–8 and 16–18) were sung or chanted by the whole chorus of priests and possibly the congregation also. The central portion (9–15) appears to have been taken partly by the precentor (9, 11, 14) and partly by the priests (10) or the congregation (15) or both (12, 13); responsive singing is mentioned in Ezr. iii. 11.

Contrasting themes such as God and man, the exaltation and humility of the Lord, the abnormality and convulsions of nature, have been dealt with previously in this group of Psalms. But no greater antithesis could be found than that which is here brought forward—the absurdity and helplessness of man-made idols, set over against the majesty, wisdom and benevolence of Yahweh. Cf. Ps. cxxxv. 13–21; Is. xliv. 6–20; Hab. ii. 18, 19. The same contrast is thrice made in Je. x. 1–16.

Unto thy name give glory (1). 'The name' gradually came to mean something more than the manifestation of the Lord, that by which He was known. It was increasingly personified (cf.

'Wisdom' in Pr. i–ix) and equated with Yahweh Himself (cf. Is. xxx. 27ff.; Je. xiv. 9; Mal. iii. 1; and note Ex. xxiii. 21). *Where is now their God?* (2). The taunt of the heathen concerning the invisibility and sometimes the non-intervention of Yahweh was a continual hurt to His people (cf. Ps. xlii. 3 and 10; Joel ii. 17b). *Our God is in the heavens* (3); i.e. He has a habitation which is superior to earthly limits. He is invisible but active, whereas idols are inert although obvious. *Whatsoever he hath pleased* (3) would include Israel's humiliation in Babylon.

The carved and graven images of the nations, fashioned by the hands of men who themselves have been created, are destitute of faculties to match their appearance; they cannot even do what their worshippers do. Two different words are used in the Hebrew text for *speak* (5, 7). The first denotes sensible speech, i.e. the utterance of oracles; the second an inarticulate noise. With verse 8 cf. Rom. i. 23–25; Rev. iii. 17.

The triple appeal to *Israel, house of Aaron, ye that fear the Lord* (9–11) recurs in Ps. cxviii. 2–4, and, with an additional phrase, in Ps. cxxxv. 19, 20. The third group is generally taken to mean those Gentile proselytes to whom reference is made in 1 Ki. viii. 41; Ezr. vi. 21; Is. lvi. 6. The response (12, 13), probably by a full chorus of voices, gives the assurance of divine blessing to each of the three groups of worshippers. The priestly blessing, 'The Lord increase you' (14, RV), was very desirable for a small community of settlers (cf. Dt. i. 11). These responsive exhortations and blessings are concluded by a united chant (16, 17) which takes up the thought of verse 15b and dwells upon the theme of creation, the heavenly estate of the Lord, the earthly realm of human history (cf. Gn. i. 28), and the silence of former generations now in the grave (*Sheol*, here eternal *silence*; cf. Ps. xciv. 17, vi. 5, lxxxviii. 10ff.). *But we* (18). The words are emphatic and have the meaning 'we who are alive'.

PSALM CXVI. NOT UNTO ME, O GOD

See General Introduction above to Psalms cxiii–cxviii

The inclusion of this peculiarly personal song in a group of liturgical Psalms points to the essentially inward nature of worship offered by individuals who are prompted by their own experiences. The unknown author of Ps. cxvi speaks of a time of severe illness and despondency out of which he was brought by the Lord. He was well acquainted with the Davidic Psalms, especially Ps. xviii.

a. Introduction (1, 2)

The emphasis is on *I love* (1); cf. Ps. xviii. 1. *He hath inclined his ear* (2); cf. Ps. lxxi. 2, lxxxviii. 2.

b. A despairing cry is answered (3–9)

The sorrows (RV 'cords') *of death* and *pains of hell* or narrow straits of Sheol (2) express a sense of serious restriction and imminent peril. The psalmist kept on calling upon the Lord whose *name*, or revealed nature, is *gracious, righteous* and *merciful* (4, 5; cf. Ps. ciii. 8, cxi. 4, cxiii. 1n.).

The simple (6); i.e. 'guileless' as in Ps. xix. 7 (cf. Mt. xi. 25). He was cast into deep dejection, but through the Lord's salvation he was brought to a place of perfect *rest* (7). The Hebrew word is in the plural, denoting complete rest. His gratitude (8, 9) is framed within the terms of Pss. xiii. 6, lvi. 13. *Walk before the Lord* (9), like Abraham (Gn. xvii. 1); in contrast to the 'straits of death' in verse 3.

c. Despair and deliverance (10–19)

His disillusionment concerned men, not God. Even when he spoke impulsively, as in the panic when expected help failed (Ps. xxxi. 22), and declared *All men are liars* (11), i.e. 'vain is the help of men' (cf. Ps. lx. 11), and when he bemoaned his condition, saying *I was greatly afflicted* (10), he none the less was trusting in God even as he thus spake. The exact translation of the Hebrew text of verse 10 is uncertain (see RV). A possible rendering is '*I believed* (i.e. I held to my faith), even when I had to say, I am greatly afflicted'. Paul in 2 Cor. iv. 13 follows the LXX. The subsequent vindication of that faith prompted him to consider what form his devotion to the Lord should take. The drink offering (Nu. xxviii. 7ff.) would be offered when next he went to the temple (14) to fulfil his vows and publicly testify that Yahweh was his rescuer. And as his deliverance had been in miniature like that of Israel from Egypt, he would drink wine from the cup at the next Passover with especial thankfulness (13; cf. Lk. xxii. 7ff.). *Salvation* (13) is in the plural in Hebrew; cf. 'rest' in verse 7.

The psalmist is one of the Lord's *saints* (15), i.e. 'beloved ones' (Heb. *ḥasid*), for whose welfare He (Yahweh) is specially solicitous; death is not lightly permitted to snatch them away. *Truly* (16) is the same Hebrew word as *I beseech thee* (4); i.e. the psalmist is eager, offering his devotion unto the Lord as a bondservant (cf. Ps. lxxxvi. 16; also Jas. i. 1; 2 Pet. i. 1; Rom. i. 1). *Son of thine handmaid* (16) is a parallel expression of *thy servant* (cf. lxxxvi. 16). *The sacrifice of thanksgiving* (17); see Lv. vii. 11ff. The repetition (18) of the intention to join in public worship (14) serves to stress the importance of this obligation.

PSALM CXVII. ALL YE NATIONS

See General Introduction above to Psalms cxiii–cxviii

This doxology is akin to Ps. c. Its comprehensiveness offsets the individual prayer of Ps. cxvi. *All ye nations;* i.e. all Gentiles, everyone (note Rom. xv. 11). *Great toward us;* lit. 'has prevailed and proved mighty on our behalf'; *gabhar*, used also in Ps. ciii. 11, is translated 'prevailed' in Gn. vii. 18ff. (cf. Rom. v. 20, 21). The divine attributes of *truth* and mercy are respectively associated with Jews and Gentiles by Paul in Rom. xv. 8. Among other Psalms with a world view may be mentioned xlvii and lxvii.

PSALM CXVIII. HIS MERCY ENDURETH FOR EVER

See General Introduction above to Psalms cxiii–cxviii

This hymn, expressive of a people's spiritual elation, is a processional song for varied voices. Verses 19, 20, 26 and 27 point to a festive approach to the temple gates and a subsequent entrance into the court of the priests as far as the altar of burnt offerings. The occasion cannot be precisely determined, but it would correspond with the particularly joyful celebrations described in Ne. viii. 13–18 when the rejoicing which was customary at the feast of tabernacles was intensified by the community's success over the Samaritans and their completion of the city walls (cf. Ne. vi. 16).

a. Invocation (1–4)

The Psalm commences and concludes with a phrase that had evidently become a liturgical formula. Cf. Ps. cvi. 1, cvii. 1. See also its use on memorable occasions at the temple (e.g. 1 Ch. xvi. 34; 2 Ch. v. 13; Ezr. iii. 11. It is elaborated in Ps. cxxxvi). Its use on this occasion (Ne. viii. 13ff.) would be a fulfilment of Je. xxxiii. 11. For the triple call to praise in verses 2–4 see Ps. cxv. 9–11.

b. The approach to the temple gates (5–19)

Some of these verses were probably sung by a precentor from the temple choir who led the procession of worshippers up to the sanctuary. He voiced the feelings of each one, and also personified the spirit of the community. The other verses would be sung in chorus by the people following him.

i. **The leader (5–7).** *Distress* (5); i.e. 'straits' as in Ps. cxvi. 3. The reference is to the restrictions of captivity which are replaced by restoration to freedom (cf. Ps. xviii. 19). *The Lord*, Heb. *Jah*, the Deliverer from Egypt (cf. Ps. lxviii. 4). Verses 6 and 7 commence with the same words, lit. 'The Lord is for me', freeing me from fear (cf. Pss. lvi. 4 and 11, cxii. 8), as one of my helpers. *With them that help me* (7); the meaning is that the Lord is his (great) helper.

ii. **The chorus (8, 9).** The allusion is to the Samaritans' local opposition and their intrigue at the Persian court. The restoration of temple and city had been approved by Artaxerxes but it was repeatedly hindered and completed only through the direct approval of the Lord (cf. Ezr. v. 5).

iii. **The leader (10a, 11a, 12a).** *All nations;* i.e. the nations around. The Samaritans were of mixed origin (see Ezr. iv. 9), and their resistance to the Jews had been reinforced by Ammonites, Philistines and Arabians (see Ne. iv. 7).

iv. **The chorus (10b, 11b, 12b).** The refrain which forms the second part of each of these verses would have been chanted by the worshippers.

v. **The leader (13–15).** The opposition of their neighbours had been like the earlier obstruction of the Red Sea; so their recent triumph recalled the ancient song of victory—verse 14 is a quotation from Ex. xv. 2. The word *tabernacles* (15), RV 'tents', continues the analogy, but denotes a permanent dwelling as in Ps. lxxviii. 55, not the temporary booths used at the feast of tabernacles.

vi. **The chorus (16).** A further echo from Moses' song. See Ex. xv. 6, 12.

vii. **The leader (17–19).** The small community is personified; they feel the main crisis is over and that their re-establishment is secure. Yet so grievous had been their chastening that it must have been the Lord's doing that they have not wholly perished. *Chastened* (18); cf. Ps. xciv. 8–11n. At this point the procession would have reached the temple gates and halted to ask permission to enter and worship Jah (cf. Ps. xxiv. 7ff.; Is. xxvi. 2).

c. Within the temple court (20–26)

i. **The Levites (20).** The voices of the waiting Levites are heard as they swing open the gates and announce the condition of entry—righteousness (see RV; cf. Ps. xv. 1, 2, xxiv. 3, 4).

ii. **The leader (21, 22).** Upon entering the court of the Lord the precentor announces the purpose of the procession in words reminiscent of verse 14. He also adds the statement about the chief cornerstone, presumably the topmost stone (cf. Zc. iv. 7). Whether or not this had been necessarily, or disgracefully, neglected by the builders until at last it was needed to crown the structure, the subject is intended as a metaphor of the godly Israelites, despised, ignored and ill-used by other peoples until the master builder (23) placed them in their present position as an essential part of His tabernacle which was amongst men (Ex. xxix. 45, 46). Note the New Testament use of this idea in Mt. xxi. 42; Acts iv. 11; Eph. ii. 20; 1 Pet. ii. 7.

iii. **The chorus (23–25).** Hence the crowd of worshippers exclaim with delight and awe at the fact of their presence in the outer sanctuary, recognizing that to God alone they owed that day of rejoicing (23; cf. Ne. vi. 16, viii. 17). The Hebrew of *Save now* (25) has passed into English as 'Hosanna'. The word 'now' is not used here in a time sense, but as a particle of emphasis (cf. Ne. i. 11).

iv. **The priests (26).** The plea for blessing and prosperity is answered by the priests assembled before the altar. The phrase *the name of the Lord* should be joined with *blessed*, thus, 'Blessed in the name of the Lord be everyone that entereth' (cf. Ps. cxxix. 8).

d. Thanksgiving and praise (27–29)

Possibly every voice joined in the ascription of praise 'The Lord is God' (27, RV); i.e. is 'the Mighty One'. But the meaning of the words which follow is uncertain; it is most improbable that the sacrificial animals were tied to the projections (horns) at the four corners of the altar, and the words indicate some action that is a climax for the worshippers. An alternative reading is 'Order ('set forward', as in 1 Ki. xx. 14) the festival procession with boughs, even unto the horns of the altar', beyond which only priests could proceed. When this is done the leader of the people's worship makes confession of Israel's faith (28; cf. Ex. xv. 2), whereupon all who are assembled unite in the final praise (29).

PSALM CXIX. LOVE FOR THE LORD AND HIS LAW

This extraordinary poem is an elaborate, ingenious and passionate meditation upon the law of the Lord. This should not be confused with any legal code. The Hebrew word is *torah*, meaning primarily 'instruction' or 'teaching'. It stands here for the will of God as known to Israel. It was dominated by Moses but not confined to his original teachings. The Psalm has an acrostic pattern; each of the twenty-two letters of the Hebrew alphabet is made the initial letter of eight successive verses, hence 176 verses in all. The major feature, however, is the melodious repetition of eight synonyms of the will of God, viz. *law*, the *torah*; *testimonies*, general principles of action; *precepts* (*piqqudim*), particular rules of conduct; *statutes* (*huqqim*), social regulations; *commandments* (*miṣvah*), religious principles; *ordinances* (*mishpatim*), the right judgments which should operate in human relationships; *word* (*dabhar*), the declared will of God, His promises, decrees, etc.; *word* (*imra*), the word or speech of God as it is brought to light amongst men. A frequent variant of the usual eight synonyms is *way* (*derek*). There can be little doubt that these were largely derived from Ps. xix. 7–9. One or other of these terms occurs in every verse of the Psalm, except verse 122; but they have no methodical sequence from stanza to stanza. The author's passionate devotion to the Lord overrides the artificial arrangement. The will of God is not observed and described so much as expressed from a rich experience. The psalmist's life is shown to be interwoven with truth irrespective of his mood.

It is not known who wrote the poem, although there appear to be several personal allusions in it. Probably it was written by a close adherent of Ezra the scribe. However it is not primarily biographical, nor does its length entail a chronological sequence of moods. The primary significance of its magnitude is the absorbing passion of a heart concentrated upon that highest good which is revealed in God (cf. Phil. iii. 7–14). The religious motive in the Psalm, as distinct from its literary structure, is the attempt to express the experience of suffering and chastening which comes to a man who holds to an implicit and loving faith in the Lord whose will

and word are good and true (cf. Rom. vii. 9–13; Heb. xii. 5–11).

Apart from the first and final sections, the other twenty may be grouped in pairs although the divisions are not always pronounced.

a. The way of the Lord is good (1–8)

Undefiled (1); RV 'perfect'; i.e. wholehearted, and therefore blameless (cf. Gn. xvii. 1). *The way* (1); the divinely appointed course of their conduct (cf. 2 Ch. vi. 14c; contrast Gn. vi. 12). *The whole heart* (2); full concentration of mind and will. See also verses 10, 34, 58, 69, 145. *His ways* (3); a variant of the usual eight synonyms. *Have respect unto* (6); i.e. learn with a view to obeying (cf. Jas. i. 25).

b. Prayer for the Lord's help (9–24)

The psalmist prays for the Lord's help in the difficulties attending a holy life and during the dangers of persecution. This expected aid will include enlightenment concerning His will. *Word* (9); Heb. *dabhar*. *Word* (11); Heb. *imra*: see Introduction. *Hid* (RV 'laid up') *in my heart* (11); i.e. not as a memory, but as a treasure continually employed (cf. Jb. xxiii. 12). *Blessed art thou* (12); men can bless God in this sense by furthering His name through their consecrated lives. *With my lips* (13); cf. Dt. vi. 6, 7. *Open* (18); i.e. unveil (cf. 2 Ki. vi. 17; 2 Cor. iii. 14–16). *Wondrous things* (18); Heb. *pala*, always used of God's works, e.g. Pss. xxvi. 7, lxxxvi. 10. *Stranger* (19); RV 'sojourner'; i.e. 'an alien'. The sense is not so much brevity of occupation (cf. Ps. xxxix. 12) as uninstructedness in the laws of the realm; hence the request *hide not thy commandments*. The sense of verse 21 is probably as follows: proud and wilful sinners are always rebuked, i.e. by divine judgment; but even they who err unintentionally are cursed, i.e. liable to punishment which any sin entails (see RV mg.). *Princes* (23); the rulers of the local community (cf. verse 161).

c. A plea for strength (25–40)

Burdened by sorrow, he pleads for strength and assurance through the ministry of the word; also for a truly penitent heart to preserve him amidst temptation. *Cleaveth unto the dust* (25); i.e. is dejected by reason of griefs. See verse 28 and cf. Ps. xliv. 25. In verse 26 the psalmist refers to a previous prayer (cf. Ps. xxxii. 5); verses 26b, 27 give his present prayer. Notice the contrast between 'the way of falsehood' (29, RV) and 'the way of faithfulness' (30, RV). The Wisdom Literature has many instances of this imagery (e.g. Ps. i. 6; Pr. iv. 14–19; Mt. vii. 13, 14). *Enlarge my heart* (32); i.e. relieve it of anxieties and set it free to serve (cf. Mt. vi. 31ff.). The harmony of divine will and human choice is expressed in verse 35, 'Make me to tread thy pathway, for I delight in it.' He pleads to be safeguarded from the enticements of material gain and false values (cf. Mt. xxvi. 41). *Fear* (38); i.e. godly reverence (cf. RV). The Hebrew word here differs from that in verse 39; cf. RV. *My reproach which I fear* (39); i.e. he was apprehensive of succumbing to men's upbraidings and taunts, thereby denying that the ordinances (*mishpatim*) of the Lord were good and satisfying. *Quicken me in thy righteousness* (40). He seeks renewal of strength, basing his plea on the faithfulness of God to His covenant promises.

d. A plea for power (41–56)

The psalmist prays for power through a discernment of the mercy, truth and salvation of the Lord: in this way he will be able to bear public testimony in confidence. 'An answer' (42, RV); i.e. his own experience of the Lord's mercy. If God did not come to him in this manner (cf.the inward witness of the Spirit, Rom. viii. 14–16), he would be unable to testify concerning the word of truth; i.e. the way of the Lord would remain true, but the psalmist would lack direct and present experience thereof. Possessing the freedom which accompanies a consciousness of divine mercy and salvation (45) he would not be overawed even by kings (46; cf. Mt. x. 18, 19). *My hands . . . will I lift up* (48) in adoration and desire (cf. Ps. xxviii. 2).

'Remember . . . because thou hast made me to hope' (49, RV; cf. verse 43). The Lord had *quickened* (50) him previously and that was a precedent and platform for hope. *Horror* (53); i.e. hot indignation (note verse 136); intense and tearful concern at the existence and potency of wickedness. *House of my pilgrimage* (54), or 'sojourning'; i.e. his earthly environment (cf. verse 19; 1 Ch. xxix. 15). 'This I have had' (56, RV); i.e. the major blessing of his life had been the experience of keeping the will of God. *Because* should rather be 'that' (cf. RV mg.).

e. Devotion to the Torah (57–72)

These verses are an affirmation of devotion to the Lord which is so unshakable that even affliction only serves to further his appreciation of the Torah. *My portion* (57); i.e. his supreme blessing (cf. Pss. xvi. 5, lxxiii. 26). *I intreated thy favour* (58); i.e. I have sought thy presence. *Thought on my ways* (59); scrutinized my conduct with a view to hastily remedying any defects. *Bands* (RV 'cords') *of the wicked* (61); i.e. the schemes and snares of his enemies (cf. verse 110). *Teach me good judgment* (66); i.e. train me to have a right discernment of good and evil (cf. Heb. v. 14). *I was afflicted* (67); an allusion to the effect of some earlier sin which caused him subsequent distress and produced a crisis in his life. See verse 71, and cf. Is. xxxviii. 17, RV, 'It was for my peace that I had great bitterness'. *Their heart is as fat as grease* (70); i.e. their heart is gross, as if turned to fat. It had become insensitive to God, the very opposite to the psalmist's attitude (70b–72).

f. A plea for light (73–88)

The psalmist prays for enlightenment by his Creator, especially because persecution has im-

perilled his life, though not his hope and trust. *Made me and fashioned me* (73); cf. Ps. cxxxix. 14–16; Jb. x. 8–11, xxxi. 15. Verse 74 may be rendered, 'Let them that fear thee be glad when they see me'; i.e., let them rejoice in God's answer to my prayer (cf. verse 79). The personal distress of the psalmist in no wise invalidated the righteousness of God. His chastisements are inseparable from His essential purpose of mercy which the sufferer now prays to become a comfort to him (75, 76). Others who have been perplexed by his affliction will then return to him (79).

Details of his distress are now given (cf. Pss. lxix. 8ff., cii. 4ff.). *Fainteth* (81); i.e. faileth, as also his eyes (82). He pines away and becomes exhausted through the delay of relief. *Bottle in the smoke* (83); i.e. an empty wineskin, hung up in the rafters, and become black and shrivelled. *Digged pits* (85); i.e. constructed hidden snares in his path (see Ps. lvii. 6). He appeals to God's righteousness and justice for deliverance from those who threatened to ruin him.

g. O how love I thy law! (89–104)

These verses express praise for the unchanging Lord and for His faithfulness, combined with love for His precepts, to which the psalmist declares he owes his preservation. *Settled in heaven* (89); i.e. is immutable, wholly independent of earthly change (cf. Ps. lxxxix. 2). Indeed earth, even as heaven, abides in a state of continual preparedness to obey His law (90, 91). *Perfection* (96) means all earthly completeness. Earthly phenomena come to *an end*, however complete they may seem. They have limits of size, scope or survival; but the commandments of the Lord are infinite (cf. Jb. xi. 7–9). The love of these (97) is the key to wisdom (98); hence he has more understanding by love than by learning from his teachers and experienced instructors (99, 100). The psalmist refers to teachers who have not derived their learning from God's law. He is showing the superiority of the law as a guide to life. *Thou* (98) is emphatic. It is God who has instructed him (cf. Jn. xvi. 13ff.).

h. Thy word a lamp (105–120)

Although harassed and threatened, he trusts in the word of the Lord to lead him in the way of holiness. Any oppression by evil-doers only strengthens his belief in divine righteousness and in the ultimate condemnation of the wicked. In verse 106 follow RV. *My soul . . . in my hand* (109); i.e. is precariously placed (cf. Jb. xiii. 14). *As an heritage* (111); a possible meaning is that he had replaced the traditional heritage of. Canaan, now under foreign domination, by a spiritual inheritance. *I hate vain thoughts* (113); better, as in RV, 'them that are of a double mind', i.e. vacillating (cf. 1 Ki. xviii. 21; Jas. i. 6–8). *My flesh trembleth* (120); i.e. shudders through thinking of the divine judgment upon *the wicked of the earth* (119).

i. Above fine gold (121-136)

In this section the psalmist presents his sufferings to God as evidence of an urgent need and is simultaneously grieved at heart for all who are heedless of His word. He claims the attention of God because he has done as God (121; cf. Ps. xxxiii. 5, lxxxix. 14); yet if that should be disallowed, he rests his claim upon divine mercy (124) and his humble readiness to learn better. *It is time for thee, Lord, to work* (126). The situation is critical and calls for immediate intervention by God; i.e. to pronounce sentence upon the wicked (cf. Je. xviii. 23b). *Therefore I esteem* (128). The Hebrew text is difficult. The LXX renders 'therefore according to all thy precepts I direct (my steps)'. *Wonderful* (129); i.e. exceptional, as in verse 18. *The entrance of thy words* (130); lit. 'the doorway, or opening, of thy word'. In eastern houses, most light comes through the doorway because windows are few and small. *I opened* (RV 'opened wide') . . . *and panted* (131); i.e. in eager expectancy. *As thou usest to do* (132); lit. 'according to judgment'; i.e. as is thine own law. The psalmist bases his plea on what God's law declares.

j. Upright are Thy judgments (137-152)

This section speaks of the truth of God's law and contains an importunate prayer for more enlightenment and divine companionship. God's word, like Himself, is righteous, and faithful (137, 138); *very pure* (140); i.e. tried and tested; and eternal (152; see RV). *My zeal hath consumed me* (139), by intensifying the antagonism of his enemies (cf. Ps. lxix. 9). The intensity of the psalmist's prayers increases as the poem continues. *I prevented the dawning . . . the night watches* (147, 148); i.e. I forestalled them. It has been suggested that if the psalmist was a Levite the reference is to the night watches in the temple. Before his watch began he was already awake in meditation.

k. Seven times a day (153-168)

The psalmist makes a passionate plea for deliverance and for the power to persist in his devotion to the Torah. *Plead my cause* (154); i.e. defend me in the proceedings which my many enemies have instituted against me; see opening verses of Ps. cix. *Was grieved* (158); i.e. felt disgusted with them, as the Hebrew word implies. *Thy word . . . from the beginning* (160); i.e. in its entirety. RV reads, 'The sum of thy word is truth'. *Lying* (163); RV 'falsehood'; a reference to idolatry. *Great peace* (165); either inward calm because of dwelling upon the truth of God, or outward ease because God rewards those who love His 'law'. The claim to integrity (166-168) was also made by the authors of Pss. vii. 3, 4, xvii. 3, 4, xxvi. 1-4.

l. Let my soul live (169-176)

These closing verses are an importunate cry for companionship and for the care of the great shepherd. *Utter praise* (171); i.e. pour forth continually. *Let thine hand help me* (173); RV 'be ready to help me'. The psalmist here beseeches divine aid on the ground of his joyful devotion; previously he has requested it because of his dedication to a life of obedience and because of his need of deliverance from peril. *I have gone astray* (176); a reminiscence of verse 67. *Thy commandments* (176). The poem ends on one of its eight principal notes. Observe, however, the pronoun *thy*. The psalmist's intense love is for the Lord Himself and therefore for all the avenues which express or reveal His will.

GENERAL INTRODUCTION TO PSALMS CXX-CXXXIV: THE 'SONGS OF ASCENTS'

These fifteen Psalms are each entitled 'A Song of Ascents' (RV; AV *Degrees*). The significance of the phrase is uncertain. Different explanations have been suggested as, for example, that they formed a liturgy associated with the fifteen steps between two of the temple courts on which a choir of Levites sometimes stood to sing; or that they celebrate the fifteen years added to Hezekiah's life, the promise of which was accompanied by the sun's shadow receding ten steps (lit. 'degrees') down the great staircase which Ahaz arranged to lead down to the temple from the king's house (see Is. xxxviii. 7, 8; 2 Ki. xvi. 17, 18; Ne. xii. 37). The LXX title is 'A Song of the steps'. A third suggestion is that they are a collection of songs which the exiles sang on returning to Jerusalem from Babylon. A fourth explanation is that the phrase has no historical basis, but denotes the literary style of several of the poems, viz. in a series of verses, each one being built upon a few words of the preceding verse so that the thought progresses by well marked stages. This repetition and expansion is well shown in Ps. cxxiii.

None of these theories is satisfactory, but it is now generally assumed that these Psalms were songs frequently used (after the return from exile) by worshippers going up to Zion for the three great festivals of the Jewish year. Even so, some of the poems are hardly in keeping with the spirit of such pilgrimages (e.g. Pss. cxx, cxxx, cxxxi). Most of the poems reflect the moods and conditions of the early years of the return from exile; but some might find a suitable setting in the siege of Jerusalem by Sennacherib and its relief (Is. xxxvii–xxxviii; note Is. xxxviii. 20).

Whatever the precise meaning of the superscription, one thing is evident; this collection of Psalms constitutes a distinctive group, and is, in itself, a miniature Psalter. This is shown by the variety of themes, authors and probable dates of origin. Also some such purposive arrangement seems to be suggested in that the final Psalm (as does Ps. cl for the whole Psalter) constitutes a benediction to close the anthology. Another parallel between this section and the whole Psalter is the way in which it can be divided into five groups each consisting of three Psalms. The first two groups deal with the source and principles of worship, i.e. external pressure on the godly soul, expectant trust in the intervention of God, and the realization of the tremendous stability, power, and righteousness in Him; thought is also focused on the choice of Zion as the hinge on which turn the Lord's purposes for men. The third group has more in common with the Wisdom literature; the viewpoint is much more general, outward and philosophical than in the other twelve songs; there is no mention of divine mercy, redemption or forgiveness, nor of prayer, the services in the sanctuary, nor the house of David; the emphasis on home and family life is peculiar to this group. The fourth group is intensely personal and devotional, but there is no inner surge of faith and gladness as in the first two groups; the theme is the discipline of patience. The last group is dominated by the concepts of divine choice; the covenant, the community, and the sanctuary; there is a very real sense of the inheritance of the historic past. (The description of the temple service in Ecclus. l. 11–21 could be read as a background of these 'Songs of Ascents'.)

The ascription of the Davidic authorship to Pss. cxxii, cxxiv, cxxxi, cxxxiii is not recognized by many of the old versions and it cannot be strictly held (save possibly in the case of Ps. cxxxi) on account of many grammatical features characteristic of a much later period. None the less they echo the spirit of David.

PSALM CXX. DELIVER MY SOUL

See General Introduction above to Psalms cxx–cxxxiv

This prayer for relief was prompted by a pervasive atmosphere of untruth and deceit; it is the cry of a man (or a community) who is spiritually exiled, and feels as Truth would feel amid a society of liars and perjurers (cf. Jn. viii. 43–46). For the emphasis in the Psalter upon the heinousness of abusing the gift of speech and perverting the word, see references under verse 2 below. It is generally understood that the campaign of slander here mentioned was the Samaritan propaganda directed against the reconstruction of temple and walls (cf. Ezr. iv. 1ff. and Ne. iv. 1ff.).

In my distress I cried unto the Lord (1). This may refer to an earlier plea and response which encourages the psalmist to plead again (2ff.); alternatively, the first verse may be a summary rehearsal of the whole Psalm. *Lying lips . . . deceitful tongue* (2). Cf. Pss. v. 9, x. 7, xii. 2–4, xxxvi. 1–4, lii. 2–4, lxiv. 1–4. The particular occasion here may be that mentioned in Ne. vi. 5–14. *What shall be given . . . what shall be done?* (3), RV 'done more'; i.e. what condemnation will fall upon thee for what is past, and what further punishment for a continuance of the practice? The phrase is common in Hebrew. See, e.g., 1 Sa. iii. 17, xx. 13. The answer is given

in the next verse. Divine judgment will be as the sharpened arrows of a warrior. *The mighty*; i.e. God, whose word is an arrow (Ps. vii. 12, 13). *Juniper* (4); RV mg., 'broom'. The roots of these shrubs were used for fires which burnt much longer than the usual thorns and dung used in treeless areas. Hence the phrase became a metaphor for hot and prolonged judgments (cf. Ps. cxl. 10). *Mesech* (5); a people living in what is now western Persia and Armenia (cf. Ezk. xxvii. 13, xxxviii. 2). *The tents of Kedar* (5); the nomads of Arabia beyond Moab and Ammon (cf. Jdg. viii. 11a). Both terms are used metaphorically to denote the barbarous society in the midst of which the psalmist lived. Possibly there may be an allusion to the mixed origin of the Samaritans (cf. Ezr. iv. 9, 10; Ne. iv. 7). The sense of alienation, *I am for peace: . . . they are for war* (7) was particularly distressing to those who had eagerly returned 'home' to the district around Jerusalem.

PSALM CXXI. GOD MY HELPER

See General Introduction above to Psalms cxx–cxxxiv

This song implies a situation of uncertainty, but any possibility of danger is offset by the boundless and unquestioning trust in the power and watchfulness of the Lord. The first verses should be read as in RV. 'I will lift up mine eyes unto the mountains', i.e. around Jerusalem (Ps. cxxv. 2), as a sentry watching for possible danger: 'From whence shall my help come?' Then follows the confident answer, 'My help cometh from the Lord, who made the mountains and all else.' This confidence toward God is elaborated by a meditation upon His watchful protection. 'He cannot possibly allow insecurity to affect you' (3a; the Hebrew gives this emphasis); and His vigilance on behalf of Israel is ceaseless (3b, 4; cf. 2 Ch. xvi. 9; Ps. xxxiii. 13, 14; Pr. xv. 3; Heb. iv. 13). *The Lord is thy keeper* (5) as He promised to Jacob (Gn. xxviii. 15). *Shade upon thy right hand* (5). 'The right hand' was a synonym for the south or sunward side; it also stood for the place of privilege and representation (cf. Ps. xvi. 8, cx. 5). His presence as a shade protecting from the heat of the sun, and from the rays of the moon, safeguards from all outward danger (cf. Dt. xxviii. 22ff.; Jon. iv. 6ff.). *Preserve thee from all evil* (7); i.e. comprehensively. *Going out . . . coming in* (8); usually the daily activities centred in the home and fields (cf. Dt. xxviii. 6); but also and especially the journeying to Zion on pilgrimage. In short, the Lord 'keeps' (see RV) constantly, personally, temporally, morally, spiritually, effectually, eternally.

PSALM CXXII. THE HOUSE OF GOD

See General Introduction above to Psalms cxx–cxxxiv

This salutation to the city of Zion is best understood as uttered within the temple precincts.

The poem expresses a sense of fulfilment both personal and corporate, the climax of a pilgrimage, and the finality inseparable from God's purposes in the house of David and the house of the Lord. The words *of David* in the title are not given in the LXX, the Targums, and many ancient versions.

Our feet shall stand (2); RV 'are standing', lit. 'have become standing'; i.e. they had come to stand within the city gates and still stood there thrilled by the experience. *A city that is compact together* (3) may mean the compact appearance of the walled city, in contrast with its former desolation when the exiles first returned to it. Or, since the words *compact together* mean 'joined to itself', and are often used of human fellowship, the phrase may convey the idea that Jerusalem was the node of Jewish life, the spring and centre of their corporate unity. This latter meaning is favoured by the following sentence about the regular pilgrimages of *the tribes of the Lord* (presumably a reference to the short period before the divided kingdom, but after David's capture of the city). *Go up* (4) is better read 'went up', for there were no thrones of the house of David after the exile. The journeys were for, or as, 'a testimony unto Israel' (4, RV); i.e. showing that they were bound by a covenant (cf. Ps. lxxxi. 3, 4). *Thrones of judgment* (5); i.e. the administration of justice on behalf of the Lord was entrusted to kings (cf. 1 Ki. vii. 7; Ps. ix. 4 and 7, lxxii. 1ff.). In the closing verses (6–9) meditation is replaced by prayer and self-dedication. *Palaces* (7); i.e. chief buildings as in Ps. xlviii. 13; there were no royal residences in the city at this time. After praying for material prosperity on the revived city (6, 7), the pilgrim finally declares the purpose of his visit. *I will seek thy good* (9); i.e. the welfare of the city. This he will do for the sake of his fellow-Israelites (8a), but most of all for the sake of the house of the Lord (*Yahweh*) our God, the place of His dwelling.

PSALM CXXIII. BE GRACIOUS UNTO US

See General Introduction above to Psalms cxx–cxxxiv

None of the psalmists sat in the seat of the scornful (Ps. i. 1), but in many of their prayers they showed themselves very conscious of the society of proud and arrogant men. The humiliation of the godly by sinners is a frequent topic in the Psalter (e.g. Pss. xvii. 10, 11, xxii. 6–8, xxxv. 19–26, xliv. 13–16, lxix. 4–12, cii. 3–10). This particular prayer seems to reflect the exasperation and anguish of heart amongst the Jews when the resistance of the Samaritans was so mocking and powerful (cf. Ne. ii. 19, iv. 2–4). In that the opposition was by intrigue, scorn, contempt, the warfare of lying and deceitful tongues, there is an obvious similarity to Ps. cxx.

Thou that dwellest (RV 'sittest') *in the heavens* (1), as sovereign ruler (cf. Ps. ii. 4). *Look unto the hand* (2); i.e. of authority and sustenance. *Exceedingly filled* (3); i.e. satiated beyond ability to bear. *Those that are at ease* (4); i.e. the Samaritans. The thought, but not the circumstance, is expanded in Am. vi. 1–6.

PSALM CXXIV. A SONG OF DELIVERANCE

See General Introduction above to Psalms cxx–cxxxiv

This Psalm is a series of tableaux depicting rescue from danger. It may refer to the exiles' first reaction to the news of permission to return, or to the final discomfiture of Sanballat and Tobias as the restoration of the city and temple was carried through (Ne. vi. 15, 16), or to some other relief from a great menace, such as Hezekiah's deliverance when Sennacherib abandoned the siege of Jerusalem (cf. Is. xxxvii. 33ff.). Verses 1–5 give utterance to the nation's consciousness that the deliverance was Yahweh's doing. Verses 6–8 express their thanksgiving and confidence in Him.

Of David, in the title, is very doubtful, for it is not given in many old versions; but the imagery is Davidic. That view of the nation's historical vicissitudes which perceives therein the sure hand of the Lord (1) is typical of later times. In verse 2 the contrast between *the Lord* (of creation; see verse 8) and *men* (lit. *adam*, i.e. of the earth) is emphatic. *Swallowed us up quick* (3); RV 'alive'; i.e. suddenly and overwhelmingly as in Nu. xvi. 32, 33. The second metaphor is of a mountain torrent in flood (cf. Pss. xxxii. 6, lxix. 1, 2, xciii. 3, 4). The third metaphor, *as a prey to their teeth* (6), can also be traced in other Psalms, e.g. xxii. 13–20, lxxix. 7 (note Is. xxxviii. 13). The final imagery, that of a bird escaping from a net (7), is used in Pss. xci. 3 and cxli. 9.

PSALM CXXV. ABIDING SECURITY

See General Introduction above to Psalms cxx–cxxxiv

A deep conviction of security and of the unchanging power and faithfulness of the Lord seeks expression in this song. It is a declaration amid worldly difficulties of the reality and relevance of the invisible realm where God is and does good. The Psalm was written in Jerusalem during some period of restlessness and tediousness. Evidently this had overcome many of the fainthearted amongst the community so that they had turned aside to do as other workers of iniquity, and would be led forth to the like judgment. This description best fits the period just after the war of nerves between the Samaritans and the returned exiles in Jerusalem (cf. Ne. vi. 9; Ezr. ix. 4 and 10–14). A similar strong sense of security might have been expressed by Hezekiah (cf. Is. xxxvii. 33, 35). The Psalm falls into two parts: an expression of confidence in God (1–3) and a prayer and warning (4, 5).

Verse 1 is more than a simile. *They that trust in the Lord* are not only as abiding as Mt. Zion, *which cannot be removed*, but, in a spiritual sense, they are Mt. Zion (note Gal. iv. 24–26; Heb. xii. 22). In a historical sense they have a covenant with God which is the counterpart of His choice of Zion (e.g. Ps. lxxviii. 68, 69). In a physical sense, as a community, they are as secure as the upland of Zion itself; both have been created by the Lord (cf. Is. liv. 10; note Phil. iv. 7). The fixity and immutability of this relationship between the Lord and His people is like that between a city and its milieu (cf. Joel iii. 17, 18); i.e. it goes far beyond an individual's experience, it is *even for ever* (2). This truth is borne out by the emphatic prophecy that the sceptre of foreign rule (3, RV) shall not rest or stay permanently over *the lot of the righteous* (the Promised Land) lest, if it did, a general failing of faith should occur among the righteous (3). *Do good unto . . . those that be good* (4). Retribution operates positively as well as negatively (cf. Pss. xxxiv. 10, lxxxiv. 11; Lk. viii. 15; Rom. ii. 10; Heb. xiii. 21). The glory of goodness lies in its power to disclose reality. *Lead them forth* (5); i.e. 'lead them away'. No more realistic punishment could be imagined than a repetition of the exile; but that would yet befall all workers of evil.

PSALM CXXVI. SOWING AND REAPING

See General Introduction above to Psalms cxx–cxxxiv

Each group of three songs (except the last) is introduced by a plaintive poem. This one is outstanding because laughter, joy, gladness and singing have a prominent part in it, although the poem as a whole conveys a sense of tearfulness tinged with disillusionment. It certainly belongs to the period when the Babylonian captivity had ceased and the hopes of the faithful had grown almost into ecstasy as they foresaw a world-wide wonderment at the marvellous working of the Lord. Yet when they returned to their homeland they were faced with the stubborn consequences of their long exile in the form of derelict fields and townships. The pressure of exile was removed, but captivity had left an imprint on their environment which was inescapably dreary. The agricultural imagery of the second half of the song was peculiarly relevant although it covered much more than the natural difficulties of re-establishing a rural community around a ruined city. First, the settlers were short of food because of the poverty of the area and its neglect; hence the sowing of seed fit for food would be peculiarly hard for those who had resumed other pursuits in the old city. Secondly, the risk attendant upon seedtime and harvest was very marked at this period because of inadequate equipment, and the natural over-draft of the soil's long neglect. Similar, but not so severe, conditions had prevailed after the Assyrian invasion in Hezekiah's time (cf. Is. xxxvii. 30), and Haggai speaks plainly of the dearth of good crops after the return (Hg. i. 10, 11, ii. 19). Thirdly, the whole process of natural growth, the discipline of giving in order to get, was a forceful reminder of the law of consequences, and what would be more present to the people than that the nation's recent exile had been a reaping of what had been sown for centuries? (cf. Zc. i. 4).

The Psalm falls into two parts: the joy of the people at their great deliverance (1–3) and prayer that their present needs may be supplied (4–6).

Turned again the captivity (1); i.e. the Lord brought back those that returned to Zion. For the laughter of incredulity (2) cf. Gn. xvii. 17, xxi. 6. The comment of the nations would be to the effect that the Lord had demonstrated His amazing goodness to (or with) these men (3). The exiles' eager anticipation may have been quickened by such prophecies as Joel ii. 21–27; Am. ix. 11ff. *Turn again our captivity* (4) may mean either free us from the rigours and hardships of our present lot, i.e. restore our welfare and our rural economy, or bring back from Babylon further exiles to reinforce our endeavours. *Streams in the south* (4); i.e. the seasonal watercourses of the dry region south of Judaea known as the Negeb. The condition of Israel was like the Negeb in drought; but as the rains come, and the streams flow down in flood, so may the Lord restore His people's fortunes! *Bearing precious seed* (6); RV 'bearing forth the seed'; i.e. casting out handfuls. For New Testament comments on this theme cf. 2 Cor. ix. 6–11; Gal. vi. 8, 9.

PSALM CXXVII. SONG OF WORK AND FAMILY

See General Introduction above to Psalms cxx–cxxxiv

This Psalm is declared by many to be composite, i.e. two Psalms joined in one. The themes in the two parts are certainly different, verses 1 and 2 speaking of the indispensable need of God's favour, and verses 3–6 of the blessings of a large family. But even if originally separate, when thus joined they fit together as a unity. The Psalm breathes the spirit of arduous toil and social consciousness which is characteristic of all pioneer settlement. At such times the physical component of life becomes dominant—the clearing of wastes, tilling of the soil, building of homes, maintenance of food supplies, and the establishment of a family to augment manpower and strengthen the community, especially in emergencies when hostilities occur. Over these necessary and typical aspects of early settlement the psalmist has thrown the vitality and sovereignty of the Lord. The whole Psalm may be regarded as an expansion of the proverb 'The blessing of the Lord, it maketh rich, and he addeth no sorrow with it' (Pr. x. 22), with the additional comment that human failure to recognize the divine basis of life does not negate it but misapplies and ultimately misses it wholly. Life then becomes vain, purposeless, ineffective, futile (cf. Rom. viii. 20).

The words 'of Solomon' (RV) in the title are omitted in the LXX. Some commentators have taken the statement together with *build the house* (1) as referring to Solomon's erection of the temple. There is no good ground for this interpretation. The poem aptly describes the period of reconstruction when the exiles returned to Jerusalem. *The house* means any dwelling and *the city* means any city. Neither one nor the other can be built without God (cf. 1 Cor. iii. 9). *Labour* (1); i.e. work till weary. Long hours, enthusiasm and determination are insufficient of themselves. *So he giveth . . . sleep* (2); better, 'in sleep' as in RV mg., meaning either that which men seek laboriously the Lord gives to His beloved even as they sleep, i.e. satisfaction, security, and sustenance (cf. Mk. iv. 27); or that which it is God's pleasure to give to His beloved does not depend wholly on their zeal and ability, for He imparts His blessing to them even when they sleep.

That conception and birth are not caused solely by human activity is repeatedly stated in Scripture, e.g. Gn. xx. 18, xxx. 2; Ru. iv. 13; 1 Sa. i. 5ff.; Lk. i. 13ff. In verse 4 read as in RV 'children of youth'; i.e. born when the parents are young. *In the gate* (5); the place of lawsuits and disputes (cf. Ps. lxix. 12; Jb. xxix. 7ff.; Is. xxix. 21). The meaning is that a man with many sons has a strong position in the community, and will not be put to shame if he has to contend at law with those who are his enemies.

PSALM CXXVIII. THE REWARDS OF A GODLY LIFE

See General Introduction above to Psalms cxx–cxxxiv

The Psalm falls into two parts, describing the blessings of the God-fearing man, first in his work and home (1–3) and then in national and family prosperity (4–6). If the return from Babylon could be regarded as a second exodus from Egypt (e.g. Ps. cxxiv), so could the re-settlement in Judaea be thought of as a re-enactment of Noah's reoccupation of a derelict world. Hence the theme of this song is the blessing upon those who emerged from their captivity in the ark, 'be fruitful, and multiply, and replenish the earth' (Gn. ix. 1, 7).

Eat the labour of thine hands (2). The enjoyment of a successful harvest was a token of divine blessing (contrast Dt. xxviii. 38, 39). *Thy wife . . . a fruitful vine* (3); i.e. needing support yet providing that which maketh glad a man's heart. *By the sides of thine house* (3); better, as in RV, 'in the innermost parts of thine house', i.e. that part of the home always allotted to women. *Olive plants* (3); symbolic of vitality. Finally, while the foundation of the Lord's blessing is personal godliness (1, 4), its sphere is peculiarly related to Zion where Yahweh is

enthroned, and the welfare of the family is inseparable from the prosperity of Jerusalem.

The benediction 'Peace be upon Israel' (6, RV; see end of Ps. cxxv) helps to distinguish this central triad of poems.

PSALM CXXIX. ISRAEL'S AFFLICTION AND THE DISCOMFITURE OF HER FOES

See General Introduction above to Psalms cxx–cxxxiv

There is no indication of a specific historical event in this 'litany of afflicted Israel'. The introductory phrases open a perspective which reaches back to the bondage in Egypt (RV 'from my youth up'; cf. Ho. xi. 1) with its whips of the overseers (Ex. iii. 7, v. 14, vi. 9). Usually the historical retrospect was intended to clarify the continuity of the divine choice of Israel (e.g. Ne. ix. 6ff.; Pss. lxviii, lxxviii, cv, cxxxvi; Ho. xi. 1ff.), and here, in spite of the strong metaphor in verse 3, the dominant thought is that of Israel's survival (2b) because no wickedness could long prevail against the righteousness of the Lord as it was believed to be established in Zion. The Psalm falls into two parts: a review of the past history of Israel (1–4) and a prayer against the present haters of Zion (5–8).

The first line of the poem is repeated after 'Let Israel now say' (RV) in order to allow a full response by the pilgrims right from the commencement of the song (cf. Ps. cxxiv. 1). Verse 3 is a vivid metaphor of cruelty and oppression practised to the full. Israel's enemies treated the nation as men do a ploughed field, leaving it covered with long furrows. There may be a reference to the lashes of the overseer's whip upon their backs. Cf. Is. li. 23. In verse 4 the metaphor changes to that of an ox bound to the plough in servitude. The Lord has released them from this bondage. Yet when Israel regained their freedom and returned home it was to find in the Samaritans new sources of hatred against Zion. Let these wither as grass in a rooftop cranny, where there is no depth of soil, which can never mature and be harvested as hay or corn. *Filleth not his hand* (7); i.e. the reaper (7, RV) cannot seize it with his left hand as he cuts it with a sickle in his right. The imagery is continued in the final verse. Such occasional and haphazard growth could never be associated with the voices of greeting and response in the harvest field (see Ruth ii. 4). The implication is, 'let those who oppose the existence and prosperity of Zion never be able to bring their schemes to fruition.'

PSALM CXXX. LIFTED FROM THE DEPTHS

See General Introduction above to Psalms cxx–cxxxiv

The Psalm is in two parts: prayer based upon God's mercy (1–4) and expectant faith quickened by waiting upon God (5–8).

This penitential plea for divine forgiveness is almost certainly a personal prayer which was found so to express the national remorse during captivity that it was adapted for general use by the addition of the last two verses where the personal pronouns are replaced by *Israel*. Alternatively, verses 7 and 8 may be regarded as an expression by the penitent of a hope so sure that he calls upon his people to share in it. The Psalm begins in the depths of distress, and ends on the heights of confident hope. Similar instances of faith triumphing over despondency are found in Pss. iii, vi and xiii.

Out of the depths (1); i.e. a frequent metaphor for intense need and critical danger (cf. Ps. lxix. 1, 2, 14, cxxiv. 5; Jon. ii. 4–6). *Mark* (3); i.e. keep for reckoning (cf. Mal. iii. 16; Jb. xiv. 17). *Lord . . . O Lord* (3); Heb. *Jah . . . Adonai*. In the court of divine justice none could stand or survive examination. *Mayest be feared* (4); i.e. the Lord's forgiveness enables men to reverence and obey Him. *I wait . . . my soul doth wait, My soul waiteth* (5, 6), a repetition indicative of passionate concentration based upon His word or promise to forgive and redeem. The duplication of the last phrase in verse 6 (see RV) adds further emphasis to this intent turning to the Lord. The communion which is so desired is characterized by the certainty and reality of the Lord's mercy or love (cf. verse 4) and His unlimited power fully to redeem from sin.

PSALM CXXXI. SCHOOLED IN HUMILITY

See General Introduction above to Psalms cxx–cxxxiv

This breath of true humility has some resemblance to the previous Psalm in that it is intensely personal except in the final verse where Israel is mentioned. There is no reason why its Davidic authorship should be doubted though it is impossible to associate it definitely with any episode in his life. It might reflect his reaction to his brother's unkind comment (1 Sa. xvii. 28) for it is most appropriate to his early years.

Haughty . . . lofty (1); the heart is seen in the eyes (cf. Ps. ci. 5; Pr. xxx. 13). *Neither do I exercise myself* (1); i.e. my walk and manner of life is not among great things in court, army or community. *I have behaved* (2); better, as in RV, 'stilled'; the meaning is to make smooth by levelling. His emotional desires (here called 'my soul'), once so eager and clamant, have been kept serene and quiet, even as a child fully weaned will rest contented on the breast which it formerly craved to possess. Confident security has replaced restless ambition (cf. Col. iii. 15).

PSALM CXXXII. THE OATH OF DAVID AND THE OATH OF THE LORD

See General Introduction above to Psalms cxx–cxxxiv

This song is unlike the previous Songs of Ascents not merely in its length, but in its appeal to two historical covenants, and in its themes of tabernacle and throne. A fragment of it (verses 8–10) has been incorporated into Solomon's dedicatory prayer as given in 2 Chronicles (see 2 Ch. vi. 41, 42). It is in two parts.

a. The oath of David (1–10)

Remember David (1); better, as in RV, 'remember for David'. The psalmist requests that the hazards and troubles which David encountered in capturing Jerusalem and bringing thither the ark (cf. 2 Sa. vi. 8–10; 1 Ch. xxi. 13 and 30) be remembered by the Lord 'for' him, i.e. in blessing to his dynasty. Particular attention is called to David's deep concern for the glory of the name of the Lord (cf. 2 Sa. vii) which was so strong that, though he inhabited the tabernacle of his house, he could not rest there with contentment and satisfaction. He made a vow to the 'Mighty One of Jacob' (2, RV, as also verse 5; cf. Gn. xlix. 24) because at that period 'the Lord had given him power over all his enemies'. The king's desire was honoured by God but its fulfilment was prohibited (cf. Is. lxvi. 1, 2a).

The antiphonal singing of this song may have followed the division, verses 1–5 and 6–9. Verses 6 and 7 certainly represent the eager response of the people of David's time when David first undertook to fetch the ark from the neighbourhood of Kirjath-jearim (lit. 'the city of the woods'; see 1 Sa. vii. 1, 2). *We heard of it* (as being) *at Ephratah* must be interpreted in the light of its actual sojourn for twenty years in the house of Abinadab (cf. 2 Sa. vi. 2–5), i.e. Ephratah must have been a name of that district. *We will go into his tabernacles* (7); i.e. 'dwelling places'; the word is plural (as 'habitations' in verse 3 mg. and Ps. xliii. 3), either as a simple form of emphasis, or as a collective term which echoes Dt. xii. 5, 11 and 21, etc. For the tabernacle rested at Gilgal, Bethel, Shiloh and Kirjath-jearim before reaching Zion. *Footstool* (7); i.e. the ark (cf. 1 Ch. xxviii. 2) which was below His invisible presence. *Arise, O Lord* (8); an echo of the frequent cry in the wilderness (cf. Nu. x. 35; note Ps. lxviii. 1).

b. The oath of the Lord (11–18)

This covenant was God's response to David's desire. It replaced the king's conception of a permanent, stone building to house the presence of the Lord (who preferred a movable dwelling), with a more enduring expression in human flesh (11, 12) of the Lord's power and steadfast purpose (cf. Ps. lxxxix. 19–37), i.e. the chosen dwelling of the Lord was personal not architectural. (Cf. Stephen's speech in Acts vii; cf. also Jn. i. 14, RV; 2 Cor. vi. 16; Heb. ix. 11; 1 Pet. ii. 4–7.) Nevertheless a peculiar relationship was affirmed between the Lord and a physical locality, i.e. Zion; this was *for ever* (13, 14). Usually the city, the sanctuary, and the site are equivalent and synonymous, but this divine election may be limited to the topographical feature of 'Mount Zion' as distinct from the habitable city (cf. Pss.

ii, lxviii. 16, lxxviii. 68; Joel iii. 17, 18). The poetical books of the Old Testament insist on the close association of the physical world with its spiritual Creator (e.g. Pss. xxix, lxxviii, civ; Jb. xxxviii—xxxix).

Note the close parallelism of thought between the two parts of the song. To the prayer 'Move to thy resting place, clothe thy priests with righteousness, let thy saints shout for joy, turn not away the face of thine anointed' (8–10), there is made the complete answer 'This is my resting-place for ever, her priests will I clothe with salvation, her saints shall shout aloud for joy, I have ordained a lamp (to burn for ever) before mine anointed' (14–17). For the metaphors in verse 17 cf. Lk. i. 69; 1 Ki. xi. 36 and notes on Ps. cxlviii. 14.

PSALM CXXXIII. THE BLESSINGS OF BRETHREN DWELLING IN UNITY

See General Introduction above to Psalms cxx–cxxxiv

This is a poem about communal sympathy and brotherly kindness. It is usually assumed that the dwelling together here spoken of refers to the gathering together of the people at the yearly feasts. The Hebrew word for dwell (lit. 'sit') might certainly be used of such a temporary assembling. There is, however, an alternative view that the Psalm may have been written to encourage the returned exiles to settle in Jerusalem. Unity was very desirable among the settlers who had returned to the neighbourhood of Jerusalem (note Ne. xi. 1). It could be greatly fostered by regular centralized worship (cf. Ezr. iii. 1). Moreover, the unity of a common blood and tradition needed to be reinforced and augmented by amity and close proximity. The psalmist's emphasis is upon the advantages of a close and compact settlement.

He illustrates this in two ways. First, it is like the special consecrating oil which, in the case of the High Priest, was poured upon his head and spread over all his person down to the hem of his garments (cf. Ex. xxix. 7; Lv. viii. 12). That is to say, unity is a rare and blessed thing, never more so than when its influence spreads to the whole of society. *The skirts of his garments* (2); lit. 'mouth of his garments', which may refer to the collar of Aaron's robe. The image of unity is preserved in that the oil would reach the two onyx stones on Aaron's breast, bearing the names of the twelve tribes.

In the second place it likens this unity to the refreshing dew, heavy as that on high Hermon, and falling also on Zion, which is so important in regions like Palestine where rainfall alone is often barely enough for good harvests. (Note Haggai's reference to its need, Hg. i. 10, 11.) *The blessing, even life for evermore* (3). See notes on Ps. cxxxii. 14–17. The promise to the nation was one of renewed and continuing life.

PSALM CXXXIV. A PRAYERFUL GREETING AND GRACIOUS RESPONSE

See General Introduction above to Psalms cxx–cxxxiv

This doxology closes the miniature Psalter of the Songs of Ascents (cf. Ps. cl). The first two verses (chanted by the retiring congregation) are a benediction upon the few priests and attendants who remain in the temple throughout the night (1 Ch. ix. 33). They were not simply guardians and watchers but maintained some form of worship. For example, they are referred to as 'standing' (cf. Dt. x. 8; 1 Ch. xxiii. 30), and 'lifting up hands' (cf. Pss. xxviii. 2, cxli. 2). The last verse was their final response ere the congregation of pilgrims dispersed. *The Lord that made heaven and earth* (3); i.e. the God of all power. *Bless thee out of Zion* (3). *Thee* is singular; i.e. the blessing was addressed to each worshipper.

PSALM CXXXV. BLESS YE THE LORD

Although this anthem is not included in the preceding anthology of songs used by pilgrims journeying to Jerusalem, it has an obvious association with the Songs of Ascents and with other Psalms of corporate praise. It can be regarded as an expansion of the final song in the group, for Ps. cxxxiv is virtually repeated in verses 1, 2 and 21. On the other hand the central portion (3–20) incorporates many features of the Egyptian Hallel (Pss. cxiii—cxviii) especially from Ps. cxv. The whole poem is very largely a mosaic of earlier Psalms, and there can be little doubt but that it was composed for public occasions of festive worship, and that it was deliberately designed to evoke memories and associations of other songs of praise. The probable period would be when centralized worship was resumed under Ezra's leadership. The general pattern of thought is fairly clear.

a. Prologue (1–6)

A general introduction consisting of three couplets which deal with Israel's privileges in worship (1, 2), the divine election of Israel (3, 4), and finally the full sovereignty of the Lord (5, 6). *I know* (5); the strength of this personal affirmation is to be seen in the subsequent verses. *Above all gods* (5); cf. Ex. xx. 3; Dt. x. 17; also Pss. lxxxvi. 8, xcv. 3, xcvii. 9. With verse 6 cf. Ps. cxv. 3.

b. The Lord and His people (7–20)

The three introductory ideas are considerably developed, but not in the same sequence. Moreover, they are so handled as to focus all upon the peculiar relationship between Israel and the Lord.

i. **God's governing activity in nature and history** (7–12). *He causeth the vapours* (7); i.e. clouds; cf. Je. x. 13; Jb. xxxvi. 26–29, xxxvii. 3,

9–12, 15, 16, xxxviii. 22–28. This is the background to the exclamation of verse 3, 'the Lord is good'. For verses 8 and 9 see Ex. xii. 12 and 29; Pss. lxxviii. 51, cxxxvi. 10. This is part of the ceaseless echo of Ex. xv and illustrates the other thought of verse 3, 'to praise Him is pleasant'. *Who smote great nations* (10); cf. Dt. vii. 1. Sihon and Og were early and outstanding examples; cf. Nu. xxi. 21–35. This action is the counterpart of verse 4a, 'The Lord hath chosen Jacob'. *Gave their land for an heritage* (12); cf. Ps. lxxviii. 55 and cxxxvi. 21, 22; for the kingdoms of Canaan cf. Jos. xii. 7. This twelfth verse is rooted in verse 4b, 'Israel is his peculiar treasure'.

ii. The absolute supremacy of the Lord over the gods of all other nations (13–18). *Thy name . . . endureth* (13); cf. Ps. cii. 12. *Judge* (14); i.e. govern righteously (implying deliverance); cf. Dt. xxxii. 36. The emphasis here on *all generations* (13) is a corporate expression to balance the personal assurance of verse 5a, 'I know that the Lord is great'. *The idols of the heathen* (15) are man-made; contrast verse 5b, He is 'above all gods'. *They speak not . . . see not . . . hear not* (16, 17); the antithesis of verse 6a, 'What he pleaseth that hath he done'. Verses 15–18 are similar to Ps. cxv. 4–8. *They that make them are like unto them* (18); the complete lack of effect upon their makers is without exception, whereas in verse 6b the Lord's power is without limit.

iii. The high calling of the Lord to Israel (19, 20). These two verses balance the first two: *Bless the Lord*—'Praise ye the Lord'; *O house of Aaron*—'O ye servants'; *O house of Levi*—'Ye that stand in the house'; *Ye that fear the Lord*—(Ye that stand) 'in the courts of the house'. This call to worship is the same as Ps. cxv. 9–11, but the addition of the house of Levi emphasizes the three groups of worshippers, and also implies the triple structure of the temple enclosures.

c. Benediction (21)

The conclusion inverts the benediction of Ps. cxxxiv. 3. In that the Lord centres His blessings on Zion (Ps. cxxxii. 13–16), and distributes them through Zion (Ps. cxxxiv. 3), so should He be praised with particular fervour at Jerusalem.

PSALM CXXXVI. MERCY AND MAJESTY

Just as Ps. cxxxv is a development of the conclusion of Ps. cxxxiv, so also Ps. cxxxvi may be regarded as a response to Ps. cxxxv. 19, 20. Indeed, the two Psalms are very closely related. The principal characteristic of this national hymn, which distinguishes it from other national anthems such as Pss. lxxviii, cv and cvi, is the regular refrain, *For his mercy endureth for ever*, a liturgical phrase much used elsewhere (e.g. 1 Ch. xvi. 41; 2 Ch. v. 13, vii. 3; Ezr. iii. 11; Pss. cvi, cvii and cxviii). This refrain was probably sung by the congregation in response to the sentences sung by the Levites, or by the Levitical choir in response to the chanting of one precentor. If the recurrent chorus is removed a short Psalm of praise remains which extols the goodness of the Lord. There are five sections to the poem.

a. Introduction (1–4)

Note the four phrases *The Lord is good* (1), *God of gods* (2), *Lord of lords* (3), *who alone doeth great wonders* (4). They may be said to serve as themes for the following four stanzas, but the order is inverted. With verses 2 and 3 cf. Dt. x. 17. With verse 4 cf. Ps. lxxii. 18.

b. A God who doeth great wonders (5–9)

Stretched out . . . above (6). The earth was regarded as floating on the waters of the deeps; cf. Ps. xxiv. 2, cxxxv. 6; Is. xlii. 5; Gn. vii. 11; Jb. xxxviii. 8, 16. *Great lights . . . to rule* (7–9); as in Gn. i. 14–16.

c. He is Lord of lords (10–15)

These verses may be divided into three pairs of twin phrases stressing the superhuman phenomena of selection (for death, and for freedom), strength (to grasp, and to sunder), success (in bringing through, and in throwing down). Alternatively they may be considered as two groups of three phrases (verses 10–12 and 13–15), each group extolling the contrast between God's treatment of Egypt and of Israel. In verse 13 see RV.

d. He is God of gods (16–22)

The Lord is shown acting in history to establish His people. The examples given illustrate His divine leadership through the years. The gods of the heathen were overthrown and their territory given to Israel.

e. The Lord is good (23–26)

In these closing verses His goodness is acclaimed first in Israel's deliverances from their *low estate* (23) and many 'adversaries' (24, RV). This is probably a panoramic concept of the trend of the nation's history, but with a particular reference to the exile and return. Then the writer recalls His benevolence toward all creatures whom He sustains in life (cf. Pss. civ. 27, 28, cxlv. 15, 16; Jb. xii. 7–10). The final expression *God of heaven* continues the idea of comprehensiveness. Contrast *all flesh* (25) with *us* (23). It also knits together the second or main portion of the poem (cf. 5, 26).

PSALM CXXXVII. JERUSALEM, EDOM AND BABYLON

This lament, at first poignant but finally indignant, expresses the reaction of Jewish exiles when they first hopefully returned to Zion only to be shocked by its derelict condition. This contradiction of mood is reflected in the poem; in fact it is its chief feature. There are two parts: one looking to the past (1–4), the other to the future (5–9). Each has two phases of thought, one associated with the Jews themselves and the other with their enemies.

In verses 1, 2 and 5, 6 the river plains of Babylon (cf. Je. li. 13) stand in contrast to the upland city of Jerusalem, and the idea of enforced cessation of music in Babylon contrasts with willingness to suffer dumbness if Jerusalem be forgotten in their hearts. *We sat down, yea, we wept* (1); cf. Jb. ii. 12, 13; Ezr. ix. 3. The harp was usually the instrument for joyous songs (cf. Is. xxiv. 8; 2 Sa. vi. 5). *Wasted us* (3); i.e. humiliated us. They had taken their harps in the hope that they might find comfort in song. But the mocking demands of their tormentors (RV mg.) made it impossible. To have sung a temple chant or *the Lord's song* (4; cf. 2 Ch. xxix. 27) for the entertainment of an alien people would have been profanity. *Let my right hand forget* (5); i.e. in the sense of 'become paralysed'.

The songs of Zion, which were refused in a strange land, are thus replaced by retribution besought upon foreign peoples (7–9). The former captivity in Babylon is set alongside the present freedom in Judaea; the exiles' earlier dreams and desires are contrasted with their city's actual decay and distress; tears of remorse are exchanged for terrible anger; the silence of a profound grief that was irked by their captors' mirth is matched by the curse of dumbness invoked upon a loyalty that is not stirred by Zion to its highest joy. The antithesis reaches its climax when the memory of those in Babylon who tormented the exiles to sing the remembrances of the Lord is balanced by a malediction upon those in Edom who treacherously desired the complete removal of the Lord's city. *Rase it* (7); i.e. 'make it bare', leave not one stone upon another. Their wrath towards the Edomites was reinforced by an age-long feud that went back to the days of Jacob and Esau. Many prophets besides Obadiah had spoken vehemently of Edom's malicious hatred of the children of Jacob (cf. Is. xxxiv; Je. xlix. 7–22; Ezk. xxv. 12–14; Am. i. 11). Their gleeful co-operation when, *in the day of Jerusalem* (7), the city was sacked by Nebuchadnezzar, was bitterly resented. Babylon was hated because it had been the agent of their downfall. The plea for a just recompense to this heathen nation is expressed in terms of 'an eye for an eye, a tooth for a tooth'. As they had cruelly and murderously served the Jews, so would they also be served (9). (See *Introduction*, p. 414.)

PSALM CXXXVIII. A SONG OF THANKSGIVING

The eight poems cxxxviii–cxlv are entitled *Of David*, but their authorship is not quite clear. The LXX adds 'of Haggai and Zechariah' to the title of Ps. cxxxviii, suggestive of a revision in the restoration period. Ps. cxxxix is so outstanding that it is not easy to imagine how it was overlooked when the Davidic poems were first collected to form the basis of Books I and II of the Psalter. Moreover, it has many linguistic characteristics of a much later period. To a lesser extent the same can be said of the remaining six Psalms. Undoubtedly all this group is Davidic in thought, and if they were not originally by his hand they have been modelled upon his works. Ps. cxxxviii may well be intended as a companion to David's prayer in 2 Sa. vii. 18–29.

The structure of the Psalm seems to be similar to that of Ps. cxxxv; i.e. an introductory statement (1, 2) which is subsequently expanded phrase by phrase as follows: e.g. *I will praise thee with my whole heart;* the reason for this desire to 'give thanks' (RV) to the Lord is expressed in verse 3. *Before the gods* (i.e. 'in the presence of the mighty rulers') *will I sing praise;* the result will be that these same *kings of the earth* (4) will join in the ascription of praise to God. *I will worship toward thy holy temple,* inspired by the greatness of God's glory (5b) and encouraged by the fact that He has *respect unto the lowly* (6). In a similar way the psalmist's confidence in God's care and protection (7, 8) seems to underlie the ascription of thanksgiving in verse 2b. (See RV.) God, he knows, will fully complete His purposes for him.

PSALM CXXXIX. INDEPENDENCE OR IDENTIFICATION

This is one of the finest poems in the Psalter; it is outstanding both theologically and psychologically. Its literary structure is simple, four stanzas each of six verses. But the pattern of thought is more complex and could be likened to a parabola, for there is a movement away and back again; the slow crisis occurs at the centre and the conclusion inverts the commencement. In it we overhear someone in the process of realizing life's most transforming experience, the apprehension of 'the otherness' of God who is personal, omnipresent, omniscient and holy.

a. Irksome sense of limitation (1–6)

The psalmist is overheard as he whispers to himself, so to speak, about his reaction to the revelation of God. 'The essence of the encounter has produced an irrefutable and revolutionary consciousness that over against me, beyond, beneath and around me, there is Another, a Person infinitely greater than myself in every positive respect. Because He cannot be changed, I must take up an attitude toward Him; because I am wholly in His power, my attitude to Him must affect my whole being and my future destiny.' The opening *Thou* is emphatic. *O Lord, thou hast searched me, and known me* (or 'knowest me') (1). The result of God's investigation is perfect knowledge, comprehending every possible form of my activity and being. *My thought* (2); a word occurring only in this Psalm (see also verse 17). *Thou compassest* (3); RV 'searchest out'; see also RV mg. The thought is that *my path* (i.e. my going forth to labour) is minutely examined by God. My goings forth and my returnings, and my whole conduct and speech (4), casual, impulsive or deliberate, are familiar to Him. Verse 4 may be rendered 'The word is not yet on my tongue, but lo!, etc.'. *Beset* (5); i.e. 'besieged or hemmed in'. God has enclosed me between birth and death. *Laid thine hand upon me* (5); this might be rendered 'laid me on thine outspread palm'. The psalmist feels bound, limited and imprisoned precisely because he realizes that God knows him so intimately, directly, thoroughly, critically and inescapably (cf. Heb. iv. 13). Such knowledge is beyond human comprehension.

b. Search for escape in space (7-12)

'The feeling of oppression which has been induced by the immensity and intensity of thy knowledge compels me to seek for an escape by any means and in any realm (7). If I try to flee or evade thee by distance (8-10) or darkness (11, 12) it is found to be impossible; neither height nor depth, sky nor grave (*hell*, RV 'Sheol') are beyond thee; and to rest lifeless in my tomb would be as noticeable to thee as though I stormed the gate of heaven (8; cf. Am. ix. 2). Thou art not only above, below and beyond wherever I may seek refuge—even though I have the swiftness of the dawn and reach the furthest isles of the sea—but thou art everywhere (9; cf. Acts xvii. 27, 28). Consequently thou art always able to reveal thyself, and thy hand can continue to lead me in compassion or hold me in wrath (10). But if I cannot leave thy presence behind me, maybe I can hide. Yet no darkness could conceal anything from thee nor make the slightest difference to thy vigilance. There is no thing nor quality but is transparent to thee; mere physical immensity or obscurity are spiritually negligible.'

c. Search for escape in time (13-18)

In his search for a way of escape from God it almost seems as though the psalmist is saying: 'All my life I have been within thy view, thy reach and thy knowledge. My only hope lies in my unconscious life. I cannot trace its present extent but I can go back to that initial period when, within my mother's womb, I had no knowledge of my own existence and maybe then thou also wast unaware of me' (cf. Jb. iii).

It is here that the theme begins to swing round for a return. In this final possibility the psalmist finds his sense of freedom and worship. This is not due to any escape from God, but to the discovery that his existence has been caused by God. The emphatic *Thou* of verse 13 is an echo of verse 2 and the beginning of a fresh journey. *Possessed my reins* (13); i.e. made (as in Gn. xiv. 19) the place of my inmost feelings. This revelation of his origin balances the previous disclosure of God's nature and being; it restores the poise of his life but on a transformed basis. Adoration and praise now spring to his lips (14). He perceives that true self-consciousness is

possible only when he realizes his creaturely existence in relation to God.

From the marvel of his physical origin under the skilled hand of God he derives three ideas:

First, the Lord intends good toward him. He is His creature and, if He took so much care and lavished so much skill on his individual origin, what will He not do for his welfare? Verses 15, 16 are an excellent summary of antenatal development: the first secret knitting together, early growth, formation of a skeleton 'frame' (RV), the fabric of flesh clothing the whole and growing day by day. *In the lowest parts of the earth* (15) primarily refers to the concealing womb, which is here compared to the nether world, a place of darkness and mystery. *Thine eyes did see my substance* (16); i.e. my imperfect substance or embryo. A different word in Hebrew from that translated *substance* by the AV in verse 15 (cf. RV). The remainder of verse 16 may be rendered 'and in thy book were they all written, even the days that were fashioned (or foreseen) and for it (my physical origin) there was one (fixed) among them'.

Secondly, the goodness of the Lord exceeds his understanding. One consequence of his formation at the hand of God is that he cannot elude or exhaust Him; he is wholly entangled in the web of His purposes, and these *thoughts* of the Lord are *precious* to him (17). In that God has made him man, He made him for a good end. Forgetting his former fears the psalmist now perceives so many possible ends that he loses count (18; cf. Ps. xl. 5; note also 1 Cor. i. 30; Eph. i. 3-12).

Thirdly, the good purpose of God towards him implies prolonged communion with Him. *When I awake* (18) does not imply an awakening after death (see notes on Ps. xvii. 15), but simply 'whenever I awake from the unconsciousness of sleep I find myself still with thee'.

d. A startling and vigorous reaction (19-24)

It should be noticed that each stanza has closed with an expression of wonderment and awe. In relation to the whole poem the last stanza serves in the same way. The contrast of mood is so abrupt as to jolt the receptive mind and intensify the impression created by the Psalm. Hitherto the poem has been intensely personal. But the author lived in a society of men not all of whom were aware of the divine Majesty. No sooner do his thoughts turn to the realm of normal life than the psalmist perceives the anomaly of God's detailed knowledge of every heart and His continuous leniency toward the ungodly. Hence his exclamation, *Surely thou wilt slay the wicked* (19). It may have been the presence of such evil men which first precipitated that desire to escape which was reorientated by the revelation of the Lord (1-12). The forthright language of verses 19 and 20 is expressive of a strong character who has been so invigorated by a new conception of divine power and goodness that he bursts out in vehement denunciations of those who practise evil schemes under the cloak of 'the name' which they take in vain. He has now become so eager for God's fellowship that he identifies himself with God in His abhorrence of the wicked (cf. Lk. x. 16). *Am not I grieved?* (21); better, as in RV mg., 'do not I loathe?'

Surprisingly enough the psalmist now becomes aware of the existence of that for which he had previously sought in vain. The change from meditation to activity has evoked in him an intensity of feeling (21, 22) that surprises him and he wonders whether in his zeal for God he has acted on human, fallible, independent and questionable motives of which he was previously unaware. Thus he pleads with God to do what he himself failed to do—to search him through and through (cf. 1 Cor. ii. 10, 11). The motive of such an investigation is not that he himself might utilize any possible territory for his soul's independence, but that, if God found such, He should purge it of that peril by His abiding presence.

This conclusion is in complete contrast to the initial mood. But the range of thought has been so wide in its contact with God and the unknown that no better or more positive conclusion could have been made. *Try me, and know my* (wandering or disquieting) *thoughts* (23); cf. Ps. xxvi. 2. *Any wicked way* (24); better translated as 'any way that would become hurtful or grievous'. *Way everlasting* (24); i.e. the path of the righteous. It is not necessarily an aspiration to immortality.

PSALM CXL. DELIVER ME FROM WICKED MEN

This prayer for divine protection against scheming enemies has much in common with the spirit of Pss. lviii and lxiv, and it may have been composed with those Davidic models in mind. It is not possible to say when it was written or what circumstance in David's life it was intended to reflect. The Psalm falls into five parts, the first three of which terminate with *Selah*.

a. The attack of lying propaganda (1–3)

The prayer for deliverance (1) is expanded by a description of the evil men whose speech threatens the psalmist with war or 'bitter strife'. The theme is illustrated by references to their secret intentions (they 'devise evil in their heart'), their attempts to stir up strife, and their pointed and poisoned words (see introduction to Ps. cxx).

b. The secret plans of the wicked (4, 5)

This prayer for protection is amplified by an account of the wicked men whose hidden works endanger the psalmist. He recounts their plans to make his feet slip or stumble, to cause him to fall foul of snares or nooses (*cords*), and to become caught in nets and traps (*gins*). The imagery is of hunting birds and beasts. While his enemies would never act literally in these ways, the contrast with the metaphors of plots and poisons in verses 1–3 suggests that there is here

a reference to some actual deeds, some cruelly contrived co-ordination of circumstances.

c. An appeal to the Lord for protection (6–8)

The prayer is threefold: 'Give ear, O my God'; 'strengthen me, O Lord my Saviour'; 'Frustrate, O Lord, the devices of the wicked.' These three phrases are the core of the whole poem. *Thou hast covered my head* (7); i.e. with a helmet. Cf. the reference to 'war' in verse 2. *Further not his wicked device* (8). This verse anticipates and explains the malediction which follows. Let not God allow wicked men to succeed in their desires lest they become powerful and arrogant ('exalted'); if that occurred the godly would be doubly oppressed.

d. Retribution (9–11)

The psalmist meets the wicked intentions of the hearts of the wicked by the desire that the evil of their lips (3) should recoil upon them and become true in them (9). He counters their hidden deeds (4, 5) with a desire for their unconcealable destruction, as plain as the fire which fell on Sodom (cf. Ps. xi. 6), and as irremediable as the deep waters of the flood. The word rendered *deep pits* by the AV occurs only here and possibly means 'deep floods': contrast Is. xliii. 2. Finally he declares that the inescapable principle of righteousness ensures the ultimate failure of every slanderer and the eventual overthrow of every violent, evil man. *An evil speaker* (11); lit., as in RV mg., 'a man of tongue'. They who hunted without mercy shall themselves be hunted; those who sought to make him stumble shall themselves be smitten down.

e. The assurance brought by the Lord's presence (12, 13)

The psalmist concludes with a note of confidence, *I know* (12). Although he is surrounded by foes, he can trust the Lord to uphold his cause. He can even begin to give thanks, not merely for deliverance out of all his troubles, but for the gracious privilege extended to the upright —as distinct from his ungodly foes—of dwelling in the presence of the Lord (13). See Ps. xvi. 11; cf. 2 Tim. iv. 16–18; 1 Jn. iv. 4ff.).

PSALM CXLI. DEDICATION UNTO RIGHTEOUSNESS

This is a prayer for strength of purpose amidst difficulties. The psalmist feels he is imperilled by hidden forces beyond his control. Outwardly there are the secret snares and temptations (4) of wicked men; inwardly there is an impulsive heart liable to resist the rebuke of friends (5), and capable of evil things. There is also an uncontrollable tongue (3), ready in a moment to speak in disparagement and complaint about G.d (for the mischief of speech see introduction to Ps. cxx). Apart from the introduction (1, 2) the Psalm falls into a double prayer (3, 4 and 8, 9) enclosing a passage of obscure meaning.

a. Introduction (1, 2)

The RV reading 'have called' (1) indicates that the psalmist has already been in prayer. The appeal for God to hasten His attention to the psalmist's voice is a frequent element in Davidic Psalms, e.g. xxii. 19, xxxviii. 22, xl. 13, lxx. 5. The association of prayer with sacrifice and incense (2) is clearly described in Ps. lxvi. 13ff. Verse 2 implies worship away from the tabernacle and without the actual evening offering. He prays that his prayer might be as acceptable to God as if it were offered in the temple.

b. Precaution against ungodliness (3, 4)

The psalmist's strong aversion to the ways of wickedness does not give him immunity from similar speech and desire. He pleads for divine power to prevent any lapse from righteousness on his part through the enticements of evil. *Their dainties* (4) would be physical luxuries acquired by unjust methods.

c. Steadfast under extreme provocation (5–7)

In one sense this passage may be regarded as a parenthesis, the prayer of verses 3, 4 being resumed in verses 8, 9. In these verses the psalmist envisages two extreme tests of steadfastness. On the one hand, the righteous may correct and reprove him, in which case he is not to be proud or resistant but to take their action as a kindness; i.e. 'as choice oil upon the head' which is intended for his welfare (cf. Ps. civ. 15, cxxxiii. 2). Throughout such an experience his prayer will continue to be directed against evil deeds (*calamities*); i.e. he would pray to be kept from partaking of the nature and action of evil men. The other extreme would be when wicked princes (*judges*) 'have been hurled down by the sides of the rock' (cf. 2 Ch. xxv. 12) and their (reading with RV mg. 'their' for 'our') bones are scattered where they entered into Sheol. Even so he would not boast or become proud, for the populace (*they*) would still hear his words that *they are sweet*, i.e. pleasant, honouring to God (cf. 2 Sa. xxiii. 1). Alternatively, retaining the word 'our' in verse 7, the verses may mean that the psalmist's friends have been extensively murdered (indeed, following the AV, their bones strew the ground like chips of wood when a log is being trimmed with an axe, or, following the RV, their bones are spread over the furrowed earth like seed on newly ploughed ground), and shall be precursors of a resurrection (cf. Is. xxvi. 19; Je. viii. 1, 2; Ezk. xxxvii. 1–14). Nevertheless, even then he would not become bitter against God, nor adopt the ungodly manners and motives of evil men. Possibly the obscurity of these three verses is due to our ignorance of some historical event to which they refer.

d. A prayer of consecration (8–10)

These final words should be read in conjunction with verses 3, 4. *Leave not my soul destitute* (8); i.e. do not pour out my life as theirs has been

(7, RV mg.; cf. Is. liii. 12). *Snares* and *gins* (9) are mentioned in Ps. cxl. 5. With verse 10 cf. Ps. vii. 15.

PSALM CXLII. 'GOD BE WITH ME'

The reference to *the cave* (see title) may be compared with that in the title to Ps. lvii. 'Maschil' probably refers to a type of musical accompaniment. The tenses throughout the Psalm are present, not past (see RV). The prayer falls into three stanzas and the last verse is a climax to the whole.

a. His plea (1–3a)

The psalmist's loneliness intensifies his yearning for the Lord. To Him he cries aloud (*with my voice*), pours out his *complaint* (see title of Ps. cii), and makes known his *trouble*. Yet he knows that God knows about him even when his spirit faints under the surge of distress. The last word, *path*, introduces the next section.

b. His path (3b–5)

The theme changes from the act of prayer to the course of experience—'the way wherein I walk' (3, RV). Somewhere in the winding pathway of his life there is a snare laid by unfriendly men. But it is his loneliness rather than his peril which burdens his soul. He has no companion, no one at his right hand on whom to depend. The way is unknown and leads to desolation. There is no refuge other than in the Lord. The last words, *land of the living*, introduce the next section.

c. His prison (6, 7)

After declaring that the Lord is his only portion in this life the psalmist proceeds to describe how limited and feeble that life is. He is *brought very low*, held by persecutors who are stronger than he, imprisoned in spirit, if not physically confined to the cave. Hence his call to God, *Attend unto my cry*. The three final phrases impart poise and serenity to the poem and show the readjustment of life which ensues from God's active presence. They outweigh the entire previous experience marked by complaint, loneliness and confinement.

PSALM CXLIII. 'LORD, HEAR MY CRY'

There is a close resemblance in mood and phrase between this Psalm and the previous one. There has been a considerable borrowing from other Psalms, especially in verses 5–9. The prayer is in two halves.

a. The platform of prayer (1–7a)

This appeal to the Lord is based upon His *faithfulness* and *righteousness* (1); i.e. His adherence to His promises (as in 2 Sa. vii) and His justice. The latter is not viewed as necessitating strict and impartial judgment, for then the psalmist, together with all living men, could never *be justified* (2), i.e. acquitted. Cf. cxxx. 3. The appeal is to divine righteousness as forgiving love (cf. Rom. iii. 21–25). There can be no good purpose in appealing to Him for attention and aid unless there is complete reliance upon His mercy (cf. Jb. ix. 2–23).

The cause of the appeal is rooted in the psalmist's distress. *For* (3) refers back to *hear . . . give ear* in the opening sentence. He is oppressed in spirit by *the enemy*. His life has been crushed to the ground so that he has lost all power to act or resist; his opponent (the group of enemies or the spirit of evil is individualized to enhance the sense of combat) has made him *to dwell in darkness* (3), RV 'dark places' (cf. Ps. lxxxviii. 6). This may mean he is as good as dead and in Sheol, or that he is already approaching the gloomy entrance to the grave (see 7b; Ps. xxiii. 4); or it may refer to imprisonment and peril as when David was surrounded by Saul's forces (see Pss. xiii. 3, xvii. 9 and 11, lvii. 4). The phrase *as those that have been long dead* (3) has the sense of 'oblivion' (cf. Ps. lxxxviii. 4, 5; La. iii. 6). *My heart . . . is desolate* (4); i.e. numbed, appalled.

The inspiration of the prayer comes from the psalmist's remembrance of the Lord's activity. *The work of thy hands* (5) refers to God's interventions in his earlier years (cf. Ps. xcii. 4), as well as to His miraculous deeds in Israel's past (cf. Ps. lxxvii. 5–12). This so intensifies his yearning for the presence of God that he feels like a parched garden withering for lack of rain (cf. Pss. xlii. 1, lxiii. 1). His extremity is so critical that if the Lord is to save him He must act immediately. *My spirit faileth* (7); lit. 'is at an end'. If God continues to withhold the light of His favour the psalmist will die. Verse 7a may be taken as a climax to this part of the Psalm.

b. The programme of deliverance (7b–12)

A series of phrases from many Psalms has been arranged here to form a detailed course of action which the psalmist desires the Lord to carry out on his behalf: 'Be quick, smile upon me, bless me, direct me, save me, teach me, accompany me, thus quicken or invigorate me, and destroy my persecutors.' There is first a desire for communion with God. Apart from His *face* (7), i.e. His presence, there can be no full life (cf. Dt. xxxi. 17, 18) or serenity (cf. Ps. xxx. 7, civ. 29), whereas conscious participation in His *lovingkindness* strengthens the bond of trust. The psalmist then expresses a desire for direction linked with a statement of his own submissiveness and need for security (cf. Ps. v. 8). Such guidance is the Godward side of full committal to the Lord. The desire for instruction which is next stated (10) is inseparable from following a leader (cf. Ps. xxv. 4, 5). The good or gracious Spirit of the Lord will yet lead him in a plain or level country (10, RV mg.; cf. Is. lxiii. 13, 14), and renew the pulse of his life because of the name of the Lord (11).

The fourth and final aspect of this prayer relates to the psalmist's circumstances rather than to his own career. It is a request for salvation, for complete freedom from his powerful enemies (see verse 3), on the ground that God is responsible for his welfare because he is His servant (12). The meaning may be that he can therefore claim a better end than that merited by the ungodly; or, that he is entitled to deliverance because God's honour would be impugned if His servant were to succumb to affliction.

PSALM CXLIV. FROM PERIL TO PROSPERITY

This joyful hymn contains a large number of phrases from other Psalms. It is Davidic in style; but although the title given in the LXX associates the song with the defeat of Goliath, there is little internal evidence to support that period. The Psalm has two main parts, the first and largest being a composite song of praise and peril. The dominant note throughout is one of joy. The psalmist rejoices in a former deliverance for which prayer had been offered and he anticipates a future prosperity which shall be idyllic in every respect.

a. Deliverance (1–11)

The first two verses are praise for power. *The Lord my strength* (1); RV 'rock'. Cf. Pss. xviii. 1, 2 and 31, xxxi. 2, 3. *Teacheth my hands to war* (1); this is also based on Ps. xviii (see verse 34). The description of God as a refuge (2) is frequent in Davidic Psalms. See, e.g., Pss. xviii. 1, 2, lxi. 3, 4. *Subdueth my people* (2); cf. Ps. xviii. 47.

The next six verses (3–8) belong to a former prayer for deliverance. They are repeated here in order to enhance the quality of freedom and delight. The first thought is of man's insignificance (3, 4; cf. Pss. viii. 4, xxxix. 11, cii. 11). The second thought is of divine power before which all creation trembles (5, 6; cf. Pss. xviii. 7, 14, civ. 32). The third thought is of personal peril needing divine intervention; 'stretch forth thine hands . . . rescue me' (7, RV; cf. Pss. xviii. 16, lxix. 1 and 14). The fourth thought is that of the nature of his peril. His enemies (RV 'strangers', as Ps. xviii. 44) are moved by falsehood, i.e. vanity and untruth (8; cf. Pss. xii. 2, lii. 2–4, cxx. 2).

Verses 9, 10 have the same spirit of joy and vigour as verses 1, 2, only the imagery of conflict is abandoned for that of music (cf. Ps. xxxiii. 2, 3). The words *the hurtful sword* (10b), i.e. the sorrows of warfare, allow the resumption of the former train of recollection and verse 11 virtually repeats verses 7b, 8. But the past experience has lost its hold and the psalmist turns to visions of the future.

b. Anticipation (12–15)

These verses are a preview of bliss. The scene is built up progressively from the family, through food resources and flocks, to avenues of trade, an ordered and stable civil life, and finally, the intangible, elusive but powerful spirit of a nation *whose God is the Lord* (15). *Our sons . . . as plants grown up* (12); i.e. in their youth our sons shall be as saplings (cf. Ps. cxxviii. 3). *Our daughters . . . as corner stones* (12), or corner pillars, carved and ornamented as found in palaces; i.e. stately and beautiful. *In our streets* (13); RV 'in our fields'. The picture is one of prosperity through absence of war, drought and pestilence. *There be no breaking in* (14); i.e. no siege and breach of a city by a foreign army, nor any forced evacuation or loud lament in the marketplaces (see RV). Verse 15 is taken from Ps. xxxiii. 12. Cf. Ps. cvi. 5.

PSALM CXLV. IN PRAISE OF GOD, THE KING

This Psalm is a preface to the final group of Psalms which together constitute the grand conclusion to the whole Psalter. The exuberant praise of this poem is paralleled by the comprehensive benediction of Ps. cl. The poem has an acrostic structure, but one letter has been omitted; a verse beginning with the letter 'Nun' should occur between verses 13 and 14. Most of the phrases have been taken from other Psalms, but nowhere else is there such a piling up of phrases descriptive of the greatness of the Lord. There is no marked pattern of thought, but the treatment of one theme by a series of couplets almost gives the impression of two similar Psalms having been intertwined. The psalmist speaks in the name of the nation.

My God, O king (1); i.e. Israel's God is the king of all the earth. Verse 3 is based on Ps. xlviii. 1 or xcvi. 4. His greatness is too vast for anyone to search it out, but it is disclosed in His mighty acts on behalf of His people. *I will speak* (5); better, as in RV, 'meditate'. *The glorious honour* ('splendour') *of thy majesty* (5) is alluded to also in Pss. xxi. 5, xcvi. 6, civ. 1. His *wondrous works* of deliverance (5) and awe-inspiring acts of judgment (6) are spoken of in Pss. lxvi. 3 and 5, cvi. 22. *Abundantly utter the memory* (7); i.e. 'pour forth ceaselessly the fame'. Verse 8 is derived from Ex. xxxiv. 6; see also Pss. lxxxvi. 15 and ciii. 8. The triple *all* in verses 9 and 10 is indicative of the unlimited scope of the psalmist's vision and belief. Verse 12, with its change from 'thy' to 'his', may be regarded as a fragment of the saints' praise mentioned in verse 10. The theme of comprehensive power is extended in verse 13 to include all time. This verse is found also in Dn. iv. 34.

The Lord's goodness in lifting up those who are downcast (14) is a frequent topic in the Psalms. See, e.g., Pss. xxxvii. 24, cxlvi. 8. Verses 15, 16 are based on Ps. civ. 27, 28 (cf. Ps. cxlvii. 9). *Holy* (17); better, as in RV, 'gracious'. Verse 18 incorporates Dt. iv. 7. Verses 19 and 20 link together *fear* (reverence) and *love*; for in the true praise of God our apprehension is met with His mercy, and our delight is sobered by His majesty. The final verse anticipates the final Psalm: *let all flesh* praise the Lord. Cf. Ps. cl. 6.

GENERAL INTRODUCTION TO PSALMS CXLVI–CL: 'THE GREAT HALLEL'

The songs cxlvi–cl form an elaborate and comprehensive doxology to the whole Psalter. The element of petition and of personal need disappears entirely; the historical factor in the nation's experience is reduced to a minor rôle. These Psalms are essentially 'praise-hymns', and this characteristic is plainly indicated in the 'Hallelujah' which is both prologue and epilogue to each song in the group. In every case it is the Lord who is praised, but the divine attributes and activities which evoke this sustained adoration vary from one poem to another.

Because the adoration of God is concerned with His pre-eminence, and with creation's richest experience in worshipping Him, there are many similarities of thought and expression between this group of songs and the groups comprising Pss. xcv–c and cxiii–cxviii. Notice also the way in which Ps. cxlv as a preparatory meditation is the counterpart of Pss. cxi and cxii.

PSALM CXLVI. GOD IS MY HELP

See General Introduction above to Psalms cxlvi–cl

Here the psalmist dedicates his whole life (*while I live, while I have any being*) to the praise of the Lord (2; cf. Ps. civ. 33). The major stimulus for this action is the futility of trusting in any man who may be in a position to help. *Princes* (3); i.e. rulers such as Ahasuerus in Est. i. 21. This is the same thought as in Ps. cxviii. 8f., but it is augmented here by the allusion to the brevity and insecurity of human life (cf. Ps. civ. 29; Gn. iii. 19). *Thoughts* (4); i.e. 'purposes'. On the contrary, *the Lord his God* (5) has been known from of old (*God of Jacob*), He made heaven and earth, and moreover He is eternally true (6; Ps. cxix. 160; Je. x. 10; Jn. iii. 33, xvii. 3). The existence of injustice, affliction and sorrow are not signs of His fallibility; rather they are occasions for the exercise of His grace. The eight phrases of compassion in verses 7–9 can be paralleled elsewhere and also illustrated from the Gospels. Notice how Yahweh ('the LORD') occurs five times at the beginning of successive sentences in verses 7–9. The psalmist's devotion is reinforced also because he knows that God has made the way of the wicked to end in ruin. In conclusion he declares that the Lord who is his helper (5), and his praise (2), will also be his King. Of His divine dominion there shall be no end (cf. Pss. x. 16, c. 5), and it shall be centred in Zion (cf. Pss. xcix. 2, cii. 15, 16 and 21, 22).

PSALM CXLVII. GOD OF LOVE AND POWER

See General Introduction above to Psalms cxlvi–cl

The exhortations to praise the Lord in verses 1, 7 and 12 indicate three aspects of His glory.

Although the psalmist's praises begin and end in the realm of human life, especially of Israel (see verses 2, 3 and 19, 20), they are mainly concerned with God's activity in the whole realm of the natural order. In this respect the Psalm is a companion to the previous song where the emphasis is on human experience rather than upon physical power. Pss. ciii and civ give comparable emphasis to these two respective spheres of divine love and power.

a. Praise God because He is righteous in purpose and mighty in power (1–6)

The invocation, which makes worship a delight rather than a duty, is similar to that in Ps. cxxxv. 3. The Lord is to be praised for bringing about the reconstruction of ruined Jerusalem, for leading thither a despised remnant, and for being compassionate toward their misery and disappointment. *Outcasts* (2); cf. Ne. i. 9; Is. lvi. 8. With verse 3 cf. Is. lxi. 1–3. The measure of His greatness is shown by the sudden change of thought from the few disheartened exiles to the innumerable stars of heaven with which the early promise concerning them had been linked (Gn. xv. 5). The Lord has counted (or determined) the number of the stars and He giveth (or *calleth*) them (*by*) *their names* (4; cf. Is. xl. 26). His understanding is beyond man's reckoning (5; cf. Is. xl. 28). Having followed the thought of His infinite power and wisdom the psalmist now returns for a moment to the original theme of the Lord's graciousness to weak men and His righteous vigilance on their behalf. *Lifteth up* (6); RV 'upholdeth'. Cf. Ps. cxlvi. 8, 9.

b. Praise God who provides food in the earth (7–11)

There is none else beside the Lord. He alone doeth all things necessary for natural life— clouds and rain, grass growing beyond sight or use by man, food for beasts and birds (cf. Jb. xxxvi. 26–29, xxxviii. 26, 27, 39–41). Yet He is not primarily concerned with the physical qualities of His creatures such as the *strength by the horse* (cf. Jb. xxxix. 19–25) or the agile *legs of a man* (cf. Ps. xxxiii. 16); i.e. the powerful war horse, and the strong warrior, firm of foot (10). His pleasure is in the heart's response of reverence and faith (11; cf. Je. ix. 23, 24; Ze. iv. 6). A similar parallel and distinction occurs in Mt. vi. 26–30.

c. Praise God because He has prospered Zion and governs the world in wisdom (12–20)

The invocation is addressed to Jerusalem, and although the LXX associates Haggai and Zechariah only with verses 12–20, the whole Psalm may have been connected with the public rejoicings when two choirs made a circuit of the rebuilt walls and assembled in the temple (Ne. xii. 27–43). God had blessed the city with defences (cf. Ne. vii. 3), a renewed family life (cf. Ps. cxxvii. 4, 5), the stability of peace within the boundaries of its life and interests, and with

ample supplies of good grain (13, 14; cf. Ps. cxxxii. 15). Verses 15–18 are unusual. The conditions here described would be exceptional in Judaea, and the psalmist may be using this fact as an illustration of God's exceptional treatment of Israel—not merely in choosing to reveal His word to them (19) but in dealing with them in ways unlike other nations (20); i.e. sending His word (15) to freeze their life in captivity, then sending His word (18) to thaw them into fresh movement. *Ice like morsels* (17); i.e. hailstones like crumbs, and cold before which none can stand. This may be an allusion to the seventh plague (cf. Ex. ix. 25; Ps. lxxviii. 47). The imagery of frost and thaw as being the word and breath of God is also found in Jb. xxxvii. 6 and 9, 10, xxxviii. 22 and 29, 30.

PSALM CXLVIII. HEAVEN AND EARTH, PRAISE YE THE LORD

See General Introduction above to Psalms cxlvi–cl

This hymn develops and extends several ideas in the previous Psalm. The association of the divine word, sent forth like snow yet nourishing the seed (cf. cxlvii. 15 and 8), with the subsequent jubilation of mountains and forests (cxlviii. 8, 9) is found also in Is. lv. 10–13. The theme of creation's praise was introduced into Ps. xcvi. 11, 12, and it is envisaged as a climax to all history in Rev. v. 13. The Psalm falls into two parts. But praise is called forth from heaven (1–6) and from earth (7–14) for different reasons. In the case of heavenly creatures, energies or principles, the source of praise lies in God's creation of them; in the case of earthly phenomena and life the cause lies in God's own immeasurably glorious being.

a. Celestial adoration (1–6)

Divine worship is first involved *in the heights* of heaven (1), where the *angels* and the *hosts* of the Lord serve Him continually (2; cf. Pss. ciii. 20, 21, civ. 4). *Hosts* (RV 'host') may refer to the multitude of spirit beings or to the stellar bodies; both are created, brilliant, harmoniously ordered, far beyond earth, yet able to affect the minds of men. Jb. xxxviii. 7 links them together. The *heavens of heavens* (4) implies the widest possible inclusiveness in the call to praise God (cf. Dt. x. 14; 1 Ki. viii. 27; Ne. ix. 6).

These celestial powers are to praise Him ceaselessly (cf. Rev. iv. 8) because they are unmistakable and permanent evidence (6a) of God's creative word of power (cf. Ps. xxxiii. 6). Moreover their subjection to His law (*decree*), which cannot be transgressed (6b; cf. Je. v. 22), demonstrates the continuity and wisdom of His work.

b. Terrestrial adoration (7–14)

Heaven's worship has its counterpart in that which comes *from the earth* (7); but whereas praise had ranged from the high angelic powers to the very waters above the heavens, it now extends from the waters of the deep ocean (*deeps*, cf. Ps. cxxxv. 6) to the royal princes of all the earth. *Dragons* (7) are the sea monsters of Gn. i. 21. Verses 8–10 cover all phenomena of sky and landscape; all cultivated (*fruitful trees*) and natural vegetation (*cedars*), all wild and domestic animals (*beasts* and *cattle*), all life that crawls or soars. As in Gn. i, man is the culmination of the natural order and his original dominion over all creation (cf. Gn. i. 28, 29) is echoed in the first words of verse 11, *Kings of the earth*. The call, *Let them praise* (13), includes all humanity irrespective of age, sex or status. Unlike heaven the basis of earth's worship is not in the natural or created order, but it is grounded in God Himself. *The name of the Lord* (13) is to be praised because He alone is exalted and only He has the supreme glory which transcends both earth and heaven. Moreover, *his people* who are *his saints* (i.e. Israel; cf. Ex. xix. 6; Ps. l. 5), *a people near unto him* (14; cf. Dt. iv. 7), have a peculiar cause to praise Him because 'He hath lifted up the horn', i.e. given to them the outward mark of honour and power (cf. Ps. lxxv. 10; La. ii. 3; Mi. iv. 13; Dn. viii. 5, 21).

PSALM CXLIX. THINE IS THE GLORY AND THE POWER

See General Introduction above to Psalms cxlvi–cl

The fourth poem in this group of five develops the theme stated at the end of the preceding Psalm. But it is distinguished from all the others by the note of victory and by the shadow of a condemnation cast over the nations. In this respect it may be compared with Ps. xcix (in the group xcv—c), in which worship is offered unto the great and terrible name of Him 'that tookest vengeance'. The song is in two parts.

a. Praise expressed with beauty (1–4)

'The assembly of the saints' (1, RV), i.e. the godly remnant of Israel that is gathered for worship (cf. Pss. cxlviii. 14, cvii. 32), sings *a new song* because they have been redeemed and restored from virtual death (cf. Ps. xcvi. 1, xcviii. 1; see also Rev. v. 9 and xiv. 3). They 'rejoice in their Maker' (cf. Ps. xcv. 6), not merely because He created their existence, but because He shapes their calling and destiny. In a double sense they are His workmanship (cf. Ps. c. 3; Eph. ii. 10). They also rejoice in *their King* (2; cf. Ps. xlvii) because Zion, whither they have been restored, is the perpetual throne of their sovereign Lord (cf. Pss. xlviii. 2, xcix. 1, 2, cii. 21, 22). Furthermore, this praise to God is to be expressed through the bodily action of dancing and making music, as well as by word of mouth (cf. Pss. xxx. 11, xxxiii. 2, 3; Je. xxxi. 4ff.). This unrestrained exuberance shown through the whole personality has its origin in the Lord's *pleasure* (4). He has changed their garments of humiliation for the beauteous adornment of salvation (cf. Is. lxi. 3).

b. Praise expressed with power (5–9)

The *saints* are to praise God not only in corporate worship (1) but in the place of habitual seclusion and repose—*upon their beds* (5). Both places are now devoid of danger and regret. *The high praises of God* (6) are to be vocal and instrumental, but the harp and tambourine (3) are to be replaced by a *twoedged sword* (6); i.e. the concept of beauty in action is changed to that of authority in action. The kingdom of God (2) is characterized by power as well as by glory (cf. Mt. vi. 13b).

There is no doubt that the psalmist gives to the two-edged sword a physical significance (cf. Ne. iv. 13 and 21, 22); Israel's praise will be by service as well as ceremony, by military success as well as music and singing, through defeat of their enemies in addition to dances before the Lord. On the other hand (cf. 2 Cor. x. 4) the conjunction of the phrases *in their mouth, a sword,* allows a symbolical exegesis such as is found in Ps. xlv. 2, 3; Is. xlix. 2; Eph. vi. 17; Heb. iv. 12; Rev. i. 16, xix. 15. However interpreted, whether against the background of Nehemiah's work, as anticipating the temporal nature of messianic judgment, or as symbolical of the spiritual triumph of truth, the Psalm plainly assigns *honour* (9) to the saints of God, in the sense either that He is their sole source of honour or that their work expresses His honour.

PSALM CL. PRE-EMINENT PRAISE

See General Introduction above to Psalms cxlvi–cl

It is not known whether this splendid doxology was specially written to mark the end of the Psalter, or whether it had a previous and independent existence. Its twelvefold 'Hallel' (praise) reflects the unity of Israel's tribes, and the only phrase which is not preceded by this word (verse 6) is the final and most comprehensive of all.

Praise is offered first and last to Jah ('Hallelujah'), the covenant God of Israel (cf. Ps. lxviii. 4; Ex. vi. 3). He is identical with El, the powerful God who rules the created universe (cf. Ps. xix. 1; Dt. x. 17) and dwells *in the firmament of his power* (1); i.e. the initial phase of creation whereby God 'extended' space is the primal demonstration of His mighty power (cf. Gn. i. 6–8; Jb. xxxvii. 18). If *in his sanctuary* is a parallelism for *firmament* (as in Pss. cii. 19, xi. 4), then this praise is to be heard in heaven (cf. Ps. lxviii. 33, 34). On the other hand if *sanctuary* is intended to be a contrast to *firmament* it must be taken to mean the temple (cf. Ex. xxv. 8; Pss. lxxiii. 17, lxxiv. 7), where He has been pleased to make His name to dwell (cf. Pss. lxviii. 16, cxxxii. 13, 14). The dual habitation of the Lord, in the heaven of heavens and the house in Zion, is frequently mentioned in 1 Ki. viii (cf. Ps. xcix. 1, 2; note Is. lxvi. 1, 2). God is to be praised throughout the universe because of His glory (*excellent greatness*) and

His power (*mighty acts*). Verses 3–5 were probably accompanied by an orchestral crescendo as the named instruments successively joined in the music. The *trumpet* blast of the ram's horn was to be followed by the sound of *psaltery* and *harp* (cf. 1 Ch. xxv. 1) and the small drum or tambourine used by dancers (cf. Ps. lxviii. 25). To the sounds of stringed instruments were added the notes of 'the pipe' (RV; i.e. flutes and clarinets) and the clash of brass *cymbals* (cf. 1 Ch. xv. 19). *Everything that hath breath* (6); i.e. all sections of the congregation, indeed all mankind and probably all forms of life (as in Ps. cxlviii. 7–12), are to unite in this act of fullest praise to the Lord.

LESLIE S. M'CAW.

THE PROVERBS

INTRODUCTION

I. AUTHORSHIP

The general title is 'The Proverbs of Solomon the son of David'. At several points in the book, however, rubrics occur giving the authorship of different sections. Thus sections are ascribed to Solomon at x. 1 and to 'the wise' at xxii. 17 and xxiv. 23. At xxv. 1 there is the interesting rubric, 'These are also proverbs of Solomon, which the men of Hezekiah king of Judah copied out'; chapter xxx is introduced as 'the words of Agur the son of Jakeh' and chapter xxxi is 'the words of king Lemuel', or, rather, of his mother.

The Rabbis said 'Hezekiah and his company wrote Isaiah, Proverbs, the Song of Songs and Ecclesiastes' (Baba Bathra 15a); in other words that they edited or published them. As regards Proverbs, it is doubtful if this Rabbinic statement had any other basis than the rubric at xxv. 1.

The scepticism which since the nineteenth century has minimized the Solomonic element seems now to be on its way out. For a review of some modern criticism of Proverbs, with a searching examination of it, see E. J. Young, *An Introduction to the Old Testament*. Formerly, the Wisdom literature as a whole was often ascribed to a post-exilic date. Now due recognition is being given to the Wisdom poetry not only in prophetic but in pre-prophetic writings (cf. Jdg. ix. 8f.). For example, W. Baumgartner writes: 'Since it cannot, therefore, have just sprung up in post-exilic times as the successor of Law and Prophecy, such late datings call for careful re-examination' (*The Old Testament and Modern Study*, edited by H. H. Rowley, 1951, p. 211). The result of this re-examination by critical scholars has led, generally speaking, to a more serious view of the rubrics being taken.

Let us consider the authors named there.

a. Solomon

In Proverbs, wisdom is not simply intellectual, it involves *the whole man*; and of this wisdom Solomon at the zenith of his fame is the embodiment. He loved the Lord (1 Ki. iii. 3); he prayed for an understanding heart to discern between good and evil (1 Ki. iii. 9, 12); his wisdom was God-given (1 Ki. iv. 29), and was accompanied by deep humility (1 Ki. iii. 7); it was put to the test in practical matters, such as just administration (1 Ki. iii. 16–28) and diplomacy (1 Ki. v. 12). His wisdom was pre-eminent in the East (1 Ki. iv. 30f., x. 1–13); he composed proverbs and

songs (1 Ki. iv. 32) and answered 'hard sayings' (1 Ki. x. 1); much of his lore was drawn from nature (1 Ki. iv. 33).

We take it that the collections in Pr. x—xxii. 16 and xxv—xxix come substantially from him. There may, of course, be Solomonic elements elsewhere in the book. Even so, this can be only an inspired selection of his wisdom, for there are not nearly 3,000 proverbs in the whole book (cf. 1 Ki. iv. 32).

b. The wise

The nations of the ancient East had their 'wise men' whose functions extended from state policy to education. (For Egypt, cf. e.g. Gn. xli. 8; for Edom, cf. Ob. 8.) In Israel, where it was known that 'the fear of the Lord is the beginning of knowledge', 'the wise' had a more important function also. Je. xviii. 18 shows that in his time they were on a par with prophet and priest as an organ of God's revelation. But, just as the true prophets had to contend with prophets and priests with unworthy motives, so many of 'the wise' compromised their function to declare the 'counsel of Jehovah' (Is. xxix. 14; Je. viii. 8, 9).

There are at least two collections of 'the sayings of the wise' in Proverbs: these are xxii. 17—xxiv. 22 and xxiv. 23–34. Perhaps chapters i—ix, containing, as they do, an exposition of the aim and content of 'the counsel of the wise', come from a like source. It is virtually impossible to date these collections. Probably they represent the distilled wisdom of many who feared God over a considerable period. But much of it is certainly of an early date. E. J. Young suggests that it may even be pre-Solomonic (*op. cit.*, p. 302).

c. Hezekiah's men

From 2 Ch. xxix. 25–30 we learn that Hezekiah took care to restore the Davidic order in the temple, the Davidic instruments and the Psalms of David and Asaph. No doubt a revival of interest in the 'classic' wisdom of Solomon was another outcome of his reformation, a revival prompted, not by antiquarianism, but by the desire to explore again the wisdom of one who had supremely loved Jehovah. And so the Solomonic collection of chapters xxv—xxix was edited and published. A. Bentzen (*Introduction to the Old Testament*, Copenhagen, 1949, Vol. II, p. 173) makes the interesting suggestion that this collection had until that time been preserved in oral form only.

d. Agur the son of Jakeh

We do not know who Agur was. It is possible that we ought to render the word translated 'prophecy' in the AV of xxx. 1 as 'of Massa'. Massa was an Arab tribe descended from Abraham through Ishmael (Gn. xxv. 14), and the eastern tribes were famous for their wisdom (1 Ki. iv. 30). But this reading is by no means certain.

e. King Lemuel

This king's mother is given as the source of xxxi. 1–9, but he is likewise unknown, though here again we may read 'prophecy' as 'of Massa'. We need not suppose him to be the author of the magnificent poem on The Perfect Wife (xxxi. 10–31) which forms an appendix to the book.

II. DATE

So much for the individual collections. When were they brought together in the book as we know it? The earliest time for this is fixed by the reference to Hezekiah's men: while the knowledge that Ben Sira (c. 180 B.C.) shows of it (Ecclus. xlvii. 17) means that it was already established and venerable in his day. Beyond this, we have no outside evidence. Perhaps the most likely time for publication would be soon after the return from exile in the settlement in which 'Ezra the scribe' played such a part, when Israel desired 'the fear of the Lord' to dominate her education.

III. FORM AND CONTENT

The word translated 'proverb' (*mashal*) comes from a root which seems to mean 'to represent' or 'be like'. Its basic meaning is therefore a comparison or simile. Its germ may be an analogy between the natural and spiritual worlds (cf. 1 Ki. iv. 33 and Pr. x. 26). The same word is aptly translated 'parable' in Ezk. xvii. 2. The word, however, was extended to sayings where no such analogy is evident, and came to designate a short pithy saying or byword (cf. 1 Sa. x. 12).

But the proverbs in this book are not so much popular sayings as the distillation of the wisdom of teachers who knew the law of God and were applying its principles to the whole of life. The LXX title of the book, *Paroimiai*, which might be Latinized *obiter dicta*, gives a good idea of the contents. These are words by the way for wayfaring men who are seeking to tread the way of holiness.

A glance at the RV will show that the whole book is cast in poetic form, generally in couplets. Chapters i—ix and xxx—xxxi are connected poetic addresses of some length. In the rest of the book the proverbs are mostly short, detached sayings, each complete in itself.

IV. THE PROVERBS OF ISRAEL AND OF OTHER NATIONS

Just as the law given through Moses did not mean that the whole common stock of Semitic law had to be abandoned, so the wisdom of Solomon and like men did not supersede all the lessons learned by the children of the East. But in the case of law and of wisdom alike, what was common to Israel and her neighbours was revolutionized by divine sanctions and by adoption into the life of a people in a special relationship with God.

But when due weight has been given to this, and to the fact that Agur and Lemuel were perhaps non-Israelites, we need not accept the arguments of those who see in Proverbs wholesale borrowings from non-Israelite sources. Evidence of this is often found in the close parallels between the Egyptian 'Wisdom of Amen-em-ope' and Pr. xxii. 17—xxiv. 22; and the difficult sentence 'Have I not written unto thee excellent things?' is rewritten 'thirty things', as in Amen-em-ope, who has thirty chapters. For a consideration of this see the commentary *in loc*. Where Egyptologists differ so widely on the date of the book it is perilous to make dogmatic statements. We need only note that Griffith, the discoverer, dates it c. 600 B.C. when 'the wise' had been active in Israel for centuries. There are good grounds for believing that Amen-em-ope was indebted to Proverbs. (Those who are interested in following up this matter should see the translation of Amen-em-ope in *Ancient Near Eastern Texts relating to the Old Testament*, edited by James B. Pritchard, Princeton, 1950, pp. 421–424. Its dependence on Proverbs is maintained by R. O. Kevin, *The Wisdom of Amen-em-apt*, Philadelphia, 1931.)

The world-wide reputation of Solomon which brought the Queen of Sheba to investigate his wisdom is an early example of the way in which wisdom was a bridge by which Israel penetrated the higher thought of her neighbours. But, while it would be untrue to say that the Egyptian proverbs are devoid of deep religious feeling, in their sanctions they are far away from the canonical Wisdom literature. 'Do not lean on the scales, nor falsify the weights, Nor damage the fractions of the measure' says Amen-em-ope (chapter xvi). But our book says: 'Divers weights, and divers measures, both of them are alike abomination to the Lord' (xx. 10). And that makes all the difference.

V. THE USE OF THE BOOK OF PROVERBS

Principal Wheeler Robinson described Old Testament wisdom as 'the discipline whereby was taught the application of prophetic truth to the individual life in the light of experience' (*Inspiration and Revelation in the Old Testament*, p. 241). It is this that makes the book perennially relevant. It is a book of discipline: it touches on every department of life and shows it to be the direct interest of God. Wisdom does not consist in the contemplation of abstract principles governing the universe, but in a relationship with God of reverent knowledge issuing in conduct consonant with this relationship in concrete situations. The man who refuses this is, frankly, a fool. And wisdom must dominate the whole life; not only a man's devotion, but his attitude to his wife, his children, his work, his business methods—even his table manners. It has been well said that 'For the writers of Proverbs . . . religion means a well-furnished intellect employing the best means to accomplish the highest ends. The feebleness, the shallowness, the narrow, contracted views and aims, are on the other side' (W. T. Davison, *The Wisdom Literature of the Old Testament*, p. 134).

There is ample evidence that our Lord on earth loved this book. Every now and then we get an echo of its language in His own teaching: for instance in His words about those who seek the chief seats (cf. Pr. xxv. 6, 7), or the parable of the wise and foolish men and their houses (cf. Pr. xiv. 11), or that of the rich fool (cf. Pr. xxvii. 1). To Nicodemus He reveals the answer to the question posed by Agur the son of Jakeh (cf. Pr. xxx. 4 with Jn. iii. 13). And He reminds those who, like the undiscriminating 'fools' of Proverbs, do not recognize Him or His message that 'wisdom is justified of her children' (Mt. xi. 19).

Our Lord, in fact, used in His parables exactly the method of teaching found in Proverbs. The Hebrew *mashal* is best rendered into Greek as *parabole*, 'parable'; and the same Greek word would translate the Hebrew *ḥidhah*, 'dark saying' or 'riddle'. Hence in Mk. iv. 11 we see that, to those who do not recognize Him, everything connected with the kingdom appears in the form of riddles or dark sayings, which they hear but do not interpret.

Was it from his company with our Lord that Peter derived his fondness for Proverbs? At any rate, his letters show a close acquaintance with the book (cf. 1 Pet. ii. 17 with Pr. xxiv. 21; 1 Pet. iii. 13 with Pr. xvi. 7; 1 Pet. iv. 8 with Pr. x. 12; 1 Pet. iv. 18 with Pr. xi. 31; 2 Pet. ii. 22 with Pr. xxvi. 11). Paul also quotes from and echoes the book (cf., e.g., Rom. xii. 20 and Pr. xxv. 21f.), and when he speaks of 'Christ the power of God, and the wisdom of God' (1 Cor. i. 24), Pr. viii floods rich meaning into his words. Heb. xii. 5f. commands us not to forget 'the exhortation that speaketh to us as sons', that we despise not the chastening of the Lord. The quotation is from Pr. iii. 11f. It gives us a picture of the true nature of the book, a study in the paternal discipline of God.

The sayings, like our Lord's parables, need to be pondered to be fully appreciated, and it is probably best to consider each separately, reading only a few at a time. 'A number of small pictures crowded together upon the walls of a large gallery are not likely to receive much separate attention from the visitor, especially if he be paying a short visit in a hurry' (Davison, *op. cit.*, p. 126). Conversely, it is important to remember that each saying is part of a whole body of teaching. To take a proverb quite apart from its relationship to the whole and to seek to apply it to any situation may be quite misleading.

VI. TEXT AND VERSIONS

There are many difficulties and obscurities in the Hebrew text, particularly in the main Solomonic section, as we might expect in a document so ancient. Recent philological discoveries, however, warn us against hasty emendation. The LXX is less help here than in some books, as it has a literary character all its own. (For details, see G. Gerlemann, in *Oudtestamentische Studien*, *deel* VIII, edited by P. A. H. de Boer, Leiden, 1950.)

OUTLINE OF CONTENTS

I. THE BOOK'S TITLE, PURPOSE AND MOTTO. i. 1–7

II. THIRTEEN LESSONS ON WISDOM. i. 8—ix. 18

III. THE FIRST BOOK OF SOLOMON. x. 1—xxii. 16

IV. THE BOOK OF THE WISE. xxii. 17—xxiv. 22

V. SAYINGS OF THE WISE: ANOTHER COLLECTION. xxiv. 23–34

VI. THE SECOND BOOK OF SOLOMON. xxv. 1—xxix. 27

VII. THE SAYINGS OF AGUR. xxx. 1–33

VIII. THE SAYINGS OF LEMUEL. xxxi. 1–9

IX. APPENDIX: THE PERFECT WIFE. xxxi. 10–31

COMMENTARY

I. THE BOOK'S TITLE, PURPOSE AND MOTTO. i. 1-7

This is the longest title of any Old Testament book. The ascription to Solomon does not mean that he wrote the whole book (cf. xxiv. 23, xxx. 1, xxxi. 1) but reminds us that the greater part stems from him and that he was the greatest figure in the proverbial lore. Verses 1-6 form a single elliptical sentence: 'The proverbs of Solomon . . . written down that you may know . . .' The reader is invited to learn from the book *wisdom* (the nature of which is explained as the book proceeds) *and instruction* (2), i.e. discipline. This latter word conveys the whole idea ef spiritual education (it is the word translated 'chastening' in Heb. xii. 5). *Of wisdom* (3); better, as in RV, 'To receive instruction in wise dealing'. *Justice, and judgment, and equity* (3) are characteristics constantly demanded by the prophets, and are features of the rule of God and His Messiah (see e.g. Is. v. 7 and xi. 4). Verse 4 shows that this wisdom is available for the youngest and most inexperienced (cf. Is. xxxv. 8), verse 5 that those who have already drawn deep of wisdom's well will yet find abundantly more. *Simple* (4) probably means 'open to every influence'. *Shall attain unto wise counsels* (5) is suggestively translated by the LXX as 'shall acquire a steersman'. This idea is implicit in the Hebrew root. The book is also written to provide a key to all the proverbs of wise men (6; cf. Mk. iv. 13). The precise meaning of the word translated here *the interpretation* is uncertain; cf. RV 'a figure'. It is translated 'a taunting proverb' in Hab. ii. 6, its only other occurrence in the Old Testament.

Verse 7 forms a sort of motto for the book, and describes its foundation principle. *Beginning* (Heb. *reshith*) implies both starting-point and essence. Without the knowledge and fear of Jehovah, the One true God, the wisdom which affords guidance for the whole of life cannot begin to be acquired. The motto is repeated, slightly differently, at ix. 10.

It is worth comparing these verses with Is. xi. 1-5, where most of the gifts here set out are shown to be attributes of the Messiah and the outcome of the presence of the Spirit of God.

II. THIRTEEN LESSONS ON WISDOM. i. 8—ix. 18

The address 'My son' begins each lesson except the last, which is given by Wisdom herself. The family relationship may be in mind, but it is more likely that a master is addressing his disciple.

a. The first lesson (i. 8-33)

i. Shun evil companions (i. 8-19). The disciple is urged to follow the teaching he received from his parents as a child. *Hear* (8), as often in the Old Testament, means 'obey'. The Hebrew word for *law* (*torah*) has here its primary sense of 'teaching', as is shown by the parallelism. The chains in verse 9 are, of course, ornamental (cf. Gn. xli. 42). The content of this teaching is described for us in the book of Deuteronomy; see especially Dt. iv. 9, vi. 7, xi. 19, xxxii. 46. A lawless state of society is depicted in verses 10-19. Organized robbery with violence seems to have been endemic in Palestine throughout the biblical period (cf., e.g., Hos. iv. 2, vi. 8f.; Ps. x. 8ff.), and even in the firmly governed Palestine of our Lord's day was established enough for Him to base a parable upon it. It is plain from these verses that the desperadoes would not stop at murder to gain their booty. The apparent meaning of verse 12 is a sudden murderous assault: they will pounce upon their victim as avidly as Death devours hers. But the invitation to an equal share in their ill-gotten gain (14) is to be consistently refused (15). Verse 16, which is not in the LXX, occurs again at Is. lix. 7. The metaphor in verse 17 is difficult. It seems best to follow Oesterley and interpret the *bird* of the instructed disciple: being forewarned, he will avoid the snare of joining such evil company, just as no bird walks into a net that he has watched being laid. But the suggestion, favoured by Toy and earlier writers, that the bird represents the robbers, who are blind to everything but gain and do not notice the trap laid under their very eyes, is certainly possible. Verses 18-19 speak of the inevitable fate of those who enrich themselves in this way. When they lie in ambush for others they are, unknown to themselves, compassing their own destruction. *So are the ways of every one . . .* (19); i.e. 'this is the outcome for everyone . . .'

ii. Wisdom's unheeded appeal (i. 20-33). This is the first of the sections in which wisdom is personified. Wisdom which has its origin in the fear of God invites the people at large to learn: but the great mass of mankind refuse to listen, despite the fact that in doing so they bring ruin and distress upon themselves. We are reminded of the manner in which the prophets pleaded with Israel to 'seek Jehovah and live', and met with stubborn lack of understanding. Indeed, there is much in this section that is reminiscent of the teaching of Hosea and Isaiah and Jeremiah. Verses 20, 21 describe the manner of Wisdom's proclamation. Read verse 20 with RV: 'Wisdom crieth aloud in the street; She uttereth her voice in the broad places.' The prophets also proclaimed their message in the streets and public places: cf. Je. v. 1; Is. xx. 2. *The openings of the gates* (21) were the places where public and private business was transacted and courts held (cf. Ru. iv. 1ff.). Verses 22, 23 give Wisdom's appeal. Three classes who pay no heed are named. *Simple* (22). The root seems to mean 'open to influence', whether good or bad; in origin the word is morally neutral (cf. verse 4). But the people in question refuse the proffered wisdom and thus remain 'simple': so the word comes (as in English) to have an unenviable connotation. *Scorners* (22; Heb. *leṣim*) are a class we shall meet again. They are Wisdom's worst enemies, arrogant, cynical and defiant. *Fools* (22) are represented as hating the knowledge which alone can save them from disaster. There are three words in Proverbs translated 'fool': the *nabhal* is churlish, dull intellectually and, usually, morally. The *'ewil* is always morally bad; he is not only stupid, but licentious (see vii. 22 in its context). There is not much to choose between him and the *kesil*, which is the word used here. Toy sums up the *kesil* as 'one who is insensible to moral truth and acts without regard to it'.

Verse 23 may be taken in either of two ways. It is possible that the fools' are instructed to turn and face Wisdom's reproof, and the *words* which Wisdom makes known are contained in verses 24–33. But it is far better, bearing in mind the 'How long?' of verse 22, to take this as a last appeal to the heedless to receive knowledge. *Turn you* is often used in the sense of 'repent' in the prophets, and that is surely the meaning here. The 'spirit of wisdom' is associated with the Messiah (Is. xi. 2), and is a privilege of Messiah's people (Eph. i. 17).

Verses 24–32 describe the general reaction to the appeal and the dire consequences. For calamity will certainly follow such disobedience, and then it will be too late to seek the aid of heavenly Wisdom. The Wisdom they rejected will laugh in their faces as they have so long laughed at it; the memory of despised knowledge will be bitter to those who are perishing. *Your fear* (26, 27) means 'the thing that shall cause your fear'. *They shall seek me early* (28); read with RV 'diligently'. The search for Wisdom induced by the final calamity will be in vain, a note of severe finality which stamps many of our Lord's parables of the kingdom. Note that again *knowledge* and *fear* of God are linked (29). In verse 32, the simple, exhorted to turn *to* God (cf. verse 23), have turned away from Him, and this will bring about their destruction. *Prosperity* (32); better, as in RV mg., 'careless ease', i.e. the fruit of prosperity. The parable of the rich fool in Lk. xii. 16–20 is sufficient commentary here. There is no denial of the fact that the fool may temporarily prosper.

Verse 33 holds out the promise of true security for those who do obey Wisdom's voice.

b. The second lesson (ii. 1–22)

i. The search for wisdom and its reward (ii. 1–9). This section stresses three things: that wisdom requires diligent search (1–5), that it is none the less God-given, and not the result of mere human effort (6), and that God watches over and keeps in His will those who receive it (7–9). The principles involved here are implicit in Solomon's dream in Gibeon (1 Ki. iii. 5–15)

and are made explicit by Paul in Phil. ii. 12, 13. *Heart* (2) has a wider meaning in Hebrew than in English, as it relates to the intellectual and moral faculties as well as to the emotional. The pupil is being exhorted to apply all his powers in the quest for understanding, until he can be said to be shouting out aloud for it (3). In verse 4 the emphasis is probably less on the fact that silver has to be mined and that the treasure requires intensive search than on the fact that both are immensely valuable. Our Lord takes up and develops this thought, applying it to the search for the kingdom of heaven (Mt. xiii. 44). The literal meaning of *layeth up* (7) is 'hideth away'; but we may note that He hides it away *for* and not *from* the righteous. In verse 8 read with RV 'That he may guard the paths of judgment, And preserve the way of his saints'. In other words God Himself becomes a shield for His people in order that He may see that what is perfectly right is constantly maintained. 'Preserve' means 'to watch over': God watches over the path His people take, both to protect them in it and to keep them in the right way. *Saints* (8) represents those who loyally render to Jehovah the love due to Him in the covenant between Him and His people. The virtues named in verse 9 are reflections of His will: see i. 3n.

ii. Some benefits of wisdom (ii. 10–22). The protection which the possession of wisdom affords is enlarged upon. The *discretion* which is promised (11) contains the idea of purposefulness. Verses 12–19 mention classes from whose pernicious ways those who have received wisdom may escape. First there is *the evil man* (12). The AV rendering suits the context better than the RV 'from the way of evil'; but in either case compare the petition in the Lord's prayer, 'Deliver us from evil' or 'from the evil one'. There is *the man that speaketh froward things* (12); lit. the man who speaks things turned upside down, i.e. the liar. Such men are crooked and perverse (13–15). We might translate verse 14, 'Who rejoice to do evil, And delight in the perverseness of evil'. Above all, there is *the strange woman* (16), against whom many warnings are given in the book. See further on v. 3. Here, at least, the warnings are against the allurements of the adulteress who has known the law of the true God (17). *Guide* (17) is an unwarranted translation; 'friend' (RV) is more exact. But from a passage like Je. iii. 1–4 we see clearly that the word was used to designate the marriage partner. Not only does the strange woman sin against the husband she married in her youth; in doing so she sins against God, to whom, as an Israelite, she is bound in a covenant relationship. It is He who has ordained the marriage covenant, and He who has laid down as part of His covenant, 'Thou shalt not commit adultery' (Ex. xx. 14). *Her house* is a steep descent all the way down to *death* (18), and her victims do not 'attain unto' (so, rightly, RV) the ways of life which all men desire to reach.

After this long digression, verse 20 picks up

again the thought of verse 11. Not only will God's gift of wisdom protect from these evil ways; it will enable a good and upright manner of life to be followed. *Land* (21) and *earth* (22) represent the same Hebrew word. The primary reference is to 'the land which the Lord thy God giveth thee' (cf. Ex. xx. 12; Ps. xxxvii. 9–11). But the significance does not stop there, as is shown by our Lord's beatitude, based on Ps. xxxvii. 11, 'Blessed are the meek, for they shall inherit the earth.'

c. The third lesson (iii. 1–10)

The theme is 'trust and obey'. Observance of the teacher's words is urgently enjoined (1, 2), as a source of long life and peace. The primary reference is to long life on earth, often regarded in the Old Testament as a great good; observance of the fundamentals of right living will enable a man to avoid the worst snares and pitfalls of life. But 'commandments with promise' (cf. Eph. vi. 2) take a deeper significance as God's revelation unfolds, and our Lord declares that His words are spirit and life (Jn. vi. 63). *Law* (1; Heb. *torah*) again has the sense of 'teaching'.

This theme is developed in verses 4–10, and the content of the life-giving teaching referred to in verse 1 is outlined. First *mercy and truth* (3) must be maintained. This expression means more than appears on the surface. *Mercy* (*ḥesedh*) is a word which is hard to understand apart from the idea of *covenant*. It represents *covenant*-love, and the full range of what that means we see from the Great Commandment and the one like unto it (Dt. vi. 5 and Lv. xix. 18). *Truth* (Heb. *'emeth*) means 'firmness' and hence 'trustworthiness', 'stability', 'faithfulness', and eventually what faithfulness demands—reality and truth. So the Lord is 'faithful and true' (Rev. xix. 11): the one quality implies the other. 'Mercy and truth' are often linked in the Old Testament, and Toy well says they are 'the expression of perfectly good relations between man and man, or between man and God'. Above all, they are divine attributes (Ps. xxv. 10). Perhaps the best explanation is given by the well-known lines:

> *Mercy and truth are all His ways,*
> *Wonders of grace to God belong.*

The advice to *bind* these qualities to oneself (3) may be paralleled by the command (Dt. vi. 8) to bind on God's covenant commandments, a constant reminder of His requirements. But men require more than to be reminded; and so mercy and truth are to be written upon their hearts, their very minds (cf. Je. xxxi. 33). The outcome of this is stated in verse 4. The combination of *favour* and *good understanding* has caused difficulty to the LXX and Vulgate translators and to many modern commentators. The RV mg., by a slight change in the Hebrew, reads 'favour and good repute'. Taking the text as it stands, the evident meaning is that the practice of 'mercy and truth' will bring about not only divine and human favour, but divine and human recognition

as possessing true understanding. We find the great example of this in Lk. ii. 52.

In the second place faith is enjoined; faith which includes trust in God (5), acknowledgment of Him in every department of life (6) and reverent awe of Him (7). Leaning 'upon' (so RV) one's own human understanding, setting a high value on one's own wisdom (cf. Is. v. 21), and living on easy terms with evil are the antithesis of this trusting dependence on Jehovah. To *direct thy paths* (6) is to make the ways straight or plain, clearing obstructions. The word is used in Is. xl. 3 of clearing the highway in the desert. The effect of such faith as is described is also physically beneficial. For *navel* (8), LXX reads 'body', representing a Hebrew text different in only one letter. In any case, this translation well conveys the sense of the verse. Finally, the pupil is instructed that the reverence due to God involves giving on the part of His worshippers. The *substance* with which he *honours* Jehovah (9) is his wealth, or revenue. He need not fear that this will finally involve him in loss (10; cf. Mal. iii. 10–12). The teaching is cast in agricultural terms. The reference to 'firstfruits' in verse 9 looks back to the law in Dt. xxvi, where the worshipper annually takes of the firstfruits of his produce and remembers with joy and gratitude God's redemption of Israel and His continuing goodness—the Old Testament harvest festival.

d. The fourth lesson (iii. 11–20)

The theme of this section is the delights of wisdom, a development of the recurring theme in the third lesson that the teaching brings a rich reward. But first comes a warning that God in His love may bring adversity as well as prosperity upon His children (11, 12). Bacon's dictum, 'Prosperity is the Blessing of the Old Testament; Adversity is the Blessing of the New; which carrieth the greater Benediction, and the Clearer Revelation of God's favour', must be qualified by such passages as this. The rendering in Heb. xii. 6, 'For whom the Lord loveth he chasteneth, and scourgeth every son whom he receiveth', follows the LXX, which has read the same Hebrew consonants with different vowels to obtain the word 'scourgeth'. (Cf. 2 Sa. vii. 14.)

With this warning, the teacher expounds blessings which follow the possession of wisdom. All around him men were engaged in the all-absorbing pursuit of riches and honour. He is therefore at pains to show (13–18) that heavenly wisdom is a thing infinitely more precious than all those things that men seek after, and, indeed, holds the key to the things most desired by them (17), things which are added as a by-product of the search for wisdom. We may note in verse 14 the germ of yet another of our Lord's parables: that of the pearl of great price (Mt. xiii. 45, 46). The phrase *tree of life* (18) suggests that wisdom is a constantly growing source of life to those that attain her. Some allusion is suggested to the tree of life in Gn. ii, iii and Rev. ii and xxii.

Perowne (Cam. Bible) points out that the tree of the knowledge of good and evil was a tree of death.

Verses 19 and 20 show further the glory of wisdom by describing its exalted status before God, and that it was His guiding principle in creation, and by it 'He that doeth all things well' upholds the universe, whether in the great and catastrophic events (the reference to the breaking up of the depths points back to Gn. vii. 11), or in the day-to-day moistening of the earth. *Dew* (20) possibly includes rain, as Toy suggests; cf. Jb. xxxvi. 28. See further the notes on chapter viii.

e. The fifth lesson (iii. 21–35)

The theme is again the manifestations and effects of wisdom, a further development of the two previous lessons. Sound wisdom and discreet purposefulness (see ii. 7n.) will be life and health and peace (21–26). *Them* (21) refers to *sound wisdom and discretion*. The word translated *soul* (Heb. *nephesh*) in verse 22 seems, though this is disputed, to have meant originally 'throat', and thence 'living being', 'person', 'self', 'life'. *So shall they be life unto thy soul* means, then, 'they shall be life to you'. Bearing in mind the parallelism, however, it is possible that *nephesh* has here its original sense of *throat*, and is used by synecdoche for the whole body. In verse 23 RV mg. reads, more literally, 'thou shalt not dash thy foot'. The injunction *be not afraid* (25) when the ruin of the wicked comes may be linked with the numerous passages of hope and encouragement to the godly with which the prophets mingle their announcements of impending judgment for the nation's sin (see, e.g., Is. x. 24ff.), and with our Lord's words to His people when catastrophe overtakes the world (Lk. xxi. 28).

Verses 27–35 consist of short detached proverbs like those in sections III, IV, V and VI, all illustrating the theme already set out in this lesson. James tells us that heavenly wisdom is pure, peaceable, gentle, easily intreated, full of mercy and good fruits, without uncertainty or insincerity, and that it has a diabolical parody whose marks are envy and strife. This is illustrated by the teacher's precepts. The first enjoins prompt payment of debts (27). The Hebrew reads 'withhold not good from the owners (*ba'alim*) thereof'. The LXX may be right in interpreting this of the poor rather than of creditors. The phrase is difficult, but not sufficiently so to warrant the emendations sometimes proposed. The second orders prompt and whole-hearted generosity (28; cf. Jas. ii. 16). The third and fourth warn against unprovoked attack (29, 30). *Securely* (29) means 'trustfully'. The fifth warns against envy (31). *The oppressor* may prosper. To the prophets it was only too obvious that he often did. But his unjustly gained wealth is not to be coveted, nor his methods imitated.

The last group of proverbs (32–35) brings these injunctions into relation with the fear of the Lord. One way of life is hateful to Jehovah: the other leads to real harmony with Him (32). Oesterley happily renders *secret* 'familiar and confidential intercourse'. On the one way God's curse rests, on the other His blessing (33; cf. Dt. xi. 26–28). God rewards with His favour humility, not arrogance (34; cf. the allusions to this verse in Jas. iv. 6 and 1 Pet. v. 5). It is the wise, i.e. the righteous, just, and humble, who eventually receive honour, not the *fools* (35; Heb. *kesilim*, see i. 22n.). The last clause of verse 35 is difficult, the word *promotion* being obscure, but the AV rendering, with its touch of irony, has at least virility and pungency, which most of the suggested emendations do not possess.

f. The sixth lesson (iv. 1–9)

This section contains a little piece of auto-biography. Consumed with desire for the moral and spiritual health of his pupils, the teacher tells of his own father's wise instruction, proved by the experience of his own life, in the effort to impress upon them the urgency of obtaining above all things the 'wisdom that is from above'.

Verse 1 shows the teacher taking up the position of a father to his pupils. RV 'Hear, my sons' is more literal (the word is the same as that which begins all the other lessons), but AV *children* conveys the idea better. He relates how concerned his own parents were for his welfare. *I was my father's son*, with the parallelism that follows, implies that the teacher's father took particular care over his son's education. Whether the whole of verses 4–9 represents the father's words, or whether the teacher is in the later sentences applying them, we cannot tell. Once more, the acquisition of wisdom is seen to provide life (4), protection (6), honour (7) and adornment (9). *Wisdom is the principal thing; therefore get wisdom* (7). The AV translation here cannot be warranted, for the Hebrew has only 'the beginning of wisdom is—get wisdom'. This is often abandoned by commentators as unintelligible, but Perowne points out the similarity with the message of ii. 1–5, especially if ii. 5 is interpreted in the light of i. 7, and the sentence may well be a compression of that message. For *with all thy getting* (7) read with RV 'with all thou hast gotten', and cf. Mt. xiii. 44–46.

g. The seventh lesson (iv. 10–19)

The theme is 'Abhor that which is evil'. Once more the teacher opens with an urgent injunction to his pupils to be teachable and maintain their grip on the lessons they have learned (10–13). Once more, the possession of wisdom will confer long life (10). They have already learned from his teaching in what direction wisdom lies (11). For *right paths* (11) it is better to read with RV 'paths of uprightness', i.e. of moral conduct of life. The wisdom which shows itself in such conduct will be a sure guide into true liberty (12). To be *straitened* is 'to be in difficulties', a word expressive of the hampered and restricted movements of those who leave 'the way of wisdom' and 'the paths of uprightness'. The urgency of gripping this discipline is well illustrated in the accumulation of expressions in verse 13. Oesterley renders the last phrase 'because wisdom is all in all to a man'.

Verses 14–19 contain warnings to shun the by-paths followed by the wicked (14, 15), a description of the men who follow them (16, 17) and vivid, contrasting pictures of what it is like to follow the true road (18) and the by-paths (19). Verse 17 probably refers to the wicked gaining their sustenance by wickedness and violence (cf. xx. 17), though it may also mean that evil was their food and drink and constant enjoyment (contrast Jn. iv. 34). In verse 18 the AV is more literal, but the RV mg. 'the light of dawn' conveys the right idea. 'As the sun climbs the heavens, shining brighter and brighter, from the first faint glimmer of dawn till he reaches his meridian height and appears to stay there firm and motionless: so is the path of the righteous. His sun standeth still at last in the heavens, and hasteth not to go down for the whole everlasting day' (Perowne). The *perfect day* is 'high noon'. With this verse cf. Is. ii. 5.

h. The eighth lesson (iv. 20–27)

The theme is 'Cleave to that which is good'. Yet another appeal to heed the teacher's life-giving instructions (20–22) is followed by an appeal to maintain heart (23), speech (24), eyes (25) and feet (26, 27) in the direction that leads to life.

In verse 21 the teacher shows that it is not enough to hear wise instruction: it must be assimilated, pondered, kept at the centre of man's being. Cf. Ps. cxix. 11 and Lk. ii. 19. *To all their flesh* (22) means 'to the flesh of every one of them'. Verse 23 gives the key to this whole series of lessons. Wisdom leads to life, but fundamentally wisdom originates, not in the following out of a collection of wise precepts, but in the heart, the focus of the mind and will and the fountain of action. (For the Hebrew connotation of *heart* see ii. 2n.) What backsliding Israel needed was '*an heart* to know God' (Je. xxiv. 7). Our Lord's words on this subject which caused such offence (Mt. xv. 10–20) draw out the teaching of this verse. For *with all diligence*, RV mg. 'above all that thou guardest' is preferable. In verse 26 instead of *ponder* read 'make straight' with LXX and Heb. xii. 13 (cf. RV). This is now the acknowledged sense of the word here; a removal of all that can be a moral hindrance is implied. But that is not all. The pupil is also bidden to see that his ways are *established* (26). The root means 'to make firm'. The road, having been cleared of obstacles, is then to be made firm, and thereafter there must be no deviation from it (27).

i. The ninth lesson (v. 1–23)

The theme is wisdom applied to the relations between the sexes. After an opening appeal for close attention (1, 2) the teacher proceeds to a description of the *strange woman* and her allurements (3–6), an injunction to avoid her (7, 8), a warning of what befalls her victims (9–14), a call to cherish holy love (15–19) and a reminder that God is watching continually (20–23).

The *strange woman* is a figure who often appears in the book (cf. ii. 16, vi. 24, vii. 5, xx. 16, xxiii. 27, xxvii. 13). Broadly speaking, there are four different views of the meaning of the phrase: first that it represents Israelite harlots or adulteresses, described as 'strange' because they have no right to the relationship portrayed; secondly that *strange* has its usual meaning of 'foreign', and Canaanite or Phoenician women are meant (we know that sacred prostitution was practised in Canaanite religion); thirdly that the reference is to a foreign cult, perhaps of Astarte the goddess of love, with a strong sexual element, met with in trade relations with neighbouring countries; fourthly that the whole is allegorical, and refers to the seductions of Greek philosophy or religion. Of these, the first explanation is the simplest, the most natural, and the one that best meets the statements in ii. 17, vii. 19f.

End (4) most naturally refers to the judgment of those who have relations with her. *Wormwood* (4) is used in the Old Testament as a symbol of suffering (see e.g. Dt. xxix. 18; Je. ix. 15). *Hell* (5) represents Sheol, 'the grave' (RV mg.) or abode of the departed. Verse 6 is difficult and obscure, but recent philological discoveries throw some light upon it. If we may follow Prof. G. R. Driver in seeing the true meaning here of the word translated *ponder* as 'to examine, search out' and Prof. D. Winton Thomas in his demonstration that the Hebrew *yada'*, usually translated, as here, 'to know', sometimes means 'to be still', 'to be quiet', we may translate 'Lest she should examine carefully the path of life; her ways are unstable and she is not at rest'. The LXX and other versions read 'not' instead of *lest* at the beginning of the verse, which would make the sense clearer.

Verses 9–14 describe the conclusion of the 'Rake's Progress'. The picture in verses 9, 10 seems to be of the adulterer, his bodily strength sapped, his worldly goods gone, spending his remaining years as a slave in another's house. *Cruel* (9) is masculine singular. More terrible, however, are the pangs of his remorse (11–14), which has come too late. *I was almost in all evil* (14) means either 'I have had the narrowest of escapes from the supreme penalty which might have been inflicted for this sin' whether death (cf. Lv. xx. 10) or otherwise; or 'I have committed the depths of evil even though a member of the holy congregation of Israel'. In this latter interpretation the phrase *congregation and assembly* is viewed as a corporate designation for Israel as the people of God, and the fact that the sin was committed in the midst of such a people would constitute an aggravation of it (cf. Heb. xii. 15). The whole passage is an illustration of i. 26ff. where wisdom is represented as 'laughing' when those who have rejected her realize their error.

From this warning of the evil consequences of sin, the teacher passes to positive instruction on the joy and sacredness of a pure marital life, in terms similar to those of the Song of Solomon. To the Oriental the love-song is a sacred thing, and there would be nothing indelicate in the terms in which he speaks. Verse 15 urges the learner to delight in his own wife as opposed to 'the strange woman'. If we retain the AV rendering of verse 16 the meaning is that 'purity of married life will diffuse itself abroad like streams from a fountain' (Perowne); but the context is better suited by the RV, 'Should thy springs be dispersed abroad, And rivers of waters in the streets?' involving a return to the warnings in the last section against promiscuity. The fountain is *blessed* (18) when enjoyed with respect to the laws of God: *the wife of thy youth* is 'the wife. you married when young', early marriage being customary in Old Testament times.

Verses 21–23 again bring all the precepts taught into relation with the covenant of the living God. He watches over every life (21). The best sense is given by rendering *pondereth* as 'scrutinizes' (see note on verse 6). The rebel rapidly becomes a victim of his own rebellion (22), the reason being that he has not heeded the divine discipline (23). In this verse the RV 'for lack of instruction' is much to be preferred to AV *without instruction* (cf. Hos. iv. 6). Such is the teacher's final deterrent from sin. For the thought of the passage cf. Eph. iv. 17–19.

j. The tenth lesson (vi. 1–19)

This lesson is based on the principle enunciated in v. 22. Three examples are taken of the process there described, and a list of seven deadly sins is added.

i. The surety (vi. 1–5). In early days, Israel's commercial law was straightforward. Borrowing was necessary only for particular emergencies, and so the taking of interest from a fellow-Israelite was strictly forbidden (e.g. Lv. xxv. 36), and if a garment was taken as security for a loan, it was to be returned by nightfall to serve as a blanket (Ex. xxii. 25–27). With the growth of civilization and foreign trade relations, the practice of suretyship seems to have grown up, a man accepting responsibility for the debts of another. The action of *The Merchant of Venice* revolves, of course, round this or a similar custom. Perhaps further research will throw more light upon what was actually involved. At any rate, in our book it is uniformly condemned. Davison probably points to the root of the objection when he says: 'The use of money is an index of character . . . The young man who enters into such monetary engagements as are condemned in the Proverbs is in the first place morally weak, in the second place practically dishonest, and in the third place will probably entail much suffering upon those who have deserved better at his hands' (*The Wisdom*

Literature of the Old Testament, pp. 193f.). It is worth noticing that Proverbs is especially concerned with surety transactions involving strangers (foreign traders?); see e.g. vi. 1, xi. 15, xx. 16, xxvii. 13.

Stricken thy hand with a stranger (1) refers to the act ratifying the transaction. The surety is, like the wicked man of v. 22, trapped by his own folly. In the verses that follow he is urged to make every effort to free himself, importuning, if need be, the one on whose behalf he has made the pledge to release him.

ii. The sluggard (vi. 6–11). In *The Pilgrim's Progress* Sloth, in company with Simple and Presumption, is seen by Christian asleep by the wayside. By teaching 'others to presume that they should do well at last', Sloth and his companions cause others to follow their example. But when Christiana passes by, she sees them 'hanged up in irons a little way off'. This picture is true to that given in Proverbs. A proverb from nature, such as Solomon made (1 Ki. iv. 33), is used to shame the lazy man into action (6–9), but if he heeds not, his slumber will soon be rudely interrupted (10, 11) by the stark fact of poverty and need—another example of a fool caught in the toils of his own folly (v. 22). *One that travelleth* (11) is rendered 'robber' by RV: a good translation would be 'highwayman'.

iii. The 'man of Belial' (vi. 12–19). A brief but vivid portrait is sketched of what A. D. Power well calls 'The Perfect Bounder' (12–14). Perverse, deceitful, divisive and vicious, he too will eventually be overthrown as a result of his sin (verse 15).

A naughty person (12) is literally 'a man of Belial'. 'Belial', meaning 'without profit', is perhaps the only genuine compound word in Hebrew: it is often used in the Old Testament to denote wickedness (e.g. Jdg. xix. 22), and Paul uses it as a title for Satan (2 Cor. vi. 15). *He speaketh with his feet* (13) is a literal translation; RV mg. reads 'shuffleth'. In either case insincerity is implied. For *teacheth* (13) read with RV 'maketh signs'.

The next section (16–19) also relates to the man of Belial. The seven deadly sins enumerated as things that God hates are marks of 'the bad lot'. He sins with his eyes (13, 17), hands (13, 17), heart (14, 18) and feet (13, 18); he is a divider and mischief-maker (14, 19). We have other 'numerical proverbs' in chapter xxx. Perhaps this was originally a didactic form for classroom use, and ran 'What six things does Jehovah hate? . . .'

k. The eleventh lesson (vi. 20–35)

The theme is the seventh commandment. The exordium treats of the guidance offered by sound teaching (20–23); and solemn warnings are uttered against the specific sin of adultery (24–35).

Commandment and *law* in verse 20 refer to parental teaching: in verse 23 they seem to refer to the law of the covenant. It was this law, however (cf. Dt. vi. 6, 7), which was the content of the home teaching of the godly Israelite. The divine law, taught and expounded, provides clear guidance for life. Oesterley makes a distinction between *commandment* as the lamp and the *law* as the source of light, and compares the way in which John the Baptist is called a lamp (Jn. v. 35) and Jesus Christ the Light (Jn. i. 8f.). At all events God's law is to be inwardly held and outwardly manifested (21), guiding and controlling all activities (22).

It is stressed that the law and discipline and correction in the light of it (cf. 2 Tim. iii. 16) afford protection from the *strange woman* (24). Here a case might be made out for an allegorical interpretation, and when we remember that the figure of an adulteress is often used in the Old Testament to describe sinful Israel (cf. Hos. ii) and that James uses it to describe the worldly Christian (Jas. iv. 4), it is clear that the reach of these chapters is far beyond sexual misconduct. Nevertheless the way in which detail is relentlessly pressed home requires us to believe that the teacher means his words to be taken literally.

Her eyelids (25) were probably painted (cf. 2 Ki. ix. 30, mg.). It is not clear whether in verse 26 the teacher distinguishes two types of immoral woman. If this is so, the verse says that a man may be brought to poverty (*a piece of bread*) through a prostitute, but runs the risk of his life (by social or legal action) through consorting with an *adulteress* (lit. 'a man's wife'). Probably, however, the same woman is referred to in both parts of the verse. *Bosom* (27) means the fold of the garment across the chest. Verse 29 brings us again to the thought of the living God. RV renders *shall not be innocent* by 'shall not be unpunished'. To be held 'not innocent' in Old Testament thought inevitably means punishment. Verse 30 is rather obscure. The simplest explanation is that if a thief who steals to feed himself, though much less despicable than an adulterer, has still to make restitution in full measure (sevenfold is probably a general, not an exact term), how much more shall the adulterer pay the penalty? Only in his case he is destroying himself (32; *soul* is to be understood thus); he can expect condign punishment and public disgrace (33), and will receive no quarter from the wronged husband (34); unlike the thief, he can make no restitution (35).

l. The twelfth lesson (vii. 1–27)

The theme, like that of the previous lesson, is the peril of adultery. First there is the customary exhortation to observe and ever keep in mind the paternal teaching which is the way of life and is particularly proof against the strange woman (1–5). The relationships mentioned in verse 4 depict the close personal knowledge of wisdom that the teacher desires in his pupils: *kinswoman* implies family intimacy (cf. Mt. xii. 50).

There follows a passage of superb vividness giving an eyewitness account of how a young man fell a prey to the strange woman (6–23). This forms the bulk of the lesson, verses 24–27 pointing the moral. The picture of the victim is skilfully sketched. He is one of *the simple ones* (7; see i. 22n.). This is illustrative of the fact that one who is simple in the negative sense, without formed ideas of good and evil, is in peril of becoming a fool and a reprobate if he remains uninstructed. From verse 8 we learn that he spent the time from twilight to midnight walking the streets near her house. The woman is lustful and restless, impudent of face (an excellent translation!) and quite shameless. She introduces a subtle religious pretext (14). Under the law of the peace offering (Lv. vii. 11ff.), the flesh of the animal had to be eaten by the worshippers on the same day as the sacrifice, or, in the case of a vow, on the following day. The woman, having made her vows to Jehovah, now invites the youth to share in the sacrificial feast. She claims to have looked for him specially to share her table (15). She paints in glowing colours 'the pleasures of sin' (16–18), and their extraordinary luck in that the *goodman*, i.e. her husband, is away for some time. Actually in the Hebrew she calls him simply 'the man', possibly what Toy calls 'a refined sneer'. In verse 20, for *the day appointed* read 'new moon' with RV. After some hesitation (implied in verse 21) the youth suddenly capitulates (22). 'Suddenly' (RV mg.) is better than *straightway*. The text in verses 22, 23 is notoriously difficult. The rendering *as a fool to the correction of the stocks* is obtained only by transposing the word order and the unwarranted assumption that the word translated *stocks* can bear that meaning. The LXX has an additional line: ' . . . as an ox is led to the slaughter, and as a dog to his chain, or as a stag by an arrow is struck through the liver'. Whatever the true rendering, the sense is clear: the young man's fate is sudden and drastic, though the form it takes is left to the imagination.

Having reached this dramatic climax, the teacher closes the lesson with a few solemn sentences. The casualties caused by the strange woman have been innumerable (26). *Many strong men* (RV 'a mighty host') have been slain by her. In other words, 'Let him that thinketh he standeth take heed lest he fall'. It is a strange irony that it was his 'strange wives' that led to Solomon's own decline from wisdom (1 Ki. xi. 1–8).

m. The thirteenth lesson (viii. 1–36)

The lesson, after a brief introduction by the teacher (1–3), is given by personified Wisdom herself: and with it we reach the high-water mark of the series. In severe contrast with the shuffling, dusk-loving, seductive manner of the woman of the last lesson, Wisdom clearly and with dignity and in the most public places pleads with men to receive her and declares the treasures of her reward (4–21). Wisdom's part in creation is then set forth (22–31), and she adds her own exhortation to cleave to her in verses 32–36.

This chapter with its personification of Wisdom was interpreted Christologically from the earliest Christian centuries. Certainly Paul (cf. e.g. 1 Cor. viii. 6; Col. i. 15–18), the writer to the Hebrews (cf. Heb. i. 3) and John (cf. Rev. iii. 14) see in it terms which have their full meaning only in 'Christ the power of God, and the wisdom of God' (1 Cor. i. 24). Theophilus of Antioch, the first Christian writer to use the word 'Trinity' of the Godhead, speaks of 'God, His Word and His Wisdom' (*Ad Autolycum* ii. 15); like other second-century writers he is not clear on the division of functions between Son and Spirit. We may believe that the fathers were justified when they saw in the personification of Wisdom a foreshadowing of that revelation made clearer in the New Testament of three hypostases in the One God. As Archdeacon Perowne says, 'The vivid and august personification falters not on its way, till it presents to us rather than predicts Him, who is "the Wisdom of God", "the Only Begotten of the Father" and "the Son of His Love"; who "became flesh" and "dwelt among us", because from all eternity His delights had been with the sons of men' (*The Proverbs*, Cam. Bible, p. 31). Finally we may note that our Lord Himself refers to the personified Wisdom of God (Lk. xi. 49) in speaking of the prophets and apostles, the mouthpieces of God's wisdom, who were consistently rejected by God's people.

i. Wisdom among men (viii. 1–21). In the most conspicuous places (2, 3) Wisdom addresses the whole of mankind (4). Once again we see that discerning shrewdness (*prudence*) is offered to the *simple*, and even hardened *fools* (*kesilim*, see i. 22n.) still have a chance to learn (5). Wisdom's words are true, straightforward and sincere (6–9). With verse 9 we might compare Mt. xiii. 16. She offers a rich reward: far richer than the things for which men spend their lives (10, 11).

Wisdom then explains further what she is. Read in verse 12: 'I, Wisdom, have made prudence my dwelling, and acquire knowledge and discretion' (cf. RV). The meaning will then be that Wisdom is demonstrated in actual life by discernment (*prudence*) and possesses the other forms of understanding spoken of in i. 4. Wisdom identifies herself with the *fear of the Lord* (cf. i. 7), which is said to involve hatred of evil (13). Among her other possessions are *counsel* and *strength* (14; RV 'might'), qualities of kingship which are seen in their fullness in the King Messiah (Is. ix. 6, xi. 2). This leads naturally to Wisdom's part in guiding rulers (15, 16). *Justice* (15) implies righteous government. Solomon himself asked for wisdom to guide him in his rule (1 Ki. iii. 5–12). Wisdom is accessible when sought (17; cf. Lk. xi. 9–13): for *early* here read with RV 'diligently'. Wisdom confers great riches upon those that love her (18–21), the greater because they are righteously obtained (18, 20). That her blessings are more than simply material is shown by the contrasts in verse 19. *Durable* (18) occurs nowhere else in the Old Testament:

RV mg. suggests 'ancient'; Koehler (*Lexicon, in loc.*) 'hereditary'.

ii. Wisdom with God (viii. 22–36). Wisdom speaks now of her part in creation. Since the time of the opening of the Arian controversy in the fourth century verse 22 has been one of the most discussed passages in the Old Testament. The main point at issue is, what is the meaning of the word *qanah*, translated *possessed*? The LXX has 'The Lord created me', and the Arians used this as one of their main proof-texts for their thesis that Christ was a created being. They were confuted on other grounds, but it was also shown that the Hebrew here did not bear this meaning. *Possessed*, the rendering of the English versions, would mean that from the beginning God's wisdom was with God: God is called the *possessor* (root *qanah*) of heaven and earth in Gn. xiv. 19, 22. C. F. Burney, in his article 'Christ as the Arche of Creation' (in *Journal of Theological Studies*, vol. 27, 1926, pp. 160ff.), adduces evidence that the meaning is 'begat': a rendering which would bring the passage to bear as closely on the doctrine of the Eternal Generation of the Son as it did in the days of Arius. In any case, the reference here is not to Wisdom's being the first created being, for His wisdom is surely inseparable from God: rather should we understand from it that Wisdom was with Him from all eternity. *Set up* (23) may refer to God's appointment of Wisdom for her task. The word is used in the sense of consecrate. Originally meaning 'to pour out' it came to mean 'to consecrate by pouring libations'. Wisdom preceded all created things, even the primeval depths (24). But that is not all. Wisdom is not only present at, but is the mediatrix of creation (30). Human craftsmanship is the product of wisdom (Ex. xxxv. 31); so also is the craftsmanship that formed the worlds. 'The versatility of the mind of man is but an image of the versatility of its archetype' (Cheyne, *Job and Solomon*, p. 118). For *as one brought up with him* (30) read with RV 'master workman'. As pointed at present (*'amon*), there is no parallel for the word. The RV rendering involves re-pointing as *'ommon* (cf. Ct. vii. 1). Others would re-point *'emun*, 'nurseling', or 'ward', which would also make good sense; but the RV rendering fits the whole context better. It is not an insuperable objection that Jehovah Himself is presented throughout as the Maker. We may easily in the same context speak of the owner, the architect and the builder all 'building' the same house. Wisdom rejoiced over the advancing creation, and her joy was complete when it was ready for mankind to live there (31). A more literal rendering would be 'sporting in the inhabited world of His earth'. With the whole passage cf. ch. iii. 19, 20.

In the concluding verses Wisdom speaks like a teacher and addresses her audience as 'sons' (32; so read for *ye children*), reminding them again that to love her brings life (35) and to hate her, death (36). *Sinneth against me* (36); better, as in RV mg., 'misseth me'. The Hebrew word 'to sin' meant originally 'to miss', i.e. 'to miss the mark': this original meaning is better here, where the contrast is with *whoso findeth me* (35). To miss Wisdom is to wrong oneself: to hate her is suicide (36).

n. Summary of the thirteen lessons (ix. 1–18)

Some of the main topics dealt with in chapters i—viii are summarized in the form of a picture of Wisdom and Folly each inviting men to a banquet.

i. The seven pillars of Wisdom (ix. 1–12).

Once more personified, Wisdom is now seen as a gracious hostess. There has been much speculation about the *seven pillars* (1). They have been made to represent things as various as the seven days of creation, the seven liberal arts, and even the first seven chapters of Proverbs (see the list in Toy, I.C.C., *Proverbs*, p. 185). It is argued by Toy and others that there is no special significance in the number *seven*, which may have been the usual number of pillars in the house-style of the period. Such a house has, however, been found only in recent years—Sennacherib's New Year festival house. (Reference by A. Baumgartner, in *The Old Testament and Modern Study*, edited by H. H. Rowley, p. 215f.) Following a hint by A. D. Power (*Sidelights on the Book of Proverbs*) we may possibly think of the seven pillars as Knowledge, Discretion, Sound Wisdom, Prudence (AV sometimes 'subtilty'), Counsel, Instruction and Understanding. Each of these attributes occurs frequently in the book; each is a facet or manifestation of wisdom, comprehended in it, but not exhausting it; each a pillar by which the house of Wisdom is supported.

Within her house Wisdom has laid a magnificent feast (2) and despatched her maids to call the guests (3). She goes herself (3–6) to call whosoever will to her banquet. There is a special place for the uninstructed *simple* and for the ignoramus (4); they may yet receive life and understanding (6). *Forsake the foolish* (6) is better read 'Forsake, ye simple' (cf. RV mg.). They are being called to a clear-cut decision. The LXX, however, is closer to the AV, 'forsake senselessness'. There is an evident connection between this Great Supper and that described in Lk. xiv. 16ff.

There follow comments, still by Wisdom herself, on the impossibility of making any impression upon the scorners by such an invitation as she was extending to the simple. The contrast in verses 7–9 is not between those invited and those not invited to the banquet, but between the reactions of the scorner and the teachable man to the holy discipline imparted by Wisdom. This, too, is an element in our Lord's teaching (cf. Mt. vii. 6). See also i. 4, 5 and i. 22 and the commentary there. Verse 10, with its repetition of the motto of the book (i. 7), gives the reason for this difference of reaction. Wisdom begins with the fear of God; the cynical scorner can therefore never learn. For *the holy* (10) read with RV 'the Holy One'.

ii. Folly's feast (ix. 13–18).

Folly is also personified—as a harlot. Brazenly, she invites the simple to her feast. She makes her invitation as widely known as does Wisdom (cf. verses 14, 15 with verses 3, 4). But whereas Wisdom offers a feast indeed and of her own preparation (5), Folly offers a paltry meal, stolen, illicit and clandestine (17), and her guests go to their death (18).

A foolish woman (13); lit. 'a woman of folly'; read with RV mg. 'Folly'. For *simple* read with RV mg. 'simplicity'. Folly is simplicity itself in its worst form, without moral sense. For *and knoweth nothing* (13) it seems better to follow Prof. D. Winton Thomas (*Journal of Theological Studies* (New Series), vol. 4, 1953, p. 23f.) and translate 'and is ever restless'. See v. 6n. In verse 18 *hell* is *Sheol* or 'the grave'.

We may note that the invitations of both Wisdom and Folly are directed to the simple and ignorant (4, 16). The wise, though they may still grow in wisdom (8, 9), and the scorner (7) need no invitation.

III. THE FIRST BOOK OF SOLOMON. x. 1—xxii. 16

This is much the largest collection in the book. It is estimated that it contains 374 proverbs. Whether the collection was made by Solomon himself, by a member of his court, or by a later collector, we have no means of knowing. But the exact figure quoted in 1 Ki. iv. 32 suggests that collections may have been made in his lifetime, so that this may be one.

Most of the proverbs are of one type, consisting of two lines, the second pointing a contrast to the first. The arrangement is not quite so haphazard as may at first appear. Often a series of proverbs on the same or a similar subject, or demonstrating the same principle, may be grouped together; or the repetition of a catchword or catchphrase may be the link between proverbs on different subjects. But the proverbs were spoken at different times and there is often no connection between them. It must be stressed that the titles at the heads of sections are only approximate guides to the contents for the sake of convenience.

a. The rewards of right and wrong living (x. 1–32)

For the title, *The proverbs of Solomon*, see the *Introduction*, p. 515. Just as the lessons sometimes begin with an exhortation to follow parental teaching (e.g. i. 8, vi. 20), the collection opens with a proverb about the response to this teaching (1). *Foolish* is more than 'stupid'; the son is a *kesil* (see i. 22n.). Verse 2 speaks of the reward of uprightness. *Treasures of wickedness* are riches gained by wickedness: *righteousness* is right living. The prophets frequently speak of oppression, cheating and exploitation of the weak as denials of the righteousness God demands in His people. The catchword *righteous* introduces the next proverb (3) dealing with God's supply of the physical needs of His people (cf. Mt. vi. 11, 33), and His frustration of the evil desires of the wicked. *Soul of the righteous* stands for 'the righteous man'; for *substance* read with RV 'desire'; in the Old Testament the word always denotes an evil desire.

Verses 4 and 5 deal with the reward of laziness and of industry. *With a slack hand* (lit. 'palm') conveys the idea of the hand hanging loose.

Verses 6–11 revert to the theme of the rewards of the righteous and of the wicked. From the parallelism we would expect *violence covereth the mouth of the wicked* (6) to refer to reproaches or blows about the mouth which will follow for him as assuredly as blessings on the 'head' of the righteous. The word *ḥamas*, however, is used elsewhere only of wrongful treatment. If we keep the text as it stands, it seems better, therefore, to understand it exactly as in verse 11; violent, vicious language envelops the mouth of the wicked. His punishment is then implied by comparison rather than stated. Verse 7 shows that the effects of righteousness and of wickedness continue on earth after death. In verse 8 the meaning is that those who are wise-hearted do heed the commandments of Wisdom, but those who do not bridle their tongue will be overthrown. In verse 9 *shall be known* is 'shall be found out' (cf. 2 Tim. iii. 9). In verse 10 *winketh with the eye* refers to crafty and insincere conduct. The LXX and Syriac both read 'But he that rebuketh openly maketh peace' instead of *but a prating fool shall fall*. This may be the better reading. In verse 11 the antithesis is between the righteous who 'is a source of inspiration and encouragement to his fellows on life's way just as the wayside well is a source of refreshment and renewed vigour to the weary traveller' (Oesterley) and the wicked whose mouth is covered with ugly and noxious language. We may note that, as in vi. 12f., righteousness and wickedness may be manifest in the heart (8), mouth (6, 8, 10, 11), feet (9) and eyes (10).

The catchword *covereth* introduces a very deep saying on love and hatred (12). Cf. 1 Pet. iv. 8; Jas. v. 20. and 1 Cor. xiii. 7 RV mg. There follow two sayings on wise and foolish talk and their respective rewards (13, 14). In verse 13 for *understanding* read with RV 'discernment'; in verse 14 for *lay up* read 'reserve' (A. D. Power); for *is near destruction* read 'is an impending calamity'. The idea is that, while wise men conceal what they know, a fool ('*ewil*, see i. 22n.) is likely to blurt out his stupidity and endanger himself and others in consequence.

The catchword *destruction* leads to an observation on wealth and poverty (15). *Destruction* is probably meant to suggest the threat of imminent disaster, e.g. the insecurity of the poor, particularly in the social revolution taking place in Solomon's time. When the first half of the saying is repeated at xviii. 11, however, it is shown that this is not the whole story, that the rich man's wealth is not in itself a sufficiently strong city.

Two proverbs (16, 17), joined together by the word *life*, speak of the fruit of right living and of wickedness, and the relation of holy discipline (*instruction*, see i. 2n.) to this. In verse 17 read with RV mg. 'He is a way of life that heedeth instruction; But he that forsaketh reproof causeth to err'. One item in the reward of right and wrong living is the effect their example has on others.

Four proverbs (18–21) follow, all connected with speech. The first shows that it is evil to hide hatred hypocritically and bad to manifest it in slander. The second warns against empty babbling; the third contrasts the value of the speech of those who live aright and those who do not; the fourth develops this thought. *Feed* (21) is the word commonly used for a shepherd's care of his sheep: the righteous by virtue of their speech become pastors; the fools die for lack of the wisdom the righteous are able to impart to others.

Verse 22 brings a proverb on the unadulterated blessing of Jehovah. The AV text is preferable here to RV mg. which has 'And toil addeth nothing thereto' as the second half. Verse 23 speaks of a fool's sport. Verses 24 and 25 return to the principal theme in this section, the punishment in store for the wicked and the blessing of the Lord laid up for the righteous. *Fear* (24) stands for 'thing feared'. For *as the whirlwind passeth . . .* (25) read 'when the whirlwind passeth the wicked is no more'. With this verse cf. the parable in Mt. vii. 24ff.

Verse 26 introduces us to the sluggard once more (cf. vi. 6). We are told of the effect of such 'a wicked and slothful servant' (cf. Mt. xxv. 26) upon his master. The converse is seen in xxv. 13.

The rest of the chapter (27–32) is devoted to six more proverbs on the fate of the righteous and wicked. We see life (27), joy (28), strength (29) as blessings of the righteous. In verse 29 read 'The way of the Lord is a stronghold to the upright: But He is destruction to the workers of iniquity' (cf. RV). The *way of the Lord* is His way of dealing with men. Verse 30 takes further the principle expressed in Ex. xx. 12, and is taken further again by our Lord in Mt. v. 5. Verses 31, 32 are more particularly concerned with the speech of righteous and wicked (cf. Jas. iii. 5ff.). For *bringeth forth* (31) read with RV mg. 'buddeth with'.

b. Some aspects of wickedness (xi. 1–31)

Verse 1 deals with honesty, and brings commercial and business practice into direct relation to the law and will of God.

The next aspect of wickedness dealt with is pride (2), and the affiliation between wisdom and humility is pointed out. Verse 3 contrasts the integrity of the upright with the crookedness and distortion (the literal meaning of the word translated *perverseness*) of rebels. *Transgressors* (RV 'they that deal treacherously') usually stands in the Old Testament for those who break or revolt against the covenant with Jehovah.

Five proverbs follow (4–8) which deal with the relation of righteousness to wickedness. The first (4) shows that in the day of wrath—be it at death, a sudden calamity, or the great judgment day of the Lord spoken of by the prophets (cf. Is. x. 3; Am. v. 18)—it is righteousness that delivers, and not riches. This is one of many passages in the book which express eternal principles, limited in their scope under the old covenant and flooded with new meaning for the Christian. The second proverb deals with the respective paths of the righteous and wicked (5), the one clearing his way of obstacles as he goes (for *direct*, RV mg. reads 'make straight or plain'), the other hopelessly stumbling. The noun cognate with *perfect* is the one translated *integrity* in verse 3, where the thought is similar. Verse 6 carries this thought still further. It is perhaps better to render the word translated *naughtiness* as 'desires' (see x. 3n., where the same word occurs). It is their evil desires which ensnare and overthrow the rebels. Verses 7 and 8 continue the comparison, the first speaking of the time after death, the second of their lifetimes. *And the hope of unjust men perisheth* (7); lit. 'And expectation of strength perisheth' (cf. RV mg.), i.e. hope based on human strength fades completely away. No book in the Bible is more concerned with eschatology than is the book of Proverbs.

Verse 9 concerns the *hypocrite*, i.e. 'the godless man' (RV), or slanderer. Through knowledge the righteous will finally be saved from him. Delitzsch remarks in his commentary that the godless becomes a 'lightning conductor' for the righteous.

Two more proverbs (10, 11) speak of the effect of these two classes of people upon the community. *City* (10); Heb. *qiryah*, a walled township. Oesterley rightly points out that the verses belong to a date when Israelite cities were governed by Israelites, i.e. before the exile. The whole township rejoices at the prosperity of the good man and the fall of the evil. A city is ennobled by the presence in it of men who are blessed of God and overthrown by the presence of wicked men (11). An illustration of this principle may be seen in Gn. xviii, where God is about to overthrow Sodom and Gomorrah for the great sin of their inhabitants, and then prepares to spare Sodom for the sake of any righteous persons who may be found there. In the verse in Proverbs city-rulers are probably especially in mind.

Verse 12 declares how unwise it is to show open contempt of anyone: the wise man keeps his thoughts to himself. Verse 13 shows another aspect of wickedness, the tale-bearer who betrays secrets, and contrasts him with the man of *a faithful spirit* —i.e. one who is absolutely trustworthy. Verse 14 speaks of the need for counsel in government (RV renders *counsel* as 'wise guidance') and of the value of taking extensive advice. Cf. xv. 20, xxiv. 6. The proverb would have been especially relevant soon after Solomon's death (cf. 1 Ki.

xii. 1–14). Verse 15 deals with the menace of suretyship (see vi. 1n.). 'None ever knew so well that "He who hateth suretyship is sure" as He who having counted the cost became for us "the surety of a better covenant" ' (Perowne, *op. cit.*, p. 30. The reference is to Heb. vii. 22). Verse 16 has a comparison instead of the usual antithesis. A gracious woman wins and keeps renown as surely as violent men seize their booty. We may note in passing how much the book has to say of the true glory of womanhood and how much honour it pays to the wife and mother.

Five proverbs (17–21) deal with various aspects of good and evil. There is the man who shows mercy (17), i.e. keeps the covenant obligations which lay upon him that he shall love his neighbour as himself. In doing so he does good to himself, whereas the cruel man brings trouble upon himself. Then the wicked man whose present prosperity is deceptive, as it will not benefit him for ever, is contrasted with the righteous whose reward is certain (18; cf. Gal. vi. 7). The idea is plainer if we read with RV 'earneth deceitful wages' for *worketh a deceitful work*. Verse 19 is difficult, as the Hebrew, which reads simply 'as righteousness to life' in the first half, is so compressed: but the general sense must be as RV renders it. The perverse, who are hateful to God, are contrasted with those of upright life (20) and then, once more, we are reminded that the wicked will be punished and the *seed of the righteous*—i.e. righteous people as a whole—will be preserved (21). *Though hand join in hand* represents the Hebrew 'hand to hand', an obscure expression which is probably a strong asseveration.

Verse 22 gives us a brief word about a beautiful woman without taste (a literal rendering) or modesty. Verse 23 speaks of the desire of the righteous which is only for good, and the *wrath* (lit. 'outpouring') that the wicked may expect.

Three proverbs inculcating generosity follow. Wealth is not conditional on miserliness (24) but rather the reverse (25); and the practice of keeping back food from sale in order to run the price up (cf. Am. viii. 4–6) is denounced (26).

Five proverbs dealing with rewards and punishments conclude this section. Those who seek goodwill find God's favour; those who look for trouble will find more of it than they bargained for (27). It is useless to trust in riches (28). The man who creates disturbance in his own home can expect to lose everything and may be reduced to slavery in consequence (29); the result of righteousness is 'life more abundant', which flourishes like a tree (30). *He that winneth souls is wise* (30) would be better translated 'a wise man taketh souls', remembering that *souls* here will stand for 'people' or 'lives'. True, the verb 'to take' when used with *nephesh* (soul) normally means 'to take away', but that would be nonsense here. The meaning surely is that the wise man by his example gains the lives of other men, so that his righteousness is a *tree of life* to others as well as himself (cf. Mt. iv. 19). Both righteous and wicked will receive their desert on earth (31). The LXX took this to mean that both will be *punished* for their sins; i.e. if the righteous are to be punished (for even they have sinned), how much more the sinner? It is the LXX rendering that is taken up by Peter in 1 Pet. iv. 18.

c. Contrasts in conduct (xii. 1–28)

The first contrast is between the reactions of different men to discipline (1). The next two are between good and bad men (2, 3). The one receives God's favour, the other His condemnation. *Condemn* (2) is a legal term; literally 'He will cause to be wicked', i.e. He will reckon him as wicked. A contrast between good and bad wives is pointed by verse 4, a contrast which reveals how much depends on the wife in the home. We may see the full development of the thought of 'a virtuous woman' in xxxi. 10–31.

Three contrasts between the righteous and the wicked follow, contrasts in their intentions (5), their words (6) and their ultimate fate (7; cf. Mt. vii. 26). Verse 8 contrasts the commendation awarded to men who possess some wisdom and the state of the man of distorted mind who possesses none. Verse 9 means either, 'It is better to be of low social status and still have enough to keep a servant than to have a high opinion of oneself and go hungry', or with the LXX, by a slight change in vowel points, 'It is better to be humble and be your own servant', i.e. work for your own living.

Verse 10 shows that the contrast between a righteous and a wicked man extends to his treatment of animals. Verse 11 sets against the industrious peasant working his own piece of ground the man who wastes time in useless pursuits. (For *vain persons* read 'vain things'.) Verse 12 is difficult: the Hebrew has only 'The evil man has desired the net of the wicked, but the root of the righteous gives'. It is easier, though not necessarily correct, to read with LXX 'The desires of the wicked are evil, but the roots of the righteous are firm'.

Two proverbs on rewards and punishments come next. The wicked man entangles himself in the snare of his own wicked words, while the righteous, though falling into trouble, is able to escape (13); and men will be rewarded according to their words and their acts (14; cf. Mt. xii. 36; 2 Cor. v. 10). These are followed by two proverbs on the fool (Heb. *'ewil*): his conceit is contrasted with the teachableness of the wise (15); and the way in which his anger bursts out at once as soon as he is vexed is set against the self-control of the wise man in the face of an insult (16).

Verses 17–19 represent three contrasts in speech: the true witness who declares what is right (this is the meaning of the phrase *sheweth forth righteousness*) and the lying evidence; the sharp-tongued who wound with their speech (cf. Ps. cvi. 33) and the helpful, healing conversa-

tion of the truly wise; the permanence of true words and the transitoriness of a lie.

The next proverb takes these thoughts further. Not only do the wicked speak lies; their mind is deceitful, a contrast to the joy and peace of those who offer wise guidance (20). Verse 21 reverts to the fate of righteous and wicked. It is better with RV to transpose the words *evil* and *mischief*.

Two more proverbs deal with contrasts in speech: between lying and true dealing (22), and between modest concealment of learning and blatant exposure of folly (23). The next proverb (24) contrasts the outcome for hard-working and for lazy workmen: the one attains responsibility, the other finds himself under the lash in a labour gang. A delightful word on sympathy follows. Translate: 'Anxiety in the heart of a man maketh it droop; But a kindly word maketh it rejoice' (A. D. Power).

The sense of verse 26 is clearly that good men are a help and bad men a hindrance to others on the path of life, but the Hebrew of the first half is obscure. In the next proverb we return to the sluggard (27). We see him, having stirred himself sufficiently to catch an animal in the hunt, too lazy to cook it. Others connect the word translated *roasteth* with an Arabic root used as a hunting term, in which case the proverb says that the sluggard is too lazy to hunt his food. By contrast 'the precious substance of men is to the diligent' (so RV renders a difficult sentence); i.e. it is the industrious who prosper. The closing verse of the chapter is another commendation of the upright living as the pathway to life. Again the Hebrew is difficult, and the versions understand an antithesis between *the way of righteousness* and the way that leads to death.

d. Life and discipline (xiii. 1–25)

The wise man and the cynic are marked out by their attitude to paternal discipline (1). The pure speech of a good man will be rewarded (cf. xii. 14), but the 'appetite' (such is the meaning of *soul* here) of rebels against the covenant of Jehovah is for violence (2). Verse 3 continues the theme of the need for discipline in speech: *openeth wide his lips* suggests a vulgar grin (see Koehler, *Lexicon*, article *pshq*).

Discipline is applied to one's attitude to one's work (4) and to telling the truth (5). The respective effects of right and wrong living on life's journey are recalled (6). Then come two proverbs on riches. The natural interpretation of verse 7 is that a contrast is made between true and false riches. A man may be wealthy and not 'rich toward God' or he may be poor and yet account himself to have great treasures (cf. Lk. xii. 21). We cannot separate this from the thought of Him who 'though he was rich, yet for your sakes he became poor' (2 Cor. viii. 9), in whom the verse reaches its greatest height of meaning. RV mg. renders *maketh* in each case by 'feigneth', making the antithesis between extravagant display and miserliness. But this is a much less likely reading. Verse 8 shows that poverty as well as wealth has its advantages: the rich man can fall back on his wealth to get him out of difficulty. The poor man is less likely to be exposed to those difficulties, or, perhaps, he has 'nothing to lose but his chains'.

Verse 9 brings us another contrast between the righteous and the wicked. Verse 10 illustrates this principle laid down in the particular aspects of pride and modesty. There follow observations on prosperity gained by wrong means and by industry (11); on the deleterious effect when something longed for is postponed and the deep source of pleasure when the *desire* (i.e. the thing desired) does come (12), and on the perils of despising the *word* of God (13), not necessarily to be confined to the law of Moses, but certainly including it (cf. Is. xxx. 12f.).

Three proverbs on the nature of wisdom follow. The first describes the refreshing and revitalizing character of wise teaching (14), for this is the sense in which *law* (Heb. *torah*) is to be understood here. The second (15) states the way in which God treats the wise and the rebel (AV *transgressors;* cf. Acts ix. 5), and the third the way in which the discerning man and the fool (*kesil*) show themselves in their true colours (16).

Verse 17 contrasts undependable and trustworthy messengers (for *health* understand 'security'). The results of refusing and of heeding discipline are set out in verse 18. Verse 19 may be paraphrased: 'Although there is nothing more sweet than to gain a high and noble desire, fools (*kesilim*) will not leave their evil ways to do that: to do so would be hateful (an *abomination*) to them.' Verse 20 shows another aspect of the divine discipline. The development of wisdom is affected by the familiar company a man keeps. Two more proverbs (21, 22) speak of the eventual outcome for wicked and righteous.

Verse 23 is very obscure. One MS has 'the wicked' instead of *the poor* (the two words in Hebrew look much alike), which gives good sense: however the wicked may seem to be flourishing, his harvest will not finally profit him because it has been obtained 'without judgment', i.e. unrighteously. But this is by no means a certain reading. Cf. Jas. v. 1–6. Verse 24 speaks of the need of paternal discipline. Cf. Heb. xii. 6–9. This and similar passages (e.g. xix. 18, xxii. 15) show how seriously the education of children in righteousness was taken under the old covenant. Verse 25 tells of the satisfaction of the righteous and the frustration of the wicked.

e. Life and the fear of the Lord (xiv. 1–35)

Verse 1 takes us back to chapter ix and the houses of Wisdom and Folly. The reference cannot be to the literal building of houses, which could hardly be women's work, but it may well have a reference to family life which may be 'built' or 'plucked down' by the wisdom or lack of wisdom of the wife and mother. Verse 2 shows that the 'uprightness' and 'perverse

ways' so often mentioned in the book are ultimately dependent on the attitude to Jehovah. Verse 3 deals with wise and foolish talk. The point behind verse 4 is probably, 'No oxen, no stable-cleaning; but also no ploughing, and therefore no corn.' Next we have a proverb on true and false witnesses (5) and one on the scorner (6). He cannot find wisdom when he seeks it, because his cynical arrogance leaves no place for 'the fear of the Lord' (see ix. 10n.). Two more proverbs on the fool follow (7, 8).

Verse 9 is another of the obscure verses in this very ancient section of the book. Taking the Hebrew as it stands, we may read 'A guilt offering mocks at fools': i.e. the sacrifices for sin which fools offer mock them by their ineffectiveness (cf. Is. i. 11ff.). But there is a strangeness in this conception which suggests that we cannot at present understand fully what the writer meant by this proverb.

The isolated proverb in verse 10 on the ultimate solitude of the human heart in its joys and sorrows is of rare beauty. Incidentally, it goes against the allegation sometimes made that the wisdom teachers were concerned purely with outward conduct, and also illustrates that *heart* in this book, as in English, does sometimes emphasize the emotions rather than the intellect and will.

In verse 11 we return to the theme of the establishment of the upright and the overthrow of the wicked. Verse 12 is entitled 'the misleading signpost' by A. D. Power. In the second half of verse 13, on laughter, read 'may be' for *is*. Other proverbs in this section deal with rewards and punishments (14), gullibility and discernment (15), and prudence (15). The wise man is cautious and does not court disaster, while the fool loses his temper (so AV) or behaves insolently (cf. RV) in his vain self-confidence (16). Then come proverbs on short temper and malice (17), the inheritance of the simpleton and the shrewd (18), retribution (19), neighbours (20, 21), doing good and evil (22), labour and gossip (23), the adornment of wise men and fools (24), true and false witnesses (25–27). A true witness *delivereth souls* (25), i.e. 'saves lives' and, above all, lives in *the fear of the Lord* (26, 27).

Verse 28 is an observation on government. Verse 29 concerns keeping one's temper. Verse 30 contrasts mental composure (read with RV mg. 'tranquil' for *sound*) with the corroding effect of envy on the person who harbours it. Verse 31 condemns exploitation of the poor, which is said to be a direct affront to God. Verse 32 deals with the fate of the wicked and righteous. The text says that the righteous has hope after death. To say that the text must be wrong because such a hope had not yet arisen in Israel (see e.g. Toy, Oesterley) is arguing in a circle. Though the scope of the teachers of wisdom was normally within this world, that is not to say that 'no one may climb to the mountain tops to greet the dawn' (O. C. Whitehouse, *Isaiah*, Cent. Bible, p. 100, in another connection).

Verse 33 is another proverb about the manifestation of wisdom and folly. For *in the midst of fools* read with RV 'in the inward part of fools', i.e. their folly. Verses 34 and 35 are proverbs for Solomon's court. The true glory of a nation is in its corresponding with the righteous law of God. Of proverbs about the king, such as verse 35, R. F. Horton says, 'The study of the things concerning the king is to the thoughtful reader of the Proverbs a study of the things concerning Christ. The ideal elements speak of Him; the actual shortcomings cry out for Him' (*The Book of Proverbs*, Expositor's Bible, p. 327).

f. The path of life and the secrets of a cheerful heart (xv. 1–33)

Verses 1–7 concern folly and wisdom, particularly as these are manifest in speech. The controlling thought is that of God's omniscience and constant watch on life (3). In verse 4 read 'a breaking of spirit' (cf. Is. lxv. 14 and mg.) for *a breach in the spirit*.

Verses 8–17 are concerned with the way of life and once more the thought of the proverbs is dominated by the knowledge that God who looks into the unknown abode of the dead watches the thoughts of men (11). For *Hell and destruction* (11) RV reads 'Sheol and Abaddon'. Among items pointed out are God's refusal to accept sacrifices offered by wicked men (cf. Is. i. 11f.) and His delight in the prayer of the righteous (8), and the cheerfulness, even in straitened circumstances, which the man who fears God may enjoy (15–17).

Verses 18–33 consist of *obiter dicta* for the path of life. That path is pointed out in verse 24, translated by A. D. Power 'The path of life is upward for the prudent so that he may turn aside from Sheol below'.

g. The Lord's watch on life (xvi. 1–33)

Wise thoughts and plans (*the preparations of the heart*), as well as their expression, come from Jehovah (1; note that AV is to be preferred here to RV). A man may be satisfied with his righteousness, but Jehovah is the final judge of this (2; cf. 1 Cor. iv. 4). All purposes and plans should therefore be committed to (lit. 'rolled upon') Jehovah (3). Jehovah made everything for His own purpose: and He will fulfil His purpose for the wicked when He brings about the day of evil for them (4). The phrase is compressed. There is no sense of an arbitrary predestination of men for this day of evil. The thing that God hates is a proud mind (5; for *though hand join . . .* see xi. 21n.). *Mercy and truth* (6), i.e. covenant love and faithfulness (see iii. 3, 4n.), are the means of purging (lit. 'covering') sin, just as love is stated to be at x. 12. This is not put forward as a formal principle of atonement; it expresses God's basic requirements under the covenant with Israel (cf. Mi. vi. 6–8; Hab. ii. 4), and is linked very closely with a forsaking of evil caused by reverent awe of God. It also well expresses the *response* to atonement, i.e. faithfulness and

departure from evil, occasioned by fear of God and grateful love toward Him. Note that, whatever man may plan, it lies in God's power to overrule it (9).

Verse 10 gives an ideal picture of the king (see xiv. 35n.). *A divine sentence* is literally 'divination'. The idea is that the king when he delivers a righteous judgment speaks oracularly, like a prophet, and the result is that his mouth does not revolt against justice. This prepares us for the portrait of the messianic King with his divine judgment (cf. Is. ix. 7, xi. 3, 4). Verses 12–15 also deal with the king. How far short of this ideal the actual royal house fell is revealed in history. But the portrait remained, to be drawn more clearly by the prophets and fulfilled in the Kingship of Christ. On the phrase *messengers of death* (14) Perowne remarks, 'The reckless fury of the Eastern despot . . . is but the abuse of the awful justice of the Archetypal King' (*op. cit.*, p. 115).

Exhortations to gain wisdom and forsake sin, and proverbs about humility, trust, gracious speech, the 'bad lot' (27; cf. vi. 12n.), the gossip, the violent man, honourable old age, and self-control make up verses 16–32. Verse 33 ends the chapter on the same note as it began. The lot is cast into the lap from whose folds it is to be shaken out; but it is God who determines what it says. The background is doubtless the sacred lot (cf. Jos. vii. 14–18), but the meaning intended is far wider. God disposes; there is no such thing as chance. Two obscure passages may be noted. In verse 20 read with RV 'He that giveth heed unto the word shall find good'. The man who deals wisely with the Word of God (i.e. obeys it) will have his reward. Verse 26 may be read 'The appetite (lit. 'soul') of the labourer labours for him'. Perowne points out that this is lifted to a new level by Jn. vi. 27. Verse 25 occurs also at xiv. 12.

h. Bad men and fools, with some others (xvii. 1–28)

The *sacrifices* (1) are used by metonymy for the feast enjoyed by the worshippers where the whole animal was not burnt. See vii. 14n. Ironically enough an outstanding illustration of the point made in verse 2 occurred very soon after Solomon's death when his own 'wise servant', Jeroboam, divided the inheritance with Solomon's own 'son that caused shame', Rehoboam, and took the lion's share (see 1 Ki. xii). Verse 3 is another example of the way in which right conduct is treated in Proverbs—not in isolation, but in the light of the fact that it is God with whom we have to do. The process used by God to try men's hearts is as drastic as that used to refine gold (cf. 1 Pet. i. 7). There can be no superficial ethics where this is a foundation principle. With verse 5 cf. xiv. 31.

The *gift* (8) is probably a bribe (cf. verse 18). In verse 10 for *more* read with RV 'deeper'. The *cruel messenger* (11) is the messenger of the rebel's doom, the avenger, whether human or angelic.

The probable meaning in verse 14 is that quarrelling begins with a very slight friction, like a trickle through a tiny hole in a bank, so that it is wise to break off before it is aggravated. But some of the words are obscure. Verse 15 refers to legal procedure. Verse 16 has been taken to suggest that 'the wise' took a fee for their instruction, but this is not necessary. The point is simply that wisdom is an inward thing that requires a heart inclined to it.

i. Some perils and blessings of life (xviii. 1-24)

Among the perils are the separatist (1; called by A. D. Power 'The Selfish Individualist'), the self-parading fool (2), miscarriage of justice (5), the quarrelsome and hurtful talk of fool and gossip (6-8) and the sluggard (9).

The righteous in their distress can call upon *the name of the Lord*, which represents His power and majesty, and be safe there (10). The rich man's wealth may indeed be his fortification (11; cf. x. 15), but a very insecure one it is compared with the *strong tower* of the righteous. It is a high wall only in his imagination (so RV renders *conceit*). With verse 12 cf. xvi. 18 and xv. 33.

Verses 13-24 number some manifestations of wisdom and folly, and some of the blessings of life, such as a buoyant spirit (14), a good wife (22) and a true friend (24). There are other observations: however manly the spirit, once broken, the burden is intolerable (14); we have another reference to the ominous power of the bribe (16); a subtle and gently humorous reminder to hear both sides of a question (17; the immediate reference is clearly to a legal action); a comment, as it seems, on the use of the lot to decide a dispute (18); a note on the lethal power of the tongue (21); a note of compassion, met often in the law and the prophets, for the downtrodden poor (23). The text of verse 19 is uncertain. LXX has 'a brother helped by a brother is like a strong high city'.

j. Studies in character (xix. 1-29)

This section contains a series of memorable thumbnail sketches. For the upright pauper (the Hebrew word is used of extreme want) and the worthless rich (1) cf. xxviii. 6. In verse 2 read with RV mg. 'desire without knowledge is not good, and he that hasteth with his feet misseth his way'. We see how folly can make a man fume against God (3), how riches and graft gather popularity (4, 6), and glimpse the isolation brought by poverty (4, 7). Verse 7 is the only three-lined proverb in the first book of Solomon. The LXX has two couplets instead, but is very confused.

The somewhat loose connection of ideas in verse 10 is avoided if, following D. Winton Thomas's identification of a second root with the same characters as that translated *delight* (*Journal of Theological Studies*, Vol. 38, 1937, p. 400), we translate: 'Administration is inappropriate for a fool; Much less appropriate for a servant is rulership over princes.'

Another proverb on self-control (11) is followed by another on royal wrath and favour (12) and a summary of the worst trials of a husband and father (13). This is immediately balanced (14) by the assertion that, while a man may inherit his home wealth from his ancestors, a good wife is the direct gift of God. Giving to the helpless is described as 'lending to Jehovah' (17; cf. Mt. xxv. 34ff.). It is not sufficient to avoid oppression: the wise man extends real help. The Hebrew of verse 18 is involved: the second half runs 'and unto the killing of him lift not up thy soul'; AV does not grapple with this and RV 'set not thy heart on his destruction', evidently meaning 'do not chasten him till he dies', is incongruous. The probable intention of the clause is to warn against destroying him by over-indulgence, i.e. by not correcting him. Verse 19 is also very compressed and obscure. Taking the two parts of verse 22 together, we gather that the measure of a man's kindness is what he desires to do: a poor man who desires to give help, but cannot, is infinitely preferable to the man who, though better off, makes only unsubstantiated professions of desire to help. In verse 24 read with RV 'the dish' for *his bosom*. The man concerned is so lazy that having dipped his hand, Oriental fashion, in the dish, he cannot be bothered to take it to his mouth. An innocent hyperbole, no doubt! On verse 25 Toy remarks: 'when bad men are punished, the morally ignorant are warned.' The Hebrew in verse 27 has 'Cease, my son, to hear instruction to err . . .'. RV gives the best explanation: 'Cease . . . to hear instruction only to err . . .', i.e. Do not listen simply in order to forget it again.

k. Means and ends (xx. 1-30)

Wine and *strong drink* (1) are personified in the drunkard, who becomes a blasphemer (lit. 'scorner', see i. 22n.) and brawler. Verse 4 reintroduces the sluggard who finds it too cold to plough and then looks in vain for the crop next summer (see RV mg.). Verse 6 declares that many boast of their kindness, but that it is desperately hard to find a man who will under all circumstances be absolutely trustworthy. *Faithful* here has much of the connotation that it has in the New Testament (cf. 1 Cor. vii. 25). After this verse 9 presents a further challenge and shows the radical view of sin which is taken in the book. *The hearing ear, and the seeing eye* (12) introduces a compressed proverb. 'Not only the organs of hearing and sight, but their functions are the work of God (cf. xvi. 4). The implication is that what the ear listens to, and what the eye rests upon, should be right and pleasing to God' (Oesterley). Verse 13 is another warning against idleness, which produces penury. Verse 14 is a piece of observation of commercial practice. The buyer complains that the article is trash, and when he has bought it boasts to others of what a good bargain he has got. For the practice of suretyship (16) see vi. 1f. The command here is addressed to the creditor. *Take his garment* refers to the security that has been offered by the surety (cf. Ex. xxii. 26f.). *Take a pledge of him* (16); i.e. hold him responsible for strangers (*strange woman* is a less likely reading). Cf. xxvii. 13.

Bread of deceit (17) represents sustenance gained by dishonest means. With verse 18 cf. Lk. xiv. 31. Verse 25 is difficult, but it is best to read with RV 'It is a snare to a man rashly to say, It is holy . . .' The warning will then be against making rash vows: dedicating something to God by the formula 'It is holy' and then 'making inquiry', i.e. regretting the action. Cf. 'Corban'; Mk. vii. 11n.

The spirit of man (27) is what marks him off from the beasts. An animal can have a *nephesh* (soul), but it was into man's nostrils that God breathed the *ruaḥ* (spirit or breath) of life. That very fact means that even in fallen man God has His *candle* whereby He searches the inner man (cf. 1 Cor. ii. 11), bearing witness to Himself by the lamp of conscience, illuminating the dark corners of the heart. In verse 28 *mercy* and *truth* (see iii. 3n.) are once more marks of the ideal king, and the covenant mercy of God secures his throne—*'Teneo et teneor'*. 2 Sa. vii. 12f. throws much light on what such a statement would have meant to Solomon. In verse 30 the RV reading makes good sense; but the text is uncertain.

l. Response in life to the law of God (xxi. 1–31)

The king's heart is directed by God as firmly as the irrigator cuts and controls the channels (1). Cf. verse 2 with xvi. 2. Verse 3 expresses a thought which is often encountered in the prophets. For *plowing* (4) read with RV 'lamp', the symbol of an individual's prosperity (cf. xiii. 9). But the verse is obscure. The text of verse 6 is likewise uncertain, but the general sense is clear enough. Riches may be obtained by deceit, but they will be transient and their possession will lead to destruction. In verse 7 the language suggests that the violence of wicked men will sweep them up, as into a net. In verse 8 read 'Very crooked is the way of a man laden with guilt'. A. D. Power's paraphrase of verse 9 is effective: 'It is better to dwell in an attic on the roof, than in a double bedroom with a nagging wife.' Verse 12 is another proverb with syntactical difficulties. The point seems to be, however, that the righteous take warning from the overthrow of the house of the wicked. Verse 16 speaks of the fate of the backslider: *he shall remain* (better, 'he shall rest') in the assembly of the Shades. Verse 18 reminds us of Is. xliii. 3, 4, where Egypt is stated to be the ransom for Israel. 'There is a kind of substitution; a ransom is paid to enable the righteous to escape and the ransom is the person of the wicked' (Horton, *op. cit.*, p. 152). Verse 21 is an Old Testament adumbration of our Lord's 'Seek ye first . . .' (Mt. vi. 33). *Righteousness* and 'covenant-love' (*mercy*) are things particularly required in God's covenant-people (Mi. vi. 6–8) and those that seek them, says the wise man, will have 'all these things', including *life* and *honour*, added unto them.

As all wisdom, understanding and counsel stem from God, there is no possibility of using them effectively against His purposes (30). And, whatever preparations are made for battle, deliverance comes from Jehovah (31). For *safety* read with RV 'victory' or RV mg. 'deliverance'. 'Two companion proverbs . . . Nothing avails against, nothing without, God' (E. H. Plumptre, *Proverbs*, Speaker's Commentary).

m. Cause and effect in the spiritual realm (xxii. 1–16)

In verse 1 read 'favour is better than silver . . .' The proverb seeks to express the value of a good reputation. Verse 2 is a reminder that all men have a common origin and a common responsibility to God, whatever barriers may exist between them on earth. Verse 4 sums up several of the main lessons of the book in a few words. The connection between *humility*, the sense of dependence expressed in piety, and the *fear of the Lord* is very close. Cf. xxi. 21.

Just as the rich lord it over the poor, so the borrower, with an equally enforced dependence, is under constant obligation to the person from whom he has borrowed (7). The word *servant* need not be taken literally. With the thought in verse 8 cf. Gal. vi. 7. *The rod of his anger shall fail* suggests that the time is coming when this menace of a man will lose his capacity for exercising his anger (cf. Is. x. 5 for the meaning).

The sluggard presents two more of his ever-interesting excuses for doing no work (13). He will not go into the country for fear of meeting a lion; and he will not go out in the town in case he is murdered in the street. On *strange women* (14) see notes on v. 1ff. Verse 16 is a dark saying indeed. Taking the text as translated in the AV, it can mean 'The man who gains his wealth by exploiting the poor, and the man who gains his by fawning upon the rich, will alike be reduced to poverty'. This gives coherent sense, but calls for some imagination.

IV. THE BOOK OF THE WISE.
xxii. 17—xxiv. 22

See the *Introduction*, pp. 515 and 516. There is more connection between the sayings in this group than in the previous collection. There are considerable parallels to the Egyptian teaching of Amen-em-ope, especially in the section xxii. 17—xxiii. 11, and a literary dependence on the Egyptian is frequently too easily assumed by some commentators. Amen-em-ope is a much more ordered and systematic document than 'the sayings of the wise', and it is difficult to see how a compiler would spoil, by such unsystematic treatment, the connection of the 'thirty chapters' of the Egyptian sage.

a. What to avoid (xxii. 17—xxiii. 11)

A short exordium (17–21) calls for the attention of the pupil to the words of the wise that his teacher has drawn up for his instruction (17), calls him to make them part of himself (18) and declares their aim is to establish in him trust in Jehovah (19). *Have not I written to thee excellent things?* (20) is a real crux. The Hebrew word is *shilshom*, which means 'three days ago'. The LXX and Vulgate render it 'in threefold form', so that Origen was able to support his threefold approach to exegesis by this verse. The AV translation *excellent things* is based on the assumption that the word was used to denote the chief of three persons in a chariot and thus came to mean 'pre-eminent, excellent'. Amen-em-ope, however, has the words: 'Consider these thirty chapters; they delight, they instruct; they are chief among all books . . .' The Hebrew word for thirty is *sheloshim*, and so it is suggested that this originally stood in the text, and that the writer, modelling himself on Amen-em-ope, had written 'thirty things', i.e. proverbs. As it is, despite Gressmann's work, not all have been able to agree that there are indeed thirty proverbs in the 'Book of the Wise' and certainly not more than a third of them have parallels with Amen-em-ope. Some have parallels with other works, such as the Babylonian *Proverbs of Aḥikar*. For all the attraction of the reading 'thirty things' and the admitted difficulty of *shilshom* a good deal of reserve is needed. The rendering favoured by the earlier commentators, 'formerly' (see RV mg.), cannot be discarded, as it is possible in sense and grammar. The teacher would then be referring to some earlier work or course of lessons. In strict grammar another particle, *temol*, would be necessary; perhaps this has dropped out.

xxii. 22—xxiii. 11 mention things which the wise man must avoid. First, exploitation of the poor (22, 23): *oppress the afflicted in the gate* (22) means to use legal action against them: it stresses that Jehovah is their advocate and avenger. Secondly, the 'infectiousness of bad temper' (24, 25); thirdly, suretyship (26, 27; these verses have no Egyptian parallels); fourthly, violation of boundaries (28; cf. Dt. xix. 14). Verse 29 speaks of the promotion of the conscientious. Amen-em-ope, who was a civil servant, seems to have taken particular care to preserve this parallel.

The sage's instructions proceed with a passage on table manners (xxiii. 1–3); an injunction to avoid the restless and unsatisfying quest for riches (4, 5), then a delightful passage on the miser at home (6–8). The phrase *an evil eye* occurs only here and at xxii. 9 in the Old Testament. It is used of people with a grudging spirit. Conversation with a fool is not recommended (9), and another solemn warning is added not to encroach on the rights of the helpless (10, 11). On their side is a strong *redeemer* (Heb. *go'el*), God Himself. The *go'el* in the Old Testament is the kinsman who holds or acquires the right and responsibility to avenge blood (Nu. xxxv. 19) and redeem property (Ru. iv. 4) and generally to protect the interests of his dead kinsman's family.

b. What to look for (xxiii. 12–25)

After an appeal to heed instruction (12), corporal punishment is enjoined (13, 14). An admonition on wisdom is then added (15–21). In this *the fear of the Lord* is an important part (17). With verses 15, 16 cf. 3 Jn. 4. The pupil is to remember that *there is an end* (18), i.e. that there will be an eventual reward; is not to *envy* sinners (17) or to join revellers in their carousings (20, 21). He is to honour his parents (22), and procure the truth and wisdom at any price (23).

c. Snares pointed out (xxiii. 26—xxiv. 2)

The address *My son, give me thine heart* (i.e. 'attend to me carefully') introduces warnings against sensuality (27, 28), drunkenness (29–35), and bad company (xxiv. 1, 2).

d. Studies in wisdom and folly (xxiv. 3–22)

The acquisition of wisdom and knowledge is compared to the building and furnishing of a house (3, 4). The relation between knowledge and strength is sketched (5–7; cf. xi. 14, xx. 18). The fool dare not speak in the *gate*, the centre for business and legal transactions (7). In verse 9 read 'fools' for *foolishness*. Verse 11 is a command to help those in danger of death, whether by unjust judgment, or, more likely, by the oppression of the poor at the hands of wealthy men (so Oesterley); or, perhaps, at the hands of a lawless society such as that pictured in i. 10ff. If this duty is neglected, God will know (12).

A just man falleth seven times (16); i.e. into calamity, not into sin. In contrast to the righteous, who may be cast down time and time again and each time recover, the wicked 'are overthrown by calamity' (so RV). A single disaster is sufficient to crush them. Even so, one must never gloat at the fall of an enemy (17, 18). *Turn away his wrath from him* (18) 'is not to be understood as affirming that God will cease punishing a wicked man because another man is pleased at the punishment; the full form of the expression is "turn from him to thee", and the stress is to be laid on the "to thee" ' (Toy). This full form of expression is denied by some commentators.

Verses 21, 22 speak of 'the powers that be'. The words *them that are given to change* (21) are very uncertain. The word is intransitive, and the meaning 'revolutionaries' cannot be got out of the Hebrew. The LXX has 'do not disobey either of them'. It is perhaps best to read with Toy, 'Fear thou God and the king; Anger not either of them; For the ruin they inflict is sudden, And the destruction they send unforeseen.' Cf. 1 Pet. ii. 17.

V. SAYINGS OF THE WISE: ANOTHER COLLECTION. xxiv. 23–34

For the title read with RV 'These also are sayings of the wise'. Verses 23–26 deal with legal procedure. Verse 26 sounds a strange scene for a court of law: but it is possible that the word translated *kiss* may bear the sense of 'equip' that it can in post-biblical Hebrew. The rendering would then be something like: 'He that equippeth his lips (i.e. with wisdom) shall give a right answer.' Verse 27 is often taken to mean that an adequate means of living should be secured before marriage. This seems to restrict the application unnecessarily, especially as among the Hebrews early marriage was customary as a matter of course. What is involved in 'preparing thy work without' is surely, as Perowne says, counting the cost and preparing the materials (cf. 1 Ki. vi. 7; Lk. xiv. 28). Cf. verse 29 with verse 17. Verses 30–34 show us the sluggard asleep and his vineyard a wilderness, and the words of vi. 6–11 are repeated with a new and ominous note.

VI. THE SECOND BOOK OF SOLOMON. xxv. 1—xxix. 27

For the title and verse 1 see the *Introduction*, p. 515.

a. Instructive comparisons (xxv. 2–28)

Verses 2–7 deal with matters connected with the court. The ways of God are inscrutable, and this reflects His glory. The king, on the other hand, has a duty to 'get to the bottom of a thing', and that is his glory (2). But the king, too, has something unsearchable about his purposes (3), for he is God's vicegerent. With verses 6, 7 cf. Lk. xiv. 8–10. *Whom thine eyes have seen* belongs to verse 8 (read, 'what thine eyes have seen').

Litigation is the subject of verses 8–10. *Strive* (8) means 'plead in the lawcourt'. The warning is against bringing contentious and ill-advised actions which will only turn to the shame of the person bringing them.

Verses 11–14 provide four similes. For *pictures* (11) read 'baskets'. What the fruits in question were we cannot say. Verse 14 refers to the man who is always boasting about what he gives but in fact gives nothing. The warning in verse 17 is plainly directed against overstaying one's welcome. To rely on an unreliable man when trouble comes is like walking on a sprained ankle (19). The most effective vengeance is to do good to one's enemy (21, 22; cf. Mt. v. 44; Rom. xii. 20). With verse 24 cf. xxi. 9.

b. Types of fool and scoundrel (xxvi. 1–28)

Verses 1–12, with one possible exception, form a Book of Fools. The word in each case is *kesil* (see i. 22n.). The exception is verse 2. Read, with RV, 'as the sparrow in her wandering, as the swallow in her flying, so the curse that is causeless lighteth not'; i.e. the curse that is unjustified never does any harm, a refutation of a superstition held, no doubt, by the *fools* in question here, that they were able to harm the righteous by their curse. The apparent contradiction in verses 4 and 5 caused trouble to the Rabbis (*Tractate Shabbath*, 30b). The official answer

given then was 'one refers to the things of the law, and the other to worldly affairs'. It is more likely, however, that the difference is simply between profitless arguing with a fool at his own level (4) and occasionally, lest he should think that he cannot be answered, meeting his prating with wisdom (5).

To use a fool as a messenger is to injure oneself by his unreliability (6; *damage* is lit. 'wrath'). A proverb (i.e. a *parable*) is hopelessly out of place when spoken by a fool (7, 9; Moffatt conveys the meaning of verse 9: 'like thorny branches brandished by a drunkard'). To honour a fool is as foolish as tying a stone in a sling so that it cannot come out (8). In verse 10, the Hebrew text is obscure. The AV rendering is quite unwarranted. RV renders 'As an archer that woundeth all, so is he that hireth the fool and he that hireth them that pass by'; i.e. the man who hires good and bad workmen indifferently is like an archer shooting off his arrows indiscriminately. But this, too, is very uncertain. With verse 11 cf. 2 Pet. ii. 22. But after all that is said of the fool, it is stressed that he has more hope of redemption than the man blinded with self-conceit (12; cf. Rom. i. 22).

Verses 13–16 give a short 'Book of Sluggards'. In verse 15 for *grieveth* read 'wearieth'. See notes on xxii. 13, xix. 24.

Verses 17–28 give us a 'Book of Scoundrels'. There is the busybody who interferes in other people's quarrels (17), the practical joker (18, 19), the gossip (20–22), the hypocrite (23–28). In verse 22 and in the parallel at xviii. 8 read with RV 'dainty morsels' for *wounds*. Follow RV also in verse 23. For *those that are afflicted by it* (28) read simply 'the afflicted'.

c. Remarks on human relations (xxvii. 1–27)

In this miscellaneous collection of detached proverbs, the main subjects dealt with are love, friendship and human relations. With verses 1 and 2 cf. Jas. iv. 13–16. For *heavier* (3) read 'more burdensome'. *Secret love* (5) is that which does not show itself in administering necessary reproof. In verse 10 the second and third parts should be taken together. The sense then runs: 'Do not desert a family friend: when you need help there is no need to call to your aid a relation, from whom you may be separated by a great distance; the family friend close at hand will be a surer help.' The high importance attached in Old Testament times to the duties and claims of blood relationship might sometimes become exaggerated, which would give rise to a warning like this.

A good pupil makes a glad master (11). With verse 12 cf. xxii. 3 and with verse 13 cf. xx. 16. Verse 14 probably refers to loud-mouthed and insincere adulation. *Rising early in the morning* refers not to the hour at which this is given but to the zeal which accompanies it. For the expression cf. Je. vii. 25. Note the RV rendering of verse 16. If correct, it would mean that this impossible woman is as intractable as the wind and as slippery as oil. Verse 17 declares that character and intellect are developed by human relationships. With verse 18 cf. Mt. xxv. 21. Verse 19 means that as water gives a true reflection of a face, so the hearts of men essentially correspond with one another. Verse 20 declares that men's ambitions are as insatiable as Death (lit. Sheol and Abaddon; see xv. 11). Verse 21 gives a test for character, a man's reaction to praise, unless, as RV mg. suggests, the test is what he praises.

Verses 23–27 are a short treatise on the pastoral life, the purpose no doubt being to encourage this industry, the real backbone of Israel's prosperity, and to discourage the corrupting influences of other ways of making money which were superficially more attractive.

d. Pure religion (xxviii. 1–28)

Verse 1 speaks of the effect of a good and a bad conscience. The saying in verse 2 would have had a great deal of appositeness when Hezekiah's men copied it out, for the northern kingdom of Israel had tottered to its ruin after constant changes of king and dynasty. Verse 3 would also have been in point in Hezekiah's time. The reference is, no doubt, to the hard-hit landlord or official endeavouring to secure his income by oppressing those even poorer than himself. The result is general starvation. There is no need to emend *poor man* to 'rich man' as is often suggested. Obedience is stressed as a condition of true knowledge (4, 5; cf. Jn. vii. 17). With verse 6 cf. xix. 1. The extortioner and usurer (a forbidden practice in Israel; cf. Lv. xxv. 36f.) will lose his gains to a more just man (8). With verse 9 cf. xv. 8. In verse 11 it is best to follow Winton Thomas and translate the word rendered *searcheth him out* as 'despiseth him'; i.e. the poor man despises this false pretension of the rich man to wisdom. For *a man is hidden* (12) read with RV 'men hide themselves'. *Covereth* (13) means, of course, not 'atones for' but 'hides up'. Cf. 1 Jn. i. 8–9. *Feareth* (14) is not the word used in the phrase *the fear of the Lord*; but it is used of fear of God (e.g. Hos. iii. 5), so the reference here may well be to fear of Him rather than of sin.

Verses 15, 16 deal with the wicked ruler. The subject of verse 17 is manslaughter; it is the only proverb in the book which is in prose. With verse 19 cf. xii. 11. For *innocent* (20) read 'unpunished' (see vi. 29n.). The reference in verse 21 is to partiality in the law courts: the meaning is that a man will betray justice for the smallest bribe (*a piece of bread*). For *an evil eye* (22) see xxiii. 6n. In verse 24 what is condemned is doubtless attempts by children to obtain their parents' property. Though foreign to the whole spirit of the Mosaic law, there was no specific legislation against it, so that the son might say, *It is no transgression* (cf. Mk. vii. 10–13). Verse 25 deals with the contrast between the grasping man (Heb. 'wide of soul'; RV 'of a greedy spirit' is better than AV *of a proud heart*) and the man

who trusts God for his sustenance; verse 26 takes the thought further. With verse 28 cf. verse 12; no doubt wicked rulers are especially in mind.

e. God and Society (xxix. 1–27)

With verse 3 cf. Lk. xv. 13, 30. *Judgment* (4) refers to the exercise of perfect justice on the part of the ruler. For *he that receiveth gifts* (4) it is better to translate with Winton Thomas 'a covetous man'. *Snare* (6) implies that the evil man by his sin has laid a trap for himself, in contrast to the rejoicing in view for the righteous.

Scorners set a city on fire (8; cf. RV); the presence of wise men, however, turns wrath from it. The scene in verse 9, as the terminology shows, is a lawsuit or debate: the fool tries to cover up his shallow case by blustering. In verse 10 follow RV for the second half: 'And as for the upright, they (i.e. the bloodthirsty) seek his life.'

A new aspect of a ruler's effect on his people is given (12), and one of his functions as king is pointed out (14). With verse 13 cf. xxii. 2, and for the meaning see Ps. xiii. 3; Mt. v. 45. Verse 15 may have had a poignancy for Solomon, for Absalom had been such a child (1 Ki. i. 6).

Perish (18); better, 'break loose'; cf. RV, 'cast off restraint'. The same word, as Perowne points out, is used in Ex. xxxii. 25, and the affair of the golden calf is an historical illustration of the meaning of this verse. *Vision* (18; Heb. *hazon*) is the normal word for the prophetic revelation (cf. Is. i. 1; Je. xiv. 14); *law*, which is seen to be parallel with it, is the revealed law of God. The law, the prophets and the wisdom literature meet in this verse. Where the revealed will of God, as expressed in His Word, is not kept constantly in view, His people break loose from their allegiance. Again this is a word which Hezekiah may well have taken to heart. With verse 22 cf. xv. 18. In verse 23 read with RV 'He that is of a lowly spirit shall obtain honour' (cf. Mt. v. 3; Lk. xiv. 11). *Cursing* (24) refers to the judge's adjuration in a case that any who have knowledge of the crime should give evidence. If a man withholds knowledge of a crime, his offence is as bad as that of the criminal itself.

VII. THE WORDS OF AGUR. xxx. 1–33

We do not know who Agur the son of Jakeh was, or where he flourished. Perhaps he was, like Job and Balaam, a non-Israelite who had knowledge of the true God. For *prophecy* (1) RV mg. reads 'of Massa', thus making Jakeh an Ishmaelite. But there is no need to adopt this reading; the RV 'oracle' on the whole is preferable. Cheyne points out that the not dissimilar speech of Eliphaz in Jb. iv. 12–21 is also oracular (*Job and Solomon*, p. 117).

a. The knowledge of God (xxx. 1–4)

RV mg. re-points the vowels to read after *the man spake*: 'I have wearied myself, O God, and am consumed.' This alteration is of little help: it is better to keep AV and assume that *Ithiel* and *Ucal* were Agur's disciples. Verses 2–4 contain Agur's longing after the knowledge of God. He confesses his utter ignorance of Him (2, 3), an ignorance which he shares with the rest of mankind (4). He has reflected on the immensity of natural forces, and stood amazed before Him who is behind them. There may be a tinge of sarcasm in his opening words. He was confronted by those who professed to know all about God and His dealings.

In verse 3 *the holy* stands for 'the Holy One'. Enoch and Elijah ascended into heaven: none had been known to return from thence (4). Our Lord answers this question in Jn. iii. 13. As to *his son's name* (4), the sequence shows that the subject is not God, but the hypothetical person who has scaled the heights to look upon Him, and has precisely measured His creation

b. The Word of God (xxx. 5, 6)

God's Word is pure, and must not be mixed with human speculation, which may be proved to be utterly wrong. Cf. Ps. xviii. 30. The name of God in verse 5 is *'Eloah*, occurring in Proverbs only here.

c. A prayer (xxx. 7–9)

The wise man prays to be preserved from the temptations of wealth and of poverty alike. For *take . . . in vain* (9) the Hebrew has 'handle', i.e. profane by sinful action.

d. Another man's servant (xxx. 10)

For the fullest application of this detached aphorism cf. Rom. xiv. 4.

e. Four classes of person (xxx. 11–14)

Generation in each case stands for 'class' or 'type' of person.

f. Four insatiable things (xxx. 15, 16)

The difficult thing about this section is the reference to the *horseleach* (15) which prefaces it. According to A. E. Shipley (Preface to Harding and Moore, *Fauna of British India*—reference from Miss G. Gnanadickam) leeches were never used medicinally by the Hebrews. The same authority interprets verse 15 of the children of the local veterinary surgeon! The Palestinian haemopis does not attack man. Probably the sentence here simply denotes yet another 'insatiable thing'.

g. The turbulent son (xxx. 17)

This is another detached aphorism. The *eye* is chosen as the organ whereby unfilial conduct is demonstrated. The implication is that the corpse will lie unburied for the birds to feed upon. Cf. Dt. xxi. 18–21.

h. Four wonderful things (xxx. 18–20)

The wonder is often supposed to lie in their leaving no trace behind them. If this is so, the examples—the serpent, particularly—seem curiously chosen. The wonder seems rather to lie in the movement. Similarly it seems that *the way of a man with a maid* (19) refers not, as is often supposed, to the act of procreation, but to the idyllic growth of love. *The way of an adulterous woman* (20) is also 'wonderful', though but a parody of the last. She covers up her sin and calmly says she has done nothing wrong.

i. Four intolerable things (xxx. 21–23)

Two examples of incongruity are taken from each sex. *Filled with meat* (22) stands for 'rich and prosperous'.

j. Four little things (xxx. 24–28)

All four are also wise. The *ant* does what the sluggard will not do (cf. vi. 6). The *conies* (26) are obviously not rabbits, as the mention of their habitat shows: 'rock badgers' is the favoured translation. The *locusts* go in ordered ranks, without jostling each other (cf. Joel ii. 7, 8). For *the spider taketh hold with her hands, and . . .* (28) read with RV mg. 'The lizard thou canst seize with thy hands, yet . . .'

k. Four comely things (xxx. 29–31)

In each case it is the stateliness which is in view. In verse 31 the Hebrew is difficult; it is best to follow RV mg. in reading 'the king, when his army is with him'.

l. A closing admonition (xxx. 32, 33)

Strife is to be avoided by the acknowledgment of wrong done. *Lay thine hand upon thy mouth* (32) is to denote a silent admission of blame.

VIII. THE SAYINGS OF LEMUEL. xxxi. 1–9

See the *Introduction*, p. 516 and on section VII. King Lemuel's 'oracle' (so RV rightly renders *prophecy*) is in the form of a short treatise on the duties of kingship, learned from his mother. Is it possible that Lemuel was an Ishmaelite whose mother came from Israel?

The 'oracle' warns against lust (3) and intemperance (4–7), and urges righteous rule and justice to be given to the needy (5, 8, 9).

Son of my vows (2); i.e. a son granted in response to my vows (cf. 1 Sa. i. 11). Verse 8 implies that the king is to befriend those who are unable to help themselves whether by miscarriage of justice or by straitened circumstances.

IX. THE PERFECT WIFE. xxxi. 10–31

This forms an appendix to the book. It is a beautiful acrostic poem, the first verse beginning with the first letter of the Hebrew alphabet and each of the remaining twenty-one letters coming in turn. The poem speaks for itself. Side by side with all that Proverbs says about 'the strange woman', 'the teaching of a mother' and the honour and dignity of womanhood are constantly exalted. Our book fittingly closes, therefore, with the ringing praise accorded to the perfect wife by her husband and children (29–31).

W. A. REES JONES.
ANDREW F. WALLS.

ECCLESIASTES

INTRODUCTION

I. STYLE

Ecclesiastes is in many respects an enigmatic book. Disjointed in construction, obscure in vocabulary, and often cryptic in style, it baffles the understanding of the reader. It contains a number of words which are not found in the rest of the Old Testament and whose meaning it is hard to determine with precision. It makes allusion to incidents, customs and sayings which would be easily understood by its original readers but to which we have no clue. It contains apparent inconsistencies which make it difficult to ascertain what the author's own view is. These contrasts have led some to suppose that an original book has been worked over and 'bowdlerized' by several hands. The way in which the writer has put together his material suggests that it was not meant to have any connected sequence of thought running through it. The book may be a collection of fragments or jottings, like Pascal's *Pensées*, with which it has often been compared.

In spite of all its difficulties and obscurities, however, the book exercises a powerful fascination. It is at once apparent to the discerning reader that here is a penetrating observation and criticism of the human scene. The profundity of such of the writer's observations as we can immediately comprehend lures us on to plumb his deeper insights, as once Socrates, delighted with the wisdom of Heraclitus speaking clearly, was led to seek a deeper wisdom in his obscurities.

II. INTERPRETATION

The crucial problem presented by the book is that of its place within the canon of Scripture. There were some among the Jews who disputed its right to be included among the sacred books from the beginning, and its presence among them has been a source of bewilderment to many Christians since. Those who think that the prevailing tone of the book is one of disillusionment and despair, tempered only by a modified Epicureanism, must indeed find it hard to see how it can be reckoned among those which are able to make us wise unto salvation through faith which is in Christ Jesus.

Some recent studies of the book, however, have shown this popular understanding of it to be superficial, and have led to a truer appreciation of the peculiar standpoint of the writer. This is probably indicated by his chosen name, *Qoheleth* 'the Preacher' (Ecclesiastes is the Greek equivalent of this). The word is connected with *qahal*, the public assembly, and it suggests the kind of wisdom delivered by the speaker to those in the outer court, as distinguished from the 'hidden wisdom' which is known only to those who have been admitted to the mystery of God (1 Cor. ii. 7). *Qoheleth* writes from concealed premises, and his book is in reality a major work of apologetic or 'eristic' theology. Its apparent worldliness is dictated by its aim: *Qoheleth* is addressing the general public whose view is bounded by the horizons of this world; he meets them on their own ground, and proceeds to convict them of its inherent vanity. This is further borne out by his characteristic expression 'under the sun', by which he describes what the New Testament calls 'the world' (*kosmos*). His book is in fact a critique of secularism and of secularized religion. For secularism need not be irreligious, and the religion of the Jews tended to be unduly secular and to forget the transcendence of God (v. 2). As such, it has an abiding message, and not least for our own time when secularism dominates the minds of men as perhaps never before in history, and religion has gone far to conform and seeks to commend itself as a means to the amelioration of life 'under the sun'. The book of Ecclesiastes discharges an indispensable function within the canon of Scripture by providing the corrective against all attempts to reduce religion to a mere tool of secularism.

The fatal weakness of secularist utopianism is, as has been said, that it takes insufficient account of the twin facts of evil and death. The eyes of Ecclesiastes are fully open to the vanity and the corruption to which the creation is subject (Rom. viii. 20ff.), and the whole book has been aptly described as an exposition of the curse of the fall (Gn. iii. 17–19). The writer sees how these two facts bracket the whole of life under the sun with a negative sign and defy all attempts to force it to yield either sense or satisfaction by itself.

But though the tone of the book is preponderantly negative, it is a mistake to brand Ecclesiastes as a sceptic or an apostle of despair. The melancholy refrain, 'Vanity of vanities, all is vanity', is not his verdict upon life in general, but only upon the misguided human endeavour to treat the created world as an end in itself. He knows all the time that it has a positive significance; how indeed could he take it upon himself to utter such destructive criticism if he did not know? This secret he keeps in the background, except for a hint here and there, because his immediate concern is to dispel all

538

false and illusory hopes which possess the minds of men and of which they must be purged before they can be brought to the hope which is sure and stedfast and which entereth into that within the veil (Heb. vi. 19). 'In order that men may be able to find the true happiness, he destroys with merciless blows the false happiness which they continually seek in the world and which yields them only unhappiness' (G. Kuhn, *Erklärung des Buches Koheleth*, 1926). But he knows that the world can yield happiness and enjoyment, as witness his frequent exhortations to seek it (ii. 24, iii. 12, 22, v. 18, ix. 7, xi. 9), and that we can find in the world a life-work which is worth while (iii. 12f., ix. 10); otherwise the counsels he offers for life and conduct in this world would be meaningless.

The significance of the world is that it can become a medium for the revelation of God's goodness, wisdom and righteousness. It is only when man treats it as an end in itself, and makes it his chief end to gain the world, that it turns to vanity. But there is a way in which man can accept life under the sun, with its gifts and withdrawals, its apparent irrationalities and injustices, and that is 'from the hand of God' (ii. 24, v. 18-20). Plainly this is not scepticism or pessimism; it is faith. As it has been expressed by a modern writer, in whom something of the spirit of Ecclesiastes lives again, faith has always protested that 'all things would be absurd if their meaning were exhausted in their function and place in the phenomenal world, if by their essence they did not reach into a world beyond this'; and it has always 'trusted the inward vision, which discerned behind nature a something more divine than nature, *in recessu divinius aliquid*' (W. Macneile Dixon, *The Human Situation*, pp. 40f.). Ecclesiastes is a sceptic only in so far as he rejects the pretension of human wisdom to elucidate the work of God (iii. 11, viii. 17). He

knows that we walk by faith, not by sight; and he exhibits the necessary humility or reserve of faith in face of the transcendent wisdom of God, of whose eternal providence he is firmly assured (iii. 14).

The characteristic complexity of his thought with its apparent contradictions or its 'counterpoint' (W. Vischer, *Der Prediger Salomo*, 1926) shows clearly in his utterances on death. On the one hand he speaks of death as the final reduction of life under the sun to nothingness (iii. 19f., ix. 4-6, xi. 8). But to say that he regards death as final extinction is to fail to do justice to another strain in his thought. He repeatedly affirms the certainty of divine judgment (iii. 17, xi. 9, xii. 14), and he remains assured, in spite of all the injustices of life under the sun, that 'it shall be well with them that fear God' (viii. 12). His position resembles that of Ps. xlix. Like the psalmist he is opposed to any specious immortality erected upon premises derived from life under the sun. The psalmist's verdict, 'Man being in honour abideth not: he is like the beasts that perish' (Ps. xlix. 12), is echoed in Ec. iii. 18: 'I said in mine heart concerning the estate of the sons of men, that God might manifest them, and that they might see that they themselves are beasts.' But over against this the psalmist sets 'the great "But God"' (Ps. xlix. 15; cf. Eph. ii. 4), and in the light of it he modifies his first conclusion: 'Man that is in honour, and understandeth not, is like the beasts that perish' (Ps. xlix. 20). The significant phrase in Ecclesiastes, 'by themselves they are beasts', surely indicates that he knew of this understanding which alone gives man pre-eminence above a beast (iii. 19). At all events, his resolute denial of all human possibilities at least clears the way for the new possibilities of God, and entitles us to speak of Ecclesiastes as standing before the threshold of the resurrection.

OUTLINE OF CONTENTS

As has been pointed out above, the book defies any logical analysis, and therefore no Outline of Contents is presented. The paragraphs, into which the book divides itself, have been indicated by the insertion of headings, which have been lettered consecutively throughout.

COMMENTARY

a. Introduction (i. 1-11)

i. **The title (i. 1).** *The Preacher.* For the probable meaning of this term see the *Introduction.* The author does not really claim to be Solomon but places his words in Solomon's mouth. We may compare the practice of ascribing written works to famous historical personages which was a familiar literary device in antiquity. It was intended to indicate the type, or genus, of literature to which a work belonged. It was not intended to deceive anyone, and none

of its original readers would in fact have been deceived.

ii. **The text of the discourse (i. 2).** *All is vanity.* 'All' for those he addressed, but not for himself; for how could Ecclesiastes pronounce all to be vanity, unless he knew of some validity, some sure ground to which his spirit clung? His object is not to counsel despair, but to refute secularism on its own ground.

iii. **Existence a vicious circle (i. 3-11).** Ecclesiastes goes direct to the heart of the matter without preliminary skirmishing. The world assesses life in terms of profit and loss. But what profit can a man win that he must not finally lose? 'Thou fool, this night thy soul shall be required of thee: then whose shall those things be, which thou hast provided?' (Lk. xii. 20). The pursuit of wealth stands confuted by man's mortality, as the world itself knows well; for its own poets and philosophers have told it often enough. But men endeavour to screen themselves from the icy wind of mortality by the thought of their posterity and the continuing race. 'Their inward thought is, that their houses shall continue for ever, and their dwelling places to all generations; they call their lands after their own names' (Ps. xlix. 11). They seek a pseudo-immortality in the fancied perpetuity of their works, or in 'minds made better by their presence', or in 'leaving footprints on the sands of time', or in the idea of 'progress'. But there is nothing to support this in the course of nature, which is circular, as Ecclesiastes points out (5–7), or in the course of history, which endlessly repeats itself (9, 10). Progress is ever accompanied by regress. It is only the actors and the scenery that change; the pattern of history remains the same, 'little more than the register of the crimes, follies and misfortunes of mankind'.

b. **The failure of all attempts to give meaning to existence (i. 12—ii. 23)**

i. **The philosophical attempt (i. 12–18).** Man cannot rest content with a meaningless existence. There is within him an irresistible urge to find rhyme or reason in it; for he is a 'thinking reed' (Pascal). God has implanted in man this unquenchable longing for order and system. Yet it only adds to man's torment; for the jig-saw puzzle of life cannot be completed; some of the parts are missing (15). The attempt to frame a complete philosophic system can be achieved only by doing violence to reality, by 'making that which is crooked straight'. The last word of human wisdom, as some of the wisest have realized, is to confess that we know nothing, that the key to the final mystery eludes our grasp. Such is the wisdom of the Tao Te Ching:

> 'Thirty spokes together make one wheel;
> And they fit into "nothing" at the centre:
> Herein lies the usefulness of a carriage.
> The clay is moulded to make a pot;
> And the clay fits round "nothing":
> Herein lies the usefulness of the pot . . .
> Thus it is that, while it must be taken to be advantageous to have something there,
> It must also be taken as useful to have "nothing" there.'

The wisdom which ends in this 'hole at the centre' must needs be vexation of spirit, until it finds 'the wisdom that is from above' (Jas. iii. 17), 'the hidden wisdom, which God ordained before the world unto our glory' (1 Cor. ii. 7).

ii. **The sensual attempt (ii. 1, 2).** Why bother your head trying to puzzle out the meaning of existence? Have 'a good time', enjoy the pleasures life affords (1). Listen to Mephistopheles:

> 'Grau, teurer Freund, ist alle Theorie
> Und grün des Lebens goldner Baum.'

But no need to waste words on the madness of this experiment; for it quickly belies its promise.

> 'Pleasures are like poppies spread,
> You seize the flower, its bloom is shed.'

The pleasure-addict cannot escape the 'morning after' and the revulsion of satiety.

iii. **The cultural attempt (ii. 3–23).** The failure of the quest for wisdom and the quest for pleasure suggests a compromise, a middle way which avoids one-sided extremes and aims at a rich, varied and balanced life. This is culture. The cultured man is he who lays hold on all the riches of life, pleasure, wisdom and action, and seeks to blend them into one harmonious whole. He soon learns the 'paradox of hedonism' and finds his pleasure, not in sensuality, but in the full exercise of his faculties of mind and will (10). But he cannot finally escape the quiet hour of reflection and self-questioning which comes after the day's labour is done; and then 'the native hue of resolution is sicklied o'er with the pale cast of thought'. Has he attained the true prize of life? Is his reward commensurate with the labour expended? It is certain that wisdom is relatively superior to folly; for the wise man makes a better job of life than the fool. But this relative is cancelled out by the absolute of death, a fact which seriously challenges the worth of wisdom. There is a paradox about wisdom: wisdom means looking forward. While the fool, like the grasshopper, lives for the moment, the wise man, like the ant, dips into the future; he takes his bearings from tomorrow, and endeavours to plot his course accordingly (14). Yet this wisdom is most hazardous; for it is not in our power to foresee, still less to control, the future. 'Thou knowest not what a day may bring forth' (Pr. xxvii. 1). And the wisest plans may be confounded:

> 'The best laid schemes o' mice an' men
> Gang aft agley.'

What can the man do . . . ? (12). This would appear to have been a proverbial saying, and its meaning can only be guessed at. It has been suggested that the sentence has been misplaced.

c. **The wisdom of creation (ii. 24—iii. 15)**

Is there any way out of the dilemma in which we find ourselves placed as between wisdom and folly? Only by a new wisdom, a wisdom which has a different standpoint and orientation; not the wisdom of this world, nor of the princes of this world (nor, we may add, of the proletariat of this world), but the wisdom of God in a mystery (1 Cor. ii. 7). The first axiom of this wisdom is that the creation and its bounty are to be enjoyed. Any wisdom which denies this in the interest of its own man-centred system is presumption. True wisdom proceeds from the given fact of our creatureliness in the midst of creation. Here we are and 'the world is so full of a number of things' to be enjoyed. This is the decree and the gift of God (ii. 26).

But it is not an easy wisdom; for it must forswear system. A systematic world-view, a *Weltanschauung*, would be possible only if we occupied the centre from which we could survey the whole and see it in its true perspectives. But that is the position of the Creator, not of the creatures. From our creaturely position under the sun we see, as it were, the reverse of the tapestry with many confused lines and loose threads. To seek to unravel it from our standpoint is to become involved in an endless labyrinth. This also is vanity and vexation of spirit.

The beginning of our wisdom is the fear of the Lord (Ps. cxi. 10; Pr. i. 7), and one element of it is the recognition of the divine election in the difference of the times and seasons. Theoretically all times are equal, but this is true only when they are emptied of their contents. We have no experience of empty time. Every time comes to us charged with its own particular challenge and opportunity; and the wisdom of life is to discern the time (Lk. xii. 56), the *kairos* (Rom. xiii. 11), the decisive moment (Ec. viii. 5, 6), the moment on which 'the accent of eternity falls'. 'There is a tide in the affairs of men.'

This incalculable, unrationalizable feature of history and experience is a sore perplexity to man. For man is not merely a creature of time; there is within him that which transcends time: 'Man has Forever.' He seeks to stand back from the time-process and to discern the plan and pattern of the whole. But he is too deeply immersed in it to succeed; the end and the beginning elude him. The tension between Today and Forever in the life of man cannot be completely resolved. Yet man can find Forever in Today by gratefully accepting the gifts of God and doing His commandments.

Also he hath set the world in their heart (11). The Hebrew word, which is here rendered *the world*, uniformly bears the sense of 'for ever' and is so rendered elsewhere in this book, e.g. verse 14. It is best to translate it 'eternity' (with RV mg.), or simply to keep the literal rendering (with Browning) 'for ever'.

d. The righteousness of God (iii. 16—iv. 3)

The moralistic interpretation of life breaks down on the hard fact of human wickedness. The hankering after a moral order is deeply rooted in the heart of man, but it makes him prone to two common delusions. One is the pathetic belief, widely entertained in our time, that order is secured by organization. Even so shrewd an observer as Lenin succumbed to this belief. But the wickedness which makes organization necessary does not stop short at the portals of organization. The egoism which taints individuals taints governments not less, but rather more; for organization magnifies power (iv. 1),

and power is amoral. Then, *quis custodiet custodes?* (who will take care of the caretakers?). The other attempted solution is the theory of a moral government of history: 'The mills of God grind slowly . . .' This is a more respectable notion, perhaps; yet, in spite of its immense popularity, it yields no real satisfaction to the moral demand. For even if it were true, it requires for its display a canvas so much larger than the brief span between the cradle and the grave. What comfort is the thought that 'The mills of God grind slowly' to those whose life is altogether ground between the upper and the nether millstones?

'*O dreadful thought if all our sires and we
Are but foundations of a race to be.*'

A moral view of life, resolutely pursued, leads to the conclusion that men are beasts. 'Man that is in honour, and understandeth not, is like the beasts that perish' (Ps. xlix. 20). But what about his 'immortality'? 'Who knoweth the spirit of man, whether it goeth upward?' (Ec. iii. 21, RV). What is there in man by himself to suggest that his destiny is so very different from that of the beasts? 'That the soul of man is in its own nature Eternall, and a living Creature independent on the body; or that any meer man is Immortall, otherwise than by the Resurrection in the last day (except *Enos* and *Elias*) is a doctrine not apparent in Scripture' (Hobbes, *Leviathan*, xxxviii).

God is the Judge. But the righteousness of God is not subject to our judgment. As the righteousness of God, it belongs to His time, though it may be hidden from ours. He who does not understand this has no choice but to esteem death better than life.

e. The vanity of life (iv. 4–16)

i. Of industry, idleness and contentment (iv. 4–6). What is the motive that inspires human industry and enterprise? It is the desire to do a little more than survive, to outstrip one's rivals, to excel in the competitive struggle. But the attainment of this desire does not yield the satisfaction it promises; for it excites the envy of others, and anxiety lest they should overtake him besets the leader in the race. Without this desire to excel, man would not be man. Yet the irony of it is that it is often the least enterprising, the *fool* (5), the 'finite clods untroubled by a spark', who obtain the most satisfaction. There must be some happy mean between these extremes. Read verse 4 with RV mg., 'Then I saw all labour and every skilful (or successful) work, that it cometh of a man's rivalry with his neighbour'. *Eateth his own flesh* (5). Eats what meat he has without coveting that of others. It is not a reference to the autophagous tendency of idleness, as the English words suggest; this hardly suits the context.

ii. Of solitude and society (iv. 7–12). Can the motive of profit in human enterprise be balanced by that of benefit to society? Can it be urged that 'unrestricted private enterprise' is conducive to the common good? It is difficult to maintain this when it is observed how strongly the profit motive operates in those who have no society and do not give twopence for it. It is doubtful, indeed, whether one who has no ties of family can have any real feeling for society. On the other hand, where the sense of solidarity is strong, the satisfactions it yields are of a different sort.

iii. Of popularity (iv. 13–16). Of all the glittering prizes life holds out, surely the vainest is popularity. The promise of youth is always preferred to the petrifaction of age (as witness the studied illusion of perennial youth in contemporary fashions). But youth inevitably becomes age, and then it must endure the pain of seeing the fickle fancy of the mob turn elsewhere.

This passage is highly cryptic, and it is impossible to interpret it with assurance. It seems to contain an allusion to some historical episode with which its contemporary readers would be familiar: a decrepit old monarch succeeded by a brilliant youth who romantically issued from prison amid universal enthusiasm but who rapidly fell into disfavour.

f. The vanity of worship and service (v. 1–9)

i. Wisdom and folly in the worship of God (v. 1–7). Surveying the vanity of all things under the sun, Ecclesiastes turns his critical eye upon religion; for secularized man is by no means averse to religion; only, his is a religion which is secularized and humanized. This is the great pitfall of religion, against which warning is given. For there is an inveterate tendency in men to seek to 'make use of God' (Deo uti, Luther), to subject God to themselves and their own concerns, to treat Him as an ally, an anodyne or an insurance agency. Characteristic of this man-centred religion is its verbosity; its anxiety to say its say is reflected in a never-ending stream of reports, statements, pronouncements, pamphlets, etc. But it loses the ear for the word of God. The word of God is not the echo of our words. It is His own word, His word of judgment and of grace, and before it we must be silent and listen. In our approach to God it is necessary to remember 'the otherness of God', and respect 'the infinite qualitative difference between God and man' (Kierkegaard).

Keep thy foot (1). The sense is excellently conveyed in the popular modern expression 'Watch your step'. The angel (6). The priest or minister. Wherefore should God be angry . . . ? (6). It is pre-eminently against human infidelity that the wrath of God is revealed.

ii. Of the civil magistrate (v. 8, 9). The fear of God is coupled (naturally) with respect for authority in the state. Cf. 1 Pet. ii. 17. For there is no power but of God: the powers that be are ordained of God. Not that the ruling powers are beyond reproach. On the contrary, there is corruption at every stage of the political hierarchy. Even the highest in the land is not free from sin. Thus the existence of injustice and oppression is not to be marvelled at; for the remedy for this lies not in any human authority. Yet there is a relatively best form of government; and Ecclesiastes expresses his preference for a patriarchal monarchy, where the king is intimately acquainted with the concerns of his (agricultural) subjects—a judgment which is no doubt sound in its emphasis on agriculture and its implied rejection of bureaucracy, but difficult of application to large, industrialized states.

Higher than the highest (8). The term is ambiguous, perhaps intentionally. Looking up the ladder of authority we may, according to our vision, see only 'the powers that be', or we may see above them Him who will 'judge the fatherless and the oppressed, that the man of the earth may no more oppress' (Ps. x. 18). Moreover the profit of the earth . . . (9). The best rendering would seem to be: Profitable for a land in general is a king devoted to the tilled field.

g. The vanity of riches and human destiny (v. 10—vi. 12)

i. Of wealth and acquisitiveness (v. 10—vi. 9). The fancied satisfaction of mammonism, which conceives of man's life as consisting in the abundance of the things which he possesseth and identifies his state with his estate, is a mirage which continually recedes; for the lust of acquisitiveness, once unleashed, becomes insatiable, and the appetite grows with eating. Capitalism can thrive only on an expanding market, and the circle of supply and demand, however expanded, remains a circle; it cannot be squared. Further, acquisitiveness brings anxiety; for wealth is uncertain (1 Tim. vi. 17), the bubble of prosperity bursts, and slump follows boom. Finally, the rich man dies, and what good is all his wealth to him then?

Are we then to commend ascetic renunciation? By no means. The good things of the world are God's gifts to be enjoyed by us with thankfulness and contentment. The key to enjoyment is to substitute grace for grab. 'For every creature of God is good, and nothing to be refused, if it be received with thanksgiving' (1 Tim. iv. 4). Experience shows that the art of enjoyment usually comes readiest to those least cumbered with worldly goods, while those who possess 'all the advantages' may miss it.

He shall not much remember . . . (20). He who is in correspondence with God, he whose chief end it is to glorify God and enjoy Him, can live in the present and enjoy the gifts of God today, without anxious thoughts for the morrow. Cf. Mt. vi. 33, 34. And also . . . have no burial (vi. 3). It has been suggested that this clause has been misplaced and that it belongs to verse 5; it would certainly seem the more likely end of an untimely birth than of one who begot a hundred children, where it is oddly inappropriate.

ii. Of human destiny (vi. 10–12). The nature and destiny of man are determined by One mightier than he, and he cannot contend with his Maker or add to his stature one cubit. All his endeavours to find enduring substance in this transitory life issue in vanity, and leave him facing the final question.

h. The wisdom of death (vii. 1–14)

Ecclesiastes sets forth a wisdom of life which takes full account of the great negatives, adversity, sorrow and death. He who would live wisely must lay death to heart and integrate it with his view of life. The wisdom which would see 'life steadily and see it whole' must see death also; it 'exacts a full look at the worst'. The modern flight from death, shown by the avoidance of serious consideration of it in popular thought and even of all mention of it in polite conversation, as if death were a sleeping dog one could pass on tiptoe, is the index of a view of life to which death has no meaning save that of an irrational brute fact which rudely interrupts man's efforts and aspirations. Man's hopes today are bound up with a progressive postponement of death and the dream of its eventual elimination. If Ecclesiastes is able to look death fearlessly in the face, it can only be because he sees it, not as a simple negative, but as a 'horizon', a line marking 'the threshold of metaphysical possibilities' and pointing to a hidden dimension of life. The lessons which he recommends us to gather from the sterner disciplines of experience may be described as a kind of chessboard wisdom: instead of complaining bitterly that the board is all black, or sighing for 'the good old days' when it was all white, this wisdom consists in patient acceptance of its real condition as the ultimate fact which we can know, but which points beyond itself. It is a mistake to suppose that the fatalism of Omar is the only, or the only logical, inference to be drawn from the chessboard character of life.

Verses 11, 12 are difficult to understand in their present context and may have been displaced. Alternative positions suggested for them are after verse 14 and after verse 21.

i. The excellence and difficulty of wisdom (vii. 15–29)

i. 'Critique of practical reason' (vii. 15–22). The attempt to reduce the raw material of life to system by means of moral principles breaks on the anomalies of experience. The consistent application of morality plays havoc with life, which will not be forced into this Procrustes bed. There is need of humility and restraint in both the thought and the practice of morality. It must be remembered that all moralities are conditioned by man's finitude and tainted by his sin. We must be careful to avoid moral pride. 'Moral pride is the pretension of finite man that his highly conditioned virtue is the final righteousness and that his very relative moral standards are absolute. Moral pride thus makes virtue the very vehicle of sin' (Niebuhr, *Human Nature*, p. 212).

ii. 'Critique of pure reason' (vii. 23–28). The attempt to reduce the raw material of life to system by means of theoretical ideas breaks down likewise. The most penetrating wisdom cannot reach the final harmony in which the discords of existence are resolved; every attempt comes to grief on the problem of evil, '*das radikal Böse*', in the human heart. Ecclesiastes finds the most obstinate manifestation of evil in the female of the species (26); for him the wisdom of Socrates miscarries on the problem of Xanthippe.

iii. The fall (vii. 29). The conclusion, which is the utmost to which human wisdom can attain, is that man has fallen from the state in which God created him, and through his cleverness has brought about his own undoing. The irresolvable antinomies of life have their focal point in the fact that man is at variance with himself.

j. The powers that be (viii. 1–9)

The logical inference from the universality of human corruption would be anarchy ('Jack's as good as his master'). But political wisdom is not a logical science, it is a psychological art. It is guided not by what is logically sound and consistent but by what is relatively opportune (5). Thus an authoritarian order of society may be irrational and even evil (9b); nevertheless, loyalty to it is preferable to insurrection. Cf. Rom. xiii. This is hardly an acceptable doctrine nowadays; yet it is a profound challenge to those who identify change with progress. The idea of reform was no doubt strange to the mind of the writer, who construes criticism of authority as simple insurrection. But his reflections are no less applicable to it. The inability to see the outcome of any proposed change places the *onus probandi* upon those who advocate or instigate it. It is a fact that reforms which are designed to remove one evil often put others in its place; and long-term policies are called in question by the short term of human life. The real problem of life is urgent and cannot be postponed; for the time is limited. 'Now's the day, and now's the hour.' We know not if we shall see tomorrow—and 'what good is it to the primeval horse that one of its descendants wins the Derby?' (K. Heim).

To his own hurt (9), i.e. to that of the ruled, not of the ruler.

k. The reversal of human judgments (viii. 10)

The precise meaning of this very difficult verse cannot now be recovered. About a dozen different interpretations have been proposed. But if we accept the rendering of RV as approximately correct, the thought would seem to be the fallibility of popular judgments either as detected by the writer's own acuter eye or, more probably, as reversed by posterity.

l. The hidden righteousness of God (viii. 11–17)

The mills of God grind slowly—so slowly that men may easily suppose they do not grind at all. The universe appears indifferent to moral distinctions, and Ecclesiastes is well aware of the difficulties of a too facile acceptance of the

Jewish 'philosophy of history' and of attempts to discern divine judgments in the course of events (14). Nevertheless he *knows* of the certainty of judgment, even though it be not manifest in the things that are seen and temporal, and for this cause he faints not and can even laugh at despair (15). Here he shows, more clearly perhaps than anywhere else in the book, that his own soul has an anchor within the veil.

m. More of the wisdom of death (ix. 1–10)

Life is a course in which all must run together, all must take the same hurdles and the same hazards, and all come to the same end. There is no anticipation of the judgment, no discrimination in favour of those who 'run the way of God's commandments'; men can turn the race into a wild stampede with apparent impunity. Nevertheless there is a judgment; there are some who are in God's hand, whose works are accepted of Him, and who may devote themselves with a single heart to the task of the moment without anxious thought for the morrow. So long as the race is running there is hope for all, even for those who appear most hopeless; the knowledge that they must die may make the living wise; but for those who have passed the limit hope is gone; for them the day of grace is past, and 'the door is shut' (Mt. xxv. 10).

n. Negative corroborations (ix. 11–18)

The wisdom which looks for light beyond the horizon of death receives confirmation from the darkness and confusion of the scene on this side. So, from his scanning of the horizon, Ecclesiastes *returned, and saw under the sun, that the race is not to the swift, nor the battle to the strong* (11). So true it is that we walk by faith, not by sight. 'Faith is of things which do not appear. And so, that there may be room for faith, it is necessary that all things which are its objects should be hidden. They cannot, however, be more remotely hidden than under their contrary objects, feelings and experiences' (Luther, *De servo arbitrio*). What counts in the world's judgment is wealth and self-advertisement; genuine, unostentatious merit goes unrecognized, unrewarded. This Ecclesiastes describes ironically as the wisdom which he saw under the sun and it seemed great to him (13). *One sinner destroyeth much good* (18). This clause introduces the next series of reflections.

o. Of folly and wisdom (x. 1–7)

Wisdom is excellent, but it is at a disadvantage in comparison with folly, which produces disproportionately large effects. A little leaven of folly can vitiate a whole lump of wisdom, and a single fool can undo the work of many wise men. Further, folly is more immediately evident; it proclaims itself on the street. When folly manifests itself in high places, the course of wisdom is patience and conciliation. Least said is soonest mended. If it be argued that this would justify

a policy of appeasement, Ecclesiastes would answer that the wise man is guided by time and judgment (viii. 15). There is a time to keep silence and a time to speak (iii. 7). That folly does invade high places is proved by the familiar observation that fools are exalted to honour and dignity in the state, and true worth passes unrecognized. *The rich* (6). Ecclesiastes probably means those of hereditary wealth, the aristocracy, as distinguished from the *nouveaux riches*.

p. Counting the cost (x. 8–10)

The general import of these gnomic utterances, which may have been current proverbs, would seem to be that no change can be effected without risk, and especially that anyone who interferes with established institutions is liable to get his fingers burned. Before embarking on any such enterprise it is well to count the cost and make sure that one has adequate skill and resources at his command (cf. Lk. xiv. 28ff.).

q. Words and deeds (x. 11–20)

i. The wise man and the fool (x. 11–15).
Ecclesiastes here touches on the notorious talkativeness of folly and the capacity of mischief that is inherent in it. Cf. Jas. iii. 5, 6. To know *how to go to the city* (15) would appear to have been a proverbial expression for practical wisdom or effective action. The fool can talk plenty, but he is incapable of action.

ii. Slothfulness at court (x. 16–19).
Ill fares the land when Sybaritism prevails at court. *The son of nobles* (17). Perhaps a *double entendre*, made possible by the Hebrew idiom which employs the periphrasis 'son of' to form a descriptive adjective: when the king's character and conduct are of a nobility consistent with his birth.

iii. Reverence due to the king (x. 20).
This warning against seditious talk and 'dangerous thoughts' accords well with Ecclesiastes' attitude of detachment towards politics. It is not a counsel of acquiescence in injustice or oppression but rather a warning against incurring unnecessary risks. Where there is neither the will nor the power to mend matters, mere grumbling and disaffection are foolish.

r. Directions for charity (xi. 1–6)

If some of the political counsels of the previous chapters have a somewhat conservative, quietistic, 'Lutheran' ring, Ecclesiastes' dialectic now takes a bold, venturesome, 'Calvinistic' turn, as if to show once more that the conduct of life cannot be based on a single principle, but the wise man has regard to 'time and judgment'. In commercial enterprise risks must be taken, and he who will not venture until he has an absolutely safe proposition will wait for ever (4). The future is always unpredictable; accidents will happen to the best regulated businesses; and no one knows by what 'act of God' (5) the most careful calculations may be upset. The course of wisdom is not to put all our eggs in one basket and not to stake our all on one card but to reduce the risk by dividing it (2).

Cast thy bread upon the waters . . . (1). It is fairly certain that the primary reference of the words, as Delitzsch has shown, is to the seaborne corn trade. But Ecclesiastes undoubtedly uses this form of commercial adventure to illustrate the course which wisdom suggests in other fields of life, such as the practice of uncalculating charity, to which the words have been commonly understood to refer. Cf. Lk. xvi. 9.

s. Respice finem (xi. 7, 8)

A wise recognition of the uncertainty of the future makes the present all the more important. The present is the only time at our disposal. Tomorrow is in God's hand: we know not what it shall bring forth. It is on today that 'the accent of eternity' (Heim) lies. Like Christ's 'Take no thought for the morrow', this does not imply disregard of the future. On the contrary, it is made possible only by a true regard for the future, viz. the recognition that the future is God's. The Epicurean philosophy which says *carpe diem*, 'gather ye rosebuds while ye may', contains an element of profound truth, and it is not so very far removed from what Paul says about 'redeeming the time' (Col. iv. 5) and 'serving the time' (Rom. xii. 11, reading *kairo* for *kurio*).

t. Counsels to youth (xi. 9—xii. 8)

i. Rejoice (xi. 9, 10). A corollary of Ecclesiastes' emphasis on the present is his counsel to youth to enjoy the season of youth while it is theirs, not to seek to put old heads on young shoulders nor to try to prolong youth beyond its term, but to accept youth with its blessings and opportunities in the sober recognition that youth and age alike are of God's appointment and both are subject to His judgment. *Rejoice . . . in the sight of thine eyes* (9). There is nothing in these words to warrant the interpretation that Ecclesiastes is recommending youth to sow *wild* oats; nor can we deduce from them any support for the current idolization of youth, with its ridiculous sartorial illusions. *But know thou* (9). 'The great But', in which the wisdom of the Bible is crystallized (Barth). 'All the ways of a man are clean in his own eyes; *but* the Lord weigheth the spirits' (Pr. xvi. 2).

ii. Remember (xii. 1-8). Man is a creature of time. In the end his creatureliness asserts itself unmistakably in his dissolution. Surely it is elementary wisdom to take account of this ultimate 'horizon' (Heidegger) in any attempt to construe the pattern of existence. Ecclesiastes recommends the frank recognition of our creatureliness even in youth, at the time when it is least apparent and life seems unquenchable. It is only when seen in this perspective that youth can be rightly understood and rightly enjoyed. The 'problem of youth' which bulks so large in our time is in great measure the conse-quence of a false perspective, a blurring of the horizons, the playing of blind man's buff with death, which is one of the chief follies of the age.

Remember now thy Creator (1). It is to be noted how Ecclesiastes shows his hand here. The prospect of age and death yields him, not *memento mori* (remember thou must die), but *memento Creatoris* (remember thy Creator). By this he clearly distinguishes himself from all sceptics, cynics and Epicureans, with whom he has often been confused.

The following verses (2-7) contain a figurative description of the decay and dissolution of life, but the imagery is difficult to interpret in detail. The picture of the approaching storm (2) may be intended to suggest the approach of death in a general way or more particularly the decay of the inner faculties. The imagery of verses 3, 4 is most probably intended to represent the decay of the bodily organs, *the keepers of the house* being the hands, *the strong men* the legs, *the grinders* the teeth, *those that look out of the windows* the eyes, *the doors* the ears. The remaining clauses of verse 4 seem all to refer to the decay of the powers of speech and song. *He shall rise up at the voice of the bird* (4). If *he* means an old man, this would involve the abrupt insertion of a literal statement in the middle of an elaborate allegory. But apart from that, it is not true that the old rise up at the voice of a bird. The old are less easily roused than the young, especially as they are often deaf (*the doors shall be shut in the streets*)! It is probable that the text is corrupt and the original was to the effect that the voice of the old becomes weak and tends to resemble the treble chirp of a bird.

The allegory is abandoned in verse 5, and literal description takes its place: The old are afraid of heights, and they are timid of venturing forth at all. In view of the great and fantastic variety of interpretations that have been suggested for *the almond tree*, *the grasshopper*, and 'the caper-berry' (rv; *desire*, av), it seems best to follow Wetzstein and Hertzberg and take the three clauses literally as descriptions of phenomena of spring and summer: the almond tree blooms, the grasshopper loads itself (with food) and the caper-berry bursts forth—but all these gladdening sights mean nothing to the old man who, after the dissolution of his earthly house (3; cf. 2 Cor. v. 1), goes to his long home.

The allegory is resumed in verse 6. The figures of *the silver cord* being loosed and *the golden bowl* broken would seem to refer to the dissolution of soul and body. The life of man is likened first to a golden bowl (containing oil for a lamp) suspended by a silver cord, then to a *pitcher* with which water is drawn from a well. The lamp and the pitcher were both familiar symbols of life in antiquity. *The spirit shall return unto God who gave it* (7). Ecclesiastes would seem to have advanced somewhat beyond the position of iii. 21, but his words here, while suggestive, are not such as to form the foundation of a hope of immortality. He is viewing the dissolution of body and spirit from the standpoint of 'under the sun', and he simply states that each returns to the source from which it sprang, the body to the dust and the spirit to God (Gn. ii. 7). As to the final destiny of the spirit after its return to God, it is not his concern to speak of that.

Vanity of vanities . . . (8). The author 'has made all earthly things small, and at last remains seated on this dust-heap of *vanitas vanitatum*' (Delitzsch). His argument, like all things under the sun (i. 3–11), has come full circle, and he repeats the theorem which he set out to demonstrate (i. 2) with an air of finality, as if to say *quod erat demonstrandum*.

u. Epilogue (xii. 9–14)

The remainder of the book consists of an editorial postscript in the form of a 'commendatory attestation' (Plumptre) of the writer and an attempt to sum up the conclusions of his teaching. Does this come from the same hand as the rest of the book, or was it added by another? The question has been much debated. The change from the first to the third person suggests a change of author, but since the author's name *Qoheleth* (Ecclesiastes) is a pseudonym in any case, it may indicate only that he now steps forward and makes a brief curtain-speech, as it were, in his own name. We may compare Kierkegaard's editorial notes to his own pseudonymous works. There is no change in the vocabulary and style of the epilogue, which bears a strong resemblance to that of the rest of the book (even in the obscurity of the metaphor in verse 11). It has been questioned whether any writer would speak of himself in terms of 9, 10, which, it is suggested, betray the hand of an admiring follower. But this is to attribute the literary fashions of our day to an age when they were very different. In the ancient world authorship was held of small account, so small indeed that the names of many of the authors of antiquity have been lost. The question men asked of a book was not 'Who wrote it?' but 'What does it say?', and there was no need for an author to make a profession of modesty, since his work was not regarded as a personal achievement or a feat of virtuosity. Even in our own time there have been exceptions to the fashion of literary modesty (which is largely humbug), notably Mr. Bernard Shaw, who sometimes spoke of himself in much more flattering terms than Ecclesiastes, and with less ground.

The most important question is whether verses 13–14 are a just summation of the teaching of the book, or, as some allege, a tendentious simplification, made with a view to commending it to orthodox readers. It is certainly difficult to see how any statement of a positive duty for man could be logically deduced from the premise that all things under the sun are vanity. But this is not the logic of Ecclesiastes; for he does not seek the premises of human duty in human theory or of moral values in the 'idea' of God. However much he stresses the difficulties of what man is to believe concerning God, he *knows* (viii. 12) that these difficulties do not suspend or abrogate the duty God requires of man; and it may be with a view to correcting any rash inference that might be drawn from his theoretical conclusion that he lays his final emphasis on the practical duty of man. The enigma of life may be insoluble by wisdom, but *solvitur ambulando*.

The words of the wise are as goads . . . (11). Though acceptable, they have their sting. The following comparison is typically obscure. The *nails* are usually understood to be tent-pegs, and the *masters of assemblies*, who are compared to them, are either the great teachers or the great teachings assembled in their works; the *one shepherd* can hardly be other than God, who is the author and source of true wisdom. The general idea would seem to be that it is the teachings of the masters, drawn from the fountain-head, which gives stability and strength to life. A final warning is given against intellectualism (12), directed in the first instance perhaps against the exaggerated pretensions of 'wisdom' in the literature which goes by that name. Ecclesiastes does not despise the intellect (ix. 17, 18), but he is aware of its limitations (viii. 17).

The whole duty of man (13, 14). This is not the practice of the theory that all is vanity. But Ecclesiastes knows that practice will not wait upon theory or life upon understanding. Theory and practice will remain at variance so long as we are under the sun. The reconciliation, the resolution of the discord awaits the time when faith will give place to sight and every hidden thing will be revealed. So we may say of the last words of Ecclesiastes, *spirant resurrectionem* (they foreshadow the resurrection).

G. S. HENDRY.

THE SONG OF SOLOMON

INTRODUCTION

In the sacred volume which brings to us the hope-kindling message of the love of God, the Song of Solomon is the only book that has love for its sole theme. The subject is handled with great skill and insight in a series of dramatic canticles, centring in a single pair and linked by the appearance and reappearance of subordinate groups such as 'the daughters of Jerusalem' (i. 5, ii. 7, iii. 10, v. 8, 16) and the 'watchmen' (iii. 3, v. 7), and the recurrence of significant refrains (e.g. ii. 7, iii. 5, viii. 4; ii. 17, iv. 6; ii. 16, vi. 3, vii. 10). The canticles are embellished by rich Oriental imagery and contain very beautiful descriptions of natural scenery.

I. AUTHORSHIP

The title may mean either that the Song is composed by Solomon or that it is about him. Tradition uniformly favours the former interpretation. Some modern scholars, however, have maintained that the large number of foreign words used in the poem would not occur in the literature of Israel before the post-exilic period. Others think, with Driver, that the widespread contacts of Israel with foreign nations during the reign of Solomon would sufficiently account for the presence of these words in the book. If this view is accepted, and if it is assumed that there are only two principal characters in the Song, there does not appear to be any substantial reason for setting aside the traditional view of the authorship. But if Ewald is followed in holding that there is a shepherd lover in addition (see below), belief in the authorship of Solomon is scarcely tenable and it is impossible to name the writer.

II. INTERPRETATION

Devout Jews from the first century regarded the Song as an allegory portraying the relations of Jehovah and Israel. In the second century, Rabbi Akiba affirmed that it was a gift of inestimable value to Israel and the holiest of all sacred writings. Christian exegesis, since the days of Origen, has seen in the imagery of the book the representation of the love of Christ and His Church. Delitzsch held that the Song is a dramatic dialogue in which Solomon and the Shulamite are the principal characters. Their love typifies the love of Christ and the Church.

Ewald, as indicated above, took a different line of interpretation. He identified 'the beloved' with a shepherd lover to whom the maiden was betrothed, prior to her being captured and brought to the palace by some of Solomon's servants. After she has successfully resisted all the king's endeavours to win her affections for himself, she is set free and joins her lover, with whom she appears in the final scene. Those who adopt this interpretation see in Solomon a type of the world and in the shepherd lover a type of Christ. The maiden represents the faithful soul loyally persevering in faith, love and obedience despite the pressure of temptation, and enduring as seeing the invisible. On this view the various sections of the Song may be understood as follows:

i. 1—ii. 7. The maiden recalls her beloved in the palace where Solomon promises to adorn her with jewels.

ii. 8—iii. 5. The maiden recollects a visit her beloved once paid her and a dream that followed it.

iii. 6—iv. 7. The maiden is again visited and praised by Solomon.

iv. 8—v. 1. Unmoved, the maiden remembers the words of her beloved and anticipates their marriage day.

v. 2—vi. 3. The maiden relates a dream and describes her beloved.

vi. 4—vii. 9. The maiden receives a further visit from Solomon, who makes a fresh attempt to win her affection.

vii. 10—viii. 3. The maiden, maintaining her loyalty to her absent lover, longs for his society.

viii. 4-14. The maiden returns home with her beloved and declares her faithfulness.

For further study of this alternative interpretation readers are referred to the outline, notes and questions contained in the I.V.F. Bible Study Course, *Search the Scriptures*, pp. 234ff.

Attempts have been made to show the existence of a chorus in the Song but they fail to convince owing to the absence of rubrics in the book itself. The theory that the Song is a collection of 'wasfs', or songs intended to be sung at a marriage, while it may throw some light on the structure of parts of the poem, breaks down on account of the evident unity of the book.

OUTLINE OF CONTENTS

This commentary takes the view that there are only two principal characters and therefore divides the book according to the analysis set out below.

I. THE SHULAMITE'S LONGING AND SATISFACTION. i. 1—ii. 7

II. THE BELOVED'S VISIT AND THE SHULAMITE'S DREAM. ii. 8—iii. 5

III. SOLOMON'S PROCESSION AND SONGS. iii. 6—v. 1

IV. THE SHULAMITE'S TARDY WELCOME AND PROLONGED SEARCH. v. 2—viii. 3

V. THE SHULAMITE AND THE BELOVED CONVERSE. viii. 4–14

COMMENTARY

I. THE SHULAMITE'S LONGING AND SATISFACTION. i. 1—ii. 7

a. The title (i. 1)

The song of songs, which is Solomon's (1). For 'song of songs' cf. 'holy of holies', 'vanity of vanities'. It means the best of songs. Solomon composed 1,005 songs (1 Ki. iv. 32). Stuart supposes that the five, additional to the thousand, are the five divisions of the Song of Solomon, which he adopts. Durham takes the title to mean the best song in Scripture; and Bernard remarks of the Song, 'Grace alone teaches it and experience alone can learn it'. The use of a different form of the relative pronoun here from that found elsewhere in the book has led to the conjecture that the title may be the work of a later hand. It is not, however, necessary to fall back on this explanation. The distinction between the title and the rest of the book might be a sufficient reason.

b. The Shulamite recalls the charm of her Beloved and her own unattractiveness (i. 2–6)

Him (2). Unnamed as in the case of a person or thing of which the heart and mind is full. Cf. Jn. xx. 15; 2 Tim. i. 12. *Wine* (2). Cf. Ps. civ. 15; Pr. xxxi. 6, where it is regarded as gladdening and reviving; see also Ps. iv. 7. Christ's love is better than what is most satisfying and cheering apart from it. In the desire of the Shulamite we may see a prayer for fresh knowledge and experience of the love of Christ. The Church having already had evidence of its uplifting and gladdening influence is encouraged by the recollection of past kindness to ask for further favour. Cf. Ps. lxiii. 1–5. *Because of the savour* (3). 'Thine ointments have a goodly fragrance' (RV). There is in the Hebrew a play on the words for ointment and name. Cf. Ec. vii. 1. *Ointments* (3). Unguents or perfumes were specially valued in the East on account of the heat. Particular uses were the anointing of priests (Ex. xxx. 23–25) and the welcoming of guests (Ps. xxiii. 5; Lk. vii. 38). The use of very costly ointment in this latter connection was a mark of unusual esteem (cf. Jn. xii. 3). Kings collected and used perfumes of rare composition and fragrance. See iii. 6 and cf. 2 Ki. xx. 13. *Name* (3). The name recalls what he is. The recollection has an effect upon the spirit similar to that of sweet perfume on the senses. The anointing oil of Old Testament times typified the work of the Holy Spirit, who came upon Christ without measure. The knowledge of Christ is compared by Paul to perfume (see 2 Cor. ii. 14). *Virgins* (3). Attendants of the bride. Mystically they are the regenerate and sanctified. Cf. Mt. xxv. 1; 2 Cor. xi. 2; Rev. xiv. 4. *Draw me* (4). In verse 2 she expressed the desire that her Beloved would come to her; now her wish is that she may be drawn after him. Cf. Ps. lxiii. 8; Je. xxxi. 3; Jn. vi. 44. *Brought* (4). A recollection of past favour. Cf. Ps. xlv. 14; Jn. x. 16.

Daughters of Jerusalem (5). The reappearance of this group at ii. 7, iii. 10, v. 8, 16 is one of the proofs of the unity of the Song. They are interested onlookers. According to the allegorical interpretation, they represent inquirers after Christ (Stuart). *I am black* (5). Bedouin women are said to contrast themselves still, in this way, with city dwellers. The Shulamite compares the swarthy colour of her skin to the dark goat-skin or camel-hair tents of the sons of Ishmael, but she likens her attractions to the many-coloured curtains of Solomon. The following verse explains the cause of the dark hue, which is temporary. *Mine own vineyard* (6). That is, her complexion. The language is suggestive of the sin, suffering and sorrow which sometimes darken the lot of the Church, or the believing soul, although it is still attractive in God's sight because of imputed righteousness and the inward work of grace. The request for undeserved blessing is fittingly accompanied by acknowledgement of unworthiness and failure.

c. The Shulamite requests and receives guidance (i. 7, 8)

Tell me (7). This verse introduces the pastoral imagery frequently employed in the book. The shepherdess was a familiar figure in the East

548

(cf. Rachel, Zipporah). Not content to wait until evening, she desires to meet with him at the noonday rest. *Where thou feedest* (7). Rather 'where thou dost pasture (thy flock)'. *As one that turneth aside* (7). 'As one veiled' (RV). It is difficult to assign a suitable meaning to the word so rendered. Aglen's reading 'as one blindfold' is, perhaps, best. *If thou know not* (8). These words are probably spoken by the Shulamite's companions. They who would meet frequently with Christ must seek Him in the well-worn paths of faith, obedience, service and worship.

d. The Beloved declares his admiration and promises gifts (i. 9–11)

Love (9). 'Friend' (RV mg.). *Ra'yah* is found only in this book and in Jdg. xi. 37. Cambridge Bible compares the French use of *ami* between lovers. *A company of horses* (9). The feminine form translated thus may be either collective, or mean 'my filly'. Since, however, comparisons with a collective form occur elsewhere (e.g. vi. 10, 12), it appears better to follow the AV. In Solomon's time Egyptian horses were greatly in demand for royal use (see 1 Ki. x. 28, 29). The comparison itself, although not in line with Western taste, is common among the Arabs, who rear particularly graceful breeds of horses. *Rows of jewels* (10). 'Plaits of hair' (RV). 'Braided plaits' (Moff.). The comparison with the chariot horses is probably in the background, since the heads of Egyptian horses were adorned with coins and silver ornaments. The fashion referred to may resemble that used by Egyptian women, who divide the hair into numerous plaits, which are allowed to hang down the back, having tassels with small gold or silver ornaments attached to them. Persian ladies use a head-dress formed by two or three rows of pearls, which pass round the head and hang down the cheeks. *Chains of gold* (10). RV and Moffatt render 'strings of jewels'. Thomson, in *The Land and the Book*, comments on the fondness of Arab women for 'an endless variety' of chains 'among other jewels'. *Borders of gold* (11). 'Borders' is the same word rendered 'rows' or 'plaits' in verse 10. Jordan translates 'circlets of gold with silver points'. However much grace the Church may have received and may exhibit, Christ has more to bestow, to make her more acceptable to Himself.

e. The Shulamite expresses her satisfaction with her Beloved (i. 12–14)

Sitteth at his table (12). 'Sat' (RV). 'Lies on his divan' (Moff.). *Spikenard* (12). A costly perfume, prepared by drying the shaggy stem of an Indian plant, early imported into Palestine. *Bundle of myrrh* (13). 'Bag' (RV mg.). Myrrh was obtained from a low thorny acacia-like tree, found in Arabia Felix. A white fluid oozes from the bark when punctured, which hardens into the myrrh of commerce. It was supposed to have disinfecting properties and reviving power and was sometimes carried in a small bottle or satchel

suspended round the neck and worn day and night. Cf. Ps. xlv. 8. *Camphire* (14). 'Henna-flowers' (RV). Henna is a small shrub, bearing clusters of white and yellow blossoms with a rich fragrance. It was found in Palestine at Engedi near the Dead Sea. It was used to give a delicate tint to hands and feet.

f. The Beloved praises the loveliness of the Shulamite (i. 15)

Doves' eyes (15). 'Thine eyes are as doves' (RV). The species referred to and often mentioned in the book is the rock pigeon. The ideas suggested are those of constancy, grace and tenderness. Cf. Mt. x. 16.

g. The Shulamite expresses her pleasure in the Beloved and her surroundings (i. 16, 17)

Our bed is green (16). 'The green sward' (Moff.). *Rafters* (17). The word is not found elsewhere and the meaning is uncertain. LXX gives 'panelled ceilings'. Cedars and firs are elsewhere mentioned together as emblems of majesty (cf. Is. xxxvii. 24; Ezk. xxxi. 8). It is probably a woodland bower rather than the interior of a palace that is to be thought of. The fresh fragrance of their resting-place suggests the pleasure and profit of their fellowship. Cf. Ps. xxiii. 2, 3. As the Shulamite gained satisfaction from the words and presence of her Beloved, so the Church may find encouragement in the commendation and promises of Christ. He will reveal Himself to her more fully as she diligently seeks Him and the realization of His presence and grace will stimulate her faith, love and loyalty.

h. The Beloved compares himself and the Shulamite to flowers, suggestive of beauty and grace (ii. 1, 2)

I am the rose of Sharon (1). The earliest Fathers, the old English Bibles, the French, Italian and Portuguese Bibles and most older commentaries assign these words to the Beloved. More recent scholars are agreed in understanding them as spoken by the Shulamite. It is difficult to decide between these opinions but, on the whole, the former view appears the more probable. 'Sharon' is best understood as a proper name. Cf. Is. xxxv. 2. A place bearing this name and famed for the plant mentioned lay to the south of Carmel on the Mediterranean coast. The word translated 'rose' appears, from its derivation, to denote a bulbous plant. The sweet-scented narcissus, which is a favourite with Orientals, is, perhaps, to be preferred to others suggested. LXX and Vulg. translate simply 'flower', while Moffatt reads 'a blossom'. *Lily* (1). The word so rendered occurs seven times in the book. The Arabs apply it to any brilliantly coloured flower. In v. 13 the lips are compared to lilies and most commentators interpret the reference as being to the scarlet anemone. Cf. Mt. vi. 29. *Valleys* (1). Stuart thinks a definite place near Sharon, where the royal cattle were pastured, is intended. Cf. 1 Ch. xxvii. 29. In these verses, according to the older view, Christ presents Himself as an object of admiration and delight. *Among thorns* (2). The thorns, with which the anemone is not infrequently surrounded, serve to emphasize its beauty. This is the point of the contrast.

i. The Shulamite tells of her delight in the fellowship of the Beloved (ii. 3–6)

The apple tree (3). The apple tree does not now flourish in Palestine, south of Lebanon. Cf., however, the article by Dr. Law in Hastings' *Dictionary of the Bible*. Many favour the AV, but others point out that the pleasing appearance, satisfying shade and sweet fruit suggested in the context are all answered by the apricot. Here again, however, as Masterman says (Hastings' *Dictionary of the Bible*, one-vol. ed.), the time of its importation from China is uncertain. As Christ looks upon the masses of mankind, so many of whom forget God, the Church in their midst, purchased by His own blood, justified by faith, indwelt by the Holy Spirit and endeavouring to serve Him, is specially delightful to Him. On the other hand, the true Church esteems none more highly than her divine Lord, on account of the splendour of His character, the sufficiency of His salvation and the satisfaction of His friendship. *Banqueting house* (4). Lit. 'house of wine', which might describe any place where wine and food are served to travellers. The AV rendering suggests the interior of a palace. The words are no doubt a figure for the enjoyment of love. In the allegorical interpretation they stand for public ordinances and the Lord's Table in particular. To the Church the place honoured by the Lord's presence and His gracious self-disclosure in word or sacrament becomes a spiritual banqueting house. *Banner* (4). A variety of explanations is given. Fausset remarks, 'Love is the name of God. It was revealed in the cross. This banner rallies round us the forces of omnipotence.' *Flagons* (5). 'Cakes of raisins' (RV mg.). It is supposed by some that cakes made from flour kneaded with grape juice, which fermented in baking, are referred to. Cf. Je. vii. 18, xliv. 19. AV translates 'flagons of wine' also in Ho. iii. 1 and 2 Sa. vi. 19, following Rabbinic commentators. *I am sick of love* (5). Stuart cites the case of John Welch of Covenanting times, who during his last illness was 'so filled with the sensible enjoyment of God' that he was sometimes heard to use in prayer the words 'Lord, hold thine hand; it is enough; thy servant is but a clay vessel and can hold no more'. *His left hand* (6). RV mg. reads this as a wish. Older interpreters distinguished the left hand as the hand of providence and the right as the hand of grace.

j. The recurring charge to the daughters of Jerusalem (ii. 7)

Roes, and . . . hinds (7) are typical in Eastern poetry of womanly beauty. They are noted for timidity. *That ye stir not up, nor awake my love* (7). Allegorical interpreters, following the AV,

understand the charge as meaning 'Grieve not the Spirit'. RV translates the latter part 'nor awaken love, until *it* please'. Morgan follows this rendering and comments that the words should be written in flaming letters in every hall where young people congregate. This refrain occurs again at iii. 5 and viii. 4, marking a break in the Song and leaving the happy pair together, as here, on each occasion.

II. THE BELOVED'S VISIT AND THE SHULAMITE'S DREAM. ii. 8–iii. 5

a. The Beloved heard and seen (ii. 8, 9)

At the beginning of this canticle the Beloved takes the initiative. Verses 8–17 are among the most beautiful in the book. They rank in literary merit with the best love poetry in the world. After wintry months devoid of fresh life and growth, the stirring vigour of the Syrian spring follows, of a sudden, upon the early rain. The earth rapidly assumes a mantle of bright green, intermingled with the varied colours of innumerable flowers. The newly clad woodland comes alive with song, amid which can be discerned the persistent mournful note of the turtle. It is then that the voice of the Beloved is heard. The whole picture is suggestive of a season of spiritual revival. *The voice* (8). For the thought cf. Jn. x. 4, v. 28. *Our wall* (9). Allegorically the wall has been variously explained as sin, the law, our mortal condition. *Looketh forth* (9). 'Looketh in at' (RV). The words may mean either 'in' or 'out from'. The former is better. *Shewing himself* (9). The original means 'making himself look brightly'. His attractiveness is seen but imperfectly. Thus he is described as being near at hand, but only partially revealed.

b. The Beloved's invitation (ii. 10–15)

Winter (11). The rainy or cloudy season. *Rain* (11). Heb. *geshem*. This is the heavy winter rain as opposed to *malkosh*, the later and lighter rain, which continues for six weeks longer. *The flowers* (12). The sudden appearance of spring flowers in Palestine has often been remarked upon. *Singing* (12). In early spring nightingales and others of the warbler species fill the woods with sweet song. *Turtle* (12). This is our own turtle, which is migratory in Palestine, appearing in large numbers by the second week of April, and pouring forth sad soothing notes from dawn to sunset. Allegorical commentators compare the Baptist's summons to repentance before the Bridegroom's voice is heard. Cf. also Je. viii. 7. *Putteth forth* (13). 'Ripeneth' (RV). The Arabic form of the word means 'reddeneth'. The figs referred to remain unripe on the trees during the winter and rapidly ripen in spring, developing before the leaves on old wood. Cf. Mt. xxi. 19. *The vines with the tender grape* (13). 'The vines are in blossom. They give forth their fragrance' (RV). The Rabbis say the word means the tender grape when it first appears. In April, however, there is scarcely any appearance of fruit. But 'blossom' is another meaning of the word and is more suitable here. *Dove* (14). The rock pigeon, which always selects lofty cliffs and deep ravines as its resting-place. Cf. Je. xlviii. 28. *Clefts of the rock* (14). The word, as appears from the Arabic, means a place of refuge. *In the secret places of the stairs* (14). 'In the covert of the steep place' (RV). *Foxes* (15), or jackals, both of which are destructive in vineyards. The allegorical interpreters explain the reference as pointing to subtle sins often in evidence at times of spiritual revival or progress.

c. The Shulamite's declaration and desire (ii. 16, 17)
He feedeth among the lilies (16). 'He feedeth his flock among the lilies' (RV). The words may also mean 'the shepherd among the lilies'. *Until the day break* (17). 'Until the day be cool' (RV). 'Till the cool of the dawn' (Moff.). Some understand 'daybreak'; others 'evening'. *Bether* (17). AV, following the Gk. versions, makes this a proper name and some identify it with Bithron, a region east of Jordan. Cf. 2 Sa. ii. 29. The word occurs in Gn. xv. 10 and Je. xxxiv. 18, 19 in the sense of animals divided at the making of a covenant. RV mg. gives 'mountains of separation'. Either of these renderings is preferable to other conjectures.

d. The Beloved missed, sought and found (iii. 1–5)
Many commentators understand these verses to be the description of a dream. *By night* (1). Lit. 'by nights'. Moffatt translates 'night after night'. Samuel Rutherford, quoted by Aglen (Ellicott's Commentary), says 'As nights and dews are better for flowers than continual sun, so Christ's absence, at times, giveth sap to humility and putteth an edge on hunger and furnisheth a fair field to faith to put itself forth'. *Broad ways* (2). There were broader spaces at the crossings and gates in the narrow streets. *Watchmen* (3). The city guard moved silently about the streets questioning and dealing with suspicious persons. In the Bible the word sometimes means prophets or pastors. Cf. Is. lxii. 6; Je. vi. 17. *But a little* (4). Christ is, as a rule, found near the means of grace. *Mother's house* (4). This implies confessing him openly. 'Mother' has been variously understood, as e.g. the Church, the nation, the Jews, mankind. For the recurring charge of verse 5 see the note on ii. 7 above.

III. SOLOMON'S PROCESSION AND SONGS. iii. 6—v. 1

a. Solomon's approach, with a description of his palanquin (iii. 6–11)
In this central section the Beloved is twice named King Solomon and the Shulamite is six times called spouse. Neither of these modes of reference appears elsewhere in the book. The description of the procession may indicate that the king is on the way to the Shulamite's house, to lead her either to betrothal or marriage. With the question in verse 6 cf. Ps. xxiv. 8, 10; Is. lxiii. 1. We are reminded of Jesus returning in the power of the Spirit from the wilderness of the temptations to make His voice heard as that of the bridegroom.
Who is this? (6). The pronoun is feminine for neuter and refers to 'litter' (7; see note below). Cf. Gn. xxxiii. 8. Lit. 'Who is all this camp?' *Wilderness* (6). This means wide open spaces, with or without pasture, as distinct from cultivated land. Older commentators refer the words to Israel's approach to Canaan. *Pillars of smoke* (6). Incense was burned before important processions. Fausset finds here a suggestion of the atonement and intercession of Christ. *Perfumed with myrrh . . .* (6). These words describe the richest perfumes the East could furnish. Frankincense is the gum of an Indian tree, obtained by slitting the bark. *Behold his bed* (7). 'Behold, it is the litter' (RV). Moffatt translates "Tis the palanquin'. *Valiant* (7). Cf. 2 Sa. xxiii. 8. *Chariot* (9). LXX has *thoreion*, 'litter'. The word *appiryon* probably means 'palanquin' but is different from that used in verse 7. The derivation is uncertain. *Wood of Lebanon* (9). This would be cedar and cypress. *Pillars* (10). The supports of the canopy. *Bottom* (10). Moffatt translates 'back', and this rendering is supported by the Gk. and Lat. versions. *Purple* (10). Rather 'red', sometimes 'dark red'. *Paved* (10). RV mg. has 'inlaid'. Moffatt adopts another reading and renders 'inlaid with ebony'. Cambridge Bible translates 'wrought as a mosaic from love on the part of the daughters of Jerusalem'. If AV be followed, cf. Lk. xxiii. 28.
Crown (11). Costly crowns were worn at weddings. The custom was abolished in the time of Vespasian. This verse was probably sung by the bride's companions, going to meet the bridal procession. *Day of his espousals* (11). This day or a day in the past; probably the latter. Historically the daughters of Jerusalem, or Zion, saw Christ crowned with thorns, indirectly by the will of the Jewish race from which He sprung as regards His human nature. But in a brighter and better day the Jewish Church, turned to the Lord, will unite with all the saints in ascribing Him glory as Redeemer.

b. Solomon's first song (iv. 1–7)
This is a song, after the pattern of the 'wasf', commonly sung at Syrian marriages still. It was sometimes imitated, where only a love song was intended. It is a type of description appreciated in the East, though it may not in all respects commend itself to Western taste. *Thou hast doves' eyes within thy locks* (1). Better, as in RV, 'Thine eyes are as doves behind thy veil'. The dove is an emblem of guilelessness and purity. Jordan supposes that the veil referred to covered the eyes, which shone through it. *As a flock of goats* (1). The colour of goats is usually black. *That appear from mount Gilead* (1). 'That lie along the side of mount Gilead' (RV). The word rendered

appear from' in the AV is of doubtful meaning. The sense is the similarity between the masses of the dark hair hanging down, probably in braids, and the flock of goats as seen on the hillside. Gilead was the name of the mountain range, east of Jordan, between the north end of the Dead Sea and the Sea of Galilee. It was a region affording much good pasture land, especially in the south. *Thy teeth are like a flock* (2). Cf. vi. 6. The point of the comparison is the white appearance of the newly shorn and washed flock. The teeth are white, they correspond perfectly in the lower and upper jaws and are complete in number. *Like a thread of scarlet* (3), or cochineal; i.e. thin red lips. *Thy temples are like a piece of a pomegranate* (3). Both temples and cheeks are probably included in this term. The pomegranate is used by the Eastern poet for purposes of comparison in the way the Western poet might use the apple. *The tower of David* (4). The building meant cannot be identified. The word rendered 'armoury' is difficult. Cheyne, altering the text, translates it 'shield'. Margoliouth takes it as a proper name and translates 'builded towards Talpioth', a village in the plain of Damascus. Moffatt has 'adorned with trophies'. The many jewels on the neck are compared to the trophies hung on the walls of the tower. *Until the day break* (6). Cf. ii. 17n. *Mountain of myrrh* (6). No particular place can be identified, but the words may mean 'a garden of spices on high ground'.

c. Solomon's second song (iv. 8–15)

Come with me (8). LXX, Vulg., and Luther, reading a change in the pointing, render 'to me'. The descriptions suggest places of danger. *Look from* (8) is probably better rendered 'depart from' in this context. *Amana* (8) is Abana (cf. 2 Ki. v. 12); i.e. either Amanus, a spur of the Taurus, or the district through which the river Amanah flowed. *Shenir* (8) is one of the three peaks of Hermon. The Amorites called it Senir and the Sidonians Sirion. Cf. Dt. iii. 9; 1 Ch. v. 23; Ps. xlii. 6. *Honeycomb* (11). Honey, dropping of its own accord, represents here pleasant speech. Cf. Pr. xvi. 24. *The smell of Lebanon* (11). Fragrant aromatic shrubs are plentiful in the Lebanon region. *A garden inclosed* (12). A common metaphor in Eastern poetry. Cf. Pr. v. 15–21. 'Inclosed' is a strong word meaning 'locked and bolted'. *A spring shut up, a fountain sealed* (12). The fountain is the source of the spring. The figures suggest Christ's exclusive claim to the supreme place in the affections of life. *Thy plants* (13). Better 'shoots'. Comparisons with trees and fruit are frequent in 'wasfs'. *Orchard* (13). The Heb. word *pardes* occurs only here and in Ne. ii. 8 and Ec. ii. 5. LXX renders *Paradeisos*. It is regarded by some as a mark of the late origin of the book. The word appears to be from a Persian source. *Saffron* (14). This word occurs here only, but the Arabic makes the meaning clear. The *Crocus saturus* is meant. Saffron is obtained by drying the pistil and stigma of the flower in the sun and then beating them to powder, which is used as a condiment. *Calamus and cinnamon* (14). The first is an aromatic cane found in India and Arabia Felix. The second is produced when the inner rind of a tree in the laurel family is separated from the outer bark and dried in the sun. It is a native of Ceylon. *Aloes* (14). This costly perfume has an aromatic odour when burned. It is obtained from eagle wood, which attains a height of 120 feet. The habitat of the tree is Northern India and Cochin China. In folksongs the allusions are as a rule homely, whereas the trees in this paradise are all exotics. The fruits of the Spirit are not native to the sinful heart. *A fountain of gardens* (15). Budde's translation, 'the fountain of my garden is a well of living water', is supported by LXX. Cambridge Bible renders 'Thou art the fountain of my garden'. She is the source of his delight and refreshment. Christ takes pleasure in the graces of the Church and when at length He presents her to Himself she will be a glorious Church without spot or wrinkle.

d. The Shulamite's appeal (iv. 16)

The bride speaks throughout. The north wind is the cool wind, the south wind is warm. The influence of both is needed in turn. The sometimes contrary activities of the Holy Spirit in the soul are suggested. They contribute to the same end, fruitfulness and fragrance.

e. Solomon's response (v. 1)

Eat, O friends (1). Some interpreters understand this to mean an invitation to the marriage: others take it to be an appeal to sympathize with the joy of the wedded pair. Stuart says the feast meant is not the marriage feast but the feast of espousal.

IV. THE SHULAMITE'S TARDY WELCOME AND PROLONGED SEARCH. v. 2—viii. 3

a. The Beloved's unexpected visit and departure (v. 2–6)

I sleep, but my heart waketh (2). Cf. Mt. xxvi. 40, 41, xxv. 5. *My head is filled with dew* (2). The dew of Palestine is usually very heavy. For the whole description of the appeal for admittance cf. Rev. iii. 14ff. *Coat* (3). LXX has *chiton*, i.e. the garment worn next to the skin. Like the man begging for bread at midnight, the Beloved has arrived at an unexpected and somewhat inconvenient hour. But the excuses are slight. The picture is one of slumber, sloth and self-indulgence.

By the hole (4). Eastern houses had an aperture above the lock for the insertion of the key, which was large enough to admit the hand. There might also be an opening through which the occupant of an apartment might look and speak. *Bowels* (4). We would say 'heart'. The idea is of deep compassion or strong desire. *Sweet smelling myrrh* (5). Myrrh that dropped naturally from the tree without incision and was most prized.

It was probably a token of welcome. *When he spake* (6). Stuart renders 'for his word'. Ewald suggests 'as he turned away'.

b. The Shulamite searches for and describes her Beloved (v. 7–16)

Watchmen (7). Cf. iii. 3n. She was misunderstood and wronged rather than helped. *Veil* (7). Century Bible and Cambridge Bible translate 'mantle', as RV. *I charge you* (8). Stuart comments that a seeking soul may find Christ before a deserted believer finds restored fellowship. *What is thy beloved?* (9), i.e. 'What sort of beloved?' The question gives occasion for the description which follows. Meditating on Christ's excellences is a means of kindling faith and love. *White and ruddy* (10). Cf. 1 Sa. xvi. 12; La. iv. 7. *Chiefest* (10). Lit. 'a standard bearer', i.e. eminent. *Bushy* (11). LXX renders 'palm buds'. 'Curled' may be a better translation. *Doves* (12). The pupil and iris of the eye surrounded by white form the point of comparison. *Fitly set* (12). Lit. 'setting in fulness'. The allusion is probably to the full round eyes which Orientals so greatly admire. *His cheeks are as a bed of spices* (13). The beard is perfumed. Cf. Ps. cxxxiii. 2. The beard in the East is a sign of strength and honour. *Lilies* (13). A red flower. Cf. ii. 1n. *His hands are as gold rings . . .* (14). Moffatt translates 'His fingers are golden tapers tipped with topaz pink', i.e. the fingers are delicately rounded and have beautiful nails. Some prefer, however, to render 'his hands *have* gold rings . . .'. *Beryl* (14). Heb. *tarshish*, a stone of Tarshish; either the topaz or chrysolite, found at Tartessus, an ancient city in Spain, between the mouths of the Guadalquiver. Cf. Ex. xxxix. 13. *Belly* (14). Better 'body'. *Bright ivory* (14). Ivory as treated by the sculptor closely resembled in colour the skin of the Eastern. The neck, breast and arms, so far as not covered by the robe, are meant. Literally the words mean 'a work of ivory' or 'wrought ivory'. Cf. Heb. x. 5. *Sapphires* (14). Some take the blue veins showing through the skin to be the ground of this description. Other commentators think a jewelled girdle is implied. Cf. Rev. i. 13. Sapphire, in Scripture, is suggestive of heaven. Cf. Ex. xxiv. 10. *Pillars of marble* (15). Marble treated with oil, as it sometimes was, would take on a flesh tint. The image is that of strength. *His countenance is as Lebanon . . .* (15), i.e. his aspect is majestic and noble. *His mouth* (16). Cf. Pr. xvi. 21; Ps. xlv. 2. *He is altogether lovely* (16). The literal translation is 'all of him is desirableness'. Christ revealed by the Holy Spirit is wholly attractive to the gracious soul. Century Bible cites a 'wasf' from Dalman's collection showing close resemblances in language with this section of the Song.

c. The Shulamite, questioned regarding her Beloved's whereabouts, replies and claims him for herself (vi. 1–3)

An impression has been produced on the daughters of Jerusalem by the description of the bridegroom. They desire to join in the search (1) but she declares that his affections are hers alone. She speaks with confidence although he is still absent. The fact that she knows where he has gone lends support to the suggestion that in v. 2–8 she was recounting a dream.

d. The Beloved addresses the Shulamite in words of ordinary praise (vi. 4–10)

Tirzah (4). This city was a place of importance and beauty. It was the seat of a Canaanite prince (Jos. xii. 24). Jeroboam I made it his capital (1 Ki. xiv. 17; cf. xv. 33). It ceased to be the capital when Omri, in the sixth year of his reign, built Samaria (1 Ki. xvi. 23, 24). The reference to it along with Jerusalem has been taken by some as an indication of a late date for the poem, either during the period when Tirzah was capital, or when, after the restoration from exile, hatred of Samaria might prevent its being selected. But all that is required is a town remarkable for strength and beauty. *Jerusalem* (4). Cf. La. ii. 15. The Shulamite is frequently compared to localities (see vii. 4, 5). Contrast Is. xlvii. 1 and Rev. xxi. 9. *An army with banners* (4). Lit. 'a bannered host'. LXX translates 'a terror as a ranked phalanx'. For the thought cf. Ex. xvii. 15; Ps. xlviii. 2–4. *Overcome* (5). The word is found elsewhere only in Ps. cxxxviii. 3. The usual meaning would have reference to the bewitching power of the eyes. LXX renders 'agitate', whence the meaning 'make spirited' is suggested. The looks of faith and love prevail with Christ. Verses 5–7 repeat with little variation the description of her beauty given in iv. 1ff., where see notes.

Threescore queens . . . (8). The underlying reference is to the polygamous practices of kings and wealthy persons. No special significance is to be attached to the numbers mentioned. Some have taken the group as representing various degrees of faith in the one Church; others with greater probability see a reference to worldly powers. *My dove . . . is but one* (9). The King of glory has but one bride, though a countless number make up the Church. *As the morning* (10). Or 'as the dawn', i.e. lovely and promise-bearing. The light of the moon is brighter than the light of the dawn; the light of the sun most splendid of all.

e. The Shulamite recounts her recent experience (vi. 11–13)

Nuts (11). Walnuts, which are commonly grown in North Palestine. Allegorically the garden of nuts has been taken to be the Word of God which yields its sweetness to those who use it diligently and prayerfully. *My soul made me like the chariots of Amminadib* (12). 'My soul set me among the chariots of my princely people' (RV). 'Amminadib' has never been identified. It is, therefore, common to take the word in two parts, as meaning 'princely people'. It might be better rendered 'companions of a prince'. Budde understands the reference to be to the 'wedding chariot' and renders 'While I was wandering . . . Hardly conscious of my deepest feeling my prince came and set me on the wedding car'. The verse is thought to be the most obscure in the Song, but the spiritual suggestion of an unexpected uplifting of soul or sudden experience of divine light and favour is sufficiently evident. This is probably the climax of the quest begun at verse 7 of the previous chapter.

O Shulamite (13). LXX renders 'maid of Shunem'; 'n' and 'l' are sometimes interchangeable in Palestinian names. Shunem was a place on the slopes of the eastern end of Little Hermon. Some think there may be a reference to Abishag as a type of beauty or to the bride's home. To take it as 'daughter of peace' seems preferable. *The company of two armies* (13). 'As upon the dance of Mahanaim' (RV). The AV takes the word as a dual. Cf. Gn. xxxii. 2. Mahanaim, a stronghold in North Gilead, was for a time Ishbosheth's capital. Perhaps there is an allusion to Jacob's vision. Century Bible translates 'a dance of two companies', and Moffatt 'the sword dance'. Stuart renders 'the conflict of Mahanaim' and takes the meaning to be 'the conflict of two armies', the flesh and the Spirit. By 'two armies' Durham understands 'an excellent army'. Cheyne alters the text to read 'a lily of the valleys'. On the whole, the rendering of the AV is preferable and the supposed reference to the 'sword dance', common at Eastern weddings, is improbable.

f. The Beloved praises her as a prince's daughter (vii. 1-9)

How beautiful (1). Cf. Is. lii. 7; Lk. xv. 22; Eph. vi. 15. *Prince's daughter* (1). Cf. Ps. xlv. 13. The words suggest the nobility of the new birth and the resulting enrichment of character. *Joints* (1). Cambridge Bible renders 'thy rounded thighs'. The point might thus be a comparison between the graceful movement and some pendulous ornament. But keeping the AV we have, on the allegorical view, a striking description of the unity of the Church brought about by the Holy Spirit. Cf. Eph. iv. 16. *Navel* (2). The word thus translated usually means the lower part of the body. Stuart renders it 'girdle clasp'. A goblet is thought of as most beautiful when filled with liquor. *An heap of wheat* (2). Heaps of wheat, decorated with flowers, were placed in parallel rows on Eastern threshing-floors. The colour of wheat was believed to be the most beautiful the body could have. The reference, however, may be to the embroidery of the dress. Cf. Ps. xlv. 13, 14. *Tower of ivory* (4). Decorated with ivory. Cf. Ps. xlv. 8. The ideas suggested are freedom and beauty. *Fishpools* (4). AV follows Vulgate but is not supported by the Hebrew. Better 'pools' as in RV. *Heshbon* (4) was the ancient capital of Sihon. It later belonged to Reuben but, in Isaiah's time, was in the hands of Moab. Many reservoirs were found among its ruins. The comparison seems to point to depth and clearness. *Bath-rabbim* (4). Lit. 'daughter of multitudes', indicating the number

passing through the gate. *Tower of Lebanon* (4). A well-known watch-tower is no doubt intended. The word 'nose' may also mean face. So the description may refer to a courageous countenance. *Carmel* (5). It appears better to keep the proper name than to render 'crimson' as AV mg. This mountain appears from the north towering over the surrounding country in solitary grandeur and is a fit symbol of majesty. *Hair* (5). Black hair has sometimes a purple sheen. Cf. iii. 10n. *The king is held in the galleries* (5). For 'galleries' cf. i. 17n. An alternative rendering is 'a king caught and bound by thy tresses'. The figure of the lover held in the locks of the beloved is common in Eastern poetry and is found in English literature. *Palm tree* (7). Tamar, the word for 'palm', was commonly a girl's name, this tall and graceful tree being regarded as a type of female beauty. It is also a type of the Church, or the believer. Cf. Ps. xcii. 12. *Apples* (8). The fragrance of the apple is highly appreciated in the East. *And the roof of thy mouth* (9). The reference is probably to speech. Wine revives the faint. The gospel proclaimed by the Church quickens the dead and restores the living.

g. The Shulamite invites him to accompany her to the open countryside (vii. 10—viii. 3)

Let us go forth into the field (11). Pastoral language is resumed, and the Shulamite is the speaker. The words of the request have been taken allegorically to suggest the desire of the Church to go forth into the highways and hedges in self-denying quest of the lost and in company with the Son of Man, who came to seek and to save the lost. But meanwhile she will not be unmindful of the development of grace within herself. If service is to be sustained and fruitful it must be accompanied with a due proportion of prayer and self-examination. *Mandrakes* (13). They belong to the potato family and have a cup-shaped flower of purple colour. The fruit resembles the plum, has a peculiar fragrance and was supposed to save from barrenness (cf. Gn. xxx. 14n.). Their presence fixes the time as May. *At our gates* (13). The allusion is to fruit stored on shelves. Cf. Jn. xv. 8.

O that thou wert as my brother (viii. 1). Only a brother having the same mother and a father's brother's son have the right to kiss a maiden among the Bedouin. Cf. Gn. xxix. 11. The desire expressed is for public acknowledgment of love. *My mother's house* (2). She wishes to bring him to her home. They render Christ good service who introduce Him to their family circle and freely acknowledge Him in home life. *Who would instruct me* (2). Better, perhaps, 'thou wouldest instruct'. *Juice of the pomegranate* (2). Sherbet made from pomegranate juice is a popular drink in the East. *His left hand* (3). The desire for intimate fellowship with the Beloved expressed in this verse appears to pass into realization in the following one in which the charge to the daughters of Jerusalem again occurs (see ii. 7, iii. 5). Compare how frequently, in the Psalms, the spiritual blessing desired is presently spoken of as realized.

V. THE SHULAMITE AND THE BELOVED CONVERSE. viii. 4–14

a. With the Beloved by her side the Shulamite declares her love, faithfulness and resolution (viii. 4–12)

Who is this . . .? (5). Questions are used in the Song to arrest attention and to fasten it upon some important picture. Cf. iii. 6. The words recall Israel. Love supports and leads to rest. We are also reminded of the Church and the believer. On their part there is dependence and heavenward progress. *Thee* (5). 'Thee' and 'thy' are masculine, but many commentators follow the Syriac, which makes them feminine. Some allegorical interpreters, following the AV, have seen a reference to the service rendered to Jesus at the cross, whence His dead body was conveyed by secret disciples to the tomb. It may be better, however, to take the pronouns as feminine. The description then points to the place where she was inspired with love.

Set me . . . (6). This verse may be regarded as one of the finest descriptions of love ever penned. *Seal* (6). Cf. Je. xxii. 24; Hg. ii. 23. The seal worn suspended from a cord round the neck, or as a bracelet, was a symbol of something dear. The earliest form, found at Babylon, was cylindrical. The seal would remind him of her, even when he was away from her. Cf. Is. xlix. 16. *Love is strong as death* (6). Death cannot overcome it, though so powerful to conquer and destroy. It failed to overthrow the love of Christ and the martyrs. The victory is with love in the case of every true believer, but it is love sustained by Christ. *Jealousy is cruel as the grave* (6). The grave is all-devouring; so is jealousy, which will brook no rival. The Church and the believer should be jealous for the honour of Christ. He is jealous for His own rights. *A most vehement flame* (6). Lit. 'a flame of God'. This is the only place where the name of God occurs in the book. It may be understood in the sense of the AV or we may translate with Ewald 'its flames are as the flames of Jehovah'. *It would utterly be contemned* (7). Or 'they would utterly despise him'. There can be no substitute for love. Christ's love alone can satisfy the soul. It reaches His people by way of the sacrifice of the cross. He will be satisfied with nothing less than their love in return.

We have a little sister (8). Some scholars take this statement as recalling the words of the brothers in earlier days with reference to the Shulamite herself. The allegorists understand them as a prophetic allusion to the Gentile Church, which was in due time to share all the privileges at first reserved for the Jews. *If she be a wall* (9). The wall and door are taken by some interpreters as meaning chastity and its opposite. The meaning then would be that if she proved virtuous they would provide for her a suitable marriage; otherwise they would take the greater precautions. Allegorists, however, understand the reference to be to the acceptance on the part of the Jewish Church of God's calling of the Gentiles, building them into the living temple and opening to them the door of faith. *I am a wall* (10). This is a declaration on the part of the Shulamite of her virtuous character and maturity. On the allegorical view it is seen as an acknowledgment by the Gentile Church of God's goodness to her in preparing her to welcome the gospel.

Solomon had a vineyard (11). If Solomon here is a type of Messiah, the interpretation of this section is seen in the parables in Is. v. 1ff. and Mk. xii. 1ff. *Baal-hamon* (11). The place has not been identified. It must have been noted for fertility. Aglen translates 'a vineyard was to Solomon as Lord of a multitude'. *A thousand pieces of silver* (11). Shekels are intended. Cf. Gn. xx. 16. It was not unusual for vineyards to be hired out in portions. Cf. Is. vii. 23. The allegorists point out that this bargain was unfulfilled by the Jewish Church and see in the following verse the transference of the vineyard to the Gentiles. The Gentile Church, while regarding it as her sphere of service, is to have due regard to the fact that it is the Lord's vineyard. The words are a declaration that His concerns will henceforward have first place.

b. The Beloved about to depart asks that he may hear her voice (viii. 13)

Thou that dwellest in the gardens (13). Words spoken by the Beloved. Prayer to Christ is not to be restrained, while the Church engages in service among men.

c. The Shulamite desires that his return may be hastened (viii. 14)

The mountains of spices (14). These suggest the heavenly place, where Jesus engages in intercession on the ground of His finished work. The prayer of this verse recalls the words with which the book of Revelation closes, 'Even so, come, Lord Jesus.'

W. J. CAMERON.

ISAIAH

INTRODUCTION

See also the General Article 'The Prophetical Literature of the Old Testament', p. 45.

I. ISAIAH, THE MAN

Amongst 'the goodly fellowship of the prophets' Isaiah stands forth regal and pre-eminent. In the majesty and originality of his thought, as also in the superlative quality of his speech, he is unique in the Old Testament. None can so worthily be called the 'evangelical prophet' as he. His name means 'Jehovah saves' or 'Jehovah is salvation', and through days of crisis and disaster, unprecedented in the history of his people, he constantly recalled to faith in the One who alone could deliver. In hours when hope seemed dead he was an inspiration and a challenge to the drooping spirits of the men of Judah. His ministry was a long one, continuing from the time of his call to the prophetic office in the reign of Uzziah, king of Judah, on through the reigns of Jotham, Ahaz and Hezekiah, with a possible short period of service during the time of Manasseh. All through these years he was a statesman who read the broad meaning of events in the big political issues of the time, as well as the appointed and chosen prophet of the Lord proclaiming the divine purpose with unfaltering conviction and passionate heart.

His father's name was Amoz (Is. i. 1, ii. 1), and there is a Jewish tradition that he was a brother of king Amaziah; in which case Isaiah would be the cousin of king Uzziah. It is of course impossible to be certain of this, but there are clear indications that Isaiah did indeed have definite opportunity for immediate and regular entrance to the royal house, as well as having the ear of the most influential people of his day. Despite this, he remained the simple and undaunted spokesman for Jehovah, and for this—so tradition again affirms—was ultimately put to death, in the wicked reign of Manasseh. He was married, his wife being called by himself 'the prophetess' (Is. viii. 3); to them were born two sons, Shear-jashub (Is. vii. 3) and Maher-shalal-hash-baz (Is. viii. 3), their names being given to them as portents of what was to come and as a reinforcement of the prophet's predictive message. Apart from this, little else is known of his personal history save what is contained in the book itself. It is not possible to affirm with exactness the duration of his ministry; we do know that for at least forty years he continued to labour, from the last year of Uzziah in 740 B.C. to the fourteenth of Hezekiah in 701 B.C., and that all through this period of time his call and challenge were unremitting and persistent, and his aim ever clear and definite—the establishment of the worship of the Lord in righteousness and truth amongst the chosen race.

II. FORMATIVE INFLUENCES

The most outstanding and lasting influence in the life of Isaiah was undoubtedly his own personal and direct call to the ministry of the prophet's office within the temple precincts after the death of Uzziah. This is recorded for us with a beauty and brilliance that clearly indicate the power with which the vision affected him all through his ministry. It is probably true to say that in all the literature of Oriental peoples, nothing has ever been found to surpass the grandeur and dignity of this immortal passage in Is. vi. Upon the youthful Isaiah as he enters the temple precincts there bursts this awe-inspiring sight—the uplifted Lord, the celestial train, the mystic seraphim, the shekinah of holiness, the voice of commission to the prophet prostrated before the majesty thus revealed, the divine authentication of his coming ministry. In the midst of the disturbed and uncertain political scene, he learns with all the power of direct revelation that the Lord God is enthroned on high, and that the seal of His commandment now rests upon him. From that there was no escape. Even though it meant bringing to the peoples of his day a message that they would not receive, there could be no going back from the glory of the revelation thus given. Thus it was that Isaiah came forth from the temple with a new vision and a new sense of the high and holy hazards of the mission entrusted to him and of the office he must now assume.

Prior to this outstanding and determinative experience, there was the effect of the ministry of Amos and Hosea which must have been fresh in the memory and experience of the youthful Isaiah. In times of national need there had been in Israel, as in Judah, the message of the Lord at one time or another through the voices of the prophets, and traces of the distinctive elements of their messages are to be found in the words of Isaiah. To one with a set purpose of heart to walk in the way of the Lord these voices must have brought an incalculable measure of inspiration, and the warm and moving words of the evangelical prophet as he points to the Redeemer of all Israel are reminiscent of the accents in which these earlier servants of Jehovah had proclaimed the divine call.

Besides these, Isaiah must have been profoundly stirred by the massive movements of the times. During the reign of the good king Uzziah, Judah was at-peace for many years and knew little of the difficulties in which the northern kingdom was involved. There was the outward appearance of peace and piety. But underneath, and at the very heart of the nation's life, there was an unrest and a pronounced turning away from the reality of the worship ordained for them in the covenant. (See Appendix I to Kings, 'The Religion of Israel under the Monarchy'.) Abroad, the horizon was already dark with omens of invasion and crisis; and for all the chosen people Isaiah must have seen clearly, in the most formative period of his life, that unless there was a turning to the Lord there could be nothing but disaster ahead. In a certain sense, we are all the products of our environment; we come to the hour of testing either to be measured to its magnitude and to determine its direction, or else to be moulded by its titanic force. In the case of Isaiah, we have one of the most striking cases of the hour being matched with the man and of a voice being raised at the very moment of the greatest need for the telling forth of the counsel of God.

To the task to which he was called, Isaiah was able to bring a superlative gift and felicity of expression and an insight that under God was to become the medium of the most intimate and profound truths of revelation. Thus uniquely endowed for the ministry to which he was called and trained in the school of experience for the coming test, in the year that king Uzziah died and when the throne which for so long had been occupied with such distinction was once more vacant, the prophet was ready for the high commission of the uplifted and transcendent Lord, and was not disobedient to the heavenly vision.

III. CHRONOLOGY

See also Appendix III to Kings, 'The Great Empires during the Period of the Monarchy'.

745	Tiglath-pileser III ascends the throne of Assyria.
740	Death of Uzziah. Succession of Jotham to the throne. Vision of Isaiah and commission of the prophet to the ministry of the Holy One of Israel.
736	Death of Jotham. Succession of Ahaz to the throne. The northern kingdom allies with Syria to attack Judah.
734–732	Tiglath-pileser attacks and invades Israel and Syria. Visit of Ahaz to Damascus.
727	Ascension of Shalmaneser to the throne of Assyria in the place of Tiglath-pileser.
725	Enthronement of Hezekiah in succession to Ahaz.
722	Ascension of Sargon II to the throne of Assyria in the place of Shalman-

eser. Capture of Samaria. The captivity of Israel.

711	Sargon invades Syria. Ashdod is captured.
709	Capture of Babylon.
705	Sargon is murdered. Sennacherib succeeds.
701	Sennacherib's invasion of Judah.

IV. THE JUDAEAN KINGS DURING THE LIFE OF ISAIAH

Isaiah was born during the reign of the good king Uzziah, and it was in the last year of that monarch's life that he received the call to the prophetic office. The character of Uzziah was acknowledged by all to be of an exemplary kind, and in every way he showed a spirit of true piety and honour for the things of God, although, in his later years, the king suffered from leprosy due to an act of overweening pride (see 2 Ch. xxvi. 16–21). During his reign, the nation as a whole enjoyed times of prosperity and temporal development, and it was with the sorrow of the nation that he passed from the scene at a time when his presence seemed needed the most. The worship of Jehovah was encouraged, but he was not sufficiently strong to secure the destruction of the high places where idolatrous practices were continued. His reign must be ranked as one of the most outstanding of the southern kingdom. After him there came to the throne Jotham his son, who had already acted as regent in the time of Uzziah's segregation. He walked in the ways of his father and under him the people continued to worship the Lord Jehovah after the manner of the commandment, though still the asherim and places of idolatry were allowed to remain. To the superficial view there might have appeared evidence of true and deep devotion, but in reality it was not so. On every side there was a rapid and spontaneous growth of the spirit of luxury and indulgence, and in the midst of this it is not surprising that the spirit of true piety was declining steadily. (See Appendix I to Kings, 'The Religion of Israel under the Monarchy'.) Following him there arose Ahaz, whose whole reign was a chronicle of disaster and destruction (see 2 Ki. xvi). With an absolute abandon, Ahaz gave himself over to the overthrow of the ordained order of worship, broke the commandment in almost every detail, destroyed the temple worship and finally closed the doors of the house of God. In the most calculated manner he conspired to obliterate the memory of the service of the Lord of all Israel, the Redeemer and the Holy One. All that he did was as a goad to the devout and outspoken prophet Isaiah. He came forth and publicly rebuked the king for his extravagances in religious things, reproved him for his sin, and arraigned him before the people as an enemy of the true way. All to no avail. His warnings and advice were disregarded by the nation, led by the king himself. Then came

Hezekiah. Unlike his father, Hezekiah endeavoured in many ways to revive the worship of the sanctuary; he did his best to abolish idolatry and to deliver the people under him from the power of foreign dominion. Under him, Isaiah came into his own and was regarded with very great favour. He was given every opportunity for the use of his keen and divinely inspired power of discernment into the facts of the contemporary situation. But the seeds of the nation's past folly were now beginning to come to fruition and it was actually too late to institute reforms that might be effective and wholesome. The overthrow of the nation which Isaiah had for so long prophesied was at hand and nothing could delay it.

It will be readily seen, therefore, that the prophet's task during the days of his long and active ministry was no easy one. The commission given to him in the day of his call was amply fulfilled, for the message that he brought was indeed a message of doom, and the prophecy then made, that he would bring the word of the Lord which would be heard and not understood, was fulfilled to the very letter. The glory of the life of Isaiah is that he did not shirk the issue when the call came to him. Throughout those dark years, as the nation went on steadily and with ever-increasing momentum towards the precipice and disaster, he continued to proclaim the word of the Lord and to stand as a rock of truth in the midst of the swirling tides of the world's infidelity and irreligion.

V. AUTHORSHIP: THE SPECIAL PROBLEM OF CHAPTERS XL—LXVI

a. The problem stated

This great section of the book of Isaiah has presented sharp critical problems for many years and no study of the book as a whole would be complete without reference to this matter. For nearly a century the Isaianic authorship of chapters xl to lxvi has been defended, questioned, denied. Names such as 'The Babylonian Isaiah', 'The Deutero-Isaiah' and 'The Great Unnamed' have been ascribed to this section of the book and are now commonplaces in the field of study. Many will readily admit with Professor A. B. Davidson that the question 'is one of fact and criticism exclusively, and not a matter of faith and practice'. It will probably also be admitted that on both sides judgment has been influenced by the student's attitude to predictive prophecy. Our aim in this short introduction will be to state as objectively as possible the chief arguments adduced in support of the two main contentions, since nothing is to be gained by ignoring the case put forward by those who disagree with us.

In Hastings' *Dictionary of the Bible* G. A. Smith writes: 'Chapters xl to lxvi have no title and make no claim to be by Isaiah. xl to xlviii plainly set forth the ruin of Jerusalem and the exile as having already taken place. Israel is addressed as if the time of their servitude to Babylon were exhausted and their deliverance is proclaimed as immediate. Cyrus is named as their saviour and is pointed out as already upon his career, and blessed with success by Jehovah. For, as part of an argument for the unique divinity of the God of Israel, Cyrus, "alive and irresistible, and already accredited with success, is pointed out as the unmistakable proof that former prophecies of a deliverance for Israel are already coming to pass. Cyrus, in short, is not presented as a prediction, but as a proof that a prediction is being fulfilled. Unless he had already appeared and was on the point of striking at Babylon, with all the prestige of unbroken victory, a great part of xl to xlviii would be unintelligible." There is thus a very clear date for these chapters; they must have been written between 555 B.C., Cyrus' advent, and 538 B.C., Babylon's fall.'

Such a quotation presents in the most lucid form the situation confronting the student of Isaiah. Further, it is most important to note the different viewpoints of the two main divisions of the book. In chapters i—xxxix, for instance, the prophet is clearly addressing his own generation, confronting a contemporary situation with the living message of his God; but chapters xl—lxvi are addressed to a generation a century and a half after his time, the captives in Babylon. There is no doubt that the Spirit of God could well have used Isaiah to speak to a distant generation, and prediction is an incontrovertible element in prophecy. But those who regard these chapters as coming from a later hand argue that this is straining judgment, and in large measure going contrary to the normal procedure of the prophets of Israel through whom the divine Word came in power to a living situation. With chapters xl—xlviii so evidently setting forth the ruin of Jerusalem and the exile as having already taken place, is it not to be assumed as probable, they say, that the message addressed in these verses to the children of Israel comes from the voice of one dwelling among them?

b. Arguments in favour of the unity of the book

Within the compass of this work, which is not of a specifically critical nature, it is not possible to make any detailed study of this problem. But the outstanding points on both sides of the question may with profit be summarized.

In favour of the unity of Isaiah all evidence that can be adduced from outside sources is unanimous. External evidence is all in favour of the unity of the book. It is only within the last hundred years that any question at all has been raised. Until then the unhesitating belief of the Jewish community and the Christian Church had regarded the whole work as proceeding from the pen of Isaiah the son of Amoz. The LXX gives no hint of any kind of dual authorship. In no better way has the old belief been recounted than by the son of Sirach who tells of the record of the days of Hezekiah and says that Isaiah the prophet . . .

> *Saw by an excellent spirit what should come to*
> *pass at the last;*
> *And he comforted them that mourned in Sion.*
> *He shewed the things that should be to the end*
> *of time,*
> *And the hidden things or ever they came.'*
> (Ecclus. xlviii. 24–25, RV)

Side by side with this are to be set the many passages from the New Testament where reference is made to Isaiah and his words are quoted. 'Isaiah the prophet' is spoken of irrespective of the part of the book from which the words are taken. The actual references are divided almost equally between the two sections of the book, those to the latter part being slightly the more numerous. This in itself is a confirmation of the view of the external evidence and that of the tradition of the Fathers.

The argument from language is always difficult, and great debate has taken place upon the considerations raised by words and phrases that are common to both sections, as also upon those that are peculiar to one or the other. Into this it is impossible to enter, though some brief comment must be made on the significance of the special appellation of Jehovah as the 'Holy One of Israel'. This phrase is found in both sections of the book, but occurs hardly anywhere else in the Bible canon. As being one of the outstanding descriptions of God common to both sections, this is a matter of primary importance.

Too great reliance must not be set upon the evidence of subtle and intricate distinction in style and language as between the two sections. To say, for example, that the word for 'righteousness' occurs about seventeen times in the second part and only four or five times in the first; that the word for 'work' or 'reward' is found five times in the second and not at all in the first; that the word meaning 'also', or something akin to that, recurs no less than twenty-two times in the first and not at all in the second; to say all that and much more is in itself to prove little, since a whole catalogue of words and phrases peculiar to both sections could easily be compiled. The very distinction between the two sections in the type of message being given in itself calls forth a distinctiveness of language. Where the first section is characterized by a spirit of tremendous energy and drive, chapters xl to lxvi are full of moving pathos, suffused with solemn beauty and carried forward on the wings of deep, eternal harmony. Like all great poetry there are passages in which repetition and duplication of phrase are found; but to the unbiased student the very grandeur of the message of redemption and messianic hope, as distinct from straightforward history or a record of coming judgment upon the nations around, will appear as sufficient cause for any distinctiveness in style and language. As to literary style,

even Dr. Driver, who selects eighteen words or phrases in chapters xl to lxvi, has to yield twelve of them as having parallels in the first section. Indeed, sober criticism has advanced that this question of diversity in style has been immensely exaggerated. It is found that there are more than three hundred words and expressions which are common to both the alleged 'former' and 'latter' sections of Isaiah, and which find no place whatsoever in the later prophecies of Daniel, Haggai, Zechariah and Malachi.

Another element which must be kept in mind in the present discussion as favouring the unity of the book is that the local colouring in the second section, as much as in the first, is mostly, and very strikingly, that of Judaea. On this, the following quotation from Angus and Green's *Bible Handbook* (p. 502) is worthy of note:

'Rocks, mountains, and forests are in the prophet's landscapes; the horizon of his view extends to the islands of the sea; the flocks are those of Kedar; the rams those of Nebaioth; the trees are the cedar and the acacia, the pine and the box, with the oaks of Bashan and the woodland heights of Carmel. In particular, that terrible section which describes the lingering idolatries of Judah (lvi. 9—lvii. 21) places the scene of them "in the torrent-valleys, under the cliffs of the rocks, among the smooth stones of the stream". "As there are," writes Dean Payne Smith, "no torrents, but only canals, in the flat, alluvial soil of Babylonia, so there are no torrent-beds there; but these form a common feature of the landscape in Palestine and all mountainous countries." '

Evidence such as this cannot be passed over lightly and it is the present writer's view that the manifestation of local colouring, as being so remarkably Palestinian, overweighs any evidence of apparent allusion to facts and incidents of Babylonian life in the later chapters.

Furthermore, whatever may be said of the rest of the later chapters, those which contain the awesome section describing the carnal idolatries of apostate Israel are so completely divorced from all that we know of Babylonia and the Jewish exile there, that they must be referred to another place and period. It is beyond question that there is very much in Israel's earlier history and her dealings with the nations around her borders from which material could have been culled for these dreadful passages.

The question must also be faced: How did so distinguished a prophet as that of the writer of Is. xl—lxvi disappear completely into the unknown? The carefully kept records of the Hebrew Church know nothing of another author. In several of the collections, as has been pointed out, Ezra and Nehemiah were bound together but were never confused by the Jew; their separate identity was always maintained. It would surely be one of the most amazing literary marvels of all time if the author of a book so majestic and sublime should be unnamed and the race in whose language he wrote and whose scribes were so exact in their compilation of records should without question have identified him with one of their most outstanding prophets.

In recent years further weight has been given to the arguments for unity through the discovery of the Dead Sea Scrolls. In them there is no break in the MSS of Isaiah between the end of chapter xxxix and the beginning of chapter xl. As a matter of fact chapter xl begins on the last line of the page. Obviously no final conclusions can be drawn from this, but as an element in a cumulative argument it must be considered important.

One final word. We do not know exactly under what circumstances Isaiah lived in the latter days of his life. Under threat of death at the hands of the godless Manasseh (2 Ki. xxi. 16), he may well have been forced out of the glare of public life into the shelter of some secluded retreat. This would present a situation rather similar to that in which John wrote the book of Revelation on the Isle of Patmos. He too looked far into the future and wrote of what he saw. Might not this prophet, Isaiah, son of Amoz, faced with the decline of true religion in his own Jerusalem, 'the home of God's elect', have found the Spirit of the Lord leading him to see and declare the deathless hope of the true children of Zion and to proclaim for generations yet unborn the matchlessness of the salvation of his God?

c. Arguments against the unity of the book

It must, however, be readily admitted that the great preponderance of critical opinion is against the unity of the book. Indeed Professor W. L. Wardle, writing in Dr. Peake's Commentary, goes so far as to say of these latter chapters of Isaiah: 'No critical conclusion is more certain than that they belong to a later period.' The evidence in favour of this may be fairly summarized as follows.

The greatest problem of all lies in the change of situation, time and place which shows itself in chapter xl. To all appearances the prophecies which begin there seem to be spoken to the captive children of Israel in Babylon and at a period of their captivity when deliverance seems imminent. If these words are from the pen of Isaiah, he is obviously no longer a preacher of righteousness to his own generation but a seer, caught up to a plane of vision where he beholds events that will come to pass a century and a half later. His words of prophecy thereby become a legacy to generations still unborn and not the inspired utterance of one caught in the tide of contemporary events together with his brethren.

There is obviously nothing impossible in this, though it differs somewhat from the usual practice of the prophets. While many will readily admit that prediction of the future is an essential and integral part of prophecy, it yet seems to them that such a facing of a situation only to arise a century and a half later is so exceptional as to be, failing conclusive evidence to the contrary, highly improbable. In a supplementary note to his work on Isaiah, Professor Cheyne quotes the words of Dean Bradley, before the University of Oxford in 1875, where he sketches this predictive view in most graphic language:

'The Isaiah,' he says, 'of the vexed and stormy times of Ahaz and Hezekiah is supposed in his later days to have been transplanted by God's Spirit into a time and a region other than his own . . . He is led in prolonged and solitary vision into a land that he has never trodden, and to a generation on whom he has never looked. The familiar scenes and faces, among which he had lived and laboured, have grown dim and disappeared. All sounds and voices of the present are hushed, and the interests and passions into which he had thrown himself with all the intensity of his race and character move him no more. The present has died out of the horizon of his soul's vision . . . The voices in his ears are those of men unborn, and he lives a second life among events and persons, sin and suffering, and fears and hopes, photographed sometimes with the minutest accuracy on the sensitive and sympathetic medium of his own spirit; and he becomes the denouncer of the special sins of a distant generation and the spokesman of the faith and the hope and passionate yearning of an exiled nation, the descendants of the men living when he wrote in the profound peace of a renewed prosperity.'

When we are studying passages that make reference to the existing condition of the land, it is normal to assume that we are reading the words of a contemporary. But this position is completely reversed if we accept the unity of Isaiah. Had chapters xl to xlviii come to us anonymously, they would most naturally have been assigned to the period of the captivity. In chapter xli the writer touches with a sure brush on a historical situation and very soon is delineating it most clearly. Cyrus, the deliverer, is presented as a world figure, and in xliv. 24—xlv. 25 we find a whole set of prophecies dealing with his work and mission. It is argued that if this is predictive writing by Isaiah of Jerusalem it is an absolutely exceptional utterance with no parallel in all other prophetic literature. In this context it is also pointed out that these chapters nowhere claim Isaiah's authorship and are, indeed, separated from the rest of the work which is clearly his by a historical narrative of some length.

In his recent discussion of the entire subject Professor C. R. North deals at length with the Suffering Servant of 'Deutero-Isaiah'. Two quotations may profitably be given here. 'As long as it was believed that the Book of Isaiah was entirely the work of an eighth-century Prophet, it was natural to assume that those portions of it which have an exilic background must be prophecy in the predictive sense of the word. Accordingly the Messianic interpretation of the Servant seemed obvious. But no sooner was there talk of a Babylonian Isaiah than Christian scholars began to adopt the view that had long prevailed among the Jews, namely, that the Servant was the nation Israel.' (From the chapter entitled 'Christian Interpretations: From Doederlein to Duhm'.) Again, on p. 207, he writes: 'The fundamental objection to the traditional Messianic interpretation is that it is wedded to a too mechanical doctrine of inspiration. This seems to put it out of court as unworthy of serious consideration. The Prophet is a mere amanuensis, and what he writes has no relevance to the circumstances of his own time. Moreover, if this implies that he "sees" in advance One who was not to come for another five or six centuries, it raises the difficult philosophical problem whether there can be an actual prevision of history.'

These are large claims and demand much greater and more detailed study than this work can give. They do, however, in succinct and emphatic form express the standpoint of the critical school concerning the question now under discussion. It may fairly be asked, however, whether a doctrine of inspiration which does not include the possibility of vision to the very ends of history can be regarded as adequate. And furthermore, is not the messianic hope among the greatest of the influences which moulded, preserved and purified the spirit of Israel? Could there be such a hope without prophetic prevision?

It is frequently pointed out that Cyrus is presented, not only as a fact of history visible before their eyes, but that this fact is adduced as proof of the fulfilment of prophecies of long ago. It is this fact which makes it difficult to accept the argument that here the prophet is using what is called the 'prophetic perfect'—viz. that in the eagerness of his speech and the certainty that certain things must come to pass, he employed a form of speech implying that the events have already taken place. George Adam Smith puts the argument thus:

'It is not only that the prophecy, with what might be the mere ardour of vision, represents the Persian as already above the horizon and upon the flowing tide of victory; but that, in the course of a sober argument for the unique divinity of the God of Israel, which takes place throughout chapters xli to xlviii, Cyrus, alive and irresistible, already accredited by success, and with Babylonia at his feet, is pointed out as the unmistakable proof that former prophecies of a deliverance for Israel are at last coming to pass. Cyrus, in short, is not presented as a prediction, but as the proof that a prediction is being fulfilled. Unless he had already appeared in flesh and blood, and was on the point of striking at Babylon, with all the prestige of unbroken victory, a great part of Isaiah xli to xlviii would be utterly unintelligible.'

Passing from the study of the historical situation it might be noted that the very evidence of apparent lack of Babylonian local colour is in itself adduced as a strong argument for the exilic date. Exiles of every age and race are accustomed to live in the spirit of the home for which they long. The very brokenness of their hearts makes it impossible for them to become true citizens of an alien society and instinctively thoughts arise of other scenes. So too would it be for the Jewish people, banished as they were from Zion, city of their God. And, furthermore, much of the literature of their people would be before them and their souls would be steeped in its beauty and grandeur. These, and not the barren, level plains of the land of their captivity, would be the fountainhead of their inspiration when they spoke.

All that is self-evident. But it is also urged by some that the absence of local colour from the prophecy of Isaiah has been greatly exaggerated. Here, for example, is a statement of the contrary kind: '. . . break after break of Babylonian light and shadow falling across our path—the temples, the idol-manufactories, the processions of images, the diviners and astrologers, the gods and altars especially cultivated by the characteristic mercantile spirit of the place; the shipping of that mart of nations, the crowds of her merchants; the glitter of many waters, and even that intolerable glare, which so frequently curses the skies of Mesopotamia (xlix. 10). . . . The beasts he mentions have for the most part been recognized as familiar in Babylonia; and while the same cannot be said of the trees and plants he names, it has been observed that the passages, into which he brings them, are passages where his thoughts are fixed on the restoration to Palestine' (G. A. Smith, *The Book of Isaiah*, II, pp. 13f.).

Finally it is urged that the contrast between Jeremiah and the book of Isaiah in regard to the form of the prediction of captivity is quite unique if indeed chapters xl—lxvi are from precaptivity days. Jeremiah spoke of exile and of the certainty of deliverance, but always in the future tense. Both of these he openly and distinctively predicted but with a reserve and reticence about details which, it is said, are quite inexplicable if these later chapters of Isaiah had already been written and by such an outstanding prophet as Isaiah. The appeal addressed by the prophet is to a people long-suffering under the hand of God; and it is to men and women whose conscience has been quickened and convicted by the chastening power of hardship and sorrow that the hope of deliverance comes and the deliverer, Cyrus, is proclaimed as the instrument of their God.

d. A summary of the evidence

In favour of a divided authorship we have seen that there is no directly explicit evidence in the book itself to prove that it was all by the prophet himself; that chapters xl—lxvi at no point claim to be from the pen of Isaiah, and that they represent the exile as not only having taken place but actually nearing its end with Cyrus about to accomplish the fall of Babylonia. Furthermore, such other evidence as is available —the language and style of writing, the theology and standpoint of the prophet's message—in no way conflicts with the theory of a later date. There is the further issue raised by some of a too mechanical theory of inspiration which makes the prophet to write of things irrelevant to his time and speak of the Suffering Servant of God as One far removed from the contemporary scene.

On the other side, in favour of the unity of the book, we have noted that external evidence is all in favour of unity; that the argument from language is as effective in favour of unity as of disunity, if not more so; that the local colouring is pre-eminently that of Judaea; that there are certain sections in chapters xl—lxvi which even on the critical view must be pre-exilic; and that the disappearance of such a remarkable author from the scene of history and the field of literature is hard to be explained.

We have already referred to Dr. A. B. Davidson's standpoint in the opening paragraph of this section. His final conclusion is stated in the following way: 'Such questions ought to be kept as far away as possible from all interference with the articles of religion. How can it affect one's religious condition whether he believes Isaiah to be the single author of the prophecies attributed to him or to have had others joined with him? And I wish to say that I think we ought to repudiate and resent the attempts that are made to make the question one of religious belief, and to endeavour so to place the question that it does not become so.'

While that is so, it remains true that 'the almost unanimous acceptance during twenty-five centuries of the Isaianic authorship of the entire book of Isaiah can only be accounted for by the fact that such a view of it is fully in accord with the conception of Prophecy set forth in the Bible as a whole' (O. T. Allis, *The Unity of Isaiah*, p. 122). If prediction is accepted as a fundamental element of the prophet's message, if the address to his contemporaries is the pointing forward to the One who was to come, and if, as illustration of the mighty providential movements of history, God makes him to see in advance that which is to be in order that he might with greater effect preach to his people, and also that the record in times subsequent might authenticate the prophetic word, then the conclusion is inevitable that the book is indivisible.

NOTE: *The passages of verse translation quoted in this commentary are largely taken from* Isaiah in Modern Speech *by J. E. McFadyen (1918), by kind permission of the publishers, Messrs. James Clarke and Co. Ltd.*

OUTLINE OF CONTENTS

The book of Isaiah falls naturally into the two distinct sections of chapters i—xxxix and chapters xl—lxvi. These parts must be treated separately and consideration given to each of them individually. See Section V of the Introduction.

CHAPTERS I—XXXIX

I. PROPHECIES CENTRED ON JUDAH AND JERUSALEM. i. 1—xii. 6

II. PROPHECIES DIRECTED AGAINST FOREIGN AND HOSTILE NATIONS. xiii. 1—xxiii. 18

III. ISAIAH'S APOCALYPSE: THE JUDGMENTS OF JEHOVAH AGAINST THE WORLD'S SIN. xxiv. 1—xxvii. 13

IV. PROPHECIES CONCERNING THE RELATION OF JUDAH AND JERUSALEM TO EGYPT AND ASSYRIA. xxviii. 1—xxxiii. 24

V. PROPHECIES PROCLAIMING THE DOOM OF EDOM AND THE REDEMPTION OF ISRAEL. xxxiv. 1—xxxv. 10

VI. HISTORICAL APPENDIX: ISAIAH'S LIFE AND ACTIVITY DURING THE REIGN OF HEZEKIAH. xxxvi. 1—xxxix. 8

CHAPTERS XL—LXVI

VII. DELIVERANCE FROM THE DOMINION OF BABYLON. xl. 1—xlviii. 22

VIII. REDEMPTION THROUGH SUFFERING AND SACRIFICE. xlix. 1—lvii. 21

IX. THE TRIUMPH OF THE KINGDOM AND THE UNIVERSAL DOMINION OF JEHOVAH. lviii. 1—lxvi. 24

COMMENTARY

CHAPTERS I–XXXIX

I. PROPHECIES CENTRED ON JUDAH AND JERUSALEM. i. 1—xii. 6

a. The argument of the Lord (i. 1–31)

i. **The title and superscription (i. 1).** The verse evidently refers to the first twelve chapters only and not to the whole book, as Judah and Jerusalem are mentioned as the subjects being dealt with.

The question has been raised as to the point in time referred to in the chapter. From verse 7 we see that the horrors of a terrible invasion have come upon the land, and all the signs would seem to point to this being the invasion of Judah by Sennacherib in 701 B.C. In that event this chapter has been chosen and written as an introduction late in life by Isaiah. The scene that confronts him as he gazes upon the world of his time is sufficiently representative to warrant the portrayal of it as typical of all Israel's attitude to the word and the will of Jehovah. As George Adam Smith says: 'It is a clear, complete statement of the points which were at issue between the Lord and His own all the time Isaiah was the Lord's prophet. It is the most representative of all Isaiah's prophecies, a summary perhaps better than any other single chapter of the Old Testament, of the substance of prophetic doctrine, and a very vivid illustration of the prophetic spirit and method' (*Isaiah*, p. 4).

ii. **Introduction (i. 2–9).** This introduction of Isaiah is in the form of a great trial. It is 'The Great Arraignment', as Ewald calls it, of the chosen people. God is at once the plaintiff and judge. Heaven and earth are called to support the complaint (2); and the prophet is the witness in chief. Against the chosen people the charge that is brought is one of absolute rebellion arising from their evil and unnatural heart. It is from this that all the evils that have come upon the land directly develop. Though by the mouth of the prophets Amos and Hosea the word of the Lord God had reached them, they had not hearkened: and their perversity had led to many blatant breaches of the moral law. The ultimate issue of such a condition is that the One by whom they have been created and kept is unknown and the misery that has fallen upon the land is eloquent testimony to the reality of this departure from the faith.

The Lord hath spoken (2). It is significant that, at the very commencement of this book, Isaiah emphasizes the fact that the authentic message of the Lord God is to be found here. Cf. Ps. 1. 4; Dt. xxxii. 1. In this statement of rebellion the emphatic pronouns should be noted: 'even My children, those whom I have reared, even *they* have rebelled.' *The ox . . . the ass* (3). The very beasts of the field are able to show a more natural and perfect habit of dependence and devotion than the chosen people of the Lord. *The Holy One of Israel* (4). This phrase and name

for God we do not find before the time of Isaiah. It is probably one of his own coining. The vision that came to him within the temple precincts was of One high and lifted up (vi. 1), of One pre-eminently holy (vi. 3): and it was no doubt from that inspiration at the very beginning of his ministry that Isaiah continued to speak of God as 'the Holy One of Israel'. It is not possible to assess all that the phrase meant for Isaiah, but it was the word of one who had seen the Lord and whose entire subsequent ministry was devoted to the bringing of his people to a like sense of the majesty and the power of the One whom he himself had seen within the sanctuary. The glory and the beauty of holiness are here enshrined, and all within the personality of the covenant-making God.

Ye will revolt more and more (5). The RV has this in the form of a question and gives thereby a better sense: 'Why will ye be still stricken, that ye revolt more and more?' *Your country is desolate . . .* (7). At least three invasions of the sacred soil of Judah took place during the lifetime of Isaiah. One of them was by the combined forces of Israel and Syria about 734 B.C., and the others by the forces of the Assyrians, the first under Sargon in 712 B.C. and the other under Sennacherib in 701 B.C. (See Appendix III to Kings, 'The Great Empires during the Period of the Monarchy'.) The Syrian attack is referred to in chapter vii, and the others in chapters xxii and xxvi. *As overthrown by strangers* (7). A variant reading suggested by Ewald gives a much stronger effect: 'as the overthrow of Sodom.' *Daughter of Zion* (8). A personification; the Holy City is here referred to. This is a not uncommon form in the more poetical writings of the Old Testament. Cf. 2 Ki. xix. 21; Ps. xlv. 12. Cheyne points out that in La. ii. 8 the phrase seems to mean the city without the inhabitants; while in Mi. iv. 10 it appears to mean the inhabitants without the city. The picture is of the desolate Jerusalem watching over the ruins that are left after the surging tide of battle and invasion has receded into the distance. In verse 8 the various pictures of the *cottage* ('booth', RV), the *lodge*, both rude shelters erected in the fields at the time of harvest, and the *besieged city* are all pictures of loneliness. *We should have been as Sodom* (9). That is, we should have been totally destroyed. Thus early, Isaiah introduces the significant phrase the *remnant* (9). The divine promise that reaches down from the ages past is of the continuity of the chosen race and of the One who would come forth from the midst of the people of Israel. The emphasis is upon the sovereignty of the purpose of God. It is the Lord who 'leaves' the remnant: it is by His grace that the entire nation is not overthrown in a catastrophe similar to that which engulfed Sodom and Gomorrah. See note on vii. 3.

iii. Formalism in worship and the divine demand (i. 10–17).

In this section of his prophecy Isaiah sets forth the multiplicity of the ways in which the children of Israel, here boldly styled the *people of Gomorrah* (10), were seeking the favour of the Lord God, and yet not in any way satisfying the high and holy standard of the commandment. Oblations, new moons, sabbaths, incense, the blood of bullocks and the fat of rams, the appointed assembly and the solemn meeting (11–14): here were all the outward trappings of the religious life, but the essential heart of the faith was lacking and the people were observing a vain show without the spirit that was the fulfilment of the entire law. Over against this terrible denial of the faith, the prophet sets forth the eternal law and the demand of the Holy One of Israel (16, 17). Righteousness and the fulfilment of the commission to attend to such needs as those of the fatherless and the widow were the fundamental things. This is one of the noblest of the sayings of Isaiah and has often been compared with the stern and unequivocal prophecies of Amos (cf. Am. v. 15, etc.).

To tread my courts (12). This reading does not give the full atmosphere of the original, which infers an insult; the sense is of 'trampling' the courts of the Lord (see RV). To come before the throne of the Lord God with all the outward appearance of deep piety, while the heart is far removed from the One who reigns there, is an insult to heaven and an affront to all the glory of the revelation of the divine power and holiness. *Appointed feasts* (14). These were the feasts set in the very heart of the law and commandment of God. When separated from the heart condition that made them to be the expression of a love and devotion seeking after God, even the sabbath, the feast of Pentecost, the feast of the Passover, of trumpets, of tabernacles, the day of atonement, all alike became hateful to Him and an offence to His glorious commandment. *Blood* (15); Heb. 'bloods', i.e. stains of blood. *Wash you, make you clean* (16). Ceremonial purification is not enough; it must be accompanied by positive reformation. *Seek judgment* (17); RSV 'seek justice'. This verse introduces us to some of the social evils which Isaiah was at pains to condemn. Cf. verse 23 below.

iv. Conditions of blessing (i. 18–20).

In these words the crux of the matter is presented to the people. Note should be taken of the emphasis in Isaiah upon the power of reason. 'God reasons with man—that is the first article of religion according to Isaiah. Isaiah lays more stress upon the intellectual side of the moral sense than on the other, and the frequency with which in this chapter he employs the words *know, consider, reason*, is characteristic of all his prophesying' (G. A. Smith, *Isaiah*, p. 10). *Come now, and let us reason together* (18). Cheyne translates this by the expression: 'Come now, let us bring our reasoning to a close.' In other words, there is only one ultimate answer to the

rebellion of man, and that is the free forgiveness of God. Such an offer of pardon as is here made is not the continuance of reasoning together, but the ending of argument and the settlement of dissension. *Scarlet . . . crimson* (18); practically synonymous terms for a bright red colour derived from the cochineal insect. They are clearly chosen to provide an emphatic contrast to the colour of snow and of natural undyed wool.

v. Judgment and redemption (i. 21–31).

This supplementary passage at the end of the first chapter is a concentrated expression of the certainty of the divine judgment for all who disobey and rebel (21–24, 28–31) and of the assurance of the redemption of the Lord that will be real and not delayed (25–27). Affliction will most certainly come, but it will be overruled for good and the Lord God will redeem Zion and the remnant of the people.

Thy princes are rebellious . . . (23). The way in which the ruling classes had given themselves over to corruption and oppression is always boldly drawn by Isaiah. The disease was from the head down through the entire body politic. See verse 17n. above. *Purely purge* (25); i.e. 'thoroughly' or 'absolutely'; lit. 'with alkali'; the metaphor is taken from the smelting process (see RSV). Cf. verse 22. In the alloying of silver *tin* or 'lead' was wont to be used. The *oaks* and *gardens* (29) were associated with pagan worship and ritual. *The maker of it* (31); rather, as in RV, 'and his work'. Luther translates it in this way.

b. Description of the glory of the messianic age (ii. 1—iv. 6)

Chapters ii—iv form by themselves a little book of prophetic and inspired sayings. There are here six short oracles and all most probably come from the earliest part of the prophet's ministry.

i. A messianic prophecy (ii. 1–4).

This passage is repeated in Mi. iv. 1–4 (see notes). The picture is of the messianic age when the Holy City shall be the city to which all the nations shall resort for the learning of the true way, and the reign of universal peace will be ushered in by the people's obedience to the revealed word of the Lord God (2, 3). Then shall justice be established and the divine law run throughout the earth (4).

The word . . . (1). Once again the prophet emphasizes that his message is *concerning Judah and Jerusalem*. As it was here that the chosen remnant was to be, it was in accordance with the fitness of things that the particular outlook of the author should be always coloured by reference to these places. *The mountain of the Lord's house* (2); i.e. Mount Moriah, on which the temple was built. Here the prediction is emphatic that the true worship of the living God shall in the end, *in the last days*, prevail over all other forms of worship or religious devotion which, by their very nature and separateness from the authentic revelation, are false and unsatisfying. *Many people* (3). Rather 'many peoples' (RV);

i.e. 'nations'. *Out of Zion* (3). This of course was literally fulfilled to the very letter. It was in the Holy City that our Lord suffered rejection, and it was from the upper room in that same city that the word went forth to all the nations. Cf. Jn. iv. 22; Lk. xxiv. 47, 49. *Among the nations* (4). The correct sense is 'between the nations' (RV). The causes of all things making for strife will be adjudicated by the Lord God and His Messiah, and the Word given shall become the arbitrament instead of the power of the armed might of men. With verse 4 cf. Joel iii. 9, 10n.

In view of the importance given to the Holy City and to Mount Zion in this passage, it has often been suggested that it is probably a very late insertion into the text, and that a post-exilic date should naturally be given to it. To argue so is to stress doctrinal and critical pre-suppositions to the breaking-point. The prophet who received the message from the Lord God within the temple precincts and went forth from thence with the word of the living God upon his lips could not but have had a most acute aware-ness of the significance of the Holy City in the purposes of God; and as the vision dawned upon his mind of the glory that was yet to be under the reign of the Prince of Peace, it would seem to him that there was only one spot where that could most fittingly be accomplished, namely, the Holy City.

ii. The day of the Lord: judgment and testing (ii. 5–22). This vision of future blessing is followed by a renewal of the indictment upon the chosen race (5–9). Then follows a description of the form of the judgment that will of necessity fall upon them as they persist in turning from the Lord God (10–22). As a mighty storm shall this day of the Lord gather force and come sweeping down from the north to the sea coast, engulfing and crushing in its course all the high and the lofty things from the cedars of Lebanon (13) to the ships of Tarshish (16). Thus will the pride of man be brought low and his sin be punished.

O house of Jacob . . . (5); the transition verse from the picture of the universal dominion of the Lord to the description of the sin of Judah. *Therefore* (6); RV 'For'. The following verses are the reasons urged by the prophet for the return to the Lord God. Only if they *walk in the light of the Lord* (5) will the foregoing prophecy be capable of fulfilment. Four great causes are here given for the divine displeasure: association with foreign peoples (6), slavish imitation of such foreign peoples in their heathen practices (6), dependence on mere financial and warlike re-serves (7), and the worship of idols (8). *Please themselves in* (6). Rather, as in RV, 'they strike hands with (make a compact with) the children of strangers', i.e. the heathen. *Therefore forgive them not* (9). Translate 'and thou dost not for-give them'. With verse 10 cf. verses 19 and 21.

Ships of Tarshish (16), i.e. the largest ships that were known: the kind that made the long voyage to Tarshish. Tarshish was perhaps the Tartessus in Spain, though others are of the opinion that

it was in Italy and that its people were the Tyrrhenians or Etruscans. See xxiii. 1n. *All pleasant pictures* (16). There have been many suggestions for variant readings, but the sense is quite clear. The implication is that all objects of desire are to be overthrown. *The idols he shall utterly abolish* (18); RV 'the idols shall utterly pass away'. Here is the great and dramatic climax for which the prophet looks. In the consummation of the mighty acts of Jehovah, the overthrow of all alien and false divinities will be absolute and entire. Nothing shall stand when He appears (cf. Mal. iii. 2). *They shall go into the holes of the rocks* (19); cf. verses 10 and 21. The picture is of a people fleeing from their homes before an invader, and trying to escape into the shelter of the hills (cf. Rev. vi. 15, 16). The destruction will be so entire that those who have been the devotees of the idolatrous practices of the heathen will in their disgust and loathing cast them to the very pests of the field and the house (20). *Cease ye from man* (22); i.e. from all trust in man alone. Only in the Lord Jehovah is there power and sufficiency and abiding strength.

iii. Oppression and anarchy (iii. 1–12). Having denounced the heathen practices and self-reliance of the people, the prophet deals in chapter iii with social evils and private luxury. In verses 1–12 he foretells a terrible time of anarchy that is to come upon the land, for the Lord will take away the rulers and all who might guide the people (1–3). So absolute will this be that men will look all over the land for someone to be their ruler and guide, but all in vain (4). This is the awesome reward that comes upon the spirit of disobedience and sin, upon the respect of persons that is shown by the people of the land and upon their Sodom-like shamelessness in their sin (5–9). The sole hope lies in righteousness. Blessing shall be to the righteous; woe to the wicked; each shall inevitably reap as they have sown (10, 11). Oppression and greed as shown by the nobles of the land must pass or there will never be hope for a better day. The position at court is so bad that the very rulers are themselves ruled by the ladies of the court and act as children (12). Anarchy is absolute over all the land.

The stay and the staff (1). Two genders of the same noun are used here, as in Ec. ii. 8; Na. ii. 12, according to the Hebrew idiom for representing all kinds of things. In this case the reference is to all kinds of supports, such as food, and then to the other things here mentioned, government, law and order, peace. *The cunning artificer, and the eloquent orator* (3). RSV 'the skilful magician and the expert in charms'. A reference to the superstition which existed. *Thou hast clothing* (6). Either the meaning is that poverty is so rife that it is something to discover one with a garment suitable for a special purpose, or that 'mantle' (see RSV) here refers to a robe of office, so that, in thus accosting his neighbour, the man is speaking to one who has previously been a ruler in the land. *Healer* (7); RV mg. 'binder up';

cf. i. 6. *Provoke the eyes of his glory* (8); cf. lxv. 3. RSV renders 'his glorious presence'. *The shew of their countenance* (9); RV mg. 'their respecting of persons'.

iv. **The judgment of the Lord (iii. 13–15).** In these words the prophet presents the Lord God arising in judgment and dealing with the rulers of the people who have so grossly mismanaged the business of government. The cry of the oppressed has reached the ear of the most High and He has come down to deliver and save them. Princes and rulers are thus now called to account: they who were the keepers of the vineyard have abused their position of privilege and have made private gain the be-all and end-all of life. The very judgment that has been meted out by them to the poor and the oppressed will come down upon them in yet greater measure. *Ye have eaten up the vineyard* (14). *Ye* is emphatic: 'Ye . . . the elders and the rulers . . . even ye.' The figure of a vineyard is a favourite one in Scripture. Cf. v. 1–7.

v. **Judgment on the daughters of Zion (iii. 16— iv. 1).** Here is the climax of this message of judgment and doom. Even the women of Jerusalem are involved in this terrible condition of affairs; they, equally with the men, will be overthrown in the day of the Lord (16, 17). The power of the picture here presented is made all the greater by the contrast with the luxury to which they were accustomed (18–24). As Amos attacked the women of Samaria for their wanton oppression of the poor and their conduct of themselves thereafter (Am. iv. 1–3), so here Isaiah assails the haughtiness and the disdain of these women of the Holy City (16). Here is the picture that the world has almost always known —abject poverty existing alongside luxurious living and haughty extravagance. For their part in this, these women are to be overtaken in the judgment that will come and on them will fall a terrible and loathsome plague (17). Not only will they be the victims of a noxious form of illness, but upon them will come the awful curse of the East, the unmarried state (iv. 1).

In the list (18–23) of the forms of dress and adornment worn by the women of Jerusalem, many objects are included that were worn by the heathen goddess Ishtar. The passage should be read in RV or RSV where some of the articles are more clearly identified. *Cauls* (18); RSV 'headbands'. *Tablets* (20); RV 'perfume boxes'. *Wimples, and the crisping pins* (22); RV 'the shawls, and the satchels' (RSV 'handbags').

vi. **Vision of comfort and peace (iv. 2–6).** This section of the book is brought to an end, as so often the great addresses of the prophet are summarized and completed, with a vision of comfort and peace. It is once again worth asserting that there is no ground whatsoever in the text itself for placing this later than the time of Isaiah. Here is the promise of glorious consummation and life (2, 3). Here is the divine answer to the wrongs of man. The land will yet be covered with fruit and vegetation for the chosen remnant of the Lord (2). Righteousness and truth will reign in the citadels of the land; the peoples shall be clean and the pillar of fire and of cloud will once again be the glory of the nation and its sure defence (3–5). In the midst of all there will be the tabernacle of the Lord, and the seeking heart will there find solace, comfort and eternal rest (6).

The branch of the Lord (2), or 'sprout of the Eternal' (see RV mg.). Cf. Je. xxiii. 5, xxxiii. 15; Zc. iii. 8, vi. 12. In these passages it is obvious that there is reference to One who will rule and guide in righteousness, one of the family of David, a servant of God. This can be none other than the Messiah, who would usher in a day of high and gracious blessing to all the land. As G. A. Smith says, 'From the blackest pessimism shall arise new hope and faith as from beneath Isaiah's darkest verses that glorious passage suddenly bursts like uncontrollable spring from the very feet of winter.' *Written among the living* (3); RV mg. 'unto life'; i.e. included in God's list of the remnant. *Upon all the glory shall be a defence* (5). Rather, as in RV, 'over all the glory shall spread the canopy', i.e. of divine love and protection.

c. God's judgments upon sin (v. 1–30)

This chapter begins in the form of a lament, with the theme of the story of the Lord's vineyard (1–7). In a passage of outstanding power and sublimity, the prophet addresses his hearers gathered around him and skilfully leads them to assent to the judgment which he is to make upon the nation. The sudden change of the rhythm in verse 7 and the use of assonance in the verse accentuates the strict and incisive message of the minister of Jehovah. Then follows a sixfold woe; the sentence of the everlasting love upon the greedy landowners (8–10), the drunkards (11–17), the unbelievers (18, 19), the foes of the moral order (20), the self-confident and worldly-wise men (21), the dissolute and unjust judges (22–24). Then comes the stern and unequivocal statement that the Lord God will Himself summon the terrible and unwearied hosts of the Assyrians to destroy the land of Judah (25–30).

i. **The parable of the vineyard (v. 1–7).** In these verses the prophet re-emphasizes the message of the previous chapters. Judah is apostate, and this is at once the sorrow of God and the cause of her overthrow and condemnation. All that could be done to make the vineyard bear good fruit has been done; but all to no avail (2, 4). Nothing remains but to uproot the defences of the vineyard and to destroy all that pertained to it in the past (5, 6). The application of verse 7 follows inevitably and with awful force.

My wellbeloved (1). 'My friend'; i.e. Jehovah. The object of the introduction in this form is to secure the attention of the bystanders for the message that is to follow. *A very fruitful hill* (1). Lit. 'upon a horn, a son of fatness'. The meaning of the text is that the peak on which the vineyard is set is most fertile: the sunny side of the rocky slopes were always the ones chosen for the cultivation of the vine. Note the emphasis on the intention of permanence in the work and plan of the beloved. Fertility, in the clearing of the stones; production and development, in the making of the winepress, which would be hollowed out of the rock; defence, in the building of the walls, hedges and towers. This marvellous intent of God concerning Israel is clear all throughout the sacred word. 'O that thou hadst hearkened to my commandments! then had thy peace been as a river, and thy righteousness as the waves of the sea' (xlviii. 18). *I will . . . command the clouds* (6). From the closing words of this verse it is clear that the prophet has been speaking of the Lord God. The keeper of the vineyard is the Lord of the whole earth. *Oppression . . . . a cry* (7). Here is the specification of that which has been given in the parabolic form of *wild grapes* (2, 4). The *cry* is the plea for help of those who are oppressed.

ii. Denunciation of the evil-doers and the declaring of woes (v. 8–24). Six woes are here pronounced upon specific evils. In the first (verses 8-10) the grasping landowners are denounced for the way in which they are continually striving to extend the limit of their possessions by the grinding under of the poor and the landless. In their greed they were driving the ancient possessors from their lands and making for themselves large and extensive estates. Soon there will come the inevitable recompense. The land will be desolate and the reaping from the soil will turn out scanty and inadequate. *Acres* (10). This word means literally 'yokes': a 'yoke' was as much as could be ploughed by a yoke of oxen (i.e. two oxen) in a single day. *One bath* (10). A liquid measure with the equivalent of an *ephah* of dry measure, roughly about eight gallons. The amount is ridiculously small for so large an area of ploughed land. *Homer* (10). About eighty-three gallons. The yield therefore is to be barely a tenth of the amount sown.

The second woe (verses 11-17) consists of a stern denunciation of all who give themselves over to rioting and dissipation. By such conduct the nation is steadily being brought to ruin and the gates of bondage are opened for the captive to enter (13, 14). To leave God out of calculation in the ordering of life is to court certain destruction and to lead the people on to the inescapable doom of the wicked. *That they may follow strong drink* (11). Isaiah refers several times to drunkenness, which suggests it was prevalent. See verse 22 and cf. xix. 14, xxiv. 20, xxviii. 1, 7. *Are gone into captivity* (13); RSV 'go into exile'. The tense is the 'prophetic perfect'. *Hell* (14), i.e. Sheol or Hades, 'the grave'. Cf. Jb. xi. 8, xiv. 13.

In the third woe (verses 18, 19) the prophet addresses himself to those who attach themselves to sin and blatantly call on God to make Himself known in judgment. Their very actions are like cords pulling the results of sin down upon them. Cf. the words of G. A. Smith: 'This figure of sinners jeering at the approach of a calamity, while they actually wear the harness of its carriage, is very striking.' *A cart rope* (18); i.e. a strong rope, suggesting the enormity of the sin.

The fourth woe (verse 20) is directed against those who by their words and behaviour seek to overthrow the established moral order. The last two phrases are really an illustration of the first.

The fifth woe (verse 21) is directed against those who in their own wisdom endeavour to order their lives. Self-confidence is the crime of foolish hearts, who leave God out of account in their planning. The spirit of dependence is the only thing that can keep the heart right in the sight of God.

The sixth woe (verses 22–24) seems to be spoken against corrupt judges who are described ironically as 'heroes at drinking wine, and valiant men in mixing strong drink' (RSV). It is, however, their rejection of the law and their despising of God's word rather than their drunkenness which is here chiefly in view (cf. verses 11, 12 above). Such men shall be as the stubble burned in the fire and as a rotten plant with no possibility of bloom. The denial of justice to the righteous is a recurring theme (cf. i. 17, 23n.).

iii. The wrath of God (v. 25–30). This is the final stroke of divine judgment. In the past there have been indications of the scope and the power of the coming judgment of an avenging deity; now this is given the final emphatic and colourful word. In these magnificent verses we see an irresistible foe coming down upon the nation and overwhelming her from the ends of the earth. No name is mentioned here of the invading force, but the natural reference is of course to the massed might of the Assyrian armies, which, mighty as they were, were ultimately to be eclipsed by a yet greater power, the power of Babylon. Down upon the defenceless cities of Judah will they come with unwearied feet and in serried array (27), with their horses and chariots poised for decisive battle (28) and their battle-cries making the hearts of all before them faint for fear (29, 30). Thus is the ultimate and terrible judgment of the Lord God fulfilled for all time and the people who have forgotten His commandment are consumed and themselves forgotten.

Nations (26). Read 'nation'. See RV mg. and cf. Am. vi. 14. *Will hiss* (26); RSV 'whistle'; i.e. to call to the invading nation to the attack. *Horses' hoofs . . . like flint* (28). The horses of the ancients were not shod; the suggestion is that the invader would not be handicapped through the horses going lame. *Carry it away* (29); a reference to the Assyrian practice of depopulating conquered cities. *Like the roaring of the sea* (30). The metaphor and atmosphere have changed here. The picture is of an angry sea over which there is settling a darkness that can be felt. The sun is under eclipse and the light of heaven is shadowed and strange. The whole scene is one of cataclysm and chaos. So ends the path of the sinning heart and the sinning nation.

d. The call of Isaiah (vi. 1–13)

Tidings of the death of king Uzziah have reached Isaiah and, in an agony of grief and sorrow mingled with a sense of the difficulties and hazards that the nation must now face, he enters the courts of the temple that he might seek after the Lord. It is then that the vision recounted in this chapter breaks upon him. Where, a short time before, he had been oppressed with the sense of the forsakenness of the land and the emptiness of the throne, he now sees the Lord God high and lifted up, and the entire power of the universe at His immediate command (1). Pre-eminent in all his thoughts and sense at this time there comes the realization of the holiness of the God of all the earth (2–4), and smitten with the consciousness of his own sin and unworthiness he cries out that he is lost (5). Then comes the message of saving mercy. There flew one of the seraphim and touched his lips with a live coal taken from off the altar (6), and the almighty words of sovereign love are spoken to his heart (7). It is only after this absolute pardon that the commission to the task of working for the Lord God is given, and the prophet hears the voice of the Lord calling for one to go at His command (8). That message is indeed a message of doom to the chosen race and not one that anyone could lightly undertake (9–13); but there within the precincts of the house of God the youthful Isaiah accepts the challenge of God and goes forth with the divine ordination resting mightily upon him.

I saw also the Lord (1). In the midst of all the unrest and turmoil he saw that God was 'keeping watch above His own'. *The Lord* (1). Cf. Jn. xii. 41, where 'his glory' implies the reading of the Targum here: 'I saw the glory of the Lord.' The manifestation of divinity here is clearly seen in the Person of the Lord Christ, the Son of God. The divine revelation is ever to man through the Person of the only-begotten Son of the Father. 'No man hath seen God at any time.' As so often in the days of the Old Testament patriarchs and saints, there is here the eternal activity of the God of all the earth mediated to man through the eternal Son. *Throne* (1). The emphasis is upon the certainty of the sovereignty of the Lord God. There is but one Ruler of the ceaseless round. *Train* (1), i.e. the 'train of His royal robe'. *The seraphims* (2). There is a diversity of translation for this word. Some translate 'burning ones' or 'fiery serpents' (xiv. 29, xxx. 6); while others translate it by 'exalted or noble ones'. They were obviously in this case winged figures, human in form, for they are represented as having hands, feet and voices. Their ceaseless ministry was the praising of the Lord and the showing forth of the divine glory. *One cried unto another* (3). The antiphonal chant: 'in responsive song they called the one to the other'. *Holy, holy, holy* (3). The repetition expresses great emphasis. Cf. Je. vii. 4, xxii. 29; Ezk. xxi. 27.

Here we see the intensely spiritual content of the vision. Henceforth for Isaiah all the old concepts under which he had been nurtured are to glow with a new and a yet more fervent flame. In the midst of a people who were more and more giving themselves over to the pursuit of things that were not of God and could not in any way be squared with a high and holy sense of His glory, Isaiah now sees that the fundamental of all fundamentals concerning the God of Israel is that He is holy. Henceforth for him God is 'the Holy One of Israel'. *Smoke* (4). Most probably a symbol of divine wrath and anger. *Woe is me!* (5). The effect upon the prophet is immediate and overwhelming. United with the nation in all its turning from the Lord and in the grasp of his own sinful desires and ways, Isaiah can only count himself *undone. A man of unclean lips* (5). Cf. Jb. xl. 4, 5. The vision of God in His holiness is the great creator of a sense of unworthiness and defilement before Him. It was no doubt because Isaiah felt that his life's work was to be the proclaiming of the message of the Lord God that he feels here the sinfulness and unworthiness of his lips for this exalted service. His particular sense of need is immediately met by the action of one of the seraphim (6). *Purged* (7). 'Atoned for'. For the use of fire as purifier, cf. Nu. xxxi. 22, 23; Mal. iii. 2; Mt. iii. 11.

The message to be given is one of solemn judgment. The people are to hear and to see, but are not to understand the implications of the message. They are to grow blinder and blinder; their hearts are to be hardened and not softened; the nation is to be destroyed as *a teil tree* (RV 'terebinth'), *and as an oak* (13). *Yet in it shall be a tenth, and it shall return, and shall be eaten* (13); RSV 'Though a tenth remain in it, it will be burned again'. The thought is one of complete devastation. But even so there is still promise. The very stump of the tree shall flourish and grow, and the remnant (*the holy seed*) that remains to the people shall yet be gathered again into the service and the dominion of the almighty Redeemer of Israel. This phrase, *the holy seed*, is missing from LXX but is found in the Dead Sea Scroll of Isaiah.

e. The message of the Lord to Ahaz (vii. 1–25)

This chapter belongs to the period of the war between Judah and the Syro-Ephraimite coalition. Under the imminent threat of attack the king of Judah, Ahaz, is terrified and in great perturbation (1, 2). To him the prophet comes with the message of the Lord that if he will but trust there will yet be deliverance (3–9). With a view to restoring the faith of the wavering king Isaiah gives him the opportunity of asking a sign of Jehovah (10, 11), but he refuses (12), and then there is given to him the sign spoken by the prophet, the sign of Immanuel (13–16). This is followed by a description of the awful manner in which Judah herself is to be ravaged in the coming days (17–25).

i. The prophet's word to the frightened king (vii. 1–9). The message with which he is sent is that of confidence in God. *Rezin . . . and Pekah*

568

(1). Cf. 2 Ki. xvi. 5, 6; 2 Ch. xxviii. 5–8. *Syria* (1). Syria in our English Bible is the 'Aram' of Hebrew. Damascus was the chief city of the Aramean states and played the main rôle in their destinies. *Confederate with* (2); lit. 'Syria resteth on Ephraim'. As Ephraim was the leading tribe of Israel, it came to be used as synonymous for the whole state. It was from the advanced base of Israel's territory that the king of Syria planned to make his invasion.

Shear-jashub (3); lit. 'a remnant shall return'. This has not to do with the disaster that shall overtake the armies of Judah. One of the most important doctrines of Isaiah is that of the remnant. Out of all the people who have turned from the Lord, there shall be a remnant that shall find its way back to the light and rejoice in the salvation of the Lord God. Here, in thus giving this name to his son, Isaiah is asserting the reality of both judgment and mercy. The race of the faithful shall not be wholly cut off from the earth. A remnant, only that, but none the less a real generation of the faithful, shall survive under the good hand of God, and shall fulfil His will.

Fear not . . . the two tails of these smoking firebrands (4). The emphasis is that those firebrands that once could have been dangerous are now almost impotent, no better than mere smoking stumps. Thus Isaiah shows his contempt for them. *The son of Tabeal* (6). Nothing is known of this man. It is significant that the prophet knows the plan of campaign so completely as to be aware of the person whom they are planning to set on the throne. The name is Aramean, and thus it probably refers to some puppet of the king of Syria.

The head of Syria is Damascus . . . (8). The sense of this and the next verse is this: 'You look at the seeming might of Aram and of Israel. Be not afraid of them. Their heads are only Rezin and the upstart son of Remaliah. But Jerusalem is the head of Judah, and the head of Jerusalem is Jehovah.'

Within threescore and five years (8). These words are regarded by some commentators as a gloss by a later writer: it is argued that the prophets did not normally date their predictions in this precise way. But cf. Je. xxv. 12, 13. Certainly this number of years is that which saw the final destruction of the power of Israel. Under the hammer blows of the invasions of Tiglath-pileser and the later introduction of foreign colonists by Esar-haddon, the power of the northern kingdom was utterly annihilated. *If ye will not believe . . . established* (9). There is a very striking word-play in the original which it is hardly possible to reproduce in translation. The following are some attempts to give the effect of the original. 'No faith, no fixity'; 'No strong trust, no trusty stronghold'; 'No confiding, no abiding'. G. A. Smith paraphrases by the sentence: 'If ye have not faith, ye cannot have staith.' The words are addressed to Ahaz and those of his followers who were showing signs

of being unconvinced by the message of the prophet.

ii. The king's refusal and the sign (vii. 10–16). In order to confirm to the heart and conscience of the king the truth of his words, Isaiah tells him to seek a sign of Jehovah (11). Afraid lest this might commit him to some alteration of the foreign policy that he has been following, the king refuses to do so (12), but the sign none the less is given (14). It is the sign of the coming of a child with the great name *Immanuel* (14). Therein is the certainty of hope that the eternal God has not deserted His people, but that throughout the entire field of their experience He is watching and guarding and overruling to His glory.

Sign (11). Not necessarily miraculous. A sign is a sensible pledge, a token of the truth which the prophet had offered in the name of Jehovah. *Neither will I tempt . . .* (12). Here is pure subterfuge and hypocrisy. The king has been expressly commanded to ask this sign, and not to do so is to refuse the very help of heaven.

Behold, a virgin shall conceive . . . (14–16). This is one of the greatest passages of Isaiah and one around which the storms of controversy and discussion have raged unceasingly in latter times. Here only a few points can be stressed; for a fuller examination of the question the larger and more detailed works should be studied. The question is whether we have here detailed and emphatic reference to the coming of the Messiah and to the manner of His birth; or whether we have here a strictly limited reference to the fact of the presence in power of the almighty Jehovah. In considering the matter, it must be borne in mind that so very often in the Old Testament prophecy has a double reference, an immediate and an ultimate fulfilment. In the verses 15, 16 there is quite obviously envisaged an early deliverance. The birth of the child with the sacred name of Immanuel ('God with us') is token of the fact that deliverance is sure. But beyond that there is the certain and ultimate promise of the salvation of Jehovah on the behalf of His people Israel. Only through the coming of the Son of God and the reality of the incarnation did the way open for the fulfilment of this latter and more absolute deliverance. It is the opinion of the present writer that it is quite impossible to separate this passage from a messianic connection. Let it be granted that the word translated 'virgin' (Heb. *almah*) need not have that exclusive connotation, and that the prophet is thinking in the first instance of an immediate occurrence. It remains true, none the less, that the redemption of the children of Israel and of all the human race is accomplished by One who bears the name 'Immanuel', and of whom it is recorded, by the express teaching of that selfsame One, that the prophets wrote and spoke of Him (cf. Lk. xxiv. 27).

With reference to the coming kingdom of which Isaiah speaks (see vii. 16–18, viii. 8), Delitzsch has made the following comment: 'If

Isaiah here, in chapters vii–ix, looks upon Assyria absolutely as the universal world Empire, this is so far true seeing that the four empires from the Babylonian to the Roman are really only the unfolding of the beginning which had its place in Assyria. And if here, in chapter vii, he thinks of the son of the virgin as growing up under the Assyrian oppressions, this is also so far true, since Jesus was actually born in a time when the Holy Land found itself under the supremacy of the universal Empire, and in a condition which went back to the unbelief of Ahaz as its ultimate cause.' There seems to be no adequate reason for not finding the ultimate fulfilment of the prophecy of these words in the Person of the Messiah, the Son of God.

iii. The ravaging of Judah (vii. 17–25). Now the prophet takes up the burden of the message of judgment on the land over which Ahaz reigns. Hostile armies that shall invade the land will leave it desolate and alone. The pictures used to enforce the message are overpowering in their intensity and graphic description: like flies and bees (18), as a hired razor (20), like a people reduced to the level of desert existence (19, 21, 22), and finally the picture of the land utterly waste with thorns and thistles luxuriating where once the fertile land had blossomed in beauty and power (23–25). *The fly . . . the bee* (18). The suggestion is of a numberless host. The fly is peculiarly appropriate to the land of Egypt, for there the moist heat produces them in abundance. *Hiss* (18); i.e. to call by whistling; cf. v. 26. *A man shall nourish a young cow* (21). The population to be left will be so scanty that a few cattle will yield an *abundance of milk* (22). *Silverlings* (23) are silver shekels.

f. The certainty of judgment (viii. 1–22)

i. The rejection of the prophet's counsel (viii. 1–18). This chapter continues the tale of the certainty of judgment and the futility of fighting against the counsel of Jehovah. Damascus and Samaria are to fall; that is ordained in the set purpose of the Highest (4). So is Isaiah commanded to take a large placard and write upon it in Hebrew and Aramaic, that all may read it, the name *Maher-shalal-hash-baz* ('speed-spoil, hurry-prey'). Witnesses have to be taken to authenticate the fact of the prophecy, so that when the time comes for fulfilment all the land might know that the Lord indeed has spoken by the mouth of His prophet (2). The name is to be that given to his son, for before the child will be able to utter his first words the destruction of Damascus and Samaria by the Assyrians will be an accomplished fact (4). This is not all. Judah too is involved in the coming overthrow, and the judgment of the Lord is sure, though the ultimate purpose of the God of Israel will not be frustrated (5–8). It is God alone that is to be feared, and if that is done no confederation of opposing kings need excite alarm (9–15). That is the burden of the message of the prophet and, faced as he is with the evident rejection of the message,

he feels that it will be idle for him to continue his ministry. This is the occasion for his withdrawing himself, and in the company of his disciples he waits for the manifestation of the will and the salvation of the Holy One of Israel (16–18).

A great roll (1); RV 'a great tablet'. *A man's pen* (1); i.e., as in RV mg., 'in common characters'. The board for the placard has to be large, and thus the effect is that of great clarity and simplicity in the message to be proclaimed. God's message to man is never covered up under any distorting camouflage. *Call his name . . .* (3). On the meaning of the name see notes above. The child is to be the sign to the times of the coming judgment and the impending chastisement of Syria and the ten tribes. *The spoil of Samaria* (4). Samaria was overthrown in 722, ten years after the downfall of Damascus. *The waters of Shiloah* (6). The same waters as those of the pool of Siloam. The gradient along which these waters came was easy, and so they flowed quietly and without rush. In thus comparing these waters with the mighty Euphrates (see verse 7n.), they were comparing their own little kingdom with the mighty kingdom of Assyria. *Rejoice in* (6). This does not make the best sense, and a very slight alteration of the original can give the reading 'and are in terror of'. RSV renders 'melt in fear before'. *The river* (7) is the Euphrates. The comparison between the river and the Assyrian people is very apt, as it was wont to overflow its banks and to erupt over the surrounding countryside. J. E. McFadyen translates verse 8 thus:

> 'On it shall sweep over Judah,
>   An overflowing flood
> That shall reach as high as the neck.
> But Jehovah's outstretched wings
>   Shall cover the breadth of the land;
>   For with us is God.'

The fact of the presence of the Lord God, as Isaiah is never tired of pointing out, is the great pledge of the triumph of the forces of righteousness over the enemies of Israel.

Associate yourselves (9); RV, following an alternative reading, 'Make an uproar'. The prophet again emphasizes the futility of opposition to Judah. The sovereignty of the will of Jehovah is absolute and complete and His will shall be done. Cf. the use of the name *Immanuel* in verse 8 with the phrase *God is with us* in verse 10. *Say ye not, A confederacy* (12). The command is not to accept the forms of security that were being offered in the realms of foreign diplomacy. Only in the will and the protection of Jehovah were there truly eternal safety and deliverance. For those, however, who disobey and refuse to accept this divine protection, there can be no escape from the destruction that comes forth from His presence, greater by far than that wrought by Rezin or Pekah. The simple warning is not to accept the popular vocabulary and outlook. *A stone of stumbling* (14). Notice the way in which this statement is quoted in Rom. ix. 33 and 1 Pet. ii. 8.

Bind up the testimony (16). In view of the rejection of his words by the people at large the prophet resolves to concentrate on his disciples, to fasten his message in their hearts, and to await with patience the evidence of the working out of the divine plan. *My disciples* (16). In these words we see that around the prophet there were gathered a number of like-minded men who followed his lead and accepted his counsel. *The children whom the Lord hath given* (18). These are, of course, Shear-jashub (see vii. 3n.) and Maher-shalal-hash-baz (viii. 3). These names were prophetic of the mercy and the judgment of the Lord, and taken together with the prophet's own, which meant 'Jehovah saves', they had a universal meaning concerning the eternal purpose. The words are thus applied to the Messiah. Cf. Heb. ii. 13.

ii. Further detached oracles (viii. 19–22). The text here is in many places obscure and the meaning cannot be determined with exactitude. See RV and cf. RSV. Verses 19, 20 are a rebuke to those who were giving themselves over to spiritism and a command to turn only to the record of the Word of God for guidance and light. Verses 21, 22 show a man crossing a lonely desert, but by reason of the greatness of the way he loses heart and curses God and the king. *For the living to the dead* (19). Rather, as in RSV, 'Should they consult the dead on behalf of the living?' Here is a message for every age that has turned for enlightenment on the question of the life after death to the cult of spiritism. No light has ever come from this source and the essence of the Christian faith expressly forbids such a search. *No light in them* (20); rather, as in RV, 'surely there is no morning for them'. *Curse their king and their God* (21). That is, curse their evil lot by their king and their God, instead of humbling themselves under the hand of God. *And look upward* (21). This should be joined in sense with the following verse.

'They shall lift up their eyes to the heaven above,
They shall look to the earth beneath;
But nought shall they see save distress and
    anguish,
And thick impenetrable gloom.'

g. Prophecy of Christ's birth and kingdom (ix. 1–7)

These words are the climax of all that has gone before, and in this vision of a righteous and prosperous king reigning over a people emancipated and delivered out of terrible bondage we have a fitting and moving consummation to the foregoing pictures of judgment and overthrow. In the midst of judgment, as Isaiah is ever reminding his hearers, there is the promise and the certainty of the deliverance of the Lord God Himself. So much so that even those parts that have suffered the most are those that will rejoice the most in the salvation of the Lord (1, 2). This

is one of the most moving passages of Scripture. Beginning with a call to the people to rejoice in that a new day is dawning for the oppressed nations and peoples of the earth (3, 4), the prophet proceeds to show how this is to be. The king, for whom all Israel has longed and waited, is to begin His reign, and the whole earth is to know the power of His dominion and the inspiration of His saving and redemptive government (6, 7). Peace (7) is to be the dominant feature of His reign; the trappings and weapons of war 'shall even be for burning, for fuel of fire' (5, RV). So great and mighty is this king who is to come that no one title of majesty is sufficient to describe Him, and the wealth of significant names that are given to Him include that of 'mighty God' (6). These words lie at the very heart of one of the greatest messianic prophecies. *Zebulun and . . . Naphtali* (1). Districts of northern Israel which were ravaged by Tiglath-pileser in 734 B.C. It is upon this darkness of overthrow and calamity that the light of the salvation of the most High is to arise. Translate: 'In the former time He brought into contempt the land of Zebulun and Naphtali, but in the latter days hath He covered with glory the land held by the nations beyond the Jordan on the way to the sea.' The perfect tenses here are prophetic, i.e. future in sense. *Thou hast multiplied . . . and not . . .* (3). Obviously not a correct development of the sense. It should read 'Thou hast multiplied . . . and hast increased its joy'. The words for 'its' and 'not' in the original are identical in sound though different in form. *The day of Midian* (4). Cf. Jdg. vi—viii. On that occasion, the Midianites were overcome by the mighty powers of the children of Israel under the leadership of Gideon, powers which were the very manifestation of the Lord God Himself. The sudden destruction then meted out to the enemies of the Lord is to be typical of the destruction of those who oppose the coming of the Prince of Peace. *For every battle of the warrior . . .* (5). Rather, as RV, 'For all the armour of the armed man in the tumult, and the garments rolled in blood, shall even be for burning, for fuel of fire.' Cf. McFadyen's translation:

'Every boot of thundering warrior,
Every war-cloak drenched in blood,
Is destined for the burning,
Shall be fuel for the fire.'

For unto us a child is born . . . (6). It is manifestly impossible to associate these words of majestic prophecy with any other than the Messiah Himself, and the Christian Church throughout the centuries has found here the certain attributes of the living and victorious King of the hearts of men, the only One able to deliver and to save the soul in its desperate plight and to lead man into the new and better way of the commandment of God. *Wonderful, Counsellor* (6). These words should be taken together. *The mighty God* (6). This One who is to come is no mere man; there is the authentic stamp of divinity upon Him. *The everlasting Father* (6). One whose fatherhood over His people will never come to an end. But there is more than that involved. Literally the words mean the 'Father of eternity', One who in His own being is eternal and is thus able to give the gift of eternal life to others. As in this passage we have such an One associated with the coming of a child, there is here clear and decisive reference to the incarnation and to the union of the divine and the human in the Person of the Christ. *The Prince of Peace* (6). That is the culmination of the titles and it is the greatest of all great boons that the Son of God brings to men, 'peace with God'.

h. The doom of Israel (ix. 8—x. 4)

From the message of peace and deliverance for the elect remnant the prophet returns to speak of the desolation that is to fall upon northern Israel. She has learned nothing from the dreadful experiences of her past history (9, 10, 13) and dire doom must therefore be her lot (11, 12). This passage is an artistic unity, consisting of four strophes, each of which concludes with the words 'For all this his anger is not turned away, but his hand is stretched out still' (12, 17, 21, x. 4). Cf. v. 25. In these verses the prophet declaims against the pride of Israel and her over-weening ambition, threatening her with the loss of her territories and population, as well as with anarchy and civil war. It is a terrible account of the certainty of judgment and the folly of not learning from the past. It is not certain whether the passage refers to what still lies in the future or to something that has already taken place. In general, perhaps, it reads best if it is taken to refer to events that are still to come and not as a reading back of the lessons of the past. The passage is one of the earliest of the prophecies of Isaiah, for according to ix. 11 Syria is at war with Ephraim and the coalition of 735 has therefore not yet taken place.

i. **The loss of territory (ix. 8–12).** The past calamities that have come upon the people have not resulted in their turning back to the Lord (9, 10); now there comes an even sharper word from the Ruler of the earth (11, 12). As G. A. Smith says: 'They did not feel the Lord shaking their land, so He sent their enemies to steal it from them. The Syrians before, and the Philistines behind; and they devour Israel with open mouth. What the earthquake had been for appalling suddenness, this was for lingering and harassing—guerilla bands, armed raids, the land eaten away bit by bit. Yet the people do not return to the One that smote them: neither seek they the Lord of hosts.' *Ephraim and the inhabitant of Samaria* (9). The counterpart of 'inhabitants of Jerusalem, and men of Judah' in v. 3. The prophecies are similar in type.

ii. **War and defeat (ix. 13–17).** The disaster that is to come on the land under the fiery judgment of Jehovah will leave none outside its sway and sweep. In the guilt of the rulers the entire nation

shares; *every one is an hypocrite . . . and every mouth speaketh folly* (17). The devastation of war that now engulfs the land shows forth in all the nakedness of utter reality that there is none exempt from the grand arraignment for condemnation. *Shall have no joy in their young men* (17); i.e. the wrath of Jehovah will be manifested in that He will suffer even the cream of the youth of the land to be destroyed in battle.

iii. **Anarchy at home (ix. 18–21).** Like the burning of a prairie fire (18, 19), the incredible wickedness of the people has spread on every hand. All that has come to pass has still failed to turn the hearts of the people to the Lord and now the prophet's eyes are opened to see that 'God's wrath is but the blast that fans men's hot sins to flame'. In the consequent famine that comes upon the earth, the victims are seen feeding upon themselves (20).

iv. **Climax of the calamity (x. 1–4).** This is the final strophe in this poetic description of the coming calamity. It consists of another of the oft-repeated charges of bad administration of justice by those who were the appointed judges of the land (1, 2). As a result of all such turning from the path of rectitude and truth, there is at the end of the road they have chosen the sure abode of the captive and the dark night of separation from the land where righteousness has been so sadly lacking (3, 4). *The desolation which shall come from far* (3); cf. v. 26. *Without me they shall bow down* (4); rv 'They shall only bow down'; rsv 'Nothing remains but to crouch'.

i. The doom of Assyria (x. 5–34).

i. **The two plans: Assyria's and Jehovah's (x. 5–15).** This prophecy reveals Isaiah's supreme conception of the sovereignty of Jehovah in history. Under the influence of Ahaz the nation was looking to Assyria for help. Isaiah, intent on instructing his spiritual children, proclaimed that Assyria would be the instrument under God to scourge His people.

> '*Ho Assyria! Rod of mine anger,*
> *And staff of mine indignation.*
> *Against an impious nation I send him,*
> *A people that sore hath provoked Me to wrath*' (5, 6).

In doing so, however, she would be so exalted with a sense of her own greatness as to ascribe her victories to her own strength and ability, and to regard her divinities as greater than those of her vanquished foes (8–11, 13, 14). Such arrogance and overweening pride, intent only on destruction, and making her completely blind to the real purpose of Jehovah, will turn upon herself. After the divine purpose has been fulfilled upon Zion and Jerusalem she will be punished herself and great will be her overthrow (12). Her folly lay in not recognizing her mission and her limitations and called forth the cry of Jehovah:

> '*Shall an axe boast over the man that wields it,*
> *Or saw treat with insolence him that doth handle it?*

As if ever a rod could swing him that doth lift it,
Or staff of wood could brandish a man' (15).

The staff in their hand (5); i.e. in the hand of the Assyrians. They who were to be the means of the overthrow and chastisement of Israel were themselves but a *rod* in the hand of God. *An hypocritical nation* (6); i.e. Judah. *Howbeit he meaneth not so* (7). The meaning is that Assyria does not regard herself as merely an instrument. She regards herself as all-powerful and in complete control of all her acts and designs. *Calno ... Damascus* (9). All these towns had been taken by Assyria. They were on the line of march from Nineveh to Jerusalem. *Found* (10). Read, with RV mg., 'reached'.

> '*My hand hath seized those kingdoms*
> *With images more than Jerusalem's;*
> *And shall I not do to Jerusalem*
> *And to her images also,*
> *As I have done to Samaria,*
> *And to her idols as well?'*

The Assyrians' supposition is that Jehovah is merely a deity of a particular land, inferior even (10) to the deities of some of the other lands they had conquered. (See Appendix I to Kings, 'The Religion of Israel under the Monarchy'.) *Fruit of the stout heart* (12); i.e. the wicked and sinful conduct growing from their pride and arrogance of the heart. *Bounds* (13); i.e. boundaries. By the rapid advance of her armies frontiers have been obliterated. Verse 14 is another implied slight to Jehovah. The nation's God should protect them as a bird protects her nest. *Shall the axe . . .* (15). The boast of the Assyrian is here made to appear ridiculous by the use of a grotesque simile. See the rendering of this verse given above.

ii. The fate of Assyria and Judah (x. 16–23). In the midst of all the judgment of Jehovah upon His people by means of the Assyrian, the remnant of the faithful will be preserved and saved. The pomp and arrogance of men that seek the overthrow of the chosen race will be thwarted, and still in Zion will Jehovah maintain a remnant true to His name and obedient to His will. *Therefore* (16); i.e. because of the attitude adopted by the Assyrians in verse 15. Verses 16–19 should therefore be interpreted as describing their eventual destruction, not Judah's.

iii. Comfort of Zion: the assurance of Assyria's destruction (x. 24–34). The prophet proceeds to make the promise still more emphatic and asserts again the certainty of Jehovah's care (24). The message is reinforced by a dramatic description of an invading army making its irresistible way against Jerusalem (28–32), but being completely destroyed by Jehovah just when total victory seems in its grasp. The destruction of the Assyrian is likened most tellingly to the fall of a forest in a raging storm (33, 34).

The indignation shall cease (25). Translate:

> '*For yet a little while,*
> *My fury will be spent,*
> *And mine anger shall have an end.'*

A scourge . . . his rod (26). The sense is that as Jehovah in days of old raised a rod against Egypt to punish her, so will He act against Assyria. *Because of the anointing* (27). The meaning is obscure, as is the text. It has been translated 'the yoke (of Israel) is broken by reason of fatness'. The figure is that of a fat ox, which bursts from and leaves his yoke. McFadyen, with Duhm (and RSV), reads 'Rimmon', a place east of Bethel, adding another to the catalogue of place-names.

> '*His burden shall pass from thy shoulder,*
> *His yoke press thy neck no more.*
> *From Rimmon he hath gone up,*
> *He hath come as far as Ai'* (27, 28).

He (28); i.e. the Assyrian army. These verses are full of word-play difficult to reproduce in translation. They describe an imaginary march of the Assyrian host upon Jerusalem from the north and its ultimate destruction.

j. The blessedness of Israel in latter days (xi. 1–16)

i. The Messiah: His Person and His kingdom (xi. 1–9). Judah's enemy having been destroyed, the prophet returns to speak of the Messiah and commits to the inner circle of faithful souls this wonderful prediction of the messianic kingdom. First he describes the character of the Messiah, born of the house of Jesse (1), and portrays His supernatural qualities (2).

> '*The spirit of wisdom and insight,*
> *The spirit of counsel and might,*
> *Of the knowledge and fear of Jehovah.'*

There follows a revelation of the methods of His government (3–5). He shall have no need of the type of guidance that men normally need, for He will not 'judge after the sight of His eyes, nor decide by the words that are poured in His ears' (3). Next there is shown in glowing words the results of His reign. Paradise comes to all animal creation and the whole world rejoices in an entire cosmic redemption (6–8). Over all the works of God's hands peace shall rest and 'the earth shall be filled with the knowledge of the Lord, as the waters cover the sea' (9).

A rod out of the stem of Jesse (1); RV 'a shoot out of the stock of Jesse'. *A Branch* (1); Heb. *netser*; the root of the name Nazareth. Cf. Mt. ii. 23. *He shall not judge after the sight of his eyes* (3). What the eyes see often misleads and what the ears hear is not all the truth. In the messianic kingdom, government and decisions are the result of perfect understanding. This is the natural outflow of a life which, in G. A. Smith's phrase, 'draws its breath in the fear of the Lord'. *Reprove with equity* (4); i.e. settle with equity. *Cockatrice' den* (8); RV mg. 'adder's den'. With this picture of the animal creation sharing in the blessings of the messianic kingdom cf. Ho. ii. 18 and Rom. viii. 18ff.

ii. The triumphal return (xi. 10–16). The prophecy is brought to a climax with the promise that from lands far distant and near Jehovah will gather His ransomed people home to the land of their fathers (10–12). The return will be in the nature of a triumphal march down one mighty prepared highway and it will be to the 'root of Jesse standing as ensign to the people' that all the tribes and nations shall resort (10). *The second time* (11). The first was the deliverance from Egypt. In verse 11, after the mention of Assyria, the other countries then threatening Judah are referred to in geographical order as encircling Palestine. They are to be regarded as referring to the whole earth. *Pathros;* southern Egypt. *Cush;* Ethiopia. *Elam;* southeast of Babylonia. *Shinar;* Babylonia. *Hamath;* on the Orontes, 110 miles north of Damascus. *The sea* is the Mediterranean. The complete fulfilment of the prophecy still tarries and will be when 'all Israel shall be saved' (Rom. xi. 26). *An ensign for the nations* (12). Note the universality of prophecy. Here is the redemption of the Gentiles (cf. verse 10). *Outcasts* is masculine, *dispersed* is feminine, in the Hebrew. *The tongue of the Egyptian sea* (15) is the Red Sea. *The river* (15) is the Euphrates.

k. Song of thanksgiving (xii. 1–6)

The hymn of thanksgiving which now follows will be sung by the redeemed people of God *in that day* (1) when Jehovah will have accomplished His sovereign purpose. There are two movements. In the first (verses 1 and 2) the nation herself, redeemed by great mercy and mighty acts, is heard singing the praises of her God. In the second (verses 3–6) the prophet is addressing the nation thus delivered. The Psalm is a counterpart to the song in Ex. xv, sung by the children of Israel after their deliverance from Egypt.

Wells of salvation (3). No doubt there is an allusion here to the water so miraculously supplied to the children of Israel when crossing the wilderness. *Declare his doings among the people* (4). Another evidence of the universality of the divine redemption. The chosen people are saved in order that they might tell forth the message to the nations everywhere. *This is known . . .* (5). Rather, as in RV, 'let this be known'. *Great is the Holy One of Israel in the midst of thee* (6). Here is the chief reason for the strength of the city and the joy of the people. It is that the One who is great in the midst of her is holy. In the midst of the city of God, the kingdom of heaven, the Great One is the Holy One. That separation from evil ensures His victory in His warfare and guarantees the permanence of His kingdom. This is therefore the supreme note in the song which celebrates His reign.

II. PROPHECIES DIRECTED AGAINST FOREIGN AND HOSTILE NATIONS.
xiii. 1—xxiii. 18

In this section there are ten 'burdens' (or oracles; see note below) concerning the nations, and one

which concerns Jerusalem. All of them lay stress upon the fact of the sovereignty of Jehovah and that it is He who overrules the affairs of the nations. This is the supreme value of their messages.

a. Concerning Babylon (xiii. 1—xiv. 23)

This magnificent poem consists of two movements quite distinct in style, namely, xiii. 2–22, which prophesies the plundering of Babylon by the Medes (17), and xiv. 4b–23, a song of triumph to be sung by the Jews to celebrate the downfall of their foes. The two sections are loosely joined together by a few verses (xiv. 1–4a) in a different metre. The poem in its entirety is a description of a proud, overweening and relentless power being destroyed by the might of Jehovah. Graphically the prophet pictures the hosts mustering against this ruthless nation which has so completely held the world in its grasp. Jehovah Himself calls His forces to battle (4). Thus is encompassed the downfall of the enemy of God. Where formerly she exulted in her glory (19) desolation reigns (20–22), and her people are scattered to the four winds of heaven (14).

Burden (1), or 'oracle'. The word is usually applied to threatenings, though not always. In Pr. xxx. 1 and xxxi. 1 the word *massa* is translated as 'prophecy' in AV and 'oracle' in RV. See Zc. ix. 1n. *The nobles* (2); i.e. the Babylonians. *I* (3); i.e. Jehovah. *My sanctified ones* (3); RV 'my consecrated ones'. Leaders of the armies are being called by Jehovah Himself and are mustering for the battle. *The golden wedge of Ophir* (12). Rather, as in RV, 'pure gold of Ophir'. So terrible will be the judgment, survivors will be few and men will become rarer than gold. *It shall be as the chased roe* (14). Or rather, 'gazelle which is frightened.' *Owls* (21); RV 'ostriches'. *Satyrs* (21); RV mg. 'he-goats'. *Dragons* (22); RV 'jackals'.

Verses 1–4a of chapter xiv are a connecting link between the picture of overthrow and the song of triumph which is to follow. The return of Israel to her own land is sure and she will be joined by others in the worship and service of Jehovah (1, 2). In the day when this rest from labour and tumult has been given them, this song shall be sung tauntingly over the king of Babylon (3, 4).

The picture in xiv. 4b–23 is of the eclipse, overthrow and death of the Babylonian tyrant. The colours of the poetry and imagery are superb and awesome. In order to render with dramatic force his particular theme of the vanity of human arrogance, the prophet employs the idea of Sheol (9, 11, 15, RV), that state after death which swallows up all living. There dwell the shades of departed men, able to greet new arrivals in their dim abode (10, 11) and with consciousness sufficient to wonder at the fall of such a mighty one (12). Here was one who had thought to climb the slopes of the immortals (13, 14) and now he is, just like themselves, brought low in death (10, 15). The very fact of his presence amongst them is supreme evidence of his downfall and overthrow. Nothing could be more absolute. On earth his lot is blood, slaughter, squalor and death (16, 17); in Sheol a place amongst the community of shuddering ghosts (18–20).

The following translation of verses 4–21 in its verse form will be more helpful than a fuller commentary.

How stilled is the tyrant become!
  How stilled is his insolent fury!
Broke hath Jehovah the rod
  Of the godless, the sceptre of despots,
Which smote the people with passion
  with stroke unremitting,
Which trampled the nations in anger
  with tread unrelenting.
At rest is the earth, all is quiet,
  They burst into singing.
Yea the pines at thy fate are rejoicing,
  And Lebanon's cedars, saying,
'Since low thou art lain there appeareth
  No woodsman out to destroy us.'
               (Verses 4–8)

Sheol beneath is a-shuddering,
  She waiteth for thine arrival;
Stirring the shades up to greet thee,
  All who were monarchs on earth.
Bidding rise up from their thrones
  All the kings of the peoples.
All of them answer and say to thee,
  'So thou too art feeble as we are,
Like unto us art become.'
Thy pride now to Sheol is levelled—
  The strumming of harps:
Under thee scattered are maggots,
  Thy coverlet worms.
              (Verses 9–11)

How art thou fallen from heaven,
  Lucifer, son of the morning,
How art thou cut to the earth
  Thou who didst lay low the nations.
And thou, thou didst say in thine heart,
  'Into the heavens I'll ascend,
Over God's stars set my throne,
  Sit on the mount of assembly,
In the farthest parts of the North.
I will climb o'er the peaks of the clouds
  And rival the Most High.'
But, ah! thou art brought down to Sheol,
  To the very depths of the pit.
            (Verses 12–15)

They who behold thee are gazing,
  gazing upon thee intently,
'Is this the mighty earth-shaker?
  Is this the shaker of kingdoms?
That made the earth like a desert,
  That tore down her cities,
That freed not the prisoners from fetters
  To return everyone to his home?'
All kings of nations, aye, all of them,
  Lie in their tombs full of honour.
But thou! thou art cast from thy grave

Like a branch that is loathsome.
Shrouded in slain, the sword-pierced,
  Like a carcase trampled by feet,
  Going down to the floor of the pit.
Thou shalt not be joined unto them
  Where they lie buried;
For thou hast ruined thy land
  And hast slaughtered thy people.
Never again be it mentioned
  The seed of this evil-doer.
Slaughter prepare for his children
  To atone for the guilt of their father;
Lest they rise up and possess the land
  Filling the face of the world with cities.
            (Verses 16–21)

b. Concerning Assyria (xiv. 24–27)

Here is the emphatic oath of Jehovah that the Assyrian power shall be broken (24, 25). The plan is formed and nothing can withstand its consummation (26, 27). The language is akin to that of x. 24–27. *In my land* (25). The death-blow against Assyria was struck in the highlands of Judaea.

c. Concerning Philistia (xiv. 28–32)

This burden was uttered in the year that king Ahaz died (28). Representatives from Philistia (29, RV: *Palestina*, AV) were in the city at the time (32), having come to Judah to solicit help, or possibly to offer an alliance with the Jews. It was this which called forth the burden of the prophet. Philistia is warned not to rejoice over the fact that one Assyrian king is dead (see note below), for a worse one shall arise (29). Philistia will be discomfited; her doom is sure (31). But Zion shall stand, for 'Jehovah hath founded Zion' (32). This was a declaration that no safety was to be found in alliances with nations which were corrupt and that the salvation of Jerusalem was sure, for it was founded by God. This demanded the maintenance by Zion of a true relationship with its Founder.

The rod of him that smote thee (29). The reference is most probably to Assyria. It is not likely that the 'rod' has reference to the royal house of Judah. *Howl, O gate* (31), i.e. city-gates, meaning the cities themselves. *Smoke* (31). No doubt the smoke of war, the smoke of mighty encampments and burning villages. *None shall be alone* (31); RSV 'There is no straggler in his ranks'. In other words, discipline will be perfect.

d. Concerning Moab (xv. 1—xvi. 14)

These two chapters contain one connected oracle concerning the Moabites. A glance at the history of this people will aid the understanding of the oracle. After the death of Solomon the Moabites had transferred their loyalty from Judah to Israel but later, after the death of Ahab, they broke away, refusing to pay the annual tribute (2 Ki. iii. 5). Jehoram, Ahab's son, aided by Jehoshaphat of Judah, made war against Moab. The capital, Ar, was captured and Kir, their chief fortress, was destroyed (2 Ki. iii.

25). Memories of the terror caused by the invaders at that time are recalled in xv. 1–9. The same kind of situation will arise again; but through the prophet deliverance is promised if they will only submit to the authority of Judah.

Chapter xv has for its theme the disaster of Moab. As before, it will be 'in a night', i.e. with startling suddenness (1). Two of her cities are laid waste and she is brought low in desolation and impotence. There can be no gainsaying the righteousness of the judgment, for she has been both proud and wicked. Notwithstanding all, the suffering of the people of Moab touches the heart of the prophet and he cries out for them (5).

Chapter xvi is remarkable for several things. First of all there is an exhortation given to her to send tribute in her grief to the mount of the daughter of Zion (1). There follows a call to Zion to shelter the outcasts of Moab and espouse her cause (3; see RV mg.). Verses 4, 5 hold out the way of deliverance and the benefits which will be hers under the messianic reign. This is wonderful indeed, for it reveals that the outlook of the prophecy is so enlarged as to take in the wider purposes of God for the ultimate deliverance of all nations. The oracle continues with a reference to the one great factor which will be an obstacle to this, the arrogance of Moab (6). This pride will not only keep their country in ruin, but will make it impossible for them to prevail in prayer at their own sanctuary (12).

In the night (xv. 1); RV 'in a night'; i.e. suddenly and without warning. *He* (2); i.e. 'the people of Moab'. *Bajith* (2); the house, i.e. the temple of their God. Cf. xvi. 12.

His life shall be grievous . . . (4). The verse can be read thus:

'*Heshbon and Elealah cry out,*
Their voice reaches Jahaz:
Whereat Moab's loins are a-shaking,
Her soul is a-trembling.'

My heart shall cry (5). Here is the true prophetic spirit. This is the true evidence of sympathy and co-operation with God. Here too is the promise of mercy for Moab, despite her pride and arrogant spirit. *An heifer of three years old* (5). The Hebrew probably represents a place name. See RV. *Shall they carry away* (7), i.e. the Moabites themselves. This is the final demonstration of their plight. They take what they can salvage from the ruin of their homes and cross the frontier stream into the land of Idumaea. *The brook of the willows* (7). Probably the brook at the southern end of the Red Sea which formed the boundary between Moab and Edom.

The lamb (xvi. 1); RV 'the lambs'. This is the call to the men of Moab to put themselves again under the protection of Judah. This would be done in the first instance by bringing the normal tribute of lambs. See 2 Ki. iii. 4. *Sela* (1). Capital city of Edom where the Moabites had taken refuge. *The fords of Arnon* (2). Cf. Nu. xxi. 13.

Take counsel (3). Sometimes understood as the entreaty of the Moabites to the men of Judah to give them the aid of their counsel and protection. Under this interpretation verses 4 and 5 are a continuation of this appeal to the 'dwellers in Zion' to espouse their cause and grant them aid. There are considerable difficulties in this view, not the least being that this puts words full of light as to the principles of the messianic kingdom into the mouths of the men of Moab. It would appear much more natural to regard verse 3 as the call of the prophet to the men of Judah to begin devising means at once of delivering the outcast and the refugee, and verses 4 and 5 as constituting the prophet's message to Moab as to the way by which she may be delivered.

Verse 6 may be rendered:

'*We have heard of the pride of Moab,*
She is utterly proud—
Of her haughtiness, anger and pride,
Of her baseless pretensions.'

The foundations (7); RV 'raisin-cakes'. These were connected with the culture of the vine. 'The cakes of pressed grapes' is a likely translation. In verse 8 the great vine-culture of Moab is represented under the image of a single vine. The vine was one of the principal products of the land. *As the years of an hireling* (14); i.e. 'no more, no less'. The years of the hireling were strictly measured, and so shall the judgment of the Lord God be.

e. Concerning Damascus and Northern Israel (xvii. 1–11)

At the time of this oracle Israel was leagued with Damascus so as to protect herself against Assyria. The policy of Judah, on the other hand (a policy which Isaiah resisted with all his powers), was that of seeking the aid of Assyria against the coalition threatening from the north. In this burden the prophet foretells the destruction of Damascus (1–5), and shows thereby how vain is the hope on which Israel sets her trust (8). What would happen would be that Israel would be left a mere remnant (6). As a result of this judgment men would turn to God again and cease trusting in their own policies. This oracle must have been spoken early in Isaiah's ministry, perhaps in the very first year of Ahaz, about 735 B.C. Fulfilment came through the invasions of Tiglath-pileser (2 Ki. xv. 29) and Shalmaneser (2 Ki. xvii).

Aroer (2). Cf. Jos. xiii. 16, 25, where two Aroers are referred to; these may be the cities of Aroer here noted as forsaken. *The fortress* (3); i.e. Damascus, which helped to protect the northern kingdom from the Assyrians. *They shall be as the glory . . .* (3). In other words, 'their fate shall be as Israel's fate'.

Verses 4–6 describe the destruction of Ephraim under the figures of wasting disease, reaping of grain and the gathering of olives. *Valley of Rephaim* (5). Cf. Jos. xv. 8. Lit. 'the valley of giants'. It lay south-west of Jerusalem and was famous for its fertility. *Gleaning grapes shall be left in it* (6). Translate:

> Like gleanings that are left
> When the olive tree hath been beaten,
> Four or five on the boughs of a fruit tree;
> Thus saith Jehovah, the God of Israel.

The groves (8); RV 'Asherim'. These were poles of wood representing female goddesses, generally found in association with Canaanite altars, but also used in the debased Jehovah worship which the prophets condemned. (See Appendix I to Kings, 'The Religion of Israel under the Monarchy'.) *Images* (8); 'pillars of the sun.' These were also used in the worship of Baal, although the exact meaning is doubtful. RSV renders 'altars of incense'. *Pleasant plants . . . strange slips* (10). 'Plants of Adonis and strange vines'. The figurative allusion is to Israel's acceptance of foreign practices, cults and alliances.

f. Prophetic soliloquy (xvii. 12—xviii. 7)

This section can well be taken as a whole and regarded as an oracle in two movements, each introduced by the exclamation 'Ah!' (xvii. 12 and xviii. 1, RV). In this setting the oracle is a prophetic soliloquy in the midst of the burdens of the nations, occasioned by the presence of Ethiopian ambassadors at the court of Judah (xviii. 1, 2). The presence of these foreigners causes the prophet to voice his awareness of the tumult of the nations round about (xvii. 12, 13). The vanity of all such tumult, however, is manifest to the servant of the Lord: *God shall rebuke them* (xvii. 13). The eternal providence stands firm as a rock amidst the swirling sea of the world's tempestuous fury. The onrushing hosts, although they be the instruments for a time of divine judgment, are overwhelmed in a night and utterly destroyed (14). This is the figure of the first movement, that of a mighty storm. The second movement introduces another figure. It is that of stillness, the stillness of the heat and the dew (xviii. 4). These are necessary to ripen grain and produce the harvest. And the very silence of God is seen as a preparation of His judgment and vengeance upon guilty nations, just as the clear heat of the sunshine and the still dews of the morning develop and compel the harvests of nature. The inactivity of heaven is only seeming. In the midst of the silence there is 'beholding': 'For thus hath the Lord said unto me, I will be still, and I will behold in my dwelling place; like clear heat in sunshine, like a cloud of dew in the heat of harvest' (xviii. 4, RV).

Woe to the multitude (xvii. 12). Rather 'Ah, the uproar of many peoples' (RV). *And behold at eveningtide trouble* (14). These verses are commonly understood of Sennacherib's rush upon Jerusalem, and this particular verse is an exact summary of the sudden break-up and speedy retreat of his army from before Jerusalem (see 2 Ki. xix. 35).

The land shadowing with wings (xviii. 1); RV 'the land of the rustling of wings'; i.e. Libya and Ethiopia. 'The buzzing of innumerable flies is the great feature of this whole region and may be employed as an emblem of the motley and swarming population.' *Go, ye swift messengers* (2). Omit the word *saying* inserted by the AV and RV and treat the remainder of the chapter as the message given by Isaiah to the ambassadors to take back with them. *Scattered and peeled* (2). 'Tall and bronze-skinned' (McFadyen); cf. RV and see also verse 7. *I will take my rest* (4). 'Though the mills of God grind slowly, yet they grind exceeding small.' *When the bud is perfect* (5). Just when the nefarious design is almost complete, God will intervene and destroy it utterly. *In that time* (7); i.e. when the Assyrian is defeated the Ethiopians will bring gifts to Zion, to the Lord of hosts.

g. Concerning Egypt (xix. 1–25)

This oracle is in two parts. Of them G. A. Smith writes: 'The first fifteen verses describe judgment as ready to fall on the land of the Pharaohs. The last ten speak of the religious results to Egypt of that judgment, and they form the most universal and missionary of all Isaiah's prophecies.'

The first section (1–15) bears the usual marks of complete catastrophe which we have seen in the foregoing oracles. The wrath of Jehovah and His fearful judgments will make desolate the whole land (1). The religion of Egypt will fail (3) and the people themselves, lacking the solace of its faith and mystery, will plunge into civil strife (2), which will end in complete despotism (4). After this, physical calamities will follow swiftly. The Nile will dry up and all native prosperity will thereby come to an end (5–10). Existence itself will be jeopardized. The wisdom lore of their people will prove unavailing (11–13) and the land will suffer and fear under its load of misfortune (14, 15). Such is the overthrow by divine judgment which the prophet sees coming upon Egypt.

The second section (16–25) of the oracle is altogether different in tone. It foretells the effect upon Egypt which will ultimately be revealed when Jehovah will have finished His strange work. Egypt is seen turning to Jehovah (21); the worship of Jehovah is established within her borders (19). Deliverance is brought to her by a saviour sent by Him (20). Jehovah will deal with Egypt by the twin method of smiting and healing (22). That however is not all. Beyond all that has been revealed of Egypt's deliverance and redemption, the prophet speaks of a still more glorious result. The ancient foes of Israel, Egypt and Assyria, are seen joined together by Israel. Israel's national territory becomes the open highway across which they pass in amicable association with each other. The three states are united in the one grand alliance with the common worship of Jehovah as the great cement of their union (23–25).

I will set . . . (2). On the death of Tirhakah, who at the time of this oracle was on the throne, Egypt was cursed with a period of internal strife, ending in the dismemberment of the land into twelve separate states, all subject to Assyria (4). *The waters shall fail from the sea* (5), i.e. the Nile. In the annual overflow of its banks the Nile has all the appearance of a sea. Cf. Na. iii. 8. McFadyen translates verses 5–7:

'The sea shall be drained of its water,
  The river be parched and dry;
Its branches shall dwindle and stink,
  And the arms of the Nile shall be parched.
Reeds and rushes shall wither,
  The sedge on its brink shall shrivel;
And all that is sown by the Nile
  Shall be withered and whirled into nothing.'

They that work in fine flax (9). A notable industry of Egypt, then and now. Moisture, so essential to their craft, would disappear with the drying up of the sea. *They shall be broken . . .* (10). The translation and meaning are alike uncertain. See RV, 'And her pillars shall be broken in pieces, all they that work for hire shall be grieved in soul.' *Zoan* (11). A great and ancient city in the Delta, on one of the eastern branches of the Nile. *Where are they?* (12). This interrogatory method is very characteristic of the latter chapters of Isaiah. Cf. xli. 22, 26, xliii. 9, xlv. 21, xlviii. 14. *Noph* (13). Egyptian, 'Men-nophri'. Gk. 'Memphis'. *Head or tail, branch or rush* (15). Cf. ix. 14. 'Branch' should be translated 'palm-branch'. The thought is that no matter from what state of society the efforts are made, they will all alike fail.

The city of destruction (18); i.e. the city in which the temple of the sun (*heres*) has been destroyed (*heres*); evidently a pun on the name of Heliopolis ('city of the sun'). *The language of Canaan* (18) ('the lip', AV mg.) is north-west Semitic, i.e. Hebrew. *A highway* (23). The road from Assyria to Egypt led through the land of Israel. *In that day shall Israel be the third* (24); i.e. all three nations shall be equally joined together in the bonds of amity. *My people . . . the work of my hands . . . mine inheritance* (25). This is the high-water mark in that element of prophetic utterance which saw the ultimate end of the processes of the work of Jehovah in the overcoming of the opposition of the nations and their inclusion in the realized kingdom on earth.

h. Warning against the folly of an alliance with Egypt (xx. 1–6)

The date of this oracle can be definitely fixed, for Sargon's own inscriptions regarding the attack on Ashdod give it as 711 B.C. It tells how Isaiah went barefoot and not fully clothed for three years through the streets of Jerusalem as a sign against Egypt (2). His message in doing so was that no help could be derived from Egypt or Ethiopia against the Assyrian attack (5). His wretched appearance was a sign and symbol of what would happen to Egypt as a result of Assyria's triumph over her (3, 4). The need for the message was clear, for it is evident that the rulers of Jerusalem had given up hope of receiving aid from Assyria and were now toying with the idea of allying themselves with Egypt. This, cried the prophet, was futile, for Egypt herself was doomed to overthrow by Assyria. In the final words of the oracle we have a reinforcement of the teaching (6). The inhabitants of the coastland, namely Palestine as a whole, see the futility of such expectation and cry out: 'And we, how shall we escape?' The outcome of the prophecy was revealed in subsequent history just as Isaiah had so clearly spoken.

Ashdod (1). One of the five cities of the Philistines. *Tartan* (1). The official title for the commander-in-chief. *Like as my servant* (3). For similar acted prophecies cf. Ezk. iv and v. *Isle* (6); RV 'coastland'; i.e. Palestine. Translate: 'If this be the fate of those to whom we have fled in expectation of help and deliverance from the king of Assyria, how shall we escape?'

i. Concerning the wilderness of the sea (xxi. 1–10)

This oracle announces, but also laments, the fall of Babylon. In this prophecy Isaiah regards Babylon as he has just been regarding Egypt: quite useless to Judah, because certain to go down before the might of Assyria (1, 2). And should the Jews think of turning back to Egypt after Assyria has dealt with her and turned to settle with Babylon, Isaiah tells them that it is no good, for Elam and Media are joined with Assyria in the attack on Babylon. The attack is quite unexpected, for there she is preparing the table, eating and drinking (5). So suddenly is the call given to her warriors to arise to battle: 'Arise, ye princes, and anoint the shield' (5). Isaiah shrinks from beholding what is done but goes to his watch-tower at the commandment of the Lord (6). At length tidings come and the message is heard: 'Fallen, fallen is Babylon' (9). The oracle ends with Isaiah protesting that this, however unpalatable it may be, is the certain message from Jehovah (10). As the monuments reveal, the prediction refers to the overthrow of Babylon by Sargon about 710 B.C.

The desert of the sea (1). Delitzsch writes of this: 'The land on which Babylon stood was a "midbar", a great plain running to the south by Arabia Deserta, and so intersected by the Euphrates and canals, as well as by marshes and lakes, that it floated, as it were, in the sea.' *It cometh* (1), i.e. the noise of the attack upon Babylon. *Elam* (2). Province of Susis, south of Assyria. *Eat, drink* (5). The tables are ready. Here is a scene from within the city gates. There is no alarm as yet and the inhabitants are busy eating and drinking. *Arise, ye princes* (5). This is the sudden call to arms at the onset of the Assyrian foe. The prophet recoils from thinking of the scene of carnage and destruction and at the commandment of Jehovah (6) retires to the watch-tower to await tidings and to declare from that place whatever is revealed. *And he cried, A lion* (8); RV 'He cried as a lion', i.e. as though wild with anxious waiting. Others read, by a simple change of letter, 'Watchman'. *O my threshing . . .* (10). This is language of infinite pathos.

> '*Ye my folk that were threshed,*
> *Like the corn on the floor,*
> *I have told you my message*
> *From Israel's God,*
> *From Jehovah of hosts.*'

They had been hoping for other news, news that Assyria would be vanquished in battle. But the prophet must speak whatever is revealed, no matter how unpleasant the hearing of it may be.

j. Concerning Dumah (xxi. 11, 12)

Dumah, which means silence, is used as an anagram for Edom. This no doubt for a double reason: that silence is wont to cover their land and that this silence is symbolic of the silence of decay under whose peril they are lying. The message is indefinite. Perhaps it might be said that the very indefiniteness is the message. Out of the silence of the dark there comes a question: 'Watchman, what of the night?' (11). That is the mental attitude of Edom, one of inquiry concerning her future. The answer given is purposefully indefinite also; it is that there are signs of morning and night (12). The meaning surely is that Edom by her own attitude or choice would decide whether she would come to the morning or the night. A more definite answer may be given them later on, if they will return again. *He calleth* (11); RV 'One calleth'. *What of the night?* (11). The sense is easily lost in the AV. The question that is asked is 'How much of the night is already passed?' The sense may be that Edom feels the night is lasting intolerably long.

k. Concerning Arabia (xxi. 13–17)

The prophet now passes from Dumah to their near neighbours, the Dedanites, who were travelling merchants (13). The dislocations caused by war and the insecurity which follows to distant places are seen oppressing them (14, 15). At the time of the Assyrian attacks the merchants have to leave the normal trading routes and lodge in the forests (13). Fugitives from war-scarred areas are entertained and from the blight there seems no escape. But worse is to come. These fugitives are but the advance parties of great armies that within a year will spread havoc across the land of the children of Kedar (16, 17). This is the word of Jehovah and nought can gainsay it. *Dedanim* (13). Merchants of Dedan; a trading tribe of north-western Arabia. The interruption of their caravans and the necessity imposed on them of leaving the highway and lodging in the thickets is a proof of the disrupted nature of the land caused by war. *Tema* (14), south of Dedan. *The years of an hireling* (16). See xvi. 14n. *Kedar* (17). A general designation for all the north Arabian tribes.

l. Concerning the valley of vision (xxii. 1–25)

The prophet now turns from his oracles concerning the nations around Palestine and speaks of the condition of things in Jerusalem itself. There are two sections, the first (1–14) dealing with the people in general and the hopeless condition of things to which they have brought themselves, the other (15–25) dealing with matters of policy and the direction of the affairs of the city by its rulers.

The opening words are addressed to a city that has gone riotously wild, all for no reason (1). Why are you thus rejoicing, demands Isaiah, when you have nothing to celebrate? (2). Away with your mad riot and foolish holiday! For a day of perplexity and blank confusion is upon you by the very ordination of Jehovah, and that in this very place, the valley of vision, the very home of prophecy (3–5). Turning to the foe for a brief glance, the prophet describes their appearance (7). But this had not sent them back to their God, the only sure Defence in an hour of trouble. They have looked to the forest-houses, the arsenals of Solomon, to the fortifications around the city, but not to Jehovah (8–11). The Lord had called them to weeping and penitence, but instead they responded with drunken revelry (12, 13). For this absolute forgetfulness of God there can be no forgiveness (14).

Only his unconquerable assurance in the survival of the remnant can have made Isaiah turn to the next section of his message to Jerusalem. For though he has thus foretold the destruction of his fellow-countrymen, yet he now proceeds to speak of ways and means of securing a better condition of things within the city. This he does by demanding that Shebna, the mayor of the palace, should be removed from office (15–19). Though his wrongdoing is not specifically mentioned, he was no doubt the leader of the party desiring alliance with Egypt. Isaiah demands that he be superseded and Eliakim, son of Hilkiah, put in his place (20–23). That this was done is evident from the fact that when Assyria stood before the gates Eliakim held the office and Shebna the second place (2 Ki. xviii. 18; Is. xxxvi. 3, 11, 22). In the closing lines of the oracle the prophet addresses Eliakim, warning him of the dangers of his high office (24, 25). The entanglements of family and indolent dependants may be so great as to encompass his own fall. Indeed the prophet states that this will actually occur. 'His family will hang upon him with all their weight, offspring and offscourings, all the little vessels, from the vessels of cups to the vessels of flagons. In that day, saith Jehovah of hosts, shall the peg that was knocked into a firm place give way and down shall come in ruin all who had depended upon it; for Jehovah of hosts hath spoken it' (24, 25).

The valley of vision (1); i.e. Jerusalem. It is the place of vision for it is the very home of prophecy. In the present state of affairs the city is surrounded by a great army, to see which all the inhabitants of the city climb to the roof-tops and other vantage points. *A . . . joyous city* (2). The city, instead of turning in penitence to Jehovah, had indulged in a wild riot of wine and song. *Not slain with the sword* (2). The prophet speaks thus scathingly, endeavouring to shame the people of the city. They have no cause for joy as have those whose sons have fallen in battle facing the foe. The death that stalks the city streets is that of pestilence and hunger. *Bound by the archers* (3); lit. 'made prisoners without the bow', i.e. without resisting. *A day of trouble* (5). The cumulative force of the description is telling: disappointment, perplexity, the knowledge that it is ordained by Jehovah, the destruction of the last rampart, and only the hills left to which to cry for help. *The house of the forest* (8); i.e. the house of the forest of Lebanon, so called from its cedar pillars. It was a part of the palace at Jerusalem, and partly served the purpose of an armoury.

Verses 9–11 are a prose addition. J. E. McFadyen translates: 'Ye collected the waters of the lower pool, ye counted the houses of Jerusalem, and demolished them (to secure material) for the fortification of the wall, and ye made a reservoir between the two walls for the water of the old pool.'

In verse 17 see RV and RV mg.

m. Concerning Tyre (xxiii. 1–18)

The chapter divides into two sections. The first (1–14) is a dramatic poem describing the destruction of the great Phoenician city, Tyre. There are three stanzas in the elegy, opening with a description of the mariners of Phoenicia, putting in at Cyprus on their homeward voyage, and hearing with consternation tidings of the awful fate which has befallen Tyre (1–5). The port to which they had hoped to come at the end of their voyage is no more (6–11). Sidon is called to lament the fate of her offspring and the prophet reveals that what has come to pass is by the act of Jehovah of hosts (12–14).

The second section (15–18), which is in prose form, tells how the desolation will last for a period of seventy years. At the end of that time Tyre will again be restored to prosperity and wealth, for Jehovah will visit her (17). No evidence will be found, however, of any alteration in her ways. As she was before, so shall she continue to be; a harlot, delighting in meretricious practices, trafficking with all the kingdoms of the world. Then follows the word: 'And her merchandise and her hire shall be holiness to the Lord' (18). This obviously does not mean that Tyre will conduct her business on principles that are holy; the very reverse has just been stated. What is signified is that under divine pressure her gains will not be preserved for her own use but devoted to the services of the people of God.

Tyre (1). This ancient city, a colony of Sidon (4), was located on the coast of Syria and was built partly on the mainland and partly on an island off shore. For a long time it was a great commercial centre, its ocean-going traffic extending to the limits of the seas. Many colonies were formed from it (see verse 7: 'whose feet in the olden time bore her to settle afar'). G. A. Smith says of this chapter: 'Isaiah's chapter on Tyre is of the greatest interest. It contains the prophet's vision of commerce the first time commerce had grown vast enough to impress his people's imagination, as well as a criticism of the spirit of commerce from the standpoint of the God of righteousness.' *Ships of Tarshish* (1). Cf. ii. 16n. The situation of this port has been much discussed. Some regard it as the celebrated Phoenician colony of Tartessus on the Atlantic coast of Spain, not far from the modern Cadiz. Others hold that it was in Italy and that its people were Tyrrhenians or Etruscans. *Land of Chittim* (1); i.e. Cyprus. *Sihor* (3); i.e. the Nile. Translate:

'Whose cargo was wheat from the Nile
And revenue trade with all nations.'

Be thou ashamed, O Zidon . . . (4). McFadyen translates:

'O Sidon, thou Mother of cities,
Thou stronghold of ocean,
In shame take up this lament.
"The youths that with anguish I bore and
brought up
And the maidens I reared, are no more."'

As at the report (5). 'When the tidings come to Egypt.' *Her merchandise* (18). This wealth shall be used for the benefit of the people of Jehovah.

III. ISAIAH'S APOCALYPSE: THE JUDGMENTS OF JEHOVAH AGAINST THE WORLD'S SIN. xxiv. 1—xxvii. 13

a. World judgment (xxiv. 1–23)

With this chapter we pass into a new section of the book of Isaiah. Chapters xxiv—xxvii form one particular prophetic utterance and have been aptly described as 'Isaiah's apocalypse'. In the oracles of the nations which have just been recorded, the prophet had looked beyond his own nation and seen and spoken of the peoples that surrounded her on every side. At the centre, however, of all his thought was the chosen race and its place in the economy of Jehovah. In this section a still wider outlook is taken and the whole earth is regarded as being visited by God. Again, however, the people of God are central and in all the judgments that befall the land their deliverance and salvation is secure.

Chapter xxiv begins with a statement (1) that the desolation which is to come upon the earth is the work of Jehovah. Why this is so is next made clear; it is because of the sins of men (5). The act of God is the operation of the very laws which man has disobeyed. It is this which makes stale all earth's boasted pleasures (6–12). For a little, amid all the cataclysm of nations and empires, the voice of the redeemed is heard in praise of Jehovah (13–16), but this again is submerged in the wail of distress from suffering men. 'Ah, misery, misery me, cried I, for the robbers are robbing and robbing still. Terror and pit and snare are upon thee, O inhabitant of the earth. Broken, utterly broken, is the earth' (16, 17). Thus are the judgments of Jehovah abroad in all the earth; nor do the rulers and principalities of evil escape (21). Judgment, irrevocable and dire, will fall upon the race that has broken the divine decrees. Through it all, Jehovah will be moving forward to the consummation of history when His kingdom shall be established 'in Mount Zion, and before his ancients gloriously' (23).

Behold, the Lord maketh the earth empty (1). The words are those which are used for cleaning a dirty dish. The thought is expressive and thorough. The rest of the chapter is illustration of this upturning and emptying of the earth. *In the fires* (15). Lit. 'in the lights'. This probably means 'in the land of light', i.e. the East (RV). *My leanness, my leanness* (16). Better, as in RV, 'I pine away'. The judgment is not confined to the earth. Its effects reach to the heavens and to the *host of the high ones that are on high* (21). This must surely refer to powers of evil which have been activating the course of evil upon the earth.

b. Thanksgiving and triumph (xxv. 1-12)

The activity of Jehovah in His day will be not merely to destroy all that defiles and disfigures His creation; not merely to subdue all false authority, both spiritual and human. Over it all will shine the blessed light of His deliverance of the poor and the needy (1–5). His activity will be redemptive and enlightening. No wonder, then, that following upon the theme of destruction (xxiv) this clear-ringing strain of joyful thanksgiving should be lifted from the hearts of those who know Him and who have been kept in the midst of all His judgments in perfect peace. Indeed it appears from verse 9 that the prophet thinks that the very judgments will be a means of revealing Jehovah and proving that through Him alone is salvation possible.

In the centre of the chapter occurs the wonderful promise that death will be swallowed up in victory (8), all the more remarkable because immortality is not a thought which comes much to the surface in the Old Testament. Cf. also xxvi. 19n.

Of chapters xxv—xxvii G. A. Smith writes: 'These chapters stand in the front rank of evangelical prophecy. In their experience of religion, their characterizations of God's people, their expressions of faith, their missionary hopes and hopes of immortality, they are very rich and edifying.'

Faithfulness and truth (1); lit. 'in perfect faithfulness'. They are proved to be faithful by being fulfilled. *A city* (2). Probably used generically without any special reference to any particular city. The contrast is an extreme one between what man devises and what is in the plan of God. *Palace of strangers* (2). A very slight change in the Hebrew makes it possible to read 'palace of pride'. *The poor . . . the needy* (4). 'In these chapters God's people are described by adjectives signifying spiritual qualities. Their nationality is no more pleaded, only their hunger and thirst after God . . .' (G. A. Smith). *Branch* (5); RV 'song'. *In this mountain* (6); i.e. mount Zion. Cf. xxiv. 23.

He will destroy (7). This is one of the most blessed of the promises contained in the chapter. That veil which hangs over the spirit of man and makes it so hard for him to apprehend divine truth will be taken away. The illumination thus granted will bring to light things miraculous and immortal. It is significant that the next verse after this promise deals with the reality of immortality and the destroying of death. *The rebuke of his people* (8). Cf. 1 Cor. xv. 54; Rev. vii. 17, xxi. 4. *Moab* (10). This country, always active against Judah and as such a typical enemy of the chosen race, is here symbolically regarded as portraying the enemies of Jehovah.

c. Gratitude and hope (xxvi. 1-21)

This chapter is another song of praise celebrating the triumphs of true faith in Jehovah. The worship and testimony of a restored and converted Israel are beautifully described. First the company of the redeemed is heard in the exultation of the song of salvation (1); then a voice is heard from heaven, crying: 'Open ye the gates, that the righteous may enter who keep the faith' (2). The blessedness of those that enter thus is described: they are kept in perfect peace, for their minds are stayed upon Jehovah (3); they are strong, for with Jehovah is everlasting strength (4); their way is the way of uprightness, for the most Upright directs their path (7). Then follows the passionate statement of the yearning of the righteous soul after its God (9), and the assertion that only by thus seeking after Him will truth be known. Out of the remembrance of the days that are past and the dominion of other powers over the spirit, the soul cries out in prayer (13).

The climax is reached in the last few verses of the chapter where, after again recalling the darkness of the way that has been travelled, the grand affirmation of faith is made: 'Thy dead shall live; my dead bodies shall arise. Awake and sing, ye that dwell in the dust' (19, RV). This is the most wonderful message yet recorded in this section of the prophecy. In the previous chapter the truth of immortality has been disclosed in the word 'He hath swallowed up death for ever' (xxv. 8, RV). But this goes even further. This is an emphatic statement of the resurrection of the body. Here is the precursor of the full intimation of the great Christian doctrine of immortality. Little wonder that the heart of Israel exults in song (19). The dweller in the dust may well sing, even though surrounded by the wrath and indignation of great and divine judgments.

In that day (1). The repeated recurrence of this phrase in this section of the prophecy should ' noted (see xxiv. 21, xxv. 9, xxvi. 1, xxvii. 1, 2, 12, 13). The day is throughout the day of Jehovah, in which He works His mighty purpose to its grand climax. *Thou . . . dost weigh the path* (7); RV 'direct the path'; RV mg. 'level'. *Therefore* (14). Rather 'for that purpose'. *The dew of herbs* (19). Lit. 'a dew of lights', i.e. it is a heavenly, supernatural awe which rests upon the called of God. *Come, my people . . .* (20, 21). A brief glance, from the security of the sanctuary of the peace of God in the heart of the trusting spirit, to the world of tribulation and anguish where God's judgments are at work. The peace of God is within this sea of trouble.

d. Climax of apocalypse of judgment and grace (xxvii. 1–13)

This last chapter of Isaiah's apocalypse is a prediction of the gracious and happy effects the events already spoken of will produce. After a renewed assertion that all the foes of righteousness and all thwarters of the divine purpose will be destroyed (1) there is introduced a vision of restoration for all the earth through the instrumentality of God's own people. Under the figure of the vineyard (used so tragically in chapter v to speak of the failure of Israel) the prophet speaks of the fruitfulness of Israel as a blessing for the whole earth. Formerly only wild grapes had been produced and the vine, thus failing in its natural function, was given over to processes of judgment. Now the vine is exceedingly fruitful (6). Through judgments, the glorious ideal has been discovered. Just for a little (7–11) the prophet recalls the chastisements she has suffered, and asserts that they have been tempered with mercy and loving-kindness. He affirms, too, that in putting away all her other trusts in false and material things she shall find the forgiveness she needs. The chapter ends with a great trumpet call whereat the exiles from every land arise and make for Zion to worship Jehovah there upon His holy mountain (12, 13).

Leviathan (1). Three empires are envisaged: Assyria (*the piercing* (RV 'swift') *serpent*, for the Tigris flowing swiftly); Babylonia (the *crooked serpent*, for the winding Euphrates); and Egypt (*the dragon*, for Rahab; cf. li. 9 and see note on xxx. 7). *A vineyard* (2). The prophet refers to Israel as a delightful vineyard over which Jehovah stands guard and from which He is gathering the fruit. All pestilential things are by Him removed from it. *Fury is not in me* (4). The sense is that Jehovah can cherish no wrath against His vineyard, but against the briars and thorns, symbol of the enemies of Israel, He will move swiftly for their destruction. *Or let him take hold* (5). This is the alternative to destruction. It is still possible for Israel's foes to make peace with Israel's God. *Them that come* (6). Rather, as in RV, 'in days to come'. McFadyen translates verses 7, 8:

'*Hath Israel been smitten so sorely,*
As those that smote her have been smitten?
Or hath she been slain without remnant.

As those that slew her have been slain?
By dismissal and exile alone
Doth Jehovah contend with her:
He hath swept her away with His blast
That blows fierce in the day of sirocco.'

The ways of Jehovah with His chosen people have been ways of mercy. The chastisement has ever been moderate and designed to bring her to Himself. But forgiveness and restoration are dependent upon renunciation of all pagan worship (9; the sense is clearer in RV).

Yet (10). Read with RV 'For'. *The defenced city* (10). An illustration which the prophet introduces to stress his point regarding the need for turning from idols to serve Jehovah. This is an elaboration of verse 7. The smiting of them that smote Israel is much greater than that of Israel herself. *The Lord shall beat off . . .* (12). RSV renders 'In that day from the river Euphrates to the Brook of Egypt the Lord will thresh out the grain, and you will be gathered one by one, O people of Israel.' The meaning is that over all the territories whither the divine writ runs, the grain will be carefully separated from the chaff, the true Israelites will be separated from the rest. As a husbandman gathers his olives from the trees, so will the Lord gather His own from every land.

IV. PROPHECIES CONCERNING THE RELATION OF JUDAH AND JERUSALEM TO EGYPT AND ASSYRIA.
xxviii. 1—xxxiii. 24

In chapter xxviii we return to the prophet's direct public ministry. From the far-flung cataclysms of universal judgment Isaiah turns to deal again with the local and immediate situation. In chapters xxviii—xxxiii there are six distinct addresses, all beginning with the word 'Woe'. In each the prophet's anger is hot against the defeatist and unwarranted policy which sought help from Egypt. As ever, the vision of Jehovah, high and lifted up, keeping watch over His own people and perfecting His own purpose, is clearly in the prophet's eye and all the currents of day-to-day policy are viewed in the light of that sovereign truth. For the religious implications of political alliances see Appendix II to Kings.

a. First 'Woe' message (xxviii. 1–29)

G. A. Smith writes thus of chapter xxviii: 'This is clearly one of the greatest of Isaiah's prophecies. It is distinguished by that regal versatility of style, which places its author at the head of the Hebrew writers. Keen analyses of character, realistic contrasts between sin and judgment, clever retorts and epigrams, rapids of scorn, and "a spate" of judgment, but for final issue a placid stream of argument banked by sweet parable—such are the literary forms of this chapter, which derives its moral grandeur from the force with which its currents set towards faith and reason. The truths are revelant to every day in which luxury and intemperance abound, in which there are eyes too fevered by sin to see beauty in simple purity, and minds so surfeited with knowledge or intoxicated with their own cleverness, that they call the maxims of moral reason commonplace and scorn religious instruction as food for babes.'

The chapter opens with the prophet appearing among the rulers of Jerusalem (see verse 7), bidding them lift their eyes from their drinking cups and look north to Samaria (1–4). Doom is certain for that city and it cannot be long before it is an accomplished fact. That was surely apparent even to them. In reply they railed upon him: 'To whom does he mean to teach knowledge, and impart his revelation?' (9). The prophet replies, taking the very words of their taunt, and saying that the storm now threatening Samaria will not exhaust itself there, for Samaria's sin is the sin of his hearers as well (11–13).

From this he moves on to deal with the folly of thinking that clever policies of alliance with Egypt or treaties with Samaria will be of any avail to avert catastrophe (14, 15). Their very agreements were 'compacts with death and covenants with Sheol' (15). None can be saved from these things by making pacts with them! Jehovah will Himself annul the covenants that are thus made and will perform His strange work of judgment (18–20); the destruction which is ahead is to cover the whole earth (22). The chapter closes with a parable which offers some brighter tones to the over-all picture (23–29). Even as the farmer using harrow for the soil and flail for the corn is working always to a steadfast plan, so is Jehovah, even amidst deluge and strife, working out His eternal purpose of good for His children.

The crown of pride (1); i.e. the city of Samaria, capital of the northern kingdom. The city 'crowned' a hill which rose in the midst of a fertile valley. O. C. Whitehouse thus comments: 'The prophet describes Samaria as the head of a drunken reveller, encircled with a wreath of fading flowers.' *A mighty and strong one* (2); i.e. the Assyrian. *A crown of glory* . . . (5). As so often in the midst of prophecies of doom, the prophet recalls for the faithful remnant the great messianic hope. Verses 5 and 6 should be contrasted with verses 3 and 4. *They also have erred through wine* (7); i.e. Jerusalem is as guilty as Samaria. *They err in vision* (7); i.e. the prophet. *They stumble in judgment* (7); i.e. the priest. Verses 9, 10 contain the contemptuous answer of the people of Jerusalem to the words of the prophet. In their wild revelry they mock him and his message, making play with the rough edge of uncouth speech the word that he brings to them. O. C. Whitehouse thus translates:

'*With his law upon law, law upon law,
Saw upon saw, saw upon saw,
Here a little, there a little.*'

With stammering lips . . . (11). Isaiah now starkly threatens them with the fact that if they will not listen to his speech they will be forced to listen to the same message from the unaccustomed speech of foreign soldiers in their streets. He describes it in the same way as they have mockingly described his message to them. *This is the rest* (12). Only in abstention from foreign alliance and in complete trust in Jehovah and His word will true rest be found for the land and for the soul.

A stone (16). Here is a reminder, graciously introduced in the midst of so many dark and dreary prophecies of doom, of the ancient promise to the family of David. On this they must rest, for the word is sure. This prophecy is quoted several times in the New Testament (e.g. Rom. ix. 33; Eph. ii. 20; 1 Pet. ii. 6–8). *Shall not make haste* (16). G. A. Smith thus comments: 'This destruction that looms is to cover the whole earth. So stop your running to and fro across it in search of alliances. He that believeth will not make haste. Stay at home and trust in the God of Zion, for that is the one thing that shall survive.' *Judgment* . . . (17); i.e. 'I will make justice the measuring line.'

From the time that it goeth forth (19); RV 'as often as it passeth through'. *The bed is shorter . . .* (20). Godless policies are insufficient to give rest. Life can find true rest only under divine government. The immediate application is to Egypt; the alliance with them (called a *covenant with death* in verse 18) will not 'cover' the situation. *His strange work* (21). It is strange, for He is to arise against His own people as formerly He arose against their enemies. In the parable of verses 23–29 the farmer's methods are typical of Jehovah's in His dealings with the nations. The effect of the parable is to soften the sentence of judgment just made. *Fitches* (25, 27); RSV 'dill'.

b. Second 'Woe' message (xxix. 1–14)

Chapter xxix continues the theme already hinted at in the previous chapter—the folly of making alliance with Egypt. There are two sections in it, comprising the second and third of the 'Woe' messages of the prophet.

In verses 1–14 the prophet addresses the city of Jerusalem under the name of 'Ariel'. His address is again one of condemnation. The city is debauched and idle, frivolous and idolatrous. The days to come will see her besieged on every side, Jehovah Himself being the instigator of the attack (2, 3). Before Jehovah can make her His own, He will have to attack and reduce her to the dust (4). In that day 'Ariel' will be a true name for her (see note below). Then suddenly, as so often noted before, the foes before her gates are seen as the small dust of earth, driven and scattered away (5, 7, 8). The effect of this message upon the people is graphically pictured in verses 9–12. They were utterly dazed, like men rudely wakened from sleep and unable to read a message thrust into their hands. The root cause of this is that they have no effective personal knowledge of the Lord whom they profess to serve (13).

Religious formalism has destroyed the fine susceptibilities of their natures which otherwise might well have heard and understood the commandment of heaven. More catastrophic measures will still be necessary to ensure that the divine purpose is not thwarted (14).

Ariel (1). A name for Jerusalem. It is used with a particular reference to its root meaning, which is most probably 'hearth of God' or 'altar hearth'. The sight of the great altar with its bleeding victims in the court of the temple may well have given the prophet the idea of the name, more especially as he foresees Jerusalem dripping with blood like the altar itself, her slain lying everywhere throughout the city streets. *Where David dwelt* (1); lit., as in RV, 'where David encamped'. *Add ye year to year* (1); i.e. 'add a year to a year'. In other words, 'in a year from now . . .' *It shall be . . . as Ariel* (2); i.e. the city itself will be worthy of its name, one great altar of the slain. *The multitude of thy strangers* (RV 'foes') (5). As so often, this message of the destruction of Israel's foes softens the sternness of the message of doom for the city of Jerusalem.

c. Third 'Woe' message (xxix. 15–24)

The prophet now turns to the politicians, the schemers and plotters, ever hatching deep designs and thinking that they do it in perfect secrecy; doing it as though God Himself could be kept out of account (15). How foolish is such imagination, for the real planning is in the hand of God! Compared with their puny attempts, how vast and grand is His work! (17). Such wonderful work will be done not just to satisfy the desire of the human heart for the sight of a miracle but for the blessing of the deaf and blind (18), the meek and the poor (19); for the overthrow of the scorner and the casting down of the tyrant (20, 21); for making Israel worthy of her God and her fathers (22). Israel has been a nation quite unworthy of all the best of her past, but when this work is done, then will true religion flourish (23).

Seek deep (15); i.e. seek to hide their designs deep. This is no doubt a reference to the political schemers who were hatching the design in secret for alliance with Egypt. *Is it not . . .?* (17); lit. 'Assuredly but a while, a very little while.' *Lebanon* (17) is proverbial. The meaning is that the wild and the cultivated land shall change places. Cf. the casting off of the Jewish nation and the ingathering of the Gentiles (Rom. ix—xi). *The words of the book* (18); i.e. the book of revelation and prophetic promise hitherto sealed to them. In other words, 'the Gentiles shall hear.' J. E. McFadyen translates verses 20, 21:

'For then shall the tyrant have vanished,
 And then shall the scoffer have ceased;
And those that were zealous in sin
 Shall all have been rooted out,
With those that have falsely condemned
 And sought to entrap the judge,
 And quibbled to injure the innocent.'

d. Fourth 'Woe' message (xxx. 1–17)

This chapter leads us still further into the negotiations with Egypt for a treaty of alliance and calls forth more of the scorn of the prophet upon the folly and fatality of such a course of action. This message is addressed to the people as a whole, now classed as 'rebellious children' (1). Previously they had evidenced a lack of trust in Jehovah in seeking alliance with Egypt; persistence in this policy after direct and distinctive warning against it by the prophet is pure rebellion.

The prophet pictures the embassy on its way to Egypt in direct contradiction of all that had been commanded by Jehovah (1, 2). The useless caravan is seen (6), sent with its tribute from Judah to Egypt, asses and camels struggling through the desert, a 'land of trouble and anguish', and all for 'a people that shall not profit them' (5). What is the reason for this calamity? Why should the people of Jehovah be thus seeking the help of a hopeless alliance? The prophet is not in doubt. It is the fruit of rebellion against God (8, 9). The people had refused to listen to the word of the Lord and had demanded 'smooth things' (10). Falsehood and irreverence had made them blind to Egypt's real character and made them turn their backs upon God and His prophet (11). Vainly the prophet calls to them, pointing again to the true way of deliverance and safety (15). To that the answer was 'No' (16). They elected to fly at the enemy, to pursue them on horses obtained from Egypt. Very well, says the prophet, you shall fly, but away from the enemy; your boasted swiftness will be the swiftness of headlong flight (16, 17).

His princes (4); i.e. the princes of Judah. *Zoan* (4). See xix. 11n. *Hanes* (4), south of Memphis. The two names indicate the northern and southern limits of Egypt. *They were all ashamed* (5). A slight change in the original gives the more natural reading, 'all of them laden with gifts for a people that cannot profit them'. Verse 6 gives a picture of the caravan crossing the desert on its ill-starred expedition. *Their strength is to sit still* (7). G. A. Smith comments on this difficult verse: 'The Hebrews had a nickname for Egypt. They called her Rahab—Blusterer, Braggart. Ay, says Isaiah, catching at the old name and putting it to another which describes Egyptian helplessness and inactivity, I call her Rahab Sit-still, Stormy-Speech, Stay at Home—that is her character; for Egypt helpeth in vain and to no purpose.' *Table* (8); RV 'tablet'.

e. Forgiveness, prosperity and triumph (xxx. 18–33)

Because of Israel's disobedience Jehovah has to 'wait' to be gracious (18). His mercy, so sovereign and free, will redeem and save His people. The words that follow (19–26) are amongst the most beautiful of all Isaiah's writings. There is no set argument in them, only flash after flash of divine revelation. Window after window is opened and from every one a new vista of glory is seen.

Gifts of God will verily be received sufficient for every need: an abiding home; comfort for all sorrow (19); bread of adversity, but with it divine revelation (20); guidance most sure (21); hatred of idolatry, so that all idols will be cast away for ever (22); the increase of the earth (23–25); light and glory (26).

All that is still in the future. Meantime the Assyrians are massing and the noise of their approach grows louder and louder (27, 28). Yet in the night of dereliction there shall be the song of solemn gladness, a song in the night as when a holy feast is kept (29). This is the song of confidence in God; and soon the clouds and thunders of war are seen and heard moving away from the Holy City in pursuit of the fleeing Assyrian (31, 32). The Assyrian power will go up in smoke and flame at the last (33).

Thy teachers (20). This should be read in the singular 'thy teacher' (see RV mg.). Obviously it means Jehovah Himself. *Ye shall defile* (22); i.e. 'ye shall regard as polluted and defiled'. *As an overflowing stream* (28). Here are three metaphors: of a flood, a sieve and a bridle. *With the sieve of vanity* (28); i.e. to nothing. The night of *holy solemnity* (29). The Passover was celebrated at night and songs were then sung. *Which smote with a rod* (31) refers to *the Lord*. Translate:

'*At the thunder voice of Jehovah,*
When He is smiting with the rod,
Shall Assyria quail with terror.'

In every place where the grounded staff shall pass (32); RV 'And every stroke of the appointed staff'. The strokes of divine destiny will fall each one after the other to the songs of rejoicing sung by the ransomed people of Jehovah. *Tophet* (33). A place of burning. *For the king* (33); i.e. the king of Assyria.

f. Fifth 'Woe' message (xxxi. 1—xxxii. 20)

In the fifth 'Woe' message, which covers chapters xxxi and xxxii, the prophet reiterates his great theme of the activity of the government of God revealing itself, as already seen, in both punitive and restorative ways. In effect, it is a repetition of what has been said before. The same principles and the same effects are outlined in new forms though spoken at a time which called for still greater urgency, for the politicians of the Jews were now more deeply involved in intrigue and events were moving faster.

i. Folly of trusting in Egypt (xxxi. 1–9). It must be supposed that at the time of this prophecy the alliance was already taking concrete shape and that the negotiators from Judah were elated at the prospect of its completion. In this tense situation Isaiah utters a new 'Woe', condemning them for setting their reliance on the horses and chariots of Egypt and never giving a thought to the God of Israel (1). 'Yet He too is wise', as well as the politicians, says the prophet, and all the cleverness of human arrangement is of no avail (2, 3). Nevertheless God is ever ready

to save what is worth saving. Around Jerusalem will He cast His shield and she shall be saved, while the foes of His will shall be utterly removed (4, 5). Let Israel in the light of this great truth turn again to her God and await His will (6). *As birds flying* (5). Cf. Dt. xxxii. 11, 12.

ii. Character of the messianic age (xxxii. 1–8). Chapter xxxii continues the fifth 'Woe' message of the prophet. The Assyrians having been thus disposed of, Isaiah again speaks of the great question of the future of his own people when they shall have entered into the full blessedness of the divine plan. In words of the loftiest eloquence he describes the establishment of the truly glorified society. First of all its king will reign in righteousness (1), giving care and protection to all who are in need (2); thus the foundation of the society will be sure. There follows the statement that public opinion will be cleansed and that personal influence, not material gain, will be the fountain force of the entire order (3, 4). True aristocracy of character will be known (5). All this comes as a result of the presence of *a king* (1) and of *a man* (2). Of this G. A. Smith writes: 'The rising of a conspicuous character alone can dissipate the moral haze; the sense of his influence will alone fill emptied forms with meaning. So Christ Jesus judges the world by His simple presence; men fall to His right hand and to His left.' *The vile person* . . . (5); lit. 'No more shall a fool be called noble, no more shall a knave be called princely'.

iii. Warning to the women of Jerusalem (xxxii. 9–20). In the midst of this wonderful description of the glory that is to be, the prophet turns aside to make an impassioned appeal to the women of Jerusalem. Once before he had done so (iii. 16–26), for well he knew their influence with the rulers of the city. Now he calls to them to weep and lament over the destruction which impends for the city of their fathers. In doing so, he challenges them with utter thoughtlessness and superficial, ignorant ease (9, 11). They have been quite heedless of previous warnings and remain unmoved by every impassioned appeal. He calls them to consider the dire menace that is hanging over them; their careless gaiety is so out of place in the light of the destruction of their beloved homes (13). But he does not linger on this theme, passing quickly to speak again of future regeneration and the blessing of the land under the hand of God. That shall be 'when the spirit of God is poured from on high' (15). Then there shall be a truly secure land and a righteous people. The vision is not yet accomplished; the rending storm has still to be passed through (19). But the vision is none the less sure. The storm will pass (20).

g. Sixth 'Woe' message (xxxiii. 1–24)

This chapter, containing the sixth and last of the 'Woe' messages, deals with the overthrow of the power of Assyria. There is little doubt that the prophecy refers to the disappearance of the Assyrians from before the walls of Jerusalem.

It is a chapter of great heights. Isaiah hurls the woe of the Lord against the Assyrians and with supreme assurance prophesies their immediate destruction. G. A. Smith suggests that part of this chapter was written on the eve of the deliverance and part immediately after morning broke upon the vanished host. In this view the opening words fit the very moment of the crisis: 'Woe to thee, thou spoiler, whom none hath despoiled' (1). There comes next a prayer of the prophet for strength in the hour of need (2), and this is followed by a graphic picture of the sovereignty of God and the eternal providence which, with justice and righteousness, filleth Zion (3–5). In the presence of such enemy forces at the gates the nation is helpless.

In verses 7–12 we see the envoys of the enemy demanding the surrender of the city and the sorrow of the defenders who have to treat with them; the grief of the land at this plight is colourfully portrayed. But then is heard the voice of Jehovah (10), and with this everything changes. All the might of the foe is as nothing when Jehovah has arisen.

The second section of the chapter (verses 13–24) is a picture of the amazed populace beginning to realize their deliverance. Foremost in all that happened was that God became real to them (14), and conviction of sin fell upon the people. They had seen the reality of the divine fires of judgment and as they watched and saw the fire devouring the Assyrian host their conscience smote them and they cried: 'Who among us shall dwell with the devouring fire?' To that the answer came clear and terse: 'He that is righteous . . . he shall dwell on high' (15, 16). This is a unique illustration of the message of a previous chapter (xxvi. 9; cf. xxxii. 1, 16, 17). There follow (17–24) some dramatic fragments describing the wild sense of deliverance with the departure of the enemy from the city. So there passes from sight the besiegers of the city with their foreign speech and wild accoutrements (19), the king may again appear (17), and the far reaches of the land out to the distant horizon are open to be traversed once more (17). Jerusalem is redeemed. (20); the temple is safe (20); Jehovah is its defence (21, 22); sickness vanishes (24); the people rejoice in a divine forgiveness (24).

Woe to thee that spoilest (1); i.e. the Assyrian. *O Lord, be gracious unto us* (2). The prayer of the prophet in the midst of the people for the people's deliverance and salvation. The prayer continues in verse 3, where the prophet recalls the might of Jehovah by which the nations are scattered. *Your spoil . . .* (4). The prophet's address is here to the Assyrians. He asserts that the Jews will soon gather the spoil of the Assyrians as locusts clear the fields. *Their valiant ones* (7); i.e. the Assyrian envoys. *Ambassadors of peace* (7); i.e. the Jewish negotiators with the tribute. *The highways lie waste* (8). A picture of the desolation caused by the onward march of the foe. *He hath broken the covenant* (8). This refers to the Assyrian king's scornful disregard of his promise

in sweeping his armies back upon Judah. *Lebanon . . . Sharon* (9); i.e. the most fertile districts are laid waste and barren. *Ye shall conceive chaff . . .* (11). A picture of human futility. *Your breath, as fire. . .* (11); i.e. the pride and arrogance of the Assyrian would encompass their destruction. *As the burnings of lime: as thorns* (12). Twin pictures of utter and speedy destruction. *Meditate terror* (18); RV 'muse on the terror'; i.e. the sight of the hated enemy lording it at the gates of the city, counting and weighing the tribute. *The receiver* (18); i.e., as in RV, 'he that weighed the tribute'. *I am sick* (24). Suffering will end with the ending of sin.

V. PROPHECIES PROCLAIMING THE DOOM OF EDOM AND THE REDEMPTION OF ISRAEL. xxxiv. 1—xxxv. 10

Chapters xxxiv, xxxv, which are the last of this section of the book of Isaiah, again lift the eyes to the furthest horizons. Just as immediately after the burdens of the nations prophecies concerning the whole world were spoken (chapters xxiv—xxvii), so now again, after the 'Woe' messages, the same rule obtains. Once more the searchlight rests upon desolation, the theme of chapter xxxiv, but the triumphant song of restoration is soon heard again, and with that glad note the section closes.

a. Universal judgment for the nations (xxxiv. 1–4)

These verses are purely apocalyptic in character. The wrath of Jehovah is seen proceeding against all nations of the earth because of their sins. Not only shall the earth perish (2, 3), but the heavens also shall be rolled up like a scroll (4). *He hath utterly destroyed them* (2). Rather 'He hath doomed them to destruction'.

b. Destruction of Edom (xxxiv. 5–17)

From the universal horizons of destruction, the prophet returns to address Edom as the symbol and centre of all antagonisms to Zion. Edom had ever taken the wrong side in the quarrel of Zion with the nations of the earth. Of this G. A. Smith writes: 'Israel, conscious of his spiritual calling in the world, felt bitter resentment that his own brother should be so vulgarly hostile to his attempts to carry it out. This is what we must remember when we read the indignant verses of chapter xxxiv. Let us remember that this chapter, for all its fierceness, is inspired by Israel's conviction of a spiritual destiny and service for God, and by the natural resentment that his own kith and kin should be doing their best to render this futile.'

It is upon this entire attitude of opposition to the revealed will of God that the vengeance of God is seen to fall (8). The spirit which is 'Edom' can end only in annihilation. Concerning this Dr. Campbell Morgan has written: 'It is at least a most suggestive fact that when our Lord, the one perfect flower and fruit of Israel's race, was here exercising His earthly ministry, an

Idumaean, that is an Edomite, in the person of Herod, was reigning over the people; and it is more than suggestive in that relation, that he is the one human being in whom Christ had nothing to say. Once He sent him a message full of contempt. When at last He was in his presence, He spoke no word to him. God makes no terms with that for which Edom stood. Its portion is destruction.'

The picture of destruction and desolation in the chapter is awesome and terrifying. Slaughter, a ravaged land haunted by wild beasts, carrion reptiles and demonic creatures, utter doom— these are the elemental colours in its lurid portrayal. And the end is sure: 'No one of these shall fail' (16). *Bathed in heaven* (5). The idea is that the sword of the Lord is bathed in the wrath of heaven. Cf. Is. lxiii. 1–6; Ob. 1–21. *Lambs and goats . . . rams* (6), i.e. the common people. *Unicorns . . . bulls* (7), i.e. the rulers, nobles and princes of the people. *Shall come down* (7); i.e. to destruction. *The streams thereof* (9). The streams of Edom. The whole district is volcanic in nature. The association of the near cities of Sodom and Gomorrah and the destruction which fell upon them is obviously in mind. *The cormorant and the bittern* (11). Rather, as in RV, 'pelican and porcupine'. *Stones of emptiness* (11). Translate:

> 'Jehovah will stretch out upon her
> The measuring-line of Chaos,
> And the plummet of Destruction.'

Dragons . . . owls (13); RV 'jackals . . . ostriches'· *The screech owl* (14); RV 'night monster'. *The great owl* (15); RV 'the arrowsnake'.

Seek ye out of the book of the Lord (16). Isaiah's own title for his prophecies. The time will come, he says, when all that is here predicted for Edom will be demonstrably fulfilled. *Cast the lot . . . divided . . . by line* (17). Just as Canaan was divided by lot and line to the children of Israel in their tribes, so is this land just described the haunt of wild and pestilential beasts, to be divided unto them.

c. The joy of the redeemed (xxxv. 1–10)

We now come to the concluding note of the first part of the book of Isaiah. It is set here in utter contrast to the desolation of the previous chapter and sings of the joy that is to be for exiles brought home from afar and the glad establishment of the ransomed of the Lord in Zion. The chapter begins with a recognition of the wilderness, the dry land and the desert, but only to speak of them in the light of what they are to become—fragrant with fruitful valleys and rejoicing flowers (1, 2). Then comes the message of Jehovah to the people that await His appearing and salvation (3–10). They are to be strong, for their deliverance is sure (4); miracles, surpassing all they have ever dreamed of, will be worked on their behalf (5, 6); wonders, too, on the road back home across the desert of their pilgrimage, will be theirs to behold (6, 7); the highway home will be plain,

safe and trodden only by the holy in heart (8, 9); the arrival in Zion will be with 'songs and everlasting joy' (10).

Thus does Isaiah lead to the climax of vision which was ever with him. The end is sure; it is Zion, city of God, where the divine order is blessedly realized. None ever saw the corruption of life more surely or denounced it more uncompromisingly. Often, perforce, his message has been dirgelike and gloomy, but it has never reached to the depths of despair. That could not be, for he was ever seeing 'the Lord, high and lifted up' above the storms and tempests of life and history. Such a vision banished fear and foreboding and set faith triumphant upon the throne. Through every day of travail and darkness, through the long night of weeping and desolation, he saw the day of Jehovah ahead. That day would dawn when the full revealed will of heaven would be done; of that there could be no doubt. Ultimate triumph was inevitable, since God was God. The processes leading to that day might be those of wrath and consuming fire, but the end would be light and life, the gladness of a great ransom, the casting out of all pollution, the realization of a regal redemption, the songs of a mighty army of the children of God. It is this vision and its triumph which this chapter celebrates.

For them (1). These words should be omitted. *Rose* (1); RV mg. 'autumn crocus'. *It shall be for those* (8); better, as in RV mg., 'He shall be with them.'

VI. HISTORICAL APPENDIX: ISAIAH'S LIFE AND ACTIVITY DURING THE REIGN OF HEZEKIAH. xxxvi. 1—xxxix. 8

The following four chapters are a historical interlude set between the first and second parts of the book of Isaiah. They are practically a transcription of 2 Ki. xviii. 13—xx. 19 (see notes there), except for Hezekiah's song of thanksgiving in xxxviii. 9–20. They record incidents in the reign of Hezekiah and fill in the context of a number of the prophecies.

a. The Assyrian threat to Jerusalem (xxxvi. 1—xxxvii. 38)

All happened as Isaiah had foretold and the attack was defeated by the intervention of God, as he had said it would be. Here we have an account of the coming of the army of Sennacherib (1–3) and the speech of Rabshakeh, his chief of captains (4–10), in which he cleverly endeavours to undermine the morale of the people. It is folly, he urged, to trust in Egypt, the staff of a broken reed (6); as for Jehovah, Hezekiah the king has deliberately turned his back upon Him (7)—a subtle misrepresentation of facts. The envoy then addressed the people on the wall directly (13), pointing out the greatness of the victories of the king of Assyria and the futility of trying to withstand him. No word was returned by them to this (21) and the Jewish representatives went to the king with their sad tale (22).

Hezekiah immediately sent messengers to Isaiah (xxxvii. 1–5). To the king it was apparent that all human help had failed and he therefore appealed to the prophet to intercede with Jehovah on behalf of the people against the Assyrian. The answer was immediate and comforting; Jehovah would intervene and the Assyrian would return to his own land, there to fall by the sword (6, 7). Rabshakeh, on returning to his master, found him engaged in war with Libnah and under threat also of war with Ethiopia (8, 9). His hand was thereby forced and he had to return, but not without a further endeavour to intimidate the people and king of Jerusalem by letter, in which he openly defied Jehovah (10–13). This letter the king took and laid before the Lord (14–20), and the prophet brought to him the divine answer (21–35). In this the deepest sin of Assyria is shown to be the fact that they were exalting themselves *against the Holy One of Israel* (23). God has known all their thoughts; and His purpose, so plainly revealed before, cannot be thwarted. *I will turn thee back* (29). To this assurance of judgment on the enemy there is added the promise that the Assyrian will not be allowed to enter the city nor shoot arrows therein (33–35). The chapter closes with an account of the destruction which fell upon the Assyrian host in the morning (36). The divine intervention was mysterious, but resulted in complete victory.

b. Hezekiah's sickness and recovery (xxxviii· 1–8)

The details of this illness and its sequel are more fully recorded in the account in 2 Ki. xx and should be noted there. It is a record of divine intervention on behalf of the people's head just as miraculous as had been the intervention on behalf of the people against the Assyrian.

c. Song of thanksgiving (xxxviii. 9–22)

Then follows a song of thanksgiving sung by the king after his recovery. It is a moving message of a man who had been to the very gates of death and been brought back therefrom. First of all, he recalls his illness (10–14), and records the darkness and sadness of those bitter moments

when hope had almost gone. *I shall not see the Lord* (11). Cf. verse 18. Death was dreaded, even by the faithful Israelite, because it was believed that it cut him off from God. *Pining sickness* (12). See the RV translation of this whole verse. In the second half of the song he proceeds to speak of the deeper spiritual values of his suffering and pain. He sees his deliverance as a token of the everlasting mercy (17), and joined with that wonderful fact is this other gracious act of God: *thou hast cast all my sins behind thy back* (17). As one commentator has said: 'Never did a man bring richer harvest from the fields of death. Everything that renders life really life— peace, dignity, a new sense of God and of His forgiveness—these were the spoils which Hezekiah won in his encounter with the grim enemy. He had snatched from death a new meaning for life; he had robbed death of its awful pomp. At the end of his course he saw the throne of God and all his life thenceforth became one grand ascent thither.'

d. Prophecy of Babylonian captivity (xxxix. 1–8)

Here is the record of failure on the part of the king and of the rebuke of the prophet Isaiah. The cause was vanity: the king of Babylon sent messengers to Hezekiah after he had learned of his illness, and in his pride and gratification at this gesture of kingly friendship Hezekiah proceeded to show them everything of his treasure both in his palace and kingdom (2). The act itself may have been innocent enough, but there was the intent behind it of impressing Babylon with a sense of his power and wealth and of thereby making favourable terms for alliance of war. It is against this that Isaiah speaks. All that has been shown will be carried to Babylon one day and nothing shall be left (6). It was a sad message and one that the king received as from Jehovah. The act he sees to have been foolish and boastful; it lacked caution and sobriety; and the stern rebuke of the prophet he receives with shame as he sees with sorrow the dark shadow of captivity cast upon all his household. Chapter xxxix is here set beside chapter xxxviii to show how fatally easy it is for men to fall from their high vows. 'The hardest duty of life is to remain true to the Psalms of our deliverance as it is certainly life's greatest temptation to fall away from the sanctity of sorrow.'

CHAPTERS XL–LXVI

We now enter upon the second great section of this book. For a discussion of the special problems connected with it see Introduction under 'Authorship'.

VII. DELIVERANCE FROM THE DOMINION OF BABYLON. xl. i—xlviii. 22

a. Prologue (xl. 1–11)

In these immortal words the theme that God will restore the exiles to their own land is introduced. This is the chief subject of the prophet's utterances right to the end of chapter lv. Nothing in all the sacred writings of the Jewish people can

surpass these passages for sublimity of thought, felicity of expression and majestic depth of spiritual understanding. Here is unconquerable hope and unquenchable joy. The thrilling tidings that he is called upon to bear transport the prophet and give to him words winged with divine and holy inspiration.

This sovereign message of divine comfort serves as prologue to the second portion of the book of Isaiah. In it herald voices are heard breaking into the night of doubt and trial, and crying aloud that the period of divine punishment is near an end. First of all it is the prophets who are addressed (1, 2), as they are urged to speak to the people; but very soon all Israel is summoned to proclaim the glad tidings (9). The New Testament is our authority for applying the words of this prophecy to the coming of the divine Redeemer (cf. Mt. iii. 1–3), and only so can the full implications of these great prophecies be met. At the same time, the message of divine comfort to hearts sore distressed is one of the greatest and most fundamental elements in the gospel.

Speak ye comfortably to Jerusalem (2); lit. 'speak ye to the heart of Jerusalem'. *Jerusalem* means the chosen people in captivity. In verse 9 *Zion* is similarly used. *Double* (2). Probably this means abundant or in full measure. The penalty paid is amply sufficient. *Prepare ye the way of the Lord* (3). This is taken from the Eastern custom of sending men to prepare the way before a monarch's visit. It was to fulfil a mission such as this that John the Baptist came, 'to make ready a people prepared for the Lord' (Lk. i. 16, 17). *The voice said, Cry* (6). The prophet now makes clear that this word of comfort is in no way dependent upon man's own endeavours; it is altogether of sovereign and divine mercy. *All flesh is grass* (6), and vain is the hope of man who trusts therein; but in the Lord God Almighty there is abiding and plenteous redemption and in the midst of all changing things His word standeth for ever (8). In verses 10, 11 God is revealed as both infinitely strong and infinitely tender; and it is this mighty fact that calls Zion to rejoice greatly.

b. Supremacy of Jehovah over the nations (xl. 12—xli. 29)

i. God the omnipotent (xl. 12–26). Moving on from the preceding passage the prophet speaks in fuller detail and with greater emphasis of the God from whom deliverance is to come. The Lord God Jehovah is alone God. His majesty and sovereignty are illustrated first in His creative power (12), then by His omniscience and foreknowledge (13, 14), and again by the complete insignificance of all other things over against Him (15–17). This is the Lord Almighty from whom deliverance is to come. How foolish, therefore, are man's attempts to create similitudes of the divine image! Molten images and graven stones, the dumb creations of the pagan races of the earth, can never express His majesty and glory (18–20). Here is sounded the great recall to the eternal fact of divine revelation, that God is a Spirit and His glory He will not give to another. That this is so is also clear from the evidence of His own handiwork in the universe of His creation as well as in His sovereign dealings with all mankind.

Lebanon is not sufficient . . . (16). Here the prophet's imagination expands most splendidly.

The idea is that for such a God no sacrifice is adequate: not all the cedars of Lebanon are enough for altar fires; all the countless beasts that roam through her forests are insufficient for sacrifice. Our debt to God is greater than any conceivable sacrifice can pay. *To whom then will ye liken God?* (18). God being thus infinitely great, the folly of trying to fashion any likeness of Him is the more apparent. *Upon the circle of the earth* (22); better, as in RV mg., 'above'. God's transcendant glory is being stressed. *They shall not be planted* (24). Rather, as RV mg., 'scarcely are they planted, scarcely are they sown, scarcely hath their stock taken root in the ground, when he bloweth upon them, and they wither.'

ii. God the hope of His people (xl. 27–31). The chapter begins with the assurance being given to the heart of Israel that their God was certain to redeem and restore them; it now draws to its magnificent close, bidding them hope in the Lord, who is so mighty and merciful. Though the fulness of His promise be delayed, yet His people should trust in Him and thus trusting they will find their God is near to save with an uttermost salvation.

My way (27); i.e. the hard and difficult way being trod. *My judgment* (27); i.e. the bitter disregard of essential rights by the oppressors of the people of God. This was the cry of the people in their exile: God had forgotten them and His promise was but a dream. Verses 28–31 are the prophet's unequivocal answer to all such words of defeat and despair. God rules on high and His arm is around His own; therefore faint not, nor fear.

iii. God the sovereign Lord of history (xli. 1–7). Having thus spoken the word of almighty consolation to the captive people of God, revealing Himself as the sovereign Lord and Saviour, Jehovah now turns to the nations of the world and issues His manifesto, at once challenging and inescapable. This chapter is introductory to the main movement of this theme, the central proclamation following in chapter xlii. But here the essential notes of preparation are seen, God addressing the heathen and appealing to them from the signs of the times and from the facts of contemporary history which are open to every man's memory and reason. 'Chapter xli is, therefore, the natural complement to chapter xl. In chapter xl we have the element in revelation which precedes history; in chapter xli we have history itself explained as a part of revelation' (G. A. Smith). All history is the workshop of God and Jehovah here demonstrates that none other than He is Master therein.

Here is the challenge of God to the nations concerning the advancing foe from the East, in which He states that this powerful one is under the government of His will (2), and satirizes the attempts of men to secure safety by the manufacture of still more idol deities (6, 7). *Let the people renew their strength* (1). It is not necessary to alter the rendering at all for the sake of a parallelism in thought. The idea is that God's challenge to the world is over against a mustering of the world's forces at large. Let all the earth in its panoplied strength keep silence at the word of Jehovah. *Raised up* (2). Not the usual word for this; rather 'forced', stirred up', 'impelled'. *The righteous man* (2). Though here as yet unnamed, the reference is apparently to Cyrus (cf. xliv. 28, xlv. 1), who is presented as the divine agent for the punishing of sinful idolatries and the liberating of Israel. *From the east* (2). Persia lay to the east of Babylon. Cyrus was born prince of a small province called Anshan, and Media was conquered by him in 549 B.C. The Lydian Empire, whilst under the rule of Croesus, fell to his armies in 540 B.C. and Babylon was overthrown in 538. The onward sweep of his mighty victories makes a well-nigh incredible picture in its immensity. *He pursued them* (3). Translate: 'He pursueth and passeth unharmed. Nor toucheth the ground with his feet'; i.e., so swiftly does he march, it seems that the very ground is passed over. Verses 5–7 contain a graphic picture of the terror which the rise of Cyrus and his great victories struck into the hearts of the nations around and before him. With only their idols to turn to, they began to make new ones and thereby tried to encourage each other against the imminent attack of their foe. These verses are rich in their sarcasm as well as in their vivid picture of the hopeless plight of those who know not the true God. *The isles* (5); an expression often used to describe the islands of the Mediterranean and the low-lying coastal section of Palestine. In these chapters, however, it has the sense of distant lands in general. *Ready for the sodering* (7). Rather, as RV, 'saying of the soldering. It is good.'

iv. God the protector of Israel (xli. 8–20).

Jehovah once again addresses His people, assuring them of His constant presence and blessing (8–10, 13, 14). While all other nations of the known world are busy trying to avert the disaster that is looming ahead, Israel may rest calm and undistrubed, for Jehovah their God is ever watching over them in power and mercy. From the days of Abraham and the patriarchs she has been the servant of Jehovah (9); and shall He not still remember her and enable her to see the victory over all her foes? Divine election implies divine succour and salvation. Even yet the desert will blossom as the rose and all shall see that this is the work of the Holy One of Israel (18–20).

From the chief men (9); rather, as in RV, 'from the corners thereof'. Ur of the Chaldees, whence Abraham came, was to the Palestinian view at the extremities of the world. *I have . . . not cast thee away* (9). Israel must not think that the exile implies any absolute rejection of the chosen race. This is discipline and not abandonment by their God. *Thou worm Jacob* (14); in captivity they felt about as insignificant and as helpless as a worm.

v. God's challenge to the idols (xli. 21–24).

These verses picture Jehovah addressing the idols which men have made. 'Give proof of your divinity', He says, 'by prophesying what is to be' (23). Not only so, they are asked to cite any case in which a former prediction of theirs has come true (22). Prediction is here made a test of divinity. In other words, they are challenged to come and be tested by facts. 'Here is history needing an explanation and running no one knows whither. Prove your divinity by interpreting or guiding it. Cease your ambiguities, and give us something we can set our minds on. Or do something, be it good, be it evil—only let it be patent to our senses. For the test of godhead is not ingenuity or mysteriousness, but plain deeds which the senses can perceive, and plain words which the reason and conscience can judge' (G. A. Smith).

The latter end of them (22). The idols are here asked to produce as a proof of their worth past predictions that have come literally true; or else clear and unmistakable foretelling of what is to be. *Do good or do evil* (23); 'do something or other' (Moff.) .

vi. Jehovah's explanation of history (xli. 25–29).

In these verses we return to the theme of verses 1–7. Here is the definitive statement that the coming of this mighty victor is by the will and act of Jehovah (25). Since none of the other so-called divinities can give answer to the challenge of the times and say what is and what is to be, Jehovah Himself declares His explanation of history, and claims its events for His doing (26, 27). And what is more, the very fact of the failure of the rest, whether gods or men, to foretell the future is a proof of their vanity (28, 29).

One from the north (25). The scene of action has changed from the east to the north; this was the exact course that Cyrus' onward march of triumph took. Media lay to the north of Babylonia; Persia was to the east. Starting from Persia Cyrus moved north to the conquest of Media, then west to the overthrow of Lydia and finally south to destroy the power of Babylon. (See map on p. 363.) *Shall he call upon my name* (25). To what was said at the beginning of the chapter concerning Cyrus, this is now added, that in the hour of his greatest triumphs he shall recognize that they have been granted him by the power of Jehovah and not by any of the other pagan deities so widely worshipped (cf. Ezr. i. 2). *Who hath declared . . .?* (26). A further emphatic affirmation that all this is beyond the powers of the idol divinities. Verses 26–29 have been cleverly rendered by J. E. McFadyen as follows:

'But who from the first hath announced this
     That so we might recognize it?
Or who hath aforetime declared it
     That now we must own to its truth?
There was none that announced or declared it,
     Not one heard a word from you.

It was I who first told it to Zion,
     And gave the glad news to Jerusalem.

I looked all around—there was no one;

*Not one of the gods could give counsel
Or answer to ought that I asked them.*

*See! One and all, they are nothing,
And nothing can they do:
Their idols are wind and waste.'*

c. The 'Servant' passages

With chapter xlii we reach a distinctive stage in the thought of the prophet Isaiah. Having dealt with the great themes of the majesty and sovereignty of God and having addressed himself to both his own people and the nations of the earth, he now proceeds to reveal to them the means by which the divine will is to be done. Israel is to learn what is the mighty purpose that her God has for her to fulfil; the nations of the world must know the truth that God is to reveal unto them. With the sure touch of inevitability the prophet therefore continues to speak of these things and to refer in particular to the Servant or Minister by whom the blessed will and purpose of heaven is to be completed. This brings us to an examination of the 'Servant' passages of our prophecy and some consideration must be given to this important matter.

In these passages (xlii. 1–9, xlix. 1–9, l. 4–9, lii. 13—liii. 12) we are brought to one of the most outstanding sections of all the divine revelation. Not only are they unique in character but, as has been truly said, they 'are allied with all that is greatest in the scheme of the divine revelation'. In thought and teaching they are linked more closely with the New Testament than any other Old Testament scriptures.

Who is this Servant by whom this work of such importance is to be done? It is clear that the prophet intends that He should be brought before us with all the urgency that his pen can command and that next to Jehovah Himself He occupies the most important place in the book. At the very points where the prophet is emphatic about the sovereignty and sure succour of Jehovah for His people, he also introduces the Servant as the certain agent of the outworking of that divine plan. Furthermore he paints the picture with such definition of detail and such felicity of expression that at times the sovereign God is for the moment forgotten and the Servant comes to dominate the complete canvas.

It would be natural therefore to think that this very Minister of Jehovah would be defined most absolutely in name; but that is not the case. Controversy has raged around this subject incessantly. Is He a person or a personification? Have we here a figurative representation of ideal Israel? Or of one of the prophets? Or is this the prophet himself speaking of himself? These and many other suggestions have been made, together with this still mightier affirmation that the Servant is none other than the Messiah, the Lord of Israel's salvation,

What are we to say of this? This at any rate, that any interpretation that does not lead to Him who in His very Person fulfilled the prophecies most wonderfully is clearly inadequate.

He alone is the Servant of whom God speaks to men when He calls mankind to listen. As Dr. Campbell Morgan writes concerning this passage: 'That the reference was to Cyrus is so palpably absurd a suggestion, we need not stay to argue it. That it referred to Israel as she then was, is equally impossible to believe. That it referred to a spiritual element within Israel then existing, is a suggestion that breaks down in that such an elect remnant, which undoubtedly did exist, did not accomplish what is attributed to this Servant of Jehovah. To say that it is ideal Israel, is to say that no part of the forthtellings has yet been fulfilled, for the simple reason that such an ideal Israel is still non-existent. There can be only one interpretation which satisfies the reason, to say nothing of the heart; and that is that Matthew was right when he deliberately declared that this foretelling found its fulfilment in Jesus (see Mt. xii. 15–21). As against that, it has been argued, "the Servant is invariably spoken of as having a present existence". And why not? It is certain that our Lord and Master, the Son of God, who became His Servant for redemptive purposes, had then a present existence. To suggest that this prophet had no appreciation of the fact is to lower the conception of the divine nature of the prophetic word. When Jehovah calls men to keep silence before Him, it is always that He may say unto them "Behold, My Servant"; and there is only One who can be so described.'

d. First 'Servant' passage: His office (xlii. 1–9)

Under the inspiration of the Spirit of God, the Servant will truly fulfil the glorious purpose for which He is called (1). Judgment (RSV 'justice'; see note below) will be His work, and this will He do without the accustomed demonstrations of human power which others so blatantly display (2, 3); there will be no ceasing from the great struggle until the work is done (4). The name of Jehovah will be spread abroad throughout the world by Him and His glory will be made known (5–9); the Servant of the Lord will know in all this ministry the gracious upholding of the God of all the earth (6).

My servant (1). As has been already noted, in an absolute sense this can only be related to the Messiah, the Son of God. But no doubt there was also in the mind of the prophet some sense of the divine mission resting upon the Israelites to celebrate the triumph of their God wherever they went. As in this day of grace the Church represents her Lord and Head, so Israel, and in particular those men and women of true faith and piety within the wider nation, could be a minister of the name of Jehovah to the world in its blindness and need. He who is supremely the Servant of Jehovah has in all ages been seeking those who would perform His purpose of love amongst men. *Smoking flax* (3). A wick that burns dim. *He shall bring forth judgment unto truth* (3); RV 'in truth'. The idea is that He shall fully and faithfully set forth the law and thereby vindicate His righteous cause. *He shall not fail* (4). In this phrase there is an emphatic repetition of the words just used of the reed and the wick. However frail or low-burning others may be, this will not be true of Him. He shall not be dimmed nor be bruised. As J. E. McFadyen translates, 'all erect and aglow shall He be.' However tender He may be, it will not connote weakness, but rather a strength that cannot be daunted. *Shall wait* (4). More probably 'are waiting'. The prophet sees the whole of the heathen world to its uttermost fringe waiting for the glad tidings of the salvation of Jehovah.

Verses 5–9 are a development of this great utterance just made. Behind the Servant's ministry is the might of Jehovah by whom the heavens were made; He shall be the One through whom ultimately all nations shall be bound into one great fraternity in the love of God.

e. Song of triumph (xlii. 10–17)

Such glad tidings as this cannot but make the heart rejoice and sing with exultation the songs of the Lord's salvation. This song, begun by the redeemed of the Lord in praise of Him (10–13), is carried forward, so inspired is the prophet by his theme, by Jehovah Himself (14–16). In glorious anthropomorphism the Lord God speaks of the way in which He is about to burst upon His people to save and deliver.

Kedar (11); the name of Ishmael's second son; here perhaps used for Arabia generally. *The inhabitants of the rock* (11), or 'of Sela' (RV); i.e. Sela's inhabitants. Sela was the stronghold of Edom. *I will destroy and devour at once* (14); rather, as in RV, 'I will gasp and pant together'.

f. The divine call to repentance (xlii. 18–25)

It is ever the goodness of God that leads to repentance, and having here revealed His Servant and the redemption He is to bring, having begun the new song that His coming inspires, Jehovah now calls to Israel in her weak and pitiable condition to give ear and come unto Him (18, 23). A great part of the appeal is based upon the facts as they are. Israel should not be thus; God had meant her for glory, but she has chosen the lesser way and sorrow has become her lot (19–22). The very greatness of her calling in the beginning makes her fall seem the greater. But she will yet find, if she will but turn unto the Lord her God, that with Him there is plenteous redemption and that His compassions fail not. It is altogether of grace unmerited that this will be. It is for the honour of His word and in order to show His righteousness that God will do this (21).

Who is blind . . .? (19). In LXX and Old Latin this verse begins: 'Who is blind but my servants, and deaf but their rulers?' 'Deaf' and 'blind' in verse 18 are also plural in Hebrew. The nation must here be in view, still unaware of its high calling. Cf. xlviii. 8. *He that is perfect* (19); RV 'he that is at peace with me'. Probably this should be interpreted as 'he that is admitted to

covenant relationship with Me'. *Blind* (19). This word in the last phrase should be 'deaf' (cf. verse 20); so certain MSS have it. *The Lord is well pleased for his righteousness' sake* (21). Rather, as in RV, 'it pleased the Lord, for his righteousness' sake, to magnify the law, and make it honourable'. Israel, on the other hand, had turned away from that high road of life and blessedness and had come to be a people despoiled and broken. They who, having received such a revelation, should have gone to the very heights of the purpose of God are found grovelling in the dust, captive and disobedient. In all this awful condition the need is seen more clearly for the coming of that Servant who will not fail as this one has and who in His own Person and work will 'magnify the law and make it honourable'. None other but He could do that; none else but He has done it.

g. God's invincible power and forgiving grace (xliii. 1—xliv. 5)

In chapter xliii, as in the next two also, a series of messages from Jehovah are given, all of which are dependent upon and flow naturally from the central proclamation of the previous chapter, 'Behold, my servant.' The manifesto of Jehovah's purpose has just been issued and there now follows the definitive interpretation of matters resulting from that mighty utterance; all of these particular sayings are begun with the words 'thus saith the Lord'. Chapter xliii has four such messages.

i. Jehovah the redeemer of Israel (xliii. 1–9). In these great verses Jehovah assures Israel that not only in creation and redemption but also in gracious providence He will uphold and sustain her through all the way that she has to go. Her sorrow and her gathering again to the land of her heart's desire are watched over and determined by a deep purpose of love.

But now . . . (1). These words constitute a link between the manifesto of Jehovah just recorded and the sayings that He is now about to propound. The messages are all dependent upon the proclamation. *I have redeemed* (1). The eternal present; God's purpose and action are eternally one. *I gave Egypt . . .* (3). This refers to the coming defeat and overthrow of Egypt and the neighbouring kingdoms by the power of Persia. They were conquered in the reign of Cambyses. *Honourable* (4). Rather 'honoured', i.e. honoured by her connection with her God. The RV gives the arrangement of the sentence as follows: 'Since thou hast been precious in my sight, and honourable, and I have loved thee; therefore will I give men for thee, and peoples for thy life.' *For I have created him for my glory* (7). Rather 'whom I have created for my glory, whom I have . . .'

ii. Israel to be Jehovah's witness to the world (xliii. 10–13). This second saying affirms that Israel will fulfil their function of being the witnesses of Jehovah because of what He is and of what He will accomplish (10, 11). Once again the telling argument from prophecy is repeated and the assurance given that the divine promise shall not fail (12, 13). This particular saying is related to the former in that the contrast between Israel being truly the witness of Jehovah and the other nations of the earth being quite incompetent to speak any affirmative word is so decisively drawn.

And my servant (10). The sense is that in being His witnesses they are His servant also. *That ye may . . . believe . . .* (10). Perhaps better translated 'that they . . .' The sense is that Israel is Jehovah's witness so that 'they', the heathen, may know and understand that beside Him there is no Saviour. *Who shall let it?* (13); RV mg. 'who shall reverse it?'

iii. **Jehovah the destroyer of Babylon (xliii. 14, 15).** Babylon, like Egypt, is to be cast down and overthrown by the might and majesty of Israel's God. This is the first unequivocal announcement of the fall of Babylon (cf. xlvi. 1—xlvii. 15) and, like the prophecy concerning Egypt also, the decisive and sure reason for the overthrow is that Israel might be redeemed. Since God is her Redeemer, Creator, King, all other opposing forces will be blotted out as and when it pleases Him. *Whose cry is in the ships* (14). The text is here somewhat dubious, though the general sense is plain. 'Whose cry' refers to the cry of their boasting or exultation. The RV renders 'in the ships of their rejoicing'.

iv. **Jehovah's new work: a mighty act of un merited grace (xliii. 16–28).** After referring back to the great record of divine deliverance in the days of the exodus and relating the mighty acts of God then and there done (16, 17), the promise is given that the work of deliverance from Babylon will be greater even than that. This will be *a new thing* of God's own working (19), and the bitter wilderness of Israel's present suffering will blossom forth into the praise of her Redeemer (20, 21). And all this gracious act of restoration will not be due to any merits of her own, for she has none. In fact she has failed signally in all that God has commanded her (22, 23). *Thou hast made me to serve with thy sins* (24); RSV 'you have burdened me'. God forgives and forgets her sins (25) as an act of His own free grace. And it is grace itself that planned the mode of her punishment and sorrow (28, RV mg.).

v. **The dependableness of God (xliv. 1–5).** In chapter xliv we have another three of the messages of Jehovah. They are, like the messages of the previous chapter, linked with the proclamation 'Behold, my servant' by the words 'Yet now'. This must be borne in mind as they are read. The first of these is a message of comfort to Israel telling her not to fear (2), because her God is about to pour His Spirit forth upon her seed (3–5).

Jesurun (2). The word is also found applied to Israel in Dt. xxxii. 15, xxxiii. 5, 26. The meaning is most probably 'the upright one'. It is for this purpose that Israel has been formed by her God, that she should be to the divine wisdom and righteousness what a man's hand is to a man. This is the mystery of redemption. In all these messages the thoughts of creation and redemption are pre-eminent; but creation is ever moving towards redemption. Israel is therefore shown as a nation as she actually is (indicated by the name Jacob, 'Supplanter'); but side by side with that is the Israel whom God sees as righteous. *Water . . . floods* (3). These denote the influences of the Holy Spirit. Verse 5 is a picture of Gentiles turning to Jehovah.

h. **The utter folly of idol worship (xliv. 6–23)**
In these verses the prophet returns to a theme which has been already heard (xl. 18–20, xli. 5–7, 21–24), but now finds its most terrible and devastating expression. False gods are here mocked (9–11); the method by which they are made (12–14); the futility of their being (15–17); the emptiness of their claims (18–20); and the children of God are called upon to remember these things (21). Verses 21–23 renew the promise to Israel of complete forgiveness. All creation is called upon to witness and to rejoice over the redemption which Jehovah has wrought.

He is hungry (12). The idea latent in this expression is how can that which is made by one who suffers from hunger and thirst be compared with the self-sufficient God. No more thorough condemnation of idolatry has ever been written. The reader is asked to consider who it is that makes the idols, then to consider all the hammerings, etc., the image suffers; and lastly the fate of the substance of which it is composed, the cooking of the workman's dinner.

i. **Cyrus named as the instrument of God (xliv. 24 —xlv. 25)**

i. **The choice of Cyrus (xliv. 24–28).** In these last verses of chapter xliv the prophet again speaks of the sovereign creative activity of Jehovah and His government of all the earth (24–27), and proclaims once more that Cyrus is the God-appointed instrument for the fulfilling of the divine will (28).

That saith to the deep, Be dry (27). This is usually taken as referring to the device Cyrus used in order to capture Babylon. By means of an engineering feat he diverted the waters of the Euphrates river from its course through the city and made his soldiers to enter through the dry bed of the river thus made. *My shepherd* (28). An epithet commonly used of kings, but most fittingly of Cyrus as one who was to gather the scattered sheep of the house of Israel from many lands. This is the first occasion on which Cyrus is specifically mentioned by name. Josephus (*Ant.* 11. 1, section 2) records that Cyrus was shown this prophecy on his entry into Babylon and resolved to become the fulfiller of it. Cf. Ezr. i. 2–4.

ii. **Jehovah's address to Cyrus (xlv. 1–10).** In chapter xlv four closely related messages take up the theme that Cyrus is the God-appointed agent of the divine will. This man whom God has raised up will perform the divine pleasure, and woe to all who oppose the government he shall establish. The salvation that waits for Israel is an everlasting one and victory all the way along will be her portion when Jehovah has wrought the work He plans.

Having proclaimed that Cyrus is to be the shepherd of Israel, God now addresses him in person (1). He is to be raised up for this mighty task and will fulfil the work appointed for him, even though he knows not what it is that he is actually doing, nor why (4, 5). Unparalleled conquest will be his, for the doors shall be opened for him by the hand of God and the bars of iron that might impede his progress will be ruthlessly destroyed (2, 3). Woe will be to him that refuses him who is sent (9, 10).

His anointed (1). The only instance where this word is applied to a Gentile. With the designation 'the shepherd' (xliv. 28) also applied to him, it becomes clearer than ever that Cyrus is in some sense regarded as a Gentile forerunner or type of the Messiah. He is anointed of God for this mighty task. *I will loose the loins of kings* (1). This is the opposite of girding for the fray. The idea is that the kings opposing will be weakened by God that they might not be able to stand against this man whom He has raised up for His service. *The gates of brass* (2). Herodotus says that these gates of Babylon numbered one hundred. All these are to burst open and reveal the hidden treasures buried in the vaults and secret places of the city. The countries conquered by Cyrus were among the richest in the world. Croesus, king of Lydia, was one of the wealthiest men of olden times; his riches indeed became proverbial. Babylon itself was no doubt even more so. *That thou mayest know* . . . (3). Cyrus is to learn by experience that God, the Lord, is with him, and that He is the God of Israel. *I have surnamed thee* (4), i.e. with the titles of 'shepherd' and 'anointed'. *I girded thee* (5). Contrast the 'loosening' of verse 1. *I form the light, and create darkness* (7). In contrast to the Persians, who had twin divinities governing the world between them, Ormuzd, the good spirit of light, and Ahriman, the bad spirit who creates the dark, Jehovah proclaims that He is sovereign Lord of all, both darkness and light. The evil and darkness here referred to obviously mean the judgments of Jehovah that fall upon the rebellious children of disobedience. *Drop down, ye heavens* . . . (8). A poetical description of the joy that is to be when this shall have been accomplished. On the other hand, in verse 9, there is presented a picture of the sorrow for those who refuse to obey and to accept the divine commandment.

iii. Reaffirmation that Cyrus is divinely appointed (xlv. 11–13). *Ask me of things to come* . . . (11). It is often suggested that this verse should be in the form of a question: 'Of things that are to come do ye impudently question Me, and concerning the works of My hands will ye lay commands upon Me?' (See also RSV.) The suggestion thereby conveyed is that it is a wrong

thing for Israel thus to question God. But has not the entire emphasis of the preceding chapters been on the sovereignty of God in being able to foretell the things to be while all other divinities are dumb? It is fully in accordance with the context of these chapters to translate it as an appeal of Jehovah to His people to ask and seek for guidance. While the clay cannot turn to the potter and demand an explanation, this is the very thing that God asks His people to do, to stop doubting His designs and in humility to seek for the illumination they need concerning His ways and their ways.

iv. Victory and everlasting salvation for Israel (xlv. 14–17). The promise is now given that the days will come when the wealthiest nations of the earth will come as suppliants to Jerusalem, seeking the knowledge of the true and living God (14). The salvation with which Israel will be saved will be such as to draw the rest of the known world unto her for light and the knowledge of the truth (15–17).

Thus saith the Lord . . . (14). It is important to note that the address is now made to Israel. *The Sabeans* (14). Cf. xliii. 3. Herodotus mentions the extraordinary height of the Sabeans (Book iii. 20). The sense is that the greatness of the moral conquest of Israel is seen the more clearly in the stature of those who will come seeking. *A God that hidest thyself* (15). In these rapturous words the prophet bursts out into an adoring cry of praise at the splendour of the prospect being opened out before him as he receives the word of the God of Israel. Mercy is in all the mystery that has been Israel's lot. God has been hidden, but the full revelation of His blessed will now impends and the only answer is the answer of speechless adoration. So does Paul exclaim in Rom. xi. 33–36 at the realization of the magnificent programme of the eternal purpose.

v. Jehovah's longing for the salvation of the whole earth (xlv. 18–25). *I have not spoken in secret* (19). The speech of God is not like that of the oracles of the heathen, but is plain and clear. The revelation of Jehovah has not been kept secret nor has Israel needed to search in vain for the salvation of her God. The event verifies the speech, and Israel, if she will but seek, will assuredly find. *All the ends of the earth* (22). This is synonymous with all the peoples of the earth. *Unto me every knee shall bow* (23). An obviously messianic prediction. Cf. Rom. xiv. 11; Phil. ii. 10.

j. Prophecy concerning Babylon (xlvi. 1–xlvii. 15)

i. The majesty of Jehovah in the overthrow of Babylon (xlvi. 1–13). The gods of Babylon are now contrasted with the God of Israel and their downfall celebrated. Bel and Nebo, the chief divinities of Babylon, are carried off on the backs of weary animals (1, 2). Gods such as these are no use for the helping of their devotees, for they are carried off into captivity along with them. Here is majestic imagery and deep poetic inspiration. With the true eye of inspired vision the prophet pictures these gods as being borne along by 'weary beasts', carried about by the men who made them, set in place wherever they appoint, unable to depart therefrom and altogether quite incapable of doing anything to uplift and save (6, 7). On the contrary, the God of Israel is One who makes and carries His chosen race (3, 4). Of this Dr. Campbell Morgan says: 'An idol is a thing which a man makes and has to carry. The true God makes a man and carries him.' This is the message the prophet has to impress upon his countrymen, not without difficulty, as we may judge from the reference to the 'stouthearted' (12).

Bel . . . Nebo (1). Babylonian divinities. Compounds of these names are found in such names as Belshazzar and Nebuchadnezzar. Nebo was the god of Borsippa near Babylon, and Bel the city god of Nippur. Bel is a Babylonian variant of Baal, while Nebo corresponds to the Greek Hermes and the Egyptian Anubis. Borne by me (3). While all Babylon must carry its gods, Jehovah carries Israel. The mother-love of the Eternal is here revealed, as also the tender solicitude with which Jehovah watched over His people from the day on which He first called them out to be the instrument of His will. To whom will ye liken me? (5). With verses 5–7 cf. xl. 18–20, xliv. 9–20. With verses 8–11 cf. xli. 21–23. The appeal to prediction as a proof of the truth of their claims is here again advanced. Shew yourselves men (8); i.e. act as men should act, men with reason and memory; act rationally and do not be carried away with any or every varying tide of opinion. A ravenous bird (11). This is another reference to Cyrus and he is called this because of the extent and rapidity of his conquests. The image is one of speed, strength and destructiveness. Xenophon records (Cyrop. 7. 1, 4) that Cyrus had an eagle as his standard. Ye stouthearted (12), i.e. those who are obstinate in belief. The LXX has this translated as 'ye that have lost heart'; the variant is interesting, but the original is nearer to the sense of the entire passage.

ii. The coming fall of Babylon (xlvii. 1–15). Now the prophet turns to utter a masterly taunt-song over Babylon's destruction. It is foretold by likening the city to a woman who, after having enjoyed unparalleled luxury, is thrown outside to poverty and shame (1–3). She who has ruled in the past will now serve as a menial and will eat the bread of sorrow. In the course of the song the prophet refers to the sorceries and enchantments in which Babylon had trafficked from youth (9, 12–15). He challenges her too in the day of her distress to call upon those in whom she has trusted and boasted. Even if she does so appeal it will avail nothing; they are dumb and helpless and the fire of the divine wrath will consume them all (14, 15).

I will not meet thee as a man (3). The text is obscure and many attempts at emendation have been made. Luther's version translates 'No one can resist me.' Delitzsch has it 'I will take vengeance and not spare men'. McFadyen, 'For vengeance I will take, irrevocable vengeance'. König's translation, 'No man shall intervene', is an attractive alternative, though there is no exact parallel in the sentence. The sense of the passage as a whole is not in doubt. Calamity un-diluted awaits the city and nothing will avail to help. As for our redeemer (4). Here is another of those joyful exclamations of the true children of God who, conscious of the overruling providence of Heaven, rest secure amidst all the chaotic conditions of the world around. I was wroth . . . (6). The speech of God. While it is true that Israel had sinned and Babylon was the chosen instrument of her punishment, yet Babylon will be rewarded according to her own cruelty and overweening ambition. I have polluted mine inheritance (6); i.e. the holy land has been defiled by its conquerors. That dwellest carelessly (8). The Babylonians openly mocked at Cyrus when he came against them; they thought that their defences were sufficient for any period of time. Widow . . . loss of children (8). The image is that of the passing away of the alliances on which she has built her trust; while in the destruction that will overwhelm her the teeming population of her streets will be removed. In a moment in one day (9). This was literally fulfilled on 3 November, 538 B.C. As the Cylinder of Cyrus, which records his conquest of Babylon, says: 'Without battle and without fighting Marduk (the chief god) made him enter into his city of Babylon.'

Laboured from thy youth (12). This reference carries the mind back to the beginnings of Babylon, which were near Babel, where men attempted to frustrate a divine purpose by federating against God (Gn. xi. 1–9). This action was the result of traffic with evil conceptions and evil spiritual forces; and this process has run right through history. Monthly prognosticators (13); RSV renders 'Those . . . who at the new moon predict what shall befall you'. There shall not be a coal (14). The sense is that this will not be a mere fire for warming oneself, but a devastating avalanche of flame that will consume and burn all before it.

k. God's gracious providence and mercy (xlviii. 1–22)

This great chapter is a beautiful celebration of the divine mercy which always determines the activity of the majesty and might of the Lord God Jehovah in the fulfilment of His will. This mercy is in spite of all the wilful refusal of Israel to hearken to the word of their God; they are still the house of Jacob, though called by the name of Israel (1); they do not act in righteousness and truth for all their lip-service to these sovereign factors of life and destiny. Mercy weeps over the persistent rebellion of the people beloved and over the consequent lack of prosperity that is their lot. Would they but hearken to the manifesto of Jehovah and the messages He has sent, their peace would be as the river and their righteousness as the waves of the sea (18). Not to do so is to discover what is eternally written in the heavens of God, that there is no peace for the rebellious and wicked heart (22).

i. The certainty of divine fulfilment of predicted things (xlviii. 1–11). *The waters of Judah* (1). Judah is here referred to as it was the royal tribe of the Messiah and was to give its name to the entire people of Israel. The waters refer to the channel of blessing designed to flow from the one great fountainhead. *Thy neck is an iron sinew* (4). Cf. Ex. xxxii. 9. *Mine idol hath done them* (5). This suggests that many Israelites were ensnared by the pagan worship of their captors. *Thou hast heard* (6). The appeal is again made to prediction fulfilled. 'You have heard; you now see it before your eyes; why will you not admit and confess that this is indeed the act of Jehovah?' *Thine ear was not opened* (8); lit. 'from olden time your ear was not opened'. *Not with silver* (10), i.e. the refining fires through which Israel has gone have been more intense than that for silver. It has been with the burning fury of fierce affliction; yet in spite of that she is still impure. *Chosen* (10); better, as in RV mg., 'tried'.

ii. Divine sovereignty revealed through Cyrus (xlviii. 12–16). Here is a renewed declaration that Jehovah is God alone and that His mighty will is to be accomplished by the man of His choice. *The Lord hath loved him* (14), i.e. Cyrus. This is the most explicit statement of God's attitude towards the man of His choice for this mighty task of liberating the Jews. *And now the Lord God, and his Spirit, hath sent me* (16). This should properly read: 'And now the Lord God hath sent me and His Spirit.' The Spirit is a second object and not a second subject. Many think that this verse is misplaced, but without textual justification. Calvin stressed the view that the clause is introduced parenthetically, the prophet referring to himself as having been commissioned by his God with this mighty proclamation to the people of God. In thus claiming commission he likewise claims that the power of the Spirit of God is with him as he comes to the task.

iii. The blessing of obedience (xlviii. 17–19). This is the great and ever-recurring lament of the Lord's eternal love over the beloved's rebellion (cf. Ps. lxxxi. 13).

iv. A call to declare what God has done (xlviii. 20–22). *They thirsted not* (21). The exodus from Babylon will be a time of singing and will repeat the ancient wonders and the miraculous interventions of Jehovah that Israel knew when coming forth from Egypt. *There is no peace . . .* (22). See lvii. 21n.

VIII. REDEMPTION THROUGH SUFFERING AND SACRIFICE.
xlix. 1—lvii. 21

To pass from chapter xlviii to chapter xlix is to move from one great division of the prophecy to another. Having made clear in the preceding chapters that Jehovah is Lord God alone, the prophet no longer needs to stress His sovereignty over the idols of the surrounding nations. In the same way Cyrus now passes from the scene, as he has been sufficiently shown as the anointed minister of God for the fulfilment of His historic will amongst men. Two mighty themes now begin to dominate the book: one, the Servant of the Lord; and the other, the glorious future that awaits Israel.

a. Second 'Servant' passage: His task (xlix. 1–6) See general introductory remarks on the 'Servant' passages, p. 591. This chapter opens with the voice of the Servant relating how He has been called to His task. The nations are called to listen and give ear (1) as He declares His sense of vocation (1–3). In spite of past rejection (4) the future is secure since it is in the hand of God (4). As He speaks, the Servant is conscious that the service to be rendered is very difficult; He sees the failure of His mission in His rejection by His nation. This rejection, however, will work in blessing for the Gentiles; and ultimately not only Israel but the whole earth will be brought to Him (5, 6).

Listen, O isles, unto me (1). Here is the word of the Servant of Jehovah to the world. To none other than to the Messiah, the Son of God, who in the fulness of time came forth from the Father to redeem and save the sons of men, can this saying be suitably or fully applied. Only He was able to bring in that better order whereby the nations of all the earth could be brought to the only living and true God. The nation Israel and the religion of Judaism were quite unadapted for a world-wide use. Their form of sacrifices was centred too completely upon Jerusalem. It is the Anointed of the Lord God who came to save the world, in whom men from all races and climes are drawn together into the one great fellowship where there is 'neither Jew nor Greek, male nor female, bond nor free'. *My mouth* (2), i.e. my speech. Cf. Heb. iv. 12. The beautiful and pointed language is eloquent of the fact that this word is indeed that very word of God that alone can pierce through the dividing walls of man's stubborn defences and bring the light of life. Cf. Jn. vi. 63; Rev. i. 16. *Thou art my servant* (3). Here is fresh evidence that it is indeed the Messiah who is in view; for in the words that follow (*Israel, in whom I will be glorified*) we see the utter necessity for Him to come forth. Another had before borne that name, meaning 'ruled by God'; but he had failed to fulfil that ideal. The nation had likewise borne that name, but in its history God had not been glorified. Now to Another the name is to be given and in Him the purpose will be fulfilled: God will be glorified in Him. Through Him too the nation Israel will eventually, in spite of all past failures, realize its high destiny. *Then I said, I have laboured in vain* (4). The fulfilment of the divine plan seems to begin in failure. So it was with our Lord: He was 'despised and rejected' (liii. 3). The path by which He came to His throne was the lowly one of suffering and grief. But the sure end of the way was never in question. His cause was 'safe with Jehovah, and His recompense was with His God' (4).

To bring Jacob again to him (5). The distinction here made between the Servant and the nation Israel is quite definite. *Though Israel be not gathered* (5). The RV reads here 'and that Israel be gathered unto him'. That makes this phrase a continuation of the functions that the Messiah Servant will fulfil when He comes. The clause that follows becomes, as a result, a sort of parenthesis: 'for I am honourable in the sight of Jehovah, and my God is my strength.' This parenthesis is inserted by some modern commentators immediately after verse 3. *It is a light thing . . .* (6); RV 'it is too light a thing'. The call of Jehovah to His Servant is to a work that will spread far beyond the bounds of Israel and reach to the uttermost parts of the earth. *My servant to raise up the tribes of Jacob* (6). Once again there is the separation between the nation and the Servant. Only the most arbitrary form of exegesis can make it seem that in this the Servant is actually Israel the nation. It is said that we can speak of Britain's duty to herself; and also that in this case it is the Israel of the captivity that is to become the restorer of the Israel of the dispersion. But surely this is straining the meaning unnecessarily. J. E. McFadyen goes further and says: 'Probably the words "that thou shouldest be my servant" should be omitted. Besides being metrically superfluous, they have the effect of making the Servant a person, whose task it is to save the nation. But elsewhere it is the nation Israel that is the Servant; so probably here.' That is quite unwarrantable. There is no ground whatsoever for the removal of these words from the sacred text. Excision is not exposition. 'That thou shouldest be my servant' surely refers to the Messiah of Jehovah, to Him who alone, after all the failures of the nation and others that before have borne the name of Israel, will be able to redeem and save with an everlasting salvation.

b. Jehovah addresses the Servant (xlix. 7–13)

The Servant has been made to suffer rejection, but in due time He will be raised up so that kings and princes shall see that He is the chosen of the Lord (7–9). There follows the picture of the exiles, travelling across the long lines of the desert wastes, strong in the help of their God, redeemed out of the bondage in which they have long been held (10–13).

To him whom man despiseth (7). G. A. Smith translates this as follows:

'*Thus saith Jehovah,*
Israel's Redeemer, His Holy,
To this mockery of a life, abhorrence of a nation, servant of tyrants.'

To him whom the nation abhorreth (7). 'The object of contempt and abhorrence to the Jewish people.' *To a servant of rulers* (7). He who once subjected Himself to the dictation of unrighteous rulers shall receive the homage of kings. In all these words Jehovah is speaking directly to the Servant Himself. *In an acceptable time . . .* (8). Cf. 2 Cor. v. 18—vi. 2, where Paul takes up this saying of Isaiah and applies it to the times of the Messiah. *They shall not hunger nor thirst . . .* (10). Cf. Rev. vii. 16. *The land of Sinim* (12). There can be no absolute certainty as to what is here signified. The sense, of course, is clear that from the wide bounds of the wastes men and women will press into the kingdom of the Messiah and find life and light therein. The prevailing conception for a long time was that Sinim meant the land of China, and this must not be ruled out. Others interpret it as referring to Assouan in the south of Egypt, where there was a large Jewish colony. Cf. Ezk. xxix. 10, xxx. 6.

c. Salvation and restoration secured for Zion (xlix. 14–26)

Though Zion may doubt God's power and picture herself as a forsaken child, Jehovah graciously reaffirms His love and care for her. Even in captivity the people will multiply so that when they return their number will cause surprise and there will hardly be room for them. *I have graven thee . . .* (16). An allusion to the ancient custom of tattooing. *Nursing fathers* (23) are those entrusted with the upbringing of other people's children. See, e.g., 2 Ki. x. 1ff.

d. Jehovah's omnipotent love (l. 1–3)

These verses are a continuation of the section in the latter part of chapter xlix (see especially xlix. 14–16). The marriage bond between the exiles and their God is literally unbreakable. *Where is the bill of your mother's divorcement?* (1). Israel had been faithless, but even so God had not annulled the covenant with her. They have been sold into bondage, not because Jehovah wished to gain some advantage from this, but because of their transgressions. Why, then, does no one answer when He calls to them in mercy? His power and love are eternal and boundless. Have they forgotten the miraculous deliverance from Egypt?

e. Third 'Servant' passage: His obedience and trust (l. 4–9)

See general introductory remarks on the 'Servant' passages, p. 591. Once again we hear the voice of the Servant of Jehovah as He answers the call of Jehovah. We have seen already (xlix. 1–6) that He is conscious that the ministry to which He is called is one that will involve much suffering and pain, and that only through suffering will Israel be redeemed. In this section, this consciousness has deepened and some of the forms of the suffering begin to be seen. It is not until chapter liii is reached that the full intensity of messianic suffering comes to light, but much is here revealed; in particular it is the consciousness of the sufferings that His enemies will inflict upon Him that is dwelt upon. The New Testament references to this whole passage are its best commentary.

It is instructive to note the physical features that are dwelt upon: the smiting, the plucking off of the hair, the shame and the spitting (6). It is to such experiences that the call of Jehovah is made. It is in regard to such experiences that the Servant is heard to say: 'Mine ear hast thou opened, and I was not rebellious, neither turned away backward' (5). Between the Servant and Jehovah there is no conflict, but the most perfect agreement (7–9).

The Lord God hath given me (4). Great gifts of Jehovah to His Servant are here detailed: a power to instruct in the way of God (4); the spirit of obedience and meekness (5); the spirit of confidence in God and of strength in Him (6, 7); the consciousness of God with Him in all His work and ministry (8, 9). *To them that plucked off the hair* (6). Cf. Mt. xxvi. 67, xxvii. 26, 30; Jn. xviii. 22. *They all shall wax old as a garment* (9). This reference to the natural decay of the enemies of the Servant is doubly significant. Not only is there a sublime assurance of the powerlessness of those who would oppose, but it implicitly proclaims the Servant's belief that He will not likewise perish. Cf. Heb. i. 11, 12 for contrasts. If the Servant were Israel this would be an almost impossible assumption, namely, that Israel is indestructible. In the mouth of the Son of God, the anointed Messiah, such a declaration is entirely fitting and part of the great elemental truth of revelation. In li. 6–8 the same metaphor is employed of the passing of heaven and earth as contrasted with the eternal stability of God's righteousness.

f. Blessings to follow the work of the Servant (l. 10—lii. 12)

i. An exhortation to faith (l. 10, 11). In these words of exhortation the truth of the preceding 'Servant' song is applied as an encouragement to the faithful and a warning to the godless. Those who are 'in the dark' and know it are called to trust. Those who are self-sufficient and direct their walk according to their own wisdom will find *sorrow* at the end of the journey.

ii. Three words to the elect remnant (li. 1–8). These three messages, each beginning with the words *Hearken unto me* (1, 4, 7), are addressed to the elect remnant of souls, who, through all defection from the true way, have continued to love righteousness and to walk therein. The faithful are summoned to look to the rock (1–3), to attend to the law, which is salvation (4–6), and to know no fear (7, 8). *Look unto Abraham* (2). As Abraham went forth from Mesopotamia to become the father of a great nation, so shall those who are his true descendants go forth to found it anew. As in him all nations were blessed, so in the revived Israel will the whole earth find help and salvation. *I will make my judgment to rest* (4); i.e. I will establish my law. *The heavens shall vanish away* (6). The

heavens, in the multitude of their starry host, were to Abraham a sign of the children that would yet be his in posterity (cf. Gn. xv. 5, xxii. 17). Now to the redeemed of Israel they are but a sign of transitoriness and of the sufficient and eternal salvation in their God.

iii. The nation's cry is answered by Jehovah (li. 9–16). These verses comprise the first of three messages, each beginning with the words *Awake, awake* (cf. li. 17, lii. 1). The nation cries for the intervention of God (9–11), and is answered by words of comfort and encouragement (12–16). *Rahab . . . the dragon* (9); i.e. Egypt and Pharaoh. Cf. Is. xxx. 7; Ps. lxxiv. 13. As the supreme example of Jehovah's might psalmists and prophets continually refer to the miraculous exodus from Egypt (10, 15), and to the wonders of His creation (13). *The captive exile hasteneth* (14). Rather:

'Soon shall the captive be freed,
He shall not end in death and the pit,
Nor suffer for lack of bread.'

In this verse Israel is compared to a famished prisoner in a dungeon. But God's salvation shall reach him who, bent under such chains, is perishing from hunger, for His power is boundless. *I have put my words in thy mouth* (16). Repeated xlix. 2 and lix. 21. The words clearly suggest pre-existence of the Servant.

iv. The cry of Jehovah to His people (li. 17–23). The second message is from God Himself, as He shows His people the sufferings that result from sin and promises deliverance. *Which hast drunk at the hand of the Lord* (17). A most forceful manner of describing the condition of Israel's hopelessness and reproach under the hand of God. The thought is picked up again in verses 21–23, where the cup is taken from Israel's trembling hand and given to those who have trampled over her.

v. The call of Jehovah in reply to His people (lii. 1–12). The cry of the people had been 'Awake awake, put on strength, O arm of the Lord' (li. 9). Now the Lord answers, *Awake, awake; put on thy strength, O Zion* (1), and once more redemption full and everlasting is covenanted to them. The triumphant establishment of the kingdom of God is then celebrated in words of great beauty and power. All this is what the prophet sees as he realizes that the Servant of Jehovah is to work the work of God (9, 10). All things will be fulfilled which the eternal will has planned, and the redeemed of the Lord will yet be made to walk in the light of the countenance of Jehovah, their God (11, 12).

Put on thy beautiful garments . . . (1). A divine challenge and promise. The purity of the Israel of Jehovah's love when she has been cleansed will be of surpassing excellence. Verses 3–6 are in prose form, unlike the verses surrounding them. In them the prophet speaks of Jehovah's concern for His honour which has been so completely degraded by Israel's apostasy.

What have I here? (5), i.e. in Babylon. Lit. 'What do I here?', meaning 'I have nothing to do with this place'. *How beautiful . . .* (7). Though Zion was laid low at the time of this prophecy, yet to the faithful heart of Judah the watchman upon the walls proclaims the coming of the longed for 'Herald'. *Eye to eye* (8). More exactly: 'they shall see, eye to eye, how Jehovah comes back to Zion.' The sense is that with the clearness of vision which a man has looking into the eyes of another, the captives shall behold the coming One. 'They see the Eternal face to face as he returns to Sion' (Moff.). *The Lord hath made bare his holy arm* (10); i.e. He hath prepared for action, for the deliverance of His people Israel. *The Lord will go before you* (12). Note the parallels with the exodus story. Cf. Ex. xiii. 21, 22, xiv. 19, 20.

g. Fourth 'Servant' passage: His life and suffering (lii. 13—liii. 12)

See general introductory remarks on the 'Servant' passages, p. 591. This great passage constitutes the fourth and last of the 'Servant' songs. In it all the leading ideas of the others are gathered up and are presented in a complete and coherent picture of the life, service, sufferings and triumph of the Servant of Jehovah. The many New Testament references to it should be studied.

i. Introductory summary (lii. 13–15). These verses are an introduction to the main movement in the presentation of the Servant, and they are actually a crystalline summary of the whole of chapter liii. The movement is from triumph (13) through suffering (14) to victory and exaltation (15). This, be it noted, is a summary from the divine standpoint of what in chapter liii is given from human observation. Here is seen suffering incomparable and triumph most glorious. The pathway to the throne is one of grief, in which 'many were astonied at thee' (14). The appalling spectacle of Him in His sorrow and suffering is thus graphically described. It is the more emphasized by the words that occur in parenthesis: 'his visage was so marred more than any man, and his form more than the sons of men' (14). Through this, however, He moves forward to the consummation of the purpose of God and the triumph eternally ordained for Him.

Exalted and extolled (13). Cf. the third 'Servant' passage (l. 4–9) where the emphasis was on His suffering. Here we begin with His victory and exaltation. *As many were astonied at thee* (14). The sense is that in the very manner ('like as') in which men were moved at the sight of His sufferings, so shall they be stirred and startled at the spectacle of His glory. *His visage . . .* (14). This is a short parenthesis introduced in order to explain the reason for the astonishment on the faces of the beholders. The literal rendering is indeed very terrible: 'So marred from the form of man was His aspect that His appearance was not that of a son of man.' Thus is recorded

the effect of the agonies of suffering and shame inflicted upon Him. *So* (15). This corresponds to the 'As' of verse 14. *Sprinkle* (15). Generally now regarded as a mistranslation. The word should be taken as meaning 'startle'. See RV mg. He who once startled all men by the sight of His sufferings will again amaze them by His triumph and exaltation. *Kings shall shut their mouths* (15), i.e. in wonder. They will be unable to speak as they look at this spectacle of triumph come out of suffering.

ii. His life and suffering unto death (liii. 1–9). After the foregoing introduction, the prophet proceeds to develop his vision of God's plan for the redemption of the world. The world to be redeemed is startled and dismayed at the sight of this strange suffering and, to begin with, imagines that such suffering must be from the hand of God. Further contemplation, however, of the blameless life that the Servant has lived makes it clear that in undergoing such reproach He is actually suffering because of others. In this recognition there is also born a consciousness that the very beholders are implicated in the matter; they see that He has suffered unjustly and that they ought themselves to have suffered instead. When He has suffered unto death, however, they see that this was part of the will of God, part of the strange way of destroying evil and bringing in perfect righteousness. It is by this way that He comes to the conqueror's reward. Only thus shall many be turned away from their unjust ways to the paths of peace and life.

The whole chapter is pregnant with mystery. Here we are introduced to the suffering Servant of Jehovah in a way which 'can only make the lips dumb, and bow the soul to the most complete prostration of wonder and amazement'. So great is the revelation that 'pity is impertinent; and sympathy is irreverent'. One can only sense that here is the greatness of the mystery of the mighty act of God in time as in eternity. Before this vision of the suffering Saviour we can only watch, wonder and adore.

For the purposes of study these nine verses may be divided into three short sections. We have presented to us first the rejected Person (1–3), then the vicarious Sufferer (4–6), and finally, the atoning Lamb (7–9). For the tenses of the verbs see RV. See also notes on particular words and phrases below.

In presenting the rejected Person the prophet clearly shows Him first as seen by God and then as seen by men. 'He grew up before him as a tender plant' (2, RV). Thus is described in a beautiful simile all that is suggested by eternal youth; but that, however, was not how man saw Him. In immediate and striking contrast there follow the words 'and as a root out of a dry ground'. There is here no suggestion that the Servant was lacking form, or comeliness, or beauty. What is stated, and emphatically, is that man was blind to His beauty. All is summarized concerning His Person in the words: 'He was despised, and rejected of men; a man of sorrows, and acquainted with grief' (3, RV).

Following upon this sight of Him as personally rejected the prophet shows that the sufferings He bore were vicarious in their power (4–6). Looking at Him men had imagined that all this was a visitation of God upon Him: *smitten of God, and afflicted* (4). So had the same philosophy mastered the thinking of the friends of Job; they had thought him afflicted by God as being a sinner, but they were wrong. *He was wounded for our transgressions, he was bruised for our iniquities* (5). Where men had seen no beauty in Him because they were blind, so here they see no real ministry in His sorrow because their minds were unillumined by the light from above. The great truth is here proclaimed by the prophet that the suffering is vicarious and the agony avails.

The next three verses (7–9) lead us to the holy place of sacrifice. Here the Lamb makes atonement: silent in the midst of the wrong being done Him; led forth to be *cut off out of the land of the living* (8); made to be the atonement for the transgressions of the people. This is the climax of the presentation of the personal Sufferer and the vicarious Sufferer; He is the atoning Lamb who was stricken *for the transgression of my people* (8).

Who hath believed our report? (1); better, as in RV mg., 'that which we have heard'. The reference is to the earlier 'Servant' passages with their incredible messages of suffering and reproach. This complaint is a confession of penitence. The voice is the prophet's, speaking in the name of the people. At the same time there is a strong suggestion of incredulity: 'Who could have believed such a report?' *As a root out of a dry ground* (2). Nothing in the nation's past could give hope of such greatness; nor was there aught in the time or surroundings of the Saviour's birth to account for Him. *Acquainted with grief* (3). C. R. North translates 'acquainted with sickness', i.e. leprosy; a picture of the Saviour's contact with sin. Cf. 2 Cor. v. 21. *We did esteem him stricken* (4). The Servant was bearing the sins of the beholders who had imagined that He was being smitten of God for His own sins. Cf. Mt. viii. 17. *The chastisement of our peace* (5), i.e. the chastisement by which our peace with God is won. *Who shall declare his generation?* (8). 'And as for his generation, who among them considered that he was cut off out of the land of the living?' (RV); or, with C. R. North, 'and on his fate who reflected?' *His generation* (8), i.e. His contemporaries. *With the rich in his death* (9). The rulers of the people had thought that the Servant should be buried disgracefully as a criminal, but the wonderful providence of His God overruled that and He was buried with the rich (RV 'a rich man') in His death (cf. Mt. xxvii. 57–60).

iii. **The glorious issue of His sufferings (liii. 10–12).** At verse 10 the note changes and we come to the setting forth of the triumph of the Lord. It commences with the words 'Yet it pleased the Lord to bruise him', and in this way our contemplation is lifted to the level of the divine will. The Servant suffers thus because God willed that in this way many would be brought to righteousness through His obedience. And beyond the darkness of the sorrow and the shadow of death is shown the radiance of resurrection. He will live to see a spiritual offspring and come to the throne of the conqueror renowned.

It pleased the Lord (10), i.e. it was the eternal purpose of God. *When thou shalt make his soul* ... (10). Many translations of this verse have been offered. Cf. RV, RV mg. and RSV. The general meaning is quite clear. Out of death and the sacrifice thus made will come the newness of resurrection life and the holy seed of the redeemed Church of God. *The pleasure of the Lord* (10), i.e. the purpose of God, which is the salvation of man. *He shall see of the travail of his soul, and shall be satisfied* (11). This is largely an extension of the thoughts of verse 10. In no greater way can the soul of the redeemed be made to marvel than through the reading of such a verse. The Dead Sea Scroll supports the reading of LXX: 'in the midst of His travail He shall see light.' Cf. Heb. xii. 2. *By his knowledge* ... (11). Either 'by the knowledge which as Saviour and Servant He possesses of the will of God, of His righteousness and the way of salvation, and which by imparting to men gives to them a like understanding of the divine path', or 'by knowledge of Him, such a knowledge of Him as will produce faith and thereby save the life'. *Divide him a portion* (12). Here are the fruits of victory given to the Servant.

h. **The future glory of Jerusalem (liv. 1–17)**

The opening word of this chapter is the fitting follow-on from the words that have just been spoken. If the Servant is to see of the travail of His soul and be satisfied, there is nothing else that the redeemed can do than rejoice with Him in His exaltation and triumph. The chapter is a great anthem of assurance in which the sovereignty of the Servant is celebrated concerning the gathering again of the chosen nation and the ransoming of the Holy City. The entire programme of redemption is governed by the restoration of Israel to her former glory, to her fellowship with God (1–4). This union is truly indissoluble, as is that of a wife to her husband (5, 6). Never again will the covenant of the Eternal be removed from her (7–10). Thus will the whole earth be reached and the will of Jehovah be perfectly fulfilled.

There follows a glorious description of the Holy City as it will be when this has been done (11–17). Jerusalem will be rebuilt as a city of great beauty and the internal spiritual life of the inhabitants will correspond to the external glories and splendour of her walls, pinnacles and gates.

Enlarge the place of thy tent (2). The sudden return of so many from afar calls for an increase in accommodation. Jerusalem is here compared to a large tent; to peoples accustomed to the pastoral life of the East the metaphor of enlarging the tent, together with lengthening the cords and strengthening the stakes, would be peculiarly appealing. *Thou shalt break forth* (3). A picture of universal expansion. Zion's inhabitants will overflow south and north, peopling the deserted cities of the Gentiles. The suggestion is clearly of a great spiritual force that will erupt beyond the life of Zion itself and spread in saving strength into the lands of others. *The shame of thy youth* (4); i.e. the bondage of Egypt. *The reproach of thy widowhood* (4); i.e. the captivity of Babylon. *The God of the whole earth shall he be called* (5). This is the ultimate of vision. It is towards this that all else will inevitably move. The eternal counsel knows no turning. *The Lord hath called thee* (6). The love that now recalls Israel is great and everlasting; against this the period of seeming rejection is not worthy of mention (7, 8). *As the waters of Noah* (9). This time of exile has been to Jehovah as a second flood. As He sware to Noah that the waters would not again encompass the earth, so now He swears that His wrath will not engulf His people. *For the mountains shall depart* (10). Rather 'the mountains may depart'.

With fair colours (11). More correctly 'in stibium'; this was a kind of paint formed from antimony with which the Hebrew women painted their eyelashes. The suggestion all through is of a surpassing glory greater than all that of the Babylonian kingdom. Cf. the description of the Holy City, the new Jerusalem (Rev. xxi. 19–20). *Taught of the Lord* (13). Cf. Jn. vi. 45. *They shall surely gather together . . .* (15). The sense here is that of the saying of our Lord: 'It is impossible but that offences will come: but woe unto him, through whom they come!' (Lk. xvii. 1). Translate: 'Men may quarrel, but it is not of Me: whosoever quarrels with thee shall fall because of thee', i.e. his shall be the ruin that strives with thee. *I have created the smith* (16), the one who fashions the *weapon* of verse 17. Since God is the creator of such men, the faithful need not fear them.

i. An appeal to embrace salvation (lv. 1–13)

After the song of triumph in the assurance of the salvation of Jehovah, there comes the great appeal of the prophet, a mighty and gracious invitation to embrace the impending salvation (3, 6, 7). The opening phrases picture life in its dissatisfaction and hunger (1, 2), while the closing passage depicts the satisfactions of the everlasting mercy (8–13). The oracle is the appeal of the prophet to men to pass from the one to the other by coming to the Lord their God and finding His blessed will. Rightly to embrace this proffered mercy will demand a complete change of mind and heart, for the ways of God are as different from the ways of man as the heavens are high above the earth (8, 9). The way by which man can thus repent and turn unto the Lord his

God is made clear in the words of verse 4: *Behold, I have given him for a witness to the people, a leader and commander to the people.* This can refer to none other than to the same suffering Servant whose work and sacrifice we have been studying in the chapters immediately preceding. It is by the way of the travail of His Servant that the Lord God can have mercy and abundantly pardon. It is through Him who has borne the sin that the sin can be put away for ever.

Ho, every one that thirsteth (1). Cf. Jn. iv. 10ff. The condition of the soul apart from the grace of God can surely be described no more adequately than one of thirst, hunger and unrewarding, fruitless labour. *Hearken diligently unto me, and eat* (2). Very often when two imperatives are found together in Hebrew they are really conditional in their effect: 'If ye hearken . . . ye shall eat.' *Hearken diligently* represents the intensive adverbial use of the infinitive absolute in the Hebrew: 'Hearken indeed.' *Incline your ear* (3). The re-emphasis on this recalls the words of the New Testament, 'faith cometh by hearing' (Rom. x. 17), as also 'Take heed what ye hear' (Mk. iv. 24). *The sure mercies of David* (3); i.e. the blessings that were so surely promised to David. There can be no doubt that the ultimate end of the promise is the Messiah and the salvation that He will bring. So Paul interprets it when, speaking of the resurrection of our Lord, he quotes this promise as one of the 'sure mercies' promised aforetime to David (cf. Acts xiii. 34). *A witness to the people* (4). David in his day was a witness and a leader of the peoples, but the complete fulfilment of all the promises made to him will come only when great David's greater Son appears. The Son of God is a 'Witness' of heavenly things and of the salvation that awaits the soul that follows Him: He is also a Leader and Commander of those that follow Him in all the ways of His determining. *A nation . . . nations* (5). These are unspecified. Cf. the 'other sheep' (Jn. x. 16). The address is to the Leader of the peoples. He shall be glorified, for He is the Son of God and shall be declared to be so with power; and because the Lord His God, the Holy One of Israel, who is eternally true to His promise, will give Him glory by giving Him the heathen for His inheritance.

Seek ye the Lord . . . for he will abundantly pardon (6, 7). These verses describe the true path of conversion: repentance; return to God from the ways of sin; the mercy of God; and the divine pardon. The ultimate ground for confidence is in God, who is not like men, but who in thought and purpose transcends them absolutely. Man's forgiveness is uncertain and imperfect; God, however, can *abundantly pardon*. *As the rain . . .* (10, 11). The promise is as sure as the very facts of nature in its mystery and power. *Ye shall go out with joy . . .* (12). The picture is one of unadulterated joy as those that have been redeemed by the hand of the Lord come to the habitation He has prepared. The wilderness will be left behind and gardens of light and beauty will welcome them as they advance. Cf. xxxv. 9.

j. The purposes of Jehovah (lvi. 1—lvii. 21)

Chapters lvi and lvii constitute one message and bring to a close the section of the prophecy that deals with the presentation of the Servant of Jehovah as the Prince of Peace. 'Where chapter lv expounds the grace and the faithfulness of God in the return of His people, and asks from them only faith as the price of these benefits, chapter lvi adds the demand that those who are to return shall keep the law, and extends their blessings to foreigners and others who, though technically disqualified from the privileges of the born and legitimate Israelite, had attached themselves to Jehovah and the law' (G. A. Smith). The promise is here made also that there shall not be one who in any way has suffered loss for the sake of the faith of Israel who will not receive at the hand of the Lord Himself comfort and great gladness of heart (lvi. 1–8). There follows a most scathing denunciation of those watchmen who are untrue to their proper function and give themselves over to the excitements of strong drink (lvi. 9—lvii. 2).

i. A word of assurance to those that believe (lvi. 1–8).

Here the prophet pronounces a word of cheer to those in danger of being excluded from the benefits of the house of Israel. *My salvation is near to come* (1). This verse obviously connects this prophecy closely with the preceding chapter. The keeping of *the sabbath* (2) is explicitly mentioned because this was one of the things that still could be fulfilled even in a land where all other religious practices had to be annulled except prayer and fasting. Its essential value in the maintenance of the very spirit of religion amongst men is, of course, implicitly held. It is perhaps introduced here as an example of fulfilling the conditions of the covenant which would lead to blessing. *The son of the stranger . . . the eunuch* (3). These men were excluded from the congregation of Israel by the law (cf. Dt. xxiii. 1). Now all this is to pass and all barriers are to be removed. The work of the Servant has been to break down all divisive factors, and the way is open for all to enjoy the favour of the divine mercy. God's house will be *for all people* (7). *An everlasting name* (5). Cf. the Ethiopian eunuch, who has been given an immortal place in the Church of Christ, greater by far than could ever have been in any other way. See Acts viii. 26ff.

ii. The leaders of Israel rebuked (lvi. 9—lvii. 2).

Beasts of the field (9); so are described the enemies of the flock of God who yet act as the instruments of the divine judgment and correction. *Watchmen* (10). This describes the leaders of the people, whose duty it was to watch and guard them from all evil. Instead of doing so and acting as true watchdogs of righteousness, they have grown idle, sleepy, sensual and gross and quite unfit for their exalted tasks. *From his quarter* (11); rather, as in RV, 'from every quarter'. *Come ye* (12). The invitation is from one of these false watchmen to a two-day revel. *The righteous perisheth* (lvii. 1). During this orgy and riot the good and true pass unnoticed from the scene. Their passing is at once a gracious providence and solemn warning to the ungodly.

iii. Denunciation of an apostate community (lvii. 3–13a).

The prophet now turns to castigate those who, in spite of all revelations of the love and mercy of Jehovah, have persisted in following idolatrous practices. His grand indictment rebukes them for a religious and political unfaithfulness so characteristic of their long history in the Holy Land. Gross idolatries and spiritual whoredoms have been committed in the land; because of these things destroying judgments will inevitably be visited upon them. *But draw near . . .* (3); Heb. 'But as for you, draw . . .' A new audience is now addressed. *Slaying the children* (5). Child sacrifice was associated with the worship of Molech. See 2 Ki. xvi. 3, xvii. 17. *Among the smooth stones* (6). The reference is to anointed stones which were set up by the heathen as objects of worship. Such idols became the 'lot' and 'portion' of the idolatrous Jews. *Thou wentest to the king* (9); Heb. *melek*. These words may refer to spiritual pilgrimages to foreign shrines; or to Molech, the god of Ammon; or to political envoys. *Even unto hell* (9); i.e. to the very lowest of degenerate activity. *I will declare thy righteousness* (12); i.e. expose the hollow claims that they make in their specious profession. *Thy companies* (13); RV 'them which thou hast gathered'. The meaning is doubtful. RSV renders 'your collection of idols'. The wind shall blow them away.

iv. 'The lofty One that inhabiteth eternity' (lvii. 13b–21).

By contrast with what has gone before the promise of return in order to possess the land again is renewed to those who trust in God. Everything which at present obstructs the way and prevents this will be removed. Cf. the similar thought in xl. 3. In contrast with the idols and their impure worshippers, the God who promises this is the high and holy One, who nevertheless condescends to work on behalf of those who are contrite and humble in spirit (15). *And shall say* (14); or 'One shall say'. Cf. xl. 3. *For the spirit should fail before me* (16). The very frailty of man is the reason given for the mercy and forbearance of God. *I create the fruit of the lips* (19). Cf. Heb. xiii. 15. Link these words with the last phrase of verse 18. The meaning is that the grace of thanksgiving will be given by God to them that are mourning, both to them that are afar off in exile and to them that are near. *There is no peace, saith my God, to the wicked* (21). This, the climax of the section, is similar to that which closed the passage xl. 1—xlviii. 22, and demonstrates the divine purpose of peace for man. There is a significant difference of name for God in these two phrases. In the section dealing with the purpose of peace, the affirmation is made by 'Jehovah', which is the title of grace. In this present section, dealing with the Prince of Peace, the affirmation is made by 'Elohim', which is the name of absolute might. God in grace purposes peace. When He makes it possible through His suffering Servant, His might insists on the terms. But even by the way of that travail there is no peace for those who refuse to hearken and who persist in wickedness. The sea, with its restless movement, caused by tide and wind, is a most apt description for them.

IX. THE TRIUMPH OF THE KINGDOM AND THE UNIVERSAL DOMINION OF JEHOVAH. lviii. 1—lxvi. 24

We now enter upon the last of the three principal sections of this great second portion of the book of Isaiah, and the subject-matter is that which we would naturally expect. Having spoken of the eternal purpose of Jehovah of peace for His people, and having revealed Him through whom alone that peace can be discovered, the Servant of the Lord, the Prince of Peace, the prophet now proceeds to demonstrate the type of life that must be lived out by those brought into the fellowship of this gift of peace. The subject essentially now is 'The Programme of Peace'.

a. Rebukes and promises to Israel (lviii. 1—lix. 21)

Chapters lviii and lix make up one movement in this theme. The former treats of the true and false worship of Jehovah, and deals with subjects such as fasting and the sabbath. Chapter lix rebukes the gross sins of the people, who are called to penitent confession and pointed to the place where deliverance and absolution are found. The prophet is charged to declare to the people of God their transgression and sin. He sternly rebukes them for observing the ritual of religion while failing entirely to produce its results. He repudiates the value of an attitude of humility and lowliness before God, when, in their dealings with their fellow-men, there was an absence of compassion and justice. Only by turning from their sinful ways and by a vitalizing of their religious services could they find the power and grace of their God and the national blessings covenanted unto them from times gone by.

i. Fasting without repentance and reform is hypocrisy (lviii. 1–12).

The people, complaining that their fasts have brought no material benefit, are told that their fasting is a hollow pretence. The ritual of fasting was observed, but the real self-denial of loving ministry was completely lacking (1–5). If they would but find the true spirit of service they would be lifted on to a higher plane of life, the life planned and blessed of God (6–12).

Cry aloud, spare not, . . . shew my people their transgression (1). This is the charge laid upon the prophet to declare. It is to be a message of condemnation and conviction. *Yet they seek me daily* (2). The outward form of worship was

there, but their hearts were far from God; they were but self-seekers in all they did. *Wherefore have we fasted?* (3). Here is the real heart revealing itself. They had thought they would obtain God's approval by virtue of their mere act of fasting. *Behold . . . ye find pleasure* (3); i.e. you carry on your business and see to it that your servants are rigorously employed during this time of so-called devotion. See RV mg. *Ye fast for strife and debate* (RV 'contention') (4). Fast days are distinguished by quarrelling and fighting. *To make your voice to be heard on high* (4); i.e. fasting like yours is not the kind that will make your prayers to be heard at the throne of grace. *Is it such a fast that I have chosen?* (5). Render 'Would such be the fast that I choose —a day when a man afflicts himself?' Mere asceticism is nothing. It is the spirit that gives life to this as to all things else. There follows in verse 6 a statement of the kind of fasting that their God demands. Freeing of slaves, remission of debts, distribution of good to the needy, and other such acts are those that are well pleasing to God and will call forth His gracious benediction. *From thine own flesh* (7); i.e. from thine own kith and kin. They should not shun them, though they be poor and needy. *Putting forth of the finger* (9); i.e. pointing with the finger, a sign of bitter contempt.

ii. The rightful observance of the sabbath (lviii. 13, 14).

There was no greater way of uniting the people of Israel when exiled from their own land than the keeping of the sabbath. Divine blessing is ever covenanted to those who maintain the sanctity of the day of rest. *Turn away thy foot* (13); i.e. do not tread the holy day with the feet of week-day work. *The holy of the Lord* (13). An unusual form of description of the sabbath, but one peculiarly appropriate. *Pleasure* (13). Again this should be read as 'business'. Cf. verse 3. *To ride upon the high places of the earth* (14). Cf. Dt. xxxii. 13.

iii. Sin a barrier to the divine purpose (lix. 1–8).

The message of this chapter is similar to that of the previous, with this difference. Whereas in the former the people are brought face to face with their sins, here the message is that these very sins are hindering the fulfilment of the divine purpose. They may be tempted to think that God is powerless to help (1); but the real trouble is that their iniquities have separated them from Him and only in returning in penitence will they find again the desired grace (2). *Your hands are defiled with blood* (3). The sins of the community are many and great: murder, deceit, perjury, and deliberate following after evil ends. Verses 5 and 6 contain a figurative account of their evil acts. Their schemes are profitable neither to themselves nor to those who oppose them. *Their feet run to evil . . .* (7). Cf. Rom. iii. 10–18. With verse 8 cf. lvii. 21n. The people must learn the lesson that sin erects a barrier total in its effect between the soul and God, and while sinning is so widespread there need be no looking for the salvation of heaven.

iv. The confession of the people (lix. 9–15).
Therefore (9). The sins which are about to be described are the reason for their sorrowful plight, and not that mentioned in verse 1. Having delivered his rebuke the prophet accepts it, so to speak, for himself and the nation, and confesses the people's transgressions. *Judgment* (9). Here and in verse 14 the word has the idea of 'justice', i.e. God's actions on behalf of His people against their oppressors. The word translated *justice* by the AV (9, 14) is better rendered 'righteousness' (RV). *Truth is fallen in the street . . . truth faileth* (14, 15); so complete is the destruction of all that savours of righteousness and holiness, that any who resolve to depart from evil immediately become marked men for ruin (15).

v. The almighty deliverance of Jehovah (lix. 16–21). The climax of the chapter is reached in the manifestation of the divine deliverance and succour in response to the cry of the people. When things are at their worst and there is none to help, the Lord God Himself comes in might to deliver and save the inheritance of His people. Only by such active intervention of God can the situation be saved at all.

No intercessor (16); rather, as in RV mg., 'none to interpose'. *He put on righteousness . . .* (17). Here Jehovah is represented as a warrior putting on armour for the struggle. The weapons are taken from the armoury of His eternal, holy love. Cf. Eph. vi. 13–17. *When the enemy shall come in like a flood* (19). Rather, as RV, 'he shall come as a rushing stream, which the breath of the Lord driveth'. With verse 21 cf. Je. xxxi. 31ff. and its New Testament references.

b. Assurance of the fulfilment of God's purposes (lx. 1—lxi. 11)

This is a prophecy of great beauty, thrilling with the joy of a great assurance that the purpose of God is so triumphantly to be fulfilled in the earth. Jerusalem is to be rebuilt and to Zion will come the nations round about, rejoicing in her restoration and finding the everlasting light of life.

i. The gift of light (lx. 1–3). The call in the opening verse is to Jerusalem, not as she then was nor as she ever has been since, but to the Jerusalem that yet shall be when she is restored in glory and beauty. Then will the city be the centre of the world's light, for the glory of the everlasting God will rest upon her and will radiate around the world. This coming of the blessing of God is nothing less than the coming of the new dawn. Though all the earth around be shrouded still in darkness, yet on His elect people the divine light will shine. The immediate outcome of this will be that the nations around will flock to rejoice also in the light that is shining.

ii. The enlargement of Jerusalem's borders (lx. 4–9). The exiles return from their captivity and swell the numbers of those who worship Jehovah in the Holy City. Verse 5 describes the tumultuous joy of the nation as this happens. It might be rendered thus:

'*At the sight of them thou shalt be radiant,*
  The heart shall tremble and throb;
For the wealth of the sea shall be turned unto thee,
  Unto thee shall the nations come in with their treasures.'

Ephah (6) is a Midianite tribe, and the Midianites were famed for the multitude of their camels. *Sheba* lies in the southern part of Arabia. *Kedar* and *Nebaioth* (7) are sons of Ishmael and are pastoral tribes in northern Arabia. *The ships of Tarshish* (9). See ii. 16n.

iii. Jerusalem to be built again (lx. 10–14). Those very people who had destroyed the city and carried its inhabitants away into exile will come and help in the building of her walls once more (10, 14). When rebuilt the gates will not be shut by day nor night (11), a symbol of absolute security under the blessing of her God, and also implying the warmth of the welcome that will be given to those that seek an entrance therein. *That their kings may be brought* (11). Either as captives, or else marching at the head of their peoples in full and glad acceptance of the blessings to be found in the Holy City.

iv. Blessings in the everlasting light of Jehovah (lx. 15–22). *Whereas thou hast been forsaken* (15). Better 'instead of thy being forsaken'. In the new city *brass* and *iron* will be replaced by *gold* and *silver* (17), a figure expressing its great prosperity. *Officers . . . exactors* (17); RSV 'overseers . . . taskmasters'. Peace and righteousness will become the governors of the entire civic life. With this section cf. the description of the new Jerusalem in Rev. xxi.

v. The anointed messenger (lxi. 1–3). This chapter continues the predictions of the future glory of Zion as portrayed in chapter lx. The speaker is the Servant of the Lord; of that there can be no doubt, from the use our Lord made of these very words at the beginning of His ministry (cf. Lk. iv. 18, 19). The subject is once again the city of God and the people of God as fulfilling the divine purpose. The mission of the Servant is here stated to be threefold: to announce to the faithful that the time of their trials and suffering is ended (1); to announce the commencement of the age of God's favour; and to announce the vengeance of Jehovah (2). Great messianic blessings are described as flowing from the ministry of the Servant of Jehovah, who is anointed with the Spirit of the Lord God.

Liberty (1). The word suggests the jubile year of Lv. xxv. 10. *The acceptable year of the Lord* (2), i.e. the year of the Lord's good pleasure. *The day of vengeance of our God* (2). We cannot read these verses without reference to the use made of them by our Lord. God's work of mercy cannot be divorced from the eternal, divine justice, and therefore that which is a day of favour for some must be a day of vengeance for others. It is significant that our Lord, when He spake these words, stopped at the phrase 'the acceptable year of the Lord'. He did not read the next, for it was not yet applicable. He had not come to proclaim vengeance, but life. The time will yet come, however, when the day of mercy will end. That it will be followed by a day of righteous judgment all Scripture asserts. *Beauty* (3). Strictly 'a garland' (RV).

vi. Blessings of the faithful (lxi. 4–11). There follows a further detailed description of the new age and the restored people. New centres of activity with strangers serving the chosen people are outlined (4, 5). All Israel will be a kingdom of priests serving their God in holiness and deep devotion (6). Thus serving God they will receive from the subservient nations the tribute paid normally by lay people to the priesthood of the land. *But ye* (6). The words are most emphatic. Over against the others performing the necessary manual tasks, Israel will be the ministers of the sanctuary. The text of verse 7 is doubtful, though the meaning obviously is that a double recompense for the sorrows of the past will be the portion of Israel. *I hate robbery for burnt offering* (8). Read with RV: 'I hate robbery with iniquity and I will give them their recompence in truth.' *Their seed shall be known* (9). The divine blessing makes the people of God distinctive and separate from the rest of the world. *I will greatly rejoice* (10). Here the prophet, in the name of the people, rejoices in such untold blessing that is to be poured forth. Such gifts as salvation, righteousness and praise cannot fail to make the heart sing.

c. The results of the work of the Servant (lxii. 1—lxiii. 6)

i. The restoration of the forsaken (lxii. 1–5). The determination of the Servant to continue His ministry towards the desired consummation of the restoration of Israel is again displayed, though there is no doubt at all as to the ultimate result. 'As the bridegroom rejoiceth over the bride, so shall thy God rejoice over thee' (5); the salvation is as sure as that. The nation will yet be ruled in righteousness and crowned with the visible favour of God.

The speaker is again the Servant. Here is heard something of that eternal determination that made Him empty Himself and be 'found in fashion as a man'. *A new name* (2); given to correspond to the new character. *Forsaken . . . Desolate . . . Hephzibah . . . Beulah* (4). Four names are employed here: 'Azubah' and 'Shemamah', meaning forsaken and desolate, 'Hephzibah' ('my delight is in her') and 'Beulah' ('married'). The names were probably common female names. *Thy sons* (5). The consonants of the text can be vocalized to read 'thy Builder' instead of 'thy sons'. The text will then read:

'For even as a youth weds a maiden,
   So thy Builder shall wed thee:
And as bridegroom rejoiceth in bride,
   So thy God shall rejoice over thee.'

Jehovah is the Builder of the new Jerusalem.

ii. Watchmen on the walls (lxii. 6–9). The watchers on the walls are charged to take no rest from their holy vocation of prayer, as Jehovah's remembrancers. While that is necessary, however, and demanded of the watchers, the issue in this is also not in doubt, for Jehovah has committed Himself by His oath to perform His purpose. *Watchmen* (6). Those appointed by God to be the guides of the people. Cf. lvi. 10; Ezk. iii. 17, xxxiii. 7. The peculiar ministry of prayer is obviously intended. *Ye that make mention* (6); i.e. 'ye that remind . . .' The Mazkir or Remembrancer was a regular official in Oriental courts.

iii. Total restoration (lxii. 10–12). The call is now made to make the final preparations for the return of the exiles. This, too, is of course ensured, in that the divine proclamation *thy salvation cometh* (11) has gone out to the end of the earth. This is the ultimate goal of the work of redemption, as it will be when the purpose of Jehovah is fulfilled. The nation shall be known as *The holy people, The redeemed of the Lord* (12). The issue and the triumph is the holiness of the people; the way of consummation is that of the redeeming activity of Jehovah. The city is to be known as *Sought out* (12). This is the work of divine grace. That which was formerly so waste and sinful will be redeemed unto holiness and, in its power and beauty, will become the desire of others. The nations of the earth will yet come to see a beauty in holiness to which they are now blind. Cf. Jeremiah's description of the city in Je. xxx. 17.

iv. God's judgment upon His enemies (lxiii. 1–6). The prophet sees One returning from Edom, with garments dyed from Bozrah; One glorious in apparel and marching in might (1). He asks *Who is this?* and receives the answer immediately and definitely: *I that speak in righteousness, mighty to save* (1). That calls forth the second question: 'Why are thy garments red with blood?' (2). To that the answer was equally immediate and utterly final. It is that the return is from battle with the enemies of righteousness and truth. This is the day of vengeance of the Lord, as foretold in lxi. 2, which was to follow upon the year of Jehovah's favour (4). The vision is evidently of the Servant of Jehovah consummating the work appointed. The winepress is trodden, thereby forcing the evil fruit of ungodliness to manifest itself. The great work of total redemption is accomplished by His unaided might (5).

Edom . . . Bozrah (1). After the vision of Israel's glory given in chapters lx—lxii, there follows the counterpart of the destruction of all her foes. Edom was proverbially her chief enemy, though so near to her in relationship, and it is natural that once again, as in chapter xxiv, she should be chosen as the great type of the enemies of Jehovah. That she is only typical is seen from verse 6, where the *people* (RV 'peoples') are to be overthrown. Bozrah was a chief city of Edom. *Dyed* (1). Rather, as RV mg., 'crimsoned'. Verse 3 has to do with destruction of evil and not with atonement for sin. It is *their blood* that is upon the garments of the Warrior-Redeemer, and not His own.

d. Prayer for divine mercy and pardon (lxiii. 7—lxiv. 12)

The prophet now breaks out in thanksgiving and prayer. It is as though he thoroughly understood the necessity for the action thus taking place in verses 1–6, associates himself completely with it, and prays that it might be accomplished. The prayer commences with praise for past loving-kindness (7–9), then continues with a confession of the nation's rebellious nature and an acknowledgment of the discipline which corrected it and the deliverance which followed it (10–14). The blessedness of the divine presence, however, had never been wholly removed and the fellowship, though often marred, had never been destroyed (15–19). The prayer continues in chapter lxiv with a cry for the manifestation of divine power on behalf of righteousness (1–3), and then becomes a meditation on the marvel of the ways of Jehovah (4–12). New confessions of sin and unworthiness break through the theme of the prophet's thoughts and new cries to the Lord his God to have pity upon the desolation of the people of His choice, and the land given to them from of old.

In Luther's version lxiii. 7 is the commencement of chapter lxiv. *Children that will not lie* (8); i.e. children who will not be rebellious and false to the One from whom they receive all that is righteous and good. *The angel of his presence* (9). So often is the presence of Jehovah referred to from the earliest times. Cf. Ex. xxxiii. 14. *Vexed his holy spirit* (10). Cf. Ex. xxiii. 20, 21 and other passages. *Then he remembered* (11); i.e. Israel remembered. It is the remembrance of past mercy that makes the heart bold to seek it anew. *That led them by the right hand of Moses* (12). The RV is more exact: 'that caused his glorious arm to go at the right hand of Moses.' *Doubtless thou art our father* (16). This is the great plea, the Fatherhood of God. *Why hast thou made us to err* (17). The thought here seems to be that God's judgment on the people has resulted in some of them hardening their hearts and in further ungodliness. *From thy fear* (17); RSV 'so that we fear thee not'.

Oh that thou wouldest rend the heavens (lxiv. 1). The plea is for another mighty divine intervention as in the days of old. The imagery of verses 1–3 is drawn from the descriptions of other mighty moments in the history of Israel, when Jehovah revealed Himself in great power and glory. Cf. Ex. xix. 16–18; Jdg. v. 4, 5; Hab. iii. 3ff.; Mi. i. 3, 4; Pss. xviii. 9, lxviii. 8. *As when the melting fire burneth* (2). Rather 'as fire setteth brushwood ablaze'. *Neither hath the eye seen* (4). Cf. 1 Cor. ii. 9. *In those is continuance* (5). In Luther's version the translation reads: 'Thou wast angry because we sinned and continued long therein; and yet we are saved.' This gives

very good sense to the verse. *We all are the work of thy hand* (8). Here the reference is to the work of God in creation. It is another appeal to the great mercy of God. Surely He will not cast off that which His own hands have made. *For these things* (12). The sense is that, with things in such a condition as they are, it is unthinkable that Jehovah can hold His peace any more.

e. The answer of Jehovah (lxv. 1–25)

The opening verse is significant, pointing again to the fact that in the moment of their asking Jehovah is found, even though it is trouble that has forced them to turn to Him and not any spontaneous desire of their heart. The very trouble that is upon them has come as a result of their failure to seek His face before. The first seven verses of the chapter amplify this theme of the resolute failure of the people to answer the divine call, and the relationship between this and the trials they are facing is clearly defined. They had never really sought after Jehovah. It was He that had sought after them, and they had refused to listen (2). Such iniquity has separated them from Him. From this the answer becomes again a promise of glorious restoration (8–25). In the impending judgment the faithful will be secure (8–10), while the faithless will be utterly cast off (11–15). The chapter moves forward to a description of the prosperity yet to come to Jerusalem and the people of God through the fulfilment of His purpose. New heavens and a new earth (17) will be created, and new inheritors of the grace of Jehovah will inhabit them. Restored in spirit, man will find himself in a world transfigured, and sorrow and weeping shall be done away (19).

Them that sought me not (1). Cf. Rom. x. 20. *A rebellious people* (2); i.e. Israel. *That sacrificeth in gardens* (3). This refers to worship under trees, a practice derived from Canaanite religion. This meant by-passing the temple worship. *Which remain among the graves* (4), for spiritualistic rites. *Stand by thyself* (5); i.e. a self-righteous attitude, now typified in the word 'Pharisaism'. *As the new wine is found in the cluster* (8). As men preserve the clusters of grapes, thinking of the gladness which the new wine brings, so will Jehovah not destroy them all, but will preserve the godly for the seed of a future nation. *Valley of Achor* (10). Cf. Jos. vii. 24. *Sharon* is on the west and Achor on the east of Judah. The blessing would therefore cover the whole land.

Ye are they that forsake the Lord (11). Translate:

'But ye that forsake Jehovah,
And forget My holy mountain,
That spread forth a table for Fortune,
And pour out mixed wine unto Destiny,
I destine you for the sword,
Ye shall all bow down to the slaughter.'

'Fortune (Gad) and 'Destiny' (Meni) (see RV of verse 12) were Semitic deities in whose service the apostate Jews participated. Tables were spread for the gods and bread and wine were set before them. *Will I number* (12), referring back to the god 'Meni' (number) just mentioned. *My servants shall eat . . .* (14, 15). Note the principle of discrimination which is ever kept. *He who blesseth himself* (16). He who invokes a blessing for himself shall do so by the God of truth and faithfulness, the God who fulfils alike threats and promises. *New heavens and a new earth* (17). With this passage cf. Rev. xxi. 1–5. *The sinner being an hundred years old shall be accursed* (20). The idea is that for a sinner to die at the same age as the youngest is clearly a mark of God's judgment on him. Notice the similarity between these verses and some of the earlier messianic descriptions. For example, cf. verse 25 with xi. 6–9.

f. Epilogue (lxvi. 1–24)

This chapter is in the nature of an epilogue, summarizing and carrying out the principles of the rule of Jehovah as they apply to all the ages to come. First of all there is the keynote of the sovereignty and omnipresence of God; none can escape from Him. No temple ever built can contain Him (1–4). He divides between the true and the false, between the corrupt and the pure, and from Him none can escape. Because of this universal sovereignty of Jehovah, Zion will be increased and Jerusalem will be saved (5–14). All evil men and them that have defiled themselves in any way will be destroyed and consumed together (15–17). In verses 18–22 we have the grand climax of the announcement throughout the world of Jehovah's glory. The new heavens and the new earth which Jehovah will fashion will revolve around Him as, moon by moon and sabbath by sabbath, they worship before Him (23). In that blest estate evil will be cast out and destroyed, an eternal warning to the godly of the tragedy of apostasy from the living God.

Heaven is my throne (1). A picture of the omnipresence of God. *All those things hath mine hand made* (2), i.e. heaven and earth. What is important is not a building, but a humble and contrite (or 'broken') spirit. *He that killeth an ox . . .* (3). It is spiritual religion alone which is desired by God, and the point of this verse is that sacrifices which unspiritual worshippers offer to God are as displeasing to Him as are heathen rites, such as the slaying of a man or the breaking of a dog's neck. *Let the Lord be glorified* (5). The ironical speech of the persecutors of the faithful. The answer of the prophet is *they shall be ashamed* (5). *The city* (6), i.e. Jerusalem. *She travailed* (7), i.e. the new Jerusalem. Such a passage illustrates here the work of the Church of Christ and its first birth on the day of Pentecost. Three thousand were converted on the very day of its formation, and the tidings of the gospel speedily ran over all the known world. *Purify themselves in the gardens* (17). Cf. lxv. 3, 5. *To Tarshish, Pul, and Lud . . .* (19). G. A. Smith writes of this verse: 'To far Spain, and the distances of Africa, towards the Black Sea and to Greece, a full round of the compass.' *From one new moon to another* (23). Regularly and unfailingly. *Their worm shall not die* (24). Cf. Mk. ix. 44.

W. FITCH.

JEREMIAH

INTRODUCTION

I. HISTORICAL BACKGROUND

When God called Jeremiah in 626 B.C., Assyria, the world's mistress, had made Judah a subject under tribute. Twenty years later, however, Assyria crumpled up almost overnight; its capital, Nineveh, was stormed after an appalling siege and, seeing all was lost, the last reigning monarch preferred to perish in the flames of his palace with his court and slave-attendants rather than surrender.

Potentially, the throne of Assyria lay open to any master-soldier of the day. Necho of Egypt marched his forces into North Palestine, encountered and put to death Josiah, king of Judah, at Megiddo in 606 B.C., subdued Syria, and then set out for the Euphrates. He met his master, however, in the person of Nebuchadnezzar of Babylon, who routed his forces at the historic battle of Carchemish and drove him back to his own frontiers, thereby putting an end for the time being to Egyptian ambition to rule the East. Thus it came about that Judah, hitherto subject to Assyria, now passed automatically under the control of Babylon.

After the tragic death of Josiah, his people anointed Jehoahaz, his son, king in his stead. Necho deposed him, however, in favour of Jehoiakim, his brother, assuming that he would better further Egyptian interests. How sound this judgment was Jehoiakim's treatment of Jeremiah makes clear. After Carchemish Nebuchadnezzar gave no attention to Judah, possibly because the disaffection in Babylon needed his immediate return once he had dealt effectively with Egypt. Jehoiakim, in the meantime, resting upon Egyptian promises of massive help, made a bid for independence from Babylon. Thereupon, in 596 B.C., Nebuchadnezzar, having consolidated his power at home, attacked Jerusalem, took captive Jehoiachin, the rebel's son and now his successor, and bore him and some of his people away in Judah's first captivity. At the same time he put Zedekiah on the throne.

Egypt dared not risk war with Babylon. Instead she sought to weaken through disaffection the bonds imposed by Nebuchadnezzar upon Syria and Palestine. Necho was succeeded in Egypt by Psamtik II, and presumably it was he who sought to persuade these countries to enter a league with Egypt against Babylon. Zedekiah was one of those approached on this score, and there clearly seems to have been a pro-Egyptian party at court. Hananiah, the prophet, was especially prominent. But Jeremiah set his face steadfastly against the proposal. See, for example, chapter xxviii with its oracle of the iron yoke.

Jeremiah vigorously opposed these officials of the cult. As the spokesman of Yahweh, he denounced them as false prophets, asserting that their pro-Egyptian activities were contrary to His will and would be tragic in their outcome. Undoubtedly they regarded themselves as true patriots, and it is clear that their fierce hatred of Jeremiah was that he, in their judgment, stood out a self-confessed disloyalist. By calling them 'false prophets' Jeremiah does not necessarily imply that they were vicious men, but rather that their intuition or judgment was not initiated by Yahweh. His charge against them is that Yahweh has not sent them, but they have come forward on their own initiative. Therefore their word will not come to pass. There, then, was the falsity. They spoke in Yahweh's name when He had not commissioned them. From all this it is clear that sincerity is not enough; only the divine inspiration constitutes a man a prophet.

Whether Nebuchadnezzar had received a direct report of disaffection or only rumours one cannot say, but Zedekiah was summoned to meet him and to report on home conditions. His return implied that he had given pledges of loyalty. The pity was that, seemingly, he had not the moral courage and strength to withstand the influence of such pro-Egyptian plotters as Hananiah and his confederates. Jeremiah consistently urged him to remain faithful to his plighted word. But when Hophra became Pharaoh in 589 B.C., in succession to Psamtik II, the Egyptian influence in the court gained headway and through its secret plotting Zedekiah was finally induced to break faith with Nebuchadnezzar. Egypt was slow to move in support and the Babylonian monarch besieged Jerusalem again in 587 B.C. At length the Egyptian army appeared and the Babylonians lifted the siege for the time being. That was the occasion of Jeremiah's arrest as a deserter to the Chaldeans (cf. xxxvii. 11–15).

The resumption of the siege seems to have brought matters to a head. Jeremiah was positive that his intuitions were of God, that He had revealed to him His purposes of making Babylon the instrument of His will. Trust in Egypt, therefore, could pave the way only for disaster and exile. On the other hand, his enemies used Yahweh's name in support of their pro-Egyptian policy. Consequently they held that his attitude and word weakened the national will to fight. That struggle stands out crucially in the person of Zedekiah. He stood between the two influences and was moved now to this side, now to that. It is customary to assert that he was a weakling, unable to make up his mind and face the consequences. It is clear that Jeremiah was not able to sway him sufficiently to make him abide by his oath of loyalty to Nebuchadnezzar. The 'false prophets' won the day and he took the plunge. For that indecision and belated action he paid bitterly. Egypt proved to be a broken reed, the resumed siege was successful, the Babylonian was ruthless, and to his own heartbreak Jeremiah saw the bitter fulfilment of his revelation.

The book gives details of Jeremiah's personal history up to his enforced departure into Egypt. Then the darkness sets in, relieved, if at all, only by traditional rumour. There is nothing to establish a final conclusion as to his fate. One Christian tradition is that some five years after the fall of Jerusalem he was stoned to death at Tahpanhes by the Jewish people who even then refused to share his vision and his faith.

II. JEREMIAH'S MESSAGE AND TEACHING

Politically, as we have seen, he lost. But spiritually he won a major victory. He shared the faith of Amos and Hosea, that, though idolatry and disloyalty to Yahweh must invite punishment, yet Israel and Judah were not finally outcast from the grace of God. He shared with those prophets too the faith that exile as a discipline would be remedial, not wholly tragic. The state, *qua* state, was doomed; but faith in Yahweh and Yahweh's faith in His chosen people would abide and outlive the crucial shock. Again, he saw that the old covenant, centring in the temple and its ceremonial worship, was ineffective; thus he was led to see that Yahweh would write a new covenant within the heart of the 'remnant', through which vital religion would persist and prove a blessing beyond national frontiers.

When the book of the law, found by Hilkiah in the ruins of the temple, brought about reformation under Josiah in 621 B.C., it seems clear that, at first, Jeremiah shared that king's enthusiasm, and lent his influence as aid. It seems equally clear, however, that later he distrusted that revival as too facile and superficial to meet the demands of Yahweh. The great need was for a change of heart and that was feasible only in a people whose faith was in Yahweh alone. That centrality of faith the generation of Jeremiah refused to give.

It has been urged by many scholars that Jeremiah with other prophets was against all sacrificial ritual, regarding it as not commanded by Yahweh and, indeed, repugnant to Him. Jeremiah's attitude is better understood, however, as teaching that, if a sacrifice were not a true index of a worshipful and repentant heart, then that sacrifice would be invalid, and therefore contrary to Yahweh's desire and will. Sacrifice, at the best, could only be the means to the spiritual end of a repentant return to Yahweh. It could not be a sufficient end in itself.

III. AUTHORSHIP

This is a very complicated issue and there is not space in a brief introduction to deal with it adequately. For a statement of the conservative position and a summary of critical views see E. J. Young, *Introduction to the Old Testament*. The book itself describes the putting into writing by Baruch the scribe of prophecies uttered by Jeremiah (see especially xxxvi. 32) and states that 'there were added besides unto them many like words'. Baruch seems to have acted generally as Jeremiah's faithful amanuensis and, it may be noted, went down into Egypt with him (Je. xliii. 6).

The prophecies themselves are not in chronological order and this can be confusing to the western mind with its logical approach to such matters. For a scheme of probable dates for the various chapters see the analysis provided in G. T. Manley's *The New Bible Handbook*. The matter is further complicated by the fact that there are very wide differences between the Hebrew and LXX texts of this book, more so than in any other. These differences do not apply to words only, but affect the order in which the material is presented. For a brief analysis of the divergences and a suggested explanation see E. J. Young's *Introduction to the Old Testament* to which reference has already been made. Where the LXX version seems to throw light on the Hebrew text this has been noted in the body of the commentary.

IV. THE CHARACTER OF THE PROPHET

Jeremiah was indeed a man of God, accessible to every spiritual influence, capable of deep emotion, a man of clear eye and candid judgment. He could be neither bought nor cajoled. He followed the way of his mind, supported as it ever was by the worshipping spirit within him. He was God's man from first to last, and therefore a true patriot to the bitter end. He was not blind to the sin and folly of his people. He read, with deep bitterness, the iron nexus of sin and penalty, and foresaw exile as the inevitable and irrevocable judgment, unless there was a change of heart. For that change he wrought without reserve. In essence he was a mediator through love of country and faith in Yahweh. Hence the vehemence of his emotion and word, now against his people, now beseeching his God. Hence his isolation, his agony, his crucial inner conflicts. His passion became his light, and that made his task clear, though repellent. He saw doom but not final disaster. Both Israel and Judah had a future in God. He would be their righteousness. There would be a new covenant. In God he read promise, not futility, hence 'he endured as seeing Him who is invisible'. In this gaunt, clamant figure we can see what God dare ask of a man, and what such a man may give. The discovery of the real Jeremiah may well be the rebirth of the discoverer.

OUTLINE OF CONTENTS

This extensive book does not lend itself readily to any satisfactory division, and therefore any analysis is, in the main, a subjective judgment. A fairly reasonable division would be into two books, the first closing at chapter xxv and the second from chapter xxvi to the end. The reason for this is that, on the whole, prophetic oracles govern the first half and narrative mainly the second.

ORACLES CONCERNING GOD'S CHOSEN PEOPLE. i. 1—xxv. 38

I. THE PROPHET'S CALL. i. 1–19

II. THE NATION'S SUMMONS. ii. 1—vi. 30

III. THE ILLUSIONS OF TEMPLE SECURITY. vii. 1—x. 25

IV. JEREMIAH AND THE COVENANT. xi. 1—xii. 17

V. THE FIVE WARNINGS. xiii. 1–27

VI. SHADOWS OF DOOM. xiv. 1—xxi. 14

VII. KINGS AND PROPHETS OF JUDAH: THE VISION OF THE END. xxii. 1—xxv. 38

HISTORICAL NARRATIVES. xxvi. 1—lii. 34

VIII. PROPHECIES AND EVENTS DURING JEHOIAKIM'S REIGN. xxvi. 1–24

IX. THE SANITY OF THE PROPHET. xxvii. 1—xxix. 32

X. A FUTURE AND A HOPE. xxx. 1—xxxiv. 22

XI. PROPHECIES AND EVENTS DURING JEHOIAKIM'S REIGN. xxxv. 1—xxxvi. 32

XII. PROPHECIES AND EVENTS DURING ZEDEKIAH'S REIGN. xxxvii. 1—xxxix. 18

XIII. PROPHECIES AND EVENTS IN JUDAH. xl. 1—xlii. 22

XIV. PROPHECIES AND EVENTS IN EGYPT. xliii. 1—xliv. 30

XV. JEREMIAH'S MESSAGE TO BARUCH. xlv. 1–5

XVI. PROPHECIES AGAINST FOREIGN NATIONS. xlvi. 1—li. 64

XVII. A RETROSPECT. lii. 1–34

COMMENTARY

ORACLES CONCERNING GOD'S CHOSEN PEOPLE. i. 1—xxv. 38

I. THE PROPHET'S CALL. i. 1–19

a. Information about the prophet (i. 1–3)

Jeremiah's call was grounded in a profound sense of God's initiative. It was as though he had been predestined to the office of prophet as from his birth, indeed before conception, a case of spiritual determinism. Verses 1, 2 give home details with date of call. *Anathoth* (1); modern Anata; some three miles north-east of Jerusalem. *The thirteenth year of his reign* (2); i.e. 626 B.C. *The carrying away of Jerusalem captive* (3);

i.e. 586 B.C., when Nebuchadnezzar destroyed the city. Jeremiah's ministry continued beyond this date and lasted for about fifty years in all.

b. The consecration of the prophet (i. 4–10)

The word of the Lord came (4). Verses 3 and 4 suggest it was not sudden but persistent (Heb. *way'hi*, 'continued to come'). *Sanctified* (5) implies one set apart, not to be stressed ethically though that would naturally follow.

His commission (6, 7) was equally clear. The

contrast drawn is that of shrinking from the task and being inspirited for it. He is the most psychological of all the prophets on record. He protests *I am a child* (6; LXX, 'too young'), implying that he lacks power because of his youth. But his objection is overruled in the moment of protestation. He therefore submits with the full consent of his personality—a typical Jeremiah attitude since, once known, the will of God comes first. God *touched* (9) his lips thereby making him His deputy, with power to destroy or to re-create. It is this dual commission which explains what has been so often a puzzle to earlier commentators, viz. Jeremiah's pessimism and hope. His pessimism does not spring from a sense of inexorable fate, but of inevitable catastrophe if there be a departure from faith and loyalty. Yet, should even the worst happen, Jeremiah knows that that judgment will be but God's prelude to a nobler day. As with the other prophets, prophecy was conditional; there would be the repeal of judgment given a change of heart in the nation.

c. The declaration to the prophet (i. 11–16)

The call of Jeremiah is immediately associated with two visions. These may have been granted to verify his call and encourage him. Revelation authenticates his commission. Through these visions God makes a declaration to the prophet and through him to the people. The vision of the *almond tree* (11) introduces the reader to Jeremiah's love and apprehension of nature as a revealing agent of God. There is a play on two Hebrew words here, *almond tree* (Heb. *shaked*) and 'wakeful' (Heb. *shoqedh;* RV 'watch over'). The almond tree is the first to awake in spring; so Yahweh is as one awaking, rising up in judgment. *A seething* (lit. 'blown upon') *pot* (13), RV 'caldron', was a large vessel used for various purposes such as cooking or washing. The direction is given as northwards implying that from that quarter judgment was to be expected. The text is difficult, but the sense is clear. *Shall break forth* (14; lit. 'be opened'); follow the LXX reading 'be blown upon', intimating that Yahweh will make a northern people the agent of His judgment. The reason is idolatry (16) which is disloyalty, involving a tension of 'two masters', Baal versus Yahweh.

d. The exhortation to the prophet (i. 17)

Jeremiah's dismay (17) as the content of prophecy comes home to him is countered by the command to be fearless.

e. The consolation for the prophet (i. 18, 19)

The consolation is to the effect that Yahweh will be with him, thus making him impregnable (19).

II. THE NATION'S SUMMONS. ii. 1—vi. 30

After Jeremiah's call and strengthening visions, he records that *the word of the Lord* came to him (1). All his discourses are inspired by God.

This section contains two oracles (ii. 1—iii. 5 and iii. 6—vi. 30).

a. Jeremiah's first message (ii. 1—iii. 5)

i. **The declaration to Israel (ii. 1-3).** Israel was once as the bride of Yahweh (2), as fair as she was pure, *holiness unto the Lord* (3; cf. Ho. ii. 2-20).

ii. **The expostulation with Israel (ii. 4-13).** Yahweh challenges Israel's memory of His gracious provision for them (6, 7) to prove that it was not He who had broken tryst. It was they who *defiled my land* (7); it was their prophets who *prophesied by Baal* (8), the chief god of the Phoenicians which had been introduced into Israel after Solomon's alliance with that nation. *Chittim* (10); the people of Kition, a town in Cyprus. Some scholars connect Chittim with the Hittites. *Kedar* (10) represents the East just as Chittim represents the West. Verses 11 and 12 summarize the horror of the prophet at his people's apostasy. Unlike even pagan nations, who remained true to their gods, Israel had preferred 'profitless' gods to Yahweh, their own God. Even the heavens were aghast at such sacrilege. The symbol *broken cisterns* (13) implies stagnant water easily leaking away through cracks, in contrast to that of a perennial (lit. *living*) spring.

iii. **The humiliation of Israel (ii. 14–19).** This paragraph shows how sin overtakes a nation. Free-born Israel is to become a slave. *Homeborn slave* (14); there were two kinds of slaves, those acquired by purchase and those born in the house of the master and so his permanent possession. Disloyalty to God is not only an evil thing; it brings bitter loss as well (15). It also leads to dependence on alien alliances, with consequent spiritual and moral corruption. *Noph and Tahapanes* (16); Egyptian cities. The former is the Hebrew name for Memphis, the capital of Lower Egypt not far from modern Cairo. Disaster, with its bitterness, must be the tragic teacher, since *my fear is not in thee* (19). *Sihor* (18) means 'muddy river' and seems to refer to the Nile.

iv. **The degeneration of Israel (ii. 20–28).** *Playing the harlot* (20). Cf. verse 2. Idolatry is frequently likened by the prophets to unfaithfulness in marriage. *A noble vine* (21). Cf. Is. v. 1-7 for a parallel use of this metaphor. Verses 22–25 describe the ingrained nature of their iniquity and their wilful determination to continue in their sin. Jeremiah likens them to a desert creature in heat, whose desire is so great that any mate that wants it can find it without wearying itself. It is as though the female were pursuing the male. *I have loved strangers* (i.e. other gods), *and after them will I go* (25). Their desire to share in the idolatrous practices of the heathen nations was so great that they were determined nothing should prevent them from doing so.

In the time of thy trouble (28). The testing hour which was coming would shame them into seeing how useless these stocks and stones are. Like a caught thief they would be found out (26, 27; see also verse 36). Their plea for help (27) would be inevitably rejected because of the falsity of their protestations of innocence (see verses 23 and 35).

v. The explanation to Israel (ii. 29–37). God explains the reasons for Israel's misfortunes. *We are lords* (31); RV 'we are broken loose'. In spite of the Lord's goodness to them (see verses 6, 7) they had asserted their complete independence of Him and failed to show even ordinary human gratitude (32).

vi. The exhortations to Israel (iii. 1–5). The plea is that Israel should return to Yahweh. Here idolatry is again treated under the figure of harlotry (cf. also verse 20). In the case of marital infidelity they recognize that there is no easy repentance. Their unfaithfulness to God has been gross in the extreme and openly flaunted. Yet they seem to think that they have only to show signs of wishing to return (see RV mg. in verse 1) for the Lord to welcome them back with open arms (5). In verse 5 see RV and RV mg. This is what they are saying and at the same time deliberately continuing in the evil practices which their Lord abhors. *Arabian* (2); i.e. nomad. *Latter rain* (3); the early rain comes in the autumn, and the latter in the spring. These are very necessary to make the grain swell and grow. *From this time* (4); probably from Josiah's reformation.

b. Jeremiah's second message (iii. 6—vi. 30)

Though the general theme of the two discourses is the same, viz. the apostasy and idolatry of Israel, there is nevertheless one marked difference. In the first discourse no hint of forgiveness is given; here in the second a distinct assurance of pardon is held out, provided repentance is genuine and heartfelt.

i. The unfavourable contrast between Judah and Israel (iii. 6–10). The prophet sees that *backsliding Israel* (6; lit. 'apostasy Israel', two nouns signifying Israel as the personification of apostasy) has been sent into exile as a judgment on her adultery; yet Judah reads no warning to herself. On the contrary, she feigns loyalty, but there is no evidence of genuine conversion (6–10). *Feignedly* (10); the reformation under Josiah did not go very deep; Judah returned but only feignedly, i.e. superficially.

ii. The urgent call to Israel (iii. 11–18). Israel, broken and exiled, is told to repent. *Treacherous Judah* (11); in spite of greater privileges, such as a succession of kings of the same family, the temple, the Levites, and the warning example of Israel, Judah proved faithless. *Turn, O backsliding children* (14). The ground of the divine appeal is the gracious relationship which God has chosen to bear with His people. *For I am married unto you* (14; lit. 'I am a husband'; cf. xxxi. 32). Two metaphors are used—*children . . . husband*. The people are children that have left their father's house and a wife that has been divorced. In line with Isaiah and Micah, Jeremiah knows that

God 'delights in mercy'. If they return in penitence He will bring them back to worship at home in Zion. *At that time* (17); when Israel returns to the Lord and from the exile, Jehovah's glory in the midst of the people will eclipse the glory and manifestation of the presence associated with the *ark of the covenant* (16). The prophet looks forward to a time when Jerusalem will be purified from all idolatry. Jeremiah seems to have lost faith in Judah, yet retracts such pessimism in the hope that after exile Judah and Israel shall be responsive to their God and come again to their heritage (18).

iii. The unconditional return of the people to Yahweh (iii. 19—iv. 4). Somehow, also, optimism prevails that Judah's exile is to secure Israel's salvation. But Jeremiah cannot avoid seeing faithless perversion with all its dread aftermath, the penalty of apostasy. Yet he hears a kind of weeping antiphony in the north, penitent children and the forgiving, healing God crying and soothing in turn (21, 22). Both Israel and Judah are here envisaged, or maybe Judah is here a synonym for Israel. *Upon the high places* (21); a common place for mourning. It was upon the high places that Israel's sin was committed and it is upon the high places that the voice of penitence is heard. *For shame hath devoured* (24); lit. 'the shame', i.e. Baal-worship. The prophets often call Baal 'bosheth', i.e. 'shame', for Baal worship was Israel's shame. The heart-broken confession of verse 25 is answered by Yahweh in terms which reveal the consistently conditional nature of salvation. *We lie down* (25); RV reads 'Let us lie down'. *If thou wilt return . . . return unto me* (iv. 1). *Abominations* (1); the word is first found in Ho. ix. 10, and is applied in Jeremiah and Ezekiel to the false gods and all that pertains to their worship. Moral reformation is not enough; there must be an inward circumcision of the heart, a cleansing of the life in the presence not of self, or society, but of God. Thus *if thou wilt put away, . . . then* (on this condition rests deliverance) *shalt thou not remove* (1); RV 'then shalt thou not be removed', i.e. away from God's presence; alternatively *remove* may be rendered 'wander', the salvation being 'thou shalt not wander away from God'. The gravity of spurning the offer to return is revealed in verse 4. The sinful nation chose to rebel and history records how bitter the harvest was, even the *fury* of Jehovah which came *forth like fire* (4).

iv. The unheard-of calamity upon the land (iv. 5–31). The coming invasion (5–18). Jeremiah pleaded for a deep repentance, but his hope was blasted. Of an inward return to God there was no outward sign. The prophet had no alternative but to pronounce judgment. The appointed scourge *from the north* (6) is already on the threshold. The prophecies which deal with these agents of Yahweh's vengeance continue to the close of chapter vi. *Blow ye the trumpet* (5); Heb. *shophar*. The horn-blast was a signal of grave danger. The lion has come out of his lair (7). He is the fierce destroyer of nations and cities, a reference in all probability to Nebuchadnezzar. *Ye shall have peace* (10). This verse has caused bewilderment and difficulty. Jeremiah never prophesied that Jerusalem would have peace. The LXX reads: 'And they shall say,' i.e. the false prophets of verse 9, who told the people to expect peace. *A full wind* (12) is another metaphor of destruction. It is the sirocco from the desert, a hot scorching wind, cyclonic and merciless. Such must be Yahweh's action upon the guilty land. The same grave judgment appears in different figures of speech, *clouds . . . chariots* and *horses . . . swifter than eagles* (i.e. griffons or vultures) (13). The desolating doom is heralded from Dan, the northern limit of the land, and the warning voice is echoed from Mount Ephraim as near as ten miles from Jerusalem (15). *Watchers* (16); i.e. besiegers who will daily watch the city and its inhabitants.

In verses 19–22 the prophet has an unparalleled vision of inevitable judgment beyond his endurance. Note the pain of his soul (19, 20), the question of his mind (21) and the answer of his God (22). His words literally writhe in the agony which tortures him. *My bowels, my bowels! I am pained at my very heart* (19). The heart is the seat of intelligence, while the bowels, according to Hebrew psychology, are the seat of the emotions. But Jeremiah is under no illusion. The judgment is just. It is the dark entail of sin upon an abandoned people. The imagery here (23–26) is so stark that a shudder vibrates throughout. The prophet's description is one of the most vivid and moving in sacred literature. World chaos has overtaken the cosmos; mountains reel, man vanishes, birds have fled out of the sky, and the fertile earth has become a desert—it is the blast of God, the divine super-atomic bomb. We are back in Gn. i where all is darkness and confusion. 'I have spoken', says Yahweh, 'and I have not repented (LXX reading); I have purposed, and will not turn back from it' (28). Such dread finality of sin involves the whole world. Jeremiah saw nothing but irremediable travail, bereft of hope. All these grim predictions were fulfilled in the final overthrow of Jerusalem in 586 B.C.

Some authorities consider that this second message of Jeremiah begun at iii. 6 is composed of several oracles, some indeed written at Anathoth and others at Jerusalem. Be that as it may, there is a definite unity in the message which justifies a continued treatment. There is the same emphasis upon the hardened sin of a besotted nation and the inevitable doom of a holy God waiting to be gracious if only the people would repent.

v. The corruption of Jerusalem (v. 1–9). In v. 1–31 the city is seen under a relentless moral investigation. If this section is in true sequence the prophet attempts a vindication of the severity of God, i.e. a valid theodicy. As Diogenes of Greece, he feels that were one to search Jerusalem, no honest man would be found to affect the doom—poor (4) and rich (5) alike are impious in life and deed. *Run ye to and fro through the streets of Jerusalem* (1). The quest is in vain, hence the nation is as defenceless as a townsman in a forest of wild beasts (6). The inhabitants of Jerusalem, indeed, had sunk down to the level of beasts. When God had full-fed them (7) they prostituted His bounty and became like full-fed stallions in their lust (8).

vi. The call to the destroyer (v. 10–19). The optimism of the negligent is portrayed in verses 10–18. God's agents are to carry through the task of purging (10, 11), yet the doomed (12–17) cherish the fallacy in blind hope that Yahweh will take no action. *Go ye up* (10); a call to the enemy to start his work. *They have belied the Lord, and said, It is not he* (12); lit. 'not he'; i.e. He will do nothing along the line of Jeremiah's prophecy. The text here is difficult, but the reason previously given must be applicable here, viz. their prophets are false men, and as futile as they are false, since they neither see nor urge that sin must be followed by repentance if they are to be saved. *Whose language thou knowest not* (15); difference of speech was always a cause of dread and uneasiness in the ancient world, for appeals for mercy would be fruitless when made in an unknown tongue. *Their quiver* (16); a remarkable comparison. Like the grave their weapons are never satisfied.

vii. The stubbornness and folly of the people (v. 20–31). This section deals with God as the moral Governor on the one hand and His rebellious people on the other. God's world is unable to break loose from His unswerving, sovereign will (22); only His people have that liberty (23, 24); a lone *differentia* for ever characterizing man. *The sea* (22); the prophet uses the sea to illustrate the might and majesty of God. Is such a God to be trifled with? If the sea is feared—and who does not fear it?—is not He to be feared? *Revolting . . . rebellious* (23); not only are the people backsliders, they are openly hostile.

In 26–31 the prophet has three classes of people in mind: the rich who oppress the poor, the false prophets who deceive, and the priests who rule by their means. The nation sits loosely to the divine will, with the evil consequence that neither justice is done nor is there any desire that prophet and priest be other than what they are—liars and false guides. *And my people love to have it so* (31). Evil, if practised long enough, is accepted by the rank and file as inevitable.

viii. The investment of Jerusalem (vi. 1–5). The conclusion of Jeremiah's second message is the inevitable doom imminent upon such an impenitent and incorrigible nation. The destructive agent appointed by God is about to invest Jerusalem. The note of alarm is again sounded. Evil 'peeps out' from the north, nothing less than tragic ruin. The prophet personifies destruction here as it overhangs the city. The warning trumpet-blast is to sound forth from Tekoa and also from Beth-haccerem (1). *Children of Benjamin* (1); this may be a call to the members of his own tribe, of whom there must have been many in the capital, or it may mean the whole city of Jerusalem. *Tekoa* (1); this place lies some twelve miles south of Jerusalem. There seems to be a play on the words 'strike' and 'blow' which have the same letters as the word Tekoa. *Sign of fire* (1); lit. 'lift up a flame', i.e. as a signal: it probably took the form of a beacon. *Beth-haccerem* (1); found only here and in Ne. iii. 14. Lit. 'house of the vineyard'; now usually identified with a place called 'Frank mountain' which forms a conspicuous eminence such as would be very suitable for a beacon. As the enemy approaches from the north, these places south of Jerusalem are to prepare to guide the fugitives in their flight from the capital. *The shepherds* (3); the enemy from the north is likened to shepherds with their flocks, eating up the grass on every side; everything will be devoured and nothing left. *Prepare ye war* (4); lit. 'sanctify ye war'; i.e. offer sacrifices to ensure success. The exhortation calls for hostilities to begin, and it is the enemy outside the city walls that thus heartens himself. Their persistence is such that, if the day attack fails, the evening will bring victory (4, 5). The prophet predicts in the name of the Lord that the victory shall be absolute and final.

ix. The coming ruin (vi. 6–15). *Hew ye down trees* (6); trees were cut down to construct siege works, but this verse also indicates the devastation the enemy will cause. Under the figure of a vineyard, the gatherers go over and over gleaning the very last grape and leave the vineyard desolate (9). Israel has not even a 'remnant' left and Judah faces a like extinction and exile. But the tragedy of the day is that in the gathering gloom the optimism of the religious leaders persists. *Turn back* (9) is addressed to Nebuchadnezzar, or in general to the leader of the besieging army. *Houses . . . fields . . . wives* (12); these coming evils are similar to those mentioned in Dt. xxviii. 30. *Healed also the hurt* (14); lit. 'breach'. The rupture between the holy God and the sinful nation is lightheartedly and superficially doctored. But the day of visitation is at hand.

x. Jehovah's appeal and Judah's disobedience (vi. 16–21). An appeal comes again from the Lord to the people through the prophet to seek *the old paths* (16). With the promise contained in this verse cf. Mt. xi. 29. Jeremiah based all his appeals on the experience of the past. They refuse. Heaven and earth therefore are set against them as witnesses. *Sheba* (20) lies in the south-west of Arabia, a country noted for its incense; cf. vii. 21. *I will lay stumblingblocks* (21); to Jeremiah, as to his predecessors, there were no such things as intermediary causes; all was ascribed to God.

xi. The enemy's cruelty and the people's incorrigibility (vi. 22–30). Once more to arouse the nation from its fatal optimistic apathy the enemy is vividly described in terrifying terms. *Fear is on every side* (25); cf. xx. 10, xlvi. 5, xlix. 29; Jb. xviii. 11; Ps. xxxi. 13; hence the fugitives are advised not to go *by the way* (25); i.e. by the open road. *Make thee mourning* (26);

i.e. 'mourn for thyself'. Verses 27–30 present the prophet's dark intuition. His function is freshly realized as *a tower* (RV mg. 'trier') *and a fortress* (27). The metaphors are difficult and the RV mg. should be followed. Jeremiah felt that his task would be as a 'refiner of silver', but now it is borne upon him that his 'fire' has failed to refine the national silver from its dross; i.e., unlike the mineral refining, the human will can refuse the purging 'fire'. God gives such a soul over to its choice. The apostle Paul pictures this wilful obstinacy on the part of the Gentile nations (Rom. i. 18–32). *The bellows are burned* (29); the RV reads 'the bellows blow fiercely'; cf. ix. 7. *Reprobate silver* (30); better, 'refuse' or 'rejected silver'. This dark shadow closes the second message of Jeremiah and the first section of his prophecy.

III. THE ILLUSIONS OF TEMPLE SECURITY. vii. 1—x. 25

To Judah the temple was sacrosanct and therefore impregnable to all attack. If the worse came to the worst, Yahweh would undoubtedly intervene to save the city in which He had set His name. Jeremiah here states the very reverse. Shiloh was also held to be inviolate, yet it was overthrown. The 'temple sermon' given here makes no mention of the alarm and fury it created. In xxvi, however, such information is given among the historical summaries of the second division of the book, together with the peril to the prophet consequent upon his fearless witness. If the assumption that chapter xxvi belongs to the same period as these 'temple sermons' is correct, then the time would be 608 B.C., the beginning of the reign of Jehoiakim. This section is Jeremiah's third message, and is in two parts.

a. The temple sermon (vii. 1—viii. 3)

The prophet's summons to the people to gather at the temple gate is shorter in the LXX than in the Massoretic Text: 'Hear the word of the Lord, all ye of Judah.'

i. A warning (vii. 3–20). The address opens with a warning. Let the nation take heed of the fate of Shiloh. *Stand in the gate* (2). The prophet is to proclaim his message at one of the temple gates and the people are to fill the outer court separated from the inner court by its own gates. The occasion may have been one of the great festivals, when there would have been normally a great concourse of people at the temple gate. *Your ways and your doings* (3); 'ways' has reference to settled habits; 'doings' to separate acts which go to form them. *The temple of the Lord* (4); the threefold repetition is for the sake of emphasis. Cf. Christ's 'Verily, verily, I say unto you'. The temple is God's house and His peculiar possession (10; Heb. 'whereupon my name is called'). The temple, therefore, would itself be an appeal to the people to be as holy as its symbolism suggested, i.e. as 'set apart'. If that be not so, then Yahweh would abandon the temple and thus the nation (a reality which also Ezekiel sets out in his prophecy), the result being overthrow and exile. If, however, they repent, then God will be with them. The words *I will cause you to dwell in this place* (3) can be rendered 'then will I dwell with you', i.e. in the temple. The moral issue is clear: the temple as 'a den of robbers' is no temple of His presence; like Shiloh it is deserted; the ark is impotent by itself to save Israel. *Steal . . . murder* (9); the verbs are in the infinitive in Hebrew, a mood which is used to present the action in the strongest terms. *We are delivered* (10); the RV is clearer. The people evidently imagined that by performing the religious rites they were delivered from the abomination to which the prophet so often referred. *Den of robbers* (11); i.e. a place of retreat between acts of crime and violence. Cf. Mk. xi. 17; Lk. xix. 46. *Shiloh* (12); the place lies on the main high road from Jerusalem to Shechem. The ark was placed there in the days of Joshua. Its destruction is nowhere described in the Old Testament. Ps. lxxviii. 60 says God forsook it. Verses 16–20 seem to interrupt the temple address unless they are an interlude symbolizing the calamitous end of impenitent profane rebellion. *Queen of heaven* (18); called Ishtar by the Babylonians, and apparently worshipped chiefly by women. The words 'cakes' and 'queen' have a foreign appearance in the Hebrew and are probably meant to indicate the foreign origin of the cult.

ii. Obedience not sacrifice (vii. 21–28). Jeremiah proclaims the truest principle of obedience. The burnt offering according to Levitical law was wholly consumed, but in the case of other sacrifices portions were eaten by priests and worshippers. If, however, it was a matter of mere ceremony, then the burnt offering would be 'common' not 'spiritual', since it would not be indicative of a repentant heart: hence it might be eaten, having lost spiritual validity. Verse 22 is classical. Critical thought holds, in the main, that what Jeremiah is proclaiming is that the entire ritual scheme of sacrifice had never been instituted by God. A conflict between prophet and priest is supposed. The tide of thought, however, is slowly turning against that extreme position. What Jeremiah is fiercely denouncing here is the sacrifice that does not symbolize the repentant heart and that does not issue in righteous conduct. Apart from ethical obedience no sacrifice is efficacious. The whole prophetic movement condemns the empty ritualism. The covenant between Yahweh and Israel was based upon the Decalogue, and it had also the honour of occupying the holiest place in the sanctuary. *Obey my voice* (23); this is not an exact quotation; the nearest to it is Ex. xix. 5. Obedience to the moral law was always put first. *But they hearkened not* (24); this is difficult to reconcile with ii. 2, unless ii. 2 be taken to refer to the period immediately following the exodus and vii. 24 to refer to a period, say, towards the end of the

wilderness wandering. *In the imagination of their evil heart* (24); lit. 'stubbornness'; cf. iii. 17. The shorter form in the LXX of verses 27, 28a is preferable: 'And thou shalt say to them this word.'

iii. National mourning (vii. 29—viii. 3). The call to the people to lament is because Jehovah has rejected that generation. No person is named in verse 29, but the verb is feminine in the Hebrew and this points to Jerusalem or the nation as personified. The symbol of deep mourning was the cutting off of the hair (lit. 'thy crown'); cf. Jb. i. 20; Mi. i. 16. Some have seen in this a reference to the Nazirite vow (Nu. vi. 7). Jerusalem has broken her vows, and so, like a faithless Nazirite, she might as well cut off the hair, which was his symbol and badge. *They have set their abominations* (30); 2 Ki. xxi. 5 tells that Manasseh profaned the temple in the manner here described. *Tophet* (31) (LXX 'high place') probably means 'fireplace' (*tephath*); cf. Is. xxx. 33. To mark the people's sense of horror at the heathen custom of infant sacrifice the vowels of the original *tephath* were changed so that the word was read and spoken as *tophet*. This was a parallel process whereby the term *melek* (king) became *Molech*, a heathen deity, i.e. by using the vowels of *bosheth* (shame). This latter term too was often substituted for *Baal* (lord), e.g. Ish-bosheth for Ish-baal. To the idol Molech child-sacrifices were offered and to Yahweh worshippers the term Molech, signifying 'shame', fitly expressed their abhorrence. The valley of Ben-Hinnom lay over against the Kidron valley. It was here that such awful sacrifices were made, and thereby passed on to the valley (*ge*) of Ben-Hinnom the appellation of shame. The agonizing vision of Jeremiah was that that foul place overflowed with dead bodies. That shameful worship was thus interlocked with death—their sanctuary was to become their cemetery. Fitly, therefore, in verse 31, Jeremiah says that its origin never came from God's heart. Gehenna (*ge*, valley), a synonym for hell, derives itself from this place-name. *None shall fray them away* (33); i.e. 'frighten them'.

They shall bring out (viii. 1). Many suggestions have been made to explain this barbarity: **1.** It was deliberate and intended as an insult to the defeated, who were thus shown to be incapable of defending either 'the ashes of their fathers' or the 'temple of their God'. **2.** It was done in the hope of finding spoil, for great treasures were often buried with the dead. **3.** It was done accidentally, in digging a hole in order to light a fire, or **4.** in the erection of earthworks for the siege. The first is the most likely. All had sinned and all would be punished, including the dead. The doctrine of future punishment has not been fully developed, hence the punishment of the dead in the form visualized here. *They shall spread them* (2); the heavenly bodies whom they have worshipped will be impotent in the day of judgment.

b. The disobedience and idolatry of the people (viii. 4—x. 25)

Some authorities consider this section to be the metrical counterpart of the temple sermon with which Jeremiah begins his third message.

i. Mournful music (viii. 4–17). Three notes are struck as from a harp of doom. Verses 4–7 sound the note of an evil mind, stubborn against repentance. Birds obey the unknown, instinctive law of migration, but Yahweh's people refuse to obey the heart's deepest instinct for the eternal home. *Rusheth* (6); lit. 'overfloweth'. Two metaphors (that of a fiery steed and a torrent) are combined.

Verses 8, 9 tell us that the scribe and the wise set the people on a false road. The 'law' (*torah*), better 'direction', would rightly point and lead to God, but through their false 'direction' they lead people away from Him. This 'direction' may have been the false teaching that sacrifice in itself, apart from ethical obedience, was adequate. On the other hand, it might mark, according to some scholars, Jeremiah's dissent from the centralization of sacrifice ordered by Josiah as the priestly reform in accordance with Dt. xii. 1–7. In the absence of precise statement, it remains ambiguous. *Scribes* (8). This is the first time that scribes are referred to as a professional class in the Old Testament. They were evidently active as a class in Josiah's time (2 Ch. xxxiv. 13) and may have had their origin in the reign of Hezekiah (cf. Pr. xxv. 1).

Verses 10–12 are not found in the LXX and are almost identical with vi. 12–15. In verses 13–17 we have the stark note of doom; *no grapes on the vine, nor figs on the fig tree, and the leaf shall fade* (13); not even a 'remnant' to save the faith alive. Such will be the effect of 'the foe from the north', that is, of course, if there be no return to Yahweh. The starkest judgment is still conditional. *Our God hath put us to silence* (14); lit. 'hath decreed our ruin'. *Gall to drink* (14); the mg. reads 'poison'. This of course is a metaphor. Life will be bitter. *Dan* (16) was in the far north and had already been reached by the enemy. Nor will the enemy be appeased. He will not be charmed (17) as snakes are charmed.

ii. The sick heart (viii. 18—ix. 26). This is a deeply moving passage. It tells of the heartbreak of the prophet as he envisages the inevitable disaster about to overtake his people. Verse 18 is difficult. The literal rendering is 'Oh, my brightness in sorrow, my heart is sick', but the meaning is clear—'incurable is my sorrow', as supported by the LXX, and expressed in the RV⟩ 'Oh that I could comfort myself against sorrow! my heart is faint within me'. The Hebrew means 'severely' or 'loathsomely' ill. *The harvest is past, the summer is ended* (20). Harvest and summer are distinct seasons. The field harvest lasted from April to June. Later came 'the ingathering of summer fruits' (RV mg.). Jeremiah speaks to the people of what will happen when the seasons pass. Zion no longer has the Presence; there is no harvest to meet the oncoming famine, no

physician to heal the sick. The prophet would weep as perennially as the spring flows. *I am black* (21); I am in mourning. *Gilead* (22) was a mountainous district beyond Jordan, and was among the first of the Israelite territories to fall to the enemy. *Balm* (22); the produce referred to by the original is not known with any certainty. It is mentioned as early as Gn. xxxvii. 25.

The mood changes (ix. 2–8) from overwhelming pity to an apposite bitterness. The people are a race of traitors. Could his loyalty consent, Jeremiah would abandon the whole breed. Further, all such corruption must entail the holy reaction of God's judgment. The dirge of his heart is resumed (9–11). Verses 12–15 teach again the harvest of disloyalty and false worship. *Walked therein* (13); this refers not to God's voice but to His law, both mentioned in this verse. *Wormwood . . . gall* (15); these two always appear together and stand, as a metaphor, for some disagreeable experience. The people shall be subjected to the bitterest woes.

Probably verses 16–21 reveal another element in the prophet's heartsickness—a touch of irony respecting professional mourners. What can such women avail (cf. 2 Ch. xxxv. 25; Mt. ix. 23) when death (personified) climbs in at the window? The only rest his heart can know is that beyond wisdom or strength stand the mercy and justice and righteousness of God (23, 24). These things are His delight. *Our dwellings have cast us out* (19); RV reads 'they (the enemy) have cast down our dwellings'. Cf. 2 Ki. xxv. 9.

The oracle (25, 26) seems to be detached here, yet in it the moral incisiveness of Jeremiah appears: Judah, though circumcised, lacks inner dedication, hence lies under the penalty of being a pagan, and so punishable for sin as the nations about her. Actually ritual perfection may involve ethical damnation. This passage anticipates Paul's teaching in the distinction between the circumcision of the flesh and that of the heart. *All that are in the utmost corners* (26); lit. 'all those corner-clipped'. The RV reads 'all who have the corners of their hair polled'. The reference appears to be to the custom of certain Arab tribes who cut their hair in a circular form in honour of Bacchus (Her. iii. 18). The habit is forbidden in Lv. xix, 27.

iii. The impotence of idols (x. 1–16). This passage contains a scathing polemic against the very conception of idolatry by one who has known it at first-hand, himself being held in awe only by the monotheistic faith cherished by the best of his people. Some scholars wonder if this passage, suggesting a different background, comes from the hand of Jeremiah. Or is it Isaiah? The style is similar to that prophet, who set Yahweh as Creator of all in striking contrast to the impotent gods of Babylon. It is an open question. *The signs of heaven* (2); i.e. heavenly portents, comets, meteors, etc. The pagan people laid great stress on these. Verses 6 and 7 are omitted in the LXX. *The stock is a doctrine of vanities* (8); lit. 'an instruction of vanities is the tree itself'. The RV has 'the instruction of idols, it is but a stock.' The meaning is that the instruction of idols is no better than the idols themselves. Idolatry is destitute of moral and spiritual force. *Tarshish* (9) was the extreme limit of the ancient world. The LXX has 'Carthage'; many identify it with Tartessus in Spain. *Uphaz* is found only here and in Dn. x. 5. It is often identified with Ophir, which was proverbial for its gold. The LXX omits verse 10. In verse 16 Israel is said to be *the rod of his inheritance;* better, as RV, 'the tribe of his inheritance'. The polemic itself is impressive. The prophet saw the gods as blocks of wood, inert, dumb, and scorned them as a scarecrow in a garden patch whose only use lay in such mean service, not a holy power that could discipline the rebellious human heart. Idolatry everywhere invites the same biting irony.

It is interesting to note that the single verse 11 is written not in Hebrew but in Aramaic, which leads scholars to think it is a marginal gloss inserted in the text to furnish the Jews with a reply to those who would tempt them to idolatry. Verses 12–16 are repeated in li. 15–19.

iv. Exile is imminent (x. 17–25). The note of doom here gathers up that in ix. 22. The community, as a corporate personality, is bidden to pack her slender bundle for the desolate march to exile. *Gather up thy wares* (17); i.e. prepare for the flight. The Hebrew word 'wares' occurs here only. *O inhabitant of the fortress* (17); the RV reads better: 'Thou that abidest in the siege.' *I will sling* (18); a very strong metaphor: the only place where it means driving a people into exile. The desolation of the people's heart is expressed in verses 19, 20. This is all the dire issue of the bad leadership of the leaders (lit. shepherds), who having lost touch with Yahweh were unable to shepherd the people to safety. The old home was to become a jackal lair (22). In verse 23 the prophet acknowledges his limitation; in verse 24 he makes his supplication; and in verse 25 he pleads for vindication. As Moses in the days gone past, so Jeremiah intercedes for his people (23, 24). *O Lord, correct me, but with judgment* (24). His 'me' is not the personal self, but the nation whose doom is breaking his heart. *Judgment* here means 'in just measure'. Verse 25 is repeated in Ps. lxxix. 6, 7. The prophet appears to turn in anger upon a nation summoned by God to carry out His retributive purpose over Judah (25). Paradoxically, this anger is feasible and just.

IV. JEREMIAH AND THE COVENANT. xi. 1—xii. 17

This section contains the fourth message of Jeremiah with an appendix (xii. 7–17). The covenant here probably infers the discovery of 'the Book of the Law' (2 Ki. xxii. 8), generally assumed to be the book of Deuteronomy, under the influence of which in 621 B.C. Josiah called for the rededication of the nation, with centraliza-

tion of worship at Jerusalem. This meant the discontinuance and obliteration of worship at the local shrines throughout the country. His sense that it was God's command, with a curse upon all who would not submit, marks, presumably, Jeremiah's feeling that the Josian reformation was of God and therefore might be effectual. It is impossible to determine the period of this discourse. But apparently Jeremiah had not yet left his native Anathoth, for he discovers a plot against him (xi. 18–21), a plot which may have occasioned his leaving the place.

a. The burden of Jeremiah's fourth message (xi. 1—xii. 5)

i. The covenant (xi. 1–5). *Hear ye the words of this covenant* (2). Jehovah had made it with His people at Horeb, and they had promised obedience. It marked their deliverance from *the iron furnace* (4; Heb. *kur*; a smelting oven symbolic of acute suffering; cf. Dt. iv. 20; 1 Ki. viii. 51; Is. xlviii. 10). Jehovah commanded the prophet thus to advocate the covenant and to both the injunction and the terms of the covenant the prophet replies, *So be it, O Lord* (5); 'Amen, O Yahweh'. *A land flowing with milk and honey* (5). Outside the Pentateuch this expression occurs only in Jeremiah (who uses it twice, here and in xxxii. 22) and in Ezk. xx. 6, 15.

ii. Incompatibility of religion and force (xi. 6–8). The LXX deletes verses 7, 8 except *yet they obeyed not* (8). *I will bring* (8); RV 'I have brought'. One feels that Jeremiah affirmed the king's vision and desire, but it is doubtful whether he consented to the force with which Josiah carried it through. Jeremiah as an idealist was also a realist. He saw that an external covenant is null and void unless it wins inner consent. Sincere conversion alone would bring this about and in this case it was lacking; hence Jeremiah's sense of forfeiture of blessing.

iii. The old sin returned (xi. 9–17). This passage records the lure of the old sin of the fathers and its inevitable judgment. When force is absent, superficial reformation casts off its ethical camouflage and returns post haste to the old worship and hoary iniquity. *A conspiracy* (9); not necessarily a formal one; all it means is that, in spite of all that has taken place, the people were determined to go on their idolatrous way. Verse 10 is evidence that the time came when Josiah's reformation ceased to be even outwardly operative. In Jehoiakim's reign the people with their king returned to idolatry as 'the sow to the mire'. Hence Jeremiah sees that religion that is void of force bears no redeeming influence, so judgment was now nearer than ever (11, 12). Yahweh brings judgment upon the false gods they worship, and they, gods and people, are impotent to avert it. *Pray not thou for this people* (14) is a solemn prohibition to the prophet against any intercession for the idolatrous nation, who shamefully worshipped Baal. Most of this verse is found in vii. 16. The corruption has gone too far; only judgment can purify the nation.

My beloved (15); i.e. Judah. Verse 16 can be understood only with the assistance of the LXX, the gist of which means that ritual minus reality is anathema to the holy God of Israel. *Olive tree* (16); a very common tree in Palestine. Hosea (xiv. 6) uses a similar metaphor for Judah. This olive tree is barren and so is given to the flames, i.e. to judgment.

iv. **The wrath of Anathoth (xi. 18–23).** This description of plots against Jeremiah by the folk of his home town is introduced abruptly. In this short paragraph there are three scenes: in the first the people speak (19); in the second the prophet speaks (20); and in the third God speaks (21–23). Anathoth was the home settlement of the priestly house of Abiathar, close friend of David, deposed by Solomon in favour of the younger rival house of Zadok, who from that time exercised priestly dominance in Jerusalem. Thus they came into great power, wealth and influence. Here then were all the elements essential to bitterness. Wrath is incurred in a village such as Anathoth whenever a son or kinsman departs from local sentiment, especially when it favours or appears to favour the opposing side. Religion at its worst in such an hour breeds a merciless anger. Thus when Jeremiah, bred of the Anathoth priesthood, supported, as a prophet, the deposition of all village sanctuaries (as for a time almost surely he did), he inferentially willed the suppression of that shrine at Anathoth. It was a deadly hurt. Abiathar had borne priestly rank and privilege before the birth of Zadok! Love can turn to hate, given adequate provocation. How bitter that hate was against Jeremiah can be inferred from the appeal he made to Yahweh's tribunal. He pleads that the desires and intentions of his village enemies be scorned and judged by that very tribunal. His own innocence (19) was that of a lamb, unwitting of peril. *Fruit* (19) perhaps should be amended to 'sap' (Heb. *leah*, instead of *lehem*). *Reins* (20) means emotion. *Heart* (20) is the seat of intelligence or reason.

v. **The problem of godless prosperity (xii. 1–5).** Jeremiah concludes his fourth message by addressing himself to the age-long problem of the success of the wicked. The prophet is among the boldest of any generation who have stood up in their suffering and interrogated the divine sovereignty on the issue of prosperity attending the labour of the godless and impious. Anger (3, 4) burns within him against the murderous intentions of his antagonists at Anathoth, these prosperous wicked! But God is not at the mercy of man's questionings, no matter what the anomalies of human life. Jeremiah receives no direct solution to his problem, but rather the command to gird his loins for a yet greater tax on his faith and courage. The earlier suffering, which is likened to a race against fellow-athletes, is but a preliminary discipline for a much sterner struggle. If that contest was too much for him, how will he fare if he be matched against race-horses? (5). And if, when the land was peaceful,

he was distressed, what will his reaction be in the difficult times which lie ahead (signified by *the swelling of Jordan*)? *Thou hast planted them* (2). The metaphor of a tree is applied to the whole nation in 2 Sa. vii. 10; here it is applied to the wicked. *The swelling of Jordan* (5; Heb. *ga'on*, swelling, pride, majesty), connoting the wild, luxuriant and beast-infested growths of the hot marshy land on the bank of the Jordan (cf. xlix. 19, l. 44; Zc. xi. 3).

b. **Yahweh's lament (xii. 6–17)**

In verses 6–11 God speaks to Jeremiah; in verses 12–17 God speaks through Jeremiah. This section is an appendix to the fourth message of Jeremiah just concluded. The prophet's sorrow, as that of Hosea, with whom he shares not a few characteristics, led him to feel that it had its counterpart in God. This divine lament in its historical setting is recorded in 2 Ki. xxiv. 1, 2, where detail and date are given (598 B.C.). *Mine house* (7); probably here used in the wider sense of 'my land' rather than the temple. *As a lion* (8); Judah has roared against the Lord as a lion would do and has taken up a hostile attitude. *Speckled bird* (9); as birds attack other birds of unfamiliar plumage, so Israel, differing from other nations, was attacked by them. *My vineyard* (10); the nation is described under various metaphors—house, heritage, dearly beloved of my soul, vineyard. The pastors, i.e. leaders, have destroyed the vineyard initially, and the enemy from without has destroyed it finally. The *evil neighbours* (14) are predicted (14–17) to share the exile fate of Judah; these Syrian, Moabite and Ammonite aggressors will likewise be punished through the agency of the common foe, Babylon, unless they worship the living God and learn *to swear by my name* (16). Again the conditional character of prophecy is to be marked.

V. THE FIVE WARNINGS. xiii. 1–27

The date of these warnings is obscure. Verses 18, 19 probably refer to Jehoiachin and his mother, queen Nehusta (597 B.C.). The first portion, pregnant with disaster, might cover the period of his father, Jehoiakim, hence 608–597 B.C.

a. **The first warning (xiii. 1–11)**

This is conveyed by the symbol of the ruined loincloth. It is an acted parable teaching through warning that idol worship is the utter ruin of real worship in corruption of soul. Yahweh's worship on the other hand was a praise and a glory and inner creation. There are four movements in connection with this parabolic warning: first, the prophet is told to get a girdle (verses 1, 2); secondly, he is commanded to take it to Euphrates (verses 3–5); then he is told to fetch the girdle from Euphrates (verses 6, 7); and finally the parable is explained (verses 8–11). The first three were preparatory; the fourth was explanatory. Jeremiah's ordered destination is ambiguous. Euphrates can hardly refer to the great river of that name, some 250 miles from Jerusalem. The likelihood is that the town mentioned was actually Parah, about three miles from Jeremiah's home town Anathoth. (The Hebrew word *Perath* is the name of the Euphrates.) Of course, if it was a vision, not an actual journey, then distance has no relevance.

b. The second warning (xiii. 12–14)

Verse 12 contains the parabolic warning; verse 13 explains it. The imagery of the wine jar bears the warning that just as strong drink confuses a man's walk and thought, so will Yahweh's judgment be. He will fill the men of Judah with drunkenness and they shall dash against each other and be destroyed. Drunkenness is the dethronement of the alert mind so essential to decision in an hour of crisis. The inhabitants of Jerusalem will have neither wits nor strength to defend themselves or know friend from foe (cf. xxv. 15–28; Ezk. xxiii. 31–34; Is. li. 17; Ps. lx. 3).

c. The third warning (xiii. 15–17)

Here Jeremiah warns his people against arrogance toward Yahweh. *Be not proud* (15). The Greeks held that pride, *hybris*, invited the stroke of the gods. *The dark mountains* (16; lit. 'the mountains of twilight') refers to the plight of travellers overtaken by night before reaching a friendly inn. *Give glory* (16); this is a Hebrew idiom for 'confess your sins' (cf. Jos. vii. 19).

d. The fourth warning (xiii. 18, 19)

The contemptuous response to Jeremiah's messages was the cause, in their lofty pride, of the people's downfall. Hence the prophet's command to address the royal house personally and directly. *Humble yourselves, sit down* (18); RV mg. 'sit ye down low'. The king and the queen mentioned are, probably, Jehoiachin and Nehusta his mother (c. 597 B.C.). *The cities of the south* (19), i.e. Negeb, the name of the barren district in the south of Judah. The cities of this desert territory are noted as the furthest away from the invasion, thus emphasizing the completeness of Judah's captivity, *all of it, wholly* (19).

e. The fifth warning (xiii. 20–27)

The last warning of judgment makes it plainer than ever that doom is due to obdurate sins. The final words convict. Verse 21 is obscure. Driver's translation is 'What wilt thou say when he shall set over thee as head those whom thou hast thyself taught to be friends unto thee?' There were times when the Babylonians had been friends and allies of Judah. For instance, Hezekiah had courted the friendship of Merodach-baladan. There may be some such reference to it in this verse. 'Woe unto thee, O Jerusalem! thou wilt not be made clean; how long shall it yet be?' (27, RV). The proverb of verse 23 is well known and axiomatic. The point is that sin may become so habitual as to involve destiny; the nexus of sin and penalty is unchangeable and unbreakable. The appositness of such penalty is that it shall be inflicted by those with whom Jerusalem has coquetted.

VI. SHADOWS OF DOOM. xiv. 1—xxi. 14

This section contains the fifth, sixth and seventh messages of Jeremiah with appendices. Events in the life of the prophet are also interspersed.

a. Jeremiah's fifth message (xiv. 1—xv. 9)

This oracle deals with the plague of drought and the vicarious intercession of the prophet.

i. **The desolation of the land (xiv. 1–6).** The desolation of the land was complete. It was upon the country as a whole (2), upon the nobles (3), upon the ground (4), and upon the many beasts (5, 6). The word of the Lord came to Jeremiah concerning the drought and all its devastating consequences, which inspired the prayers of the prophet. Drought is a terror in the East. The root trouble, *because there was no grass* (5, 6), is expressed twice.

ii. **The supplication of the prophet (xiv. 7–9).** The description is poetic. The prophet takes up the imagery as a fit symbol of spiritual drought. The living God abandons the people to their sin; He remains no longer than a night, like a wayfaring man (8). *Leave us not* (9) is the climax of the intercession.

iii. **The intimation of the Lord (xiv. 10–12).** To forbear prayer (11) is an inexorable command. *Sword . . . famine . . . pestilence* (12); the combination occurs seven times in Jeremiah.

iv. **The declaration concerning false prophets (xiv. 13–16).** Jeremiah can only plead (13) that the prophets have lied to the people, have predicted a false peace. Such liars were not his ambassadors; they prophesied in their own godless authority. Yet—and here is the drama—the people willed to be deceived, therefore this punishment must fall on deceivers and deceived alike.

v. **The lamentation of the true prophet (xiv. 17–22).** As Abraham of old for Sodom, so Jeremiah dares still to intercede. He takes high ground. *Break not thy covenant with us* (21), he pleads. Still further, Jeremiah rests upon the divine name and character and the relation of Jehovah to His people. *Art thou not he, O Lord our God? therefore we will wait upon thee* (22). Israel had broken covenant, but Israel's God—never!

vi. **The declaration of the Lord (xv. 1–9).** But the Lord is adamant. He replies to the prophet's prayer. Moses and Samuel of old interceded, *yet my mind could not be toward this people* (1); cf. Ex. xxxii. 11–14, 30–32; Nu. xiv. 13–24; Dt. ix. 18–20, 25–29; 1 Sa. vii. 8, 9, xii. 19–25; Ps. xlix. 6–8. Doom is appointed for Judah, by sword, dog, vulture, and wild beast (3). *I will fan them* (7); RSV 'I have winnowed them'. *She that hath borne seven* (9). Jerusalem, which has been so prolific and prosperous, will be bereft of her children (7).

b. Dialogue appendix (xv. 10–21)

Jeremiah becomes introspective. Anguish moves him that he has become a curse to his people, but Yahweh strengthens him and will yet vindicate him. Verse 11 is difficult. The RV differs considerably from the AV and makes the reading much clearer. Verses 12–14 signify exile. *I will make thee to pass* (14); RV 'I will make them (i.e. the treasures) to pass'. But the words are applicable to both Jeremiah and the treasures. The utter loneliness of God's man (15–18) is here given expression. He has to side with the Lord against his own kinsfolk, as though against his own heart and will. *Thou hast filled me with indignation* (17). His cry is desperate. He has reached extremity. *Why is my pain perpetual?* (18). Is Yahweh to be to me as a lying stream (i.e. as a spring that dries up in drought)? The Lord replies. The end of all this dialogue is a pledge of vindication if his obedience is unbroken: if thou bringest out *the precious from the vile* (19, 'common'); i.e. make clear the eternal difference between good and evil, *thou shalt be as my mouth* and continue to be my prophet. Verses 20–21 are a substantial repetition of i. 18–19.

c. Jeremiah's sixth message (xvi. 1—xvii. 18)

The burden of this message is emphasized by the divine order to remain unwed. Doom is to overshadow the land, for sin harvests its unrepealed penalty. *Thou shalt not take thee a wife* (xvi. 2), for children born in Judah shall die even without burial. *Grievous deaths* (4); lit. 'deaths of sickness', i.e. death by wasting diseases, a famine. All shall be devoured by birds and beasts. The prophet is to keep aloof from *mourning* (5), lit. 'shrill crying' such as is produced by sorrow, from festivity (8) and from home (9). Idolatry is the cause, and punishment is inevitable, i.e. exile (13). *Where I will not shew you favour* (13); surely severity itself. *Tear themselves* (7); the RV reads 'Neither shall men break bread for them in mourning'. This may be a reference to the funeral feasting, which, originally, was probably a communion with the dead. *The cup of consolation* (7) was similarly served as a refreshment at funerals. *A land* (13); the Hebrew has the definite article, 'the land'. The people were not ignorant of the land to which they would go. Verses 14, 15 seem displaced, a scribe's interpolation, perhaps, of some joy after exile. Alternatively, they may be an outburst relieving the deadly pressure upon the prophet's heart. These verses recur in xxiii. 7ff. The threats of verses 9–18 now continue after the break of the previous two verses 14, 15. The shadows deepen. Like fish and beasts, only captivity and death await the condemned citizens of Jerusalem. Later, even pagans shall share the city's refuge in Yahweh. This is Jeremiah's faithful expectation when doom is past, perhaps a parallel to the relieving optimism of verses 14, 15. *They shall know that my name is The Lord* (21); i.e. 'Jehovah'. *Fishers* (16). Amos uses a similar

metaphor (Am. iv. 2); so does Habakkuk (Hab. i. 15) and Ezekiel (Ezk. xii. 13). *Double* (18); cf. Is. xl. 2; it means 'ample'. *Defiled . . . mine inheritance* (18); idols were, after all, dead things and as such polluted the land, God's inheritance.

Judah's sin is as the indelible writing of a pen of iron or a diamond point (xvii. 1). The iron stylus was used for cutting out inscriptions on hard surfaces like rock or stone (cf. Jb. xix. 24). The diamond point was used to cut the equally hard diamond. The truth is that the nation is in the same category of hardness, whose sin is inscribed permanently upon its heart. As durable and lasting shall be the penal fires of Jehovah (4). *Their groves* (2); i.e. the asherim. See note on 1 Ki. xiv. 23. *O my mountain* (3); this is generally taken to mean Jerusalem. *For sin* (3); i.e. on account of sin. Following the description of Judah's sin (1, 2) and Judah's judgment (3, 4) comes a contrast between the man who trusts man (5, 6) and the man who relies on God (7, 8). The desperate condition of the human heart apart from spiritual diagnosis and healing is described in verses 9, 10. *Desperately wicked* (9); RV 'desperately sick'. In xv. 18 and xxx. 12 the word is translated 'incurable'. The rich fool is photographed in verse 11. *Shall serve them* (11); RV reads 'They (riches) shall leave him', i.e. the sick man. Throughout Scripture the term 'fool' refers to moral folly not to intellectual foolishness. The sensitiveness of Jeremiah is revealed in his closing words. They are a cry for vindication. *Written in the earth* (13); a figure for that which is unenduring: 'they shall disappear, like writing on the sand'. *Pastor* (16); elsewhere this word is applied to kings or rulers; here it is applied to the prophet himself.

d. Sabbath appendix (xvii. 19–27)

As in the previous discourse, there is an appendix. It concerns the sabbath and is a change from poetry to prose. It also raises the question of chronology. To the prophet who, as in honour bound, loved the sabbath, its desecration must have suggested the divine displeasure. *The gate of the children of the people* (19), at which Jeremiah is bidden to stand and instruct all burden-bearers entering on the sabbath, cannot be identified among the city, palace, or temple gates. The prohibition of verse 27 suggests one of the city gates. For the closing words cf. xxi. 14, xlix. 27, l. 32; Am. i. 3—ii. 5.

e. Jeremiah's seventh message (xviii. 1–17)

i. An illustration (xviii. 1–10). This discourse is associated with the prophet's commanded visit to the potter's house, where he understood the mind of God. He comprehended, through the operations of the local potter, the divine potter at work with His human clay. Here we have a parable on the familiar Eastern craftsman. Jeremiah's inspired and intuitive understanding of Yahweh's creative work with His human material furnishes the message. The seer watched again more purposively than ever before the potter's *work on the wheels* (3); lit. 'the two stones', upper and lower. He particularly noted, for it may have occurred more than once, the failure to make a vessel. This marring could be attributed to the potter's carelessness or clumsiness, the crude machine, or some flaw in the clay itself. Whatever the perversion the potter persevered and made the recalcitrant clay into another vessel. So the Lord, who has no obstructions save the human clay, is master also of the clay, shaping it to the purpose in His mind, whether one of meanness or grandeur. If the material fails to respond precisely to the shaping pressure, it is remoulded. The parable is a vivid picture of divine sovereignty. Human freedom as philosophically reasoned out is here neither thought of nor denied. *Deus vult!* The ethical and spiritual inference is seen by Jeremiah (5–10). *Cannot I do with you as this potter?* (6). The prophet works out the content of his intuition, for God is speaking to him. If a nation does evil then inevitably Jehovah will repent of the good wherewith He promised He would benefit it.

ii. The declaration (xviii. 11a). The message is clear. Exile is the new mould into which the nation is to be shaped. The condition is as clear.

iii. The exhortation (xviii. 11b, 12). 'Return . . . mend.' The first draws attention to the initial process, the other to the more continuous one. The Lord's moulding will is all of grace, provided the national mind ceases to be rebellious and becomes responsive and obedient.

iv. The expostulation (xviii. 13–17). Jeremiah, instructed by the Lord, warns the men of Judah and the inhabitants of Jerusalem of the evil of the stubborn mind. The sin of the people is as irrational as it is tragic. Familiar elements of nature even may be cited as their judges: *the snow of Lebanon* (14) and the running stream (14) are stedfast, but Yahweh's people forget Him and worship gods that actually have no existence. *Vanity* (15); figurative of nothingness. In disaster, therefore, Yahweh's face is turned from them (cf. ii. 27).

f. Reactions (xviii. 18–23)

At the conclusion of Jeremiah's seventh message we have recorded two reactions, first in the case of the audience and second in the case of the speaker.

i. The hostile hearers plot against the prophet's life (xviii. 18). Cf. xi. 18–23, xii. 1–6, xv. 10, 11, 15–21. This is the second plot against Jeremiah. The first was made by the people of Anathoth (xi. 19ff.). Jeremiah's enemies were confident that his dire prophecies would fail and that through priest, wise men, and cultic prophets, they would secure his downfall. *Let us not give heed to any of his words* (18). As read in the AV this implies that the murderous conspirators intend to ignore Jeremiah's predictions and exhortations. The LXX, however, omits the negative, giving a better sense, viz. to watch all the prophet's utterances and secure treasonable evidence against him out of his own mouth.

ii. The sensitive prophet cries out for vindication (xviii. 19–23). The retributive fury of this passage is so vehement that many think it is quite unlike Jeremiah. But the exception may prove the rule. The prophet is transparent. His very soul is laid bare. He hides nothing. The provocation is more than he can bear. The surface interpretation of egotistic imprecation may be discarded. Here is a cry that the divine cause, which the enemies so ruthlessly scorned, may be vindicated by the overthrow of their fancied security and power. In the first part of the prayer the emphasis is on himself; in the second half it is on his enemies.

g. Jeremiah's eighth message (xix. 1–15)

i. The method used (xix. 1, 2). This oracle like the previous one is parabolic. He is to act his message in two places, in the valley of Ben-Hinnom and in the temple court. Jeremiah is ordered to go to *the valley of the son of Hinnom* via the gate of potsherds, or broken shards (*Harsith*) (2), accompanied by the elders of priests and people, taking with him an *earthen bottle* (1). There are textual difficulties in this section, but the meaning is clear.

ii. The message given (xix. 3–15). Jeremiah was to empty out the contents of an earthen bottle, then break it, thus symbolically conveying thereby that even so would Yahweh penalize their idolatry and wrongdoing. Verses 4 and 5 have already occurred in substance in vii. 31, 32. The LXX does not have the phrase *for burnt offerings unto Baal* (5). *I will make void* (7); lit. 'empty out', a play on *earthen bottle* (1). The Hebrew words are cognate. *They shall bury them in Tophet* (11); the LXX omits this part of the verse. The same symbolic action of breaking the empty vessel is to be repeated *in the court of the Lord's house* (14). Thereafter warning is to be given to the people and sentence of doom pronounced.

h. Jeremiah in the stocks (xx. 1–6)

Pashur . . . the priest . . . chief governor (Heb. 'ruler'; RV 'chief officer') *in the house of the Lord* (1), in savage reaction smites and imprisons Jeremiah in the stocks. In that priestly circle, the prophet was an incarnate menace against their reiteration that, if Babylon attacked them, Egypt would compel him to lift the siege. The night made Pashur think again, with the result that he freed Jeremiah. If he did so to induce him to change or soften his message, he was soon disillusioned. Men, such as the prophet, do not change their message with a change in circumstance. All through history the opportunist in office has been rudely taken aback by the granitic quality of God's spokesman. Tragically therefore Jeremiah renamed Pashur as *Magor-missabib* (3; Heb. 'terror on every side'; AV mg. 'fear round about'). The meaning is that when the Babylonian victory shall prove how false was his prophecy of security, he shall be seen as responsible for such an incredible disaster, a false prophet, not only in his own eyes, but in the eyes of all his friends (4).

i. Jeremiah's complaint (xx. 7–18)

This is a unique psychological passage in canonical prophecy, a passage tremendous with feeling, a soul laid bare. Yahweh had compelled him to be a prophet. If he forbore the word of doom, it would be as a flame within him, a tension beyond endurance. His friends taunt him as 'a terror on every side'. His perennial stimulus is that the Lord is with him as a mighty man. In the end his enemies will lose the fight. *My familiars* (10); lit. 'men of my peace', i.e. acquaintances, those to whom he should normally say *Shalom*—peace be with you. Verses 14–18 reveal the breaking point. The words here do not seem to fit in easily. They suggest an even darker day, being grim words of utter breaking. They indicate a time when he would be more outcast from his people than he had ever been, yet had to watch the doom engirdle them. How sure of His man God must have been when He made such a soul plough so lonely and desperate a furrow! The point is that they reveal the soul of a man of God in expostulation against his fate, but a soul submissive, reverent, obedient and loyal.

j. Jeremiah's ninth message (xxi. 1–14)

The prophet's word here is another warning that Jerusalem will fall. In xxxvii. 3–10 there is a similar account, but it is not a doublet. It deals with the temporary raising of the siege by the Egyptians, only to be resumed later on with greater intensity and agony. Here we have the siege in its initial phases.

i. Jeremiah's message to Zedekiah (xxi. 1–7). First comes the plea of Zedekiah (1, 2). He sends Pashur (not the official so named in chapter xx) to entreat Jeremiah's intercession. The prophet replies to Zedekiah as instructed by Jehovah. With all the authority of one divinely commissioned Jeremiah announces *Thus saith the Lord God* (4). The answer is that Yahweh has willed that the Babylonians be agents of His judgment, with no quarter given; verily *he shall smite them with the edge of the sword* (7). The king, his court and people, all who survive the horror of the siege, its famine and pestilence, will be handed over to Nebuchadnezzar. Death will be the fate of those who will not surrender. The city will be burned to the ground.

ii. Jeremiah's message to the people of Jerusalem (xxi. 8–10). The figure of two ways comes from Dt. xxx. 15, 19. *For a prey* (9); i.e. escape with his bare life.

iii. Jeremiah's message to the royal house (xxi. 11–14). This consists of an exhortation (11, 12) and a declaration (13, 14). Such as are in authority to judge are to deal justly lest Yahweh's anger be as a consuming fire. *In the morning* (12); the early morning was the usual time for this, but it might also mean the king was to make justice his first, his primary concern.

Inhabitant (13); the Hebrew word is in the feminine, and the reference is obviously to Jerusalem, but why Jerusalem should be thus described is not clear.

VII. KINGS AND PROPHETS OF JUDAH: THE VISION OF THE END. xxii. 1—xxv. 38

a. Kings of Judah (xxii. 1—xxiii. 8)

This section contains a series of prophecies relating to contemporary kings of Judah; whether uttered by Jeremiah in sequence or not we cannot say.

i. Introductory (xxii. 1–9). King and people alike are to execute judgment and mercy, especially to the most needy: otherwise the house of David will become a waste. Yahweh pledges Himself by the most solemn oath that disobedience will be punished by desolation, viz. *I swear by myself* (5); cf. comment on formula in Heb. vi. 13–18. The house of David, under the figure of Lebanon forest, is to be gutted with fire. Again unrepentant idolatry is the reason. *Thy choice cedars* (7); these were the leaders of the nation.

ii. Shallum (xxii. 10–12). Josiah, whose death at Megiddo (608 B.C.) was a major disaster to the reformation movement, is not to be mourned for. *Weep not for the dead* (10), but rather for Shallum, i.e. Jehoahaz, who died in Egypt as an exile after reigning only three months (2 Ki. xxiii. 36—xxiv. 7). He was the first ruler of the southern kingdom to die in exile. The whole sense of verse 10 is that it is better to die on the battlefield than to die in captivity.

iii. Jehoiakim (xxii. 13–23). This king's father had been a reformer, but he did evil in the sight of the Lord. Josiah was just, his son unjust; Josiah acted as the father of his people, his son faithlessly exploited their basic rights; one was a man of austerity, the other one of ostentation; the former died the death of a hero, the other had the burial of an ass, lacking funeral ceremony (cf. 2 Ki. xxiv. 6). Verses 20–23 may apply to some unknown king. *Lovers* (20); means 'allies'. 'Lebanon . . . Bashan . . . Abarim' (20, RV) were mountains overlooking Israel and Judah beginning from the north and working down the eastern boundary.

iv. Jehoiachin (xxii. 24–30). This prophecy about Jehoiachin or Coniah appears to be the combination of two of Jeremiah's oracles, the first (verses 24–27) of future captivity, the second (verses 28–30) of captivity actually experienced. The whole is a lament for Jerusalem laid waste through the shortsighted policy of her kings. Jehoiachin and his mother are 'hurled forth' to die as exiles. The prophecy was fulfilled and is described in 2 Ki. xxiv. 8ff. In 597 B.C. Nebuchadnezzar came up against Jerusalem and Jehoiachin, his mother, and all the royal house went out to him and were taken to Babylon. After thirty-seven years in captivity he was released.

v. Pastors or rulers (xxiii. 1–8). The next in

order should have been the last king Zedekiah. Some think that Jeremiah refrained from prophesying against him by name, but the oracle implies him above all the others. It is a condemnation of false *pastors* (1) that do not shepherd but destroy and scatter their flock, as if their sheep were prey and they themselves wild beasts. *Driven them away* (2); true shepherds do not drive but lead their sheep. Yahweh will gather His *remnant* (3) and raise up shepherds who will feed not ruin His flock. Jeremiah's conviction is that Yahweh will raise up a Davidic king whose name will be indicative of his nature, *Yahweh Tsidkenu, The Lord our Righteousness* (5, 6). He will lead home a new 'exodus', the northern exiles sharing in it (7, 8). *The days come* (5); this phrase occurs sixteen times in Jeremiah and only five times elsewhere. *Branch* (5); i.e. a shoot, sprout. The Hebrew word *tsemach* designates that which sprouts from the roots of a tree. The figure here is of a tree that has been felled showing fresh life.

b. Prophets of Judah (xxiii. 9–40)

The former paragraph dealt with rulers in the state; this one deals with the religious leaders.

i. Jeremiah's distress because of the false prophets (xxiii. 9). Here Jeremiah has an unnerving vision. It is as distressing as though his heart was broken, all his bones become as those of a man overcome by excessive drunkenness. Note the threefold *because*. *Because of the prophets . . . because of the Lord . . . because of the words*.

ii. The sins of the false prophets (xxiii. 10–15). Over against Yahweh's holiness *both prophet and priest are profane* (11). Penalty is inevitable (10, 11). The prophets of Jerusalem are worse than those of the north. *The prophets of Samaria* (13) were idolaters; the prophets of Jerusalem were, in addition, immoral. And if judgment came upon the former, how much more will it come upon the latter. Their profanity is as that of Sodom and Gomorrah. They make it easy to sin (13–15).

iii. The condemnation of false prophets (xxiii. 16–20). They prophesy out of their own profane heart and have no word from Yahweh. None of them has stood in His council and heard His speech. Verses 19, 20 seem to break the sequence of thought; some have suggested that they are a misplaced repetition of xxx. 23, 24.

iv. The illegality of the false prophets (xxiii. 21–32). Jeremiah's condemnation of the prophets continues and their false, futile and illegal mission exposed (23, 24). Yahweh did not send them, nor had He spoken to them. They preach their own illusions. His presence is inescapable. The 'lie in the soul' (Plato) cannot be Yahweh's revelation, even though a prophet name His name. A prophet akin to Baal has no lot with Yahweh. The dreams of the false prophets are to be clearly distinguished from the Word of God as chaff is from wheat (28). The Lord is against all that is false: by His word it shall be destroyed.

v. The disgrace of the false prophets (xxiii. 33–40). There follows a play upon the word *burden* (33); Heb. *massa*. On the true prophet a word of Yahweh is a burden he must deliver. To the rebel such a word is burdensome, and mockery is substituted for reverence. Because there is no word or burden of Yahweh the judgment is that of a perpetual shame. The LXX, Syr., and Vulg. emendation 'I will lift you up' is preferable to *I will utterly forget you* (39) as it is in keeping with the meaning of 'burden'. Verse 37 is omitted by the LXX.

c. Two baskets of figs (xxiv. 1–10)

Here we note Jeremiah's apprehension of the vision (1–3) and Yahweh's explanation of it (4–10). Under the imagery of good and bad figs Jeremiah contrasts the exiles of 597 B.C. and the home folk under Zedekiah. *The good figs, very good* (3) stand for the exiles; *the evil, very evil* (3), too bad to be eaten, symbolize Jerusalem. The exiles are to be restored (4–7); the homefolk to be destroyed (8–10). The exiles are to be wholly reborn of heart and to become Yahweh's people. *In the land of Egypt* (8); Necho probably took a number of Jews with Jehoahaz into Egypt, though nothing is known of any Jewish settlement there until later.

d. Vision of the end (xxv. 1–38)

In the crucial battle of Carchemish (605 B.C.) the Babylonians defeated the Egyptians and thereby put an end to Pharaoh Necho's domination over Palestine. It was one of the decisive battles of history. In it Jeremiah clearly read Yahweh's will. The Babylonians were the 'foes from the north' harnessed by Yahweh to carry out His judgment over Judah.

i. A confirmation (xxv. 1–14). *The thirteenth year of Josiah* (3) was the year of Jeremiah's call (626 B.C.; cf. i. 2). *Rising early and speaking* (3) is a nomad idiom for an early start on a journey. Jeremiah saw that the people had not responded to Yahweh's initiative, but had vexed Him to their own hurt (7). *My servant* (9) is not in the LXX but its meaning evidently is 'my instrument'. The Babylonian king and his allies would lay waste the land and carry off into exile whom he willed. *Families of the north* (9). The Babylonian Empire, as its predecessor, the Assyrian, was made up of many races, many 'families'. The duration of exile *seventy years* (11) is a round number. Babylon is overthrown under judgment (12–14). Not only is judgment to come through Babylon, but judgment will come also upon Babylon. This section is absent from the LXX. Its appropriate reference is to chapter 1.

ii. A condemnation (xxv. 15–33). The wine cup (15–22) is the symbol of Yahweh's inescapable wrath over Judah and other nations. Babylon is His agent. *As it is this day* (18) is lacking in the LXX. *All the mingled people* (20) means the foreign settlements in Egypt who had been established there for various reasons, trade for instance. *In the utmost corners* (23); the

Hebrew runs 'corner-clipped', or 'having the corners of the hair polled', and signifies a ritual shaving of the hair (cf. ix. 26, xlix. 32). Observe that the fury of the Lord begins with Jerusalem, and extends to other nations, who also deserve the divine chastisement. Fearlessly Jeremiah declares the day of Yahweh in which *a noise shall come even to the ends of the earth* (31). The Lord *will plead with all flesh* (31), which means that He will bring them into the court of His righteousness, 'plead' being a legal term. The metaphor is changed (32) and Yahweh as a roaring lion symbolizes one bringing in war over the earth. His victims are 'unhonoured and unsung' (33).

iii. **A lamentation (xxv. 34–38).** The midnight hour of judgment has arrived and the prophet strikes once again the sad note of lament. *The days of your slaughter . . . are accomplished* (34); the RV reading is clearer: 'the days of your slaughter are fully come'. In the same breath the metaphor changes from that of a flock ready to be slaughtered to that of a pleasant vessel to be broken in pieces. *The fierceness of the oppressor* (38); the RV again has 'the fierceness of the oppressing sword'.

HISTORICAL NARRATIVES. xxvi. 1—lii. 34

VIII. PROPHECIES AND EVENTS DURING JEHOIAKIM'S REIGN. xxvi. 1–24

This chapter contains the story of two prophets—Jeremiah and Urijah.

a. Jeremiah's danger (xxvi. 1–19)

Six distinct scenes bring out the contents of this paragraph.

i. **God speaks (xxvi. 1–3).** God tells Jeremiah to go to the court of the temple to declare to the people the word of Yahweh.

ii. **Jeremiah speaks (xxvi. 4–7).** Cf. vii. 1–15. This passage is a toning down of the severity of the earlier passage.

iii. **The priests and false prophets speak (xxvi. 8–11).** The Shiloh disaster, a divine judgment on the nation, is used by Jeremiah as symbolic of the coming destruction of the present temple. This unites priest and the cultic prophets (the LXX calls them 'false prophets') in a plot against him. The falsity of their message to the people lay in its stress on the immunity of the city and temple from danger, despite the idolatry of the day. At first the people were carried away by the enthusiasm and action of the priests and false prophets and turned against Jeremiah (9). Later on, the same people changed their mind and sided with the prophet (16). A crowd can be easily swayed.

iv. **Jeremiah speaks to the princes and people (xxvi. 12–15).** The grievance of the charge levelled against Jeremiah in the assembly of princes and people lay in his denial of the community of the temple and of Jerusalem. His 'apologia' was that he had been sent by Yahweh to proclaim that, failing repentance on their part, the whole state stood in stark peril. His evident sincerity, plus prophetic fearlessness, caused a division between princes and people on the one hand, and between priests and cultic prophets on the other.

v. **The princes speak (xxvi. 16).** The accused is exonerated. This must have come as a blow to the priests and their associates. Even the common people had decided to change sides.

vi. **The elders speak (xxvi. 17–19).** The elders recall the incident of Micah in the reign of Hezekiah who had uttered a similar warning. The historic reference, intimating again the conditional quality of prophecy, prevented immediate peril to Jeremiah. *Mountain of the house* (18) is a synonym for the temple.

b. Urijah's death (xxvi. 20–24)

On the human side Jeremiah owed his life to the intervention of powerful and influential friends. Urijah was not so fortunate. The extradition and murder of this man indicates how near Jeremiah stood to death. The fickleness of the people and the loyalty of an influential friend stand out in contrast (24). For a number of years Jehoiakim was a vassal of Egypt and this explains the ease with which *the king sent men into Egypt* (22). And so both prophets were saved: one for service, the other from service. Some are left and some are taken, but always for a purpose. Urijah was fetched from Egypt, Jeremiah was later taken into Egypt; both died for their loyalty and devotion to their God.

IX. THE SANITY OF THE PROPHET. xxvii. 1—xxix. 32

These three chapters, which relate to the reign of Zedekiah, may originally have been a pamphlet circulated among the Babylonian exiles to disabuse their mind of a speedy return from exile. Nowhere else, in the same degree, does the same balance of Jeremiah's mind stand out so clearly as here. The background is already familiar. The first captivity in 597 was an accomplished fact; Zedekiah was on the throne on the sufferance of Babylon. But inside and outside the country many were plotting against Nebuchadnezzar. In these chapters Jeremiah sets himself the task of denouncing and correcting the notion that, somehow, it was possible to overthrow the power that had become supreme in the Eastern world. The prophet addresses on this subject the neighbouring nations, Zedekiah the king, the priests and prophets, and the exiles themselves!

a. The prophetic word (xxvii. 1–22)

i. **A message to the Gentile kings (xxvii. 1–11).** Jeremiah's cited symbolism of the yoke lays bare the plot as futile and ineffective. Though verse 1 reads *In the beginning of the reign of*

Jehoiakim, verses 3, 12 and 20 make it clear that what is meant is Zedekiah, not Jehoiakim. It is almost certainly a scribal error. The verse is omitted in the LXX. In this message the prophet first refers to God's sovereignty and then to Nebuchadnezzar's sway. Verse 7 is also lacking in the LXX.

ii. A message to Zedekiah (xxvii. 12–15). This consists of an exhortation to submit to Nebuchadnezzar and a declaration concerning the false prophets. The falsity of these prophets lies in the fact that they speak on their own initiative, with no higher source of information.

iii. A message to the priests (xxvii. 16–22). This message too consists of an exhortation and a declaration. The Massoretic Text and the LXX harmonize only in the common prophecy that the sacred vessels will be carried into captivity. The LXX text is more terse and probably original (cf. 2 Ki. xxiv. 13). The sacred vessels referred to in verse 16 were those carried away with Jehoiachin in 597 B.C. Jeremiah counters the facile optimism of the false prophets with the word that they also will experience captivity.

b. Prophets in conflict: Jeremiah and Hananiah (xxviii. 1–17)

This chapter shows large divergence between the Massoretic Text and the LXX. Usually the differences are unnecessary expansions in the Hebrew of the terse form in the LXX. The chapter contains four speeches, two by Hananiah and two by Jeremiah.

i. Hananiah's proclamation (xxviii. 1–4). As here, the question is always crucial whether a prophet is true or false. Hananiah had heard Jeremiah proclaim exile for the rebellious nation. In fierce reply Hananiah says that Yahweh had spoken the contrary to him, and he symbolizes that correction in the broken yoke (4).

ii. Jeremiah's declaration (xxviii. 5–9). Jeremiah's answer is ironic: 'Yahweh indeed perform that prophecy!' His tone would convey to the hearer his utter repudiation of such fancied security. Unlike Hananiah, he knew that only a change of heart would avert disaster. In any case, only the confirmation of Hananiah's prophecy could establish its validity. To Jeremiah the issue was doom, not peace or security, since he saw that Hananiah and his fellow cultic prophets betrayed a total ignorance of Yahweh's requirements. The question of truth or falsity did not turn upon sincerity alone, but upon experiential insight and obedience. The principle was tragically clear: one might be utterly sincere and yet be damned.

iii. Hananiah's demonstration (xxviii. 10, 11). Dramatically Hananiah demonstrates his point by breaking the yoke which he had taken from Jeremiah; so would Nebuchadnezzar's power be broken within two years. *Jeremiah went his way* (11). Why did Jeremiah not answer immediately? Much has been written about this. The probable answer is that Jeremiah sensed that it was not the right moment. The crowd must have been greatly impressed by Hananiah's message. Moreover, there may have been danger to Jeremiah's life. He withdrew to allow the emotional atmosphere to cool before making his answer. Perhaps he also wanted more time to think over his reply.

iv. Jeremiah's denunciation (xxviii. 12–17). Jeremiah came out of his silence and meditation with the issue clarified in his mind; Yahweh had confirmed his intuition; therefore, Hananiah must be wrong and, therefore, false. *The Lord hath not sent thee* (15). To Jeremiah it bore the gravity of a death sentence; there also lay Jeremiah's enduring strength, and he must go on, despite the greatest danger, since he has been sent. 'He endured as seeing him who is invisible.'

c. The crucial letter (xxix. 1–32)

A fairly large contingent of captives had been carried to Babylon in 597 B.C.; among them was Jehoiachin the king, his household, a company of priests and some prophets. News had reached Jeremiah that certain false prophets among the exiles were prophesying a speedy return to the land. Jeremiah writes this letter lest the exiles be carried away by the superficial, non-factual optimism of Hananiah and his friends. Patience to wait Yahweh's restoration would be the great factor and it must not be endangered by precipitate action. Faith in God's tomorrow is the great principle involved—patience with its expectancy, not the inertness of despair, nor the suicide of folly. In this message the prophet first addresses an exhortation and then makes a declaration. In his exhortation to the people (4–9) he tells them to carry on the normal activities of life as far as possible. The declaration which follows (10–32) includes four groups of people: those already in captivity (10–14), those about to follow them (15–19), the false prophets in Babylon, of whom two—Ahab and Zedekiah —are named (20–23), and Shemaiah (24–32).

Neither hearken to your dreams which ye cause to be dreamed (8). The Massoretic Text is not so good as the LXX 'which ye dream'. Neither deluded prophet nor personal dream must lead them astray. Seventy years is the horizon-limit. Yahweh will give them a future (lit. 'a latter end') and a hope. Moreover, He is accessible to them even in Babylon. How sure Jeremiah was! Verses 14 and 16–20 are absent from the LXX. See xxiv. 1–10 which suggest that this latter section is a dittography of that passage. Verse 15 has its fit connection with verse 21.

And of them shall be taken up a curse (22); Heb. *qelalah*. A play on the words *Qolaiah*, the father of Ahab (21) and *qalah, roasted* (22), is probably intended. The text of verses 24–32 is confused; the LXX and Syr. also differ from it. The meaning, however, is clear. The question is raised why Jeremiah was not restrained from sending such a distracting letter. Zephaniah read this complaint to Jeremiah, who thereupon pronounced judgment upon the sender and his house.

X. A FUTURE AND A HOPE. xxx. 1—xxxiv. 22

Chapters xxx—xxxiii are an interruption of Baruch's biography of Jeremiah. xxix. 11 might well, as a prelude, head these words of vision and hope: *For I know the thoughts that I think* (lit. 'the purposes which I purpose') *toward you, saith the Lord, thoughts of peace, and not of evil, to give you an expected end* (lit. 'a latter end and a hope'). Up till now the tone of Jeremiah's prophecies has been gloomy in the extreme. True, from time to time a gleam of light fell upon the dark path of God's people, but that was an exception rather than the rule. These chapters present a remarkable change. Though we still hear the thunder of judgment in the distance, on the whole the sky is clear, and the message is one of hope. This is rather remarkable, for chapters xxxii and xxxiii were written in the tenth year of Zedekiah, i.e. on the very eve of the final collapse. From the internal evidence it appears that chapters xxx and xxxi were also written at that time. What an extraordinary situation! Jeremiah is in prison, famine and pestilence rage in the city, and the Babylonian army is battering against the wall of Jerusalem. This was Judah's midnight hour and the people needed hope and comfort. In this dark hour God has a message for His people. The message is that the nation is not to perish. More than that, the time will come when even the Gentile nations will acknowledge God's truth, and when a righteous branch will arise from the house of David whose name will be the Lord our Righteousness. Having led the people so long in a dry and barren desert, the prophet brings them at last, if only for a time, to a little green oasis.

The whole theme is germane to the spirit of Jeremiah. The section forms a minor collection, though scholars are divided as to whether the chapters as they stand came originally from the pen of Jeremiah. The prophet, however, is prominently here, both as to spirit and expression.

a. The book of consolation (xxx. 1–24)

i. Restoration assured (xxx. 1–11). The chapter opens with a declaration of the restoration (1–3). There must be discipline, but not final disaster (4–11). What Hananiah sought symbolically to do, but without the right or the power to accomplish it, Yahweh in His great mercy would yet perform (8). Hence the call to the fearlessness of faith, since in the hour of cosmic judgment He would save His people. *The time of Jacob's trouble* (7) could be applied to the immediate situation, though it has a much longer period in view—the whole period of the captivity. The reference to *David their king* (9) does not mean that David the son of Jesse will be raised from the dead; it refers to an ideal king of the house of David.

ii. Wounds and healing (xxx. 12–17). Israel's wounds have been dealt to her by Yahweh at the hands of a merciless enemy. They are the result of her iniquity (15) and apart from divine intervention are incurable (12, 15). She has been deserted by all her associates, which helps to emphasize the hopelessness of her position. But verses 16, 17 introduce what is almost a paradox, as so often happens in Jeremiah. *I will restore health unto thee* (17). Those who have spoiled Israel shall themselves be spoiled, and wounds which are incurable shall be healed.

iii. Restoration (xxx. 18–24). Beyond exile there is home. There is a lilt in this section, as though spring was bursting out of severe winter. This is the equivalent of Is. xxxv, but in the imagery and spirit of Jeremiah. There shall be the laughter of children, and their overlord shall be their own kith and kin. He shall have priestly access to the Presence, and they shall know that they are Yahweh's people. Thus the prophet envisages a fivefold restoration—restoration of the heathen (17), restoration to the land (18), restoration of prosperity (18–20), restoration of an ideal king (21), and restoration to God's fellowship (22). Matthew Arnold's phrase 'there is a power, not ourselves, making for righteousness' is apposite to verses 23, 24, dealing with the principle of righteousness.

b. Restoration and the new covenant (xxxi. 1–40)

This whole chapter deals with the restoration, prosperity and peace of Israel—both kingdoms. There is not a dark cloud in the sky; the vision is bright and glorious.

i. Grace in the wilderness (xxxi. 1–6). Northern Israel (Ephraim) is to be restored, rebuilt and cultivated anew. Fittingly, there is a call to end the schism between north and south in the presence of Yahweh, the God of the whole nation (6). Verses 1–22 deal mainly with the northern kingdom; verses 23–26 mainly with the southern kingdom; and verses 27–40 deal with both kingdoms. Many explanations have been offered of verse 2. It is, however, probably best to take it in a prophetic sense, i.e. it describes something that is yet to take place as if it had already taken place. *Wilderness* in that case will mean the captivity. *When I went to cause him to rest* (2) is probably equivalent to 'when the time comes for God to be on the move to give them rest', i.e. peace in their own land.

ii. Joy after exile (xxxi. 7–14). Instead of the Massoretic Text *save thy people* (7), the LXX is preferable: 'hath loved'. This is a sense of realization, not a prayer. Their return with tears of repentance is answered in salvation (8–10). That in itself becomes a message to the nation, a ringing cry of joy, a satisfied heart, a satiation in Yahweh's country.

iii. Rachel comforted (xxxi. 15–17). An imaginative prophetic touch of Rachel the 'Beloved' in her grave weeping afresh over the exile of her sons Joseph and Benjamin. But Yahweh wipes away her tears in the pledge of restoration. *Ramah* (15) is about five miles north of Jerusalem.

iv. Conscience and prayer (xxxi. 18–22). The same prophetic intuition hears Ephraim awaking to the call of conscience, with Yahweh as mother-father yearning over him. There is some doubt concerning the original text, with a double sense of 'turn' in verse 19. A number of scholars would render 'After I turned (from thee) I repented'. When conscience is heard, a man is not far from God. *Set thee up waymarks* (21); i.e. signposts for the returning exiles. *A woman shall compass a man* (22); probably, originally, a proverb whose meaning has been lost.

v. Judah the blessed (xxxi. 23–26). When these better days come, that is what recreant Judah is to be—the blessed of Yahweh. The prophet records how sweet to his heart this day-dream had been (26).

vi. Yahweh the Re-creator (xxxi. 27–30). Once the discipline and its suffering is over, Yahweh will be intent again upon re-creating His people. Only in inevitable action is He ever destroyer; fundamentally He is Creator. In that new day justice shall see to it that only the wilful sinner suffers the due reward of his deed. Verse 29 refers to a doctrine which was very prominent and which was based on the idea of the solidarity of the tribe or nation. This doctrine is known as 'corporate personality'.

vii. The new covenant (xxxi. 31–34). The prophet had been compelled to see that the Mosaic covenant, even at its best, had been only external. In the new age (33) Yahweh would make an enduring covenant, one written upon the heart, and enforceable from within, not an imposition from without. Man's personal experience of the mercy of Yahweh would yield a finer response to Him, a law created through fellowship, instinct with reverential knowledge. Forgiveness would create gratitude, and out of that would emerge that finer obedience which obeys, not through fear of penalty, but through a surge of love; a new covenant in a re-created nature. This was the very nerve of Jeremiah's vision and prayer and hope. Moses was the means of an external covenant; Jeremiah the proclaimer of an internal covenant; Jesus, the Messiah, was to be the Creator of the eternal covenant, of which Jeremiah was a fit forerunner. Here is seen, therefore, the continuity of God's sovereign grace, conveying through covenant deep forgiveness of sin, a richer experience of God Himself in such fellowship, issuing in a finer brotherhood among men. A vision and a hope and a dedication.

viii. Permanence (xxxi. 35–37). Two pledges are seen here: that Israel shall endure, the world itself being an illustration. The perseverance of Israel rests on the persistence of Yahweh.

ix. The polluted converted (xxxi. 38–40). A prophecy, the realization of which Nehemiah was to see and in which he was to have a share. Jerusalem would be rebuilt, the valley of Hinnom, polluted by Baal worship and refuse, would be purified; and the city and its environment would be made sacred for life and worship—in short, Jerusalem will be rebuilt (38), Jerusalem will be extended (39), and Jerusalem will be sanctified (40).

c. The future bravely pledged (xxxii. 1–44)

The next two chapters are dated—the tenth year of Zedekiah, i.e. a short time before the final collapse of Jerusalem. But, in spite of the encircling gloom, the prophet maintains a steady and impressive optimism, optimism not in the immediate deliverance of Jerusalem but in the final purposes of God. Chronologically, this chapter should have followed chapters xxxvii and xxxviii.

The chapter can be roughly divided into two parts. In the first the prophet of God is prominent; in the second the God of the prophet is prominent.

i. The prophet of God (xxxii. 1–25). We note three things about him: his imprisonment, his optimism and his supplication.

Verses 1–5 describe the prophet's imprisonment. This paragraph is actually an introduction to the next one. The enemy was besieging the city and the prophet was deemed too pro-Babylonian to be left at liberty. For his realistic vision they have no room either in mind or heart. *Until I visit him* (5); visitation may mean either consolation or punishment. As it turned out, visitation in Zedekiah's case meant penalty.

Verses 6–15 speak of the prophet's optimism. Jeremiah had stressed that there would be no total destruction, since Yahweh had resolved on a remnant to serve His unchanging purpose. The intuition that he would be tested on this point of faith came through his cousin Hanameel's offer to sell the field at Anathoth, now in possession of the enemy. He felt that the revelation known to him must also be experienced by the people, hence the care he took in drawing up and safeguarding the documents of transfer and purchase. There are three scenes in this paragraph. In the first we see God and Jeremiah (6, 7), in the second Hanameel and Jeremiah (8–10) and in the third Jeremiah and Baruch (11–15). The *sealed* and the *open* (11) mean probably a double copy, papyrus or clay-tablet, with a view to preserving the fact of purchase, even should the outer copy be destroyed. In classical history there is a similar record. When Hannibal the Carthaginian was besieging the gates of Rome, the field on which his camp stood was sold at its highest figure in the Roman Forum.

Verses 16–25 contain the prophet's prayer. In the first part of the prayer the prophet dwells on the God of the people (17–22), and in the second part, on the people of God (23–25). There is an underlying anxiety in Jeremiah's heart.

ii. The God of the prophet (xxxii. 26–44). God sees the perplexing thoughts of His servant and makes a declaration concerning Judah's immediate fate, which is dark, and concerning Judah's ultimate fate, which is bright.

Judah's immediate fate (26–35) is grim enough. The disease has advanced so far that a drastic operation is imperative. In every generation it is required that God's men justify His ways with men. The sanity and balance of every generation rest just here. So here, Jeremiah, as by the voice of God Himself, reads out the history of His people—idolatrous the whole way through, hence the compulsion to discipline them unto righteousness. 'The Judge of all the earth must do right', and it is the burden of His men that it be so expressed. The duty is categorical; the issue tragic or redemptive. Even now redemption may lie through tragedy.

Judah's ultimate fate (36–44) is bright and glorious. Discipline there must be, but it will not be final disaster. There will be a restoration of the people to the land, and there will be a restoration of the land to prosperity. Moreover, there will be a regeneration of heart and soul and the people will not depart from their God. 'Standeth God within the shadow, keeping watch above His own.'

d. Reiteration of restoration and future happiness (xxxiii. 1–26)

This chapter continues the general theme of Israel's restoration and all that such a restoration will imply. The paragraph of verses 14–26 is not found in the LXX. Many critics regard it as late and not from the pen of Jeremiah. The theme of the chapter is a threefold restoration: the restoration of the people to the land; the restoration of the land to prosperity; and the restoration of the Davidic king.

i. The restoration of the people to the land (xxxiii. 1–8). The text presents many difficulties. *The maker thereof* (2); not of the prison, which is the subject in the previous sentence, but of the plan which God is unfolding to the prophet. The LXX reading of the verse is 'The Lord who made the earth and formed it to establish it.' Verse 3 seems an addition. Verse 5 is hard to translate with certainty. Cornill's reconstruction of the verse reads: 'The houses which are broken down, against which the Chaldeans come with mounts and swords to fight and to fill them with the dead bodies of men . . .' When the wrath has passed, peace shall return, and a cleansed and pardoned people will become a glory to God, manifest as such to all nations.

ii. The restoration of the land to prosperity (xxxiii. 9–13). These verses present a very striking contrast between what is and what shall be, what the land has become through the sin of man, and what it will become through and by the mercy of God. Instead of desolation there will be prosperity; instead of sorrow joy. The people are in their homes, prosperity is in the land, joy is in their hearts, and praise is in the temple. One other thing is needed to complete the happy picture, and that is an ideal king, and to such an ideal king the next paragraph introduces us.

iii. The restoration of the Davidic king (xxxiii. 14–26). The Davidic line shall be restored, and David's Son shall rule justly as of old. To such an extent shall this be that the name of Jerusalem shall be *The Lord our rightousness* (16). The Levitical sacrificial order shall be restored to its primacy. The permanence of the Davidic reign

and the Levitical order rests upon the persistence of Yahweh's cosmic ordinances, i.e. upon His word and power. The compassion of Yahweh for His disciplined and distressed people shall obliterate the taint of rejection flung at them by the onlooker and enemy. In a narrow nationalistic sense this promise has not been fulfilled, but in a spiritual and wider sense it has. Jesus Christ is 'the root and the offspring of David' (Rev. xxii. 16), and to Him—and to Him alone—the title 'The Lord our Righteousness' can be applied.

e. King and people addressed (xxxiv. 1–22)

i. A message to king Zedekiah (xxxiv. 1–7). In this message the prophet first makes a declaration to the effect that both the capital and the king will be delivered into Nebuchadnezzar's hands. Nebuchadnezzar, king of Babylon, will enter Jerusalem as victor, and Zedekiah, king of Judah, will enter Babylon as the vanquished. To the declaration, however, the prophet adds a word of consolation (4, 5); Zedekiah will not be killed, but will die in peace, i.e. in his captivity.

ii. A message to the people (xxxiv. 8–22). When the city's danger came to a head in the siege, the king induced his people by solemn oath to emancipate their Hebrew slaves in the hope that such an action would effect God's blessing. When the siege was temporarily lifted by the Egyptian allies this solemn pledge was broken and the slaves were forcibly brought again into servitude. Such were the circumstances, such is the background to this prophetic message. The action of the people was a breach of faith with the 'law of release' (Dt. xv. 12). It was also a profanation of the name of God, since they had pledged their action in His name. Not only had the people broken God's law but also their own promise, adding perjury to treachery. *At the end of seven years* (14); actually at the end of six years (the LXX reads 'six'). For the Hebrew counting of this kind both the first and last items were reckoned in. The prophet declares that the people shall be removed (17–21), and that the enemy shall return (22). He saw at once that such a breach of faith invited the retribution of Yahweh. As they had perjured themselves by such an action and had riveted bondage again upon Hebrew kith and kin, so Yahweh would lift from them His own protection, with the result that they themselves would become slaves under such ruthless masters as sword, pestilence and famine, until their condition would become the horror to *all the kingdoms of the earth* (17). *When they cut the calf* (18) stood for the ritual of some Semitic contracts (cf. Gn. xv. 9–20) and was an unspoken symbolic word that, if they broke pledge, then let retribution follow.

XI. PROPHECIES AND EVENTS DURING JEHOIAKIM'S REIGN. xxxv. 1—xxxvi. 32

In these two chapters we return again to the reign of Jehoiakim. Chronologically they follow on chapter xxvi. Why these chapters have been arranged in this order we cannot tell.

a. The lesson from the Rechabites (xxxv. 1–19)

i. The prophet and the Rechabites (xxxv. 1–11).
Jeremiah is instructed by God (1, 2) to go to the encampment of the Rechabites, to bring them (or probably their representatives) into one of the chambers in the temple, and to give them wine to drink. Jonadab had been the ancestor of the Rechabites, and to meet, as a nomad, the Baal-worship associated with the settled agriculturist and city dweller, he had disciplined his folk to forswear vine-culture and house-building, forbidding thereby the drinking of wine. They were to maintain the austerity of nomad life. As a Kenite tribe they had thrown in their lot with Israel. The advent of the Babylonians had driven them into the city.

Jeremiah does what he is bidden to do (3–5), and the Rechabites' reaction (6–11) is that, to a man, the people refused to drink wine.

ii. The prophet and the people (xxxv. 12–19).
That action the prophet had foreseen, and he now used it to show by way of contrast the practice of Judah. In verses 12–15 we have the prophet's expostulation; this is followed by a declaration (16, 17), which in turn leads to the pronouncement of blessing upon Jonadab's house (18, 19). *I have spoken* (14) is emphatic, putting in strong contrast the success of Jonadab with his people and the failure of Yahweh with His.

b. The writing of the roll (xxxvi. 1–32)

i. The first writing (xxxvi. 1–26).
In the fourth year of Jehoiakim (604 B.C.) God commanded the prophet to make a more permanent record of his public utterances, with a view to securing repentance in the hearts of the people (1–3). In response to His divine command Jeremiah secured the services of his associate, Baruch, and he recorded what the prophet dictated (4–8). Since Jeremiah was hindered from public speaking, he bade Baruch act as his deputy. *From my mouth* (6) is therefore equivalent to 'as my mouth'. His purpose in all this was that Judah should return from her evil way before judgment fell. Again, note the conditional nature of prophecy.

On a certain feast day Baruch read the roll to a large concourse of people, and we may well imagine the consternation the message caused (9, 10). Michaiah, who was present and heard what Baruch read, gave an abstract of the threatening nature of Jeremiah's prophecy to the princes of Judah (11–13). On questioning, Baruch, who had been summoned to appear before the princes with the roll, replies that he had written the roll at Jeremiah's dictation (14–19). The whole matter is reported to the king (20–26). Thus on one day there seem to have been three readings of the roll—before the people, before the princes, and before the king. The inference, therefore, is that the roll could not have been very lengthy. When the matter was

reported to the king, he must have felt that it was a state affair. As soon as a few columns were read, his anger was immediate, and against the intercession of the princes he flung them into the fire. The king next commanded that the prophet and his scribe be apprehended, but in vain, for *the Lord hid them* (26). Jeremiah had insisted on subordination to Babylon, but this symbolic scorn on the king's part was evidence enough that he was intent upon a contrary policy (cf. 2 Ki. xxiv). This strong reaction of the king seemingly banished the fear of the princes, roused as they had been by the private reading of the roll.

ii. The rewriting of the roll (xxxvi. 27–32).
Prophecy, other than false, has seldom come to heel at a king's threat. Times without number the prophets of Israel have had as part of their duty the discipline of king and court. So in this instance. The burning of the roll brought but a quickened sense that a second must be written, with necessary additions, including an indication of the fate awaiting the impious king. God must have the final word. The fulfilment of verse 30 regarding the *dead body*, a parallel to xxii. 19, is not actually recorded in history. As a detail it has little significance.

XII. PROPHECIES AND EVENTS DURING ZEDEKIAH'S REIGN. xxxvii. 1—xxxix. 18

In these three chapters the emphasis first falls upon the prophet and his captivity (xxxvii—xxxviii), and then upon the king and his captivity (xxxix).

a. The prophet's incarceration and preservation (xxxvii. 1—xxxviii. 28)

i. Jeremiah's answer to Zedekiah's request (xxxvii. 1–10).
Zedekiah had been appointed king at Babylon's instigation, doubtless after having given pledges of loyalty. Largely through the Egyptian influence at court, coupled apparently with his own instability of character, he became disloyal to him. Religiously, he would have said that he was a servant of Yahweh, yet, like his people, he must have been disloyal in matters of faith. Instability of nature and of faith led on, naturally, to instability in state policy, a kingly Reuben, 'unstable in all his ways' (cf. Gn. xlix. 3, 4). The advance of Egyptian troops temporarily raised the siege (5), but Jeremiah is at pains to proclaim that this is not decisive (10). If the Babylonians had only wounded troops, they would win in the end (cf. xxxiv. 1ff.).

ii. Jeremiah's arrest and detention (xxxvii. 11–21).
In the meantime Jeremiah attempted to go out of the city, presumably to inspect the property he had purchased from Hanameel. He was arrested and charged as a traitor, a likely superficial judgment in view of his attitude and word, thereby suffering his first imprisonment. 'Dungeon house' (house of the pit) has the unsavoury sense of an underground cell. Summoned by the king to a secret interview (17–21), Jeremiah stood by his prophecy that Yahweh had

purposed the supremacy of Babylon. That being so, why was he as His servant and spokesman treated as a traitor against His people? Not he, but the other prophets were false who had prophesied the overthrow of Babylon. He is removed to the guardroom, not sent back to the dungeon, and his food was authorized.

iii. **Jeremiah is cast into a dungeon (xxxviii. 1-6).** This chapter is chronologically ambiguous. Some have suggested that it is a different version of the earlier events, but from another hand. The same elements are in it: similarity of question and answer, a like release and guardroom imprisonment. Yet the differences are fairly strong: the guardroom would give him sufficient liberty to speak as recorded in verses 2 and 3. Zedekiah had not, so far as we can see, the calibre to go against his advisers; the rescue has elements of realism in it, while the king had sufficient authority to prevent the prophet being put to death, even though he could not effect his release.

In verses 1-3 Jeremiah presents the issue squarely before the people, who doubtless were able to converse with him in the relative seclusion of the guardroom. In the eyes of the princes, however, who bore the burden of the city's welfare and survival against attack, Jeremiah's counsel of surrender to the enemy meant a weakening of morale amounting to treason (4). In our own time men have been executed for similar attitudes and statements. It has never been, probably never will be, easy to establish in political quarters the priority of religious principle and vision over statecraft. The mistake the princes made was due to the fact that they could not see that Jeremiah spoke with an authority above his own person and mind. He stood, under that authority, for the better welfare of his people, in that he stood for the divine discipline of their sin, leading on to a truer and finer life. Exile was inevitable and essential to root idolatry out of their mind and spirit. The Babylonians were the unconscious agents or servants of Yahweh's will. How hard it is for men who have never shared such vision to accept a message of this kind, the history of man supplies vast evidence. The princes, on the ground of statecraft, were in the right to silence Jeremiah, even to the extent of ordering his execution. This they did not accomplish, but they brought sufficient pressure upon Zedekiah not to interfere in their imprisonment of Jeremiah in a cistern so filthy with mire as to ensure death unless release came fairly quickly. This appears to have been Jeremiah's third imprisonment.

iv. **Jeremiah is saved by Ebed-melech (xxxviii. 7-13).** Ebed-melech, a royal Ethiopian slave-eunuch, had the faith and courage to intercede with Zedekiah to lift him out of the cistern, and re-lodge him in the guardroom—the fourth imprisonment, reckoned by number of changes. Altogether these changes strike a strong note of providence (cf. xxxvi. 26, *the Lord hid them*). Ebed-melech was promised safety when the Babylonians took Jerusalem.

v. **Jeremiah is interviewed by Zedekiah (xxxviii. 14-26).** The desperate king again summons the prophet and swears on oath that he shall not be put to death for being candid. The prophet therefore puts before him the dread alternatives. Either go out in surrender to the Babylonians or suffer the worst when the city is captured and set on fire. Zedekiah expresses his fear of mockery if he does so surrender—the unhappy word of a weak, unstable mind. That had been the inner tragedy of Zedekiah: he could not implement in action what his own mind acknowledged as wise and sound. On that Jeremiah intones a dirge which presumably he had heard in a day-dream (22). Verse 23 seems to be Jeremiah's additional emphasis, the last phrase of which in Hebrew is particularly impressive: 'And thou shalt burn this city with fire.' The LXX, Syr., Vulg., and Targum give the passive sense. Although this account in the Versions should doubtless be accepted, nevertheless it was Zedkiah's indecision and lack of courage that actually brought about the ghastly result. Quite frequently it is not positive evil that does most harm, but the cowardice of an otherwise good man. Zedekiah wins our sympathy through pity roused at the massacre of his family and his own blindness, but it is at the cost of respect. No one can stand at the salute.

vi. **Jeremiah is questioned by the princes (xxxviii. 27, 28).** Zedekiah pledges Jeremiah to silence as to the purport of the interview, and Jeremiah with a half-truth allays the suspicions of the princes. *They left off speaking with him* (lit. 'were silent from him'); *for the matter was not perceived* (27) infers that there had been no eavesdropper near the interview.

b. **The collapse of Jerusalem and the captivity of Judah (xxxix. 1-18).**

i. **The collapse of the city (xxxix. 1-3).** The last hour has arrived. For some eighteen months the city had held out against the might of Babylon, but the inevitable hour could not be postponed indefinitely. Weakened by a long and merciless siege without and decimated by famine within, Jerusalem at last surrendered.

ii. **The capture of the king (xxxix. 4-8).** Though he had to give up the city, Zedekiah had not yet given up the hope of life. With the few defenders who were left he escapes and makes his way towards Jericho. But the hour of judgment had come for him and flight was impossible. He is overtaken near Jericho and then taken to Riblah to Nebuchadnezzar. Judgment is meted out to him and his family. His fate is a cruel one (6, 7).

iii. **The captivity of the people (xxxix. 9, 10).** This was the final captivity of Judah. In 597 B.C. king Jehoiachin and part of Jerusalem had been carried away; now, eleven years later, the rest of the city follows suit. But not quite. A small remnant, *the poor of the people* (10), are left behind to make a new start.

iv. **The release of the prophet (xxxix. 11-14).**

Judgment was given to the king of Judah, captivity to the remnant of Jerusalem, the country to the poor of the land, and freedom to Jeremiah the prophet. Such was Babylon's dealing with Judah. Jeremiah is set free and is given into the generous care of Gedaliah, the son of a friend.

v. The message to Ebed-melech (xxxix. 15–18). This is an appendix to chapter xxxix and is clearly in its wrong position, which is after xxxviii. 7–13, the passage recording his ingenuity and high courage in rescuing Jeremiah from the cistern fouled by mire in which he was either to die of starvation or be poisoned by the filth. *Men of whom thou art afraid* (17) is ambiguous, unless it implies the princes out of whose power he had rescued Jeremiah. *Thy life shall be for a prey unto thee* (18) is a Hebrew idiom meaning personal security. Just as they reasoned that an evil man in the end would fall a prey to that evil, so good would ensure a good man's deliverance.

XIII. PROPHECIES AND EVENTS IN JUDAH. xl. 1—xlii. 22

The prophecies to and events among the remnant left behind by the Babylonians clearly fall into two parts: those taking place in Judah (xl—xlii) and those taking place in Egypt (xliii—xliv).

a. The release of the prophet (xl. 1–6)
Jeremiah had remained in Jerusalem and was rounded up and put in fetters with others destined for deportation to Babylon. He was released on arrival at Ramah on the authority of the Babylonian commander. Clearly information had been lodged with this officer as to the identity of Jeremiah and his king's will concerning him. He is given the choice of going to Babylon with promise of the king's special favour (lit. 'set mine eyes upon thee') or going where he would. Verse 5 suggests that that second alternative would be to remain with Gedaliah. The first phrase of this verse, however, is omitted from the LXX, and no clear emendation of the Hebrew is feasible. However, his choice is his own, presumably either Jerusalem or Mizpah with Gedaliah. Verses 2, 3 would most certainly not be the direct speech of a Babylonian, but recast by the writer according to his own faith. The contrast is that all Jeremiah's work was in the name of Yahweh; on the other hand, he did yeoman service to the Babylonian cause, and his release was his reward.

b. The return of the fugitives (xl. 7–12)
Gedaliah was now governor of the land, and his new task, now that the leading men had been taken into exile, was to see that farmers and peasantry settled down amicably to secure the harvest out of which the tribute money would be paid to their new masters, the Babylonians. Hence a phase of that new task would be to come to terms with the 'forces of the field', i.e. the guerilla bands, each of which had its own leader.

That Gedaliah was a Jew would be a great factor in their pacification. His initial words (9, 10) were such as to win a measure of confidence and loyalty. His sane and cordial policy was underscored by what is reported in verse 12.

c. The warning of a plot (xl. 13–16)
Gedaliah was the soul of honour, but unfortunately for him one of the guerilla leaders, Ishmael, had been suborned by the Ammonite king, Baalis, to overthrow Gedaliah's policy and effect his murder. Johanan, another guerilla leader, was aware of this plot, but Gedaliah felt it was too foul to be substantial. Seemingly Gedaliah had overlooked two congruent factors: first, that Ishmael was of the royal house of David, and hence his superior in status. A slight thrown upon Ishmael may thus have created something of jealousy upon which Baalis was able to play. The other factor may have been that in Ishmael's eyes Gedaliah was a traitor to the cause by assuming this post under the Babylonians. Like many other high-souled men in history, before and after his time, Gedaliah lacked the ability to sift the spirit of treachery from that of loyalty, and thereby paved the way for the assassin's stroke.

d. The execution of the plot (xli. 1–9)
The deadly nature of Ishmael's proffer of loyalty is seen in that he used the normally sacred hour of Eastern hospitality to carry out the murder. The clauses *and the princes of the king* (1) and *and the men of war* (3) are lacking in the LXX but, if correct, mean that both Jews and Chaldeans who formed Gedaliah's bodyguard were all wiped out by Ishmael's men. One marvels at Ishmael's lack of insight, since Gedaliah's death was a major loss to his people, but jealousy and suspicion blind and brutalize. A murderer has usually no scruples regarding life, and in verses 4–9 we have a ruthless example of it. The pilgrims were bringing meal and vegetable offerings to the site in Jerusalem on which the ruined temple had stood, for such must be the meaning of *the house of the Lord* (5). Their shaven beards and rent garments and gashed bodies symbolized their distress over the desecration and destruction of the house of God. The spirit of murder is often also accompanied by that of hypocrisy, as here in Ishmael's *weeping all along as he went* (6). Greed of gain also marks such a character. Ten of the pilgrims saved themselves by revealing a cache of valuable food supplies. It is remarkable that so slight a force, eleven men in all, was able to butcher seventy out of eighty men, surprise possibly being the explanation. The sentence 'by the side of Gedaliah' (9, RV) is inexplicable, but the LXX helps us by adding 'was a great pit', i.e. probably a cistern. The reference to Asa recalls that he built this cistern to supply his garrison at Mizpah with water (cf. 1 Ki. xv. 22).

631

e. The abduction of the remnant (xli. 10)

The uselessness of all these murders is shown by the fact that Ishmael had to flee to Ammon, taking captive with him the rest of the refugees in Mizpah entrusted to the oversight of Gedaliah, including Jeremiah and Baruch. *The king's daughters* (10) presumably refers to some direct or indirect relationship to the royal house.

f. The rescue of the remnant (xli. 11–18)

Johanan was as prompt in his pursuit of the murderers as he had been in warning Gedaliah against them. Though he failed to capture Ishmael, he secured the release of his prisoners. *Men of war* (16) appears to be at variance with what is in verse 3, viz. Ishmael's slaughter of them at Mizpah. Probably we should read 'men, and women, and children' as in xliii. 6. Fear dissipates sound judgment, especially if, as here, it follows the murder of so important an official as Gedaliah. Presumably at the caravanserai (see RV mg.) of Chimham (17) the final intention was argued out that to go to Egypt would be safer for them than to remain and undergo examination by the Babylonians later on.

g. The remnant consults Jeremiah (xlii. 1–6)

Jeremiah must have been gravely exercised in mind over this request, since his word *I will keep back nothing from you* (4) is impressive. His hesitation, however, is met by the promise that they will abide by Yahweh's command, for on such obedience they felt their welfare rested. Indeed, according to verse 5, they invoke His judgment if they break troth: *The Lord be a true and faithful witness between us.*

h. Jeremiah's message to the remnant (xlii. 7–22)

For ten days Jeremiah remained silent, but when at last he spoke he left no doubts in the minds of the people who had consulted him as to what God's message was. He begins with an exhortation and assurance. They have nothing to fear from the Babylonians, and if they stay in the land God would prosper them (7–12). For *return* (12) of the Massoretic Text and the AV, the emendation of the Syr. and Vulg. is preferable, 'cause to settle'. Following the exhortation to remain in the land comes a solemn word of warning (13–18). Refusal to follow the divine leading involves the divine displeasure with all its dire consequences. There will be no safety in Egypt; a similar calamity to that which had overtaken their city would overtake them in Egypt. But the prophet already knows by some intuition what the mind of the people is and begins an expostulation with the men who had asked him to inquire of Jehovah (19–21). Instead of *dissembled* (20) the LXX has 'ye have done evil against'. The prophet's message ends with a solemn declaration (22).

XIV. PROPHECIES AND EVENTS IN EGYPT. xliii. 1—xliv. 30

a. The flight of the remnant (xliii. 1–7)

The leaders of the remnant presumably listened in silence to Jeremiah till he had finished and then gave their considered reply. If, instead of the unidiomatic term *saying* (2) (Heb. *omerim*) we accept the judgment of several scholars and read 'defiant' (Heb. *hammorim*), and with the LXX delete *proud* (2), we get the following: 'Then spake Azariah . . . and all the defiant men'. That probably gives us the true picture. It was not so much a case of pride as of fear or panic, defiance being an apt psychological outcome. Guerilla forces often fear the ruling force against which they stubbornly fight, and here it expresses itself in the charge of falsehood against Jeremiah upon whose verdict earlier they had promised to rest. The charge against Baruch of plotting to deliver them to death or exile has the same origin. The LXX tersely clarifies the difficult phrase *that were returned from . . . in the land of Judah* (5) by reading 'that were returned to sojourn in the land of Judah', and chapter xl. 11, 12 supports this. The company followed the lead of Johanan and not of Jeremiah. *Tahpanhes* is now named Daphne or Defenneh (cf. ii. 16), a city on the Egyptian frontier within the eastern delta, on the Palestine-Egypt road.

b. Jeremiah's message to the remnant (xliii. 8—xliv. 14)

This is Jeremiah's first recorded message to the remnant in Egypt. It is in four parts:

i. An announcement of what Nebuchadnezzar would do in Egypt (xliii. 8–13). At first Jeremiah gave no direct answer. He probably knew that such panic could not be fitly answered by mere words. They compelled him to go with them, and he must have sought guidance on the road down. That came to him at Tahpanhes. Just how he carried it out is difficult, for all the texts—Massoretic, LXX, Vulg., etc.—throw up varying differences. The terms 'brickwork' and 'mortar' (9, RV), are uncertain as to their precise meaning. The former is probably a case of dittography. If we make the slight change of one consonantal omission, as suggested by several texts (*ballat*), we can then translate 'and hid them secretly' instead of the difficult *and hide them in the clay in the brickkiln* (9). For Jeremiah, doubtless, had to take these great stones and effect the symbolism in dead of night, with no one but his awe-struck countrymen to mark his toilsome work. Thereupon he proclaimed the inwrought meaning. They had fled from Nebuchadnezzar to find, as they thought, secure shelter in Egypt. But all is in vain, since Nebuchadnezzar is to conquer that land and upon the stones there hidden build his throne. The stones, then, represented Babylon, and the clay Egypt. Egypt now appears strong and hides Babylon for the moment from the eyes of the fugitives, 'but soon the clay will vanish, and the hard stones, the

Babylonian Empire, will be set up in Egypt in the presence of these very men who are striving to escape from it'. This is in accordance with the LXX and Syr. approved reading 'he shall set up'. For *I have hid* (10) the LXX gives 'ye have hid'. If acceptable, the inference is that they have hidden themselves, though all in vain. Their flight therefore from the will of Yahweh is futile, since He has summoned from afar these unconscious agents to effect His disciplinary purpose. Earlier Jeremiah had been silent at their word, and now they are silent at his; it is the silence of a new fear as they hear this note of dark destiny. A fragmentary inscription confirms the fact that Nebuchadnezzar invaded Egypt in 568 B.C., Amasis then being Pharaoh, and overthrew its defenders. Josephus also records the tradition that he then deported to Babylon the Jews he captured there. *Beth-shemesh* (13) means 'house of the sun'. In Greek *Heliopolis*.

ii. A reminder of what God had done in Judah (xliv. 1–6). The clash of opinion is fierce in this chapter. Jeremiah thrusts upon the minds of the Jews then in Egypt the truth that penalty always interlocks with sin. They had burned incense to the 'queen of heaven' (Astarte, the 'Great Mother' of antiquity), and thereby the anger of Yahweh had fallen athwart the land of Judah. (Fifth-century papyri give us a picture of these Jewish colonies.) *Migdol . . . Tahpanhes . . . Noph . . . Pathros* (1); apparently some time must have elapsed since the flight into Egypt to enable the fugitives to establish themselves in all these places.

iii. A denunciation of their sins (xliv. 7–10). In spite of all God's judgments, in spite of the many red lights of their history, the remnant had gone blindly ahead, ignoring the warnings of the past. Instead of *wives* (9) the LXX reads 'princes'.

iv. A declaration of judgment (xliv. 11–14). The message which the prophet had to proclaim for so many years to the nation as a whole, he had now to proclaim to the small remnant in Egypt. Judgment would be their lot just as it was the lot of Jerusalem; from it there will be no escape.

c. The answer of the remnant (xliv. 15–19)
Post hoc, ergo propter hoc. The clash of opinion is here very evident. The men refuse to listen to what Jeremiah tells them. They ascribe all success to the queen of heaven, and apparently connected all their troubles and misfortunes with the reformation of Josiah. At the head of verse 19 the LXX and Syr. have this additional phrase 'And all the women answered and said'. Some of these were accompanied by their husbands, others not so accompanied.

d. Jeremiah's last message (xliv. 20–30)
This is the prophet's last recorded message and it is full of realism. Instead of *Ye and your wives* (25) the LXX rendering is preferable—'Ye women'. So, addressing these women, Jeremiah reaffirms the contrary truth, and goes so far as

to say that so dire shall Yahweh's answer be to such a denial of His presence and action that, on account of such worship, His name shall disappear from the mouth of every man of Judah dwelling in Egypt (26). The nemesis of idolatry is that in the end a remnant shall escape to know whose word stands fulfilled—His or theirs (28). As a sign, even Pharaoh, whose protection they had sought, shall fall into the hands of his enemies. Herodotus (ii. 161) records the fall of this monarch. ('Apries' to Herodotus, 'Hophra' in history.) He was put to death in 564, several years after his dethronement. Amasis was Pharaoh in 568 when Nebuchadnezzar attacked Egypt.

This whole chapter reveals the realism of Jeremiah, based on his insight, compared with the superficial inferences of two fellow-countrymen. They argued that, in the pre-reformation, when they worshipped the Asherah, fortune favoured them; since then disaster covered the land. It was the wrath of the 'Great Mother'. To Jeremiah it was the disciplinary work of God. With this chapter also ends Baruch's biography of Jeremiah. History has left no trace of what happened to the prophet after the encounter with the remnant related in this scene.

XV. JEREMIAH'S MESSAGE TO BARUCH.
xlv. 1–5
A careful reading of xxxvi. 1–8 shows that this chapter should really have followed that section rather than here at the end of the biography of Jeremiah. It is a poignant word. Baruch is stricken with sorrow at having to record the nexus of sin and penalty. Jeremiah had to remind him that Yahweh's sorrow vastly exceeded his own; that being so, how could Baruch seek his own well-being? Enough that in the end he will win through the disaster that has overtaken the rebellious and the impious. God's gift of bare life is adequate. The *thou* of verse 5 is emphatic. The LXX omits 'and this in the whole land' (4, RV). As it stands it is unintelligible. Many scholars believe that a better reading would be 'I will smite (*akkeh*) this whole land'.

XVI. PROPHECIES AGAINST FOREIGN NATIONS. xlvi. 1—li. 64
The LXX inserts these chapters in the middle of xxv, which position suits these oracles better than here. The fact that they are there inserted as a collection suggests their original separateness. Various scholars have argued just how much or little non-Jeremiac additions are here contained, and the issue is still an open question. In the matter of detail, recourse must be made to fuller commentaries. What must be maintained is that Jeremiah's spirit and hand are here pertinent. Jeremiah was not only concerned with the lot of his own people; his prophecy has a wider range.

a. Against Egypt (xlvi. 1–28)

Jeremiah begins with Egypt, because they were of old Israel's oppressors and of late their deceivers.

i. The battle of Carchemish (xlvi. 1–12).

Egypt's ambition was checked and humbled at the battle of Carchemish. This was one of the most decisive battles of history, on whose bitter field the dream of Pharaoh Necho of Egypt crashed into ruin. First the verses thrill as the spirit of an exultant army confronts the foe on the eve of battle; then comes the panic of a smitten army as it breaks up in flight. As nowhere else, perhaps, these verses reveal the insight of Jeremiah's mind as it bears on political implications of his day, revealing also the sanity and clarity of his thinking. He sees in the Babylonian crown prince, Nebuchadnezzar, the will and the force to overthrow the environing enemies of Israel, Egypt included. Thus the line of Yahweh's will lay clear—peace must be made with him as Yahweh's new and strange scourge of nations. It is a day of Yahweh. The Hebrew of verse 5 is somewhat unusual; the LXX omits the verb 'to see' and reads, 'Wherefore are they dismayed?' This makes the meaning clearer. The *Lydians* (9) were probably a people dwelling on or near the border of Egypt. The three nations mentioned in this verse supplied contingents to the Egyptian army and were probably Egypt's allies (cf. Ezk. xxx. 5).

ii. Missing the flood-tide (xlvi. 13–26).

With piercing insight Jeremiah saw that the overthrow at Carchemish left Egypt open to later invasion. Behind that Egyptian collapse, on foreign soil and on home soil, Jeremiah saw the will and act of God. *Migdol . . . Noph . . . Tahpanhes* (14) were border cities of Egypt, in the direction of Asia; *Noph* (i.e. Memphis) was for a time the capital of Lower Egypt. Verse 15 is clearer in the LXX than in the Massoretic Text: 'Why is Apis fled?' (Apis, the sacred bull of Egypt, incarnation of Osiris, the god of Egypt). 'Thy strong one (lit. 'thy choice calf') stood not, because Yahweh did thrust him down.' Better follow the LXX or Vulg. in verse 17, and read the imperative for the perfect tense of the Massoretic Text: 'Call ye the name (Heb. *qir'u shem* for *qar'u sham*) of Pharaoh "crash", "noise".' In such symbolism Pharaoh's name is recast as 'crash', with the addition that this exultant soldier and ruler failed to come in time. In war as in politics, 'there is a tide in the affairs of men which, taken at the flood, leads on to fortune.' He was 'found wanting' in the hour of the ordeal.

As Tabor is among the mountains . . . (18); i.e. Nebuchadnezzar towering above all others. Pharaoh must yield before him, even as other mountains must yield in majesty to Tabor and Carmel. For *destruction* (20) the RV mg. 'gadfly' is preferable; a touch of imagery for the Babylonian attack, descriptive of a biting charge causing wild flight. Instead of *cometh; it cometh* (20) (RV 'is come, it is come'), read with LXX, Syr., etc. 'upon her'. In the crucial hour of battle, Egypt's mercenaries are but as calves in the hands of the butcher. The imagery of verses 22, 23 is ambiguous. If with the LXX we read 'a hissing serpent' we have an effective contrast, a sound of an incredible weakness where the roar as of a lion is necessary, the snake creeping back into its hole. The hiss of enmity is ineffective, as the Babylonians come on as an army of wood-cutters levelling Egypt as a forest appointed for timber felling. In Egyptian thought the snake is royalty symbolized. *Multitude* ('Amon', AV mg.) *of No* (25) is the chief god of Thebes, the capital of Upper Egypt. The LXX omits the phrase *and Pharaoh, and Egypt, with their gods, and their kings* (25). The hint of Egypt's restoration (26) possibly implies that Yahweh is only destroyer for a time; there will be re-creation in His time.

iii. A message of comfort (xlvi. 27, 28).

These verses are a repetition of xxx. 10, 11, a note more in line with the thought and style of Isaiah than Jeremiah. It has been suggested that in both places they may be an addition. The main argument against their validity here is that they assume the captivity as having already taken place. But it is quite in keeping with Jeremiah's thought to look ahead and see the future as an accomplished fact. So certain was he of its fulfilment that he speaks of it as already fulfilled.

b. Against the Philistines (xlvii. 1–7)

The Philistines were of course Israel's own enemies. Their power had been considerably reduced in the days of David, but they apparently managed to maintain their nationhood until the days of the Babylonians. The day of their débâcle, then, is a phase of the day of Yahweh. *Caphtor* (4), i.e. Crete, the original home of the Philistines (cf. Am. ix. 7), indicates that disaster has overwhelmed the Philistines at home. *Before that Pharaoh smote Gaza* (1). When Pharaoh smote Gaza is not known. It may have been on his way to the engagement with Josiah in which the latter was killed, or it may have been on his way back, or perhaps some other occasion. *Waters rise up out of the north* (2). Waters sometimes signify calamities, and sometimes multitudes of people and nations. Here they signify both. The Babylonians *out of the north* will come as a mighty flood, and that will mean calamity as far as the Philistines are concerned. *Baldness* (5) suggests completion of disaster, as a sign of deep mourning, as does also the 'gash' or cuttings in the flesh. The LXX reads 'Anakim', a tall people, for *their valley* (5) in the AV and Massoretic Text. The Anakim were connected with the Philistines (cf. Jos. xi. 22). They were a giant race and dwelt near Hebron in prehistoric times. By accepting *it* (AV, LXX, Syr., Vulg.) for 'thou' (Massoretic Text) verses 6, 7 serve as a kind of antiphony: one voice (6) is the bitter cry of the Philistines under the stroke of Yahweh, and the other (7) is the prophetic intimation that the stroke is Yahweh's judgment.

c. Against Moab (xlviii. 1-47)

The country of Moab was the elevated and rich plateau which lay east of the Dead Sea. Prof. Driver says: 'Originally (Nu. xxi. 26) the Moabite territory extended as far north as Heshbon, to the north-east of the Dead Sea, but the Israelites, after their conquest of the country east of Jordan, considered the territory north of Arnon to belong to Reuben (Jos. xiii. 15-21), and regarded the Arnon as the border of Moab. But Reuben did not ultimately remain in possession of the district allotted to it; and so here, as in Is. xv—xvi, many of the cities assigned in Jos. xiii. 15-21 to Reuben are mentioned as occupied by Moab.' The poem is perhaps the most highly finished production of Jeremiah's writings. If one makes a comparison with Is. xv and xvi, extensive borrowing is inescapable. Both the Isaiah passages should be carefully studied, especially xvi. 6 (cf. 29).

i. **Yahweh versus Moab's god, Chemosh** (xlviii. 1-10). The arrogance of Moab is founded on its god, thus both god and the priests of Moab are to be driven into exile (7, 8). *Woe unto Nebo* (1); i.e. the city of that name, not the better-known mountain of the same name. *Misgab* (1); this place is mentioned nowhere else. The word signifies 'a high retreat' and was probably the name of a fortress. *Heshbon* (2) was an ancient and famous city on the east of Jordan: Joshua allotted it to Reuben, but in Jeremiah's time it was in the hands of Moab. *Madmen* (2) is nowhere else mentioned. The LXX, Syr., Vulg. read: 'Yea, thou (i.e. Moab) shalt be utterly brought to silence'. The LXX should perhaps also be followed in 4b: 'Its cry can be heard as far as Goar'. This place lay at the extreme south-east end of the Dead Sea, and the implication, according to this reading, would be that the cry of Moab is thus heard from one end and the other. *For in the going up of Luhith . . .* (5); better, 'men climb the pass to Luhith in tears'. *Lives* (6) means 'living souls', for the term *nephesh* is the 'breath-soul' animating the body, not incarnate within it, as in Greek thought. *Thou hast trusted in thy works* (7); i.e. in thy undertakings, measures of defence, etc. The LXX has 'in thy fastnesses', and this may be the original reading. *No city shall escape* (8) has perhaps primary reference to the capital city of Moab. *The plain shall be destroyed* (8); i.e. the extensive elevated plateau on which most of the Moabite cities lay.

ii. **A contrast in judgment** (xlviii. 11-15). *Israel* (13) had trusted in the Bethel sanctuary in which Yahweh was represented by the golden bull, but in vain. Moab had had an immunity from judgment, as wine that had not been changed from vessel to vessel to save it from contamination of the lees (i.e. dregs); but now in the judgment of exile *Moab shall be ashamed of Chemosh* (13), a god who in time of peril was impotence itself against the power of Yahweh, the living God. The only clear meaning of verse 15 is that of spoliation

iii. **The calamity of Moab** (xlviii. 16-25). So

dire is Moab's distress that even her enemies are moved to sympathy. *Staff* and *rod* (17) are figures of strength and authority; both will disappear in the day of judgment. *Daughter* (18) is a figure for population. *Dibon* (18) lay on two hills (hence *come down*), some thirteen miles east of the Dead Sea. It was here that the famous Moabite Stone was found in 1868. The loss of security and might is seen in verse 25; *horn* is a figure of power.

iv. **Moab's antagonist** (xlviii. 26-34). Moab is to be drunk, not with her famous wine, but by the terror of her antagonist, Yahweh. The LXX reading of verse 26 is: 'Moab has clapped his hands (i.e. in derision) but himself shall be derided.' Their earlier derision of Israel has come home to roost in judgment. Cf. verse 29 with Is. xvi. 6. The RV gives a better and clearer reading of verse 30. The first person, as consonant with the whole section, is required in verse 31 ('I will mourn'). Cf. also with Is. xv. 5, xvi. 7, 11. Instead of *men* (31) read 'raisin cakes', made of raisins and ground meal for festival use at religious gatherings. Cf. verses 32, 33 with Is. xvi. 9, 10. The LXX corrects *even to the sea of Jazer* (32) to 'as far as Jazer'; this latter was probably a town north of Heshbon, but this is only conjectural (cf. Is. xvi. 8). Instead of *none shall tread with shouting* (33) read 'the treader shall not tread'. Cf. Is. xv. 4-6 with verse 34. *The waters also of Nimrim shall be desolate* (34). The meaning apparently is, they will be dried up, their sources being stopped by the enemy (cf. 2 Ki. iii. 25).

v. **The wail of Moab** (xlviii. 35-39). The cause of it is God. He will end Moabite worship (35), followed by that people's moaning cry (36-38). Yahweh has shattered Moab as a vessel no longer fit for service (38b), and Moab is a shame and derision (39). *That offereth in the high places* (35); read with LXX 'him that goeth up to the high place'. In verse 36 for *mine heart* the LXX has 'harp of Moab', but the Massoretic Text is more germane to Jeremiah's nature, which had not become petrified by hate, but remained sensitive even to an enemy's hurt. Cf. Is. xv. 3 with verse 38. Read the imperative mood, 'Lament ye', instead of *They shall howl* (AV) or 'how do they howl' (RV) in verse 39.

vi. **Yahweh has the last word in judgment** (xlviii. 40-47). The LXX omits from verse 40 the words *Behold . . . Moab. He shall fly as an eagle* (40); properly a griffon-vulture; here a figure of the foe, Nebuchadnezzar. *Kerioth* (41) was an important city of Moab; it is mentioned also in Am. ii. 2. Verses 45-47 are absent from the LXX. Verses 45b and 46 are based, with slight variations, upon Nu. xxi. 28 and xxiv. 17: Balaam's oracle against Moab is about to be enacted. Verse 47 may well reflect the pity of Jeremiah's heart as reflecting that of Yahweh. Wrath is always God's 'strange work', and mercy is ever native to His heart. Moab is to be thrust under fierce discipline, not doomed to destruction.

d. Against Ammon (xlix. 1–6)

This short paragraph contains two distinct thoughts: the condemnation and the restoration of Ammon. The condemnation of Ammon (1–5) is due to its greed in robbing Gad of some land at an unstated time. The territory of Gad was on the east of Jordan, and the country of the Ammonites lay east of that. Instead of *their king* (1, 3) the LXX, Syr., and Vulg. read Milcom; this was the name of Ammon's national god (1 Ki. xi. 5, 33), but the Hebrew could also mean 'king'. Rabbah was their capital city on the river Jabbok. *Heap* (2), Heb. *tell*, is a mound consisting of ruins of any formerly inhabited site, whether city or village. *Her daughters shall be burned with fire* (2) is a figure for the surrounding towns or villages. The LXX has 'her high places'. *Heshbon* (3) appears to be out of place here, for it was known as a Moabite city, and *Ai* (3) is an unknown place. *Thy flowing valley* (4) is omitted by the Syr. and has the appearance of a dittography. Glorying in the valley (4) probably means esteeming highly its fertility, which was made possible by the waters of the river Arnon. The prophecy ends on the note of restoration (6). Once again this judgment is not to be complete, for Yahweh will bring back Ammon from captivity.

e. Against Edom (xlix. 7–22)

Edom, Israel's traditional foe, lay to the south of Moab. Many of the expressions used in Jeremiah's prophecy appear also in Obadiah. The common passages may be based upon some older prophecy, which both Obadiah and Jeremiah adapt in their own way. Unlike the prophecy against Ammon, there is no message of hope and restoration for Edom: judgment will be final and complete. The LXX omits the interrogation in verse 7, and is preferable. *Teman* (7) was a tribe of Edom in the north of the country; here it stands for the whole people. *Dwell deep* (8) is a synonym for escape by seeking out some impregnable refuge. *Esau* (8); also represents Edom (cf. Gn. xxv. 30). *Dedan* (8) was a south-eastern neighbour (cf. Ezk. xxv. 13). Only those who *dwell deep* will escape Edom's oncoming disaster. *I have made Esau bare* (10); i.e. all the fortresses of Edom are laid bare and he has no hiding-place; in short, there is no escape from judgment. *Drink of the cup* (12); i.e. the cup of Yahweh's anger. If Israel has to drink of this cup, surely Edom cannot hope to escape it. *Bozrah* (13), a city in the north of Edom, about twenty miles south-east of the Dead Sea. The physical topography is referred to in verse 16. Stanley gives a good description of it in his *Sinai and Palestine* (pp. 88ff.). The figure of Sodom and Gomorrah, which in l. 40 is applied to Babylon, is here applied to Edom (18). With verse 19 cf. also l. 44. As a lion comes up from the thick growth of semi-tropical vegetation fringing the banks of Jordan, so the enemy will swoop upon Edom and its cities (19); and as a lion scatters a flock, so the enemy will scatter the inhabitants of Edom (20).

f. Against Damascus (xlix. 23–27)

The scene of judgment now shifts to the north, to Damascus, the ancient capital of Syria. Damascus and her dependent cities shall be seized with panic and shall become disquieted with terror as the turbulent sea. Her proverbial fertility and beauty are to be wasted by fire. *Hamath . . . Arpad* (23); two cities named together in Is. x. 9, xxxvi. 19 and xxxvii. 13. Hamath was approximately 110 miles north of Damascus, and Arpad some ninety-five miles north of Hamath. For *sorrow* (23) read 'disquiet' or 'care'. The term *sea* (23) is to be understood figuratively, since Damascus was far from the sea (cf. Is. lvii. 20). Verse 25 is spoken by a native of Damascus. Cf. verse 27 with Am. i. 4.

g. Against Kedar, or the Arabians (xlix. 28–33)

A like threatened doom that can be escaped only by flight. Kedar was an Ishmaelite tribe, nomadic and wealthy in flocks and herds, skilled in archery, altogether representative of desert tribes, whom Nebuchadnezzar conquered. *Hazor* (28) is given as a dwelling-place (33) and may have been the Arabic settlement south of Palestine. *Their curtains* (29); i.e. their tent hangings. *A purpose against you* (30); the Hebrew text has 'them'. *Arise* (31) is addressed to the assailants of Hazor. *That dwelleth without care* (31); lit. confidently.

h. Against Elam (xlix. 34–39)

The uniqueness of this oracle lies in its being dated in Zedekiah's reign, when the first deportation had taken place. Elam was situated east of Babylon.

i. Against Babylon (l. 1—li. 64)

These two chapters contain a long and impassioned prophecy against Babylon. The oracle presents many difficulties. The critical view is that it is not from the hands of Jeremiah, though many of his familiar terms are used. The argument against the Jeremiac authorship may be stated as follows. First, the historical situation cannot be that of the fourth year of Zedekiah, i.e. 593 B.C. (cf. li. 59, 60). The Jews are already in exile (l. 4, 17, li. 34), the temple has suffered violence (l. 28, li. 11), and, moreover, the end of Babylon appears in sight (l. 8, li. 6, 45). Secondly, the point of view is not that of Jeremiah in 593 B.C. From chapters xxvii—xxix we learn that round about that time Jeremiah was opposing the false prophets who prophesied that Nebuchadnezzar's yoke would be broken in a very short time, and exhorted the exiles of the first deportation to settle down for a considerable period of time. These chapters, however, assume that Babylon's fall is at hand. Thirdly, it is said that the temper is not that of Jeremiah. He was convinced that the Babylonians were God's agents for the punishment of Judah—a work which had not yet been accomplished in the fourth year of Zedekiah. These chapters on the contrary reveal an anti-Babylonian spirit and a deep satisfaction at the prospect of their approaching fate.

The suggestion is therefore made that this oracle may have been the work of an unknown prophet who was acquainted with the writings of Jeremiah and who used many of his expressions. The time would probably have been towards the close of the Babylonian Empire, say 538 B.C. A later editor of the book of Jeremiah prefixed it to li. 59–64, which was Jeremiah's original oracle against Babylon, consisting of a forecast in very general terms of Babylon's downfall. Those who take this view point out that in the LXX the ascription is absent from l. 1.

Young (*Introduction to the Old Testament*) feels that 'there is no sufficient reason for denying the Jeremianic authorship'. If the 593 date for these chapters is accepted Jeremiah 'is simply placing himself in the future and portraying the temple as destroyed'. Alternatively, and more probably, they are, Prof. Young suggests, an expanded form of his original message against Babylon 'prepared in Egypt under divine inspiration after the sanctuary at Jerusalem had actually been destroyed'. This would also explain the allusions to the exile.

Babylon is taken (l. 2) is the prophetic future tense: the prophet sees in vision the doom as already consummated. *Bel* (2) is a title of Merodach (i.e. Marduk, the supreme god of Babylon), meaning Lord. *Out of the north* (3) is a cryptic saying suggestive of the sinister hidden quality of the north, or as referring to the Persian conqueror, since Media was north of Babylon. In the confusion occasioned by this disaster, Israel, now moved to penitence and covenant loyalty, is given the chance to escape (4–8). *Let us join ourselves* (5); the Heb. reads 'they shall join themselves'. *We offend not* (7); contrast this with ii. 3. *The habitation of justice* (7); lit. 'homestead'. *The hope of their fathers* (7); this is the reading of the LXX; the Hebrew text adds, 'Yahweh'. *As the he goats before the flocks* (8); i.e. leading the way.

Yahweh summons the spoilers against Babylon (9–13). These verses speak of the spoilers of Babylon, the sin of Babylon, and the consequences for Babylon of her sins. 'The mills of God grind slowly, yet they grind exceeding small.' *Your mother* (12); Babylon is regarded as the mother of the individual citizens (cf. Ho. ii. 5, where the 'mother' is Israel). *It shall not be inhabited* (13); the Hebrew reads 'it shall not sit'. Babylon's attackers are bidden to raise the battle-cry as they smite her into impotence (14–16). *She hath given her hand* (15); i.e. submitted herself. *They shall flee every one to his own land* (16); this apparently alludes to the many foreigners settled in Babylon. Israel and Judah are to be restored when Babylon, as Assyria earlier, suffers judgment (17–20). Restoration shall inaugurate a fresh beginning, the remnant will be forgiven, and the sin will be forgotten. *I will punish the king of Babylon . . . as I have punished the king of Assyria* (18). Babylon over-

threw Assyria, and was herself overthrown by Medo-Persia. *His soul shall be satisfied* (19); the soul in Hebrew psychology was regarded as the seat, or organ, of appetite.

The enemy is again invited to attack Babylon (21–27). *Merathaim* (21) is evidently meant to signify Babylon. South Babylonia was known as *nar Marratim* ('land of the bitter river'), and *Merathaim* may be based upon that. *Pekod* (21); a people of Babylonia, bordering on Elam. *Pakad* in Hebrew means 'to punish' or 'to visit', and the prophet may have mentioned the place seeing he had punishment in mind. *Great destruction* (22); Heb. 'a great breaking'. *Thou hast striven against the Lord* (24); lit. 'excited thyself against the Lord'. *The weapons of his indignation* (25) is a figure for the nations who unconsciously perform God's will and purposes. *Open her storehouses* (26); i.e. her granaries or fodder-stores. *Bullocks* (27) signifies young warriors led to utter defeat (cf. Is. xxxiv. 7). The escape of Yahweh's people (28) has a dual inference: His providence over them on the one hand, and on the other His punishment of Babylon for their desecration of His temple. The proud stumble and fall, with no chance or escape, and with fire to complete what bow and sword had begun (29–32). *Thy day is come* (31); the LXX has 'the time of thy visitation has come'. Israel and Judah may be enslaved, yet they have a redeemer, and He is strong. That Lord of hosts is peace to them but disquiet to their oppressors (33, 34).

Verses 35–40 describe the doom and utter desolation of Babylon. Everyone and everything will feel the bitterness of the avenger's sword. *A sword is upon the liars* (36); an allusion probably to the false prophets and diviners who promised Babylon security. *They shall dote* (36); i.e. become foolish. *A drought is upon her waters* (38); the LXX and Syr. have 'a sword'. The Hebrew for 'sword' is *hereb*, and that for 'drought' *horeb*. The drought would be a sword, and a sharp one at that. Verses 41–43 are repeated from vi. 22–24, but the sense is changed. Verses 44–46 are repeated from xlix. 19ff., where they are applied to Edom. In xlix. 19 the lion signifies Nebuchadnezzar; here it signifies Cyrus.

Babylon's destroyer (li. 1–6) is as one winnowing chaff from grain, a synonym of judgment for that nation's crime against the Holy One of Israel. Israel and Judah have their protector. Let Israel escape when He exacts the due of guilt. *That dwell in the midst of them* (1). The RV reads 'Leb-kamai' which means 'the heart (or 'midst', 'centre') of them that rise up against me'. *Fanners* (2); this is the reading of the LXX, the Targum, and the Vulg., but the Hebrew text has 'strangers' (*zarim* for *zorim*). The reading of verse 3 is difficult, and its original meaning is obscure. *Their land* (5) apparently refers not to Judah but to the land of Babylon, though it was true of both.

An oracle of bitter irony is contained in verses 7–10. There may be balm in Gilead, but not for Babylon. Her judgment reaches up to the judgment-bar of Yahweh. *The nations are mad* (7); i.e. bewildered and helpless. *Fallen and destroyed* (8); Babylon is broken like a cup. *If so be she may be healed* (8); the words are meant ironically. Yahweh's strange work is described in verses 11–14. He calls a nation that knows Him not to carry out His will to wrath. It is to make an end as though it were destiny incarnate. *The kings of the Medes* (11); it was the Medes and Persians who destroyed the Babylonian Empire. *Make the watch strong* (12); i.e. blockade it closely. *Watchmen* (12), here, does not mean those who 'look out' but those who guard or blockade the city. *Caterpillars* (14); probably locusts. Verses 15–19 are an interpolation from Je. x. 12–16, but adduced to show the impotence of Babylon's gods to save her. The reference in verses 20–24 is probably to Cyrus, as Yahweh's unconscious agent in the humbling of Babylon; but they could also be applied to Babylon herself as Yahweh's earlier instrument of judgment on Judah. *Battle axe* (20); lit. a 'shatterer'; something that dashes in pieces. Cf. Na. ii. 1; Ezk. ix. 2. Verses 25, 26 are either an interpolation originally referring to a mountainous tribe such as Edom, or they are introduced figuratively of Babylon, which was actually built on a plain. *A burnt mountain* (25); i.e. barren and desolate as an extinct volcano.

Yahweh's trumpet summons His agents to effect His decree of judgment against Bablyon (27–32). The runners (31, 32) are the bearers of the tidings of her doom. *Prepare the nations* (27); Heb. 'sanctify'. *Ararat* (27); the Urartu of the Assyrian inscriptions, corresponding to the modern Armenia. *Minni* (27); the Mannai of the Assyrian inscriptions, south-east of Lake Van. *Ashchenaz* (27); a people somewhere near the above two. *Their might hath failed* (30); Heb. 'dried up'. *The passages are stopped* (32); lit. the 'crossing places', i.e. the fords across the Euphrates. *The reeds* (32) had something to do with the defences of Babylon.

The inevitable harvest is declared in verse 33. The drama of the eternal courtroom is given in verses 34–37. Zion states her case against her aggressor—spoliation, maltreatment, wrong, exile, physical injury. Yahweh makes her case His own. As a result, Babylon, the fabulous garden of the East, becomes a jackals' lair, a scorn and a desolation. *I will dry up her sea* (36); this may be a reference to the great lake which Nebuchadnezzar constructed for the defence of Babylon.

Verses 38–44 describe the final end of Babylon. *Sheshach* (41) is a synonym for the city (cf. xxv. 26). In verse 39 the LXX rendering 'be stupefied' is more likely than the AV *that they may rejoice*. For *I will make their feasts* (39) the Syr. has 'I will poison', etc. Verses 45–48 appear fragmentary and reduplicative. The LXX omits them. The Syr. rendering of verse 49, 'Babylon's slain ones shall fall in all the earth', is preferable to the AV *at Babylon shall fall the slain of all the earth*. If, in addition, we read 'Babylon shall fall for the slain of Israel', the meaning becomes clear. Babylon is about to fall for the slain of Israel just as, for Babylon, the slain of all the earth had fallen. The summons to Israel therefore is to remember Yahweh and Jerusalem and its desecration.

Yahweh's twofold oracle against Babylon is recorded in verses 52–58. Babylon's idols and high-soaring buildings are to meet their match (52–53). The crash of doom (54–57) is a fitting recompense from Yahweh, with whom destiny finally rests. In the hour when Babylon needs her best men at their fittest, they are made drunken by the wrath of Yahweh. *Mount up to heaven* (53); lit. 'cut off', i.e. making herself inaccessible. This is the regular meaning of the Hebrew word rendered 'fortify'. Fenced or fortified cities were cities that were 'cut off'.

In verses 59–64 we have Jeremiah's charge to Seraiah. 'Quarter-master' is preferable to 'chief chamberlain' (59, AV mg.), as the official charged with the king's comfort at any halting-place at nightfall (lit. 'prince or captain of a resting-place'; cf. Nu. x. 33). Seraiah probably was a brother of Baruch, being a son of Neriah, the son of Maaseiah, as in xxxii. 12. *They shall be weary* (64), or 'shall weary themselves', is absent from the LXX and is probably a dittography from verse 58. *Thus far . . . Jeremiah* (64b) is commonly understood as a compiler's note added to separate the foregoing from chapter lii, which is practically identical with 2 Ki. xxiv. 18ff. and xxv. 21, 27–30.

XVII. A RETROSPECT. lii. 1–34

This closing chapter deals with the fortunes of king Zedekiah, the city of Jerusalem, the sacred vessels of the temple, and of king Jehoiachin. See li. 64n. above. Presumably it was included with a view to rounding off the book of Jeremiah. The intention, probably, was to show the validity of the prophecies in that they were fulfilled, unlike the prophecies of the false prophets. A curious contrast, however, is that no mention is made of the Babylonian king's command to safeguard Jeremiah, such as we find in xxxix. 11–14, while in verses 17–23 a detailed account is given of the temple equipment which is not mentioned in chapter xxxix. The appointment of Gedaliah and his subsequent assassination are also omitted.

a. Zedekiah's final captivity (lii. 1–27)

Zedekiah rebelled, was overthrown, and the Babylonian monarch inflicted upon him, his family and his people the terror that had haunted the soul of Jeremiah in prospect. Verses 4–16 were given in chapter xxxix. 1–10, and a parallel of the whole section is found in 2 Ki. xxiv. 18—xxv. 21. Verses 31–34, touching the fate of Jehoiachin, are also given in 2 Ki. xxv. 27–30. The famine of verse 6 is dated, but not dogmatically. Verses 10b and 11b are not found in 2 Kings. For a comparison of the two accounts see the larger commentaries. *Certain of the poor of the people* (15) is not found in 2 Kings, and may be deleted here, since it apparently contradicts verse 16 and may have been taken by error from that verse. *Without weight* (20); i.e. not actually weighed.

b. Conclusion (lii. 28-34)

Verses 28-30 are omitted from the LXX but need not be deleted, especially when its reserve as to number is considered. On these three deportations, more exhaustive commentaries should be read, since there are inherent difficulties. *In the seven and thirtieth year* (31); i.e. 561 B.C. *Evil-merodach* (31); he succeeded Nebuchadnezzar and reigned for two years (561-559 B.C.). *Before him* (33) is a synonym for the royal table. *A portion* (34); lit. 'a matter of a day in its day'.

F. CAWLEY.

LAMENTATIONS

INTRODUCTION

I. TITLE

The fuller title 'The Lamentations of Jeremiah' is found in LXX and Gk. Uncial MSS. But the Talmud and Rabbinical writers refer to it simply as 'Lamentations' (*qinoth*) or 'How!' ('*ekhah*), the opening word in the Hebrew.

II. POSITION IN CANON

In keeping with the longer title, LXX places the book immediately after the prophecies of Jeremiah, as in our English versions. In the Hebrew Bible it is not to be found among the prophetical writings but occupies the middle position among the five Festival Rolls (Megilloth) which immediately follow the three poetical books in the Hagiographa or third division of the Hebrew canon. Each of the Megilloth was read at an annual festival, Lamentations being read on the ninth day of Ab (about mid-July), the anniversary of the destruction of the temple by Nebuchadnezzar king of Babylon. In the Talmud, the poetical books and the Megilloth are rearranged in what appears to be a chronological order, viz. Ruth, Psalms, Job, Proverbs, Ecclesiastes, Song of Solomon, Lamentations, Daniel, Esther, etc.

III. AUTHORSHIP AND DATE

The tradition that Jeremiah composed these poems goes back to the position and title of the book in LXX, where it is introduced by the words: 'And it came to pass, after Israel had been carried away captive, and Jerusalem had become desolate, that Jeremiah sat weeping, and lamented with this lamentation over Jerusalem and said . . .' It is also asserted in Syr. Targum and in the Talmud (Baba Bathra) that 'Jeremiah wrote his own book, Kings, and Lamentations'. In 2 Ch. xxxv. 25 reference is made to this prophet's lamentations over the death of king Josiah which are there stated to have been written down and to have become 'an ordinance in Israel'; with this cf. La. iv. 20 and ii. 6. But our present book concerns not so much the death of a king as the destruction of a city, and iv. 20 could equally well refer to Zedekiah in spite of his unworthiness (cf. the sentiment in 2 Sa. i. 14, 21). Nevertheless Jeremiah as the weeping prophet (see Je. ix. 1, xiv. 17–22, xv. 10–18, etc.) might conceivably be held to be the author also of Lamentations, were it not for the fact that there are certain difficulties in accepting this view. The style is much more elaborate and artificial than that of Jeremiah, and in chapters ii and iv is more like that of Ezekiel. Chapter iii recalls Pss. cxix and cxliii. The attitude to foreign powers implied in iv. 17 is certainly not that of the 'collaborationist' Jeremiah and does not reflect the prophet's own experience.

Many, therefore, regard the author as a younger contemporary of Jeremiah, who, like him, was an eyewitness of the heart-rending calamities which befell Jerusalem at the time of her capture by the Babylonian armies in 587–586 B.C. Others consider chapters ii and iv as the work of an eyewitness (note the writer's concern for the fate of the children in ii. 11, 12, 19, 20, iv. 4, 10), *c*. 580 B.C., to which have been added, perhaps from different sources, the national lament of chapter i, the personal lament of chapter iii, and the prayer of chapter v. The date of this material may be about 540 B.C. Some would place the whole collection much later and make the book refer to the siege of Jerusalem in 170–168 B.C. by Antiochus Epiphanes or even by Pompey in 63 B.C., but this is very improbable. In favour of the traditional dating in the period of the exile is the despondent note throughout which suggests a time before the rise of Cyrus the Persian. There is also the fact that this particular period of Babylonian history is noted for its threnodies or dirges over fallen cities. Cuneiform inscriptions are extant in which 'the daughter of . . .' is bidden lament her lot (cf. ii. 1). The technique may thus have been learnt by the Jews in exile.

IV. STRUCTURE

Rabbinic commentators refer to 'the seven acrostics' and it will be noticed at once that each chapter has twenty-two verses, corresponding to the number and order of letters in the Hebrew alphabet, with the exception of chapter iii which has sixty-six, each successive letter having three verses allotted to it instead of one. This alphabetical arrangement is said to show that 'Israel had sinned from aleph to tau', i.e., as we should say, from A to Z, just as in Ps. cxix the implication is that the law should command a man's whole attention and desire. In chapter v, however, the successive letters of the alphabet are not employed, although some scholars contend that this must have been so originally.

The first four poems make use of the halting rhythm known as the dirge (*qinah*), i.e. 3 : 2, which is also found in Jeremiah.

OUTLINE OF CONTENTS

I. FIRST ODE. i. 1–22

    a. The desolation of Jerusalem (i. 1–7)
    b. Sin brings suffering (i. 8–11)
    c. A cry for compassion (i. 12–22)

II. SECOND ODE. ii. 1–22

    a. The Lord is an enemy (ii. 1–9)
    b. The horrors of famine (ii. 10–13)
    c. Prophets false and true (ii. 14–17)
    d. A call to supplication (ii. 18–22)

III. THIRD ODE. iii. 1–66

    a. The cry of the afflicted (iii. 1–21)
    b. The mercies of God (iii. 22–39)
    c. A call for conversion (iii. 40–42)
    d. The sorrows of sin (iii. 43–54)
    e. Comfort and cursing (iii. 55–66)

IV. FOURTH ODE. iv. 1–22

    a. Then and now (iv. 1–12)
    b. The consequences of sin (iv. 13–20)
    c. Edom shall not escape (iv. 21, 22)

V. FIFTH ODE. v. 1–22

    a. An appeal for mercy (v. 1–10)
    b. The shamefulness of sin (v. 11–18)
    c. God's eternal throne (v. 19–22)

COMMENTARY

I. FIRST ODE. i. 1–22

a. The desolation of Jerusalem (i. 1–7)

The opening words of this 'political funeral song' (Gunkel) depict Jerusalem as a woman bereaved of her husband and children and from whom *all her beauty is departed* (6) through persistent sorrow. So, many years later, a Roman coin, which commemorates this same city's destruction by Titus in A.D. 70, shows her as a woman sitting under a palm-tree and bears the inscription 'Judaea capta' (cf. verse 3). She upon whom has been centred so glorious a heritage of spiritual and prophetic religion is now brought to utter desolation *for the multitude of her transgressions* (5).

All her friends (2), those surrounding nations to whom she had looked for help, have failed her miserably, and her streets and places of assembly, whether for merchandise (*her gates*) or for the joyous solemnities of worship, are now deserted (4). *Her princes* (6), i.e. Zedekiah and his courtiers (2 Ki. xxv. 4; Je. xxxix. 4, 5), have turned tail and fled away.

b. Sin brings suffering (i. 8–11)

The hint given in verse 5 is now taken up and developed, and eventually becomes one of the major themes of the book. *Jerusalem . . . is* *removed* (8). She 'is become as an unclean thing' (RV), because she *hath grievously sinned* (8). Her sufferings are not unmerited. She has failed to remember *her last end* (9), i.e. to consider the consequences of her actions, until it has become too late. Countless warnings have gone unheeded, and now she is reaping the fruits of her iniquity. But even while her plight is thus being graphically described, she is pictured as beginning to cry out to God, and her cries break in upon the poet's meditations (9b, 11b).

c. A cry for compassion (i. 12–22)

Zion's first supplicating sobs have already been overheard in the previous section. Now not only the casual passers-by (12), but all nations (18) and, lastly, the Lord Himself (20), are asked to ponder, with sympathetic understanding, the grievous affliction which has been thus placed upon her. The words in verse 12 have long been associated with our Lord in His passion. Although Christ deprecated sympathy for Himself (Lk. xxiii. 28), He identified Himself so closely with human sin and its consequences (2 Cor. v. 21) that, as these prophetic words suggest, He would have us consider the significance of that identification.

The language in verse 15 recalls that of the great festivals of the Jewish year. But instead of

x

the favoured people of Israel, their enemies are summoned to a feast, the object of which is not the praises of God for His bounty in vintage or harvest, but the crushing of the Jews themselves in the winepress of affliction. Yet there is no complaint against the divine justice, no problem of theodicy as in the book of Job. *The Lord is righteous* (18); and so it is to Him that resort is made, for all human aid is ineffectual (17, 19, 21). He may punish, but He will bring comfort to those who are led to recognize the reasons for such punishment. And even the very instruments of the divine judgment will themselves be judged by Him whose way is perfect (Ps. xviii. 30). We have here a vivid demonstration of faith in God's sovereign power, wisdom and grace.

II. SECOND ODE. ii. 1–22

a. The Lord is an enemy (ii. 1–9)

With gruesome details of scenes which he himself had witnessed the poet describes in this elegy *the day of the Lord's anger* (22). God Himself seemed to have become pre-eminently Judah's enemy (5, RV), for all these terrible happenings were but the outworking of His wrath. He, and not a mere human foe, was responsible for them. The temple (*the beauty of Israel*) and the ark with its mercy-seat (*his footstool*; cf. 1 Ch. xxviii. 2), as well as the forts and palaces and the humble dwellings of the people, had been cast to the ground and destroyed (1, 2). Even *his tabernacle*, the place of all places where mercy might confidently be awaited, had been *violently taken away* (6), thereby showing the powerlessness of outward ritual to avert God's judgments from a guilty people. God 'makes plans to destroy' (8): a striking testimony to His sovereign activity. Nebuchadnezzar and his Babylonian armies are completely ignored! The capture of Jerusalem, so far from being a defeat for Jehovah, was a victory for His righteousness. See Is. xlii. 24f. for the absolute supremacy of God. The wrath of God, His judicial displeasure against iniquity, is no idle term, but an awesome reality for those who render themselves liable to it. This fact makes the cross of Christ even more significant (Rom. iii. 25f.).

b. The horrors of famine (ii. 10–13)

The plight of innocent children (11, 12) is a theme which recurs in verses 19–21 and in iv. 4, 10. The writer evidently could not get the harrowing scenes out of his mind. The elders or heads of families who shared in the administration were powerless to do anything. Grave magistrates and light-hearted maidens alike were reduced to grief-stricken silence (10). Suffering such as this is always a profound mystery; but even a child cannot be considered in isolation. 'It is monstrous to charge the providence of God with the consequences of actions that He has forbidden' (W. F. Adeney). Consider also Christ's own words in Lk. xiii. 1–5. For verse 13, see RV. Trouble has burst in upon Zion like the

sea forcing its way through a breach in a sea-wall; nothing can stand against it.

c. Prophets false and true (ii. 14–17)

Thy prophets (14). This would seem to refer, not to Jeremiah or Ezekiel, who were now presumably in Egypt and Babylon respectively, but to the prophets left behind in Judah who, unlike them, were visionless (9) and afraid to expose the true cause of Zion's calamity, *thine iniquity* (14). They were men who had gone about saying 'bad luck' instead of crying 'repent!'. Their words were mocking words, little different from the taunts of the hostile spectators of the city's desolation (15, 16) and utterly apart from the fearless messages of the true prophets in accordance with which God was now fulfilling *his word that he had commanded in the days of old* (17). These shallow optimists with their *false burdens* (14) had no light to shed on the present situation.

In verses 16, 17 the usual order of initial letters is reversed and *Pe* precedes '*Ayin*, as it does also in chapters iii and iv, but not in chapter i (which may be a sign of difference of authorship). The quaint Rabbinic explanation of this feature is that 'Israel spoke with the mouth (*Pe*) what the eye ('*Ayin*) had not seen', i.e. illicit things. *Horn* (17) is the usual symbol of strength.

d. A call to supplication (ii. 18–22)

The suffering city is not only bidden to cry to the Lord (19), but words are put into the suppliant's mouth (20–22). Verse 18, however, is a little obscure. To whom does *their* refer? If to the adversaries of the previous verse, then verse 18 must begin with an insolent shout of triumph at the God of the Jews. But the succeeding words hardly seem appropriate to that end, and why is the wall addressed, and not God? We should also expect, in Hebrew, the link-word 'saying' between the statement and the cry. Many, with Calvin, prefer to take the first phrase absolutely; i.e. 'the heart of the Jews cried . . .'. Then the elegist himself speaks, urging his fellow-countrymen first of all to give free vent to their surging emotions and then to turn their griefs into prayer. He himself gives them the lead in verses 20–22. Godly sorrow that worketh repentance will, in the end, secure their deliverance (2 Cor. vii. 10).

The *wall* (18) must mean the citizens within the wall, and *the night* (19) is either the time of undisturbed reflection or a picture of sorrow itself. In verse 22, instead of summoning worshippers to a festival, God has called together His *terrors round about* (cf. Je. xx. 3, AV and RV mg.) and so encircled His people that *none escaped nor remained*.

III. THIRD ODE. iii. 1–66

a. The cry of the afflicted (iii. 1–21)

This chapter with its acrostic in triplets concentrates on the personal sufferings of the writer, although he is speaking, no doubt, 'as the typical representative of his people' (T. H. Gaster). Through all his agony there breathes a spirit of quiet resignation and confidence, especially in the second section (22–39). This is a finished product of literary art, although it is possible to detect a lack of cohesion here and there owing to the exigencies of the alphabetical framework. But in more ways than one, this poem brings us to the very heart of the book. As a foreglimpse of Christ's passion it has affinities with Is. liii and Ps. xxii.

Once more, in a series of suggestive metaphors, the sufferings are directly attributed to God: *He hath led me* (2), etc. In verse 6 see RV. One of the most striking figures here given is that of God as a huntsman, winging His arrows (RV mg. 'the sons of his quiver') against the prey (12, 13). He has also given stones instead of bread; hence the broken teeth of verse 16. But in verses 19–21 the way is prepared for a different and complementary portrait of the Almighty.

b. The mercies of God (iii. 22–39)

That such a beautiful expression of assurance in God's unfailing mercies should be found in Lamentations and in such a context is indeed remarkable and carries its own rich consolations. Cf. verse 57. *His compassions fail not* (22). Targum and Syr. have: 'The Lord's mercies, verily they cease not . . .' They are adapted to each day's requirements (cf. Dt. xxxiii. 25, 26). In verses 25ff. the poet universalizes his own experience and inculcates the duties of watchful expectancy and glad submission. 'Let him sit alone and keep silence' (28, RV), let him put his mouth to the dust like a beaten slave (29); for the infliction will pass (31), in that it does not represent God's final will for a man (32, 33). If God is so just that He cannot tolerate the illtreatment of captives, the perversion of the courts of law, or sharp practices in business (34–36), then any sufferer can afford to be patient (26). Evil too (i.e. trouble, not moral wickedness) is subject to God's control and has no independent existence (38). God is supreme (37), and can use trouble for beneficent ends. No man alive can contend that his sufferings are entirely undeserved (39). To meet them in the way suggested will turn them into means of blessing. Cf. Ps. cxix. 71.

c. A call for conversion (iii. 40–42)

'The goodness of God leadeth thee to repentance' (Rom. ii. 4). In true prophetic vein the elegist puts himself alongside his countrymen and entreats them to return to the Lord and to seek reconciliation with Him. Let them examine themselves (40) in the light of His commandments which they have *transgressed* (42), and let the lifting up of their *hands unto God in the heavens* be accompanied by the lifting up of their hearts also, i.e. let their prayers for pardon be true and sincere. Let them know too what it feels like to be unpardoned, to be under God's judgment still (42b), and they will come to appreciate all the more the wonder of His forgiveness.

d. The sorrows of sin (iii. 43–54)

The sense of dereliction which precedes every genuine conversion is then described. There comes to the soul a chastening apprehension of the wrath of God against sin and of the barrier which sin has erected between it and Him (44). The effects of sin are fully acknowledged and heartfelt grief ensues. But God is no longer regarded as an implacable enemy. His tender mercy is in view and is keenly awaited (50) by the one who had seemed beyond the reach of all help (52–54). These last moving verses suggest an actual physical experience on the part of the writer, but if so, it was an experience different from that of Jeremiah who was placed in a dry dungeon by his own people (Je. xxxviii. 6). *The daughters of my city* (51) may be the villages outside Jerusalem which were also devastated.

e. Comfort and cursing (iii. 55–66)

Out of the depths of self-despair the prayer of the penitent sinner reaches the heights of heaven. Casting himself upon the name or character of Jehovah (55), He finds that God is by his side as advocate and redeemer, with words of consolation on His gracious lips (56–58). With this section cf. Ps. lxix.

But while admitting the validity of God's judgments he cannot find it in his heart to excuse those who have been the instruments of them. They too must be punished: *Give . . . thy curse unto them* (65). Such an imprecation at this juncture may strike a jarring note, but it is well to remember that the infliction of suffering upon another man may, in the providence of God, lead that man to come to a recognition of his own sins and to seek the Lord, but it does not, on that account, render the instigator of the suffering less amenable to God's laws. The writer appears to be speaking under considerable provocation.

IV. FOURTH ODE. iv. 1–22

a. Then and now (iv. 1–12)

A series of bitter contrasts between Jerusalem in her glory and Jerusalem in her shame. Two parallel passages (1–5, 6–11) are brought to a conclusion in the reflection of verse 12, and the execution of this section is most artistic.

Verse 1 recalls the burning of the temple by Nebuzaradan in 2 Ki. xxv. 9. At such a time even the tender offices of motherhood were in abeyance. Children received worse treatment than the offspring of jackals (3, RV) or the young of the careless ostrich (see Jb. xxxix. 13–17). Sodom perished in a moment by the hand of God; Zion must undergo a long and weary punishment, meted out to her by the hands of men (6). Those normally conspicuous because of their rank or calling (7; *Nazarites*, AV; 'nobles', RV) are no longer *known in the streets*; they are indistinguishable from all the rest (8). Verse 12 is at one and the same time an illustration of arrogant self-confidence and of subsequent disillusionment.

b. The consequences of sin (iv. 13–20)

The prophets and priests who had failed to proclaim God's true word are involved in a fearful nemesis. They are treated as lepers and hurried out of the city. Even the heathen are asked to give them no shelter (15), for they are guilty men, against whom the prophet Jeremiah had spoken so often (Je. vi. 13, viii. 10, xxiii. 11, 14), and they had helped to *shed the blood of the just* (13; cf. Je. xxvi. 20–23). The people too are brought to realize that trust in an earthly ally (such as Egypt, Je. xxxvii. 7) was doomed to disappointment (17), nor could the possession of the Davidic kingship be taken as a guarantee of divine blessing and protection (20). *The anointed of the Lord* (20) is Zedekiah, Judah's last tragic king, whose fate is described in 2 Ki. xxv. 4–7. Thus ecclesiastical leaders, politicians, the king himself, have all been powerless to avert God's judgments from the guilty nation whose *end is come* (18).

c. Edom shall not escape (iv. 21, 22)

At the time of Jerusalem's capture, Edom had sought to enrich herself at her kinsmen's expense (Ob. 10–16), and her conduct at that time had been bitterly resented (Ezk. xxv. 12–14; Ps. cxxxvii. 7–9). But the Jews could console themselves with the thought that, whereas their own punishment was now accomplished (22; cf. Is. xl. 2), that of Edom was still to come: *the cup also shall pass through unto thee* (21). And when it did, it would be a sign of returning mercy for Judah. *Uz* (21), the home of Job, is probably mentioned here as showing the extent of Edomite domains. *He will discover thy sins* (22). 'Discover' is the opposite of 'cover', the usual word for 'forgive'.

V. FIFTH ODE. v. 1–22

a. An appeal for mercy (v. 1–10)

Although there are twenty-two verses in this chapter, the acrostic arrangement is missing. Here is a prayer which may reflect conditions a little later than the actual destruction of the city, and which is an impassioned congregational entreaty for divine mercy. Although God is responsible for the calamity, yet it is to Him that the sorrowing people instinctively turn for help. Was it not He who had given them their *inheritance* (2)? Their present forlorn state, in which they were compelled to purchase the bare necessities of life from their captors (4) and to seek their bread in the wilderness at the peril of their lives from marauding Bedouin (9), was a plea to God to restore them, for His own name's sake, to their rightful position in the land, so that they would no longer be under the rule of servants, i.e. Babylonian satraps who were often promoted slaves of the king's household (8). The sentiment in verse 7 is in line with the second commandment. Generations of mankind do not live in watertight compartments, and children normally have to bear, i.e. reap the consequences of, their parents' misdoings (cf. Ex. xx. 5n.; Dt. v. 9n.). That this does not, however, override personal responsibility is made clear in such passages as Ezk. xviii. 1–4.

b. The shamefulness of sin (v. 11–18)

One more glance at the awful retribution which the people of God have brought upon themselves by their persistent transgression of His laws. But the mood is one of sorrow, not resentment. All thoughts of personal revenge are absent, for the rightness of God's judgment has been freely acknowledged and the issue is left in His own hands. The poet, in the name of his people, has won through to contrite humility and patient submission. For *young men to grind* (13) was dishonouring as being women's work (cf. Jdg. xvi. 21). *Foxes* (18) are of course jackals (RV mg.).

c. God's eternal throne (v. 19–22)

The last look is reserved for the throne of God which still abides even though the throne of the Davidic dynasty has been sent crashing to the ground. Only in God is there hope for the stricken people. A great longing for reconciliation and renewal breathes through the petition of verse 21. This in turn intensifies the realization of present forsakenness (20, 22). Suffering has done its work, the prodigal has come to himself and is ready to arise and go to his Father.

Thou hast utterly rejected us (22). See AV and RV mg. It is possible to render 'unless Thou hast . . .' (which God forbid!).

L. E. H. STEPHENS-HODGE.

EZEKIEL

INTRODUCTION

I. AUTHORSHIP, DATE AND CIRCUMSTANCES

The three problems are all bound together in regard to this writing. The book is composed mainly in the first person and purports to come from the prophet Ezekiel, who is stated to be one of the Jewish exiles deported with King Jehoiachin in 597 B.C. (i. 1f.). The narrative is punctuated by progressive marks of time, beginning at the fifth year of the captivity, 593 B.C. (i. 2), continuing up to the twenty-fifth year when chapters xl—xlviii were written (xl. 1; xxix. 17ff., written in the twenty-seventh year, was later inserted by the prophet at that point for a specific reason; see commentary notes).

Until recent times the authenticity of the book was largely unquestioned but in the present century it has provided fair game for the ingenuity of some scholars. Their labours, on the other hand, have served to set forth clearly the nature of the problems presented by the book and enabled their successors the more intelligently to approach them.

Of the two chief difficulties in the way of accepting the genuineness of Ezekiel, the first may be dealt with summarily. It is held that this prophet, like his forbears, was a preacher of doom, and nothing else. All the pre-exilic prophets set themselves against the popular eschatology of their day and pronounced only judgments against Israel. How, it is asked, could a prophet in one breath proclaim judgment for sins, and in the next bestow wonderful promises on the sinful people? Some further maintain that the idea of an age of bliss came from Persia, so that all passages which speak of it must be dated after the exile, when the Israelites had been in contact with that nation. On this view a considerable portion of Ezekiel has to be pronounced late interpolation, and such is Hölscher's position. His disciple, von Gall, has applied the same criterion to all the prophets; the postulated process of gradual editing of the prophetic books, in which successive 'accretions' to the text take place in successive generations, evokes sheer wonder at the ingenuity of the scheme, but it is far too complicated to be real. Most scholars reject the notion that the hope of a kingdom of God was the sole property of the Persian nation; that hope was also indigenous to Israel.

It is hard to understand why the prophets could not have predicted a restoration after judgment; that they saw only chaos is no more to be inferred from their prophecies of doom than

it can be said that Jesus saw nothing but ruin for the chosen people when He foretold the destruction of Jerusalem (Mk. xiii. 2). From the biblical evidence it is hard to resist the dictum of Gressmann, 'World renewal necessarily follows upon world catastrophe.' Ezekiel himself provides the best answer to the question, 'How could a prophet conjoin threat and promise with any effect upon his hearers?' Apart from the development observable in the general trend of his prophecies—first judgment (i—xxxii), then consolation (xxxiii—xlviii)—he mingles the two in such a way as to create a sense of shame in the very moment of promise. See especially Ezk. xx. 42ff.: 'Ye shall know that I am the Lord, when I shall bring you into the land of Israel . . . And there shall ye remember your ways, and all your doings, wherein ye have been defiled; and ye shall lothe yourselves in your own sight for all your evils that ye have committed.' (The whole passage xx. 33–44 should be carefully read, where a species of remnant-doctrine is also observable.) It may be added that this general position is being adopted by a growing number of Old Testament scholars; for further details the student is referred to the standard works on Old Testament theology and eschatology.

The second major consideration is more important and has occasioned most of the later theories regarding Ezekiel. Whereas the prophet lived in Babylonia he constantly addresses the Jews left in Jerusalem. He enacts symbolic prophecies for their benefit which, nevertheless, they could not see; he knows their situation perfectly; he describes events which he witnesses happening in Jerusalem and its neighbourhood, e.g. the idolatries of the elders in the temple (chapter viii), the sudden death of one of their number (xi. 13), Zedekiah's attempted escape from Jerusalem by night (xii. 3–12), Nebuchadnezzar consulting omens at cross-roads on the way to the city (xxi. 18ff.) and later encamping outside Jerusalem (xxiv. 2). That a man living in Babylonia could witness events of this order in so remote a place as Jerusalem seems nonsense to a scientific age like ours; it is therefore argued that some other solution must be found. Either Ezekiel actually lived in Jerusalem, not Babylonia, and this book incorporates his genuine prophecies with those of a later redactor who made out that he lived as an exile (so Herntrich); or the whole situation is fictitious and the work is comparable to the pseudonymous apocalyptic writings of later Judaism, belonging actually to the age of Alexander (so Torrey). Of these two alternatives, hardly anyone takes the latter seriously, but the former commands considerable attention and is accepted by Oesterley (*Introduction to the Old Testament*, pp. 324–325). Cooke, however, voices the feeling of many critics when he says that it is just as hard to believe in the highly imaginative redactor as to accept the statements in the text (I.C.C., p. xxiii). Consequently he accepts the authenticity of the book in the main; and the consensus of modern scholarship is with him. Guillaume has further related this extraordinary gift of second sight possessed by Ezekiel to other similar phenomena in the Old Testament, and even in the modern Bedouin world. By his researches he has enabled us better to understand a type of mind which has little in common with modern Western civilization (*Prophecy and Divination;* see especially pp. 155–158). If this controversy has served no other purpose, therefore, than to throw into relief the truly amazing character that was Ezekiel's, it will not have been in vain.

Ezekiel ministered, then, to the nation, both that part in exile and those left in the homeland, in the period just prior to the fall of Jerusalem and after. He was a younger contemporary of Jeremiah; judging from the echoes of the senior prophet in his book, he must have had considerable contact with him.

II. CONTENTS

As the outline of contents shows (see below), the book is constructed on a clearly defined plan, the subjects of each section being mainly adhered to. After the introductory vision of chapters i—iii, Ezekiel concentrates almost exclusively on laying bare the iniquity of his people. He pitilessly drags their sins to the light and pronounces the judgment of God on them. By symbolic actions, parables, fiery oratory and logical statement he reiterates his theme of the wickedness of the nation and its inevitable destruction. The repetition of denunciation and threat of doom is so constant as to make the reader recoil in horror, all the more so in that, whereas other prophetic works light up their threats with promises, this element is largely lacking in the first section of Ezekiel's book. When he does allow a ray of hope to shine through, it usually glows a fiery red, so that the restoration spoken of is a shameful one and not in joy (see, e.g., xvi. 53–58, xx. 43, 44). In this, as in other respects, Ezekiel has affinity with the author of the book of Revelation, for both works set forth, as none other in their respective Testaments, the unmitigated terror of God's wrath.

The second section (chapters xxv—xxxii) confines itself to oracles against the nations of Israel's environment, both the petty states that plundered the people in their hour of distress and the greater nations of the day. Here Ezekiel's poetic imagination soars to its height; we are given some of the most vivid word pictures of the

Old Testament in his oracles against the prince of Tyre and Pharaoh of Egypt. It is curious that Ezekiel is silent as to the fate of Babylon, the chief destroyer of Jerusalem. Some believe that, since this nation must have figured in Ezekiel's prophecies of doom, it must be symbolized by Gog in the prophecy of chapters xxxviii, xxxix. There is, however, no hint of this in the text and everything seems to point against the identification. One can but feel that, like Jeremiah, Ezekiel regarded Nebuchadnezzar as a servant of Jehovah and so regarded his actions as divinely ordained; unlike Jeremiah, however, Ezekiel received no subsequent word concerning Babylon and so left the issue with God.

The turning-point in Ezekiel's ministry is occasioned by the arrival of a messenger from Jerusalem, announcing the city's fall (xxxiii. 21). In face of the consistent scepticism of the people towards his preaching, this event constituted the divine confirmation of his ministry. Henceforth people flocked to hear him (xxxiii. 30). He was now free to give himself to the task of rehabilitating the scattered nation and this forms the theme of chapters xxxiii—xxxvii.

It has been a long-standing perplexity that, after the restoration of the nation in the messianic era, Ezekiel should have spoken of a further uprising of foreign powers against Israel (xxxviii, xxxix). There are nevertheless cogent reasons lying behind this teaching and we cannot see any necessity for denying it to Ezekiel. See introductory notes to these two chapters in the commentary.

The conclusion of the book (xl—xlviii) is the product of a devout mind that has long and affectionately pondered over the worship of Israel in her coming age of bliss. We are here forcibly reminded that Ezekiel was a priest as well as a prophet. As such he combined in himself the two great streams of Israel's tradition. In a land purged of uncleanness, the ideal worship in an ideal temple is set forth for the observance of an ideal people.

III. CHARACTERISTICS

Two features of Ezekiel's personality have already been mentioned, viz. the vividness of his imagination and his unique powers of telepathy, clairvoyance and prognosis. These combine with an overwhelming sense of the transcendence of God to produce passages of literature that in many ways seem alien to the modern mind, but which richly reward investigation. How many, for example, are so bewildered by Ezekiel's account of his inaugural vision in chapter i that they read no further? Yet that chapter, once grasped, is seen to be highly significant and of great spiritual value, as the Jews themselves recognized. (A saying in the Mishnah records that the Chariot, i.e. Ezk. i, and the Creation, i.e. Gn. i, are the two matters to be expounded only to a prudent person; Hag. ii. 1, quoted Cooke, p. 23.) Similar observations could be made concerning many obscure and neglected passages in Ezekiel.

In certain directions Ezekiel pioneered movements of thought which were destined to develop into the characteristic features of later Judaism. He was the first to state with dogmatic clarity the truth of individual responsibility. By the frequency of his visions and the ecstatic nature of many of his utterances, and especially by his prophecies concerning Gog and the future kingdom, he shaped a type of prophecy that in due course led to the apocalyptic movement. Ezekiel is thus the bridge between prophecy and apocalyptic. Further, by his priestly training he was naturally more interested in worship than in evangelism; consequently the missionary spirit, so evident in the latter chapters of Isaiah, is largely absent from his writings. In all these matters, viz. individual responsibility, apocalyptic prophecy and the by-passing of the Gentile in contemplating the kingdom of God, Judaism went much further than Ezekiel and in certain directions actually produced a caricature of his teaching. (See, e.g., the introductory notes to chapter xviii in the commentary.) It is as unjust, however, to blame Ezekiel for these unfortunate developments, as it is to blame Daniel for the puerilities of some apocalyptic writings, or St. Paul for the doctrine of predestination to damna-tion. Where Ezekiel and Daniel were silent, or at most implicit, Judaism became explicit and exaggerated; just as some people's logic drives them to a position which most Christians believe St. Paul would have disowned. It is unfortunate in the highest degree, therefore, that many biblical scholars should disparage Ezekiel as being retrogressive in its doctrine. On the contrary, this book makes an important contribution in the providence of God to the unfolding revelation of God in the Bible. It needs to be studied with a greater sympathy than some moderns are at present inclined to accord it.

Finally, it may perhaps be mentioned that in some places the text of Ezekiel has suffered badly in transmission. To sort out the difficulties would demand more space than is allowable in a commentary of this compass. Only the more important corrections have been pointed out in the exposition. The interested student is recommended to the very useful commentary by G. A. Cooke in the I.C.C. While in many respects it goes further in the matter of conjecture than conservative scholars would generally allow, it is nevertheless characterized in the main by a commendable sobriety of judgment. The present writer has not hesitated frequently to draw upon it.

OUTLINE OF CONTENTS

ISRAEL'S SIN AND IMPENDING JUDGMENT. i. 1—xxiv. 27

I. THE CALL OF EZEKIEL. i. 1—iii. 27

II. FOUR ACTED PROPHECIES. iv. 1—v. 17

III. PROPHECY AGAINST THE MOUNTAINS OF ISRAEL. vi. 1-14

IV. ISRAEL'S IMMINENT DOOM. vii. 1-27

V. JERUSALEM'S SIN AND JUDGMENT: ITS ABANDONMENT BY GOD. viii. 1—xi. 25

VI. PROPHECIES AGAINST JERUSALEM. xii. 1—xxiv. 27

PROPHECIES AGAINST FOREIGN NATIONS. xxv. 1—xxxii. 32

VII. PROPHECIES AGAINST SURROUNDING TRIBES. xxv. 1-17

VIII. PROPHECIES AGAINST TYRE. xxvi. 1—xxviii. 26

IX. PROPHECIES AGAINST EGYPT. xxix. 1—xxxii. 32

THE RESTORATION OF ISRAEL. xxxiii. 1—xlviii. 35

X. THE RESPONSIBILITY OF PROPHET AND PEOPLE. xxxiii. 1-20

XI. THE TURNING-POINT IN EZEKIEL'S MINISTRY. xxxiii. 21-33

XII. THE RETURN OF ISRAEL TO HER OWN LAND. xxxiv. 1—xxxvii. 28

XIII. PROPHECY AGAINST GOG. xxxviii. 1—xxxix. 29

XIV. TEMPLE AND PEOPLE IN THE KINGDOM OF GOD. xl. 1—xlviii. 35

COMMENTARY

ISRAEL'S SIN AND IMPENDING JUDGMENT. i. 1—xxiv. 27

I. THE CALL OF EZEKIEL. i. 1—iii. 27

a. The vision of the glory of God (i. 1–28)

It is not known from what epoch Ezekiel dates *the thirtieth year* (1), whether Babylonian or Israelite. Origen thought it represented his own age. *The fifth year of king Jehoiachin's captivity* (2), however, fixes the date as 593 B.C. Evidences of Jewish settlements have been found at Nippur on the river *Chebar* (1), known to the Babylonians as 'The Grand Canal'; that Ezekiel should receive in such a place *visions of God* (1) would be revolutionary to many of his compatriots, whose feelings rather found expression in utterances such as Ps. cxxxvii.

Like others before him, Ezekiel's call to the prophetic office came with a vision of God. But, as frequently in prophetic ecstasy (cf. Acts x), the nature of the vision was conditioned by the environment of the recipient. In this case it was the approach of a storm cloud by which God revealed Himself to Ezekiel (4). The blackness of the cloud, the unnatural fiery glow and the lightning flashes provided the framework for the manifestation of the greater glory of God. (See Guillaume, *Prophecy and Divination*, pp. 155–156, and compare the following report of a storm on the Euphrates: 'Dense masses of black clouds, streaked with orange, red and yellow appeared coming up from the WSW, and approaching us with fearful velocity . . . The clouds by this time were quite terrific. Below the darkest of them there was a large collection of matter, of a dark crimson colour, which was rolling towards us at an awful rate . . . All became calm and clear as before, and barely twenty-five minutes had seen the beginning, progress and termination of this fearful hurricane.' Chesney, *Narrative of the Euphrates Expedition*, quoted by Cooke in I.C.C., p. 10.) Note the repeated term *likeness* (5, 10, 13, etc.); Ezekiel can suggest only parallels to the figures of his vision. The *living creatures* (5) with their *wheels* (15) form an unearthly chariot for the throne of God. The comment of the Rabbis on the faces of the living creatures (10) is frequently quoted with approval: 'Man is exalted among creatures; the eagle is exalted among birds; the ox is exalted among domestic animals; the lion is exalted among wild beasts; and all of them have received dominion, and greatness has been given them, yet they are stationed below the chariot of the Holy One' (*Midrash R. Shemoth*, 23, on Ex. xv. 1). Cf. Rev. iv. 7.

The wheels (15, 16) enabled the chariot to travel anywhere, a needful reminder for the exiles (see note on verses 1, 2). Viewed from Ezekiel's position, they seemed to revolve within each other; their construction was as though one wheel were in the midst of another (see RV mg.), though actually there were only four wheels,

each separate, standing at the four corners of a square. The movement of the wheels (17) is unimaginable if we have ordinary vehicles in mind; this is a supernatural chariot! *Their rings* (i.e. 'rims') *were full of eyes* (18). These eyes denote intelligence, for *the spirit of the living creature was in the wheels* (20). *Likeness of the firmament* (22); better, 'platform'; *raki'a* is translated firmament in Gn. i, but its fundamental meaning 'something made firm and flat by stamping' is here in mind. It serves as the basis for Jehovah's throne (26) and is borne by the living creatures.

Note that in verses 26–28 the prophet will not say he definitely saw Jehovah, only a *likeness as the appearance of a man* or *the appearance of the likeness of the glory of the Lord*. (There is the 'large face' and the 'small face' of God, says the Talmud, and man is given to see the latter only; cf. Jn. i. 18.) Nevertheless that which Ezekiel saw was sufficient to overwhelm him; cf. Is. vi. 5; Dn. x. 8, 9; Rev. i. 17.

b. The prophet's call and commission (ii. 1—iii. 3)

The title *son of man* (1, 3, etc.) applied to himself is characteristic of Ezekiel and emphasizes his status as mere creature over against the majesty of the Creator. It is used by God in addressing the prophet, not by Ezekiel of himself, apparently to show that his duty is to be the mouthpiece of the divine will and nothing more. *They . . . shall know that there hath been a prophet among them* (5) finds its counterpart in the oft-repeated phrase 'they shall know that I am Jehovah'. Both truths are to become apparent by God fulfilling the prophet's predictions; cf. xxxiii. 32, 33; Dt. xviii. 21f.

The prophet is bidden not to share the rebelliousness of his nation by hiding from them the messages God will declare to him (8). That God should have directly touched the mouth of Jeremiah (Je. i. 9) but given *a roll of a book* to Ezekiel (9) illustrates the difference between the two prophets; the former declares the immanence of God, the latter His transcendence. The writing on the book *within and without* (10), contrary to normal usage, indicates the fulness of its contents. *Lamentations, and mourning, and woe* (10) is a fair description of the major part of Ezekiel's prophecy. His message was not changed until, according to the promise of verse 5, God fulfilled his words in the destruction of Jerusalem (xxxiii. 21f.).

Eat this roll (iii. 1). There is nothing mechanical in this mode of inspiration; that Ezekiel must masticate the roll shows he must make its message his own. Despite the nature of the message, its taste to the prophet was *as honey for sweetness* (3), for 'it is sweet to do the will of God and to be trusted with tasks for Him'

(McFadyen). Note the variation in the experience of the New Testament apocalyptist (Rev. x. 10).

c. The commission emphasized (iii. 4–15)

The prophet is not sent to a foreign nation (5), nor to the heathen world in general (6); if it had been so they would have listened. But Israel will listen neither to a prophet nor to God Himself (7). A people 'deep of lip and heavy of tongue' (5, RV mg.) indicates 'a people whose speech sounded guttural and thick to Hebrew ears' (Cooke). The traditional obduracy of Israel is referred to by our Lord in Mt. xi. 21–24; Lk. iv. 24–27. With verses 8 and 9 cf. Is. l. 7; Je. i. 17–19.

To them of the captivity (11). Ezekiel's mission, although directed to all Israel (4), is now specified as immediately intended for his fellow-exiles. This would be necessitated by his circumstances; but the writing of the book, or even of its separate parts, would make his message available to the whole nation.

The departure of the chariot of glory leaves the prophet in a reaction of *bitterness* and *heat of . . . spirit* (14). But he is compelled to start on his prophetic ministry. He moves to Tel-abib, the 'house of green ears', a chief centre of the exiles. It takes him *seven days* to recover from the effects of the vision (15).

d. The prophet as watchman (iii. 16–21)

I have made thee a watchman (17). A watchman's task was to warn a city of impending danger; so Ezekiel must warn his people of the disaster shortly to overtake them. The passage has in mind the catastrophe about to fall on Jerusalem, but the prophet would no doubt apply it generally. Its importance lies in the relationship to be established between Ezekiel and his hearers; he is responsible for them individually and must warn each man as a faithful pastor (18, 20); they are individually responsible for their actions and their fate, for God will deal with them as moral persons, not as a unit (19). This is a revolutionary conception and marks a significant step in the process of revelation. See notes on chapters xviii and xxxiii. 1–20.

e. Silence enjoined (iii. 22–27)

Ezekiel is commanded to remain in his house (24), perhaps owing to a threat of violence (25). Dumbness will come upon him (26), except when Jehovah opens his mouth in prophetic utterance (27). If this episode is in place here, Ezekiel's ministry is a private one, which only they receive who come to his house (cf. viii. 1), until tidings of the fall of Jerusalem reach him (xxxiii. 21, 22). Some feel that this comes strangely after the preceding commission; they suggest that this paragraph may be misplaced and belongs to a later period of Ezekiel's ministry. If that be so, verse 27 relates to a specific occasion when God shall cause the prophet's dumbness to cease (see xxxiii. 21, 22). The suggested transference is not impossible, especially as the previous paragraph finds a fuller exposition in xxxiii. 1–20.

On the other hand, the passage receives a good meaning where it stands now and may be allowed to retain its place: 'his freedom of movement will be restricted by the exiles . . . God will restrain his utterance, suffering him to speak only when specially directed to do so' (Wardle).

II. FOUR ACTED PROPHECIES.
iv. 1—v. 17

a. The siege of Jerusalem (iv. 1–3)

The *tile* (1) used by Ezekiel would be of soft clay, the drawing would be carved by means of a stylus; when it was finished the clay would be baked as a brick. Presumably the operations of verse 2 were to be inscribed on the tile. The *iron pan* (3) perhaps portrays the strong fortifications set up against the city.

b. The exile (iv. 4–8)

The prophet lies on his side, bearing Israel's *iniquity*, i.e. the chastisement for the iniquity, for the period of the exile (4). LXX reads 190 in verses 5 and 9 instead of 390 and is probably correct. From verses 5, 6, 9 we gather that Ezekiel was to lie 150 days on his left side and forty on his right; the period from the deportation under Tiglath-pileser in 734 B.C. (2 Ki. xv. 29) to the taking of Jerusalem in 586 was 148 years, i.e. roughly 150 years, while the forty years (general designation of a generation) for Judah roughly corresponds to the period 586 to 536, the time of Judah's exile in Babylon. Cooke suggests that the figure 390 was due to a copyist interpreting *the iniquity of the house of Israel* (4) as the whole period of Israel's sinning. According to the chronology of the book of Kings, the period from the division of the kingdom under Rehoboam to 586 was 394½ years.

c. The famine (iv. 9–17)

Two thoughts about the approaching famine are to be distinguished here: the scarcity of food (9–11, 16, 17) and the uncleanness involved in eating it in a foreign land (12–15). The curious mixture of grain in verse 9 merely implies shortage and is not to be compared with Lv. xix. 19. For *fitches* read, as in RV, 'spelt'. *Twenty shekels* (10) is about nine ounces; *the sixth part of an hin* (11) about two pints. *The dung* (12) used in the baking of bread was for fuel. To Ezekiel, brought up as a priest, human excrement was too revolting; in response to his prayers (14) he was allowed to use *cow's dung* (15), which is still used for fuel by Bedouin. With verse 13 cf. Ho. ix. 3f.; Am. vii. 17. All lands outside Canaan were unclean and their products likewise, for Jehovah was not worshipped in them.

d. The slaughter (v. 1–4)

Shaving the head was a figure for catastrophe; see Is. vii. 20; Je. xli. 5. Here the act represents the fate of the inhabitants of Jerusalem; they were to be burned, slain and scattered (2); the sword pursuing those that flee the city (2c) indicates the completeness of the destruction. Of the few that truly escape (those bound in Ezekiel's skirt, verse 3) some shall yet perish (4), so that the remnant is very small indeed. Ezekiel thus does hold to a doctrine of the remnant (see also vi. 8–10, ix. 8, xi. 13), in spite of the asseverations of some to the contrary; but it is wholly subordinated to his message of judgment until the fall of Jerusalem, after which it becomes his dominant theme.

e. An exposition of the signs (v. 5–17)

Jerusalem is the centre of the world, alike by her position and privilege (5; cf. xxxviii. 12). This makes her excess of wickedness over the nations more heinous (cf. xvi. 47f.; Je. ii. 10f.). The argument of verse 7 implies that the nations about Israel walked according to such light as they had, but Israel had not; God accordingly would requite the sins of His people *in the sight of the nations* (8), both as an example and vindication of His holiness. With verse 10 cf. Lv. xxvi. 29 and Dt. xxviii. 53, prophecies fulfilled in the event (La. iv. 10). *Pestilence and blood* (17) are one plague; we thus have the four scourges of Lv. xxvi, *famine, evil beasts, pestilence, the sword*. They occur again in xiv. 21 and figure in the plagues of the book of Revelation (Rev. vi. 7, 8).

III. PROPHECY AGAINST THE MOUNTAINS OF ISRAEL. vi. 1–14

Ezekiel addresses the country under the figure *the mountains of Israel* (2), since they formed its chief feature; it is, indeed, 'a central mountain range sloping down to the narrow plains by the Mediterranean and the Jordan' (Toy). Moreover, *mountains* and *hills* (3) are usually associated by the prophets with idolatry (e.g. Is. lxv. 7; Je. iii. 6; Ho. iv. 13). *Rivers* (3); RV 'watercourses', RV mg. 'ravines'. These and the *valleys* were used for impure rites and the worship of Moloch (see Je. vii. 31, 32). *High places* (3) were originally lofty sites, but came to denote sanctuaries wherever situated; there were many of these in the land where worship was ostensibly offered to Jehovah, but actually differed little from that of Israel's neighbours. Apparently the reforms of Hezekiah and Josiah had been in vain (2 Ki. xviii. 4, xxiii. 5). *Images* (4; RV 'sun-images'; Heb. *hammanim*) were probably images of Baal hamman, 'the glowing Baal', and so were not really representations of the sun god, though the cult may have been connected with sun worship in the temple (see viii. 16f.). *Ye shall know that I am the Lord* (7). A phrase characteristic of Ezekiel; it occurs in verses 10, 13, 14 and about sixty times elsewhere. The motive for Jehovah's action is always the acknowledgment by the nations of His sole deity and power.

I am broken with their whorish heart (9); read with RV mg. 'I have broken their whorish heart'. God breaks the heart by sorrow to bring

about repentance. *Smite . . . stamp* (11). The actions of Ezekiel seem to express exultation rather than horror (see xxi. 17, xxii. 13, xxv. 6). *Alas!* is better rendered Aha! (LXX, *euge, euge*; i.e. Bravo!), as though the prophet exults in the coming judgment. His concern is the vindication of Jehovah's honour rather than the fate of sinners. Cf. Rev. xix. 1–4. The destruction of idolaters *among their idols* (13) will reveal the impotence of the latter and convince the survivors that Jehovah alone is God. *Diblath* (14), RV 'Diblah' (situated east of the Dead Sea in the south), is almost certainly a misreading of Riblah (lying far north by 'the entrance to Hamath', xlviii. 1), the Hebrew *d* and *r* being almost identical. 'From the wilderness to Riblah' thus represents an equivalent of the better known phrase 'from Dan to Beersheba'.

IV. ISRAEL'S IMMINENT DOOM. vii. 1–27

There are four short oracles in this chapter (verses 2–4, 5–9, 10–11, 12–13), followed by an exposition of their common theme (verses 14–27). As *the end* (2) is stated to be immediately impending, and the date given in i. 1 leaves seven years to the fall of Jerusalem, it is likely that this chapter was written later. The date at the head of a section does not necessarily embrace everything that follows till the next date is given.

The oracle is directed to *the land of Israel* (2), yet verses 5–7, 10, 12 appear to have the day of the Lord with its universal significance in mind. It is therefore better to translate the concluding phrase of this verse by 'the four corners of the earth' as in Is. xi. 12. The judgment upon Israel is set against the background of the judgment of the nations. Note the play of words, as in verse 6, *the end* (*hakkes*) *is come* or 'awakes' (*hekis*).

An only evil (5); i.e. a final evil. *The time is come, the day . : . is near* (7). That this is a reference to the day of the Lord seems clear from a comparison with xxx. 3; Dn. xii. 1; Joel i. 15; Mal. iv. 1.

Verses 10 and 11 record a rhythmic oracle which gives the core of the prophecy. All is ripe for judgment, 'the tree has burst into leaf and flower!' (Cooke). The *rod* and *pride* probably refer to the king of Israel and his court. Cf. the frequent usage of the word 'rod' for the sceptre of Israel (e.g. xix. 11).

The buying and selling in verses 12 and 13 appears to be of property, the seller either doing it against his own inclination (cf. 1 Ki. xxi. 1-16) or at a bad price. The prophet says the one need not be glad, nor the other sorry, for both will shortly be involved in catastrophe. Many have thought that verse 13 refers to the law of jubile (Lv. xxv. 10f.), and it may be so. Otherwise the prophet is continuing the thought of verse 12; buying back of ancestral lands is unthinkable, for 'the nation will be broken up and questions of property will cease to have interest' (Toy).

Comparing the last clause of verse 19 with

verse 20, the uncleanness of *their silver and their gold* (19) is due to their being lavished on idols. In verse 20 read as follows: 'the beauty of its ornament (i.e. the idol) they set in majesty, and they made the images of their abominations . . . therefrom' (see RV mg. and cf. Is. xxx. 22). Such idols Jehovah will give to the invaders (21). *Make a chain* (23) may be a command to the prophet to perform a symbolic act, otherwise its meaning is unknown. A threefold division of the people religiously is indicated in verse 26: *the prophet* for the immediate word of Jehovah; *the priest* for instruction out of the law; *the ancients* (or 'elders') for advice on civil matters. Verse 27 gives a threefold division socially: *the king, the prince* (i.e. 'princes'; the singular is collective as in xxii. 6) and *the people of the land.*

V. JERUSALEM'S SIN AND JUDGMENT: ITS ABANDONMENT BY GOD. viii. 1—xi. 25

a. The idolaters in the temple (viii. 1–18)

The date (verse 1) is August-September 592 B.C., fourteen months after Ezekiel's inaugural vision (i. 1). For *the appearance of fire* (2; Heb. *esh*) LXX reads as in i. 26, 27 'the appearance of a man' (Heb. *ish*). Ezekiel is carried in vision to the temple and views idolatries taking place there. This is no pictorial reconstruction of the prophet, based on reports received from others, but a description of things seen by means of a supernaturally heightened gift of 'second sight'. The distance between Babylonia and Jerusalem makes the episode astonishing, but it is not without parallel in the Bible. Cf. 2 Ki. v. 26, vi. 8–12; Is. xxi. 6–10. The *image of jealousy* (3) (i.e. an image which rouses Jehovah to jealousy) may have been an 'asherah' (sacred pole). Manasseh had set up such an image (*semel*, the unusual word here used) in the temple and later removed it (2 Ch. xxxiii. 7, 15). This may have been the same idol replaced. The translation *chambers of his imagery* (12; Heb. *mashkith*) is doubtful. LXX reads 'their secret chamber', as good a conjecture as most now made. Cf. ix. 9; Is. xxix. 15.

Tammuz (14), a Babylonian deity, was the god of vegetation, whose death at the time of great heat was mourned annually, and whose resurrection was celebrated in spring. The traditional time of mourning was the fourth month (named, accordingly, 'Tammuz'), but as this vision took place in the sixth month the ritual may have been modified among the Jews of this time. *They worshipped the sun* (16). Sun worship was practised by the Canaanites, but lately had been reintroduced from Assyria (2 Ki. xxiii. 5, 11; Je. viii. 2). *Between the porch and the altar* (16) was the place where the priests offered prayer (Joel ii. 17), with their faces, of course, towards the temple; in this spot, *with their backs toward the temple*, the adoration of the sun took place, as complete a renunciation of Jehovah as possible. Cf. 2 Ch. xxix. 6.

They put the branch to their nose (17) represents a form of idolatry that can be paralleled in Babylonian and Persian rites. (For the various explanations possible consult the larger commentaries.)

b. The judgment of Jerusalem (ix. 1–11)

If RV mg. be followed in verse 1, the executioners are addressed directly, 'Draw near, ye executioners of the city!' *Six men* with the man *with a writer's inkhorn* (2) make a group of seven; they are doubtless angelic beings. Cf. the seven angels who stand before God (Rev. viii. 2, 6), who are also revealed as executors of God's wrath. *Set a mark* (4). The righteous are marked (the word signifies, strangely, a mark in the shape of a cross) to distinguish them from idolaters and to secure for them Jehovah's protection. Cf. Ex. xii. 23; Rev. vii. 3–8, xiii. 16–18, xiv. 1. *Begin at my sanctuary* (6); cf. 1 Pet. iv. 17. *The residue* (or 'remnant') *of Israel* (8) denotes the inhabitants of Jerusalem. The northern kingdom had gone into captivity in 722 B.C., and Judah had suffered a partial captivity in 597. In contrast to his cry in vi. 11, and to his usual attitude of complete sympathy with the divine judgments on Israel, Ezekiel here pleads for mercy on his erring countrymen. The answer is given in verses 9, 10; the guilt of the land is so heinous, its punishment cannot be averted. *The Lord hath forsaken the earth* (9); RV mg. 'land'; i.e. Jehovah has deserted His people, as is evidenced by their continual troubles. There is accordingly no obligation on their part for continued loyalty to Him. It did not occur to these apostates that their adversity was the righteous judgment of Jehovah upon their wickedness.

c. The burning of Jerusalem (x. 1–22)

The *throne* (1) is empty (cf. ix. 3); the cherubim wait for Jehovah to remount and depart. The destroyer of the city is *the man clothed with linen* (2), who formerly marked off the faithful for preservation; all seven angels are thus ministers of vengeance, as in Rev. viii. 1—xi. 15. *Cherub* (2) is a collective term for the four cherubim, as in ix. 3. We are told nothing of the destruction of the city, other than that the commissioned angel took fire from the midst of the cherubim (cf. Is. vi. 6) *and went out* (7). The vision was prophetic of the fires that actually destroyed Jerusalem in 586 B.C. (2 Ki. xxv. 9); but more significant than the prediction is the revelation of the identity of the Destroyer, God Himself. The purpose of the repetition of verses 9–22 is but to impress this very fact; for the description of the glory of God and the chariot had already been given in chapter i. Its recurrence here in detail underlines the startling fact that the God, whom men thought to be inseparably bound to His sanctuary and city, is to destroy them both and abandon their ruins. Owing to the vagaries of later copyists, some of the description of verses 9–22 is confused and difficult to follow. For example, 11a speaks of the wheels, 11b apparently has the cherubim in mind; verse 13 would read better after verse 6; the first face in verse 14 should be 'ox' not *cherub*, as in i. 10 (unless we follow Rabbi Resh Lakish, 'Ezekiel besought the Merciful One with regard to it (the ox face) and He changed it into a cherub'!); verse 15 interrupts the sequence and anticipates verses 19, 20. *The glory of the Lord departed* (18). Jehovah leaves the temple by *the east gate* (19); xi. 22, 23 records His departure from the city altogether.

d. Judgment of conspirators in Jerusalem (xi. 1–13)

This city is the caldron (3). This statement shows the drift of these men's thoughts. The city walls would protect them as a cauldron protects flesh from the fire; the warnings of the prophets, therefore, could be ignored. The first clause may be taken to imply, 'Our present occupation must be war, not the building of houses; let us fight it out' (see RV). This interpretation, however, reads much into the text. LXX renders, 'Have not houses recently been built?', reflecting, perhaps, the jubilation of the princes on having overcome the effects of the 597 invasion, and implying that there was no cause for worry now. If RV mg. is followed, 'Is not the time near to build . . .?', we are to understand an attitude of defiance to prophetic warnings, a flagrant act of disbelief in their veracity. *Your slain . . . they are the flesh* (7). The only people who are to enjoy the security of the city will be the slain victims of the plotters; the latter are to be led out (9) and executed on the borders of the land (10). See the fulfilment of this (2 Ki. xxv. 18–21). Verse 13 is an integral part of the vision but presumes that the event actually occurred while Ezekiel was 'looking on'. The phenomenon is to be compared with the vision of the idolaters in the temple (chapter viii), that of the beginning of the siege of Jerusalem (xxiv. 2), the death of his wife (xxiv. 16), and the cessation of his dumbness (xxiv. 25, 26; cf. xxxiii. 21, 22).

e. Promise of restoration (xi. 14–25)

Thy brethren (15) are Ezekiel's' fellow-exiles from Judah; *all the house of Israel* (15) are the descendants of those transported from northern Israel in 722 B.C. (cf. xx. 40, xxxvi. 10). *Get you far from the Lord* (15). The sneer of the remnant still in Jerusalem reflects the old notion that Jehovah's power was limited to His land; to be away from it was to be cast off from Jehovah (cf. 1 Sa. xxvi. 19). The promise of God in verse 16 negates such an idea.

The glory of the Lord (23) removes entirely from the city (cf. x. 18, 19). Many exegetes believe the two visions in xi. 1–21 occurred later than the rest of chapters viii–xi, and have been placed here because they concern events seen in the temple and the apostates of Jerusalem. Admittedly xi. 1–13 comes strangely after the description of the destruction of the people in chapter ix and the burning of the city in chapter x; the message of restoration (xi. 14–21) would

also better fit the period immediately prior to the doom of the city. It is, however, unwise to dogmatize either way on the matter.

VI. PROPHECIES AGAINST JERUSALEM. xii. 1—xxiv. 27

a. Portrayal of the imminent exile (xii. 1–20)

A rebellious house (2); i.e. the exiles among whom the prophet lives; they are as obtuse as the Jews at Jerusalem! Verse 5 gives an illustration of the desperation of the besieged and of the ruin of their property; see 2 Ki. xxv. 4. *Cover thy face, that thou see not* (6). An allusion to Zedekiah's flight and fate. See verse 12 RV which reads 'He shall not see . . . with his eyes'. The LXX translates as passive, 'that he might not be seen by the eye'; i.e. the covering of the face serves for a disguise. But the verse is also prophetic of the punishment inflicted by the Babylonians upon the king, who was blinded at Riblah and taken captive to Babylon (2 Ki. xxv. 5–7). *They shall know* (15); i.e. the escaped of Jerusalem, who will know that Jehovah is Lord when they experience these horrors according to prophecy. The nations among which they travel will also know it (16), for this demonstration of Jehovah's might will convince them that He alone is God. The object of leaving survivors from the catastrophe is solely for the honour of Jehovah's name.

The acted prophecy of the hardships of the siege (17–20) is akin to iv. 9–17 (see especially iv. 16, 17). The symbolic actions of the earlier passage, however, represent the scarcity that will prevail in the siege; this stresses the terror of those days.

b. Prophets and people (xii. 21—xiv. 11)

This passage consists of a group of five oracles dealing with prophecy, true and false, and with the attitude adopted by the people in reference to it.

i. **Scepticism rebuked (xii. 21–28).** Two oracles (verses 21–25, 26–28) supply reasons for popular disbelief in prophecy. The first is expressed in the proverb, *The days are prolonged, and every vision faileth* (22); i.e. time passes but the many threats of doom never come to pass (cf. 2 Pet. iii. 4). The element of delay would have been aggravated by Jeremiah's ministry. For the past thirty 'years he had announced the coming judgment of Jerusalem; events had apparently discredited him. Ezekiel's answer from God is, *The days are at hand, and the effect of every vision* (23). The second objection came from those who accepted the truth of prophecy, but regarded it as applying to *times that are far off* (27). The same answer is returned to them, *There shall none of my words be prolonged* (RV 'deferred') *any more* (28).

ii. **Denunciation of false prophets and prophetesses (xiii. 1–23).** False prophets were a menace by reason of their opposition to the true word of God and their propagation of untruth (2, 3). Cf. Jeremiah's struggles against them (Je. v. 30,

31, xiv. 13-18, xxiii. 9-40, xxix. 8-10, 21-23). For the test of the validity of a prophet's ministry see Dt. xiii. 1-5, xviii. 21, 22. *Thy prophets are like the foxes* (4); i.e. they were mischievous and destructive. With verse 5 contrast 1 Sa. xxv. 16. *Divination* (6) is the obtaining of an oracle by the reading of omens and drawing lots; cf. xxi. 21. *The writing of the house of Israel* (9); i.e. the register of citizens in the coming age of blessedness. Cf. the earlier use of the idea in Ex. xxxii. 32f. and the developed symbol in Lk. x. 20; Rev. xx. 15.

Untempered mortar (10ff.); Heb. *taphel*, better translated 'whitewash'. False prophets merely whitewash the insecure walls (see RV mg.) of the state instead of strengthening it. When God shall shatter the wall, they will be buried beneath its ruins. In verse 15 read as in verse 12, 'It shall be said unto you, The wall is no more . . .'

The false prophetesses sewed bands (not *pillows*) upon all wrists (18), a process of sympathetic magic which either fastened power upon the consulter, or symbolized the power of the sorceress to bind her victims. The head coverings (*kerchiefs*) served a similar purpose, though the derivation of the term (*mispachoth* from an Akkadian root *sapahu*, to loose) suggests the opposite power of loosing from the influence. *Souls* (18ff.); i.e. 'persons'; there is no thought of distinguishing between the spirit and the man. Render the last clause of verse 18 as a statement, 'You hunt the persons of my people but your own persons you keep alive.' Translate verse 19 'Ye have profaned me (because the sorceresses invoked Jehovah's name in their rites) with handfuls of barley and with crumbled pieces of bread'; the latter were not given as a reward but were used for divining the future, just like the liver of a sacrificial victim. Verses 20-23 describe the fate of all those who practise divination of this kind. False prophetesses share the judgment of false prophets.

iii. **Idolatrous inquirers (xiv. 1-11).** *Then came certain of the elders* (1). It is likely that exiles frequently came to Ezekiel, waiting for a word from God that might fall from him (cf. xxxiii. 30). Like the heathen, these elders thought that they could worship some god beside their own (3, 4); they had not learned the meaning of 'I the Lord thy God am a jealous God' (Ex. xx. 5; see also Ezk. xvi. 38, 42). *I the Lord will answer him that cometh* (4); RV 'him therein'; Jehovah will use no intermediary to reply to such a man. His speech will be in deeds of judgment, as in verses 12f. *Separateth himself from me* (7); lit. 'dedicateth himself away from following me'; cf. Ho. ix. 10. As people so prophet; both alike were corrupt (9). Only a *deceived* prophet would give an answer as from Jehovah to idolaters, and both would bear their punishment. Some interpret the 'deception' of a prophet by Jehovah as an instance of the Old Testament overlooking of secondary causes; i.e. the deceived state of the prophet is due to his own perversion of conscience, but since the consequences of sin,

equally with the moral law, are of God's ordering, one may say that the deception is brought about by God. Such a train of argument, however, would sound strange to Ezekiel. Cf. Ezk. iii. 20; 1 Ki. xxii. 21f.

c. **The rationale of judgment (xiv. 12-23)**

In verses 12-20 a general principle is laid down, that the judgment of a wicked people is not averted by the righteousness of a few; verse 21 applies the principle to Jerusalem. To illustrate and emphasize it, three notable examples of righteousness are adduced: Noah (who saved his family, Gn. vi. 8), Daniel (who saved his friends, Dn. i. 6-20?) and Job likewise (Jb. xlii. 7-10). The achievements of these men are not to be cited as examples of the habitual leniency of God. When Jehovah sentences a guilty land, the righteous will deliver themselves only. Possibly Ezekiel had heard that the men of Jerusalem looked for the city to be spared on the basis of the story of Abraham's intercession for Sodom (Gn. xviii. 23f.); the prophet replies, 'This is the principle on which God acts; if it is true generally, *how much more* in Jerusalem's case (21), which has no Noah, Daniel or Job!' Cf. Jeremiah's similar assertion of the uselessness of intercession for Jerusalem, even from Moses and Samuel (Je. vii. 16, xv. 1-4). For the principle of individual responsibility here implied, cf. chapter xviii.

Daniel (14, 20). Expositors have long questioned as to whether the man of this name is the Daniel of the book named after him, presumably a contemporary of Ezekiel, or a patriarch of similar antiquity to Noah and Job. That the Phoenicians knew of such a person is attested by the reference to him in the Ras Shamra tablets, *c*. 1400 B.C. That his name is spelt there as in Ezekiel, and not as in Daniel, indicates it may be the patriarch who is here meant.

The escaped remnant would show, by their corrupt lives, how just was the judgment of Jerusalem and so set at rest the minds of the exiles. *Ye shall see . . . and ye shall be comforted* (22).

d. **A vine for burning (xv. 1-8)**

This parable suggests that certain Israelites had compared themselves, as Isaiah had done for a different purpose, to the vine among the trees, the choicest among the nations in God's sight. Ezekiel corrects such a notion. Israel is but a wild vine of the forest (not a cultivated one, as elsewhere in the Old Testament); far from being better than other trees, it is useless for anything but fuel. As the wild vine is appointed, as it were, by nature, to be burned, so is Jerusalem destined for destruction (6).

e. **A faithless woman (xvi. 1-63)**

This discourse seeks to show, in allegorical fashion, that Israel's history constitutes 'one unbroken record of black apostasy' (McFadyen). It is in four movements: 1. An adaptation, perhaps, of a popular story concerning a foundling baby that became a queen (3–43). **2.** Jerusalem's notorious sisters, Samaria and Sodom, are righteous in comparison with her (44–52). **3.** Jerusalem can be reinstated only in conjunction with these formerly despised sister communities (53–58). **4.** Penitent Jerusalem will receive a new covenant from God (59–63). For the comparison of Jerusalem to a faithless wife, cf. Is. i. 21; Je. iii. 1f.; Ho. ii. 2–23. The allegory is developed with a candour that tends to shock the Western mind, but it is normal to the Oriental outlook.

Amorite . . . Hittite (3). 'The genealogy is moral, not ethnical' (Toy). Nevertheless the Aramaean ancestors of Israel were kin to the Amorites (or Canaanites) and made affinities with certain of the Hittites. Normal care was denied to this child (4). 'Heathen by parentage, it received heathen treatment at its birth' (Cooke). *I spread my skirt over thee* (8). For this custom see Ru. iii. 9. In the allegory it may be referred to the covenant at Sinai, while verses 9–14 could be applied to the increasing prosperity of the nation up to the days of Solomon. For *badgers' skin* (10; RV 'sealskin') read 'leather'; cf. Ex. xxv. 5.

The evil process described in verse 15 began when Israel adopted the Canaanite sanctuaries of Palestine (cf. xx. 28; Je. ii. 5–7). The actions described in verse 18 represent the treatment accorded to idols on festal occasions. *Thy sons and thy daughters . . . these hast thou sacrificed* (20). Though Josiah stamped out this evil practice for a time (2 Ki. xxiii. 10) it is likely that it was revived in the desperate days of the siege. Verse 26 is a reference to Israel's perennial tendency to look to Egypt for help; cf. Is. xxx. 1–5, xxxi. 1–3. Similarly verse 28 refers to dependence on Assyria (2 Ki. xvi. 7f.; Ho. v. 13, viii. 9), and verse 29 to reliance on Chaldea, i.e. Babylonia (2 Ki. xx. 12f.).

Verses 35–43 describe the punishment of Jerusalem; it will be like that of a harlot, humiliation and death (see verse 38).

Jerusalem's sin is not only as bad as that of her heathen predecessors (44, 45), not only of the same order as that of the wicked cities of Samaria and Sodom (46), but even worse than these (47–51). To her unutterable shame she will later be forced to confess it (52). It is not necessary to assume that Israel's deeds were of a worse character than those of Samaria and Sodom; doubtless the heinousness of her guilt was felt to be accentuated by the uniqueness of her privilege as the betrothed of Jehovah. Cf. Am. iii. 2.

The promise of restoration (53–58) is put in such a way as to be of little comfort to Jerusalem. She can be reinstated only along with Samaria and Sodom, who will be consoled by the shame-faced recognition accorded to them by their erstwhile proud and self-righteous neighbour.

I will remember my covenant (60). This is the one bright spot in this gloomy sky. Jehovah will make an everlasting covenant with her such as

shall completely restore the broken relationship and give back her former position. This is the 'new covenant' of Je. xxxi. 31f. See also Ezk. xxxvii. 26; Is. lix. 21, lxi. 8.

f. The vulture and the vine (xvii. 1–24)

A great eagle (3); Heb. *nesher*. As Jb. xxxix. 27–30 and Mi. i. 16 show, this is the griffon vulture; here it symbolizes Nebuchadnezzar. *Lebanon* is the hill country of Judah; *the highest branch of the cedar* (3) is Jehoiachin, king of Judah (2 Ki. xxiv. 10–16). *A land of traffick* (4) designates Babylonia. Zedekiah, son of Josiah, was made king by Nebuchadnezzar in place of Jehoiachin (2 Ki. xxiv. 17). The location 'beside many waters' (RSV) denotes Palestine; cf. Dt. xi. 11. *A spreading vine* (6). The metaphor changes from that of the cedar. Cooke links this sentence to verse 5 and by a change of vowels reads 'that it might grow and become a spreading vine'. Nebuchadnezzar set Zedekiah on the throne to be a submissive vassal. *Another great eagle* (7). This other vulture is Pharaoh Hophra; see Je. xliv. 30.

Verses 11–21 interpret this figurative language. Zedekiah is denounced for turning to Egypt for help against Babylon (15). The prophets speak unitedly against Israel resorting to Egypt for aid, though their reasons vary (see, e.g., Is. xxx. 1–5, xxxi. 1–3; Je. ii. 36). It was not the political inexpediency of the revolt that drew forth Ezekiel's wrath, but Zedekiah's abandonment of his oath to Nebuchadnezzar (15–18). From verse 19 it is clear that Zedekiah must have invoked Jehovah's name in the oath; to break it was to disgrace the sacred Name (cf. Jos. ix. 15–20). For another instance of Zedekiah's breaking of an oath see Je. xxxiv. 8–22.

Verses 22–24 really form an additional parable in which the figures of verses 3, 4 are differently applied. The *tender one* taken *from the top of his young twigs* (22) is the Messiah of the house of David (Je. xxiii. 5f., xxxiii. 15), who will be planted by Jehovah on Mount Zion and protect the nation restored from exile. For the image of a tree sheltering beasts and birds cf. xxxi. 6, 12; Dn. iv. 12, 21; Mk. iv. 32.

g. Retribution and responsibility (xviii. 1–32)

The teaching of this chapter, summarized in verse 20, needs to be set in the context of the whole book to be judged fairly. Its chief purpose is to vindicate the justice of God, and it has a particular crisis in mind. The prophet's contemporaries alleged that they were being punished for the sins of the previous generation. Ezekiel declared that God does not work in that way, but holds each man accountable for his deeds and will requite him accordingly. This is a foundation principle of revealed religion. Ezekiel was the first to state it clearly. That it can be abused is unquestionable, especially if men divorce the individual from society. But the prophet does not do this; he usually has the whole nation in mind, and indeed it is difficult to reconcile this chapter with his predictions of the utter destruction of Jerusalem (e.g. v. 12, vii. 10–27, xi. 7–12), so real is the unity of the nation to him. Ezekiel's teaching has many facets; they should be viewed together to be truly appreciated. The divorcing of this principle from its context led men to argue that a man's condition reflects God's judgment upon him, so that adversity is the fruit of sin and prosperity the result of righteousness. Against this distortion of Ezekiel's teaching the book of Job is directed, but none could fairly say that it was aimed at the book of Ezekiel.

The proverb (2) was current in Jerusalem (Je. xxxi. 29) and came from there to the exiles in Babylonia. In verse 4 the principle is stated in brief. Then, in illustration, Ezekiel takes the case of three generations, a righteous man who continues in his righteousness (5–9), his son who behaves wickedly (10–13), his grandson who repudiates the evil of his father (14–17). In verse 20 the principle is elaborated; every man shall receive a just requital for his conduct. Ezekiel primarily has in mind the coming judgment of Jerusalem and the restoration to follow; but he would regard it as capable of general application. *If the wicked will turn . . . he shall not die* (21). A man is not only free from the sin of his father; he may be free from his own past if he so wishes. He can repent at once. Kraetzschmar declares verse 23 to be 'the most precious word in the whole book of Ezekiel'. Cf. 1 Tim. ii. 4; 2 Pet. iii. 9. *Make you a new heart* (31); cf. xxxvi. 26, 'a new heart also will I give you'. The same dual truth is expressed in Phil. ii. 12, 13.

h. Dirge over kings (xix. 1–14)

Two elegies are joined together in this chapter; in the first the rulers of Judah are pictured as lions (1–9), in the second as branches of a vine (10–14). If the two poems were written at the same time, the second is predictive (see note on verse 14); but if verse 14 describes past events, the second poem was written later, being modelled on the earlier one and so conjoined to it.

i. **The lioness and her whelps (xix. 1–9).** *Thy mother* (2) is the nation Israel or, more strictly, Judah, as in verse 10. The *young lion* (3) represents Jehoahaz, who was bound by Pharaoh Necho after a reign of only three months and was carried off to Egypt in 608 B.C. (4; see 2 Ki. xxiii. 31–34). *Another of her whelps* (5). Jehoiakim, brother of Jehoahaz, succeeded him on the throne, but is passed over in silence because he had a peaceful end. Jehoiachin, the son of Jehoiakim, is here described. After three months as king he was taken by Nebuchadnezzar to Babylon in 597 B.C. (9; see 2 Ki. xxiv. 8–16). A double application may be seen in verses 8, 9; not only were lions captured in this manner, for the sport of Assyrian kings, but conquered princes were also confined in cages to be a public spectacle.

ii. **The vine and her rods (xix. 10–14).** Verses 11 and 12 should be read, with the Greek, Latin and Armenian versions and RV mg. in part, as mentioning a single rod; but it is uncertain as to which ruler is meant, whether Jehoiachin, as in verses 5–9, or Zedekiah, as in verse 14; the former interpretation seems preferable. *A rod of her branches* (14); i.e. Zedekiah who is held responsible for the destruction of Jerusalem inasmuch as the city would have been spared had he submitted to the Babylonians. Cf. Je. xxxviii. 20–23.

i. History of apostate Israel (xx. 1–44)

The situation is similar to that of chapter xiv; elders come *to inquire of the Lord* (1) through Ezekiel. As in xiv. 3 they had 'taken their idols into their heart', so here the prophet reads the intention of conforming to the idolatry of their environment (32). The answer of Jehovah on both occasions is judgment on the idolaters (xiv. 7, 8, xx. 33–39). This review of Israel's history sets forth Israel's fortunes in Egypt (5–9), in the wilderness (10–26), in Canaan (27–29), in the present (30–32), traversing another wilderness (33–39), resettled in Palestine (40–44). The date (verse 1) is July–August 591 B.C., eleven months after that given in viii. 1. *I . . . lifted up mine hand* (5); i.e. to enforce the oath (cf. Gn. xiv. 22; Dn. xii. 7; Rev. x. 5–7). *They rebelled against me* (8). We have no information of an act of rebellion in Egypt, unless Ex. v. 21 be in view. There may have been other traditions of this period of Israel's history, current in Ezekiel's day, upon which he draws. *I wrought for my name's sake* (9); i.e. so that His reputation among the nations should not suffer through apparent inability to fulfil His word (cf. Nu. xiv. 16; Dt. ix. 28).

Their heart went after their idols (16); cf. Ex. xxxii. 1–6; Nu. xxv. 1–3. *Statutes that were not good . . .* (25). A reversal of the normal purpose of Jehovah's laws; see verse 11. The sacrificing of children (26) was evidently regarded as a fulfilment of the law of Ex. xiii. 12, an interpretation which the prophet appears to view as due to judicial blindness from God (cf. xiv. 9n.; Is. vi. 10–12 and Cooke's note in I.C.C., pp. 218, 219). Translate verse 29 'What is the high place (*bama*) whereunto you are the comers (*ba'im*)?'

In verses 33–38 judgment is mingled with mercy. Jehovah will lead His people out from the land of exile, as He brought them out of Egypt long ago (34); the guilty will perish in the desert as on the former journey (35–38; cf. Ho. ii. 16, 17). The picture of the future redemption as a second exodus is frequent in the prophets. See, e.g., Is. xli. 17–20, xliii. 16–21; Je. xxiii. 7, 8; Mi. vii. 15–17.

The surviving righteous of Israel will return to their land and worship Jehovah (40–44). By this redeeming act Jehovah will make Himself known as God alone, both to the Gentile world (41) and to Israel (42). As in xvi. 61–63 the promise is tempered with the reminder of their former sinfulness (43, 44).

j. The sword of the Lord (xx. 45—xxi. 32)

A new chapter commences at xx. 45 in the Hebrew text; our English translators have followed the ancient versions in their division of the chapters. Four oracles are here conjoined: the destruction of Jerusalem as by fire and sword (xx. 45—xxi. 7); the song of the sword (xxi. 8–17); Nebuchadnezzar at the cross-roads (xxi. 18–27); the judgment of Ammon (xxi. 28–32). If verses 21, 22 afford another example of Ezekiel's clairvoyant vision (cf. chapter viii), the chapter dates from 588 B.C., when Nebuchadnezzar marched on Jerusalem.

The south (46) is Palestine; although west of Babylonia, it is so described because the caravan route traversed the Euphrates and then went southward through Syria. Doth he not speak parables? (49). This saying reflects the scepticism of the people rather than their inability to interpret what Ezekiel said to them. But in xxi. 3ff. the prophet uses a plainer figure to ensure that all understood the meaning of his former proverb. Sigh, therefore (6). This acted prophecy is intended to show the way the news of the catastrophe will be received; cf. xii. 17–20.

'A wild ode to the avenging Chaldean sword' is the description given by Toy to verses 8–17. Certain of the verses, especially 10 and 13, are difficult of elucidation owing to faulty transmission of the text. Smite therefore upon thy thigh (12); i.e. to express grief (cf. Je. xxxi. 19). In verse 14 follow RV. The 'deadly wounded' is Zedekiah as in verse 30. See note on verse 25.

Appoint thee two ways (19). Ezekiel is to draw (on sand?) two roads starting from a common point, i.e. Babylon, and diverging outwards, one leading to Jerusalem and the other to Rabbah (RV), capital city of Ammon. Nebuchadnezzar is seen at the cross-roads (21). He uses divination to ascertain which road to take. Arrows were used in the same way as lots; one marked 'Jerusalem' and another 'Ammon' would be shaken in a quiver and one drawn out. Liver, owing to its connection with blood, was regarded as the seat of life; the colour and marks on that of a sacrificed sheep provided omens of the future. Images (RV 'teraphim') were small human-shaped images; cf. 1 Sa. xix. 13, 16. Unto them (23); i.e. to the men of Jerusalem who believe the divination is false. With verse 25 cf. verse 14. Profane; RV 'deadly wounded'; some prefer to translate this 'dishonoured'. I will overturn . . . (27). The monarchic succession and the state are to be brought into ruin till Messiah comes. The latter half of the verse quotes Gn. xlix. 10, 'until Shiloh comes'; read 'until he whose it is (shello) come'.

The language of verses 28–32 is reminiscent of verses 9, 10; but here the sword is that of Ammon drawn against Israel at the time of Nebuchadnezzar's attack; Jehovah will blot out the memory of Ammon (32), a contrast to Israel's future destiny (xx. 40–44).

k. Arraignment of Jerusalem (xxii. 1–31)

Three oracles are to be distinguished: the sins of the city of bloodshed (1–16); the smelting of Israel (17–22); the indictment of 'the classes and the masses' (McFadyen) (23–31). Jerusalem by its guilt has caused its full number of days and years to draw near (4). The versions read 'thy day' and 'the time of thy years' (cf. xxi. 23). The princes (6) abused their authority by committing judicial murders (cf. 2 Ki. xxiv. 3, 4). To their power (6); read as in RV 'according to his power'. Men that carry tales (9); RV 'slanderous men', i.e. informers who got rid of their enemies by false accusations. I have smitten mine hand (13); a sign of scorn (cf. xxi. 14, 17). In verse 16 see RV. The versions read 'I shall be profaned through thee'; see xx. 9n.

In the second oracle Israel is unrefined ore (18); Jehovah smelts it in the furnace, but dross is the only result. Brass, and tin, and iron, and lead (18) are the precipitates of the ore when first smelted, from which the silver is afterward separated. The real point of the figure is the judgment involved in the idea of smelting. Unlike other prophets who use this figure, Ezekiel excludes the possibility of refinement; his generation is but slag! (cf. Ps. cxix. 119).

There is a conspiracy of her prophets (25). LXX reads 'whose princes' (nasi instead of nabi). If this be accepted, Ezekiel indicts the whole gamut of society in Jerusalem, the 'princes' (25; i.e. members of the royal house), priests (26), 'nobles' (27; Heb. sarim, i.e. officials and heads of important families), prophets (28), and the ordinary people (29). I sought . . . but I found none (30). None of the official leaders stood for righteousness and the true welfare of Israel. Ezekiel naturally considered Jeremiah, whom those leaders persecuted, as one apart (cf. Is. lix. 16, lxiii. 5).

l. Oholah and Oholibah (xxiii. 1–49)

The chapter is in two parts. Verses 1–35 give the allegory of the two sisters, Samaria and Jerusalem, using similar figures as that in chapter xvi (see notes there). But whereas the earlier poem had in mind the evil influences of Canaanite religion, here it is the making of foreign alliances that is condemned. Verses 36–49 are an appendix, developing the allegory in a different manner, possibly with a different situation in mind. Here the two sisters are viewed together and are indicted for Moloch worship and profaning the sanctuary and sabbath (37–39); the foreign alliances appear to be those with countries bordering on Israel (42) rather than with distant empires.

The two names (see verse 4, RV) are identical in meaning, being coined feminine forms of ohel, a 'tent'. They may have in view tents associated with false worship (see xvi. 16). The RV forms of the names should be followed. With all their idols she defiled herself (7). Political alliances usually involved the adoption of the cults of the superior power. Samaria had made alliances with Assyria (5ff.) and Egypt (8); Jerusalem went further and approached the Babylonians also (14–18). Assyrian worship (12) was popularized by Manasseh and remained in the city till its fall (see 2 Ki. xxi. 1–9; Je. xliv. 15–19). *Sent messengers . . . into Chaldea* (16). The occasion is unknown, unless it be that recorded in 2 Ki. xxiv. 1. In verse 20 Judah's request for Egyptian aid against the Babylonians is in mind, Je. xxxvii. 7f. *Pekod, and Shoa, and Koa* (23) were tribes east of the Tigris. *Naked and bare* (29). This stripping of Oholibah represents the devastation of Jerusalem.

Verse 40 describes a petition to a distant people for help, perhaps against the Babylonians. *Sabeans from the wilderness* (42); better, as in RV, 'drunkards from the wilderness'. These would be Israel's near neighbours, Arabs, Edomites, Moabites, etc. (cf. Je. xxvii. 3f.). *The righteous men* (45) can hardly be Babylonians (cf. vii. 21–24); they are the few men of Jerusalem who remain faithful to Jehovah and condemn the national policy. Oholah and Oholibah will be judged as adulteresses (47; see Dt. xxii. 23, 24).

m. The beginning of the end (xxiv. 1–27)

There are three connected themes in this chapter: the parable of the rusty caldron (1–14); the sign of the death of Ezekiel's wife (15–24); the end of the prophet's dumbness (25–27). Reckoning from Jehoiachin's captivity, the date (verse 1) is January, 588 B.C. See 2 Ki. xxv. 1.

The knowledge of the siege (2) again illustrates Ezekiel's supernaturally heightened gift of clairvoyance. The setting down and announcement of this date would constitute a public confirmation of his prophetic office when news filtered through at a later date. *Set on a pot* (3). Perhaps Ezekiel was actually preparing a meal in a caldron when the word of God came to him, declaring this to be symbolic of the judgment of Jerusalem. The use of the figure is wholly opposite to that in xi. 3. *Bring it out piece by piece* (6). The meat is not to be eaten but thrown away, symbolic of the scattering of the people. The last clause of this verse implies that lots were drawn in 597 B.C. as to who should go into captivity; this time there will be no option. The city is like a caldron whose 'rust' (6, RV; i.e. 'bloodshed'—not *scum* as in AV) will not be removed. The only recourse is to set the caldron upside down on the fire and melt it away (11). Jerusalem must be destroyed to be cleansed (12–14).

Ezekiel's wife will die suddenly *with a stroke* (16), or 'plague' (cf. Nu. xiv. 37). He is to hide his grief and show no mourning (17). The day following his wife's death he carried out his normal occupations (18). That caused his fellow-exiles to ask the meaning of his conduct (19). It is explained in verses 20–24 Jerusalem and its sanctuary are as dear to them as a wife to a husband; when they hear of its destruction, and the loss of their relatives, they too must bow in silence before God; it is His just judgment.

Read verses 25–27 as one sentence: 'In the day when I take from them their strength . . . in the day he that escapeth shall come . . . in that day shall thy mouth be opened.' A considerable lapse of time is to occur between verse 25 and verse 26. Cf. Je. lii. 5–7 with Ezk. xxxiii. 21. The divine restrictions on Ezekiel's ministry are to cease when the messenger from Jerusalem arrives. See note on iii. 26.

PROPHECIES AGAINST FOREIGN NATIONS. xxv. 1—xxxii. 32

The denunciations of Jerusalem are complete. Before recounting his predictions of restoration (xxxiii–xlviii), the prophet inserts this group of oracles against Israel's enemies (although some of them belong to a later date) to indicate that all hostile powers must be broken before Israel could be reinstated in glory.

VII. PROPHECIES AGAINST SURROUNDING TRIBES. xxv. 1–17

a. Ammon (xxv. 1–7)

Although at the Babylonian invasion Ammon joined with Edom, Moab and others in persuading Zedekiah to revolt (Je. xxvii. 1–11), at the fall of Jerusalem they seized Israelite cities (Je. xlix. 1f.), and instigated the murder of Gedaliah (Je. xl. 14). Ezekiel makes no mention of these things, only of their malicious joy at Israel's distress (3, 6). Note that in verse 3 the prophet speaks of the desolation of Jerusalem as a past event.

b. Moab (xxv. 8–11)

Jeremiah denounces Moab for its arrogancy and rebellion against Jehovah and derision of Israel (Je. xlviii. 25f.). Zephaniah speaks of their plundering the Jews (Zp. ii. 8). Ezekiel denounces them for their scornful rejection of Israel's claim to be a nation apart, in view of her relation to Jehovah (8).

c. Edom (xxv. 12–14)

For the malice of Edom against Israel at the fall of Jerusalem cf. Ezk. xxxv. 10–15; Ob. 10–16; Ps. cxxxvii. 7.

d. The Philistines (xxv. 15–17)

We have no information of their behaviour towards Israel in this period other than this passage. Cherethites at one time had formed part of David's bodyguard (2 Sa. viii. 18, xv. 18, xx. 7). See note on Jdg. iii. 3.

VIII. PROPHECIES AGAINST TYRE. xxvi. 1—xxviii. 26

The facts of the contemporary situation account for the prominence given by Ezekiel to Tyre.

The Babylonians were about to lay siege to the city. What would be the result? 'On patriotic and religious grounds the Jewish exiles felt themselves to be involved in the issue. Ezekiel has no doubt that it will end in Tyre's overthrow and extinction (xxvi); he anticipates its ruin in a magnificent dirge (xxvii); and threatens its king with retribution (xxviii)' (Cooke).

a. The overthrow of Tyre (xxvi. 1–21)

Tyre exults over Jerusalem's fate, for she had been 'the gate of the peoples' (2, RV). Caravan traffic from north to south would have been subject to taxation by the Jews. *As the sea causeth his waves to come up* (3). Tyre was built upon a rock island 'in the heart of the seas' (xxvii. 4, RV), a position which facilitated trade and made it seemingly impregnable. *Her daughters . . . in the field* (6) are its dependent mainland towns. Ezekiel always spells the name of the Babylonian monarch *Nebuchadrezzar* (7); this approximates more closely to the Babylonian original *Nabukudurri-usur*, 'Nebo protect my boundary'.

This description of the campaign in verses 8–12 presupposes the erection of a mole from the mainland to the island, a procedure probably adopted by Nebuchadnezzar (cf. xxix. 18n.) and certainly by Alexander with complete success in 332 B.C. 'The pillars of thy strength' (11, RV) would be those associated with the worship of Melkart, the god of Tyre. *The isles* (15) are coasts and islands of the Mediterranean with which Tyre traded. *I shall bring thee down . . . into the pit* (20). Tyre is to be brought down to Sheol. For *I shall set glory in the land of the living* (20) LXX reads 'thou shalt not stand in the land of living', which more accords with the context.

b. Lament over Tyre (xxvii. 1–36)

The elegy proper (verses 3–9a, 25b–36) likens Tyre to an expensively equipped ship, filled with goods, which was wrecked by a storm and lamented by those that held an interest in it. The central section (9b–25a), describing the merchandise of Tyre, does not maintain the imagery; but that is insufficient reason for denying its authenticity. The whole chapter has deeply influenced the author of the book of Revelation, who applies its imagery to the anti-Christian empire of his own day (Rev. xviii).

Senir (5) was the Amorite name for Hermon (Dt. iii. 9). *Chittim* (6; RV 'Kittim') originally denoted Cyprus, but 'isles of Kittim' came to represent the islands and coasts of the Mediterranean. *Lud* (Lydia?) and *Phut* (10) (on the African coast of the Red Sea) are placed together because of similarity of sound, not because of their supposed proximity. The three names suffice to show that Tyre's mercenaries came from all parts of the ancient world. *Gammadims* (11) perhaps hailed from northern Syria. *Tarshish* (12) is Tartessus, a port in southern Spain. *Javan* (13); Ionians in Asia Minor. *Tubal, and Meshech* (13); situated in east Asia Minor (see xxxviii. 2n.). *Togarmah* (14); Armenia.

Dedan (15); an Arab tribe in Edom. *Minnith* (17) in Jdg. xi. 33 is an Ammonite town. By a slight regrouping of the consonants the term 'spices' is gained. *Pannag* (17); perhaps a loan word from Akkadian, *pannigu*, which is a kind of meal or cake (Cooke). *Dedan* (20), associated with Arabians, is not to be confused with the Dedan of verse 15. *Sheba* (22) was 1,200 miles south of Jerusalem in southern Arabia (cf. 1 Ki. x). The towns of verse 23 were in Mesopotamia.

In verses 25–27 the imagery of the poem is resumed; the good ship Tyre sinks with all hands lost. For *the east wind* (26) cf. Ps. xlviii. 7, but it may be an allusion to Babylon. Verses 29–34 describe lamentation of the sailors at Tyre's loss. Cf. Rev. xviii. 17–19. *The inhabitants of the isles* (35) may refer particularly to *the merchants among the people* (36); cf. verse 3. For the lamentations of the kings and merchants cf. Rev. xviii. 9–17.

c. Dirge for the king of Tyre (xxviii. 1–19)

The prince of Tyrus (Ithobal II) is addressed (2) as representing the city; his self-exaltation to the status of deity is typical of the pride of the people. Tyre's impregnable position on a rock reminds him of the mythical mountain of God (14, 16); as God reigns supreme there, so securely is he enthroned *in the midst of the seas* (2). *Daniel* (3); see xiv. 20n. *The deaths* (intensive pl.; RV 'death') *of them that are slain* (8) is one without burial. Since the Phoenicians practised circumcision, *the deaths of the uncircumcised* (10) were shameful, involving a dishonourable position in Sheol.

In verses 11–19 Ezekiel seems to have adopted for his threnody a popular story, presumably current in Tyre as elsewhere, of a primal being who dwelt in the Garden of God in splendour and purity but was subsequently driven out through pride; so shall the king of Tyre shortly fall from his glory. It looks like a highly mythological version of the story in Gn. iii, but the prophet does not hesitate to use it since it was well known and admirably suited to his purpose. *Thy covering* (13); i.e. 'dress'; Babylonian gods were frequently dressed in robes ornamented with jewels. Nine stones are enumerated here; LXX has twelve and they are identical with those of the High Priest's robe (Ex. xxviii. 17–20); perhaps the three missing stones dropped out of the Hebrew text by accident. After the list, read 'of gold was the workmanship of thy tabrets and ouches' (Cooke).

In verse 14 the LXX reads 'with the cherub . . . I set thee', and again in verse 16, 'the cherub destroyed thee', variations which materially alter the story but which are generally adopted by expositors. The moral of the story is applied first to the king (17) and then to the city (18). Both will be brought to utter ruin.

d. Prophecy against Zidon (xxviii. 20–26)

Zidon is to share the fate of its neighbour. Elsewhere the two cities are spoken of together (e.g. Is. xxiii; Joel iii. 4f.). Verses 24–26 state the theme not only of chapters xxv—xxxii, but also of the section dealing with Israel's restoration (chapters xxxiv ff.); the destruction of Israel's enemies is necessary both to the establishment of Israel in the kingdom of God and the demonstration to all nations of the sole deity of Jehovah.

IX. PROPHECIES AGAINST EGYPT. xxix. 1—xxxii. 32

These oracles come from the period of the siege and conquest of Jerusalem (587–585 B.C.), except xxix. 17–21 which was written in 571 B.C.

a. The fall of Egypt (xxix. 1–16)

The date (verse 1) is January 587 B.C. *Pharaoh* (2) is addressed (like the king of Tyre in chapter xxviii) as representing the genius of his people. Gunkel argues, with considerable cogency, that Ezekiel in verse 3 makes Pharaoh use the speech of the chaos-dragon of the waters (see Haupt's note in Toy) and not simply of a crocodile; his fate (4, 5) is thus similar to that of the monster in the Tiamat story; see further on xxxii. 2–8. With verses 6 and 7 cf. Is. xxxvi. 6.

In verses 8–12 the allegory is applied. Egypt will suffer a like fate to Israel, devastation and dispersal among the nations for forty years. Read 10b as RV mg. 'from Migdol to Syene'; these cities were the northern and southern limits of Egypt.

Like Israel, Egypt is to be restored (13–16), but not to a position of glory: it will be *the basest of the kingdoms* (15).

b. Nebuchadnezzar's wages (xxix. 17–21)

The date (verse 17) is April 571. This is the latest in the book and indicates that this oracle has been added as an appendix. Nebuchadnezzar worked hard to take Tyre; heads were *made bald* and shoulders sore through the toilsome construction of a mole from the mainland to the city (18). *Yet had he no wages* from Tyre (18). The city capitulated but there was little booty; the Tyrians had plenty of time to ship away their valuables. Jehovah would recompense his 'servant' (Je. xxvii. 6) by giving him the spoils of Egypt. Nebuchadnezzar invaded Egypt *c.* 568. Israel will be restored to power once more (21). The fulfilment of these prophecies will open the prophet's mouth in thanksgiving and renewed prophetic ministry; and the criticism of his hearers over the incomplete fulfilment of his prophecy on Tyre would be silenced.

c. Egypt's day (xxx. 1–26)

In verses 1–19 is described the approach of the day of the Lord on Egypt, in verses 20–26 the breaking of Pharaoh's might by Nebuchadnezzar. *Woe worth the day* (2); i.e. 'Alas for the day!' See note on vii. 2 and cf. Joel ii. 1, 2; Zp. i. 15. Verse 5 gives a list of Egypt's provinces and allies who are to share its ruin. *The mingled people*

(*'ereb*) are not Arabs (*'arabh*) but foreigners living in Egypt (cf. Je. xxv. 20); the same word denotes the 'mixed multitude' in Israel (Ex. xii. 38) and foreigners in Babylon (Je. l. 37). For *Chub* (RV 'Cub'), an unknown name, LXX reads *Lub*, i.e. Libya. *The men of the land that is in league* is an unknown nation confederate with Egypt; it is unlikely that it means Israel, as LXX implies and RV mg. would encourage.

The destruction of Egypt is described in detail (13–19), principal towns being singled out for particular mention. Instead of *images* (13; RV mg. 'things of nought'; Heb. *elilim*), LXX reads 'chiefs' (Heb. *elim*), a reading favoured by many commentators. *Aven* (17; i.e. 'nothingness') is a contemptuous pronunciation of 'On', the two words being spelt alike in Hebrew. It was famous for its sun temple, hence its name 'Beth-shemesh' ('House of the Sun') in Je. xliii. 13 and its Greek name Heliopolis ('City of the Sun'). At *Pi-beseth* the cat-headed goddess Ubastet was worshipped.

The oracle of verses 20–26, dated April 587 B.C. (verse 20), takes its rise from Nebuchadnezzar's defeat of Pharaoh Hophra, characterized as a breaking of Pharaoh's arm and consequent weakening of his power (21). This will be followed by a further defeat that will completely overthrow the Egyptian monarch (22f.).

d. The mighty cedar Pharaoh (xxxi. 1–18)

The allegory has three movements: verses 2–9 are a description of Pharaoh, representing Egypt, under the figure of a lofty cedar; verses 10–14 describe the destruction of the great tree, and verses 15–18 the reaction to this event on the part of the rest of the nations. Both this chapter and the next have parallels with Is. xiv. 4–20. Mention of *the deep* (4), *the garden of God* (8) and *Eden* (9, 18) indicate the probability of a background similar to that of chapter xxviii (where see notes).

In verse 3 read 'Behold there was a cedar in Lebanon'. The initial letter of *t'asshur* (cedar) fell out and produced *'asshur*, i.e. Assyria. The context clearly shows that Pharaoh is in mind. For *thick boughs* (3) read with LXX and RV mg. 'clouds'. The figurative language of verses 5 and 6 is frequently used to indicate the greatness of a kingdom (cf. xvii. 23; Dn. iv. 11, 12; Mk. iv. 32).

Pharaoh's sin is pride (10), the failing of most tyrants (cf. xxviii. 6; Is. xiv. 13f.; Dn. xi. 12). The fall of Pharaoh is to be a warning to all nations against committing the same fault (14). *The mighty one of the heathen* (11) is Nebuchadnezzar, *the terrible of the nations* (12) his armies. The imagery of verses '15 and 16 portrays the effect of Pharaoh's doom on the nations left on earth. If with LXX we omit in verse 16 *in the nether parts of the earth*, the figure is carried out consistently; the rival nations were *comforted* in that they were freed from Egypt's domination. *They also went down into hell* (17) should perhaps be regarded as a prophetic perfect 'they also will go down'.

For *hell* read, as in RV mg., 'Sheol'. Pharaoh is to join in Sheol the *uncircumcised* and the *slain* in battle (18). Since the Egyptians practised circumcision and, even more than the rest of the Orient, paid lavish attention to burial, this involved the uttermost of disgrace—inclusion amongst the lowest ranks of the underworld.

e. Lament over Pharaoh and Egypt (xxxii. 1–32)

The first lamentation (1–16) deals primarily with Pharaoh, the second (17–32) with the nation's descent to Sheol, though in both poems the thought passes imperceptibly from ruler to people. The former poem itself divides into two, verses 2–10 describing the fate of the water monster Pharaoh, verses 11–16 the desolation of Egypt by the king of Babylon. The date (verse 1) is the end of February 585 B.C., eight months after the fall of Jerusalem.

Thou art like (2); RV 'Thou wast likened'; this may better be translated from another root of the same spelling (*damah*) 'thou art destroyed'. There is no connection between this reference to *a young lion* and the following allegory; it serves only as an introductory remark. *Thou art as a whale* (or 'the monster') *in the seas* (2). Most commentators believe this refers simply to the crocodile, as also xxix. 3–5. It is more likely an echo of the chaos-monster allegory, which told how the monster Tiamat, personification of the waters, fought against heaven and was destroyed

by Marduk. From its body was made the material creation, but some of it is reserved for food for man (2 Baruch xxix. 4). The story is applied to any tyrannous peoples (e.g. Is. xxvii. 1; Dn. vii), but especially to Egypt (Is. xxx. 7, li. 9, 10), thereby showing both their evil character and sure fate. Its use here explains the extraordinary language of verses 4–8.

The prophet then passes from the judgment of the king (11, 12a) to that of the nation (12b–15); the allegorical language seems to be maintained in verses 13, 14, the agitated waters settle down and become clear again; that neither man nor beast further troubles them is a sign of desolation.

The month of verse 17 is presumably the same as that of verse 1, the *word* coming fourteen days later. In the verses that follow the prophet portrays Egypt going down to the land of the departed, consequent upon her destruction. Egypt must do this at the bidding of the prophet (19, 20). There they will find the armies of great nations of the past, Assyria, Elam, Meshech with Tubal (22–27), together with hostile nations of the present, Edom, *the princes of the north* (i.e. lands bordering on Phoenicia) and Zidon, all which are evidently to be destroyed (29, 30). When Egypt perishes from the judgment of God, then Pharaoh will at least have the cold comfort of knowing that his is not the only empire that has gone to the grave (31)!

THE RESTORATION OF ISRAEL. xxxiii. 1—xlviii. 35

X. THE RESPONSIBILITY OF PROPHET AND PEOPLE. xxxiii. 1–20

The interpretation of this passage depends on its true context. If, as many hold, verses 21, 22 should determine the whole chapter, then this section relates to God's judgment on sinners prior to the re-establishment of Israel in the glorious kingdom. To 'die' is to depart this life before the restoration; to 'live' is to enjoy the privileges of the kingdom. On this reading, xx. 33–42 forms an excellent parallel. If, however, verses 2ff., 10, 20 imply the last desperate stages of the siege of Jerusalem, and the consequent despair of the nation, then this constitutes a final warning to the people. Perhaps the latter is the preferable alternative.

The parable of verses 1–6 is drawn from the custom of setting a watchman on the city wall in times of danger to look for the approach of the enemy. The dread responsibility of the watchman's position is here chiefly in mind. With verse 6 cf. Gn. ix. 5. With similar seriousness Ezekiel is to view his office at this critical juncture of the nation (7–9). These verses repeat iii. 17–19, on which see notes.

As the watchman has a responsibility to sound the alarm, so the people have a duty to respond. Verse 10 implies both an admission of the justice of the nation's misfortunes and an attitude of despair (see RV). Ezekiel calls them to renewal of

faith and hope by stressing the grace of God (11), the importance of one's present state rather than one's past life (12–19) and the possibility of immediate repentance and forgiveness (11, 14–16, 19).

XI. THE TURNING-POINT IN EZEKIEL'S MINISTRY. xxxiii. 21–33

The day for which Ezekiel had waited for seven years! From now on he is free to devote himself to the ministry of building up instead of pulling down and so to develop the message he has but hinted at earlier (see, e.g., xvi. 60ff., xvii. 22ff., xx. 33ff.). The date (verse 21) is probably based on the Babylonian reckoning of years as beginning with spring; that in Je. xxxix. 2 reckons in years beginning in autumn, so that July 586 B.C., the date of the fall of the city, is the eleventh year of the captivity on Jeremiah's reckoning and the twelfth on Ezekiel's. The news of the capture of the city thus reaches Ezekiel six months later. For Ezekiel's dumbness, see notes on iii. 26. Verses 23–29 contain a message of judgment on the Jews left behind in the homeland. For a similar situation cf. xi. 14ff.

Talking against thee (30); better, as in RV, 'talking of thee'. Verses 30–33 give us a glimpse of the popularity enjoyed by the prophet, no doubt intensified by the fulfilment of his message. But the enthusiasm of the people is shallow; his word is not obeyed by them. In verse 31 instead of *with their mouth they shew much love*, LXX reads 'lies are in their mouth'. Ezekiel is like one of the love-songs which they delight to hear (32, RV mg.); but probably we are to understand that he is like a singer of such, rather than the song itself. *When this cometh to pass* (33) they will realize the personal truth of his words. The reference here is not to judgment but to the redemption and conditions of its enjoyment which henceforth dominate his preaching.

XII. THE RETURN OF ISRAEL TO HER OWN LAND. xxxiv. 1—xxxvii. 28

a. Helpless sheep and faithless shepherds (xxxiv. 1–31)

The allegory, apparently a development of Je. xxiii. 1–4, is in two sections: the rapacious rulers of Israel, who must bear responsibility for the plight of the people (1–16); God's dealings with the nation itself (17–31).

The shepherds (2), as appears from the end of verse 4, are Israel's rulers, especially those who but lately had governed the nation. For the figure cf. Ps. lxxviii. 70ff.; Is. xliv. 28, lxiii. 11; Je. ii. 8; Zc. xi, xiii. 7. *My sheep wandered* (6); *my flock became a prey* (8). A symbolic description of Israel's oppression (by such powers as Assyria, Egypt, Babylon) and of the dispersion after the fall of Jerusalem. With verse 5 cf. 1 Ki. xxii. 17; Mt. ix. 36. *I will bring them . . . and gather them* (13). The exiles are to be brought back from all lands whither they have gone (including Egypt, Phoenicia and Arabia, as well as Babylonia) and settle down under the government of Jehovah. The tenderness of Ezekiel, so largely concealed in his prophecies, is well seen in this description of God's beneficent rule as Shepherd of His people (14–16). Cf. Lk. xv. 3–7; Jn. x; Heb. xiii. 20; 1 Pet. ii. 25; Rev. vii. 17.

At verse 17 the figure changes. The prophet turns from the kings to lesser officials who nevertheless tyrannize over their fellow-countrymen. This verse may have suggested to our Lord His parable of the sheep and goats (Mt. xxv. 31ff.). The teaching of the whole passage reminds us of xx. 37, 38; restoration is mingled with judgment. *I will set up* (23); cf. 2 Sa. vii. 12; Am. ix. 11. *One shepherd* (23) implies one flock (not two as formerly); see xxxvii. 24 and cf. Jn. x. 16. He is to be another *David* (24) through whom God rules; cf. xxxvii. 25, xlvi. 1–18. Note that his appearing is consequent upon the salvation wrought by God. That salvation is achieved by the Messiah is a distinctively New Testament doctrine, adumbrated only in the latter part of Isaiah. The *covenant of peace* (25) is between the land and the people, and is linked with the removal of the *evil beasts*, which would multiply in the period of exile; cf. Lv. xxvi. 4–6 and a similar covenant in Ho. ii. 18. Only then would it be safe for a man to *sleep in the woods* (25).

A plant (RV 'plantation') *of renown* (29); the word is a collective singular, implying plantations

so fruitful as to become famous. With LXX and Latin omit *men* in verse 31 and read 'Ye are my sheep . . . and I am your God'; cf. Rev. xxi. 3.

b. The extirpation of Edom (xxxv. 1–15)

The insertion of this oracle of doom in prophecies of restoration is explained by Edom's attempted occupation of Israel and Judah (10). Since Israel's restoration depends on her return to the land, Edom must first be overcome; such a judgment is demanded by the cruelty (5, 6) and blasphemy (10–13) of this ancient foe of Israel.

Mount Seir (2) is properly the mountain range south of the Dead Sea; but it also denotes the country of the Edomites. Edom's *perpetual hatred* (5) towards Israel goes back to the origins of the two nations (Gn. xxvii. 41). The former had evidently assisted the Babylonians in the slaughter of 586 B.C., characterized as 'the time of the iniquity of the end' (5, RV; cf. xxi. 25, 29). Edom claimed the territory of Judah and Israel as her own possession (10). Since this was looked upon as Jehovah's inheritance ('the Lord's land', Ho. ix. 3) and was to be again taken up by Him (xlviii. 35), Edom's claim was nothing short of blasphemy (12) in the eyes of the prophet; cf. verses 12, 13; Ob. 12. Verse 14 indicates that Edom will have no part in the kingdom of God.

c. Restoration and regeneration (xxxvi. 1–38)

Israel's external recovery is dealt with in verses 1–15, her internal renewal in verses 16–38. As in vi. 1–7 *the mountains* (1) stand for the country itself, for they are its most prominent feature. But whereas in chapter vi the 'mountains' were denounced, here they are consoled with promises of blessing. The derisive *enemy* (2) denotes the petty states bordering on Israel (see chapter xxv), but with special reference to Edom whose hatred has been the subject of chapter xxxv. The *jealousy* of Jehovah (5) is evoked by the nations' seizure of His land and their scorning of His people. The same jealousy that brought requital on Israel (xxiii. 25) brings judgment upon them and leads Israel to a glorious reinstatement (xxxix. 25). The end of the exile is *at hand* (8). This is the normal prophetic outlook on the redemption of the end-time, both in the Old Testament and New Testament (cf. Hab. ii. 3; Rom. xiii. 12; 1 Pet. iv. 7; Rev. i. 3, xxii. 10). *All the house of Israel* (10) will enjoy restitution, not one tribe only (cf. xxxvii. 15f.). *Thou shalt no more henceforth bereave them* (12); i.e. by the four sore judgments; see xiv. 21.

Israel's name was bound up with that of Jehovah (21, 22); their condition therefore reflected on the honour of their God. The nations thought that Israel's distress was due to Jehovah's impotence (20); their restoration to blessedness in their own land would make all see that Jehovah's government was characterized by holiness, not by weakness, and so His name would be revered by all (23). The conception is integral to Ezekiel's thought and is moral in the highest degree. The cleansing from sin, though described in the language of ceremonial (5), is figurative for moral renewal; cf. Zc. xiii. 1. The *new heart* and *new spirit* (26) are practically synonymous, occasioned by the gift of God's Spirit; it is not to be rationalized as simply the inspiration of a new disposition, but is a supernatural gift. The bestowal of the Holy Spirit is frequently associated by the prophets with the coming of the new age (cf. xxxix. 29; Is. xliv. 3, lix. 21; Joel ii. 28, 29; Acts ii. 16f.). The passage is Ezekiel's counterpart to the 'new covenant' of Jeremiah (Je. xxxi. 31f.). *I will multiply the fruit* . . . (30). Supernatural fertility of the land is a mark of the kingdom of God; cf. verse 35; see also xlvii. 1–12; Is. xxxv. 1, 2, lv. 13; Zc. viii. 12. The population also will be increased (38), so that cities shall be as crowded as the streets of Jerusalem used to be when sacrificial animals thronged them at the great festivals.

d. Resuscitation and reunion of Israel (xxxvii. 1–28)

Ezekiel predicts the political revival of his nation (verses 1–14) and the reunion of its two divisions (verses 15–28).

Whether the prophet in verse 1 sees the *valley* (or 'plain') in vision, or whether he is impelled by the Spirit to go to this place to receive a vision (as in iii. 22), is not clear. The dry bones (2) indicate an army slain in battle. To the despondent of Israel the nation seemed to be in a similar state. Both the question and answer of verse 3 reflect the hopelessness of the situation (cf. verse 11, xxxiii. 10); nothing but a stupendous act of God could effect a restoration. In verse 9 the same Hebrew word *ruach* signifies both *wind* and 'spirit' (see RV mg.). The phrase *the four winds* (9) is an Akkadian idiom for the four quarters of the earth (see Cooke, I.C.C., p. 400). The breath of God does not come from the winds, in the sense of identity with them, but comes from the ends of the earth; translate therefore, 'Prophesy unto the breath, prophesy . . . and say to the breath . . . Come from the four quarters, O breath, and breathe upon these slain.' Cf. the Greek *pneuma* and the ambiguity in Jn. iii. 8 (RV mg.) arising therefrom.

The interpretation of the vision changes the figure by regarding the Israelites as buried in graves (12) instead of scattered on the ground. This is a prediction of the reintegration of Israel's political life, not of a literal resurrection of the dead. Some expositors are eager to point out that the doctrine of resurrection was unknown in Israel at this time. It is pertinent to ask, however, whether it is more likely that the dogma of resurrection originated from this passage, as many believe, or whether the passage is not rather an application of the idea of resurrection with which Ezekiel was already acquainted. It seems extraordinary, in view of the later teaching on resurrection, that a prophet should coin this figure with no knowledge whatever of the doctrine. Probability would indicate that it is a

figurative use of a conception already current in his circles.

In verses 15–28 Ezekiel enacts a symbol. Two sticks, representing the southern and northern kingdoms of Israel (Judah and Joseph being respectively their chief tribes), are joined to form one stick, symbolizing the unity of the nation on its return to the homeland. At that time the house of David shall rule over the united nation for ever (22, 24, 25; see notes on xxxiii. 23, 24). It is sometimes pointed out that this never happened in the post-exilic history of Israel; but the prophet is looking for nothing less than the advent of the messianic kingdom, when the tabernacle of God shall be with His people (27; see Rev. xxi. 3). At that time the nations shall recognize the power of Jehovah through His redemption of His people (28).

XIII. PROPHECY AGAINST GOG. xxxviii. 1—xxxix. 29

These two chapters are unique in Old Testament prophecy in that they describe an uprising of foreign powers against the people of God after the commencement of the messianic kingdom. The prophet has already predicted the coming blessedness of Israel (xxxiii—xxxvii); he now portrays the nation as long settled in their land and transformed into a prosperous community (xxxviii. 8, 11, 12, 14), a condition which, according to his earlier teaching, involves their prior repentance, regeneration and political revival (xxxiii—xxxvii). Whereas he had said that Israel's restoration was 'at hand' (xxxvi. 8), he says that Gog shall be mustered *after many days . . . in the latter years* (xxxviii. 8). The motive underlying the prophecy is the necessity of earlier prophecies concerning the destruction of hostile Gentile powers being fulfilled (xxxviii. 17, xxxix. 8) and for the nations of the world to learn the power, holiness and sole deity of Jehovah (see note on xxxix. 7). The author of the book of Revelation has both used these chapters to vivify his description of Armageddon prior to the millennium (Rev. xix. 17, 18), and adapted their essential idea so as to make it a final rebellion of the godless of humanity at the end of the millennium, before the new creation (xx. 7–9). In comparing the two writings it should be remembered that Ezekiel knew nothing of a new creation nor of a new Israel which was to inherit the kingdom; if John was to incorporate the prophecy he had of necessity to change its form. In conformity with his usage of Old Testament prophecy generally, he has not hesitated to do so.

Gog (2); perhaps from 'Gagaia', home of barbarians, mentioned in the Amarna letters. It is the name of the leader. *Magog* is both his land (as here) and people (xxxix. 6). In Rev. xx. 8 Gog and Magog symbolically represent the godless nations of the whole world. *Meshech and Tubal* (2) are always coupled together, in secular as well as biblical writings (see, e.g., Gn.

x. 2; Ezk. xxvii. 13, xxxii. 26); the reading of AV and RV mg. *chief prince of Meshech and Tubal* is therefore preferable to that of RV 'prince of Rosh, Meshech and Tubal'. Meshech and Tubal were probably east of Asia Minor and are usually identified with Phrygia and Cappadocia; their equation with Moscow and Tobolsk, and Rosh with Russia, is unsupportable. *Libya* (5), RV 'Put', is East Africa. *Gomer* (6) is linked with Magog in Gn. x. 2. They were called Gimirrai by the Assyrians and Cimmerians by the Greeks. Originating north of the Black Sea, by Ezekiel's time they had settled in Asia Minor. Their name survives in Gamir, Armenian name for Cappadocia. *Togarmah* (6), north-east of Asia Minor, is Armenia. From Ezekiel's point of view it appears to be 'in the uttermost parts of the north' (6, RV) just as, to the author of *Psalms of Solomon*, Rome was regarded as 'the uttermost part of the earth' (Ps. Sol. viii. 16).

After many days (8); the invasion is not to occur for a long time. Cf. Is. xxiv. 22. *The latter years* (8) indicates the period of the kingdom (cf. Is. ii. 2). Israel, long settled in peace in her own land, has no fear of attack and so dwells in *unwalled villages . . . without walls, and having neither bars nor gates* (11; cf. Zc. ii. 4). Merchants and slave dealers all over the world are interested in the forthcoming campaign (13).

Gog's destruction will be by earthquake (19, 20), mutual strife (21) and plagues like those on Egypt at the exodus (22, 23); it is presumed that Israel will be brought safely through these calamities as in that former time. The reference to the earlier prophets in verse 17 would be to such passages as Zp. iii. 8; Je. iii. 6; and perhaps, seeing that the prophets spoke *in old time*, to prophecies known to Ezekiel but which have since perished.

Verses 1–20 of chapter xxxix cover the same ground as xxxviii. 2–4, 14–23 (see especially the commencement of the two chapters). The repetition is made to emphasize the marvellous nature of the deliverance; the number of weapons burned by the Israelites and the long time taken to bury the dead show the immensity of Gog's armies, while the feast for birds and beasts stresses the completeness of the victory. Both Israel and the nations will learn of Jehovah's greatness through this judgment (7). This is a recurring theme of the prophecy (cf. xxxviii. 16, 23, xxxix. 6, 13, 21–23, 25–29).

The burial of Gog and his hosts takes place in a valley east of the Dead Sea (11–16); strictly this is outside the borders of Israel in the kingdom of God (xlvii. 18), but it is sufficiently close to serve as a memorial of honour for the victorious nation. The removal of all trace of corpses is necessary for the complete cleansing of the land (cf. Nu. xxxv. 33, 34; Lv. v. 2).

The picture of Jehovah's feast (in verses 17–20) serves to underline the terrible destruction of Gog and his hosts. It entails a change of figure, for bodies cannot be both eaten and buried, but the inconsistency is so slight, and in any case

vanishes in the light of verses 14, 15, that it seems a hazardous ground for suggesting that the picture comes from another hand and relates to the Persian or Greek age. Verses 21 and 22 stress the supreme lesson to be learned by Israel and the nations. Israel's captivity and Gog's destruction alike reveal the holiness of God and His unfailing grace towards His people.

Verses 25–29 are a concluding summary of Ezekiel's prophecies of restoration: God will certainly perform His word to Israel and bring glory to His name in all the earth.

XIV. TEMPLE AND PEOPLE IN THE KINGDOM OF GOD. xl. 1—xlviii. 35

The concluding chapters of Ezekiel's writing form a strange contrast to the furious oratory of the earlier prophecies. In reality they are the essential complement to the judgments he had enunciated. Ezekiel was a priest as well as a prophet. It was his joyful task to balance the prophecies of the ruin of the temple, the departure of Jehovah and the scattering of the nation with a detailed prediction of the rebuilding of the temple, the return of Jehovah to His people and the reorganization of the national life. It was not sufficient to declare that the nation was to return and erect another temple; they must be instructed how to build it. To ensure the holiness of temple, people and worship alike, detailed instructions are issued by the prophet which were the fruit of both prolonged vision and reflection. If their reading is tedious to us, we must remember that, to the Jewish mind, it was impossible to bestow too much trouble and thought on the place whose name is 'Jehovah is there' (xlviii. 35). Such was the spirit in which these chapters were written. It needs little imagination to realize that among Ezekiel's companions in exile they would excite as much interest and discussion as anything he had as yet issued.

A word must be added concerning the interpretation of these chapters. It need hardly be said that Ezekiel has here advanced plans which he expected to be carried out to the letter. To make them a deliberately symbolic description of the worship of the Christian Church is out of the question. Nor was the vision thought of as something to be fulfilled in normal conditions, as chapter xlvii shows; it was a plan for the era of God's kingdom. Some expositors, accordingly, look for a rebuilding of the temple at the second coming of Christ and an exact fulfilment of all Ezekiel's predictions in the kingdom of Christ. This view is challenged by certain fundamental principles of the New Testament. 1. The atonement of our Lord has nullified all sacrifices for ever (Heb. x. 18). 2. The heirs of the kingdom are no longer the Jewish nation but the Church, the new Israel in which the old Israel may find its true place (Mt. xxi. 43; 1 Pet. ii. 9, 10). 3. John in the Revelation adapts these chapters to describe the Church in the kingdom of God (Rev. xxi. 9—xxii. 5) and removes from them all traces of

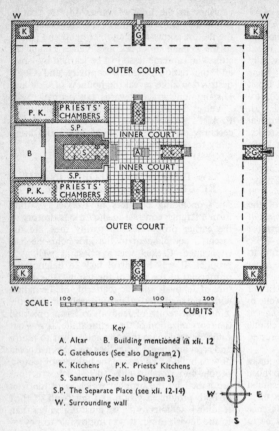

W   W

OUTER COURT

P. K.   PRIESTS' CHAMBERS

S.P.

INNER COURT

B   S   A

INNER COURT

S.P.

P. K.   PRIESTS' CHAMBERS

OUTER COURT

K   G   K

W   W

SCALE: 100   0   100   200   CUBITS

Key

A. Altar   B. Building mentioned in xli. 12
G. Gatehouses (See also Diagram 2)
K. Kitchens   P.K. Priests' Kitchens
S. Sanctuary (See also Diagram 3)
S.P. The Separate Place (see xli. 12-14)
W. Surrounding wall

W ⊕ E
S

1. THE TEMPLE AREA

Judaism. To speak of a 'double fulfilment' of all
these things at the same time, so that there are
two reigning Israels in the kingdom, two New
Jerusalems, each having a river of life and trees
of life, etc., two rulers from David's seed, an
earthly and heavenly Sovereign, and so on, is to
demand credence in the incredible. The conclusion of Ezekiel's prophecy, therefore, is to be
regarded as a true prediction of the kingdom of
God given under the forms with which the prophet was familiar, viz. those of his own (Jewish)
dispensation. Their essential truth will be embodied in the new age under forms suitable to
the new (Christian) dispensation. How this is to
be done is outlined for us in the book of Revelation (xxi. 1—xxii. 5).

a. The plan of the new temple (xl. 1—xlii. 20)

It is impossible in the limits of this
commentary to attempt a full exposition of Ezekiel's description of
the future temple. This must be left
to the longer works. The reading of
his plans will be greatly facilitated
if each paragraph is checked against
the accompanying drawings.

Ezekiel is transported in vision to
Mount Zion where his angel guide
greets him (xl. 1–4). The first thing that
meets his eye is the wall surrounding
the temple precincts (5; see Diagram
1). Passing through a massive gateway
on the east side, built in similar style
to many he had seen in Babylonian
temples (6–16; see Diagram 2), he
comes into the outer court about which
was a pavement and thirty rooms set
apart for the use of people during
festivals (17–19). On the north and
south sides there are gateways similar
to the one by which he had entered
(20–26). In the four corners there are
kitchens for the people (marked 'K'),
but these are not described until xlvi.
21–24. He walks through another large
gateway into the inner court, which
is at a higher level (note the references
to *steps* in verses 26, 31 and 34), and
views the arrangements made for preparing sacrifices as well as certain
rooms set apart for the priests (28–47).
Here also there are gatehouses on the
south (28–31) and on the north (35–37).
The temple proper is now described,
first the porch (48, 49), then the nave
or 'holy place' (xli. 1, 2), then the 'most
holy place' (3, 4). See Diagrams 1 and 3.
Round the north, west and south sides
of the temple are rooms in three storeys,
thirty on each floor, presumably to be
used for utensils, stores, etc., needed
for the service of the temple (5–11; these
rooms are marked 'C' on Diagram 3). West of the temple
lies a separate building (marked 'B') whose
purpose is not mentioned, but which may have
been for storage (12). The total measurements of
the temple and its immediate surroundings are
supplied (13–17), and a description of the interior
of the temple follows in verses 18–26. For *the
place that was left* (11) see Diagram 3 ('M'); for
separate place (12–14) see Diagram 1 ('SP').
North of the temple in the inner court are
two blocks of three-storey buildings, one twice
the length of the other. The larger is to be used
by priests for eating sacrifices (xlii. 13), the
shorter for dressing rooms (14). Similar buildings
are on the south side of the temple (xlii. 1–14;
see Diagram 1, 'Priests' Chambers'). Next to
these are Priests' Kitchens (marked 'PK') but

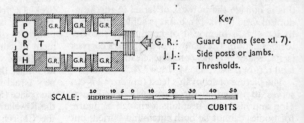

P O R C H

G.R.   G.R.   G.R.

T   T

G.R.   G.R.   G.R.

SCALE: 20   10   5   0   10   20   30   40   50   CUBITS

Key

G. R.:   Guard rooms (see xl. 7).
J. J.:   Side posts or Jambs.
T: Thresholds.

2. A TYPICAL GATEHOUSE

they are not described until xlvi. 19, 20. The whole temple enclosure is measured at 500 cubits (15–20, reading with the LXX 'cubits' instead of *reeds*).

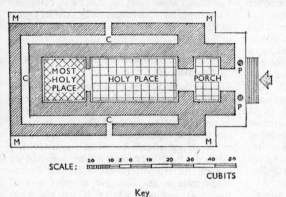

SCALE:

CUBITS

Key

C: The cells or side-chambers (see xli. 5-11).

M M M M: The marginal area of the temple platform described in xli. 11 as 'the place that was left'.

P P: The Pillars (see xl. 49).

3. THE SANCTUARY

b. Jehovah's return to the temple (xliii. 1–12)

As a fitting conclusion to his survey of the temple, Ezekiel sees Jehovah returning in splendour by the gate through which He had earlier departed (x. 19ff., xi. 23), henceforth never to leave it again (7a). The prophet is told that in the future the shame of placing graves of Israelite kings next to the sanctuary must cease (7b), Whereas in the past the palace had been contiguous to the temple, separated from it only by a wall (8), the whole of Mount Zion was to be 'holy of holies' (12).

c. The altar (xliii. 13–27)

The altar is described in verses 13–17, the procedure of its consecration in verses 18–27. Toy's summary of this description of the altar admirably clarifies its obscurities: 'it comprises a base twenty-seven feet square and eighteen inches high, with a moulding about nine inches wide; on this is set a square of twenty-four feet, three feet high; on this a square of twenty-one feet, six feet high; and above this the hearth, eighteen feet square and six feet high, on which the victim was laid; at the four corners are the horns, eighteen inches high, originally, perhaps, projections to which the victims were tied.' This translation of Hebrew measurements into English, however, obscures the fact that they are evidently symbolic: Cooke points out that the topmost altar-hearth was twelve cubits square and the height, including the horns, was also twelve cubits.

d. Levites and priests (xliv. 1–31)

After the introductory paragraph concerning the permanent closure of the east outer gate (1–4),

the main topic of the chapter is discussed, viz. the status and offices of the two chief classes of priests. Formerly the menial work of the sanctuary had been done by aliens, probably prisoners of war (cf. Ezr. viii. 20; Zc. xiv. 21). This, declared Ezekiel, had been an offence to God and must cease (6–9). Foreigners were to be replaced by the former priests of the country sanctuaries, the 'Levites', who had been responsible for much of Israel's religious declension (10–14). This procedure at once solved the problem as to how foreign labour could be avoided and pronounced a judgment on the Levites for their conduct, for they were henceforth excluded from the higher priestly functions.

The priests the Levites were of the line of Zadok (15), who was made principal priest by Solomon when Abiathar and his family were excommunicated from the priestly office (1 Ki. ii. 26, 27, 35). They had continued ministering in the temple of Jerusalem from that time onwards, and despite their aberrations (cf. chapter viii) were regarded as having perpetuated the true worship of Jehovah. Their obligations and duties are outlined in verses 15–27, their rights of maintenance in verses 28–31.

For the problems entailed in estimating the relations between Ezekiel, Deuteronomy and the 'Priestly Code', consult the larger commentaries. See also G. T. Manley, *The New Bible Handbook*, pp. 229, 230, and G. C. Aalders, *A Short Introduction to the Pentateuch*, chapter X.

e. Oblations and offerings (xlv. 1–xlvi. 24)

An oblation of the land is to be offered to Jehovah (1), a territory about eight miles square. Of this land a strip, two-fifths of the length, was for the priests, in the centre of which was the temple (1–4); a further strip northwards of the same size was for the Levites (5) and the remaining fifth southwards was designated for the city (6). East and west of this square, stretching to the Jordan and Mediterranean respectively, was the prince's territory (7, 8). The whole scheme appears to be directed to the safeguarding of the sanctity of the temple, making it in very truth a 'holy of holies'. A warning to the prince and his sons not to oppress the people as their forbears had done (9; cf. 1 Sa. xxvi. 19; 1 Ki. xxi. 19) is followed by a statement of the right standards for weights and measures (10–12), a source of perpetual trouble both in those and comparatively modern times. Verses 13–17 outline the revenues to be paid to the prince for provision of the regular sacrifices. Two annual festivals are to be observed, the Passover in the first month (21–24) and the feast of harvest or tabernacles in the seventh (25). A kind of day of atonement is to precede each festival (18–20).

In verse 20 the quotation from the LXX in RV mg. is to be followed, 'so shalt thou do in the seventh month, on the first day of the month'.

Sabbath, new moon and daily offerings are detailed in xlvi. 1–18, with the privileges and obligations of the prince. While the prince, like the rest of the populace, was not permitted to enter the inner court, he was allowed to take up a position on the *threshold* of the east inner gate (i.e. the west end of the gate, facing the inner court) so as to observe the sacrifices more closely (1, 2). He is to make stated offerings every sabbath (4, 5) and every new moon (6, 7). In verse 8 it is again stressed that he is not to enter the inner court. When the temple is crowded at feasts, worshippers must pass through the temple courts from gate to gate and not leave by the gate through which they entered (9); this applies even to the prince (10).

The enactment concerning the prince's bequeathing of his property (16–18) appears to be a limitation of his powers, both to ensure that his territory remains in the royal family and to prevent his seizure of commoners' lands (cf. xlv. 9n.). *The year of liberty* (17) is more likely to be the fiftieth year, the year of jubile (Lv. xxv. 13–15), than the seventh, the sabbatic year (Ex. xxiii. 10–11; cf. Ex. xxi. 2).

Kitchens for the use of priests (19, 20) and people (21–24) are now described, the former being situated at the north-west and south-west of the inner court (marked 'PK' on Diagram 1, p. 664), adjacent to the three-storey buildings running parallel to the temple (xlii. 1–14); the latter are placed in the four corners of the outer court (marked 'K' on Diagram 1). The kitchens for the people are themselves spoken of as *courts* (22, 23); they comprised 'a low wall surrounding each of these four corners; on the ground below and within these walls, recesses were made for the hearths or *boiling places* where the meals were cooked' (Cooke). This whole paragraph would suitably follow xlii. 20 and may have dropped out from that place.

f. The river of life (xlvii. 1–12)

The prophet sees a river emerging from beneath the door of the temple and flowing eastwards (1), leaving the temple area just below the outer eastern gate. (Note that Ezekiel has to make a detour to reach that point; see xliv. 1, 2.) Passing along its banks, he traces its course till, from being a mere trickle (3), it becomes a deep river (5). In this formerly desert land trees in abundance grew on either side of the river (7), yielding a perpetual cycle of fruits and healing leaves (12). The water is fresh, sweetening even the waters of the Dead Sea and enabling fish to multiply wherever it flows (8–10), a point doubtless made in reference to the fact that fish carried down to the Dead Sea by the Jordan are thrown up on the shores dead.

This description is to be taken literally, but it may also have been intended to show that the source of the nation's blessing in the New Age will be none other than Jehovah in His sanctuary. Many other lessons may be learned by the Christian, while John in the New Testament Apocalypse has characteristically used its figures to portray the spiritual blessings of the Church in the age of consummation (Rev. xxii. 2).

g. Boundaries and allotments of the land (xlvii. 13 —xlviii. 35)

The northern border runs from the Mediterranean Sea, just north of Tyre, to a point near Damascus (15–17); the eastern border is formed by the Jordan and the Dead Sea (18); the southern from a little below the Dead Sea to the mouth of the so-called river of Egypt (19, RV; this is not the Nile; consult a Bible map and see below); the western border is formed by the Mediterranean Sea (20). No territory east of Jordan is included, neither is the old ideal regarded that the borders of Israel stretch from the Nile to the Euphrates (see, e.g., Gn. xv. 18; Ex. xxiii. 31). This may be due to Ezekiel's aiming at 'concentration rather than extension' (Cooke); the prophet was anxious that there should be no contamination of the Holy Land by Gentile influence (cf. xliv. 9). On the other hand, the granting of full participation in the inheritance to *the strangers that sojourn among you* (22, 23) is more generous than anything else in Old Testament legislation in these matters (but cf. Lv. xix. 34, xxiv. 22; Nu. ix. 14).

The disposition of the land (xlviii. 1–35) is dominated by the position of the temple and its lands; seven tribes are placed north of the oblation (1–7) and five south (23–29). This, together with the transference of the 'two and a half tribes' east of Jordan to the west side, has involved a change in the allotment from that of former times (cf. Jos. xiii—xvii). Especially noteworthy is the removal of Judah from south to north. It has been suggested that 'the tribes descended from Leah and Rachel are brought nearer to the oblation than those descended from the handmaids Bilhah and Zilpah (Gn. xxxv. 23–26), as though the more privileged positions were determined by relative purity of blood' (I.C.C., p 531).

The oblation (8–22) has already been described in xlv. 1–8. In both chapters we should probably read cubits instead of *reeds* in the measurements; see notes on xlv. 1–8 and cf. xlii. 15–20n. It is inferred that Jerusalem is to be populated by members drawn from all the tribes of Israel (19). Ezekiel draws special attention to the oblation, city area and city itself being *foursquare* (20, 15, 16). This feature also impressed John, who however added that the height of the city was also of the same measurement as the length and breadth, so making the city a perfect cube, a tremendous 'holy of holies' (Rev. xxi. 16). The gates similarly find a place in John's city (cf. verses 30–34 with Rev. xxi. 12, 13), but they intersperse twelve apostolic foundations (Rev. xxi. 14); the city is a Christian, not a Jewish, institution!

The whole description of the land and people in the kingdom of God is fittingly concluded by the declaration of the name that is to be given to the City of God, *Jehovah Shammah, The Lord is*

there (35). The unfolding of this theme is the constant delight of the New Testament Apocalyptist, who again and again mentions the presence of God as the chief joy of the heavenly city (Rev. xxi. 1—xxii. 5; cf. especially xxi. 3, 4, 7, 22, 23, xxii. 3–5).

G. R. BEASLEY-MURRAY.

DANIEL

INTRODUCTION

I. POSITION IN CANON

In the Hebrew Bible the book of Daniel is found in the third division, the *Hagiographa*, rather than in the second, in which the prophetical books occur. The reason for this is not that Daniel was written later than these prophetical books. In some lists, it may be noted, Daniel was included in the second division of the Canon. The reason, however, why the book of Daniel came to be placed in the position which it now occupies lies in the status of the writer in the Old Testament economy.

The authors of the prophetical books were men who occupied the technical status of prophet; that is, they were men specially raised up of God to serve as mediators between God and the nation by declaring unto the people the identical words which God had revealed unto them. Daniel, however, was not a prophet in this restricted, technical sense. He was rather a statesman at the court of heathen monarchs. As a statesman, he did possess the prophetical *gift*, even though he did not occupy the prophetical *office*, and it is in this sense, apparently, that the New Testament speaks of him as prophet (Mt. xxiv. 15). Daniel therefore was a statesman, inspired of God to write his book, and so the book appears in the Old Testament Canon in the third division among the writings of other inspired men who did not occupy the prophetical office.

II. PURPOSE

At Mount Sinai in the wilderness the God of heaven and earth set His affection in a peculiar way upon Israel, choosing her to be His people and declaring that He would be her God. He thus entered into a covenant relationship with Israel, and manifested this relationship by a mighty act of deliverance. His purpose for the nation was that it should be a 'kingdom of priests' and that God should be its ruler. Thus the theocracy (rule of God) was established. Israel was to be a holy nation, a light to lighten the Gentiles and to bear the saving knowledge of the true God to all people.

To this high purpose, however, Israel was not faithful. After being in the Promised Land for a time, she exhibited dissatisfaction with the fundamental principles of the theocracy by asking for a human king so that she might be like the nations round about. An evil king was first given to her, and then a man after God's own heart. David, however, was a man of war, and so it was not until the peaceful reign of Solomon that the temple, the external symbol of the kingdom of God, was built. After the death of Solomon the northern tribes rebelled and renounced covenant promises. From this time on, both in the northern and southern kingdoms, wickedness characterizes the people, and God announces His intention to destroy them (cf. Ho. i. 6; Am. ii. 13–16; Is. vi. 11, 12, etc.). The instruments which the sovereign God employed to carry out His purpose of bringing the theocracy to an end were the Assyrians and Babylonians. Under the power of these nations the theocratic people were carried into captivity, and the exile or period of 'indignation' came (Is. x. 25; Dn. viii. 19). The exile itself gave way to a period of expectancy and preparation for Messiah's coming. It was revealed that a period of seventy sevens had been determined by God for the accomplishment of the messianic work (Dn. ix. 24–27). The book of Daniel, a product of the exile, serves to show that the exile itself was not to be permanent. Rather, the very nation which has conquered Israel will herself disappear from the scene of history, to be replaced by another, in fact by three more human empires. While these kingdoms were in existence, however, the God of heaven would erect another kingdom which, unlike the human kingdoms, would be both universal and eternal. It is thus the purpose of the book of Daniel to teach the truth that, even though the people of God are in bondage to a heathen nation, God Himself is the sovereign and ultimate disposer of the destinies both of individuals and of nations.

This truth is taught by means of a rich use of symbol and imagery, and the reason for this characteristic is to be found in the fact that the revelations made to Daniel were in the form of vision. Daniel may thus be called an apocalyptic work, but it towers far above the post-canonical apocalypses. The only work which may justly be compared with it is the New Testament book of Revelation. Essentially, Daniel exhibits the qualities of a truly prophetical book, and its imagery is used for a didactic purpose.

III. AUTHOR

The book of Daniel is a product of the exile and was written by Daniel himself. We may note that Daniel speaks in the first person and asserts that revelations were made to him (Dn. vii. 2, 4ff., viii. 1ff., 15ff., ix. 2ff., etc.). Since, however, the book is a unity, it follows that the author of the second part (chapters vii—xii) must also have composed the first (chapters i—vi). The second chapter, for example, is preparatory to chapters vii and viii, which develop its contents more fully and which clearly presuppose it. The ideas of the book reflect one basic viewpoint, and this literary unity has been acknowledged by scholars of different schools of thought. Daniel reflects the Babylonian and Persian background, and the alleged historical objections (to be discussed in the commentary) are not really valid. Lastly, an indirect approval of the genuineness of the book seems to be found in the following New Testament passages: Mt. x. 23, xvi. 27ff., xix. 28, xxiv. 30, xxv. 31, xxvi. 64.

In the Christian Church it has been traditionally maintained, because of the claims of the book itself, that the historical Daniel was the author. The first known doubt to be cast upon this view came from Porphyry of Tyre (born *c.* A.D. 232–233), a vigorous opponent of Christianity, who maintained that the work was the product of a Jew living at the times of the Maccabees. During the eighteenth and particularly the nineteenth centuries, Porphyry's view seemed to come into its own in the world of scholarship. It was widely maintained that the book of Daniel was the work of an unknown Jew, living at the time of Antiochus Epiphanes. The reasons for this were the remarkable accuracy with which these times are described in Daniel, the supposed historical inaccuracies in the book, and the alleged lateness of the language of the prophecy. Sometimes too, it would seem, an attitude of aversion toward the supernatural character of the book led men to seek to deny its true prophetic character. Recently, however, perhaps largely as a result of Hölscher's study ('Die Entstehung des Buches Daniel' in *Theologische Studien und Kritiken*, xcii, 1919, pp. 113–138), there has been more of a tendency to recognize the antiquity of much underlying material in Daniel. It is still maintained—wrongly, we believe—that the book in its present form comes from the second century B.C., but that much of the material, particularly in the first part, is very much older.

It may be well briefly to consider some of the historical objections that have been raised against the book of Daniel.

In the first place it is said that the usage of the term 'Chaldean' betrays an age later than the sixth century B.C. In the book of Daniel this term is employed in an ethnic sense to denote a race of people, and it is also used in a more restricted manner to indicate a particular class, namely, the wise men. This latter usage, however, it is argued, did not arise until long after the time of Daniel. In answer it may be said that Herodotus (*c.* 440 B.C.) speaks of the Chaldeans as a caste in such a way as to show that this must have been the case for years before his time. Since extra-biblical references are so few, we do not know enough to assert that the representations in Daniel are in error.

It has also been charged that Daniel would never have been admitted into the Babylonian priesthood or have been made its head. A careful reading of the prophecy, however, shows that Daniel merely exercised political authority (ii. 48, 49). There is no evidence that he was admitted or initiated into any religious caste. If the book of Daniel really is late, how can we conceive of the late author depicting Daniel as entering a heathen caste?

It has sometimes been maintained that there are no extra-biblical allusions to the account of Nebuchadnezzar's madness and that therefore the narrative is not historical. However, the historian Eusebius quotes from Abydenus a description of the last days of Nebuchadnezzar in which the language is such that it implies that something strange had occurred toward the end of the king's life. There are certain similarities in this account with what is stated in Daniel. In Berossus also (recorded in Josephus, *Contra Apionem*, i. 20) there is a reflection upon the fact of the king's madness. It should be pointed out, however, that even if there were no extra-biblical reflections upon the fact of Nebuchadnezzar's madness, this in itself would not mean that the biblical account was unhistorical.

Objection to the Danielic authorship of the book has also been advanced on the ground that the Aramaic language in which a part of the book is written belongs to a time after that of Daniel. While there is nothing in the Aramaic usage of Daniel which in itself would preclude Danielic authorship, it seems most likely that the character of the Aramaic is that which may be called 'Reich' or 'Kingdom' Aramaic; i.e., which was introduced into the Persian Empire by Darius I. Does this fact, however, rule out Daniel as the author? Not at all. It is quite possible that the Aramaic in which Daniel is written is simply a working over or modernizing of the Aramaic in which the book was originally composed. The question of the authorship of the book must be settled on grounds other than that of the language in which the book is written.

IV. LITERATURE

The student will find a complete exposition of the modern point of view in the commentary by James A. Montgomery (The International Critical Commentary Series). This same viewpoint is also expressed in the learned articles of H. H. Rowley. The present writer has sought to expound the book from the viewpoint of orthodox Protestantism in *The Prophecy of Daniel* (Grand Rapids, 1949).

OUTLINE OF CONTENTS

I. DANIEL RAISED TO POWER. i. 1–21

II. THE KING'S DREAM INTERPRETED BY DANIEL. ii. 1–49

III. THE EPISODE OF THE FIERY FURNACE. iii. 1–30

IV. A SECOND DREAM INTERPRETED BY DANIEL. iv. 1–37

V. BELSHAZZAR'S FEAST AND THE MYSTERIOUS HANDWRITING. v. 1–30

VI. DANIEL IN THE LIONS' DEN. v. 31—vi. 28

VII. DANIEL'S VISION OF THE FOUR BEASTS. vii. 1–28

VIII. DANIEL'S VISION OF THE RAM AND THE HE GOAT. viii. 1–27

IX. DANIEL'S PRAYER. ix. 1–23

X. THE PROPHECY OF THE SEVENTY SEVENS. ix. 24–27

XI. THE VISION OF GOD. x. 1—xi. 1

XII. THE REVELATION OF THE FUTURE. xi. 2–20

XIII. THE TIMES OF ANTIOCHUS AND THE ANTICHRIST. xi. 21—xii. 3

XIV. THE CONCLUSION OF THE PROPHECY. xii. 4–13

COMMENTARY

I. DANIEL RAISED TO POWER. i. 1–21

a. Nebuchadnezzar's expedition (i. 1, 2)

In the third year of . . . Jehoiakim (1). According to Jeremiah (xxv. 1, xlvi. 2) the expedition of Nebuchadnezzar against Jerusalem took place in the fourth year of Jehoiakim. Daniel, however, evidently employs the Babylonian method of reckoning, in which the first year is regarded as following the year of the king's accession to the throne. Hence, the first year would equal the second year of the Palestinian reckoning, and the third year (Babylonian reckoning) and the fourth year (Palestinian) would be equated. There is therefore no conflict with Jeremiah. *Jehoiakim king of Judah* (1). He was placed on the throne by the king of Egypt. He was a wicked king who, in his fourth year, became a subject of Nebuchadnezzar, and three years later revolted. He reigned for eleven years and was followed by his son Jehoiachin. See 2 Ki. xxiii. 36—xxiv. 9; Je. xxii. 18, 19, xxxvi. 30.

It is not stated that Nebuchadnezzar attacked Jerusalem as king. Rather, he is here called *king of Babylon* proleptically. Note also that Daniel does not say that Nebuchadnezzar took Jerusalem, as some critics have asserted. It may be, as Berossus (Josephus, *Contra Apionem* i. 19, *Antiquities* X. xi. 1) has said, that word reached him of the death of his father, and he returned to Babylon to take up the kingdom.

b. The Jewish youths at the Babylonian court (i. 3–16)

The etymology of the word *Ashpenaz* (3) is uncertain. The man, however, was a chief marshal or officer at the court. In verse 3, three different classes are not mentioned; rather, the phrase *children of Israel* is general, and the other two, *of the king's seed, and of the princes,* are explicative. The meaning is 'Israelites, both of the royal seed and of the nobles'. Among these the king desired those who possessed a sound mind in a sound body (4), and who could, therefore, the more efficiently serve at the court.

In order to accomplish this design, the king appointed a *daily provision* (5; RV 'portion') both of his food and wine. In verse 6 the Hebrew youths are introduced, and we learn that their names were changed. Daniel *purposed in his heart that he would not defile himself* with the daily portion (8), the reason being that this food and drink had evidently been consecrated by a heathen religious rite, and to have eaten it would be, in Daniel's opinion, to have been guilty of idol worship. Daniel therefore approached the chief eunuch, and God made the officer favourably disposed toward him (9). The *Melzar* (11; evidently an official who was under the chief eunuch; see RV) granted Daniel's request, and at the end of the appointed time the appearance of the youths was better and they were fuller in flesh than those who had partaken of the king's appointment (15). Thus began the triumph of God's power and grace in Babylon.

c. The first triumph of grace in Babylon (i. 17-21)

The lives of the four youths were in the hands of God. He gave to them *knowledge* (17), that they might discern between the false and true in their instruction, which lay in the fields of *learning* (i.e. literature) *and wisdom* (17) (i.e. science). Daniel also attained unto readiness or facility in the interpreting of dreams or visions. This mention of *visions and dreams* (17) is an accurate reflection upon the Babylonian background of the book.

Verse 21 does not mean that Daniel continued only *unto the first year of king Cyrus*. Rather, since the first year of Cyrus was the year which marked the close of the exile, it is mentioned to show that Daniel continued even to this time. The language does not imply that he did not continue beyond this time.

II. THE KING'S DREAM INTERPRETED BY DANIEL. ii. 1-49

a. Nebuchadnezzar's dream (ii. 1-16)

In the second year (1). This phrase is thought by some to conflict with the three-year period of training mentioned in chapter i. But the phrase 'three years' (i. 5) need refer only to portions of years (cf. e.g. 2 Ki. xviii. 9, 10; Je. xxxiv. 14; Mk. viii. 31), so that the first year of training could comprise part of the year of Nebuchadnezzar's accession, and the third year part of the second year of his reign (Babylonian reckoning). The king was so disturbed by the dream that *his sleep brake from him* (1). Hence he immediately summoned those whom he believed able to tell the meaning of his dream. These men desired to know the dream that they might interpret it (4). The word *Syriack* (4), i.e. 'Aramaic', seems designed to call attention to the fact that from this point on to the end of chapter vii the language of the book is Aramaic. It may be, however, that the word serves to indicate the language in which the Chaldeans spoke to the king. Some critics have asserted that such a statement could not be historical, but in the light of the recently discovered (1942) Aramaic letter of Adon, such an objection can no longer stand (cf. F. F. Bruce, 'More Light on Daniel's First Verse' in *Bible League Quarterly*, No. 203, 1950, pp. 6-8).

With respect to the Aramaic used in the book of Daniel, it may be said that there is nothing in it which in itself could preclude usage by Daniel. If, however, the present Aramaic should prove to be later, it would not affect Danielic authorship, but would merely show that the original Aramaic had been brought up to date by a later writer. It is difficult to determine why two languages are employed in Daniel, but Daniel himself probably wrote thus, employing the Aramaic, or language of the world, for those sections of his book which deal principally with the histories of the world empires, and the Hebrew for those sections which develop the future of the people of God and His kingdom.

The reason why the king will not relate the dream is not that he has forgotten it (verse 5 should be rendered '. . . the thing is certain with me, etc.', not *the thing is gone from me*), but that he wants to test the wise men. *Ye shall be cut in pieces* (5). The cruelty contained in this threat was widespread in antiquity, and characterized the dealings of the Babylonian kings. The Chaldeans declare their inability to tell and interpret the dream, asserting that such knowledge can be found only with the gods *whose dwelling is not with flesh* (11). By this confession the Chaldeans make reference to God, for even in dark heathendom there has remained the persuasion that God exists (cf. Rom. i. 21). The king, however, was enraged and ordered the wise men to be slain (12, 13). Daniel judiciously intervenes and asks for time (14-16).

b. Daniel's prayer (ii. 17-23)

The interpretation is called a *secret* (18), since it is that which cannot be obtained by unaided human reason. In response to the revelation, Daniel blesses God in prayer. To God belongs *wisdom*— He is omniscient and all-wise—and *might*, for He governs all things (20). The course of history lies in God's hand, who changes times and seasons, and the destinies of rulers also are at His disposal. When true wisdom is found among men, it is a gift of God, and true understanding is also from Him (21). He reveals *the deep and secret things* (22), namely, the wondrous works of God for the salvation of men. It is this sovereign God to whom Daniel utters his thanksgiving.

c. The interpretation of the dream (ii. 24-49)

When Daniel reappears before the king he seeks to make clear that he has not come to the interpretation of the dream in his own power, but gives the glory to God (28). The dream is eschatological; i.e. it has to do with the *latter days* or, in other words, with the messianic age (cf. Acts ii. 16, 17; 1 Tim. iv. 1; Heb. i. 1). Daniel relates the content of the dream by describing the colossus which the king saw, the various parts of which were of different metals. The head of gold is identified as Nebuchadnezzar himself, and this probably means that we are to understand the Babylonian Empire as represented by its great king. Other parts of the image are said to stand for other kingdoms.

Different interpretations of this imagery have been offered. Most critical scholars who deny the authenticity of Daniel believe that the four empires represented by the colossus are Babylon, Media, Persia and Greece. It has been maintained by some of the advocates of this position that, since Media did not exist as a separate empire after the fall of Babylon, the book of Daniel is therefore in error. There are, however, strong reasons for rejecting this identification (see *The Prophecy of Daniel*, pp. 275-294). Objections to this view will be pointed out as the exposition proceeds. From time to time conservative scholars have identified the kingdoms as Babylon, Medo-Persia, Alexander's Empire, and the successors of Alexander. But for the most part the traditional conservative position has been to identify them as Babylon, Medo-Persia, Greece and Rome. This is the only position which interprets verse 44 correctly, a verse which distinctly states that the messianic kingdom will be erected in the days of the kingdoms already mentioned. The first two views assume that the messianic kingdom will be erected *after* the four human empires, and this is definitely counter to the teaching of verse 44.

The dispensationalist teaching interprets the ten toes of the image as representing a time when the Roman Empire will be revived and will be divided into ten kingdoms. It may be noted, however, that no mention is made of the number of toes.

The stone *cut out without hands* (34) represents the Messiah and the growth of the messianic kingdom, which kingdom is described as being eternal and of divine origin (44), and thus standing in contrast with the human and temporal empires of the colossus.

God is a God of gods . . . (47). Nebuchadnezzar's confession does not really rise above the level of polytheism. He recognizes the superiority of Daniel's God, but does not yet adore Him as the true God.

It need not be thought that Daniel's advancement (48) would necessarily involve him in the superstitions of Babylon. We may be sure that a man of his sterling devotion to God would keep himself free from such defilement.

III. THE EPISODE OF THE FIERY FURNACE. iii. 1-30

An image (1). It was customary for the Assyrian kings to erect statues of themselves. That this was a statue of Nebuchadnezzar himself, however, is not expressly stated. It may be that Daniel's identification of the king as the head of gold (ii. 38) and his own satisfaction at the number of his conquests (among which Jerusalem itself might now probably be included) led Nebuchadnezzar to become filled with pride, and to erect this statue so as to honour both his god and himself. *Of gold* (1). The statue need not have been made of solid gold, but may have been gold plated. It is also possible that it may have rested upon a pedestal, and been in the form of an obelisk which at its base was nine feet in breadth. The grotesqueness of the statue is no argument against the historicity of the account, and an evidence of genuineness is seen in the employment of the Babylonian sexagesimal system. *The plain of Dura* (1) is a broad place between mountains, the exact location of which has not been determined, although the word

duru (an enclosing wall) is fairly common in Babylonian.

Objection to the authenticity of Daniel has been raised because of the presence of alleged Greek words in verse 5. The names of three of the musical instruments (namely, those translated *harp, sackbut* and *psaltery*) have sometimes been regarded as Greek. If they are Greek words, so the argument runs, then surely Daniel would not have known them, since he lived so long before the rise of Greek culture. If, however, these words are really of Greek origin, it does not follow at all that Daniel could not have used them, since Greek culture had spread very early, and there were Greek soldiers in Nebuchadnezzar's armies (see *The Prophecy of Daniel*, p. 87).

The unjust character of the charge against the companions of Daniel should be noted (12). They are said to be Jews, thus stressing the fact that they are foreigners, with the possible implication that, being foreigners, they would not be loyal. Note further the statement that the king has honoured these Jews, the implication being that they were lacking in gratitude. The question has been raised why Daniel is not mentioned in this chapter. Various suggestions have been offered by way of answer, but none of them is satisfactory. Since the Bible at this point does not mention Daniel it is useless to speculate upon the matter.

In rage the king commands the three accused men to be brought before him and gives them an opportunity to deny the accusation (14). Verse 16 offers some difficulty, and we may best translate the latter part of it, '. . . we have no need with respect to this matter to make defence before thee'. In other words the three acknowledge the truth of the accusation and, rather than defend themselves, are willing to rest their case in the hands of God. Verse 17 does not cast doubt upon God's ability to save, but rather stresses His *ethical* ability, i.e. if God in His good pleasure can deliver, He will do so.

In response Nebuchadnezzar orders the furnace to be heated seven times beyond what was wont, and the three were cast into the flames (19). Verse 25 presents the king's astonishment when he sees in addition to the three Jews one in the furnace like 'a son of the gods'. Through the opening at the bottom of the furnace the king saw a fourth Person, and, although speaking from the viewpoint of one steeped in Babylonian superstition, he recognizes the presence of a supernatural Being, one of the race of the gods. The heathen king, of course, could not recognize the true identity of the One before him. Some have thought that it was an angel who appeared in the furnace, but more likely we have to do with a pre-incarnate manifestation of the Son of God.

In the deliverance of the three a mighty miracle was performed by God. A miracle is an act, performed in the external world by the supernatural power of God, contrary to the ordinary course of nature (although not necessarily performed against the ordinary means of nature) and designed to be a sign or attestation. A miracle, therefore, is not to be regarded merely as a mighty work, but as a mighty work designed to attest God's redemptive purposes. The miraculous deliverance from the fiery furnace was designed to show the sovereignty of the true God over the nation which had taken Israel captive. Nebuchadnezzar acknowledges the superiority of Israel's God *because there is no other God that can deliver after this sort* (29). Although he has advanced beyond what he said in ii. 47, he has not yet spoken from a heart of true faith.

IV. A SECOND DREAM INTERPRETED BY DANIEL. iv. 1–37

a. Nebuchadnezzar's dream (iv. 1–18)

The doxology (1–3) with which chapter iv begins presents certain difficulties, since its language exhibits familiarity with biblical thought, and this would be strange, it is maintained, on the part of a heathen monarch. But it must be remembered that Daniel had exerted an influence upon the king, and the theocratic language of the edict is probably due to Daniel's influence.

Nebuchadnezzar states that he had dreamed a dream which the Chaldeans could not interpret, but Daniel *in whom is the spirit of the holy gods* (8) interpreted the dream. This particular phrase may be paraphrased, 'that which pertains to true deity is to be found in Daniel'. Perhaps the reason why the king did not immediately summon Daniel was, not that he had forgotten Daniel, but that he realized that the dream had to do with humiliation which he would suffer at the hands of Daniel's God. He wants to have nothing to do with Daniel's God, until driven to Him by extreme necessity.

In verses 10–18 the content of the dream is related. *In the midst of the earth* (10); i.e. the tree occupied upon earth a central position so that it would attract attention. Evidently the king in this symbolism recognized himself. *A watcher and an holy one* (13); i.e. a watcher who was holy; only one individual is intended. The language is that of paganism, for it is the king who speaks. Probably the king, in mentioning the vigilant, has reference to angels known to him from the Babylonian religion. In verse 16 the stump of the tree is personified. Its heart is to be changed 'away from' that which is human. This is to be done until *seven times* (or periods of time, the length not being stated) *pass over him*. Since the length of the times is not stated, we are not warranted in identifying the duration in terms of years. The king interprets the decree as of *the watchers* (17), but this pagan interpretation is repudiated by Daniel, who says that it is *the decree of the most High* which has come upon the king (24).

b. The interpretation and fulfilment of the dream (iv. 19–37)

Upon hearing the dream Daniel was perplexed, for he himself wished the king well, but realized that the dream contained the announcement of a judgment upon the king from God. *For one hour* (19); the phrase is an idiom; it does not mean that Daniel was astonished for an entire hour. We may render correctly 'for a moment'. Daniel then interprets the dream and advises the king as to what must be done if the period of tranquillity before the judgment is to be lengthened (27). It is generally assumed that, if Nebuchadnezzar repents, the threatened calamity will be averted. The text, however, does not mention an averting of the predicted judgment. The thought appears to be that the judgment threatened will come in order to bring Nebuchadnezzar to the knowledge of the true God (25). However, if he repents of his sins he will enjoy a longer period of tranquillity.

Jerome and many following him have interpreted verse 27 as though it said, 'Redeem thy sins by almsgiving, and thine iniquities by showing mercy to the poor.' This of course teaches salvation by the merit of human works, and such a thought is foreign, not only to this verse, but to the entire Bible. Daniel's words do not mean 'Redeem thy sins by almsgiving' but *break off* (i.e. 'cease') *thy sins*, by means of doing righteously. In other words, we have to do here with a command to repent, to turn from evil and to do good. It is a perversion of the text to force it to teach the doctrine of salvation by human merit.

Verse 30 should be noted because it so accurately reflects Nebuchadnezzar's attitude. He was primarily a builder, rather than a warrior, and his own statements, preserved upon the cuneiform inscriptions, show his pride in the city and palace which he rebuilt. The judgment came upon Nebuchadnezzar as predicted, and he was driven from men, acting like an animal, apparently suffering from the disease known as lycanthropy (33). At the end of the predicted time the king's reason returned to him, and from a heart of faith he praised the true God (34–37).

V. BELSHAZZAR'S FEAST AND THE MYSTERIOUS HANDWRITING. v. 1–30

The fifth chapter of Daniel, although it has often been attacked as inaccurate in its statements, is nevertheless noteworthy for its accuracy.

There was a time when the name Belshazzar proved to be a difficulty to expositors since his name was not known from the monuments. Hence, while some sought by various means to identify him, others denied his existence altogether. However, the name of the king, as the subsequent discussion will point out, has been found upon cuneiform tablets, and there can be no question about his historicity. The Bible is thus shown to be accurate in its mention of Belshazzar.

Belshazzar the king (1). This statement has been criticized (most ably by Prof. H. H. Rowley,

'The Historicity of the Fifth Chapter of Daniel' in *The Journal of Theological Studies*, Vol. XXXII, pp. 12-31), since Belshazzar never reigned as sole king, and is never designated as king (*sharru*) in the cuneiform inscriptions. Furthermore, it is maintained that there is no evidence to show that Belshazzar ever ruled upon the throne as a subordinate to Nabonidus his father. In reply to these charges we may note, first of all, that the Aramaic word *malka* (king) need not have the connotation of monarch or sole king (see R. D. Wilson, *Studies in the Book of Daniel*, 1917, pp. 83-95). Furthermore, one of the cuneiform documents expressly states that Nabonidus entrusted the kingship to Belshazzar. Now, it follows that if a kingship has been entrusted to a man and that man administers the affairs of the kingship, he is acting as a king. It is precisely that which Belshazzar did. Although on the cuneiform documents Belshazzar is consistently designated 'son of the king', yet he is also set forth as performing regal functions (see *The Prophecy of Daniel*, pp. 115-118, for evidence). In all probability there was a co-regency between Nabonidus and Belshazzar in which Belshazzar occupied a subordinate position. Since, however, he was the man upon the throne with whom Israel had to do, he is designated king in the book of Daniel. No valid objection can be raised against this usage.

Great feast (1). Here again we meet the accuracy of this chapter, for great feasts were characteristic of antiquity. The word *thousand* must evidently be considered as a round number, and serves to indicate the size of the banquet. It was the custom at Oriental feasts for the king to sit on a raised platform, apart from the guests. So in the statement that Belshazzar drank *before the thousand* (1) we have another instance of the accuracy of the chapter. In verse 2 Nebuchadnezzar is said to be the *father* of Belshazzar, and since this seems not to have been so, some commentators have considered the text in error. However, since the use of the word 'father' in the Semitic languages was vague, there need not be an error here. The word 'father' was capable of being employed in at least eight different ways, and it may be that it is used here merely in the sense of ancestor.

The plaister of the wall (5). Excavations have shown that the palace wall did have a thin coating of painted plaster. This plaster was white, so that any dark object moving across it would stand out distinctly. By the sight of the hand, the king was startled out of his stupor of drunkenness, and he promised that the man who could read the writing would be made *the third ruler* (or 'Triumvir') *in the kingdom* (7). The word translated *third ruler* means 'one of three', and these would include, in the order of authority, Nabonidus, Belshazzar, Daniel. The use of the word implies that Belshazzar himself was only second in the kingdom. It is a mark of accuracy such as would be almost inconceivable if the book of Daniel were a product of the second

century B.C. *The queen spake and said* (10). This fact of the queen addressing the king also attests the remarkable accuracy of the present chapter. In Babylonia the queen mother held the highest rank in the royal house. Because of her intervention Daniel is summoned. He rejects the king's rewards and after preaching to the king concerning his wickedness (18-23) proceeds to interpret the strange writing (25-28). Each of the words contains a double sense: *MENE*, numbered; i.e. God has numbered (*mena*) the days of the kingdom; *TEKEL*, a shekel, indicated that Belshazzar was weighed (in the balances) and found deficient; *PERES*, thy kingdom is divided (*peres*) and given to the Medes and Persians (*paras*). The word *paras* would seem to point out that the Persians were the dominant power to whom Babylon would fall. When Daniel read the writing he read *UPHARSIN* (25), but in giving the interpretation he employed the form *PERES* (28). The *U* is the Aramaic conjunction 'and', which would be omitted when the interpretation was being given. *Pharsin* is a plural form, whereas *peres* is singular. Upon the basis of some ancient versions it would seem that *peres* is the original form, and the plural, *pharsin*, may possibly be accounted for as the work of a scribe who may have had in mind the word for Persians (*paras*).

VI. DANIEL IN THE LIONS' DEN.
v. 31—vi. 28

Verse 31 of chapter v really belongs to chapter vi, and is so treated here. The mention of *Darius the Median* constitutes a problem, since Darius is unknown from secular history. Attempts have been made to identify him with Cambyses, Astyages, Cyaxares and Gobryas, but, in the present writer's opinion, these attempts are not convincing. The period of the downfall of Babylon is somewhat obscure, and it is possible that Darius was some hitherto unknown figure, who may have been entrusted with the kingship by Cyrus. Although his identity has not yet been established, this in itself does not indicate that he is not an historical figure. Nor does it follow that the writer of Daniel conceived, as has been charged, of a separately existing Median Empire after the fall of Babylon. Darius is said to be a Mede, merely because he was of Median ancestry; it is not stated that he was king of the Medes. In this very context (v. 28) the Medes and Persians are brought together, and in vi. 8 *the law of the Medes and Persians* (not merely the Medes) is mentioned. All the evidence in the book of Daniel points to the fact that the kingdom which followed Babylonia was Medo-Persia and not the Medes alone.

Darius appointed 120 'satraps' (1, RV) or 'kingdom-protectors' to care for the newly conquered country. The statement is not out of harmony with secular history. Since Daniel in his position distinguished himself (3), jealousy appeared among the others and they sought a means of destroying him. *Assembled together* (6); the phrase may better be rendered 'they came in concert', i.e. they acted in harmony. *Ask a petition* (7); i.e. a religious request, since the king would be regarded as the sole representative of deity. Many critics, since they regard such an action as impossible during the days of the Persian kings, believe this account to be unhistorical. However, while there may be difficulties in the account, at the same time the king may very well have been overcome by the subtle flattery of the proposal and so yielded to it. The foolish and wicked action of the king, however, did not cause Daniel to be unfaithful to God. In continuing to pray (10), Daniel was not guilty of ostentation, but evidently so prayed that he would be found out only by those who were willing to spy upon him.

Objections have been raised against the account of the den of lions which have been based upon the assumption that the den must have been constructed in a particular way. In all probability there was an opening at the top through which Daniel had been lowered into the den, and through which the king later spoke with Daniel, and also an opening at the side through which the lions were fed. It was probably such a side entrance which was closed by the stone and seal; the entrance at the top was evidently too high for any man to escape through it. In the punishment of the accusers (24) we need not assume, as some commentators have, that 120 satraps, together with their wives and children, were cast into the den. The body of accusers was likely rather small, and these, as instigators of the attack upon Daniel, were doubtless the ones who were punished. Note the phrase, *those men which had accused* (i.e. 'slandered') *Daniel* (24), which seems to single out the guilty from the rest. We must not assume that the author of this noble account would introduce into it an absurdity, such as would be the case if all the satraps and their families had been thrown into the den, and were said to be in the power of the lions before reaching the bottom of the pit.

The accuracy of the account should be stressed, since it was in accordance with Persian custom to punish the relatives of a man because of his crime. The chapter closes with the statement of Daniel's prospering *in the reign of Darius, and in the reign of Cyrus the Persian* (28). The designation of Cyrus shows that he was of different racial ancestry from Darius, who was a Mede. The kingdom, however, over which both reigned was the same; there was not first a Median and then a Persian kingdom. It was one kingdom, administered first by a Mede and then by a Persian.

VII. DANIEL'S VISION OF THE FOUR BEASTS. vii. 1–28

a. The vision described (vii. 1–14)

The subject of this chapter is the same as that of chapter ii. The dream which Daniel saw and

the *visions of his head* (1) were not those which originated in his head or brain, but rather, those which came to his head and were intellectually apprehended. The dream and visions were special, divinely imposed revelations, as the remainder of the chapter assumes. We are dealing, then, not with an ordinary dream of Daniel's, but with a revelation from God.

In the dream *the four winds of the heaven strove upon* (RV 'brake forth') *the great sea* (2). The sea represents humanity (cf. verse 17); it is not the Mediterranean or any particular sea that is intended, but simply the vast, limitless deep. The four cardinal winds symbolize heavenly powers, and these heavenly powers set the nations of the world in motion.

The first beast to arise from the sea corresponds to the head of gold of the image (ii. 32). The symbolism of the *lion* and *eagle's wings* (4) represents Babylon, as may be seen from Je. iv. 7, xlix. 19; Hab. i. 8; Ezk. xvii. 3. It is difficult to see how a writer, living long after the destruction of the Babylonian Empire, could have learned of this imagery. Babylon is represented by the most kingly of creatures. The change which came upon the beast evidently has reference to the event of Nebuchadnezzar's madness and his subsequent restoration. Both outwardly and inwardly, a humanizing process takes place.

The second beast to arise from the sea has a double-sided aspect. The feet on one side were raised for the purpose of going forward, whereas the feet on the other side were not thus raised (5). The beast is commanded to devour the flesh which is already in its mouth. Attempts have been made to identify the three ribs, but it is probably best to regard the number as a round one and not to seek for specific identifications.

The third beast which arises from the sea is a *leopard* or 'panther', an animal noted for speed and agility. *Upon the back of it* (6); the phrase may also be rendered 'upon its sides', and it may be that, like the representations of winged beasts from Babylon, the beast had wings upon its sides. The wings evidently denote swiftness. *Four heads* (6). These stand not for the four Persian kings mentioned in Dn. xi. 2, nor for the four successors of Alexander's conquests, but rather, in order to symbolize the universal character of the kingdom, for the four corners of the earth. In Dn. ii. 39 it was stated that this kingdom 'shall bear rule over all the earth'.

The fourth beast is introduced with particular solemnity. It is nondescript, for in the animal realm its likeness could not be found. The description stresses the beast's destructive character. *Diverse* (7). In the Aramaic a participle is employed, which we may translate 'was acting diversely'. There are three points in the appearance of this fourth beast which call for special notice: first, the beast itself is mentioned; second, the ten horns upon the beast's head; and third, the little horn. It would seem, therefore, that, because of the order of statement, we have to do with the unfolding of a history. After beholding the beast,

Daniel was contemplating the horns, and then beheld *another little horn* (8). The horn is described as 'little', but constantly acted as though it were big. Thus a contrast appears. This little horn does not grow in size, as does that mentioned in chapter viii. The description of the horn as little serves to call attention to the eyes and the mouth, which speaks blasphemous and presumptuous things against God.

Verse 9 introduces a heavenly scene of judgment. *Were cast down;* better, as in RV, 'were placed'. The thought is that the thrones were placed in preparation for the judgment. The *Ancient of days*; the literal meaning of the phrase is 'one advanced in days'. The Figure upon the throne therefore was that of an aged, venerable Person. The symbolism is intended to signify that God is seated upon the throne, ready to pronounce judgment. The scene of judgment is majestically conceived, and the tenseness with which one anticipates the pronouncement of judgment is heightened by the fact that throughout the preparation of the scene Daniel hears the mouth of the little horn speaking presumptuous things (11). In the vision the judgment falls first upon the fourth beast, a judgment which utterly destroys it. When the little horn is destroyed, then the power of the fourth kingdom disappears entirely (11). The first three beasts which were seen in the vision lose their power to rule, but are nevertheless allowed to continue alive until the coming of the time which God had determined (12).

Verse 13 introduces a new aspect to the scene, for the judgment is not concluded by the destruction of the beasts but includes also the establishment of the kingdom of *the Son of man. With the clouds* (13); i.e. in accompaniment with the clouds. This description is intended to express the deity of Him who comes with the clouds, for it is a symbolism expressive of judgment (cf. Is. xix. 1; Pss. civ. 3, xviii. 10–18; Mt. xxiv. 30; Mk. xiii. 26; Rev. i. 7). Read 'a son of man', not *the Son of man*; we may render literally, 'the likeness of a son of man'. It is a figure in human form, as distinguished from the beasts which represented the four kingdoms of men. It is not explicitly stated that the figure was a man, but that he was the likeness of a man. Thus, he is a human-like Personage, and so distinguished from the beasts which arose from the sea. The heavenly figure is escorted majestically before the Ancient of days, and an eternal and universal kingdom is given unto Him (14).

It is now necessary to inquire as to the interpretation of the vision. Three views may be noted.

1. Among scholars who do not hold to the Danielic authorship of the book it is generally thought that the four beasts which arise from the sea stand for the following kingdoms: Babylon, Media, Persia and Greece. Since such an order of kingdoms never occurred historically, it is consequently assumed that at this point the book of Daniel is guilty of an historical error. There are several arguments adduced by those who favour the identification of the kingdoms just mentioned. For one thing it is maintained that if Rome, instead of Greece, is intended by the fourth beast, then the prophecy does not agree with history. When in A.D. 476 the historical Roman Empire came to an end, ten kingdoms did not arise from it. Therefore, it is argued, the fourth beast does not signify Rome. In opposition to this line of reasoning, however, it may be said that the number ten is not to be pressed and taken literally; it is a round number, and the symbolism of the ten horns merely has reference to a second phase in the history of the beast. It may further be pointed out that those who see in the fourth beast a reference to Greece have great difficulty also in identifying ten kings or kingdoms. In fact, such identification cannot be made. Attempts are usually made to discover ten *successive* kings after the death of Alexander, whereas the emphasis of the symbolism of the ten horns is not upon succession but upon contemporaneity; the ten horns exist during a second phase of the beast's history.

It is further maintained that the little horn of chapter vii is to be identified with the little horn of chapter viii. Now this latter horn is expressly identified (viii. 23) as a king who shall arise from Greece, and therefore it is concluded that the little horn of chapter vii must also arise from Greece and hence the fourth beast must represent Greece and not Rome. However, in reply to this two things may be said. In the first place, the description of the little horn of chapter vii and that of the horn of chapter viii shows beyond any shadow of a doubt that they are not intended to be identified. If anyone will list the characteristics of each of these horns and will note carefully what is said about each, he will be impressed with the dissimilarity of the two. Secondly, if one will compare carefully all that is said in chapter vii concerning the nondescript beast (verse 7) with the description of the the he goat (Greece) in chapter viii, he will discover how essentially different the two are. They differ with respect to origin, nature and destiny.

It is also argued that Darius is portrayed as a Median who ruled after Belshazzar and before Cyrus. However, such a charge is not quite accurate; nowhere in Daniel is it stated that Darius ruled before Cyrus. Furthermore, it has been claimed that Darius is called a Median and Cyrus a Persian, and thus a racial distinction is emphasized. However, the racial distinction has to do with the men themselves and not with the kingdom over which they reigned, which kingdom in the book of Daniel is the kingdom of the Chaldeans. Lastly, it has been argued that according to Dn. v. 28 the kingdom is to be divided between the Medes and Persians.

With respect to these arguments it should be noted that although Darius is identified as a Mede, it does not at all follow that the empire over which he ruled was Median. Such a deduction is a *non sequitur*. Also, when it is said that the kingdom will be divided (v. 28), the meaning is that its present form (the form which it had when Belshazzar was king) would be broken and it would be given to the enemy, the Medes and Persians. The verse does not mean that part of the kingdom will be given to the Medes and part to the Persians. In the light of the above considerations, therefore, we feel constrained to reject the identity of the four beasts which finds Greece represented by the fourth beast. (Note: The student who wishes to read a capable defence of the identification outlined above should procure H. H. Rowley's *Darius the Mede and the Four World Empires*, 1935. For the conservative position see *The Prophecy of Daniel*, pp. 275-294.)

Advocates of the position outlined above find the identification of the heavenly Figure like a Son of man in the people of Israel, 'the saints of the most High'. In support of this interpretation appeal is made to vii. 18, 27 where it is stated that the kingdom is given to the saints. However, the saints receive it as a trust from the Son of man to hold it for ever. The Son of man is presented as a supernatural Figure and therefore He is not to be identified with the saints. Rather, they as kings reign in His kingdom.

2. The second interpretation is that held by the dispensationalist school of thought. This agrees with the traditional view in identifying the kingdoms as Babylon, Medo-Persia, Greece and Rome. It is believed, however, that there will be a revived Roman Empire which will be divided into ten kingdoms, and so the ten horns of the beast are compared with the ten toes of the image in chapter ii. This ten-kingdom period is said to occur after the return of Christ for His people. The little horn signifies a prince of the revived Roman Empire who will be Satanically inspired. We must, however, leave the detailed discussion of this view for consideration in connection with ix. 24-27.

3. The interpretation which the present writer believes to be correct is the following. Since the four beasts arise from the sea (mankind), they therefore represent kingdoms which are of human origin and consequently are both temporal and non-universal. The first beast stands for Babylonia. The second, as its double-sided character shows, stands for Medo-Persia, and not for Media alone. The third represents Greece. The fourth beast itself symbolizes the historical Roman Empire.

As for the ten horns, they stand for kingdoms which are to exist during the second phase of the beast's history. It does not necessarily follow that these kingdoms must arise *immediately* after the downfall of Rome, but only that they may be able to trace their origin back to Rome. They are contemporary only in the sense that they exist during this particular period; they need not be actual contemporaries.

As this second period comes to a close a third period is introduced by the appearance of the little horn. From the symbolism it is not possible to tell whether this little horn represents a man, a government, a coalition of governments or an ideology. He will oppose the saints until the judgment of God brings about the complete destruction of the fourth beast.

The kingdom given to the Son of man is not of human, but of divine origin, and is both universal and eternal. The heavenly Figure does not represent the saints, but, as the symbolism shows, is a divine Personage. It was this vision that our Lord had in mind when He referred to Himself as the Son of man.

b. The interpretation of the vision (vii. 15-28)

I Daniel was grieved in my spirit (15). In the vision itself Daniel introduces himself in order to show how he was affected by what he had seen. *The saints of the most High* (18); not the Jews in distinction from the heathen, but the redeemed, i.e. true believers, who are to be a kingdom of priests, a holy nation (Ex. xix. 6). They do not found the kingdom themselves but receive it as a trust from the Son of man, to whom the kingdom was given. *Judgment was given* (22). This verse expresses the ultimate outcome of the war which the little horn wages against the people of God. The judgment is one which God makes on behalf of His people, so that they are in eternal and secure possession of the kingdom. A *time and times and the dividing of* (RV 'half a') *time* (25). These words characterize the intensity of the little horn's persecution. The length of period indicated by the word *time* is not stated, and consequently we are not warranted in identifying it as a year. The expression itself is chronologically indefinite, yet the meaning is quite clear. The power of the little horn will appear for a time, and then for two times. Thus there is expressed symbolically a doubling of the intensity of the little horn's power. It would seem that this power would continue to grow, and we should expect this to be signified by the words four times, thus making a total of seven, symbolizing complete and perfect triumph upon the part of the persecutor. Instead, however, we find mention of 'half a time', and thus learn of the sudden end of the power of the little horn, an end brought about, we believe, by divine judgment and the return of the Lord from heaven.

VIII. DANIEL'S VISION OF THE RAM AND THE HE GOAT. viii. 1-27

a. The vision described (viii. 1-14)

At Shushan in the palace (2); RV mg. 'Shushan the castle'. This was Susa, the capital of Persia, which in the Old Testament is constantly designated the 'fortress'. We are not to think of Daniel as actually present in Persia and beholding the vision there, but rather while beholding the vision (2) he was present in the vision in Susa. *A ram* (3); the ram with the two horns represents Medo-Persia (see verse 20). The butting of the ram (4) symbolizes the rapid conquests of the Persian kings. *An he goat* (5); the he goat stands for Greece (see verse 21), and the *notable* (or 'conspicuous') *horn* represents the first king, namely, Alexander (see verse 21). The symbolism of the he goat smiting the ram (7) signifies the Grecian conquest of Medo-Persia. *The great horn was broken* (8); by this the death of Alexander is symbolized. The four horns which arose in its place (8) represent the four kingdoms into which Alexander's empire was broken, namely, Macedonia, Thrace, Syria and Egypt. In verse 9 the horn which comes forth is not actually described as little, but is said to have 'gone forth from littleness'; i.e. the state of being little. From small beginnings the horn then grew to great power. *The pleasant land* (9); this is a designation of Canaan, the Promised Land (cf. Je. iii. 19). *Host of heaven* (10); i.e. the stars (cf. Je. xxxiii. 22); the symbolism has reference to the saints, who are the objects of attack. *The prince* (11); i.e. God Himself. The 'acting greatly' (*magnified himself*) toward God consisted in the removal of the temple sacrifices. In verse 14 the length of the desolation which the horn causes is stated as *Unto two thousand and three hundred days;* lit., as in RV, 'evenings and mornings'. The figures given do not mean 1150 days, but, as the AV translates, 2300 days. The expression evening-morning (probably based upon Gn. i) means a day. This entire period of the abominations of Antiochus would extend from about 171 B.C. to 165 B.C., and then the sanctuary would be restored.

b. The interpretation of the vision (viii. 15–27)

As Daniel in his mind was seeking to understand the vision an angel in the likeness of a man stood before him (15). In verse 19 see RV; 'the appointed time of the end' refers not to the end of all things, nor to the final judgment, but to the end of the time when afflictions will fall upon Israel. *The last end of the indignation* (19); i.e. the end of the period when indignation has fallen upon God's people. It is the period of the appearance of Antiochus Epiphanes. *Of fierce countenance* (23); i.e. one of unyielding countenance; the reference is to Antiochus. *Understanding dark sentences* (23); i.e. one who was a master of dissimulation. *Without hand* (25); i.e. without human hand. It is God who will bring to an end the power of the tyrant.

IX. DANIEL'S PRAYER. ix. 1–23

Books (2). This term evidently has reference to the Scriptures. From the study of Jeremiah Daniel learns that the period of exile will endure for seventy years (Je. xxv. 12). He therefore turns to the Lord in supplication because of the sins of his people. In verses 4–14 Daniel makes acknowledgment of Israel's guilt, and in this acknowledgment includes himself. Verses 15–19 constitute a plea for God's mercy and forgiveness. While Daniel is still engaged in prayer Gabriel comes from God to make Daniel wise in understanding (20–23).

X. THE PROPHECY OF THE SEVENTY SEVENS. ix. 24–27

This remarkable section declares that a definite period of time has been decreed by God for the accomplishment of the restoration of His people from bondage. The general theme, namely, the decreeing of a period of seventy sevens, is stated in verse 24, and the details are worked out in the three subsequent verses. It will be necessary to discuss the meaning of practically every word in this brief section. *Seventy weeks* (24). The word which is usually translated weeks is more accurately rendered 'sevens'. It means a period divided into sevens, the precise length of this 'besevened' period not being stated. The word comes first in the Hebrew, and we may paraphrase, 'a period of sevens, in fact, seventy of them.' *Are determined*; i.e. the sevens were decreed by God as the period in which the messianic redemption was to be accomplished. *Upon;* i.e. with respect to Daniel's people and Jerusalem, the holy city. The revelation of this decreed period thus has direct reference to Daniel's prayer. The time of the exile is almost concluded, what then lies in store for God's people? In answer it is revealed that with respect to these people a period of seventy sevens has been determined in which their salvation is to be accomplished.

The seventy sevens have been determined for the express purpose of bringing about six results, three of which are negative and three positive. *To finish* (RV mg. 'to restrain') *the transgression;* transgression which hitherto has lain open and bare is to be sealed up and put away, so that it may no longer be considered as in existence. *To make an end of sins, and to make reconciliation for iniquity.* The language implies that a necessary sacrifice will be offered, upon the basis of which iniquity will be forgiven. Thus, the negative result to be obtained is the abolition of the curse which separates God from man. The nature of this curse appears in the use of the words transgression, sins and iniquity.

The three positive results are now described. *To bring in everlasting righteousness.* This righteousness is to be brought in from without, namely, from God through the Messiah. The expression corresponds with the first; the transgression is removed and in its place is introduced the everlasting righteousness of God which, as we learn from the New Testament, is received by the believer through faith alone. *To seal up the vision and prophecy* (RV mg. 'prophet'). The reference is to the Old Testament dispensation, during which the prophet was the representative of God before the nation, and the vision was one of the means by which God made known His revelation to the prophets. A prophet was an Israelite who was raised up of God as an accredited spokesman, to deliver God's words to the people. God made His will known to the prophets by means of dreams and visions (see Nu. xii. 1–8). The entire prophetic institution was typical of the great Prophet to come, and, since it was under Moses, partook of the preparatory character of the Old Testament age. When this method of revelation ceased, the Old Testament dispensation itself was at an end, and it is this which is signified by the sealing of vision and prophet. *To anoint the most Holy* (RV mg. 'a most holy place'). This difficult phrase, which literally translated is 'a holiness of holinesses', apparently has reference to the enduing of the Messiah with the Spirit of the Lord. It will thus be seen that the six objects to be accomplished are all messianic, and it may be noted that when our Lord ascended to heaven every one of these purposes had been fulfilled.

In verses 25–27 the details of the period of seventy sevens are set forth. Verse 25 states the beginning of the period and the length of time until the appearance of the Messiah. Daniel is commanded to know and to *understand* the message. *From the going forth of the commandment.* The translation simply means 'word'. The text has reference to 'the going forth of a word' from God, not to the issuing of an edict on the part of a Persian monarch. At the same time the effects of the going forth of this word appeared in human history, and this was during the first year of Cyrus, when he permitted the Jews to return to their land. The *terminus a quo*, therefore, of the seventy sevens, was the year 538–537 B.C. This word which proceeded from God had reference to restoring the city of Jerusalem to its former condition. *Unto the Messiah the Prince;* RV renders 'unto the anointed one', i.e. one who is both anointed and also a prince, or, in other words, one who is priest and prince. There is only One to whom these words may apply, even Jesus who is the Christ. From the *terminus a quo* of the prophecy until the appearance of an anointed one is said to be 'seven sevens and sixty and two sevens'. It is possible that the seven sevens stand for the period between the first return from exile under Zerubbabel and the completion of the work of Ezra and Nehemiah, and the sixty-two sevens for the period between that time and the first advent of Jesus Christ. The sevens should be regarded as symbolical numbers.

Verse 26 deals with that which is to take place after the expiration of the sixty-two sevens. Two events are mentioned, but it is not stated whether these are to occur during the seventieth seven or not, nor how long after the expiration of the sixty-two sevens they will be. In the first place it is said that an anointed one (AV *Messiah*) will *be cut off.* This anointed one is to be identified with the anointed one of verse 25. The reference is to the death of Christ, who was 'cut off' by crucifixion. *But not for himself;* RV 'and shall have nothing'. By this expression the utter rejection of the Christ, both by man and God, is set forth.

Secondly this verse mentions the fate of *the city and the sanctuary* (i.e. Jerusalem and the temple), which are to be destroyed by *the people of the prince that shall come.* This seems to be a clear prophecy of the destruction of Jerusalem under Titus Vespasianus. *Unto the end,* i.e. of the destruction, war and desolation will continue.

He shall confirm the covenant (27); better translated 'he shall cause the covenant to prevail'. The Hebrew words are unusual. They are sometimes interpreted as though they meant simply 'to make a covenant'. Such an interpretation, however, is incorrect, for it does not do justice to the original which can only mean to cause a covenant 'to prevail', or 'to make a covenant firm'. The implication is that the covenant is already in existence and that its terms and conditions are now to be made effective. Who is the one that causes the covenant to prevail? Many find the subject in *the prince that shall come* of verse 26, and refer this, either to Antiochus, or to the Roman ruler of a future, revived Roman Empire. However, the word prince is there in a subordinate position, and it is very unlikely that this word should be the subject in verse 27. It is better to regard the subject as the Messiah, since He has been the most prominent Person in this passage. The covenant which is to prevail is the covenant of grace wherein the Messiah, by His life and death, obtains salvation for His people. The seventieth seven (a symbolical number) thus has reference to the time of our Lord's earthly life. *In the midst of* this seven the Messiah, by means of His death, causes the Jewish sacrifices to cease (cf. Heb. viii. 13).

For the overspreading of abominations he shall make it desolate; better, as in RV, 'upon the wing (RV mg. 'pinnacle') of abominations shall come one that maketh desolate.' As a result or consequence of the death of the Messiah one making desolate (i.e. the Roman prince Titus) appears 'upon the wing of abominations' (i.e. the pinnacle of the temple). By this language the complete destruction of the temple is signified. This state of destruction will continue *even until the consummation* or 'full end', which has been determined by God, has been poured upon the desolate (i.e. the ruins of Jerusalem and the temple).

This prophecy of the seventy sevens is one of the most difficult in the entire Old Testament, and although the interpretations are almost legion, we shall confine ourselves to the discussion of three which may be regarded as of particular importance.

1. Those who do not hold to the absolute trustworthiness and divine authority of the Scriptures refer the passage to Antiochus Epiphanes. The desolation described in verse 27 is therefore one caused by Antiochus; the anointed one of verse 25 is usually thought to be the priest Onias III, and the entire passage is deprived of any messianic character. The objections to this type of interpretation, however, are so serious that it cannot possibly be regarded as correct.

2. A very widespread interpretation today is that of the dispensationalist school of thought. The advocates of this view naturally differ

among themselves in some respects, but their position is essentially as follows.

The beginning of the seventy sevens is usually taken to be the 20th year of Artaxerxes, which is said to be 445 B.C. (see Ne. ii). The period of seven sevens refers to the restoration from exile and the rebuilding of Jerusalem, and the period of sixty-two sevens carries one on to the triumphal entry of Christ.

The promises made in verse 24, however, according to this view, were not fulfilled at Christ's first advent, and the seventieth seven does not immediately follow the sixty-ninth. Instead there intervenes a long parenthesis which is known as 'the Church age', a time that was not revealed to the Old Testament prophets. When this parenthesis has run its course Jesus Christ will return for His people, and the seventieth seven (seven years in length) will begin.

The prince of verse 26 will make a covenant with many Jews for one seven. In return for allegiance to himself he will permit them to erect their temple and perform sacrifices. In the midst of the seven (i.e. after $3\frac{1}{2}$ years) he will violate the covenant, and a fierce persecution will break out which will last for the remaining $3\frac{1}{2}$ years of the seven, when Christ will return with His saints to reign for one thousand years. From the exposition outlined above it will be seen that the present writer considers that the difficulties which this view entails are very great.

3. The traditional messianic interpretation entails less difficulty than do the others and at the same time does justice to the language of the text. Upon this view the seventy sevens serve as a symbolical number for the period that has been decreed for the accomplishment of the messianic salvation (verse 24). In verse 25 we are taught that two segments of time elapse from the issuing of a word from God to rebuild Jerusalem until the appearance of Christ. After these two segments have elapsed, the Messiah will be cut off by death and Jerusalem and the temple will be destroyed by the Roman armies of Titus. The Messiah, however, will cause the Jewish sacrifice to cease by means of His death, and He will do this in the midst of the seventieth seven. As a consequence, the temple will be destroyed, and the destruction will continue until the end appears which has been appointed by God. The precise point of termination of the period of seventy sevens is not revealed. The emphasis, rather, is not so much upon the beginning and termination of this period as it is upon the great results which the period has been set apart to accomplish.

XI. THE VISION OF GOD. x. 1—xi. 1

The revelation recorded in this chapter was given to Daniel in *the third year of Cyrus* (1), which shows that he continued in Babylon even beyond the time mentioned in i. 21. Why he did not return to Palestine with Zerubbabel is not stated. It may be noted that Daniel mentions his Babylonian name *Belteshazzar*, apparently out of a desire, now that the Babylonian Empire has been overthrown, to preserve his identity among his own people.

The time appointed was long. See RV. In all probability the meaning is 'for a long time', since the word *saba*, which is translated 'warfare' in the RV, has now been found on the tablets from Mari in the sense of 'time'. At the time when the revelation was made to Daniel he was engaged in mourning, doubtless occasioned by reflection upon the sins of his own people. *Behold a certain man* (5); the revelation is a theophany or pre-incarnate appearance of the eternal Son. The language of the description reminds one of the language of Ezk. i (cf. also Rev. i. 13-15). The vision produced upon Daniel an effect of weakness (8).

Daniel, a man greatly beloved (11). Cf. ix. 23. By the assurance that he is beloved of God Daniel is encouraged and prepared to hear the message, which, he is told, has to do with the *latter days* (14), i.e. the messianic age. It is first related (20) that the Speaker will *fight with the prince of Persia* (i.e. the spiritual power behind the gods of Persia), and when the Speaker is victorious (*when I am gone forth*, i.e. victorious from the struggle), the prince of Greece will next come and must be opposed. Only Michael is at hand to help, even as, in the first year of Darius the Mede, the Speaker helped him (x. 21, xi. 1; cf. verse 13). Thus, there are to be severe trials in store for God's people.

XII. THE REVELATION OF THE FUTURE. xi. 2-20

Verse 2 means that three kings are to arise after Cyrus and the fourth after them will arouse all the kingdom of Greece. The kings therefore must be Cyrus, three yet to stand—Cambyses, Smerdis and Darius Hystaspis—and the fourth, Xerxes. *A mighty king* (3); i.e. Alexander the Great. When Alexander has come to power, his kingdom shall be broken. When he died in Babylon he was but thirty-two years of age. At his death his twelve generals divided the gains among themselves. For a time Aridaeus, a guardian of one of Alexander's children, ruled, but soon the empire was broken up into four divisions.

The king of the south (5); i.e. the king of Egypt (cf. verse 8). The dynasty which ruled in Egypt after the breaking up of Alexander's kingdom was known as Ptolemaic, whereas that which ruled in Syria was known as Seleucid. The king of the south is Ptolemy Soter (322-305 B.C.), and the prince mentioned is Seleucus. *The king's daughter* (6); i.e. Berenice, the daughter of Ptolemy, who married Antiochus II, yet was unable to maintain herself against a rival wife, Laodice. Antiochus finally divorced her and Laodice encouraged her sons to murder Berenice. *A branch of her roots* (7). Berenice's brother (i.e. from her ancestry) will come against the army of the north and succeed in putting Laodice to death. The Scripture then continues, relating the various struggles and wars between the Ptolemies and Seleucids until the appearance of Antiochus Epiphanes.

XIII. THE TIMES OF ANTIOCHUS AND THE ANTICHRIST. xi. 21—xii. 3

A vile (RV 'contemptible') person (21). With this language Antiochus Epiphanes is introduced. By means of flattery he won to himself the kings of Pergamus, and the Syrians gave in to him. He was a master of cunning and treachery, so that his contemporaries nicknamed him Epimanes (madman) instead of the title which he himself assumed, Epiphanes (illustrious). The prince of the covenant (22). The identification of this prince is not certain, but the language seems to refer to some prince who stood in covenant relation with Antiochus. He shall come up (23); a general statement of Antiochus' rise to power. Peaceably (24); RV 'in time of security'. When men think that all is secure he will slip in. He will take the fattest (i.e. 'richest') provinces and fortresses of the land of Egypt.

Verses 25–28 describe Antiochus' first campaign against Egypt, a campaign in which the Egyptian Ptolemy could not stand because of the treachery of those who should have supported him. Antiochus (27) shows hospitality toward his enemy, but actually violates the custom of Oriental hospitality by means of lying words. On his return Antiochus sets his heart against the holy covenant (28), i.e. the land of Palestine.

Verse 29 describes another campaign against Egypt, which is the third. Apparently there had been yet another campaign on which the book of Daniel is silent. It should be noted, incidentally, that this entire account is related in the future. According to the writer these events had not yet taken place, but are to occur in the future. The account, therefore, purports to be true prophecy.

He shall be grieved, and return, and have indignation (30). The presence of the Romans caused Antiochus to leave Egypt and so, in rage, he turned his attention toward Palestine. On the sabbath Jerusalem was attacked, and a heathen altar was erected on the altar of burnt offering. Certain apostate Jews are perverted (32) and serve to carry out the conqueror's designs, but many among the Jews, the true elect, suffered death rather than yield to Antiochus (cf. 1 Macc. i. 62). At this time men of true faith were able to instruct others, although they should suffer greatly (33).

The little help (34) which helped the faithful apparently refers to Judas Maccabaeus. Some of the wise who follow him will stumble because of the severity of the persecution. At the same time Judas' rebellion proved to be successful,

and on December 25, 165 B.C., the altar of the temple was rededicated.

Verses 36–45 are of peculiar interest. Many expositors believe that they continue the description of Antiochus. There is a difficulty in such a position, however, since the death of Antiochus was quite different from that which is herein described. The interpretation which may be called traditional in the Christian Church is to regard these verses as referring to the Antichrist. Antiochus who persecuted the Church shortly before the first advent of Christ may be regarded as typical of the Antichrist who will persecute the Church before the second advent of Christ.

Verse 36 states that the king will magnify himself above every god, a description which does not well apply to Antiochus. Likewise it is difficult to see how Antiochus showed disrespect for the gods of his fathers (37). The language of verses 40–45 teaches that at the end of the present age the Antichrist will engage in fierce conflict. He will finally take a stand between the sea and the glorious holy mountain (i.e. Zion) where he shall come to his end.

When these events take place, those who are found written in the book (xii. 1) will be delivered. The reference is to the elect, those predestinated unto everlasting life. The persecution of the Antichrist will cause many to fall. Those who are written in the book, however, will be delivered. This is true also of those who sleep (2). Many of them (the reference is to those who have died during the tribulation—not to all who are dead) shall arise, some to everlasting life and some to eternal reproaches. The reference here is not to the general resurrection but rather to the fact that salvation will be not only for those who were alive but also for some who lost their lives during the persecution.

XIV. THE CONCLUSION OF THE PROPHECY. xii. 4–13

Daniel is commanded to protect the words just revealed until the time of the end. The knowledge of God's purposes is in the world in the Scriptures, and men shall travel to and fro in vain, not seeking in the one place where the truth may be found. Verse 7 refers again to the length of Antichrist's power and to his end (see note on vii. 25). The numbers of verses 11 and 12 must be taken symbolically, the 1290 days symbolizing the period of Antiochus' persecution, and the 1335 days apparently symbolize the whole period of persecution unto the consummation. He who endures throughout this period will be blessed. Daniel himself is assured of his salvation, and that he shall stand in his lot at the end of the days (13). May this same destination be that of all who read these words.

EDWARD J. YOUNG.

HOSEA

INTRODUCTION

I. AUTHOR

Hosea, whose book stands at the beginning of the scroll of the twelve prophets, marks a new stage in Hebrew prophecy, for he is the first, or one of the first, prophets to put his prophecies in writing. And no nobler book could written prophecy desire for its beginnings.

The prophet seems to have been a native of the northern kingdom. At any rate, he seems to be very well acquainted with its geography and the details of its political, religious and social life. The great bulk of the book is claimed by his interest in the kingdom of Israel; the references to its southern sister are scarce. His ministry as a prophet was a prolonged one; and of this the list of kings which stands at the beginning of his book is sufficient evidence. Why the prophet should start his list by giving first the names of the kings of Judah, is difficult to say. He may have done it to show his respect for the lawful, Davidic line of kings who ruled in Jerusalem (cf. viii. 4). In all probability his main ministry extended from the last years of Jeroboam II's reign (782–741 B.C.) to the fall of Samaria (722).

II. CONTENTS

The contents of the book are a mirror of the political, social and religious conditions prevailing in Israel in the days of the prophet. The last decades of the life of the northern kingdom were marked by a frantic and senseless change of policies—now courting the favour of Assyria, now trying to bribe Egypt. Instead of putting their trust in their God, the leaders of the nation tried to save the country by means of political schemes which, by the very nature of things, were destined to lead to disaster.

The religious leaders of the people proved themselves to be equally unworthy. The form of religion prevailing in Hosea's day was an amalgam of the worship of Jehovah and the idolatrous religion of Canaan. (See Appendix I to Kings, p. 333, 'The Religion of Israel under the Monarchy'.) In this mixture only Jehovah's name was retained; the ritual was wholly taken from the corrupt practices of the Baal-worship. The worship itself had a corrupting effect on the people as it was closely connected with acts of gross immorality. The situation was made even worse by the priests whose only concern was to promote their own material interests, which they did not hesitate to do by encouraging the people to indulge in their sins, thus increasing the priests' revenue from the sin offerings.

Under such conditions it is not strange that the moral and religious standards of the people were much lowered. A vivid, if very sad, picture of this stage of affairs is given in the enacted parable of the tragedy of Hosea's family life. The prophet had married a maiden, who, with the lapse of time, proved faithless. The names which the prophet gave to his wife's children are signs of the increasingly acute agony through which he passed. In spite of all her wickedness, however, and although her sin led her to be the slave-concubine of another man, the prophet reclaimed her as his lawful wife, and his attitude to her thereafter is a beautiful equilibrium of loving tenderness and severe judgment. And such are the contents of his book. Passages of unsurpassed tenderness and harsh judgment are intermingled with each other to show God's feelings for His erring people. The theme around which the whole message of the prophecy is revolving is God's complaint that His people lack knowledge, and by this term we are to understand not simply a theoretical knowledge, but a close, warm contact of the heart of the people with God's loving heart.

The book falls into two parts. Chapters i—iii contain the story of his family tragedy. Chapters iv—xiv contain the application of this story to the life of the people, to whom a series of prophecies are addressed, now branding their sins, now addressing to them a loving call to repentance.

OUTLINE OF CONTENTS

I. THE MAKING OF THE PROPHET. i. 1—iii. 5

II. ISRAEL'S MORAL CORRUPTION. iv. 1—viii. 14

III. THE INEVITABLE JUDGMENT. ix. 1—xi. 11

IV. ISRAEL REPROVED BY GOD. xi. 12—xiii. 16

V. REPENTANCE AND RESTORATION FORETOLD. xiv. 1–9

COMMENTARY

I. THE MAKING OF THE PROPHET.
i. 1—iii. 5

This first division is biographical. It reveals the domestic tragedy of Hosea's career. His wife, although so dearly loved by her husband, became unfaithful to him and welcomed other lovers. It seems even that some of the children she bore did not belong to him. But the prophet's love persisted and eventually won her back to his heart and home. He redeemed her from the abysmal moral depths into which she had fallen. No wonder Hosea has been called 'the prophet of the sorrowful heart'. But God had ordained this trying experience to be the medium of the revelation of His love to His faithless people Israel. 'God hid a gospel in the heart of Hosea's sufferings.'

a. His home life (i. 1–9)

The beginning of the word of the Lord by Hosea (2). Since from the list of the kings in verse 1 it can be gathered that Hosea's ministry lasted at least forty years (i.e. from before 741 to 701 B.C.), the events of this chapter take place in Hosea's early youth. It is worth noticing that, according to the prophet, the *land*, not the people, *committed great whoredom* (2); the people that were established in Canaan, not the people in the wilderness, departed from the Lord.

Go, take unto thee a wife of whoredoms (2). There are two main points of interest in this difficult passage. Did God actually order His prophet to take unto himself as a wife an unchaste woman, or do we have here only a cataleptic vision of something which never actually occurred in his life? And, if we have a real experience of Hosea's, was Gomer unchaste before she became his wife or did she lapse into immorality afterwards? The answer to the second question may shed some light on the first. It is more natural to accept that Gomer was chaste at the time of her marriage: this would fit in with the symbolical use God makes of His prophet's family life in the realm of His relations with His own people. (See ii. 15, 'as in the days of her youth . . .', i.e. when Israel was pure in her relations with God.) This leads us to believe that it was an actual experience Hosea passed through. The objection that in such a case God would have ordered His prophet to commit an immoral act is not conclusive, because the objection would hold true even in the case of a vision. Even in a vision, God would not countenance an immoral state of things. It is more natural to accept that God ordered His prophet to marry a chaste maiden who in His foreknowledge He knew would lapse into immorality —a perfect picture of Israel's relations with her God

Call his name Jezreel; for yet a little while, and I will avenge the blood of Jezreel upon the house of Jehu (4). This is a reference to the slaughter of the house of Ahab by Jehu. The prophet condemns this act, though it had been ordered by God (2 Ki. ix. 1-10), for Jehu had committed it in the wrong spirit. His motive was not to obey God, but to promote his own ambition. *Loruhamah* (6); i.e. 'unpitied'. This name, given to the second child, reveals Hosea's rising suspicions about his wife's immorality, though not his certainty; for otherwise he would have terminated the state of marriage before the birth of the third child. The name of the child is a picture of the divine displeasure with the apostasy of Israel. *For I will no more have mercy . . .* (6). For the actual fulfilment of the promise in verse 7 see 2 Ki. xix. 35-37. *Lo-ammi* (9); i.e. 'not my people'. The suspicions of the prophet are now confirmed and this name of the third child suggests the complete severance of the marriage bond. Notice the ominous climax formed by the names of the children. First the punishment; then the withdrawal of the divine affection; and lastly the complete estrangement.

b. A vision of hope (i. 10, 11)

Here we have one of the transitions from darkness to light, from the threatenings of the divine justice to the promises of the divine love, of which this prophet is very fond. For a literal fulfilment in Christ of the promise in verse 10 see Rom. ix. 25, 26 and 1 Pet. ii. 10. *Out of the land* (11) is not necessarily the land of exile. The people will go forth united.

c. Guilty Israel (ii. 1–5)

He, who in chapter i had followed his household tragedy in silence, now gives vent to his feelings of anger and indignation against his wife. This is a fine picture of the prophet, in whose heart anger and love, complaint and hope, are mingled together. For *out of her sight* (2) read, as in RV, 'from her face'. The phrase suggests the shameless character of her immorality. In the middle of verse 3 the prophet leaves, for a moment, his own household tragedy in order to deal with the tragedy of Israel's apostasy from her God. The two pictures of the stripping of the adulteress and the destruction of the vegetation of the land intermingle with each other, a symbol of the spiritual impoverishment which attends the sinner. In verse 5 the second clause explains the first. The adultery of Israel consisted in the fact that she attributed to other gods the gifts she received from her God.

d. The way of suffering (ii. 6–13)

In verse 6 notice the rapid change of persons— a sign of the language of anger. *I will hedge up thy way* (6). The reference is to God's chastisement which has as its purpose the bringing back of the wanderer. The first effect of this chastisement is to intensify Israel's worship of the Baals. (Notice the intensive forms of the Hebrew verbs:

ridephah, biqshatham.) Later, however, there comes the cry of repentance, *I will go and return* (7), reminiscent of the cry of the prodigal in the 'far country'. *For she did not know* (8). This lack of knowledge is, according to Hosea, the root of all evils in Israel's relations with God. The idea recurs repeatedly (see iv. 6, vii. 9; cf. ii. 20, vi. 6). *I gave her corn* (8). The emphatic 'I' (Heb. *anoki*) corresponds to the equally emphatic 'she' (Heb. *hi*) of the opening of the clause. The divine *my* in verse 9 answers the sinner's *my* in verse 5. *Will recover* is more correctly 'will deliver'; i.e. God's gifts will be delivered out of the wrong uses to which they have been put. So also the feasts of Jehovah, which had been retained in the north and given new, idolatrous associations, would be made to cease (11). *My rewards* (12); lit. 'a harlot's hire', picturing the utter degradation of Israel.

e. Apostasy and mercy (ii. 14–23)

Therefore (14) introduces a logical connection, hardly expected, between the foregoing apostasy of the people and the divine mercy which attends it, as if the former were the explanation of the latter. The sin of man creates, so to speak, in the divine nature the need of mercy and grace. Cf. Rom. v. 20. *The valley of Achor for a door of hope* (15). As in the days of Achan, so now a new door of hope can be found only in the expiation of the nation's sin. *And she shall sing* (15); better, 'she shall respond', i.e. to the call of God. *Ishi . . . Baali* (16). Both words have the same meaning: 'my husband'; the use of the latter, however, is condemned because of its evil associations. The covenant of grace in verse 18 corresponds closely with the curse of verse 12. After the restoration of Israel's relations with her God in the spiritual sphere there follows the harmony in the sphere of nature. Physical evil disappears after the spiritual and moral evil is done away with. *And thou shalt know the Lord* (20). As a result of the people's repentance, God betroths Israel unto Himself anew. The intimate knowledge of God is the last and best jewel in the dowry which the new Israel brings to her God. A beautiful chain of responses is presented in verses 21, 22, leading from the heaven of blessings back to the earth of need.

In the words *I will sow her* (23) there is a play on the name Jezreel and the double meaning of its root (*zara*). In i. 4 it was used in the sense of scattering; here it is used in the sense of sowing. The curse is turned into a blessing, which embraces, at the end of the verse, the names of the other two children as well.

f. Divine and human love (iii. 1–5)

The command to *love a woman* (1) must mean the same woman, his wife Gomer. The prophet is bidden not simply to take back his wife, but to go on loving her. Notwithstanding Israel's fall, God loves her still. Some scholars, however, regard chapters i and iii as parallel accounts of the same event, in the third and first person

respectively. But this seems unlikely in that the comparison with Israel (iv. 15) suggests that Gomer was not an adulteress when Hosea first took her and there is no hint of purchase in a slave-market in i. 3. *Beloved of her friend* (1); better, 'of her companion', i.e. her 'husband' (RV mg.). This rendering of *rea'*, finding support in Je. iii. 20, is more compatible with what follows, *yet an adulteress*. The love of her husband aggravates her crime. The *flagons of wine* (1) are, more correctly, 'raisin cakes' (*ashishe anabhim*), used for idol sacrifices. *So I bought her* (2). The point of difficulty is why should Hosea be in the need of buying back his wife? Of all conjectures the most plausible is that she had deserted him and had become the slave-concubine of some other man. The utter unworthiness of Gomer heightens the mercy shown to her; a fitting emblem of God's love to His people. *Fifteen pieces of silver* (2) would, together with the presumed value of one and a half homers of barley, be the price of a slave (see Ex. xxi. 32). In the phrase *thou shalt not be for another man* (3) the word *another*, not found in the Hebrew text, is superfluous. By *man* is meant her husband, and this gives a natural explanation to the, otherwise difficult, second clause of the verse. The meaning of the verse is that, because of the former abuses, in punishment, Gomer is deprived, for a time, even of the lawful uses of her natural instincts. This finds its natural application in the punishment which befell Israel (see verse 4) in her being deprived, during the time of exile, of her civil and religious institutions, both true and false.

II. ISRAEL'S MORAL CORRUPTION.
iv. 1—viii. 14

These remaining chapters contain the prophecies of Hosea. His messages to his age come through his own sorrowful experience. They flow together and a clear-cut division into logical sections is not easy to make.

a. Like people, like priest (iv. 1–19)

The lack of *truth* and *mercy* (1), both of which have reference to man's relations with men, is the result of the lack of *knowledge* which has reference to man's relations to God. Man's relations to God are always the governing principle in his behaviour to his fellow-man; ethics always rely on theology. Verse 2 paints a picture of complete anarchy. The sins enumerated here are the natural consequences of the spiritual state of the people described in the previous verse. Thus the lack of truth has begotten the *lying* and *stealing* and the lack of mercy has begotten the *killing. Therefore shall the land mourn* (3). Cf. Rom. viii. 22. Nature itself groans under the consequences of man's sin. *Yet let no man strive* (4). To do so is useless because of the hardened hearts of the people, who have committed the sin of withstanding God's priest (cf. Dt. xvii. 12, 13). *The prophet also shall fall* (5). The reference is clearly to the false prophet (cf. 1 Ki. xxii. 6f.).

The repudiation in verse 6 is confined by some to the priests among the people; but the opening words of the verse would suggest that the whole people is addressed here regarded as the priest of God (cf. Ex. xix. 6). In verse 8, on the other hand, the priests in the strict sense of the word seem to be denounced. There is here a sad play of words: for *ḥaṭṭath* means both 'sin' and 'sin offering', and those greedy priests who wished the sins of the people to be multiplied, so that their share in the sin offerings (Lv. x. 17) should also be increased, were literally living on the sin of the people. This verse contradicts the theory that the system of sacrifices came into existence after the return of the people from the Babylonian exile.

They shall eat, and not have enough (10). Sin brings its own punishment by not yielding the satisfaction expected. The priest, though eating the sin offering of the people, remains hungry; and in spite of his committing whoredom (a detail of the Baal worship introduced into the worship of Jehovah) he remains childless. *Their staff declareth unto them* (12). This is a reference to a pagan custom of divination by means of the position of a rod which was thrown on the ground. That God's people should fall victims to such superstitions is a cause of bitterness to Him.

Beth-aven (15); i.e. a house of falsehood or idolatry. The prophet ironically uses the word instead of 'Bethel', the house of God. The second part of verse 16 is probably to be understood as a question to which a negative answer is expected. Alternatively the *large place* may be taken as meaning the wilderness where no pasture can be found. On this interpretation the prophet is using bitter irony: the 'largeness' of their freedom from God will become the 'largeness' of the wilderness. *Ephraim* (17). As the largest of the northern tribes the name seems to be used by the prophet at times as a synonym for Israel. In verse 18 the text is very difficult. Probably it should be translated: 'when their drunkenness is over, they commit harlotry.' In verse 19 the meaning seems to be that the punishment which all this sin incurs takes away its culprits suddenly in its wings.

b. Pride and contempt (v. 1–14)

In verse 2 the text is very difficult. By a slight change of the Hebrew (reading *setim* for *shetim*) it can be made to read: 'The apostates have sunk deep in the slaughter; but I am a punishment to them all.' *They will not frame their doings* . . . (4). A better rendering would be 'their works do not allow them to return to their God' (cf. RV). The sins of the people have gained such a dominion over them that they have lost the power to repent and turn unto God. Cf. Heb. vi. 3–6.

The pride of Israel (5) can be taken either in the good sense, denoting God as the true pride of Israel, or in a bad one, i.e. the arrogance of the people which is the evidence of their sin. The latter is the more probable meaning. Their pride and contempt for God are further evidence of the loss of the power of repentance referred to in the previous verse. They shall *seek . . . but they shall not find* (6). The climax of the tragedy of the people is that when at last they shall recover the power of repentance it will come too late and be fruitless. They will seek God in vain. Cf. Heb. xii. 17. *Now shall a month devour them* (7). Judgment will fall upon them swiftly. Hosea calls for the alarm to be sounded (8) to warn the people of the coming punishment.

Like them that remove the bound (10). This removal of the bound (RV 'landmark') does not refer to the oppression and exploitation of the poorer people by the rich, against which other prophets have raised their voice (cf. Is. v. 8; Mi. ii. 2), but rather to the Syro-Ephraimite war, during which Judah took advantage of the northern kingdom's weakness to make some easy conquests at her sister's expense.

He willingly walked after the commandment (11). A human commandment is obviously meant here, probably the setting up of the golden calves in the northern kingdom. The LXX renders it 'after the vain things'. *King Jareb* (13) is probably a nickname which the prophet attached to a king of Assyria. The meaning is 'King Contender'.

c. A superficial profession of repentance (v. 15—vi. 11)

I will return to my place (15). In this verse God declares that He will withdraw His presence until a true repentance takes place. An important question is whether vi. 1–3, which the prophet places on the lips of the people, is an expression of genuine repentance or the superficial presumption on the part of the people that God will forget and forgive. The latter is the more probable in view of the characteristic lack of any expression of recognition of their sin on the part of the people, and bearing in mind God's contemptuous description of the people's goodness in verse 4. *In the third day* (vi. 2). Some Protestant interpreters have seen in this an allusion to our Lord's resurrection. This is rather doubtful. More probably it means 'a short time', in which sense it was used by our Lord in Lk. xiii. 32. *Then shall we know, if we follow on to know the Lord* (3); a better rendering would be 'Let us know and pursue the knowledge of the Lord' (cf. verse 6). *And thy judgments* . . . (5). This is an obviously defective rendering of the Hebrew. The LXX, by another division of the consonants, has: 'My judgment shall go forth as the light.' *I desired mercy, and not sacrifice* (6). The prophet denounces not sacrifices as such, but the notion that a formal and dead adherence to a religious system is enough to please God (cf. 1 Sa. xv. 22).

They like men have transgressed the covenant (7); more accurately, as in RV, 'They like Adam have transgressed . . .'. The parallel case of Adam's breaking his covenant with God stresses the fact that God's people have broken His covenant all too easily. *There* (7); probably some locality notorious for its idol-worship. *So the company of priests murder in the way by consent* (9); read, as in RV, 'So the company of priests murder on the way toward Shechem'. Shechem was one of the refuge cities, which makes the crime of the priests all the more horrible.

The *harvest* of Judah (11), which will take place 'when I shall return the captivity of the people' (and not *when I returned*, etc.), will be a harvest of blessings and not, as most commentators suggest, one of sorrow; for, unlike Ephraim, Judah would have a remnant which would form the nucleus of a restored community.

d. Iniquity discovered (vii. 1–16)

A vivid description is here given of the extent to which sin had corrupted the national life of the people. *An oven heated by the baker* (4); an apt picture of sensual lust. The continuous feeding of the fire up to the time of kneading is a picture of the perseverance of the people in evil-doing. A better rendering of verse 5 would be 'On the day of our king (probably the day of his coronation or some other civic festival) the princes have made themselves ill with the fever of wine'. *He stretched out his hand . . .* (5) probably means 'he enjoyed the fellowship of . . .'

The prophet addresses his protest not against the particular foreign policy of his country, pro-Assyrian or pro-Egyptian, but against the fact that Israel was seeking her safety in a system of foreign alliances and not in her faith in God. A further image from the bakery is introduced. *A cake not turned* (8), and therefore burned on one side and left unbaked on the other; it is a symbol of the great progress made by God's people in matters of worldly wisdom to the point of their being burnt by it, which was not followed by a corresponding progress in the spiritual sphere. This also is an accurate picture of modern society. Twice the prophet expresses his grief over the fact that Israel *knoweth not* the sad state of her present condition (9). This is the natural consequence of Israel's ignorance of God, of which the prophet complains elsewhere (cf. ii. 8, vi. 6). One who is not acquainted with God's nature and character eventually loses contact with the real state of his own nature and character. *The pride of Israel* (10); see v. 5n.

Without heart (11); better, as in RV, 'without understanding'. As the dove which, deserting its nest, flies aimlessly here and there, so does Israel fluctuate between Assyria and Egypt and will eventually be caught in the snare of this foolish policy (12). *Though I have redeemed them, yet they have . . .* (13). The 'I' and 'they' are both emphatic in the Hebrew text, which marks the height of the people's sin of ingratitude. *When they howled upon their beds* (14). A more plausible reading, by a slight change of the consonants of the Hebrew text (reading *mizbechotham* for *mishkebhotham*), is 'when they howled at their altars'. *They assemble themselves* (14). The LXX renders 'they cut themselves'. This, together with

the above emendation of the text, reminds one of the picture of 1 Ki. xviii. 28. *I have bound* (15); better, 'I have trained'. See also RV. *Like a deceitful bow* (16). As the archer cannot rely on a bow that is defective to send the arrow to its aim, so God cannot rely on Israel to fulfil her mission.

e. Reaping the whirlwind (viii. 1–14)

The house of the Lord (1) is not the temple in Jerusalem, and certainly not the idol-worshipping Samaria, but the people of Israel (cf. Ezk. iii. 1). The claim that *we know thee* (2) is made in the same superficial mood in which the profession of vi. 1–3 was made, and calls to mind our Lord's words in Lk. xiii. 26, 27. *Israel hath cast off the thing that is good* (3); i.e. her own real interest; for one who does not 'know God' is in danger of not recognizing, and therefore repudiating, the things that concern her most. The setting up of kings without divine authorization (4) refers to the schism effected by the establishment of the northern kingdom under Jeroboam I. The fact that this had been predicted by the Lord's prophet and permitted by God does not alter the nature of the action, as being contrary to the divine plan for Israel.

Thy calf, O Samaria, hath cast thee off (5); more accurately, as in RV, 'He (i.e. God) hath cast off thy calf.' This is the divine answer to Israel's action in verse 3. In both cases the verb used contains a suggestion of utter contempt. In verse 7 a principle is set down, according to which the measure and kind of punishment meted out to man is determined by man's own sin. Cf. Gal. vi. 7. Notice the three progressive stages through which punishment proceeds to its terrible climax. In verse 10 it is difficult to say whether *them* means the Assyrians or the Israelites. The word translated *sorrow* should be rendered 'abstain' or 'delay'. Thus the most probable rendering is: 'I will gather them together and for a short time they will abstain from rendering the tribute money to the king of princes.' Such a delay in the payment of tribute took place under king Hoshea (2 Ki. xvii. 4).

The multiplication of altars in which Ephraim had indulged (11) was in itself a sin, as being forbidden by the law (Dt. xii. 5–14). In the statement *I have written to him the great things of my law* (12; better 'the myriads of my laws'), Hosea shows himself acquainted with a substantial code of written laws, a fact which does not favour the theories of modern criticism. The threat of a *return to Egypt* (13) foreshadows the exile, for Egypt here stands as the symbol of the land of exile and bondage. The building of *temples* (14) like the making of altars (11) was again a contravention of God's law.

III. THE INEVITABLE JUDGMENT.
ix. 1—xi. 11

a. The certainty of exile (ix. 1–17)

Thou hast loved a reward (1). Cf. ii. 5 and Je. xliv. 17. The fertility of the land had been associated in Israel's religion with the worship of the Baalim. The celebration of harvest and other festivals were occasions when gross immorality was practised, which would give force to the prophet's description of unfaithfulness to Jehovah in terms of sexual infidelity.

The new wine shall fail in her (2); lit. 'shall lie to her', just as Israel has lied to her God. In other words the reward which Israel seeks will not be forthcoming. Verse 3 is a clear announcement of coming exile. *They shall eat unclean things* (3). Meat could be eaten only in connection with a religious festival. In Assyria, therefore, where no altar of the Lord existed, all meat would be polluted from a religious point of view. For the same reason they would not be able to offer the usual libations at sacrifices, and the drinking of wine under such circumstances would pollute them. *Bread of mourners* (4); cf. Nu. xix. 14; Dt. xxvi. 14. The thought is again that their food would be unclean, satisfying their hunger (RV renders *bread for their soul* as 'for their appetite'), but unsuitable for presenting before the Lord. A climax is reached in verse 5. If their being deprived of the daily sacrifice would be a source of sorrow, how much more sorrowful for the exiled people would be the omission of the great festivals of the Lord. *The pleasant places for their silver* (6); RSV renders 'their precious things of silver'. The picture is one of complete desolation with *nettles* and *thorns* overgrowing the sites of their former homes (cf. x. 8). The prophet represents himself as driven *mad* (7) by sorrow on account of the multitude of the iniquity of the people. In verse 8 the reference is probably to the false prophets, who are 'spies with my God, a fowler's snare upon all the ways of Israel'. But see RV and RSV, where the suggestion is that the people seek to ensnare the prophet because of their hatred of his God.

As in the days of Gibeah (9). For the awful crime committed at Gibeah see Jdg. xix. The point of these verses is that Israel is behaving now only as she has always behaved in the past. In spite of God's delight in her (in view of the lateness of the fig harvest the first ripe fruit was specially valued; cf. Je. xxiv. 2), 'they consecrated themselves unto the shameful thing' (10, RV) at Baal-peor (see Nu. xxv). *That shame* (10); i.e. Baal. In verse 11 follow RV and cf. viii. 7 where, in reverse order, a similar climax of complete loss is foretold. See also verses 12 and 16. In verse 13 the Hebrew is uncertain. We might follow the leading of LXX and translate: 'Ephraim, as I saw, gave their children to the murderer.' A moving dilemma of the patriotic heart of the prophet is presented in verse 14. It can be interpreted either as an imprecation or as an intercession: this latter would have the meaning that it is better for children not to be born than to be handed over to death. *Gilgal* (15) was the centre of that false worship which Hosea is so concerned to denounce. Cf. iv. 15, xii. 11. *Out of mine house* (15); i.e. the holy land.

Israel will be driven from her home like a harlot. *My God* (17). A sad appropriation of God by the prophet, implying an alienation of the people from Him.

b. Sowing and reaping (x. 1–15)

Israel is an empty vine (1); more correctly 'a vine which empties itself'; i.e. pours forth the abundance of its fruit (see RV). This is supported by the LXX. Israel had often been compared to a vine, and our Lord Himself made use of this figure (Mt. xxi. 33). The fruit spoken of here is material prosperity, and the point of the divine complaint is that the more prosperous Israel became, the more she gave herself over to idol-worship. *Their heart is divided* (2); RSV renders 'false'. *We have no king* (3); this suggests a period of anarchy. The loss of the ruler is first deplored, but, on second thoughts, even if there were a king, what would he do for the nation? A figure of terrible picturesqueness follows (4b). Israel has ploughed her field, only to receive in its furrows the hemlock of divine judgment.

The calves of Beth-aven (5). The feminine gender is used for both words to express the abhorrence of the prophet (since the Hebrews knew no female deity) and as a piece of mockery. The weak female deities which the people adopted are causing them some anxiety! This anxiety was proved to be well founded by the fate which befell those 'deities', as described in the following verse. The Gk. and Syr. versions read 'calf' for *calves*. For *Beth-aven* see iv. 15n. For *Jareb* (6) see v. 13n.

As the foam upon the water (7); better, 'like a chip, or splinter, upon the water'. The picture conveyed in the words *they shall say to the mountains, Cover us; and to the hills, Fall on us* (8) (cf. Lk. xxiii. 30; Rev. vi. 16) becomes even more suggestive when it is remembered that on the mountains and the hills, now invoked by the people, there were the altars at which they sinned against their God. The people will be buried under the ruins caused by their sin, which has, for its pattern, the outrage at Gibeah (see ix. 9n.).

There they stood (9); RV mg. 'there have they continued'. The heart of the descendants of the perpetrators of that awful crime had not changed; they obstinately stood their sinful ground. *When they shall bind themselves in their two furrows* (10); better 'when I shall bind them for their two transgressions'. The reference is to the two calves at Dan and Bethel. The bitter irony of the present state of things is that Israel, by being bound to the yoke (see RV mg.), are found to have exchanged places with the beasts of burden which they have made their gods. *I passed over upon her fair neck* (11); RSV 'I spared her fair neck'. This verse describes Ephraim as a spoilt heifer which prefers the easy work of threshing the corn. But the Lord is now about to put on her the yoke of hard circumstances. This thought leads the prophet to urge the people to make the right response to these punishments. If, while they are under their yoke, they break up their fallow ground, God's mercies will come upon them as a rain. In the past their ploughing has been wickedness and their trust has been in themselves. It is very uncertain as to what historical events verse 14 refers. Probably *Shalman* is an abbreviation of Shalmaneser, who came up against Samaria in the days of king Hoshea (2 Ki. xvii. 3). *So shall Bethel do unto you* (15). Notice that it is not God who punishes His people, but their own sin (personified in the idolatrous Bethel) that will bring about its own punishment.

c. The triumph of God's mercy (xi. 1–11)

In between the thunders of imprecation the prophet introduces one of the parentheses of tender love, of which he is so fond. God recalls once again the happiness of His early relations with Israel. These, however, soon deteriorated. *As they called them, so they went from them* (2). The first 'they' stands for the prophets of God, the second for Israel. Although God had so tenderly called Israel unto Himself, yet Israel had turned unto the Baals. The parenthesis of tenderness, introduced in verse 1, is brought to a beautiful climax in verses 3 and 4. *I was to them as they that take off the yoke* (4) implies that the divine mercy is waiting to bring to an end the punishment foretold in x. 11. The promise that Israel *shall not return into the land of Egypt* (5) does not contradict viii. 13 and ix. 3, as there 'Egypt' is spoken of figuratively, as the symbol of slavery, while here it is spoken of literally. The word for *branches* (6; Heb. *badh*) means literally 'a pole' or 'a stave'; hence some render it 'his bars', 'his defences'. This is more probable. Others take the word in a figurative sense and translate 'his princes'.

How shall I give thee up, Ephraim? (8). The divine dilemma of the conflict between divine justice and divine mercy finds expression in one of the most beautiful passages of Hebrew prophecy. *Admah* and *Zeboim* (8) were two cities which were destroyed together with Sodom and Gomorrah (cf. Dt. xxix. 23). Verse 9 gives the outcome of the dilemma of the previous verse. God's mercy has won the battle. *I will not enter into the city* (9). By a simple change of vowels in the Hebrew this becomes 'I will not enter in wrath', which seems preferable. Verses 10 and 11 both speak of the return of the people after exile. The former pictures a lion calling its cubs back to it. The latter uses the imagery of birds returning after migration.

IV. ISRAEL REPROVED BY GOD.
xi. 12—xiii. 16

a. Israel's unfaithfulness compared with Jacob's trust (xi. 12—xii. 14)

The chapter division is unfortunate here. The new train of thought, which is once more occupied with Israel's sin, begins in verse 12.

Ephraim feedeth on wind (xii. 1). Wind is the symbol not only of vanity but also of destruc-

tion, as in the case of *the east wind*, which follows (cf. xiii. 15). Notice the vacillating element in the policy of Israel: at one time the favour of Assyria is being courted; then oil is being sent to Egypt, as a gift, to secure her support.

Even while in his mother's womb, Jacob was ambitious for God's blessing, and this he earnestly sought when he grew up, until he found Him at Bethel, the very place where his descendants sinned against their God. This example of earnestness is offered now to Jacob's descendants to show them how far they had departed from the example of their believing progenitor and also to point them to the way in which they should seek the Lord (6). *He is a merchant* (7); the word literally means 'Canaanite'; the Canaanites had so much distinguished themselves in commerce as to lend their name as a synonym for 'merchant'. On the other hand the use of 'Canaanite' is characteristic: Jacob's descendants had so much degenerated as to exchange the name 'Israel' for 'Canaanite'. Israel has a false basis of self-defence: he points to the riches he has acquired as a sure sign of God's favour to him (8; cf. Rev. iii. 17). In its context a threat, rather than a promise, is suggested in the words *as in the days of the solemn feast* (9). Their homelessness in exile is likened to the living in booths during the feast of tabernacles. The fact that God had repeatedly spoken to Israel through His prophets, who had *used similitudes* and a language easy to understand, aggravated Israel's sin (cf. Is. v. 4). *Is there iniquity in Gilead?* (11). The question is asked in order to provoke an emphatic affirmation. For *Gilgal* see ix. 15n. *Their altars are as heaps in the furrows of the fields* (11). In the train of this iniquity there follows disaster, which scatters in the fields the debris of Israel's idolatrous altars.

In verses 12 and 13 the prophet looks back to Israel's ancestors once again in order to make a contrast between Jacob's simplicity of life and his rebellious descendants' luxurious existence, and, also, to stress God's care for His people. Jacob was preserved, but the present generation shall bear the punishment of their guilt.

b. Swift and inevitable doom (xiii. 1–16)

The most probable rendering of verse 1 is: 'When Ephraim spoke, there was trembling . . . but he sinned through Baal and died.' The period of Israel's prosperity, when everyone showed her respect, is contrasted with the period of her destruction. *Kiss the calves* (2); i.e. as a sign of homage. The swiftness of Israel's coming destruction is set forth in four successive pictures: the morning cloud, the early dew, the chaff, and the chimney smoke (3). The *chimney* is really the window (see RSV) through which the smoke escaped.

I did know thee in the wilderness (5). A slight change of the Hebrew consonants gives a more plausible rendering (supported by LXX): 'I shepherded thee.' This is in better agreement with the context. Prosperity had resulted in drawing away from God (6; cf. Dt. viii. 11ff.). *As a leopard by the way will I observe them* (7). A slight emendation of the Hebrew gives the reading of the LXX and other versions: 'As a panther on the way to Assyria.'

Verse 9 should be rendered, as in RV: 'It is thy destruction, O Israel, that thou art against me, against thy help.' In verse 10 also the RV gives a better rendering (supported by LXX and other versions): 'Where now is thy king, that he may save thee?' The verbs in the next utterance should be in the present tense: 'I give', 'I take' (frequentative imperfects in the Hebrew). The reference is thus not to the elevation of Jeroboam I to the throne, but to the whole succession of kings in the northern kingdom. To say that *the iniquity of Ephraim is bound up* (12) implies that it is carefully collected and stored up for the day of judgment, and is an answer to the claims of some of the prophet's fellow-countrymen that God, who has taken their nation in His special favour, will forgive and forget their sin, as an evidence of which they brought the prosperity in which they thought they were living (cf. verse 15). Against this superficial estimate of their sin the prophet is placing that terrible hoarding of punishment.

The anguish of the prophet then expresses itself in a swift change of imagery. First the travailing woman in the midst of the birth-pangs; then the child which is not brought to birth at the right time. Both foreshadow the impending destruction. The second image is the symbol of the lack of timely repentance on the part of the people, which might have saved their country.

In verse 14 a small change in the order of consonants of the Hebrew gives the reading 'Where is thy plague, O death? Where is thy sting, O Sheol?' This is supported both by LXX and by the quotation in 1 Cor. xv. 55. The meaning of the verse is difficult. Is it an un-expected flash of mercy? If so, the last part of the verse should be read in the light of Rom. xi. 29, where it is clear that 'repentance' means a change of mind on God's part; i.e. 'I will not change my mind about that'. *Though he be fruitful* (15). This play on Ephraim's name, which means 'fruitfulness', brings forth in a more sinister light the utter fruitlessness of the people.

V. REPENTANCE AND RESTORATION FORETOLD. xiv. 1–9

This last chapter is an undisturbed record of God's tender mercy to a repentant people. *So will we render the calves of our lips* (2). 'Instead of sacrificial oxen, we shall offer our lips'; i.e. the confession of our guilt. (Cf. Ps. li. 17–19.) Verse 3 confesses the three chief sins of Israel: reliance on Assyria; reliance on Egypt (the 'land of horses'); and idolatry. The repentance is accepted and God moves graciously to help them in love and mercy. *He shall grow as the lily* (5) because the lily is the symbol of the purity which will take the place of corruption. Casting forth *his roots as Lebanon* (5) is the symbol of the lasting nature of Israel's happiness. This thought is a beautiful contrast to xiii. 15. *The scent thereof* (7); better rendered 'the memorial thereof'. It is to be noted that the two memorials of the redeemed Israel are *corn* (bread) and *wine,* a foreshadowing of another, greater memorial. *From me is thy fruit found* (8). A repetition of the play on Ephraim's name (see xiii. 15n.), whose sinister character is now swallowed up in the divine source of the people's fruitfulness. The words *he shall know them* (9) are an epitome of the whole prophecy. God's chief complaint against His people was that they did not 'know' Him. Now that they have become wise, they will know *the ways of the Lord* and they *shall walk in them* (9).

G. A. HADJIANTONIOU.
L. E. H. STEPHENS-HODGE.

JOEL

INTRODUCTION

I. STYLE

The book of Joel is one of the literary gems of the Old Testament. It is built up with care and dramatic effect and here and there throughout its chapters are beauties which shine brilliantly and even dazzle the imagination. W. G. Elmslie has drawn attention to this in *The Expositor*, Fourth Series, Vol. 3, p. 162: 'If there is a book in the Bible that is a masterpiece of literary art, it is the Book of Joel. There are other Prophets who write with greater passion and greater power, who rise to loftier altitudes of divine revelation; but there is hardly a writer in the Old Testament who shows proof of so careful, and detailed, and exquisite pains to give his work literary polish, finish and beauty.'

'Joel's style is pre-eminently pure. It is characterized by smoothness and fluency in the rhythms, roundness in the sentences and regularity in the parallelisms. With the strength of Micah, it combines the tenderness of Jeremiah, the vividness of Nahum, and the sublimity of Isaiah' (A. R. Fausset).

II. DATE

The book presents the student with many problems and perhaps the first and most important is to determine where to place it among the other Old Testament prophets. This difficulty can be better realized when it is known that it has been placed in nearly every period of the prophetic dispensation. From the simple fact that no mention is made of Assyria or Babylonia, it is assumed that Joel exercised his ministry before the rise of the former or after the decline of the latter. There is, therefore, almost universal agreement that the book is to be placed either among the very first of the prophets or among the last of them. It is true that many modern scholars favour the very late date, but this is not by any means universal and several factors seem to suggest that the very early date is well within the bounds of possibility. Among these factors are first the portrayal of the kingdom. All mention of a king is hushed to a pianissimo, which would confirm the view that the period is that of Joash who, although king, was yet a minor with Jehoiada as regent (2 Ki. xii. 1ff.). Alongside this, in Joel we find the priesthood held in the highest honour and regard. The worship of the temple was sedulously maintained and the darkest aspect of the disaster caused by the drought and by the locusts was the fact that the daily offerings could no longer be made

(i. 9). Religion must have been generally practised when nothing seemed worse than that. These facts, to begin with, would fit in with the time of Joash's minority.

In the second place, moreover, there is no reference whatever to the northern kingdom, so near geographically and so interrelated with Judah at a later period. If we choose the early date it seems natural that, in view of all that Judah had suffered at the hands of Athaliah, the infamous daughter of Ahab (2 Ki. xi. 1ff.), there would be but scanty reference to Israel in the appeals of the prophet to the southern kingdom.

A third feature supporting an early date is that the condemnatory passages would seem to be a relic of Israel's more warlike days and not of those of her enfeebled period of declension, which would have been her condition if the prophecy was as late as some critics consider it to be.

A further argument for the earlier date is to be found in the cross-references which may be observed between the prophecies of Joel and Amos. It has, of course, been argued that Joel has borrowed from Amos; but from the character of these various references it is arguable, if not conclusively provable, that the opposite was the case, namely, that Amos began to prophesy where Joel left off (cf. Am. i. 2 with Joel iii. 16; Am. iv. 6 with Joel ii. 12; Am. ix. 13 with Joel iii. 18). This point is fully worked out in Kirkpatrick's *Doctrine of the Prophets*, pp. 63–65. To all this may be added the fact that, by the time of Amos, the idea of 'the day of Jehovah' was a commonplace one and, in keeping with the apparently close connection of Amos and Joel, it would seem that it was familiar simply because Joel had made it so in his earlier ministry.

There are, in conclusion, a number of allusions to historical events which, if rightly interpreted, seem to demand an early date. Joel iii. 17, 19, which speak of strangers 'passing through' the land and accuse Egypt and Edom of shedding 'innocent blood', might well refer to Shishak's invasion of Judah (1 Ki. xiv. 25) and the revolt of the Edomites in the reign of Jehoram (2 Ki. viii. 20–22). Again, Joel's charge against the Phoenicians and Philistines (Joel iii. 4, 6) may be compared with the Chronicler's account of Philistine raids in the reign of Jehoram of Judah (2 Ch. xxi. 16), and the oracles of Amos against both nations (Am. i). There is also in the mention of the 'valley of Jehoshaphat' (Joel iii. 2) a possible reference to that king's defeat of Moab,

Ammon and Edom in the valley of Berachah (2 Ch. xx. 26). All these would be in keeping with Joel's traditionally early place in the Canon, a position which is not airily to be dismissed as entirely fortuitous since it is undeniable that the present arrangement was, at the time, intended to be chronological.

All this is not to infer that there are not arguments in favour of placing Joel after the return from captivity. The main reasons advanced for this may be put as follows. The general nature of the language and style, it is said, and, in particular, the wording of iii. 1, 17, would seem to demand that the book be subsequent to the destruction of Jerusalem in 586 B.C. The absence of any references to the northern kingdom suggests that it was, in fact, no longer in existence as a separate political entity. The absence of any reproof for national sins and especially for idolatry is inconsistent with the state of things existing in pre-exilic times. The hostile attitude adopted to other heathen nations is more characteristic of the later period when Jewish nationalism became more narrowly exclusive. The predominance of the priesthood in everyday affairs and the ardent devotion for the temple sacrifices were not so typical of the pre-exilic period but really belong to later days in the smaller, more tightly knit community of returned exiles.

The argument from style and language is, at best, a very unreliable one and, in the case of the prophets, there are other factors as well as the purely personal one to complicate the whole matter. 'The remains of Hebrew literature are too scanty for us to decide with certainty what was and what was not possible in a particular period. The uniformity of the Massoretic punctuation has obliterated many distinctions of pronunciation which would have served as landmarks' (Kirkpatrick, *op. cit.*, p. 72). The reference in iii. 1 to 'bringing again the captivity' need not necessarily mean that the words were spoken during or after the exile; they were also used by Amos (ix. 14) and Hosea (vi. 11) and are quite consistent when used by prophets who saw clearly beyond the disasters which they prophesied would come.

Neither can the absence of any reference to the northern kingdom be considered conclusive; for while hopes of reunion were held by others of the early prophets, none of them stood so near in time to the bitter and cruel despotism of Athaliah as did Joel, and it was to be expected that any references to that part of the land from which had come such a cruel and wicked ruler should be allowed to fade into the background. Furthermore, in connection with the absence of reproof for national transgression we cannot assume that the days which followed the return were free from blameworthy sins, political and ecclesiastical. Ezra, Nehemiah and Malachi found plenty against which to speak. To try to fit Joel into this situation raises as many difficulties as it professes to solve. The same might

also be said of the argument that the whole attitude of the book is marked by the bigoted nationalism which sprang up later. Nothing conclusive can be built on this. Indeed, this argument can be turned round the other way. The earlier prophets are either silent (Hosea) on the subject of the heathen, or interested only in their final overthrow (Amos), while the later can see a remnant being saved out of every nation under the sun.

Of the priestly predominance and the tendency to ritual which are claimed as characteristic of post-exilic times it need only be said that this is liable to appear in every age when vital religion dies down. That it was not unknown in the days of the early prophets can be seen from Is. i. 11-15. There are, therefore, solid reasons for supporting the traditionally accepted early date of Joel's prophecy. However imposing and impressive are the arguments against it, they seem to involve us more and more in adjusting our facts to the theory of a later date, and to create greater difficulties than they resolve.

III. THE AUTHOR

Of Joel himself we know little more than that he was the son of Pethuel (i. 1) and that, in all likelihood, he lived in Jerusalem. The many references to it reveal a great love for it as well as an intimate knowledge of its history and worship (i. 14, ii. 1, 15, 32, iii. 1, 2, 6, 16, 17, 20, 21). 'Joel', which means 'Jehovah is God', was a favourite name (1 Sa. viii. 2; 1 Ch. vi. 36, vii. 3, xi. 38, xv. 7, xxvii. 20). From i. 13, 14, ii. 17 it might be deduced that he was not a priest. He lived and prophesied at a time when the people of Judah had not fallen into that extreme depravity which, in later times, drew down upon them such heavy chastisement. This would seem to place him either early in the reign of Joash or between those of Joash and Uzziah (2 Ki. xi. 17, 18, xii. 2-16; 2 Ch. xxiv. 4-14). He was also probably contemporary with Hosea and Amos, and as they addressed Israel, so he addressed Judah. If this was so, it was probably just after the evil and idolatrous reign of Athaliah, the infamous daughter of a wicked pair, Ahab and Jezebel (2 Ki. xi), when, under the influence of Jehoiada (2 Ch. xxiii. 16-21, xxiv. 14, 18), something in the nature of a religious revival was taking place.

IV. CIRCUMSTANCES

It so happened that in the providence of God the land was literally laid bare by a plague of locusts, there being such a scarcity of food as to cause the meat offering and the drink offering to be withholden from the house of God (i. 13). 'But although such a plague may in the first instance have aroused the prophet's extreme apprehension and stirred his soul to its lowest depths, still we rise up from the perusal of his words convinced that they refer to some greater anxiety yet to come, some incursion of enemies who would inflict terrible ravages upon the land, leaving it desolate and bare behind them, after the manner of these locusts' (S. L. Warren in *Ellicott's Commentary*, p. 437).

Joel appears in Jerusalem to declare that this invasion of locusts is a picture of a visitation of God in His wrath and judgment. He calls for an act of national repentance, a solemn fast (ii. 12), and urges the leaders of religion to show a good example (ii. 15–17). He then prophesies the return of God's favour and the prosperity of the land (ii. 18–20) and the removal of their enemies (ii. 21–27). After this he is caught up, in a way that has no meaning apart from divine inspiration, to describe the outpouring of the Holy Spirit which should follow (ii. 28–32). 'This is that which was spoken by the prophet Joel' was Peter's verdict on the day of Pentecost (Acts ii. 16). Lastly, Joel is led on to prophesy the final destruction of all the enemies of God and His people (iii. 1–21).

V. INTERPRETATION

The foregoing description of the contents of the book of Joel presupposes an answer to a question which is not universally admitted. Was Joel describing an actual plague of locusts then afflicting his nation? Or was he predicting some such plague to come in the future? Was he speaking of real locusts at all or not? Or was he predicting that surrounding nations would invade the land after the manner of a plague of locusts? Even these questions do not exhaust the possible lines of interpretation. There remains the further question as to whether or not the locusts are 'eschatological locusts' and not historical ones. Those who hold that this is so affirm that there is here no history at all; all is ideal, mystical and apocalyptical.

It would appear even to a casual reader that chapter i, for example, is clearly intended to be historical. G. A. Smith declares that 'its figures are too vivid, too actual to be predictive or mystical. And the whole apocalyptical interpretation wrecks itself on the same verse as the allegorical, viz. i. 16, in which Joel plainly speaks of himself as having suffered with his hearers the plague he describes' (*The Twelve Prophets*, Vol. 2, p. 395). On the other hand 'the language of the book is too aggravated and too ominous tō be limited to the natural plague . . . under the figure of locusts he must be describing some more fateful agency of God's wrath upon Israel' (*ibid.*, p. 390).

It therefore appears obvious that in an actual visitation of locusts the prophet sees an approaching invasion of neighbouring armies. The locusts have come; the invasions are yet to come. Moreover, it seems evident that from these things the prophet is led on to speak of the judgments of the 'day of the Lord' which are more searching than any physical plague. The book is therefore partly historical and partly predictive.

OUTLINE OF CONTENTS

I. HISTORY. i. 1—ii. 17

    a. The plague of locusts described (i. 2–12)
    b. The priests appealed to and advised (i. 13–20)
    c. The forebodings of the prophet (ii. 1–11)
    d. The appeal to the people (ii. 12–17)

II. PREDICTION. ii. 18—iii. 21

    a. The blessings of the immediate future (ii. 18–27)
    b. The blessings of the distant future (ii. 28–32)
    c. The ultimate destruction of all the enemies of God (iii. 1–21)

COMMENTARY

I. HISTORY. i. 1—ii. 17

The son of Pethuel (1); LXX 'Bethuel'. Apart from this we know little or nothing about Joel himself. It may be assumed from ii. 1, iii. 2, 6, 16, 17 that he was an inhabitant of Jerusalem and from i. 13, 14, ii. 17 that he was not a priest. In assuming the latter it should be pointed out, however, that some scholars interpret his frequent references to sacrifice, to the temple, and to the priests as inferring that he was a priest himself.

a. The plague of locusts described (i. 2–12)

Much controversy has taken place between commentators in an effort to determine whether we have here an actual historical happening or a prophecy under a figure. There is no reason to suppose that this chapter is either allegorical or symbolical. The description of the plague is so vivid and realistic as to suggest that it was real and actual, and indeed present before Joel's very eyes. Moreover in i. 16 there is an undoubted reference to a contemporary situation and any attempt to deny the historicity of the actual plague is, as Dr. George Adam Smith points out, 'wrecked' on this verse. (See *Introduction* above.)

The plague which has come upon them is without parallel in their history (2) and so remarkable that it deserves to be remembered and recounted (3). It seems to have consisted of successive swarms of different types of locusts, of which naturalists say there are as many as ninety varieties. There are ten Hebrew words referring to locusts in the Old Testament, and here, in i. 4 and in ii. 25, four different words are so used. They are *arbeh, gazam, yeleq, hasil*, translated respectively *locust, palmerworm, cankerworm* and *caterpiller.* Do these speak of a fourfold plague? 'A consideration of the book of Joel as a whole does not show that the ravages of four different insect pests are referred to but rather a single one, and that one the locust. These words may therefore be regarded as different names of the locust, referring to different stages of development of the insect' (I.S.B.E.). Others think the use of these four words represents four successive swarms or four swarms in successive seasons. The exact meaning of this fourfold description is, however, uncertain. Those who favour any sort of allegorical interpretation say that the 'locusts' of chapter i are the 'heathen' of chapter iii and that these four varieties of i. 4 represent 'the four sore judgments' with which Ezekiel was instructed to threaten Jerusalem and which were the four foreign invasions by the Assyrians, Chaldeans, Macedonians and Romans. All this is scarcely vital. The important thing is surely simple and plain and has been clearly stated by A. B. Davidson in *The Expositor*, Third Series, Vol. 7, p. 199. 'Whether he means to describe locusts in general by such names, mentioning four to express universality, or whether he means to describe the same swarm of locusts according to the advancing stages of its growth, is not of much consequence to decide . . . The prophet uses the various names—all denoting locusts— not strictly to describe distinct classes, but to indicate that many and successive swarms have invaded the land; and, put into prose, his language means, what one swarm hath left another hath eaten, and so on.'

Those who have witnessed or experienced a plague of locusts affirm that what is here described in i. 4–10, 17–20 and ii. 2–11 is so accurate and true that in the first place it is pure description without any poetic hyperbolism. G. A. Smith has several such accounts in *The Twelve Prophets* (Vol. 2, pp. 399–403) and he adds: 'These extracts prove to us what little need Joel had of hyperbole in order to read his locusts as signs of the day of Jehovah.'

Verses 5–12 serve to point out to all classes in the community the gravity of the situation. In the first place their most valued luxuries are denied them. This is not the greatest calamity in the eyes of the prophet although it is to many in his nation. *Drunkards* (5) are reminded that the vines are ruined (7). This is the only specific sin

laid to the charge of his countrymen by Joel. Secondly, the public worship of God is interrupted through lack of offerings (9, 10). This is a greater evil to the prophet, and he voices his indignation by using the figure of a young wife bereaved and in mourning (8). Thirdly, the very means of subsistence are also cut off (11, 12). This is the worst of all and the hearts of all are failing them. Dr. R. F. Horton in the Cent. Bible points out that the word translated *dried up* (10) can be more truly rendered 'ashamed'. This also applies to verse 12 where the same word occurs twice as *withered*. So in this graphic way Joel makes men and crops and fields mourn together.

b. The priests appealed to and advised (i. 13–20)

In this tremendously powerful passage, the prophet appeals to the priests, urging them to *call a solemn assembly . . . and cry unto the Lord* (14). Notice the play on the words 'my God' and 'your God' in verse 13. The prophet's God is one who calls for repentance; the priests are in danger of thinking of Him merely as One who demands the drink offering and the meat offering. The country is famine-stricken and Joel seems to see this as a precursor of further destruction coming from the Almighty, for which he uses the phrase *the day of the Lord* (15); see ii. 1n. Even the beasts gasp and groan in their dismay and hunger (18). What the locusts had left, the excessively hot weather has finished off (19). Perhaps we are to think here in verse 19 of the heat and drought which accompany the locust plague. But it is possible that the locusts themselves are typified as fire, consuming the herbage. See Clarke's description of the *Gryllus migratorius* (Clarke's *Travels*, Vol. i, p. 438): 'it has red legs and its inferior wings have a lively red colour which gives a bright fiery appearance to the animals when fluttering in the sun's rays' (Cent. Bible, pp. 93, 94). But *the rivers of waters are dried up* (20) definitely suggests an excessive drought in which the distress of *the beasts of the field* is itself a prayer to God (20). *O Lord, to thee will I cry* (19). Joel himself is driven to his knees by it all.

c. The forebodings of the prophet (ii. 1–11)

Chapter ii follows much the same line as chapter i; but instead of filling in the details of the desolation which the plague has brought, it is mainly taken up with a description of the attack of the locusts themselves. The drought and the story of the aftermath of the visitation are the prominent features of chapter i; but the appearance of the locusts and the onward progress of their march almost completely fills the canvas in chapter ii. So vividly is this picture drawn for us that some commentators think it entirely excludes the allegorical interpretation (e.g. A. B. Davidson in *The Expositor*, Third Series, Vol. 7, p. 206). This antithesis is not necessary. This second description of the locusts, this time on the march, need not be regarded as a description of soldiers under the form of locusts; but it is obvious that the description of the locusts is given in preparation for the prophecy of social, political and religious disaster which is about to fall on the nation.

i. A call to repentance (ii. 1–3). *Blow ye the trumpet* (1). This instrument (Heb. *shophar*) was used almost exclusively for warlike purposes. It gave the signal 'to arms' (Jdg. vi. 34; 1 Sa. xiii. 3; 2 Sa. xx. 1); it warned of the approach of the enemy (Am. iii. 6; Ezk. xxxiii. 3ff.; Je. iv. 5, vi. 1); it was heard throughout a battle (Am. ii. 2). The prophet uses it here to show the seriousness of the situation. *The day of the Lord* (1). This phrase, which is introduced also in many other passages, has confused many by the apparently conflicting senses in which it is used. Is it present or future? Has it to do with a concrete human situation or is it an apocalyptic finale to the drama of history? Its sense here would seem to be that set out by A. B. Davidson (*The Expositor*, Third Series, Vol. 7, pp. 201, 202): 'Now unquestionably the day of the Lord is connected by the prophet with the other plagues but it is not confounded with them. These plagues are not the day of the Lord; they are but heralds and omens of it. The day of the Lord is the moment when He grasps the reins which He seems to have held slackly before, when the currents of His moral rule, which have been running sluggishly, receive a mysterious quickening and the Lord's work upon the earth is at last fully performed . . . Naturally any severe judgment or calamity awakened the thought of it and it seemed the advanced post of the final terrors.' There was so much about the locust plague to make it natural to connect the two. For example, *A fire devoureth before them* (3). Many travellers, some of them unacquainted with the biblical allusion, have described the country visited by locusts in this same way, e.g., 'A few months afterwards, a much larger army alighted and gave the whole country the appearance of having been burned. Wherever they settled it looked as if fire had devoured and burnt up everything.' Pusey gives an impressive list of travellers in many countries who saw the same thing and remarked on it in the same way (*Commentary*, p. 113).

ii. The locusts' onward march (ii. 4–11). *As the appearance of horses* (4). Attention has often been drawn to the striking resemblance which the locust bears to a horse. When magnified, it has even been said to be like a well armed horseman (Cam. Bible, p. 90). There is an Arabic saying to the effect that 'in the locust, slight as it is, is the nature of ten of the larger animals, the face of a horse, the eyes of an elephant, the neck of a bull, the horns of a deer, the chest of a lion, the belly of a scorpion, the wings of an eagle, the thighs of a camel, the feet of an ostrich, the tail of a serpent'. The various features of a locust invasion are faithfully recorded here. First the tremendous noise which they make (5), and the terror which they strike in those about

to be afflicted with them (6). Pliny speaks of 'the nations looking up with anxiety lest they should cover their lands' (*Nat. Hist.*, xi. 35). *All faces shall gather blackness* (6); better, as in RV, 'all faces are waxed pale'. Then their 'marshalled order' is noticed (7). They act under a common impulse. *They shall not break their ranks* (7); or 'they change not their caravans' (Cent. Bible), or 'each on his own track' (Moff.). They are inviolable to any weapon that may be used against them (8). 'Weapons are useless against them, because of their numbers; though millions are destroyed the rest march serenely on over their fallen comrades. Trenches filled with water to hinder them are quickly filled with drowned bodies and crossed; fires lighted to impede them are quenched by the ashes of the cremated. Armies have literally been led out in swarms; but in vain' (Cent. Bible, p. 97). This makes them irresistible (9). *They shall enter in at the windows like a thief* (9). Some commentators have suggested that our Lord and His apostles had this passage in mind when they used this same simile to describe the coming of the day of judgment (cf. Rev. xvi. 15; Mt. xxiv. 43, 44; 1 Thes. v. 2; 2 Pet. iii. 10). The reference to disturbances in the solar system (10) seems to suggest that more is meant here than physical phenomena accompanying the plague of locusts, and that Joel is about to set forth some of the things which the invasion, just experienced, presages and illustrates. See ii. 31 and iii. 15, and compare our Lord's own description of the things which herald the coming of the Son of man in Lk. xxi. 25, 26. *The Lord . . . before his army* (11). Jehovah is pictured as marching at the head of these irresistible forces of destruction, issuing His commands.

d. The appeal to the people (ii. 12–17)

Who can abide it? (11) appears to suggest that there is no hope; *the day of the Lord is great and very terrible* so that no one is able to endure it. But the prophet hastens on with the assurance that it is not too late to turn away His righteous anger by earnest turning unto God. It must, however, be *with all your heart* (12). The *heart*, as used here, is not to be thought of as the centre of the emotions and passions. In Hebrew psychology it was more generally thought of as the centre of moral, spiritual and intellectual life. It is supremely the organ of moral purpose and resolve. Moreover, their repentance is to be accompanied *with fasting, and with weeping* (12); i.e. with every sign of grief for their sins. God is greater than they know, kinder than they imagine, and gracious towards them in their unworthiness (13). *He will return and repent* (14); better, as in RV, 'he will turn' (Heb. *shubh*); i.e. the same word as in verse 12. This is a strong statement and it would seem at first to set aside the scriptural doctrine of the immutability of God. The Bible invariably asserts that God is unchangeable in His nature and perfections, in His knowledge, will and purpose. He is always the same. He is not a man, that He should repent (1 Sa. xv. 29). On the other hand, it never represents the unchangeableness of God as a dead immobility out of all relation to man and the world. His knowledge, will and purpose are never conceived of as conditioned or determined by men's acts; but He is shown to sustain a different relation to the godly and to the wicked, and to the same individual at different times according as he is godly or wicked. It is just because God is unchangeable that in His dealings with men He must seem to vary His course as they vary their conduct. He will yet send them *a blessing* (14); and the prophet's passion for God's glory is seen in that the greatest blessing He can conceive of is a good harvest which will enable a *meat* (RV 'meal') *offering and a drink offering* to be offered again in the temple.

Verses 15–17 repeat the call to prayer of i. 13, 14, but here there are three important differences. In chapter i the appeal was to a negligent priesthood alone; but here everyone is summoned—men, women, children and even the newly married bride and bridegroom who, in ordinary circumstances, were granted a year's exemption from public duty (Dt. xxiv. 5). If need be, the young couple were to rise up from the bridal festivities; the word *closet* (16; Heb. *chuppah*) is rather 'canopy' or 'pavilion', and undoubtedly refers to the special bridal tent which even in modern times is erected for the wedding. A second difference is that here they are called not to answer for their iniquities, as in chapter i, but rather in expectation of God's mercy. The *trumpet* (15) is not, as in ii. 1, a warning of the approach of danger, but rather a call to a religious assembly. The great reason given here for this 'national day of prayer' was lest *the heathen should rule over them* (17), or, as Moffatt puts it, lest they 'be a byword among pagans' (see RV mg.). Joel was anxious lest the plight of God's holy nation should provoke the heathen (note that he is here identifying the locusts with the heathen) to say that Israel's God was either no God at all, or that He was either unwilling or unable to keep them. This calumny Joel could not easily endure. It was false to fact, to experience and to the covenant.

II. PREDICTION. ii. 18—iii. 21

Then will the Lord be jealous (18) is obviously a turning-point in the book. It clearly sounds a distinct, new note. The RV reads 'Then was the Lord jealous'; this would mean that the day of fasting and prayer had been held, the Lord had heard and forgiven them, and was now as zealous to bless them as before He seemed swift to chastise. 'The future tenses of the AV are grammatically indefensible' (Cam. Bible, p. 58). Nevertheless, all that follows seems clearly to be yet in the future; some in the more or less immediate future and some in the dim distance of the 'last days'.

It is a law of Old Testament prophecy that

prophecy is conditional, unless it be expressly stated to be absolute. Up to this point Joel has come to them with a message of impending judgments and now, when the people have repented, he says 'it shall not be'.

a. The blessings of the immediate future (ii. 18–27)

These are promises of temporal benefits. Verses 18–20 contain the promise of immediate relief from their troubles. God is *jealous* (18). His power has been doubted, His honour impugned, and the fact that the heathen reproach His people calls for His intervention. He will not allow them to be for ever afflicted but will bring them complete relief. Verses 21–27 promise an early return of the land to health and prosperity. Joel here prophesies that God will send prosperous days after the invasion is over and their repentance is proved. The thick darkness (ii. 2) has gone; the land, or better still the ground, which mourned (i. 10) is now bidden to *be glad and rejoice* (21); the groaning beasts (i. 18) are now bidden to *be not afraid* (22); the barren fields and orchards (i. 7, 10–12) now *yield their strength* (22). Where there was no rain (i. 20) there is now abundance (23); where there was no wheat, wine and oil (i. 10) there is a superabundance (24). The damage done by the locusts (i. 4) is to be repaired and the loss restored (25–27).

In this passage the prophet takes up his stand as if some of his predictions had already taken place. This use of the 'prophetic' past, which describes what is yet to be as though it had already happened, is seen in verse 23. Here, instead of the AV, *he will cause to come down for you the rain*, the RSV reads 'he has poured down for you abundant rain'. The RV tries to convey the sense by using present tenses here. 'The future tense is unjustifiable as a translation but it is an entirely correct interpretation' (Cam. Bible, p. 61). The prophet already saw God giving them *the rain, the former rain, and the latter rain* (23), that is, the three rainy seasons in Palestine. The *former rain* is the showers of October and the first part of November. The *rain* is the main bulk of rain and falls from December to February. The *latter rain*, which is most appreciated of all because it helps to ripen the fruit and outlast the drought of summer, comes in April. The result of these would be an abundance of the things they have lost by reason of the locusts (24–26) and the vindication of God's honour as seen in a prosperous and reverent people (26, 27).

b. The blessings of the distant future (ii. 28–32)

These blessings are spiritual and pertain not to material things but to the realm of God's rule in the hearts of men and nations. This particular section, which forms a separate chapter in the Hebrew, is a prophecy that there would be an outpouring of the Holy Spirit of God before there would be any visitation of final judgment on the world. These verses owe their utterance here to several causes. W. G. Elmslie points out

(*The Expositor*, Fourth Series, Vol. 3, p. 177) that Joel felt that Israel needed more than a penitence born in the midst of austerity and famine. She also needed to be transformed, sanctified and made conformable to the mind and will of God. This could come about only if God would send down His Spirit into the hearts of His people. Then, in his unrolling of the canvas of the nation's history, the prophet was predicting that before the judgment of the world God would send forth His Spirit so that His people could achieve His kingdom in the world. This was, of course, what actually happened in Jerusalem (Acts ii. 1–14) on the day of Pentecost after our Lord's ascension. This event puzzled many who tried to understand it. But Peter's own inspired comment, 'This is that which was spoken by the prophet Joel', assured them that what was happening was nothing less than what had been predicted, and he went on to quote Joel ii. 28–32.

At this stage in the book the events of the recent past begin to fade away and to be lost in a foreshadowing of future history and even of eschatological and apocalyptic events. It is as if one were looking at a great range of mountains the peaks of which are clear enough but whose exact relation in distance from each other is quite indistinct. So, as Dr. R. F. Horton says: 'Pentecost looked nearer than it was, and the hills of blessing, which even we have not yet reached, seemed in that evening light of prophecy already glowing on the horizon' (Cent. Bible, p. 104).

Verses 30, 31 do not appear to be connected with the events of the day of Pentecost and some Bible expositors are led to declare that there will be a further world-wide outpouring of the Holy Spirit before the great day of the Lord. But Peter did most certainly identify the whole passage ii. 28–32 with the day of Pentecost. Moreover Joel may not have caught the full significance and connection of the images which he used; other writers of apocalypse did not. Therefore we may conclude that what we have here is a prophecy of the coming of the Holy Spirit at the beginning of the 'last days' (Acts ii. 16–21), the days of the gospel of Jesus Christ, and after that shall follow for all the enemies of God swift and terrible judgment from on high.

c. The ultimate destruction of all the enemies of God (iii. 1–21)

When I shall bring again the captivity of Judah (1). Not necessarily a reference to the return from exile. RSV translates 'When I restore the fortunes of Judah'. See *Introduction* under 'Date'. *The valley of Jehoshaphat* (2). The identification of this spot is uncertain and not really important. Jehoshaphat means 'Jehovah judges', which indicates the symbolical meaning of the term. See verse 12 and cf. verse 14 where the same place is called 'the valley of decision', i.e. God's decision as to their judgment. The picture is one of retribution for the cruel oppression of God's

people. *They have cast lots* (3). Captives were allocated to the soldiers in this way and were used to satisfy their physical appetites.

Verses 4–8 relate specifically to the Phoenicians and the Philistines (see RV). Their theme is that these nations shall be recompensed for their action in selling Jewish slaves to *the Grecians* (6), by having their own sons and daughters sold to *the Sabeans* (8; RV 'the men of Sheba'), a country just as far away in the opposite direction. If we accept the early date for Joel this is the first biblical reference to the Greeks. As the Phoenicians were a maritime people its introduction is quite natural here.

Verse 9 resumes the thought of verse 2. The nations are almost mockingly called on to make what preparation they can to defend themselves against the Lord who not only sits to judge them (12) but who also executes the judgment. *Beat your plowshares into swords* (10). The exact opposite of Is. ii. 4, a fact which serves to emphasize the difference in the fate awaiting the heathen and the godly. In verse 13 the figure is changed. The destruction of the wicked is likened to reaping and to the treading of the winepress. Cf. the similar use of this imagery in Rev. xiv. 15–20. *Multitudes in the valley of decision* (14). See note on verse 2. With verse 15 cf. ii. 10n. *The heavens and the earth shall shake* (16). Cf. Hg. ii. 6 and Heb. xii. 25–29. The object of this judgment is that all men shall *know that I am the Lord your God* (17; cf. ii. 17).

Linked with this judgment on the heathen is the restoration of Israel expressed in verse 18 in terms of those natural blessings which, after the locust and drought of the earlier chapters, would most readily conjure up a picture of happiness and prosperity. In contrast with the coming desolation of Egypt and Edom, *Judah shall dwell for ever* (20).

This chapter clearly deals with events of great moment for the Jews and the world. Commentators differ as to its meaning.

It is regarded by some as an imaginative and poetical description of the literal triumph of the Jewish people over their surrounding and traditional enemies. Those who argue this suggest that verse 2 could hardly be interpreted in any other way. But, as has been pointed out above, the 'valley of Jehoshaphat' has probably a symbolical rather than a literal meaning. The whole tenor of the description suggests that Joel had more than a local national victory in mind.

Others regard this passage as a literal description of events to take place at the time of the 'end', when the wicked will be destroyed in actual battle, followed by the full restoration of the Jewish people. That this chapter can be interpreted in this way must be recognized. Historically speaking, the judgment of God will follow the day of grace, which we might even term 'the day of the Holy Spirit' (cf. ii. 28–32). 'The outpouring of the Spirit is the precursor of judgment. Is that not a startling transition? Not at all. As soon as God's people have been divinely fitted to accomplish their task, as soon as God's servants are prepared completely to achieve His kingdom on earth, then the end of all things is at hand. The plenitude of the Spirit put into the Church means the finale of our world's history . . . and those who call on the name of Jehovah and whom Jehovah calls to be His own, pass through it unscathed and saved' (W. G. Elmslie, *The Expositor*, Fourth Series, Vol. 3, p. 177).

A third view which relates Israel to the Church and which sees in this chapter the fortunes of Israel and the fortunes of the Church, the Israel of God, merging together is one for which most, perhaps, can be said. Those who expound the text in this way see symbolized in the victories here described the overthrow of all those who are opponents of the gospel of grace. The passage is therefore a prediction of the progress of that gospel in this age culminating in its complete victory. As Pusey remarks on the statement *Judah shall dwell for ever* (20): 'Not earthly Judah, nor earthly Jerusalem; for these must come to an end, together with the earth itself of whose end the Prophets well knew. It is then the one people of God, the true Judah, the people who praise God, the Israel which is indeed Israel. Egypt and Edom and all the enemies of God shall come to an end, but His people shall never come to an end' (*Commentary*, p. 145).

J. T. CARSON.

AMOS

INTRODUCTION

I. THE HISTORICAL BACKGROUND

Amos, one of the greatest of the so-called 'minor' prophets (Cornill calls him one of the most wonderful appearances in the history of the human spirit), prophesied in the days of Uzziah, king of Judah, and Jeroboam II, king of Israel. It is impossible to determine the exact year of his prophecy, but it was probably round about 760 B.C. The reference to the earthquake (i. 1), which apparently had been a memorable one (cf. Zechariah's allusion to it in Zc. xiv. 5 long afterwards), does not help much to fix an absolutely certain date.

In 803 B.C. Adad-nirari III of Assyria inflicted a crushing defeat on the Syrian confederacy. This weakening of Israel's northern neighbour and Assyria's subsequent preoccupation elsewhere gave Jehoash and his son Jeroboam II a supremacy in northern Palestine and Syria probably unknown by any of their predecessors. Israel was free again to appropriate new territory, and this she did with great zest, particularly at the expense of Syria. All the main trade routes were in her hand, and Samaria, the capital, became a meeting-place of merchants who travelled between Mesopotamia and Egypt. Here caravans met from the various parts of the eastern world, and she became the emporium of goods of every type. The increased commercial activities brought Israel enormous gains, and a powerful merchant class grew up which had wide repercussions upon the rest of the inhabitants.

This commercial prosperity gave rise to a very large building programme of 'winter houses with summer houses' (iii. 15), and of 'houses of ivory'. Samaria had many palaces (iii. 10) belonging not only to the king himself, but to the rich merchant-princes who had grown rich through trade. These great houses became ere long the depository of every type of luxury (iii. 12, vi. 4). The chance to get rich made the merchants eager to increase their profits both by fair means and by foul. They were impatient with the sabbaths and the new moons (viii. 5). In this unholy traffic they were urged on by their wives who demanded more and more luxuries (iv. 1).

The dictum 'money corrupts' was truly exemplified in the northern kingdom during the days of Jeroboam II. The desire for wealth had disastrous results both for the merchant and for the poor peasant. The rich merchant-princes became demoralized, corrupt and unjust; the poor were oppressed, robbed and ill-treated. Amos belonged to the poor peasant class, and he probably knew from bitter experience to what indignity the poor and oppressed had been put. The rich were getting richer, and the poor were getting poorer. What property the smallholder might have had he was compelled to sell by the sheer force of unpleasant circumstances. For him there was no justice in the land. The money-lenders took men's very clothes as pledges for debt. Judges were influenced by bribes, and that meant victory for injustice and defeat for truth (viii. 6). No honest witness could be found in the courts. 'The honest man was bullied out of truth and property and life.' Pity became a rare quality, and the poor stood with their backs to the wall (ii. 6). The independent small-holder, the peasant-proprietor, was fighting a losing battle. The small plots of land were absorbed into the larger estates.

As far as religion was concerned, the shrines at Bethel and Gilgal, especially at Bethel, were crowded with worshippers. Baal worship had certainly been suppressed by Jehu, Ahab's successor, but the spirit, if not the form, had remained in the authorized shrines where Jehovah was supposed to have been worshipped. Here the oppressor of the poor, the rich luxuriating in their luxuries, worshipped with a dulled or dead conscience. Outwardly all was done according to rule, but there was no true worship as we understand worship today. Israel had ceased to live before God, as she had done in the desert under Moses, and was now merely living towards God. The shrines may have been crowded with worshippers, but God was not there. Superstition and immorality had taken the place of godliness and sincerity. Religion was utterly divorced from conduct, and it was some time before Israel could be made to understand that these two must go hand in hand. (See Appendix I to Kings, p. 333, 'The Religion of Israel under the Monarchy'.)

Jeroboam's kingdom, then, was a land of contrasting extremes: the rich were very rich and the poor were very poor. In such conditions dissatisfaction and restlessness were bound to grow. As subsequent events showed, the country was ripe for civil war. After Jeroboam's death there were three kings in one year. Revolution followed revolution, and in a few years' time part of the kingdom of Israel had vanished, the rest holding on to a precarious independence depending on the goodwill of Assyria. Such social conditions could not endure indefinitely; they had, indeed, the sentence of death in themselves. Amos was one of those men who realized this. He saw the dark cloud of judgment on the horizon. There were social, moral and political forces at work which would perform the will of God and execute the judgment that had already been passed. Israel was, indeed, 'a basket of summer fruit' (qayits), and her end (qeyts) could not be delayed (viii. 2).

II. THE PROPHET

Amos was a native of Tekoa, a small town some six miles from Bethlehem. He was not a courtier like Isaiah, or a priest like Jeremiah, but a herdman and a dresser of sycomore trees. From the similes which he frequently uses it is plain that he was fully and personally acquainted with the hardships and perils of a shepherd's life. Life was difficult and there were few luxuries. On the other hand, his trade will have taken him to towns and important market-places where, no doubt, he will have met caravans from many lands. A man of his calibre will have always had an open ear for tidings of men and their doings in other places. Hence his surprising amount of knowledge of other lands and people. As the opening chapters of his book show, he knew a great deal of the history, the origins and deeds of the surrounding nations. Out of such experiences, and moulded by his personal observation of conditions in the land, there grew and developed a hard, stern man, a great fighter, a veritable champion of the poor.

Though not of the line of prophets, nor of the school of prophets, he was called, like Elijah, from the daily round of his duties to the dignity of the prophetic ministry. There was no doubt in his mind, nor did he leave any doubt in other men's minds, that he was called of God, even as Moses had been called when engaged in a similar occupation. With Amos it was not a case of turning prophet in order to earn his living; it was a case of leaving his living to act as a prophet. He makes no attempt to hide his past life or employment, and he was not ashamed to make known his lowly birth. The fire of God was burning in his soul, and, as with the apostle Paul centuries later, it was a case of 'Woe is unto me if I speak not'. He saw the corruption, the sin and the shame of the people whom God had brought out of Egypt, and there could be no keeping silence. The path in which he was called upon to walk was not of his choice. The God of the ends of the earth, with whom he had communed often and long in the solitude of the Tekoan desert, had a message for His rebellious people in the north, and it was through Amos that this message of justice and judgment was to be announced.

III. THE PROPHET'S MESSAGE

Amos' burden was one of almost unrelieved judgment and punishment. Though in the last few verses of the book there is a note of optimism, revealing the wideness of God's mercy in a restored Davidic throne, yet the whole message of this intrepid messenger of God must be set in the context of imminent disaster. He certainly was not a tickler of the popular ear, but kept his eye on the divine message he had to proclaim. National sin leads to national judgment, and the greater a nation's privilege and opportunity has been, the greater must also the judgment be.

As far as Jeroboam's Israel was concerned, everything outwardly appeared in order, but doom was hanging over all. As a lion is ready to spring on his prey, so Jehovah was ready to visit His people in judgment. The whole land would feel the impact of that judgment. Again and again warnings had been sent to Israel, but all to no avail. This time there could be no mercy, no turning back. Where people go on flouting the will of God they must take the consequences.

In addition to the moral corruption which had issued in social oppression and legal injustice, there was the matter of the false shrines at Bethel and Gilgal. But God loathes all this fulsome ritual. He has no use for their feasts, their festivals and their rich offerings. It is all a mockery; it is all foreign to Him. In the desert of old there was none of this. How far Amos was influenced against the worship of Bethel and Gilgal by the fact that he was a southerner we need not inquire now. There can be little doubt, however, that these shrines, set up shortly after the split of the Solomonic kingdom, were regarded by every true, 'orthodox' southerner as abominations unto the Lord. These shrines, the prophet announces, will be utterly destroyed. Already Jehovah stands by the altar (ix. 1–4) and will bring the place down to utter ruin.

For these sins—expressed man-ward in social oppression and injustice, and God-ward in abominable practices at Bethel and Gilgal—there can be but one thing—the utter rejection of Israel. If privilege is the measure of responsibility, then Israel's rebellion was unpardonable. God had brought Israel out of Egypt, led her through the desert and given her possession of a fair land, as well as prophets out of her midst. The punishment for her transgression must be proportionate; therefore Israel will be utterly rejected. The fact that Jehovah had brought Israel out of Egypt would now mean no more than the other fact that He had brought the Philistines from Crete and the Syrians from Kir. The sentence is already passed, and judgment will be executed speedily. Like the roller of a threshing-floor He will crush the whole nation (ii. 13–16).

The message of Amos is based on the firm inner conviction that Jehovah is a God of righteousness. This righteousness is in conflict with and has declared war upon the unrighteousness of man. The issue of this conflict will result in the severest judgment for man. The teaching of Amos is ethical in character, but, like the other eighth-century prophets, he did not base his teaching on what was good and right in man, but on what he had come to know of the nature of

God. 'Sin', therefore, with Amos is more than transgression, more than a mere moral lapse from some established code; it is rebellion against God. Israel stood in a covenant relationship to Jehovah. This relationship laid duties upon Israel, and her sin lay in repudiating the duties inherent in this God-man relationship. Israel had rebelled against Jehovah.

Though a southerner, the message of Amos was directed to and against the northern kingdom. He was, in fact, the last prophet to northern Israel. On the whole, he says very little about his own people. This silence, however, must not be construed as meaning that the southern kingdom was free from those sins which the prophet saw in the north and which he so vehemently denounces. He was called to speak to Israel which was ripe for judgment, and he confines himself almost exclusively to that part of the country.

But Amos had also something to say about the surrounding nations. While condemning Israel for sinning against a law which God had made known to her, he applied a quite different standard to the nations which did not stand in a covenant relationship to God. What Amos saw in the surrounding nations was the heart-breaking spectacle of a cruelty which ignored all human rights, which denied all pity, and which made the relations of the nations like those of wild beasts. Whichever way the prophet looked, he saw one thing absent—man's natural pity for his fellow-man. What made the matter worse was the trivial advantage such conduct brought. Gaza sold a whole village into slavery to make a little money. The king of Moab burns the bones of an enemy to gratify his revenge. And so the story goes on. Man's sense of fellowship with man had disappeared. Such a world could not continue, for the very basis for a continuation did not exist.

Though Amos had no academic training, he was not surpassed by any of his successors in vividness, vigour and simplicity of speech. His style is simple, yet full of energy and elegance. Professor Robertson Smith defends Amos as a master of pure Hebrew style. The terms he employs were all familiar to his contemporaries, for his observations are all drawn from every-day life. No other prophet has furnished us with such metaphors from nature in such fresh, vivid and rich variety. He refers to iron sledges of the thresher (i. 3); hurricanes (i. 14); the cedars and oaks with their deep roots (ii. 9); the hungry lion roaring in the forest (iii. 4); the snared bird (iii. 5); the shepherd coming to the rescue of the lamb (iii. 12); hooks and fishers' netting (iv. 2); partial showers (iv. 7); mildew and blight, hills and winds and sunrise, stars, mourning husbandmen, earthquakes, eclipses, corn sifted in a sieve, refuse of wheat, mended booths, etc.

Such was this great 'minor' prophet. Living close to God he knew His will and had His message. Though unpopular, as, indeed, almost every prophet of Israel was, he proclaimed with an undying zeal the message Jehovah had entrusted to him, for, with Martin Luther, Amos would have said 'I can do no other, so help me God'.

OUTLINE OF CONTENTS

I. PROLOGUE. i. 1, 2

II. DECLARATION OF THE NATIONS' DOOM. i. 3—ii. 16

    a. Damascus (Syria) (i. 3–5)
    b. Gaza (Philistia) (i. 6–8)
    c. Tyre (i. 9, 10)
    d. Edom (i. 11, 12)
    e. Ammon (i. 13–15)
    f. Moab (ii. 1–3)
    g. Judah (ii. 4, 5)
    h. Israel (ii. 6–16)

III. PROCLAMATION OF THE PROPHET'S MESSAGE. iii. 1—vi. 14

    a. The first discourse (iii. 1–15)
    b. The second discourse (iv. 1–13)
    c. The third discourse (v. 1—vi. 14)

IV. REVELATION OF GOD'S DESIGN. vii. 1—ix. 10

    a. The vision of the devouring locust (vii. 1–3)
    b. The vision of the consuming fire (vii. 4–6)
    c. The vision of the searching plumbline (vii. 7–9)
    d. Historical interlude (vii. 10–17)
    e. The vision of the basket of summer fruit (viii. 1–14)
    f. The vision of the Lord upon the altar (ix. 1–10)

V. EPILOGUE. ix. 11–15

COMMENTARY

I. PROLOGUE. i. 1, 2

The words of Amos (1). There is only one Amos in the Old Testament and that is the writer of this book. His occupation was that of a herdman or shepherd. The word used is not the usual word *roeh* but *noqed*, and means the herdman of a peculiar breed of desert sheep with short legs and ugly faces but highly valued for their wool. The word is found again only in 2 Ki. iii. 4, where it is translated 'sheep-master' (RV). 'Viler than a naqqad' is still an Arabian proverb of contempt. *Which he saw* (1). The word *chazah* was used for the specific prophetic vision. The scope of his message was *concerning Israel*. Amos was God's prophet to the northern kingdom, and he was the last prophet that kingdom had. The prophet received his vision in the days of Uzziah (*c.* 791–740 B.C.), king of Judah, and Jeroboam II (*c.* 793–753 B.C.), king of Israel. In the next sentence this prophecy is narrowed down to *two years before the earthquake*. It is impossible, however, to fix the precise year of this particular earthquake, but that it had left a profound impression is witnessed by the fact that after many decades Zechariah refers to it (xiv. 5). *The Lord will roar* . . . (2). God is about to speak dramatically, and when He speaks certain consequences will follow. The word *roar* (*sha'ag*) means the roar of the lion as he leaps upon his prey. God's judgment, as Amos saw it, was not a long way off, but was already on the way and would be presently revealed with all its dire consequences. Moreover, it would not be from Bethel or Gilgal, but *from Zion*, the centre of religious authority, and *from Jerusalem*, the very dwelling-place of Jehovah, that His voice would be heard. One of the consequences envisaged is that *the top of Carmel shall wither* (2). Carmel, a promontory by the sea, 1,200 feet high, south of the Bay of Acre, and the scene of Elijah's great exploits, is reckoned the most fruitful and striking hill in the north. Its name, 'garden-land', testifies to its fertility. Little wonder the shepherds will lament, for if Carmel is to wither through drought what other pastures can there be left in the land?

These opening verses give the substance of Amos' message. No matter how safe the lamb may appear to be in its fat pastures, the lion's roar indicates how deceptive appearances may be. Israel was feeding in rich pastures, and all appeared, outwardly at least, to be safe, but that was not the case. Judgment is imminent and, moreover, it is inescapable.

II. DECLARATION OF THE NATIONS' DOOM. i. 3—ii. 16

Like most other prophets, Amos has his oracles against foreign nations. Unlike the other prophets, however, he introduces them so that they precede and lead up to an indictment of his own people. One by one they are named, their sins are cited, and they are condemned. The formula in each case is the same: first their crimes are named and then the consequences are proclaimed. The sins, in almost every case, are sins of foreign relationships—wanton war, massacre and sacrilege. His occupation will have taken Amos to many market-places where he will have met caravans from many lands, and in this way he will have learned a great deal of the nations surrounding Israel and Judah. By exposing and denouncing these barbarous outrages, Amos prepares the way for the real word of judgment that is to come for Israel, whose sins are even greater, for they are sins, not so much against other people as against their own kith and kin. Moreover, Israel's sin was greater than that of the surrounding nations because her privileges and her light had been so much greater.

a. Damascus (Syria) (i. 3–5)

For three transgressions . . . and for four . . . (3). Attempts have been made from earliest times to find symbolical meaning in these numbers, but it probably is a literal translation of an idiomatic expression meaning 'for many crimes'. Moffatt has 'crime upon crime', and T. H. Robinson 'for so many crimes'. The whole of Syria is meant by this reference to its capital Damascus. This was the most important of Israel's neighbours and stood in the line of Assyrian conquest. For many years before Jeroboam II Israel had been engaged in deadly conflict with Syria, and the mention of Damascus would at once have arrested attention. The formula *I will not turn away the punishment* (lit. 'I will not turn it back') is repeated in i. 6, 9, 11, 13, ii. 1, 4, 6. *Threshing instruments* (3) in the East were, and in many places still are, carved slabs, studded with iron teeth, drawn by horses or mules over heaped corn. In this way the straw was chopped into little pieces and the grain released. In some such cruel way had Syria treated (*threshed*) Gilead. When this barbarity was perpetrated is not stated, but probably it was done by Hazael when he conquered Gilead in the days of Jehu and Jehoahaz (2 Ki. x. 32ff.).

I will send a fire . . . (4). *Fire* is here a symbol of war. Judgment will involve both the dynasty and the people of Syria. Hazael and Ben-hadad were the two most cruel oppressors of Israel. The prophecy that their dynasty would perish must have brought peculiar pleasure to Israel. *I will break also the bar* (5); i.e. Damascus would be laid open to the enemy (cf. Dt. iii. 5). The *plain of Aven* (lit. 'valley of idolatry') has been variously identified. Prof. G. A. Smith identifies it with Baalbek; some think the reference is to the broad and fertile oasis of Damascus itself. *House of Eden* (5). There was a place called Bitadini (Assyrian for 'house of Eden') on the middle Euphrates, and some Bible scholars hold that this is a reference to that place. But the context demands some place in the region of Damascus, which even today is the paradise of the Arab world. *Shall go into captivity* (5) probably refers to the Assyrian policy with regard to native peoples, which was captivity. *Kir* remains unidentified (the Vulg. has 'Cyrene'). According to Am. ix. 7 it was the original home of the Syrians. They were to return to it when they ceased to be a nation.

b. Gaza (Philistia) (i. 6–8)

From the far north the prophet next turns to the south. Gaza was the most southerly of the cities of the Philistines, on the edge of the desert, and at the junction of caravan routes. It was probably its strategic situation which involved the place deeply in the slave traffic. Though this oracle is addressed against Gaza in particular, it is, no doubt, meant for the whole of Philistia. *They carried away captive* . . . (6). A typical instance of brutality. It is not stated who the captives were, nor is the occurrence dated, but they were sold to the Edomites. Raids of this kind were, no doubt, frequent enough in those days (cf. 2 Ch. xxi. 16). As in the case of Damascus, judgment will come not only to Gaza but to the strongholds of the Philistines as well, and the whole country will be visited and overwhelmed by the fire of war.

c. Tyre (i. 9, 10)

The crimes of Tyre (representing the whole of Phoenicia, as Gaza did Philistia) were selling slaves, and forgetting *the brotherly covenant* (9). Slave traffic flourished not only among the Philistines but among the Phoenicians also. It is difficult to say what *the brotherly covenant* meant. Perhaps it referred to the covenant between Hiram and Solomon (1 Ki. v. 12, ix. 13), or maybe to some later covenant. The punishment is again *fire*, i.e. war (10). Tyre was destroyed by the Assyrians, and later again by Nebuchadnezzar. Alexander the Great captured it and sold 30,000 of its inhabitants into slavery.

d. Edom (i. 11, 12)

Edom has already been mentioned twice (i. 6, 9) as a partaker in the crimes of other nations; now the thunderstorm breaks over it. *He did pursue his brother* (11); i.e. Israel. *Cast off all pity* (11; lit. 'stifled his compassion'). The perpetual and unrelenting nature of this hatred is emphasized. There was always great enmity between Israel and Edom, particularly after the exile. The punishment here, as elsewhere, is again fire (war). *Teman* (12; cf. Ob. 9) was apparently a district in northern Edom, and *Bozrah* a city of some importance.

e. Ammon (i. 13–15)

The crime of Ammon (13) is particularly brutal and revolting, but it appears to have been quite common in Semitic warfare (cf. 2 Ki. viii. 12; Ho. xiii. 16; Na. iii. 10), and has not been altogether unknown in our day. To enlarge their border they made war on unborn children. The consequences are that Rabbah, their capital, a city some twenty-five miles north-east of the north end of the Dead Sea, will be taken by storm and will be destroyed (14), and the king and the princes will go into captivity (15).

f. Moab (ii. 1–3)

If the Ammonites were guilty of the crime of declaring war on the unborn child, the Moabites were guilty of the crime of declaring war on a corpse (1). Moab's crime may have been against Israel's bitter foe, the Edomites; nevertheless, the prophet condemns it for it was a shameful crime against humanity. The desecration of the body was a great sacrilege in the eyes of the ancient world. The soul (*nephesh*) in Semitic thought was so identified with the body that to burn the one meant to destroy the other. The consequence is that *fire* (war) . . . *shall devour the palaces of Kerioth* (lit. 'cities'). It has been suggested that Kerioth, the capital of Moab, may have consisted of several absorbed small towns like London, hence the plural. Moab will perish amid tumult, amid the din and crash of battle, and her *judge*, or ruler, probably a vassal king appointed by Jeroboam, together with the princes and nobles, will likewise perish.

g. Judah (ii. 4, 5)

Judah's crime, it will be observed, is not, as in the case of the other nations, against man; it is against God (4). His law is *despised*, and as a consequence His commandments are *not kept*. *Their lies* (4); i.e. their false gods. The punishment follows the pattern of the other oracles. *Fire* (war) will be sent to all Judah, but particularly to Jerusalem, where its *palaces* (probably all big houses) will be destroyed.

h. Israel (ii. 6–16)

Having paved the way by drawing Israel's attention to certain cruel sins of which their neighbours were guilty, and having presumably stirred up their righteous indignation against them, the prophet now comes to what is his main purpose, namely, the denunciation of Israel's own sins and crimes. A fuller list of these is given in Israel's case than in that of any other nation. The first crime is that of slavery: *they sold the righteous for silver* (6). The law allowed a poor man to sell himself into slavery (Lv. xxv. 39; Dt. xv. 12), but it did not sanction the sale of an insolvent debtor, which is evidently what is meant here (2 Ki. iv. 1; Ne. v. 5). The poor man was sold *for a pair of shoes* (6), or 'for an old song' as we might say. Another sin is greed. The rich are so rapacious that they even *pant after the dust of the earth on the head of the poor* (7). The poor man (Heb. *dallim*, i.e. 'weak', 'drooping', 'thin') casts a handful of dust on his head in token of his misery, but the greedy landowner is even after that, so great was the land-hunger of the rich. The iniquity of injustice follows next. The powerful and greedy rich *turn aside the way of the meek* (7; Heb. *anawim*); i.e. the humble followers of Jehovah (Is. xi. 4), and for them there was no justice in the courts. Added to all the above crimes, there was the evil of immorality. Sanctuary prostitution was a regular feature of the Canaanite cults and had evidently found its way into the shrines of Israel. Dt. xxiii. 17 strictly forbade this evil practice. *Clothes laid to pledge* (8). The reference seems to be to forfeited pledges, and the old charge of rapacity is here again. To rapacity and inhumanity is added the evil of intemperance (8b, 12a). Verses 9–12 present Israel's sin of indifference to and forgetfulness of all that Jehovah had done to the Amorites whom He had displaced, and to Israel whom He had brought out of Egypt, led through the desert and brought into the Promised Land. In addition, God had raised up inside the nation prophets and Nazarites—consecrated and ascetic lives. For the law of the Nazarites (better, as in RV, 'Nazirites') see Nu. vi. 1–21. They were the separated, consecrated ones, and took the vow of total abstinence. The crowning sin was that of intimidation (12b); their prophets were *commanded* (intimidated) not to prophesy, so that their dulled conscience might not be disturbed. *Behold, I am pressed under you* (13). This might mean that Jehovah is pressed and burdened under the weight of His people's grievous and manifold sins (Is. xliii. 24), or, following RV, it might mean that God will grind the nation down 'as a threshing-wagon pressed down hard upon the sheaves which filled the threshing-floor' (N. H. Snaith). But the first interpretation may stand, for sin has consequences not only for the sinner; it deeply affects God Himself. Verses 14–16 describe the inescapable judgment that will fall upon all. Neither for the swift of foot, nor the strong, nor the warrior, nor the horseman will there be any escape. This headlong flight is the result of the severity of the storm of vengeance which had rolled over the surrounding countries and was now reaching Israel in all its fury. The forecast was fulfilled in the Assyrian invasion.

III. PROCLAMATION OF THE PROPHET'S MESSAGE. iii. 1—vi. 14

In the next four chapters Amos proclaims, in greater detail, the vital message God had given him for Israel. The substance of it has already been given in the Prologue and more especially in ii. 6–16. Here the theme is worked out in greater detail. The message, which is one of almost unrelieved doom, takes the form of three discourses which open with the words *Hear this word* (iii. 1, iv. 1, v. 1).

a. The first discourse (iii. 1-15)

i. Amos justifies his claim to be heard (iii. 1-8). After so daring and revolutionary an announcement of judgment in verses 1 and 2, striking at

all the pride and boast of a privileged people, Amos proceeds to explain his appearance on the scene. Such daring words demand some authentication of the prophet's authority, and in verses 3–8 he gives, in a series of brief figures, the ground on which he claims he should be heard. Every effect has its cause; his appearance in Israel has also its cause. The illustrations drawn are mostly from desert and agricultural life. Some scholars have suggested that the expression *of all the families of the earth* (2; Heb. *adamah*; lit. 'ground') has been used on purpose 'to stamp the meanness and mortality of them all'. *Can two walk together . . .?* (3). It is not likely that two men will meet in a trackless desert. If they do walk together, it may be safely assumed that this is so because of a prior appointment. *Will a lion roar . . .?* (4). The ominous roar of a lion means the lion has sprung upon his prey, for the hunting lion is silent till his quarry is in sight. The inference is that Amos' voice is a sign that Jehovah's judgment has come. *Can a bird fall . . .?* (5). The snare is the trap which springs and catches the bird when it has touched the bait, and the point of the image is that, as the captured bird proves the snare, so the prophet's voice of doom is an indication of God's design. *Shall a trumpet be blown . . .?* (6). When the *shophar* (horn) was blown, people knew there was some significant meaning behind it. The same was true of some calamity befalling a city: it was a sign that Jehovah had permitted it for some good reason. By means of these interrogative thrusts Amos prepares the ground for his real point: *the Lord God hath spoken, who can but prophesy?* (8). Here is the climax of this section. Amos' appearance as a prophet in Israel has its cause: God has spoken to his soul; he can do none other. 'A man does not choose to be a prophet; he is chosen.'

ii. The appeal for witnesses (iii. 9, 10). *Assemble yourselves . . . behold . . .* (9). The heathen neighbours are called to witness the strife within Samaria, caused by the ruthless rapacity and greed of the rich. There is violence and robbery, and the victims, no doubt, are the defenceless poor. The rich who *store up violence and robbery in their palaces* (10) are so debased that they seem incapable of doing what is right.

iii. The announcement of judgment (iii. 11-15). The agent of this judgment is described as *an adversary . . . round about the land* (11); i.e. a foe who shall surround the land and blockade it on all sides. In *c.* 734 B.C. Tiglath-pileser overran Gilead and Galilee and in *c.* 724 B.C. Shalmaneser overran northern Israel. Samaria was surrounded for three years and finally taken. The palaces were spoiled, and the rich and delicate were taken into captivity. The nature of this judgment included diminution of strength (11) and the deportation of the people (12). This latter point is vividly illustrated by the shepherd-prophet. Samaria will be almost completely destroyed. As a shepherd can sometimes do little except, maybe, recover the barest remnants of a sheep, so none, except a few odd survivors, will escape the general doom. The mention of Damascus at the end of verse 12 raises a difficult point. Damascus was, of course, the capital of Syria and has already been dealt with by the prophet. Some translate it 'So shall the children of Israel who dwell in Samaria escape with the corner of a couch or with the Damascus-cloth of a divan' (so Ehrlich and others; cf. RV). The whole picture is one of utter wretchedness for the few survivors of Samaria. The last two verses of this chapter indicate the extent of judgment. The sacred shrines of Bethel, built by Jeroboam I after the division of the kingdom, will share the doom of Samaria: there will be complete and utter desecration of the altar. The fate which will overtake the rich will also overtake their mansions. The *winter house* (probably built for cold weather), together with the *houses of ivory* (probably inlaid with ivory; but cf. 1 Ki. xxii. 39), shall perish. To the shepherd-prophet who knew the hardships of the poor, and who slept under God's open heaven, these elaborate dwellings must have appeared the very incarnation of pride, self-indulgence and departure from God.

b. The second discourse (iv. 1–13)

i. The women of Samaria (iv. 1–3). This discourse opens with a fierce and scathing denunciation of the rich women of Samaria. The sarcasm is unsurpassed. These opulent, greedy women are likened to fat, sleek cows—prize cows, we might say—of *Bashan*, which was famous for its pastures and breed of cattle and sheep (cf. Dt. xxxii. 14; Ezk. xxxix. 18). They care for nothing except their easy life and lazy luxury. In their mad rush for more food and drink they trample upon all that is fragile and fine. The poor are oppressed and the needy are crushed. This may not have been done directly, but it was done indirectly—through their husbands—for idle luxury at one end means oppression and poverty at the other.

But, as in all the other oracles, this denunciation of crime is immediately followed by an announcement of dire consequences. *The Lord God hath sworn by his holiness* (2). The idea conveyed by the word *holiness* (*qodesh*) was reserved for Jehovah alone. The expression, therefore, is equivalent to 'by Himself'. The punishment will be captivity. The women of Samaria will be led, through open breaches in the wall; and moreover, as unruly cattle are led with hooks in their nostrils, so these women will be led away with *hooks* and their *posterity* (probably their daughters) *with fishhooks*, i.e. hooks like fishhooks. In the Assyrian monuments captives are portrayed as being dragged with hooks in their mouths. The expression *cast them into the palace* (3) has caused commentators a great deal of difficulty. For the word *palace* some versions have Harmon, some Armenia, and others still Mount Rimmon

(see RV). In any case, some unpleasant fate is indicated.

ii. The worship of Samaria (iv. 4, 5). In this oracle the prophet attacks with biting sarcasm the empty ritualism of the schismatic shrines of Israel. The worshippers were very punctilious in the performance of the ritual, even though the moral and spiritual reality had gone out of it. The denunciation is similar to Isaiah's reproach of Judah (Is. i. 10ff.). Such empty, meaningless mockery, divorced from all morality, can only *multiply transgression* (4). *Bring your sacrifices every morning, and your tithes after three years* (4b). They were quite correct in bringing their morning sacrifices, but the reading *after three years* is difficult. Some read 'every three days' (see RV); the suggestion is that they spend three days on their tithes, one at each of the three great feasts; i.e. the feasts of unleavened bread, of harvest and of ingathering. The whole scene at Bethel and Gilgal was one of feverish activity and earnest zeal—*this liketh you* (5). The worshippers were very correct in all that pertained to their worship, but their hands were polluted and their hearts were evil.

iii. The impenitence of Israel (iv. 6–13). In the next few verses we have a series of five oracles, each telling of some disaster which had come upon Israel in the natural world, and each ends with the same refrain which tells of Israel's impenitence—*yet have ye not returned unto me, saith the Lord*. The first oracle deals with famine. *I have given you cleanness of teeth* (6); i.e. because there was nothing to eat and they have not been stained with food. Some ancient versions have also 'dullness', suggesting that the teeth are blunt from disuse. The second oracle deals with drought (7, 8). The word for rain is *geshem* and must, therefore, mean the heavy October rains, the 'former rains' of the Old Testament. The heavy autumn rains had not arrived by the time the lighter spring rains were due; this meant disaster for the whole country. Verses 7b and 8, however, seem to imply that the drought was not universal. Thomson on one occasion found the ground round the Jordan valley like a desert, while at Tiberias the whole country was a paradise of herbs and flowers (*The Land and the Book*, p. 395). This partial rainfall seems to be characteristic of Palestine. *Wandered* (8); more accurately 'tottered', or 'staggered' (like a drunk man), in the weakness of thirst. The third oracle has blight for its theme (9). The scourges mentioned here were frequent enough in Palestine to serve as a reminder of judgment. *Palmerworm* (Heb. *gazam*) is the locust. Next comes the plague (10), which is said to have had its origin in Egypt (cf. Is. x. 24, 26). *Your young men have I slain with the sword* (10) may refer to some local invasion by an unnamed foe. The slaughter of the young men, probably left unburied for a time (cf. *the stink of your camps*), may well have been the cause of the pestilence. In any case, the affliction was dreadful, but it left Israel quite impenitent. The last oracle deals with earthquake (11). The earthquake may well be the one referred to in i. 1. This was recent enough and would still be fresh in the minds of the people. Many perished in it, as people did when Sodom and Gomorrah were overthrown (Gn. xix. 24–28), and others, like firebrands, were plucked from the burning.

All these visitations had failed. God is, therefore, going to do something fresh, and Israel is exhorted to *prepare to meet* her God. The *thus* of verse 12 evidently refers to what was said in iii. 11. The last verse is a doxology. The God Israel is to meet is the Creator of the visible (*mountains*) and the invisible (*wind*); who knows what is in man; who can change the existing order of things; and who is superior to all *the high places of the earth*. There can be no trifling with such a God.

c. The third discourse (v. 1—vi. 14)

i. The tragic fall of Israel (v. 1–3). Amos' third discourse opens with a brief dirge, in poetic form, in which he bewails the tragic fall of Israel. *The virgin* (2) (which in Isaiah means Jerusalem and occasionally some other city, but is here applied to the whole of Israel), whom Jehovah loved, *is fallen*, or 'dashed' (Heb. *nitshah*) on the ground. Not only has she been crushed to the ground; she is abandoned. She cannot rise again, for there is none to raise her up. *The city that went out* . . . (3); a regular phrase for going to war. Apparently in this period the host went out, not as in old times by tribes and families, but by towns and villages. No wonder the prophet laments! for what land can continue where nine-tenths of its man-power is lost in battle?

ii. The passionate appeal of Jehovah (v. 4–15). Tragic as the fall of Israel may be and beyond the help of man, there is still hope for her in Jehovah, who can bring something out of nothing (cf. iv. 13), if only she will seek Him (4). The appeal is stated negatively and positively. *Seek not Beth-el . . . Gilgal . . . Beer-sheba . . .* (5). These places are helpless. They will not be able to save themselves, so how, by implication, can they save others? 'Gilgal shall taste the gall of exile' (G. A. Smith), and Bethel shall become iniquity (Heb. *aven*). Hosea actually calls the place Beth-aven (Ho. iv. 15), i.e. 'house of iniquity'. But *seek the Lord* (6). The reason for the appeal is next given—*ye shall live*, and *lest he break out like fire*. The fire is God's judgment, and woe to *the house of Joseph* (Ephraim and Manasseh) if it breaks out, for then it will consume all and none will be able to quench it (6). *Ye who turn* . . . (7); i.e. the people generally. *Wormwood* (bitterness) is a Palestinian plant regularly used as a synonym for bitterness. Few things can be more bitter than the award of a corrupt and bribed court. This same theme is continued in verses 10–13, but as he urges these men and women to *seek him* (8) the prophet introduces a majestic description, in the form of a doxology (cf. iv. 13), of Him who makes the appeal. The

lips are those of the prophet Amos, but the voice is the voice of Jehovah Himself. He is the Creator of things above, the Transformer of things around (8), and the Defender of the exploited (9).

They hate him . . . (10). The *gate* was the great meeting-place, the centre of business, like the Roman forum, and the place where the elders used to sit to administer justice (Dt. xxi. 19). Both Jeremiah (xvii. 19, xix. 2) and Isaiah (xxix. 21) rebuked at the gate, and doubtless Amos will have done the same. But such witnesses were hated and loathed. Verse 11 describes, almost in a sentence, the sin and punishment of the rich. By robbing the poor of their very bread, and by crushing them, the rich were able to build fine houses and plant pleasant vineyards. But judgment will overtake them, and they will neither be able to dwell in their houses nor enjoy the fruit of their vineyards. The sins of the rich are not only numerous, they are immense (12). Not only are the poor crushed down and robbed, but the just are afflicted and bullied. What chance for justice can there be? Bribes are given by those who can afford them, and corrupt judges are influenced by them. The *prudent* or wise man feels it best to *keep silence;* the times are so evil (13). The results of a search for the good are next indicated (14, 15). Life and the assurance of Jehovah's presence will follow. Above all, if the seeking is accompanied, as it should be, by a genuine hatred of evil and a deep love of that which is good, issuing in justice, Jehovah may be gracious to *the remnant of Joseph* (15).

iii. The dark day of Jehovah (v. 16–20). Having described Israel's tragic fall and God's passionate appeal, Amos next describes Jehovah's dark day. The prophet knows that Israel's only hope lies in a genuine return unto the Lord, but all along he seems to feel that there is not much chance of this happening. The evil is too deep-seated. Though judgment could be averted, on conditions, it is not likely to happen. The *day of the Lord* (18) is on the way, and when it comes it will bring not light but darkness. There will be wailing in the streets (of towns and cities) and in all the highways (of the country). The professional mourners will be called upon to wail, and the husbandman, who has no professional skill in wailing, will, nevertheless, be called upon to join them (16). In the city, in the country, in the vineyard—it will all be the same. Nor will there be any escape from it (19).

iv. The empty worship of Israel (v. 21–27). The unhallowed cultus of the northern shrines was evidently practised most assiduously. The *feast days* (21; Heb. *haggim*; i.e. the three feasts at which every male had to appear—cf. Ex. xxiii. 14, 17), the *burnt offerings*, the *meat offerings*, the *peace offerings* (22), were all there, except justice. The evil of this worship lay in the separation of religion from morality. The prophet's message in its pure essence is summed up in verse 24. All the prophetic passion is here. It was God's supreme message to that age of corrupt social morals. In the desert, the golden age to which the prophets looked back with great longing, there was none of this elaborate ritualism, Amos appears to imply; and yet it was a time when God had lived with His people. *Moloch and Chiun* (26), or probably more correctly 'Saccuth and Kewan', were Assyrian gods. By her sin and evil ways Israel had, by implication, made the Assyrian gods her own. The prophet visualizes captivity for Israel in Assyria, *beyond Damascus* (27). She would presently take up these idols in the land of her captivity, and so make explicit what before has been only implicit.

v. The callous rich of Israel (vi. 1–6). The prosperity and comparative peace of the country, together with the flourishing worship at Bethel and the other shrines, had engendered a false political confidence. The people, and particularly the wealthy merchants, were *at ease* (1). This deadly 'ease' had apparently spread to the southern kingdom also, for *Zion* (1) is coupled with Samaria in the prophet's indictment. But, apart from the brief mention of Zion, his concentrated attack is on the callous rich of Samaria who, because of the social position which wealth had given them, regarded themselves as the *chief of the nations, to whom the house of Israel came* (1); i.e. men of mark who, as nearly always, set the fashion and whom the rest of the country seek to imitate.

The prophet next bids the people take a look at *Calneh, Hamath* and *Gath*, three of the neighbouring *kingdoms* upon whom judgment has fallen (2). Do these callous, indifferent and beguiled rich, he asks, really think that they are better than these kingdoms, and that they can escape judgment? Is their border larger than the border of the rest of the people? Do they really think themselves to be safe when all the rest, inside and outside Israel, are in danger? Then follows a terrible exposé of the sins of these rich. The evil day is put far away, out of their minds; they refuse to think about it, but this only brings the *seat of violence*, the day of crisis and judgment, nearer and makes it all the more certain (3). They sleep on ivory beds and are sprawled out on divans—customs for which the shepherd-prophet could entertain only the greatest contempt (4). Looseness of gesture goes with looseness of morals (Horton). Their food consists of 'fresh lamb and fatted veal' (Moff.). They *chant* (Heb. *parat*, lit. 'bawl') like drunkards who attempt to sing to their orchestra. As David introduced music for divine worship, so these drunkards are inventing instruments to accompany their bawling at their drinking-bouts (5). They drink wine by the bowlful and anoint themselves with the best of ointments, but remain indifferent to and are not grieved for the affliction of Israel—the affliction of all the oppressed poor around and the greater affliction that was looming ahead for them all. These rich had all they wanted—wealth, ease, luxury, religion; but they did not have the one thing

they needed—a heart of pity and compassion. Politically and economically Israel was prospering, but morally she was rotting.

vi. The impending judgment upon Israel (vi. 7–14). Verse 7 announces the nature of this judgment—it is captivity. In this judgment the rich will retain their pre-eminence; they will be among the first to go (7). The outcome of their judgment will be the cessation of all banquets (7). But, though the rich will be the first to feel the impact of judgment, it will not be confined to them. The whole of Samaria will be delivered up, for God abhors the city with all its palaces which were the pride of Israel (8)— 'the vainglory which had displaced the true glory' (Prof. M. A. Canney). The next two verses give the results of the overthrow of Samaria. The scourge will be so severe that there will be scarcely a survivor. A kinsman visits the house with a friend to bury the bones of a relation. To the question 'Have you any more there?' the answer of the friend who has been searching the house is 'No'. 'Hush!' says the kinsman. God has been angry; that is plain enough. Such devastation only His wrath could bring about. There must be no mention of His name (10). By the commandment of Jehovah *the great house* (of the rich) will be reduced to fragments, and *the little house* (of the poor), standing as it does in the path of the hurricane, cannot altogether escape the blow and will suffer rents (11).

Verse 12 gives once again the reason for this judgment—the perversion of justice. It is senseless to expect horses to run over precipices, and just as senseless to plough with oxen on similar ground: both would end in disaster. In the first part of this verse 'there' has been inserted in the AV and RV to make sense of what is otherwise almost unintelligible in the Hebrew. The word translated *oxen* is, in addition, the only example of the plural of what is normally a collective noun in the singular (i.e. *b'qarim* for the usual *baqar*). The plural ending can, however, be detached and made to read *yam* (sea), leaving *bqr* to be pointed in the ordinary way. The sentence would then read 'Will one plough the sea with oxen?' (i.e. *babaqar yam* instead of *b'qarim*) and this reading has been followed in the RSV. Israel has been guilty of such crazy behaviour. She has turned justice into poison and righteousness into hemlock or wormwood. Now she must take the consequences—judgment (12). Iniquity, such as Israel was guilty of, is not a thing to gloat over, and yet that is what she has done (13). She was also boasting of her power (13), but Jehovah was raising up *a nation* (Assyria) against her, and no power of hers will avail in that day (14). *A thing of nought* (Heb. *Lo-debar*) and *horns* (Heb. *Karnaim*) were towns in Gilead, and many commentators believe that this verse (13) refers to these two towns which Jeroboam II had taken from Syria. Israel was rejoicing in and boasting about her success. Whichever way we interpret it, Assyria was coming against Israel and would afflict her from *the entering in* (i.e. frontier) *of Hemath unto the river of the wilderness*. In other words, Assyria would oppress Israel from her most northerly boundary (Hamath) to the river of the wilderness, probably the wady of Egypt, the traditional southern limit of Israel; in short, the whole land.

IV. REVELATION OF GOD'S DESIGN.
vii. 1—ix. 10

The third part of Amos consists of a series of five visions which are in nature a revelation of God's design with regard to Israel in view of her rebellion and impenitence. The third vision is followed by an historical interlude (vii. 10–17). Jehovah's design, as the prophet has already indicated more than once, is judgment. At first, owing to Amos' intercession, it is averted (vii. 1–6), but as the visions unfold it becomes obvious that it is inevitable (vii. 7–9); moreover, it is imminent (viii. 1–14) and inescapable (ix. 1–10).

a. The vision of the devouring locust (vii. 1–3)

The Lord God shewed unto me (1). Revelation on God's part becomes vision on the prophet's part. *Grasshoppers* (1); i.e. locusts, which have been one of the most frequent and also one of the most destructive of the plagues of Palestine. *Latter growth* (1). The first 'growth' starts in October and continues through the winter; the *latter growth*, therefore, comes in the spring after the 'latter rains'. It was this latter and richer growth which the locusts had devoured. This was a terrible calamity, for the next pastures would not be due until the autumn. The *king's mowings* (1) were evidently a tribute levied by the kings of Israel.

The vision of the plague is followed by the prophet's prayer for forgiveness, and the prayer, in turn, is followed by God's pardon: *it shall not be* (3). The unnamed 'it' is evidently the same as that so often referred to in chapter i, namely, the Assyrian invasion.

b. The vision of the consuming fire (vii. 4–6)

The prophet's second vision is that of a great consuming fire which will not only destroy a portion of the land, i.e. Jehovah's promised land to Israel, but one which will devour *the great deep* (4; Heb. *tehom*). This is the primeval deep of creation, the vast gathering of waters on which the earth was supposed to float, the source of all the fountains and rivers. It follows that if this great deep were to be devoured, the source of all springs and rain-supply would disappear. This would mean drought, and the unwatered land would soon perish.

As in vii. 1–3, the prophet's vision of the plague is followed by a prayer, and the prayer leads to Jehovah's pardon.

c. The vision of the searching plumbline (vii. 7–9)

The first two visions were of calamity in the sphere of nature, but this next one lies in the sphere of religion and politics. The nation's whole fabric is so rotten that final collapse is inevitable. God Himself sets the plumbline. Israel is measured, is weighed and is found wanting. So convinced is the prophet of inevitable judgment that he cannot even pray for respite. *The high places* (9), i.e. the sacred places of Palestine, largely taken over by Israel with a large admixture of the original pagan rites, will become desolate; so will also the official shrines at Bethel, Gilgal, etc. The pillars, supporting Israel's religious edifice, Jehovah's measuring line finds altogether crooked, and the storm of judgment will lay them all low. The same applies to the political structure; it is hopelessly bent and unstable and must inevitably fall in the day of Jehovah's wrath—*I will rise against the house of Jeroboam* (9).

d. Historical interlude (vii. 10–17)

It is probable that this third vision was delivered by Amos to the people at the shrine of Bethel. And it was at this point that Amaziah, the priest of Bethel, interrupted him. 'The priest, who was conscious of no spiritual power with which to oppose the prophet, gladly grasps the opportunity afforded him by the mention of the king, and fell back on the invariable resource of a barren and envious sacerdotalism: "He speaketh against Caesar"' (G. A. Smith). First Amaziah turns to the king, *Amos hath conspired against thee* (10). Recalling perhaps that Jeroboam's own dynasty in the time of Jehu, about a hundred years before, had been put in power by the prophetic guilds under Elisha, no wonder Amaziah became apprehensive. But this time there is more to it. Not only is the country's king to go, but the king's country is to go too—the whole land is to go into captivity (11). No wonder the land, according to the priest of Bethel, could not bear the weight of this oracle. But, whatever the reasons, whether a sense of his own security or just mere contempt for the message of this shepherd-prophet, Jeroboam evidently took no notice of Amos. Amaziah next turns to the prophet (vii. 12, 13). He is told to return to his own country and to earn his bread there, taking it for granted that Amos was a professional prophet. Amaziah appears to use the word *seer* (12; Heb. *ḥozeh*) in a contemptuous sense: 'away with you, visionary.' Bethel is the king's chapel and palace; they did not want a prophet from Judah.

Amaziah having finished his accusations against Amos, it is now the prophet's turn to answer the priest (14–17). First Amos has an explanation (14, 15). He has had no connection with any prophets; he was a shepherd and a gatherer of sycomore fruit. God had called him from his flock and had commissioned him to go to Jehovah's own lost flock. But the man who had had no past connections with prophets was destined to have a very definite and vital connection with prophets in the future. Next comes a twofold declaration (16, 17): one concerns Amaziah and his family, and the other concerns Amaziah's country. The priest's command not to prophesy, *drop not thy word* (16), is contrasted with Jehovah's command, *Thus saith the Lord* (17). With bitter and stinging emphasis the prophet describes the consequences to the priest's family of invasion and defeat. His wife will be a harlot in the very city where for so long she had been the chief lady, his children will be slain, and he himself will perish in *a polluted land*, on unclean soil, i.e. a foreign land. As for the country, it will be divided, and the inhabitants will go into captivity.

e. The vision of the basket of summer fruit (viii. 1-14)

In this vision the prophet returns to the imminence of judgment. It was perhaps the word *end* (Heb. *qeyts*) which brought to Amos this vision of summer fruit (Heb. *qayits*). Israel is like a basket of over-ripe summer fruit, ready to decay. *The end is come upon my people* (2). God had often shown pity and had been patient with His people. Again and again judgment had been deferred, but this time the decision is final and irrevocable, *I will not again pass by them* (2). Some of the results of this judgment are indicated in verse 3. Instead of singing there will be howling in *the temple* (or 'palace'; *heykhal* is occasionally used of a royal palace and could have that meaning here). Outside are the bodies of the slain everywhere, and these shall be cast away in silence without burial.

Amos now returns to the main theme of his prophecy—the unparalleled greed of the rich, the unbearable oppression of the poor, and the inevitable judgment of heaven. The greedy rich landowners seek to *swallow up the needy* (4). It probably means they are buying up his smallholding and so inevitably make him their slave. So greedy are they that they can scarce wait till the sabbath and the new moon are passed. False balances and measures are used to sell their grain, giving as little as they can for as much as they can extract (5), 'making big money' by buying the poor man 'for an old song' and selling him as a slave. Not only that, but *refuse* was sold for good grain (6).

After the brief denunciation of such unparalleled greed of the rich merchants comes the announcement—this time with great relentlessness—of the certainty, completeness and consequences of judgment (7-14). The certainty of judgment lies in the fact that Jehovah who has *sworn by the excellency of Jacob* (probably a synonym for the sacred name) will not forget their wicked works (7). The completeness of judgment is indicated in the words *it shall rise up wholly as a flood* (8). It will overwhelm the land as the overflowing of a river may overwhelm the surrounding countryside. Israel shall be cast out, shall be swept away from her own land and be drowned, i.e. disappear in a foreign country, as the Nile overflows its banks and carries away all loose objects into the sea (8).

The rest of the chapter deals with some of the consequences of this judgment. First of all, there is darkness (9). An eclipse of the sun took place in 763 B.C. and may well have inspired this passage. But the prophet is obviously thinking of a day yet future. The day of judgment, so near and inevitable, will be a dark day indeed for the people of Israel. It will be a worse darkness than any eclipse of the sun could produce. Next there will be *mourning* (10). The judgment that came did indeed produce such mourning (cf. Ps. cxxxvii. 1, 'By the rivers of Babylon, there we sat down, yea, we wept, when we remembered Zion'). Nor was it an ordinary mourning that was indicated, but *as the mourning of an only son*. No language can express the poignancy and bitterness of such sorrow. *Famine* is another consequence of Jehovah's judgment (11). Only this time it is *not a famine of bread, nor a thirst for water*; it is a spiritual famine—a famine for the Word of God, that very word which Israel had despised and rejected. But his bread will not be found no matter where it may be sought (12). 'In the famine for the Word of God the young suffer most' (Horton). Old people, looking back, can live on memory; it is otherwise with the young: they will faint, and there will be nothing to revive, let alone to feed the inner man (13). The final consequence of judgment will be the complete destruction of all idolaters. Those who *swear by the sin of Samaria*, i.e. by the golden calf set up by Jeroboam I; or by the 'way to Beersheba' (see RV), as Moslems swear by the 'sacred way to Mecca', *shall fall, and never rise up again* (14). Their idols will be utterly unable to help them in the dark and dreadful judgment day.

f. The vision of the Lord upon the altar (ix. 1-10)

In this last vision the prophet envisages final and inescapable judgment. Amos sees Jehovah, not like Isaiah, 'high and lifted up', surrounded by angels and archangels, holding out a message of hope for the unclean, but alone, *standing upon the altar*, and the command is *Smite* (1). All along judgment had been declared and was imminent. Now the crucial moment has come. Judgment in the vision begins with the house of God—the shrine at Bethel, the centre of Israel's national worship, the very spot which the religious Israelite regarded as the dwelling-place of Jehovah, sacred and inviolable. This will demonstrate that Jehovah is not there at all. *Smite the lintel* (1; RV 'chapiters'). As the roof of the house is supported by pillars, the capitals of the pillars are to be smitten first, so as to ensure the collapse of the whole building. The picture is that of a temple full of worshippers: the whole building suddenly collapses upon them. Some, who at the time may chance to be outside, flee terror-stricken, but they *shall not flee away*; any who for the moment may have escaped *shall not be delivered* (1). Judgment will overtake them even though they dig deep down into the earth or climb up into the very skies (2). Neither the top of Mount Carmel, which was an asylum where cattle were protected by religious sanctions (cf. Robertson Smith's *Religion of the Semites*), nor the depth of the sea, where the dreaded leviathan or sea-monster is (AV *serpent*), can hide them from the hand of God (3). Even in captivity—'to Israel as terrible a distance from God's face as Sheol itself' (G. A. Smith)—they would not be safe, for the sword of judgment has a mandate to slay them there. Such is the inescapable judgment, for Jehovah's eye is no longer upon them *for good* (4).

In the following verses the emphasis shifts from the judgment to the Judge Himself. The judgment will be and must be as depicted because of the omnipotence of the Judge: He is the *Lord God of hosts* (5). When God touches the land, then judgment will be as already described in viii. 8, like a mighty, overwhelming flood, like the overflowing waters of the Nile (5). Verse 6 is a picture of the many-storeyed palace of Jehovah, reaching 'terrace after terrace high into the sky'. But, though His dwelling-place may be on high, He works on earth and for the good of man. As far as the naked eye of man can see, He has established His *troop* (Heb. *aggudah*, i.e. 'vault' or 'bundle', i.e. something bound), the vast hemispherical vault of the sky, like a huge cupola, upon the earth. The water of the sea He draws up (*calleth for*; cf. v. 8) and then pours it out again upon the earth as rain.

The next verse makes it plain that, though Israel's Judge stands in a special relationship to her, this relationship depends for its continuance upon Israel's loyalty and faithfulness. It is true that Israel was brought out of Egypt to be His special people, but this particular relationship was based not so much upon this fact as upon the covenant that was established later in the desert. After all, God had also brought the hated Philistines from Crete (*Caphtor*) and the Syrians from *Kir* beyond Damascus (7). The prophet's universalism springs from his conception of universal morality. Because Jehovah was exalted in righteousness, He was Ruler and Judge of all mankind. But the God of all the earth who was watching the destinies of all nations could not excuse Israel's sins on the ground of a covenant relationship. His eyes were *upon the sinful kingdom* (8), and sins committed against light must be punished severely. The kingdom would be utterly destroyed, but a remnant will remain (8). This is such a new note in the prophecy of Amos, that many scholars are unprepared to admit this final section as genuine. But there is nothing inconsistent here. The judgment proclaimed throughout is ruthless, severe, all-embracing, inescapable; but the dark, dark sky has a few stars. The judgment of Israel will be in the nature of a sifting process. *I will sift the house of Israel among all nations, like as corn is sifted in a sieve* (9). All the chaff will perish (*All the sinners of my people shall die*), but the good grain will be saved (10).

V. EPILOGUE. ix. 11-15

The theme of this closing section is restoration. Notice the key phrases *I will raise; I will bring; I will plant*. The few rays of light of the last two or three verses give place to the sunrise of a new day as the prophecy ends. Dark indeed has been the midnight of his message, but dayspring is at hand. The remnant of the captivity shall become the spearhead of a new nation. There shall be a great restoration; and, first of all, a restoration of the Davidic house (11). This will be the glory of an undivided kingdom, when north and south will once again be under one king as in the days of David. The breaches shall be healed and the ruins shall be rebuilt. This is followed by the restoration of the kingdom (12). Israel shall again possess what is left (*the remnant*) of Edom and of all the other nations whom Jehovah will conquer. *The heathen, which are called by my name* (12) is probably a reference to all the countries which David had conquered. The restoration of the Davidic family and the country will also mean the restoration of the land (13). So fertile will be the soil that *the plowman shall overtake the reaper*, preparing the soil for the next harvest. In other words seedtime and harvest will follow in rapid succession, and no interruption of this process through drought or any other plague is envisaged. The hills, normally barren, shall also make their contribution to the prosperity of the people, for they shall yield their harvest of grapes—*shall drop sweet wine* (13). And, finally and supremely, there shall be the restoration of the captivity (14, 15). Cities shall be rebuilt and shall be inhabited; vineyards and gardens shall be planted and the fruit thereof enjoyed; Israel herself shall be planted as a tree in the land given to her by Jehovah, and no disaster shall ever uproot her again. The night of tragedy and judgment shall be passed for ever from the face of the land, for Jehovah, Israel's God once more (*thy God*), has willed and spoken it.

O. BUSSEY.

OBADIAH

INTRODUCTION

I. AUTHOR AND DATE

The title of this little prophecy—the shortest book in the Old Testament—is 'The vision of Obadiah' (1). Who this Obadiah was we have no means of knowing. The name means 'servant of Jehovah', and is met with a number of times in the Old Testament, but there is nothing to connect this prophet with any of the others so called. For the use of the word 'vision' to describe the contents of a prophecy, and as throwing light on the way in which the prophet received his message, compare the opening verses of Isaiah, Ezekiel, Amos, Micah, Nahum and Habakkuk; see also Nu. xii. 6.

The prophecy is 'concerning Edom'. Edom is denounced for her pride, especially for her lack of brotherly kindness towards Judah, and her judgment in the day of Jehovah is predicted along with that of all the nations.

As for the date of the prophecy, we may refer it to some time after the destruction of Jerusalem by Nebuchadrezzar, king of Babylon, in 586 B.C. This event seems to be clearly alluded to in verses 11-14, and 'the captivity of Jerusalem' which followed is mentioned in verse 20.

There are marked similarities both in ideas and phraseology between the first part of Obadiah (verses 1-8) and Je. xlix. 7-22, a passage which belongs to the years before the fall of Jerusalem. Literary critics do not agree on the exact relationship between the two passages. Some argue for the direct dependence of one on the other. But while Je. xlix is almost certainly earlier than Obadiah, and while the passage in Obadiah shows some signs of having been derived from another source, yet in certain respects the Obadiah passage appears the more original of the two. For this reason many critics hold the hypothesis that both Jeremiah and Obadiah are making use of an earlier prophecy. This is not inherently unlikely, as the character and doom of Edom was a constantly recurring theme among Hebrew prophets.

II. EDOM AND JUDAH

The eponymous ancestor of the Edomites was Esau (see Gn. xxxvi. 1, 8, 9). His relations with his twin brother Jacob, father of Judah, are described in Gn. xxv—xxxvi. Even while the children struggled together within the womb of their mother it was told her by the Lord that 'two nations are in thy womb and . . . the elder shall serve the younger' (Gn. xxv. 22f.). Subsequently Esau is portrayed as one 'who for one morsel of meat sold his birthright' and who thus

became the type of a 'profane person' (Heb. xii. 16), insensitive to spiritual values. He was born within the covenant, but he failed to appreciate the privilege which was his by right, and he failed also of the accompanying blessing. God's estimate of Jacob and Esau respectively is most succinctly expressed in the declaration, 'I loved Jacob, and I hated Esau' (Mal. i. 2f.; cf. Rom. ix. 13).

The Herods of the New Testament were Edomites, and were true to type. Notice how they showed themselves insensitive to spiritual truth, especially as it was embodied in Jesus Christ, the perfect representative of Jacob and Judah. (See esp. Mt. ii; Lk. xiii. 31f., xxiii. 8ff.; Acts xii. 21ff.)

Gn. xxxvi. 8 tells us that 'Esau dwelt in Mount Seir'. Mount Seir is often used as a synonym for the whole of Edom, which became the land of Esau's descendants. Edom is the area directly south of the Dead Sea, especially the mountainous country east of the Arabah (i.e. the depression connecting the Dead Sea with the Gulf of Aqabah). The southern part of Edom is the region of Teman, also sometimes used in the Old Testament as a synonym for the whole land, and Edom's two principal cities are Bozrah and Sela (Petra); the latter means 'rock' in both its Hebrew and Greek forms.

From Ezion-geber on the Gulf of Aqabah 'the king's highway' ran through Edom northwards. It was along this highway that Moses wanted to lead the children of Israel. The account of Edom's refusal to give the necessary permission is found in Nu. xx. 14-21 (cf. Dt. ii. 1-18). The antagonism continued after the settlement in Canaan (see, e.g., 2 Sa. viii. 14; 2 Ki. xiv. 7; 2 Ch. xxviii. 17), and we find the prophets denouncing Edom continually. For the principal anti-Edom prophecies see Is. xxxiv. 5; Je. xlix. 7-22; La. iv. 21f.; Ezk. xxv. 12-14, xxxv; Joel iii. 19; Am. i. 11f. A vivid picture of judgment being visited on Edom is given in Is. lxiii. 1-6, and some time later we find a backward look to Edom's destruction in Mal. i. 2-5. There were recrudescences of the power and influence of Edom after the close of the Old Testament period, but today the remarkable ruins at Petra are all that is left of Edom's greatness.

For Edom's part in the sack of Jerusalem in 586 B.C. see especially Ezk. xxxv. 5, 12, 15 and Ps. cxxxvii. 7. This participation by Edom is not mentioned in the historical books, though it would easily fit into the picture as we see it, e.g., in the marauding raids described in 2 Ki. xxiv. 2.

Esau and Edom occupy a place of profound

significance in the divine revelation of truth. That significance is brought into sharp focus in this small prophecy of Obadiah. 'The background of the picture presented to us by Obadiah is Jacob; the foreground is Esau. Jacob and those descended from him are seen passing through suffering, which is of the nature of chastisement, to ultimate restoration. Esau is seen proud, rebellious, defiant, moving towards ultimate destruction' (G. C. Morgan). We may rejoice that, in the day of the Lord, 'the kingdom shall

be the Lord's' (21), but we should no less be warned by Esau's example, for, after all, 'was not Esau Jacob's brother?' (Mal. i. 2). In the New Testament the writer to the Hebrews exhorts us to be 'looking diligently lest any man fail of the grace of God; lest any root of bitterness springing up trouble you, and thereby many be defiled; lest there be any . . . profane person, as Esau . . . For ye know how that afterward, when he would have inherited the blessing, he was rejected' (Heb. xii. 15ff.).

OUTLINE OF CONTENTS

I. IMPENDING DOOM ON EDOM. Verses 1–9

II. EDOM'S BEHAVIOUR TOWARDS JUDAH. Verses 10–14

III. JUDGMENT ON EDOM AND ALL NATIONS IN THE DAY OF THE LORD; JUDAH'S RESTORATION. Verses 15–21

COMMENTARY

I. IMPENDING DOOM ON EDOM.
Verses 1–9

This opening section of the prophecy of Obadiah, which describes some terrible disaster apparently about to overtake Edom, is prefaced by the words: *Thus saith the Lord God concerning Edom* (1). Jehovah does not actually speak until verse 2, and the form of the intervening passage, *We have heard a rumour from the Lord* . . ., suggests that Obadiah is here quoting an earlier prophetic oracle which he believes has come near to fulfilment. It is interesting, therefore, that most of this section appears almost word for word (though not in the same order) in Je. xlix. 7ff. Obadiah is perhaps quoting from Jeremiah, whom he may have heard preaching in Jerusalem, or both prophets may be employing an earlier prophecy; Jeremiah and Obadiah were assuredly not the first to speak of Edom in such a way. (See also *Introduction*.)

The immediate occasion of Obadiah's utterance, and for which he draws on the words of an earlier prophet, seems to be indicated in verse 7. This verse, which has no parallel in Jeremiah, gives the idea (though the Hebrew is somewhat obscure in details) that Edom's own neighbours and confederates were turning against her. 'The men of thy covenant' and 'the men of thy peace', to give a literal rendering, were either treacherously hostile or were yielding none of their expected assistance. In this situation Obadiah saw the appropriateness of the words . . . *an ambassador is sent among the heathen* (i.e. the Gentile nations), *Arise ye, and let us rise up against her* (Edom) *in battle* (1).

The chief ground of Edom's proud confidence was her almost impregnable position. The Edomites were not the first nor the last to put

their trust in a rocky fortress city. But neither their strong position nor their wit (Edom was renowned also for her wisdom) could deliver them now. No matter how high Edom should go, to inaccessible eagle's eyrie, or among the very stars, yet God would bring her *down to the ground* (3). *The rock* (3) is the capital Sela (later Petra).

A picture of the completeness of Edom's coming destruction is given in verse 5. Had it been a case of an ordinary raid by a band of robbers, there would have been plenty left to salvage. *Robbers by night*, depending on speed and surprise, would take only a limited amount of booty, and so steal only *till they had enough*, much as grape-gatherers leave plenty of gleanings behind them. But Edom, by contrast, is 'cleaned right out', as we should say, and the utter devastation evokes the prophet's exclamation: *how art thou cut off!*

Another picture of the completeness of Edom's destruction is in the exposure of all the *hidden things* contained in her inaccessible and mysterious strongholds (6). All is *searched out* and laid bare. Since the judgment of Edom is here seen in the context of the final judgment of *the day of the Lord* (15), its characteristics are the more worthy of study. It is always part of the judgment of God to 'bring to light the hidden things of darkness' (1 Cor. iv. 5). Edom gloried in her wisdom, might and riches (cf. Je. ix. 23ff.). But her 'hidden treasures' (RV) will be *sought up* (6), her *wise men* destroyed (8), and her *mighty men* dismayed (9).

II. EDOM'S BEHAVIOUR TOWARDS JUDAH. Verses 10–14

Why was all this to befall Edom? The reason is given in verses 10, 11: *For thy violence against thy brother Jacob*. 'The name *Jacob* is expressly used (in place of Israel or Judah) in order to recall the relationship between the nations. In Dt. xxiii. 7 the claims of kinship between the two peoples are urged upon Israel; but Edom had shown no reciprocal sense of brotherly relationship' (G. W. Wade). Not only did this age-long antagonism date back to the time in the wilderness when Edom refused to give Israel passage through his border (Nu. xx. 20f.), but, as verse 11 shows, it reached a head in the sack of Jerusalem by Nebuchadrezzar in 586 B.C. The participation of Edom on this occasion was long and bitterly remembered by the Jews. In exile by the rivers of Babylon they cried: 'Remember, O Lord, the children of Edom in the day of Jerusalem; who said, Rase it, rase it, even to the foundation thereof' (Ps. cxxxvii. 7).

Verse 11 clearly looks back on the destruction of Jerusalem, when Edom had stood *on the other side*. This expression may imply aloofness, i.e. a failure to render the assistance she ought to have given (as the priest and Levite 'passed by on the other side' in the story of the Good Samaritan), or, what is more likely, it implies active opposition.

The AV renders verses 12–14 as a series of reproofs, *thou shouldest not have looked . . . neither shouldest thou have rejoiced*, etc., whereas the AV mg. and the RV render as prohibitions, 'look not . . . rejoice not', etc. The latter represents the actual construction of the Hebrew, but this is a rhetorical device, and the AV is right in seeing that in fact they have a past reference. These verses, then, may be taken as describing the actual part taken by the Edomites in the sack of Jerusalem. First they gloated insolently and without pity over the fall of Jerusalem (12); then they *entered into the gate* of the city and joined in the looting (13), and finally they took up positions where they prevented fugitive Jews from escaping and even rounded up any they could find unapprehended (14).

Note the use of the word 'day', especially in such phrases as *the day of thy brother* (12). Cf. 'the day of Jerusalem', as already quoted in the passage from Ps. cxxxvii. 7. 'The expression *day* is often thus used to denote the occurrence of either good or bad fortune in connection with some place or person' (Wade). Jerusalem was to have another 'day' (Lk. xix. 42), the time of her visitation, but she knew it not. *The day of the Lord*, on the other hand, which the next section of Obadiah introduces, is the day of Jehovah's final and uninhibited vindication of His own righteousness.

III. JUDGMENT ON EDOM AND ALL NATIONS IN THE DAY OF THE LORD; JUDAH'S RESTORATION. Verses 15–21

The day of the Lord (15) is one of the great themes of the Old Testament. Its character is emphasized rather than its exact time, although it is the ultimate issue of history and is often spoken of as imminent. Since 'the Lord alone shall be exalted in that day' (Is. ii. 11) it is a day of just retribution on all 'the nations that forget God' (Ps. ix. 17). Among these Edom shall suffer: *as thou hast done, it shall be done unto thee* (15).

Verse 16 seems to be an ironical thrust. The prophet, recalling the way in which the Edomites caroused and drank in Jerusalem after the plunder of the city, declares that the heathen nations shall drink indeed, but it shall be such a drinking and swallowing down as shall make them *as though they had not been*.

In Jehovah's judgment on the nations, however, there shall be one safe place: *upon mount Zion shall be deliverance* (17). Here, 'they that escape' (AV mg.) of the exiles of Judah shall congregate. The phrase *there shall be holiness* refers not to moral quality but to security from defilement and so from assault of the heathen, as in Joel iii. 17. Best of all, the saved remnant of *the house of Jacob* will be reinstated in the territories which God had given them of old.

It is interesting to notice that in the next verse *the house of Joseph* is mentioned alongside *the house of Jacob*. This means that there is to be a restoration of the northern kingdom of Israel as well as of the southern kingdom of Judah.

Historically, it was only through a faithful remnant of the single tribe of Judah—indeed through the single faithful Israelite, Jesus Christ, 'the Lion of the tribe of Juda' (Rev. v. 5) —that God's saving purposes were carried out. But by His death the Christ of God was to 'gather together in one the children of God that were scattered abroad' (Jn. xi. 52), and in God's purposes His chosen people, the spiritual Israel, will ultimately stand complete in all its tribes. It is the fully restored nation of the children of Israel which will consume as a flame the whole house of Esau.

The full extent of Israel's 'possession' of its inheritance is given in verses 19 and 20. Not all the details are clear, and the passage may be somewhat corrupt in Hebrew, but a glance at the main physical divisions of the kingdom on a map and at such a passage as Je. xxxiii. 13 will help to give the general sense well enough. *The south* is to this day known by the Hebrew term, the 'Negeb', and is the area south of Hebron towards the wilderness of Paran. The second division, called *the plain* in the AV, is the lowland lying roughly west of Hebron towards the sea. The actual seaboard was occupied by the Philistines who had come there in the twelfth century, after the Israelite entry into Canaan. The third division of Judah ought to be the hill-country, and it has been conjectured that the next sentence of verse 19 has lost its original subject and that (here with some support from the LXX) it should be restored to read 'they of the hill country shall possess Ephraim and the hills of Samaria'.

The text of the following verse is even more uncertain, but on the whole it seems best to take it as a reference to the future of the two principal groups of exiled Hebrews: first, those deported by Sargon after the fall of Samaria in 721 B.C. (*this host of the children of Israel*), and secondly, *the captivity of Jerusalem*, i.e. those carried off by Nebuchadrezzar in 586 B.C. The former group will occupy the land of *the Canaanites* (i.e. the Phoenicians; cf. Mt. xv. 22 and Mk. vii. 26), since their original area is now occupied by Jews from the southern kingdom. The latter group will occupy the cities of the Negeb, which the Jews who occupy Edom have vacated (19). The *Sepharad*, which is given as the place of this latter captivity, cannot now be identified. Locations have been suggested in Mesopotamia, Asia Minor and Spain. It was no doubt a group of exiled Jews in which Obadiah and his hearers had some special interest.

The final verse of Obadiah's prophecy gathers together the main themes of the book in two fine affirmations. First, there is the actual execution of judgment on Edom by *saviours*, whose headquarters are in Jerusalem. In regard to the Jews they are deliverers or defenders (cf. Jdg. ii. 16 and Is. xix. 20), and in regard to the Edomites they are executors of justice.

Finally, *the kingdom shall be the Lord's*. The people of God never doubted that Jehovah was ruling as King, 'be the earth never so unquiet' (Ps. xcix. 1, Prayer Book Version), but they awaited the full expression and acknowledgment of His sovereign rule. See Dn. ii. 44 and vii. 27, and especially Rev. xi. 15, where the people of God still rejoice in the assurance that 'the kingdom of the world is become the kingdom of our Lord, and of his Christ: and he shall reign for ever and ever' (RV).

D. W. B. ROBINSON.

JONAH

INTRODUCTION

The book of Jonah is entirely concerned with the personal dealings between Jehovah and His servant Jonah the son of Amittai. These dealings arise out of a prophetic commission and its attempted evasion. Jonah finds that God's thoughts are not his thoughts, and that his ways are not God's ways. But God will not leave Jonah to himself. In the first half of the story He lets him go to the extremity of almost losing his life, only to restore him to where he was before he attempted, by physical means, to evade Jehovah's command. In the second half of the story He lets him go to the extremity of mental and spiritual depression only to reveal to him the essential rightness of His merciful purposes.

I. THE MESSAGE AND ITS FORM

The form of the book is that of a piece of biographical narrative, similar (in style, language, atmosphere and miraculous element) to the various incidents in 1 and 2 Kings concerning Elijah and Elisha, who, indeed, were Jonah's immediate predecessors as prophets in the northern kingdom of Israel and who, like him, performed part of their work in relation to heathen peoples, Elijah to Sidon, Elisha to Syria, Jonah to Nineveh. The story of Jonah, however, is not simply an isolated incident in the prophetic history of Israel which might as well have been related in its place in the book of Kings where Jonah's ministry is mentioned (2 Ki. xiv. 25). Its message is distinct, and each part of the story is so told as to exhibit that message. For this reason, the book properly finds its place among the prophets; it is concerned with a particular revelation of the truth of God, and that revelation is closely related to prophetic experience.

The particular revelation with which the book of Jonah is concerned may be expressed in the words which form the conclusion of the story of Peter and the Gentiles in Acts xi. 18: 'Then to the Gentiles also hath God granted repentance unto life' (RV). This revelation in Jonah is so given as to emphasize, on the one hand, God's sovereign mercy and righteousness in granting Nineveh 'repentance unto life', and, on the other hand, the sinful particularism of God's servant, Jonah, in resisting this manifestation of His will.

II. HISTORICAL BASIS

Because the book of Jonah conveys such a distinctive message, many people in recent years have thought that the narrative is not historical but imaginative, and that, for example, it like the story of the Good Samaritan,

should be classed as parable. But while the latter view is clearly not impossible, it is certainly not necessary to imagine that because a book has a didactic (or, as we should prefer to say, a revelatory) purpose, it cannot at the same time be historical narrative. Acts x—xi. 18, which, we have already suggested, is in some respects the New Testament counterpart of Jonah, has a similar didactic motive. But there is no suggestion that Luke thought he was writing parable or homiletic fiction. Similarly, of course, the presence of miracle in a story is no evidence that it was not recorded as, and intended to be accepted as, historical narrative.

A smaller group of people has supposed that Jonah is an allegory of the exile and mission of Israel. Je. li. 34 is put forward as a possible basis for the story. This view is in part an attempt to explain otherwise the miraculous occurrences in the story, and it involves the theory that the book is a product of the post-exilic period. But once again, while we may legitimately see an illuminating parallel between Jonah's experience and that which was to befall the Israelitish nation, it by no means follows that the story is late or unhistorical. The books of the Bible are not fortuitous productions. The swallowing of Jonah may as well pre-figure the exile as it certainly pre-figures the burial of Christ.

Any assessment of the historical character of the book of Jonah must take into consideration the following facts. First, Jonah himself was without doubt an historical figure, a prophet of Jehovah in Israel (2 Ki. xiv. 25). Secondly, the book is in the form of straightforward historical narrative, and there is no positive indication in the book that it is to be interpreted in any other way. Thirdly, if the book is parable or allegory, it is unique and without analogy among the books of the Old Testament. Fourthly, neither Jews nor Christians have ever, until recently, regarded Jonah as anything else but a record of actual fact, whatever interpretations they have placed on its message. Finally, our Lord Jesus Christ clearly believed that the repentance of the men of Nineveh was a real occurrence, and it is most natural to take His allusion to Jonah's 'three days and three nights in the whale's belly' (Mt. xii. 40, 41) in the same way. In addition it may be urged that the whole force of Jehovah's self-vindication to Jonah demands an actual mission to a heathen city with an actual repentance and 'sparing' of it. It is not easy to believe that the challenge, 'Should not I spare Nineveh?' was presented to the people of Israel through the inspired writer as a purely hypothetical consideration.

III. DATE AND AUTHORSHIP

No certainty can be reached in regard to the date of the book. Some have argued that the entire story would have no meaning after Nineveh had actually been destroyed (612 B.C.). There is force in this argument. 'Should not I spare Nineveh?' would then be not only a hypothetical consideration, but a particularly ill-chosen one. (Jon. iii. 3 will be considered in the commentary.) The book has actually been assigned, by various prominent scholars, to every century from the eighth to the second B.C. But it should be pointed out that the chief reason why many scholars hold the book to be a product of the post-exilic period is that 'the general thought and tenor of the book . . . presupposes the teaching of the great prophets' including Jeremiah (S. R. Driver). With this highly subjective judgment we see no compelling reason to concur.

'The presence of Aramaisms in the book cannot be made a criterion for determining the date, since Aramaisms occur in Old Testament books from both early and late periods' (E. J. Young). With the linguistic evidence must also be reckoned the fact that 'there is not in them (Jonah, Joel, etc.) one certainly Persian word, nor a single Greek word' and 'not a Babylonian word not already found in the earlier literature' (R. D. Wilson). This evidence does not support the theory that Jonah belongs to the post-exilic period. S. R. Driver, who himself held the post-exilic view, admitted as a possibility that 'some of the linguistic features might be consistent with a pre-exilic origin in northern Israel' (*Introduction*, p. 301).

Jonah exercised his ministry in the reign of Jeroboam II (793–753 B.C.), and it seems most natural to suppose that the story was first committed to writing some time before the fall of the northern kingdom in 721 B.C., though there may easily have been circumstances occurring between 721 B.C. and 612 B.C., when Israel was governed from Nineveh, which prompted the wider publication of the book in that period. Nothing is said in the book of Jonah about its author. Although Jonah himself must obviously have been the main ultimate source of information for the story, there is no reason why he should have been the writer. No doubt the story soon became known in Israel, and we may presume that the sailors did their share of the telling. Chapter i has a number of signs of being derived from a source other than Jonah (like Acts xxvii). Verse 5a, for example, describes what took place while Jonah was asleep below, and verse 16 tells what the sailors did after Jonah had been thrown overboard. Presumably the ship returned to port when the storm subsided, since they were apparently not yet far out (i. 13) and in any case had jettisoned their cargo (i. 5). If Jonah likewise was returned to Joppa, it was perhaps on the basis of the sailors' information that he was able to calculate how long he had been under water.

IV. JONAH AND JESUS

A number of important scriptures should be studied alongside Jonah. In the Old Testament, for example, Je. i. 4–10 (for the prophetic commission), Je. xviii. 7–10 (for the effect of repentance on God's proclamation), Pss. cxxxix, xvi. 8–11 (for the prophet's experience). In the New Testament, Acts x—xi. 18 and Rom. ix—xi illustrate the missionary message of Jonah, and *vice versa*. But, in particular, the Gospel passages which refer to Jonah should be compared and studied (Mt. xii. 38–41 and Lk. xi. 29–32). Some points will be dealt with in the commentary. But here we may notice that Jonah is the only Old Testament prophet with whom Jesus directly compared Himself. Jesus obviously regarded Jonah's experience and mission as of great significance. It is the more interesting, therefore, to recall that both Jesus and Jonah were 'prophets of Galilee'. Jonah's town, Gath-hepher, was only a few miles to the north of Nazareth, Jesus' town. It was less than an hour's walk away. Jesus must often have gone there. Perhaps even in His day the tomb of Jonah was pointed out there, as it was later in Jerome's day. Was it here that, in the days of His obscurity, Jesus began to meditate on the significance of Jonah and of His own mission?

The Pharisees apparently overlooked Jonah when they taunted Nicodemus with the assurance that 'out of Galilee ariseth no prophet' (Jn. vii. 52). Had they searched the Scriptures more carefully, they would not have erred so exceedingly in failing also to perceive that 'a greater than Jonas is here' (Mt. xii. 41).

OUTLINE OF CONTENTS

I. THE COMMISSION GIVEN TO JONAH AND REJECTED. i. 1–3

II. JONAH'S FLIGHT AND JEHOVAH'S PURSUIT. i. 4–17

III. JONAH'S PRAYER FROM THE FISH'S BELLY. ii. 1–10

IV. THE PROPHETIC COMMISSION RENEWED AND DISCHARGED. iii. 1–9

V. TWO REACTIONS TO NINEVEH'S REPENTANCE: JEHOVAH CHALLENGES JONAH. iii. 10—iv. 11

COMMENTARY

I. THE COMMISSION GIVEN TO JONAH AND REJECTED. i. 1–3

Jonah appears as one to whom *the word of the Lord came*, i.e. as a prophet. (Cf. 2 Ki. xiv. 25 for other details of Jonah.) His assignment was as unusual as it was unwelcome, for Nineveh, mighty and famous, was capital of the heathen empire of Assyria, the constant enemy of Israel. The phrase *is come up before me* (2) pictures Jehovah as 'Judge of all the earth' (Gn. xviii. 25; cf. Gn. vi. 13).

Jonah's resignation of his prophetic commission is immediate and deliberate. The emphasis on his fleeing *from the presence of the Lord* (3; see also i. 10) does not imply a belief, like that of Naaman in 2 Ki. v. 17, that the presence of Jehovah was restricted to the soil of Israel. Verses 2b and 9 prove the contrary. Rather it indicates a withdrawal from the prophet's intimacy with Jehovah. No longer could the prophet say of his God, 'before whom I stand' (1 Ki. xvii. 1). Jonah did what Moses feared to do (Ex. xxxiii. 14, 15), and he forfeited also the 'rest' which accompanies the presence of God.

With a gesture of independence the servant of Jehovah selects a destination, Tarshish, far away at the western end of the Mediterranean Sea. Relying now on his own resources, *he paid the fare* of the ship and embarked (3). Joppa, modern Jaffa, is the only considerable port on the coast of Palestine. It is interesting that Joppa also plays a part in the New Testament story of Peter and the Gentiles in Acts x—xi. 18.

II. JONAH'S FLIGHT AND JEHOVAH'S PURSUIT. i. 4–17

Jonah's desperate attempt to evade God, even to the point of accepting death by drowning, and God's reclaiming of Jonah, occupy the largest section of the narrative. The disobedient prophet cannot escape from Jehovah. We have not yet been told why it was that Jonah chose to disobey Jehovah's command; that will be disclosed later in its appropriate place.

Here we are confronted with a fundamental fact of God's elective purposes, namely, that 'the gifts and calling of God are without repentance' (Rom. xi. 29). To all His prophets Jehovah said, as Jesus said to His apostles, 'Ye have not chosen me, but I have chosen you' (John xv. 16).

Jehovah took two steps to recover Jonah. First, *the Lord sent out* (RV mg. 'hurled') *a great wind into the sea* (4). This resulted in the terror of the sailors, the exposure of Jonah and his being thrown overboard. Secondly, *the Lord had prepared* (lit. 'appointed') *a great fish to swallow up Jonah* (17; see note below). This was the means of preserving him from death and of causing him to throw himself on the mercy of God. God's instruments here were *a great*

wind and *a great fish*. Compare other occasions when God works for His people through the manœuvring of His creatures, e.g. in the exodus.

It is instructive to study Jonah's experience in the light of Ps. cxxxix. The writer's thoughts, words and every movement are known to Jehovah. 'Whither shall I flee from thy presence?' he asks. 'If I make my bed in hell (Sheol), behold, thou art there. If I . . . dwell in the uttermost parts of the sea; even there shall thy hand lead me, and thy right hand shall hold me' (Ps. cxxxix. 7–10). So Jonah found it.

The account of the ship in distress is graphic and realistic—the violent gale, the *mariners* (5; lit. 'salts') 'of many races and religions, their panic, the excited questioning of Jonah, their reluctance to take the desperate step he suggests, their frantic rowing. The LXX adds the detail that it was Jonah's snoring as he lay asleep in *the sides of the ship* (5; lit: 'the innermost parts of the lower deck') that first attracted the ship-master's attention to the suspicious traveller.

Jonah's behaviour is set off against the behaviour of the heathen sailors. They have a strong sense of religious obligation and are amazed at Jonah's temerity in fleeing from the presence of his God (10). They are scrupulous when the ejection of Jonah appears inevitable; and when the sea is finally calmed, they show proper fear towards Jehovah (16).

Yet the incident clearly shows that Jonah is no coward. He is comparatively calm and self-possessed. He professes his faith and his guilt deliberately, and as deliberately chooses to drown rather than let others perish on his account. No doubt he regarded his impending death as Jehovah's punishment. A comparison of Jonah's behaviour with that of the characters in Acts xxvii and Mk. iv. 35–41 (and parallels) will be found instructive.

The Lord had prepared a great fish (17). Notice that the only place where the term 'whale' is used is in Mt. xii. 40 where the Greek word so translated means 'a huge fish'. G. C. Aalders (*The Problem of the Book of Jonah*) points out that there are a number of enormous sea-creatures able to swallow a full-grown man easily enough and refers to an actual case mentioned in the *Princeton Theological Review* (1927). The fish may have been the 'sperm whale', actually found in the Mediterranean, which does not have the narrowness of throat of the true whale which, in any case, is not found in such waters. The information that Jonah was incarcerated for *three days and three nights* (17), if intended literally, is not likely to have been supplied by Jonah himself, who, even had he been conscious for the whole time, would hardly have had any means of marking the passage of time. It must then have been calculated from information supplied by the sailors. On the other hand, *three days and three nights* may be only an approximate expression for a shortish period of time (cf. iii. 3 and Jos. ii. 16). The addition of *three nights* does not necessarily add to the accuracy of the expression, and we know that elsewhere 'after three days' is equivalent to 'on the third day'. Cf. the New Testament references to the duration of Jesus' entombment (e.g. 1 Cor. xv. 4). Mt. xii. 40 shows that 'three days and three nights' was regarded then as sufficiently accurate to denote a period of not more than thirty-six hours.

III. JONAH'S PRAYER FROM THE FISH'S BELLY. ii. 1–10

In this section Jonah describes his experience, ascribing salvation to Jehovah, and is restored to land. We are perhaps meant to observe the contrast of Jonah's position: he who, in the ship, apparently declined to arise and call upon his God (i. 6) is now constrained to pray *unto the Lord his God out of the fish's belly* (ii. 1).

Jonah's prayer, a Psalm in Hebrew elegiac metre, has often been declared to be an extraneous insertion. It has, however, a real appropriateness in its context, and we need not doubt that its essential content belongs to the occasion to which it is ascribed, even if its poetic form should belong to the period of reflection after the deliverance. Some of its phrases recall phrases in other Psalms but, taken as a whole, it is distinct from any other extant Psalm. Note, however, that it is a Psalm of thanksgiving to Jehovah for deliverance from death (Sheol), and not, as some critics seem to think it ought to have been, a prayer to be saved from the fish.

First Jonah describes how in his extremity his voluntary resistance to Jehovah broke down, and as the awfulness of his fate impressed itself on him he cried in desperation to his God. (Cf. Peter's spontaneous cry in Mt. xiv. 30.) *The belly of hell* (2) is the place of the dead (Sheol) (the word for *belly* is different from that used for the *fish's belly*) whose inhabitants were thought of as being cut off from God's hand and remembered no more by Him (Ps. lxxxviii. 5; read the whole of this Psalm for a description of Sheol and an understanding of Jonah's horror).

There are some grounds for thinking that the second part of verse 4 should be emended slightly so as to read 'How shall I look again . . .?' Jonah is indeed *in extremis. Thy holy temple* (4), here and in verse 7, symbolizes the place of Jehovah's presence, whence Jonah had fled. It is in extreme contrast to *the belly of hell*. At whatever shrine Jonah may have been accustomed to worship in Israel, it is probable that he who worships the God of heaven is here thinking of *thy holy temple* as 'heaven thy dwelling place' (1 Ki. viii. 39).

The sequence of thought in verses 2–7 suggests that after his desperate prayer Jonah was overcome by the water and pressure of the depths, and that the next thing he was conscious of was simply

that he was still alive. If we are to take it that his thanksgiving was uttered near the end of the three-day period, we may suppose that for most of the preceding time he was insensible, as perhaps he was already insensible when swallowed by the great fish. In that case, his was 'the further experience of Ps. cxxxix. 18, 'when I awake I am still with thee'. Jehovah had heard Jonah's prayer and had *brought up* his *life from corruption* (6). Jonah promises a sacrifice of thanksgiving, for *Salvation is of the Lord* (9).

We should note, however, that although Jonah is no doubt ready now to obey God's command, there is no evidence that he feels any compassion for the Ninevites. His experience of God's mercy only confirms him in his belief that those who *observe lying vanities* (i.e. worship false gods or idols) *forsake their own mercy* (i.e. cut themselves off from Jehovah, the only true source of succour for them) (8). This evidence of Jonah's exclusiveness, even in the midst of Jehovah's mercy, gives further point to Jehovah's remonstrance in chapter iv. But this attitude was not peculiar to Jonah. Again Ps. cxxxix has a parallel; note the similar transition of thought there from verse 18 to verses 19ff.

This Psalm of Jonah is of especial importance in the light of Jesus' reference to him in Mt. xii. 40; for the nature of the similarity between Jonah's experience and that of Christ is most clearly seen here. Thus, Jesus, the greater than Jonah, the true Servant and Prophet of Jehovah, went to the extremity of human suffering (because of the disobedience of others). What Jonah endured 'in a figure' (Heb. xi. 19—a similar figure of death) Jesus endured in reality. In His 'affliction' He went to 'the belly of hell'; all God's 'billows and waves passed over Him' (cf. Is. liii). As Jonah cried, *I am cast out of thy sight* (4), so Christ was constrained to cry, 'My God, my God, why hast thou forsaken me?' (Mt. xxvii. 46).

And yet the entombment of Jesus not only denoted the extremity of His passion (as the Creed states 'He descended into hell', i.e. Hades, or Sheol); it also emphasized the reality of His deliverance from death to life. Study Peter's Pentecostal Sermon in Acts ii, especially verses 24ff.: 'Whom God hath raised up, having loosed the pains of death: because it was not possible that he should be holden of it.' Jonah's testimony, *yet hast thou brought up my life from corruption* (6), has a striking parallel in the verse from Ps. xvi. 10 quoted by Peter in Acts ii. 27: 'Thou wilt not leave my soul in hell, neither wilt thou suffer thine Holy One to see corruption.'

IV. THE PROPHETIC COMMISSION RENEWED AND DISCHARGED. iii. 1–9

Jonah, having been restored to land at Jehovah's commandment, is commissioned a second time. Chastened by his experiences he obeys, although he is not apparently more charitably disposed

717

towards Nineveh than before. *The preaching that I bid thee* (2) emphasizes that the preacher speaks not of himself, but 'as the oracles of God' (1 Pet. iv. 11). What is true of Christ the Son, the eternal Word, must also be true of all His servants: 'he whom God hath sent speaketh the words of God' (Jn. iii. 34). See also the case of Moses (Ex. iv. 10–16), Jeremiah (Je. i. 6–9), and Jesus' disciples (Mt. x. 19, 20). Jonah knew from the beginning that he must preach the preaching that God bade him; he was a disobedient, not a false, prophet.

A note in verse 3 draws attention to the magnitude of Nineveh, and thus of Jonah's task. *Exceeding great* is literally 'great to God' or 'great before God', which is a regular way of expressing a superlative. Thus Moses is described in Acts vii. 20 (AV mg.) as 'fair to God'. There is a certain irony in its use here; it stresses God's estimate of Nineveh, which was not Jonah's.

This note, however, has caused difficulty to some people on two scores. First the verb *was* is in the perfect tense in Hebrew, and has been thought to imply that Nineveh had long since perished (thus supporting a late date for the book). Secondly, modern archaeological research does not altogether confirm the great size of Nineveh. The first difficulty is not decisive, for since the whole narrative is cast in the past, the statement that *Nineveh was an exceeding great city* need imply no more than that this is how it was when Jonah went there. (Of course it *may* be a late gloss; it would be a natural one, and such annotations by smart scribes are not unknown in ancient manuscripts. But it is curious that the people who are normally adept at discovering secondary interpolations in the books of the Old Testament prefer to leave this note as part of the text and use it as a lever to bring the date of the whole book to some time long past the fall of Nineveh in 612 B.C.) The second difficulty is likewise capable of solution. Nineveh city itself, according to the dimensions given by Sennacherib and modern surveys of its ruins (c. twelve miles), was considerably smaller than the language of Jonah implies. Gn. x. 12 (RV), however, applies the title 'the great city' to four cities in the area, of which Nineveh proper is first named and most important. Recent archaeological discoveries show that one of these, Calah, had a population of 70,000; and as this city is known by its walls to have been about half the size of Nineveh, the much doubted figure of *sixscore thousand persons* (iv. 11) is seen to be most likely a census figure of Nineveh in its prime. In later times Nineveh was calculated (by Ktesias and Diodorus) to have had a circuit of some 480 stadia, or about 60 miles, and this seems to reflect the tradition of a very large city area (though it was never bounded by a single wall, as Diodorus seems to think it was). The entire circuit of the four seats of the Nineveh district is, in fact, 61½ miles, or about *three days' journey*. Now, in addition to the note in iii. 3 which we are considering,

Nineveh is on three separate occasions described as *that great city* (i. 2, iii. 2, iv. 11) and the addition of this term may indicate that the larger area or 'district' is deliberately intended. We may compare such modern appellations as 'Greater London'. It may be significant that the term is not added in iv. 5; *the city* here is no doubt Nineveh proper, the city of *a day's journey* where Jonah had first entered (iii. 4). Here the word of Jonah's preaching came to the king of Nineveh, by whose proclamation the fast of repentance extended to all the people of Nineveh.

We do not know what other circumstances in Nineveh may have been favourable to the producing of contrition, but Jonah's preaching of imminent doom—the only actual 'prophecy' in this prophetic book—resulted in an immediate and widespread repentance. The king himself ordered a national fast. Note the curious inclusion of animals in the fast (7), as in Judith iv. 9ff., and as in the famine of Joel i. 19, 20. The very beasts of the field who cry unto the Lord are in turn the objects of His compassion, as the last words of Jonah tell us.

'The sign of Jonas' (Mt. xvi. 4) includes not only his 'death' and 'resurrection', but also his preaching, by virtue of that 'resurrection', to Gentile Nineveh. Ponder the great importance of this sign for Christ's generation (Lk. xi. 29ff. and Mt. xii. 38ff.), and for our own.

V. TWO REACTIONS TO NINEVEH'S REPENTANCE: JEHOVAH CHALLENGES JONAH. iii. 10—iv. 11

God repented of the evil (iii. 10) . . . *but it displeased Jonah exceedingly* (iv. 1). God's 'repentance' and averting of judgment is, of course, not arbitrary. It is a basic postulate of the book of Jonah that God repenteth him of the evil (see Joel ii. 13, 14n. and especially Je. xviii. 6–10). But we have reached the core of Jonah's problem. Jonah now explicitly confesses the reason, hitherto unexplained, for his first attempt to evade Jehovah's command. The question which forms the climax of the book here comes directly into view: 'Should Jehovah spare Nineveh?'

It was in the certain knowledge that God would spare Nineveh if she repented that Jonah fled to Tarshish. Now that Nineveh has repented, Jonah knows that judgment will not fall on Nineveh, and this he cannot face. He cannot reconcile himself to what he knows is the unchangeable character of God. Again he seeks death rather than see God's face and live. *Take . . . my life from me; for it is better for me to die than to live* (3). Compare Elijah's prayer in 1 Ki. xix. 4 and the grounds for it.

But Jehovah directly challenges Jonah. His question (verse 4) may be construed as 'Are you rightly angry?' or 'Are you very angry?' The force is not very different. The first is an explicit challenge to the righteousness of Jonah's behaviour. The second is more in the nature of an exclamation of surprise that Jonah should be at variance with God's mind.

In the final passage of the book (iv. 5–11), God presents His challenge to Jonah in dramatic form, in the acted parable of the gourd. By means of this parable God elicits from Jonah a confession in the matter of the gourd which implies his unrighteousness in the matter of Nineveh.

Jonah, awaiting in forlorn hope the expiry of the *forty days* of his prediction (iii. 4), is again the object of God's 'preparations'. This time a *gourd* (6), a *worm* (7) and a *vehement east wind* (8) are employed. In his depression God dealt with him thus: First He relieved Jonah's grief by providing additional shelter in the thick leafage of the tropical gourd. Next day He reversed the situation and allowed Jonah to suffer acute physical distress by destroying the gourd. Jonah was angry because the gourd perished. Though it was in no sense 'his' gourd, and was by nature short-lived, yet Jonah would have spared it, because it brought comfort to him.

And should not I spare Nineveh? asks Jehovah. Cannot Jonah see some ground for pity in the 120,000 ignorant people and the dumb beasts therein? *Persons that cannot discern between their right hand and their left hand* (11). This is probably a reference to their ignorance, as compared with the Israelite, of the law of God. The ignorance of the people and the helplessness of the cattle are not, of course, the sole ground for the exercise of Jehovah's mercy, but they are mentioned to show how lacking, even in common sympathy, Jonah's religious exclusiveness has made him. Selfishness, blindness, unrighteousness: these are progressively revealed by the parable as Jonah's sins.

The last word is with God, 'whose property is always to have mercy', and the book of Jonah is another signpost to the full revelation of the salvation of God, which, in His sovereign mercy and grace, was to be 'a light to lighten the Gentiles' (Lk. ii. 32). The evangelical message of the book may be expressed in the words of St. Paul: 'What shall we say then? Is there unrighteousness with God? God forbid. For he saith to Moses, I will have mercy on whom I will have mercy, and I will have compassion on whom I will have compassion' (Rom. ix. 14, 15).

D. W. B. ROBINSON.

MICAH

INTRODUCTION

I. DATE

The opening verse fixes the period during which Micah prophesied as being between the years 751 and 687 B.C. The same verse implies that Samaria still stands and her impending destruction is threatened in i. 5, 6, so that this section at least antedates 721 B.C., the year of Samaria's fall and of the collapse of the northern kingdom. Verse 9 seems to anticipate Sennacherib's investment of Jerusalem in 701 B.C. Human sacrifice was a feature of the dark days of king Manasseh (696–642 B.C.), but it is not necessary to suppose that Mi. vi. 7 refers to this period as these rites were also practised by king Ahaz (736–716 B.C.): see 2 Ki..xvi. 3. It would appear therefore that Micah was a younger contemporary of Isaiah: some would even regard him as Isaiah's disciple. It is interesting to note that a similar oracle appears in both prophecies (Mi. iv. 1ff. and Is. ii. 2ff.).

The fulfilment of Micah's prophecy in iii. 12 was remembered over a hundred years later. See Je. xxvi. 18 where it is stated that 'Micah . . . prophesied in the days of Hezekiah king of Judah'. No doubt his main work was done during that reign (729–687 B.C.), and he would thus be partly responsible, under God, for the spiritual revival of that time (see 2 Ch. xxx).

II. THE CRITICAL PROBLEM

A variety of material is contained in this book and the several oracles need not all have been uttered at the same time. Apart from the opening verse there are no other clear indications of dating, such as we find, for example, in Hg. i. 1, ii. 1, 10, 20, but a ministry is implied which extended over a considerable number of years. Many scholars therefore hold that any differences of style or subject-matter are readily accounted for by changing needs and by Micah's own spiritual and mental development and that it is consequently unnecessary to posit more than one author.

Others however cannot bring themselves to believe that the prophet who spoke the stern warnings and denunciations of the first three chapters can also be held responsible for the glowing vision of chapter iv or for the heartening promises of chapter v. In their opinion, also, chapters vi and vii envisage a completely different historical situation from that presupposed in the earlier prophecies. But to assert that the man who composed chapters i—iii could not have composed chapters iv and v is to impose upon Micah a degree of limitation which is quite unjustifiable. To urge that the person who speaks in chapters i—iii was too much occupied with social problems to have any interest in the visionary speculations of chapters iv and v is to fail to realize that every social reformer can persist in his tremendous task only if he has a vision of a world redeemed.

There is no need to expect an obvious connection between the various blocks of material, and within one chapter there may be found a number of utterances dealing with diverse subjects. Possibly vii. 7–20 may be an appendix later than the time of Micah, but this is by no means a certainty.

III. THE PROPHET

He is described in i. 1 as 'the Morasthite', i.e. the inhabitant of Moresheth-gath (i. 14) which, according to Jerome, was still, in his day, 'a small hamlet near Eleutheropolis'. Eleutheropolis is identified with Beit-Jibrin and stands in one of the valleys which run up from the coastal plain to the Judaean highlands around Jerusalem. Moresheth therefore would lie about twenty-five miles south-west of Jerusalem in the Shephelah country and would be about midway between the Philistine city of Gath (i. 10) on the west and Adullam (i. 15) on the east. Its relationship to Mareshah (i. 15) is not clearly known: some think them to be identical. At some time or other it seems to have been under the suzerainty of Gath or to have had some connection with that city.

Thus Micah lived in no backwater, but in the most important of the valleys, one which offered an approach to the capital from the maritime plain. From this vantage-point he overlooked the great coastal road, along which for hundreds of years had passed the armies of conquerors, the caravans of trade, and companies of pilgrims. Dwelling close to this natural bridge between Asia and Africa, with the Mediterranean as a glittering background twenty miles away, he would be in a position to see the grim drama of 721–719 B.C. when, after the fall of Samaria, Sargon proceeded to overwhelm the forces of Egypt on the coastal road at Raphia in 719. A few years later Judah joined with Edom, Moab and the Philistines in an attempt, with Egyptian aid (which never came), to break the power of Assyria; but the allies were sternly dealt with by the Tartan, Sargon's officer, and Ashdod and Gath were sacked (Is. xx. 1). Later still came Sennacherib, who on one of his inscriptions boasts that he had captured forty-six Judaean towns, and Moresheth-gath may well have been one of these.

Again, there would be no traffic between Egypt and Jerusalem which Micah did not observe. He saw Judah putting her confidence in the declining empire of the Nile; the teams of Egyptian horses and chariots in which Judah, a mountainous and unsuitable country, falsely reposed her trust; the corrupting influences of a foreign alliance; the increasing pride and unscrupulosity of the men of the capital. (See Appendix II to Kings, p. 335, 'The Implications of Political Alliances'.)

As a countryman the prophet saw in the capital of his country the fount and centre of iniquity. 'What is the transgression of Jacob? is it not Samaria? and what are the high places of Judah? are they not Jerusalem?' (i. 5). He may himself have been a farmer, and have been dispossessed of his heritage by some greedy landowner. 'They covet fields, and take them by violence; and houses, and take them away: so they oppress a man and his house, even a man and his heritage' (ii. 2). Bitter personal experience and loss may lie behind these words. Micah was possessed of a countryman's directness, depth of conviction, and rugged indignation. Yet he was capable also of lofty and beautiful utterances.

He surpasses even Isaiah in the tenderness of appeal, the lucid simplicity and the moral sublimity which accompany his greatest oracle (vi. 1–8).

Although Micah came from the countryside whereas Isaiah belonged to the capital and to the royal court, their main messages are substantially the same. Isaiah, as may be expected, has more to say about the political situation and about relations with Egypt and Assyria, but in dealing with the social and moral evils consequent upon Israel's rejection of her Lord both prophets speak with one voice. Cf., e.g., Mi. ii. 1ff. with Is. v. 8ff.; Mi. iii. 1–4 with Is. x. 1–4. The Hebrew nation was failing to fulfil her mission in the world to which God had called her (Mi. ii. 7; Is. i. 21) and must therefore be purged with judgment and refitted for service (Mi. iii. 12, iv. 6, 7; Is. i. 25–27). The challenging messages of both prophets must have profoundly influenced Hezekiah in his work of reformation.

Micah was a common name among Jews and is a shorter form of Micaiah, meaning 'who is like Yahweh?' (cf. Michael, 'who is like God?'). It is noteworthy that Micah's prophecy begins with the words of an appeal made by an earlier namesake (1 Ki. xxii. 28). Thus Micah deliberately links himself with the earlier champion of the truth.

OUTLINE OF CONTENTS

I. THE WRATH TO COME. i. 1–16

II. MICAH'S DENUNCIATION OF THOSE WHO WORK EVIL. ii. 1—iii. 12

    a. The grasping landowners (ii. 1–11)
    b. Rulers, prophets and priests (iii. 1–12)

III. THE MOUNTAIN OF THE LORD. iv. 1–5

IV. ORACLES OF BLESSING AND JUDGMENT. iv. 6—v. 1

V. THE COMING OF THE REDEEMER. v. 2–15

VI. THE LORD'S CONTROVERSY WITH ISRAEL. vi. 1—vii. 20

    a. A supreme appeal (vi. 1–8)
    b. The sin of the city denounced (vi. 9–16)
    c. The prophet laments the existing corruption (vii. 1–6)
    d. Confession and doxology (vii. 7–20)

COMMENTARY

I. THE WRATH TO COME. i. 1–16

Like other prophets (e.g. Obadiah) Micah opens with a statement of judgment to come. He bids the people hear the charges of God against them, with the amphitheatre of the whole earth as court house (2). God will come to judge His people and the earth shall melt before Him (3, 4). Whether this refers to an actual earth-tremor (cf. Am. i. 1) or is poetic imagery is not certain. The reason for the threatened visitation is *the transgression of Jacob* and *the sins of . . .*

Israel (5). The centres of sin in both the Israelite kingdoms are the capital cities of Samaria and Jerusalem. The prophet gives a grim picture of the devastation which hangs over them. Samaria in the north will be like a heap of rubble, like a bombed city of modern times (6). The *images* and *idols*, paid for and supported by the proceeds of immorality, will be destroyed (7). By declaring that he will give vent to extreme expressions of grief (8), Micah is probably seeking to underline the urgency of his message. Cf. Is. xxii. 4; Je. ix. 1ff.

The danger now threatens Jerusalem (9–16). The Assyrian army sweeps along the coastal plain towards Egypt, turns round, rushes up the river valley in which Micah dwelt, overwhelms one town after another, and finally reaches the walls of Jerusalem. It is instructive to compare this passage with Is. x. 28–34. In Isaiah we have a description, by a man within the city, of the onrush of the enemy from the northern quarter. In Micah, a man outside the capital gives an account of the enemy sweeping past him from the south-west.

There is a play here on the Hebrew names of towns which defies translation into English. G. A. Smith, Pusey and others have made the following suggestions. *Declare ye it not at Gath* (10; cf. 2 Sa. i. 20); the radicals of the verb 'to declare' and of the town-name Gath are similar. It might therefore be rendered 'tell it not in Tell-Town'. So with *Aphrah* which means 'dust': 'in the house of dust, roll thyself in the dust'. For an attempt to translate these allusions into English see Moffatt.

Lachish is described as *the beginning of the sin to the daughter of Zion* (13). According to G. A. Smith, the prophet is challenging the inhabitant of that town to *bind the chariot to the swift beast* because it was closely connected with the chariot traffic. It was the mistaken policy of both Israel and Judah to purchase large quantities of horses and chariots from the Egyptians. The nation was thereby encouraged to believe that she was becoming a military power, but, all the time, she was only straining her financial resources. For however suitable chariots might be for the flat lands of the Nile, they were quite out of place in the mountainous terrain of Judah. Moreover, such a panoply of war was causing the nation to look to herself and to her allies rather than to Jehovah. For this reason the prophets of Jehovah viewed the chariots with disapproval and regarded them as a source of error.

It is suggested that at Lachish, on the coastal plain, the newly purchased horses and chariots were halted and rested before finally passing on to Jerusalem. In this way Lachish could be spoken of as *the beginning of the sin to the daughter of Zion*. In verse 15 follow RV and read 'the glory of Israel shall come even unto Adullam'. Cf. Is. ii. 19. This repeats the thought of verse 3. *Make thee bald* (16). To shave the head was a sign of mourning. Cf. Is. xxii. 12.

II. MICAH'S DENUNCIATION OF THOSE WHO WORK EVIL. ii. 1—iii. 12

a. The grasping landowners (ii. 1–11)

Jehovah's case against His people is continued, but instead of a general verdict of doom upon Israel and Judah, particular classes who have provoked that doom are singled out for execration and some idea is given of the social and religious life of Judah and of the evils from which the nation was suffering.

Rich upstarts in the city desire country estates. They lie awake at night scheming how to acquire land. In the morning, they use influence in appropriate quarters (1). With the help of a crooked legal procedure, peasant landowners are forcibly evicted and a number of farms are joined together to form a sizeable estate (2). These unfortunate people are compelled to become casual labourers, or beggars, or to sell themselves as slaves. The nation thereby loses its vitality, for this independent peasant class is its real backbone. The problem is also religious as well as economic, and the same evil is denounced by Isaiah (Is. v. 8). Cf. the story of Naboth's vineyard in 1 Ki. xxi.

After the indictment (1, 2) these grasping landowners are warned that their punishment will fit the crime. The lands which they have filched from other people will be taken away from them (4). None of them shall be able to take up an allotment of land in Israel (5).

Prophesy ye not (6). Angered by this straight speaking, they tell Micah to be quiet; but the prophet answers bitterly that it is because they do not care to be made to feel uncomfortable that they wish him to desist. Or the whole of verse 6 may be taken as the words of the rich men who, when remonstrated with, reply with confused cries: 'Stop your prophesying! They are prophesying (at us)! They shall do no such thing! Will their reproaches never cease?'

Undeterred by the unfavourable reception of his message, Micah tries to reason with them. Are their ways God's ways? If they are really Jacob's people, why is not the work of God's Spirit seen in their lives? *Are these his doings?* (7). They can expect the blessing of God only if they act uprightly. He then confronts them with some of their recent actions to show how far short they have fallen of God's requirements. They behave as enemies to those who trust them, and rob them of their very garments (8). They turn women and children out of their homes (9). The prophet concludes this part of his message of condemnation and warning with an appeal for action. He summons them to arise from their sinfulness. For if they remain sunk down in their present evil, slothful condition, it will eventually destroy them (10).

But the people do not want a prophet of righteousness. They want a jolly fellow, babbling *of wine and of strong drink* (11), a popular ministry in the worst sense of that word. They will get the sort of preacher they deserve. Like people, like priest.

NOTE. *Verses 12 and 13 appear to belong to a different period from the foregoing and succeeding passages and will be treated along with the kindred section in v. 2–4 (q.v.).*

b. Rulers, prophets and priests (iii. 1–12)

King, princes, nobles, judges: the whole glittering throng of those who hold administrative and judicial positions in the state is now addressed (1–4). *Is it not for you to know judgment?* (1). The *raison d'être* of such people is service. They have been put into high positions of authority in order that they may serve the people and dispense justice to every man. Instead, they are abusing their office, and robbing the very people whom they are supposed to be protecting (2). They enjoy good food and luxuries while others starve (3). The description is so vivid that one can almost see the cheek-bones of the poor standing out from their drawn faces. 'Pinched peasant faces peer between the words' (G. A. Smith). But God will punish their oppressors. He will not deliver them in their hour of need (4).

As for the false prophets (5–8) who minister so acceptably to the rich (ii. 11), they *make my people err*. They no longer teach the commandments of God. Only to those who feed them well do they unctuously say 'peace'. But God will bring them to judgment. *It shall be dark unto you* (6). He will give them darkness of mind so that they will be unable to read the signs of the times. When men ask them for counsel, there shall be *no answer of God* (7). This is the nemesis of commercialized preaching. Preaching which distorts and suppresses truth for reward is ultimately unable to discern the truth and to declare it. In contrast there is the true prophet, whose words are with power, for he has upon him the *spirit of the Lord* Himself (8). His are no honeyed utterances, but he brings a message of judgment upon *transgression* and *sin*.

In the last great oracle of this chapter (9–12) Micah gathers up all that he has so far said and hurls it at those whom he has been denouncing. The nation's leaders are dishonest. They are trying to build a prosperous city and a prosperous nation, but at the expense of the lives of the poor (10). The *heads . . . the priests . . . the prophets* (11). The political, ecclesiastical and religious leaders are all corrupt and all desire one thing—money. Yet with bland satisfaction they imagine that God cannot be otherwise than pleased with such respectable people as they are! So there comes the terrible ultimatum: *Therefore shall Zion for your sake be plowed as a field, and Jerusalem shall become heaps, and the mountain of the house as the high places of the forest* (12), i.e. like mounds in a wood which mark where ruined buildings lie. We are not surprised to read in Je. xxvi. 18 that this utterance had made a very deep impression, and, in view of its actual fulfilment, was still well remembered over a century after Micah's own time. His stirring words not only led to an immediate reformation, but the quotation of them was instrumental in saving the life of the prophet Jeremiah when he, for uttering similar truths, was in danger of being put to death in the reign of Jehoiakim. It is an interesting example of the continuing life and power of God's Word.

It is noteworthy that these three oracles (verses 1–4, 5–8, 9–12) are regular in structure. First, there are the people addressed; secondly, the evil they commit; thirdly, the judgment that will fall upon them.

III. THE MOUNTAIN OF THE LORD.
iv. 1–5

The prophet, lifting his eyes away from the sordid abuses which surrounded him, no longer gazes at the cloud of impending judgment but beholds afar off a glorious vision of the last days (1–4). A like vision is recorded in Is. ii. 2–5 in very similar words. The question arises whether the oracle was original to Micah or to Isaiah, or whether it was an independent oracle used by both of them. Micah seems to give the vision in a fuller form and his text is in a better state of preservation. But it seems unlikely that Isaiah, the older of the two, would have borrowed from his younger contemporary, and if he did borrow, why did he not make an exact quotation? Perhaps God taught the same truth to both men through a common source, and the great importance of the passage is therefore signified by its double attestation.

In contrast with the punishment which will soon overtake Zion for the sins of the people, there is this dazzling vision of the supremacy of God's house in the last time. It rises 'on mountain tops above the hills'. Towards it the nations converge. Rivers of people, having their beginning afar off, and growing in ever-increasing volume, *flow unto it* (1). Nations exhort one another to seek the guidance of God's law. Recognizing that they cannot settle disputes by themselves, they desire to be taught God's ways and to walk in them (2). So Zion will become the legislative centre for the whole earth, and all disputes will be brought before the God of Jacob. Strong nations, who would otherwise be unchecked in their aggressions, will accept His rebuke; nor will distance lessen His authority. They will scrap their armaments in which once lay their confidence and pride, and will turn the metal into implements of peace. No longer will they declare war on one another; the energy, ingenuity and wealth, once devoted to learning war, will now be directed to more constructive and profitable ends (3). So tranquil will the earth become that every man shall dwell in peace. 'The key keeps the castle and the bracken bush the cow.' The old days of guards, raids and terrors by night will have become things of the past, for *none shall make them afraid* (4). The nations will be able to develop their lives undisturbed. God pledges His word that every man shall be in safety and peace is assured because the Word of the Lord is the universal law.

Such is the great vision vouchsafed to both prophets. There is nothing impossible in its content. Already it is an ideal dimly apprehended by individuals, if not by nations. Given the premises of verses 1 and 2, that the house of God be supreme and that the law of God be obeyed, universal tranquillity and universal security must follow.

Unfortunately, the supremacy of God's house and of His law is not yet a matter of world-wide recognition. We are still at the stage of verse 5, which may be translated: 'For all people walk everyone in the name of his god, but we will walk in the name of our God for ever and ever.'

IV. ORACLES OF BLESSING AND JUDGMENT. iv. 6—v. 1

Having implied, in moving terms, the distressed condition of the exiled people of God, the prophet now holds out the wondrous promise that *in that day* (6) they will be reintegrated into a kingdom over which *the Lord shall reign* in Mount Zion for ever (7). Then in two further oracles he speaks of the afflictions and exertions which must befall Jerusalem before the promised *kingdom shall come* (8). In the first (8–10) Zion is compared to a *tower of the flock* (8), one of those walled enclosures with folds around for sheep which are to be found in the wide pasturelands of the holy land. But even her walls will cease to be a protection, and her inhabitants will be forced to *dwell in the field*, and then in *Babylon* (10). But there too the Lord shall redeem them. This reference to Babylon is a remarkable prediction since, when Micah wrote, Assyria was the chief enemy power.

In iv. 11—v. 1 Jerusalem is again seen to be besieged, but now the tables are turned on her oppressors and the opposing nations will be threshed like wheat. However, in this process Israel's own leader or *judge* (v. 1) shall suffer severe indignities.

V. THE COMING OF THE REDEEMER. v. 2–15

With this section we include ii. 12, 13. Verse 2 begins a new chapter in the Hebrew Bible. It and the next verse reveal the expectations of longing Israel. A Deliverer shall come *to be ruler in Israel*. His birth in Bethlehem implies that He will be another David and so be a true shepherd of God's people (4, RV). This remarkable prophecy has had both a literal as well as a spiritual fulfilment in the birth of our Lord Jesus Christ at Bethlehem (Mt. ii. 5, 6), and there may be a reference to the incarnation in verse 3. He who is here looked for is clearly no ordinary, earthly man. He is clothed with timeless dignity, *whose goings forth have been from of old, from everlasting* (2). The work which the Deliverer will do will be of a pastoral character, and He will be the shepherd of the people. *He shall stand* (4); carefulness, confidence and strength are here implied. *And feed* (4); RV 'and shall feed his flock'; i.e. He will nourish His people, leading them in pastures of tender grass and beside the waters of quietness, through the grace and power of God. He shall be regarded with awe and reverence, because He is kingly, and bears the name of the Lord, and His fame shall spread abroad unto the ends of the earth.

In his capacity as shepherd the coming ruler is also described as a *breaker* (ii. 13), i.e. one who removes obstacles and opens up a way. God's people are pictured as sheep penned up in a narrow fold (ii. 12) and longing to be set free; the breaker not only flings wide the gate but pulls down part of the wall to facilitate their release. He then passes on in front of them as their divinely appointed Leader and Lord.

With such messianic visions the prophet Micah helped to keep alive through weary centuries the hope of a Saviour in the hearts of longing Israel. He apprehended one essential rôle of the deliverer, which was that of shepherd, and in the unusual thought of the breaker he reveals to us another aspect of the many-sided glory of the Son of God.

Verses 5 and 6 form in Hebrew a strophe of ten lines. They envisage a different and more immediate historical situation than the foregoing. The word *man* supplied by the AV in verse 5 is better omitted. Read, 'this shall be the peace'. Invasion is anticipated, and with good reason, from Assyria. An indefinite number of national leaders, seven or eight, shall be raised up against the invader, so that the enemy is beaten back into his own country (5, 6). But then the several leaders are merged into one; *thus shall he deliver us* (6).

Verses 7–9 consist of a poem which has for its theme the remnant of Jacob, upon whom the King will bestow His own lion-like strength. The two strophes begin with an almost identical phrase, *and the remnant of Jacob shall be . . . in the midst of many people* (8). One aspect of the people is given in the first strophe; they are free and beautiful as summer rain, gentle, refreshing, sparkling, elusive. In the second strophe they are represented as being strong, terrible, kingly, irresistible. These two strophes form one poetic gem.

Then follows, in verses 10–15, an account of those things in which Israel vainly trusts instead of in her King, viz. *horses* and *chariots* (10), *strong holds* (11), *witchcrafts* and *soothsayers* (12), *graven images* (13), *groves* (14), i.e. wooden poles erected to symbolize the Canaanite deity Astarte (14). A necessary prelude to reformation in Israel is the removal of these idolatries in the power of Jehovah. Still in a so-called Christian country men mistakenly rely upon such false sources of confidence. Instead of trusting in the power of God, they set their confidence in wealth, in the strength of worldly position, and in unworthy forms of religious faith but little removed from superstition.

VI. THE LORD'S CONTROVERSY WITH ISRAEL. vi. 1—vii. 20

a. A supreme appeal (vi. 1–8)

There are few passages in the Old Testament where the simplicity of true religion is brought home to the heart and conscience of every man more clearly than it is here. As in the opening passages of the book, the Lord invites His people to reason with Him in the presence of the everlasting hills (1). He appeals to the mountains, those silent and unchanging spectators of human history, and before this majestic and lofty court of inquiry he proceeds to state His case (2). He does so with great tenderness (3), and in words through which there breathes a warm evangelical appeal. He gives the people the opportunity to make known their grievance (3c), but before they do so He recalls to their minds past mercies which they may be in danger of forgetting (4, 5). So far from wearying them, the Lord has wonderfully redeemed them. He reminds them of the deliverance from Egypt (4), the greatest event in Israel's history and the outstanding fact in the national consciousness, the occurrence of which had made them a nation, and to which in thought psalmists and prophets always returned. Not only has the Lord redeemed them and given them great national leaders (4), but He has shown His righteousness and love by causing them to be blessed when their enemies would have cursed them (5). So ends the Lord's statement of His case.

One is conscious of a break in the passage at this point, of a change in the form of thought, and this causes some to think that verses 6–8 may have had an existence independent of their present setting. However, taking the passage as a whole, Israel is now represented as answering the Lord with a counter-challenge. What worship and what service does the Lord really require? Does He desire a meticulous observance of the Levitical law? (6b). Does He wish it to be fulfilled in an excessive and lavish manner by holocausts of herds and *rivers of oil*? (7a). Does He desire the people to show a frenzied and non-moral devotion to Him comparable to the fanaticism of some of the heathen peoples round about, such as moved the worshippers to offer human sacrifice? (7b). While the sacrifices mentioned in verse 6 seem to be in keeping with Mosaic requirements, those of verse 7 go beyond anything that is laid down in the Pentateuch, where we find the sacrifice of the firstborn definitely forbidden (e.g. Lv. xviii. 21). We seem therefore to have moved on to heathen practices.

The controversy is closed by the Lord's own declared answer (8). Among the many truths taught in this verse is the lesson that ritual offerings, even the Levitical ones, are valueless unless they express a sincere movement of the heart towards God, of which the true outward symbol is an honest character and a humble bearing in the sight of men. In any case, the value of a ritual offering does not consist in its amount or in its excess, but in the state of mind with which it is accompanied, and which may exist without it.

Nevertheless, it would be wrong to infer from this that Micah is here ranging himself against sacrifice as such. There is not present here the antithesis so much emphasized by many modern critics between the prophetic and priestly elements in Hebrew religion. For Micah, *to walk humbly with thy God* would include the reverent keeping of the ceremonial as well as the moral laws of the Pentateuch. The prophet is simply putting first things first and showing that, after all, a holy walk with God is the best evidence of genuine religion. The sacrificial system was never meant to be an end in itself, but was intended to assist the inner resolution of a man's mind by a series of specific, overt acts which must have their significance interpreted in terms of actual holy living to make them effective.

Of verse 8 one may say that here is the simplicity of true religion. In this one saying Micah comprehends the salient points in the teaching of the other great prophets, Amos, Hosea and Isaiah. Along with Christ's teaching, this word of Micah is a sufficient rule of life for Christian men.

b. The sin of the city denounced (vi. 9–16)

The remainder of this chapter condemns the commercial sharp practices which had become so prevalent in Israel. Micah here addresses himself to the business men of the city (9) who were engaged in commercial dishonesty (10, 11), blustering and lying (12). He proclaims the eternal truth that businesses so built up will not endure and that profits so gained will not be enjoyed (13–15). With verse 15 cf. Ho. viii. 7. Some of these verses might well be posted up, like the Factory Acts, in business premises, so that merchants and business men might read and inwardly digest them. The city magnates are condemned for keeping *the statutes of Omri* and *all the works of the house of Ahab* (16). From this it would appear that oppressive and violent customs, characteristic of the dynasty of Omri, had been raised almost to the level of statutory law by the time of the eighth century. Of all the works of Ahab's house the unjust acquisition by Ahab himself of the vineyard of Naboth was, as has already been noted, an outstanding example.

c. The prophet laments the existing corruption (vii. 1–6)

Micah describes years spiritually lean. Judah and Jerusalem are like a garden after the fruit has been picked. The show of leaves is fair enough, but one searches in vain for solid fruit (1). Judah is morally barren. *There is none upright among men* (2). One preys upon another. To do evil is not an occasional lapse or sudden yielding to temptation on the part of an individual; it is a deliberate policy in which prominent men cooperate: 'they weave it together' (3, RV; cf. iii. 11). There is no one upon whom a man may rely and even those who at first sight appear promising in goodness prove to be disappointing. They have become sharp in their self-interest; everyone is barbed *as a brier* (4). So there afflicts the members of this society the inevitable nemesis of isolation, for where none may be trusted, each must stand alone, and it is every man for himself. Shattered are the closest ties of friendship and kinship. Society disintegrates, because its members do not fulfil the conditions of mutual good faith upon which social life depends (5, 6). This passage describes a period of informers and persecution, such as obtained in the time of king Manasseh.

d. Confession and doxology (vii. 7–20)

From the sordid moral failure and corruption of society around him, the prophet lifts his eyes to God's eternal verities (7). In great words he affirms the hope which lights up the darkness of affliction for every believer (8). How many good men, hard pressed in the strife against overwhelming evil, have asserted their faith in ultimate victory in these valiant words of verse 8, as John Bunyan in his *Pilgrim's Progress* makes Christian do, when almost overthrown in the struggle with Apollyon!

He confesses that God's treatment of His people is just (9). With sudden spirit he rebukes his nation's enemies (10). Then, regaining his calm, he foresees a day when the exiled children of Jerusalem will come back to her (11, 12). But even then things will not be easy (13). But, once more, the figure of a shepherd and his flock comes into the prophet's mind, and he appeals to God to show His pastoral carè (14). The great days of old will return, for God has not changed; and with a repentant people He will do wonders in the eyes of the nations (15–17).

The book closes on a great note. The last three verses are a Psalm in praise of the timeless mercy of God. The prophet soars above all local considerations, and furnishes every generation of worshipping men and women with words in which to bless Him who *retaineth not his anger for ever, because he delighteth in mercy* (18).

A. Fraser.
L. E. H. Stephens-Hodge.

NAHUM

INTRODUCTION

I. THE DATE

The prophecy of Nahum anticipates the fall of
Nineveh. The prophet speaks of the fall of the
city with a clarity and an intimacy possible only if
the event were almost immediate. This dates the
prophecy of Nahum shortly before the fall of
the city in 612 B.C. The prophet also mentions
the sack of No, that is No-amon or Thebes
(iii. 8), as an accomplished fact. This city was
pillaged by king Ashurbanipal of Assyria about
666 B.C. The prophecy may therefore be dated
between these two events. Another small piece
of internal evidence suggests that the date may be
fixed more precisely as being shortly after the
Josianic reformation of 621 B.C. There is one
reference (i. 15) which suggests that the importance of observing religious ceremonies was fresh
in the minds of the people of Judah at this time.
We may therefore tentatively place the prophecy
between 621 and 612 B.C. The prophet was
therefore a contemporary of Zephaniah, Habakkuk and Jeremiah.

II. THE MAN

The writer is described as 'Nahum the Elkoshite'.
The name Nahum means 'consolation', 'comfort'
or 'relief'. While the primary message of Nahum
is the impending doom of Nineveh, a necessary
consequence of the fall of the Assyrian tyrant was
the relief of the oppressed Judah. In that sense
the message of Nahum justified the name of the
prophet. He had no word of judgment or of
condemnation for his own people, but only of
comfort. He declares in the name of the Lord,
'Though I have afflicted thee, I will afflict thee no
more. For now will I break his yoke from off
thee, and will burst thy bonds in sunder' (i. 12,
13).

'Elkoshite', the supplementary designation of
the prophet, indicates that Nahum was closely
connected with a locality known as Elkosh. Four
locations are suggested for this place. Jerome
says that Elkasch (*Het kesai*) was a little village
of Galilee, and that it was shown to him by a
guide. Another suggestion is Capernaum in
Galilee, the name of which is a transliteration of
two Hebrew words, meaning 'village of Nahum'.
A third identification is that of Alqush near
Mosul in Assyria which is locally claimed as the
prophet's native home. Fourthly, Pseudepi-
phanius maintains that 'Elcesei' was a village of
Judah.

Of these four traditions, the third does not go
back earlier than the sixteenth century. Con-

cerning the first two there is no evidence within
the text to suggest a Galilean environment for
Nahum. Of course, if we accept the tradition that
Nahum was a deported exile in Nineveh itself,
one would not look for traces of a Galilean background. But it appears that in New Testament
times no tradition existed that Nahum came from
Galilee (cf. Jn. vii. 52, which, however, overlooks
Jonah). This origin for the prophet may be
doubted on other grounds. The fourth suggestion
connects Nahum with Elkash 'of the tribe of
Simeon'. In that case, Elkash may be located
near Beit-Jibrin, between Jerusalem and Gaza.
It will be noted that evidence points to the fact
that Micah also came from this neighbourhood.
This region seems to have been productive alike
of piety and of genius.

III. HIS MESSAGE

The primary note of Nahum's message is
'Vengeance is mine: I will repay, saith the Lord'.
'God is jealous, and the Lord revengeth' (i. 2).
The word 'jealous' here means the zeal, or the
intense feeling, of God towards His enemies.
Nahum apprehended and declared with passionate insistence the one truth that the wrath
of God is provoked by wickedness. He bears long
with men, but His anger is eventually aroused.
Then He punishes those who have provoked
Him. He strikes and makes an utter end. The
wrath of God is terrible and inescapable. He
who divides the storm-darkened sky with spears
of lightning and cracks the rocks is an awful
adversary. Puny man is nothing before Him.
Men may take counsel with themselves. They
may say 'We are strong. Who can throw us
down?' God will deal with them. No matter how
strong they may be, no matter how many
helpers they may have, God will inflict upon them
a death-blow. There have been others stronger
than they. These were overthrown. So shall the
enemies of God always be overthrown.

In addition, Nahum singles out two sins in
particular for denunciation. There is first the sin
of ruthless military power. As a result of this
evil, blood is shed in rivers, nations are annihilated, institutions are destroyed, and war is
waged with every kind of ferocity (ii. 11–13). Of
the people who so violate the decencies of human
life, it is declared, 'Behold, I am against thee,
saith the Lord of hosts.' The other sin which
Nahum denounces is unscrupulous commerce.
The surrounding nations are corrupted so that
they may minister to the luxuries and vices of

the conquering city. Merchants, motivated by greed for gold, sell their wares in a city lusting for fine things. Morality and honesty are allowed to perish so that wealth may be acquired and pleasures enjoyed (iii. 1-4). On this sin, also, the same judgment is passed with sombre simplicity. 'Behold, I am against thee, saith the Lord of hosts' (iii. 5).

To his own people Nahum declares that messengers with good tidings are already on their way. As an expression of gratitude for the destruction of the oppressor, the people of Judah are to observe the religious seasons and scrupulously to discharge the obligations of their faith (i. 15).

IV. HIS SIGNIFICANCE AS A PROPHET

Like Cato, the Roman senator, who closed every speech in the senate with the words *Carthago delenda est* ('Carthage must be destroyed'), Nahum is obsessed with one idea, *Nineve delenda est*. His gaze is fixed on Nineveh and her sins. Though sincere, intense and effective, he has not much to say of the inwardness of true religion. He does not call for a personal and national return to righteousness, rather than the observance of religious fasts, as does Amos (Am. iv. 4, 5). He does not seek to win his own people with the tenderness of Micah (Mi. vi. 3). He does not proclaim mercy for all men, even for Nineveh, with the breadth of vision and the wide charity of the book of Jonah.

Nevertheless, limited as Nahum's message may have been, his place among the prophets is secure. The date at which his prophecy was composed may help to explain his apparent lack of concern with the sins of his own people, his omission to point out their moral and spiritual obligations, and his seeming lack of charity towards Nineveh itself. If the prophecy were composed just before 612 B.C. (the fall of Nineveh), then it was not long after the Josianic reformation (621 B.C.). It is true that Jeremiah saw that the reforms were not sufficient; but Nahum may have felt that the nation was now on the right road. The disillusionment brought about by Josiah's untimely death in 609 B.C. had not yet taken place and the relief felt at the impending destruction of Nineveh was such as to blot out for Nahum all other considerations.

The prophecy of Nahum has been well called 'the cry of an outraged conscience'. It is a passionate assertion that justice in its stern retribution will prevail. This truth he declares with insistence. He proclaims its moral necessity. He envisages its accomplishment with unrivalled lucidity. He foresees the completeness of its fulfilment. In the great corpus of truth taught by the twelve prophets, this truth is particularly the property of Nahum, and if his prophecy is the prophecy of one idea, at least he presents that idea with much power and complete effectiveness.

OUTLINE OF CONTENTS

There are three odes corresponding to the three chapters:

I. AN ALPHABETIC ACROSTIC. i. 1-15

    a. The book's title (i. 1)
    b. The poem (i. 2-8)
    c. The punishment of enemies (i. 9-15)

II. A THREEFOLD PICTURE. ii. 1-13

    a. The siege (ii. 1-6)
    b. The sack (ii. 7-10)
    c. The overthrow (ii. 11-13)

III. A WAR SONG. iii. 1-19

    a. The wickedness of Nineveh (iii. 1-7)
    b. Comparison with Egypt (iii. 8-15)
    c. The irremediable doom (iii. 16-19)

COMMENTARY

I. AN ALPHABETIC ACROSTIC. i. 1-15

a. The book's title (i. 1)

The burden of Nineveh. Primarily that which is taken up with, or concerning, Nineveh; then, that which is weighty concerning Nineveh; finally, that which is spoken concerning Nineveh.

The word *burden* followed by a place-name as an objective genitive frequently denotes a pronouncement of a threatening and condemnatory nature against that place. But this is not invariably so. In Zc. xii. 1 we find 'the burden of the word of the Lord for Israel', where the threat is not to Israel, but to the enemies of Israel.

b. The poem (i. 2–8)

There are a number of poems in the Bible which have each verse, or perhaps each line, beginning with successive letters of the alphabet. Pss. cxi, cxii and, notably, Ps. cxix are examples of this arrangement, the purpose of which was probably to act as a kind of *aide-mémoire*. In some cases, as in these verses, the whole alphabet is not employed.

The distinctive peculiarity of the poem, with its successive initial letters, is of course lost in translation. An indication of the working out of the scheme, however, may be given here. *Aleph; God is jealous* (2). *Beth; The Lord hath his way in the whirlwind and in the storm* (3). *Gimel; He rebuketh the sea, and maketh it dry* (4). The letter *Daleth* cannot be traced. *He; The mountains quake at him* (5). *Waw; And the earth is burned at his presence* (5). *Zain; Who can stand before his indignation?* (6). *Teth; The Lord is good* (7). *Yodh; He knoweth them that trust in him* (7). *Kaph; He will make an utter end of the place thereof* (8).

Some critics make the liturgical hymn include verse 9. If that be the case, the order of the clauses requires to be reversed, as at present the first begins with *Mem* and the second with *Lamedh*. In the revised order, they read *Lamedh; Affliction shall not rise up the second time. Mem; What do ye imagine against the Lord? He will make an utter end.*

The theme of this poem is the certainty and the severity of God's vengeance upon the heathen, and it begins with a very forceful statement of this fact (2). With cumulative repetition, the prophet affirms and re-affirms that the Lord *will take vengeance*. He declares that just because the anger of the Lord is slow to gather, it will be slow to dissipate. He *will not at all acquit the wicked* (3), but will hold them responsible and will judge them. It is all too easy to lose sight of these moral truths. Only too readily do men think that, because wickedness is allowed for a time, it is therefore condoned. A passage such as this is a reminder that God's anger is directed against all unrighteousness and that, without repentance, there is no cheap and easy forgiveness.

To convince his audience of the terror of the Lord, Nahum points to the phenomena of physical nature and in vivid language paints a picture of storm, whirlwind, drought, earthquake and fire (4, 5). These all reveal the power of the mighty God and, confronted with them, even the boldest of men become aware of their own insignificance. *Who can stand before his indignation?* asks Nahum, *and who can abide in the fierceness of his anger? his fury is poured out like fire, and the rocks are thrown down by him* (6).

Nahum then states the moral implications of the power of God, both for the righteous and for the wicked. Just because God is so strong, He is a safe refuge for those who *trust in him* (7). He knows who these are and will not forget them. On the other hand, He is mighty to smite the wicked. He knows them also, and His vengeance will not fail. Their doom is certain (8).

c. The punishment of enemies (i. 9–15)

In this arrangement we have separated verse 9 from the liturgical hymn, although, as we have pointed out above, a number of critics include it in the hymn. Working on the theory that Nahum did not compose the alphabetic acrostic, but that it was added later to his prophecy, these commentators consider that verses 10 and 11 are the first genuine verses of Nahum. Some, indeed, wish to place verses i. 10, 11 after verse 1 of chapter ii, thus making these verses part of the war song describing the attack upon Nineveh.

There is, however, a close connection between these verses and those which have preceded them. The same theme is handled and the two thoughts previously noticed are worked out, i.e. the punishment of the enemies of the Lord and consequent relief to those whom they have oppressed.

While the vengeance of God threatens them, God's enemies are not yet subdued in mind. They still refuse to believe that He will smite. But He is about to deal with them. His punishment of them will be complete and final. He will not need to strike *the second time* (9). In describing this judgment Nahum uses a metaphor which is a favourite with the prophets (see Is. v. 24; Joel ii. 5; Ob. 18) and one likely to appeal to the imagination of an agricultural people. God's enemies will be gathered together as thorns and consumed as fire burns the dry straw after harvest (10; cf. Mt. xiii. 30).

There is one . . . a wicked counsellor (11). Nahum seems to see the evil of the Assyrian people summed up in the person of one of their leaders. He is so contemptible that especial shame is reserved for him (14). His family will cease to be, his gods will be thrown down and he himself will be put to death.

As a consequence of the overthrow of the enemies of the Lord, there is relief for His oppressed people (12c, 13). The arrival of this good news is declared in a picturesque and beautiful fashion. Perhaps it was because good news must of necessity be brought to Jerusalem over mountain roads that it was announced [by the prophets in this form (cf. Is. lii. 7). *Behold upon the mountains the feet of him that bringeth good tidings, that publisheth peace!* In gratitude for this deliverance, Judah is exhorted to cultivate her religious life (15). Along with this section may be taken ii. 2. *The Lord hath turned away;* better, as in RV, 'the Lord bringeth again'. The meaning might be expressed thus: 'the vine of Judah shall bloom afresh as the vine of Israel, although the spoilers have spoiled him and destroyed his tendrils.'

Thus Nahum deals with his theme of the overthrow of Nineveh in a general and introductory manner. He has given the setting in relation to the justice of God and to the oppressed people of Judah. In the remaining two chapters he turns to his subject in particular and in detail, setting forth its accomplishment in word-pictures of battle, unrivalled in Hebrew literature.

II. A THREEFOLD PICTURE. ii. 1-13

a. The siege (ii. 1-6)

The enemy is come up against Nineveh (1). These verses may be dated after the death of the great Assyrian ruler Ashurbanipal in 626 B.C. The Medes, a hardy Aryan people, had settled in the area between the Caspian Sea and Assyria. Under their king Cyaxares, they were pressing on the older Semitic peoples, who were enervated by luxury. Now they were approaching the gates of Nineveh. Nahum, with bitter mockery, exhorts the Ninevites to prepare defensive measures. *Scarlet* (3) was a favourite colour with the fighting men of Media. Their shields are red, as are their cloaks. The whole scene is lit by the light of torches, carried by the chariots in the darkness of the early morning before the assault. *Fir trees* (3; lit. 'cypresses'); RV renders 'spears'. The RSV corrects the text and translates 'the chargers prance'. The chariots roll along the broad ways in the large built-up areas which surround the central fortifications of Nineveh. So numerous are they that they thrust and press one against another (4). Picked men are chosen for the attack. They come forward at a stumbling run. *The defence shall be prepared* (5), RV 'mantelet'; i.e. a movable defence, under cover of which they make ready for the final assault. Then, having captured the sluices and water gates controlling the river Chaser which flowed through the city, they suddenly open them, so allowing a great flood of water to pour down on the buildings. Foundations are loosened and in this way the palace is literally *dissolved* (6).

b. The sack (ii. 7-10)

Huzzab (7); i.e. the queen, or, perhaps, the female representative of a goddess. Attempts have been made to regard the word as a verb (see AV and RV mgs.) but it is better to take it as a proper noun. Her female attendants follow her as she is *led away*. They moan in their distress like doves cooing in a wood and beat upon their breasts (7). For many years Nineveh has been a reservoir of trade and wealth into which has been flowing from all quarters streams of goods and gold. Nineveh has thus become like *a pool of water* fed by many tributaries (8). She has a heterogeneous population, held together only by the opportunities to acquire wealth which the power of Nineveh gives them. When the blow falls there is nothing to make these people cohere. They rush in every direction, as waters break out when a dam bursts. A few try to rally the defence crying *Stand, stand*, but the inhabitants flee wildly, without looking back (8). House-to-house plunder begins. *Silver, gold, pleasant furniture*, the accumulated wealth of centuries, are looted (9). The sacked city stands empty. The few terrified survivors look sadly on the ruins (10).

c. The overthrow (ii. 11-13)

Nahum closes the ode with a magnificent picture of a pride of lions which has been destroyed. *Where is the dwelling of the lions?* (11). In vivid words he describes their fearlessness, strength and rapacity. But now the den is forsaken and the menace a thing of the past. So the Lord has finally dealt with Nineveh. She also was cruel and blood-thirsty. But her brood has been smoked out and slain with the sword. She will not prey upon the surrounding nations any more.

Thus ends the first of two powerful odes on the fall of Nineveh. In the closing verses of this poem the emphasis seems to be laid on the ruthlessness and aggressiveness of Nineveh. Of all empires, Nineveh had been one most unashamedly founded on force and cruelty. Nahum teaches that force will be destroyed by superior force; 'for all they that take the sword shall perish with the sword' (Mt. xxvi. 52).

III. A WAR SONG. iii. 1-19

a. The wickedness of Nineveh (iii. 1-7)

Other aspects of Nineveh's wickedness are indicated, namely her commercial unscrupulosity and evil influence (1). Her sins are punished in 'the battle of the streets' (2, 3). These verses are a superlative example of Nahum's powers of description, and form one of the most vivid battle scenes in Hebrew literature. The confusion and noise as the chariots and horsemen attack, the glint of the sun on armour and weapons, the huddled dead lying in heaps about the streets, so thickly strewn that the advancing troops stumble over the bodies. What a grim picture it is!

Nahum then speaks of the city of Nineveh under the simile of a harlot (4-7). This metaphor for sinful nations and cities was a favourite one with biblical writers. Sometimes it was used to describe idolatry. The people of Israel worshipping other gods were compared to an adulterous woman (Lv. xvii. 7). It was also used of their action in imitating the ways of the Gentiles (Ezk. xxiii. 30). It condemned the practice of superstitions associated with idolatry (Lv. xx. 6). Finally, as here, it was applied to the exchanges of trade which the Gentile peoples carried on among themselves. It is evident that after her conquests Nineveh endeavoured to build herself up as a centre of world commerce. Presumably this was for the sake of the wealth and luxuries to be gained thereby. She approached people with her wares. She deceived them by her lies. She enervated them with her luxuries. Like a harlot she corrupted them with her immoralities. For these sins also will she be punished. Instead of honour, she will be a *gazingstock* (6). Instead of fine living and soft clothing, she will be humiliated with every circumstance of degradation (5, 6).

b. Comparison with Egypt (iii. 8–15)

To convince Nineveh of the certainty of her doom, Nahum reminds her of the fate of *populous No* (8), i.e. 'No-amon', or Thebes, which fell despite its strength. This town, described by Homer (*Iliad* ix. 383) as hundred-gated, was the most ancient and most honourable in Upper Egypt. Of great extent, it was beautified with temples, obelisks and sphinxes. It was situated on both banks of the Nile, the waters of which were led to the gateways of its temples by canals. The wonders of this mighty place may still be seen by visiting Karnak and Luxor. Nahum refers to its mighty river and canals whèn he writes of it that it *was situate among the rivers, that had the waters round about it* (8). In addition to its natural strength, No-amon formed powerful alliances. Ethiopia, a poor and backward country, but producing vigorous Sudanese warriors, was closely connected with her. Egypt stood between Thebes and her Assyrian foes in the north. No-amon was also helped by Put and Lubim, generally taken as signifying Libya (9). Put is translated as *Libyas*, both in the Vulg. and in the LXX. Yet, in spite of all this, the cruel Assyrians themselves overthrew No-amon (10). A like fate shall overtake Nineveh. She will reel and stagger under her misfortunes. The brightness of her glory will be clouded over. *Thou also shalt seek strength* (11); i.e. she will attempt to form defensive alliances just as Thebes did. But the forts of her outer ring of defences are ready to fall. Just as a man shakes a fruit tree and collects the over-ripe fruit which falls easily, so will the enemy gather up her forts (12). Her people have no stomach for resistance. They will open the gates to the enemy. The enemy will give their defences to the flames that they may never resist again (13).

As in ii. 1, Nahum then ironically bids the city make ready for war. Let them lay in a water supply that will not become exhausted during a long siege. Let them build ramparts and repair the breaches in the towers. Let them go to the clay pits, dig out the clay, mix with it straw, set it in moulds, fire it in the kilns, and repair the walls with it (14). Such measures, though very necessary, were somewhat late, when the enemy was at hand. The great buildings of Nineveh will be given to the flames. The sword will cut down her chief men. The city will be stripped bare as a field is denuded by the *cankerworm* (15), i.e. the locust.

c. The irremediable doom (iii. 16–19)

The prophet takes up this figure of the locust, one of the facts of nature familiar to oriental minds, and serving for a favourite literary illustration. Having already applied it to the ravages of the invading army (15a), he now uses it to describe the numbers of Nineveh's citizens (15b, 16). The captains of the city are as many as grasshoppers or locusts. Her military men are gathered within her like a swarm of grasshoppers, gathering together for warmth in the bushes on a cold day. But when the sun shines forth, they will scatter. There will not be one to be seen. As the locusts suddenly disappear, rising in clouds to seek new fields, so will the men of war in Nineveh's evil day take flight in every direction (17).

Thy shepherds slumber (18). Hence the people are *scattered upon the mountains* like lost sheep with none to gather them into the fold. The picture is of a helpless nation deprived of all its leaders. *There is no healing of thy bruise* (19). For Assyria there is no hope of a 'remnant'. This is the end. And the *bruit* (i.e. 'news') of her overthrow will cause satisfaction in all places where her wickedness has been experienced.

A. FRASER.

HABAKKUK

INTRODUCTION

I. THE AUTHOR

We know nothing about Habakkuk apart from his book, and even here he does not give us his genealogy or tell us when he prophesied. The name itself is akin to an Assyrian word which signifies a plant or vegetable. In the LXX it appears as *Ambakoum*. Jerome derived it from a Hebrew root meaning 'to clasp' and said 'he is called "Embrace", either because of his love to the Lord, or because he wrestles with God'. Luther and many modern commentators have favoured the same derivation. It is certainly not unfitting, for in this little book we see a man, in deadly earnest, wrestling with the mighty problem of theodicy—the divine justice—in a topsy-turvy world. The same sort of conflict meets us in the larger book of Job.

Habakkuk is the first prophet to arraign not Israel but God. The book contains a soliloquy between himself and the Almighty. What baffles him is the apparent discrepancy between revelation and experience. He seeks an explanation. No direct answer is given to his query, but he is assured that patient faith will win the day (ii. 4). He expresses this faith very vividly in iii. 17-19, where the sentiment finds a more recent echo in William Cowper's hymn: 'God is His own interpreter, and He will make it plain.'

Because of the musical arrangement of chapter iii, some have thought that Habakkuk was a Levite. It may be that he was a member of a professional guild of prophets attached to the temple (1 Ch. xxv. 1). He is the only one of the canonical prophets who styles himself a 'prophet' (i. 1), and this is thought to indicate professional status.

Habakkuk appears in the Apocryphal story of Bel and the Dragon as the one who rescued Daniel from the lions' den for the second time; but this is only legend.

II. DATE AND OCCASION

In i. 6 we are told that God is raising up the Chaldeans (i.e. the Babylonians) as an instrument of punishment. This no doubt refers to the revived kingdom of Babylonia which overthrew the weakened Assyrian Empire at the close of the fifth century B.C. Nineveh was destroyed in 612 B.C. and Nebuchadnezzar king of Babylon defeated Pharaoh-Necho of Egypt at Carchemish in 605.

Three years before this battle, Pharaoh-Necho slew Josiah king of Judah at Megiddo (2 Ki. xxiii.

29, 30; 2 Ch. xxxv. 20ff.) and set up puppet kings on the throne of Judah, but neither he nor they were any match for the growing power of Babylon, and so, for the next twenty years, Judah was at the mercy of the Chaldeans and was finally carried away into captivity in 586 B.C.

The prophecies of Habakkuk clearly refer to this period and may have been delivered either before or after the battle of Carchemish. In both cases Habakkuk would be a contemporary of Jeremiah (627–586 B.C.).

In favour of the earlier date is the suggestion in i. 5 that the raising up of the Chaldeans is still future and, at the time of the prophet's speaking, is still a thing to be wondered at (E. B. Pusey, for instance, dates the prophecy as early as the end of the reign of Manasseh, i.e. as far back as the phrase *in your days* in i. 5 will allow); in favour of a date after 605 is the detailed description of Chaldean methods of warfare as something already well known (i. 7–11).

The reign of the evil king Manasseh had been 'an age to try the faith of pious souls' (Kirkpatrick). The reformation under king Josiah (637–608 B.C.) had proved ineffectual and 'so the iniquity and perverseness (i. 3) of backsliding Judah must be punished. For this God is raising up the Chaldeans.

This is the general view of scholars. Some, however, refer i. 2–4 not to backsliding Judah but to some heathen oppressor. The oppressor may be Chaldea herself; if so, the text must be re-arranged so that verses 5–11 precede verses 2–4 (Giesebrecht) or are eliminated (Wellhausen). Or the oppressor may be Assyria: so Budde, who places verses 6–11 after ii. 2–4 and dates the prophecy just after 625 B.C. when Nabopolassar the Chaldean made himself independent of Assyria. But in this case why is Assyria not mentioned? Thirdly there is Egypt: so G. Adam Smith, who compares i. 2–4 with 2 Ki. xxiii. 33–35.

But Habakkuk's complaint in i. 12—ii. 1 is not that God is using one heathen nation to punish another, but that He is using a heathen nation to punish Judah. In spite of the rediscovery of the law in the temple in 621 B.C. (2 Ki. xxii. 8; cf. Hab. i. 4), the people of Judah are bent on violence and injustice. The rearrangement of the text to suit a particular theory is always a questionable expedient. It seems safer to take the text as it stands and refer i. 2–4 to the people of Judah.

A conservative critic, W. A. Wordsworth, puts

the delivery of the prophecy a century earlier and makes Habakkuk the contemporary of Isaiah, with whose prophecies he finds many affinities in Habakkuk. The peg-date is then the capture of Babylon by the Chaldean, Merodach-baladan, in 721 B.C. Others, with a certain amount of support from the Greek versions, omit the word 'Chaldeans' in i. 6 altogether, or else, with Duhm, substitute for it the word 'Kittim', i.e. Cypriot Greeks, and so place the book in the days of Alexander the Great, c. 333 B.C. Such views demand considerable tinkering with the text and are not very feasible. But it is interesting to note that the recently discovered Dead Sea Scroll which contains the Habakkuk commentary, although lacking the first half of i. 6, has this note about it: 'interpret (this) of the Kitti'im, whose fear is upon all the nations.' This, however, may only be a 'modern application' of an older situation.

It seems best then to put the date of Habakkuk at about 600 B.C., or a little earlier.

III. TEXT AND COMPOSITION

The meaning of the Hebrew text is not always clear and the LXX has a few interesting variations, e.g. the great assertion in ii. 4 is in one text of the LXX 'through and through Messianic' (T. W. Manson). See note *in loco*. Uncertainty as to whom various passages refer has led many critics to rearrange the text, and, in some cases, to divide the authorship. To some, Habakkuk is the author of chapter iii and the compiler of chapters i and ii; to others he is the author of chapter i and most of chapter ii, whereas chapter iii is a late poem of the Persian or Maccabean period. But many, like Kirkpatrick, J. Paterson and others, prefer to look upon the book as an artistic and connected whole.

It would seem that the prophecy was intended to be read rather than heard (see ii. 2). It is more in the nature of a meditation or speculatory poem than a sermon or harangue. The Psalm in chapter iii was evidently meant to encourage God's people in time of adversity.

OUTLINE OF CONTENTS

I. INTRODUCTION. i. 1

II. THE FIRST COMPLAINT. i. 2–4
  Why do the sins of God's people go unpunished?

III. GOD'S ANSWER. i. 5–11
  I am about to punish: the Chaldeans are My instrument.

IV. THE SECOND COMPLAINT. i. 12—ii. 1
  How can a holy God use an unholy instrument?

V. GOD'S ANSWER. ii. 2–4
  Insolence will be punished also, and patient faith will have its reward.

VI. THE FIVE WOES. ii. 5–20
  Against aggression, self-assertion, violence, inhumanity and idolatry.

VII. A VISION OF JUDGMENT. iii. 1–19

COMMENTARY

I. INTRODUCTION. i. 1

The theme is greater than the man, hence the briefest mention of the prophet's name and status together with his *burden*, i.e. prophetic utterance, or oracle. This word is practically synonymous with 'revelation': thus *did see* (as a 'seer'); cf. 2 Ki. ix. 25.

II. THE FIRST COMPLAINT. i. 2–4

How long shall I cry? (2). The prophet speaks as the conscience of the nation. He is troubled at the presence of iniquity among God's people to the detriment of all religious institutions. *The law* (i.e. *torah*) *is slacked* (4). Why does not God intervene?

Such a question could arise only in Israel. Only to men who believe in one God who is both holy and good and is at the same time the omnipotent creator and upholder of the universe can there be any real problem of theodicy. The dilemma 'if God, then why evil?' is no dilemma to those who believe in a pantheon of warring deities whose morals are hardly different from those of men and women. The thought of God's undeviating righteousness at once creates a tension in the light of everyday experience and demands an explanation. There are times in some men's lives when this tension becomes particularly acute, as here. *The wicked doth compass about the righteous* (4); surround him as an enemy with a view to causing his ruin.

III. GOD'S ANSWER. i. 5–11

The Chaldeans, who are already wreaking destruction on surrounding nations, are to be turned against Judah and to become, in God's hands, an instrument of chastisement. This is the *work* which the people of Judah *will not believe* (5), so incredible will it appear. For the Chaldeans worship their own strength (11) and with them might is right. They are a law unto themselves (7b) and mock at all authority (10). For *among the heathen* (5; Heb. *bagoyyim*) read 'ye wrongdoers' (Heb. *bôgh'dhîm*), or 'faithless creatures' (Moff.). In verse 8 the second *their horsemen* may be omitted. *Eagle* (8) is, of course, the vulture. Verse 11 is obscure. For *and offend* RV reads 'and be guilty', but this is meaningless as it stands. Perhaps punctuate after 'sweep by' (RV) and then emend the text and translate 'and his spirit (i.e. purpose) changes and he sets up an altar to his god' (I.C.C.), i.e. reading *wayyâsem*, 'and he sets up', instead of *w'âshem*, 'and he is guilty'. W. A. Wordsworth translates 'I will appoint him whose power is his God's', i.e. the messianic king.

IV. THE SECOND COMPLAINT. i. 12—ii. 1

If the Chaldeans idolize their own brute strength, how can they be used by a God who cannot, by His very nature, *look on iniquity* (13; RV 'perverseness')? If He uses them, then He must be like them, treating men as if they were *the fishes of the sea* (14) to be captured and slaughtered at will, the only consideration being the pleasure derived from their destruction (15ff.). The revealed nature of God and the actual object of Chaldean worship seem dead against the assumption that God can use the Chaldeans. The prophet can see no possibility of contact from either side. God must vindicate Himself. *I . . . will watch to see what he will say* (ii. 1). The prophet is deeply conscious of the urgency of the situation. 'He has a post to hold, a rampart to guard' (G. Adam Smith).

We shall not die (12). The Talmud has 'Thou shalt not die', which makes better sense. It is not necessary to regard the second half of this verse as an intrusion (*sic* I.C.C.). It is the fact that *thou hast ordained them for judgment* which creates the problem for Habakkuk. The LXX has a different rendering. In verse 16 there is a pun on the word *net* and the word 'accursed thing' which are practically the same in Hebrew.

What I shall answer (ii. 1). So Heb., LXX, RV. But probably read 'what He shall answer'. The person has been changed by some scribe out of a sense of reverence. The thought of God standing at the bar of human justice is certainly staggering.

V. GOD'S ANSWER. ii. 2–4

Chaldea, God's instrument of chastisement, is herself under God's judgment and will not escape the just penalty for her misdeeds. Arrogance and faithfulness each have their own reward, as those who wait will see.

At first sight, there does not seem to be anything very inspiring about this assertion. Some have even doubted whether it constitutes a 'revelation'. But, as has been pointed out, there is more here than meets the eye, and the use of this passage in the New Testament shows it to be indeed a pregnant one.

But whatever treasures the statement in 4b was later made to disclose, one thing is immediately clear, and that is that the prophet himself has been given the realization that the only lasting element in an unstable, wicked world is character. Tyranny, greed and pride are all self-doomed; only integrity lasts on.

Make it plain upon tables (2). Clay tablets were used in Babylonia (cf. Is. viii. 1). *That he may run that readeth it* (2); a Hebrew idiom. The meaning is: 'that he may read it quickly (whoever sees it).' *The just shall live by his faith* (4). This great theme is developed by St. Paul in Rom. i. 17; Gal. iii. 11, and by the author of the Epistle to the Hebrews in Heb. x. 38. The first half of the verse is differently rendered by the LXX which has: 'if he, i.e. the promised deliverer who *will surely come* (3), draw back, my soul hath no pleasure in him.' This version is reproduced in Heb. x. 38 but the clauses are there inverted. LXX continues 'but the just shall live by my faith'. The 'my' is omitted in Heb. x. 38. The Hebrew text of Habakkuk (cf. also Rom. i. 17; Gal. iii. 11) has 'his faith' (so also AV, RV) and the reference is, not to the Messiah who is to prove His identity by courageous fidelity to His commission, but to the believing soul who in 'faith' has the touchstone of perseverance. *Live* is used in the pregnant sense of enjoying God's favour with or without temporal benefits.

Here 'faithfulness' rather than 'faith' is in view; the term is wider than in Paul or Hebrews. But 'this faithfulness must spring from faith: hence Paul's insight is a true one' (Kirkpatrick). Calvin says *ad loc.*: 'the prophet here speaks of the state of the present life. What has this to do with the salvation of the soul? But whatever benefits the Lord confers on the faithful in this life are intended to confirm them in the hope of eternal inheritance. Hence when Habakkuk promises life in the future to the faithful, he no doubt overleaps the boundaries of this world, and sets before the faithful a better life than that which they have here.'

VI. THE FIVE WOES. ii. 5–20

These verses contain five predictions of the doom of the 'puffed up' soul. Cf. the six woes of Is. v. 8ff. Note the recurring phrase *because of men's blood . . .* in verses 8, 17, which may originally have been a refrain concluding each of the five woes. Some critics regard the last three woes as later additions, but S. R. Driver regards all five as authentic. Verses 5, 6a are introductory, but the text of verse 5 is corrupt. See the RV and RV mg. readings. Perhaps an adverbial clause 'as with wine' originally stood here.

a. Woe against aggression (ii. 6–8)

The two Hebrew words rendered *thick clay* (6) when joined together form one word which means 'debts'. RV reads 'pledges'. The spoiler will himself be spoiled.

b. Woe against self-assertion (ii. 9–11)

Set his nest on high (9). As birds build in the top of tall trees, so he seeks to put himself out of the reach of harm. For *beam* (11) LXX has 'beetle' (Gk. *kantharos*). Perhaps a mistake for camphire, the resin from the pine, which, like drops of blood, cries out against the oppressor. The root of the Hebrew word may be 'to dig' or 'to carve', thus it may refer to carved images—'dumb idols crying out for a manifestation of the living God' (W. A. Wordsworth). See Lk. xix. 40.

c. Woe against violence (ii. 12–14)

With verse 12 cf. Mi. iii. 10. Habakkuk is probably quoting from this passage. *Blood* may mean human sacrifice (see 1 Ki. xvi. 34). The meaning of verse 13 is that, since God alone can 'stablish a city' (Ps. cxxvii. 1), all human attempts to do so, however violent, are foredoomed to failure. *For* means 'only to satisfy'. Verse 14 is a free quotation from Is. xi. 9.

d. Woe against inhumanity (ii. 15–17)

That puttest thy bottle to him (15). RV renders 'that addest thy venom thereto'. By omitting one letter in Hebrew the phrase would become 'from the cup of thy fury' which makes better sense. *For the violence of* (RV 'done to') *Lebanon* (17). It is uncertain what particular invasion is referred to, unless this be the nearest to Judah that the Chaldeans had yet penetrated.

e. Woe against idolatry (ii. 18–20)

What profiteth the graven image? (18). For the sentiment cf. the latter half of the book of Isaiah. *It shall teach* (19). RV detaches this from the previous sentence and renders 'Shall this teach?' So RSV 'Can this give revelation?' *But the Lord is in his holy temple* (20). 'The prophet passes by contrast from the contempt of the dumb and helpless idols to the thought of the living God' (S. R. Driver). Thus we are prepared for the theophany of chapter iii.

VII. A VISION OF JUDGMENT. iii. 1–19

The tenses in this chapter are uncertain and may be past, present or future. The prophet seems to draw on all the great stories of the past history of Israel, particularly the exodus and the defeat of the Canaanites at the river Kishon (Jdg. iv and v). He pleads for a repetition of these mighty deliverances—*revive thy work* (2). Or else we have here an expression of his faith (cf. ii. 4) in God's present activity, in spite of everything to the contrary (see especially verses 17–19). God is even now coming to judgment.

The genuineness of this chapter has been called in question. There are no specifically Chaldean features. The calamities in verses 17ff. seem natural rather than due to enemy action. In chapter ii the downfall of the Chaldeans is to be brought about by natural causes; in chapter iii by divine intervention. But this is to point the contrast too sharply and it is better to see in this chapter an example of that 'faithfulness' by which the just man is enabled to look beyond present frustrations to eternal justice ceaselessly at work in the world.

Shigionoth (1). Cf. the title of Ps. vii. The Hebrew root *SGN* means 'reel'. Thus a wild, dithyrambic song. But the LXX here implies 'Neginoth', i.e. 'stringed instruments', as in verse 19. *In the midst of the years* (2). The LXX has 'in the midst of the two creatures', an interesting reading which in Pseudo-Matthew, one of the Apocryphal Gospels, is regarded as a prophecy of the nativity; hence the ox and the ass in conventional pictures of the infant Saviour.

God came from Teman (3). For the tenses see note above and RV mg. Teman was a district of Edom; hence Edom itself. Cf. Am. i. 12. *Paran* (3); part of the Sinai region; cf. Dt. xxxiii. 2. See also Jdg. v. 4, 5; Ps. lxviii. 7, 8. *He had horns* (4); better, as in RV, 'he had rays', probably an allusion to lightning flashes. God's coming is pictured as a storm rolling up from the south and breaking upon Palestine and its neighbours. *Hand* (4); i.e. 'side' as in 1 Sa. iv. 13 where the Hebrew is lit. 'by the hand of the way'. *There* (4); i.e. 'in that place'. *Measured the earth* (6). The LXX has 'the earth quaked'. Cf. RV mg. The suggestion is of an earthquake accompanying the storm. *Cushan* (7); a Midianite or Arabian tribe (cf. Nu. xii. 1 mg.). Otherwise Cushan-rishathaim (Jdg. iii. 8, 10), or Kishon (Jdg. iv. 7).

Verse 9 is very obscure. 'Nearly a hundred translations of this verse have been offered' (Delitzsch). *The sun and moon stood still* (11). A poetical description of their being hidden by the dark storm clouds. *Thou wentest forth* (13); RV mg. may be thinking of God's promised deliverance from the oppressor which Micah regards as already accomplished, so certain is it. *The neck* (13) may be part of a building; cf. Is. viii. 8. *The head of his villages* (14). RV, following the Vulgate, renders 'the head of his warriors'. The Hebrew is uncertain. Verse 16 is again difficult. For *that I might rest* Wellhausen suggests 'I will take comfort'. See also RV mg. This assurance or determination to wait quietly for the day of trouble to fall upon the aggressor (see RSV) probably lies behind the beautiful expression of 'living by faith' given in verses 17, 18. It is the knowledge that eventually he *will rejoice in the Lord* which enables Habakkuk to endure present discontent. Thus he discovers the answer to his initial questioning.

The last phrase of verse 19 appears in the LXX as 'that I may conquer by his song'. The *chief singer* (RV 'Chief Musician') was the master of the temple music.

L. E. H. Stephens-Hodge.

ZEPHANIAH

INTRODUCTION

I. AUTHOR AND DATE

The book of Zephaniah is the ninth of the books of Hebrew prophetic literature. In many respects it is a typical 'minor prophecy' but it marks 'the first tingeing of prophecy with apocalypse'. Zephaniah is a matter-of-fact man, sober and restrained, but he is not devoid of impressive powers of imagination and strong realistic figures of speech. It is certain that he was a young man, most likely not more than twenty-five years old, when he began to prophesy. He was contemporary with Jeremiah among the prophets, and with the good Josiah of Judah among the kings. Some scholars (e.g. Kirkpatrick, *Doctrine of the Prophets*, p. 237ff.) would say that Nahum was also a contemporary of Zephaniah and that Zephaniah appeared toward the end of the former's ministry which was, of course, concerned solely with prophecies regarding the city of Nineveh. With this all will not agree, for, it is argued, the destruction of Nineveh did not take place till 612 B.C. and Nahum must be regarded as prophesying nearer to that event than in the period covered by 640–621 B.C., which is the period within which Zephaniah must have appeared. (See note on this in Ellison, *Men Spake from God*, p. 70.)

The appearance of Jeremiah seems to have followed soon after Zephaniah's earliest prophecies. There are those who aver that they were practically the same age, but there is no proof of any close collusion between them. Indeed, at certain points, Jeremiah saw the weakness and danger of Zephaniah's sweeping and lightning-like revival. Doubtless he rejoiced in the reforms which Zephaniah's preaching prompted at the hands of Josiah, but Jeremiah seemed to see further—perhaps because he lived longer—and to view some of the reformation as a mere outward form, a fashionable gesture to a popular movement, and not a sincere, spiritual purification with qualities of permanence about it.

Zephaniah was the first prophet for a couple of generations. It was probably seventy years since any of the voices of the prophets of the period of Assyrian ascendancy—Isaiah and Micah—had been heard. The fate of Samaria in 721 B.C. had brought a solemn reminder of God's might and majesty and righteousness. It may have been that the fifty years before the reign of Josiah had sounded a new depth of degeneracy and barrenness in the history of Judah. In any case, Zephaniah's youthful vigour and zeal were qualities needed by the situation in which he was called to serve and they are easily discernible in his book. The forthrightness and the unsparing tone of the pronouncements of judgment are typical of a young man possessing strong convictions and manifesting an unusual degree of moral sensitiveness and earnestness. The reforming zeal of the young king Josiah (639–609) was well matched by the earnest preaching of the new young prophet. They were both 'come to the kingdom for such a time as this' and their youthfulness and the difficult years which moulded them fitted them well to play a worthy rôle in this new era. Dr. George Adam Smith suggests that Zephaniah's name, which means 'Jehovah has guarded (or hidden)', may indicate that his birth took place in the killing time of Manasseh (*The Book of the Twelve Prophets*, Vol. 2, p. 47). It is certain, at any rate, that when, in the providence of God, Zephaniah stepped to the front of the stage of events in Judah, it marked the beginning of a new line of prophets which was to contain Jeremiah, Habakkuk, Obadiah and Ezekiel (and Nahum, if the later date for that prophet is accepted), all of whom were to seek to save Judah from the fate which had already overtaken the northern kingdom. It is therefore possible to say with certainty that the main body of the book is to be associated with the reformation connected with Josiah which took place in 621 B.C., and it is reasonable to suppose that Zephaniah's preaching was one of the contributory causes of it. We may conclude, therefore, the probable date about 627 B.C.

II. CIRCUMSTANCES OF ITS UTTERANCE

As already indicated, the circumstances in which Zephaniah was called to prophesy were, at one and the same time, perilous and promising. During the long reign of Manasseh (696–642), the evil son of the good king Hezekiah, the moral and religious state of Judah had sadly deteriorated (2 Ch. xxxiii. 1–11). Throughout his reign he had opposed the revival of religion which had marked his father's reign. He had built again the altars which his father had thrown down and restored the debasing nature worship associated with the worship of Baal. Superstition, worship of the stars and even human sacrifice became part of a religion of outward form and ceremony devoid of inward reality, and without spiritual or ethical convictions. (See Appendix I to Kings, p. 333, 'The Religion of Israel under the Monarchy'.) It is possible to portray all this as 'the mark of a desperately earnest soul seeking blindly to propitiate the mysterious divine powers—the fanatical return to the religion of his grandfather' (I.S.B.E.), but it was, at the best, an externalism and a religious syncretism which paid too much deference to the Assyrian

736

overlords and it was sheer, headlong wickedness to the prophets. Those who had tried to preserve the purity of the worship of Jehovah were rewarded for their pains with persecution and even death. 'Manasseh shed innocent blood very much, till he had filled Jerusalem from one end to another' (2 Ki. xxi. 16).

It is true, of course, that from this attitude Manasseh repented before his death and 'humbled himself greatly before the God of his fathers' (2 Ch. xxxiii. 12). It is also apparent that the evil tendencies of his reign had not completely won the support of the people. Once again a remnant had not bowed the knee; there were those who wished and worked for better times. It was this factor which made the times promising as well as perilous. Josiah came to a nation, many of whom yearned for a purer religion, and were ready both to hear Zephaniah and to follow the king in his reforming zeal.

Mention must also be made of the Scythian invasion of Media and Assyria in 632 B.C. which turned their fruitful fields into a desert as if a swarm of locusts had marched past. 'War was their chief business and they were a terrible scourge to the nations of Western Asia. They broke through the barrier of the Caucasus in 632 B.C. and, pushing across Mesopotamia, they ravaged Syria and were about to invade Egypt when Psammitichus I bought them off with rich gifts' (Porter, I.S.B.E., p. 2706). The account of this invasion, which is given by Herodotus in Book IV of his History, has received some confirmation in recent researches on the subject, and it serves to account for the waning power of Assyria, enabling Josiah to carry out his reforms, and giving Babylon the opportunity to seize the ascendancy. Some scholars, on the other hand, doubt the accuracy of Herodotus' account because of the demonstrable errors which it contains and because it is our only authority for the story that they swept so far south and west as the Egyptian border. Moreover, it is argued that, since we are here dealing with 'the typical vague language of eschatology, where everything is seen through a haze of dust', the judgments here announced cannot refer to this invasion. (See Ellison, *Men Spake from God*, pp. 81, 68.) It is not essential, however, to suppose that the Scythian invasion is here portrayed, but it is reasonable to hold that, knowing of it as he most certainly would, Zephaniah should see in it a picture of what would happen if Judah persisted in her present course of rebellion against the Lord. As a matter of fact the Scythian invasion does not seem to have touched Judah at all; her ultimate oppressor and instrument of God's judgment was Babylon.

III. ZEPHANIAH'S MESSAGE

Zephaniah was an inhabitant of Jerusalem. This is obvious from certain references to specific parts of the city which could have been made only by one well acquainted with them (cf. i. 4, 'from this place'; see also i. 10, 11, 12). In the city he observes a populace, bent on living by force and fraud among themselves, and idolatrous and sceptical towards God. His early prophecies are, on that account, almost unrelieved gloom; the dark line in the face of God is very clearly seen in the picture we have in i. 1—iii. 8. From that point onward a new note is sounded, the hope of universal salvation and ultimate restoration for Judah. The section iii. 9–20 is so different from what precedes it that some scholars would dissociate it from the rest of the book; but there is no real reason why this should be done. It is true that the great burden of Zephaniah's prophetic preaching was about judgment, swift, imminent and disastrous, on Judah and the surrounding nations. Yet we often find that those who discern most clearly God's judgments abroad in the world are those who also see the rainbow of His love and mercy arching the horizon of the future. And while Zephaniah foretold the judgments upon Judah, he foresaw them as a necessary purgative essential to Judah's becoming the blessed of the Lord and His handmaiden to the whole world.

OUTLINE OF CONTENTS

I. GENERAL PROPHECY OF GOD'S JUDGMENTS. i. 1—ii. 3
    a. Judgment declared (i. 1–6)
    b. Judgment defined (i. 7–13)
    c. Judgment described (i. 14–18)
    d. Judgment may yet be avoided (ii. 1–3)

II. DETAILED PROPHECY OF GOD'S JUDGMENTS. ii. 4—iii. 8
    a. Philistia (ii. 4–7)
    b. Moab and Ammon (ii. 8–11)
    c. Egypt (ii. 12)
    d. Assyria (ii. 13–15)
    e. Jerusalem (iii. 1–8)

III. BLESSING PROMISED. iii. 9–20
    a. To the remnant of Judah (iii. 9–13)
    b. To the whole Israel of God (iii. 14–20)

COMMENTARY

I. GENERAL PROPHECY OF GOD'S JUDGMENTS. i. 1—ii. 3

a. Judgment declared (i. 1–6)

The book opens with the more or less usual biographical note, a kind of author's signature (cf. Ho. i. 1; Zc. i. 1; Am. i. 1), although here it is unusually long and detailed. G. A. Smith points out that it is not usual in the Old Testament to carry a man's genealogy beyond his grandfather except for some special purpose, or in order to include some ancestor of note (*The Book of the Twelve Prophets*, Vol. 2, p. 47). If this is really so here in the call of Zephaniah, it raises the interesting problem whether the Hezekiah referred to was the good king of Judah (2 Ki. xviii; 2 Ch. xxix) or not. In spite of the fact that the words 'king of Judah' are omitted after his name, there seems no insuperable difficulty in the matter, for he was outstandingly great and his fame needed no such tag to denote who he was. That being so, it follows first that Zephaniah was a very young man. Four generations separate him from his illustrious ancestor so that G. A. Smith's conclusion seems sound, 'In 627 Jeremiah calls himself but a boy and Zephaniah can hardly have been out of his teens' (Je. i. 6, 7). It also follows that Zephaniah came of royal stock and this adds interest to his 'condemnation of the royal house for their aping of foreign manners and for the high-handed wrongs practised by their retainers' (Cam. Bible, p. 96).

An alternative to this 'royal prince' theory about Zephaniah is that of Sellin, according to which *Cushi* (1), which means 'Ethiopian' (i.e. Egyptian), would indicate that Zephaniah's grandfather had been an ardent pro-Egyptian in the dark days of Manasseh and had given his son this name, a rather strange one for a Hebrew. It would immediately call for an explanation here in view of the fact that in Dt. xxiii. 8 no Egyptian or Ethiopian could be admitted to the Jewish community unless he could show a pure Jewish pedigree for at least three generations. Zephaniah's line of descent, therefore, is traced back three more generations and it is this which accounts for its unusual length rather than any royal dignity attaching to the name of Hezekiah, who would be styled 'king of Judah' if the person referred to were that well-known figure in their not so distant past.

In the days of Josiah . . . king of Judah (1) might, of course, mean anything from 639 to 609 B.C., but the whole tone of i. 2—iii. 8 is such as to suggest that these prophecies must have been delivered before Josiah's great reformation in the eighteenth year of his reign, i.e. in 621 B.C. (2 Ki. xxii. 3). Other views which conflict with this have been advanced. Two typical points raised centre in two references. First the phrase *remnant of Baal* (4) might imply that the reformation was well past, and secondly *the king's*

children (8; RV 'sons') are referred to as if they were grown men. It may be said, however, that the former phrase is a doubtful reading (LXX has *the names of Baal*) and that the latter one could mean nothing more than the royal family in general. Moreover, the particular vices and practices condemned in this book are exactly those which Josiah wiped out. There can be little room for doubting that the phrase referred to has to be placed within the period between 630 and 621 B.C.

The judgment predicted is directed against Judah and especially against *the inhabitants of Jerusalem* (4). This visitation, referred to in verse 7 as *the day of the Lord*, is represented as destroying everything 'from off the face of the ground' (2, RV), cattle, fowl, fish of the sea, and man being mentioned in turn. Even idols, which seems to be the sense of *makhsheloth* translated *stumblingblocks* in AV and RV (cf. Ezk. xiv. 3, 4, 7), will not escape and those wicked men who worship them will not be spared.

Jerusalem seems to be regarded by the prophet as the fountain-head of the rampant evil and idolatry of the period. When God acts in such judgments, He begins at the house of God. All traces of the worship of Baal, the god of the Phoenicians, would be *cut off* (4). The last vestige of it (which seems to be the sense in which *the remnant of Baal* is to be understood) would disappear and the 'Chemarim' (2 Ki. xxiii. 5), the black-robed priests of Baal, and the unfaithful priests of Jehovah would be destroyed together (4). In addition to the false priests, false worshippers of every class would be destroyed. They are described in verses 5 and 6. First, *them that worship the host of heaven upon the housetops* (5). This was doubtless some astrological superstition, which is never alluded to by the prophets to the northern kingdom, and which seems to owe its power in Jerusalem to the influence of Assyria. Then *them that . . . swear by the Lord, and that swear by Malcham* (5); i.e. those who seek to amalgamate the true worship of Jehovah with the pagan cults of their neighbours. *Malcham* means 'their king' and is thought to refer to Molech, the Phoenician god, whose worship with its atrocious child-sacrifice (2 Ki. xxiii. 10; Je. vii. 31) was to be found in Judah in Zephaniah's time. It is thought to be Canaanitish in origin (Dt. xii. 29–31, xviii. 9–14). Ancient tradition has tried to connect Molech with Milcom, the national god of Ammon; there is little to substantiate this idea (H.D.B., 617, 627). Finally *them that are turned back . . . that have not sought* (6); i.e. those who do not concern themselves with God, and are wholly indifferent. Cf. verse 12, 'settled on their lees', and see note there.

b. Judgment defined (i. 7–13)

Whether these false worshippers take notice of Him or not, the Lord Jehovah will come in *the day of the Lord* (7). *He hath bid* (RV 'sanctified') *his guests* (7). In His sovereignty He has already sanctified (consecrated), or appointed, those who would destroy Israel.

Doubtless, in this passage, Zephaniah has in view some terrible visitation of the providence of God, or some approaching enemy such as the Scythians. But 'this fact should not lead us to suppose that the prophets call any great visitation of God by the name of "the day of the Lord" ' (A. B. Davidson in Cam. Bible, p. 113). G. A. Smith points out that 'to Zephaniah, the day of the Lord begins to assume what we call the "supernatural". The grim colours are still woven of war and siege, but mixed with vague and solemn terrors from another sphere by which history appears to be swallowed up . . . In short, with Zephaniah the day of the Lord tends to become the Last Day. His book is the first tingeing of prophecy with apocalypse' (*The Twelve Prophets*, Vol. 2, p. 49). Hence this message may have immediately in view some such threat as the Scythians, who advanced from their northern strongholds to threaten Assyria and Egypt; but it clearly looks beyond it to the judgments of the end.

In the previous verses Zephaniah has already indicated some of the sections of the community in Jerusalem on whom the judgment will fall. He now includes the godless aristocracy (8) with their aping of foreign ways and fashions. *Strange apparel* (8) is lit., as in RV, 'foreign apparel'. In the second place he warns those guilty of *violence and deceit* (9). *Leap on* (RV 'over') *the threshold* (9). This has a reference to the priests of Dagon who avoided treading on the threshold of his temple because the idol had fallen upon it (1 Sa. v. 5) (Cam. Bible, p. 115). Verses 11–13 are aimed at those who in their luxury appear independent of God and His claims upon them.

This whole passage reveals Zephaniah's close acquaintance with Jerusalem and its landmarks, viz. *the fish gate* (10), *the second* (10; RV 'the second quarter'), a part of the city on the north side from which direction danger would later threaten, and *Maktesh* (11), some 'hollow place' (as the word is rendered in Jdg. xv. 19), again in the northern side of the city, where they would be pounded by their foes as in a mortar (see RV mg. and cf. Pr. xxvii. 22). His use of *Kena'an, merchant people* (11; RV 'the people of Canaan'), reveals acquaintance with the usage which identified the 'Canaanite' with 'merchant'. Cf. Ho. xii. 7n. It is doubtless in that sense we are to understand it here.

All of these classes will be resolutely sought out for punishment. Not one will escape when God comes to *search Jerusalem with candles* (12; Heb. 'lamps'), punishing those who have degenerated morally and spiritually and have become a byword for sloth and indifference (cf. Je. xlviii. 11, 12). *Settled on their lees* (12); lit. 'thickened on their lees' as in RV mg. The phrase is a picture of wine which has been standing undisturbed for a long time. The prophet uses it to describe those who, for want of the humbling discipline of the worship of God, have become 'thickened' and insensitive towards Jehovah. What a revelation the coming judgment will be for those who think of God as morally indifferent, saying to Him, *The Lord will not do good, neither will he do evil* (12); in other words, 'The Lord never does anything' (Moff.). In verse 13 the phrase *they shall also build houses* . . . was a common one signifying that they shall not enjoy the fruit of their labours (Cam. Bible, p. 117).

c. Judgment described (i. 14–18)

This passage describes, in some detail, the *day of the Lord*. It was to be a *day of wrath*, of *desolation*, of *darkness and gloominess*, of *clouds and thick darkness*, of *trumpet and alarm* (15, 16). There is no more vivid description of the 'day of the Lord' than here. Doubtless, like that 'day' spoken of by Amos, Hosea, Isaiah and Micah, and most fully of all by Joel, these prophecies were partially fulfilled in the judgments which fell on Judah and the surrounding nations of the sixth century B.C. But it must be clear that this application of the passage does not exhaust its meaning. It is not necessary for us to believe that Zephaniah's words were literally fulfilled in the consequent judgments which fell on Judah and her neighbours. Actually they were not, because they await the 'day' when universal judgment will be visited upon all wickedness and the wrath of God be poured out upon all who know not God and obey not the gospel of our Lord Jesus Christ. That will be a day of wrath and weeping and distress for all the wicked; it was the Vulgate version of verse 15, *Dies irae dies illa*, which inspired the opening words of the well-known medieval hymn by Thomas of Celano (*c*. A.D. 1250) on the last judgment. The description which follows here has features in common with the other prophets. With the physical display of clouds and thick darkness (15) cf. Am. v. 18, 20; Is. xiii. 10; Joel iii. 15; with the sense of alarm (or shouting) (16) cf. Am. i. 14, ii. 2; men will be utterly unable to escape and their hoarded treasures will be of no value (cf. Ezk. vii. 19; Is. xiii. 7) against the *fire of his jealousy* (18; cf. Na. i. 2; Ezk. xxxvi. 5, xxxviii. 19) until He shall make a *speedy riddance* (RV 'terrible end').

d. Judgment may yet be avoided (ii. 1–3)

O nation not desired (1). Here the prophet appeals to Judah; RV renders 'O nation that hath no shame'; 'O people unabashed' (G. A. Smith); 'not desirable, unworthy of the grace or favour of God' (Calvin). They are called on to gather themselves together (Heb. *qashash*, i.e. 'to gather straw or sticks'). 'Huddle and cower, ere you become like drifting chaff' (Moff.). The actual rendering of verse 1 is obscure and Ellicott prefers to read simply 'Bend yourselves, etc.' But if the exact text is uncertain the sense is clear. It is a solemn summons to the nation to penitence, reminding them that the opportunity for repentance was passing and the 'day' was rushing on them all like a threatening storm. They could seek Jehovah by humbling themselves and by observing His righteous judgment, and thus, by seeking Him in the face of their approaching desolation, they might yet be *hid in the day of the Lord's anger* (3).

The Scythian invasion of southern and western Canaan did not include Jerusalem in its sweep; in the providence of God they were hid from this danger. Now when Zephaniah is moved to foretell another cataclysm of a similar type, but more directly involving Jerusalem, he cannot get away from the ideas which the Scythian invasion suggested; neither can he get away from the belief that God in His mercy will find a° way of escape, not indeed for all, but for the *meek* (3) or, better still, the humble. *Anaw*, the Hebrew word used here, is the word used so often in the Psalms and by the prophets to describe the devout worshippers of Jehovah, and it carried with it the suggestion of an attitude towards God rather than towards men. The meek man is not necessarily the weak man, but one who bows, or humbles himself, under the hand of God, as opposed to the 'proud' and 'the evil-doers'.

There is no mention of the mercy of God here, it is true. Zephaniah's gospel appears sternly moral as he commands them to seek righteousness and meekness. But we are not to understand that he has quite forgotten or thinks otherwise than that

> *'Tis from the mercy of our God*
> *That all our hopes begin.*

II. DETAILED PROPHECY OF GOD'S JUDGMENTS. ii. 4—iii. 8

The authenticity of almost every verse in this passage has been called in question by one critic or another. Chapter i is written in elegiac measure; here the measure is broken in parts and abandoned in verses 8–12. Certain words found more often in post-exilic writings occur here and there, and a difference in tone is thought to betray another hand. All these objections are inconclusive and can be answered. Certain words, e.g. the use of 'meek' and 'meekness' as religious terms, do undoubtedly appear more frequently in the post-exilic Psalms and prophets, but this does not prove that they might not have been so used in Zephaniah's time (cf. Ex. x. 3; Nu. xii. 3; Is. ii. 9; Mi. vi. 8).

The objections to the verses 8–15 are finely summarized in F. C. Eiselen's art. in the I.S.B.E., p. 3145. It is claimed that Moab and Ammon (4–7) were far removed from the route taken by the Scythians along the sea coast. Secondly, a destruction of Jerusalem is presupposed in verses 8 and 10. Thirdly, the prophet's attitude to Judah (9, 10) is apparently different from that in chapter i. Lastly, *qinah* or elegiac metre is broken

in verses 8–11 after predominating in the remainder of the passage.

Against these objections it may fairly be said that, if the view is maintained that the prophet is not predicting the Scythian invasion but some subsequent one like it, some of these difficulties vanish at once. For example it would solve the first difficulty easily, although it is also to be remembered that what the prophet is announcing in chapter i is a universal judgment of which any invasion, even if it were the Scythian, is only a figure. The second objection does not seem entirely valid. As regards the third, it is to be observed that the promises are only to the *remnant of the house of Judah* (7) which is consonant with the judgment announced in chapter i. The break in the elegiac measure in verses 8–11 may or may not indicate some imperfection in the text. Or it may be explained by the fact that, in oratory of this kind, consistency in the use of a certain metre is not to be insisted upon.

The whole passage ii. 4–15 is a series of prophecies about certain neighbouring nations and those, like Ethiopia (12), who represent the distant lands. The conjunction *for* (4) connects it with the world-wide judgment proclaimed in the first chapter.

a. Philistia (ii. 4–7)

According to Herodotus (i. 103–106) this nation lay in the path of the Scythians invading from the north, but that invasion did not spread far from the coastal plain. The prophecy, however, has in mind an area of country bigger than that, as is seen again in verses 8–11. This prophecy predicted that this region, which was rich in tillage land and in people, would be reduced, as is seen again in verses 8–11, to one devoid of population and fit only for sheep. *Gaza shall be forsaken* (4); in the sense of depopulated. Note the play on words here. In the Hebrew verse 4a reads 'azzah 'azubhah and verse 4b 'eqron te 'aqer. Ashdod would be driven out by a surprise attack (interpreting *at the noon day* as meaning 'when least expected'), or by a bold and swift stroke that would be over and done with 'by noon day'. *The Cherethites* (5; cf. 2 Sa. viii. 18) were a Philistine clan, apparently occupying the sea coast. 'The Philistines are said to have come from Caphtor (Am. ix. 7; Dt. ii. 23; Je. xlvii. 4) which may be Crete' (Cam. Bible, p. 122), and in consequence the LXX translates the name 'Cretans'. *Canaan, the land of the Philistines* (5) was to be destroyed like the early inhabitants of the land (cf. Jos. xiii. 2, 3), and the narrow strip of coastline land would become *dwellings and cottages for shepherds, and folds for flocks* (6) that would 'couch by night in the houses of Ashkelon, and pasture beside Ekron' (7, Moff.). The use of the name 'Canaan' as synonymous with Philistia occurs nowhere else in the Old Testament, although in Egyptian inscriptions and in the Old Testament it is used in a sense which covers this as well as other low-lying parts of Palestine.

b. Moab and Ammon (ii. 8-11)

The prophecy denounces 'the loud-mouthed arrogance' of Moab and Ammon and nothing can be more drastic and destructive than the picture of their desolation in verse 9, viz. *the breeding* (RV 'possession') *of nettles, and saltpits* (cf. Jdg. ix. 45), *and a perpetual desolation* (cf. Ho. ix. 6). The disappearance of Moab and Ammon took place long before the coming of Christ, but it did not take place till long after the reign of Josiah or even Jehoiakim. The completeness of the disappearance of Moab's former glory in accordance with this prophecy has often been the comment of modern archaeologists.

c. Egypt (ii. 12)

Egypt is here called Ethiopia, G. A. Smith thinks, on account of its long subjection to Ethiopic dynasties. Others find the reason for it in the close connection existing between Egypt and Ethiopia as allies in time of war (cf. Je. xlvi. 2-9; Ezk. xxx. 5-9). This prophecy was fulfilled when Nebuchadnezzar conquered Egypt in the thirty-seventh year of his reign, 568 B.C.

d. Assyria (ii. 13-15)

The elegiac measure (15) is renewed here where we have the prediction of the utter destruction of the Assyrian Empire, 'the climax and fount of heathendom'. This happened in 612 B.C. 'It was 230 years since Israel first felt the weight of Assyria's arms. It was more than a hundred since her hosts had swept through Palestine and for at least fifty her supremacy had been accepted by Judah. Now the colossus began to totter. As she had menaced, so she was menaced. The ruins with which she had strewn western Asia, to these were to be reduced her own impregnable and ancient glory. It was the close of an epoch' (G. A. Smith, *The Twelve Prophets*, Vol. 2, p. 66). *Bittern* (14); Heb. *qippodh*. RV renders 'porcupine'. The LXX has 'hedgehog'. Smith observes that it is birds which would naturally roost on capitals and therefore 'bittern' is the better rendering. Those who favour 'hedgehog' say that so great will the desolation be that the pillar-capitals would be lying strewn on the ground; the vacant windows will echo to the song of the birds and the inner glories of the mansions of Nineveh will be laid bare to the curious gaze of the idle passer-by and to the ruinous effect of wind and weather. Moffatt translates verse 14b thus: 'Owls hoot in her windows' (here reading *qom*, 'owl', for *qol*, 'voice') and 'ravens on her door-steps' (here reading for *horebh*, 'desolation', the LXX choice of '*orebh*, 'raven'). It is certain that nothing seemed more improbable when it was first uttered; but so it happened even as the prophet foretold. The nation which ruled the world was brought to nothing. The place which was once the centre of pride and glory became nothing more than 'a few mounds and monuments in a wilderness, at which the traveller shakes his head'. So fickle is earthly glory and uncertain her

rewards. The phrase *shall hiss, and wag his hand* (15) is expressive of intense scorn and contempt. (Cf. Ezk. xxvii. 36; La. ii. 15, 16; Na. iii. 19.)

e. Jerusalem (iii. 1-8)

The city is charged with impurity and injustice (1), with disobedience and haughtiness towards the prophets (2a), with indifference to, and independence of, God (2b). All her leaders are alike guilty, the *princes* of violence and cruelty, the *judges* of greed and deceit (3). Follow RV in this verse and read 'they leave nothing till the morrow'. The very *prophets* are *light and treacherous persons* (4), or, better, 'braggarts and traitors' (G. A. Smith). 'The figure expressed by "light" is that of the boiling over of water (Gn. xlix. 4; Jdg. ix. 4) and the word characterizes the prophets as vapourers, extravagant and arrogant in their own imaginations and conceits' (A. B. Davidson, Cam. Bible, p. 129). *Treacherous* has undoubtedly the idea of disloyalty or falsehood toward God. In the book of Proverbs it is often used as a parallel to 'wicked' and carries the idea of one who acts untruly to the moral law. This would make the charge one of immoral conduct (cf. Je. xxiii. 14, xxix. 23).

Moreover, the entire city had forgotten that the Lord, who can do no unrighteousness, was in her midst (5). 'Morning by morning does his justice dawn' (Moff.). How foolish then of Jerusalem to be proud and arrogant when He who has 'wiped out nations, ruining their ramparts, emptied their streets till none walks there' and destroyed their towns so that there is 'not a soul to inhabit them' (6, Moff.) is ready to cut off the erstwhile holy city. To these nations an appeal had been made to be humble under the mighty hand of God and to accept His discipline (7). He would have been gracious to them but they heeded not and so perished. Hence Zephaniah appeals in the name of God to Jerusalem to turn to Him (8), for He will surely destroy everything that rises up against Him.

Two things are worthy of note in this passage. Up to this point we have not had the same keen ethical sensitiveness such as Micah had; there have been only a few indirect references to social sins (e.g. ii. 3). But here Zephaniah shows that they were far from being forgotten. Indeed, it would seem as if he had kept this to the end. To Zephaniah, as to the other prophets, social unrighteousness was the height of iniquity, the supreme sin, the unanswerable indictment of their corrupt worship of God. Secondly, there is little doubt that 'the tinges of apocalypse' begin to appear here. Zephaniah is soaring far above and beyond the iniquities of Judah and the nations, and even beyond the events of the impending future to the time and judgment of the End.

III. BLESSING PROMISED. iii. 9-20

a. To the remnant of Judah (iii. 9-13)

These verses speak of a day when, as a result of God's disciplinary judgments, there would be world-wide conversion. With God, judgment is not an end in itself. He does not punish gratuitously. His judgment is always just, and here it is seen accomplishing a beneficent, redeeming purpose. These verses refer, in the first instance, to the chastened and humble remnant, *an afflicted and poor people* (12), who would come up from captivity after their city had been destroyed by the Chaldeans. But a wider application of the passage is certainly in view for, as throughout the whole book, we find the vision of the prophet is world-wide. The judgment of the day of the Lord's anger would fall upon all (ii. 4–15) and, in the same manner, the blessings of the gospel would be as universal as the judgments (ii. 11, iii. 9, 10). The Hebrew text of verses 9, 10 is not clear, and much discussion has been given to its admissibility after verses 1–8. The meaning of the passage is, however, obvious, viz. that from Ethiopia, which was considered the end of the earth, and beyond, there would be those to whom God would give a purified lip (which is the literal meaning of the phrase, *a pure language*) so that they might all, Jew and Gentile (cf. Is. lxvi. 19, 20), call upon the name of the Lord in a new and better covenant, and serve Him *with one consent* (Heb. 'with one shoulder').

b. To the whole Israel of God (iii. 14–20)

The final verses are in so different a strain that some scholars steadfastly maintain that they belong to the later days when the remnant came back from exile to their own land. Even if this were so, it would not be inconsistent with the fullest inspiration of the book as a whole; but the possibility of their being Zephaniah's authentic voice is far from being disproved.

The prophet is doubtless speaking here in poetic vein of the great days which were ahead when the Lord would be King over His redeemed people (cf. Is. xliv. 6) and they would have no more trouble. By his use of the 'prophetic' perfect (see verse 15) he projects himself into the future and describes the things which are not yet a reality as though they had already taken place. The Lord would be among them, a warrior to rescue them (cf. Is. xlii. 13), One who would thrill with joy over them, renewing His love, and exulting with a festal song (so Moff. in verse 17). Furthermore, we may conceive of the prophet looking down through the centuries to a day of universal blessedness for the Israel of God. This magnificent note of prophecy is also heard in the later chapters of Isaiah, but it is a vision as yet only dimly seen and partially understood. 'He has not yet found the vision great enough for his song. He has the music; he has not yet found his theme and the prophetic word has to move forward to a vaster conception of redemption before it can rise again to its ancient majesty' (Orchard, *Oracles of God*, p. 123).

J. T. CARSON.

HAGGAI

INTRODUCTION

Haggai, first of the restoration prophets, has no recorded history. He was 'the Lord's messenger' (i. 13) and his testimonials are safely stored with his divine Employer. The message, not the messenger, is of prime importance. God, not His prophet, dominates the page.

I. DATE

It is impossible to fix with accuracy the period covered by the life of Haggai. It has been conjectured by some that he had seen the temple of Solomon. The conjecture is founded on ii. 3— 'Who is left among you that saw this house in her first glory?' This would mean that the prophet was at least eighty years old when his message was delivered. But the language of the verse, unsupported by other evidence, will hardly bear this interpretation. It is much more likely that he was born during the time of, and possibly in the land of, the captivity. The period of greatest probability would therefore be the first half of the sixth century B.C. His message, however, is so closely linked with contemporary history that it can be definitely fixed as being delivered in 520 B.C. His age at the time is conjecture and we can only infer that God deemed it irrelevant. The dates so prominent in the prophecy refer, as dates always do, to passing things, but behind these we get a well-focused picture of the dateless character and requirements of God.

II. AUTHOR

Jerome explains the name Haggai to mean 'festive' (from *haj*, the 'festive' or 'exuberant one'). This, unless Reinke's surmise is true that it can be accounted for by the fact that he was born on some outstanding feast day, would suggest both divine guidance of his parents and, under the circumstances of the times, a strong faith on their part in the choice of a name for their infant son. They seem to have realized that though he might sow in tears yet he would one day reap in joy. The prophecy in the name was at any rate fulfilled, for Haggai was one of the few prophets who had the inexpressible pleasure of seeing the fruits of his message ripen before his very eyes.

We are left entirely to his own writings to form our estimate of the man. A couple of references in Ezra merely refer to him as 'Haggai the prophet'. There are no poetic flights of fancy in his book. His style is even considered by some to be dull and prosaic. But there is a terseness, directness and brevity in what he has to say. This brevity has led some to consider that we may have the message here only in condensed form. It may equally well be true that this characteristic, in common with the others, furnishes proof that the prophet was a messenger plain, straightforward and direct. The man, however, is shrouded in the work. He is characteristically God's prophet, speaking on God's behalf and establishing a kind of postal service between God and His people.

III. THE TIMES

Haggai had a very clearly defined work to accomplish. His task differed from, and was in some respects more narrowly limited than, that of either the former prophets or of his contemporary, Zechariah. Circumstances were different from those of pre-captivity days. When earlier prophets delivered their messages, the house of the Lord was there with all its outward glory, an honoured heritage from the past. The ceremonial observances were rigidly kept, so far as outward forms went. So meticulously observed in fact were they that the Almighty betimes grew 'weary' of the starkly dead formalities. When the people's religion thus ran to weeds they were inclined to look with self-satisfaction and deluded pride at their magnificent buildings and say, 'The temple of the Lord, The temple of the Lord, The temple of the Lord, are these' (Je. vii. 4). The call of the prophets was therefore a Spirit-inspired and sometimes anguished cry for a due appreciation by the people of spiritual values and for actions in keeping with their God-given religion. Attachment to the material and the formal had been getting first priority in their lives. (See Appendix I to Kings, p. 333, 'The Religion of Israel under the Monarchy'.)

Now those buildings are in ruins and the pendulum has swung to the other side. There is not even sufficient interest in the outward to impel the people to rebuild the temple.

IV. THE MESSAGE

The specialized, God-given task of Haggai is to galvanize them into action in a new effort in that direction. Arguments from past or future used by him are focused on that task.

Contemporary with and complementary to the work of Haggai was that of Zechariah. The very zeal and enthusiasm of Haggai for the material reconstruction of the house of God might tend to divert the people's thoughts from the God of the house and the glory of the coming Messiah. There was certainly room for Zechariah's message as well. We would, however, be doing Haggai a grievous wrong if we considered that material things were his only care or, as some will have it, that he was interested only in 'bricks and mortar'. The surgeon who specializes in foot diseases is not unmindful that the heart and bloodstream are vital to the health of the whole body and essential even to the success of his own efforts to heal a particular limb. No more was Haggai forgetful that the whole of vital religion lay behind the special work of the moment; and in his God-given revelations there was sufficient to justify him, in company with all his fellow-prophets, in searching 'what or what manner of time the Spirit which was in them did signify'. He saw the day of Christ afar off and was glad. He saw the restoration of the temple as a link in God's great chain of events. He saw in Zerubbabel, his prince, a living link in the human chain of the seed of David which was to reach unbroken to the Messiah's coming (Mt. i. 12ff.). He saw the glory of a kingdom into which one day the nations would flow and 'the earth would be filled with the glory of God as the waters cover the sea'.

The work to which God called both rulers and people of Judah through Haggai was the recommencement of an unfinished task (see Ezr. iv). The 50,000 exiles, who had taken advantage of the decree of Cyrus and had returned from Babylon to the homeland, had undertaken the rebuilding of the temple. The work, however, had been stopped owing, ostensibly at least, to the fierce opposition and bitter persecution by 'the people of the land', those plantation settlers who had come in during the exile to fill up the gaps in a depleted population. The real reason, however, was deeper rooted than this, viz. the lethargy of God's people. For about sixteen years the Lord's house lay 'waste', the sadness of the scene being intensified by the signs of the abortive attempt at reconstruction. Suddenly to this lethargic people Haggai comes, like a dispatch-rider from the headquarters of the supreme commander, and dramatically presents his message. Incidentally the record of God's providential dealings with His people reveals to us the key to the solution of the world's food problem. Condensed into Christ's words it would read, 'Seek ye first the kingdom of God, and his righteousness; and all these things shall be added unto you' (Mt. vi. 33).

OUTLINE OF CONTENTS

I. A MESSAGE FOR PRINCE AND PRIEST. i. 1, 2

II. A MESSAGE FOR THE PEOPLE. i. 3–12

III. A MESSAGE OF ENCOURAGEMENT TO ALL. i. 13, 14

IV. A MESSAGE FOR PRINCE, PRIEST AND PEOPLE. ii. 1–9

V. AN APPEAL TO ALL FOR THOUGHTFUL MEDITATION. ii. 10–19

VI. A PERSONAL MESSAGE FOR THE PRINCE AS DAVID'S SUCCESSOR. ii. 20–23

COMMENTARY

I. A MESSAGE FOR PRINCE AND PRIEST. i. 1, 2

This message came *in the second year of Darius* (1). This was Darius Hystaspes. The date is therefore 520 B.C. The year fits the events into their niche in history. The month and day mentioned serve as a point of comparison with the dates that follow, and thus mark the progress of the work.

Zerubbabel was then *governor of Judah* (1). The word translated *governor* (*pehāh*) is a foreign word and is a reminder that Judah is subservient to an alien power. This does not lessen responsibility to God. The fact that the message is addressed to Zerubbabel conjointly with Joshua, *the high priest*, shows that the civil ruler in his own department, equally with the ecclesiastical

ruler in his, has a responsibility for the welfare of the kingdom of God.

There is rebuke in the phrase *This people* (2). God does not say 'My people'. Sin estranges. The people were saying *The time is not come* (2). For this perennial excuse possibly one of several, or a combination of several, arguments would be used. It was harvest time and therefore the people were too busy. The harvests were poor and therefore times were hard. The work had been stopped sixteen years ago by the fierce opposition and persecution of 'the people of the land' and this opposition would flare up again on any attempt to resume the task. Counting from the final destruction of Jerusalem (586 B.C) the prophesied seventy years of captivity (Je. xxv. 11, 12) were not yet quite complete. The people were therefore waiting for God's time. This last, by lending an air of sanctity to their excuse, would give a breather to their stifled consciences.

The message that follows, addressed directly to the people (10), plainly suggests that the real hindrance lay in the lethargy of the nation. It is character—not want of time, or unsuitable times, or even opposition—that hinders the progress of God's work. There is no suitable time to men who are uninterested. Every time is suitable to those who are in line with God's wishes.

II. A MESSAGE FOR THE PEOPLE. i. 3–12

This oracle is of even date with the message just given to the nation's leaders. God answers the objection raised by asking a question, *Is it time for you, O ye, . . .?* (4). RV renders 'for you yourselves', i.e. a people like you and with a history like yours. There is rebuke in this very mode of address, *O ye*. The people are non-descript when they should have been manifesting themselves as the people of God.

Note the contrast between *cieled houses* and *this house lie waste* (4). A *cieled* house is one comfortably and ornamentally lined with timber. As timber was scarce in Judah's land *cieled houses* were a sign of luxury and expense. They formed a vivid contrast to the stone foundations of the Lord's house unfinished and weather-beaten by exposure to the elements during the last sixteen years since the attempt was first made to rebuild. A house, as distinct from a tent as a dwelling-place, or from an altar alone as a place of worship, denotes an abiding habitation. *Cieled houses* with the house of God lying waste imply therefore that the people desired to remain in the land in luxury, but had no anxiety that God, to whom they owed their return (Ps. cxxvi), should abide with them.

Consider your ways, says God (5, 7). Lit. 'Set your heart on your ways'. This is a kind of refrain throughout the prophecy. In Hebrew psychology the 'heart' signifies thought or attention. Facts would speak to them if only they would listen and attend. Their efforts towards self-induced prosperity have proved a failure. See verse 6. Every gift seems to go un-blessed. There is poverty even in the midst of plenty. Wages are earned but the earners reap no more enjoyment from these than if they had poured them into *a bag with holes* (6). The heart-rending futility of it all! 'Ponder this,' says God. 'Ask yourselves "Is there not a reason for it?" and does not that reason lie in your own manner of life?' *Go up to the mountain* (8), comes the command. This hardly waits for the logical result of their pondering. It is a command which calls for obedience irrespective of whether or not the result of such pondering leads them to connect their poverty with their forgetfulness of God. Is it that God would have them do His will as revealed by Him, out of love and with a noble faith, and not merely as a necessary condition of

material prosperity? 'Try the big experiment,' says God. 'Do My will. Seek first the glory of My house. Then you will by actual experience know how blighted fortunes can be changed to true prosperity' (see ii. 18f. and cf. Jn. vii. 17). Compare *Ye* (9) and *I* (11). God does not leave the people to draw false conclusions. He states the facts plainly. The people had made strenuous efforts, but they forgot that God has the last word in a nation's prosperity. *I did blow* (9); *I called for a drought* (11). Not chance, but God is supreme food controller.

Results soon followed. All three parties addressed obeyed the message. In their obedience there is recognition of God as their supreme Lord, of Haggai as His prophet and of the sweet reasonableness of the demands made. *Their God* (12). Note the return of the possessive pronoun and the closer relationship implied.

III. A MESSAGE OF ENCOURAGEMENT TO ALL. i. 13, 14

Then spake Haggai . . . in the Lord's message (13). This is a different description of the method of delivery, but the message comes from the same source. Heavenly power is wrapped in the words *I am with you* (13). This is the fact that has cheered men to do the world's greatest deeds. Cf. Moses (Ex. iii. 12, xxxiii. 14), Gideon (Jdg. vi. 16), Jeremiah (Je. i. 8). Under the same promise Christ's soldiers have battled and will battle to the end (Mt. xxviii. 20). Evidence of His presence was soon felt, *The Lord stirred* (14). God works through instruments, but the work is His. He works in us as well as along with us. We are not only fellow-labourers, but God-empowered workers in His kingdom. With what joy the prophet must have written verse 15. A wonderful building scheme had been not only conceived but put into effect in a couple of dozen days!

IV. A MESSAGE FOR PRINCE, PRIEST AND PEOPLE. ii. 1–9

There is a winsome graciousness about the timing of this message. It arrived on the last day of the feast of tabernacles (cf. Lv. xxiii. 34). This was usually a festival of gladness and thanks-giving for harvests safely home. This year the crops are poor. The people are despondent. The old men, as they look at the results of a month's work on the temple, are inclined to be retrospective and to compare present condi-tions with the glories of the past. There were fewer such old men now to weep than when the foundations were first laid (Ezr. iii. 12, 13) but their grief was no less intense. And the old men's pessimism tempers the young men's morale. Into their gloom comes God's message to but-tress their failing spirits by a renewed assurance of His presence with them (4, 5; cf. i. 13), with the obvious assumption that, where He is, difficulties cannot count.

Who is left? asks the prophet (3). Well-nigh

'the allotted span' of life has elapsed since the temple was destroyed. Few alive have seen it. *In your eyes . . . nothing* (3). Comparison with the former temple is almost sure to lead to a wrong estimate, because the man of eighty will not see with the same eye as he did as a child of twelve; the present work is only partly finished; and the true glory of any house of God lies not in an ornamented structure alone. Glory and glitter are not synonymous terms. The true glory of the temple lay in what it was—'My house'—not in what it was like. The command *be strong* (4) is the same for all three sets of people. Their tasks may differ, but the spirit in which they are to be undertaken is the same for prince, priest and people.

There is an unpolished practicability about the prophet's utterances. Terse and insistent comes the exhortation, *Be strong . . . work* (4). Cf. Jos. i. 6. In close connection with the above command stands the reiterated promise of God's presence, *For I am with you* (4). It is no excuse for idleness, but rather an incentive to toil, and the only guarantee of the success of the efforts of all parties. *The word that I covenanted . . . my spirit remaineth* (5), or 'abideth'. Both the AV and RV supply the words 'according to' at the beginning of this statement. The RV translates the second part of the verse 'And my spirit abode'. This addition of words gives the sense, though the cryptic style of the original is perhaps more impressive. God's presence with His people is not the outcome of a new promise but the fulfilment of an old covenant by a God who never changes and never fails to keep His word.

When ye came out of Egypt (5). The statement here seems historically inaccurate. The covenanters who had literally come out of Egypt were dead. Many generations had come and gone since the days of emancipation from Egyptian bondage. But God is the God who 'keepeth covenant . . . to a thousand generations'. The individuals pass but the nation remains. National covenants cannot die of old age. This covenant made with Israel in the days of their release from Egypt is counted by God as still in force in the days of Haggai. 'I am still with you, ready to fulfil My part of the contract,' says God. 'Are you ready to fulfil yours?' (See Ex. xix. 5, 6.) There is here a latent call to consider their ways. What connection is there between their forgetfulness of the covenant and their ruined country and want of material prosperity (i. 6)? Why Babylon's tears at all? Was it not because they had been untrue to the covenant and so missed the glory of what they might have been?

A searching question for individuals or nations always is, How true have I been to my covenant with God? The failure is never on His side. 'I am with you according to the word that I covenanted.' 'Consider your ways.'

Yet once, it is a little while (6). Lit. 'Once again and speedily'. Whilst opinions differ as to the events referred to in the context, the fact is patent that God claims supreme control among all nations and uses the 'shakings' for the advancement of His own kingdom. Cf. the shaking of the kingdoms of Persia, Greece and Rome before Christ's advent. A phrase which has lingered in our religious vocabulary is worthy of special note—*the desire of all nations* (7). Much as the hearts, especially of those who have found Him who is all their desire, would wish to follow ancient Jewish expositors and find a personal reference here to the Messiah, and great as would be the truth that would be thus expressed, the difficulty in so rendering the words seems insuperable. Though the noun is singular, the verb (*bau*, they shall come) is in the plural. The LXX translates 'the choice things of all the nations shall come', or perhaps 'the choice nations of all the nations'. See also RV. The construction of the sentence suggests that this happening not merely follows upon, but is the result of, the shaking of the nations. Whilst such 'shakings' were to be the precursor of and accompaniment to the coming of the Messiah, they could hardly be spoken of as the cause of the coming. The statement of verse 8 would seem to suggest that the influx is to be the silver and gold which, though they are in the hands of the nations, are yet under the control of God and will be brought when and as He wishes (cf. Ezr. vi. 8-10).

This will ensure *the glory of this latter house* (9), or 'the latter glory of this house' (RV). 'This house' refers to God's temple, whether built by Solomon or rebuilt by Zerubbabel or by Herod. It was 'mine house' even when lying 'waste'. The latter glory will exceed even that of the first building. *In this place will I give peace* (9); i.e. the grumblers of verse 3 will be silenced. The chief glory is not in gold and silver and hewn stone. The heart as well as the eye will find enjoyment. The deep-seated need of man will be met—peace. *This place* is first of all Jerusalem, the place where God's house stands. But the vision is widened for us today. The Prince of Peace has come. On His authority we know that 'neither in this place nor yet in Jerusalem shall men worship'. The spiritual temple of God is everywhere and peace still has its home there (Eph. ii. 16ff.). It is worthy of note how this section illustrates God's method of cheering the tried or the despondent by the promise of better things to be. His own Son endured the cross 'for the joy that was set before him' (Heb. xii. 2). Cf. Gn. iii. 15, xii. 2; Jn. xiv. 1.

V. AN APPEAL TO ALL FOR THOUGHTFUL MEDITATION. ii. 10-19

Two months have elapsed since the previous message. Meanwhile, we may assume, the work has been proceeding, the people being stimulated by a fresh voice co-operating with that of Haggai in its appeal for a turning back to God. Zechariah has now uttered his plea (Zc. i. 1, 3). Only a new love to God will impel the people to new zeal in building His house. Verses 11-14 form a background for their thoughts as they are asked further to 'consider' their way. See verses 15, 18. Consideration is now to be of their future path rather than of the past.

Ask now the priests (11). Go to the proper source of authority. Make sure of your premises before drawing conclusions. God is willing to reason with His people. Cf. Is. i. 18. The facts adduced are taken from well-known and established principles of the law. With Paul we might perhaps say 'Doth not even nature itself teach you?' We know that a touch of the polluted thing will defile the clean. A touch of the clean cannot, however, purify the defiled (Lv. v. 2). *So is this people* (14). Mark again the separation of defilement—not 'my people'. The people have been polluted by disobedience and by their lethargy in the rebuilding of the temple. Therefore everything they touch is polluted and consequently the blessing of God has been withheld from their work and possessions (see verses 16, 17). No good deed can merit the reversal of the curse, yet such is the marvellous grace of God and such His wondrous reward to those who keep His commandments that it will be noticeable that the improvement in their material prosperity synchronizes with the beginning of their obedience to God's command, even to the very day of laying the foundation of the house of the Lord. The prophet asks *Is the seed yet in the barn?* (19). It was not merely by intelligent anticipation based on favourable signs of a good year that Haggai was able to forecast an abundant harvest. Before the seed is sown he foretells it. On the rains of the ninth month and onward depended much of the fruitfulness of the following year. 'Do not consider it mere coincidence,' pleads God by His prophet. 'Mark well the very date of the change in your conditions. Consider . . . *from this day will I bless you*' (19).

VI. A PERSONAL MESSAGE FOR THE PRINCE AS DAVID'S SUCCESSOR. ii. 20–23

Twice in the same day God sends by His prophet (cf. verse 10). There is the urgency of love behind this. This second message of the twenty-fourth day of the ninth month has in it all the optimism of the God of hope and the confidence of the God of power. Neither heaven nor earth can withstand Him. Behind all upheavals is His hand. *I will shake*, says God (21). Lit. 'I am shaking'. It is a present and continuous process.

The convulsions of the Persian Empire, e.g. in the days of Darius, turned out to the advantage of the Jews. Darius was anxious to conciliate the Jews as subjects who had not rebelled, and equally to pursue the policy of Cyrus. So he confirmed the edict of Cyrus that the temple should be rebuilt. But the prophecy widens indefinitely. It visualizes the *kingdoms of the heathen* (22). Haggai gets a vision of tottering kingdoms with God's kingdom ruling over all. The 'I wills' are arresting. *I will overthrow : . . I will destroy* (22). Again, *will I take . . . and will make* (23). There lies behind these statements the quiet assurance of omnipotence.

Not by direct interference but by the process of events is God's plan fulfilled: *by the sword of his brother* (22). Yet there is no contradiction between this and the 'I will' of the previous part of the verse. 'Verily thou art a God that hidest thyself.' He works through others but it is He who works. Zerubbabel is given a beautiful promise, *as a signet* (23). The signet ring was very precious in the eyes of Orientals. It was likewise the sign of authority. There is beauty in the use of this symbol in connection with the promised restoration of Zerubbabel to the throne as descendant of David. Jeconiah's rejection had been made known by Jeremiah in these words, 'As I live, saith the Lord, though Coniah the son of Jehoiakim king of Judah were the signet upon my right hand, yet would I pluck thee thence' (Je. xxii. 24).

The promise therefore amounts to this: I will count thee most precious and will give thee a position of great authority. Both preservation and preferment are implied. And he owes it all, not to merit but to God's choice: *I have chosen thee* (23). As Abram and David and Solomon were selected, so Zerubbabel falls into line in the noble succession of the chosen ones in whose 'seed' the promises find their highest fulfilment (Mt. i. 12, 13). For behold, a greater than Zerubbabel is here. In the Messiah will be the completed vision. Of Him who sits for ever on David's throne it is said, 'He shall be great, and shall be called the Son of the Highest: and the Lord God shall give unto him the throne of his father David: and he shall reign over the house of Jacob for ever; and of his kingdom there shall be no end' (Lk. i. 32, 33). God has chosen Him 'as a signet'.

J. McILMOYLE.

ZECHARIAH

INTRODUCTION

Zechariah was the son of Berechiah and the grandson of Iddo. Ezra refers to him as 'the son of Iddo' (Ezr. v. 1, vi. 14), but this apparent discrepancy is simply removed by the assumption that Berechiah died before Iddo, and that Zechariah succeeded his grandfather in the headship of David's priestly course. Ezra's reference to him as the *son* of Iddo is to be understood in the more general sense of descendant.

Together with his contemporary, Haggai, Zechariah aimed at encouraging the Jews in the work of rebuilding the temple, which work had been in suspense since the first year of Cyrus (538 B.C.; see *Introduction* to Commentary on Haggai). The two main divisions of the book, namely, chapters i—viii and chapters ix—xiv, are so dissimilar in style and historical standpoint,

however, that it has become common to assign these divisions to different authors. But these admitted dissimilarities can well be accounted for without surrendering belief in the unity of authorship. For in i—viii the prophet is principally concerned with contemporary events, particularly the rebuilding of the temple; while in ix—xiv he deals with such future events as the coming of Messiah and the glory of His reign. Naturally, therefore, the former division is historical in style, whereas the latter is apocalyptic. It is probable also that the first part of the prophecy belonged to Zechariah's early life, and the second to his old age. The internal evidence of the book is favourable, as W. H. Lowe so clearly shows, to the post-exilic origin of both divisions, as well as to a unity of authorship.

OUTLINE OF CONTENTS

I. THE INTRODUCTORY MESSAGE. i. 1–6

II. THE EIGHT VISIONS. i. 7—vi. 8

III. THE SYMBOLIC CORONATION. vi. 9–15

IV. THE DEPUTATION FROM BETHEL. vii. 1—viii. 23

V. THE RESTORATION OF JUDAH AND THE DESTRUCTION OF HER ENEMIES. ix. 1—x. 12

VI. THE REJECTION OF THE SHEPHERD-KING AND ITS CONSEQUENCES. xi. 1—xiii. 9

VII. THE FINAL VICTORIES OF THE SHEPHERD-KING. xiv. 1–21

COMMENTARY

I. THE INTRODUCTORY MESSAGE. i. 1–6

The opening words of the prophecy are chronologically important, indicating, as they do, that Zechariah's commission came to him 'in the second year of Darius' (Hystaspes), or sixteen years after the Jews, by the permission granted in the decree of Cyrus, began to return to Palestine. The date is, therefore, 520 B.C. The prophet's first words to his countrymen are in the strain of remonstrance. Their zeal for the restoration of the temple had abated (cf. Hg. i). This slackening in effort was a clear symptom of a deteriorating spiritual condition, a departing in heart from God. For this very sin the Lord had been *sore displeased* (2; lit. 'angry with anger', denoting great indignation) with their fathers, and had sent them into captivity. Both their fathers and

the former prophets (4), who had forewarned them of the captivity, were dead; but God's words had *taken hold* (6), i.e. been fulfilled. The rhetorical questions in verse 5 would serve as a reminder, not only of the steadfastness of God's purpose, but also of the brevity of life and the transiency of its opportunities. A great work called for their attention, and there was no time for postponement.

II. THE EIGHT VISIONS. i. 7—vi. 8

a. The first vision (i. 7–17)

The call to repentance is immediately followed by a narration of the first of the eight visions which make up the earlier part of the prophecy.

This vision was given in the eleventh month of the Jewish year, the month Sebat, whereas the call to repentance was issued in the eighth month (see verse 1).

The scene of the first vision was a low-lying valley where grew a grove of *myrtle trees* (8). The characters in it are *a man riding upon a red horse* (8), who is referred to as *the angel of the Lord* (12), and *the Lord* (13), a company of riders upon horses *red, speckled* and *white* (8), an interpreting angel (9), and the prophet himself.

The rider of the red horse is clearly more than man or angel; He is the divine Mediator, the Lord Jesus Christ, appearing in this scene as the Protector of His people. The fact that He and the company around Him are mounted suggests both strength and speed; and the colours of the horses are taken by some to signify various dispensations of divine providence—the red horses denoting bloodshed and battle; the white, peace and victory; the speckled, or bay, an intermediate condition in which there are elements of strife and unrest, and yet of peace and prosperity.

Puzzled by the vision, the prophet turned to the interpreting angel asking *O my lord, what are these?* (9). In this instance, the interpretation was given by *the man that stood among the myrtle trees* (10), i.e. *the angel of the Lord* Himself (11). *These are they*, He explains, alluding to His followers, *whom the Lord hath sent to walk to and fro through the earth* (10). The hosts referred to then report to their Leader on their errand. *All the earth*, they said, *sitteth still, and is at rest* (11). This description fits in well with the contemporary situation. The calm which precedes the storm was upon the nations which composed the Persian Empire. This situation favoured the Jews in that it provided opportunity for the rebuilding of the temple. But the tidings were not altogether good, for Haggai, whose prophecy is complementary to that of Zechariah, had proclaimed this message from the Lord, 'Yet once, it is a little while, and I will shake the heavens, and the earth, and the sea, and the dry land' (Hg. ii. 6). It was in such a time of unrest that the prosperity of Jerusalem was to be restored; and the announcement that the earth was *at rest* indicated that Haggai's 'little while' was not yet spent.

The Angel of the Lord, having received the report of His horsemen, became intercessor for His waiting people. For *these threescore and ten years* (12) they had been in bondage in Babylon. Few had availed themselves of the opportunity to return which was given in the decree of Cyrus, and *Jerusalem* and *the cities of Judah* were in a sorry condition. *How long*, He pleads, true to His character as Mediator, *How long wilt thou not have mercy . . .?* His intercession is addressed to the eternal Father, but we do not hear His reply. The Lord who answered *with good words and comfortable words* (13) was the Intercessor Himself. The sudden transition from *the angel of*

the Lord to the Lord, which we have in verses 12 and 13, is not unusual (cf. Ex. iii. 2 and 4).

The comforting message spoken by the Angel of the Lord to the interpreting angel became the substance of the message which the prophet was commanded to deliver to his fellow-countrymen. God was not indifferent to their plight; He was 'zealous' for them 'with a great zeal' (14). The peaceful quiet which prevailed among *the heathen that are at ease* (15) must not be taken to indicate that He had overlooked their wickedness. He had been *but a little displeased* with Judah, and had used their enemies as a whip wherewith to scourge them. But they had *helped forward the affliction* (15), i.e. they had exceeded their commission, taking full advantage of the opportunity for plunder and oppression that the situation gave them. The time of Judah's recovery was at hand, however. The temple was to be built, Jerusalem to be restored and extended, and the cities of Judah to be numerously and prosperously inhabited (16, 17).

Many writers take the view that the myrtle trees in this vision (the myrtle being indigenous to Palestine) symbolize the Jews. The situation of the trees *in the bottom* of a valley may suggest their lowly condition at the time of the vision; but while that suggestion is not wanting, their position is clearly intended to symbolize their security (cf. Ps. cxxv. 2). Few and feeble though they were, they enjoyed the protection of the Angel of Jehovah and His mighty hosts.

It will be noticed that there is a threefold promise in the message of the interpreting angel: *My house shall be built . . . a line shall be stretched forth upon Jerusalem*, and *My cities through prosperity shall yet be spread abroad* (16, 17). The first of these predictions was fulfilled in the sixth year of Darius, i.e. four years after the time of this vision; the second was fulfilled some seventy years later, when Jerusalem was rebuilt by Nehemiah; and the fulfilment of the third prediction is to be found in the history of the Jews under the Hasmonean princes. The concluding assurance, that the Lord should *yet comfort Zion* (17), probably relates to that still more distant event—the coming of Him who is referred to by Luke as 'the consolation of Israel' (Lk. ii. 25).

b. The second vision (i. 18–21)

The vision is self-explanatory. The Lord had already declared His intention to settle accounts with the oppressors of His people. Those oppressors are represented here by *four horns* (18), symbolizing, it would seem, the four powers, Assyria, Egypt, Babylon and Medo-Persia, which had *scattered Judah, Israel, and Jerusalem* (19). The horns may be of less particular application, however, and may symbolize the four points of the compass, to signify that God would deal with the enemies of His people, from whichever quarter they might arise.

After four horns, the prophet saw four

carpenters (20); better 'artificers' (RV 'smiths'); these artificers symbolized the powers whereby God was to fulfil His promise of vengeance upon Israel's enemies. They were to *fray*, or wear down as by filing, the horns which had scattered God's chosen people (21).

c. The third vision (ii. 1–13)

This vision follows in direct sequence from the two that preceded it. The Lord had declared His purpose to rebuild Jerusalem and restore her prosperity. Now He gives a glimpse of the Jerusalem that was yet to be.

In this vision, Zechariah beheld a young man with a *measuring line in his hand* (1), whom he asks *Whither goest thou?* (2). The young man's reply recalls the promise in i. 16: 'a line shall be stretched forth upon Jerusalem.' At this stage the interpreting angel left the prophet's side to go in pursuit of the man with the measuring-line and bid him desist from his purpose. As he did so he was intercepted by another angel whom he directed to run after the man with the measuring-line and give him the message regarding Jerusalem that is recorded in verses 4 and 5, while he himself remained near the prophet to interpret.

The view that the *young man* referred to by the angel (4) was Zechariah himself hardly fits into the circumstances of the vision. For instance, it is difficult to understand why the second angel should be directed to run back to Zechariah, or why the interpreting angel should charge the second angel with the duty of interpreting the vision, since that function belonged so properly to himself. It is much easier to see the need for haste on the part of the second angel when we take the view that he was directed to overtake one who had already set out on his errand. On the view that Zechariah was the young man referred to, the need for this haste is not so apparent, nor indeed is it evident why the message of the interpreting angel should be given to Zechariah through the agency of the second angel since he was near enough to overhear what passed between the two angels. Zechariah had questioned the man with the measuring-line in regard to his purpose; now he must hear the interpreting angel's message to him, and, in turn, proclaim it to his fellow-countrymen.

It was indeed a most heartening announcement that the interpreting angel made, and one that agreed with what had already been foretold in regard to the coming glory of Jerusalem and the confusion of her enemies. Jerusalem was to be *inhabited as towns without walls* (4; Heb. *perazoth*). Many of the citizens, failing to obtain dwelling within the bounds of the old city, would require to build outside the walls. But, even so, they were to be perfectly secure; *For I, saith the Lord, will be unto her a wall of fire round about* (5). Within the all-encircling rampart of divine omnipotence they would dwell in safety. Moreover, the promise was added, *I will be the glory in the midst of her.* The Lord who had dwelt between the cherubim in the temple in the past would again glorify Jerusalem with His presence.

The promise of renewed favour to Jerusalem is followed by a summons to the Jews who were still in Babylon to *flee from the land of the north* (6) and return to their own country. Some regard the words which follow, *for I have spread you abroad as the four winds of the heaven*, as a promise of future extension; but the support of the context is given rather to the view that they relate to their past dispersion. Haste is urged for two reasons: first that the returning exiles might share in Jerusalem's promised prosperity; and secondly that they might escape the doom of Babylon. The words *after the glory* (8) may refer back to the glory promised to Jerusalem in verse 5, and may signify that after God had shed the promised glory upon Jerusalem He would visit her enemies with destruction, as He had threatened to do. But the fact that there is no article in the original before 'glory' does not favour such an interpretation. The more probable meaning is 'in pursuit of glory hath He sent me'; i.e. God was now to glorify Himself by punishing the oppressors of His people, so making manifest His unswerving righteousness and inflexible justice. Those nations, by *touching*, in a hostile sense, His people, had touched the *apple*, or 'pupil', of his eye. So Henderson understands these words, referring the possessive pronoun to *the Lord of hosts* (8) rather than to the enemy.

The shaking of the hand, or fist (9), is a well-recognized attitude of threatening. The tables were to be completely turned upon the spoilers; the people whom they had spoiled were in turn to spoil them. The interjection *Be silent* (Heb. *has*, corresponding to our word *hush!*) at the beginning of verse 13 gives a special impressiveness to the announcement that God was already *raised up out of his holy habitation* to intervene on behalf of His people. The reference in verse 11 to the *many nations* who were to be added to Israel probably carries the prophecy into messianic times.

d. The fourth vision (iii. 1–10)

The earlier visions promised great prosperity to Jerusalem; but the promise was conditional upon moral and spiritual reformation on the part of the people. That is the central lesson of this vision. *Joshua*, the 'Jeshua' of Ezra (ii. 2, iii. 2), was of priestly descent. His grandfather, Seraiah, is designated 'the chief priest' (see 2 Ki. xxv. 18–21). Josedech, or Jehozadak (see 1 Ch. vi. 14, 15), the son of Seraiah, the father of Joshua, was taken away as a prisoner to Babylon, where, probably, Joshua was born. The High Priesthood was revived in Joshua after the captivity. It is in his capacity as High Priest that he appears in this vision, where he is the representative, not only of the priesthood, but also of the nation.

The reference of the words *and he shewed me* (1) is not quite clear. The allusion may be to the interpreting angel or, more probably, to Jehovah by whom all the visions were given. The sight presented to the prophet was indeed a disquieting one. Israel's High Priest was seen standing before the angel of the Lord or, as He is alternatively designated, 'the Lord' (cf. 1, 2), utterly unfit to engage in his holy duties; for his *filthy garments* (3) symbolized sin—his own, and that of the people whom he represented. The scene suggests the setting of a Jewish legal trial, where the accused faced the presiding judge, and the pursuer stood at his right hand to accuse him.

Joshua was about to take up his duties as High Priest in the restored temple when 'the adversary' (2; Heb. *haṣṣatan;* the use of the article shows that 'Satan' is not here a proper name) intervened to accuse him; but he was immediately silenced. It may be inferred from the reference to Jerusalem in the Lord's rebuke (2) that the accusation was to be directed not only against Joshua personally but also against the entire nation. The Lord who has *chosen Jerusalem* had plucked it as *a brand out of the fire* of the Babylonian furnace, a fact which indicated that His people were precious to Him and destined to a great future. Vain, therefore, were the accusations of the adversary!

Verses 4 and 5 describe the transformation of Joshua. The angels who stood by were directed to take away his filthy garments and clothe him with clean raiment. This change was announced by the Angel of the covenant Himself as signifying that his iniquity had been made to pass from him (4) and that he was now fit to take up high-priestly duties, in token whereof the mitre of priesthood was set upon his head. The charges connected with his office were delivered to him by the *angel of the Lord* who *stood by* to superintend the proceedings (5). Joshua must walk in the ways of the Lord, i.e. cultivate personal holiness; and keep the charge of the Lord, i.e. be faithful in his office (7). Upon condition of dutiful obedience he is promised first that he shall *judge* God's 'house', an expression which probably denotes more than that he should have the principal charge of the temple; for the term 'house' is often used to signify the nation (cf. Ho. viii. 1). Secondly he will be given *places to walk among these that stand by* (7), a promise which refers not only to a higher ministry after death but also to the fact that, as a faithful High Priest, he would be a co-worker with the angels in the fulfilment of the purposes of God.

This message to Joshua has also a reference to the coming of Messiah. The Angel of the Lord, speaking for God the Father, *the Lord of hosts* (7), announces His purpose to bring forth *the BRANCH* (8). This messianic title is of fairly frequent occurrence (see Is. xi. 1, iv. 2; Je. xxiii. 15); likewise the term *servant* (see Is. xlii. 1, lii. 13). Here the two designations are conjoined, *my servant the BRANCH*. The promise of His coming is foretold to Joshua and his fellows because they

were *men wondered at*, or rather, 'men of sign' or 'type' (8), the priesthood being symbolical of Messiah's ministry of mediation and reconciliation.

The messianic strain of this passage is continued in the reference to the *stone . . . laid before Joshua* (9). The immediate reference is probably to the head-stone of the temple; but the ultimate reference is to Christ, the 'chief corner stone' of the spiritual house (see 1 Pet. ii. 6) The meaning of the *seven eyes* upon this *one stone* is not so clear as to permit of dogmatic assertion. There is ground for the view that the eyes were to be sculptured upon the stone in symbol of the perfection of Him who 'hath the seven Spirits of God' (Rev. iii. 1); but the better view, we think, is to understand the words as a promise that 'the seven eyes (i.e. the perfect watchfulness and care—seven being the number of perfection) of God shall be fixed upon this stone; that He will never, so to speak, take His eyes off either type or anti-type, till His purpose respecting them is accomplished' (Cam. Bible, p. 83). This view is confirmed by iv. 10.

I will engrave the graving thereof (9). 'These gravings represent the gifts and wounds of Christ, in allusion to the polished corners of the temple' (Trapp). 'It pleased the Lord to bruise Him' (Is. liii. 10). Thus 'the stone that the builders refused' became 'the head stone of the corner'. Messiah's sufferings were to result in the removal of *the iniquity of that land in one day*, with the eventual return of peace and prosperity to a penitent people.

e. The fifth vision (iv. 1–14)

The special importance, for Zechariah, of this vision is indicated by the manner in which it was brought to his notice. The interpreting angel roused him from a reverie, or sleep, with the question, *What seest thou?* (2). The principal object in his vision, on this occasion, was *a candlestick all of gold*, having a central bowl, from which proceeded seven feeding-pipes, one to each of the seven lamps which branched out from the central stem. The structure of this candlestick was different from that in the tabernacle and, later, in the temple (see Ex. xxv). The central shaft was, in this case, surmounted by the bowl, or reservoir, from which the lamps were fed, and around which they were grouped. The bowl itself was fed continuously with oil from two olive trees which stood, one on each side of the candlestick.

The significance of this vision was not immediately perceived by the prophet, and he inquired of the interpreting angel concerning it. The angel expressed surprise at his question, but proceeded with the desired interpretation, which takes the form of a message to Zerubbabel, the master-builder of the temple. The vision was the illustration of the message. The resources of human *might and power* were largely lacking to Zerubbabel and his helpers, and the obstacles which stood in their way were so mountainous as to make success appear impossible. But it was not by the 'might and power' of man that the supply of oil to the seven lamps was maintained; the olive branches, through the golden pipes, *empty the golden oil out of themselves* (12). Similarly, by the supply of the Spirit, symbolized by the oil, success should attend the exertions of Zerubbabel. The hands which had laid the foundations of the temple would yet place the *headstone* in position amid the joyous acclamations of the people (7). This message to Zerubbabel serves also for the encouragement of the Church in later times.

There is a caution in verse 10 against despising *the day of small things.* Several who had been engaged in the work of reconstruction had abandoned the task, and others had weakened the hands of the builders who had continued at work by stressing the utter inadequacy of their resources. The question *who hath despised the day of small things?* implies the answer that God does not despise it. The *seven* referred to in this verse are 'the eyes of the Lord'. The passage would be better rendered 'they shall rejoice, even these seven eyes of Jehovah', etc. This rendering agrees with the message of the angel of the Lord to Joshua, 'upon one stone shall be seven eyes' (iii. 9). The work proceeds under the perfect watchfulness and care of Jehovah. His Spirit shall stir up the people and provide Zerubbabel with all needed help for the undertaking, and His eyes shall rejoice at the sight of the plummet in the hand of His own appointed overseer of the work. The mountainous obstacles shall be overcome in His strength, and the task joyously completed.

Having received this general explanation of the vision, Zechariah desired a more particular explanation of one special feature of it, namely, the two *olive trees.* The answer of the interpreting angel is regarded by some to be intentionally obscure as signifying that the *two anointed ones,* or rather 'sons of oil' (RV), are two mysterious agencies or agents near to God and beyond human knowledge. This view, however, hardly fits in with the angel's rejoinder to the prophet's admission of ignorance, *Knowest thou not what these be?* (13). We prefer the view that the reference is to Joshua and Zerubbabel, 'sons of oil' in the sense that they were Spirit-filled men, who stood *by the Lord of the whole earth* (14), and were ordained by Him to be channels by which His blessing was to be communicated to the Church and nation. They stood *by the Lord* in their official character and, as the olive tree receives its fatness from the Lord, so these ministers of God, in Church and State, derived their spiritual influence from Him, and were used by Him to communicate His blessings to the people. The lamps fed in this manner would never go out for lack of oil. The continuity of the Church of God is guaranteed by this vision. Christ, her Head, unites Priesthood and Kingship in Himself, and she receives all needed grace out of 'His fulness' (cf. Jn. i. 16).

f. The sixth vision (v. 1–4)

Again the scene changed, and there appeared to the eyes of the prophet an inscribed roll of great dimensions, flying through the air (1). The fact that it flew in its extended state indicated that public attention was claimed for its contents; its message was for all to see. The nature of that message was indicated to the prophet by the interpreting angel. It was *the curse that goeth forth over the face of the whole earth* (3), or rather, 'land', signifying the land of Judah. Two sins in particular are mentioned as being denounced in the roll, stealing and perjury, these, probably, being most prevalent among the Jews at that time. It is not to be concluded, however, that the curse was pronounced against these sins alone. The commandments violated by these transgressions were representative of the whole law (cf. Jas. ii. 11).

The penalty of these transgressions was to be exile; for the passage translated *shall be cut off as on that side according to it* (3) is better rendered 'shall be cut off "from hence" ' (see RV mg.). The curse was to be of a most penetrating nature, entering into the transgressor's house, resting upon his goods there, and consuming the very timber and stones of the structure. Such a punishment would suit the offence for which Haggai, Zechariah's contemporary, rebuked his fellow-countrymen. They were dwelling in their 'cieled houses' while the house of the Lord was allowed to 'lie waste' (Hg. i. 4). A blight from the Lord would therefore settle upon all the labour of their hands.

g. The seventh vision (v. 5–11)

Directed again by the interpreting angel to take note of what was coming into view, Zechariah now saw *an ephah* (lit. 'the ephah'). The ephah was a Jewish measure, roughly corresponding to our bushel. The mouth of this measuring-vessel was covered by a circular lid of lead (Heb. *kikkar*, rendered *talent* in AV and RV, signifies primarily something round and flat) which, when raised, revealed that a woman was sitting within. This woman was the *resemblance*, or 'personification', of the wickedness of the whole land. Having *cast it* (RV 'cast her'; i.e. the wickedness of the land, personified in the woman) *into the midst of the ephah* he closed the measure with its covering of lead (8).

Thereupon, *there came out two women* with *wings like the wings of a stork* (9), who lifted the ephah and bore it swiftly away. It is unnecessary to raise questions as to why the bearers of the ephah were women. No special meaning is assigned to them in the passage of Scripture in which they appear, and conjecture is precarious, tending sometimes to lead away from the principal lesson of the vision. Their number is easily understandable. A measuring vessel, especially when full, would require two bearers, one on each side. The *wings* of the bearers suggest celerity of motion.

The removal of the ephah prompted the prophet to inquire as to its destination. It was to be borne away, replied the interpreting angel, to *the land of Shinar* (11), i.e. Babylonia. There, a house was to be built for it, and there it was to find a lasting habitation.

While many writers consider that this vision forecasts the dispersion of the Jews by the Romans, Babylon being mentioned symbolically as the land of their former exile, C. H. H. Wright's view is probably the more correct one, namely, that 'the picture represents sin and transgression as removed from the land of Israel' and 'driven into the land of the world-power which was antagonistic to God'. 'The vision teaches that even in the administration of restored Israel, the spirit of lawlessness will still exist, but that it will be restricted in its operations' (G. C. Morgan).

h. The eighth vision (vi. 1–8)

In this vision, which is probably the most obscure one of the series, Zechariah beheld *four chariots*, drawn by horses of different colours, appearing from between two *mountains of brass*, or copper (Heb. *nechosheth*). On inquiring of the angel as to what these chariots represented, he was told that they were the *four spirits* (RV 'winds'; cf. Je. xlix. 36) of heaven, *which go forth from standing before the Lord of all the earth* (5) as servants to execute His commands. The chariot drawn by the black horses went toward the north country; and the chariot with the white horses followed it. That drawn by the *grisled* (or *bay*) horses went toward the south country, and were subsequently commissioned to *walk to and fro through the earth* (7). No mission is assigned to the chariot with the red horses.

The four chariots may be taken as symbolizing the divine agencies—for the time being held in check—which were to be released upon the world for the fulfilment of God's plans concerning His people. The varied nature of these agencies is indicated by the different colours of the horses. (See exposition of the first vision.)

The *mountains of brass* are symbols of immutability and strength. 'The Prophet no doubt understood by these mountains the providence of God, or His hidden counsel, by which all things have been decreed before the creation of the world; and hence he says, that they were mountains of brass, as they could not be broken' (Calvin).

The fact that the red horses are mentioned first, and yet are not sent out, suggests that their work was already done. The Persian wars had already subdued and wasted the Chaldeans—the oppressors of the Jews. The black horses were now about to *go forth into the north country* (6), i.e. to Babylon. The revolt of Babylon, in the reign of Darius, brought fresh sorrow upon the Chaldeans. When the mission of the chariot with the black horses was finished, the interpreting angel, speaking in the name of Jehovah, declared that His spirit was now *quieted* in the north country (8). God had declared His intention to punish 'the heathen that are at ease' (i. 15), who had oppressed His people; and now that

His judgments had been executed upon Babylon (the vision, of course, is prophetic) His wrath is appeased. The mission of the white horses to the north country is probably symbolical of the return of peace after war.

In the reference to the *grisled and bay* horses (3, 6 and 7) the translation is somewhat faulty. 'Spotted' and 'strong' would be better. They went, first, *toward the south country*, and desired that their commission might be extended. This was granted, and they *walked to and fro through the earth* (6 and 7). The *south country* mentioned was probably Egypt and Arabia, the direction in each instance being taken as from Judaea. The sending of these horses to the *south country*, and beyond, was 'to show that the punishments of Egypt and Arabia . . . should be somewhat mixed and mitigated; they should be in better case than Babylon; yet not so good as that the Jews should dream of a happy estate in those countries; but rather repair to Judaea, and there keep them; since those that are out of God's precincts are out of His protection' (Trapp).

III. THE SYMBOLIC CORONATION.
vi. 9–15

The series of visions being ended, God commanded the performance of a symbolical action in confirmation of their message. Naming certain individuals, who were probably men of distinction among the returned captives, the Lord charged Zechariah to meet with them in the house of one named Josiah, in Jerusalem. From these men of the captivity he was to receive silver and gold, which may have been part of the restored treasure, or an offering sent by the Jews still in exile for the restoration of the temple and its worship. With these precious metals he was to make crowns, probably two in number, and set them upon the head of Joshua the High Priest. In this coronation, Joshua is to be regarded as a typical person, for it is not to be supposed that he, any more than any of his predecessors, was both priest and king. He was a type of Christ, in whom the two dignities of priesthood and kingship were to be united. Drawing attention to the fact that it was the High Priest, and not the civil ruler, who was selected to wear the two crowns, Wardlaw remarks, 'It is the priest that is to wear the regal, not the prince to wear the sacerdotal. This has the important meaning—that it was to be by the execution, to the divine satisfaction, of His priestly work, that He was to obtain, in reward, His kingly crown.'

The significance of the coronation was declared by Zechariah in a message given him by the Lord. The proclamation *Behold the man whose name is The BRANCH* (cf. iii. 8) does not signify that the person so designated was actually present, but rather that he was symbolically represented. The various things said of the Branch are in full accord with messianic prophecy elsewhere. *He shall grow up out of his place* (12), or rather, 'He shall sprout forth from under himself', implies the growth of the Christian Church from Christ, the root-stem. *He shall build the temple* (12); the emphatic repetition of this statement signifies that the temple, then in course of construction in Jerusalem, was but the symbol of the true temple, the 'spiritual house' referred to in 1 Pet. ii. 5. The fact that in iv. 9 it is promised that Zerubbabel shall complete the temple, whereas here the glory of that achievement appears to be made over to Joshua, has led to the advancement of the view that the name of Zerubbabel stood originally in vi. 11, but was subsequently replaced by that of Joshua in view of the disappearance of Zerubbabel from the narrative, owing, perhaps, to his having been deposed by the Persians. This view is not supported by the evidence, however; nor is such an explanation required. The reference in iv. 9 is to the literal temple, which was to be completed by Zerubbabel, an event which was to be regarded as a sign and pledge of the completion of the spiritual temple. But the reference in vi. 11 is to the spiritual temple, the Church, of which The BRANCH, represented by Joshua, was to be the author and finisher. The disappearance of Zerubbabel from the narrative serves to bring out more clearly the typical character of Joshua. Christ, reigning upon the throne of His Church, His kingdom, shall *bear the glory* of the combined offices of Priest and King; *and the counsel of peace shall be between them both* (13)—i.e. between the two offices united in Him. In virtue of this fusion of offices in Christ, there is also a *counsel of peace*, a lasting reconciliation, between God and His people.

The coronation of Joshua completed, the event was commanded to be held in lasting remembrance by those who had witnessed it, and the crowns to be deposited in the temple as a token of divine promise concerning the coming of the true Priest-King and Temple-Builder.

The concluding words of this message are also in messianic strain. As contributions to the building of the literal temple had come from afar, so contributions to the building of the spiritual house were to be brought in from many lands. The declaration that these things would come to pass if they (the Jews) would *diligently obey* the voice of the Lord their God (15) does not mean that the fulfilment of these promises was conditional upon their obedience. What is meant is that the Jews themselves would be partakers of these gospel blessings only if they believed and obeyed. Their disobedience did not prevent the coming of Christ, the completion of His undertaking as Redeemer, and the ingathering of the Gentiles. But by it they shut themselves out from participation in gospel blessing.

IV. THE DEPUTATION FROM BETHEL. vii. 1—viii. 23

a. The question (vii. 1–3)

There was an interval of two years between the giving of the first of the visions to Zechariah and the events which he records in this chapter (cf. i. 1 and vii. 1). Now, once more, the word of the Lord came to him for the benefit of Israel. *When they had sent unto the house of God* (2). Better, as in RV, 'Now they of Bethel had sent'. The giving of this message was occasioned by the arrival at Jerusalem of a deputation from Bethel. We prefer the view that *beth-el* here signifies the town so named rather than *the house of God*, i.e. the temple. *Beth-el* is nowhere used in Scripture for the temple. The purpose of the deputation was to inquire as to whether they ought still to observe a national fast which had been instituted in the time of the captivity. The persons named in verse 2 were probably the leaders of the deputation who came, with certain others, to worship at the temple, and to put their question regarding this fast of the fifth month to the priests and prophets in Jerusalem. The fast referred to was evidently a self-imposed one, commemorating the destruction of the temple. Circumstances were now changed; ought they therefore to discontinue the fast?

b. The answer (vii. 4–14)

The answer is marked by severity, and put in the form of searching questions which imply the charge that both their fasting and feasting during their captivity were devoid of religious motive, and were therefore unacceptable to God. Their deputation was shown to be unnecessary, for God had already expressed His mind on mere will-worship in the inspired utterances of *the former prophets* (7; cf. Is. i. 10–15). All the calamities which had befallen Judah are shown to have been the direct consequence of their fathers' disregard of these prophets, a summary of whose teaching is given in verses 9, 10. In verse 9 follow RV and read 'Thus hath the Lord of hosts spoken'. Their obduracy had brought *great wrath from the Lord* upon them (12). When He had laid a restraining hand upon them in providential circumstances they had *pulled away the shoulder* (11), an action denoting extreme perverseness.

The punishment was made to fit the offence. God had cried to them, and they had refused to hearken; in their time of adversity they cried to God, and He refused to hearken (13), and dispersed them *among all the nations* (14).

c. A promise of restoration (viii. 1–17)

In the opening part of viii God reaffirms His goodwill toward His chosen people and their land. His *jealousy* (or 'zeal') for Jerusalem manifested itself in a *great fury* (2) against her enemies. For a time, Jerusalem had become a city of deceits and perverse counsels, and the Lord had withdrawn His presence. Now, however, He promises to return and *dwell in the midst of Jerusalem* (3), thereby reaffirming His purpose previously expressed (see i. 16). The blessings attendant upon His indwelling are enumerated. *Jerusalem shall be called a city of truth* (3) in respect of its being the special centre of revelation and worship. Moreover, temporal prosperity was to result from spiritual loyalty. The scene drawn in verses 4 and 5 is one of security and tranquillity. The inhabitants reach a ripe old age in peace and contentment, and see their children, and children's children, playing blithely in the streets.

Now, such a picture would be difficult for the returned remnant to envisage. Jerusalem's prosperity was at a low ebb. The family life of the inhabitants of the city had been largely disrupted by the captivity. Such a restoration as was promised would seem *marvellous* (6) to the point of incredibility. God's question *should it also be marvellous in mine eyes?* clearly implies a negative reply. With God all things are possible. He repeats His promise to bring back the Jews from every region whither they had been scattered, and to renew His old-time favour to them; *they shall be my people, and I will be their God* (8; cf. Je. xxxi. 33).

Verses 9–13 are designed to encourage the temple builders. The exhortation begins and ends with the words *Let your hands be strong*, and to strengthen them in the work He reminds them that the promises to which they were then hearkening were spoken by the same prophets, and upon the same authority, as were the encouraging promises which they had heard when the foundations of the temple were laid (9). They were already beginning to reap the reward of their endeavours. *Before these days* (10), i.e. the days when the work of restoration was begun at the instigation of Haggai and himself, the normal reward of their ordinary toil was withheld, with resultant want and unrest (cf. Hg. i. 6); but since the resumption of the work conditions had markedly changed for the better. The Lord announced His intention to continue His favour to them in yet greater measure (cf. verse 12 with Hg. i. 10, 11). As they had been an object of cursing among the heathen who had led them captive, so now they would be an example of blessedness (13). But to inherit the promise they must deal faithfully with each other, and execute righteous judgment in their legal assemblies, eschewing malice and false swearing (16, 17).

d. Feasts instead of fasts (viii. 18–23)

In these verses a more particular answer to the deputation from Bethel is given. It refers, not only to the *fast of the fifth* month, which was the subject of the inquiry, but also to the *fast of the fourth month*, which commemorated the opening of the gates of Jerusalem to Nebuchadnezzar (Je. xxxix. 2, 3 and lii. 6, 7); *the fast of the seventh*, in which month Gedaliah was assassinated (cf. 2 Ki. xxv. 22–25); and *the fast of the tenth*, when the siege of Jerusalem by Nebuchadnezzar began.

God now promised His people such joy as would change their former fast-days into festal-days; but upon condition that they would *love the truth and peace* (19). The subsequent sorrows

of the Jewish nation were due to their non-observance of this condition.

The promises contained in the remainder of the chapter look forward to a more remote period; for the gathering of the nations to Jerusalem *to seek the Lord* and to pray before Him (22) was not realized in any period of Jewish history. Calvin remarks, 'The temple was built for this end and purpose—that the doctrine of salvation might continue there, and have its seat there until the coming of Christ; for then was fulfilled that prophecy in the hundred and tenth Psalm, "The sceptre of Thy power shall God send forth from Sion". The Prophet here teaches us that Christ would not be the king of one people only . . . but that He would rule through the whole world.'

V. THE RESTORATION OF JUDAH AND THE DESTRUCTION OF HER ENEMIES.
ix. 1—x. 12

a. The judgment upon Syria (ix. 1, 2)

In earlier passages of this prophecy, God had declared His wrath against the oppressors of His people. These oppressors are now mentioned specifically, and His judgments upon them are proclaimed. The word *massa'* (1) means a *burden* (so AV); and also an 'oracle' (so RV). It is probably from the root *nasa'*, to 'lift up'—hence to 'lift up the voice', particularly when the pronouncement is of a 'burdensome', or threatening, character. The phrase *Damascus shall be the rest thereof* (i.e. of the judgment threatened in the divine oracle) indicates that Syria, of which Damascus was the chief city, was the particular nation against whom the first of the judgments mentioned in this chapter was directed. The reference to Syria as *the land of Hadrach* is not quite clear. 'Hadrach' has been taken to be the name of a Syrian king, a Syrian god, a Syrian town or district, and a derivation from 'Hadar'— a general name of the kings of Syria. We take the third suggestion to be the most probable of these views. 'It is now certain that there was a city called Hadrach in the neighbourhood of Damascus and Hamath, although its exact site is not known' (Rawlinson). *Hamath* (2), which 'bordered' upon Damascus both in respect of territorial proximity and spiritual affinity, was to share its 'burden'. The second clause of verse 1 is obscure, but probably signifies that when these threatened judgments upon the cities and districts mentioned take place, the eyes of the nations, as well as of the tribes of Israel, *shall be toward the Lord* in awesome contemplation of His just judgments. The agencies of the punishment inflicted upon Syria were the armies of Alexander the Great.

b. The judgment upon Tyre (ix. 3, 4)

The 'wisdom' ascribed to Tyre and Sidon (see verse 2) was of a purely worldly character. By their merchandise these cities had become enormously rich; but great wealth was matched by great wickedness. Tyre, which was situated on an island about half a mile from the mainland, did *build herself a strong hold* by encircling herself with great walls. But although the inhabitants of Tyre felt secure in their defences, the calamities foretold in these verses actually came upon them. Alexander, in his determination to reduce the city, constructed, through almost incredible difficulties, an artificial mole which connected the island with the mainland, and utterly destroyed the proud city. (Cf. Ezk. xxvi. 17.)

c. The judgment upon Philistia (ix. 5-8)

The land of the Philistines lay closely adjacent to Tyre, and the tidings of the fall of Tyre would naturally cause alarm to the less strongly fortified cities which lay in the path of the conqueror. *Ashkelon shall see it* (i.e. the fall of Tyre), *and fear; Gaza . . . shall . . . be very sorrowful,* and 'shall tremble very much'; likewise Ekron, *for her expectation* (that Tyre would be able to halt the invader) *shall be ashamed* (5). Gaza, whose ruler at that time seems to have borne the title of *king,* was to lose her kingly status; Ashkelon was to be stripped of inhabitants; a 'mongrel people' (for the word *mamzer,* translated *bastard,* more correctly denotes one born of mixed parentage, of unlawful union) were to inhabit Ashdod; and the pride of Philistia was to be utterly crushed.

And I will take away his blood out of his mouth . . . (7). This signifies a change in religious observance on the part of the nation. The Philistines did not observe the restriction placed upon the Jews with respect to eating blood (see Lv. vii. 26, 27); so that the statements in this verse, taken together, indicate a change of spiritual loyalty on their part. The remnant left should be *for our God,* and should become merged with the Jews (as in the case of the Jebusites) following the religious customs of the people with whom they associated. *And he shall be as a governor in Judah* means, not that the Philistines should become pre-eminent among the Jews, but that their mode of government would be similar to that of the chosen people among whom they settled. The tribes of Israel were divided into units of thousands, each unit under a governor —hence the frequent references to the 'thousands of Israel'. A similar arrangement was to obtain among the merged Philistines.

We have the testimony of Josephus that such an incorporation of Philistines among the Jews did actually take place.

Verse 8 contains a promise of protection for the Jews while neighbouring lands were being devastated by the invader. *House* here signifies 'family' (the house of Israel) rather than the temple. The expression *now I have seen with mine eyes* signifies favourable regard, as in Ps. xxxiii. 18.

d. The coming King (ix. 9-12)

At this point a sequence of more distant events appears to the prophet's eyes. He witnesses the advent of a Conqueror whose triumphs should be more glorious and lasting than those of Alexander or any other military hero. For the reference to Christ in verse 9 is direct and immediate. The Jews are called upon to welcome their King who comes for their salvation. His character is described. *He is just;* no stain of unrighteousness rests upon His victories, His administration or His character. He is *lowly,* coming, not with the arrogant mien of a man of war, but with the gentleness of one whose conquests are aimed at the establishment of peace. He is mounted, not on a prancing warhorse, but on the animal favoured by the man of peace. Here we have an exact forecast of Christ's triumphal entry into Jerusalem (see Mk. xi. 7ff.).

The use of the term *Ephraim* in verse 10, as denoting the ten tribes of the northern kingdom, has led some to the view that this part of the prophecy belongs to the pre-captivity period, inasmuch as the ten tribes are not so designated in the post-captivity writings. But this argument is quite inconclusive. In viii. 13, which is acknowledged as post-captivity, the old distinction of the 'house of Judah' and 'house of Israel' appears. There does not seem to be any good reason therefore why the familiar name 'Ephraim' should not be used still of the 'house of Israel' when it is referred to as a separate entity. 'Ephraim' and 'Jerusalem' are specifically mentioned here as if to stress that the whole land was to enjoy the promised blessing. For *I will cut off the chariot* (10) does not signify a military disaster, but rather an act of disarmament by a people whose lives and liberties were no longer threatened.

The description of the coming King's dominion as extending *from sea even to sea, and from the river even to the ends of the earth* (rather, 'to the borders of the land') may have a primary reference to local geographical boundaries, the seas being the Dead Sea and the Mediterranean (i.e. east to west); and the 'river' perhaps the Euphrates, in which case the 'borders' referred to would be those of the south. But as applied to Messiah's kingdom in its ultimate extension the description signifies earth's utmost bounds. Compare this verse with Ps. lxxii, where the rule of Solomon, the peaceful king, is made the type of the far greater kingdom of Messiah.

Speaking more particularly to Jerusalem, for he is still addressing the *daughter of Zion* (9), the prophet likens her in her captive state to prisoners held in a pit *wherein is no water* (11). Captives so treated were faced with the prospect of a horrible death. Extinction would have been the fate of the Jews were it not for the blood-sealed covenant of God with their fathers (see Ex. xxiv. 8) in virtue of which they are described as *prisoners of hope* (12) and exhorted to turn to the *strong hold* (probably Zion with its natural fortifications) to receive *double* their former prosperity from God's hand.

e. The restoration of Judah (ix. 13-17)

The RV has, and rightly we think, a full stop at the end of verse 12. Verse 13 introduces a new topic. The construction of this verse is rather obscure in the Hebrew, but the general meaning seems to be that God will use Judah and Ephraim as instruments of aggression against the heathen powers, a reference, probably, to the victories of the Jews over the Seleucidae in the Maccabean period. In the promised victories, the hand of the Lord was to be seen. The statements in verse 14 may mean that the very powers of nature were to be employed for the defeat of His people's enemies, or simply that their weapons were to be used of God (cf. Jdg. vii. 20).

The efficacy of God's help to His chosen people is the subject of verse 15. He shall empower them to *devour* their enemies, as a wild beast devours its prey. They shall 'subdue the stones of the sling' (mg.). The idea seems to be that the stones slung at them shall fall short of their mark, or shall be so lacking in force as to do no harm. They shall trample them under foot in their onset (see RV). The figure of the devouring wild beast is continued where the prophet speaks of them as drinking the blood of their enemies. The *bowls* were the vessels which held the blood of the sacrifices, and the *corners of the altar* were always abundantly sprinkled with blood.

In verse 16 the preciousness of God's people is brought out under two figures. They are His *flock*, they are also *as the stones of a crown* or 'dedicated stones', *lifted up as an ensign*, or better 'shining from on high'. It is not quite clear whether the exclamation in verse 17 refers to Israel's goodness and beauty as the favoured of the Lord, or to the goodness and beauty of the Lord Himself. The concluding phrase of the verse seems to favour the former, for it is an added promise of such prosperity as would impart cheerfulness, or virility.

f. Encouraging prospects (x. 1–5)

The promise of temporal prosperity with which chapter ix ends is continued and expanded in this chapter. 'Corn' and 'wine' are the Lord's gifts, and the people are exhorted to look to Him for the *latter rain*, which fell in March or April, and which served to swell the grain then approaching maturity. In verse 1 the RV reading of 'lightnings' is better than *bright clouds*. The *latter rain* was often accompanied by thunderstorms.

The injunction to look to the Lord is enforced by the reminder of the disastrous results of looking to false gods. The *idols* (lit. *teraphim*) had *spoken vanity* (2), and those who divined by means of these images had been misled and had comforted others with vain promises. The result of their having recourse to this form of false worship was that they *went their way* (in the sense of straying) and were *troubled*, or rather 'afflicted' (RV), because they had no shepherd to tend them. Their rulers and priests who ought to have been 'shepherds' to them had served them ill, thereby bringing God's anger upon themselves. The term *goats* in verse 3, used also in Ezk. xxxiv. 17, refers to the principal men of the nation. In Is. xiv. 9 the same word is rendered

'chief ones'. In their dire straits, the Lord Himself became the Shepherd of His flock and made the house of Judah as His *goodly* (or 'majestic') *horse*—the horse being regarded as an emblem of beauty and strength (cf. Jb. xxxix. 19–25). In this passage the prophetic perfect, the equivalent of the future, is used. In the fixity of the divine purpose, the promised transformation was as good as effected.

Verse 4 confirms what has already been promised of Judah. Out of that favoured tribe was to come *the corner*, or corner-stone (lit. that which projects), an allusion to the ruler of the people. The *nail* (4; Heb. *yathedh*) signifies the hooked peg built into the wall of the house, on which household utensils or implements of war were usually suspended (cf. Is. xxii. 23). The suggestion here is reliability. Out of Judah were to come also the chief warriors of the nation, alluded to as *the battle bow*. The word *oppressor* signifies 'exactor' (RV), and the meaning is that Judah was to exact tribute from her vanquished enemies.

Such great princes and leaders did indeed spring from Judah in the Maccabean period, but the ultimate reference of the promise is to the 'Lion of the tribe of Judah', by whose almighty aid the Church is to expand until the last remaining rebel is subdued.

g. The return of the nation (x. 6–12)

In verse 6 the survivors of the ten tribes are spoken of as *the house of Joseph*, as in Am. v. 6 and Ob. 18, and promised lasting replacement in their former possessions; *their children shall see it* (7). The words *I will hiss for them* (8) form a promise of favour. The *hiss* or 'whistle' referred to is that of the shepherd summoning his sheep, or of the bee-keeper gathering his swarm. Where, in verse 9, God speaks of sowing them among the people, the reference is probably to the future dispersion of the Jews and to its good effect. There would be fruit of this sowing. Though scattered because of their sins, the divine purpose was to turn the curse into a blessing. We learn from Acts how the dispersed Jews of those days became the means of helping forward the missionary enterprise of the infant Church. The Jewish synagogues situated among Gentile peoples afforded opportunity for the preaching of the gospel and yielded small bands of converts who became active in the work. But on a much larger scale shall the 'dispersed of Israel' be used in future days when they shall turn to the Lord. Dispersed though they are, God's watchful care is over them. They have not lost their identity as a people; they still *live with their children* (9) and await the promised restoration. Their past deliverances from Egypt and Assyria are taken as the symbol of their future ingathering. The imagery of verse 11 is drawn from the exodus. As no barrier was allowed to stand in their way then, whether sea, river, or enemies, so again there would be no thwarting of God's purpose.

The expression *they shall walk up and down in*

his name (12) signifies that the conduct of the restored people would be in accordance with the will of God.

VI. THE REJECTION OF THE SHEPHERD-KING AND ITS CONSEQUENCES.
xi. 1—xiii. 9
a. The destruction of Jerusalem (xi. 1-6)

This chapter provides a companion picture to that of chapter x. But the pictures are in contrast. In chapter x we see a nation prospering under divine blessing, whereas here we see it deteriorating and hastening to ruin under divine wrath. Coming, as it does, in immediate sequence to promises of favour, this passage has the appearance of being out of its true context; but such is not the case. It is clearly intended to warn the Jews that, notwithstanding the glory of Israel's ultimate destiny, God would not let their wickedness go unpunished. Here, then, the destruction of Jerusalem by the Roman armies is foretold.

The chapter opens dramatically. Many commentators have taken verse 1 as an apostrophe addressed to the temple—the materials of which were in such large measure the products of Lebanon that it might well, in a figurative sense, be addressed *O Lebanon*. But it is probably more accurate to refer these words to the region of Lebanon rather than to the temple, and to regard verses 1-3 as a description of the land devastated by the Roman armies. The invaders were to come from the north, thrusting their way through the forests of Lebanon and driving southwards through Bashan and the Jordan valley, spoiling the *glory* of the shepherds, the rich pasture-land, and the *pride of Jordan* (3), the dense Jordan thickets. The fall of the mighty cedar of Lebanon and the destruction of the *forest of the vintage* (2) (better 'inaccessible forest') was an indication that nothing could withstand the invader. If the cedar fell, so would the trees of lesser grandeur; the coming calamity would extend to all classes in the nation.

The root cause of this catastrophe is revealed to be the misconduct of the people and their 'shepherds', or rulers, toward the great Shepherd sent by God to feed His flock. The prophet is required to assume the character, first of the long line of God's faithful shepherds who had laboured among His chosen people, and later, of the Good Shepherd Himself. His charge was to feed *the flock of the slaughter* (4), i.e. 'destined to slaughter', whose *possessors* (rather 'buyers') sold and slew without compunction or awareness of guilt (5). These rulers, civil and ecclesiastical, were so lacking in patriotic and religious fervour as to have no sense of responsibility for the people entrusted to their care.

The picture of an oppressed Israel is one that found realization in various periods of their history; and God's interventions, as described in verses 6 and 7, were of frequent occurrence. Repeatedly He had raised up faithful 'shepherds'

over them and had punished their adversaries. The *inhabitants of the land* (6), or 'dwellers in the earth', are the various peoples who oppressed the Jews, as distinguished from the *flock of slaughter* (7) who were the objects of God's special care. The enemies of Israel were to be given up to civil dissension and to the despotism of ruthless kings.

b. The rejection of the Good Shepherd (xi. 7-14)

As commanded by God (see verse 4), and representing the Good Shepherd of Israel, the prophet then undertook the feeding of the flock. The names of his staves are significant (7). *Beauty* would be better rendered 'Grace', as indicating the favour of God towards His people. *Bands*, or 'Binders', signifies union, in particular the fusion of the kingdoms of Judah and Ephraim into one nation. These, then, were to be the benefits of a right conduct toward their true Shepherd, favour from God and unity among themselves.

In demonstration of his care for the flock, the prophet records his removal of three of the unfaithful under-shepherds—*in one month* (8). It is really unprofitable to seek for any three persons in particular to whom these words may refer. Calvin takes the removal of the three shepherds merely to signify that God 'took the greatest care of His flock, for He loved it, and omitted nothing necessary to defend it'.

But despite all the care bestowed upon the nation, the Shepherd's service was not appreciated. And here Zechariah clearly represents Christ. His people returned His kindness with enmity, until His soul *lothed* (better 'was weary of') *them* (8); and He resolved to leave them to their fate, some to perish, and the rest to be so divided as to accomplish each other's destruction (9). In symbol of changed relationship, the staff *Beauty* was *cut asunder* (10) to signify the withdrawal of His favour, and the abrogation of a 'covenant' or engagement in virtue of which *all the people*, or nations, were restrained from molesting His people. In the tribulation resulting from the breaking of that covenant of favour, the *poor of the flock* (11), i.e. the godly remnant, recognized the fulfilment of God's word.

Prior to His withdrawal from the flock, the Good Shepherd asks for His hire (12), the incongruity of such a demand being obviated by the consideration that the 'flock' consists of men. He asks as one who cares little whether His demand be met or not. By such a demand, He reveals His displeasure with them; and they, in their response, indicate their contempt of Him by weighing for His hire *thirty pieces of silver* (12).

Up to this point, the prophet has spoken as the representative of the Lord, but now the Lord Himself speaks, commanding His representative to cast the insulting hire (ironically described as a *goodly price*) *to the potter in the house of the Lord* (13). The unworthiness of the price is shown by its being cast to the tradesman who made the least valuable of all vessels (cf. 2

758

Tim. ii. 20). It is not necessary to assume that he was actually present when the money was cast to him. It was cast *in the house of the Lord* because the Lord was the real object of the insult.

In Mt. xxvii. 10 this symbolical incident of the Shepherd is shown to have been fulfilled in the betrayal of Christ. The price agreed upon between the representatives of the nation and the betrayer was 'thirty pieces of silver', which sum was later cast down in the temple by the remorseful traitor, and subsequently expended in the purchase of the 'potter's field'. In Mt. xxvii. 9 this prophecy is assigned to Jeremiah. The easiest way to account for this seeming discrepancy is to attribute it to a scribal error. But it is not improbable that 'Jeremy' here is a generic covering the whole corpus of prophetic books, for the accepted order of them in Matthew's time placed Jeremiah first.

The second result of the rejection of the Shepherd is indicated in the breaking of the staff called *Bands* (14). The *Beauty* of the flock was already gone; its unity would now depart also.

c. The unfaithful shepherd (xi. 15–17)

Having already acted the part of the Good Shepherd, the prophet is now called upon to impersonate an unfaithful shepherd. It is not necessary to read any special meaning into the phrase *the instruments of a foolish shepherd* (15). The difference was not so much in the instruments as in the shepherd. The people were to be punished for rejecting the Good Shepherd by being put into the charge of an unfaithful shepherd who would have no concern for those who were *cut off* (i.e. separated from the body of the nation), nor for the *young* (rather, 'dispersed'), nor for the *broken* (or 'wounded'), nor yet for those who stood still (i.e. the whole, as opposed to the *broken*). Instead of tending them, he was to devour them as his prey.

By the unfaithful shepherd in this passage is to be understood the Roman oppressor, who destroyed the Jewish state and mercilessly harassed the Jews subsequent to their rejection of Christ. But the *idol*, or useless (rv 'worthless'), *shepherd* must bear responsibility for his own actions, and be dealt with accordingly (17). The *sword* may be taken as signifying affliction generally. The false shepherd's *arm*, the symbol of his strength, was to be completely enfeebled; and his *right eye*, the symbol of his discernment, was to be *utterly darkened* by a judicial blindness.

Here then we have a forecast of the sufferings of the Jews subsequent to their rejection of Christ and of the ultimate downfall of their oppressors.

d. God's defence of Jerusalem (xii. 1–9)

We have already commented on the significance of *massa'* (1) as denoting an oracle—usually of a threatening nature (see ix. 1n.). Here, however, the *burden*, or 'oracle', is not 'upon' or 'against' (*bh*) Israel, but 'for' or 'concerning' ('*al*) Israel,

whose enemies were to be severely punished by the Lord because of their ruthless treatment of His people.

This new prophecy begins with a sublime unfolding of divine majesty. The words about to be spoken were to constitute a proclamation from the throne of eternal Sovereignty. The resources of the universe were at the Lord's disposal for the accomplishment of His purposes. Israel, though rejected because of her rejection of the Good Shepherd, was yet to be delivered from the power of her oppressors and exalted over them.

The figures used to represent the invincibility of Jerusalem are striking. It is to be made *a cup of trembling* (2), or staggering, to the besieging forces. They thirst to drink of the city's contents, but the draught intoxicates and stupefies them. Again, Jerusalem is to be a *burdensome stone* (3) to its enemies. The figure may be taken from a weight-lifting contest. The lift proves too much for the contestants, and the stone drops from their grasp, lacerating and wounding them.

The clause *when they shall be in the siege both against Judah and against Jerusalem* (2) is difficult; but the rendering which, in the light of the context, appears most probable is 'and also over Judah it shall be (i.e. the favour promised in verse 1) in the siege against Jerusalem'. 'God will not only be guardian of the city alone, but also of the whole of the holy land' (Calvin). Because God was to *open* His *eyes upon the house of Judah*, a figure denoting favourable regard, her enemies were to be put to confusion; the horses smitten with *astonishment* (or 'stupefaction') and with blindness; the riders with *madness* or frenzy (4).

Beholding the confusion of the attackers, the *governors*, or princes, of Judah, speaking for all the people, shall gladly acknowledge that they owe their safety, under God, to the inhabitants of Jerusalem (5).

But the princes of Judah were also to share in Jerusalem's triumph; and, in this connection, another group of arresting metaphors is used. They shall be *like an hearth* (or pan) *of fire among the wood, and like a torch of fire* (or firebrand) *in a sheaf* (6), the wood and sheaves representing their enemies, who would be devoured by them. The result of this conflagration among Jerusalem's enemies would be that the city would survive and continue *in her own place* (6).

In the deliverance thus wrought, the *tents of Judah* (7) were to have the first benefit. This phrase denotes the people of the countryside as distinct from the inhabitants of the city. The dwellings of the former were unfortified, whereas those of the latter were strongly walled. But, as we have seen, the princes of the undefended people were to be as firebrands among the besieging forces, and to distinguish themselves in the conflict, thus precluding all boasting on the part of the *house of David* (i.e. the princes) and of *the inhabitants of Jerusalem* against their weaker brethren (7). The glory of the deliverance belonged neither to Judah, nor to Jerusalem, but to the Lord. By His help, the feeblest of the people should be *as David*, when David was at the height of his power; and the princes *as God*, rather 'as a god', or as *the angel of the Lord* (8) before the people. 'The general meaning is that the Lord God will strengthen the weakest and give additional elevation, honour, and influence to the highest, and add divinely to the might of the mightiest, so that no opposing power shall ever stand before them, any more than when that divine angel of the covenant was commissioned to be their conductor and guardian of Whom Jehovah said, MY NAME IS IN HIM' (Wardlaw).

In this picture of the impregnable city Jerusalem represents the Church. The literal Jerusalem was to be laid waste by the Romans, as it had been on former occasions by other enemies; but the spiritual Jerusalem shall never know defeat by the 'gates of hell'.

e. The penitent people (xii. 10–14)

The crowning mercy of God to His chosen people is now mentioned. He will send a plentiful effusion of the *spirit of grace and of supplications* (10) upon them which will bear fruit in penitent prayer. But 'sight of sin must precede sorrow for sin' and their 'sight of sin' comes through looking upon Him *whom they have pierced* (10). The pierced One is undoubtedly Christ Himself (see Jn. xix. 36); but the change from the first person to the third in this passage creates some difficulty, and various explanations have been advanced. But such transitions are not uncommon in the prophetic books. Hitzig, however, explains the transition 'simply from the identification of the Sender with the Sent' (cf. Mk. ix. 37; Lk. x. 16).

The comparisons made of this mourning indicate both its intensity and generality. It shall be as the mourning of a parent over the death of an only son, or a firstborn child; and as the mourning of the nation over the death of king Josiah. Hadadrimmon is believed to have been a city situated in the valley of Megiddo, where Josiah was slain (see 2 Ch. xxxv. 22). Although Jerusalem only is mentioned (11) as being involved in this mourning, it is clear from the verses that follow that, in this instance, the city stands for the nation.

Wardlaw, and others, regard the families specifically mentioned in verses 12, 13 as representing the leading classes of the people: *the family of the house of David*—the royal lineage; *the family of the house of Nathan*—the prophetic line; *the family of the house of Levi*—the priesthood; and *the family of Shimei*—the whole assemblage of the scribes or teachers. The mention of their wives as mourning *apart* is in reference to the practice of males and females sitting and worshipping separately. The mourning extends to all classes individually—the leading families mentioned, and *all the families that remain* (14).

This mourning for Christ began almost immediately after the crucifixion (see Lk. xxiii. 48). The number of mourners greatly increased on the day of Pentecost, and subsequently; and shall continue to grow until 'all Israel shall be saved'. These prophecies have a special reference to the spiritual Israel of God; for repentance is a necessary part of Christian experience.

f. The cleansed land (xiii. 1–6)

There is an obvious connection between this chapter and chapter xii in that it deals with the moral reformation which should follow after penitential sorrow. Mourning for sin is followed by cleansing from sin.

The *day* (1) is the same as that in xii. 11; and the piercing of the rejected Messiah is, in effect, the opening of the *fountain*. This verse 'exhibits the two grand doctrines of the gospel—justification and sanctification' (Henderson). The grace of the Spirit of Christ is needed for the latter, as the virtue of the blood of Christ is needed for the former. The apostle John, with the genius of the mystic, sees a connection between this twofold figure and the 'blood and water' that issued from the pierced side of Jesus (Jn. xix. 34). Blood was needed for atonement, as the countless sacrifices of the Old Testament indicated; and the Spirit was required for sanctification, as the many washings of the law showed; and both issue from the same fountain. The fountain was opened by anticipation from the beginning, and on the ground of what Christ was to accomplish by His atoning death believers who lived under the Old Testament dispensation were saved. But when Christ died the fountain was opened in reality. The term *fountain* denotes fulness; and the mention of it as being opened *to the house of David and to the inhabitants of Jerusalem* (1) signifies that it was to be available to all, from the princely family to the humblest dweller in the royal city.

This cleansing was to be marked by moral reformation. The idols were to be *cut off*—their very names banished from memory. The false prophets, and the unclean spirit by whom they were actuated, were to be expelled (2). So great should be the zeal for pure doctrine that the very parents of any false prophet who might yet remain should rise up against him and destroy him in their deep abhorrence of the sin of speaking *lies in the name of the Lord* (3; cf. Dt. xiii. 6–11, xviii. 20). Such would be the discredit cast upon the false prophet that he would become ashamed of the things of which he formerly boasted. No longer would he wear a *rough* (or 'hairy') *garment to deceive* the people into regarding him as a prophet (4). The description of Elijah as 'an hairy man' (2 Ki. i. 8) probably had reference to his rough mantle of camel's hair or sheepskin—a form of dress that succeeding prophets appear to have affected in imitation of him.

To cast off all suspicion from himself, the false prophet would now try to pass himself off as a serf of the fields, engaged from his youth in the humbler tasks of husbandry (5). And if one should still regard him with suspicion, because of certain wound-marks in (better 'between'; Heb. *ben*) his hands (i.e. upon his breast or back), he would attribute these, not to the cause which they suspected, viz. idolaṭrous worship (cf. 1 Ki. xviii. 28), but to wounds sustained in the house of friends. The reference may be to lacerations made by mourners in their own flesh when they visited bereaved friends (although the practice was forbidden among the Jews; see Lv. xix. 28) or to wounds 'received by him on the occasion of some carousal with boon companions' (Wright).

g. The purifying chastisement of Israel (xiii. 7–9)

At verse 7 the prophecy takes a new turn, although it is directly continuous from the earlier part of the chapter. Jehovah summons His sword to smite His Shepherd, whose official character is first described, and then the constitution of His Person. He is Jehovah's *shepherd* entrusted with the charge of His flock. In His Person, He is uniquely suited to His task, being a *man* and yet Jehovah's *fellow* (7). The word *gebher*, rendered *man*, is emphatic, indicating that the Shepherd is a man *par excellence*; while the word *'amith*, *fellow*, contains the idea of fellowship on equal terms. The smiting of any mere Jewish ruler, which is the interpretation favoured by some writers, could not therefore be regarded as the ultimate and true fulfilment of this prophecy.

The immediate result of the smiting of the Shepherd is next shown: *the sheep shall be scattered* (7). The significance of these words is revealed in Christ's application of them as recorded in Mt. xxvi. 31. This prophecy may also refer to the dispersion of the Jews after the siege of Jerusalem by Titus, notwithstanding that at the time they were Messiah's enemies.

The flock were not to be left in their scattered condition, however, for the prophecy proceeds, *I will turn mine hand upon the little ones* (7); rather 'I will turn back my hand over (Heb. *'al*) the humble ones'. This action is to be understood in a gracious sense, as in Is. i. 25 and xl. 11. The Shepherd was smitten as the substitute of the flock, and for His sake the scattered sheep were to be re-gathered and lovingly protected by the very hand that had wielded the sword against the Shepherd. By the resurrection of Jesus Christ from the dead, God rallied the dispersed disciples, and by the execution of the commission given to them, and through them to the Church in all succeeding ages, the 'outcasts of Israel' are to be 'gathered together' (Ps. cxlvii. 2).

But although the smiting of the Shepherd was 'by the determinate counsel and foreknowledge of God', the action of those who crucified Him was none the less their own on that account. It was by 'wicked hands' that He was 'crucified and slain'; and the righteousness of God

demanded that justice should be executed. Hence the concluding prediction of this chapter. It is not necessary to interpret the *two parts* and *third part* mentioned in verses 8 and 9 with literal exactness. The two facts made clear are that there was to be a widespread destruction and slaughter among the rejecters of the Good Shepherd, and that a remnant was to be spared. Even this remnant would have to endure severe chastisement, but the figure of the refiner and his crucible (9) makes it clear that the fiery trial is to have a glorious issue. God will again speak to Israel in terms of covenant grace and say *It is my people*, and they, refined and purified by their long tribulation, will respond *The Lord is my God*. Punished for their rejection of the true Shepherd (xi. 16), they shall be blessed on their penitent return to Him.

VII. THE FINAL VICTORIES OF THE SHEPHERD-KING. xiv. 1–21

a. The rout of Jerusalem's enemies (xiv. 1–15)

In this chapter the subject of chapter xiii is expanded. The opening words are addressed to Jerusalem, the capture of which city, with the horrors attendant upon such an event, are described in verse 2. So completely shall the city be taken that the enemy shall sit down in the very midst of her to divide the spoil. *All nations* (2), generally speaking, were represented in the invading army, for Rome was the mistress of many lands.

But the judgment of God against Jerusalem was to recoil eventually upon the heads of those who were the ministers of His wrath against her (3), and it is significant that the decline of the Roman Empire dates from the fall of Jerusalem.

The striking and sublime figure of verse 4 promises divine intervention to facilitate the escape of the favoured remnant from the city. The Lord was to fight against His people's enemies *as when he fought in the day of battle* (3). There may be a reference here to what happened at the Red Sea when the Egyptians pursued after Israel at the exodus. Moses quietened the host with the assurance, 'Jehovah shall fight for you, and ye shall hold your peace' (Ex. xiv. 14). As on that occasion He divided the sea for them, so enabling them to escape, so now He would, as it were, divide the mountain for them for the same purpose.

The figure of the cleft mountain indicates the direction of their flight. Half of the mountain was to remove northwards and the other half southwards, thus leaving a valley running east and west. *Azal* (5) is probably a place-name, perhaps the Beth-ezel mentioned in Mi. i. 11. It is by no means uncommon for 'Beth' in a place-name to be omitted.

The *earthquake* referred to in verse 5 is not recorded in any of the historical books of the Old Testament; but Amos mentions it in a way which indicates that it was a disaster of such importance as to furnish a date from which other events were reckoned (Am. i. 1).

In describing the coming of the Lord to deliver His people and smite their enemies, the prophet changes abruptly from the third person to the second—*The Lord my God shall come, and all the saints* (better 'holy ones' or 'angels') *with thee* (5). So clear is his vision of this great event that he addresses Jehovah as actually present and describes the salvation which should ensue from His coming. In that day 'there shall not be light, the bright ones shall contract themselves' (6; RV mg.). This signifies a dimming of the light by the contraction of the heavenly bodies, with the resultant condition of the deep gloom of a heavily overcast day. The duration of this condition shall be *one day which shall be known to the Lord* (7), i.e. a continuous period of mingled light and darkness enduring, not for 'one day' of twenty-four hours, but for a time, the measure of which is known only to the Lord. And then at 'evening time', when usually darkness deepens, the light shall suddenly brighten, and instead of dusk shall come dawn.

Here we have a picture of the condition of the Christian Church from the time of the fall of Jerusalem until the present hour. It has been a long and cloudy day, with some periods brighter than others, but without any period of absolute darkness or of perfect light. When this 'day' shall approach its close, instead of the darkness becoming denser, as might be expected, the light will grow brighter, and the glory of the Lord will illumine the world. This illumination will be marked by joy and blessing; for that appears to be the meaning of the figure in verse 8 where Jerusalem is represented as the watershed of *living waters*, i.e. pure and gushing waters, *half of them* flowing *toward the former sea*, and half *toward the hinder sea*, unaffected by drought of summer or frost of winter. Instead of *former* and *hinder* seas, the RV more correctly reads 'eastern sea' and 'western sea', i.e. the Dead Sea and the Mediterranean Sea. The general meaning of this figure is that the water should flow in all directions, and throughout the world, Palestine being the symbol of the wider area, bringing life and fertility wherever it came.

The blessings symbolized by the perennial streams of living water are the outcome of the return to God on the part of the people. There shall be *one Lord* (9); i.e. idols shall be disowned and abolished; *and his name one;* i.e. His name alone shall be invoked and adored.

When the great King is thus acknowledged, His royal city shall attain to outstanding prominence. That is the significance of the exaltation of Jerusalem described in verses 10–12. *Turned as a plain* (10). Henderson connects this figure with that of the *living waters* (8), flowing throughout the land from Jerusalem. 'Every obstruction shall be removed which prevents the free and full flow of the living waters throughout the world. What is high shall be levelled, and

what is low shall be elevated.' To say that this levelling was to take place *from Geba to Rimmon* is the equivalent of saying that it was to cover the whole land, from north to south—these towns marking roughly the northern and southern extremities of the kingdom of Judah. The exalted city is to be *inhabited in her place* (10); i.e. its former boundaries shall be occupied to the full. *Benjamin's gate* (alternatively, 'the gate of Ephraim') was situated in the centre of the old northern wall. From this gate the wall ran westward to the *corner gate*, and eastward to the *place of the first gate*, which is identified with the 'old gate' of Ne. iii. 6. *The tower of Hananeel* was situated in the north-east corner, near the 'first gate', and the *king's winepresses* were on the south side of the city, in the king's garden (see Ne. iii. 15). In this verse, therefore, we have the breadth of the city from east to west and from north to south.

The security of the city is next indicated. There should be no more *utter destruction* (11), mowing down, of the inhabitants. Their defence would be in the hands of the Lord. The picture drawn in verse 12 is both graphic and appalling. A plague from the Lord smites the serried ranks of Jerusalem's enemies suddenly, while they are *on their feet*. The eyes turned with evil intent upon the city and the tongues which uttered blasphemous defiance against her shall *consume away* (12). Moreover, they are thrown into such confusion that they turn their swords against each other and become an easy prey to the defenders of Jerusalem and the men of Judah. The very horses and beasts of burden belonging to the enemies of Jerusalem are afflicted by the destroying plague, and the would-be spoilers are themselves utterly spoiled (13–15).

b. Jerusalem's ultimate glory (xiv. 16–21)

But the destruction of Jerusalem's enemies is not universal. The spared remnant of those who went up against Jerusalem shall go up again to the royal city, this time *to keep the feast of tabernacles* (16). We are not to conclude from the statement that they shall go up *from year to year* for this purpose that the rites of Judaism are to be given a place in the Christian economy. The language used is figurative, and the particular feast mentioned is the fittest of all Jewish festivals to illustrate the prophet's meaning. The feast of tabernacles was a harvest festival, and thus a fitting symbol of the ingathering of the heathen to the kingdom of God. Moreover, as it was a feast of remembrance to the Jews, commemorating Israel's sojourn in the wilderness, so to the ingathered Gentiles it should also become a feast of remembrance recalling the times in which they dwelt in the wilderness of ignorance and idolatry. To Jew and Gentile, now united in a common loyalty to Christ, it would serve also as a reminder that they were 'strangers and pilgrims' in the earth, whose citizenship was in heaven. Grateful recollection, adoring praise, and joyful anticipation—all of which are associated with the feast of tabernacles—are abiding elements in Christian worship.

But a recalcitrant section of the spared remnant have yet to be dealt with. Their failure to join in the worship of Jehovah would be requited by the withholding of the rain which was needful for the support of life (17). Verse 18 is somewhat obscure. Egypt is specially mentioned among the enemies of Jerusalem, probably because the Egyptians were the first oppressors of the Jews, and because, since their land was irrigated by the Nile, the withholding of rain from Egypt might seem but a light disadvantage. The threatened plague would come upon them in common with all other peoples who would neglect *to keep the feast of tabernacles,* and they too would suffer want as a result of the withholding of rain from their own land and from the lands whose streams fed their river.

In the closing verses of the prophecy we are given a picture of a Jerusalem wholly consecrated to Jehovah—a picture in which the holy city is the symbol of the Christian Church regnant in the world. The distinction as between secular and sacred is done away, for everyone and everything is now consecrated to the Lord's purposes. The *bells,* or plates, of the horses bear the same inscription as the mitre of the High Priest; the pots and common vessels of the Lord's house shall be holy as the *bowls before the altar;* all shall be consecrated to holy purposes.

By the *Canaanite* (21), some writers understand 'trafficker' (RV mg.) or merchant; and the word will bear that meaning (see Jb. xli. 6). In this sense the passage may mean that marketing in the holy courts, as in Jn. ii. 13–16, would be unknown, or, more probably, that there would be no more mercenary priesthood. But it is also possible to take the word as referring to all the frequenters of God's house. The ancient inhabitants of Canaan had been a corrupt people, whence the name Canaanite was sometimes given in reproach to Israel in times of backsliding (see Ezk. xvi. 3). The city of God should no longer be polluted by the ungodly and profane: 'There shall in no wise enter into it any thing that defileth, neither whatsoever worketh abomination, or maketh a lie: but they which are written in the Lamb's book of life' (Rev. xxi. 27).

G. N. M. COLLINS.

MALACHI

INTRODUCTION

I. DATE

It is not possible to fix the date of Malachi with any exactness. We know from his references to the temple and the priests that he lived after the return from the Babylonian exile and after the rebuilding of the temple (516 B.C.). The reference in i. 3 to a raid on Edom is not helpful as many such raids occurred in the fifth and fourth centuries. Nor is the 'governor' in i. 8 necessarily a Persian governor. However, the state of affairs during the prophet's ministry is similar to that presupposed by the reforms of Ezra and Nehemiah, and many scholars are of opinion that the book was written shortly before the coming of Ezra. This date (c. 460 B.C.) is very generally accepted.

II. BACKGROUND

The Jews had returned from exile with high hopes. Inspired by Haggai and Zechariah, they had rebuilt the temple. This building did not have the glory of the original one which had been destroyed by the Babylonians, but it served its purpose. As the years passed, the Jews became disillusioned. The promised prosperity did not return. Life was hard. They were surrounded by enemies, such as the Samaritans, who sought to thwart them at every opportunity. They suffered from drought and bad crops and famine.

They began to doubt the love of God. They questioned the justice of His moral rule. The evil-doer is good in the sight of the Lord, they said. They argued that there was no profit in obeying His commandments and walking penitently before Him, for it was the evil and self-reliant who prospered.

III. THE PROPHET'S MESSAGE

The prophet proceeded to answer them and to show them that this scepticism was hypocritical. If adversity was their lot, it had befallen them, not in spite of their godliness, but because of their sinfulness. There was the corrupt worship of the priests, for example. They were irreverent and extremely perfunctory in their temple duties. They gave a bad lead to the people who brought blemished offerings, even after promising good ones. The very Gentiles offer worthier sacrifice. The people were also transgressing, the men divorcing the wives of their youth, and contracting foreign marriages. Sins of all kinds prevailed: sorcery, adultery, dishonesty, oppres-sion of the weak and general ungodliness. How could they expect to prosper when the country was rotten with such practices?

Malachi, in true prophetic strain, condemned the sins and summoned the people to repentance. If they would purify their worship, obey the law, and pay their tithes in full, God's blessing would follow. In sounding forth this call, the prophet revealed that he had a lofty conception of God. God was the majestic Lord of hosts; His decrees and judgments were irresistible; His love was holy and unchanging.

Malachi found ultimate salvation for his people not in their repentance but in the Lord's action. The great day of the Lord would dawn. It would purify and vindicate the godly and destroy the wicked. That day would be prepared for by the coming of the prophet Elijah.

IV. THE MAN

All that we know of the prophet himself we have to infer from his utterances. He was a true prophet. He spoke with full authority. He could say, 'Thus saith the Lord of hosts.' He had an intense love for Israel and for the services of the temple, and a high conception of the tradition and duties of the priests. It has often been said that, while other prophets emphasized morality and inward religion, Malachi laid stress on worship and ritual. While this is true on the whole, we have to note that he was not altogether forgetful of Israel's moral obligations (see the formidable list at iii. 5), and that, for him, ritual was not an end in itself, but the expression of the people's faith in the Lord.

His style is simple and direct, and marked by the frequent occurrence of the words 'Yet ye say'. Perhaps this is more than the rhetorical method of the writer; it may have had its origin in the protesting and questioning cries of the hecklers, when he first delivered his message on the streets.

V. NEW TESTAMENT QUOTATIONS

Only three passages are referred to or quoted in the New Testament, viz. i. 2f., iii. 1, iv. 5f. The first of these, 'I loved Jacob, and I hated Esau', contains an idea that has proved somewhat offensive to modern taste. Yet it is difficult to avoid holding some doctrine of election in view of the many statements in the Bible and of the facts of human experience. Truly one is often taken and another left. It is in support of the doctrine of the election of the true Israel that Paul quotes the verse in Rom. ix. 13.

VI. THE END OF PROPHECY

With Malachi the curtain was rung down on prophecy until the coming of the Baptist. The living and powerful words of the prophets were heard no more. The scribes and the priests became the central religious figures. The age of creativeness had given way to the age of learning. The Jews had now a large body of literature, and its exegetes, those who expounded it, were the new channel of the voice of God. Of this coming situation, in which religion was mainly legalistic, we have a clear sign in the book of Malachi.

OUTLINE OF CONTENTS

I. THE SUPERSCRIPTION. i. 1

II. THE LORD'S LOVE FOR ISRAEL. i. 2-5

III. ISRAEL'S DISHONOUR OF THE LORD. i. 6—ii. 9

IV. CONDEMNATION OF DIVORCES AND FOREIGN MARRIAGES. ii. 10-16

V. THE COMING JUDGMENT. ii. 17—iii. 6

VI. REPENTANCE BY TITHES WILL BRING BLESSING. iii. 7-12

VII. THE COMING VINDICATION OF THE GODLY. iii. 13—iv. 3

VIII. CONCLUSION. iv. 4-6

COMMENTARY

I. THE SUPERSCRIPTION. i. 1.

Burden; something taken up solemnly on the lips, especially a divine oracle. See note on Zc. ix. 1. *Malachi.* The name means 'my messenger'. There has been considerable discussion as to whether this was the real name of the prophet. If so, it may be the contracted form of Malachiah, 'the Lord's messenger', on the analogy of Abi for Abijah ('Jehovah is my father') and Uri for Urijah ('Jehovah is my light').

II. THE LORD'S LOVE FOR ISRAEL. i. 2-5

Yet ye say (2). The prophet employs the vivid method of question and answer eight times (cf. i. 6, 7, ii. 14, 17, iii. 7, 8, 13). Men are asking for a proof of the Lord's love. It is to be found in the favour He has shown *Jacob* (i.e. Israel), and in the overthrow of Edom, a people originally sprung from Jacob's twin brother *Esau*, but in more recent years Israel's hated foe (2, 3). *Yet I loved Jacob.* See Rom. ix. 13. Edom has suffered utter and final desolation and, in the future, her waste places will be a witness of her wickedness and of the Lord's anger. The reference in verse 3 is to some recent calamity that had befallen Edom, probably at the hands of the Nabatean Arabs who drove the Edomites from their old territory of Mount Seir to the district south of Judah, thereafter called Idumaea. *Whereas* (4); RV mg. reads 'though'. *The Lord of hosts* (4). This title occurs over twenty times in the book. *The border of wickedness* (4). The thought is that when men of a future generation see the desolation, they will conclude that Edom must have been desperately wicked to merit such punishment. Israel, on the other hand, will have indisputable proof of God's sovereign care. Verse 5 may be rendered, 'The Lord is great above the territory of Israel' (I.C.C.).

III. ISRAEL'S DISHONOUR OF THE LORD. i. 6—ii. 9

A son honoureth his father (6). In Israel this attitude towards one's father was stressed above all others. To think of God as Father, therefore, should result in honouring His authority and majesty. *My fear* (6); i.e. reverence for Me, of the sort that is due to a master from a servant. But the priests *despise my name* (6). *Ye offer polluted bread . . .* (7). This is not an answer to the preceding question but a second predicate descriptive of the priests, which is explained in verse 8. They despise His name in thinking that *the table of the Lord is contemptible* (7), and they pollute Him by their blemished offerings. For *thee* (7) the LXX and Targum read 'it', as also in verse 8. *The blind* (8). Every sacrificial victim had to be unblemished (see Dt. xv. 21, etc.). *Is it not evil?* (8); better, as in RV, 'it is no evil', and understood as expressing the sentiments of the priests. *Governor* (8); possibly Persian; the priests were bringing offerings to the altar which they would not dare present to the civil ruler. *Accept thy person* (8); lit. 'lift up thy face', i.e. 'to assure thee of his favour'. So their efforts to entreat God's favour will avail nothing if they bring such gifts to Him. *This hath been by your means* (9). Read with Exp. Bible, 'When things like this come from your hands, can He accept your persons?' In verse 10 follow RV and read, 'Oh that there were one among you that would shut the doors, that ye might not kindle fire on mine altar in vain!' Better to close the temple doors and to have no sacrifice at all than offer this vain worship. *Shall be* (11). Read each time with RV 'is'. The point is that in the prophet's day the very Gentiles were offering worship which was more sincere than that in Jerusalem. *In that ye say* (12). Cf. verse 7; it is their attitude rather than their actual utterance that the prophet has in mind. *Snuffed* (13); i.e. 'sniffed'. The priests find the temple services boring, and the people, following their example, are stingy and deceitful. *Cursed be the deceiver* (14). We are reminded of the story of Ananias and Sapphira in Acts v. Dr. M. Dods quotes very appositely from Pirke Aboth i. 16, 'Say little and do much. Be like Abraham, who only promised a morsel of bread, but fetched a calf tender and good.'

This commandment (ii. 1); i.e. the teaching of the subsequent verses. If the priests do not pay heed to it, they will be cursed. *Your blessings* (2). Probably the priestly benedictions, though some would understand the phrase as meaning the personal advantages enjoyed by the priests. *Your seed* (3); i.e. your posterity. For the last phrase the LXX reads 'Behold, I remove the shoulder from you', i.e. incapacitate you from your function of blessing. The German Bible has the interesting reading, 'it shall remain stuck to you'. The obvious meaning of the verse is that the priests will be openly disgraced and thoroughly discredited unless they learn to be worthy representatives of God's covenant with Levi (4). In verses 5–7 the nature of true priestly service is indicated. *Peace* (5) means here 'general prosperity' (cf. Nu. xxv. 12). A better rendering of this verse is, 'My covenant was with him; life and peace—I gave them to him; fear—and he feared me, and was afraid before my name.' The covenant promised prosperity in return for true reverence. *The law of truth* (6); i.e. true instruction. When this was given by the priest many were converted from wickedness. *Equity* (6); i.e. 'uprightness', the opposite of *iniquity*. *He is the messenger* (7). The priest, as well as the prophet, is the Lord's messenger with the duty of imparting *knowledge*, i.e. of the Lord and of His commandments.

Ye have corrupted the covenant (8); i.e. 'broken' it. This they have done by showing partiality and generally doing the opposite of what was expected of them. Little wonder that they were despised by the people (9).

IV. CONDEMNATION OF DIVORCES AND FOREIGN MARRIAGES. ii. 10–16

Have we not all one father? (10). The fact that Israel has in God a common Father and Creator ought to bind them closely together, and make them despise any treachery that tends to break the unity. But Judah has *dealt treacherously* (11) and profaned the Lord's sanctuary with he foreign marriages. *Holiness* (11), i.e. 'sanctuary' means either the temple or the holy people (cf Je. ii. 3). A *daughter of a strange god* (11) is a woman of another religion. Verse 12 may be read thus: 'May the Lord cut off to the man who doeth this the caller and the called' (see RV). The latter phrase is idiomatic and means 'all his posterity'. There are two ways of understanding verse 13. The *weeping* may be that of the divorced wives, as a consequence of which the worship of the people is not acceptable before the Lord. Or, reading 'because' for *insomuch that*, the weeping may betoken the renewed efforts of the zealous but impenitent people to procure the Lord's favour, after their offerings have been rejected by Him.

The wife of thy covenant (14); i.e. 'the wife to whom thou hast vowed loyalty'. The meaning of the first half of verse 15 is very obscure. Oesterley suggests: 'Did not One make us and preserve our spirit alive? And what does the One desire? A godly seed!' The point here is that when an Israelite marries a non-Israelitish woman, the religion of the offspring is more likely to be that of the mother than of the father. *He hateth putting away* (16). Malachi leaves his hearers in no doubt as to the Lord's attitude to these divorces, so justifying his call to them to *take heed* (15). *For one covereth violence with his garment* (16). Read with RV 'and him that covereth his garment with violence'. When a man claimed a woman as his wife, he cast his garment over her (cf. Ru. iii. 9). In this verse, therefore, 'garment' has to be understood in the sense of 'wife'.

V. THE COMING JUDGMENT.
ii. 17—iii. 6

The people have *wearied the Lord* (17) by saying that He delights in the evil-doer and by doubting the justice of His rule. The attitude expressed in this verse has to be understood against the background of the hardships of the post-exilic years. *My messenger* (iii. 1). In view of iv. 5, it is natural to interpret this as Elijah. In Mt. xi. 10, 14 our Lord quotes the first part of this verse and identifies Elijah with John the Baptist. This identification shows that the words of prophecy must not be taken too literally. Cf. also Lk. i. 17. The general meaning is that Malachi prophesies a revival of prophecy before the coming of the Lord: this was fulfilled in the ministry of John the Baptist, who was a true prophet and who prepared the way for the mission of Jesus Christ. *Messenger of the covenant* (1). The phrase is to be taken in apposition to *the Lord, whom ye seek*; for 'messenger', therefore, read 'angel', the Hebrew word having this double meaning. The day of the Lord is a day of darkness and not light (cf. Am. v. 20), yet its purpose is to purify rather than to destroy.

Contrast iv. 1. *Fullers' soap* (2). A 'fuller' was a bleacher of cloth. In the Anglo-Saxon Gospels John the Baptist is called 'the Fuller'. *The sons of Levi* (3). Judgment will begin at the house of the Lord in the person of the priests, purifying them to fit them for their high function (4). Verse 5 shows that the prophet is concerned about the morality of the people as well as their worship. The coming Judge will expose and condemn evil-doers of all kinds. *That turn aside the stranger* (5). As the 'stranger' was liable to have few friends to protect him and to ensure that he received justice, special concern was shown for him in the law (cf. Lv. xix. 10, 33). *I change not* (6). The Lord's love for Israel is unchanging, and so Israel is not destroyed (cf. La. iii. 22).

VI. REPENTANCE BY TITHES WILL BRING BLESSING. iii. 7–12

Malachi now calls the people to return to the Lord and to the observance of His ordinances. For *ye said* (7) read, as in RV, 'ye say'. *Tithes* (8); see Lv. xxvii. 30; Nu. xviii. 21. They have been robbing God by withholding from Him His dues. This has brought down a curse upon them. Note that in verse 9 *me* is emphatic in Hebrew. *All the tithes* (10); this suggests that some people had ceased tithing. The Hebrew may also be translated 'the whole tithe', which would mean that the people had been keeping back part of what they should bring. Times were admittedly bad, but Malachi calls them to prove God by bringing to His house what the law demanded. Then the *windows of heaven* would be opened (a phrase which suggests that they had been experiencing drought and bad crops), and there would be more than enough for all. *That there shall not be room enough to receive it* (10). The Hebrew is lit. 'until there is no sufficiency', which is understood as meaning 'until there is no more need'. For the *storehouse* see Ne. xiii. 5. *The devourer* (11); i.e. the 'locust'. *Cast her fruit* (11). The cause of this would be mildew and blasting (I.C.C.). When the surrounding nations see the prosperity which will follow liberality towards God, they will rightly judge that it is the Lord's action in blessing His people.

VII. THE COMING VINDICATION OF THE GODLY. iii. 13—iv. 3

Stout (13); i.e. unyielding, insistent. The attitude of the people to God has been one of defiance.

Spoken (13); the form of the verb in Hebrew is the Niphal, which is used of reciprocal action. The meaning is that they have spoken to one another, perhaps in little groups. Among themselves they have questioned the profitableness of serving God loyally, and have imagined that it is the evil-doers who are prosperous. *Walked mournfully* (14); i.e. in penitence for any failures to obey the Lord's commands. *They that work wickedness are set up* (15); i.e. made prosperous. The next phrase should be read as in RV: 'they tempt God, and are delivered.'

In verse 16 some, following the LXX, would read, 'Such things spake they that feared the Lord to each other.' But it is better to follow the Hebrew as in the AV translation. The words in verse 14 are the complaints of the sceptics. The faithful refuse to be moved by these arguments and seek to deepen their fellowship with each other and to reassure themselves of God's justice. Their names and records were written down in the Lord's *book of remembrance. In that day* . . . (17). RV reads 'in the day that I do make, even a peculiar treasure'. G. A. Smith translates 'in the day when I rise to action'. As God's special treasure the faithful will be spared the judgment which will fall on the ungodly. *Return, and discern* (18); i.e. 'discern again'. There will be a restoration of the moral order that obtained in the pre-exilic days. The wicked shall be punished, burnt up like stubble (iv. 1); the godly, on the other hand, shall be justified and healed, as in the rays of the sun (2). *Grow up* (2); RV 'gambol'. The suggestion is of a joyful, vigorous and care-free life. *In the day* (3); see RV and notes on iii. 17 above.

VIII. CONCLUSION. iv. 4–6

Horeb (4); i.e. Sinai. The people are exhorted to remember the law of Moses. With this verse we might compare the ending of Ecclesiastes: 'Let us hear the conclusion of the whole matter: Fear God, and keep his commandments.' For *Elijah* (5) see note above on iii. 1. The coming of this prophet will reconcile fathers and children and avert the threatened curse. The estrangement between the older and younger generations, which seems to be implied here, was probably due in part to the laxity about the marriage bond which Malachi has already denounced. These closing verses indicate that both the law and the prophets have their part to play in preparing for the coming of the Lord. Cf. Mk. ix. 4; Lk. xxiv. 44.

J. T. H. ADAMSON.

PART THREE

THE NEW TESTAMENT

THE GOSPEL ACCORDING TO MATTHEW

• INTRODUCTION

See also the General Article, 'The Fourfold Gospel', pp. 58–63.

This Gospel is known to us from the vellum codices of the New Testament dating from the fourth and fifth centuries, from papyrus fragments of an earlier date, from early versions, for example the Syriac and the so-called Old Latin, and from quotations from patristic writers from the second century onwards. The questions of its text and transmission are bound up with those that concern the New Testament as a whole.

I. AUTHORSHIP

Like the other three Gospels the book is anonymous. The name of the apostle Matthew (see ix. 9, x. 3) has, however, been traditionally connected with it since at least the second century. There are extant in the *Historia Ecclesiastica* of Eusebius, who wrote early in the fourth century, quotations from Papias, a second-century bishop (iii. 39), from Irenaeus, Bishop of Lyons in the second century (v. 8, 2), and from Origen the 'Christian scholar of the third century' (vi. 25), which agree in stating that this Gospel was written by Matthew for Hebrew Christians in Hebrew (by which these writers no doubt mean Aramaic). Eusebius adds his own testimony to the same effect twice in the course of his history (iii. 24, 6 and v. 10, 3). Well attested as the Aramaic original thus appears to be, no trace of it has survived. The earliest quotations from the Gospel are in Greek, and no scholar today doubts that the Gospel in Greek in its present form was in existence in the second half of the first century. Although no author's name is mentioned in the Gospel, there is at least one piece of internal evidence which confirms the traditional authorship. The account of the call of Matthew in ix. 9 is followed by that of a meal taken by Jesus in the company of publicans and sinners (ix. 10ff.). This begins with the words *kai egeneto autou anakeimenou en tē(i) oikia(i)* (ix. 10). This reads as if the meal took place in Jesus' house, for the last three Greek words quoted above are best rendered in English 'at home'. The parallel account in Mk. ii. 15, however, makes it clear that the feast took place in Levi's (that is, Matthew's) house. There the reading is *en tē(i) oikia(i) autou*, in his house. The alternative sense in Mt. ix. 10, agreeing both with Mark and with the facts as they are obviously conveyed to us by both evangelists, is

that 'at home' means 'in my (that is, in the author's) house'. Here, therefore, is a phrase that betrays the identity of the author.

II. SOURCES OF THE GOSPEL

The dominant hypothesis among scholars at the present day is that Mark's Gospel was the earliest written and that Matthew and Luke based their own work partly upon Mark (which according to this hypothesis they incorporated *in toto*, though with editorial variations), and partly upon other unknown sources, to which they had access. This may or may not be so. The evidence in its favour may be read in such a classical work on the subject as Canon Streeter's *The Four Gospels* (5th impression, 1936). See also the General Article, *The Fourfold Gospel*, p. 61. We may well agree that the principal points in our Lord's teaching, with the facts of His life, ministry, death and resurrection, were passed down among the Christians from the first in an oral tradition and that this may have taken a more or less fixed form in consequence of its use in the catechizing of candidates for baptism. The preface to the third Gospel appears to confirm that attempts had been made from time to time to incorporate this tradition in writing (Lk. i. 1, 2). We can readily understand that later Christian writers, including our evangelists, would have made use of such oral and written material. Yet there are certain further considerations with regard to the first Gospel. If the author was Matthew, he was an eyewitness of much that he records, as was not the case with the other two synoptists. The tradition that he wrote in Aramaic may be based upon the possibility of his having composed notes or memoranda of our Lord's sayings in his native language for his own use and for those to whom he went preaching. We need not exclude the possibility of these notes having been made actually contemporaneously with the Lord's ministry, nor of their having had a wide use as the basis of much subsequent oral and written tradition.

It seems certain that at least by the second century Matthew's Gospel had taken its place as the first of the four. The present writer feels that the natural inference is that at that time it was considered to have been the first written. Such a tradition may well have been based upon, or confirmed by, two obvious facts. The first is that the Gospel was written for the Hebrew Christians of Palestine who constituted the earliest Christian communities. The internal evidence that it was written for them is strong and lies in such facts as the references to Jerusalem as 'the holy city', the references in v. 21, 22 to the Sanhedrin and the synagogue Courts, the special respect paid to the Mosaic law (v. 17–19), the rabbinic language of xvi. 19, xviii. 18, and above all the use made of Old Testament prophecy. The second fact that may well have contributed to the placing of this Gospel as the first among the four follows on from the first. It forms a connecting link with the Old Testament and thus a fitting introduction to the New. At the outset it links itself with the Old by carrying the pedigree of Christ to David and Abraham. We may notice also that much of the great discourse known as the Sermon on the Mount, which is so placed in the New Testament as to constitute a foundation for Christian ethics, is occupied with a careful, even elaborate explanation of the relationship of the new gospel ethic with that of the law. In all early Greek MSS of the New Testament this Gospel is placed first of the four and in the great majority the Gospels are placed first in the New Testament.

III. PURPOSE OF THE GOSPEL

The evangelist's object is obviously to place on record a connected account of the birth, ministry, passion and resurrection of Jesus Christ. He arranges his material around five great discourses of our Lord's: the Sermon on the Mount (v. 1—vii. 27); the charge to the apostles (x. 5–42); the parables (xiii. 1–53); the discourse on humility and forgiveness (xviii. 1–35); and the apocalyptic discourse (xxiv. 1—xxv. 46). (See also notes on p. 62.) The evangelist makes his framework clear by the repetition of the same formula at the end of each of these addresses, i.e. 'It came to pass when Jesus had ended these sayings . . .' The intervening portions are occupied with accounts of miracles and other events so grouped and arranged as to make them easy to memorize. The opening portion before the first discourse (chapters i—iv) consists of the birth and infancy stories, the ministry of John

the Baptist, the baptism and temptation of the Lord and a general introduction to His ministry. The climax of the passion and resurrection immediately follows the last of the five discourses. The evangelist makes frequent use of proof texts from Old Testament prophecy and, indeed, interprets Old Testament prophecy as having its fulfilment in Jesus Christ in a manner that must have been very convincing to a Palestinian Jew of the first century and has been followed since by the Christian Church.

The following sections are peculiar to Matthew: the birth and infancy stories (i. 18—ii. 23); the general introduction to the Galilean ministry (iv. 23–25); the reference to Is. liii. 4 (viii. 17); the healing of the two blind men and of the dumb demoniac, with the reference to sheep having no shepherd (ix. 27–38); the invitation to the heavy laden (xi. 28–30); the reference to Is. xlii. 1–4 (xii. 15–21); the parables of the tares, the hid treasure, the pearl of great price and the drag net (xiii. 24–30, 34–50); the general reference to the ministry of healing (xv. 29–31); the discovery of the coin in the mouth of the fish (xvii. 24–27); the reference to children and their angels (xviii. 10, 11); the teaching on reconciliation, prayer and forgiveness (xviii. 15–35); teaching on eunuchs (xix. 10–12); the parable of the labourers in the vineyard (xx. 1–16); the parable of the two sons (xxi. 28–32); the denunciation of the Pharisees (xxiii); parts of the apocalyptic discourse, which is fuller in this Gospel than in the other synoptists (xxiv); the parable of the ten virgins (xxv. 1–13); the judgment of the sheep and goats (xxv. 31–46); the suicide of Judas (xxvii. 1–10); the resurrection of the saints (xxvii. 52, 53); the setting of the watch at the tomb (xxvii. 62–66); the rumour of the theft of the body and the great commission (xxviii. 11–20).

The evangelist has a distinct style of his own of which one of the more obvious features is the lack of detail in the description of events. His accounts incline to be summary and details are run together. This may be clearly seen by contrasting his accounts of the healing of the centurion's servant (viii. 5–13) and the raising of Jairus' daughter (ix. 18–26) with the parallel accounts in Luke. His background and approach are naturally Semitic.

OUTLINE OF CONTENTS

I. THE BIRTH AND INFANCY OF JESUS CHRIST. i. 1—ii. 23

II. THE PREPARATION FOR JESUS' PUBLIC MINISTRY. iii. 1—iv. 17

III. THE BEGINNING OF THE PUBLIC MINISTRY. iv. 18–25

IV. DISCOURSE I. THE SERMON ON THE MOUNT. v. 1—vii. 29

V. MIRACLES. viii. 1—ix. 34

VI. THE APPOINTMENT OF THE TWELVE. ix. 35—x. 4

VII. DISCOURSE II. THE CHARGE TO THE TWELVE. x. 5—xi. 1

VIII. JOHN THE BAPTIST AND CHRIST. xi. 2–24

IX. A GOSPEL INVITATION. xi. 25–30

X. A DISPUTE WITH THE PHARISEES. xii. 1–45

XI. JESUS AND HIS FAMILY. xii. 46–50

XII. DISCOURSE III. TEACHING BY PARABLES. xiii. 1–53

XIII. JESUS IN HIS HOME TOWN. xiii. 54–58

XIV. THE DEATH OF JOHN THE BAPTIST. xiv. 1–12

XV. MIRACLES. xiv. 13–36

XVI. CONTROVERSY WITH THE PHARISEES OVER RITUAL.
    xv. 1–20

XVII. FURTHER MIRACLES. xv. 21–39

XVIII. CONTROVERSY WITH THE PHARISEES AND SADDUCEES.
    xvi. 1–12

XIX. SIMON PETER'S CONFESSION. xvi. 13–20

XX. THE FIRST ANNOUNCEMENT OF CHRIST'S SUFFERINGS.
    xvi. 21–28

XXI. THE TRANSFIGURATION. xvii. 1–13

XXII. THE HEALING OF THE DEVIL-POSSESSED BOY. xvii. 14–21

XXIII. THE SECOND ANNOUNCEMENT OF CHRIST'S SUFFERINGS.
    xvii. 22, 23

XXIV. THE TEMPLE TAX. xvii. 24–27

XXV. DISCOURSE IV. TEACHING ON HUMILITY AND FORGIVENESS.
    xviii. 1—xix. 2

XXVI. TEACHING ON DIVORCE IN ANSWER TO THE PHARISEES.
    xix. 3–12

XXVII. THE BLESSING OF CHILDREN. xix. 13–15

XXVIII. RICHES AND SALVATION. xix. 16—xx. 16

XXIX. THE THIRD ANNOUNCEMENT OF CHRIST'S SUFFERINGS.
    xx. 17–19

XXX. THE REQUEST OF JAMES AND JOHN. xx. 20–28

XXXI. THE HEALING OF THE TWO BLIND MEN. xx. 29–34

XXXII. THE EVENTS OF THE LAST WEEK OF THE MINISTRY.
    xxi. 1—xxiii. 39

XXXIII. DISCOURSE V. THE LAST DAYS. xxiv. 1—xxv. 46

XXXIV. THE PASSION, DEATH AND RESURRECTION. xxvi. 1—xxviii. 20

COMMENTARY

I. THE BIRTH AND INFANCY OF JESUS CHRIST. i. 1—ii. 23

a. The ancestry of Jesus (i. 1–17)

The book of the generation (1); i.e. His pedigree or ancestry. *David* (1). The purpose of tracing our Lord's ancestry to David is to show that the promises made to David that he should be an ancestor of the Messiah are fulfilled in Jesus Christ (see 2 Sa. vii. 12–16; Pss. lxxxix. 29, 36, 37, cxxxii. 11). *Abraham* (1). Similar promises were made to Abraham (see Gn. xii. 7, xiii. 15, xvii. 7, xxii. 18; Gal. iii. 16).

Thamar (3). She was a foreigner and a woman of doubtful morality (see Gn. xxxviii). *Rachab* (5) was also a foreigner and originally a wicked woman (see Jos. ii. 1; Heb. xi. 31). *Ruth* (5). She was a Moabitess. See the book of Ruth for her story. *Her that had been the wife of Urias* (6); i.e. Bath-sheba (see 2 Sa. xii. 10, 24). The fact that she is described in this way suggests a deliberate reminder of her sinful association with David.

Solomon (7). It is probable that this genealogy traces not the natural descent (for which see Lk. iii. 23–38), but the royal and legal, in right of which Jesus Christ was heir to David's throne. *Ozias* (8); i.e. Uzziah (Is. vi. 1; 2 Ch. xxvi. 1), also called Azariah (2 Ki. xiv. 21). Three generations are omitted here (see 1 Ch. iii. 11, 12) in order to make the table conform to the evangelist's arrangement (see verse 17). This was a recognized feature of genealogies and is not due to inaccuracy. It is possible that generations are also omitted in the first and third sections of the table (verses 2–6, 12–16). *Jechonias* (11). He is also called Jehoiachin (2 Ki. xxiv. 8) and Coniah (Je. xxii. 24, 28) and was debarred from having any descendant upon the throne of David (Je. xxii. 30). Jesus Christ was not a natural descendant of his. *Carried away to Babylon* (11). The reference is to the seventy years' captivity.

Joseph the husband of Mary (16). The wording is carefully chosen to avoid giving the impression that Joseph was the natural father of Jesus Christ. As the husband of Mary he was His legal father, and the one through whom the right to David's throne was transmitted. The marriage of Joseph and Mary took place after the conception but before the birth of Jesus Christ. *Fourteen generations . . . fourteen generations . . . fourteen generations* (17). The genealogy was purposely arranged in this way by the evangelist in order to be memorized easily. The Greek particle *oun*, translated *so*, implies this artificial arrangement. The sentence means, 'This makes all the generations . . . to be fourteen generations'.

b. The birth of Jesus (i. 18–25)

Espoused (18). This means that she was already bound to Joseph, although they were not yet actually married. Unfaithfulness after espousal was regarded as adultery. *Of the Holy Ghost* (18). Conception was by the miraculous operation o God the Holy Ghost, whereby 'the Word be came flesh'. *Make her a public example . . . pu her away privily* (19). These two courses wer open to him by Jewish law and custom. A ma of Joseph's character would naturally incline t the second. *While he thought* (20). Knowin Mary's good character, he was naturally greatl puzzled. *The angel* (20); better 'an angel', as i RV. The intervention of the angel should no make the story less credible. It was essentia under the circumstances, as no husband coul be expected to believe the fact of the virgin con ception unless the truth were revealed to hin supernaturally. *In a dream* (20). Dreams wer often recognized in the East as importan channels of revelation, and still are so today *Son of David* (20); the normal Hebrew way o saying 'descendant of David'. *JESUS* (21). Th Greek form of the Hebrew Jeshua, Joshua o Jehoshua, meaning 'the Lord saves'. *He shal save his people from their sins* (21); i.e. from thei guilt and penalty as well as from their grip an power. This is a great foundation statement o the gospel standing at the outset of the Nev Testament.

That it might be fulfilled (22); i.e. the statemen of the prophet made the events inevitable. *Of th Lord by the prophet* (22); better, as in RV, 'b the Lord through the prophet'. The Lord i the source or author of the prophecy. The pro phet is the mouthpiece or channel. This was th Jewish view of prophetical inspiration. It wa also the view of the Christian Church unti challenged by the liberalism of the nineteentl century. Wherever the phrase 'by the prophet occurs the better rendering would be 'througl the prophet'. *Behold, a virgin . . . his nam Emmanuel* (23); quoted substantially from th Alexandrine Greek version (LXX) of Is. vii. 14 In the Greek the phrase *God with us* is taker from the LXX version of Is. viii. 8, where it is a translation of the Hebrew *Emmanuel*. This is the second of two outstandingly importan statements of the gospel, both of them found within the scope of three verses (see above or verse 21). This statement reveals that Jesus is God. The whole Christian revelation may be said to be founded on these three verses.

Knew her not (25). The language carefully safeguards the fact of the virgin birth. It implies, however, that, after the birth of Jesus, Joseph and Mary lived a normal married life. *Her firstborn* (25). These words are not found in the MSS that are considered the best and most accurate and should probably be omitted as they are in RV. They imply that Mary had younger children and at least prove that at the time this phrase crept into the text in the early centuries of the Christian era no difficulty was experienced in believing this fact. For the names of the Lord's brothers see Mk. vi. 3.

c. The story of the wise men (ii. 1–12)

Bethlehem (1). This was the village where king David was born. It was not the home of Joseph and Mary. For the reason of their journey there see Lk. ii. 1–5. It lies a little south of Jerusalem. *Judaea* (1); i.e. the Roman province of Judaea and southernmost of the three provinces into which Palestine west of the Jordan was divided. *Herod the king* (1). He came from an Idumaean (Edomite) family and was king, under the Romans, of the whole of Palestine. He is usually known as Herod the Great. *Wise men* (1). Most likely they were astrologers belonging to a class of men similar to the Chaldeans mentioned in Dn. ii. 2. They probably came from Mesopotamia. Though legend has grown round them, nothing is known of the circumstances of their journey beyond what is told us in this Gospel. *Born King of the Jews* (2). This phrase is an echo of Jewish messianic expectations. *His star* (2); see also verse 10. No certain grounds exist for a decision between the view that this was a peculiar astronomical phenomenon or a supernatural manifestation. *To worship him* (2). It appears from this that the wise men regarded Him already as a divine Being.

The chief priests and scribes (4). The religious leaders were the natural people to whom to turn. The scribes (Heb. *sopherim*, Gk. *grammateis*) were the official interpreters of the Mosaic law and constituted a sort of order of religious scholars. *Christ* (4); the Greek rendering of the Hebrew *Messiah*. Both mean 'anointed one'. Jewish kings and priests were anointed as a sign of their consecration, and the ceremony gave them a special sanctity. *And thou Bethlehem . . . my people Israel* (6). The quotation is from Mi. v. 2, but does not come from the LXX nor is it apparently intended as a literal translation of the Hebrew. The religious leaders undoubtedly understood the passage as a prediction of the birth of the Messiah, as also has the Christian Church.

The house (11). The holy family was no longer in the stable of the inn at Bethlehem. As the incident may have taken place at any time during the two years after Jesus' birth (see verse 16), they may even have been in Galilee. The fact that Herod later slew the children in the Bethlehem area was due to the prophecy and not to information given him as to where the infant Jesus had been found. *Worshipped* (11). The wise men must have received a very complete revelation with regard to the Person of Christ. *Gifts* (11). The three kinds of gifts are generally regarded as symbolic of Christ's threefold office as King, Priest and Prophet.

d. The flight into Egypt (ii. 13–23)

The angel (13); better 'an angel', as in RV. *Herod will seek the young child* (13). The family may have moved already from Bethlehem and so would have escaped the slaughter there. But it would have been difficult to remain hidden while still in Palestine. *The death of Herod* (15). This took place in the year 4 B.C. Owing to miscalculation the years of the Christian era, which were not reckoned until the fourth century A.D., commenced from four to six years after the birth of Christ. *Out of Egypt have I called my son* (15). This quotation is taken from the Hebrew of Ho. xi. 1. In the

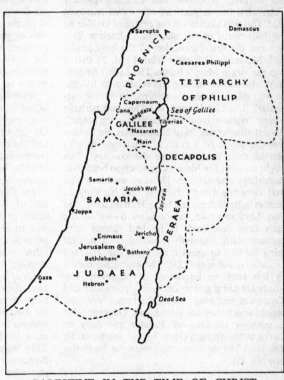

PALESTINE IN THE TIME OF CHRIST

original context the passage refers to the redemption of Israel from Egypt by Moses. There was a hidden meaning implanted in the passage by the Holy Spirit, which is here brought out by the evangelist.

According to the time (16). This seems to imply that the visit of the wise men took place when the Lord was nearly two years old. See note above on verse 11 and cf. verse 7. The quotation in verse 18 is taken substantially from the LXX and perhaps partly from the Hebrew of Je. xxxi. 15. The context in Jeremiah contains a promise of resurrection and restoration to their mothers of the infants murdered by Herod. Ramah was a town that belonged to Benjamin (see Jos. xviii. 25), whose territory was immediately north of Jerusalem. Rachel, wife of

Jacob and mother of Benjamin, stands as the symbol for the Benjamite mothers. *The land of Israel* (20); i.e. Palestine. *Archelaus* (22). He was the son of Herod the Great. On his father's death in 4 B.C. Archelaus succeeded to the provinces of Judaea, Samaria and Idumaea, the rest of Herod's dominions going to other sons (see map on p. 775). He was a notorious tyrant. *The parts of Galilee* (22). Galilee was the northernmost of the three sections of Palestine. It had formed part of the dominions of Herod the Great, but on his death did not go to Archelaus but to his brother Herod Antipas, another son of Herod the Great. Antipas was not called king but *tetrarch*, a Greek title meaning literally 'ruler of a fourth part'. *A city called Nazareth* (23). This was situated in the centre of Galilee on the hills north of the plain of Esdraelon. This was not the first connection of the holy family with Nazareth. It is clear from Lk. i. 26 that it was the virgin Mary's home. The Lucan nativity story also shows that she had relatives in Judaea. In Mt. xiii. 55 Joseph is referred to as 'the carpenter'. The Greek word is *tektōn* and perhaps means 'stone-mason' as much as 'carpenter'. Recent discoveries have shown that Bethlehem was the centre of a guild of stone-masons who carried their craft all over the country. This might account for Joseph's connection both with Bethlehem and Galilee. He may well have felt that after the Lord's birth it was his duty to remain in Bethlehem and bring Him up there, and may have reversed his decision owing to the facts here described. If he had former connections with Nazareth it would be a natural thing for him to select it for his home. *He shall be called a Nazarene* (23). The evangelist means by this term an inhabitant of Nazareth. The words are not a quotation from a particular Old Testament prophecy; hence the rather indefinite way in which they are introduced. The evangelist is perhaps thinking of Isaiah's prophecy of Christ as the Branch (Heb. *netser*; see Is. xi. 1). The term has no connection with the Nazarites (see Nu. vi).

II. THE PREPARATION FOR JESUS' PUBLIC MINISTRY. iii. 1—iv. 17

a. The ministry of John the Baptist (iii. 1–12)

See notes on Mk. i. 1–8; Lk. iii. 1–20. Cf. also Jn. i. 6–34. *In those days* (1); i.e. about twenty-eight or thirty years after the events last described. *John the Baptist* (1). He was the son of Zacharias and Elisabeth and a cousin of the Lord, called and consecrated from birth to be Christ's forerunner (see Lk. i. 5–25, 57–80). *The wilderness of Judaea* (1); i.e. the eastern tract of the province of Judaea, lying east of the main mountain ridge and west of the Dead Sea. It was not a sandy desert, but was insufficiently fertile to repay cultivation. *Repent* (2). The root idea of this great gospel word is a change of heart and mind towards sin. The term 'conversion' emphasizes the same change in its Godward

attitude. *The kingdom of heaven* (2). This expression is peculiar to Matthew, who uses it where the other evangelists say 'kingdom of God'. The change is due to Matthew's Jewish background and outlook, it being regarded among the Jews as blasphemous to refer to God by name. Thus they substituted a term such as 'heaven'. The kingdom of God meant the sovereignty or rule of God which Jewish messianic expectations looked to see set up over Israel. By the words *is at hand* the Baptist meant that the advent of Jesus was to introduce the new order. *The voice of one crying . . . make his paths straight* (3). These words are quoted from the LXX in Is. xl. 3, and thus explain that passage as a prophecy of John the Baptist. John was a 'voice', the one purpose of his preaching being to point men to Jesus. He was to prepare the way by calling men to repentance and thus making them ready to receive the Lord. *Locusts* (4). The reference may be perhaps, to locust beans. But locusts were eaten by the very poor.

Were baptized (6). The form that baptism took in John's day or subsequently is never defined in the New Testament. It may have been immersion. On the other hand it may be that the baptizer and the one to be baptized stood together in the river while the former poured water on the latter's head. *Confessing their sins* (6); no necessarily to John, but to God.

The Pharisees (7). They were the most important of the Jewish religious sects which had arisen in the inter-Testamental period. Their aim was to stress and defend the Jewish religious outlook as opposed to the Hellenistic, when the latter was gaining much ground in the East through the influence of the Seleucid, or Greek kings of Syria. The name is a Hellenized form of Heb. *Perushim*, 'separated ones'. Their name for themselves was *ḥasidim*, 'pious ones'. They stood for a scrupulous observance of the letter of the Mosaic law, but regarded rabbinic tradition a on a level with the Old Testament Scriptures. They were the ritualists of the Jewish Church. *Sadducees* (7). They were the next great Jewish sect after the Pharisees and probably originally came into being as a reaction against them. Their name derives, perhaps, from Heb. *ṣaddiq* 'righteous'. They taught that virtue was to be practised for its own sake, not for reward, and from this premise they went on to deny the existence of a future world. They were the rationalists of the Jewish Church.

The wrath to come (7); i.e. the day of judgment *Fruits* (8); RV 'fruit'. This was the token of true repentance. The gospel message is that entry into the kingdom of God is not the privilege of a particular race or nation, but is open to all on the grounds of repentance and faith. Jewish privilege belonged only to Old Testament day (see Gal. iii. 28, 29). *These stones* (9); i.e. the stones that lay around on the ground. The Baptist means that the Jewish nation possessed no more privilege in the eyes of God by reason of descent from Abraham than did the stones

And now ... (10). This is a picturesque and vivid way of saying the same thing as Jn. iii. 18, 'is condemned already'. *The fire* (10); i.e. the bonfire that burns up the rubbish. *Whose shoes I am not worthy to bear* (11). John felt himself unworthy to perform even a menial task for the Lord Jesus. His well-known humility is expressed in Jn. iii. 30. *With the Holy Ghost, and with fire* (11). The Holy Ghost and the fire are identical. He is the fire of God that burns up the dross in the believer's life and sets him ablaze for God. The Holy Ghost fell upon the whole Church on the day of Pentecost and is available for every believer since. Pentecost probably constituted the baptism here foretold by the Baptist (see Acts ii. 33). The distinctive characteristic of the Christian believer is that he is led by the Spirit of God (see Rom. viii. 14). *Purge his floor* (12); i.e. threshing-floor, as in RV. The *fan* was used for winnowing. This act of judgment is in process throughout the gospel age as the wheat and chaff are separated by acceptance or rejection of the gospel. It is consummated at the last day. *Gather his wheat* (12); see xxiv. 31. *Unquenchable fire* (12); i.e. fire that will never be put out until its purpose is accomplished (see Is. xxxiv. 10; Je. vii. 20, xvii. 27; Ezk. xx. 47, 48).

b. The baptism of Jesus (iii. 13–17)

See notes on Mk. i. 9–11; Lk. iii. 21, 22. *Suffer* (15); i.e. let, allow, or permit. *To fulfil all righteousness* (15). His baptism was a step that must be taken in order to accomplish the whole of God's righteous purpose. Though He needed no repentance and had no sins to confess, Jesus, by submitting to baptism, took the sinner's place. This symbolic act was an illustration of the greater baptism (see xx. 22) which He was to undergo at Calvary, where He was to fulfil God's purpose in sending Him into the world by representing the sinner. *Unto him* (16). These words are omitted in some texts. *He saw* (16). This appears to mean that Jesus saw the dove (a symbol of gentleness), but it is clear from Jn. i. 31–34 that John also saw it. *The Spirit of God* (16). All three Persons of the Holy Trinity were either visible or audible to human eyes and ears at this sacred moment. This does not mean that Jesus was not one with the Spirit from birth and indeed from eternity past. The Spirit now came to equip Him for His public ministry. *This is my beloved Son* (17). We ought not to take these words to mean that the Father was now proclaiming Jesus to be His Son for the first time, or that Jesus was now for the first time aware of His unique relationship with the Father. He was aware of it in childhood (see Lk. ii. 49). The same proclamation was made by the Father at the time of the transfiguration (xvii. 5).

c. The temptation of Jesus (iv. 1–11)

See notes on Lk. iv. 1–13; Mk. i. 12, 13. *Then* (1); i.e. immediately after His baptism. There is a close connection between the baptism and the temptation. By the former Jesus dedicated Himself to the way of the cross. In the latter the devil presented to His mind ways of carrying out His ministry which would have avoided the cross. *Led up of the Spirit* (1). This crisis was brought upon Jesus by the direct will of God. It was not a test on God's part to see if Jesus would fall, but a demonstration of the impossibility of His falling. The reason for His going *into the wilderness* (1) was that He needed to face this great testing alone.

The devil (1). This is one of the names of the original serpent of the Garden of Eden who brought about the fall of man (Rev. xii. 9). He is 'the prince of this world' (Jn. xvi. 11) and 'the prince of the power of the air' (Eph. ii. 2). It is sometimes difficult in these scientific days to believe in the reality of a spirit world, but there is nothing contrary to reason in what the Bible tells us of an invisible world of intelligences who, in a way of which we know nothing, have access to our minds with suggestive power. The teaching of the Bible as to the personality of the devil is consistent from Genesis to Revelation. *When he had fasted* (2). The necessity for this is not clear. It may have been part of the demonstration that at His weakest the Lord could meet and conquer the devil at his strongest. It may have accompanied a time of intense prayer.

Command that these stones be made bread (3). The temptation had a wider scope than an appeal to personal hunger. It seems to have been a suggestion to avoid the cross by becoming a popular social reformer. *It is written* (4). Each time when tempted the Lord appealed to Scripture. This is a fundamental example of the use of 'the sword of the Spirit' (see Eph. vi. 17). *Man shall not live by bread alone* ... (4). The words are quoted from the LXX of Dt. viii. 3. The purpose of the quotation seems to be to indicate that man has spiritual needs in addition to material and that Jesus' first duty, therefore, must be to preach the Word of God. The word 'alone' shows that the material needs were not to be wholly neglected. There is therefore no inconsistency when we find our Lord working such miracles as the feeding of the five thousand (xiv. 13–21).

Taketh him up (5); doubtless in thought and suggestion. See verse 8n. *The holy city* (5). This expression occurs twice in this Gospel and not at all in the other three. This possibly indicates that the Gospel was first addressed to the inhabitants of Jerusalem. *A pinnacle* (5); RV 'the pinnacle'; RV mg. 'the wing'. The reference is probably to the flat roof or parapet of the wing of the temple. *Cast thyself down* (6). The temptation seems to have been to choose the life of a popular wonder-worker. *It is written* (6). The devil can quote Scripture when it suits him. This means that the Scripture was known to Jesus and was running in His mind, and the temptation came to misapply it. The quotation is from the LXX of Ps. xci. 11, 12. It is interesting that this Psalm, the only passage of Scripture recorded as being quoted by the devil, goes on immediately to promise victory over him. *Thou shalt not tempt the Lord thy God* (7); a quotation from the LXX of Dt. vi. 16. To tempt God appears here to mean to take a risk that is not in accordance with the will of God, and then to dare, or attempt to force, God to preserve from disaster. A man might put his hand in the fire and complain that God had not kept him from being burnt.

An exceeding high mountain (8). The fact that there is no mountain from which all the world can be seen proves that these experiences of our Lord were subjective. *Will I give thee* (9). The Bible occasionally shows us the devil as responsible for the government of the empires of the world. *Worship me* (9). The temptation seems to have been to avoid the cross by establishing a kingdom by force, a procedure that would have been popular with, and intelligible to, the Jews. *Satan* (10). This means in Hebrew 'adversary'. Satan is a prosecuting counsel, accusing the children of God in the court of heaven. For this name see Rev. xii. 9. For his activity see 1 Ch. xxi. 1; Jb. i. 2; Zc. iii. *Thou shalt worship . . . shalt thou serve* (10); a quotation from the LXX of Dt. vi. 13. It establishes one of the fundamental principles of scriptural religion.

d. Jesus' residence in Capernaum (iv. 12–17)

John was cast into prison (12). For the circumstances of his arrest and death see xiv. 1–12. The city of Capernaum where Jesus now settled was a Roman settlement near the Sea of Galilee and the centre of the Roman government of Galilee. *Zabulon . . . Nephthalim* (13). For the borders of these tribes see Jos. xix. 10–16, 32–39. The quotation in verses 15 and 16 is adapted from the LXX of Is. ix. 1, 2. *Great light* (17). Cf. Lk. ii. 32; Jn. viii. 12, xii. 46. *Repent* (17). The Lord took up the message of John the Baptist. Cf. iii. 2 and x. 7.

III. THE BEGINNING OF THE PUBLIC MINISTRY. iv. 18–25

a. The call of the four disciples (iv. 18–22)

See notes on Mk. i. 16–20 and cf. Lk. v. 1–11. *Simon called Peter* (18). For the probable circumstances of the change of name see Jn. i. 42 and cf. Mt. xvi. 18. *I will make you fishers of men* (19). This promise is linked with the earliest expression of the gospel call and suggests that the main work of the Christian in the world is to win others for Christ. *Mending* (21). Not necessarily mending, but getting ready for use. *They immediately left the ship and their father* (22). Following Jesus may require the abandonment of occupation and the severance of family ties. It is in any case a call to wholehearted allegiance.

b. A preaching and healing ministry (iv. 23–25)

In their synagogues (23). These were the halls in provincial towns where the Jewish congregations met for prayer and praise on the sabbath, and for instruction and the administration of justice on other days. Their use dated from the days of Ezra and Nehemiah. *The gospel of the kingdom* (23); i.e. the good news that God's rule was being set up. *Healing all manner of sickness* (23). Note that this healing ministry was undertaken by our Lord through sheer compassion, in fulfilment of prophecy, and as part of the credentials of His Messiahship. *Syria* (24); i.e. the Roman province north of Palestine. *Possessed with devils* (24). Demon possession was common in the time of our Lord. Its nature is a mystery, but it exists in heathen countries today and is thought by some to account for some of the cases in the asylums of civilized nations. In spite of rationalistic objections the Bible-believer can do no other than accept it as a fact, as did our Lord. For further information the bigger Bible dictionaries and encyclopaedias should be consulted. *Those that had the palsy* (24); i.e. paralytics. *Decapolis* (25) was a district of ten Greek cities, mostly lying east of Jordan, and extending as far north as Damascus. The phrase *beyond Jordan* probably means the district of Peraea which coincided with the Old Testament Gilead.

IV. DISCOURSE I. THE SERMON ON THE MOUNT. v. 1—vii. 29

A shortened form of this sermon is found in Lk. vi. 20–29, where see notes. It is also probable that the teaching it gives was repeated on other occasions.

a. Christian character (v. 1–12)

He went up (1). This was probably in order to avoid the crowds and to find a quiet opportunity for teaching His disciples. See Lk. vi. 17n. *Was set* (1); better, as in RV, 'had sat down'.

Blessed (3); i.e. 'happy'. *The poor in spirit* (3); an allusion to Is. lvii. 15. The gospel begins here with those who realize their need and are ready to rely upon Another for the necessities of spiritual life. Verse 4 is an allusion to Is. lxi. 3 and Ps. cxxvi. 5. The reference is to those who are under conviction of sin, or who 'sigh and cry' over the sinful state of the world. It is also applicable to Christians who are suffering persecution or reproach for their faith. The comfort is given by faith in our hearts now and later will be openly received in the world to come. The word *they* in verses 4–9 is emphatic. *The meek* (5); i.e. the unselfish. The word *inherit* (5) implies membership of God's family. *The earth* (5); i.e. the 'new earth wherein dwelleth righteousness' (2 Pet. iii. 13). It is important to remember that both in Hebrew and Greek the same word means 'earth' and 'land', so that prophecies in the Old Testament about the land may be fulfilled in the new earth. For this verse see Ps. xxxvii. 11. *The pure in heart* (8); an allusion to Ps. xxiv. 4, li. 10, lxxiii. 1. God requires purity in the essential being, and this can be obtained only by the new birth. *See God* (8). This they do by faith now and face to face then. Cf. Jn. xiv. 9; 1 Jn. iii. 2. *The peacemakers* (9). Primarily the reference is to those who in Christ make peace between God and man by bringing men to accept the reconciliation of the gospel. There is also doubtless a reference to peace between man and man. *The children* (9); better 'sons', as in RV. Verses 10–12 would leave the hearers in no doubt as to the likely attitude of the world to the gospel. The Christian is consistently represented in the New Testament as one liable to be persecuted.

b. Christian witness (v. 13–16)

Note that in verses 13 and 14 the word *Ye* is emphatic. The function of salt which seems to be in mind here is that of preserving from corruption. *Ye are the light of the world* (14); i.e. in the sense of reflecting the light which had shone into their hearts. See verse 16 below and cf. Jn. viii. 12 and 2 Cor. iv. 5, 6. *A bushel* (15); better 'the bushel', as in RV, a vessel kept in every house for purposes of standard measurement. *A candlestick* (15); better 'the lampstand'. *Glorify* (16) has the sense of ascribing praise to God.

c. The relationship of the gospel to the law (v. 17–48)

The law (17). This was the common Jewish name for the first of the three divisions of the Hebrew Scriptures, i.e. the five books Genesis to Deuteronomy. The term was sometimes used, however, in a wider sense. See verse 18 below. *The prophets* (17). Strictly the reference is to the second of the divisions of the Hebrew Scriptures, consisting of the books Joshua to 2 Kings and Isaiah to Malachi. But by the use of the expression 'the law or the prophets' our Lord is probably referring here to the whole Old Testament (cf. vii. 12). Jesus fulfilled the law in His life by perfectly keeping it, in His teaching by promulgating an ethic of love which fulfils the law (Rom. xiii. 10), and in His death by exhausting its sanctions.

Jot (18); i.e. the Hebrew letter *yod*, the smallest in the alphabet. The *tittle* was a 'tail' or flourish attached to letters of the Hebrew alphabet, in some cases making an essential difference between one of the characters and another. By the phrase *the law* the whole of the Old Testament is probably meant. The Lord here teaches a very high view of biblical inspiration, and indicates clearly that the gospel is founded upon the Old Testament. *The least in the kingdom of heaven* (19). It does not seem certain whether our Lord means by this 'of no value in the kingdom' and is referring to those who never enter it at all, or whether He is teaching a difference of status and reward among the saved in the final state. See xviii. 1–6. The former alternative is perhaps the more probable. *Except your righteousness shall exceed* (20). The Lord is here emphasizing the necessity for genuineness and reality in the spiritual life. *Enter into the kingdom*

of heaven (20). This is the same thing as to have everlasting life (see e.g. Jn. iii. 16).

By them (21); better 'to them', as in AV mg. and RV. *Thou shalt not kill* (21). This is the sixth commandment of the Decalogue, quoted from the LXX of Ex. xx. 13. The Greek word refers only to the taking of human life. *In danger of the judgment* (21, 22); i.e. liable to be brought before the local council which met in the synagogue and was subordinate to the Great Council of Seventy, or Sanhedrin, at Jerusalem. *Whosoever is angry* (22). Our Lord means that the real sin is committed in the heart before the stage of outward action is reached. In God's sight he is as great an offender as the man who kills. The Mosaic law could restrain only outward actions; Jesus deals with the evil heart of man and transforms it (see Rom. viii. 3, 4). In this sense His ethic fulfils the law because it deals with the root of the matter and enables the aims of the law to be carried out. *Without a cause* (22). This expression is omitted in some good MSS. It occurs in RV mg. but is omitted by the RV and RSV. *Raca* (22); i.e. 'vain fellow', a Hebrew expression of contempt (see 2 Sa. vi. 20). *The council* (22); i.e. the Sanhedrin, or Great Council of Seventy. The Lord uses this judicial grading to make clear the degree of gravity of the offence. *Thou fool* (22). This represents the Greek word *More*. It seems probable, however, that the original word was the Hebrew *moreh*, which is an expression of condemnation. Its use would imply a murderous hatred. *Hell fire* (22); Gk. *tēn geennan tou pyros*. Gehenna was the Hellenized form of the name of the valley of Hinnom at Jerusalem in which fires were kept constantly burning to consume the refuse of the city. This is a powerful picture of final destruction.

Bring thy gift (23); i.e. offer a sacrifice to God in accordance with the Mosaic law. *First be reconciled* (24). God cannot receive the worship, or accept the person, of anyone who is not in a right relationship, so far as he is aware, with all others. Cf. the words of the Church of England Communion Service, 'Ye that . . . are in love and charity with your neighbours, . . . draw near with faith'. *Agree with thine adversary* (25). The stern principle lying behind verses 25 and 26 is expressed even more forcibly in Mt. vi. 14, 15 and xviii. 23–35. See notes there.

By them (27); better 'to them'. The words are omitted by RV and RSV. *Thou shalt not commit adultery* (27). This is the seventh commandment of the Decalogue, quoted from the LXX of Ex. xx. 14. Adultery is the taking of another man's wife. The term never refers in the Bible to the unfaithfulness of a husband to his wife unless, of course, it includes the former. *Whosoever looketh* (28). It seems clear that the Lord does not mean to condemn here natural sexual attraction but the lustful look, perhaps with special reference to a married woman. *In his heart* (28). This is the seat of sin. The wicked action is the product of the wicked heart. As in the case of the sixth commandment, the Mosaic law dealt with the outward acts, whereas Jesus deals with the inner motive.

Offend (29); i.e. 'ensnare' or 'entrap'. This root meaning of the word should be borne in mind whenever it occurs. *Pluck it out, and cast it from thee* (29). Get rid of sinful desire at whatever cost. The language of verses 29 and 30 constitutes a vivid figure of speech. *Thy right hand* (30). The hand stands for action, whereas the eye stands for desire.

Whosoever shall put away his wife (31, 32). Verse 31 is a summary of the direction recorded in Dt. xxiv. 1. In contrast to Moses our Lord forbids divorce absolutely. From His further teaching on the subject in xix. 3–9 we learn that the Mosaic enactment accommodated itself to the evil nature of man. As Jesus came to deal specifically with that evil nature, He repudiates this accommodation and restores the primitive standard. *Saving for the cause of fornication* (32). This clause is frequently misunderstood in the sense that unfaithfulness on a wife's part gives legitimate ground for divorce and is thus supposed to be a modification of the absolute prohibition found in Mk. x. 11; Lk. xvi. 18. There is, however, no contradiction whatever between the two. *Fornication* (not 'adultery') refers to unfaithfulness on the part of a woman before marriage. If this is discovered subsequent to marriage, the Lord's words oblige the husband to put the woman away because in God's sight there has been no marriage. The present writer believes that Scripture teaches that every woman belongs by nature in God's sight to the first man with whom she has sexual intercourse, and to 'marry' her during the lifetime of that man is to commit adultery. *Causeth her to commit adultery* (32); i.e. makes her out to be an adulteress. In accordance with the above the husband who divorces his wife proclaims to the world that she belonged to another before 'marrying' him.

By them (33); better 'to them'. The remainder of the verse is a combination of the laws to be found in Ex. xx. 7; Lv. xix. 12; Nu. xxx. 2. *Swear not at all* (34); i.e. take no oath at all. To reduce the sense to a prohibition of profane language is to do violence to the original (Gk. *mē omosai*) and to rob the passage of meaning. The Mosaic law allowed oaths with proper safeguards as a protection against the dishonesty of the human heart. Our Lord has come to deal with the human heart, so that oaths are no longer necessary, and He is able to restore the primitive standard and forbid them altogether, thus accomplishing (fulfilling) the purpose of the law. See Jas. v. 12. *Neither by heaven . . . nor by the earth . . .* (34, 35). The words are taken from Is. lxvi. 1. *Jerusalem* (35); notice the emphasis upon the capital city in this Gospel. *The city of the great King* (35); the phrase is from Ps. xlviii. 2. Jerusalem in Palestine still possessed this prerogative till the Lord's death and resurrection. Now there is a 'new Jerusalem' (Gal. iv. 26). *Cometh of evil* (37); that is, the necessity for oaths was due to the evil nature of man, as in the case of divorce above, which the law was powerless to deal with (Rom. viii. 3).

An eye for an eye . . . (38). This is taken from the LXX of Lv. xxiv. 20. This is the law of retaliation. It was not so much a command to the injured person that he must take this equivalent as a direction to the judges that an injured person might retaliate up to the point of equality, and no further. *That ye resist not evil* (39); RV 'resist not him that is evil'. The Mosaic law of retaliation illustrated the perfect justice and righteousness of God. Our Lord commands that an injury must not be righted. In the view of the present writer the moral basis on which He issues this command is that He Himself exhausted on Calvary every sanction of the law, righted all wrongs and in His own Person suffered all vengeance, retribution and requital. His ethic of non-resistance is inextricably bound up with His atoning death. If He had not once and for all satisfied the justice of God, such an ethic would have no moral basis. If an ethic of justice and righteousness only (as opposed to love and non-resistance) were retained after Calvary (as it too often is practised and retained), the effect would be to deny the finished work of Christ. *Compel* (41); a reference to the Roman custom of staffing the postal system by obliging civilians to carry the letters.

Thou shalt love thy neighbour (43). See Lv. xix. 18. *Hate thine enemy* (43). These words do not occur in the Old Testament, but their spirit is there (see for instance Dt. xxiii. 6). *Love your enemies* (44). The command to love was present in Lv. xix. 18, but the context clearly shows that it was limited in scope to a fellow-Israelite. Under the gospel all barriers are broken down (Gal. iii. 28; Col. iii. 11). This limitation is therefore removed and the command applies universally. The New Testament teaches its application internationally (Lk. x. 25–37), socially (Jas. ii. 1–9) and personally (Rom. xiii. 8–10). Note the RV rendering of this verse. *The children* (45); RV 'sons', implying likeness. Regeneration is moral. *Publicans* (46); i.e. the local tax collectors (Gk. *telōnai*), rendered inexactly in Vulg. *publicani*, whence 'publicans'. The *publicani* in reality the tax-farmers at Rome who put up the taxes of various sections of a country to auction. The subordinates again let out the taxes to local collectors, who extorted all that they could from the people. By the Jews these collectors were regarded as traitors, and their name became a byword for all that was vilest. *What do ye more than others?* (47). The implication behind this question is the secret of the Christian ethic. Love does more than it need do. *Publicans* (47). A better reading here is *ethnikoi*, 'Gentiles'; see RV. The term means those outside the covenant, who could not be expected to know better. *Be ye therefore perfect* (48). This is an adaptation of Lv. xix. 2. The point seems to be that the Christian believer must guide his life by the perfect, ethical standard of the gospel in contrast to the limited standard of the law.

d. Almsgiving, prayer and fasting (vi. 1–18)

Alms (1). Another reading is 'righteousness' as in RV. *To be seen* (1). The reference is to the Pharisees, whose religion was hypocritical. *Of your Father* (1); better 'with', as in AV mg. and RV. *They have their reward* (2); i.e. they have it already, and so will miss it in the future. *Let not thy left hand know . . .* (3); i.e. keep it secret even from those dearest and nearest to you. The word *openly* (4) is omitted in some texts; see RV here and in verse 6.

Hypocrites (5); lit. 'play-actors'. The word does not necessarily imply conscious imposture. It describes a religion that is outward and ritual. Verse 6 is adapted from the LXX of 2 Ki. iv. 33 and Is. xxvi. 20. *Use not vain repetitions* (7); a reference to the long formal prayers used by the Pharisees without much thought as to their meaning. *Your Father knoweth* (8). Some texts read 'God your Father' as in RV mg. Prayer, therefore, should not consist of informing God of our wants.

After this manner (9). See note on Lk. xi. 1–4. This parallel passage has 'When ye pray, say' (Lk. xi. 2). The prayer that follows is, therefore, intended both as a pattern and for repetition. *Our Father* (9). Only a child of God, that is, one who has been born again, can rightly pray this prayer. *Hallowed* (9); i.e. regarded with holy reverence. *Thy name* (9); i.e. God's character or essence; what He really is. *Thy kingdom come* (10); it will come when the last enemy is destroyed, at the Lord's return (see 1 Cor. xv. 24–28). *In earth as it is in heaven* (10); the RV reading 'as in heaven, so on earth' is probably better. The fulfilment will be in the 'new heavens and earth' (cf. 2 Pet. iii. 13). *Daily* (11); Gk. *epiousion*. The word seems to be unknown outside this and the parallel passage in Luke. It does not mean 'daily'. Scholars are not agreed whether it means 'for today' or 'for tomorrow'. See Lk. xi. 3n. *Debts* (12); all sin constitutes a debt to God. *As we forgive* (12); not 'because', but 'in the same way as'. *Lead us not . . . deliver us* (13). The idea seems to be the same as that expressed in Lk. xxi. 36. *For thine is the kingdom . . . Amen* (13). These words are omitted in some texts (see RV). They constitute an affirmation of faith, and are a fitting end to the prayer.

It is striking that the only phrase in the prayer picked out for special comment by our Lord is the one dealing with forgiveness (14, 15). As in Mk. xi. 21–26, the ethic of love and forgiveness is inseparable from justification by faith. To accept God's free grace with a clear conscience involves the realization that Christ suffered the penalty for sin on the cross. This means that we cannot properly exact any more punishment or retribution from the sinner, but must freely show love and forgiveness to all. Cf. Mt. xviii. 32–35. *When ye fast* (16). The context associates the fasting with prayer and, like prayer, it is a secret matter between the individual and his God.

e. A warning against worldly-mindedness (vi. 19–34)

Cf. Lk. xii. 13–21, 33, 34. *There will your heart be* (21). To have a heart in heaven means to be utterly devoted to the interests of Christ. *Light* (22); RV 'lamp'. *The eye* (22). It stands here for interests, desires, ambitions, the direction in which the attention is attracted. The sentence means that these are an indication of the whole character of a man's life. *Single* (22); i.e. entirely devoted to the interests of Christ and the service of God. *But if thine eye be evil* (23); i.e. if the mind is set upon wrong things. For the use of the expression 'evil eye' see Dt. xv. 9; Pr. xxviii. 22. *If therefore the light . . . be darkness* (23); a most graphic way of describing a heart which is dead to the things of God. *Ye cannot serve God and mammon* (24). Double-mindedness is an impossible attitude; there can be no spiritual sitting on the fence. Service that is not wholehearted is not the service of God at all. *Mammon* is an Aramaic word meaning 'wealth' and stands here for money and worldly interests. *Take no thought* (25); i.e. do not worry. The expression meant this in seventeenth-century English. With this passage cf. Lk. xii. 22–31. *Life* (25); Gk. *psychē*, 'soul'. The word 'soul' in the Bible is not used in the sense in which we normally use it, a sense that derives from Plato, but as equivalent to Heb. *nephesh*, which means the 'person' or 'self'. It is sometimes used in the sense of the natural life or self life, as opposed to the spiritual life (see Heb. iv. 12). The soul is the seat of the emotions and appetites, and throughout the Bible eating and drinking are regarded as functions of the soul, as here. *Behold* (26); i.e. 'study'. *Are ye not much better* (26); RV 'of much more value'. *Can add one cubit unto his stature* (27); a difficult phrase. The Greek word is *hēlikia*, which does not mean 'stature' but 'age' (see RV mg.). A cubit is about half-a-yard and does not make sense with 'stature'. An expression equivalent to 'half-an-inch' is required. A possible meaning well adapted to the context is 'can add half-a-yard to his life's journey'.

Consider (28); 'study' as in verse 26. *Solomon in all his glory* (29). For Solomon's life see 1 Ki. i–xi; 1 Ch. xxv iii—2 Ch. ix; for his glory see especially 1 Ki. x. 4–7. *Seek ye first the kingdom of God . . .* (33). This is one of the great, fundamental, familiar phrases of this Gospel. To seek the kingdom of God means to strive to enter it ourselves, and then to bring others into it. God's *righteousness* is the perfect righteousness of Christ which He imputes to every believer (see Rom. iii. 21, 22). *All these things shall be added unto you* (33). The reference is primarily to the necessities of life listed in verses 25, 31, and with which it is so easy to become completely preoccupied. *The Gentiles* (32) are here mentioned as providing an example of this unspiritual, worldly attitude. God undertakes to supply the essential needs of all who fulfil the conditions laid down, and often provides *much more* (30). In view of this, as verse 34 shows, it is wrong for a Christian to worry about the future. The present will supply him with enough opposition and temptation.

f. A right relationship with others (vii. 1–12)

With verses 1–5 cf. Lk. vi. 37–42. *Judge not* (1); i.e. do not criticize others. We are not to attempt to assign responsibility, or to make distinctions in our attitude or behaviour to others, but to treat all, especially the unconverted, with the fullness of love. There is a legitimate judgment which is a family affair and extends to those inside the Church (see 1 Cor. v, especially verses 3, 12, 13). Our Lord here lays down a general principle. Verse 2 expresses the same thought as vi. 14, 15, where see notes. *A mote* (3) is a speck of dust or small splinter; a *beam* is a plank. There is an intentional exaggeration designed to bring home the force of the teaching.

Verse 6 seems to be a warning against an entirely promiscuous preaching of the gospel. Care should be taken to ascertain God's will in the matter of the choice of persons to whom to witness. The idea is the same as that found in Pr. ix. 7, 8, xxiii. 9. Verses 7 and 8 are one of the outstanding New Testament promises with regard to prayer. Cf. Lk. xi. 9–13. *If ye then, being evil* (11); notice that the Lord here endorses what has since been formulated as the doctrine of original sin. *Good things* (11). The parallel passage in Luke has 'the Holy Spirit' (Lk. xi. 13). Verse 12 lays down the great principle known as 'the golden rule'. It is the practical expression of Christian love. The initial word *therefore* emphasizes the connection between a right relationship to God and a right relationship to man. The practice of this principle is necessary because of the goodness of God in giving the good things to those that ask. The former follows from the latter. *For this is the law and the prophets;* cf. Rom. xiii. 8–10. See also Mt. v. 17n.

g. The gospel appeal (vii. 13–23)

Strait (13); i.e. 'narrow' as in RV. The gate is narrow because there is room for nothing in the Christian life but single-eyed devotion to the Master's cause and the dedication of the whole being and possessions to it. The exclusion of self-interest and separation from worldly cares and amusements make the gate and way narrow. *Broad* (13); i.e. able to accommodate the crowd. *Life* (14) is here contrasted, as so often in the Bible, with destruction (13). These are the two alternative destinies of man. *Few* (14). This is one of the mysteries of God's providence, but its truth has been attested in experience in each succeeding generation of mankind. Only a minority has found salvation. In the aggregate, however, there will be 'a great multitude' (Rev. vii. 9).

False prophets (15); i.e. teachers of error who claim divine authority for their teaching. *In sheep's clothing* (15); i.e. pretending, and possibly believing themselves, to be true Christians. *Ravening wolves* (15). They are eager to turn

men away from the path of salvation, and so to destroy them by the propagation of false doctrine. *Ye shall know them by their fruits* (16). They will be recognized not so much by their conduct (many teachers of error live outwardly blameless lives) as by their teaching. *Hewn down, and cast into the fire* (19). They will be cut off from the Christian Church and finally destroyed in the second death.

Not every one . . . shall enter into the kingdom of heaven (21). There must have been at this stage of our Lord's ministry many 'hangers-on', who made an outward profession of discipleship, but were insincere and self-seeking. It is possible to have some sort of relationship with the Lord Jesus Christ which is not the saving relationship. Profession without possession is a real danger. *Doeth* (21). A life of service and holiness is the only ultimate test of true regeneration. *In that day* (22); i.e. on the day of judgment. *Have we not prophesied in thy name?* (22); an allusion to Je. xiv. 14, xxvii. 15. It is possible to be a leader or teacher in the Christian Church and yet be deceived regarding one's own salvation. This fact explains much that has happened in Christian history. *Cast out devils* (22). The same is true in the case of moral reformers. *Wonderful works* (22); Gk. *dynameis*; better 'mighty works', as in RV. Men of great influence and power do not escape this condemnation. *Profess* (23); Gk. *homologēso*, meaning 'admit' or 'acknowledge'. *Depart from me, ye that work iniquity* (23); a quotation from Ps. vi. 8, taken substantially from the LXX. Sinful conduct is the evidence of an unregenerate heart.

h. Acceptance or rejection of the gospel (vii. 24–27)

Cf. Lk. vi. 46–49. *Doeth* (24); cf. verse 21. The emphasis is still on obedience. *A rock* (24); better 'the rock', as in RV. Cf. 1 Cor. iii. 9–11. The parable contrasts the eternal loss of those just described with the stability and ultimate victory of the true disciple. Contrast the buildings of Wisdom and Folly in Pr. ix.

i. The effect of the Sermon (vii. 28, 29)

When Jesus had ended these sayings (28). This is the formula with which the five discourses, around which the Gospel is built, all end. See xi. 1, xiii. 53, xix. 1 and xxvi. 1. See also the note in the *Introduction* on the construction of the Gospel. *The people* (28); better 'the multitudes', as in RV. In this and in the reference to *the scribes* in the following verse there is an implied contrast between the attitude of the crowds and that of the rulers. See also Jn. vii. 47–49. *One having authority* (29); i.e. it was clear that He knew what He was talking about and was not concerned with merely repeating the traditional interpretations of the law. *Not as the scribes* (29). This is usually interpreted as setting Jesus in a class apart from the scribes. There are, however, some indications that Jesus was Himself actually regarded as a scribe, and in that case the words mean 'not as the scribes usually do'. Some good texts add the word *autōn*, read by the RV in its rendering 'their scribes'. If this word formed part of the original text, the former interpretation must be the correct one. The insertion of the word, if it did not, goes to show that in very early days the former interpretation was regarded as correct or tended to be imposed on the text.

V. MIRACLES. viii. 1—ix. 34

a. The cleansing of a leper (viii. 1–4)

See notes on Mk. i. 40–45; Lk. v. 12–14. *Make me clean* (2). By the law of Moses ceremonial uncleanness attached to leprosy. See Lv. xiii especially verses 45, 46. *Jesus . . . touched him* (3); a remarkable action, which normally would bring ceremonial uncleanness. In the case of Jesus, on the contrary, cleansing was brought to the leper. *See thou tell no man* (4). The purpose of Jesus in giving this command, as He did on several occasions, has been variously interpreted. It is probable that He did not wish crowds to be attracted by miracles alone without spiritual hunger, or to appear in the rôle of a popular wonder-worker. *Shew thyself to the priest* (4); i.e. in obedience to the Mosaic law (see Lv. xiii). *Offer the gift that Moses commanded* (4). The Mosaic directions for the cleansing of the leper, which are typical of Christ's atonement, are to be found in Lv. xiv. 2–32. *For a testimony unto them* (4); i.e. as evidence to the priest that the leper had been cleansed.

b. The healing of the centurion's servant (viii. 5–13)

A rather fuller account of this miracle is given in Lk. vii. 2–10, where see notes. *A centurion* (5). The rank of a centurion was between that of an officer and a non-commissioned officer. Perhaps the nearest modern equivalent is that of regimental sergeant-major. The position was one of considerable responsibility. *Servant* (6); Gk. *pais*, i.e. 'boy', as in RV mg. The word was used with much the same variety of sense as modern English 'boy'. It could mean 'child' or 'servant'. *Sick of the palsy, grievously tormented* (6); i.e. 'paralysed and greatly afflicted'; the phrase does not necessarily mean that he was in great pain. *The centurion answered and said* (8). The centurion was not personally present, as is plain from the parallel account in Lk. vii. 1–10. The answer was given through messengers. For a similar use of the word 'said' see xi. 3. *Servant* (9). Here the word means 'slave'. *He marvelled* (10); a very human trait. *So great faith* (10). In likening Jesus to himself as one *under authority*, he indicated that he believed that Jesus had all the power of God behind Him and that His *word* would be instantly obeyed even in the realm of illness and death. *From the east and west* (11). The words are taken from Ps. cvii. 3 (LXX). Cf. also Is. xlix. 12, lix. 19; Mal. i. 11. The Lord is referring to the gathering

in of Gentiles through the gospel culminating in the final gathering together at His coming. *Sit down* (11); i.e. recline at table. The ancients reclined at meals on low couches, resting on the left elbow. This Eastern picture of the world to come as a great banquet is used by our Lord again in the parables of the wedding feast (Mt. xxii. 1–14) and of the great supper (Lk. xiv. 15–24). *The children of the kingdom* (12); i.e. those to whom the kingdom really belongs, that is, the Jews. *Outer darkness* (12); i.e. destruction, the second death. *There shall be weeping and gnashing of teeth* (12). 'There' is emphatic. The phrase looks back to Ps. cxii. 10. *As thou hast believed* (13). Faith is always the measure of blessing.

c. The healing of Peter's mother-in-law (viii. 14–17)

See notes on Mk. i. 29–34 and cf. Lk. iv. 38–41. *Laid* (14); i.e. lying in bed, the bed being a mattress placed on the floor. *Ministered unto them* (15); i.e. attended to their needs. This observation is included, perhaps, to stress the immediate and complete nature of the cure. *He cast out the spirits* (16); i.e. evil spirits, meaning the devils or demons. These beings belong to a higher and invisible world which our scientific knowledge has not yet pierced so that we know nothing of their nature and characteristics. See also iv. 24n., ix. 32n.

With his word (16); better 'with a word', as in RV. *By Esaias* (17); RV mg. 'through Isaiah'. *Himself took our infirmities, and bare our sicknesses* (17). This is taken from the Hebrew of Is. liii. 4. It is an important quotation which establishes the meaning of the first sentence of Is. liii. 4, which refers to the ministry of healing and not to Calvary. The meaning is obscured in the AV of the Old Testament passage, and the sentence is mistranslated in the LXX. It appears from Mk. v. 30 and Lk. viii. 46 that there was a physical cost to the Saviour in healing.

d. The cost of discipleship and the stilling of the storm (viii. 18–27)

See notes on Mk. iv. 35–41; Lk. viii. 22–25, ix. 57–62. *He gave commandment to depart* (18). The Lord often wished to escape the crowds, partly perhaps in order to be alone with God, and partly perhaps for the disciples' sakes. *A certain scribe* (19); Gk. *heis;* RV mg. 'one scribe'. The scribes are nearly always spoken of in the plural. *Master, I will follow* (19). These words have an underlying spiritual meaning in addition to the literal. See Rev. xiv. 4. *Master* is lit. 'Teacher'. Notice that our Lord did not make it easy to follow Him, but insisted on the counting of the cost. *The Son of man* (20). This is the title by which our Lord most frequently referred to Himself. It was probably taken originally from Dn. vii. 13, where it has a messianic significance. In the vision of Daniel the kingdom of the Son of man followed and superseded those of the four wild beasts. In the apocalyptic thought of our Lord's day the title was used for the Messiah.

This is undoubtedly the aspect which the Lord emphasized by its use. By applying it to Himself He was testifying that He was the Messiah. *Another of his disciples* (21). We must infer from this that the man who found difficulty in following unconditionally was a professed disciple. *Bury my father* (21). This probably means to stay at home until the father's death. *Let the dead bury their dead* (22); a rather difficult answer. It probably means that we are to leave the people of the world to live the ordinary life of the world and to devote ourselves to the urgent business of the kingdom. Notice that the claims of Christ have precedence over the highest that life can give, even the claims of one's family. See Mt. x. 37n. *Tempest* (24); Gk. *seismos*, 'a disturbance'. *His disciples* (25). 'They' is the better reading, as in RV. Note that the RV, following the better texts, also omits *us. Fearful* (26); Gk. *deiloi*, 'cowards'.

e. The healing of the Gadarene demoniacs (viii. 28–34)

See notes on Mk. v. 1–20; Lk. viii. 26–39. *Gergesenes* (28); a better reading is 'Gadarenes' as in RV. Gergesa was a town on the eastern shore of the Sea of Galilee whose site is said to be that of some modern ruins known as Kersa. The town was included in the district of Gadara which took its name from that of a town of the same name, one of the cities of Decapolis. The whole was included in the larger administrative district of Gerasa, whose centre was the town of Gerasa in Gilead. *Two possessed with devils* (28). The mention of two demoniacs is peculiar to Matthew, the parallel passages in the other synoptists mentioning only one. A possible explanation is that the case of the one was outstanding in view of his conversation with Christ and subsequent witness in the district, so that he would be the only one of the two of whom the evangelists Mark and Luke had heard. The evangelist Matthew, on the other hand, even if he was not himself present (his call is described in chapter ix), was intimate with those who had seen the double cure. See also notes on xx. 30, xxi. 7. *What have we to do with thee* (29); Gk. *Ti hēmin kai soi.* The meaning seems to be, 'What is there in common between us?' and a better translation would perhaps be 'What have you got to do with us?' The question was an expression of resentment at intrusion. *To torment us before the time* (29). In the New Testament this word *basanisai* does not seem to be used in its earlier, narrower sense of 'to torture', but to express the wider meaning of 'to cause suffering' or 'loss' in any way. Note that the evil spirits appear to be aware that retribution awaits them in the future. *An herd of many swine* (30). Swine were unclean animals by the ordinances of the Mosaic law. To keep them was illegal for the Jews. *The whole herd . . . perished* (32). This is the only recorded miracle of our Lord which was destructive of animal life.

The fact that He granted the demons' request is not easy to understand. The principle involved may be that those who are knowingly disobedient, as was the case of the pig-breeders, deprive themselves of divine protection and place themselves at the mercy of the forces of evil. Perhaps this is an instance of limiting the Holy One of Israel (Ps. lxxviii. 41). See Mk. v. 11–13n. *They besought him that he would depart* (34). The incident ends in tragedy. The people preferred their business to the Saviour.

f. The healing of the paralytic (ix. 1–8)

See notes on Mk. ii. 1–12; Lk. v. 17–26. *He entered into a ship, and passed over* (1). Jesus never stays where He is not wanted. *His own city* (1); i.e. Capernaum (see Mt. iv. 13). *Seeing their faith* (2). This suggests that effective faith can be exercised on behalf of another. *Thy sins be forgiven thee* (2). Jesus attended first to the man's spiritual need, which of course was the greater. RV renders 'are forgiven'. *This man blasphemeth* (3). The supposed blasphemy lay in the claim to forgive sins. Jesus knew instinctively in His own heart, without being told, the nature of their wicked reasoning and asked a pointed question. It is left unanswered and the answer is not easy. It may be that the scribes, who regarded Jesus as an impostor, thought it easier to say glibly 'Thy sins are forgiven', because no outward result could be observed. In the face of this the implication may be that it is, in fact, an easier task to deal with man's physical needs than with his spiritual. Another answer may be that both alike are equally easy with God. *Power* (6); Gk. *exousian;* i.e. 'authority' or 'right'. *They marvelled* (8); better texts read 'they were afraid', as in RV.

g. The call of Matthew (ix. 9–13)

See notes on Mk. ii. 13–17; Lk. v. 27–32. *The receipt of custom* (9); i.e. the toll-booth in the street where the tax-collectors sat to receive the taxes and dues. *In the house* (10); Gk. *en tē(i) oikia(i)* meaning 'at home'. It might mean Jesus' home, but we know from the other synoptists that the house was Matthew's (Mk. ii. 15; Lk. v. 29, where the expression used is *en tē(i) oikia(i) autou*, 'in his house'). The only possible alternative meaning of the expression in Matthew's Gospel is that the owner of the house was the one who was writing. This then is a piece of internal evidence for the Matthean authorship of the Gospel. *Publicans* (10). See v. 46n. *Whole* (12); i.e. 'strong', as in RV mg. *I will have* (RV 'desire') *mercy, and not sacrifice* (13). These words are taken from the LXX of Ho. vi. 6, *and not* meaning 'in preference to'. The same principle is expressed by Samuel in a well-known passage (1 Sa. xv. 22). The quotation is lit up with a fresh glory as Jesus applies it to the salvation of sinners. *The righteous* (13). The word is ironic. It means the self-righteous. Scripture tells us that 'there is none righteous, no, not one' (Rom. iii. 10). *To repentance* (13). The more trustworthy texts omit these words (see RV) but their omission seems to be a loss.

h. The question of fasting (ix. 14–17)

See notes on Mk. ii. 18–22; Lk. v. 33–39. *Oft* (14). Some texts omit this word. See RV mg. The principle taught by our Lord here is that fasting is not an end in itself, but is to be practised only under appropriate circumstances. The Pharisees' fasting was part of the righteousness which the Lord had just condemned (see verse 13 above). *The children of the bridechamber* (15); i.e. the wedding guests. *As long as the bridegroom is with them* (15); i.e. while the wedding festivities last, which might be for some days. *When the bridegroom shall be taken from them* (15). This is an allusion to His own death and ascension. Note the RV reading.

In verses 16 and 17 the principle expressed is that Jesus Christ has come to bring in a new dispensation altogether, which cannot be fitted into the forms of the old Jewish economy. The rule of the law must go, that grace may have free play. *New cloth* (16); i.e. unbleached. RSV reads 'unshrunk'. *Bottles* (17); i.e. skins, which were frequently used in the East as containers for liquids. The strength of fermentation of the new wine would be too much for partly worn or old, inelastic skins and they would break.

i. The healing of the woman with the issue and the raising of the ruler's daughter (ix. 18–26)

See notes on Mk. v. 22–43; Lk. viii. 41–56. *A certain ruler* (18); i.e. a magistrate. We know from the other synoptists that his name was Jairus. *Worshipped* (18). This suggests that he seemed to sense Jesus' divinity. *Is even now dead* (18). In the other Gospels we are told that she was dying when the father first came and that on the way to his house he was met by messengers who announced that she had died. Matthew combines these two phases into one.

I shall be whole (21); Gk. *sōthēsomai*, 'I shall be saved'. The use of this word for the restoration of physical health makes it easier to understand that these miracles are pictures of spiritual healing. *Daughter* (22); the usual mode of address from a rabbi. *Be of good comfort* (22); Gk. *tharsei*, 'cheer up'. *Thy faith hath made thee whole* (22); Gk. *sesōken se*, 'has saved thee'. See verse 21n. The incident is an outstanding illustration of faith in action.

Verse 23 describes the usual scene in an Eastern house where someone lay dead. Mourners were hired to make a noise. *The minstrels* were flute-players (see RV). *The maid is not dead, but sleepeth* (24). The Lord meant that her death had been turned into a temporary sleep by the fact that He was shortly going to raise her. On the same principle the dead in Christ are said to be asleep in view of the certainty of their resurrection. *Took her by the hand* (25). Perhaps He did this so that she should not be startled on such a tremendous awakening.

j. The healing of the blind and dumb men (ix. 27–34)

Cf. xii. 22, 23, xx. 30–34. See also Lk. xi. 14–26. *Crying* (27); better 'crying out', as in RV. *Thou son of David* (27). This appears to have been an expression in use at the time that implied Messiahship. The blind men had apparently put their faith in Jesus as the Messiah. *Into the house* (28). This may have been His own home in Capernaum, or, perhaps, Matthew's house as in verse 10. *Believe ye . . .?* (28). Notice the emphasis laid in this, as in other miracles, upon faith. *See that no man know it* (30). See note on viii. 4. For verse 31 see also Mk. i. 45, vii. 36. This disobedience may have made the Lord's ministry more difficult and brought around Him large crowds with no spiritual hunger, thus contributing to the necessity of His use of parables (see chapter xiii).

In verse 33 notice the connection between spiritual evil and the physical disability. By *the prince of devils* (34) is meant Satan. See xii. 24–37.

VI. THE APPOINTMENT OF THE TWELVE. ix. 35—x. 4

See notes on Mk. iii. 13–19; Lk. vi. 12–19. *Fainted* (36). The RV, following another reading, translates 'were distressed'. *As sheep having no shepherd* (36); quoted from Nu. xxvii. 17. The words are taken substantially from LXX, but with an altered construction. See also Ezk. xxxiv. 5. Verses 37 and 38 constitute one of the great missionary passages of the New Testament. Cf. Lk. x. 2; Jn. iv. 35–38.

Power against unclean spirits (1); i.e. authority over demons, as RV. *Apostles* (2); Gk. *apostolōn*. In the original this is not the technical term that it early became in the course of Christian history, but simply means 'missionaries'. It is applied to the twelve men who are called in verse 1 by the more general term of 'disciples' when they are commissioned for a special work. Note that their twelve names are arranged in six pairs, which perhaps correspond to the arrangement in which they were sent out on their mission. See Mk. vi. 7. Cf. also Acts i. 13.

The first, Simon (2). Peter heads all four lists of the Twelve (cf. Mk. iii. 16; Lk. vi. 14; Acts i. 13). In the Gospels and Acts he is the most prominent and it may well be that he exercised a natural leadership among them. It does not follow from this, however, that his leadership was ever passed on to successors. *Bartholomew* (3) is generally considered to be identical with the Nathanael of Jn. i. 45–51. *Lebbaeus, whose surname was Thaddaeus* (3). Better texts, followed by RV, read simply 'Thaddaeus'. Luke gives his name as Judas (vi. 16; Acts i. 13). *Simon the Canaanite* (4). This does not mean an inhabitant of Canaan. A more correct term is the RV 'Cananaean'. Simon had been a member of the nationalist party known as 'Zealots' (Heb. *qanna*, hence Gk. *kananaios*, 'Cananaean'). The party had resisted Herod the Great and was ready to resist all foreign rule by force of arms. They were a kind of *maquis*. *Judas Iscariot* (4). The name Iscariot may mean a member of the tribe of Issachar, or an inhabitant of Kerioth (Jos. xv. 25), or the one who carried the purse (from Aram. *secariota*, 'purse'), or the one who was strangled (from Heb. *iscara*, 'strangling'). The second is the most probable.

VII. DISCOURSE II. THE CHARGE TO THE TWELVE. x. 5—xi. 1

See notes on Mk. vi. 7–13; Lk. ix. 1–6. *The way of the Gentiles* (5). There were Greek cities in Galilee which lived a separate life from that of the Jews. The apostles were to confine themselves to the Jewish towns. *The Samaritans* (5). They occupied the central portion of Palestine between Judaea' and Galilee. They were descended from the Eastern peoples imported by the Assyrians after the destruction of the northern Israelite kingdom, with a certain mixture of native Israelite blood. Since the days of Nehemiah they had been the bitter enemies of the Jews. Cf. Jn. iv. 9. *The house of Israel* (6). This term is not confined in either Old or New Testament to the ten northern tribes. *The kingdom of heaven is at hand* (7). This was the message of John (see iii. 2n.) and of Jesus Himself (iv. 17). *Provide* (9); better 'Get', as AV mg. and RV. *Purses* (9); Gk. *zōnas*, i.e. 'girdles', as in RV mg. The fold of the robe of the girdle acted as do our pockets. *Scrip* (10); better 'wallet', as RV. It was a small bag. *Coats* (10); Gk. *chitōnas*, the outer robe or tunic, corresponding to the Roman toga. *Staves* (10); RV 'staff'. The Greek is singular. With this Lk. ix. 3 agrees. The meaning of Mk. vi. 8 is perhaps that they were to have one walking-stick between a pair. Perhaps our Lord did not wish them to look like ordinary travellers. *The workman is worthy of his meat* (10). They were to rely upon the gifts and hospitality of those to whom they preached. These words are quoted in 1 Tim. v. 18 in their Lucan form.

Inquire (11); better 'search out', as in RV. The accepted code of Eastern hospitality was such that many offers of accommodation would probably be received. But they were not to rely for hospitality upon any who rejected their message. *Salute it* (12); i.e. with the customary greeting of 'Peace', which explains the meaning of verse 13. *Shake off the dust of your feet* (14). This was a symbolic act of rejection and condemnation. Not even the dust of the wicked city was to cling to them. *Verily* (15); Gk. *amēn*, a transliteration from the Hebrew meaning 'truly' and giving emphasis to the statement that followed. *Sodom and Gomorrha* (15). For the story of the destruction of these cities see Gn. xix. See also Ezk. xvi. 49, 50; Jude 7. For an application of this statement to Capernaum itself see Mt. xi. 23, 24. Verse 16 refers to the meekness and outward defencelessness of Christians against their enemies in the world. *Wise as serpents* (16); cf. Gn. iii. 1. The phrase emphasizes the amount of wisdom needed since the serpent was commonly regarded as the wisest of beasts. The quality of the wisdom to be shown is very different, as the next phrase shows. For an example of such wisdom in action see 1 Cor. ix. 19–23. Notice that it is because of the fierce opposition that these qualities are to be exercised.

With verses 17ff. cf. Mk. xiii. 9–13; Lk. xii. 11, 12, xxi. 12–19. *Take no thought* (19); RV 'be not anxious'. *It shall be given you* (19). As the next verse shows, this will be by the inner prompting of the Holy Spirit. *The brother* (21); in both cases the definite article is better omitted as in RV. *Children shall rise up against their parents* (21). This is a summary of Mi. vii. 6. *For my name's sake* (22); i.e. because you belong to Me. *But he that endureth to the end shall be saved* (22); i.e. perseveres in a life of faith.

It has been suggested that in the latter part of verse 23 the Lord was referring to a meeting with the apostles later during the course of His ministry. But such an interpretation seems out of harmony with the meaning attached in this Gospel and throughout the New Testament to the conception of the coming of the Son of man. These rather difficult words seem to lift the commission here given to the apostles out of purely local circumstances and prove its application to the missionary work of the whole Church in every generation. As a matter of history it is still true today that there are Jews who need the gospel and who listen to it when it is preached to them. *Have gone over* (23); better 'end', or 'finish', as in AV mg. In verse 24 our Lord means that, when engaged on the same work as Himself, His disciples must not expect better treatment than He has received.

Beelzebub (25); Gk. *Beelzeboul* or *Beezeboul*. The spelling with final 'b' occurs in Syriac and Old Latin versions. The name refers to an evil demon and is most probably a contemptuous name for Satan. Its origin is not known. The first part represents Heb. *Baal*, lord. The second part may be derived from Heb. *zebul*, house. In this case Satan would be called 'the lord of the house' (of demons). There is an obvious reference in the immediate context to this; sense. Others have thought that the name is derived from *Baal-zebub*, lord of flies, a heathen god referred to in 2 Ki. i. If this is so, the final letter was perhaps changed to 'l' in order to suggest Heb. *zebel*, which means 'dung' or 'filth'.

Fear not . . . (28). The worst that our enemies can do is to destroy our physical life, but this does not prevent a blessed resurrection to life everlasting. To God, however, belongs the power of 'the second death', which is eternal destruction. By *soul* is meant the personality or personal identity. The contrast here made is between this world and the next. *Hell* (28); i.e. Gehenna, as in RV mg., a description of 'the second death'; see v. 22n. *A farthing* (29); Gk. *assariou*, the Roman *as*, equal in the time of our Lord to one-sixteenth of the denarius, and worth about a halfpenny or less. *Without your Father* (29); i.e. without His being concerned.

Confess me (32); i.e. acknowledge that he belongs to Me. In the long run secret discipleship is an impossibility. But, as verses 34–39 show, open confession of Christ leads to division and conflict, first and chiefly in family life. See the parallel passage in Lk. xii. 49–53. The message of 'peace on earth' proclaimed by the angels at the Lord's birth is not to be fulfilled outwardly in this world. It is fulfilled in the hearts and attitude of those who believe, and perfectly in the world to come, the 'new earth'. *A sword* (34); a vivid figure of division, and so rendered by Luke (xii. 51). Verses 35, 36 are taken from Mi. vii. 6. The words come apparently from the Hebrew, with reminiscences of the LXX. Verse 37 teaches that every man must choose between even his nearest and dearest personal relationship on the one hand and Christ on the other. Cf. Mt. xv. 4 and see Lk. xiv. 26n. *Worthy of me;* fit to follow me, and so in verse 38. Verses 38 and 39 are repeated in xvi. 24, 25; see also Mk. viii. 34, 35; Lk. xi. 23, xiv. 26, 27; Jn. xii. 25. *Taketh not his cross* (38). This is the first mention of the cross in the Gospel and, therefore, in the New Testament. It was the custom for the condemned man to carry his cross on the way to execution. There is plenty of evidence that the Lord anticipated the mode of His own death. These words come as the climax of His warning to the apostles that their mission would involve arrest and persecution, culminating in condemnation to death, as in His own case. These important words have also a deep spiritual significance and constitute the basis of the apostle Paul's teaching about the identification of the believer with the cross of Christ (see e.g. Gal. ii. 20). *Findeth his life* (39); i.e. gains, or gets something out of it for himself. For *life* see vi. 25n. Here the word means the 'self-life', or 'natural life', as opposed to the spiritual life. *Shall find it* (39); i.e. in the world to come. A life emptied and poured out in the service of Christ in this world will find its full enjoyment and expression then in life everlasting.

In the name of a prophet (41); i.e. 'as a prophet'. *A prophet's reward . . . a righteous man's reward* (41); i.e. the reward due for receiving a prophet or a righteous man respectively. *These little ones* (42). As used here this is perhaps a general term for weaker disciples, or disciples in general.

With xi. 1 compare the similar expression in vii. 28, where see note.

VIII. JOHN THE BAPTIST AND CHRIST. xi. 2–24

Verses 2–19 are parallel with Lk. vii. 18–35, where see notes. *In the prison* (2). This imprisonment has already been mentioned (see iv. 12), but the circumstances leading up to it are not described until xiv. 3–12, where the manner of John's death is also recounted. *The works of Christ* (2); i.e. His miracles. *Two* (2); Gk. *duo*. Some texts

read *dia*, which is adopted by the RV and translated 'by'. *He that should come* (3); i.e. the Messiah of Old Testament prophecy whose coming John had proclaimed. *The blind receive their sight* (5); an allusion to Is. xxxv. 5, lxi. 1, where, with some of the other miracles mentioned in this verse, this is stated to be one of the works to be performed by the Messiah. John would understand the allusion. *The poor have the gospel preached to them* (5); another allusion to a prophecy in Isaiah (lxi. 1) concerning the Messiah. Again John would understand the reference. In verse 6 the RV renders 'find none occasion of stumbling in me'. RSV translates 'takes no offense at me'. *A reed shaken with the wind* (7); i.e. a commonplace event which no one would go out of his way to see. *But what went ye out for to see? A prophet?* (9). The RV reading with its different punctuation is a good alternative and perhaps gives greater emphasis. *More* (9); Gk. *perissoteron*, i.e. 'much more', as in RV. The quotation in verse 10 is from Mal. iii. 1. Only the first few words follow the LXX. John was the foreordained forerunner of the Saviour and, as verse 11 implies, the last of the Old Testament prophets (see also verse 13). He belonged to the Old Testament dispensation. This latter verse may be interpreted in various ways. The weakest believer who has the light of the knowledge of the glory of God in the face of Jesus Christ risen from the dead is in a more privileged position than was John. The expression *them that are born of women* meaning 'mortal men' also gives to the saying an emphasis upon life in this world. John may be the greatest of all in this life; but no position in this life can be compared with the glory of the life to come. Or again, we may ask what made John the greatest among mortal men. Was it that he alone of all men, as recorded in iii. 16, 17, perceived with his senses all three Persons of the Holy Trinity at the same moment? If so, the saying may mean that this will be the common experience of even the least in the life to come.

The kingdom of heaven suffereth violence (12); Gk. *biazetai*. The meaning of this saying and the connection of verses 12–14 with the preceding and following contexts are very difficult. The line of thought seems to be as follows: John threw open the kingdom of heaven (by baptizing sinners) to those who would never before have been supposed fit to enter it. He was the culminating point of Old Testament witness. He was the fulfilment of the prophecy of the coming of Elijah. If *biazetai* is in the passive voice, the saying with the sentence immediately following seems to mean that beginning with John the heralds and messengers of the kingdom are treated with violence and persecuted. There is no need to support this view by supposing (as has been done) that the words are not the words of our Lord at all, but those of an editor looking back to the days of John through a generation or two of early church history. The expression 'from the days of John the Baptist until now' can quite well mean 'from the days when John was preaching'. On the other hand in a parallel passage in Lk. xvi. 16 the verb *biazetai* is in the middle voice. If that were the case here the saying would mean that the kingdom of heaven is pressing its way on in the world and communicating its force and enthusiasm to those who receive and enter it. *This is Elias, which was for to come* (14); see Mal. iv. 5, 6. Our Lord here distinctly states that this prophecy of the coming of Elijah was fulfilled in John the Baptist. This is a valuable hint that we are not to literalize Old Testament prophecy. The meaning of Mal. iv. 6 seems to be that John was to form a link between the Old Testament and the New.

This generation (16) refused to exercise its capacity to hear, but made excuses for disregarding both John and Jesus. Our Lord likens them to children playing out of doors. Some interpret verse 17 as describing first a game of 'weddings' and then a game of 'funerals'. Others regard the verse as describing a kind of 'nuts-and-may' game which required suitable responses. The application to His hearers' contrary attitudes to John (18) and Himself (19) is obvious. *But wisdom is justified of her children* (19). Some better texts read 'works' for 'children' (see e.g. RV). 'Children' is the reading in the parallel Lucan passage, and may have been introduced from there. On the other hand 'works' may be a gloss on 'children'. The meaning of either word is the same, i.e. 'results'. The saying means that the wisdom of both John and Jesus, in adopting differing modes of life, was justified in either case by its results.

The denunciation of Galilean cities which follows (20–24) is recorded by Luke but in a different connection. See Lk. x. 13–16. *Chorazin* (21) was about an hour's journey north of Capernaum. *Bethsaida* was on the west of the Sea of Galilee about three miles south-east of Chorazin. *Tyre and Sidon* (22) were both on the Mediterranean coast of Syria, beyond the northern boundary of Palestine. In verse 23 note the different and possibly better reading in the RV. The saying is an allusion to Is. xiv. 13, 15, where it is spoken of the king of Babylon and probably refers to Satan. *Hell* (23); Gk. *Haidou*, corresponding to Heb. *Sheol*. It means 'the grave'. For verse 24 see x. 15.

IX. A GOSPEL INVITATION. xi. 25–30

Answered (25). The words that follow are the response of Jesus' heart to the circumstances just described. *Thank* (25); Gk. *exomologoumai*; lit. 'acknowledge'. *Babes* (25); i.e. spiritual babes, who receive God's revelation in simple faith. With verse 27 cf. Jn. iii. 35, xvii. 2. Verses 28–30 are a figure which would appeal immediately to an agricultural community. The *yoke* (29) probably represents the teaching of Christ, and there is an implied contrast with the burdensome teaching of the Pharisees (see Mt. xxiii. 4). *Ye shall find rest unto your souls* (29). The words

are taken from Je. vi. 16. The LXX has 'Ye shall find purification unto your souls', and is corrected in the Gospel to the meaning of the Hebrew. *Easy* (30); Gk. *chrēstos*, meaning 'good' or 'kind'. The passage is peculiar to Matthew's Gospel.

X. A DISPUTE WITH THE PHARISEES. xii. 1–45

a. The sabbath (xii. 1–21)

See notes on Mk. ii. 23—iii. 6; Lk. vi. 1–11. *The sabbath day* (1); i.e. the seventh day of the week, corresponding to our Saturday. It began at sunset on Friday and lasted till the following sunset. *Corn* (1); better 'cornfields', as in RV. *That which is not lawful* (2). The Pharisees had burdened the sabbath with a multitude of detailed observances which were not laid down in the Mosaic law. Apparently what they objected to in this case was the rubbing of the ears in the hands. *Have ye not read?* (3). The passage referred to is 1 Sa. xxi. 1–6. The point is that in a case of necessity the provisions of the ceremonial law might rightly be overruled. *The shewbread* (4). For this see Lv. xxiv. 5–9. The loaves were placed on the table in the holy place in the tabernacle each sabbath, and when taken out were eaten by the priest and his family. For the allusion in verse 5 see Nu. xxviii. 9. The priests prepared the sacrifices on the sabbath in spite of the general prohibition of work. If the necessities of temple worship permitted the priest to *profane the sabbath*, there was all the more reason why the service of Christ should allow a similar liberty. *I will have mercy, and not sacrifice* (7). See ix. 13n. The application of this principle, which is that ethics are more important than ritual, is easily seen in the present context. Verse 8 asserts that Jesus Christ has the right to interpret the Mosaic ordinances, which may not interfere with His service.

Withered (10); i.e. paralysed. *Better* (12). RV translates 'of more value', which is preferable. Notice in verse 13 how the power to obey was given with the command to act. *Held a council* (14); better, 'took counsel', as AV mg. and RV. Verses 18–21 are taken from Is. xlii. 1–4, slightly abridged towards the close and mainly following the Hebrew, though the LXX is followed in the last sentence. *My servant* (18). In the original Old Testament passage the reference is to Israel, i.e. the true Israel of God. This true Israel is gathered up in the Person of the Messiah. See also Is. xli. 9. *He shall shew judgment to the Gentiles* (18); a prophecy that the righteousness of God would be made known to the Gentiles by the gospel. Verses 19 and 20 refer to the gentleness of Jesus. He never clamoured for a hearing or wrangled in debate. He never brushed aside or trampled on the weakest faith or the wounded conscience. *Till he send forth judgment unto victory* (20); i.e. till the final triumph of righteousness.

b. Exorcism and the Pharisees' blasphemy (xii. 22–37)

See notes on Mk. iii. 22–30; Lk. xi. 14–22. *Is not this the son of David?* (23); a messianic title; see ix. 27n. *Beelzebub* (24). See x. 25n. Here Beelzebub seems to be identified with Satan. *Jesus knew* (25); Gk. *eidōs*; He realized, or understood, the true meaning of their thoughts. *Your children* (27); better, 'sons', as in RV. The reference is probably to the disciples of the Pharisees. For an example of the Jewish practice of exorcism see Acts xix. 13–16. *The kingdom of God* (28). Matthew's usual expression is 'the kingdom of heaven'; see iii. 2n. They mean the same thing. *Is come unto you* (28); i.e. has come upon you unawares. The Lord's power over the demons was evidence that He was the Messiah. Verse 29 is difficult. Its meaning seems to be that the Lord's power over devils shows that Satan had already been bound. The binding probably took place when the kingdom of God came, that is, perhaps, when the Lord overcame Satan's temptations in the wilderness and entered upon His public ministry. Satan is 'spoiled' by the capture of souls from him for Christ by the gospel. *He that is not with me is against me* (30). There is no middle course. Everyone either gathers souls with Christ or scatters them from God. In Mk. ix. 40 we have the converse truth stated. The present passage applies to any teaching which is positively unscriptural: that in Mark should be borne in mind when confronted, for example, with denominational differences.

The blasphemy against the Holy Ghost (31). This sin is deliberate rejection of Christ and His salvation, the only sin that by its very nature puts a man beyond the pale of forgiveness. The reference is probably to Nu. xv. 27–31, where we read that the sin offering was for those who sinned 'through ignorance', not for those who sinned 'presumptuously'. To act presumptuously was to reproach (RV 'blaspheme') the Lord. See Mk. iii. 28, 29n. and cf. Lk. xii. 10. At first sight the contrast in verse 32 may seem strange. The reason for it seems to be that it is the Holy Spirit who brings the offer of salvation to the heart of man. *The tree is known by his fruit* (33). The point of this verse seems to be that the good works done by Christ were evidence of His goodness and should have prevented any such blasphemous saying as that spoken by the Pharisees. But the illustration of the tree is double-edged and as verse 34 shows proves the wickedness of the Pharisees as well as the goodness of Christ. *By thy words* (37). Words are not the cause of justification or condemnation, but the evidence of either.

c. The sign (xii. 38–45)

•See also Lk. xi. 29–32 and cf. Mk. viii. 11, 12. *Answered* (38). The thought carries on from the previous verses. In view of the Lord's claims the Pharisees ask for evidence, though they should have seen it in the miracles. The word *adulterous*

(39) means unfaithful to God; it was a metaphor frequently used in the Old Testament. *The prophet Jonas* (39). For the prophet's story see the book of Jonah. The reference in verse 40 is to the LXX of Jon. i. 17. *Three days and three nights* (40). The actual period was from Friday evening to Sunday morning. The expression means that three periods of twenty-four hours, Friday, Saturday and Sunday, were wholly or partly covered. *The whale's belly* (40). This is the only occurrence of the English word 'whale' in connection with the story of Jonah. The Greek word means 'a great sea monster'. *The men of Nineveh* (41). Notice that our Lord places them on the same level of historical reality as those whom He was actually addressing. *The queen of the south* (42); i.e. the queen of Sheba. For her story see 1 Ki. x. Our Lord is contrasting her eagerness to hear the wisdom of man with the refusal of His hearers to listen to one *greater than Solomon* (42). Notice also the claims made by our Lord in verses 6 and 41.

Verses 43–45 seem to be a reference to the fact that, though the Jews were cleansed by the Babylonian exile from idolatry, their unbelief and hardness of heart had produced in them a worse moral condition than when they were idolaters before the captivity. Cf. Lk. xi. 24–26.

XI. JESUS AND HIS FAMILY. xii. 46–50

See notes on Mk. iii. 21, 31–35; Lk. viii. 19–21.

XII. DISCOURSE III. TEACHING BY PARABLES. xiii. 1–53

a. The parable of the sower (xiii. 1–23)

See notes on Mk. iv. 1–20; Lk. viii. 4–10. *In parables* (3). A parable is an illustration of spiritual truth in the form of a story. Verse 11 shows that they were primarily intended for those completely ignorant of spiritual truth. (See notes on verses 13, 14 below.) The disciples, however, understood and so did not need parables to catch their attention. The contrast is brought out by the word *you*, which is emphatic. The interpretation of this particular parable is provided by our Lord in verses 18–23.

The mysteries (11). The word has the sense of secrets, into which one must be initiated in order to be able to understand. Verse 12 seems to express a law of the spiritual world. Compare the father running to meet the prodigal son as soon as he set out to return (Lk. xv. 20), and the hardening of Pharaoh's heart by God after he had refused to listen (Ex. viii. 32, ix. 12). *They seeing see not* (13). Spiritual things mean nothing to those who have only natural understanding, even when they hear them, just as a horse may gaze at the beauty of a sunset without knowing it to be there. See 1 Cor. ii. 14. Verses 14 and 15 are taken word for word from the LXX of Is. vi. 9, 10. The passage comes in the context of the prophet's call. It describes the state of the people to whom he was sent and directs him to

789

make it known to them. As in Isaiah's time, so in that of our Lord, the Jews deliberately shut their eyes against spiritual truth. See Mk. iv. 12n. The blessing of verse 16 is explained by the fact that light had dawned in the coming of Christ which had been unknown in Old Testament times.

The word of the kingdom (19); i.e. the gospel message. *Anon* (20) means 'at once'. *He is offended* (21); i.e. ensnared in the trap set for him by Satan. *The care of this world* (22); i.e. the anxiety or worry which preoccupation with worldly interests so often brings. *Also* (23); better, as in RV, 'verily'. The expression in the Greek almost corresponds to present-day 'actually'. Note that the bearing of fruit is again the test of reality (cf. vii. 24). To 'understand (19, 23) means to grasp, believe and appropriate

b. Other parables (xiii. 24–53)

i. The parable of the tares (xiii. 24–30). *The kingdom of heaven* (24). The meaning of the expression here is the method of God's working during the gospel age. This, as the interpretation given by our Lord in verses 37–43 clearly shows, is what the parable is intended to reveal. *Tares* (25); i.e. 'darnel'. It is a large kind of rye-grass which grows as a weed among corn crops. It closely resembles the common rye-grass until its ear appears. If the seed is ground with the corn the resulting flour is poisonous.

ii. The parable of the mustard seed (xiii. 31, 32). Cf. Mk. iv. 30–32; Lk. xiii. 18, 19. *The least* (32). The seed of the mustard plant is commonly very small. *Herbs* (32); Gk. *lachanōn;* i.e. plants or vegetables. In Palestine the mustard plant grows many feet high. *The birds of the air come and lodge in the branches thereof* (32). This phrase is taken from several Old Testament passages (cf. Ezk. xvii. 23, xxxi. 5; Ps. civ. 12; Dn. iv. 12, 21). It resembles substantially the LXX of Dn. iv. 21. These references provide the clue to the meaning of the parable. In Ezk. xvii the 'tree' is the new Israel. This is the 'kingdom of heaven' of the parable. But in Ezk. xxxi and Dn. iv the tree is respectively the Gentile world Empires of Assyria and Babylon. The parable accordingly foreshadows the growth of the Church into a world power, as in fact took place and reached its climax during the Middle Ages. If we add to this the interpretation of the birds given to us in verse 19 above, namely, that they represent the wicked one, we have a perfect picture of the apostasy of the visible church. That is more likely to be the meaning of this set of parables than the spread of the gospel in a good sense. But see Mk. iv. 30–32n.

iii. The parable of the leaven (xiii. 33). *Leaven;* i.e. yeast, or any substance that causes fermentation. Leaven wherever symbolic in the Bible (e.g. xvi. 12; 1 Cor. v. 8) is consistently a symbol of evil. This fact brings the interpretation of this parable into line with what has been suggested above for the parable of the mustard tree. *A measure* (Gk. *sata,* corresponding to the Heb.

seah) was equivalent to about a gallon and a half.

iv. The parable of the tares explained (xiii. 34–43). The quotation in verse 35 is taken from Ps. lxxviii. 2. The first clause is from the LXX, the second from the Hebrew. Note that the evangelist takes the statement in the Psalm as a prophecy of Christ. *Declare* (36); better, 'explain', as RV. *Children* (38); RV 'sons'. The meaning is 'those who belong to the kingdom' and 'to the wicked one' respectively. *Things that offend, and them which do iniquity* (41). This is an allusion to the Hebrew text of Zp. i. 3. In the Greek *iniquity* is *anomian,* i.e. lawlessness. *A furnace* (42); better, as in RV, 'the furnace'. *Shall the righteous shine forth* (43); an allusion to Dn. xii. 3. The point of the parable and its explanation is not that Christians should be tolerant of evil. It is rather a call to consider this present life, in which evil so often seems to predominate, in the light of that final victory of the righteous which is here described.

v. The parables of the hidden treasure and the pearl of great price (xiii. 44–46). *Again* (44). Some texts omit this; see RV. Verse 44 has been interpreted as referring to our Lord Himself, giving all that He had to buy the treasure consisting of His people. Others see it as a reference to the sinner giving everything to obtain salvation. There are no doubt elements of truth in both these interpretations. This twofold interpretation also applies to the parable of the pearl of great price.

vi. The parable of the drag net (xiii. 47–50). Note that in this case an interpretation of the parable is immediately given. Its meaning is very similar to that of the parable of the tares. When the net is cast by the evangelist it brings in those who are truly converted and also those who only profess to be. *At the end of the world* (49) a great gathering in and casting out will take place.

vii. Conclusion of the discourse (xiii. 51–53). *Is instructed unto* (52); better, as in RV, 'hath been made a disciple to'. *Things new and old* (52). The disciples were to be themselves teachers bringing out new truths from the store of what they had learnt from the Master and at the same time revealing the inner beauty and true meaning of the Old Testament teaching. For verse 53 see note on vii. 28.

XIII. JESUS IN HIS HOME TOWN. xiii. 54–58

See notes on Mk. vi. 1–6; cf. Lk. iv. 16–30. *Own country* (54); this probably means His native place Nazareth and not Capernaum (cf. iv. 13). *Astonished* (54); i.e. amazed or astounded; it is a strong word in the original. *Carpenter's son* (55); the Greek word can also mean a stone-mason. See note on ii. 23. Mark reads 'Is not this the carpenter?' As Joseph's name is not mentioned it is presumed by many commentators that he had already died. *His brethren* (55). There is no reason to suppose that these and the sisters mentioned in the following verse were not children of Joseph and Mary. Note how the *unbelief* (58) of those who thought they knew Him best limited the power of God.

XIV. THE DEATH OF JOHN THE BAPTIST. xiv. 1–12

See notes on Mk. vi. 14–29; Lk. ix. 7–9. *Herod the tetrarch* (1); i.e. Herod Antipas, son of Herod the Great. He had ruled Galilee and Peraea since his father's death. For the meaning of 'tetrarch' see ii. 22n. *Servants* (2); Gk. *paisin;* lit. 'boys'. *John the Baptist . . . risen from the dead* (2). This superstition seems to have been fairly widespread. Lk. ix. 7 suggests that Herod was not the originator of the rumour. Cf. Mt. xvi. 14.

Herodias (3). She had been the wife of Herod's half-brother, Philip; not Philip the tetrarch (Lk. iii. 1), but another brother of the same name. It does not seem to be known who her parents were. *The daughter of Herodias* (6); Salome. She was the daughter of Herodias by Philip, and afterwards married her uncle, Philip the tetrarch. *Charger* (8); a dish. Notice that the events of this chapter are not described in chronological order, but in a way in which they can best be retained in the reader's memory.

XV. MIRACLES. xiv. 13–36

a. The feeding of the five thousand (xiv. 13–21)

This is the only miracle recorded by all four evangelists. See notes on Mk. vi. 30–46; Lk. ix. 10–17; Jn. vi. 1–15. *When Jesus heard of it* (13). This links the miracles which follow with the death of John as far as time sequence is concerned. From the standpoint of verses 1, 2 Matthew is recounting events which took place in the past. Here as elsewhere the writer's aim is not to tell the story in chronological order but to give it in a way in which it can best be retained in the reader's memory. *People* (13); 'multitudes', as in RV. *The time is now past* (15); probably the time for the evening meal. *Loaves* (17). These were small loaves like rolls. *Sit down* (19). They would recline on the left elbow, the normal way of taking a meal. *Baskets* (20); Gk. *kophinous*, small baskets carried on the arm and used, for instance, for shopping. See Lk. ix. 17n. The miracle is an illustration of feeding on Christ in our hearts by faith in His Word. See Jn. vi. 27–59 for our Lord's discourse on the 'bread of life' which arose as a direct result of this miraculous feeding.

b. The walking on the water (xiv. 22–36)

A mountain (23); RV 'the mountain'. *In the midst of the sea* (24). Notice the variant reading in the RV mg., which may be original. *In the fourth watch of the night* (25); i.e. between three and six o'clock in the morning. *It is a spirit* (26); Gk. *phantasma*, a ghost or apparition. *It is I* (27); Gk. *egō eimi*, lit. 'I am'. This is the divine name. See Ex. iii. 14.

Peter answered him (28). This action of Peter's is recounted only by Matthew. The story is very characteristic of this impetuous disciple. *To go* (29); RV 'to come'; RV mg. 'and came'. *Boisterous* (30); RV omits this, but see RV mg. *Thou art the Son of God* (33). In Aramaic the use of this expression would imply recognition of the deity of Jesus. *Gennesaret* (34); probably the plain to the north-west of the Sea of Galilee. Peter's stepping out of the boat at the call of Jesus is a vivid illustration of faith in action at the call of the gospel and of the conflict between faith and sight which so often arises in the Christian's experience.

XVI. CONTROVERSY WITH THE PHARISEES OVER RITUAL. xv. 1–20

See notes on Mk. vii. 1–23. *Of Jerusalem* (1). It appears that the central religious leaders came to investigate the ministry and teaching of Jesus. *The tradition of the elders* (2). The Jews of our Lord's time believed that, in addition to the written law of Moses, there was an oral law given to Moses on Sinai and passed down from him by word of mouth till it reached the Great Synagogue or Council of Elders which succeeded Ezra after the return from the exile. This council lasted till 291 B.C. and seems to have been the source of the many accretions to the law of God which have been found in Judaism ancient and modern. *Wash not their hands* (2). The washing consisted of pouring a trickle of cold water over the outstretched hands. The Jews were not concerned with cleanliness but with ritual. *Why do ye also transgress?* (3). The Lord here shows that additions to the Word of God ultimately contradict it. *Honour thy father and mother* (4). This is the fifth commandment of the Decalogue. See Ex. xx. 12; Dt. v. 16. *He that curseth . . . let him die the death* (4); taken from the LXX of Ex. xxi. 17. *It is a gift* (5). It was possible for a Jew by a legal quibble to dedicate his property to the temple, thus avoiding the necessity of supporting his parents, although he could continue to enjoy the proceeds himself. Notice the RV rendering of these two verses. 'He shall not honour his father' (6, RV) means 'he need not honour . . .' Notice that the Lord interprets the command to honour our parents in a practical sense. For children it means to obey them (Eph. vi. 1–3) and for adults to support them. Our Lord condemns this common practice based on tradition since it completely defeats the purpose of the law (6). *Commandment* (6); Gk. *entolēn*. Alternative readings are *nomon*, 'law', and *logon*, 'word'. The last is adopted by the RV and is perhaps most likely the original. Verses 8 and 9 are from Is. xxix. 13 and follow the LXX where it differs from the Hebrew.

Defileth (11); i.e. makes him profane. The term is a technical one. The idea in Judaism was that to eat the wrong sort of food deprived a man of holiness and ultimately, therefore, of acceptance with God. The Jewish leaders take offence at this deliberate contradiction of their own teaching. In two vivid pictures (13, 14) our Lord tells His disciples that the Pharisees have no real mission from God and are themselves blind. They and all that their religion stood for would be destroyed.

Peter, acting on behalf of the others, asks for an explanation of the saying which had given such offence. Our Lord proceeds to elaborate the teaching for their benefit. *Draught* (17); Gk. *aphedrōna*, a rare word meaning here a drain or cesspool. *They defile* (18). The *they* is emphatic. *Evil thoughts* (19); i.e. evil schemes. *Blasphemies* (19); not only blasphemy in the modern, narrow sense of the word, but also criticism or libel of others.

XVII. FURTHER MIRACLES. xv. 21–39

a. The Syro-Phoenician woman's daughter (xv. 21–28)

See notes on Mk. vii. 24–30. *Tyre and Sidon* (21); see xi. 22n. The word translated 'coasts' in this verse means 'districts'. This is the only known occasion during His ministry that our Lord went outside the boundaries of Palestine. *A woman of Canaan* (22); better 'a Canaanitish woman', as in RV. The woman was a Gentile and descended from the Canaanites who inhabited Syria and Palestine before the conquest of the latter by Joshua. By *children* (26) our Lord means Jews, and by *dogs*, Gentiles. Our Lord's attitude was intended to test the woman's faith.

b. The feeding of the four thousand (xv. 29–39)

See notes on Mk. vii. 31—viii. 10. It is perverse to say that this miracle is identical with that of the five thousand (xiv. 13–21) and that we have here only a duplicate account. If one Gospel had mentioned only the five thousand and another only the four thousand, such a view might have been difficult to refute. But both Matthew and Mark include the account of both events and do so in such a way as to indicate that they quite clearly thought of them as two separate miracles. *Glorified* (31); see ix. 8n. *Baskets* (37); Gk. *spyridas*, i.e. store-baskets, which would be larger than those mentioned in xiv. 20; see xvi. 9, 10n. *Magdala* (39); the correct reading is probably Magadan. It has been suggested that this was a suburb of Tiberias. These miracles of feeding show clearly our Lord's compassion and His willingness to meet men's physical as well as their spiritual needs. Perhaps the best comment is supplied by James (see Jas. ii. 14–17).

XVIII. CONTROVERSY WITH THE PHARISEES AND SADDUCEES. xvi. 1–12

See notes on Mk. viii. 11–21. *Adulterous* (4). The word is probably used in a spiritual sense, meaning 'unfaithful to God'. *The sign of the prophet Jonas* (4); see on xii. 39–41.

The other side (5); i.e. of the Sea of Galilee. For verse 9 see xiv. 17–21 and for verse 10, xv. 34–38. It is interesting to note that the different words used in these accounts for baskets (see notes on xiv. 20 and xv. 37) are both used here, a point of difference which clearly underlines the fact that they were two completely separate events.

XIX. SIMON PETER'S CONFESSION. xvi. 13–20

See notes on Mk. viii. 27–33; Lk. ix. 18–21. *The coasts of Caesarea Philippi* (13). This was a town in the extreme north-east of Galilee, near the source of the Jordan. *Coasts* means 'district'. Verse 14 shows that public opinion placed our Lord on the highest human pedestal by identifying Him with one of the national heroes of the past. *John the Baptist* (14). Herod himself was a victim of this particular superstition; see xiv. 2n. From xxi. 26 we know that he was held in high esteem as a prophet by the people. The coming of Elijah (*Elias*) was prophesied by Malachi (Mal. iv. 5) and the Jews often linked the name of Jeremiah with the prophet foretold in Dt. xviii. 15. *Thou art the Christ* (16). Simon Peter recognized and acknowledged openly our Lord's deity. He may have been speaking for all the disciples. Verse 20 suggests that it was a conviction which they all now shared.

Thou art Peter, and upon this rock I will build my church (18); the Greek word used for 'rock' is *petra*, and there is, of course, a deliberate play upon the name Peter, Gk. *Petros*. The Roman Catholic interpretation of this passage is that Peter was the foundation stone of the Church, that he had a primacy among the apostles, that he became Bishop of Rome, and that his primacy was passed on to his successors, the popes. The verse will scarcely bear the first of these propositions and certainly none of the others. Protestant interpreters, with some patristic support, have tended to identify the rock with Peter's faith or confession, or with our Lord Himself. The most straightforward interpretation seems to be that Peter is meant by the rock, but that he is not the exclusive foundation. For the twelvefold foundation of the Church see Eph. ii. 20; Rev. xxi. 14. This view seems borne out by the fact that the same words are spoken to all the disciples in xviii. 18 as are spoken to Simon Peter in xvi. 19.

The word here translated *church* (Gk. *ekklēsian*) means a chosen assembly. It seems never to be used of an outward organization, but of 'the whole company of faithful people', the sum of the regenerate. This is the first occurrence of the word in the New Testament. It is used in the LXX to represent Heb. *qahal*, 'congregation'. *The gates of hell shall not prevail against it* (18). The common interpretation of this passage has been, and still is, that the powers of evil will never prevail against Christ's Church. While this is true, the real meaning seems to be that death will never finally overcome believers, but that all of them will ultimately rise. The word *hell* (Gk. *haidēs*) really means 'the grave' (cf. Heb. *Sheol*). *The keys of the kingdom of heaven* (19). This means that Peter would have the right to enter the kingdom himself, would have general authority therein, symbolized by the possession of the *keys*, and by preaching the gospel would be the means of opening the kingdom of heaven to all believers and shutting it against unbelievers. The book of Acts shows us this process at work. By his sermon on the day of Pentecost (Acts ii. 14–40) Peter opened the door of the kingdom for the first time. See also Acts viii. 14–17, xv. 7. The expressions *bind* and *loose* were common in Jewish legal phraseology with the meaning of 'declare forbidden' and 'declare allowed'. Peter and the other disciples (see xviii. 18) were to continue on earth the work of Christ in preaching the gospel and declaring God's will to men, and were armed with the same authority as He Himself possessed. Christ in heaven ratifies what is done in His name and in obedience to His word on earth. *They should tell no man* (20). The revelation was to remain the property of the disciples until after the Lord's resurrection. Cf. xvii. 9n. The word *Jesus* in this verse is better omitted (see RV).

XX. THE FIRST ANNOUNCEMENT OF CHRIST'S SUFFERINGS. xvi. 21–28

See notes on Mk. viii. 34–38; Lk. ix. 22–27. *From that time forth* (21). The disciples' faith was now proved by Peter's confession to be sufficiently established to warrant the announcement of the sufferings. Thus, from this point onwards, our Lord's ministry takes on a somewhat different complexion as He seeks to prepare His followers for the suffering which awaited Him and which would so disappoint their hopes. *Elders* (21); i.e. the religious leaders. The word probably denotes members of the Sanhedrin. *The third day* (21). Jewish reckoning was inclusive. The three days were Friday, Saturday and Sunday.

Be it far from thee (22). Notice the marginal readings of both AV and RV. The sentence seems to mean literally 'Have mercy on yourself'. Peter's instantaneous reaction to our Lord's new teaching shows how foreign to their way of thinking was this conception of His suffering. *Satan* (23). The Lord recognized in Peter's words a repetition of the temptations to avoid the cross which He had undergone in the wilderness. The word translated *offence* means a trap or snare. *Savourest* (23); Gk. *phroneis*. The word is very difficult to translate. It occurs in Rom. viii. 5; Phil. ii. 5. It means to adopt and maintain an attitude of mind upon which the life and actions are based. It almost corresponds to our expression 'to have a (certain) outlook'. With verses 24, 25 cf. x. 38, 39. *Deny himself* (24); i.e. refuse his own claims upon himself. *Take up* (24). The meaning is 'lift up'. It is a stronger word than that used in x. 38, and implies a lifting of the

cross on high, so that all may see it. *His own soul* (26); Gk. *tēn psychēn autou*, the same word as that translated 'life' in the previous verse. To lose one's soul or life means to perish. See vi. 25n., x. 39n. *He shall reward every man according to his works* (27). The words are adopted from the LXX of Ps. lxii. 12 and Pr. xxiv. 12, *kata tēn praxin* being substituted for *kata ta erga*, a change that emphasizes the whole course of life rather than individual actions. This great fundamental moral principle of the Old Testament is made more explicit here by our Lord in explaining that it will find its fulfilment at His return. Both Old Testament passages are suggestive in their context, that in Proverbs being particularly heart-searching. Verse 28 has caused much difficulty and needless misunderstanding. Its fulfilment may be looked for in the transfiguration which follows immediately (an occasion on which the apostle Peter asserts that the three disciples saw Christ's coming; cf. 2 Pet. i. 16), and also in the Lord's resurrection and subsequent glory (see xxvi. 64).

XXI. THE TRANSFIGURATION. xvii. 1–13

See notes on Mk. ix. 2–13; Lk. ix. 28–36. *Peter, James, and John* (1). These three disciples were sometimes admitted to scenes not witnessed by the others. The number three was amply sufficient for witness by the law of Moses. *Apart* (1); i.e. privately, by themselves. *Was transfigured* (2); i.e. His form or appearance was changed. *Moses and Elias* (3); the representatives respectively of the law and the prophets. See Jude 9, where Moses' resurrection is implied, and 2 Ki. ii. 11 for the account of Elijah's being taken up into heaven. *It is good for us to be here* (4). Peter wished to retain the vision and situation and so suggests building *tabernacles* or 'tents'. *A voice* (5); i.e. the Father's voice. For the words spoken compare iii. 17. *Tell the vision to no man* (9). Presumably the other disciples were included in this ban. Cf. also the prohibition of xvi. 20. As our Lord draws near to the cross He seems to have avoided deliberately any popular uprising in His favour which might have resulted if the disciples had proclaimed what they now knew. Cf. Jn. vi. 14, 15.

The point of the disciples' question in verse 10 seems to be that, supposing that Jesus' resurrection meant the end of the world and the inauguration of the kingdom, they thought it would be necessary for Elijah, of whom they had been reminded by seeing him on the mountain, to come and appear publicly first. Our Lord's answer is a quotation from Mal. iv. 5, 6, where the coming of Elijah was prophesied. For the meaning of *restore all things* (11) see Lk. i. 17. He then repeats what He has told them already that the prophecy foretelling the coming of Elijah was fulfilled in John the Baptist. See xi. 14n. He does not name him directly but recalls his suffering and compares with it the treatment which will be accorded to Himself (12).

XXII. THE HEALING OF THE DEVIL-POSSESSED BOY. xvii. 14–21

See notes on Mk. ix. 14–29; Lk. ix. 37–42. *Lunatick* (15); Gk. *selēniazetai*, 'moonstruck'. The RV has 'epileptic'. *Sore vexed* (15); Gk. *kakōs echei*, 'is very ill'. *How long shall I suffer you?* (17); i.e. 'can I endure you?' *Unbelief* (20); Gk. *apistian*. A better reading is *oligopistian*, 'little faith', as in RV. *As a grain of mustard seed* (20). This seems to mean that faith, once implanted in the heart, grows naturally like a living organism. *This mountain* (20); i.e. any seemingly impossible obstacle or difficulty that stands in the Christian's way. There may also be an allusion, by implication, to the disappearance of the Jewish economy and, later, of the heathen Roman Empire. Note that verse 21 is omitted by the more reliable texts. It seems to have been interpolated from Mk. ix. 29.

XXIII. THE SECOND ANNOUNCEMENT OF CHRIST'S SUFFERINGS. xvii. 22, 23

See notes on Mk. ix. 30–32; cf. Lk. ix. 43–45. *While they abode* (22); notice the RV mg., which is the reading of the texts considered most trustworthy. At this time our Lord seems to have been moving unostentatiously from place to place and preparing His disciples for the final journey to Jerusalem, the record of which begins in xix. 1. This further announcement of His coming suffering is no more understood by the disciples than the first. The accounts in Mark and Luke show that they began to feel a vague foreboding of trouble, but did not dare to ask for further enlightenment. It is in this sense that *they were exceeding sorry* (23). RSV renders 'greatly distressed'.

XXIV. THE TEMPLE TAX. xvii. 24–27

Tribute money (24); Gk. *ta didrachma*, lit. 'two drachmae', a technical term for the tax of half a shekel, which every Jew over twenty was expected to contribute to the upkeep of the temple. The amount was about fifteen or eighteen pence. *Prevented* (25); used here with its seventeenth-century meaning of 'anticipated'. *Of strangers* (26). It was the subject races which were taxed first and most heavily. The *children*, i.e. the king's own race, were *free*. The Lord Jesus Christ was the Lord and owner of the temple, and therefore it was not for Him to pay the tax. Action based on this fact might obviously be misunderstood, however, and under such circumstances our Lord would not give offence by seeming to be a law-breaker. But note that in any matter where a fundamental principle was at stake, our Lord did not tone down His message in order not to offend. Cf. xv. 10–14. *A piece of money* (27); Gk. *statēra*, the silver tetradrachma, equivalent to the shekel and therefore the exact amount of the tax for two persons.

XXV. DISCOURSE IV. TEACHING ON HUMILITY AND FORGIVENESS. xviii. 1—xix. 2

This is the last great discourse before the journey to Jerusalem. From Mark we learn that it was given 'in the house' (Mk. ix. 33; cf. Mt. xvii. 25), probably Peter's, and that it arose because of jealousy of one another which had manifested itself in their conversation on the way to Capernaum.

a. Humility (xviii. 1–20)

See also Mk. ix. 33–37; Lk. ix. 46–48. *A little child* (1). Perhaps a member of Peter's family. *Be converted* (3); Gk. *straphēte*, 'turn', as in RV. It means a turning of the whole life and person towards God, exactly what takes place in a genuine conversion, as we use the word in modern times. *Become as little children* (3). The point of this lies not so much, perhaps, in the faith, humility and simplicity of children, as in the conception of starting life over again in regeneration. *Receive . . . in my name* (5); i.e. on the ground that the child belongs to Me.

Verses 8 and 9 form an interlude, in the general theme, dealing with 'offences' (lit. 'snares'). They are substantially a repetition of verses 29, 30. See the notes on these verses. *Hand, foot* and *eye* stand respectively for action, conduct and desire. *Everlasting fire . . . hell fire* (8, 9); i.e. the second death. See v. 22n.

In verse 10 the theme of humility is resumed, reinforced by the conception that the lack of humility constitutes an 'offence'. *Their angels . . . behold the face of my Father* (10). This statement is made as an additional reason for honouring and not despising children. The reference may be to a guardian angel assigned to each child, or at least each believing child, in the sense in which angels are spoken of in Heb. i. 14, waiting in the Father's presence in heaven for His commands concerning the child. Some regard it as a reference to an exact image of the child present in the spiritual world of reality, a sense in which the phrase appears in Acts xii. 15, where we would say 'It is his ghost'. But those who used the term in this sense, e.g. the Christians in Acts xii. 15, probably did not believe in the idea more seriously than we do when we talk about a person's 'ghost'.

Note that the more reliable texts omit verse 11 (see RV). The loss from this context of so beautiful and familiar a statement is sad, but the omission is probably correct. It is hard to see why, if originally there, it should ever have been omitted, but not so difficult to understand that it could have been inserted from Lk. xix. 10, where it belongs, in order to make less apparently abrupt the connection between verses 10 and 12. For a rather fuller version of the parable of the lost sheep see Lk. xv. 3–7. *Perish* (14). Notice that the verse does not exclude such a possibility but merely states that God does not wish it. *Thy brother* (15). Probably we are not intended to confine the meaning of these words to a Christian brother, but to extend it to mean anyone else. *Tell him his fault* (15); i.e. bring the matter home to him. The last phrase of verse 16 is taken from Dt. xix. 15, substantially from the LXX. This just and sensible principle of the Mosaic law is thus brought over by our Lord into the New Testament and established for the advantage of the Christian Church. *Neglect* (17); better, 'refuse', as in RV. *As an heathen man and a publican* (17); i.e. as those who would not be admitted into the Church. The obstinate sinner is to be cut off, at least temporarily, from Christian fellowship. Examples of this are to be found in 1 Cor. v. 4, 5 and 1 Tim. i. 20. For verse 18 see xvi. 19n. The promise is here addressed to all the disciples. Verse 19 is one of the great gospel promises with regard to prayer. But note the close connection of the verse with those that precede and that which follows. The promise is specifically given to a gathering of disciples with Christ *in the midst* (20), called to discipline an erring brother (17). Their authority to do this is re-stated (18) and the promise can be claimed because they are acting on behalf of the Father, in the name of the Son. *In my name* (20); i.e. claiming and using My authority.

b. Forgiveness (xviii. 21—xix. 2)

Then came Peter (21). The theme of the following verses leads on fairly easily from verses 14–17, since the idea of 'gaining thy brother' implies forgiving him when he repents. The section is peculiar to Matthew. *Seventy times seven* (22). This means an infinitely large number of times and is equivalent to 'always'. The idea is expressed in this way to contrast with Peter's 'seven', which limited forgiveness. *Ten thousand talents* (24); a very large sum, probably at least £2,000,000. *Payment to be made* (25). The sale of the servant and his family would not, of course, bring in enough to pay the enormous debt; but this is not the point of the parable. *An hundred pence* (28). The reference is to the Roman denarius and the total value would be probably about £3. The contrast with the 'ten thousand talents' of verse 24 is very marked. *Tormentors* (34); Gk. *basanistais*. The meaning is probably 'executioners'. For verse 35 and the whole teaching of the parable see notes on vi. 14, 15. Notice how true forgiveness 'from the heart' that is, from a heart made clean and regenerate, is one of the signs of true faith. The same truth, is expressed from the opposite angle in Eph. iv. 32.

Verse 1 of chapter xix indicates the close of another division of the Gospel. See vii. 28n. With verse 2 it describes very briefly a journey from Galilee into the district of Judaea *beyond Jordan* (i.e. Peraea) which must have taken a considerable time and into which the events of Lk. ix. 51—xviii. 34 must largely be fitted. The teaching and incidents which follow in xix. 3— xx. 34 also took place during the stay in Peraea.

XXVI. TEACHING ON DIVORCE IN ANSWER TO THE PHARISEES. xix. 3–12

For every cause (3); i.e. for any reason at all. The point of this question is that there were two schools of thought among the Jewish rabbis on the matter of divorce. One denied that it was admissible except on the grounds of unfaithfulness or immorality; the other allowed it on trivial pretexts. *He which made them* (4). Some texts read 'he which created them'. The reference is to the LXX of Gn. i. 27. *And said* (5). The statement that follows is not attributed to God in Genesis but occurs in the course of the narrative (see Gn. ii. 24). Yet our Lord attributes it to the Creator. This reveals His view of the inspiration of Scripture. *One flesh* (6). This seems to teach that they are made one by the sexual act. In His pronouncement on the subject the Lord goes back over the head of Moses to the primitive revelation in Eden.

The further question raised by the Pharisees (7) is an allusion to Dt. xxiv. 1. Jesus answers that the Mosaic law was accommodated in some respects to the sinful nature of man. *Except for fornication* (9). See v. 32n. *Committeth adultery* (9); RV mg. 'maketh her an adulteress'. It seems best to follow this alternative MS reading which makes the saying parallel with v. 32 (where see notes).

It is not good to marry (10). The disciples mean that, if a man is to be indissolubly bound to his wife, it is safer for him not to undertake marriage at all. The connection of thought between the earlier verses and verses 9 and 10 is difficult. The words *this saying* (11) may refer to our Lord's statement in verse 9 about the indissolubility of marriage. In that case his statement about eunuchs in verse 12 is intended as an illustration of the possibility of Christian men exercising self-restraint. If they can do so to the extent of abstaining from marriage, they can do so to the extent of holding fast the marriage tie. Or the words *this saying* may refer to the remark of the disciples in verse 10. The Lord's words in verses 11 and 12 then simply mean that there are those capable of conforming to the disciples' idea that abstinence from marriage is best. *Made themselves eunuchs* (12). Misunderstanding of these words in a literal sense in an age of asceticism has brought about tragedies in Christian history from time to time. The words refer to abstention from marriage for the sake of the gospel. The principle involved is seen in 1 Cor. vii. 25–38. *He that is able to receive it . . .* (12). This seems to refer to the disciples' statement in verse 10 and not to go back to the Lord's statement about the indissolubility of marriage. It should be noted that this verse does not glorify celibacy, but implies that only those who are truly eunuchs can accept the disciples' saying. Those who, for the kingdom of heaven's sake, are able to set aside all desire for marriage may be called to celibacy. But unless a man can do this the inference is that he would be wiser to marry normally.

XXVII. THE BLESSING OF CHILDREN.
xix. 13-15

See notes on Mk. x. 13-16; Lk. xviii. 15-17. *Little children* (13); RSV omits 'little'. They do not seem to have been infants but of an age to come to Christ when called tò do so. *Of such* (14); i.e. of childlike persons.

XXVIII. RICHES AND SALVATION.
xix. 16—xx. 16

For verses 16-29 see notes on Mk. x. 17-31; Lk. xviii. 18-30. *Good Master* (16). The more reliable texts omit the word 'good'. See RV where the next verse is also better rendered 'Why askest thou me concerning that which is good?' The AV reading, *there is none good but one*, follows Mark and Luke. In saying this the Lord is not denying His own deity, but impressing upon His questioner the implications of calling Him good. *If thou wilt enter into life, keep the commandments* (17). The point of this statement is, of course, that the questioner supposed that he was keeping them. It is not a statement of the gospel. It is made plain everywhere in Scripture that no one is capable of keeping the commandments. For verses 18 and 19 see Ex. xx. 12-16; Dt. v. 16-20; Lv. xix. 18. The quotation is from the LXX. The young man was wrong in supposing he had kept the commandments (20), especially that of love to his neighbour, but he felt a sense of need. *If thou wilt be perfect* (21); cf. v. 48n. *Sell that thou hast, and give to the poor* (21). In its context this command is not a general instruction to all Christians to lead a life of poverty. Our Lord called on the man to take this step because it provided the surest test of his genuineness. But the command is in line with the principle derived from other Scriptures (see e.g. Lk. xii. 33) that the Christian ought to possess only what is necessary for his everyday needs and those of the work for God on which he is engaged. *Hardly* (23); i.e. with difficulty. There are three possible interpretations of verse 24. First, both the camel and the needle's eye may be regarded as literal. Secondly, it is supposed thàt the word translated 'camel' really means 'rope', the needle's eye being again taken literally. Thirdly, camel is taken literally, but the needle's eye is regarded as the name of the small gate beside the main gate of Jerusalem which a camel could pass only by unloading all its burden, kneeling down and being pulled or pushed through. The last of the three seems to the present writer the most probable. In any case the sense is clear and was quickly grasped by the disciples (25). *Beheld* (26); looked at. *With God all things are possible* (26). The words are an allusion to Gn. xviii. 14; Jb. xlii. 2; and Zc. viii. 6. Salvation is impossible by human effort. It is a supernatural act of God.

We have forsaken all (27). Peter is contrasting himself with the rich ruler who has just refused to give up anything. *What shall we have therefore?*

is a reference to the Lord's promise of 'treasure in heaven' (21). Our Lord deals graciously with this question, but in the parable which follows (xx. 1-16), He warns against adopting ordinary earthly standards when judging such matters. See verse 30n. below. *In the regeneration* (28); Gk. *palingenesia*. The reference is to the renewed world of the future, the 'new heavens and new earth'. *Ye shall also sit . . . judging* (28). Cf. 1 Cor. vi. 2, 3; Rev. iii. 21. *Or wife* (29). Some texts omit these words; see RV. *An hundredfold* (29). Some texts read *pollaplasiona*, 'manifold', as in RV mg.

The point of the statement in verse 30 (repeated in xx. 16) is that reward in the world to come depends upon God's grace and faith in Christ, not upon the quality or quantity of service. Note how the parable illustrates and drives home this fact. It is peculiar to Matthew. *A penny* (xx. 2); i.e. the Roman denarius. Its value used to be reckoned as about 8½d. With the fall in the purchasing power of sterling it would now be worth more. *Standing idle in the marketplace* (3). It was the usual place to wait when seeking employment. The times mentioned in verses 5 and 6 were twelve midday, three o'clock and five o'clock respectively. *And whatsoever is right, that shall ye receive* (7). The texts which are considered more reliable omit these words (see RV). *Beginning from the last unto the first* (8). Notice the connection with xix. 30 and xx. 16. This is the main theme of the parable.

Verse 15 shows that, everything being of grace, God has the right to give or withhold at will. We must take care that this goodness of God does not provoke us to complaint. The point of verse 16 is that all Christians receive the same, the reward being everlasting life given on the ground of Christ's death for them. By earthly standards of judgment, expressed clearly in verses 11, 12, such action is regarded as putting the last first and the first last. *For many are called, but few chosen* (16). Some texts (see RV) omit these words. They make, however, good sense and refer back to the Lord's words in xix. 23-26, where He speaks of the difficulty that many experience in believing and obeying the gospel because their minds are fixed on what they can get for themselves, whether in this world or the next.

XXIX. THE THIRD ANNOUNCEMENT OF CHRIST'S SUFFERINGS. xx. 17-19

See notes on Mk. x. 32-34; Lk. xviii. 31-34. The journey to Jerusalem is now resumed after the stay in Peraea (see xix. 1, 2n.). As the final events of His life draw nearer, our Lord again seeks to enlighten His disciples. Again they failed to understand, as is evidenced by the request of Zebedee's sons which immediately followed. But the fulfilment of these detailed predictions would strengthen their faith when the time came. Compare the angel's words in xxviii. 6.

XXX. THE REQUEST OF JAMES AND JOHN. xx. 20-28

See notes on Mk. x. 35–45. *Zebedee's children* (20). From Mt. iv. 21 we know that the two sons were the apostles James and John. *Grant* (21); better, 'command', as in RV. The request and the indignation of the others which followed (24) show that the disciples were still thinking in terms of the setting up of an earthly kingdom, in spite of the clear prediction of suffering and death which our Lord had just made. Some texts (see RV) omit the last part of our Lord's question in verse 22 and it may have been inserted from the parallel passage in Mk. x. 38. The same is true of verse 23. The cup and the baptism both refer, of course, to our Lord's suffering and death. *Shall be given to* (23); better, 'is for', as in RV. *Let him be* (26). Here and in verse 27 the better reading is probably 'shall be' as in RV.

To be ministered unto (28). It is not wrong to accept ministry. Christ accepted it. But it was not the purpose of His life and should not be ours. *His life* (28); Gk. *tēn psychēn autou*, lit. 'his soul'. *A ransom* (28); Gk. *lytron*. This important phrase provides one of the few occasions on which the doctrine of substitutionary atonement is mentioned in the synoptic Gospels. It implies a price paid for the deliverance of captives. Of course neither God nor the devil, as has been suggested at various times in the past, received any pecuniary or other advantage by our Lord's death. The price lay in the necessity for His life to be laid down. His life thus became the cost of our redemption.

XXXI. THE HEALING OF THE TWO BLIND MEN. xx. 29-34

See notes on Mk. x. 46–52; Lk. xviii. 35–43. *Two blind men* (30). Mark and Luke speak only of one; see viii. 28n. *Rebuked them, because they should hold their peace* (31). The AV phrase is awkward and the RV scarcely less so. The meaning is 'severely charged them to be silent'. In verse 34 follow RV.

XXXII. THE EVENTS OF THE LAST WEEK OF THE MINISTRY. xxi. 1—xxiii. 39

a. The triumphal entry into Jerusalem (xxi. 1-11)

See notes on Mk. xi. 1–10; Lk. xix. 29–39; Jn. xii. 12–15. *Bethphage* (1); a village near Bethany about a mile east of Jerusalem and apparently hidden from it by the summit of the Mount of Olives which was the hill on the east of Jerusalem. *The Lord hath need of them* (3). The account of these closing events in our Lord's life shows that there were men and women in Jerusalem and its neighbourhood who recognized Jesus as Lord. They may have become disciples during the earlier Jerusalem ministry described by John. The quotation in verse 5 is a combination of Is. lxii. 11 and Zc. ix. 9, taken substantially from the LXX. *Thereon* (7); that is, on the clothes. *Hosanna* (9) is a Hebrew term meaning 'Save, Lord', and occurs in 2 Sa. xiv. 4 and Ps. cxviii. 25. From the following verse of this Psalm the acclamation *Blessed is he that cometh in the name of the Lord* is taken. In verses 10 and 11 there is a contrast between the men of *the city*, who were ignorant of our Lord's identity, and the *multitude* who were able to answer their question. There were probably many Galileans in the latter who had come up for the feast and who already knew our Lord through His preaching and healing ministry in the north.

b. The cleansing of the temple (xxi. 12-17)

See notes on Mk. xi. 15–19; Lk. xix. 45–47. *The temple* (12); Gk. *to hieron*, i.e. the whole temple area on Mount Moriah including all the precincts and courts. Note that some texts omit the words *of God. Moneychangers* (12). Temple dues could be paid only in sacred coinage, and it was necessary to change one's money. The selling of doves was, of course, for purposes of sacrifice. In His condemnation (13) our Lord quotes from the LXX of Is. lvi. 7 and Je. vii. 11. *They were sore displeased* (15). It was not just our Lord's popularity that angered them: the title 'Son of David' which the children kept calling out implied Messiahship. The cavils of the enemy were, however, stilled by the children's praise, as is suggested by the context of the Psalm from which our Lord quotes (Ps. viii. 2).

Bethany (17) was a village on the eastern shoulder of the Mount of Olives, a little more than a mile east of Jerusalem. It was the home of Lazarus and his sisters.

c. The withering of the fig tree (xxi. 18-22)

See notes on Mk. xi. 12–14, 20–26. Notice the AV mg. in verse 19. It was the only fig tree visible. *Leaves only* (19). The fruit of the fig tree appears in February before the leaves, which are not formed till April or May. Thus there should normally have been some fruit on the tree. *Let no fruit grow on thee henceforward for ever* (19). The context immediately following seems to point to the barren fig tree being selected by our Lord as an illustration of difficulties or obstacles in the way of the gospel or of the spiritual life. *Presently* (19) has here its seventeenth-century meaning of 'immediately'. *How soon is the fig tree withered away!* (20). A better rendering is that of the RV, 'How did the fig tree immediately wither away?' For verse 21 see xvii. 20n.

d. A dispute with the Pharisees in the temple (xxi. 23—xxii. 14)

See notes on Mk. xi. 27—xii. 12; Lk. xxi. 1–19.

i. **Our Lord silences His questioners** (xxi. 23–27). The point of the Lord's question seems to be that, since John preached without their authority, He Himself might also teach without it.

ii. The parable of the two sons (xxi. 28–32).

This parable is linked with the preceding verses by the reference to John in verse 32. The priests and elders had not believed him (25); the people, on the other hand, regarded him as a prophet (26). It may be noticed that in verse 32 our Lord in effect answers the question which He Himself had put. *Son* (28); 'child', as in RV mg. *Kingdom of God* (31). See xii. 28n. *In the way of righteousness* (32); i.e. to lead you along the way of righteousness. *Repented not* (32). The Pharisees were like the son who pretended to be obedient but did not obey. The publicans were like the son who at first disobeyed but afterwards repented. They thus became acceptable to God.

iii. The parable of the wicked husbandmen (xxi. 33–46).

See notes on Mk. xii. 1–12. *Planted a vineyard . . . built a tower* (33). The words are adapted from the LXX of Is. v. 1, 2. The *husbandmen* represent the Jewish religious leaders; the *servants* the Old Testament prophets. Thus the parable describes the persecution and rejection of the prophets by the nation's civil and ecclesiastical leaders, which was about to be followed by their rejection of God's Son Himself.

Our Lord's quotation in verse 42 is taken exactly from the LXX of Ps. cxviii. 22, 23. The stone is Jesus Christ. The story is a picture of His rejection by the Jews, only to become the foundation stone of the Christian Church by the act of God in raising Him from the dead. Because of unbelief and disobedience the Jews are rejected and their privilege given to *a nation* (i.e. the Christian Church) *bringing forth the fruits thereof* (43). For an explanation of the whole passage see 1 Pet. ii. 4–10.

The first clause of verse 44 probably refers to those who are *broken* (RV 'broken to pieces') by coming to Christ, to be re-made into new creatures in Him; the second clause refers to those who are finally destroyed by Him on the day of judgment.

iv. The parable of the wedding garment (xxii. 1–14).

Cf. Lk. xiv. 16–24. This is a parable which illustrates the gospel dispensation, God's grace, the rejection of it by the Jews and the calling of the Gentiles. *Made a marriage* (2). The Eastern custom was for the marriage festivities to be held in the home of the bridegroom, not in that of the bride. The wedding was the responsibility of the bridegroom's parents. *The highways* (9); RV 'the partings of the highways'. The original *tas diexodous tōn hodōn*. seems to mean 'crossroads'. *Both bad and good* (10). The visible professing church consists of both. *Wedding garment* (11). This was the proper dress for the wedding feast and was provided for each guest by the host. *And take him away* (13). These words are omitted in the more reliable texts (see RV). *There shall be weeping and gnashing of teeth* (13); see viii. 12n. In the context the meaning of verse 14 seems to be that there have been many who have heard the gospel, or been members of the visible church, but only a few whose hearts are right with God.

e. A question about tribute to Caesar (xxii. 15–22)

See notes on Mk. xii. 13–17; Lk. xx. 20–26. *The Herodians* (16). They were a party that favoured the dynasty of Herod and stood for the Roman connection. They cared little or nothing for religion and were normally opposed bitterly by the Pharisees. The statements recorded in verse 16 were insincere and intended as hypocritical flattery. Their question (17) was intended to place the Lord in a dilemma. If He said yes, He could be held up to the people as a traitor. If He said no, He could be denounced to the Roman authorities. *Caesar* (17); i.e. the Roman emperor and head of the Roman state. Caesar was the family name of Julius Caesar, the first man who aspired to autocracy, and was taken over from him by his adopted son, afterwards the Emperor Augustus. It soon came to be regarded as a title. *Penny* (19). See xx. 2n. *Render therefore unto Caesar . . .* (21). The Lord means that we are to give the civil magistrates all that is due to them, so long as it does not interfere with the honour due to God.

f. The Sadducees and resurrection (xxii. 23–33)

See notes on Mk. xii. 18–27; Lk. xx. 27–40. *The Sadducees* (23); omit 'the', as RV. See iii. 7n. *Moses said* (24); see Dt. xxv. 5, 6. This is known as the law of levirate marriage. An early instance occurs in Gn. xxxviii. 8, and the LXX of this passage is echoed in the present quotation. *Knowing* (29); i.e. understanding the meaning of. *The power of God* (29). This power was especially evident in resurrection; cf. Rom. i. 4; Eph. i. 19, 20. *Nor are given in marriage* (30); Gk. *oute gamizontai*. When the subject of the verb is the woman, as is probably intended here, the meaning is 'to give oneself in marriage', i.e. 'to wed'. Cf. the way in which different words are used for the man and the woman in Latin and modern French. The meaning of the verse is literally 'neither the men nor the women marry'. *The angels of God* (30); better, simply 'angels', as in RV. The point is that angels do not reproduce their kind. There is no need to infer from the Lord's answer that families will not be united in the world to come.

g. Further controversy with the Pharisees (xxii. 34–46)

See notes on Mk. xii. 28–37. *Tempting him* (35); i.e. trying to catch Him out. Our Lord's reply to the question (37) is adapted from Dt. vi. 5 where the original commandment is found, being taken partly from the LXX and partly apparently from the Hebrew. Duty to God is the first duty of man. *First and great* (38); better, 'great and first', as in RV. *Like unto it* (39); i.e. *like* in its necessity for showing love, which means absolute devotion to the interests of another. The quotation is from Lv. xix. 18. With verse 40 cf. Rom. xiii. 10.

In spirit (43). This probably means by the inspiration of the Holy Spirit. The quotation in verse 44 is from the LXX of Ps. cx. 1. The point of the quotation lies in the expression *my Lord.* The passage is a prophecy of Christ's present session at the Father's right hand. The answer to our Lord's question lies in the fact that Christ is both God and man. There is implied here a clear claim to deity.

h. Denunciation of the Pharisees (xxiii. 1–39)

Cf. Mk. xii. 38–40; Lk. xx. 45–47. *Sit in Moses' seat* (1); i.e. occupy Moses' place of authority. *Whatsoever they bid you observe, that . . . do* (3). Bearing in mind the strictures which follow, it seems clear that this means all lawful things; i.e. it depends on the extent to which they do really 'sit in Moses' seat'. It cannot include, for example, the 'traditions of the elders' (see the condemnation of some of these in xv. 1–20). But, as the verse goes on to show, the sin of the Pharisees lay more in their evil practices than in their teaching, for they themselves did not practise what they preached. *They make broad their phylacteries* (5). A phylactery was an amulet consisting of a strip of parchment on which was inscribed certain portions of the Pentateuch and which was rolled and placed in a small metal cylinder inside a square leather case. The cases were attached by the Jews with straps to their forehead and to the back of their right hand, following a strictly literal interpretation of Dt. vi. 8, 9. They were normally worn only during prayer, but the Pharisees appear to have worn them always and to have made them especially conspicuous. *The borders of their garments* (5) were the fringes worn in obedience to Nu. xv. 38, 39. *Uppermost rooms* (6); better, 'chief place', as in RV.

Rabbi (7, 8); Gk. *Rabbei*, from Hebrew word meaning literally 'my teacher'. *Master* (8); i.e. teacher. Note that the words *even Christ* are omitted by the better texts and are probably a gloss (see RV).

Call no man your father (9); i.e. in a spiritual sense. This appears to condemn the use of the word 'Father' used in addressing the clergy in the unreformed churches, and to render of doubtful propriety the use of the word 'padre' (Italian for 'father') as a synonym for a chaplain. *Masters* (10); Gk. *kathēgetai*; lit. guides or leaders, i.e. teachers. *Servant* (11); Gk. *diakonos*, meaning minister or attendant. Verses 10–12 are very typical of our Lord's teaching. Cf. Lk. xiv. 11, xviii. 14.

Ye shut up the kingdom of heaven against men (13); i.e. you put stumbling-blocks in the way of the sinner coming to repentance and conversion. *Devour widows' houses* (14); i.e. extort money from the helpless and bring them into debt and bondage, while making an outward show of religion. *The greater damnation* (14); Gk. *perissoteron krima*, i.e. 'a more severe sentence'. But note that this verse is omitted by RV following the more reliable texts. *Proselyte* (15). The Jews recognized two sorts of proselytes: those who agreed to the so-called seven precepts

of Noah, and those who submitted to circumcision and became full Jews by religion.

Verses 16–22 give illustrations of the Pharisees' casuistry with regard to oaths. *Temple* (16); Gk. *naos*, 'sanctuary'. Our Lord teaches that all oaths are equally binding, and no man can expect to escape their consequences before God by making distinctions such as these.

Pay tithe of (23). A tithe or tenth of all produce was, by the Mosaic law, to be given for the use of the priests and Levites. See e.g. Lv. xxvii. 30. Several species of *mint* grow in Palestine. *Anise* (Gk. *anēthon*) is better rendered 'dill', as in RV mg. It grew both wild and cultivated in Palestine, its fruits being used for medicine. The seeds of *cummin*, which resemble caraways, were used as spice in seasoning. In such little matters the Pharisees are most careful to keep the law; yet they have completely overlooked its more important precepts.

Strain at a gnat (24); better, 'strain out the gnat', as in RV. The Jews strained wine before drinking it so as to avoid touching or swallowing anything unclean. *But within they are full of extortion and excess* (25). For 'of' read 'from' as in RV. The Pharisees' living was obtained by extorting wrongfully from others.

Whited sepulchres (27). Since contact with a dead body rendered a person unclean according to the Mosaic law, it was the custom to paint graves white in order to make them conspicuous, and so give the opportunity of avoiding contact with them. *The children of them which killed* (31); Gk. *tōn phoneusantōn*, 'those who murdered'; RV 'sons of them that slew'. *Generation* (33); RV 'offspring'. *The damnation of hell* (33); being judged worthy of Gehenna. See v. 22n.

That upon you may come (35). The generation to which these words were addressed represented the culminating point of the whole sinful history of the nation, beginning with the murder of *Abel* by his brother Cain (see Gn. iv; Heb. xi. 4) and going on to the murder of *Zacharias son of Barachias*. In 2 Ch. xxiv. 20, 21 we find the account of the murder of Zechariah son of Jehoiada 'in the court of the house of the Lord'. As the books of Chronicles closed the Hebrew Old Testament canon, if this is the incident here referred to, the mention of Abel and Zacharias may be intended to cover the whole Old Testament canon. The difficulty is that the Zechariah murdered in 2 Ch. xxiv was not the son of Berechiah. This Zechariah was the prophet (Zc. i. 1). Though he lived after the exile and towards the close of Old Testament history there seems no tradition or record that he was murdered. Another possibility is that the Zechariah referred to here is identical with 'Zechariah the son of Jeberechiah' mentioned in Is. viii. 2, but nothing further seems to be known of him. This passage is also recorded by Luke (Lk. xi. 49–51).

Your house is left unto you desolate (38); a reference to 1 Ki. ix. 7, 8; Je. xii. 7, xxii. 5. The Lord is predicting the destruction of the temple.

Verse 39 closes our Lord's ministry to the Jews. It foreshadows His death, resurrection and departure to the Father and indicates that He is henceforth only to be known by the new birth. *Blessed is he* . . . (39). The words are taken from the LXX of Ps. cxviii. 26.

XXXIII. DISCOURSE V. THE LAST DAYS.
xxiv. 1—xxv. 46

For xxiv. 1–51 see notes on Mk. xiii. 1–37; Lk. xxi. 5–38.

a. The coming of the end (xxiv. 1–14)

Temple (1); Gk. *hierou,* meaning the temple precincts. The prophecy of verse 2 was fulfilled in the time of the Emperor Julian who, in a futile attempt to rebuild the temple, removed even those stones that had been left .at the time of the destruction by Titus. *Thy coming* (3); Gk. *parousias,* a word used to express a royal visit. The disciples' questions show that they connected the destruction of Jerusalem with the end (or 'climax') of the world, were convinced that Jesus was Messiah, and looked for His future manifestation in glory at the end of the world to usher in the eternal messianic age. In the second and third conviction they were wholly right. In the first they were partially so. The destruction of Jerusalem was a sign that the old order was obsolete and that a new one had begun. Being still ignorant of the crucifixion and resurrection, the predictions of which they had not believed, the disciples did not understand that the new age was to be inaugurated by the Lord's resurrection and was to overlap the old. *Many shall come* (5). During the forty years between the Lord's resurrection and the destruction of Jerusalem several false Christs appeared and collected considerable followings. *These things must come to pass* (6); taken from the LXX of Dn. ii. 28; cf. Rev. i. 1, iv. 1. Note that RV, following the better texts, omits the word *all. For nation shall rise against nation* . . . (7); an allusion to Is. xix. 2; 2 Ch. xv. 6, but to the Hebrew rather than the LXX. The contexts of both Old Testament passages are instructive for the understanding of the present passage. *Famines, and pestilences* (7); Gk. *limoi kai loimoi.* It is perhaps the close resemblance of the two Greek words which has caused the omission of the latter in some texts (so RV). *Sorrows* (8); RV 'travail'. The reference is presumably to the birth pangs of the messianic age. *To be afflicted* (9); RV 'unto tribulation'. *False prophets shall rise* (11); see vii. 15, 16n. Verse 12 seems to suggest that the pull of the world will be too strong for many professing Christians. Note that endurance is an essential corollary to true conversion (13). *World* (14); Gk. *oikoumenē(i),* the inhabited or civilized world.

b. Great tribulation (xxiv. 15–28)

The abomination of desolation . . . *in the holy place* (15). This is a mysterious phrase which we might call part of the technical language of apocalyptic.

It comes from Dn. ix. 27, xii. 11, and is explained in the parallel synoptic passage (Lk. xxi. 20) as meaning the encirclement of Jerusalem by victorious armies and the subsequent destruction of the city and the sanctuary. *By* (RV mg. 'through') *Daniel the prophet* (15). The Lord here endorses the authorship of the book of Daniel by the prophet whose name it bears. *Clothes* (18); better, 'cloke', as in RV (Gk. *himation,* the outer garment). *Neither on the sabbath day* (20); a reference to the Jewish legal tradition which forbade travel beyond a short distance on the sabbath.

Verse 21 is adapted from Joel ii. 2 and Dn. xii. 1. The horrors of the siege of Jerusalem fully justified this prediction. About a million Jews were killed, mostly by crucifixion, and about two million were sold to misery and death in slavery. *Elect* (22); 'chosen'. See xxii. 14. *And shall shew great signs and wonders* (24). There is an allusion here to Dt. xiii. 1–4. The reason given in Deuteronomy for the permission of false prophets throws much light on the deeper meaning of our Lord's words. *The very elect* (24); 'even the elect', as in RV. *Secret chambers* (26); Gk. *tameiois,* lit. 'store-chambers'. The verse is a warning against running after any false prophet claiming to be the Christ who may appear in the country districts and also against believing lying rumours that the Christ is living secretly in the town. When the Son of man comes, He will be clearly manifested to everybody (27). The point of verse 28 seems to be that, just as birds of prey appear 'from nowhere' as soon as a carcase drops dead, knowing of it by instinct or a very keen sense of smell, and not needing to be told of the fact, so will all true believers be aware of the Lord's coming even though it be as sudden as a flash of lightning (27), and be gathered together to Him.

c. The coming of the Son of man (xxiv. 29–31)

Immediately after the tribulation of those days (29). The 'tribulation' did not end with the destruction of Jerusalem. In the present writer's view it includes the subsequent Christian age. There may be an intensification of it at the end of the age. The various expressions in verse 29 are again what we might call the technical language of prophecy. They are taken from Is. xiii. 10, xxxiv. 4, but not wholly from the LXX. The reference in the former passage seems to be to the destruction of the Babylonian Empire and in the latter to the final judgments at the end of the world. *The sign of the Son of man* (30). This probably means 'the sign, that is to say, the Son of man'. *Then shall all the tribes of the earth mourn* (30); an allusion to Zc. xii. 10–14. Mourning, which may now be the mourning of repentance, must on the day of judgment be the wailing of despair. *The Son of man coming in the clouds of heaven* (30); an allusion to Dn. vii. 13 where, however, the prophecy seems to be of the ascension. Here the words undoubtedly refer to the return of Christ in glory. In verse 31 notice the allusions to Is. xxvii. 13; Dt. xxx. 4; Zc. ii. 6. The Lord is referring to the event often known as 'the rapture (i.e. the sudden taking away) of the saints'. His words are amplified by the apostle Paul in 1 Thes. iv. 15–17. Notice in both passages the presence of the Lord in person, the angels or archangel, the trumpet, the rapture of the saints and the clouds.

d. A call to be ready (xxiv. 32–51)

A parable (32). The point of the parable seems to be that the events which the Lord has been describing in verses 5–28 constitute signs of the certainty and imminence of the Lord's return. There seems no scriptural warrant in this context for equating the fig tree with the Jews or for other fanciful interpretations. *It is near* (33); or, as in RV, 'he is nigh'. Verse 34 is difficult and has been explained in various ways as follows. Some regard *this generation* as meaning the generation which sees the signs of the end; others interpret *generation* as 'race' and refer it to the Jews; others think that the generation referred to is the same as that in Phil. ii. 15, and means the unconverted in general. It is best of all to take *these things* (34) as referring to the siege of Jerusalem in contrast to *that day and hour* (36), which refers to the end of the world. Cf. Lk. xxi. 32n. Verse 35 contrasts the temporal nature of the created universe with the eternal nature of spiritual truth.

But my Father only (36). The better texts insert before these words 'neither the Son' (see RV and the parallel passage in Mk. xiii. 32). This statement of our Lord's about the limitation of His own knowledge is difficult to understand. There is no implication that it was owing to the incarnation that His knowledge was limited. In Acts i. 7 it seems that these matters are still the prerogative of the Father. *The days of Noe* (37); for a description of them see Gn. vii. 7. *The one shall be taken, and the other left* (40). It does not seem clear whether one is taken to glory and the other left to judgment, or whether one is taken to destruction and the other left alive. The important point lies in the fact of the separation of the two at the end and the separate destinies involved. See xiii. 49.

The short parable in verse 43 serves as a warning against trying to press the allusions in parabolic teaching too far. For here the coming of the Son of man is likened to the coming of a thief. Obviously the story serves only to illustrate the need for keeping awake (watching) in order to be ready. For the whole passage (verses 42–51) cf. Lk. xii. 36–48 in addition to the parallel section in Mk. xiii. *Weeping and gnashing of teeth* (51); see viii. 12n.

e. The parable of the wise and foolish virgins (xxv. 1–13)

This parable shows the difference between real and nominal Christians and reinforces the call already given to be ready for the Lord's coming. *Went forth to meet the bridegroom* (1). After dark on the evening of the wedding day the bridegroom led the bride home, accompanied by friends of both, and joined on the way by others carrying lamps in honour of the bridal pair. *Gone out* (8); RV 'going out'. *Marriage* (10); RV 'marriage feast'. The festivities sometimes continued for as long as seven days. Note that the more reliable texts omit the words *wherein the Son of man cometh* (13), which are likely to have been a gloss.

f. The parable of the talents (xxv. 14–30)

See notes on Lk. xix. 11–28. This parable illustrates the state of the Church before and at Christ's second coming. *Talents* (15); roughly equal in value at the time to about £300. *Ability* (15); Gk. *dynamin*, 'power'. *Straightway* (15). This is best taken as the opening word of verse 16, as in RV. *Hard* (24); i.e. severe or merciless. *Reaping where thou . . . . hast not strawed* (24). The slave misjudged his master's character and, therefore, could not have known him well. *I was afraid* (25). The slave seems to have thought that whatever he did his master would be unjust to him. Verse 26 is not an admission on the part of the master that the servant's estimate of his character is correct. He is simply saying, 'If you thought that, then you ought to have . . .' *Exchangers* (27); 'bankers', as in RV. For verse 29 see xiii. 12n.

g. The last judgment (xxv. 31–46)

Verse 31 is an allusion to Zc. xiv. 5, based substantially on the LXX. The better texts (see RV) omit the word *holy*. It may have been inserted in order to make the quotation conform more exactly to the original. The LXX of Zc. xiv. 5 reads *pantes hoi hagioi*, 'all the saints' or 'holy ones'. The evangelist glosses *hagioi* by *angeloi*, angels. *All nations* (32); better 'all the nations', as in RV, or perhaps 'all the Gentiles'. For the same expression see xxiv. 9 and xxviii. 19. Two main difficulties arise with regard to this judgment of the nations. First, is the expression 'all nations' intended to refer to outsiders only, and if so does it mean non-Jews or non-Christians? It can scarcely mean the former as the distinction between Jew and Gentile is broken down by the gospel. And in view of the fact that there are righteous who appear at the judgment it is difficult to think that Christians are excluded. The expression is therefore probably equivalent to 'the whole world', a sense in which it seems to be used in xxiv. 9 and xxviii. 19. Secondly, is this judgment the same as that described in Rev. xx. 11–15? The latter is distinctly said to be a judgment of 'the dead' (Rev. xx. 12, 13). There is no mention made here of either living or dead as such. Perhaps no clear answer can be given to this particular query, but it is natural to suppose that the present judgment scene includes the living and the dead. The two descriptions, therefore, probably refer to the same event, the mention of the dead in Rev. xx being, in that case, only one of context and emphasis.

On the question of the present judgment appearing to be an eternal issue decided by works, it may be answered first that the works appear as evidence of nature and condition, not as meritorious in themselves; secondly that, in Rev. xx. 12, 13, works similarly appear as evidence on eternal issues; and thirdly that the atmosphere of the present scene is entirely consistent with that of the whole of this Gospel, where the emphasis is constantly placed upon reality in religion, exhibited in a life that involves taking the cross as opposed to the self-righteousness of the Pharisees. The Johannine emphasis is somewhat different from this, although, of course, not inconsistent with it. *Inherit* (34). Note that inheritance is due to being a member of a family, not due to actions. *Prepared for you from the foundation of the world* (34); prepared, therefore, long before the actions were done. Note in verses 35, 36 that the point of central importance is relationship to Christ.

My brethren (40). The brethren of Christ are believers, members of the true Church (see Heb. ii. 10–12). It does not follow from this that Christians are not present at this judgment any more than that the wise virgins (verse 2) do not represent true Christians because in the parable they are not identical with the bride.

Everlasting fire, prepared for the devil and his angels (41); not for men, who have the opportunity to be saved from it. See xviii. 8n. In verses 42–45 notice that the fault of those who are condemned lay entirely in omission. The failure was due to there being no love in their lives. Verse 46 is an allusion to the LXX of Dn. xii. 2, where the reference is to the resurrection of the dead, a hint that we are intended to regard the dead as well as the living as present at this judgment scene.

XXXIV. THE PASSION, DEATH AND RESURRECTION. xxvi. 1—xxviii. 20

These chapters describe the plot of the priests, the anointing of the Lord in Bethany, the betrayal, the institution of the Lord's Supper, the agony in the garden, the Lord's arrest, His trial before the priests, Peter's denial, the trial before Pilate and finally the crucifixion and resurrection.

a. The consultation of the priests (xxvi. 1–5)

See notes on Mk. xiv. 1, 2; Lk. xxii. 1, 2. Verse 1 indicates the end of the fifth of our Lord's discourses around which the Gospel is built. See vii. 28n. *The feast of the passover* (2). This great festival inaugurated the Jewish religious year and was kept in commemoration of the national deliverance from Egypt (see Ex. xii). Thousands of pilgrims flocked annually to Jerusalem for it. The Lord's death was the fulfilment of that of which the annual feast had been a shadow. *Betrayed* (2); RV 'delivered up'. *Palace* (3); i.e. courtyard. *Caiaphas* (3). He was a Sadducee, and had been appointed High Priest

the year before the beginning of the Lord's ministry.

b. The anointing and betrayal (xxvi. 6–16)

For verses 6–13 see notes on Mk. xiv. 3–9; Jn. xii. 1–8. *Simon the leper* (6); mentioned only here and in the parallel Mk. xiv. 3. By a comparison with Jn. xii. 1–8 it becomes a reasonable deduction that he was the father of Lazarus, Martha and Mary. *She did it for my burial* (12). The point seems to be that the action was appropriate in view of His burial which was soon to take place, and that it might be regarded as symbolic or prophetic of the burial. *This gospel* (13); i.e. the good news of the Lord's death and resurrection.

For verses 14–16 see notes on Mk. xiv. 10, 11; Lk. xxii. 3–6. *Judas Iscariot* (14); see Mk. iii. 19n. *And they covenanted with him for thirty pieces of silver* (15). These words are substantially from the LXX of Zc. xi. 12. *Betray him* (16); i.e. 'hand Him over'. The same verb in Greek is translated 'deliver' in verse 15.

c. The Last Supper (xxvi. 17–35)

See notes on Mk. xiv. 12–31; Lk. xxii. 7–38; and cf. Jn. xiii. 1–38. *The first day of the feast of unleavened bread* (17). The Passover lasted eight days in all. The day referred to here is Thursday, 13th of Nisan, when the preparations for the removal of leaven from houses began. It thus came to be popularly known as the 'first day of unleavened bread'. *Eat the passover* (17). Jewish households celebrated the Passover by a ritual meal on the evening of the fourteenth day of the month Nisan, which roughly corresponded to April. This is perhaps what the disciples supposed the Lord intended to do. The last supper, however, appears to have been eaten on the evening of the 13th (already by Jewish reckoning the 14th, as the day began at sunset). (For a note on the Johannine chronology see *Introduction* to commentary on John and introductory note to Jn. xiii. 1–38.) *Is it I?* (22); Gk. *mēti egō eimi;* 'It is not I, is it?' *He that dippeth . . . in the dish* (23). All who ate together did this. The point of our Lord's words was that the traitor was at that moment at the table. *Thou hast said* (25); i.e. 'Yes, what you have said is right'.

Jesus took bread (26). The head of the Jewish household was accustomed to do this during the Passover feast. Jesus gave a completely new significance to the action. *This is my body* (26). If the words of the Lord had intended to convey a transformation of the bread into His body they would have read 'This has become my body'. During the Passover feast the Jewish householder took bread in his hand and said, 'This is the bread of affliction which our fathers ate in the land of Egypt', meaning, of course, that the one represented the other. By His words the Lord changed the whole significance and emphasis of the feast from looking back to the typical redemption from Egypt to faith in the redemption from sin accomplished by His death.

For a clear parallel example of the use of 'is' (Gk. *estin*) to mean 'represents' see Gal. iv. 25. So also in verse 28. *The cup* (27). Three cups were passed round by the Jewish householder during the Passover meal, the third, which is probably that referred to here, being known as 'the cup of blessing'. *My blood of the new testament* (28); taken from the LXX of Ex. xxiv. 8 with allusions to Je. xxxi. 31 and Zc. ix. 11. The covenant in Ex. xxiv. 8 was sealed with blood. Some texts omit here the word *new*, though we undoubtedly have here the fulfilment of the prediction of Je. xxxi. 31. The word *testament* (Gk. *diathēkēs*) did not mean a covenant, which is an agreement between equals, but a settlement by a great or rich man for the benefit of another. As the most common form of settlement was, and still is, by testament or will, the word came to have this meaning almost exclusively. *Shed for many for the remission of sins* (28). Here is a clear statement that the death of Jesus was necessary to enable God to forgive sins. It in fact made it right, or morally justifiable, for Him to do so. *That day* (29); i.e. when He comes again in glory.

The quotation in verse 31 is taken from the LXX of Zc. xiii. 7, except that the first word *pataxon*, 'smite', is changed to *pataxō*, 'I will smite'. *Go before you* (32); lit. lead you forth, going at your head, as an Eastern shepherd leads his sheep. This does not mean that the Lord would go first to Galilee in the sense that the disciples must go there to find Him, but that He would appear to them at Jerusalem and lead them to Galilee. *Though I should* (35); better, 'Even if I must', as in RV.

d. The agony in Gethsemane and the arrest (xxvi. 36–56)

See notes on Mk. xiv. 32–52; Lk. xxii. 39–53; Jn. xviii. 1–12. *A place called Gethsemane* (36). It was a piece of private property across the brook Kidron and probably at the foot of the Mount of Olives. *My soul is exceeding sorrowful* (38). The words are from the LXX of Ps. xliii. 5. *Watch* (38); i.e. keep awake for the purpose of being ready to meet whatever might come. *This cup* (39); i.e. His suffering and death. Cf. xx. 22. Verse 41 seems to be a reflection of the experience through which the Lord Himself was passing at the moment. The word *temptation* is used more widely in the New Testament than we use it in modern English, and includes every kind of test of faith and obedience. The Lord was here being tempted to draw back from the fullness of God's will because of the tremendous cost involved in carrying it out. It was His human nature, 'the flesh' (which in His case was sinless), that shrank from the cross. His spirit was willing (i.e. eager). The same conflict occurs in some form in every disciple. *Sleep on now, and take your rest* (45). It is difficult to decide whether these words are to be taken as a literal piece of advice to take the opportunity for the sleep they needed, in which case a considerable interval must be understood to have elapsed between

these words and those that follow, or whether they are to be regarded as ironical, as many commentators suppose. In either case they strike a note of finality and indicate that the conflict in Gethsemane was successfully over. *Let us be going* (46); not to escape, but to meet the officers.

Friend (50); Gk. *Hetaire*, used also in xx. 13, xxii. 12. The emphasis of the word is on the fact that Judas was a fellow-member of the band of disciples. *Wherefore art thou come?* (50). The AV is almost certainly wrong in making these words a question. RV is better: 'Do that for which thou art come.' Perhaps they are an exclamation, *ho* being equivalent to *hoion*, 'What an errand on which to come!' *One of them* (51). It was Peter (Jn. xviii. 10). *Drew his sword* (51). The sword had been brought from the upper room where the last supper had been held (Lk. xxii. 38). *All they that take the sword shall perish with the sword* (52). This is a general principle. The Lord did not mean that every individual who resorts to force will literally perish by force, but that force would always react on the heads of those who use it. Some see in this verse, which forbids the use of force even in the only cause known to be certainly and absolutely righteous, a principle stated which forbids having resort to arms under any circumstances. *Legions* (53); the largest units of the Roman army, containing about six thousand men. Our Lord tells Peter that his use of force is not only wrong but unnecessary. Verse 54 indicates that the Lord was conscious that, in submitting to suffering and death, He was fulfilling Old Testament prophecy.

e. The trial before Caiaphas and Peter's denial (xxvi. 57–75)

See notes on Mk. xiv. 53–72; Lk. xxii. 54–65; Jn. xviii. 13–27. *Palace* (58); RV 'court', the open space round which the main buildings were built. *Servants* (58); 'officers', as in RV. Follow RV also in verses 59 and 60. The evidence which was eventually brought forward (61) was based upon the Lord's words recorded in Jn. ii. 19, 21. *I adjure thee by the living God* (63). This statement put a man on his oath and compelled an answer. The High Priest was seeking an admission which could be the foundation of a charge of blasphemy. *Thou hast said* (64); this means 'yes'. *Hereafter* (64). 'Henceforth', as in RV. The session at God's right hand began at the ascension (even, perhaps, at the resurrection). Note the allusion in our Lord's reply to Ps. cx. 1 and Dn. vii. 13. The second part of the phrase may refer as much to the ascension as to the second coming. The Jewish religious leaders would be witnesses of the victories of Christ after His resurrection as well as being present at His second coming. *Buffeted* (67); i.e. punched. Verse 68 is a sarcastic demand to be told the name and identity of those who were strangers to Him as a sign of supernatural knowledge.

Peter sat without (69). From the other evangelists we know that he was warming himself by a fire in the courtyard. *I know not what thou sayest* (70); i.e. I have no idea what you mean. *Thy speech bewrayeth thee* (73). Galileans spoke a 'north-country' dialect.

f. The trial before Pilate (xxvii. 1–26)

See notes on Mk. xv. 1–15; Lk. xxiii. 1–25; Jn. xviii. 28—xix. 16. *Pontius Pilate the governor* (2). Pontius Pilate was the Roman procurator of Judaea from A.D. 26 to 37, holding his office under the Prefect of Syria. His usual place of residence was Caesarea, but he was in Jerusalem during the festival in order to deal with any insurrection or trouble. *The innocent blood* (4); omit 'the' as in RV. *Hanged himself* (5). It may be supposed that the 'falling headlong' mentioned by Luke in Acts i. 18 happened while he was attempting to do this. *Bought* (7); in such cases the purchase was made in the name of the man to whom the money had been paid and to whom the money by a legal fiction was supposed all the time to belong. By law, therefore, the man himself purchased the field (see Acts i. 18).

Much difficulty has been felt at the mention of Jeremiah in this passage (9) on the ground that the quotation comes from Zechariah. Various ingenious theories have also been put forward to account for it. There is an allusion, it is true, to Zc. xi. 12, 13, but the words do not agree closely either with the Hebrew or the LXX. The most important addition is the word 'field', upon which the fulfilment just described by the evangelist largely hangs. This word and the conception behind it come from Je. xxxii. 6–9, a passage in which occurs the purchase of a field for so many pieces of silver. The comparison between prophecy and fulfilment, therefore, which the evangelist is attempting to make, depends upon both Old Testament passages. It is natural, therefore, that he should mention Jeremiah, who was the greater of the two and the earlier of the two, from whom also was derived the word that gave the real point to the quotation. *Barabbas* (16); the name means in Aramaic 'father's son'. There seems a designed contrast with Jesus the Father's Son. Pilate's question, *Why, what evil hath he done?* (23), comes at the end of the trial and is an incidental acknowledgment of the innocence of Christ. No wonder that Pilate tried to shift the guilt of putting Him to death from his own shoulders to those of the Jews. The dramatic answer of verse 25 marked the final tragedy in the history of the Jews. The curse which they called down upon themselves has been upon them ever since. With this assurance from them Pilate allowed his weakness and fear of a disturbance to override his sense of justice.

g. Our Lord's crucifixion and death (xxvii. 27–56)

See notes on Mk. xv. 16–41; Lk. xxiii. 26–49; Jn. xix. 2, 3, 17–37. *The common hall* (27); Gk. *to praitōrion*. This is the Latin term Praetorium. It is the technical name for the governor's quarters. *Band* (27); i.e. unit; perhaps a cohort, which consisted of about 360 men, or a maniple, which was a fraction of the cohort. *Scarlet robe* (28); Gk. *chlamyda kokkinēn*. This robe, the chlamys, was a cloak worn by military officers fastened by a buckle on the right shoulder. It was also a mark of royalty. *·A man of Cyrene, Simon by name* (32). Cyrene was a district in North Africa where many Jews lived. They had a synagogue in Jerusalem (Acts vi. 9), so that numbers of them must have been constantly there. Simon's two sons, Alexander and Rufus, afterwards became well-known Christians (see Mk. xv. 21). *Compelled* (32); Gk. *ēngareusan*. For the meaning see v. 41n. *To bear his cross* (32). The cross was carried by the prisoner, a custom which was at first followed in the case of the Lord (Jn. xix. 17), but He evidently found the weight too great for Him. The transverse bar was at this stage usually attached by a piece of rope, and was fastened in its place on arrival at the scene of execution. *A place of a skull* (33); the reason for the name is not known. The site was either that of the present church of the Holy Sepulchre, which at that time, though now not now, was outside the wall, or the hill on the north of Jerusalem usually known as 'Gordon's Calvary'. The former alternative seems in the most recent view to be the more probable.

They gave him vinegar to drink mingled with gall (34); an allusion to Ps. lxix. 21. The act appears to have been usual in the case of all who were condemned, the drink being intended as an anodyne. *Vinegar* (34); Gk. *oxos*. The better MSS read *oinon*, 'wine' (see RV). *He would not drink* (34); the Lord refused any mitigation of His sufferings. *Parted his garments, casting lots* (35). The words come from the LXX of Ps. xxii. 18. A prisoner's clothes were divided among the squad of soldiers as perquisites. Note that the latter part of the verse is omitted by the RV following the more reliable texts.

Wagging their heads (39); an allusion to Ps. xxii. 7 and Ps. cix. 25 (LXX). *Thou that destroyest . . . in three days* (40); see xxvi. 61n. *The chief priests* (41). If the site of the crucifixion was that of the modern church of the Holy Sepulchre, the priests were probably able to call across the slope from the temple precincts. *He saved others; himself he cannot save* (42). This was profoundly true in a sense opposite to that in which the priests intended it. *If he be* (42); a better reading is that of the RV, 'He is', said in mockery. *He trusted in . . . will have him* (43). The words seem to be taken from Ps. xxii. 8, but not altogether from the LXX, nor from the Hebrew, possibly a mixture of both. The priests may have had in mind the (apocryphal) book of Wisdom ii. 13, 18–20.

The sixth hour (45); i.e. twelve noon. *Darkness* (45). An eclipse of the sun at full moon was of course out of the question. It is impossible to tell whether the phenomenon was meteorological or directly supernatural.

Eli, Eli, lama sabachthani? (46); Aramaic, and probably the actual words that came from the Lord's lips. The form Eli is, however, reminiscent of Hebrew. *My God, my God, why hast thou forsaken me?* (46); substantially from the LXX of Ps. xxii. 1, but with the Greek vocative form *Thee* for the LXX *ho Theos.* In this cry we plumb the depths of the atonement. Christ was accursed by God as the sin-bearer (see Gal. iii. 13). *Elias* (47); i.e. the prophet Elijah. Verse 48 is another allusion to Ps. lxix. 21. It is possible that this action was intended in mockery.

The veil of the temple was rent . . . to the bottom (51). This was clearly symbolical of the end of the separation between God and man. The strange incident recorded in verses 52, 53 is told only in this Gospel. It is possible that the evangelist himself came face to face with one of these risen saints. The strangeness of the story is heightened by its omissions. We are not told what happened to the saints between the Lord's death and His resurrection, nor what happened to them afterwards. Presumably their graves remained empty and they were translated to heaven. It is possible, though not accepted by a majority, that the words 'his resurrection' mean 'his raising of them'. This would mean that the appearances of the saints in Jerusalem took place on the afternoon of the crucifixion, but it does not explain what happened to them subsequently.

Mary the mother of James and Joses (56). She is traditionally represented as sister to Mary the mother of Jesus.

h. Our Lord's burial (xxvii. 57–66)

See notes on Mk. xv. 42–47; Lk. xxiii. 50–56; Jn. xix. 38–42. *Arimathaea* (57); probably in the hill country of Ephraim in central Palestine. *Linen cloth* (59); i.e. a shroud. *In his own new tomb* (60). Rich people frequently had their tombs constructed during their lifetime. The entrances to tombs were ordinarily secured in the way described by rolling across the entrance a stone which moved in a groove.

Note that verses 62–66 are peculiar to Matthew. *The next day* (62); i.e. Saturday, the Jewish sabbath. *The preparation* (62); Friday. The words *by night* (64) are omitted by the more reliable texts, as in RV. *Ye have a watch* (65); perhaps 'Take a guard', as in RV mg. *And setting a watch* (66); the original language of this verse is a little obscure. These words perhaps mean 'in the presence of the guard'.

i. Resurrection (xxviii. 1–20)

See notes on Mk. xvi. 1–20; Lk. xxiv. 1–12; Jn. xx. 1–31. *In the end . . . of the week* (1). This note of time may be interpreted in two ways. It may mean late on Saturday evening as the sabbath was giving place at sunset to the first day of the week, which began at that hour by Jewish reckoning. For this use of Gk. *epiphōskein* see Lk. xxiii. 54. If this is what the evangelist means, the visit of the women took place on Saturday evening, the earthquake and descent of the angel took place during the night and the women are understood (not stated) to have returned in the early morning of Sunday (verse 5). Secondly it may mean 'after the sabbath' and refer to the actual dawn of Sunday morning. In that case the earthquake took place as the women were approaching in the twilight of dawn, and the women on arrival saw the guards lying prostrate and the angel seated on the stone. It should be clearly understood that the purpose of removing the stone was not to let the Lord out, an unnecessary proceeding, but to let the women in. The second alternative of the two mentioned above is much the more probable.

Answered (5); i.e. answered their looks of amazement and bewilderment. The word *ye* is emphatic. *The Lord* (6); the better texts omit these words and read 'he lay'. *He goeth before . . . ye see him* (7). These words appear to mean that the Lord would go at the head of His disciples like a shepherd. They need not exclude appearances in Jerusalem. See xxvi. 32n. *As they went to tell his disciples* (9). The better texts omit these words, as in RV. *All hail* (9); Gk. *Chairete,* the ordinary word for greeting; cf. our 'Hello' or 'Good morning'.

Large (12); Gk. *hikana,* a considerable sum. *Secure you* (14); Gk. *humas amerimnous poiēsomen,* 'rid you of anxiety'.

Power (18); Gk. *exousia,* authority. *Teach* (19); Gk. *mathēteusate,* 'make disciples of' or 'gather disciples from'. *In the name* (19); better 'into the name'. *Teaching them to observe* (20). This is more than head knowledge. *Unto the end of the world* (20); or 'of the age', that is, till He comes again. How slow and reluctant we have all been to carry out this commission. The existence of millions in the world today who have never heard the Saviour's name is a disgrace to us all.

BASIL F. C. ATKINSON.

THE GOSPEL ACCORDING TO MARK

INTRODUCTION

See also the General Article, 'The Fourfold Gospel', pp. 58–63.

I. AUTHORSHIP

The Gospel does not refer to its author. Yet the authorship of Mark, the attendant of Peter, has never been seriously questioned. There is little doubt, also, that this Mark is the 'John whose surname was Mark', who is mentioned eight times in the New Testament. He was a relative of Barnabas (Col. iv. 10), and the statement in 1 Pet. v. 13 may mean that he was converted through Peter.

Evidence for the Markan authorship is abundant in the writings of the Church Fathers of the first four centuries. Papias, Justin Martyr, Irenaeus, Clement of Alexandria, Tertullian, Origen, Eusebius and Jerome all refer to it.

II. DATE AND PLACE OF WRITING

In fixing the date of the second Gospel, opinion differs widely within the limits of the thirty-five years from A.D. 40 to 75. But it is now almost universally agreed that Mark is the earliest of the Gospels. On the one hand, the statement of Irenaeus that Mark composed his Gospel 'after the departure (*exodos*) of Peter and Paul' would indicate a date not earlier than A.D. 68 and not later than A.D. 70 when Jerusalem was destroyed, assuming that 'departure' here means death, which it possibly may not. Dr. Vincent Taylor favours A.D. 65–67, and thinks 'attempts to date the Gospel earlier are precarious'. On the other hand, the relation of Mark to the other synoptics, particularly Luke which antedates Acts (Acts i. 1), tends to throw the date back into the fifties. A date somewhere between A.D. 50 and 55 would represent a position midway between extremes.

Most scholars, following ancient testimony, favour Rome as the place of writing. Dr. Graham Scroggie thinks that 1 Pet. v. 13 tends to confirm this, if indeed 'Babylon' stands for Rome. Other suggestions have included Alexandria, Caesarea and Syrian Antioch.

The Gospel was probably written for Gentile readers in general, but particularly for Romans. Old Testament quotations and allusions are relatively few; Aramaic expressions are interpreted (e.g. v. 41); Jewish customs are explained (e.g. vii. 3, 11); there are some Latin words. The general tone, depicting the Lord's ceaseless activity and His power over demons, disease and death, is such as would appeal to Roman readers, whose interest was in deeds rather than words.

III. MARK AND PETER

A tradition which dates from Papias (A.D. 70–130) says that behind the record of Mark's Gospel there is in fact the preaching and authority of the apostle Peter. The statement of Papias (preserved by Eusebius) is that 'Mark, having become the interpreter of Peter, wrote down accurately all that he remembered of the things said and done by the Lord, but not however in order'. This tradition is confirmed by other patristic writers and 'is so sound', says Dr. Vincent Taylor, 'that if we did not possess it, we should be compelled to postulate something very much like it.' This does not mean that Mark was little more than a scribe or amanuensis, or that he did not make use of material from other sources, including his own reminiscences; for it is evident that the author, though not an apostle, was nevertheless very close to the events he narrates, and there are all the marks of originality in his record. His order or arrangement of the material is evidently criticized in the Papias tradition; and it appears from the Gospel itself that this is homiletical rather than chronological.

The internal evidence for the influence of Peter is equally clear:

The Gospel begins at the point where Peter became a disciple, and gives no account of the nativity.

The Galilean ministry is prominent, centring particularly on the district around Capernaum, Peter's home.

The vividness of the narrative suggests the first-hand acquaintance of an eyewitness.

Details such as the benediction at Caesarea Philippi and the walking on the water, which tend to present Peter in a favourable light, are omitted; while others less favourable, such as the denial, are related with exceptional fulness.

IV. SOURCES

In view of the established priority of Mark, inquiries into the sources which lie behind this Gospel have not been nearly so successful as in the case of Matthew and Luke. In regard to the oral tradition, much work has been done during the last thirty-five years in the field of Form-Criticism, of which Martin Dibelius is one of the originators. Form-Criticism postulates the existence, prior to any written Gospel which we now possess, of comparatively small tradition cycles (mostly oral, though some may have been written and be such as Luke's preface mentions). The nomenclature for these cycles differs with various critics. B. S. Easton divides the material into Sayings-groups, Parables, Dialogues, Miracle Narratives and Passion Narratives. Vincent Taylor distinguishes Pronouncement Stories, Miracle Stories and Stories about Jesus. The very diversity of these analyses points to the danger that lies within them, namely, that the isolation of these groups must be purely subjective since there is no external check such as Textual Criticism supplies. If we are to explore behind the documents, any plausible hypothesis may be put forward. On the other hand, there is value in the claim of the Form-Critics that the Gospel was 'preaching' before it was a written record. Much of the material tended in the course of time to assume well defined forms for mnemonic and catechetical purposes, and there may be traces of this in Mark's topical grouping.

This oral tradition is largely Semitic in its colouring and atmosphere. The presence of a quite considerable Aramaic element in Mark's Greek indicates this, though it is probably insufficient to justify the conclusion, strongly maintained by C. C. Torrey and others, that the Gospel is a translation from an Aramaic original. What is of importance is that this fact undoubtedly enhances the historical value of the record, inasmuch as Mark, though Gentile in his sympathies, nevertheless stood very near to the original Jewish Christian tradition.

In regard to documentary sources, the main question is whether Mark knew of and used the elusive document known as Q. In the opinion of Canon Streeter, it almost certainly antedated Mark, and some consider there are traces of it in Mark. Beyond this vague possibility, however, nothing more can be said. Attempts have been made to show the existence of an earlier edition or draft behind our Gospel, known as 'Ur-Markus', or Original Mark, but these may be dismissed as at best hypothetical and highly subjective.

Summarizing, we may say that the principal source of this Gospel is the preaching and teaching of Peter, whose sermon at Caesarea (Acts x. 34—43) is practically a résumé of it. This was supplemented by other oral tradition'of a general kind and by Mark's own reminiscences, together with perhaps some documentary material.

V. THEOLOGY

a. The Person of Christ

It has frequently been said that Mark's presentation of the Person of Christ is that of the Servant of Jehovah (Is. lii. 13—liii. 12), while, correspondingly, Matthew presents the King, Luke the Man, and John the Son of God. Several features suggest this, such as the absence of genealogy and the predominance of deeds over teaching. The title 'Son of man', which occurs fourteen times, is in most cases (e.g. viii. 31, ix. 9, 12, 31, x. 33, 45, xiv. 21, 41) to be interpreted in terms

of this conception. Nevertheless, as Mark asserts in his very first verse, the lowly Servant is also beyond all doubt the Son of God, whose ministry was authenticated by mighty works. The divine attestation of this at the baptism and the transfiguration (i. 11, ix. 7) is unequivocal. Dr. Vincent Taylor considers this the most fundamental element in Mark's christology, which he says 'is a high christology, as high as any in the New Testament, not excluding that of John'.

The Messiahship of Jesus is seen in Mark to be in the nature of a carefully guarded secret, at least until the confession of Peter (viii. 30). This was doubtless to avoid the peril of the popular national and materialistic conceptions with which the expectations of the Jews invested the title, and to secure for it an ethical as well as an apocalyptic content. The term 'Christ' occurs only seven times, and in no instance does Jesus use it of Himself.

b. The work of Christ

The two metaphors of x. 45 and xiv. 24 indicate the two main lines of teaching. Our Lord's life, laid down sacrificially, is 'a ransom for many' and 'the blood of the covenant'. The former effects deliverance from sin and judgment, while the latter provides covenant relationship and fellowship between God and men. This is not to say that in Mark these conceptions are worked out into anything like a developed doctrine. Still less is there any justification for thinking that the ransom saying is an indication of Pauline influence. 'If we find the same thought in Paul,' says Dr. James Denney, 'we shall not say that the evangelist has Paulinized, but that St. Paul has sat at the feet of Jesus.' All the synoptists mention the three occasions when Jesus made deliberate attempts to initiate the disciples into His approaching passion; but Mark especially notes the varying attitude of the disciples (viii. 31f., ix. 31f., x. 32).

c. Eschatology

The eschatology of the Gospel is contained chiefly in two passages, viii. 38—ix. 1 and xiii. 1–37, where Jesus seems to have had in view two widely separated events, the destruction of Jerusalem in A.D. 70 and His personal return in glory. Nevertheless it has also to be said that Mark's view of the kingdom of God is predominantly eschatological. The primary ideas in this conception are, first, of the kingly rule or sovereignty of God, and then of a realm or community which may be entered (ix. 47, x. 23). Sayings of the latter kind may carry a future meaning as well, but in others, such as xiv. 25 and xv. 43, the reference to a future consummation is unmistakable.

d. Affinities with Pauline teaching

Reference has been made above to the suggestion that Mark was subject to Pauline influence. This has been strongly debated on both sides for many years. An examination of the vocabulary and ideas of this Gospel undoubtedly betrays much that is common to Mark and Paul, but it could with equal truth be claimed that such common ground belongs in fact to early Christianity as a whole. And it still remains that many of the distinctively Pauline words and doctrinal concepts, such as righteousness, justification by faith, union with Christ, life in the Spirit and others are entirely absent from Mark. The most we are entitled to say is that Mark lived and wrote in a Roman and Pauline environment, and may have been acquainted with some of the earlier Epistles. But as Dr. Vincent Taylor says, 'he has neither recast nor obscured the historic tradition. His Jesus is the Jesus of Galilee.'

NOTE: *For a map of Palestine in the time of Christ see p. 775.*

OUTLINE OF CONTENTS

I. THE PREPARATION. i. 1–13

    a. John the Baptist (i. 1–8)
    b. The baptism of Jesus (i. 9–11)
    c. The temptation of Jesus (i. 12, 13)

II. THE GALILEAN MINISTRY. i. 14—ix. 50

    a. The call of the first disciples (i. 14–20)
    b. The first sabbath in Capernaum (i. 21–45)
    c. The beginnings of opposition (ii. 1—iii. 6)
    d. The Twelve appointed (iii. 7–19)
    e. Charges against Jesus (iii. 20–35)
    f. Parabolic teaching (iv. 1–34)
    g. Mighty works (iv. 35—v. 43)
    h. Rejection at Nazareth and the mission of the Twelve (vi. 1–13)
    i. Herod and John the Baptist (vi. 14–29)
    j. Miracles and teaching in Galilee and beyond (vi. 30—viii. 26)
    k. Messiahship and suffering (viii. 27—ix. 29)
    l. Rebukes and warnings (ix. 30–50)

III. THE JOURNEY TO JERUSALEM. x. 1–52

    a. On marriage and divorce (x. 2–12)
    b. On childhood (x. 13–16)
    c. On riches (x. 17–31)
    d. The third prediction of the passion (x. 32–34)
    e. The request of James and John (x. 35–45)
    f. Blind Bartimaeus restored to sight (x. 46–52)

IV. THE PASSION WEEK. xi. 1—xv. 47

    a. The entry into Jerusalem and opening events (xi. 1–26)
    b. Teaching in Jerusalem (xi. 27—xii. 44)
    c. The prophetic discourse (xiii. 1–37)
    d. The passion narrative (xiv. 1—xv. 47)

V. THE CONSUMMATION. xvi. 1–20

    a. The resurrection (xvi. 1–8)
    b. The epilogue (xvi. 9–20)

COMMENTARY

I. THE PREPARATION. i. 1–13

a. John the Baptist (i. 1–8)

See notes on Mt. iii. 1–12; Lk. iii. 1–20. Cf. also Jn. i. 6–34. The opening verse is probably intended by Mark as a title to the whole book. *The gospel* (1), however, is not the book itself but its contents, 'the good news about Jesus Christ'. It is possible to treat verses 2, 3 as a parenthesis, thus connecting verse 1 directly with verse 4: 'The beginning of the good news about Jesus Christ the Son of God . . . was John who baptized in the desert . . .' This is attractive, and brings out the suggestion that the good news of the Messiah's coming began in a religious revival, not, as was commonly expected, in a political upheaval. It tends to subordinate, however, the importance of the Old Testament quotation; and the RV arrangement, which places a full stop at the end of verse 1, leaving it as the title, is to be preferred.

In the prophets (2); MS authority favours 'in Isaiah the prophet' (RV). The former is an obvious correction to account for the fact that the first quotation is from Mal. iii. 1, and not from Isaiah. The important phrase is *in the wilderness* (3), which is taken up in verse 4. Mark may have named Isaiah as the author of this (Is. xl. 3), at the same time including the Malachi quotation for its obvious suitability. Both prophecies are introduced to show the nature of John the Baptist's mission, as a preparation for the Messiah's coming. Both speak in their original setting of a drawing near of Jehovah to His people, yet they are here significantly applied to Jesus Christ.

The quality and influence of John's preparatory ministry are further indicated. It was a preparation of the hearts of men, and notable for its moral power; a *baptism of repentance* with a view to *the remission of sins* (4). The Greek word for repentance (*metanoia*) originally denoted 'change of mind', but in the New Testament it assumes the deeper meaning of a deliberate coming to one's senses, resulting in a change of conduct. This aspect of John's ministry is more fully described in Lk. iii. 1–20 (see notes). The whole province of Judaea was affected; Jesus Himself came from Galilee (9), but that Judaea should be so deeply stirred was a measure of the power of John's mission. The confession of sins was probably oral, an open avowal, after which the one who had confessed was plunged (*baptizō*, the intensive form of *baptō*) in the waters of the river, as a representative action.

John's clothing and food (6) indicated frugality and separation from worldly interests. His dress was characteristic of the prophets, and particularly of Elijah (2 Ki. i. 8) whom John resembled in other respects also (Mk. ix. 13). Locusts, though tolerated as food only by the poorest, are said still to be eaten roasted or salted by the Bedouin. The testimony of John is centred in the *one mightier than I* (7) who was at hand, and whose baptism should be not with water but with the Holy Spirit (8). That this would characterize the days of the Messiah was also in accord with Old Testament teaching (Is. xliv. 3; Ezk. xxxvi. 26f.; Joel ii. 28f.).

b. The baptism of Jesus (i. 9–11)

See notes on Mt. iii. 13–17; Lk. iii. 21, 22. Jesus appeared at Jordan simply as one of the many who came to John's baptism. Matthew records the surprise and diffidence of John (iii. 14, 15), but upon our Lord's insistence John took the sacred body and immersed it in the waters. *Straightway* (10); the first instance of Mark's favourite adverb, occurring forty-one times. As Jesus emerged, a threefold experience set Him apart from all others and marked Him as having a unique relation to God. First, He saw *the*

heavens opened (10), i.e. being rent asunder (*schizomenous*, present participle), signifying open vision of heavenly things (cf. Jn. iii. 12, 13; Is. lxiv. 1). Secondly, He saw *the Spirit like a dove descending upon him* (10). That the dove was something visible, and more than a poetic simile of the gentleness of the phenomenon, is clear from Luke's addition, 'in a bodily shape' (Lk. iii. 22). An interesting suggestion connects this with Gn. i. 2, where the Spirit is seen hovering like a bird over the primeval waters. Thirdly, the voice of the Father was heard from heaven, bearing witness to His Son (11); so also in ix. 7 and Jn. xii. 28. The words are reminiscent of Ps. ii. 7 and Is. xlii. 1. There is thus a clear revelation of the Trinity here, but the final focus is on the Son; for, although God is a Trinity, man's first encounter with Him must always be in Christ.

It is noteworthy that Jesus made no confession of sin, and although He received John's baptism, the early Church remained unshaken in its faith in His absolute sinlessness. For Him, the baptism was firstly the fulfilment of all righteousness (see Mt. iii. 15n.); secondly, an act of identification, in which He was 'numbered with the transgressors' (Is. liii. 12); thirdly, an act of dedication to His ministry.

c. The temptation of Jesus (i. 12, 13)

See notes on Mt. iv. 1–11; Lk. iv. 1–13. Information about this must have come from Jesus Himself. Mark's account is exceptionally brief, which is the more remarkable in view of his evident interest in the victory of the Son of God over the powers of darkness. All the synoptists agree in emphasizing the close proximity of the baptism and the temptation. Edersheim (*Life and Times of Jesus the Messiah*, i, p. 281) suggests that, in the former, Jesus was active, in the latter passive, driven by the Spirit; in the former case He fulfilled righteousness, in the latter His righteousness was tried. Before ever He entered upon a ministry whose purpose was to challenge and ultimately to break the power of Satan in others, that enemy had to be met and defeated on the battle-ground of His own life. Cf. Heb. ii. 18, iv. 15. The loneliness of the struggle is reflected in the words *and was with the wild beasts* (13; a detail noted only by Mark), and its severity in the fact that *angels ministered unto him* (cf. Lk. xxii. 43). No merely psychological explanation is adequate. The encounter was real, Satan was real, and the angels were real. In a lesser degree, every disciple, called to some high task, must expect similar conflict and may enjoy similar victory. Mark considers it unnecessary to say who was the victor.

II. THE GALILEAN MINISTRY.
i. 14—ix. 50

a. The call of the first disciples (i. 14–20)

i. **The ministry of Jesus (i. 14, 15).** Cf. Mt. iv. 12–17; Lk. iv. 14–44. According to Mark this began *after that John was put in prison* (14), which implies that there was an interval between Jesus' baptism and His Galilean ministry. But what Jesus did in that period Mark does not say. The Gospel of John, in this as in other matters, supplements the synoptic record (see Jn. i. 19—iv. 42). Jesus began to proclaim the good news from God, that the time of waiting was at an end and the long-expected kingdom of God was at hand. In view of its advent, men everywhere were required to *repent* and *believe* (15). These are the two key words of the Gospel on its human side. The *kingdom of God* (15) is the rule of God in the hearts of men and in society.

ii. The call of Peter, Andrew, James and John (i. 16–20). See notes on Mt. iv. 18–22 and cf. Lk. v. 1–11. The choosing and training of the Twelve, who were to share with Him the proclamation of the good news and to continue it after His ascension, was a matter of vital importance in the ministry of Jesus. The two pairs of brothers here had all met Jesus before (see Jn. i. 15–42), and had believed that He was the Messiah. Now He calls them to the further step of leaving their fishing in order to follow Him wholly. Their calling as fishermen would have provided good training in the patient endurance necessary for the work of winning men for Christ. Nevertheless, more is needed, and if they will now follow Him, He declares *I will make you to become fishers of men*. Christ calls men, not so much for what they are, as for what He is able to make them become, if they are prepared to obey Him.

b. The first sabbath in Capernaum (i. 21–45)
This compact account of the day when Jesus first came forward in his town and ministered in his own home would be related with especial personal interest by Peter. It bears all the marks of personal reminiscence and of the evidence of an eyewitness. A parallel account is given in Lk. iv. 31–44.

i. The cure of a demoniac in the synagogue (i. 21–28). Much emphasis is placed upon the teaching ministry of Jesus in Mark; see ii. 13, iv. 1, vi. 2, 6, 34. *Synagogue* (21) is strictly a Greek word meaning 'a bringing together' or 'an assembly'; but it was often used, as here, for the building in which the congregation met. Of the origin of synagogues nothing is known. The service in them was largely instructional; but they were also courts of justice (Lk. xii. 11, xxi. 12), where punishment could be inflicted (Mt. x. 17). It was the custom for the President of the synagogue (*archisynagōgos*) to arrange who should read and expound the Scriptures each sabbath, and at this stage of His ministry this provided Jesus with manifold opportunities, for wherever He went He would be invited to teach. Paul was similarly invited later. The authoritative tone of Jesus' teaching contrasted sharply with the utterances of Jewish teachers who invariably appealed to tradition or to the sayings of famous rabbis.

While Jesus was thus speaking, either His very presence or His utterance, or both, provoked an outburst from a demon-possessed man Demon-possession is a phenomenon specially associated with the period of our Lord's presence on earth. It is referred to only twice in the Old Testament, and twice in the New Testament outside the Gospels; and it is clearly distinguished from mental disorders. The demons were real, and knew of the messianic office of Jesus long before the disciples were aware of it, although they were never allowed to proclaim the fact (see verse 34 and Jas. ii. 19). Jesus had but lately challenged the prince of evil (13); little wonder that the subordinate spirits of wickedness realized they had now met their conqueror (24). The authority of the Saviour's word is now seen not only in the quality of His doctrine but in His power to command; for at His word the unclean spirit, having convulsed the man, though, as Luke the physician tells us (Lk. iv. 35), without harming him, came out of him. Jesus never touched a demoniac in order to deliver him; the spoken word sufficed. The people watched in awe, and then broke out into a buzz of conversation (27, RV). Quickly the fame of Jesus spread throughout the region.

ii. Peter's mother-in-law healed (i. 29–31). See Mt. viii. 14, 15; Lk. iv. 38, 39. *The house of Simon and Andrew* (29) became almost a headquarters for Jesus from this point, when He was in Galilee (see ii. 1, iii. 19, ix. 33, x. 10). In Jn. i. 44 we are told that these two brothers belonged to Bethsaida. They may have moved in the meantime. On the other hand, there are some who think that this Bethsaida was the fishing quarter of Capernaum. 1 Cor. ix. 5 confirms that Peter was married, and that later, possibly, his wife accompanied him in ministry. To him, this occasion in his own home was unforgettable. The rapidity and completeness of the cure is indicated by the fact that, without any of the exhaustion and debility generally consequent upon such a fever, the restored woman *ministered unto them* (31) at the sabbath meal after the synagogue service.

iii. Healing after sunset (i. 32–34). See Mt. viii. 16, 17; Lk. iv. 40, 41. The sabbath ended at sunset; it then became possible to move the sick without infringement of the law. The physically sick are classified separately from the demon-possessed (32, 34). People began flocking towards the door of the house, and soon a dense crowd was formed (33). Jesus did not fail them, for the divine compassion and power are always put forth in response to the appeal and acknowledgment of human need.

iv. Departure to solitude and a tour in Galilee (i. 35–39). Cf. Lk. iv. 42, 43. It was an unexpected development that from the midst of such scenes Jesus should arise *a great while before day* (35; lit. 'very much at night') and slip out of the town before others were awake. The story is related from the point of view of those within the house who discovered He was gone, and who at once felt He was discarding valuable opportunities in Capernaum without realizing how widely He was sought after. Simon Peter at once began to lead and with his friends *followed after him* (36; lit. 'hunted Him down'—a strong word occurring only here in the New Testament but frequently in LXX, e.g. Ps. xxiii. 6). The determining motives of Jesus' withdrawal were the desire for communion with His Father (35) and the need to preach elsewhere (38). He could not be monopolized in Capernaum. *Therefore came I forth* (37) refers not to His departure from the town but to His mission from the Father (Lk. iv. 43).

v. **The cleansing of a leper (i. 40–45).** See notes on Mt. viii. 1–4 and Lk. v. 12–14. The miracles of healing apparently aroused particular excitement, and there was the danger, so common in our own day, that this type of ministry would eclipse the more fundamentally spiritual work of the gospel. So we find no mention of healing in verse 39. This case of a leper, however, evoked the Lord's compassion and was of a type that cannot be explained on any basis of 'suggestion' or 'faith-healing' so called. The leprosy of the Bible varied considerably in malignity, some skin diseases being classed as such. With the leper's *If thou wilt* (40) should be compared the father's 'if thou canst' in ix. 22. Leprosy is never said to be healed in Scripture, always cleansed. *Jesus, moved with compassion, put forth his hand* (41). 'It was owing to His compassion for mankind that He had a hand with which to lay hold' (Plummer). Having first experienced the power of Christ, the man is then able to fulfil the requirements of the law (Lv. xiv. 2–20). This is the order of Christian experience (Rom. viii. 1–4). His ability to do so is *a testimony unto them* (44), that is, either to the priests or the people in general. For the reason just stated, the leper was strictly bound to silence (44). His disobedience necessitated a temporary change in the Lord's sphere of ministry from town to country (45).

c. **The beginnings of opposition (ii. 1—iii. 6)**

i. **The paralytic and forgiveness (ii. 1–12).** See notes on Mt. ix. 2–8 and cf. Lk. v. 18–26. This incident is the first of a series in this section, showing the gradually mounting hostility to Jesus which was now appearing among the scribes and Pharisees. The rumour went round Capernaum that Jesus had returned and was at home again. *The house* (1) was almost certainly Peter's, the one previously mentioned (i. 29). Like many Palestinian houses, it would have an outside staircase leading to a flat roof. While Jesus was within, speaking *the word* (2; almost a technical term for 'the good news'; cf. iv. 14, 33; Acts viii. 4, xi. 19, etc.) to the crowd who had gathered again, four men arrived carrying their paralysed friend, and with commendable earnestness and resolution to overcome all obstacles mounted the roof and began to break through it. Luke mentions 'the tiling' (Lk. v. 19). Then they

lowered the man on his mattress to the feet of Jesus. The plight of some needy souls is such that the sympathetic faith of believing friends is required to bring them to Christ (cf. v. 36, ix. 24). Their common task of mercy would also have created an interesting bond between the four friends themselves.

When Jesus saw their faith (5), that is, the faith of all five, He immediately responded, but in an unexpected way. He by no means taught that every case of affliction results from sin (cf. Jn. ix. 2; Lk. xiii. 1–5), but as the Great Physician He diagnosed this case unerringly. The man's physical condition had a fundamentally spiritual cause. The conclusions of much modern psychotherapy are thus anticipated. Jesus' pronouncement of forgiveness (5) should be read as in RV, 'Thy sins are forgiven'. It was not a pious wish, as AV might suggest, or even a declaration, but an authoritative action. Jesus Himself forgave the man. This authority is the crucial question in the story. The scribes were right when they asked *who can forgive sins but God only?* (7); but their question was a challenge to the deity of Christ. He answered this first by replying to their thoughts without anything being said (8); He who knows the hearts of men can pardon their sins. Secondly, He provided a test. The claim to forgive sins could not be substantiated by any result; but the power to heal could be demonstrated at once. If therefore He can cause the man to walk, let them *know that the Son of man hath power on earth to forgive sins* (10). Son of man is a title used exclusively by our Lord of Himself, and originating probably in Dn. vii. 13. Opinions differ widely as to its precise meaning, though most expositors believe it had messianic significance. At least it seems to convey the idea of the essential and representative humanity of Christ. But that the Son of man has power *on earth* to forgive indicates that He had not, by incarnation, been emptied of divine prerogatives. The forgiven man was then enabled to arise and walk, for divine forgiveness is always accompanied by power to discontinue sinning, that is, to 'walk in newness of life' (Rom. vi. 4).

ii. **The call of Levi (ii. 13–17).** See notes on Mt. ix. 9–13; Lk. v. 27–32. The identification of Levi with Matthew the publican (Mt. ix. 9) and author of the first Gospel is practically beyond doubt, though none of the four lists of apostles gives the name Levi. That Jesus *went forth again by the sea side* (13) suggests a recurrence of the circumstances of i. 16 in which yet another is called to join the apostolic company. Levi was an official in the service of the tetrarch of Galilee, Herod Antipas. *The receipt of custom* (14) is, literally, his toll booth, where doubtless others of his profession (cf. verse 15) were with him at the time. His renunciation of a lucrative calling was greater than that of the fishermen, since it was final, whereas they could on occasion return to their fishing. His call illustrates the grace of the Lord in choosing a despised tax-collector to be an apostle, but also the wisdom of the Lord, for Levi probably knew both Aramaic and Greek, and 'the only thing he took with him out of his old occupation was his pen and ink' (Alexander Whyte).

Levi's first missionary act was to entertain Jesus in his house and invite his colleagues and acquaintances to meet Him. Lk. v. 29 confirms that the house was in fact Levi's, and there is the suggestion that it was spacious by comparison with the humbler home of Peter. But the meal table is regarded in the East as the place of most intimate fellowship. The next ground of offence therefore to the Pharisees is the close association of Jesus with moral and social reprobates in this way. This time they voice their objection to the disciples (16). Jesus' answer reveals the irreconcilable difference between Himself and them, and precipitates the conflict which is eventually to end in His death. The message of Christ is essentially redemptive, a message to the masses of the unwashed, ignorant and erring. He is the physician to the sin-sick soul, and He looks for the response of confidence and committal (Rom. iii. 21–24).

iii. The question of fasting (ii. 18–22). See notes on Mt. ix. 14–17; Lk. v. 33–39. Only one fast day, the great day of atonement, was prescribed by the law (Lv. xxiii. 27–29; Acts xxvii. 9). Others, however, had been added to such an extent that fasting had become a feature of religious life in our Lord's day (cf. Lk. xviii. 12). *Used to fast* (18); rather, were actually observing a particular fast, and that perhaps even while Jesus was feasting (15). In reply to this third objection, Jesus points out the incongruity of such behaviour. His companionship with the disciples constitutes a situation as joyous as a wedding feast. *Children of the bridechamber* (19) is a Hebraism which may mean either groomsmen or wedding guests. To impose upon this new situation of the gospel the religious observances of the old Judaism is as incongruous as applying a patch of undressed cloth to an old garment, or pouring unfermented wine into hard, inelastic wineskins, and as disastrous in its results. This was precisely the mistake of the later Judaistic teachers, against whom Paul's polemic is directed in the Epistle to the Galatians (e.g. Gal. iv. 9–10). But days will come when Jesus will be violently *taken away from them* (20; Gk. *aparthē;* this word is found only here and in the parallel passages), a first hint of the cross. On the subject of fasting, it may be said that Jesus sanctions it without enjoining it (Mt. vi. 16–18). The essence of it is self-discipline; not the formalism of the ascetic or monastic, but the voluntary subordination of the physical to the spiritual (cf. 1 Cor. ix. 24–27).

iv. Jesus' attitude to the sabbath (ii. 23—iii. 6). See notes on Mt. xii. 1–14; Lk. vi. 1–11. Two incidents illustrate the fourth objection, one which is frequently levelled against Jesus in the Gospels (cf. Lk. xiii. 10–17, xiv. 1–6; Jn. v. 1–19, ix. 1–41), namely, His attitude to the sabbath.

The disciples, walking through the cornfields, were doing what was quite allowable on any other day (Dt. xxiii. 25); but the Pharisees classed it as reaping, which was forbidden on the sabbath (Ex. xxxiv. 21). In answer, Jesus quoted as a precedent no less a person than David, whose greatness was acknowledged. The fourth commandment (like all the rest) was given, not for the sake of imposing religious restrictions, but to meet man's physical and spiritual need. *In the days of Abiathar* (26) is thought by most commentators to be incorrect and a possible later addition, since the High Priest in question was actually Abimelech, father of Abiathar (1 Sa. xxi. 1ff.). But textual evidence is not decisive against the reading 'Abiathar'. The Old Testament context suggests that Abiathar was one of a considerable number who exercised priestly functions at Nob during Abimelech's high-priesthood, and most of whom were slain by command of Saul very shortly after the occasion here referred to. *And he said unto them* (27) rather indicates the conclusion of the cornfield incident and that Mark has here appended the saying of Jesus as generally relevant. The sabbath has been given for man's benefit. Therefore the Representative Man may decide how it can best be used. Under His influence it has been changed to another day of the week and made available to all nations. We disregard it to our loss and peril.

The second incident introduces a positive note. The sabbath should be devoted not merely to rest and passive inactivity, but to works of love and mercy (cf. Jn. v. 16, 17). *To save life, or to kill* (iii. 4) has a double significance. The rabbis themselves admitted that relief might be given to a sufferer when life was in danger, and being in danger was interpreted liberally. On the other hand, they were using the sabbath with murderous intentions, plotting to kill Jesus. Which was more appropriate to the day, His healing or their plotting? Nowhere else is *anger* (5) attributed to Jesus; Mark is fond of recording His human emotions, and this is doubtless the testimony of an eyewitness who observed His look. It was not, however, personal rancour, but anger accompanied by grief *for the hardness* (or 'blindness') *of their hearts* (5). The healing of this man provoked the final cleavage between Jesus and the religious authorities; it was the parting of the ways. So bitter was the opposition aroused that the Pharisees, ardent nationalists, were ready to join forces with their deadliest opponents, the Herodians, who were quislings of a kind, in a common effort to destroy Jesus (6).

d. The Twelve appointed (iii. 7–19)

See notes on Mt. x. 1–4; Lk. vi. 13–16. Because of the imminent danger, Jesus with His disciples withdrew to the Sea of Galilee. He never exposed Himself to danger unnecessarily, and in view of His ministry such precaution was right and proper. A graphic and lifelike description follows (7b–12) of the crowds who were attracted by His works of healing. Two multitudes seem to be indicated, one from Galilee and the other from remoter places. Almost the whole of Palestine is represented in the latter group, with the exception of Samaria; which shows how widespread the fame and influence of Jesus had by this time become. Indeed the crowds almost fell upon Him (10) in their eagerness to touch Him, especially *as many as had plagues* (Gk. *mastigas*, lit. 'scourges'). The word, which occurs also in v. 29, 34; Lk. vii. 21; Heb. xi. 36, suggests distressing bodily diseases inflicted as a divine chastisement. It is a wholesome thing when such affliction drives people to Christ. The purpose of the boat (9) was probably the purely practical one of enabling Him to cope with the situation. He did not apparently use it on this occasion as a pulpit; but cf. iv. 1. Reference is again made to works of exorcism, and for the third time we learn that the demons who recognized Jesus were forbidden to make Him known (11, 12; cf. i. 24, 25, 34). Great happenings draw great multitudes, and where human need is truly met there is no lack of seeking souls. Moreover, Jesus was never unequal to the increasing demands made upon Him.

From the lake Jesus went into the surrounding hill country, where Luke tells us (Lk. vi. 12) He spent the whole night praying in preparation for the momentous task of choosing the Twelve. This was the first step in organizing the Church, and from this point the teaching and training of these men became a matter of paramount importance to our Lord. The 'Twelve' quickly became an official designation, used sometimes even when not all were present (1 Cor. xv. 5). They were chosen in absolute sovereignty; Jesus called *whom he would* (13), i.e. according to His pleasure, not theirs. But in free will they responded and *came unto him* (13). Their appointment involved communion and companionship, *that they should be with him;* commission, *that he might send them forth to preach* (14); and delegated authority, *to have power to heal* (15). Some important manuscripts insert the words 'whom He named apostles' in verse 14; but there may be an interpolation from Lk. vi. 13. See Mt. x. 2n.

The list is given four times in the New Testament (cf. Mt. x. 2–4; Lk. vi. 14–16; Acts i. 13) with slight variations in the order. But three groups of four are distinguishable, headed in each list by Peter, Philip and James the son of Alphaeus. Judas Iscariot is always last. Five of the twelve (Peter, Andrew, James, John, Matthew) have appeared in the narrative before (i. 16, 19, ii. 14). The origin of the name *Boanerges* (17) is obscure, most explanations being in the nature of attempts to account for Mark's phrase, *The sons of thunder*, which at least has the merit of appropriateness in the light of Lk. ix. 54. Philip's first contact with Jesus is recorded in Jn. i. 43. 'Bartholomew' is a patronymic (i.e. son of Talmai, a name which occurs in 2 Sa. iii. 3). He has anciently been identified with Nathanael (Jn. i. 45), for John never mentions Bartholomew, and the synoptists never mention Nathanael. But the identification, though probable, is not certain. All that we know of Thomas comes from the fourth Gospel. James the son of Alphaeus is so called to distinguish him from James the son of Zebedee; he may be the same as James the Little (xv. 40). Nothing is known of Thaddaeus, for whom Luke substitutes the name of another Judas (Lk. vi. 16; Acts i. 13); the two may, of course, be the same. *Simon the Canaanite* is a mistranslation, corrected in RV to 'Cananaean' (probably from Heb. *qanna*, 'jealous' or zealous, and correctly interpreted in Lk. vi. 15 as 'the Zealot'; cf. RV mg.). See Mt. x. 4n. The title *Iscariot* (lit. 'man of Kerioth', a place whose site is uncertain) applied to Judas indicates that he was the only apostle who was not a Galilean. Here were twelve typical men, no two alike, and all imperfect; yet, with one exception, there was a place for each in the fellowship of Christ.

e. Charges against Jesus (iii. 20–35)

The lake (7) and the mountain (13) are left, and Jesus with His disciples enters *into an house* (19). Here opposition arises from two quite different sources: from His family (20, 21, 31–35) and from the scribes (22–30). It is evident that we are to understand *his friends* (21; lit. 'those belonging to Him') to be the same as the relatives mentioned in verse 31. So that verses 22–30 represent an interlude going on in the house, while His family were outside seeking contact with Him. This at least is a more natural and satisfactory explanation than that the material has been editorially assembled in this way by the evangelist. The opposition from the family was in the nature of well-intentioned, but misguided, remonstrance. *He is beside himself* (21) means not that He has lost His reason, but that He is suffering, as we should say, from religious mania and has become eccentric. A similar charge was more than once brought against Paul (Acts xxvi. 24; 2 Cor. v. 13), and is often made against an earnest Christian.

On the subject of *his brethren* (31) the literature is extensive, but three main views have been held. They were either own brothers by blood, or half-brothers, the sons of Joseph by a former wife, or cousins, the sons of Mary the wife of Clopas and sister of the Virgin Mary. The second and third alternatives have been argued by some, principally Roman Catholic writers, in the interests of the dogma of the perpetual virginity of Mary. The available evidence is unfortunately not conclusive; but the fact that Jesus had own brothers is the most natural inference from such passages as Mt. i. 25 and Lk. ii. 7. From a doctrinal point of view it would, moreover, emphasize the reality and completeness of the incarnation. See also Lk. viii. 19n. and Mt. xii. 46–50. Mary the mother of our Lord appears only here in Mark, and the absence of any reference to Joseph suggests that he was dead. The answer given by Jesus (33–35), when at last the message from without reached Him, does not in any way depreciate the sacredness of family relationships, but asserts that the ties which bind the spiritual family of God are even deeper and dearer, and are based upon obedience to the will of God. This is, so to speak, the germ truth out of which grew the early Church.

The opposition from the scribes (22) was more serious and resulted from bitter hatred and jealousy. See notes on Mt. xii. 22–37; Lk. xi. 14–22. They were attributing the work of the Holy Spirit to Satan. The name, Beelzebub, is of uncertain spelling and derivation; it may originate in 2 Ki. i. 2, 16, where Baal-zebub means 'Lord of flies'. But the AV spelling occurs in no Greek MS; some have Beezebul, others Beelzebul. It is no less uncertain whether the name is the same as Satan or represents an inferior evil power. The charge of the scribes seems to have been made behind the Saviour's back, for He *called them unto him* (23) in order to answer them. In reply, He showed first the sheer absurdity of such an allegation (23–27), then warned of the awful consequences which would result (28–30). There is nothing so illogical as unbelief. The gradation in verses 24–26 is noteworthy—kingdom, house, Satan. The smaller the community the more fatal the division. In an individual, division is a contradiction in terms. The saying about blasphemy against the Holy Spirit (28, 29) is one of the most challenging utterances of Jesus. Wrongly understood it has caused untold distress. On the other hand it must not be explained away. The unpardonable sin is not an isolated act or utterance, but an attitude of defiant and deliberate rejection of light, a preference of darkness to light (Jn. iii. 19). Jesus did not say the scribes had committed it; only that they came perilously near, and were *in danger of eternal damnation* (29; lit. 'involved in (Gk. *enochos*) an eternal sin'). Such an attitude of wilful unbelief might rapidly harden into a condition where repentance, and therefore forgiveness, became impossible. But 'of all religious teachers no one was less inclined than He to minimize possibilities of forgiveness and amendment and the boundless resources of divine grace' (Vincent Taylor).

f. Parabolic teaching (iv. 1–34)

See notes on Mt. xiii. 1–23; Lk. viii. 4–10. This chapter introduces a new departure in the teaching ministry of Jesus, namely, His adoption of the parabolic method. The change coincides significantly with a shifting of the principal objective of His teaching from the multitudes to the Twelve whose training He is now taking in hand. The people are still in view, but they have hitherto been far more attracted by His works than by His words. They came for physical healing but are as yet unresponsive to His spiritual teaching. *By the sea side* (1) once more, therefore, Jesus first secured a measure of detachment by withdrawing into a boat (possibly

the same one as in iii. 9), and using it as a pulpit from which to address the crowd assembled on the shore facing the sea. The word 'parable' means literally the placing of two things side by side for purposes of comparison; hence, the illustration of truth in the spiritual realm by a story in the earthly or natural realm. Yet a parable was more than a mere illustration to enlighten. The word *Hearken* (3) (preserved by Mark alone), followed by the repeated injunctions to hear (9, 23, 24), suggests that parables were designed to provoke serious thought. They were also moral weapons to surprise and stir the conscience. Nathan's parable to David (2 Sa. xii. 1–14) may be compared as an Old Testament example of this. The parable of the sower (3–8), recorded by all three synoptists, reflects the immediate situation in which Jesus found Himself in His preaching, and at the same time enunciates principles which hold good for all time in regard to the preaching of the word. *Stony ground* (5) is not ground full of stones, but with rock close to the surface so that there is *no depth of earth*. Such ground is common in Galilee. The emphasis of the story is on the abundant harvest (8), despite initial discouragement (cf. Jn. iv. 35; Mt. ix. 37). Mark alone of the evangelists preserves this emphasis by using the singular (*some fell . . .*) of the three failures, and the plural (*other fell . . .*) of the one success: Gk. *ho men* (4); *allo* (5); *allo* (7); *alla* (8). The seed on the good ground was the most abundant.

Before giving the explanation of the parable to the Twelve alone (10), Jesus makes a further statement about the purpose of parabolic teaching in answer to their question. Verse 12 has for long presented a difficulty to expositors. The Old Testament reference is to Is. vi. 9, 10, and on the face of it it seems to suggest that the purpose of parables is twofold, first to reveal the truth to disciples, secondly to conceal it from *them that are without* (11), as a judgment or chastisement upon their blindness. And certainly this receives support from the reference to *the mystery of the kingdom of God* (11), for in the New Testament the word 'mystery' has the sense of 'an open secret', made known by revelation (cf. Eph. iii. 3, 4; Col. i. 27), but previously hidden. Nevertheless this interpretation has been felt to be so intolerable by some expositors that they have preferred to surrender the verse as an authentic saying of Jesus, regarding it, and the explanation which follows (13–20), as secondary tradition enshrining later Christian beliefs. Other attempted interpretations are that this judgment upon unresponsive hearers is in fact merciful, delivering them from the guilt of rejecting plain truth, or that Mark's compressed style here creates the difficulty, and that the word *That* (12) is a loose equivalent for 'in order that the Scripture might be fulfilled' (cf. Mt. xiii. 14).

The basic assumption which all expositors seem anxious to secure is certainly right, namely, that the ultimate purpose of a parable is to help and not to hinder the apprehension of the truth.

But beyond this we may say that it belongs to the very nature of revelation that the capacity to receive it depends upon the prior surrender and obedience of the will. 'Come and see' (Jn. i. 39, 46) is the order of Christian experience; moral conquest must come before intellectual enlightenment. The disciples had so surrendered to the sovereignty of Jesus and could therefore know (11). If temporarily parables concealed the truths of the kingdom from the outsider on the intellectual plane, it was only in order that moral conviction might first be secured with a view to intellectual enlightenment afterwards. There are many who through intellectual pride would like to have it otherwise, but it cannot be (cf. Mt. xi. 25ff.).

The interpretation of the parable of the sower (13–20) is given as a specimen, to provide canons of interpretation for other parables, much after the manner of a teacher who, when teaching something new, works an example on the blackboard. The first part of verse 13 should probably be taken as a statement, and the distinction preserved between the two words 'know' which are different in Greek. 'You do not understand (*ouk oidate*) this parable; how then will you come to know (*gnōsesthe*) all My parables?' The kingdom is to be propagated by the sowing of the word (14). This conception is fundamental to all evangelism; the task of the evangelist is not merely by means of cogent argument or persuasive eloquence to induce others to think in a certain way, but to sow living seed of the word of God in the soil of human hearts. The germ of the new life is in the Word, and without its implantation no one ever became a Christian (1 Pet. i. 23). There are things that hinder the reception of the word: hard-hearted indifference (15), lack of spiritual depth (16f.), preoccupation with the cares and riches of the world (18f.). But where the word is heard, understood and believed, the harvest is sure (20). The reference to *Satan* (15) is strong evidence that Jesus taught the existence of a personal power of evil, for He could easily have explained the birds (4) as impersonal temptations. In verse 16 there is no confusion between the seed and the soil. We commonly speak of land being sown, that is, planted with seed; which is the sense here.

Two groups of sayings (21–23 and 24, 25), each introduced by the formula *And he said unto them*, further explain the parabolic method with special reference to the moral responsibility of the hearers. The statement about the *candle* (21), better 'lamp', as in RV, confirms the view of verse 12 taken above, that the ultimate purpose of a parable is to enlighten and reveal, even if it temporarily conceals. A bushel is a vessel for measuring seed. The second group (24f.) teaches that response to the truth is the condition of receiving further truth. Where there is no response, even the power to respond is diminished; like the atrophy of a physical faculty through disuse. See Lk. viii. 16n. and cf. Mt. v. 15, x. 26.

The parable of the seed growing secretly (26–29) is the only parable peculiar to Mark. Its principal emphasis is upon the fact that the word of God will do its own work in human hearts if given the chance in right conditions, in exactly the same way as *the earth bringeth forth fruit of herself* (Gk. *automatē*) (28; cf. Is. lv. 10f.; 1 Cor. iii. 6f.). Human instrumentality is limited to two things, first sowing and finally reaping (Jn. iv. 35, 38). Between these initial and final activities it is a matter of confidence in the vitality of the seed and in the fruitfulness of the interaction between seed and soil.

The expression used to introduce the third parable of the kingdom, that of the mustard seed (30ff.), is unique: *with what comparison shall we compare it?*, lit. 'in what parable are we to place it?', as though the parable were a kind of wrapper to contain the truth. This parable may be viewed in one of two ways, as showing either the expansion of the kingdom from insignificant beginnings, or (as Dr. Campbell Morgan held) its development into abnormal proportions so that the fowls of the air (spirits of wickedness) find lodgment in it. The latter view has the merit of a certain consistency in the use of the symbols (e.g. the birds represent evil both here and in the parable of the sower), and it may be said that history supports it. For it was when, under the Emperor Constantine, the Church gained an imperial position and patronage it was never intended to have that it became corrupt. See Mt. xiii. 32n. On the other hand, the traditional view is the simpler, and accords better with the general atmosphere of the chapter which is one of optimism and confidence in the ultimate prosperity of the word of God.

A statement by the evangelist (33, 34) finally summarizes the purpose and principle of parabolic teaching. The kingdom of God was so different from prevalent notions about it, and the parables were well fitted to dislodge these popular ideas where direct statements would not have been received. The nature of the kingdom was declared to the people by comparison rather than by definition. But to His private disciples privately (34; Gk. *kat' idian de tois idiois mathētais*) Jesus gave fuller instruction.

g. Mighty works (iv. 35–v. 43)

The series of parables is followed by a series of miracles, as though to suggest that the works of Jesus vindicate His words. What He does confirms what He says. A similar arrangement is found in Matthew, where these and earlier miracles are recorded as following the Sermon on the Mount (see Mt. viii.).

i. The stilling of the storm (iv. 35–41). See notes on Mt. viii. 18–27; Lk. viii. 22–25. Jesus decided to cross the lake from west to east. This may have been either to disperse the crowd or to find a new sphere for His ministry, or perhaps for both reasons. *Even as he was* (36) refers back to verse 1. After some hours of teaching the multitude and the disciples, He was too weary even to help in sending the people away. The sudden storm is characteristic of the region round the Sea of Galilee, where the movement of the air currents causes the wind to sweep with tremendous violence down the narrow gorges that descend to the shore from the surrounding hills. It is Mark alone who preserves the vivid detail that *he was in the hinder part of the ship, asleep on a pillow* (38). The pillow was probably a rower's wooden or leathern seat used as a head rest. There is a note of resentment and reproach in the disciples' question, paraphrased by Moffatt, 'Teacher, are we to drown, for all you care?' Jesus therefore awoke, and said to the sea, *Peace, be still* (lit. 'be silent, be muzzled'; the latter word is the same as in i. 25). The story illustrates first the divine authority of Jesus over the forces of nature; He is superior even to a storm which caused experienced fishermen to panic with alarm. It also shows His true and real humanity, for He had evidently toiled up to and almost beyond the limit of His strength. On no other occasion is His sleeping mentioned; but He needed sleep, just as He needed food. Again, some have thought the story was intended to bring a message of peace to a storm-tossed Church in the time of persecution. The disciples were in the path of obedience, but even obedience brings no immunity from trouble. Dangers beset the Church even when engaged in carrying out the Master's commands. Nevertheless there is no ground for cowardice or craven fear. They should have known enough of Him by now to enable them to trust and believe that neither could the Messiah perish in a storm, nor would He allow them to perish because they had obeyed Him. 'Have ye not yet faith?' (40, RV).

ii. **The Gerasene demoniac (v. 1-20).** See notes on Mt. viii. 28-34; Lk. viii. 26-39. It is not clear to what part of the opposite shore Jesus crossed over. 'The country of the Gerasenes' (1, RV) represents the best reading here, though 'Gadarenes' is found in Matthew. At only one point on the eastern shore of the lake is there *a steep place* (13), and there are no rock-hewn tombs in the vicinity of this; but tombs built on the ground (cf. Lk. xi. 44) may possibly be meant.

The fulness of detail in this account illustrates Mark's particular interest in this type of miracle of exorcism, which exhibits the authority and power of the Lord Jesus Christ even in the spirit realm. It has also been pointed out how the narrative seems to be arranged in scenes in which the centre of interest shifts from the man (1-10) to the herd of swine (11-13), then to the townspeople (14-17) and back again to the man (18-20), almost like a little drama in four acts. First the demoniac is described as to his strength (4). Man had tried to tame him as a beast is tamed, but the external remedies of coercion and restraint had failed. His life was one of misery to himself, for he knew neither rest nor sleep, but only ceaseless outcry and self-laceration (5). His recognition of Jesus and acknowledgment

of His authority seem to have been a common feature of these cases (cf. i. 24, iii. 11), and shows that no merely psychological explanation can account for the facts. This man was more than a case for the psychiatrist. The expression *the most high God* (7) is one used repeatedly in Scripture by Gentiles (Gn. xiv. 18; Is. xiv. 14; Dn. iii. 26; Acts xvi. 17) and suggests that the man was not a Jew. The population on this side of the lake was probably of a mixed character, for Jews would not have been found keeping swine. It is remarkable that in a frantic appeal to Jesus not to inflict immediate punishment the unclean spirit used the same formula, *I adjure thee by God* (7), that was employed in exorcisms.

Two explanations have been given of the question *What is thy name?* (9). First, the ancient belief that knowledge of the name gave power over an adversary. Alternatively, and more probably, it was to recall the man to a sense of his own personality apart from the demon. *Legion* was a Latin word, which to people under Roman domination would suggest numbers, strength and oppression. He felt himself to be a conglomeration of evil forces, without moral unity, and this divided personality is reflected in the alternating singular and plural pronouns on his lips (9). For the expression *out of the country* (10), Lk. viii. 31, RV has 'into the abyss', which suggests that what the spirits feared was complete disembodiment.

The ethical implication of Jesus' action in regard to the swine (11-13) has given rise to much discussion. Was it not wanton destruction of property with consequent heavy loss to the owners, and did Jesus anticipate the result, or did He not? Those who accept a psychological explanation of demon possession are obliged to account for the panic of the swine by saying that in the paroxysm which accompanied his deliverance the man struck terror into the herd and drove them down the cliff. The more satisfactory view, however, is that the destruction of the swine was permitted by the Lord as an ocular demonstration to the demoniac that the demons had in fact departed from him, and to confirm his faith. The sacrifice of brutes and property is justifiable where the sanity and lives of persons are at stake.

Three phrases describe the completeness of the transformation wrought in the man by the grace and power of Christ: he was *sitting* instead of restless, *clothed* instead of naked, *and in his right mind*, sober instead of raging (15). Thus does Jesus expel the spirits of anger, pride, selfishness, impurity and the like from the lives of men, restoring them to spiritual health and clothing them with the garments of salvation. But the townspeople, filled with alarm in the presence of the supernatural, and probably fearing, as so many have done since, that if Jesus stayed yet other things might have to go, *began to pray him to depart* (17); and He will never stay unwanted. The prayer of the man was very different (18); but Jesus' answer was contrary to His usual practice of enjoining silence in such cases (cf. iii. 12). The reason was probably that, in this country beyond Jordan, there was not the danger of the miracle being used for political purposes, as in Judaea. *Decapolis* (20) was, as the name implies, a group of ten Greek cities, all except one being east of the lake.

iii. The raising of the daughter of Jairus and the healing of the woman with an issue of blood (v. 21–43). These two miracles, the one within the other, illustrate the Lord's authority over disease and death. See notes on Mt. ix. 18–26; Lk. viii. 41–56. It will be convenient to consider the story of the woman (verses 25–34) first. Her malady was one which made her ceremonially unclean and would convey the uncleanness to all who came in touch with her (Lv. xv. 25). For this reason, probably, she approached Jesus from behind, in order not to be seen. It was an ancient belief that even handkerchiefs and aprons carried from the person of a healer possessed healing power (cf. Acts xix. 12), and similarly his shadow (Acts v. 15). Having touched the Lord's garment, the woman was instantly cured, but He would not allow her to escape without a fuller understanding of what had taken place. His inquiry, *Who touched my clothes?* (30), seems therefore to have had a twofold purpose. First He desired the information; for although He was aware that the power proceeding from Him had gone forth in conscious response to the touch of faith, there is no need to suppose that He exhibited supernatural knowledge where information could be obtained without it. Secondly, He wished to elicit her open confession (cf. Rom. x. 9, 10). What follows is an interesting lesson in the nature of true faith. The impatient remonstrance of the disciples (31) shows that there is a world of difference between thronging Jesus and touching Him in personal faith out of a deep sense of need and a conviction of His saving power. It is still true that, while multitudes throng Jesus, it is the few who touch Him. Calvin pointed out, moreover, that the words of verse 34 do not encourage a belief in the efficacy of relics! We may go further and say that no outward 'sacrament' is efficacious apart from faith in the living Christ. There was no magical power resident in the garment. Again, although Jesus attributes the woman's cure to her faith, nevertheless in the New Testament view faith is no mere subjective experience, but something which derives its virtue from the object in which it rests, 'a spiritual experience which begins in a venture of spirit and is constituted and made effective by God Himself' (Vincent Taylor).

The delay caused by the intrusion of the woman must have been an agonizing test of faith to the ruler of the synagogue, who had approached Jesus by the lakeside and, casting aside his dignity in the acuteness of his distress, had fallen at His feet (21f.). This was only intensified when a message from his house

suggested that it was already too late, *Thy daughter is dead* (35). It is not quite clear whether Jesus overheard this message, or ignored it. The RV takes the latter view. The word *heard* (36; Gk. *parakousas*) means 'to refuse to hear' in the LXX and in Mt. xviii. 17. Perhaps both meanings are implicit here. Jesus overheard the message and deliberately set it aside in giving a word of assurance to Jairus. For the first time Jesus took with Him Peter, James and John (37), who were later present also at the transfiguration (ix. 2) and in Gethsemane (xiv. 33). This was not for favouritism; but first because in sovereignty He had chosen them for special service; and secondly, perhaps, because they emerged as a nucleus of the most responsive among the apostolic band. The crucial question in the story is the meaning of the words, *the damsel is not dead, but sleepeth* (39). Some expositors take the view that whereas Matthew (ix. 18) and particularly Luke (viii. 53, 55) plainly imply that the child was dead, the Markan saying, which is earliest, is ambiguous and could mean that she was only in a coma or trance-like sleep. On the other hand this is by no means decisive. The scorn of the people (40) rather points to the contrary. So also does the injunction to silence (43), which may among other reasons have been designed to forestall the suggestion that He was right after all; she was only asleep. It is better to conclude that here is in fact the germinal truth of later Christian teaching about death. As God sees it, it is a sleep from which there is to be an awakening (1 Thes. iv. 13, 14). Our knowledge of the other world is limited, but it is within reach of the Saviour's voice and our dead are safe in His keeping. His authority extends beyond the grave. This is particularly true in regard to little children. The apostle Peter evidently observed his Master's technique on this occasion very closely, and the story of Dorcas in Acts ix. 36–43 not only invites an interesting comparison, but well illustrates the great truth of Jn. xiv. 12.

h. Rejection at Nazareth and the mission of the Twelve (vi. 1–13)

For verses 1–6 see notes on Mt. xiii. 53–58. *His own country* (1) is clearly Nazareth, as the context indicates. This visit is to be distinguished from that described in Lk. iv. 16–30, which took place a year earlier. Jesus had left Nazareth as a private individual; now He returned as a rabbi, surrounded by His scholars, presumably to give His own folk a further opportunity. But the result was the same as before; their jealousy was aroused. It was inconceivable that one of their fellow-villagers could have any mission from heaven. The reason for this attitude is stated in verse 6 as *their unbelief.* The fact of His wisdom and power was undeniable (2), but they questioned the divine origin of these things, the implication being that when the obviously supernatural does not come from God it must emanate from the devil. This is the essence of unbelief, the stubborn refusal to accept the evidence and admit the presence and power of God; and nothing so inhibits the power of God. That *he could there do no mighty work* (5) is one of the boldest statements in the Gospels, but it clearly shows that our Lord's miracles were not mere magic; they were vitally related to the moral condition and faith of the people. Though He is omnipotent, God in His sovereignty will not act for blessing in the face of human rebellion. Of the family mentioned in verse 3, James afterwards became president of the church in Jerusalem (Acts xv. 13; Gal. ii. 9, 12) and author of the Epistle of James; Juda the author of the Epistle of Jude. Little is known of the others or of the sisters.

For verses 7–13 see notes on Mt. x. 5–40; Lk. ix. 1–6. This mission of the Twelve is said by Matthew (ix. 35–38) to have originated in the Master's compassion for the people, which led Him to bring in at this point as 'fellow-labourers' those whom He had chosen and was training for the purpose. At the same time this first preaching tour may have been of the nature of an experiment forming part of the training itself. They would learn much from it, as, for example, that Christ's power extended beyond His presence and could even be delegated to them; that God could supply their temporal needs; that their commission was one of moral dignity and authority. They were to go in twos for the sake of witness (Dt. xix. 15; 2 Cor. xiii. 1) and fellowship. Their equipment was to be simple and serviceable, avoiding either extreme of slovenliness or extravagance. The exception of the staff (8) is peculiar to Mark. The *scrip* was a bag for provisions. Hospitality was to be accepted where offered; but where it was refused they were to 'shake off the dust . . . for a testimony against them' (11, RV; 'as a warning to them', Moff.). This action did not express personal resentment; it was symbolic of the fact that the place was to be regarded as heathen, the intention being to provoke thought and lead to repentance. Verse 11b (*verily . . . city*) is omitted by the principal uncial MSS and has been added here by assimilation to Mt. x. 15. The threefold ministry of the Twelve is summarized in verses 12 and 13, as preaching repentance, exorcising demons and healing the sick. Anointing with oil is mentioned only here, Lk. x. 34 (a case of medicinal use) and Jas. v. 14. It is probably to be thought of here as an accessory to miraculous healing and a stimulus to faith.

i. Herod and John the Baptist (vi. 14–29)

See notes on Mt. xiv. 1–12; Lk. ix. 7–9. Herod Antipas was the son of Herod the Great (Mt. ii. 1ff.) and Malthace. The title *king* as applied to him is at best one of courtesy or local custom. He was actually 'tetrarch', or ruler of a fourth part, in Galilee and Peraea, under the overlordship of Rome, and is invariably so described by Luke. For *he said* (14) the better reading is 'they said' or 'people were saying'. Of the varying

reports of Jesus which reached the ears of Herod, pangs of conscience probably led him to fix on the first as the most likely, *that John the Baptist was risen*, and that was why supernatural powers were at work in Him. Mark now narrates retrospectively and with some fulness the circumstances which led to the murder of John. This not only throws light upon the character of Herod, but seems to be a kind of interlude before proceeding to the account of Jesus' further ministry in Galilee, within Herod's jurisdiction, and beyond it into Gentile territory. According to Josephus, the scene of John's imprisonment was Machaerus, a combined fortress, palace and prison just north-east of the Dead Sea. Herodias was in fact the niece of Antipas, being the daughter of Aristobulus his half-brother; she had married yet another half-brother whom Josephus calls Herod, but who may also have borne the name Philip (17). John had repeatedly rebuked Antipas for this union on the grounds of Lv. xviii. 16, xx. 21, with the result that Herodias nursed a grudge and was only restrained from carrying out her fell desire by Herod himself, whose conscience was evidently not yet completely dead. Verse 20 should be read as in RV: 'Herod . . . kept him safe. And when he heard him, he was much perplexed.' It is the picture of a vacillating moral weakling, torn between his respect for John and his passion for Herodias. *Chief estates* (21) should be 'leading men' or 'notables of Galilee'. The *daughter of the said Herodias* (22) was Salome. A few very important MSS have the reading 'when his daughter Herodias came in' (see RV mg.); but in the first place a daughter of Antipas and Herodias could be only about two years old, and secondly it is hardly credible that Herod could find pleasure in the degrading of his own child in a voluptuous dance, for such it was. The story is after the manner of the oriental potentate and should be compared with Est. v. 2f. *Charger* (25) is old English for a flat wooden trencher or dish. There is reason for thinking that Herod Antipas is an example of one who had committed the unpardonable sin (iii. 29). He had persistently and deliberately trifled with the truth as John gave it to him, and when later Jesus Himself appeared before him for the first and only time (Lk. xxiii. 7–11) Jesus had nothing to say to him. That silence is most significant for, had he been responsive to any entreaty, the Lord would surely have spoken.

j. Miracles and teaching in Galilee and beyond (vi. 30—viii. 26)

i. The return of the disciples (vi. 30–34).

Here and here only are the Twelve called *apostles* in this Gospel. They have fulfilled their mission and now resume their rôle as disciples, having still much to learn. They report to the Master and are taken aside to recuperate. Cf. Lk. ix. 10. The position of the *desert place* (31) is thought by most commentators to have been the northeast side of the lake. There is a time for rest as well as for work in the service of Christ. But, as so often, the seclusion of both the Master and His disciples is invaded by the claims of human need, and once more His deep compassion is the source of the events which follow (34). This compassion reflects the very heart of Jehovah in a picture of surpassing tenderness. Cf. Je. xxiii. 1–4; Ezk. xxxiv.

ii. The feeding of the five thousand (vi. 35–44). This miracle has the distinction of being the only one recorded by all four evangelists. See Mt. xiv. 13–21; Lk. ix. 10–17; Jn. vi. 1–15. The suggestion of the disciples (36) was perhaps not wholly in the interest of the people. They had been disappointed of their time apart with Jesus and may have been hungry themselves (cf. verse 31). The answer of Jesus must therefore have come as a seemingly impossible challenge; and the word 'ye' is very emphatic: 'they are not to go away; you are the ones to feed them' (37). Such words come as a lasting rebuke to the helplessness of the Church, in face of a starving world, and regarding her own paltry resources with dismay. Yet it is evident that the need can be met if the Lord is allowed to direct the use of those resources. Estimates of the worth of a 'denarius', or penny, necessarily vary owing to the changing values in the purchasing power of money; but it was a day's wage for a working man, and the point of the computation in verse 37 is that a sum far greater than the disciples had with them would be hopelessly insufficient. Mark's description of what followed (39f.) is singularly vivid. The people were arranged in an orderly fashion *by companies* (Gk. *symposia symposia*, lit. 'drinking parties') *upon the green grass . . . in ranks* (Gk. *prasiai prasiai*, lit. 'garden beds'). They resembled garden beds in their bright colours against the green background. The purpose of this, however, was rather the practical one of dividing up the assembly into manageable groups so as to avoid confusion and secure that all were served 'decently and in order' (1 Cor. xiv. 40). Attention has been drawn to the similarity of verse 41 to xiv. 22, as though to suggest that the meal in the wilderness was in some sense an anticipation of the Last Supper. That may be so, but probably the safer view is that these simple actions were usually associated with any meal on the part of the host, and were later invested with new and richer meaning by the Lord in the fellowship of His disciples. The manner of the miracle alone is left unrevealed, as to whether the multiplication took place in the hands of the Lord or of His disciples. Various attempts have been made by the rationalists to dispose of the miraculous element altogether, by supposing that the numbers are exaggerated, or that the crowd were persuaded to share their provisions; in which case it is difficult to see why so ordinary an event has been preserved in a fourfold record. Everything depends upon the view we take of our Lord's Person. If He was in fact incarnate deity, there is no real difficulty in believing that

He wrought on this occasion a creative act, as the evangelists clearly supposed. The *baskets* (43; Gk. *kophinoi*) were provision-baskets carried by travelling Jews to avoid eating Gentile food. Cf. viii. 8, 19, 20. *Fragments* were not crumbs, but surplus broken portions. In the light of John's account, which leads on directly to the great discourse about the bread of life, we are left in no doubt as to the meaning of the story. Jesus is not only the Giver of life; He is the Support and Sustainer of it, as indispensable for Christian living as daily bread for the body, the complete satisfaction and nourishment of the believing soul who daily, hourly feeds upon Him in the heart by faith.

iii. The walking on the water (vi. 45–52). See notes on Mt. xiv. 22–33; Jn. vi. 16–21. By comparison with the earlier story of the stilling of the storm (iv. 35–41), the central feature here is the fact that Jesus walked upon the sea. There He was in the boat with the disciples; here they were alone, having been compelled by Him to embark *while he sent away the people* (45). The reason for this compulsion appears from John's remark (Jn. vi. 15) 'that they would come and take him by force, to make him a king'. The disciples would have been delighted if they had done so, for this was precisely what they had always hoped for. But Jesus recognized it to be a moment of supreme peril necessitating the immediate dispatch of the disciples and His own retirement into solitude and prayer (46). It was the temptation of Lk. iv. 5–8 all over again. There is a geographical difficulty about Bethsaida (cf. verse 53 and Jn. vi. 17), which has led some scholars to conjecture the existence of a western Bethsaida as a kind of fishing suburb of Capernaum and distinguishable from Bethsaida Julias to the north-east. But the simplest solution seems to be that the disciples set out to cross the bay, and were blown off course and out to sea, eventually making for Gennesaret on the western shore. It is remarkable that Jesus did not immediately intervene. The disciples struggled for some hours until *the fourth watch of the night* (48); or three o'clock in the morning according to the Roman reckoning which Mark is using. Even then Jesus *would have passed by them*. This is entirely after the manner of His conduct on other occasions (cf. Lk. xxiv. 28; Jn. xi. 6) and we may infer that His purpose was to test their faith. Mark is careful to tell us that *they all saw him* (50); it was no subjective delusion or hallucination, but someone objectively visible to the whole company. Yet such was their blindness of heart (52; cf. Rom. xi. 25; Eph. iv. 18) that even the miracle of the loaves afforded them no basis for further understanding. The human heart can be unbelievably obtuse in spiritual matters.

Here once more objections have been raised to the miraculous element, first on the ground that the intervention of Jesus does not meet any desperate need, for the disciples were not in jeopardy; secondly, and more seriously, because the story has been held to support a Docetic view of the Person of Christ, that His body was heavenly and not truly human. But if Jesus was only wading through the surf, there was no cause for terror, neither could He have conversed with them (50), nor is there any adequate explanation of the words *in the midst of the sea* (47). Furthermore we cannot dogmatize upon what would be possible or impossible for a unique Personality such as His.

The omission of the story of Peter's stepping from the boat (Mt. xiv. 28–31) points to the influence of the apostle himself on the Markan narrative. As we have seen (*Introduction*, p. 806), he is careful to avoid incidents which might tend to magnify him. Many of the Christians at Rome and elsewhere probably felt they were making little headway against the contrary winds of persecution, and the record of this incident would bring untold consolation to them, assuring them of the presence and power of their Lord.

iv. Ministry at Gennesaret (vi. 53–56). See also Mt. xiv. 34–36. Gennesaret was a fertile and populous plain, lying south of Capernaum. The scene here so graphically described marks the climax of the Galilean ministry. As Jesus moved through the district, the people followed Him, carrying around their sick upon pallets. Sometimes they were too late and missed Him; then they carried the sufferers from place to place until they overtook Him. Their desires apparently did not rise above the healing of the body; and as there is no mention of any further teaching here, it seems that Jesus gave Himself unreservedly to them to do as much as they would let Him.

v. Teaching about cleansing (vii. 1–23). See also Mt. xv. 1–20. The first four verses provide further evidence that this Gospel was written for Gentile readers, for the Jewish customs in regard to ceremonial ablutions are carefully explained. These washings were not for the purpose of cleansing in the hygienic sense but for the removal of ceremonial defilement. *Defiled* (2; Gk. *koinais*, translated 'common', Acts x. 14, 28, and 'unclean', Rom. xiv. 14) was a technical term for what was ceremonially unclean to Jews because of Gentile associations. In verse 3 the superior but more difficult reading for *oft* (Gk. *pykna*) is 'with the fist' (Gk. *pygmē*), as RV mg. This is variously rendered 'diligently' (RV), 'up to the wrist' (Moff.). In this section three groups of people are addressed; a hostile group of critics (1), the people (14) and the disciples (17f.). The Pharisees raised the question of *the tradition of the elders* (3, 5). In reply Jesus stated that human tradition can never have the same authority as the Word of God. There were times when the scribes made even more of it than of the commandments, preferring, as so many still do, religious ritual to that which is inwardly moral and spiritual. It is an ancient attitude of the human heart, aptly described by Isaiah (Is. xxix. 13), for human nature is basically the same in every generation. Jesus then cited an outstanding example which is not purely hypothetical (10–13). Indeed some think there may have been some contemporary *cause célèbre* of the kind, which was current gossip. It related to the Corban vow. The law concerning duty to parents was plain, but the Jews, with characteristic sophistry, had devised a means of evading it, even under the cloak of piety. A son could pledge his money to be paid into the temple treasury. This could be done in an ideal sense without any actual payment being made, or the payment could be deferred until after his death. He could even do it in a fit of anger, and could then tell his old parents in their time of need that he could offer them no help, since his money was *Corban* (11), i.e. dedicated under oath. *Corban* is a transliteration of a Hebrew word meaning an offering or gift devoted to God.

Having answered the Pharisees on the subject of tradition versus commandment, Jesus now turned to the whole company to deal with the question of defilement. This He did in a parabolic saying (15) which is revolutionary in its religious implications and was destined to liberate Christianity from the bondage of legalism. On the one hand, nothing external can pollute a man; on the other, the real source of all impurity is within, a matter not of the hands but of the heart. The disciples did not at the time understand, and therefore asked the Lord privately about it (17).

Verses 18–23 are an expansion of the two parts of the saying in verse 15. According to the best reading (which represents a difference of one letter) the last phrase of verse 19 should read, with RV, 'This he said, making all meats clean'. Jesus ended the old distinction between meats clean and unclean. This comment may well be a reflection of Peter's in the light of his experience at Joppa (Acts x. 9–16). In the catalogue of vices that follows, Mark begins where all sin begins, in the realm of thought. Gal. v. 19–21 may be compared. Of the last five, *lasciviousness* is the licentious behaviour that shocks public decency; the *evil eye* is malignant envy; *blasphemy* is rather slander or 'railing' (RV); *pride* is the superiority complex of Lk. xviii. 9; while *foolishness* is that moral inanity that treats sin as a joke.

vi. The Syro-Phoenician woman (vii. 24–30). See also Mt. xv. 21–28. The significance of this and the following two miracles is that they took place on Gentile or pagan territory, whither Jesus had gone not only to avoid a premature clash with the hostile Jews, but primarily to secure some privacy with His disciples (24). His undertaking of a brief Gentile ministry also foreshadows the universal scope of the gospel. The woman is introduced (26) by her religion, she was *a Greek*, and by her nationality, a Phoenician of Syria, Syro-Phoenician being a term used in distinction from Liby-Phoenician or Carthaginian. These Phoenicians came from the Canaanites, and Matthew (Mt. xv. 22) so describes her.

We might indeed ask, Was she the first heathen convert to Christ? The apparent roughness of the Lord's answer to her plea for the healing of her daughter admittedly arises from the fact that she was a stranger to the covenant, but none the less brings into focus the question of the sovereign grace of God in election, which at first sight looks like divine favouritism. But election is merely the method of God's initiative in salvation. 'Particularism is a stage towards a wider universalism in God's plan' (E. Y. Mullins). Cf. Eph. ii. 11–18. God seeks to save not as few but as many as possible. The stage of the wider universalism has not yet been reached, but it is foreshadowed in Christ's treatment of the woman. Her answer (28), which so clearly evinced her faith and earnestness, seized upon two things. First, the term *dogs* (Gk. diminutive *kynaria*, 'little dogs', household companions, not outside scavengers) has not the opprobrium we associate with it. She assented to His estimate and drew her own conclusion. Secondly, His word *Let the children first be filled* (27) led her to expect that her own turn would come eventually. Some modern expositors regard this story as a case of supernatural or telepathic knowledge rather than miraculous healing. But it seems clear that Mark, followed by Matthew, intended us to understand that Jesus healed at a distance, the only example in this Gospel of His doing so.

vii. The healing of the deaf mute (vii. 31–37).
See also Mt. xv. 29–31. If the best reading is accepted, verse 31 must read 'he went out from the borders of Tyre, and came through Sidon unto the sea of Galilee, through the midst of the borders of Decapolis'. So RV. The geography of this is difficult, as a glance at the map will show. It involves a long detour proceeding first northward, then eastward and southward. Most of the attempts that have been made to account for this long journey, or otherwise explain the text, are speculative and unsatisfactory. We cannot do more than surmise that Jesus may thus have tried to gain the necessary seclusion for the instruction of the Twelve, which He had twice previously failed to secure (cf. vi. 31–34, vii. 24). For *Decapolis*, see v. 20n. Once more Jesus was near the country of the Gerasenes, where in the meantime the healed demoniac had been bearing his testimony and thus acting as a pioneer. The people of the district accordingly brought to Jesus another helpless soul, who *was deaf, and had an impediment in his speech* (32; Gk. *kōphon kai mogilalon*). He was not necessarily dumb, but a stammerer. (A well supported variant reading, *moggilalon*, describes him as 'harsh of speech'.) The account in verses 33, 34 is full of vivid and interesting detail of the method employed to restore him; first the retirement from the crowd, perhaps to avoid distraction and unnecessary publicity (cf. verse 36); secondly, the various means of contact, including the use of saliva which was supposed to be remedial, but in this case was designed to

evoke in the man the co-operation of faith (cf. viii. 23; Jn. ix. 6); thirdly, the upward look and the sigh or groan, an indication of the Lord's deep feeling and compassion and an example of those human emotions in Him which Mark delights to record; fourthly, the actual Aramaic word used which could easily be read from the lips by a deaf person. The whole is undoubtedly a parable for the Christian. Dumbness usually results from deafness. If our ears are open to listen to the word of the Lord, then our tongues will surely be unloosed in praise, prayer and testimony.

viii. The feeding of the four thousand (viii. 1–10).
See notes on Mt. xv. 32–39. The chief question which arises is whether this narrative is a doublet of the feeding of the five thousand (vi. 35–44). There is admittedly considerable agreement, even verbally; and it is argued that the disciples must have been incredibly stupid to have asked such a question as that in verse 4, in the light of their earlier experience. On the other hand there are differences which ought not to be minimized. The period of *three days* (2) is much longer than in the case of the 5,000, which occupied hardly a day. In the earlier narrative the dismissal of the crowd is urged by the disciples; here it is rejected by Jesus on His own initiative. The variation in the numbers, though not of the same importance, is nevertheless not negligible. But particularly striking is the difference in the word used for *baskets* (8). Here this is *spyris*, an affair woven of twigs or rushes, of the kind carried by Gentile merchant-men and large enough to contain a man (Acts ix. 25). The basket of the earlier occasion was the Jewish provision-basket (Gk. *kophinos*); see vi. 43n. These two kinds are carefully distinguished by Jesus in verses 19, 20; see also Mt. xvi. 9, 10n. It is scarcely satisfactory therefore to dismiss these differences as mere modifications of the tradition, and we may be pardoned for suspecting embarrassment when it is suggested that Mark, who usually adheres closely to the original tradition, has nevertheless allowed homiletical or other impulses to colour the record of the Lord's words in this case. Of the perplexity of the disciples, Trench (*Notes on the Miracles, ad loc.*) appropriately says: 'It is only the man of a full-formed faith, of a faith which apostles themselves at this time did not possess, who argues from the past to the future, and truly derives confidence from God's former dealings of faithfulness and love (cf. 1 Sa. xvii. 34–37; 2 Ch. xvi. 7, 8).' The stubbornness and dullness of the human heart frequently appears in Scripture (cf. Ex. xiv. 31 with xvi. 2, 3) and was evidently a source of grief to the Lord here (17–21). The significance of this occasion seems to be that Jesus was still among Gentiles, to whom the bread of life is to be offered as well as to the Jews. The identity of *Dalmanutha* (10), a name which occurs only here, is unknown. Mt. xv. 39 has 'Magadan' (RV) or 'Magdala', which suggests a crossing once more to the western side of the lake.

ix. The demand for a sign from heaven (viii. 11–21). Verses 11–13 should be compared with Mt. xvi. 1–4, where Jesus condemns the Pharisees for their failure to discern the signs of the times. They were insincere in their demand, and far more anxious to secure material for proving Jesus was not the Messiah than to be convinced that He was. Cf. also Mt. xii. 38–42; Lk. xi. 29–32. Signs on earth were not wanting, and Jesus' saying to the disciples (19–21) implies that both miracles of feeding were of that order. But it is a *sign from heaven* that is required; a voice, or a wonder in the sun or moon, would be more convincing, so they suggest, than the meeting of human need. Yet would it? There is none so blind as those who refuse to see, and to the moral perversity that shows itself in these Pharisees Jesus has nothing more to say. The words *and he left them* (13) mark a tragic abandonment.

The occasion is used to warn the disciples of those corrupting influences which more than anything cause blindness of heart (15). Cf. Mt. xvi. 5–12. We learn from Lk. xii. 1 that the leaven of the Pharisees was hypocrisy; the leaven of Herod was probably worldliness and sensuality. But even the disciples were completely missing the inner spiritual meaning of their Master's teaching and supposed that He was referring to some specific kind of leaven about which the Pharisees were very punctilious. Their condition, however, was not that of the Pharisees, for which there was nothing but abandonment; it was rather spiritual dullness which called for and met with infinite patience from the Lord. There is consolation in this. The keynote of this passage therefore is the all-important one of spiritual discernment, a faculty all too rarely possessed even by disciples. It is a matter of the heart rather than the head (17), of moral sympathy rather than intellectual erudition. Cf. 1 Cor. ii. 9–16; Eph. i. 17f.

x. A blind man healed at Bethsaida (viii. 22–26). There are remarkable similarities between this miracle and that of the deaf mute (vii. 31–37). They are the only miracles peculiar to Mark. In each case, the sufferer was isolated from the crowd, spittle and the touch of the hand were used, and undue publicity was to be avoided. But in one notable feature this work of healing was unique, in that the cure was gradual. The man looked up and said 'I see men; but they look like trees, walking' (24, RSV); and a second touch was required to restore his sight completely. This highly distinctive detail alone confirms the historical character of the incident. It is difficult to resist the conclusion that Mark has introduced the narrative here with a purpose. The disciples were at this time rather like the blind man in the first stage of his recovery. But a note of hope is sounded. There is thoroughness in every work of Jesus and He will not be satisfied short of perfection. What He has begun He will finish; and presently, after the second touch of His Spirit at Pentecost, they will see all things clearly.

k. Messiahship and suffering (viii. 27—ix. 29)
From this point the narrative becomes dominated by the thought of the approaching passion, of which there are three definite predictions (viii. 31, ix. 31, x. 33f.).

i. The confession of Peter and the first prediction (viii. 27–33). See notes on Mt. xvi. 13–23; Lk. ix. 18–22. Caesarea Philippi was the most northerly town reached by Christ. It is to be distinguished from Caesarea Stratonis on the western coast, the seat of Roman government frequently mentioned in Acts. There Jesus put to the disciples two questions: first a general one (27) which elicited the information that men recognized in Him someone outstanding, but no more. The second challenged them personally (29), and Peter, as spokesman for them all, made the tremendous affirmation that He was the Messiah, promised and predicted of old. Significantly the Lord's benediction upon Peter at this point is omitted. Peter had doubtless preserved a modest silence about it. But the parallel account in Mt. xvi. 13–23 should again be compared. After the blindness of the Pharisees and the dullness of the disciples, Jesus rejoiced to find the light of revelation beginning to dawn. They were beginning to see, but, as the sequel shows, their vision like that of the blind man was by no means clear yet. Nevertheless those who knew Jesus best reverenced Him most. With human characters it is not so; familiarity often breeds contempt; on approach the halo becomes dim. The reverse was the case with Christ.

This confession is the crisis point both of the teaching of Jesus and of the Gospel record. Jesus Himself had been aware of His messianic mission at least from the beginning of His public ministry and probably before (cf. Lk. ii. 49); aware too of the suffering involved and of the necessity of the cross which had shadowed His pathway from the first (Jn. ii. 19, iii. 14). But only at this decisive point did He begin to speak of it plainly (32). And from this point Mark's narrative becomes governed by the one purpose of establishing the thesis that Jesus was not taken unawares but that the course of events was foreknown, and indeed was part of the predetermined counsel of God (Acts iv. 28).

The disciples were right as to the fact, but wrong in what they understood by it. The Old Testament prophets foreshadowed the Messiah in two ways, as triumphant (Is. xi) and as suffering (Is. liii); cf. Lk. xxiv. 26; 1 Pet. i. 10, 11. The Jews cherished the material and political implications of the former and conveniently ignored or rejected the spiritual implications of the latter. And at this stage even the disciples shared the common view. Jesus therefore *began to teach them, that the Son of man must* (Gk. *dei*, of the divine decree) *suffer* (31). The disciples were obviously staggered by this revelation, and Peter, probably after some deliberation on the matter, drew the Lord aside and *began to rebuke him* (32). Through Peter's lips Jesus recognized a voice He had heard before (Lk. iv. 5–8). It is a solemn reflection that a well-meaning but unspiritual disciple can become the tool of Satan. The goal of true discipleship is complete conformity to the divine mind, as revealed in Jesus, savouring *the things that be of God* (33); Gk. *phroneis ta tou theou.* Paul uses a similar expression in Col. iii. 2. Those things are further developed in what follows.

ii. **The conditions of discipleship (viii. 34—ix. 1).** See notes on Mt. xvi. 24–28; Lk. ix. 23–27. The first mention in Mark of the *cross* is here (34), and with its familiar Roman associations the word must have fallen upon apostolic ears far more startlingly than it does upon ours. For the follower it means precisely what it meant for the Lord; not mere inconvenience or discomfort, but death. The mind of the disciple in relation to the world is defined in this way. He will experience an essential antagonism resulting in persecution, and he will exhibit non-resistance to that persecution (Jn. xv. 19; Gal. vi. 14). He will accept the last consequences of obedience and take the last risk. In relation to himself his attitude will be that of self-denial, which means the complete dethronement of self that the life may be Christ-centred. In relation to his Lord, he will follow in submission to His will (34). Paradoxically such surrender and submission is the surest and most abiding gain; whereas the self-realization and self-expression so dear to the modern mind is to lose one's own soul. And once lost, what has a man to *give in exchange* (Gk. *antallagma,* a marketable equivalent) to redeem it? The loss is irrevocable (37).

But lest such stern doctrine should utterly discourage, Jesus went on to speak of His coming (viii. 38) and His kingdom (ix. 1). Although suffering awaited the Son of man, nevertheless that other strand of messianic prophecy which spoke of His victorious reign should not go unfulfilled. The precise meaning of ix. 1 remains somewhat uncertain. Four possible interpretations which have been suggested are: the transfiguration; the resurrection and ascension; the destruction of Jerusalem in A.D. 70; Pentecost and the beginning of missionary enterprise. If the first of these be accepted the words amount to little more than an assertion that some of the disciples would still be alive six days hence, which seems pointless. Of the other three the last is probably most satisfactory. The disciples eventually came to see that the cross which was now such a stumbling-block to them was in fact the sign and secret of conquest over the hearts of men, and thus of the coming of the kingdom. On the basis of the rather speculative idea that the designation 'Son of man' denotes the elect community (a view advanced by some expositors), Vincent Taylor (*Gospel According to St. Mark, ad loc.*) says: 'A visible manifestation of the rule of God displayed in the life of an Elect Community is the most probable form of His expectation'. This may be so, in this particular context, though we prefer to think that

'the Son of man' should be interpreted personally rather than communally.

iii. **The transfiguration (ix. 2–8).** See notes on Mt. xvii. 1–8; Lk. ix. 28–36. This is the second occasion on which the Lord took the three disciples into special intimacy with Himself (cf. v. 37). The *high mountain* (2) is nowhere named but is generally conjectured to have been Mount Hermon (9,200 feet), about twelve miles north-east of Caesarea Philippi. The time was probably at night (Lk. ix. 32), though Luke is careful to emphasize that the disciples were thoroughly awake when it happened. Hypotheses advanced in explanation of the phenomena of this event differ widely, ranging from those which attribute no more than a legendary or symbolic value to the story, or explain it as a resurrection story read back into the earthly life of Jesus, to the other extreme of the spiritualists who claim it as a séance. In reply to the latter it may be pointed out that there was no communication from Moses and Elijah to the disciples, and the subject of discussion was the cross (Lk. ix. 31), not usually a topic at séances! The behaviour of Peter is thoroughly true to life and argues strongly for the historical character of the narrative, as does also the appropriateness of the story in its context. Dr. Campbell Morgan considered that what the disciples saw was not the effulgence of deity but the glory of sinless and perfected humanity, that the Lord at that moment was ready to return into heaven again, without dying (for death is the result of sin, and He was sinless), but 'for the second time turned His back upon heaven, in order that, as perfected Man, He might share in the mystery of human death'. But the transfiguration, while an event of tremendous significance in itself touching the Person of Jesus, also played an important part in the spiritual education of the disciples and profoundly impressed the early Church (2 Pet. i. 16–18). It confirmed their faith, which may well have begun to waver after the revelations of viii. 31, 34. It showed that in fact the conception of a suffering Messiah was not contrary to the Old Testament revelation, but accorded well with the testimony of the Law and Prophets of whom Moses and Elijah were representatives. It urged the importance of listening to the Lord (7) when He spoke of His approaching passion (cf. Dt. xviii. 15); this Peter had been unwilling to do (viii. 32).

iv. **The descent from the mount (ix. 9–13).** See notes on Mt. xvii. 9–13. For the last time we meet the command to keep silence, this time with the resurrection as a time-limit. The concealment of the Lord's Messiahship had been necessary because of the current political and materialistic expectations. But once He had died and risen again, the danger of seeing in Him a Messiah of this world was over. The question of verse 11 arose from the presence of Elijah at the transfiguration. In reply the Lord made two things clear: first that 'Elijah' had already come in the person of John the Baptist and had been rejected and killed. *As it is written of him* (13) must refer to the persecutions Elijah endured (1 Ki. xix. 1–3). John had found his Ahab and Jezebel in Herod and Herodias. Secondly, the Son of man would suffer the same fate as His forerunner. Verse 12b should be read, with RV, as a direct and not an indirect question.

v. The epileptic boy (ix. 14–29). See notes on Mt. xvii. 14–21; Lk. ix. 37–42. The contrast between the glory of the mountain and the scene of human tragedy and failure in the valley has often been observed and is probably intentional. In view of verse 9 we conclude that it was the opportuneness of the Lord's unexpected arrival that occasioned the amazement of the people (15), rather than any remaining traces of the celestial glory. Modern medical science would probably regard the case as one of epilepsy; but that is not incompatible with the view that the malady was caused by the presence of a demon with whom Christ directly deals. We have already noted Mark's special interest in such miracles of exorcism (see on i. 21–28 and v. 1–20), and his account here is distinctive for its wealth of vivid detail. The group in the valley represents the world in miniature: youth in the grip of evil, parental anguish, nine disciples to whom the necessary power had been given (vi. 7) so that they ought not to have failed, but who, for certain reasons they were later to learn, were helpless before the challenge of this need, and finally *the scribes questioning with them* (14), a collection of critical and hostile religionists. It is easy to criticize the failure of others and do nothing ourselves. Before such a situation the Lord first expresses His distress, describing the whole company as an unbelieving generation (19). Cf. Heb. xii. 3. Nevertheless, infinite forbearance is His, *How long shall I suffer you?* and infinite compassion, *bring him unto me* (19). It is remarkable that Jesus should have left the boy in his distress while He engaged in conversation with the father (20–24). This was evidently to lead the father to the point of faith first. The word *believe* should be omitted from verse 23 (see RV). Jesus takes up the father's doubting words, *if thou canst* (22), and flings them back at him. The father responds to the challenge, *Lord, I believe* (24), but feeling the very weakness of his faith casts himself all the more upon Jesus. *The people* in verse 25 (RV 'a multitude') are not necessarily the same as the crowd in verse 14 from whom apparently Christ and the father had withdrawn while the boy was being fetched.

If we have failed, the wisest thing is not to set up a committee of inquiry, or even to discuss our problems among ourselves, but to ask the Master, privately. This the disciples did. Comparing Matthew's account here (Mt. xvii. 19–21) we find the Lord gave three reasons for failure: lack of faith—unbelief deterred them from using the power they had been given; lack of prayer—perhaps they were so stunned by the announcement of the cross that they forgot to

pray and were thus out of touch with God; lack of self-discipline (fasting). The words *and fasting* (29) are omitted by Codices Sinaiticus and Vaticanus, and are said by some to have been added in the interests of early asceticism. But the evidence against them is not conclusive. The meaning is that only prayerfulness and strict self-discipline can make a man competent to deal with such cases.

l. Rebukes and warnings (ix. 30–50)

i. **Second prediction of the passion (ix. 30–37).** See notes on Mt. xvii. 22, 23, xviii. 1–6; Lk. ix. 43–48. At this point the final journey southward towards Jerusalem and the passion begins. The reason for the secrecy preserved was probably twofold: first the fact that the Galilean ministry was now ended; secondly, the desire to instruct the disciples. *For he taught his disciples* (31); that is, His coming passion was the constant theme along the road. The second prediction of the cross follows (cf. viii. 29–31). *Delivered* (31) has reference to the divine action rather than the treachery of Judas. The thought is that of Paul in Rom. viii. 32. Once more the disciples failed to comprehend, *and were afraid to ask him* (32). Undoubtedly the reason was their preoccupation with prospects of political power (34). Their dispute may have arisen out of the privilege accorded to the three who were specially chosen to witness the transfiguration. Such is human nature that even the highest spiritual privileges may engender pride. The cardinal sin is pride, and there are times when God has to take drastic steps to secure that humility in us which is of paramount worth to Him (cf. 2 Cor. xii. 7). 'Humility is the ornament of angels, and pride the deformity of devils' wrote William Jenkyn, an old Puritan. The Lord's answer (35–37), first in plain words, then by means of a child as an object lesson, is at once an encouragement to all parents and teachers and any who have the care of little children, and at the same time a rebuke to proud ambition.

ii. **Lessons in discipleship (ix. 38–50).** These verses contain a miscellaneous collection of sayings of Jesus, which are distributed in various forms and different contexts in the other Gospels. This suggests that, while they are all genuine, they have nevertheless been assembled editorially here by Mark and were not necessarily spoken on the same occasion. If we look for some common theme linking them together, we may say that there are two groups, the first (verses 38–42) dealing with the duty of mutual charity and toleration, and the second (verses 43–50) dealing with the need for personal discipline. The first governs the disciple's attitude to others, the second his attitude to himself. Towards others he must be charitable, towards himself strict. Unlike the exorcists of Acts xix. 13–16, the man described by John (38) was at least sincere and successful, in however defective a way; and if lives are being blessed and delivered from the power of evil, such work ought not to be hindered. There is no more forthright rebuke of ecclesiastical intolerance than this. Even a much less spectacular service from the right motive shall earn its reward (41). Possibly the disciples' discouragement of the man had in fact caused him to stumble and this accounts for the stern warning of verse 42. A *millstone* (Gk. *mylos onikos*) is one large enough to require an ass to turn it. The language of the second group of sayings is obviously figurative. 'We must shrink from no spiritual surgery to save the life of the soul' (J. D. Jones). The word *hell* (43, 45, 47) is the Greek *geenna*, which must be carefully distinguished from another word normally so rendered in av, namely *Hades*, the abode of departed spirits (Lk. xvi. 23). *Geenna* is a loose transliteration of the Hebrew *Ge-Hinnom*, 'the valley of Hinnom', a gorge just outside Jerusalem which had in ancient times been the scene of human sacrifices (Je. vii. 31), but later, during the reforms of Josiah (2 Ki. xxiii. 10), became the refuse heap of the city. It was a natural metaphor for the place of future punishment. At least fourteen or fifteen possible explanations have been advanced of the obscure verse 49, the latter half of which should probably be omitted (as in rv) on the textual evidence, as being an attempt to explain the preceding statement on the basis of Lv. ii. 13. It is probably a challenging word on the purifying value of suffering, which would be particularly relevant to the church at Rome facing persecution. In which case, the fire of verse 49 has nothing to do with that of verse 48 (which is destructive rather than purificatory), and *every one* (49) means every disciple. The connection of verse 50 seems to be purely verbal and artificial, for *salt* here is used in its more familiar sense of the grace of Christian character.

III. THE JOURNEY TO JERUSALEM.
x. 1–52

The geography of the first verse is complicated somewhat by textual uncertainty. What is probably the best reading has 'the borders of Judaea and beyond Jordan' which may mean the region of southern Palestine on both sides of the river. At all events, the teaching and incidents here described are to be thought of as taking place in the course of the journey.

a. On marriage and divorce (x. 2–12)

See also Mt. xix. 3–12. Once again the question put by the Pharisees was malicious, *tempting him* (2). Divorce was a matter of dispute at the time, and there were two distinct schools of thought. The Mosaic enactment (Dt. xxiv. 1–4) stated that a husband was allowed to give his wife a writing of divorcement if he had found some unseemly thing in her. The question turned upon what constituted an unseemly thing. The school of Shammai maintained the strict interpretation of this, that the marriage bond was indissoluble except in the event of the wife's infidelity. That of Hillel took the liberal view allowing divorce

for almost any cause. In reply, Jesus first pointed out that Moses' legislation was a concession to human weakness and rightly introduced to regulate divorce in a defective state of society (5). Secondly, He took them back beyond Moses to God's ideal at the beginning, from which we discover that marriage was instituted as the divine ideal for man and woman, and that the bond is permanent and indissoluble (6–9). When, later, His disciples questioned Him in private about the matter, He took them further in order to indicate that in this particular the sexes are on equal terms. Jewish law did not allow a wife to divorce her husband. Verse 12 is therefore an innovation. It is not possible to comment exhaustively on this complicated question as it affects modern society. Something depends upon the view we take of the exceptive clause introduced by Matthew (Mt. v. 32, xix. 9). Suffice it to say that, while the teaching of Jesus to unbelievers moves on one level and, without in any way lowering the divine ideal, can be interpreted as endorsing the Mosaic concession, yet to the disciples it moves on a higher level at which, undoubtedly, the individual believer must reckon with it. Paul's development of the subject in 1 Cor. vii. 10–16 is designed to meet the new situation in the Church of the post-marital conversion of one partner. The individual Christian need not be left in doubt. But 'for its own protection and well-being society will do well to be guided by His positive teaching in defining grounds for divorce which threaten personal and family life' (Vincent Taylor).

b. On childhood (x. 13–16)

See Mt. xix. 13–15; Lk. xviii. 15–17. The subject follows naturally from that of marriage, which leads modern commentators to think that its insertion here is topical. It is difficult to resist the attractiveness of the older suggestion, however, which associates the children with the house in verse 10. They 'were brought to Him to say good-night, and receive His blessing before being sent to bed' (Salmon). The Lord is the Defender both of womanhood and of childhood; and when the disciples, true to their materialistic ideas of the kingdom, attempted to drive the children away, *he was much displeased* (14). This is the only occasion where this word (Gk. *aganaktein*, implying anger) is predicated of Jesus. The disciples had a wrong estimate both of the worth of a child and of the nature of the kingdom. As to the first, it is not necessary for a child to become an adult before participating in the kingdom; rather the reverse is the case, the adult must be converted, turn back, and become a child (cf. Mt. xviii. 3). As to the second, the kingdom is not a matter of achievement or merit; we must *receive the kingdom of God* (15) as a gift, and this is where the child has the advantage. The point is not that it is innocent or humble, which it may not be, but that it is receptive and willing to be dependent upon others. And so Jesus took up the children *and blessed them* (16). It is a delightful picture conveyed by the strong compound word in Greek (*kateulogei*), occurring nowhere else in the New Testament: 'He blessed them fervently, again and again.'

c. On riches (x. 17–31)

See notes on Mt. xix. 16–29; Lk. xviii. 18–30. It is Luke who tells us that this man was a 'ruler', though of what seems uncertain. His youth is rather against his being ruler of a synagogue. There are several indications of the attractiveness of his character, apart from his own words (20) which constitute no mean claim (cf. Phil. iii. 6). Mark adds the details that he *came . . . running, and kneeled* (17), which suggests both eagerness and respect. But his form of address, *Good Master*, was a very unusual one, quite unknown among Jews to a rabbi, and perhaps intended as a fulsome compliment. In Mark the expression *eternal life*, so common in the Johannine writings, occurs only here and at verse 30, and whether it has in this passage the full Johannine connotation of a present possession is at least doubtful. In the mind of the young man it probably had an eschatological meaning of life in the age to come, which a man inherits. Verse 30 confirms this. Of such life he could feel no sense of security despite all he had attempted to do. In answer, Jesus took up a word the man had used, and threw it back upon him for consideration (cf. ix. 23n.). The theological implications of this answer (18) have been variously understood. Many of the Fathers and some modern commentators have taken the view that Jesus was trying to lead him to a perception of His divinity; as much as to say 'God alone is really good; and as you do not believe I am God, but only a teacher, I cannot accept that epithet from you'. But it is extremely doubtful whether the man would have understood this at all. Strictly, the theological implications are secondary; and in so far as there are such, the meaning probably is that in an absolute sense goodness belongs to God the Father alone. By contrast, the goodness of Jesus was in some sense subject to growth and testing in the circumstances of the incarnation wherein He learned obedience by the things which He suffered (Heb. v. 8). So H. R. Mackintosh (*The Doctrine of the Person of Christ*, p. 37). But the primary bearing of the words is upon the need of the man who, despite his sense of insecurity for the future, nevertheless felt himself to have attained a measure of goodness judged by the standards of the law (20). What he now expected was to be told to undertake something difficult and exceptionally meritorious, to make good anything that might be lacking. It is this popular idea of meritorious goodness, than which there is no sin more subtle, that our Lord attacks. The lesson to be learnt is that human attainment, such as he relied upon, can produce nothing 'good' in God's sight (Rom. vii. 18). It is still true that perfect obedience to the law without failure or deviation would mean eternal life; but see Jas. ii. 10, 11. In fact this man was breaking the first and greatest commandment; for his possessions were his god. Therefore Jesus administers to him a liberal dose of the law as his 'schoolmaster' to bring him to Christ that he might be justified not by works but by faith (Gal. iii. 24). The command to sell his possessions is accordingly not of general application; it concerned this man in particular. Neither did Jesus promise him eternal life in return for the sacrifice of his riches; but only a secure treasure in return for an insecure one. The way of life is to dispose of anything that hinders and then to follow continuously (21; Gk. *akolouthei*—present imperative). It is quite possible to part with one's possessions in some good cause without becoming a follower (1 Cor. xiii. 3). We do not know whether this man ever thought better of it and returned. An interesting conjecture is that he did, and that his name was Barnabas.

In verses 23–27 some textual variations should be noted. First, in verse 24 the words *for them that trust in riches* should be omitted (so RV mg., RSV). Secondly, the Western Text reverses the order of verses 24 and 25. With these alterations the conversation moves smoothly and logically to the climactic statement in verse 27. The disciples were astonished when Jesus pointed out how difficult it is for a rich man to enter the kingdom, for it was the prevalent opinion in Judaism that riches were a mark of divine favour, as with Job. (Verse 25 is familiar Eastern hyperbole and need not be otherwise explained.) When He went on to repeat the statement in tender tone (*Children*, 24) but stronger form, that it is difficult for anyone, rich or poor, they were even more amazed. But, after all, it is the fundamental proposition of the gospel that salvation is with men impossible, but not with God (27). It is the gift of God which money cannot buy; for rich and poor alike it is a miracle of divine grace.

In the meantime Peter had been making some characteristic mental calculations and began to compare himself and his fellows favourably with the rich man (28). *We* is emphatic. Jesus in reply used figurative language to state the truth that He will be no man's debtor either in time or eternity (29, 30); but neither will He encourage a bargaining spirit among those who profess to follow and serve Him. Hence the warning added (31), which may be compared with Mt. xx. 1–16 in the same context.

d. The third prediction of the passion (x. 32–34)

Cf. Mt. xx. 17–19; Lk. xviii. 31–34. The journey draws near to its close, and we have depicted here, in an atmosphere of deepening solemnity, a striking procession—Jesus walking ahead, alone, after the manner of an oriental shepherd (cf. Jn. x. 4); then apparently two separate companies, the Twelve, awestruck, and further back a group of casual followers who have an indefinite presentiment that something is impending (32a; cf. Moff). Once more the Twelve are drawn aside and the unwelcome subject renewed, this time in the most explicit terms of all (32b–34). For the first time it is made clear that both Jews and Gentiles are to have a hand in this thing, the Jews to condemn and the Gentiles to execute. The latter, had the disciples understood it, is tantamount to a disclosure that His death would be by crucifixion. Matthew (Mt. xx. 19) so records it.

e. The request of James and John (x. 35–45)

See notes on Mt. xx. 20–28. From such solemn reflections the transition to this ambitious request is almost abrupt. Nothing could better illustrate the danger of having a mind pre-occupied with petty thoughts of self at a time when big things are happening in the spiritual realm. Matthew puts the request into the mouth of the mother of James and John. She was Salome, and seems to have been the sister of Christ's mother (xv. 40; Mt. xxvii. 56; Jn. xix. 25). James and John would therefore be first cousins to Jesus. What has been well described as 'the first ecclesiastical intrigue for high places in the Church' doubtless began as a family attempt to steal a march on Peter, the third member of the inner trio. But Jesus, as Bengel finely put it, was dwelling on His passion, knowing that He was first to have others on His right hand and on His left; and all the time their minds were in another world. Using therefore the poetic terms of the cup and the baptism, familiar from the Old Testament (Ps. xi. 6; Is. li. 17; Pss. xlii. 7, lxix. 1, cxxiv. 4, 5), as descriptions of suffering and immersion in overwhelming sorrow, He tried to lead them to see what lay between Him and His glory and therefore between them and the realization of their desire. Their bold assertion *We can* (39) is as ignorant as their request; but Jesus took them at their word as they both lived to discover afterwards (Acts xii. 2; Rev. i. 9). Nevertheless the place of their ambition was in the right of the Father alone to bestow, and that not by favouritism but on the basis of fitness of character (40). As little could an umpire promise the first two prizes to two runners in a race, as could Jesus promise to them the chief places in the kingdom. They might indeed obtain them, but it would be because they were worthy and not as a personal favour.

When the ten heard it (41) they displayed little better grace than the ambitious two, for they were by no means content to be last. Yet again, therefore, Jesus took them all aside to repeat the lesson they had already been taught (ix. 33ff.) and to put to them in plainest terms the essential difference between worldly greatness and spiritual greatness. In the world—and the words are as true a reflection of society in this modern age as in any—men delight to domineer and 'lord it' (42, RV and Moff.) over one another, using personal influence to secure private advancement. In the kingdom, true greatness flows from lowly and voluntary service.

But the unique fact about Jesus is that without any exception He practised what He preached; He is the embodiment of His own ethic. We therefore find these principles gathered up now in a saying concerning Himself which is one of the most important in the Gospels, and certainly the key verse of this Gospel (45). For the suggestion that the saying is unhistorical and a product of Pauline influence see *Introduction*, p. 807. It is one of the earliest explicit statements of the purpose of Christ's coming, and defines His work as being in two parts: first *to minister* and secondly *to give*. This, we may note in passing, also provides a simple division of this Gospel, the first part as far as x. 31 dealing with the ministry or service of the Son, and the remainder dealing with the ransom or sacrifice of the Son. Our main interest, however, centres in the remarkable phrase *a ransom for many* (Gk. *lytron anti pollōn*). There is little doubt that Jesus has in mind the predictions of Is. liii, which tell of the work of the Suffering Servant of Jehovah in order to redeem men from evil. The figure of ransom means to deliver by paying a price and should be understood in the light of other sayings of Jesus which imply that the soul of man may become lost or forfeit. Here, for example, is the divine answer to the humanly unanswerable question of viii. 37. Jesus came 'to lay down His own life as a ransom price that those to whom these forfeited lives belonged might obtain them again' (James Denney, *The Death of Christ*, 1951, p. 33). The word *ransom* (*lytron*) occurs elsewhere only in compounds; e.g. 1 Tim. ii. 6 (*antilytron hyper pantōn*), where also it is followed by a different preposition of less intensive force. The use of the Greek preposition *anti* in this case clearly indicates the substitutionary character of the work of Christ. The force of the two prepositions together may be well illustrated by the action of a signatory for an illiterate person. He does what the other cannot (*hyper*, on behalf of) and what the other therefore need not (*anti*, instead of). The word *many* (*pollōn*) is a probable allusion to Is. liii. 11, 12, and is intended not to limit the scope of the atoning work of Christ as though it applied to many but not all, but to show how a multitude shall derive blessing from the solitary offering of the One (cf. Rom. v. 19). The early Fathers pressed the analogy of this ransom saying too far, by speculating as to who received the price, God or the Evil One. The results were grotesque, even as the speculation is illegitimate. A metaphor is intended to convey only a fragment of the truth.

f. Blind Bartimaeus restored to sight (x. 46–52)

Cf. Mt. xx. 29–34; Lk. xviii. 35–43. There are divergent details in the three accounts of this story which have for long exercised the ingenuity of the harmonizers. Matthew (Mt. xx. 30) speaks of two blind men, while Luke (Lk. xviii. 35) places the incident at the approach to Jericho instead of when Jesus was leaving the city. These differences do not affect anything vital, being such as one would expect to find in all evidence given by trustworthy witnesses. And this is doubtless a case where, if all the facts were known, there would be no difficulty of reconciliation.

Besides being in all its details an excellent parable of the gospel, the healing of the blind man was a work of messianic significance (Is. xxxv. 5), and is evidently introduced here by Mark with that in mind. Bartimaeus addressed Jesus by a messianic title, *son of David* (48), and is the first in this Gospel to do so. The whole incident was a prelude to the public presentation of the Messiah. Yet despite this movement of the divine programme and purpose which took Jesus steadily towards Jerusalem, it is remarkable that He was halted by this impassioned cry of need (49). God is always responsive to such a cry characterized, as this was, by determination (48), definiteness (51) and faith (52). The vivid picture, drawn in a few rapid strokes in verse 50, is peculiar to Mark. At first the question put by Jesus, *What wilt thou that I should do unto thee?* (51), sounds superfluous to a blind man; but it probably had the twofold purpose of making him define his need, and also of demonstrating to the crowd that this time he was not merely begging for money. The same question had been put previously to James and John (36), but received a very different response. This was Christ's only visit to Jericho.

IV. THE PASSION WEEK. xi. 1—xv. 47

a. The entry into Jerusalem and opening events (xi. 1–26)

With the exception of the last few verses dealing with the ascension, the entire remainder of the Gospel from this point is occupied with the narration of events which took place within the space of eight days. By comparison, the events recorded hitherto cover a space of three years. This disproportionate literary ratio is preserved more or less by all the evangelists, and is an indication of where the emphasis lay in the gospel of the early Church. In the language of Dr. James Denney, the centre of gravity in apostolic preaching was not Bethlehem but Calvary; not the life of our Lord, but His death; not His example but His expiation; not His teaching but His atonement.

i. **The triumphal entry (xi. 1–11).** Cf. Mt. xxi. 1–11; Lk. xix. 29–39; Jn. xii. 12–15. *Bethphage* (1) is named by all synoptists in this connection, but the name occurs nowhere else in the Old Testament or New Testament, although it is frequent in rabbinic literature, and means 'house of figs'. Its locality is uncertain. Neither is it clear whether *the village over against you* (2) is Bethphage or Bethany, though it might well be either. There is no need to understand verse 2 as indicating supernatural knowledge on the part of Jesus; the simpler view is that He had an arrangement with the owner, who was perhaps

an anonymous disciple like 'the goodman of the house' (xiv. 14). *Whereon never man sat* was one of the general conditions of consecration to Jehovah (Nu. xix. 2; 1 Sa. vi. 7). Plummer points out that the virgin birth and the burial in a new tomb are facts of the same kind. Some expositors prefer to regard *the Lord* (3; Gk. *ho kyrios*) as referring to the owner of the animal, as we might say, 'its master', on the ground that the title is not used of Jesus at all until after the resurrection, and then only by Luke and John. But there is an air of artificiality about such a message being put into the mouths of the disciples, and it was after all Jesus Himself who needed the colt. He regards Himself as having a certain sovereignty over the possessions of His followers even though He will not take them by force. With this agrees well the variant reading represented by RV mg.: 'And straightway he sendeth him back hither.' Jesus promised to return the colt as soon as possible. Such was His poverty that even for this occasion He had to borrow an animal to ride upon. But it was not a mark of His humiliation that the animal was an ass, for an ass is quite in keeping in biblical thought with a royal personage coming peaceably, and this is indeed the real significance of the triumphal entry.

It represented first a fulfilment of Zc. ix. 9, recognizable as such by the people; secondly, an open and deliberate assertion of Messiahship; the hour was approaching when He would be rejected and the issue must now be made plain. Either He is King, or a mistake lies at the roots of His life. He must be rejected as Messiah-King. The need for concealment was now past. Thirdly, the manner of His entry expressed the character of His Messiahship, for here was in fact no military conqueror upon a war-horse, or political revolutionary of the kind the Jews expected. His purpose was not the overthrow of Rome but the breaking of the power of sin. The cry *Hosanna* (9) is a transliteration of the Hebrew of Ps. cxviii. 25, 'Save now'. It is remarkable that Mark does not translate it, but it had probably become a general expression of praise and salutation, as familiar in common parlance as 'Rabbi'.

On arrival in the capital city Jesus went at once to the temple, which He is depicted as surveying with authority. His work had to do not with the politics and wars of Israel, but with its religion. Finally, He retired to Bethany for the night (12). This was His procedure every night of the passion week, camping out on the Mount of Olives (cf. Mt. xxi. 17).

ii. **The barren fig tree (xi. 12–14, 20–26).** Cf. Mt. xxi. 18–22. In Mark this story is in two parts, divided by that of the temple cleansing. The miracle has aroused criticism from modern scholars on two grounds: first the unreasonableness of our Lord's action in looking for figs at Passover time, secondly that such an action associated with His own hunger is both unlikely and unworthy of Him. The usual explanation is to say that a parable like that of the fig tree in Lk. xiii. 6–9 has reappeared in factual form; against which it has to be said that neither the details nor the meaning are the same. As to the first of the two objections, the probable explanation is that the fig tree in Palestine bears an early crop of immature fruit, like green knobs, which appears before the leaves. These are known as *taksh*, and are the common food of peasants. Their absence was clear indication of the barrenness of the tree. As to the second objection, we may note that this was Christ's only miracle of judgment, performed 'in mercy to man, on an inanimate object, to teach a moral lesson' (T. M. Lindsay). The fig tree was a symbol of the Jewish nation, which abounded in the leaves of religious profession but was barren of the fruits of righteousness. Its cursing was prophetic of the fate of the Jewish authorities who were now about to reject their Messiah.

The following day, Peter was startled by the rapidity with which the Lord's word had taken effect (21), and from the incident Jesus drew for His disciples a lesson on the effectiveness of prayer (24). Prevailing prayer turns upon two conditions, one governing our relation to God and the other our relation to others. The first is faith (22). *Have faith in God* (Gk. *echete pistin theou*) means 'Have a faith which rests on God'. With such you will be able to challenge and remove mountains of obstruction in the way of God's purpose. With verse 23 cf. Zc. iv. 7. The second is forgiveness (25, 26). The words apply, of course, to the spirit and attitude of the believer when he prays. They do not make God's forgiveness of the sinner, in the evangelical sense, depend upon the sinner's forgiveness of others first (see Eph. iv. 32).

iii. **The cleansing of the temple (xi. 15–19).** See notes on Mt. xxi. 12–17; Lk. xix. 45–47. The tendency among some modern scholars is to identify this incident, recorded by all the synoptists at the beginning of passion week, with that placed by John right at the beginning of the ministry (Jn. ii. 13–17), though whether Mark's or John's placing of it is the correct one is a matter upon which opinion is sharply divided. By far the most satisfactory solution is that Jesus cleansed the temple twice. There is nothing improbable about this; indeed it is likely that the evil would revive after a first cleansing. It would agree also with John's general plan of supplementing the synoptists, and would account for important differences of detail (e.g. the scourge) in his narrative.

The sight that met His eyes the previous evening (11) must have led Jesus to take this course. But it was also yet another function of the Messiah (see Mal. iii. 1–4). The scene of action was the Court of the Gentiles where there was a market for the sale of temple requisites and an exchange to provide Jewish coinage, since the temple dues might not be paid in heathen money. These apparently reasonable amenities had opened the door to extortion by the hierarchy and to all the contentious bargaining of an oriental bazaar where the pilgrims were defrauded. There were also those, apparently, who used the precinct as a short cut between the city and the Mount of Olives (16), a detail noted only by Mark. We may well picture the confusion caused by Jesus' action, and just as we are entering upon the period when He meekly surrendered to His foes it is valuable to be thus vividly reminded of His capacity for moral indignation. Having cleared the market, He began to teach (17), basing His teaching upon two Old Testament passages, Is. lvi. 7 and Je. vii. 11, the former of which, significantly, has special reference to the provision of a place of prayer and worship for the Gentiles. Yet in face of this, the authorities were still powerless to take any immediate action because of the popularity of Jesus with the multitude (18). But every day during this last week, when He was a 'wanted man', *he went out of the city* as evening fell (19).

b. **Teaching in Jerusalem (xi. 27—xii. 44)**

i. **The question of authority (xi. 27–33).** Cf. Mt. xxi. 23–27; Lk. xx. 1–8. *They come again to Jerusalem*, probably later in the same day as verse 20. It was the Tuesday, and, in view of all that follows, it has been called 'The day of questions'. Such drastic interference as the cleansing of the temple quite naturally led the Jewish leaders to call Jesus to account on the question of His authority. If He claimed Messiahship, He should in their view have attacked the Romans first, not the Jews. *These things* (28) refers not only to the events of the previous day, but also to the whole career of Jesus which they considered had been one continual conflict with lawful authority. Yet their question was put not from the motive of protecting the public from an impostor. They sought to trap Him fatally. For Him to claim divine authority would, so they thought, amount to blasphemy; to claim authority as son of David would be treason against Rome; to disclaim all authority would prove Him an impostor. His reply (29) was in no sense an evasion or clever piece of fencing. It was merely tracing the issue a stage further back, for the right answer to His question would also answer theirs and would, moreover, show whether they had any capacity to test moral authority. John the Baptist had borne testimony to Jesus as the Messiah. If they acknowledged him to be a prophet with divine authority, the answer to their question was plain, and they would see that the authority of Jesus was derived from the same source. The ministry of John was one of high public importance upon which men in their position should be competent to pronounce. When therefore they pleaded ignorance on a matter of such magnitude they virtually abdicated from their office as teachers of the nation, and had no further right to question the authority of Jesus. Our Lord, therefore, did not reply to their question directly. Instead He provided the complete answer in the parable that follows.

ii. The parable of the wicked husbandmen (xii. 1–12). See also Mt. xxi. 33–46. The chapter division here is unfortunate, since the parable arises out of the challenge of the chief priests. Its scope is remarkably comprehensive, covering the centuries of Israel's past history, depicting the present situation of conflict, and pointing to its future issues. As a national symbol of Israel, the vineyard was familiar from the Old Testament (Is. v. 1–7) and would quickly be so understood. The hedge (Gk. *phragmos*) to give protection from wild animals, the *place for the winefat* (Gk. *hypolēnion*), a vessel or trough to gather the juice of the pressed grapes, and the *tower* (Gk. *pyrgos*), a wooden booth on a high platform for a watchman, are all necessary elements in the story exhibiting collectively the care bestowed by the landlord, but without further significance individually. The lesson is, first, that to this nation has been sent through the centuries a succession of servants in the Old Testament prophets, culminating in John the Baptist, all of whom have looked for the fruits of repentance and righteousness (cf. Lk. iii. 8). Last of all has come One who is not merely another in the line of servants, but the only begotten and beloved Son and Heir, invested with all the authority of His Father (6). At verse 7 the parable becomes prophetic, first of the cross involving the rejection of the Messiah by His own people, secondly (9) of the judgment that would overtake the nation at the destruction of Jerusalem in A.D. 70, thirdly (10, 11) of the final triumph and exaltation of the Son. The words *and will give the vineyard unto others* (9) refer to the extension of Israel's privileges to the Gentiles (cf. Mt. xxi. 43). The change of figure from the vineyard to the corner stone (10) makes possible the allusion to the resurrection, for where the slain son could not be revived, the rejected stone can be exalted. The Old Testament reference is to Ps. cxviii, the 'Hosanna' Psalm, part of which had been sung at the triumphal entry (xi. 9, 10). *Builders* are experts who should have known better. It has been objected against the parable that the behaviour of the husbandmen is contrary to natural probability. But is it any more unnatural or unreasonable than the unbelief it is meant to illustrate?

iii. On tribute to Caesar (xii. 13–17). See notes on Mt. xxii. 15–22; Lk. xx. 20–26. For the second time the Pharisees are found in alliance with the Herodians who were their political opponents (see iii. 6n.). Their common purpose was *to catch* (Gk. *agreusōsin*, a hunting metaphor, 'to snare, entrap') *him in his words* (13). Their question, put with flattery, concerned the Roman taxes so hateful to the Jews as a sign of their subjection. It involved the usual dilemma wherein an affirmative reply would disgust the people and a negative one would bring Him into trouble with the Romans. Jesus' answer is one of several on this 'day of questions' which display His unassailable wisdom and perfection, and one which has profoundly influenced all subsequent thought on the ethical problem of the attitude of the Christian to the State. The whole principle laid down turns on the change of wording from *give* (15) to *render* (17). 'It was not a question of giving what might lawfully be refused, but of paying what was lawfully claimed. The tribute was not a gift but a debt. Caesar gave them the inestimable benefit of stable government; were they to take it and decline to pay anything towards its maintenance?' (Plummer). Duty to God and duty to the State are not incompatible; we owe a debt to both, and it is certainly possible to be a good Christian and a loyal citizen. This answer would be of particular interest to Mark's Roman readers, since it acquits Christianity of the charge of disloyalty to the State. We may compare the teaching of Paul in Rom. xiii. 1–7.

iv. On the resurrection (xii. 18–27). See notes on Mt. xxii. 23–33; Lk. xx. 27–40. This is Mark's only reference to the Sadducees whom he introduces with a word of explanation (18). They were a priestly aristocracy, less numerous than the Pharisees and less popular. Religiously they were the rationalists of the day, although conservative in their attitude to the Scriptures in the sense that they denied the validity of the oral tradition which the Pharisees held to be binding. They took their stand particularly upon the authority of the Pentateuch. They were therefore as obnoxious to the Pharisees on religious grounds as were the Herodians on political grounds. But the Pharisees were willing to work with either for the destruction of Jesus. It may be, however, that the Sadducees now hoped to succeed where their adversaries had failed. Their question was less dangerous than the previous one, being a matter of exegesis and speculation rather than politics, doctrinal rather than ethical. The fantastic story they told was doubtless intended to draw Jesus into ridicule. It was based on the law of levirate marriage in Dt. xxv. 5–10, the purpose of which was to prevent the eventuality of a man dying without posterity —a calamity of the first order to a Jew. Our Lord's reply deals first with the manner of the resurrection (24, 25), pointing out that marriage on the physical side, to which the levirate law relates, is relevant only in the world where death prevails and so makes necessary the perpetuation of the race. Life in the next world is not a mere repetition of present conditions. In one sense, the particular question of the Sadducees is of little concern to us today, but objections arising from the difficulty of conceiving a resurrection are still current. It is argued that a resurrection would involve conditions that are incredible. The answer to all such objections is the plain one, *Ye know not . . . the power of God* (24). The Lord then proceeds from the manner to the fact of the resurrection (26, 27), skilfully drawing His proof from the Pentateuch so greatly cherished by the Sadducees.

Long after the patriarchs had died, God spoke of Himself as enjoying a relationship with them which remained intimate and permanent. 'The passage suggests the one consideration which above all others confirms the modern Christian in his belief in life after death; for to him this hope is based, not on Platonic arguments concerning the nature of the soul, but upon the experience of communion with God' (Vincent Taylor, *ad loc.*).

v. On the first commandment (xii. 28–34). See Mt. xxii. 34–40, 46; cf. Lk. x. 25–28. This further question, a moral one, is obviously introduced here by Mark as having been asked on the same occasion; it is not inserted merely for topical reasons although belonging chronologically to the Galilean ministry, as some have suggested. The scribe exhibited qualities not apparent in other questioners. He was sincere and intelligent; yet this did not suffice to bring him into the kingdom. His question—lit. 'What kind of commandment (Gk. *poia entolē*) is first of all?'—presupposes a difference in importance between commandments or classes of commandments. Rabbis divided the precepts of the law into 'weighty' and 'light', but the allocation of them into these categories caused much debate. Or possibly the scribe had in mind the distinction between moral and ritual commands (cf. verse 33). The answer of Jesus is remarkable for the fact that it brings together two widely separated Scriptures (which, so far as we know, have never been so associated by any other writer in Scripture or beyond it) to sum up the duty of man. Yet both were very familiar. The first, Dt. vi. 4, 5, was called the *Shema*, and would normally be recited twice daily by the questioner himself. It was the commandment actually worn in phylacteries, and sometimes nailed to doorposts in literal obedience to Dt. vi. 8, 9. The second is given in the exact words of the LXX from Lv. xix. 18. The two are summed up in the one word 'love', first toward God, then toward man; love conceived not as an emotional sentiment but as an active principle embracing the entire personality (30). It is probably true to say that in modern times men lay great emphasis on love to man, or philanthropy, but are inclined to forget the requirement of love to God. Our Lord links the two and gives primacy to the latter. 'Philanthropy' is no substitute for 'religion', but should flow from it.

vi. On the Son of David (xii. 35–37a). Cf. Mt. xxii. 41–45; Lk. xx. 41–44. It is the turn of Jesus Himself to ask a question. The reason He does so is not, as some have suggested, to deny His birth in Bethlehem from the line of David, but to teach that He is in fact far more than 'son of David'; He is Lord. To do this He quotes from Ps. cx. 1, the Davidic authorship of which is generally denied by modern criticism. An interesting critical problem is therefore raised, and it is surprising to what subtleties of argument critics will allow themselves to be driven rather than jettison the theory that the Psalm is not Davidic. It is impossible to state the position fully here, but we may observe that, whereas in other instances the validity of our Lord's pronouncements on questions of Old Testament authorship may be held not to affect His argument, in this case His whole argument turns upon it. It 'is not drawn from the august language of the Psalm, but from David's relationship to the Messiah, and crumbles to pieces if he is not the singer' (Alexander Maclaren). We hold, therefore, that our Lord's attribution of the Psalm to David must foreclose the question of authorship for all who accept His authority. (See also Edersheim, *Life and Times of Jesus the Messiah*, ii, pp. 405f.)

vii. A warning against the scribes (xii. 37b–40). See Lk. xx. 45, 46; cf. Mt. xxiii. 1–39. That *the common people*, or rather 'the great multitude' (RV mg.), the mass of the people, *heard him gladly* (37) is a statement which belongs probably to what follows rather than to what precedes. His teaching still attracted crowds. They were fascinated by His wisdom and perhaps enjoyed seeing the rout of the professional teachers. But nearly all, under pressure, were later prepared to consent to His death. Not all the scribes were equally bad (cf. verse 34), but the general tendency of their class was in the direction of ostentation, avarice and hypocrisy. Let simple folk beware of religion of this kind; moral and spiritual power counts for far more than *long clothing* (38; Gk. *stolais*, 'robes') and officialdom.

viii. The widow's two mites (xii. 41–44). See Lk. xxi. 1–4. This choice story brings welcome relief after the heat of controversy, for here is one who, in the simplicity of her lowly worship, gave to the Lord her all. It is no doubt in place here as to its historical setting, but possibly the saying about devouring widows' houses (40) gave it a topical appropriateness as well. *Jesus sat over against the treasury* (41; Gk. *gazophylakion*; cf. Jn. viii. 20). It is not certain that there was a building so called; but along the colonnade which surrounded the Court of the Women there were thirteen chests with trumpet-shaped openings (Heb. *shopharoth*) provided for the offerings of the worshippers. At some vantage point in full view of this part of the temple Jesus sat, probably wearied by the prolonged disputations of the day. There is a wealth of meaning in the one word *how* (41), for the lesson of the whole story is that our Lord's first concern is not what men give but how they give it. Money in itself has no value in the kingdom of God; so Jesus refused to count totals but looked at the motives of the donor (cf. 2 Cor. viii. 12). Therefore when His eye fell upon the solitary figure of a poor widow who *threw in two mites* (42; Gk. *lepta*, the smallest copper coin in use) which Mark, for the benefit of his Roman readers, computes in terms of Roman coinage as equivalent to a farthing (Gk. *kodrantēs*, a transliteration of the Latin *quadrans*), He called the attention of the disciples to her. In answer to the question how Jesus came to know the amount of her gift, we may reply that He may have discovered by quite ordinary means which are not disclosed, or, as some prefer to think, by supernatural knowledge; but in any case the question is irrelevant to the story. The essence of all true giving is sacrifice, and the value of every gift relative, not absolute.

c. The prophetic discourse (xiii. 1–37)
See notes on Mt. xxiv. 1–51; Lk. xxi. 5–38. It is not possible within the scope of our present purpose to discuss at any length the state of criticism in regard to this great chapter, which is sometimes called the 'Little Apocalypse'. For some time it was a widely accepted hypothesis that the core of the chapter was a small Jewish or Jewish-Christian apocalyptic writing. Two considerations, however, tend to discredit the idea. First, certain characteristics of true apocalyptic are wanting. There is none of the highly figurative language of Daniel or Revelation, featuring strange beasts and visions; also, while apocalyptic is predictive to the almost entire exclusion of moral exhortation, the latter is present here in a marked degree throughout. Secondly, as Edersheim has shown, contemporary Jewish opinion regarding the end-time was utterly different from anything expressed here. Moreover, it is significant that this discourse of our Lord on Mount Olivet is recorded by all the synoptists at considerable length and with substantial agreement as to the main details; they further agree in placing it at the same point in our Lord's ministry (see Mt. xxiv. 1–51; Lk. xxi. 5–38). This indicates that the early Church recognized and accepted it as part of the original gospel tradition.

i. The question of the four disciples (xiii. 1–4). As was His custom at the close of the day, Jesus left the temple and the city. On the way, an unnamed disciple drew attention to the magnificence of the temple buildings. We may imagine that the temple, larger than York Minster, and having a façade of gold, would present a most imposing spectacle from the Mount of Olives. Some of the stones measured as much as thirty feet in length. To the Jew, nothing seemed so stable as this building, the symbol of God's presence with His people. Little wonder that the disciples were astounded to be told that the great edifice should be completely overthrown. Four of them, therefore, the two pairs of brothers who were called at the beginning (i. 16–20), put to Jesus in private a twofold question as to the time and the sign (4) of this terrible calamity. It is not quite clear what *all these things* refers to, and Matthew (Mt. xxiv. 3) expands the question into a threefold one looking on to the end of the age. In any case, from this question flows the discourse that follows in which two major events seem to be in view throughout: first the immediate event in the fall of Jerusalem in A.D. 70, and secondly the ultimate event of the return of Christ in glory. It has frequently been observed that there is a kind of perspective

in the point of view of prophecy, whereby crises of history are seen like mountain ranges portrayed upon a canvas, one behind another, without any cognizance of the tracts of territory between. This chapter, with its two great crises in view, between which already nearly 1900 years have intervened, is an illustration of this principle, and this fact should be borne in mind when seeking to interpret it.

ii. Warnings to disciples (xiii. 5–13). See notes on Mt. xxiv. 4–14; Lk. xxi. 8–19. Some take the view that this section derives from a group of sayings relating to the 'coming' of Christ, or Parousia (a word found only in Mt. xxiv in the Gospels), rather than to A.D. 70, and that therefore it is no part of the original answer to the question in verse 4. It is obvious, however, that Mark intends us to take it as the answer, and we prefer to think that Jesus spoke these words, as He so often did, first for the disciples there present, but also with an eye to the future needs of the Church. He is, as it were, using the events associated with the immediate crisis to foreshadow those connected with the ultimate crisis, and this explains why the two are interwoven so closely. *Jesus . . . began to say, Take heed* (5). The words not only state the main lesson of the chapter (cf. verses 9, 23, 33) but also emphasize the true purpose of all biblical prophecy, which is not speculative but practical, not to enable us to forecast the future but to interpret the present, not to satisfy curiosity but to deliver from perplexity. The disciples are warned against deception. There would be impostors in the religious sphere (6), commotions in the political and international field (7–8a), and calamities in the physical realm (8b); but such things are incidental to the course of the age, and are not necessarily to be taken as the signs of the end. Rather are they *the beginnings of sorrows* (8; Gk. *ōdinōn*, 'birthpangs'). A second warning follows (9–13) against spiritual failure in view of what will happen to them personally and within the Christian community. This paragraph brings vividly before us a truth which is often lost sight of in modern times, namely, that the rôle of the Christian Church during this age is unquestionably one of suffering. Indeed the Church has never flourished better than at those times when it has been an illicit society driven underground. Worldly favour and prosperity, as in the days of Constantine, have always had an enervating and enfeebling effect upon it. One of the first to fulfil the prediction of verse 9 was Saul of Tarsus, as a persecuting Jew and then as a persecuted Christian (Acts ix. 1, 2; 2 Cor. xi. 24). Verses 10 and 11 significantly place the preaching of the gospel in this context of suffering, a context which it undoubtedly has in the book of Acts, where the greater part of apostolic preaching was not before respectable congregations gathered for the purpose, but in courts of justice. Verse 11, therefore, offers no encouragement to the unprepared preacher; it is a promise to those suddenly called upon to defend their faith in the face of persecution, that they may count upon the moment-to-moment guidance and inspiration of the Holy Spirit. To *endure unto the end* (13) probably means not to the end of the age, as in verse 7, but to the uttermost (cf. Jn. xiii. 1), an endurance which is complete. Endurance, therefore, is one of the keynotes of Christian life and witness in this age. It is very often much easier to be busily engaged in work and action than it is to endure with patience (cf. Heb. x. 32-39, xii. 3, 4; Rev. i. 9). The expression to *be saved* (13) is used here, of course, in an eschatological sense.

iii. **The two crises of the future (xiii. 14-27).** See notes on Mt. xxiv. 15-31; Lk. xxi. 20-28. A new section of the prophecy seems to begin here. Having answered the questions of verse 4 thus far in a general, rather negative manner, pointing to certain phenomena which are not signs of the end, Jesus now speaks of a particular notable event, and of the proper behaviour of the disciples when it comes to pass. *The abomination of desolation* (14; Gk. *to bdelygma tēs erēmōseōs*) is an expression which comes from Dn. ix. 27, xi. 31, xii. 11. In Old Testament usage an 'abomination' is any idolatrous person or object such as would excite the disgust and abhorrence of the Jew. Cf. 1 Ki. xxi. 26; 2 Ki. xvi. 3, where the same Greek word occurs in the LXX. The fact that Mark here deliberately, though ungrammatically, connects a masculine participle, *standing* (Gk. *hestēkota*), with this neuter noun indicates that a person is in view. We conclude therefore that the first reference in this verse is to the profanation of the temple by the Romans in A.D. 70; this is confirmed by Lk. xxi. 20. Nevertheless the meaning of the words is not exhausted by this, and Jesus was probably referring in a secondary sense, for the benefit of the future Church, to the appearing of Antichrist. The context supports this, for the language of verses 19, 20 is certainly eschatological and far too emphatic to apply only to the circumstances of the siege of Jerusalem, however terrible. *Where it ought not* (14) is an intentionally vague expression, since more precise terms would perhaps have been politically dangerous for Mark's readers. *Let him that readeth understand* may be either the words of Jesus calling attention to the passage in Daniel, or those of Mark calling attention to this saying of Jesus; most probably the latter since the words *spoken of by Daniel the prophet* should be omitted here, with RV, having been inserted by assimilation to Mt. xxiv. 15. Verses 15-18 present a series of vivid illustrations of the need for instant flight as in conditions of war. Prayer for temporal advantages to facilitate escape is enjoined (18). *Winter* (18) may perhaps better be rendered 'stormy weather'. Just prior to A.D. 70 the Christians of Jerusalem did in fact make their escape in this way and Eusebius, the Church historian, tells us that they fled to Pella, in Peraea, east of Jordan. Verses 21-23 are thought by some to be a doublet of verses 5f., derived from a different

source and reflecting a doctrinal situation in the early Church similar to that of 2 Thes. ii. 9. There is, however, no inherent improbability in the suggestion that what is undoubtedly the chief practical lesson of these prophetic utterances should have been thus reiterated and expanded by our Lord. His technique as a teacher is no less perfect than His technique as a physician.

From this point Jesus goes on to speak of the second great crisis yet future, namely, the return in glory of the Son of man. The impression is conveyed that this follows soon upon the tribulation of verses 14-23, which again leads us to think that the latter has an eschatological significance and was by no means limited to the happenings of A.D. 70. How far the language of verses 24, 25 is to be understood symbolically of political and international convulsions, as most commentators of the past fifty years have understood it, is difficult to decide. Much that used to be relegated unhesitatingly to the realm of apocalyptic may now, in an atomic age, be seen to have rather the semblance of sober truth and grim reality; and it would be unscientific, to say the least, to affirm that these words may not refer to objective phenomena in the form of cosmic disturbances prior to the return of Christ. *The Son of man coming in the clouds* (26) is a clear reference to Dn. vii. 13. Early in His ministry Jesus began to use the title 'Son of man' of Himself (see ii. 10n.), but here for the first time the connection with the prophecy in Daniel is apparent. Amid much that is perplexing in the details of such a chapter as this, the one fact that stands out with crystal clarity is the ultimate triumph of Jesus; the suffering Messiah shall eventually enter into His glory, although the use of the third person here, *then shall they see* (26), rather intimates that those whom He is addressing will not live to see it. The gathering together of the *elect* (27) by the angels (cf. Heb. i. 14) suggests that the divine purpose in verse 10 will have been accomplished in the meantime.

iv. **Parables and sayings on watchfulness (xiii. 28-37).** See notes on Mt. xxiv. 32-51; Lk. xxi. 29-36. This is the practical application of all that has gone before. The *parable of the fig tree* (28) draws attention once more to what is the true purpose of prophecy (see on 5), not that disciples may prophesy, but that they may with spiritual insight discern the unfolding of God's purpose in the moving spectacle of events. Verse 30 is a saying of acknowledged difficulty, preserved by all three synoptists. Two meanings seem possible: either that the Jewish race will survive until the end of the age, or that Jerusalem would be destroyed within the lifetime of the generation then living. This latter actually happened and is the more probable meaning; although Swete, *ad loc.*, concedes in regard to the word *generation* (Gk. *genea*) that it may have been purposely employed because it was capable of being understood in a narrower or a wider sense. Clearly we are to learn from verses 30, 31 that the fact of Christ's personal return is unalterably sure. The following verse (32) shows that the time alone is uncertain, being locked in the counsels of the Father, so that even the Son in the voluntarily accepted limitations of His incarnation does not share the secret. The necessity for vigilance and prayerfulness is therefore reiterated (33). The parable of *the master of the house* (34, 35) helps to define vigilance not as a leaving of our duties, but a faithful doing of them, in the expectation that the Master will one day examine our work (1 Cor. iii. 13–15; 2 Cor. v. 10). The chapter concludes with a plain assertion that these injunctions belong not to that generation alone, but to every generation of the Christian Church. 'What the Church of the New Testament has been and is, that her Lord and Master made her, and by no agency more effectually than by leaving undetermined the precise time of His return' (Edersheim).

d. The passion narrative (xiv. 1—xv. 47)

i. The plot to betray Jesus (xiv. 1–11). See notes on Mt. xxvi. 1–16; Lk. xxii. 1–6; Jn. xii. 1–8. We treat this paragraph as a whole because verses 10, 11 are directly connected with verses 1, 2, and the intervening story of the anointing has evidently been introduced here by Mark with the twofold purpose of throwing into relief the treachery and avarice of Judas and of showing that the incident was at least one factor in his turning traitor. For here he heard Jesus speak quite plainly of His burial (8) and perhaps at last realized that his cherished hopes of material power and advancement were doomed. The chronology of events on the Thursday and Friday of passion week presents one of the most difficult problems in the Gospels. What is clear is that those events moved according to divine programme, not human design. The priests evidently planned (1) to arrest Jesus after the feast of the Passover to avoid an insurrection (2). But the unexpected offer of Judas Iscariot simplified matters considerably so that they were able to act without further delay. They had secured a competent agent whose responsibility it now was, instead of theirs, to find an opportunity to arrest Him (11). Thus it came to pass that the divine plan was followed, and Jesus, 'the Lamb of God', yielded up His life on the great festival day. There is therefore discernible in Judas an amazing fusion of divine sovereignty and human free will. The latter must not be surrendered in an attempt to soften his guilt. Jesus must suffer; but Judas need not have been the traitor; he opened the door to Satan (Jn. xiii. 27) and well illustrates the solemn principle enunciated in Heb. vi. 4–8 that there is a supreme peril in enjoying spiritual privileges and failing to respond.

The lovely story of the anointing is placed by John 'six days before the Passover' (Jn. xii. 1). His precision in dating it is not likely to be erroneous, and we conclude that Mark, followed by Matthew (Mt. xxvi. 6–13), has sacrificed the chronological order for homiletical reasons. It is John also who identifies the woman with Mary of Bethany. *Simon the leper* (3) was probably one who had been healed; he may have been related to Lazarus and his sisters. C. C. Torrey makes the interesting suggestion on the basis of the Aramaic that the word for *leper* should in fact be 'jar merchant', the two words in Aramaic having identical consonants. The identity of name has led some, even as far back as Origen's time, to confuse this narrative with that in Lk. vii. 36–50. But whereas the difficulty of believing in two such anointings is infinitesimal, that of believing that Mary of Bethany was ever 'a sinner' is enormous. Moreover Simon was one of the commonest of names. The meal was probably the special festive meal of the sabbath. At that last feast of fellowship Mary alone among the disciples and guests seemed to discern how near the end was. Whether she fully appreciated the significance of her action at the time may be questioned; for it is probably true of most service and worship offered in pure devotion to Christ that it possesses a worth and meaning beyond our understanding. So far as we know, Jesus' body received no other anointing for burial; cf. xvi. 1. When therefore this fact came home to her, how great would be her joy! In humility, love and faith she exemplifies 'the fellowship of his sufferings' (Phil. iii. 10). *An alabaster box* (3) would probably be a fragile unguent flask with a long narrow neck. *Ointment of spikenard* (Gk. *myrou nardou pistikēs*) is lit. 'ointment of genuine nard', though the precise meaning of the expression is uncertain. That it was of special quality and value is clear. *Three hundred pence* (5) represents a sum of money roughly equivalent to a labourer's wage for the greater part of a year, the penny or 'denarius' being a day's wage.

ii. The Last Supper (xiv. 12–25). See notes on Mt. xxvi. 17–29; Lk. xxii. 7–23; cf. Jn. xiii. 1–35. *The first day of unleavened bread, when they killed the passover* (12) was the day we know as Good Friday, 14th Nisan. But according to Jewish reckoning this day began at sunset the day before. The events of this paragraph therefore took place on the Thursday evening. The question of whether the supper was in fact the Passover meal remains unsettled despite prolonged discussion on both sides. The synoptic tradition, as here, clearly indicates that it was. On the other hand, John with precision and consistency (Jn. xviii. 28b, xix. 31) places the Passover on the Friday evening after the crucifixion. There is hardly likely to be any better solution than to conclude, as most scholars now do, that Jesus, knowing that He could not observe the Passover at the proper time, kept it a day in advance. It is attractive to believe, accordingly, that 'Christ our passover' (1 Cor. v. 7) was sacrificed for us at the very hour when the Passover lambs were slain in the temple. In preparation for the feast *Jesus sendeth forth two of his disciples* (13), whom Luke names as Peter and John (Lk. xxii. 8), into the city to look for *a man bearing a pitcher of water*. This was unusual since normally only women carried such pitchers (Jn. iv. 7). The man would evidently be a servant, and on following him they would be led to the owner, with whom it seems Jesus had a previously arranged understanding about the use of the room. This is rather implied in the question, which should be read with RV, 'The Master saith, Where is my guest-chamber?' (14). For security reasons it was necessary that both the identity of this anonymous disciple and the location of the venue should be a well-kept secret. The *large upper room* (15) would be furnished with such necessities as table, couches for reclining, basin, water and towel (Jn. xiii. 4f.). The disciples would complete the preparations for food. Perhaps the most significant detail is that there is no mention of a lamb being provided or consumed, and it is very improbable that there was one. There would be no need of a typical lamb when the true Lamb of God was present and about to be offered the very next day.

As they sat and did eat (18); originally the Passover lamb was eaten standing (Ex. xii. 11), but this custom had long been abandoned, and the feast was now celebrated reclining in token that the people were no longer slaves but free, enjoying the security of the land of promise. The disclosure of the betrayal (18–21) is made with startling plainness, yet not, according to Mark's account, in such a manner as to name the traitor. We depend upon John (Jn. xiii. 26) for the knowledge that this information was secretly given to the beloved disciple. The enormity of the crime is indicated by the fact that, to the Oriental, the fellowship of a meal was specially sacred, and hostile action against one with whom one ate bread was absolutely precluded. Cf. Ps. xli. 9. In this case Judas not only ate with Jesus; he dipped with Him in the dish, even more intimately (20). *The dish* (Gk. *tryblion*) was probably the bowl of sauce into which pieces of unleavened bread were dipped, assuming that the meal was in fact the Passover. Verse 21 clearly states both the divine sovereignty and human responsibility to which we have already referred (see on 1, 2, 10, 11), and places the latter squarely on the shoulders of Judas. 'The divine necessity for the Passion was no excuse for the free agent who brought it about' (Swete).

Mark's account of the institution of the Lord's Supper (22–25) is concise almost to the point of obscurity, but it brings before us the second main line of teaching in the Gospel concerning the work of Christ (see *Introduction*, p. 807, and x. 45n.). The following points are clear. First, *Take, eat* (22) indicates that His death with its benefits was a gift which His disciples must appropriate, and that this appropriation is of a most intimate kind comparable with the assimilation of food and a partaking of its nourishment and efficacy. Secondly, His death is the inauguration of *the new testament* (24) or covenant of

grace prophesied by Jeremiah (Je. xxxi. 31–34). Moses had spoken of 'the blood of the covenant' (Ex. xxiv. 8) in connection with the old covenant which Jehovah made with Israel at Sinai. Centuries later Jeremiah revealed the terms of the new covenant, namely, divine forgiveness and indwelling, but he said nothing about its ratification by blood. This would strike Hebrew ears as unusual, for among Oriental peoples any kind of covenant or agreement between two people, such as, for example, two Bedouin of the desert, would be sealed in some way by blood. It is as though Jesus now completed the picture outlined by Jeremiah; the new covenant would be sealed in His blood. *Shed for many* (24; cf. again x. 45) once more echoes Is. liii. 11, 12. Jesus thought of His death as a vicarious sacrifice for men. The expressions *this is my body* (22) and *this is my blood* (24), though literally rendered in the AV, are perhaps as well translated by Moffatt as by any: 'Take this, it means my body . . . This means my covenant-blood.' 'Our Lord's human body was present and His blood had not yet been shed. Therefore all carnal ideas respecting the meaning of these words are excluded' (Plummer). Thirdly (25), Jesus looked forward beyond His death to His risen life and to the perfect fellowship of the consummated kingdom. The table of the Lord has a forward aspect towards the consummation as well as a backward reference to the cross.

iii. **Peter's denial foretold (xiv. 26–31).** See notes on Mt. xxvi. 30–35; cf. Lk. xxii. 34; Jn. xiii. 36–38, xviii. 1. *When they had sung an hymn* (26); it was probably the second part of the Hallel (Pss. cxv—cxviii). As Jesus foretold the betrayal, so now, on the way from the upper room to the Mount of Olives, He foretells the denial by Peter. The words of Zc. xiii. 7 will find fulfilment in the case of Himself and His disciples. A time of testing will come upon them as a result of which the faith of them all will give way. Nevertheless beyond the dark hour He will meet them again in Galilee. Jesus scarcely ever referred to His death without looking beyond it. Peter protested, as once before (viii. 32f.), and Jesus' reply is in the most solemn terms, *Verily I say unto thee* (30). *This day, even in this night* brings the denial within the space of the next few hours. It is well to remember that all the disciples (31b) associated themselves with Peter's vehement protestations.

iv. **The agony in Gethsemane (xiv. 32–42).** See notes on Mt. xxvi. 36–46; Lk. xxii. 39–46. Again the privileged three are taken and there are several points of similarity between this scene and the transfiguration. With verses 37–40 cf. ix. 5f.; Lk. ix. 32. *Sit ye here* (32) is spoken to the eight who are left near the entrance. While still in the company of the three He *began to be sore amazed, and to be very heavy* (33; Gk. *ekthambeisthai kai adēmonein*). These are words supremely difficult to translate. They express the utmost degree of unbounded horror and suffering. Little is said in Scripture about the soul

(Gk. *psychē*) of the Lord Jesus, but when He says *My soul is exceeding sorrowful unto death* (34) the deep anguish of His humanity becomes evident. So great was it that He was driven from them a short distance—Luke says 'about a stone's cast' (Lk. xxii. 41), where they could both see and hear—to seek the face of His Father. *Abba* (36) is Aramaic for 'Father'. The addition of *Patēr* (*Father*) is probably not a translation by Mark. Some think the two words together are a very early liturgical formula of address in prayer. But it is more likely that they reflect a natural prayer habit of Jesus Himself, which some of His disciples caught and transmitted (cf. Rom. viii. 15; Gal. iv. 6). In any case they are a reminder that our faith had its origin among a bilingual people. We shall never know exactly what was *this cup* from which Jesus shrank in such horror. It was certainly more than physical suffering, otherwise many a martyr has since shown greater courage than He. We may say that it was the agony to His sinless soul of being 'made sin' (2 Cor. v. 21) and exposed to the divine judgment on sin, of tasting in all its bitterness that death which is the wages of sin that those who trust in Him might never taste it (Heb. ii. 9). This is something beyond the range of human experience altogether, since He alone was sinless. The words *nevertheless not what I will, but what thou wilt* (36) are the crucial point in Gethsemane. Doctrinally they illustrate the important truth that there was in Jesus a real human will, distinct from, but always submissive to, the will of His Father. Experimentally they mark the point of His triumph, so that the victory of the cross was in fact won in prayer in the garden beforehand and Jesus went to Calvary victoriously. Man's arch-enemy wrought sin and death by asserting his will against God (Is. xiv. 13, 14); Jesus wrought salvation by submitting His will to God. Acceptance of the will of God is always victory, whereas self-will inevitably leads to defeat.

The picture of the sleeping disciples is in sharp contrast with that of Jesus at prayer. Peter is addressed as the one who had protested that he would die with Jesus; yet now he had not the strength to watch for an hour. There was clearly an element of conflict with Satanic powers in the garden. The earlier temptations of our Lord's ministry were here renewed in a last titanic assault, the intensity of which He felt. Knowing full well that victory in temptation was to be won only at the price of vigilance and prayer, He warned the slumbering disciples of their own need (38). *Sleep on now, and take your rest* (41); it is possible that we are to understand an interval of time here, during which Jesus Himself watched over them.

v. The arrest of Jesus (xiv. 43–52). See notes on Mt. xxvi. 47–56; Jn. xviii. 1–12; cf. Lk. xxii. 47–53. Few details in history have so powerfully impressed the minds of men as the fact that Judas betrayed the Son of God with a kiss. In verse 45 an emphatic form of the verb (Gk.

katephilēsen; RV mg. 'kissed him much') is used, as though to suggest more than usual fervour and affection. *One of them that stood by* (47); this anonymous person is referred to by John (Jn. xviii. 10) as Peter, and the servant's name is given as Malchus. Luke alone (Lk. xxii. 51) records the healing of the ear. *A certain young man* (51). Why is this curious incident mentioned? Many commentators favour the suggestion that the young man was Mark himself, who thus, as it were, 'paints a small picture of himself in the corner of his work' (Zahn). If, as some also have conjectured, he was the son of 'the goodman of the house' (14; cf. Acts xii. 12), his appearance at this juncture is even more intelligible. Becoming aware of the noise and the lights in the garden near at hand, he took the first thing that came to hand as a covering and ran out to see what was happening. No good reason can be shown for the recording of the incident unless it is based on personal reminiscence.

vi. The trial before the High Priest (xiv. 53–65). See notes on Mt. xxvi. 57–68; Jn. xviii. 13, 14, 19–24; cf. Lk. xxii. 54, 63–71. The combined synoptic record makes it clear that the trial of Jesus was in two parts, one ecclesiastical before the Jewish authorities as here related, the other civil before the Roman governor as related in the next chapter. Again, the ecclesiastical trial seems to have been in two parts, the first of an informal and preliminary character at midnight, and the second before a full official meeting of the Sanhedrin in the early morning (xv. 1). Luke's account (see Lk. xxii. 54–71) is clearer than Mark's in this respect. The whole proceeding transgressed the requirements of Jewish law in several particulars. The meeting of the Sanhedrin by night was in itself illegal, as was also the suborning of witnesses. *The high priest* (53) was Caiaphas (Mt. xxvi. 57) who held office A.D. 18–36. Nothing is said by Mark about Annas (cf. Jn. xviii. 13). Peter's affection for his Lord evidently reasserted itself to a degree (54), but to follow *afar off* is in any circumstances to invite disaster. From this point the narrative consists almost entirely of sayings, questions and answers, and seems to lack the usual artless details which characterize the record of eye-witnesses. This may be due to the fact that no disciple was an immediate witness of the trial, though Jn. xviii. 15f. suggests that the beloved disciple and Peter were in the vicinity. The efforts of the council were at first unavailing. The witnesses did not agree, and Jesus kept silence. The High Priest therefore sought to force an issue, and put to Jesus a point-blank question about His claim to Messiahship (61). Thus challenged, Jesus for the first time in the Gospel acknowledged who He was, using the language of Ps. cx. 1 and Dn. vii. 13. *The high priest rent his clothes* (63); for his own misfortunes he was forbidden to do so (Lv. xxi. 10), but in his official capacity he protested in this way against any utterance regarded as blasphemous. The Talmud prescribes the exact manner in which it must be done. His question, *What need we any further witnesses?*, reveals 'the satisfaction of the conspirator . . . through the distress of the official' (Plummer). *They all condemned him to be guilty* (Gk. *enochon*, 'worthy of', RV mg. 'liable to') *of death* (64), but had no power to inflict the penalty; only Pilate could do that. That members of the supreme court could behave in the manner described in verse 65 shows the malignity with which they had come to judge their prisoner.

vii. **Peter's denial (xiv. 66–72).** See notes on Mt. xxvi. 69–75; Lk. xxii. 55–62; Jn. xviii. 15–18, 25–27. It is well to remember that this particular account comes without doubt from the recollections of Peter himself and is accordingly related with singular fulness and vividness. That *he began to curse and to swear* (71; Gk. *anathematizein kai omnynai*) does not, however, mean that he used profanity; but rather that he affirmed on oath. He called down the 'anathema' of God upon his head if what he said was not true. *When he thought thereon, he wept* (72; Gk. *kai epibalōn eklaien);* the exact meaning of the Greek words has long constituted a difficulty. Perhaps the best attempt is RSV, 'he broke down and wept.'

viii. **The trial before Pilate (xv. 1–15).** See notes on Mt. xxvii. 1–26; Lk. xxiii. 1–25; Jn. xviii. 28—xix. 16. *Straightway in the morning* (1); Gk. *euthys prōi;* i.e. as soon as it was lawful to transact business, a brief and formal meeting of the Sanhedrin was convened to confirm the proceedings of the irregular midnight session and to get the matter dealt with by the Roman governor before the Paschal lambs were killed in the afternoon. The delivering of Jesus to Pilate initiated the civil trial. Pontius Pilate was procurator of Judaea under the legatus of Syria from A.D. 26 to 36. Normally he resided in Caesarea but came to Jerusalem for the Passover season to ensure order at a time when national feeling ran high. He is represented in secular history as corrupt and cruel, but the Gospels seem to take a less unfavourable view of him. Mark's account here does not hide the deplorable weakness of the man but, at the same time, seems designed to exonerate him as far as possible and place the ultimate responsibility for the crucifixion squarely upon the Jews. It would be of particular importance to Roman readers to learn that, in the eyes of the Roman officer, Jesus was held to be innocent and could not be condemned as a political agitator. *King of the Jews* (2); the hierarchy had evidently framed the charge with this political flavour since a claim to Messiahship would be meaningless to Pilate. *Thou sayest* (2) is an answer which assents without necessarily agreeing to the meaning which Pilate would attach to his question. Verse 3 suggests that the priests felt their case was not going too well, so they multiplied accusations. The general course of the proceedings becomes more intelligible if we compare the more detailed account given by John (Jn. xviii. 28—xix. 16). There we discover that Jesus explained to Pilate in private that His kingdom was not of this world. Nothing is known of the custom referred to in verse 6 beyond what is told us in the New Testament. *Barabbas* (7) means 'a son of a father' and the name invites a contrast with 'the Son of the Father'. In the parallel passage, Mt. xxvii. 16, there is an interesting variant reading 'Jesus Barabbas', which was originally rejected by Hort as a corruption. At that time, however, the Koridethi manuscript of the Gospels and the Sinaitic Syriac Version, both of which contain it, were unknown. Vincent Taylor, therefore, concludes that 'There is good reason to think that it is original in Matthew . . . and to conjecture that it was read in Mark'. Barabbas was just the type of political insurgent the hierarchy had wanted to see in the Messiah, one who would use force where Jesus had refused to do so. But at verse 8 the crowd comes into view and Pilate began to discern that the real crime of Jesus was not hostility to Rome, which Jews would not normally resent, but that He had been too popular and the priests were envious of Him (10). He therefore hoped that a proposal to release Jesus in honour of the feast would be welcomed by the people. The amazing fickleness of the crowd, stirred up as they were by the chief priests (11), is thought by some to be almost incredible. But it was undoubtedly a profound shock to them to see the supposed Messiah a helpless prisoner in the hands of the heathen procurator. There was a violent change of feeling, psychologically characteristic of a mob, and they were quickly ready to clamour for the punishment of the impostor. *Willing to content the people* (15); the lasting shame of Pilate is that he chose expediency above principle. Multitudes have done, and are doing, precisely the same thing since. The punishment of scourging usually preceded crucifixion. It was a brutal torture, inflicted with whips of leather loaded with metal or bone. One infliction of it often proved fatal. John seems to suggest that Pilate resorted to it in the hope that the Jews would be satisfied (Jn. xix. 1). Even so it was a flagrant breach of Roman justice in the case of an uncondemned man.

ix. **The crucifixion (xv. 16–41).** See notes on Mt. xxvii. 27–56; Lk. xxiii. 26–49; Jn. xix. 17-37. Jesus was handed over to the soldiers who made sport with Him. *Praetorium* (16) is translated 'hall of judgment' in Jn. xviii. 28; it was probably part of the residence of the procurator, which some think was in Herod's palace in Jerusalem. The *purple* (17) may have been a soldier's faded cloak which looked like purple. In all this they acted out of contempt, not so much for Jesus, perhaps, as for the Jewish nation whose King He claimed to be. It is not said (20) that they eventually removed the crown of thorns as well as the purple, but it is probable that they did. Plummer points out that the centurion would not have allowed the mockery to continue when the march to the place of execution began. Pictures of the crucifixion are therefore misleading when they represent the Saviour as wearing the crown of thorns. Perhaps the dominant impression left upon the mind by this account of the mockery is that of the intense loneliness of Jesus. *Simon a Cyrenian* (21); Cyrene is in North Africa. There was a strong colony of Jews there and Simon may have been one of them, arriving in Jerusalem for the Passover; or he may have been a Gentile stranger. The mention of his sons indicates that they had become disciples. We know nothing further of Alexander, but Rufus may be the Rufus of Rom. xvi. 13, a member of the church in Rome. *The place of a skull* (22) was probably so called from the contour of the ground. *Wine mingled with myrrh* (23) was an opiate or anaesthetic. But Jesus refused to meet death with His mental faculties clouded. Had He received the potion, we might never have had the words from the cross.

In all the Gospels the actual crucifixion is narrated in the most straightforward manner and with marked restraint. Our Lord's physical sufferings are not dwelt upon, for nothing is gained by gruesomeness. Moreover, the physical pain was only secondary to the bitter desolation of spirit which He experienced because of sin. *It was the third hour* (25); that is, nine o'clock in the morning. Various explanations have been advanced to explain the apparent disagreement with Jn. xix. 14 (where see note). But John is probably reckoning from midnight, in which case he merely states that Jesus was still before Pilate at 6 a.m. *The superscription* (26) accords with Roman custom; all four evangelists record it but no two agree exactly as to the wording. Mark's version, however, is basic to all and preserves the words that were so particularly offensive to the Jews (cf. Jn. xix. 21). The *thieves* (27) occupied the places for which James and John had asked (x. 37). Verse 28 should be omitted on decisive textual evidence. Mark does not as a rule concern himself with the fulfilment of Old Testament Scripture, and the interpolation is based on Lk. xxii. 37 and Is. liii. 12. The mocking words of the chief priests, *He saved others; himself he cannot save* (31), constitute 'one of the supreme ironies of history' (Vincent Taylor). He could have come down from the cross, but did not. His staying there was our salvation; and that salvation costs us nothing because it cost Him everything. All the synoptists record the darkness from noon until 3 p.m. (33). Though brought about by natural causes, the timing of it was clearly supernatural. It could not have been the darkness of a solar eclipse, for, as Origen pointed out, it was full moon. The cry of dereliction (34) is the only word from the cross recorded by Mark and Matthew. It is preserved in the Aramaic, but it is not improbable that Jesus actually quoted the words of Ps. xxii. 1 in the Hebrew. Mark translates the Aramaic into Greek for the benefit of his readers. We may not fathom the depths of the saying, for it brings us to the very heart of the atonement. But it is important that we do not interpret the words merely of the feeling and subjective consciousness of Jesus, as though the dereliction were not a fact. This is the tendency among modern scholars. But the view of the older theologians (e.g. R. W. Dale, *The Atonement*, p. 61f.) is to be preferred as the correct one, namely, that since God cannot look upon sin (Hab. i. 13) He hid His face when our sin was laid upon His sinless Son. Jesus, the sinner's substitute and sin-bearer, was in fact forsaken that we might never be (Heb. xiii. 5). This was indeed the supreme and unparalleled sorrow from which He shrank. To affirm that such a view is inconsistent with the love of God (so Vincent Taylor, *ad loc.*) is to emphasize the love of God at the expense of His holiness. *Jesus cried with a loud voice, and gave up the ghost* (37); none of the evangelists says He died. Mark's expression is simplest: He 'expired' (Gk. *exepneusen*). But even here the loud cry confirms what is even more clearly expressed by the others, that His death was not the result of natural causes or of exhaustion. It was a voluntary act, and therefore unique. Before any natural cause became fatal, and at the moment of His own choosing, He delivered up His Spirit, so that Pilate marvelled that He was already dead (cf. Jn. x. 17f.). *The veil of the temple was rent in twain* (38); this again is recorded by all the synoptists. It would be observed and reported by the priests, of whom afterwards many believed (Acts vi. 7). Upon the Hebrew mind such a momentous happening must have made a tremendous impression after centuries of tabernacle and temple worship in which the holy of holies had been closed to all except the High Priest on the day of atonement. Its meaning for us is clearly set out in Heb. x. 19ff. *The centurion* (39), whom tradition has named as Longinus, and who was stationed directly opposite the cross where he saw all that happened, was evidently impressed by precisely those peculiarities about our Lord's death that we have noted above (on verse 37). Though his words may not have meant for him all that we read into them, nevertheless he stands at the close of the Gospel story as the first among the heathen to be drawn to faith in Christ by the power of His death. The women at the cross surpassed the disciples in their devotion (40f.), and may even have supplied to the evangelist some of his information concerning the crucifixion. Salome was the mother of James and John (Mt. xxvii. 56). Mark does not mention the mother of our Lord.

x. The burial (xv. 42–47). See notes on Mt. xxvii. 57–61; Lk. xxiii. 50–56; Jn. xix. 38–42. The burial of Jesus occupied an important place in the creeds of the early Church because it proved the reality of His death (see 1 Cor. xv. 3f.). *The preparation* (42) is the technical term for the Friday before the Jewish sabbath, as Mark explains for his Gentile readers. An additional reason for urgency in burying the body of Jesus was the law of Dt. xxi. 22f., commanding the burial of criminals before nightfall on the day of execution. Joseph is described as 'from' (Gk. *apo*) Arimathaea, probably because he had ceased to reside there, and had settled in Jerusalem. The location of Arimathaea is unknown. The tomb (Mt. xxvii. 60), and possibly also the garden containing it, were his. As a member of the Sanhedrin that had driven Pilate to condemn an innocent person to ·death, his action would indeed require courage (43). But reverence and love for the Master prevailed in him. Mark alone records the questioning of the centurion (44f.).

V. THE CONSUMMATION. xvi. 1-20

a. The resurrection (xvi. 1-8)

See notes on Mt. xxviii. 1-20; Lk. xxiv. 1-12; Jn. xx. 1-31. *When the sabbath was past* (1). Complete silence hangs over this sabbath except for the brief statement of Lk. xxiii. 56 that they rested that day. The accounts of the resurrection differ in details as all genuine eyewitness evidence does; but the main outlines of the day's events agree. The first visit was made by women who came very early. *At the rising of the sun* (2) is thought to be difficult in view of Jn. xx. 1, 'when it was yet dark.' Torrey repunctuates and connects the phrase with verse 3: 'When the sun was risen and they were saying . . .' But something depends upon the point of view from which the events are narrated. The actual resurrection was unseen by human eyes, and the first sign of it was the removal of the stone (4). Angels appeared before Jesus Himself was seen (5). Mark leaves us to infer that the *young man* was an angel. Jesus was first seen by Mary Magdalene (9).

Evidence for the resurrection is unimpeachable. The tomb was empty and no one could produce the body. His friends could not have stolen it and His foes would not have done so. If further evidence is needed we may find it in the very existence and survival of the Christian Church. We may with profit compare here Paul's enumeration of the consequences that result from the dire hypothesis, 'If Christ be not risen . . .' (1 Cor. xv. 14-19). In verse 7 the words *and Peter* are peculiar to Mark and constitute one of the evidences of the connection between this Gospel and the apostle. Peter would cherish the fact that, despite his grievous fall, his risen Lord showed special remembrance of him.

b. The epilogue (xvi. 9-20)

These last twelve verses present one of the major textual problems of the New Testament. The principal facts are as follows. The two Codices Sinaiticus and Vaticanus omit the whole section, though their scribes possibly knew of it. Four other MSS of less weight supply an alternative and much shorter ending, and three of them add an explanatory note. Most other uncial and cursive MS, together with Versions and patristic writers, support the inclusion of xvi. 9-20. Conybeare found in an Armenian MS of the tenth century a note ascribing the verses to Aristion, the disciple of John of whom Papias speaks. This

would mean that they are at least very early (perhaps A.D. 100), even if non-Markan, and have something of the authority of John. The transition from verse 8 to verse 9 is abrupt and there is a change of subject. Mary Magdalene is introduced as a stranger in verse 9, despite her appearance in verse 1. Instead of the vividness of detail so characteristic of Mark, we have here a kind of résumé or summary of the resurrection appearances.

The generally accepted view is either that the Gospel was very early mutilated at the last page, or that Mark was unable to finish, perhaps owing to the rising tide of persecution. There remains the possibility, however, that Mark intended to end abruptly at verse 8 and this has been argued with some force recently by R. H. Lightfoot (*The Gospel Message of St. Mark.* O.U.P. 1950, chapter vii).

An interesting theory, which would fit the facts, is that when the Gospels of Matthew and Luke appeared, by reason of their greater detail and interest they eclipsed Mark in popularity with the result that the latter was discarded in obscurity for a time. Shortly afterwards, when the church at Rome began to be interested in the preservation of its records, the only copy of Mark which could be found was mutilated at the end and this became the parent of future copies, the present conclusion being supplied to round it off. The passage contains four sections. The appearance to Mary Magdalene (9-11); the appearance to two travellers (12f.; cf. Lk. xxiv. 13-35); the appearance to the eleven (14-18); and the ascension and the session on high (19, 20).

In another form (12); the risen body of Christ had powers which it did not possess before the passion. The term *the eleven* (14) is used in a collective sense to designate the apostolic company irrespective of the exact number. Though upbraided for their unbelief, they are given the great missionary commission. *He that believeth not shall be damned* (16); better, as in RV, 'condemned'. It is noteworthy that no mention of baptism is made in this negative member of the pair. of clauses. It is unbelief which leads to condemnation, not absence of any ritual observance. With verse 18a cf. Acts xxviii. 3-5.

Verses 19 and 20 indicate the fact that from one point of view our Lord's work on earth, of which this Gospel is the record, is finished: he *sat on the right hand of God*; from another point of view it is to continue through the Church which is His mystical body: *they went forth . . . the Lord working with them.* And so the Gospel which pre-eminently sets forth the power and activity of the Son of God on earth closes with the revelation of the unfinished task of the Church on earth. That task still awaits completion, but the same Lord still works with those who obey His command, *confirming the word with signs following.*

C. E. GRAHAM SWIFT.

THE GOSPEL ACCORDING TO LUKE

INTRODUCTION

See also the General Article, 'The Fourfold Gospel', pp. 58–63.

I. AUTHORSHIP

The authorship of the third Gospel has been attributed to Luke, the friend of Paul, by the whole Christian Church throughout the ages. This tradition can be traced back without interruption to the middle of the second century, and nothing has been found in the records of the early Church to indicate that the book was ever ascribed to any other writer. The internal evidence is in harmony with this objective testimony.

Luke's name does not appear in the Gospel, and it occurs only three times in the New Testament. Paul alone mentions Luke, and in doing so he throws some light upon him. He was a physician (Col. iv. 14), and that implies that he was a man of culture and education. His literary culture appears in the classical preface to the Gospel (i. 1–4), in which he follows the manner of the Greek historians. Traces of his medical knowledge appear throughout the book: see iv. 23, 38, v. 12, viii. 43, xiii. 11, xxii. 44. He seems to have been a Gentile, for he is not included in the list of those 'who are of the circumcision' in Col. iv. 10, 11. He was one of Paul's fellow-labourers (Phm. 24), and the only companion the apostle had during his last imprisonment in Rome just before his martyrdom (2 Tim. iv. 11).

Luke was the author of the Acts as well (Acts i. 1, 2), and although his name does not occur in that book either, yet the course of his companionship with Paul can be traced in the passages where the first personal pronoun is used. These 'we' sections begin when Paul was at Troas on his second missionary journey (Acts xvi. 9, 10). There is some probability in Sir W. M. Ramsay's theory that Luke was the 'man of Macedonia' in Paul's vision and belonged to Philippi, although tradition says that he belonged to Antioch. He accompanied Paul and his party from Troas to Philippi, and seems to have remained there when Paul and Silas went on into Greece. The third person is resumed at that point in the narrative, and it is continued until Paul revisited Philippi on his third missionary journey some years later (Acts xx. 5, 6). Then Luke takes up the first person again as he goes on with the story, and continues to use it to the end of the book, except when telling of Paul's imprisonment in Caesarea. This shows that Luke was the apostle's constant companion from the time he left Philippi on his last journey to Jerusalem, and that he remained in Palestine within easy reach of Paul until he was able to join him again on the voyage to Rome.

II. DATE AND PLACE OF WRITING

The two years of Paul's enforced stay in Caesarea would afford Luke ample time and opportunity to gather the material for his Gospel. At this time, if not before, his purpose to write a Gospel must have been conceived, and it would be the most natural thing for him, when he found himself in Palestine, to follow the steps of Jesus up and down the land. The date of the book cannot be determined exactly, but there is no valid reason for placing it at a later period. The Gospel was written before the Acts, for Luke calls it 'the former treatise' (Acts i. 1); and the Acts does not take us beyond Paul's two years' imprisonment in Rome, that is, to about the year 62. All these circumstances make it probable that the Gospel was written at Caesarea about A.D. 60.

III. THE WRITER'S AIM

The book is addressed to a private Christian called Theophilus (i. 1–4), who must have been a man of some prominence, but is otherwise unknown. It was intended, of course, for a wide circle of readers, and the fact that 'Theophilus' is a Greek name would indicate that Luke had in mind the Greeks of the Roman world. They were the people among whom Paul's missionary labours were carried on.

Luke writes as a historian and sets his narrative in the frame of contemporary history. It begins 'in the days of Herod, the king of Judaea' (i. 5). It mentions the imperial decree that brought Joseph and Mary from Galilee to Bethlehem (ii. 1). In the course of the story Luke pays careful attention to dates and marks of time (e.g. i. 26, ii. 21, 42). When he begins the account of the Lord's public ministry he notes the years of the reigning Caesar and the age of Jesus, and takes a survey of the civil and religious rulers who were specially concerned with Palestine (iii. 1, 2, 23).

This Gospel presents Jesus as the ideal Man and as the Saviour of all classes of men. Here we see Him pass through all the stages of a normal human life, from infancy through boyhood to mature manhood. Here He is seen touching human life on all sides, entering the domestic life of the people and moving among all classes of society. Luke makes it clear that the sympathy of Jesus went out especially to the poor, who compose the vast majority of mankind, and to women, on whom both Jews and Gentiles in that ancient world looked down.

The universal gospel which Paul preached would give Luke the basis for the portrait that he draws of the Saviour, and his own calling as 'the beloved physician' would give him a sympathetic understanding of the nature and needs of men. Thus Luke was peculiarly well qualified to be the author of such a book as this.

NOTE: *For a map of Palestine in the time of Christ, see p. 775.*

OUTLINE OF CONTENTS

I. PREFACE. i. 1–4

II. THE ADVENT OF THE SAVIOUR. i. 5—ii. 52

    a. The announcement of John (i. 5–25)
    b. The announcement of Jesus (i. 26–38)
    c. Mary's visit to Elisabeth (i. 39–56)
    d. The birth of John (i. 57–80)
    e. The birth of Jesus (ii. 1–20)
    f. The infancy of Jesus (ii. 21–39)
    g. The boyhood of Jesus (ii. 40–52)

III. THE SAVIOUR'S PREPARATION FOR HIS MINISTRY. iii. 1—iv. 13

    a. The preaching of John the Baptist (iii. 1–20)
    b. The baptism of Jesus (iii. 21, 22)
    c. The lineage of Jesus (iii. 23–38)
    d. The temptation of Jesus (iv. 1–13)

IV. THE MINISTRY IN GALILEE. iv. 14—ix. 50

    a. Up to the call of the first disciples (iv. 14–44)
    b. From the call of the first disciples to the choice of the Twelve (v. 1—vi. 11)
    c. From the choice of the Twelve to their first mission (vi. 12—viii. 56)
    d. From the mission of the Twelve to the departure from Galilee (ix. 1–50)

V. THE JOURNEY TO JERUSALEM. ix. 51—xix. 28

    a. The first stage of the journey (ix. 51—xiii. 21)
    b. The second stage of the journey (xiii. 22—xvii. 10)
    c. The third stage of the journey (xvii. 11—xix. 28)

VI. THE MINISTRY IN JERUSALEM. xix. 29—xxi. 38

    a. The entry into Jerusalem and the cleansing of the temple (xix. 29–48)
    b. Teaching daily in the temple (xx. 1—xxi. 4)
    c. Foretelling the destruction of the temple (xxi. 5–38)

VII. THE DEPARTURE OF THE SAVIOUR. xxii. 1—xxiv. 53

    a. The final preparations (xxii. 1–13)
    b. The Last Supper (xxii. 14–38)
    c. The agony and the betrayal (xxii. 39–53)
    d. The Jewish trial (xxii. 54–71)
    e. The Roman trial (xxiii. 1–25)
    f. The crucifixion (xxiii. 26–49)
    g. The burial (xxiii. 50–56)
    h. The resurrection morning (xxiv. 1–12)
    i. The risen Lord (xxiv. 13–43)
    j. The farewell instructions (xxiv. 44–53)

COMMENTARY

I. PREFACE. i. 1–4

Luke begins his Gospel with a simple and modest introduction, finely phrased, which tells of the care he took to secure fullness and accuracy for his narrative, and of the end he had in view. His purpose was to set forth the historical foundation of the Christian faith.

Many have taken in hand (1). This statement is the only positive information we possess about written records lying behind the synoptic Gospels. These narratives have all perished. *Those things which are most surely believed* (1); rather, 'those matters which have been fulfilled' (RV), i.e. the established facts of the gospel. *Having had perfect understanding of all things* (3); rather, 'having traced the course of all things accurately' (RV). Luke distinguishes himself from the *eyewitnesses* (2) but claims to have made a thorough investigation. *Most excellent Theophilus* (3). The title indicates a man of official rank. It occurs three times in the Acts (see xxiii. 26, xxiv. 3, xxvi. 25, RV).

II. THE ADVENT OF THE SAVIOUR.
i. 5—ii. 52

These chapters contain the most complete account in the New Testament of the facts connected with the incarnation. They record a series of events beginning before the birth of Jesus and taking us on into His growing boyhood. There is a peculiar beauty and a joyous atmosphere in these opening scenes of the Gospel story.

a. The announcement of John (i. 5–25)

The first scene takes place in the temple, the centre of the Old Testament system. *The course of Abia* (1), or Abijah, to which Zacharias belonged, was one of the twenty-four courses into which David organized the priests (1 Ch. xxiv. 10). Each course was on duty in the temple for a week every six months, and incense was offered twice every day, at the morning and evening sacrifices. The narrative tells of the righteous character of the aged and childless couple (5–7), and of the angel's appearance to Zacharias as he ministered at the altar of incense (8–12). He informed the priest that his wife Elisabeth was to have a son, whom he should name John; and then he described the life John would live and the ministry he would fulfil (13–17). When Zacharias expressed doubt because of the advanced age of himself and his wife, the angel disclosed his own name and high position, and pronounced a temporary judgment upon the priest for his unbelief (18–20). The narrative goes on to record the fulfilment of both the judgment (21, 22) and the promise announced by the angel (23–25).

In the days of Herod (5). Usually, but wrongly, called Herod the Great. He was an Edomite by race and a Jew by religion; he ruled over the Jews from 37 to 4 B.C. *His lot was to burn incense* (9). It was only once in a lifetime that a priest could obtain this honour, and the number of priests was so great that many of them never obtained it. *Into the temple* (9). The inner sanctuary (Gk. *naos*) as distinguished from the temple structure (Gk. *hieron*). *Were praying without* (10). The people stood waiting in the court outside the sanctuary, but within the temple walls, while the clouds of incense arose within, symbolizing their prayers.

Thy prayer is heard (13). Zacharias had no doubt prayed for a son in the past, but in that solemn service when, as priest, he offered the supplications of the people his prayer would be that of all devout Israelites—for the coming of the Messiah. The angel was announcing the first step in the answer to that prayer. *Thou shalt call his name John* (13). The name means 'the grace of Jehovah'. The dispensation of grace in distinction from that of the law was about to begin (cf. Jn. i. 17). *In the spirit and power of Elias* (17). The angel's words recall the closing prophecy of Malachi (iv. 5, 6). The New Testament begins where the Old Testament ends. Malachi's prophecy was fulfilled in the person of John the Baptist (Mt. xi. 14, xvii. 12, 13). *I am Gabriel* (19). He had been sent on two former occasions to Daniel, whose prophecies were concerned with the advent of the Messiah (Dn. viii. 16, ix. 21). *To take away my reproach* (25). That of being childless, keenly felt by every Hebrew wife. See Gn. xxx. 23, where Rachel uses the same words.

b. The announcement of Jesus (i. 26–38)

From the temple in Jerusalem the narrative takes us to the home of a humble maiden in a Galilean village. The same angel who announced the coming birth of John was sent to Nazareth to announce a more transcendent birth. He greeted Mary with a salutation that puzzled her, and she wondered what it meant (26–29). He told her that she had found favour with God and should bring forth a son, whom she was to name Jesus. In Him should be fulfilled the promise God gave David of a throne and an everlasting kingdom (30–33). In answer to Mary's wondering question, the angel conveyed to her the explanation, with delicate reserve and holy joy, that God was to be the Father of her Son (34, 35). Then he encouraged Mary by telling her about Elisabeth, and Mary's final words express the humble submission with which she put herself at God's disposal (36–38).

Call his name Jesus (31). The name is the Greek form of 'Joshua' and means 'the salvation of Jehovah'. It was revealed to Joseph also (see Mt. i. 21). *How shall this be?* (34). Mary's question does not imply any doubt or unbelief as did that of Zacharias (see verse 18), but simply innocent surprise. *The Holy Ghost shall come upon thee* (35); in His capacity as the creative power of God (Gn. i. 2). The incarnation was the beginning of a new creation. *That holy thing* (35), free from all taint of sin. Jesus was not born as a member of Adam's fallen race, but as the sinless Head of a new race. *Shall be called the Son of God* (35). The angel's words base the divine Sonship of Mary's child on His conception by the divine Spirit. This does not imply, nor does it exclude, His prèexistence. Its result is seen in the consciousness of the Fatherhood of God which Jesus possessed from His earliest years. Mary's simple words in verse 38 are a sublime expression of her faith and self-devotion. She accepts the sacrifice involved—such a sacrifice of her reputation as is revealed in what Joseph intended to do with her before the matter was revealed to him (Mt. i. 19).

c. Mary's visit to Elisabeth (i. 39–56)

Mary went up to Judaea with lively eagerness, and Elisabeth greeted her with an inspired salutation of intense feeling (39–45). Mary's song breathes a calm, deep repose, and a profound sense of exaltation (46–55). It is modelled on Hannah's song (1 Sa. ii. 1–10), and contains several quotations from the Psalms. Mary seems to have remained with Elisabeth until John was born (56).

Filled with the Holy Ghost (41). The prophetic spirit of the old covenant came upon Elisabeth and she recognized Mary as the mother of the Messiah (43). *And Mary said* (46). Her first words express the state of her soul and reveal the high spiritual plane on which she had been living.

d. The birth of John (i. 57–80)

The circumstances attending the birth and naming of the child made a profound impression on the people round about (57–66). The song of Zacharias is modelled on the prophecies and is full of the idea of redemption. It shows that the spiritual significance of the messianic age, which was now being ushered in, was well understood by the devout souls in Israel (67–75). He expresses his joy at the part assigned to his own son in this work, and then the song overflows with a closing thanksgiving for the messianic salvation (76–79). The historical conclusion of the narrative, telling of the growth of John and the preparation for his ministry (80), agrees with the statement in verse 66 that *the hand of the Lord was with him.*

Laid them up in their hearts (66); a characteristic expression of Luke's (cf. ii. 19, 51), showing that he gathered some of his information from the people actually concerned in the events he narrates. *To give knowledge of salvation* (77). This was the purpose of John's work as the forerunner. The people had a false idea of the salvation which the Messiah was to bring. John was to give them the true idea as consisting in spiritual deliverance from the dominion of sin. *The dayspring from on high* (78); an allusion to Mal. iv. 2, a beautiful figure to describe the dawn of the new age.

e. The birth of Jesus (ii. 1–20)

The story opens with a historical note about an imperial decree for taking a census of the Roman world (1–3). When this was put into operation in Palestine it brought Joseph and Mary from Nazareth to Bethlehem to be enrolled in their ancestral city; and there the Saviour of the world was born (4–7). Heaven's interest in the event was manifested by the news an angel brought to the shepherds in the open country, and by the praise of a heavenly host accompanying the message (8–14). The shepherds found the new-born babe by the sign the angel gave them, and then spread abroad the angel's message about the child (15–17). Luke goes on to tell of the impression produced among those who heard the story, and implies that there was a great contrast between the momentary and superficial wonder of the people and the profound thoughts and feelings of Mary (18–20).

Caesar Augustus (1); the first of the Roman Emperors, who reigned from 31 B.C. to A.D. 14. *Should be taxed* (1); lit. 'should be enrolled'. The decree was for the taking of a periodical census as the basis of taxation. *This taxing was first made* (2); rather, 'This was the first enrolment made' (RV). The first application of the decree in Palestine was being made when Jesus was born. Luke mentions Cyrenius (Quirinius) as governor of Syria at the time because that Roman province exercised a measure of supervision over the kingdom of Herod. See also note on Acts v. 37.

The city of David (4); Bethlehem, six miles south of Jerusalem, was David's birthplace and original home (1 Sa. xvii. 12, 58). *To all people* (10); lit. 'to all the people', pointing to the Jews as the first recipients of the joy. *Christ the Lord* (11). Thus does the angel declare the new-born babe to be the promised Messiah.

The song of the angels as given in the RV (14) is in two symmetrical parts, and presents two corresponding scenes. It is literally: 'Glory in the highest (heavens) to God, and on earth peace among men of good will.' The phrase 'men of good will' is a Hebraism, and means men who are the objects of God's good will. Verse 19 throws light on Mary's character and also indicates that Luke obtained his information from her.

f. The infancy of Jesus (ii. 21–39)

His parents brought the child to the temple in Jerusalem and carried out all that the law required in the case of a first-born son (21–24). The song of Simeon is marked by suppressed rapture and profound spiritual insight. He represents himself as a watchman now released from duty because the messianic hope, for which he was commanded to wait, has appeared (25–32). His address to Mary shows that he had some insight into the meaning of the prophecies that foreshadowed the sufferings of the Messiah (33–35). The aged prophetess Anna confirmed his testimony regarding the child (36–38). Joseph and Mary returned to Nazareth after every prescription of the law had been fulfilled (39).

To present him to the Lord (22). All the first-born in Israel belonged to God because of the deliverance in Egypt on the Passover night (Ex. xiii. 2). A first-born son had to be redeemed by a sacrificial offering (Nu. xviii. 15). The offering of Joseph and Mary was that which the very poor were allowed to substitute for a lamb (Lv. xii. 8). *The fall and rising again* (34); i.e. the ruin of some and the salvation of others. *Them that looked for redemption in Jerusalem* (38). Simeon and Anna represent the devout people in Israel as distinguished from the carnally minded Jews. There seems to have been an expectation among them at this time that the advent of the Messiah was approaching.

g. The boyhood of Jesus (ii. 40–52)

He grew in body, mind and spirit from childhood (40), through boyhood into young manhood (52). His human nature was perfect and complete at each stage of its development. When He was twelve years old, the age at which a young Jew became a member of the congregation of Israel, Jesus was taken up to the Passover in Jerusalem for the first time. The incident that occurred on this occasion reveals the unique and sinless nature of the growing boy (41–51). *The feast of the passover* (41). This feast commemorated the deliverance of Israel from Egypt (Ex. xii. 1–20). It was held in the spring of the year and its celebration, which included the feast of unleavened bread, lasted eight days. *In the company* (44). It would be a troop of Galilean pilgrims travelling in a caravan. When they halted for the night Jesus was missed. *After three days* (46). After one day out and one day back, He was found on the third day in one of the courts of the temple, where He had spent each day in His eagerness to learn from the doctors of the law, who were accustomed to give public instruction at the feasts. *Wist ye not?* (49). The answer of Jesus is an expression of surprise. There was something about Him which He was surprised His parents did not know. Both the AV and the RV paraphrase, rather than translate, the indefinite phrase of the original Greek, 'in my Father's things'. He had always been occupied with His Father's affairs and had no interests of His own to engage Him. This was what His parents might have known. Here is revealed the inner life of a child who had no self-will. His words do not imply a consciousness of His own divine nature, but rather the consciousness of an unfallen human nature. This accounts for His parents not understanding what He meant (50). *Was subject unto them* (51). This expresses the attitude of Jesus' life in Nazareth for the next

eighteen years (iii. 23). Joseph is not mentioned again, no doubt because he was not living when Christ's public ministry began. Jesus worked at Joseph's trade (Mt. xiii. 55; Mk. vi. 3), and, being the eldest son in the family, would carry the burden of the home after the father's death.

III. THE SAVIOUR'S PREPARATION FOR HIS MINISTRY. iii. 1—iv. 13

The transition from Jesus' private life in Nazareth to His public ministry in Israel was marked by two unique events in His experience which constituted His special preparation for His task —the baptism and the temptation. Luke begins his account of these events with a reference to the rulers of the time (iii. 1). See the map of Palestine on p. 775. Tiberius was associated with Augustus in the rule of the Roman Empire for two years before the latter died, which would make his fifteenth year A.D. 26. Judaea was under the direct rule of the Roman governor Pontius Pilate, whose province included Samaria as well as Judaea. It was one of four parts into which the dominion of Herod the Great had been divided. Hence the title tetrarch, 'ruler of a fourth part', was given to the rulers of the other three parts. Herod, known as Antipas, and Philip were sons of Herod the Great. The realm of the former included Peraea, the district east of the lower Jordan, as well as Galilee. That of the latter lay east of the upper Jordan and the Sea of Galilee. Nothing is known of Lysanias, who ruled over a small political division between Damascus and Mount Hermon. The heads of the Jewish hierarchy were Annas and Caiaphas (iii. 2). Annas had been deposed by the Romans in A.D. 15 but was still High Priest in the eyes of the Jews. His son-in-law Caiaphas was the official High Priest.

a. The preaching of John the Baptist (iii. 1–20)

See notes on Mt. iii. 1–12; Mk. i. 1–8. Cf. also Jn. i. 6–34. Having received a call from God, John began to preach repentance in the region of the Jordan and used baptism as a sign of repentance, thus fulfilling a prophecy of Isaiah's (2–6). He warned the crowds who came to be baptized to bring forth fruits proving their repentance, and gave them practical directions to forsake their besetting sins and do the particular duty that was required of them (7–14). In the midst of the general wonder he awakened, John told them why he baptized with water and announced that the Messiah was coming after him and would baptize with the Holy Spirit and execute judgment (15–17). Luke then completes his account of the Baptist at this point by telling how his ministry was abruptly terminated by imprisonment at the hands of Herod, whose wickedness he had reproved (18–20). Cf. Mt. xiv. 1–12; Mk. vi. 14–29.

The voice of one crying (4). The general sense of the passage, quoted from Is. xl. 3–5, is a call to prepare a highway through the wilderness for the coming of a king. *The wrath to come* (7). The people thought that the judgment of the Messiah was to be executed upon their Gentile oppressors. John warned them of a coming judgment for the Jews themselves, and declared that it was imminent. *I indeed baptize you with water* (16). There is an emphasis in the original on both *I* and *with water*. That was all that John could do. Then he points the contrast between his own baptizing with water and the Messiah's baptizing with the Holy Spirit. This is noted in all the Gospels (Mt. iii. 11; Mk. i. 8; Jn. i. 33), and is also mentioned by Jesus after the resurrection (Acts i. 5). Obviously there was an intended parallel between John's baptizing with water and the subsequent outpouring of the Holy Spirit at Pentecost. The rite John introduced was based upon the promises of the prophets (Is. xliv. 3; Ezk. xxxvi. 25–27). *And with fire* (16). This refers to the purifying power of the Spirit's work, while water refers to its cleansing power.

b. The baptism of Jesus (iii. 21, 22)

See notes on Mt. iii. 13–17; Mk. i. 9–11. In being baptized, Jesus dedicated Himself to God as the representative Man in order to receive the power of the Holy Spirit for carrying out His messianic task. Luke gives only a brief summary of the event, but he adds the important feature that Jesus was *praying* at the time. It is implied that the descent of the Holy Spirit upon Him was the answer to His prayer. The prayer life of Jesus stands out in this Gospel. There are nine other instances of prayer in the Lord's life mentioned by Luke alone (v. 16, vi. 12, ix. 18, 29, xi. 1, xxii. 32, 44, xxiii. 34, 46). *Thou art my beloved Son; in thee I am well pleased* (22). This was the Father's acceptance of the self-dedication of the Son and His approval of the preceding thirty years of private life.

c. The lineage of Jesus (iii. 23–38)

This differs from the genealogy in Mt. i. 1–17 (q.v.) because it gives the line of Mary instead of the line of Joseph. Luke traces the human ancestry of Jesus back through David and Abraham to Adam—thus showing His connection not only with Israel, as Matthew does, but with all mankind as well. The two lines differ between David and Joseph. Matthew traces the royal line of David from Solomon down to Joseph, showing Jesus to be the legal heir of David. Luke traces Mary's ancestry back to Nathan, another son of David (31), showing that Jesus was 'of the seed of David according to the flesh' (Rom. i. 3). Mary's name is not mentioned, but Joseph is called the son of Heli (23) as being his son-in-law. Luke ends his genealogy by calling Adam *the son of God* (38). In him humanity had its first beginning as a result of a creative act of God. In Jesus humanity had a new beginning by another creative act.

d. The temptation of Jesus (iv. 1–13)

See notes on Mt. iv. 1–11; Mk. i. 12, 13. This mysterious experience took place immediately after Jesus had received the fullness of the Holy Spirit at His baptism and was the first outcome of that experience (1). It was an attack on the attitude of complete surrender to God which He had then taken, and a subtle attempt on the part of the devil to introduce the element of self-will into the work of the Messiah. Jesus refused to have the matter referred to Himself at all, and met each separate appeal of the adversary in the light of the will of God as revealed in His Word. Luke gives the three temptations in an order different from Matthew's (see Mt. iv. 1–11). It is probable that they were all presented to the mind of Jesus at one time, and that He separated the different elements of the one great temptation and gave them this objective form in order to tell the disciples of a subjective experience that was too profound for any human mind to understand.

If thou be the Son of God (3); an allusion to the voice Jesus heard at His baptism. *It is written* (4). Jesus did not reply as the Son of God, but as the representative Man, giving an answer which any man can give. All His quotations are from Deuteronomy (viii. 3, vi. 13, vi. 16). *That is delivered unto me* (6). Jesus did not deny the claim Satan made here; elsewhere He recognizes it (cf. Jn. xii. 31, xiv. 30, xvi. 11). The subtlety of this temptation lay in the fact that the devil offered to put his own enormous influence in the world at the disposal of Jesus for the promotion of the messianic kingdom. *For it is written* (10). The devil did not misquote the Scripture (Ps. xci. 11, 12), but he misapplied it to make it mean presumptuous reliance on God and not faith. *All the temptation* (13); rather, 'every kind of temptation', the whole round of temptation to which the Lord's human nature was open (cf. Heb. iv. 15). *For a season* (13). The devil may have returned to the attack from time to time; but Luke probably alludes to his final assault in Gethsemane (Jn. xiv. 30; Lk. xxii. 53).

IV. THE MINISTRY IN GALILEE.
iv. 14—ix. 50

Luke's account of the Lord's Galilean ministry begins with Nazareth, His home town, and ends with the transfiguration, the real consummation of His human life. During this period He gathered a group of disciples around Himself, and it may be divided into four parts, marked by steps in their calling and training.

a. Up to the call of the first disciples (iv. 14–44)

After an introductory statement about the return of Jesus into Galilee, we are told of a visit to Nazareth and a sabbath in Capernaum.

i. The return to Galilee (iv. 14, 15). Jesus came back into Galilee and entered upon a ministry of teaching in the synagogues, carrying it on in the power which He had received at His baptism. His fame spread throughout the whole province, which at that time was densely populated. *In the power of the Spirit* (14). All the evangelists tell us that the Holy Spirit came upon Jesus at His baptism, but Luke alone goes on to show how this experience influenced His life. There are four references to it in this chapter (see verses 1, 14, 18).

ii. **A visit to Nazareth (iv. 16–30).** Coming to His own city, Jesus taught on the sabbath in the synagogue there. He read from Is. lxi. 1, 2 and applied the prophecy to Himself, thus explaining the change that had taken place in His life since He left His home to go down to John's baptism. The people bore witness to the gracious character of His message, but when He mentioned cases of God's favour being shown to Gentiles they were enraged and made an attempt to do away with Him. The passage is peculiar to Luke, and it is doubtful whether this is the same visit as that recorded by Matthew (xiii. 54–58) and Mark (vi. 1–6) later in the ministry.

As his custom was (16). This throws light on His previous private life. Every Jewish community had its synagogue for the reading and teaching of the law and for the worship of God. It was customary to stand when reading the Scriptures and to sit when teaching. *He began to say* (21). There is a solemn emphasis about these words in their context. When Jesus sat down, showing that He intended to teach, a hushed and eager expectation took possession of the people. Then He broke the silence with an amazing claim. *Is not this Joseph's son?* (22). He was one of their own townsmen and had been brought up among them. Why should He show such grace and make such claims?

iii. **A sabbath in Capernaum (iv. 31–44).** This passage is parallel with Mk. i. 21–39, where we have the most complete account of a sabbath day's work in the life of Jesus. See notes there. Luke tells of the casting out of an unclean spirit in the synagogue (31–37), the restoration of Peter's wife's mother from a fever in his home (38, 39), the healing of a crowd of sick people in the city in the evening (40, 41), and the departure next morning for a tour in Galilee (42–44). Cf. Mt. viii. 14–17.

Came down (31). Capernaum was on the shore of the Sea of Galilee which lies 680 feet below sea level, while Nazareth was in the hill country of Galilee. *A spirit of an unclean devil* (33). This is a typical instance of demon possession and of Christ's method of dealing with it. Demons belong to the kingdom of Satan, which was especially active when Christ was among men. *When the sun was setting* (40); marking the end of the sabbath day, when the people could now carry their sick.

b. **From the call of the first disciples to the choice of the Twelve (v. 1—vi. 11)**

Jesus had been winning adherents by His preaching, but had not yet formed a band of personal followers. Now He began to attach to Himself regular disciples. During this period the religious leaders began to show their opposition to Him.

i. **The call of Simon Peter (v. 1–11).** This incident is probably the same as that recorded in abridged form in Mt. iv. 18–22 and Mk. i. 16–20. See notes there. Luke alone tells of Jesus teaching from Simon's boat (cf. Mk. iii. 9, iv. 1) and of the great catch of fishes. The surprising result which followed Simon's incredulous obedience to the Lord's command broke down his proud self-confidence and brought him to the feet of Jesus with a confession of utter unworthiness. Jesus replied with a word of encouragement and told him that he was to become a fisher of men. Simon and his partners then gave up their fishing and became followers of Jesus.

Master, we have toiled all the night (5). This was the best time for fishing. Peter expected no result, but he would let down the nets as a token of obedience to the *Master* (5). From Jn. i. 40–42 we know that he had already met Jesus. *Depart from me* (8). The result gave Peter such a new revelation of the character of Jesus, who had thus rewarded him for the use of his boat, that he saw his own character in a true light. He addressed Jesus now with the higher and holier title of *Lord*.

ii. **Special miracles of healing (v. 12–26).** During a tour among the cities of Galilee Jesus healed a leper who had appealed to Him, and the miracle resulted in a great increase of popular interest. Throngs came to be healed, but Jesus kept withdrawing from them for prayer (12–16). The miracle is described more briefly in Mt. viii. 1–4 and more fully in Mk. i. 40–45, where see notes. Luke alone describes the man as *full of leprosy* (12). The growing fame of Jesus drew the religious leaders from all over the land, and some of them were present on another occasion, when Jesus healed a paralytic who had been let down through the roof in a crowded house. They were scandalized when Jesus told the sick man before healing him that his sins were forgiven (17–24). But the people who witnessed the miracle were amazed and awed and gave praise to God (25, 26). See notes on Mt. ix. 2–8; Mk. ii. 1–12. *Shew thyself to the priest* (14). Jesus would not have the law ignored, which required the priest to give a certificate of cleansing (see Lv. xiii). *Pharisees* (17). They were a religious party who stood for the strict observance of the law as interpreted by the scribes or *doctors of the law* (17). *The power of the Lord was present to heal them* (17). It was present for Jesus to use in His miracles of healing. This indicates His dependence upon God in all His work. *The Son of man* (24). This is the phrase that Jesus always used in speaking of Himself. None of the evangelists use it of Him, and no one ever addressed Him by this title. It occurs in the Gospels about eighty times.

iii. **The discipleship of Levi (v. 27–39).** This passage is parallel with Mt. ix. 9–17 and Mk.

ii. 14–22, where see notes. Levi is also known as Matthew, the name which he uses himself. He was a collector of taxes, and was called from his toll-booth. He responded immediately, leaving his lucrative business to become a follower of Jesus (27, 28). He gave a reception to his new Master in his own home, which brought a great many of his fellow-publicans and other social outcasts and Jesus together. This gave Jesus an occasion to explain the real purpose of His mission (29–32). Then a question was raised why His disciples did not fast like the disciples of John and the Pharisees. In replying Jesus gave the first hint of His death (33–35), and followed it with two parabolic statements to show that He was not patching up the old legal system but introducing an entirely new order (36–39).

A publican (27). The publicans were of two classes—collectors of direct taxes and custom-house officers. Levi belonged to the second class. *Their scribes and Pharisees* (30); rather, 'the Pharisees and their scribes', i.e. scribes who belonged to the party of the Pharisees. The function of the scribes was to copy and explain the law. They had loaded the law with tradition, and among other things they had added many new fasts. *While the bridegroom is with them* (34). Jesus was alluding to the fact that John had called Him 'the bridegroom' and himself 'the friend of the bridegroom' (see Jn. iii. 29). *New wine into new bottles* (38); rather, 'fresh wine into new wineskins'. Two different words are used here for 'new': *neos*, i.e. new with reference to time, fresh or newly made; and *kainos*, new with reference to quality, not outworn or impaired by use. Verse 39 is peculiar to Luke. The Lord explains how natural it was that those who had come to realize the value of the old Judaism should be unwilling to abandon it for something new and untried.

iv. **Sabbath day incidents (vi. 1–11).** This passage is parallel with Mt. xii. 1–14 and Mk. ii. 23–26, where see notes. These two incidents show how the hostility of the religious authorities came to a head on the observance of the sabbath law. In the first case (1–5), the Pharisees criticized the disciples of Jesus for rubbing ears of grain to satisfy their hunger as they passed through the fields on the sabbath, for this was regarded as a breach of the law forbidding labour on that day. Jesus defended them by citing the case of David who, when he and his men were hungry, ate the sacred shewbread of the tabernacle. In the second case (6–11), He healed a man with a withered hand in the synagogue after challenging the scribes and Pharisees who were there to declare whether it was lawful to do good or to do harm on the sabbath day.

The second sabbath after the first (1). This is the rendering of a curious term (lit. 'second-first') used only by Luke, the meaning of which is obscure. It is not found in some MSS and the RV omits it. *Have ye not read?* (3); referring to the incident related in 1 Sa. xxi. 1–6. The Phari-

sees would not dare to criticize what David did. Jesus does not abrogate the sabbath law, but He claims the right as the representative Man to administer it for man's good (5).

c. **From the choice of the Twelve to their first mission (vi. 12—viii. 56)**
During this period the popularity of Jesus continued to increase and His ministry in Galilee reached its height. The section begins with the appointment of the twelve apostles, contains the most important of His Galilean discourses, and records a series of remarkable miracles.

i. **The choice of the Twelve (vi. 12–19).** Jesus spent a whole night on the mountain in prayer, and next day He chose twelve from among His disciples and named them apostles to indicate His purpose for them. Their names are the same as in Mt. x. 2–4 and Mk. iii. 16–19, where see notes, except that of Judas the son of James, who is called Thaddaeus in the other Gospels. Jesus then came down with the Twelve to a level spot on the side of the mountain, and there a large group of His own disciples and a great crowd of other people gathered about Him to hear and to be healed. *Stood in the plain* (17); rather, 'stood on a level place' (RV). There is no discrepancy between this and the statement in Mt. v. 1. Matthew's account is that of the group who went up into the mountain with Jesus; Luke describes the event from a detached point of view. It would seem that our Lord sought first the privacy of the mountain top with His disciples, and then came down to a level place and spoke in the hearing of all the people. Note the references to the 'great multitude' in Mt. viii. 1 and to the 'people' in Mt. vii. 28.

ii. **The sermon to the disciples (vi. 20–49).** In the midst of the scene just described, Jesus delivered what is usually called the Sermon on the Mount. It is fully recorded in Mt. v. 1—vii. 29 and parts of it were probably repeated on other occasions. See the commentary on Matthew for detailed notes on its teaching. Luke's account begins with a series of 'Blesseds' followed by a series of 'Woes', bringing out, on the one hand, the contrast in character between those who belong to the kingdom of God and those who live for the present world, and, on the other hand, the contrast between the happiness that is the portion of the one class and the misery that awaits the other (20–26). The next part of the discourse deals with the duties required of the members of the kingdom (27–38). Luke omits most of what Matthew reports regarding Christ's relation to the Mosaic law, which would have little meaning for his Gentile readers. What he emphasizes is the teaching that love is the principle of the kingdom and the distinguishing quality of its members. For verses 37ff. see notes on Mt. vii. 1–5. Then come several pointed sayings and practical illustrations showing how this principle is to be maintained (39–45). For verses 43–45 see notes on Mt. vii. 15–20. The sermon closes with a warning to His hearers of the consequences of not heeding His words (46–49). Cf. Mt. vii. 24–27.

Blessed be ye poor (20). Jesus is addressing His disciples and means that their actual poverty is a blessing because it helps to preserve their dependence on God and so fit them for His kingdom. *And immediately it fell* (49). The word for 'immediately' (*eutheōs*) is frequent in Mark, but rare in Luke. The RV always renders it 'straightway'. An equally good rendering would be 'thereupon', bringing out the idea of sequence which is always implied.

iii. Two works of power (vii. 1–17). After the sermon to the disciples Jesus returned to Capernaum (1), and there a centurion appealed to Him for his servant who was at the point of death, and Jesus healed him. See also notes on Mt. viii. 5–13. Luke's story of the miracle is much fuller than the condensed account given by Matthew, which represents the centurion as doing himself what Luke says he did through a deputation of Jewish elders (2–5). As Jesus approached the house He was met by friends of the centurion, who had sent them to express his own unworthiness to receive the Lord or even approach Him, and also his conviction that a word from Him would suffice, because his experience of the authority of a military commander led him to regard the authority of Jesus as similar in its reach (6–8). When Jesus heard this, He marvelled and declared that the faith of this Gentile far surpassed any faith He had found among the Jews. When the friends returned to the house they found the servant completely restored (9, 10). *Who was dear unto him* (2). It was characteristic of Luke to note this. All the centurions mentioned in the New Testament have something recorded to their credit (Mt. xxvii. 54; Acts x. 1, xxii. 26, xxvii. 43). *My servant* (7); lit. 'my boy', a term of affection.

The raising of the widow's son at Nain is recorded only in Luke (11–17). Nain was about twenty-five miles from Capernaum out on the plain in the southern part of Galilee. The desolate state of the widow who had lost her only son touched the compassion of Jesus. He stopped the funeral procession, called the young man back to life, and restored him to his mother. The miracle overawed the people, and the fame of Jesus was spread still more widely. *The Lord* (13). Luke seems to use this title purposely here: the Lord of life is meeting death.

iv. A message from John the Baptist (vii. 18–35). This passage is parallel with Mt. xi. 2–19, where see notes. John sent two of his disciples to Jesus enquiring whether He was the one whose coming was expected. At that very time Jesus performed many miracles of healing, and He sent John's disciples back to tell their master what they had seen and heard (18–23). When they were gone Jesus spoke to the people about John and pronounced the highest praise upon him. He was much more than a prophet, for he had the unique honour of being chosen of God to introduce the Messiah. As such John is the greatest of all men, and yet the least member of the kingdom of God is greater than he (24–28). At this point Jesus summed up the result of John's ministry as twofold, a general movement among the common people and open opposition on the part of the rulers (29, 30). Then He went on to liken the people of His own generation to children in the market-place, finding fault with their companions because they cannot get them to play at any kind of game. They call John a demoniac because he practises asceticism, and they call Jesus a glutton and winebibber because He does not do so (31–35).

Art thou he that should come? (19). The question does not imply a complete failure in John's faith; but he had probably expected Jesus to follow a different method when he bore witness to Him as the Messiah. *Go your way, and tell John* (22). Jesus describes the works John's disciples had seen Him do in the very words which the prophet Isaiah had used of the messianic age (Is. xxxv. 5, 6); John, a prophet himself, would understand what Jesus meant. *There is not a greater prophet than John the Baptist* (28); rather, 'there is none greater than John' (RV). Jesus is not comparing the Baptist with all other prophets, but with all other members of the human race. In so doing He reveals the true standard of greatness—nearness of relationship to Himself. The meaning of verse 35 is that divine Wisdom is vindicated by her own children, the faithful minority who welcomed the Baptist and the Messiah, not by the unbelieving majority who rejected them.

v. In the house of Simon the Pharisee (vii. 36–50). This incident is recorded by Luke alone. The anointing of Jesus by the sinful woman (36–38) is to be distinguished from the anointing in Bethany recorded by the other evangelists (cf. Mt. xxvi. 6–13; Mk. xiv. 3–9; Jn. xii. 1–8). Jesus answered the unspoken thought of the proud and supercilious Pharisee by telling the parable of two debtors (39–43), and then applying it to his case and the woman's. His indifference toward his guest and his failure as a host were in sharp contrast with the affection and the behaviour of the woman (44–47). The final word which Jesus spoke to her indicates that the love she had shown Him sprang from her faith in Him and this faith in Him implied that her sins were forgiven (47–50).

At his feet behind him (38). The sandals were removed at meals and the guests reclined on their elbows with their feet stretched out behind them. *Five hundred pence, . . . fifty* (41). The two debts would represent about £50 and £5 respectively. *Seest thou this woman?* (44). In this and the next two verses Jesus mentions three acts of courtesy with which a host usually received a guest. Simon had ignored them all and the woman had performed them. In drawing out the contrast between Simon and the woman, the words of Jesus rise into the rhythmic parallelism of Hebrew poetry. *For she loved much* (47). The proof of her forgiveness, not the reason for it.

vi. Another tour in Galilee (viii. 1–21). Luke describes a feature in the Lord's ministry at this period which is not mentioned elsewhere. He and the Twelve formed a travelling company, going about with the message of the kingdom of God; and another company, composed of women of means, arranged for their reception and support (1–3). This group of women followed Jesus even to the cross (see xxiii. 49). Luke continues this section with the parable of the sower and its interpretation (4–15), given more fully in Mt. xiii and Mk. iv (where see notes), and several other parabolic sayings (16–18). Then comes a brief account of the incident that occurred when Jesus' mother and brethren came seeking Him and could not reach Him for the crowd (19–21), which is recorded also in Mt. xii. 46–50 and Mk. iii. 31–35.

Mary called Magdalene (2); i.e. Mary of Magdala, to distinguish her from Mary of Bethany and other Marys. The name was a common one. She is not to be identified with the sinful woman of vii. 36. *He spake by a parable* (4). Luke has already used the term 'parable' of several brief sayings of Jesus, but this is the first of the more elaborate parables which now become more common in our Lord's teaching. They are stories or illustrations from the natural world and from everyday life which He used to set forth the spiritual world and the spiritual life. See notes on Mt. xiii. 1–23; Mk. iv. 1–20. *A sower went out to sow* (5). His seed fell on four different kinds of ground, and the teaching of the parable rests on the differences in the ground. It might be called the parable of the four soils. *The mysteries of the kingdom of God* (10). Those aspects of it which cannot be discovered by human reason and are understood only in the light of divine revelation. *That seeing they might not see* (10). Christ's purpose was to put the truth in such a way that it would be hidden from those who were unwilling to welcome it, but be full of meaning to those who wished to understand it. See Mk. iv. 12n.

No man, when he hath lighted a candle (16). The connection between this and the preceding verses lies in the fact that by answering the question of the disciples (9) Jesus had lighted a candle within them, and they must not hide it but spread its light to others. If they do this they will get more light. The sayings which Luke has grouped together here are scattered in three different places in Matthew (v. 15, x. 26, xiii. 12).

His mother and his brethren (19). See notes on Mk. iii. 20, 21, 31–35; cf. Mt. xii. 46–50. The family of Joseph and Mary consisted of four sons and at least two sisters, all born after Jesus (Mt. xiii. 55, 56; Mk. vi. 3). They did not yet believe in Him (Jn. vii. 3–5) and probably thought He was beside Himself (Mk. iii. 21).

vii. A series of typical miracles (viii. 22–56). All the synoptic Gospels record these four miracles and in the same order. See notes *in loc.* Matthew's account is the briefest and most compact (viii. 23–34, ix. 18–26), and Mark's the longest and most detailed (iv. 35—v. 43). They are representative miracles and belong to the four different realms in which Jesus wrought His mighty works. The stilling of the storm on the sea manifested His power over the natural world (22–25); the deliverance of the Gadarene demoniac manifested His authority over the spirit-world (26–39); the healing of the woman who touched His garment showed His power in the realm of our physical nature (40–48); and His raising of the daughter of Jairus revealed His authority over the realm of death (49–56).

Rebuked the wind (24). The same word is used of the way in which He dealt with the fever of Peter's wife's mother (iv. 39). Behind all the disturbances of nature and the ills of our physical frame Jesus saw His own great foe. *Being afraid* (25). The disciples were overwhelmed with awe in the presence of a supernatural power they had not seen in their Master before.

What is thy name? (30); addressed to the man to arouse in him a sense of his own personality. See Mk. v. 9n.

One only daughter (42). Luke alone mentions this touching fact, as he does in the case of the widow's son (vii. 12), and again later in the case of the demoniac boy (ix. 38). *Who touched me?* Our Lord's question gave the woman an opportunity to make a voluntary confession and not to go away with a stolen blessing. He would not leave His work with her unfinished, even under the urgent pressure of Jairus's appeal.

Peter, and James, and John (51). These three formed an inner group within the Twelve, whom Jesus chose to be with Him on several special occasions (see Mt. xvii. 1, xxvi. 37).

d. From the mission of the Twelve to the departure from Galilee (ix. 1–50)

This section brings the Galilean ministry to its consummation. It includes several events of supreme importance, especially Peter's great confession and the Lord's transfiguration.

i. The mission of the Twelve (ix. 1–9). Luke's account of the commission of the Twelve (1–6) is substantially the same as Matthew's (x. 5–15) and Mark's (vi. 7–13), except that Matthew gives a fuller report of the instructions Jesus gave them and Mark tells us that He sent them forth 'by two and two'. See notes *in loc.* The stir caused by this mission throughout Galilee brought the fame of Jesus to the notice of Herod Antipas, who was perplexed by what he heard and tried to get an interview with Him (7–9; see Mt. xiv. 1–12n. and Mk. vi. 14–29n.).

Take nothing for your journey (3). This mission of the apostles was limited to Israel, and as the messengers of the Messiah they were worthy of the people's support.

ii. The feeding of the five thousand (ix. 10–17). When the apostles returned with their report, Jesus took them apart for retirement to the north-east side of the lake, but the people followed Him and interrupted His plan. Yet He gave them a welcome and ministered to them.

When evening came the Twelve suggested that He send the people away to get food and lodging in the surrounding villages. Instead, He had the disciples feed them with what they had themselves, five loaves and two fishes. He made the people sit down in groups of fifty, and after blessing the food He gave it back to the disciples to distribute among them. All were satisfied, and twelve baskets were filled with the fragments that remained. The special importance of this miracle is marked by the fact that it is the only one recorded in all the four Gospels. The parallel accounts are Mt. xiv. 13–23, Mk. vi. 30–46 and Jn. vi. 1–15, where see notes.

The city called Bethsaida (10). Not 'the city of Andrew and Philip' (Jn. i. 44), which was on the west side of the lake, but Bethsaida Julias, which was on the east side of the upper Jordan in the territory of Philip the tetrarch. *About five thousand men* (14). Matthew adds 'besides women and children', but of these there would be very few. *Looking up to heaven, he blessed them* (16). All four accounts note this, seeing in it the secret of the power displayed. *Brake, and gave* (16). The Greek verbs are in different tenses; *brake* indicates a single act, and *gave* a continuous one. As the food was being distributed, it was being multiplied. *Twelve baskets* (17). The word means a wallet (Gk. *kophinos*), which was carried by Jews when travelling to avoid buying food from Gentiles.

iii. Peter's confession of Christ (ix. 18–27). This passage is parallel with Mt. xvi. 13–28 and Mk. viii. 27–38, where see notes. Luke does not mention the place where the incident occurred but he tells us that Jesus was praying at the time. Peter's answer to the question Jesus put to the disciples about Himself is given briefly and is followed at once by the Lord's prediction of His rejection and death at the hands of the Jewish leaders and His subsequent resurrection (18–22). Luke omits Jesus' commendation of Peter and the statement about His Church, and records only His warning to the disciples how they were to follow Him. They must take up their cross and be prepared to lose their life for His sake. If they should be ashamed of Him they would not share in His glory when He comes (23–27).

The Christ of God (20). The first confession of Jesus as the Messiah made by any of the disciples. But the people were not yet ready for this announcement because of their carnal views of the kingdom. *Take up his cross* (23); the first mention of the cross in Luke. It must have startled the disciples, for they well knew that a cross was not carried merely as a burden, but as something on which to be put to death. *Shall come in his own glory* (26); Christ's first reference to His second advent. His statement in verse 27 may mean that the transfiguration, which was to occur soon afterwards, would forecast the glory of His kingdom (cf. 2 Pet. i. 16–18).

iv. The transfiguration (ix. 28–36). This marked the highest point in the life of Jesus. It was the culmination of His sinless and perfect humanity,

for death had no claim upon Him. Luke's account of the scene throws further light upon the record in the parallel passages (Mt. xvii. 1–7 and Mk. ix. 2–8). Jesus was praying when His transfiguration took place, and the theme of His conversation with Moses and Elijah was 'his departure (rv mg.) which he should accomplish at Jerusalem'. He might have crowned His earthly life as the Son of man by departing by the way of the mount of transfiguration, but He turned back to go by the way of the cross and so accomplish the redemption of the world. The voice which came out of the cloud that finally overshadowed the scene expressed the Father's approval of the Son's self-surrender.

Into a mountain (28). The context in the other accounts identifies it as Mount Hermon, whose snow-capped top, over 9000 feet high, can be seen from many parts of Palestine gleaming like gold in the sunlight. *Moses and Elias* (30); representatives of the law and the prophets. *Who appeared in glory* (31). Not as immaterial spirits, but in bodily form as Jesus was. Elijah had been translated bodily into heaven (2 Ki. ii. 11), and Jude 9 implies that the body of Moses had been raised from the dead. *His decease* (31). The word is *exodos*, a 'way out', and does not refer to His death alone, but to His resurrection and ascension as well. This theme would be of peculiar interest to both Moses and Elijah because of their own experience.

v. The close of the Galilean ministry (ix. 37–50). The transfiguration was followed next day by a miracle at the foot of the mountain (37–42). Jesus cured a demoniac boy whom the disciples He had left there the day before had tried to cure but could not. The parallel accounts in Mt. xvii. 14–21 and Mk. ix. 14–29 (see notes) bring out more fully the reason for their failure, but Luke marks the human interest of the scene in the father's pathetic appeal for his *only child* (38) and in the tender touch that when Jesus cast the demon out of the boy He *delivered him again to his father* (42). *How long shall I be with you?* (41). These words reveal a sense of homesickness in the heart of Jesus. He felt the contrast between the unbelief and perversity of the human race and the holy devotion of the heavenly world from which He had come.

Luke's account of the Galilean ministry comes to a close with another prediction of the passion (43–45; cf. Mt. xvii. 22, 23; Mk. ix. 30–32), an object lesson in humility (46–48; cf. Mt. xviii. 1–5; Mk. ix. 33–37), and a warning against intolerance (49, 50; cf. Mk. ix. 38–40).

V. THE JOURNEY TO JERUSALEM.
ix. 51—xix. 28

The narrative contained in this part of the Gospel is almost wholly peculiar to Luke. In Matthew the story is limited to two chapters (xix, xx) and in Mark to one (x). The journey occupied several months. In the course of it Luke mentions three times that Jesus was on

His way to Jerusalem (ix. 51, xiii. 22, xvii. 11). This would indicate three stages in the journey. It is probable that these were separated by different visits to Jerusalem, for John's Gospel shows that Jesus was in the city on two occasions during this period before the final Passover. These occasions were the feast of tabernacles in the autumn (Jn. vii. 2, 10, 37) and the feast of the dedication in the winter (Jn. x. 22, 23).

a. The first stage of the journey (ix. 51—xiii. 21)

The first incident related shows that Jesus set out first on the direct road through Samaria and then crossed over the Jordan into Peraea and journeyed south through that district.

i. Rejected in Samaria (ix. 51–62). Jesus sent messengers into Samaria to prepare for His arrival. He had passed through Samaria once before and had been welcomed there (Jn. iv. 39, 40), but then He was on His way from Jerusalem. Now one of their villages refused Him hospitality because He was on His way toward Jerusalem. James and John drew a rebuke from the Lord for desiring to call down fire from heaven upon it (51–56). Three incidents occurred as they went on their way in which Jesus showed His knowledge of the hearts of men in dealing with would-be but doubtful disciples (57–62; cf. Mt. viii. 19–22).

The time . . . that he should be received up (51); lit. 'the days of his taking up', a reference to the ascension. *He stedfastly set his face* (51). The fixed set purpose of the Lord's bearing at this time is noted in Mk. x. 32. *Let the dead bury their dead* (60). Leave the spiritually dead, whose interests are only in this life, to attend to the duties of earthly society.

ii. The mission of the seventy (x. 1–24). As Jesus sent the Twelve into the northern parts of the province because the labourers were so few and the harvest was so great (Mt. ix. 37—x. 1), so now for the same reason He sent a much larger number of His disciples into the southern parts through which He was about to travel (1, 2). The charge He gave them was similar to that given to the Twelve (3–12). It closes with a denunciation of the impenitent cities in Galilee (13–16), which Matthew records in another connection (see Mt. xi. 20–24).

Whither he himself would come (1). They were to precede Jesus Himself and announce that the kingdom was at hand in the person of the King. *Salute no man by the way* (4). Because of the urgency of their mission, they were not to waste time in the long and complicated salutations of the wayside (cf. 2 Ki. iv. 29). *The labourer is worthy of his hire* (7). Paul quotes these words as Scripture in 1 Tim. v. 18, which implies that the third Gospel was published before the Epistle was written. *Go not from house to house* (7). Another warning against wasting valuable time by accepting numerous invitations.

The joy which these disciples manifested on their return evoked an exultation on our Lord's part which is unique in the life of the Saviour.

He saw in their success a symbol and earnest of the complete overthrow of Satan (17–20). Then He went on to express His joy that the truths of His new order were being revealed to the simple, and to congratulate His disciples that they had seen them. While doing this He made one of those sublime assertions of divine power and authority that flash out again and again from His teaching (21–24). *Rejoiced in spirit* (21). The verb is a very strong one and means that Jesus showed exultant joy. The RV rendering, 'rejoiced in the Holy Spirit', means that He was filled by the Holy Spirit with a rapturous joy which led Him to give utterance to the words which follow.

iii. The Good Samaritan (x. 25–42). The occasion of this parable was a practical question put by a lawyer who asked what he should do to inherit eternal life, implying that it could be secured by the performance of some one act. Jesus referred him back to the law which, as a lawyer, he should know. The lawyer showed that he rightly understood the law by quoting the heart of it as summed up in love to God and to one's neighbour (Dt. vi. 5; Lv. xix. 18). Jesus approved the answer and added, *this do, and thou shalt live* (28), implying that life consists in the continuous performance of acts of love. This touched the lawyer's conscience and put him on the defensive, and he asked another question: *And who is my neighbour?* (29).

Jesus replied by telling the story of a Samaritan, which was probably taken from real life, for He would hardly represent a priest and a Levite as so callous if there had been no actual incident to justify His doing so. The parable illustrates the true operation of the law of love. *Went down* (30). The road from Jerusalem to Jericho descended more than 3000 feet in less than fifteen miles through gorges that were infested with robbers. *A certain Samaritan* (33); the representative of a despised race, while the priest and the Levite represented Jewish orthodoxy and respectability. *When I come again* (35). The 'I' is very emphatic: 'I, and not the wounded man, will repay thee.'

Jesus shifted the lawyer's ground from the self-interest implied in his question to interest in others by asking, when He had finished the story, *Which now of these three . . . was neighbour?* (36). If a Samaritan could prove himself a true neighbour to a Jew by showing mercy to him, then all men are neighbours.

The exquisite picture of Jesus in the home of Martha and Mary, which follows the parable and is preserved by Luke alone, may have been inserted here to supplement the answer Jesus gave to the lawyer's question about eternal life. Practical benevolence such as that of the Samaritan is not enough. It must be combined with communion with the Lord. This was *that good part* (42) which Mary had chosen. *A certain village* (38). From John's Gospel we learn that it was Bethany (see Jn. xi. 1). *Came to him* (40). Martha made an impatient movement, losing her temper sufficiently to reproach Jesus and indirectly rebuke Mary. *But one thing is needful* (42). Many dishes were not required; just one would suffice. It was fellowship Jesus valued, not entertainment.

iv. A lesson on prayer (xi. 1–13). On one occasion when Jesus had been praying, He was asked by one of the disciples to teach them to pray, and He gave them as a model what we know as the Lord's Prayer (1–4), in a somewhat shorter form than Matthew's record of it in the Sermon on the Mount (see notes on Mt. vi. 9–13). Probably Jesus taught it to the disciples on different occasions. The word rendered *daily* (Gk. *epiousion*) is found nowhere else in Greek literature, and its precise meaning is therefore uncertain. It has been found, however, in a document from Egypt in a context which suggests the meaning 'daily rations'. Probably the best way to render it is 'bread for the coming day', i.e. if used in the morning, 'today's bread', and if in the evening, 'tomorrow's bread'.

He followed this model prayer with an encouragement to pray in the parable of the importunate friend (5–8). Three persons are to be distinguished: the host—*which of you* (5)—with nothing to supply his guest; his neighbouring *friend* (5) who has abundance; and his guest—*a friend of mine* (6)—who has come to him needy and hungry. The parable teaches its lesson by contrasting the reluctance of the selfish friend who has to be roused by importunate asking with the willingness of the bountiful God. Jesus added an exhortation to the disciples to persevere in prayer, and supported it by an appeal to their own understanding of a human father's nature (9–13). For this last section see also Mt. vii. 7–11. Observe that the gift of *the Holy Spirit* (13) implies all other good gifts (cf. Mt. vii. 11).

v. That generation denounced (xi. 14–36). Having cured a dumb demoniac, Jesus was accused of complicity with Beelzebub and was challenged for a sign to clear Himself of the charge (14–16). He first refuted the charge by an appeal to common sense (17–19). Then He gave the true explanation of His cures: the power of God was present with Him and the kingdom of God had come among them (20–22). See notes on Mt. xii. 22–30; and cf. Mk. iii. 22–30. *Beelzebub the chief of the devils* (15). This name, probably from that of the Philistine deity mentioned in 2 Ki. i. 2, was applied by the Jews to Satan. The name Baal-Zebul ('lord of the high place') appears as the name of a Canaanite deity as early as the Ras Shamra tablets (*c.* 1400 B.C.). *A strong man* (21); i.e. Satan. *A stronger than he* (22); i.e. Christ. Thus Jesus foreshadows His victory over Satan. He went on to point out the impossibility of being neutral in the conflict between Himself and Satan (23).

The case of a demoniac who has been cured and allows himself to become possessed again is likened to that of the sinner who repents of his sin but does not let the Spirit of Christ come in (24–26). Cf. Mt. xii. 43–45 and see note there.

At this point an incident occurred which illustrates the deep impression the Lord's words were making upon the people (27, 28). As they thronged around Him Jesus denounced the Jews of His day as *an evil generation* (29) for seeking a sign, and declared that no sign should be given it but that of Jonah. It would be condemned in the final judgment by the queen who came to hear the wisdom of Solomon, and by the Ninevites who repented at the preaching of Jonah. They would condemn by their example the Jews of that day who had a greater than Solomon and Jonah in their midst (29–32). With these verses cf. Mt. xii. 38–42; Mk. viii. 11, 12. Those whose spiritual vision had not been darkened by impenitence and indifference had no need of a sign from heaven. They were illumined by a light that was shining all around them—the light shed by Christ Himself (33–36). For verse 33 see notes on Mt. v. 14–16. For verse 34 see notes on Mt. vi. 22, 23.

vi. Denunciation of the Pharisees and lawyers (xi. 37–54). A Pharisee who had asked Jesus to dine with him was surprised at His not performing the usual act of ceremonial washing (37, 38). This led Jesus to rebuke the Pharisees for the externalism of their religious practices and for their vainglorious spirit (39–44). A remark interposed by one of the lawyers present led Him to denounce them also and to foretell the doom that would fall upon that generation (45–52). When Jesus left the Pharisee's house He was followed by His foes and there was a great commotion around Him (53, 54).

Had not first washed (38); lit. 'was not first baptized'. The reference is to ceremonial cleansing and not ordinary washing. *Such things as ye have* (41); lit. 'the things that are within'. The reference is probably to the contents of *the cup and the platter* (39). The way to keep them clean is to give of their contents to the poor.

One of the lawyers (45); i.e. one of the scribes. Their profession involved the interpretation of the law. *The wisdom of God* (49); i.e. God in His wisdom. *The blood of Zacharias* (51). A reference to the murder of Zechariah recorded in 2 Ch. xxiv. 20, 21. The books of Chronicles come last in the Hebrew Canon and Genesis comes first, and so the two murders Jesus mentions appear at the beginning and the end of the Jewish Bible. See Mt. xxiii. 35n. *To catch something* (54); i.e. something which they might twist and misinterpret in order to bring an accusation against Him.

vii. A series of discourses (xii. 1—xiii. 9). This section contains a number of Christ's utterances which are found in different parts of Matthew, either in the Sermon on the Mount (Mt. v—vii), or in the charge to the Twelve (Mt. x), or in the Olivet prophecy (Mt. xxiv). Luke records them here as one continuous series of discourses with breaks at verses 13, 22 and 54.

Jesus addressed His first words to the disciples in the hearing of the multitude. He warned them against *hypocrisy*, the characteristic spirit of the Pharisees (1–3). He encouraged them with the assurance of God's loving care in this world (4–7). *Fear him* (5); i.e. God, not Satan. We are nowhere told to fear the devil, but to resist him stedfastly (Jas. iv. 7; 1 Pet. v. 9). He promised them a recompense of glory in heaven which would be denied to those who denied Him (8–10). Note that blasphemy against the Holy Spirit is not a specific sin, but constant and persistent opposition to God's grace seeking to reach man through the Holy Spirit (10). After that God can do no more for man. See Mt. xii. 31n.; Mk. iii. 29n. The disciples were not to be anxious before persecuting tribunals, for the Holy Spirit would aid them in their testimony (11, 12). See Mt. x. 17–20; Mk. xiii. 9, 11n.

A covetous request from a man in the crowd (13) brought a rebuke from Jesus. *Man* (14). There is a stern tone in this form of address. He declined to interfere in the affairs of civil life and uttered a warning against covetousness (14, 15), following it with the parable of the rich fool. The ground of the rich man was blessed with a plentiful harvest, but he had no thought for God and was forming plans for the enjoyment of his wealth for many years to come when God called him suddenly to his account. Such is the man who lays up treasure for himself and does not acquire the riches of God (16–21). Note how the first personal pronouns in the rich man's thought vividly depict his character.

After this interruption Jesus once more turned to the disciples. They were not to be anxious, but to trust in their Father's loving care (22–30). See notes on Mt. vi. 25–34. *The nations of the world* (30); i.e. the heathen. The disciples of Jesus should not act like those who do not know God as their Father. They were to seek His kingdom (31), for it was the Father's good pleasure to give them the kingdom, and they were to have their treasure in heaven (31–34). *Sell that ye have, and give alms* (33). The fulfilment of this precept lies in the principle that followers of Christ should sit loose to earthly possessions (see Mt. vi. 19–21; 1 Cor. vii. 29–31). They were to be always ready, like servants waiting for their master's return (36–38). His coming would not be announced beforehand: He would come when unexpected (39, 40). *He shall gird himself . . . and serve them* (37); describing the gratitude that Christ will manifest in rewarding His servants in the coming kingdom (cf. Rev. iii. 20, 21).

Then Peter said (41). As the spokesman of the Twelve he asked whether the promise Jesus had made in verse 37 was for them alone or for all the disciples. Jesus did not answer directly, but threw the responsibility of answering it back on the disciples themselves. He reminded them of their special responsibility to be faithful and wise stewards during their Master's absence, and warned them against being unprepared for His return (41–48). Then He gave voice to the emotion that filled His heart in view of the moral divisions which He was to cause on the earth (49–53). *And what will I, if it be already kindled?*

(49). A difficult passage: probably Jesus meant, 'How I wish that it were already kindled.' The fire would purify and cleanse, as well as destroy. *I have a baptism* (50). The baptism of suffering to be accomplished in Gethsemane and on the cross (cf. Mt. xx. 22). *Peace on earth* (51). It is only in His coming kingdom that Christ is to be the Prince of Peace. In the present world His followers are promised tribulation. Cf. Rev. vii. 14.

Addressing the people once more, Jesus denounced them for not recognizing the significance of what was happening in the world. If they did they would seek reconciliation with their opponents before the final crisis made it too late (xii. 54–59). Then He uttered three warnings of judgment which Luke alone records. Two of them were based on recent incidents (xiii. 1–5). Although there is no record anywhere else of the massacre mentioned in verse 1, such incidents were not uncommon under Roman governors. The third is the parable of the barren fig tree, in which Jesus pictured the failure of Israel to respond to God's patient dealing with the nation and foreshadowed its coming judgment (xiii. 6–9). The fig tree represented Israel in the Old Testament (see Je. xxiv. 3; Ho. ix. 10). The owner corresponds to Jehovah as the God of Israel, and the vine-dresser to Jesus as the Messiah.

viii. The last synagogue scene (xiii. 10–21). This incident is peculiar to Luke and is the last recorded visit of Jesus to a synagogue. The ruler of the synagogue, angry because Jesus had healed the infirm woman on the sabbath, attacked Him indirectly by charging the people not to come for healing on the sabbath day. Jesus exposed his hypocrisy and so put him to shame before the people (10–17). *He called her* (12). This was unusual; generally those whom He cured came to Him. Probably He wished to call her will into action as He delivered her body from the *spirit of infirmity* (11) that bound it. *Whom Satan hath bound* (16). Jesus regarded God's great foe as the cause of human sickness and bodily impurity (cf. 1 Cor. v. 5; 2 Cor. xii. 7).

Seeing how the people rejoiced at what He was doing, Jesus repeated the parables of the mustard seed and the leaven, which describe the twofold result of the presence of the kingdom of God in the world, the one as producing a large visible organization from a small beginning, the other as exercising a hidden pervasive influence in human society (18–21). These parables were spoken first in the sermon of parables recorded in Mt. xiii. See Mt. xiii. 31–33; cf. Mk. iv. 30–32.

b. The second stage of the journey (xiii. 22— xvii. 10)

At this point a break seems to have occurred in the journey. After that Jesus continued His steady progress toward Jerusalem, teaching at every city and village as He went on His way (22). During this period He uttered some of His greatest parables.

i. Warnings on the way (xiii. 23-35). Jesus was asked by one of the company whether few are to be saved. He did not answer directly, but urged the people to attend to the matter of their own salvation; for the time would come when it would be too late, and they would find themselves shut out. He added a prediction of the calling of the Gentiles, when people from all parts of the world would enjoy the blessing of the kingdom (23–30). For verse 24 see Mt. vii. 13, 14n. An attempt was made by some Pharisees to frighten Jesus with a threat from Herod through whose territory He was travelling (31). It failed to divert Him from His purpose. *Tell that fox* (32). Jesus saw the cunning of Herod behind the warning of the Pharisees. He would go on fulfilling the work given Him to do till He had finished it in Jerusalem (31–33). But this thought led Him to utter a lamentation over the city which had so often refused to receive His ministry. She had rejected the salvation He offered her, and now her people were left to the desolation that was coming (34, 35) and which fell upon the city in A.D. 70. *Until . . . ye shall say* (35). This solemn utterance seems to mean that the return of the Lord awaits the national repentance of Israel (cf. Acts iii. 19–21).

ii. A sabbath meal in a Pharisee's house (xiv. 1-24). In this scene, which is peculiar to Luke, we are shown something of Jesus' indoor life and familiar table-talk. They had a man with the dropsy there and were watching to see if Jesus would heal on the sabbath day (2). The refusal of the lawyers and Pharisees to answer His question betrayed their bad faith (3, 4). After healing the man and sending him away, He exposed their hypocrisy by asking another question which they could not answer (5, 6). Jesus marked how the guests took the chief seats for themselves, and He gave them a lesson in humility, clothing it in the form of a recommendation to intelligent self-interest (7–11). Then He gave His host a lesson on charity toward the poor and needy, promising him a reward in the resurrection of the just (12–14). This drew a remark from one of the guests about the blessedness of sharing in the feast of the kingdom of God. Then Jesus spoke the parable of the great supper to show how little this privilege was appreciated. The man who made the supper bade many, but when he sent his servant to tell them that all things were ready they proceeded to excuse themselves. The parable depicts the indifference of the Jews to spiritual things, their rejection of the gospel, their exclusion from the kingdom, and the subsequent calling of the Gentiles (15–24). Cf. Mt. viii. 11, 12.

And, behold (2). This verse vividly describes the Lord's immediate realization of the whole meaning of the scene before Him. Verse 11 is one of our Lord's characteristic utterances; it is repeated in Lk. xviii. 14 and Mt. xxiii. 12. *The resurrection of the just* (14). In the light of Lk. xx. 35 this expression implies a double resurrection, first of the just and then of the rest of

mankind. *Come; for all things are now ready* (17). This represents the first gospel message to the Jewish nation as uttered by John the Baptist, Jesus, and His apostles (see Mt. iii. 1, 2, iv. 17, x. 7). *The streets and lanes of the city* (21). This represents the outcasts of Israel, the publicans and sinners. *The highways and hedges* (23). The country districts beyond the city, representing the Gentile world. *Compel them to come in* (23); rather, 'constrain them' (RV), using persuasion, not compulsion.

iii. The conditions of discipleship (xiv. 25-35). As Jesus resumed His journey great crowds followed Him. They were disposed to believe that He was the Messiah, but they misunderstood the nature of the kingdom and the conditions of discipleship. These Jesus now pointed out. The disciple of Jesus must bear the cross after Him (25–27). He must count the cost of following Him to the end (28–32). He must renounce all that he has for Christ's sake and maintain the spirit of self-sacrifice, so that the salt of his life may not lose its savour (33–35).

He turned, and said (25); a dramatic touch. Jesus made a deliberate attempt to check the unthinking enthusiasm of the crowds. *And hate not his father, and mother* (26). To be taken in the light of Mt. x. 37 and xv. 4. Jesus often stated a truth in a startling way and left it to the common sense of His hearers. *Bear his cross* (27). Accept what he has to endure as a means of putting his own self-life to death. *Forsaketh not all that he hath* (33). In the sense of being no longer dependent on it. The disciple must renounce everything that would prevent his dependence on Christ alone. Cf. Mt. x. 38, 39, xvi. 24, 25; Jn. xii. 25.

iv. Three parables of grace (xv. 1-32). These three stories form a connected series and are found in Luke alone. They were the Lord's answer to the contemptuous remarks of the Pharisees and scribes about His association with publicans and sinners (1, 2). The parables of the lost sheep (3–7) and the lost coin (8–10) set forth the seeking love of God and depict the aspect of grace shown in the work of the Son and of the Holy Spirit. The third parable sets forth the pardoning love of God and depicts the aspect of grace as manifested by the Father. It is in two parts. The first tells of the prodigal son (11–24) and reveals the attitude of God's heart toward the world of sinners. The second part tells of the elder brother (25–32), depicts the spirit of the Pharisees and scribes in their murmuring against Jesus, and reveals God's attitude to them.

The whole chapter is full of singular beauty. The note of joy rings through it. Each of the first two parables ends with a refrain which reflects the joy of heaven over the salvation of the sinner. The third parable, which occupies two-thirds of the chapter, seems to rise into poetry as the story approaches its close. Each of its two parts ends with a refrain, which expresses the father's joy over the finding of his lost son and reflects the Father-heart of God.

Rejoice with me (6). Great joy seeks sympathetic fellowship. We have here a charming picture of simple village life. *Which need no repentance* (7); an ironical reference to the Pharisees and scribes. Jesus accepts their estimate of themselves for the sake of the truth He is emphasizing. *Ten pieces of silver* (8); lit. 'ten drachmas', which would be worth about eight shillings, but in purchasing power much more. *Joy in the presence of the angels of God* (10). The joy of God Himself. The point of both these parables is the value of the individual soul to God. Note the phrase *one sinner that repenteth* (7, 10).

The portion of goods that falleth to me (12). In Jewish law this would be one-third of his father's estate: the elder son received a double portion (Dt. xxi. 17). *To feed swine* (15); an unspeakable degradation for a Jew. *The husks that the swine did eat* (16). The pods of the carob tree, used for feeding swine in Mediterranean countries. *Robe . . . ring . . . shoes . . . fatted calf* (22, 23). These were intended not only to supply the wants of the son but to give him a place of honour in the home. *Thou never gavest me a kid* (29). *Me* is emphatic. Not even a kid, much less a fatted calf, was given to him to enjoy himself with his friends. *This thy son* (30); spoken contemptuously. He would not say 'my brother'. *Son, thou art ever with me* (31); lit. 'child', a tender word. *Thou* is emphatic. *This thy brother* (32); a gentle rebuke. The brotherly relation remains as well as the fatherly. This best of all stories ends with the rhythmical cadence of the refrain corresponding with verse 24.

v. Two parables of warning (xvi. 1–31). These two parables are also peculiar to Luke. They have to do with the use of this world's wealth. One was spoken to the disciples and the other to the Pharisees.

In the parable of the prudent steward (1–8) Jesus drew a lesson for the disciples from the man's foresight in providing for his future. The steward was not acting dishonestly in cutting down the debts that were owed his master, for in each case it is implied that he would make up the amount out of his own wealth. This is involved in the very lesson Jesus bases on the parable (9). It is the wealth that is in our own possession we are to use in making friends, not the wealth of another man fraudulently used. The steward is called unjust with reference to the primary charge of wasting his master's goods, not with reference to his dealings with his master's debtors. He was commended *because he had done wisely* (8); he used his present wealth to make provision for the future. Jesus was describing the kind of wisdom the people of this world show in providing for their earthly future in order to point a lesson for *the children of light* (8) in providing for their eternal future. He then goes on to enforce the lesson of the parable with some further comments (9–13). *A steward* (1); he would have the entire

management of the rich man's estate. *His lord's debtors* (5). They paid their debts in kind and the steward had sometimes received more from them than he had put down in his accounts, thus increasing his own wealth. This time he will accept less from them than they owe in order to curry favour with them. *An hundred measures of oil* (6). This measure was the Hebrew *bath*, which held about nine gallons. *An hundred measures of wheat* (7). This is a different measure, the Hebrew *cor*, which equalled about ten bushels.

The lord commended (8); RV 'his lord', i.e. the rich man, who evidently knew what the steward had done. *The unjust steward* (8); lit. 'the steward of unrighteousness', describing his general character. *The children of this world* (8); lit. 'the sons of this age', the world as it now is. *The children of light* (8); lit. 'the sons of the light', those who have received the light of the new age. *The mammon of unrighteousness* (9). Money or worldly wealth tends to promote unrighteousness, but the disciples of Christ have to use it for the sake of the kingdom of God. *When ye fail* (9); rather, 'when it shall fail' (RV), i.e. when it comes to an end, as it surely will. *They may receive you* (9). The word *they* does not necessarily refer back to the word *friends* but is probably used in an impersonal or general sense. *That which is another man's* (12); i.e. earthly riches, which we have only in trust and cannot keep. *That which is your own* (12); i.e. spiritual riches, which we possess for ever.

The Pharisees scoffed at this teaching and Jesus reminded them that God saw through their self-righteous pride. The old dispensation was being superseded by the kingdom of God in which the law would be completely fulfilled (14–18). Jesus then illustrated these principles by the parable of the rich man and Lazarus, in which He pictured the consequences that follow the wrong use of earthly riches. The parable contains two scenes, one on earth and the other in another world, which are set over against each other. In the scene on earth (19–22) a striking contrast is drawn between the rich man and the beggar, first in life and then in death. The other scene is in Hades (RV), the world where all the departed go to await the final judgment. Here the contrast is completely reversed, and between the two men there is a great gulf fixed. Of the two interviews composing the scene one relates to the rich man's lot after death (23–26) and the other to that of his five brethren on earth (27–31).

Who were covetous (14); rather, 'lovers of money'. The Pharisees regarded their wealth as a special reward for their meticulous observance of the law. *The law and the prophets* (16); implying that a new dispensation began with him. *Every man presseth into it* (16). People were unwilling to enter in by the narrow gate (Mt. vii. 13) and were trying to force themselves in some other way. In verses 17 and 18, which seem to have little connection with what precedes, Jesus contrasts the teaching of the law with the spirit of the Pharisees.

A certain beggar named Lazarus (20). The name is the Greek form of the Hebrew *Eleazar* and means 'God helps'. It was probably intended to indicate the beggar's faith in God. *Moreover the dogs came* (21); aggravating his misery, for dogs were not domesticated and were regarded as unclean. *Into Abraham's bosom* (22); not a synonym for Paradise, although it meant being there. The expression is taken from the idea of a banquet where each man, reclining on his elbow, is in the bosom of the man to his left. Lazarus is supposed to be seated next to Abraham (cf. Jn. xiii. 23). *And was buried* (22). The angels are not mentioned: they did not attend the rich man in his death.

I am tormented in this flame (24); symbolically describing the agony of inflamed desires which now cannot be satisfied. *Son, remember* (25). The memory of the past is not drowned in the other world. *But now* (25); RV 'But now here', marking the contrast of both time and place. *A great gulf fixed* (26). The word means a yawning chasm. *So that* (26); rather 'in order that'. The chasm was fixed for the purpose of making an impassable separation between the two classes in the other world.

vi. Further teaching for the disciples (xvii. 1–10). This passage contains four brief sayings addressed to the disciples, which appear to have no connection with the preceding discourses. They deal with the greatness of the sin of causing others to sin (1, 2), the duty of forgiving a sinning brother if he repents (3, 4), the power of even the smallest faith (5, 6), and the fact that obedience and good works imply no merit on our part and give us no claim on God (7–10).

It is impossible (1); i.e. morally impossible in the present sinful condition of the world. *Offences* (1); 'occasions of stumbling' (RV), causes of sin. *One of these little ones* (2). Jesus called even the apostles by the tender name of 'children' (Jn. xiii. 33) and his reference here is primarily to His own disciples. *Seven times* (3); the number of completeness, hence an unlimited number of times. *Increase our faith* (5). This request of the apostles probably arose from a consciousness of their own natural inability to fulfil the moral requirements that Jesus had just laid down. *Faith as a grain of mustard seed* (6). It was not a question of additional faith, but of genuine faith. See note on Mt. xvii. 20 and cf. Mt. xxi. 21; Mk. xi. 23. *This sycamine tree* (6). The expression shows that Jesus was teaching in the open air and pointed to the tree as He spoke. The sycamine seems to have been a general name for different kinds of mulberry trees. *Having a servant* (7). There is no harshness implied in the behaviour Jesus describes. He is simply appealing to the customs of ordinary daily life in which servants were usually bondslaves. The whole social and economic order of the world of Christ's time was based on the system of slavery. *Unprofitable servants* (10). Not in the sense of being worthless, but as doing nothing to bring

their master extra profit for which payment was to be expected.

c. The third stage of the journey (xvii. 11—xix. 28)

For the third time Luke tells us that Jesus was moving on towards Jerusalem. This part of the journey brings Him to Bethany just before the triumphal entry into the city. His addresses during this period are pervaded with the thought of His second advent.

i. The ten lepers (xvii. 11–19). These men cried out to Jesus for mercy, and He bade them go to the priests. This implied a promise of cleansing, and their faith was shown in their obedience. Jesus expressed His disappointment with the nine who took their cure as a matter of course, and rewarded the grateful Samaritan with an additional blessing.

Stood afar off (12). This was in accordance with the law which required the leper to dwell apart from others and cry 'Unclean, unclean' (Lv. xiii. 45, 46). *Go shew yourselves unto the priests* (14); i.e. to get certificates of cleansing according to the law (Lv. xiii). *This stranger* (18); RV mg. 'this alien'. The Samaritans sprang from the mixture of the Israelites with the heathen people who were brought in by the Assyrians after the fall of the northern kingdom (2 Ki. xvii. 24).

ii. The coming of the kingdom (xvii. 20–37). Asked by the Pharisees when the kingdom of God was coming, Jesus replied that it was not coming with any visible sign; 'for lo,' He went on to say, 'the kingdom of God is in the midst of you' (20, 21, RV mg.), referring to Himself and the life He was living among them. Then He turned to the disciples and spoke of the future of the kingdom. The days would come when they would long for His coming, and He warned them not to be led astray by false rumours, for it was to be a visible and universal event after He had suffered and been rejected (22–25). People will be living their everyday lives when the Son of man is revealed, and only those will be ready for Him who have not identified themselves with the interests of this world, for then earthly relations will suddenly be completely severed (26–36). In verse 31 Christ describes in pictorial terms the attitude of indifference to worldly interests which His disciples would require to take in order to be ready for His return. To the question which the disciples asked (see verse 37) Jesus replied with a general statement which meant that, wherever the conditions were fulfilled, there the agents of judgment would appear. *The eagles* (37); i.e. vultures, who swoop down in flocks from a clear sky upon any dead body lying on the ground.

iii. Two parables about prayer (xviii. 1–14). Luke alone records these parables. That of the importunate widow (1–8) was told to the disciples as a sequel to the preceding discourse, and teaches the necessity of persevering prayer in view of the second coming. The argument is this: if an unrighteous judge will give a just judgment in the case of a helpless widow in whom he has no interest because of her ceaseless pleading, how much more will the holy God answer the unwearied cry for justice of His own chosen people? If He does not interpose to deliver them immediately, it is because He is long-suffering to their oppressors. The parable of the Pharisee and the publican (9–14) was addressed to some members of the company following Jesus who manifested a haughty spirit of self-righteousness. Both men were alike in going up to the temple to pray, but quite different in the spirit and purpose of their prayers. The Pharisee thanked God he was not like the rest of men, and recited his meritorious works. The publican pleaded with contrition for mercy as a sinner. His prayer was answered, but not that of the Pharisee.

A widow (3). Of all classes widows were the most helpless and defenceless in the world of the time. *Avenge me* (3); rather, 'do me justice' (RV mg.). *Though he bear long with them* (7). His forbearance is shown, not to His elect, but to their oppressors. *Shall he find faith?* (8); lit. 'the faith', the kind of faith that persists in prayer.

Stood (11). This was the usual posture of the Jews in prayer, but the word seems to be used here to indicate that the Pharisee took a conspicuous place. *Of all that I possess* (12); rather, 'of all that I get' (RV). It was his income he tithed, not his capital. *Standing afar off* (13); a very different attitude from that of the Pharisee. *A sinner* (13); rather, 'the sinner'. He is thinking of himself alone and not of others. *Justified* (14); i.e. accounted righteous. It is the word that Paul uses so often. It occurs five times in Luke, twice in Matthew, and not at all in Mark or John.

iv. Incidents in Peraea (xviii. 15–34). At this point Luke's narrative joins the narratives of Matthew (xix. 13) and Mark (x. 13). See notes there. The incidents recorded are: the blessing of the babes brought to Jesus (15–17), the interview of Jesus with the rich ruler on the question of eternal life (18–23), His conversation with the disciples about it afterwards (24–30), and a final prediction of what was to happen to Him at Jerusalem (31–34).

What shall I do? (18). The same question was asked by the lawyer in x. 25. Both men thought that eternal life could be won by some meritorious deed. *Why callest thou me good? none is good, save one* (19). The ruler had used the word *good* superficially and thoughtlessly. Our Lord reminds him that God is the only source of all goodness. Even Christ's goodness is dependent on His union with the Father (Jn. v. 19). Cf. the alternative account of this conversation preserved in the RV text of Matthew. *All these have I kept* (21); not a hypocritical statement, but it reveals a superficial view of what the commandments require. *Yet lackest thou one thing* (22). Jesus put the test of self-renunciation to the rich ruler in the only way he could understand it.

A camel . . . a needle's eye (25). For three possible interpretations see Mt. xix. 24n. The present writer feels that the words are to be taken in their obvious meaning. They express in metaphorical terms what is naturally impossible. *Who then can be saved?* (26). The apostles were almost dismayed by the Lord's words. His answer means that salvation itself, not only for the rich but for anyone, is a work of God's miraculous grace beyond the reach of any human effort.

Unto the Gentiles (32). This is the first time Jesus has mentioned them in announcing His death. It is the third and most detailed of His predictions of His suffering. *The third day he shall rise again* (33). Jesus usually followed the announcement of His death with a prediction of His resurrection.

v. Jesus at Jericho (xviii. 35—xix. 10). When Luke's account of the miracle of the healing of the blind man is compared with the accounts in Matthew (xx. 29–34) and Mark (x. 46–52), it appears that two blind men were healed. One of them heard the travelling company of pilgrims entering Jericho as he sat by the wayside begging and was told that Jesus of Nazareth was passing. Next day, he and another blind man took their places by the roadside where Jesus would be leaving Jericho, and as soon as they heard the company approaching one of them cried out appealing to Him as the son of David. The crowd resented the interruption, but Jesus had them brought near and rewarded their faith by giving them both their sight. *Thou son of David* (38). The use of this messianic title implied strong faith on the blind man's part. The people had only said *Jesus of Nazareth* (37).

The story of Jesus' visit to the house of Zacchaeus the publican (xix. 1–10) is peculiar to Luke and is full of human interest. The device to which Zacchaeus resorted as a man of small stature in the crowd shows that he had an unusual eagerness to see Jesus. To this Jesus responded in an unusual way by making Himself the guest of Zacchaeus. The crowd criticized this action of Jesus, but it resulted in a complete revolution in the life of the publican and in the salvation of his house. *The chief among the publicans* (2). This is the translation of one Greek word which occurs nowhere else. Probably it means a commissioner of taxes. *Zacchaeus stood, and said* (8); indicating the solemnity of the statement he was about to make. It was the result of his personal contact with Jesus Christ. *The half of my goods I give to the poor* (8); an act he carried out there and then. *I restore him fourfold* (8). This was one of the extreme penalties imposed by the law when a man was compelled to make reparation for a robbery (see Ex. xxii. 1; 2 Sa. xii. 6). Zacchaeus imposes the penalty upon his own unjust exactions as a publican.

vi. The parable of the pounds (xix. 11–28). Two reasons are given to explain why Jesus spoke the parable at this time (see verse 11). There was evidently increasing excitement among the pilgrims as they drew nearer to Jerusalem, and they were expecting that Jesus would set up the messianic kingdom there at once. The parable represents the Lord's departure from the world as necessary in order that His kingdom should be established, and it indicates how His disciples were to be occupied during His absence and how He would reward them when He returned. Each of the ten servants was given the same sum. The pound, therefore, must represent what all believers have in common, either the grace of salvation or the gospel as a trust (cf. 1 Thes. ii. 4; 1 Tim. i. 11). The parable describes the attitude of the Jews toward their messianic king, and closes by depicting Him. With this passage cf. Mt. xxv. 14–30.

To receive for himself a kingdom (12); a prophetic announcement of the Lord's enthronement in heaven in preparation for the establishment of His kingdom on earth. *Ten pounds* (13). The pound was not a coin but a sum of money. Its value was not quite £4. *Occupy till I come* (13). The Greek word means 'do business'. *His citizens* (14); representing the Jews, to whom the messianic kingdom by promise belonged, as distinguished from 'his servants', who represent the disciples. *Had gained by trading* (15); rather, 'what business he had done'. The original expression does not involve the idea of gain. *I feared thee* (21). His attitude was wrong. He was devoid of devotion to his lord, and this vitiated all his conduct. Verse 25 probably marks an interruption on the part of the people to whom Jesus was speaking. It shows how keenly they were listening to the story and how impressively He was telling it. In that case verse 26 is His reply to them and verse 27 the continuation of the parable.

VI. THE MINISTRY IN JERUSALEM.
xix. 29—xxi. 38

Jesus had been in Jerusalem on several occasions before and taught in the temple, but John alone tells of these visits. The present section deals with His final ministry there and it is parallel with Mt. xxi. 1—xxv. 46, Mk. xi. 1—xiii. 37 and Jn. xii. 1–36, where see notes. Luke connects the events he records immediately with the temple, which is mentioned eight times in the course of the narrative.

a. The entry into Jerusalem and the cleansing of the temple (xix. 29–48)

For verses 29–44 see notes on Mt. xxi. 1–11; Mk. xi. 1–10; Jn. xii. 12–15. Jesus deliberately presented Himself in the nation's capital as the promised Messiah by a specially arranged public entry. All the details emphasize the solemnity which He attached to the event. The sending of the two disciples for the colt indicates a deliberate plan on His part. When they brought the animal for Him to ride upon He was treated with royal honour (29–36). As He moved on He became the centre of enthusiastic homage from

a multitude of people. He accepted their messianic salutations and rebuked the Pharisees for suggesting that He stop them (37–40).

Bethphage and Bethany (29). The first name was probably that of the district in which the village of Bethany lay. *Ye shall find a colt* (30). Jesus was preparing to enter the city in the way that Zechariah announced the Messiah would come (see Zc. ix. 9). *The Lord hath need of him* (31). The owner of the colt was doubtless one of the Lord's unknown friends, who, like Lazarus (Jn. xi. 3), do not appear in the narrative in any other way.

When He came within sight of the city He uttered a lamentation over it and foretold its coming destruction (41–44). Cf. Lk. xiii. 34, 35. Then He entered the temple, cleansed it of its unholy traffic, and established Himself there as a teacher. See notes on Mt. xxi. 12–16; Mk. xi. 15–18. At the same time the religious authorities were planning to put Him to death but were restrained by His great popularity (45–48). According to Mark the cleansing of the temple took place on the day after the triumphal entry. Luke gives no note of time, but links these two events together as part of one great messianic act.

Wept over it (41). The word *eklausen* implies wailing or audible weeping, different from the weeping of Jn. xi. 35 where the word *edakrusen* means that He shed silent tears. *The time of thy visitation* (44); the whole period of opportunity given her by the presence of Christ in the land, and His various visits to the city. *Into the temple* (45); the whole temple, including its various courts. In the large outer court, called the court of the Gentiles because they were permitted to enter there, the sale of animals required for sacrifice was carried on by the hierarchy for their own profit, and it had become a scandal. This noisy traffic hindered the quieter use of the temple for worship.

b. Teaching daily in the temple (xx. 1—xxi. 4)

i. *The rulers silenced* (xx. 1–8). See notes on Mt. xxi. 23–27; Mk. xi. 27–33. One day the Jewish rulers came upon Jesus and asked Him what kind of authority He had for what He was doing. He replied by asking them a question about the source of John the Baptist's authority which would have led to the answer to their own question. They exposed their failure as religious guides by saying they did not know. Therefore Jesus refused to answer their question. *The baptism of John* (4). This question was quite relevant and should be settled first, for John had introduced Jesus as the Messiah and testified as to His divine authority.

ii. *The parable of the wicked husbandmen* (xx. 9–19). See notes on Mt. xxi. 33–46; Mk. xii. 1–12. This parable was addressed to the people and depicted the sin of the religious leaders and foreshadowed the judgment that was coming upon them. They realized that the parable was directed against themselves, but their fear of the people restrained them from arresting Him. *Planted a vineyard* (9). The figure is taken from Is. v. 1–7, where Israel is God's vineyard. The husbandmen in the parable represent the religious rulers of Israel and the servants sent from time to time represent the prophets. *I will send my beloved son* (13). After the triumphal entry the Lord's teaching about His own divine dignity becomes more explicit. *Give the vineyard to others* (16). This is not primarily a reference to the Gentiles, although they are involved, but to a new Israel composed of both Jews and Gentiles, 'the Israel of God' (Gal. vi. 16). The kingdom was taken from the official rulers and given to His own disciples (Lk. xii. 32), who formed the nucleus of the new nation bringing forth the fruits of the kingdom (Mt. xxi. 43).

He beheld them (17); a striking touch. He fixed His eyes upon them, thus giving special solemnity to His quotation from the Scriptures. *The stone which the builders rejected* (17); from Ps. cxviii. 22. This was one of the Hallel Psalms sung at the Passover and was regarded as messianic. *The head of the corner* (17); not the keystone of an arch, but the corner stone of a building where two walls meet. *Whosoever shall fall upon that stone* (18); i.e. stumble upon it in unbelief. *On whomsoever it shall fall* (18); i.e. in judgment.

iii. Paying tribute to Caesar (xx. 20–26). See notes on Mt. xxii. 15–22; Mk. xii. 13–17. They watched Him, however, and sent spies who sought to ensnare Him in His words that they might accuse Him to the Roman governor. With fulsome compliments they asked Him if it was right to give tribute to Caesar. The craft of this question lay in the attempt to put Jesus on the horns of a dilemma. If He answered 'yes', the Pharisees would expose Him to the people, who hated the Roman yoke. If He answered 'no', they would accuse Him of treason against Rome. The answer of Jesus was perfect, meeting every aspect of the question put before Him. It also means that the claims of God and of the state are not mutually exclusive.

iv. The Sadducees and the resurrection (xx. 27–40). See notes on Mt. xxii. 23–33; Mk. xii. 18–27. Then came some of the Sadducees with a question about a hypothetical case intended to make the resurrection appear foolish. They were the aristocratic party among the Jews. Although not as numerous as the Pharisees, they held the highest offices. They did not believe in an after life and lived for this world alone. Jesus answered their question in such a way as to show that they did not understand the resurrection life and also that an after life was implied in the writings of Moses whom they had quoted. *Moses wrote unto us* (28). See Dt. xxv. 5–10. *At the bush* (37); i.e. in the passage telling of the bush that burned with fire (Ex. iii. 6). The Sadducees accepted the authority of Moses but not that of the prophets. The argument here is that when God speaks of Himself as 'the God of Abraham, and the God of Isaac, and the God of Jacob', after they had

died in their bodily state, these patriarchs must now be living in another state.

v. A stern denunciation (xx. 41–47). See notes on Mt. xxii. 41–45, xxiii. 1–36; Mk. xii. 35–40. Jesus brought His public teaching to an end and silenced His adversaries by asking a question based on Ps. cx. 1. Having quoted David's statement in calling the Messiah 'Lord', Jesus put the question *How is he then his son?* (44). The failure of the Jews to answer it showed that their idea of the Messiah was quite inadequate. The Lord's argument rests upon the Davidic origin as well as the messianic character of the Psalm. If it did not come from David, then our Lord's words could have no weight for us now, whatever weight they might have had with His hearers then. *Beware of the scribes* (46). Luke gives a very brief summary of the Lord's terrible denunciation of the scribes and Pharisees which is recorded at length in Mt. xxiii.

vi. The widow's mite (xxi. 1–4). See notes on Mk. xii. 41–44. The incident is not recorded by Matthew. *The treasury* (1) was in the Court of the Women, which was entered from the Court of the Gentiles. It consisted of a number of chests for receiving the voluntary gifts of the Jews. Mark indicates that the commendation of the widow's action was especially addressed to the disciples.

c. Foretelling the destruction of the temple (xxi. 5–38)

See notes on Mt. xxiv. 1–51; Mk. xiii. 1–37. Both Matthew (xxiv. 3) and Mark (xiii. 3, 4) tell us that this prophecy was spoken on the Mount of Olives after Jesus had left the temple for the last time. Luke simply records the occasion which called it forth and the question the disciples asked as to the sign when the destruction of the temple would come to pass (5–7). Jesus first warned them against being led astray by false signs, and went on to describe what would occur after His departure. There would be national commotions and public calamities (8–11), but *before all these* (12) they themselves would be persecuted both by Jews in the synagogues and by Gentiles in the courts. This would give them opportunities for testimony (13). *I will give you* (15). The position of *I* in the original gives emphasis to these words. Christ Himself undertakes to give His disciples the divine help they need to make their defence and bear their testimony. They are to trust Him. They would be betrayed and hated and some of them would suffer martyrdom, but they would be saved by their patient endurance (16–19). Cf. Mt.-x. 17–22; Mk. xiii. 9–13; Lk. xii. 11, 12. Verse 18, since it comes after the statement that some of them will be put to death, must be taken as a proverbial expression for complete spiritual security. *Possess ye your souls* (19); lit. 'win your souls', i.e. attain your eternal salvation.

Next Jesus spoke of the sign that would announce the approaching destruction of Jerusalem. When the disciples saw armies gathering around the city, they were to flee from it with all speed, for the long-foretold judgment upon Israel was about to fall and the age-long subjection to the Gentiles was about to begin (20–24). *Compassed with armies* (20); lit. 'being encompassed'. When the process of investing the city was completed it would be too late. *Flee to the mountains* (21). The early Church historian, Eusebius, says that when the Roman armies came into Judæa, 'the whole body of the church at Jerusalem, having been commanded by a divine revelation, removed from the city and dwelt at a certain town beyond the Jordan, called Pella'. *These be the days of vengeance* (22); a reference to the many Old Testament prophecies of judgment upon Israel which were now to be fulfilled in the destruction of the city and the temple. The fall of Jerusalem at the hands of the Romans in A.D. 70 brought the whole Mosaic dispensation to a tragic end. Then began 'the time of Jacob's trouble' (Je. xxx. 7) and the 'great tribulation' of Israel (Mt. xxiv. 21). *The times of the Gentiles* (24); the age during which the Gentiles are given opportunities for receiving the gospel.

After this reference to the fall of Jerusalem, Jesus passed on to tell of His own coming in power and glory. The signs of its approach would be distress among the nations and alarming commotions in the whole world system. When these things began to happen believers were to lift up their heads, for the consummation of their salvation would be drawing near (25–28). When they see the trees sprout forth they know that summer is near; so when they see these things come to pass they will know that the kingdom of God is just at hand (29–33). *With perplexity* (25); rather, 'in perplexity for the roaring of the sea and the billows' (RV). The physical signs described in this verse are used in Old Testament prophecy as symbols of the violent overthrow of national systems and great empires (Is. xiii. 10; Ezk. xxxii. 7). *Then shall they see* (27); that is, not till then. A hint that the second coming would not take place in the lifetime of the disciples. *Coming in a cloud* (27) —reappearing from the cloud which 'received him out of their sight' at the ascension (Acts i. 9–11). It means coming out from the heavenly world. *Your redemption draweth nigh* (28). The consummation of salvation is the redemption of the body (Rom. viii. 23, xiii. 11). *This generation shall not pass away* (32); the generation then living. The statement in this verse has special reference to the question the disciples asked in verse 7, and is the only place in the prophecy where Jesus answers the question directly. The destruction of the temple was then only one generation away. Cf. Mt. xxiv. 34n.

But let them take heed lest that day come upon them unawares, for it will come suddenly upon the whole human race. Let them watch and pray that they may not be involved in the judgment, but be able to stand before the Son of man when He comes (34–36). The prophecy is followed with a brief statement of the way Jesus spent the last days and nights of His public ministry (37, 38).

VII. THE DEPARTURE OF THE SAVIOUR. xxii. 1—xxiv. 53

These chapters tell how Jesus accomplished His departure from the world by the way of the cross, the resurrection, and the ascension. They are parallel with the last three chapters of Matthew and the last two of Mark and with chapters xiii—xxi of John. The notes on these parallel accounts should be consulted.

a. The final preparations (xxii. 1–13)

See notes on Mt. xxvi. 2–5, 14–19; Mk. xiv. 1, 2, 10–16. While the leaders of the Jews were plotting how to put Jesus to death without causing a tumult, Judas Iscariot made a bargain with them to betray his Master (1–6). When the day of the Passover sacrifice came, Jesus sent Peter and John into the city to prepare the Passover meal. They would meet a man bearing a pitcher of water, whom they were to follow to the house he was going to, and the head of the household would let them have a large furnished upper room in which to get the Passover ready (7–13).

The feast of unleavened bread (1); so called because the Jews were required to remove all leaven from their houses before it began (see Ex. xii. 15). *The chief priests and the scribes* (2). The two rival religious parties were now united against Jesus. The chief priests were Sadducees and the scribes were associated with the Pharisees. *The chief priests and captains* (4); the two groups of temple authorities concerned in the bargain. The captains were the officers of the temple guard, which was a body of Levites.

b. The Last Supper (xxii. 14–38)

See notes on Mt. xxvi. 20–25; Mk. xiv. 17–31; and cf. Jn. xiii. 1–38. When the time came Jesus sat down with the apostles, telling them that He had eagerly looked forward to this occasion, for He would not eat the Passover with them until it should be fulfilled in the kingdom of God (14–18). Then He instituted the service that was to commemorate the sealing of the new covenant by His death. While doing this He announced the presence of the traitor at the table and pronounced his doom (19–23).

To eat this passover (15). This probably means that it was not the actual Jewish Passover but one that was intended to supersede it—a Passover of far higher significance. There is no mention of a lamb at the Last Supper. He was instituting a service to commemorate the reality which the old symbol only prefigured. *Until it be fulfilled in the kingdom of God* (16); in the spiritual banquet of the fellowship of the saints with their Saviour. *He took the cup* (17); rather, 'he received a cup' (RV); it was handed to Him. It was probably one of the cups handed round during the ritual of the Passover meal, of which there seem to have been several. *The new testament in my blood* (20); properly, 'the new covenant' (RV), a reference to the promise of the new covenant in Je. xxxi. 31. The old covenant, that of the law, was ratified by the shedding of blood at Sinai (Ex. xxiv. 7, 8). This new covenant, that of the gospel, was about to be ratified by His blood.

In the course of the supper a dispute took place among the disciples as to which of them should be accounted the greatest. Jesus rebuked them by declaring that the standards of greatness in earthly kingdoms were reversed in His kingdom, for He Himself was among them as a servant, and then promised that because of their loyalty to Him in His humiliation He would give them high places in His kingdom (24–30). He went on to say that they were to be subjected to a test at Satan's hands, and directed a special warning to Peter in connection with it, adding an encouraging word, but foretelling that disciple's threefold denial of his Master (31–34). He proceeded to prepare them for the new conditions they should meet in the world after He had been put to death, but they misunderstood His figurative reference to a sword and He dismissed the subject with a brief and final word, *It is enough* (35–38).

Sit on thrones (30). This figurative language means fellowship with Christ in the rule of His messianic kingdom. *Satan hath desired to have you* (31); rather, 'obtained you by asking'. He obtained permission to put the apostles to a test, as in the case of Job (Jb. i. 12, ii. 6). Jesus prayed specially for Peter as the leader of the band and as one in the greatest need of help. *When thou art converted* (32); 'when once thou hast turned again' (RV). After the resurrection Peter was restored to the leadership of the apostles in the scene recorded in Jn. xxi. 15–17. *I tell thee, Peter* (34). Addressing His boastful disciple by this significant name Jesus reminds him that rock-like strength is not to be found in self-confidence. *Here are two swords* (38). Peter had one of them and used it in Gethsemane (see Jn. xviii. 10).

c. The agony and the betrayal (xxii. 39–53)

See notes on Mt. xxvi. 36–56; Mk. xiv. 32–52; Jn. xviii. 1–12. Luke's account of the agony is the briefest of the three (it is not recorded by John), but he alone tells us that an angel from heaven appeared to Jesus, *strengthening him* (43), and that His sweat was like *great drops of blood* (44). In his story of the betrayal and arrest (47–53), Luke alone tells of the way Jesus healed the ear of the High Priest's servant. The Lord's command, *Suffer ye thus far* (51), was a flash of inherent power and dignity, compelling them to pause till He performed this act of mercy before yielding Himself up to them.

Being in an agony (44). The only adequate explanation of the experience of Jesus as described in this verse is that His whole nature shrank from the mysterious burden of the world's guilt which was being laid on Him (cf. 2 Cor. v. 21; Is. liii. 6). *One of them* (50). John tells us it was Peter and gives the servant's name (Jn. xviii. 10). *This is your hour and the power of darkness* (53). With these words Jesus surrendered.

d. The Jewish trial (xxii. 54–71)

See notes on Mt. xxvi. 57—xxvii. 2; Mk. xiv. 53 —xv. 1; Jn. xviii. 13–27. Jesus was first taken to the High Priest's house, where He was mocked and reviled (54–65). In the course of this scene Peter, who had followed the crowd and was sitting in the midst of a group around a fire in the court, was repeatedly challenged as a follower of Jesus and each time boldly denied Him. While he was speaking the cock crew and *the Lord turned, and looked upon Peter* (61). This brought the Lord's prediction to his remembrance and he went out weeping bitterly. At daybreak the Jewish Council held a meeting (66–71). Before the assembled rulers of the Jews Jesus declared that He was on the way to His glory, and, in answer to their question, confessed that He was the Son of God.

In the midst of the hall (55); RV 'in the midst of the court', around which the rooms of the house were arranged and into which they opened. During the Passover season the nights get cold, for Jerusalem is 2400 feet above sea level. *He is a Galilean* (59). Peter's provincial dialect betrayed him (see Mt. xxvi. 73).

Hereafter (69); rather, 'from henceforth' (RV). This can only mean 'from the present time onward'. Jesus is thinking of the glory into which He is going by the way of the cross, the resurrection and the ascension. *Art thou then the Son of God?* (70). His answer was an affirmative reply, and for this claim they condemned Him to death. But to get the death penalty inflicted the Roman governor had to condemn Him too, and the only accusation Pilate would listen to was that of high treason.

e. The Roman trial (xxiii. 1–25)

See notes on Mt. xxvii. 2–26; Mk. xv. 1–15; Jn. xviii. 28—xix. 16. Bringing Jesus before Pilate, the Jews laid a political charge against Him, accusing Him of perverting the nation from loyalty to Rome by claiming to be a king. In answer to a question by Pilate, Jesus confessed that He was the king of the Jews, but Pilate saw at once that He was innocent of treason and told the Jews that he did not find Him guilty (1–4). This made them more urgent in their accusation, and they charged Jesus with stirring up sedition from Galilee throughout the whole country. Learning that Jesus was a Galilean, Pilate sent Him to Herod, who was in Jerusalem at the time of the Passover (5–7). Herod was delighted because his desire to see Jesus was now gratified. But Jesus answered none of his questions, nor the vehement accusations of the chief priests and scribes who had followed Him. Herod subjected Him to mockery at the hands of his soldiers and sent Him back to Pilate. This resulted in a reconciliation between the two rulers who had been estranged (8–12).

When Jesus appeared before Pilate again, the governor called together the Jewish rulers and people and informed them that neither he nor Herod found anything worthy of death in Jesus, and he proposed to scourge Him and let Him go. But they demanded instead the release of Barabbas, a rebel and murderer (13–19). Pilate again declared that he found no ground for the death penalty, but in the face of his repeated protests they kept clamouring for the crucifixion of Jesus. At last he yielded to their will, released the murderer, and delivered Jesus over to be crucified (20–25).

The whole multitude (1); i.e. the whole Sanhedrin; the people had not yet gathered. *Led him unto Pilate* (1). The Roman governor's headquarters were in Caesarea, but at the time of the Passover he usually came to Jerusalem to preserve order among the Jewish crowds. *To the people* (4). This is the first mention of them. They had gathered in a crowd, attracted by the procession of the Sanhedrin. *Who himself was also at Jerusalem* (7). Herod's headquarters were at Tiberias, but he conformed to the national religion and attended the Passover to gain favour with his subjects. Verse 17 is omitted by the RV, but the statement is found in both Matthew and Mark. It appears that the Romans had given the Jews the privilege of asking for the release of one prisoner at the time of the Passover. *The third time* (22). Pilate's repeated attempts to release Jesus indicate the deepening impression made upon him by the strange prisoner before him. *Him that for sedition and murder* (25). By repeating these words from verse 19 and adding the words *to their will*, Luke emphasizes the enormity of Pilate's act.

f. The crucifixion (xxiii. 26–49)

See notes on Mt. xxvii. 32–56; Mk. xv. 21–41; Jn. xix. 16–37. As Jesus was led out a foreign Jew on his way into the city was impressed into the service of carrying the cross after Him. A group of women in the crowd kept bewailing and lamenting Jesus, and He turned and told them to weep not for Him but for themselves and their children because of the judgment that was coming (26–31). In describing the scene at Calvary, Luke adds several incidents not found in the other Gospels, among which are the prayer of Jesus when they were nailing Him to the cross (32–38), His word to the penitent thief who appealed to Jesus to remember him when He came into His kingdom (39–43), His loud cry at the moment of His death, and His final prayer (44–46), and the consternation and sense of remorse manifested by the crowds that were drawn by curiosity to the sight (47–49). *A Cyrenian* (26). Cyrene was the principal town of a district in North Africa, and the Jews of that place had a synagogue in Jerusalem (Acts

vi. 9). *Daughters of Jerusalem* (28). They were not the women who had followed Jesus from Galilee, but inhabitants of the city. No women ever appear in the Gospels as enemies of Christ. Verse 31 was probably a proverb of the time. On the lips of Jesus it means, 'If the Romans deal thus with One whom they admit to be innocent, how will they deal with those whom they find to be guilty?'

The place called Calvary (33); lit. 'the skull'. There is a low rocky hill just outside the Damascus Gate which has the appearance of a skull when viewed from the city wall. *Father, forgive them* (34); a prayer not only for the Roman soldiers, but for the Jews as well. This is the first of seven utterances from the cross, three of which are recorded by Luke alone (34, 43, 46), three by John alone (Jn. xix. 27, 28, 30) and the other one by Matthew (Mt. xxvii. 46) and Mark (Mk. xv. 34). *In letters of Greek, and Latin, and Hebrew* (38). These were the three languages used in Palestine then. The superscription is given differently in all four Gospels. When they are put together we have: 'This is Jesus of Nazareth, the King of the Jews.'

One of the malefactors (39). Matthew and Mark say that both the robbers 'reproached' Jesus (*ōneidizon*), but Luke tells us that only one of them 'railed' on Him or used insulting language (*eblasphēmei*). The conversation of the penitent robber would have special interest for Luke as illustrating the fact that salvation is always open to all. *In paradise* (43); a Persian word for a park or pleasure ground. It is used by Jesus, not to describe an intermediate state, but to assure the penitent of heavenly bliss.

About the sixth hour (44); i.e. midday. *Over all the earth* (44); rather, 'over all the land', the land of Judaea. The darkness could not have been caused by an eclipse of the sun, for the Passover was held at full moon. *The veil of the temple* (45); the veil that separated the Holy Place from the innermost sanctuary. The rending of this veil would be well known to the priests, many of whom afterwards became believers (Acts vi. 7). *Cried with a loud voice* (46); probably the word 'It is finished' (Jn. xix. 30), which was really a shout of victory. The prayer which follows is a quotation from Ps. xxxi. 5, and shows how the Scriptures filled the mind of Jesus. *He gave up the ghost* (46); lit. 'He breathed out', implying an act of His own will. The loud cry indicated that Jesus did not die of exhaustion. All the evangelists seem deliberately to avoid saying 'He died'. The words they use mean that He gave His life away. His death was voluntary in the absolute sense of the term. The extraordinary events that accompanied it marked its unique and supernatural character. *All his acquaintance* (49). In contrast with the Jerusalem crowds, who went off in apparent remorse for the strange tragedy which they had shared in and were now awed by, His own faithful Galilean followers remained on the scene to the end.

g. The burial (xxiii. 50–56)

See notes on Mt. xxvii. 57–61; Mk. xv. 42–47; Jn. xix. 38–42. Joseph of Arimathaea, a member of the Jewish Council who had not voted for the condemnation of Jesus, and who was looking for the messianic kingdom, having secured permission from Pilate, buried the body of Jesus in his own new tomb. The women from Galilee followed and saw where the body was laid. They went home and prepared spices and ointments, and then rested over the sabbath.

A good man (50). John says that he was a secret disciple of Jesus, and also that Nicodemus was associated with him in the burial of Jesus (see Jn. xix. 38, 39). Probably neither of them had attended the meeting of the Sanhedrin. *The preparation* (54). The day when preparation was made for the sabbath—our Friday.

h. The resurrection morning (xxiv. 1–12)

Cf. Mt. xxviii. 1–20; Mk. xvi. 1–20; Jn. xx. 1–31. The women from Galilee came with their spices at early dawn on the first day of the week and found the stone rolled away and the body gone. In the midst of their perplexity two angels appeared and told them that Christ was risen, and reminded them of His prediction that He should be crucified and rise again the third day (1–7). The women returned and told the apostles, who at first would not believe. Peter, however, ran to the tomb to see for himself, and went home wondering what had happened (8–12).

The Lord Jesus (3). This is the only time this combination occurs in the Gospels except in the RV of Mk. xvi. 19. It is frequent in the Acts and the Epistles. The early Christians called Jesus 'Lord' when they came to realize that He was actually Jehovah manifest in the flesh (1 Cor. xii. 3). *Mary Magdalene* (10). All the evangelists tell of her presence at the tomb. John mentions no other women and says that Jesus appeared to her first. All the Synoptic Gospels give the names of other women besides.

i. The risen Lord (xxiv. 13–43)

The story of the walk to Emmaus and the manifestation there, which is noted briefly by Mark (xvi. 12, 13), is narrated at some length by Luke. It occurred in the afternoon of the resurrection day. Nothing is known of Cleopas, whom Luke mentions, probably because he got the story directly from him. What the two disciples said to Jesus when He drew near to them reflects the perplexity and wonder that had taken possession of them all because of what was told them by the women (13–24). As they walked on toward Emmaus, Jesus gave them a talk on the central theme of the Old Testament, *the things concerning himself* (25–29). The meal to which they sat down when they arrived at the village was not the Lord's Supper, but something in His manner of breaking the bread and blessing it opened their eyes to recognize Him. Then He vanished from their sight, such was the mysterious nature of His body. They hurried back at once to Jerusalem and found the apostles and other disciples gathered together and telling the news of the resurrection (30–35). Immediately afterwards Jesus Himself stood in the midst of the group and greeted them with a salutation of peace. In order to calm their fears and prove His identity, He showed them His wounded hands and feet, and then, to put them at their ease, He asked for something to eat (36–43).

Art thou only a stranger in Jerusalem? (18); rather, 'Dost thou sojourn alone in Jerusalem?' Only a solitary stranger would have missed hearing of what all Jerusalem was talking about. *Beginning at Moses* (27). The meaning is that Jesus began with the books of Moses and went on through the Prophets book by book, expounding the messianic passages in the whole Old Testament. *The things concerning himself* (27). Obviously Jesus found Himself in the Old Testament. *He vanished out of their sight* (31). He became invisible and thus passed from their sight. His resurrection body was not subject to the laws of the natural world. He was living now on another plane of being.

Hath appeared to Simon (34). There is no record of this interview of the risen Lord with the disciple who had denied Him. It was too sacred to be recorded. But Paul refers to it as the first of His appearances to any of the Twelve (1 Cor. xv. 5). *Handle me, and see* (39). Jesus meant that He was not a bodiless spirit, but the same Person He was before His death, the Master whom they supposed they had lost. We are not to infer from the words *flesh and bones* that He was referring to the composition of His resurrection body. Nor are we to infer from His subsequent request for something to eat that He needed food. The mystery of His resurrection body is beyond our comprehension because it is beyond our experience. *They yet believed not for joy* (41). This psychological touch reveals Luke's profound insight into the feelings of the disciples that night.

j. The farewell instructions (xxiv. 44–53)

Luke follows his narrative of the appearances of Jesus on the day of the resurrection with a summary of the instructions He gave to the apostles during the forty days that followed. It contains their missionary commission and closes with a command to wait in Jerusalem until they were *endued with power from on high* (49). Then comes a brief account of the ascension, and the Gospel closes with the great joy which that transcendent event produced among them. While waiting for the Holy Spirit, the disciples were *continually in the temple, praising and blessing God* (53).

In the law of Moses, and in the prophets, and in the psalms (44). These phrases correspond with the threefold division of the Hebrew Canon into 'the Law, the Prophets and the Writings'. *Beginning at Jerusalem* (47). This had been foretold in the Old Testament: 'Out of Zion shall go forth the law, and the word of the Lord from

Jerusalem' (Is. ii. 3; Mi. iv. 2). *The promise of my Father* (49). Probably an allusion to His own farewell words in the upper room (Jn. xiv. 16, 17, xv. 26). The Old Testament prophets also foretold the outpouring of the Holy Spirit (Is. xliv. 3; Joel ii. 28). *Carried up into heaven* (51).

There His enthronement took place at the right hand of God (Acts ii. 33; Heb. i. 3). He was seated at the centre of ultimate power that He might administer the redemption which He had accomplished.

J. McNicol.

THE GOSPEL ACCORDING TO JOHN

INTRODUCTION

See also the General Article, 'The Fourfold Gospel', pp. 58–63.

I. AUTHORSHIP

It is generally acknowledged that the author of the Gospel was a Palestinian Jew, but many commentators do not accept his identification with John the apostle. Evidence in favour of this traditional identification is, however, strong. The Gospel claims to be the testimony of an eyewitness. The disciple whom Jesus loved, who was present at the last supper and later at the crucifixion and the empty tomb, is the disciple who 'testifieth of these things' (Jn. xxi. 24). These facts concerning the eyewitness point, by a process of elimination, to John the apostle.

Internal evidence points decisively in favour of the identification of the beloved disciple with John the apostle. His knowledge of Jewish customs, feasts and topography is unquestionable. Many critics, however, believe that the author of the Gospel was a certain John the Elder, who was a disciple of the apostle. This claim is based upon the evidence of Papias, Bishop of Hierapolis, who appears to refer to two Johns in his *Exposition of the Oracles of the Lord*, one of whom he calls 'the Elder'. Others endeavour to pay some respect to the traditional view by suggesting that John the Elder acted as amanuensis for the apostle. The testimony of the *Alogoi* is also adduced as evidence that the apostle John was not the author. This is the name given to a rather obscure sect who refused to accept the view that the Gospel was his work and who were severely criticized by Irenaeus. Their views have been given an importance much greater than they deserve. Space does not permit a thorough treatment of the problem of authorship in a commentary of this kind. For brief but very adequate studies see F. F. Bruce, *Are the New Testament Documents Reliable?* (I.V.F.), and H. P. V. Nunn, *The Fourth Gospel* (Tyndale Press).

II. RELATION TO THE SYNOPTIC GOSPELS

Some have felt that there is difficulty in reconciling the presentation of Christ in the fourth Gospel with the portrait given in the synoptic Gospels. There appear to be differences in the scene and duration of the ministry of Jesus and in the content of His teaching. It is easy, however, to exaggerate these differences. Jn. vii. 1 shows that John knew of the Galilean ministry with which the synoptists are chiefly concerned. They, in their turn, confirm a ministry at some time in the south of the country since they refer to disciples there (cf. Mk. xi. 3–6, xiv. 12–16). The account of this Jerusalem ministry as given in John's Gospel is entirely feasible. It extended over roughly three years, while in the synoptists the ministry lasted a year.

The general chronology of the passion week does seem to differ from that of the synoptists. In John, for example, the incident of the anointing precedes the triumphal entry into Jerusalem and took place six days before the Passover. The crucifixion itself occurs before the Jews have eaten the Passover meal on the 14th Nisan, while the synoptists assume that Christ ate the meal with His disciples. Most of the problems in this respect can possibly be traced to our present inability to unravel some of the time relations owing to the incompleteness of data. It must be remembered that the Gospels were presentations of Christ; not 'biographies' in the modern sense of the term. (See also note on Jn. xiii. 1–38.)

III. DATE AND PLACE

In arriving at a date the following facts need to be taken into account. Since Ignatius knew the Gospel, it must have been written before A.D. 115; on the other hand, if Mark and Luke were used in its composition, the date must be later than A.D. 85. A fragment of the Gospel found recently in Egypt is dated A.D. 130–150. From this it is clear that it must have been issued some years earlier to account for its circulation in that country at that date. In addition, another fragment of Gospel extracts which is dated c. A.D. 110–150 makes use of the fourth Gospel. We may therefore conclude that the Greek Gospel was probably written between A.D. 90 and 110, although it is possible that the epilogue (xxi. 1–25) may have been written somewhat later. If we accept the suggestion of an Aramaic source, this, obviously, must be earlier still and was probably written not later than A.D. 70. (See Burney, *The Aramaic Origin of the Fourth Gospel*.) As regards the place of writing, Irenaeus spoke of the apostle residing in Ephesus and tradition has always connected the Gospel with that city.

IV. MEANING OF THE GOSPEL

The principle of interpretation is of importance to us in seeking to unfold the meaning of this

Gospel. It is a record of the revelation of the Word made flesh and must be studied in its own historical context. For this purpose the analyses of critical interpretation can be very valuable. But the literary structure, the unity of teaching, the development of the claims of Christ, the clear transcript of the consciousness of Jesus in relation to great themes demand a *theological* exposition. The Gospel is such a unity theologically that it is becoming increasingly felt that this principle of interpretation gives the key to its inner significance. The theological teaching arising out of the seven signs, the messianic claims of Christ, the controversies between Jesus and the Jews and the revelation of the unbelief of the Jews lead up to the final events in the ministry of Christ.

The keynotes of the Gospel are life, light and love. Christ comes to give a fuller, more abundant life to men. He is the light that was in the world, in conflict with its darkness, and the source of man's true life. The sacrifice of His life for the world was the expression of God's love to men.

In the prologue, we have the identification of the historic Jesus with the eternal Word who was with the Father. While the ancestry of the terminology may be thought to show the influence of Hellenistic thought, its main inspiration comes from the Old Testament conception of the Word. The Word was personified in Old Testament philosophy, and in the prologue we have an extension of this thought. The idea of 'the Word' being made 'flesh' was really completely alien to Greek thought.

NOTE: *For a map of Palestine in the time of Christ, see p. 775.*

OUTLINE OF CONTENTS

I. PROLOGUE. i. 1–18

II. JOHN THE BAPTIST AND THE FIRST DISCIPLES. i. 19–51

III. FIRST SIGNS AND DISCOURSES IN JUDAEA, SAMARIA AND GALILEE. ii. 1—iv. 54

IV. FURTHER SIGNS AND DISCOURSES IN GALILEE, AND THE BEGINNING OF THE CONTROVERSY WITH THE JEWS. v. 1—vii. 52

V. THE WOMAN TAKEN IN ADULTERY. vii. 53—viii. 11

VI. FURTHER TEACHING AND INCREASING OPPOSITION. viii. 12—x. 42

VII. THE RAISING OF LAZARUS AND ITS EFFECT ON THE JEWS. xi. 1–57

VIII. THE CLOSE OF OUR LORD'S PUBLIC MINISTRY. xii. 1–50

IX. FINAL DISCOURSES AND THE HIGH-PRIESTLY PRAYER. xiii. 1—xvii. 26

X. OUR LORD'S PASSION AND RESURRECTION. xviii. 1—xx. 31

XI. EPILOGUE. xxi. 1–25

COMMENTARY

I. PROLOGUE. i. 1–18

The prologue to the Gospel is no mere preface or introduction but a declaration of the central theme which underlies the teaching of the Son of God, namely, the incarnation of the Word. The evangelist is giving the necessary background to the life and redeeming action of the Word made flesh. The prologue is poetical in form and structure and constitutes a hymn to the Word of God.

a. The Word in relation to being (i. 1, 2)

In the first verse we have a clear echo of the opening verses of the Old Testament and also a clue to the Johannine concept of the *Logos*. In Gn. i. 1 we are pointed to God's creative act, but in Jn. i. 1 we are pointed to the Word who existed before creation. The thinking of the writer is steeped in the Old Testament, and the evangelist is not to be thought of as borrowing a term or form which was current in Hellenistic philosophical thought. He is setting forth an idea whose ancestry is to be traced to Jewish teaching concerning the Word of God. The *Logos* is a Being whose existence lies beyond time. His eternal pre-existence is implied. *The Word was with God* (1). The preposition 'with' (Gk. *pros*) implies relation and distinctness. Used with the accusative it means not merely co-existence, but directed intercourse. Plummer suggests 'face to face with God'. *The Word was God* (1). This cannot mean that the *Logos* was God in the exclusive sense, for that would identify Him with the totality of divine existence and attributes, yet more is stated than the fact that He 'was divine', which is the sense given by the Moffatt translation. There is implied a definite claim to deity. The substantive *theos* is placed first, which gives it emphasis, and is without the article. The *Logos* is thus identified with God in the sense that He partook of the divine essence and nature and, by virtue of such a relation, can be regarded as God. In verse 2 John gathers into one whole the three clauses of the first sentence. The verb *was* is used in its absolute sense of 'being' as distinct from 'becoming'. His being was timeless and un-created.

b. The Word in relation to creation (i. 3–5)

The emphasis is now laid on the 'becoming' and it is equated with the creative process. The Word is the instrument of creative activity, for *all things were made by him* (3); lit. 'through him all things were made'. The ultimate source is the Father and no intermediary agents had any part in the work of creation, a belief held by the Gnostics. Note that RV mg. gives a different punctuation in verses 3, 4: 'And without him was not anything made. That which hath been made was life in him; and the life was the light of men.' The possibility of creative development apart from Him is excluded. This reading, which is undoubtedly the earlier, emphasizes the thought that all created things are sustained by Him and cohere through a principle of life derived from Him. He is the underived fountain of life; all forms of existence and energies of life have their source in Him. 'The source of life is necessarily the source of light' (Cam. Bible). *The light shineth in darkness* (5). The thought of the evangelist is now extended to the spiritual sphere. Man has received spiritual illumination. Such endowment springs from the life that is grounded in the Word of God. The connection between life and light is drawn by the Psalmist (Ps. xxxvi. 9; cf. also 1 Jn. i. 5). The light shines in the world and is in conflict with the spiritual darkness caused by man's disobedience and ignorance. The witness of divine truth has never been quenched. The light is inextinguishable,

unconquerable: 'the darkness overcame it not' (5, RV mg.).

c. The Word in relation to history (i. 6–13)

The Word is now considered in His historical relations. His coming was heralded by John, who is not in this Gospel distinguished as the Baptist, an incidental witness to Johannine authorship which should be linked with the fact that the apostle John is never mentioned by name. He arose to bear witness to the light and through his witness lead men to a living faith in the coming One (6, 7). John was 'the lamp that burneth and shineth' (Jn. v. 35, RV), but he was only a reflection of the true, underived light which was then 'coming into the world' (9, RV mg.).

We need not regard verses 6–8, with some commentators, as the work of a redactor who wished to exalt the Christ at the expense of the Baptist. The introduction of these verses and their apparent abruptness in this context can be explained by reference to the historic situation. The testimony of the Baptist is integral to the context. At the same time, the evangelist asserts John's subordination to the Word, who must take precedence.

The light was creatively present in the world prior to any incarnation. He had revealed Himself immanently in a world which existed through Him and yet did not recognize Him (10). He had, moreover, revealed Himself historically to His own people Israel and they did not receive Him (11). We note the progressive manifestation of the Word. He *was* (2); *He was in the world* (10); *He came unto his own . . .* (12). His own people refused Him a welcome. The tragedy of opposition to Him becomes apparent. But those who do receive Him enter upon a new relationship as *sons of God* (12). This filial relationship is possible through spiritual re-birth. 'They were reborn into a condition which could in no way be accounted for from within or from below' (Scott Holland, *The Fourth Gospel*, p. 139). This experience is not attained as a result of a natural process involving the will of the flesh and the will of man (13). It is not achieved through any inherent faculty in the possession of man, but through a new birth from God.

d. The Word incarnate (i. 14–18)

There is a striking correspondence between the essential declarations of verse 1 and verse 14. The Word who was in the beginning became man; the Word who was with God dwelt among men; He who was God was full of grace and truth. The eternal Word is now identified with the Christ of history. *The Word was made flesh, and dwelt among us* (14). Note that the mention of flesh excludes Docetism and other views of modern times that are akin to it. Our Lord assumed a real human body; He is declared to have tabernacled in the midst of men. The essential being of God shines forth in Him who is incarnate grace and truth. The majesty and the power of God become veiled in flesh.

We beheld his glory (14). John the evangelist is speaking for the original eyewitnesses of the glory of God. The concept must be subjectively considered. It was moral and spiritual grandeur (Plummer). This glory is further defined as 'the glory as of an only begotten from a Father' (14, RV mg.). 'The glory of Jesus corresponds with the uniqueness of His Sonship' (Hoskyns, *The Fourth Gospel*). The words *as of* may introduce a comparison in the sense that His Sonship is different from that of ordinary sons (as in verse 12). 'The glory of the incarnate Word was such glory as the only Son of the eternal Father would derive from Him and so could exhibit to the faithful' (Bernard, I.C.C.). *Only begotten* (14). The Word *monogenēs* is a synonym for the word 'beloved' with the significance of 'an only son', and does not mean 'begotten'. His glory was manifested not only in majesty and power (the Old Testament conceptions of glory), but in grace and truth. Grace and truth as characteristic attributes of the incarnate Word probably answer spiritually to the life and light of the eternal Word in verse 4.

John bears witness to the Sonship of Jesus (15–17), and his witness is a prophetic reinforcement of the testimony of the eyewitnesses to the glory of the Word. His is but a herald's voice. He knew his own limitations and declared that He who followed him did in fact precede him. *Before me* (15). *Prōtos* refers both to time and place and as used by John is a recognition of the uniqueness of Jesus as to authority, pre-existence and dignity. This testimony is also confirmed by all believers who have received *of his fulness* (16), a fulness of divine attributes and grace. *Grace for grace* (16). *Anti* means 'instead of' or 'in exchange for'. 'Each blessing appropriated became the foundation of a greater blessing' (Westcott). Every grace that was used and appropriated was repeated in fuller measure.

The thought of grace suggests a contrast between Moses the prophet of Israel and Jesus the Christ, who is now mentioned by name for the first time (17). The evangelist contrasts the law of Moses, requiring obedience from man and yet powerless to give life, with the grace that forgives and the truth that sets free. God had now revealed Himself in Christ and is no longer hidden. If God was hidden from men, it was in the splendour of divine self-concealment through the very excess of light. Now He is known through His Son who is the light of the world. The reading *monogenēs theos*, 'God only begotten' (18, RV mg.), has overwhelming evidence in its favour. *Theos*, as in verse 1, is used without the article and refers to Jesus. God has been revealed by His Son who is predicated with deity in that He partakes of the divine nature. The other reading, *the only begotten Son* (18, AV), emphasizing the uniqueness of His Sonship, is required in the immediate context to define the phrase *which is in the bosom of the Father*. The

meaning is clear: the Lord has once and for all declared the Father to men. He is the perfect 'exegesis' of God.

II. JOHN THE BAPTIST AND THE FIRST DISCIPLES. i. 19–51

a. The witness of John to Christ (i. 19–34)

The historical introduction to this Gospel opens with the testimony of the Baptist. Jn. i. 19—ii. 11 gives us the detailed report of an eventful week in the inauguration of the ministry of Jesus. The witness of John is linked up with the significant identification of the Word with the Christ who was in the world to declare the Father. The purpose of the writer is clearly evident in the selection of incidents which begin to reveal the tragic cleavage between those who believe in His name and those who do not. The witness of the Baptist is made against a background of an incipient opposition and prejudice, and the arrival of a deputation of priests and Levites from Jerusalem who come to question him concerning baptism and the claims which he made (19). This is no dramatized setting lacking basis in historical reality. The particularity of detail, such as the mention of the Levites, the precise dating, the location of the site where the inquisition took place, shows regard for fact. The narrative could come only from one who was an eyewitness. *Bethabara* (28); RV correctly 'Bethany'. As no such place as Bethany was known *beyond Jordan* in Origen's time, he apparently altered it to Bethabara, a reading which passed into later MSS.

The priests and Levites authoritatively demand *Who art thou?* (19). John in his reply denies that he is the Christ, or Elijah, or the prophet predicted by Moses (20, 21; cf. Dt. xviii. 15ff.). They again press him to tell them who it is that he claims to be (22). He declares that he is but a voice *crying in the wilderness* (23; cf. Is. xl. 3); his mission was preparatory. On further interrogation, he asserts that his rite of baptism was purificatory, disclaims all personal authority and dignity, and bears witness to the worth of One already present. The words in verse 27 *who . . . is preferred before me* (AV) are found in a variant reading and omitted in the RV translation.

The embassy departs, having heard the witness of John to the Messiah. On the second day the Baptist sees Jesus and proclaims Him to be the *Lamb of God, which taketh away the sin of the world* (29). The Johannine narrative presupposes the baptism of Jesus, which took place presumably before the arrival of the deputation. The Baptist has talked with Jesus and the vocational significance of the coming of the Messiah has burned itself into his soul. The *Lamb of God* may refer either to the paschal lamb of Ex. xii, the lamb of the morning and evening sacrifice of Ex. xxix. 38–46, or the lamb of Is. liii. 4–12. There is also the lamb of Gn. xxii. 7. The conception of the Messiah as the Lamb of God taking away the sin of the world involves a view of His death which embraces sacrificial, vicarious and redemptive aspects. Jesus is the Lamb of God, 'the property of God by whose complete obedience the normal sacrifices in the temple . . . were fulfilled' (Hoskyns). There is an almost certain reference to the Isaiah passage. In RV mg., where the Lamb of God 'beareth' the sin of the world, there is included the thought of the removal of sin through vicarious 'bearing'. The redemptive aspect is also implicit in the thought of the suffering of the paschal lamb with whom Jesus is often identified.

Many modern commentators believe this great utterance to be a later evangelical interpretation placed upon the lips of John and so imposed upon the narrative. It is objected that the universal significance of the redemptive act of Jesus was utterly outside the appreciation of the Baptist. The saying must preferably be understood, however, as one of those flashes of divine revelation by which John the Baptist, like many a prophet before him, possibly spoke better than he knew. Some suggest that John must have brooded over the Old Testament Scriptures, especially the Isaiah passage, where the universal significance of the Messiah's work is emphasized. There is some evidence for this in that the circle to which Simeon and Anna belonged must have thought over such things in their Scriptures (see, e.g., Lk. ii. 32 and Is. xlii. 6, xlix. 6).

John then once more points to the Messiah who came after him in point of historical manifestation but who was before him in point of dignity and priority (30). *I knew him not* (31) implies John's unwillingness to trust his own verdict on such a matter. There is no contradiction here to the words of Mt. iii. 14. John is saying here that he had not the knowledge that Jesus was the Messiah. Then John received a revelation from God. *Like a dove* (32). The appearance of a dove (Luke insists on the objective fact; Lk. iii. 22) was a heavenly token confirming the abiding descent of the Spirit upon the Son of God. Through this sign John received the assurance that Jesus was indeed the Messiah and he thus interprets His Messiahship in terms of Sonship (34). There is no warrant here for the view that it was not until this moment that Jesus was constituted the Son of God.

b. The calling of the first disciples (i. 35–51)

On the morrow, i.e. the third day (the precise time and day are indicated), John sees Jesus walking, and in the presence of his disciples, one of whom was Andrew, he repeats his witness: *Behold the Lamb of God!* (36). Two of the disciples then go over to Jesus (37). Who is the one not named? He is usually regarded as John the son of Zebedee. The two pairs of brothers, Simon and Andrew, John and James, constituted the original nucleus of discipleship. There is deliberate allusiveness of reference in the suggestion that Andrew was the first to bring his brother to Jesus, implying that John also brought his brother to Jesus. The name

of the disciple is suppressed, but it seems reasonable to identify him with the beloved disciple.

Jesus asks them: *What seek ye?* (38). They address Him as teacher and express a desire to spend the day with Him (38). They follow, and abide with Him. This is no haphazard movement towards Christ. They are persuaded to follow Him as there flashes upon them the wonder of His personality. *We have found the Messias* (41) cries Andrew, as he brings Simon to Jesus. Under the scrutiny of Jesus, Simon receives a new name. *Cephas* (42), the Aramaic name of which Peter, a rock, is the Greek counterpart, was suggestive of his real character. To receive a new name was to enter upon a new relation with God. Cf. Gn. xxxii. 28. (For the call to leave home and to follow Jesus see notes on Mt. iv. 18–22; Mk. i. 16–20; cf. also Lk. v. 1–11.)

The circle is now widening and in verses 43–51 we have the call of Philip and Nathanael. On the morrow, i.e. the fourth day, Jesus is minded to set out on a journey to Galilee (43). He finds Philip, who in turn finds *Nathanael* (45). Nathanael was identified very early with the Bartholomew of the synoptic narrative, because his name was coupled with that of Philip. Philip makes the confession that Jesus is the Christ, He who was foretold by Moses and the prophets. *Son of Joseph* (45). This is not a sign that the author was unaware of the miraculous birth; that is already implied in the prologue. The term was the designation by which our Lord was generally known. Nathanael is frankly incredulous that any good can come out of Nazareth, let alone the Messiah, but Philip bids him *Come and see* (46), 'the profoundest apologetic' (Godet, quoted by MacGregor). Jesus reads his character as one *in whom is no guile* (47): there is here, perhaps, an implied contrast with Jacob, from whom, of course, the Israelites derived their name. He tells Nathanael that He knew him before Philip ever called him (48). There is claimed for Jesus the power to read the hearts of men. The *fig tree* (48) was a place of resort for meditation. Nathanael is deeply impressed and acclaims Jesus as *the Son of God* and *the King of Israel* (49). Jesus tells him that, because of his experience and his faith, he would be granted a deepened understanding and a clearer vision of the nature and character of the Messiah's work (51). Jesus uses the term *Son of man* in connection with His Messiahship, supplying what was defective in Nathanael's confession. The vision of the glory of the Son of man was to be the reward of faith. The vision of Jacob is recalled (Gn. xxviii. 12), and Jesus describes the new messianic order which He was to usher in with His coming.

III. FIRST SIGNS AND DISCOURSES IN JUDAEA, SAMARIA AND GALILEE. ii. 1—iv. 54

a. The witness of Jesus to the Jews (ii. 1—iii. 21)

i. The marriage in Cana (ii. 1–12). The miracle at Cana of Galilee was the first of Christ's 'signs' (11, RV). The question that faces us here is whether the evangelist's motif is historical or allegorical. The story itself bears the hallmark of historicity, as can be evidenced by its minuteness of detail. There can also be no doubt that the historical details lend themselves to allegorical interpretation. The story of this miracle had an undoubted foundation in an incident which clearly manifested the glory of the Lord. While no discourse follows this 'sign' as we find after the other 'signs', it is the evangelist's intention nevertheless to associate the 'sign' with spiritual interpretation and significance in relation to the new age about to be ushered in. The miracle thus becomes a sign of that new age. The detail of 'six waterpots of stone set there after the Jews' manner of purifying' (6, RV) suggests a messianic purification.

The third day (1); i.e. three days after i. 43. *Woman, what have I to do with thee? mine hour is not yet come* (4). In answering thus Mary's appeal Jesus was not disrespectful to His mother, for the word 'woman' does not necessarily imply rebuke. His answer was, however, in the nature of a refusal. The hour for manifesting forth His glory as the Messiah had not yet come. 'Mine hour' has also the deeper meaning of His death and glorification (cf. vii. 30, viii. 20, xii. 23, 27). Mary is persistent in her faith and does not give up hope (5). Jesus then commands the servants to fill to the brim with water the six large stone jars which were standing by. The jars when full would contain over 100 gallons. A change takes place in the water. *The governor of the feast* (8), i.e. the steward (8, RV mg.) or head waiter, tastes the wine and, calling the bridegroom, expresses surprise at its excellent quality and asserts that the new wine is better than the old.

This was the first of the *miracles* (11; 'signs', RV) that Jesus did. It may be noted, in passing, that this verse is conclusive evidence against the apocryphal stories of childhood miracles. The Greek word used here, *sēmeion*, is to be distinguished from *dynamis*, an act of power, and *ergon*, a work. The miracles in the fourth Gospel are always 'signs' rather than 'acts of power' or 'works'. They are related for their evidential value. Jesus had thus manifested His glory and borne witness to the new messianic age. He who has appeared in the flesh will introduce a new order into the world. *And his disciples believed on him* (11). Belief is here the consequence and result of the miracle; in the Synoptists it conditions the miracle.

Interposed between the narrative relating to the two signs is the account of a visit to Capernaum (12). Since a little time had yet to elapse before the Passover in Jerusalem, they travelled down from the hill country to this town, which lay at the north end of the Sea of Galilee. Capernaum is generally identified with the modern Tell Hum. Jesus was accompanied by His mother, brothers and disciples.

ii. **Cleansing of the temple (ii. 13-22).** The time of the Passover was at hand and Jesus, accompanied by His disciples, went up to Jerusalem to keep the feast. This is the first of the 'Passovers' that are mentioned in this Gospel. It is a fitting occasion for the public inauguration of His ministry. He visits the temple and finds that within the sacred enclosure in the court of the Gentiles a market has been established for the sale of animals required for the sacrifices (14). The money-changers sit there changing Roman currency into Jewish. Jesus is stirred in His soul and is moved with flaming indignation at such profanation of the temple of God. He takes a scourge made of twisted rushes and 'cast all out of the temple' (15, RV). The wrath of the Lamb is a reality.

The exactness of statement and the precision of detail bespeak the eyewitness. The oxen and the sheep are driven out, the money of the changers is poured out on to the ground, and the doves are removed at the command of Jesus. *Make not my Father's house an house of merchandise* (16). We cannot fail to note the specific relation which Jesus has thus claimed for Himself. The significance of His act is messianic. 'The record is a commentary on Mal. iii. 1f.' (Westcott). The Lord has come suddenly to His temple. Judgment has begun at the house of God. The zeal that Jesus has revealed is a messianic characteristic. He protested against the irreverence and unspirituality of the temple worship. His act may be interpreted as a messianic purification of the whole sacrificial system, an act which had the sanction of prophetic zeal. *His disciples remembered that it was written, The zeal of thine house hath eaten me up* (17); RV '. . . shall eat me up'. The force of this word 'eat up' is expressed in words like consume, destroy. There may be here a veiled reference to the death of Jesus. 'The purification of which this action is a sign depends upon the sacrifice of His body' (Hoskyns and Davey, *The Fourth Gospel*).

The Jews demand a sign, for they recognize the import of His act. They ask for a visible attestation of His authority (18). They receive an answer veiled in metaphorical language which has no meaning for them: *Destroy this temple, and in three days I will raise it up* (19). They will kill Him, but He will set up again the sanctuary they have destroyed. The difficulty of this verse is due to the double reference in the verbs 'destroy' and 'raise'. The verb 'destroy' has the double meaning of loose, as of destruction of a building, and the dissolution of the body; while the verb 'raise' can mean either raising a building or house or the setting up of a sanctuary; hence the idea of raising up a body. The double meaning of the verbs creates the possibility of double interpretations with resultant obscurity. Jesus gives the sign of resurrection as His authority for purifying the temple. The Jews suppose Jesus to have referred to the literal temple which was in process of being built. The building of the temple was initiated *c.* 20 B.C. and completed in A.D. 63. Forty-six years had elapsed since the commencement of the building, thus bringing the date up to A.D. 26 or 27. The Jews were not familiar with the idea of the sanctuary or temple of the body.

Was Jesus simply claiming to set up a new spiritual religion? The significance of this incident is linked up with its chronological position. Many commentators regard the incident as antedated and identify it with the synoptist incident at the culmination of His ministry (cf. Mt. xxi. 12, 13; Mk. xi. 15–17; Lk. xix. 45, 46). This identification was based on the improbability of two separate incidents taking place, one at the beginning of His ministry, the other at the end. The two incidents have many points of concurrence, but the minuteness of detail, the fitting character of the incident as an inaugural act on the part of Jesus and the Johannine interpretation of the significance of the act argue for its retention in its present position at the beginning of the ministry of Jesus. There is nothing historically or chronologically improbable in John's account. John the evangelist finds its greatest significance in the fact that for him it provides the key to the understanding of the controversy between Jesus and the Jews (Hoskyns).

iii. The new birth (ii. 23—iii. 21). The background for the discourse on the new birth is that of the insufficiency of a faith based on external signs (23). Jesus could not trust Himself to those whose faith was only superficial, for He had a perfect knowledge of their motives (24, 25), and this is exemplified in the story of the interview with Nicodemus.

Nicodemus, a member of the Sanhedrin (*a ruler of the Jews*, 1), visits Jesus *by night* probably in order to avoid compromising his position. He recognizes that Jesus is a teacher sent *from God* (an emphatic phrase, distinguishing Him from teachers qualified by passing through the schools), and is evidently impressed with the signs which Jesus does (2). He therefore asks our Lord to clarify His teaching, especially regarding the kingdom of God. Jesus makes the reply: *Except a man be born again, he cannot see the kingdom* (3). The Greek word *anōthen*, translated 'again', may also be translated 'from above'. The reply of Jesus contains the very heart of the theme of this chapter. It affirms the necessity of such a radical change of heart that it is conceived of in terms of a birth from above. A faith based on miracles is insufficient and leaves the inner core of a man's life untouched. Inward renewal alone will enable a man to share in the purposes of the kingdom. Nicodemus wonders how anyone who has passed through all the developing processes of life can be reborn (4). Jesus then reveals the true nature of this new birth and defines the conditions by which it is obtained (5, 6). He means no physical birth, but a creative act of God within the soul. The conditions of entrance into the kingdom are fulfilled when one

repents and is inwardly purified. *Of water and of the Spirit* (5). It seems probable that our Lord's primary reference in the allusion to water was to John's baptism, but the rest of His sentence warns that the outward rite was insufficient without the inner quickening of the Spirit. Some commentators see here a clear reference to Christian baptism. It is not quite certain that this is a correct understanding of our Lord's words, but in any case this verse cannot be adduced to support baptismal regeneration. Some expositors decline to see any reference to baptism in the word 'water' at all, and assume that our Lord was speaking about the cleansing effects of the Word of God (cf. this thought in Eph. v. 26). The most probable interpretation, however, is that our Lord is alluding to the necessity for repentance (John's baptism of water) and the necessity for faith (His own baptism of the 'Spirit', which brings faith). *That which is born of the flesh is flesh* (6). Spiritual life is not transmitted by ordinary generation; it is not identifiable with any fleshly existence. There is no evolution from flesh into spirit. It need cause no wonder then that spiritual birth is the necessary pre-condition of entrance into the kingdom (7). *The wind bloweth* . . . (8); 'The Spirit breatheth' (RV mg.). The same Greek word is used for both wind and Spirit. As the presence of the wind is known by its effects, so the Spirit is evidenced by His operation. The movements of the Spirit are sovereign. The origin and destiny of the believer in whom the Spirit of God has wrought His own creative work is unknown to the world (8).

Nicodemus cannot understand this teaching (9) and Jesus expresses surprise at his ignorance (10). Jesus then declares, associating Himself with His disciples and the whole prophetic testimony of the past, that they have seen and known of the work of the Spirit and so are able to bear witness to His activity (11). If the Jews reject His witness concerning earthly things, though their source lies in heaven (a reference to His teaching on the new birth), how will they receive heavenly things concerning the ultimate revelation of His eternal counsels? (12). No one had ascended into heaven, yet God had willed that there should be a descent from heaven to earth (13). Jesus has come from heaven with a perfect knowledge of God, to reveal God to men. *Which is in heaven* (13). This clause is omitted in the oldest MSS.

Jesus then proceeds to tell Nicodemus of the *heavenly things* (12). *As Moses lifted up the serpent* (14). He illustrates His great theme of the descent of the Son of man into flesh by an Old Testament incident (cf. Nu. xxi. 8, 9). As the dying Israelites turned their eyes towards the brazen serpent and received life, even so men under the condemnation of sin would receive eternal life and healing through the uplifted Saviour (14). The reference is quite clearly to the death of Jesus. In the consciousness of Jesus, death as a divine necessity was embraced as the means of bringing redemption to the world

(15). His death was determined not by the will of man but by the love of God, who gave His only begotten Son, a sacrifice for the world, all-embracing in its universality (16, 17). *The world* (16) is the theatre of God's redemptive purpose.

Do verses 16–21 give us the very *logia* of Jesus or do they give us the evangelist's interpretation of the mission of Christ? It is unquestionable that the evangelist has entered deeply into the mind of Jesus, and, if these are not His *ipsissima verba*, they certainly contain the very heart of the glorious evangel. We have, however, no justification for concluding that these verses were not His own in the context in which they are given to us.

To believe *in the name of the . . . Son of God* (18) is to put one's confidence in His work. Those who do not do this are condemned already (18). The divine mission is asserted to be a work of salvation. The Son of man came to save the world, yet the world has been judged by His coming (17, 19). Salvation and judgment meet in His person. Thus Nicodemus receives a new interpretation of an Old Testament incident to illustrate God's love to men expressed in the death of His Son, and also a new emphasis on an eschatology which emphasizes its 'realized' nature. Salvation and judgment are present realities. Light has come into the world and men have loved the darkness rather than the light (19). *Every one that doeth* (RV mg. 'practiseth') *evil hateth the light* (20). Unbelief is due essentially to an evil disposition that shuns the light. Faith is the practice of the truth; it is obedience and gravitation to the light; it welcomes the divine scrutiny (21). The work of Christ thus sifts out the good from the evil. This is the 'judgment' (19, RV; Gk. *krisis*), that Jesus has entered the world. The appearance of Jesus constitutes a crisis in the life of the world and compels men by the very nature of things to come to the light or to abide in darkness.

b. The final witness of John the Baptist (iii. 22—iv. 3)

These verses present to us a picture of concurrent baptisms which does not appear to accord either with tradition or the synoptic presentation of the respective missions of Jesus and John. A solution to this problem has been found in regarding the narrative as a redactive interpretation fitted into a dramatized framework for an apologetic purpose; namely, that of revealing the superiority of Christian baptism to a rite of legal purification. But there is no valid reason for regarding the narrative as containing any historic improbability. We believe that 'at this point the work of Jesus and the forerunner met' (Westcott). The disciples baptized in Judaea (22) while John baptized in Aenon (23). *John was not yet cast into prison* (24). The occasion for the final testimony of the Baptist to Jesus is provided by a dispute between the disciples of John and a Jew (25, RV) concerning a question of purification. John's disciples are jealous because of the popularity of Jesus (26). John in his magnanimous reply attributes such success to God's favour (27) and reminds his followers again of the preparatory nature of his mission and of his own subordinate relation to Jesus (28). He illustrates this relationship by a simile which springs from the Old Testament conception of the relationship between God and His bride, Israel (see, e.g., Is. liv. 1–10). John is but *the friend of the bridegroom*, and his duty is to procure the bride for the bridegroom and to make all the necessary preparations for the wedding, to arrange the contract of marriage and to stand before the bridal chamber until he hears the bridegroom's voice. It was a matter of joy to John that the people were gathering to Jesus, for it was the seal to his own ministry (29). 'The joy of the forerunner is, in the picture of the Gospel, not weakened by the fact that the work of Jesus is to culminate in an act of sacrifice (i. 29)' (Hoskyns, *The Fourth Gospel*, Vol. 1, p. 249). *He must increase, but I must decrease* (30). 'He must wax, I must wane' (Moff.). As the morning star is eclipsed by the glory of the rising sun, so John the herald must give way to the Christ.

The thought in verses 31–36 becomes more abstract. It seems highly probable that these verses represent the reflections of the writer. The Messiah is heavenly in origin, and hence is unique and supreme. He contrasts the heavenly character of the Messiah's work with that of the Baptist, whose place of origin was the earth (31). The teaching of Christ also corresponds to His heavenly origin. His teaching was the witness of what He had both *seen and heard* of the Father, a witness which no unillumined man on earth can possibly receive (32). The man, however, who is born of the Spirit puts the Word of God to the test, authenticating it in his own experience. For *hath set to his seal* (33) read, as in RV, 'hath set his seal to this'. Christ represents God to man and is His messenger, and to trust Him is to assert the truth of God. God has given the Spirit in full measure to Jesus, in contrast with the partial endowment given to earlier prophets (34). To the Son also has been given supreme authority, the secret of which is the Father's love for Him (35). The evangelist's testimony concludes with a message of life and judgment. Christ is significant for the life of men and their attitude to Him will determine their final destiny. Belief on the Son secures for a man the possession of a life which is eternal. But *he that believeth* (RV, 'obeyeth') *not the Son shall not see life; but the wrath of God abideth on him* (36); 'God's anger broods over him' (Moff.). The final destiny of the disobedient is the experience of the wrath of God. Final impenitence and disobedience mean enduring punishment.

Jesus quits Jordan and returns to Galilee (3), knowing that the movement of the crowds towards Him will provoke the hostility of the Pharisees (1). This return to Galilee may have been the beginning of the ministry recorded in the synoptic Gospels. *Though Jesus himself baptized not* (2). This plain assertion appears to contradict Jn. iii. 26. The explanation of this apparent contradiction is that, although Jesus did not Himself baptize with water, He invested the material act of baptism with its real significance. Possibly the disciples did not apprehend its Christian significance, but Jesus provided the rite with its proper form from above (Jn. iii. 5).

c. The witness of Jesus to the Samaritans (iv. 4–42)

i. **The water of life (iv. 4–19).** The sequence of thought becomes apparent in the history that follows. If water purifies, it is true also that it satisfies thirst. The reference to Samaria is in line with the wider implications of the faith of Jesus. The mission of Jesus includes the non-Jewish peoples of the world. Jesus now goes north. In order to avoid the detour through Peraea it was necessary to take the north road from Jerusalem to Galilee, passing through Samaria *en route. And he must needs go through Samaria* (4). We read in these words also the sense of a compelling constraint which arose out of the urgency of His mission. He comes to *Sychar* (5), usually identified with Askar, a little village in the neighbourhood of Shechem. The traditional site of the well lying at the foot of Mount Ebal has much to commend it as the authentic location. Jesus is exhausted by the journey and sits down alone on the kerb of the well, for His disciples had gone into the village to find food (8). *It was about the sixth hour* (6); i.e. about noon. John is here using the Jewish method of reckoning. It should be noted, however, that in chapter xix he uses the Roman.

Jesus requests a drink of water from a Samaritan woman who had come to the well to draw water (7). The woman's reply, which takes the form of a question, reflects surprise and hesitation (9): surprise that a Jew should request a drink of water from a Samaritan; hesitation because of the known hostility that existed between Jew and Samaritan. *For the Jews have no dealings with the Samaritans* (9) is an explanatory comment most likely by the evangelist. There was acute antagonism between Jews and Samaritans dating from the return of the Jews from exile and the erection of a rival Samaritan temple on Mount Gerizim. The Samaritans claimed descent from the ten tribes and a pure religion derived from the law of Moses.

Jesus, seeking to awaken within the woman a sense of need, and also to quicken her interest, tells her of a better gift than He had already asked of her, a gift which He would have been willing to bestow upon her had she desired it. It is the gift of *living water* (10). The woman is surprised that He is able to produce the flowing waters of a stream (for so she interprets His gift of 'living water'), especially when Jacob had failed (11, 12). The sense of mystery which Jesus had introduced in His reference to living water leads Him to the truth which He communicates in His claim to satisfy man's thirst for ever. The water of Jacob's well can satisfy thirst only for a moment (13), but He can give the gift of eternal life springing up in the soul and fully satisfying man's inner thirst (14).

The woman conceives of this living water as something magical and calculated to make life easy and comfortable, and makes the request, *Sir, give me this water . . .* (15). Jesus, realizing that the exposure of her sin will alone awaken a sense of personal guilt, bids her call her husband (16). The woman's reply, which reveals her evasive embarrassment, gives Jesus an opportunity of confronting her with her sin (17, 18). The woman confesses, realizing that she is in the presence of One whose knowledge is not merely intuitive but supernatural: *Sir, I perceive that thou art a prophet* (19).

ii. **The new worship (iv. 20–26).** In these verses there emerges the controversial issue regarding worship. The woman, probably wishing to divert the attention of the 'prophet' from her guilty secrets, points to Mount Gerizim and broaches the burning question of the validity of the Gerizim worship (20). Significantly enough, the place of worship is important for one whose guilt has been exposed. Jerusalem or Gerizim? The woman's motives are probably mingled as she brings up this question. In His answer Jesus presents a conception of worship which is not limited to any one place (21). Claiming superiority for the Jewish faith, *for salvation is of the Jews* (22), as against the Samaritan faith with its worthless rites, He defines the true nature of worship in verse 23. The locality is irrelevant. What matters is spiritual reality. The messianic hour has struck, abolishing all racial differences. Worship is personal and spiritual, offered to God in the realm of the Spirit. The conditions of true worship are defined as being inward reality and sincerity of purpose. *God is a Spirit* (24). Follow RV mg. and RSV and omit the article. The Greek places Spirit first, so giving it emphasis. Spirit is what God essentially is.

The woman, conscious of the sublimity of the truths Jesus has proclaimed, asserts that she prefers to wait for the fuller revelation which the Messiah will bring (25). Jesus then dramatically reveals Himself as the Messiah: *I that speak unto thee am he* (26). This assertion is entirely relevant in this context of His conversation with the Samaritan woman, for the hour of the establishment of the messianic kingdom has struck. The revelation was withheld from the Jewish nation until the supreme hour of crisis.

iii. **The faith of the Samaritans (iv. 27–42).** The disciples now appear and the conversation is interrupted (27). The woman, excited with the discovery she has made, hurries back to the village to share it with the people of Sychar (28, 29). The One who had exposed her heart and her conduct must surely be *the Christ* (29).

The expression of surprise on the part of the disciples and the abandonment of the pitcher by the woman are significant literary details. The woman so quickens the interest of her fellow-Samaritans that they too set out to see Jesus (30).

In the interval the disciples prepare the food they have bought and they invite Jesus to share the meal (31). Jesus, exalted in spirit by His self-giving to the woman, replies that He has food of which they know nothing (32). Jesus was speaking in a manner which required spiritual interpretation. The disciples interpret His words literally (33), and He then explains that He obtained refreshment and sustenance through His obedience to the will of God. He bids His disciples lift up their eyes and behold the neighbouring fields, for the Samaritans were approaching. *Four months* (35). This suggests that this event took place about mid-December. By contrast with the normal course of nature the seeds sown in the heart of the Samaritan woman are already bearing fruit. The harvester waits the allotted time in the course of nature before he receives his reward, whereas the disciples are now reaping a harvest already. The sower is able to rejoice with the reaper (36). The time-interval has been bridged and the disciples are able to reap the fruits of His labour, proving the truth of the saying, *One soweth, and another reapeth* (37). The disciples thus enter into the labours of others (38).

The climax of the narrative is reached in the faith of the Samaritans, for, on account of the woman's testimony, many believe on Him (39). They urge Him to abide with them (40). Jesus stayed with them two days and far more of them believed, because of what He had said Himself (41). Faith is no second-hand experience received from hearsay and the testimony of others, but a living trust that rests upon the word of Christ. The Samaritans recognize Him to be *the Saviour of the world* (42). This is no later interpretation placed upon the lips of the Samaritans, but the recognition of the aspect in which Christ the Messiah was revealed to them.

d. Healing of the nobleman's son in Galilee (iv. 43–54)

The miracles of healing are also 'signs' of the messianic kingdom. Cf. Is. xxxv. 5, 6. Jesus has witnessed to Judaism concerning the new age. At Cana of Galilee He changed water into wine, thus manifesting His glory (ii. 1–11). His other signs in Jerusalem (ii. 13–22) formed the background of His discourse to Nicodemus concerning the new birth (ii. 23—iii. 21), the necessary preparation for admission into the new kingdom. In His conversation with the Samaritan woman He declared that the messianic hour of true worship had come without distinction of place or class (iv. 23). The act of healing recorded in this chapter is also significant as a sign of this new age and is here linked up with the former sign in Cana (ii. 1–11).

After a stay of two days with the Samaritans, Jesus left for Galilee (43). He states His reason for going there: *For Jesus himself testified, that a prophet hath no honour in his own country* (44). This would almost seem a sufficient reason for not going. Hence certain commentators, following Origen, identify the 'country' with Judaea (Westcott, Plummer, Hoskyns). Bernard (I.C.C.) regards verse 44 as 'a gloss introduced by John or by some later editor from Mk. vi. 4 suggested by the mention of Galilee but not apposite in this place'. In the context it does appear to apply to the region of Judaea. The reason for going to Galilee would then be the inhospitality and hostility of the people of Judaea. It is, however, difficult to arrive at a conclusive verdict as to the location intended by the evangelist. Jesus receives 'a great welcome in Galilee' (45).

The incident of the healing of the nobleman's son has many points of affinity with the healing of the centurion's servant (cf. Lk. vii. 1–10). One can trace certain philological resemblances in the use of certain phrases such as *he was at the point of death* (47; cf. Lk. vii. 2). The miracles are both effected at a distance, and the faith of the nobleman corresponds to the faith of the centurion. But in the Johannine narrative the word of healing by which the miracle is effected is spoken at Cana, and not at Capernaum. There is an evident dissimilarity also in the detail of the story which we cannot attribute to a free rendering of the synoptist narrative. Plummer adduces eight very marked points of difference. A *nobleman* (46; RV mg. 'king's officer'), of the court of Herod, who had probably heard of the former 'sign' of Cana of Galilee, travels all the way from Capernaum, a distance of roughly twenty miles, and begs Jesus to come down to Capernaum and heal his son (47). But Jesus rebukes the faith that merely rests on signs and wonders (48). The official merely repeats his plea for his boy's life, for he believes that the presence of Christ can heal the child (49). Jesus will not reject even the little faith that he had, so He bids him go his way, for *thy son liveth* (50). The official accepts the assurance given him and believes His word. On the next morning, as he returns to his home, he meets his servants who inform him of his son's recovery (51). He inquires when his son showed signs of improvement and discovers that the fever left him at the very moment that Jesus had spoken, *Thy son liveth* (53). The sequel to the narrative is expressed thus: *and himself believed, and his whole house* (53).

IV. FURTHER SIGNS AND DISCOURSES IN GALILEE, AND THE BEGINNING OF THE CONTROVERSY WITH THE JEWS.
v. 1—vii. 52

Many modern commentators (e.g. MacGregor, Bernard) transpose chapters vi and v so that chapter vi follows chapter iv. It is assumed that this transposition gives a better chronological sequence to the incidents related in chapters v and vi. Then the reference in vi. 1 to Jesus going away to the other side of the sea of Galilee would follow naturally after the incident related in iv. 46–54. Likewise the feast of which mention is made in v. 1 would be identified with the Passover of vi. 4, and the reference in vii. 21 which obviously refers to a miracle performed by Jesus would be brought closer to the Bethesda incident. Such proximity to the incident, however, is not necessary. The miracle performed was such that it could easily be singled out for the controversy it caused. Thus it fits into its own context in vii. 21. The identification of the Passover feast with the feast mentioned in v. 1 is based upon an old MS reading 'the feast of the Jews' (RV mg.). It is preferable to accept the better attested reading, *a feast of the Jews* (AV, RV). It is clear that vi. 1 introduces a definite stage in the mission of Jesus. It is difficult to determine the exact chronological sequence. We are told that Jesus went to Galilee after the events recorded in chapter v. There follows the abrupt declaration that He went away to the other side of the sea. This sudden withdrawal on the part of Jesus would seem, however, to coincide with the events described by the synoptists, the sad news of the death of the Baptist, and the return of the Twelve from their mission (cf. Mt. xiv. 13; Mk. vi. 31, 32; Lk. ix. 10). The motive for the withdrawal of Jesus was the desire for peace. The location chosen was Bethsaida on the other side of the lake (Lk. ix. 10). Jn. vi. 1 would therefore seem to have followed the events described in the synoptics. The Galilean ministry of Jesus ends in vii. 2, so it is highly probab'e that the ministry of Jesus in Galilee took place between chapter v and vii. 2 and mainly in chapter vi, which describes two important miracles, the feeding of the 5,000 and the walking on the sea.

A modification of the order, which transposes chapter vi to follow chapter iv, may certainly give a clearer connection between the events, but it is not warranted by the external evidence at our disposal. The evangelist's purpose, moreover, is to select miracles for the sake of the discourses to which they lead. It was not his purpose to give a clear chronological sequence to all the different events in the mission of the Messiah. Thus certain events and periods are telescoped and brought together. In the first four chapters Jesus has borne witness to the establishment of a new messianic age. His miracles are signs of that new age and His discourses affirm the new birth and new worship which are essential characteristics of that new messianic ministry. He has already given evidence of His life-giving power. Now the writer is concerned to show the nature of the opposition and hostility between the Jews and the Messiah until the controversy culminates in final and deliberate rejection of the Messiah's claims. In chapter v the controversy arises over the healing of the impotent man.

a. Healing of the impotent man and the ensuing controversy (v. 1–47)

i. The act of healing (v. 1–9). *After this* (1). 'After these things' (RV). The phrase expresses a sequence in the mind of the writer. *A feast of the Jews* (1, AV, RV). Cf. RV mg. and see note above. There is real difficulty as to the identification of this feast. Westcott believes it to be the feast of trumpets. Century Bible identifies it with the feast of Purim, in view of the apparent reference to spring in Jn. iv. 35 and the approach of the Passover in vi. 4. The evangelist's intention, however, is clear. He emphasizes the coincidence of the visit of Jesus with a Jewish feast when the city would be thronged with people. It was also the sabbath (9, 16).

Jesus went up to the pool which was situated by the sheepgate (2, RV). The word for 'gate' or *market* is omitted in the Greek text. The pool was called *Bethesda*, which means 'house of mercy', so named because of the porticos which were built there as shelters for the crippled. (RV mg. has 'Bethsaida', or 'Bethzatha'. It is difficult to determine the exact form and origin of the word. Bethzatha, 'house of olives', is accepted by many and was located north of the temple. Bethsaida, 'house of fishing', is unacceptable.) The spring was intermittent and was believed to have healing powers. The concluding clause of verse 3 and verse 4 (*waiting for the moving of the water . . . of whatsoever disease he had*) are omitted in the best MSS and may be a later interpolation designed to explain verse 7. It is, of course, possible that these clauses formed part of the original text and were omitted 'to avoid giving support to popular pagan practices connected with sacred pools' (Hoskyns, *The Fourth Gospel*, quoting Robertson Smith). The *moving of the water* (3) would be due to the activity of angels. We do not question that there are unseen energies and powers which operate for the healing of man in ways we are unable to trace.

Jesus singles out a man who had waited a long time by the water (5, 6). He was crippled by an inveterate disease and his case appeared hopeless. Jesus, who knew that the man had been a long time in that case, takes the initiative and asks him: *Wilt thou be made whole?* (6). The impotent man has acquiesced in his condition for so long that he has almost lost the desire to become whole again (7). The question of Jesus is designed to arouse him from his apathy and to awaken a sense of expectation and hope. The reality and completeness of the miracle effected is emphasized by the man's immediate obedience (9).

ii. Antagonism of the Jews (v. 10–18). The miracle had happened on the sabbath day and, in the view of the rulers, constituted a breach of the law which was stringently guarded by the Jews (Je. xvii. 21). The man is questioned, probably by members of the Sanhedrin, who charge him with breaking the sabbath (10). *He that made me whole . . . said* (11). The man's defence is simple but conclusive. 'The authority of the One who wrought the miracle seemed to him to outweigh legal enactment' (Westcott). 'The cripple knew His power but not His name' (Hoskyns). Jesus had slipped away as the crowds gathered (13). He meets the restored man later in the temple and emphasizes the moral significance of the act of healing (14). The miracles of Jesus had an ethical and spiritual intention: inasmuch as a principle of righteousness was involved in the act of healing, there must be no lapse into sin. The restored man goes away and, evidently under a sense of obligation, reveals to the Jews the fact that Jesus had healed him (15). 'And for this cause did the Jews persecute Jesus, because he did these things on the sabbath' (16, RV). This is the first open declaration of antagonism to Jesus.

Our Lord's defence is based on His unique filial relation to the Father: *My Father worketh hitherto, and I work* (17). 'My Father worketh even until now' (RV). God has always been at work for man and there is no rest from such activity. 'Sabbaths have never hindered the Father's work; they must not hinder the Son's' (Plummer). The Son claims co-operation with the Father and His work is co-ordinate with the Father's. The healing activity of Jesus on the sabbath was no violation of the law but a spiritual fulfilment of its true intention. The Jews realize that Jesus has claimed a unique relationship with the Father, a unity of being and activity which is nothing less than a claim to equality with God, which to them is sheer blasphemy (18).

iii. The divine Sonship of Jesus Christ (v. 19–29).

Jesus now answers the charge of blasphemy: *The Son can do nothing of himself, but what he seeth the Father do* (19). 'The relation between the Father and the Son is so intimate that even the Son of God can do nothing of Himself' (Bernard, I.C.C.). 'Their will and working are one' (Clar. Bible). Hence the perfect identity and harmony between the will of the Son and the will of the Father. The Father's love of the Son is the authority for His mission and from that love have issued the works which He has done, and there shall also issue *greater works than these* (20). Verse 21 defines the nature of the 'greater works': the spiritually dead shall be quickened. The mission of Jesus is thus distinguished as 'life-giving'. The Son has also been given the prerogative of *judgment* (22). The life-giving and judging functions of the Son cohere. In the exercise of these prerogatives, the Son is the ultimate revelation of the Father, whose object it is that all men should finally honour the Son. To reject the Son is to dishonour God Himself (23). The thought is developed in verse 24. Acceptance of the word of Christ and faith in the Father who has sent the Son are the conditions of eternal life, which is viewed as a present possession, not as a future prospect. *And shall not come into condemnation* (24). 'And cometh not into judgement' (RV). The

idea of a future judgment in the eschatological sense is not discounted, but it is over for those who believe the word of Christ. In verse 25 those who are dead spiritually will hear the voice of Christ and live. The Father, who is the source of life, has given to the Son *to have life in himself* (26). In the prologue the Word had life and was a source of life in Himself (i. 4); now this attribute is transferred to the historic Christ, who has been invested with authority to execute judgment, *because he is the Son of man* (27). Christ as the Son of man is the judge of man. 'A son of man' (RV mg.) most probably refers to His humanity, stressing the fact that He became a man. It is possible, though doubtful, that the reference is messianic; this thought is further developed in verses 28, 29, where the final consummation is in view. The line of thought is clearly eschatological. There will be a final judgment when the good shall be separated from the evil (29).

iv. Four witnesses to His deity (v. 30–47).

The claim of Jesus was based upon His unique relationship with the Father. His authority is not exercised independently. His judgment reflects His perfect knowledge of the thoughts of the Father (30, 31).

His claims do not rest on His own witness alone. His authority authenticates itself through the intimacy of His relationship with the Father, and thus His witness rests upon the Father's testimony. *There is another that beareth witness of me* (32), and that other was God Himself. The Jews had been demanding external evidence and questioning His authority. Now Jesus comes down from the higher level of witnessing authority and urges grounds of witness that might prevail with them (34). John bore witness of Him; he was 'the lamp that burneth and shineth' (35, RV), and they were glad to rejoice in his witness to the truth. John was not 'the self-luminous light (i. 8), but the lamp which must first be kindled and which can shine only by burning itself out' (MacGregor, *Moffatt Commentary*). The Jews rejoiced in his light perhaps more like children, but disregarded the stern seriousness of his call to repentance.

I have greater witness . . . (36). Jesus now appeals to the witness of the works which God the Father enabled Him to perform. These acts were visible attestations and corroborations of His Father's presence and power. He draws attention also to the permanent and continuous witness of the Father to Him in the Old Testament Scriptures. The Jews, however, were blind to the glory of God and deaf to His call. They were slaves to the letter of the law and could not appreciate the inner meaning of the Scriptures, sufficient proof of which could be found in their failure to believe in the Messiah (38). *Search the scriptures* (39); RV 'Ye search the scriptures'. If we take the verb as an indicative we have the sense that they studied the Scriptures, believing that a mechanical obedience to the precepts of the law would bring them eternal life. If we take the verb in the imperative we have the sense that they were not wrong in searching the Scriptures in the hope of eternal life, but they completely misunderstood the Scriptures and could not find the Christ to whom they bore witness. *Ye will not come to me* (40). It was He alone who could give life, yet they rejected Him. Jesus accuses the Jews of unbelief. He rebuts their charge of egoism and throws it back upon themselves (41, 42). He receives no credit nor glory from men as they do. The fact that the love of God is not in their hearts is the root of their unbelief and hostility. They would welcome the arrogant claims of false prophets, yet they reject the One who comes with a commission from the Father (43). It was no wonder then that they would not receive Him, for they cared not for the credit that comes from God. He will not condemn them before God: one of their own race will accuse them, *even Moses, in whom ye trust* (45); RV 'on whom ye have set your hope'. They regarded Moses as their defender and mediator, but he would become their accuser because of their disloyalty to the essential meaning of the Mosaic dispensation which pointed to the Christ. If they had appreciated the real content of the law of Moses, they would have welcomed Him (46); but if they could not enter into the teaching of Moses, how could they ever be led to accept the words of Jesus Christ? (47).

b. Feeding of the five thousand and discourse on the bread of life (vi. 1—vii. 1)

i. Five thousand are fed (vi. 1–14). This is the only miracle recorded by all four evangelists. See notes on Mt. xiv. 13–23; Mk. vi. 30–46; Lk. ix. 10–17. 'The record of a critical scene in Christ's work in Galilee follows the record of a critical scene at Jerusalem' (Westcott). 'The evangelist has described and explained the unbelief of the Jews at Jerusalem. He now proceeds in spite of Jn. iv. 45–54 to expose the unbelief of the Galileans' (Hoskyns). The two signs which are recorded in this chapter provide the framework for the discourse on the bread of life. The miracle of the feeding of the five thousand takes place *after these things* (1) and when *the passover . . . was nigh* (4). While it is almost impossible to determine the precise chronological sequence of these events, it is nevertheless most likely that the Galilean ministry of Jesus as given in the synoptic presentation can be telescoped within the orbit of Jn. vi. The episodic narrative of chapter vi contains 'the essence of the Galilean ministry' (Westcott).

The feeding of the five thousand in the synoptic narrative took place after the return of the disciples from their missionary labours and the sad intimation of the murder of the Baptist. The multitudes were being won over by the benevolent ministry of Jesus, who went about doing good, and were pursuing Him from place to place. We read that He wished to have a time of quiet (cf. Mt. xiv. 13; Mk. vi. 31; Lk. ix. 10).

The Johannine narrative differs from the synoptic in particularity of detail. It bears the authentic evidence of an eyewitness. *The passover . . . was nigh* (4) is a detail which explains the presence of the large crowds and gives a clue to the spiritual understanding of the miracle. Jesus sees the crowds approaching and suggests a meal (5). He takes the initiative and discusses the matter with Philip, possibly to test Philip, *for he himself knew what he would do* (6). Philip's answer is businesslike and calculating (7). He does not regard the situation in the light of faith and in the Lord's ability to meet the needs of the people. It has been suggested that the preciseness of the answer presupposes previous meditation on the problem and this sum represented their entire resources. *A lad* (9); Gk. *paidarion;* i.e. 'a little lad'. *Barley* (9) was the food of the very poor. This all helps to emphasize still further the disciples' own insufficiency. Jesus bids the disciples 'make the people sit down' (10, RV). There are two words in this verse translated 'men' by the AV. The first may be rendered 'people', and the second, which is more particularly masculine in significance, may possibly represent heads of households, by which method the people had possibly been seated on the ground. Jesus blesses the supply available and in a miraculous way it is multiplied to the people (11). John records the command of Jesus to gather up the fragments, and twelve baskets were filled to the brim with broken pieces of bread (12, 13). The wonder of the multitude deepens and they recognize the messianic significance of the miracle: 'This is of a truth the prophet that cometh into the world' (14, RV); i.e. the prophet of Dt. xviii. 15. The miracle possibly reminded the people of the provision of manna centuries before. See the discussion that follows later in the synagogue.

ii. Christ walks on the water (vi. 15–21). Mark tells us that after the miracle of the feeding of the five thousand Jesus constrains His disciples to take ship and depart from the scene of the miracle (Mk. vi. 45). John supplies the reason (15): the people would have carried Him away and acclaimed Him as their king at the approaching feast. Jesus, having first of all withdrawn His disciples from the dangerous enthusiasm of the crowd, retires to a mountain for prayer and communion (15). The disciples were expecting Jesus to rejoin them later, possibly at Bethsaida (Mk. vi. 45), but 'Jesus had not yet come to them' (17, RV). When He fails to appear, the disciples set out in the direction of Capernaum and are overtaken by a storm. When they are roughly half-way across, they see Jesus walking on the sea and all are terrified at the sight. He reassures them with the words *It is I; be not afraid* (20), and they willingly take Him aboard.

iii. Teaching on the bread of life (vi. 22–59). The immediate sequel to the two 'signs' is the pursuit of Jesus by the multitude. John is silent about the 'sending away' of the multitude, but we infer that the departure has not been complete, for many remain at the scene of the miracle (22). They cross over on the following day and to their astonishment find Jesus there before them (24, 25). *Ye seek me . . . because ye . . . were filled* (26). Jesus condemns their attitude to Him; it is unspiritual and based upon material considerations. They have sought Him for material refreshment. 'Work not for the meat which perisheth, but for the meat which abideth unto eternal life' (27, RV). He bids them appropriate the spiritual nourishment that He alone can give, and appeals to the divine authentication of His mission: *for him hath God the Father sealed* (27). 'For him the Father, even God, hath sealed' (RV). They appreciate the fact that such a gift can verify itself only by the accompaniment of works. They inquire what they are to do (28). Jesus replies that the work required of them is faith in Him whom God has sent (29). They accept the claim that He has made, but they insist that the invisible gift of faith requires an external act of proof. They demand a sign from heaven to confirm His claim to give life (30). Will He usher in the new messianic age with a miracle such as the provision of manna from above? (31; cf. Ex. xvi. 15). The Lord answers their inferences by denying that Moses gave the manna, and by implying that in any case it was not 'bread out of heaven' in the true spiritual sense. *My Father giveth* (32). The tense is present continuous in contrast with the aorist *gave*.

Our Lord further defines the true bread as *he which cometh down from heaven* (33). The Jews desire this bread, thinking it to be some miraculous provision from heaven (34). Jesus replies that He is *the bread of life* (35), in whom the believer will find satisfaction for his inner hunger. The Galileans have seen Him, but have not believed, and hence are forfeiting the gift of eternal life through their unbelief (36). Their motive in pursuit of Him is purely material. Faith is the motive which leads to Him, and those who have faith are the Father's gift to Him. *All that the Father giveth me* (37). There is nothing haphazard in the elective choice of the Father who draws men to Himself (cf. verse 44). The gift is irrevocable, for *him that cometh to me I will in no wise cast out* (37). *I will raise him up* (40). Resurrection is a necessary corollary of the gift of *everlasting life. The last day* (40). See also verses 39, 44, 54. This was a familiar eschatological concept with the Jews referring to the time of Messiah's full vindication and glory. Cf. Jn. xi. 24.

The Jews take exception to the claim that He is the bread which came down from heaven on the ground of His lowly origin and earthly parenthood (41, 42). The answer of Jesus (43–51) catches up the thought of His digression on the blessedness of those who truly believe in Him (36–40). Only those who are drawn and enlightened by the Father will come to Him (44), and such enlightenment comes through the action of God Himself. *The prophets* (45); i.e.

the section of the Old Testament Scriptures known by that name. *And they shall be all taught of God* (45). Cf. Is. liv. 13; Je. xxxi. 34; Mi. iv. 2. The direct vision of God is of course the prerogative of the Son (46). Jesus then renews His claim to be the *bread of life* (48) and solemnly declares that to believe in Him is to possess eternal life (47). He contrasts the manna which had been given in the wilderness with the bread that He can give: the manna could not prevent death (49), but whoever eats of the bread of life that He gives will never die (50, 51). He has in His own person the life principle that abides for ever and is not as the manna which perishes. Jesus then identifies this spiritual bread which He gives with the giving of His flesh, which is *for the life of the world* (51). The impartation of His divine nature is to constitute the food of man.

The Jews are now utterly incredulous and they wrangle with one another (52). The discourse moves to its climax and Jesus further amazes them by the declaration of verse 53 (see RV). His claim to give His flesh for the life of the world is now invested with sacrificial significance. The language is figurative and many commentators have attached sacramental meaning to the figures used, for in the sacrament of the Lord's Supper we have a symbolical representation of the eating of the body and the drinking of the blood of the Lord. In the context, however, the primary ideas are confined to the redemptive character of the death of Jesus and the benefits resulting from an appropriation of the spiritual values of His death; only secondarily to the manner in which men may partake of these benefits. *Whoso eateth my flesh . . .* (54). Jesus declares that partaking of the values of His life and death results in the immediate possession of eternal life and the certainty of future resurrection. *For my flesh is meat indeed, and my blood is drink indeed* (55); RV mg. 'For my flesh is true meat and my blood is true drink'. His flesh and blood are real nourishment for the soul. A close, intimate union results from the assimilation of His nature (56), such union being the counterpart of the union existing between Father and Son (57). Verse 58 summarizes the preceding teaching and verse 59 adds the historical detail as to the location where the discourse was given.

iv. The effect on the disciples (vi. 60—vii. 1). The evangelist records the opposite results of this discourse. The presentation of His claims and the revelation of the Christ as the living bread of God broken for humanity provoke unbelief. *This is an hard saying* (60). Even the disciples found it difficult to understand His doctrine and were offended in Him. His supernatural knowledge of their thoughts leads Him to say to them: 'Doth this cause you to stumble? What then if ye should behold the Son of man ascending where he was before?' (62, RV). The thought here is that the fact of His ascension into the Father's presence will remove any idea of a material feeding on Christ's flesh and blood and show that spiritual participation in His merits and achievements is what is here intended. The cross and resurrection are facts integral to the revelation. A spiritual response to these facts is mediated through the words of Jesus, which are *spirit and . . . life* (63). Material flesh cannot evolve into spiritual life. Spiritual appropriation is the work of the Spirit. The words of Jesus embodied in His discourse are life-giving, creating spiritual desire and life in the soul.

The unbelief of the disciples was no surprise to Jesus, for He foresaw their disloyalty, and the treachery of Judas was known to Him (64; cf. xiii. 11). It was for that reason that He has emphasized the Father's power in securing the spiritual response of those who truly believe (65). This discourse marked a climax in the ministry of Jesus, for *from that time* (RV 'upon this') *many of his disciples went back* (66). The sifting power of the words of Jesus reveal who are truly His. Jesus then turns to the nearer circle of His disciples with the question *Will ye also go away?* (67), and finds loyalty and emergent conviction in Peter's grand acknowledgment: *Lord, to whom shall we go? thou hast the words of eternal life* (68). Peter's confession is reinforced by the united testimony of His disciples: 'And we have believed and know that thou art the Holy One of God' (69, RV). Peter speaks for them all, but there is treachery in their ranks. It is, however, foreseen by Jesus (70; cf. note on verse 64). *Judas Iscariot the son of Simon* (71). 'Judas the son of Simon Iscariot' (RV). Iscariot probably means 'man of Kerioth', in which case Judas is the only disciple who was not a Galilean. The evangelist sorrowfully adds that he is to betray Him. Such an act can proceed only from one who is *a devil* (70; cf. vii. 20n.). The tragic contrast is deepened by the fact that he is one of the Twelve.

Jesus had withdrawn for a season from the active opposition of the Judaean Jews, resulting from the healing of the impotent man. He now walks in Galilee, awaiting the hour of His manifestation (vii. 1).

c. The feast of tabernacles (vii. 2–52)

i. The decision to visit Jerusalem (vii. 2–13). The tension now shifts from Galilee to Jerusalem, and we are told that the *feast of tabernacles* is at hand (2). The brethren of Jesus wish Him to reveal His power in a spectacular way and so authenticate His messianic claims to the people; so they urge Him to attend the feast of the tabernacles in Jerusalem, knowing that there would be great gatherings of the people (3, 4). This festival commemorated the life of the Israelites as a people dwelling in tents in the wilderness. The feast was also made a time of joyous thanksgiving for the ingathering of the harvest because it took place in the month of September or October (cf. Lv. xxii.. 34ff.; Dt. xvi. 13–15). The reply of Jesus to His brethren is similar in character to that given to His mother (6; cf. ii. 4): the hour of His manifestation to men has not yet come. He is referring to His death and glorification. They can go to the feast at any time, since they are in sympathy with the spirit of the world. But He has antagonized the world by His witness to the truth, revealing essentially evil character of the world (7). *I go not up yet unto this feast* (8); RV mg. 'I go not up unto this feast'. The 'yet' is probably an interpolation to explain the apparent contradiction between His statement and His subsequent action. The verb 'go up' may have the deeper meaning of ascension. Tabernacles, a feast of joy for work accomplished, is not yet meaningful for Him. His thoughts move on towards the Passover.

In the end Jesus also goes up to the feast, *but as it were in secret* (10), i.e. not to give a public demonstration of His power. We receive intimation of suppressed excitement, of whispered opinions and much speculation, for He has become a figure of national interest. Some say that He is a good man, others that He is misleading the people. None dare to speak their minds or opinions for fear of the Jews (11–13).

ii. Teaching in the temple (vii. 14–39). The sudden appearance of Jesus at the feast and His teaching in the temple cause amazement and wonder. *How knoweth this man letters . . . ?* (15). The Jews marvel at His undoubted scholarship and wisdom, yet they know that He has not been trained in the rabbinic schools. Jesus replies that His teaching has not originated from Himself; it has come from a higher source (16) and it will verify itself as divine teaching to those who will obey it (17). *If any man will do* (RV 'willeth to do') *his will, he shall know of the doctrine* (17). Moral obedience to the truth matters more than intellectual apprehension. It is the canon of spiritual reality and supplies the key to the understanding of His teaching. The proof that the teaching is not of Himself lies in the disinterestedness of His motives. The authority of His teaching rests also on the fact that He *seeketh his glory that sent him* (18). The reason for their rejection of His teaching is not far to seek. They have violated the law which Moses gave them. If they had obeyed the spirit of that law, they would not now be seeking to kill Him (19). They are utterly unrighteous. *Who goeth about to kill thee?* (20). The citizens are ignorant of the real intentions of their leaders, and reject such an interpretation with scorn, believing that He has *a devil* (20), i.e. is 'possessed'.

Jesus then reminds them of the miracle which He had performed on the sabbath day on a previous visit to Jerusalem (cf. v. 1–16). They had all marvelled then (21–23). *Therefore* (22); RV 'For this cause'. This has reference to the fact that follows. As circumcision is prior to the law, it has the power to override the law in any clash that arises between the two. Such a clash inevitably arises if the eighth day after birth falls upon a sabbath. If, then, they permit the rite of circumcision, which symbolizes the partial restoration of a man's nature, why are they so infuriated when He has made a man *every whit whole* (23)? They judge according to appearance and so cannot appreciate that His action has not only been in keeping with the spirit of the law but is in very truth a fulfilment of it (24). *He speaketh boldly* . . . (26). The citizens of Jerusalem are amazed at the boldness with which Jesus vindicates Himself, and they imagine that, as a consequence, the rulers themselves will become convinced of the truth of His teaching. Yet they know His place of origin and He does not fulfil the tests and conditions of Messiahship. He has come openly, yet the advent of the Messiah is to be shrouded in mystery (27).

Jesus, deeply moved by their misunderstanding, picks up their statement: *Ye both know me, and ye know whence I am* (28). They know His origin, but they are ignorant of the purpose of His mission and of the Father who sent Him. *But I know him* . . . (29). Their failure to recognize His claim does not shatter His own conviction of His divine origin and mission. The significance of His claim is not lost upon them: realizing its purport, they seek to arrest Him, but *no man laid hands on him* (30), for the appointed hour of His passion was not yet (cf. vii. 6, viii. 20). The people, however, are on His side. Their faith rests on His *miracles* (31; RV 'signs').

The Pharisees, jealous of this popular movement in favour of Jesus, instigate the *chief priests* (32), i.e. the priestly members of the Sanhedrin, to procure His arrest. Jesus beholds the officers who had been sent to arrest Him and confronts them with the cryptic utterance: *Yet a little while am I with you, and then I go unto him that sent me* (33). Jesus realizes that this attempt on His life is the beginning of the end. He will soon take His departure along the God-directed way of death. The day of opportunity is still in their grasp, but the time will come when they will sorrowfully seek His help but will not find it; they will not be able to follow Him into heaven (34). The Jews are puzzled at this enigmatic utterance and suppose that He envisages a continuance of His mission elsewhere *among the Gentiles* (35); RV 'among the Greeks'. Their very caricature of His words contains the truth of the course this gospel will take after His death at their hands. They speak words of judgment and condemnation, the significance of which is hidden from them.

In the last day, that great day of the feast (37). This was an additional day of special ceremonies and, apparently, the daily libation of water from the Pool of Siloam (which had marked the other seven) was not repeated. The water was ceremonially poured out from a golden vessel to commemorate the provision of water in the wilderness. To fill up the omission, as it were, *Jesus stood and cried, saying, If any man thirst, let him come unto me, and drink* (37). Jesus here claims to give 'the water of life' to all who believe. Verses 37, 38 admit of a double punctuation. The punctuation in AV and RV, where the stop is placed after 'let him . . . drink', has the

effect of applying the citation to the believer. The believer himself becomes a source of life to others. Cf. Jn. iv. 14. The other punctuation refers the citation to Christ: 'Let him drink that believeth on me . . . Out of his (i.e. Christ's) belly shall flow rivers of living water'. There is a possible reference here to Dt. viii. 15, 16: 'water out of the rock of flint.' The reference is more likely to the Spirit, who would be given to men in all fulness when His task would be accomplished. The glorification of Jesus would result in an outpouring of the Spirit (39).

iii. **Increasing controversy (vii. 40–52).** As a consequence of His words, there is a cleavage amongst the people. Some believe Him to be the prophet spoken of by Moses (40; cf. Dt. xviii. 15); others *the Christ* (41), i.e. the Messiah Himself. Others, ignorant of bare facts that the evangelist does not trouble to correct, say that the Messiah should come from Bethlehem (cf. Mi. v. 2). Some would have laid violent hands upon Him, but dare not (44).

The story returns now to the failure of the officers to arrest Him. They are questioned by members of the Sanhedrin and urge as their defence the authority with which He spoke (46). Cf. Mt. vii. 28, 29. The Pharisees are scornful that they should have allowed themselves to be so misled and they assert proudly that none of their own number has been so misguided (48). The common people who were ignorant of the law came nevertheless under its bane and curse because of their violation of it (49).

Nicodemus, the member of the Sanhedrin who had secretly visited Christ (cf. iii. 1–21), protests against such illegal procedure and reminds them that they have not given Him a fair hearing (51). Nicodemus is scornfully silenced with the charge that he, too, is acting like an ignorant Galilean and that no prophet had ever arisen out of Galilee (52; cf. verse 41, i. 46).

V. THE WOMAN TAKEN IN ADULTERY. vii. 53—viii. 11

There is overwhelming external and internal evidence against the traditional theory that this story was written by John. The evidence of the oldest MS and Versions (with the single exception of Codex D) and also the evidence of the Fathers is against its insertion in the fourth Gospel. The story definitely breaks the sequence of the narrative. Yet it is unquestionable that it forms part of the authentic tradition of the Church. Internal evidence would bring it into line with the synoptic Gospels in point of a similarity in style and phraseology. The story very early became current as a true episode in the ministry of Jesus and was accepted because of its antiquity and authority. It has no theological relevance, however, in ts present context and, as Temple says, 'was probably introduced here as an illustrative gloss on the words "I judge no man" (viii. 15).'

The incident in all likelihood takes place in

the last days before the passion of Jesus. Jesus goes to the temple during the day and at night He goes to the home in Bethany or to the Mount of Olives. One morning, as He is teaching in the temple, the Jews bring to him a woman who has been taken in adultery (3, 4). They wish to place Jesus in a dilemma (6) and ask Him concerning the punishment which should be meted out to the delinquent (5). If Jesus recommends mercy, He will find Himself in opposition to the law of Moses. If He recommends stoning, they know that His judgment will conflict with the civil law of Rome, which alone claims the right to inflict the death penalty. Jesus makes a gesture on the ground which has the effect of discomfiting the Jews (6). The gesture means that He will not pronounce judgment, but they ignore His action and persist in their questioning (7). Jesus then says: *He that is without sin among you, let him first cast a stone at her* (7), and continues writing on the ground. The Jews realize that their own condemnation is being recorded, and they depart from the silent Presence (9). They perceive that they have been judged in the inner motives of their hearts. Jesus has removed the problem from its legal aspect and brought its moral significance to bear on their lives.

Jesus and the woman are now alone, for all the others have withdrawn. He asks her concerning her erstwhile accusers and their condemnation of her (10). He Himself will not speak the word of condemnation, but He bids her sin no more (11). He does not treat sin lightly nor condone it in any way, for the righteousness of God condemned the sin. The lesson He taught the Jews is that human beings are not the agents of the punishment of God. 'The truth in Him rebuked the lie in the scribes and Pharisees. The purity in Him condemned the lust in her' (C. J. Wright, *The Mission and Message of Jesus*, p. 795).

VI. FURTHER TEACHING AND INCREASING OPPOSITION.
viii. 12—x. 42

a. The debate with the Jews continued (viii. 12–59)

i. Discourse on the light of the world (viii. 12–20). Jesus is teaching in the temple; His position is noted in verse 20. He makes the great claim to be *the light of the world* (12). Light, like water, is a thought which is integral to the character of the feast of tabernacles. The ceremony of lighting the four great candelabra in the Court of the Women, commemorating God's guidance of His people by the pillar of fire, affords a likely background to the claim of Jesus. It is also true, however, that the metaphor of light, which entered largely into the thought of the Hebrew writers, may have been in the mind of Jesus Himself. The Messiah is to be a light unto the Gentiles (Is. xlii. 6). The metaphor conveys the ideas of illumination and witnessing. Jesus Christ is the light of the world, dispelling the evil characteristics of darkness and witnessing

to God's final revelation to men. *He that followeth* . . . (12) refers probably to the pillar of fire, while the association of 'light' and 'life' reflects Ps. xxxvi. 9.

The Pharisees question the validity of His witness on the ground that it is self-evidenced (13). While Jesus accepts the truth of the principle of evidence involved, He reminds them of certain objective facts concerning His origin and destiny which make His case as it were exceptional (14). His witness to Himself arises out of His unique self-consciousness. Their judgment is *after the flesh* (15). The word 'judgment' admits of different shades of meaning, having reference to witness, condemnation and knowledge. Their judgment of Him was superficial (15). *I judge no man* (15). This does not deny our Lord's place as Judge of all, but merely asserts that the emphasis of His present mission is not that of judgment. Yet His presence in the world constitutes a challenge, and men are condemned if they reject Him (cf. iii. 19). Hence His judgment is finally authoritative and just, satisfying all legal requirements (Dt. xvii. 6). There is the double witness, His own and His Father's (16, 18). Their flippant challenge to Jesus to reveal the other witness reveals their blind ignorance (19). His life and mission attest the union of Father and Son. The Jews do not attempt to arrest Him, for His work had not yet been accomplished (20; cf. vii. 8, 30).

ii. Consequences of unbelief (viii. 21–30). The word 'therefore' (21, RV) links up the preceding discourse. Jesus develops His claims and reveals the true nature of unbelief and its destiny: *ye . . . shall die in your sins* (21). The Jews are still incredulous and scornful. Jesus again declares that they will be unable to find Him when He goes, and the Jews think He contemplates suicide. The explanation of their failure to follow Him lies in the fact that 'in origin, affinities and outlook they belong to two different worlds' (MacGregor, *Moffatt Commentary*).

Christ is the eternal *I am* (23), and faith in Him becomes the potent determinant of destiny. The repeated solemn declaration, *ye shall die in your sins* (24), follows. They ask Him who He is. *Even the same that I said unto you from the beginning* (25). 'How is it that I even speak to you at all?' (RV mg.) is probably the best translation of this verse. The Latin versions have given rise to the AV and RV translations. The Greek text admits, however, of many interpretations. Westcott, Brooks, MacGregor follow RV mg. translation. Other commentators maintain that the phrase 'the beginning' is to be taken as a variant for 'at the beginning', which if accepted gives the sense: 'I am what I have even told you at the beginning' (Hoskyns, RV). The other alternative translation is 'I am primarily what I am telling you' (Bernard, I.C.C.).

Jesus has much *to say and to judge* (26); i.e. He must pronounce judgment. He has already spoken of the doom awaiting those who die in their sins (cf. verse 21). The thought here is resumptive of verse 16. His judgment is true because it is the judgment of the Father (26). But the Jews cannot understand His allusion to His Father (27), nor will they understand these truths until He is *lifted up* (28). He refers to the approaching consummation of His ministry which is to end in death. He asserts once more His consciousness of union with the Father and His obedience to His will (29). The darkness and ignorance of the Jews are relieved by the statement regarding those who *believed on him* (30).

iii. **True freedom and true sonship (viii. 31–51).** Jesus now addresses Himself to those who are disposed to listen to Him. His teaching will further sift them, and if they are truly sympathetic they will be led into a fuller faith. Thus it is possible to reconcile the initial sympathy evinced by the Jews with their final enmity and antagonism. The severity of the tone of Jesus, the inexorable demands of righteousness, the challenge of His teaching, the demanding nature of true discipleship combine to present the truth in such a way that their basic attitudes stand revealed. The presentation of that truth reveals the unstable foundations on which many based their faith. It also reveals the true nature of His controversy with the Jews.

If ye continue in my word (31). True discipleship involves an abiding in the Word. Only by such abiding would they penetrate into the inner core of His teaching and receive the knowledge of the truth which would make them free (32). Practical obedience to the truth is the key to its understanding. The continuous experience of God's presence is true liberty.

The Jews interpret freedom in a political sense (33): they are *Abraham's seed* and have never yet been *in bondage to any man*. The Jews had indeed known periods of successive bondage to Babylonians, Egyptians, Persians and Romans, but they had never accepted slavery. Jesus is speaking of an inner freedom. A slave is one who is mastered by sin (34), and by virtue of his slavery to sin he has no right in his master's house (35). Only the son of the house has the right. The unbelieving Jews are not entitled to receive the promises of God and remain in His house, because of their slavery to sin. *Ye shall be free indeed* (36). True spiritual freedom is obtained through the Son, and those who are set free abide in His fellowship. The Jews are the physical descendants of Abraham (37, 39), but this is not the same as being his 'children' (cf. Rom. ix. 7). They do not recognize the One who stands in their midst as the concrete expression of God's will and truth, but seek to kill Him. In that respect they are at one with the unbelieving body of the nation. *My word hath no place in you* (37); RV 'My word hath not free course in you'. His words meet with opposition. He has followed His Father's example and they are following their father's example. The emphasis is placed on the difference of origin: *my Father . . . your father* (38). The Jews protest again that their father is Abraham, and Jesus

contrasts the two fathers. Their actions demonstrate that they do the works of their own father, but their works do not correspond with the nature of their father Abraham (39, 40). *The truth, which I have heard of God* (40). Jesus identifies His teaching with God, and this provokes their antagonism. They demonstrate that they are not *born of fornication* (41), hinting perhaps at an irregularity in the birth of Jesus. The words are better interpreted, however, as a disclaimer of the suggestion that they had been guilty of an idolatrous relationship with God. They were probably thinking of the Samaritans. But Jesus is emphasizing spiritual kinship and not physical descent. If they are truly God's children, they will be like their Father and will love Him (42). Their actions betray their evil paternity. They are of their *father the devil*, who was *a murderer from the beginning*, and who *abode not in the truth* (44); RV 'stood not in the truth'. The devil hates the light. He lies, and so expresses his true nature, 'for he is a liar, and the father thereof' (44, RV). The Gnostics saw in this latter phrase a reference to the Demiurge, 'the father of the serpent'; but there is no warrant for such an interpretation. What the phrase means is not that the devil has a father who is also a liar, but that he himself is the father of lies.

Jesus challenges them to find any moral blemish in Him (46). He stands in their midst, the living embodiment of truth. Surely such a concrete manifestation of divine righteousness will lead them to a living faith in Him. The explanation of their unbelief lay in the fact that their parentage was *not of God*, but of the devil (47). The Jews then retort that He is mad and no true Jew, but *a Samaritan* (48), the product of an illegitimate faith, i.e. a heretic. Jesus replies that they dishonour Him (49). His actions spring from His desire to honour God, not to glorify Himself (50; cf. vii. 18). *There is one that seeketh and judgeth* (50), i.e. who will vindicate the Son.

iv. **Increased antagonism of the Jews (viii. 52–59).** The Jews are now quite convinced that He is possessed of a devil. They interpret His words *shall never see death* (51) literally. Was He greater than Abraham and the prophets? (52, 53). Jesus repudiates the charge of self-glorification and replies that He is prompted only by the desire to fulfil the Father's will (54; cf. verse 50, v. 31, etc.). He knows the Father, but they cannot recognize Him (55). God will be glorified in Him through His unique knowledge of His Father (for were He to deny this, He would deny the validity of His mission); and through His loyalty to the commission He has received He is keeping His word (55).

Abraham rejoiced to see my day (56), i.e. the day of the Messiah. He anticipated Christ's coming and received assurance of the fulfilment of the promises. Abraham, however, not only foresaw the advent of Christ but he is able now to rejoice in His day. The implication is that Abraham still has a conscious existence and is thus able to enter into the joy of His advent. The Jews ask Jesus if He has seen Abraham, for He is not yet fifty years old (57). The dramatic reply of the Christ contains the tremendous claim to pre-existence: *Before Abraham was, I am* (58). The contrast between the verbs *ginomai* and *eimi* is the contrast between the created and the unbegotten. Jesus claims that He is the eternal 'I am'; His life partakes of the timeless quality of deity. The Jews realize the significance of His claim: absolute pre-existence means equality with God. This to them is blasphemy, so they take up stones to kill Him, but Jesus hides Himself and passes through their midst. The concluding words in verse 59 (*going through . . . so passed by*) appear to be a later addition to the text.

b. The healing of the blind man and the ensuing controversy (ix. 1–41).

i. The act of healing (ix. 1–12). The narrative in chapter ix follows the discourse in chapter viii and describes an act of healing which is characteristic of the new messianic age. Jesus sees a man *blind from his birth* (1) and the disciples ask Jesus: *Master, who did sin, this man, or his parents . . . ?* (2). Some Jews believed that, if blame was to be attached to a sufferer, sin must have been committed pre-natally either in his mother's womb or in some previous existence. They also believed in the retributive visitation of parents' sins upon their children. Jesus does not treat the matter as a problem for discussion, but regards it as an occasion for manifesting His glory (3). He thereby seems not to admit the point of any such necessary connection. 'The question for us is not where suffering has come from but what we are to do with it' (*Expositor's Greek Testament*). Suffering thus becomes an occasion for divine action. Jesus is conscious of the urgency of the situation. Note the RV rendering of verse 4. The 'we' may refer to the co-operation of Father and Son or to the identification of the Son and His disciples. But this mission and relationship to the Father are on an entirely different plane from His relationship with the disciples (cf. v. 17). The time is short: while He is *in the world* (5) He is the source of light (cf. viii. 12). He illustrates this truth by the act of healing which follows. *He spat on the ground . . . made clay . . . anointed the eyes . . .* (6). The significant elements in the cure were the anointing of the man's eyes with spittle, which was popularly supposed to have a curative effect, and the application of clay to the eyes. These actions were designed to elicit faith. The command to go and wash his eyes in *the pool of Siloam* follows (7). The pool was situated in the Kidron Valley to the south-east of Jerusalem. The real significance of the pool lies in its name. It is interpreted here as meaning 'Sent', a title of Jesus (cf. xiii. 16). Its meaning in the context seems to be 'sending': a reference to the flowing waters of Shiloah (cf. Is. viii. 6). There are realistic details in the narrative which suggest the evidence of the man himself. The neighbours

are so surprised at the cure that they become unsure of the man's identity (8, 9). When the man affirms his identity, they ask him how he received his sight (10). He describes the process whereby the cure was effected and attributes his cure to *a man that is called Jesus* (11).

ii. Further controversy with the Jews (ix. 13–34). The way is prepared for the ensuing controversy by the reference to the use of clay on the sabbath day (14). The spotlight becomes focused again on one of the crucial issues between Jesus and the authorities. For them, the act of healing involved a violation of the law, so the man is brought before a local synagogue council or Beth-Din (13). Some of the Pharisees asserted that such a sign could not be effected by one who was not from God (16). To settle the differences between the various groups, an appeal is made to the man himself to declare his belief. He believes Jesus to be *a prophet* (17). Hitherto the Pharisees have believed in the cure, but now they seek to discredit its reality and they call in the man's parents, who establish both the identity of their son and the fact that he was born blind (20). They are afraid to declare the cure lest they be excommunicated (22), and so they refer the matter to their son (21, 23). The Pharisees had made up their minds about Christ and they bring pressure to bear upon the man to declare his error. *Give God the praise* (24); RV 'Give glory to God'; i.e. by speaking the truth. Cf. Jos. vii. 19. The man insists on the absolute genuineness of his cure: *one thing I know, that, whereas I was blind, now I see* (25). Further questioning elicits no inconsistency in the man's story. He becomes tired of the cross-examination and, losing his patience, asks them sarcastically if their interest is leading them also to the way of discipleship (27). The Pharisees revile him and accuse him of being a disciple of Jesus; they themselves are disciples of Moses (28). They question the origin of Jesus and His authority (29). The man is amazed that they should be ignorant of the origin of One whose power could effect such miracles. He is emboldened by their evident discomfiture, and once again he asks them in ironical tone how anyone could perform such miracles apart from God's help. God listens to those who worship Him and do His will (30–33). The incoherent rage of the Pharisees finds expression in abuse, for the man's argument is unanswerable (34).

iii. The spiritual application of the sign (ix. 35–41). The man is cast out. The phrase used is somewhat too vague to mean formal excommunication. He is found, however, by Jesus who asks him the question, *Dost thou believe on the Son of God?* (35). The reading 'Son of man' (RV mg.) has the support of the oldest MSS. The man understands the significance of the title, but does not know to whom it refers (36). Jesus declares His Messiahship (37), whereon the man believes and worships Him (38). At this act of adoration Jesus is moved to declare the spiritual application of the sign: *For judgment I am come into this* *world* (39). The mission of Jesus was not specifically one of judgment (cf. iii. 17, viii. 15), but judgment is the inevitable result of His coming (v. 22 has reference to the act of judging). A ju cial process is at work whereby those who feel no need of Christ are confirmed in their darkness and ignorance, whilst those who come to the light receive fuller vision. There were listening certain Pharisees who think it incredible that they should be included among the blind (40). Jesus replies to them on their own ground: they could be excused the blindness of ignorance, but never the blind self-satisfaction which prevented them from seeing the truth. Their condemnation would be all the greater because of their privileges. *Therefore your sin remaineth* (41). Follow the RV, omitting the 'therefore'.

c. The allegory of the good shepherd (x. 1–21)

We have in this allegory a continuation of the words of Jesus to the blind Pharisees. The 'sign' of the healing of the blind man provides a fitting background to it. A transposition of the section x. 19–29 to follow ix. 41 which some commentators suggest is unwarranted. The imagery in the allegory is complex, but it crystallizes as the argument develops. Jesus presents a metaphor which is consistent and gives His interpretation of it. The form of teaching used is defined as *paroimia* (6), not *parabolē;* i.e. allegory rather than parable. The distinction between these two forms of teaching should not be overemphasized. *Paroimia*, which means more than a 'proverb' (6, RV mg.), is an extended use of metaphor. Chapter ix had closed with solemn words of warning to the Pharisees. In x. 1 the *Verily, verily* amplifies the preceding discourse in the form of an allegory.

The Pharisees had shown themselves to be in no position to lead others (cf. verse 4). The Eastern *sheepfold* (1) is a walled enclosure; access into it is obtained by means of a *door.* The sheep are driven into the enclosure and watch is kept over them during the night by a porter who guards the entrance. The shepherd returns in the morning and to him the porter opens the door (3). The robber would seek to climb over the wall from some other direction (1). The method of entrance declares the true shepherd (2). Moreover, sheep recognize the shepherd's voice, for it is known to them (3, 4). The approach of the robber causes instant consternation amongst the sheep, for they do not recognize his voice (5). The true shepherd knows his sheep, for he has named them, and he leads them out (3). 'The helplessness of the sheep is contrasted with the free action of the shepherd, for their freedom depends upon his action, and they are thus constrained to freedom' (Hoskyns and Davey, *The Fourth Gospel*, Vol. 2, p. 432). The shepherd goes before his sheep to guide them and the sheep follow him (4).

The Pharisees cannot perceive the import of this allegory. They cannot see that their behaviour in excommunicating the man whose blindness had been cured is contrasted with that of the shepherd who has received and welcomed him. Their failure to understand is evidence of their complacent blindness. The pastoral imagery used is quite familiar to them, but they are unable to understand its true meaning (6).

Jesus now proceeds to interpret the allegory. He says that He is *the door of the sheep* (7). This was frequently the case with the Eastern shepherd who himself lay down with his body across the gap of the sheepfold, and so made himself 'the door'. MS evidence against the translation 'I am the shepherd of the sheep' is conclusive. Jesus is the door, a door of entrance and exit; a door by which we obtain access into the Father's presence (xiv. 6), and through which we pass into liberty, life and service. Jesus sets aside the spurious authority of the Pharisees who have unwarrantably arrogated to themselves positions of leadership. 'In relation to the fold, Christ is the door' (Westcott). Jesus contrasts His own claim to be the door of the fold with the pretentious claims of false shepherds: *All that ever came before me are thieves and robbers* (8). This has the more probable reference to the wolves with whom the true shepherd always waged conflict, the whole hierarchical set-up that obscured the teaching of God and substituted the traditions of men for the commandments of God. The sheep know them to be impostors, wolves in sheep's clothing, and so they are not beguiled. Jesus alone is the door of the sheep (9). He alone can mediate salvation: 'not the Pharisees but Jesus could admit to or reject from the fold of God' (*Expositor's Greek Testament*). *Go in and out* (9) expresses utter freedom of action, sustenance and safety. Cf. Nu. xxvii. 15–21.

The aims of the thieves and of the Christ are then contrasted. *The thief cometh not, but for to steal, and to kill, and to destroy* (10). His object is to exploit others; his aims are in the end destructive. Christ came in order that they *might have life, and . . . have it more abundantly* (10); RV mg. 'may have abundance'. The idea of an overflow of grace is stressed. His purpose is to bestow upon them 'the abundance of all that sustains life' (*Expositor's Greek Testament*). Cf. Ps. xxiii. 1. Jesus now designates Himself as the good shepherd who lays down his life for the sheep. The death of Jesus is a voluntary act. *The good shepherd giveth his life . . .* (11); RV 'layeth down', lit. 'risketh'. 'It is the staking or risking his life when danger approaches rather than its actual loss that the metaphor seems to require . . .' (Brooks). The idea of a sacrifice of life is by no means foreign to the message of the context. The adjective 'good' can have a variety of meanings: beautiful, noble, competent. The metaphor is now extended from the door to the shepherd, from the false teachers as robbers to the 'hirelings'. The transition would be natural to the Hebrew mind.

JOHN X. 12-36

The hired shepherd who tends the flock for mercenary ends deserts it on the approach of danger (12). He has no true regard for the flock, for they are not his own (13), and so the flock falls a prey to the wolves. The good shepherd knows his own and by virtue of the reciprocal knowledge that exists between them (14) is willing to surrender his life for their sakes (15). The understanding between the shepherd and the sheep is a counterpart of the mutual knowledge existing between Father and Son. *Other sheep I have* (16). There are others, Gentiles, who will share in the benefits of His sacrifice. *Them also I must bring* (RV mg. 'lead') . . . *and there shall be one fold, and one shepherd* (16); better, as in RV, 'and they shall become one flock, one shepherd'. Wycliff followed the translation in the Vulgate. There may be many folds but there can be only one true flock.

The Son has power not only to lay down His life, but also to take it up again (17). His death was not an accident, due to circumstances over which He had no control. His decision to lay down His life was voluntary. He is, moreover, able to take it up again; a reference to His resurrection. His death is divinely determined although His action is free, because it is the necessary condition of His Father's love (17). He has a commission from the Father and He is dependent on the Father (cf. v. 30). The idea of His 'taking up his life' accords with the teaching of other passages which attributes the resurrection of the Son to the agency of God. The Jews are further divided at these words (19). Some say that He is mad; others that this is not the language of a lunatic. Others recall the miracle of healing: *Can a devil open the eyes of the blind?* (21).

d. The feast of dedication (x. 22–42)

The drama is now nearing its climax. Discourse after discourse has been given. The storm is gathering around Him and now, in His discourse at *the feast of the dedication* (22), our Lord makes another appeal.

And it was . . . the feast (22); RV mg. 'At that time was the feast', suggesting a connection with the preceding passage. We note that the chronological framework in John is provided by the sequence of feasts. The feast of dedication (Heb. *chanuccah*) took place in December and was instituted to commemorate the restoration of the temple services in 165 B.C. by the Maccabees after its desecration by Antiochus Epiphanes. The narrative opens with suggestive details regarding the occasion on which Jesus gave His discourse. He is walking in the temple, in Solomon's porch, when the Jews gather round Him (23, 24). They are determined to force Him to give a definite answer to their questions. They urge Him to make a clear pronouncement regarding His messianic claims. *How long dost thou make us to doubt?* (24). 'How long dost thou hold us in suspense?' (RV). If He is the Messiah, let Him declare Himself. The Greek

verb used in verse 24 is the same as is used in verse 18 where it means to take away life. Hence, 'How long dost thou continue to take away our life?' 'The Jews understand the peril without perceiving that it is necessary in order that they may fulfil their true destiny' (Hoskyns, *The Fourth Gospel*). The implication is clear: the safety of the nation hinges upon the ministry of Christ. This is the deeper meaning that lies behind Caiaphas' proposal in xi. 50.

If thou be the Christ, tell us plainly (24). The Jews think that the time is opportune for an unequivocal declaration of His authority, if He is indeed all that He claims to be. Jesus replies that He has already declared Himself, but their unbelief and lack of vision have prevented them from recognizing His works as the self-evidencing criteria of Messiahship. They were not His sheep, for *my sheep hear my voice, and I know them, and they follow me* (27), and so they receive *eternal life* (28; cf. verse 10). *Neither shall any man pluck them out of my hand* (28). This verse teaches the eternal security of the believer, though it does not discourage spiritual effort and vigilance. *My Father, which gave them me, is greater than all* (29). The RV mg. reading appears to be better attested: 'that which my Father hath given unto me is greater than all'. 'The unity of the church is strength invincible' (Clar. Bible). Cf. vi. 39, xvii. 2. 'The life of eternity which is the Father's gift to Jesus is "greater" than every potency of earth' (C. J. Wright). The RV mg. translation accords with the teaching in vi. 39. The RV translation emphasizes the fact that the Father is the ultimate source of the authority on which the security of His children rests. *I and my Father are one* (30). The evangelist does not define the nature of the union between Father and Son. Augustine considered that the verb *esmen* ('we are') refutes Sabellianism, and *hen* (the neuter form of 'one') refutes Arianism. The Jews interpret this as a claim to absolute authority, which to them is nothing less than utter blasphemy; so they take up stones to kill Him (31; cf. viii. 59). Jesus appeals to them on the ground of His good works; *for which of those works do ye stone me?* (32). They stone Him, they say, not for His good works, but for His blasphemous claim to such unique fellowship with the Father. He is then making Himself God (33).

Jesus replies with a two-pronged argument. The one is in effect an appeal drawn from the Old Testament (34–36), while the other arises out of the character of His mission (37, 38). If Jewish rulers were called 'gods' (Ps. lxxxii. 6), by virtue both of the commission they received from God and of an authority and consecration to office which rested on the divine Word which could not be broken (35), how can they designate the Christ, who has been consecrated and sent into the world by the Father, a blasphemer? (36). If it is the case that the Jewish representatives were designated 'gods' by virtue of their commission, how much more true is it of Him who has been consecrated by the Father? The Son of God has been dedicated to a task of redemption. Death is His final sanctification (xvii. 19). It is interesting to note that the word 'dedication' used in connection with the feast (22) is different from that used in connection with the dedication of Jesus (36). The former refers to the dedication of a thing, the latter to the dedication of a person.

The second line of argument is that His actions are consistent with His teaching. His *works* are of themselves sufficient for faith and constitute evidence in favour of His claims (38). The testimony of His works leads to an understanding of His claim to union with the Father: 'that ye may know (aorist) and understand (present) that the Father is in me, and I in the Father' (38, RV).

Jesus escapes from their attempt to arrest Him, and retires beyond Jordan (39, 40). His withdrawal to Peraea, the scene of the Baptist's early ministry (i. 28), is significant. Jesus stays there about two months, until the time of the Passover draws nigh. Many come to Him there, adducing John's faithful witness as their motive for coming (41). The unbelief of the Jews is thus subtly contrasted with the faith of those in the region of Jordan who remembered John's testimony to Jesus.

VII. THE RAISING OF LAZARUS AND ITS EFFECT ON THE JEWS. xi. 1–57

The historicity of this story is challenged by most critics. It is maintained that its omission by the synoptic writers can be adequately explained only on the assumption that the incident was not known to them. But the argument from 'omission' is never a safe one. It is asserted, moreover, that its inclusion in the Johannine narrative suggests allegorical creation which is made to subserve the evangelist's purpose. It is of course conceded by the critics that the original basis of the story was historical, but that it was so freely worked upon by the dramatizing mind of the author that it becomes exceedingly difficult to disentangle the strand of the historical from that of the allegorical. The circumstantial details which we normally accept as affording evidence of the historical accuracy of a narrative then become no more than vivid touches reconstructed by the author's imagination for purposes of emphasis and embellishment.

We believe that the narrative bears on the face of it the *imprimatur* of historical accuracy. It portrays a miraculous deed occurring in the realm of historical, observable action. The miracle *per se*, apart from the length of time the body lay in the ground, is no more remarkable than the raising of the widow's son at Nain. Its omission from the synoptics is adequately explained by the fact that, as an event occurring near Jerusalem in the final days, it was outside the cycle of events recorded by these writers, who were concerned more with Galilee than Jerusalem. The narrative fits coherently into the Johannine scheme and occurs as the final, culminating sign which manifested the glory of the Son of God. There are admitted difficulties as to the sufficiency of the historical basis of the narrative, but there is no necessity to accept the limitations of an allegorical interpretation which would also leave many difficulties unexplained.

a. The death of Lazarus and teaching about the resurrection (xi. 1–31)

In John's Gospel this incident marks the climax of the public ministry of Jesus. John has portrayed the nature of the conflict between Jesus and the authorities. The storm is now about to break over His head.

While in Peraea, Jesus hears of the illness of Lazarus of Bethany, brother of Mary and Martha. Mary is identified with the unknown woman of Mk. xiv. 3–9 who anointed the feet of Jesus in the house of Simon (2). Lazarus is designated as one whom Jesus loved (3, 5). His name (Heb. *Eleazar*) means 'God is my help'. Jesus hears the message but declares that the issue will not end in death, but in an occasion which will display the glory of the Son (4). The *sickness* of Lazarus would be a link in the chain of circumstances that were leading to the cross. Jesus abides two days *in the same place where he was* (6). To ask why Jesus delayed is beside the mark. He delays in accordance with the Word of God, not in order to test the women's faith.

Jesus then proposes to journey *into Judaea again* (7). The disciples seek to dissuade Him from going there, as they know that He will encounter the determined opposition of the Jews (8). Jesus in His reply states a general principle in God's economy: *Are there not twelve hours in the day?* (9). He has a task to fulfil and time to do it (cf. ix. 4). When the allotted time runs out, the night of His passion is at hand. The subsidiary idea of a man outrunning his appointed hour and so stumbling in the darkness of disobedience because he has lost the light of guidance (10; cf. 1 Jn. ii. 10, 11) is also present. Jesus then states the purpose of His journey: *I go, that I may awake him out of sleep* (11). The disciples interpret the word 'sleep' literally and remark that *he shall do well* (12; RV 'will recover') and that it is therefore unnecessary to go to him. Jesus tells them plainly that *Lazarus is dead* (14); they will now behold a miracle that will increase their faith in Him, and He rejoices for their sakes that He was absent from the scene of death; *nevertheless let us go unto him* (15). Thomas, believing that their departure into Judaea will mean death for them all, loyally bids the others accompany Him, *that we may die with him* (16).

Jesus arrives in Bethany and finds that Lazarus has been *four days* in the tomb (17). He also finds many Jews there who have come from Jerusalem to console the bereaved (19). Martha hastens to meet Jesus, while Mary sits *still in the house* (20).

This reveals clearly the difference in the temperaments of the two women. *Lord, if thou hadst been here . . .* (21). There is no real reproach in Martha's word to Jesus, but an admixture of faith and hope. She had faith that He could have saved her brother, and that even now He has the power to recall him from the grave. Jesus assures her that her brother will *rise again* (23). Martha, a devout Jewess, believes in the certainty of a final resurrection, but that belief does not console her immediate grief (24).

Jesus then confronts Martha with the tremendous fact that He Himself is *the resurrection, and the life* (25). Resurrection was not merely a distant prospect, but a present, life-giving power incarnate in Jesus. Jesus Himself is the life that man needed. 'He does not say, "I promise", or "I procure", or "I bring", but "I am" ' (Westcott). The believer survives death by virtue of the gift of eternal life which is his by faith (26). Death has no power over the believer, whose life is hid with Christ in God (cf. Col. iii. 1, 3). Jesus then puts the searching question: *Believest thou this?* (26). Belief in this truth is essential to the spiritual appreciation of the miracle of resurrection. Martha declares what she does believe (27). Her confession is true to her own understanding of the functions of the Messiah, but it falls short of the declaration Jesus has made concerning Himself.

Martha then departs to call her sister and tells her quietly that *the Master* (28; RV mg. 'the Teacher'; the name by which He was known in the household) has come and is calling her. The Jews, however, witness the departure of Mary, presumably to mourn at the grave, and follow her (31).

b. The miracle and its significance (xi. 32-44)

Mary finds Jesus and falls at His feet (32). She uses words that the sisters had often spoken to each other (cf. verse 21). Her grief is such that she can say no more. Jesus is deeply moved by the *weeping* (33; lit. 'wailing') of Mary and of the Jews, and He *groaned in the spirit, and was troubled* (33); RV mg. 'was moved with indignation in the spirit, and troubled himself'. The significance of the emotion revealed by Jesus has been variously interpreted. Many commentators think His emotion was due to the intensity of His sympathy. He felt the poignancy of the sisters' grief and revealed His own identification with their sorrow. Others believe that His pent-up emotions were released in the presence of the fact of death. Some believe that the hypocritical weeping of the Jews provoked Him to indignation.

The passionate intensity of His emotion, as on the other occasion when He wept outside Jerusalem (cf. Lk. xix. 41), is due partly to the sorrow caused by the unbelief of the Jews (their entrance upon the scene at this juncture is significant), and also in the historic context to the costliness of the miracle He is about to effect. He is moved to deep emotion, yet His emotion is disciplined. Jesus is the Son of God, manifesting in His life the love and compassion of God. The explanation of His grief by the Jews contains an unintentional truth: *Behold how he loved him!* (36).

Jesus weeps at the tomb, and some of the Jews question the reality of His grief (37). Jesus again groans in His spirit. 'Their sneering scepticism rouses His indignation afresh' (Clar. Bible). He stands before the burying-place and commands the removal of the stone (39); but Martha thinks this unnecessary, as *by this time he stinketh* (39). Jesus rebukes her unbelief with the declaration that she is to see *the glory of God* (40; cf. verses 4, 23) in the triumph over death. He lifts up His eyes, and thanks God in anticipation of His answer to His prayer: *I knew that thou hearest me always* (42). God's action would confirm the divine union existing between Father and Son. The answer to His prayer was certain and inevitable, but 'because of the multitude which standeth around I said it, that they may believe that thou didst send me' (42, RV). There is a necessary distinction between the prayer which was in accordance with the Father's will and the public thanksgiving which was made for the sake of the people (cf. xii. 30).

Jesus then calls Lazarus by name (significantly, in view of His words recorded in v. 25, 28f.), and bids him come forth. Lazarus comes forth immediately. So the story ends and silence falls. We do not hear of the immediate reactions of those most closely concerned. Jesus has, however, by this sign revealed His glory.

c. The Jews plan our Lord's death (xi. 45-57)

This is the final sign given to the Jews, and the division between them now becomes very marked. Many of those who witnessed the miracle believe on Him (45), while others who are hostile depart to relate all to the Pharisees (46). The Sadducees and Pharisees, forming a coalition, summon a council. *What do we?* (47). They feel that instant action is necessary; the Christ has been performing miracles while they have remained inactive. They fear they will be dispossessed and deprived of their prerogatives by the Romans if prompt action is not forthcoming to curtail the revolutionary activities of this Jesus (48). *Caiaphas, being the high priest that same year* (49). This does not imply an annual election of high priests, but merely draws attention to the notable character of that year. Caiaphas takes command of the situation, brushes aside their reasonings, and advises death. It is expedient that Jesus be handed over to the authorities and die for the people; only so will the nation be saved (50). To allow Him to live is to jeopardize their existence as a people. The irony of the situation lies in the fact that he as High Priest should give utterance to the great truth that Jesus should die for the whole nation, and the evangelist adds, in proleptic anticipation of the ingathering of the Gentiles, *and not for that nation only, but that also he should gather to-*

gether in one the children of God that were scattered abroad (52).

The council decides upon the death of Jesus (53), who meanwhile retires to Ephraim, twelve miles north of Jerusalem, and tarries there, for He is aware of their declared hostility (54). The Passover is drawing nigh and great numbers are going up to Jerusalem to perform the necessary rites of purification (55). Many are wondering if He will *come to the feast* (56). The Jewish authorities have also made their preparations, and they have given orders that the arrival of Jesus in the capital be immediately reported to them (57).

What a contrast is presented between the quiet withdrawal of Jesus to Ephraim and His undisturbed serenity and the confused plotting of the ecclesiastical hierarchy!

VIII. THE CLOSE OF OUR LORD'S PUBLIC MINISTRY. xii. 1–50

a. The anointing at Bethany (xii. 1–8)

In John, the incident of the anointing takes place after the decision of the authorities to arrest Jesus and their renewed plotting against His life. The dating, detail and general emphasis of the incident differs from that given in Mk. xiv. 3–9; Mt. xxvi. 6–13; cf. Lk. vii. 37–50. The problem here is both critical and chronological. John's account of the incident approximates very closely to the Lucan account of the anointing of Jesus by a woman who was a sinner. This occurred a long time before His death. In John's account, we can trace also a clear Markan-Matthean background. John, however, identifies the unknown woman with Mary, the sister of Martha. The view held in the Latin church is that the same Mary anointed Jesus twice, once when she was arrested on her path of sin and later at Bethany.

John dates the incident *six days* (1) before the Passover; Mark, two days (Mk. xiv. 1). The chronological difficulty is bound up with the uncertainty of the date of the crucifixion. Westcott dates this incident on the 8th Nisan, as strong reasons could be adduced in favour of the crucifixion falling on the 14th Nisan. Jesus would thus have arrived on the last Jewish sabbath before the Passover. Others date the incident on Monday the 10th Nisan, the day on which the lamb was set apart. In John, this incident precedes the triumphal entry.

The feast is held in Bethany, in the house of Simon (cf. Mk. xiv. 3). Martha serves and Lazarus is present (2). Mary takes *a pound of ointment* (3). *Spikenard* (3). The meaning of the Greek word *pistikē* is not certain. It often means drinkable, and may be an adjective of local significance. Moffatt translates it 'real', for the nard was often adulterated. Mary anoints His feet and wipes them also with her hair (3). Judas Iscariot protests against such extravagance and demands why the money so wasted was not *given to the poor* (5). He is not moved by philan-

thropic concern for the poor; his intention is mercenary, for he carries the box and as treasurer can easily carry away the money. *Bare what was put therein* (6). Gk. *bastazō* ('carry away') corresponds to the English verb 'lift' with its double meaning. Jesus explains why Mary has not given the money to the poor: 'Suffer her to keep it against the day of my burying' (7, RV). Mary has reserved the remainder of the ointment in anticipation of His passion. This preliminary act of devotion is contrasted with the calculating motives of Judas. Judas could have given prudential reasons for inhibiting such extravagant giving; Mary would have found it difficult to give a rational explanation of her action. Thus the contrast between Mary's love, which pours itself at His feet in recognition of His coming sufferings, and the covetousness of Judas slowly maturing into hatred is heightened.

b. Triumphal entry into Jerusalem (xii. 9–19)

The people have heard of the miracle that has taken place (9). The chief priests and Sadducees are furious at the sensation that has been caused and they plan to kill Lazarus also, for he is a living refutation of their denial of the possibility of resurrection (10, 11).

The pilgrims who crowd the streets become excited. They go forth to meet Jesus with palms in their hands and give Him a spontaneous welcome to the capital (12, 13). See notes on the parallel accounts in Mt. xxi. 1–11; Mk. xi. 1–10; Lk. xix. 29–40. Their cry of welcome is taken from Ps. cxviii. 25, 26. *Hosanna* (13) is a Hebrew expression meaning 'Save now'. Their tumultuous messianic welcome is accepted by Jesus, who comes seated on *a young ass* (14), the symbol of peace. He wishes to impress upon them both the character in which He comes to them and the nature of His kingdom. The evangelist quotes the words of the ancient prophecy (15; cf. Zc. ix. 9) which is now being fulfilled, and notes that the significance of Jesus' action is fully understood only in the light of the events that follow (16). The city populace also join in the general acclamation, for they too have heard the testimony of the Jews who were present at the raising of Lazarus (17, 18). *Behold, the world is gone after him* (19). The general jubilation convinces the chagrined Pharisees of their own weakness in face of a power so irresistible.

c. The Greeks' inquiry: Calvary foreshadowed (xii. 20–36)

Certain Greeks (20), i.e. Gentile-born proselytes, come to Philip with the request: *Sir, we would see Jesus* (21). They come to Philip, probably because he is of *Bethsaida of Galilee* (21), a place where many Greeks have settled. When Jesus hears of the inquiry of the Greeks from Andrew and Philip, He gives utterance to teaching which is the veritable transcript of His consciousness. He addresses Himself to the crowd and declares that the hour of His glorification is at hand (23).

He sees in the approach of the Greeks a firstfruit of the harvest to be reaped through His dying. The corn of wheat must *fall into the ground and die* (24) if it is to bear fruit. His mission must culminate in death if He is to receive a harvest of redeemed souls. His travail must precede His satisfaction (cf. Is. liii. 11). The Son of Man is thus glorified through the sacrifice of His life, for sacrifice is the law of life and the guarantee of life eternal. The saying of verse 25 is found in all the Gospels. See, e.g., Mt. x. 39; Mk. viii. 35; Lk. ix. 24. This law is thus applied to those who follow Him in the path of obedience. They will ever be with Him and will be honoured by the Father (26).

Now is my soul troubled (27). Jesus shrinks at the prospect of His sufferings, but He receives assurance from heaven that the way of obedience to the cross is the way of ultimate glorification (28). The Father ratifies publicly the obedience of His Son. When the people speculate as to the noise they have heard (29), Jesus declares that the voice has significance for them. *The judgment of this world* (31) is near and its *prince* (a title for the devil) will be dethroned. A new kingdom will be ushered in through the 'lifting up' of the Son. His victory on the cross will ensure a universal response (32, 33). The people are perplexed, for they cannot reconcile their conception of the Messiah with the words of Christ, believing that the Messiah would appear from heaven and abide for ever. They ask: *Who is this Son of man?* (34). Jesus appeals to them to walk in the light while He is with them, and to believe in the light. He warns them that it is possible to walk in darkness and reject the light (35, 36). To believe in Him is to be spiritually enlightened.

d. The response to the teaching of our Lord (xii. 37–50)

Jesus departs and the evangelist sums up the significance of their rejection of Him: they were hardened in their hearts and spiritually blind. The rejection of Jesus by the Jews is shown to be in the line of prophetic fulfilment (38–41; cf. Is. liii. 1, vi. 9, 10). Yet there were some who believed in Him, but who would not confess Him for fear of excommunication (42, 43).

Verses 44–50 give us a summary of the significant elements in the discourse of Jesus, and reveal the true nature of belief and unbelief. Belief in Christ is identified with belief in God (44). The vision of Christ is the vision of God (45). Faith in Christ dispels all darkness. He came *to save the world* and not to judge it (47), yet the attitude of men to Christ is significant for salvation or judgment (48). The teaching of Jesus does not originate from Himself, but from God (49). He has spoken what God has commanded Him. The Word and will of God expressed through the Son bring eternal life (50). The Jews had rejected the teaching of God and denied Him. Their unbelief is exposed; they stand under the condemnation of God.

IX. FINAL DISCOURSES AND THE HIGH-PRIESTLY PRAYER. xiii. 1—xvii. 26

a. The eve of the crucifixion (xiii. 1–38)

The precise dating of the last supper and the crucifixion is the major difficulty of Johannine chronology. Whereas the synoptic Gospels place the supper on the 14th Nisan, John dates it one day earlier. John's dating seems preferable for the following reasons. The enemies of Christ resolved not to arrest Him on the feast day; a trial on a feast day would have been illegal; carrying of arms would also have been illegal; linen was purchased and spices prepared—both unlikely on a feast day. Some scholars hold that in the year of the crucifixion the Sadducees observed the feast a day later than the Pharisees. This may perhaps account for the appearance of disharmony.

i. The washing of the disciples' feet (xiii. 1–20).

The scene is the upper room where Jesus partakes of a meal with His disciples. Jesus knows that the hour of His passion is at hand. John does not describe the institution of the Lord's Supper (see Mt. xxvi. 20–35; Mk. xiv. 17–31; Lk. xxii. 14–38) but, instead, an act which is truly interpretative of the value of His death. The washing of the disciples' feet is intended to signify more than a lesson in divine condescension, for the event occurs in the context of a saying relating to the approach of His hour and in the reference to the treachery of Judas. Note that the betrayal is said to have been by inspiration of the devil (2; cf. verse 27 and Gn. iii. 15).

Jesus rises from supper and, having *laid aside his garments* (4; the Greek verb *tithēmi*, to lay aside, is used in Jn. x. 11 with reference to the 'laying down' of life), He takes a towel and girds Himself. He then begins to wash the feet of the disciples, a menial action which should have been performed by a slave, or by one of the disciples themselves, as soon as they came in. When Peter protests (6), Christ tells him he will understand the meaning of His action afterwards (7). To Peter's renewed protest (8) Jesus again makes answer, and Peter then desires to have *feet*, *hands*, and *head* all washed (9). Peter, however, is mistaking symbol for reality. Verse 10 appears to mean that the washing of the feet is sufficient and declares a complete purification. He who has bathed completely before leaving home needs only to wash his feet on arrival at his host's house. *Ye are clean, but not all* (10). Judas, however, is not spiritually clean, although he has had his part in the act of washing.

Jesus then explains the meaning of the act. The disciples call Him Teacher and Lord; He has performed the action of a slave, thus expressing His complete humiliation. The act of humiliation was the condition of man's salvation. He enjoins upon them a like self-abasing humility (14, 15) and He goes on to reveal the nature of true authority. The slave is not greater than his master, nor the commissioned servant greater than him that sent him. Let them find their true happiness in following His example. He speaks of Judas who will shortly betray Him (18); yet the Scripture must be fulfilled. He tells them now so that they will remember afterwards and the remembrance of His word will confirm their confidence in their commission (19). They are His messengers, and whosoever receives them receives Him and His Father (20).

ii. The unmasking of Judas (xiii. 21–30). Jesus, troubled by the presence of Judas, declares that one of the disciples will betray Him (21). In the ensuing consternation, Peter motions to the disciple *whom Jesus loved* and who reclines on the Lord's right hand (*on Jesus' bosom*, 23), and asks him if he knows the traitor. To him, leaning back on His bosom, Jesus says He will reveal the identity of the traitor by giving him *a sop* (26), i.e. by taking a morsel of bread, dipping it into the dish and giving it to him—a mark of special honour which will also constitute a last appeal to Judas. He gives it to Judas, saying *That thou doest, do quickly* (27). The deed has already been perpetrated in his heart. The word of Jesus to Judas is not understood by the disciples, who think that Jesus has commissioned him to give money to the poor (29). *And it was night* (30). There follows the withdrawal of Judas into the night. He is thus banished from the scene of light and retires into darkness.

iii. A new commandment given (xiii. 31–38). On the night of the betrayal Jesus gives His valedictory teaching. Many commentators feel that the words 'Arise, let us go hence' (xiv. 31) mark a definite change of scene. But the change does not take place until chapter xviii, so it is felt that a clear case for transposition is indicated. We do not feel that any such rearrangement of text is warranted by MSS evidence. The words constitute a pause in the discourse, unless there is indeed an intermediate change of scene from the upper room to the temple courts at the end of chapter xiv, in which case the figure of the vine in xv. 1 would be suggested by the golden vine which trailed over the temple porch.

After the departure of Judas, Jesus readdresses Himself to His disciples and declares that the hour of His glorification is at hand. God is glorified in the death of the Son. The glorification of the Son of man lies not only in the present; a glory in the future awaits Him on the fulfilment of His divine mission (32). 'As God is glorified in the messianic work of the Son, so the Son shall be glorified in the eternal blessedness of the Father' (Cam. Bible). Jesus uses a term of endearment, *Little children* (33), as He tells them of His imminent departure. But they are not finally separated from Him, as will be the case with the Jews. Jesus gives His disciples a new commandment of love, giving as the reason 'even as I have loved you' (34, RV). The distinguishing mark of their discipleship and hence its test is to be revealed in their love for one another (35). Peter then asks, *Lord, whither goest thou?* (36), and receives the answer that he cannot follow Him now, but afterwards. Peter's renewed inquiry and

rash enthusiasm are met by words of prophetic warning (38).

b. The last discourse (xiv. 1—xvi. 33)

i. Christ comforts the disciples (xiv. 1–15). Jesus refers now to the purpose of His departure and to their destiny. In words of tender compassion, He bids them be unafraid. *Ye believe in God* (1). 'Believe in God, believe also in me' (RV mg.) brings out the imperatives. Jesus bids them put their trust in God and in Him. In His Father's house are many *mansions* (2); RV 'abiding places'. He goes to prepare a place for them. His departure is necessary, for it means that He will come again to receive them that they may be ever with Him. This 'receiving' has been variously interpreted as at death, at the resurrection, or eschatologically. See Acts vii. 59; 2 Cor. v. 8; Phil. i. 23. They know that His departure is by the way of death. Thomas protests that they know not His destination nor the way thereto. Jesus replies that He is Himself *the way, the truth, and the life* (6). The goal is the knowledge of the Father, which He alone can give. To know Him is to know the Father.

Philip asks for a theophany, a visible manifestation of the unseen God, thinking that a physical appearance of deity would yield indisputable proof of His existence (8). (Observe how this reference to the misunderstanding of the disciples bears out the authenticity of the record.) But to see Jesus is to see the Father. Jesus claims union with the Father, a union which His works confirm as real, for both words and works are not His own but His Father's (10). His works should have convinced them of the truth of His claims. Belief in Him would enable them to do even greater or more extensive works than His own (12). The departure of Jesus to the Father would secure for them the release of the Spirit, through whose enabling they would accomplish great deeds. His presence with the Father would enable Him to grant them whatever they asked in His name (13, 14). The Father is thus glorified in the triumphs of the Son effected through the prayer of the disciples. Their obedience to Him is the evidence of their love (15).

ii. The promise of the Holy Spirit (xiv. 16–31). He would also send them *another Comforter* (16). RV mg. 'Advocate'; Gk. *paraklētos*. The word is used four times in this Gospel and once in the first Epistle of John. The literal meaning is 'one called to the side of', 'one called to assist in a court of witness'; hence the translation 'advocate' in 1 Jn. ii. 1. The function of the Spirit is to convince (Jn. xvi. 8); to bear witness to (xv. 26): to teach (xiv. 26). The translation 'Comforter', used first of all by Wycliff, meant 'Strengthener' and has the advantage of stressing the active force of the word. 'Advocate' is to be preferred on etymological and linguistic grounds. The old translation is relevant, however, in present context and in the perspective of this Gospel. The Comforter is one who strengthens not only by consolation but by the revelation of the nature and work of Jesus. This verse confirms the distinct personality of the Spirit. The Spirit of truth will remain with them. He is the other Paraclete whom they know. The world does not recognize the Spirit of truth and cannot receive Him (17).

Their final consolation will be His own advent. *I will not leave you comfortless* (18); RV 'desolate'; RV mg. 'orphans'. He gives the disciples the promise of an appearance which will be a seal of His essential union with the Father. He is referring to His resurrection appearances. Their obedience to His commandments will be the test of their love and the proof of their union with Him. Their reward for such obedience will be a manifestation of the risen and glorified Christ (21). Judas Thaddaeus (not the betrayer) is perplexed by the thought of a manifestation limited to the disciples (22). The answer of Jesus points out the true nature of His kingdom and defines the conditions of His manifestation. Love is the condition issuing in obedience to the word and spiritual fellowship with God: *If a man love me, he will keep my words . . . and we will . . . make our abode* (lit. 'mansion') *with him* (23). There can be no obedience without love. In these verses Jewish transcendentalism is left far behind.

Jesus tells the disciples that the 'Paraclete' would bring His teaching to their remembrance. The work of the Comforter is 'more than a reminiscence of the *ipsissima verba* of the Son of God; it is a living representation of all that He had once spoken to His disciples, a creative exposition of the gospel' (Hoskyns and Davey, *The Fourth Gospel*, Vol. 2). To the disciples, disturbed in spirit, Jesus leaves the legacy and gift of His peace, a peace which the world can neither give nor take away (27). They need not fear, for has He not told them of His approaching departure to the Father, a fact which should bring them joy and gladness? Jesus is returning to the Father and His return will secure for them the effectual benediction of His peace. He tells them all this beforehand, for the event will confirm their faith (29). *My Father is greater than I* (28). This is a comparison of office and function, not of personal worth and dignity, and should be interpreted in the light of its context. There is no reference here to the creation of the Son with the implication of His inferiority to the Father, but to a necessary condition of the incarnation. Jesus points out that the Father is the ultimate goal to which He returns by the way of humiliation and death.

Jesus pauses in His discourse. There is scarcely time left for words. *The prince of this world* (30) is at hand to do his evil works, yet he will avail nothing against Him, for there was nothing in Him to which the prince of the world could lay claim. Yet He must suffer and the cross will reveal to the world His love for the Father (31). *Arise, let us go hence* (31), linked up with 'I will no more speak much with you' (30, RV), may constitute a period of pause in His discourses.

iii. **The allegory of the vine (xv. 1–17).** The metaphor of the vine has as its scriptural background the simile of Isaiah (Is. v. 1–7) and the teaching of Jesus regarding the believer's union with God. Jesus is *the true vine* of God, and the Father is *the husbandman* (1); the branches live only as they abide in organic union with the vine. All useless branches are cast aside and the fruitful shoots are pruned in order that they may bear more fruit (2). In God's pruning process worthless branches are cut off (as in the case of Judas). The true believers are pruned through the Word and their experience of union with the vine (3). *Abide in me, and I in you* (4). Such abiding will issue in abounding fruitfulness (5). Without the Son, they are powerless. Verse 6 emphasizes the fate of the severed branches (cf. Ezk. xv. 2–4); verse 7 is an expansion of the phrase 'abide in me'. The characteristic feature of such an organic union is that an aswer is given to all requests, for they are asked in His name and in line with the Father's will. God is glorified in such fruitfulness (8), and the fruits of love and obedience are the marks of true discipleship. The Son's love to the disciples has been grounded on the Father's love to the Son (9). The pattern of their love and obedience rests on the relation between the Father and the Son (10). Cf. Jn. x. 15, xiv. 20. Love and joy characterize the spiritual union of the disciples with their Lord. His joy is also theirs (11). He bids them love each other for the reason that His love is set on them, a love which fulfils the highest test by the voluntary sacrifice of His life (13). This text has often been used as an illustration of the human love that reaches to a sacrifice of life for others. In the actual context, the emphasis is upon the uniqueness of the thing sacrificed, namely the life of the Son of God, who dies voluntarily for His friends. They are His friends, if they do the things which He commands (14). He calls them no longer bondservants but friends, for a servant has no knowledge of his lord's aim and purpose. They are His friends, to whom He has made known *all things that I have heard of my Father* (15). They have been uniquely initiated into the Father's purpose and have received divine truth and teaching. He has chosen them, revealing that the initiative lay with Him, and has sent them forth into the world to carry out His work (16). Theirs is a divine call which must ever be the inspiration of their work and the source of its continuing fruitfulness (16). Whatsoever they shall ask in the name of the Father will be given them.

iv. **Consequences of union with Christ (xv. 18–27).** Obedience to Jesus will incur the hatred of the world. Like their Master, they must expect persecution and hostility if they are to remain loyal to His name (21). Jesus cannot find excuse for those in the world, for He spoke unto them, yet they hated Him, and hatred of Him is hatred of the Father. It is hatred *without a cause* (25; cf. Ps. xxxv. 19, lxix. 4), for the Scripture must be fulfilled. Their contact with Jesus served only to evoke their evil passions and bitter antagonisms.

Jesus then speaks of the mission of the Comforter (26, 27; see xvi. 1–15n.). Their keeper is the Spirit of truth, who comes from the Father and bears witness to the revelation of truth in Jesus. The disciples also, by virtue of their fellowship with Him, have been entrusted with the same witnessing commission. Their authority rests on their spiritual experience (27).

v. The mission of the Holy Spirit (xvi. 1–15). Jesus has spoken these words in order that they may be prepared to face the hatred of the world and the probability of martyrdom, for His sake (1, 2). The perverted zeal of the world will seek to compass their death in the interests of truth, but really because it is ignorant of the Father and the Son. He warns them beforehand of a time of suffering, so that in the hour of tribulation they may remember His words (4). Now He is returning to the Father and they are too overcome with grief to ask Him concerning the purpose of His departure. But it is expedient for them that He should go away (the Greek verb emphasizes the idea of departure); for if He goes (the verb suggests a goal in view, the act of proceeding to the Father), He will send the Comforter (7). *Because I go to my Father* (10). The stress is laid on the idea of withdrawal. He must go away, for His departure will procure for them the Paraclete, whose mission into the world will be directed to the great issues of *sin, and of righteousness, and of judgment* (8). His convicting power will unmask sin and reveal its true nature in terms of unbelief (9). The Paraclete will also vindicate the righteousness of Christ. The righteousness of Christ will be vindicated by the Father's acceptance of Him. The victory of the risen Christ is the guarantee of the final overthrow of the prince of this world (11). Judgment is the inevitable issue of the divine act of redemption.

These truths are imperfectly understood by the disciples, but a fuller disclosure of the truth will result from the teaching of the Paraclete. The Paraclete will guide them into all truth (13). The Spirit does not speak of Himself (cf. v. 19, vii. 17f.): He will declare and interpret the significance of the acts and events which constitute God's final revelation to men. He will also witness to the fulfilment of His purpose in the future. He will glorify the Son by making known His work (14, 15).

vi. Joy after sorrow (xvi. 16–24). Jesus now directs His thoughts to the sorrow of the disciples, who grieve at the prospect of His departure (16). His physical presence will be withdrawn, but a spiritual presence would be realized in the works of the Spirit, beginning at Pentecost and continuing in the life of the Church. The disciples think that the expression *a little while* contradicts His declaration concerning His departure to the Father (17, 18). Jesus perceives their confusion, but meets their perplexities not by any endeavour to remove them,

but by an assertion of His own conviction. Their sorrow will be transmuted into joy (20). Their sorrow is comparable to the pains of travail, which are only temporary; when the child is born, fear departs and there is joy (21). Their joy also will be born out of their spiritual anguish. He will come again after His death and their joy no one would take from them (22).

In that day they will not be asking the questions that occasion their present perplexity. There is a distinction between the Greek verbs *erōtan*, 'to ask questions', and *aitein*, 'to make request', in verse 23. They will make their requests in accordance with the will of God. He bids them ask in that deeper sense and assures them of the joy of receiving an answer.

vii. Victory after failure (xvi. 25–33). So far He has spoken to them in proverbs, veiling His teaching in symbolical language, but the hour is coming when He will speak plainly. In that day they will pray with perfect knowledge of His will by virtue of their fellowship with the Father through the Spirit. Indeed, Jesus says: *and I say not unto you, that I will pray the Father for you* (26). The interceding advocacy of Christ is not presented here as the ground of their praying. The Father Himself loves them for their love of His Son. Their union with the Father is intimate because they have believed in the divine mission of His Son. Absolute devotion and love to Christ becomes the complement of the Son's intercession with the Father. The disciples express their faith in Him (29–31), but the basis of their faith is insufficient. Verse 30 is an immature declaration. Jesus questions the validity of their confidence by the prophecy of their desertion (32). His confidence is in the Father's will, for the Father is ever with Him. Jesus reveals that the foundation of faith must be based on His victory over the world and His triumph over the forces of darkness. He bids them have courage and *be of good cheer* (33).

c. The prayer of consecration (xvii. 1–26)

This chapter contains the prayer which Jesus offers on the eve of His crucifixion in the presence of the disciples. It is uttered either in the upper room or in the courtyard below, or possibly in the temple courts. The leading thoughts of the prayer spring from the teaching given in chapters xiv—xvi.

i. Our Lord's prayer for Himself (xvii. 1–8). Jesus prays with the consciousness that the hour which had not come in Jn. ii. 4, vii. 6, and which was drawing nigh in xii. 23, has now come. It is the hour of His glorification through death. *Glorify thy Son, that thy Son also may glorify thee* (1). He prays that, by completing the act of redemption which will secure man's salvation, glory may come to both Father and Son. The 'eternal life' made possible through this mutual glorification is defined as knowing God through His Son Jesus Christ (3). Jesus now prays that He may pass on to that state of exaltation and glory which He enjoyed with the

Father in a pre-existent life (5). Note the evidence here for the pre-existence of the Son. See also verse 24. He has perfected the work given Him to do (4, 6). This perfection of work is identified with the annunciation of the name of God to the disciples: *I have manifested thy name* (6). His mission is limited to those whom the Father has given Him. They recognize that the source of His teaching is from above and that His mission originated with the Father.

ii. **His prayer for the disciples (xvii. 9-19).** Jesus pleads the unity and reciprocity of knowledge between Father and Son as the ground of the disciples' assurance that they belong to God (10). Jesus is glorified through their faith. But He must go to the Father while they must continue in the world. He prays that they may be kept from all evil (11, 15), that their unity may reflect the unity that exists between Father and Son. Various readings are found in verse 11. The AV translation may well be correct, which accords with Jn. vi. 37 and xvii. 24, or it may less easily be read as 'keep them in thy name which thou hast given me' (RV). In this sense He prays that the disciples may be true to Him. They have been loyal to Him in the flesh with the exception of Judas, *the son of perdition* (12). This phrase is possibly a Hebraism signifying the fact that Judas is doomed to perish for his sinful deed. No doctrine of predestination to judgment is here implied. Our Lord prays also that they may share the joy of His completed mission (13). He has given them His word, and to accept His word has been to antagonize the world (14). He prays not for the removal of the disciples from the world, for that would obstruct the divine purpose, but that they may be kept from all evil in the world. Note the RV rendering of verse 15, 'keep them from the evil one', and cf. xiii. 2, 27. Our Lord now solemnly consecrates His disciples to their mission, and 'He prays that the divine Father will consecrate them in that whole life of truth incarnate in Himself' (C. J. Wright). The disciples are to remain in the world to fulfil the Father's mission (18). Jesus now consecrates (*sanctify*, 19) Himself to the sacrificial death that lay before Him. His consecrating word makes His death effective, a death which likewise ensures the consecration of those for whose sakes He died.

iii. **His prayer for the Church (xvii. 20-26).** The prayer of Jesus is extended to include all those who shall become His followers through the effective labours of the disciples (20). He prays for their unity, that it may be a counterpart of the unity of Father and Son (21). A spiritual organic unity will convince the world of their mission. To achieve such unity, there must be a sharing in the glory of the Son. The manifestation to the believer of the Father's love to the Son unites all in a perfection of unity. The perfection of all blessedness is to be with Him, to behold the ineffable glory that was His from all eternity. 'It is the prayer that the *ecclesia militans* may become the *ecclesia glorificata*'

(Hoskyns). The world has not known the Father (25); to the disciples, however, Jesus has revealed Him, and in His final petition He prays that they may share in that same love which the Father has for His beloved Son (26).

X. OUR LORD'S PASSION AND RESURRECTION. xviii. 1—xx. 31

a. The trials and crucifixion (xviii. 1—xix. 42)

i. **The arrest (xviii. 1-11).** See notes on Mt. xxvi. 36-56; Mk. xiv. 32-52; Lk. xxii. 39-53. The hatred of the Jews reaches its climax. Jesus crosses *the brook Cedron* (1); RV mg. 'winter-torrent'; it was dry for part of the year. John omits the prayer of the agony (cf. Mt. xxvi. 36ff.; Mk. xiv. 32ff.; Lk. xxii. 39ff.). Judas leads a *band of men* (3; lit. 'cohort of soldiers') equipped with lights and weapons to the garden. The mention of these *lanterns and torches* (3) is evidence of an eyewitness account. The evangelist records the voluntariness of the surrender of Jesus (4); He reveals His identity in the words *I am he* (5). The soldiers and Judas are temporarily disconcerted by this majestic utterance of Jesus and fall to the ground. Jesus repeats His question: *Whom seek ye?* (7), and receives the same reply from the soldiers. They may arrest Him, but not the disciples (8), who effect their escape and the Scripture is fulfilled (9). Jesus deprecates the impulsive action of Peter and reproves him. He then surrenders Himself: *the cup which my Father hath given me, shall I not drink it?* (11).

ii. **The ecclesiastical trial and Peter's denial (xviii. 12-27).** See notes on Mt. xxvi. 57—xxvii. 2; Mk. xiv. 53—xv. 1; Lk. xxii. 54-71. Jesus is bound and taken before Annas, the father-in-law of Caiaphas. (Annas had been deposed from the High Priesthood by Valerius Gratus, Pilate's predecessor as procurator, but continued to exercise control from the background.) Simon Peter and the disciple *known unto the high priest* (15)—presumably John—follow Him. The account of this examination before Annas is not given in the synoptist narrative, and it was probably an informal inquiry at Annas' house. John records a trial before Annas at night and another before Caiaphas in the morning. Meanwhile John gains admission into the court (15) and uses his influence to secure the admission of Peter, who, when challenged, denies three times that he is a follower of Jesus (17, 25, 27). When questioned as to the nature of His teaching, Jesus asserts that it is known to all: *ask them which heard me* (21). Jesus is ill-treated for His supposed insolence to Annas, who had been High Priest before, so that it would be natural enough to call him by his old title (22), but Jesus' answer is irrefutable (23). He is sent to Caiaphas. Peter could have spoken regarding the teaching of Jesus, but instead denies his Master (25-27).

iii. **The civil trial (xviii. 28—xix. 16).** See notes on Mt. xxvii. 2-31; Mk. xv. 1-20; Lk.

xxiii. 1–25. After being taken to the residence of Caiaphas and tried there by the Sanhedrin, He is led to *the hall of judgment* (28; the praetorium, or governor's residence). The Jews remain outside for fear of defilement, for they have not yet eaten the Passover. Pilate wants to know the charge that is being made against Jesus (29). The Jews evade the question. They wish him to confirm their decision, but Pilate would leave the matter with them since they will not specify an accusation. The Jews would have stoned Jesus if they could, but they could not do so legally (31). Other acts of Jewish mob murder are not a contradiction of this legal position. The Roman authorities developed the use of the blind eye. Pilate then interrogates Jesus regarding the charge made against Him: *Art thou the King of the Jews?* (33). Jesus asks Pilate whether his question implies personal recognition of His Kingship or mere hearsay (34). After Pilate's scornful disclaimer and his question, He points out the true nature of His kingdom (36). It is not of this world, is not established by earthly might, but is a spiritual kingdom based on truth. Observe that when answering the High Priest Jesus speaks in Jewish eschatological phrases, but to Pilate he appeals to truth. Pilate dismisses His claim with a jest (38).

Pilate goes out to the Jews, declares his conviction as to the prisoner's innocence (38), and suggests a compromise by releasing the Christ and keeping Barabbas. The Jews cry out for the release of Barabbas (40). Pilate, wishing to save Jesus from death and at the same time to placate the Jews, suggests a lighter penalty. He has not the courage, however, to acquit Jesus outright. He inflicts upon Him the punishment of flagellation in the hope that it will satisfy the Jews (xix. 1). The soldiers add mockery to the scourging (2, 3). This scourging was part of the capital punishment, but here it seems to have been inflicted without formal judgment on Pilate's part. Pilate presents Jesus, wearing a crown of thorns and purple garments, to the crowd, asserts his faith in His innocence and exclaims, *Behold the man!* (5), an enigmatic word expressing both pity and contempt. When the Jews cry out for the crucifixion of Jesus, Pilate in exasperation thrusts the responsibility of His death upon them. The Jews then accuse Jesus of blasphemy, a crime worthy of death in accordance with their law (Lv. xxiv. 16). Pilate has scruples and he hesitates and turns to Jesus with a question which receives no answer (9). Pilate reminds Jesus of his authority. Jesus reminds Pilate that his authority is derived from a higher source; to abuse his authority is to be guilty of sin, but the greater sin attaches to those who have delivered Him up. The Jews are held responsible and Judas also who betrayed Him (11). Pilate's determination is weakened by the veiled implication of disloyalty to the emperor (12). He then brings Jesus out, sits down on the raised tribunal and gives sentence. It is the preparation of the Passover, Friday. *About the*

sixth hour (14). If Roman reckoning is used here, as seems likely, the time would be 6 a.m., which agrees with the times indicated in Mk. xv. 25 and 33 where the Jewish method of measuring the hours is used. The Jews cry out *Away with him . . .* (15). Pilate's sarcastic rejoinder, *Shall I crucify your King?* (15), provides the spark which lights up the crowning apostasy of the Jews, for they have deliberately disowned their King. We note the relevance of the adverb: *Then delivered he him . . .* (16).

iv. The crucifixion (xix. 17–37). See notes on Mt. xxvii. 32–56; Mk. xv. 21–41; Lk. xxiii. 26–49. Jesus carries His cross to Golgotha, where He is crucified between two thieves. The site of Calvary is traditionally held to be in the Church of the Holy Sepulchre; others prefer the place known as Gordon's site, which is a skull-shaped mound outside the city. Pilate places a trilingual superscription above His head (19, 20). He refuses to modify the text on being approached by the Jews. The differences in the title as appearing in the synoptic Gospels are probably due to the differences of language employed or quoted. John adds details regarding the dividing of the garments and the casting of lots for the seamless robe not found in the Synoptics. The significance of the action was that it constituted an unconscious fulfilment of Ps. xxii. 18 (23, 24).

The callousness of the soldiers is contrasted with the sorrow of the women who stand by the cross. Mary, another sister, probably Salome, Mary the wife of Cleophas and Mary Magdalene are there (25). Jesus beholds His mother and commends her to the care of the beloved disciple. This disciple is also bidden to protect His mother (26, 27). Her own unbelieving sons are passed by.

After an interval, Jesus, knowing that His mission is fulfilled, says *I thirst* (28). The soldiers take a sponge dipped in vinegar and bring it to His mouth. When Jesus has received the vinegar, He cries *It is finished* (30), bows His head and gives up His Spirit.

The Jewish leaders desire the bodies to be removed, as it is the eve of the sabbath. To hasten death, it was customary to break the legs of malefactors. This was done in the case of the two thieves, but Jesus was already dead. A soldier thrusts his spear into the side of Jesus and *forthwith came there out blood and water* (34). Interpretation differs as to the significance of the effusion of blood and water. We cannot doubt the veracity of the evangelist's testimony. It was plainly miraculous and not to be explained away naturalistically. The 'blood' and 'water' symbolized the redemptive and cleansing mission of Jesus realized through the outpouring of the Spirit (30). Cf. 1 Jn. v. 8.

The decision not to break the legs and the piercing of His side were fulfilments of Old Testament prophecies (Ps. xxxiv. 20 and Zc. xii. 10). The oracular testimony of John is irrefragable: 'He that hath seen hath borne witness . . . and he (Gk. *ekeinos*) knoweth that he saith true' (35). This 'he knoweth' probably refers to Christ, for *ekeinos* is so used in the Epistles of John. It means more than a solemn asseveration and has the force of our phrase 'God knows'.

v. The burial (xix. 38–42). See notes on Mt. xxvii. 57–61; Mk. xv. 42–47; Lk. xxiii. 50–56. Two secret disciples come to Pilate with another request. Joseph of Arimathæa and Nicodemus, both members of the Sanhedrin, bring with them spices to embalm the body of Jesus. As the Passover day begins at 6 p.m., a hurried preparation is made and Jesus is embalmed according to the Jewish custom. He is bound in linen clothes and laid to rest in a tomb nearby (42).

b. The resurrection (xx. 1–31)

See notes on Mt. xxviii. 1–20; Mk. xvi. 1–20; Lk. xxiv. 1–12. The resurrection appearances of Jesus are centred on Jerusalem. The evangelist selects certain scenes which provide a background for His appearances. These scenes are episodic in form.

i. The empty tomb (xx. 1–10). The sabbath has interrupted the work of embalming, so on the first day of the week, the first Easter, Mary Magdalene arrives at the tomb and, finding the stone removed from the entrance, assumes that the body has been removed. It seems possible that she was accompanied by the other women and subsequently became detached from them. She hastens to tell Peter and the beloved disciple, who both run to the sepulchre. The details in the narrative suggest the historical reminiscence of an eyewitness. When Peter enters the tomb he finds the linen clothes still stiff with spices, but the napkin which covered the Lord's head has fallen flat or has been carefully rolled up and put aside. John then enters himself and realizes that Jesus has risen. No pilferer would have left the shrouds in this condition. The supreme miracle has occurred.

ii. Appearance to Mary Magdalene (xx. 11–18). Mary returns to the tomb and remains there weeping. Two angels sit in the place where the body has lain. In answer to their question, *Why weepest thou?* she gives her reason (13). She likewise answers another, whom she supposes to be the gardener. She then hears her name pronounced and recognizes the Lord (16). She clasps His feet, but the Lord forbids further touch. *Touch me not* (17). The force of the imperative is more clearly brought out in the translation 'cease touching me'. The reason the Lord gives is that He has not yet ascended unto the Father. For that event she must now begin to prepare herself by ceasing to cling too closely to the physical form of her Master. He then commissions her to declare to the disciples His coming glorification, which now carries with it the promise of their own. In His invitation to the eleven to touch Him (Lk. xxiv. 39), a different Greek word is used which implies 'handling' rather than 'clinging', and the motive behind the two touchings is quite different.

iii. Appearance to the disciples (xx. 19–23). The disciples are hiding in Jerusalem. The Lord comes to them through shut doors and stands in their midst with words of peace on His lips (19). His body was not a phantom, but was what Paul calls 'a spiritual body' (1 Cor. xv. 44). The account is told in such a way that we are to read it as a fulfilment of the promises made by Jesus in His final discourses. He imparts His peace (xiv. 27), and their joy is fulfilled (xv. 11). He sends them into the world and breathes upon them the Spirit. This is in anticipation of the real bestowal of the gift at Pentecost. *Whose soever sins ye remit* . . . (23). Commentators differ as to whether this commission is to be limited to the disciples. He gives them power to remit and retain sin. By virtue of their close fellowship with Him, they are empowered to act in His name as the channels of His forgiveness and to be the agents of the remission or retention of sin. The power bestowed is one of authoritatively declaring forgiveness on the basis of the sin-bearing death of Christ. His authority was intrinsically theirs because of the Spirit's presence in their lives. Authority is not given only to those specially ordained, but the whole Church has an authority derived from the presence of the Spirit in her life and from the teaching of her Head.

iv. Appearance to Thomas (xx. 24–31). Jesus again appears to His disciples and salutes them with His peace. This time Thomas is present. He had declared his refusal to believe unless he be shown the print of the nails in His hands and His riven side. Jesus stands before him, revealing the evidences of His passion, and invites Thomas to touch the marks in His hands and thrust his hand into His side. Thomas then passionately declares his faith and makes the great acknowledgment: *My Lord and my God* (28). This cry is not an ejaculation to the Father, as Unitarians maintain, but a confession by a great sceptic of the deity of Christ. The narrative leads up to this crowning confession, which witnesses to a faith that rises above the necessity of being shown tangible proofs of the passion. Jesus declares that sensuous evidence is an insufficient ground of faith: *blessed are they that have not seen, and yet have believed* (29).

The evangelist now concludes with a statement of the purpose of his narrative (31), which is to secure the faith in Christ of his readers, even though they may be among those who 'have not seen'. Any reading of this Gospel which does not lead to faith in the deity of Christ and the receiving of eternal life is a misreading of it.

XI. EPILOGUE. xxi. 1–25

Many commentators believe that this chapter was not written by the evangelist. It is clearly an appendix, but the similarity in emphasis, structure and phraseology with the rest of the

Gospel is strong evidence in favour of its authorship by the same writer.

a. Appearance at the Sea of Tiberias (xxi. 1-14)

The resemblance between this narrative and Lk. v. 1-11 need not necessarily suggest John's dependence upon the Lucan narrative. Acting on Peter's suggestion, six disciples, including Thomas, Nathanael, the sons of Zebedee, and two unnamed disciples, set out on a fruitless night's fishing on the Sea of Tiberias. In the early morning, Jesus stands on the shore and addresses them tenderly: 'Children, have ye aught to eat?' (5, RV). Their answer is negative, so He bids them cast the net on the right side of the boat. A simple obedience to His word brings results beyond all expectation. The beloved disciple then recognizes the Lord and tells Peter, who throws himself into the sea (7). When the others arrive, they find a meal already prepared and are commanded to bring of the fish which they have taken. Peter drags the net ashore. They are invited to *Come and dine* (12). RV 'Come and break your fast'. This was the third time Jesus had manifested Himself to the disciples, the other two appearances being recorded in Jn. xx. 19ff. and xx. 26ff., and the purpose of the miracle is to show the condition upon which alone the work of disciples as fishers of men is to be effected.

b. Peter's commission (xxi. 15-23)

The figure of the capture of fish is now replaced by the figure of a shepherd and his sheep, which symbolizes the extension of the disciples' mission to that of shepherding. Peter had denied his Lord three times. The questions of the Lord elicit a threefold affirmation of his love. *Lovest thou me . . .?* (15). The verb used by the Lord is *agapaō*, which suggests a love involving deliberateness of choice. Peter replies with the verb *phileō*, which is a love involving personal affection, a lower form of love. In verse 17 Jesus uses Peter's word, thus causing him sorrow. If the difference of connotation in the verb be accepted, we note a lowering in the demands of the Lord. We note also the growing humility of Peter. The verbs are used interchangeably, however, in other connections. The Lord commissions Peter to feed the lambs, to shepherd the sheep and to feed His young sheep (Gk. *probatia*, (young sheep)).

Peter questions the Lord concerning the destiny of the beloved disciple 'which also leaned back on his breast' (20, RV), but is rebuked. Peter is to follow the Lord, who says of the beloved disciple: *If I will that he tarry till I come, what is that to thee?* (22). This saying was interpreted to mean that the disciple would never die. The purpose of the author is to correct that misunderstanding. Some critics maintain that John had already died and that it is the author's intention to reconcile the fact of his death with the prediction of deathlessness.

c. Conclusion (xxi. 24, 25)

The last two verses of the Gospel are added by unknown persons who declare that 'the disciple which beareth witness of these things' is the author of this Gospel (24, RV). This disciple is one of the seven persons who went fishing (2), and is also the disciple whom Jesus loved (20). *We know that his testimony is true* (24). To whom are we to attribute this additional testimony? Many (e.g. Lightfoot) attribute it to the inner group of the disciples and others to the Ephesian elders associated with John in his work. Others maintain that John himself is speaking for all. The readers are reminded of the fragmentary nature of the work. Verse 25 contains no mere hyperbolical statement, but a confession of literary inadequacy confronted with a task so great. The world could not contain the record of the incarnate act of redemption which had its source in the eternal purpose of God. This verse was omitted from his text by Tischendorf, but his action was successfully challenged. There is no documentary evidence for omitting it.

A. J. MACLEOD.

THE ACTS OF THE APOSTLES

INTRODUCTION

See also the General Article, 'The Primitive Church', p. 64.

The book of the Acts is the sequel to the third Gospel, and written by the same author, Luke, the beloved physician and companion of the apostle Paul (cf. Col. iv. 14). The external evidence of various writers from the second century onwards is unanimous and adequate on this point, and the internal evidence of the style, outlook and subject-matter of the two books is equally satisfactory. (See *The Acts of the Apostles: The Greek Text with Introduction and Commentary*, by F. F. Bruce (Tyndale Press, London, 1952), pp. 1ff.)

Acts, like the third Gospel, is dedicated to a certain Theophilus (cf. Lk. i. 3 with Acts i. 1). The third Gospel is the 'former treatise' of the opening sentence of Acts. Theophilus appears to have been a person of some distinction, as he is accorded the title 'most excellent', elsewhere given to the Roman governors of Judaea (Acts xxiii. 26, xxiv. 3, xxvi. 25). He had already acquired some information about the Christian faith, and it was to provide him with a more accurate account of its trustworthiness that Luke in the first instance wrote his history of Christian beginnings, carrying the story from the nativity of John the Baptist and Jesus (*c.* 8–6 B.C.) to the end of Paul's two years' detention at Rome (*c.* A.D. 61).

Thus, Luke and Acts are not really two works, but two parts of one work; and the brief preface to the Gospel (Lk. i. 1–4) is intended to apply to both parts. It has been suggested by some scholars that Luke projected a third volume, but the arguments advanced for this belief are not conclusive.

I. DATE

The date of the twofold work is a matter of dispute; some would put it as late as A.D. 90; but the weight of evidence seems to the present writer to favour an earlier date, probably not long after the last event of which Acts tells. Acts ends on a note of triumph, as has often been pointed out, with Paul proclaiming the gospel at Rome, in the heart of the Empire, without let or hindrance; but, even so, it is not easy to believe that Luke would have dropped no hint about what happened to Paul later, if indeed he wrote after Paul's death. It also seems probable that he wrote before two important events—the Great Fire of Rome in A.D. 64, with the ensuing persecution of Christians by Nero; and the Jewish war, A.D. 66–70, culminating in the destruction of Jerusalem and the temple, with the extinction of the Jewish priesthood and cultus. It is difficult to suppose that the atmosphere of Acts would have been exactly as we find it if, at the time of writing, these epochal events lay in the past instead of being yet future.

Very early in the second century, the four Gospels, which hitherto had circulated separately, began to be bound up together in one collection. This led to the separation of the two parts of Luke's history. The second part soon began to circulate independently, under the title 'The Acts of the Apostles'. There is some textual evidence that the separation of the two parts led to a slight readjustment at the end of Luke and the beginning of Acts; possibly at this time the former was rounded off by the addition of the words 'and was carried up into heaven' in Lk. xxiv. 51, which naturally involved the addition of 'was taken up' in Acts i. 2. If this be so, some discrepancies which have been noted between the ascension stories of Luke and Acts disappear, for there would then be no record of the ascension in the former.

II. LUKE THE PHYSICIAN

Luke was not himself a personal companion of Jesus before the cross. He was, according to a strong and variously attested early tradition, a native of Syrian Antioch, and in that case we may take it that his acquaintance with Christianity dated from the early days of Christian witness in that city, when the gospel was first preached on a large scale to Gentiles and the first Gentile church was established. For Luke appears to have been a Gentile. In Col. iv. 10f. Paul sends greetings from three friends, Aristarchus, Mark and Jesus Justus, whom he calls his only Jewish fellow-workers. And as he then goes on in verse 14 to send greetings from three others—Epaphras, Luke and Demas—we conclude that they were Gentile Christians.

There are several touches about Luke's history which betoken the Greek outlook. Sir William Ramsay suggested that he was a brother of Titus, and whether or not this suggestion can be based on 2 Cor. viii. 17–19 (where Origen thought the 'brother whose praise is in the gospel in all the churches' to be Luke: cf. the Collect for St. Luke's Day), it is at least a possibility. For we remember that Titus also was a Greek from Antioch (Gal. ii. 1–3), and that, although it is evident from the Epistles that he played a very important part among Paul's companions, he is never mentioned in Acts.

III. SOURCES OF INFORMATION

What, then, were Luke's sources of information as he traced the course of all things accurately from the very first? For part of the narrative of Acts, of course, he was himself present at the events. This he indicates delicately but unmistakably by his sudden transition from the third person to the first person plural in xvi. 10, xx. 5, xxvii. 1, three verses which mark the commencement of what we call the 'we' sections. And as most of the second half of Acts, even apart from these 'we' sections, is devoted to the activity of Paul, Paul's beloved physician had ample opportunity for first-hand information about these events.

He had many other possible informants about events in the earlier days of the Church's life, before Paul's conversion, as well as about the events narrated in his Gospel. A native of Antioch must have met many who could tell him about those beginnings, such as Barnabas and even possibly Peter (cf. Gal. ii. 11); and he had special opportunities of amplifying his knowledge during the two years when Paul was kept in custody in Caesarea (Acts xxiv. 27). In that city lived Philip the evangelist, with his four prophesying daughters, who are mentioned by later writers as informants about persons and events in the infant Church. In Jerusalem, Luke stayed with Mnason, one of the original disciples (Acts xxi. 16), he met James the Lord's brother, and it is thought by some that he may even have met the Lord's mother and heard from her own lips the story of the holy nativity which he narrates at the beginning of his Gospel.

IV. COMPOSITION

He probably employed a good part of the two years at Caesarea in setting in order the material thus gathered. And when he accompanied Paul to Rome, he may have found other informants there. At one time, at least, during Paul's Roman imprisonment Mark and Luke were together in his company, and some have argued from internal evidence that Luke amplified what he had already collected from information supplied by Mark, whose own Gospel, based on the preaching of Peter, is said by some ancient writers to have appeared in Rome. This view, as it affects the third Gospel, is known as the Proto-Luke hypothesis; but it may well be that Luke was indebted to Mark also for some of the information contained in the early chapters of Acts.

V. HISTORICAL CHARACTER

Luke's sources of information were second to none in value, and he well knew how to use them. The resultant work is a marvel of histori-

cal accuracy. Unlike the other historical writers of the New Testament, Luke sets his history in the framework of contemporary imperial events. He is the only New Testament writer who so much as mentions a Roman Emperor's name. His pages are full of references to provincial governors and client kings. A historian who does this sort of thing must do it carefully if he does not wish to be exposed as inaccurate; Luke emerges from the severest test with flying colours. What has struck several critics most is the familiar way in which he moves among the multiplicity of varying titles borne by officials in the cities and provinces of the Empire, getting them right every time. Almost as striking is the deft way in which, with a few touches, he paints the true local colour of the widely differing places mentioned in his narrative.

The most detailed and thorough-going vindication of the historical accuracy of Luke's writings was provided, as is well known, by Sir William Ramsay, who devoted many years to intensive archaeological research in Asia Minor. When he went out there first in the eighties of last century, he accepted the then current Tübingen theory that Acts was a late and unhistorical production of the middle of the second century; and it was not apologetic interests, but the evidence of archaeology, that compelled him to recognize that Luke's writings reflect the conditions, not of the second century but of the first, which were very different, and reflect these with unsurpassed accuracy. Ramsay sums up Luke's qualities as a historian in these words:

'Luke's history is unsurpassed in respect of its trustworthiness. . . . Luke is a historian of the first rank: not merely are his statements of fact trustworthy, he is possessed of the true historic sense; he fixes his mind on the idea and plan that rules in the evolution of history; and proportions the scale of his treatment to the importance of each incident. He seizes the important and critical events and shows their true nature at greater length, while he touches lightly or omits entirely much that was valueless for his purpose. In short, this author should be placed along with the very greatest of historians' (*The Bearing of Recent Discovery on the Trustworthiness of the New Testament* (1915), pp. 81, 222).

Ramsay's thesis is frequently regarded as exaggerated, but students of Acts who ignore his unique contributions to the study of that book impoverish themselves and their pupils. 'Every reader of *St. Paul the Traveller* knows with what a wealth of detail Ramsay brings out the historical value of innumerable passages in Acts' (W. F. Howard, *The Romance of New Testament Scholarship* (1949), p. 151).

An illustrious contemporary of Ramsay who also did much from quite a different viewpoint to establish the historical worth of Luke's writings was Adolf von Harnack of Berlin. (See his *Luke the Physician* (1907), *Acts of the Apostles* (1909), *Date of the Acts* (1911).)

VI. THE PALESTINIAN ATMOSPHERE OF THE EARLY CHAPTERS

The earlier chapters of Acts reflect a different atmosphere from the later chapters. When Paul sets out on his missionary journeys, we breathe the fresh air of the wide spaces of the Roman Empire; but in the earlier part of the book the writer is dealing with events in Jerusalem and other parts of Palestine, and there is in many places a clearly discernible Semitic atmosphere. Some sections of these earlier chapters show strong linguistic evidence of having been translated into Greek from Aramaic sources; indeed, one eminent Semitic scholar, Professor C. C. Torrey, of Yale, has written a short work, *The Composition and Date of Acts* (1916), to prove that the whole of Acts down to xv. 34 was translated from a single Aramaic document; and while he has greatly overstated his case, yet he has amassed some weighty evidence for the Aramaic origin of much in these chapters, especially in the reports of the apostolic preaching.

VII. APOLOGETIC INTEREST

While the primary and stated object of Luke's history was to provide Theophilus with a trustworthy account of the origin of Christianity, other aims can be detected. One obvious one is to demonstrate that the Christian movement was not a menace to law and order throughout the Roman Empire. Luke demonstrates this by citing the testimonies of imperial representatives. As Pilate pronounces our Lord 'not guilty' of the threefold charges of rebellion, sedition and treason (Lk. xxiii. 4, 14, 22), so, when similar charges are brought against His followers, Luke shows what ill success they meet. The praetors of Philippi, it is true, imprison Paul and Silas because of a threat to property interests, but have to release them with a humble apology for their high-handed excess of jurisdiction (Acts xvi. 19ff., 35ff.). The politarchs of Thessalonica are content to find citizens of that place who will be guarantors for the missionaries' good behaviour (Acts xvii. 6-9). Gallio, the proconsul of Achaia, the brother of the influential Seneca, who was Nero's tutor and adviser in the early years of his rule, refuses to listen to the charges made against Paul by the Corinthian Jews, recognizing that they are not charges of which Roman law takes cognizance, but internal questions of Jewish theology (Acts xviii. 12–17). At Ephesus, Paul enjoys the goodwill of the Asiarchs, the chief men of the cities of the province of Asia (Acts xix. 31); and when a riot is aroused by the outcry of property interests *versus* the threat implicit in Christianity against the cult of Ephesian Artemis, the town clerk of the city testifies that Paul and his companions have been guilty of no indictable offence in relation to the worship of the great goddess (xix. 35–41). At Jerusalem, Paul's bitterest enemies do their best to procure his condemnation by the Roman governors Felix and Festus,

with conspicuous ill success; Festus and the petty king Agrippa II agree that he has committed no offence worthy of death or imprisonment, and that he might have been set free had he not, in order to secure a fairer trial than he feared he might receive in Palestine, appealed to the supreme tribunal of the Emperor in Rome (Acts xxvi. 32). And Acts ends on a triumphant note, with Paul in custody, it is true, but yet prosecuting his missionary work unmolested in the Imperial City itself. It is unlikely that this triumphant note would have been so unqualified if Luke had written after the commencement of the Neronian persecution or the execution of Paul.

VIII. JEWISH OPPOSITION

It could not be denied, however, that wherever Paul and his companions had gone, trouble had risen. If the new movement was really as innocent as Luke maintained, how had it so invariably been attended with so much unrest? With the exception of the incident at Philippi and the riot at Ephesus, Luke explains this trouble by the opposition fomented in almost every place by the Jews. In the Gospel it is the Jewish Sanhedrin, led by the Sadducean chief priests, who overbear Pilate's desire to acquit Jesus and force him to condemn Him. So in Acts it is Jews who are the fiercest enemies of the gospel in almost every place visited by Paul. In Damascus, Jerusalem, Pisidian Antioch, Iconium, Lystra, Thessalonica, Berea, Corinth, it is his own fellow-countrymen who form the greatest hindrance to his work. They deeply resented the way in which Paul, as it seemed to them, poached on their preserves by visiting the synagogues and enticing away those Gentiles who attended worship there, and who, the Jews hoped, would one day become full proselytes. The bulk of the Jews, in city after city to which Paul went, would not have Jesus as the Messiah themselves, and were enraged when the Gentiles accepted Him; and while Acts records the steady advance of the gospel in the great Gentile communities of the Empire, it records at the same time its progressive rejection by that nation to which it was first offered.

IX. THEOLOGICAL EMPHASIS

On the theological side, the dominating theme of Acts is the work of the Holy Spirit. Right at the beginning of the book, the promise of the Spirit is made by the risen Lord, and this promise is fulfilled for the Jews in chapter ii, and for Gentiles in chapter x. The apostles proclaim their message in the power of the Spirit, manifested by outward supernatural signs; the converts' acceptance of the message is likewise attended by visible manifestations of the Spirit's power. This probably explains what some have felt to be a difficulty in Acts—that the Spirit is received by some believers after repentance and baptism (as by the Jews who believed on the day of Pentecost, ii. 38), by some after baptism and the imposition of apostolic hands (as by the Samaritans in viii. 15ff. and the Ephesian disciples in xix. 6), and by others immediately on believing, before baptism (as by Cornelius's household, x. 44). What Luke is thinking of in each case is not so much the invisible operation of the Spirit in the soul as His outward manifestation in speaking with tongues and prophesying.

Indeed, the whole book might well be called, as Dr. Pierson called it in the title of his exposition, 'The Acts of the Holy Spirit'. The Holy Spirit controls the whole work; He guides the messengers, such as Philip in chapter viii and Peter in chapter x; He directs the Antiochene church to set Barnabas and Saul apart for the work to which He Himself has called them (xiii. 2); He guides them from place to place, forbidding them to preach in Asia or enter Bithynia, but giving them clear indications that they must cross to Europe (xvi. 6–10); He receives pride of place in the letter from the Apostolic Council to the churches of Syria and Cilicia: 'It seemed good to the Holy Spirit and to us' (xv. 28). He speaks through prophets, foretelling for example the famine of the days of Claudius and Paul's arrest at Jerusalem (xi. 28, xxi. 11), just as He spoke through the prophets of Old Testament days (i. 16, xxviii. 25). It is He primarily who appoints the elders of a church to be its overseers (xx. 28). He can be lied to (v. 3), tempted (v. 9), and resisted (vii. 51). He is the primary Witness to the truth of the gospel (v. 32).

X. THE MIRACULOUS ELEMENT

It has been held against Luke that he is too fond of miracles. This objection will have little weight with those who accept the supernatural origin of Christianity. Luke does not relate miracles for the sake of the miraculous; to him, as to the other Evangelists, they are important because they are signs as well as wonders—signs, that is, of the inauguration of the New Age, signs of the Messiahship of Jesus. For just as Jesus in the Gospels performs these signs and mighty works in His own Person, so it is He who, in Acts, performs them from heaven by His Spirit in His representatives, as they act in His Name and by His authority.

It is noteworthy, too, that the miraculous element is not scattered at random throughout the book; it is more prominent at the beginning than at the end, and that is what we should expect in any case. 'Thus we have a steady reduction of the emphasis on the miraculous aspect of the working of the Spirit which corresponds to the development in the Pauline Epistles; it seems reasonable to suppose that Luke is here reproducing his sources faithfully.' (Cf. W. L. Knox, *The Acts of the Apostles* (1948), p. 91.)

When we consider how scanty is our knowledge of the progress of Christianity in other directions during the years A.D. 30–60, and in all directions during the decades that followed those thirty years, we may estimate our indebtedness to Acts for our relatively detailed knowledge of its expansion along the road from Jerusalem to Rome during the period which it covers.

OUTLINE OF CONTENTS

I. THE BIRTH OF THE CHURCH. i. 1—v. 42

    a. The forty days and after (i. 1–26)
    b. The day of Pentecost (ii. 1–13)
    c. The apostolic preaching (ii. 14–36)
    d. The first Christian church (ii. 37–47)
    e. A miracle and its consequences (iii. 1—v. 42)

II. PERSECUTION LEADS TO EXPANSION. vi. 1—ix. 31

    a. Appointment of the seven and the activity of Stephen (vi. 1–15)
    b. Stephen's defence and death (vii. 1—viii. 1a)
    c. Philip and the Samaritans (viii. 1b–25)
    d. Philip and the Ethiopian chamberlain (viii. 26–40)
    e. Conversion of Saul of Tarsus (ix. 1–31)

III. ACTS OF PETER: THE GENTILES BROUGHT IN. ix. 32—xii. 24

    a. Peter in Western Palestine (ix. 32–43)
    b. Peter and Cornelius (x. 1–48)
    c. The other apostles approve Peter's action (xi. 1–18)
    d. The first Gentile church (xi. 19–30)
    e. Herod Agrippa and the Church (xii. 1–24)

IV. ANTIOCH BECOMES A MISSIONARY CHURCH. xii. 25—xvi. 5

a. The evangelization of Cyprus (xii. 25—xiii. 12)
b. Paul's address at Pisidian Antioch (xiii. 13–41)
c. Reaction to the gospel at Pisidian Antioch (xiii. 42–52)
d. Iconium, Lystra and Derbe (xiv. 1–28)
e. The apostolic letter from the Council of Jerusalem (xv. 1—xvi. 5)

V. THE AEGEAN SHORES EVANGELIZED. xvi. 6—xix. 41

a. Over to Europe: the gospel in Philippi (xvi. 6–40)
b. Thessalonica and Berea (xvii. 1–15)
c. Paul in Athens (xvii. 16–34)
d. Paul in Corinth (xviii. 1–28)
e. Ephesus and the province of Asia (xix. 1–41)

VI. HOW PAUL REALIZED HIS HOPE OF SEEING ROME. xx. 1—xxviii. 31

a. Paul sets out for Palestine (xx. 1–38)
b. Miletus to Caesarea (xxi. 1–14)
c. Paul in Jerusalem (xxi. 15—xxiii. 35)
d. Paul in Caesarea (xxiv. 1—xxvi. 32)
e. Paul's journey to Rome (xxvii. 1—xxviii. 31)

COMMENTARY

I. THE BIRTH OF THE CHURCH.
i. 1—v. 42

a. The forty days and after (i. 1–26)

In the first five chapters we have a series of scenes, or cameos, as they have been called, of the primitive Christian community in Jerusalem. The book opens where Luke's Gospel left off, with the risen Lord appearing to His disciples at intervals during forty days, directing them to wait in Jerusalem until they should receive heavenly power, and then to act as His witnesses in Jerusalem, Judaea and Samaria, and to the ends of the earth. It has been pointed out that this threefold geographical indication (i. 8) forms a sort of Index of Contents to Acts, for this is the order in which Luke describes the gospel spreading. The words of Christ, *Ye shall be witnesses unto me*, are noteworthy as being a quotation from Is. xliii. 10; the implication is that these words of the great Old Testament prophet are fulfilled in the disciples of Jesus; they form both the remnant of the old Israel and the nucleus of the new.

Then comes the account of the ascension, after which the disciples, 120 strong, wait in Jerusalem for the fulfilment of the promise of the Spirit, and meanwhile fill the vacancy left in the number of the Twelve by the defection of Judas, for whose fall they find Old Testament prediction (cf. Mt. xxvii. 9f.; Jn. xvii. 12).

The former treatise (i. 1); i.e. the third Gospel, also addressed to Theophilus (Lk. i. 3). Who *Theophilus* was we cannot be sure, but he appears to have been a Roman citizen of equestrian rank, and possibly of administrative position, as the title 'most excellent' (Lk. i. 3) suggests. *All that Jesus began both to do and teach* (1). Since the subject-matter of the third Gospel is summed up thus, the implication is that this new volume is to deal with what Jesus continued to do and teach after His ascension—by His Spirit in His followers. *Being seen of them forty days* (3). Hence in the Christian calendar Ascension Day falls on the fortieth day after Easter. But Jesus' exaltation to God's right hand, which is what Ascension Day really commemorates, did not await the fortieth day after His triumph over death. In the primitive apostolic message His resurrection and ascension, which together constitute His exaltation, are viewed as one continuous movement. The fortieth day merely marked the last time on which He vanished from His disciples' sight after a resurrection appearance: the series of frequent though intermittent visitations was now brought to an end with a scene which brought home to them their Master's heavenly glory. We should not imagine that the intervals between these appearances were spent by Him in some earth-bound condition. The *things pertaining to the kingdom of God* (3). This brief statement was expanded by the Gnostics to represent Jesus as imparting esoteric teaching such as the Gnostic schools maintained. But 'the kingdom of God is conceived as coming in the events of the life, death, and resurrection of Jesus, and to proclaim these facts, in their proper setting, is to preach the Gospel of the Kingdom of God' (C. H. Dodd). No doubt the bearing of Jesus' passion and triumph on the message of the kingdom was now made plain to the disciples. *Ye shall be baptized with the Holy Ghost* (5). Cf. John's own prediction in Mk. i. 8. *In like manner* (11). Possibly with particular reference to the *cloud* (9); cf. Lk. xxi. 27 (Mk. xiii. 26); Mk. xiv. 62. The list of apostles in verse 13 agrees with that in Lk. vi. 14ff., with some variation in order, and the omission here of Judas Iscariot.

Now this man . . . (18). Verses 18 and 19 must be regarded as Luke's parenthesis, not as part of Peter's words to his fellow-disciples. *Falling headlong* (18), or 'swelling up'. *The field of blood* (19). Cf. Mt. xxvii. 8.

The quotations in verse 20 are from Pss. lxix. 25 and cix. 8. *Beginning from the baptism of John . . .* (22). The period is that of Jesus' public ministry, covered by the apostolic preaching (cf. Acts x. 37) and by the Gospel of Mark. The outstanding qualification is that the new recruit to the Twelve must be *a witness . . . of his resurrection* (22). *Joseph called Barsabas* (23). Of him Papias relates, on the authority of Philip's daughters, that he suffered no harm after drinking snake-venom (cf. Mk. xvi. 18). *Matthias* (23). There is no further record of him to which any serious attention need be paid. *And they gave forth their lots* (26). Deliberate selection and prayer played their parts in this appointment as well as the lot. The lot was a sacred institution in ancient Israel and was a well-established means for ascertaining the divine will (cf. Pr. xvi. 33), being in fact the principle of decision by Urim and Thummim. This is the first and last occasion of the employment of the lot by the apostles; it belongs, significantly enough, to the period between the ascension and Pentecost; Jesus had gone, and the Holy Spirit had not yet come. But if there are better ways of appointing the right men to ecclesiastical responsibilities, there are also worse ways. *And he was numbered with the eleven apostles* (26). The idea that Paul was divinely intended to be the twelfth, and that the apostles here wrongly anticipated God's plan, betrays a misunderstanding of the unique character of Paul's apostleship.

b. The day of Pentecost (ii. 1–13)

The day of Pentecost, the festival of the weeks (cf. Lv. xxiii. 15; Dt. xvi. 9), which fell on the fiftieth day after the passion Passover, found the little community gathered together in one place. Suddenly they were seized by the Holy Spirit from heaven, while visible and audible signs accompanied the effusion of the promised heavenly Gift. There was a sound as of a *mighty wind* (2); and *cloven tongues like as of fire* appeared, and *sat upon each of them* (3). But more impressive was the outburst of *glossolalia*, speaking with tongues, as the disciples were heard praising God in languages and dialects diverse from their native Galilean Aramaic, but recognizable by visitors to the feast as those which some of them spoke. Most of the visitors would speak the common Greek dialect (the *Koinē*) except those from eastern parts (Parthia, Media, Persia, Mesopotamia, Syria), who would speak in Aramaic dialects.

There were dwelling at Jerusalem Jews, devout men, out of every nation under heaven (5). According to rabbinical tradition, the feast of weeks was the anniversary of the giving of the law at Sinai, and on that occasion the voice of God was heard by every nation on earth (seventy in all, by rabbinical reckoning). But Gentiles are not in view here; even if, with

Codex Sinaiticus, we omit *Jews* from this verse, the word *devout* (Gk. *eulabēs*) is used in the New Testament only of Jews; it is Jews from every land of the Dispersion that are intended. *We do hear them speak in our tongues the wonderful works of God* (11). The reversal of the curse of Babel is probably in the narrator's mind.

c. The apostolic preaching (ii. 14–36)

The Galilean dialect was so distinctive and difficult for non-Galileans to follow that the disciples' release from the peculiarities of their local speech and their sudden capacity for speaking in tongues understood by the motley crowds then in Jerusalem could not fail to be remarked. When once the attention of the people had thus been attracted, Peter seized the opportunity to stand up with the other apostles, and address all who were within earshot (14). The words of his address are noteworthy, for they show the pattern regularly followed in the primitive apostolic preaching, or *Kerygma*, the pattern or outline which can also be traced as the original framework of our gospel tradition. This pattern shows four main features: first, a narrative of the public ministry and passion of Jesus; secondly, the divine attestation of His Messiahship in the resurrection, of which the speakers claim to be eyewitnesses; thirdly, 'testimonies' from the Old Testament proving Jesus to be the Messiah; and lastly, exhortation to repentance and faith.

These features can be traced fairly clearly in this speech of Peter, delivered at a time when the events leading up to the crucifixion were fresh in the minds of his audience. The change in Peter since the night of the betrayal has often been remarked upon; here he straightly charges his audience with the guilt of delivering their Messiah over to 'the hands of wicked men' (i.e. the Romans) and putting Him to death.

The use made by Peter of Old Testament testimonies is striking: his *This is that* (16) proclaims that the time has now come of which the prophets testified. For example, the words of Ps. xvi. 10, 'Thou wilt not leave my soul in hell; neither wilt thou suffer thine Holy One to see corruption', ascribed by the Hebrew and Septuagint texts to David's authorship, cannot, he argues, refer to David himself, for everyone knows that David did die, his soul *was* left in Sheol, the abode of the dead, and his body did see corruption. To whom, then, do the words refer? Not to David, but to Him whom David prefigured, 'great David's greater Son', the messianic King.

Thus far, every rabbi in Jerusalem would have agreed with Peter. But, he goes on, there has been only one Person of whom these words could be truly spoken—Jesus of Nazareth; for although (as all knew) He died, yet His soul was not left to Hades, nor did His flesh undergo corruption; He rose from the dead, 'and we are witnesses of this,' he adds; 'we saw Him alive.' Therefore Jesus of Nazareth, crucified by men, raised from the dead by God, is the true Messiah; the stone which the builders rejected has become head of the corner. Later we find the same argument drawn from Ps. xvi by Paul at Pisidian Antioch (Acts xiii. 35–37). But Jesus not only died and rose; He also ascended into heaven; Peter and his companions had seen Him go up. And this fulfilled another Davidic Psalm, Psalm cx. 'Jehovah said unto my Lord, Sit thou at my right hand, until I make thine enemies thy footstool.' Who was raised to God's right hand? Not David, but King Messiah: that this Psalm was messianically interpreted at that time is plain from the incident of Mt. xxii. 41ff. This, too, corresponded with the actual facts about Jesus of Nazareth; He was therefore undoubtedly Lord and Messiah.

The prophet Joel (16). The quotation is from Joel ii. 28–32. The physical phenomena of verses 18, 19 may have reminded the hearers of the strange darkness of Good Friday afternoon and its accompaniments. But, while the whole section of Joel's prophecy of the Day of the Lord is quoted, the outstanding point of comparison with the present situation is *I will pour out of my Spirit upon all flesh* (17). *The determinate counsel and foreknowledge of God* (23); i.e. as revealed in Old Testament Scripture, especially, no doubt, in Is. liii (cf. Lk. xxiv. 26, 46). The guilt of those who engineered Christ's death was none the less, but it was overruled by God for the achievement of His saving purpose. *For David speaketh* (25). The following quotation, from Ps. xvi. 8–11, is given for the sake of the words 'Thou wilt not abandon my life to Hades, nor allow thy Holy One to experience destruction', which were fulfilled in the resurrection of Jesus. The variation between the form of Peter's quotation and that given in AV and RV of Ps. xvi is due largely to the fact that the LXX is followed here. *He hath shed forth this* (33), i.e. the Holy Spirit, upon His disciples. When Luke speaks of the Spirit as coming upon people, he usually thinks, not of His silent inward operation in the soul, but of those of His operations which are attended by visible and audible manifestations. *David is not ascended* (34); better, 'It was not David that ascended . . .' *Both Lord and Christ* (36). For the triumph and exaltation of Jesus as confirming His messianic sovereignty cf. Rom. i. 4; Phil. ii. 9–11.

d. The first Christian church (ii. 37–47)

Convinced by the power of Peter's argument, the multitude were conscience-stricken; realizing that they were guilty of the blood of the Lord's Anointed, they cried, 'What are we to do, brothers?' and received from Peter the assurance that forgiveness and the gift of the Holy Spirit would be granted them by God if they repented and were baptized in the Name of Jesus as Messiah. The generation as a whole had proved perverse, but there was a place for a believing remnant; having previously quoted from Joel ii. 32 the words *Whosoever shall call on the name*

of the Lord shall be saved (21), Peter now urged his hearers to save themselves thus from that perverse generation, and so effective was his exhortation that three thousand believed the good news and were baptized, thus forming the first Christian church.

Then follows a picture of the primitive Christian community, gathering daily in various homes to break the bread, meeting publicly in the temple (apparently in the colonnade called Solomon's, to judge from iii. 11 and v. 12), adhering to the apostolic teaching and fellowship, and increasing in number day by day, praising God and enjoying the favour of all the people. The miracles which,· when wrought by Jesus in His own Person, had been 'signs' of the advent of the messianic age, continued to be performed by Him from heaven through His disciples as they acted in His Name, providing additional proof that the divine kingdom had invaded the present age, for these mighty works were indeed 'powers of the age to come'.

Repent, and be baptized (38). This command seems to have caused no surprise to Peter's hearers; they had probably some familiarity with the practice of baptism. Christian baptism is, like John's, baptism in water, accompanied by repentance, but it is administered in the Name of Jesus and associated with the gift of the Spirit. Like John's, it has an eschatological reference, but it betokens the realization of that to which John's baptism pointed forward. Cf. verse 39 with Is. lvii. 19; Joel ii. 32. *The apostles' doctrine and fellowship* (42). The fellowship was shown in the *breaking of bread, and in prayers* and also in the community of goods (45f.). *Daily* (46). This adverb modifies every verb in the sentence. *And the Lord added . . .* (47). Translate with Weymouth: 'Also day by day the Lord added to their number those whom He was saving'—not that a continuous process of salvation in each individual is here in view, but a continuous procession of individuals who, one after another, accept the offered salvation and are incorporated in the saved community.

e. A miracle and its consequences (iii. 1—v. 42).

i. **The cripple cured (iii. 1–26).** In chapter iii Luke goes on to give an example of these 'wonders and signs' (ii. 43), narrating one which had interesting consequences. The apostles and the other believers continued to be observant Jews, and attended the temple regularly. One afternoon, as Peter and John went to the temple at the time of the evening oblation (about 3 p.m.), they were about to pass through the 'Beautiful Gate', the Nicanor Gate of Corinthian bronze which led from the Court of the Gentiles to the Women's Court, when their attention was attracted by a man lame from birth, who lay there to beg alms from people who passed through the gate. Peter commanded him to stand up and walk, invoking the authority of Jesus the Messiah of Nazareth. When he had helped him to rise to his feet, the cripple walked, and, overjoyed with his new-found strength, he raised his voice in praise to God, jumping about so that all the people round about noticed him. Naturally, it created a great sensation, as everybody knew the cripple who had sat so long begging at his usual station. When a crowd had collected in Solomon's colonnade, Peter improved the occasion by proclaiming Jesus as the Messiah, rejected and crucified by the Jewish people, but now risen from the dead and offering remission of sins and fulfilment of the prophetic promises to Israel. And the healed man stood by, a powerful witness to the truth of Peter's words, for it was by the power of the Name of Jesus that he had been cured, and his cure was a patent messianic 'sign', for they could remember how Isaiah had prophesied of the messianic age: 'Then shall the lame man leap as an hart' (Is. xxxv. 6).

At the hour of prayer (1). The stated times for prayer were early morning, the time of the morning sacrifice; afternoon, the time of the evening sacrifice; and sunset. Josephus (*Ant.* xiv. 4. 3) says that sacrifices were offered in the temple 'twice daily, in the morning and about the ninth hour.' *Which is called Beautiful* (2). The gate is probably to be identified with what the Mishna calls 'Nicanor's Gate' and with the gate of Corinthian bronze described by Josephus as 'far exceeding in value those plated with silver and set in gold' (*Jewish War*, v. 5. 3). *The porch that is called Solomon's* (11), which ran the whole length of the east side of the outer court (cf. Jn. x. 23).

His Son Jesus (13); better, as in RV, 'his Servant' (Gk. *pais*) (so in verse 26 and iv. 27, 30). The expression harks back to the Servant of Jehovah portrayed in Is. xlii. 1ff., lii. 13ff. With the present statement that God *hath glorified his Son* (i.e. Servant) cf. Is. lii. 13, 'Behold, my servant . . . shall be exalted and extolled' (LXX *doxazō*, the same verb as is used here). *The Holy One and the Just* (14); two messianic designations. *The Prince of life* (15). 'Prince' represents Gk. *archēgos*, 'pioneer', appearing also in Acts v. 31; Heb. ii. 10, xii. 2. *And his name . . .* (16). Perhaps render: 'And by faith in His name He has healed this man whom you see and know.' *Through ignorance* (17); i.e. they did not know that it was their Messiah whom they were putting to death. *That Christ should suffer* (18). It is not explicitly prophesied in the Old Testament that the Messiah will suffer; this statement is based on Jesus' own identification of the Suffering Servant with the Messiah and His acceptance and fulfilment of Messiahship in that sense (see ii. 23n.).

When the times of refreshing shall come (19). The sense probably is that the Jews' acceptance of Jesus as Messiah would speedily be followed by those conditions of world-wide blessing which the prophets had described as characteristic of the messianic age. *Until the times of restitution of all things* (21). For *restitution* read 'establishment' or 'fulfilment'. The sense is: 'until the time when all that God has spoken through the prophets has been fulfilled.' *For Moses truly said* (22). The quotation is from Dt. xviii. 15ff., a favourite messianic 'testimony' in the early Church; cf. vii. 37; also Jn. i. 21, vi. 14, vii. 40. Jewish Christians in particular in the early centuries A.D. looked on Jesus as a second Moses. *Him shall ye hear* (22). The words 'hear him' in the heavenly Voice at the transfiguration (Mk. ix. 7; Lk. ix. 35) probably echo this Deuteronomic injunction. *All the prophets from Samuel* (24). Samuel is here regarded as first of a series of prophets (cf. 1 Sa. iii. 20). There is no record of any messianic prophecy by Samuel, but the general sense here is that the days which had now arrived marked the consummation of all that the prophets had foretold. *Saying unto Abraham* (25). The following words are a free quotation from Gn. xii. 3, xviii. 18, xxii. 18. *Having raised up his Son* (i.e. Servant) *Jesus* (26). Here and in verse 22 *raised up* may refer, not to Christ's resurrection, but to God's raising Him up as a Deliverer to Israel, as in xiii. 22 He is said to have 'raised up David' (see also xiii. 33n.).

ii. The rise of persecution (iv. 1–22). But such a commotion was by no means to the liking of the temple authorities, who seized the two apostles and put them in custody till the following day, when they were brought for examination before the Sanhedrin. The high-priestly party, who dominated the Sanhedrin, were mostly Sadducees, and it is noteworthy that their grievance was that the apostles 'taught the people and proclaimed in the case of Jesus the resurrection from the dead'. Besides, the ruling caste, anxious to maintain peaceable relations with the Romans, looked with great disfavour on every messianic movement, whether political or spiritual. But they could find no legal fault with the apostles, especially in the presence of the once-lame man, whose cure was a strong testimony in their defence.

Peter, bold as ever, pressed home his accusation where it most properly belonged, warning the Supreme Court that the same Name by which the cripple had received bodily health was the only Name through which they could receive from God spiritual health. This boldness was the more surprising on the part of 'laymen', untrained in the rabbinical schools; but these men had been disciples of no ordinary teacher, who had Himself excited the surprised comment: 'How knoweth this man letters, having never learned?' (Jn. vii. 15).

The captain of the temple (1); the *sagan*, who was head of the temple police and superintended arrangements for the preservation of order in and around the buildings. *Preached through Jesus the resurrection from the dead* (2). It is significant that it was the adherents of the Sadducean party who objected most strongly to the apostles' preaching, in view of their insistence on the resurrection of Jesus, which naturally involved the general principle of resurrection, repudiated by the Sadducees (see xxiii. 8). *The number of the men* (4), i.e. of the males. *Their rulers, and elders, and scribes* (5). In other words, the Sanhedrin, the supreme court of the Jewish nation, consisting of seventy-one elders, including the High Priest, who was president by virtue of his office. *Annas the high priest, and Caiaphas* (6). Cf. Lk. iii. 2. Annas was senior ex-High Priest, having held the office from A.D. 6 to 15; his son-in-law Caiaphas (cf. Jn. xviii. 13) was now High Priest (A.D. 18–36). But Gk. *archiereus* is used not only of the High Priest strictly so called, but also of the chief priests in general, i.e. members of the wealthy families from which the High Priests at this time were regularly selected. *And John, and Alexander* (6). Neither of these can be identified with certainty. *This is the stone . . .* (11). Quoted from Ps. cxviii. 22, another common early Christian 'testimony', used in this sense by Jesus Himself (Mk. xii. 10; Lk. xx. 17). *Ignorant men* (13). The Greek word here used, *idiōtēs*, appears in later Hebrew and Aramaic as a loanword (*hedyoṭ*) meaning 'unskilled', 'untrained', which is no doubt the sense here. *They took knowledge of them, that they had been with Jesus* (13), i.e. they recognized that this was the explanation of the otherwise inexplicable boldness and eloquence of men who had enjoyed no rabbinical education. *They conferred among themselves* (15). It is noteworthy that no effective attempt seems to have been made by the Sanhedrin to disprove the central affirmation of the apostles' proclamation, the resurrection of Jesus; yet, if they thought there was a reasonable chance of success, would they not have done so?

iii. Continuous expansion (iv. 23–37). In the absence of any reasonable ground for punishing Peter and John, the Sanhedrin dismissed them, forbidding them with threats to speak any more in the Name of Jesus. But the net result was a further increase in the Church, which now numbered five thousand men, not to speak of women. The original pooling of property continued, by which the richer members made provision for the needs of the poorer. Among these richer members Barnabas, a Levite of Cyprus, receives special mention for liberality.

Lord, thou art God, . . . (24). The opening words of this prayer probably illustrate early Christian liturgical practice, based on Jewish liturgical forms. The phraseology of the exordium echoes such Old Testament passages as Ex. xx. 11; Ne. ix. 6; Ps. cxlvi. 6. *Who by the mouth of thy servant David hast said* (25). The original text is longer, and may be rendered: 'Who didst say through thy servant David our father, the mouthpiece of the Holy Spirit.' *Why did the heathen rage . . . ?* (25). Quoted from Ps. ii. 1, 2. The application of this Psalm to the future Messiah appears first in the seventeenth 'Psalm of Solomon' (*c.* 50 B.C.). *Thy holy child Jesus* (27). Here and in verse 30 *child* is to be rendered 'Servant' (Gk. *pais*, the same word as is rendered 'Son' in iii. 13, 26). *Whom thou hast anointed* (27), i.e. 'whom Thou hast made Messiah'. *Both Herod, and Pontius Pilate* (27), representing 'the kings . . . and the rulers' of

verse 26 respectively, as *the Gentiles, and the people of Israel* (27) correspond to 'the heathen . . . and the people' (lit. 'peoples') of verse 25. *Herod* is Herod Antipas, tetrarch of Galilee (4 B.C.–A.D. 39); the occasion referred to is that of Lk. xxiii. 7–12. *For to do whatsoever . . .* (28). Cf. ii. 23 for the foreordained character of the death of Christ. *The place was shaken* (31). The phenomena of Pentecost were repeated (cf. ii. 2f.).

They had all things common (32). The reference to the community of goods (cf. ii. 44f.) is repeated here to introduce the incidents of Barnabas and of Ananias and Sapphira. *Barnabas (which is, being interpreted, The son of consolation)* (36). This is the idiomatic Semitic use of 'son' in a phrase indicating a man's character. If 'consolation' is the best rendering, the name may be Aram. *bar-nawḥa* ('son of refreshment'), but probably we should render it 'son of exhortation' (cf. xi. 23) and recognize in the second part of the name Aram. *nebu'a* ('prophecy').

iv. Ananias and Sapphira (v. 1–16). But in such a large company, especially at such a time of enthusiasm, there must almost inevitably be some black sheep; and the case of Ananias and Sapphira illustrates the temptations to which less spiritual members were liable. (It also illustrates Luke's honesty, in not glossing over this unfortunate incident.) That the pooling of property was purely voluntary is plain from Peter's question to Ananias: 'Whiles it remained, was it not thine own?'; the sin consisted not in keeping back part of the money received for their estate, but in pretending that the part which they handed over was the whole. And the lie told to the Church was reckoned as told to God the Holy Spirit.

The story has given offence to many; one commentator, for example, finds it 'frankly repulsive'. But we need not make Peter guilty of their death; he told them plainly that they had been trying to cheat God, and the shock produced by the sudden sense of the enormity of such a crime caused their death. Sapphira had the additional shock of having the news of her husband's sudden death so bluntly broken to her. The whole story fits exactly into the picture of spiritual exaltation prevailing in the infant Church. The tragedy had a salutary effect on those who might light-heartedly have joined the popular movement; but even so the progress continued.

Kept back part of the price (2). The Greek verb *nosphizomai*, used here, is the verb used in the LXX of Jos. vii. 1, of Achan's misappropriation of part of the consecrated spoil of Jericho. If the Gospels are the 'Torah' of the New Testament, Acts is its book of Joshua, and there are a number of striking parallels between Joshua and Acts, though beneath rather than on the surface. *To lie to the Holy Ghost* (3). The sovereign presence of the Holy Spirit in the Church is so real that any action done to the Church is regarded as done to the Spirit, just as any action taken by the Church is predicated of the

Spirit (cf. xv. 28). The language of verses 3 and 4 makes it clear that the Holy Spirit is viewed as a divine Person. *To tempt the Spirit of the Lord* (9). The idea is that of seeing how far one can go with impunity. Ananias and Sapphira discovered that they had gone too far. *Upon all the church* (11). This is the first occurrence of *church* in Acts (the word is absent from the best texts of ii. 47). The word (Gk. *ekklēsia*) has its background in the LXX, where it is used of the 'congregation' (Heb. *qahal*) of Israel: see vii. 38n. The followers of Jesus are the new people of God, continuators and successors of the old 'congregation of the Lord', formerly restricted to one nation, but now about to be thrown open to all believers everywhere. *The rest* (13). This has been emended to 'the rulers' by M. Dibelius; to 'the elders' by C. C. Torrey; to 'the Levites' by A. Hilgenfeld and A. Pallis, the latter of whom also reads 'hinder them' (Gk. *kōlysai autous*) for *join himself to them* (Gk. *kollasthai autois*).

v. A further attempt at persecution (v. 17–42). A second attempt by the priestly authorities about this time to inhibit the Christians met with as little success as the previous one. This second attempt is interesting because in the account of it we are introduced to the great rabbi Gamaliel the Elder, pupil of Hillel and teacher of Saul of Tarsus. Gamaliel's moderating advice to let the new movement alone, lest it might prove to be of God, was followed for the time being, although the apostles this time had an opportunity of rejoicing that they had been counted worthy to endure stripes for the honourable Name which they proclaimed. But before long a new departure within the Christian community gave the authorities an opportunity to institute a really thoroughgoing policy of suppression.

But the angel of the Lord by night opened the prison doors (19). The angel of the Lord represents Gk. *angelos Kyriou*, the phrase which in LXX renders Heb. *mal'akh Yahweh*, the supernatural messenger who manifests God's presence to men, and who may be spoken of as God, being an extension of God's personality. It is unlikely that Luke has this particular idea in mind. Certainly he wishes to indicate that the agency of God was behind this opening of the prison doors, but this would be as true if the doors were opened by secret sympathizers with the apostles as if an angel came down from heaven to let them out. Cf. xii. 7ff. for the similar experience of Peter himself. On the present occasion all the apostles appear to have been locked up. *All the words of this life* (20). In Aramaic one word represents both 'life' and 'salvation'; the expression used here is thus almost identical with that in xiii. 26. *All the senate* (21); i.e. the Sanhedrin (Gk. *gerousia*, 'body of elders'). *The officers* (22). Probably Levites of the temple police force. *This man's blood* (28). We can probably trace thus early a reluctance on the part of the Jewish religious leaders to refer to Jesus by His personal name

(cf. J. Jocz, *The Jewish People and Jesus Christ*, 1949, p. 111, for the persistence of this tendency). *We ought to obey God rather than men* (29). Cf. iv. 19; cf. also the words of Socrates to his judges: 'I shall obey God rather than you' (Plato, *Apology* 29d). *The God of our fathers raised up Jesus* (30). See iii. 26n. for the sense of 'raised up' here. These words introduce the fourth summary of the primitive apostolic preaching in Acts; the three previous ones come in ii. 22–36, iii. 13–26, iv. 10–12. Note how the emphasis is regularly pointed on the contrast between the hearers' action and God's, so here: *whom ye slew . . . Him hath God exalted* (30, 31). *Hanged on a tree* (30); harking back to Dt. xxi. 22, 23, where the divine curse attaches to such a death (cf. Acts x. 39; Gal. iii. 13). *We are his witnesses . . . and so is also the Holy Ghost* (32). Note the continued existence of the apostles' personal testimony (cf. i. 8, 22, ii. 32, iii. 15, iv. 33), with which the witness of the Spirit in them is here combined (see v. 3n.). *Gamaliel* (34). The most illustrious rabbi of his day and leader of the Pharisaic party in the Sanhedrin. The Pharisees were a minority in that body, but they enjoyed the support and confidence of the people to such a degree that their judgment had to be respected by the Sadducean majority. *Theudas* (36). The only insurgent named Theudas of whom we know from any other source was a magician who, according to Josephus (*Ant.* xx. 5. 1), led a band of his adherents to the Jordan, promising to divide it that they might cross dryshod, but was attacked and killed by soldiers sent against him by the procurator Fadus. This incident is to be dated *c.* 44, whereas Gamaliel's speech was delivered ten or twelve years earlier. Gamalie.'s Theudas (who in any case antedates the revolt of Judas in A.D. 6) is probably one of the innumerable insurgents who infested Palestine after Herod the Great's death in 4 B.C. *Rose up Judas of Galilee in the days of the taxing* (37). When Judaea was reduced to the status of a Roman province in A.D. 6, Quirinius, imperial legate of Syria, held a census there with a view to assessing the amount of tribute to which the new province would be liable. Judas and others, regarding this action as a prelude to enslavement and as a dishonour to God, the only true King of Israel, raised the standard of revolt. The revolt was crushed, but the party of the Zealots kept its spirit alive until the outbreak of the Romano-Jewish War in A.D. 66. *Refrain from these men, and let them alone* (38). 'The doctrine preached by Gamaliel is sound Pharisaic teaching; God is over all, and needs no help from men for the fulfilment of His purposes; all men must do is to obey, and leave the issue to Him' (J. A. Findlay). Cf. the dictum of a later rabbi: 'Every assembly which is in the name of heaven will ultimately be established, but that which is not in the name of heaven will not ultimately be established.' *To teach and preach Jesus Christ* (42). Better, 'to teach and proclaim the good news that the Messiah was Jesus'.

II. PERSECUTION LEADS TO EXPANSION. vi. 1—ix. 31

a. Appointment of the seven and the activity of Stephen (vi. 1-15)

A new departure in the narrative of Acts is marked by the introduction of the name of Stephen. Stephen appears first as one of the seven officers who were appointed to supervise the distribution of largesse from the common fund to the poorer members of the community. At a very early stage, the Church attracted Hellenistic Jews (i.e. Greek-speaking Jews from outside Palestine as well as Aramaic-speaking Palestine-born Jews; and before long complaints arose that the widows of the latter group were being favoured in the daily 'hand-reaching'. It is significant that the seven officers chosen by the community and appointed by the apostles to supervise this business all bore Greek names, being probably themselves Hellenistic Jews. Two of the seven, Stephen and Philip, were destined to leave their mark on the Church far beyond the bounds of this special function to which they were appointed. Stephen seems to have had an exceptionally far-sighted comprehension of the total breach with Judaic worship which the new movement logically and ultimately involved. In this he blazed a trail later trodden by Paul and especially by the writer to the Hebrews.

The Twelve had kept the respect and goodwill of the Jerusalem populace; they attended the temple services regularly, and appeared outwardly to be observant Jews whose only distinction from others was that they believed and proclaimed Jesus to be the Messiah. But a new note was heard in the debates in the Hellenistic synagogue which Stephen attended, a note which envisaged the abolition of the temple cultus and the institution of a new and more spiritual form of worship. If the charges made by Stephen's accusers are garbled, yet we are not at a loss to discover the real trend of his arguments; the speech preserved for us in chapter vii is not so much 'Stephen's apology' (such a defence was but little calculated to lead to an acquittal, as Stephen well knew), as a reasoned exposition of his teaching about the transitory nature of the Jewish worship. Now, the people of Jerusalem lived on the temple; contributions came in from Jews all over the world to maintain the cultus; the crowds of pilgrims who regularly came up to the great festivals provided an immense revenue for the city. An attack on the temple was, therefore, in their eyes, an attack on their livelihood. The rulers at once saw their opportunity, and arraigned Stephen on a popular charge. The indictment against him was practically the same as that against his Master at an earlier date (Mk. xiv. 58), and against Paul at a later date (Acts xxi. 28); it was alleged that he meditated the destruction of 'this holy place'.

A murmuring of the Grecians against the Hebrews (1). The *Grecians* (or rather 'Hellenists') were Greek-speaking Jews, mainly belonging to the lands of the Dispersion; the *Hebrews* were Aramaic-speaking Jews, most of whom, like the apostles themselves, were native-born Palestinians. *Their widows were neglected in the daily ministration* (1). From the common pool in which the property of the wealthier members had been placed (ii. 45, iv. 34, 35) daily distribution was made to those who were needy, among whom widows would naturally figure prominently. *Look ye out among you seven men* (3). It is evident from the names of the seven that they were Hellenists; one of them, indeed, was not even a Jew by birth, but a proselyte from the Gentile city of Antioch. They were probably recognized as leaders of the Hellenistic community in the primitive Jerusalem church. Note that even for such practical duties as fell to their lot spiritual endowment is required as well as a good reputation and general wisdom (3). While they were appointed on this occasion as almoners, the ministry of those of their number of whom we have any further account was not restricted to this form of service. *Nicolas* (5). According to Irenaeus (who may depend on Papias), the Nicolaitans of Rev. ii. 6, 15 took their name from him; the truth of this cannot be determined. *They laid their hands on them* (6). The seven were selected by the rank and file; the imposition of apostolic hands confirmed this selection, commissioned the seven for their special work, and expressed the apostles' fellowship with them in the matter. *A great company of the priests* (7). Many of the ordinary priests were humble and pious men, unlike the wealthy ecclesiastical politicians of the high-priestly families. *There arose certain of the synagogue . . .* (9). Probably one synagogue is meant, although five, four, three and two have been understood by various commentators. As it was attended by *them of Cilicia*, it may have included Saul of Tarsus among its members. *Libertines* (9). Probably Jewish freedmen or descendants of freedmen from the various places mentioned; Deissmann suggests freedmen of the imperial household. There is not sufficient reason to reject the text here for the attractive emendation 'Libyans' suggested by Beza, Tischendorf and Dibelius. *Brought him to the council* (12), i.e. the Sanhedrin.

b. Stephen's defence and death (vii. 1—viii. 1a)

Arrested and put on trial before the Sanhedrin, the Supreme Court of the Jewish nation, over which in those days the High Priest presided, Stephen stated his case in the form of a historical review, a form not uncommon among the Jews. The two chief themes of his speech are, first, that the nation, from the days of Abraham onwards, had always been intended to sit loose to any one locality of earth; a movable tent was therefore a fitter shrine than a permanent building; and secondly, that the nation, from the time of Moses onwards, had always rebelled against God and opposed His messengers, a course of action which had culminated in their slaying of 'the righteous One'. Any line of argument less likely to conciliate his judges could hardly be imagined. After one or two angry interruptions, which Stephen countered in true prophetic vein, he was prevented from finishing his speech, thrown out of the building and stoned. Whether his death was a simple act of lynch-law or an excess of jurisdiction on the part of the Sanhedrin is not quite clear; probably it partook of the nature of both. Although the procurator's ratification was technically necessary for the execution, he was at the moment in Caesarea, his usual residence, and Caiaphas and Pilate certainly had a mutual understanding by virtue of which Pilate could be trusted to turn a blind eye when convenience required. (It was most exceptional that a Roman governor should leave the same High Priest in office for the whole period of his procuratorship, as Pilate left Caiaphas.)

Then said the high priest (1), acting as president of the court. *When he was in Mesopotamia, before he dwelt in Charran* (2). Charran (spelt 'Haran' in the Old Testament) was a flourishing city in the first half of the second millennium B.C., to which the life of Abraham belongs. According to the Received Text of Gn. xi. 31—xii. 5 (see RV for correct translation), it was after Abraham's arrival in Haran that the words quoted here in verse 3 were spoken. But Philo and Josephus agree with Stephen that Abraham received a divine communication before going to Haran (cf. Gn. xv. 7; Neh. ix. 7). *Yet he promised* . . . (5). Cf. Gn. xvii. 8. *And God spake on this wise* . . . (6). Quoted from Gn. xv. 13f. *Four hundred years* (6). Rabbinical exegesis reckoned four hundred years from the birth of Isaac to the exodus. *And serve me in this place* (7). These words come from Ex. iii. 12, where they are spoken to Moses and where the place referred to is Horeb. The conflation of separate quotations is characteristic of Stephen's speech as here summarized. *And he gave him the covenant of circumcision* (8); cf. Gn. xvii. 10, xxi. 4. 'Thus, while there was still no holy place, all the essential conditions for the religion of Israel were fulfilled' (Lake and Cadbury).

And the patriarchs, moved with envy, sold Joseph into Egypt (9). The narrative from here to verse 34 consists largely of a cento of passages from Gn. xxxvii—Ex. iii. *He sent out our fathers first* (12). For *first* read 'the first time', as distinct from *the second time* (13). *Threescore and fifteen souls* (14). The Received Hebrew Text of Gn. xlvi. 27; Ex. i. 5; Dt. x. 22, enumerates seventy persons, including Jacob himself and Joseph and his two sons; the number seventy-five comes from the LXX of Gn. xlvi. 27 and Ex. i. 5; it omits Jacob and Joseph, but reckons nine sons to Joseph. *And were carried over into Sychem* (16); i.e. Shechem. Jacob was buried in the cave of Machpelah at Hebron (Gn. xlix. 29ff.); Joseph was buried at Shechem (Jos. xxiv. 32). *In the sepulchre that Abraham bought for a sum of money of the sons of Emmor the father of*

Sychem (16). Abraham bought the cave of Machpelah at Hebron from the Hittites (Gn. xxiii. 16); Jacob bought the land at Shechem which he gave to Joseph (and where Joseph was buried) from the sons of Hamor (Jos. xxiv. 32). Not only separate quotations (see verse 7n.) but separate incidents are conflated in Luke's summary of Stephen's speech.

Till another king arose, which knew not Joseph (18); probably a reference to the foundation of the XIX Dynasty (c. 1320 B.C.). *Exceeding fair* (20); lit. 'fair to God'. *Pharaoh's daughter took him up* (21); i.e. adopted him. Eusebius calls her Merris; cf. Meri, daughter of Rameses II by a Hittite princess. *And Moses was learned in all the wisdom of the Egyptians* (22). Stephen is more moderate than the generality of Hellenistic Jewish writers, who represent Moses as the founder of all science and culture, and indeed of the whole civilization of Egypt. *And was mighty in words and in deeds* (22). Moses disclaims eloquence in Ex. iv. 10, but the reference here may be to written words. Josephus (*Ant.* ii. 10) preserves a legend of his prowess in martial deeds. *When he was full forty years old* (23). Ex. ii. 11 says simply 'when Moses was grown'. *For he supposed his brethren would have understood* . . . (25). This explanation of his action is not given in the Old Testament. Philo, like Stephen, regards Moses' championship of the Israelites at this point in his career as a settled policy. And note the parallel here: Moses appeared as a messenger of peace and deliverance and was rejected; Jesus in due course was treated the same way. *He begat two sons* (29); i.e. Gershom and Eliezer (Ex. ii. 22, xviii. 3, 4). *There appeared to him in the wilderness of mount Sina* (i.e. Sinai) *an angel of the Lord* (30). Stephen emphasizes that God is not tied to one city or land; He appeared to Abraham in Mesopotamia and to Moses in the wilderness, in the land where he *was a stranger* (29). This *angel* is the messenger of the divine Presence, who speaks as God (32). *I have seen, I have seen* (34); better, 'I have certainly seen'. *The same did God send to be a ruler and a deliverer* (35). The rejected one is God's appointed saviour: this pattern recurs in the careers of Joseph, Moses and Jesus. *By the hand* (35), i.e. by the agency.

A prophet shall the Lord your God raise up . . . (37). This citation from Dt. xviii. 15 (see iii. 22n. above) helps further to point the parallel between Moses and Christ. *This is he, that was in the church in the wilderness* (38). Probably an allusion to Dt. xviii. 16 (immediately following the words quoted in the previous verse), where mention is made of 'the day of the assembly' (Heb. *qahal*, LXX *ekklēsia*) at Horeb. As Moses was with the old *ekklēsia*, so Christ is with the new *ekklēsia*, but it is still a pilgrim church, 'the church in the wilderness'. *With the angel which spake to him* (38). In Ex. xxxii. 34 God says to Moses, 'mine Angel shall go before thee'; but later, at Moses' insistent request, He makes a more personal promise, 'My presence (i.e. 'I myself', so LXX *autos*) shall go with thee' (Ex. xxxiii. 14). In Jubilees i. 27, ii. 1, however, an angel speaks with Moses at Sinai (see verse 53n. below). *And they made a calf in those days* (41). See Ex. xxxii for the narrative of this.

Then God turned, and gave them up to worship the host of heaven (42). This statement is not based, apparently, on the Old Testament narrative of the wilderness wanderings, but seems to be an inference from the passage from Am. v. 25–27 quoted in verses 42, 43. In the Received Hebrew Text of Amos, the people of Israel are warned that the Assyrian king will deport them 'beyond Damascus', and that they will carry thither the very instruments of that idolatry for which this calamity is about to overtake them. In the LXX (quoted here with variations) this idolatry—the worship of the heavenly host, especially of the planet Saturn—is dated as early as the wilderness period. *Have ye offered to me . . . in the wilderness?* (42). The Greek wording makes it plain that the answer is 'No'. It was not Jehovah but heathen astral deities that they worshipped. *The tabernacle of Moloch* (43). In contrast to *the tabernacle of witness* (44). The Hebrew means 'Sakkut your king', Sakkut being an Akkadian name of the god of the planet Saturn. *The star of your god Remphan* (43). The AV of Amos has 'Chiun', a form of Kaiwanu, an Assyrian name of Saturn; in the LXX (quoted here) the Assyrian name is replaced by an Egyptian name for the same planetary god, represented here by *Remphan* (RV 'Rephan'). *Beyond Babylon* (43). Stephen has the Babylonian captivity in mind, as was natural for one speaking in Jerusalem, and therefore substitutes 'beyond Babylon' for Amos's 'beyond Damascus', which referred to the earlier Assyrian captivity.

The tabernacle of witness (44). So called because it enshrined the 'witness' or 'testimony' which God gave to Israel, consisting of the tables of the Law—whence the ark which housed them is also called 'the ark of the testimony' (e.g. Ex. xxv. 22). *According to the fashion that he had seen* (44); quoted from Ex. xxv. 40 (cf. the development of this idea in Heb. ix. 1ff.). *Brought in with Jesus* (45); i.e. Joshua (cf. Heb. iv. 8). *Unto the days of David* (45). The process of dispossessing the Canaanites, begun under Joshua, was not completed until David's time; besides, and more especially, successive generations had the tent handed on to them until the reign of David (2 Sa. vii. 6; cf. 1 Ch. xvii. 5). *Desired to find a tabernacle for the God of Jacob* (46). Cf. Ps. cxxxii. 5. Several excellent textual authorities have 'the house of Jacob' here, but this reading gives awkward connection with verse 47, *But Solomon built him an house*. There is emphasis upon *house*—a fixed house as distinct from a movable tent. Stephen regards the building of the temple as a retrograde step, and counters the idea that God could dwell in a house with the quotation from Is. lxvi. 1, 2 (49, 50). Other divinities might be so conceived of, but not *the most High* (48). This unmistakable attack on the most cherished centre of the national religion probably caused an explosion of anger, which drew forth the denunciation of verse 51.

Ye stiffnecked . . . (51). The language of the denunciation is thoroughly Old Testament; cf. Ex. xxxiii. 5; Lv. xxvi. 41; Dt. x. 16; Is. lxiii. 10; Je. iv. 4, vi. 10, ix. 26; Ezk. xliv. 7. *They have slain them which shewed before of the coming of the Just One* (52). Cf. our Lord's accusation in Mt. xxiii. 29–37 and the implication of His words in Mk. xii. 2–8; Lk. xiii. 33, 34. *Who have received the law by the disposition of angels* (53); lit. 'by angelic ordinance'. For the mediation of the law through angels cf. Gal. iii. 19; Heb. ii. 2. The idea does not appear in the Old Testament, but is found in Jubilees i. 29, Testament of Dan vi. 2, Josephus (*Ant.* xv. 5. 3), and Philo (*On Dreams*, i. 141ff.).

When they heard these things . . . (54). They cut his speech short; they had heard more than they desired. *Jesus standing on the right hand of God* (55). We should not press the idea of His *standing* here in contrast with the more regular mention of His being seated at God's right hand. *I see the heavens opened, and the Son of man standing on the right hand of God* (56). This is the only New Testament occurrence of the title 'the Son of man' outside the Gospels (the expression in Rev. i. 13, xiv. 14 is different). Many members of the Sanhedrin must have been reminded of the words of Jesus Himself (Mk. xiv. 62) which drew forth their verdict of blasphemy. *The witnesses laid down their clothes at a young man's feet, whose name was Saul* (58). It was the witnesses' duty to cast the first stones. The mention of Saul suggests that he played some responsible part in the proceedings, which is confirmed by viii. 1a. *Lord, lay not this sin to their charge* (60). Contrast the dying prayer of Zechariah in a similar situation (2 Ch. xxiv. 22). *And Saul was consenting unto his death* (viii. 1a). This could, but does not necessarily, mean that he was a member of the Sanhedrin. Cf. xxii. 20, xxvi. 10.

c. Philip and the Samaritans (viii. 1b–25)

The execution of Stephen was now the signal for a much more thorough campaign of repression. The large community of believers in Jerusalem was scattered throughout Palestine and even beyond its borders, although the apostles, who perhaps were not identified in the popular mind with the activity of Stephen, stayed in Jerusalem. The dispersion, however, did much more good than harm to the cause; those who were thus scattered carried the good news with them and disseminated it everywhere, even as far north as Syrian Antioch, which led to a remarkable development in that city in a few years' time. But nearer home a fresh departure was made almost immediately, for another member of the seven, Philip, left Jerusalem for Samaria, and began to evangelize its schismatic, half-Jewish population. Hitherto the gospel had been preached to pure Jews only. But Philip's evangelism was remarkably successful and, when news of it came to the apostles, Peter and John were sent there on a mission of inquiry. (Did John remember his earlier proposition with regard to the Samaritans in Lk. ix. 54?) The arrival of the two apostles confirmed the genuineness of the Samaritans' conversion, and the converts received the Holy Spirit. The episode of Simon Magus at this point is interesting, among other things, because in later Christian literature he appears as the father of all heresies.

They were all scattered . . . except the apostles (1). It appears from the sequel that the Hellenistic believers were the chief target of the persecution, perhaps as being more closely associated with Stephen. From this time until A.D. 135 the church of Jerusalem seems to have been almost entirely composed of 'Hebrews'. *Made havock* (3), i.e. 'ravaged', as a wild beast does the body of its victim. *The city of Samaria* (5). The city called Samaria in the Old Testament was restored by Herod the Great with the new name Sebaste. A variant reading, 'a city of Samaria', appears in several authorities; if it is right, the city in question might be Gitta, said by Justin to have been the native place of Simon Magus. In any case, the preaching of the gospel to Samaritans represented a widening of its scope (cf. i. 8). *A certain man, called Simon* (9). Simon Magus is said in later times to have visited Rome and other parts, where he secured a large following; the Simonians are known to have survived to the third century at least. *The great power of God* (10); lit. 'the power of God which is called great'. This may mean that he claimed to be the Grand Vizier of the Most High. *Simon himself believed also* (13). This need not be pressed to mean that he received the gift of 'saving faith'. He was simply convinced of the potency of the Name of Jesus when he saw the mighty works wrought by its means.

They sent unto them Peter and John (14). For some time the Jerusalem apostles exercised general supervision over the widespread work of evangelization. *Prayed for them, that they might receive the Holy Ghost* (15). Evidently they had not received the Holy Spirit at baptism; not, at least, in the Lucan sense (which regularly involves the manifestation of some spiritual gift). *They were baptized in the name of the Lord Jesus* (16); lit. 'into the name of the Lord Jesus', an expression found in Acts only here and at xix. 5. The person so baptized bears public witness that he has passed into Christ's ownership. *Then laid they their hands on them, and they received the Holy Ghost* (17). It has frequently been held that this apostolic action was confirmation, considered as an act, distinct from baptism, in which the gift of the Spirit is bestowed. But the evidence of the New Testament is against this interpretation; Paul, for example, takes it for granted that all baptized believers have the Spirit of God (cf. Rom. v. 5, viii. 9; 1 Cor.

xii. 13). (Such a contradiction in terms as an 'unbaptized believer' is not contemplated in the New Testament.) Not until the rite of Christian initiation itself became divided was any separation between baptism and confirmation envisaged. On this occasion we probably have an act of recognition and incorporation of the new community of Samaritan believers into the larger community of the apostolic Church, the imposition of apostolic hands being an act of fellowship, which was attended by manifestations of the Holy Spirit in the new converts. (See G. W. H. Lampe, *The Seal of the Spirit*, 1952, pp. 64ff.) *He offered them money* (18). He thereby gave the term 'simony' to the ecclesiastical vocabulary. *The gall of bitterness* (23); probably a Semitizing genitive, meaning 'bitter gall'; quoted from Dt. xxix. 18 (cf. Heb. xii. 15). *The bond of iniquity* (23). Cf. Is. lviii. 6. *Come upon me* (24). The 'western' text adds 'who never stopped weeping copiously', an adjective clause which is tacked on awkwardly at the end of the sentence instead of coming immediately after its antecedent 'Simon'. *And they . . . returned to Jerusalem* (25); i.e. probably Philip as well as the two apostles.

d. Philip and the Ethiopian chamberlain (viii. 26–40)

Once the work in Samaria was well established, Philip was sent by the Holy Spirit to make contact with the treasurer of Candace, queen-mother of the Ethiopians (Nubians), who reigned in Meroe, between Assuan and Khartoum. He had been on pilgrimage to Jerusalem, and was now returning south in his chariot. His perplexed reading of the great prophecy of the Suffering Servant in Isaiah gave Philip the opportunity of preaching Jesus to him from this very passage—most appropriately, because this, more than any other part of the Old Testament, colours our Lord's language about His life mission, as well as the language of a number of the New Testament writers. When this new convert had been sent on his way rejoicing, Philip continued his northward journey along the coast road to Caesarea, where we meet him next with his family over twenty years later.

And the angel of the Lord spake unto Philip (26). The language of this section is curiously reminiscent in places of the Elijah and Elisha narratives of the Old Testament. *Gaza, which is desert* (26). Old Gaza had lain deserted since its destruction in 93 B.C.; New Gaza, built in 57 B.C., was by the sea, a little south of the old city. *Candace queen of the Ethiopians* (27). The king was deified as child of the sun-god and regarded as too holy for secular functions; these were discharged for him by his mother, who bore the dynastic title *Candace*. *Had come to Jerusalem for to worship* (27); probably as a 'God-fearer' (see x. 2n. below). *Heard him read the prophet Esaias* (30). The ancients habitually read aloud. *The place of the scripture which he read was this* (32). The words are from Is. liii. 7, 8, in the LXX (this explains the differences between the

English here and in the Old Testament, which represents the Received Hebrew Text). He had no doubt procured a scroll of Isaiah in Greek in Jerusalem. *Of whom speaketh the prophet this? of himself, or of some other man?* (34). The answers that have been given to this question throughout the centuries would fill a volume. Yet no answer is so satisfying as that which Philip gave, when he *began at the same scripture, and preached unto him Jesus* (35). *And Philip said . . .* (37). Philip's stipulation and the eunuch's response do not form part of the original text (they first appear in the 'western' recension); but they do reflect early Christian baptismal procedure. *The Spirit of the Lord caught away Philip* (39). The 'western' text has: 'the Spirit of the Lord fell upon the eunuch, and the angel of the Lord caught away Philip'. But even if the best attested text does not explicitly speak of the eunuch's receiving the Spirit, this is probably implicit in the statement that *he went on his way rejoicing. Azotus* (40). The Old Testament Ashdod, twenty miles north of Gaza. *Till he came to Caesarea* (40). The seaport on the Mediterranean coast, about fifty miles north of Ashdod, built by Herod the Great *c.* 13 B.C. Here Philip appears to have settled down and brought up a family (cf. xxi. 8).

e. Conversion of Saul of Tarsus (ix. 1-31)

The ringleader of the campaign of repression which followed Stephen's death was Saul of Tarsus, destined to become one of the greatest men of all time. Although born a Roman citizen in the Greek city of Tarsus in Asia Minor, he was brought up by his Jewish parents not as a Hellenist but as 'a Hebrew of Hebrews' (Phil. iii. 5, RV), being sent to Jerusalem to be trained at the feet of Gamaliel, the great leader of the Pharisees whom we have already met as a counsellor of moderation. The pupil showed little of his teacher's moderation. As a Jew of Cilicia, he may well have attended the synagogue where Stephen debated, and heard those arguments which were bound to undermine the whole religious structure of Judaism. Saul's mind, as penetrating as Stephen's, saw the irreconcilability of the old order and the new, and he set out on his career as a vigorous champion of the old order, resolved to stamp out the revolutionary movement.

At Stephen's martyrdom he seems to have played some official part, and thereafter, wherever the believers fled in their dispersion, he pursued them, not only in Palestine itself, but even to Damascus. To the synagogues of that city he carried a letter from the High Priest, authorizing him to arrest and bring to Jerusalem any who might have sought refuge in the ancient Syrian city. The writ of the High Priest was respected in the synagogues of the Empire, and his authority in religious matters was upheld by the Roman power. It was on his journey to Damascus that Saul was confronted by the vision of the risen Christ which wrought such a

revolution in his life, and made him thenceforward the most valiant champion of the faith he had hitherto sought to destroy. 'The conversion and apostleship of St. Paul alone,' in the view of the eighteenth-century statesman George, Lord Lyttelton, 'duly considered, was of itself a demonstration sufficient to prove Christianity to be a divine revelation'; and when we consider the implications of this event, we may well agree. Luke realized the importance of Paul's conversion, for, despite his limited space, he relates it in some detail three times, once in the third person (chapter ix), and twice as narrated by Paul himself (chapters xxii and xxvi).

The way was prepared for Paul's entertainment by Christians in Damascus by the Lord's appearing to Ananias. The Lord's words to him describing Paul as a 'chosen instrument' have stuck to Paul ever since. In later years he recognized that, without his knowing it, he had been set apart by God for the work of the gospel even before his birth (Gal. i. 15f.; Rom. i. 1). Jewish by birth and education, he was also a Roman citizen, and his privileges as such stood him in good stead more than once. While the influence of the educational atmosphere of his native Tarsus upon him has often been exaggerated, it need not be minimized to the point of vanishing altogether.

His conversion and baptism were immediately followed by his bold proclamation of Jesus as the Son of God in those very Damascus synagogues to which he had been accredited by the High Priest for a very different purpose. But his activities there and in the neighbouring territory of the Nabataean king Aretas IV (the 'Arabia' of Gal. i. 17) roused so much opposition that at last he had to be smuggled out of a city which had become too hot to hold him, the local Jews perhaps combining with the local representative of Aretas in order to catch him.

On his return to Jerusalem in the third year from his conversion, he spent a fortnight with Peter, and also met James the Lord's brother (Gal. i. 18f.). His contact with these and other Christians was facilitated by Barnabas, who presumably knew him before and could vouch for his sincerity. But when he began to do in the Jerusalem synagogues what he had done at Damascus, he had again to be got away for his own safety, and was escorted to the coast and shipped off to Tarsus; and 'then', says Luke, 'the Church had peace' (ix. 31). The first wave of persecution seems to have died down with the conversion of the leading persecutor.

The high priest (1). Still, probably, Caiaphas. *If he found any of this way* (2). Better, 'any of the Way'. 'The Way' was a primitive Jewish-Christian idiom denoting Christianity (cf. xix. 9, 23, xxii. 4, xxiv. 14, 22). It was probably in the main refugees from Judaea, rather than native Damascene believers like Ananias, that Saul went to arrest. *It is hard for thee . . . And the Lord said unto him* (5, 6). These words have been imported into this context from the parallel passages in xxii. 10 and xxvi. 14; cf. RV. *Hearing a voice* (7), i.e. hearing Paul's voice: 'but they heard not the voice of him that spake to me', he says in xxii. 9. *Ananias* (10). His character is described by Paul in xxii. 12. He appears to have been a native of Damascus, who knew of the outbreak of persecution in Jerusalem only by hearsay (13). We have no account of the establishment of Christianity in Damascus; it may have been carried there from Galilee. *The street which is called Straight* (11); now called the Darb al-Mustaqim. *Hath seen in a vision* (12). We can distinguish three early visions of Paul: on the way to Damascus (4ff.); in the house of Judas (12); and on his return to Jerusalem (xxii. 17ff.). *From the chief priests* (14). See iv. 6n. above. *All that call on thy name* (14); i.e. those who invoked Jesus as Lord (cf. ii. 21). *How great things he must suffer for my name's sake* (16). He was to endure many times over what he had made others endure, and that for the sake of the same Name. But in the kingdom of Christ suffering for the King is a sure sign of His favour and an earnest of His reward. *Putting his hands on him* (17); not only as a token of fellowship, greeting him as a fellow-Christian (*Brother Saul*), but also because Ananias, albeit a 'private' Christian, was acting for the time being as the Lord's duly appointed commissioner to Saul. *Be filled with the Holy Ghost* (17). Such filling was necessary for the prophetic ministry described in verse 15; the sequel (20–22) makes it plain that the particular manifestation of the Spirit shown in Saul was the supernatural power of his missionary preaching. *As it had been scales* (18); better, 'a scaly (or flaky) substance'. *Arose, and was baptized* (18). We are probably to infer that (unlike the Samaritans in viii. 16) Saul had received the Holy Spirit before he was actually baptized. *Then was Saul certain days with the disciples which were at Damascus* (19). Whether this was before or after his visit to Arabia (the Nabataean kingdom) mentioned in Gal. i. 17 cannot be ascertained. Luke's chronological indications here are vague; we know from Gal. i. 18 that the events of verses 26ff. took place in the third year after Paul's conversion. *That he is the Son of God* (20). It is significant that the only occurrence of this title in Acts should be in the report of Saul's first preaching. While the divine Sonship of Messiah is a corollary of Ps. ii. 7, Paul's use of the title here probably marks an advance on the designation of Jesus as Lord and Messiah hitherto (e.g. ii. 36). *Proving* (22). The Greek word (*symbibazō*) probably suggests that his method of proof was to place the prophetic Scriptures alongside the events which fulfilled them. *The Jews took counsel to kill him* (23). According to Paul himself, in 2 Cor. xi. 32, 'the governor under Aretas the king kept the city of the Damascenes with a garrison, desirous to apprehend me'. The situation was probably as has been suggested in our summary on p. 911. *Brought him to the apostles* (27). The term is used in a wider sense here. According to Gal.

i. 18, 19, the only apostles (in a stricter sense) whom he saw were Peter and James the Lord's brother. *Disputed against the Grecians* (29), or 'Hellenists'; no doubt in the very synagogue or synagogues which had witnessed Stephen's similar activity. *Then had the churches rest* (31). The best texts have 'church' (singular) with the following verbs in the singular accordingly.

III. ACTS OF PETER: THE GENTILES BROUGHT IN. ix. 32—xii. 24

a. Peter in Western Palestine (ix. 32–43)

A sign of the peace is seen in Peter's evangelization of the semi-Gentile territory in the Plain of Sharon and his visits to Lydda and Joppa, in both of which he performed miracles of healing. The fact that he lodged in the latter town with a man who followed the unclean occupation of a tanner shows how he was becoming more emancipated in his relations to the ceremonial law.

The saints which dwelt at Lydda (32). Obviously there were Christians at Lydda and Joppa before Peter visited these places (cf. verse 36). *Sick of the palsy* (33); i.e. paralysed. *Make thy bed* (34). The Greek might alternatively mean 'get ready to eat'; this would accord with the interest which Luke and other New Testament writers elsewhere show in the nourishment of convalescents. *Saron* (35); the coastal plain of Sharon. *Tabitha* (36); Aram. for 'gazelle'; in Gk., *Dorcas*. *When they had washed* (37); a reference to the Jewish custom of 'purification of the dead'. *Shewing the coats and garments* (39). The 'middle voice' of the Greek verb indicates that they were wearing them at the time. *He tarried . . . with one Simon a tanner* (43). Simon lived by the shore (x. 6), perhaps because he required sea-water for his tanning, and Peter, as a fisherman, might naturally choose a lodging in this part of the town.

b. Peter and Cornelius (x. 1–48)

A great step forward had still to be taken, and it was at Joppa that Peter learned the lesson that nothing cleansed by God should be called common or unclean. Was it in the light of this lesson that he added to our Lord's teaching on meats the comment, 'This He said, making all meats clean', reported in Mk. vii. 19 (RV)? At any rate, having learned this lesson, he had immediately to put it into practice when he was invited to visit the Roman centurion Cornelius at Caesarea and make known the good news to him and his household. This is another episode to which Luke obviously attached high importance, for, after telling it in chapter x, he repeats it in chapter xi, where Peter himself tells the story, and reverts to it in chapter xv, again in the mouth of Peter.

Cornelius as well as Peter had been divinely prepared for the new move. Cornelius, a member of the class referred to by Luke as 'God-fearers', who attached themselves to the spiritual and monotheistic Jewish worship in the synagogues without becoming full proselytes and members of the commonwealth of Israel, was instructed in a vision to send for Peter. When Peter entered his house and began to proclaim the divine action in the cross and resurrection of Christ, a further proof of divine guidance was afforded in the sudden possession of the Gentile household by the Holy Spirit, manifested by the same outward signs as on the day of Pentecost. There was this difference: at Pentecost those who were baptized received the Spirit; now Cornelius and his family were baptized because they had already received the Spirit. Without this obvious mark of God's favour, Peter might have hesitated to go so far as to baptize them.

A centurion of the band called the Italian band (1). A centurion had the status of a non-commissioned officer with the responsibility of a captain. Centurions were the backbone of the Roman army; it is striking that something is recorded to the credit of all the centurions mentioned in the New Testament. *The Italian band* (properly 'cohort', Gk. *speira*) may be identical with the 'second Italian cohort of Roman citizens' for which there is inscriptional evidence in Syria in A.D. 69. *One that feared God* (2); i.e. a 'God-fearer', one of a class of Gentiles who gave general adherence to the Jewish faith, worship and practice without submitting to circumcision and becoming full proselytes. *Are come up for a memorial* (4). The verb 'are come up' may suggest the burnt offering (Heb. *'olah*, lit. 'ascending'). The Greek word *mnēmosynon*, rendered 'memorial', is used in Lv. ii. 2ff., LXX, for that part of the meal offering which was presented to God. For the sacrificial efficacy of such conduct as that of Cornelius cf. Ps. cxli. 2; Phil. iv. 18; Heb. xiii. 15, 16.

About the sixth hour (9); i.e. midday. *Trance* (10), or 'ecstasy' (Gk. *ekstasis*), a state in which a man, so to speak, 'stands outside' himself. *A certain vessel* (11); lit. 'a certain object'; the Greek word (*skeuos*) is quite indefinite. *A great sheet* (11); suggested to Peter's subconscious mind possibly by the awning spread over the roof or a sail on the western horizon. *The four corners* (11). The Greek word *archē*, here rendered 'corner' (lit. 'beginning'), was used in medical parlance for the end of a bandage, and in nautical language in the sense of 'rope'. *All manner of fourfooted beasts* . . . (12). The better texts omit *and wild beasts* here and transpose *of the earth* to follow *creeping things*. For the resultant threefold division of the animal world cf. Gn. vi. 20. (The Received Text here is influenced by xi. 6.) *Not so, Lord* . . . (14); cf. Ezekiel's protest (Ezk. iv. 14). The Jewish food laws were based on Lv. xi. These laws, in their ceremonial application, were now abrogated explicitly as they had been implicitly in Jesus' teaching in Mk. vii. 14ff.

The Spirit said unto him (19). The Spirit of inner prophetic monition. *I have sent them* (20). This raises a question about the relation between the Spirit now speaking within Peter and the apparently external angelic manifestation to Cornelius. *Which were sent unto him from Cornelius* (21). The best texts omit these words. *Was warned from God* (22); lit. 'received an oracular communication' (Gk. *chrēmatizō*). *Certain brethren from Joppa* (23). They were six in number (xi. 12). *And as Peter* . . . (25). The 'western' text amplifies this verse: 'And as Peter was drawing near to Caesarea, one of the servants ran ahead and announced that he had arrived. Then Cornelius ran out and met him. . . .' *Worshipped him* (25), or 'paid homage to him' (Gk. *proskyneō*) does not necessarily connote divine honours. *Four days ago* (30); by inclusive reckoning. On day one Cornelius received his vision; on day two Peter received his, and Cornelius's messengers came to him; on day three Peter and the others set out from Joppa; on day four they arrived at Caesarea. *Thou hast well done that thou art come* (33); an expression of gratitude; i.e. 'Thank you for coming.'

God is no respecter of persons (34). Cf. Dt. x. 17; Rom. ii. 11; Eph. vi. 9; Col. iii. 25. The sense is: 'God has no favourites.' Divine election does not imply partiality; God's grace extends to Gentiles as freely as to Jews. To us this is a truism, but it was a revolutionary thought to Peter. *The word which God sent unto the children of Israel* . . . (36). From here to the end of verse 43 we have the fullest summary of the apostolic message in Acts. Its scope extends from the ministry of John the Baptist to the resurrection, and looks on to the judgment. The present summary bears the marks of fairly literal translation from Aramaic. *Throughout all Judaea* (37); here used in the wider sense of Palestine (cf. Lk. iv. 44, RV mg.). *God anointed Jesus of Nazareth with the Holy Ghost* . . . (38). 'Anointed' carries with it the more formal idea 'made Messiah'; the occasion intended is our Lord's baptism. Cf. Is. lxi. 1, quoted in Lk. iv. 18. *In the land of the Jews* (39); i.e. all Palestine, like Judaea in verse 37. *Who did eat and drink with him* (41). This emphasized the reality of His bodily resurrection. Cf. Lk. xxiv. 41, 43 (and in Acts i. 4 'being assembled together with them' should perhaps be rendered 'eating with them'; Gk. *synalizomenos*). *Ordained of God to be the Judge of quick and dead* (42). This goes back to the 'Son of man' vision of Dn. vii. 9ff. *Remission of sins* (43). The chief Old Testament prophecy promising remission of sins through Christ is Is. liii.

The Holy Ghost fell on all them which heard the word (44). As Peter himself suggests in verse 47 (cf. xi. 15), this event reproduced the descent of the Spirit on the original band of disciples in Acts ii. The occasion has been well described as 'the Pentecost of the Gentile world'. No routine procedure would have availed for so unprecedented a situation as the acceptance of the gospel by Gentiles; an unmediated act of God was required. *Magnify God* (46); cf. ii. 11, 'speak . . . the wonderful works of God'. *He* commanded them to be baptized in the name of the Lord (48); better, 'in the name of Jesus Christ', the same expression as in ii. 38. It is nowhere hinted that anything was said to these Gentiles about the necessity or even desirability of circumcision.

c. The other apostles approve Peter's action (xi. 1–18)

The news travelled quickly to Jerusalem, and when Peter arrived back there he found himself obliged to answer the criticisms of his fellow-apostles. Stephen's activity had been bad enough, in the eyes of men who, while followers of Jesus, were still orthodox Jews; but that the prince of the apostles himself should so outrage sacred convention was too bad altogether. The apostles apparently still enjoyed a measure of popular favour, but they were likely to lose it, too, if it became known that their leader had fraternized with the uncircumcised. It is probably more than a coincidence that, not long after this, Herod Agrippa I made a bid for popularity by laying violent hands on two of the apostles, and also that very soon James, the Lord's brother, appears as leader of the Jerusalem church.

However, when Peter told of his experience of the Lord's guidance, and of the outpouring of the Holy Spirit in the house of Cornelius, asking, 'What was I, that I could withstand God?', the apostles were convinced that he had acted rightly and praised God for His grace to Gentiles. *They that were of the circumcision* (2). The more 'rigorist' party in the Jerusalem church are probably intended here, although the same phrase in x. 45 means simply Jewish Christians. *Whereby thou and all thy house shall be saved* (14). Additional to the version in x. 22. The 'house' included not only the family in the modern sense, but all who were under the authority of the head of the house—slaves, attendants, and so forth. Cf. xvi. 15, 31ff., xviii. 8. *John indeed baptized with water . . .* (16). The words of the Lord in i. 5. *Also to the Gentiles* (18); better, 'even to the Gentiles' (in Jewish eyes, the most astounding token of divine grace).

d. The first Gentile church (xi. 19–30)

The other apostles might well approve Peter's action, for about the same time there took place a great work with far-reaching results at Antioch, in the north of Syria, to which some Hellenistic Jews had made their way in the course of the dispersion which followed Stephen's death. The atmosphere of Antioch was as different as could be from that of Jerusalem. In this busy northern capital, a commercial city where European and Asiatic met, where Greek civilization touched the Syrian desert, men naturally got their rough corners rubbed off, and religious differences which loomed so large in Judaea began to look far less important. It was here, then, that some of these Hellenists, not content with preaching Jesus in the synagogues to their fellow-Hellenists, began to preach Him to Gentile Greeks as well,

with the result that a great number of these embraced the new faith, so that the second Christian church to be founded had a considerable Gentile element, and the disciples first received the name 'Christians' there.

When news of this innovation reached Jerusalem, the apostles, wishing to look into it, sent just the right man for the job, Barnabas, 'the son of exhortation', as his name means. He went to Antioch, and, instead of being scandalized at the mingling of Jew and Gentile, he rejoiced at so astounding a token of God's grace, settled down among them, and did all he could to help this new church and build it up. But the work grew apace, and Barnabas, casting about in his mind for a suitable helper, bethought himself of Saul, who had been for some years now in Tarsus and the surrounding regions. So he went and fetched Saul, and made him his fellow-worker, and both of them continued to promote the great work which God had inaugurated in Antioch.

It was about this time that the prophet Agabus announced in the church at Antioch that great and widespread dearth was to be expected. The Roman historian Suetonius confirms that the reign of the Emperor Claudius was marked by constant seasons of unfruitfulness. Josephus tells us that about the year 46 Palestine was hard hit by famine, and that the Jewish queen-mother of Adiabene, in Northern Mesopotamia, bought corn in Egypt and figs in Cyprus to relieve the necessities of the Palestinian Jews. At the same time Barnabas and Saul were sent to Jerusalem by the Antioch church, bearing to the mother church the proceeds of a special collection which the daughter church had made to help the Palestinian Christians in their distress. The Jerusalem church seems to have been afflicted with chronic poverty; later on we shall find Paul organizing collections in the Gentile churches founded by him for the relief of the poverty of the Jerusalem church. It was probably during this famine-relief visit of Barnabas and Saul that the events of Gal. ii. 1–10 took place; the 'revelation' according to which they went up (Gal. ii. 2) will then be the prophecy of Agabus (Acts xi. 28), and the words of Gal. ii. 10 are specially applicable to this visit: 'They desired us to remember the poor, which very thing I had indeed proved zealous to do.'

Now they which were scattered abroad (19). These words take us back to the same point of departure as we have in viii. 4, which begins with the same expression. *Phenice* (19); i.e. Phoenicia (Tyre, Sidon, etc.; cf. xxi. 3ff., xxvii. 3). *Antioch* (20). The former capital of the Seleucid kingdom, now the seat of government of the Roman province of Syria, and the third largest city in the world (Rome and Alexandria being first and second). *Spake unto the Grecians* (20). Whether the true reading here be 'Grecians' (Hellenists) or 'Greeks' (so RV; Gk. *Hellēnes*), the meaning certainly is that Greek-speaking Gentiles were now evangelized. *They sent forth Barnabas* (22), just as they sent Peter and John to Samaria (viii. 14). *Then departed Barnabas to Tarsus, for to seek Saul* (25). Saul had spent the time since ix. 30 in various parts of the united province of Syro-Cilicia, in which Tarsus and Antioch were both situated (Gal. i. 21). *And the disciples were called Christians first in Antioch* (26); lit. 'they did business under the name of Christians', i.e. became commonly known by this name. Only from Gentiles could they have received this name (meaning 'Christ's people'), for 'Christ' was a mere personal name in Gentile ears, whereas to Jews it meant 'Messiah' and they would not have called the followers of Jesus 'Messiah's people'.

In these days (27); i.e. during the year that Barnabas and Saul spent in Antioch (26). *Agabus* (28). He reappears in xxi. 10 in a 'we' section of Acts. *Throughout all the world* (28); i.e. the Roman world. *In the days of Claudius Caesar* (28). Claudius was Emperor from A.D. 41 to 54. It is not clear how long before the famine the prediction was made. Probably the Antiochene Christians set aside money systematically until the time of need actually came, and then sent Barnabas and Saul as their delegates to take the accumulated sum to the Christians at Jerusalem.

e. Herod Agrippa and the Church (xii. 1–24)

A new wave of persecution broke over the Jerusalem church, and this time the apostles, far from being immune, were the chief object of attack. Herod Agrippa I, the grandson of Herod the Great, had received a large grant of territory in and near Palestine from his lifelong friend the Emperor Caligula (37–41), together with the title of king; and Claudius (41–54) added to that territory the regions of Judaea and Samaria. During his brief reign over Judaea (41–44), Herod, despite his faults, proved a studious patron of the Jewish faith, and maintained friendly relations with the religious leaders of the people. It is said that on one occasion, when reading the law at the feast of tabernacles, he burst into tears as he read Dt. xvii. 15 ('one from among thy brethren shalt thou set king over thee; thou mayest not put a foreigner over thee, which is not thy brother'), for he remembered the Edomite origin of the Herod family; but the populace cried out: 'Be not distressed; thou art our brother!'

The story of his execution of James the Zebedean, and his arrest of Peter, is well known. The words, 'because he saw it pleased the Jews', are significant, for reasons already suggested. The idea that John suffered martyrdom at the same time as James rests on the flimsiest foundations, in spite of the vigour with which some New Testament critics have pressed it. Peter's escape from prison, and his unexpected visit to the house of Mary, where the believers were praying for him, are narrated with a masterly vividness. Where Peter went from Mary's house (xii. 17) is uncertain; there is no good ground for the tradition that he went to Rome at this time. His words, 'Tell James and the brethren',

suggest that by this time James, the Lord's brother, had attained a special status in the Jerusalem church.

Soon after this, Herod's death took place under circumstances of dramatic impressiveness which are related by both Luke and Josephus. The two historians differ in details, but agree on the main features; as for their differences, we may quote the German historian Eduard Meyer: 'In outline, in date, and in the general conception, both accounts are in full agreement. By its very interesting details, which are by no means to be explained as due to a "tendency" or popular tradition, Luke's account affords a guarantee that it is at least as reliable as that of Josephus.'

Then were the days of unleavened bread (3). The days of unleavened bread commenced on Passover eve, Nisan 14, and lasted till Nisan 21 (cf. xx. 6). Nisan 14 fell in that year (A.D. 44) on May 1—an unusually late date owing to the intercalation of a second month of Adar that year from March 19 to April 17 inclusive. *Four quaternions of soldiers* (4). One quaternion for each watch of the night. Peter was in the custody of four soldiers at a time, of whom two were probably on guard at either side of him, and two at the door. *After Easter* (4), or rather 'Passover'. The Passover strictly speaking was celebrated on Nisan 14, but the term was sometimes used in a more general sense, to cover the festival of unleavened bread as well (cf. Lk. xxii. 1); that is the sense here. *And, behold, the angel of the Lord came upon him* (7); cf. verse 19. Probably the most remarkable modern parallel to Peter's release is the story of Sadhu Sundar Singh's mysterious release from a well in which he was locked by a Tibetan ruler (told by Streeter and Appasamy, *The Sadhu*, pp. 30f.). But 'Peter thought it was all a vision until he found himself safe and sound. The Sadhu thought the rescuer was a man until he disappeared' (L. E. Browne). *When they were past the first and second ward* (i.e. guard), *they came unto the iron gate that leadeth unto the city* (10). 'There were obviously three gates and three wards to pass (Peter was allowed to pass the first and the second, being taken presumably as a servant; but no servant would be expected to pass beyond the outermost ward at night, and a different course was needed there)' (Ramsay). So the street-gate opened *of his own accord* (lit. 'automatically'; Gk. *automatē*); how, we are not told. But the whole inserted description reflects the account of an eyewitness, including the 'western' addition 'and went down the seven steps' inserted after *they went out*. Peter was probably imprisoned in the fortress of Antonia, north-west of the temple area. *He came to the house of Mary the mother of John, whose surname was Mark* (12). This house appears to have served as a meeting-place for one group of Jerusalem Christians; it is an attractive suggestion that it was the house in which the last supper was held. The group associated with James the Lord's brother seems to have had another meeting-place (17). *To hearken* (13); better, 'to answer the door' (Gr. *hypakouō*). *It is his angel* (15); i.e. his guardian angel or spirit counterpart, capable of assuming his appearance and of being mistaken for him. The Iranian *fravashi* conception is a parallel. Cf. also the reference to children's angels who behold the face of God (Mt. xviii. 10n.). *Beckoning unto them with the hand to hold their peace* (17); another eyewitness touch. *Went into another place* (17). This may simply mean that he went into hiding, 'went underground'. He told nobody at the time where he was going, and Luke could not find out in later years where he had actually gone.

That they should be put to death (19); lit. 'led off' (presumably to execution). Herod probably suspected them of collusion in a plot to rescue Peter. *Their country was nourished by the king's country* (20). The Phoenician seaboard depended on Galilee for its food supply, as in the days of Hiram and Solomon (1 Ki. v. 9ff.). *Upon a set day* (21). Josephus says it was a festival in honour of the Emperor Claudius (*Ant.* xix. 8. 2), possibly on his birthday, August 1. This might well have afforded an occasion for public reconciliation between Herod Agrippa and his Phoenician neighbours. *Arrayed in royal apparel* (21). 'He put on a robe made of silver throughout, of marvellous weaving' (Josephus). *The people* (22); Gk. *dēmos*; i.e. the city populace of Caesarea. *It is the voice of a god, and not of a man* (22). According to Josephus, his flatterers, addressing him as a god, said: 'Be gracious to us: hitherto we have reverenced thee as a man, but henceforth we acknowledge thee as more than a mortal.' *The angel of the Lord smote him* (23). For this Old Testament expression cf. 2 Ki. xix. 35. *Because he gave not God the glory* (23). He accepted the divine honours from his flatterers, instead of ascribing them to God. *He was eaten of worms* (23). A medical colleague diagnoses his malady as a hydatid cyst. *And gave up the ghost* (23); five days later, at the age of fifty-four. The persecutor dies; the cause he persecuted survives in increasing vigour (24).

IV. ANTIOCH BECOMES A MISSIONARY CHURCH. xii. 25—xvi. 5

a. The evangelization of Cyprus (xii. 25—xiii. 12)

On the return of Barnabas and Saul from Jerusalem to Antioch, they took with them Barnabas's cousin Mark, and continued for some time to minister to the church as had been their custom. In addition to Barnabas and Saul, the most gifted teachers of that church, there were three others: Lucius of Cyrene; Simeon, surnamed Niger ('the Black'), whom we are tempted to connect with Simon the Cyrenean of Lk. xxiii. 26; and Manaen, the foster-brother of Herod Antipas. This Manaen was possibly the grandson of another Manaen, mentioned by Josephus as a favourite of Herod the Great. It was perhaps from him that Luke received much

of his special information about the family of the Herods.

But the Holy Spirit had further work for the Antioch church to do, and He called upon them (presumably using one of their prophets as His mouthpiece) to release Barnabas and Saul for the special work to which He had called them. It is worth noticing that it was the two ablest ministers of the church who were thus set apart for what we should call 'foreign missions', though such an expression is not really applicable to a time when almost all the civilized world was politically united under Rome.

Acquiescing in the divine will thus expressed, the church sent forth the two men, expressing their fellowship with them by the imposition of hands. Mark went with them as their *minister* (5), which has been taken to mean that they availed themselves of his knowledge of the gospel story; he was probably one of the 'ministers of the word' mentioned in Lk. i. 2. Having set sail from Seleucia, the port of Antioch, they landed

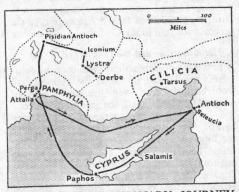

PAUL'S FIRST MISSIONARY JOURNEY

in Cyprus, Barnabas's native island, and traversed it from east to west. When they came to Paphos, the western capital, there occurred a passage-of-arms between Paul and the magician Bar-jesus, who belonged to the entourage of Sergius Paulus, the proconsul of the province. He seems to have been the sort of pet magician whom some great men liked to keep, and he was probably afraid that, if Sergius paid too much attention to the missionaries, his own days as court magician would be numbered. Ancient commentators delighted to point out that the magician's temporary blinding was intended by Paul to have the same effect as his own three days' blindness at Damascus had. Ramsay shows reason to believe that some members of Sergius's family were Christians in later generations.

Barnabas and Saul returned (xii. 25), i.e. to Antioch. *Salamis* (xiii. 5). On the east coast of Cyprus, the chief town of the island, and the seat of government of the eastern half. *The deputy* (7); better, 'the proconsul'. The Romans had annexed Cyprus in 57 B.C. *Sergius Paulus* (7). Probably identical with a man of the same name who appears on a Roman inscription as a curator of the Tiber earlier in Claudius's reign. *Elymas the sorcerer (for so is his name by interpretation)* (8). This does not mean that 'Elymas' is equivalent to 'Bar-jesus', but that Elymas, being a Semitic word, means 'sorcerer' (Gk. *magos*). *Saul (who also is called Paul)* (9). From this point the apostle is regularly given his Roman cognomen Paul (Lat. *Paullus*) instead of his Hebrew birth-name Saul, the former being more appropriate when the story is moving into a predominantly Gentile environment. *The deputy . . . believed, being astonished at the doctrine of the Lord* (12). It has been suggested that the proconsul's courtesy was mistaken for conversion, but a matter-of-fact Roman official was the very man to be convinced by the act of power which accompanied the teaching (cf. Lk. iv. 32).

b. Paul's address at Pisidian Antioch (xiii. 13-41)

From Cyprus the company sailed across to Asia Minor, where Mark left them and returned to Jerusalem. His reasons are not given; perhaps he resented the way in which his cousin Barnabas was falling into second place. When they set out from Antioch, it was *Barnabas and Saul* (2); when they left Cyprus, it was *Paul and his company* (13). Whatever his reason, Mark went back; Barnabas himself seems not to have minded; he was an outstanding example of the old saying:

> It takes more grace than I can tell
> To play the second fiddle well.

Barnabas and Paul, left alone, now struck up country (Ramsay thought this was because Paul had caught malaria in the low-lying country near the coast, though this is only speculative). They arrived at Pisidian Antioch, a Roman colony in the province of Galatia, and stayed there some time. Roman colonies played an important part in Paul's plan of campaign in all his missionary journeys. With true strategic instinct he picked out for intensive evangelization the important points along the main highways between Jerusalem and Rome. Another constant feature of his method is seen at Pisidian Antioch, where they tackled the local Jewish synagogue first. 'To the Jew first' was Paul's constant programme everywhere.

On the first sabbath after arriving at Pisidian Antioch they went into the synagogue; and after the reading of the law and the prophets the rulers of the synagogue invited the strangers to pass on any word of exhortation they might have for the company. Paul stood up to speak, and the summary of his address is given at some length, probably to show the sort of synagogue sermon he was accustomed to preach throughout the Empire. He narrated the deliverance wrought by God for the nation of Israel at the exodus, and outlined their history from Moses to David. Then he passed from David to the promised Messiah of David's seed, and declared that the promised Messiah had appeared in their day in the person of Jesus, whose death and well-

attested resurrection proved Him to be the Messiah foretold in Hebrew Scripture. Like Peter at Pentecost, he argued that the words of Ps. xvi. 10, 'Thou wilt not suffer thy Holy One to see corruption', could not apply to David himself, who did 'see corruption', but to the descendant of David who had in these last days, as a matter of evidence, risen from the dead. The sermon ended with an application to the present situation of the warning of the prophet Habakkuk on the eve of the Chaldean invasion: *Behold, ye despisers, and wonder, and perish . . .* (the word 'despisers' is quoted from the LXX, where it replaces 'among the nations' in the Hebrew text).

Antioch in Pisidia (14). It was not 'in' but near the border of Pisidia (one of the regions of the province of Galatia); render 'Pisidian Antioch'. *After the reading of the law and the prophets* (15). The law was read through according to a fixed lectionary; readings were selected from the prophets with some resemblance or relation to the preceding lesson from the law. *The rulers of the synagogue* (15). These made arrangements for public worship, and invited suitable members of the congregation to read the lessons and give the address. *Ye men and brethren* (15). As elsewhere in Acts, this expression should simply be rendered 'Brethren'.

Men of Israel, and ye that fear God (16). These words indicate the two elements in the congregation, the Jews and the Gentile 'God-fearers' (see x. 2n.). *Suffered he their manners* (18). Some texts, with a change of one letter in the Greek verb thus translated, read 'he carried them like a nurse' (cf. Dt. i. 31). *Seven nations* (19). See Dt. vii. 1. *About the space of four hundred and fifty years* (20). This time-note is misplaced in AV and really covers the time from the beginning of the patriarchal sojourning to the occupation of the land (cf. RV). *Cis* (21); i.e. Kish. *I have found David . . .* (22); quoted from Ps. lxxxix. 20 and 1 Sa. xiii. 14. *When John had first preached . . .* (24). Verses 24-31 contain an outline of the apostolic preaching similar to that in x. 36-43. *I am not he* (25); i.e. the Messiah. Cf. Jn. i. 20, 21. *They took him down* (29); a generalizing plural. In the Gospels Joseph of Arimathaea and Nicodemus are said to have done this. *Unto us their children* (33). Read 'to us and to our children' (F. H. Chase). *He hath raised up Jesus again* (33). Omit 'again'; the reference here is to God's raising up Jesus as Messiah in the sense in which He *raised up* David as king (22); contrast verse 34, where the resurrection is in view: *he raised him up from the dead. Thou art my Son, this day have I begotten thee* (33); quoted from Ps. ii. 7. The day of the king's anointing 'was ideally the day in which he, the nation's representative, was born into a new relation of sonship towards Jehovah' (F. H. Chase); the day of Jesus' baptism is probably intended here (when He was addressed by God, 'Thou art my Son . . .'). *I will give you the sure mercies of David* (34); quoted from Is. lv. 3. The 'holy and sure blessings' (RV) promised to David find their fulfilment in Christ through His resurrection. *All that believe are justified* (39). It is noteworthy that only in this sermon of Paul's does the concept of justification find explicit expression in Acts. Faith in Christ brings a completely righteous status in God's presence, such as the law could never afford. *Behold . . .* (41); cf. Hab. i. 5 (which itself echoes Is. xxix. 14).

c. Reaction to the gospel at Pisidian Antioch (xiii. 42–52)

Paul's address had been listened to with special interest by the Gentiles who attended the Jewish place of worship, the 'God-fearers', as Luke calls them, who, without becoming proselytes, were attracted by the pure worship of Judaism, and even kept the Jewish law to some extent, e.g. by observing the sabbath. These were greatly attracted by Paul's proclamation of forgiveness of sins through Christ, and begged that he should address them again next sabbath. These people, indeed, formed the main nucleus of Paul's converts in most of the cities he went to, as he offered them through Christ equal rights before God with Jewish believers, without the necessity of observing the Jewish ceremonial law and becoming proselytes.

Their adhesion to Paul naturally aroused the envy of the Jews of the dispersion, who resented his drawing after him those Gentiles for whose ultimate conversion to Judaism they hoped. Such envy was speedily aroused at Pisidian Antioch, for the 'God-fearers' spread the news around, and next sabbath nearly the whole Gentile population of the colony attended the synagogue. When the Jews manifested their annoyance, Paul announced that since they reckoned themselves unworthy of the eternal life which he proclaimed, he would concentrate on the Gentiles—a process which was to be repeated in city after city. But such opposition was stirred up by the Jews that Paul and Barnabas had to leave the city, not, however, before a number of the 'God-fearers' had confessed Christ and been formed into a church.

Religious proselytes (43). It is disputed whether actual proselytes or 'God-fearers' are meant, but if it be the latter (as is suggested by the word rendered 'religious', Gk. *sebomenoi*), then this is the only place where such people are called *proselytes*, a word elsewhere used in its strict sense. *Everlasting life* (46). Gk. *zōē aiōnios*, representing the Jewish expression 'the life of the age to come (the resurrection age)', which believers in Christ receive while still living temporally in the present age. *I have set thee to be a light of the Gentiles . . .* (47). This quotation from one of the Isaianic Servant Songs (Is. xlix. 6) implies that the mission of the Servant of the Lord, inaugurated by Jesus, is continued by His followers. *As many as were ordained to eternal life* (48); cf. verse 46. The verb rendered 'ordained' may here have the sense of 'inscribed', 'enrolled'. Cf. Rev. xiii. 8, xvii. 8.

d. Iconium, Lystra and Derbe (xiv. 1–28)

The next city to be visited was Iconium where, in the same manner, the apostles entered the synagogue, and as a result of their preaching a large number both of Jews and Gentiles believed. But they were soon forced to leave Iconium in the same way as Antioch. Persecuted in one city, however, they fled to another, and betook themselves to Lystra, another Roman colony, where the healing of a lame man by Paul provoked an outburst of religious enthusiasm among the native Anatolian population. Fancying that their city was again being favoured by a visit from the supreme god and his chief herald, as it had been in mythological narrative, they prepared to pay the missionaries divine honours. Recent archaeological research has revealed that in that region Hermes (Mercurius) was associated with the worship of Zeus (Jupiter).

When the apostles discovered what was afoot (the use of the Lycaonian vernacular had prevented their grasping the full situation at first) they succeeded with much ado in dissuading them, and Paul improved the occasion by instructing them in the truth about the one true Creator who had revealed Himself in creation and providence. This short summary of his speech resembles the longer account of his Athenian speech (xvii. 22–31); and if in chapter xiii we have a sample 'synagogue sermon' of Paul, we have here a sample sermon delivered to pagans which, when taken along with the Athenian speech of chapter xvii and the arguments of Rom. i. 18—ii. 16, shows us the proper function of 'natural revelation' as a *praeparatio evangelica*.

The visit to Lystra was abruptly cut short by a visit from Jews of Pisidian Antioch and Iconium, who stirred up a riot in which Paul, so recently acclaimed as the messenger of the Immortals, was manhandled and cast out of the city as dead. When he revived (this is narrated in such a way as to suggest miraculous intervention), they went on to the neighbouring city of Derbe. After repeating their programme there and founding another church, they made their way back through Lystra, Iconium and Pisidian Antioch, encouraging the new disciples and placing the young churches on a stable basis by the appointment of elders in each. Some modern missionaries would think it hardly wise to confer presbyteral ordination on 'native' Christians so recently converted from heathenism! But we should not overlook the pluck of the apostles in revisiting cities from which they had so lately been expelled with every circumstance of outrage and brutality. From these cities they made their way to the coast, preaching the gospel *en route*, until they reached Attalia, from which they took ship for the River Orontes and Syrian Antioch. See map on p. 916 for the complete outline of this first missionary journey.

Iconium (1). The modern rail-junction of Konia, then the easternmost city of the Phrygian region of the province of Galatia. *Together* (1);

918

better, 'in the same way' (as in Pisidian Antioch). Verse 2 is recast thus in the 'western' text: 'But the Jews' synagogue-leaders and rulers stirred up persecution against the righteous, and made the Gentiles' minds ill-disposed towards the brethren. But the Lord soon gave peace.' This recasting is no doubt intended to smooth the transition from verse 2 to verse 3, but it involves a double persecution. Verse 2 is really parenthetical, preparing the way for verse 5, and *therefore* at the beginning of verse 3 is resumptive, to be rendered 'So, then'. *With the apostles* (4). Barnabas was no more one of the Twelve than Paul was, but he was probably, like him, a witness of the resurrection, and in any case they were both commissioners (Gk. *apostoloi*) of the church in Syrian Antioch. *Fled unto Lystra and Derbe, cities of Lycaonia* (6), i.e. they crossed the regional frontier from Phrygia into Lycaonia, another region of Roman Galatia. *They called Barnabas, Jupiter; and Paul, Mercurius* (12). The names of the gods given by Luke are 'Zeus' and 'Hermes', the Greek forms; *in the speech of Lycaonia* (11) native Anatolian names were no doubt used. An altar near Lystra records the dedication to Zeus of a statue of Hermes by men with Lycaonian names; another altar in the vicinity is dedicated to the 'Hearer of prayer' (presumably Zeus) and Hermes. Ovid's tale of how these two gods were hospitably entertained unawares by Philemon and Baucis has also its setting in these parts. *Because he was the chief speaker* (12). Hermes had a title similar to this in the Egyptian mysteries. *The priest of Jupiter, which was before their city* (13), i.e. the priest of the temple of Zeus which lay in front of the city gate (the temple of Zeus Propolis). *That ye should turn from these vanities unto the living God* (15). Cf. 1 Thes. i. 9 for very similar language. *Who in times past . . .* (16). Cf. the reference to 'the times of this ignorance' in xvii. 30. *From Antioch* (19); i.e. Pisidian Antioch. *Having stoned Paul* (19); cf. 2 Cor. xi. 25, 'once was I stoned'. *Derbe* (20); from a Lycaonian word meaning 'juniper'. *And that we must through much tribulation enter into the kingdom of God* (22); a transition from indirect to direct speech. Translate: 'saying, "Through much tribulation . . .".' Here 'the kingdom of God' is something yet to be realized. *Attalia* (25); modern Antalya, at the mouth of the Cataractes; it was the chief port of Pamphylia. *All that God had done with them* (27); an expression emphasizing that the apostles were but God's agents, or even instruments. (Cf. the title of Müller's *Narrative of the Lord's Dealings with George Müller*.) *Long time* (28); lit. 'no small time' (a characteristic Lucan idiom); probably about a year.

e. The apostolic letter from the Council of Jerusalem (xv. 1—xvi. 5)

i. The letter issued (xv. 1–29). The churches founded by Paul and Barnabas during this journey are the Galatian churches to which Paul's letter is addressed. He had not long left

them when a crisis arose among them through the activity of Judaizers who urged upon them the necessity of adding circumcision and observance of the ceremonial law to their faith in Christ. News of this coming to Paul at Antioch, he wrote them an urgent letter: 'I marvel that you have *so soon* turned away to a different gospel' (Gal. i. 6). The Epistle, written at white heat, reveals his loving anxiety lest these new-born children should be beguiled from the simplicity of Christ and his indignation against those who were troubling them.

The same issue became a live one at Antioch, too, about this time. The Gentile mission based on Antioch was bound to result in predominantly Gentile churches; and the more extreme Jewish party in the Jerusalem church saw that they must act at once if they were to act at all. So a campaign was organized, not only in the new churches of the Galatian province, but also in Antioch itself, the citadel of Gentile Christianity, urging the wholesale adoption of the Jewish law by all Christians as an indispensable condition of salvation and of fellowship with their Jewish fellow-believers.

What happened at Antioch is described by Paul in Gal. ii. 11ff.; so vigorously did the Judaizers press their point of view that even Peter, who was in Antioch at the time and knew perfectly what the rights and wrongs of the matter were, was drawn into an alarming appearance of 'play-acting', as Paul calls it, for he withdrew from the society of Gentile Christians. This action, though Peter may have justified it on grounds of expediency, was bound to have a devastating effect; even Barnabas of all people was inclined to follow suit, and Paul dealt drastically with the situation, charging Peter outright with dissimulation. His rebuke had a salutary effect; at the ensuing Council of Jerusalem Peter supported Paul's arguments in an uncompromising manner.

But the problem raised by the Judaizers had to be dealt with and settled, if the Christian Church was to avoid the risk of being split right at the beginning into two bodies, a Jewish and a Gentile. So the church at Antioch sent delegates to the apostles and elders at Jerusalem, and the question was thoroughly discussed by them in the meeting known as the Council of Jerusalem. In spite of the arguments of the Pharisaic party in the church, the weight of Peter's authority, supported by Barnabas and Paul's narrative of God's blessing on the Gentile mission, and finally by James's judicious summing-up, swayed the mind of the Council in the liberal direction.

No conditions were to be imposed on the Gentile Christians for salvation or admission to full Christian fellowship, save that condition which God Himself had accepted as sufficient, faith in Christ. Once that principle had been established, it was easier to deal with the practical question of social intercourse. It would manifestly be an act of courtesy and grace on the part of Gentile Christians to respect certain Jewish scruples; and the finding of the meeting was therefore conveyed in a letter to the church at Antioch and her daughter churches, asking them to abstain from food which had been sacrificed to idols, from blood and from flesh from which the blood had not been properly drained (*things strangled*), and to conform to the lofty and divinely appointed Jewish code of relations between the sexes. It is nonsense to say, as some have said, that Paul would never have accepted such conditions for his Gentile churches. Where principles were at stake, Paul was uncompromising; where these were not compromised, he was the most conciliatory of men, and there are several places in his letters where he urges upon his converts and others this very duty of respecting the scruples and consciences of others (cf. 1 Cor. viii. 1ff.; Rom. xiv. 1ff.).

Certain men which came down from Judaea (1). Probably the same as those referred to in Gal. ii. 12, 'certain came from James' (though there is MS authority for reading 'certain' there as singular: 'someone came from James'). Cf. verse 24. *Certain of the sect of the Pharisees which believed* (5). There was nothing to prevent a Pharisee from accepting Jesus as Messiah while retaining the distinctive Pharisaic tenets, but he tended to be a legally minded Christian. (Paul, of course, was the great exception to this tendency.) *It was needful to circumcise them, and to command them to keep the law of Moses* (5). By 'them', of course, Gentile converts are meant. It is not clear whether 'needful' means 'needful for salvation absolutely' or 'needful for recognition by and fellowship with Jewish Christians'. Probably these Pharisees would have considered this a distinction without a difference.

The apostles and elders came together (6). It seems from verse 12 (*all the multitude*) that other members of the Jerusalem church were present, although deliberation and decision rested with the leaders. *That the Gentiles by my mouth should hear the word of the gospel* (7); a reference to the Cornelius incident (see chapter x). *Giving them the Holy Ghost, even as he did unto us* (8); cf. x. 47, xi. 15-17. *Purifying their hearts by faith* (9). 'Purifying', like *giving* in verse 8, is in Greek a simultaneous aorist participle, and both participles denote the same event: as those Gentiles believed the gospel, the Holy Spirit came upon them, cleansing their hearts (cf. x. 15, 'what God hath cleansed'). *A yoke . . . which neither our fathers nor we were able to bear* (10). The obligations of the Jewish religion are frequently referred to as a 'yoke' by the rabbis (cf. the words of Jesus, 'my yoke', Mt. xi. 29, 30). Peter's words probably represent the general attitude of the Jewish rank and file towards the practicability of keeping the law. *But we believe . . .* (11). This verse probably means: 'But by the grace of the Lord Jesus we are saved by faith just as they are.'

James answered (13). James appears by this time to be the acknowledged leader of the Jerusalem church, and one who commanded the loyalty of the legalists. *Simeon* (14), i.e. Peter; Simeon represents Heb. *Shim'on* more accurately than Simon does. *To take out of them a people for his name* (14); from among the Gentiles, that is, as well as from the Jews. This verse has been given an exaggerated 'dispensational' significance far beyond the implications of its context. *To this agree the words of the prophets* (15). The quotation is from Am. ix. 11, 12 (LXX), with variations at the beginning and the end. As the presence of believing Jews in the Church fulfilled the prediction of the restoration of David's tabernacle, so the presence in it of believing Gentiles fulfilled Amos's reference (LXX) to 'the residue of men' and 'all the Gentiles'. *Saith the Lord . . .* (17). The words which follow and conclude the quotation should run: 'who maketh these things known from the beginning of the world' (RV); cf. Is. xlv. 21.

That they abstain (20). In the Received Text, which should be retained, the conditions laid down for social intercourse are in the main food laws; the *fornication* here prohibited may denote breaches of the Jewish marriage law of Lv. xviii (fornication in the general sense was in any case absolutely forbidden to all Christians). The 'western' text, here and in verse 29 (and xxi. 25), turns these conditions into ethical regulations—abstinence from idolatry, fornication (in the general sense) and bloodshed—and adds a negative form of the golden rule: 'and that they should not do to others what they do not wish to have done to themselves'. The 'western' reading reflects a time when the Judaizing controversy was gone and forgotten. *For Moses of old time hath . . .* (21), i.e. there is no danger that the Mosaic law will be forgotten, as it is regularly made known in synagogues throughout the Gentile world. *It seemed good to the Holy Ghost, and to us* (28). So completely Spirit-possessed is their consciousness that the community is regarded as the very mouthpiece or vehicle of the Spirit.

ii. The letter received (xv. 30—xvi. 5). The letter was taken to Antioch by two Jerusalem Christians, Judas and Silas, who accompanied the delegates from Antioch on their return journey. The reception of the letter at Antioch caused great satisfaction.

Then Paul and Barnabas agreed to revisit the churches evangelized on their former journey, but disagreed about Mark. Barnabas refused to forgo the company of his cousin, and the upshot of the dissension was that instead of one missionary tour there were two: Barnabas and Mark going to Cyprus again, while Paul took Silas, who had the double advantage of being a member of the Jerusalem church and a Roman citizen, and with him went through the cities of Asia Minor visited on the previous journey, delivering to the churches copies of the apostolic decree.

At Lystra they were joined by Timothy, whom Paul circumcised that he might be more useful in the work of the gospel. Lesser minds have not been slow to charge Paul with inconsistency here (or else to deny the truth of Luke's statement); but Paul was in truth loyal to a higher consistency, the consistency described in 1 Cor. ix. 19–23. He fought against any suggestion that Christians should be circumcised in order to complete their salvation; but Timothy had been brought up by his Jewish mother and grandmother to be a Jew religiously in every point but circumcision. To the Gentiles he was therefore a Jew; but to the Jews he was a Gentile because, his father having been a Greek, he was not circumcised. Therefore to regularize his position Paul circumcised him; it was better that he should be clearly one thing or the other than betwixt and between.

Notwithstanding it pleased Silas to abide there still (34). This verse, taken over by the Received Text from the 'western' text, is no part of the original, and is therefore rightly omitted from

PAUL'S SECOND MISSIONARY JOURNEY

RV; it contradicts verse 33, but was interpolated in an effort to explain why Silas appears again at Antioch in verse 40; it is simple, however, to suppose that Paul sent for him to Jerusalem. *The contention was so sharp* (39); lit. 'there was such friction' (Gk. *paroxysmos*). It is idle to apportion blame between the two apostles; Mark's later development proved that Barnabas had right on his side, but probably Mark would not have developed thus in Paul's company. *Paul chose Silas* (40), who is called Silvanus in the Pauline Epistles and in 1 Pet. v. 12. It appears from xvi. 37 that he was, like Paul, a Roman citizen. *Syria and Cilicia* (41). The double province mentioned in verse 23.

A certain disciple was there (xvi. 1); i.e. in Lystra, the common factor in *Derbe and Lystra* (1) and *Lystra and Iconium* (2). *A certain woman, which was a Jewess* (1). She is called Eunice in 2 Tim. i. 5. On her 'mixed' marriage, Ramsay suggests that the Phrygian Jews were less exclusive than those of Palestine.

V. THE AEGEAN SHORES EVANGELIZED. xvi. 6—xix. 41

a. Over to Europe: the gospel in Philippi (xvi. 6–40)

As the three made their way in the direction of Ephesus, they were conscious of a succession of heaven-sent inhibitions which barred this road to them, and turned them north until they found themselves in the Aegean port of Troas, another Roman colony, where they were joined by a fourth companion, Luke, the writer of the narrative.

At Troas Paul had the night vision which led the whole company to conclude that God was calling them to go across to the European mainland with the gospel. So they sailed across the north Aegean and landed at Neapolis in Macedonia, the modern Kavalla, and went inland to the colony of Philippi. Here they settled, for Paul knew the value of planting a church here, near the eastern end of a great Roman highway, the *Via Egnatia*, which connected the Aegean with the Adriatic. The city's status as a Roman colony was perhaps in Paul's mind when at a later date he reminded the Philippian Christians that they were 'a colony of heaven' (Phil. iii. 20).

There was apparently no synagogue in Philippi, presumably owing to the lack of the requisite minimum of ten men; but they found by the River Gangites a place *where prayer was wont to be made* (the AV probably represents the better reading here), and spoke to the women who came together there. One of these, Lydia from Thyatira, traded in the purple dye for which her native town had long been famed. When she heard the gospel, she believed, was baptized with her household, and persuaded the four missionaries to accept the hospitality of her home.

Lydia is the first of three people in Philippi whose experience of the power of Christ in their lives is specially mentioned; and the three are so different that they might almost have been deliberately chosen to show how that power was able to bring peace and deliverance to the most diverse types. The second was the fortune-telling slave-girl who persisted in shouting unsolicited testimonials after Paul and his friends in the Philippian streets until Paul in the Name of Christ exorcized the spirit that possessed her. Unfortunately from her owners' viewpoint, he exorcized their means of gain as well, and this led to Paul and Silas being dragged before the praetors—the grandiloquent name by which the two chief magistrates of this and other Roman colonies liked to call themselves—with the complaint: 'These men are Jews, troubling our city continually, and teaching customs which it is not right for Roman citizens like us either to allow or to practise.' It is noteworthy that on the two chief occasions in Acts where Gentiles oppose the gospel, it is because of its threat to vested financial interests, the other occasion being at Ephesus.

Paul and Silas were seized not only because they were the two leaders of the party, but also possibly because they looked much more Jewish than did Timothy, who was Greek on his father's side, or Luke, who was probably a complete Greek. The praetors, without inquiring carefully into the allegations, commanded the two men to be beaten with the rods of the lictors, the attendants of senior Roman magistrates, and to be securely imprisoned. But while the two missionaries were praising God aloud at midnight, in spite of their cramped and painful situation, an earthquake loosened the bars of the prison and the bonds of the prisoners, and the jailer, probably an ex-soldier, awakened in spirit as well as in body, found himself indebted for the preservation of his life and the salvation of his soul to the men whom a few hours previously he had locked in the stocks.

The praetors, sending next morning to release the prisoners, found the tables turned on them, for they learned what in yesterday's excitement they had omitted to ascertain, that the men were Roman citizens, and therefore legally protected against such shameful treatment as had been meted out to them. So they had to eat humble pie and ceremoniously conduct the two missionaries out of prison. Soon afterwards Paul, Silas and Timothy left, apparently leaving Luke behind to help the new church, which quickly became a church worthy of emulation.

Phrygia and the region of Galatia (6); rather, the Phrygian region of the province of Galatia. They turned northwards through this territory after the way into the province of Asia was barred. Their original intention probably had been to follow the main road westwards to Ephesus. *The Spirit suffered them not* (7). Read 'the Spirit of Jesus . . .'. *A man of Macedonia* (9). It is idle to inquire how Paul knew him to be a Macedonian; his words, *Come over into Macedonia, and help us*, were sufficient indication. *Immediately we endeavoured . . .* (10). These words mark the beginning of the first 'we' section of Acts, which continues to verse 17. *Philippi* (12); so called after Philip of Macedon who re-founded it as a fortified city, *c.* 350 B.C. It was made a Roman *colony* when Antony and Octavian settled their veterans there after the battle of Philippi in 42 B.C. *The chief city of that part of Macedonia* (12). Read 'a city of the first division of Macedonia' (Macedonia was divided by the Romans into four administrative areas).

Which worshipped God (14), i.e. a 'God-fearer'. *Possessed with a spirit of divination* (16); lit. 'having a python-spirit'. 'Pythons' were people supposed to be inspired by Apollo, the 'Pythian' god, whose chief oracle was at Delphi (also called Pytho), where he was believed to be embodied in a snake (the 'Python'). *Servants of the most high God, which shew unto us the way of salvation* (17). These religious terms were as current in Greek as in Jewish circles at this time. Among the Gentiles 'salvation' (Gk. *sōtēria*) was the object of many vows and prayers to the 'most high God' (Gk. *theos hypsistos*) and other 'saviour gods' (Gk. *theoi sōtēres*), and was held out to initiates in the mystery religions. *The magistrates* (20); more accurately, 'the praetors' (which is the sense of Greek *stratēgoi* used as a civil title). They were the two senior collegiate magistrates of the colony. The more general Greek term for magistrates (*archontes*) is translated *rulers* at the end of verse 19. *Rent off their clothes* (22); i.e. the clothes of Paul and Silas. *And commanded to beat them* (22). The word rendered *beat* means strictly 'beat with rods' (cf. 2 Cor. xi. 25, where Paul says he received this treatment on two other occasions as well). The rods were those which the praetors' attendants, the lictors, carried in bundles (*fasces*) as a badge of office. *Made their feet fast in the stocks* (24). This served as an instrument of torture, as well as of security, for it had more than two holes for the legs, which could thus be forced far apart, causing great discomfort and pain. *Paul and Silas prayed, and sang praises unto God* (25). 'The legs feel no pain in the stocks when the heart is in heaven,' says Tertullian. *Would have killed himself* (27); since, presumably, he was answerable for the prisoners' safe keeping, and not even an earthquake could relieve him of his responsibility. *We are all here* (28). This suggests that the two missionaries were able to exercise some moral control over the other prisoners. The jailer and his actions could be seen from within, silhouetted in the doorway, although the prisoners in the darkness were invisible to him. *What must I do to be saved?* (30). It is difficult to say how much he meant by this expression, but the salvation he actually received was full salvation, resulting from his acceptance of *the word of the Lord* (32). *Washed their stripes; and was baptized* (33). 'He washed them from their stripes, and was himself washed from his sins' (Chrysostom). *With all his house* (34) is an adverb (Gk. *panoikei*) which modifies *rejoiced* as well as *believing*. For the whole household's becoming Christian cf. the stories of Cornelius (xi. 14), of Lydia (xvi. 15), and of Crispus (xviii. 8). *The serjeants* (35); i.e. the lictors; lit. 'rod-bearers' (Gk. *rhabdouchoi*). *Uncondemned* (37); Gk. *akatakritos*, which probably represents here Lat. *re incognita*, 'without investigating our case'. By a series of laws (the Valerian and Porcian Laws) Roman citizens were exempt from all degrading forms of punishment. *Desired them to depart* (39). They could not expel Roman citizens from a Roman city, but only request them to leave; the responsibility of protecting two unpopular Roman citizens was apparently more than they felt able to undertake.

b. Thessalonica and Berea (xvii. 1-15)

Paul and his company continued along the Egnatian road to Thessalonica, the capital of Macedonia, where they stayed long enough to found a new church. The message on which this church was founded is made plain in 1 Thes. i. 9, 10. But after Paul had made known the gospel in the synagogue for three successive sabbaths, showing from the Scripture lessons that Jesus was the Messiah, the Jews who opposed him accused him before the politarchs —the name given here and in a number of inscriptions to the chief magistrates of this and some other Macedonian towns. Paul had to leave the city in a hurry, perhaps because Jason, his host, had to go bail for his departure. Continuing south, he came to Berea, and found its Jewish community more amenable than that of Thessalonica; but Thessalonian Jews followed him there and stirred up the people against him. So he was escorted by brethren from Berea to Athens, where he waited for Silas and Timothy, who had remained behind. (The course of events at this juncture must be reconstructed by comparing this passage of Acts with 1 Thes. ii. 17—iii. 8.)

Amphipolis (1), a bridgehead position on the Struma, and *Apollonia*, between the Struma and the Vardar, were Macedonian cities on the Egnatian road. *Thessalonica* (1), made a free city by the Romans in 42 B.C., was the capital of the Roman province of Macedonia. *Opening and alleging* (3); i.e. opening the prophetic Scriptures and setting alongside them the recent historic events which fulfilled them. *Christ must needs have suffered* . . . (3). For this emphasis cf. Lk. xxiv. 26, 46. *The devout Greeks* (4); i.e. the 'God-fearers'. *Lewd fellows of the baser sort* (5); i.e. 'loafers', 'corner-boys'. *The rulers of the city* (6). Gk. *politarchai*, a word not found in classic literature, but attested epigraphically. Thessalonica was governed by a board of five magistrates so named in the Augustan Age. *These that have turned the world upside down* (6). The word (Gk. *anastatoō*) suggests subversive revolutionary agitation. *Another king* (7); or 'another emperor'. The charge as framed was of the most serious character and could not be ignored. *When they had taken security of Jason* (9). Jason and his associates went bail for Paul's good behaviour, which in this case involved his leaving Thessalonica, a situation referred to in 1 Thes. ii. 18.

Berea (10). A city of Thessaly. *More noble* (11); i.e. more liberal or open-minded. *As it were to the sea* (14); rather, 'as far as the sea', perhaps to Methone or Dium, where he took ship for Piraeus, the port of Athens.

c. Paul in Athens (xvii. 16-34)

Paul's residence in Athens is reported by Luke in a manner which rings true in the ears of classical students. Several centuries earlier this city had been reproached by its statesmen for being more interested in hearing the latest news than in attending to matters of more pressing importance (cf. xvii. 21). Nothing is said of Paul's aesthetic appreciation of the sculptures of Pheidias, or of any feelings stirred in the breast of this champion of Christian liberty by the knowledge that this was the cradle of democracy; to him the sight of the beautiful city of Cecrops brought sorrow as he beheld it so full of idols. Here he discoursed not only with the Jews in the synagogue, but also with the Athenians in the market-place, the *Agora*, the centre of Athenian life, where he disputed with the followers of the two illustrious schools of the Stoics and the Epicureans, the former of whom pursued self-sufficiency as the highest good, the latter pleasure. To these Paul appeared as *a setter forth of strange gods* (18), and they brought him before the Court of the Areopagus to expound his teaching.

This was the most ancient institution of Athens, founded, according to tradition, over a thousand years before by the city's patron goddess Athene. When Athens became a democracy in the fifth century B.C., much of the power of this court was broken, but it retained great moral prestige, which tended to increase under the Romans; and there is evidence that at this time one of its functions was to examine and license public lecturers.

Paul's speech before this body, as reported by Luke, followed lines not unlike those of his speech at Lystra (xiv. 15-17). Beginning with a reference to an altar dedicated TO THE UNKNOWN GOD (a type of altar-dedication at Athens to which other writers testify), Paul declared that his mission was to make this unknown God known to them; and he went on to describe His work in creation and providence, using language borrowed from some of the Greek poets, such as Epimenides of Crete (*For in him we live, and move, and have our being*) and Aratus of Cilicia (*For we are also his offspring*).

Paul then argued that God should not be worshipped after the idolatrous fashion of Athens and the pagan world in general, and that, whereas hitherto God had overlooked the ignorance of men, a change had come now in that He was commanding all men everywhere to repent, in view of the coming judgment of the world, proof of which had been publicly given, seeing that the Man appointed to execute this judgment had been raised from the dead. (For this emphasis on the Manhood of Christ in connection with His judging the world cf. Dn. vii. 13; Jn. v. 27.) The audience listened interestedly enough until Paul spoke of resurrection. This they could not stomach. The immortality of the soul was a commonplace of several of their philosophical schools, but the resurrection of the body was to them as absurd as it was undesirable. It is still as much a stumbling-block to many as it was to the Athenians, but it is integral to the Christian faith.

Wholly given to idolatry (16); i.e. full of temples and images of pagan deities. *Devout persons* (17); i.e. 'God-fearers'. *Epicureans* (18). These took their name from Epicurus, the founder of this school (341–270 B.C.); *Stoicks* were so called from the Painted Stoa (colonnade) where Zeno, their founder (340–265 B.C.), taught his disciples. *Babbler* (18); Gk. *spermologos*, an intellectual cheap-jack, a retailer of scraps of second-hand philosophy (a word of characteristic Athenian slang). *Jesus, and the resurrection* (18). These may have been taken by the Athenian populace as the names of two new-fangled divinities. *Areopagus* (19). Not here a place, but a body of men, the Court of the Areopagus. *For all the Athenians . . . spent their time in nothing else, but either to tell, or to hear some new thing* (21). Several examples of this characterization of the ancient Athenians can be found in classical literature. *Mars' hill* (22); lit. 'Areopagus'; here as in verse 19 the men, not a place, should be understood. *Too superstitious* (22), or 'very religious' (RV). *TO THE UNKNOWN GOD* (23). See on this N. B. Stonehouse, *The Areopagus Address* (Tyndale New Testament Lecture, 1949), pp. 15ff. *Ignorantly* (23), i.e. confessing Him to be unknown to you. *Dwelleth not in temples made with hands* (24). Cf. vii. 48, and see R. A. Cole, *The New Temple* (Tyndale New Testament Lecture, 1950). In the words of verse 25 the Epicureans would find confirmation of their view that the divine Being has no need of anything that men can give, and the Stoics of their view that He is the source of all life. *Hath made of one blood* (26). The best texts omit 'blood'; the reference will then be to the 'one man' from whom, in the Bible, all men are descended. This contradicted the cherished Athenian belief that they themselves were sprung from the soil of Attica. *Hath determined the times . . . and the bounds of their habitation* (26). Cf. Dt. xxxii. 8. *For in him we live, and move . . .* (28). This quotation from Epimenides is interesting for several reasons. For one thing, Epimenides was supposed in Greek legend to have advised the erection of 'anonymous altars' in and around Athens; for another, a further line from the same context is quoted in Tit. i. 12. In the context referred to, Epimenides addresses the Supreme God:

'They fashioned a tomb for Thee, O holy and high One,
The Cretans, always liars, evil beasts, idle bellies!
But Thou art not dead; for ever Thou art risen and alive,
For in Thee we live and move and have our being.'

Winked at (30), i.e. overlooked; cf. Rom. iii. 25, 'the passing over of sins done in former times'. *He will judge the world in righteousness* (31); based on such Old Testament passages as Ps. xcvi. 13. *Whom he hath ordained* (31); cf. x. 42. *When they heard of the resurrection of the*

dead (32). The tragedian Aeschylus had described the god Apollo as saying, on the occasion when the Court of the Areopagus was founded by the city's patron goddess Athene, 'But when the earth has drunk up a man's blood, once he is dead there is no resurrection' (the same Greek word *anastasis* being used as in Paul's preaching). This, in Athenian eyes, was higher authority than Paul's. *Dionysius the Areopagite* (34). A member of the Areopagus Court. The body of Neoplatonic literature ascribed to this Dionysius is actually several centuries later than his time.

d. Paul in Corinth (xviii. 1–28)

i. The church founded (xviii. 1–17). Paul's next move was to Corinth, a great commercial city with a double harbour. After its destruction by the Roman general Mummius in 146 B.C., it had lain in ruins for 100 years, until Julius Caesar refounded it as a Roman colony in 46 B.C. It had long enjoyed an unenviable reputation for loose morality, and it was only with difficulty that the church soon to be founded there kept this at bay; yet Paul knew the importance of leaving a strong 'cell' of the new community in this city, and he spent eighteen months there. There he met Aquila and his wife Priscilla, who were to prove such a help to him in his subsequent labours.

At first, with some success, he made the local synagogue his base of operation, but when Jewish opposition made it impossible to continue there, he availed himself of the hospitality of Titius Justus, a 'God-fearer' who lived next door to the synagogue. (Ramsay supposed, probably rightly, that this man's full name was Gaius Titius Justus, and that he was 'Gaius mine host' of Rom. xvi. 23 and of 1 Cor. i. 14.)

As Paul went on proclaiming the good news at Corinth, many believed, including the ruler of the synagogue, Crispus (cf. 1 Cor. i. 14). His Jewish opponents, however, did not slacken their efforts to hinder him, and soon accused him before Junius Gallio, the Roman proconsul of Achaia, of illegal religious propaganda. Gallio is an interesting figure; he was the much-loved brother of Seneca, the Stoic philosopher and tutor of Nero. There is inscriptional evidence that he governed Achaia from 51 to 52. He saw through the specious pleas of Paul's accusers. If Paul had contravened Roman law, he said, he would listen to them, but as the question seemed to concern only Jewish beliefs and interpretations, it did not fall within his jurisdiction. Ramsay emphasizes the importance of Gallio's decision both as a precedent for other governors and as a sign in Paul's eyes that Roman government could be relied upon to protect the liberty of Christian preachers, in which confidence he later appealed to Caesar himself.

The scene which followed Gallio's rebuff to the Jews, the beating of the ruler of the synagogue by the Greek mob, shows how near the surface anti-Jewish feeling lay in those days. If this Sosthenes is the same as that of 1 Cor. i. 1, then he, like his predecessor Crispus, ultimately became a Christian. Another eminent Corinthian convert was Erastus, the city treasurer (Rom. xvi. 23), whose name has been identified with great probability in a Corinthian inscription.

Pontus (2). A province of northern Asia Minor, on the south shore of the Black Sea. *Priscilla* (2); the diminutive and familiar form of her name; Paul regularly refers to her, more formally, as 'Prisca'. *Claudius had commanded all Jews to depart from Rome* (2); all Jews, that is, who were not Roman citizens. According to Suetonius, he expelled them 'because they were constantly rioting at the instigation of Chrestus', probably a distorted allusion to disputes between Christian and non-Christian Jews at Rome. The expulsion may be dated *c*. 49–50. *Tentmakers* (3). The word may mean, more broadly, 'leather-workers'. It was regarded as proper for a rabbi to practise a manual occupation, so as not to make monetary profit out of his sacred teaching. *Every sabbath* (4). The 'western' text adds, 'inserting the name of the Lord Jesus' (i.e. as an interpretative expansion in the readings from the prophets). *Was pressed in the spirit* (5); better, 'proceeded to devote himself entirely to the preaching', his material necessities being supplied by gifts which Silas and Timothy brought from the Macedonian churches. *Blasphemed* (6). 'Spoke evil of the name of Jesus.' *One that worshipped God* (7); i.e. a God-fearer. *With all his house* (8). Cf. xi. 14, xvi. 15, 31ff. *No man shall set on thee to hurt thee* (10). This promise was fulfilled in the failure of the attack described in verses 12–17. *A year and six months* (11). Probably from autumn 50 to spring 52.

When Gallio was the deputy of Achaia (12). For 'deputy' read 'proconsul' (cf. xiii. 7, 12, xix. 38). An inscription at Delphi, recording a proclamation of Claudius, makes it probable that Gallio was appointed to his proconsulship in July, 51. The Roman province of Achaia included all Greece south of Macedonia. *This fellow persuadeth men to worship God contrary to the law* (13); i.e. he propagates a *religio illicita*, a cult not licensed by Roman law. *I will be no judge of such matters* (15). Previously Jewish opposition had had recourse to mob violence or to city magistrates; it now attempted to influence a higher court, the provincial magistrate, against the apostles. Gallio's decision that the gospel was a form of Judaism, which was a religion specifically protected by Roman law, could not be allowed undisputed validity for long, but as a precedent it did afford protection to Christianity for ten vital years. *Gallio cared for none of these things* (17); i.e. he turned a blind eye to the behaviour of the pagan crowd, who followed up the proconsul's snub to the local Jews by assaulting one of their leading representatives.

ii. Paul leaves Corinth and Apollos arrives (xviii. 18–28). In the spring of 52 Paul left Corinth and paid a short visit to Jerusalem, at the Passover season. On the way he called at Ephesus, but could not stay there at the time, in spite of the pressing invitation of the synagogue. He promised, however, to return, and kept his promise in the autumn. Meanwhile great interest was aroused in the synagogue at Ephesus by an Alexandrian Jew named Apollos, well versed in the Old Testament Scriptures and also in the story of Jesus, comparison of which with the Old Testament convinced him that Jesus was indeed the Messiah; and with his powerful reasoning he expounded this teaching in the synagogue. Aquila and Priscilla, who had accompanied Paul from Corinth to Ephesus, heard him and, as he knew only of the baptism of John, they taught him the way of the Lord more accurately, benefiting from the teaching they themselves had received from Paul. When Apollos was about to pursue his journey to Greece, they commended him to the church of Corinth; and so powerful was the assistance he gave the Christians there that Paul could write to them later: 'I planted, and Apollos watered' (1 Cor. iii. 6). Although some Corinthians tried to make him a party leader in rivalry to Paul, it is clear that there was no party feeling between Paul and Apollos themselves (cf. 1 Cor. xvi. 12).

Having shorn his head in Cenchrea: for he had a vow (18), i.e. Paul. The vow was a temporary Nazirite vow, perhaps one of gratitude for the promise of verses 9, 10. Cf. Acts xxi. 23, 24. Cenchreae (the better spelling) was the eastern (Aegean) port of Corinth: cf. Rom. xvi. 1. *Ephesus* (19). An ancient Greek city, at this time capital of the province of Asia and chief commercial centre of Asia Minor. *I must by all means keep this feast that cometh in Jerusalem* (21). This is a 'western' addition to the original text, but no doubt gives the true reason for Paul's hasty departure. The feast was probably Passover, which in A.D. 52 fell early in April, and as the seas were closed for navigation until March 10 there was the less time to spare. *Gone up* (22); i.e. to Jerusalem. *Went over all the country of Galatia and Phrygia* (23); lit. 'the Galatian region and Phrygia', revisiting the churches founded on his first missionary journey in Asia Minor.

Born at Alexandria (24), and perhaps therefore given to the allegorizing interpretation of Scripture, like Philo. *An eloquent man* (24); rather, 'a learned man' (RV). *Fervent in the spirit* (25); i.e. full of enthusiasm. *The things of the Lord* (25); i.e. the gospel story. *Knowing only the baptism of John* (25). His knowledge of the gospel may have come from a Galilean source rather than from the Jerusalem apostles. *When he was disposed to pass into Achaia* (27). According to the 'western' text, some Corinthian visitors in Ephesus heard him there and persuaded him to accompany them back to Corinth.

e. Ephesus and the province of Asia (xix. 1–41)

i. Ephesus evangelized (xix. 1–20). Paul, having paid his visit to Palestine, returned overland to Ephesus and settled down there for some two and a half years, from the autumn of 52 to the spring of 55. There a great work was accomplished, radiating out from Ephesus to other cities of the province of Asia, such as Colossae, Laodicea and Hierapolis. The effect of the preaching is vividly portrayed by Luke in a few cameos. First we meet the twelve 'disciples' who knew only John's baptism and had never heard of the Holy Spirit; perhaps these were the fruit of Apollos's earlier preaching. Then we have Paul's withdrawal from the synagogue to the lecture-hall of Tyrannus where, according to one textual tradition, he lectured daily from 11 a.m. to 4 p.m., during the heat of the day, after having presumably spent the earlier hours of the morning tent-making. The mighty works wrought through Paul at Ephesus led to encounters with the local magicians, and we have the vivid description of the sons of Sceva. The

PAUL'S THIRD MISSIONARY JOURNEY

burning of the magic scrolls reminds us that such scrolls were so closely connected with Ephesus in the ancient world that they were commonly called *Ephesia grammata*, 'Ephesian letters'.

Having passed through the upper coasts (1). Paul, instead of taking the main route to Ephesus by the Lycus and Maeander valleys, appears to have taken a higher road farther north, approaching the city from the north side of Mt. Messogis. *Disciples* (1). This word standing alone means not 'disciples of John' but 'disciples of Jesus', whatever the defects in their knowledge might be. *Have ye received . . .?* (2). Better, 'Did you receive the Holy Spirit on believing?' *We have not so much as heard whether there be any Holy Ghost* (2), with special reference to the Holy Spirit as sent at Pentecost in Acts). *John verily baptized . . .* (4); cf. i. 5, xi. 16. *That they should believe on him which should come after him* (4); cf. Jn. i. 26ff., iii. 25ff. There are striking agreements between John and Acts in their accounts

of John the Baptist and of the Holy Spirit. *They were baptized in* (into) *the name of the Lord Jesus* (5). The same expression as in viii. 16. This is the only instance of re-baptism recorded in the New Testament. *And when Paul had laid his hands upon them, the Holy Ghost came on them* (6), as happened to the Samaritan converts in viii. 17.

Spake evil of that way (9); better, '. . . the Way', i.e. the gospel, as in ix. 2. *Disputing* (9); better, 'conducting discussions' (Gk. *dialegomai*). *In the school of one Tyrannus* (9), which served much the same purpose in Ephesus as the house of Titius Justus did in Corinth. The 'western' text adds 'from the fifth to the tenth hour', the midday recess when Tyrannus himself did not use his lecture-room. *Two years* (10). Probably two years and a few months, which with the *three months* of verse 8 approximate to the *three years* of xx. 31. *All they which dwelt in Asia* (10), i.e. in the Roman province of that name, and especially in the area round Ephesus. Probably all seven churches addressed in Revelation (Rev. i. 11), as well as those at Colossae and Hierapolis (Col. iv. 13), were founded in these years. *Handkerchiefs or aprons* (12). Two words of Latin origin: *sudaria* (lit. 'sweat-rags'; cf. Lk. xix. 20; also Jn. xi. 44, xx. 7) and *semicinctia* (articles which Paul would use while engaged in 'tent-making').

We adjure you by Jesus (13). The use of this name and other Jewish names in pagan exorcism is attested by papyrus scrolls of magic spells which have come down to us. *Chief of the priests* (14). Luke is probably quoting, but not confirming, Sceva's account of himself. A Jewish High Priest was believed to know the secret pronunciation of the ineffable Name of Israel's God, and so to be in command of a specially potent spell. *Confessed, and shewed their deeds* (18); i.e. their spells; to divulge these was to render them useless. *Curious arts* (19); i.e. magical practices. *Books* (19); i.e. scrolls of papyrus or parchment. *Pieces of silver* (19); drachmae ('shillings').

ii. The riot at Ephesus (xix. 21–41). The most vivid scene of all in Luke's narrative of Paul's Ephesian ministry is the riotous assembly in the great open-air theatre of the city, lately excavated and estimated to have had room for 25,000 people. The local guild of silversmiths, who drew a comfortable income from the sale of silver images of the great goddess Artemis set in silver niches, were alarmed for the prospects of their craft at the sight of so many people becoming Christians and, disguising this alarm as concern for the honour of the goddess, they called an indignation meeting. The indignation spread to the general public, who ran into the theatre and staged a pro-Artemis and anti-

Jewish riot. (Notice the humour of verse 32.) Paul himself was prevented from entering the theatre by the Asiarchs, the chief men of the cities of the province, from whose ranks the high priests of the imperial worship in Asia were drawn. Alexander, a local Jew, tried to address the mob, perhaps in order to dissociate the Jewish community from the objects of the popular resentment. But the mob, in no mood to make fine distinctions, howled him down, and kept up for two hours the cry 'Great is Diana (Artemis) of the Ephesians'. At last the town clerk, greatly agitated lest the Roman authorities should lay severe penalties on the city for this riotous behaviour, persuaded them to be quiet and go home, telling them that if they had any complaint against these men they should lay it before the authorities in the proper manner.

To go to Jerusalem (21), along with the delegates of his Gentile churches who were carrying gifts from these churches to the Jerusalem Christians. *I must also see Rome* (21). Cf. Rom. i. 11ff., xv. 23ff. for Paul's plans. Ramsay finds here 'the clear conception of a far-reaching plan' to visit Rome on his way to evangelize 'the chief seat of Roman civilization in the West' (i.e. Spain), and regards this decision as a crisis in Paul's career. *Timotheus* (22). Cf. Phil. ii. 19 for this mission of Timothy to Macedonia. *That way* (23). 'The Way', as in verse 9. *Diana* (24). It is unfortunate that this Roman name has been used by the translators for Greek Artemis, the great goddess of Ephesus (a local form of the great mother-goddess worshipped from time immemorial in Asia Minor), whose temple was one of the seven wonders of antiquity. *Whom all Asia and the world worshippeth* (27). Over thirty places throughout the world have been enumerated where the cult of Ephesian Artemis was venerated. *Gaius and Aristarchus, men of Macedonia* (29). Read with some MSS, 'a man of Macedonia', referring to Aristarchus; Gaius belonged to Derbe in Asia Minor (xx. 4). These two may have been Luke's informants for this incident. *Into the theatre* (29). The open-air theatre of Ephesus could accommodate 25,000 persons and was a convenient place for meetings of the citizen body, regular or irregular. *The chief of Asia* (31); lit. Asiarchs. It is noteworthy that Paul found sympathizers in the highest ranks of Ephesian society. *The townclerk* (35); Gk. *grammateus*. He was chief liaison officer between the free municipal administration of Ephesus and the Roman provincial government. *A worshipper of the great goddess Diana* (35); better, 'Temple Warden of Great Artemis'—a much prized title borne by the city. *The image which fell down from Jupiter* (35); i.e. from the sky; presumably a meteorite, in which the semblance of the 'many-breasted' goddess was discerned. *Robbers of churches* (37); i.e. temple-robbers. *There are deputies* (38); i.e. proconsuls; the generalizing plural is used because Junius Silanus, proconsul of the province, had recently been assassinated (late in 54) and his successor

had not yet arrived. The proconsul presided at the assizes (*the law is open* should be rendered 'assizes are held'). *In a lawful assembly* (39). The regular assembly (Gk. *ekklēsia*) of the citizens met three times a month. Rome would not tolerate an irregular and riotous assembly like the present one. *To be called in question* (40); i.e. by the Romans.

VI. HOW PAUL REALIZED HIS HOPE OF SEEING ROME. xx. 1—xxviii. 31

a. Paul sets out for Palestine (xx. 1–38)

i. **The apostle sails with the delegates (xx. 1–16).** After the conclusion of his time in Ephesus, Paul spent some time in Macedonia and Greece, during which he travelled to the borders of Illyricum (the modern Albania and Yugoslavia), as we learn from Rom. xv. 19. He had organized collections, as an outward sign of fellowship, in his Gentile churches, for the poor Christians in the Jerusalem church; and in the spring of 57 he set sail for Palestine with the delegates whom these Gentile churches had appointed to present their gifts. His intention was, after paying this visit to Jerusalem, to leave the Eastern Mediterranean for the Western, calling on the Roman church on his way to Spain (xix. 21; Rom. xv. 23ff.). Luke rejoined him at Philippi and accompanied him to Jerusalem, and we have a detailed narrative in the first person plural of the voyage to Palestine. The visit to Troas throws some interesting light on Paul's practice when he visited a church; we notice incidentally that his sermons (or rather dialogues) were not of the twenty-minute order, and even if his discourse was interrupted by a momentarily fatal accident, yet, after Paul's reassuring words about the young man, the meeting went on till daybreak.

Embraced them (1). Read 'exhorted them and took his leave of them'. *He came into Greece* (2); i.e. into the province of Achaia (cf. xix. 21 and see xviii. 12n.). *And there abode three months* (3); mainly at Corinth, where early in A.D. 57 he wrote his Epistle to the Romans. *And there accompanied him . . .* (4). The names are those of delegates from the Pauline churches on both sides of the Aegean, who were carrying their churches' gifts to the Christians at Jerusalem (cf. xxiv. 17; 1 Cor. xvi. 1ff.; 2 Cor. viii. 1ff.; Rom. xv. 25ff.). *Sopater* (4); perhaps the Sosipater of Rom. xvi. 21. *These going before tarried for us at Troas* (5). They crossed from Cenchreae, presumably, while Paul and Luke crossed from Philippi.

We sailed away from Philippi (6). It is noteworthy that this new 'we' section (xx. 5—xxi. 18) begins where the former one finished (xvi. 17)— at Philippi, where Luke may have spent the whole intervening period. *After the days of unleavened bread* (6). In A.D. 57 they ended on Thursday, April 14. *Upon the first day of the week, when the disciples came* ('we were gathered', RV) *together to break bread* (7); i.e. to celebrate the Eucharist; probably it was their practice to do this each Sunday evening. In the event it was Monday morning before they 'broke the bread' (11), for Paul *continued his speech until midnight* (7). *There were many lights* (8). The resultant smoky, oily atmosphere would increase Eutychus's proneness to sleep. *The third loft* (9); i.e. the third storey. *Was taken up dead* (9). Luke, as a physician, probably satisfied himself that this was so. *His life is in him* (10); probably implying that life had returned to him. Cf. 1 Ki. xvii. 22; 2 Ki. iv. 34, 35. *Broken bread* (11); lit. 'broken the bread'; the article points back to verse 7 and indicates that now at last they celebrated the Eucharist as they had intended to do. *And eaten* (11). This refers to their taking food in addition to the eucharistic breaking of the bread. *They brought the young man alive* (12). Eutychus evidently recovered consciousness just before Paul's departure. *Minding himself to go afoot* (13). The sea route from Troas to Assos was longer than the land route, as it involved the rounding of Cape Lectum. *Mitylene* (14). The chief town of the island of Lesbos. *And tarried at Trogyllium* (15). This clause is absent from the best texts, but the statement is inherently probable. *Paul had determined to sail by* (i.e. 'past') *Ephesus* (16). He probably made this decision at Troas, and so chose a fast ship which took the straight course across the mouth of the Ephesian gulf, in order to reach Palestine in time.

ii. **Paul's address to the elders of Ephesus (xx. 17–38).** The meeting at Miletus between Paul and the elders of the Ephesian church is important because it contains the one record in Acts of Paul's addressing a Christian audience. Its authenticity is strongly supported by its similarity to Paul's Epistles, the more so as there is no evidence that Luke was acquainted with these. The address throws light both on the course of events in the recent past and on Paul's misgivings for the future, although nothing shifted him from his determination to carry out the work divinely allotted to him and to finish his course with joy.

From Miletus he sent to Ephesus (17). A distance of some thirty miles. *Temptations, which befell me by the lying in wait* (lit. 'plots') *of the Jews* (19). Cf. the reference to Alexander the coppersmith in 2 Tim. iv. 14, which may be relevant here if he is the Alexander of xix. 33. It is plain, besides, from references in the Corinthian Epistles (cf. 1 Cor. xv. 30–32; 2 Cor. i. 8–10) that Paul was exposed to serious danger during his Ephesian ministry, over and above the danger occasioned by the riot of xix. 23ff. *Both to the Jews, and also to the Greeks* (21); cf. Rom. i. 14ff., iii. 9. *Repentance toward God, and faith toward our Lord Jesus Christ* (21). For this summary of Paul's message cf. xxvi. 20; Rom. x. 9ff.; 2 Cor. v. 20ff. *Bound in the spirit* (22); i.e. under the constraint of the Spirit (cf. xvi. 6, 7). *The Holy Ghost witnesseth in every city* (23). Speaking through the prophets in various churches (cf. xxi. 4, 11). Compare the appre-

hensions expressed in Rom. xv. 31a. *To testify the gospel of the grace of God* (24). This is evidently identical with *preaching the kingdom of God* (25). *I know that ye all . . . shall see my face no more* (25). His intention, if he survived the foreseen dangers at Jerusalem, was to go to Spain. Whether in fact they did see him again must remain uncertain. *I am pure from the blood of all men* (26). For the general idea cf. Ezk. xxxiii. 1–9. *The Holy Ghost hath made you overseers* (28); i.e. 'bishops' (Gk. *episkopos*). In the first century A.D. 'elder' (cf. verse 17) and 'bishop' are practically interchangeable terms. *Which he hath purchased with his own blood* (28). Or '. . . with the blood of His own One', '. . . of His Well-beloved'. *Grievous wolves* (29). This refers to one class of false teachers; another class is indicated in verse 30. *Three years* (31); see xix. 10n. *The word of his grace* (32). 'This message of the free bounty of God is the word which has the greatest effect on the heart of man, and so it is *able to build up* the church' (Rackham). *An inheritance among all them which are sanctified* (32); cf. xxvi. 18; Eph. i. 14; Col. iii. 24. *These hands have ministered unto my necessities* (34). Spoken no doubt with an appropriate gesture. Cf. 1 Cor. ix. 15ff.; 2 Cor. xi. 7ff.; 1 Thes. ii. 9; 2 Thes. iii. 7ff. *It is more blessed to give than to receive* (35). This saying is not recorded in the Gospels, though its general sense can be paralleled there. It seems that collections of the sayings of Jesus were already current.

b. **Miletus to Caesarea (xxi. 1–14)**

When Paul and his companions left Miletus they continued the journey to Palestine and landed at Tyre, where their ship was to unload. The picture of their departure from Tyre, escorted to the ship by the Christian families of that city, fast friends after a week's acquaintance, shows how firm a bond primitive Christianity was. As Paul went from one port to another, indications of the danger lying ahead of him in Jerusalem became more and more ominous; the Tyrian disciples, speaking by inspiration, begged him not to continue his journey there, and at Caesarea the prophet Agabus reappears to foretell plainly what is going to happen to him. But 'none of these things move me', Paul had said at Miletus, and so he said still. We must not infer that he was wrong in going on; these friends tried to dissuade him because they foresaw the risks to which he would be exposed at Jerusalem, but they seem to have recognized that Paul's movements were divinely guided when they acquiesced in his decision, saying, *The will of the Lord be done.*

At Caesarea we meet Philip again, after leaving him there at the end of chapter viii. Now we find him at home with his four prophesying daughters; and, as we have already seen, Luke was probably indebted to them for some of his information about the gospel story and the history of the early Church, if not during the few days they spent in Caesarea at this time, then during Paul's two years' detention there.

Coos (1); better 'Cos'; an island of the Dodecanese; *Rhodes* (1) is the largest island of that group; *Patara* (1) is a port of south-west Asia Minor. *Discovered*(3); Gk. *anaphainō*, apparently a nautical term for sighting land. *And finding disciples* (4); Gk. *aneuriskō* implies that they had to seek them out. The Tyrian church was probably planted during the Phoenician mission of xi. 19. *Ptolemais* (7); Old Testament Acco, modern Acre or Akka. At this time it was a Roman colony. *Four daughters* (9). Some at least of Philip's daughters spent their old age in the province of Asia, where they were renowned as authorities on persons and events belonging to the earliest days of Christianity (cf. Eusebius, *Eccl. Hist.* iii. 31, 39, v. 24).

Agabus (10). Cf. xi. 27, 28. His sudden appearances and disappearances are 'not fiction, but real life' (Lake and Cadbury). *He took Paul's girdle, and bound his own hands and feet* (11). Acted prophecy of this kind was common in the Old Testament (cf. 1 Ki. xi. 29ff.). *So shall the Jews at Jerusalem bind the man . . . and shall deliver him into the hands of the Gentiles* (11). The general sense, but not each detail of the prophecy, was fulfilled; in the event Paul was delivered by the Gentiles from the Jews. *The will of the Lord be done* (14). Cf. the words of Jesus in Gethsemane. There is a (probably intentional) series of parallels between this account of Paul's last journey to Jerusalem and our Lord's last journey thither.

c. Paul in Jerusalem (xxi. 15—xxiii. 35)

i. The apostle in trouble (xxi. 15–30). From Caesarea Paul and his companions went up to Jerusalem, and the party lodged with Mnason, one of the original believers, probably a Hellenist, in whose house the Gentile Christians would be sure of a welcome. When the delegates called on James and the elders of the Jerusalem church they were welcomed; but these good men were clearly troubled because of the exaggerated rumours that had reached Jerusalem about Paul's attitude to the law. They admitted that the position with regard to Gentile believers had been defined at the apostolic Council, but they wished Paul to give the lie in a practical manner to the report that he was dissuading *Jewish* Christians from keeping the law and from circumcising their children. Paul himself, so far as we can tell, continued to observe the law throughout his life, especially in Jewish company, and his consent to take the advice of James on this occasion and share the purificatory ceremony of four men who had taken a temporary Nazirite vow and pay their expenses was entirely in keeping with his settled principle: 'To the Jews I became as a Jew, that I might win Jews' (1 Cor. ix. 20). We may compare his own vow of Acts xviii. 18, which involved the shearing of his hair. He has been quite unnecessarily castigated for such actions by people whose ideal seems to be that lower brand of consistency which has been called 'the virtue of small minds'.

The carrying out of this duty involved his presence in the temple, and there he became the object of a hue and cry raised by some Jews from the province of Asia who recognized him. Having seen him in the city with a Gentile Christian from Ephesus, they imagined that he had taken this man into the temple. A riot broke out at once, the mob dragged Paul out of the temple, beating him all the time, and as soon as they were outside, the gates were shut.

Our carriages (15); RV 'our baggage'. But the single Greek word *episkeuasamenoi*, translated 'we took up our carriages', might mean here 'having hired horses'. *An old disciple* (16); RV 'an early disciple' (Gk. *archaios*); it suggests that he was a foundation member of the Church. Translate: 'bringing us to Mnason of Cyprus, one of the original disciples, with whom we were to lodge.' *Paul went in with us unto James; and all the elders were present* (18). Apparently none of the original apostles was now resident in Jerusalem. James (the Lord's brother) is the undisputed leader of the Jerusalem church.

How many thousands (20); lit. 'how many myriads (tens of thousands)'. We may too easily underestimate the strength of early Jewish Christianity. *Zealous of the law* (20); i.e. 'zealots for the law'. *The customs* (21); i.e. those ordained by Jewish law, 'received by tradition from Moses' (cf. vi. 14; Gal. i. 14). *Be at charges with them* (24); i.e. 'pay their expenses'. Cf. Nu. vi. 14, 15 for the nature of these expenses. *We have written* (25). A reference to the apostolic letter of xv. 23–29.

Were almost ended (27). Rather, 'were going to be fulfilled'; the following events took place about the beginning, not the end, of the seven days. *That teacheth all men every where against . . . this place* (28). Cf. the charge brought against Stephen (vi. 13). *Brought Greeks also into the temple, and hath polluted this holy place* (28). Into the outer court anybody might go; but further penetration was forbidden to Gentiles on pain of death. The Roman government ratified the death sentence passed by the Sanhedrin for this offence even when the trespasser was a Roman citizen. Notices in Greek and Latin were fixed to the barriers separating the outer and inner courts, warning Gentile visitors against further ingress; one of these notices, found in 1871, is now in Istanbul, while another, found in 1935, is in the Palestine Museum. By the letter of the law, Trophimus (29) would have been the guilty party had the charge been true, although Paul would have been guilty of aiding and abetting him.

ii. Paul fails to pacify the Jerusalem mob (xxi. 31—xxii. 29). Above the temple stood the fortress of Antonia, in which a Roman garrison was stationed. Hearing of the riot the captain of the garrison sent down soldiers, who rescued Paul from being lynched. Even so, the mob thronged them to such an extent as they ascended the steps to the fortress that they had to carry Paul to prevent him from being pulled down. At the top of the steps stood the captain, who imagined that Paul was an Egyptian agitator, who had presented himself to the people some time previously in the guise of a second Moses, and who had aroused deep popular resentment when he left his followers to be cut to pieces by Felix's soldiery while he himself escaped. He was, therefore, surprised when Paul addressed him in Greek, and requested leave to speak to the people.

Having obtained leave, Paul stood on the steps and addressed the people below, not in Greek but in the Aramaic vernacular. Silence fell as they heard themselves addressed in their native tongue, and Paul told them of his upbringing at the feet of Gamaliel in that very city, his persecution of the Christians, his conversion near Damascus, where he stressed the part played by Ananias, 'a devout man according to the law'. They listened to all this with quiet interest, but when Paul went on to tell of his commission to evangelize the Gentiles their fury burst out afresh, and the captain, at his wits' end, ordered Paul to be scourged, so that he might find out the true reason for the trouble. Paul, however, protested his Roman citizenship and thus escaped the scourge, which was a much more murderous instrument than the lictors' rods of Philippi.

Went about (31); RV 'were seeking'. *The chief captain of the band* (31); i.e. the military tribune in charge of the auxiliary cohort which was stationed in the fortress of Antonia (*the castle* of verse 34). *When he came upon the stairs* (35). Two flights of steps led down from the fortress to the outer court of the temple. *Art not thou that Egyptian . . . ?* (38). The story of this Egyptian agitator is told by Josephus in his *Jewish War*, ii. 13. 4f., and *Jewish Antiquities*, xx. 8. 6. *Four thousand men that were murderers* (38); RV 'assassins'. The reference is to the *sicarii* ('dagger-men') who specialized in assassinating Romans and pro-Roman Jews. This figure of 'four thousand' is more probable than Josephus's 30,000. *In the Hebrew tongue* (40); i.e. in Aramaic.

They kept the more silence (xxii. 2); as though a bilingual Irish or Welsh audience, expecting to be addressed by an unpopular politician in English, suddenly realized that he was using the Celtic vernacular. *Taught according to the perfect manner of the law of the fathers* (3). Paul here emphasizes all those features in his career which would appeal to their religious nationalism. *The estate of the elders* (5); i.e. the Sanhedrin. *They heard not the voice of him that spake to me* (9). See ix. 7n. *And he said, The God of our fathers hath chosen thee . . .* (14). These words of Ananias are not given in the other accounts of Paul's conversion, but we may compare the words spoken by the Lord to Ananias in ix. 15, 16. Ananias communicated to Paul the revela-

tion he had received from the Lord concerning him. There is no basic contradiction between this account and Gal. i. 1, 12, where Paul maintains that he did not receive his apostolic commission from man. There Paul is concerned to show that he received his gospel and the authority to proclaim directly from God, not from the Jerusalem apostles. Ananias acted simply as the mouthpiece, or messenger, of Christ to Paul. *Be baptized, and wash away thy sins* (16). These verbs are in the Greek middle voice and might be rendered: 'Get yourself baptized and get your sins washed away'. *Calling on the name of the Lord* (16); i.e. 'invoking His name' by confessing it in baptism; such invoking the name of Christ appears to have been involved in baptism in (or 'with') that name (cf. ii. 38, x. 48). *When I was come again to Jerusalem* (17). This was in the third year from his conversion (see ix. 26; Gal. i. 18). *Make haste, and get thee quickly out of Jerusalem* (18). In ix. 29, 30 the Jerusalem brethren, getting wind of a plot against Paul, take him to Caesarea. This is not the only place in Acts where action is taken in simultaneous response to divine revelation and human advice. *And I said, Lord, they know . . .* (19). Paul argues that he is the very man to persuade the Jews, because they must remember how wholeheartedly he persecuted the Christians and must therefore realize that the reasons for his change of attitude are overwhelmingly cogent. *I will send thee far hence unto the Gentiles* (21). And so he went back to Tarsus, and in that neighbourhood and later in Antioch he had ample opportunity to fulfil his commission to evangelize Gentiles.

They gave him audience unto this word (22); i.e. the word 'Gentiles'; this reminded them of their grievance. *Threw dust into the air* (23). 'In England mud is more frequently available' (Lake and Cadbury). *Is it lawful for you to scourge a man that is a Roman, and uncondemned?* (25). Paul at once protests his Roman citizenship, which exempted him from this treatment. (Thus far he had mentioned only his Tarsian citizenship; xxi. 39.) A non-citizen might be scourged in order to make him admit the truth. As in xvi. 37, *uncondemned* means 'without having my case investigated'. *With a great sum obtained I this freedom* (or 'citizenship') (28). This may be sarcastic: 'I know how much it cost me to buy Roman citizenship; if a man like you can claim it, it must have become cheap of late.' The officer's Gentile name 'Claudius' (xxiii. 26) suggests that he had become a citizen in the reign of Claudius. *But I was free born* (28). How Paul's father or earlier ancestor acquired Roman citizenship we do not know. Ramsay suggests that some citizens of Tarsus received Roman citizenship from Pompey (c. 64 B.C.), and for a century before that there had been a considerable Jewish element in the citizen body of Tarsus. We are insufficiently informed on the way in which a man might prove at short notice the truth of his verbal claim to be a Roman citizen.

iii. Paul before the Sanhedrin: he is sent to Caesarea (xxii. 30—xxiii. 35).

A Roman citizen must be treated with scrupulous regard to the due processes of law, so next day the captain brought Paul face to face with the Sanhedrin. Ananias, the High Priest, behaved in a thoroughly disgraceful manner; and it is excessively squeamish to censure Paul for his plain speaking to him (for which, indeed, he apologized to the official, if not to the man), or for his throwing the apple of discord between the Sadducees and Pharisees. It was just the question of resurrection that made all the difference, for to Paul the general resurrection in which Pharisees believed hung upon the resurrection of Christ. A Pharisee might become a Christian without ceasing to be a Pharisee (cf. xv. 5); a Sadducee could not become a Christian and remain a Sadducee.

The captain, as far as ever from learning what the real cause of the trouble was, dismissed the meeting and ordered Paul to be taken back to the fortress. His troubles were not lessened when he learned of a plot against Paul's life, and so he sent him off to Caesarea at dead of night, under a well-armed escort, to Felix, the Roman procurator of Judaea.

The chief priests and all their council (30), i.e. the Sanhedrin, in which the chief-priestly Sadducean families played an influential part. If Paul had broken the Jewish law in a matter of which Rome took cognizance, it was the Sanhedrin's business to try and sentence him, and the Roman governor's to ratify a capital sentence. *I have lived in all good conscience before God* (xxiii. 1). Cf. Phil. iii. 6. *The high priest Ananias* (2). Ananias, son of Nedebaeus, a notoriously unscrupulous and avaricious politician, was High Priest from 47 to 58. *God shall smite thee* (3). Some have seen the fulfilment of these words in Ananias's assassination by nationalist insurgents in 66. *Contrary to the law* (3). Jewish law presumed a man's innocence until his guilt was proved. *I wist not . . . that he was the high priest* (5). Does he mean 'I didn't think that a man who spoke like that could possibly be the High Priest'? *Thou shalt not speak evil of the ruler of thy people* (5). Quoted from Ex. xxii. 28. *Of the hope and resurrection of the dead I am called in question* (6). The resurrection of Christ, the foundation of Israel's hope, as he saw it, was central to Paul's gospel. *The Sadducees say that there is no resurrection* (8). Cf. Mk. xii. 18 and parallels. *Neither angel, nor spirit* (8). 'What they rejected was the developed doctrine of the two kingdoms with their hierarchies of good and evil spirits' (T. W. Manson). *The Pharisees confess both* (8), i.e. both resurrection and angels and spirits. *Let us not fight against God* (9). These words are missing from the original texts; they have been supplied by the later Byzantine text. *So must thou bear witness also at Rome* (11), thus confirming Paul's own purpose. *Under a curse* (12); i.e. by a solemn oath, breach of which would automatically incur the divine wrath against perjurers. *The chief priests and*

elders (14). Not the whole Sanhedrin, as appears from verse 15 (*with the council*), but that part of it which was most hostile to Paul. *Paul's sister's son* (16). The first reference to any member of Paul's family; we wish we knew more about them. *Make ready . . . to go to Caesarea* (23). The escort consisted of heavy-armed infantry, cavalry, and light-armed troops, the three constituents of the Roman army. Caesarea was the headquarters of the provincial administration of Judaea. *Felix the governor* (24); i.e. Antonius Felix, procurator of Judaea A.D. 52–59. *The most excellent governor* (26). The title 'most excellent' (Gk. *kratistos*, equivalent of Lat. *egregius*) was given primarily to members of the equestrian order, from which such procurators were normally drawn (Felix was an exception). It is given in Acts also to Festus (xxvi. 25) and in Lk. i. 3 to Theophilus. *With an army* (27); i.e. with an 'armed force'. *Having understood that he was a Roman* (27). A delicate manipulation of the truth; it was rather later that Lysias learned this fact! *I sent* (30). The 'epistolary aorist' in Greek. The English idiom requires 'I am sending'. *Antipatris* (31) was about ten miles north of Lydda and twenty-five miles south of Caesarea (mod. Ras el-'Ain). *They left the horsemen to go with him* (32). The road from Antipatris ran through open country, inhabited mainly by Gentiles. *Herod's judgment hall* (35); lit. 'praetorium', a palace in Caesarea, built for himself by Herod the Great, and now serving as official headquarters for the procurator.

d. Paul in Caesarea (xxiv. 1—xxvi. 32)

i. Paul and Felix (xxiv. 1–27).

Felix, a man of ignoble birth, a freedman who had attained high station because his brother Pallas was an influential favourite at the imperial court, has been pilloried for all time in the cutting epigram of Tacitus: 'he exercised the authority of a king with the mind of a slave.' His present wife was Drusilla, the younger daughter of Herod Agrippa I, and they both knew something of Christianity, though their interest was strictly academic.

A few days later, a delegation from the Sanhedrin, led by the High Priest and assisted by the services of a second-rate orator called Tertullus, went down to Caesarea to state their case against Paul. Tertullus began his speech with a magnificent flourish, but it tailed away in a very lame and impotent conclusion, Paul being indicted only in general terms, not unlike those in which Christ was accused before Pilate (Lk. xxiii. 2).

To each of Tertullus's charges, however, Paul opposed a categorical negative, telling exactly why he had come to Jerusalem and what he had done since coming there, insisting again that the whole difference between him and his opponents hinged on this question of resurrection, which was no new-fangled notion of his own, but one which had been handed down from his fathers. If we realize the centrality of the resurrection in

Paul's gospel, we shall not quibble at this statement of his case.

Felix adjourned proceedings until Lysias, the captain, could come down from Jerusalem to give his evidence. Meanwhile he and his wife Drusilla availed themselves of Paul's presence in Caesarea to summon him frequently to their presence for theological discussion. Although their interest was academic, Paul's was not, for he seized the opportunity to discourse on three subjects which both his hearers badly needed to hear about—righteousness, self-control, and coming judgment—so much so that Felix trembled, but did no more about it. He kept on postponing a decision on Paul's case, hoping to receive money for releasing him, until after two years he was recalled to Rome; and knowing that the Jews were likely in any case to send an adverse report of his term of office to imperial headquarters, he decided to ingratiate himself with them at least to the extent of not releasing Paul, but leaving him in custody for his successor Festus to deal with.

Seeing that by thee we enjoy great quietness (2). Felix's procuratorship was marked by severe attempts to suppress insurgent bands, and so great was the consequent disaffection that only by courtesy could the ensuing conditions be described as 'quietness'. The Jews of Jerusalem had, however, co-operated with Felix in putting down the Egyptian mentioned in xxi. 38. *A pestilent fellow, and a mover of sedition among all the Jews throughout the world* (5). Tertullus represents Paul as a disturber of the peace in terms which were calculated to suggest that he was another insurgent leader of the class that Felix had so energetically suppressed, but more dangerous than most, because his activities were of wider range. It was easy to portray the spiritual messianism of the gospel as a form of militant and political messianism (cf. xvii. 6, 7). *The sect of the Nazarenes* (5). The most natural explanation is that the Christians received this appellation after Jesus the Nazarene; but other explanations are current, such as that the term means 'observants'. In Hebrew and Arabic Christians are still known as 'Nazarenes'. *Whom we took . . . to come unto thee* (6–8). This passage is a 'western' reading which has found its way into the Received Text; although not attested by the best authorities, it bears strong marks of genuineness. The reproachful reference to the *great violence* (7) with which Lysias took Paul away from his Jewish enemies when they were about to judge him according to their law is an even grosser manipulation of the facts than Lysias himself had practised in his letter to Felix (xxiii. 27). *Twelve days* (11). From the time-notes which are fairly full in this part of Acts (cf. xxi. 15, 18, 26, 27, xxii. 30, xxiii. 11, 12, 23, 32, xxiv. 1), we conclude that the seven days of xxi. 27 were only beginning when Paul was arrested. *The way which they call heresy* (14). Christians spoke of their movement as 'the Way', for to them it was the true fulfilment of

Israel's faith and the one way of salvation. Non-Christians called it 'a sect' (RV)—a party within Judaism (but much less respectable than the parties of Sadducees, Pharisees, and so forth). The Greek word is *hairesis*, used of 'the sect of the Sadducees' (v. 17) and of 'the sect of the Pharisees' (xv. 5). *Both of the just and unjust* (15). This is the only place in the New Testament where Paul refers definitely to a resurrection of the unjust (cf. Jn. v. 28, 29; Rev. xx. 12ff.). *To bring alms to my nation, and offerings* (17). The sums contributed by Gentile churches for the relief of the Jerusalem Christians. *Except it be for this one voice* (21). He is not blaming himself for his words before the Sanhedrin (he has just repeated the same argument before Felix, verses 14, 15); but he maintains that the one charge that can properly be brought against him is a theological one. *Having more perfect knowledge of that way* (22); i.e. 'having a fairly accurate knowledge of "the Way" '—possibly derived from *his wife Drusilla, which was a Jewess* (24), a daughter, in fact, of 'Herod the king' of xii. 1. (Felix, despite his low birth, married into distinguished families; his three successive wives were all princesses, one of them a granddaughter of Antony and Cleopatra. Drusilla was his third. They had a son, Agrippa, who perished in the eruption of Vesuvius of A.D. 79.) *When I have a convenient season, I will call for thee* (25). He did this rather frequently, moved partly by theological interest of a strictly detached character, and partly by financial expectations (26). Laws against bribery were more often violated than observed by Roman provincial administrators. Ramsay argued that there must have been a considerable improvement in Paul's financial position about this time; there is not much evidence for this, but he no doubt received gifts of money from the Gentile churches which he had founded. *But after two years Porcius Festus came into Felix' room* (27). Felix was recalled because of his violent but ineffective intervention in riots between the Jewish and Gentile inhabitants of Caesarea.

ii. Paul appeals to Caesar (xxv. 1–12). Festus, a more upright man than Felix, arrived in his province some time in A.D. 59; and after a few days went up from Caesarea, the seat of government, to Jerusalem to meet the High Priest and Sanhedrin. These lost no time in bringing up Paul's case, hoping that Festus in his inexperience would allow them to have their way with Paul. Festus did not accede to their request that Paul should be sent up to Jerusalem, but invited them to come down to Caesarea and state their case against him. This they did after eight or ten days, making charges which they could not substantiate, and to which Paul returned uncompromising negatives. Then Festus, perplexed and wishing to do the Jews a favour at the outset of his term of office, asked Paul if he were willing to go up to Jerusalem to be tried before him there; and Paul, afraid lest the weakness of Festus might again expose him to danger from his bitterest enemies, made a far-reaching decision, and, availing himself of his privilege as a Roman citizen, he appealed from the provincial tribunal to Caesar himself to be tried before the supreme court of the Empire. His previous experience of Roman justice probably made him confident of getting an impartial hearing there. Festus gladly seized this opportunity of avoiding the responsibility of making a difficult decision; his only trouble now was to know how to frame the report which he should send to Rome with Paul.

When Festus was come into the province (1). We have no information about Festus outside the writings of Luke and Josephus. His administration was not marked by the excesses of his predecessor and successors, but it was of short duration, being terminated by his death in A.D. 61. *Nor yet against Caesar* (8). In addition to answering the old charges of offences against the Jewish law in general and of profaning the temple in particular, he also rebuts the charge of activity against the Emperor's interests (see xxiv. 5). *Wilt thou go up to Jerusalem?* (9). The suggestion seemed reasonable enough; as the alleged crime was committed at Jerusalem, Jerusalem might seem the most appropriate place to have the charge examined, and Festus himself proposed to act as judge. But Paul was afraid that this one concession to the Sanhedrin might lead to others. *I stand at Caesar's judgment seat* (10), the procurator being the Emperor's representative. *I appeal unto Caesar* (11). The right to appeal to the Emperor, which every Roman citizen enjoyed, arose out of the earlier right of appeal to the sovereign Roman people, traditionally dating from 509 B.C. The right was usually exercised by appealing against a magistrate's verdict, but might be exercised at any earlier stage in the proceedings, 'claiming that the investigation be carried out at Rome and the judgment pronounced by the Emperor himself' (Schürer). The present Emperor was Nero (A.D. 54–68)

iii. Agrippa the Younger visits Festus (xxv. 13–27).

A way out of his difficulty soon presented itself to Festus. On the borders of his province was the petty kingdom of Herod Agrippa II (son of the Herod of Acts xii. 1), whose capital was at Caesarea Philippi, famed in Gospel story. He and his sister Bernice, the elder sister of Drusilla, were about to pay their respects to the new imperial representative, and Agrippa was known to be an expert in all matters affecting the Jewish religion. Among other things, he had the right of appointing the Jewish High Priests, and had the custody of the ceremonial robes worn by them once a year on the great day of atonement, and hence has sometimes been called, not very accurately, 'the secular head of the Jewish Church'. So when he and his sister came to Caesarea, Festus sought help from Agrippa in framing his report on Paul; it was necessary that he should grasp the gravamen of the Sanhedrin's accusation in order

to communicate it to the Emperor, but all that he could make out was that the trouble concerned 'a certain Jesus, who was dead, whom Paul affirmed to be alive'. Paul had made his main point clear enough, in spite of the procurator's lack of comprehension! Agrippa was interested and expressed a desire to see the man himself. So next day Festus, Agrippa and Bernice seated themselves in state, in the company of the procurator's entourage and the chief men of Caesarea. Paul was then brought before them, introduced by Festus to Agrippa, who gave him permission to state his case.

Agrippa and Bernice (13). This Agrippa was only seventeen at the time of his father's death in A.D. 44, and so Claudius was dissuaded from appointing him to succeed his father as king of Judaea, but a few years later gave him a kingdom north-east of the Lake of Galilee, which Nero enlarged. Bernice figures later in Roman history, when the crown prince Titus wished to marry her (c. A.D. 75) but changed his mind in view of popular disapproval at Rome. *Their own superstition* (19); RV 'their own religion'. As Agrippa professed the Jewish religion himself, Festus would not have referred to it before him in disparaging terms. *Augustus* (21). A title of honour, 'His Majesty'. *Chief captains* (23); i.e. 'military tribunes'; there were five cohorts at Caesarea, each in charge of a military tribune. *My lord* (26); i.e. the Emperor. *After examination had* (26). A Latinism in the English versions; render 'after holding an inquiry'.

iv. Paul's speech before Agrippa (xxvi. 1–23).

Paul proceeded to state his case with no reluctance, saluting the distinguished audience and congratulating himself on so illustrious an opportunity of making known the message which it was his life's mission to proclaim. This speech may well be called Paul's *Apologia Pro Vita Sua*. Here for the third time we have the story of his conversion, told for the second time by himself. The differences between his narration here and that to the Jerusalem mob in chapter xxii are mainly differences of emphasis; on each occasion he emphasized those aspects of the story which were likely to interest his audience at the time. The present speech may be divided into exordium (2, 3); his stand as a Pharisee for the hope of Israel, which involves the belief in resurrection (4–8); the account of his persecuting zeal (9–11); the heavenly vision (12–18); his life of obedience thereto (19, 20); his arrest (21); the substance of his preaching (22, 23). The Greek style of the original is unusually elegant, as befitting this distinguished audience.

Point by point Paul tells his story, insisting throughout that the hope which he proclaims is the ancestral hope of his whole people, that he preaches no other things than what Moses and the prophets said would happen, namely, that the Messiah was to suffer and rise from the dead, and that light and salvation were thereby to be offered both to the Jews and to the Gentiles.

Paul stretched forth the hand (1); i.e. in a gesture of salutation. *Before thee* (2) is emphatic. *Our religion* (5); Gk. *thrēskeia*, i.e. 'cultus', 'ritual' (referring to the external manifestations of religion); a different word from that used by Festus in xxv. 19 (*deisidaimonia*). *The promise made of God unto our fathers* (6). Paul has in mind the promise made in particular to Abraham, Isaac and Jacob, of world-wide blessing to come through their progeny. This promise was fulfilled in Jesus, and especially by His resurrection. *Our twelve tribes* (7). Cf. Jas. i. 1. Paul knows nothing of the figment of ten 'lost' tribes. *For which hope's sake . . . I am accused of the Jews* (7). Omit 'the', reading '. . . I am accused by Jews', with emphasis on *Jews*. That they, of all people, should show hostility to one who proclaimed that on which the fulfilment of their ancestral hope depended was preposterous. *Why should it be thought a thing incredible with you, that God should raise the dead?* (8). There is no textual justification for moving this verse to a position between verses 22 and 23, as Nestle and Moffatt do. 'With you' is again emphatic: 'with you Jews'. The hope of Israel was bound up with the resurrection of Christ. *When they were put to death* (10). As in the case of Stephen (viii. 1). *I gave my voice* (10); lit. 'I cast my vote'. *Compelled them . . .* (11); rather, 'I tried to compel them . . .' (this is the force of the Greek imperfect). *To blaspheme* (11); to say 'Jesus is anathema' (1 Cor. xii. 3) or something to the same effect. *Unto strange cities* (11); i.e. cities outside Palestine, such as Damascus. *When we were all fallen to the earth* (14). In the other versions of the incident, only Paul is said to have fallen. *In the Hebrew tongue* (14); i.e. in his Aramaic mother-tongue. *It is hard for thee to kick against the pricks* (14). The picture is that of an ox kicking out against the goad and only causing itself more trouble by doing so. The expression is proverbial and can be paralleled in several places. The words throw considerable light on Paul's mental condition, especially (no doubt) after the stoning of Stephen. Verses 16-18 summarize the communications which Paul received from the Lord on the Damascus road, through Ananias in the house of Judas, and later in the Jerusalem temple. *Stand upon thy feet* (16). Cf. Ezk. ii. 1, where Ezekiel's commission contains these words. Ezekiel, too, had fallen to the ground when he first saw 'visions of God'. *Both of these things which thou hast seen . . .* (16); better, 'of the visions which you have both had of me and will yet have of me'. *Delivering thee . . .* (17). Cf. Je. i. 8, where Jeremiah hears similar words when receiving his prophetic commission. *To open their eyes* (18). Cf. Is. xlii. 7. Paul is called to continue the mission of the obedient Servant inaugurated by his Master (cf. xiii. 47). The remaining words of this verse are characteristically Pauline and can be abundantly paralleled from his Epistles. *Works meet for repentance* (20); 'works worthy of their repent-

ance', i.e. works which would show that their repentance was genuine. Cf. Mt. iii. 8; Lk. iii. 8. *Went about* (21); i.e. 'tried'. *That Christ should suffer, and that he should be the first that should rise from the dead* (23). This verse seems to consist of headings from a collection of messianic 'testimonies': 'Is the Messiah to suffer? Is He first by the resurrection of the dead to proclaim light to the (Jewish) people and to the Gentiles?' By these headings Luke summarizes the arguments from the Old Testament which Paul pressed upon Agrippa to demonstrate the truth of his gospel.

v. Festus, Agrippa and Bernice make up their minds about Paul (xxvi. 24-32). As Paul went on in this vein, Festus, who had been vainly trying to follow the drift of his argument, interjected the observation that his great learning must have driven him mad. Paul was quick to defend himself against the charge of madness, and assured Festus that Agrippa could, if he would, bear witness to the truth of his words, since the subject of all his preaching was also the subject of Old Testament prophecy, and Agrippa himself believed the prophets. His direct appeal to the king put that gentleman in a dilemma. He had followed Paul's talk with interest enough, but he did not want even to appear to commit himself to agreement with Paul and thus lose face with Festus and the others. On the other hand, he did not wish to forfeit Jewish favour by appearing not to believe the prophets. So he laughed off Paul's appeal.

The court then rose, and Festus, Agrippa and Bernice, conferring with one another, agreed that at any rate Paul had done nothing deserving either death or even imprisonment, and that he might have been liberated there and then had he not appealed to Caesar.

Much learning doth make thee mad (24). Festus found himself completely out of his depth, and could only conclude that Paul, while obviously extremely learned, had been carried by his learning over the narrow frontier that divides erudition from insanity. 'Many educated people hold the same view about eschatology today, but history is against them and Festus, and proves that whether eschatological hope be true or false, it is no proof of insanity' (Lake and Cadbury). *This thing was not done in a corner* (26); a proverbial tag. The early Christian preachers regularly insisted that the historical foundations of their gospel were matters of public knowledge (cf. ii. 22). *I know that thou believest* (27). The implication is that anyone who knows and accepts the truth of the prophetic writings, as Paul is persuaded Agrippa does, must inevitably agree with Paul's conclusions. But Agrippa is not to be manœuvred into an appearance of supporting Paul's case, nor can he afford to disclaim belief in the prophets. So he says, 'In short, you are trying to persuade me to play the Christian'—for that is the true sense of his words in verse 28. And Paul replies (29): 'The short and the long of it is, I could pray that you and all the others here today were what I am, apart from these manacles' (holding out his chained hand). *This man doeth nothing worthy of death or of bonds* ('imprisonment') (31). Luke emphasizes again this official testimony of the law-abiding nature of Christianity and its preachers. *This man might have been set at liberty, if he had not appealed unto Caesar* (32). But as he had appealed, the legal procedure must take its course. We need not, with J. V. Bartlet, detect an ominous note in the 'if' clause.

e. Paul's journey to Rome (xxvii. 1—xxviii. 31)

i. The voyage begins (xxvii. 1–12). The narrative of the voyage and shipwreck of Paul is as graphic a piece of descriptive writing as any in the Bible. It has been called 'one of the most instructive documents for the knowledge of ancient seamanship'. (*The Voyage and Shipwreck of St. Paul*, by James Smith, 4th edition, 1880,

allies, it was Abraham—Abraham the man of faith, Abraham the 'unpractical' man from the viewpoint of secular business methods—who seized the opportunity and proved the man of the moment.

Luke, Paul's fellow-traveller on this occasion, looked at the sea with the eye of a Greek, and tells us what he saw. Together with Luke and Aristarchus, Paul set sail from Palestine under the command of a centurion named Julius, a member of the corps of imperial couriers. Paul, with his ready capacity for making friends, soon won the favour of this Roman officer (it is remarkable how the centurions in the New Testament are uniformly presented in a favourable light); and this favour was to stand him in good stead not only at Sidon at the beginning of the voyage, but to even better purpose at the journey's end, when the soldiers were for killing the prisoners to prevent their escape.

They sailed to Myra in their first ship, which

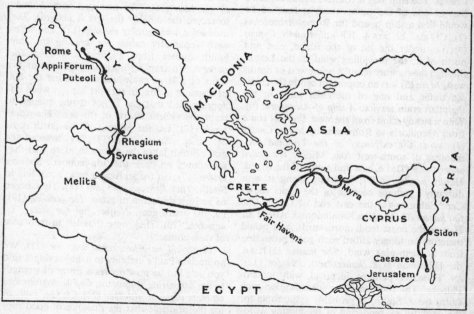

PAUL'S JOURNEY TO ROME

remains an indispensable handbook to the study of this chapter.) We need not allegorize it as a picture of the rise and progress of religion in the soul or of the history of the Christian Church in order to derive spiritual profit from it.

It is, above all, valuable to us for its portrayal of the character of Paul in circumstances in which the real man is most likely to be revealed. We have seen him in many rôles, but here we see him as the practical man in an emergency. Not once or twice the world has had to thank the great saints and mystics for providing that help in critical times which realistic, practical men of affairs were unable to give. When Lot had to be rescued from Chedorlaomer and his

was calling at the ports of the province of Asia. There they transhipped to a vessel of the Alexandrian corn fleet. Egypt was the great granary of Rome, and the fleet which served the corn trade between these two places was a State service. Sailing became dangerous in the Mediterranean after 14 September, and ceased altogether for the winter after 11 November; and before they reached Fair Havens, a harbour on the south of Crete, the day of atonement ('the fast' of verse 9) was already past; it fell on 5 October in A.D. 59. As it was thus getting late for safe sailing, a ship's council was called, at which Paul, as a distinguished passenger and experienced traveller, was apparently present. He urged them strongly to remain where they were, at Fair Havens, but the shipowner and the helmsman thought they might be able to make Phoenix, another and more commodious port farther west along the south coast of Crete. The centurion, who, as the principal officer on board, had the last word, naturally accepted the advice of the experts rather than Paul's, and so they set sail for Phoenix.

That we should sail into Italy (1). The 'we' narrative is resumed, and continues to xxviii. 16, but Luke was probably not far away from Paul during his two years' custody in Palestine. *Augustus' band* (1); 'The Emperor's Cohort'. We have evidence that a similarly named cohort (*Cohors I Augusta*) was in Syria in the time of Augustus, but here we have probably to do with the imperial corps of officer-couriers (*frumentarii*) detailed for communication service between the Emperor and his provincial armies. *A ship of Adramyttium* (2), a port in Mysia, opposite Lesbos. The ship was a coaster; Julius expected that at one of the ports which it touched he would find a ship bound for Rome. *Aristarchus* (2). Cf. xix. 29, xx. 4. *We sailed under Cyprus* (4); i.e. under the lee of the island, east and north of it, the prevailing wind in the Levant through the summer months being west or north-west. *Myra* (5) was an important centre for cross-sea traffic and one of the chief ports of the Egyptian grain service. *A ship of Alexandria* (6). With a steady wind from the west, the best route from Alexandria to Rome was by Myra. *Cnidus* (7) lay at the extremity of the Triopian promontory of south-west Asia Minor. *We sailed under Crete* (7); i.e. east and south of the island. *Hardly passing it* (8); 'coasting along it with difficulty', perhaps because of the rocks round Cape Salmone (at the east end of Crete). *The fair havens* (8). Modern Kalolimonias. After Fair Havens the coast tends northwards, and would therefore no longer afford such good protection from a north-west wind. *The master* (11); i.e. the helmsman (Gk. *kybernētēs*). *Phenice* (12); RV 'Phoenix', perhaps identical with modern Phineka. The more popular identification with Lutro (so J. Smith) is probably responsible for the doubtful RV rendering of the closing words of the verse: 'looking north-east and south-east'. RV mg. reads 'down the south-west wind and down the north-west wind'.

ii. Storm and shipwreck (xxvii. 13-44). Before they could make the port of Phoenix, however, a typhonic wind blew down upon them from Mount Ida, in Crete, from the north-east, and drove them away from the Cretan coast. With great difficulty they got the dinghy on board (in normal weather it was towed astern), and, having jettisoned part of the cargo, they contrived, by careful tacking, to avoid being driven on the quicksands off the Libyan shore. They continued for a fortnight in a west-north-west direction through the central Mediterranean, until all hope of safety was given up—by all except Paul, who stands out as the one man on board able to take charge of this hopeless situation and inspire his fellow-passengers with encouragement and fresh hope. The confidence which he had derived from an angelic visitant he sought to pass on to them, and encouraged them to take food.

Paul's confidence was justified; they found that they were approaching land, and although, by reason of the ship's prow being caught fast in a spit of sand and the stern being beaten by the waves, the vessel broke amidships, yet all on board escaped safe to shore, 276 in all.

There arose against it (14); better, 'there rushed down from it', i.e. from the island. *A tempestuous wind* (14); lit. 'a typhonic wind'. *Called Euroclydon* (14). Better, 'Euraquilo' (RV), a hybrid formation, from Gk. *Euros* ('east wind') and Lat. *Aquilo* ('north wind'). *We let her drive* (15); 'we scudded before it'. *Clauda* (16); RV 'Cauda', modern Gavdho, Ital. Gozzo, in the vicinity of which the Battle of Cape Matapan was fought on 28 March, 1941. *We had much work to come by the boat* (16). 'We managed with difficulty to secure the dinghy' (i.e. get it aboard). *They used helps, undergirding the ship* (17). The 'helps' were apparently cables for bracing the ship. Smith quotes from Falconer's *Marine Dictionary*: 'To frap a ship is to pass four or five turns of a large cable-laid rope round the hull or frame of a ship, to support her . . . when it is apprehended that she is not strong enough to resist the violent efforts of the sea.' *The quicksands* (17); i.e. the Syrtes, off the north coast of Africa. *Strake sail* (17); RV 'lowered the gear'. Smith takes the phrase to mean that they sent down on deck the 'top-hamper'. *So were driven* (17); on the starboard tack, according to Smith. *They lightened the ship* (18). They began to jettison the cargo of grain. *The tackling* (19); i.e. the spare gear. *Neither sun nor stars . . . appeared* (20). They were thus left in ignorance of their course.

Ye should have hearkened unto me (21). We appreciate Paul's inability to avoid saying 'I told you so'; but he now proves a tower of strength to his despairing shipmates. *God hath given thee all them that sail with thee* (24). Cf. Gn. xviii. 26 for the principle that the presence of good men is a protection to a community. *We were driven up and down in Adria* (27); better, 'while we were drifting through the sea of Adria', i.e. the central Mediterranean. (This is not the Adriatic Sea, which was then known as the 'Gulf of Adria'.) *They drew near to some country* (27); lit. 'some land was approaching'. Possibly they could hear the breakers. *And sounded . . .* (28). The soundings agree with the direction of a ship passing Koura on her way into St. Paul's Bay, Malta. *They cast four anchors out of the stern* (29); i.e. to act as a brake. Anchoring by the stern on this occasion meant that the prow was kept pointing to the shore. *Except these abide in the ship* (31). Paul's presence of mind appears again. Had the sailors made good their escape, there would not have been enough skilled hands to work the ship. *Cut off the ropes of the boat* (32); i.e. 'cut away the falls of the dinghy', possibly misunderstanding Paul's advice. They certainly prevented the sailors from getting away, but also made the business of getting ashore more difficult.

Ye have . . . continued fasting (33). Cf. verse 21, 'after long abstinence'. This would be due to a variety of reasons, such as the difficulty of cooking, spoiling of food by seawater, seasickness, etc. *Gave thanks* (35); Gk. *eucharisteō*. Some have conjectured that the Christians on board made this meal a Eucharist. *Two hundred threescore and sixteen souls* (37). The Vatican manuscript says 'seventy-six', but there is no improbability in the larger figure. In A.D. 63 Josephus sailed for Rome in a ship which had 600 on board (and it too was wrecked in the Sea of Adria). *They lightened the ship* (38); i.e. by jettisoning the rest of the grain cargo (cf. verse 18). *A certain creek with a shore* (39); lit. 'with a sandy beach'. *The rudder bands* (40); i.e. the lashings of the steering-paddles. *The mainsail* (40); rather 'the foresail' (Gk. *artemōn*), a small sail on the foremast. *A place where two seas met* (41). This was the narrow channel between Malta and Salmonetta (Smith). *Some on broken pieces of the ship* (44); or possibly, 'some on the backs of members of the crew' (lit. 'on some of those from the ship').

iii. **Winter in Malta (xxviii. 1–10).** When the shipwrecked party landed, they found that they had arrived at the island of Malta, an appropriate name, for it is a Phoenician word meaning 'refuge'. The natives received them hospitably, and lit a fire to warm and dry them. Paul again shows a practical turn of mind; he gathers sticks to keep the fire going, even though one of the sticks turned out to be a snake, torpid through the cold. When the heat of the fire thawed it, it fixed on Paul's hand, and there is quiet humour in Luke's description of the natives' reaction, first thinking he was a murderer whom Justice had resolved to destroy, if not by the sea, then by the snake, and then seeing no harm come to him after he shook the beast into the fire, changing their minds and concluding that he was a god.

But although he was not a god, yet both Paul and Luke proved very useful guests during the three winter months they spent in Malta. First Paul healed of dysentery the father of Publius, the chief man of the island. Then others were tended by Paul and Luke and, when at last they left, the islanders paid them many honours, which in this context may mean honoraria.

Then they knew that the island was called Melita (1). If the sailors did not recognize Malta at first, it may have been because they were accustomed to landing at Valletta. *The barbarous people* (2); i.e. 'the natives'. Greeks and Romans used the term 'barbarians' of all who did not share their civilization. *There came a viper out of the heat* (3). Cf. T. E. Lawrence, *Revolt in the Desert*, p. 107: 'When the fire grew hot a long

black snake wound slowly out into our group; we must have gathered it, torpid, with the twigs.' It has been suggested that the snake was a *Coronella austriaca*, which looks like a viper but is not poisonous. There are now no poisonous snakes in Malta. *Vengeance* (4); better, 'Justice' (Gk. *dikē*), personified as a deity. *They looked when he should have swollen* (6); better, 'they kept on expecting him to swell up'. *Said that he was a god* (6). M. Dibelius finds a different attitude in the narrative here from that shown in xiv. 14ff., where Paul and Barnabas cry out with horror at the ascription to them of divine honours. This overlooks the humour of the situation as Luke sees and describes it. *The chief man of the island* (7); lit. 'the first man (Gk. *prōtos*) of the island'. Both Greek and Latin inscriptions confirm the accuracy of this title in a Maltese context. *Came, and were healed* (9). 'The whole story of the abode of the narrator in Malta is displayed in a medical light' (Harnack). *Many honours* (10). Gk. *timē* may mean 'honorarium' here, as in 1 Tim. v. 17.

iv. **The last lap (xxviii. 11–16).** The voyage to Italy was completed early in A.D. 60 in another ship of the Alexandrian grain service, which had 'The Heavenly Twins' as its figure-head. They disembarked at Puteoli, where they were entertained for some days by Christians. Then they proceeded to Rome, and as they travelled along the *Via Appia*, they were met, while still forty miles away from the city, by a delegation of Roman Christians who had walked that distance to greet the apostle and escort him to the capital. There he was handed over to an official called the stratopedarch, probably the commander of that corps of imperial couriers in which Julius was a non-commissioned officer.

A ship of Alexandria (11). Probably it also belonged to the grain fleet. *Which had wintered in the isle* (11); probably in the harbour at Valletta. *Whose sign was Castor and Pollux* (11); Gk. *Dioskouroi*, 'The Heavenly Twins'. Ships, like inns, took their names from their figure-heads. *Syracuse* (12) was on the east coast of Sicily. It was the chief city of that island, with a double harbour. *We fetched a compass* (13); better, as in RV mg., 'we cast loose'. *Rhegium* (13). This was Reggio di Calabria, a Greek colony in the toe of Italy. *Puteoli* (13), Modern Pozzuoli, then the principal port of south Italy, and one of the two chief ports of arrival of the Alexandrian grain fleet (the other being Ostia). *Appii forum, and The three taverns* (15). Both these places were situated on the Appian Way; Appii Forum was a market town about 43 miles south of Rome, The Three Taverns (*Tres Tabernae*) was a station about 33 miles from Rome. *He thanked God, and took courage* (15). He might well be glad for this assurance that he was not friendless in the Eternal City. He had assured the Roman Christians three years previously of his desire to see them; now, in circumstances then unforeseen, he found his desire fulfilled. *The centurion delivered the prisoners to the captain of the guard* (16). This clause, which came into the Byzantine text from the 'western' text, is absent from other texts and therefore from RV. The 'captain of the guard' (Gk. *stratopedarchos*) might be the commander of the Emperor's praetorian guard (*praefectus praetorii*)—at this time Afranius Burrus—or, more probably, the commander of the corps of centurions detailed for imperial communication service (*princeps peregrinorum*), whose headquarters in Rome were on the Caelian Hill. *Paul was suffered to dwell by himself with a soldier that kept him* (16), to whom he would be lightly chained by the wrist.

v. Paul in Rome (xxviii. 17–31). Paul's interview with the Roman Jews sums up one of the themes of Acts, the general rejection of the gospel by the Jews. Paul, as usual, gets the last word, 'generally with devastating effect', says one commentator, and the last word on this occasion is that quotation from Is. vi. 9, 10 which our Lord similarly used in the days of His flesh (cf. Mk. iv. 12; Jn. xii. 40).

The other and chief theme of Acts is summed up in the closing words of the book, which depict Paul spending two years at the heart of the Empire, receiving all who visited him, proclaiming the kingdom of God and teaching the story of the Lord Jesus without let or hindrance. At last, by mysterious paths, his desire had had its fulfilment: 'I am ready to preach the gospel to you that are at Rome also' (Rom. i. 15). 'The victory of the Word of God,' says Bengel, 'Paul at Rome, the apex of the Gospel, the end of Acts. . . . It began at Jerusalem; it ends at Rome. Here, O Church, thou hast thy pattern; it is thine to preserve it and guard thy deposit.'

Not that I had ought to accuse my nation of (19). He confines himself strictly to the defensive; he will make no complaint against the Jewish people. *For the hope of Israel I am bound with this chain* (20). For his constant emphasis on this point cf. xxiii. 6, xxiv. 14, 15, xxvi. 6, 7. *We neither received letters . . .* (21). The Jerusalem authorities may have judged it hopeless to pursue their case against Paul in Rome, since they had such small success at home. In any case, the Roman Jews would be anxious to dissociate themselves as far as possible from the prosecution of a Roman citizen who had won favourable verdicts from Festus and Agrippa. *As concerning this sect, we know that every where it is spoken against* (22). They had probably had more experience of Christianity in Rome itself than they were prepared to admit at the moment (see xviii. 2n.). *They departed* (25); better, 'they began to break up'. *The salvation of God is sent unto the Gentiles . . . they will hear it* (28). This is a recurrent theme from first to last in the record of Paul's ministry in Acts (cf. xiii. 46). *And when he had said these words . . .* (29). This verse (absent from RV) is a 'western' reading which was taken over by the Byzantine text. *Two whole years* (30). They were the years A.D. 60 and 61, probably long enough for the case to go by default. Roman law was severe on frivolous prosecutions and his opponents in Palestine may have judged it safest to drop the matter. *In his own hired house* (30); better, 'on his own earnings', 'at his own expense'. *Preaching the kingdom of God, and teaching those things which concern the Lord Jesus Christ* (31). Cf. verse 23. 'In the conjunction of these words the progress of doctrine appears. All is founded upon the old Jewish expectation of a kingdom of God; but it is now explained how that expectation is fulfilled in the person of Jesus, and the account of its realization consists in the unfolding of the truth concerning Him. The manifestation of Christ being finished, the kingdom is already begun. Those who receive *Him* enter into *it*. Having overcome the sharpness of death, He has opened the kingdom of heaven to all believers' (T. D. Bernard).

F. F. BRUCE.

THE EPISTLE TO THE ROMANS

INTRODUCTION

See also the General Article, 'The Pauline Epistles', p. 68.

I. THE CHRISTIAN CHURCH AT ROME

a. Its origin

The fellowship of saints in Rome is expressly stated by Paul not to be of his own founding (i. 10–15, xv. 20–22). It is the exception to the apostle's rule not to build on another man's foundation (2 Cor. x. 16). Churches established by his co-workers Paul reckons as his own. By whom, how and when the church at Rome came into being forms one of the problems of early ecclesiastical history. The tradition that Peter was the founder is not accepted, but the denial does not exclude the fact that this leading apostle was certainly at some time or other in Rome and there suffered martyrdom. But when Paul wrote his letter to the Roman church it is evident that Peter was not in the city. Had this alleged head of the Church been in Rome surely Paul would have mentioned the fact, or indeed never address- ed an Epistle to this church at all. It is believed that the church at Rome must have originated in the witness and labours of Christians who were Empire citizens in the habit of travelling to and from the metropolis. It is not unlikely that the work of evangelization was commenced by the 'sojourners of Rome, both Jews and pros- elytes' (Acts ii. 10). These witnesses of Pentecost would in after days be assisted by Christians from Syrian Antioch, Ephesus and Corinth and thus augment the fellowship. By the time Paul wrote his letter to the church at Rome the Christian community would be of a goodly size.

b. Its character

The church at Rome was evidently composed of both Jews and Gentiles. As Paul does not address any special ecclesiastical dignitary or any persons with recognized authority, it is deduced that there was no central organization. The church is believed to have included at least four different congregations, viz. in the home of Aquila and Priscilla on the Aventine; in the Imperial Palace; in the house of Hermes; and in the home of Philologus (see xvi. 3–15. See also Dr. A. C. Mackinnon, *The Rome of St. Paul*, pp. 73ff.).

If Palestinian Christian Jews founded the fellowship they would evangelize first among their own countrymen, who formed a colony in Rome and had many synagogues. The apostle throughout the Epistle implies Jewish readers by addressing them particularly and by many allusions to the Old Testament (there are about sixty direct quotations) and to the history of the children of Israel.

Again Paul certainly has in mind Gentile readers who would form the majority of the Christian community. He addresses such in the opening chapter (i. 1–15). Cf. also xv. 14–16 and xi. 13, where there is the unambiguous statement 'I speak to you Gentiles, inasmuch as I am the apostle of the Gentiles'. It is also significant that the greater number of the names cited in chapter xvi are of Greek or Roman origin. Thus the Roman Christian church was composed of both Jewish and Gentile members, the latter being the more numerous and possibly to a great extent accepting Christianity by way of previous con- version to Judaism. Hence Paul was justified in quoting from the Old Testament and engaging in the problem of the Jewish race.

II. THE PLACE AND DATE OF WRITING

There is no dubiety about the geographical origin of this Epistle. Paul in his third missionary journey awaited the delegates from the Gentile churches, who bore the offerings for the relief of the destitute Jewish Christians in Jerusalem, at Corinth (see Acts xx. 2, 3n.). We read of this collection in 1 Cor. xvi. 1–4 and 2 Cor. viii, and of the apostle's last visit to Jerusalem in Acts xxiv. 17, after all the delegates had arrived at Corinth. Some of the names given in the last chapter of the Epistle, such as Phebe, the deaconess of Cenchrea, the port of Corinth, 'Gaius mine host' (cf. 1 Cor. i. 14), 'Timotheus my workfellow' (cf. 2 Cor. i. 1), 'Erastus the chamberlain of the city' (cf. 2 Tim. iv. 20), have a very definite association with Corinth. Such a careful and well- reasoned Epistle as Romans could have been penned only when Paul was able to stay in a comparatively fixed abode for some period of time. He remained at Corinth for three months, according to the testimony of the historian Luke (Acts xx. 3), which fulfils the necessary conditions for writing.

An indication of the time of composition is given in chapter xv, where the apostle reveals that he is about to sail to Palestine, bringing with him the 'collection for the poor', and that then he hopes to be free to visit Rome, and after- wards Spain. This points to the close of the third missionary journey and the last visit to Jerusalem. It was on the eve of his departure to Jerusalem that Paul finished his letter and addressed it to Rome. Regarding the exact chronology of Paul's life and work no authority can be dogmatic, but the limits of the last visit to Jerusalem are carefully fixed as from A.D. 56 to 59, the earliest and the latest possible dates.

III. THE OCCASION OF WRITING

Why did Paul write to the church at Rome, especially as neither he nor any of his fellow-workers had founded it, nor had he ever previously visited it? The answer to this question involves the question of the form of the Epistle. Is it a theological treatise or simply a letter occasioned by circumstances in the career of Paul? It may be both in some degree, but the point is whether the apostle originally sat down to expound the gospel he preached or took up his pen to write a letter which imminent affairs dictated. The view has been held that Paul felt that his days were numbered and he wished to leave to posterity a definite and final statement of his teaching. That the apostle's doctrine in his day was misunderstood and assailed, that it never lacked critics (especially from the ranks of Judaism), and that it had never had a systematic presentation, may be conceded. The suggestion is, therefore, that Romans was the last will and testament of the great apostle to the Gentiles. Moreover, it is argued that the Roman church was just the right repository for this authoritative document. The logical and theological form of the Epistle, which is the most systematic and closely reasoned, the most doctrinal of all Paul's letters, affords no little ground for the formal theory. But that Romans is a theological treatise is going too far. Note the following arguments against this hypothesis of a studied manifesto of Pauline theology.

There is every indication in the Epistle that Paul was addressing a live Christian community out of circumstances which gave reality to his letter.

There is no real justification for suggesting that the apostle felt that 'the sands of time were sinking' and his career about to close so that he must leave his theological system to posterity. Rather, at the time at which he wrote, Paul's eyes were looking to the future of a new missionary enterprise.

Does Romans, in any case, set forth the complete teaching of the apostle? Is there not more of the Pauline theology in his other Epistles which the occasion of writing to the Romans did not immediately educe?

Paul's purpose in writing is definitely stated in the letter and he has no reason to conceal any theological ambition. He writes to intimate his true intention to visit the Roman Christians (see i. 10–13) in order to impart to them as an apostle of Jesus Christ 'some spiritual gift' (cf. xv. 29). He makes the best of all his available contacts as chapter xvi reveals. Paul also plainly declares that his coming to Rome falls within a

larger plan (see xv. 15–24). He has completed as far as lies within his power the evangelization of the Gentiles eastward; now he sets his face to a new missionary enterprise westward. He writes to engage their co-operation in this scheme since Rome is a real strategic centre and the Roman fellowship an influential group in that direction. All the doctrinal part of the Epistle was penned for this very purpose, that the Roman church might apprehend the greatness of divine grace and the wideness of God's mercy, so amazing and so all-embracing that evangelization on his part (and on theirs also) was absolutely imperative.

IV. THE TEXTUAL PROBLEM

The question here is whether the letter is a complete whole and composed all at the same time by the apostle, or whether any other author has had his writing incorporated at an earlier or later date. The problem arises from four points:

A short form of Romans was in circulation during the second and third centuries. Textual evidence shows that we have MSS ending with chapter xiv.

The Epistle as we now read it has various endings. 'Now the God of peace be with you all. Amen' (xv. 33). 'The grace of our Lord Jesus Christ be with you all. Amen' (xvi. 24). 'To God only wise, be glory through Jesus Christ for ever. Amen' (xvi. 27).

In the shorter recension the doxology which appears in our English versions at xvi. 25–27 is found at the close of chapter xiv. Some MSS insert it at the close of both chapter xiv and chapter xvi. Intrinsically also its genuineness has been doubted by some as not being in Paul's usual style.

The personal greetings of chapter xvi are alleged to be inappropriate to the circumstances since Paul was a comparative stranger to the Roman church. They suit rather the church at Ephesus.

In the face of these objections the integrity of the Epistle is still maintained. The solution of the textual problem is probably found in the belief that the heretic Marcion (who flourished at Rome A.D. 154–166) deliberately expunged the last two chapters because chapter xv gave Judaism a preparatory function in the furtherance of the gospel. See, e.g., verse 4: 'For whatsoever things were written aforetime were written for our learning, that we through patience and comfort of the scriptures might have hope.' Moreover, chapter xv has at least five quotations from the Old Testament, while chapter xvi was of no importance to Marcion's views, being neither for them nor against. The longer version, according as we now read it, is accepted as the original version, since the shorter version ending at chapter xiv manifests a bias against the Old Testament. As for chapter xvi with its list of names, there appears a certain fitness in their mention considering that Paul's purpose was to create as many contacts as possible, while Rome was as suitable for the home of Paul's friends as Ephesus, even apart from the hypothesis of Ephesus as the origin of many of the Pauline Epistles. The view here accepted is that we have in Romans a complete letter written at one time by the apostle from Corinth and handed down to us in all its integrity. All theories of textual disintegration fall to the ground in face of the unity of the message.

OUTLINE OF CONTENTS

I. THE PROLOGUE. i. 1–17
a. The address (i. 1–7)
b. Thanksgiving and prayer (i. 8–12)
c. Personal explanations (i. 13–17)

II. THE PRINCIPLES OF THE GOSPEL. i. 18—v. 21
a. Gentile 'righteousness' (i. 18–32)
b. Jewish 'righteousness' (ii. 1—iii. 20)
c. Divine righteousness (iii. 21–31)
d. Abrahamic righteousness (iv. 1–25)
e. Believer's righteousness (v. 1–21)

III. ETHICAL PROBLEMS RAISED BY THE GOSPEL. vi. 1–23
a. The charge of licence (vi. 1–14)
b. The charge of lawlessness (vi. 15–23)

IV. THE CHRISTIAN AND THE LAW. vii. 1—viii. 39
a. Law is valid only in lifetime (vii. 1–6)
b. Law and sin are not synonymous (vii. 7–25)
c. Law is vanquished by grace (viii. 1–39)

V. THE PROBLEM OF JEWISH RIGHTS AND PRIVILEGE. ix. 1—xi. 36
a. The absolute sovereignty of God (ix. 1–29)
b. Jewish responsibility in the historical situation (ix. 30—x. 21)
c. The merciful purpose of God (xi. 1–36)

VI. CHRISTIANITY IN PRACTICE. xii. 1—xv. 13
a. Introduction (xii. 1, 2)
b. Personal ethics (xii. 3–21)
c. Political ethics (xiii. 1–7)
d. Personal ethics (xiii. 8–14)
e. The strong and the weak (xiv. 1—xv. 13)

VII. EPILOGUE. xv. 14—xvi. 27
a. Paul's justification for writing (xv. 14–21)
b. Plans for future journeys (xv. 22–33)
c. Greetings to friends in Rome (xvi. 1–16)
d. A final admonition (xvi. 17–20)
e. Greetings from Corinthian brethren (xvi. 21–23)
f. A concluding doxology (xvi. 25–27)

COMMENTARY

I. THE PROLOGUE. i. 1–17

a. The address (i. 1–7)

The salutation is briefly 'Paul to all the called in Rome'. The form is similar to that adopted in all the Pauline letters as it was the regular epistolary style of the first century. We have many examples of such letter-writing in the Greek, and all follow the same pattern, first the writer's name, then the reader's, followed by the greeting. This formula is varied in the Pauline literature according to circumstances. Here, as addressing a church which he has neither founded nor hitherto visited, Paul presents his credentials. He is *a servant of Jesus Christ* (1; lit. 'a slave'), one whose very life is that of unwavering loyalty and undisputed obedience, the chattel, the property of Jesus Christ. The apostle belonged to the class whose ears were bored and whose liberty was in their slavery. Among the various Greek words in the New Testament translated 'servant' this word *doulos* is the strongest and most frequent. It is interesting to remember that the rank of the slave depended upon his master. *Called to be an apostle* (1); lit. 'one sent', 'a messenger' and so rendered in 2 Cor. viii. 23; Phil. ii. 25. This is a divine selection, an imperative summons to function which may not be disobeyed. In the biblical biography this call normally follows the call to repentance and surrender in faith and the call to follow the Lord in manner of life. The special calling here is apostleship. Paul consistently maintained his direct call to this high office (cf. 'not of men, neither by man', Gal. i. 1). The dignity was normally mediated through the living Church. The title belonged primarily to the Twelve whose distinction was that they were with Jesus in the days of His flesh. Later it was given to other church leaders and preachers (cf. Acts. xiv. 14). *Separated unto the gospel of God* (1). Thus Paul further introduces himself. He is consecrated or 'set apart' to the service of the gospel. Dedication is the human response to the act of selection, and these ideas must be distinguished. The separation is all of God. He consecrates His servants who in turn dedicate themselves to Him.

We now have an example of Paul's habit of 'going off at a tangent'. In most of his salutations and elsewhere he expands his thought as ideas chase after each other in swift succession. Here the word 'apostle' leads to the 'gospel' which, in its turn, leads him into a passage of great Christological value. The style is both telegraphic and telescopic. He proceeds to define the gospel of God as divine (1), predicted (2), and Christo-centric (3–5).

The gospel is not man-made; it is from above. This is the emphasis of the preposition in the phrase *of God* (1); Paul has in mind here its origin. Before proceeding to describe what the gospel is about, the apostle affirms the continuity of his message with the revelation given previously to the Jewish people. It is in line with all the promises of the prophets of old; it is rooted *in the holy scriptures* (2); i.e. the Old Testament.

The main feature of the gospel is that Jesus Christ is its all in all. Accordingly Paul is captured by his apprehension of the Lord who first apprehended him in risen power. In this Christological passage (verses 3–5) Paul stresses first the incarnation, since that must be the starting-point of the gospel message. But His coming *according to the flesh* (3) was a fulfilment of messianic prophecy and so his statement in verse 2 is justified. Secondly, *according to the spirit of holiness* (4), i.e. in respect of His moral perfection, He has been manifested to be from all eternity the Son of God through the miracle of the resurrection. The AV *declared* (4) has behind

it the Greek 'determined' or 'appointed', suggesting the predestinated career of the pre-existent Christ in His redemption of the world.

This great gospel, divine, predicted and Christocentric, becomes the rule for Christians as such. The unity of writer and readers is *Jesus Christ our Lord* (3). Note Paul's use of the personal, the official and the universal names of God's Son who is Saviour, Messiah and King. Through Him the Romans receive *grace*, and Paul, in addition, *apostleship* (5). Grace, which is the favour of God to undeserving sinners, is the new relationship to God in which believers stand. The end of the Pauline endowment of apostleship is the *obedience to the faith* (5), or trusting submission, of all the Gentiles to the Saviour of the world. Paul is the apostle of the Gentiles and hence interested in the Romans both as potential and actual sharers of divine grace. Thus he infers his claim to address them. *To all that be in Rome, beloved of God, called to be saints* (7). There is evidently a Christian fellowship in the metropolis, one dear to God's heart whose destiny is newness of life unto moral perfection. The address proper concludes with a benediction which is the combination of Greek and Hebrew ideas, *grace* and *peace*.

b. Thanksgiving and prayer (i. 8–12)

The apostle expresses his gratification concerning the Roman Christians, every one of them, because their faith is not hid in a secret corner but is public property. They have been faith's heralds to such an extent that God, whom he so worships in his spirit by preaching His Son, is witness to his continual mention of them in his prayers. The burden of his petitions is that God would speed him in due course to a meeting with them, if it be His will, the reason underlying the request being twofold. He wishes to establish them by imparting to them a spiritual gift, and also to share with them the comfort of mutual faith, theirs and his.

c. Personal explanations (i. 13–17)

The Roman Christians must know that, though so far prevented from doing so, Paul had often proposed to visit them in order to see the same spiritual work done among them as had already been done among other Gentiles. He feels his debt to civilized as well as to uncivilized, to wise as well as to fools. His commission is to preach the gospel to all men and, so far as his personal eagerness is concerned, he feels that he owes Rome a debt of evangelization, for he is proud (note the meiosis, *not ashamed*) of preaching the gospel, which is able to save everyone who believes, Jew or Greek, though the Jew has the first claim and interest (16). In the gospel God's justification (see introductory note to section II) is disclosed from faith to faith—believers make believers! This too had been revealed to the prophets (cf. verse 2) as is shown by Habakkuk's words *The just* (i.e. the justified) *shall live by faith* (17; cf. Hab. ii. 4).

II. THE PRINCIPLES OF THE GOSPEL.
i. 18—v. 21

The apostle has now glided into the doctrinal part of his letter and has embarked upon a discussion of the principles of his gospel. The subject of the treatise was stated in verse 17 as *the* (RV 'a') *righteousness of God revealed from faith to faith.* This great theme is the very heart of the Epistle, even as it was of the gospel which Paul preached. Simply expressed, it is 'justification by faith alone'. The apostle's personal problem, not primarily of his mind but of his practice, was the question, 'How can I be right with God?' Before the arresting experience of the Damascus road Paul had essayed to solve the problem in the Jewish way, by doing right, i.e. by establishing right relations with God by fulfilling the law of God. The method had proved hopeless. No mortal man has ever been sinless, much less positively holy, keeping all the commandments of God. All Paul's theology was experiential, and he discovered that by the way of faith in the finished work of Christ he was set right with God. He was not rectified or put right by himself; he did not get right with God, but was put right by 'a righteousness of God'. This is the meaning of justification. The apostle's terms for 'just', 'justification' and 'righteousness' (*dikaios, dikaiōsis* and *dikaiosynē*) all come from the same root. Justification by faith, therefore, means righteousness by believing, the entrance into a proper relationship with God through faith in the revealed gospel of Jesus Christ.

It is for this blessed reason in his own experience that Paul is not ashamed of the gospel of God. Some Jews at Rome might stumble at it and some Gentiles consider it foolishness (1 Cor. i. 23); but to the apostle this selfsame gospel is real dynamite (*power*), a spiritual force, a manifest activity of God in his own life, bringing salvation in its most comprehensive sense to body, mind and soul, both here and hereafter. This divine activity within human experience, this entrance into and maintenance of a right relationship with God, is the gist of the apostle's whole message. As the theme of the righteousness of God is developed it involves, in the course of the letter, the doctrines of justification, sanctification and predestination, which emerge from Paul's exposition and defence of it.

a. Gentile 'righteousness' (i. 18–32)

The 'righteousness' of the human race is in fact unrighteousness. The absolute moral ideal is the righteousness of God which can come only from God and be revealed, or made known, only through the gospel of Jesus Christ. Paul accordingly draws a vivid picture of the unrighteousness of the Gentile world, describing both heathen religion (*ungodliness*) and heathen morality (*unrighteousness*). Upon both *the wrath of God is revealed* (18) equally as His righteousness is revealed (see verse 17). The idea of judgment is frequent in the Old Testament as an integral part of the righteousness of God in dealing uprightly with His own people and with the Gentile world. Paul's Jewish readers, at least, would be well aware of the implications of this term 'the wrath of God'.

i. Heathen religion (i. 18–25).
The pagan world of Paul's day worshipped idols after the likeness of both men (Athens) and beasts (Egypt). This polytheism was the religious outcome of rationalism. The Gentiles became *vain in their imaginations* (21); i.e. futile in their philosophies. The Gk. *dialogismos* is usually rendered 'thought' or 'reasoning' and once in this Epistle 'disputation' (xiv. 1). Only here have we in the AV the translation 'imagination'. (Cf. Mt. xv. 19; Mk. vii. 21; Lk. ii. 35, v. 22, vi. 8, ix. 46, 47, xxiv. 38; 1 Cor. iii. 20; Phil. ii. 14; 1 Tim. ii. 8; Jas. ii. 4.) 'Reasoning' approaches nearest to the idea of the root verb which means 'to consider or balance accounts', or simply 'to reason'. This vainglorious theorizing led to idolatry, for their obscuring or holding down the truth (18; see RV) caused them to drift away from God and to devise ignoble substitutes for Him (23). They should know better! They ought to know what is knowable; God has revealed it to them Himself. His hidden hand is discernible right from the beginning. God has always had a witness both in nature and in conscience. There is no excuse for their ignorance. Paradoxical as it is to talk about seeing what cannot be seen, the invisible things of God, *even his eternal power and Godhead,* 'God in action and in essence', have never been concealed from man (20). Thus Paul condemns the Gentile philosophies as estranging men from God, who is the truth, and as issuing in the foolish worship of idols. In verse 25 note the RV reading 'exchanged the truth of God for a lie' and see 2 Thes. ii. 11n.

ii. Heathen morality (i. 26–32).
An impure religion results in an impure life. This ghastly picture of heathenism is corroborated by the writers of Paul's day. It was an age of unabashed vice and anti-social sin, a period of unspeakable moral decadence. The inevitable judgment of God fell upon those who preferred human reason to divine revelation. The apostle three times asserts the divine abandonment, *God gave them up* (24, 26, 28). It has been observed that this desertion is definitely punitive, not merely permissive in the sense that God allowed the heathen idolators to give Him up, nor just privative in that He quietly withdrew His grace. It is a positive punishment for culpable ignorance and wilful sinfulness.

The divine judgment was an inevitable sequence, a harvest of the seed sown (27). The heathen world was given over to lust in the unnatural use of their bodies in sexual perversions (26, 27) and finally to *a reprobate mind* (28). Observe the play upon the words here. Even as the heathen *did not like* (*edokimasan*) *to retain God in their knowledge, God gave them over to a reprobate mind* (*adokimon noun*); i.e. just as these foolish and filthy idolaters disapproved of God so God abandoned them to a disapproved conscience. The Greek term *adokimos* originally refers to the testing of metals; those which do not stand the test are therefore 'disapproved'. The adjective is rendered by three English words: 'rejected' (Heb. vi. 8), 'castaway' (1 Cor. ix. 27) and 'reprobate' (Rom. i. 28; 2 Cor. xiii. 5, 6, 7; 2 Tim. iii. 8; Tit. i. 16). Verse 32 indicates that the sins which are condemned are not the result of sudden yielding to temptation, but are indulged in deliberately and are encouraged in others.

b. Jewish 'righteousness' (ii. 1—iii. 20)

Like the 'righteousness' of the heathen world, the 'righteousness' of the Jews is also a miserable unreality and failure. With greater privileges than the Gentile, the Jew nevertheless has not attained to justification. Before entering upon his indictment of Israel, the apostle declares two preliminary principles—the impartial judgment of God (ii. 1–11) and the universality of moral obligation (ii. 12–16).

i. The impartial judgment of God (ii. 1–11).
Verse 11 sums up the first principle upon which Paul bases his charge against his own people. When the Jews play the critic of righteousness, as they are always doing, they condemn themselves, for these judges do the same things themselves. It is a postulate with Paul that all the Jews agree to the undisputed righteousness of God in judgment (see verse 2). Hence the divine verdict is according to the moral reality (*truth*) of the case, quite apart from privilege or profession. The apostle abolishes the false assumption that the Jewish people are exempt from universal judgment on the ground of integrity or because they are less sinful than the pagan world. Even the fact of national privilege does not exempt them from judgment (cf. Mt. iii. 9; Jn. viii. 33; Gal. ii. 15). If this has not yet fallen upon the Jewish practitioners of the selfsame sins as the heathen it is only because of the divine *forbearance* (4). God's seeming indifference to sin is due wholly to His *longsuffering*, the aim of which is to induce repentance. The wealth of grace—*the riches of his goodness*—and the wealth of wrath—*treasurest up unto thyself* (5)—are set in solemn contrast. Every man will be judged according to his deeds, Jew and Gentile alike. Hard impenitence is an investment in divine wrath at compound interest to be realized on *the day of wrath* (5). Cf. Is. xiii. 6; Ezk. xxx. 3; Zp. i. 7; see also New Testament references to 'the day of the Lord' (e.g., Acts ii. 20; 1 Cor. i. 8; 2 Cor. i. 14; 1 Thes. v. 2). On that day the divine righteousness in judgment will be manifest as strictly just, recompensing every man according to his works. If these are the fruit of patient well-doing in search of glory, honour and incorruption, the result is eternal life (7). But factiousness (see RV), disobedience to the truth and obedience to unrighteousness culminate in wrath and passion, in trouble and anguish, for every soul of man that works evil, particularly for the Jew (who

should know better), but also for the Greek (8, 9). Thus the impartiality of the divine judgment is demonstrated. None is exempt.

ii. The universality of moral obligation (ii. 12–16).
All are accountable unto God for judgment whether, like the Jews, they possess the Mosaic law or, like the Gentiles, the 'natural' law written on the conscience of men who are all made after the divine image. All have a valid standard for trial, for it is not he who possesses law that is reckoned righteous but he who practises it. The Jews may not pride themselves in their Torah, for it does not matter whether one has or has not a law. Our actions are the criterion of judgment. Every man has a *conscience* (15; Gk. *syneidēsis*), a moral consciousness, a co-knowledge between the act and its ethical value, or between man and God as ultimate truth or reality. (Paul uses the term in this Epistle also in ix. 1 and xiii. 5, and several times in his other letters.) If he attends to this conscience it will infallibly accuse or acquit him, particularly when on the day of God all secrets shall be read and judged by Jesus Christ (16). Paul's gospel is here again affirmed to be Christocentric, which is indeed its chief characteristic.

iii. The indictment against the Jews (ii. 17–29).
Having thus prepared the way by affirming both impartiality and universality in divine judgment, the apostle proceeds to his specific charge against the self-assumed righteousness of the Jews. They, equally with the Gentiles, have not lived up to their light, and their light was greater than that of the Gentiles. In fact the Jewish gift of divine revelation was reckoned to mean privileged practice as well as privileged possession. Paul refers to two things in which the Jews prided themselves, the law (verses 17–24) and circumcision (verses 25–29), although they neither obeyed the law nor were really circumcised in heart.

Thou art called a Jew (17); rather, as in RV, 'bearest the name of a Jew', or 'callest thyself a Jew'. The emphasis is upon their nationality. The name 'Hebrew' implies origin and language; 'Israelite' recalls their relation to God and religion; 'Jew' speaks of the race in distinction from the Gentiles. The enumeration which follows of advantages included in the gift of the law is somewhat satirical, for the apostle implies that the Jew has perverted his privileges. *Restest in the law* (17). Paul's word *epanapausis* suggests complacency. The Jew was the chosen of God, and the gift of the Torah was a proof of the fact. Hence possession was considered to be enough without worrying about practice. *Makest thy boast of God* (17); Moff. 'priding yourself in God'. He is charged with a wrong idea of his relationship with God. True, he might glory in God (cf. Je. ix. 24) but not arrogantly. The Jew behaved with a conscious superiority over other races which were regarded as 'lesser breeds without the law'. He claimed to be so intimate with God through his possession of the law that he knew the divine will. *Approvest the things that are more excellent* (18); lit., as in AV mg., 'triest the things that differ'. The meaning is that the Jew claims to be able to discern right and wrong and the shades of moral value between lesser and greater good (cf. Phil. i. 10). Because of all these advantages of the law the Jew prided himself upon his ability to guide, teach and judge others. *A guide of the blind* (19; cf. Mt. xv. 14, xxiii. 16) was probably a proverbial phrase. *An instructor of the foolish* (20); i.e. the infants in religious knowledge such as the Gentiles appeared to the Jews. Such proud claims all rested upon the possession of *the form of knowledge and of the truth in the law* (20). Did Paul mean that the Jew really had the secret of the Lord, the fount of all knowledge and truth, for the term *form* (Gk. *morphōsis*) implies the outline, delineation, 'the full embodiment', of the essential form (Gk. *morphē;* cf. Phil. ii. 6, 7)? Or did he imply here, as the context would suggest, that the Jew had only the semblance of the true *morphē* through his own failure to fulfil it? The apostle uses the term *morphōsis* only in this passage and in 2 Tim. iii. 5 where it is put in contrast to *dynamis*, 'power'. Certainly the gift of revelation was real; but the point is that the Jew, by his obedience, could have had a fuller insight into it, and, in spite of his boast, was in fact but a poor guide, light, corrector and teacher of the heathen.

Arising from this there follows in verses 21–24 a fearless exposure of the unrighteousness of the Jews. 'Well, Mr. Teacher-of-others, do you teach yourself? You preach against stealing, are you a thief yourself?' etc. *Dost thou commit sacrilege?* (22); RV 'Dost thou rob temples?' This was evidently a crime for which the Jew was sometimes blamed (cf. Acts xix. 37). 'The man who abominates idols should not rob heathen shrines and so make an idol of covetousness' (Ward). In verse 24 Paul quotes freely from Is. lii. 5 (LXX). Jewish inconsistency of profession and practice and their boasting of God's favour while showing an utter disregard for His standard of morality must cause God's name to be dishonoured among the heathen. *Circumcision verily profiteth* (25). Paul admits the advantages of this peculiar and distinguishing rite in which the Jew also boasted and for which he was despised by the Gentiles. Circumcision has its points, but only if the law is kept. If that is transgressed, then circumcision becomes uncircumcision. Similarly, if the uncircumcised man keeps the requirements of the law, surely his uncircumcision should be accounted to him for circumcision? The man who is by nature uncircumcised (as was the non-Jew), and fulfils the law, shall judge the Jewish transgressor of the law. Paul bluntly declares that the upright Gentile in his uncircumcised state is as good as the disobedient, though circumcised, Jew. *Letter* (27, 29); Gk. *gramma*. In the first case the reference may be to the letter of circumcision, the literal commandment; but it probably means the letter of the law which is definitely the meaning in verse 29, thus emphasizing the outwardness of the law. Paul has in mind here 'the written word as an external authority in contrast with the direct influence of the Spirit as manifested in the new covenant' (G. Abbott-Smith, *Greek Lexicon*). Paul employs the same contrast in vii. 6 and 2 Cor. iii. 6; cf. Acts vii. 51. The idea of a *heart* circumcision (29) belongs also to the Old Testament (cf. Dt. x. 16; Je. iv. 4, ix. 26; Ezk. xliv. 7). Hence, *he is not a Jew, which is one outwardly* (28). Thus Paul clearly demolishes the alleged righteousness of the Jew.

iv. Jewish objections answered (iii. 1–20). Such reduction of Jewish righteousness to unrighteousness could not pass unchallenged. The criticism of the apostle's condemnation (verses 1–8) may come from his opponents, or perhaps arose in Paul's own mind, as he reasoned out his grave charge against his race. In this Epistle especially Paul introduced a fancied objector to whose casuistical arguments he gives a reply (cf. iv. 1ff., vi. 1ff., vii. 7ff.). The unseen heckler's objections are four.

1. If the Jews are equally condemned with the Gentiles and are as grievous sinners, what is the good of their privileges, what profit is there in circumcision? Paul replies that in spite of the fact that the Jews abuse their favours, nevertheless such remain for their proper acceptance and world-wide witness. Here he refers only to the highest of all their blessings (he lists others in ix. 4, 5); they are entrusted by God to be 'the repository of revelation'. The term *logia* (*oracles;* cf. Acts vii. 38; Heb. v. 12; 1 Pet. iv. 11) refers particularly to the utterances of God on Mount Sinai and His promises of a coming Messiah.

2. If the Jews are not right with God what of all God's oracles and promises to them? Is not God going back upon His word? Paul repudiates the argument. The faithlessness of *some* (3; Paul is charitable in saying 'some') does not impugn the faithfulness of God. It is obvious that if a covenant is broken by the unfaithfulness of one party, the honour of the other is unimpaired. *As it is written* (4). The quotation is from Ps. li. 4 (LXX). While human faithlessness prevails, nevertheless the divine character is vindicated in all God's pronouncements about sin.

3. One objection grows out of the other. The heckler continues questioning the justice of God in punishing sinners. If the unrighteousness of the Jews 'is only a foil to set off the righteousness of God', and if the failure of the Jewish nation serves only to accentuate by contrast the uprightness of God, can God honourably condemn such serviceable sinners? Paul dismisses the idea as preposterous and declares it to be virtually a denial of God's prerogative to bring the world to any sort of judgment. If our wrongdoing commends God's righteousness are we to say that God is unjust in applying wrath to us? *Who taketh vengeance?* (*I speak as a man*) (5); i.e. 'Pardon my very human expression; it is perhaps too bold an anthropomorphism'.

4. If my sinfulness, persists the objector, serves to glorify the holiness of God, this fact not only strikes at the root of the divine title to judge me, but condones my sin. Note how, in Paul's presentation of the objection, the *truth of God* is contrasted with the *lie* of the Jews (7); i.e. the divine fidelity to all promises and revelation is set over against Israel's unbelieving faithlessness and practical falsehood. Why am I still adjudged a sinner? the objector argues. The logical conclusion surely is *Let us do evil, that good may come.* Paul reveals here that some had slandered him in declaring this immoral maxim to be part of his doctrine. These traducers are dismissed in a word: their doom is righteous (8).

These four questions are not handled by the apostle at any length here, but they crop up again later. Objections **1**, **2** and **3** are treated in chapter ix, while objection **4** is dealt with in chapter vi.

In the remainder of this section (verses 9–20) Paul continues his exposure of Jewish unrighteousness. He points out that it is condemned by Scripture as sternly as the Gentile unrighteousness. Both Jews and Gentiles are sinners. The apostle appeals to the absolute authority of the Word of God, universally admitted by the Jews, and gives a mosaic of Scripture verses in proof. With two exceptions these are all taken from the Psalms and are quoted from the LXX. These passages of Scripture represent the law, and they all apply to the Jew in his unrighteousness. The conclusion of this section is stated in verse 20. The failure of the Jew to find justification was due to his adopting the wrong method; indeed no one living can hope to get right with God in this way, for *by the deeds of the law there shall no flesh be justified.* Verily, the law brings hopelessness, for it creates a conscience of sin, a realization of what it means to God and man, to the Judge and the judged.

c. Divine righteousness (iii. 21–31)

Paul now proceeds to describe *the righteousness of God* (21; cf. i. 17), the method by which he himself became right with God. Note the following characteristics.

It is apart from the law (21). The law reveals what duty God requires of man (whether it be contained in the law, the prophets and the writings, or more specifically in the law or Pentateuch) and demands moral effort or works for man's justification. The righteousness of God comes without the law's fulfilment.

Secondly, it is attested by the law (21). The previous mosaic of Scripture passages (iii. 10–18) was taken chiefly from the writings, the third section of the complete Torah: now the apostle makes the testimony of the law complete by referring to *the law and the prophets* (21). The new way of being right with God is really not new at all, but was actually foretold in rites, types and predictions throughout the Old Testament.

In the third place God's righteousness is provided in Christ through faith (22–25). It is

for all who believe, *by faith of Jesus Christ* (22). The Greek has the genitive case here and is thus capable of being rendered either subjectively or objectively. The divine righteousness may be achieved by the faith of the Saviour even up to the cross, which strong faith was an integral element in the atoning value of His supreme sacrifice. Again, and in harmony with the New Testament usages, this faith is projected towards Jesus as object, and so becomes faith in the Redeemer. *All have sinned, and come short of the glory of God* (23). *Glory* (Gk. *doxa*) is the visible brightness and splendour which emanates from the perfect character of God. This is the Shekinah glory of the Old Testament (cf. ix. 4; Ex. xvi. 10, xxiv. 16f., xxix. 43, xxxiii. 18, 22, etc.) and in the New Testament is expressed in the incarnate life of Jesus, the Word or expression of the Father (see Jn. i. 14; 2 Cor. iii. 18, iv. 6). In respect of God's glory all men *come short*. The Greek *hysterein* means 'to fall behind', 'to be inferior', 'to suffer want' (cf. Mt. xix. 20; 1 Cor. viii. 8; 2 Cor. xi. 5; Phil. iv. 12). This universal deficiency is one view of sin. Both in reality and consciousness all are far removed from the blazing light of the divine perfection.

But in face of this universal sinfulness, justification is free or by grace (24). Christ is a propitiation propounded by God. Faith is the channel. Christ's blood is the price accepted, in the divine forbearance, in virtue of which man's sins to date are passed over. Paul expresses the ground of righteousness in two pregnant phrases: *through the redemption that is in Christ Jesus* (24) and *a propitiation through faith in his blood* (25). The Greek *apolytrōsis* means 'release effected by payment of a ransom', hence redemption, emancipation or deliverance. The word for propitiation, *hilastērion*, is the neuter of an adjective derived from the verb *hilaskomai*, which has three meanings: to placate, conciliate or appease someone; to be propitious or merciful; or to make propitiation for. The New Testament uses the two last renderings (see Lk. xviii. 13 and 1 Jn. ii. 2). The idea is not that of conciliation of an angry God by sinful humanity, but of expiation of sin by a merciful God through the atoning death of His Son. It does not necessarily exclude, however, the reality of righteous wrath because of sin. Christ is therefore a means of satisfaction for sin, this expiation being effected by the death of Jesus, *the blood* signifying the principle of life sacrificed (cf. Gn. ix. 4; Lv. xvii. 11; Dt. xii. 23). Hence the RV 'through faith by his blood' is preferred to the AV *in his blood*. Justification on such grounds has nothing to do with man's moral effort nor his spiritual merit. It is bestowed *freely by his grace* (24). In other words we are acquitted for nothing, without price, and out of the undeserved love of God towards sinners. Because of this new method of getting right with God, men's sins in the past were overlooked and in the present are delayed in punishment (25), all with perfect righteousness on God's part.

The fourth characteristic of God's righteousness is that it is divinely just (26–31). The apostle now expands his last phrase *to declare . . . his righteousness* (26). God is not only just, as always; He can also justify, or put into right relationship, those who have faith in Jesus, though apart from Christ they have no right to such justification. God is righteous; and because of His eternal and intrinsic righteousness (not in spite of it) reckons righteous the sinner who *believeth in Jesus* (26). On this basis of justification by faith alone the apostle challenges the boasting of the Jew. There is no room for it. *By what law?* (27); i.e. on what grounds is it excluded? Paul uses the term 'law' in a number of different ways. It stands for the Torah and for the Pentateuch; here it means an established principle. The rule *of works* (27) does not banish boasting, for many a Pharisee was full of self-glorification. But the rule of faith does absolutely exclude any such exultation. The definite conclusion of the whole matter is that a man is put right with God by faith quite apart from any fulfilment of the law (28). This principle of faith at once abolishes the wall of partition between Jew and Gentile; God is the God of both if they believe. And such belief is the *sine qua non* which only God can bestow. *By faith . . . through faith* (30). The expressions merely emphasize the contrast between circumcision and uncircumcision. There is no difference in the quality or in the method of faith. So, if there is one God, there is one people whose hallmark is faith. God looks past circumcision to faith in the Jew, and equally past uncircumcision to faith on the part of the Gentile. Both really display the same 'trade mark'. Moreover, Paul adds, in such faith the law is not side-stepped but established. God is not being soft or sentimental. His justice is satisfied.

d. Abrahamic righteousness (iv. 1–25)

Paul now takes Abraham as a test case, in which he shows the relation of the new system of justification to the Old Testament teaching. He imagines the objector asking where in this discussion Abraham stands. Is he a 'faith' man or a 'works' man? This is a crucial point, but the apostle demonstrates beyond doubt that the patriarch was justified by faith and not by deeds of the law. The ground of the argument is Gn. xv. 6: 'And he believed in the Lord; and he counted it to him for righteousness.' The review of Abraham's life reveals three realities.

i. His righteousness was wholly by faith (iv. 1–8). It was universally accepted by the Jews that Abraham was uniquely righteous and had better grounds than most to boast. But such glorying is inadmissible in the sight of God (2). Scripture says *Abraham believed God, and that was reckoned to him for righteousness* (3; see Gn. xv. 6). Now, if a man works, his wages do not depend on his employer's goodwill, but on his employer's indebtedness to him (4). But if he doesn't work, merely believing in Him who justifies the sinner, his faith is counted for righteousness (5).

The sacred writer to the Hebrews echoes the Old Testament view in verses 8–19 of chapter xi. Abraham's faith is outstanding and he had an illustrious niche in this author's temple of fame. It is noteworthy that James in his Epistle (ii. 23) also quotes Gn. xv. 6, adding 'and he was called the Friend of God'. Paul and James arrive at the same conclusion from entirely different points of view. When James declares 'Was not Abraham our father justified by works?' (ii. 21), his aim is to commend good works as the necessary proof and essential fruit of faith. Paul's task, on the other hand, is to condemn good works as the ultimate ground of salvation and to deny to them any merit in getting right with God. The apostle continues to emphasize that this new system of justification, which is his gospel, has its roots in the Old Testament by showing that David is also a 'faith' man; for he expresses the blessedness of those who are reckoned righteous apart from any merit accrued by works (Ps. xxxii. 1, 2). This state of the highest happiness is not pronounced upon the forgiven by David, but by God Himself. The Psalmist is merely recording the blessed fact, even though with personal exultation, out of his own experience.

ii. Abraham's righteousness was independent of circumcision (iv. 9–12). The order in the experience of the patriarch was first faith, then justification, then circumcision. The Jews have reversed the order, putting the rite first. Taking the idea of blessedness as his link, the apostle shows that Abraham possessed this fruit of faith previous to his circumcision (10). *He received the sign of circumcision, a seal* (11). The rite itself was the token, or confirmation, of the covenant made by God with Abraham (cf. Gn. xvii. 1–14; Acts vii. 8). On this ground the patriarch is *the father of all them that believe* (11), whether circumcised or uncircumcised (cf. 2 Pet. i. 1). In the face of orthodox Jewish teaching, Paul asserts one of the vital principles of his doctrine, the open door for the Gentiles, the universal privilege of justification by faith.

iii. Abraham's righteousness was independent of the Mosaic law (iv. 13–22). Paul's next point is that Abraham was reckoned right with God some four hundred years before the law came into existence, before ever it was promulgated from Mount Sinai. *The promise, that he should be the heir of the world*, was not given to either the patriarch or his posterity by way of law, but by way of *the righteousness of faith* (13). The 'heir of the universe' is interpreted as the sum of all the promises which Abraham received as revealed in Gn. xii. 3, 7, xiii. 15, 16, xv. 1, 5, 18, xvii. 8, 19, and mentioned in Acts iii. 25 and Gal. iii. 8. These promises included the gift of a son and heir, a countless posterity, the Messiah, and His universal kingdom. Observe the way in which our Lord, in one of the beatitudes, spiritualized the idea of world inheritance by stating that the meek should inherit the earth (Mt. v. 5). Had those of the law inherited it, faith would have been *made void* and the promise *of none effect* in securing righteousness (14). Law, however, can bring only the sense of sin, guilt and penalty; for remove the law and sin is gone (15). Accordingly faith, not law, is the basis of Abraham's righteousness in the sight of God.

The apostle argues similarly in Gal. iii. 17ff., but the logic there is more legal and historical, whereas here it is more doctrinal. Law and grace are two incompatible spheres. Hence the promise is confirmed to all the seed, not just to that sprung from the law, but also that sprung from faith (16). By this faith Abraham becomes the father of all believers, Gentiles as well as Jews. In a physical sense the promise is given that he shall be father of all (Gn. xvii. 5); but Paul is thinking here of a universal spiritual fatherhood. Abraham, the father of the faithful, appears before God as the representative of all believers, Jew or Gentile (16, 17).

Note the two arresting and apposite divine attributes which Paul adds here: *God, who quickeneth the dead, and calleth those things which be not as though they were* (17). God's life-giving power is seen in the miracles of Abraham's procreation of Isaac (19; cf. Heb. xi. 12, 'and him as good as dead'), by the deliverance of Isaac upon the sacrificial altar (cf. Heb. xi. 19, 'God was able to raise him up, even from the dead') and by the resurrection of Christ (24). The second attribute may be rendered, 'Who also speaks of, or summons, non-existents as if they were really existents.' The reference is to the unborn sons, the future posterity of father Abraham, when historically he was childless.

Again Paul eulogizes the faith of the patriarch. *He staggered not . . . but was strong in faith* (20), meaning that in reference to the divine promise Abraham did not vacillate in unbelief but was empowered by faith (RV 'waxed strong through faith'), thus bringing glory to God's name by his full faith in the divine ability to fulfil this promise. The conclusion of this test case of Abraham is the assertion with which it began, that his faith was imputed to him for righteousness (22; cf. verse 3).

The apostle now prepares for his greatest theme, the believer's righteousness. This acceptance of Abraham, the father of the faithful, is recorded that we might also believe and claim the righteousness of God through Jesus, who was offered up for our transgressions and resurrected for our justification (23–25).

e. Believer's righteousness (v. 1–21)

The apostle now passes more into the subjective or experimental sphere. Some consider this chapter to be a devotional parenthesis since it is based on Paul's own experience of God's dealings with him. But the great theme of justification by faith is being here further developed. 'Paul never contemplates the possibility of a justification which was not invariably followed by a sanctification: justification and sanctification are for him inseparably connected in fact.' The one is the wicket-gate, preliminary absolution; the other the long road to the heavenly Jerusalem. The apostle unites himself with all believers and speaks for them. On the firm foundation of being right with God the blessed effects of justification are declared (1–5). Then, in poetic style, there follows the guarantee of such blessedness (6–11). To this is added the method of justification as men of faith realize it through the new Head of the race (12–21).

i. The benefits which justification brings (v. 1–5). *We have peace with God* (1). Those justified by faith secure peace with God. The best attested texts have the subjunctive instead of the indicative mood in the verb *echōmen*, the only difference being the long or the short vowel. Hence the hortative rendering of the RV, 'let us have'. But as Paul seldom mingles his teaching and his preaching, the meaning is the milder exhortation 'we should have', and so 'we do have' (cf. I.C.C., p. 120). We actually enjoy, as men of faith, peace with God. It is a new relationship with God which is not a question of mere feeling but of fact. Secondly, *we have access* (2). The believer does not enter into favour with God on his own merit. The idea of access is introduction into the presence-chamber of the king. This presentation before the royal throne is effected by one near the monarch himself. Here it is Jesus who leads us unto God (cf. Eph. ii. 18, iii. 12). The apostle describes the active favour of the Father to believers by the term *grace* (2; cf. Gal. v. 4; 1 Pet. v. 12). The justified are ushered into a state of grace which brings security and confidence. A third blessed result of being right with God is joy, a triumph based on hope and victorious over tribulation (2, 3). Believers exult *in hope of the glory of God* (2). They glory in the glory (cf. iii. 23) which one day will be the crown and consummation of all things for the justified. They also boast even in trial, because trouble is productive of many fine qualities in believers, who know that sufferings produce patience, and this endurance (cf. ii. 7) leads to a tested character, and this proved experience (cf. 2 Tim. ii. 3) brings forth hope. (Paul uses this 'chain-catalogue' style again in x. 13–15; cf. also 2 Pet. i. 5–7.) This high hope does not carry disgrace nor prove illusory (cf. 2 Cor. vii. 14, ix. 4) because the souls of believers are flooded with God's love, which is in fact the presence of the Paraclete (5). The justified become conscious of God's love toward them through the indwelling Spirit. (Cf. the blessedness of the man to whom God reckons righteousness apart from works; iv. 5–8.) Note that this is Paul's first reference in this Epistle to the Holy Spirit.

ii. The security of the believer (v. 6–11). The believers who are set right with God enjoy their new relation with God, their standing in grace, with perfect security. It is guaranteed on the one hand through the death of Jesus Christ upon the cross (6–8), and on the other through the risen life of the same Saviour (9–11). *Christ died for the ungodly* (6; cf. verse 8). Christ's death on the cross was for us first *when we were yet without strength* (6); i.e. when we were weak and impotent to save ourselves by legal merit, and were indeed the ungodly (6), sinners (8) and enemies (10). Secondly it was for us *in due time* (6). This right season, the 'psychological moment' of the world's clock, is frequently expressed by Paul (cf. 'Gal. iv. 4; Eph. i. 10; 1 Tim. ii. 6, vi. 15; Tit. i. 3). For us, then, in the fulness of time, Christ died, even though we not only had nothing to commend us, but in very truth had everything to condemn us. In verse 7 the apostle makes a contrast between the righteous and the good man. For the one type hardly any would die; for the other some might venture the sacrifice. The *righteous man* is he who keeps the law, 'a model of stern duty'. The *good man* is he who in spirit and disposition exceeds the just demands of the law (cf. Mt. v. 20).

Much more then (9). Paul continues his assertion of the security of the believer's righteousness with a triumphant *a fortiori* argument. The love of God toward us as undeserving and rebellious sinners is testified by the sacrifice of His Son on our behalf, a death upon the cross which brings us into a completely new relation with Him. This amazing love of God in putting us right with Himself is the greatest fact of our salvation, greater than our new life. God achieved reconciliation *by the death of his Son* when we were in a state of unbelieving hostility (10). Much more, then, shall God be able to keep us in peace with Himself as His friends by the *life* of His Son. If God can accomplish our justification, beyond doubt He can also accomplish our sanctification. The idea is all of life, the believer's life through the Saviour's life. Paul does not use the term 'sanctification' in his measuring of the greater and the great. His contrast is between justification and salvation. But the latter term has just this meaning of progressive holiness. In union with Christ as a living Lord we are empowered to live the holy life of moral and spiritual overcoming so that we, in our sanctified personality, escape the wrath of God on the judgment day through the merit and mediation of Jesus Christ.

This finished work upon the cross, which puts believers right with God and involves their being kept right through the life of Jesus, is the constant spring of intense joy (11). This relationship is termed the *atonement* (RV 'reconciliation'). The Greek *katallagē* means 'change' or 'exchange'; hence, when predicated of persons, a change from enmity to friendship, a reconciliation. This implies a change of attitude on the part of both God and man. The necessity of change on the human side is obvious; but many theologians deny any need for such on the divine side. God's love is abiding and He in Himself is unchangeable. But note that the apostle speaks of a reception by us (Gk. *elabomen*) of a reconciliation freely given to us by God. Implicit in the doctrine of justification is the changed attitude of God toward the sinner on the ground of the merit of Jesus Christ.

iii. A righteousness of grace (v. 12–21). The apostle now concludes this section of the believer's righteousness by emphasizing that it is in truth a standing in grace, for it is accomplished through grace (verses 15, 20). The channel of justification is through one Person by the free gift of God, a principle which leads Paul to discuss the two heads of the human race, Adam and Christ (cf. 1 Cor. xv. 21f.). Note the construction of the passage. After stating the truth of the universality of sin and its penalty through Adam (12), the apostle digresses in a parenthesis (13–17), and resumes his argument in verses 18, 19. We have in verse 12 a grammatical anacoluthon. There is no sequel to the 'as' clause which depicts Adam as the type of Him who was to come. This 'as' does not find its sequel until verse 18, after the parenthesis had dealt with some difficulties.

The crucial passage is verse 12, where the doctrine of the relation of the one to the many is set forth. Special emphasis is laid upon the two prepositions used in the Greek, *dia*, 'through', and *eis*, 'into', whereby a channel and a passage are indicated. Through one man as channel sin passed into the world (*kosmos*), and through sin, as its penalty, death. The world hitherto had been pronounced by the Creator 'very good', but now, by Adam's transgression, both sin and death had entered in. The point which Paul makes is that all are involved in the sin of Adam, all have sinned in him and with him. Humanity is not simply accounted as having sinned and just legally charged with Adam's sin, but all are declared to have actually and actively sinned with Adam.

This dogmatic statement leads the apostle into a parenthesis where he faces two difficulties. The first is that up to the time of Moses the law had not been declared. As there was no law there could be no sin. He lets that go, admitting that *sin is not imputed when there is no law* (13); i.e. is not regarded as guilt involving penalty. In the second place he argues that, law or no law, sin's penalty was in operation from Adam's time. The universality of death nobody could deny, and Paul adheres to the doctrine that death is the sentence of God upon sin, although there was no law until Moses' day, and although those penalized did not sin after the likeness of Adam's sin, i.e. eating the forbidden fruit (14). Commenting upon this verse 14 some argue for the universality of sin but not for its originality. This would be to deny our oneness in Adam, which is the type of the oneness of the redeemed in Christ.

Up to this point Paul is describing the comparison between Adam and Christ. Both by a single act influenced the whole race. Now follows the contrast. The effect of Adam's sin is death; the effect of Christ's righteousness is life. But Paul does not put it that way. He states that the result is abounding, or overflowing, grace or *the gift by grace* (15), which is further defined in verse 17 as *the gift of righteousness*. The sentence was of one unto the condemnation of all; the free gift was of many transgressions unto a pronouncement of *justification* (16). The Greek *dikaiōma*, not the usual *dikaiōsis*, rendered simply *justification*, means a judicial utterance, or decree, or act of justification or putting right with God. The same Greek word occurs in i. 32, ii. 26, viii. 4, which the RV renders 'ordinance' in each case. The contrast between Adam and Christ is further developed in verse 17 where the one establishes a reign of sin and death, the other a reign of grace and life. The connection with Christ annuls for eternity the sinful connection with Adam.

Paul now links up with the principle posited in verse 12, restating it and adding the other limb of the parallelism, *even so by the righteousness of one the free gift came upon all men unto justification of life* (18). *The offence of one . . . the righteousness of one* (18). The Greek can be rendered 'one offence' ('trespass') and 'one act of righteousness'. The difference is between agent and act. The contrast which is in view suggests that the AV rendering is preferable.

The sum of the whole comparison and contrast between Adam and Christ is stated in verse 19 as the conclusion of the argument that the believer's righteousness is one of grace. It leaves us, however, with the problem of the relation of Adam and Christ to mankind whereby sin on the one hand and grace on the other are transmitted. Imputation is a legal conception and does not completely satisfy. The theory of federal headship is helpful. Paul elsewhere teaches that this spiritual headship of Christ antedates the physical headship of Adam (cf. Eph. i. 4; Col. i. 15–17; see also Jn. i. 1–5). Yet by his deductions from it the apostle indicates a closer relationship, for humanity has no power of choice to commission its representative. The scientific fact of the solidarity of the race gives the best solution. As the whole lies in the germ, the oak in the acorn, so all humanity resides in Adam and, by grace through faith, also in Christ. As we are a physical, so also are we a spiritual organism.

Paul concludes this section of the believer's righteousness with an appended note on the function of the law. 'Enter the law as an accessory, that the trespass might be multiplied; but where sin was multiplied, grace was multiplied the more exceedingly, that as sin was king in death, so too grace, through righteousness, might be king unto eternal life through Jesus Christ our Lord.' Grace is not the end. It leads through righteousness to its consummation, eternal life.

III. ETHICAL PROBLEMS RAISED BY THE GOSPEL. vi. 1–23

Paul now proceeds to defend the doctrine of justification by faith against the charge that it is incompatible with ordinary morality. He does so by affirming the doctrine of sanctification. This is not merely a theoretical sequence to justification; it is a vivid fact in the apostle's experience. As verses 1–11 show, Paul knew not only what it meant to be put right with God, but also what it was to be kept right. See also vii. 7–25. 'He prized Christ's Spirit as the power of holiness as highly as Christ's sacrifice as the reason for his forgiveness.' This ethical problem takes two forms. First, does not being reckoned righteous by God simply encourage sin? Secondly, does it not result in lawlessness?

a. The charge of licence (vi. 1–14)

Paul's doctrine of justification, the objector argues, implies 'the more sin, the more grace'. If more sin means more grace, why not continue to live in sin? Paul's reply centres in the fact of the believer's union with Christ. This mystical relationship with the Saviour is here set forth for the first time in this Epistle. The apostle's characteristic thought is illustrated by the rite of baptism in the mode of immersion. The three actions therein are symbolic: into the water—death; under the water—burial; out of the water—resurrection. To be *baptized into Jesus Christ* is to be brought into union with His death (3), His burial (4) and His resurrection (5). Burial is really a confirmation of the fact of death. Christ's death was concerned with sin. It was a sacrifice by which sin was put away (cf. Heb. ix. 26). *He died unto sin once* (10); i.e. once for all (cf. 1 Pet. iii. 18; Heb. vii. 27, ix. 12, 28, x. 10). His resurrection marked His entrance upon a new life 'apart from sin'. The believer, accordingly, passes through the same experiences. It is the way of sanctification, the destined issue of justification. God not only puts us right, but keeps us right with Himself. His righteousness is first imputed, then imparted to us. Paul has been dealing so far with the Godward side of sanctification through faith-union with Christ. Now, in verses 12–14, he declares the manward aspect. Moral effort is necessary in the progressive righteousness of the believer. The believer must not present his members as *instruments of unrighteousness* (13). This is a case of continual sinning (Gk. *paristanete*; continuous present tense). The second presentation, as *instruments of righteousness*, is 'an act of choice' (Gk. *parastēsate*; completed past tense) whereby believers definitely yield themselves to a life of holiness, although such cannot be continually sinless. 'Do not go on presenting your limbs to sin as weapons of unrighteousness. Present yourselves outright (once for all) to God.'

The transition to the next aspect of the ethical problem is found in verse 14, where Paul exults in the certainty of progressive righteousness, and cries: 'Sin shall not lord it over you. Ye are not under law, but under grace.' The 'Thou shalt not' of the law must give place to the power of the Spirit.

b. The charge of lawlessness (vi. 15–23)

This gospel of 'the righteousness of God' results, it is again alleged, in utter disrespect of law. This is the special Judaistic arraignment against Paul's doctrine of grace. Why! the law may now be disregarded and sin can be indulged. This is the heresy of antinomianism.

Paul's answer to this objection against free grace is that, while it is true that the believer is not under law but under grace, this does not mean that he is lawless. He owes allegiance to God. There are two possible masters to lord it over us—sin or God (16). To make his point the apostle takes an illustration from the slave-law of the time. (He is using the term *doulos*, 'slave', all the time, translated by the AV as *servant*.) A slave could buy his freedom by paying his price to the temple, i.e. he gave his purchase money to some god or goddess and in this way claimed his freedom; but the gold actually went, via the temple, to the master. Thus the deity ransomed the slave from the owner and the slave went free, although still the slave of the god. In a similar way the believer is free in the sense that he has become God's slave. He is not an irresponsible person without a master, for Jesus is Lord of all his life. The apostle realizes the inadequacy of the analogy but reminds his readers that he speaks *after the manner of men* (cf. Gal. iii. 15) and owing to *the infirmity of your flesh*, i.e. their immaturity (19). Paul closes his argument by an appeal to the results or fruits of the two services, sin or righteousness. The one issues in shame and death; the other in sanctification and life eternal.

IV. THE CHRISTIAN AND THE LAW. vii. 1–viii. 39

Another difficulty involved in the apostle's doctrine of 'the righteousness of God' as a free gift, or 'justification by faith alone', was the position of the law. The law was almost worshipped by the Jews and it was sheer blasphemy to assert that faith should take its place. To this question of the abrogation of the law Paul now addresses himself.

a. Law is valid only in lifetime (vii. 1–6)

The illustration is used of the emancipated widow released from the law of her husband on his death. She is free to marry again. The law is superseded and is no longer valid or operative in this case. Similarly believers are made *dead to the law by* (RV 'through') *the body of Christ* (4); i.e. either on account of the cross or through the Church. This second interpretation of the phrase is to be preferred. The 'you' becomes 'we' (4) by coming to belong to the body of Christ, the totality of whose members, or limbs, constitutes the body of which Christ is the Head. The point of the analogy is that the believer, being dead to the law, is free to be united to the risen Lord. The apostle here substitutes the law for sin, deadness to which, accompanied by life unto

righteousness, was his teaching in the previous chapter. He stresses now the emancipation through death. *In the flesh* (5), the contrast to which is 'in the spirit', describes the life of sinful indulgence. *The motions of sins* (5) means 'sinful passions' (RV). The two states of slavery are again contrasted in the phrases *newness of spirit* and *oldness of the letter* (6); they represent the state of grace and the state of law.

b. Law and sin are not synonymous (vii. 7–25)

Paul, as we have seen, has substituted 'law' for 'sin' in his argument. This fact gave rise, either in his own mind or in that of his critics, to the question *Is the law sin?* (7). Are these two things identical? The regenerate man dies to sin and self, and so to law. What then is the relation between sin and law? The apostle defines the connection between the two from his own personal experience. This section is accordingly highly autobiographical, although some commentators have thought that Paul is speaking quite generally. The better view is that it is the regenerate man who is speaking from his own experience. We have no picture of unregenerate experience *per se*, but rather the righteous man's retrospect, for he alone is in a position to assess the slavery of sin. Paul regards his own experience as typical. The true relationship between law and sin is set forth as threefold.

i. The law reveals sin (vii. 7, 8). *I had not known lust* (evil concupiscence or coveting), *except the law had said* (7). Were there no law we would be unconscious of sin's vitality, and so of sin's existence. This is really an ethical commonplace, so very commonplace that it is ignored. *Sin, taking occasion* (8, 11). Sin, like a military strategist, made the law a sort of 'base of operations'. This is the literal sense of the Greek word *aphormē* when applied to warfare. It means a 'starting-point', and so, metaphorically, an 'occasion', 'incentive', 'opportunity' (cf. 2 Cor. xi. 12; Gal. v. 13). The soul, ignorant of the prohibitions of the law, is happy in unrecognized sin; but when the knowledge of sin comes then sin arouses rebellion against the law, which keeps on saying 'Thou shalt not', and so sin works *all manner of concupiscence* (8); RV 'coveting'.

ii. The law stimulates sin (vii. 9–13). Once, says Paul, I lived free from any consciousness of sin. I really lived apart from the law. *But when the commandment came* (i.e. a particular injunction of the law), *sin revived* (Gk. *anazēn*, 'to leap into life'), *and I died* (9). The apostle's experience was that the law, decreed to promote life (cf. x. 5; Lv. xviii. 5) by obedience, turned out to be death to him. Indeed, through the law, sin beguiling him (cf. Gn. iii. 13; 2 Cor. xi. 3; 1 Tim. ii. 14) slew him (11). This death does not mean atrophy or paralysis of this or that living function. It means wholesale death, the kind of thing that drove Paul to a frenzied persecution of the Way, to a mania of hatred towards it, which the Lord alone 'cured' by the vision on

the Damascus road. Every law-begotten covetousness (i.e. evil 'concupiscence') must have leapt into a new heinousness as the Christian looked back upon the frenzied baiter and persecutor, as Paul indeed looked back upon Saul, and understood the misery of his hatred. The apostle will not allow that the law, in whole or in part, is anything but holy, just and good (12). Its purposed effect is life. Only when perverted by sin and made subservient to its deceit does the law work death. Sin is the mischief that waylaid and slew Saul. The divine intention was to show sin in its true colours, as already declared (13; see verses 7, 8). But sin turned God's blessing, the law, into a curse.

iii. The law creates a conflict with sin (vii. 14–25). The apostle reaches now the very core of his bitter experience. He confesses that he sees the better way, and approves thereof; but he follows the worse. He realizes the difference between the nature of the law and his own nature. *Spiritual* and *carnal* (14) are opposites: one is of the Spirit, the other of the flesh. Paul continues in a classical picture of divided consciousness to sketch his inner conflict between what psychologists term the organized and disorganized self. The real self centres in an ideal, in Paul's case Christ, or the good and holy law. Sin, personified in the graphic and emotional portrait, is the disorganized self and definitely not Paul as he longs to be. When doing what he does not approve he declares *it is no more I that do it, but sin* (20), identified here with his lower or disorganized self. The apostle's experience provides a principle which is enunciated in verse 21, and one which operates all through life. 'To be saved from sin a man must at the same time own it and disown it; it is this practical paradox which is reflected in this verse' (James Denney). The emotional expression of this inner conflict and divided consciousness culminates in a cry of distress or despair (24). Paul lives again his experience, which he presents as typical, of being the convicted sinner. *O wretched man that I am! who shall deliver me from the body of this death?* (24). The body is the instrument of sin and destined to die; so repulsive is sin, and death so much its synonym, that Paul agonizes to be rescued from this death's body which, in his horror, he feels it to be. Then follows the swift reaction in a paean of praise, as salvation floods his soul. 'Thanks be unto God through Jesus Christ our Lord.'

c. Law is vanquished by grace (viii. 1–39)

The law, while thus exposing and exciting sin and splitting the self, is still in its purpose holy and good. The law is the friend of men if it could be allowed to operate, but it is *weak through the flesh* (3). However, through Christ, it is strong and condemns sin in the flesh, for Christ is absolutely righteous and He dwells within us. We are also in Christ and by this union fulfil the law (1, 4). Christ's obedience is our obedience. We satisfy in this way the claims of the law and

render it powerless. So in this chapter the apostle proceeds to chart the course of the Christian life in which grace triumphs over law and believers find deliverance from sin.

i. The failure of law (viii. 1–4). The previous system of life through obedience to the law had manifestly never been successful. Now it is made good by the incarnation of Jesus and the presence of the Spirit. Law is unable to confer benefits, but what the law failed to do, grace accomplished through Christ and the Holy Spirit. The overcoming life begins here and now in the absence of any sentence for being in the wrong with God. United with Christ, the believer is acquitted and is free for ever from the law of sin and death. The just requirement of the law, a righteous life, is accomplished not 'by' us but *in* us (4). This is *what the law could not do* (3). The idea is more of the inherent inability of the law to do anything in the direction of a holy life, than merely of its impotence to do what Christ accomplished. The failure of the law is absolute. The new law under which we are brought is *the law of the Spirit of life in Christ Jesus*, and this law emancipates us *from the law of sin and death* (2). Sin is foreign to human life. It is an intrusion. By sending His Son *in the likeness of sinful flesh* (3) God dealt with sin. Paul does not here imply that Jesus was incarnate in sinful flesh, as if all flesh were tainted or corrupt with sin. The evangelists are very definite about the advent of our Lord as regards the manner of His birth. The holiness of the child is marked both as originated by the Holy Spirit and as itself holy (cf. Lk. i. 35). Our Saviour's flesh was the true, unfallen humanity of the divine intention. Our Lord's body was only 'in the guise of sinful flesh' (Moff.), not in sinful flesh itself which is our legacy from Adam. The Pauline point here is that the Father sent His Son to deal with sin in the very same circumstance and sphere in which our human race in Adam had been worsted. This engagement with sin implies all that Jesus was, said and did to condemn sin in His own body on the tree (cf. 3, RV, 'as an offering for sin'; cf. also iii. 25). Flesh was the realm of sin; but in the case of believers God put that sphere of influence out of court, the death of the Son annulling the power of sin over saints completely and permanently. Man in Christ is free for ever from the law of sin and death. The just requirement of the law (4), a righteous life, is accomplished not through the law (for it has failed) but through grace.

ii. The triumph of grace (viii. 5–13). The apostle proceeds to describe the grace-life as one of the Spirit and to contrast it with the life of the flesh under the law. The old life has its interests and absorptions in fleshly things, but the new in spiritual things. If our life accords with the flesh, the yellow streak will run through our mental outlook. If the spiritual element prevails, the analogous results will be seen in our spiritual alignments. The sum of the matter is *to be carnally minded* (RV 'the mind of the flesh') *is death*; *but to be spiritually minded* (RV 'the mind of the Spirit') *is life and peace* (6). On the one hand death is the result of the flesh-life: on the other life flows from the Spirit-life. The underlying reason is plain. The carnal life is hostile to God, frustrating the divine ideals for humanity. It is self-centred and at war with God. By its very nature it is powerless to submit itself to the law of God (7). Living in the world of self as supreme it cannot please God (8). The flesh, in fact, is the seat of revolt against God. John's synonym for the flesh in this Pauline sense is 'the world' (cf. Jn. xvi. 8–11, xvii. 6, 9). It is life without God in it: one of egotism, self-indulgence and disobedience to the light of conscience.

Paul now turns directly to his readers and addresses them as Christians in whom the Spirit dwells (9). The motive power behind the spiritual life is the indwelling Holy Spirit. Hence the victory of grace over law; for by grace, through faith, the Spirit is in them and they in the Spirit. Here mark Paul's characteristic preposition 'in', which he uses in the metaphorical sense of union or communion with God in Christ through faith (e.g. viii. 11, ix. 1; 1 Cor. iii. 16; cf. 1 Thes. iv. 8). *The Spirit of God . . . the Spirit of Christ* (9) are used interchangeably, showing the equality and functions of the one Godhead. The Father is the source of all grace; the Son, the channel; the Spirit, proceeding from both the Father and the Son, the agent. The criterion of the Christian is this indwelling, divine motive power, apart from which dynamic there can be no communion with God. *The body is dead because of sin* (10). These words have been interpreted as meaning either that our bodies are destined to death as the penalty of sin; or that our bodies, united with Christ, share in the death of the cross and so are reckoned dead and the penalty paid; or that our bodies are dead to us as the instruments of sin. Body and flesh are used in the same sense, being contrasted with spirit. This last interpretation appears the best as being most in harmony with the context (cf. the phrases 'the body of sin', vi. 6, and 'the body of this death', vii. 24). *Because of sin . . . because of righteousness* (10). This is another way of expressing the triumph of grace over law. Nothing but death is in the old way of sin, but all life pulses through the new way of righteousness, or justification, that stupendous thing which God does for us, in the doing of which we ourselves have neither part nor competence. Such justification, the pure judicial assignment of righteousness to us on God's part, is the basis of such moral righteousness as results from receipt of the blessings of Christ. The statements made in verse 11 about the Spirit are analogous to those made in verse 10 about Christ. This makes the verse most important for the Trinitarian conception of God, so vital and indispensable to true Christian knowledge.

Verses 12 and 13 form a hortatory aside. The brethren at Rome are admonished, along with the preacher himself, not to go on living to the lower self, as if that were a necessity (cf. i. 14, xiii. 8), but to continue to live to the Spirit, causing death to all selfish actions and so gaining, not death, but real life.

iii. **The goal of grace** (viii. **14–17**). Sonship with God is the glorious end of all grace's triumph. *Led by the Spirit of God* (14). Those whose lives are controlled by the Spirit are in fact, from the moment of their reception of the Spirit, in filial relationship with the Father. They hold a rank which entitles them to privilege. (Cf. Peter's conception of Christians as a royal priesthood in 1 Pet. ii. 9.) The voluntary opening of the heart to the indwelling rule of the Spirit at conversion places them beyond the stage of reverting to a state of slavery to fear (15). In the old life they lived in fear of the curse of the law. *The spirit of bondage* (15) is neither the human nor the divine spirit, but rather a temper, mood or state. The corresponding phrase *the Spirit of adoption* (15) is 'delicately ambiguous' and can mean either the permanent condition of sonship, or the human spirit conscious of filial relationship, or the Holy Spirit as the Creator of actual sonship.

The Spirit itself (16) is a permissible translation from the Greek: but as there is ample evidence from the Scriptures that the Holy Spirit is a Person, and as this personality is an accepted article of Christian faith, 'the Spirit himself' (RV) is equally correct and more apposite. Sonship means an adopted state, a position conferred upon one to whom it is not natural. It is by Christ's act of grace that Christians are in such a relationship. The Jews had no such custom of adoption, but it was common to both Romans and Greeks.

Paul does not go out of his way to deny any doctrine of universal fatherhood, but definitely teaches the necessity of Christian sonship, the relationship to God as Father in Jesus Christ through the Holy Spirit. This sonship is no mere official recognition of a filial tie, a title only. It is an actual fact. We are sons with a right to say *Abba, Father* (15), as sharing the sonship of the eternal Son. This cry heavenwards is a combination of Aramaic and Greek, the two spoken tongues of the period. The same double interjection is found in Mk. xiv. 36 and Gal. iv. 6. It is probable that our Lord used this formula and the apostles followed His practice. The cry under intellectual or spiritual emotion reveals the naked soul of the believer and is spontaneously accompanied by the corroborating testimony of the Holy Spirit to real sonship (16).

Paul now advances in his exultant thought, *and if children, then heirs* (17; cf. iv. 14). The idea of inheritance runs through both Old and New Testaments (cf. Nu. xxvi. 56; Ps. xxv. 13; Is. lx. 21; Mt. v. 5, xxi. 38; Gal. iii. 29, iv. 7). The advent of the indwelling Spirit is the earnest, or forecast, of the believer's inheritance (cf. 2 Cor. i. 22, v. 5; Eph. i. 14). Christ is God's Son, hence we are His fellow-heirs, *heirs of God, and joint-*

heirs with Christ (17). Christians have a common inheritance with Christ, which they will share in due course. In verse 17b Paul may be quoting a familiar saying of the early Church (cf. 2 Tim. ii. 11–13) that believers experiencing adoption are co-heirs with Christ if indeed 'they share His sufferings that they may share His glory too'. The Christian's life is a reproduction of the life of Christ. *We suffer with him* (17) implies the communion of cross-bearing or self-sacrifice; not that our experiences are redemptive in themselves but we 'fill up that which is behind of the afflictions of Christ' (see Col. i. 24n.).

iv. **The glory which shall be revealed (viii. 18–27).** In his ecstasy over the victory of grace Paul has soared far beyond the richest possibilities of law. He is entranced in a realm which the law could never know. The idea of suffering does not overwhelm him (18). The apostle has no doubts about the 'hardness' needed for following Christ (cf. Paul's sufferings in Acts xix. 23–41, xx. 18–35; 2 Cor. i. 3–11, vi. 4–10, xi. 23–33). As little does he doubt that the glory to come will far outbalance present sufferings. This future glory or ultimate manifestation of God in Christ will be no mere objective vision alone, but a subjective transformation of the believer's character (cf. 2 Cor. iii. 18; 1 Jn. iii. 2). The assurance of future glory is not a passing emotion of optimism. Paul confirms his confidence with three testifying facts.

First he points to the organic unity of creation (verses 19–22). Paul here states a scientific fact viewed theologically. Man and nature are so closely related that, as by man's sin nature suffered with him, so by free grace in putting man right with God nature also shares the hope of righteous readjustment or perfect completion. *The creature was made subject to vanity, not willingly* (20). Man fell of his own free will, but the universe (Gk. *ktisis*, meaning 'creation', not *creature* as in AV) automatically and not voluntarily was corrupted with him, according to the decree of God. Its fate was to be made *subject to vanity* (20), or cursed with futility, dissatisfaction or incompleteness, yet not without hope of deliverance. Man's redemption will mean for the whole of sighing nature the fulfilment of the prophecy that the desert shall blossom as the rose. The apostle strikes again the main theme of the passage, that this present grace of possession of *the firstfruits of the Spirit* awaits the future *redemption of our body* (23). In a like earnest expectation to that of the visible world, Christians who experience the 'earnest' of the Spirit, the foretaste of His transforming power, also sigh for the deliverance of the body from sin and sin's environment. The resurrection will be the final stage of sonship with God.

Paul now proceeds to call as his second witness the Christian's conscious hope, which by its very nature proves the reality of future glory (verses 24, 25). It is another ground of assurance. *For we are saved by hope* (24). Paul by emphasizing hope in this way does not thereby discard or minimize the pre-eminent function of faith in the believer's salvation. Some prefer to render 'in hope' so as to avoid misunderstanding, but 'by hope' and 'through faith' serve the same purpose. Faith is the definite means of salvation and hope can emerge only within the faith-attitude. The point which the apostle is making here is that by its very nature hope testifies to the fact of future glory. Hope is no longer hope if it can realize the consummation for which it looks. Our duty, then, is to wait for the end, to endure, to exercise patience. We are saved, yet full salvation still lies ahead.

The help of the Holy Spirit is the third witness to the full realization of adoption, the third ground of assurance that grace will become glory (verses 26, 27). *Likewise the Spirit also helpeth our infirmities* (26). Paul is fortified in his faith in the believer's final glory by the experience common to all Christians of the Spirit's operation in furthering all prayerful aspiration towards the realization of complete adoption as sons of God. If God is thus involved in our movement towards the glorious consummation, then the end is no delusion but a wonderful reality. The term *helpeth* (Gk. *synantilambanetai*) is in the original a very forcible word, being compounded with two prepositions, *syn*, 'along with' and *anti*, 'over against', as prefixes to the verb, *lambanein*, 'to take hold of'. The metaphor is of a helper supporting the weight in co-operation with the bearer and at the opposite end of the burden. *Infirmities* refer to the weaknesses of the Christian in his ignorance or part comprehension of the will of God, *for we know not what we should pray for as we ought* (26). Here the specific help of the Spirit is realized. His intercession is within us; the intercession of the Saviour is at God's right hand (Heb. vii. 25). The Paraclete, not merely beside us but dwelling within us, strengthens us by energizing and inspiring the inarticulate longings of the soul towards a full sonship of imparted righteousness as the fruit of imputed righteousness. Divine intercession gives utterance to our sighs and the intervention prevails: our great longing for the consummation is borne to the Father's throne. *He that searcheth the hearts* (27) is God Himself who is omniscient, knowing the direction and movement of the Spirit in His inspiration of human aspirations. But even more specifically the Father knows this *mind of the Spirit* (27), for it is His own mind.

v. **The sovereign will of God guarantees grace (viii. 28–30).** The human and divine Spirit, harmonized into one will, are in fact, Paul asserts in this paragraph, realizing the all-embracing will of God. In view of such divine working in us and on our behalf, we are aware that to them that love God all things co-operate for good, that is, to those who are effectually *called according to his purpose* (28). The eternal will is behind the called, who not only hear the call but obey it. What is established in the divine foreknowledge and foreordination inevitably reaches the divine goal for the divine glory, which includes the blessed state of the elect. This eternal purpose and plan is to make believers *conformed to the image of his Son* (29), who is Himself the perfect image of the Father (cf. 1 Cor. xv. 49; 2 Cor. iii. 18, iv. 4; Col. i. 15), so that He is the firstborn among a host of brethren. *Firstborn* (29) implies not mere priority but pre-eminence within the host of redeemed brethren. Paul reveals the stages of the divine decree and its accomplishment. The eternal order operating in space is foreknowledge, then fore-ordination. The predestination is based upon the 'knowing beforehand'. The several stages tele-scope out from one another. The term 'to foreknow' (Gk. *proginōskō*) means 'to unite oneself before with someone' (Cremer, p. 161). The idea is a personal and pre-temporal associa-tion, and in the dynamic not static sense, for it is the prolific origin of subsequent activities. Thus 'to foreknow' anyone is to enter into com-munion with a view to conferring special favour upon him, while 'to foreordain' decides that this special favour will take the shape of sonship in Christ. Foreknowledge according to the biblical usage of the verb 'know' (cf. Pss. i. 6, cxliv. 3; Ho. xiii. 5; Am. iii. 2; Mt. vii. 23; Jn. x. 27; 1 Cor. viii. 3; Gal. iv. 9) implies favour or grace as the eternal beginning of all the other processes of salvation, an interpretation which accords with the whole Pauline theology. Then the divine decree passes over into time and is manifested as calling, justification by faith, and finally glorification (30). This miraculous consumma-tion, planned in eternity, is worked out in our believing hearts with the promise of an issue in our creaturely praises in the state of sanctification here and glory hereafter.

vi. A hymn of praise (viii. 31–39). With a triumphant paean of praise Paul concludes his review of the course of the Christian life, which lives in a realm beyond the grasp and power of law. If God be in our destiny nothing else matters. To us who are of the faith-family He gave His own Son, and with the greater gift the lesser is certainly included. *Spared not his own Son* (32) is reminiscent of Abraham's sacrifice (Gn. xxii. 16). The apostle continues from this all-inclusive promise of limitless blessing by reverting to his first statement in verse 1. 'There is therefore now no condemnation.' There are two main questions to which the thought of the hymn is subordinated. First, *Who shall lay any thing to the charge of God's elect?* (33) and second, *Who shall separate us from the love of Christ?* (35). If God justifies, can anyone dare to accuse the chosen of God? And again, if Christ Himself died for the faithful, rose again for them, and now at God's right hand is their continual Advocate, is there any possible power to sever the love-link between the Saviour and the saved? There can be no charges and there can be no dissolution of redemptive bonds.

Paul in his ecstatic confidence now defies every conceivable antagonism. There are two classes of frustrating opponents. First he lists temporal adversities (35) experienced generally by those professing Christ who, suffering with Him, shall also share His glory. The sufferings are real indeed as the apostle well knows (cf. xvi. 4; 1 Cor. iv. 11, xv. 30; 2 Cor. xi. 26, 27; cf. Acts xii. 2), and he quotes to prove his case Ps. xliv. 22 (LXX). Secondly, there are spiritual powers recorded almost with derision because of the futility of their attempts to separate from the love of Christ. They are catalogued in twos and threes alternately: *death, nor life, nor angels, nor principalities, nor powers* (RV reads 'powers' after 'things to come' and Moff. renders 'powers of the height or of the depth'), *nor things present, nor things to come, nor height, nor depth, nor any other creature.* Christ has conquered all enemies and put them under His feet. The glorious consummation of this victory is 'that God may be all in all' (cf. 1 Cor. xv. 24–28).

V. THE PROBLEM OF JEWISH RIGHTS AND PRIVILEGE. ix. 1—xi. 36

Paul at this point appears to have reached his climax and all is ready for the practical applica-tion of his teaching on how to be right with God and how to keep in the same reconciled relation-ship. He has successively expounded the doc-trines of justification, sanctification and glori-fication. But there emerges another problem, the Jewish question. The apostle must have faced this difficulty many times. Stated simply it is this: This new gospel of 'faith-righteousness' in place of 'law-righteousness', which opens the door of salvation for the Gentiles, abolishes the covenant rights and privileges of the Jewish race and, moreover, passes them by as the channels of revelation. The Jews are not only reduced in the order of grace but altogether rejected. What value has their history been and what is their future to be? Historical facts and the Pauline gospel do not appear to agree; hence the apostle's gospel of a new way of life must be false. No preaching could alter the place of the Jews in the revelation of God.

Paul felt this objection keenly. It meant that he was accused of being no genuine apostle and his gospel was being treated as entirely untrue. This was not, however, the sharpest sorrow. The tragedy of the Jews was that they had been left outside the progressive revelation of God and cut off from the economy of grace. He therefore addresses himself to this historical problem. It was obvious that the people of God were losing their place in the kingdom and that the Gentiles were now filling it. The gospel given to the heathen people was being readily received and it appeared as if Israel was now neither being saved nor being serviceable. When the Gentiles were in their sin, Israel had the revelation of God. They were God's own chosen people. Elected and rejected! How can this be? He essays the solution in three assertions. The first deals with the absolute sovereignty of God (ix. 1–29), the second with Jewish responsibility in the historical situation (ix. 30—x. 21), and the third with the merciful purpose of God (xi. 1-36).

a. The absolute sovereignty of God (ix. 1-29)

i. Paul's personal sorrow (ix. 1-5). As a preface to dealing with the main problem, Paul expresses his own anguish at the state of the Jews. *I say the truth in Christ* (1). This is the apostle's solemn oath. His Judaistic adversaries charged him with insincerity; hence his vehement defence. In it he reveals himself as a true patriot. He loved his race and was unashamed to call them *my brethren, my kinsmen according to the flesh* (3). He is proud of the Jewish privileges and recounts them with a certain flourish, the greatest of all being that Christ sprang from the Jewish stock (5). The genuineness of the apostle's disappointment that his own race was not fulfilling its function and accepting its Messiah is evidenced by his noble wish *that myself were accursed from Christ for my brethren* (3; cf. Moses' prayer, Ex. xxxii. 32, 33).

ii. God is not unfaithful in His promises (ix. 6-13). This is the substance of the first objection. Paul begins his reply by denying that *the word of God hath taken none effect* (6). The promises which he has already mentioned (4) are not broken but fulfilled to the true Israel. God's Israel is henceforth contrasted with Judaism, hitherto the official heir of Abraham, but now rejected owing to its lack of faith and its refusal to accept the claims of the Messiah. The apostle makes his point by distinguishing between spiritual and carnal sonship with illustrations from the patriarchal history. Had history given the whole Jewish race a claim upon God, reversing what seems more normal, God's claim upon them? Because they were the seed of Abraham are all Jews the children of God? Paul declares that God in the exercise of His sovereign will has decreed that faith, not heredity, is the eternal principle of sonship. Within God's redemptive purpose the actual promises of God to Sara and Rebecca were fulfilled. God was free to exercise His selective grace in the case of the patriarchs, for He alone is the originator of its purpose. Righteousness then is *not of works, but of him that calleth* (11), thus excluding all human merit. Jacob and Esau were not differentiated on the ground of their life and character, for Jacob was chosen before the twins were born (11, 12). *Jacob have I loved, but Esau have I hated* (13) must be interpreted in the sense of nations, not individuals, which is the original reference in the two Old Testament quotations (Gn. xxv. 23; Mal. i. 2, 3). Moreover, 'love' and 'hate' are not the grounds of election as we understand these subjective feelings. God is not arbitrary in His choice and cannot be charged with irrational favouritism. The emotional terms indicate rather a national function and destiny. Judah, not Edom, was elected for progressive revelation in history. This meaning may be supported by the rendering 'Jacob have I loved, but Esau have I

loved less' (cf. Gn. xxix. 30-33; Mt. x. 37; Lk. xiv. 26; Jn. xii. 25).

iii. God is not unrighteous in His dealing (ix. 14-24). The Judaistic objector (real or imaginary) now advances his accusation that if Paul's gospel is true then God has been unrighteous. Paul deals first with the suggestion that God is unfair in His choice (verses 14-18). He expresses himself vehemently in his categorical denial of this charge: *God forbid* (14). Let no one say this! Mercy and pity are entirely of God. So much is this so that we cannot understand, but can only accept their incidence as being His will. This is no new doctrine. It was revealed of old time to Moses (Ex. xxxiii. 19, LXX). Neither human purpose nor human effort enters into divine election. *It is not of him that willeth, nor of him that runneth* (16). God alone acts alone. It just is and no human can hinder it! *Pharaoh* (17) is but a medium to enable God to display His power in that monarch and to publish His own holy name far and near. Of His own will absolutely God shows mercy; of the same will He hardens men. Note that in verse 18 the verb used for will is *thelō*, not *boulomai*. The latter is the firm term for will denoting determined purpose. Paul uses it sparingly and prefers the former word, as here, which permits a bigger background in the divine character than bare volition (cf. Eph. i. 5, 11). It is God as our Father in Christ Jesus who wills one way or the other, not stark, cold, divine will. In a word it is God who wills, not an unknown Will that wills.

Paul now proceeds to deal with the charge that, if what he has said is true, then God is unjust to blame (verses 19-24). If God is absolutely free to elect for better or worse, as Paul has now demonstrated, what of human responsibility? Since none can withstand this omnipotent divine will, sin is not voluntary (19); hence the sinner is not blameworthy. Paul replies that this argument is out of court. The creature may not find fault with the Creator, although the reverse stands. Who is anyone to 'speak back' to God? The thing formed simply cannot quarrel with God over its formation (20). The apostle introduces the illustration of the potter and the clay (cf. Is. xxix. 16, xlv. 9, 10, lxiv. 8; Je. xviii. 6). It is the potter's prerogative to make out of the same lump of clay *one vessel unto honour, and another unto dishonour* (21), one a work of supreme art and another a homely article (Moff. 'one vessel for a noble purpose and another for a menial'). Cf. 2 Tim. ii. 20. 'What answer will you make now?' Paul challenges his opponent. If God wishes, on the one hand, to display His wrath and manifest His power, that is His will and He will await His time to reveal it. If God wishes, on the other hand, to publish His mercy in His election to salvation, that is again a matter of His good pleasure.

The contrast is vividly expressed in the terms *vessels of wrath* (22) and *vessels of mercy* (23). The sovereign will of God in relation to the latter is an eternal preparation for glory. Can it be likewise interpreted that the former are pre-destined pre-temporally to destruction? The vessels of wrath are the disobedient, with whom God is justly angry and upon whom there comes the nemesis for sin. Are they also prepared beforehand for eternal loss? Note, in the first place, that the two verbs are themselves differ-ent. The vessels of mercy are *afore prepared* (23), Gk. *proētoimasen*, while the vessels of wrath are *fitted* (22), Gk. *katērtismena*; lit. to render 'fit' or 'complete', with the perfect participle giving the sense of 'equipped' or 'perfected'. God is not stated to be the agent of the 'fitting'. The con-dition is stated simply as historical fact. Hence some would prefer the rendering 'fit for destruc-tion', i.e. 'ripe and ready for destruction' (Moff.). Secondly, note that the prefixes of the two parallel verbs are different—*pro*, signifying beforehand, and *kata*, signifying intensity of the action of the verb. It is legitimate to deduce from this that in the case of the disobedient the stress on the eternal aspect is missing. The mystery of predestination must remain, yet there appears here no warrant for any dogma of predestination to damnation, while the parallel foreordination to glory is stated with no uncertainty. In the third place it seems clear from Paul's language and thought that, while in the case of the vessels of mercy God's action was pre-preparation, in the case of the vessels of wrath He took no action but *endured with much longsuffering* (22). He was active on the one hand and passive on the other. 'God has tolerated most patiently the objects of his anger' (Moff.). Paul thus leaves his opponent without an answer; for no mortal man can reply either to the right of God in election or to His exercise of that right. There is no answer; but nevertheless the character of God remains irreproachable.

iv. God's election confirmed by the Scriptures (ix. 25–29). In this whole section dealing with the Jewish question the apostle probably has in mind more particularly the Jewish Christians in Rome. He therefore turns naturally to the law and the testimony for confirmation of the state-ments he has made. To corroborate his conclu-sion that the divine will is absolutely free to include Gentiles and reject Jews (25, 26), and to create an election within the election, Paul quotes freely first from Ho. ii. 23 (LXX) and i. 10 (LXX) and secondly from Is. x. 22, 23 (LXX) and i. 9. Here the doctrine of 'the remnant' is introduced to be treated further in xi. 1–10 (where see notes).

b. Jewish responsibility in the historical situation (ix. 30—x. 21)

In this defence of the legitimacy of his gospel, the gist of which was the new way of justification by faith, not works, Paul has routed all charges by the thunder of a high and inscrutable predesti-nation. His opponent is silenced, but the apostle feels that the Jew will now take refuge in an attitude of fatalism. To avoid a drift into deter-minism Paul now turns to examine the question of human responsibility. The Jewish question is therefore reviewed, not now from the divine standpoint as previously, but from the human standpoint. Paul asserts that the Jews them-selves are to blame for their rejection by God as the media of revelation to the world and (which is even more tragic) as sons of God themselves.

i. The Jews sought law-righteousness instead of faith-righteousness (ix. 30—x. 13). The Jews are responsible for their own apostasy. It is they who reject God, not God who rejects them. A vivid contrast is drawn between the Gentiles who had only the light of conscience and the Jews who possessed a special revelation. The one secured salvation by faith, even acceptance by God; the other lost the way of life by relying upon the observance of law. *They stumbled at* (i.e. 'took active offence at' or 'showed irritation at') *that stumblingstone* (i.e. 'the stone which causes stumbling or offence') (32). The reference is to the cross (1 Cor. i. 23), a seeming shame which the Jews could not endure as being the destiny of their Messiah.

Paul cannot get over the plight of the Jews. His *heart's desire*, longingly laid before God, is for their salvation (x. 1). Their appetite for religion is strong. But this zest is *not according to knowledge* (2); their action arises from their *being ignorant* (3). Paul does not mean that the Jews are unenlightened and without revelation of the righteousness of God. Rather they have not paid careful attention to (Gk. *epignōsis*) and have ignored (Gk. *agnoeō*) God's righteousness. Their ignorance is culpable. Their keenness is not in question; but they have not fully grasped the crucial point that God has a righteousness above the righteousness of the law. They do not see that Christ is the end of the law, now super-seding its sway and gaining its goal (4). Christ is the real righteousness; that of the Mosaic law might be enough if it could be kept, for law-righteousness must be kept (5). But faith-righteousness is a thing totally other. It is applied righteousness when applied by God to man.

Paul now portrays for his readers the divine method. His first point is that the way of salva-tion is not difficult and remote but near and easy (verses 5–10). He quotes from Dt. xxx. 11–14 and places an interpretation on the words with reference to Christ which he is careful to indicate. Christ is ever available to faith and so likewise is the gospel. Verses 9 and 10 indicate the form taken by the earliest Christian creed. Cf. Paul's reply to the question of the Philippian jailer in Acts xvi. 31. Salvation is a matter of personal trust in a living Saviour, which will be evidenced by open confession. The actions of belief and witness are complementary and Paul could hardly envisage one existing without the other. The quotation in verse 11 is repeated from ix. 33 and is itself taken from Is. xxviii. 16. It follows naturally on the thought that those who believe will also be proud to confess. Paul then picks on the word *Whosoever* to introduce his second point, that the way of salvation is within the reach of all, Jew and Gentile alike (verses 11–13). This universality of the gospel is emphasized by a further quotation from Joel ii. 32 which leads inevitably to the conclusion that, if they do not *call upon the name of the Lord* (13), the Jews are themselves responsible for their fate.

ii. The Jews are without excuse in their unbelief (x. 14–21). Israel cannot validly object that there has been lack of opportunity or warning. In the first place the gospel, this righteousness of God by faith, has been universally preached (18). The Jews may allege, by way of exoneration of their unbelief, that the preaching of the gospel has never reached them (14). Paul replies by a series of questions and answers laced with the words of prophecy (see Is. liii. 1; Ps. xix. 4; Dt. xxxii. 21; Is. lxv. 1, 2). In the second place lawgiver and prophet alike have issued a warning that Israel would reject God's message (19–21). The Jews cannot plead ignorance of their attitude. They cannot say it was not told them. God provoked this nation and angered it by what was not a nation, a nation void of understanding (Dt. xxxii. 21). And Isaiah, who asserts that God was found of them that sought Him not, and revealed to them that did not ask for Him (Is. lxv. 1), has recorded that Israel, on the contrary, rebuffed God's approach by their disobedience and contradiction.

c. The merciful purpose of God (xi. 1–36)

Paul now proceeds to consider more carefully whether the historical fact of the apostasy of the Jews and their consequent dereliction by God does necessarily amount to a final, absolute rejection of Israel. He comes to the conclusion that it does not, and glows with hope as he reasserts the fact of the believing remnant, the election within the election. Further, he is confident that, as the Jews have led to the conversion of the Gentiles, so the Gentiles will be the agents of the conversion of the Jews. The issue of the divine purpose will be to include all under grace.

i. The rejection of the Jews is partial, not complete (xi. 1–10). *Hath God cast away his people? God forbid* (1). The apostle with some heat repudiates the very idea that the disobedience of Israel was tantamount to God's rejection of His own people. It may have appeared as if this were indeed the end of Paul's argument, but the apostle rejects it in strong language. The very idea of an all-inclusive casting away of God's own chosen and favoured people is as blasphemous to him as to the Judaizers. God did not wholly reject. The issue of a total abandonment, which the historical situation seemed also to uphold, was avoided by reference to the past. Paul selects the case of Elijah (1 Ki. xix). It is parallel to the present situation. The prophet had good cause to condemn Israel then and to despair of its destiny; but God corrected his pessimism by the revelation of the remnant.

However stubborn a people may be at any time, there is always room for God's elected remnant. God still had grace for Israel. Election is by grace. If it were of works, there could be no grace. *The election hath obtained it, and the rest were blinded* (7). Israel as a whole failed to get right with God, but the true election secured this righteousness of God. The rest were 'hardened' (RV for *blinded*) according to the purpose of God (cf. ix. 18); i.e. 'a spirit of stupor' (8, RV; cf. Is. xxix. 10) was given them, a sort of spiritual insensibility. By quoting Ps. lxix. 22, 23 Paul places them on a level with David's own adversaries (9, 10).

ii. The rejection of the Jews is only temporary, not final (xi. 11–15). Again pressing the high predestination of God, the objector seems to ask 'Was it the purpose of God to make the Jews stumble in order that they might fall? Did the Almighty cause this irretrievable tragedy?' (11). Paul once more protests *God forbid.* The fall was not an end in itself but had in view a larger issue. The ruin of Israel was not final. One great result of their defection is the salvation of the Gentiles which is, in its turn, a goad to Israel's jealousy (11). The apostle still abjured any facile dogmatism such as his adversaries would spin from the situation. He still falls back upon an ultimate justification of God against plain appearances. If Israel's *fall* is the world's wealth and their loss the Gentiles' gain, then, *a fortiori,* a much greater blessing may be anticipated from their return. The word *fall* (Gk. *paraptōma*) is a moral concept suggesting trespass; hence *fulness* (Gk. *plērōma*) must also have an ethical meaning, although the Greek term is quite neutral, signifying 'completeness'. The context suggests a perfect consummation of faith, a spiritual goal which does not exclude material success. In verse 13 follow the punctuation of the RV. What Paul is saying is addressed to the Gentiles. But he wants them to understand that one of the reasons why he makes so much of his special commission as an apostle to them is that his brethren may be made jealous and in this way find salvation for themselves. Verses 13–15 thus repeat the thought of verses 11 and 12. This idea of the interaction between Jews and Gentiles is then further enlarged by an illustration.

iii. The figure of the olive tree (xi. 16–24). Paul begins with two metaphors in his mind: the piece of dough offered as a heave offering (Nu. xv. 19–21) consecrating the whole, and the holy root consecrating the branches. He passes over the first, however, and develops only the second (cf. Je. xi. 16; Ho. xiv. 6). The figure of the olive tree serves the twofold purpose of warning the Gentiles against boastful pride, and of substantiating Paul's Jewish optimism. The Gentiles are prone to adopt a supercilious attitude towards the Jews because of the gift of the righteousness of God by faith which they have received. Paul therefore applies the illustration first to them. It happens that branches are broken off, and wild olive strains are grafted in among them. In consequence the grafted shoots feed on the fatness of the original roots. Hence Paul insists that Gentiles should not 'glory' over themselves as the olive's branches (18, RV), for the branches are supported by the root and not *vice versa*. Faith does not presume upon privilege. *Be not highminded, but fear* (20). God punished the Jews, the natural branches. Therefore the apostle warns the Gentiles, the grafted branches, lest this severity take the place of His goodness toward them (22). Paul then applies his illustration to the Jews (23, 24). His hope for their future is presented as being perfectly natural by the *a fortiori* argument of *how much more* (24) can the natural branches, once cut off, be grafted back into their own olive tree. If only Israel would give up their persistent unbelief, *God is able to graff them in again* (23). Here Paul implies a spiritual, if not a horticultural, reality; the original branches are more akin to the tree than the wild shoots and should therefore be easier to graft into the stock from which they were originally taken.

iv. The fulness of both Jew and Gentile (xi. 25-32). Thus may be seen, Paul continues, the purpose of God working upwards through apparent severity to a beneficent goal, the restoration of all. He calls attention to *this mystery* (25). In Paul's period, the age of 'the mystery religions', the meaning of the word was a secret known only by the initiated. But by the term as applied to the Christian faith Paul means a secret, hidden in the past, but now revealed openly (cf. xvi. 25; 1 Cor. ii. 7; Eph. vi. 19; Col. ii. 2; 1 Tim. iii. 9). Here the particular sense of the mystery is the new light shed upon the unbelief of the Jews. The historical situation was now to be viewed with a different interpretation. This defect of Israel was not to be their last condition; for restoration was the divine will. The apostle desires the Jews to mark well this issue, lest in the pride of their own wisdom they arrive at the wrong conclusion. *Blindness in part is happened to Israel* (25). The RV again reads 'hardening' (cf. verse 7); the Greek is *pōrōsis*, from *pōros*, a stone, hence 'a covering with a callus'. Here the agent of the hardening is not mentioned. It is merely a historical fact morally interpreted. The partial hardening of Israel finally issues in their salvation as eternally decreed. *Until the fulness of the Gentiles* (25); i.e. until the 'great multitude' of Rev. vii. 9 is complete. The suggestion is that there will be little response to the gospel on the part of the Jews while the Gentiles are being brought into the kingdom. *And so all Israel shall be saved* (26). This conclusion taken together with verse 32, *that he might have mercy upon all*, is not infrequently interpreted as Pauline universalism. In what sense does the apostle use such terms? In verse 32 the word *all* evidently refers to the unbelieving Jews and the unbelieving Gentiles who have now come into the kingdom by their repentance and faith. In verse 26 *all Israel* could mean either the true spiritual Israel or the people

taken as a race. Some commentators, bearing in mind statements such as those in ix. 6-8 in which Paul stresses the spiritual nature of the true Israel, interpret the word here as referring to the true and eternal seed of Abraham which includes, of course, both Jews and Gentiles (cf. Gal. vi. 16). Others point out that in the following verses Paul seems to have clearly in mind the Jews as a race and feel that 'Israel' must therefore be interpreted in this sense in verse 26. In that case Paul is envisaging a future from the 'present time' of verse 5 until the historical Israel is saved. Some, again, would interpret this of the Jewish nation as a whole. Others feel that the phrase should not be regarded as so all-embracing and that it has the same meaning in relation to the Jews as has the term 'fulness of the Gentiles' in relation to non-Jews; i.e. *all* means 'all those who, in the purpose of God, will turn in faith to Christ'. To interpret it as referring to a universal salvation conferred upon men and women in view of their physical birth irrespective of their belief would be to contradict what Paul has plainly taught elsewhere (see, e.g., ii. 28, 29). *The gifts and calling of God are without repentance* (29); i.e. the unchanging God never regrets His promises or falters in His purpose, a fact which in verses 26 and 27 Paul corroborates from Is. lix. 20, 21 and xxvii. 9. From the gospel standpoint the Jews are objects of God's hostility, *they are enemies* (28); but from the point of view of 'the election' *they are beloved* (28). Actively and at the 'present time' the Jews are against Christ in the Gentile interest; passively, i.e. on historical considerations, they are beloved in the covenant sense. Disobedience characterizes both Jews and Gentiles in God's sight and even in this there is a purpose; it is so that God may have mercy on both, for neither party can really claim any pre-eminence over the other. Mercy apart, there is nothing for either Jew or Gentile.

v. Doxology (xi. 33-36). The apostle has now ended his argument. He has vindicated the justice and mercy of God in the rejection of the Jews and the election of the Gentiles on the basis of the merciful purpose of God. He has shown how even unbelief and sin are overruled for good. Paul ceases his arguing and concludes with praise. The eternal decrees of God are beyond man's understanding, but they are both wise and good. The divine acts are all-mysterious. If God condemns, who shall question or annul the decree? We behold His works in redemption, but the 'how' of them utterly baffles; for, after all, He is God unsearchable, inscrutable. All things originate from Him, continue through Him, and arrive at their consummation unto Him, for His glory. This ascription of praise is called forth from the apostle's heart; this noble doxology 'stands in simple grandeur like one of the patriarchs' pillars (cf. Gn. xxviii. 18, xxxv. 14) set up in remembrance of some special revelation of the goodness and majesty of God'.

VI. CHRISTIANITY IN PRACTICE.
xii. 1—xv. 13

a. Introduction (xii. 1, 2)

The apostle has completed the doctrinal sections of the Epistle dealing with principles and problems. He has set forth how to get right and how to keep right with God. He has defended this free righteousness of God against all objections. Now he seeks to explain the life of faith in practice and to impress upon his readers the duty of Christian living. The righteousness of God accepted by the believer is an inward experience which must have an outward expression. The *therefore* of verse 1 marks the transition from the defended doctrines of justification, sanctification and election to applied Christianity. At root the Christian life is one consecrated to God, lived not in conformity to the world but in 'transformity' to God. The apostle's approach to the Roman Christians is a model for all true preachers. *I beseech you therefore, brethren* (1); cf. for the same appeal Eph. iv. 1; 1 Tim. ii. 1; 1 Cor. iv. 16. Note that *the mercies of God* (1) form the ground of the appeal. They are collectively all that Paul has described in God's compassionate dealing with sinners of both parties, Jews and Gentiles. The demand is for a *reasonable service* (1), i.e. a spiritual worship, or offering, in contrast to the sacrifice of brute beasts, a moral rather than a ceremonial surrender to God (cf. 1 Pet. ii. 5). This consecration involves both body and mind. That Paul urges the Roman Christians to present their *bodies* (1) may be because of an existing tendency to belittle the flesh and to abuse the earthly temple as evil in essence. The Christian view of the body as sacred and as the servant of the soul is unique among the religions of the world. The yielding of the life in holy living is well-pleasing to God (cf. xiv. 18; Phil. iv. 18). This *living sacrifice* also includes the mind which, however, must first be renewed before it can be offered (2). This is a miracle of transformation, a readjustment to both temporal and eternal realities. The ideas conveyed by the terms used to express nonconformity and transformation are striking. The first has the root *schēma*, implying external semblance; the other is derived from *morphē*, meaning essential and radical likeness. The consequence is the recognition of God's will as right and fit and ideal.

After this exordium dealing with the fundamental principle of Christian living, self-sacrifice and devotion to God, the apostle proceeds to apply the law in four main sections of exhortation.

b. Personal ethics (xii. 3–21)

In this section the apostle evidently has in mind relations with both Christians and pagans. His admonitions are given spontaneously without any attempt at logical presentation; yet many characteristically group themselves together.

i. **The exercise of gifts (xii. 3–8).** *Through the* *grace given unto me* (3); Moff. 'in virtue of my office'. Paul declares that talents which come from God ought to be used with humility. He who is specially endowed is tempted to fancy himself and become self-important; hence the apostle warns that such must take himself seriously and avoid conceit. The sane view is grounded on the fact of the givenness of gifts from God and on the truth of mutual interdependence as *God hath dealt to every man the measure of faith* (3). This latter idea of faith-distribution as the norm of endowments leads the apostle to refer to the figure of the body and its members (4, 5; cf. 1 Cor. xii. 12; Eph. iv. 16; Col. i. 18). He is clearly thinking of the Christian community as a social organism with the various members co-operating in mutual service. There follows a list of seven illustrative gifts functionally correlated (6–8). *Prophecy* (6), i.e. inspired utterance of truth, or preaching (cf. 1 Cor. xv. 1), is to be exercised *according to the proportion of faith*. This may mean either that the more full of faith a man is, the better will be his preaching, or that his utterance must always be in harmony with his creed (interpreting the word 'faith' objectively). *Ministry* (i.e. deacons' work, service in things material rather than spiritual), *teaching* and *exhortation* are three gifts which are to be used each in its place; otherwise they will be ineffectual (7, 8). Giving or liberality to be exercised *with simplicity* (8), i.e. without any parade (cf. 2 Cor. ix. 11, 13; Jas. i. 5) and purely because of the need for the gift (following the RV rendering 'with liberality'). *He that ruleth* (8); i.e. he that has authority or leadership due to his ability. The reference may be to the home (cf. 1 Tim. iii. 4, 5, 12) or to the congregation (cf. 1 Thes. v. 12; 1 Tim. v. 17). *He that sheweth mercy* (8); i.e. is active in glad ministry to others (Moff. renders 'the sick visitor must be cheerful'). The phrase expresses the general idea of Christian kindness.

ii. **The law of love expressed in various activities (xii. 9–13).** Love, which is really the ruling principle of Christian living, is more than an emotion and of firmer nature than mere sentimentality or pure philanthropy. The Greek term *agapē* implies a quota of intellect and volition as well as feeling. It is akin to the divine quality behind 'the mercies of God' (1) and all His redemptive intervention in the destinies of a lost world. If this love be *without dissimulation* (9), i.e. void of hypocrisy and pure and sincere in its outflowing, then it will find activity in various forms. Love will produce loathing of evil and hungering after good (9). Also it will inspire a mutual affection for kindred souls (10). *In honour preferring one another* (10) is a phrase capable of several possible interpretations. It may mean putting the interests of others before our own, or being forward to pay honour to others, or eagerly surpassing others in praiseworthy works. *Not slothful in business* (11) appears to refer to secular matters alone; but the RV rendering 'in diligence not slothful' is more correct, and gives the phrase a wider application (cf. Mt. xxv. 26). The idea is that love, if allowed to rule, will never allow enthusiasm to flag. *Fervent in spirit* (11) is memorably rendered by Moffatt as 'maintain the spiritual glow', the reference being not to the divine but the human spirit. *Serving the Lord* (11); i.e. the Lord Jesus Christ. Some MSS read *tō(i) kairō(i)* for *tō(i) Kyriō(i)*, hence the rendering 'serving the opportunity' (RV mg.; cf. Eph. v. 16). The apostle continues the manifold manifestations of the dynamic of love in Christian living by citing cheerfulness in the reality of the Christian hope, endurance in suffering, perseverance in prayer, sharing the needs of Christian brethren and the practice of hospitality (12, 13).

iii. Additional maxims of Christian ethics (xii. 14–21). In this further list of moral precepts Paul may have non-Christians more in mind. Some certainly are definitely relative to those outside the fellowship of the Church. Verse 14 echoes our Lord's teaching in the Sermon on the Mount (Mt. v. 44). 'Share your fellows' joys and sorrows' admonishes the apostle (15). *Be of the same mind* (16); lit. 'mind the same things' (cf. 2 Cor. xiii. 11; Phil. ii. 2, iv. 2), i.e. never alter your Christian attitude to your fellows. Beware of selfish ambition. 'Aspire not to lofty tasks but follow the stream of lowly duties' (Prof. David Smith). Beware of self-conceit (cf. Pr. iii. 7). Never return ill for ill (17; cf. Mt. v. 43, 44; 1 Cor. xiii. 5, 6; 1 Thes. v. 15; 1 Pet. iii. 9). *Provide things honest* (17); better, as in RV, 'Take thought for things honourable in the sight of all men'; i.e. either consider the best things of any philosophy or religion in your cosmopolitan environment (cf. Pr. iii. 4; 2 Cor. iv. 2, viii. 21), or think nobly of all men, or aim to be above reproach in the eyes of all (Moff.). To be at peace with all men is the next admonition, attached to which is the concession *as much as lieth in you* (18), i.e. so far as it depends upon you.

Paul arrests his sermon with the homiletical address *dearly beloved*, to impress upon his readers that he sees them living at Rome, even as he dictates his Epistle. This last injunction on vengeance is an important point, he seems to say. *Give place unto wrath* (19). This means either that we should leave it to God to exercise wrath as declared in Dt. xxxii. 35, or that we should let the principle of retribution inherent in the moral universe pursue its course (reading 'the wrath'; cf. i. 18), or that we should give place to our own or our enemy's anger, i.e. 'let tempers cool'. The first affords the best interpretation. The attitude of the Christian under the rule of love must be one of mercy, the very opposite of retaliation. *Thou shalt heap coals of fire on his head* (20); i.e. give him a burning sense of shame. The verse is a quotation from Pr. xxv. 21, 22 (LXX). Therefore let good triumph over evil (21).

c. Political ethics (xiii. 1–7)

In this second section of admonitions Paul passes from purely personal matters to the realm of political ethics, and declares the Christian's duty to the State, a subject most relevant to his Roman readers. The apostle's view of the State in relation to the believer presents the principle of Christian submission which has ever been recognized as the mind of God and obligatory upon the Church. The grounds of this obedience to secular powers can be expressed under three headings.

i. Civil government is a divine institution (xiii. 1, 2). *Every soul* (1). Paul exhorts the Roman Christians, not as a social community merely, but as individuals, to be subject to the Roman rule. The apostle had always found the Roman high officials to be just and helpful, but this fact does not wholly account for an inspired dictum on political relations. It is the divine revelation for the Church in all ages, for which rational grounds are afforded. The first is that all authority is derived from God ultimately, and therefore the present powers have divine origination and sanction. Government has a place in the purposes of God. Theologically this is the doctrine that both Church and State are factors in the kingdom of God, each having its own particular function. The believer who resists earthly authority is, in fact, disobeying God. For such disaffection the rebel will acquire judgment. It has been plausibly suggested that in Paul's thought were both Jew and Gentile are visualized as possible, if not actual, resisters. The Jew in his religious assertiveness and the Gentile believer in his Christian dogmatism might both indulge in some hot-headed fanaticism against *the powers that be* (1). Such conduct is condemned.

ii. Civil government is ordained to promote good and to prevent evil (xiii. 3, 4). Obedience to secular powers is further commanded because of its service to the very righteousness of God which is the Epistle's theme. Twice here Paul describes the secular authority as *the minister of God* (4), continuing the idea of divine appointment into that of its purpose. A Christian must obey the magistrate because, in God's hand, his business is to keep order, commending the good and punishing the evil. Only evil-doers need tremble before the judges of the earth, for they are on the side of righteousness.

iii. Civil government has the approval of the Christian conscience (xiii. 5–7). Obedience to the powers that be is a Christian's duty, not only because of the inevitable penal consequences of resistance, but for conscience' sake. The moral constitution of the believer approves of the workings of the moral constitution of the State. Hence, taxes due as citizens of Rome or as a subject people must be paid (6). Indeed the apostle, enlarging the scope of the obligation, declares that all dues are to be honoured (7; cf. Mt. xvii. 25; Mk. xii. 17; Lk. xx. 25).

d. Personal ethics (xiii. 8–14)

Paul at this point reverts to exhortations in relation to one another after the style of chapter xii. He has just said 'Render to all their dues', which carries him back to the fundamental principle of all ethics, the law of love. The Christian has one debt, spoken of by Bengel as 'his immortal debt'. Origen says, 'It is our duty always to pay and always to owe this debt of love.' Love is the one obligation which fulfils all obligations. It realizes the end of all law (cf. Gal. v. 14). To reinforce this exhortation to love Paul reminds his readers of the approaching return of our Lord. The imminence of the Parousia is cited as one of the strongest motives for Christian living. *Knowing the time* (11); RV 'season', which gives the sense. It is the definite age before the second coming, the period yet to pass until the Lord appears again according to promise (cf. Mk. i. 15; 1 Cor. vii. 29; Heb. ix. 9). The admonition is to *awake* (11), to be up and doing, living more intensely the Christian life in its dynamic love. The end of the 'opportunity' is near, drawing ever nearer every day. The RV introduction of the word 'first' before *believed* (11) emphasizes rightly the aorist tense of a definite time, that of conversion. The aroused condition of the believer under the stimulus of the signs of the times will result in three resolute duties of higher living. First, *put on the armour of light* (12; cf. 2 Cor. vi. 7; Eph. vi. 13; 1 Thes. v. 8), the negative of which is abjuring all evil deeds which are associated with the night-time of ignorance. Secondly, *walk honestly* (13). Conduct must be as seemly as in the open day. Light is contrasted with darkness in verse 12, and here day with night, since the admonitions are being based on the passing of night-time and the nearness of the day of the Lord. Thirdly, *put ye on the Lord Jesus Christ* (14), the negative of which is refusing all provision for the lower man and his lusts. Christ is here conceived as the complete panoply of the believer (cf. Gal. iii. 27).

e. The strong and the weak (xiv. 1—xv. 13)

Paul now addresses himself to the special situation in the Roman fellowship of which he had been reliably informed. There are always brethren in every church who entertain imperfect conceptions of Christian truth combined usually with a certain doggedness for their defective creed. These are not to be browbeaten. Their conscience, partially enlightened as to the liberty which Christians enjoy in Christ, must be reverenced, and the conduct of the other members of the society of believers must not hurt them. On the other hand such troublesome brethren must not criticize the rest, advance their views as standards and demand uniformity. Evidently the apostle was familiar with this type of mind, as brethren were found in other churches under his inspection, especially in Corinth (cf. 1 Cor. viii. 1—x. 33) and Colossae (cf. Col. ii. 16–23). Two of the vexed questions upon which difference of opinion arose in Paul's time were the keeping of the sabbath and the eating of flesh. Probably the church at Rome refused membership to those who held eccentric views and Paul was endeavouring to advance the milder policy that they should be accepted upon confession of the essentials of the Christian faith and afterwards instructed in the Lord. Many had scruples in these matters and the apostle seeks to avoid schism in the church and to counsel toleration under the law of love.

i. The weaker brother is not to be despised (xiv. 1–12). Paul first of all stresses the point that every man must have his own reasoned convictions. He will regulate his conduct thereby with intellectual and moral honesty and suffer his neighbour to do likewise. He lives not in the presence of his fellow-men, but before the Lord at whose judgment seat we shall all stand. *Weak in the faith* (1) implies a lack of balance in discerning between the essentials and non-essentials of saving and sanctifying faith. Paul with apostolic authority commands the reception of such weak brethren into the Christian fellowship, but *not to doubtful disputations* (1); i.e. without entering into critical discussions or condemning their scruples. Prejudices of such minor importance are not sufficient grounds for denying sacramental privileges. Paul proceeds to note the two problems at issue, flesh-eating (3, 4) and holy days (5). There is the case of the ex-Jew, presumably, who is still in favour of kosher meat and differs from the ex-pagan who believes he can eat any flesh if he desires. It is not clear whether flesh is abstained from purely *per se*, or whether there is the added taint of consecration to idols (1 Cor. x. 25). It is likely that both elements entered into the prejudice. At any rate there must be no criticism between eater and non-eater. Before God alone and not his fellow-men the eater *standeth or falleth* (4), i.e. is acquitted or condemned, or, if taken subjectively, is morally unshaken in his liberty or becomes immoral in licence. But Paul adds that the freeman shall be in no danger, for the Lord can preserve him, having already *received him* (3). The other question is to be solved in the same spirit of liberty and toleration. One man holds by the sanctity of special days, another considers all are the same. Each should settle his own way of regarding such matters so long as it is *unto the Lord* (6). This motive of service rectifies observance or non-observance. Paul becomes gripped with this normative principle of the inspiration of service and expands it in verses 7–12. The Lordship of Christ is supreme and all-inclusive of life and death and judgment. When Christians remember that each *shall give account of himself to God* (12) other matters will assume the right perspective.

ii. The weaker brother's conscience must be respected (xiv. 13–23). Paul passes from his wise counsel to the Roman Christians not to judge one another to the suggestion that their critical faculty could be better employed by being turned upon themselves. They ought never to put temptation in the way of the weaker brethren by parading their own liberty in the matter of eating and drinking. Such freedom in the presence of those whose conscience disapproved might become a hindrance or *an occasion to fall* (13), i.e. a snare in the path of moral progress. Action taken against the light of conscience, however poor that light may be, is moral failure. When the apostle states that he believes that no meat is *unclean of itself* (14), he is referring simply to edible food under the ban of the ceremonial law or custom. Some think differently and for them, as for all, their view must regulate their conduct. The motive for deferring in this way to a weak brother's opinion is the ruling principle of love which Paul has already expounded (xii. 9–13), and to which he now joins the fact that such a one is beloved of the Lord and a sharer in the benefits of His atoning death (15). *Destroy not* (15). Paul uses this strong term to describe the final result when a weak brother is caused to act against his own conscience. To allow one's *good* (16), i.e. one's liberty, to grieve and destroy others in this way would cause the gospel to be evil spoken of. As far as the kingdom of God is concerned love is more important than questions of eating and drinking, and its expression in righteousness, peace and joy is the thing which matters most. Paul here is evidently combating the Jewish materialist conceptions of the messianic kingdom. *Destroy not* (20); a different word from that used in verse 15. It is the opposite of *edify* (19). RV renders 'Overthrow not'. The principle of total abstinence in all things that give offence is commended as the Christian's rule in living the life of faith-righteousness, lest a brother be tempted, not so much unto carnal degradation, as unto moral and spiritual ruin by suppressing his conscience. In verses 22, 23 follow RV. In some circumstances our faith may have to be expressed not openly but secretly in our communion with God. The happy man is the one whose conscience is clear. But the one who acts against his conscience condemns himself. Faith is the all-important factor. To change one's behaviour in such a matter without believing that it is the right thing to do is, in fact, sin (23).

iii. **A plea for unity (xv. 1–13).** The apostle now warns against the unwisdom of division, urging unity within the church at Rome, especially as regards the questions of Christian liberty and Gentile privilege. Basing his counsels upon the teaching already given he pleads for mutual understanding and helpfulness between those whose views and practice differ in the matters he has discussed. The *strong* (1). This is the first time that the apostle uses this term to describe those whose conscience enjoys the greater light, although the idea was implicit in his use of the term 'the weak' (cf. xiv. 1) to describe their opposites. The idea is one of moral ability, which serves not only its possessor but also others who may need support. True oneness of heart can be achieved in two ways, both of which are essential. First, it is the duty of the strong to bear with the weak and not to assert themselves. Egotism must be shunned. The life of self-sacrifice was the example set us by Christ, for even He *pleased not himself* (3). In confirmation of the point he is making Paul quotes from a messianic Psalm (lxix. 9); this leads him to assert the value of Scripture in its inspiration towards Christian living (4; cf. 2 Tim. iii. 16).

The second way of achieving unity is for the strong, representing the authorities of the church, to admit the weak into their fellowship. This duty the apostle had already urged (xiv. 1), using the same terms *receive ye* (7), for after all it is Christ who receives us all, strong or weak. Glory then be to God!

Paul then reminds the church at Rome that the mercy of God is extended to both Jew and Gentile alike. On this ground he exhorts to unity between circumcised and uncircumcised. That the fellowship at Rome should be split, or in any wise suffer, because of this universalism of the gospel is unthinkable. Christ was equally a servant to Jew and Gentile alike. By His life and work our Lord confirmed to the circumcision the promises made to the patriarchs (cf. ix. 4, 5). But the promises made to the uncircumcision in the Old Testament are similarly confirmed so that *the Gentiles might glorify God for his mercy* (9). Paul avers that all are 'one in Christ Jesus'. To prove to the Jews this sublime truth, the 'mystery' of his Epistle, Paul adds several Old Testament quotations; see Ps. xviii. 49 (LXX); Dt. xxxii. 43; Ps. cxvii. 1 (LXX); Is. xi. 10 (LXX). Paul then concludes the section by a benedictory prayer. *The God of hope* (13); cf. verse 5, 'the God of patience and consolation' (RV 'comfort'), and verse 33, 'the God of peace'. These are all qualities which God gives to believers. Cf. also xiv. 17.

VII. EPILOGUE. xv. 14—xvi. 27

a. Paul's justification for writing (xv. 14–21)

The apostle has now come to the conclusion of his noble Epistle. He begins his closing section with a reference to his own vocation as the explanation of his writing to the Roman Christians. With supreme tact he commends their spiritual maturity and ability in mutual self-help. He is persuaded that they are *full of goodness* (14). His letter is simply a reminder of truths they have learned already, even though he had not been their teacher. His boldness in addressing them arises from the fact of his apostleship to the Gentiles. Paul describes his divine commission in terms of the priesthood (16): *minister* (Gk. *leitourgos*; lit. 'a priest'; cf. Heb. viii. 2), *ministering* (Gk. *hierourgōn*; rendered by RV mg. 'ministering in sacrifice') and *offering up* (Gk. *prosphora*) are three sacerdotal terms. In the exercise of his preaching ministry as the prophet of God he is also a priest, offering the sacrifice of the Gentiles made righteous unto God and consecrated by the Holy Spirit. The same metaphor of offered sacrifice is used in xii. 1, 2 and Phil. ii. 17 with the same association of assured acceptance.

The success of his work among the Gentiles is

another mark of his apostolic commission upon which Paul rests his authority to write this Epistle. His mission has prospered, not through Himself but through Christ working in him. These miracles wrought *by the power of the Spirit of God* (19) are the only ones of which he is free to speak. He refers to his field of labour as *from Jerusalem, and round about unto Illyricum* (19); i.e. 'the north-west coast of the Adriatic with its hinterland, extending perhaps even into the Roman province of Macedonia'. Most of the Roman eastern provinces are meant, although there is no record in the Acts of Paul's missionary travels in Illyria. The apostle, while not an individualist, is diffident about mentioning the labours of others; his policy had always been to pioneer with the gospel and not to *build upon another man's foundation* (20), a rule he also states in 2 Cor. x. 15, 16. The figure of a foundation he also uses in 1 Cor. iii. 10 and Eph. ii. 20. Paul justifies his missionary strategy to go to the regions beyond by a citation from Is. lii. 15.

b. Plans for future journeys (xv. 22–33)

Dealing with more personal affairs, Paul now alludes to his future plans. The breaking of all this new ground has hitherto prevented a visit to Rome. But now the work has been covered and, having for many years longed to visit them, he hopes soon to come *en route* to Spain. Indeed the apostle expects the assistance of the Roman Christians to further his missionary enterprise in the West. *If first I be somewhat filled with your company* (24). He will not leave them until he has had the opportunity of satisfying some of the longing to have fellowship with them which he has already expressed in verse 23.

Meanwhile Jerusalem calls for his ministry as the bearer of alms from Macedonia and Achaia for the poor. The Hebrew Christians have shared with the Gentiles their spiritual treasures; it is therefore the duty of the new converts to contribute in temporal things to the needs of the mother church. With this charitable commission fulfilled, Paul plans to visit Rome on his journey to Spain. He arrived at Rome in circumstances never envisaged in his plans; but his confidence that his coming would be *in the fulness of the blessing of the gospel of Christ* was abundantly fulfilled (29). We do not know whether he ever reached Spain.

This more personal section ends with an apostolic charge that they should pray to God for him. His requests are, first, that he might be delivered from the unbelievers (RV 'them that are disobedient') in Judaea, i.e. the Jews who were still rejecting the claims of their Messiah; secondly, that he might find his missionary contribution acceptable to the Jerusalem saints; thirdly, that his western visit might be unto edification by God's will, with the blessed result of rest both for the Roman Christians and for himself. *Be refreshed* (32) is rendered by RV 'find rest'. As later events show, Paul's wish was far from being fulfilled. His experience, both in

Jerusalem and Rome, was very different from his peaceful dreams. With verse 33 cf. verses 5 and 13.

c. Greetings to friends in Rome (xvi. 1–16)

As Heb. xi has been termed the 'picture gallery' of Old Testament saints, so we may call Rom. xvi the 'picture gallery' of New Testament believers. It may be thought strange that Paul, who had never been to Rome, should yet have so many friends there. But the Jews of the first century (as of every century afterwards) were a commercial and migratory people. They moved along the trade routes and followed the markets. The commendations and salutations were to saints either going to, or living at, Rome. The greetings are varied, each giving a true index of the work performed and of the character won. One third of the names on this historical roll are those of women, revealing the prominent place women held in the church at Rome. Paul was a pioneer in the recognition of the function of women in Christian service and his attitude has been much misunderstood in this sphere. His testimonial to *Phebe* (1, 2) is most honourable. She is described as a *sister*, i.e. in the spiritual family of the Lord, suggesting equality of privilege with the brotherhood, as a *servant* of the church at Cenchrea, i.e. a deaconess (cf. Phil. i. 1), and as a *succourer* (Gk. *prostatis*, 'patroness'), implying that she was a lady of means who worked among the dock-population at the port of Corinth. It is believed that Phebe was on her way to Rome and Paul entrusted his precious Epistle to her care for safe delivery. *Priscilla and Aquila* (3) are a married couple whom Paul met at Corinth (Acts xviii. 1–3) on his first visit there; being of the same trade (they were tentmakers), the apostle lodged with them. We read of them further in Acts xviii. 18, 19, 26; 1 Cor. xvi. 19; 2 Tim. iv, 19. Apparently they had risked their lives for Paul's sake in some unrecorded incident which was well known to all the churches. Note how these churches are united with Paul in this expression of gratitude. Here, as in four out of the six instances in the New Testament, the wife's name (RV 'Prisca') precedes her husband's, the reason being unknown. *The church that is in their house* (5) is included in Paul's salutation. In the early Church there were at first few, if any, church buildings. Groups of Christians met in houses of prominent believers or in other available rooms (cf. Mt. xxvi. 18; Acts xii. 12; 1 Cor. xvi. 19; Col. iv. 15; Phm. 2). This is the first of five groups of believers in Paul's list; but the only one referred to definitely as a church (see verses 5, 10, 11, 14, 15). *Epaenetus* (5) is marked as a special friend and one of the first of Paul's converts in *Achaia* (i.e. Corinth), as was Stephanas (1 Cor. xvi. 15). But note that the RV, following the best MSS, reads 'Asia'; in this case he would be an Ephesian convert. *Mary* (6) is mentioned for her conspicuous service, either to Paul (AV *on us*) or to the Roman church (RV 'in you'). *Andronicus and Junia* (7) are *kinsmen* or, rather, fellow-countrymen (cf. ix. 3), i.e. Hebrews like Paul. *Junia* could refer either to a man (Junias) or to a woman. Three interesting pieces of further information are given. They had been *fellow-prisoners* with Paul, probably implying simply imprisonment for Christ's sake and not a period of confinement with the apostle in the same prison. They were *of note among the apostles*, i.e. outstanding apostles themselves in the wider sense of mission-preachers (cf. Acts xiv. 14; 1 Cor. xv. 7; 2 Cor. viii. 23, xi. 13). They were *in Christ before me*, i.e. they became converts to the new way of faith-righteousness before Paul had his own experience of the Damascus road. *Amplias* (8), a contracted form of Ampliatus, a slave name, is unknown, as also are *Urbane* (Urbanus is also a slave name) and *Stachys* (9) and *Apelles* (10), who is distinguished as a well-tried Christian (cf. 1 Cor. xi. 19; 2 Cor. x. 18, xiii. 7). *Aristobulus' household* (10) is the second group of Christians listed. This noble was a grandson of Herod the Great, who lived privately at Rome. Those belonging to him, aptly rendered 'his household', including officials and slaves, had a Christian fellowship among them. *Herodion* (11), as his name implies, belongs to Herod and probably is included in the household of Aristobulus. He may have been a leader in the group already mentioned (10). Along with Andronicus and Junia he is described as a *kinsman* of Paul. Hence, if we exclude Mary, who may have been a Jewess, there are only three Jews of the church at Rome in the catalogue of commendation. Similarly among the greetings from Corinth given later in this chapter (verses 21-23) there are only three other Hebrews. The household of *Narcissus* (11) contains the third group of Christians mentioned. *Tryphena and Tryphosa* (12) were probably twin sisters whose names mean 'Delicate' and 'Dainty' ('Dainty' and 'Disdain', according to Denney's suggestion). Paul records, perhaps with a touch of humour, that in spite of their names they are 'toilers in the Lord'. Another lady, *Persis*, is honoured in this verse. The name occurs in an inscription as that of a freed woman. *Rufus* (13) is perhaps the Cyrenian noted in Mk. xv. 21. The apostle refers to him as *chosen*, or 'elect', in the sense of being set apart for distinguished service. His mother at some time or other evidently 'mothered' Paul and so is included in the greeting. Now follows another group of believers, the fourth in this roll of honour, the most important of them being named—*Asyncritus, Phlegon, Hermas, Patrobas, Hermes* (14). A fifth company of saints, if not actually a church, comes next. The prominent members are mentioned—*Philologus* (lit. 'lover of wisdom'), *and Julia*, supposed to be husband and wife, with their family *Nereus, and his sister, and Olympas* (15). *An holy kiss* (16) is referred to by Paul in 1 Cor. xvi. 20; 2 Cor. xiii. 12; 1 Thes. v. 26. Another name is 'a kiss of love' (1 Pet. v. 14, RV). To salute with a kiss was the usual Eastern manner of greeting. The apostle now closes his roll of honour by greetings to the Roman saints from *the churches of Christ* (16). This is the more general phrase which Paul adopts (RV 'All the churches of Christ'). He claims to speak sometimes in their collective name (cf. xvi. 4; 1 Cor. vii. 17; 2 Cor. viii. 18, xi. 28). His practice, however, is to localize the fellowship, while generalizing the members, e.g. 'all the saints' of such and such a church (e.g. 2 Cor. xiii. 13; Phil. iv. 22). Once he writes 'the churches of Asia' (1 Cor. xvi. 19).

d. A final admonition (xvi. 17-20)

This warning against false teachers is as surprising in its interruption as that inserted in the Philippian letter (iii. 2). It is suggested that at this point of the Epistle Paul took the pen from his scribe to add his name as its credential of genuineness (cf. 1 Cor. xvi. 21-24; Gal. vi. 11-18; 2 Thes. iii. 17, 18). Then the pastoral emotion arose in the apostle's heart and he could not refrain from a last word of exhortation. Such an interpretation would suit a normal situation. On the other hand some advance the idea, as in the case of the church at Philippi, that something unusual had happened, perhaps the advent to Rome of the very false teachers against whom Paul feels urged to warn. It is not definitely known who these were. The Judaizers were always hostile to the apostle and dogged his footsteps. The trend of the warning seems to suggest the Antinomians, whose immoral licence was based on the doctrine 'the more sin, the more grace'. Paul exhorts the Roman saints with an impressive imperative, *mark them* (17); i.e. so as not to follow them. In Phil. iii. 17 the term is used positively as a call to follow a good example. The evil of these false teachers lies not merely in their doctrine but in their divisive influence. They cause *divisions and offences* (17), i.e. 'dissensions and hindrances' (Moff.). Paul's experience in other churches leads him anxiously to this warning. He appears to know these disturbers well. Their aim is not to glorify the Lord but to benefit themselves (18). He charges these deceivers with selfish egotism. They are 'slaves of their own base desires' (Moff.); cf. Phil. iii. 19. They also exercise the accomplished art of flattery and trap the unwary. Paul commends the fidelity of the Roman church to the traditional Christian faith which is already widely known. Further his ideal for them (cf. Mt. x. 16) is his motive in this warning (19). The appropriate title *God of peace* (20; cf. xv. 33) is used in this exhortation to beware of those who cause divisions and offences. Paul is confident that the Maker of peace is stronger than the destroyer of peace and soon Satan shall be thrown under the feet of the Roman saints that they may trample upon him (cf. Gn. iii. 25; cf. also 2 Cor. xi. 13-15).

e. Greetings from Corinthian brethren (xvi. 21-23)

Paul had interrupted his long list of salutations with a warning he felt a strong urge to give.

Now he seeks a conclusion. His companions at Corinth, where he is writing, wish to associate themselves with the apostle's greetings. Whether it is because they are prominent saints or have some connection with Rome is not revealed. Timothy (21) is well known as an intimate associate and 'fellow-labourer' in the gospel. *Lucius, and Jason, and Sosipater* are three of Paul's fellow-countrymen who are with him at Corinth, just as he has three Hebrew friends in Rome (7, 11). The three Corinthian Jews may be identified as Lucius of Cyrene, connected with Antioch (Acts xiii. 1), Jason, Paul's host at Thessalonica (Acts xvii. 5-9), and Sopater of Berea who went with Paul from Corinth to Asia (Acts xx. 4). It appeared to the amanuensis that Paul had now finished and so he added his own name *Tertius* (22) to the salutations. However, the apostle remembers some more people interested in the brethren at Rome and so he puts in a postscript (23). *Gaius* is described as *mine host*; clearly Paul had found a lodging with him during his stay at Corinth. He is probably the same person whom Paul baptized along with Crispus (1 Cor. i. 14). The name is found in Acts xix. 29, xx. 4; 3 Jn. 1. But he is also host of *the whole church*, i.e. the church at Corinth. Its gatherings were, presumably, held in his house. *Erastus* (23) is a high official in Corinth, the treasurer of the city, and certainly a Christian. He is most likely to have had some civil connection with the imperial city. The same name is mentioned in Acts xix. 22 and 2 Tim. iv. 20. *Quartus* (23) is an unknown brother. The benediction of verse 24 is omitted by the RV in accordance with the best MSS. See the *Introduction* p. 940.

f. A concluding doxology (xvi. 25-27)

While not always concluding an Epistle with a doxology, Paul has composed several (cf. xi. 36; Gal. i. 5; Eph. iii. 20; Phil. iv. 20; 1 Tim. i. 17). The ascription of praise is here offered to God in two aspects of His perfection. He is *of power to stablish* (25) and is also *God only wise* (27). This divine ability has already been referred to in the Epistle (i. 16, xiv. 4). God's omnipotence is redemptive through the gospel for it is 'the power of God unto salvation'. This conception, which was early emphasized in the Epistle, is now, at its close, proclaimed after the inspired exposition of the gospel entrusted to the apostle. This gospel is described as *the preaching of Jesus Christ* (25); i.e. the offer of a faith-righteousness in place of a works-righteousness on the ground of the finished work of reconciliation through the life, death and resurrection of Jesus Christ. It is also *the mystery, which . . . now is made manifest*, a reference to the inclusion of the Gentiles in the privileges of the righteousness of God. It is also *by the scriptures . . . made known* (26), i.e. attested. The gospel, Paul all along maintained, had been proved by the Scriptures of the Old Testament (cf. i. 2, iii. 21, ix. 1—xi. 36). The prophets of old were commissioned by the eternal God to declare His will of salvation to all men, *for the obedience of faith* (26). RV renders 'unto obedience of faith' implying that faith and obedience are synonymous (cf. i. 5). The idea emerges in i. 5, vi. 16 and xvi. 19. The RV mg. suggests 'obedience to the faith', giving the objective rather than the subjective interpretation of the term 'faith'. Paul also throughout his Epistle conceives of the divine omnipotence in its redemptive aspect as an inward force in the believer whereby he is able to stand. The power to stablish the Roman saints is an inner experience whereby he is upheld (xiv. 4). Thus, in this concluding doxology, the characteristic concepts of Paul's teaching are repeated: the new way as the real consummation of the old, the effectual call of God to His servant in both dispensations to reveal His will, the universalism of the gospel, and the one condition, 'faith'. *Only wise* is another phase of the divine character which evokes the adoration of the apostle. The wisdom of God in the Pauline thought is not mere speculation, or philosophy, beyond the ken of human understanding. It is rather an attribute wherein Paul sees the mercies of God toward sinful men, practically designed and achieved through Jesus Christ. Such wisdom is the sole prerogative and property of God. Hence eternal glory be to God! *Laus deo*. Amen.

G. T. THOMSON.
F. DAVIDSON.

THE EPISTLES TO THE CORINTHIANS

INTRODUCTION

See also the General Article, 'The Pauline Epistles', p. 68.

I. PAUL'S CONTACTS WITH CORINTH

The gospel was brought to the city of Corinth, the chief city of Achaia, within twenty years of the crucifixion. It was a city containing a mixed population of native Greeks, Roman colonists, and Jews. It was on a main trade-route between west and east, and so had a ceaseless stream of traffickers, with an accompanying restlessness of spirit and outlook. There are clear indications in our two Epistles to the Corinthians of the effect such an atmosphere had on Christians there.

We read about two of Paul's visits to Corinth in Acts xviii and Acts xx. 1–3. He also corresponded with the church there on several occasions, and had letters and communications from them (see 1 Cor. vii. 1, 2 Cor. ii. 4). The apostle's relations with the Corinthian church seem to have been of a very close and personal character. He was the first to plant the gospel there (1 Cor. iii. 6 and iv. 15), and he watched the growth of the church with intense personal interest. There were peculiar difficulties. Great enthusiasm was combined with much liability to error, party feeling often ran high, and the apostle seems to have had his detractors who sought to undermine his influence. This comes out very clearly in our second Epistle.

The first visit to Corinth was made in what we usually term Paul's second missionary journey. He arrived there after his visit to Athens, and at once preached in the synagogue (Acts xviii. 4). He encountered such opposition from the Jews that he was led to make the declaration: 'Your blood be upon your own heads; from henceforth I will go unto the Gentiles' (Acts xviii. 6). These words would seem to imply disputation about the guilt of crucifying Jesus. That the apostle made the cross his special subject at Corinth is borne out in our first Epistle: 'I determined not to know any thing among you, save Jesus Christ, and him crucified' (1 Cor. ii. 2). Whether his experience at Athens had led to this decision we can only conjecture; but it might possibly be the case.

At the same time there were some converts from among the Jews. First of all there was Aquila and his wife Priscilla. They were not Corinthians, but were living there, and Paul resided with them (Acts xviii. 1–3). Then there was Crispus, who was no less than the 'chief ruler of the synagogue' (Acts xviii. 8). He believed and all his house. Thirdly there was Sosthenes (1 Cor. i. 1), who may be he who is described in Acts xviii. 17 as the 'chief ruler of the synagogue'. If so, like Crispus, he had been converted to faith in Christ. Later he travelled with Paul and was with him in Ephesus, and the apostle includes his name in the salutations sent to the church in Corinth in the first Epistle (1 Cor. i. 1). Paul's main success, however, was among the Corinthians themselves, of whom we are told that 'many . . . believed' (Acts xviii. 8). Also, God told him in a vision, 'I have much people in this city' (Acts xviii. 10). Jewish opponents continued to persecute Paul, and eventually brought him before Gallio, the deputy, or Roman proconsul, of Achaia (Acts xviii. 12). Gallio gave them no satisfaction, the whole incident recoiling on the head of Sosthenes, then the chief ruler of the synagogue, through a counter anti-Jewish demonstration of the Greek population (Acts xviii. 17). The mention of Gallio as proconsul gives us reason for dating Paul's first visit to Corinth in the early fifties of the first century, for Gallio's proconsulship may be reckoned to have begun in the summer of A.D. 51, or at the latest in A.D. 52. The apostle remained there for some eighteen months (Acts xviii. 11), which gave him a good opportunity of building up the church there. It was not his longest stay at one place, as we read of his being over two years in Ephesus afterwards (Acts xix. 10).

II. THE NUMBER OF PAUL'S VISITS

How often did the apostle visit Corinth again? Only one other visit is recorded in Acts, namely in xx. 1–3. No details are given, but it was a visit immediately prior to his final visit to Jerusalem, and therefore may be taken as his last visit to the city. So we have a record in Acts of his first and last visits. In the Epistles before us, the apostle speaks as if this last visit was really a third visit (2 Cor. xiii. 1). Some ambiguity exists, however, on this point, because a promised visit was cancelled (2 Cor. i. 23). Whether still another visit was made we are not explicitly told, and the matter can hardly be settled with certainty. We do know that Paul had to write severely to the Corinthians about their behaviour (2 Cor. ii. 4), and he postponed the promised visit so that he might not be present to blame them even more severely than in his letter (2 Cor. i. 23). If this promised visit was not undertaken, then there was no intermediate visit.

III. THE DATE OF THE EPISTLES

The value of discussing this point is simply for the reconstruction of the circumstances that led up to the writing of 1 and 2 Corinthians. We know that Paul stayed for eighteen months at Corinth on his first visit, then crossed by sea to Ephesus, visited Jerusalem and Antioch, travelled round his earlier scenes of missionary activity in Asia Minor, and then came again to Ephesus where he stayed over two years (Acts xviii. 11, 18–23, xix. 1). He wrote 1 Corinthians from Ephesus, perhaps about a year after his arrival there in, say, 55 A.D. It was written partly to condemn the growth of factions amongst them, of which he had heard through members of the family of Chloe (1 Cor. i. 11); partly to censure the Corinthians in connection with an act of gross immorality committed by one of them, and against whom they had not taken sufficiently strong action (1 Cor. v. 1–8); and partly to answer some questions about which the Corinthians had written seeking his advice (1 Cor. vii. 1). It would seem that Timothy was already on his way to Corinth when Paul wrote this Epistle (1 Cor. xvi. 10), so that the Epistle must have been taken direct to Corinth by some other messenger.

We next know for certain that some time after Paul had written this Epistle (though it was not the first letter that Paul had written to the Corinthians, as we know from 1 Cor. v. 9), he himself set out for Corinth via Macedonia (1 Cor. xvi. 5). While this was the plan he finally adopted, he had previously talked of going first to Corinth, then to Macedonia, and back again to Corinth. He refers to this previously declared intention (2 Cor. i. 15, 16) because it would seem that some had taken offence at his change of plan, and tried, by disparaging reference to it, to undermine his influence with the Corinthians. We might therefore conjecture that the messenger who took 1 Corinthians to Corinth returned at once to Ephesus with a very serious report of the state of the church there. Whereupon Paul, instead of visiting Corinth at once, wrote a hurried letter (which has not come down to us), in which he scolded the Corinthians rather severely, and which he sent to Corinth by the hand of Titus. (See 2 Cor. ii. 3, 4, 9, vii. 5–16.) This left Paul much burdened in mind and most eager to know as soon as possible how the Corinthians had responded to such reproof. Titus was to return via Macedonia; and Paul left Ephesus and went first to Troas, and then on to Macedonia, in order to meet Titus the sooner. When he did so, he was overjoyed to learn from Titus that the scolding letter had had a most beneficial effect, and that the Corinthians had entirely come round to see his point of view (2 Cor. ii. 12–14). Thereupon he wrote the letter which we call 2 Corinthians, and sent back Titus with it, together with two other brethren (2 Cor. viii. 16–24). They delivered the Epistle and also completed the gathering of a collection that was being made at Corinth for the 'poor saints at Jerusalem' (2 Cor. viii. 11). 2 Corinthians was therefore written from Macedonia and expressed Paul's joy at the turn of events at Corinth. In it, however, the apostle also did not hesitate to drive home the lessons of the 'quarrel', elaborating upon it in the last four chapters (x—xiii. 10).

This reconstruction is conjecture, and is not accepted by all in this form. Some hold that this severe letter mentioned in 2 Cor. ii. 3 is our 1 Corinthians; others suggest that 2 Corinthians as we have it is made up of two or three sections taken from different Epistles written by the apostle to the Corinthians at different times. Such distinct sections are said to be: i—ix, with the exception of vi. 14—vii. 1, and x—xiii. 10. Such a possibility cannot be altogether overlooked, and we shall refer to it again later. But this view is not absolutely necessary, and good arguments can be brought forward in favour of the unity of 2 Corinthians as it stands. In any case the Pauline authorship of the whole is unquestioned.

Eventually Paul himself arrived at Corinth from Macedonia, and spent three months there. He had to escape Jewish persecution once again, and left Corinth by land instead of by sea, as was his intention at first (Acts xx. 3). As far as we know, the apostle was never at Corinth again.

IV. EXTERNAL EVIDENCE

In later times Clement of Rome addressed an Epistle to the church of Corinth from the church of Rome. This was about A.D. 95, and in it he mentions an Epistle of Paul which can be identified with 1 Corinthians. This early mention makes 1 Corinthians one of the best authenticated Epistles in the New Testament. Possibly the earliest reference to 2 Corinthians is to be found in the writings of Irenaeus and Clement of Alexandria, both towards the end of the second century; but the genuineness of the Epistle has never been questioned.

V. THE CHURCH AT CORINTH

The church at Corinth was formed first of a few Jews and many Gentiles, as has been already mentioned. Their weak and strong points may be learnt as we study Paul's letters to them. In neither of these Epistles, however, nor in the account of Paul's visits to Corinth given in the Acts, are we told what exactly happened in the church to occasion the severe rebuke that was administered to them. We know there was a case of incest of a peculiarly bad kind (1 Cor. v. 1–5);

also there was a case of one 'who had done wrong' (2 Cor. vii. 12), if indeed these were two different persons. But we would gather that there was an even more general reason than these to cause disquiet to the apostle, namely, some movement that questioned Paul's apostleship, and set up a counterclaim of its own (see 2 Cor. xi. 1–6). We are left in the dark, then, as to the exact development of events.

Let us put together as much as we can. From the Acts we know that Apollos also visited Achaia (and therefore certainly Corinth, the capital city) and preached there acceptably (Acts xviii. 28). Also he is mentioned by Paul with commendation in 1 Corinthians—'Apollos watered' (1 Cor. iii. 6). It is interesting to note that his was one of the names chosen to designate a party—'I of Apollos' (1 Cor. i. 12). From what we read of him in Acts, he seems to have been a well-instructed Jew who became a believer and was an eloquent speaker. He was evidently not responsible for the creation of the 'Apollos party', any more than was Paul for that called after his own name. Timothy, Titus and Silas also laboured with Paul at Corinth (see Acts xviii. 5 and 1 and 2 Corinthians *passim*).

An interesting speculation has arisen as to whether Peter ever visited Corinth, because of the mention of a 'Cephas party' (1 Cor. i. 12). No mention, or hint, of such a visit occurs anywhere in the New Testament. What then, in particular, can the Cephas party have stood for? This is a question we cannot answer with certainty; but from the fact that Paul himself in his Epistle to the Galatians declares 'I withstood Peter to the face' (Gal. ii. 11), it is possible that news of this disagreement on a major matter of principle reached Corinth, and some there championed Peter. The issue then would be the strict observance of Jewish law by all Christians.

VI. PAUL'S PURPOSE IN WRITING

Now the temperament of the population at Corinth, consisting as it did of people drawn from several races, lent itself to party divisions. Even the Christians were affected by this sectarian spirit and used the names of outstanding leaders, and even of Christ Himself, to denote their different divisions. Against this the apostle has to write very strongly, and the first four chapters of 1 Corinthians are devoted to showing the wrongness of the party spirit among Christians. Paul traces the root cause of these divisions to a false conception of wisdom on the one hand and of the Christian ministry on the other. The divisions were wrong not only because of the bitterness engendered, but also because the teachers, whose names the different parties took, were not themselves in opposition to one another. It was otherwise among the non-Christian population of Corinth, where teachers of really different views did exist. It is recorded, for instance, by Publius Aelius Aristides in the second century, that in every street in Corinth you met a 'wise man', who had his own solution to the problems of life. This partisanship may be linked to a natural tendency among the Greeks for a certain mental levity; also a curiosity about the mysterious which was satisfied with many possible explanations without necessarily deciding upon the one true explanation. (Cf. Acts xvii. 21.) Lest the Christian community should follow this tendency, the apostle writes with vigour, 'Is Christ divided? was Paul crucified for you?' (1 Cor. i. 13).

But so far we have considered only the party names mentioned in 1 Corinthians. All of these names were of genuine and good men, and the trouble was not caused by them but by the Corinthians themselves in using their names for party purposes. In 2 Corinthians we find a different situation, for now a group of other 'apostles' has appeared undermining Paul's influence. These are dealt with in the last four chapters of this Epistle and, as he writes about them, Paul is led to use great plainness of speech. He sets down their attitude. 'His letters, say they, are weighty and powerful; but his bodily presence is weak, and his speech contemptible' (2 Cor. x. 10). Against these Paul has to speak about himself in a way which obviously hurts him. 'What I do, that I will do, that I may cut off occasion from them which desire occasion' (2 Cor. xi. 12); and 'That which I speak, I speak it not after the Lord, but as it were foolishly, in this confidence of boasting' (2 Cor. xi. 17). There follows a list of experiences in Paul's own life of which we should not have known except for these mischief-makers in the church at Corinth. So good has come out of evil. But even of greater interest to us as we contemplate these things is the fact that the apostle kept on communing with this factious group of Christians; he did not dismiss them as impossible folk, but carried out our Lord's injunction, 'despairing of no man' (see Lk. vi. 35, RV mg. and Gk.). And in the midst of these words of personal controversy we can sense the spirit of Christian love and the outworking of the principles expressed in 1 Cor. xiii. 'I will very gladly spend and be spent for you; though the more abundantly I love you, the less I be loved' (2 Cor. xii. 15).

VII. TWO LETTERS OR THREE?

Let us here make a digression to consider whether these chapters (2 Cor. x—xiii) are not misplaced in their present position, and should rather be regarded as a separate letter, and indeed as the letter referred to in 2 Cor. ii. 3, 4. Let us give Paul's own description of this letter:

'I wrote this same unto you, lest, when I came, I should have sorrow from them of whom I ought to rejoice; having confidence in you all, that my joy is the joy of you all. For out of much affliction and anguish of heart I wrote unto you with many tears; not that ye should be grieved, but that ye might know the love which I have more abundantly unto you.'

Now, if we turn straight from reading these words to chapter x, we can appreciate the force of the above question. The chapter begins:

'Now I Paul myself beseech you by the meekness and gentleness of Christ, who in presence am base among you, but being absent am bold toward you: but I beseech you, that I may not be bold when I am present with that confidence, wherewith I think to be bold against some, which think of us as if we walked according to the flesh.'

Later, in xi. 2 and 3 we read:

'For I am jealous over you with godly jealousy: for I have espoused you to one husband, that I may present you as a chaste virgin to Christ. But I fear, lest by any means, as the serpent beguiled Eve through his subtilty, so your minds should be corrupted from the simplicity that is in Christ.'

These sentiments, it is thought, fit Paul's description of the letter so well that many commentators conclude that these chapters are the letter in question, and therefore are chronologically earlier than chapters i—ix. The present arrangement, however, is found in all MSS, and no evidence whatever is forthcoming to indicate that the last four chapters did not originally belong to the first nine. The question can therefore be discussed only from internal evidence, and a unanimous opinion has not been reached. In favour of the present order being correct, it can be pointed out that chapters i—ix, though recording joy, also contain reproof (see, for example, i. 23). This indicates that the matter is not yet entirely out of mind, and the warning tone of the last four chapters can appropriately follow. Again, the tone of x—xiii is not all hostile, and might be thought to be hardly severe enough for the description of the scolding letter. Genuine love and anxiety also mark these chapters (see, for example, xii. 20: 'For I fear, lest, when I come, I shall not find you such as I would, and that I shall be found unto you such

as ye would not'). When these qualities of each section are borne in mind, the total attitude in each section is not so very different that the latter cannot conceivably follow the former.

Did the apostle succeed in restoring Christian fellowship between himself and the church of Corinth, and also within the church itself? Those who place chapters x—xiii prior to chapters i—ix can answer, Yes. If we feel that we must take the chapters in the order in which we have them, we can still believe that Paul, through the Holy Spirit, will once again have been 'consoled and comforted' as he was on previous occasions (see 2 Cor. i. 1–14).

VIII. THE TEACHING OF THE EPISTLES

The church at Corinth was thus at once a source of joy and of anxiety to the apostle. The two Epistles which we possess are characterized by a spirit of intense personal concern on the part of the writer for the Corinthian Christians. This personal concern prevented him from developing any one line of doctrine, as, for instance, in Galatians; or a systematic presentation of the way of salvation as it is in Christ Jesus, as in Romans (though it is interesting to recall that Romans was written at Corinth). Many doctrinal topics are touched upon, some of them being of primary importance to the understanding of the Christian faith. There are sections dealing with the nature of human and of divine wisdom (1 Cor. i—iv); the doctrine of Christian behaviour (1 Cor. v, vi, viii, ix, xi); the Christian doctrine of marriage (1 Cor. vii; cf. 2 Cor. vi. 14—vii. 1); the institution and meaning of the Lord's Supper (1 Cor. x, xi. 17–34). There is teaching concerning the unity of the Church (1 Cor. xii, xiii, xvi. 1–9; 2 Cor. viii, ix); spiritual gifts (1 Cor. xiv); the resurrection (1 Cor. xv) and the Christian ministry (2 Cor. iii—vi. 10, x—xiii. 13). From this list it will be seen what a very great loss the Church would have suffered had these Epistles never been written or not been preserved.

I CORINTHIANS: OUTLINE OF CONTENTS

I. INTRODUCTION. i. 1–9
    a. Greetings to the Christians in Corinth (i. 1–3)
    b. Thanksgiving for the grace given to them (i. 4–7)
    c. Confident hope concerning them (i. 8, 9)

II. DIVISIONS IN THE CHURCH. i. 10—iv. 21
    a. Statement of the facts (i. 10–17)
    b. The root cause of the divisions: A wrong conception of wisdom (i. 18—iii. 4) and a wrong conception of the Christian ministry (iii. 5—iv. 13)
    c. Concluding appeal to end the divisions (iv. 14–21)

III. MORAL FAULTS IN THE LIFE OF THE CHURCH. v. 1—vi. 20
    a. Laxity in dealing with a case of incest (v. 1–13)
    b. Lawsuits before heathen judges (vi. 1–11)
    c. The sin of fornication (vi. 12–20)

IV. ANSWERS TO QUESTIONS. vii. 1—xiv. 31

a. Marriage (vii. 1–40)
b. Meats offered to idols (viii. 1—xi. 1)
c. Public worship — the principles at stake (xi. 2—xiv. 40)

V. THE GOSPEL OF THE RESURRECTION. xv. 1–58

a. Summary of the facts (xv. 1–19)
b. Consequences of the facts (xv. 20–34)
c. The nature of the resurrection body (xv. 35–49)
d. Immortality (xv. 50–58)

VI. FINAL INSTRUCTIONS. xvi. 1–24

a. Systematic giving (xvi. 1–9)
b. Concerning Timothy, Apollos and Stephanas (xvi. 10–18)
c. Greetings and closing prayer (xvi. 19–24)

I CORINTHIANS: COMMENTARY

I. INTRODUCTION. i. 1–9

a. Greetings to the Christians in Corinth (i. 1–3)

The apostle adopts the usual form of Greek salutation, in which the writer's name comes first. He describes himself as one who has been *called to be an apostle of Jesus Christ through the will of God* (1). He was very conscious of the hand of God in his calling. Knowing the account of Paul's conversion (see Acts ix. 1–16), we can appreciate why the apostle constantly referred to it, both directly (see e.g. Acts xxii. 1–16) and indirectly in his epistolary salutations. We may also infer that Paul is concerned to emphasize his God-given apostolic commission and authority especially when writing to churches where, as in Corinth, there was a tendency on the part of some to disparage it. *Sosthenes our brother* (1). He delights to join the name of another Christian with his own, always thinking in terms of the fellowship with others in the gospel (cf. 2 Cor. i. 1 and his other Epistles). (For Sosthenes, see *Introduction*.) *The church of God which is at Corinth* (2) is the striking way the apostle speaks of the group of Christian men and women of Corinth; they are the local representatives of the one Church of God. *Sanctified in Christ Jesus* (2), i.e. set apart, or dedicated to God, by being brought into union with Christ Jesus. The tense of the Greek word for 'sanctified' indicates a continuous state consequent upon a past experience of sanctification. *Called to be saints* (2) again indicates that the Christian's standing is from God, not gained by his own merits (see note on Phil. i. 1). *All that in every place call upon the name of Jesus Christ our Lord* (2). The Church of Christ is universal, 'catholic', and yet there is an intimate feeling between each part, and each individual, and Christ—*both their's and our's* (2). We may use the descriptive phrases in verse 2, following the words *church of God*, as giving the doctrine of the Church, and the method of describing membership of the Church. Note the sequence—'of God', 'sancti-

fied,' 'called', 'call upon', 'theirs and ours'. The Church is God's creation, for Him and by His will. Its members are sanctified, set apart for God's use; they are called—the word also implying empowered—to be saints; and they continually call upon the name of Jesus Christ, conscious that others in other places are doing the same, thus not thinking that they alone constitute the whole Church, or that they alone possess Christ. *Grace . . . peace* (3); the first is the fountain from which our salvation flows, the second the reward of personal trust in God. *God our Father, and . . . the Lord Jesus Christ* (3). The association of the name of Jesus with that of God the Father in such incidental phrases as this gives us more than formal statements could do: an assurance of the apostolic belief in the deity of Jesus Christ. The doctrine of the Holy Trinity is not derived from isolated texts; we believe it underlies the whole of the New Testament. Occasion to refer to it again will be found as we proceed (see especially the notes on chapter xv).

b. Thanksgiving for the grace given to them (i. 4–7)

The apostle says that he continually thanks God for the results of the preaching of the gospel in Corinth, through which the grace of God was received by many (4). He had been told by God, 'I have much people in this city' (Acts xviii. 10), and this was a source of great joy to him. *Which is given* (4) should be 'which was given' (see RV), indicating a definite experience in the past. This has resulted in an enrichment of their lives, their speech, and their knowledge (5), in accordance with the testimony which the apostle gave of Christ, which was then confirmed in them (6). The Corinthian Christians exhibited a full Christian faith, and lived in the expectation of Christ's return (7). The apostle would teach us to regard this expectation as the climax of the Christian faith. It is indeed so; and its widespread

971

neglect today is a measure of the departure from the apostolic faith of the Church. Cf. the attitude of the 'scoffers' in 2 Pet. iii. 3, 4.

In thanking God for the grace given to the Corinthians, we notice that the apostle refers to 'utterance' and 'knowledge' as special gifts of the Corinthian Christians. This is significant in the light of what is written later in the Epistle. For instance, we learn in chapter xiv the apostle's mind on the subject of speaking with tongues. He encourages rather that they should 'prophesy', that is, give utterance to the gospel message. Also, in this Epistle we have a discussion of true, and false, 'knowledge' (see verses 18ff.). The Corinthians, then, by their intellectual activity were raising new questions upon which there was need of apostolic guidance.

c. Confident hope concerning them (i. 8, 9)

Jesus Christ . . . confirm you unto the end (7, 8). 'Confirm' means to strengthen the grace already given so as to make it endure to the end. The result will be that they will be blameless, unimpeached, *in the day of our Lord Jesus Christ* (8), that is, when Christ shall return as judge. *God is faithful* (9). God's promises can be utterly relied upon. That is why trusting God is both the test, and the joy, of the true Christian. *Ye were called* (9). The assurance that it is God who calls us *unto the fellowship of his Son Jesus Christ* (9) removes many fears depending upon reliance on self. This thought has received the attention of many Christian teachers. The phrase, *fellowship of his Son*, is a way of describing the Church, and its use here is significant in view of the party feelings that had arisen at Corinth, about which the apostle was soon to speak rather forcibly. Christians should have fellowship one with another because each has fellowship with Christ.

II. DIVISIONS IN THE CHURCH. i. 10—iv. 21

a. Statement of the facts (i. 10–17)

Verses 10–17 come somewhat as a shock. The 'saints' are quarrelling amongst themselves! How can we explain it? Saintliness in the New Testament represents primarily a status before God, but should also be manifested in holiness of life. This requires deliberate training and self-discipline. *By* (or 'through') *the name of our Lord Jesus Christ* (10). To recall the divine Master is the way to make one ashamed of one's sins. Even Paul did not presume to correct the saints in his own authority. *That ye be perfectly joined together in the same mind and in the same judgment* (10). 'Mind' and 'judgment' can perhaps be distinguished by taking the first to mean agreement in thought, and the second agreement in decision or purpose. *It hath been declared unto me . . . by them . . . of Chloe* (11). Some of the Christians of Corinth were grieved by the party feelings, and appealed to Paul. Chloe is not elsewhere mentioned. *I am of Paul; and I of Apollos; and I of Cephas; and I of Christ* (12). What was

the particular teaching, or viewpoint, of each of these parties cannot be determined with certainty. Perhaps they were simply used as terms of personal loyalties, though the party *of Christ* is very hard to explain along these lines. Various suggestions have been made—that those *of Paul* were a group which emphasized freedom from the Jewish law, perhaps even more than Paul himself did; those *of Apollos* were those who were influenced by the rhetoric of Apollos, who came from Alexandria, a centre of Jewish rhetoric; those *of Cephas* might be the opposite of the Paulinists, men who took their stand on the Jewish law and ceremonial (see *Introduction*); and those *of Christ* might be Christians who claimed the name of the Saviour in an exclusive way for themselves. But all this is conjecture, and in any case is incidental to the main message of the section, which is to avoid fine distinctions leading to mere verbal differences. (See again in 2 Cor. x. 7–18.)

The apostle deals with the situation in a very effective way. *Is Christ divided? was Paul crucified for you?* (13). The union of Christians is found in Christ, it will never be found by agreement in theories. *Were ye baptized in the name of Paul?* (13). The rite of baptism might be misinterpreted as something the minister of baptism does through his own virtue (see verse 15). The apostle thanks God (for present purposes) that he baptized very few. *Christ sent me not to baptize, but to preach the gospel* (17). This is not intended as a disparagement of baptism, but as emphasizing that the preaching of Christ which Paul did could not possibly give occasion for any to say that he thereby attached converts to himself. And this preaching was unadorned by worldly rhetoric, *wisdom of words* (17), which was the test applied to successful public speaking in the world of Paul's day. But Paul eschewed it, because the saving force of his message did not lie in wisdom of words, but in the *cross of Christ* (17).

b. The root cause of the divisions: A wrong conception of wisdom (i. 18—iii. 4) and a wrong conception of the Christian ministry (iii. 5—iv. 13)

i. True and false wisdom contrasted (i. 18—ii. 5).

The preaching of the cross is to them that perish foolishness (18). Natural man, that is, man as he is born into the world, cannot believe the serious consequence of sin, and so cannot enter into the need for receiving Him who was 'made sin for us' (2 Cor. v. 21). A thing appears foolish to the natural man when it does not fit in with his preconceived ideas. *Unto us which are saved is the power of God* (18). The Greek tenses in these two phrases give: 'Them that are perishing . . . us which are being saved', as in RV. Each phrase represents a class. The New Testament teaches that the 'saints', that is, true believers, are in the saved class, but they are not yet fully sanctified. Sanctification is a process.

The apostle now goes on to estimate the nature

and value of worldly wisdom, and to contrast with it the nature and value of the wisdom which is to be found in Christ Jesus. *Hath not God made foolish the wisdom of this world?* (20). All man-devised philosophical systems, which either leave God out or define Him after man's own imagining, end in nothingness, foolishness. 'Canst thou by searching find out God?' (Jb. xi. 7). *The world by wisdom knew not God* (21). The apostle enlarges upon the false trails pursued by man in the latter part of Rom. i. A comparison of the two passages might be made. It is true both that the universe itself manifests God (this is the message of Rom. i), and also that man cannot come to a true knowledge of God by natural gifts alone (this is the message of 1 Cor. i). *The foolishness of preaching* (21). The Greek word for 'preaching' here means the 'message'. It refers to the bare facts, as we might say, of the Christian story, the contents of the gospel. These seemed 'foolish' (because most unusual; e.g. the virgin birth, the resurrection) to the Greek contemporaries of the apostle. They seem foolish also to many today, because the Greek mode of thought (roughly speaking rationalistic) has persisted in Europe. *Them that believe* (21). 'Believe' in the New Testament does not usually imply intellectual assent in the first place; rather personal trust *plus* obedience. Taking the events of the gospel as from God, and therefore trusting fully in them, one enters upon a state of salvation. *The Jews . . . a sign, the Greeks . . . wisdom* (22). This sums up the racial characteristic of each in a word. The Jews were miracle-hunters. We may recall our Lord's attitude to miracles. He tried to hide them, if anything. The wisdom of the Greeks was an intellectual activity. No one can deny the high intellectual perception of the Greek philosophers, and also the nobility of much of their writing. Yet all this has no saving power for mankind as a whole. Something else is needed, in the presence of which the highest human thought is seen to be a powerless possession. That something is *Christ crucified* (23). It is a *stumblingblock* (23) to the Jews, for several reasons. In itself the cross is a sign of ignominy and defeat. Also, it touched an uneasy spot in the Jewish conscience. It is the reverse of a triumphant Messiah, setting up a 'glorious kingdom here and now'. It is *foolishness* (23) to the Greeks, because it does not appear to have intellectual explanation. But there are some *Jews and Greeks* who have already found it to be the *power of God, and the wisdom of God* (24). It is the power of God, because sin, man's hitherto undefeated foe, is conquered by it; it is the wisdom of God, because it shows that God knew the real nature of man's failure and provided for it. And the apostle ends by declaring triumphantly that the *foolishness of God* (so thought) *is wiser than men; and the weakness of God is stronger than men* (25).

Following upon this, it is not surprising that *not many wise men after the flesh, not many mighty, not many noble, are called* (26). Their ideas were already fixed in another channel. On the contrary, God has 'exalted the humble and meek'. He has chosen *the foolish things . . . the weak things . . . and base things . . . things which are despised . . . yea, and things which are not* (27, 28) to show His power. If God can exalt things which men have rejected as useless—both things and people—then God is omnipotent. *That no flesh should glory in his presence* (29). The first step in mankind's recovery is the discovery that apart from God man has no ground of existence whatever. Verses 30 and 31 sum up the apostle's thought. They might be paraphrased as follows: 'You Christians do, however, recognize your dependence upon God; for you are children of God in Christ Jesus, that is, through His merits and His association of you with Himself. Jesus Christ stands to us as the true wisdom which comes from God; also He represents absolute righteousness and holiness, and complete restoration to perfection, on our behalf. Wherefore we follow the truth as it is written, He that glorieth, let him glory in the Lord.' (See Je. ix. 23, 24.)

The apostle Paul himself followed this course. *When I came to you, I came not with excellency of speech or of wisdom* (ii. 1). He shunned all natural powers. His purpose was to declare the *testimony of God* (1). The RV, following another reading, translates 'mystery of God'. The word 'mystery' in the Greek New Testament carries with it the meaning of something being revealed —not, as with us, something which completely puzzles us. The point of Paul's teaching here is that God reveals Himself to those who approach Him in Christ—the theme, of course, of the whole New Testament. The knowledge of God is 'mysterious' then in this sense that the natural man working through his own faculties cannot receive it (see later on verse 14). The word 'testimony', which occurs in other Greek MSS, would emphasize rather the outworking of the knowledge of God in Paul's own life. Paul's work in Corinth as an evangelist was marked by an absence of show and display—it was *in weakness, and in fear, and in much trembling* (3). He concentrated wholly on presenting the Person of Christ (for the reasons already enumerated in i. 30) and Christ's work for us on the cross—the event in the life of Christ which required the most understanding. *My speech and my preaching was not with enticing words* (4). The Corinthians looked for oratory in a preacher. They had yet to learn the vanity of all human wisdom, on the one hand, and the convicting *power* of the *Spirit* (4) on the other. The apostle's weakness was actually a help to the demonstration of the Spirit's power. (See also 2 Cor. xii. 9—'My strength is made perfect in weakness'.) It had the value that the Corinthians were not led to exalt Paul in their minds, but God—*your faith should not stand in the wisdom of men, but in the power of God* (5).

ii. True wisdom defined (ii. 6–13). *We speak wisdom among them that are perfect* (6). Paul is speaking about the things of God to the people of God. True wisdom originates in God, and its whole content is derived from God. 'The fear of the Lord is the beginning of wisdom.' (See also Jb. xxviii. 28.) Human wisdom, in contrast, has numerous starting-points, and equally diverse contents, so that there is no unity in it. *Perfect* is a term applied in the New Testament to believers. It may almost be regarded as a technical term. A believer is 'perfect' because he is a new creature in Christ, in whom he shares Christ's own perfection in the eyes of God. It does not imply sinlessness while the believer is still in the flesh. 'If we say that we have no sin, we deceive ourselves' (1 Jn. i. 8). The word is probably introduced in this context to stress the fact that, in Christ, the believer has an experience of the ultimate realities. *Princes of this world* (6). The word is 'rulers', and the thought may be the way the people of the world follow the fashion set by those in authority. Such fashions get great publicity but eventually *come to nought* (6). (Some commentators take 'princes of this world' to mean angels; e.g. Satan is sometimes so described.) In contrast the *wisdom of God* is hidden (7), it is spoken in a *mystery* (see ii. 1). It is hidden in the very nature of the universe, *ordained before the world* (7) with a view to *our glory* (7), that is, both bringing us into glory and bringing glory to us. *None of the princes of this world knew* (8) this glory, for their attitude to Christ would otherwise have been different— *they would not have crucified the Lord of glory* (8). Note this title of Christ. 'Glory' is another technical word in the New Testament meaning an attribute of God which He bestows upon believers. That it is something beyond the natural capacity of man to conceive is expressed in verse 9—*Eye hath not seen*, etc. These words are not to be found in the Old Testament exactly as they occur here, but seem to be a combination of Is. lxiv. 4 and lxv. 16, 17. This is an instructive illustration of Paul's knowledge of, and free use of, the Old Testament. *Revealed them unto us by his Spirit* (10). This verse declares the need for the guidance of the Spirit in understanding the things of God. Just as man understands his fellow-man through the sharing of a common *spirit* (11), so man can understand God only through the communion of the *Spirit of God* (11). This verse is interesting in presenting the thought of communication through a common 'spirit'.

The word 'spirit' in the Bible is not easily defined, meaning at times little more than 'influence', but at other times being used in a way which indicates the full, distinct, third Person of the Holy Trinity. Verse 11 might be used as the starting-point of an investigation in the matter. *We have received, not the spirit of the world, but the spirit which is of God* (12). Here the Greek word for 'world' is different from that used in verse 7 above. There the word had the meaning of 'an age' (of time); here it has the meaning of 'the ordered universe'. The phrase *spirit of the world* means the spirit or 'outlook' of

our human civilization. *Are freely given* (12). The Greek tense is past, 'were freely given'. The revelation of God has been completely given in the historical Jesus, and so is a past event, but with ever-present potentialities. This true wisdom of God *we speak, not in the words which man's wisdom teacheth, but which the Holy Ghost teacheth* (13). It is a different type of wisdom altogether, containing different conceptions and so acquiring different expression. *Comparing spiritual things with spiritual* (13). Within the ambit of this spiritual wisdom, there is opportunity for comparisons of one part with another.

iii. **Why so many fail to apprehend (ii. 14—iii. 4).** *The natural man receiveth not the things of the Spirit of God* (14). There is not in 'the natural man' the Spirit of God to enable him to apprehend. *He that is spiritual* (15). This gives us the contrast with the 'natural man'. The contrast is made between man as an intelligent being (but fallen) and man as a spiritual being (regenerated by the Spirit). *Judgeth all things . . . judged of no man* (15). The regenerate man, having the Spirit of God in him, has the capacity to be able to judge all things in a true light—in the light of truth; but is himself outside the 'ken' of the natural man. Moffatt gives: 'No one can read what he is.' The reason is that the natural man does not know *the mind of the Lord* (16), but believers have *the mind of Christ* (16), for Christ dwells in them by faith (see Col. iii. 16).

The apostle turns from the contemplation of this lofty theme to his readers, the Corinthian Christians. They are not yet fully surrendered to the working of the Holy Spirit. They are *carnal, even . . . babes in Christ* (iii. 1). He has had to feed them *with milk, and not with meat* (2) and even still they need this kind of nurture. *Ye are yet carnal: for whereas there is among you envying*, etc. (3). The presence of party strife was an indication that the Holy Spirit was not given full charge of the Corinthian church. The Greek form of the word 'carnal' differs slightly in verse 1 from that in verse 3. In verse 1, the word means 'fleshly', 'made of flesh'; in verse 3, it means 'fleshly in character', 'carnally minded'. Those who are newly-born of the Spirit still retain their natural desires for a greater or less time. This is not blameworthy. But to remain carnally minded, that is, still retaining the judgments of the world, this is blameworthy. To do so is to *walk as men* (3). And the world is always following party-cries—*I am of Paul . . . I am of Apollos* (4).

This section as a whole (i. 18—iii. 4) teaches that the Christian is given power by the Spirit to judge all things. This teaching however does not imply that the Christian religion is a form of experience or of thought which is in opposition to the workings of man's natural faculties, such as reason and feeling. Later, in chapters xii and xiv, the apostle warns his readers against an anti-rationalism in spiritual things. Again, this teaching, while it does maintain that the Christian life is lived in the Spirit, nevertheless does not imply that it is a life of mysticism divorced from ordinary human concerns. Paul himself was possibly the most practical-minded of the apostles.

iv. **Ministers are of no account in themselves** (iii. 5–9). The second root cause of the divisions is now considered by the apostle. Not only have they a wrong conception of wisdom: they also have a wrong conception of the ministry. *Ministers by whom ye believed* (5). The minister is of no account in himself, and indeed it is dangerously wrong if he looms at all on the horizon of the believer's faith, because he is only such as God has made him—*as the Lord gave to every man* (5). *I have planted . . . watered; but God gave the increase* (6). The first two verbs are in a tense expressing completed action in past time, whereas the third (*gave*) is in the imperfect tense, denoting continuity of action. The change of tense is noteworthy. *Are one* (8). Paul and Apollos are not divided between themselves; also, their ministrations for God, though differing in character, are part of the same process. Each, however, has his own part to play, and *shall receive his own reward* (8). *God's husbandry* (lit. 'tilled land'), *God's building* (9). These are favourite metaphors in Christian teaching, and worth pondering over. God is the Master-Gardener, the supreme Architect.

Apollos, who is mentioned here, is also mentioned in Acts xviii. 24–28. A cultured Alexandrian, with some knowledge of Christianity, he came to Ephesus and was further instructed by Aquila and Priscilla, Paul's intimate friends. He seems to have been particularly anxious to go to Corinth, whence Paul, Aquila and Priscilla had recently come, and was recommended to the brethren there by letter. He at once started teaching in the synagogue at Corinth that Jesus was the Messiah. He must have been a distinguished speaker to give his name to a party at Corinth. Did he unintentionally introduce the party spirit there? Paul shows no sign of feeling that Apollos has been opposing him—*he that planteth and he that watereth are one*—so that we must dismiss this idea. It was not the ministers who were at fault in this case. Paul's use here of his own name and that of Apollos might be simply for the sake of example: that this is so is possibly indicated by verse 6 of chapter iv.

v. **Ministers are responsible for the character of their work** (iii. 10–17). *The grace of God which is given unto me* (10). Paul, though he calls himself a *masterbuilder* (10), yet receives his instructions and his power from God. The work is God's, a thought which both allays over-anxiety on the part of the minister, and also inspires him with the great dignity of his work. *I have laid the foundation . . . which is Jesus Christ* (10, 11). Cf. Eph. ii. 20n. The only foundation of Christianity is Jesus Christ. No theory or system of thought, even one in which Jesus Christ may be given a place, may be substituted. *If any man build . . .* (12). Using the metaphor of building, the apostle compares the works of Christian ministers to *gold, silver . . .* (12). Some is precious work, durable work; some is worthless and will not stand the test. *It shall be revealed by fire* (13). Gold, silver and precious stone can pass through fire unharmed; wood, hay, stubble are consumed by fire. So the works of some Christian ministers stand, that of others disappear. Notice Paul's change of metaphor from building to naming materials which illustrate durability or the reverse, when subjected to fire. *The day shall declare it* (13). Probably the apostle means only the day of testing, not the day of judgment. Cf. Rom. xiv. 10–12. *Receive a reward . . . suffer loss* (14, 15). When we are 'in Christ Jesus' (see Rom. viii. 1), we can do work for God which He will value and reward accordingly; the nature of the reward is not here revealed. *He himself shall be saved; yet so as by fire* (15); lit. 'through fire', as RV. Paul is anxious to distinguish between the minister and his work. His work may perish—as stubble is consumed in fire; but the believing minister will be saved, 'yet so as through fire'. This may simply be a proverbial Greek phrase meaning 'by a hairbreadth escape', it being a coincidence that the picture of fire is used to describe the testing of the work, and the same word is found in this phrase. The apostle would regard a Christian who has no work to show as one to be pitied, because he has missed the joy of service for the Master.

These verses (13–15) are admittedly strange on first reading, and have been interpreted in ways other than that given above. The crucial points are *the day* (13) and *saved . . . by fire* (15). Is the 'day' the Day of Judgment? If so 'fire' would be the judgment of God; and such a metaphor is indeed used in the Old Testament, and again by our Lord in His reference to Gehenna. Following along this line, the Roman Church uses verse 15 to support its doctrine of Purgatory. But, as is so often the case with supposed scriptural support for its distinctive doctrines, the phrase *saved . . . by fire* is taken entirely out of its context. Its context is the Day of Judgment (if this supposition be accepted), *not* an intermediate state between death and judgment. The passage cannot possibly give a doctrine of purgation of believers after death.

The explanation adopted previously is very simple, and is based upon the view that 'the day' means some such thing as the occasions of trial which occur each day; 'fire' is then used with two meanings, the one simply as an illustration of something that gives a very severe test, the other derived from a Greek proverb.

Exhortation of the believer to good works is to be found everywhere in the New Testament, beginning with the teaching of our Lord, such as, 'Let your light so shine before men, that they may see your good works, and glorify your Father which is in heaven'. Also, the attachment of reward to such good works is taught by our Lord—'he shall in no wise lose his reward'—

and taken up in the apostolic writings. Consequently the present passage fits in completely with general New Testament teaching; only its phraseology is peculiar.

Ye are the temple of God (16). Elsewhere, the apostle describes the individual believer as indwelt by the Holy Ghost—'your body is the temple of the Holy Ghost' (1 Cor. vi. 19), but here he applies this to the whole Christian church at Corinth. *If any man defile . . . him shall God destroy* (17). This is in contrast to the thought in verse 15, where a faulty Christian worker is saved, though his work is destroyed. Here, one who mars God's temple is himself destroyed by God. We might compare this thought with our Lord's teaching about causing a believer to stumble (see Mt. xviii. 6). The word for 'defile' is the same Greek word as is translated 'destroy' in the same verse. The RV translates accordingly.

vi. Warnings against boasting and against judging (iii. 18—iv. 5). *If any man . . . seemeth to be wise* (18). This verse is a good example of the forthright speaking of the apostle. Paul could speak to those who boasted about their education, because he had had a 'university education' himself. He knew from experience the vanity of human speculation on the real meaning of life and the universe. *Let him become a fool* (18). The apostle's advice was to turn rigidly away from such human wisdom, *For the wisdom of this world is foolishness with God* (19). Part of the penalty of the fall is the vitiation of all human activity—everything man does 'before the grace of Christ' (see Anglican Article XIII) is tainted with sin. Two quotations follow; the first is a free quotation of Jb. v. 13—the only direct quotation from that book in the New Testament—and the second (verse 20) is from Ps. xciv. 11.

Let no man glory in men (21). As the next verse shows, Paul still has in mind the party strife referred to in i. 12 and iii. 4. Each group was clearly claiming for itself a monopoly of truth and wisdom, and boasting in the particular leader it had appreciated. But these great leaders are really servants and each belongs to the whole church. By permitting such sectarian groups to flourish the Corinthian Christians are showing that they have no conception of the extent of their possessions in Christ. They have a Master in whom to glory, even Christ Himself, to whom they belong and who Himself belongs to God. (For this last phrase *and Christ is God's* see note on xv. 24–28.). This warning against 'hero-worship' should be carefully noted. Glorying in a man is at the root of much sectarianism.

Ministers . . . and stewards (iv. 1). The thought of the apostle passes from one aspect of the case to another. From pointing out that ministers in themselves are nothing, and that it is a foolish thing to name oneself the follower of a human teacher, he now passes to the consideration that he (and Apollos) are ministers of Christ—Christ's name gives them a status which must not be underestimated. He uses the metaphor of stewardship. A steward, having unrestricted access to his master's possessions, must needs be honest, and must have personal loyalty to his master (2). The one whose judgment the steward really values (or fears) is that of his master—*with me it is a very small thing that I should be judged of you . . . he that iudgeth me is the Lord* (3, 4). The steward cannot even trust his own judgment of himself; he might be unaware of his own failings (4). The apostle's advice, therefore, is for Christians to desist from passing judgment on one another, and leave such judgment for Christ when He comes, and *then shall every man have praise of God* (5). It is a significant part of Paul's presentation of the gospel that the Lord will come as judge. A clause in the Nicene Creed keeps this thought before us—'I believe . . . that He shall come again with glory to judge both the quick and the dead.'

Thus the apostle presses home his teaching concerning Christian ministers. His whole conception rests on Christ, whose ministers they are. All believers are Christ's, and ministers are those by whom they believed (iii. 5).

vii. The example of the apostles (iv. 6–13). *Transferred to myself and to Apollos* (6). Since the first reference to the various divisions in i. 12, Paul has omitted all reference to leaders other than himself and Apollos. From xvi. 12 we may infer that the matter had been discussed with Apollos, and he, no doubt, concurred in Paul's decision to use them both as an illustration of human frailty in order to show the Corinthians that they were *not to think of men above that which is written* (6). This probably refers to Scripture and means that our view of man should be biblical. The word might be taken to mean that we must not 'esteem men above what is written (i.e. manifest) in their characters'. By exalting *one* (say Paul) *against another* (say Apollos) they were pandering to their own pride. The foolishness of such pride is pointed out in the verses that follow. *What hast thou that thou didst not receive?* (7). This thought cuts the ground from under all such boasting.

Now ye are full . . . (8). Paul is speaking ironically. Such boasting regarding their status as believers is quite out of keeping with true spirituality. *I would to God ye did reign* (8). A fervent prayer for the coming of God's kingdom which throws into even greater relief the description which follows of his present sufferings. *Spectacle* (9); a reference to the gladiatorial contests in the arena. He pictures all the world and even angels looking on while the apostles, a feeble band, are brought in last to fight to the death. With some irony he contrasts still further the claims of the Corinthians with the actual experience of the apostles who are despised and treated like slaves. *Labour, working with our own hands* (12). See Acts xviii. 2, 3 and cf. 1 Thes. ii. 9 and 2 Thes. iii. 8. Cf. also 1 Cor. ix. 18. *Being reviled, we bless* (12). The apostles put into practice our Lord's teaching in the Sermon on the Mount. See Mt. v. 44. The attitude of the Corinthians was apparently very different. See

vi. 7. The words *filth* and *offscouring* in verse 13 have sacrificial associations. Paul may be inferring that all this degradation was on behalf of others. The whole of this passage reveals the apostle's intense feeling and his great concern for these Corinthian Christians.

c. Concluding appeal to end the divisions (iv. 14-21)

As my beloved sons I warn you (14). This shows Paul's true feeling towards the Corinthians. *In Christ Jesus I have begotten you through the gospel* (15). Paul here explicitly claims to have been the first to preach the gospel in Corinth. The same is probably true of Greece as a whole. See Acts xvi. 6-11, xviii. 1-18. He can therefore demand their attention and loyalty with special justification—*be ye followers of me* (16). He has, indeed, sent Timothy to them to remind them of what he had taught them, and which they had evidently forgotten (17). *Puffed up* (18). This word is rather distinctive of the Epistle, being used six times (iv. 6, 18, 19, v. 2, viii. 1, xiii. 4). It indicates the adoption of an attitude of superiority over others. This is the very antithesis of the Christian spirit. *Not the speech . . . but the power* (19). The apostle's attitude towards these is a challenging one. Let them be tested, and see if their power to act is as great as their boasting would suggest. *The kingdom of God is not in word, but in power* (20). Our membership of the kingdom is demonstrated by the power of God in our lives, not in mere lip profession. *Shall I come . . . with a rod?* (21). The apostle adopts an authoritative attitude, and is quite ready to deal in a disciplinary manner with them, if necessary. His actions, however, spring from a real anxiety as to the spiritual well-being of the Corinthians, and not from a domineering spirit, as is seen by his following words, *or in love, and in the spirit of meekness* (21). The choice rests with them.

III. MORAL FAULTS IN THE LIFE OF THE CHURCH. v. 1—vi. 20

a. Laxity in dealing with a case of incest (v. 1-13)

The apostle turns abruptly to comment on the moral laxity of the Corinthian Christians. First, there is a notorious case of a Christian man having taken his father's wife. We may suppose that the father was dead; nevertheless the action was contrary to Old Testament marriage laws, which still are binding on the Church. Moreover, it was an action which even Gentiles would not countenance (see verse 1). But the most amazing thing was that the Corinthian church was accepting the situation without comment! *Ye are puffed up, and have not rather mourned* (2). *I . . . have judged already* (3), says Paul. This is a case where there is no need to hesitate in condemnation; there are no possible extenuating circumstances. In very solemn words the apostle instructs the church what to do—*In the name of our Lord Jesus Christ . . . deliver such an one unto Satan for the destruction of the flesh* (4, 5). The

church is to call a solemn assembly and, conscious of the power of the Lord Jesus Christ (note the full title used here) in its midst, is to 'deliver to Satan' the offending brother. Paul himself will be with them, *and my spirit* (4). This may mean that the apostle will be spending the time in earnest prayer. *Deliver such an one unto Satan.* In New Testament teaching Satan is the 'prince of this world' (see Jn. xii. 31). But he has power only over the 'flesh' (Jb. ii. 5, 6; Lk. xiii. 16; 2 Cor. xii. 7). In 1 Tim. i. 20 (RV) we read: 'Hymenaeus and Alexander; whom I delivered unto Satan that they might be taught not to blaspheme.' These references show that Satan was allowed by God to inflict bodily suffering upon men, which might have the result of leading to repentance.

We must admit that we should greatly hesitate to do today precisely what the apostle commanded the Corinthians to do. We might excuse ourselves by suggesting that the Church of the apostolic age had to take special action under certain circumstances in order definitely to establish the fact of the power of the risen Lord. The apostolic Church, too, was a small body, relatively speaking, and consequently much more intense in spiritual matters (or capable of being such under apostolic guidance).

But while today we may find it difficult to think in the precise terms used here by the apostle, that is no reason why we should not take to heart and put into practice the advice he gives, namely, to excommunicate from the congregation one who is a notorious evil-liver. Looking ahead to verse 11, we see a list of sins which should be so treated. Any member of the church who sins in this way should be openly condemned in the congregation, have pointed out to him that he is held by Satan in such practices, and be shunned by other Christians in the hope that he will be brought to realize the gravity of the position and repent, so that his *spirit may be saved in the day of the Lord Jesus* (5). This is discipline indeed, and of a type which is unfamiliar these days!

Leaven (6). Here the term is used as a symbol of corruptible human nature. If an element of corruption is allowed to remain in the church, the whole church will become corrupt. *Purge out therefore the old leaven* (7). The use of the word reminds him of the whole ceremony of the Passover in Old Testament religion, and he is led by the Spirit to see in it an illustration of the Christian dispensation. Christ is *our passover* (7) and He is *sacrificed for us* (7). *Therefore let us keep the feast . . . with sincerity and truth* (8). The Israelites of old were specially alert and prepared spiritually and morally for the observance of the Passover. So also ought Christians to be at all times in the continuous age of Christ's Passover.

Further to this matter, the apostle refers in verse 9 to advice he had given of the same kind in a previous Epistle, namely, *not to company with fornicators.* He makes clear now that his meaning was that they must not have fornicators in the church company. He acknowledges that Christians must mix with the fornicators, the covetous, and the extortioners (10), while they live in the world. But *if any man that is called a brother be a fornicator*, do not eat with him (11). This reference to a former letter is of much interest. As far as we know none of it has been preserved for us, unless (as some think) 2 Cor. vi. 14—vii. 1 is part of it.

The apostle ends by again stressing the need for the Church to maintain discipline in its own ranks—*them that are without God judgeth* (13). And so he urges the Corinthians to *put away from among yourselves that wicked person* (13).

b. Lawsuits before heathen judges (vi. 1–11)

This passage teaches that if Christians have quarrels amongst themselves they should have them judged by fellow-Christians, and not before heathen judges (1). But it is an indication of lack of spiritual understanding that there should be such feelings at all amongst brethren. Christians who are injured should suffer rather than seek retaliation (7). Cf. iv. 12, 13, where, no doubt, he had this situation in mind.

The saints shall judge the world (2). *We shall judge angels* (3). These striking statements are not inventions of Paul. Our Lord teaches in Matthew's Gospel that the apostles 'shall sit on twelve thrones, judging the twelve tribes of Israel' (Mt. xix. 28). See also Rev. xx. 4, 'And I saw thrones, and they sat upon them, and judgment was given unto them.' Such judgment by the saints will even be exercised over angels, or spirit-beings. Belief in angels is, of course, present throughout Scripture, and has been held by Christians all down the ages. For teaching regarding their function and position see Heb. j and ii.

Set them to judge who are least esteemed in the church (4). These words have been variously interpreted. They might be ironical. They might mean that even the least esteemed Christian is worthier as a judge than a heathen man. They might refer to heathens 'who are least esteemed', that is, not esteemed at all, in the church. The present writer would favour the first suggestion because the apostle proceeds to direct the Corinthians to pick out wise men (5) among them as judges. It would seem from their present foolish behaviour that such men were indeed least esteemed among them.

The apostle proceeds to warn the Corinthian Christians that if they continue in the sins which marked their life before conversion, they will *not inherit the kingdom of God* (9, 10). The sins enumerated here indicate the low moral standard of life at Corinth before the coming of the gospel. *But ye are washed, . . . sanctified, . . . justified* (11). The gospel, however, raised those who accepted it to a new status before God. But the old sins cling hard, and some Corinthian Christians had not yet availed themselves of the power of the Holy Spirit in the life of a believer to throw them off. There may be a reference here to the rite of baptism (cf. Acts xxii. 16). Sanctification and justification are both aspects of regeneration.

c. The sin of fornication (vi. 12–20)

Verse 12 contains the whole philosophy of the Christian attitude towards earthly things. (We use the word 'earthly' rather than 'worldly'. The former word means things pertaining by nature to this earthly life; the latter means human civilization as developed by man without reference to God.) *All things are lawful*, says the apostle, *but all things are not expedient*, or 'helpful' (RSV); and furthermore, though lawful, he is taking care not to *be brought under the power of any*. It may not be expedient, therefore, to partake of some earthly things at certain times; and at no time is indulgence in them to lead to enslavement by them.

Now it is clear that feasting and fornication were both closely associated with idolatry, and those who exercised their freedom with regard to the one might claim an equal freedom with regard to the other. Paul therefore shows that his principle of liberty given in verse 12 does not apply to things definitely wrong in themselves. As regards food, it and the body are made for each other and will both eventually perish or 'be brought to nought' (Gk.). Eating or not eating is, therefore, a matter of indifference. Fornication, however, is in a completely different category. The body is not made for it, *but for the Lord* (13), as is proved by the fact that *God . . . will raise up us* in the resurrection (14). The bodies of Christians are indeed *members of Christ* (15), through a spiritual union with Him (17), and should be instruments for Christ to use. How can a Christian indulge in an act which hands over the body to a harlot? for this is what fornication involves (16). Flee away from fornication, then, says the apostle (18). Every other kind of sin is exterior to the body, but this one is a sin affecting the body, and to be guarded against with special care. To put it another way, the Christian is indwelt by the Holy Spirit, and in the deepest sense he is not his own (19). A great ransom price was paid for him, and he is to glorify God for this by making himself, in body and spirit, the instrument of God (20). Notice Paul's repeated *know ye not?* (15, 16, 19), remembering that his readers were clearly rather proud of the fulness of their Christian knowledge and wisdom.

This passage gives us the Christian doctrine of the body, and prepares us for the belief in the resurrection of the body, which is so fully set forth in chapter xv. The passage also outlines the principle of Christian liberty, a subject which is taken up again in chapter viii (*q.v.*). The underlying fact governing the exercise of Christian liberty is that the Christian has been redeemed by the precious blood of Christ, and so belongs to Him. His commitment to Christ is deeper than it ever was to the 'world', to which he belonged before his acceptance of redemption.

IV. ANSWERS TO QUESTIONS.
vii. 1—xiv. 31

a. Marriage (vii. 1–40)

i. **The apostle's own opinion concerning marriage (vii. 1–9).** The apostle now turns to answer questions asked him by the Corinthian church. The first concerns marriage and the mutual duties of man and wife. He states quite clearly *it is good for a man not to touch a woman* (1). For Paul the fellowship he had in Christ with other Christians completely met that human need of fellowship normally met by marriage. Indeed it was more than met, for, to the apostle, Christian, or spiritual, fellowship was a fellowship even deeper than marriage. Nevertheless he recognizes that, 'because of the temptation to immorality' (2, RSV) existing in a heathen city like Corinth, there were strong reasons why his own feelings in the matter should be overruled. Paul is not taking here a low view of marriage. He is writing within the context of the existing state of affairs. What he says must be interpreted within that context. He proceeds to give advice concerning the married state. A man and a woman joined together in marriage have a duty to consider the bodily needs of each other. A false asceticism may actually give Satan an opportunity for leading one or other into sin. *I speak this by permission* (6). Read as in RV, 'by way of permission'. Paul does not mean that he is permitted, but not commanded, by the Spirit to say this; but that his suggestion that men and women might marry is not to be regarded as an order but only as permission to do so. His real desire is given in verse 7. But here again he realizes that men and women have varying capacities and gifts, so that he would be the last to judge a brother, or to insinuate in the smallest degree his own superiority.

Better to marry than to burn (9). The apostle here indicates degrees of Christian morality— better to marry, but best to remain unmarried so that one may devote oneself wholly to the things of Christ. Theologians have elaborated a theory of the 'double standard' from such a consideration, that is, one standard for ordinary Christians and another for 'experts'. The whole monastic system springs from this conception. The evangelical view of Christianity prefers not to make this distinction, because it inevitably leads to belief in the acquiring of merit by the 'religious'. This is contrary to the basic principle of redemption, as understood by evangelicals. While it must not be denied that the monastic system has led some members of it to a high degree of sanctity and the accomplishment of wonderful works for Christ, the evangelical feeling is that, on balance, the system comes down on the other side. The fact that the Roman Catholic Church openly teaches a doctrine of merit, in conjunction with the extensive practice of monasticism, seems to justify the evangelical in his opinion on the matter. Although we need not hesitate to say with Paul that one line of action is superior

spiritually to another, we must refrain from codification and from forming institutions of 'superiors'. The discussion of these matters forms the study of moral and ascetic theology.

ii. **God's commandment against divorce (vii. 10, 11).** The apostle states in uncompromising terms the lifelong character of the marriage vow. In doing so he is careful to remind the Corinthians that he is quoting the direct teaching of Christ. *Let not the wife depart from her husband: but and if she depart, let her remain unmarried; . . . and let not the husband put away his wife* (with a view to marrying another). The apostle interprets our Lord's teaching, therefore, as allowing separation, but not divorce.

iii. **Concerning unbelieving partners (vii. 12–16).** *Speak I, not the Lord* (12). Paul now turns to deal with a problem which had not been the subject of any specific command of our Lord. What is to be done when one partner in a marriage is a believer and the other still a heathen? There must have been many such in Corinth, and cases constantly occur in the mission field today. He advises Christians not to separate from their unbelieving partners, unless these latter depart of their own volition (12, 13, 15). This advice strikes us at once as being charitable and Christ-like. The apostle makes some further comments upon it: *the unbelieving husband is sanctified by the wife, and the unbelieving wife is sanctified by the husband: else were your children unclean; but now are they holy* (14). Commentators are not agreed as to how much meaning we are to put into these words. Do they mean that the unbeliever, by reason of his or her marriage union with a believer, shares with the believing partner sanctified status before God, and, further, that the children born of such a union (and, *a fortiori*, of a union of two Christians) are in some way holy (e.g. without the stain of original sin)? Do they mean that, because relations with an unconverted partner are sanctified (i.e. hallowed) in the subjective world of the believer's thought and life, there is nothing wrong in sustaining such already existing marriages to which he refers? If the connection were not sanctified in this way then the children, too, would be an offence to God (*unclean*), but *now are they holy*, i.e. there is no wrong attaching to them just because they are children of such a 'mixed' marriage. Or thirdly, do they simply mean that, as Christ is stronger than Satan, so the believing partner will be the dominating influence in the home and bring into it a high degree of sanctity, so that, in fact, the children are brought up to be holy? The present writer favours this third view. It stimulates believing partners into home evangelism.

If, however, the unbelieving partner chooses to depart, *let him depart* (15), says the apostle. The marriage bond for the Christian does not require that an effort must be made to maintain the relationship under such circumstances. There is no certainty that the result would be the salvation of the unbelieving husband or wife

(16). He concludes with an acknowledgment that each individual case must be decided in the light of the gifts and calling of God so that the decision rests finally between the individual and his Lord (17). See verses 7, 20, and 24 where the same thought is brought out.

iv. **The need to continue in the state in which we are called (vii. 17–24).** Each individual, Paul teaches, has his own gift or position in society by divine providence. He should seek to live to God's glory in the place where God has put him rather than seek or expect great change because he has become a Christian. Examples are given: circumcision or uncircumcision (18); servant (slave) or free (20). The Christian attitude is to remain in his particular state as far as outward appearances are concerned, but *therein abide with God* (24). This will make all the difference as regards the meaning the 'state' holds for the person concerned. Circumcision, for instance, is nothing in itself, nor is uncircumcision any handicap. The essential thing is to observe the commandments of God as set forth by Christ (19). Again, he who was a slave when he was called is not to mind that; although, if his freedom is offered him, he should avail himself of it. This question of human status is not the important thing. For the Christian slave is spiritually free in Christ and the free man voluntarily makes himself Christ's servant when he believes. *Ye are bought with a price; be not ye the servants of men* (23). The first words are an echo of vi. 20. Since they belong to Christ, believers will no longer slavishly follow human judgment in such matters. The Christian spirit transcends earthly handicaps knowing that the circumstances of life are all under God's control.

v. **A special problem: the marriage of virgins (vii. 25–40).** There is some difficulty in discovering whether Paul is here addressing married persons who have refrained from the physical consummation of marriage (suggested by the AV), or answering the question 'Ought Christian fathers to give their daughters in marriage?' which seems to be the meaning of the RV. See especially verses 36–38. If the passage is interpreted in the first way, the answer given is that the man who feels that he would be wiser to marry is at perfect liberty to do so. If, however, he can remain steadfast to his purpose—and his partner likewise—then he *doeth better* (38). The present writer, however, regards the passage as answering the question regarding the responsibility of fathers in the matter of the marriage of their daughters. In replying Paul seizes the opportunity of recalling and repeating what he has said earlier about marriage generally and about the need for glorifying God in that condition of life in which His call found us. *Art thou bound unto a wife? seek not to be loosed. Art thou loosed from a wife? seek not a wife* (27). This principle applies to women as well as to men and is developed in its twofold application in the following verses. Celibacy is to be preferred, but the apostle fully realizes that that is

not everybody's gift. If all the circumstances suggest that the daughter should be allowed to marry, let her marry. But those who are able to remain unmarried do better (36–38).

The teaching of the passage as a whole is clear enough. It is a dissuasive from marriage in the interest of fuller Christian service. The apostle, who, of course, was fully aware of the way in which a man and his wife can labour together, each enriching the work of the other, makes it plain that he is expressing his own personal opinion—*I give my judgment* (25)—and is careful not to be dogmatic or to lay down hard and fast rules. *The time is short* (29) refers probably to the hope of our Lord's return and certainly has behind it the idea that the opportunity to serve the Lord will quickly pass. This is not a time for caring *for the things of the world* (33, 34) and for putting wife or husband first as married men and women do. Pioneer work often demands special sacrifices and there are still tasks in the mission field today which can be undertaken only by those without family ties or responsibilities.

Verses 30 and 31 elaborate this thought that those who are serving the kingdom must free themselves from worldly cares and ambitions. We weep because of earthly loss or disappointment. We rejoice because in some way we have achieved success. We buy and lay up comfort and treasure for ourselves. In all these ways we show that we have set our affections upon things on the earth. Paul's command here is exactly the same as that given to the Christians at Colossae. 'Set your affection on things above' (Col. iii. 2). It is spiritual values and qualities which are truly lasting. *The fashion of this world*, all those external things in which we take so much interest, *passeth away* (31).

The section concludes with an answer to another question regarding the remarriage of widows. So long as her husband is alive, the wife is bound to him. This is the position *by law* and it covers presumably the case of separation suggested in verse 15. But if the husband dies, she is free to marry again. But even so she is not to rush into a second marriage. It is to be *in the Lord* (39). And in Paul's judgment, not only will she be happier if she avoids remarriage, but he gives this advice as one who is convinced that this is what the Holy Spirit would have him teach.

b. **Meats offered to idols (viii. 1—xi. 1)**

i. **The principle enunciated (viii. 1–13).** In this chapter the apostle deals with a problem arising out of the circumstances of the times in which the Corinthians lived, and about which the Corinthians had asked him in their letter. Food sold publicly in the market might have been previously connected with idol worship. Was it all right for Christians to use it? Paul uses the occasion to enunciate a principle, namely, that, while the whole of life is derived from God, yet a curtailment of its use may be necessary for the

Christian in order not to offend a weaker brother, that is, to cause him to stumble.

Knowledge puffeth up, but charity edifieth (1). Students of philosophy will be acquainted with various theories of knowledge. The apostle, as a former university student himself, was acquainted with such theories as were current in his day. But in the first three verses of this chapter he indicates that belief in God is a factor in our thinking which will determine the whole of our attitude to life. Mere knowledge will make a person puffed up, but a genuine love of one's fellow-men will lead one to seek their edification. Without such love, knowledge is thus an unsocial factor. Again, one must be careful to recognize that man cannot know anything fully (verse 2), because all things have their ultimate essence in God, and the finite cannot comprehend the infinite. But although we cannot fully know God, we can *love* Him. There follows the assurance that He knows us, with all that such knowledge implies (3).

An idol is nothing (4). Having delivered this warning the apostle takes up again the point raised in verse 1. They are right in teaching that all idols and, indeed, all so-called gods and lords are nothing (4). *There is but one God* (6). This verse is like a formal statement of belief, and is often used as an example of an early creed. However, it is hardly a creed in our own sense of the term, namely, a formal statement of faith issued authoritatively by the Church. In order to meet this particular problem and under the inspiration of the Holy Spirit Paul sums up for his readers in these words the uniqueness of the Father and the Son. *Of whom . . . by whom* (6); lit. 'of whom . . . through whom'. He distinguishes between the relation of the Father and that of the Son to creation. The Father is the source of all things; the Son gives meaning to all things. In this connection see Col. i. 16, 17.

Not in every man that knowledge (7). Those who have not this knowledge of the oneness of God will react in a different way towards an idol. Since they believe in the idol, their consciences will rightly be troubled if they eat food that has been offered to it.

The whole of this passage is addressed to those who were rejoicing in their emancipation from such bondage. In order to demonstrate their *liberty* (9) they were probably prepared to go out of their way to eat this meat, feeling that such a testimony would commend them to God. Paul negatives this idea: partaking or abstaining will not make those who are freed from superstition either better or worse (8). But their liberty may *become a stumblingblock to them that are weak* (9). A warning must therefore be given. Brethren who are not so well established in the faith may see a fellow-Christian sitting *at meat in the idol's temple* and themselves be persuaded against their conscience to join in eating *things which are offered to idols* (10). For them this would be tantamount to joining in the idol worship. So their Christian life and testimony would be ruined (11). To cause a Christian to defile his conscience in this way is to *sin against Christ* who died for him (11, 12). This is why, *if meat make my brother to offend, I will eat no flesh while the world standeth* (13).

The topic raised in this chapter, though expressed with reference to the particular situation at Corinth, is of perennial interest to Christians. It throws light, for instance, on the question of fasting. The apostle would obviously teach that mere fasting, unaccompanied by a spiritual disposition towards God, is useless. He himself often fasted—'in fastings often' (2 Cor. xi. 27)—but it was of necessity in the course of his work for the kingdom. Again the principle can be applied to cover actions—for example, in the realm of pleasure or entertainment—which to us are harmless but which might offend the 'young' Christian. If by our careless behaviour we wound their consciences, we *sin against Christ* (12). It is a solemn thought.

ii. Disciplined freedom (ix. 1–27). This chapter must be seen as part of the wider section now under review (viii. 1—xi. 1), in which the apostle is dealing with a question which he has been asked by the Corinthians. The question, on the surface, seemed to be simply one concerning the eating of meats offered to idols. But we seem driven to infer that the Corinthians, in asking the question, made some unfriendly comments about Paul and his manner of life whilst he was among them. Paul does not hesitate to speak very plainly as he deals with this tendency to belittle his apostleship, to question his attitude towards the receiving of material reward for preaching the gospel, and to throw doubt, perhaps, upon the success of his preaching.

In reply, the apostle boldly claims apostleship and personal freedom, freedom to live as did the other apostles. He too had seen the Lord, and he himself had brought the gospel to Corinth (1) so that the fact that they were Christians was a proof of his apostleship (2). The degree to which he had been moved by their criticism is seen by the quick repartee with which he defends himself in verses 4–6.

He next enunciates the principle that *they which preach the gospel should live of the gospel* (14). Those who follow the secular callings of soldier, husbandman or herdsman are all paid their wages (7), and rightly so (8). Even the ox is allowed by law to eat in return for its work, a sign to the farmer that the hope of harvest which prompts his sowing shall not be disappointed (9, 10). Paul then transfers this last thought to his work as a preacher of the gospel. A spiritual seed is sown, but that does not mean that there should be no physical reward (11). In the service of the temple at Jerusalem, the priests were supported by the gifts and sacrifices which were brought (13). It is therefore quite clear that the labourer in God's harvest is worthy of his hire. This is as Christ Himself ordained (14) when sending out the seventy (see Lk. x. 7). Now it would seem as if the apostle had not taken advantage of these privileges in the past, and did not intend to do so in the future (12 and 15). This was not because he had any doubts about his apostleship but so that he could continue to proclaim the gospel *without charge* (18) to all who would hear. This was what he gloried in, not in the preaching itself. For there was a divine urge goading him on to proclaim the message of God. *Woe is unto me, if I preach not the gospel!* (16). In one sense he has no choice in the matter, for *a dispensation* (stewardship) *of the gospel is committed unto me* (17). But since he also undertakes the task willingly (a sign of this is his refusal to accept payment), he has the great reward of seeing the gospel proclaimed without hindrance as far as money is concerned.

The apostle reveals to us some of his methods of working in his ministry for Christ. We have already seen that he makes *the gospel of Christ without charge* (18); he has also made himself *servant unto all* (19); he has approached each group from its own background—Jews, those under the law, those without the law, the weak (20-22); he is *all things to all men* (22). When speaking of those without the law, he describes his own position as—*not without law to God, but under the law to Christ* (21). This phrase is worth remembering as a balancing concept to the freedom that is properly Christian.

Finally, the apostle compares the work of the Christian ministry to a race in which all run, but only *one receiveth the prize* (24). Success requires that we should be *temperate in all things* (25), and decisive in action, *not as one that beateth the air* (26). So the apostle says: *I keep under my body* (27); he does not let it play an important part in his life. *Lest . . . I myself should be a castaway* (27). The Greek word means 'rejected after testing'. In Rom. i. 28 it is translated 'reprobate', and explained as meaning 'being filled with all unrighteousness, fornication, wickedness'. The apostle is thus teaching the need for self-discipline in the Christian life, otherwise the passions of the body will dominate once more, and we shall become like the unregenerate. This statement raises the question of Christian 'assurance'; i.e. once a man is regenerate in Christ, can he subsequently be lost? Scripture on the whole gives us many assurances, that once we accept Christ, He will keep us safe to the end (e.g. Rom. viii. 38, 39, to give a statement from the same apostle). At the same time, such a passage as the one before us teaches us the need for constant vigilance that we fall not again into the ways of the ungodly. (Other passages of similar import are 1 Cor. x. 12; Gal. v. 4; Heb. iv. 11, x. 38, 39.) Some commentators, interpreting the word 'castaway' as 'rejected' (i.e. for the prize, cf. verse 24), regard the passage as meaning simply that under certain circumstances one who has ministered to others may lose his reward. (For an expression of the doctrine that a Christian might lose his reward see iii. 10-15.) The metaphor, drawn from the

Olympic Games, would at once appeal to Greek readers.

iii. The overcoming of temptations (x. 1-15). The apostle follows up his exhortation to strive hard to control fleshly lusts with a reference to early Jewish history, the wanderings in the wilderness. He shows how God had of necessity to punish those who fell into evil ways in those days, even though they had shared in the outward signs of belonging to Israel. Note the repetition of the word 'all'. *All . . . under the cloud, and all passed through the sea . . . all eat . . . all drink . . . but with many* (i.e. the majority) *God was not well pleased* (1-5). What a warning for nominal church members! Again, we may note that the apostle refers to these early Israelites as *our fathers* (1). Israel and the Church have a common ancestry. *Under the cloud* (1). A reference to the account in Ex. xiv. 19ff. *Baptized . . . eat . . . drink* (2, 3). The apostle finds analogies to the two Christian sacraments of baptism and the Lord's Supper in Israel's experiences. *Rock that followed them* (4). We need not assume that Paul is adopting here the rabbinical legend that the water-bearing Rephidim rock journeyed onwards with the Israelites. This is unthinkable. It is possible, however, that Paul is alluding to the fancy and giving it a spiritual turn as a picture of Christ in an allegorical fashion. Lightfoot comments that it was the streams, not the rock, that followed them. *Our examples* (6) (also in verse 11, *for ensamples*). Old Testament history is not only of value as a record of past events, but also as an instructor in the knowledge of God. Paul urges his readers to take warning from what happened to the children of Israel and not to commit the same sins. *Upon whom the ends of the world are come* (11). The word for 'world' here signifies 'ages'. The thought may be of the world as a series of epochs; or, as relating to various strands of history such as the 'age of Israel', the 'age of the Gentiles'. In this case the 'ends of the world' would mean some such thing as the climax or outcome of past history. *Lest he fall* (12). A thought similar to that of ix. 27. Note that the warning is to one who *thinketh he standeth.* Assurance must be based on reliance on God's promises and one's faithful adherence to the conditions implied in them. Temptation is always present to draw men away from true living. But God guards the Christian in this matter, and, if he is relying on God, he will find a way of escape opened for him by God (13). *Flee from idolatry* (14). This refers back to the question of meats offered to idols. The apostle's advice is to keep away from such associations. His insertion of the words, *I speak as to wise men* (15), taken as ending this section, indicates that he wishes to stimulate their minds in the matter and to arouse their attention.

iv. The Lord's Supper and pagan feasts (x. 16-22). He proceeds now to speak of the Lord's Supper and to teach that participation in it should utterly preclude any idea of participation in pagan sacrifices. This section gives us an authoritative scriptural way of describing what the Lord's Supper is. *The cup of blessing . . . is . . . the communion of the blood of Christ. The bread . . . is . . . the communion of the body of Christ* (16). These words should be known by heart by every Christian. To partake of the Lord's Supper, then, is to come into spiritual contact with the sacrifice of Christ on Calvary. The unity of Christians is also symbolized in the Lord's Supper—*we . . . are one bread, and one body* (17). The apostle illustrates the matter further by reference to *Israel after the flesh* (18), that is, historical Israel. By eating of the sacrifices, as they did in Old Testament times, they all were united by the altar (18). Can a similar illustration be drawn from Gentile sacrifices? Yes, although the idol is nothing in itself, Gentile sacrifices are clearly offered to devils, not to God, and the same principle of unifying those who take part is involved. Therefore Christians must not take part in Gentile sacrifices (20). They are united round *the Lord's table* (21). (Note this title; it is in contrast with the Old Testament *altar* (18), as well as with the *table of devils*.) Otherwise, they run the danger of provoking *the Lord to jealousy* (22). For the use of the word 'jealousy' in this connection, see the second commandment (Ex. xx. 4–6).

This passage teaches a high view of the sacrament, and no Christian should dream of teaching otherwise. False teaching arises only when attempts are made to define the sacrament in terms of change imparted to the bread and wine in themselves; or when power is claimed for one particular class of ministers as against all others. Neither of these things is even hinted at in Scripture. The due and proper ordering of the administration of the Lord's Supper is another matter.

v. Conscience, one's own and one's neighbour's (x. 23—xi. 1). The apostle returns now to the topic of the consideration of one's neighbour's conscience already dealt with in chapter viii and drives it home by reference to a 'dinner party' (27). *Whatsoever is set before you, eat* (27). If, however, someone declares that *this is offered in sacrifice* (28), *eat not*, because the man who reveals this fact associates the meat with idol worship. The question as to the use of, or abstinence from, alcoholic liquor might be considered in the light of this verse. The apostle would abstain for the sake of the conscience of his friend, but obviously underlines the principle of freedom—freedom under the control of the grace of God (30 and 31). What was expressed negatively in viii. 12 is expressed positively in verse 31. *The Jews . . . the Gentiles . . . the church of God* (32). A threefold division of mankind which still serves. In Corinth the division would have been easily perceived. *Followers of me, even as I also am of Christ* (xi. 1). It is as the apostle follows Christ, seeking to give no offence so that many may be saved, that others are to follow him.

c. Public worship—the principles at stake (xi. 2—xiv. 40)

i. Men and women in the congregation—their different standing (xi. 2–16). In this section Paul is giving instructions with regard to the proper deportment of Christian men and women. Although on first reading some of his statements are difficult to understand (see e.g. verse 10), yet, as we reflect on the passage, we can see the importance of his general teaching and its need in the present day. The social customs which provide the background for his thought are, of course, different from ours; but the factors involved are the same, namely, modesty, propriety, orderliness.

The head of every man is Christ (3). This verse sets the whole matter in its proper perspective. Paul enunciates a great basic principle in the order of creation, and applies this principle to the solution of the matter in hand. *Head covered* (4). Covering of the head is a sign of subjection. Man, as created in God's image (7), need not be 'covered' in the presence of other creatures (perhaps including angels), but it is appropriate that women should be so, in that, by God's ordinance, she is subject to man. *Shorn* (6). In a woman this was at that time a sign of disgrace indicating that she was an adulteress. *Woman for the man* (9). Scripture gives us a conception of marriage in which, although the wife is to obey the husband, yet the husband's duties towards the wife safeguard her from arbitrary domination (see e.g. 1 Pet. iii. 7).

For this cause ought the woman to have power on her head (10). 'A sign of authority on her head' (RV). There have been many interpretations of this difficult verse. The simplest seems also the most natural. The previous verse has stated that woman derived her origin from man and was created on his account. To cover her head was an acknowledgment (or 'sign') of this divine order in the work of creation, a symbol of her husband's power. *Because of the angels* (10). A phrase obscure to us but probably well understood by the Corinthian Christians at the time. Some link this verse with the account of the union of 'sons of God' and 'daughters of men' in Gn. vi (where the LXX has *angeloi* for the AV 'sons of God'), but the point of such a reference is not very clear. A simpler interpretation is to see here a reference to the fact that the Jews and the early Christian Church thought of angels as being present in their worshipping assemblies. Where they in all their holy order are assembled, recognition of the divinely constituted order of creation should be shown by every worshipper. Paul enforces his argument with an appeal to natural custom and common sense. *Doth not even nature itself teach you* (14). We should therefore translate his advice into terms relevant to present-day customs, in order to secure conditions which will similarly produce modesty, propriety and orderliness.

ii. The observance of the Lord's Supper (xi. 17–34). Paul turns now to the important matter of how the Lord's Supper is to be observed in the Church. In apostolic times it was regularly preceded by the 'love feast' (Gk. *agapē*), in order, no doubt, to make the parallel closer with the Last Supper itself. In accordance with custom each member would bring his own food. In contrast with ordinary social gatherings, rich and poor would be meeting together in this Christian feast, so that there would be a considerable discrepancy in the amount of food supplied by each. But instead of pooling the food, each kept for himself what he had brought, with the shameful result described in verse 21. Thus the feast, intended to foster a family spirit, was completely failing in its object, and the apostle practically advised its discontinuance even at this early date (see verse 22).

Because of these abuses Paul declares he cannot praise the Corinthians in this matter (17). This is in contrast to the praise he was able to accord them for observing 'the ordinances' he had given them (see verse 2). He refers again to the existence of parties amongst them (18), and adds: *there must be also heresies among you, that they which are approved may be made manifest among you* (19). Heresy is not only holding a wrong opinion, but definitely choosing it and taking sides over it. God's purpose in allowing these factions is to make manifest those who are *approved* by Him. Paul then declares that what they are doing when they come together is not a proper observance of the Lord's Supper at all (20). By permitting excess, by allowing some to go hungry and by causing the poorer members to feel ashamed, they *despise . . . the church of God* (22). This phrase may be linked with verse 29, RV, bearing in mind that the phrase *come together in the church* (18) does not refer, of course, to meeting in a church building, but describes the special and solemn nature of this gathering. It is the failure to *discern* or estimate the body (i.e. the Church) at its true value which is condemned throughout this passage.

The apostle's full account of the institution of the Lord's Supper (notice that he declares it was *received of the Lord*) is the form which has been followed in Church worship ever since (23–25). The term 'eucharist' is the Greek word meaning 'to give thanks' (24), and is sometimes used for the Holy Communion. *This is my body* (24). All 'carnal' ideas of participation are excluded by the fact that our Lord was alive when He said this, i.e. it was before His death. The *body* and *blood* of Christ are received after a 'spiritual manner'. *Broken for you* (24). See RV and cf. Lk. xxii. 19. The word 'broken' is not well supported. *This do* (24). These words are not in Matthew and Mark; the command rests, therefore, on the testimony of Paul. His words presuppose the practice in the Church and are understood as from the Lord Himself. *In remembrance of me* (24, 25). The repetition is impressive and gives us the scriptural reason for the observance of the Lord's Supper. It is to remember the Saviour, in all the events of His life, but chiefly

in His death for us on the cross; and, in remembering Him, to feel His presence with us. The Lord's Supper is thus a 'remembrance' of Christ and a 'communion' with Christ. *Testament* (25) is the same as 'covenant'. The terms 'Old Testament' and 'New Testament' are derived from this verse. *Ye do shew* (26). The word in the Greek means 'proclaim', and is the same as used in ix. 14. The observance of this ordinance is thus the 'great preacher of the death of Christ' and a witness to the world of the devotion of Christians to their Lord, and their reliance on His death *till he come* (26). *Guilty of the body . . .* (27). This verse is a solemn warning against thoughtless participation in the Lord's Supper. The words mean guilty of a crime committed against the sanctity of the body and blood of the Lord. Such a one puts himself on the side of those enemies of Christ who crucified Him. This memorial service is given us by Christ Himself and to abuse it leads to *damnation* (29) or 'judgment' (RV). It should be noted that *unworthily* (27, 29) does not mean 'unworthy', for we can never be anything but that. The exact meaning of verse 30 is obscure. It may be interpreted metaphorically as a description of their spiritual ineffectiveness; or it may be linked with the 'judgment' of verse 29 and interpreted as a description of the physical evils which result from their excesses and which are the outward signs of God's condemnation. Verse 31 urges alertness in keeping a watch over ourselves—our motives and our thoughts—being *chastened* (schooled), but not *condemned* (32). The apostle ends with an exhortation to conduct all such gatherings of the Church in a decent and orderly manner with the promise that he will deal further with the subject when he next visits them (33, 34).

The fact that Paul devoted so much space to teaching concerning the Lord's Supper shows its importance in the Christian life. At the same time, let us keep a proper perspective in the matter. There are very few direct references to the sacrament apart from the Gospels and this Epistle. Its institution by our Lord and His command to do it in memory of Him lead us to give it a central place in our Christian life. But to make it the one focus of our devotional life upsets the spiritual balance and, as we know from a study of Church history, leads to grievous error and superstition.

iii. Spiritual gifts and their use in the congregation (xii. 1–31). This chapter gives us a vision of the functioning of the Church as a body with many members, having different parts to play but all harmonizing together because they are unified by the 'one Spirit' (13). This Spirit is the Holy Spirit. Formerly, when they were Gentiles, they were led this way and that with no goal or object in life (2); but now, the fact that they call Jesus 'Lord' proves that they are led by the Spirit; and contrariwise, it is only by being so led that anyone can recognize Jesus as the Lord; the Holy Spirit (*Ghost* is the older English word for Spirit), and He alone, bears witness to Christ (3).

What Christians must learn is that the Holy Spirit uses different men in different ways, imparting different gifts to each (4). Likewise with Jesus Christ (the *Lord* of verse 5), there are different ministries (AV *administrations*) which He exercises towards men, and with God (the Father) there are different *operations* which He undertakes in the world (6). But the diversities proceed in each case from a single divine Person (cf. Eph. iv. 4–7n.)

If this interpretation of these verses is accepted it is clear that we have here an important statement bearing on the doctrine of the Trinity. But the apostle's thought is highly suggestive, and this may not be the only way of taking it. For instance, one might regard the terms *Spirit*, *Lord* and *God* as all referring to the Holy Ghost, so as to give a full doctrine of His distinct personality and His nature as deity.

Let each, then, profit by the manifestation of the Spirit in himself, and also use this for the profit of the whole Church (verses 7ff.). This 'sharing' principle is much stressed in the New Testament, not only by Paul, but also by the other writers. The Church, as he is about to show, is a body in which this close partnership should be manifested. Some of the Spirit's gifts are listed in verses 8–10 and may be compared with the list in verse 28. Note the contrast between *wisdom* and *knowledge* (8), and the way in which many of the gifts seem to fit the particular needs of the early Church. *Prophecy* (10) is not so much foretelling the future as proclaiming the truth generally.

In verse 12 the apostle practically gives the title of 'the Christ' to the Church (the AV and RV leave out the definite article which is present in the Greek), though this is amplified in verse 27 to the more familiar title, *the body of Christ. Baptized into one body* (13). The reference here is either to the act of baptism as the confession of faith, or the act of the Holy Spirit by which believers, irrespective of race or class, are put into the body. The verses which follow seem rather to confirm the second of these meanings since it is the Holy Spirit who is the invisible source of the oneness of the visible community of the baptized. *Drink into one Spirit* (13). Not impossibly a reference to the Lord's Supper. The two gospel sacraments were notable rites in the apostolic Church and must have been much thought about. The alternative reading 'drink of one Spirit' (RV) brings out the idea of each convert being made a partaker of the Holy Spirit (cf. Heb. vi. 4).

Verses 14–26 take up the idea of the Church as a body (see verse 12) and elaborate it in a kind of parable. Paul's aim is still to emphasize the thought of essential unity, and he does this by a threefold *reductio ad absurdum*. First he shows how foolish it would be for any member to rebel and claim independence (14–16); secondly he conjures up the absurdity of a body which consisted only of an eye or an ear (17); thirdly, and arising from this, he indicates how ridiculous it would be if none of the members could be distinguished from each other but were all the same (19). The Church, like the body, is a living organism, not a mechanical organization, and each member has a necessary part to play. In view of the 'divisive spirit' which existed in Corinth, it is interesting to note the stress here on the interdependence of the various parts, both in suffering and joy (26), the need for those members *which seem to be more feeble* (22), and the tempering together of *honourable* and *less honourable*, and *comely* and *uncomely* (23, 24). *Bestow* (RV mg. 'put on') *more abundant honour* (23). The reference may be to the use of clothes to cover those parts of the body other than the head, hands and feet.

God hath set some in the church (28). The Church is God's and therefore He orders it Himself. In view of this it is clearly wrong that there should be any quarrelling or jealousy over the offices to be filled. With verse 28 cf. verses 8–10 and Éph. iv. 11–13n. The list is instructive and shows a relation of office to the contemporary situation. *Apostles*, for instance, have since passed away. *Prophets;* see note on verse 10. *Teachers* may have been those who instructed the new converts. *Helps;* perhaps the 'interpreters of tongues' (cf. verse 10 and xiv. 27, 28), but the word is capable of a much more general application. *Governments;* RSV 'administrators'. It is relevant to point out that no office of priesthood, such as was conceived in later Church history, is envisaged here or in Eph. iv.

Covet earnestly the best gifts (31). The danger which arises when the interdependence and equal worth of all members is stressed is that proper and legitimate ambition may be stifled. But obviously any such 'coveting' must be done in a spirit of Christian love, and this thought the apostle proceeds to elaborate in the next chapter.

iv. The basis of all is love (xiii. 1–13). The whole of this chapter is really a parenthesis, the main theme of the apostle's argument being taken up again in chapter xiv. The thought of *a more excellent way* which seems to have come into his mind suddenly in xii. 31 is expanded in exalted language into a 'Hymn of Love' in which he points out that even the gifts of the Spirit, to which he has referred already in xii. 8–10 and 28–30, are nothing worth if love is lacking. In xiii. 1–3 he refers to some of these gifts, listing them, perhaps, in the order of importance favoured by the Corinthians. In verses 4–8a he elaborates what he means by love by describing what it will and what it will not do. The contrast with the prevailing code of ethics in cities such as Corinth must have been startling. The list is also influenced, no doubt, by the recent behaviour of the church which in earlier chapters he has been seeking to correct. In verses 8–13 he proceeds to draw a comparison between the gifts which they so greatly valued and the virtues which, by their actions, they despised. The former are restricted by our human limitations, are of value only for the service of the Church on earth and will pass away with the coming of the kingdom. The latter are eternal in quality. He illustrates the thought by comparing their present spiritual experience to childhood with its imperfect speech, understanding and reasoning power. *When that which is perfect is come* (10) it will be like entering into manhood. The same thought is developed in a further illustration. It is as though we are at present looking at a metal mirror from some distance away. The image is blurred and to make it out is like attempting to answer a riddle (Gk. *ainigma*, a dark saying). But *then* (referring back to verse 10) we shall see clearly *face to face. Now abideth* (13). The reference is not to a point of time, as in the previous verse, but to the point reached in his argument. *The greatest of these* (13). Love is not only superior to the gifts which have been considered but is supreme also among the graces.

The AV translation of the Gk. *agapē* as *charity* is misleading in view of our present-day use of the word. (See e.g. verse 3a.) Love in the thought of the apostle is an attitude of the heart, of the mind and of the will. In other words it actuates the whole of man's personality. It is to be distinguished from mere sentiment and, of course, from ordinary human affection. Christian love is possible only in one who lives in the power of the indwelling Christ. The theme is developed strongly by the apostle John in his writings. See e.g. 1 Jn. iii. 13–24, iv. 7–21.

v. Speaking with tongues (xiv. 1–40). This practice of speaking in a tongue was apparently common at Corinth and was obviously a highly prized gift. The only other references to the subject are in Acts, although it is not certain that what Luke describes (e.g. in Acts ii. 4–11) was a manifestation of the Spirit exactly similar to the gift dealt with here. The AV, by inserting the word *unknown* (which is not in the Greek), gives the impression that the speaking was in a language or languages foreign to the speaker. More probably Paul is referring to ecstatic utterances, expressing feelings rather than logical thought, which were completely unintelligible to the hearers (2) unless 'interpreted' (5). Indeed the speaker might not know himself the meaning of the utterances and is urged to pray for the ability to interpret (13). If neither he nor anyone else can interpret he is to keep silence in the public meetings of the church and to use the gift only in his own private communion with God (28). There is no suggestion that the gift was one which would enable the gospel to be preached in other languages.

The apostle's aim is to show that by attaching too much importance to this gift they are likely (as a church) to lose that *edification, and exhortation, and comfort* (3) which result from the exercise of the gift of prophesying. He does not decry the gift of tongues: he himself has it in greater measure than they (18). But for very practical reasons he urges them to desire rather that gift which enables the recipient to reveal the truths of the gospel and to teach sound doctrine. By such means is the Church profited (6).

He uses three illustrations to drive home his point. Different musical instruments each have their distinctive tone; otherwise it would be impossible to tell one from the other (7). In addition, each instrument, for example a trumpet, must be played intelligently, otherwise no one will understand or appreciate the music (8). Thirdly, if thoughts are to be conveyed from one person to another it must be in words which are understood by the hearer. All words have some meaning (10) but it is like trying to hold a conversation with a foreigner if the meaning of the words used is not known (11).

The application of this follows in verses 12–19. Paul turns from contrasting the gift of tongues with that of prophesying in order to give practical instructions on its use. His one concern is that the church shall be edified. Obviously such a result can follow only if the ministry is understood by all those present, including 'anyone who lacks the gift' (16, Weymouth. Cf. RSV mg.).

For a moment he pauses to remind them that even in this matter of understanding there are degrees. He even introduces a little moral exhortation, 'in malice be ye babes' (20, RV). He then returns to his first theme and contrasts once more prophesying and speaking in a tongue. The quotation in verse 21 referred to as *in the law* is actually from Is. xxviii. 11, 12. The 'Law and the Prophets' formed a closely knit system of revelation to the Jews and the term law is used comprehensively here. The reference is to God's use of the Assyrians as a sign to His people after they had refused to listen to the clear message of the prophets. Verse 22 must be interpreted within this limited context. *Tongues are for a sign . . . to them that believe not* (22), convicting them of God's power but bringing no message of hope. On the other hand *prophesying serveth . . . for them which believe* (22). With hearts prepared they hear God's voice and obey it.

An entirely different approach is made to the subject in the next three verses. The unbeliever of verse 23 is really the same person as the believer of verse 22, but at an earlier stage. Paul shows how he comes to faith not through the use of the gift of tongues, but through the convicting power of the gospel clearly preached. The hardened sinner of verse 22 who is compared with the children of Israel who would not hear (21) is not in view in verses 23–25.

How is it then, brethren? (26). 'What lessons are we to draw from all this?' In summing up the apostle seeks to establish some order among the customary confusion of their gatherings. As regards tongues, let not more than two or three exercise this gift at any one meeting and let them do it singly. Even so this may be done only if there is someone to interpret (27, 28). Similarly the prophets must be prepared to submit to the judgment of others and to give way to one another. By control over his own spirit (32), however, a prophet can learn to wait his turn to speak. With verse 33 cf. verse 40.

Let your women keep silence (34). This should

be linked with the last clause of verse 33. In addition to the confusion described in verse 26, the church at Corinth has been allowing the women to take part in the public gatherings contrary to the custom of the Church generally. With some sarcasm Paul asks in verse 36 whether they are the originators of the gospel. These verses refer probably to the main public gatherings of the church and the prohibition is to be understood in the light of the teaching already given (see chapter xi) on the order of creation. The danger of bringing shame and disrepute on the Church by a misuse of liberty contrary to local custom may also be present in the apostle's mind. In xi. 5 he has inferred that women may prophesy and pray in public. But these may have been smaller and more informal meetings such as the prayer meeting which took place in the house of Mark's mother (Acts xii. 12).

Verse 37 is a clear claim to inspiration. The test of a man's spiritual knowledge is his acceptance of these commandments. Verse 38 as translated in the AV suggests that if anyone refuses to acknowledge these instructions he is so wilfully ignorant that Paul refuses to bother with him. An alternative reading is followed in the RSV and translated 'If anyone does not recognize this, he is not recognized'. Compare this with viii. 2, 3. The final verses are a return to xii. 31 and xiv. 1 and sum up the whole matter.

V. THE GOSPEL OF THE RESURRECTION. xv. 1–58

a. Summary of the facts (xv. 1–19)

The apostle now moves on to one of the most glorious themes in all his writings—the assurance of the resurrection for believers. *The gospel* (1). Its cardinal points should be noted. Christ's death *for our sins* (3), His burial and His resurrection (4). The tense in Greek implies Christ's present resurrected state. These events are facts of history and took place *according to the scriptures* (3, 4), i.e. in fulfilment of Old Testament prophecy. *Unless ye have believed in vain* (2). This anticipates the argument he is about to bring forward. The statement is purely hypothetical. It is expressed more fully in verse 17.

The multitude of witnesses for the resurrection (for it was a multitude relative to the needs of ordinary testimony) are recalled (5–8). This passage is the earliest extant written statement we possess of the historical evidence for Christ's resurrection. *After that* (6, 7); *last of all* (8). The list seems to be in chronological order. The Gospels record nine separate appearances of the risen Lord. There is no parallel biblical reference to the appearances to the five hundred at once and to James. Since in the Gospels our Lord was not recognized by his brethren, and in the Acts James appears as an apostle, the reference to this special resurrection appearance is significant. *One born out of due time* (8). Paul is contrasting his own conversion with that of the other apostles. Theirs was the result of long

association with Christ. His was a sudden, overwhelming experience. *Am not meet to be called an apostle* (9). Cf. Eph. iii. 8n. A word of penitence for his former persecution of the Church is followed by all the greater joy in that *the grace of God* enabled him to work *more abundantly than they all. What I am* (10); not 'who I am'. Paul seems to be referring to character and attainment.

How say some among you that there is no resurrection of the dead? (12). News has reached Paul that there is false teaching in the church on this subject. Cf. 2 Tim. ii. 17, 18. The Athenians, we know, rejected the idea of resurrection (see Acts xvii. 32), and Corinth may have been influenced by this Greek teaching. Among the Jewish converts, too, may have been some who had been influenced by the attitude of the Sadducees. Cf. Acts xxiii. 8. Paul's aim is to show that such a denial is contrary to the facts, and to point out what the logical implications of it are.

If Christ be not risen (14). Better, as in RV, 'If Christ hath not been raised', and similarly throughout this passage. The resurrection is part of the gospel (4, 12). But a denial of human resurrection must involve a denial of Christ's resurrection (16). The implications for them and the apostles are clearly shown. Their hope of salvation is vain (14, 17; cf. verse 2) and their teachers, whose word they have trusted, are not merely mistaken but deliberately false in their testimony (15). *Of God* (15); Gk. *kata*, 'against'. Paul means he would be making God false, misinterpreting Him, and so bringing something 'against' Him. In addition, if there is no resurrection, those who have died trusting in Christ are really on a level with the beasts that perish (18). We have also to assume that God is allowing us to have hopes in Christ which can never be fulfilled — a pitiable state of affairs. *Most miserable* (19); in Greek not a superlative but a comparative and meaning 'the more to be pitied'. He implies that believers have denied themselves what people call pleasure here, and have no happiness beyond.

b. Consequences of the facts (xv. 20–34)

But now is Christ risen (20). Paul sweeps away the hypotheses and returns to the solid fact of the resurrection. *In Adam . . . in Christ* (22). This contrast between the old and the new, between Adam as representing fallen humanity and Christ as the head of all the redeemed, is a favourite theme of Paul's. In one form or another it appears in a number of his Epistles (cf. Rom. v. 12–19; Eph. iv. 22–24; Col. iii. 8–11). He returns to the thought later in the chapter. *Every man in his own order* (23). Paul indicates a sequence in the events leading up to the end (cf. 1 Thes. iv. 13–17), but gives no indication of time intervals. In verses 24–28 he carries our minds beyond the bounds of space and time to the final victory of Christ culminating in God's being *all in all* (28). Notice how the personal pronoun 'he' in these verses sometimes refers to God the Father, sometimes to God the Son. '(Christ) must reign

... for (God) hath put all things under (Christ's) feet ... It is manifest that (God) is excepted, which did put all things under (Christ) ... The Son himself shall be subject unto (God) that put all things under (Christ).' The relation between Christ and the Father expressed in this passage is of the greatest interest in our formulation of the doctrine of the Holy Trinity. We are given a view of the 'subordination of the Son'— to use the theological term—but this does not conflict in any way with belief in the full deity of Christ, who shares with the Father the 'substance' of the Godhead. The 'subordination' is of office, not of person. The reference is to His work as Redeemer and as King of God's kingdom. He has been appointed to these rôles by the Father (27). Cf. 1 Cor. iii. 23.

Baptized for the dead (29). A difficult phrase which has been variously interpreted. Some see here a reference to a local custom of being baptized vicariously on behalf of some relative or friend who had died believing in Christ but unbaptized. It is known that such baptisms did take place during the second century. They were chiefly associated, however, with heretical sects and there is no reference to the practice as early as this. If this is the meaning it should be noticed that Paul in no way associates himself or his readers with such baptisms. He refers to those who practise this rite in the third person and his aim is simply to indicate that what they teach (i.e. their denial of the resurrection) is inconsistent with what they do (since the dead are now beyond such help). Another explanation is to interpret the phrase as 'baptized for the sake of the dead', i.e. as a result of the witness which they gave during their lives or by their deaths. This relates the inconsistency to the act of baptism itself and the stress is on its symbolism of death and resurrection. A similar meaning is obtained if we suppose that throughout the verse Paul is thinking of the symbolism of baptism and is not referring to those who have died physically at all. The person who is baptized is acknowledging that he is dead with Christ and in this sense baptism is only 'for the dead'. (Cf. Rom. vi. 1–11 where this thought is developed.) On this view the phrase *for the dead* is inserted by Paul only because he wants to remind them forcibly of this symbolism.

The hope of the resurrection also explains the willingness of Christians to endure suffering in this world. *I die daily* (31). The implied corollary of this is that he is also raised to life daily. Contrast this with *to morrow we die* (32) and the materialistic and Epicurean outlook on life which Paul ironically suggests we might well have if resurrection were not a fact. This verse should be punctuated as in RV. *After the manner of men* (32); RSV 'humanly speaking'. *Fought with beasts* (32). No doubt used figuratively of the fierce opposition he encountered. There is one word only in the Greek—'fight-with-wild-beasts'. *Evil communications* (33.) A quotation from a Greek poet, Menander. RSV translates 'Bad com-

pany ruins good morals'. Paul, fully realizing the corrupting nature of the teaching he has sought to counter, concludes the section with a challenge to righteous living. *Some have not the knowledge of God* (34). Evidence of a 'mixed' church.

c. The nature of the resurrection body (xv. 35–49)

The apostle uses well-known facts of nature to show the reasonableness of belief in a higher form of life in the resurrection state. He is reasoning 'by analogy'. It should be clearly understood that he is not seeking to prove the resurrection in these verses. He is meeting the case of the person who agrees with the logic of his previous argument but is worried by the questions put forward in verse 35. *Thou fool* (36). See RV. The chiding is gentler than the AV translation suggests. By three analogies Paul shows that identity of matter is preserved in a variety of form. Corn is still corn whether it be seed or plant, flesh is still flesh whether it be human or belonging to some kind of animal; matter is still matter whether it exists in the earth or in the sun, moon or stars. He seizes on the last illustration to drive home his point. The difference is a difference in form, *in glory* (41). So also the resurrection body differs from the natural body. As a seed is sown, so man is born; as the seed dies, so does he; as it enters into new life as a plant, so is he raised in glory. The words *natural* and *spiritual* are not to be thought of as expressing the 'material' of which the bodies are made, but as stressing their adaptability. The 'spiritual body' has some kind of germinal connection with the 'natural body' though the development is glorious beyond our comprehension, and the 'spiritual body' is perfectly adapted to the full life of a glorified spirit. This contrast between natural life and spiritual life leads him again to contrast Adam *a living soul* and Christ *a quickening* (or 'life-giving') *spirit* (45). The contrast is worked out in some detail (45–49). Verse 49 may be read as in RV mg. 'let us also bear the image of the heavenly'. It would be in keeping with Paul's method for him to urge that we should begin now to 'put on Christ', and to round off his analogy with this practical application.

d. Immortality (xv. 50–58)

The two realms having been clearly discerned, it remains to state the antithesis between them and to show how it is overcome. *I shew you a mystery* (51); i.e. something which has been hidden but is now revealed. Paul here leaves the realm of natural knowledge, where analogy is possible, and describes the future coming of Christ from the point of view of a believer on earth (cf. 1 Thes. iv. 13–18). By analogy he has already shown that those who died will *be raised incorruptible*. By revelation he teaches the corollary of this that those who are alive at our Lord's coming will *be changed* (52). *Trump* (52). The trumpet was the instrument for giving a command, like the bugle of today. It is used metaphorically but with a reference to Old Testament usage as in Ex. xix. 16. *Death is swallowed up in victory* (54). From Is. xxv. 8. Death is pictured as a monster unable to hold those who have already become its victims and foiled of those Christians who are alive at Christ's return. This victory in which Paul rejoices, regarding it as already present, is *through our Lord Jesus Christ* (57). *The sting of death* (56). See Ho. xiii. 14. For a development of Paul's teaching regarding sin, the law and death see Rom. iv and v. Sin gives death its power and itself derives its power from the law. *Be ye stedfast* (58). Here again is the practical application of the doctrine. The words *in vain* take us back to his original hypothesis. Because the Corinthians have not believed in vain (cf. verse 2) they can be sure that their labour in the Lord will not be vain. Faith in the resurrection, therefore, becomes the greatest protection against instability and the greatest incentive to service.

VI. FINAL INSTRUCTIONS. xvi. 1–24

a. Systematic giving (xvi. 1–9)

Collection for the saints (1). This collection was for the poor at Jerusalem and was a project dear to Paul's heart. Cf. 2 Cor. where chapters viii and ix are largely devoted to it. See also Acts xxiv. 17. *The first day of the week* (2). Already, it seems, this day was of special significance for Christians. *Lay by him in store*. Either put on one side at home a sum proportionate to what one has received, or else bring it to the central treasury of the church. In either case it is clear that regular, proportionate giving is urged. *Whomsoever ye shall approve* (3). The reason for this care is given in 2 Cor. viii. 20, 21. *I do pass through Macedonia* (5). Better, as in RSV, 'I intend to pass through Macedonia'. The apostle is not referring to where he is at the time of writing. This is given as Ephesus in verse 8, where in spite of all difficulties there were tremendous opportunities which demanded his presence.

b. Concerning Timothy, Apollos and Stephanas (xvi. 10–18)

Verses 10 and 11 serve to strengthen the impression regarding Timothy's character which is derived from a study of Paul's letters to him. Paul is very solicitous for the welfare of his 'dearly beloved son'. Verse 12 shows that, in spite of the divisions in the church, Paul was in no way jealous of Apollos. Perhaps Apollos himself stayed away lest the position should be aggravated. See also *Introduction*.

Watch ye . . . (13, 14). These words sound like the concluding exhortation of the Epistle. The return to the thought of doing everything *with charity* shows how convinced Paul was that this was the solution of all their practical difficulties.

Stephanas . . . Fortunatus . . . Achaicus (17); members of the Christian community at Corinth who had brought news of the church to Paul and may have been the bearers of the letter containing the various questions which Paul has sought to answer. When they return they are to be recognized as helpers and labourers in the gospel with Paul.

c. Greetings and closing prayer (xvi. 19–24)

The apostle is the link between the Christians in different parts and by conveying greetings from one group to another stresses their membership one with another. Aquila and Priscilla had been with Paul at Corinth and are now with him at Ephesus. *Holy kiss* (20). An Eastern method of greeting taken up and used by the Church. It is still practised on special occasions in the Eastern Orthodox Church. *Mine own hand* (21). It seems to have been Paul's custom to add a final salutation in his own handwriting, so setting his seal upon the letter. *If any man love not the Lord* (22). Personal love for Jesus Christ is the essence of Christianity. *Anathema* (22). A Greek word meaning 'cast aside' or, more forcibly, 'accursed'. *Maranatha* (22). Probably Aramaic, meaning 'Our Lord, come!' The closing benediction is distinctively Pauline.

The note placed at the end of the Epistle indicates the opinion held at the time the Authorized Version was first issued (1611). As stated in the *Introduction* it is now thought that the letter was written from Ephesus, not Philippi, and was sent by the hand of Titus.

W. C. G. PROCTOR.

II CORINTHIANS: OUTLINE OF CONTENTS

For the general introduction to this Epistle see p. 967.

I. THE APOSTLE'S RECENT TRIALS AND TRAVELS. i. 1—ii. 13

    a. Greetings (i. 1, 2)
    b. God comforts His people (i. 3–11)
    c. Paul denies that he has been fickle (i. 12–22)
    d. Personal reasons for not visiting Corinth (i. 23—ii. 4)
    e. A call to forgive (ii. 5–13)

II. THE NATURE OF THE CHRISTIAN MINISTRY. ii. 14—vi. 10

a. The triumph of the gospel (ii. 14—iii. 6)
b. The gospel's greater and open glory (iii. 7—iv. 6)
c. The heavenly treasure in earthen vessels (iv. 7-18)
d. The earthly and the heavenly house (v. 1-10)
e. The ministry of reconciliation (v. 11—vi. 10)

III. A PERSONAL APPEAL. vi. 11—vii. 16

a. Let affection be mutual (vi. 11-13)
b. A call to separation (vi. 14—vii. 1)
c. Paul rejoices in their repentance (vii. 2-16)

IV. THE COLLECTION FOR THE POOR IN JUDAEA. viii. 1—ix. 15

a. Titus will organize the collection (viii. 1-15)
b. Arrangements for the collection described (viii. 16—ix. 5)
c. Principles of Christian giving (ix. 6-15)

V. PAUL'S APOSTOLIC AUTHORITY. x. 1—xiii. 10

a. Paul defends himself against false charges (x. 1-18)
b. The character of Paul's ministry (xi. 1-15)
c. Paul's defence based on his life and work (xi. 16—xii. 11)
d. Paul's love and concern (xii. 12-21)
e. Paul's closing appeal (xiii. 1-10)

VI. CONCLUSION. xiii. 11-14

II CORINTHIANS: COMMENTARY

I. THE APOSTLE'S RECENT TRIALS AND TRAVELS. i. 1—ii. 13

a. Greetings (i. 1, 2)

It is of interest to compare the opening sentences of this Epistle with those of 1 Corinthians. We notice the omission of the word 'called' from the phrase 'called to be an apostle' (1 Cor. i. 1). The longer phrase was suitable in a first letter. Similarly he had described the Corinthians in the first letter as 'called to be saints' (1 Cor. i. 2). Their status and calling is now well known and need not be repeated. They are simply *the church of God which is at Corinth* (1). In the first letter the apostle is more general in his associating the church at Corinth with the whole Church in 'all that in every place call upon the name of Jesus Christ' (1 Cor. i. 2). Here he directs their attention to the Christians beside them—*all the saints which are in all Achaia* (1). This is a good reminder that Christians should be in fellowship with other neighbouring Christians as well as being linked in Christ to those afar off.

b. God comforts His people (i. 3-11)

Paul proceeds to strike the keynote of this Epistle—the need for reconciliation, a merciful attitude one to another, and a mutual comforting of one another—by describing God as the *Father of mercies, and the God of all comfort* (3). His own immediate personal experiences in Ephesus (see 1 Cor. xv. 32; Acts xix) give special significance to the words in verses 4 and 5. *Abound* (5).

To the apostle, to suffer for Christ was the greatest joy, as it made him feel more close to Christ; and his constant experience was that the grace of God did in such cases all the more abound (see also iv. 10). *Same sufferings* (6). The apostle attributes to the Corinthians the same feelings of sorrow and grief over the estrangement as he himself experienced, and also trusts that they now enjoy the same comfort from God. *Our hope of you is stedfast* (7). To hold a high opinion of a fellow-man, however he may have temporarily failed, is a great help in his restoration. *Despaired even of life* (8). The uproar at Ephesus threatened the apostle's life (see Acts xix), but the experience made him realize once again that his welfare was in the hands of God. *Sentence* (9); RV 'answer'. As far as his human nature was concerned, death seemed inevitable.

c. Paul denies that he has been fickle (i. 12-22)

Testimony of our conscience (12). The Epistles as well as Acts show that Paul was consistently conscientious in his behaviour. *Simplicity and godly sincerity* (12). The Greek is 'holiness and sincerity of God'; that is, the holiness and the sincerity that God gives by His grace. *Fleshly wisdom* (12). See notes on 1 Cor. i. 18-25 and ii. 6-16. *None other things* (13). The apostle teaches and writes the same things with consistency. *Your rejoicing* (14). Paul seems to have felt a specially close spiritual relationship with the Corinthians, and by this comment hopes to make them as glad about him as he is about them. *Day of the Lord Jesus* (14); a general expression signifying the manifest triumph of Christ as Saviour and judge. It embraces all that is taught in Scripture about the second coming and judgment.

Second benefit (15). Paul had hoped to visit Corinth, to go up to Macedonia from there, and return to Corinth, thus giving that city a double call (see *Introduction*). Some of the Christians in Corinth seem to have resented his failure to keep to his plan. *The flesh* (17). Unreliability in carrying out a task is characteristic of 'fleshly men'. Paul asserts emphatically that he is not a 'yes and no' man. *God is true* (18). There is no unreliability where God is concerned, and Paul sets the same high standard for himself. The preaching of the gospel among them, carried out by Paul, Silvanus and Timothy, was a positive and definite thing. For in Christ all the promises of God come to fruition. God too, says Paul, established *us with you* (21), and *hath anointed us* (21), and *sealed us* (22); that is, God put His mark upon us as His property. He gave us the *earnest of the Spirit in our hearts* (22), i.e. a token payment in advance, or a token sample of the power of the Holy Spirit.

d. Personal reasons for not visiting Corinth (i. 23—ii. 4)

To spare you (23). Paul postponed his visit to let his feelings subside, and he does not hesitate to use language calculated to persuade men of his sincerity. *Dominion* (24). The apostle does not claim any ultimate authority over the Corinthians as regards their faith, but rather sets himself alongside of them as a fellow-believer. *Faith* (24). The Greek word includes the ideas of personal trust and obedience. *Come again* (ii. 1). In view of the New Testament evidence, only two visits to Corinth are certain. Therefore *come* here might have to be given a wider interpretation and taken as referring to a communication from Paul, either by letter (no longer extant?) or by message. *Wrote* (3). This lends support to the view that there was a letter which is now lost (see *Introduction*).

e. A call to forgive (ii. 5–13)

If any have caused grief (5). The apostle is not too explicit here in apportioning blame, thus showing a kindly Christian spirit. Christians should not keep alive the memory of wrongs that are passed and forgiven. Follow the RV rendering in this verse and notice that Paul asserts that the wrong affects the whole church. He may be suggesting that the church had not sufficiently taken the disgrace to heart. *Ye ought rather to forgive* (7). The Christian should be ever ready to forgive (as he has been forgiven by God). This is in accordance with our Lord's teaching. *Swallowed up with overmuch sorrow* (7); too severe chastisement is discouraged. *Confirm* (8); i.e. 'ratify', make sure the penitent knows he is fully restored.

We may infer that this was to be done by receiving him back into the fellowship of the church as a repentant sinner. *To this end also did I write* (9). The 'lost letter' evidently was an exhortation to the charitable handling of this grievous affair, the details of which are unknown to us. *In the person of Christ* (10); the Greek is 'in the presence of Christ', signifying a consciousness of Christ being present and approving. The phrase implies 'acting on Christ's behalf', and is a further reference to the official reinstatement of the offender by Paul, acting for Christ the King and Head of the Church. *Satan* (11); the adversary would gain an advantage over the church by the continuance of feelings of severity.

Troas (12). The apostle recalls his recent travels to let the Corinthians know that all the time he was seeking only to do God's will, and was not (as might appear to outward judgment) going back on his promise to visit them. The account in Acts xx is very brief and gives no details. It simply relates that Paul, after the uproar at Ephesus, 'departed for to go into Macedonia. And when he had gone over those parts, and had given them much exhortation, he came into Greece, and there abode three months' (Acts xx. 1–3). The present Epistle was written from Macedonia during the period of time referred to in these verses.

II. THE NATURE OF THE CHRISTIAN MINISTRY. ii. 14—vi. 10

The apostle breaks off the narrative suddenly and speaks of the nature of the Christian ministry. We may suppose him much troubled in mind concerning the Corinthians, and how they would take his rebuke, received by them in the 'lost Epistle'. But, as he contemplated this, he is led to see the wonderful nature of the ministry Christ has committed to him, and proceeds to speak about it. In doing so, he both glorifies God 'who hath given such gifts unto men' (Eph. iv. 8), and also raises the level of the dispute between himself and the Corinthians to a lofty plane.

a. The triumph of the gospel (ii. 14—iii. 6)

Thanks be unto God (14). In his letters Paul is continually finding cause for such thanksgiving. In this Epistle cf. viii. 16, ix. 15. *To triumph* (14); lit. 'lead in triumph', as in RV. The ancient custom of leading one's beaten foe in a triumphal procession may have been in the apostle's mind. So he rejoices that the believer is so 'led in triumph' by Christ. *Savour* (14) is a word originally connected with sacrifices and is introduced here as Paul remembers the incense used in triumphal processions. The apostle has spread abroad the knowledge of God just as the incense-bearer spreads the fragrance of the incense. But the preaching of the word has a double effect. To those who accept the message and are *saved* (15) it brings life; to those who refuse to listen it is in effect a *savour of death*

(16), since as a result of their refusal they *perish* (15). *Sufficient* (16). As Paul contemplates such a powerful influence as this emanating from himself, he humbly acknowledges his insufficiency and his dependence upon God (see also iii. 5). *Many, which corrupt the word of God* (17). The apostle will not diminish in any way the full gospel message to make it more acceptable to human thought. This process had already started in his day. *In Christ* (17). Paul's whole life, thought and actions were centred in Christ. This is a favourite Pauline form of expression (cf. Gal. ii. 20).

Epistles of commendation (iii. 1). For the practice of commending teachers to other churches in this way see Acts xviii. 27. It would seem that teachers had visited Corinth who bore such letters, perhaps from the elders in Jerusalem. Paul is arguing here that it was not the possession of such documents that guaranteed the truth of the teacher's ministry. A better means of judging was by the fruit of his work. So the converts of his ministry at Corinth were his epistle and, if properly read, sufficient commendation. From the use of the word *again* (1) and the repetition of the phrase in v. 12, it would seem that the teachers who opposed him were accusing him of having 'commended himself', and were suggesting that this was not a very reliable credential compared with the letters they carried. Later, in x. 12, Paul turns the charge round and levels it against them. *Epistle of Christ* (3); a striking phrase referring to the message proclaimed by the witness of the believer's life when he is controlled by the *Spirit of the living God*. The thought leads on to a reference to the old covenant, which was also written by God, and the laws of which were exterior to men. This is then contrasted with the new covenant, which is an inward work, operating in the realm of mind and spirit. *Fleshy tables . . .* (3); better, as in RV, 'tables that are hearts of flesh', which brings out more clearly the reference to Ezk. xi. 19. The whole phrase recalls Je. xxxi. 33. *Our sufficiency is of God* (5). The minister is nothing (see 1 Cor. iv); God is the effective operator. In this and the following verse Paul answers the question he asked in ii. 16. *Testament* (6); the Greek is 'covenant'; Latin versions use *testamentum*, hence the English word. The Bible speaks of the 'old covenant' and the 'new covenant' to describe the law, on the one hand, and God's gift of grace through Jesus Christ, on the other. *Letter . . . spirit* (6). These words contrast the former dispensation with the latter. Judaism had become the following of a law, but Christianity is the living of a life. A ministering of precepts must be deadening owing to the inability of man to conform to what is written ('the letter'); but the message of salvation brings life by means of the spiritual, or life-giving, qualities attaching to the gospel through the Holy Spirit. Paul still has in mind here passages such as Je. xxxi. 31–34 and Ezk. xi. 19, 20.

b. The gospel's greater and open glory (iii. 7—iv. 6)

Ministration of death (7). By referring to the law of Moses in this way, the apostle is recalling that death was the outcome of man's failure to keep the law. Nevertheless, the inauguration of this ministry was accompanied by much glory— the glory of Sinai, and also the glory reflected on the face of Moses. This is because the law reveals the will of God. *Rather glorious* (8). The gift of life will abound still more to the glory of God, because mercy and love are now combined with righteousness in man's knowledge of God. *Condemnation . . . righteousness* (9). Under the law, man was condemned because of his proven unrighteousness. In Christ, man receives a righteousness, not his own, which is perfect in the sight of God. This is ministered with much greater glory. *Plainness of speech* (12). The apostle makes no reserve in his preaching; nor does he need to dress up what he has to say. The message of the gospel is a superlative case without any human adornment. *Vail* (13); a reference to Ex. xxxiv. 32–35. *The end* (13). The thought in the apostle's mind seems to be that Moses veiled his face so that the Israelites would not see the transitoriness of the dispensation thus inaugurated, by the fading of the glory. But they failed to perceive either the purpose of the law or the newer and greater dispensation which would follow. *Done away in Christ* (14). Paul was given the special commission by God to proclaim the fulness of Christ; that is, that He was the fulfilment or the 'end' (see Rom. x. 4) of the law; so that he who had Christ had, in Him, all the righteousness demanded by the law. (This theme is more fully worked out in Galatians and Romans.) *It* (16). Understand as referring to 'their heart' in the previous verse. *The Lord* (17); i.e. the Lord Christ. Paul seems to be using the word *Spirit* here in the sense in which he has employed it in verses 6 and 8 above, so that there is still the implied contrast with the 'letter'. *There is liberty* (17); i.e. the consciousness of the restraining and condemning nature of the law is taken away. Christians no longer desire to break the law; they are imbued with the spirit of the law. *Are changed* (18); the RV reads 'But we all, with unveiled face reflecting as a mirror the glory of the Lord, are transformed into the same image from glory to glory, even as from the Lord the Spirit'. This teaches us that the man who has turned to Christ and reflects Him in his life is transformed more and more in glory, by Christ who is the Spirit. The law contains the mind of the Spirit.

We faint not (iv. 1). The apostle was ever conscious of the glory of the ministry of the Christian gospel, and aware that human beings, in their own strength, were unworthy of it; hence his repeated assertion that God gives the grace (or mercy) for the ministry, and so upholds the glory of the ministry by His own power. *Not walking in craftiness* (2). No human argumentation suits the commending of the gospel to the world; such inevitably becomes 'craftiness'. *Handling the word of God deceitfully* (2). The Greek verb translated 'handling deceitfully' continues the idea of craftiness, i.e. human manipulation with an end in view other than the truth. Cf. iii. 12n. above. The phrase *the word of God* can be interpreted broadly as the revelation of God. That it refers primarily here to the gospel message we need not doubt; but it would also embrace the revelation of God in the old covenant, which is the background of the gospel; and so it could ultimately be interpreted (by us today) as referring to the Bible as a whole. *Commending ourselves to every man's conscience* (2). The gospel commends itself to all except wilful wrongdoers, and the Christian should be a man whose life all can commend. *Hid* (3). The word for 'hid' is the word used in iii. 13 for 'veiled' and the thought is linked on to that passage. *The god of this world* (4); RV mg., 'of this age'. The reference is to the present temporal order. The Bible ascribes this rôle to Satan. (See 1 Cor. v. 5n.) *The light of the glorious gospel of Christ* (4); RV 'the light of the glory of the gospel of Christ'. The work of the god of this world is directed towards the object of turning men away from the light. Paul once again draws attention to the 'glory' of the gospel, perhaps with the ministration of the law still in mind. *Image of God* (4). 'No man hath seen God at any time; the only begotten Son, which is in the bosom of the Father, he hath declared him' (Jn. i. 18). In 1 Cor. xi. 7, Paul declares that man is 'the image of God', going back in thought to Gn. i. 26. Sin has marred the image in all mankind; but it is seen again, perfectly, in Christ. *Light to shine* (6); a reference to Gn. i. 3. Christ, the light of the world (Jn. viii. 12), shines in the heart of the believer. Spiritual illumination is the accompaniment of regeneration, and this in turn originates in Christ. The point of the verse in Paul's argument is that it is God who has shined; therefore any unbelief in men is due, not to obscurity in the message, but to wilful hostility of men. Because the true light now shines, Paul proclaims it.

c. The heavenly treasure in earthen vessels (iv. 7–18)

Verse 7 again expresses the real source and power of the Christian ministry. The minister is an *earthen vessel*. See iii. 5 above. *Distressed* (8); RSV 'crushed'. *Cast down* (9); RV 'smitten down'. Paul's life was full of affliction. Yet, in spite of his suffering, his attitude is that it could all have been much worse. He refuses to allow his faith to be shaken. *Bearing about in the body the dying of the Lord Jesus* (10). This is the way the apostle is able to interpret the afflictions he endured as he ministered in the name of Christ. His Master had suffered great afflictions in the days of His flesh, and the disciple is ready to experience like afflictions; for in them, and through them, he feels the presence of Christ with him, turning these deadly afflictions into triumphant victory.

This being so, *the life also of Jesus* (10) is manifest in the disciple's body, that is, in his earthly experiences. Verse 11 reiterates the thought. *Death . . . life* (12). The apostle's arduous life is contrasted with the fruit of salvation manifested in his converts.

I believed (13). The same Greek root as for 'faith'. Personal trust in God leads to testimony for God, even if that testimony includes the recounting of afflictions. The psalmist had the same experience. (See, e.g., Ps. cxvi. 9–11.) *For your sakes* (15). The apostle again expresses his particular desire for the salvation of the Corinthians. *Perish* (16); RSV 'wasting away'. *Inward man* (16). The spirit of Paul was waxing stronger and stronger in his labours for Christ, in spite of the toll which affliction was taking of his physical powers. Verses 17 and 18 express confidence in God's care for the believer. They do not contain a 'philosophy of suffering', that is, they do not explain the cause or purpose of suffering; but they do express the assured knowledge of the reality of things eternal against which the things temporal are of slight account (cf. Rom. viii. 18). A wealth of meaning lies behind Paul's use of the phrase *our light affliction* (17) to describe all that he himself had suffered.

d. The earthly and the heavenly house (v. 1–10)

Chapter v is closely connected with the last chapter, and develops further the thought of the eternal glory of the believer in contrast to his present temporal life. *Building of God* (1). Paul goes into greater detail than most other New Testament writers in his teaching about the personal resurrection of believers. The earthly home of the spirit of man is likened to a *tabernacle*, or 'tent', but the heavenly house to a *building* (1). *Heavens* (1); i.e. the spiritual regions where God dwells. The plural is a Jewish usage. Scripture gives us this word to describe the 'place' and the 'state' of a soul in bliss. It is not incorrect to say that nothing is revealed about heaven except the blessedness of those who are brought there by Christ. This is enough as a spur to faith. *Not for that we would be unclothed* (4). Paul's desire is not death, but that experience of 'victory over death' which is to be the happy lot of believers who are alive at Christ's coming (see 1 Cor. xv. 50–55). *Wrought us for the selfsame thing* (5). God has prepared believers for a heavenly life, with accompanying qualities of 'bodily' existence. *At home in the body . . . absent from the Lord* (6). The close union with Christ after death, or at His coming, in comparison with which this life may be described as being 'absent' from Him, is the thought that prompts this statement. *Faith . . . sight* (7). These words indicate the difference between the two states. *Wherefore we labour* (9). Notice that the apostle did not let the contemplation of the heavenly state hinder his undertaking the work for Christ which needs to be done in this earthly state. *Judgment seat* (10). The Greek word means 'award throne' and was used of the Olympic Games. The 'judgment throne of God' in Rev. xx. 11 is a different word. The idea of awards for the faithful is clearly taught by our Lord (consider, e.g., the parable of the talents, Mt. xxv. 14–30), and also in the New Testament writings generally. The word *appear* (10), too, suggests an appearance for awards, not for judgment. The word is more accurately translated as 'made manifest' in RV (as in verse 11 of AV). The Greek word translated *receive* (10) is a word with a variety of meanings, one being to 'supply', to 'carry off', to 'gain'. The sense thus would be that Christians, working for Christ, may accomplish some things that are *good*, but some that are *bad* (lit. 'worthless'). Of what kind they are will be revealed when 'we are made manifest before the judgment seat of Christ'.

e. The ministry of reconciliation (v. 11—vi. 10)

The apostle passes on to indicate the effect of Christian ministry in the lives of men and women who pay heed to the gospel. The apostle pleads with his readers to accept the reconciliation that God has provided through Christ. *Terror of the Lord* (11); i.e. the fear of God, reverence for God. *Persuade* (11). Our arguments, he says, are for men, but God knows our inner mind. *Made manifest in your consciences* (11). At this point Paul seems to revert to the thought of iii. 1, 2. He hopes that the Corinthians perceive the sincerity of his ministry. This is what should commend his work to them. Cf. x. 18. *Glory* (12); lit. 'boast'. Some had been leading the Corinthians to despise Paul and his companions, because they lived under such hardships. But an examination of the apostle's inner life will give them all the answer they need for those whose boast is only in externals. Cf. x. 7 RV and see note on x. 12. By verse 13 the apostle probably means to convey to the Corinthians that, whether he appears mad or sober, he is God's minister, and he is not affected by his detractors' opinion of him. Perhaps the words were chosen to cover two types of criticism. Some may have said that he was an ecstatic; others that he was too *sober* or unassuming.

The verses which follow give us a valuable insight into the apostle's understanding of Christ's death. He begins by saying that *the love of Christ constraineth us* (14); that is, the love that Christ exhibited for the human race in dying for them holds the apostle fast in his allegiance to such a Saviour. If the Saviour died thus *for all* (14; lit. 'on behalf of all'), they should reckon themselves as having died too; for Christ represents supremely the whole human race. (See Col. i. 17, 'in him all things consist'.) Therefore they *should not henceforth live unto themselves, but unto him* (15). Notice the repetition: 'One died for all' . . . 'he died for all' . . . 'him which died for them'. The death of Christ for the salvation of men is the supreme revelation of the love of God, and it should 'hold us in'

('constrain' us). *Know we no man after the flesh* (16); that is, making the fleshly, or earthly, life the standard of our judgment. *Christ after the flesh* (16). Christ too lived an earthly life, but we no longer think of Him in such terms. *Know we him no more* (16). Not only has Jesus passed into the realm of spirit, but also the revelation of who He was—the Son of God—makes earthly knowledge of Him take a subordinate place. Later heretical thought, known as 'docetism', dismissed Christ's earthly life as unreal; but this is far from the apostle's meaning here. *A new creature* (17); the believer, too, has entered a new realm of being. Verses 18 and 19 express God's plan of reconciliation of the world to Himself, which opens this new realm to men. *Reconciled* (18). It is God Himself who does away with the sin of the world. It is the atonement which makes possible reconciliation (see also Rom. v. 10). *Not imputing their trespasses* (19). This is an act of God which indicates the depth of His love and mercy for weak human beings. Christ has taken upon Himself the whole burden of sin, so that man is freed from having to answer for his own sinful past. *God . . . in Christ, reconciling* (19). Note the RV rendering, which omits the comma. This verse is not so much a proof text of our Lord's deity (God was in Christ) as a statement that God was reconciling in Christ. *Ministry of reconciliation* (18). *Word of reconciliation* (19). By describing his ministry in these two ways, the apostle emphasizes the elements of 'declaration' (word) and 'application'.

Ambassadors for Christ (20). Behind all the apostolic activity was the consciousness of the Person of Christ. The apostle here uses a word which indicates a position of highest honour bestowed by the living Christ Himself. *We . . . beseech you . . . be ye reconciled to God* (20). This was the great desire of the apostle for all mankind. He appeals to men to accept God's reconciliation which He has wrought in Christ. Our Lord's death was effective not merely to remove man's hostility to God, but also to deal with the divine necessity requiring that God should turn from man. The way is now open for men to enter into God's forgiveness. God has *made him* (i.e. Christ) *to be sin* on our behalf (21). Probably a unique phrase in literature, appropriate to the fact that it describes a unique event. Christ was not made to be a 'sinner', but to be *sin*. He therefore bore no personal punishment, although He did bear the full penalty for the sin of the whole world. (The reader should refer to Gal. iii. 13 and Rom. viii. 3 for other Pauline expressions of the same revealed truth.) He bore this *for us* (21) that we might be released from sin and so be reconciled to God. This reconciliation too has a positive significance, for by it we are *made* (RV 'become') *the righteousness of God in him* (21); i.e. be regarded by God as righteous, though not yet actually so. This is the doctrine of justification. There is a parallelism between Christ's being made sin, though Himself sinless, and the believer's being regarded as righteous from the initial moment of belief.

The apostle now sums up in general terms the work and character of a minister. *In vain* (vi. 1); i.e. without its effect being shown in one's life. Verse 2 is a quotation from Is. xlix. 8, which is a messianic prophecy. *Day of salvation* (2); i.e. the epoch in which salvation is present because it has been brought in by Christ. *Ministry be not blamed* (3). The apostle realizes that the misbehaviour of his converts will be used to discredit his ministry of the gospel to them. In verses 4–10 he describes the nature and character of the ministry which he has exercised. *In all things approving ourselves* (4); RV 'commending ourselves'. Cf. iii. 1, 2, v. 12. Here is the answer to those who have questioned his credentials. In all circumstances Paul and his companions have shown that they have 'received not the grace of God in vain', and so constitute an example for the Corinthians. Through all kinds of difficult experiences (4, 5) and in spite of untrue charges and contrary opinions expressed about them (8, 9), their genuineness has been proved by the spiritual quality of their lives (6), the truth and force of their message (7) and their reaction to the sufferings inflicted upon them (9, 10). This is the way in which the true minister of God commends himself to the attention of his hearers.

III. A PERSONAL APPEAL. vi. 11—vii. 16

a. Let affection be mutual (vi. 11–13)

The apostle now turns in a personal way to the Corinthians and makes an earnest appeal for a return of affection and frankness between them. *Ye are not straitened in us* (12); that is, 'We do not give you a small place in our affections; rather ye yourselves restrict the affection which you might enjoy from us'. *Bowels* (12); a Jewish phrase to indicate the seat of the affections. We say 'heart'. *Recompence* (13); that is, 'give to me as I am giving to you'. Paul wishes to speak to them about matters that might offend, but first reassures them of his love for them.

b. A call to separation (vi. 14—vii. 1)

This section seems somewhat isolated, as the personal theme is taken up again in vii. 2ff., which links up with the thought of vi. 13. The subject-matter here is marriage with unbelievers, a topic which was also discussed in 1 Cor. vii. 10ff. The apostle strongly exhorts Christians not to mix with unbelievers in the sense of sharing in their lives. Marriage is, of course, the supreme way of sharing in the life of another; but the apostle would appear to widen the scope of his exhortation as the passage proceeds. *Belial* (15); that is, Satan. *Ye are the temple of the living God* (16). This is one of the great revealing phrases of Scripture, conveying a wonderful revelation in a few pregnant words. God dwells in the hearts and lives of believers, and God has no fellowship with Satan. Therefore believers cannot tolerate companionship with unbelievers in their distinctive activities. *Come out* (17). A quotation from Is. lii. 11, which is there addressed to the priests. Just as the priests of Israel were to be strictly 'clean', so now all Christians are to be so, for they are all 'priests'. The apostle enlarges the thought of the passage from Isaiah by a reference also to Ezk. xxxvii. 27. *Flesh and spirit* (vii. 1). The whole man must be kept clean.

c. Paul rejoices in their repentance (vii. 2–16)

Receive us (2); the Greek is more vividly rendered by 'make room for us' (RV mg.). We return to the theme raised in vi. 13. The apostle recounts his anxiety about the quarrel between him and them which he felt when he had proceeded to Macedonia, and was there awaiting the coming of Titus. This passage helps us to make a conjecture as to the occasion and circumstances of the writing of the present Epistle, and has been made use of in the *Introduction* (q.v.). He had written a severe letter to them which he despatched probably through Titus. As soon as it was gone, he felt he had overdone it, and might have lost the Corinthians altogether. *I do not repent, though I did repent* (8). His joy knew no bounds when he learnt from Titus that the Corinthians had received the letter in a spirit of true repentance (see verses 4, 6, 9, 13). *Not to be repented of* (10); the repentance which leads to salvation is never to be regretted (see RV). *The sorrow of the world worketh death* (10). When the world's pleasures fail, as they inevitably do, the end is despair, death. *His cause* (12); the exact nature of the wrongdoing is not told us. Whether this present reference is to the same incident as that recorded in 1 Cor. v. 1 is uncertain. *Our care for you* (12); the reading is 'your care for us' as in RV. The apostle continues to rejoice in the 'falling out, which all the more has endeared' and which has revealed to the Corinthians how much they cared for him. In this the Corinthians have shown an example of the right response to the gospel, how the grace of God works in the restoration of relations of love.

IV. THE COLLECTION FOR THE POOR IN JUDAEA. viii. 1—ix. 15

a. Titus will organize the collection (viii. 1–15)

The passage now before us is of great interest, though the subject-matter, namely, a 'special collection', might appear to be of no permanent importance. The interest, however, lies in the fact that the apostle exhorts the brethren of Achaia to add their offering to that of the brethren of Macedonia, to help the material needs of the poor saints at Jerusalem. Thus we learn from the Scriptures that we have a duty towards our poorer brethren in the Lord; and that the fulfilment of this duty can have rich spiritual significance.

It was not in circumstances of prosperity that the saints in Macedonia made this collection. They were in *a great trial of affliction* and *deep poverty* (2) when they gave liberally and, indeed, *beyond their power* (3). Then they were anxious to pass on their gift by the hands of Paul and his companions, regarding the giving of the gift to the saints at Jerusalem as the expression of *fellowship* (4). *Titus* (6). Titus was the organizer of a similar collection among the Corinthians. The apostle exhorts them to show the same zeal in this practical Christian matter as they did in such things as their *faith*, *utterance*, *knowledge*, and *diligence* (7), matters of a more 'spiritual' character. The apostle obviously regarded the full Christian life as embracing both kinds of activities. He admits, however, in verse 8 that he has no authority to demand the collection from them, but only to give them the opportunity of proving *the sincerity of your love* (8). Verse 9 sums up in a wonderful way the whole purpose of the incarnation. Christ's position of glory with the Father is sacrificed by Him so that He may bring us aid. Cf. Phil. ii. 6, 7. So ought we to sacrifice something to aid others. For this use of our Lord's life and death as an example see also 1 Pet. ii. 20, 21. *A year ago* (10). A note of time which helps to place the writing of this Epistle chronologically. Evidently at that time the Corinthians had undertaken the making of such a collection; the apostle now prompts them to carry it out. Perhaps he enlarges somewhat on this subject in order to get them occupied on a practical matter as a safe antidote to their quarrelling over matters which should now be forgotten. *A willing mind* (12). Cf. our Lord's commendation of the widow who gave 'of her want' a very small sum indeed (Mk. xii. 41–44). No one can give what he does not possess. It is the spirit in which the giving is done at which our Lord looks. Notice, also, that there should be *an equality* (14) in the sense that no one should be overburdened in the giving if there is not a corresponding need in the receiver. Others should not be unduly *eased, and ye burdened* (13). Another occasion may arise when the transaction should be reversed. *He that had gathered much* (15). This is a free quotation from Ex. xvi. 18.

b. Arrangements for the collection described (viii. 16—ix. 5)

This passage shows the apostle's organizing powers and his knowledge of human nature. Titus is one of those who will organize the collection. But another *brother* (18) will help him, and perhaps still one or two more (see ix. 5). The 'brother' mentioned in verse 18 is unknown to us, but evidently he was well known to the Corinthians, for his *praise is in the gospel throughout all the churches* (18). Further-more, he was elected by the churches to travel with Paul (19). It might conceivably be Barnabas or John Mark, of both of whom these words would be true. Others have suggested Luke and Apollos. *Your ready mind* (19). The Greek is 'our'. The meaning is virtually unaltered. Verses 20 and 21 show Paul's desire that the destination of every penny should be clearly known. *Our*

brother (22). Another unknown Christian. *I have* (22). There is no Greek verb in the text. This is supplied to make a sentence. 'He has' might give a better meaning. If we allow ourselves a little liberty, we may think of this brother as a Christian 'accountant', and his enthusiasm would be increased by a good response from the Corinthians, for he allied his accountancy with evangelism. *Titus . . . messengers of the churches* (23). Titus is given the certificate of being Paul's personal emissary, not a servant to Paul in status, but evidently devoted to the great apostle and helping him gladly; 'mine own son after the common faith' is the way Paul describes him in Tit. i. 4. The Greek word for 'messengers' is 'apostles'. Its use in a general sense here would seem to indicate that the word had not yet assumed the specialized sense which we attach to it. These were men who were appointed by local church councils and sent forth to convey greetings and instruction to other churches or evangelize new areas. They were 'travellers for Christ'.

The apostle has evidently been speaking to the Macedonian Christians of the zeal of the Corinthians concerning the collection; but knowing the weakness of human nature, and perhaps fearing the consequences of the quarrels which had arisen, he takes the precaution of sending this group of messengers ahead; so that when he comes, accompanied perhaps by some Macedonians, the collection will be ready, and will come up to expectation. *Ye had notice before* (ix. 5); note AV mg. 'Which hath been so much spoken of before', or RV 'aforepromised'. *As of covetousness* (5). The apostle has taken great trouble to lift the act of giving to a high spiritual level.

c. Principles of Christian giving (ix. 6–15)

The apostle proceeds to describe the spirit in which Christians should give for the needs of others and how the grateful receiving of such gifts by these others should lead them to prayer on behalf of the donors. Thus a two-way blessing is created, and the apostle glorifies God as he contemplates this blessed result.

He which soweth sparingly (6). This is a message taken from nature and applied to the spiritual life. If we scatter seed sparingly, our crop will be scant. So if we draw back, or are grudging, in our Christian service, the harvest will be light. Verse 7 gives us the spirit of such service. *Cheerful giver* (7). The Greek word is 'hilarious'. This connotes a spirit of real enjoyment sweeping away all restraint. *God is able* (8). Man's giving is not from his own products, but out of things God has already given to him. The Bible reminds us of this in many places—'Of thine own have we given thee' (1 Ch. xxix. 14). In verse 9 the apostle quotes from Ps. cxii. 9. The Psalm describes the manner of life of a righteous man. He shall be rich in his house, and shall himself give to others. He shall not fear evil tidings, for his heart is fixed in God. In other words, the Bible teaches that the man of God will not suffer need, but actually will have sufficient to give to others. *Minister bread* (10); the RV gives the meaning more clearly: 'He that supplieth seed to the sower and bread for food, shall supply and multiply your seed for sowing, and increase the fruits of your righteousness.' *Is abundant . . . unto God* (12). God has so constituted human life that our service for each other leads to blessing to ourselves, and is itself to God's glory, who is the Creator of all things. *Experiment* (13); i.e. 'proof'. *Professed subjection unto the gospel of Christ* (13). The saints, who will receive the gift, will welcome it all the more because it springs from the acceptance of the gospel by the Corinthians. *Long after you* (14). A bond of love is created by these gifts. *Thanks be unto God* (15). The contemplation of all these results makes the apostle rejoice in his spirit for the working of God in human hearts. *His unspeakable gift* (15). Cf. viii. 9. The apostle's mind naturally rises to the thought of God's generosity to men in His gift of Christ, a thought which can never find fully adequate expression.

V. PAUL'S APOSTOLIC AUTHORITY.
x. 1—xiii. 10

In chapter x we enter an atmosphere totally different from that of the previous one. For this reason some believe that this section is part of the lost letter in which the apostle spoke so severely to the Corinthians that he feared he would lose their friendship altogether by it (see vii. 8n.).

a. Paul defends himself against false charges (x. 1–18)

The points in this present chapter which are raised by the apostle as needing defence are first, that his presence when amongst them is *base* (1), but when absent he writes in a *weighty and powerful* manner (10); and secondly, that he walks *according to the flesh* (2). Obviously some detractors had arisen who tried to undermine his authority. Perhaps they were not Corinthians, but other 'travelling apostles' who were seeking to win support for themselves by speaking ill of others. Such persons would have known of Paul's writings not only to the Corinthians but to other churches too, and so the term *letters* (10) might have a wider significance than the Corinthian letters. They sought to make an unfavourable comparison between these 'weighty documents' and the insignificant appearance and manner of speech of the apostle who wrote them. We may ascribe jealousy to this statement, and need not take it as expressing reality. The man who almost persuaded king Agrippa to become a Christian, or who could silence a mob by his speech, is not likely to have been *weak* and *contemptible* in his speech (10). We know something today of the power of propaganda—the constant repetition of lies which eventually are accepted as truth because they have been repeated so often. These detractors were propa-

gandists of this type. The apostle challenges the Corinthians to weigh the matter again.

With regard to the second charge the apostle distinguishes walking *after the flesh* from walking *in the flesh* (3). The latter is of necessity while a man is in this life. The meaning of the former phrase would be to live for this world and to observe its standards. In the present case it would seem to refer to Paul's manner of preaching the gospel and his habit of self-support as contrasted with a more elaborate presentation of religion and the acceptance of hospitality, as if by right, by certain other 'apostles' who visited Corinth (see xi. 13). On first sight, we should apply the description of 'walking after the flesh' to those 'apostles' rather than to Paul. But it is a distinctive feature of false propaganda that it attributes its own failings to those whom it persecutes. We can understand from the various allusions in this Epistle that these apostles made a great show and display which impressed some people. Paul, on the other hand, was humble and meek in his personal bearing, always considerate of others and ever loath to press his own rights. The acceptance of this false propaganda forced the apostle to recount his sufferings for Christ, which could not be paralleled by the false apostles.

With this general introduction in mind we can now look at the passage in detail. *Meekness and gentleness of Christ* (1); the gospel narrative confirms this. The apostle seeks to display the characteristics of his Master. *The weapons of our warfare are not carnal, but mighty through God to the pulling down of strong holds* (4). The word 'carnal' here may be understood primarily to refer to methods adopted by 'natural' men for the overcoming of their enemies or the achievement of their purposes. From verse 5 we gather that it is of thought and behaviour that the apostle is chiefly thinking. In this realm, argumentation, bullying and compulsion are the methods of natural men. *Strong holds* may be taken as referring to opinions strongly advocated by the holders. These must be examined in the light of the knowledge of God, and cast down if false. Every thought is to be brought into captivity *to the obedience of Christ* (5). The apostle clearly has in mind a section in the Corinthian church against whom he fears he may have to take a very strict line. It is the last thing he wishes to do, but he will not shrink from doing so if necessary.

Do ye look . . . after the outward appearance? (7); probably better translated as a statement, 'Ye look . . .' as in RV. The thought links on again to his argument in v. 12ff. Those who glory in this way make special claims to belong to Christ (cf. the reference to the 'Christ party' in 1 Cor. i. 12), but Paul is just as much His. *For though I should boast somewhat more* (8). The reference may again be to one of the criticisms levelled at him. RSV translates 'even if I boast a little too much'. *Commend themselves* (12). This seems to have been a charge levelled against Paul by visiting preachers (cf. iii. 1, v. 12). Paul now turns it back on his detractors. His own spiritual experience made him shrink from anything in himself that might be commendable; he utterly debased himself because he was so conscious of the change in him made by the grace of God acting in his life. But in the present instance he is forced to speak as a man to men, and to recount his own deeds and behaviour. *Even unto you* (13). The apostle is going to relate the experiences he has had which are the background out of which, as it were, he eventually was granted the privilege by God of preaching to the Corinthians. The apostle thus hopes that he may now be able to go forth even unto *regions beyond you* (16). If we refer to Rom. xv. 19–24, we find that the apostle contemplates visits to western Greece, Rome and even Spain. *In another man's line* (16); RV 'in another's province'. Verse 17 implies that Paul himself is ascribing the glory to *the Lord*. Verse 18 should be read in the light of iii. 1, v. 12, x. 12.

b. The character of Paul's ministry (xi. 1–15)

The apostle now launches out into a discourse well calculated to show up these false teachers. He does this because he is *jealous over* the Corinthians (2) and is greatly disturbed by the thought that they might be led astray. He wishes to present them *as a chaste virgin to Christ* (2), i.e. as a people whose faith has not been contaminated by falsehood. He is anxious that their minds should not be *corrupted from the simplicity that is in Christ* (3). Note that the RV inserts the words 'and the purity' after the word *simplicity*. RSV renders 'led away from a sincere and pure devotion to Christ'. In view of the modern critical attitude towards the early chapters of Genesis it is of great interest that Paul mentions the account of Eve's temptation by the serpent in this verse. The apostle was very fond of Old Testament references. Several times in his Epistles he refers to Adam (e.g. 1 Cor. xv; Rom. v) and references to Abraham, David and other Old Testament characters are also frequent.

The apostle now upbraids the Corinthians for their patient listening to false preachers. *Ye might well bear with him* (4); rather 'ye are very patient', used no doubt ironically. *Rude in speech* (6). The phrase means not following the rhetorical rules of the schools. Paul challenges the Corinthians to consider whether ultimately he did not lead them to deeper things than these other *chiefest apostles* (5), a phrase which is also ironical. The word for *chiefest* is really an adverb. The meaning is those who were more than mere messengers. They posed as authorities themselves.

The apostle refers to the fact that he did not make himself a charge upon them. Some were foolish enough to think on this account that the gospel he preached was less valuable. With verse 7 cf. xii. 13. *Robbed other churches* (8). Paul is really indicating that he did not receive wages at all for preaching the gospel. If what was given him for his support by other churches was to be regarded as 'earnings', then he had in

effect 'robbed' them since the service given was not to them but to the Corinthians. Thus he reduces the whole argument to absurdity. His needs were always met; and if he did not in fact receive anything material from the Corinthians, it was because the Macedonian Christians had supplied most of his needs. In particular we learn from Acts xviii. 5 that Timothy and Silas were instrumental in conveying this help to the apostle. For the general principle enunciated in these verses see notes on 1 Cor. ix. 1–27. *Found even as we* (12). This is a challenge to the false apostles to make their own living.

Satan . . . his ministers (14, 15). The New Testament teaches us that we have an active spiritual adversary in this world, namely, Satan; and that he enslaves men to be his ministers. Their 'gospel' would be presented as a 'gospel of righteousness' in order to trap the unwary. It is essential for all who would be truly saved to know that righteousness comes to them only through faith in Christ Jesus, not of their own works, lest any man should boast (see Eph. ii. 9), and to use this knowledge as a test of any teaching presented to them.

c. Paul's defence based on his life and work (xi. 16—xii. 11)

The apostle now proceeds to make his defence by recounting the hardships through which he had passed. He recognizes that what he is going to do is *not after the Lord* (17). It is not contrary to anything fundamental, but merely not in accordance with the usual practice of Christians, who do not boast. *Ye suffer fools gladly* (19). The apostle is possibly being gently ironical in this verse. Superior people can allow a little liberty to inferior breeds! But, says the apostle in verse 20, do realize what you are allowing these false apostles to do to you. RSV renders the first part of verse 21 'To my shame, I must say, we were too weak for that!' Paul is suggesting, again ironically, that he had not dared to go to such lengths, and that they are reproaching him for such weakness. He then proceeds to compare his qualifications as an apostle with those of their other teachers and to recount his experiences as a minister of Christ. From the narrative in the Acts, we have enough information to enable us to identify some of the incidents referred to in verses 23–27.

As a fool (23). The apostle regards this kind of argument as foolish, and unbefitting a Christian; but it was forced on him. *Care of all the churches* (28). Paul's monumental labours for Christ are indicated in this phrase. He was an indefatigable worker, both physically (in his constant travels), and mentally (in his numerous Epistles), and spiritually. His example is a spur to all missionary endeavours. In verses 32 and 33 reference is made to his exciting escape from Damascus. This is narrated for us in Acts ix. 24, 25. The apostle here mentions *Aretas* (32) by name. This would be Aretas IV, king of the Nabatean Arabs. This is the only place where we learn that he also held sway over Damascus. Secular history does not record this fact.

Continuing the record of his experiences, he turns now to the realm of *visions and revelations* (xii. 1). In this connection, understanding the words *I knew a man in Christ* (2) as really referring to himself, the apostle becomes reticent, and verbally dissociates himself from the experience. The nature of the experience is beyond what is common to man and we have to leave it as it is told to us, without attempting to explain it or find a parallel to it. *Third heaven* (2); that is, where God dwells. The 'first heaven' was used to denote the atmosphere in which the birds fly; the 'second', the region of the sun, moon and stars. *Paradise* (4). A word used in Jewish cosmology for the third heaven regarded as the abode of the blessed. *Unspeakable words* (4); i.e. ideas communicated to him apart from the usual means of speech. *Not lawful for a man to utter* (4). This is the apostle's spiritual perception of the sacredness of his experience. The deeper things of the spirit are not able to be explained in human language.

In verse 5 the apostle expresses again his own personal unworthiness of this experience, and desires rather to appear to be none other than what a man sees him to be (6). Paul rather rejoiced that in himself he was nothing, perhaps even positively unattractive, so that there should be no detraction of interest from the message itself which he preached. *Thorn in the flesh* (7); some bodily complaint which the apostle had continuously. It did not incapacitate him for his work, but was like a 'thorn' giving pain at times. Notice the apostle's attitude towards it. He prayed for deliverance from it *thrice* (8; cf. Mt. xxvi. 36ff.) and received the answer that God's grace was sufficient for him (9). In other words God promised that it should never overcome him so as to prevent his work for God. The incident is full of interest for Christian workers who are handicapped in some way. It also has a bearing on the subject of sickness and the healing ministry; not that we should be discouraged from expecting healing in answer to prayer, but we should see that sometimes God may have a purposè in withholding a complete recovery. The spiritual condition of the patient is more important than his physical wholeness. Prayer for the sick is a Christian ministry which is always accompanied with blessing. In Paul's case he actually took *pleasure in infirmities* (10) as well as in other torments, for in them all he felt the *power of Christ* (9) resting on him. In this experience he is able to say, *in nothing am I behind the very chiefest apostles* (11); perhaps another ironical reference to the self-advertising apostles, who so prided themselves on their credentials (cf. xi. 5, 13).

d. Paul's love and concern (xii. 12–21)

In this section the apostle declares that his whole desire is the edification of the Corinthian church. It is no self-glory that he seeks, and anything he did was done out of love for them. The whole passage is suffused with irony as he takes up again some of the accusations levelled against him and reveals their absurdity. See, for example, verse 12. *I seek not your's, but you* (14). This was the apostle's policy. Material things had no attraction for him, because he already possessed something of the riches of Christ. *The third time* (14). See below on xiii. 1. *I will very gladly spend and be spent for you* (15). Tireless service was his willing attitude towards them, and yet it seems to him that, in spite of his longing for their affection, the more he reveals his love for them the smaller is the response. *Being crafty, I caught you with guile* (16). These qualities Paul all along repudiates, but here he caustically takes the words out of the mouths of his detractors and says, in effect: 'So I caught you with guile, did I?' He then makes his own refutation of so vile an insinuation in the words that follow (17, 18).

Though a thoroughgoing idealist (as we should describe the apostle in present-day speech), nevertheless he was also a thoroughgoing practical person. He does not hesitate to say, in verses 20 and 21, what might be the case in reality when next he comes among them. He realizes that many who have sinned in the way of *uncleanness and fornication and lasciviousness* (21) might not have repented; and it is the apostle himself who will then feel humiliated. So much does the true disciple of Christ come into union with his divine Master that he too feels the griefs of Christ over sinners.

e. Paul's closing appeal (xiii. 1–10)

Third time (1). We may understand the three visits as the one recorded in Acts xviii. 1, the abandoned visit (see i. 16), and the visit now in view (see *Introduction*). The apostle knows there are still members of the Corinthian church persisting in sin (2). The situation in Corinth was admittedly a very difficult one for Christians due to the surrounding low standard of morals, and the apostle is having a severe struggle trying to rescue them from the grip of sin. In verse 7 we have again one of those peculiarly intense revelations of spiritual reality which characterize the writings of Paul and the other New Testament books. *Though he was crucified through weakness, yet he liveth by the power of God* (4). To see Christ led to the cross would be to see someone apparently overcome by His enemies and powerless in their hands. But this very scene of weakness was in reality the power of God—for in it God took to Himself the sting of sin, endured its poison, and rose triumphant over it. In enduring the effect of sin, which is death, He appeared weak. But it was the weakness of One who knew His own strength; One who could afford to be weak because of His great strength. *We also*, says the apostle, *are weak in him; but we shall live with him* (4).

Even at this late stage of their Christian history the apostle is prepared to challenge them to examine themselves whether they *be in the faith* (5). No Christian is beyond the value of such self-examination. It deepens faith, where the faith is already true faith. *Reprobates* (5). This word conveys the idea of rejection after testing. No man is rejected by God without being tested, and only then if he is found 'fitted to destruction' (Rom. ix. 22). The apostle brings the Epistle to a close by an exhortation to honesty (7), leading to *perfection* (9). *Sharpness* (10). Paul is anxious that all causes of friction should be removed before he arrives at Corinth and that they will respond to his written exhortations. There will then be nothing which he will have to destroy or tear down when he comes to them.

VI. CONCLUSION. xiii. 11-14

This Epistle gives us the beautiful words of 'The Grace', as it has come to be used wherever Christians gather together for prayer (14). The beautiful Bible word *grace* has a breadth of meaning ranging from the simple idea of 'help', through the idea of 'favour' and 'unmerited reward', to the conception of 'indwelling character'. Christ helps us in our lives; He favours us greatly, turning evil to good for us; and He dwells in us so that we reflect His character to the world. The clause *the love of God* may be taken as referring to the love of the Father; 'God so loved the world, that he gave.' Such a love, in its willingness to give and to forgive, is to be present too in the lives and actions of Christ's disciples. The word for *communion* is also translated 'fellowship' in the New Testament. The primary reference here is to that fellowship which the Holy Spirit creates among all those who are 'in Christ'. We must always remember that the Holy Ghost is a Person, not a mere influence. He is the 'other advocate' whom the Father has sent in the Son's name, according to Christ's own promise in Jn. xiv. 26. He dwells in the midst of believers, and constitutes them the Church of Christ. He is also the personal companion of each individual Christian, comforting, that is, strengthening him, and also making him aware of his spiritual union with Christ, and in Christ with all believers.

W. C. G. PROCTOR.

THE EPISTLE TO THE GALATIANS

INTRODUCTION

See also the General Article, 'The Pauline Epistles', p. 68.

I. OCCASION AND THEME

The genuineness of this Epistle was never questioned in the early Church, and the most extreme and radical New Testament criticism regarded it as indubitably Pauline. It is a passionate vindication, vigorous and uncompromising, both of the gospel of the grace of God and of Paul's own authority as an apostle of Christ who had commissioned him to preach that gospel. Paul's soul is at white heat as he writes, because he is perturbed to the very depths of his being by the grave crisis which has arisen in the Galatian churches. These Galatians, most of them Gentiles who had heard Paul's preaching and believed, no doubt, in Christ for salvation, had now most hastily (i. 6) adopted the insidious suggestion of certain Judaizing teachers, who had told them that they must be circumcised and observe the Jewish law. Paul's soul recoils in horror from such an idea as obscuring the vital truth of the all-sufficiency of Christ for salvation; and he writes this Epistle to save his beloved converts from being fatally led astray. The Epistle, as Godet says, 'marks an epoch in the history of man', because 'it is the ever precious document of his spiritual emancipation'.

II. ITS TEACHING

The transition from Judaism to Christianity was a slow process with some of the early Jewish believers. There were Pharisees who believed (Acts xv. 5), and some of these taught that, before a Gentile could become a Christian, he must first become a Jew, by submitting to circumcision and by undertaking to observe the Jewish law, ritual as well as moral. Some of these stricter Jewish Christians had gone to the Galatians with such unsettling teaching. Such Judaizing teachers dogged Paul's steps all his life. As late as about A.D. 62 we find them plotting against him at Rome, so that he is moved to write, with something of the fire that blazes in this Epistle, some very scathing words about them, and to set over against them, as in Gal. vi. 16, the true Israel, who worship by the Spirit of God (RV), who glory in Christ Jesus, and who have no confidence in the flesh, who rely upon no outward privilege (Phil. iii. 2, 3, Moff.). In this Epistle Paul strongly emphasizes the all-determining efficacy of faith, as shown in the case of Abraham, the typical believer (iii. 6–9), who, as Paul says elsewhere, was a believer, and

was therefore justified, before he was circumcised (Rom. iv. 10ff.).

On two subjects the Epistle lays very marked emphasis, the cross and faith. The great words of Habakkuk, 'The just shall live by faith', are quoted (iii. 11). The law was a slave-attendant who exercised over men stern discipline till Christ came, till the era of faith dawned, in which by faith we become sons of God (iii. 24—iv. 7). Christ died to redeem us from the curse of the broken law of God (iii. 13), and all who rest on Him alone for salvation are 'justified' or accepted with God, who gives to them His Holy Spirit, shedding abroad in their hearts filial love and holy confidence (iii. 14, iv. 6). To go back to the law would mean relapsing into the immaturity and the restrictions of spiritual childhood (iv. 9). The heart of the message of the Epistle is to be found in ideas like these, as will be shown in the exposition.

The law was later in time than the promise made to Abraham, and it was given to intensify the sense of sin (iii. 15ff.); the law fulfils its function, therefore, when it brings us, deeply convicted of sin, groaning under the curse of the broken law (iii. 10), to Christ, in whom alone is there justification before God. Thus, like Paul, by means of the law we die to the law, as a source of justification, in order that we may live the new life in the Spirit (ii. 19ff.). The Holy Spirit, dwelling in the believer, brings him back to the law, as the eternal standard of personal righteousness, and enables him more and more to live in accordance with that standard (see comments on v. 13–25). To submit to circumcision would indeed mean for the Galatians a retrograde step: it would mean going back to trust in a merely fleshly ordinance, after having known better things. They must throw off completely the entangling yoke of bondage to the ceremonial law (v. 1), and having begun in the Spirit they must continue in the Spirit, so as to possess all the spiritual wealth that is treasured up for them in Christ (iii. 2, 3).

III. DESTINATION AND DATE

To whom was the Epistle sent? and when was it written? These questions have caused much discussion in modern times.

In 25 B.C. Augustus formed the Roman province of Galatia. He used as a nucleus the country of Galatia (so called because a tribe of

Gauls had settled there in the third century B.C.), with its southern boundary about the centre of Asia Minor, and added to it part of Pontus on the north-east, part of Phrygia on the south-west, and most of Lycaonia on the south. These southern and south-western districts were, politically and commercially, far the most important part of the province, as they were well provided with roads. The question that arises here is this: Are the Galatians to whom Paul wrote the descendants of the Gauls in the northern part of the province, whose chief city was Ancyra (the modern Ankara), or are they the Christians of the cities evangelized by Paul on his first missionary journey, Pisidian Antioch, Iconium, Lystra and Derbe, all of which came within the comparatively new province of Galatia?

The 'north Galatian theory' has been advocated by Lightfoot, Chase and others. The great exponent of the 'south Galatian theory' in recent times was Sir William Ramsay, who has been followed by a host of others. For various reasons this latter theory appears to be, on the whole, the more reasonable. In his *Historical Commentary on Galatians* Ramsay sets forth in a very interesting way the parallels between Paul's address at Pisidian Antioch (Acts xiii) and this Epistle, and declares that the coincidences are so striking as to make each of the two documents the best commentary on the other.

In 1 Pet. i. 1 'Galatia' beyond any doubt means the Roman province. Many have argued that Paul, with his keen sense of Roman citizenship, would be almost certain to use that word in the same way. Ramsay, Zahn and others hold that Paul always adopts the imperial standpoint and writes like a Roman. His use of terms such as Achaia, Macedonia, Syria and Cilicia is regarded as consistently imperial; so, most likely, with Galatia.

If Paul ever visited north Galatia, the first time he could possibly have gone there was at the time mentioned in Acts xvi. 6, and the narrative there does not support the suggestion that he engaged in a missionary campaign. It seems rather to mean that he passed through only the western fringes of the country. Furthermore, the period referred to in Acts xvi. 6 was after the Jerusalem Council of the year 50, when the question of circumcision was discussed and settled. A strong argument against the north Galatian theory emerges here. If the Galatians to whom the Epistle was written are to be sought in north Galatia, then, when Paul preached to them, he would have had the authority of the decrees of the Council already at his back (Acts xvi. 4). It is also unlikely that at that date Judaizing teachers insisting on circumcision

could have made such an impression on the Galatians, as they evidently had made judging from the Epistle. This seems to imply that the Epistle must have been written before the Jerusalem Council, a conclusion to which Calvin came long ago and which is the view of many today. If so, Galatians is the earliest of Paul's Epistles, and was perhaps written in the year 49, shortly after his return from his first missionary journey, perhaps in Antioch.

There is no direct mention anywhere in the New Testament of the founding of churches in north Galatia and it seems strange to seek the Galatians of this Epistle in the hypothetical churches of north Galatia, and to leave the well-known churches of south Galatia, which must have been dear to Paul's heart as the sphere of his first great missionary campaign, without any share in his correspondence, as we must leave them if the north Galatian theory be correct. (See also comment on ii. 13.)

The visit of Paul to Jerusalem, mentioned in Gal. ii. 1–10, is here taken to be the visit mentioned at the end of the eleventh chapter of Acts. The meaning of Gal. ii. 1 seems to be that the visit mentioned there took place fourteen years after Paul's conversion (see comments). The visit mentioned in Acts took place, probably, in the year 46, or early in the year 47, and there is nothing to prevent our believing that Paul's conversion took place as early as the year 32. The visit mentioned in Galatians took place 'in consequence of a revelation' (ii. 2, Moff.); the visit mentioned in Acts took place in consequence of a revelation made to Agabus (Acts xi. 28ff.). The visit referred to in Galatians resulted in a *private* conference between Paul and the other apostles; the Council of the year 50 (Acts xv) was a meeting of the whole Church to discuss more formally, in public, after several more years of missionary work among the Gentiles, the question of how the Gentile converts were to be treated, and to come to what may be called an official decision on that problem. The Council came to the same decision with regard to circumcision as that arrived at in the private conference, and Paul mentions this private conference in order to indicate to the Galatians that the question of circumcision had been settled in principle some years before he wrote to them. Finally, as C. T. Woods says, in his *Life, Letters, and Religion of Paul*, 'in Gal. ii. 11 we learn that Peter at Antioch vacillated about the Judaistic question and led Barnabas to do the same. This is intelligible after a private conference at Jerusalem: it is almost impossible after the Council, where St. Peter had committed himself in a public speech, and after the first missionary journey, where Barnabas had taken up a final attitude towards the question of circumcision.'

OUTLINE OF CONTENTS

I. HISTORICAL AND APOLOGETIC. i. 1—ii. 21

    a. Opening salutation (i. 1–5)
    b. The only gospel (i. 6–10)
    c. Paul's gospel derived not from men, but from God (i. 11–24)
    d. Paul's apostleship recognized in Jerusalem (ii. 1–10)
    e. Paul's rebuke to Peter (ii. 11–14)
    f. Justification and union with Christ by faith (ii. 15–21)

II. DOCTRINAL AND ARGUMENTATIVE. iii. 1—iv. 31

    a. An appeal to experience and to Scripture (iii. 1–9)
    b. The curse and the blessing (iii. 10–14)
    c. The real function of the law (iii. 15–23)
    d. In this era of faith we are sons of God (iii. 24—iv. 7)
    e. The foolishness of wishing to be again in bondage (iv. 8–11)
    f. A call to remember their first reception of the gospel (iv. 12–20)
    g. The allegory of Abraham's two sons (iv. 21–31)

III. PRACTICAL AND HORTATORY. v. 1—vi. 18

    a. A call to hold fast to freedom (v. 1–12)
    b. The works of the flesh and the fruit of the Spirit (v. 13–26)
    c. Burden bearing (vi. 1–5)
    d. Sowing and reaping (vi. 6–10)
    e. Conclusion (vi. 11–18)

COMMENTARY

I. HISTORICAL AND APOLOGETIC.
i. 1—ii. 21

a. Opening salutation (i. 1–5)

The salutation opens with an emphatic assertion of Paul's apostolic authority, and it is so phrased as to give a succinct statement of the central truth of Christianity, the atoning death of Christ. Thus, this fundamental truth of which the Epistle will have so much to say meets us right at the outset.

Not of men, neither by man (1); RV 'not from men (as the ultimate source), neither through man' (as the channel). Cf. i. 12. If Galatians be Paul's earliest Epistle, it may be the earliest New Testament writing; and if so, the fact is the more noteworthy that in its opening verses it places Jesus the risen Lord on the divine side of reality, over against men, and alongside God, as the source of grace and peace. *Grace . . . and peace* (3); the former is the free, unmerited favour of God to sinful men; the latter is its fruit and realization in the believing soul. Christ, in obedience to the eternal, sovereign *will of . . . our Father,* freely *gave himself* (to death) *for our sins* (4). The purpose of His death was *that he might deliver us* (or 'rescue us') *from* (out of) *this present evil world* (or 'this present age, with all its evils', a rendering which brings out the emphasis suggested by the order of the words in the Greek). These 'evils' are described clearly in Eph. ii. 1–3: see notes there. How His death

effected our salvation will be explained more fully later on. To turn away from the cross of Christ, the sinner's only hope, was the height of foolishness. The Galatians were doing that (cf. ii. 21, v. 4). *Glory* (5); rather 'the glory', as in RV; i.e. the glory which is pre-eminently God's: God is 'the God of glory' (Acts vii. 2). The great salvation wrought by Christ makes that glory to shine forth resplendently. Cf. Phil. ii. 11; Eph. iii. 21.

b. The only gospel (i. 6–10)

It is striking that Paul does not, as in other letters, begin by praising his readers but plunges at once into a condemnation of the Galatians for so quickly forsaking the gospel of the grace of God for something else which was no gospel at all. He severely condemns certain false teachers, the fountainhead of the mischief, who were disturbing the peace of the Galatian churches and corrupting and perverting the gospel of Christ. He most emphatically declares that there is only one gospel. Loyalty to Christ constrains him to use very strong language.

Removed (6); rather 'removing' (RV); 'hastily shifting' (Moff.). This process was going on even as Paul was writing. The verb is used for migrating from place to place (Heb. xi. 5), and for a change in religion and morals (1 Ki. xxi. 25, LXX). *Into* (6); rather 'in' (RV). It is in the realm of grace that the call of God operates, not in that of works or ceremonial observances. *Another gospel: which is not another* (6, 7). Two words are used in Greek, the first meaning a gospel of a different kind (Gk. *heteron*), and the second meaning another numerically (Gk. *allo*). The so-called gospel to which they were turning was indeed no gospel at all, for there is only one gospel. *Trouble* (7). The verb occurs frequently in New Testament with the meaning 'to disturb mentally' (Mt. ii. 3; Jn. xiv. 1; Acts xv. 24). *Pervert* (7); 'turn round, change to the opposite'. *Though we . . . preach . . . If any man preach* (8, 9); i.e. 'If anyone should preach' (subjunctive)—an almost inconceivable supposition; 'if anyone is preaching' (indicative)—wonder of wonders, it has happened, and it is still going on. *Let him be accursed* (8, 9). On Paul's very strong language here there are some mordant comments in James Denney's *The Death of Christ*, chapter III. Such strong condemnation arouses our curiosity, and makes us long to know what exactly was the false teaching which so deeply moved the apostle.

Verse 10 is parenthetical, in allusion to some taunt of his opponents that he sought men's favour. The meaning seems to be: 'For am I now (in utterances like these) seeking the favour of men, or of God? If any one has ever said such a thing about me (namely, that I seek men's favour) can they say it now? Whatever men may think of me, I desire only to please Christ, whose bondslave I am, and to be loyal to His gospel at whatever cost.'

c. Paul's gospel derived not from men, but from God (i. 11–24)

Paul's gospel was given to him by special revelation (11, 12). His previous education could never have led him to such a gospel (13, 14). God revealed His Son in him, and when that happened, Paul conferred not with other human beings, but departed into Arabia for lonely communion with God (15–17). When at last he visited Jerusalem for the first time since his conversion, two to three years after that event, his intercourse with those who were apostles before him was neither close nor prolonged, and he left Jerusalem then without being known even by sight to the mass of the believers.

Not after man (11); or 'not according to man'. His gospel was not the kind of teaching that the heart of man could ever have imagined. Neither the original gift (12), nor the later detailed instruction in its meaning, was from man. *Revelation* (12). The word means 'unveiling'. In view of verse 16, it seems probable that the meaning is 'an unveiling of Jesus Christ'. The veil was drawn aside which hides Christ from mortal view. *Conversation* (13); 'manner of life' (RV), i.e. conduct, behaviour, as often in New Testament (cf. Eph. iv. 22; 1 Pet. i. 15, 18, ii. 12, iii. 1, 2). *The Jews' religion* (13); rather 'Judaism' (Moff.), which is here contrasted with *the church of God*. *Beyond measure* (13); this strong expression occurs also in Rom. vii. 13; 1 Cor. xii. 31;

2 Cor. i. 8. *Wasted* (13); the same Greek verb occurs in verse 23 and in Acts ix. 21 ('destroyed'), with reference to Paul's persecuting activities. The RV throughout renders 'made havock of'. The verbs *persecuted* and *wasted* are imperfect tenses, indicating a course of action which continued until his conversion. *Profited . . . above* (14); 'outstripped' (Moff.). *Many my equals*; 'many of mine own age' (RV); his youthful contemporaries in the school of Gamaliel, among whom he was an outstanding leader and hero (Acts vii. 58). *Of my fathers* (14). Paul's parents were strict Pharisees (Phil. iii. 5), and all the influences which had played upon him in his home made his conversion to Christianity most unlikely.

Separated (15). Paul means that, before his birth, he had been set apart by God to a special purpose, like Jeremiah (Je. i. 5); cf. Rom. i. 1. It is well to note how word after word emphasizes the fact that his conversion was altogether the work of God: viz. *It pleased God* (or, as in RV, 'it was the good pleasure of God'), *separated, called, his grace. To reveal his Son in me* (16). When the veil was drawn aside (12) Paul saw Christ as the Son of God, at the right hand of power, decisively proved to be that by His resurrection (Rom. i. 4). That was daybreak in his heart (2 Cor. iv. 6). *Flesh and blood* (16); cf. our Lord's words to Peter (Mt. xvi. 17). *Apostles before me* (17). Paul was an apostle, possessing absolutely the same authority as the original disciples: he had seen the risen Lord (1 Cor. ix. 1, xv. 8).

Arabia (17); probably some part of the Arabian deserts, within easy reach of Damascus. That he went as far away as the Sinaitic Peninsula, as some have supposed, is extremely doubtful. His desire, one supposes, was to be alone with God, for meditation and thought. There is no mention of this sojourn in 'Arabia' in Acts ix. We may conjecture that Paul preached 'certain days' in Damascus (Acts ix. 19–22), went to Arabia, then returned to Damascus entering on the 'many days' of Acts ix. 23, these days forming a great part of the 'three years' mentioned in the next verse here. *After three years* (18); almost certainly, three years after his conversion, for from that date Paul reckoned everything worthwhile in his life. *To see Peter* (18); RV 'Cephas', which is the true reading here. Note the RV mg. translation here, 'to become acquainted with'; 'a purpose very different,' says Beet, 'from a desire to obtain apostolic sanction for his work.' *James the Lord's brother* (19), so described to distinguish him from James, the son of Zebedee, who at that time was still alive. Whether this James is here called an apostle is a moot point. He may be, in the wider sense in which the word seems sometimes to be used, as, for example, when applied to Barnabas (Acts xiv. 4, 14). James was not one of the original disciples of Jesus (Jn. vii. 5), but he is seen here in close association with them in Jerusalem. The risen Lord appeared to him (1 Cor. xv. 7), and that appearance, very likely, brought about his conversion. There is no valid reason to keep us from believing that James was the son of Joseph and Mary. (On this whole problem, see Dr. Wm. Patrick's book, *James the Lord's Brother*, and the elaborate excursus in Eadie's Commentary.) *Before God, I lie not* (20). Paul's opponents had, no doubt, misrepresented the purpose of Paul's visit: hence his strong language here. *Syria and Cilicia* (21) are adjoining provinces. They were far away from Jerusalem, so that for long Paul was unknown to the Christian churches of Jerusalem and its neighbourhood (22). That Paul preached in his native province, as well as in Syria, and made converts, may be deduced from the mention of the churches of Syria and Cilicia in Acts xv. 41. *They had heard* (23); more literally, 'they were hearing'. *They glorified God in me* (24). Already Paul was beginning to be recognized as a typical example of Christ's redeeming power (1 Tim. i. 16).

d. Paul's apostleship recognized in Jerusalem (ii. 1–10)

When Paul was next in Jerusalem, it was fourteen years after his conversion. He went there, not summoned by Peter and the rest, as though they possessed authority superior to his, but in obedience to a direct command received from the Lord; and when there, he acted as one who was on terms of equal authority with the original disciples. After a perfectly friendly conference, a division of fields of service was agreed upon, and hands were cordially clasped in ratification of the agreement reached. The same gospel was to be preached to Jew and Gentile, on the same terms, but there were to be different spheres of service— that was the gist of the agreement.

Fourteen years after (1); i.e., almost certainly, after his conversion. Fourteen years of Christian life and service lay behind this visit, which is, most probably, to be identified with the visit in connection with famine relief work recorded in Acts xi. 28–30 and its date was probably about the year 46. *By revelation* (2); 'in consequence of a revelation' (Moff.), i.e. urged by supernatural light from God. *Privately* (2). A full discussion in public might have given some of the 'false brethren' the opportunity of making extreme speeches, with mischievous results. *To them which were of reputation* (2); 'the authorities' (Moff.); 'the acknowledged leaders' (Ramsay). *Run . . . in vain* (2). 'What concerned Paul was whether his whole missionary work, past and present, should be rendered "useless", should be made "to lead nowhere"—as it would have been had the Jerusalem Church insisted that Gentile Christians must accept circumcision' (Moffatt Commentary). The figure of the foot-race was a favourite one with Paul (cf. especially 1 Cor. ix. 24; Phil. iii. 13, 14 ; 2 Tim. iv. 7). Verses 3–5 are among the most difficult in the New Testament to interpret. As Lightfoot says: 'The thread of the sentence is broken, picked up, and again broken.' Farrar and others

have thought that Titus was actually circumcised. F. C. Burkitt (*Christian Beginnings*, p. 118) says: 'Who can doubt that it was the knife which really did circumcise Titus that has cut the syntax of Gal. ii. 3–5 to pieces?' Those who think thus understand Paul as meaning that, though he yielded on this point, it was not by compulsion: Titus was not *compelled* to be circumcised. But that seems a very forced construction of Paul's language. It is far more natural to understand him as meaning that Titus most definitely was not circumcised. 'But even my companion Titus, Greek though he was, was not obliged to be circumcised' (Moff.). See article 'Was Titus Circumcised?' by A. B. Bruce, *The Expositor*, First Series, Vol. xi, 1887. *And that because of . . .* (4). The demand that Titus should be circumcised was resisted 'because of the false brethren' (RV), in order to prevent the disastrous consequences that would have followed the granting of such a demand. The metaphor Paul uses is that of spies or traitors introducing themselves by stealth into a camp. The verb *spy out* (4) occurs in the LXX of Jos. ii. 2; 2 Sa. x. 3.

These who seemed (RV 'who were reputed') *to be somewhat* (6). The verb, which is the same word as that in ii. 2, is really a present tense; i.e. 'those who are looked up to as authorities' (Lightfoot). *Person* (6); lit. 'face'. It is not because of any merely external privilege, in their personal intercourse with the Lord, that these 'authorities' are what they are. *Added* (6); RV 'imparted'. They imparted no fresh knowledge to Paul, they saw no defect whatsoever in his gospel. *Was committed* (7); RV 'that I had been intrusted with'. The same word and thought are found in 1 Thes. ii. 4; 1 Tim. i. 11; Tit. i. 3. The perfect tense is used here, indicating that this trust was in Paul's hands permanently. *In Peter . . . in me* (8). Rather, as in RV, 'for Peter . . . for me'. *Who seemed to be pillars* (9); RV 'who were reputed' (same word again; cf. ii. 2, 'to be pillars'. Whatever be the meaning of our Lord's words to Peter at Caesarea Philippi (Mt. xvi. 18), they did not give him pre-eminence in leadership. James and John shared with him the responsibility and the privilege of being 'pillars' of the Church.

e. Paul's rebuke to Peter (ii. 11–14)

So far was Paul from being inferior to Peter that, at Antioch, Paul sternly rebuked him for inconsistent behaviour. Of this incident there is no mention in Acts. 'The omission is instructive, for it bears out the impression, which the Epistle itself conveys, that the collision was a transitory incident, and had no lasting effect on Church history' (*Expositor's Greek Testament*). As to when this incident occurred, we are left in the realm of conjecture. Probably it was somewhere in between the events of the preceding verses and the Council of Acts xv; and the 'certain from James' (12) are identical with the 'certain men from Judaea' (Acts xv. 1), who are described by James himself as 'certain which went out from us' (Acts xv. 24), but whose policy James repudiated.

Peter (11); the correct reading is again 'Cephas', as in RV; so also verse 14. The 'man of rock' sadly belied his name on this occasion. *He was to be blamed* (11); rather, as in RV, 'he stood condemned', i.e. by his inconsistent conduct. In verse 12 note the imperfect tenses, 'he began to draw back and hold aloof' (Moff.).

Barnabas also (13); 'even Barnabas' (RV), the largehearted. An important argument in favour of the south Galatian theory (see *Introduction*) may be found here. Barnabas was with Paul only on the first missionary journey.

f. Justification and union with Christ by faith (ii. 15–21)

Paul leaves the dispute at Antioch far behind and soars to lofty regions of thought and experience. Justification is by faith in Christ, not by works of law. Paul is crucified once for all and for ever with Christ, and thus possesses the life that is life indeed by faith in the Christ who died for him and now lives in him. If righteousness comes by works of law, then the death of Christ was superfluous, it was without sufficient cause.

Paul passes from the incident at Antioch, 'to discuss the question on its merits, yet at first having still in mind the Antioch situation and mentally addressing Peter, if not quoting from what he said to him' (I.C.C.). Both he and Peter, Jews as they were, had discovered that salvation could never be attained by 'works of law' (16, RV mg.): it must come *by the faith of Jesus Christ* (16), faith which has its origin in Him and which rests on Him alone (cf. Rom. iii. 26). That great Pauline verb, 'to justify', emerges here. Justification is more than forgiveness of sins; it is defined as follows in the Westminster Shorter Catechism: 'Justification is an act of God's free grace, wherein He pardoneth all our sins, and accepteth us as righteous in His sight, only for the righteousness of Christ imputed to us, and received by faith alone'. It is the opposite of condemnation (cf. Rom. viii. 33, 34).

The argument in verses 17 and 18 is very condensed. Paul is answering a supposed objection that faith in Christ makes Jews to be no better than Gentile sinners, and that therefore Christ is an agent of sin. 'Away with the thought!' he says; 'on the contrary I would make myself a transgressor if I were to return to the law as a means of justification.' *God forbid* (17); may it never be! Ten times in his Epistles Paul uses this strong expression to repel with the utmost horror some suggestion that has been made: cf. such passages as Rom. iii. 4, vi. 2, vii. 7. *For* (19); this establishes the foregoing statement: 'In abandoning the law as a source of justification, I was only following the leading of the law itself. The law itself, by its exacting demands which I could never fulfil, convinced me of the utter impossibility of being justified by it. I died to the law, that I might live unto God, who justifies

me freely by His grace, because of what Christ has done in my room and stead.'

It has been said that when we arrive at verse 20 it is as though we had passed suddenly from a scarred battlefield to a lovely garden. This verse is indissolubly linked with the preceding one. Paul explains how and where he died, and he explains the nature and source of the life he now lives. *I am crucified*; RV 'I have been crucified'. It is a perfect tense that is used, and it suggests a death the effects of which abide for evermore. *Nevertheless I live*; rather, 'and it is no longer I (with emphasis on 'I') who live, Christ lives in me' (Moff.). 'The best exposition here is that given by Christ Himself, in His statement about the vine and its branches (Jn. xv). The branch, though living and flourishing, has no life properly its own, the life it has and lives is properly of the vine. The theological explanation here is, that when men come to die with Christ on the cross, He comes to live in them by the Spirit' (Macgregor). *The life . . . faith*; more literally, 'the life which I now live in flesh, in faith I live'; i.e. the life lived in the flesh has its hidden root elsewhere. *The faith of the Son of God*; cf. note on ii. 16 above. *Gave himself*; RV 'gave himself up'. The love is eternal; the supreme exhibition and proof of that love is in the cross. There the Son of God (cf. iv. 4) gave Himself up to a death in which there was a curse (cf. iii. 13). *Me*. We have here a moving example of appropriating faith. 'Remember, I'm the sinner whom Jesus came to save.' The life which Paul now enjoys is a gift of God's undeserved favour (21). It is a life of acceptance in God's sight as righteous in Christ. *Frustrate* (21); 'annul' (Moff.). Paul implies that those *do* annul the grace of God who think that acceptance with God can ever be theirs by their own works; if so, then 'Christ died for nought' (21, RV); 'uselessly, without sufficient cause' (Lightfoot).

II. DOCTRINAL AND ARGUMENTATIVE. iii. 1—iv. 31

a. An appeal to experience and to Scripture (iii. 1–9)

Paul appeals to the experience of the Galatians. Christ crucified has been vividly presented to them and it is by faith in Him that they have received the Spirit. Do they really mean to go back to carnal ordinances? Abraham was justified by faith; and it is only those who live by the principle of faith who are his true children.

Foolish (1); 'senseless' (Moff.); the same word as in Lk. xxiv. 25. *Bewitched* (1); this word was often used by the Greeks of deceiving by magic, sometimes with the 'evil eye'. 'So strange is their spiritual blindness that Paul assumes that someone has thrown a spell over them; and asks who the magician is' (Beet). *Evidently set forth* (1); RV 'openly set forth'; RSV 'publicly portrayed'. Those who heard the gospel with faith in their hearts (2, 3) received far richer blessings than those under the law could ever receive; they received the Holy Spirit. To begin 'with Spirit' and to seek maturity of experience 'with flesh' is to stultify themselves and to violate the law of real progress. *Suffered* (4). Some would take this verb (Gk. *paschō*) as referring to spiritual experience: so Moffatt, 'Have you had all that experience for nothing?' But the verb seems to occur nowhere else in the New Testament in that sense, and it is more likely that the reference here is to persecutions endured. *In vain* (4); 'for nothing' (Moff.); a different word from that used in ii. 21. *Ministereth* (5); RV 'supplieth'; the suggestion is one of lavish abundance. It is God who does this; according to iv. 6, He sends forth the Spirit of His Son into the hearts of His sons.

We note again the emphasis laid on faith, leading up to the appeal to Abraham as the typical believer (6). Gn. xv. 6 ('the great text of Genesis', as Luther described it) is quoted not only here, but also in Rom. iv. 3; Jas. ii. 23. Abraham was promised a seed countless as the seaside sand. Who are they? Those who are *of faith* (7), 'they whose starting-point, whose fundamental principle is faith' (Lightfoot). *The scripture, foreseeing . . .* (8); a remarkable personification. *Would justify*; quite literally 'is justifying'. That is God's perpetual and unvarying method. The gospel as preached to Abraham announced blessing for all nations, and that through faith. The quotation made here is a fusion of Gn. xii. 3 and xviii. 18. *Faithful Abraham* (9), or, 'believing Abraham' (Moff.). Faith was the essential characteristic of Abraham's religion, and is typical of all true religion.

b. The curse and the blessing (iii. 10–14)

Those who remain under the law can expect only the law's curse. Christ died in order to redeem us from that curse, so that, instead of the curse, the blessing promised to Abraham, the blessing of the promised Holy Spirit, might come to all nations through faith.

Those who seek salvation by *works of the law* (10) soon discover that they have attempted an impossible task. The curse of the broken law rests on them (Dt. xxvii. 26 is quoted). It was never intended that the blessing should come through the law but *by faith* (11). One of the greatest Old Testament utterances (Hab. ii. 4) is quoted. See also Rom. i. 17; Heb. x. 38. *The law is not of faith* (12); lit. 'out of faith'. It does not start on a principle of faith, but is opposed to it. *Redeemed* (13); lit. 'bought us out', the same verb as in iv. 5. The infinite cost of our salvation is suggested. *Being made* (13); better, as in RV, 'having become'. *A curse* (13). This is a strong statement, reminding us of an even stronger one in 2 Cor. v. 21. 'He made our *doom* His own. He took on Him not only the calling of a man, but our responsibility as sinful men. It is in this that His work as Redeemer lies, for it is in this that the measure, or rather the immensity, of His love is seen' (Denney, *The*

Death of Christ, I.V.F. ed., p. 92). *For us* (13). The Greek preposition used is *hyper*, 'on our behalf'. This verse, however, seems to demand the idea of substitution. A. T. Robertson says, in his *New Testament Grammar*, that only violence to the context can get rid of that idea here. Jn. xi. 50 is another verse where this preposition carries with it the idea of substitution: so also 2 Cor. v. 20 and Phm. 13. *For it is written . . .* (13). The quotation is from Dt. xxi. 23. Christ died the death of the worst malefactor, a death with a very evident curse in it, so closely did He identify Himself with the chief of sinners. *Tree* (13); 'gibbet' (Moff.). To Christ the curse, to all nations the blessing promised to Abraham (14). That blessing is the blessing of justification, as the context shows. This is one result of the atoning work of Christ; another is the presence of the Holy Spirit in the believer (cf. Acts ii. 33). *The promise of the Spirit* (14); or, 'the promised Spirit'. For the promise see such passages as Ezk. xxxvi. 27 and Joel ii. 28.

c. The real function of the law (iii. 15–23)

The promise is a fact prior to the law and is the original and the essential element in the purpose of God. The law was only a temporary provision; it is not contrary to faith, but was given in order to prepare men for the era of faith.

Brethren (15). A touch of tenderness, as if to mitigate the severity of much that has been written. *I speak after the manner of men* (15); 'To take an illustration from human life, my brothers' (Moff.). *Disannulleth* (15); RV 'maketh it void'; the verb is the same as in ii. 21. *Addeth* (15); 'adds fresh clauses' (Lightfoot).

In verse 16 Paul has often been accused of making a wrong application of the words which he quotes from Genesis. The truth may rather be, that his critics have not seen so deeply into the things of God as he has. Is he not here suggesting to us this idea, that the whole of the Old Testament looks forward to the coming of an individual, the Christ, who sums up in Himself the covenant people and in whom the Israel of God are blessed with all spiritual blessings? Christ and His people are one, as Paul will explain more fully later on (iii. 27–29). If the inheritance could be shown to be dependent on the keeping of the law, that would abrogate and annul the promise. *Gave it* (18); 'hath bestowed it (the inheritance) as a free gift' (Lightfoot). The perfect tense indicates that the effects of the promise endure.

Wherefore then serveth the law? (19). Better, literally, as in RV, 'What then is the law?' Its inferiority comes out in three ways. First, instead of justifying, it condemns; *it was added* to bring out more clearly the sinfulness of human nature and to deepen the sense of sin in the human heart (cf. Rom. iii. 19, 20, v. 20). Secondly, it was in force only for a time. Thirdly, it did not come directly from God: there was a double interposition, angels and Moses. For *angels*, cf. Acts vii. 53 and Heb. ii. 2. *God is one* (20). It has been said that there are over 250 interpretations of this puzzling verse; but that is surely an exaggeration. The meaning of the first clause seems clear enough: the very idea of a mediator implies two parties. Of the second clause an interpretation along the lines suggested by Lightfoot seems satisfactory. God dealt with Abraham singly and directly, without a mediator. 'Unlike the law, the promise is absolute and unconditional. It depends on the sole decree of God. There are not two contracting parties. There is nothing of the nature of a stipulation. The giver is everything, the recipient nothing.' *God forbid* (21); cf. ii. 17n. The law was never intended to communicate life or to bestow righteousness.

The scripture (22); see, e.g., such passages as Dt. xxvii. 26, quoted in iii. 10, and Ps. cxliii. 2, quoted in ii. 16; similar passages are quoted in Rom. iii. 10–18. *Hath concluded* (22); RV 'shut up'; 'consigned all without exception to the custody of sin' (Moff.). The same verb is used in iii. 23 (*shut up*) and in Rom. xi. 32; also in Lk. v. 6, of the net enclosing the fish. The law shut up men in its prison-house, thus bringing home to them a sense of the guilt and power of sin. *Faith* (23); lit. 'the faith'; i.e. the faith referred to in verse 22, the faith which justifies; cf. verses 11 and 14. *Kept* (23); RV 'kept in ward'. The imperfect tense describes the ceaseless activity of the law as a warder. The same verb (Gk. *phroureō*) is used of the guarding of Christians in 1 Pet. i. 5; it is used literally of the guarding of a city in 2 Cor. xi. 32.

d. In this era of faith we are sons of God (iii. 24—iv. 7)

The law led us to Christ, in whom we found justification by faith. The state of nonage is over: we have come of age and have attained to the stature of sons and heirs of God.

Schoolmaster (24); RV 'tutor'; 'the law acted the part of a tutor-slave to lead us to Christ' (Wey.). The law thus held us as *paidagogos*, 'child-leader', from which comes the English word 'pedagogue'; it occurs also in 1 Cor. iv. 15. It describes a trusted slave in ancient families of the better class who conducted the children of the family to and from school. He had this supervision over them between the ages of seven and seventeen, and he guarded them from evil society and immoral influences. The function of the law is discharged when it conducts us to Christ and leaves us with Him, not merely to receive instruction, but, above all, to receive redemption, which carries with it full sonship. *Ye are all the children* (26); rather, as in RV, 'ye are all sons'. The commas should be as in RV: 'ye are all sons of God, through faith, in Christ Jesus'. It is not all men indiscriminately who are sons of God, but those only who have true faith, and who are in vital union with Christ. *Baptized* (27); the only reference to baptism in this Epistle. Baptism had been for these Galatians a moment of intense spiritual crisis: they had been baptized *into Christ*. *Have put on* (27); RV 'did put on'; i.e. in the moment of baptism. For the

figure, cf. Eph. iv. 24; Col. iii. 10; and especially Rom. xiii. 14. It means here to have Christ's standing before God. Their baptism not only signified and sealed but also made more real to them the fact that they were one with the crucified and risen Lord.

There is neither (28); RV 'there can be neither'; 'there is no room for' (Lightfoot and Moff.). In the Jewish Prayer Book we find these words: 'Blessed art Thou, O Lord our God, King of the Universe, who hast not made me a heathen. Blessed art Thou . . . who hast not made me a bondman. Blessed art Thou, who hast not made me a woman.' Paul has travelled far from the standpoint of that prayer, which probably goes back to his time. Duncan (*Moffatt Commentary*) suggests that we might say today that there is no room for 'white man and coloured man, master and servant, capitalist and wage-earner, man and woman. Such distinctions, of course, exist in the natural world, but they can now no longer be regarded as ultimate'. *One* (28); RV 'one man'. 'One heart beats in all: one mind guides all: one life is lived by all' (Lightfoot). *Christ's* (29). They are members of Christ; one might say, part of Christ (cf. Eph. v. 30). As such, they are heirs, but *according to the promise*, not by the law.

In chapter iv the thought that before the coming of Christ the human race was in the period of its minority is still further pursued but from a slightly different angle. *Child* (iv. 1); the word in the Greek used by Paul in opposition to 'man' in 1 Cor. xiii. 11, and in opposition to 'perfect' or 'full grown' in 1 Cor. xiv. 20. *Tutors* (2); RV 'guardians', i.e. guardians of his person. This is the only instance of the use of this word by Paul; elsewhere in the New Testament it occurs only in Mt. xx. 8 and Lk. viii. 3, and refers to a steward of a household or of lands. *Governors* (2); RV 'stewards'; 'trustees' (Moff.), i.e. guardians of his property. This word occurs often in the New Testament, in the sense of 'steward', literally in Lk. xii. 42, xvi. 1, metaphorically in 1 Cor. iv. 1; 1 Pet. iv. 10. In Rom. xvi. 23 it denotes the 'treasurer' (RV) of Corinth. *Elements* (3). The word here used describes in 2 Pet. iii. 10 and 12 the physical elements, fire, water, etc. Most of the early Fathers understood the word to refer to the sun, moon and stars, and iv. 9, 10 has been thought to lend some support to that idea. The word also means the first principles or rudiments of any subject (as in Heb. v. 12), and this is the more likely meaning here and is adopted in RV ('rudiments'). The translation 'elemental spirits' is given by Moff. and RSV. No instance of the use of the word in that sense can be found in either classical or Hellenistic Greek. It is difficult to see what real grounds there are for so subtle and bizarre a notion, when a simpler translation is ready to hand, and finds strong support in other New Testament passages. In Heb. v. 12 the context clearly demands the meaning 'rudiments'. In Col. ii. 8 and 20 the rudimentary religious teaching of certain heretics seems to be contrasted with 'all the treasures of wisdom and knowledge' which are in Christ (Col. ii. 3). Here, the association of the word with *children* seems to fix on it the idea of 'rudiments'. The heathen nations were in the lowest infant class, and the teaching enjoyed by the Jews was but rudimentary in comparison with the revelation given in Christ.

The fulness of the time (4); cf. Mk. i. 15. It was the time appointed by the heavenly Father (cf. iv. 2), and we can see that it was the exactly right moment by studying the condition of the world, politically, morally and religiously, when Christ came. *Sent forth* (4). The verb conveys the idea of God sending forth the Son from Himself, from the state of pre-existent glory (cf. Jn. xvii. 5). *His Son* (4); the same phrase as in Rom. i. 3. Similar phrases occur in Rom. viii. 3 and 32. *Made* (4); RV 'born'; i.e. 'coming to be'. He was sent forth from God, born of a woman, and so truly human. The reality of the incarnation is the idea emphasized. We cannot regard the phrase as definitely alluding to the miracle that was involved in the birth of Christ, although the great German scholar Zahn has strongly defended that idea, and the mention of the mother alone is certainly remarkable. *Under the law* (4). The Lawgiver submits Himself to the yoke of His own law, to keep it in all its precepts and also to bear its curse (iii. 13). 'He came from a land beyond the stars, from a heaven above the heavens . . . We may gather up the evangelic teaching on this majestic theme in three short statements: He came forth from God; He came down from heaven; He came in the flesh' (D. M. McIntyre, *Christ the Lord*, p. 65). *Redeem* (5). This, as already explained, He accomplished in the cross (iii. 13). *The adoption of sons* (5); or 'as sons'. God in His grace has taken into His family those who before belonged to a very different family (Jn. viii. 44), and has given them 'a right to all the blessings and all the privileges of the children of God'. Such blessings and privileges can be enjoyed only by those who have been redeemed.

Sent forth (6); same verb as in iv. 4. The presence and operation of the Holy Spirit in the heart are sure evidence of sonship (cf. Rom. viii. 14-16). *The Spirit of his Son* (6). The Holy Spirit is given by the Father through the intercession of the Son (Jn. xiv. 16), is sent by the Son from the Father (Jn. xv. 26), and bears witness to the Son (Jn. xv. 26 and xvi. 14). Cf. such phrases as 'the Spirit of Christ' (Rom. viii. 9), 'the Spirit of Jesus Christ' (Phil. i. 19) and 'the Spirit of Jesus' (Acts xvi. 7, RV). *Your hearts* (6); the true reading is 'our hearts', as in RV. 'You Galatians are sons, but so are we Jews.' *Crying* (6); the word denotes a strong cry and describes earnest, importunate prayer. *Abba, Father* (6). This expression occurs again in Mk. xiv. 36 and Rom. viii. 15. *Abba* is Aramaic for 'Father'. We may find here an illustration of what Paul has been saying (iii. 28) of the oneness of all believers in Christ; 'for *Abba, Father,*

unites Hebrew and Greek on one lip, making the petitioner at once a Jew and a Gentile' (Macgregor). See I.C.C. on Rom. viii. 15 and article 'Abba' in H.A.C. *Thou* (7). Paul brings this matter home to each individual believer. *Then an heir of God through Christ* (7). The true reading here seems to be, as in RV, 'Then an heir through God', or 'all owing to God' (Moff.).

e. The foolishness of wishing to be again in bondage (iv. 8-11)

Or rather are known of God (9). Cf. Jn. xv. 16 and 1 Jn. iv. 10. 'God knew them ere they knew Him, and His knowing them was the cause of their knowing Him' (Eadie). For this knowledge, which holds within it the secret of life eternal, cf. Mt. vii. 23; Jn. xvii. 3. *How turn ye?* (9), or 'are ye turning?', as of a process still going on. *Weak and beggarly elements* (9), or 'rudiments' (RV); cf. iv. 3n. *Weak*, because powerless to 'redeem' (5), *beggarly*, because they can bring no increase of spiritual wealth to those who are heirs of God (7). The spiritual wealth of the children of God is referred to over and over again in the New Testament (1 Cor. i. 5, iii. 21-23; 2 Cor. viii. 9; Jas. ii. 5). *Ye observe* (10); 'ye minutely, scrupulously observe', striving to omit none. Various Jewish ordinances are mentioned: *days*, i.e. sabbaths, fast-days, feast-days; *months*, i.e. the new moons (cf. 2 Ki. iv. 23); *times* (or seasons), i.e. the annual festivals, such as the Passover, Pentecost, etc.; *years*, i.e. the sabbatical years. No support can be found here for the idea that the sabbath law has been abrogated by Christ. What Paul is condemning here is the scrupulous observance of the Jewish sabbath, with all its Pharisaic strictness, and the scrupulous observance of other Jewish sacred days, as a means of salvation. *I am afraid of you* (11); better, 'I am afraid for you'. *In vain* (11); same word as is used in iii. 4.

f. A call to remember their first reception of the gospel (iv. 12-20)

Be as I am (12); or 'become as I am', free from Jewish ordinances. *I am as ye are* (12); or 'I became as ye are'; i.e. I threw off the yoke of the Jewish law in order to bring myself to the level of my Gentile converts. *Ye have not injured me at all* (12); rather, as in RV, 'ye did me no wrong'; i.e. in the old and better days, but, on the contrary, you treated me as described in verses 13 and 14. *Through infirmity of the flesh* (13); rather, as in RV, 'because of an infirmity of the flesh'. It was because of some bodily ailment that he came to preach the gospel to the Galatians. Ramsay's theory is an interesting one, viz. that Paul's 'infirmity of the flesh', which he takes to be the same as the 'thorn in the flesh' of 2 Cor. xii. 7, was an attack of malarial fever brought on while he was in the low-lying, swampy district of Perga in Pamphylia (Acts xiii. 13), which made him push north to the bracing air of the mountains. Other suggestions are weak eyesight or epilepsy; but no one knows with certainty.

At the first (13); 'on my former visit' (Moff.), probably on the outward journey, as opposed to the return journey (Acts xiv. 21–24). The better reading in verse 14 is that which underlies the RV rendering, 'that which was a temptation to you in my flesh'. There was some symptom in connection with Paul's illness which made him a humiliating spectacle and this might have tempted the Galatians to treat his preaching in a contemptuous manner, but their reaction to it was very different. *Rejected* (14); lit. 'spat out'. It is interesting to remember that it was in south Galatia that Paul and Barnabas were taken for divinities (Acts xiv. 12).

Where is then the blessedness ye spake of? (15); rather, as RV, 'Where then is that gratulation (or felicitation) of yourselves?' Verse 15 has been used to buttress the theory that Paul's 'thorn' was weak eyesight, but the words are almost certainly metaphorical. *They* (17); i.e. the Judaizing teachers. *Zealously affect you* (17); rather, as in RSV, 'make much of you'. So also in the following verse. *But not well* (17); RV 'in no good way', i.e. with no good motive. *Exclude you* (17); RV 'shut you out', i.e. from the Church of God. By insisting on circumcision the false teachers were in fact shutting out the Galatians from Christ (cf. v. 4, RV). *That ye might affect them* (17); RSV 'that you may make much of them'. Paul's meaning in verse 18 is: 'I do not grudge the attention that is paid to you, provided that it be for a good purpose. I am appealing for a share in your affections, and would they were as warm towards me now as when I was with you.' *My little children* (19); a sudden outburst of very warm affection. This is the only instance of this phrase in Paul; it is frequently found in John. Paul says that he has a greater claim to their love than these others because they owe to him their new life in Christ (cf. 1 Cor. iv. 15). The same anguish of spirit which he felt when he preached to them is present in him again, in view of their spiritual peril. *Formed* (19). The purpose of the new birth is that the Christian life and character should grow from more to more: would the new teaching to which they had listened contribute to that growth? *Change my voice* (20); 'alter my tone' (Moff.). 'If you and I could only come face to face would we not speedily be on the old footing again?' As it is, he is 'perplexed' (RV) about them.

g. The allegory of Abraham's two sons (iv. 21–31)

It is written (22); a general reference to Gn. xvi and xxi. 1–21. *Which things are an allegory* (24); lit. 'are allegorized'. To those who really *hear* (21), they say something distinct from the meaning that lies on the surface of the story. *For these are* . . . (24); i.e. they represent typically. Cf. such passages as Mt. xiii. 37–39, xxvi. 26, 28; 1 Cor. x. 4. *Which gendereth to bondage* (24); RV 'bearing children unto bondage'.

For this Agar is mount Sinai in Arabia (25). The RV mg. gives a reading which is found in many MSS, and is adopted by Lightfoot and

others, 'for Sinai is a mountain in Arabia', i.e., as Lightfoot comments, 'in the land of bondsmen, themselves descended from Hagar'. *Answereth to* (25); lit. 'stands in the same row or file with', 'belongs to the same category'. Jerusalem was in political bondage and also in spiritual bondage, not having received the freedom Christ offered to her. *The mother of us all* (26); RV 'our mother'. For Jerusalem as the mother of believers see Ps. lxxxvii. Believers are already citizens of the heavenly Jerusalem (Lk. x. 20; Phil. iii. 20; Heb. xii. 22). *It is written, Rejoice* . . . (27); a quotation from Is. liv. 1 (LXX), a passage which predicts the vast increase of Jerusalem's children. Under the figure of a wife neglected and barren the desolation of the exile is described, and Jerusalem is promised a day of blessing and increase. Isaiah's prophecy is spiritually fulfilled in the ingathering of the Gentiles into the Church of God (cf. Is. xlix. 18–23). From Is. liv. 2 William Carey preached his famous missionary sermon.

The allusion in verse 29 seems to be to Gn. xxi. 9, but the imperfect tense here ('was persecuting', 'went on persecuting') hints at the fact that the incident mentioned in Gn. xxi. 9 was no isolated one. *What saith the scripture?* (30); the reference is to Gn. xxi. 10. The essential meaning, no doubt, as given by Lightfoot: 'The law and the gospel cannot co-exist; the law must disappear before the gospel.' Verse 31 is a summing up of the passage (21–31), and it leads right on to the exhortation in the next verse. We should note the stress laid throughout on *free, freewoman, freedom*. On this passage we may remark that this one clear example of inspired spiritualizing of the Old Testament does not justify any general use of the allegoric method of scriptural interpretation.

III. PRACTICAL AND HORTATORY.
v. 1—vi. 18

a. A call to hold fast to freedom (v. 1–12)

The true reading of verse 1 seems to be as in RV, 'With freedom (RV mg. 'for freedom') did Christ set us free: stand fast therefore . . .' Some would link this verse to the preceding verses as the conclusion of Paul's argument. *Stand fast* (1). Paul uses this verb again in 2 Thes. ii. 15; 1 Cor. xvi. 13; Phil. i. 27, iv. 1. *The yoke of bondage* (1); lit. 'a yoke', as in RV; i.e. any yoke, whoever may try to impose it. Cf. Acts xv. 10, and contrast Mt. xi. 29, 30. *I Paul say* (2); i.e. with all the authority of an apostle of Christ, and as one who knows from bitter experience the truth of what I say. Submission to circumcision would mean going back to the method of seeking salvation by law-works (3), and would thus mean accepting the obligation to keep the whole law, which requires a perfect fulfilment of all its precepts (iii. 10).

Christ is become of no effect unto you (4); RV 'Ye are severed from Christ'. The Greek verb *katargeō* is translated 'abolish' in 1 Cor. xv. 26 (RV) and 'bring to nought' in Heb. ii. 14 (RV). The

AV has 'destroy' in both places. It denotes here the cessation of all connection. In Rom. vii. 2 and 6 Paul uses it of the wife who is 'discharged from the law of the husband' by his death, and so of Christians who are 'discharged from the law' (RV). *Ye are fallen* (RV 'fallen away') *from grace* (4); i.e. the special grace of justification on condition of faith. *For* (5); the true character of the children of God is seen in us who through faith have a spiritual (AV), or Spirit-given (RV), expectation of the glory that is to be. *Wait for* (5). A verb which Paul uses frequently (see 1 Cor. i. 7; Rom. viii. 19, 23, 25; Phil. iii. 20). All these passages point to the glory awaiting the people of God at the coming of Christ. *The hope of righteousness* (5) is the hope associated with, or inspired by, righteousness, the hope which is ours because we are justified (cf. Rom. v. 2 and Col. i. 27). The children of God now possess righteousness in Christ, and it holds within it the promise of coming glory. (Cf. 'the hope of the calling' in Eph. i. 18, iv. 4.) *For in Jesus Christ . . .* (6); i.e. once you have become a Christian that which has power is not outward man-wrought differences of the flesh, but an inner Spirit-wrought activity of faith which manifests itself in love. *Which worketh by love* (6); RV 'working through love', the love in which the whole law is fulfilled (14). 'In these words,' says Bengel, 'stands all Christianity.' They 'bridge over', as Lightfoot says, 'the gulf which seems to separate the language of St. Paul and St. James. Both assert a principle of practical energy, as opposed to a barren, inactive theory.' For *faith, hope* and *love* in close combination see 1 Thes. i. 3; Rom. v. 1-5; 1 Cor. xiii. 13; Col. i. 4.

Ye did run well (7); better, as in RV, 'ye were running well'. Again, as in ii. 2, we have a metaphor from the foot-race. *Hinder* (7). This is a metaphor from military operations, suggesting the idea of the breaking up of a road in order to arrest the progress of an advancing army. *This persuasion* (8); 'this sort of suasion' (Moff.). *Him that calleth you* (8); i.e. God, as in i. 6 and 15. The verb is in the present tense as in 1 Thes. v. 24. God called them, in the crisis of conversion (i. 6), but He is still calling them to loftier heights of vision and knowledge. Are they listening to Him, or to another voice, a deceptive voice? Verse 9 is a proverb, quoted also in 1 Cor. v. 6. The reference may be either to a person, the hinderer (7), or the troubler (10), or, and perhaps more likely, to an infusion of false teaching which, however small it seems, will spread and work infinite mischief. *I* (10), 'who know you so well, who remember your former zeal' (Lightfoot), have good hopes for you in spite of all. *Troubleth* (10); the same verb as in i. 7.

Yet (11); RV 'still', as in the days before his conversion, as perhaps some had wickedly said. *Offence* (11); RV 'stumblingblock'. The Greek word *skandalon* means 'the trigger of a trap', then a 'trap' or a 'snare', and so anything that trips, catches and hinders. *Ceased* (11); RV 'done away'; the same verb as in v. 4. These words are

of course ironical. Paul is still preaching Christ crucified (ii. 20, iii. 1, 13, vi. 14), who is to Jews a stumblingblock (1 Cor. i. 23); that is why he is persecuted. *Cut off* (12); RV 'would even cut themselves off', i.e. 'sever themselves from all connection with the Church'. Ramsay adopts that interpretation, but nearly all modern scholars favour a more drastic, indeed a startling, translation, that given in RV mg. and RSV, 'mutilate themselves'. Why stop at circumcision, why not go all the way in physical mutilation, like the priests of the goddess Cybele in the Galatian region? The verb is that found in Dt. xxiii. 1 (LXX). *Trouble* (12); RV 'unsettle', a verb which does not occur in classical Greek, but was used in the vernacular, as is proved, for example, by its use in a letter of the date A.D. 41, found in Egypt. It occurs twice elsewhere in the New Testament (Acts xvii. 6, xxi. 38) of fomenting social disorder.

b. The works of the flesh and the fruit of the Spirit (v. 13-26)

For (13); i.e. I may well use such strong language about those who are unsettling you (12), *for* you were called 'for freedom' (RV). *Occasion* (13); a word peculiar to Paul in the New Testament, denoting in Rom. vii. 8, 11 and 2 Cor. xi. 12, as here, an opening for sin. It was applied in military language to a base of operations. For a similar exhortation see 1 Pet. ii. 16. *By love serve one another* (13), so obeying the teaching of Christ (Mk. x. 44). This method of love (14) is a better way of keeping the law than to be circumcised (3); indeed, it is the only way (cf. verse 6). We have the same thought in Rom. xiii. 8. *Bite and devour* (15). The ferocious strife of warring sects in the Church results in mutual destruction. *Walk* (16); i.e. live your life day by day. This verb is often used in that sense by Paul; see Rom. vi. 4, viii. 4; 1 Cor. iii. 3; Eph. iv. 1 and 17; Phil. iii. 18. *In the Spirit* (16); RV 'by the Spirit', i.e. led by Him (cf. Rom. viii. 14 and verse 18 here).

Flesh (17). In this context the word does not mean the body, as though the seat of sin were there. It should be noted that many of the sins mentioned in 'the works of the flesh' are spiritual sins. 'Flesh' means, as Melanchthon said, 'the entire nature of man, sense and reason, without the Holy Spirit.' The child of God has the Holy Spirit in him as the source of the new life, and so there arises in him that 'irreconcilable war' of which this verse speaks. 'Have you not clear proof,' Paul seems to say, 'of the presence of these two antagonists in your heart? How otherwise can you explain the fact that you do not always obey the dictates of conscience?' Conflict there must be, but the fact remains unaltered that believers are not under the law (18). It no longer condemns them, and is not an irksome constraint in their case. Sweetly constrained by the Spirit, they do the will of God. *The works of the flesh are manifest* (19); manifest enough in that old pagan world, manifest enough today everywhere. There is no attempt in verses 19–21 to mention all possible sins; some glaring examples are given. Lightfoot classifies them under the four headings of sensual passions, unlawful dealings in things spiritual, violations of brotherly love, and intemperate excesses.

i. Sensual passions (19). *Adultery . . . lasciviousness. Adultery* is omitted in RV as not part of the true text. *Lasciviousness*; i.e. 'wantonness' (Lightfoot), open, unashamed indecency. The word occurs in Mk. vii. 22; 2 Cor. xii. 21; 1 Pet. iv. 3; 2 Pet. ii. 7 (of the men of Sodom) and elsewhere. We should remember that in that old pagan world sexual vice was provided for by public law and was incorporated even into the worship of the gods.

ii. Unlawful dealings in things spiritual (20). *Idolatry, witchcraft.* The first of these is the open recognition of false gods. For *witchcraft* RV reads 'sorcery'; Moffatt reads 'magic'; the reference is to that trafficking with the dead, and so with the powers of evil, which is so sternly condemned in the Old Testament (see, e.g., Is. viii. 20; see also Rev. xxi. 8, xxii. 15).

iii. Violations of brotherly love (20, 21). *Hatred . . . murders. Variance*; RV 'strife'. *Emulations*; RV 'jealousies'. *Wrath*; lit. 'wraths' as in RV; i.e. passionate outbursts of anger. *Strife*; RV 'factions'. *Heresies*; RV mg. 'parties', an aggravated form of 'divisions'. The word *murders* is, probably, not part of the true text and is omitted in RV.

iv. Intemperate excesses (21). *Drunkenness, revellings*; 'drinking bouts, revellings' (Moff.). The two words occur again in Rom. xiii. 13, and the second word in 1 Pet. iv. 3.

Those who practise (21, RV) such things must, in the nature of the case, be outside the holy city of God that is to be (see Rev. xxii. 15). The works of the flesh involve hard, grinding, fruitless toil, which yields in the end the wages of that death which is the antithesis of eternal life (Rom. vi. 23).

Fruit (22), by contrast, is the sure sign of healthy life in the tree, and 'the fruit of the Spirit' is the beautiful and quiet and ever progressive manifestation in conduct, even to old age (Ps. xcii. 14), of the new life communicated by Him. Paul writes not of 'fruits' but of 'fruit'; cf. 'fruit of righteousness' (Phil. i. 11, Gk.), and 'fruit of the light' (Eph. v. 9, RV). A lovely ninefold cluster of fruit is described here. 'Like the chain of graces in 2 Pet. i. 5–7 they are all linked together as though to suggest that the absence of any one means the nullity of all' (article 'Fruit' in H.A.C.). Lightfoot's threefold classification into habits of mind, social qualities, and general principles of conduct is again helpful.

i. Habits of mind (22). *Love.* The Holy Spirit inspires in the soul that love to God and to man which is the fulfilling of the law (cf. verse 14). See Paul's wonderful eulogy of love in 1 Cor. xiii. *Joy.* Deep joy of heart such as the drinking-bouts and the other works of the flesh can never

produce. This joy is joy 'in the Lord' (Phil. iv. 4), not in circumstances. *Peace.* A felt sense of harmony in heart and state towards God and man, that peace of God which guards the heart against all invading cares and fears (Phil. iv. 7).

ii. Social qualities (22). *Longsuffering.* Passive patience under injuries or wrongs. *Gentleness*; RV 'kindness'. A kindly disposition towards others. *Goodness.* Active beneficence, and thus a step in advance of kindness of disposition. No higher tribute could be paid to Barnabas than this: 'He was a good man', and that because he was 'full of the Holy Ghost' (Acts xi. 24).

iii. General principles of conduct (22, 23). *Faith.* Probably here in the sense of fidelity: cf. Tit. ii. 10, where the word is so rendered. *Meekness.* The specially Christian temper of not standing on one's rights. Our Lord associates blessedness with it (Mt. v. 5) and it is an attribute of Himself (Mt. xi. 29 and 2 Cor. x. 1). *Temperance*; RV 'self-control'. The idea suggested is that of a man keeping a firm hand on his desires and passions: the word occurs in Acts xxiv. 25 and 2 Pet. i. 6.

Against such . . . (23). The law exists for purposes of restraint, but here there is nothing to restrain (cf. 1 Tim. i. 9, 10). *Crucified* (24). Those who are Christ's have consented to the old, corrupt nature, 'the old man' (Rom. vi. 6), being nailed to the cross of Christ; they must maintain that attitude of mind. *Affections* (24); RV 'passions'. The word occurs in this sense in Rom. vii. 5. *In the Spirit* (25); RV 'by the Spirit', as in verse 16. *Walk.* A different word from that used in verse 16, a word which conveys the idea of walking in line: in classical Greek it is used of marching in battle order: Paul uses it in Rom. iv. 12 of walking in line with Abraham's faith. The idea is suggested that the guidance of the Spirit must be closely followed. *Desirous of vain glory* (26); RV 'vainglorious'. The corresponding noun occurs in the New Testament only in Phil. ii. 3, where 'lowliness of mind' is placed in striking contrast with it. This foolish striving after empty honour reveals itself in two ways, *provoking* and *envying*. The former word occurs only here in the New Testament and has in it the idea of 'challenging to combat', which may easily follow on 'envy', i.e. vexation at the superiority of others. Paul goes on to speak of a far different attitude to adopt towards brethren, even toward those of them who have grossly erred.

c. Burden bearing (vi. 1–5)

Brethren (1). Bengel says that 'a whole argument lies hidden under this one word'. *If*; RV 'even if'. *Overtaken*; 'detected' (Lightfoot), perhaps in the very act of sin, so that his guilt is beyond doubt. *A fault*; RV 'any trespass'. The same word occurs in Mt. vi. 14; lit. 'a fall beside', so that the offender has got out of the straight line of the Spirit's guidance (cf. v. 25n.). *Ye which are spiritual* (1); you who have the Spirit, are led by Him and walk by Him (iii. 2, 14, iv. 6, v. 18, 25), you in whose lives the fruit of the Spirit, with meekness as part of it, is growing from more to more. *Restore* (1). An interesting verb, which is used in various ways in the New Testament. In the classics we have it used of setting bones; in the New Testament of equipping and preparing (Heb. x. 5, xi. 3), and of mending nets (Mt. iv. 21). It is the verb translated 'make perfect' in Heb. xiii. 21 and 1 Pet. v. 10. The damage wrought in the erring brother by his trespass is to be repaired, and he is to be again fitted into his place in the body of Christ. *Considering thyself* (1); RV 'looking to thyself'. The exhortation is addressed to the conscience of each: let each consider his own liability to sin and remember that some day he may need the same merciful treatment. *One another's burdens* (2). The emphasis is on *one another's*: self-centredness is condemned. The *burdens* are such a burden of sorrow for sin as the erring brother is bearing and all other burdens of sorrow and care that may weigh down the hearts of our fellows. Here are better burdens to bear than the burden of the law, and here is the best of all laws to fulfil, *the law of Christ*.

A very different mental attitude is next described in verse 3, the attitude of laying claim to spiritual superiority to the fallen brother. Such an attitude can be taken only by one who is self-deceived. *Deceiveth himself* (3); i.e. by his own fancies. The Greek verb occurs only here in the New Testament, the corresponding adjective occurring in Tit. i. 10. All comparisons of ourselves with others should cease, and each man should aim at having his own work of sterling worth (4), and 'then he will have something to boast about on his own account, and not in comparison with his fellows' (Moff.). *Prove* (4). A verb used in the classics of testing metals and money. It occurs in that sense in Pr. xvii. 3 (LXX) and 1 Pet. i. 7. It occurs as meaning to examine and test in 1 Cor. iii. 13, xi. 28; 1 Thes. v. 21. *Another* (4); lit. 'the other'; RV renders 'his neighbour'. *Burden* (5), or 'load' (RV mg.). A different word from that in verse 2. The word used there emphasizes the weight of the burden; this word simply notes the fact that it is something to be borne (*phortion*, from the verb *pherō*, 'I carry'). There is for each man a burden of personal responsibility which he cannot shift over to other shoulders, and if he devotes his mind to it he will not have time or inclination to compare himself with others.

d. Sowing and reaping (vi. 6–10)

Taught (6). The Greek word is that from which come our words 'catechize' and 'catechism'. The reference is to oral teaching. *Communicate* (6); lit. 'go shares with'. *Good things* (6). In Lk. xii. 18 and xvi. 25 this phrase signifies worldly wealth, and it has often been so understood here; that is to say, Paul is regarded as exhorting Christians to give liberally for the financial support of their teachers. That idea may be intended, but the phrase seems capable of a wider

application. Each believer has his own peculiar burden of responsibility to bear, 'but' (as RV begins this verse) let him not forget this, that he must share with his teacher in every good work. *Be not deceived* (7); the same phrase is used in 1 Cor. vi. 9, xv. 33; Jas. i. 16; lit. 'be not led astray'. *Mocked* (7). The verb means literally 'to turn up the nose at'; it occurs only here in the New Testament; it is frequent in the LXX (e.g. Ps. lxxx. 6; Pr. xv. 20; Je. xx. 7). *Soweth* (7). In 2 Cor. ix. 6 this figure is used in connection with the spending of money, but again a wider application is surely intended here. The laws of God cannot be trifled with; He will not alter them for our benefit. What a man reaps is the inevitable result of what he sows (cf. 2 Cor. v. 10). In verse 8 the *flesh* and the *Spirit* seem to be regarded as seed-beds, and *corruption* is contrasted with 'eternal life' (RV). From Rom. ii. 7 this latter expression is seen to carry with it the ideas of 'glory and honour and immortality' (RV 'incorruption'); cf. 1 Tim. vi. 19 (RV). *Let us not be weary in well doing* (9). The same exhortation is found in 2 Thes. iii. 13. The verb suggests the idea of fainting, or losing heart; it is translated 'faint' in Lk. xviii. 1; 2 Cor. iv. 1, 16; Eph. iii. 13. *Well doing*; i.e. 'doing what is good' —such 'good' as is suggested in verses 1, 2, 6 and 10. The application here is to the best kind of sowing. *In due season* (9); i.e. at the appropriate season for reaping, not earlier. The great harvest time will be at the coming of the Lord (cf. Mt. xiii. 39; Jas. v. 7). *Faint* (9); a verb used in Mt. xv. 32 and Mk. viii. 3 of physical exhaustion, in Heb. xii. 3, 5 of relaxing effort. It seems to describe here the moral and spiritual collapse that may be caused by apparent lack of results in Christian work, or by hope deferred which makes the heart sick (Pr. xiii. 12). *Opportunity* (10); the same word as that translated *season* (9). There is one season for sowing, another for reaping: what matters now is that we should sow lavishly. *Them who are of the household of faith* (10). Macgregor suggests, as a quite literal translation, 'the domestic persons of the faith', those, Jews and Gentiles, who, through the door of faith (Acts xiv. 27), have entered into the house of God and now live there, by faith similar to Paul's (ii. 20); cf. Eph. ii. 19.

e. Conclusion (vi. 11–18)

How large a letter (11); far better, as in RV, 'with how large letters'. Paul often wrote the closing verses of an Epistle with his own hand (see 1 Cor. xvi. 21; Col. iv. 18; 2 Thes. iii. 17). This would suggest that, at this point, Paul took the pen out of the hand of his amanuensis, and wrote the eight concluding verses in large, bold characters, perhaps for the sake of emphasis. Some of the principal ideas of the Epistle are here stated again, in order to fix them more deeply in the minds of the readers. *To make a fair shew* (12); lit. 'to put on a good face', i.e. 'to make a good showing' (RSV). *In the flesh* (12); in ordinances which are bodily and external. It was not sincere zeal for the law which was the inspiring motive with these Judaizing teachers, but the unworthy desire to escape persecution. It was the preaching of the cross as the sinner's only hope, to the exclusion of all reliance on the law for salvation, which stirred up persecution (cf. v. 11). *They . . . who are circumcised* (13); RV 'they who receive circumcision', 'the circumcision party' (Moff. and Lightfoot); i.e. those who insist on circumcision as essential to salvation. They themselves do not consistently and rigidly observe all the requirements of the law. Or, Paul may mean that they most certainly have not given perfect obedience to the law which demands nothing less (iii. 10).

God forbid (14); the same strong expression as in ii. 17 and iii. 21. *By whom* (14); RV 'through which'; RV mg. 'through whom'. *Crucified* (14); finally and with abiding results; the tense used is the same as in ii. 20. The *world is crucified* to him, because it has for ever lost its power to charm; and because he also is crucified *unto the world*, the real change having taken place in himself, he is dead now to all the allurements of the world. Compare Isaac Watts' well-known hymn, 'When I survey the wondrous cross'. Verse 15, according to the true text, reads as in RV, 'For neither is circumcision anything, nor uncircumcision, but a new creature'. Cf. v. 6 and 1 Cor. vii. 19, the three passages together providing material for profitable study of the things that really count in Christianity. What really matters is not anything external, but the inward regeneration wrought by the Holy Ghost, the *new creature* or the 'new creation' (RV mg.), the same phrase as in 2 Cor. v. 17, which takes the place of the man who has been crucified.

Walk (16); RV 'shall walk'; the same word as in v. 25. *Rule* (16); i.e. the principle laid down in verses 14 and 15. The Greek word is *kanōn*, which sometimes meant a carpenter's rule or a surveyor's measuring line, and from it comes the word 'Canon' as applied to Holy Scripture as 'the only rule to direct us how we may glorify and enjoy God'. *Peace . . . mercy* (16). To the peace which he had invoked upon his readers (i. 3) Paul now adds mercy. Miserable sinners need the mercy of God (Eph. ii. 4). ' 'Tis from the mercy of our God that all our hopes begin,' and from it alone abiding peace of heart flows. *And upon the Israel of God* (16); 'even upon . . .' (Moff.). The Church of redeemed men and women is God's Israel (iii. 7, 9, 14, 29). Cf. Rom. ii. 28, 29; Phil. iii. 3; 1 Pet. ii. 9, 10. There is an allusion here to Pss. cxxv. 5 and cxxviii. 6.

Let no man trouble me (17). The Judaizers have sorely troubled him; he hopes that he has now silenced them. He has proved decisively that he is a true apostle of Christ; if further proof be desired, let them look at the scars (*marks*) of his body. 'I bear branded on my body the marks of Jesus' (RV). The Greek for 'marks' is *stigmata*. Slaves sometimes had their owner's name branded on them, and persons devoted to the service of a god were thus branded; so Paul seems to regard the scars left on his body by the stoning at Lystra in south Galatia (Acts xiv) as sure and certain proof that he was the slave of Jesus, and one who had entered into 'the fellowship of his sufferings' (Phil. iii. 10). In later Epistles Paul often describes himself as the slave of Christ (Rom. i. 1). He gloried in such 'marks', not in circumcision. *Brethren* (18). As indicated in the RV, this is the last word in the Epistle, occupying thus a position of emphasis. Paul wants the 'foolish Galatians' (iii. 1) to realize that they are still his brothers, in spite of all the hard things he has written to them. Thus, as Bengel says, 'the severity of the Epistle, taken as a whole, is softened'.

ALEXANDER ROSS.

THE EPISTLE TO THE EPHESIANS

INTRODUCTION

See also the General Article, 'The Pauline Epistles', p. 68.

I. AUTHORSHIP AND DATE

It is a well-attested and generally accepted fact that Paul was the writer of this Epistle, as the opening sentence claims (cf. iii. 1). The circumstances of the writer as revealed incidentally in the text point to its being written during Paul's imprisonment in Rome (Acts xxviii. 16, 28–31), for he speaks of himself as a prisoner (iv. 1), wearing chains (vi. 20), on behalf of the Gentiles (iii. 1). The wide imperial view of things that is taken in the Epistle accords well with this.

No special occasion or immediate purpose of writing is revealed in the Epistle, except the fact that Tychicus was to bear other correspondence into Asia (Col. iv. 7). The impulse to write was probably associated with the quiet and secure leisure which the apostle enjoyed in his imprisonment at Rome—it was little more than 'house arrest' (Acts xxviii. 16ff.). In this calm and imperial atmosphere his thought ripened, and the Spirit revealed to him more clearly than ever before a divine philosophy of world history, the high purpose of God, and the glorious destiny of the Church. Such thoughts and revelations must be expressed; and with the leisure of his long waiting for trial (Acts xxviii. 30), and the opportunity provided by the journey of Tychicus, Paul pens this noble work.

Some have thought that the Epistle was written during his imprisonment in Caesarea (Acts xxiii. 33—xxvii. 2), but Rome is much more generally accepted as the place of origin. The most probable date, therefore, that we can assign to the Epistle is A.D. 61.

II. DESTINATION

Two sets of facts combine to suggest that this Epistle was sent not to one particular church but to a number of churches within a limited area. The facts that the words 'in Ephesus' do not occur in the most authoritative manuscripts, and that the greetings which usually accompany one of Paul's Epistles to a church where he was well known (as he was in Ephesus, for he had spent over two years there, Acts xix. 10) are absent, suggest that a wider circle than that of a single church was envisaged by the writer.

Yet there are indications of a personal nature that seem to confine the Epistle within the limits of a comparatively small area. The faith of the particular group he had in mind is referred to in i. 15, and their knowledge of, and sympathy for, his circumstances in iii. 13. This group of churches was probably not very different from that addressed by John in Rev. i. 4. Among these churches Ephesus was of central importance (Rev. ii. 1), and it is probable that this Epistle became widely known mainly through the circulation of the Ephesian copy.

III. RELATION TO COLOSSIANS

The literary relation between this Epistle and Colossians is so close that these two have been called twin Epistles. Half the verses in Ephesians can be traced in language or substance in Colossians. As many as forty coincidences of thought and language can be found; yet they are so intimately woven into the fabric of each Epistle that it is impossible to believe that they are due to any attempt at imitation or forgery. Especially significant is the fact that, while similar words and phrases appear in the two letters, they often appear in different contexts and with various associations. The similarities that exist between the two can reasonably be assigned to the fact that the author's circumstances were the same in each; the differences will owe their origin mainly to the different circumstances of those to whom they were addressed. There is, for example, no controversial matter in the general Epistle to the Ephesians, such as is found in that to the individual church at Colosse (Col. ii. 16–23). If any precedence in time is to be given it would seem that Colossians was written before Ephesians, if only because in Ephesians the thought common to both is more fully developed.

Ephesians and Colossians are also similar in structure. Each is divided into a doctrinal section (Eph. i. 1—iv. 16; Col. i. 1—iii. 4), and each concludes with a practical application. The manner in which topics follow one another in the same order is remarkable: the relation of Christ to the Church appears in chapter i in each Epistle; Paul's reference to his commission (Eph. iii. 1–13; Col. i. 23–29), and the summary of doctrine at the end of the doctrinal sections (Eph. iv. 1–16; Col. iii. 1–4) are also parallel. In the practical sections we have parallel warnings against sins (Eph. iv. 17—v. 21; Col. iii. 5–17), and notable passages on human relationships under the gospel (Eph. v. 22—vi. 9; Col. iii. 18—iv. 1).

OUTLINE OF CONTENTS

The main division of the Epistle is into two parts. The first part, chapters i to iii, is mainly doctrinal; the second, chapters iv to vi, mainly practical.

I. THE ADDRESS. i. 1, 2

II. THANKSGIVING FOR BLESSINGS TO THE WHOLE CHURCH. i. 3–14

III. THANKSGIVING FOR SPIRITUAL STATE OF READERS. i. 15–23

IV. THEIR RELATION (AS SINNERS) TO CHRIST. ii. 1–10

V. THEIR RELATION (AS GENTILES) TO JEWS. ii. 11–22

VI. THE MYSTERY OF THE GOSPEL. iii. 1–21

VII. THE UNITY OF THE SPIRIT. iv. 1–16

VIII. ETHICAL ELEMENTS OF THE CHRISTIAN LIFE. iv. 17—v. 21

IX. CHRISTIAN RELATIONSHIPS IN FAMILY LIFE. v. 22—vi. 9

X. THE CHRISTIAN WARFARE. vi. 10–20

XI. CONCLUSION. vi. 21–24

COMMENTARY

I. THE ADDRESS. i. 1, 2

In the opening phrases of this uncontroversial Epistle, Paul states very simply and without special emphasis his authority for writing. It lies in the undeserved grace of God that made him *an apostle . . . by the will of God* (1). That is his supreme authority; but in other contexts he had reason to insist upon it more fully (1 Cor. ix. 1, xv. 8; 2 Cor. xii. 11; Gal. i. 1). *Saints* (1). A term having a different connotation then from the specialized meaning it has today. In its modern use it refers to pre-eminent attainment in holiness; in the New Testament it is applied simply to one who was sanctified by the Spirit (1 Cor. vi. 11), as all true believers are. Each and every Christian is therefore a saint, and should live as such. Because Old Testament believers also were 'saints' the readers here addressed are specifically defined as *the faithful in Christ Jesus*.

The Epistle opens with a benediction in terms of God's unmerited favour to men, and the peace which it brings in the heart. This is Paul's usual form of greeting. He delighted to use the composite greeting of *grace and peace* which unites the common greeting of the Greeks, 'grace', with that of the Hebrews, 'peace'. The close connection of *from the Lord Jesus Christ* with *from God our Father* (2) should be considered as strong evidence of the deity of Christ. Such incidental allusions, making Him 'equal with God' (Jn. v. 18), have an evidential value of their own.

II. THANKSGIVING FOR BLESSINGS TO THE WHOLE CHURCH. i. 3–14

The mighty surge of apostolic thought and inspiration sweeps over the narrow confines of rigid grammatical analysis and presents, as no logical process could, a conception of things that can clearly be seen to have come direct from God. It reveals an immeasurable depth and height of thought. Yet because of the generalized nature of the latter, these sentences are deprived of a very potent element in Pauline writing, the personal pronoun used as subject. Compare, for example, the warmth of personal address in 1 Thes. i. 2; 2 Thes. i. 3; Gal. i. 6; Col. i. 3; Phil. i. 3. The nearest parallel we have is in 2 Cor. i. 3–11; but the personal element appears more strongly there, and the conceptions are, in general, more mundane. This paragraph is formed in three prose strophes: the purpose of the Father (3–6); the redemption of the Son (7–12); and the sealing of the Holy Spirit (13, 14).

Salient features stand out in this paragraph. The three Persons of the Trinity appear in order: the *Father* in verse 3; the Son (*the beloved*) at the end of verse 6; and the *holy Spirit* in verse 13. The thoughts regarding each are expressed in a separate strophe which, in each case, ends with the refrain *to the praise of the glory of his grace* or *of his glory*. There is a notable emphasis on the will of God, seen in the reiteration of verses 5, 9, 11 (cf. verse 1). The central phrase is *the mystery of his will* in verse 9; and this mystery finds expression in verse 10, 'to sum up all things in Christ' (RV).

a. The purpose of the Father (i. 3–6)

The significant repetition of the preposition *in* should be noted. The doxology of verse 3 is also found in 2 Cor. i. 3; 1 Pet. i. 3. This verse forms the text of which verses 4–14 are an amplification and exposition. *Spiritual blessings* (3) are typical of the New Testament. The blessings of the Old Testament were largely temporal (cf. Dt. xxviii. 3, 5).

Heavenly places (3); there is no noun for the adjective 'heavenlies' to qualify. The expression is vague, with the vagueness not of uncertainty but of an order of things higher than we can fully comprehend. The use of the term is confined to this Epistle (see also i. 20, ii. 6, iii. 10, vi. 12). Gathering up the sense of the different passages in which it occurs we find that the term refers to the sphere of heavenly blessing (i. 3) where Christ now sits supreme over every other authority (i. 20), and to which believers themselves have been raised (ii. 6) for the display of God's glory (iii. 10). Yet it is not a sphere of perfect peace and bliss for it is inhabited by 'the spiritual hosts of wickedness' with whom the bèliever has unceasing warfare (vi. 12). The nearest we can come to an interpretation of it is 'that realm of spiritual realities in which the great forces of good and evil wage their warfare; in which also Jesus Christ sits supreme, and we representatively in Him'. It is the realm of spiritual experience—not a physical locality but a region of spiritual realities and experiences. That sin has wrought disorder in the heavenlies is implied also in Col. i. 20. How wide is the scope of the gospel as seen by Paul! The power of the gospel in us does not yet owe enough to these broad and mighty truths.

The phrase *in Christ* (3) was of Jewish origin, in the sense that 'Christ' referred to the Jewish Messiah. But in Paul's use of it the phrase has a far wider meaning than 'the Messiah of the Jews'. For Paul 'Christ' included the Messiah of prophecy, the Jesus of history and the Lord of glory who had been revealed to him on the Damascus road (Acts ix). The conception of the earthly Jesus, made so vivid in the Gospels, had been absorbed for him in the risen Lord so fully as to give rise to the purpose expressed in 2 Cor. v. 16. The preposition *in* expresses with an almost incomprehensible simplicity the union that exists between Christ and believers: it expresses far more than we can understand or appreciate, but it suggests to us something of the inwardness and depth of that mystical union (see Gal. ii. 20, RV). The full purpose of God in regard to the relationship indicated by this preposition is expressed in verse 10.

The exposition of verse 3 in verses 4–14 is not by a process of beating the thought out thinly, for the amplification is as rich in depth and height as the text. The mighty conceptions of election and of God's eternal purpose are immediately presented. The fact of election, *according as he hath chosen us in him before the foundation of the world* (4), was common knowledge and a source of pride to every Jew, for it made him a member of the chosen people of the Old Testament. Paul here refers to a principle of selection that had already been in evidence in the workings of divine providence, but that was now seen to have an extended scope; no longer was it confined to the Jewish people, but embraced Christian believers as well. Just as Israel had been the chosen people of God in the Old Testament, so Christians were the chosen people of the New Testament. Election is falsely viewed if we regard it as a narrow and selfish thing; it must be considered in relation to the end in view (see verse 9). *Before the foundation of the world* (4) takes us beyond time into eternity. This new people, the Christian Church, is not the result of a hasty, temporal expedient, but is a part of God's eternal purpose equally with the people of Israel. Christianity is no innovation but takes its place in the continuity of the divine plan. Compare 'before the world' (i.e. 'the ages') in 1 Cor. ii. 7 and 'before the world began' in 2 Tim. i. 9; Tit. i. 2. The purpose toward which election moves is *that we should be holy and without blame* (RV 'blemish') *before him in love* (4). The aim, so far as individual believers are concerned, is holiness. For the wider aspects, see verses 6 and 10. All this great work of God was done *in love*, and the divine aim is to work in us the holy love that wrought for us.

That there is nothing of blind destiny in the life of the Christian is further emphasized when Paul speaks of God 'having foreordained us unto adoption as sons through Jesus Christ unto himself' (5, RV). The sonship that man had from God by the fact of his being created in the divine image (Gn. i. 26f.) required renewing after the fall. This renewing was accomplished in the incarnate Son of God first of all (compare 'image' in Gn. i. 26f.; Heb. i. 3), and then in those who are 'in Him' by faith. Sonship is by both regeneration and adoption: the new birth alters our nature and adoption alters our relationship to God. Both are made possible for us *by* (the redemptive work of) *Jesus Christ* (5). God wrought all this *according to the good pleasure of his will*, a phrase which embodies the primary and ultimate expression of eternal purpose, beyond which we cannot go. The end at which God aims in His great work is *the glory of his grace* (6).

b. The redemption of the Son (i. 7–12)

'The sublimest exposition ever framed of the ultimate purpose of God.' Much of the New Testament is expressed in terms more familiar to a Jew than to any other, because the terms are those of his own ancient religion. *Redemption* (7) found its chief historical illustration in the exodus from Egypt which was the birth of the Hebrew people as a nation. The redemption wrought by Christ also created a new people, and this redemption was at the price of His death, or *his blood* (7) as we have it here. There is implied a state of bondage: in the Old Testament, the Israelites were held captive by the Egyptians; in the New Testament all men are captives of sin and Satan. Redemption is deliverance from captivity (see Ex. xii. 7, 13; Heb. ix. 12). *Forgiveness* (7) is so central in Christian experience that it is mentioned here as embracing the whole of it. The splendid proportions of the whole scheme of grace are nothing less than the *riches* (7) of God, flowing towards us in gifts of *wisdom* which gives us insight into reality, and *prudence* which leads us to right courses of action (8). Chapters i—iii of this Epistle demonstrate this wisdom; chapters iv—vi deal with practical matters of prudence.

The mystery of his will (9). The word 'mystery' in the New Testament has not its modern sense of something perplexing and unintelligible, but of something undiscoverable by human reason which has now been made the subject of revelation by God. It is a divine secret that has now been revealed. See notes on Col. i. 26. *Purposed in himself* (9); better, as in RV, 'purposed in him', referring to Christ, through whose work it was to take effect. *Dispensation* (10), lit. 'house management'; in the terms of our subject it refers to the carrying out by the Son of the Father's purpose when the time was ripe, i.e. in the gospel era. *Gather together in one* (RV 'to sum up') *all things in Christ* (10) indicates the totality of the universe, and not simply the Church, as in v. 23; cf. Col. i. 18. This ultimate totality is to be brought under Christ as Head: this is the hidden truth, the mystery, that is now revealed. Thus will be brought to an end the discordances and confusions of earth. But this is to be accomplished only *in Christ*. This truth is to be correlated with Jn. i. 3, 'all things were made by him', and Col. i. 16f., 'through him and unto him they have been created: in him all things consist' (see RV). The broken unity is to be at last restored, and its restoration is to be effected through Christ. How far then was He from being merely the national Messiah of Jewish expectation! Even 'the Saviour of the world' is not a great enough designation for Him: He is the Saviour of the universe. See also Rom. viii. 18–25.

In verse 11 Paul returns to more mundane things and deals with Jews (11), then with Gentiles (13), and then with Jew and Gentile (14). He does this to show the place of Jew and Gentile in the purpose of God. He states this in terms drawn from the Jewish Scriptures with which he, if not all his readers, had a perfect familiarity. Note the specially significant change here from the AV, *in whom also we have obtained an inheritance*, to the RV, 'in whom also we were made a heritage' (11). This to Paul was the fulfilment of Dt. xxxii. 8ff. *According to the purpose* (11). Matters are not really at the mercy of men. That the divine purpose is achieved, not by

outward constraint but by the inward working in the heart, is suggested by the verb *worketh*, which is really 'inworketh'. *Who first trusted* (12); a reference to the priority of Jewish Christians in the matter of time over Gentile believers (cf. Rom. ii. 10). All the first Christians, so far as we know, were Jews; and the admission of Gentiles was looked upon as quite a novelty. See Acts x and xv.

c. The sealing of the Holy Spirit (i. 13, 14)

Having indicated the historical priority of Jewish Christians in the Church Paul hastens to include the Gentiles, for most of his readers (in Asia Minor) would not be Jews. Yet they also, his Gentile readers, were chosen of God, and having *heard the word of truth* they believed; and the reality of their conversion and acceptance is assured by the power of the Spirit working in them; they were *sealed with that holy Spirit of promise* (13). This too had been a part of God's ancient promise (see Gal. iii. 14; Acts ii. 38, x. 47). The gift of the Holy Spirit to the Gentiles was both God's authentication of the Gentile converts at the time (Acts x. 47), and their foretaste of the fulness of blessing in the future. This latter is expressed in two ways. First Paul takes a metaphor from mercantile life, *the earnest of our inheritance* (14), which refers to a pledge deposited for a time and ultimately claimed back; then it came to mean an instalment and proof of the *bona fide* nature of the bargain. Secondly he tells his readers, 'Ye have been sealed unto the redemption of God's own possession' (see RV). The full emancipation of God's people is still in the future (Mal. iii. 17), but it is sure, for they are in Christ and are sealed in Him by the Holy Spirit. The refrain, *the praise of his glory*, occurring for the third time, closes this wonderful doxology.

III. THANKSGIVING FOR SPIRITUAL STATE OF READERS. i. 15–23

Wherefore (15) gathers up into one connecting word the whole revelation of God's purpose as unfolded in the previous verses (3–14). That revelation shows faith to be part of such a significant and tremendous whole that Paul cannot but *give thanks for you* (16). Paul's interest was centred in his readers' *faith . . . and love* (15). For these evidences of the spiritual state of believers he often looked with keenest eagerness (see Rom. i. 8; Col. i. 4n.; 1 Thes. i. 3; 2 Thes. i. 3; Phm. 5). On the increase of faith and love, rather than on merely outward and organizational success, we should concentrate too.

Cease not to give thanks for you (16). Paul's prayers were particular and pointed, and in them there was direct mention of the churches and the believers in which he was interested (Rom. i. 9; 1 Thes. i. 2; Phm. 4). The solemnity that Paul attaches to prayer and the encouragement he found in it are indicated by the title he gives to God (17). Though he prayed much, Paul never brought prayer into contempt by a spirit of thoughtless and irreverent familiarity. He draws encouragement and hope from the relationship of Jesus Christ and God, the Father to whom glory belongs. The prayer seeks for the believers a special gift of the Holy Spirit in relation to knowledge, a *spirit of wisdom and revelation*, not in general, but *in the knowledge of him. Revelation* here means 'unveiling' (cf. 2 Cor. iii. 12–17). Paul prays here that the experience he already had been given (Eph. iii. 3) should be granted to his readers. Elementary faith is not sufficient for the later stages of the Christian life. Paul's thankfulness of verse 15 does not preclude the prayer of verses 18ff. It is the purpose of God that knowledge, and other things too, be added to it (see 2 Pet. i. 5). *The eyes of your understanding* (18); RV reads 'the eyes of your heart'. Such wisdom is far from being mere intellectual knowledge. The mind alone cannot grasp the truth of God; the heart of man, his affections and especially his will, must all be bent to the task. Otherwise the essential part of divine revelation will escape the student, leaving only an unsatisfying and incomprehensible framework within his grasp. In this lies the explanation of much barren intellectual study of Scripture.

The prayer that his readers *may know* is now expanded in three clauses. The first refers to the past; i.e. to God's call, looked at from its stronger side, the side on which our assurance depends. The believer rests not upon his own imperfect acceptance of God's call, but upon the fact that what he has heard and responded to is the call of God the Father of glory (cf. 1 Thes. v. 24). The second clause refers to the future, the believer's glorious destiny, *the riches of the glory of his inheritance in the saints* (18). The viewpoint is still the same: it is not the aspect of the believer's inheritance that is in view but 'the riches of the glory' of God's inheritance in His people. Again, as in verse 11, the thought is that of Dt. xxxii. 9. The third reference is to the present; the power that works now in the believer and on his behalf is nothing less than 'the strength of his might which he wrought in Christ' when He raised and exalted Him (19–23; see RV). For *heavenly places* (20), see i. 3n.

Verse 21 embraces all distinctions, titles and powers of the spiritual world: all without exception are placed under the exalted Christ (cf. Col. i. 16n.). The train of thought that is found here can be traced throughout Scripture, from the original promise made by God to our first parents in the Garden of Eden (Gn. i. 26), through the prophetic renewal of the promise in Ps. viii. 4–6 (cf. verse 22), to the inspired commentary on it in Heb. ii. 6–9. Only in Christ can mankind achieve the promised destiny. Throughout his Epistles Paul emphasizes two points in regard to the relation of Christ and the Church, union and headship: Christ and His people are one, and He is their Head. In the figure here (23) this is strikingly expressed by the metaphor of a human body in which welfare depends upon the union of head and body, and also on the government of the body by the head (cf. Col. i. 18n.). In the further description of the Church, *the fulness of him that filleth all in all* (23), it is seen as something without which Christ is not complete. This is true, not from any defect in the Godhead which the Church makes up, but simply by the will of the Father who *gave him to be the head over all things to the church* (22). As He is Head of the Church, so the Church is His fulness.

IV. THEIR RELATION (AS SINNERS) TO CHRIST. ii. 1–10

In his highest flights of inspired insight and oratory Paul never loses sight of the practical end he had in view, which is the spiritual welfare of his readers. So here he returns from the contemplation of the glory of the exalted Lord to the pressing needs of those whom he addresses. The main verb of the opening sentence is to be found in verse 5, *hath quickened.* The thread of thought is somewhat broken by a lengthened explanation of what *dead* (1) means, and the implications of the state to which it refers (2, 3). It is not a physical condition, but is the spiritual state of the living brought about by *trespasses and sins* (1); although it also includes physical death which is the penalty of sin (Rom. vi. 23). In it lies the necessity of regeneration or the new birth (Jn. iii. 3) and the more abundant life (Jn. x. 10). Its origin is to be found in the fall of man and in his consequent separation from God (Gn. iii); its healing lies in union with Christ (5). Readers can best learn what Paul means by consulting their own experience in the past when their course of life was governed by the world around them, as seemed only natural and inevitable and proper at the time (2). But the hidden and unrecognized impulse of life in unregenerate days was really Satan himself, *the prince of the power of the air,* the controlling force in *the course of this world.* Satan's is not a supreme authority, which belongs to God alone; but an authority exercised by permission of God (cf. Jb. i). It is a part of the significance of the fall that mankind, hitherto under the control and guidance of God, came under the spiritual dominion and direction of Satan. Because this government of evil has so long been the rule among natural man, it is unrecognized and counted simply 'human nature'. But it is shown plainly here, without making it a source of excuse for men, that mighty spiritual forces of wickedness are in control of the natural man: they are summed up in *the spirit that now worketh in the children* (RV 'sons') *of disobedience* (2). We can then wonder but little at the past history, present state and future outlook (i.e. *the course*) of the world. Indeed, but for the restraints of God, irremediable catastrophe must long ago have overtaken mankind (see 2 Thes. ii. 7).

This is very severe doctrine, true indeed, but painful and humbling. So Paul seeks to sôften the distress it must cause by sharing the burden, and the *ye* of verse 2, indicating the Gentiles, is changed to *we* in verse 3 (including the specially favoured Jewish race). 'Among whom we also all once lived' (3, RV) is a tremendous admission for a Jew to make, but Paul had so learned Christ that he presents this confession, not as an admission unwillingly drawn from him, but as one of the profound facts of divine revelation. *By nature the children of wrath* (3); i.e. of God's wrath. This is a Hebrew idiom asserting the essential depravity in human nature following on the fall of man, commonly called 'original sin'.

The dark picture that Paul has painted of men in the state of nature under this domination is now used as the background against which the glorious riches of God's mercy are shown (4). The *ye* and the *we all* give way to *but God*; nor can anything else but the intervention of God turn aside the evil course of men's lives from inevitable and irretrievable disaster to the secure achievement of a noble destiny. *Mercy* and *love* (4) were elements in the impulse which moved God to help us; never is there any hint that there was anything in fallen man that was the cause or impulse of God's redeeming work. The ultimate reason is that of Jn. iii. 16, or as here *his great love*. The greatness of divine love is emphasized by a recurrence of the thought of man's lost and ruined condition by nature, *even when we were dead in sins* (5). The blessing bestowed upon man by the work of Christ is that of new life, for the dead need to be *quickened* before anything else can be done for them, or by them. As Jesus put it to Nicodemus, 'Ye must be born again' (Jn. iii. 7). It is only in union with Christ that men can have new life: they are raised, not by themselves, but *together with Christ*; or, as the RV mg. gives it, 'in Christ', which is the thought of i. 3, 7, 13, 20. Everything in our redemption depends on our having a close and vital relationship with Him who has wrought all things for us: His part will not fail, and it is our part to come unto Him. Here, therefore, Paul interjects a clause to indicate that all our salvation in its completeness (the verb is in the perfect tense) is owing to the free favour of God. This thought implicit in 'quickened when dead' is central in all Paul's writings.

In phrases that are parallel to those of i. 20, Paul now expresses the steps in God's work for us (6). Just as Christ died for us, so He rose from the dead for us, and for us ascended up on high; and as the Christian can truly say 'I have been crucified with Christ' (Gal. ii. 20, RV), so he is taught that he has a part in the resurrection and ascension of Christ. We too readily think of these events of resurrection and ascension and enthronement as associated with Christ alone. Here we can see how far wrong that conception is. While these experiences are yet objects of hope

for us, Jesus has really experienced them and possessed them for us. The work of Christ is our salvation and has reference not to us alone but also to a wider and vaster circle (7). Far beyond the time and conditions in which we now live it is God's purpose to show forth *the exceeding riches of his grace in his kindness toward us through Christ Jesus*. His grace and mercy to us will be held in everlasting remembrance. The phrase 'in Christ Jesus' (see RV) retains the pervading thought of union with Christ.

Paul again emphasizes the greatness of God's love in undertaking the work of man's salvation: it is entirely *by grace* (8). The word *that* has occasioned some controversy because of the difficulty of determining the grammatical connection. It has often been referred to faith, and faith has in consequence been called *the gift of God*. But it is more probable that the neuter form of *that* embraces the entire sense of the clause *by grace are ye saved through faith*. *Not of works* (9) defines more closely the sense of *not of yourselves* (8). Man's natural and almost ineradicable tendency to boast has no place in the divine scheme of salvation. The thought of this verse is illustrated and expanded in Rom. iv. 1–5. *For we are his workmanship* (10). Just as the words of Psalm c. 3 refer in similar terms to the first creation of man, so here Paul points to man's re-creation in Christ Jesus as being wholly a divine work. For the idea of a new creation, see 2 Cor. v. 17; Gal. vi. 15, RV mg. While Paul gave no place to works in the matter of regeneration (see Rom. iv as above), he insisted that they had their essential place in the life of the believer as a consequence of regeneration: *created in Christ Jesus unto* (RV 'for') *good works*. Compare Jas. ii. 14ff. There is no dispute between Paul and James, but a difference of emphasis. The works of which Paul speaks in this verse are not the outcome of the believer's own bright ideas but the guidance of God, who had 'afore prepared that we should walk in them' (RV). The Christian should live within a divinely planned economy, a way of life prepared by God. This is the true planning and the true life.

V. THEIR RELATION (AS GENTILES) TO JEWS. ii. 11–22

Wherefore remember (11) points to a train of thought that meant more perhaps to Paul than to anybody else, for he had been foremost in fighting the long battle for the recognition of Gentile Christians on an equal footing with Jewish Christians. Something of that battle would probably be known to his readers. It was chiefly to the efforts of Paul that these readers, the *Gentiles in the flesh*, owed their place and standing in the Christian Church: but for him they might have been relegated by the early Church to a subordinate status, or even to a separate and secondary Gentile Christian church. In this verse Paul stresses the great division which they had experienced in their unregenerate days, calling upon them to remember what they had been in the past in contrast to what they now are. As Gentiles they were the uncircumcision, not having in their bodies the sign of the covenant: this is the meaning of *Gentiles in the flesh* (11). Their greatest loss was not their separation from Judaism but from God. *Without Christ* (12), RV 'separate from Christ', is the opposite of 'in Christ', the keynote of this Epistle. The Jews had hope in *the covenants of promise* (of the Messiah; cf. Acts xiii. 32f.), but the Gentiles had no hope at all. A godless world is a hopeless world; the godless life is a life without hope. Here alone in the New Testament the word *atheos, without God*, is used (12). They were without God, not as having been forsaken by Him (for they were not), but as not knowing or trusting Him. It is a solemn thought that all who are not 'in Christ' are really atheists in the sight of God. How great an inspiration this should be for the spread of the evangel! On the other hand they were *in the world* (12) as Christians are 'in Christ'. In it their treasure and their heart lay (see Mt. vi. 19-21, 33).

But now in Christ Jesus (13). A similar contrast is found in verse 4, 'but God'. Their condition when their interests were centred in the world and they were 'separate from Christ' has been described; now their new condition *in Christ Jesus* is presented. The terms *far off* and *nigh* recur in verse 17 in a context that looks back to Is. lvii. 19 (cf. Dt. iv. 7). The *far off* are the Gentiles: the *nigh* are the Jews. To the blood of Christ there was ascribed in i. 7 redemption: here the emphasis is on the bringing together of those whom sin had separated by a wall of bitterness and hatred. Only in *the blood of Christ* can men and nations find the true and only possible and practicable solution to those problems of the world which centre in race and class. The figure used is one common in the Old Testament, where every compact and covenant between God and man was ratified by a sacrifice. On the individual level see Gn. xv; and on the national level, Ex. xxiv. See also Mk. xiv. 24. It would seem that in verse 14, with the force of Is. lvii. 19 growing in his mind, Paul allows it further to govern his thought and to suggest the concept of *peace* which it contains, applying t to the Person of the Lord Jesus. The action of he Saviour is seen here in bringing together those who had long been kept apart by pride and hatred; and this union is brought about, not by an external act of Christ merely, but only in fellowship with Him, for *he is our peace*, and this union is so close that the two parties become one. This is no mere armistice but an enduring peace.

The *middle wall of partition* (14) is a metaphor for all that separated Jew and Gentile, and owes its force to the existence of an actual wall in the temple which separated the court of the Gentiles (the outermost court, and that to which alone

the Gentiles had access) from those inner courts which were open to Jews. There has been found on the site of the ancient temple in Jerusalem one of the inscribed stones of this wall, on which can still be seen the threat of death on any Gentile who would intrude farther. Just as this wall in the temple was a physical barrier between Gentile and Jew, so the Mosaic *law of commandments contained in ordinances* (15) was the significant element in their moral separation (and also in the separation between men and God). But when Christ was crucified the veil of the temple was rent, indicating the end of the legal ordinances as the way of life for the believer, and opening up a direct access to God for both Jew and Gentile (cf. verse 18 with Heb. x. 19). Note the parallel passage in Col. ii. 14, where the same thought is expressed in different terms. In verse 14 we have the phrase *made both one*; but in verse 15 there is a great advance in thought, and the concept of the new creation enters. The *twain* were Jew and Gentile: the *one new man* is the Christian. Hitherto the concept of unity had in view the healing of the breach between Jew and Gentile, but now it is seen to include, and indeed spring from, the healing of the breach between men and God by the atoning work of Christ. Through this new creation peace comes; and the world is constantly finding that it cannot come otherwise. The reconciliation wrought by Christ is described in verse 16 as affecting *both*, i.e. the 'twain' of verse 15, and *in one body* is parallel to the previous 'one new man'. On Calvary Jesus put an end to the great obstacle to peace, which is enmity: He had *slain the enmity thereby*, i.e. by the cross. This is true of enmity between man and man indeed, but primarily of enmity between man and God. The thought of Is. lvii. 19 still lingers in the writer's mind.

Came (17) refers not to the incarnation but to the proclamation of the peace that had been secured by the work of Christ described in verses 14-16. This preaching of Christ, *to you which were afar off* (Gentiles) and *to them that were nigh* (Jews), was by the Spirit through apostles and teachers. It came to both these great divisions of humanity by the work of the Holy Spirit (18) who led Jew and Gentile alike, the 'one body' of verse 16, to the Father by virtue of Christ's sacrificial work. The *foreigners* (19), RV 'sojourners', were a class of residents who were recognized by law and were allowed certain definite privileges. But their very name suggested that their position was not a permanent one; they resided on sufferance only, and had no rights of citizenship. Such might have been the permanent position of Gentiles in the Church but for the powerful and successful advocacy of Paul himself. *Saints* (19) is used in its essential meaning of a people who are holy and separated in virtue of their calling. It was a coveted term among the Jews, but it is here given by Paul the wider meaning that has reference to the Christian Church, because the Christian Church has inherited both the promises and the privileges of Judaism (see 1 Pet. ii. 9).

The political metaphor now gives place to a domestic one. *The household of God* (19) as a figure of the Church has reference to a closer, warmer fellowship than is suggested by political phrases: they were members of one family. The figure then changes again, slightly this time, from the household to the structure of the house itself. In that structure the *apostles and prophets* are foundation stones (20), while the chief stone of all is *Jesus Christ himself*. Other aspects of the same truth are seen in the use of the same metaphor in a rather different way in 1 Cor. iii. 11. Cf. Is. xxviii. 16. For the relation of the new building to the old, see Acts xv. 16f., and the passage in Amos quoted there. It must be remembered that metaphors express only aspects of the truth and that many figures are required to build up a complete picture. The meaning of verse 21 is governed by the Greek word used for *temple*. Two words are translated 'temple' in the New Testament: *naos*, the central building of all, the shrine itself; and *hieron*, all the buildings within the outer walls. The use of *naos* here points to the sense (if we accept the RV) 'in whom every building (within the holy precincts) groweth into (or is built into or joined with) the most holy shrine itself'. Many authorities still prefer the AV rendering which gives the sense 'in whom all the building (the holy shrine itself, the *naos* alone is brought into the picture) groweth (as each believer is added to the structure; see 1 Pet. ii. 4) into an holy temple in the Lord'. *In the Lord* takes the place of the 'in Christ' which has occurred so frequently in the earlier verses. The influence of Old Testament conceptions is insistent. Hitherto it had been a source of pride to the Jew that God's dwelling was among them (Ex. xxv. 8); but now Christians, as they are built into the growing Church, are 'an habitation of God in the Spirit' (22, RV).

VI. THE MYSTERY OF THE GOSPEL.
iii. 1–21

Paul returns now to the subject of *the mystery* (3; cf. i. 9f. and see Col. i. 26n.), this time with special emphasis on the unique relationship it bore to his own experience. The course of thought begun in the first verse is broken at the end of it and is not resumed until verse 14, where the phrase *for this cause* recurs. The intervening verses contain what is logically a digression, but is also a noble and majestic utterance of the highest things. The line of thought that Paul had begun is overwhelmed by the recollection of how the mystery had been made known to him, 'the least of all the saints' (8, RV).

The thought expressed in *the prisoner of Jesus Christ* (1) is one that must have sweetened all the apostle's experience of imprisonment—an experience to which a man so active and earnest must have found it difficult to make a satisfactory adjustment. By accepting it as the will of his

ster, hard lot though it was, he makes the very best of it and through it glorifies and serves his Lord. Paul quietly reminds his Gentile readers that his imprisonment, which was at the instigation of Jewish hostility, was due to his advocacy of the full rights and freedom of the Gentiles in the Christian Church. The one party in this matter which he does not mention is his actual gaolers, the Romans. The sense of the conditional clause in verse 2 may be expressed by the colloquial phrase 'Surely you have heard'. Many of his readers had never seen him, but the news of his work and especially of the central revelation of which he was made a minister had gone widely abroad. *Grace* (2); not the grace of individual salvation but that of the whole wide gospel that he had received by revelation from God. This gospel was not the product of his own imagination, nor a tradition inherited from his forefathers, nor a matter passed on to him by the apostles of our Lord, but a special *revelation* from God (3). *Wrote afore in a few words* (3), i.e. in the earlier verses of this Epistle (i. 9ff.). A study of that passage would be sufficient to give his readers an inkling of his understanding in the mystery of Christ. This is not self-praise or pride, but a simple acknowledgment of God's work in him in granting him insight into the deep things of God. Though he himself had been the chief channel of communication by which God had made known this mystery, he embraces in that act of revelation the *holy apostles and prophets* (5). See, for example, the case of Philip and the Ethiopian eunuch (Acts viii. 26ff.), and the case of Peter and Cornelius (Acts x). The *prophets* here are not the Old Testament prophets but the New Testament order referred to in ii. 20.

Paul now unfolds the substance of *the mystery* more fully than he had yet done. It is, not simply that the Gentiles might have part in the common salvation, but specifically 'that the Gentiles are fellow-heirs, and fellow-members of the body, and fellow-partakers of the promise in Christ Jesus through the gospel' (6, RV). The RV reiteration of the term 'fellow-' represents a similar repetition in the original Greek of the prefix *syn-* meaning 'together with': a reiteration that is so significant that it must be preserved. It is indeed the essence of the revelation. The Gentiles were not to be saved with a salvation of their own, with meaner blessings appropriate to their outcast state; but they had part, an equal part, in the salvation which the Jew enjoyed. They were 'fellow-heirs' in relation to Jewish believers; 'fellow-members of the body' in relation to Christ the Head; and 'fellow-partakers of the promise' in relation to the historic promises of God. *The gift of the grace of God* (7). Paul was ever conscious of the wonderful work of grace that God had wrought in him (Gal. i. 15f.), and he makes frequent reference to it as in verse 8; see also Col. i. 24ff. *Less than the least of all saints* (8); a phrase of deep humility inserted lest any reader should think that there was any self-exaltation in what he says. See also 1 Cor. xv. 9. *The unsearchable riches of Christ* (8). The gospel is not simply teaching, nor a mere indication of a way of life; it is 'riches in incalculable measure'. The wide extent of God's purpose was nothing less than *to make all men see* the truth: that is the particular truth of which the apostle had in a special manner been given the 'stewardship' (9, RV mg.). The newly revealed truth was not a new thought on the part of God, nor any divergence from the original plan, forced upon Him by the course of events. It was *hid in God, who created all things* (9), and therefore existed from the beginning. But God had not made it plain until now. Besides the salvation of the Gentiles, a further purpose of this revelation of the age-old mystery is the instruction of created intelligences other than men in the *manifold wisdom of God* (10). *Heavenly places* (10); see i. 3n. The special instrument of instruction to these other-world beings is *the church*; not the individual Christian, nor the body ecclesiastic, but that unity of believers of all nations and of all eras of which Christ is the Head. God's *eternal purpose . . . in Christ Jesus* (11) had in view not men alone but 'the whole creation' (cf. Rom. viii. 19–21).

But the more immediate and personal consequence for Christ's work is that believers are by faith given holy confidence to draw near to God (12; see RV). A fresh reference to his imprisonment (13) concludes the parenthesis begun by the previous reference to it in verse 1. Paul's own unquenchable faith in God's eternal purpose is seen in his exhortation that they should not be despondent because of his sufferings for them. The ultimate end, their *glory*, must always be kept in view.

The repetition of *for this cause* (14, cf. verse 1) shows that the apostle is resuming the thought, which has been broken by the parenthesis of verses 2–13. What follows is in the form of a prayer, the ground of which is the whole wonderful work of God as he has come to know it by revelation and as he has been unfolding it earlier in chapter ii. *I bow my knees* (14). The customary attitude of prayer among the Jews was that of standing (Lk. xviii. 11); a kneeling posture was expressive of special solemnity or unusual urgency (Lk. xxii. 41; Acts vii. 60). The significance of the phrase is heightened when we note that a favourite text of Paul was Is. xlv. 23 (see Rom. xiv. 11; Phil. ii. 10). This prayer (or perhaps it should be regarded as the closing part of the prayer begun in i. 17–23) begins with a reference to *the Father* (cf. i. 17). The thought is not easily translated into English because, while our word *family* (15) is not derived from 'father', the Greek *patria* (family) is derived from *patēr* (father). The best sense is gained by taking the RV mg. 'fatherhood' and giving it not only a sense like that of 'family' but also the much wider sense demanded by the clause *in heaven and earth*. How wide the sweep of Paul's thought ever is (see also i. 10–21)! We see by this that the Fatherhood of God is not a mere metaphor drawn from human relationships. The very opposite is the case. God is the Father; the archetype of all fatherhood is seen in the Godhead, and all other fatherhoods are derived from Him.

The first petition, as in i. 17, is for the working of the Spirit in the heart of the believer (16). In i. 17 the desire is especially for knowledge (i.e. revelation); here it is especially for power (i.e. realization). In i. 19 the knowledge of God's 'mighty power' is sought; in iii. 16 Paul prays that his readers may experience that power, so that the acquirement of the knowledge sought may be made possible (18). Cf. 1 Cor. ii. 14. The second petition is for the indwelling of Christ (17). They are 'in Christ' as believers; that is their standing before God. The prayer here is that they may realize the converse of this, which is a matter of human experience and should be realized in human experience. Christ should dwell in their hearts. This is the consequence of being in Christ, and is dependent also on the exercise of *faith* by the believer. This indwelling is to be expressed in the life of Christians by love which is an essential correlative of faith (cf. i. 15n.). They are both elements in the strength needed to comprehend the revealed truth of God, and without the strength which the Spirit supplies through them the mind of man, even of the believer, must fail to grasp the revelation that God has given. Even when endowed with the fulness of spiritual strength, no single saint can by himself hope to grasp the fulness of divine truth: it is God's purpose that we should *comprehend with all saints* (18). Only the whole Church in its entirety can hope to come within sight of the fulness of God's revelation. This is a humbling thought. Because *the love of Christ . . . passeth knowledge* (19) the apprehending of it remains an ideal; it is something never attained but always capable of being more nearly approached. Knowledge is not the end of the blessing for which Paul prays, but a deeper experience still, *that ye might be filled with* (RV 'unto') *all the fulness of God.* See also Col. ii. 9. The tense of the verb *filled* (aorist) suggests that this experience is not looked upon as something gradually acquired, but is thought of as some positive experience of the believer.

There follows a mighty doxology. Paul has prayed for great things, but he is conscious that his highest thoughts and aspirations do not strain the resources of God. So he goes further, and prays that God may work far beyond the hopes and imaginings of any human heart, beyond *all that we ask or think* (20). His hope and assurance in this is the fact that the power of the Spirit of Christ *worketh in us*. God is to be glorified 'in the church and in Christ Jesus' (21, RV); the Church is the Body of which Christ is the Head, and the two here are looked upon as inseparable (see i. 23).

VII. THE UNITY OF THE SPIRIT.

iv. 1–16

Paul here hands on the torch to others. He has carried it long and faithfully. Now he is a *prisoner of* (RV 'in') *the Lord* (1). He can preach and he can write; but the sphere in which he can put into practice the principles of the gospel has been narrowed to a prison-house. It is for others, his readers, to show to the world at large how Christian truth can be carried into action in the life of every day. *I therefore . . . beseech you* (1). The standard set for the Christian life is the transcendently high one indicated by the utterance of the preceding chapters. The apostle has left his readers in no doubt that the responsibilities attending *the vocation wherewith ye are called* are very great; but always there is 'the power that worketh in us' (iii. 20), without which there can be no success and with which there can be no final failure. The 'high calling' of Christians (cf. Phil. iii. 14) is not to lead to pride. The simple, humble virtues of verse 2, which cannot be maintained by the natural heart of man, are essentials in the Christian's daily life. Pagan thought, ancient and modern, commonly treats them with repugnance, and looks upon them as vices. The Christian must take his stand on God's revealed truth, and on the power of the Spirit within to fulfil the good purpose of God in human lives that are consecrated to Him.

One great essential of the Christian spirit is the ability to make allowance for the failures of others, *with longsuffering, forbearing one another in love*. A chief aim of this course of action is the maintenance of *the unity of the Spirit in the bond of peace* (3). The many breaches that have been made in Christian unity all down the history of the Church have been due, not so much to great crimes and malevolent intentions on the part of one and another, not even to vast and profound differences of opinion, but almost wholly to the lack of these simple, essential Christian graces on which hangs the unity of all.

This unity is not one the Christian has to achieve, but one which exists already and which he is *to keep* (3). The reality of that unity is now unfolded. It is seen to be sevenfold, and the elements fall into three groups around the three Persons of the Godhead. There is first *one body*, the Church, which owes its existence and its unity to the *one Spirit*, and which moves in the power of that Spirit toward one goal of *hope* (4). Secondly there is *one Lord*, even Jesus Christ, who is the great object of the *one faith* by which men believe unto salvation, and who has given to the Church the initiatory sacrament of *one baptism* (5). Thirdly there is *one God and Father of all*, who is the supreme source of that unity (6).

The unity of the whole having been emphasized, Paul now turns to the parts that make up the whole, namely, individual Christians. These parts are not mechanically uniform but possess an individuality that God recognizes and uses in His service. Cf. Rom. xii, where similar thoughts arise. In verse 7 the apostle generalizes a truth about God's gift of grace, to which he had repeatedly referred, so far as his own experience of it was concerned, in chapter iii. (See iii. 2, 7f., where he identified his own mission to the Gentiles with this gift of grace.) Now he points to 'each one of us' (RV) as possessing a similar but individually distinct gift of grace. The difference in these gifts is not assigned to natural ability or capacity but to *the measure of the gift of Christ*. Cf. 1 Cor. xii. 1–11n. This giving of gifts is associated with the ascension of Christ (8; cf. i. 19f.). The thought here is referred to the figure of a victorious king (cf. Col. ii. 15n.) distributing the spoils of war, as suggested by Ps. lxviii. 18. In this Psalm God is viewed as leading His people in triumph through the wilderness (verses 4, 7), and through Bashan (verse 15), and then sweeping in the majesty of twenty thousand chariots to Zion (verse 17). Paul points to this Psalm as foreshadowing the triumphant ascension of Christ. (See further Jn. vii. 39 where the central gift is indicated; and cf. Acts ii.)

Paul explains his reference in verse 8 by a parenthesis in verses 9, 10. The descent here spoken of is probably that from heaven to earth at the incarnation; this is a sufficient explanation, but some would give it the more extended application suggested by 1 Pet. iii. 18f. The identity of the One who suffered humiliation on earth and then exaltation in heaven is emphasized in verse 10. This exaltation fulfilled one great purpose of God, *that he might fill all things* (see also i. 23).

In verse 11 five orders of ministry are mentioned, detailing some of the 'gifts' of verse 8. The familiar terms 'bishops', 'presbyters', 'deacons' do not appear, and it has been suggested that the reason lies in the fact that these three terms refer to local officers in the churches, while Paul has here in view the Church as a whole and therefore refers to orders that serve the Church at large. See also 1 Cor. xii. 28n. As the history of the Church progressed all the functions of ministry were drawn into the three local forms. The true significance of verse 12 depends on taking the second clause as dependent on the first as in RV (the AV makes them co-ordinate): 'for the perfecting of the saints, unto the work of ministering.' The purpose for which Christ gives to His Church such gifts as are mentioned is not that those who receive them should be His sole servants in the Church and in the world, but that, through them, every member of the Church might be inspired to serve His Lord. Yet 'the work of ministering' has been so largely confined to the officers of the churches that the Church itself, 'the body of Christ', has not been built up as it should; for only a few have wrought while a mass of church members have watched, all unconscious of their divinely ordained duty.

Edifying (RV 'building up') *of the body of*

Christ (12) combines Paul's two favourite figures of the Church, referring to its structural and its organic unity (cf. 1 Cor. iii. 16, 17, xii. 12–27n.). He is not afraid to use mixed metaphors, for he speaks of the temple as 'growing' (ii. 21), and here of the body being 'built'. On the divine side there is a unity already existing (4–6); on the human side it is something that must be attained by the Church through the right and proper use of the gifts spoken of above. Progress in *the knowledge of the Son of God* (13) is essential to the advancement of this unity. The conception of 'a fullgrown man' (13, RV) carries on this idea of unity. Our advancement is not to be along the lines of individualism, as though God's purpose were the production of great men. Individualism is to give place to a corporate oneness in which the whole will attain unto something far beyond the reach of the individual, *the measure of the stature of the fulness of Christ*. Individualism is an indication of the immaturity of childhood. This is the contrast made here; we are to be 'full-grown' men, not *children . . . carried about with every wind of doctrine* (14). The uncertainty and instability of childhood as well as its individualism are in Paul's mind. Little ships are at the mercy of wind and waves in a fashion and to an extent unknown by great vessels. The winds are a figure of the men who teach 'another gospel' (cf. Gal. i. 6–9), and who pervert the truth by their *craftiness*. *Speaking* (15) represents a verb that need not be confined to speech, but covers other forms of witness as well. In this uncontroversial Epistle Paul does not attempt either a statement of particular forms of error or a detailed rebuttal of such. He indicates a positive line of action that is calculated to be the best safeguard against the inroads of all kinds of error. Attack is the best defence. A second element here in resistance to error is the presentation of a common front to the enemy. Progress (*grow up*) is not to be along individualistic lines, but is to be governed by the demands of unity. It is to be *into him . . . even Christ* (15), a repetition of the thought in verse 13. This growth is to embrace not merely the most essentially religious elements in life, but *all things*. It is to be governed, not by the diverse wills of individual members of the body, but by him *which is the head, even Christ* (15).

In verse 16 Paul has in view the whole wonderful and complicated structure of the human body as it is solidly bound together by its appropriate bands and ligaments (see the parallel passage, Col. ii. 19, and cf. 1 Cor. xii. 12–27). In this he acknowledges and marks the place and influence of *every part* as it works 'in due measure' only (see RV): and so, by the proper functioning of the individual part, a coherent and harmonious structure is reared. Again the apostle is unable to avoid the bringing together of metaphors that indicate both structural and organic unity; both are needed in the presentation of this great truth.

VIII. ETHICAL ELEMENTS OF THE CHRISTIAN LIFE. iv. 17—v. 21

A new aspect of the Christian's *walk* (cf. verse 1) is brought before us here in a review of the ethical elements that are essential to Christian living. Notice the maintenance of this metaphor throughout chapters iv and v (iv. 1, 17; v. 2, 8, 15). Verses 17–19 present the injunction in a negative form: *not as other Gentiles walk* (17). This walk of the Gentiles is shown to be vain, dark, alienated, ignorant; and the reason given for this is 'the hardening of their heart' (18, RV; cf. ii. 12). The expression *vanity of their mind* (17) points to the fact that human reason, without the illumination of God's Spirit, inevitably leads to delusion and failure. This is a hard saying, but the history of mankind bears it out. To have the *understanding darkened* (18) is the natural state of man till the experience of i. 18 comes to him; for he is *alienated from the life of God*. The fact of the fall of man (Gn. iii) is in view here; his present state is the result, not of separation from God simply, but of active alienation. The divine life is something which we ought to have, but have not by nature. *Because of the blindness of their heart* (18); better, as in RV, 'hardness'. The word in the original indicates loss of sensation in general. *Being past feeling* (19); i.e. they have got over the pangs of conscience and now care no longer. This leads to the floodgates of evil being opened as they, of their own will, give themselves up without restraint to indulgence in every possible form of impurity as if it were the chief business of life. A similar line of thought is found in Rom. i. 21–28.

Ye have not so learned Christ (20). In this brief and emphatic phrase Paul turns the minds of his readers from these shocking thoughts to the fountain of all purity, Christ. The *if* of verse 21 is the same construction as in iii. 2, the conditional clause not expressing any doubt in the matter, but for the sake of emphasis calling on the reader to verify the statement made. It has the same sense as 'you heard him, didn't you?' *Learned . . . heard . . . taught* (20, 21); cf. Jn. vi. 45. With the phrase *the truth is in Jesus* (21), cf. Jn. xiv. 6. The instruction they have had in Christ is now indicated negatively and positively. They must have done with their former manner of life, as they would strip off a filthy garment. That old life of self-will is called *the old man*, a favourite metaphor of Paul's. Cf. Rom. vi. 6; Col. iii. 9; cf. also the conception of the first and second Adam, Rom. v. 12–19; 1 Cor. xv. 21–58. The place of *the old man* is to be taken by 'a new creation' (2 Cor. v. 17), *the new man* (24). The call for renewal is of course answered by the power of God, as we see in verse 24. The *new man* is the result of a divine work of creation, in which is fulfilled the demand expressed in another metaphor, 'Ye must be born again' (Jn. iii. 7). The new creation is like God in that it possesses *righteousness and true holiness* (in contrast to the filthiness and deceit of verse 22). The connection of verses 25–31 with what has gone before is emphasized by the use in verse 25 of the same verb, *putting away*, as was used in verse 22, *put off*. Here are the implications and consequences of putting off the old man. Five things are detailed that must be forsaken.

i. Lying (verse 25). The injunction to 'put away falsehood' (*lying*, in a wider sense than that of speech; see RV) is enforced by a quotation from Zc. viii. 16, and by an appeal to the vital union of Christians in the fellowship of the Church.

ii. Sinful anger (verses 26, 27). There is anger that is right and righteous and this fact is brought out by a quotation from the LXX version of Ps. iv. 4. Righteous anger easily passes into resentment when personal feelings begin to control it. Even as God 'will not keep his anger for ever' (Ps. ciii. 9), so men are instructed to keep their anger on a short rein: *let not the sun go down upon your wrath* (see, for the same sentiment, Dt. xxiv. 13–15). To harbour personal anger, or to keep even righteous anger overlong, is to let the devil have his own way in our lives.

iii. Stealing (verse 28). Thieving had probably been the practice of many of the Gentile converts all their lives till their conversion. In moments of temptation the habit might be carried over into the Christian life. The remedy is to forestall the temptation with honest labour, which will provide what is needed, both for personal use and even for the needs of such as are in want. An unwillingness to do an honest day's work is at the root of almost all forms of stealing.

iv. Bad language (verses 29, 30). Foul speech can become a habit so strongly ingrained that it may suddenly burst out in unexpected circumstances; see Mk. xiv. 71. Suppression is not enough, and the cultivation of the positive habit of *that which is good* is the only safe and proper course. We should try to edify or help others by our words, and not simply to entertain them with polite conversation. The position of verse 30 attaches it to evil speaking, and we are confronted by the solemn fact that by our words (of which we think so lightly) we can grieve the Holy Spirit (cf. Mt. xii. 37). Our words should not be a merely instinctive reaction to stimuli, as they too often are. The Holy Spirit should have control of them (see v. 18f.). *Whereby ye are sealed* (30); cf. i. 13n.

v. Bad temper (verse 31). Evil passions express themselves in many ways: they are every one to be *put away* in the 'putting off' of the old man.

Positive injunctions (32) fill the vacuum produced by the negative ones. An essential requirement of Christian fellowship is forgiveness, not kindness or tenderness merely, but forgiveness like the forgiveness of God. See also the emphasis in the Lord's Prayer (Mt. vi. 12–15).

In v. 1 the apostle points to the supreme example, than which there can be no higher. The RV renders literally 'Be ye therefore imitators of God'. The possibility of this being accomplished is indicated by the reference to

sonship, *as dear children*. The metaphor of walking (2) is carried forward from iv. 1, 17, a clear indication of the continuance of the same subject. As in verse 1 the measure of the believer's love is set at the greatest possible height. *As Christ also hath loved us.* He showed His love by giving Himself up *for us*, that is 'on our behalf'. Such is Christian love; not mere sentiment and feeling, but self-sacrifice. *An offering and a sacrifice* (2). The incidental nature of this reference to our Lord's atonement indicates that this view of His death was common ground between Paul and his readers. Both words are used of sacrifices which involve the shedding of blood, but when used together, as here, the word *offering* may have more particular reference to those gifts which did not involve this. The complete fulfilment in Christ of the Old Testament foreshadowings is thus indicated. *For a sweetsmelling savour* (2). Cf. Gn. viii. 21; Lv. i. 9, 13, 17, etc. A phrase taken from the Old Testament and indicating God's acceptance of the sacrifice.

It is clear that certain sins menaced the peace and security of the early Gentile believers in a special manner (3). They had been brought up in them (ii. 1–3), and evidently some professing Christians found them still a strong temptation (see especially Paul's letters to the Corinthians). The only safe course was not even to make mention of such things; the thought of evil was to be excluded as well as the act. This indeed is no more than what is due to their Christian profession. The lesser sins from which the greater develop are next condemned (4). There are many in all classes of society who would not indulge in the grosser sins but who revel in *foolish talking* and *jesting. Not convenient* (4); RV 'not befitting'; cf. 'as becometh saints' in the previous verse. The lips of Christians should constantly be filled with the praise of God; not unctuous, blatant praise which would draw forth the mockery of men, but the unceasing spirit of thankfulness which will find quiet utterance in many ways that cannot but influence the ungodly. See also iv. 29. In verse 5 Paul points out that his readers will certainly understand (the meaning of *for this ye know*) that no one who is given to the gross sins mentioned will have any part in the inheritance he has already referred to as being their portion in Christ (i. 14, iii. 6). Notice the phrase *the kingdom of Christ and of God* and see Mt. xxv. 34 and Jas. ii. 5 for the connection. Verse 6 is a warning against the power of propaganda. Today it may find special application in those who surrender to the wiles of false religionists, who may even go from door to door in their search for the unwary. See also iv. 14. This is no light matter, for *because of these things cometh the wrath of God upon the children of disobedience.*

The avoidance of sin is pressed on the readers by the consideration of their new profession (7). In their old lives of the darkness of unbelief they were *partakers with them* but now they are the light of the world (8; cf. Mt. v. 14). Again the exhortation comes to *walk* as Christians should (cf. iv. 1, 17, v. 1). *Fruit of the Spirit* (9); better, as in RV, 'fruit of the light'. Paul introduces a contrast here between this fruit and *the unfruitful works of darkness* (11). The fruit of light consists in *goodness and righteousness and truth* with an absoluteness that is expressed by *all*. *Proving* (10); by testing everything, the children of the light can avoid being deceived (cf. verse 6), and so come to know what the will of the Lord is. But the Christian is to go beyond the mere avoidance of the *works of darkness* (11); he is to expose to the influence of the light that is in him their true nature and show what they really are (the sense of *reprove;* see RSV). *It is a shame* (12); cf. verse 3n. Much that is in modern newspapers, magazines and novels adds to the difficulty of keeping a clean mind, and provides unsavoury topics for too many people; even for too many Christians. *Whatsoever doth make manifest is light* (13). This rendering by the AV overcomes a difficulty but is doubtful. RV more correctly reads 'everything that is made manifest is light'. In view of what follows it seems best to interpret this as meaning that evil, when exposed in Paul's sense, will have its nature changed. It had happened to his readers in their own experience: they should so shine that it would happen in others too. To emphasize the thought that whatever is exposed to the light is thereby changed Paul quotes some words (14), the source of which is unknown, but which may be from an early Christian hymn (cf. verse 19). They are a call to men to awake to the transforming realization of the light of the world (Jn. viii. 12). For *he saith* (14) RSV reads 'it is said'. For the last time in the Epistle the exhortation to *walk* as becometh a Christian is given (15; cf. also iv. 1, 17, v. 1, 8). They are to exercise the greatest care in this matter, and not to live thoughtlessly, as so many people unwisely do. In this way they will be able to seize every opportunity of doing good in these evil times. *Redeeming* (16); lit. 'buying out'; RSV renders 'making the most of'. The believer's aim must ever be to do *the will of the Lord* (17), and to know what this is must be his first concern. That it can be known by those who seek had long been understood (Ps. xxv. 8f.). The vivid contrast of verse 18 would not so readily have occurred to a modern Christian; but habits of drunkenness were so universal among the heathen populations from which those Gentile Christians had been drawn that such a contrast was indeed an appropriate one. See also Acts ii. 15ff. The drunken seek some supposed 'good' in their excesses, even, perhaps, what they would call 'inspiration'. The true 'good' is to be found in the filling of the Holy Spirit. That which men seek through drunkenness cannot be so found: their hopes are inevitably illusory. All that men seek in satisfaction of their needs and desires is to be found in and by the Holy Spirit. This verse reminds us of the enthusiastic spirit of early Christians. Their religion had not yet cooled into

stereotyped forms and phrases. The noisy, maudlin good fellowship of the drunken is well known, and against it Paul puts the picture of Spirit-filled Christians in a truer fellowship and with nobler songs, encouraging one another and praising God (19). It is no stereotyped form of worship he speaks of, but the spontaneous ebullition of spiritual vigour. The true praise of God is not a superficial and extravagant effervescence: it is a thing of the heart. *Hymns and spiritual songs* (19). An interesting indication that the early Church developed its own poetical expression of worship and praise as well as making use of the Old Testament Psalms. Cf. Col. iii. 16. Some commentators distinguish the two by suggesting that *hymns* may have been sung congregationally, whereas the *spiritual songs* were sung by one person only. The unceasing providence of God (20) is good and sufficient reason for such expressions of praise as have been mentioned. The self-surrender of the Christian to Christ involves a relationship to others that is humble and self-sacrificing (21). This may seem to be a curious admonition to follow an encouragement of the free expression of spiritual enthusiasm such as is found in verse 19. But it is indicative of Christian witness that its boldness is governed by a constant concern for others' feelings and welfare, and is submissive to the loving demands of circumstances and conditions (cf. 1 Cor. xiv. 26–33). The motive for submission is not to be found in those to whom we lovingly submit; we shall look in vain for it there. If we look to them alone we may find it impossible to bring ourselves to submit to them. The motive is to be found in 'the fear of Christ' (RV correctly), which is the New Testament equivalent of the Old Testament 'the fear of the Lord'. The principle stated in this verse now finds its exposition in the sections that follow.

IX. CHRISTIAN RELATIONSHIPS IN FAMILY LIFE. v. 22—vi. 9

In the intimacy of home life Christian ethics are often put to a stringent test. The good ordering of society and of all human relationships depends on a recognition of the divinely revealed principles of subordination, a thought which is developed from the exhortation given in verse 21. These principles Paul now applies to wives and husbands (22, 23), to children and parents (vi. 1–4) and to servants and masters (vi. 5–9). In each case Paul begins at the subordinate end of the scale, with those whose primary responsibility is that of obedience.

a. Wives and husbands (v. 22–33)

Wives, submit yourselves (22). The sentiment of this verse is so far removed from, and contrary to, the common thought of the world today that it must seem to some the very essence of retrogression in civilized social relationships. Have not women attained by the onward march of civilization an equality with man that has always been their natural right, but has only recently come to be recognized? The answer is that in many things, for example spiritual qualities, woman is the natural (and divinely ordained) equal of man. But in the relationships of family life God has ordained a certain order, and in this divine order the wife is to be subject to the husband. See notes on 1 Cor. xi. 2–16 and Col. iii. 18. This subordination does not imply inferiority (see note on vi. 1). The sanction that is given to encourage wives in this divinely ordained course (at which the natural heart may rebel) is found in the words *as unto the Lord*. Because this is a matter in which God has laid down the law, the course of action indicated is to be taken for His sake and as unto Him. Many otherwise insoluble problems would find their solution if this principle were applied to them. It is a divine ordinance for family life that *the husband is the head of the wife* (23), not in any despotic sense, nor in any sense of man's devising, but *even as Christ is the head of the church* (23). The husband must find the pattern of his conduct in the conduct of Christ towards His Church. In that there was no oppression, but self-sacrifice, for He is *the saviour of the body* (the 'body' being the Church as in i. 23, iv. 16). The rule is reiterated for emphasis (24).

The special responsibilities which rest on the headship of the husband are more largely dealt with than those which belong to the subordination of the wife. The heavenly pattern (cf. verses 1, 2) is still insisted on so that the love of Christian husbands for their wives is to be *even as Christ also loved the church*. The relation of the husband to the wife is not to be that of domination, but of self-sacrifice. It is well that wives should learn their lesson from the verses addressed to them, and husbands from these other verses in which they are addressed: not *vice versa*. Paul emphasizes not rights but responsibilities; and it is by fulfilling responsibilities rather than by claiming rights that harmony and happiness will be achieved.

Having introduced the thought of Christ's love for the Church, Paul is led on to develop this theme. The purpose of our Lord in giving Himself for the Church is expressed by the two terms *sanctify* and *cleanse* (26), which refer to the cleansing from sin by His blood and the consequent making holy of the cleansed people by the inward working of the Holy Spirit (cf. verse 2). It is the Church as a whole that is spoken of here, not the individuals that compose it. *The washing* (lit. 'laver') *of water by the word* (26); better, as in RV, 'with the word'. This is an almost certain reference to baptism. *The word* is either the spoken word of faith (cf. Acts xxii. 16; 1 Pet. iii. 21) or the baptismal formula (see Mt. xxviii. 19). *That he might present it to himself* (27). The metaphor of a marriage is continued here. The duty of presenting the bride to the bridegroom would normally be that of the bridegroom's friend. Cf. 2 Cor. xi. 2, where Paul regards himself in this light. Here Christ is both

the one who presents and the one who receives. *Holy and without blemish* (27). Cf. Eph. i. 4 and Col. i. 22. The words have a sacrifi ial connotation (cf. Ex. xii. 5 and 1 Pet. i. 1?), but are used here to show the perfection of Christ's work in His Church. Paul resists the urge that was ever in him to break away from all other topics to speak of the glories of his Lord, and with an effort (it would seem) returns to the subject before him, that of the duty of husbands. Such being the care and ambition of Christ in regard to His Body, the Church, so ought husbands to *love their wives as their own bodies* (28), seeking their welfare in highest things and ever striving towards a more intimate union in the deep things of God. The emphasis now passes from the idea of headship to that of a deep and mysterious oneness (29). The close and intimate union of husband and wife makes it most proper, and in the highest sense natural, that the deepest and highest love should unite them. *Nourisheth . . . cherisheth* (29); provides it with food and looks after its comfort. *Of his flesh, and of his bones* (30). The weight of textual evidence is against the insertion of these words. The strong position that Paul has taken up with reference to the close union of husband and wife might seem to demand a greater weight of evidence than mere assertion. This evidence he now provides (31) by referring to Gn. ii. 24, a passage of which the importance had earlier been indicated by our Lord (Mk. x. 6–9). The cause assigned by the 'therefore' in Gn. ii. 24 referred to the fact that 'she was taken out of man'. The cause here, 'but I speak in regard of Christ and of the church' (RV), points to a far higher sanction, the fact that *we are members of his body* (30). The New Testament sense of *mystery* (32) is 'something hidden that God has now revealed'; here it is the far-reaching revelation of the relation of Christ to the Church (cf. iii. 1–13). Again (33) Paul calls the reader's attention back to the subject of this passage, and summarizes the lessons he has sought to enforce upon husband and wife alike.

b. Children and parents (vi. 1–4)

The relationship of children and parents which in past generations had been so closely knit has in ours lost much of its solidarity and influence. Hence these words are of more importance now than ever before. The verb here (*hypakouō*), which has the sense of 'obeying orders', has an emphasis of 'literal obedience to command' that has no place in the phrase of v. 22, 'submit yourselves' (*hypotassō*), which has the sense of 'arranging in order'. *In the Lord* is a phrase that the writer does not expand or explain, but it is evident that the commands of God cannot be carried out without the grace and power that belong to the indwelling Spirit of the Lord. The law of nature itself gives authority to the parent and demands obedience from the offspring; and the law of God specifically embodies the injunction in the fifth commandment (2), and enforces it with a promise of long life and prosperity to the obedient (3). Right obedience, especially in children, is largely dependent upon the proper exercise of authority on the part of parents (4). A discipline that is harsh, or capricious, can easily discourage the child (see Col. iii. 21). If the parent recognizes that his true guide and example is the Lord, then his *nurture and admonition* (4; RSV 'discipline and instruction') will be fitting and right. Modern methods of child control, in the home, in the church, in the school, and in the juvenile court, may owe much to psychology, but hardly enough to the influence and power of the Spirit of the Lord.

c. Servants and masters (vi. 5-9)

The same word for obedience is used here in verse 5 as in verse 1, implying literal obedience to the word of command. The *servants* were really slaves, or 'bondservants' (*douloi*), but only *according to the flesh;* in spirit and conscience they were free (Gal. iii. 28). It is of greater significance now than ever that the New Testament demands that the mind and heart be left free. Modern slavery aims at the total subjection of the mind and will, as well as of the body, to the mastery of the despot. The obedience of the slave is to be in earnest, *with fear and trembling,* and not from mixed motives or for subtle ends, but *with singleness of heart;* and the high sanction of their service is that it is to be *as unto Christ.* The New Testament neither condones the system of slavery, nor demands its immediate and violent overthrow; but it sowed the seeds of many truths, the growth of which would inevitably bring social slavery to an end. And so it has come about. There is an object lesson of incalculable value in this for all who would be social reformers; especially for those who by coercion and revolution would hasten the slow, divinely adjusted speed of the mills of God. He who made man, to whom the whole human race owes its origin, knows better than any how to bring about salutary and necessary changes without destroying precious things in the process. The service of the slave is to be honest work; not with his eye upon his master, ready to idle when the surveillance has ceased, nor even with the conscientious motive of pleasing an earthly master alone. His one aim must be to please the supreme Lord and Master, Jesus Christ (6). The New Testament sets the standard very high indeed for slaves! How much more do such injunctions apply to those who work under the free and closely protected conditions of modern labour! Yet how far we are from this ideal! To the natural rewards of good and honest service, which seldom fail in the end, is added the great encouragement of a heavenly reward (8); the true worker labours not for men alone, but *as to the Lord* (7; cf. Mt. xxv. 21, 23).

Masters are to have the same spirit and the same ideals as slaves (9). That is to say, they are to do their very best for those who are under them and to seek their interests in everything; they are to be not overbearing but *forbearing,* exercising their rightful authority without threatening. See Phm. 16. The supreme reason for this attitude is the overruling factor in everything, that *your Master also is in heaven,* and He does not respect the individual rights of the master any more highly than those of the slave. The outstanding merit of this passage is that, amid social conditions in which there was much evil, no attempt is made to present a (necessarily controversial) program of social reform; but a message is given in which a basic morality and spiritual principles are laid down, applicable to the conditions existing at the time, and the effects of which will inevitably produce changes of a kind and of a degree most salutary to the welfare of mankind.

X. THE CHRISTIAN WARFARE. vi. 10-20

From giving guidance to particular classes the apostle now turns to the whole circle of the Christian community, and speaks of an external enemy from whom assaults are to be expected, unfolding at the same time the equipment that individual Christians ought to have in order to meet the inevitable assaults. Christian wives, husbands, children, parents, servants and masters are all concerned in this warfare: each has his part to play and his duty to do. Thus, at its close, the Epistle returns to the thought of divine power in men which it emphasized at the beginning (i. 19). The present tense of *be strong* (10) points, not to the need of acquiring new strength, but to the need of using the strength that Christians have through their union with Christ. *Put on the whole armour of God* (11). The word 'whole' is not found in the original, and its insertion obscures the real sense, which is 'Put on God's panoply'. 'Panoply' means 'the whole armour', but the emphasis of the original rests on the fact that it is God's. The need for God's panoply is indicated by the phrase *the wiles of the devil,* the methods and stratagems of the evil one, who 'carries on a campaign' against souls of men (see 1 Pet. ii. 11). There is an emphasis on the personal pronoun *we* at the beginning of verse 12 that distinguishes this conflict in which Christians are engaged from the common physical violence of men. Paul assumes that the Christian life is understood by his readers to be a life of conflict; his concern is to stress that it is not a physical but a spiritual struggle. The enemies of the soul are not earthly forces, nor beings on a level with man, but are the leaders of the evil spiritual forces of the universe. This is a thought that should inspire Christians to the highest and most urgent efforts. We have been warned, but all too few have taken warning. If such is indeed the state of affairs, and the human soul and affairs of mankind are open to such subtle and violent assaults, then it is little wonder that the world tosses in torment; for comparatively few have fitted themselves to resist the assaults of the evil one.

In verse 13 a second fundamental fact is laid

down. The first was that our warfare is spiritual; the second, that for such a warfare spiritual weapons are essential, and without them there can be no withstanding the powers of evil. In this sphere atom bombs are of no more value than bows and arrows. Paul's picture seems to be that of defenders resisting assault (14). Some commentators have suggested that his description is one of the forces of Christ's Church advancing against the powers of evil; but this hardly seems to be under consideration here. The figure Paul adopts was familiar to those acquainted with the Old Testament since it occurs in two passages of Isaiah; see Is. xi. 5, lix. 17. Guided by the Spirit Paul boldly applies these passages, which in the Old Testament refer to the Messiah, to those who are 'in Christ Jesus'. It is a strange paradox that *the gospel of peace* (15) should be a part of the Christian's panoply of war, but so it is. The relation of this gospel to the feet might seem strange to some, but it finds its illustration (and probably its origin) in Is. lii. 7. Cf. Rom. x. 15. *The shield of faith* (16). Of the two shields used in warfare the reference here is to the larger, heavier shield, intended to protect the whole body from weapons of the enemy. This means that the fullest protection is needed, and is available. *The fiery darts* (16) is a phrase expressive of the deadly harm that can come from the assaults of Satan. *The helmet of salvation* (17) comes from Is. lix. 17. As Christ was clad for His warfare, so is the Christian to be arrayed for his. Is. xi. 4 (see above on verse 14) is the source of the second figure in this verse. For 'breath' in the Isaiah passage we may equally well (or better) read 'Spirit': thus we have 'and he shall smite the earth with the rod of his mouth, and with the Spirit of his lips shall he slay the wicked'. See also Rev. i. 16, xix. 15 for the same figure. Here is the one weapon of offence in the Christian panoply, *the word of God*, and in it is the power of the Holy Spirit. This the Christian is to use, with complete faith in its virtue.

The word and prayer (see verse 18) are linked together in the purpose of God, and are ever to be used in conjunction. Both are needed in this warfare; our words to God, and God's words to the enemy. Prayer is not to be only the occasional exercise of the soul, but the Christian is to pray *always*, that is, on all occasions and in respect of everything; and in all we are to consult the guidance and help of the Spirit. We are to pray not for ourselves alone, but *for all saints*, and to that end are to be wakeful and alert amid the temptations of sloth and sleep. The humility and earnestness of the great apostle is seen in his earnest request for special prayer on his behalf, not indeed for ease or rest, but that he might be enabled to fulfil the purposes God had for him (19). Again in verse 20 we have a glimpse of Paul's circumstances as in iv. 1. Though an ambassador of the heavenly King and kingdom, he has been made a prisoner; but he knows that this does not relieve him of his responsibility toward God and the gospel; it may put many and great difficulties in his way, and some temptations too, but he sees that his duty still is to *speak boldly, as I ought to speak*.

XI. CONCLUSION. vi. 21–24

The mission of Tychicus is commended to his readers (21, 22). The noble character of Tychicus is evidenced in each of the few references made to him (see Acts xx. 4; Col. iv. 7; 2 Tim. iv. 12; Tit. iii. 12). He is now to be the bearer of this letter to the church in Ephesus, and from Col. iv. 7 we know that Onesimus was to be his companion. The benediction (23, 24) concludes the Epistle. The form is quite general, in conformity with the object of this Epistle and in contrast to Col. iv. 10–18. *Peace* was the ancient Hebrew greeting as *grace* was the Greek. Instead of using his favourite phrase 'grace and peace', as in i. 2, Paul here separates the two elements. How much 'peace' means as it comes from Paul's pen may be seen by a consideration of ii. 14–17, iv. 3. 'Grace' has the definite article before it in the original, pointing to the specific grace more fully named in many passages as 'the grace of our Lord Jesus Christ' (Rom. xvi. 20; 1 Cor. xvi. 23; 2 Cor. xiii. 14, etc.); see also iv. 7 and 2 Cor. viii. 9. The word *sincerity*, RV 'uncorruptness', with which the Epistle closes is elsewhere translated 'immortality' (Rom. ii. 7; 2 Tim. i. 10) and 'incorruption' (1 Cor. xv. 42, 50, 53f.). The love referred to is therefore not a love that springs from earth, but that love of God 'shed abroad in our hearts by the Holy Ghost which is given unto us' (Rom. v. 5).

W. G. M. MARTIN.

THE EPISTLE TO THE PHILIPPIANS

INTRODUCTION

See also the General Article, 'The Pauline Epistles', p. 68.

I. THE FOUNDING OF THE CHURCH

The city of Philippi was originally called Krenides (Little Fountains), but afterwards, *c.* 350 B.C., was renamed Philippi in honour of Philip of Macedon, father of Alexander the Great. It came under Roman rule about 168 B.C. when the province of Macedonia was subjugated, and in 42 B.C. it became a Roman colony (see Acts xvi. 12) or military settlement in honour of the victory of Antony and Octavian over the Republican forces of Brutus and Cassius wherein the murder of Julius Caesar was avenged. Eleven years later, in 31 B.C., Octavian, now emperor Augustus, recolonized Philippi. A Roman colony in its government and customs was modelled on Rome itself. Its magistrates were elected by the citizens and their authority within the city was supreme. Allusions to the colonial status of Philippi are found in the Epistle in i. 27 (RV mg.) and iii. 20 (RV). Hence administration of the city was entirely Roman with its praetors and lictors (Acts xvi. 35, RV mg.). The notable thing about Philippi is that it was Paul's first conquest in Europe and hence 'the birthplace of European Christianity'.

The story of the founding of the church is related in Acts xvi. The membership of the Christian congregation was mainly Greek with possibly a few Jews and Roman citizens. Women had an honourable place (Acts xvi. 13, 14).

II. OCCASION OF WRITING

There are two main reasons why the apostle wrote this letter. The first was to assure the Philippians of his grateful appreciation of their recent gifts by the hand of one of their number, Epaphroditus (iv. 10–18). The second was to adjust some of the minor disorders within the church.

Philippi seems to have been the only congregation from which the apostle accepted money. It was a token of his complete trust in their perfect understanding of his relationship with them and of both his right to live by the gospel and his spirit of independence. Evidently such communication of gifts had not happened for some long time, but the apostle, with infinite delicacy and exemplary tact, assures them it is not their fault. They 'lacked opportunity' (iv. 10), that was all. Their love and remembrance of him were as warm and vivid as they had ever been. It is probable that the leaders of the church

had acted prominently in this ministry as the apostle makes special mention in the address of the bishops and deacons. In no other Epistle are they singled out in this manner.

Epaphroditus himself was also sent as a gift to help the apostle in his prison, but at some time in his service he was taken ill and almost reached the point of death. Paul sends this living 'gift' back to Philippi, both because Epaphroditus was homesick and because a letter must be carried. It is almost certain that Epaphroditus bore a letter to Paul along with the bounty of the Philippians. This correspondence the apostle answers in our extant Epistle. An undercurrent of uneasiness on the part of the apostle's converts has been detected from the obvious anxiety of Paul to assure the Philippians of his deep gratitude. Did their beloved teacher really rejoice in their free-will offerings? Was he a little colder than usual or had they misunderstood him? Paul in memorable words set their minds and hearts at peace. The other main reason for writing, that of setting right minor disorders within the church, is probably closely related to the contents of the letter Epaphroditus had borne to Paul. The matters to which it referred would doubtless be further explained by the bearer himself. Evidently these were:

Pessimism at Philippi because of persecution there and the bad news of Paul's continued imprisonment.

Rupture within the congregation, due chiefly to sinful incompatibility of some members. Two women in particular, Euodias and Syntyche, were the cause of friction (iv. 2). There were no extreme factions at Philippi, as at Corinth, but merely minor murmurings and disputings.

Disloyalty creeping out of its dark places, fostered in his absence by Paul's Jewish enemies (iii. 2, iv. 8). This, however, was only in small degrees and Paul felt that warning was sufficient to restore the old allegiance.

III. PLACE AND DATE

Four of Paul's letters were written, as stated or indicated by themselves, when the apostle was a prisoner (cf. Eph. iii. 1, iv. 1, vi. 20; Phil. i. 7, 13, 14; Col. iv. 18; Phm. 9). The question arises as to where the captivity took place, and whether all four letters were written during the same captivity. The traditional answer is Rome; but this has been challenged, formerly in favour of

Caesarea, and latterly on behalf of Ephesus. Acts records three imprisonments, at Philippi (xvi. 23), at Caesarea (xxiii. 23), at Rome (xxviii. 30). That at Philippi was obviously too short for any literary activity. The objection against Caesarea is likewise weighty as regards the Epistle to the Philippians, in that Paul at the moment of writing was anticipating his speedy release, but in prison at Caesarea he was looking forward to a long voyage to Rome. The case for Caesarea is abandoned now almost unanimously. This leaves Rome, but not in possession of the field. More recently Ephesus has been advocated as the source of the imprisonment Epistles, and of the four letters it is contended that Philippians at least is definitely beyond dispute. The case for Ephesus as the source of the Philippian Epistle may be briefly put as presented by Principal G. S. Duncan, Prof. J. H. Michael and others.

Although there is no definite statement in Scripture of an imprisonment at Ephesus, yet no strong argument can be based upon such silence. On the contrary Paul speaks of many imprisonments in a letter (2 Cor. xi. 23) written before the imprisonments at Caesarea and Rome. The antipathy of the Judaizers was bitter enough to render possible an imprisonment as early as the Ephesian ministry. It is argued also that Paul's words in 1 Cor. xv. 30–32 and 2 Cor. i. 8–10 imply imprisonment in Ephesus.

When Philippians was written, Timothy was expected soon to visit Philippi (ii. 19). This agrees with Acts xix. 22. Paul, if released, hopes to go to Philippi (i. 27, ii. 24); but if the Epistle was written from Rome, this is in conflict with Rom. xv. 24.

Phil. i. 30 gains in significance if Ephesus be the place of writing. Paul says in effect, 'you saw me in prison at Philippi and now you hear of me in prison at . . .'. If at Rome, the apostle is putting two things together which have an interval between them of about twelve years. If at Ephesus, there had been a comparatively short lapse of time from the apostle's visit to Philippi to the summer of A.D. 54.

Phil. i. 13 has long been assumed to indicate Rome as the source, but the term *praetorium* was in common use of the official residence of a governor in any province and not merely for one supreme place at Rome. So also the phrase 'the household of Caesar' does not of necessity point to Rome, but includes all who were attached to the personal service of Caesar whether at Rome or elsewhere.

It is evident from ii. 26 that the Philippians had heard of the illness of Epaphroditus and that Paul had heard that they had heard, but the distance between Rome and Philippi renders the frequent communications between Paul and his converts indicated in the letter to the Philippians highly improbable. It would take Epaphroditus a considerable time (about a month) to encompass the journey from Rome to Philippi, while two weeks would suffice for the distance between Ephesus and Philippi.

It appears that the Ephesian hypothesis is not quite groundless, but yet not sufficiently weighty to overcome the traditional view of a captivity at Rome.

The plea of shorter distance between Ephesus and Philippi is considerably weakened when we note, as Wood and others point out, that communication between Rome and Philippi was easy and frequent, for the Macedonian city lay on the Via Egnatia, the great overland road from the Hellespont to the Adriatic.

The terms 'praetorium' and 'household of Caesar' may equally be used of Rome and Ephesus, but Rome is the place to which they more obviously refer.

If Ephesus be the source of the imprisonment Epistles and especially of the Philippian letter, it is surprising that no trace of this view is found in the early centuries.

Even if the apostle's words in 1 Cor. xv. 30–32 and 2 Cor. i. 8–10 do imply that he suffered imprisonment in Ephesus, it does not follow that the captivity Epistles were written there.

The Roman imprisonment had a specific cause for its duration, as Paul was awaiting trial; but the Ephesian imprisonment was probably a very short time in comparison; indeed the supporters of the Ephesian hypothesis actually postulate several short periods of restraint.

Finally, if the Ephesian hypothesis is correct, then i. 12–20 of the letter must find an interpretation apart from the appeal case, which Paul knew must be heard at Rome before Caesar (Acts xxv. 11).

The issue cannot be dogmatically decided and fortunately it does not disturb the apostle's abiding message. Meanwhile we may accept the Roman origination and the date A.D. 61–63. (If Ephesus, the date is given as A.D. 54–57.) The majority of those who accept Rome as the place of origin of the Epistle believe it comes last of the captivity Epistles. These certainly fall into two divisions both geographically and theologically. Ephesians, Colossians and Philemon have the same destination in the Lycus valley of Asia Minor, while Philippians has a European location. Again, Philippians stands alone among the prison letters as not involved in the incipient Gnostic heresy which obviously was infesting the churches of Asia Minor. The three letters, Ephesians, Colossians and Philemon, were probably written almost at one time, while Philippians came by itself later. That our Epistle here is of later date than the others may be supported by observing, first, that the communications between Philippi and Rome, implied in ii. 26, must have taken a considerable time; secondly, that when Paul wrote to Philippi he was well known 'in the whole Praetorium' (AV 'in all the palace, and in all other places'). He had contacted so many soldiers and others that the reason of his imprisonment was common knowledge and many became interested in his appeal to Caesar (i. 13f.).

The inference is that the Epistle to the Philippians must have been written toward the close of Paul's captivity, hence the suggested date A.D. 61–63.

IV. CHARACTERISTICS

This letter has three special features which are noteworthy. It is, first, one of the most personal of all Paul's Epistles. There is no restraint on his part. He writes more as an intimate friend than as a bishop or ecclesiastic. His opening salutation dispenses with the title 'apostle', and with perfect confidence of his place in the hearts of his readers he calls himself simply 'a servant'. The intensely biographical passage (iii. 4–14) unveils his deep spiritual experience with all the artlessness of perfect trust. As he dictates his thoughts he seems to have his friends at Philippi beside him.

This Epistle is also marked by its revelation of the person of Christ. The great Christological passage (ii. 5–11) is introduced, not indeed for the purpose of doctrinal teaching, but rather to impress the readers with the grace of humility. The supreme example of lowliness of mind is that manifested in the incarnation of Jesus, the Lord of glory. Hence the practical exhortation to possess the mind of Christ Jesus and esteem each other better than themselves. That this great unveiling of the Person of our Lord should come so spontaneously from the mind of Paul convinces us the more readily of its reality and truth.

The third feature is the dominant note of joy. The noun 'joy' (*chara*) is found five times (i. 4, 25, ii. 2, 29, iv. 1), while the verb 'to rejoice' (*chairein*) occurs eleven times (i. 18 twice, ii. 17 twice, 18 twice, 28, iii. 1, iv. 4 twice, 10). That the apostle in his humanly forlorn circumstances should write with such magnificent optimism makes the bright exhortation the more remarkable. Paul did really feel himself to be above his environment and master of the situation, his 'head bloody, but unbowed'. He was not just making a show and playing a part so that the Philippian believers might have a good example in their own peculiar hardships and personal persecutions. It was a joy 'in the Lord'. 'Rejoice with me' is a sincere, clarion call. It indicates for all time the duty of Christian optimism.

V. INTEGRITY

The genuineness of the Epistle to the Philippians is almost universally accepted. From the earliest date it has been accepted as an authentic letter from the apostle Paul to the Christian church at Philippi. It is its unity which has been challenged. Granted that Paul did write letters to the Philippians other than the one now extant, some critics advance the theory that the Epistle is composite, a combination of at least two letters. A few things suggest the probability of such a view, e.g. the use of the term 'finally' in iii. 1a; the sudden change of tone expressed in iii. 2, 'Beware of dogs'; the belated expression of gratitude (iv. 10ff.); and the double 'Amen' (iv. 20, 23). Accordingly it is suggested that in our New Testament Epistle there is present an interpolation, Pauline indeed, but belonging to another letter to the Philippians. Many scholars accept not the solution of 'interpolation' but rather 'interruption', a view which is wholly embraced here. The basal argument for a Pauline insertion by some editor is the abrupt change of tone in iii. 2. This can be satisfactorily interpreted on psychological grounds. The apostle is dictating his letter, and as he speaks news arrives of some Judaistic offensive at Philippi. This diverts his thoughts and at once he bursts forth in grave warning, 'beware of dogs, beware of evil workers, beware of the concision'. The mental habit of the apostle 'to fly off at a tangent' has long been observed by many students. As a projecting stone deflects the flowing stream, so the current of his thought could be diverted into different channels. The weakness of the interpolation theory is the difficulty, realized by its sponsors, of agreeing upon any definite termination for the alien insertion. Some say iv. 8, others iv. 9, and still others iv. 20. There are even hypotheses of three Pauline letters necessary to make the one in our hands. Such disruptive theories defeat themselves.

OUTLINE OF CONTENTS

I. OPENING SALUTATION. i. 1, 2

II. THANKSGIVING AND PRAYER. i. 3–11

III. THE SITUATION AT ROME. i. 12–26

IV. INCENTIVES TO CHRISTIAN UNITY. i. 27—ii. 4

V. THE EXAMPLE OF CHRIST. ii. 5–18

VI. APPROACHING VISITS. ii. 19–30

VII. WARNING AGAINST FALSE TEACHERS. iii. 1-21

VIII. THREE FINAL EXHORTATIONS. iv. 1-9

IX. ACKNOWLEDGMENT OF GIFTS. iv. 10-20

X. CLOSING SALUTATION. iv. 21-23

COMMENTARY

I. OPENING SALUTATION. i. 1, 2

And Timotheus (1). In this address Paul associates Timothy with himself, not in any sense as author, but as fellow-worker. He may actually have been the apostle's amanuensis. The two names are also joined in the greeting at the beginning of 2 Corinthians, Colossians, 1 and 2 Thessalonians and Philemon. Paul describes himself and his assistant as *servants of Jesus Christ*. The Greek word *douloi* is literally 'slaves', and indicates that the spiritual tie between Christ and themselves was that of bondservants, for they had given themselves to Him as Master and would not go free (cf. Ex. xxi. 5, 6). Paul does not use his title 'apostle' here (cf. 1 Cor. i. 1; Gal. i. 1), doubtless because his position was never challenged in the love-bond between himself and this church. Note the order of our Lord's names. The AV gives *Jesus Christ*, but the RV 'Christ Jesus', the order of the preferable Greek Text. This is important, for Paul is careful in this point. When the emphasis rests upon the human historical Jesus, he puts 'Jesus' first in any combination; when 'Christ' takes precedence he means the risen Jesus, the eternal Messiah.

Those addressed are *all the saints . . . with the bishops and deacons* (1). The apostle calls the Philippian converts *saints*, both because of their present justification through Christ and because of their assured end, as wholly sanctified in Him (cf. i. 6). The addition *with the bishops and deacons* makes this salutation unique. The term *episkopos*, or 'bishop', means one who overlooks or oversees, a superintendent of sorts (cf. 1 Thes. v. 12, 'them which are over you'). From the use of this term in the Pauline literature many adopt the view that an *episkopos* was present in the early Church from the very beginning and was not just a development of a later century. Others note that *presbyteros* ('presbyter' or 'elder') is the general name of a church leader in the New Testament, and are convinced that our Episcopacy is of later date. *Episkopos* and *presbyteros* are accepted as identical terms, especially as at Philippi we have *bishops* in the plural. It is sufficient here to mark the origin of the two views on church government. The term *diakonos* occurs frequently in the Gospels and Epistles and is generally translated 'servant' or 'minister', which is its meaning. In a more technical sense 'deacon' is applied to the class of church officers whose duty is concerned more with material things than with those directly spiritual (cf. 1 Tim. iii. 8). The special office may have had its origin in the election of the Seven in Acts vi, although there this name is not given to them. The greetings of verse 2 is an adapted Christian combination of the familiar Greek and Hebrew forms of salutation, *grace and peace*, which can come only from God the Father and the Lord Jesus Christ (see Eph. vi. 23, 24n.).

II. THANKSGIVING AND PRAYER. i. 3-11

An outstanding trait of the apostle's spiritual life is thanksgiving. Constantly, in every letter with the exception of the Epistle to the Galatians, he inspires his converts to the cultivation of the grace of gratitude (cf. Col. i. 12n.). Every prayer of his is suffused with this spirit. Here in verses 3-8 Paul expresses thanks to God for the *fellowship* (5) he has enjoyed with his converts at Philippi. From the very first evangelization of their city until the present time of his imprisonment this link has been unbroken. The Greek term *koinōnia*, used here, is derived from the root meaning 'to make common' and has two usages in the New Testament. It means communion, fellowship, having things in common, as in the practice of the Pentecostal church (Acts ii. 42). Also, since there can be no Christian fellowship which does not involve a 'giving' as well as a 'getting', the word is used for the idea of 'contribution' (Rom. xv. 26; 2 Cor. viii. 4, ix. 13; Heb. xiii. 16. See also Phm. 6n.). Paul's use here involves both shades of meaning, as he gives thanks for this personal comradeship with the Philippians, a union not for its own sake but a real contribution to the gospel. *In the gospel* (5); better as in RV, which gives the full force of the preposition *eis* ('to' or 'towards') and reads 'for your fellowship in furtherance of the gospel'.

Paul's thanksgiving is inspired by memory (3), expressed in prayer (4), accompanied with joy (4) and strengthened by the conviction that God Himself will make perfect His work of grace in their lives (6). The apostle feels justified in this attitude towards God and towards the Christians at Philippi for two reasons. First, *I have you in my heart* (7), an open confession of love further interpreted in verse 8, which means 'my love is great indeed, for it is just the love of Christ loving you through me': so very close is the *koinōnia* between the apostle and his Saviour. Secondly, *ye all are partakers of my grace* (7), 'partakers with me of grace' (RV); i.e. you are sharers with me of divine grace, given to me as I suffer bonds and establish the gospel by my witness here in Rome and my defence of the faith in the law-courts. The help and sympathy you are giving me make this manifest.

Paul reveals that this all-pervasive spirit of thanksgiving was constantly with him in all his devotions and led him to definite prayer. *And this I pray* (9). His word here, *proseuchomai*, is the most general and sacred term. It is unrestricted as to content, and is never used of prayer to man, but to God alone. In this letter the apostle employs two other terms for prayer, *deēsis* and *aitēma*. The former (i. 4, 19) implies entreaty of real need, supplication in urgent petition; the latter (iv. 6) indicates 'that which I have to ask for', a definite plea. All three with their peculiar shades of significance are found combined in iv. 6.

Some of Paul's prayers are preserved for us and their characteristic is a specific suitability to a need acutely discerned. In the case of the Philippians he recognized there was perfervid emotionalism of an absolutely genuine type, but that they had much need of a compensating light. He accordingly prays, not that warm love may cool, but that it may grow yet warmer, balanced by *knowledge* and *judgment* or 'moral discernment' (9). Thus love would become not an unregulated impulse, but a guiding principle with the practical end that they may discriminate differences between moral qualities, thus choosing the best. *That ye may approve things that are excellent* (10); a possible alternative rendering is 'put to the test things that differ' (cf. RV mg.) with the same ultimate vote for the highest. The result of such love and light in combination would inevitably be that the Philippians in their circumstances would know both what to be and what not to be, *sincere and without offence* to themselves or others (10). Thus the subjects of Paul's prayer, with love enriched by his intercession, would possess three things: a critical faculty (9-10a), a guileless character (10b) and an upright life (11). All the praiseworthy graces and Christian conduct of these converts at Philippi would be in perfect harmony, all uniting to *the glory and praise of God*. Note that the Greek *karpos* is singular, not plural, 'fruit' not *fruits*. The root of new life in Christ produces the one fruit of godliness or Christlikeness although in diverse human forms and features (cf. Gal. v. 22n.).

III. THE SITUATION AT ROME. i. 12-26

In this section Paul reveals several facts about himself and his gospel work at Rome. Verses 12 and 13 indicate that he was in prison awaiting his trial and the verdict might be death. His affairs (i.e. *the things which happened unto me*) about which the apostle knows the Philippians were deeply concerned, together with *my bonds in Christ* (13), combine to witness to his actual imprisonment. In verse 20 Paul reveals quite frankly how serious the situation is with alternative issues of life or death. His fearless example of unashamedly preaching the gospel even in captivity was, however, encouraging the Christians in the Roman church to evangelize more boldly.

The sphere in which the gospel is being thus furthered is described as *in all the palace, and in all other places* (13), lit. 'in the whole praetorium'. The word praetorium may mean either the headquarters in a Roman camp, or the official residence of the governor of a province, or the imperial guard, a picked body of special troops. The word is used in the second sense in the Gospels and Acts (see RSV rendering of Mt. xxvii. 27; Mk. xv. 16; Jn. xviii. 28, 33, xix. 9; Acts xxiii. 35). There is no evidence, however, that it was ever used of the Emperor's palace at Rome, and it is probable that in this place Paul refers to the Praetorian guard, which was commonly known as the Praetorium (see RV and RV mg.). It has been suggested that the word here signifies the judicial authorities before whom Paul's trial would take place, but there is no evidence in the letter that the trial was then, at the moment of writing, proceeding. Paul in his hired lodging (Acts xxviii. 30) would be guarded by a soldier of the Praetorian guard, and it is not difficult to imagine how, as one soldier after another came on duty, it would soon become known to the whole guard, and beyond it ('to all the rest', RV, and cf. the reference in iv. 22 to 'they that are of Caesar's household') that he was a prisoner for Christ's sake.

Evidently Paul was encouraging two types of preachers, some of bad and others of good will (15ff.). The former may have included some at least of the leaders of the Christian community before Paul arrived who, being out of sympathy with his views and methods, were jealous of his influence; the latter, a few big souls who truly judged the situation that Paul was no self-seeker but was devoted to the gospel. These therefore gladly gave the apostle their love and sympathy in his parlous position, and themselves ventured on a much more courageous witness. Paul's reaction to this rivalry is magnanimous. The motives for proclaiming the gospel may be mixed, even unworthy, but the all-important fact is *Christ is preached* (18).

I know that this shall turn to my salvation (19). He was confident of the issue that he would be brought safely through. The term *salvation* has a wide connotation in the New Testament, and Paul envisaged something spiritual in his temporal deliverance. Some scholars detect here a quotation from Jb. xiii. 16 which in the LXX reads 'This shall turn to me for salvation'. After passing through the strain of prison and trial, Paul believes he will be released, not simply for his own personal comfort, but much more for the triumph and furtherance of the gospel. Two factors would ensure the desired end: the intercession of the Philippians and the resources bestowed upon him by *the Spirit of Jesus Christ* (19). This last phrase is found only here in the New Testament, but there are similar expressions elsewhere which place it beyond doubt that the third Person of the Godhead is intended (cf. Acts v. 9, xvi. 7, RV; Rom. viii. 9; 2 Cor. iii. 17; Gal. iv. 6). The expression which Paul here uses implies the doctrine which was afterwards known as the 'procession' of the Holy Spirit from the Son together with the Father, as in the famous credal clause *filioque. In nothing . . . ashamed* (20). That he might make an unashamed witness to his Lord is the apostle's hope as he thought upon those two factors of his salvation, intercession and the Spirit's grace. But whatever the legal verdict of the Roman court might be, his aim is to magnify Christ either by the prolongation of his life or by his imminent death. Paul's attitude to the issue of his trial is perfect submission to the will of God, although he did feel that he would be released. But life or death will have the same result—*Christ shall be magnified* (20).

But the apostle is not superhuman, in spite of all his assurance, and he is not able absolutely to banish the possibility of death. This creates for him a dilemma: *what I shall choose, I wot not. For I am in a strait betwixt two* (22, 23). *But if I live in the flesh, this is the fruit of my labour* (22; Gk. *touto moi karpos ergou*). Various interpretations have been offered. The AV rendering means that this abiding in the flesh, this continued existence among them, is the fruit or 'reward' of his labours in the gospel. His spared life is due to him for its usefulness in the past. This rendering of the Greek and its interpretation is not satisfactory, as the apostle is the very last to consider human merit in any guise and never elsewhere uses the term 'fruit' to mean reward for work done. The RSV text is perhaps the simplest of all and conveys the general drift of the apostle's meaning: 'If it is to be life in the flesh, that means fruitful labor for me. Yet which I shall choose I cannot tell.' Dr. J. W. C. Wand's translation brings out this meaning: 'To me indeed life means Christ, and death would bring an added advantage. But so long as physical existence gives an opportunity of fruitful work, I hardly know which to prefer.'

I am in a strait betwixt two (23). The verb here is *synechomai*, which means to be constrained or pressed. It is found also in Lk. xii. 50 ('straitened'), Acts xviii. 5 ('pressed'), and 2 Cor. v. 14 ('constraineth'). Two potent forces were playing upon Paul rendering him immobile in either direction. Personally his whole heart moved to be with Christ in the felicity of perfected eternal life; but at the same time the urgent need of his converts pinned him to earthly life and privileged duty. From the expression of the apostle's mind here, terse as it is, it may with confidence be affirmed that he did not entertain any dogma of an intermediate state. His thought is more akin to the statement of the Westminster divines, that 'The souls of believers are at their death made perfect in holiness, and do immediately pass into glory; and their bodies, being still united to Christ, do rest in their graves till the resurrection'. (Cf. Heb. xii. 23; 2 Cor. v. 1, 6, 8; Lk. xxiii. 43.)

IV. INCENTIVES TO CHRISTIAN UNITY.
i. 27—ii. 4

In these verses Paul sets forth the attitude and spirit which he desires to see in the Philippian church. The key phrases are, *that ye stand fast in one spirit* (i. 27) and *being of one accord, of one mind* (ii. 2). These words emphasize the duty of Christian unity. Evidently there were at Philippi indications of disruption, probably slight, yet showing definite danger. The Philippians were the most loved of all Paul's converts, and their church was one which gave him the least concern, so true and loyal it was. But it was not perfect. Counsel and exhortation must be given. In the case of the Philippian Christians two factors were required to create complete harmony of life and testimony, namely, consistency of conduct and continuance of conflict. *Let your conversation be as it becometh the gospel of Christ* (27). Today our English word 'conversation' is in its reference limited to speech; formerly it meant behaviour, conduct, like the Latin *conversatio*. The Greek here is *politeuesthe*, 'to live as a citizen', from the root *polis*, a city. The word is found again in Acts xxiii. 1 where the point is the apostle's reference to his good citizenship as a free-born Roman. The Christians at Philippi as residents in the Roman colony (Acts xvi. 12) would understand the privileges and obligations of citizenship. As a Roman colony was intended to represent the mother city of Rome, so the church at Philippi must show in their behaviour that they were citizens of the heavenly kingdom. Hence the RV 'Only let your manner of life be worthy of the gospel of Christ'. 'Live the gospel life', Paul exhorts, for the gospel supplies both standard and stamina.

Striving together (27). Unity can be realized by sharing the same conflict. The Greek verb here is *synathlountes*; the prefix *syn* applies to the community life, and indicates striving along with one another. In verse 30 Paul affirms for their encouragement that they strive together with him also, *having the same conflict* (Gk. *agōn*; cf. iv. 3; Rom. xv. 30). This fellowship of suffering for the sake of the *faith of the gospel* (i.e. the things revealed for salvation and most surely believed) is a unifying force. It is more. It is a veritable grace of God bestowed upon the Philippians, who need not be affrighted by or shy away from persecution viewed in this light, *for unto you it is given* (29), i.e. it is granted to you as a favour. The stress of the Greek *echaristhē* rests upon the idea of givenness, *charis* (grace) being the root.

That Paul was a sufferer his converts well knew, from the first time they met at Philippi until the present imprisonment at Rome. Such was his lot for the sake of Christ. Now persecution was theirs also; hence let them *stand fast in one spirit* (27). Courage in the suffering of hostility, the apostle says, is a very clear sign of their opponents' ultimate destruction, *an evident token of perdition* (28), but for them a proof of their *salvation*, not from any human source but alone from God Himself. In other words Christian fearlessness in face of persecution begets fear in the heart of the persecutor, while it begets confidence in the heart of the suffering believer. Here *perdition* (Gk. *apōleia*) and *salvation* (Gk. *sōtēria*) are sharply contrasted: the one a terrible negative, an awful loss; the other a positive deliverance from sin and blessed security for eternity.

Paul counsels the cultivation of these formative forces of consistency and conflict in the creation of true community of spirit. He proceeds to give them two exhortations with the same aim—to fulfil his joy, and to preserve a humble mind within the fellowship. First he exhorts them to unity by a loving plea to make his heart overflow with an inner and abiding gladness, *fulfil ye my joy* (ii. 2). They had already given him cause for joy (i. 3, iv. 10), but if they would make this joy complete, let them do this thing of which he is now speaking and be united. The admonition is supported by four strong appeals (ii. 1) which the apostle, in hortatory style, believes will certainly carry weight, for surely such things are real and have moving power. Moffatt translates this verse: 'So by all the stimulus of Christ, by every incentive of love, by all your participation in the Spirit, by all your affectionate tenderness, I pray you to give me the utter joy of knowing you are living in harmony.' See also RSV.

A second admonition with a view to encouraging unity is added, the cultivation of humility. Disruptive forces will quickly abate if *lowliness of mind* be present (3). The heavenly citizenship of communal spiritual life in the Philippian church will be preserved complete if unselfishly each one, or each group of Christians, considers the affairs of his or its neighbour. To the pagan humility was a vice, not a virtue. *Strife* (3; RV 'faction') implies the formation within the church of cliques, who for the sake of party advantage try to manœuvre things their own way. *Vainglory* means the ambition of any member of the church to gain position, so as to create a following and to minister to his personal vanity.

V. THE EXAMPLE OF CHRIST.
ii. 5–18

The apostle appeals to the example of Christ as an inspiration of lowliness of mind so essential to united happy fellowship. This section has two parts, ii. 5–11 and ii. 12–18.

a. The self-emptying and self-humbling of Christ (ii. 5–11)

This is the great Christological passage of the Epistle and bears upon the incarnation of Jesus. The great truth here set forth just flowed out from the apostle's mind as he turned to the historical advent of Jesus to illustrate humility (cf. 2 Cor. viii. 9). The heart of the doctrine lies in the phrase, *but made himself of no reputation* (7), or 'but emptied himself' (RV), which latter phrase is a literal translation of the Greek *ekenōsen*, from which is derived the technical theological term *kenōsis* or self-emptying. Jesus, who existed in the *form of God* and *equal with God* (6), humbled Himself in taking upon Him the *likeness of men* (7) in place of the pre-existent form of God.

Note that in this passage there are three graded ideas: 'essence' (Gk. *hyparchōn*, Lat. *essentia*); 'form' (Gk. *morphē*, Lat. *forma*); 'fashion' (Gk. *schēma*, Lat. *figura*). Essence, existence, or being, is fundamental and must exist in some form and when once adopted always keeps to the same form. Every being has its own form. Form is the permanent expression of existence. Thus we have the form of God, the form of an angel, the form of man, and the form of a beast; all of which are immovable manifestations of being or existence. Fashion, on the other hand, is transient. The fashion or shape may change, but the form remains. Thus the fashion (*schēma*) of the world passes away but not its form (*morphē*) (1 Cor. vii. 31). Satan may transfigure himself into an angel of light, but not transform himself so (cf. 2 Cor. xi. 14). Thus our Lord existed primarily in the *form of God*, a strong affirmation of His essential deity, and in the incarnation and self-emptying He adopted the *form of a servant*, which resulted in His becoming man, His being made *in the likeness of men*.

The apostle finds in Christ the supreme example of what he has been saying in verses 3 and 4. He describes, first, the height from which Christ descended, *being* (Gk. 'being originally', cf. RV mg.) *in the form of God* (6). This denotes the essential attributes of God and implies not merely the pre-existence of Christ but His existence as God in a divine mode of being. He was, as the next clause shows, *equal with God* (6). But He did not regard this mode of being as something to be grasped (RV 'counted it not a prize'), but 'emptied himself'. The apostle, secondly, describes the depth to which Christ descended. Instead of living on an equality with God, He *took the form of a servant* (of God) as a human among men (7). Thus, *being found in fashion as a man* (Wey., 'being recognized as truly human'), He did not seek His own glory (Jn. vii. 18), but *humbled himself*, fulfilling His life as a servant in an obedience which did not stop short even at crucifixion (8). Thirdly, the apostle describes the height to which God has *highly exalted him* (9), Gk. *hyperypsōsen*, the prefix indicating a more than ordinary exaltation. God has thus set the seal of His approval upon humility, 'the mind that was in Christ Jesus'.

Thus the mode of the incarnation was self-emptying, its full significance being contained in the sentence *who . . . thought it not robbery to be equal with God* (6). Different interpretations are possible here according as we render the Greek *harpagmon* active or passive, i.e. a 'grasping' or a thing 'grasped'. Paul may be saying that Jesus did not consider His equality with God 'a grasping', 'an act of seizure', 'a robbery' (AV), i.e. something not inalienably His own already. But although thus firmly established as God's equal, He denuded Himself of all divine prerogatives and became man. Or the meaning may be that Jesus did not consider His equality with God 'a thing to be grasped', a prize, something to be 'clung to', like a miser hoarding his gold. Jesus freely divested Himself of this 'equality with God'. On this view 'equality with God' was already possessed by Christ in His pre-existent state, else it could not have been let go. A third view, also adópting, like the second, the passive sense of *harpagmon*, construes the meaning thus: Jesus did not consider 'equality with God' to be a prize, a something to be 'snatched at' and possessed for the taking (cf. the lure of Satan 'Ye shall be as gods' in Gn. iii. 5). On the contrary He emptied Himself that He might gain that equality and manifest His inherent deity by humbling Himself and becoming *obedient unto death, even the death of the cross.* This view finds more support in Heb. v. 8, 9. Christ regarded the goal as one to be reached not by His own snatching or usurpation, but by divine appointment to the way of the cross.

Whatever interpretation of this difficult Christological passage may be accepted the distinction between deity and 'equality with God' must be observed. By the way the apostle's thought runs on it is indicated that 'equality with God' refers to the exalted rank to which God raised His Son, giving Him *a name which is above every name* (9–11). This, not His deity, is the prize Christ won, by humbling Himself, by becoming man and by perfectly accomplishing the redemptive will of God.

b. Practical issue for the Philippians (ii. 12–18)

i. **Work out your own salvation (ii. 12–16).** The lowly example of Jesus in all its amazing sacrifice ought to inspire the readers to a life of devoted discipleship, especially the following of Jesus in this impressive humility. The Philippians (not all perhaps, but some of their number) were prone to high-mindedness, the fertile source of dissension. It is their immediate duty, all the more because Paul's absence means that his spiritual help is lacking to them, to work out for themselves their own salvation, to use every effort to the maximum to be delivered from their besetting sin. The exhortation is primarily to the defective group, but also to the whole Christian church at Philippi; for each individual must

labour for his own and his neighbour's perfection.

This exhortation is presented as to its mode, its ground and its purpose. *With fear and trembling* (12) describes how they are to *work out* or 'labour earnestly at' their own salvation (cf. 2 Pet. i. 10. The phrase occurs also in 1 Cor. ii. 3; 2 Cor. vii. 15; Eph. vi. 5). The setting in these three references implies anxious suspense lest relationships be ruptured, and all refer to the human sphere. In this passage the exposition is often given as in the sight of God, and the translation offered 'with meticulous reverence' (Wand) or some such rendering. This is allowable if the community bearing is not obscured.

The ground of the admonition is inspiringly asserted: *for it is God which worketh in you* (13), i.e. 'enables you' (Moff.). The emphasis rests upon the word *God*; in the Greek it is placed first. It is neither Paul who is the dynamic, nor any ideal of their own that can accomplish salvation to its completion. It is God alone. The inward, divine grace deals with both will and deed, the initiation of the effort and the very effort itself, both of which carry out the divine will, the *good pleasure* of God (13). The apostle uses this same Greek term *eudokia* in i. 15 to describe the attitude of others to himself. Here he employs it, as in Eph. i. 5, 9; 2 Thes. i. 11, of the gracious will of God.

The purpose of the exhortation to work out their own salvation is *that ye may be blameless and harmless, the sons of God, without rebuke* (15). This is to be their aim as well as the goal of the divine energizing. The life of the Philippians in the fellowship of the saints ought to be unifying, bringing together every individual, family and group, and not disruptive through giving offence. As sons of God they are destined to be *lights in the world* (15; RV mg. reads 'luminaries'). The figure is of a shining star in a dark night. Its attractive brilliance strikes the imagination of the apostle and he next sees the Philippians radiating the 'words of life', and dispelling the spiritual darkness amidst *a crooked and perverse nation* (RV 'generation'; cf. Dt. xxxii. 5).

ii. **Joy and rejoice with me (ii. 17, 18).** This is the second injunction Paul gives the converts at Philippi as the practical issue of the humiliation of the Lord Jesus Christ. The paramount thought of the apostle in this whole section is that of sacrifice as exemplified in Christ, then in himself, then in the Philippians. If the disciples at Philippi abandon their high-mindedness and crucify their pride and self-will they shall be truly the *sons of God* (15). If their faith finds expression in a Christ-like life of sacrifice and service, then Paul will know that his ministry will not be *in vain* (16) and so rejoice. Even if in addition to this living sacrifice (cf. Rom. xii. 1) of theirs, the apostle is destined to pour out his life-blood as a libation upon the sacrifice (17; cf. Nu. xxviii. 7), it is a matter of triumphant joy both for them and for him.

VI. APPROACHING VISITS. ii. 19–30

In this sixth section the apostle reveals his plans for the future. He contemplates three visits to the Philippians, one by Timothy (19–23), another by himself (24), and a third by Epaphroditus (25–30).

The decision to send Timothy is to cheer both the Philippians and himself by the exchange of news. Timothy is the right man to send and a high testimonial is given him. He alone of Paul's circle of friends and helpers is *likeminded* (20; lit. 'of equal spirit'). The heart of the apostle is full of care for the church at Philippi; but all those around Paul at the time, except Timothy, are fully taken up with their own concerns (21). Does this sweeping condemnation refer to all Paul's followers and assistants, to all the inner circle of his friends? Hardly, for where were Epaphroditus and Luke at the time? The language surely expresses more the special qualifications of Timothy to go to Philippi and the obvious self-seeking of either pagans or immature Christians hanging around Paul, than an impeachment of the apostle's fellow-workers. Timothy has won his spurs, he is a tried servant of the Lord, and a real spiritual son of his father Paul, hence the adverb *gnēsiōs*, AV *naturally*. The Greek term refers to a son 'lawfully born', 'born in wedlock' and so genuine or true. Timothy reproduces the nature of the apostle as a spiritual father, especially in his care for the Philippians. This solicitude is seen in the fact that Paul is willing to send to them the only like-minded companion whom he had at the time.

The second contemplated visit to Philippi is by Paul himself (24). He states this briefly. While ready to become a martyr for the faith, the apostle is fully confident of his release. Observe the repetition of the phrase *in the Lord* (19, 24). This is the sphere of all his plans.

The third visit which Paul has in mind is by Epaphroditus, a name occurring only in this Epistle (ii. 25 and iv. 18). It means 'charming' and probably this co-worker deserved the name, for he was much beloved by the Philippians. He is not to be confused with Epaphras (Col. i. 7, iv. 12; Phm. 23). Paul gives him five titles: *my brother, and companion in labour* (RV 'fellow-worker'), *and fellowsoldier;* then *your messenger* and your 'minister to my need' (RV). It was not willingly that the apostle let him go, but he deemed it necessary for the sake of Epaphroditus and of the Philippians and lastly of himself. There were three reasons for his return. Epaphroditus had been sick even to the point of death (27, 30), and also sick in mind and yearning to be home again, especially since he learned that his fellow-Christians were grieving over him (26). He was sent also to cheer the church at Philippi for he held some ecclesiastical position in it and his religious service was much appreciated quite apart from the place he held in the hearts of the members. Then for Paul's own sake Epaphroditus was being sent to them, a point

revealed in the phrase *that I may be the less sorrowful* (28). Probably Paul here is thinking of his friend's escape from death by the mercy of God, and his immunity from any recurrence of illness away from the perils to health existing in Rome. Also it may be that the thought of the joy of reunion and mutual explanations at Philippi between Epaphroditus and the Philippians promised the apostle some relief from his distress about their anxieties. It is probable that misunderstandings had arisen.

VII. WARNING AGAINST FALSE TEACHERS. iii. 1–21

The apostle had just dictated, *Finally, my brethren, rejoice in the Lord* (1), when something happened which turned the course of his happy thoughts into a less congratulatory stream. What this was cannot be definitely said. There may have been an interruption which prevented Paul from writing further and before he could take up the letter again a grave report came to hand. Probably it was some disturbing news from Philippi together with another increased agitation against himself in Rome. At any rate Paul begins to speak rapidly and vehemently, in obvious warning against three classes of false teachers.

a. A warning against the Judaizers (iii. 2–11)

Cf. Gal. iii. 1–29, iv. 21–31; Rom. ii. 25–29. See also the *Introduction* to Galatians. Paul, thoroughly filled with righteous indignation, gives these men names equal to their character, *dogs, evil workers, concision* (2). *Dogs* is a term of contempt. They were the pariahs of the East, the eaters of garbage in the streets. Paul infers that the Judaizers were the rank outsiders of covenant and grace, turning back upon them the very words they used of Gentiles. They did injury wherever they journeyed, and they went about with evil personal animosity. They were also the *concision* (AV and RV), 'the incision party' (Moff.), 'those who mutilate the flesh' (RSV). The Greek word is *katatomē*, a term Paul uses in contradistinction to *peritomē*, thus a parody of contempt—amputation, not circumcision. The word implies a rite bereft of faith and so a mere empty symbol, just a mutilation of the body. *Peritomē*, on the other hand, implies the real circumcision of faith, as described in verse 3— the spiritual worshippers of God, the boasters in Christ Jesus, who alone is the source of righteousness. Such put no trust in their own righteousness or in the works of the flesh.

Verses 4–11 are a biographical passage, in which Paul declares that he has all the Judaizers have, and more. He reveals how he himself might boast in terms of legalism. There are seven excellent marks: 'Whoever thinks he can rely on outward privileges, I can outdo him. I was circumcised on the eighth day after birth; I belonged to the race of Israel, to the tribe of Benjamin; I was the Hebrew son of Hebrew parents, a Pharisee as regards the Law, in point of ardour a persecutor of the church, immaculate by the standard of legal righteousness' (Moff.). Verse 9 presents the two kinds of righteousness which Paul in his life-experience knew well: the *righteousness, which is of the law* and *the righteousness which is of God by faith*, i.e. one legal, the other imputed. He rests upon Christ alone for righteousness. His great problem, which he puts into formal shape in his Epistle to the Romans, 'How can I get right with God?', is solved by faith in the risen Lord. All Paul's hereditary and religious merit, his law-righteousness, is viewed by him as *dung* (8), or 'refuse', that which is cast out as worthless. His values have come under a radical revision. The most precious treasure, he now covets, is *the excellency of the knowledge of Christ Jesus my Lord* (8). The personal pronoun singular, *my*, is very impressive. Paul is not ashamed to own his Lord.

The master thought of these verses is this experimental knowledge of the risen Lord. The apostle rings the changes upon it and reveals it to be the dynamic of all his self-renunciation, the underlying motive of complete repudiation of any self-merit whatsoever. He phrases the goal differently: *that I may win Christ* (8), that I may be *found in him* (9), *that I may know him* (10), and that *I might attain unto the resurrection of the dead* (11). These four phrases are rewarding to contemplate.

i. That I may win Christ (iii. 8). The RV renders not *win* but 'gain', thus bringing to our notice that Paul uses the same Greek term as in his previous reckoning of gains (see verse 7, RV mg.). He already has Christ, but not yet in fulness. The Christian life is a good fight of faith. Its goal is not achieved automatically.

ii. That I may be found in Him (iii. 9). Paul is here thinking above all of his standing in Christ. Brought into spiritual union with Christ (*in him*) by faith, not by law, he is safe for time and eternity. His is a full salvation, a never-ending fellowship with God the Father through Christ the Son. This personal knowledge of Christ is made still more explicit.

iii. That I may know Him (iii. 10). It is Christ Himself Paul wants to know in increasing measure, the Christ of the resurrection, and the Christ of the cross. The three pregnant phrases, *the power of his resurrection, the fellowship of his sufferings, being made conformable unto his death*, contain a wealth of meaning. The question has been raised whether they refer to the apostle's life in Christ or to his service for Him. The answer surely is that they include both. *The power of his resurrection*; not the power of the doctrine merely that on the third day, according to the Scriptures, Jesus rose from the dead, though that too is powerful (cf. Acts xvii. 31; Rom. i. 4, iv. 25); but the power of the risen life of the Saviour realized in Paul's daily life and service. (Cf. Rom. viii. 10, 11, xv. 18, 19; 2 Cor. iv. 7–11, xii. 9.) *The fellowship of his sufferings;* an experience so closely linked with the vital flow of grace from

the risen, living Lord that it comes under the same realization of Christ. One Greek article serves both the resurrection *power* and *fellowship* in suffering, thus grammatically making the two phrases one. The fellowship of Christ's sufferings is found in the experience of denial of self (Mk. viii. 35), in learning obedience (Heb. v. 8), in redemptive service (2 Cor. iv. 11, 12). *Being made conformable unto his death.* This is an inner experience which relates to the essential form (Gk. *morphē*) and not the outer fashion (Gk. *schēma*), as in Rom. xii. 2, where conformity to the world is prohibited. Cf. Gal. ii. 20, v. 24, vi. 14.

iv. If by any means I might attain unto the resurrection of the dead (iii. 11). Involved in the knowing of Christ, as Paul has grasped it, is the blessed result of rising with Christ at the resurrection of the dead. To know Christ in His resurrection power and in fellowship with His sufferings is to be on the way to glory through resurrection. The imputed righteousness of Christ becomes the imparted righteousness, for experimental knowledge of the Saviour transforms the whole life. Paul anticipates realizing the victorious, risen life of Christ in his own personality and uniting with the spirits of just men made perfect. The 'day of the Lord' will be a glorious day for the apostle. Paul has no doubt whatsoever of his destiny. The words *if by any means* do not express doubt, but rather a free purpose of heart to have part in 'the resurrection of life' (Jn. v. 29).

b. A warning against Perfectionists (iii. 12–16)

The apostle speaks of his own experience quite frankly. Some of his unenlightened converts may fancy they are perfect, but Paul denies any such complete attainment. Such conceit is tactfully condemned. *I follow after*, their spiritual father humbly confesses, *if that I may apprehend that for which also I am apprehended of Christ Jesus* (12). The RV is preferable here: 'for which also I was apprehended by Christ Jesus.' The Greek verb in the passive aorist tense (*katelēphthēn*) implies definite action in the past, a specific event in the apostle's experience, i.e. his conversion. Christ's purpose in saving him must be fulfilled by his continual pursuit in the same direction. 'I continue to lay hold because likewise I was laid hold of.' But even so, in all this consecrated life of his, Paul did not assume high sainthood. On the contrary, like a runner on the foot-track, he strained forward in the direction of the goal to win the prize of the heavenly calling in Christ Jesus. The idea of the Christian finish and its felicity is common in the Pauline literature and is summed up as the receiving in fulness all that God has given us in Christ. Cf. 1 Cor. ii. 9; Eph. iv. 13, 14; Col. iv. 12. Cf. also 1 Pet. v. 4 ('crown of glory'); 2 Tim. iv. 8 ('crown of righteousness'); Rev. ii. 10 ('crown of life').

For Paul the blessed consummation of the Christian good fight is never a solely individual experience. He reveals his own ideals to inspire his converts unto 'the perfection of the saints'. Thus he continues *Let us therefore, as many as be perfect, be thus minded* (15). It has been suggested that Paul is here being ironical: 'such among you as fancy you are perfect.' The meaning rests with the Greek word in the text, *teleioi*. Paul in his letters uses the term nine times (Phil. iii. 15; 1 Cor. ii. 6, xiv. 20; Eph. iv. 13; Col. i. 28, iv. 12; Rom. xii. 2; 1 Cor. xiii. 10). Only the first six refer to persons; 1 Cor. xiv. 20 and Eph. iv. 13 are definitely in contrast with *nēpios* (child). Hence 'mature' is a clear meaning of *teleios*. It is possible that the word was used in the early Church to describe Christians of ripe experience (cf. Heb. v. 14, RV mg.). Some would render also 'initiated', a word used in the mystery cults of the age. But the translation 'perfect' suffices when it is noted that the fulfilment of our end is possible at various stages of experience. Child perfection is different from the perfection of youth or manhood or old age. Another mode of interpretation is to view the word, as Paul uses 'saints', in the light of the end. None is perfectly perfect, but both Paul and his converts are on the road to perfection and may be so considered. Hence it is not necessary to assume sarcasm in the expression here. Paul enjoins the Philippians (with the perfectionists among them especially in mind), who fancy they have reached finality, to be *thus minded* (15), to have this point of view, i.e. of heights yet to be scaled. If his children at Philippi hold different ideas God Himself shall be their teacher; thus gently does Paul rebuke the perfectionist party. Just one thing more the apostle wants to say before he passes on. 'So far as we have gone let us keep on going' (16). Perfection is attained only by progressing from the stage already arrived at. This progress cannot be achieved in any isolation of disunion; but is made by keeping in step with one another. The Greek word *stoichein*, translated 'walk', means to march in rows or in file in the same direction.

c. A warning against Antinomians (iii. 17–21)

Paul is believed in this section to be thinking of the Antinomians (lit. those against the law or moral code). Such affect, in their excessive but spurious spirituality, to despise the flesh as evil. There is no need, on this view, to obey the law as far as the body is concerned, for the spirit is everything. Indeed the spirit strives to rid itself of its contaminating partner. This attitude to the body runs either to asceticism or to libertinism. Here at Philippi the issue evidently was the latter, that is, gross sensuality. Such ideas used as a way of life are absolutely alien to the true Christian. Paul exhorts the Philippians to follow his example (17) and to shun that of the Antinomians in their midst who make a god of their appetites (19). The gospel of Jesus Christ which he had preached to them laid the emphasis upon the spiritual, not upon the carnal, upon heavenly, not upon earthly things (cf. Col. iii. 1). Their *conversation* (RV 'citizenship', see i. 27n.)

is in heaven (20). Hence the Christian way of life is regulated by the Lord Jesus Christ, whose spiritual rule in the lives of believers involves the two facts of His coming again and the transformation of the body (20, 21). Far from contempt for the body there ought to be reverence. *Our vile body* (21). There is nothing derogatory intended here; it is only an unhappy rendering. The RV 'the body of our humiliation' follows the Greek. Even the idea of humiliation implies no more than that the body we now have is conditioned by its earthly limitations, mortality included; but it has the potentiality of exaltation, glorification, transformation into a spiritual body *like unto his glorious body* (21). The omnipotent power of the Creator-Redeemer will accomplish this.

VIII. THREE FINAL EXHORTATIONS.
iv. 1–9

The first verse here may be the conclusion of the previous section—a general appeal to *stand fast* (RSV 'firm') *in the Lord*. It may also refer to the advice Paul is about to give, so quickly does his mind move. Thus he gives three last counsels to remain steadfast, one to individuals, the other two to the church as a whole.

a. Counsels of reconciliation (iv. 2, 3)

Two distinguished ladies of the church had evidently quarrelled—Euodia (fem. as in RV) and Syntyche. Each would have a following and so disruption was being sown. Paul exhorts them to *be of the same mind in the Lord* (cf. ii. 2), and so live together in harmony. The assistance of a third party is invoked to this peaceful end. Who the *true yokefellow* thus entreated is, is not known. Likewise Clement cannot be identified. Possibly both were 'bishops' in the church at Philippi (cf. i. 1). The pictorial expression *book of life* is found only here and in the book of Revelation (cf. Rev. iii. 5, xiii. 8, xvii. 8, xx. 12, 15, xxi. 27). But cf. Ex. xxxii. 32; Ps. lxix. 28 (RV); Is. iv. 3 (RV mg.); Da. xii. 1; Lk. x. 20.

b. Counsels of rejoicing (iv. 4–7)

The keynote of the Epistle is joy. It emerges at all places. The accompaniments of rejoicing are noted here as five: sweet reasonableness (*moderation*, RV 'forbearance', RV mg. 'gentleness'); the presence of Jesus (*The Lord is at hand*, or perhaps 'is near'; His presence rather than His Parousia); absence of care; prayer with thanksgiving (see i. 9n.); and the peace of God.

c. Counsels of righteousness (iv. 8, 9)

These centre in the reckoning of the true values of life. *Think on these things* signifies 'take these things into account'. It is an appeal to the moral judgment. What are these values? The apostle gives a list of seven: real (*true*), the venerable (*honest*), the upright (*just*), the *pure*, the *lovely* ('those things whose grace attracts'), the 'hightoned' (*of good report*) and everything of moral value worthy of praise (*if there be any virtue, and if there be any praise*). Such were the things of excellence Paul valued most of all and he exhorts his converts to fill their thought-life with them as the very spring of practice. For contemplation of these things is not enough. Thought must be translated into action, along the line of Paul's own teaching and example (9). Walking thus, the *God of peace* will be with them (cf. verse 7).

IX. ACKNOWLEDGMENT OF GIFTS.
iv. 10–20

In this concluding section Paul first expresses his gratification for the generosity of the Philippian church. This noble and tactful acknowledgment is indeed the immediate occasion of the letter. Again the prisoner greatly rejoices. Now it is because of the thoughtfulness of his beloved converts. They were ever mindful of his temporal needs, but recently they had not managed to send any gift owing to lack of opportunity. Evidently the gifts he had now received at the hands of Epaphroditus had arrived most opportunely. But while rejoicing in their bounty Paul feels he must assert his complete independence of material conditions so long as he can depend upon the power of Christ within him (13). He is not a greedy man ever expecting gifts. It is the grace of liberality bestowed upon the Philippians that rejoices the apostle's heart. Some discover in verse 18 a play upon the name of Euodia to whom he refers in iv. 2 for *an odour of a sweet smell* (in the original *osmēn euōdias*, an euodian odour). It may be that Euodia had a prominent part in collecting the gifts sent through Epaphroditus. A similar play upon a name (Onesimus) is found in Phm. 11.

Paul follows his acknowledgment of the Philippian gifts with praise for their characteristic open-handedness (14–16). From the very foundation of the Christian fellowship there some years before, the Philippians had exercised constant consideration for the apostle's livelihood. They had sent time and again their free-will offerings to him. It appears that Paul made the Philippians his only benefactors. They were so loyal, and loving, and eager to give. Their many love-gifts come back to the apostle's mind as he accepts these fresh and fragrant remembrances of him. All is carried into God's presence. From the spiritual, rather than from the material standpoint, Paul declares the Philippians will be rewarded for their kindness, not as compensation indeed, but as commendation. God is the apostle's banker. 'My need you supply. Your need my God will supply' (19).

X. CLOSING SALUTATION. iv. 21–23

It is believed that these last lines of the letter were in the apostle's own handwriting (cf. 2 Thes. iii. 17; 1 Cor. xvi. 21; Gal. vi. 11; Col. iv. 18). The little phrase *in Christ Jesus* is sometimes taken with the verb *salute* and sometimes with the noun *saint* (21). It goes with the verb in Rom. xvi. 22 and 1 Cor. xvi. 19 where it is slightly changed to *in the Lord*. But the association with the noun is preferred here (cf. i. 1). *The brethren which are with me*, who send greetings, are not named. It would depend upon where Paul actually was in prison, Rome or Ephesus, but the bearer of the letter, Epaphroditus, could supply all the necessary information to the Philippian church. The RV reads 'with your spirit' in place of *with you all* (23), following the best attested text. The phrase 'with your spirit', implying that grace is desired to infuse the most inward nature, is found also in Gal. vi. 18 and Phm. 25.

F. DAVIDSON.

THE EPISTLE TO THE COLOSSIANS

INTRODUCTION

See also the General Article, 'The Pauline Epistles', p. 68.

I. DESTINATION

The Colossae of New Testament times was a city whose glory had long since departed. Its neighbours in the Lycus valley—Hierapolis and Laodicea—had by now attained to a position of far greater eminence. Colossae, the scene of a halt of Xerxes' great host during its march against Greece, was referred to on that occasion as a 'great city of Phrygia' (Herod. vii. 30); but Strabo, writing two generations before the time of Paul, calls it 'a small town'. Significant, too, is the fact that while Laodicea and Hierapolis loom large in the early records of the Christian Church, Colossae practically disappears. This led Bishop Lightfoot to write: 'Without doubt Colossae was the least important church to which any Epistle of Saint Paul was addressed.'

Besides the Phrygian population there was in Colossae a substantial number of Jews and Greeks. References such as those found in Col. i. 27, ii. 23, iii. 7 would suggest that a large proportion of the membership of the Colossian church was Gentile, while the presence of a Jewish element may be inferred from the nature of the heresy which Paul attacks in the course of the letter. There is also independent testimony to the presence of a large and influential Jewish community in the district.

'We give thanks to God . . . since we heard of your faith in Christ Jesus' (i. 3, 4); 'Epaphras . . . who also declared unto us your love in the Spirit' (i. 7, 8). These expressions and particularly the opening words of chapter ii make it clear that at the time of writing, at least, the apostle himself had not visited the church at Colossae. Nevertheless, the connection between Paul and this church was very close and cordial. Epaphras, who appears in the letter as the one through whom they had been introduced to the gospel, is represented in some MSS as having acted in this capacity on the apostle's behalf (see i. 7, RV). He was probably one of Paul's Ephesian converts. Then there was Paul's contact with the church through Philemon and now through Onesimus, the latter's slave (see iv. 9). It was on the occasion of Onesimus' return to Philemon, bearing Paul's letter to him and accompanied by Tychicus, that this letter was delivered.

II. AUTHORSHIP AND DATE

It is clear that Colossians was written at the same time as Philemon and the two letters seem to have been delivered by the same messengers.

The question of the authenticity of Colossians is therefore closely bound to that of Philemon. Baur, in rejecting the authenticity of Colossians, was forced to deny the authenticity of Philemon also. He found in Colossians ideas which he considered to belong to a later Gnosticism. But the author is compelled to use certain quasi-Gnostic terms in order the more thoroughly to overthrow the teaching of the heretics. There can be no doubt that Paul wrote Philemon (see *Introduction* to that book), and the case for attributing the same authorship to both is overwhelming. Besides this, the external witness to Colossians is very strong and scholars are generally in favour of the Pauline authorship.

The letter obviously belongs to a period when Paul was a prisoner (cf. Col. iv. 3, 18). Some commentators assign it, with its companion letters, to an early imprisonment, with the suggestion that the place was Ephesus. They point out that Paul writes in the name of himself and Timothy, and Paul had Timothy with him at Ephesus. Moreover, they argue, Paul appears to be in close touch with Macedonia and Asia Minor. Does not this point to Ephesus rather than to Rome? Again, would Paul have sent Onesimus all the way from Rome to Colossae, in view of the difficulty of travel in those days? For a detailed statement of this suggestion see the *Introduction* to Philippians.

These arguments appear strong until the traditional arguments for Rome are marshalled. Rome was the obvious place for a runaway slave like Onesimus. Moreover, the composition of these companion letters would demand a fairly protracted imprisonment, and there is no evidence of such an imprisonment at Ephesus. The crisis at Ephesus would appear to have been sharp and short. The imprisonment at Rome fulfils the conditions required for such careful and thorough writing as is found in these Epistles. There are, besides, the references in Philippians to the 'Praetorium' and to 'Caesar's household' which would immediately suggest Rome. It may be safely assumed, therefore, that the letter was written during the imprisonment recorded in Acts xxviii, probably in the year A.D. 61. (See also the General Article, 'The Pauline Epistles', p. 70.)

III. OCCASION

The letter to the Colossians was written primarily to combat a subtle and dangerous heresy.

Attempts have been made to name and identify the heresy, notable among them the attempt of Lightfoot to prove that it can be traced to Jewish Essenism. But more important than identifying the heresy is to see its underlying principles. The chief relevant passage is ii. 8–23. In this passage various elements in the heresy are mentioned or implied. The teaching is represented as a 'philosophy' (ii. 8); it probably insisted on the enforcement of the Judaistic initiatory rite of circumcision (ii. 11); it had to do with the observance of special days, such as the new moon and the sabbath (ii. 16), and with ascetic practices (ii. 16). There was also a tendency to rob Christ of the all-sufficiency of His mediation between God and man by interposing spiritual beings as a means of communication between man and deity, and worshipping these beings (ii. 18, 19).

The Jewish element in the heresy is clear enough. What can be said of the more unfamiliar angel-worshipping element? Here are discerned definite Gnostic tendencies. The basis of Gnosticism is the doctrine that matter is evil. In creation God cannot come into direct contact with matter. It is necessary, therefore, to posit a number of emanations of deity, a number of spiritual beings germinating, as it were, the first from God, the second from the first and so on until they sink lower and lower and make contact with matter possible. Only thus could God have created the universe and at the same time maintained His holiness inviolate. It follows, then, that these graded angelic beings are in control of the material universe in which man has to live. He must, therefore, enlist the support of spiritual beings who will protect him against the forces at work in the material universe. Thus the work of Christ has to be supplemented by a cult of angels.

It will be seen that the heresy is a grave one. It dares to assert the insufficiency of Christ in the work of human redemption. Paul counters this 'philosophy'—it might well be called a 'theosophy'—by asserting the absolute supremacy of Christ in the universe. Against the background of this heresy is to be seen the full import of the great passage in Col. i. 15–20, where the cosmic significance of the Person and work of Christ is so grandly set forth. Christ is not one of many spiritual beings through whom our redemption is wrought. He is head over all things, the agency of creation, the One in whom it pleased the Father that all fulness should dwell. The meaning and purpose of the universe are, therefore, known in Him.

The very heresy Paul combats accounts for the fact that this letter is more philosophical in tone than most other Pauline Epistles. But even in this letter the great thought of reconciliation is central and the great doctrine of the mystical sharing in the death and resurrection of Christ is set forth. Occasioned by one specific heresy, the letter in Paul's hands becomes a statement of vital Christian faith in its doctrinal and ethical aspects.

There is a close connection between this book and Ephesians, passages in both being virtually identical. For a note on this see the *Introduction* to Ephesians, p. 1015.

OUTLINE OF CONTENTS

I. SALUTATION AND THANKSGIVING. i. 1–8

II. PRAYER FOR THEIR SPIRITUAL ADVANCEMENT. i. 9–14

III. CHRIST IN RELATION TO GOD, THE UNIVERSE AND THE CHURCH. i. 15–19

IV. THE RECONCILING WORK OF CHRIST. i. 20–23

V. THE APOSTLE'S PART IN PROCLAIMING THAT WORK. i. 24—ii. 3

VI. WARNING AGAINST, AND REFUTATION OF, THE FALSE TEACHING. ii. 4–23

VII. THE NEW LIFE AND THE OLD. iii. 1–11

VIII. THE GARMENTS OF HOLINESS. iii. 12–17

IX. INJUNCTIONS CONCERNING DOMESTIC LIFE. iii. 18—iv. 1

X. EXHORTATION TO PRAYER, WISDOM AND CIRCUMSPECT SPEECH. iv. 2–6

XI. COMMENDATION AND CLOSING SALUTATIONS. iv. 7–18

COMMENTARY

I. SALUTATION AND THANKSGIVING. i. 1–8

In his opening sentences the apostle adopts the customary framework of salutation but, with his own deft touches, fills it with Christian content. In giving his authoritative title, particularly in the phrase *by the will of God* (1), some commentators think Paul is seeking to defend his authority against those who might question it (cf. Gal. i). In view, however, of the use of the same expression in 1 Cor. i. 1, 2 Cor. i. 1, Eph. i. 1, etc., Lightfoot inclines to the view that the expression must be taken as 'a renunciation of all personal worth, and a declaration of God's unmerited grace'. This is probably the sound interpretation. For the phrase 'by the will of God' came freely from the apostle's pen in contexts where it can have no polemical significance (cf. Rom. xv. 32). *Timotheus* (1). Timothy is often associated with Paul in the opening salutation (cf. Philippians and Philemon), and the greeting is here clearly from both. The association is dropped in verse 23. The people to whom the apostle writes are designated *saints and faithful brethren in Christ* (2). As saints, they were separated unto God, for the underlying meaning of the word is 'set apart'. Perhaps the additional and unusual title of *faithful brethren in Christ* suggests by implication that Paul is addressing only those who are steadfast in their profession. But see Eph. i. 1n. The best MSS give the greeting as 'Grace to you and peace from God our Father' (see RV), omitting *and the Lord Jesus Christ* (2). This is the only place where the name of the Father alone is mentioned in a Pauline opening benediction.

We give thanks (3). In 'giving thanks' Paul adopts the conventional Greek way of opening epistles. But it is here more than a convention. It is charged with genuine feeling and is used to lead up gradually to the main theme of the letter (cf. Eph. i. 15–23). *Since we heard* (4). This shows that Paul had to depend on reports for his knowledge of the condition of things at Colossae (see *Introduction*); clearly there was much in these reports to gladden his heart. The bringing together of *faith, love* and *hope* (4, 5) should be noted (cf. 1 Cor. xiii. 13; 1 Thes. i. 3, v. 8; and see Eph. i. 15n.). *Faith* is the essence of Christian life in its Godward or religious aspect; *love* in its manward aspect; while the whole life is based on a great *hope*, 'hope being here not so much the act of hoping as the object hoped for' (C. H. Dodd). This hope had been proclaimed to the Colossians *in the word of the truth of the gospel* (5) which they had heard before the heretical teaching arose. *In all the world* (6). This gospel bears fruit in all sorts of places and thus bears the stamp of catholicity. It is not like the fancy teaching of the false teachers who would turn the Colossian church into the rallying-point of an esoteric cult. Christian faith makes a universal appeal. This faith the Colossians had

received *in truth* (6), i.e. 'in its genuine simplicity, without adulteration' (Lightfoot). The gospel had been brought to them by Epaphras who had acted as Paul's representative. *For you* (7); follow RV and read 'on our behalf'. *Who also declared* (8). By this time he had reported back to Paul their love in the Spirit. The less pleasing parts of the report are naturally left unmentioned in this section of thanksgiving.

II. PRAYER FOR THEIR SPIRITUAL ADVANCEMENT. i. 9–14

For this cause (9) refers back to the whole of the preceding paragraph. The substance of the apostle's prayer is virtually that his readers be fortified against the false teaching (see *Introduction*). It is because of the threat to the truth from the new speculation that Paul prays that they may be *filled with the knowledge of his will in all wisdom and spiritual understanding* (9). The aim of all this is practical, that they *walk worthy of the Lord* (10). Sound doctrine is in order to right conduct. Nor is the latter possible without the former. Note the characteristic correlation of doctrine and behaviour. For Paul, Christianity is not a mere 'way of life' in the accepted modern sense, but always a way of life founded upon a doctrine. *Unto all pleasing* (10) does not mean 'pleasing everybody'. The phrase goes with *the Lord* and might be paraphrased 'pleasing God in every way'. The strengthening of the believer by the power of God which he desires for them leads to endurance, joyfulness and thanksgiving (11, 12). This latter is enjoined upon the Colossians as a Christian duty (cf. ii. 7, iii. 17, iv. 2). They have sufficient cause for thanksgiving. For God has made them competent to share the lot of the saints *in light*. The heavenly kingdom into which they have been brought is a kingdom of light. Cf. Eph. v. 8ff. Lightfoot paraphrases verse 13: 'We were slaves in the land of darkness. God rescued us from this thraldom. He transplanted us thence, and settled us as free colonists and citizens in the kingdom of His Son, in the realms of light.' It is to be noted that the word rendered *translated* (13) is used of the transportation of whole peoples from one country or district to another. There may be here the idea of a Christian 'exodus'. The kingdom into which they are transported is the *kingdom of his dear Son* and not of inferior angels. (The controverting of the heresy begins: see *Introduction*.) Cf. Heb. i. 1—ii. 8. Finding himself in this kingdom the believer is no longer subject to the *powers of darkness* (cf. Eph. vi. 12). This transportation involves a great emancipation. Verse 14 is the picture of a benefactor who sets a slave free by the payment of a ransom. It is verbally identical with Eph. i. 7, where see note.

III. CHRIST IN RELATION TO GOD, THE UNIVERSE AND THE CHURCH. i. 15–19

This is the crucial passage of the Epistle. Hitherto Paul has shown that our salvation is wrought by Christ. Bringing this fact into relation with the heresy he is attacking (see *Introduction*), Paul now seeks to prove conclusively that no angelic agencies are necessary. In order to do this, he states Christ's relationship to God and to the universe. The reader will at once recognize in Paul's treatment a close similarity to the Logos doctrine in the prologue to John's Gospel (Jn. i. 1–18).

Christ is the *image of the invisible God* (15). The word rendered *image* (Gk. *eikōn*) carries the meaning of likeness and involves representation and manifestation. Thus the God whom no man hath seen at any time becomes manifest in Christ (cf. Jn. i. 18). Paul was able to write elsewhere that Christians have beheld the 'glory of God in the face of Jesus Christ' (2 Cor. iv. 6). The writer to the Hebrews speaks of Christ as being 'the express image of his person' (Heb. i. 3). The word used here in Hebrews is different from that used here but the thought is closely related. This *image of the invisible God* is *the firstborn of every creature* (15; RV 'of all creation'). This phrase was used by the Arians to prove that Christ was a created being and not co-eternal with the Father. It would appear in the English rendering to mean that Christ is to be regarded as one, even though the earliest, of created beings. But the Greek word *prōtotokos* may denote the one prior to creation. Christ is then placed outside of creation. Moffatt renders 'born first before all the creation'. That this is the meaning here will be seen clearly from the next verse. There is also the thought that as *firstborn* he is heir of all creation.

In verses 16 and 17 note the three things said of Christ in His relation to the universe. First, He is the ground of creation (16a). This means that all created things, whether visible or invisible, owe their being to Him. This shows the true place of the hierarchy of angelic powers which the heretics were trying to set up in rivalry to Christ. The terms *thrones, dominions,* etc., were being used in current angelology. Paul uses these terms to show that 'all possible existences are included'. Owing their existence to Christ, they are all subordinate to Him. Cf. Eph. i. 21. Secondly, Christ is the ultimate goal of the universe. *All things were created . . . for him* (16b; RV 'unto him'). 'As all creation passed out from Him, so does it all converge again towards Him' (Lightfoot). Cf. Heb. ii. 10. In Christ, then, is to be found the inner purpose of the creation. Thirdly, as He is the source and goal of creation, so also in Him all things hold together (17b). The Greek word *synestēken* translated *consist* means 'cohere'. Lightfoot makes this point in an admirable sentence: 'He impresses upon creation that unity and solidarity which makes it a cosmos instead of a chaos.'

The universe, then, begins, continues and ends in Christ. This profoundly theological statement, giving the cosmic significance of Christ, is not the kind of passage we expect to find in writings in which the religious interest is uppermost. But the speculative side of the heresy at Colossae

demanded some such statement. Nor was the apostle one to think compartmentally. Even beliefs which mainly concern the spiritual life have to be co-ordinated with our view of the whole order of reality.

Having shown that no power or being can claim a place along with Christ in our conception of creation, Paul proceeds to show that no such being is to share a place with Him in the worship and life of the Church. For as Christ is the source and chief of the natural creation, so He is the head of the new creation, the Church. *The body, the church* (18). Paul elsewhere describes the Church as the body of Christ, usually starting from the function of the members and stressing their interdependence, etc. (cf. 1 Cor. xii. 12–26). In using the figure here, he starts from the idea that Christ is the head not merely in the sense that the head is the most important and controlling member of the body (cf. Eph. i. 22, 23n.) but rather in the sense that 'all the forces of the body are gathered up in the head' (E. F. Scott). His qualification to be head of the Church is put in similar terms to those used in describing His relationship to the creation. Note the parallel use of the term *firstborn* (Gk. *prōtotokos*). Through His resurrection from the dead, Christ is the first-born of the new creation. *In all things,* therefore (i.e. in all matters of both the natural and spiritual orders), He has the *preeminence*. Verse 19 provides an explanation of this absolute pre-eminence of Christ. It is because *it pleased the Father that in him should all fulness dwell*. The word *fulness* (Gk. *plērōma*) denotes 'the totality of the divine powers and attributes' (Lightfoot). In Gnostic writings the term was used to denote the sum total of the emanations of the Godhead (see *Introduction*), and it has been suggested that some such meaning had begun to attach itself to the term in the church at Colossae under the influence of the heretical teachers. Whether this be so or not, Paul's purpose in using the term in this context is clear. Christ is not one among many heavenly powers to be reckoned with. He needs no supplement. In His redemptive work we see the fulness of divine action. *Dwell* (19), i.e. 'abide permanently'.

IV. THE RECONCILING WORK OF CHRIST
i. 20–23

It will be noted that the reconciling work of Christ is all-embracing. Rom. viii. 19–22 shows that in the apostle's view even the material creation shares in the cosmic discord. And reconciliation, to be complete, must deal with *all things . . . whether they be things in earth, or things in heaven* (20). C. H. Dodd interprets: 'Through Christ God has chosen to put an end to all the distressing disharmonies within His universe and bring all under one effective rule.' This is achieved once and for all by that divine act which is the death of Christ, the full outworking of whose consequences had yet to be witnessed, cf. Rom. viii. The thought of this passage is developed more fully in Ephesians (see e.g. i. 9f., ii. 13ff.). What has taken place thus on a universal scale is to be seen in the experience of the Colossians themselves. In this complete salvation wrought by Christ and needing no supplementing by other heavenly powers, the believers themselves have shared. The former condition of the Colossian believers is described in the strongest terms—*alienated and enemies* (21). Theirs is an example of hostility overcome. The theological truth of verse 20 is seen now in evangelical experience. *In the body of his flesh* (22). These words serve to underline the truth that Christ entered fully into the life of man in order to fight sin on its own ground and that He achieved our eternal redemption by one decisive act in history. In His victory, Christ presents the believer without blemish and without a charge being levelled against him. C. H. Dodd points out that the reference in this verse is not to a moral perfection which the Colossians will one day attain. Paul is here dealing with justification by faith, and so *holy and unblameable* (RV 'without blemish') *and unreproveable* (22) refer to their present standing in Christ. Cf. Eph. i. 4, v. 27. There is, of course, one condition to be fulfilled, viz. that they maintain unsullied their faith in Him who so justifies them. They must cling to this universal gospel and not be drawn away to any fancy cult.

V. THE APOSTLE'S PART IN PROCLAIMING THAT WORK. i. 24—ii. 3

Paul never ceased to marvel at, and rejoice in, the stewardship of the gospel entrusted to him. *Fill up that which is behind of the afflictions of Christ* (24). There is no suggestion in any writing of Paul's that the sufferings of Christ are insufficient for the redemption of the world. Indeed the insistence is so constant in the other direction that any interpretation of this verse must first of all take for granted that no suffering on the part of the disciple is needed to supplement the atonement for sin. What, then, is the meaning of this phrase? Lightfoot makes a helpful distinction between the 'sacrificial efficacy' and the 'ministerial utility' of Christ's sufferings. Viewed from the latter standpoint, there is a sense in which Christ's afflictions are incomplete: '. . . the afflictions of every saint and martyr do supplement the afflictions of Christ. The Church is built up by repeated acts of self-denial in successive individuals and successive generations.' An interpretation may also be offered along the following lines: Paul in this context brings in the idea of the mystical union of the believer with Christ. The apostle thus endures his sufferings in fellowship with Christ, and these are not yet completed. These afflictions are not endured for their own sake, but *for his body's sake, which is the church* (24). *To fulfil* (25), i.e. to preach fully (cf. AV mg. and Rom. xv. 19).

The most virile religions in the Hellenistic age were those practised by select cults and known as 'mystery religions'. Worship was in two parts. There was the general worship and accepted belief; these were open to all and sundry. Then there were certain secret rites and teachings which were reserved for the select few, the chosen initiates. This esoteric element accounted for the general name 'mystery religions'. Did Paul have these religions in mind when he wrote of *the mystery* (26)? It has been pointed out that by Paul's day the word was used generally to signify a secret of any kind, and that the mere occurrence of the word would not necessarily carry an allusion to the esoteric religions. But what the apostle writes in verses 26–28 strongly suggests that he has the figure of these religions in the back of his mind, but that he uses it intentionally in a contradictory way. There is a *mystery which hath been hid . . . but now is made manifest* (26), but the idea of secrecy or reserve is entirely absent. Indeed it is explicitly excluded. For the Christian preachers *preach, warning every man, and teaching every man in all wisdom; that we may present every man perfect in Christ Jesus.* The word *perfect* was used in the mystery religions to describe the fully initiated and consequently 'mature' man (Gk. *teleioi;* cf. 1 Cor. ii. 6 and see also note on Phil. iii. 15). The whole of Christianity is for *every man* (cf. Eph. i. 9, iii. 3–9, vi. 19; see also Col. iv. 3).

And what is this mystery? Lightfoot suggests it is the offering of salvation to the Gentile world, and interprets *Christ in you . . .* (27) as referring specifically to the Gentiles. 'Not Christ, but Christ given freely to the Gentiles, is the "mystery" of which Paul speaks.' E. F. Scott, on the other hand, thinks it doubtful whether this great 'mystery' consists in nothing more than 'the inauguration of a Gentile mission'. He points out that in verses 25, 26 the term *mystery* is in apposition to *the word of God,* so that in all probability the 'mystery' refers to the inner content of the gospel rather than its spread. 'The mystery of God, hidden from all eternity and now revealed, is the indwelling of Christ in His people, whether Jews or Gentiles.' But in view of Eph. iii, the former interpretation would seem to carry more weight. This indwelling of Christ is the *hope of glory,* the promise of the believer's coming inheritance.

According to his working (29). This work of the ministry Paul undertakes not in his own strength. Here is a characteristic statement of Paul's view of the relation of grace and freedom. Cf. Phil. ii. 12, 13. *As many as have not seen my face* (ii. 1). The apostle makes it clear that his ministry and his concern embrace those whom he has not met. The letter was probably meant to be read also to the other Lycus valley churches —Laodicea and Hierapolis (see *Introduction*). Verses 2 and 3 introduce Paul's discussion of the Colossian heresy. The way of strength to the Colossians lies in a harmony of spirit (*hearts . . . knit together in love*) and a full grasp of their treasure in Christ. There are no secret *treasures of wisdom* (3) which are not in Christ Himself.

VI. WARNING AGAINST, AND REFUTATION OF, THE FALSE TEACHING.
ii. 4-23

Direct reference is now made to the teachers whose heresies occasioned the writing of the letter. The Greek *paralogizētai*, translated *beguile*, carries the idea of being led astray by fallacious reasoning (Lightfoot). Nothing is more powerful to do this than 'persuasiveness of speech' (RV). The heresy evidently commended itself because it appeared plausible on the lips of the teachers and appealed to the quasi-intellectuals. The words translated *order* and *stedfastness* (5) are military metaphors. Lightfoot paraphrases 'the orderly array and the solid phalanx which your faith towards Christ presents against the assault of the foe'. *So walk* (6); cf. i. 10 and Eph. iv. 1, 17n. There is to be no turning away from the precepts of the gospel as first received by them. *Rooted* and *built up* (7) bring out different ideas, the former being a perfect participle and the latter a present participle. 'The sustaining faith of the Christian is to be something fixed once for all—the conduct which rests upon it is to be always growing' (E. F. Scott). Note the recurrent emphasis on thanksgiving (cf. i. 12n.).

Two factors combine to make the detailed exposition of verses 8-15 extremely difficult: concentrated packing together of the essential doctrines of the faith, and the allusions to a heresy with whose details we are not familiar and of which we have no systematic statement. The main teaching of the passage is, however, beyond doubt.

Beware . . . philosophy (8). It must not be imagined that here we have Pauline grounds for a wholesale attack on philosophy as such. The words *and vain deceit . . .* would indicate the kind of philosophy (perhaps the word here should be in quotation marks) Paul has in mind, viz. an empty although plausible teaching. This teaching is *not after Christ*. It is based on human tradition, i.e. a secret system confined to a sect. Moreover it is *after the rudiments* (AV mg. 'elements') *of the world* (8). The Greek phrase *ta stoicheia*, rendered 'the elements', has an interesting history. From 'things set in a row' it came to mean the letters of the alphabet, then the rudiments of any subject, and through various stages came to be applied to the elements of the physical universe. Later it was used of the powers believed to be controlling the universe. This is the meaning given by many commentators to the word as it appears in this verse. The meaning then would be that this teaching derives from angel-worship rather than from Christ. The 'supplementing' work of these heretics is to be fiercely resisted. For Christ cannot be supplemented. In Him dwells *all the fulness of the Godhead bodily* (9). *Bodily* here is not a reference to Christ's human body. The meaning is that the fulness of deity in its totality is in Christ. As C. H. Dodd puts it: 'Bodily is "corporately" rather than "corporeally".' There is

no element of the divine nature absent in Christ. *Ye are complete in him* (10). As Christ cannot be supplemented, so the life in Christ cannot be supplemented. He is head of all powers. Having Him we need none else. (See notes on i. 17, 18 and Eph. i. 21.)

The rite of circumcision as administered in Israel is a picture of what has happened to us (11). Material circumcision was a cutting away of the flesh; spiritual circumcision is likewise a cutting away, but of the whole carnal nature, described here as *the body of the sins of the flesh* (cf. Rom. vi. 6). *Putting off* (11). Cf. Eph. iv. 22ff.

The transition from the idea of spiritual circumcision to that of baptism is a natural one. Here we have another picture of the experience of the believer. The figure used is that of immersion. There has been a burial of the believer with Christ and a rising again to newness of life (cf. Rom. vi. 4). It must not be supposed that the apostle considers that the mere act of baptism achieves this, *ex opere operato* as the phrase has it. It is 'through faith in the working of God' (RV) that meaning and validity can be given to the rite. *Dead in your sins and the uncircumcision of your flesh* (13). Are we to conclude from this statement that Paul makes uncircumcision a symbol of natural wickedness? The general trend of his teaching goes against this view. It would seem that the figure is used just to bring out the contrast between their former state and their present position in Christ. It is as though he were saying 'You were morally and spiritually dead, nor did you have even the racial token to give you hope. But now . . .'. Forgiveness (13) is the great initial blessing bestowed upon us in Christ. Paul introduces in verse 14 two figures to describe what God has done with sin and guilt. First, He has erased the note of hand (14a). The law (AV *ordinances*) is here regarded as man's debt to which he is bound. It is *against us* because it stands as a testimony to our failure, but God, in Christ, has cancelled the IOU (see RSV). Secondly, He has done more. He has taken it and cast it aside (14b). Lightfoot paraphrases: 'the law of . . . ordinances was nailed to the cross, rent with Christ's body, and destroyed with His death.' The suggestion that the reference is to the cancellation of a debt by running a nail through it and displaying it in a public place is not convincing. No evidence of such a custom exists.

In verse 15 there is a sudden change of figure. One thing emerges clearly. Christ has *spoiled principalities and powers*. The metaphor is a military one. He has fought unseen powers, stripped them of their arms and displayed them in the manner of the Roman triumph. (Cf. Eph. iv. 8 where this thought is linked with our Lord's ascension.) Hence we have no powers to fear. We are no longer submitted to bondage, whether of the law or of angelic powers.

This assertion leads on to and has an important bearing on Paul's criticism of the heresy. The Colossians are warned against mistaking shadow for substance. The heretical teachers would have them pay attention to ascetic practices and ritual none of which avail to the man who is in Christ. *Judge you* (16); i.e. 'take you to task' (Moff.). *In meat, or in drink* (16). Although the Levitical law was silent on the subject of drink, this ascetic ruling probably had a close connection with Judaism, particularly when coupled, as it is here, with the observance of holy days, new moons and sabbath days, the annual, monthly and weekly ceremonials of Judaism (cf. Gal. iv. 10). The objection to these practices is that they are, at best, merely anticipatory, *a shadow of things to come* (17; cf. Heb. x. 1). In each case 'the reality, the antitype is found in the Christian dispensation' (Lightfoot). *The body* (17); i.e. 'the substance'. Verse 18 is notoriously difficult of interpretation. In 1912 Sir William Ramsay discovered an inscription at Klaros containing the word here translated *intruding into*. The meaning in the inscription is 'he entered in', the expression being used of an initiate who had completed his course of probation. This would suggest that in this verse the apostle uses the grandiose language of these mystery cults in a tone of scorn. *Those things which he hath not seen*. The negative should be omitted (cf. RV). The phrase then refers to the 'visions' enacted before the worshipper. RSV gives the general sense of the verse: 'Let no one disqualify you, insisting on self-abasement and worship of angels, taking his stand on visions, puffed up without reason by his sensuous mind.' The trouble with such people is that they do not hold fast by Christ who, as the head of the body, gives it unity and vitality (19). The tendency then is toward disintegration. Note the implication in this figure of a direct relation between every believer and Christ Himself, without the use of intermediaries.

Wherefore if ye be dead (20). Those who have died with Christ to lower things must not know again bondage to human tradition. The prohibitions put forward by the heretics (21) show that they are still under the domination of the material. Verse 23 shares the difficulty of verse 18. It is suspected that there has been a corruption of the original text. *Shew of wisdom* would suggest that the practices have no sound doctrinal basis. Lightfoot's paraphrase of the verse probably gives the meaning as exactly as possible: 'All such things have a show of wisdom, I grant. There is an officious parade of religious devotion, an eager affectation of humility; there is a stern ascetic rigour, which ill-treats the body: but there is nothing of any real value to check indulgence of the flesh.'

VII. THE NEW LIFE AND THE OLD.
iii. 1–11

Under the figure of baptism Paul has already pointed out (ii. 12) that the believer is buried and risen again with Christ. He now proceeds to bring out the implications of this burial and resurrection. The Christian is done with the mundane things upon which the heretics concentrate. Through his resurrection with Christ he belongs to a higher world and his desires and conduct must accordingly be raised to a higher level. *Your life is hid* (3); i.e. your new life. Lightfoot paraphrases: 'When you sank under the baptismal water, you disappeared for ever to the world. You rose again, it is true, but you rose only to God. The world henceforth knows nothing of your new life . . .' Note here that the new life is comparable to that offered by the mystery religions in being 'hidden' and yet, unlike such, it does not depend upon ordinances and intermediaries. It is a life directly in God. Because of this direct relation, in contrast to the heretics' endeavour to penetrate intermediate realms (ii. 18), the Christian can freely set his mind on the things of highest heaven, where Christ sits enthroned. But although the true character of this new life is now hidden, it will shine forth in that day when the Lord shall appear (4). The day of the manifestation of Christ will be the day of the manifestation of the Christian also (cf. 1 Jn. iii. 2).

A list of things to which the Christian is dead is given in verse 5. Why, it may be asked, does the believer need to *mortify* his members if he is already dead? In answering this question something may be said of the apostle's method of argument in these matters. He consistently seeks to make the believer see the implications of his new position. The Christian must accept the new position by faith and seek by God's grace to make it objectively true. 'On the ideal or purely religious plane, the Christian by faith . . . has left the old life behind and entered the new. But Paul was realist enough to recognize that it did not by any means automatically follow that the Christian ceased to sin . . . The steady intention of mind and will is needed to make explicit in fact what is already given in principle' (C. H. Dodd on Rom. vi. 11, *Moffatt Comm.*). The classic elaboration of the thought in verse 6 is found in Rom. i. 18ff., where Paul points out the awful consequences of godlessness. There he goes so far as to say that God 'gave them up to uncleanness'. It is well to note that this terrible state which looks like the automatic outworking of sin is an expression of the reaction of the living God Himself to sin, termed *the wrath of God*. Verse 7 is characteristic of the apostle. Not once nor twice does he remind his readers of what they have been saved from (cf. 1 Cor. vi. 9–11). The reminder is usually followed immediately by a *But* (see verse 8) introducing a description of their present state and making the grace of God loom large. The putting off of *the old man* (9) and the putting on of *the new man* (10) imply a break with everything that is of the old life. See notes on the parallel passage in Ephesians (Eph. iv. 22–24). The *new man* is a creation of God, and is renewed according to that ideal of man which was originally in the mind of the Creator. The thought of the new life suggests another change, namely in the relationship of race with race and of one estate with another. These racial, religious and cultural differences are transcended in Christ. *Barbarian* and *Scythian* are not in contrast to one another, as are the other pairs in this verse. *Barbaroi* was the name given by the Greeks to those who spoke any (to them) unintelligible language, i,e. uncivilized foreigners. (The word *barbaroi* is onomatopoeic.) The Romans knew all foreign races as 'Scythians'.

VIII. THE GARMENTS OF HOLINESS. iii. 12–17

The virtues of verse 12 are to take the place of the vices of verse 8. The putting off of the old garment is to be followed by the putting on of the new. See notes on Eph. iv. 25–31 where the negative aspects are given at greater length.

Elect . . . holy and beloved (12); an allusion to the covenant relation of the Old Testament. The words apply in a new and nobler sense to the new Israel of God. This privilege is the basis of the Christian's great responsibility. *Bowels of mercies* (12). The *splanchna*, translated 'bowels', were regarded as the seat of the affections, so that the expression might be translated (as Lightfoot) 'a heart of pity'. *Longsuffering* (12); the ability to endure with patience all misunderstanding and opposition.

Quarrel (13); better, as in RV, 'complaint'. *Even as Christ forgave you* (13). The RV substitution of 'the Lord' for *Christ* is probably right and brings out the *a fortiori* argument with greater force. If the Master forgives His servants how much the more should they forgive one another (cf. our Lord's parable in Mt. xviii. 23–35)! *Above all these things* (14). Lightfoot (and others) interpret this verse as signifying that 'love is the outer garment which holds the others in their places'. The force of these words and the word *bond* is in that case obvious. *The peace of God* (15; RV 'the peace of Christ'; cf. Jn. xiv. 27) is to be the 'umpire' in all things. This is the meaning of the Greek word *brabeuetō*, translated *rule* (RV mg. 'arbitrate'). When occasions of dispute arise in the fellowship (notice the reference to *one body*), as they are prone to do, then the peace of Christ is to give the decision. This is, of course, an exhortation to cultivate the peace-loving temper.

The Christian message is to be so deeply rooted in the life that it governs the believer's thinking (16). Lightfoot uses the suggestive phrase 'inward monitor'. The prominent place which psalmody occupied in the churches of New Testament times is indicated in this verse. Some of the *hymns* and *spiritual songs* were probably spontaneous expressions of praise. E. F. Scott compares them with the unpremeditated spirituals of the negro. See Eph. v. 19n. *Do all in the name of the Lord Jesus* (17). The reference here is not to the invocation of His name. It is an exhortation to the Christian to do everything as in His presence and unto Him. The recurrent emphasis on thanksgiving echoes ii. 7.

IX. INJUNCTIONS CONCERNING DOMESTIC LIFE. iii. 18—iv. 1

The treatment here should be compared with that in Eph. v. 22—vi. 9, where see notes. The apostle writes concerning the Christian attitude to relationships within the household. These are threefold; that of husband and wife, that of parent and child, and that of master and slave. *Wives, submit yourselves* (18). If by modern standards Paul seems to fail to treat the wife on an equality with the husband, two facts must be borne in mind. In some of the churches of the time there was clearly a tendency for the women to neglect their household duties and to seek an unnatural emancipation. Cf. the various references in the Pastoral Epistles. Also the general attitude in Paul's day was to assume that all the rights were the man's. The really significant thing here is that the apostle insists that there are obligations on both sides. The injunction to children (20) is in accord with the Decalogue and the whole of Old Testament teaching. Fathers have to exercise discipline but this must not be administered in such a way as to become sheer nagging. *Discouraged* (21). The Greek means 'to lose heart'. Lightfoot paraphrases 'go about their task in a listless, moody, sullen frame of mind'.

Undoubtedly the case of Onesimus and Philemon (see *Introduction* to Philemon) prompted the statement given here (iii. 22—iv. 1) of the relationship between servants and masters. This does not mean that the character of either is to be deduced from the injunctions. The slave is to work conscientiously, remembering that all he does is done as unto the Lord. Whatever treatment the slave receives at the hands of his earthly master, he must remember that he will receive the heavenly Master's reward for work well done (25). See the notes on the parallel passage in Ephesians (Eph. vi. 5–9).

Is Paul here condoning the whole system of slavery? Is he attempting to dope the slave into accepting the injustices of the system by promising reward in heaven? Questions of this kind are best answered by placing the statements of the apostle in the context of his own day. In the eyes of the law the slave was a chattel and the question of treating a chattel fairly would seem ridiculous. And yet this is the very question raised here. The slave is to be treated with justice and equity (iv. 1), i.e. as a person having rights. And so, while Paul does not condemn the system of slavery, he seeks to establish that relationship which was eventually, in the slow working of Christian conscience, to overthrow the system itself. (See the discussion of this question under Philemon.) In verse 25 the first part probably refers to the slave, the second to the master. This accords with the connection of the sentence with what precedes it and with the verse that follows.

X. EXHORTATION TO PRAYER, WISDOM AND CIRCUMSPECT SPEECH. iv. 2–6

In this section the apostle emphasizes first the Church's duty towards its messengers. The

Colossians are asked to continue steadfast in prayer. *Watch in the same* (2); Gk. *grēgorountes;* lit. 'keep awake'. There must be no sloth or listlessness in regard to prayer. Moffatt, while not adhering too closely to the original, gives a suggestive rendering: 'maintain your zest for prayer.' Especially are they asked to pray for Paul and his colleagues 'that God may open unto us a door for the word' (3, RV), i.e. that opportunities of preaching may be given them. For *the mystery of Christ* (3) see under i. 26–28. Next Paul stresses their duty toward the 'outsider', our modern term for *them that are without* (5). He realizes, as the Colossian Christians must realize, that the most effective testimony to the power of the gospel is the life (*walk*) and conversation (*speech*) of the ordinary Christian. The wickedness of the age made the opportunities for good all the more precious and so the Christians were to buy up every passing moment (6; cf. Eph. v. 15, 16n.).

Their speech must be *with grace* (6). Paul is not thinking of linguistic style, of course. The idea is that of acceptableness. E. F. Scott suggests that in these verses the apostle may have in mind those 'well-meaning people who felt it laid on them to denounce all Pagan customs—in season and out of season—with the result that they set the world against them'. Their behaviour and talk should attract rather than repel. *Seasoned with salt* (6). The thought here is not of being preserved from evil or corruption, but of avoiding insipid and pointless argument.

XI. COMMENDATION AND CLOSING SALUTATIONS. iv. 7–18

This section is much more detailed and personal than the closing verses of Ephesians, where personal greetings are entirely absent. Paul does not need to provide details of his condition. These can be given by Tychicus who bears the letter. He has been instructed by Paul to call at Colossae for the very purpose of giving them such information. For *that he might know your estate* (8) substitute RV rendering 'that ye may know our estate'. This is better attested and fits in better with *the same purpose* which obviously refers back to verse 7. Tychicus was a native of Asia Minor (cf. Acts xx. 4) who had accompanied Paul toward the end of his third missionary journey and was later to be mentioned by him again in connection with missions to Crete and Ephesus (cf. Tit. iii. 12 and 2 Tim. iv. 12). The description of him as *a faithful minister* (7) probably refers to the service he had rendered the apostle himself. *Onesimus, a faithful and beloved brother* (9). There is no reference here to his reformation. But the commendation would convey as much to those who had known of him. *Aristarchus* (10) was a Thessalonian (Acts xix. 29). *My fellowprisoner* is taken to mean that Aristarchus had voluntarily shared Paul's imprisonment in order to minister to him. His association with Paul may, of course, have aroused suspicion and caused him actually to be made a prisoner

for a time. *Marcus* (10). This is the first mention of Mark after the rupture of Acts xv. 39. The impression of that time had evidently been wiped out. Since this is the first time Paul had written to the Colossians, the *commandments* (10), previously received by the church, must refer to some message Epaphras had sent. We know nothing else about *Jesus . . . called Justus* (11). The punctuation of the latter part of this verse needs to be amended to give this sense: 'these are the only fellow-workers of the circumcision who have been a comfort to me': cf. the complaint in Phil. i. 15, 16. *Epaphras* (12), himself a Colossian, has already been commended (i. 7f.). *Servant of Christ* (12); Gk. *doulos Christou*. Only on one other occasion does Paul use this phrase of someone other than himself (cf. Phil. i. 1), and it is to be regarded as high commendation indeed. *In all the will of God* (12). The meaning is not 'in whatever befalls you'. The thought is that they should have such a grasp of God's will that nothing will shake them. For *perfect* see note on Phil. iii. 15. Verse 14 is the source of our information that Luke was a physician. His long association with the apostle may have been due to the fact that Paul's malady, whatever it was, was his constant companion. *Demas* (14). Notice that there is no epithet of commendation. Is this omission a foreshadowing of the relationship described in 2 Tim. iv. 10?

Paul now sends greetings to people he knows in the churches which the messenger will visit. *The church which is in his house* (15). The early Christian communities had no buildings set apart for worship. It was necessary for a church in any given town to divide itself into little communities worshipping in private dwellings (cf. Acts xii. 12; Rom. xvi. 5). A more general congregation might be held in the open air. Verse 16 throws light on Paul's intentions in writing this letter. It is clear that for all their intimate character they were intended to be read aloud to a church gathering. Moreover the reference to the exchange of letters between the Colossian and Laodicean Christians shows that the Epistles were meant to have a certain amount of circulation and were not casual messages to a single group. It is probable that the Laodicean letter referred to here is now lost, although some believe it is the one known to us as 'Ephesians'. *Archippus* (17) was of the family of Philemon (Phm. 2). Perhaps he had been placed in charge of affairs in the church in Epaphras' absence.

By the hand of me Paul (18). Paul ends his dictated letter with a greeting in his own hand. Papyri of the period show that this was a fairly general custom. Also, Paul seems to have used his autograph as a sign that the letters bearing it were genuinely his (cf. 2 Thes. ii. 2, iii. 17). *My bonds* (18). Did his chains move even as he signed the letter? The sound of pen and chains together is the final sign that the preacher's chains cannot bind the word of God.

J. ITHEL JONES.

THE EPISTLES TO THE THESSALONIANS

I THESSALONIANS: INTRODUCTION

See also the General Article, 'The Pauline Epistles', p. 68.

I. BACKGROUND

Thessalonica (Saloniki) was originally called Therme, but was refounded by Cassander *c.* 315 B.C. and named Thessalonica after his wife, a step-sister of Alexander the Great. Alike in Macedonian and Roman times it was an important city. The Romans made it the capital of the province of Macedonia in 164 B.C. and a free city after the battle of Philippi in 42 B.C. Through it ran the great Egnatian Road, on its way from Neapolis on the Aegean to Dyrrhachium on the Adriatic.

Paul's first visit to Thessalonica—to be dated probably in the early summer of A.D. 50—is narrated in Acts xvii. 1-9. It was the first city where he and his companions, Silas (Silvanus) and Timothy, spent any length of time after their departure from Philippi, in the course of his 'second missionary journey'. In accordance with their regular practice, they visited the local synagogue. For three successive sabbaths Paul attempted to convince the synagogue congregation from their Old Testament scriptures that the Messiah was bound to suffer and rise again from the dead, and that Jesus was therefore the Messiah. Several of his hearers believed his message, including a large number of 'God-fearing' Gentiles. But the consequent opposition between the synagogue authorities and the missionaries led to public disorder. The city magistrates, or 'politarchs' as Luke calls them (a title which they shared with the chief magistrates of other Macedonian cities), received information that Paul and his companions were messianic agitators, such as had caused disturbances in many other places throughout the Roman Empire where there were Jewish communities, and that they proclaimed another king in rivalry to the Emperor. Such a charge was necessarily regarded with the utmost gravity. But Jason, Paul's host, and other friends whom the missionaries had made in Thessalonica, went bail for them, undertaking that they would leave the city quietly, and sent them away by night.

The young church which they were thus forced to leave behind in Thessalonica was exposed to some active persecution. Paul was very anxious for his converts' welfare, and wondered how they would stand, especially as his sudden departure prevented him from giving them all the instruction that he regarded as adequate for the establishment of an infant Christian community (cf. 1 Thes. iii. 10). But his hands were tied by his Thessalonian friends' guarantee; he could not go back at present. From Thessalonica he went on to Berea with Silas, and Timothy later rejoined him. He sent Timothy back to Thessalonica, and Silas to some other parts of Macedonia, while he himself went on to Corinth. Here, after some weeks, Silas and Timothy returned to him, and Timothy was able to report that the Thessalonian Christians, far from succumbing to the persecution with which they had been tested, were standing firm and actually propagating the gospel on their own initiative. But there were several matters on which they desired further enlightenment, especially with regard to what Paul had taught them about the return of Christ. In particular, some of their number had died since Paul left their city, and they were eager to know if these would in consequence suffer any disadvantage at Christ's return in comparison with those who would still be alive when it happened.

Paul was overjoyed at Timothy's good news, and wrote at once to congratulate and encourage his Thessalonian converts, and to deal with their practical problems. The letter which he wrote has come down to us as the first Epistle to the Thessalonians.

II. DATE, AUTHORSHIP, CANONICITY

It follows from what has just been said that this letter was written in the earlier part of Paul's stay at Corinth—say towards the end of A.D. 50. For Timothy's return from Macedonia to Corinth (bringing Paul the news from Thessalonica) see Acts xviii. 5.

Although Paul associates his two travel-companions with himself in the salutation (i. 1), the letter is really his own (cf. ii. 18, iii. 5, v. 27 for the first person singular). There has been little serious doubt of its genuineness. F. C. Baur's idea that it was written after A.D. 70 by a disciple of Paul in order to arouse interest in the return of Christ rests on subjective arguments which have failed to win general agreement. The personal note of pastoral concern and affection speaks strongly for the letter's authenticity. It was included in Marcion's Canon (*c.* A.D. 140) and in the orthodox Roman Canon preserved in the Muratorian fragment (late second century).

III. TEACHING

Paul is not concerned in 1 Thessalonians to give instruction on any one doctrine or to correct any one error—apart from his desire to complete the eschatological teaching which he had given the Thessalonian Christians during his curtailed visit to their city, and thus remove some misunderstandings and perplexities in this field. It is first and foremost a missionary's letter to his converts, and references to Christian doctrine are incidental rather than central. But for that very reason the way in which they are introduced and expressed is the more significant. We may note the following points.

a. God the Father

Paul is completely and continuously God-conscious. It is basic to his whole thought that God is the source of all and the goal of all, the One in whose presence he lives and works moment by moment. It is He who has chosen His people (i. 4); He is the object of their faith (i. 8) as the living and true God to whom they turned from unreal gods (i. 9). He imparts the authority for the apostles' bold confidence (ii. 2); it is by His permission that the gospel has been entrusted to their charge (ii. 4); it is His pleasure that they must seek and His witness that they ought to be able to invoke (ii. 5, 10). It is His will that must be done (iv. 3, v. 18); His guidance that must be followed (iii. 11). He has called His people to holy living (iv. 7) and He alone can impart to them the sanctification to which He has called them (v. 23). It is He who raised up Jesus and will bring with Him from the dead those also who have fallen asleep in Him (iv. 14), thus consummating the salvation to which He has appointed them (v. 9).

b. The Lord Jesus Christ

The spontaneous and almost unconscious way in which Christ is associated with God the Father is even more eloquent testimony to Paul's conception of the Person of Christ than a formal statement of His deity would be. The church at Thessalonica is 'in God the Father and in the Lord Jesus Christ', and he salutes them with a prayer for grace and peace 'from God our Father, and the Lord Jesus Christ' (i. 1). So also in iii. 11 'our Lord Jesus Christ' is directly and actively associated with 'God . . . our Father' in His direction of the apostles' footsteps. (Cf. also 2 Thes. i. 1, ii. 16.)

c. The Holy Spirit

The Holy Spirit is all-pervasive in the Christian life, which indeed is His creation. The gospel is proclaimed by His power (i. 5); not only is His joy imparted to those who believe it (i. 6), but He Himself is given to them (iv. 8) to accomplish His sanctifying work in their lives (2 Thes. ii. 13). In church life too He plays His part by communicating the divine will through prophetic utterances; to despise or inhibit such utterances is to 'quench the Spirit' (v. 19).

d. The apostolic preaching

The references to the message which had brought salvation to the Thessalonian Christians show that it was the same message as that attested elsewhere in the New Testament. Its basic facts are Jesus' death ('for us', v. 10) and resurrection, which have already taken place (iv. 14, i. 10), and His coming again, which is to take place at the day of the Lord, when His people, delivered by Him from the wrath to come (and sharing His resurrection if they have already died), are to live for ever with Him (i. 10, iv. 15ff., v. 1ff.). Those who believe this message turn from unrealities to the living and true God, to serve Him in the light of Christ's second advent (i. 9f.). And it is plainly shown what this serving God involves, by the plain instruction in practical Christian living here and there throughout this Epistle and the following one (e.g. iv. 1–12, v. 6ff.).

e. Pastoral responsibility

Paul reveals himself in every sentence of this letter as a true and faithful pastor, rejoicing in his flock but anxious for their welfare, confident and concerned, thanking God for them and simultaneously praying to God for them, tirelessly caring for them as a father for his children, straining his strength to the limit in order not to be a burden to them. 'Here was a new phenomenon in history, a man to whom the religious steadfastness and ethical progress of other men was a matter of life and death (see especially ii. 8, 9, iii. 6–8)' (C. A. A. Scott).

I THESSALONIANS : OUTLINE OF CONTENTS

I. SALUTATION. i. 1

II. THANKSGIVING. i. 2–10

III. APOLOGIA. ii. 1–16

IV. NARRATIVE OF EVENTS SINCE PAUL LEFT THESSALONICA. ii. 17—iii. 10

V. PRAYER FOR A SPEEDY REUNION. iii. 11–13

VI. EXHORTATION TO HOLY LIVING AND BROTHERLY LOVE. iv. 1–12

VII. CONCERNING THE SECOND ADVENT. iv. 13—v. 11

VIII. GENERAL EXHORTATIONS. v. 12–22

IX. PRAYER, FINAL GREETING AND BENEDICTION. v. 23–28

I THESSALONIANS : COMMENTARY

I. SALUTATION. i. 1

Paul, and Silvanus, and Timotheus (1). Associated with Paul in the salutation are his two friends who had collaborated with him in the evangelization of Thessalonica and were now with him at Corinth. Silvanus, the Silas of Acts xv. 22ff., was a Hellenistic member of the Jerusalem church and a Roman citizen who joined Paul as his travel-companion after the Council of Jerusalem, at the outset of the second missionary journey. (Paul gives his friends their formal names when writing about them; Luke prefers the more homely pet-names.) Timothy, a native of Lystra in Asia Minor, joined Paul and Silvanus when they passed through his home town early in their journey (Acts xvi. 1ff.).

II. THANKSGIVING. i. 2–10

Paul and his friends express their joy at the Thessalonian converts' steadfastness and energy in Christian grace and witness. The facts were known widespread, and spoke for themselves. *Faith . . . love . . . hope* (3). This triad of graces reappears in v. 8 and Col. i. 4f. (see notes) as well as in the famous passage 1 Cor. xiii. 13. The writers rejoice that these graces are manifested in the life and activity of the Thessalonians. *Knowing . . . your election* (4). They had recognized the genuineness of the Thessalonians' Christianity by the way in which they received the gospel in the beginning, and this was confirmed by the news which Timothy had brought back. *Ye became followers* (RV 'imitators') *of us* (6); in Christian behaviour as well as in the endurance of persecution. *Macedonia and Achaia* (7). These two Roman provinces together covered most of the area of modern Greece. Apart from Thessalonica itself, Philippi was the principal church in Macedonia; Corinth was the outstanding church in Achaia. *In every place* (8). Had Priscilla and Aquila (cf. Acts xviii. 1–3) told Paul that news of the church in Thessalonica had travelled as far as Rome? *They themselves* (9); i.e. the people of Macedonia and Achaia and so forth. *Ye turned to God from idols to serve the living and true God*.(9). Cf. the apostolic admonition to the pagans of Lystra 'that ye should turn from these vanities (i.e. idolatry) unto the living God' (Acts xiv. 15). This was a primary necessity when the gospel was proclaimed to Gentiles. *And to wait for his Son from heaven, whom he raised from the dead* (10). The words in which the Thessalonians are reminded of their conversion show us that the message preached to them

followed the regular lines of the primitive apostolic preaching. For the close connection of Christ's resurrection with His coming again in this preaching cf. Acts xvii. 31. The return of Christ had plainly occupied a prominent place in the apostolic preaching at Thessalonica, as it did elsewhere in the earliest days of Christianity (cf. Acts iii. 20, x. 42). *Jesus, which delivered us from the wrath to come* (10). This might be rendered more personally 'Jesus, our deliverer from the coming wrath', i.e. the divine judgment to be poured upon the earth at the end of the age.

III. APOLOGIA. ii. 1–16

Paul's conduct had been represented in an unfavourable light to the converts whom he had left behind at Thessalonica, and he now defends himself. He and his companions had made no attempt to exploit them or live at their expense; on the contrary, they had shown all gentleness and care towards them. They had worked night and day in order to earn their own living while they were busy preaching the good news and building up the new-born Christian community. And the Thessalonian Christians in turn had proved worthy converts, persevering in face of persecution just like the Christians of Palestine.

After that we had suffered before . . . at Philippi (2); a reference to the well-known events related in Acts xvi. 19ff. *Not of deceit* (RV 'error'), *nor of uncleanness, nor in guile* (3). So many wandering charlatans made their way about the Roman world, peddling their religious or philosophical nostrums, that it was necessary for the apostles to emphasize the purity of their motives and procedure by contrast with these. *We might have been burdensome, as the apostles of Christ* (6). For Paul's voluntary forgoing of his undoubted right to have his material requirements met by those for whose spiritual welfare he cared cf. 2 Thes. iii. 9; 1 Cor. ix. 4ff.; 2 Cor. xi. 7ff. Here he associates Silvanus and Timothy with himself as *apostles*, in the wider sense of the term (i.e. missionaries). *We were gentle* (7); Gk. *ēpioi*. There is a variant reading 'we were babes' (Gk. *nēpioi*); but *gentle* seems preferable, and more appropriate in the context.

Labouring night and day (9); cf. 2 Thes. iii. 7ff.; Acts xviii. 3, xx. 34. This policy not only reflected a desire to be financially independent of those among whom they ministered; it also marked them off from the ordinary religious traffickers of the day, and showed the converts a good example. *That ye would walk worthy of God, who hath called you unto his kingdom and glory* (12).

The highest of all incentives for holy living is set before them. In the New as in the Old Testament the people of God must display the character of God. By faith they had already entered the kingdom of God, but the revelation of its full glory belonged to a day yet future; they were, however, heirs of that glory, and must live accordingly.

Not as the word of men, but . . . the word of God (13). Paul was so accustomed to hearing his message denounced as man-made, not only by non-Christian Jews, but by many Jewish Christians as well, that he found it specially encouraging when it was sincerely welcomed as the good news of God. Cf. Gal. i. 11, 12n. *The churches of God which in Judaea are in Christ Jesus* (14); the original church of Jerusalem in dispersion (cf. Acts ix. 31; Gal. i. 22). *Who both killed the Lord Jesus, and their own prophets . . .* (15). The bitterness of this reference to *the Jews* (14) is unparalleled in Paul's writings and it has been suspected of being an interpolation. There is no textual basis for this suspicion, however, and the summary of their behaviour is closely in accord with the narrative of Acts. The trouble stirred up by the leaders of the Jewish communities of Thessalonica and Berea was fresh in Paul's mind. It would be foolish to imagine that the author of verses 14–16 could not also have expressed himself in the language of Rom. ix. 1–5. *Forbidding us to speak to the Gentiles* (16); cf. Acts xiii. 45. *To fill up their sins alway* (16). For the same idea cf. Mt. xxiii. 32. *The wrath is come upon them to the uttermost* (16). This has been thought by some to presuppose the destruction of Jerusalem in A.D. 70, which would mean that this section is a later addition to the letter or that the whole letter is a pseudepigraph (Baur). The Jews of the dispersion were not for the most part involved in that disaster. Paul means that by their persistent opposition to the gospel they had ensured for themselves that eschatological judgment which they might have averted by accepting it (cf. Acts ii. 38ff., iii. 19ff.). In Christian literature before A.D. 70 no very clear distinction is drawn between the destruction of Jerusalem (which, taught by their Lord, Christians knew to be impending) and the final judgments of the day of the Lord.

IV. NARRATIVE OF EVENTS SINCE PAUL LEFT THESSALONICA. ii. 17—iii. 10

It was not lack of interest that prevented Paul from staying longer with them or going back to see them; it was circumstances over which he had no control. He assures them of his longing for them and his joyful confidence in them in view of the return of Christ. It was his impatience to know how they fared that made him send Timothy back to visit them, together with his concern that their faith should be strengthened amid their afflictions. Timothy's report of their welfare and steadfastness had filled him with joy, and also with fresh longing to see them once more.

I Paul (18). Of the other signatories Timothy

had actually visited them, and Silvanus had paid a short visit to Macedonia (Acts xviii. 5), if not to Thessalonica itself. *Satan hindered us* (18). W. M. Ramsay supposed that Paul detected this subtle agency behind the politarchs' action in exacting security from Jason (Acts xvii. 9) and binding him over to prevent Paul, the alleged cause of the disturbance, from coming back to Thessalonica. *Are not even ye in the presence of our Lord Jesus Christ at his coming?* (19). If Paul's converts do him credit, he will face with joy the review of his service to take place at Christ's return (cf. Phil. ii. 16, iv. 1). This is the first occurrence of Gk. *parousia* (translated *coming*) in the Pauline Epistles. Its ordinary sense is 'presence' (cf. 2 Cor. x. 10; Phil. i. 26, ii. 12); but its eschatological sense is akin to its idiomatic usage in the Hellenistic vernacular, of the arrival of some dignitary to pay an official visit to a place. It is so used of the return of Christ eighteen times in the New Testament; the Thessalonian Epistles account for seven of these.

We thought it good to be left at Athens alone (iii. 1). Here the *we* is purely epistolary, referring to Paul himself. Cf. verse 5. For the occasion, see Acts xvii. 15ff. For *minister* (2; Gk. *diakonon*) there is a well-attested variant 'fellow-worker' (Gk. *synergon*); cf. 1 Cor. iii. 9. *We are appointed thereunto* (3). It is taken for granted throughout the New Testament that affliction is the normal lot of Christians; it is, in fact, an evidence of the genuineness of their faith and an earnest of their part in the coming glory. Cf. Acts xiv. 22; Rom. viii. 17f.; 2 Tim. ii. 12. It is noteworthy that the inevitability of *tribulation* had formed part of the apostles' instruction to the Thessalonian Christians as to others (4). What had been an acute problem to faith in Old Testament times— the suffering of the righteous—had come to be recognized as an essential element in God's purpose for His people. Since their Lord Himself had suffered, they need expect nothing else; let them rather glory in tribulation (cf. Jn. xv. 20, xvi. 33; Rom. v. 3).

V. PRAYER FOR A SPEEDY REUNION. iii. 11–13

Paul prays for a speedy reunion with his Thessalonian friends and for their increase in love and holiness in view of the return of Christ.

Now God himself . . . and our Lord Jesus Christ, direct our way unto you (11). The fact that the verb *direct* is singular in Greek, despite its compound subject, has no such theological significance as is sometimes imagined; in such a construction the verb commonly agrees with the nearer subject. But it is significant that Christ is thus associated in action with God the Father. *To the end he may stablish your hearts unblameable in holiness* (13). The second coming of Christ should provide the Thessalonian Christians, as it did Paul himself (ii. 19), with an incentive to holy living. Cf. 1 Jn. ii. 28, iii. 3. The day of Christ's return is the day when He reviews

His people's record. *At the coming of our Lord Jesus Christ with all his saints* (13); or 'with all his holy ones'. Cf. the description of the day of the Lord in Zc. xiv. 5 (LXX): 'The Lord my God will come and all his holy ones (Gk. *hagioi*, as here) with him.' This description is based on the earlier theophanic vocabulary of the Old Testament such as Dt. xxxiii. 2; Ps. lxviii. 17 (cf. also Dn. vii. 10 and the words of Enoch quoted in Jude 14f., and such words in the New Testament as those of Jesus in Mk. viii. 38; Mt. xxv. 31). Primarily therefore here, as in 2 Thes. i. 7, we may regard the 'holy ones' as attendant angels, though we may find cause in 2 Thes. i. 10 to see departed believers associated with them.

welfare of the whole community. The Greek word rendered *study* is *philotimeisthai*; lit. 'be ambitious'. It is usually supposed that exaggerated eschatological expectation (cf. 2 Thes. ii. 2, iii. 6ff.) tended to make some of them excited and restless and neglectful of their ordinary business; this would make them a charge on others and would bring the whole group into disrepute. Brotherly love therefore demanded sober and industrious habits. Paul's idea of readiness for the coming of Christ is in line with the gospel injunction, 'Let your loins be girded about, and your lights burning' (Lk. xii. 35). He himself had taught them this lesson by example as well as by precept.

VI. EXHORTATION TO HOLY LIVING AND BROTHERLY LOVE. iv. 1–12

Paul exhorts them to personal consecration and purity, especially in sexual relations. To this he adds an admonition to maintain brotherly love —superfluous as such an admonition may be in their case—and to go on diligently with their daily work and not to become a charge on others.

By the Lord Jesus (1); i.e. by His authority. *How ye ought to walk* (1); i.e. to behave; this ethical sense of 'walk' is common in the New Testament. *Your sanctification, that ye should abstain from fornication* (3). Paul lays special emphasis on this particular aspect of practical holiness because it was in the sphere of relations between the sexes that even the highest pagan ethic of the time fell far short of the Jewish and Christian standard. Fornication was widely regarded in the Graeco-Roman world as almost on the same level of ethical indifference as food and drink. Experience proved that insistent injunctions of this kind were by no means superfluous for Christians converted from paganism. *To possess his vessel* (4); RV 'to possess himself of his own vessel'; i.e. to keep control of his body rather than to live with his wife; the latter interpretation is not so appropriate here, despite the sense of 'vessel' (Gk. *skeuos*) in 1 Pet. iii. 7. *Even as the Gentiles which know not God* (5); cf. Rom. i. 24ff. *That no man go beyond and defraud* (RV 'transgress and wrong') *his brother in any* (RV 'the') *matter* (6); i.e. in the matter already referred to. Paul seems to be thinking of a trespass of this kind even within the family circle of a fellow-Christian. *Because that the Lord is the avenger of all such* (RV 'in all these things') (6); cf. Eph. v. 6. *Not called us unto uncleanness, but unto holiness* (7). In one sense believers are already 'saints', set apart by God for Himself; in another sense they must manifest this sanctification in daily life. *He therefore that despiseth* (8); i.e. he who disregards these apostolic precepts about practical purity. *Taught of God* (9); cf. Is. liv. 13; Jn. vi. 45; 1 Jn. ii. 20.

Study to be quiet, and to do your own business, and to work with your own hands (11). This is not a new subject, but belongs to the duty of brotherly love; the behaviour of one member affects the

VII. CONCERNING THE SECOND ADVENT. iv. 13—v. 11

He reassures their anxiety about the position of those of their number who have died; they will suffer no disadvantage at Christ's return, but will be raised from the dead and joined by those who are still alive, to form a united escort for their Lord. The time of His return is unknown; it is therefore necessary for His people to be continually ready and watchful.

Concerning them which are asleep (13). Some of their number had died since Paul's departure (possibly as a result of persecution); would these forfeit a share in the glory to be bestowed upon Christians at the second advent? *Even as others* (13); i.e. non-Christians; cf. Eph. ii. 3. *Which have no hope* (13); cf. Eph. ii. 12. The hopelessness of the pagan world in face of death can be illustrated by much contemporary literary and inscriptional material. *If we believe that Jesus died and rose again* (14); the quintessence of the gospel (cf. 1 Cor. xv. 3f.). *Even so them also which sleep in Jesus will God bring with him* (14); i.e. bring back from death, by resurrection. Albeit at a later date, they will rise with Jesus, sharing His resurrection (cf. 1 Cor. xv. 20ff.). The prepositional phrase *in Jesus* is literally 'through (by means of) Jesus' (Gk. *dia tou Iēsou*); the expression 'points to Jesus as the mediating link between His people's sleep and their resurrection at the hands of God' (G. Milligan). Cf. Rom. viii. 11; 1 Cor. xv. 18. Death through Jesus is but the prelude to resurrection with Jesus.

By the word of the Lord (15); i.e. on the authority of an utterance of Christ Himself. We do not find an exact equivalent to what follows in any of His sayings preserved in the Gospels, but that need not imply that Paul is quoting a private revelation made to himself as a prophet. *We which are alive and remain* (RV 'that are left') *unto the coming of the Lord* (15). If here Paul groups himself with those who would be alive at that date, yet a few years later, in 1 Cor. vi. 14 and 2 Cor. iv. 14, he groups himself with those who would be raised from the dead. His estimate of the probability one way or the other might vary from time to time, but as he did not know when the Parousia would take place, he could not know whether he would in fact be alive or dead when it happened. *Shall not prevent* (15); RV 'shall in no wise precede', or 'have any advantage over'. *The Lord himself* (16); for the emphasis cf. Acts i. 11, 'this same Jesus'. *With a shout* (16); lit. 'word of command' (Gk. *keleusma;* cf. its solitary LXX occurrence in Pr. xxx. 27, 'the locust marches at one word of command'). *With the voice of the archangel* (16); lit. 'with archangel's voice'; it is doubtful if we should think of Michael or any other individual archangel here. *And with the trump of God* (16); cf. Mt. xxiv. 31; 1 Cor. xv. 52 ('the last trump'). The shout, the voice and the trumpet may be different figures for the same event. The language reflects the theophanic passages of the Old Testament; cf. Joel ii. 1ff., especially verse 11. *The dead in Christ* (16); cf. verse 14n.; 1 Cor. xv. 18; Rev. xiv. 13. *Shall be caught up* (17); Gk. *harpagēsometha,* Lat. *rapiemur,* whence the event is sometimes called the 'rapture' or snatching away of the saints. *In the clouds* (17); cf. Dn. vii. 13; Mk. xiii. 26, xiv. 62; Rev. i. 7. *To meet the Lord* (17); Gk. *eis apantēsin tou kyriou.* When a dignitary paid an official visit or *parousia* to a city in Hellenistic times, the action of the leading citizens in going out to meet him and escorting him on the final stage of his journey was called the *apantēsis;* it is similarly used in Mt. xxv. 6; Acts xxviii. 15. So the Lord is pictured as escorted to the earth by His people—those newly raised from death and those who have remained alive. *And so shall we ever be with the Lord* (17); the climax of blessedness.

But of the times and the seasons (v. 1); Gk. *chronoi* and *kairoi,* denoting respectively the ages to elapse before the Parousia and the critical epochs marking these ages (so Milligan). *The day of the Lord so cometh as a thief in the night* (2). For the simile cf. Mt. xxiv. 43; Lk. xii. 39; Rev. iii. 3, xvi. 15. See also Lk. xxi. 34ff. for a parallel simile, and Lk. xvii. 24ff. for the general teaching. From his words *yourselves know perfectly* (2) we may infer that Paul had already given them some oral teaching to this effect, based on the words of Jesus. Paul here identifies the Old Testament *day of the Lord* with the second coming of Christ. *As travail upon a woman with child* (3). The woes preceding the inauguration of the messianic age are called in Jewish literature *ḥebhlo shel Mashiaḥ* ('the birthpangs of Messiah'); cf. Mk. xiii. 8, 'the beginning of travail'. *Children* (RV 'sons') *of light* (5); cf. Lk. xvi. 8. *Children of the day* (5); not merely a synonym for *children of light,* but marking believers out as partakers of the glory to be revealed on the day of the Lord. *Let us not sleep* (6). If we are *children of light* and *children of the day,* let us behave accordingly.

The following verses present a close parallel to Lk. xxi. 34–36. *The breastplate of faith and love; and for an helmet, the hope of salvation* (8). See i. 3 for the triad of graces, and for an elaboration of the armour metaphor cf. Eph. vi. 11ff. *God hath not appointed us to wrath, but to obtain*

salvation (9); cf. i. 10 and Rom. v. 9. There, as here, the *wrath* is the judgment of the day of the Lord. *Whether we wake or sleep* (10); i.e. whether we survive to His coming or have died. The words are the same as those above for moral watchfulness and carelessness respectively, but Paul does not mean that it will not matter in the end whether we have been watchful and sober or not! He means, as in iv. 15ff., that no difference will be made between living and dead saints at Christ's appearing; both groups will live together, and live with Christ, since He died for them. Cf. Rom. xiv. 9. 'The real point of this whole paragraph, whose motto, Watch and Pray, should be graven on the shield of every Christian warrior, is the paradox so difficult to us, but much less difficult to minds schooled in the prophets, of stressing the imminence of the Parousia while denying its immediacy' (W. Neil).

VIII. GENERAL EXHORTATIONS. v. 12–22

They are exhorted to lead orderly and peaceable lives, active in well-doing.

Know them which labour among you, and are over you in the Lord, and admonish you (12); i.e. give them practical acknowledgment by submitting to their guidance. The term *pro-istamenoi* ('those who are over you', 'leaders') used here appears also in Rom. xii. 8 of the leaders of the Roman church; they are no doubt identical with those elsewhere called pastors, elders and bishops. Presumably they had been appointed by the missionaries, like the elders of the Galatian churches (Acts xiv. 23), but there is no record of this. *Now we exhort you, brethren* (14). It may be that in this verse the leaders themselves are addressed. *Warn them that are unruly* (14); RV 'admonish the disorderly', lit. 'those who do not remain in the ranks' or 'those who play truant' (Gk. *ataktous*), referring here to 'loafers' (Moff.), who neglected their daily duty and lived in idleness; cf. iv. 11. *See that none render evil for evil unto any man* (15). The ethical injunctions of the Pauline Epistles contain clear echoes of the teaching of Jesus; cf. Rom. xii. 17. *Rejoice . . . pray . . . give thanks* (16–18). Christian life is to be lived in an atmosphere of continual joy, prayer and gratitude to God. *Quench not the Spirit. Despise not prophesyings. Prove all things* (19–21). The reference here is to the exercise of the gift of prophecy, under the impulse of the Holy Spirit, a common phenomenon in the Church of apostolic days. The gift was easily counterfeited, and called for discernment (*Prove all things*), especially on the part of the leaders. The gift itself was not to be disdained, and genuine prophecy was not to be repressed, for that would amount to 'quenching the Spirit'. *Hold fast that which is good. Abstain from all appearance of evil* (21, 22). These clauses should probably be taken together as a pair of complementary injunctions. 'Form of evil' (RV) is lit. 'species (Gk. *eidos*) of evil'. The AV *appearance of evil* is based on the other sense of *eidos.*

IX. PRAYER, FINAL GREETING AND BENEDICTION. v. 23–28

The very God of peace (23); cf. Rom. xv. 33. *Sanctify you wholly* (23); i.e. bring to completion the work of sanctification already begun (cf. note on iv. 7); the aorist optative *hagiasai* here indicates 'a "process seen in perspective", and so contemplated as a complete act' (Hogg and Vine). *I pray God your whole spirit and soul and body be preserved blameless* (23). This clause expresses the same prayer in a new way; the aorist optative is again used with the same force (*tērētheiē*). It is not certain that *spirit and soul and body* should be interpreted as teaching a formal tripartite doctrine of human nature, *spirit* being the 'God-conscious' aspect and *soul* the 'self-conscious' aspect of the inner life. One might as well deduce a formal quadripartite

doctrine from Mk. xii. 30. Verse 24 probably means that He who calls His people to holiness is He who also makes them holy. *I charge you by the Lord that this epistle be read unto all the holy brethren* (27). It is not clear why Paul so solemnly puts the recipients on oath to read the letter to every member of the community. Harnack's theory that there were two distinct groups in the Thessalonian church, one Gentile and the other Jewish, and that, while this Epistle was primarily directed to the Gentile group, Paul wished its contents to be communicated to the Jewish group as well, cannot be maintained. Possibly he wished to make sure that those members who were 'playing truant' (14) heard what he had to say. But his words may be no more than a solemn direction to read the letter at a meeting of the whole church.   F. F. BRUCE.

II THESSALONIANS : INTRODUCTION

I. DATE, AUTHORSHIP, CANONICITY

The second Epistle to the Thessalonians, like the first, is addressed 'unto the church of the Thessalonians' by 'Paul, and Silvanus, and Timotheus'. The situation with which it deals is to a large degree similar to that dealt with by the first Epistle. This suggests that it also was sent from Corinth, and not long after the despatch of the earlier letter. Like 1 Thessalonians, this letter appears too in the earliest lists of Pauline letters that have come down to us. The external evidence for its canonicity is as good as for that of the first Epistle. It is quoted by Polycarp (c. A.D. 120).

Yet several difficulties have been felt to stand in the way of accepting this internal and external evidence at face value. The style of 2 Thessalonians is said to be formal and official by contrast with that of 1 Thessalonians. This point does not amount to much; it arises from such expressions as 'we are bound' and 'it is meet' in i. 3, which really call for no special explanation—certainly not that offered by Dibelius, that 2 Thessalonians, unlike 1 Thessalonians, was written specifically to be read in church (see 1 Thes. v. 27).

More serious is the argument that 2 Thessalonians insists that certain events must precede the day of the Lord (chapter ii), whereas 1 Thessalonians stresses the unexpectedness of that day's arrival, 'like a thief in the night'. But a distinction should be made between suddenness and immediacy; Paul's words about the suddenness of Christ's return in 1 Thessalonians had been interpreted to imply its immediacy, and this made it necessary to point out that a number of things must happen first.

In describing these things, however, 2 Thessalonians uses apocalyptic language unparalleled elsewhere in the Pauline letters. We have, in fact,

a tiny apocalypse in 2 Thes. ii. 3–12. This is not an adequate argument against the authenticity of the letter, and, indeed, present-day knowledge of apocalyptic beliefs at that time, with special reference to the manifestation of Antichrist, has done much to reduce what was once felt to be a great difficulty here (see commentary below).

The similarities between the two Thessalonian Epistles have also been felt to constitute, in their way, almost as great a problem as the differences. In spite of the first Epistle's warning against restless idleness arising from excessive eschatological expectation, the same situation is implied by the second Epistle. However, if the first Epistle's emphasis on the suddenness of the Parousia had been understood to mean its immediacy, the tendency for some to 'play truant' would have been strengthened, in spite of all the admonitions to remain calm and get on with the ordinary business of life.

II. RELATION TO I THESSALONIANS

There are real difficulties in the relation between the two Epistles, and they are largely due to our very inadequate information about the circumstances at Thessalonica. Apart from the attempt to cut the knot by regarding 2 Thessalonians as a forgery, various theories have been propounded to account for the difficulty in relating the two Epistles to each other.

One of these makes 2 Thessalonians earlier than 1 Thessalonians. But this aggravates the difficulty. 2 Thessalonians does seem to imply some previous correspondence by letter (cf. ii. 2, 15, iii. 17), whereas 1 Thessalonians certainly appears to be the first letter written to the Thessalonian church after Paul's departure (see ii. 17—iii. 10). (But see T. W. Manson's article 'St. Paul in Greece', in the *Rylands Bulletin* for March, 1953, for the view that 2 Thessalonians was taken to Thessalonica by Timothy on the occasion mentioned in 1 Thes. iii. 2.)

Harnack's theory has already been mentioned —that 1 Thessalonians was written to the Gentile section of the Thessalonian church and 2 Thessalonians to the Jewish section. The apocalyptic teaching of 2 Thes. ii, it was supposed, would be more intelligible to Jews. But it is incredible that Paul of all people would have acquiesced in such a division between Gentile and Jewish Christians to the extent of writing a separate letter to each; we should certainly have found him taking the line he took at Antioch when a division of that sort began to appear there (see Gal. ii. 11ff.) and making the inculcation of Christian unity his first concern in writing to them.

Yet another suggestion is F. C. Burkitt's— 'that both Letters were drafted by Silvanus-Silas, that they were read to Paul, who approved them and added 1 Thes. ii. 18 and 2 Thes. iii. 17 with his own hand'. This suggestion does not greatly help us—in any case Burkitt intended it as

a supplement to Harnack's hypothesis—and 2 Thes. iii. 17 seems rather intended to authenticate the whole letter as Paul's own (despite Burkitt's idea that the terms of Paul's autographed postscript 'suggest that he is not wholly responsible for all the rest').

In fine, all these suggestions raise greater difficulties than the view that 2 Thessalonians was written by Paul (who added his companions' names) to the whole Thessalonian church no long time after the despatch of 1 Thessalonians, to deal with a development of the earlier situation of which fresh news had come to him. The persecution of the Christians seems to have died down, and there appears to have been no occasion to repeat his previous warning about moral purity. But the eschatological excitement had not abated—partly because Paul's words in 1 Thessalonians were misunderstood and partly through some teaching which they had received from other quarters, and which was perhaps represented as having Paul's authority. It was therefore necessary to deal more explicitly and sharply with this particular question.

II THESSALONIANS: OUTLINE OF CONTENTS

I. SALUTATION. i. 1, 2

II. THANKSGIVING AND ENCOURAGEMENT. i. 3–12

III. EVENTS TO PRECEDE THE DAY OF THE LORD. ii. 1–12

IV. FURTHER THANKSGIVING AND ENCOURAGEMENT. ii. 13—iii. 5

V. THE NEED FOR DISCIPLINE. iii. 6–15

VI. PRAYER, FINAL GREETING AND BENEDICTION. iii. 16–18

II THESSALONIANS: COMMENTARY

I. SALUTATION. i. 1, 2

Paul, and Silvanus, and Timotheus, unto the church of the Thessalonians (1). A comparison with the salutation of the first Epistle makes it as certain as anything can be that both Epistles were written to the whole Thessalonian church.

II. THANKSGIVING AND ENCOURAGEMENT. i. 3–12

We are bound to thank God . . . as it is meet (3). The alleged formality of this language has been contrasted with the language of 1 Thes. i. 2ff. and used as an argument against the authenticity of 2 Thessalonians. But if the Thessalonian Christians had protested against what they considered the excessive commendation expressed in the previous letter, Paul might well reply: 'But it is only right that we should thank God for you; it is the least we can do'; and that is the force of the wording here. *We ourselves glory in you in the churches of God* (4). This is not in-

consistent with 1 Thes. i. 8, 'we need not to speak anything'; even if there was no need, they would speak all the same. Cf. 1 Thes. ii. 20. *A manifest token of the righteous judgment of God* (5). As in 1 Thes. iii. 3f., so here, he points out that their affliction is a proof of the genuineness of their faith, and that their steadfast endurance of it marks them as worthy to inherit the divine kingdom: in them, as in their persecutors, God's righteousness will be vindicated.

To recompense tribulation (RV 'affliction') *to them that trouble you; and to you who are troubled rest with us* (6, 7). The day of Christ's return will be the day of equitable retribution and reward. The *rest* is relaxation or relief (Gk. *anesis*) after toil and conflict. In verse 7 RV renders 'at the revelation of the Lord Jesus from heaven'. The reference is to His manifestation in glory (cf. 1 Cor. i. 7; Lk. xvii. 30). *With his mighty angels* (7). Cf. Mk. viii. 38; Mt. xxv. 31; and other passages mentioned in the note on 1 Thes. iii. 13. *In flaming fire* (8). This again reflects the theophanic language of the Old Testament (cf. Ps. xviii. 8ff.; Is. lxvi. 15). *Taking* (RV 'rendering') *vengeance.* The exercise of judgment by Christ in the New Testament is based on Dn. vii. 13f.; cf. Jn. v. 27; Acts xvii. 31. *That know not God* (8); i.e. who ignore Him, 'refuse to have God in their knowledge' (cf. Rom. i. 28). *Everlasting destruction* (9); i.e. the destruction of the age to come, with the decisive implication of finality. It consists in exclusion *from the presence of the Lord,* with whom alone is 'the fountain of life'. *To be glorified in his saints* (10). This might mean His holy angels (see 1 Thes. iii. 13n.), but the parallelism with the following words, *and to be admired* (RV 'marvelled at') *in all them that believe,* suggests that Christian men and women are meant here. They are to share His glory; the 'revelation of the Lord Jesus from heaven' (7) is also the day of 'the revealing of the sons of God' (Rom. viii. 19).

That our God would count you worthy of this calling (11). This probably looks forward to the day of recompense at the Parousia, that they may on that day be adjudged to have acquitted themselves worthily of their calling; even so, it implies a prayer for their present spiritual progress. *And fulfil all the good pleasure of his goodness* (11); better, as in RV, 'every desire of goodness'. This refers to their own desires, while it is of course true that every such desire, like every *work of faith,* is produced in them by the Holy Spirit (cf. Gal. v. 22; Phil. ii. 13). *That the name of our Lord Jesus Christ may be glorified in you, and ye in him* (12). The reference again is primarily to the Parousia, but Paul's prayer would be fulfilled then only if the Lord's name were glorified in them day by day through life.

III. EVENTS TO PRECEDE THE DAY OF THE LORD. ii. 1–12

Some of the Thessalonian Christians had somehow got it into their heads that the day of the Lord had already begun. Paul explains that it must be preceded by the Great Apostasy, led by the Antichrist, who is to be brought to nought by the advent of the day of the Lord.

By the coming (1); better, as in RV, 'touching the coming'. The Greek preposition is *hyper. Our gathering together unto him* (2); a reference probably to the event described in 1 Thes. iv. 17, when those who survive to the Parousia will be 'caught up together' with those who are raised from the dead 'to meet the Lord in the air'. *Neither by spirit, nor by word, nor by letter as from us* (2); i.e., neither prophetic utterance, nor more ordinary oral communication, nor a letter purporting to come from Paul or his companions. It is not plain whether Paul suspected that a letter in his name had actually been sent to the Thessalonians without his authorization. Certainly it would be unwarranted to suppose that this remark casts any doubt on the authenticity of 1 Thessalonians. Even if 2 Thessalonians were pseudonymous, it is unlikely that its author would have intended to throw suspicion on 1 Thessalonians. Possibly the reference to the *letter as from us* alludes to false conclusions drawn from the wording of 1 Thessalonians. But more probably Paul suspected that the idea that the day of the Lord had already started had been conveyed to the Thessalonians' minds by some kind of communication claiming his authority, but he had no certain information on this point. *That the day of Christ is at hand* (2); RV 'now present', i.e. 'has already set in'. Cf. 1 Thes. v. 2. *That day shall not come* (3). This apodosis to the conditional clause has to be supplied; it means, 'the day of the Lord will not begin'. In the following clause note RV 'except the falling away come first'. The Greek word *apostasia* (whence Eng. 'apostasy'), here rendered 'falling away', means 'revolt', 'rebellion' (here religious in character). *That man of sin be revealed* (3). 'The lawless one' (cf. verse 8), otherwise called Antichrist and Belial and 'the beast from the abyss' (Rev. xi. 7), is the leader of the great eschatological rebellion against God. *The son of perdition* (3); a Hebraism, meaning here 'he who is doomed to destruction'; the same phrase is used of Judas Iscariot in Jn. xvii. 12 where it means rather 'the lost boy'. *Who opposeth and exalteth himself above all that is called God, or that is worshipped* (4); lit. 'object of worship' (Gk. *sebasma*). The language here echoes the description of the pre-Christian 'Antichrist', Antiochus Epiphanes, in Dn. vii. 25, viii. 9ff., xi. 36ff.; cf. also Rev. xiii. *So that he as God sitteth in the temple of God* (4). This part of the picture of Antichrist probably reflects the attempt by the Emperor Gaius in A.D. 40 to have his statue set up in the temple at Jerusalem. That crisis brought vividly to the minds of Christians the eschatological discourse of Jesus preserved in Mk. xiii. The words 'when ye see the abomination of desolation standing where he ought not' (Mk. xiii. 14, RV; note that a person is referred to) seemed specially applicable to the Emperor's policy. *Remember ye not . . .?* (5). An interesting sidelight on the element of apocalyptic in the early kerygma.

In verse 6 see RV. 'You know what holds him back,' Paul says, 'so that he will not make a public appearance before the time appointed for him.' The restraining agency is impersonal here, but personal in verse 7; this throws light on the meaning. The apostle is intentionally vague in writing this, but he appears to have been more explicit in his oral teaching at Thessalonica. This supports the view that the Roman Empire is the restraining agency, since it may be considered either as an impersonal power, or as embodied personally in the Emperor. After the accusation brought against Paul at Thessalonica (Acts xvii. 6f.), any allusion to the imperial power had best be as vague as possible lest the letter fall into the wrong hands. *For the mystery of iniquity* (RV 'lawlessness') *doth already work* (7). The principle of rebellion against God is already operating (e.g. in the opposition offered to the gospel in Thessalonica and elsewhere), but it is not openly enthroned in the world as it will be for the brief duration of Antichrist's domination, because 'there is one that restraineth now' (7, RV). Here is the agency that holds the spirit of godless revolt in check is personal, indicating the Emperor himself. Others, however, have regarded the restrainer as being as much an apocalyptic figure as Antichrist, e.g. the angel of the abyss (Rev. ix. 1, xx. 1); in that case, however, Paul's reference might have been more explicit. Even less plausible is the suggestion that the Holy Spirit is intended. But if the restrainer is the Emperor, we need not think that the reigning Emperor Claudius (41-54) is specifically referred to, or that Paul was thinking of Nero as Claudius's heir whose accession was held in check so long as Claudius lived. Nero was only twelve years old in A.D. 50, and some of Paul's warmest encomia of the Roman power were written after Nero came to the throne. But Paul had frequent reason to be grateful for the protection of the imperial authorities, who restrained the forces most opposed to the gospel. When such protection was withdrawn, the forces of Antichrist would be able to work their will.

Among other suggested identifications of the restraining power, mention might be made of B. B. Warfield's view that it was the continued existence of the Jewish state: 'so soon as the Jewish apostasy was complete and Jerusalem given over to the Gentiles . . . the separation of Christianity from Judaism, which had already begun, became evident to every eye; the conflict between the new faith and heathenism, culminating in and now alive almost only in the Emperorworship, became intense; and the persecuting power of the empire was inevitably let loose' (*Biblical and Theological Studies*, p. 473).

Until he be taken out of the way (7). The subject of this clause is the restrainer, but it would be considered seditious to speak explicitly of the removal of the Emperor; hence Paul's vagueness. Gk. *ek mesou genesthai*, 'to be taken out of the way', is a quasi-passive form corresponding to the active *ek mesou airein* (1 Cor. v. 2; Col. ii. 14; and cf. Lat. *e medio tollere*). Failure to recognize this idiom has led some to force upon the words here a literalist translation, 'until he (Antichrist) become (i.e. appear) out of the midst'; but that is not Paul's meaning. In verse 8 follow RV, 'And then shall be revealed the lawless one'. Here we have the normal Greek construction (*ho anomos*) corresponding to the Semitizing 'man of lawlessness' of verse 3 (RV mg.). His revealing or unveiling precedes that of the true Christ. *With the spirit* (RV 'breath') *of his mouth* (8); i.e. by His Word; cf. Rev. xix. 15. *With the brightness of his coming* (8); i.e. 'by the glory of His Parousia'. Antichrist also has his Parousia (*coming*, verse 9). For his being energized by Satan *with all power and signs and lying wonders* cf. Rev. xiii. 2, 13ff. *Because they received not the love of the truth* (10). That refusal to accept God's truth is the certain precursor of infatuation by error is similarly taught in Rom. i. 18ff. *That they*

should believe a lie (11); rather, 'the lie', the false counterpart of *the truth* of verse 12; cf. again Rom. i. 25, which is literally 'who exchanged the truth of God for the lie'. In Zoroastrianism, too, 'The Lie' (Avestan *druj*) denotes the whole system of evil.

On this whole section (verses 1-12) Geerhardus Vos's chapter 'The Man of Sin' in *The Pauline Eschatology* (pp. 94ff.) is specially deserving of study.

IV. FURTHER THANKSGIVING AND ENCOURAGEMENT. ii. 13—iii. 5

But we are bound to give thanks alway to God for you (13); cf. i. 3. *Brethren beloved of the Lord* (13); cf. 1 Thes. i. 4. *God hath from the beginning chosen you* (13); see note on 1 Thes. i. 4. We should probably understand *from the beginning* to denote the eternity of God's choice, as in Eph. i. 4. Had Paul meant the earliest days of his preaching at Thessalonica he would probably have used such an expression as 'the beginning of the gospel' (Phil. iv. 5). We should note the variant reading 'firstfruits' (Gk. *aparchēn*) for *from the beginning* (Gk. *ap' archēs*); both are well attested, but *ap' archēs* is probably to be preferred. If 'firstfruits' be read, the idea is apparently that of Jas. i. 18, a carrying over into Christian phraseology of the Jewish idea of Israel as God's firstfruits among the nations. Harnack, in line with his theory of the destination of this Epistle, took *aparchēn* to imply that the Jewish believers were the 'firstfruits' of Paul's mission at Thessalonica. *To salvation* (13). 'The thirteenth and fourteenth verses of this chapter are a system of theology in miniature. The apostle's thanksgiving covers the whole work of salvation from the eternal choice of God to the obtaining of the glory of our Lord Jesus Christ in the world to come' (J. Denney). *Through sanctification of the Spirit* (13); cf. 1 Thes. iv. 3ff.; the Holy Spirit is the Sanctifier. *To the obtaining of the glory of our Lord Jesus Christ* (14); i.e. at His Parousia. Cf. Rom. ii. 6ff., viii. 18ff., 30.

Hold the traditions (15); i.e. the things handed on to you (Gk. *paradosis*). With this term are associated two Greek verbs *paralambanein*, 'to receive in turn', 'to have handed down to one' (cf. 1 Thes. ii. 13, iv. 1; 2 Thes. iii. 6), and *paradidonai*, 'to hand on in turn', both being found in conjunction, e.g., in 1 Cor. xi. 23, xv. 3. Emphasis is laid on the continuity of the transmission of the truth of Christianity; the tradition is identical with the apostolic testimony, resting on the authority of Christ Himself. (See O. Cullmann, 'Paradosis and Kyrios', *Scottish Journal of Theology*, iii (1950), pp. 180ff.) Read the last phrase of this verse in the RV, 'whether by word, or by epistle of ours'. 'Of ours' refers to *word* as much as to *epistle*; Paul means 'whether by our oral or written teaching'. The *epistle* he has in mind is doubtless 1 Thessalonians. *Now our Lord Jesus Christ himself, and*

God, even our Father . . . comfort your hearts (16, 17). As frequently (cf. 1 Thes. iii. 11) the Lord Jesus and God the Father are united in action. Here, as in 2 Cor. xiii. 14, the Lord Jesus Christ is placed first. 'The only theological significance to be attached to the variations in order is that there is complete equality in the apostle's mind between the Father and the Son' (W. Neil).

Finally, brethren, pray for us (iii. 1); cf. 1 Thes. v. 25. *That the word of the Lord may have free course* (RV 'run') (1); cf. Ps. cxlvii. 15 ('His word runneth very swiftly'). The reference here, of course, is to the gospel, which Paul and his companions were proclaiming at Corinth. It is probably with special reference to dangers at Corinth that he requests prayer *that we may be delivered from unreasonable and wicked men* (2). The Greek word *atopos*, here rendered *unreasonable*, means literally 'out of place', hence 'untoward', 'improper', 'perverse'. Paul is thinking primarily of his Jewish opponents. *For all men have not faith* (2). This may mean 'all men do not exercise faith' (in Christ), or 'all men do not hold the faith' (i.e. the gospel). It makes no difference to the general sense here whether we understand the *fides quâ creditur* or the *fides quae creditur*, but the former is more probable at this stage. *But the Lord is faithful* (3); Gk. *pistos*, an easy transition from *pistis*, the last word of the preceding sentence; *pistos* is the first word of the new sentence in the Greek. Cf. 1 Thes. v. 24. *Keep you from evil* (3); RV 'guard you from the evil one'. Here, as in the Lord's Prayer (Mt. vi. 13), RV rightly takes the evil (Gk. *ponēros*) as personal; AV makes it impersonal in both places. *And we have confidence* (4). For similar expressions of confidence cf. 1 Thes. iv. 1, 9f., v. 11. *And the Lord direct your hearts into the love of God* (5). The Lord Jesus is the subject. The *love of God* may be either their (increasing) love for Him or (a fuller appreciation of) His love for them. It would be natural to suppose that the construction is the same as that of the following phrase, 'and into the patience of Christ' (RV); to suppose, in other words, that both genitives are subjective. The 'patience of Christ' is an attribute of Christ Himself which the writer desires to see reproduced in His people; we should therefore take 'the love of God' to be the love which God shows to men. The AV translation, *the patient waiting for Christ*, is a less natural way of understanding the words; if it were right, it would suggest that *the love of God* similarly is our love for Him.

V. THE NEED FOR DISCIPLINE. iii. 6–15

They must dissociate themselves from those of their number who refuse to work for their living.

We command you . . . in the name of our Lord Jesus Christ (6). Apostolic authority is fundamentally the authority of Christ; the apostles are His accredited ambassadors. *Every brother that walketh disorderly* (6); Gk. *ataktōs*; cf. the adj.

ataktous in 1 Thes. v. 14; here as there we have a military metaphor, denoting those who 'break rank' or 'play truant'. He reverts to the problem of those who neglect to earn their own living, instead of following *the tradition . . . received of us*. This practical aspect of the *tradition* was emphasized by example as well as by precept; for the words of verses 7–9, drawing attention to the apostles' own behaviour in this regard, cf. 1 Thes. ii. 6ff. and other passages cited in our notes there. *If any would not work, neither should he eat* (10). This may be a Jewish proverb based on Gn. iii. 17ff. Even rabbis were expected to earn their living by manual labour and not to make the teaching of the law a means of gain; thus Paul maintained himself by working in leather. *Working not at all, but are busybodies* (11). There is a word-play here in the Greek, *mēden ergazomenous alla periergazomenous:* 'Busybodies instead of busy' (Moff.); 'neglecting their own business to mind other people's' (Knox); 'minding everybody's business but their own'. *That with quietness they work, and eat their own bread* (12); i.e. the bread they have earned themselves. 'Stop fussing, stop idling, and stop sponging' (W. Neil). Cf. 1 Thes. iv. 11. *Be not weary in well doing* (13); cf. Gal. vi. 9. *And if any man obey not our word by this epistle, note that man* (14). Again the apostolic authority is stressed (cf. verse 12). It is not formal excommunication that is enjoined, but such practical expression of disapproval as will make the 'loafers' ashamed of themselves and mend their ways. But, as verse 15 shows, they are not to be treated as outsiders, 'as the Gentile and the publican' (Mt. xviii. 17); they are still brethren, members of the Christian community, responsive (it is hoped) to this brotherly discipline.

VI. PRAYER, FINAL GREETING AND BENEDICTION. iii. 16–18

Paul takes his leave of the Thessalonians with a prayer for their blessing, pointing out that his personal signature authenticates this and other letters as genuinely his.

The Lord of peace (16); He who is 'the author of peace and lover of concord'; cf. 'the God of peace' in 1 Thes. v. 23; Rom. xv. 33, xvi. 20; Phil. iv. 9; Heb. xiii. 20; also 1 Cor. xiv. 33; 2 Cor. xiii. 11. *The salutation of Paul with mine own hand, which is the token in every epistle: so I write* (17). Lest they should be misled by a letter purporting to come from him, he draws their attention to the fact that all his letters are authenticated by some words in his own handwriting at the end. For the most part, he made use of amanuenses in writing his letters (cf. Tertius, Rom. xvi. 22). There is a reference to the character of his own handwriting in Gal. vi. 11. *The grace of our Lord Jesus Christ be with you all* (18); the same benediction (with the addition of *all*) as in 1 Thes. v. 28 (and Rom. xvi. 20).

F. F. BRUCE.

THE EPISTLES TO TIMOTHY AND TITUS

INTRODUCTION

See also the General Article, 'The Pauline Epistles', p. 68.

I. AUTHORSHIP

In contrast to the Epistle to the Hebrews, which contains in its text no explicit indication of its author, these three Epistles all openly declare themselves to be letters of the apostle Paul. Early external evidence in support of this is quite strong; and there is no similar evidence against it. Present-day uncertainty on this point is entirely due to internal and theoretical considerations: these are largely unprofitable because they are inconclusive and simply create hesitation and misgiving. While both the subject-matter, and still more the vocabulary found in these Epistles, can be used to support a case against the possibility of Paul's having written them, none of this reasoning is decisive. Much can still be said on the other side, and very many responsible scholars have nevertheless still accepted the Pauline authorship. It seems, therefore, wiser for us to do the same, without attempting to set out in detail all that can be said on both sides; such discussion is not the primary purpose of this commentary.

The Epistles themselves provide us not only with justification for this attitude, but also with urgent exhortation not to turn aside to questionings which are empty of satisfying result, and which are not only without positive benefit but may serve to undermine the faith of some. (See 1 Tim. i. 4, vi. 20, 21; 2 Tim. ii. 14, 23; Tit. iii. 9.) The Epistles also have many incidental personal touches, which are too true to Paul and his circumstances to be other than genuine. Most of all, documents which claim to be something which they are not can no longer carry full weight as canonical Scripture, as the divinely inspired record of apostolic teaching; and, therefore, any who entertain such doubts about these Epistles had better leave detailed comment on their abiding Christian significance alone. It would be better for them virtually to leave such documents out of their operative Canon of Scripture until they come to a better mind and a surer faith. For our part, we accept them as Pauline, and desire with God's help to seek to understand them accordingly.

II. DATE

It is generally agreed that it is impossible to fit these Epistles within the limits of Paul's life as we know it from the Acts of the Apostles. For their explanation they demand the recognition, indeed they themselves provide the most decisive evidence, that Paul was released from the imprisonment of which we read at the end of Acts (cf. Phil. ii. 24; Phm. 22), and allowed to engage for a period in travel and active missionary work before he was again arrested and brought to Rome, this time to face martyrdom. Lack of other information makes it impossible to fix with any certainty, as some have attempted to do, the chronology and order of events of these closing years. Clearly these Epistles were written between about A.D. 62 and the date of Paul's martyrdom, which must have occurred between A.D. 65 and 68.

III. OCCASION AND PURPOSE

Here we can speak with more certainty from the plain evidence and unmistakable implications of the Epistles themselves. They are clearly personal letters, written by the apostle Paul to his intimate fellow-workers Timothy and Titus, concerning the discharge of their responsibilities of oversight, particularly in the churches of Ephesus (possibly of the province of Asia as well) and of Crete. They share many features in common and can therefore well be treated together. Their primary interest is in the preservation and propagation of the truth of the gospel, and in the promotion and healthy maintenance of corresponding consistent Christian conduct on the part of its preachers and believers.

Concern for appropriate action is made the more urgent as Paul realizes that his own day of witness is passing, and that the future of the work rests with the younger generation. He is concerned still more because he is aware of the present prevalence and certain, increasing menace of false teaching, and of its unhealthy moral consequences in perverted character and conduct. Exhortations to personal self-discipline, to faithfulness in preaching and teaching the God-given word, to the need for a becoming order in home and church life, to the importance of entrusting ministry and oversight in the congregation only to individuals of proved and established moral quality, all have the same overriding considerations in view. What matters is that the God-given gospel of saving grace should be fully possessed and faithfully passed on intact.

This can be only if those called to its stewardship are found faithful, and if they find others to whom to hand on their sacred trust. For the apostolic succession, which must be preserved, is the trusteeship of the message to be proclaimed and of the teaching to be given. Similarly, this can be only if those who are brought within the sphere of the gospel and its preaching give and sustain to the Lord of grace a response of heart reverence and sincerity, and the practice of active good works. For the faith will soon be corrupted and lost unless it be held with a good conscience towards God, and unless it works by love in active goodwill towards men.

IV. THE FALSE TEACHING

The New Testament documents reveal in many places that the first congregations of believers in Jesus as Christ and Lord were soon troubled from within by the emergence of false teachers. There is, too, a prophetic awareness (see 1 Tim. iv. 1; 2 Tim. iii. 1) that this kind of evil will get only worse as the age moves towards its consummation. In the picture language of Christ's own parable they were very conscious that within the visible church there were tares among the wheat, and that both are meant to mature and manifest a fuller development before the inevitable separation, rejection and ingathering of the day of harvest and of judgment.

These particular Epistles make plain that such evil emerges from within the professing church when men cease to give to the truth heart loyalty and submissive and conscientious obedience, and turn aside to pursue inquiries which promote only conceit and spiritual unsettlement rather than faith and establishment in godliness. Such questions are in themselves foolish and profitless; and they involve those who pursue them in active irreverence. Their study leads some to a pretentious claim to so-called knowledge, on the ground of which they oppose the truth and abandon the simple attitude of faith in it. So they become corrupted in mind, lacking in understanding, unhealthily absorbed in the kind of investigations and controversies which produce only strife. See 1 Tim. i. 4–7, 19, iii. 9, vi. 3–5, 20, 21; 2 Tim. i. 13, ii. 16, 18, 23, iii. 8; Tit. i. 10, 11, 14–16, iii. 9–11.

It is characteristic of such men to substitute for the Word and revealed purpose of God the fancies and commandments of men. For instance, they demand the renunciation of marriage and abstinence from certain foods, when God, who created all things, created them all to be used in the spirit of prayerful thanksgiving (1 Tim. iv. 3–5). Or, because they think the human body to be too material and therefore too evil to have any good, future, eternal destiny in resurrection, they assert that the resurrection of Christian faith is a spiritual quickening which has occurred already (2 Tim. ii. 18). Still worse, such men not only become insensitive to the truth, but will in the end become victims of misleading spirits and

their evil doctrines (1 Tim. iv. 1, 2). Such evil spreads destructively like a malignant disease, and demands nothing less than complete avoidance (2 Tim. ii. 16, 17).

Those who thus withstand the truth are past redemption (Tit. i. 15, 16). In the interest of the spiritual well-being of true Christian believers they must be sharply rebuked, and, if they refuse to be admonished, totally rejected (Tit. iii. 10, 11). On the other hand, those who have been misled by them and taken captive by the devil's wiles need sympathetic and patient handling to win them back to the Lord's true service (2 Tim. ii. 24–26). In neither case is direct controversy appropriate. The best answer and antidote to such a situation is positive exposition of the truth.

V. DEVELOPING FORMS OF CHRISTIAN DOCTRINE AND CHURCH ORDER

There are significant signs in these Epistles of a process of development. The content of the faith is clearly becoming crystallized in brief confessional summaries, often so framed as to present a moral challenge. So we find numerous 'faithful sayings' (1 Tim. i. 15, iv. 9; 2 Tim. ii. 11; Tit. iii. 8), which are said to be worthy of active appropriation and believing response. We find essential principles expounded and applied to particular practical problems in a form which not only can be clearly taught, but which is also meant to be pressed upon the faithful with exhortation to act accordingly.

Some points of fundamental Christian theology are explicitly emphasized in a new way in order to counter the prevalent false teaching. There is, for example, the marked emphasis on the essential nature, attributes and unity of God as the sovereign Creator and Saviour of all (see 1 Tim. i. 1, 17, ii. 3–5, iv. 4, 10, vi. 13, 15, 16; 2 Tim. iii. 13; Tit. i. 2, 3); on Christ as the only Mediator between God and men, on His Person and work, on His humanity and on His death, endured as a substitutionary ransom price, as the one and all-sufficient way of redemption, spiritual renewal and consecration to God and His service (see 1 Tim. i. 1, ii. 5, 6, iii. 16; 2 Tim. i. 10; Tit. ii. 13, 14, iii. 5, 6).

There are evidences of an ordered and more regulated congregational worship, found in references to the necessary place of reading of Scripture, exhortation and teaching (1 Tim. iv. 13), and of supplications, prayers, intercessions, thanksgivings (1 Tim. ii. 1). There are traces of hymns, of credal and liturgical fragments, of doxologies (see 1 Tim. iii. 16, vi. 13–16; 2 Tim. i. 9, 10, ii. 8, 11–13, iv. 1; Tit. ii. 11–14, iii. 4–7). Guidance is given for the proper appointment of individuals to responsible oversight and ministry, in pastoral care and exposition of the Word; and plain and detailed warning is given of the dangers latent in unwise appointments. Each local congregation, or church, is recognized as a household of God, and a divinely intended warden of, and witness for, the truth. And such congregations are likely to prove steadfast and faithful in the face of perils from within as well as from without only if diligent attention is paid to such proper procedure (1 Tim. iii. 15, RV). Yet underlying all such detailed guidance, and predominantly expressed through it, is the compelling awareness that what matters most of all is not the system but the men; the main stress is not on office and form but on genuine Christian character and on conscientious and consistent behaviour.

I TIMOTHY: OUTLINE OF CONTENTS

I. PERSONAL ADDRESS AND GREETING. i. 1, 2

II. A FORMER CHARGE REITERATED. i. 3–20

III. AN EXHORTATION TO PRAYER. ii. 1–7

IV. GUIDANCE CONCERNING PRAYING AND TEACHING IN THE CONGREGATION. ii. 8–15

V. QUALIFICATIONS FOR THE CHRISTIAN MINISTRY. iii. 1–16

VI. A SOLEMN WARNING REGARDING FALSE TEACHING. iv. 1–5

VII. TIMOTHY'S TEACHING AND PERSONAL BEHAVIOUR. iv. 6–16

VIII. SPECIAL GROUPS WITHIN THE CHURCH. v. 1—vi. 2

IX. SOME FURTHER WARNINGS. vi. 3–10

X. A SOLEMN PERSONAL CHARGE. vi. 11–16

XI. THE RIGHT USE OF MATERIAL THINGS. vi. 17–19

XII. A FINAL EXHORTATION. vi. 20, 21

I TIMOTHY: COMMENTARY

I. PERSONAL ADDRESS AND GREETING. i. 1, 2

Paul writes as *an apostle* (1), as one conscious of a mission given to him by divine appointment. He writes as a servant of Jesus, recognized as Messiah or the Lord's anointed; one might almost say he writes as an ambassador of 'King Jesus'. The form 'Christ Jesus' is characteristic of the Epistle; see RV here, and cf. i. 12, 14, 15. This commission of Paul's is an expression of God's own activity to save men, and is directed towards helping men to find sure *hope* of this salvation in Christ. Such language indicates at once that this is more than a private, personal letter. It is written to Timothy as to a genuine second-generation Christian, one of the true children in the faith of Christ, to whom Paul can look to carry on the work and witness of the gospel. Its contents concern Timothy's activity as a minister in the church, household or family of God; see iii. 14, 15. The spontaneous way in which Christ is twice coupled with God Himself in these verses implies a significant recognition of His place in the Godhead.

II. A FORMER CHARGE REITERATED. i. 3–20

a. A call to oppose false doctrine (i. 3–11)

Paul reminds Timothy of the particular task committed to him when he urged him to remain at Ephesus; he was to admonish those who are tending to turn aside to false and profitless teaching, and to recall them to sincere and devoted Christian living. It is noteworthy how quickly the churches were troubled from within by false teachers, and how Paul viewed such men with the most solemn gravity, and took deliberate and sustained precaution against their potentially fatal influence. Cf. vi. 3–5; Acts xx. 28–30; Gal. i. 6–9. The varied errors are all comprehensively described as the teaching of *other* (RV 'different') *doctrine* (3). Note that this implies a recognized 'form of doctrine' or 'pattern of teaching' (Rom. vi. 17) already generally accepted. Here the danger is lest wrong attention be paid to (probably Jewish) *fables* and *genealogies* (4), possibly fanciful additions to, and interpretations of, the Old Testament. To try to find hope in human descent or succession is inconclusive and unsatisfying, i.e. *endless* (4). Such inquiries give rise only to controversial questionings; they do not serve to establish confidence. *Godly edifying* (4); RV 'a dispensation (RV mg. 'stewardship') of God'. The meaning is either that they cannot further that dispensation of God in the gospel which offers men salvation by faith, or that they do not promote that effectual discharge of the stewardship of life, to which we are called as believers.

In contrast to these mistaken activities of some, the practical teaching of the gospel demands a response which is expressed in inner sincerity and active goodwill. The four characteristics of verse 5 are acquired in the reverse order. *Faith*, which is no mere pretence, is the foundation. This issues in the inward enjoyment of *a pure heart*, and the concern to preserve *a good conscience*, and in the outward practice of love (*charity*) towards God and men. Such love is *the end* in view, the proper goal or completion of saving faith. Cf. Acts xv. 9, xxiv. 16; Gal. v. 6. The aforementioned 'some' have not only failed to aim at and pursue this end; they also *have turned aside unto vain jangling* (RV 'talking') instead of doing, and to an activity which is valueless instead of fruitful (6). They are dominated by the desire to be authorities or *teachers of the law* (7), like Jewish rabbis. Actually they have no proper understanding of the things concerning which they thus not only talk but even make self-confident assertions. They are, therefore, a serious danger to the Christian community, capable of deceiving and misleading many.

Lest his derogatory reference to would-be law-teachers should be misunderstood, Paul introduces a statement (verses 8–11) declaring that the law is good, and that it supports and complements the gospel by forbidding everything that is opposed to its wholesome teaching. The fault lies with the false teachers, who do not use the law as God intended it to be used, i.e. to restrain and convict evil-doers. It is not intended as material for fanciful interpretation and profitless speculation on the part of the righteous or justified man. Evil-doers are here described as lacking moral standards, reverence for God, a sense of the holy, and without regard for family relations, human life, sexual purity and social good faith. As a consequence they are unruly, sinful, profane, merciless. In verses 9 and 10 Paul obviously follows the order of the Ten Commandments and bluntly specifies violations in their most extreme form. The *sound doctrine* (10), or wholesome, healthful teaching, is a phrase characteristic of, and peculiar to, the Pastoral Epistles. By contrast, false teaching is like gangrene (2 Tim. ii. 17, RV); and devotion to it a sign of spiritual sickness (1 Tim. vi. 3, 4, RV mg.). *The glorious gospel* (11); RV 'the gospel of the glory'. The genitive is one of content rather than of quality. God's glory is revealed to men in the gospel which tells men of Christ; 'the glory' is virtually a reference to Christ Himself. Cf. Jn. i. 14, 18; 2 Cor. iv. 4, 6.

b. Paul's own experience of salvation (i. 12–17)

Paul proceeds indirectly to encourage Timothy to a high yet humble view of his calling and to a sustained devotion to its discharge. This he does by a typical, parenthetical doxology to Christ and to God for his own amazing experience of divine mercy, and for his appointment by Christ to a stewardship of that gospel (note also verse 11), to which he first owed his own salvation. In the Christian experience the com-

plement to trusting Christ and to being inwardly empowered by Him is to be trusted by Him to fulfil some appointed ministry (12, RV). The word *ministry* (Gk. *diakonia*, without the definite article) is potentially very general in reference, though Paul often uses it (and 'minister', Gk. *diakonos*), as no second-century writer would have been likely to do, to refer to his apostolic office (cf. Rom. xi. 13; 2 Cor. iii. 6, v. 18, vi. 3). *Injurious* (13), Gk. *hybristēs*, describes a doer of outrage, a man given to violence. It was when Paul was showing no mercy, as one strong in the conviction that he knew what was right, that he was treated mercifully, as one whose active unbelief prevented him from understanding the truth. Such is the overflowing excess of divine grace (cf. Rom. v. 8, 10, 20), given to us in Christ Jesus, and moving us to live the characteristic Christian life of *faith and love* (14), instead of the typical sinful life of unbelief and enmity (so violently expressed in Saul before his conversion). Thus it was through a deep, personal experience of its benefit that Paul both learned and exemplified the character and the trustworthiness of that gospel which he was appointed to beseech all men to believe (as *faithful*) and to receive (as *worthy*) (15). For he still (note the significant present tense, *I am*) knew himself as *chief* of sinners (15). He knew that the purpose of the incarnation of God's Son as Messiah Jesus was to save sinners like himself. He knew that God's purpose in showing such a chief sinner as himself such utterly undeserved mercy was to make his life a *pattern* (RV 'ensample'), or exhibit, of the full extent of Christ's long-suffering kindness (i.e. towards such a violent opponent). Such an exhibit would encourage others in the future to found their confidence upon the same Saviour, and thus enter into the enjoyment of the life eternal. Verse 17 includes some noteworthy infinite and absolute attributes of God. *King eternal;* RV mg. 'King of the ages', the plural word suggesting eternity; He is sovereign over all. It may be better to understand 'is' rather than *be* in the phrase *be honour and glory*; cf. Mt. vi. 13.

c. A reminder and a warning (i. 18–20)

Paul appeals to the inspired words, which at the beginning of Timothy's ministry indicated the work and spiritual warfare to which he is called (cf. iv. 14). He then warns him of the underlying cause of that spiritual disaster to which some have already come. *The prophecies* (18) may have marked Timothy out as chosen of God for special service (see RV mg.). He was meant to find *by them* (lit. 'in them') inspiration or fortification to wage a good campaign (Gk. *strateia*) for God (18). Comparison of verses 18 and 19 with verse 5 suggests that Paul is repeating a charge originally given to Timothy concerning the importance of moral sincerity. It is because some have failed just here, and deliberately thrust away from themselves the good conscience to which they should have held fast, that they have made shipwreck with regard to the Christian faith and become heretical in their teaching. (For more detail about *Hymenaeus* (20) see 2 Tim. ii. 16–18.) Their error is so blasphemous that for their own good they have had to be severely disciplined. *Delivered unto Satan* (20); cf. Jb. ii. 6; 1 Cor. v. 5. This seems to mean to excommunicate. By putting such an one outside the sphere of Christ's kingdom or protection, he was exposed to the dominion of Satan, and particularly to his power to inflict physical disease.

III. AN EXHORTATION TO PRAYER.
ii. 1–7

Paul begins here to indicate the particular items of his general charge. He treats as of first importance the full practice of prayer *for all men* (1). It seems probable that Jewish or Gnostic heretical teaching was suggesting the restriction of salvation to a particular race, or to certain classes only. Paul, therefore, justifies his universal exhortation by a sixfold assertion. He points to the character and will of God as the universal Saviour, to His unity as the one God of all men, to His provision of the human Christ Jesus as the single Mediator between Himself and the whole human race, to the universal scope of Christ's redeeming act which was *for all* (6), to the consequent testimony to this accomplished redemption which is being given now that the proper time for it has arrived, and to his own divine appointment to a share in its proclamation as none other than *a teacher of the Gentiles* (7), i.e. one called to evangelize men of all nations alike.

The four words used for prayer (1) may be progressive as well as comprehensive, indicating the supplication of one in need, the general outgoing of prayer to God alone, confident boldness of access to God's presence to make known one's requests, accompanied by consequent thanksgiving for mercies enjoyed and prayers answered. The word *intercessions* (Gk. *enteuxeis*) has no necessary reference to others; its primary idea is of approach to a superior to make request (cf. older English meaning of 'intercession' in Je. xxvii. 18, xxxvi. 25). Such prayers should primarily be for all men's salvation; but a complementary duty, if Christians are to be free to live as they ought in this world, is to pray for rulers and for all who occupy 'high place' (RV), that by their government they may preserve peace and order. *In all godliness and honesty* (2) means with due reverence for God and with a proper sense of the seriousness of life. RV renders 'godliness and gravity'. *This* (i.e. such praying) is intrinsically good, and pleasing to God because in harmony with His will for men (3). Verse 4 does not say that God has determined that every single man must be saved; but simply that His general desire for mankind is that all alike shall enjoy salvation (cf. Rev. vii. 9, 10). This universality arises first from God's oneness. Since

He is the only God, He deals directly and in the same way with all men (see Rom. iii. 30, x. 12). *The man* (5); Gk. *anthrōpos*, 'a human being', without the definite article; RV renders 'himself man'. The very humanity of Christ and His appointment as the only mediator between God and men supply added indication that the salvation provided in Him is for men, and for all men alike. *Ransom* (6), Gk. *antilytron*, indicates a price paid for release. The preposition *anti*, 'instead of', suggests substitution; cf. Mk. viii. 37, x. 45 (Gk.). Note that what Christ thus gave was *himself* (6). *In faith and verity* (7) may indicate Paul's sincerity or, more probably, the subject of his teaching; cf. verse 4.

IV. GUIDANCE CONCERNING PRAYING AND TEACHING IN THE CONGREGATION. ii. 8–15

In all congregations it should generally be the men who lead in prayer, and those who do it should be careful to do it worthily. Similarly, in the congregation women should abstain from lavish adornment, and seek to commend themselves by their good works. They should display a becoming modesty and restraint, a quiet and submissive readiness to learn, rather than a self-assertive desire to teach. The proper place of woman in relation to man is indicated by the original order of creation; and her unfitness as a guide of the man is demonstrated by the way in which Eve was deceived and transgressed God's commandment. Woman's special calling is to motherhood; and, although there are now pain and peril in childbirth (see Gn. iii. 16), those women will be brought safely through who respond fully to the demands of the gospel.

In verse 8 Paul gives authoritative counsel which is to apply *every where* (RV 'in every place'), i.e. wherever Christians meet for worship. To 'lift up the hands' was a recognized outward expression of the attitude of prayer (see Ex. xvii. 11, 12; 1 Ki. viii. 22; Ps. xxviii. 2). The conditions of effective praying are purity (selfward), peace (manward), faith (Godward) (8). Women are to give a silent witness by their seemly dress and deportment, and by lives of active good works (9, 10). Cf. 1 Pet. iii. 1–6. *Shamefacedness*, Gk. *aidōs*, signifies a proper sense of shame which preserves one from all unbecoming behaviour; *sobriety*, Gk. *sōphrosynē*, describes a balanced and discreet self-restraint. In public worship it becomes the woman to be silent and submissive —that is part of her true dignity—not to try to take over the reins and direct the man (11, 12). So Paul does not *suffer* (RV 'permit') this; to do so would be to encourage something bad for both sexes and to violate the created order. This appeal to the mind and purpose of the Creator shows clearly that Paul is not basing what he says simply on the position assigned to woman in the society of that day. He is appealing rather to a guiding principle of universal and abiding application (see 1 Cor. xi. 2–16n.).

Further, the tragedy of the fall establishes the general truth that a woman is more easily deceived than a man; so it is out of place for her to take the lead in settling either doctrine or practice for the Christian community. (Note that it is, however, a woman's privilege to teach children and younger women; see 2 Tim. i. 5, iii. 14, 15; Tit. ii. 3, 4.) In verse 15 the change to the plural *they* follows a reference to 'woman' in verses 11–14 which is generic and collective. The concluding sentence indicates what each particular woman must actively do in order to experience the blessings of salvation in relation to the discharge of her function of motherhood. Cf. i. 5; these words *in faith*, etc., indicate the pathway of Christian obedience.

V. QUALIFICATIONS FOR THE CHRISTIAN MINISTRY. iii. 1–16

The function of oversight in or 'taking care of' the church of God (see verse 5) is a worthy task that should be well discharged. It requires a man of blameless, pure, disciplined and generous character, who manages his own home well; and particularly no recent convert, but one whose established good conduct as a Christian is well spoken of so that he may give no occasion to the devil to accuse or ensnare him either because of his own pride, or because of the reproaches of those outside the church. Similarly, those who are to serve as deacons ought first to have approved themselves by their consistent and conscientious Christian behaviour, particularly in matters of self-discipline and home management. For this similarly is a ministry which ought to be discharged well, and those who fulfil it worthily will thereby both ensure their own good standing as Christians and greatly increase the outspoken confidence with which they can commend the Christian faith.

a. The office of a bishop (iii. 1–7)

Paul's first concern here is to encourage a proper regard for the task of oversight or episcopacy (Gk. *episkopē*), and the corresponding recognition that those who are to undertake it ought to be men above reproach. *Bishop* (Gk. *episkopos*) and 'elder' (Gk. *presbyteros*) were in New Testament times alternative names for the same officer (see Tit. i. 5, 7; Acts xx. 17, 28), the first term indicating function or duty, and the second dignity or status. *The husband of one wife* (2); this phrase is variously interpreted. The parallel phrase in v. 9, *the wife of one man*, suggests that it means 'married only once'. It doubtless means a man free, as many converts to the faith were not, from all unsatisfactory sexual history or associations. *Patient, not a brawler* (3); the Greek words mean 'forbearing', or 'considerate', and 'not contentious'. Capacity for effectively controlling others will not find expression in church oversight if it is lacking in a man's handling of his own children. *Lifted up with pride* (6); RV 'puffed up'; the Greek participle means 'beclouded', and so in a confused state of mind, here due to conceit because of sudden elevation to office. *The condemnation of the devil* (6) probably refers to the judgment under which the devil came because of his insensate pride. Though, as the Greek word *diabolos* occurs in these Epistles in the sense of 'slanderer' or 'accuser' (see verse 11), some would interpret it in verses 6 and 7 in this sense. Then the phrase in verse 6 would mean 'the judgment passed upon him by the typical slanderer'; and verses 6 and 7 together would reinforce at the end the first qualification for a bishop mentioned in verse 2, i.e. 'without reproach' (RV), having a good reputation, and so not open to obvious or easy attack from 'the slanderer'.

b. The office of a deacon (iii. 8–13)

Deacons (8). The Greek word has a very general meaning, 'ministers'. But in the Christian fellowship it obviously became the special term for a class of helpers subordinate to bishops or elders; cf. Phil. i. 1. As the qualifications emphasized in this whole section are moral, and are such as ought to characterize all good Christians, much the same are required in deacons as in bishops. If, however, as seems likely, deacons did house visitation and looked after church funds, there is special appropriateness in the qualifications stressed in verse 8. *Doubletongued* means saying different things to different people to suit the occasion; or the Greek word *dilogos* can mean simply 'given to repetition', i.e. a talebearer. *Greedy of filthy lucre;* the Greek word means disposed to seek gain in base and shameful ways; cf. Tit. i. 7, 11. A *mystery* (9) is something hidden from men in general, but openly revealed to the privileged, in this case to those who have faith (cf. iii. 16). Such faith and understanding can be healthily maintained only where there is active conscientious obedience; cf. i. 5, 19, ii. 15. None should be allowed to serve as deacons unless they have first thus openly approved themselves as worthy in the eyes of all.

In verse 11 the Greek word 'women' (RV) is ambiguous. It could mean the deacons' *wives*. Here it may refer to women workers or deaconesses (cf. Rom. xvi. 1, RV). The four qualifications demanded are closely parallel to those demanded of men in verse 8; in the misuse of the tongue women are more prone to be *slanderers* (Gk. *diaboloi*). *A good degree* (13) has been interpreted of the first step on the ladder of promotion; but this does not suit the context. Some regard the 'good standing and great boldness' (RV) thus gained as pointing Godward, particularly with reference to the day of judgment and reward; cf. vi. 19; 1 Jn. ii. 28, iii. 21, iv. 17. It seems more appropriate, however, to interpret the words manward, for the main emphasis of this whole section is on the need for a worthy reputation to be gained and maintained in the eyes of men by all who are to hold office in the church. For this use of *boldness* cf. 2 Cor. vii. 4.

c. The purpose of these instructions (iii. 14–16)

How thou oughtest (15); better, as in RV, 'how men ought'. Paul is concerned to guide the behaviour of all church members, not of Timothy only, and that because of the character of the company to which they belong. The reference is to each local congregation; there are no definite articles. Every such congregation is a genuine *house* (i.e. 'temple' or 'family') and *church* of God, not occupied like a heathen temple by a lifeless idol, but enjoying the manifested presence *of the living God* (15). Also, its corporate existence and regular public meetings provide for the truth in that locality a visible witness, or *pillar*, and an enduring support. *Ground* (15). The Greek *hedriōma* seems rather to mean 'bulwark' or 'stay' (see RV mg.). Verse 16 summarizes this *truth* as a *mystery* revealed to those who have a spirit of true piety or due reverence. The common Christian confession indicates its greatness (the Greek says it is 'confessedly' great). There follows a quotation from such a confession, abruptly introduced in the Greek by a masculine relative pronoun, obviously referring to Christ; for this 'mystery' is a Person (cf. Col. i. 27). The rhythmical and antithetical phrases suggest a quotation from an early credal hymn. Pre-existence is implied and incarnation asserted. It is by what happened in the realm of His spirit (RV) that His true identity was vindicated (cf. Rom. i. 3). This manifestation of God in history disclosed new wonders even to angels (cf. Eph. iii. 10; 1 Pet. i. 12), and has provided a gospel to be preached to all nations. His consequent rewards are a company of believers gathered from earth, and His own exaltation to a permanent place of glory in heaven.

VI. A SOLEMN WARNING REGARDING FALSE TEACHING. iv. 1–5

In surprising contrast to these things (iii. 15, 16), Paul testifies that unmistakable witness has been given by the Spirit that there will be in the future, on the part of some in the church, an abandonment of revealed truth. This will be due fundamentally to the influence of evil spirits, and more immediately to the false teaching of insincere men, who will be the instruments of these evil spirits, and who will improperly insist on the necessity of abstaining from marriage and from certain foods. Such teaching directly contradicts the purpose of the Creator, particularly His purpose for fully instructed believers. For everything which God made is not only good in itself, but intended to be used by men. Nothing, therefore, is to be rejected as absolutely unusable. Rather we need to learn how we may properly and continuously sanctify things to our use in a spirit of thanksgiving, expressed to God in appropriate prayer, particularly prayer itself learnt from the written Word of God.

The Spirit speaketh (1); probably through Christian prophets, or possibly through Paul himself (cf. Acts xx. 23, xxi. 11; see also Mt.

xxiv. 11). *Latter times* (1); the Greek means 'later' (as in RV), or subsequent to the time of writing, not 'last'. *The faith* (1), with the definite article, indicates the body of revealed truth (cf. i. 19, RV; Jude 3). The *doctrines* (1) are not about devils, but they emanate from devils. Over against the Spirit and the mystery of godliness stand misleading spirits and their false teaching. In verse 2 note the alternative reading of the RV. These men are said to be either lacking in moral sensitiveness (as AV), or bearing the brand-mark of sin, that is, something known inwardly to the consciences of the individuals concerned ('their own' is emphatic), though they deceive others by their hypocrisy. The assertions of verses 3–5 are significant when studied in relation to the Gnostic and dualistic views that matter is evil and not created by God. But, while God created everything for use by men, right use depends on faith, full knowledge and an actively expressed spirit of thanksgiving. *The word of God* (5) is a common phrase for divinely inspired utterance, especially as found in Scripture. Here it suggests the use in saying 'grace' of actual Old Testament phraseology; or it may mean that such eating is sanctioned by explicit divine direction.

VII. TIMOTHY'S TEACHING AND PERSONAL BEHAVIOUR. iv. 6–16

Paul makes plain to Timothy that his calling to the service of Christ demands faithful devotion, both in his own living and in his ministry to his fellow-Christians. He must be careful both to preach what is true and profitable and himself to practise and pursue the same. The various aspects of the ministry of the Word must all be diligently discharged, and the God-given gift for such service fully exercised. Such ministry demands utter devotion. To live in this way leads to the double reward of salvation fully enjoyed by both preacher and hearers alike.

In verse 6 follow RV. It is Timothy's responsibility to set these truths (see verses 4, 5) before the Christians, to lay them down as the foundation of right practice (Gk. *hypotithemenos*). Only as he does so will his own training in, and obedience to (cf. 2 Tim. iii. 10, RV), the truth find its proper fulfilment in worthy ministry. It is, too, by such ministry that a man approves himself as *a good minister of Jesus Christ* (6). The ideas suggested by *profane* and *godliness*, and by *refuse* and *exercise thyself unto*, stand in opposition (7). One can give oneself to the good only by having nothing to do with the bad. Christ's minister must keep himself spiritually fit by appropriate nourishment (6) and exercise (7). Instead of the misleading self-discipline of asceticism (3), let him engage in proper and strenuous Christian training (cf. 1 Cor. ix. 25–27). Even at its best, bodily discipline as an end in itself is of only limited value (8). In his training the Christian minister ought rather to make *godliness* (8), or the devotion of his life to the proper worship of God, his dominant aim. The benefit thus to be gained is without limit or all-embracing; it concerns one's true spiritual *life* rather than one's physical existence (Gk. *zōē*, not *bios* as in 2 Tim. ii. 4), and it promotes its future as well as its present well-being or full enjoyment (8). Such teaching is worthy to be believed and received, i.e. acted on, by all Christians (9). It indicates the 'end' (RV) that Paul himself has in view (note the use of *we* in verse 10) in continuing to face the physical effort and endurance demanded by his apostolic labours. Also, hope of this benefit is grounded, not on any power in the physical exertion to produce such a result, but on God in His revealed character as *living* (Gk. *zōn*) and as *Saviour* (10). These characteristics assure men of His ability and His readiness to give them true life (Gk. *zōē*). While God, by His gracious providences, shows Himself active to save in His dealings with all (cf. Mt. v. 45, vi. 26), the full exhibition of all that His saving activity can mean is especially realized in the experience of believers.

This proper practice of Christian living Timothy is both to enjoin and explain (11), in order to lead his hearers to engage in it with full understanding. His relative youthfulness and natural diffidence must not be allowed to encourage any to look down on him (12; cf. 1 Cor. xvi. 10, 11). Rather, he should openly set himself before all as a model to be imitated (cf. Phil. iii. 17; 2 Thes. iii. 9), not only in his teaching, but also in his conduct and in the underlying love, faith and purity to which it obviously gives expression (12). Also, as one called to a special ministry in the congregation, he must give sustained attention (13) to its three main responsibilities: public *reading* of the Scriptures; *exhortation* or preaching (i.e. sermons); *doctrine* (RV 'teaching') or giving instruction (cf. Lk. iv. 16; Acts xiii. 15, xv. 21, xvii. 2, 3).

Nor should he forget and leave unexercised the special *gift* he has within him for such ministry (14). Note that such God-given enablement demands human co-operation for its full exercise (cf. Phil. ii. 12, 13; 2 Tim. i. 6). Timothy had been assured of the character and of the impartation of this gift by the complementary witness of both a prophetic word and a solemn ordination (cf. Acts xiii. 1–3). Note the significant reference to the corporate function of a body of local elders acting together (*presbytery*), and the combination in significant order of prophecy and symbolic action directed towards the recipient (i.e. 'word' and 'sacrament'). In verse 15 follow RV. The minister must continually give his whole mind and self to these things. Not only should he thus make 'progress' (RV), but also it should be obvious to all that he is thus growing in grace of personal character and in the fulness and quality of his teaching. These are the things to which he must unceasingly apply himself (16). Such practice by the minister is the way to ensure the full salvation of himself and

his hearers alike. Note how the minister explicitly fulfils his ministry by what he says (those he serves are described as *them that hear thee*), and implicitly completes it by how he himself lives.

VIII. SPECIAL GROUPS WITHIN THE CHURCH. v. 1—vi. 2

a. General instructions (v. 1, 2)

Ministry like Timothy's involved dealing with people and solemnly confronting them with the truth, and this duty must be discharged; but it should be *fittingly* done in true affection and with sober restraint. It does not become a relatively young minister like Timothy sharply to reprimand anyone older than himself. The word *elder* (1) refers simply to age not office. The qualification *with* (RV 'in') *all purity* (2) refers particularly to Timothy's ministry to the young women. It is part of his responsibility to exhort them, but he must watch against any development, or even suggestion, of improper interest or intimacy. In Tit. ii. 3–5 the actual training of young women is explicitly entrusted to older Christians of their own sex.

b. Instructions about widows (v. 3–16)

In rightly marking widows out for appropriate regard and care, those should be distinguished for such honour and help who are, on the one hand, really destitute, and, on the other, truly worthy. Whenever possible, widows should be provided for by their own children or families; this is an obvious Christian duty, and the church ought not to be needlessly burdened. Only those widows should be enrolled among those who fulfil ministry and receive maintenance who are sixty or over, who have been married only once and do not intend to remarry, and who are well spoken of as active in good works. Younger women are unsuitable for such appointment. They may be tempted to remarry, or fall into the snare of making house-to-house visitation an occasion for idle and harmful gossip. It is better for such to remarry and to shoulder the responsibilities of having children and running a home. In this way they may be able themselves to help widows whom the church would otherwise have to relieve.

Honour (3). This may include the provision of necessary material assistance; see verse 17 and Mt. xv. 5, 6. A genuine widow, or 'widow indeed', who needs such assistance is one without either means or relatives to support her; she is left *desolate* (5). *Nephews* (4); RV 'grandchildren'; in 1611 'nephew' meant 'grandchild'. Every widow with such relatives should be supported by them. This means that they must, as a primary duty, *learn* (i.e. make it their regular practice) to show filial piety towards members of their own family, and to give back proper recompense to their parents or forebears. Such conduct is *acceptable* (4) not only to those who thus benefit, but also 'in the sight of God' (RV).

The genuine widow, in addition to being *desolate*, will commend herself as worthy of support as one who had acquired the habits of looking hopefully to God, not men, and devoting herself to long and frequent praying (5). In contrast to this the type of woman, who wastefully or prodigally spends life and all that it brings, is not to be reckoned as actually a widow (i.e. a 'widow indeed'); for, though living, she is in God's sight already dead (6). The need to make these distinctions and to maintain a worthy standard must be definitely enforced by Timothy, with a view, not to shutting some widows out of benefit, but rather to securing that all will live irreproachable lives (7). Every Christian ought to take thought for the needs of his relatives, and most of all for those of the members of his own family. Not to do so is by act to deny the faith which with the mouth one professes. It would even make one worse than the unbelieving heathen, for he recognizes a duty in such matters (8).

In verses 9 and 10 some find the earliest and a significant scriptural reference to an 'order of widows' (often mentioned in other early Christian writings). These seem to have been 'women elders' rather than 'women deacons' or 'deaconesses' (see iii. 11n.), who can scarcely all have been over sixty. Their particular responsibilities appear to have been to care for children, particularly orphans, and the younger women; this would involve house-to-house visitation. The qualifications for enrolment are obviously strict. Such conditions seem clearly those for ministry rather than merely maintenance, unless the reference is to specially selected as well as needy widows, who are guaranteed permanent lifelong support by the local church. *The wife of one man* must mean 'married only once' and, by implication, pledged not to remarry.

Paul gives two reasons for not enrolling younger widows. In the first place it is unwise to make them pledge not to remarry. For, should they later wish to do so, such desire, otherwise innocent, will then be a rebellion against the yoke of Christ, and will make them stand self-condemned for casting off *their first faith* (12), i.e. setting aside their former pledge. Secondly, it would give them an undesirable opportunity to become talkative busybodies rather than active workers (13). The suggestion seems to be that still active, younger women, who as wives have been occupied with home management, if they are suddenly given maintenance, and possibly a ministry largely to be fulfilled by visiting other homes and by words of exhortation, may fall into the temptation to be lazy and to become talkers who make mischief by betraying confidences. Therefore, to avoid the danger of giving opponents a ground for reproaching Christians, it is better that such women should remarry and be fully occupied again with family responsibilities. Some would say that this passage implies that the experience of married life develops a woman's aptitude for some tasks and lessens it

for others; that younger women who are maintained by the church to do work as deaconesses should be spinsters, not widows; or, alternatively, that any healthy widow under sixty ought to find some kind of employment (if not a husband) rather than be given full maintenance, even as a church worker. *The adversary* (14) seems here to mean the typical human opponent, not the devil. In verse 15 Paul appeals to the witness of experience to confirm his judgment. This kind of departure from the way of Christ (11) to follow Satan has thus occurred in some cases. The insertion of *already* suggests that it has happened in the short time which has elapsed since such appointments of younger widows were first made. It is also significant as indicating that the probable date of such a reference to church organization is therefore not so late as might at first seem probable.

c. The proper treatment, discipline and appointment of presbyters (v. 17-25)

Timothy was charged with special responsibilities in connection with the elders, who were the leaders of the local churches. Some of these were also active in preaching and teaching. He is, in particular, solemnly charged (21; see RV) to beware both of wrong prejudice against, or undue partiality for, particular individuals. First, he must see that the value of the elders' service is recognized and they themselves amply recompensed (17). Secondly, discipline of some who fail may be necessary: but no accusation should be treated seriously unless it is properly supported by confirming witnesses (19); and those proved guilty of sinful practices should be openly reproved (20). Thirdly, he should make no hasty appointments, lest his own position be compromised by connection with the sinful, and he himself be defiled (22). For neither all the bad nor all the good of any man's character is immediately obvious. There are other things not so conspicuous, but discoverable by the patient and watchful investigator. In appointments to the presbyterate, therefore, it is a mistake either to receive or to reject anyone too quickly.

Elders (17). In contrast with verse 1 the reference here is to those who are set over a local church as its leaders. The following verse makes plain that the *honour* they ought to be given includes material support (cf. verse 3); also it should be *double* or 'ample'. Not only should they be given it, they should also be truly recognized as worthy of it. In verse 18 Paul quotes Dt. xxv. 4, not to enforce the letter of the law, but to appeal to the moral principle which it illustrates. Note the RV 'when he treadeth', i.e. while he is actually working (Gk. present participle). Some have wondered whether the phrase *the scripture saith* covers the second quotation, because it is found in Lk. x. 7. If so, it would be a remarkable reference to the third Gospel as Scripture. The words are more probably a well-known proverbial saying, quoted by our Lord, and here used by Paul to indicate the point of his preceding Old Testament quotation. In verse 19 see RV and Dt. xix. 15. *Them* and *all* (20) are perhaps best taken as both referring to the elders only, though the second, and some think the first also, may refer to church members in general. *Lay hands* (22). For the practice cf. iv. 14; 2 Tim. i. 6. The meaning is, 'Ordain no one with undue haste,' an injunction appropriately applying the preceding warning against partiality. Timothy will serve God and the churches well only if he keeps himself pure, and refuses to welcome the unworthy to partake in the leadership. In verse 23 see RV. In a personal parenthesis —a striking sign of the Epistle's genuineness— Paul indicates that this exhortation to keep himself undefiled need not prevent Timothy, in the interests of his health, from ceasing to be a total abstainer (note the force of *no longer*) and taking wine in moderation. *A little wine*: contrast iii. 3. Note the indication that Timothy's health was poor. *Open beforehand* (24); i.e. 'clearly evident' (see RV) or 'conspicuous'. *Going before* means 'leading the way'. *They follow after*; i.e. some men are pursued later by the after-effects of their sins, which in due course find them out. *They that are otherwise* (25) means 'good works that are not immediately evident'; these are, nevertheless, not completely concealable.

d. The duty of Christian slaves (vi. 1, 2)

These verses provide more teaching for Timothy to pass on concerning due *honour* (1; cf. v. 3, 17) to be given, this time by slaves to their masters. It will bring only dishonour on the name and gospel of God, as apparently subversive of the existing social order, if Christians who happen to be slaves fail to be good slaves. Nor, if their masters happen to be fellow-believers, ought they to cease properly to respect them as their human masters. They ought rather to serve them the better, just because those who get the benefit of their improved service are Christians. The RV is preferable in both verses. *All honour* (1) means 'full honour', honour in every form and way in which it is due.

IX. SOME FURTHER WARNINGS.
vi. 3–10

It is easy to be led astray by the worldly attractiveness of some men's teaching; and yet it stands condemned as 'different' (3, RV), or heterodox, because those who give it have clearly abandoned the fundamental spiritual loyalties, and their personal condition and conduct are unworthy. Also their teaching causes violent social strife, because it serves only to pervert men's moral judgment, to rob them of the truth, and to obsess them with the idea that the purpose of the practice of godliness is material gain (4, 5). Not that there is not great gain in true godliness, but only if one is free from covetousness (6). Since we cannot amass wealth and take it with us when we leave this world, it is for us to be satisfied here as long as we have food and clothing (7, 8). For such as set their desire on the

acquisition of wealth get enticed, ensnared, obsessed and utterly overwhelmed (9). Such love for money is a root which, if allowed to grow, produces only evils of every kind. Those who allow themselves to be occupied with it are commonly led astray from the faith, and cause themselves many troubles (10).

In verses 3 and 4 there is a contrast between teaching which is 'healthful' and teachers who are 'sick' (see RV mg.). Teaching is confirmed as *wholesome* (3), first, by having Christ as its author and, second, by the God-fearing spirit and conduct of the teacher. By contrast the false teacher stands self-condemned by his air of conceit, by his lack of understanding, and by his unhealthy obsession with the kind of discussion which only produces strife (4). In verse 5 follow RV. In the Greek the participles (not adjectives) describe permanent losses which have happened to them; their powers of moral judgment are destroyed, and they are deprived of the truth. So they now habitually suppose that godliness is a means to material gain. *Gain* (5); the Gk. *porismos* means virtually 'good business', i.e. a source of profit or way of gain. The statements of verse 7 confirm the implied attitude of the passage to material things; they are of only secondary and passing importance, not part of the true and abiding self; not transferable to the life beyond. In verse 8 see RV: the Greek verb is future indicative. It is not so much an exhortation as a dogmatic assertion that this is the way of realized contentment—in contrast to setting one's mind on acquiring wealth. *Foolish and hurtful lusts* (9); i.e. passionate desires which are doubly condemned as negatively senseless and positively injurious. In verse 10 see RV. The occupation of the mind with getting rich and the consequent stretching out of oneself in its pursuit result in both negative loss (being 'led astray from the faith') and positive damage. In contrast to the 'good business' of godliness it does not pay.

X. A SOLEMN PERSONAL CHARGE.
vi. 11–16

Paul exhorts Timothy to be true to his Christian calling, to keep clear of such ensnaring things as the love of money, and to sustain the pursuit of Christian virtues (11). Let him maintain the contest worthily to the end, that he may gain the prize. He is committed to such a course by his Christian *profession* (12). Let the recollection that God sees and will not fail to sustain, that Christ Jesus Himself has confirmed the truth Timothy has confessed by the witness of His sufferings, and is going to be manifested openly as the Judge by the all-sovereign God—let such awareness enforce Paul's charge to him not to defile or expose to reproach his Christian obedience (13–16).

It is possible here to give some of the phrases a particular interpretation. *Man of God* (11) may refer to Timothy's status as a worker; the phrase was a recognized Old Testament description for a prophet (see 1 Sa. ix. 6). Verse 12b may refer to his ordination, and verse 13 to our Lord's own faithful testimony before Pilate. Then verse 14 will be a specific exhortation to Timothy to discharge his particular ministry. However, it seems preferable to give the phrases a more general reference. *Man of God* may describe any mature Christian (see 2 Tim. iii. 17). Verse 12b may refer to Timothy's baptism. 'The good confession' (RV; note the definite article) is 'the faith' or truth then confessed, *good* describing 'the faith confessed', or Timothy's confession of it. This same *good confession* Timothy is reminded was attested as true by our Lord Himself by His death and resurrection, which took place 'under Pontius Pilate' (an equally possible interpretation of the Greek phrase, as in the Apostles' Creed). Some of the accompanying phraseology may well echo confessions of faith used in baptism. Note the reference to God as the Preserver (RV mg.), etc., and to the passion and second coming of Christ. This then means that Paul knows no better way to exhort Timothy than to address to him words applicable not only to him as a special worker but to him (as to all) as a Christian believer. In verse 12 the difference of the Greek tenses suggests *fight* as a sustained activity and *lay hold* as a decisive act. Christ's *appearing* (14; Gk. *epiphaneia*), or 'manifestation', will occur at its own proper time by the pleasure and act of God, and as a 'showing' or sign from His hand (cf. Jn. ii. 18). Verses 15 and 16 provide a significant description of the unique majesty of God. In His absolute bliss and unending life He is completely self-contained. Such things belong wholly to Him, and to Him alone. He is thus the exclusive Lord of all else. So to Him should all honour be rendered and all power ascribed.

XI. THE RIGHT USE OF MATERIAL THINGS. vi. 17–19

Rich Christians need to beware lest the possession of material wealth make them over-confident.

Their settled hope should rest, not in the wealth and its characteristic insecurity, but in God the Giver (17). They need, too, to remember that such wealth is given not to be hoarded, but to be enjoyed (cf. iv. 3–5) and used to *do good* (18). Thus to share one's good things liberally with others is the way to put by for the future something more enduring than earthly riches, and thus to possess true life (Gk. *zōē*) rather than just to have in abundance the present earthly means of livelihood (Gk. *bios*). See 1 Jn. iii. 17; Lk. xii. 15. Note the contrast between *this* (RV 'present') world (17) and *the time to come* (19); cf. Mt. vi. 19–21. In verse 17 see RV. To 'have their hope set on' brings out the force of the Greek perfect; also the warning is enforced by giving prominence in thought not to the deceptive 'riches' but to their 'uncertainty'. In verses 18, 19 see RV and RV mg. Those with earthly riches are exhorted to use them to acquire better and more enduring wealth. For this they need paradoxically in deed and heart a readiness to share their material riches with others.

XII. A FINAL EXHORTATION. vi. 20, 21

In an emphatic personal word to Timothy Paul here briefly sums up his chief, twofold concern in writing—to secure that Timothy preserves and hands on unimpaired the deposit of truth, and avoids the impious and arrogantly assertive false teaching, which has already fatally side-tracked some.

Timothy is here addressed as a steward who has been entrusted with 'the deposit' (20, RV mg.; cf. 2 Tim. i. 12, 14, RV mg., ii. 2), i.e. what Jude (verse 4) calls 'the faith delivered to the saints'. 'The (*falsely so called*) knowledge' suggests an unjustified pretentiousness which consequently attracts adherents to their own undoing as believers. *Grace be with thee* is Paul's distinctive form of Christian salutation to end an Epistle; see 2 Thes. iii. 17, 18.

A. M. STIBBS.

II TIMOTHY: OUTLINE OF CONTENTS

For the General Introduction to this Epistle see p. 1063.

I. PERSONAL ADDRESS AND GREETING. i. 1, 2

II. THANKSGIVING FOR TIMOTHY'S FAITH. i. 3–5

III. THE NEED FOR COURAGE AND FIDELITY. i. 6–14

IV. PAUL COMMENDS THE DEVOTION OF ONESIPHORUS. i. 15–18

V. A FURTHER EXHORTATION TO STEADFASTNESS AND DILIGENCE. ii. 1–13

VI. SOME RULES OF CONDUCT. ii. 14–26

VII. A WARNING OF COMING APOSTASY. iii. 1–9

VIII. A CALL TO PREACH THE WORD IN SPITE OF PERSECUTION.
iii. 10—iv. 5

IX. A DESCRIPTION OF PAUL'S OWN CIRCUMSTANCES: FINAL
GREETINGS. iv. 6–22

II TIMOTHY: COMMENTARY

I. PERSONAL ADDRESS AND GREETING. i. 1, 2

Compare and see notes on 1 Tim. i. 1, 2; Tit. i. 1–4. It is typical of Paul to ascribe his apostleship to *the will of God* (cf. the opening verse of 1 and 2 Corinthians, Ephesians and Colossians). He was overwhelmingly conscious that his appointment was of God; see Gal. i. 1, 15, 16. *According to the promise of life . . . in Christ Jesus* (1). This expresses the concern of Paul's apostleship; it was to make this promise known, and to bring men to embrace it, that he was commissioned (cf. Tit. i. 1–3). *My dearly beloved son* (2); RV 'my beloved child'; an affectionate indication of intimate association, particularly as leader and follower in work for God (cf. 1 Cor. iv. 17). Paul often spoke thus of his converts; see 1 Cor. iv. 14, 15; Gal. iv. 19; Phm. 10.

II. THANKSGIVING FOR TIMOTHY'S FAITH. i. 3–5

Paul confesses the depth of his feeling towards Timothy, feeling to which he continually gives expression in his prayers, feeling which includes the eager yearning to have the joy of seeing Timothy again, instead of the recollection of the tears which he shed when they parted. Above all, Paul says, he thanks God as he is reminded in his prayers of the sincerity of Timothy's faith, and of the similar faith of his grandmother and mother before him. (It seems best thus to make the remembrance of Timothy's faith the cause of Paul's thankfulness, and to regard the intervening clauses as describing the circumstances when this occurs. This understanding of the sense is helped by reading 'as' instead of *that* in verse 3.) In the context of this thought about Timothy Paul becomes conscious how much he too owes to his forebears, from whom he learnt to serve or worship God with conscientious sincerity (3). Both these references may be regarded, therefore, as Christian testimonies to the value of a good Jewish religious upbringing. For when Timothy was taught the Old Testament as a small child (iii. 15) his teachers had probably not yet believed in Christ.

III. THE NEED FOR COURAGE AND FIDELITY. i. 6–14

Paul reminds Timothy that he has a spiritual gift, and that God's endowments are not given to make men cowardly, but strong, loving and sober—indeed 'sobering' (RV mg.). Therefore he ought to stir up into flame the God-given fire, and in the strength of God to take his share in any suffering in which the gospel may involve him, by not hesitating to associate himself with witness concerning our Lord, and with Paul as one who suffers imprisonment on Christ's account. To enforce this appeal Paul reminds Timothy how wonderful the gospel is. For according to His own gracious purpose, and not because of anything which we have done, God has saved us. This gift of grace, already given to us before world history began, has now been openly manifested through the advent of Jesus Christ to be our Saviour and through His victory over death. In consequence, through the gospel now being preached, incorruptible life has been brought out into the light (for men to see as a reality and embrace as a possession, in contrast to previous dark uncertainty about its existence and despair of its enjoyment). This is the gospel, says Paul, which I am commissioned to preach; and it is through discharging this commission that I suffer as I do. Nor (in spite of imprisonment and the prospect of martyrdom) do I see any reason for being ashamed of it. For God is faithful and able; so (although my day of fulfilling a stewardship in the gospel is done) I am sure He will preserve what He has thus entrusted to me so that a good account may be given on the final day of reckoning. It is this outline of wholesome teaching, says Paul to Timothy, passed on by me to you, which you must make your own and preserve, in responsive faith and love to Christ Himself. Remember also that God's Spirit dwells in us to enable this stewardship to be discharged.

Wherefore (6); RV 'for the which cause'; a reference to Timothy's *unfeigned faith*. Note how Timothy is not exhorted to seek fresh grace; he is rather reminded of grace already given and exhorted to stir it up into flame (see RV mg. and 1 Tim. iv. 14n.). *Fear* (7); RV 'fearfulness', or 'cowardice'; *spirit* (7) may be interpreted as 'Holy Spirit', or it may describe the human spirit as wrought on by the Holy Spirit. The two are complementary; cf. Rom. viii. 14–16, RV. *His prisoner* (8); i.e. by His doing; cf. Eph. iii. 1; Phm. 9. Those who are saved are first called by God according to His own freely predetermined purpose; this *calling* is *holy* because by it we are brought into likeness and fellowship with Himself; cf. Rom. viii. 28–30. While these Pastoral Epistles repeatedly insist that good works are an intended fruit of salvation, they also make equally plain, in characteristic Pauline fashion, that human good works are not its cause; cf. Tit. iii. 5; Eph. ii. 8–10. *Before the world began* (9); RV, following the Greek, 'before times eternal'. Cf. AV and RV of Tit. i. 2; Rom. xvi. 25. *Abolished death* (10); i.e. brought it to nought as a power overshadowing men; the Greek *katargein* means 'to render inoperative'. *Life and immortality* (RV 'incorruption'). The latter indicates the character of the former, i.e. life completely exempt from destruction. *I have believed* (12). The Greek perfect tense used here implies a continuing attitude of trust consequent upon its decisive adoption. *That which I have committed unto him* (12); see RV mg. As the same Greek word clearly refers in i. 14 (see RV mg.; cf. 1 Tim. vi. 20) to 'the deposit' of the gospel, with which the steward is entrusted, that sense seems preferable here. But the AV interpretation is possible. An assertion by Paul of his hope of final personal salvation (cf. 1 Thes. v. 23) suits the context. His use of 'guard' and 'deposit' (RV) may have suggested their further use in a contrasted sense in i. 14.

IV. PAUL COMMENDS THE DEVOTION OF ONESIPHORUS. i. 15–18

Paul enforces his appeal to Timothy not to be ashamed of the gospel and its apostle (i. 8) in a day of persecution by reminding him both of the many who have been ashamed to be openly associated with Paul the prisoner and of one who outstandingly was not. Since Onesiphorus has shown such kindness to Paul in his need, Paul prays that the Lord will recompense him by showing kindness both to Onesiphorus's household now, and to Onesiphorus himself in the coming day of divine judgment and reward. In verse 15 render with RV 'turned away' (omitting AV *be*) which better expresses the sense. It was a decisive act of repudiation; they disowned Paul. By contrast Onesiphorus not only acknowledged and helped Paul after his arrest, but later, when he arrived in Rome, he took extra trouble to find Paul (apparently no easy task) in order again to encourage him (16, 17). Timothy, too, is well acquainted with the many ministries he performed in Ephesus (18). In this verse follow RV and omit *unto me*. Onesiphorus appears here as one separated from his household, either by absence from home, or quite possibly by death (cf. iv. 19). This does not mean, however, that Paul is praying for his present well-being as one dead, a practice completely unsupported elsewhere in Scripture. The prayer concerns not the intermediate state at all, but conduct in this life, and reward on the future day of judgment. Such desire for adequate and appropriate recompense then is one that can equally be expressed for living or dead, and is in harmony with the plain teaching of our Lord and the New Testament. See Mt. x. 33; Mk. viii. 38; and compare and contrast 2 Tim. iv. 14, RV.

V. A FURTHER EXHORTATION TO STEADFASTNESS AND DILIGENCE. ii. 1–13

Following the example of Onesiphorus, and in contrast to the failure of others, Paul exhorts Timothy to find his strength in Christ and to be prepared to suffer hardship. Two tasks supremely matter: first, that the deposit of truth, the full gospel, should be faithfully handed on to faithful men, who will in their turn teach others; and secondly, that God's purpose in giving the gospel should be fulfilled in the eternal salvation of the elect. These tasks demand for their discharge such devotion, discipline and diligence as may be seen in the soldier (3, 4), the athlete (5) and the farmer (6). They may also involve suffering, as may be seen in the actual Christian experience of the aged apostle himself. In the face of possible martyrdom, which is Paul's prospect and may become Timothy's, it is good to remember the faithfulness of God and the sure heavenly reward of present earthly sacrifice and steadfastness, as well as the corresponding shame that must follow failure.

Be strong (1). The Greek present tense and passive voice means 'be continually strengthened'. *In the grace that is in Christ Jesus* (1) indicates the sphere in which alone this is possible. *Commit* (2); Gk. *paratithenai*, from the same root as 'deposit' (Gk. *parathēkē*) in i. 14 (see RV mg.). Timothy had been solemnly entrusted with the gospel by Paul. He is charged similarly to commit it to trustworthy ministers, who will in their turn pass it on to others. *Among* (i.e. in the presence of) *many witnesses* (2) may refer to those present when Timothy was set apart to this ministry; or the phrase may mean that the content of Paul's gospel had been confirmed to Timothy 'through' (Gk. *dia*) the testimony of many others. *Endure* (3); the sense of the Greek is 'suffer with me' (see RV mg.; cf. i. 8). *That warreth* (4); Gk. *strateuomenos*, i.e. serving as a soldier. Such service demands complete detachment from ordinary worldly business, single, wholehearted devotion to obeying one's commanding officer, and fulfilment of the purpose of one's enrolment. In verse 5 see RV; the reference is to a competitor in an athletic contest. In ancient times the winner was given a crown or garland as his prize. *Lawfully* (5); i.e. according to the rules, in strict conformity to what the particular contest demands, first in training and then in actual performance. *That laboureth* and *first* (6) are significant words added to an otherwise general statement. Such partaking is in contrast to the rightly inferior participation of the indolent. These three illustrations (ii. 3–6) enforce different aspects of the challenge to utter devotion to the worthy discharge of gospel ministry.

Consider what I say (7); i.e. grasp the meaning of what has just been said, and its practical application to your own ministry. This is no empty exhortation, because the *understanding*, i.e. the ability to pass right judgment, the Lord will give. Note RV 'for' and 'shall'. *Was raised* (8); better 'is raised' or 'risen' (RV). Timothy is to find inspiration in the recollection of *Jesus* vindicated as 'Messiah' (*Christ*) not only by His human birth *of the seed of David* in fulfilment of prophecy, but much more by His resurrection from the dead; cf. Acts ii. 36; Rom. i. 1–4. He can, therefore, be called to mind as the living Lord. Such essential truth about Him is part of the gospel entrusted to Paul to be preached (and through him to Timothy); cf. Rom. ii. 16, xvi. 25; 1 Cor. xv. 1.

Wherein (9); i.e. in this very gospel preaching of mine. The word *gospel* refers to the evangelizing as well as to the evangel. *I suffer trouble, as an evil doer, even unto bonds* (9). These words emphasize the extremity of utterly undeserved indignity and shame which Paul was suffering and which Timothy must be ready to share. *Is not bound* (9); i.e. as Paul is. God's word cannot thus be confined. *Therefore* (10); i.e. on this account, for the sake of the gospel and its propagation. *I endure all things* (10); i.e. I patiently submit to every kind of experience, even the worst; cf. Heb. xii. 2. The goal in view is that those whom God has freely chosen for such a destiny may also themselves actually encounter His salvation—the salvation which is to be found in Messiah Jesus (above referred to, ii. 8) and which possesses a glory whose quality and full manifestation are eternal, not temporal.

In verses 11–13 see RV. These phrases, quoted as worthy of credence, were possibly taken from a familiar hymn, or string of aphorisms, intended to inspire faithfulness unto death and hope of sharing in Christ's eternal glory. Our entrance into that glory will correspond to our share in His sufferings here; cf. Rom. viii. 17. *If we be dead* (11); better, as in RV, 'if we died', referring to the decisive event either of spiritual crucifixion with Christ or of physical martyrdom, thought of as already past (Gk. aorist tense). Contrast 'if we endure' (12, RV; Gk. present tense), i.e. a sustained activity. Note the paradoxical contrast between the pathway and the goal—through death to life, through patient submission to sovereign sway. *If we deny him* (12; Gk. future tense); see RV; a more remote possibility is suggested; cf. Mt. x. 33. While men's failure to confess Him now will affect Christ's future acknowledgment of them, their failure to trust Him and to be true to Him does not alter His abiding trustworthiness and faithfulness; cf. Rom. iii. 3. To be false to Himself is something which even omnipotent God cannot be.

VI. SOME RULES OF CONDUCT.
ii. 14–26

There was increasing danger of attention being diverted to profitless and damaging speculation and controversy. Two men are mentioned by name who were propagating wrong doctrine about the resurrection. Timothy, therefore, must remind the Christians, and particularly those 'faithful men' (verse 2) to whom he entrusts the gospel to be preached, of such truths as Paul has just enumerated (verses 4–13). And he must solemnly charge them not to become involved in the prevalent controversies. For his own part let him rather adhere to the straightforward presentation of the truth in a way which will win God's approval, and give him, as a workman, no cause for shame in God's sight, particularly in the coming day of judgment. Let him avoid irreverent fancies, which are capable of being as harmful as an eating sore. If the overturning of the faith of some tempt him to tremble for the very survival of the Christian community, let him remember that the true Church is God's own firm foundation, but that not all who profess to acknowledge Christ as Lord are its true members. For only God knows who are truly His. Profession of the name involves the demand (to which some do not respond) to give up sin. Just as the many articles in a large house vary in quality, and some are of little or no value and unfit for honourable use, so the visible community of professing Christians is a mixed company. The individual believer, like Timothy, who has the discernment to recognize this, should seek, by diligent self-purification, to cease to belong to the class of the unworthy, and thus to become fit for honourable use in the Master's service. He should abandon self-indulgence and share the company and spiritual ambitions of sincere believers. He should refuse to engage in senseless investigations which promote only violent disagreement. As one called to the Lord's service he should not engage in controversy with those ensnared by error, but show them gentle forbearance, and meekly seek to instruct them in the truth in the hope that God may bring them to a better mind, and so they may escape from the devil who has ensnared them, and devote themselves to doing God's will.

Strive not about (or 'with') *words* (14); i.e. do not engage in controversy. The following phrases indicate its results. Negatively it is without profit; positively, instead of edifying the hearers, it overturns them, or involves them in spiritual 'catastrophe'. *That needeth not to be ashamed* (15); the Greek word may have a passive force, viz. 'not to be put to shame'; cf. Phil. i. 20, RV. *Rightly dividing* (15); lit. 'cutting straightly'; see RV and RV mg.; possibly a metaphor from cutting a straight road or furrow, and so not deviating from *the word of truth*, i.e. the gospel; cf. Gal. ii. 14. *Shun* (16); i.e. 'stand clear of', 'withdraw from'. *Profane . . . babblings* (16); i.e. talk empty of value and irreverent in spirit. *They* (16); i.e. those who give themselves to such talk make progress only in the wrong direction, in ungodliness; the spirit of irreverence grows. Such talking, when given the opportunity through their indulgence in it, spreads like a malignant sore eating away healthy tissue. *Hymenaeus* (17) is also mentioned in 1 Tim. i. 20. Belief in a physical resurrection was a difficulty to many (cf. 1 Cor. xv), especially to those who regarded all matter as evil. So they interpreted *the resurrection* (18) as a spiritual quickening or initiation already experienced, thus missing the truth themselves and upsetting the faith of others.

In verse 19 follow the RV, 'the firm foundation of God standeth'; i.e. it cannot be overturned. The reference is to the true Church of God's building; cf. Eph. ii. 19–22. Its double attestation indicates, from God's side and from man's, how its genuine members are to be distinguished and separated from the false. For light on the virtual quotations see Nu. xvi, esp. 5, 26; cf. Is. lii. 11. Note that the genuineness of others is fully known only to God, and that it is for each one who professes to acknowledge Christ as Lord to make his own election sure by appropriate action. Verse 21 reiterates the individual's responsibility to separate himself from the defilement of association with the unworthy. Note the obvious reference for Timothy to the false teachers. Verse 22 indicates complementary truths. Defilement from within, as well as from without, must be avoided, and fellowship with the sincere is to be pursued. Note the repeated indication that some inquiries are foolish and inept, or unenlightened, because they generate not edification but contention (23). *The servant of the Lord* (24); RV mg. 'the Lord's bondservant'. The term applies to any Christian (1 Cor. vii. 22), but particularly to one called to special ministry like Timothy; cf. Tit. i. 1. *Gentle . . . patient* (24); i.e. kindly in word and demeanour, and forbearing towards evil. *Apt to teach . . . instructing* (24, 25); i.e. devoted to positive exposition of the truth rather than to controversy with those who oppose it. This is how those ensnared by false teaching ought to be treated (contrast the more drastic handling of its deliberate propagators, Tit. iii. 10); for such can be won back only as God grants to them a change of mind to enter into full knowledge of the truth (25). In verse 26 see RV and RV mg. Of the three interpretations suggested RV mg. seems the best, viz. that those who have been taken alive by the devil may return to soberness, escape from his trap, and enter instead into the pursuit of God's will.

VII. A WARNING OF COMING APOSTASY. iii. 1–9

If Timothy thinks it strange that so much of evil should arise within the visible Church, Paul now desires him to learn that worse is to follow as the end approaches. The sinfulness of human self-will will find full, unrestrained expression in deed, word and thought. The practice of reverence, dutifulness, gratitude, love of kindred and covenant-keeping will cease. Men will become diabolical, uncontrolled, violent, enemies of virtue, ready to betray their fellows, reckless, misled by their own conceit. Those who profess religion will put love of pleasure before love of God; they will outwardly affect a form of reverence but deliberately repudiate its actual trans-

forming power. Men of this kind must be avoided. They are the sort who stealthily impose on and mislead weak women, who because of their sensitive conscience about wrongdoing, their readiness to be moved by emotion, their love of novelty, and their inability to grasp the truth, are an easy prey. Such men must be recognized in their true character as opponents of the truth, of a depraved mind, and in God's eyes rejected in relation to the very faith which they profess (cf. Mt. vii. 22, 23). Nevertheless there will be a limit to the progress they make; for all will see that their behaviour is manifestly insane.

In the last days (1). The Christian era as a whole is sometimes so described (see Heb. i. 2), but the reference here is explicitly to the consummation of the age. Note the future tense *shall come*, though the present tenses in iii. 5, 6 indicate that the evil later to mature was already at work. Cf. Mt. xiii. 24–30; 2 Thes. ii. 7, 8. *Perilous* (1); Gk. *chalepos*; i.e. 'difficult', 'hard to live in'. *Men* (2); the Greek has the definite article, i.e. not men or mankind generally. The whole context, especially verse 5, suggests that this manifestation of evil is to occur within the sphere of professed Christianity. It is not unenlightened heathen, but those who resist the truth and repudiate the power of the gospel who become corrupt. Cf. 2 Thes. ii. 3 where Paul teaches that 'a falling away' (Gk. *apostasia*) must happen first. In verses 2–4 note the RV rendering, 'lovers of self . . . lovers of pleasure rather than lovers of God'; i.e. they are men who put devotion to self-satisfaction in the place of pleasing God. This is of the very essence of sin and its practice, called in educational terminology 'self-expression'. *Proud* (2); Gk. *hyperēphanos*, i.e. 'haughty' (RV), arrogant, scornful of others. *Blasphemers* (2); RV 'railers', i.e. those who speak disrespectfully, whether of God or man. *Trucebreakers* (3). The Greek *aspondos* describes not so much one who breaks contracts as one who will not make any; so 'implacable' (RV). *Despisers of those that are good* (3); Gk. *aphilagathoi*, i.e. haters of all good, whether in things or people. *Heady* (4), or 'headstrong' (RV), or 'rash' (Acts xix. 36, RV). *Denying* (5); cf. 1 Tim. v. 8; Tit. i. 16. *From such turn away* (5); contrast ii. 25. These are apparently to be regarded as past redemption, and capable of doing only harm. *Silly women* (6); Gk. *gunaikaria*, a diminutive expressing contempt. For the greater ease with which women are misled cf. 1 Tim. ii. 14. *Jannes and Jambres* (8) are mentioned in a Hebrew Targum on Ex. vii. 11 as magicians who opposed Moses. This comparison may imply similar use of occult powers; see note on 'seducers' (iii. 13). *Of corrupt minds* (8); i.e. no longer able to understand the truth (cf. Rom. i. 21, 22; Eph. iv. 17, 18). With verse 9 contrast ii. 16, iii. 13. While such men will get worse in their own depravity and in their power to deceive, they will not be able to do so without their folly being generally recognized. *Their's* is a reference to Jannes and Jambres.

VIII. A CALL TO PREACH THE WORD IN SPITE OF PERSECUTION.
iii. 10—iv. 5

a. The example of Paul's own experience (iii. 10-13)

How different is Timothy's previous history from all this (i.e. iii. 1-9)! Paul reminds Timothy of his own faith and practice, and of the persecution and suffering in which his Christian service has involved him, not least in his early missionary work in Timothy's home neighbourhood. Let Timothy take to heart that this experience was typical. All who determine to live lives of true Christian devotion must expect persecution; and the more so as the contrast between the good and the evil increases, and evil men get worse, both in their own blind departure from the truth, and in their power to mislead others.

But thou hast fully known (10); lit., as in RV, 'didst follow', i.e. in responsive discipleship; cf. 1 Tim. iv. 6, RV. Paul is not boasting but reminding his devoted follower of the essentials of devotion to Christ. *Which . . . what* (11); lit. 'such (as)'. In illustration of his point Paul selects trials specially well known to Timothy, from which he first learnt that such afflictions are part of the inevitable experience of all true Christians (see Acts xiv. 19-22). This is the lesson enforced in verse 12 (cf. Mt. v. 10, x. 22; Jn. xv. 20). *All that will* (12); lit. all who are so minded or determined. *Godly in Christ Jesus* (12) is a significant description of the spirit and sphere of true Christian living, i.e. responding in reverent devotion as one enabled and constrained by a vital personal relation. *Seducers* (13); RV 'impostors'. The Greek *goētes* means 'wizards', lit. 'wailers', referring to incantation by howling; it may imply, therefore, the use of magical arts.

b. The value of the Scriptures (iii. 14-17)

What is more, Timothy knows the revealed truth of God and has been assured of its value from those who taught him as a child. His duty, therefore, is steadfastly to adhere to these things. For the sacred Scriptures in which he was taught are uniquely qualified to guide men into the experience of that salvation of God which is to be enjoyed through faith in Messiah Jesus. Not only so, every single Scripture, because it owes its origin to the creative breath or Spirit of God (Gk. *theopneustos*, 'God-breathed'; cf. Ps. xxxiii. 6), has its value for the moral education of the man of God and his thorough equipment for every kind of good work.

Thou (14); in sharp contrast to the *evil men* (13). *From a child* (15); lit. 'babe'; a reference to Timothy's instruction from very early infancy (see i. 5). *The holy scriptures* (15); lit. 'the sacred writings' (RV) or 'letters'. Used with the definite article this is a virtual technical expression (found also in Philo and Josephus) for the Old Testament. Note the significant Christian

description of their theme and purpose. They afford not just knowledge or information, but practical wisdom. *Able* (15). In Greek the word is a present participle, indicating a permanent enduring quality. In verse 16 see RV and RV mg. The meaning is that every single scripture (of those just referred to), because it is inspired of God, is also profitable; so none should be neglected. *Instruction in righteousness* (16); i.e. discipline, or education, in the way (or life) of righteousness. *Perfect, throughly furnished* (17). In Greek the adjective and the participle reiterate the same root, enforcing the idea of 'fully equipped and adapted'.

c. Paul's charge to Timothy (iv. 1-5)

In view, therefore, of his calling to ministry Paul solemnly charges Timothy before God, and in the light of the account he must render to King Jesus when He comes to judge, to preach the word, to be on the alert to do so on all occasions, whether favourable or not, and to apply its challenge to his hearers both in rebuke and in comfort with unfailing patience and comprehensive instruction. Timothy ought to do this now because a time is coming when men will not tolerate this kind of profitable teaching, but will turn from the truth to fiction and to teachers who say things to tickle their fancy. Timothy must, therefore, be always sober, prepared to suffer hardship, active in declaring the Christian good news, discharging to the full his ministry.

In verse 1 follow RV. Paul adjures Timothy by God, by Christ the future judge, by His 'epiphany', or second advent, and by His kingdom. It is an important feature of the New Testament gospel that Jesus is to judge all men, and that a day is coming when He will thus be manifested. Cf. Acts xvii. 31; Rom. ii. 16. This phrase 'judge the living and the dead' is found in early Christian creeds. *Preach the word* (2); i.e. the gospel; cf. Acts vi. 4; Col. iv. 3, RV. *Be instant* (2); i.e. be attentive, as one standing by ready to fulfil this ministry. *Reprove, rebuke, exhort* (2). Note how the word and its preacher must hurt before they can heal. *With all* (i.e. every kind of) *longsuffering and doctrine* (2). This indicates both how the minister is to handle his hearers, and how he is to choose his subject-matter. He should give varied and positive teaching, not monotonous and negative condemnation. The future prospect described in verses 3 and 4 provides added reason for preaching now on every possible occasion. *Endure* (3); i.e. 'put up with', 'have the mind or patience to receive'. Note how this hearing is wrong both in motive and interest; it is determined by selfish caprice, and directed away from the truth toward fables. In verse 5 follow RV.

IX. A DESCRIPTION OF PAUL'S OWN CIRCUMSTANCES: FINAL GREETINGS.
iv. 6-22

Paul declares that he is ready to die a martyr's death, which he knows is imminent. His life work is done; he has been true to his trust. He can look forward to that consummation of salvation which the Lord will give in that day when He comes as judge to all who have their hope thus fixed on His appearing. Of Paul's intimate friends and fellow-workers only Luke is now with him. So Paul urges Timothy to endeavour to come to him quickly, and to bring with him Mark and some of Paul's personal belongings which he left at Troas. In his imprisonment and trial Paul has had his disappointments. Demas forsook him. Alexander actually did him injury and spoke against him. No one was prepared publicly to take his side. But the Lord did not fail to enable him fully to declare the substance of what he preached for all to hear. He was preserved from being overwhelmed and silenced, and is persuaded that the Lord will bring him safely through what now lies ahead into His kingdom above. To Him is eternal glory due. Timothy is to give Paul's greetings to his special friends, and accept greetings from some who wish to send them to him. Because Paul is without those whom Timothy might imagine to be with him, let him come before winter. May he know the Lord's presence in his heart; and may the saving grace of God be with all in whose midst he is.

In verse 6 see RV and RV mg. Paul's circumstances provide added reason why Timothy should be zealous (iv. 5). Pouring out of blood (Dt. xii. 27) or wine (Nu. xxviii. 7) unto the Lord accompanied sacrifice; Paul so speaks of the shedding of his own blood (RV mg.). Cf. Phil. ii. 17. Note that what was then a remote possibility is now an immediate certainty, indeed, has already begun. In verse 7 read with RV (following the Greek) 'the' (not *a*) *good fight*; i.e. 'of faith' (cf. 1 Tim. vi. 12). *My course* (7); cf. Acts xx. 24. *The faith* (7); i.e. the gospel, or deposit of doctrine, entrusted to Paul. This he has successfully guarded (cf. i. 14). *Laid up* (8); i.e. reserved, set aside. *A* (RV 'the') *crown of righteousness* (8); either the crown is the reward for righteousness, or righteousness is the content of the crown (cf. 1 Pet. v. 4). The two ideas may be combined in that heavenly consummation of the God-given righteousness or justification, of which believers enjoy now only the firstfruits (cf. Rom. v. 1, 2). This is suggested by the fact that it is to be shared in equally by all who have had their love set on this crowning manifestation of the Lord in righteous judgment at His second advent.

Demas (10) is not charged with apostasy, but with unwillingness to face the possibility of physical suffering and death through further association with Paul the prisoner and likely martyr. Contrast his 'love of this present world' with the 'love of His appearing' (8). *Take* (11); i.e. add to your company for, or on, the journey; cf. 'take in' (Acts xx. 13). In spite of serious early misgivings about his fitness (Acts xv. 38), Paul

here (cf. Col. iv. 10) commends Mark as 'useful for ministering', perhaps in the gospel or perhaps to Paul's more personal needs. Some think Mark's probable knowledge of Latin made him particularly useful in Rome. Verse 12 implies, perhaps, that Paul needs Mark to take Tychicus's place. Paul trusted the latter more than once to carry messages and act on his behalf (see Eph. vi. 21, 22; Col. iv. 7, 8; Tit. iii. 12). *The cloke* (13); i.e. a large outer garment, apparently needed by Paul for use during the cold of the coming winter; see verse 21. *The parchments* (13); Gk. *membranai*, in origin a Latin word and meaning prepared skins of vellum, preferred to papyrus for important documents. These were especially precious to Paul. They were presumably either copies of Old Testament Scriptures, or possibly manuscripts and valuable personal documents of Paul's own. *Did me much evil* (14); i.e. 'shewed' (RV mg.) me much ill-treatment. *The Lord reward him* (14); follow RV and the preferable Gk. reading, 'the Lord will render to him', a virtual quotation of Ps. lxii. 12 (cf. Pr. xxiv. 12), implying 'It is for the Lord to recompense him accordingly (not me or you)'; cf. Rom. xii. 19. 'Meanwhile', says Paul to Timothy, 'there is need for you to beware of him.'

At my first answer (16). According to Roman legal procedure Paul had appeared once in court to present his defence. On that occasion he had to plead his cause alone. He had no advocate or supporting witnesses. Those who might have been such all deserted him, presumably through fear, not deliberate malice, as in the case of Alexander. So Paul prays that God in mercy will not reckon such failure against them. *That by me the preaching might be fully known* (17); follow RV and RV mg. The Greek verb means 'be fulfilled' or 'fully performed'; cf. iv. 5. Paul's concern was that the proclamation of the gospel should be faithfully discharged by him there in the capital city for all to hear. 'To be rescued out of a lion's mouth' (17) may have been a current phrase for deliverance out of apparently overwhelming peril. Or 'lion' may refer, either to the beasts of the amphitheatre, or to the emperor Nero, or to the devil. In 1 Pet. v. 8 to be devoured by the lion seems to mean to have one's faithful testimony silenced by surrender through fear to the devil. Cf. also the Lord's Prayer— 'deliver us from the evil (one)'—of which there seem to be further reminiscences in verse 18. *Preserve me unto* (18); Gk. *eis*, a pregnant construction. Paul's salvation is to be completed by his being brought 'into' *his heavenly kingdom*. The deliverance he expects from all evil is not from death, but through it. Note that the doxology (18) is addressed to Christ as God. The benediction of verse 22 is twofold: the first is addressed to Timothy personally, the second is the distinctive Pauline 'signature' (see 2 Thes. iii. 17, 18).

A. M. STIBBS.

TITUS: OUTLINE OF CONTENTS

For a General Introduction to this Epistle see p. 1063.

I. PERSONAL ADDRESS AND GREETING. i. 1–4

II. THE QUALIFICATIONS OF ELDERS OR BISHOPS. i. 5–9

III. A WARNING AGAINST FALSE TEACHERS. i. 10–16

IV. INSTRUCTIONS FOR VARIOUS GROUPS IN THE CHURCH. ii. 1–10

V. THE CHRISTIAN'S DUTY TO MAINTAIN GOOD WORKS. ii. 11—iii. 11

VI. PERSONAL MESSAGES AND FAREWELL GREETINGS. iii. 12–15

TITUS: COMMENTARY

I. PERSONAL ADDRESS AND GREETING. i. 1–4

Compare and see notes on 1 Tim. i. 1, 2. Paul writes as one constrained by the obligation of bond-service to God and by the authority of the commission of Christ. This service and commission concern, and are directed towards, the bringing of those whom God has chosen to save to faith in Him (cf. Acts xiii. 48; 1 Thes. i. 4–8) and to the full knowledge of the truth. Note that full instruction in the truth is an essential part of the apostolic task and that such truth is disclosed in Christ. See Mt. xxviii. 19, 20; Jn. i. 14; Eph. i. 13, iv. 20, 21. Both for its understanding and for its enjoyment this truth demands a spirit of *godliness* (1), or active reverence Godward. The foundation of confidence, first in the apostle or preacher of this truth, and then for its learner and believer, is a *hope of eternal life* (2). This foundation was firmly laid before the ages of world history began by a promise of God, who cannot deceive or utter falsehood. Cf. Nu. xxiii. 19; Heb. vi. 18; and note the sure guarantee afforded by the word of such a God. God's announcement of this word of His to men has been openly made, when the proper time for this came (cf. 1 Tim. ii. 6), in the gospel message (see RV and RV mg.). Its proclamation has been entrusted, says Paul, *unto me* (3) by the direct appointment of God Himself, as the One active to save us. In verse 4 Paul, by natural birth a Jew, greets Titus, a Greek (see Gal. ii. 3), as one brought by the faith which they now share into an intimacy of family relationship. The wording may well mean that Titus owed his conversion to Paul.

II. THE QUALIFICATIONS OF ELDERS OR BISHOPS. i. 5–9

Paul left Titus in Crete to complete the establishment of their missionary work there, and particularly to see to the appointment of elders in each local congregation (cf. Acts xiv. 23). He had not only charged him to do this, but

had also indicated how to do it properly by stating what kind of men should be appointed. These instructions he now repeats and enforces. Anyone who is to be appointed ought in character and conduct to be beyond reproach, free from incongruous moral weakness, actively given to good works and to the disciplined pursuit of personal holiness, and so unswerving in his loyalty to the truth which he has received that he can encourage many by his healthy teaching and expose the error of any who speak contrary to it. Cf. 1 Tim. iii. 1–7 and see notes there.

Titus was to *set in order* (5) any things which were deficient. Note that the same officers are called elders (Gk. *presbyteroi*), describing status as 'seniors', and bishops (Gk. *episkopoi*), describing function as 'overseers'. One congregation might have several; cf. Acts xx. 17, 28. A man's personal and family life and previous history are all important as indicating his character and determining his reputation. *Not accused of riot or unruly* (6) refers to the *children* (see RV). Note the plain indication that children of a true Christian home should not be dissolute or undisciplined, but rather themselves responsive to the gospel as believers. Irreproachable character is indispensable because the elder has to be a *bishop* (7); i.e. to exercise oversight as one answerable to God as His steward. For 'the house', or church, for which he cares is God's. The word that is *faithful* (9), and essential to 'healthful teaching' (9, RV mg.), is the word 'which is according to the teaching' (RV), or apostolic doctrine. Paul, who has himself been entrusted with that word, is supremely concerned that others, appointed to its stewardship, should first hold fast to it themselves, and then faithfully preserve and propagate it. Cf. 2 Tim. ii. 2.

III. A WARNING AGAINST FALSE TEACHERS. i. 10–16

Note the significant correspondence with our Lord's similar warnings in Mk. vii. 1–23. There is need for 'bishops' who can expose the error of those who oppose the truth (9). There are many who are active in misleading men by their false teaching, and they must be silenced. Also, Cretans readily fall for things untrue and sensual, as a true testimony of one of their own poets makes plain. So severe exposure of the false teachers and of their fanciful and man-made teaching is the more necessary if the Cretan Christians are to maintain their spiritual health. In these matters the response of the heart and the practice of the life go together. Those who through heart unbelief become inwardly defiled defile everything they touch by the way they use it. Though they may confess God with their lips, their deeds proclaim that they do not know Him. Rather in His sight they are abominable, because disobedient, and so disqualified for any good work.

The false teachers are *unruly* (10); i.e. they do not submit their minds to divinely revealed truth. *Vain talkers and deceivers* (10). They teach things which have no substance or corresponding reality (cf. Rom. i. 21, 22), and are capable of misleading the minds of men. Those who are the greatest dangers are Jews and Judaizers, propagating teaching which has its roots in Judaism (cf. verse 14). They must be silenced, both because of the damage they can do—they are the sort who can overturn the faith of whole families —and because they stand doubly condemned as teaching what is wrong and as doing it for material gain.

In verse 12 Paul quotes a hexameter line of the Cretan philosopher Epimenides, who wrote about 600 B.C. In remarkable language Paul calls him *a prophet* and endorses his *witness* as *true* (13). This affords scriptural authority for believing that in some small degree Gentile nations have had their own prophets. Note RV 'idle gluttons'. The quotation was probably well known. Certainly Cretans had in the Greek world a proverbial reputation as *liars* (12). The character of the false teaching and of those who propagate it is then radically exposed and condemned. In contrast to the gospel, which is 'of God' and *the truth*, this teaching is *of men* and consists of *fables* or mere fiction (14). Those who teach it have turned their backs on the truth. Therefore, to give heed to their teaching is to do likewise (cf. Is. xxix. 13; Mk. vii. 6-9). These *commandments* probably prohibited the use of certain things as unclean (cf. 1 Tim. iv. 3; Col. ii. 16, 21). Verse 15 means that things are pure or not in men's use (not in their judgment) of them according to their inner spiritual and moral condition. Defilement takes its rise within, not through things from without (cf. Mk. vii. 15). *Reprobate* (16); Gk. *adokimoi*, a word often used by Paul; it means 'unapproved of'.

IV. INSTRUCTIONS FOR VARIOUS GROUPS IN THE CHURCH. ii. 1-10

Having shown (i. 10-16) why the error of opponents of the truth needs exposing, Paul now indicates how 'to exhort in the healthful teaching' (see i. 9, ii. 1, RV mg.). The injunctions here given to Titus and the detailed exhortations he is to give to others all concern conduct. The best antidote to wrong teaching is positive moral exhortation and teaching which promotes spiritual health. It has already been shown that those who follow wrong teaching are first corrupt in heart, and then become so in life. Therefore those who desire by their teaching to maintain the true spiritual well-being of others must demand the consistent expression in conduct of heart-soundness within. This is the kind of exhortation to which Titus must publicly give utterance. He must direct appropriate exhortations of this kind to the different age-groups in the church. He should exhort the older women similarly to teach the younger women. He should enforce what he demands, particularly to the young men, by the example of his own personal behaviour. Thus, by the serious sincerity and irreproachable character of his ministry, he should put to shame and silence potential opponents. Those who as slaves have to serve human masters need special exhortation to show themselves obedient and faithful in order thus attractively to exhibit the worth of the gospel which declares that God is the Saviour of men.

Grave (2); Gk. *semnos*; lit. 'reverend' or 'venerable', because 'serious' in one's attitude to life, and correspondingly 'restrained' in one's behaviour or dress. *Temperate* (2); Gk. *sōphrōn*; RV 'sober-minded'; cf. verses 4, 5 (*discreet*), 6; it describes 'the well-balanced state of mind resulting from habitual self-restraint'. *Sound* (2) means 'healthy'; see i. 13, RV mg. *False accusers* (3); RV 'slanderers'; Gk. *diaboloi*; cf. 1 Tim. iii. 6, 11. *Teachers* (3); the older women are to fulfil an active teaching ministry among the younger women, but not in the congregation generally; see 1 Tim. ii. 11, 12. Verses 4 and 5 teach that Christian married women are to find their sphere of service in the family and the home as good wives and mothers, submissively recognizing their husbands as the head of the house, lest the God-given gospel be reproached for encouraging an improper freedom and disturbing domestic life (cf. 1 Tim. vi. 1). *Good* (5) means 'kind' (RV); i.e. not hard or mean in their management of the home. Cf. the use of the word in Mt. xx. 15.

Shewing thyself a pattern (7); the personal reference is emphatic; the practical 'model' (Gk. *typos*) of good living which Titus is to provide for others to look upon is himself. *Uncorruptness, gravity* (7) describe characteristics of the teacher, not the teaching; i.e. they refer to the sincerity and seriousness in which he is to give it. Further, what Titus teaches should be not only intrinsically 'healthful' but also so expressed as to be 'irreprehensible' (8). The opponent of the truth, whose aim is to slander its teachers and to propagate error, is to be put to shame by this ministry of the health-giving word and by his own inability to say anything bad about the Christian's manner of life. *Answering again* (9); RV 'gainsaying'; cf. i. 9. The Greek *antilegein*, lit. 'to contradict', can mean 'to oppose', 'to show active enmity against'. *Purloining* (10); the Greek literally means 'putting on one side for themselves'. *All good fidelity* (10); 'all', Gk. *pas*, has here an extensive force and signifies 'on every possible occasion'. *Adorn* (10); the Greek verb *kosmein* can be used of the 'setting' of a jewel, a process by which it is favourably displayed. *The doctrine of God* (not Christ) *our Saviour* (10); i.e. not the ethical precepts of our Lord, but the gospel of our salvation; see verse 11.

V. THE CHRISTIAN'S DUTY TO MAINTAIN GOOD WORKS. ii. 11—iii. 11

Paul has just indicated that it is the gospel of God's salvation which ought to be attractively set forth by the appropriate good works or Christian behaviour of those who believe it (ii. 5, 10). He now introduces two remarkable doctrinal summaries of essential features of this gospel (ii. 11–14, iii. 3–7), both of which are directed to show that a life of good works is God's purpose and the only appropriate behaviour for all who enjoy the benefits of His redeeming grace and saving mercy. Titus is told, therefore, that it is his responsibility confidently to proclaim this gospel, which is so worthy of being believed, and then authoritatively to apply its practical challenge in exhortation and rebuke to all who profess to have believed it, in order to move them to give the most careful attention to the matter of good living. This is the teaching, says Paul, which is both virtuous in itself and profitable to men. Foolish inquiries and subjects which, by contrast, are productive of nothing but strife and division should be avoided because they are obviously so unhelpful. So should any who show a perverse interest in them and will not give them up after being admonished

Hath appeared (11) (Greek aorist tense) points to one definite act, i.e. the incarnation and atoning work of Christ (cf. iii. 4). In character and purpose the grace thus manifested is 'saving' or 'bringing salvation' (see RV), and that not to Jews only, but *to all men*. Its scope is world-wide. God's saving grace brings us under a discipline or instruction which makes plain that we must live our present lives differently. Negatively, we must decisively abandon the kind of life which is dominated by no reverence for God but by mere worldly interests; positively, we must seek to live rightly in relation to ourselves, to others, and to God—i.e. *soberly, righteously, and godly* (12). In verse 14 follow RV and RV mg. This gospel also gives us a hope beyond this life which is to be anticipated as *blessed* (13); i.e. the consummation of bliss. For Christ's second advent will be an appearing (Gk. *epiphaneia*) of God's 'glory' as the first was of His 'grace' (ii. 11). Then Jesus will be

openly manifested not only as *our Saviour* but also in all the glory of His majesty or greatness as *God*. Christ's ability to be *our Saviour* depends on His one accomplished act of self-sacrifice on our behalf as a ransom price (14; cf. Mk. x. 45; 1 Tim. ii. 6). The full salvation which He thus procured means, negatively, our release from every kind of lawlessness, and, positively, our purification to be His own chosen people (see RV), devoted to good works. So transformed living is intended and possible for those who know God and His Christ as their Saviour. It is therefore rightly expected from them both by God and by men. *Let no man despise thee* (15); i.e. when you thus speak, do not allow anyone to treat what you say as unworthy of their attention.

In iii. 1, 2 follow RV. These verses give detailed instruction how, in this world, appropriate Christian good conduct should express itself in relation both to civil authorities and one's fellow-men. Christians ought to be dutiful citizens, prepared to take an active share in every kind of good activity—a particularly significant injunction here as Cretans had a reputation for being seditious. Christians ought also to act towards all with whom they come into contact in positive goodwill, refraining from attacking any by word or deed, and actively displaying a considerate and yielding spirit towards all.

What should inspire such conduct is the two-fold recollection that we ourselves were by nature as bad or *hateful* as any (3), and that God has treated us kindly and saved us when we did not deserve it. The gospel of saving grace is therefore again pregnantly stated. Verse 3 provides a general description of sinful and unredeemed human nature—what *we ourselves also were. Foolish* (3); lit. 'senseless', 'without understanding'. Sinners show how completely hateful their sinful condition must be to God, because they even hate one another. Verse 4 shows that the change in our condition is due entirely to God, to His initiative, to His kindness and active love (contrast our hate and active enmity), to His open intervention to save. Verse 5 makes it still more explicit. Our salvation is not due to any righteous works of our doing, but is wholly determined by God's mercy; the *not, we* and *His* are all emphatic. In status this salvation is made ours through the outward seal of baptism; in vital experience it comes through the inner quickening by the Spirit. (Cf. Jn. iii. 5, 'born of water and of the Spirit'.) This gift of the quickening and indwelling Spirit has been made ours by God through Christ and His saving work (6; cf. Jn. vii. 39). So the whole Trinity is active to make salvation ours. And the full gospel includes not only the gift of God's Son for our justification, but also the gift of God's Spirit to make us heirs who can, by the life which He makes ours, hope to enjoy salvation eternally (7). Cf. i. 2; Rom. viii. 11, 15–17, 23, 24; Gal. iv. 4–7. Alternatively, following RV in verse 5, one may interpret the washing of baptism as a mediating token of two benefits, *regeneration* and spiritual *renewing* (5), benefits which are possibly again referred to as *being justified* and being *made heirs according to the hope of eternal life* (7), the one giving a new status of acceptance with God (elsewhere called 'adoption', e.g. Gal. iv. 5), and the other giving the complementary blessing of new Spirit-born life. Note that *regeneration* (Gk. *palingenesia*), like our word 'naturalization', though it suggests a new birth or nature, may rather signify a change of status.

The gospel thus summarized in verses 4–7 is trustworthy doctrine and justifies Titus in confidently making the strongest assertions with regard to it (see 8, RV) in order that those who have thereby come to trust in God may give attention to the practice of *good works*. *Maintain* (8), Gk. *proistasthai*, may mean 'to be forward in', 'to devote themselves before all else to' (cf. ii. 14). Note how similar are the descriptions of harmful teaching given in verse 9 and in 1 Tim. i. 4, vi. 4, 20; 2 Tim. ii. 23. A 'heretical' man (Gk. *hairetikos*) is primarily one who causes divisions, i.e. 'factious' (10, RV mg.). This he does by 'choosing on his own' (the root idea) to depart from the truth and to follow and propagate different teaching. So 'heretical' comes to mean 'holding false doctrine'. But note the fundamental references of the word, first to the moral cause, self-will, and then to the evil consequence, division. Such a man needs not argument but admonition. *Subverted* (11); note RV 'perverted'. What makes his completely unsatisfactory moral (not intellectual) condition thus plain is his refusal to heed admonition.

VI. PERSONAL MESSAGES AND FAREWELL GREETINGS. iii. 12–15

Paul instructs Titus to join him at Nicopolis, where he intends to spend the winter. Titus is to leave as soon as either Artemas or Tychicus arrive, whom Paul says he will send—probably to take over the work in Crete for which Titus was responsible. Practical help is also to be given to expedite the journey of Zenas and Apollos, who likewise may have been going to join Paul. This instruction brings Paul back in thought to a final reiteration of his main injunction, that the Christians in Crete should learn to use every opportunity to do good works and to supply the needs of others. Only so will they be truly fruitful. Paul then sends greetings from all his companions to Titus; he himself greets all in Crete who have true Christian love for himself and his fellow-workers in the gospel. Then he adds his characteristic benediction.

Nicopolis (12). There are three cities so called, in Cilicia, in Thrace or Macedonia, and in Epirus. The last is most probably the one here referred to. *There* (not 'here') implies that Paul was not at Nicopolis when he wrote. But see the AV postscript to iii. 15. *Bring . . . on their journey diligently* (13). There are several indications in the Epistles that Christians were taught and expected to entertain and provide for Christian travellers, particularly those active in preaching. See Rom. xv. 24; 1 Cor. xvi. 6; 3 Jn. 5–8. *In the faith* (15); RV 'in faith'. This was the bond that united them. It was Christian not natural love. Cf. 1 Tim. i. 2. *Grace be with you all* (15). See 1 Tim. vi. 21n.

A. M. STIBBS.

THE EPISTLE TO PHILEMON

INTRODUCTION

See also the General Article, 'The Pauline Epistles', p. 68.

I. OBJECT AND OCCASION

The object of this Epistle and the circumstances which gave rise to it become clear as soon as the text is examined. Several supplementary details can be gathered by comparison with the Epistle to the Colossians. From the Epistle itself, however, we learn that Philemon was a convert and intimate personal friend of Paul's, seemingly well-to-do, noted for his generosity towards Christian brethren in distress. His slave, Onesimus, had absconded, probably with some of his master's money. He made his way to the distant city where Paul lay in prison, and, coming into contact with the apostle, was brought to true repentance and faith in Christ, either from paganism, or from an outward and insincere profession of Christianity. In love and gratitude he attached himself to Paul, and began to render him what personal service he could. Paul in his confinement greatly appreciated these attentions, but felt it improper to retain another man's servant. He therefore persuaded Onesimus to return to his master. A letter of explanation was clearly desirable to inform Philemon of the fact that Onesimus had, in Paul's judgment, truly repented, and to prepare the way for a complete reconciliation between master and slave. Happily the Epistle has been preserved, the only surviving example of many private letters which Paul must have written, and one that throws valuable light on his character and outlook.

II. PLACE AND DATE

The place and time of writing and the place to which it was sent are not indicated in Philemon, but its close relationship with Colossians (Col. iv. 7ff.) shows that it was written at the same time as that Epistle and, therefore, at the same time as Ephesians. These 'Imprisonment Epistles' are generally considered to belong to Paul's Roman imprisonment, mentioned in Acts xxviii. 30; and this is quite consistent with the data in Philemon. This would give a date of approximately A.D. 61 (see also p. 70). Some, who think these Epistles may have been written in Ephesus (or Caesarea), point out that it would be easier for Onesimus to reach those towns than to reach Rome, but this is no strong argument against Rome. A fugitive would wish to flee as far as possible, and would welcome the concealment afforded by the great metropolis. For a detailed statement of the arguments in favour of Ephesus as the place of writing see the *Introduction* to Philippians.

Col. iv. 7–9 shows that Onesimus was sent back by Paul to Colossae with Tychicus, and he is described to the Colossians as 'one of you'. It is natural to infer that Philemon's household resided there, though alternative suggestions of residence in some neighbouring town are not altogether excluded. Lightfoot, for example, favours Laodicea. From Phm. 2 it appears that Archippus was one of Philemon's household, and if he resided outside of Colossae this would help to explain the curiously indirect nature of the message sent to him in Col. iv. 17. That Tychicus is not mentioned in the letter to Philemon, nor Philemon in Colossians, could also be explained by supposing Philemon to have lived outside Colossae. Such points, however, can be otherwise explained, and form very insubstantial evidence against residence in Colossae.

III. GENUINENESS

This has very seldom been doubted, and then chiefly because its matter appeared too private and commonplace, which is really a strong argument against the likelihood of forgery. 'This Epistle found its place in all catalogues, from the Muratorian Canon downwards, and in all the ancient versions' (Ellicott).

IV. VIEWPOINT AND CHARACTERISTICS

The Christian attitude towards slavery is the most important subject dealt with in the Epistle, for it shows the apostle returning a slave to his master, while on the other hand demonstrating his loving sympathy for that slave. Supporters of slavery have emphasized the first fact; opponents, with much more reason, the second; for the spirit of the letter strikes at the very roots of the institution. To preach brotherly love between master and slave ultimately makes slavery meaningless. If abolition of slavery had been practical politics in those days, we may well suppose that the apostle would have been an abolitionist. It was not then practical politics, and Paul may not have foreseen that it ever would become so in this wicked world. But in God's providence abolition was eventually attained, and the influence of this Epistle played no small part in the accomplishment of this result.

The Epistle should not, however, be regarded as an intentional effort on Paul's part to conduct indirect propaganda against the institution of slavery. He is not here concerned with considerations of the rights and wrongs of slavery as such, but with the spiritual welfare of Philemon and Onesimus, and the promotion of Christian brotherhood between them. If not deliberately working for the overthrow of slavery, still less is he seeking to support it. Paul believed that Christian slaves should respect the rights of their masters according to the laws of those days (cf. Eph. vi. 5ff.). He may have been partly influenced by this general principle in advising Onesimus to return; but there is no necessity to exaggerate the extent to which he was affected by such considerations. Would he, for example, out of respect for Roman law, have told Onesimus to return to a cruel pagan master to be tortured or crucified? We have no authority for asserting that he would have done so. He doubtless knew Dt. xxiii. 15. He evidently considered the case on its merits. He knew and loved both Onesimus and Philemon; he understood the circumstances, and thought it better for all concerned that Onesimus should return; and probably Onesimus, disillusioned in the far country, thought so too.

The most significant features of the Epistle are love for the slave and insistence on the new ideal of Christian brotherhood. Where these prevail, slavery is doomed. The Epistle has often been deservedly praised for its tact and grace. An easy familiarity of tone appears here and there. Paul was, however, intensely in earnest. Matthew Henry's Commentary distinguishes no fewer than fourteen arguments in favour of reconciliation in this short letter, a sign that much thought and prayer preceded the writing of it. Luther observes how Paul in pleading puts himself in the place of Onesimus, the wrongdoer, thus imitating Christ's mediatorial work. 'For we are all His Onesimi.'

OUTLINE OF CONTENTS

I. SALUTATION. Verses 1-3

II. THANKSGIVING AND PRAYER FOR PHILEMON. Verses 4-7

III. THE PLEA FOR ONESIMUS. Verses 8-21

IV. CONCLUDING GREETINGS AND BENEDICTION. Verses 22-25

COMMENTARY

I. SALUTATION. Verses 1-3

Philemon (1) was Paul's *fellowlabourer*, doubtless in Christian work. *Our beloved Apphia* (2); read rather 'the (our) sister Apphia' (see RV and mg.); she was apparently Philemon's wife. *Archippus* (2); probably Philemon's son, and a missionary pastor in Colossae or the neighbourhood (cf. Col. iv. 17), hence called Paul's *fellowsoldier*. For Philemon, Archippus, and the place of Paul's imprisonment, see also *Introduction*. If Archippus frequently visited his father's house in Colossae, he could appropriately be saluted there, even if he normally worked and lived elsewhere. *The church* (2); the group assembling in Philemon's house for worship (see Col. iv. 15n.). The form of the salutation in verse 3 is the same as the AV rendering of Col. i. 2; but see note there.

II. THANKSGIVING AND PRAYER FOR PHILEMON. Verses 4-7

Always (4) can go either with *thank* (RV) or *making mention* (AV). The emphasis on constant thankfulness in the RV rendering seems preferable and agrees with the parallel passage in Philippians (Phil. i. 3). *Hearing of thy love and faith* (5). The reporters would be men like Epaphras (Col. iv. 12), and perhaps Onesimus.

Love and faith were qualities continually emphasized by Paul. Cf. Eph. i. 15n. and Col. i. 4. The wording here, however, raises a difficulty which is absent from the Ephesian and Colossian references. It looks at first sight as though the apostle were making his fellow-Christians (*all saints*) objects of faith along with *the Lord Jesus*, which is, of course, unthinkable. The best way of meeting this difficulty is to emphasize the change in the Greek prepositions; literally the phrase reads 'faith "toward" the Lord Jesus and "unto" all the saints', i.e. extending itself to them in beneficence and generosity. Weymouth renders 'faith . . . which you manifest towards all the saints'.

Verse 6 indicates the content of the prayers mentioned in verse 4. *Communication*; Gk. *koinōnia*, which the RV rightly renders as 'fellowship'. Actively it means 'sharing', and so has the sense of imparting material or spiritual good to others. Passively it means sharing in, or benefiting from, fellowship with Christ or with the brethren or with both (see Phil. i. 5n.). *Effectual*; i.e. operative, or effective in producing results. *By the acknowledging of*; RV 'in the knowledge of' (Gk. *epignōsis*). The word means something more than knowledge and has the sense of 'recognition' or 'clear realization'. *In you*; the RV mg. reading 'in us', i.e. 'in us

1085

Christians', is well attested and seems preferable to the AV reading meaning 'you Christians'. *In Christ Jesus;* better, as in RV, 'unto Christ'. The Greek preposition *eis* signifies movement towards rather than position in. If the 'fellowship of thy faith' (RV) is interpreted as meaning the communicating or imparting of faith by preaching, the verse would then simply be a prayer that his preaching might produce in others the knowledge referred to. More commonly, however, the phrase is taken to mean fellowship, either active or passive, arising from or connected with faith. There are then a number of possible interpretations. Philemon's charities are to lead others to realize the high possibilities of Christian attainment. Alternatively, Philemon's communion with Christ and the brethren is to lead Philemon himself to understand and aim at these attainments. Or again, Philemon's charitable activities are to be made fully operative through his deepening realization of how many noble attainments are open to Christians. The apostle prays that working in the sphere of full knowledge the communication of Philemon's faith may prove itself effective (so I.C.C.). This interpretation has the advantage of representing the growth of knowledge as taking place in Philemon himself (a view strongly supported by the parallels Col. i. 9; Eph. i. 17ff.; Phil. i. 9, 10, in all of which Paul desires growth in knowledge for his readers), while also referring to his charitable activities, which were prominent in the apostle's mind. *The bowels* (7); i.e. 'the hearts' (RV); see note on Col. iii. 12. *Refreshed* (7); the same Greek word as for 'give you rest' in Mt. xi. 28.

III. THE PLEA FOR ONESIMUS. Verses 8-21

That which is convenient (8); i.e. befitting a Christian. Paul, therefore, would not be afraid of exceeding his apostolic authority in commanding it, but he prefers to appeal to the generosity of a loving heart like Philemon's, and reinforces his appeal by emphasizing his weakness, not his strength. He is *Paul the aged, and now also a prisoner* (9). He was probably between fifty and sixty, but, worn by persecutions and labours, could truly call himself old. For *aged* some MSS read 'ambassador' (see RV mg. and RSV), but *aged* is the better attested reading and more appropriate in the context. In verse 10 the name *Onesimus* comes last in the Greek. It is tactfully reserved till Philemon has been told of Onesimus's conversion and Paul's love for him. Its meaning is 'useful'. In verse 11, therefore, a play upon words seems clearly to be in the apostle's mind. He does not make it unduly obtrusive, however, by repeating exactly similar terms, but says, as it were, 'Useful' by name, formerly unprofitable, but now true to his name 'profitable'. *Whom I have sent* (12); epistolary aorist, equivalent to 'I send'. The word *receive* (12) is not found in the best MSS but agrees with the meaning of verse 17. A more vivid translation can be secured without it,

viz. 'whom I send back to thee—even him who is my very heart' (see RV).

I would have retained: would I do nothing (13, 14). In Greek the first 'would' is a different word and tense from the second. Paul 'was wishing' to retain him but 'chose' not to do so. He was sure that Philemon, who would gladly have served him in person, would not grudge doing so through his servant, but he disliked to take the liberty of retaining Onesimus and thus compel Philemon to grant this benefit. All through verses 11-16 Paul emphasizes how profitable Onesimus has become. Verse 15 suggests that God may have purposed, through the brief inconvenience of his servant departing *for a season* (lit. 'for an hour'), to give Philemon the blessedness of receiving him back for ever. It would be deplorable if Philemon by spurning Onesimus should reject a divinely sent opportunity of eternal blessing. Paul says *perhaps*, for he cannot profess to know God's plans fully, or what Onesimus or Philemon may do in future; but he wishes Philemon to consider what seems a remarkable leading of providence. *Not now as a servant* (16). Paul's words may hint at legal enfranchisement, but this is doubtful. He concentrates on pleading that Onesimus be in fact treated like a brother, not like a slave described by Aristotle as 'a living tool'. Then by prolonged fellowship *in the flesh, and in the Lord* (16), i.e. in worldly and spiritual affairs, Onesimus will endear himself to Philemon even more than he has endeared himself to Paul during his briefer acquaintance with him. Philemon will love him better, not merely because he has known him longer in the past, and certainly not because he is his legal slave, but because he will longer enjoy close fellowship with him in Christ.

Therefore (17); the second word of the sentence in the Greek. This verse recalls that Onesimus is now worthy to be treated as a brother, so Paul can appropriately say, 'If you would wish to receive me as *a partner,* a friend related by close spiritual ties, receive him so.'

Philemon's likely sense of grievance, however, could not be ignored. He might feel wronged by the mere fact of the slave absconding, and money had probably been stolen also. *If he . . . oweth thee ought* (18) does not mean that Paul knew nothing definite about this, but he graciously avoids speaking bluntly of theft, and leaves it open to Philemon to claim what he considers right, or to refrain from claiming anything if he is so disposed. *I Paul have written it with mine own hand* (19); i.e. like a bond, promising to give any restitution required. This was surely not a mere pleasantry, but to convince Philemon that he was in earnest. It is not, however, meant to be a legally cognizable bond, but a gentleman's solemn assurance. *Albeit I do not say to thee . . .* (19). If there be any slight mock-seriousness of legal formality about these words, it is no more than to avoid the appearance of taking his own generosity too seriously. If Philemon, aggrieved, or perhaps even financially embarrassed, by robbery following upon sacrificial giving, felt it unfair of Paul to suggest forgoing all compensation, then Paul was ready to help. Though poor, he was not without resources. He hopes, however, that Philemon will be generous, reminding him that he 'owes his own self', i.e. his conversion, to his instrumentality. This was probably by direct personal contact in Ephesus.

Verse 20 is an affectionate appeal for generosity. *Let me have joy.* The verb is from the same root as the name Onesimus. *Refresh my bowels;* cf. verse 7n. Paul's *confidence* (21) was doubtless justified. If the Epistle had been disregarded it would naturally have been destroyed. *More than I say* (21). This may be a hint to liberate the slave. It is at least a request that Philemon will do the very best he can devise for Onesimus.

IV. CONCLUDING GREETINGS AND BENEDICTION. Verses 22–25

Lodging (22); i.e. hospitality, naturally in Philemon's own house if suitable. The prospect of Paul's coming would incidentally give an additional incentive for complying with his request for Onesimus. The salutations of verses 23 and 24 agree with those in Col. iv. 10–14; 'Jesus, which is called Justus' (probably unknown to Philemon) is, however, omitted. *Epaphras* is here called his *fellowprisoner;* i.e. 'of war' (it is not the same word for prisoner as in verse 1). In Colossians this designation is attached to Aristarchus, and not to Epaphras. This variation has perhaps no significance, though some have surmised that it points to Paul's friends voluntarily taking turns in sharing his confinement. A form of benediction similar to that of verse 25 was frequently used by the apostle, emphasizing the importance of the human spirit, and that the grace of Christ is what it needs. The plural possessive *your spirit* (cf. *your prayers* in verse 22) includes all those addressed in the beginning of the Epistle.

T. E. ROBERTSON.

THE EPISTLE TO THE HEBREWS

INTRODUCTION

There are several questions which it is natural to ask concerning the writing of a document of the New Testament, and which in the case of this Epistle it is impossible to answer with any certainty. While possible answers may be suggested and to some extent reasonably supported, the simple truth is that we do not know either who wrote this Epistle or to whom it was first written. Our ignorance on such points does not, however, prevent right understanding or minimize the spiritual and theological value of a document which has from the first commended itself as authoritative by its own intrinsic worth. Indeed, the only adequate answer of Christian faith to these very questions is that God Himself is the primary author and Christians of every age are the divinely intended readers. For through this Epistle God unquestionably has spoken, and still speaks, by His Spirit to His people. This is ultimately the most important vindication of its place in the canon of the New Testament.

I. AUTHORSHIP

In the Epistle itself there is no explicit indication who wrote it. Nor do early Christian writers provide us with any unanimous or convincing testimony. Tertullian is definite in his witness; he says that Barnabas wrote it. But this witness is unconfirmed; though there is still a little to be said in its favour. The man who was given a Christian name meaning 'son of exhortation' (Acts iv. 36, RV) may well be responsible for this 'word of exhortation' (Heb. xiii. 22). As a Levite he would have more than an ordinary interest in the sacrificial ritual; as a Jew from Cyprus he quite possibly had intimate contact with the Hellenistic and philosophical teaching of Alexandrian Judaism with which both the writer and his readers seem to have had some acquaintance; as one of those converted immediately after Pentecost (which may be what Heb. ii. 3, 4 refers to), he doubtless came under the influence of the teaching of Stephen, an influence which seems to persist in this Epistle.

In Alexandria, where the Epistle was accepted on its own merits, there is evidence of a growing tendency in the third century to connect it with Paul, but only rather indirectly. Clement suggested that Paul wrote it in Hebrew and that Luke translated it into Greek. Origen was prepared to think that the original thoughts were the apostle's but not the final written form and language. Such connection of the Epistle with the name of Paul commended itself widely

because it gave it welcome apostolic authority, for lack of which many hesitated to accept it as canonical. Consequently many manuscript copies came to be headed with the title 'The Epistle *of Paul* to the Hebrews'. This ascription to the apostle, however, most present-day students are not prepared to accept. The internal evidence of the Epistle itself, its language, style and contents, are regarded as conclusive against it (e.g. contrast ii. 3 and Gal. i. 12, ii. 6).

Other suggestions are wholly speculative. They include Apollos, Silas, Aquila (or Priscilla and Aquila) and Philip the evangelist. Of these Luther's suggestion of Apollos is perhaps best. From what we know of him (see Acts xviii. 24–28) he is exactly the kind of man who might have written such an Epistle. But there is no other evidence to prove that he did. When a human writer of Scripture was providentially led to hide his identity there is no need to try, and possibly little or no hope of success in trying, to discover it. It is wiser to be content not to know.

II. THE FIRST RECIPIENTS

There is no clear indication in the Epistle itself to whom it was originally written. The familiar title *To the Hebrews* goes back to the second century. The contents strongly confirm that the Epistle was written to Jewish Christians. In it there is no reference to heathenism at all; and the Old Testament Scriptures and the Levitical sacrificial ritual are treated with marked respect as possessing God-given sanction and authority. Modern attempts to suggest that the Epistle was written to Gentile Christians can be dismissed as more ingenious than convincing.

There is similarly a lack of information in the Epistle concerning the location of its original readers. Jerusalem, Caesarea, Antioch in Syria, Ephesus, Alexandria and Rome have all been suggested. The fact that the readers had not themselves heard Christ (ii. 3) tells against their being lifelong residents in Jerusalem. Their general background, while unquestionably Jewish, seems to have been Hellenistic and somewhat Alexandrian rather than exclusively Palestinian and rabbinical. They seem to have been Jews of the Dispersion, whose Scriptures were the Old Testament in Greek. The phrase 'They of (literally 'from') Italy salute you' (xiii. 24) may be interpreted to mean people away from Italy sending greetings to their homeland. If this interpretation be correct (see notes *ad loc.*) it favours the view that the recipients were a

Jewish section of the Christian community in Rome. It is perhaps significant that the earliest known quotations from this Epistle occur in a letter written by Clement of Rome about A.D. 95. Also, the reference to persecution in x. 32–34 might be a reference to the.expulsion from Rome of (Christian) Jews by the emperor Claudius about A.D. 50. See Acts xviii. 2.

It is clear from the Epistle that it was originally written to a definite group of readers. See ii. 3, v. 11, 12, vi. 9, 10, x. 25, 32–36, xiii. 7, 19, 23, 24. They knew the writer and Timothy. The writer hopes to come and see them. They had been Christians for a long time; and had been known to the writer from the beginnings of their Christian faith. From the references in the Epistle (see xiii. 24) they seem to have been a limited circle, who perhaps had a special 'house-church' meeting of their own rather than a large community which would presumably have included many more recent converts.

It seems possible to suggest (but it is only a suggestion) that the particular recipients of this Epistle were a group of Jews who had originally been members of a synagogue of the Dispersion. They were men zealously devoted to Judaism, and to Judaism as they understood it, not from lifelong residence in Palestine, but from the study of the Old Testament in Greek. They were not unacquainted with Alexandrian thought. As Jews they were originally zealous in visiting Jerusalem for the great annual feasts. Possibly it was when, as a group, they were on such a visit to Jerusalem, at or soon after the great Christian Pentecost, that they, as well as the writer, were converted to faith in Jesus as the Christ through hearing the preaching of the apostles and through seeing the visible signs of the power of the Holy Ghost (ii. 3, 4). They may even have seen and shared in the persecution that was stirred up against the church in Jerusalem by the Jewish authorities and by zealous Jews like Saul of Tarsus; which may be to what x. 32–34 refers (see Acts v. 41, viii. 3, ix. 13, 14). It may well be to the poor saints in Jerusalem that they subsequently ministered from their home base (vi. 10). Such a background to their entrance into the experience of new life in Christ would give added significance to the writer's assertion that the followers of Jesus have no earthly Jerusalem as their continuing city; rather they must go forth unto Him without the gate (xiii. 12–14). As Christians they are 'come unto mount Sion, and unto the city of the living God, the heavenly Jerusalem' (xii. 22). Here they need no longer stand in the court outside the shrine into which the High Priest alone enters, and that only once a year, but can themselves freely and continuously enter boldly through the now rent veil into the very holy of holies of God's presence.

III. DATE

This it is impossible to fix with absolute certainty, though one may say with considerable confidence that the Epistle was most probably written between A.D. 60 and 70. Its readers had been Christians quite a long time (v. 12, x. 32). Some of their original leaders had passed away (xiii. 7). On the other hand, Timothy was still alive (xiii. 23). It seems possible to argue that had the destruction of Jerusalem taken place the writer would not have omitted to refer to it, particularly as it was such a significant judgment of God on the old order of Jewish worship.

IV. OCCASION AND PURPOSE

In order to be able to assess the occasion and purpose of the Epistle we need first to appreciate the circumstances of those to whom it was written. In this connection their spiritual condition is of much greater significance than their geographical location. For knowledge about this we depend entirely on the evidence of the Epistle itself. The writer clearly contrasts the state in which his readers are with what they have been, what they ought to be, and what they seem to be in danger of becoming. As Christians they are slothful (v. 11, vi. 12) and despondent (xii. 3, 12). They have lost their initial enthusiasm for the faith (iii. 6, 14, iv. 14, x. 23, 35). They have failed to grow or, more exactly, to progress, and are seriously deficient in spiritual understanding and discernment (v. 12–14). They are ceasing to attend Christian meetings (x. 25) and to be actively loyal to their Christian leaders (xiii. 17). They need afresh to be exhorted to imitate the faith of those who have gone before (xiii. 7). They tend to be easily carried away by new and strange teachings (xiii. 9). They are in danger of coming short of God's promises (iv. 1), and drifting away from the things which they have heard (ii. 1, RV). They are even in danger of completely abandoning the faith in deliberate and persistent apostasy (iii. 12, x. 26); and this danger will be the greater if they fail to check any one of their number who may be moving in that direction (iii. 13, xii. 15). If they yield to such temptation and actually reject the gospel of Christ they can expect nothing but judgment (x. 26–31).

Particularly as those who had once been zealous adherents of Judaism, it seems very probable that they had become personally disappointed with Christianity because, on the one hand, it had brought to them no visible earthly kingdom, and, on the other hand, it had been decisively rejected by the great majority of their fellow-Jews. Further, continued attachment to it seemed only to involve them in sharing the offensive reproach of a suffering and crucified Messiah and in having to face the increasing prospect of violent anti-Christian persecution. It may well be, therefore, that they were being seriously tempted to disown Jesus as the Messiah and to go back to re-embrace the visible and preferable good which Judaism still seemed to offer to them.

That it was Judaism which thus attracted

them afresh as preferable to Christianity seems confirmed by the obvious way in which the writer sets himself from the first to demonstrate the superiority of the new covenant over the old, and to set forth particularly the outstanding excellence of Jesus, the Son of God, as compared with the prophets and angels, leaders and High Priests, who functioned in the old economy. So he shows that, while the old order was imperfect and provisional, Christianity brings perfection (vii. 19), and perfection which is eternal (v. 9, ix. 12, 15, xiii. 20). He and his readers were apparently Hellenistic Jews with some acquaintance with Greek philosophical thought, and he seems to be using ideas from these sources when he declares that the old order contained merely 'figures of the true' (ix. 24) or 'a shadow of good things to come, and not the very image of the things' (x. 1). On the other hand Christianity is the truth itself, the heavenly and ideal reality, which actually and absolutely possesses all those inherent values which these other things can at their best only reflect or prefigure. Nevertheless, since his readers recognize the divine authority of the Old Testament Scriptures, his final argument for recognizing the superiority of Christ over angels and over the Levitical priesthood, and the superiority of His sacrifice of Himself over that of bulls and goats, is the prophetic testimony of the Old Testament itself. See i. 5-13, vii. 15-22, x. 5-10.

The writer's purpose, therefore, is to make his readers fully aware, first, of the amazing revelation and salvation given by God to men in Christ; secondly, of the true heavenly and eternal character of the blessings thus freely offered to the appropriation of faith; thirdly, of the place of suffering and patient endurance by faith in the present earthly pathway to the goal of God's purpose as shown in the experience and work of the Captain of our salvation and in God's discipline of all His children; fourthly, of the awful judgment which must befall any who, knowing all this, reject it. Having striven to make them aware of these things, his complementary purpose is to stir them to act accordingly. These purposes are pursued throughout the Epistle by the use in turn of reasoned exposition, challenging exhortation and solemn warning.

V. CONTENTS

As already indicated, the contents of this Epistle are to be properly appreciated only in relation to its occasion and purpose. The writer obviously regards the Old Testament Scriptures as full of figures and anticipations of the true realities of God's purpose. Therefore he continually uses them to support, illustrate and develop his own theme. He recalls, for instance, how God brought a people out of Egypt, established a covenant with them at Sinai, and provided a priesthood and tabernacle service for the maintenance of covenant relationship. He remembers how many who thus began with God

perished in the wilderness (iii. 16, 17, RV). On the one hand they failed through unbelief to embrace God's promise and to enter into the inheritance (iii. 18, 19, iv. 2, 6). On the other hand they came under the divine judgment by disobeying the covenant regulations (ii. 2). For instance, the punishment for those who committed spiritual adultery and worshipped other gods was death (x. 28). Or, similarly, when Esau, born and brought up within the family of privilege, despised his birthright and sold it, it was lost beyond recall; there was for him no place for repentance (xii. 16, 17). From such Scriptures the writer is aware that those to whom God's light is given and God's call comes either go on with God in faith and obedience to possess the full inheritance, or by rejecting the light and disobeying the call come under judgment.

So he longs and fears for his readers; longs that they may all go on to perfection (vi. 1), fears lest any fall back from the grace of God (xii. 15, RV mg.). For they have tasted the benefits (vi. 4, 5) of the greater 'exodus' (Gk. *exodos*, Lk. ix. 31; cf. Eph. ii. 8, 14, 15) accomplished by Jesus at Jerusalem. They have been sealed and sanctified by the blood of the new covenant (see x. 29). As with the Israelites at Sinai, these things not only place upon them obligations to faith and obedience, but also set before them the opportunity to inherit the divine promise. But the dangers besetting them are also exactly similar to those besetting the Israelites under the first covenant. There is the danger of unbelief; there is the complementary danger of disobedience and apostasy, of deliberately rejecting the light and departing from the living God (iii. 12, x. 26, 38). They need, therefore, encouragement to go forward, and warning against turning back; and of these the Epistle is full.

The writer is no less persuaded that, in contrast to the first covenant, the revelation and the redemption given to men in Christ are the final truth of God. The obligation to pay heed and the assurance of complete divine provision are, therefore, absolute. These things settle either one's full salvation or one's final condemnation. So his urgent concern is to exhort his readers fully to respond, to warn them properly to take heed.

He provides a solid basis for such exhortations and warnings by an exposition in some detail of the superiority of Christ and of what is given under the new covenant to everything used or given under the old covenant. In Christ there is the final revelation of God, greater than anything hitherto given through prophets and angels, because He is Himself God the Son. In Christ there is the final reconciliation to God, because, having condescended to become true man, a partaker of flesh and blood, He went even lower and tasted death for every man, thus putting away sin by making Himself the sin offering. So the true house, or community, of God's people is being built of which Christ is the Head, and to which all who believe in Him are called to belong. But they become partakers in it only if they hold fast to their confidence through this testing wilderness experience which lies between the great exodus and the coming inheritance of the promise.

Further, this community is called to share in a new covenant, which is full of better promises, and of which Jesus has become the effective mediator by His decisive redeeming work and by His never-ending administration of its benefits. As their High Priest He has dealt with sin once for all by the one offering of His earthly, human life upon the cross. This has secured for Him as their representative not only entrance into God's presence but also enthronement at God's right hand. The separating veil which kept them out of the holy place is decisively rent. So they can come to the very throne of God and find it a throne of grace, with One there ever waiting to speak to God on their behalf. So they can look to their High Priest on the throne for grace to meet their every need and fully to perfect their salvation. So they can count on the fulfilment in them as His people of all the divine promises of the amazing new covenant. With the wonder of such privileges open before them let them hold fast to their confidence and its open confession, and press forward to a fuller experience and enjoyment of the available benefits.

One other important truth they also needed more effectively to learn. Those who would thus have dealings with God must have them by faith. He is the great unseen One, and His greatest rewards lie in the future. Indeed, the immediate outlook and one's present experience may seem both to deny His presence and to contradict the hope of His reward. Faith, therefore, is indispensable to right awareness and to steadfast continuance. Here, once again, the Old Testament Scriptures, as a God-given handbook of instruction, show by the witness of men's lives and achievements that this has continuously been true in the experience of all who have in any way pleased God and become heirs of His promises. So the writer would encourage his readers not to be turned aside by the lack in Christianity of visible glory and immediate, earthly triumph. Rather, he says, 'let us hold fast the confession of our hope that it waver not; for he is faithful that promised' (x. 23, RV). 'For we have not here an abiding city, but we seek after the city which is to come' (xiii. 14, RV). The kingdom we are given to enjoy will stand fully disclosed only when this temporal order has passed away in judgment.

Let them, therefore, find their all in Christ, in His unchanging Person (xiii. 8), in His abiding companionship (xiii. 5, 6) and in the all-sufficiency of His one atoning act outside the gate of Jerusalem (xiii. 12). Instead of yielding to the temptation to abandon Christianity and to return to Judaism, let them once for all, whatever the reproach involved, stand clear of Judaism and openly associate themselves with Jesus the crucified as their only hope (xiii. 13). For, says the writer in his final benediction, this Jesus is 'our Lord'; He is 'that great shepherd of the sheep'. (xiii. 20). All our hopes are rightly fixed on Him. Nor is such confidence vain. God has raised Him from the dead. The covenant which His death sealed is 'already in operation. God Himself is active to fulfil it. We may, therefore, count on Him to make perfect that which concerns us. So, while others may draw back— and it is well that the awful warning should be sounded—it is inconceivable that we should. Nay, 'we are not of them who draw back unto perdition; but of them that believe to the saving of the soul' (x. 39).

For further notes on the new covenant, on the priesthood of Christ and on the warning passages see Appendices I, II and III, pp. 1114-1117.

OUTLINE OF CONTENTS

Note the alternation of exposition and exhortation and the closely linked sequence of thought in the expository sections.

I. INTRODUCTION: GOD'S FINAL WORD THROUGH HIS SON.
i. 1–4

II. THE SON'S SUPERIORITY TO ANGELS. i. 5–14

III. PRACTICAL APPLICATION AND WARNING. ii. 1–4

IV. THE INCARNATION, SUFFERING AND DEATH OF THE SON OF GOD. ii. 5–18

V. THE SUPERIORITY OF CHRIST JESUS TO MOSES. iii. 1–6

VI. PERSONAL APPLICATION AND WARNING. iii. 7—iv. 13

VII. CHRIST OUR GREAT HIGH PRIEST. iv. 14—v. 10

VIII. AN EXHORTATION TO PROGRESS AND TO PERSIST. v. 11—vi. 20

IX. THE CHARACTERISTICS AND EFFICACY OF CHRIST'S ETERNAL PRIESTHOOD. vii. 1–28

X. THE EXCELLENCE OF CHRIST'S HIGH-PRIESTLY MINISTRY. viii. 1–6

XI. THE TWO COVENANTS. viii. 7–13

XII. THE MINISTRY OF THE FIRST COVENANT DESCRIBED. ix. 1–10

XIII. THE CHARACTERISTICS OF THE SACRIFICE OF CHRIST. ix. 11—x. 18

XIV. PRACTICAL EXHORTATION. x. 19–39

XV. THE TRIUMPHANT ACHIEVEMENTS OF FAITH. xi. 1–40

XVI. PERSONAL APPLICATION: A CALL TO SERVE GOD ACCEPTABLY. xii. 1–29

XVII. VARIOUS ADDITIONAL EXHORTATIONS. xiii. 1–17

XVIII. PERSONAL MESSAGES AND FINAL BENEDICTION. xiii. 18–25

COMMENTARY

I. INTRODUCTION: GOD'S FINAL WORD THROUGH HIS SON. i. 1–4

This grand opening statement indicates the great theme of the writer (cf. iii. 1). This vision of the absolute supremacy and sufficiency of Christ dominates the thought of the whole Epistle. He is superior to and supersedes all other mediators between God and men, such as prophets (1) and angels (4). Note the continuity between the Old Testament revelation and that now given in Christ. The first prepares for the second; the second consummates the first (cf. x. 8, 9). Note also that this final revelation of God is given to men not only in the incarnation of the Son, but in the Son as the fulfiller of the work of atonement for sin (cf. 1 Jn. iv. 9, 10), and that the full significance of this revelation and redemptive work is appreciated only by those who see by faith that the Christ once crucified is now enthroned, and so able to save to the uttermost all who come unto God by Him (see viii. 1, vii. 25).

In verses 2–4 there are eight successive statements about Christ. In His eternal being He is genuine, absolute Deity, the *brightness* or visible outshining of God's glory, Himself an identical expression of deity (RV mg. 'the impress of his substance'), the eternal *Son* of the Father, 'very God of very God'. In the divine ordering of the universe He is its author, sustainer and end. By Him it was made. He upholds it. He is its heir. Note that the end is seen from the beginning; the divine appointment of the Son to be the heir of the universe precedes its creation. In relation to men He is men's Prophet, Priest and King. In Him God spoke His final word of revelation; so He brings God to men (cf. Jn. i. 14, 18). In His own Person He purged our sins and finished the

work of reconciliation; so He brings men to God. He now sits enthroned at God's right hand. As the exalted God-Man He has obtained by inheritance a position far above all others (cf. Eph. i. 20, 21; Phil. ii. 9–11).

II. THE SON'S SUPERIORITY TO ANGELS. i. 5–14

In Jewish thought angels held a very important place as the mediators of God's revelation to His people. Therefore the writer sets out to demonstrate Christ's superiority to angels in order to establish the superiority of the message which He brings (cf. ii. 5–8). This he does through seven quotations from the Old Testament. The whole method is very significant. It implies, first, that the Old Testament possesses a direct relevance and a decisive authority for Christian believers. Secondly, the words quoted are ascribed not to the human psalmists and prophets, but directly to God as their author. Cf. the statement of verse 1. Thirdly, it is now possible for those who are acquainted with the final revelation in Christ to see in the words of the Old Testament a meaning and significance with reference to Christ, which could not possibly have been seen in the same way, either by those who wrote them, or by any before Christ came. Cf. 1 Pet. i. 10–12.

Son (5) is the *more excellent name* (4) by which Christ's superiority to angels is measured. The Son is superior to the angels, first, because of what He is eternally as God; secondly, because of what He has now become as the exalted God-Man. The first quotation (5a) from Ps. ii. 7 introduces both thoughts. There never was a time when the Father could not say to Him, *Thou art my Son*. But there came a day in time when by resurrection in glorified humanity He was begotten to a new status as the exalted Man. So in Acts xiii. 33 this quotation from Ps. ii is explicitly applied to Christ's resurrection. In consequence, He is not only Son in virtue of His deity; he is now exalted to be as a son ('the firstborn among many brethren', Rom. viii. 29) in virtue of His humanity. The second quotation (5b), the promise to David concerning his seed (2 Sa. vii. 14), is fulfilled in Christ as it never was, nor could be, in Solomon. Similarly, He is 'the firstborn' (6, RV) in a double sense (cf. Col. i. 15, 18), first as the only-begotten of the Father, existing before the created universe and Lord over it, and now as the firstborn from the dead, who has, as the great path-maker of salvation, opened the way for the many to enter as sons into glory (ii. 10). The third quotation (6) is made to indicate that this office of His in relation to men, both as Creator and Redeemer, will be consummated at His second coming, when He will be brought again into this 'inhabited earth' (6, RV mg.) to judge. For the prophetic vision of God coming to judge will be fulfilled in the Person of His Son. Then His deity will be openly manifested. Then all the angels shall worship Him. See Ps. xcvii. 7 (the Hebrew word 'gods' becomes 'angels' in the Greek of the LXX).

The fourth and fifth quotations (7–9) show that while angels fulfil their service (e.g. at Sinai) through wind (see RV) and fire, i.e. in the material sphere, in transitory fashion, in creaturely sub-servience to the divine pleasure, the Son is a free moral personality, Himself occupying the throne of God in righteousness for ever. Because of His righteousness as the God-Man, He has been exalted and anointed as the One to whom belongs the pre-eminence. The quotations are from Pss. civ. 4 and xlv. 6, 7. The sixth quotation (10–12) shows that, in contrast to created things, the Son is the Creator, the sovereign, un-changeable Lord. Words from Ps. cii. 25–27, addressed to Jehovah, are applied to Jesus. This implies that He is Jehovah. There will be with Him no decay nor decease. Cf. xiii. 8.

Finally, as the seventh quotation shows (13), the Son is superior to the angels not only in what He is as God but also in what God is now doing for Him as the exalted Man or enthroned Messiah. By divine appointment He is to con-tinue to occupy the throne in sure hope of com-plete triumph (Ps. cx. 1). The angels, by contrast, are sent forth from the throne to fulfil ministries on behalf of those who are to share in this glorious consummation of man's full salvation (14). *Heirs of salvation* (14); the first of a variety of expressions used by the writer to describe the people of God and their destiny (see *Introduction*, p. 1088).

III. PRACTICAL APPLICATION AND WARNING. ii. 1–4

The writer here introduces the first of his characteristic words of urgent exhortation and solemn warning (see Appendix III, 'The Warning Passages', p. 1116). This new revelation places on all who hear it a supreme obligation to give heed, an obligation which, for a number of reasons, is greater than that of obedience to the law of Moses. First, there is the known authority of that law. It was a word which could not be defied or disregarded with impunity. Under it every sin of commission (i.e. *transgression*), and every sin of omission (i.e. *disobedience* or 'failure to hear'), received its *just recompence* (2). Secondly, there is the character of the new message which is *salvation* (3), so great and of such a kind as to be amazing (cf. Jn. i. 17). The third reason is the Person of the Messenger. On the Godward side the Sinaitic law was given to Moses by angels (cf. Acts vii. 53; Gal. iii. 19); it was a medi-ated revelation. This new revelation is direct and immediate, given by the Lord Himself in Person. In the fourth place there is the decisive con-firmation of the message. In addition to having been first spoken by the Lord Himself it has been *confirmed unto us* (3) by the evidence of eye-witnesses, and also by the superadded testimony of a great variety of God-given miraculous signs and by gifts of the Holy Spirit, which in their distribution are clearly not of man's appointing but wholly according to the divine pleasure (4). Cf. Mk. xvi. 20; 1 Cor. xii. 11. Finally, there is the inevitable consequence of *neglect* (3). To drift past out of reach (1, RV) when we have the opportunity to pay heed must leave us without excuse and with no prospect but judgment. This point is made still more explicit later (see x. 26, 27). *How shall we escape?* (future indicative). Note the implied certainty of judgment to come.

IV. THE INCARNATION, SUFFERING AND DEATH OF THE SON OF GOD. ii. 5–18

In this chapter the writer deals with a difficulty which his readers might find in his teaching regarding the superiority of Jesus to angels, for to Jewish minds the place of angels was of no small importance. To them it was clear that, in the present order, angels are superior to men. For example, they stood between God and men at the giving of the law (2). If Jesus was a man, and still more if He suffered and died, how can He be said to be superior to the angels as a mediator (i. 4)? In answer these verses indicate first the fact and significance of His exaltation as man—*we see Jesus . . . crowned* (9); note the use of the unqualified human name. Secondly, they describe the divinely ordained and saving pur-pose of His preceding humiliation, together with (for God) its moral fitness and (for men) its beneficial consequences. Further, these verses indicate that not only Jesus but men—through Jesus as their High Priest and Captain of sal-vation—are called to inherit a destiny of glory and dominion.

a. Not angels, but men, are the divinely destined lords of the coming age (ii. 5–8)

All this is prophetically anticipated in Scripture. In Ps. viii it is made plain that, although man in this present world-order begins by being made 'for a little while' (RV mg.) lower than the angels, God's ultimate purpose is to give him glory and dominion, even over the angels. For the *all things* (8) include the angels. Cf. 1 Cor. vi. 3. This consummation is clearly not yet fully realized (8c). It must, therefore, still be spoken of as future; it is *the world to come* (5); i.e. 'the coming world-order' (cf. vi. 5). It is this coming consummation or completed salvation which is the writer's theme, and ought to be the Christian's constant object of hope (see x. 37–39, xi. 13–16, xiii. 14).

b. The purpose of the incarnation, suffering and death of Christ (ii. 9–18)

On the other hand, there is to be seen in the Person of Jesus a present realization of man's destiny. He, as a true man, began, like men, by being *made* (for a little while) *lower than the angels* (9). He is now *crowned with glory and honour*. Ps. viii, therefore, is thus seen to be messianic. God's purpose for man is fulfilled only through the one Man, i.e. Christ (cf. Gal. iii. 16).

Also, in relation to God's intended purpose for men, it is possible to see why the Son of God was humbled to the form of a servant. For, as man, He is crowned with glory and honour only because He has suffered death (9, RV). By a wonderful manifestation of the grace of God He became man in order that, for the benefit of mankind as a whole (i.e. *for every man*), He might thus enter into death. It was, indeed, supremely fitting (10), and an act worthy of God Himself, who is the first cause and final end of *all things*, that in order to bring sinful men into the true glory of manhood, which they had irretrievably lost, God should provide for men a Saviour of this kind. By entering into His own glory through suffering He opened up the way by which 'the many' (cf. Is. liii. 12; Mk. x. 45) can now be brought in to share the same human glory as sons of God and joint-heirs with Christ (cf. Rom. iii. 23, v. 2, viii. 29, 30). Jesus' suffering of death, therefore, was necessary completely to qualify Him to function as men's Saviour. *Captain* (10); lit. 'leader'. The same word is rendered in xii. 2 'author', which is the RV reading here.

Our Lord's work issues in His becoming the Head of a saved company or community, i.e. those whom God has given Him through and because of what He has done (cf. Jn. xvii. 2, 6, 26). The Old Testament quotations used to confirm this are remarkable. The first (12) is from Ps. xxii, a Psalm which foreshadows the cross. The constitution of the 'congregation' or *church*, with Christ in the midst revealing God to His brethren, is possible only because of His sacrifice.

The other two quotations (13) are from Is. viii. 17, 18. The first is often said to be from Ps. xviii. 2; but the LXX of Is. viii. 17, 18 suggests that this one passage is the source of both quotations. It is a place in the Old Testament where the thought of the believing remnant or 'church' distinctly emerges.

These elect *children* (14) of the divine purpose were, as men, 'sharers in flesh and blood' (RV), and, as sinners, subject to bondage and fear, held under by the devil and the power of death (14, 15). There was no hope of a redeemed community being raised up to enjoy man's intended destiny, unless this hold of the devil and of 'the gates of Hades' could be broken (see Mt. xvi. 18; Mk. iii. 26, 27; 1 Cor. xv. 17–19). This was done when the Son of God became incarnate and entered into death, not as a helpless victim but as the decisive victor. (Cf. Rev. i. 18; Rom. xiv. 9.)

This salvation is meant for men, not angels (16). Christ came to redeem *the seed of Abraham*, i.e. men of faith (cf. Gal. iii. 7, 9, 29). Note that 'doth he take hold' (RV) refers not to His becoming man, but to His work of rescue and redemption. Cf. Je. xxxi. 32 where, in the LXX, the same Greek word describes a gracious 'laying hold' in order to take out of a state of bondage. Christ could (17, 18) fully help them in this way only by entering completely as a true man into their human experience of trial. What they needed was one who could put them right with God (17) and help them to triumph over life's continuing temptations (18). So as 'the author of their salvation' (10, RV) the Son of God became a High Priest who was *faithful* in His discharge of the work of making *reconciliation* (RV 'propitiation') for the sins of the whole people of God, and *merciful*, i.e. 'compassionate', or ready to sympathize with and help the tempted, because of His own experience of human temptation. This, then, is why He trod the path of incarnation, suffering and death.

V. THE SUPERIORITY OF CHRIST JESUS TO MOSES. iii. 1–6

Moses was the human mediator of the old covenant; he was called in a unique way to God's servant. See Nu. xii. 5–8. The Israelites traced back to him their sense of status and calling as the consecrated people of God. The Christian brotherhood is similarly consecrated and called through Jesus (ii. 11), the Mediator of the new covenant. Christians, therefore, should *consider* (1), i.e. fix all their gaze, their steadfast mental attention, upon Jesus, whom they have confessed (see RV) to be their *Apostle and High Priest*. He combines in His own Person both these offices. As God, He has been 'sent forth' to reveal God to men; as Man, He has become High Priest to reconcile men to God. *Partakers of the* (RV 'a') *heavenly calling* (1). There is an implied contrast with the earthly inheritance set before those who came out of Egypt under Moses.

Jesus is like Moses in a number of ways. God made or *appointed him* (2); i.e. His status and function are divinely constituted (cf. 1 Sa. xii. 6, RV and RV mg.). He was *faithful* (2). The sphere of His work was the whole house of God (4, 6). Cf. Nu. xii. 7. Jesus also surpasses Moses and is worthy of more glory and honour. For Moses was himself part of the house in which he served, himself one of the people of God (3). But Christ is the builder of the house, Himself God (4). It was the declared task of God's anointed king to build a house for His Name (2 Sa. vii. 13); and the Church which Jesus said He would build is this 'house of God' or new 'Israel' (cf. 1 Tim. iii. 15; Gal. vi. 16). Therefore it is we Christians who are this 'house of God' (6). Again, Moses was only a servant in the house (5). Christ is set as the Son over His Father's house (see 6, RV mg.). He is its Head; by virtue of His Sonship the house is *his own* (6; cf. Mt. i. 21: 'his people'). Note that He is here called Son in reference to God (cf. i. 2); there is definite implication of Godhead. Again, Moses' work was one of preparation (5); it pointed forward to that which should come after; it witnessed to the kind of work that the coming One would do. See Dt. xviii. 15-19. Christ is the fulfilment of all that Moses foresaw. He points to none but Himself. No wonder this Epistle emphasizes so strongly, 'Consider him' (iii. 1, xii. 3). Similarly, the Old Testament house of God, in which Moses served, pointed forward to the Christian Church, that present house of God, over which Christ is set as Son.

In the latter half of verse 6 the thought turns to the personal application of what has been said. These privileges can be fully possessed only if those who have embraced the hope set before them in Christ persist steadfast until the hope is realized. They must continue in that outspoken confidence and exulting testimony (RV 'boldness' and 'glorying') which are characteristic of the new-born believer.

VI. PERSONAL APPLICATION AND WARNING. iii. 7—iv. 13

a. The danger of unbelief (iii. 7-19)

See Appendix III, 'The Warning Passages', p. 1116. The warning here is enforced by the solemn example of the failure of the Israelites in the wilderness. The comparison between Moses and Jesus given in verses 1-6 is followed by a comparison between the promise and the people under the old covenant and under the new. Moses and Christ were both faithful to the end (2). But the great majority of those who followed Moses were faithless. They all shared in the great deliverances of the Passover and the Red Sea, but later they hardened their hearts against God and perished in the wilderness. Cf. 1 Cor. x. 1-5. This provided an eloquent warning to those Jews of the first century A.D. who had seen in Jesus the Passover Lamb sacrificed and God's power manifested in His resurrection from the dead. It was clearly no new thing for the majority of the nation not to believe. Also, many of the Israelites under Moses saw God's works for *forty years* (9) and still hardened their hearts. So, at the very doors of the Promised Land, they failed to enter in. Similarly, at the time this Epistle was written, about forty years had possibly elapsed since the first proclamation of salvation by the Lord Himself. The divine origin of the gospel had been signally confirmed to these Hebrews (ii. 3, 4). Let them fear lest they, also, take offence at God's ways and come short of the promised consummation (iv. 1).

This exhortation is introduced in words from Ps. xcv. 7-11, which are quoted as spoken by the Holy Ghost, and as spoken for *To day* (7), to those who are now confronted in this new era of redemption by the new revelation given by God's voice spoken in Christ. Note the implied divine authorship and Christian purpose of the Old Testament Scriptures. Everything depends on how men hear. It is not just words but the living God who here confronts men. Cf. iv. 12, 13. To refuse to hear is to reject Him (12).

Provocation and *temptation* (8) are translations of the Hebrew names Meribah and Massah. See Nu. xx. 1-13; Ex. xvii. 1-7. The latter instance of Israel's unbelief occurred in the first, and the former instance in the fortieth, year of the wilderness wanderings. They are evidence that the hardening of heart persisted from beginning to end of the forty years. *Tempted me* (9). To 'tempt' God seems to mean seeing how far one can go in disobeying Him. Though God in His displeasure rebuked them (10) and set their error before their eyes, they still showed no understanding of the purpose of His dealings with them. They refused to repent. So God solemnly declared (11) that it was impossible for people in such a condition to enjoy the promised inheritance.

In verses 12-15 these words from Ps. xcv are taken to indicate that 'To day', while there is still opportunity to hear God's voice in the gospel (cf. 2 Cor. vi. 2), there is danger of the same peril as beset the Israelites. For God's word calls forth an inevitable reaction; men will either respond in obedience or will stubbornly reject it. The causes of failure, which ought to be avoided, are, on the one hand, *unbelief* and unfaithfulness (12), and, on the other hand, the very *deceitfulness of sin* through which men's hearts are hardened against God (13). The practical consequence of such failure is nothing less than a 'falling away' (lit. apostasy) from the living God (12). Protection against it is to be found in daily, mutual exhortation (13). Every day Christians should speak words of encouragement to one another. The many are responsible for the one; every member of the Christian community should take heed lest any one of their number becomes infected (see 12, RV). For full participation in the messianic blessings is given only to those who are steadfast in their *confidence* (14) from start to finish. Faith is the 'confidence' or 'assurance' of things hoped for (xi. 1). It must be held fast, in all the intensity of its first manifestation (cf. iii. 6), and in the face of delay, suffering and temporary disappointment (cf. x. 35, 36). In verse 14 note the antithesis of *the beginning* and *the end*; cf. xii. 2, 'Jesus, the author and perfecter of our aith' (RV).

The solemn significance of the example of the Israelites is further enforced by a series of questions. See the RV rendering of verses 16–19. Those who provoked God for forty years in the wilderness were none other than those who shared in the deliverance from Egypt, a surprising anticlimax. The reason why they were overthrown in judgment was sin. The reason why they failed to enter the Promised Land was disobedience due to unbelief. Lack of faith, then, or *an evil heart of unbelief* (12), is the obvious and fatal peril of which to beware.

b. Exhortation to enter into rest (iv. 1–13)

There is urgent reason to pay heed to the warning because, on the one hand, the divine promise of entering into God's rest still stands open, and, on the other hand, failure to embrace it may result in a loss that cannot be remedied, a permanent missing of God's best. It is possible to *come short of it* (1) or to be 'left behind'. The writer again stresses that the whole company should be on its guard lest any single individual drop out. Cf. iii. 12, 13, xii. 15.

This promise of entrance into God's rest is offered to men afresh in the preaching of the gospel of Christ (2). It is this which gives to men 'to day' opportunity to 'hear His voice'. But, as the Old Testament Scriptures make plain, when men hear the God-given word they can enjoy the blessings He promises only if they become vitally united to it by means of the response of faith (2, AV); or, following an alternative MS reading, if they believingly associate themselves with those who obey it (2, RV). And although God sware that the unbelieving Israelites should not enter in, it is clear from the present experience of Christian believers that Christ has brought the rest within the reach of His people. For those who have become believers are actually entering into this very rest (3).

This rest of God has been in existence for men to share since the creation of the world was finished; *God did rest the seventh day from all his works* (4). This rest does not consist merely of inactivity; the word describes the satisfaction and repose of successful achievement. Further, the words of Scripture which speak of this subject (Gn. ii. 2 and Ps. xcv. 11) are to be regarded as God's own word and witness on the matter. These words show, first, that God Himself rested. Secondly, and by implication, they indicate that it is clearly His purpose that men should enter into and share His rest. His word about it guarantees its certainty; God never speaks empty words. Thirdly, we are told that those to

whom the opportunity was first offered failed to embrace it because of unbelief and were by the word of the same God solemnly forbidden all hope of entrance. For *If they shall enter* (3, 5) read with RV 'they shall not enter'. Also we see that the inheritance into which Joshua led the people cannot really be the promised rest because long after the time of Joshua, in the days of David, God speaks of a fresh opportunity (*To day*) to hear His voice and to enter in.

It is clear, therefore, that God intends His people to share His own 'sabbath rest' (9, RV). This is the reward that He has reserved for them. Entrance into it means a cessation from their own works, just as God rested from the work of creation on His sabbath. In its fulness such a goal is, therefore, something which lies beyond this life. Yet those who find salvation and new life in Christ do begin to experience it here and now. So, as the writer has already said (3), those who take the decisive step and become Christian believers are entering into rest. They have begun to enjoy a blessing which is yet to be consummated. Its possession is both now and not yet. There is need, therefore, for us all to exhibit zeal and earnest endeavour in its continual pursuit (11), lest any single one of our number fall by the way, and become like the Israelites in the wilderness (cf. Lot's wife), yet another, similar example of unbelieving disobedience. It is a solemn thing to become a negative witness to the truth of God's promises by being 'left behind'. It is better to be a positive witness and to enter in. Those who have opportunity to hear His voice must become one or the other.

It is well, therefore, to consider the character of the word that confronts us, the word of Scripture and of the gospel, if we are fully to appreciate the responsibility under which hearing it puts us. For this word is God's word (12). It shares the very attributes of God Himself. It is living (*quick*), and full of activity and power to achieve. In it God Himself is active, and so it is never without result; it brings either salvation or judgment. It penetrates into a man's inmost being and, like a dissecting knife, forces open a radical division and distinction between things that differ in human life. It brings under judgment the thoughts and ideas of man's mind and will. It is the 'critic' (Gk. *kritikos*; AV *discerner*) by which all are judged. Confronted by it, man is confronted by God, before whom nothing can be concealed. Indeed, it makes us aware that all things stand stripped and bare and fully exposed to His searching glance. And it is to Him, the God from whom this word comes, that all who hear the word (Gk. *logos*) have ultimately to give back in answer their own 'word' or 'account' (Gk. *logos*). *Opened* (13); RV 'laid open'. The Greek word means 'with the head thrown back and the neck bare'. It suggests the impossibility of hiding one's face. In the final giving of account all must look at God and be looked upon by Him, face to face.

VII. CHRIST OUR GREAT HIGH PRIEST. iv. 14—v. 10

a. The Epistle's main theme stated (iv. 14–16)

As Christians *we have* (the words are emphatic) *a great high priest* (14), i.e. great in His essential nature for He is both truly man and truly God. In the fulfilment of His work as High Priest, He has 'passed through the heavens' (14, RV) into the very presence of God Himself, where He sits enthroned. Note that this enthronement is implied in verse 16; it is explicitly stated several times (see i. 3, 13, viii. 1, x. 12). Because of His humanity and earthly experience He is able sympathetically to appreciate our human limitations and trials. Let us, therefore, hold firmly to the open confession of faith in Him; and let us enter into the enjoyment of the benefits that His priestly work has made available. *Boldly* (16); i.e. with outspoken expression of our faith and our need. Let us come to the very throne of God Himself, there to find that it is a throne of grace and divine bounty where we may always obtain compassion or mercy in relation to our weakness and sin, and where we may discover grace that will afford us timely help, i.e. help suited to the need of the present hour. *Our infirmities* (15) are the weaknesses due to our finite creaturely existence, e.g. weariness, shrinking from pain, etc. These are things which the incarnate Son Himself experienced. *Yet without sin* (15) may describe either the issue of His temptations (i.e. He never fell into sin), or a difference in the way in which He was tempted (i.e. there was in Him no sinful nature, no sinful promptings from within). *Come* (16); RV 'draw near'; the Greek word here is commonly used of priestly approach to God. This privilege, formerly restricted to a select few, is now extended to all the people of God. Also it is not just a symbolic earthly shrine that we can enter, but the very presence of God.

b. Our Lord's qualifications and work as High Priest described (v. 1–10)

A High Priest is appointed to act for men in matters of Godward reference, especially to present offerings to God (1). He must be chosen from among men and be able, as a true man, fully to sympathize with men's weaknesses (2). (This qualification has already been declared to be true of our Christian High Priest; see ii. 18, iv. 15.) Also, he must not presume to take such an office upon himself; he must for such a task be called and appointed by God (4). All this (in reverse order) is declared to be true of Christ as the writer considers His divine appointment, His perfect humanity and consequent ability to sympathize, and His office and work. For it is God who, raising Him from the dead, acknowledged Him as His Son (5) and openly declared His appointment to an eternal priesthood after an order different from that of Aaron, *the order of Melchisedec* (6). He is also able fully to sympathize with men in their life in the flesh. For He Himself, though He were God the Son, learnt as man in the experience of His earthly life the full meaning of obedient submission to the will of God in the face of extreme human suffering and the power of death (7, 8). This is how He reached that human perfection, which qualified Him to enter upon His work (9). It is as thus qualified that God has solemnly ascribed to Him the title which is His due, the title of High Priest after a new eternal order (10). And it is as thus fully competent to act that He has become the one sufficient cause of eternal salvation to all who learn from Him to make a similar believing and obedient response to the will and way of God for men.

The *sins* (1) covered by the sacrifices of the law were sins due to human infirmity, not wilful sins done with a high hand. A human High Priest would be able to show understanding sympathy towards such wrongdoing because, as a man, he himself suffers from the same weakness. Also, for a similar reason, he must of necessity offer expiatory sacrifice for his own sins (3). Christ's case is, of course, different on this last point; for He was undefiled (vii. 26). But His sympathy is none the less real. One does not need to yield to temptation to be fully aware of its pressure upon the natural man. Indeed, only He who resisted to the end felt its full weight. Cf. ii. 18, iv. 15.

The Old Testament quotations of verses 5 and 6 come from two important messianic Psalms (Pss. ii. 7 and cx. 4). See comments on i. 5, vii. 1ff., and Appendix II, p. 1114).

When he had offered up prayers (7). Christ prayed particularly in Gethsemane, with earnest and urgent entreaty to be saved out of death, i.e. delivered from its power (cf. ii. 14, 15). But even though His human nature shrank from such a way forward (Mt. xxvi. 38, 39), He prayed in a spirit of reverent submission and obedient response to the will of God, as one prepared to learn—such was His 'godly fear' (7, RV)—that every circumstance and experience had its place in the Father's plan. Such praying was heard; and by the experience of such a discipline He Himself learnt the full meaning of human obedience, and was thereby perfected in His human character and in His fitness to be the cause to men of salvation eternal in quality. Men can enjoy the full benefit of His saving work only if they, too, are baptized into the same spirit, and become those who make active obedience to Christ their continual practice.

VIII. AN EXHORTATION TO PROGRESS AND TO PERSIST. v. 11—vi. 20

This rebuke and exhortation are prompted by the writer's subject (which only the mature can fully understand), by his awareness of his readers' backward condition, by his recognition of God's purpose for His children, and by the contemplation of the only ultimate alternative, namely, complete relapse and terrifying judgment. For those who share to the full in a God-given opportunity to receive His Word, and then knowingly and deliberately reject it, can expect nothing but judgment. It is impossible to do anything further to move such to repentance; they openly take sides with those who crucified the Son of God. Here (vi. 9) the writer, alarmed by such thoughts, is careful at once to state, in tender affection for his readers, that their condition is not hopeless. Their lives show the fruit of good works. But they need to be awakened to the dangers of sloth, and they need to learn to put devotion (similar to that which they have put into their good works) into persisting in believing hope until the day of full possession (11, 12). Further, God Himself, in order to remove from men's minds all possibility of doubt, has pledged His sure word by a confirming covenant oath (17). So men have in their dealings with God by faith a double ground of confidence—God's word and God's oath, both of which are incapable of being proved false (18). Finally, Jesus Himself has entered, as a forerunner, into the holy of holies, i.e. the very presence of God, having become men's High Priest after the new eternal Melchisedec order. There is, therefore, every reason and every confidence for seeking to progress into the full possession of God's promises, the laying hold of the hope set before us, by following Jesus the forerunner into the very presence of God.

a. An urgent call to go on to spiritual maturity (v. 11—vi. 12)

The truths concerning Christ's Melchisedec priesthood require much detailed exposition (11). They are *strong meat* (12, 14), or 'solid food' (RV), which can be understood or digested only by the spiritually mature. The whole subject, therefore, is difficult to expound to these particular readers because, although they are Christians of long standing, they have become slack and backward in their response to the God-given word. Note the words *dull* (v. 11) and *slothful*, RV 'sluggish' (vi. 12). *The oracles of God* (v. 12) probably means in this context the gospel, whose rudiments are indicated in vi. 1, 2. This message and the Old Testament Scriptures are thus regarded as being equally utterances of God. Cf. Rom. iii. 1, 2; 1 Pet. i. 23–25. In v. 13, 14, RV note the detailed contrast between the two types ('fullgrown men' and 'babes'), their condition ('senses exercised' and 'without experience'), and their diet ('solid food' and 'milk').

There is urgent need that Christians in this backward and slothful condition should stir themselves to active advance towards maturity rather than try to repeat the process of laying the foundation. Notice the basic nature of the actions and doctrines mentioned in verses 2 and 3. They represent the steps which the new convert would be expected to take and the essential truths which he would be required to believe. The one safeguard against slipping back and falling out is to go forward. This requires

deliberate and decisive action. Yet, paradoxically, *let us go on* (1), RV 'press on', is in the Greek a passive verb and means literally 'let us be borne along' (cf. Acts xxvii. 15, 17; 2 Pet. i. 21). 'The thought is not primarily of personal effort, but of personal surrender to an active influence. The power is working; we have only to yield ourselves to it' (B. F. Westcott. *Hebrews*, p. 145). Cf. Eph. iii. 20; Phil. ii. 13. So the writer exhorts his readers to respond and in verse 3, speaking for himself not for them, expresses the decision thus to act.

There is one necessary and very solemn qualification. Men can so act only *if God permit* (3). Some actions by the very divine constitution of things are morally *impossible* (4). If men share within the visible Church in all the blessings of the gospel, if (like those at the Red Sea deliverance, who later perished through unbelief in the wilderness) they have actually been in the company of the people who have experienced the mighty workings of God's Spirit, and so have themselves *tasted* (5) of its character, and then deliberately turn from it all and reject Christ, it is impossible to begin all over again with them and lay once more the foundation of repentance. As those who have decisively failed, or deliberately refused, to respond to divine grace there is nothing for them but judgment. Cf. 1 Cor. x. 1–5 and especially Lk. xx. 13–16. Scripture consistently teaches that the same actions of divine grace, which bring within men's grasp salvation and life, also finally settle the condemnation of those who, after sharing in the revelation, deliberately reject it. Cf. 2 Cor. ii. 15, 16. Also, it is impossible in the early stages to distinguish between the wheat and the tares, or between the seed that will wither or be choked and the seed that will bring forth fruit unto life eternal. Cf. 1 Cor. x. 12; 2 Tim. ii. 18, 19. Judgment is determined not by the beginning but by the *end*, or fruit (8). That is why this writer is so concerned that those who have begun to experience the grace of Christ should prove their genuineness by. going on to its true end. Cf. 2 Pet. i. 5–11.

Once enlightened (4). The word *once* suggests a certain absoluteness and finality, indicating something done once for all in such a way that it is of necessity incapable of repetition. It is in contrast to *again* (6). Compare its use in ix. 26, 28, x. 2, xii. 26, 27. Those so enlightened could never again become as those who had never received the light. *Fall away* (6) means not just gross sin but nothing less than deliberate apostasy, a complete rejection and disowning of the faith of Christ. As far as they are concerned (i.e. *to themselves*), such people put Christ out of their lives, or reject His claim to be the Son of God, by an action similar to that of those who got rid of Him by crucifying Him. Thus they publicly expose Christ to shame. See also Appendix III, 'The Warning Passages', p. 1116.

After such a solemn picture of inevitable doom (8) the writer hastens with real affection (only in this place does he call his readers *beloved*) to assure his readers that he is convinced that they are in no such hopeless state (9). Some therefore regard the type described in verses 4–8 as hypothetical rather than real. From verses 10–12 we learn what is indicative of true spiritual life and needful for full spiritual progress, namely, diligence, or all-absorbing zeal, in the *labour of love* (10), i.e. ministering to Christian brethren for the sake of the Father's name, the 'fulness of hope' (11, RV) in expectation of the fulfilment of God's promises, and the persistence and patient waiting of *faith* (12) until the day of realized possession.

b. Grounds of confidence to inspire steadfastness (vi. 13–20)

God's promises of salvation are the more sure because they are confirmed by an oath by God Himself. This was true from the first. When the promises were made to Abraham, God at the same time sware to fulfil them (13, 14). Abraham's confidence in God's word enabled him patiently to endure until the promise was fulfilled. The significance of oath-taking one may learn from the common practice of men (16). Its purpose is to put an end to all doubt or misgiving about a promise and to silence those who would gainsay its certainty. Its veracity and sure fulfilment are therefore confirmed by the most solemn of pledges. This commonly involves swearing by Almighty God. When men thus pledge their word to one another they virtually call upon God Himself to mediate or stand between them as a witness of their promises (cf. Jdg. xi. 10; Rom. i. 9) and to watch over their fulfilment (cf. Ru. i. 17). As Someone greater He is able to take vengeance if either party fails to keep his word. This certainty of divine vengeance makes swearing by God final as a way of confirming promises. In order to make men doubly sure of His promise God has condescended to use this method of oath-taking (17, 18). So He made Himself (since there was none greater to appeal to) a kind of third party or mediator between Himself and men. So we have a double ground of confidence, in God the Promiser who gives us His word and in God the Guarantor who confirms it by His oath. There is therefore no possibility of being deceived or disappointed.

An anchor (19) provides a peculiarly appropriate illustration. It was a recognized symbol of hope. It suggests a confidence to turn to and to lay hold of, a confidence which will hold fast and never fail because it enters into the unseen depths, the holiest of all. Also, this line of thought brings back the minds of the readers to *Jesus* and to His high-priestly office *after the order of Melchisedec* (20), the great theme which the writer has already indicated his eagerness to expound (v. 10, 11). Jesus offers us new hope because He has entered the innermost sanctuary not only on our behalf (*for us*) but also 'as a forerunner' (RV), opening the way for us to follow Him and thus enabling us to draw near to God. Cf. vii. 19 and x. 19. Also, like an anchor, He offers us a sure and an abiding confidence because in the innermost sanctuary of God's presence He abides, or remains enthroned, in contrast to the Levitical High Priest who came out and was removed by death. So He is *an high priest for ever* (20). It is this eternal quality which distinguishes the Melchisedec order of priesthood from that of Aaron.

IX. THE CHARACTERISTICS AND EFFICACY OF CHRIST'S ETERNAL PRIESTHOOD. vii. 1–28

The writer has already asserted that Jesus can be, to all who obey Him, the author of eternal salvation because He has become on their behalf a High Priest for ever 'after the order of Melchisedec' (see v. 6, 9, 10). It is this new and distinctive priestly office and work of Jesus about which he has 'many things to say' (v. 11), and which he now sets himself fully to expound. The Old Testament Scriptures themselves both provide and authorize the use of this illustration or pattern, namely, the priesthood of Melchisedec after whose order the Messiah is by divine oath declared to be a priest for ever (see Gn. xiv. 17–20; Ps. cx. 4). It is the implications of these Scriptures and the significance of this divinely ordained pattern that the writer now expounds. This new order of priesthood implies and involves difference from, superiority over, and the supersession of, the old Levitical order. Also, it makes possible (as the Levitical priesthood failed to do) the realization of the hope of all religion, namely, free access to God and full and complete personal salvation.

The record in Genesis indicates two things about *this Melchisedec*—his continual abiding and his greatness. It indicates the first figuratively by its silence, and the second factually by its statements. This means that in Scripture both what is said and what is omitted are alike important. It is very remarkable that in Genesis nothing is said about Melchisedec's ancestry; for in the Old Testament great importance is attached to genealogies, particularly of priests. Melchisedec is simply presented as a priest in his own right, not by reason of physical descent. Also, his birth and death are not mentioned. He simply appears once in the record as a living figure, and is left to abide alone and 'for ever' in the minds of readers as Melchisedec the priest. Nor is anything said of any successor to him. In all this he is made, by the very silence of Scripture, to suggest the likeness of *the Son of God* (3; note the divine title and contrast verse 22), who appeared once in history, but who is without beginning of days or end of life. Jesus is a High Priest after this order, unique and 'for ever'.

Further, the Genesis record makes plain Melchisedec's greatness. For no other than Abraham, the patriarch, gave him a tenth or tithe and selected it from the very best of the spoil. And he did this in the hour of his own victory when he might have claimed to be second to none in the land. Also, Melchisedec actually blessed Abraham, which proves that, signally favoured by God as Abraham was, Melchisedec was even greater than he. Similarly, Melchisedec is greater than the Levitical priests. They have only a legal right to take tithes from their equals. Abraham acknowledged that Melchisedec possessed an inherent right to be regarded as his superior. Also, it is possible 'so to speak' (see 9, RV), i.e. though some may think such reasoning rather unusual, to reckon that in what Abraham did Levi his descendant was involved, and so shared in acknowledging the greatness and superiority of Melchisedec. Note that Scripture pictures him as one who is a king as well as a priest (1). The combination of these two offices was to be a distinguishing characteristic of the Messiah. Cf. viii. 1 and Zc. vi. 13. Also, the meanings of the Hebrew words suggest that as 'Melchi-zedek' he is *King of righteousness*, and as King of 'Salem' he is *King of peace* (2). Note, too, the moral significance of the order here emphasized, first righteousness and then peace. Cf. xii. 11; Is. xxxii. 17; Jas. iii. 17, 18.

There is, moreover, independent proof that this Melchisedec priesthood, which belongs to our Lord, is radically different from, and far superior to, the Levitical priesthood. For there is the scriptural prophecy (Ps. cx. 4) that the Messiah is to be a priest divinely appointed according to this Melchisedec order. This scriptural indication of the need for a new order of priesthood clearly implies that the existing Levitical order has failed to achieve its intended end or true *perfection* (11). Also, the priesthood was so fundamental to the old covenant between God and His people (the whole relationship was constituted in dependence upon its ministry), that any change in the order of priesthood must of necessity imply and involve a change in the whole constitution; i.e. it implies nothing less than an accompanying new, and indeed better, covenant (12, 22).

One of the distinctive features of the new order is then noted (13, 14). Priests of the old order had to be descendants of Levi. But we know, not only from Scripture prophecy but also from the historical facts about Jesus, that He whom (so the writer implies) we confess to be the Messiah has been pleased to become a member of another tribe. For it is public knowledge that Jesus was born *of Juda* (14), a tribe with no claim to the order of priesthood appointed by Moses. Note the striking description of Jesus as *our Lord* (14). It corresponds here to the thought of Ps. cx. 1, in which David called Him 'my Lord'.

Further, the ground on which our Lord has made good His right to be Priest makes it still more obvious that there has been a complete change in the law governing the priesthood. Under the old order the necessary qualifications

both for being a priest and for performing priestly functions were all physical and external, depending on conformity to law (16). It was a matter first of physical purity by means of appropriate ritual. Under the new order Christ's necessary qualifications to be Priest and successfully to complete His priestly work are essentially spiritual and internal. They depend on the personal possession of life which cannot be destroyed (16), and on the consequent ability to complete to its finish or full perfection His work of saving men. This difference is made unmistakably clear by the description of the new Priest as one who arises 'after the likeness of Melchisedec' (15, RV). The distinctive feature of the Melchisedec priesthood is that it is *for ever* (17). The One who is to be a Priest of this order must have life which not only never does end, but never can be brought to an end (16; see RV mg.). This is why He is able to do what no Levitical priest could do. He can both bring men to God (19) and save them to the uttermost (25). For Christ's physical death as Man was no dissolution of His eternal life as God. He entered heaven as the living One and is there alive for evermore. In other words His indissoluble life made it possible for Him in and through His human death still to act and to enter in, and thus to present Himself to God as the Lamb slain. Also, it makes it certain that in God's presence He now continues alive for evermore.

Further, such a solemn introduction by God of a new priest itself cancels out the old order and proves that it was only 'foregoing' (18, RV), i.e. temporary and provisional. Indeed, in the light of what Christ has now done, we can see that the old law was completely powerless and useless. Indirectly, therefore, the writer is teaching his Jewish readers as Christians to recognize this and not to be so foolish as to trust any longer in the old Jewish order; for it has been divinely superseded by 'the bringing in thereupon' (i.e. on top of it) by God Himself of something better which does do what the old order could not do and gives us full access to God's presence (19, RV).

Again, the new priesthood is superior to the old because it has been constituted with an oath of God. This is witness that the new order of priesthood is a divine undertaking, and one that is thus doubly pledged by God's word and God's oath (cf. vi. 13–18). Therefore it cannot fail like the old. Also, being thus divinely instituted, this priesthood is *for ever* (21). The day will never come when this Priest will cease to be or His ministry cease to be effective. The divine oath implies something final, eternal, unchangeable. Therefore Jesus, who is thus given to us as the Priest of the new covenant, is to us the Guarantor of a covenant which is clearly far better than the old one (22). Note that *draw nigh* (19) and *surety* (22) probably come in the Greek from the same root. Jesus is 'the one who ensures permanently near relations with God'.

Because this Priest continues for ever, His

priesthood will never, like the Levitical, pass to someone else by reason of His death (23, 24). It is a priesthood which death cannot encroach upon. It is 'inviolable' (24, RV mg.). No one will ever draw near to God, looking to Jesus to save, and fail to find Him there, still alive and active to intervene to support their cause. And, because He thus lives for ever to function as Mediator and Priest on behalf of His people, He is able to bring to its final completion the salvation of all who thus draw near to God, trusting in Him. The present tenses of the verbs 'save' and 'draw near' (25, RV) may well suggest a sustained experience resulting from a continuous practice. He is able 'to be saving' those who 'are continually coming', i.e. those who make it a regular habit thus to draw near to God.

Verses 26–28 sum up what the writer has been saying. Our Christian High Priest is outstandingly great. Only one as great as this was fitted to meet our need and secure our full salvation. In character (26) He is towards God *holy*, towards man *harmless* (RV 'guileless'), and in Himself *undefiled*. He is free from any pollution which would incapacitate Him for the work of His office. As regards His sphere of operation He is lifted out from among sinful men by His removal to heaven, and there He is exalted to a position of the highest dignity, at the right hand of God. In contrast to the Levitical priests, He has no need repeatedly to offer sacrifices for sins. If He had, He would have to offer them *daily* (27), for His priestly work is going on every day. But all the offering necessary for sins He made 'once for all' (RV), *when he offered up himself* (27). This is a new thought (although it has already been suggested) which is to be developed later. As one whose life was not dissolved by human dying, He was able, as no other could, to be both Priest and Victim; He offered *himself*. Similarly, the new covenant is vastly superior to the old. The old was a law which appointed as High Priests weak men unable to achieve the true end of priestly ministry. The new order, which has superseded the law, is constituted by an oath of God Himself. It appoints as High Priest One who is divine, a veritable Son of God, and One who by reason of His incarnation, death, resurrection and ascension has become perfectly and permanently competent to discharge His office *for evermore* (28), *to the uttermost*, for all who *come unto God by him* (25).

X. THE EXCELLENCE OF CHRIST'S HIGH-PRIESTLY MINISTRY. viii. 1–6

The writer now comes to the crowning truth of all that he has to say, namely, that we Christians (in contrast to the Jews of the Old Testament order) have a High Priest of this outstanding kind: One who is Himself the reality, who answers to and fulfils the God-given pattern of priesthood; One whose ministry is therefore fulfilled in the heavenly sphere and not the earthly; One whose work has been consummated

in enthronement at the right hand of God; and One who is therefore able to fulfil a more excellent ministry as the mediator of a new and better covenant.

It is important to recognize that because Christ is a *minister* of the *true tabernacle* (2), and has entered for us not into some earthly shrine but into the very presence of God, the whole sphere of His ministry is to be thought of as *in the heavens* (1) and not *on earth* (4). This explains why He is invisible and not consummating His work, like the Jewish High Priest, with elaborate ceremonies in some grand and visible earthly temple—an important truth for Jewish readers to grasp. The Jewish priests who served on earth belonged to a different order, to which Jesus did not belong. Also, the order of their service, while God-given, was only a copy or shadow of the heavenly truth (5). It was Christ's work to fulfil this heavenly truth. This explains also why it was necessary for Him to die. For the pattern shows that he who would approach God as High Priest for men must have something to offer (3). So Christ offered Himself. Cf. vii. 27, ix. 14, x. 10. This offering was all accomplished and finished in one decisive action. In the Greek the aorist tense of the verb *to offer* (3) suggests a single finished act, not a continuous activity. Jesus, therefore, is not now offering. Indeed, the fact that His one offering was accepted as eternally sufficient is demonstrated by the fact that He is permanently enthroned in the place of all power (cf. x. 12, 13), and so able fully to save all who draw near to God by Him. It is this heavenly achievement and its successful consummation in enthronement which make Him the effective mediator of the wonderful new covenant. No wonder that the writer describes His ministry as being very different from the Levitical. No wonder that the possession as ours (*we have*) of a High Priest of such a kind is called 'the chief point' (1, RV), the mountain peak of revelation and redemption, the crowning truth of all.

Notice carefully the writer's distinction between the heavenly realities and their earthly copy or figurative representation (2, 5; cf. ix. 23, 24, x. 1). Because Jesus belonged to the heavenly order and not to that *on earth* (4) His offering of Himself (though He died as Man on earth) can be properly appreciated only if it is understood as done in relation to the heavenly tabernacle, and as having its consummation at the throne of God (cf. i. 3, x. 12, xii. 2). Compare the way in which Christians, though they still live on earth, are to regard themselves as belonging to heaven (see iii. 1, xii. 22, 23); and are exhorted, by following Jesus, to pass into the heavens and to come boldly to the throne of grace (see iv. 14, 16). Christian worship, like Christ's priestly work, is not 'on earth'.

XI. THE TWO COVENANTS. viii. 7–13

The very presence in the Old Testament of a promise of a new covenant is itself witness that the first covenant is not wholly satisfactory and free from fault. This promise (quoted in verse 8) is found in Je. xxxi. 31–34. What is there said indicates how the first covenant failed because the Israelites failed to abide by its conditions. This covenant, though genuine and good, was deficient in that it provided no guarantee that sinful men would continue in its faithful observance. So God declared His intention to make a new covenant by whose terms or *better promises* (6) He Himself undertook to make good the deficiency and to ensure the realization of His purpose. This purpose is that a company of people should be separated from the world, and brought into fellowship with Himself to be His people, to delight in His company, and to do His will. God is to secure this end by making His law no longer an external restraint from which men only break away, but an inner constraint (10). This change is to be effected by putting the Spirit of obedience into men's hearts, so that, like the incarnate Son, they will say, 'I delight to do thy will, O my God: yea, thy law is within my heart' (Ps. xl. 8). Such intimacy of personal dealing will give to each individual direct personal knowledge of God. No privileged intermediate class, whether of priests or prophets, will be needed to teach men about God. For all shall know Him directly (11). Knowing Him and being taught by Him personally in this way are thus to become the distinctive marks of God's true children. Cf. Is. liv. 13; Jn. vi. 45. And all this will happen because God in His mercy towards them (instead of judgment against them) will so put away their sins (cf. ix. 28) that perfect unhindered fellowship between them and Himself will become possible (12).

The foundation act of divine mercy on which all else is built is therefore the priestly work of putting away sin. The High Priest who does this, and makes it possible for men to draw near to God, thus becomes the *mediator* of this new covenant (6). This very promise of a *new covenant* (13) means that, since the days of Jeremiah, the first covenant has to be recognized as already made *old*; and this description of anything as getting ancient and becoming aged means that it may be expected soon to pass away. Thus, from their own Jewish Old Testament Scriptures, the writer provides his readers with a further decisive indication that the old covenant was only temporary, and that it was the divine intention that it should be superseded by the new covenant and itself cease to be.

XII. THE MINISTRY OF THE FIRST COVENANT DESCRIBED. ix. 1–10

The first covenant had its divinely appointed regulations of ministry and a sanctuary for their performance, a *worldly* (i.e. 'earthly') one. A tabernacle was prepared with two sections, each richly and elaborately provided with furniture necessary for the ritual ceremonies, and with symbols of God's presence, of His past dealings with His people, and of His revealed will for their lives. It is impossible here, says the writer, to comment on all these features in detail (5). The important thing on which to concentrate attention is the way in which this order of divine service furthered the one great purpose of its existence, namely, to enable men to draw near to God.

These ordinances of the first covenant allowed a select class—the priests—to go continually into the outer shrine, the holy place (6). But into the inner shrine, or holiest sanctuary of all, where the cherubim over the ark symbolized the dwelling-place and manifested glory of God Himself, access was very severely restricted. One man only could enter, the High Priest, on one day only each year, and only if he took with him the shed blood of atoning sacrifice (7). An order of worship so arranged by divine direction was a witness given by the Spirit of God Himself that the way for all God's people to enter freely into the immediate presence of God *was not yet made manifest* (8) or opened up. Note here the contrast between the divinely ordained splendour of the old order of worship, so dear to the writer's Jewish readers, and its disappointing spiritual ineffectiveness. It made nothing perfect (vii. 19). Yet, far from being valueless, it had a deep spiritual significance. For, by providing 'figures of the true' (ix. 24), it foreshadowed the character, the necessity and the benefits of the 'good things to come' (11), when the true High Priest appeared. *The golden censer* (4); more probably, as in RV mg., 'altar of incense'. The wording here (cf. 1 Ki. vi. 22) probably means not that it was itself kept in the inner shrine, but rather that it was specially connected with the ministry carried out there on the day of atonement. See Ex. xxx. 1–10; Lv. xvi. 12, 13, 18–20.

The limited and provisional character of the first covenant is still further demonstrated by the very nature of its forms of service. For the *gifts and sacrifices* (9) which were ordained by it have no moral power to purge away the defilement of sin and to make those who bring them properly fit to approach and to enjoy God's presence (i.e. the intended goal). All that they can do as *carnal ordinances* (10) is to give those who submit to them a certain external or physical 'cleanness' (13, RV), a formal or ritual status of ceremonial 'holiness'. They are, therefore, clearly temporary and provisional and meant to serve a purpose only until the time comes for them to be superseded by the realities whose character they foreshadow. It is these *good things to come* (11) which are now made available for all to enjoy through the high-priestly work of Christ. For the very forms which showed in *figure* (9), or 'parable' (RV), what was necessary to make access possible also showed that as yet the barriers were not removed for all to enter into the holiest of all (8). As long as men were kept at a distance by a veil and an outer shrine placed between them and the holiest of all, clearly they could not enjoy access to God's presence. This meant, therefore, that only by the removal of this existing order, by the rending of the veil, and the doing away with a separate outer shrine, could the people outside have open access to God's presence. The writer is, therefore, suggesting to his Jewish readers that the realization of those hopes to which the first covenant pointed forward must involve the complete abolition of the old order. As he says later of the two kinds of sacrifice (see x. 9), God has taken away the first in the act of establishing the second—the new and living way into the holiest of all (see x. 19, 20). The writer has prepared his readers' minds for this extremely radical conclusion by suggesting earlier (viii. 13) that, since the first covenant has now been made old, it may be expected to disappear.

XIII. THE CHARACTERISTICS OF THE SACRIFICE OF CHRIST. ix. 11—x. 18

The writer now describes the distinctive characteristics of the sacrifice of Christ and the great eternal benefits which are made ours by it. Following his now familiar method he illustrates and enforces these truths, first by both comparison and contrast with the Levitical forms of service and sacrifice, and then by quotation and exposition of some of the God-given prophetic words of the Old Testament Scriptures.

a. Its far-reaching consequences (ix. 11–15)

These consequences are briefly summarized. First, by His offering of Himself Christ made a decisive 'once-for-all' (12, RV; cf. vii. 27, RV) entrance into the presence of God as the High Priest of sinful men. The goal of all priestly ministry is to secure access to, and acceptance in, God's presence; to restore and to secure the unbroken maintenance of immediate and unhindered communion with God. Secondly, Christ *obtained eternal redemption* (12). He wrought a work of deliverance which set God's people permanently free from the defilement, separation from God and inevitable doom to which they were otherwise subject because of sin. Thirdly, through His blood-shedding (i.e. by reason of the inexhaustible and abiding virtue of His one sacrifice of Himself) Christ is able to purge the conscience from the paralysing power of guilt and to set men free to serve the living God (14). He thus gives us release or remission from the sins which would otherwise keep us from God so that we can serve Him in the sanctuary of His presence. Cf. ix. 22, x. 22. Fourthly, such achievements mean that He is *the mediator of the new testament*, or 'covenant' (15), who is able to guarantee to all whom God calls the actual possession of the eternal inheritance which He promises. Lastly, this result is the more sure because His death secures release from the penalty of transgressions under the old covenant (15). It clears the field for a new work of divine grace by fully settling the outstanding issues between God and His people. It

blots out all the sins of the past. It means, also, that the men of faith of Old Testament days who, through the law, could not find perfection or the actual realization of all that they hoped for, and who saw the day of God's fulfilment as still future, can now be made perfect and possess the inheritance. In other words, Christ's death was retrospective in its efficacy. It covered all the sins done before He came. Cf. xi. 13, 39, 40, xii. 23; Mt. xxvii. 51–53; Rom. iii. 25.

b. Its necessity (ix. 16–23)

Jesus had said of His death, 'Thus it must be' (Mt. xxvi. 54). But the crucifixion of the Messiah continued to be a stumbling-block to Jews. They needed much help if they were to see why it was necessary. So the writer here stresses two reasons for its necessity. First, it was required in order to dedicate, institute or ratify the new covenant. Solemnly it sanctified or set apart the person making the covenant to the keeping of its terms by thus pledging (and in this case actually performing) obedience unto death. Secondly, it was needed in order to cleanse or purify the people who are covered by the covenant and to secure for them release or remission from the sins which would otherwise estrange them from, or keep them out of, the place of God's presence. For *without shedding of blood is no remission* (22). So a sacrifice of this unique and surprising kind, a better sacrifice than under the law, the death of Christ Himself, was necessary to secure a better (moral) purification and to establish the better (and really effective) covenant.

In the references here to the necessity for death to take place in connection with a testament or covenant (16), two or three different ideas are probably combined. According to ancient practice covenants were sealed in blood, by the symbolic introduction of the death of the party or parties making it. So verses 16, 17 (see RV mg.) speak of 'death' being 'brought in' and of a covenant having validity only 'over dead bodies', i.e. probably over the divided pieces of the sacrificed victims between which such covenant-makers passed. See Gn. xv. 7–21; Je. xxxiv. 18, 19. This gave visible confirmation of a vow of faithfulness unto death, and was probably accompanied by the prayer that one's life might be similarly taken in penalty if the promise thus sealed was broken. Once the transgression of a covenant obligation had been committed, therefore, death became necessary for a second reason, to pay the penalty of such failure. So verse 22 asserts that under the old law this was the common price of redemption; *and without shedding of blood is no remission*. Further, since God's new covenant spoke of an inheritance which included the full forgiveness (or forgetting by God) of sins, this could not become available for men to enjoy until an actual death had taken place for the remissions of sins, i.e. 'for the redemption of the transgressions that were under the first covenant' (15, RV). In this connection, therefore, the new covenant operates like a will or testament (in the Greek the word used signifies both 'covenant' and 'testament'). Its good things become available for enjoyment only after the death has taken place of the benefactor who is making the disposition. For He (i.e. Christ) could make forgiveness of our sins possible only by dying and Himself paying the penalty of our sins.

c. Its finality (ix. 24—x. 18)

This offering of Himself to God which Christ has made once for all in His human death is also perfect and final. It has achieved in full completion the true end of such sacrifice. Therefore, none greater is possible; and no other is necessary. As Jesus Himself said, 'It is finished' (Jn. xix. 30). 'There is no more offering for sin' (x. 18).

i. **By it He entered into heaven itself (ix. 24).** His one act achieved what the sacrifices of the law only figuratively suggested. For the Levitical High Priest entered only an earthly, man-made shrine. Through His death Christ has won an entrance on our behalf (*for us*) as our High Priest into the immediate presence of God (cf. verses 11, 12). There He is now openly manifested before the very face of God as our representative, guaranteeing that we shall be accepted and our prayer answered when we come. It is because He is there to support our cause that full salvation is assured to all who come unto God by Him. Cf. iv. 14, 16, vii. 25; 1 Jn. ii. 1, 2.

ii. **He offered Himself (ix. 25, 26).** Cf. vii. 27, ix. 14. This was in contrast to the Levitical High Priest who entered the holiest of all *with blood of others* (25), or 'with blood not his own' (RV). He had no power himself to perform this act as a sacrifice to God; i.e. he could not offer himself. His presentation of the blood of a slain animal before God was an acknowledgment that something was necessary which he not only could not do himself, but also needed to have done on his behalf. Christ doubly excelled him. Not only did He not need any *blood of others* shed on His behalf to give Him entrance (for He was sinless); but also He made His decisive appearance on the field of human history to put away the sin of others *by the sacrifice of himself* (26). This He was able to do because, as man, He was 'without blemish' (ix. 14, RV), and as God He could as *eternal Spirit* (ix. 14), by the power of His indissoluble life (vii. 16, RV mg.), still Himself act in death and offer the sacrifice of His human life to the Father. So He was both Priest and Victim; He offered Himself to God.

iii. **He offered Himself once only and once for all (ix. 25–28).** This is proved by His non-appearance in earlier ages. For, as it is very important to recognize, He offered Himself to God on the field of history by becoming Man and offering His human body to die to bear away the sins of many. We are saved by the earthly sacrifice of His flesh and blood. Therefore, had frequent offerings been necessary, similar to the yearly repetitions of the sacrifice of the day of atonement, it would have been

necessary for Christ to have had many incarnations in order to suffer death many times. Also, if one offering availed only for a limited number, such as the generation then alive, it would *now* (i.e. in the first century A.D.) be too late to offer sacrifice for the sins of earlier generations; and so it would have been necessary soon after the creation and the fall of man for a series of incarnations to begin (26). No such series has occurred. This is objective proof that it was not necessary, and clear indication that the one incarnation and death are sufficient and final for all history—past, present and future. Christ's one appearance in the very 'consummation of the ages' (26, RV mg.) is all that is necessary to remove completely the sins of the whole world by His one sacrifice of His single human life. As He said Himself, His one soul (or human life) thus given is enough to provide ransom for the many (Mk. x. 45).

Further, this final settlement of eternal destiny by the decisive action of a single life and death in human history corresponds with, and is confirmed by, all that is revealed by God concerning the solemn responsible character and eternal consequences of all human life in this present world. For all men live and die once, and according to the deeds done in that one lifetime their eternal judgment is settled (27; cf. Rev. xx. 12, 13). Similarly Christ's single appearance in history, and His one decisive action in atonement for sin, is sufficient to secure eternal redemption and the possession of an eternal inheritance (28). There is no need of repetition. Any idea that either on earth or in heaven He must repeat or continue His offering is completely out of place. The redemption is eternal, and it has been obtained finally and for ever, not by an eternally continuous offering, but by the single decisiveness of one act in history.

iv. **By this sacrifice of Himself He actually put away sin (ix. 26b—x. 4).** This was something which it was absolutely impossible for the Levitical sacrifices to do. The purpose and the consequence of His sacrifice of Himself was to bring sin to nought, to cancel it out, to set it on one side (26b, Gk.; the old covenant is similarly 'disannulled'; see vii. 18, Gk.). Christ was offered *to bear* (or 'bear away') *the sins of many* (28). He took the burden upon Himself and removed it. It is, therefore, completely gone. When He appears the second time it will be *without sin*, i.e. completely free from its burden, as One able to complete the salvation of those who have their hopes fixed on Him (28).

In contrast to this substantial reality—*the very image of the things* (x. 1)—all that the old Jewish law had to offer was a *shadow*, or representation in outline, *of good things* (yet) *to come* (x. 1). Its sacrifices, yearly repeated, had no power to effect a permanent benefit for those who thus drew nigh to God. Rather their continued repetition was first a witness of their own ineffectiveness to complete the work of cleansing, and second a witness to the fact that those who thus used them did not gain from their use any real deliverance from a sense of guilt (1, 2). For such animal sacrifices can never *take away* sins (4). What they cannot do, Christ has actually done.

v. His offering fulfilled the will of God with regard to sacrifice (x. 5–10). It was thus that He effected the sanctification of God's people. In other words, His offering of Himself was the reality of which the sacrifices of the law were but a shadow. Because of the ineffectiveness of those sacrifices, there was an important sense (to which the Old Testament Scriptures gave expression) in which God was not satisfied with them and did not desire them. In their place they served a purpose. But the same Scriptures, which spoke of God's lack of pleasure in them, also indicated that ultimately God contemplated a better sacrifice (6–9). His will with regard to sacrifice would be fulfilled when a person, in the full freedom of personal moral choice and qualified so to act, would devote himself and his human life to doing God's will by offering his own body. Also, the prophetic Scripture teaches that this is what the Christ of God will choose to do and come to do in fulfilment of the pattern, and in obedience to the principles, set forth in Holy Scripture. (The parenthesis in verse 7 means 'according to the direction of the things therein written for my learning'.) Further, the way in which the disowning of animal sacrifices and the promise of a person to come to do God's will precede and follow one another in the same Psalm (xl. 6–8) plainly indicates that it is God's purpose that the second should take the place of the first (8, 9). For the writer's first readers this means again that, as Jews, they must recognize that, in fulfilment of the will of God, the Levitical order was now 'taken away' and openly superseded by God's own establishment of a new order in which is to be found the full and final realization of all towards which the old order pointed. For, by Christ's one offering of His human body (10), the people of God are eternally made fit for God's presence and consecrated to His service.

vi. In consequence of His one finished sacrifice Christ sits enthroned and assured of complete victory (x. 11–14). There is a striking contrast between Christ's present position and prospect and that of the Levitical priests. They continue to stand in order to continue offering their repeated sacrifices, but with no hope that they will ever *take away sins* (11). Christ is already seated, a sign that His work of offering is finished (12). What is more, He is enthroned in the place of sovereignty and power at God's right hand with the sure hope, based on the Father's own word to Him (see Ps. cx. 1; Heb. i. 13), that all His enemies are to be subdued beneath His feet (13). All this has come about through His one, final, atoning sacrifice, which is eternal in its efficacy and has secured the permanent continuance in right relation to God (perfected) of all whom it serves to cleanse from sin and to dedicate as God's people (sanctified).

vii. There is no further need or place for any more offering for sin (x. 15–18). Such a conclusion is here based on the witness to us of the Holy Spirit given in the words of a prophecy which declares the blessings of the new covenant (see Je. xxxi. 31–34). For its crowning promise is the declaration by God Himself that, once the new covenant is ratified, He will remember the sins of His people no more (17). And if sins are so completely remitted that God Himself ceases to remember them, there is obviously no need or place for any further offering to be made to secure their removal. This, then, is the conclusive proof from God's own new covenant promise that Christ's redemptive act which has established the new covenant is in itself all-sufficient and absolutely final. Henceforth there is no longer any place for any kind of offering for sin or presentation before God of Christ's one sin offering. Reconciliation has not to be made or completed by any further propitiatory offering or memorial of Christ's sacrifice; it has simply to be received by penitent faith as an already complete and available benefit of the finished work of Christ (see Rom. v. 11, RV).

XIV. PRACTICAL EXHORTATION.
x. 19–39

a. A call to steadfastness in faith, hope and love (x. 19–25)

These verses summarize the positive appeal of the whole Epistle. It is based (note the *therefore* of verse 19) on the doctrinal teaching already given about the absolute efficacy of Christ's one sacrifice and His abiding continuance in the place of sovereign ability as our High Priest. It is a call first of all to enter into the realized presence of God in confident, appropriating faith. Here the writer reinforces an appeal already made in iv. 14–16, when he introduced these themes. This is complemented by exhortations to be steadfast in the open confession of Christian hope and to be active towards fellow-Christians in love, fellowship and mutual encouragement. This brief, threefold exhortation is virtually expanded in the remainder of the Epistle. Chapters xi, xii and xiii emphasize in turn the same three themes, the expression of faith, the patience of hope, and love and good works.

The new possibility open to all Christians is that of free access to God's presence. There is a way which has been inaugurated for us by Jesus, the forerunner. This way is *new*, i.e. it did not exist under the old covenant, and it is *living* or effective (20). The veil through which Jesus opened up this way was His human flesh. For when it was broken in sacrificial death the symbolic temple veil was rent asunder (20). See Mt. xxvii. 51–53; Col. i. 20–22. So we can have joyous confidence to enter God's presence through *the blood* (i.e. the death, or accomplished and effectual sacrifice) *of Jesus* (19). Note it does not say 'with the blood of Jesus'. Christians have no longer to seek to win entrance by a fresh presentation of the sacrifice. The way stands open and unbarred. Further, as we thus enter God's dwelling-place and join the company of His family, we find we have the same Jesus as our enthroned and ever-living Priest to support our case and meet all our need (21; cf. vii. 25; 1 Jn. ii. 1, 2). What is required of all who thus come is sincerity of purpose and absolute confidence that what Christ has done avails to make ours that full purification both within and without which was symbolized under the old ritual forms by sprinkled blood and freshly washed bodies (see, e.g., Lv. viii. 6, 23). In the face of temptations to abandon their confidence because some promises remained unfulfilled, the writer appeals for a steadfast persistence in openly confessing their Christian hope (23, RV); for they have the sure guarantee of the faithfulness of the Promiser. There should also be among Christians mutual 'provocation' (a striking word because commonly used with a bad sense) to active good works by deliberately taking notice of each other's needs (24). They should not, therefore, copy the custom of some and cease attendance at Christian meetings, but rather use such opportunities for mutual encouragement, and the more so in the light of the approaching consummation and judgment (25).

b. The consequences of deliberate rebellion (x. 26-31)

The writer sees for those in the position occupied by himself and his readers only two possibilities: either to make full response, or to become deliberate rebels. Having exhorted his readers fully to respond (x. 19-25) he now considers, at least hypothetically (this may be the force of *if we*), the only alternative. Suppose that, persistently and by deliberate choice, we turn aside from what has been brought within our knowledge and our reach; what else remains for us to enjoy? The solemn answer is, first, that there is no way of atonement for sin (26) and, second, that nothing awaits us but the terrifying prospect of judgment as objects of that divine wrath which is to be displayed against all who oppose God (27). For even under the old covenant (see Dt. xvii. 2-7) a man who completely set its demands on one side in active rebellion (e.g. idolatry) suffered the extreme penalty of death without mercy (28). Does it not commend itself as fitting, even to our judgment, that an apostate from the new covenant ought to suffer a much worse penalty (29)? For consider the gravity of his offence. He has trampled down the person of Him who is, and has been confessed as, the Son of God. He has denied that there is any sacred significance to that blood which had been to him the covenant seal of his own sanctification. He has treated with proud insolence that Spirit who is Himself the author of the whole work of grace in the experience of which he had shared. Do not God's spoken words (i.e. in Scripture) make plain, also, His character as a God who executes

judgment, and who will certainly show by His judgments who are His people and who are the traitors and rebels against Him (30)? Can any prospect be more terrifying than thus to have this God against one in judgment (31)? See also Appendix III, 'The Warning Passages', p. 1116.

Sin (26) must mean here apostasy or rebellion (cf. Is. i. 2, 29, 30; Heb. iii. 12, 13; 2 Pet. ii. 21). The present tense indicates sustained persistence; the emphatic adverb, put first in the Greek, stresses that it is done *wilfully*. There remaineth no more sacrifice for sins (26); not only because the one final sacrifice has been rejected, but also because such sin is unforgivable; there is no divine provision for its remission. *The Lord shall judge his people* (30). The Old Testament idea is that God will execute judgment for or on behalf of His people. The meaning here is that He will vindicate the true by removing the false. Cf. Nu. xvi, esp. verse 5.

c. An encouragement to go forward (x. 32-39)

Having contemplated the worst, the writer now finds ground to expect and appeal for the best. If his readers are tempted to abandon Christianity because it involves them in suffering and reproach rather than fulfilment of their natural hopes, let them find inspiration to continue both in looking forward and in looking back. Let them remember from their own early experience as Christians that public exposure to reproach and trial has been, from the first, the lot of those who share this enlightenment. It is therefore no new and unexpected development. At that time their own attitude in the face of such trials showed that they fully realized that these were experiences in which, as Christians, they were called to share, and that any physical pain or material loss could be accepted with joy when compared with their heavenly and eternal gain (32-34; cf. 2 Cor. iv. 16-18). Let them also look forward and realize that their joyous Christian confidence has not been misplaced. It holds sure promise of a full reward and ought by no means to be abandoned (35). They must realize, however, that in the will of God there is a period of waiting and working and trial before the expected fulfilment can be enjoyed (36). This fulfilment will be very soon. It will be consummated by the appearance of the Coming One (37). His advent is certain; nor will He be behind His time. For those who know these things there are only two possible attitudes: to find acceptance with God and life by holding on in faith; or to withdraw one's confidence and come under God's displeasure (38). For us the latter alternative is unthinkable. We are not the sort to depart from the faith to our own destruction; we are the kind who go on believing until we reach the goal of truly gaining life for our souls (39).

Ye had compassion of me in my bonds (34); RV 'compassion on them'. The MS reading which is followed by the RV is more likely to be correct; i.e. there is no necessary reference to the writer.

In verses 37, 38 the writer does not claim to be specifically quoting Scripture; but there is obviously a free use of Old Testament phrases. *A little while* (37) is probably an echo of Is. xxvi. 20. The other sentences are from Hab. ii. 3, 4. There, according to the Hebrew and the AV, what is coming is either the vision or the advent of God thus visualized. The LXX makes the subject a person. This personal reference is made still more definite here by the addition in Greek of the definite article to the participle; the RV renders 'He that cometh'. In using the statements of Hab. ii. 4 the writer not only follows the LXX, which is a statement very different from the Hebrew, but also he transposes the two sente.ices. There is no *any man* in the Greek; the subject of both statements is the same person (see RV), suggesting that the true believer may apostatize. But the second statement is only hypothetical. The resulting couplet states the plain alternatives: to live by faith, to perish by apostasy. Just as before God there is justification and life by faith, so, if a believer deliberately withdraws from the faith attitude, he can only encounter divine displeasure and perdition. No wonder the writer adds that neither he nor they can have any intention of committing such spiritual suicide.

XV. THE TRIUMPHANT ACHIEVEMENTS OF FAITH. xi. 1–40

In x. 38, 39 the writer has enunciated the scriptural principle of faith as a way of life pleasing to God and has expressed the resolution to persist in it until the full possession of its reward is received.. He now enforces this by many scriptural illustrations, showing that, from the very beginning and throughout all history, faith has been in God's sight the one indispensable condition. of worthwhile achievement and hopeful endurance. Faith, he declares, deals essentially with things of two types, things future (or *hoped for*) and things *not seen* (1). It is equally sure of the coming fulfilment of the one and of the present reality of the other. Without such an active attitude of awareness and assurance towards God *it is impossible to please him* (6), or indeed to have personal dealings with Him (i.e. to come to God). For the very being of God Himself is the supreme unseen reality with which faith has to do; and His faithful fulfilment of His promises (cf. verse 11) and His certain rewarding of those who *diligently seek him* (6) are the great future good for which faith hopes. The one requires *evidence* (Gk. *elenchos*), the faith of verifiable certification and established conviction; the other requires *substance* (Gk. *hypostasis*, of which a possible meaning is 'title deed'), the faith of assured confidence and settled expectation (1). It is because they manifested a faith of this sort (2) that those who have gone before have had their deeds and sufferings approved by God as worthy to be recorded in Scripture. It was by their faith that they joined the company of God's witnesses (xii. 1) or 'martyrs' (Gk.). For God witnessed of them (2, 4, 5); and they thus still witness for Him. The activity of such a faith as theirs afforded something to be recorded which has an abiding message for men; it continues to provide encouragement and examples for others. Such witness, therefore, outlives the individual it concerns; and through the record of his doings his faith still speaks to others after he is dead (4).

The many witnesses of the Old Testament record are then surveyed in chronological order and in some detail. Throughout there is emphasis on their awareness of the unseen divine realities and on their assurance of the coming divine fulfilments, both in striking contrast to the visible appearance and immediate natural outlook, which seemed often completely to contradict their confidence (9, 11, 17, 18). The one sure and all-sufficient certainty is the living God and His faithful doing. So, for instance, Moses *endured, as seeing him who is invisible* (27); he counted earthly suffering and reproach preferable to worldly enjoyment and wealth, because he looked for God's sure payment of worthwhile reward (25, 26). The common experience of all these pilgrims was to see from a distance promised rewards, which they never enjoyed in this life (13). Yet they never withdrew and turned back to the world which they had left behind, because they believed in a fulfilment that was heavenly rather than earthly (14–16). These are the people whom God owns as His, condescending to be called their God.

The final emphasis is upon rewards beyond this life. True, many reached faith's goal here in open triumph (29–35a), and such victories have been of all kinds—material, moral and spiritual. Yet faith's most outstanding witnesses are the martyrs (35b–38), those who, for faith's sake, have endured great suffering, those who have died painful and shameful deaths rather than deny their faith. In them faith has shown itself victorious in indomitable endurance, in refusal to accept deliverance. Their reward, which they thus chose, lies beyond death in *a better resurrection* (35; i.e. better than restoration to life in this world such as was granted to the sons of the women of Zarephath and Shunem). Indeed, none of these old heroes of faith, worthy as they are of their place in Scripture, ever enjoyed the complete fulfilment of God's promises, because God in His providence ordained that we Christian believers should enjoy even greater privileges and share with them in the consummation (39, 40).

In xi. 1 the order of the words in Greek puts the emphasis on the objects of faith, i.e. the *things hoped for* and *things not seen*; and the inclusion of a noun (Gk. *pragmata*) in the second phrase, making explicit that these unseen things are realities, is itself a proof or *evidence* of their existence. Such faith is a primary condition of knowledge (3), particularly knowledge of the scriptural witness. It is essential to the understanding of the origin of the universe, as described in Gn. i. It is the foundation of all right thinking about those *worlds* which form the stage and setting of human history (3). For it is impossible to provide an adequate explanation simply by reasoning from what can be observed by the senses. One needs to recognize the prior and independent existence of the living God and His creative activity as the first cause. With the phrase *by the word of God* cf. 'And God said' used ten times in Gn. i; cf. also Ps. xxxiii. 6. It was the faith in which he offered it that made Abel's sacrifice (4) better than Cain's. He made a more appropriate response to the truth about God of which he was aware. It was because of his faith, thus expressed by what he gave, that he was reckoned *righteous*. It is through his faith that he still speaks (i.e. through the pages of Scripture; note the present tense, *speaketh*), witnessing to men how to please God. Note that *which* and *it* both refer back to *faith*.

Enoch (5) witnesses that faith active in a man's heart in this life so pleases God that He gives finally to the true believer escape from death and a fuller enjoyment of His own presence and glory. Such examples are sufficient to justify the generalization of verse 6, 'Without faith it is impossible to be well-pleasing unto God' (RV). For how can a man have dealings with One who is unseen, and whose chief rewards lie beyond this present life, unless he believes both that God exists and that, whenever a man thus sets himself wholeheartedly to devote himself to God, God never fails to become his rewarder or payer-back of recompense (cf. Jas. iv. 8a)?

Noah (7) is a peculiarly significant example for those privileged to hear the gospel. Out of reverence for a word from God, which spoke of impending judgment and indicated a way of salvation, he acted in obedience to the divine command, because he believed that what God said would be fulfilled. By such faith he not only himself inherited that righteousness which is God's gift to believers (note the implication that this is a thought familiar to the readers of the Epistle; cf. Rom. i. 17); he was also used as God's witness and worker to the condemnation of his generation and the salvation of others of his family.

Abraham (8) obeyed the divine call to go forth to possess an inheritance, though he did not know to what land he was going, still less what it was like. His faith was in a marked way an evidence of the unseen and a guarantee of something to be enjoyed in the future (cf. verse 1). When he actually entered the land of divine promise (9) it was to reside in it only as an outsider living in a land belonging to others. He learnt also to make his home in tents, as a man always on the move. His son and grandson entered into the heritage of the same divine promise, but no more saw its actual fulfilment than he. Yet this experience did not cause him to give up believing. Rather he looked for a supernatural fulfilment, an abiding city, built according to the design (note RV mg. 'architect') and by the working of God (10; cf. xii. 22, xiii. 14). The triumph of faith in Sarah's experience (11) was the more remarkable not only because she had been long barren (Gn. xi. 30), but still more because any such fulfilment was contrary to the time of life she had now reached. Her faith rested on God's word of promise and on His active faithfulness in fulfilling His word (cf. Rom. iv. 20, 21). The *one* (12) from whom such a vast progeny sprang was Abraham; see Gn. xv. 5; Is. li. 1, 2; Ezk. xxxiii. 24.

This experience of deferred fulfilment in the lives of the patriarchs (13–16) enabled them eventually to triumph by faith over death itself. For they learned to look beyond death for a larger fulfilment than that which their own lifetime and earthly experience could afford. So they came to realize that this life is not an end in itself but a pilgrimage (see Gn. xxiii. 4, xlvii. 9) towards a better (i.e. a heavenly) goal beyond it. It is such people with whom God has condescended openly to associate Himself and to be known as *their God* (16); cf. Mk. xii. 26, 27, and note the similar reference there to life beyond death.

Abraham's faith was tried in the demand to offer up Isaac, not only because he was peculiarly beloved as Sarah's only child (*his only begotten*), but most of all because the demand seemed to oppose the fulfilment in Isaac of the God-given promise which Abraham had already embraced, i.e. that through him Abraham's family was to be continued and multiplied (17, 18). Abraham's faith triumphed because he refused to see inconsistency or faithlessness in God. He believed God could and must resolve the problem. No solution seemed possible unless God gave Isaac back from death to become the father of children. This Abraham therefore reckoned as fully possible with God; his faith thus triumphing in a fresh way over death by the hope of resurrection (19). Such faith turned a way of darkness into a pathway of hope. *In a figure* (19), RV 'in a parable', may mean 'as it were' or it may suggest 'for a lesson', i.e. one from which Abraham learnt the kind of working to expect from God as His way of solving life's darkest problems (cf. Jn. viii. 56). Some think the reference is to such a lesson already learnt from the manner of Isaac's birth (cf. verse 12).

Isaac (20) expressed his faith in God's sovereign providence in accepting, contrary to his own natural preference and intention, that Jacob should come before Esau in blessing (cf. Gn. xxvii. 33), and in anticipating blessings of the future for their descendants. Similarly *Jacob* and *Joseph* (21, 22) looked beyond their own deaths and anticipated the *departing* (Gk. *exodos*) of the Israelites from Egypt and their return to Canaan (cf. Gn. xlviii. 21, l. 24). Jacob gave to Joseph instead of to Reuben the privilege of the firstborn, i.e. a double share, divided between his two sons. Jacob also showed his awareness of the reality and sovereignty of God by the way in which, in spite of his age and infirmity, he bowed or prostrated himself in worship on his staff (LXX) or bed (Heb.) (Gn. xlvii. 31). Joseph, like Jacob, out of regard for God's sure purpose, was concerned ultimately to be buried not amid the wealth of Egypt but in the land of divine promise. See Ex. xiii. 19; Jos. xxiv. 32.

Moses' *parents* (23) apparently saw something in their child which made them sure that it was God's purpose to preserve and use him. So, instead of killing the child through fear of Pharaoh and his order, they saved him through faith in God and His co-operating providence. What Moses refused to enjoy (24) was the princely status of a son of a daughter of the royal house. He did this because he deliberately preferred publicly to be known as one of the Hebrews, who were to his faith not a race of slaves but *the people of God* (25), i.e. a people with a divinely ordained destiny. Inevitably this meant choosing to share their hardships rather than, at the cost of apostasy from the God of the Hebrews, to enjoy the immediate but short-lived comfort and luxury of the Egyptian court. Note here the significance for the original readers of the word *sin* (cf. x. 26) and of Moses' choice to suffer rather than commit it. So having regard to the ultimate reward it would bring at God's hand he reckoned that to suffer reproach in such a cause would be a greater personal enrichment than all the Egyptians' wealth so obviously within his grasp. Such reproach is *the reproach of Christ* (26; cf. xiii. 13) because it is the typical lot in the world primarily of the Lord's anointed or Messiah (Ps. lxxxix. 50, 51; Rom. xv. 3), but also and inevitably of all associated with Him as God's elect people (cf. 1 Pet. iv. 12–16). *Not fearing the wrath of the king* (27). Ex. ii. 14 seems to contradict this; but the two are not irreconcilable. For, although Moses felt natural alarm and the need for flight, his spiritual awareness of God and of His purposes both for the Israelites and for Moses' own life made him sure that Pharaoh's enmity would not be allowed to prevail. Also, while the words *he forsook Egypt* may refer to the flight to Midian, it is perhaps more likely that they refer to the exodus. Note that the two reasons why Moses chose as he did, and persisted in his choice, were his awareness of the unseen One and his confident expectation of future reward (cf. verse 1).

Moses' faith helped the whole people to respond to God's words of warning and promise (note RV mg. rendering). Inspired by his leadership, they believed beforehand in the certainty of an impending divine judgment upon the firstborn, and in the sufficient shelter from such judgment afforded by the one divinely appointed provision, *the sprinkling of blood*. It was thus in judgment and salvation that the Lord showed who were His (cf. Ex. viii. 22). *The Red sea* (29) presented a naturally impassable barrier. It was impossible first to conceive and then to avail themselves of a way through except *by faith*.

The attempt by the Egyptian forces simply to 'try it out', without any confidence of faith in God's control, resulted only in their being overwhelmed (see RV).

The manner of Jericho's capture is another striking example of that obedience and endurance of faith, to the practice of which the writer wished to exhort his readers (30). The Israelites acted throughout in confidence in the unseen, and they held on till God's time was fulfilled (*seven days*) in the sure expectation of His certain action; nor were they disappointed. *Rahab* (31) acted as she did because she recognized the power of the God of Israel (i.e. things unseen) and the certain coming victory of His people (i.e. things future). See Jos. ii. 8–13. Her response is significant because as a woman, a Gentile and an open sinner she joined the company of those who were saved by faith. By contrast the other inhabitants of Jericho are described as 'disobedient' (RV), i.e. actively unbelieving.

Forced to summarize (32) the writer now limits himself to a selection of typical names and a list of characteristic and outstanding achievements. Among the latter there seem to be obvious references to Daniel (viz. *stopped the mouths of lions*; cf. Dn. vi. 22, 23) and to the three who were cast into the fiery furnace (viz. *quenched the violence of fire*; cf. Dn. iii. 25–28). But while many deeds which fit the other phrases used can be found in the Old Testament, it seems possible that this and the subsequent survey (35–38) also include some intended references to the doings of faithful Jews in the centuries between the Testaments, particularly in Maccabean times. The supreme achievement of faith is victory over death in resurrection. Some experienced this reward in this life; their dead were restored to them (see 1 Ki. xvii. 17–24; 2 Ki. iv. 17–37). (Note that in Scripture the recorded raisings from the dead are mostly for women; cf. Lk. vii. 11–17; Jn. xi. 1–46.) Others had the faith to hold on in unconquered but outwardly unrewarded endurance, through imprisonment and torture, and as fugitives and exiles. They accepted no earthly deliverance because it would have been enjoyed only at the price of denying their faith. Their reward lies in a *better* (i.e. a heavenly) *resurrection* in the life beyond (35). *Of whom the world was not worthy* (38). This is the actual but paradoxical truth. The world of their day treated them as not worthy to live in it; actually the world was not worthy of such men. It is for such that God has prepared a city (16). The goal towards which all these heroes of faith were moving in confident hope was one which they never reached (39). For God in His providence (40) has reserved *for us* (i.e. Christian believers) the crowning blessing and has ordained that they should not enjoy the consummation until we had been brought in to share it. Note the implication that the men of faith of Old Testament and New Testament times alike are all called to belong to the one company of God's purpose (cf. xii. 22–24).

XVI. PERSONAL APPLICATION: A CALL TO SERVE GOD ACCEPTABLY. xii. 1-29

This exhortation is based first on the supreme example and complete sufficiency of Jesus Himself as the author and perfecter of faith (verses 1-3); secondly, on the positive purpose and profit of trials under the providence of a loving heavenly Father (verses 4-11); thirdly, on the dangers of the greater (and even fatal) failure to which the slack and careless expose themselves (verses 12-17); fourthly, on the amazing privileges of grace to be enjoyed under the new covenant compared with the experiences of those who first participated in the old covenant (verses 18-24); and finally on the impending and inescapable consummation of God's dealings with men (verses 25-29).

a. The supreme example of Jesus Christ (xii. 1-3)

Having surveyed the achievements of the past heroes of faith, the writer confronts his readers with the inspiration and challenge of their example (1); let them face their contest with similar concentration and endurance. Above all, he exhorts them to find encouragement to face reproach and persecution by deliberately filling their minds with thoughts of Jesus and His triumphant achievement (2, 3). Let them fortify themselves against despondency and collapse by recalling what He endured and by recognizing that, in the face of the extreme shame and suffering of crucifixion, He had regard for the joy of the heavenly reward which He now permanently enjoys as One who is enthroned at God's right hand. Also, the manner and success of His achievement not only make possible our pursuit of the same pathway of faith, but also guarantee that He will enable us to complete what He enables us to begin. In this way, therefore, He is both the initiator (*author*) and consummator (*finisher*) of our faith. Cf. ii. 10 (where 'captain' is the same word in the Greek as 'author' here), v. 8, 9, vii. 25.

A cloud of witnesses (1). While the idea of an encompassing crowd of spectators may be included the primary reference is to their testimony. They are God's witnesses to us, who encourage us by their example. *Sin* (1, 4), in the mind of this writer, seems often to be an act of apostasy. Here the temptation is to give up the race altogether, one which is constantly put in their way, and so needing decisive rejection and unflinching resistance (cf. iii. 12-14, x. 26, 38, xi. 25). *Patience* (1); i.e. endurance. Note the recurrence of 'endure' (verses 2, 3, 7). *Jesus* (2). Note the significance of the unqualified human name (cf. ii. 9, vi. 20, vii. 22, xii. 24, xiii. 12); He is One who has Himself sustained the conflict. The *contradiction* (RV 'gainsaying') *of sinners* (3) means nothing less than the rejection of His claims in defiant rebellion. Cf. 'speaketh against' Cæsar (Jn. xix. 12).

b. The purpose of suffering (xii. 4-11)

They need to remember, he says, that their sufferings are so far light compared with those of Jesus; faithfulness has not yet cost any of them his life (4). What is more, they have forgotten the teaching of Scripture which makes plain that, as a loving Father, God uses the trials, which men have to endure in their earthly experience, for their spiritual discipline and education as His children (5). The very experience of such trials is, therefore, practical proof that God is dealing with them as His children (6, 7); it is those who are without such experiences who may well question their status in God's family (8). Admittedly such experiences are at the time unpleasant. It is important, therefore, to recognize the unseen hand that controls them, and to submit in reverence to a Father's pleasure, as children often do in their way to their earthly parents (9). It is equally important to recognize God's purpose in these trials, and the consequent profit that, in the end, they will unquestionably gain from them. This divinely intended fruit is nothing less than the increase in the life of practical righteousness and godliness (10). Such results ensue in the experience only of those who in responsive and persistent faith are prepared to submit to the unseen God, and actively to co-operate in letting the discipline do its work in the hope of worthwhile benefit.

The chastening (5ff.); the Greek word *paideia* means 'education', the training of a child, with particular reference here (as in Pr. iii. 11, 12) to discipline and reproof. In verse 7 note the RV reading, 'It is for chastening that ye endure.' This follows a Greek text different by only one letter from that on which the AV is based. It is preferable in sense, indicating why God allows trials to befall men and makes men endure them. *The Father of spirits* (9); a reference to God as the Creator of the human spirit; contrast *fathers of our flesh*. The verse implies that beings thus created can know true life only by submission to God's control. *For a few days* (10). Discipline by human parents has its limits. It is administered only during childhood; it depends upon men's uncertain judgment or mood. Divine discipline is infinitely superior; it is always imposed in men's interest and aims to make them sharers in the very holiness of God Himself.

c. The danger of failure (xii. 12-17)

They ought, therefore, to throw off despondency and face life as Christians with courage and confidence (12). For if they do not thus help one another to go forward the imminent danger is that some who are halting in their response will completely abandon the way of faith (13). On the other hand, let them seek in their fellowship to promote true holiness as well as peace with one another (14). Let them all be on the watch lest any one of their number should not only himself turn aside from God's way of salvation by grace, but also be allowed in their midst to become a perverting influence injuring the whole community (15). For this kind of failure needs to be recognized as nothing less than spiritual profanity and apostasy. It means acting like

Esau and vilely giving up one's God-given inheritance for some trifling material gain (16). Still worse, Esau's history shows that, once a God-given inheritance has been thus deliberately rejected, there can be no further opportunity of regaining it. A man who acts in such a way stands permanently condemned (17).

The full significance of verses 12 and 13 is best appreciated by comparing Is. xxv. 3; Pr. iv. 25-27; 1 Ki. xviii. 21. The whole community is exhorted to advance, to walk in an even, or straightforward, path and to avoid inconsistencies in order to help the halting to make headway (cf. Rom. xv. 1, 2). The *lame* (13) were possibly those halting between Christianity and Judaism. The danger was lest they should abandon faith in Christ, an action described in verse 15 (see RV mg.) as 'falling back from the grace of God'. *Looking diligently lest any man* (15). The Greek verb here means 'exercising oversight' or acting as 'bishops'. But the reference is to the whole community, not to special ministers. In the Christian congregation the many should care for and deal with the one. Cf. iii. 12, 13, iv. 1 (RV); Gal. vi. 1, 2. *Lest any root of bitterness . . . trouble you* (15). Cf. Dt. xxix. 18, where similar phraseology is used to describe the man who turns from the Lord to serve other gods, i.e. the apostate. Note also that such a person can bring defilement on the whole congregation. Cf. the story of Achan; see Jos. vi. 18, vii. 25. Esau's folly (16, 17) ended in despair (cf. Judas); it was impossible to alter what he had done. He had made the decisive choice which settled his destiny. Also his profanity, or lack of reverence for the things of God, was such that he was incapable of true repentance. He wept for what he had lost (the blessing), not for the sin he had committed.

d. The privileges of the old and new covenants contrasted (xii. 18-24)

As Christians they have entered under the new covenant into the enjoyment of things very different from those experienced under the old covenant by those who came out of Egypt. Those things were earthly, visible, terrifying and forbidding; these are heavenly, unseen, all-glorious and all-gracious. In the wilderness the Israelites stood in the presence of a tangible mountain and actual burning fire. The place was overshadowed by clouds and intense darkness and the violence of storm (18). They heard a trumpet sound and a voice speaking words (19). The whole experience was so terrifying that the people asked that it might cease (Ex. xx. 18, 19). Since even an animal, venturing too near, had to be stoned for sacrilege, they feared for their lives (20; see Ex. xix. 12, 13; Dt. v. 25). Even Moses himself was overwhelmed with fright (21). How different is the experience of drawing nigh to God in which, as Christians, they are called to share! They come to the unseen heavenly realities, which correspond to and actually fulfil the mere earthly types. They come to the true mountain and city of God, where God actually dwells; to hosts of angels in festal array (22); to the church of the privileged with the heavenly inheritance; to the one all-sovereign God as their Vindicator; to the spirits of the righteous (i.e. either Old Testament saints or all the faithful departed), whose bliss is consummated (23); to Jesus the Mediator of this recently established (Gk. *nea*, not *kainē*, as is usual) covenant; and to the blood of sprinkling which speaks of remission of sins in contrast to Abel's blood which cried out for vengeance (Gn. iv. 10), and so (in contrast to the voice at Sinai) offering them welcome and assured peace (24).

In the Greek none of the terms used in the two descriptive lists given in these verses is preceded by the definite article. The writer is simply describing general distinctive characteristics of the two covenants. The word *mount* (18) does not occur in the best Greek MSS; see RV and RV mg. The primary stress is on the whole character of the revelation at Sinai as something tangible (cf. 1 Jn. i. 1), rather than on its particular locality on a mountain. On the other hand, since there is an obvious opening contrast between Mount Sinai and Mount Sion, the insertion of 'mount' is appropriate and not misleading. *To an innumerable company of angels* (22); for different possible translations see RV and RV mg. The description 'tens of thousands' or 'myriads' (Greek) is commonly used of angels (cf. Dt. xxxiii. 2; Dn. vii. 10). *General assembly* (23; Gk. *panēgyris*) means a 'festal gathering' and describes the angels; it is in contrast to their terrifying manifestation on Sinai. *Firstborn* (23) expresses the idea of privilege and heirship, blessings such as those which Esau despised (16). In Greek the word is in the plural, i.e. 'firstborns'; it describes all who belong to the Church. They are the company who have peculiar rights in the heavenly Jerusalem and whose names are, therefore, enrolled in the register of its citizens (cf. Lk. x. 20; Rev. xxi. 27). Note that it is to this *church*, the one true Church in heaven, that these Hebrew Christians are come. Jesus' crowning and comprehensive work (24), as our great High Priest enthroned in heaven, is to mediate to all who come to Him all the promised blessings of the covenant now established and sealed for ever by His shed and sprinkled blood. Cf. vii. 20-22, viii. 6, xiii. 20, 21.

e. All must have dealings with God (xii. 25-29)

Let them take heed, therefore, not to seek (like those at Sinai) to withdraw from listening to Him who speaks. (Note the present tense; it is an abiding ever-present revelation. Also, from the previous verse, we know that He now speaks in mercy through the sprinkled blood.) For it is impossible to escape having dealings with Him. Those who tried to withdraw from the earthly manifestation at Sinai found that His voice literally shook the earth. Christians, by contrast, are confronted by One who speaks to them in the heavenly realms disclosing the final realities. But note that, in whatever way He speaks, it is the same God who speaks throughout (26; cf. i. 1, 2). Let them realize that it is much more impossible now to turn aside and escape having dealings with Him. For, as He has declared in prophecy (see Hg. ii. 6), God will in Christ bring His dealings with the universe to a head in a single decisive act of judgment by finally shaking both heaven and earth. Cf. Mk. xiii. 31; and note that it is His words that abide, not the universe; see also 2 Pet. iii. 7. Then this transient, temporal order will pass, and the abiding eternal order will stand revealed. We Christians are destined to share in a kingdom or sovereignty belonging to this abiding eternal order (28; cf. Dn. ii. 44, vii. 18–27). *Let us have grace* (28); see RV mg. Sheer gratitude to God ought therefore to constrain us (or, following the AV, let us appropriate the grace so abundantly available) to serve God in ways well-pleasing in His sight. In the presence of such a God and in the face of such a prospect this will be with a real sense of unworthiness and awe (cf. 2 Pet. iii. 9–14). For the God whom we are thus privileged to call 'our God' is *a consuming fire* (29; cf. Dt. iv. 24) both of zeal for holiness and of zeal against sin. Only those who thus follow after holiness will survive His judgment, see the Lord, and reign eternally with Him. See also Appendix III, 'The Warning Passages', p. 1116.

XVII. VARIOUS ADDITIONAL EXHORTATIONS. xiii. 1–17

The writer now adds (quite in the manner of Paul, cf. Rom. xii. 4–13) a variety of brief statements containing pointed practical exhortations to worthy Christian living. He includes also a warning against prevalent misleading teaching, and issues an urgent challenge to his readers finally to abandon Judaism and the earthly Jerusalem, and to find in the unchanging Jesus Christ and in His one sacrifice outside the city gate both inevitable earthly reproach and abiding heavenly gain.

He knew that his readers had been active in the past in sympathy and kindness towards their fellow-Christians (see vi. 10, x. 33, 34). He urges, therefore, the importance of maintaining such practical love between fellow-members of the Christian brotherhood (1). This should be practised not only towards familiar local brethren but also towards *strangers* or visitors from elsewhere, a ministry sometimes rewarded by enriching surprises, e.g. in the experiences of Abraham and Lot (2; see Gn. xviii, xix). Let them be particularly mindful of any in prison or suffering physical illness or ill-treatment; for Christians ought to share each other's trials, and to recognize that in this life they are all equally liable to suffer physical affliction (3). Let them also recognize that (since God has ordained it) there is nothing dishonourable about the marriage relationship and that its physical intimacy, when

rightly practised, brings no defilement. But those who engage in improper sexual relationship, whether they are unmarried or married, will find that they have God Himself against them in judgment (4).

In relation to material things the right attitude (see RV mg.) is not covetousness but contentment, learning to make do rather than always wanting more. This attitude is possible because one never faces life alone. The Lord has promised each one His personal help. He will never leave any in the lurch (5). It is therefore possible to face life with cheerfulness, and openly to confess that, with the Lord at one's side, there is nothing to fear, and no one who can harm us (6). These two verses show how Old Testament Scriptures can be quoted, and how the believer may use their words to tell his soul what God has promised, as if the assurance were addressed to him personally and individually (see Dt. xxxi. 6; Jos. i. 5), and also to confess his confidence before God and men (see Ps. cxviii. 6).

Let them find inspiration to be steadfast in the faith by remembering their former Christian leaders, by whom they were instructed in the truth of God and the gospel. Fresh consideration of the lives they lived and of the way such lives ended will help them to copy their faith (7). For Jesus Christ, whom they trusted and followed, is the same today as He was then, and will continue the same for ever. He is the one all-sufficient guarantee of salvation, 'the author and finisher of our faith' (8; cf. xii. 2).

Let them beware, therefore, of the perverting influence of other very varied and strange doctrines which are in circulation, particularly the teaching that one cannot become properly established except by partaking of special, sacred or sacrificial food (9). Such teaching stands completely condemned. It is unspiritual in principle. The good way for the heart to be established is by God's own working in *grace*, not by man's physical eating of food. But also its professed value is denied by experience. Those who have devoted themselves to such things have gained from them no spiritual profit. Our Christian altar (to use the familiar language suggested by Old Testament figures; cf. x. 19–22) is not one of which the worshippers (i.e. those who serve the true tabernacle; cf. viii. 4, 5) have any right to eat (10). Even in the corresponding Levitical figure of the earthly tabernacle the bodies of those animals, whose blood was used to make atonement for sin by being brought into the inner shrine, were never eaten; they were burnt without the camp (11). That, therefore, is how Jesus, as our great High Priest, consummated the work of saving or sanctifying the people on whose behalf He was acting: He suffered outside the gate (12). This indicates in figure that those who would embrace the benefits of His work must not trust in eating sacrificial meat, nor cling to the earthly Jerusalem (13). Rather they must be prepared to come out from the camp of Israel after the flesh; to bear the reproach of associating themselves with One who in Jewish eyes was rightly rejected because He hung crucified under the curse of God; to find their all not in meats but in Him the living Lord of grace; to find their hope not in any city of the present earthly order which must pass away, but in the true city of the living God, which is a city of the coming heavenly order which will remain (14; cf. xii. 27). Henceforth Christian worship needs no earthly holy city, no special visible temple, no priestly caste. There are sacrifices to be offered, but we are to offer them in the heavenly tabernacle through Jesus as our one great High Priest (15). These sacrifices, too, are not sacrifices of beasts but continual offerings of praise and thanksgiving to God (15; cf. Ps. l. 14, 23; Ho. xiv. 2), together with ministries of practical kindness to men (16; cf. Ho. vi. 6).

Instead of allowing themselves, therefore, to be perverted by strange doctrines, let them with a ready confidence and compliance follow the teaching of their leaders (17). For the latter have a solemn responsibility to discharge on their behalf and an account to render. Their lead is, therefore, worthy of respect. Not to follow them now is to make the leaders' task on that great day of reckoning a painful rather than a joyful one. Also it results in loss for themselves.

Verses 9 and 10 raise questions of interpretation on which opinions differ radically. In contrast to the exposition given above some think the reference to eating meats (9) has to do with distinctions between clean and unclean foods (cf. Rom. xiv. 14–21; 1 Cor. viii. 4–13; Col. ii. 16; 1 Tim. iv. 3–5). But in such cases holiness would be promoted by proper abstinence from that which is unclean; here the idea seems rather to be of a misleading suggestion of some spiritual benefit to be gained by eating meat offered in sacrifice. The Christian *altar* (10) is generally recognized to be the cross. But, as the New Testament teaches that the sacrifice of Christ is something of which Christians spiritually partake (see Jn. vi. 53–56; 1 Cor. v. 7, 8, x. 16), many prefer the interpretation that what the priests of the Jewish tabernacle could not do all Christians can do, i.e. partake of their sin offering. Further, the details of the Levitical ritual (11) and of Christ's crucifixion (12) figuratively imply that it is impossible thus to partake of Christ without completely abandoning Judaism. *To communicate* (16; Gk. *koinōnia*, i.e. 'fellowship') describes the act of sharing with others material things. In Rom. xv. 26 the sense is rendered by 'contribution'; cf. 2 Cor. ix. 13.

XVIII. PERSONAL MESSAGES AND FINAL BENEDICTION. xiii. 18–25

For the first time the writer speaks of himself, and in the first person singular. His request for prayer and his profession of integrity (18) imply an awareness that his action and attitude may be misjudged. He is personally particularly eager for their prayer that he may be enabled to rejoin them as soon as possible (19). This seems clearly to imply that he had been in the past in some way closely connected with them. His benediction (20, 21) is remarkable for its significant details and its comprehensive sweep; again it is quite Pauline in character. His words focus their thoughts on the doings of God. For them as well as for him what God has done is the ground of assurance and hope. Therefore, what God may be counted upon to do for them is the substance of his prayer. God brought up Jesus from the dead ('up' seems here the force of the Greek prefix *ana* rather than *again*). He did this to Him not just personally as His Son, but as the Leader of His people (cf. ii. 10, xii. 2), i.e. as *that great shepherd of the sheep,* and as *our Lord.* He did it to Him in relation to, and in fulfilment of, the new and eternal covenant secured and ratified by His death or *blood.* His resurrection is, therefore, decisive proof that man is reconciled to God, or able to enter glory, and that God is now active to fulfil for His people all that is promised to them under the new covenant (cf. Zc. ix. 11). In other words, He will bring them up also, as He brought up Israel with Moses their shepherd out of the Red Sea (see Is. lxiii. 11). So the writer prays for his readers that through this Jesus, acknowledged as God's *Christ,* they may know God both personally and corporately as *the God of peace* and experience His working in their lives and fellowship, enabling them fully to co-operate in the doing of His will. *Make you perfect* (21); the Greek verb *katartizō* is very suggestive. It includes the ideas of harmonious combination (cf. x. 24, 25, xii. 13, 14), the supply of what is lacking (see 1 Thes. iii. 10), and the rectification of what is wrong or damaged (e.g. it is translated 'restore' in Gal. vi. 1 and 'mending' in Mk. i. 19).

The writer claims to have written briefly, i.e. considering the vastness of the themes dealt with, and so ventures to ask for their patient attention (22). He sends them news of Timothy's liberation (23); this provides yet another indication of possible close connection with the apostle Paul. His special greetings (24) to their leaders and to the whole Christian community suggests that the letter was actually sent to a limited group of ordinary Christians. The greetings from *they of Italy* indicate plainly that the writer was in the company of Italian Christians; but the wording is not sufficiently explicit to decide whether he was writing from or to a place in Italy, though either is possible. Finally (25), the simple and sufficient Christian 'farewell', indeed its guarantee, is found in the one word *grace* and in the assurance that it is fully available for all.

A. M. STIBBS.

APPENDIX I: THE NEW COVENANT

According to this Epistle God has for His people a destiny which is variously depicted. It is described as inheriting salvation (i. 14, RV, ii. 3), as lordship in the world to come (ii. 5–10), as participation in God's house and with His Christ (iii. 6, 14, RV mg.), as entering into the rest of God (iv. 1, 11), as going on unto perfection (vi. 1), as inheriting the promises (vi. 12, x. 36, xi. 13), as receiving the eternal inheritance (ix. 15), as gaining the soul (x. 39, RV mg.), as reaching the heavenly country and the divinely prepared city (xi. 10, 16, xii. 22, xiii. 14), as receiving the kingdom which cannot be shaken (xii. 28). This destiny is to be theirs simply because they are His people and He is (and is not ashamed to be called, xi. 16) their God.

In order first to establish, and then to preserve, this special relation between Himself and those whom He is pleased to call His people God has not only given His word of promise but has also solemnly pledged Himself in covenant under the recognized covenant seal of shed blood. It is into this covenanted relation to Himself that God calls men to enter; it is with this immediately in view that He redeems them. Henceforth, for those who respond, it is according to the promises thus covenanted that men have dealings with God, obligations towards Him, and an assured ground of confidence in Him.

Although there are two covenants of this kind there is in them an essential unity and continuity. The same ultimate end is contemplated in both. The second has been introduced only because the first was ineffectual, and was, indeed, never intended to be more than a provisional anticipation of better things to come. The second supersedes the first because it completely achieves what the first failed to accomplish. Because this achievement is eternal the second covenant is the final covenant. There is no hope of some further provision of God beyond it. One of the great purposes of the writer of this Epistle is to make this plain. Christianity not only supersedes Judaism; it is God's last word to men.

The first covenant failed for two reasons. On the one hand, the people brought under it did not fulfil its conditions; they continued not in God's covenant (viii. 7–9). On the other hand, its institutions did not avail to give men true release from sin and consequent access to God's presence (x. 1–4). The very order and ritual of its tabernacle was a witness that the way into the holy place was not yet made manifest (ix. 8); its tabernacle was only a figure for the time then present (ix. 9). As a covenant it was weak and profitless (vii. 18). So, even while it obtained as the divinely ordained order, the same Scriptures which acknowledged its divine origin also prophetically anticipated the provision of something better. The very mention of a 'new' covenant was itself witness that the first covenant was to be disannulled, and was shortly to pass away (vii. 11–19, viii. 1–13, x. 5–9).

The new covenant is 'a better covenant', and one 'enacted upon better promises' (viii. 6, RV). It is effective in ways in which the first covenant was not because it provides a real redemption of transgressions (ix. 15), or putting away of sin (x. 15–18), and so makes possible full and free access to God's presence (x. 19–22). Also it provides an all-competent High Priest who, because of His 'once-for-all' finished sacrifice and His 'endless' (or 'indissoluble', RV mg.) life (vii. 15, 16, RV), has not only gained entrance for Himself and those He represents into God's presence, but sits for ever enthroned by God in the place of all power (i. 13), able to complete to its full perfection the salvation of all those who make Him their Mediator between God and themselves (vii. 25). What God has done for Him in raising Him from the dead and bidding Him sit at His own right hand in sure hope of complete triumph (x. 12, 13), is pledge and proof of the final victory of His people. For it was done by God to Him as 'our Lord Jesus, that great shepherd of the sheep'; and it was done 'through the blood of the everlasting covenant' (xiii. 20). There is, therefore, through this covenant, sealed by Christ's death, full and final remission of sins and completely assured perfection for all Christ's people (x. 8–18). There is no need for, and indeed no possibility of, failure. For under this covenant God puts His law in His people's hearts (viii. 10); and Himself works to make them perfect in every good thing to do His will (xiii. 20, 21).

The one all-sufficient guarantee of this new covenant is to be found in the person and work of its mediator and surety (vii. 21, 22, viii. 6, ix. 14, 15). Its benefits are administered by One who is enthroned on high, and who never dies; 'Jesus Christ the same yesterday, and to day, and for ever' (xiii. 8). It is, therefore, the outstanding theme or 'chief point' of this Epistle to declare that as Christians under the new covenant 'we have such an High Priest, who is set on the right hand of the throne of the Majesty in the heavens' (viii. 1).

A. M. STIBBS.

APPENDIX II: THE PRIESTHOOD OF CHRIST

In this Epistle the writer connects with Christ the ideas of 'truth' and 'perfection'. What elsewhere is only figuratively hinted at, or but partially realized, is in Christ found in actuality and fulness. Henceforth, therefore, we must not limit our Christian idea of priesthood to what we learn from the Levitical priesthood. Although the latter did foreshadow or figuratively indicate many of the fundamental essentials of all true priesthood, there are other complementary and distinctive characteristics of true priesthood which, in as far as they were foreshadowed at all in the Old Testament revelation, were foreshadowed not by Aaron but by Melchisedec. These distinctive characteristics, which belong of necessity to the perfection of Christ's priesthood, are to be appreciated over against the Levitical priesthood in terms more of contrast than of comparison.

The Levitical High Priests were weak men, sinful and mortal, needing first to offer sacrifices for their own sins, and unable to continue in office because they were inevitably removed by death (vii. 23, 27, 28). They served in an earthly shrine, a mere figure of the true (viii, 4, 5, ix. 1, 9, 23, 24). Their sacrifices were sacrifices of animals, which could never remove sin (x. 1–4); and so, under the old order, the dividing veil which shut men out from the holy of holies was never rent and done away (ix. 7, 8). The sacrifices of the day of atonement gave one man only temporary, symbolic access once a year to the inmost shrine of the divine presence; they did not give to the whole people full and abiding access to God. Also, these sacrifices had to be incessantly repeated (x. 11), and served only as a sobering reminder that something still needed to be done fully and finally to put away sin (x. 1–3). 'The way into the holiest of all was not yet made manifest' (ix. 8).

Our Christian High Priest is 'Jesus the Son of God' (iv. 14). His priesthood is of a different order because of the difference in the Person of the Priest. He is, first of all, very God of very God (i. 3), able 'through eternal Spirit' (ix. 14) to act as deity and to do things completely beyond the power of weak men. He is, on the other hand, truly Man, One who not only genuinely partook of human nature, but who also, through the experience of earthly trial and suffering, has reached a final perfection in His manhood, which has qualified Him to be for His fellow-men the author of an eternal salvation (ii. 9, 10, 14–18, iv. 15, v. 7–9). He could do what no Levitical High Priest was able to attempt. Because, as Man, He was Himself without sin, He did not need to offer sacrifice for His own sin. What is more, He was in a position to offer His own spotless human life as the sin offering for others, that is, for sinful men. Being, as God, undying Spirit, and acting in the power of indissoluble life (vii. 16, RV mg.), He was able in His one Person and two natures to act both as Priest and Victim, and in the experience of the death of His human nature deliberately to offer Himself to God (ix. 14), and to claim, as One still alive in death, entrance thereby as men's High Priest into the actual presence of God. Symbolically, as He thus offered Himself in His physical human death upon the cross (x. 10), the veil was rent (see Mk. xv. 37, 38; cf. x. 19, 20). Actually, as One acting in the true heavenly sanctuary (viii. 2, ix. 11, 12, 24) and not in the figurative tabernacle (or temple) on earth (viii. 4, 5), He thereby 'through his own blood' (ix. 12, RV), or by the act of laying down His physical human life (cf. again x. 19, 20), entered decisively and once for all into the true holy of holies, there to show Himself 'before the face of God' (ix. 24, RV) on our behalf. When He did this He was immediately accepted, hailed as victor and invited to occupy the throne at God's right hand. God further sealed His acceptance of His work as a work on behalf of sinful men by raising Him up in His humanity from the dead (xiii. 20). It is, however, probably significant that Christ's resurrection is mentioned only once in this Epistle, and that right at the end. This is because, in the earlier consideration of His offering of Himself, He is thought of, not as rising on the third day and ascending after another forty days, but as acting in the heavenly tabernacle and immediately entering the presence of God.

The enthronement in heaven of the One who entered through His own death as our High Priest is the divine proof and pledge that He has by this one act of sacrifice obtained eternal redemption for us (i. 3, x. 12, 13, xii. 2). Also, He was then declared by God, not only by His word, but by His solemn oath, to be a Priest for ever after the order of Melchisedec (v. 9, 10, vi. 19, 20, vii. 21, 22), which means, in other words, that His priesthood is royal in power because of His finished sacrificial work, and also unceasing in duration because of His divine Person. For He was seated at once upon the throne, and there remains, placed by God in the position of supreme power, able to give gifts to men (iv. 14–16), and assured by God of final victory over all His foes (i. 13).

Through such achievement as High Priest, far surpassing anything accomplished by the old order of Levitical priests, He is able to engage in a more excellent ministry as the mediator of the new covenant (viii. 6), under which sinful men who come to Him, or to God through Him (vii. 20–25), are assured in the possession of forgiveness of sins, intimate personal knowledge of God, and the transforming inner quickening of the indwelling Spirit (viii. 10–12). His ability thus to proclaim absolution and to assure His people that their sins are actually forgiven and forgotten by God is itself proof that no further offering for sin is necessary (x. 14–18). As one exalted above the heaven our Christian High Priest has no need to make fresh or further offering of Himself, or of His blood or earthly sacrifice, to God (vii. 26–28). But, as One who never dies, He is always at God's right hand to intervene on men's behalf, to speak for them to the Father (or against the adversary who would condemn them, Rom. viii. 33, 34) whenever they come to the throne of God, and thus to secure the full completion of their salvation (vii. 25). All who come can also be sure of understanding sympathy and appropriate help because He is thoroughly qualified to discharge such compassionate ministry by His own earthly experiences of suffering and trial (ii. 17, 18, iv. 15, 16, v. 2, 7, 8).

Those, therefore, who come to Him as their Mediator are assured by the royal and eternal order of His priesthood of participating in a salvation which is (like His Person and work as Priest) perfect, final and eternal. For His one sacrifice gives to all who trust Him eternal fitness for unhindered approach to God's presence (ix. 13, 14, x. 10, 14); and the final completion of the work of salvation which He has begun in them is assured by the blood of the eternal covenant, by God's resurrection of our Lord Jesus from the dead (xiii. 20, 21), and by His own undying presence as our advocate at God's right hand (vii. 25).

A. M. STIBBS.

APPENDIX III: THE WARNING PASSAGES

See ii. 1-4, iii. 7—iv. 1, vi. 4-8, x. 26-31, 38, 39, xii. 25-29. As Jews these Hebrew Christians had been used to the ideas of a succession of prophets and a continuous repetition of sacrifices for sin. They needed to be made aware of the once-for-all and final character of the revelation of God and the reconciliation to God given to men in Christ. Because the incarnate Son is God's last word to men, and because there is offered to men in Him amazing salvation by grace, those who pass Him by cannot expect to escape the coming judgment of God. No further word of saving intervention from God is to be expected. Also, since Christ's sacrifice of Himself was a decisive, 'once-for-all' achievement, there is no more offering for sin (x. 18) either by Christ in heaven or by men on earth. Neither can there be repetition of this one sacrifice (ix. 25-28), nor will there be the introduction by God of any other sacrifice (x. 26). This one sacrifice for sin, wrought once for all, is all-sufficient for ever for all God's people (x. 10-14).

Enjoyment by men of the benefit of Christ's sacrifice is similarly 'once for all' (vi. 4); it is decisive, final and eternal. Therefore (to follow one interpretation of these passages) any who have been consciously confronted by this offer of grace, and have personally shared in the proofs of its origin, and then deliberately reject the gospel of Jesus as the Christ (without of course ever truly believing and becoming regenerate) cannot be similarly brought a second time to the opportunity of repentance and faith. Or, alternatively (to follow another interpretation), those who have experienced all the characteristic blessings of God's saving grace through Christ's atoning sacrifice, and by the Spirit's work in their hearts, and have then turned aside from it all and tried to settle down to live as if such things were not true and had never happened, cannot be brought back a second time to the initial and decisive Christian response of repentance and faith. The meaning of vi. 6 may be that even to suggest that Christ virtually needs crucifying again to bring such an apostate or backslider for the second time to the place of decisive repentance and quickening by the Spirit is to put Christ and the efficacy of His one sacrifice to an open shame. The whole thing is unthinkable. Such renewal of enlightenment and repentance a second time is, therefore, absolutely impossible, just as, when many Israelites departed from God in unbelief in the wilderness, it was impossible to take them through the Passover and Red Sea deliverances a second time in order to awaken or renew their faith. For such apostates or unbelievers there was, and still is, no prospect but judgment.

The kind of failure here in view (to follow one interpretation) is nothing less than a conscious, deliberate and persistent abandonment of the Christian way of salvation, an abandonment which involves nothing less than apostasy from the living God, rejection of the word and confirming witness of God, Father, Son and Holy Ghost, treating the Son of God, as the Jews had done in Jerusalem, as One who ought to be disowned and crucified, and thus brought publicly under the curse of heaven, denying the covenant significance before God of His shed blood, and doing open insult to the Spirit who in grace pleads with men to acknowledge Jesus as Lord. Such actions are surely what our Lord called the sin of blasphemy against the Holy Ghost, which is eternal sin and never has forgiveness (Mk. iii. 28, 29). Yet it was to nothing less than a sin of this character that these Hebrew Christians were exposed, if they were being tempted to go back to where they were before in Judaism (although actually to do this was impossible), and in doing so publicly to repudiate Jesus as the Messiah and the Son of God.

It may be, however (to follow an alternative interpretation), that the writer is concerned to make plain to his unquestionably Christian readers that their present tendency to become slack, and to settle down half-way in the imagined possession of what their faith in Christ has already made theirs, is a fatal self-deception. The reason is that for those who have thus made a beginning in the way of Christian discipleship the only possible alternatives are either to go on to the full possession of faith's inheritance, or to draw back from this forward movement of God in their lives and to come under His inevitable judgment, like the Israelites who became the objects of God's wrath and were overthrown in the wilderness because they were not prepared by faith in God to go forward into the Promised Land. In that case the kind of failure here in view is that of those who, having been taken by grace into covenant relation with God, completely fail to regard its amazing privileges and overwhelming obligations with due seriousness. If those, already redeemed from Egypt, who failed to obey God's word under the first Sinaitic covenant, were removed in judgment from the company of God's people, may not those who fail to respond to the demands of the new covenant in Christ rightly expect even more severe and drastic treatment? For while, in the Christian life, God's discipline, however painful, is profitable and to be welcomed as a proof that He is dealing with us as His sons for our progress in holiness, can anything be more terrible in the life of one who is already by grace a child of God than that, in relation to his subsequent earthly conduct, God should have to deal with him in fiery and even fatal judgment?

The theological questions here involved are whether those who may thus apostatize or come under judgment ever were regenerate, and whether any man once saved can finally be lost. In answer to both questions some say emphatically, 'No'. They would compare the types mentioned in Mt. vii. 22, 23, xii. 22–32. They would argue that the very apostasy of these individuals is proof that they were never regenerate. Others say that those described in vi. 4, 5 must be regenerate; for no more decisive description of the regenerate could be given. Some would then argue that the consequent judgment on their complete degeneracy and unfruitfulness does not necessarily involve them in the loss of eternal salvation. They are, for instance, only 'nigh unto cursing' (vi. 8). Cf. 1 Cor. iii. 15, v. 5. Others, again, suppose that this suggestion that the regenerate can thus become apostate, and be finally lost, is actually only hypothetical and theoretical. Even on the human side it is much more unlikely than physical suicide, and so only to be thought of as a remote possibility; and actually on the divine side it can by grace never happen. See Jn. x. 28.

Yet Christians and all who share in the knowledge of the truth will do well to treat such solemn warnings with due seriousness. Let us remember that John Bunyan wrote, 'Then I saw there was a way to hell even from the gates of heaven, as well as from the City of Destruction.' Let us remember, also, that Paul the apostle feared lest by any means after he had preached to others, and been used to bring them to Christ, he himself should be 'rejected' (1 Cor. ix. 27, RV; the Greek is lit. 'disapproved' which AV renders 'a castaway'). Cf. 2 Pet. ii. 20, 21.

A. M. STIBBS.

THE GENERAL EPISTLE OF JAMES

INTRODUCTION

I. AUTHORSHIP

There are three men with this name mentioned in the New Testament—James, the son of Zebedee; James, the son of Alphaeus; and James, the brother of Jesus. Although the Scriptures do not make the matter certain, most scholars agree in identifying the author of this Epistle with James, the brother of our Lord. James, the son of Zebedee and brother of John, was slain by Herod (Acts xii. 2). Thereafter Peter was thrown into prison and, having been miraculously released, asked that news be sent to James and to the brethren (Acts xii. 17). James, the son of Alphaeus, is mentioned only in the lists of apostles and is possibly referred to in Mk. xv. 40. It is scarcely to be expected that one occupying so obscure a place in the Gospel narratives would be the author of this Epistle which so evidently comes from the pen of a man of outstanding, robust personality, who clearly occupied a position of authority in the Church.

There remains James, the brother of our Lord, and the references to him in the New Testament show him as a man of great influence and distinction, especially among the Jewish Christians. Our Lord appeared to James after His resurrection (1 Cor. xv. 7) and, although it is not so stated, it seems safe to assume that this refers to James, the brother of our Lord. In the light of Mt. xiii. 55 and Jn. vii. 5 we may gather that either the closing events in the life of our Lord, or His death, or this post-resurrection appearance was the means of his conversion. He is numbered among the company in Jerusalem waiting and praying for the 'promise of the Father' (Acts i. 14). Three years after his conversion Paul went up to Jerusalem with Peter and saw none of the apostles 'save James the Lord's brother' (Gal. i. 19). In the conference held at Jerusalem on the question of the admission of Gentiles to the Church, James was the presiding elder. After Peter, Paul and Barnabas had spoken he summed up the whole discussion.

His decision was adopted by the whole assembly and formulated in a letter which has some very striking parallels in its phraseology to this Epistle (Acts xv. 6–29). On the occasion of another visit to Jerusalem Paul received the right hand of fellowship from James, Cephas and John (Gal. ii. 9); and when he came up to Jerusalem for the last time he reported his work to James and the elders present with him (Acts xxi. 18ff.).

James, therefore, stood in a position of great, if not supreme, authority in the mother church at Jerusalem, presiding over the assemblies and speaking the final and authoritative word. The authoritative tone of this Epistle comports well with the position of primacy ascribed to James.

II. DATE AND PURPOSE

Neither internal nor external evidence affords much help in determining the date of the Epistle with accuracy. The contents certainly seem to indicate a primitive form of Christian organization in the Church. Mayor and other authorities argue for a very early date (about A.D. 45) on the basis of omission from the contents of any reference to the Jerusalem Council and of what was decided there. On the other hand, Wordsworth, Farrar and Ewald argue for a later date (about A.D. 62) on the ground that the Epistle was written by James shortly before his martyrdom to correct certain misinterpretations of Paul's doctrine of justification by faith. The early date, on the whole, seems to be preferable. The purpose of the Epistle is to demonstrate that faith in the Lord Jesus Christ must be applied to all the experiences and relationships of Christian disciples. It is faith in action with which James is concerned; hence his marked emphasis on the place of works in the Christian life. It would seem from the teaching of the Epistle that the Christian Jews to whom he is writing were in danger of regarding this practical outworking of faith as unimportant.

OUTLINE OF CONTENTS

I. INTRODUCTION. i. 1

II. FAITH AND TRIAL. i. 2–27

III. FAITH AND SOCIETY. ii. 1–13

IV. FAITH AND WORKS. ii. 14–26

V. FAITH AND THE CONTROL OF THE TONGUE. iii. 1–12

VI. FAITH AND WISDOM. iii. 13–18

VII. FAITH AND FIGHTINGS. iv. 1–17

VIII. CORRUPTED RICHES. v. 1–6

IX. PATIENCE ENJOINED. v. 7–12

X. FAITH AND PRAYER. v. 13–20

COMMENTARY

I. INTRODUCTION. i. 1

James. For his identity see *Introduction. Servant;* i.e. 'bondslave'. The apostles seem to have delighted to describe themselves thus. Cf. Rom. i. 1; 2 Pet. i. 1; Rev. i. 1. *To the twelve tribes;* not to the Jews as a race but to Christian Jews who, having been brought face to face with the great principle of faith, were in need of practical instruction in the art of Christian living. By the use of the word *twelve* James is not necessarily distinguishing each tribe separately. It is a collective term to denote all those of Jewish descent. *Scattered abroad;* lit. 'in the dispersion'. The letter is directed specially to those living among Gentiles outside the borders of Palestine.

II. FAITH AND TRIAL. i. 2–27

a. The Christian attitude to suffering (i. 2–4)

Temptations (Gk. *peirasmos*) signifies trials with a beneficial purpose and effect, or trials or temptations divinely permitted or sent. In some contexts, however (e.g. Lk. iv. 13), it is used of temptation by the devil. See also Jas. i. 13–15, where the verb form *peirazō* is used in the same sense. The readers were undergoing trials and testings as believing Jews who had accepted the Lord Jesus Christ as Messiah, and James exhorts them not to be grieved over their trials but contrariwise to count suffering and persecution a joy. They were proof of their sonship (Heb. xii. 6; Ps. xciv. 12) and of the reality of their faith. These temptations were *divers* (Gk. *poikilos*), i.e. 'variegated' or 'many-coloured'. The word refers to the variety of the trials rather than to their number. *The trying* (RV 'proof', lit. 'the process of testing') *of your faith worketh patience* (3). The testing may refer to the pressure of circumstances issuing from persecution. James would have these early Christians understand that such testing is an opportunity for proving their mettle and as a discipline in courage and endurance. On that account they should even welcome it (cf. Rom. v. 3). *Patience* (3, 4); i.e. 'endurance', which enables a man to resist the pressure of external circumstances. RSV renders 'steadfastness'. This grace of endurance must be given full scope till it has accomplished its work in making us *perfect and entire, wanting nothing* (4). *Perfect* has nothing to do with the perfection of sinlessness but means rather 'mature' or 'full-grown'. The Greek is *teleios*, which signifies having reached its end, complete.

When used of persons it refers primarily to physical development; then, with ethical import, to full growth or maturity. *Entire* (Gk. *holoklēros*) signifies whole, or complete in every part, or 'lacking in nothing' as James himself puts it (cf. 1 Thes. v. 23).

It has been suggested that these expressions are borrowed from the sacrifices under the law. A victim was perfect which was perfectly sound, having no disease; it was entire if it had all its members, having nothing deficient. The Christian believer is to be to the Lord what He required His sacrifices to be. He is to be wholly sanctified to the Lord of hosts.

b. The need for wisdom (i. 5–8)

Trials can be very perplexing and much wisdom is needed if we are to bear them triumphantly or if, as Paul did, we are to glory in tribulation. Wisdom signifies, in general, knowledge of the best end and of the best means of attaining it. James has in mind primarily the effective understanding of the believer's way and walk. Wisdom from above is needed to point the way and direct the course of action. Such wisdom is obtained by an utter dependence on God, expressed in prayer. Therefore, if any be deficient in wisdom *let him ask* it from God who is infinite in wisdom and gives *liberally, and upbraideth not* (5). He does not rebuke us for our lack of wisdom but delights to give according to our need and out of His boundless store. Note that the promise is accompanied by the assurance, *and it shall be given him. Liberally* (Gk. *haplōs*); i.e. simply, unconditionally and generously, with a free hand. *But let him ask in faith, nothing wavering* (6). Doubt, hesitancy about God, dependence on something or someone other than God are in reality unbelief. There must be no wavering, nor debating, nor indecision in the asking; and there must be no doublemindedness, wanting partly our own way and partly God's way. *Like a wave of the sea* . . . (6); i.e. in a state of continual agitation, rising and falling between trust in God and unbelief; veering from one course to another; showing instability and lack of divine control. Such instability is the mark of *a double minded man* (8); Gk. *dipsychos*, lit. 'two-souled', a man of divided affections and unsubdued will, wishing to secure both worlds. Such a man must not dream of receiving answers to prayers. One condition of having prayers answered is single-mindedness.

c. True riches (i. 9-12)

The poor man in an obscure position who receives the gospel is raised to high rank by his faith and therein he may find a further incentive to cheerful endurance (9). On the other hand, the rich man who has become a Christian and has learned life's true values becomes a special object of persecution and trials of various sorts and has much to lose thereby (10). He is brought to the *low degree* (9) of his poorer brethren and is required to accept what, from the worldly point of view, is a position of humiliation, membership in a poverty-stricken brotherhood. Such should rejoice and accept it as from the hand of Him who is unerring Wisdom, because he has learned to see riches in their true perspective. Worldly wealth is transitory, as short-lived as the patches of grass or the flowers of the field under the sirocco, or scorching wind, and the blazing sun which burn them up and cause their beauty of form and colour (*grace of the fashion of it*) to perish. So, also, does the rich man *fade away in his ways* (RV 'goings'), i.e. in the midst of his worldly pursuits. The converted rich brother can rejoice that he has been delivered from such a fate and has an inheritance and a *crown of life* (12) that cannot fade away. His humiliation in the eyes of the world, therefore, is not really humiliation, but a cause for deep and lasting joy. The man, whether of high degree or low degree, who endures trial and does not break down under it is truly blessed, for when he has been *tried* (RV 'approved'), *he shall receive the crown of life* (12). After probation comes reward. When the temptation is over, if the believer has stood the test and has remained steadfast to the end, he receives the victor's crown, the crown of life. This gift must not be confused with that eternal life which is the free gift of God to all who believe in the Lord Jesus Christ. The crown of life is the special reward for faithful endurance.

d. The source of temptation (i. 13-18)

Here James contrasts the kind of excuse a tempted man may make with the actual truth about temptation, and is evidently referring to an incitement to evil rather than to the testing of character which he has already discussed (see verses 3, 4). *Let no man say . . . I am tempted of God: for God cannot be tempted with evil* (RV mg. 'is untried in evil'), *neither tempteth he any man* (13). It has been suggested that this contradicts such statements as Heb. xi. 17 and 1 Cor. x. 9. But temptation in these cases came from without, whereas James is referring here to temptation or trial from within arising from uncontrolled passions and appetites. Weakness in yielding to such evil desires cannot be excused by casting the responsibility upon God (cf. 1 Cor. x. 13). The real source of temptation is to be sought not in God but in man himself. 'Each man is tempted when he is drawn away by his own lust, and enticed' (14, RV). Lust dwelt upon, or entertained in the heart, brings forth sin; for as a man thinketh in his heart so is he. It is when the

desire for self-gratification is yielded to that the deadly offspring of sin is brought forth which in turn bears the awful fruit of death (cf. Rom. viii. 6). *Sin, when it is finished* (RV 'fullgrown'), *bringeth forth death* (15). 'The sin, the child of uncontrolled desire, grows up and in its turn has a child, death' (Cam. Bible). Death is the finished product, the 'perfect work' (verse 4), of sin.

So far from God being the source of temptation, He is the author and giver of every good. He is also the *Father of lights* (17), the Creator and ultimate Source of physical, intellectual and spiritual light (cf. 1 Jn. i. 5). With Him there can be *no variableness, neither shadow of turning* (17). The sun and moon have variations. They may be eclipsed and leave us in darkness. Not so God. Every blessing we enjoy we owe to His unfailing goodness and unalterable grace and mercy. Further, God deliberately willed to make us His own choice offspring. It was His own will that we should be born by the Word of truth to be *a kind of firstfruits of his creatures* (18). James may be thinking of these Jewish Christians, now made new creatures in Christ, as the first sheaves, or pledge, of the great world-wide harvest of the redeemed (cf. Rom. xvi. 5; 1 Cor. xvi. 15). Or his thought may be that Christians are 'the pick of creation' (Gk. *aparchē*), an offering of firstfruits to God, anticipating the redemption of all things for which creation waits (cf. Rom. viii. 18-23).

e. Responsibility towards the Word (i. 19-27)

Apparently there were some Christian Jews who thought the Christian life could be promoted by discussion and who were fonder of talking than of listening. Often their speaking grew into angry debating and much ill-will was engendered which neither commended sound doctrine nor promoted holy living nor produced the fruit of righteousness. Because of what has been stated (see verse 18) it behoves us to be *swift to hear* and heed the Word, to be slow to express ourselves and, above all, to be slow to give way to anger under provocation, for such anger is never in accord with the righteousness of God which leads Him to deal justly with sin (19, 20). Further, we must lay aside *all filthiness and superfluity of naughtiness* (21; RV 'overflowing of wickedness'); every tendency to uncleanness must be put away (cf. Col. iii. 8, 9). The Word is a seed and requires clean soil in which to thrive. 'So clear away all the foul rank growth of malice, and make a soil of humble modesty for the Word which roots itself inwardly with power to save your souls' (Moff.). But hearing is useless unless it leads to a practical outcome in holy living. Having been made new creatures in Christ we must walk in obedience to the faith revealed in the Scriptures, for it is possible by sophistical argument to reason oneself into a state of carnal security and so to delude oneself (22). The mere hearer of the Word is likened to *a man beholding his natural face in a glass* (23). *Beholding* here carries the suggestion of a passing glance which leaves only a casual impression (24). The Word of God is, as it were, a mirror of the soul, showing us what we really are; and if we merely behold and make no effort to bring our lives into line with the Word, the impression is soon lost. Mere hearing of the Word leads to no permanent or practical result in the life of the hearer (cf. Rom. ii. 13).

But James recognizes that the Word is also a *law*; the man who looks carefully into it sees not only his actual self but the ideal and possibilities of the Christian life. Such an one, if he persists in his study, meditating upon God's law and putting it into practice in his daily life, will be blessed in so doing (25). *The law of liberty* (25; cf. Ps. xix. 7; Rom. viii. 2). The law of Christ brings liberty and consists not so much in restraint as in guiding and guarding the new life in Christ. The true believer delights to do the will of God, 'whose service is perfect freedom'. But though the law is a 'law of liberty' its precepts nevertheless require obedience. It requires that the man whose religion is to be real and not an empty profession should bridle his tongue (26), i.e. curb the impulse to give expression to the malice, spiteful and hasty criticism of others and acrimonious discussion already referred to. The Greek *thrēskeia* signifies religion in its external aspect, forms and ceremonies. James uses the word deliberately in order to contrast the vain with the true religion, which manifests itself in such deeds as bridling the tongue, caring for the needy and keeping clear of the worldly spirit (cf. Mt. xxv. 31–46). Widows seem to have received special care in the early Church (Acts. vi. 1). In the social conditions then obtaining the loss of one's husband could be a very severe *affliction*, leading to much suffering and temptation.

III. FAITH AND SOCIETY. ii. 1–13

In verse 1 follow the RV mg., 'Do ye, in accepting persons, hold the faith . . . glory?', the implication being that if you do you are not really Christian. An alternative interpretation is that they must not allow their progress in the Christian life to be hindered by paying undue deference to the rich and a corresponding lack of recognition of the poor.

James pictures an overdressed, wealthy man, whose jewels and gorgeous raiment proclaim his opulence, entering a Christian *assembly*, not necessarily a Jewish synagogue, although many still met in these centres where Moses was read and instructions were given in the Scriptures. At the same time there enters a poor man, clad in old clothes, shabby and stained (2). There was the tendency for the Christians to show undue deference to the rich man and to invite him to occupy a place of honour, while the shabbily dressed man was told to stand, or offered a place on the floor (3). In so doing they showed that they were drawing invidious distinctions (RV 'divided in your own mind') and

were judging people with partiality (4). 'They judged "with evil thoughts" (RV) on the principle that the costliness of a man's dress showed that he was a desirable associate' (Cent. Bible). Favouritism was characteristic of oriental judges. Because of this, all sense of Christian brotherhood was lost and the example of the Lord Jesus was ignored, for all, rich and poor alike, are precious to God. Neither costly nor shabby clothing matters in His presence. To have *respect of persons* in this way was a direct infringement of the law of Moses (cf. Dt. i. 17).

James then reminds them that God is specially gracious to the poor. *Hath not God chosen the poor of* (RV 'as to') *this world rich in faith, and heirs of the kingdom?* (5). It is a startling inquiry, indicative as well as interrogative. Though poor in this world's goods, they had faith in Christ which put them in possession of the choicest blessings and gave them the right to the kingdom of heaven. Yet these were the people whom the recipients of the Epistle were in danger of despising while they paid court to the rich. Was it not the rich who opposed the gospel and oppressed those who embraced it, especially those in less fortunate circumstances, even dragging them before the courts where the administration of justice was in a miserable state of corruption? In carrying out the persecution of the Christians, the persecutors were wont to pour out blasphemies on Christ's name and teaching (6, 7).

James now reaches the conclusion towards which he has been moving in his argument. If they fulfilled the law of the kingdom, the royal law, as set forth in Lv. xix. 18 (cf. also Mk. xii. 28–33; Rom. xiii. 8–10; Gal. v. 14), they did well. On the other hand, if they had respect to persons they committed sin and stood *convinced of* (RV 'convicted by') *the law as transgressors* (9). The apostle now anticipates a possible objection. Why make so much of this matter of respect of persons? It is only a single offence, and it is surely not to be taken so seriously. He rebuts the argument by pointing out that the whole law is broken through failure at any one point. The *royal law* is the sovereign law of God as a whole, and as a whole it demands fulfilment. One of the tests of keeping that law is our attitude to our neighbour. There is a higher law than the legal code of Moses. It is the law of freedom in Christ (see i. 25n.), the spontaneous obedience of the believer to the revealed will of God. It is by this that we shall be judged. Hence 'Speak and act as those should who are expecting to be judged by the Law of freedom. For he who shows no mercy will have judgment given against him without mercy' (12, 13, Wey.). Under the divine government men reap as they sow, and with what judgment they judge others they themselves shall be judged. In the great day, though justice might condemn every man to the utmost penalty of the law, yet God will cause mercy to triumph over judgment in bringing those into His glory who, having been forgiven themselves, are ready to forgive others and for His sake to show mercy to others (cf. Mt. vi. 14, xxv. 31–46). This leads naturally to the thought of the next section.

IV. FAITH AND WORKS. ii. 14–26

This paragraph is the crux of the Epistle and contains statements which have formed the subject of endless debates in the Church. It was this paragraph that moved Martin Luther to utter his famous stricture in which he called the letter 'a right strawey Epistle'. But the apostle's whole statement is eminently reasonable. He seeks to point the difference between a living and active faith and a faith that exists in name only. 'My brothers, what is the use of anyone declaring that he has faith, if he has no deeds to show? Can that faith of his save him?' (Moff.). There is no antagonism here between the teaching of James and that of Paul. The latter teaches that justification before God is never by deeds of the law but by faith in Christ (see Rom. iv. 1—v. 2). This is what he needs to stress as he seeks to help those who think that by keeping the law they can find salvation. At the same time he would thoroughly support James's contention that faith which has no practical output in life and conduct is a hollow mockery, and that no one is justified before God who is not justified practically before men (see, e.g., Tit. i. 16, iii. 7, 8). Faith, the root, must naturally issue in works, the fruit. James needs to stress this side of the picture since the situation which he is meeting is almost the opposite of that with which Paul is dealing in the early chapters of Romans.

To illustrate his point James draws a picture of the heartless conduct of one who dismisses shivering, starving fellow-Christians by saying simply, 'I wish you well; keep yourselves warm and well fed' (16, Wey.), yet fails to supply their bodily need. What is faith worth which can witness such suffering and not be stirred to deeds of kindness? James presided over the church at Jerusalem which suffered (and probably at the time of writing was still suffering) from the famine foretold by Agabus (see Acts xi. 28–30). He could therefore speak from experience. '"Good Wishes" is an empty phrase unless the speaker does good deeds' (Plautus). What profit is there in mere words unaccompanied by practical deeds of mercy? Religious belief, however orthodox, that does not issue in practical action is dead because it is lacking in power. The mere assent to a dogma has no power to justify or save (cf. Rom. ii. 13). 'No man is justified by faith unless faith has made him just.'

James now meets a possible objection. He supposes the case of someone arguing *Thou hast faith, and I have works: shew me thy faith without* (RV 'apart from') *thy works, and I will shew thee my faith by my works* (18). He then declares in effect that the pretence to have faith 'apart from' works of charity or mercy is utterly vain; for since faith cannot be discerned except by its

effects (i.e. good works), it follows that the man whose life produces no good works has presumably no faith.

Every morning and evening the pious Jew recited the Shema, the opening words of which are 'Hear, O Israel, Jehovah our God, Jehovah is one'. This monotheism was a fundamental article of the creed. But merely giving assent to this without any resultant deeds lifts a man no higher than the level of *devils* (RV mg. 'demons') who believe the same. Their belief is clearly worthless and they *tremble* (RV 'shudder') as they contemplate meeting the one God in judgment. Such faith, which might be described as mere intellectual belief, is not the faith that saves.

James pursues the matter no further, but has a touch of scorn for the *vain man*. The adjective in Greek is *kenos*, meaning 'empty', implying the senseless, empty-headed devotee of a religion of mere formalism. He then proceeds to give two examples of justification from the Old Testament. First he draws attention to *Abraham our father* (21; cf. Gal. iii. 6, 7), who was *justified by works* when, in complete devotion and unquestioning obedience to the command of God, he offered up Isaac (see Gn. xxii). James and Paul agree that it was when Abraham *believed God* that *it was imputed unto him for righteousness* (Gn. xv. 6); i.e. he was justified by faith before God. But when by faith he offered Isaac upon the altar he was justified by works before men as he demonstrated the reality of his confidence in God. *The Friend of God* (23); the highest character ever given to a man. God took Abraham into intimate communion with Himself, hiding nothing from him (Gn. xviii. 17), and pouring upon him His choicest blessings. It is evident from this example that Abraham's faith was not merely believing that there is a God, but a principle that led him to trust God's promises, to work by and to love and obey God's will. His works justified and proved the genuineness of his faith.

The second illustration is that of *Rahab* (cf. Jos. ii. 1ff.; Heb. xi. 31). The faith of Rahab in the God of Israel was of such a quality that it expressed itself in doing all she could for the protection of His servants.

Verse 26 is James's conclusion and summary of the whole matter. 'Death is shown by the absence of bodily activity and the presence of corruption; so faith, apart from practical holiness, shows no activity and becomes corrupt' (Cent. Bible). Genuine faith issues in good works. These do not make our standing before God more secure, but they are evidences to the faith by which we stand.

V. FAITH AND THE CONTROL OF THE TONGUE. iii. 1–12

Language is the expression of a man's thoughts and a revelation as to whether he is dominated by self-will or by obedience to God's will. James introduces this section with a warning,

'Do not crowd in to be teachers' (Moff.). There seems to have been an eagerness on the part of many to speak in public, and a failure to recognize that the fundamental qualification for teaching is learning. Perhaps, also, there was a tendency to mistake fluency of speech for knowledge. Teachers carry heavy responsibility and will be judged with special strictness on account of their influence over others. Note the RV rendering in verse 2, 'In many things we all stumble'. The Greek verb is *ptaiō*, to stumble or slip (cf. ii. 10). The danger for the would-be teacher lay in undisciplined speech leading to rash statements and displays of bad temper. James does not say that everybody deliberately misuses the tongue but that it is misused by everybody quite unintentionally at times. The man who is never guilty of a slip of the tongue, who never gives vent to an idle or vain word, is a *perfect man* (2), i.e. one fully instructed, well-balanced and well equipped to accept the responsibility of teaching others and to hold in restraint every unholy propensity. *Bridle* (2); Gk. *chalinagōgeō*, to check, restrain, control or govern. The term *the whole body* may be applied to the Church of Christ as well as to the passions and appetites. If this interpretation is adopted here it would seem to mean that the man fully instructed in divine things is equipped to exercise government in the Church of Christ.

The writer enforces his teaching on a disciplined tongue by using the illustrations of the horse and the bit (3), the ship and the rudder (4), the fire and the wood (5, 6), the untamed animals (7, 8), the fountain and the water (11), and the tree and the fruit (12). In the case of the horse, he is held in by bit and bridle and so rendered subservient to man whose strength, in comparison, is small. Its whole body is regulated by controlling the mouth. So also the ship is controlled by the use of a relatively small rudder, yet the fate of the whole ship depends on it. These two figures illustrate the great influence exercised by so small a thing as the tongue.

In verse 5b follow the RV rendering, 'Behold, how much wood is kindled by how small a fire!' A tiny spark may start a great conflagration with disastrous results, an illustration of the mischief wrought by the tongue. *A world of iniquity* (6); Gk. *ho kosmos tēs adikias*, 'the world of unrighteousness'. The Greek word *kosmos* is primarily expressive of order, and then of the world, or universe, as an ordered system; *adikia* denotes 'unrightness', usually translated 'unrighteousness'. Here, as in i. 27; 2 Pet. i. 4, ii. 20, the 'world' is that which is 'apart from and opposed to Christ; the sphere in which life is purely selfish' (Cent. Bible). The tongue, this world of mischief, is set in our members and stains the whole body, for every evil word leaves its impress upon and blots the whole character. It sets on fire *the course* (RV 'the wheel') *of nature; and it is set on fire of hell* (6). Moffatt renders 'setting fire to the round circle of existence with a flame fed by hell'. The uncontrolled tongue is

set on fire by the devil and the fire spreads to all the baser passions in man's nature.

Turning from the mischief wrought by an undisciplined tongue, James speaks about its fierceness under the figure of untamed animals. While man has been able to tame all kinds of wild creatures such as beasts, birds, reptiles and fishes, yet *the tongue can no man tame* (8). Nothing but the grace of God can bring it under subjection. It is a restless evil, that cannot be restrained or brought under any kind of government, *full of deadly* (death-bringing) *poison* (8; cf. Ps. cxl. 3). Throughout the whole of this descriptive declaration, James has particularly in mind the tongue of the slanderer, backbiter, whisperer and tale-bearer. Poisonous snakes are not more dangerous to life than are these to the peace and reputation of men. A graphic picture follows in verses 9–12 of another characteristic of the tongue, inconsistency. A man's tongue, which is capable of praising the Eternal, and setting forth His glory, is capable also of abusive raillery against his fellows who are made in the same likeness of God. While this is of general application, James doubtless had in mind the attitude of Jews towards Christians, or even of bigoted Jewish Christians towards Gentiles. They could be loud in their praises and blessing of God, but were equally ready to pour direful imprecations upon those who worshipped not after their manner, but who were yet as truly created after the same image of God as they were. See the inconsistency of blessing and cursing proceeding out of the same mouth! Surely such things should not occur. James points to nature and asks if a fountain sends out both fresh and brackish water from the same vent, a very natural figure for Palestine where salt, sulphurous and brackish springs are not uncommon. *Can the fig tree, my brethren, bear olive berries?* (12). The answer is obvious. No more can the same fountain send forth salt water and fresh. If it did, the fresh water would lose its character and be tainted with the brackish. So when praises to God and curses on men proceed from the same mouth, the praises are tainted and therefore worthless. How incongruous is such behaviour!

VI. FAITH AND WISDOM. iii. 13–18

From these impressive arguments James turns to put a question—*Who is a wise man and endued with knowledge* (Gk. *epistēmōn*) *among you?* (13). 'According to Mayor *epistēmōn* is used in classical Greek for a skilled or scientific person as opposed to one who has no special knowledge or training' (Cent. Bible). The question looks back to verse 1. James is still dealing with those who would be teachers in the Church. To such, wisdom must ever be an indispensable qualification. There is a distinction between knowledge and wisdom. A wise man is a man of faith, subject to and taught of God. It is possible to have much knowledge and little wisdom. Both are necessary in a teacher. Whether we are to understand any very marked difference between *wise* and *endued with knowledge* is of little importance. The practical point that James wishes to make is that everyone who professes a superiority which entitles him to teach others should prove it practically and modestly by his good conduct among his fellow-Christians. 'Wisdom teaches us to do, as well as to talk' (Seneca). The term *good conversation* (13), i.e. 'good conduct', means a life which manifests true goodness (see RV).

But there is a false or counterfeit wisdom which produces jealousy and rivalry in the heart. Where these exist there can be no room for glorying over someone on the ground of superior privileges (14). The falsity of such a claim is shown by the bitter railing in which they indulge against those who differ from them. That kind of so-called wisdom is not a divine gift received on the terms of i. 5–8. It is *earthly* (cf. 'the wisdom of this world', 1 Cor. i. 20), wholly lacking in spiritual illumination. It is *sensual* (RV mg. 'natural or animal'). The Greek is *psychikos* which describes man as he is in Adam (i.e. 'natural'), in contrast to *pneumatikos*, 'spiritual'. Hence this wisdom is limited to the mere physical or animal life and lacking in fellowship with the divine. It is *devilish* (Gk. *daimoniōdēs*), i.e. Satanic in origin, proceeding from or resembling demons. Its source is the same as that which setteth on fire the course of nature (see verse 6). 'Where jealousy and faction are, there is confusion and every vile deed' (RV). *Confusion* (16); Gk. *akatastasia;* i.e. disorder, disturbance, tumult; hence, as here, revolution or anarchy.

In sharp contrast to this false wisdom there stands the true. As to its origin it is *from above* (cf. verse 15). Its nature is not earthly, sensual, demoniacal; rather it is supernatural alike in its origin, nature and issue. It has a sevenfold excellence: purity, peaceableness, gentleness, conciliatoriness, mercy, fruitfulness, single-mindedness and sincerity (cf. Gal. v. 22f.; 2 Pet. i. 5–9). James directs attention to the inner characteristic of the wise, for what is inward is of primary importance. *Pure* means free from stain or defilement of any kind. He who has no inward moral purity has not begun to be wise. *Peaceable*, i.e. not given to conflict or dissension. There can be no real peace without purity or righteousness. *Gentle;* cf. Matthew Arnold's 'sweet reasonableness'. Gentleness is not so much tenderness as fairness in contrast to unreasonableness. 'The gentleness of Christ' is the Christian standard with its subjection of self-interest to higher ends. *Easy to be entreated;* i.e. open to persuasion, conciliatory, ready to be guided (Gk. *eupeithēs*, ready to obey; hence compliant). *Full of mercy and good fruits;* i.e. ever ready to take the initiative in showing pity and compassion and extending forgiveness; bringing forth good fruits (works); for a tongue controlled by divine grace can be a mighty influence for good. *Without partiality* (RV

'variance'); i.e. not given to wrangling or quarrelling over places of preferment. *Without hypocrisy;* i.e. sincere, not pretending to be what it is not, uttering words that can be depended upon (Moff. 'straightforward'). Note the RV and RV mg. renderings in verse 18. He who possesses wisdom sows the good seed which produces righteousness. He sows in peace because he is a peacemaker. 'The harvest of righteousness is sown in peace by those who make peace' (RSV).

VII. FAITH AND FIGHTINGS. iv. 1–17

a. The origin of strife (iv. 1–6)

The previous section closes with the mention of peace and righteousness. Instead of such peace, however, the people to whom James was writing had *wars and fightings* (1). The fightings (Gk. *machoi*, 'strivings') refer, in this instance, to disputes over doctrine. Their brawlings and controversies caused disorder in their assemblies, and the ultimate source of these was their passions, *that war in their members* (Gk. *strateuō*, 'to make war', from *stratos*, an encamped army). Their passions encamped in their members and possessed and controlled them like an army of occupation. Quarrels are not always caused by outward circumstances; often they are the result of inward passions. The term *lusts* (3) refers to gratification of the desire for pleasure, in this case the pleasure of wielding power over, and bringing about the humiliation of, rivals. The RV renders it simply 'pleasures' (Gk. *hēdonē*, the gratification of sinful desires) while Moffatt and RSV render it 'passion'. The meaning in any case is clear.

Ye lust, and have not (2). Cf. the sins of David (see 2 Sa. xi) and Ahab (1 Ki. xxi. 2–4). The desire becomes the master passion of a man's soul, but the natural heart is never contented or satisfied with anything the world can offer. *Ye kill, and desire to have, and cannot obtain* (2). All the fighting and wrangling disputes and all the efforts to gratify your own desires are quite unavailing and end only in futility and dissatisfaction. And the reason is *Ye have not, because ye ask not* (2). You have not made your wants the subject of earnest prayer. God has abundant supplies of grace available for those who ask. But you fail to ask and so you do not receive. And even when you do ask you do not receive because your asking is prompted by wrong motives (3). Your praying is self-centred, concerned with the gratification of your own desires, so that God cannot, in faithfulness, grant your requests. You are not asking for blessing on others, nor even that you yourselves should receive God's highest and best. Your requests are made so that you may satisfy the baser part of your nature. This is the cause of that unholy restlessness which produces confusion and strife.

Ye adulterers and adulteresses (4). See RV. The better MSS give 'ye adulteresses' only, as though God would charge us with being like an unfaithful wife. James describes the soul's unfaithfulness to God in these startling terms. Worldliness is spiritual adultery. *The world* (4) is that order of things about us, or that spirit within us, which is blind to the value and the reality of spiritual things. The worldly man is governed by the desires of the flesh or by the fashions and customs around him and refuses to acknowledge God's right to rule. It is clear, then, that the world's ways and its objectives are fundamentally at variance with the character of God and with His revealed will for His children. There are two friendships, friendship of God and friendship of the world. They are incompatible and irreconcilable and therefore we must choose which of these we will have. Notice in verse 4 the phrase *whosoever . . . will be* (RV 'would be'). In the spiritual world our choice of friends determines our enemy. A man who desires to be the friend of the world makes himself an enemy of God (see RV). 'Can two walk together except they be agreed?' (Am. iii. 3).

Verse 5 is somewhat obscure. Westcott and others, although not dogmatizing, render the first sentence, 'Do you think the Scripture speaketh in vain?' and regard the second part of the verse as an independent statement rather than the object of the verb 'speaketh', as it appears in the AV. If this arrangement is accepted, and there seems no good reason why it should not be so, James in effect asks if we can imagine that the many warnings against worldliness in verse 4 and throughout Scripture are mere empty phrases. The Scripture speaks solemnly against this evil and we refuse its warnings at the peril of our souls.

On the second part of the verse interpretations vary. *The spirit that dwelleth in us* is regarded by some as indicating the spirit of evil which, since the fall, has indwelt and corrupted the natural man and is the source from which envy springs. On the other hand, we may accept the RV mg. rendering and read, 'That spirit which he (God) made to dwell in us yearneth for us even unto jealous envy.' In this case the reference is to the gracious work of the Holy Spirit who is grieved and distressed when we prove unfaithful to Christ and to God who has blessed us so richly. He yearns over us with a holy envy or jealousy to have us wholly for Himself, for He cannot be satisfied with a divided loyalty. This interpretation seems preferable to the former. 'The word "envy" or "jealousy", though commonly viewed as evil, was yet treated at times as a parable of the finest affection (2 Cor. xi. 2; Gal. iv. 17, 18)' (Cam. Bible).

Their worldly spirit had been the root cause for God's withholding from them their request. They asked and received not because they asked amiss. But He never withholds His grace from those who ask. Indeed, to ask for grace is to receive more and more of it (6). James supports his statement by a quotation from Pr. iii. 34 (LXX); cf. 1 Pet. v. 5. Proud self-will refuses to yield to God: it feels sufficient in itself for all the moral warfare and has no need to come as a suppliant to the throne of grace confessing that the appeal of the world is too strong and only God's grace can counteract it. Such an attitude can find no acceptance with God. Rather does He *resist* it. The Greek word *antitassō*, originally a military term meaning to set in battle array against, is used in the middle voice signifying to set oneself against. God resists by leaving persistent evil-doers to pursue their determined course with eventual retribution. To such, however, who are humble enough to acknowledge Him, realizing their weakness and proneness to evil, God delights to give freely of His grace.

b. Submission to God (iv. 7–10)

Having contrasted the proud and the humble and the divine attitude of resisting the one and bestowing grace on the other, James proceeds to set forth the abiding secret of victory in the war against worldliness and sin. It consists of two activities, submission to God and resistance to the devil (7). Herein are blended perfectly the true activities of faith and works. By faith we submit to God in a fuller, deeper surrender to His will and cease to fight against Him. In the act of submission we are prepared for conflict with the evil one; and at the same time our powers of resistance are strengthened and multiplied. See also 1 Pet. v. 8, 9.

There now follows a series of practical injunctions which have special application to those who are seeking the way of God more perfectly and who no longer fight against Him. They are to *draw nigh to God*, and, as they do so, they have the assurance that *he will draw nigh* to them (8). God never refuses to meet those who sincerely seek His face. There is more involved here than drawing near to God in prayer. It means a close walk of fellowship with God even as Enoch walked with God. But such a privilege demands fitting preparation. Hence, *cleanse your hands . . . purify your hearts* (8). The latter injunction is addressed chiefly to those who were double-minded (see i. 8n.), i.e. those who were striving to maintain a loyalty to the Lord and an allegiance to the world. In their submission to God He was to be all in all (cf. also Ps. xxiv. 3, 4). The clean hands symbolize our activities; the pure heart represents the very citadel of our personality.

Then follows a call to repentance: *Be afflicted* (Moff. 'lament'), *and mourn, and weep* (9). The memory of former compromise with the world emphasized the need for deep and true repentance. Laughter, the careless, selfish, luxurious rejoicing of the world, the sport of the fool in Pr. x. 23 (cf. Cam. Bible), are to give place to *mourning*, and *heaviness* (Gk. *katēpheia*, denoting the downcast look expressive of sorrow) is to take the place of joy. Cf. Lk. xviii. 13. The true penitent does not venture 'so much as to lift up his eyes to heaven'. There is nothing uplifted about him until God's pardon and grace raise him to his feet (10). When we are humble and contrite before Him, He delights to give us the treasures of His grace. A later practice which seems foreshadowed here was for mourners and penitents to lie on the ground and roll themselves in the dust. Only when pardoned did they rise, shake themselves from the dust and clothe themselves with better garments.

c. Evil-speaking rebuked (iv. 11, 12)

To speak evil of one another, i.e. morally to fight against each other, is to offend against the majesty of the divine law. The general sense of the argument is that to speak against a brother is to condemn him, and to condemn or pass sentence is the function of a judge. This fault-finding, or evil-speaking against a brother, implies that the law is inadequate in its judgment. Besides, the law of Christ forbids judging (Mt. vii. 1f.) and, consequently, judging breaks the law. The Giver of the law is the only true and ultimate Judge, who alone has the power *to save and to destroy* (12). Who is man to dare to usurp the office and prerogative of the supreme Judge by judging his neighbour? True humility enjoins a deliberate refusal to enter into a spirit of judgment upon others, and an attitude of strict obedience to the law.

d. Planning without God (iv. 13–17)

James now turns to another form of fighting against God, viz. worldliness in the sense of planning for the future without taking God into the reckoning. The Jewish traders would go to the commercial centres of the day, e.g. Antioch, Alexandria, Damascus, Corinth, etc., and spend a considerable time in each place of business. To *buy and sell, and get gain* (13) are legitimate pursuits, but they become corrupt and immoral if conducted without any reference to God and His will and the brevity of life (cf. Pr. xxvii. 1 and Lk. xii. 16–21). *Ye know not what shall be on the morrow* (14). Life is utterly precarious, and God has not put it within the power of any of His creatures to command one moment of that which is the future. Hence the absurdity of reckoning without God. James is not condemning the making of plans for the future. Our Lord enjoins prudence and foresight. What he is condemning is the making of plans without any reference to God, and he inserts a searching question to illustrate this point. *What is your life?* he inquires (14). The very question is a rebuke, but the answer is stern and unflinching. Human life at best, viewed in the light of eternity, is only *a vapour, that appeareth for a little time, and then vanisheth away*. The apostle connects man's life with a higher will than his own and seeks to correct the false approach to human activities by reminding his readers that God's will is supreme and that their plans for the future must bear the stamp *Deo Volente*. But they have been guilty of exulting in their supposed self-sufficiency, boasting, in effect, that they could live independently of God. That man walks most safely who has the least confidence in himself. True wisdom and true humility keep God

continually in view. The argument is closed with a striking application. The apostle says, in effect, 'I have shown you what is right to do and any failure to do it on your part is, therefore, sin' (17; Moff.). The danger is that, while assenting to the abstract truth of the brevity of life and the uncertainty of the future, we shall go on practically as before with our far-reaching plans for the future without reference to the will of God. Such an attitude is of the very essence of sin. Sin consists not only in doing evil, but in failing to do the good we know. If we do not act according to the fact that we are entirely dependent upon God, we sin. 'Sin is any want of conformity to the will of God.' When He makes known His will it is our responsibility to act accordingly.

VIII. CORRUPTED RICHES. v. 1–6

This section carries a stern denunciation of the rich men who have gained their prosperity through oppression. Such are condemned, not because they are rich, but because their riches are ill-gotten, and upon them rest the marks of corruption. James calls upon them to *weep and howl for your miseries that shall come upon you*. The Orientals are very demonstrative in expressing their grief. Gold, silver and apparel (cf. Mt. vi. 19; Acts xx. 33) were the chief forms of Eastern wealth. *Corrupted . . . motheaten . . . cankered* (RV 'rusted') (2, 3). These are prophetic perfects in which the future is spoken of as though it had already come to pass. 'The inevitable fate of their wealth is set forth as if it were already realized' (Cent. Bible). In spite of all outward evidences of prosperity and brilliant success their garments were, in the divine eyes, moth-eaten and their silver and gold in which they were trusting were affected with canker and the very tarnish was a witness against them. Whether or not these words had their primary fulfilment in the woes that preceded the destruction of Jerusalem, the general principle holds good that those who seem to find security in corrupted wealth will one day have to face inevitable retribution.

The chief opposition to the Christians at this time came from the rich. See notes on ii. 1–7. Here the apostle proceeds to specify other grounds of complaint and shows how their riches have been corrupted. It is not only that they have shut up their bowels of compassion against the poor, but the just and lawful wages have been kept back from the labourers who reaped their fields (4; cf. Lv. xix. 13; Dt. xxiv. 15; Je. xxii. 13; Mal. iii. 5). In his picture of the struggle between Employer and Labour, James does not hesitate to lay the charge of fraud against the oppressors. But although the cries and appeals of the oppressed have fallen upon deaf ears as far as the oppressors were concerned, they have *entered into the ears of the Lord of sabaoth* (4). 'Jehovah Sabaoth', Lord of hosts, or Lord of armies, is a frequent appellation of God in the Old Testament and signifies His almighty power by which He governs the world, defends His people and punishes the wicked. He is not an uninterested spectator (cf. Ex. iii. 7–10). In all this the rich have simply *heaped treasure together for the last days* (3). James feels· in his soul the impending judgment on the Holy City in which the wealthier Jews were robbed of everything and a reign of terror followed which prevailed wherever Jews were found. But there is also this further suggestion that just such conditions as James here describes will largely obtain as the end of the present dispensation draws nigh.

The apostle brings a further charge against them, that of wanton luxury with its social cruelty. *Ye have nourished your hearts, as in a day of slaughter* (5). They have been so absorbed in their pampered selfish luxury that they have been fattening themselves, as it were, all unconscious of their doom, as beasts are fattened for the shambles. They are simply hoarding their money for the spoiler to seize and so will be a richer prey for him because of the treasure which they are heaping together. But that is not all. In so doing they have *condemned and killed the just* (6). The poor, pious people were at their mercy and had received no mercy. They had to live on scanty fare and anyone who defrauded them of it was regarded by God as a murderer. 'He murders his neighbour who deprives him of his living, and he who defrauds a hireling of his wages is a shedder of blood.' The poor had no means of redress and submitted without murmur to their suffering. The helplessness of the victims aggravates the guilt of the oppressors.

IX. PATIENCE ENJOINED. v. 7–12

Turning from the oppressor to the oppressed the apostle makes an affectionate appeal for steadfast endurance until *the coming of the Lord* (7). This is the blessed hope to which he would have them cling. Then shall all wrongs be righted and all oppression cease. For that day the suffering ones are to wait and in their waiting to be longsuffering even toward those who oppress them. James enforces this counsel to patient endurance with illustration and doctrine. Their patience is to take a long view. *The husbandman waiteth . . . and hath long patience* (7). The farmer tills his land, sows his seed, and then through all the trials of climate waits patiently expecting a harvest. *The early and latter rain* (7) in the Holy Land were of critical importance to the farmer, for, should they fail or be delayed, famine would be inevitable. So are they to exercise patience, strengthening and stablishing their hearts with the conviction that *the coming of the Lord draweth nigh* (8). The fact that in this very early document there should be so clear and explicit reference to the 'blessed hope' of the Church invalidates the argument that it was an afterthought that came to Christians at a late period of development of doctrine. It was a belief which was held and nourished from the day of

ascension when the angels assured the upwardgazing, if not bewildered, disciples that 'this same Jesus . . . shall so come in like manner as ye have seen him go into heaven' (Acts i. 11).

One practical outcome of this patient waiting will be the development of a spirit of cheerfulness and a deliverance from the sin of murmuring and from the irritable and censorious spirit. Such a spirit provokes and deserves judgment. James is alive to the fact that God's judgment takes strict account of the Christians' behaviour as well as of their oppressors. Besides, why should they be fretful and censorious when *the judge standeth before the door* (9), ready to judge the oppressors and succour the oppressed? As an example of those who had to stand alone, and to suffer evil, the apostle points to *the prophets, who have spoken in the name of the Lord*. His reference, no doubt, was chiefly to the prophets of the Old Testament, all of whom, almost without exception, suffered persecution. But the prophets in the Christian Church also, such as Paul, Stephen and James, were exposed to the same trials as their predecessors. 'We call those happy who were steadfast' (11, RSV; cf. Mt. v. 11).

From a general reference to the prophets who are given as an example of affliction and patience James turns to the particular illustration of Job. Job's patience is interpreted in the light of the purpose of the Lord. It was more than a courageous endurance of suffering and loss. It was a patience which had to be exercised towards his three friends who insisted that his misfortunes were the result of secret sin. The blissful conclusion at which Job arrived was that *the Lord is very pitiful, and of tender mercy* (11). Job, oppressed beyond measure, was able to say 'He knoweth the way that I take: when he hath tried me, I shall come forth as gold' (Jb. xxiii. 10): surely a triumph of faith.

In excitement and irritation (cf. verse 9) there was always the temptation to lose control of the tongue, a sin against which James has already clearly written. Hence the practical exhortation of verse 12. They were to be content with simplicity of truthful utterance and were to refrain from making any oath either in the name of heaven or of earth. They are to be so truthful and straightforward that their bare word would be sufficient.

X. FAITH AND PRAYER. v. 13–20

This closing paragraph of the Epistle contains one of its characteristic notes. All the way through James has insisted on the necessity for and the value of prayer. He has no philosophy of prayer to offer, but he himself cultivated the habit of prayer. The tradition concerning him is that his knees were worn hard as a camel's through his constant habit of prayer. His counsel to those who are afflicted (RV 'suffering'), therefore, is to *pray*, for thereby comes help and comfort. His directions to those who are cheerful is that they should praise. The word *merry* (RV 'cheerful') is the Greek *euthymeō* (from *eu*, 'well', and *thymos*, 'the soul') which signifies strong feeling emotionally or passionately. If anyone feels thus, let him remember God in his gladness and let him sing praise. Prayer and praise are to be the centres round which life is to move.

In verses 14, 15 the apostle deals with the function of prayer at the sick-bed, and these verses have given rise to much controversy. The directions James gives are important in their bearing on the life of the Christian Church. There is to be the closest possible friendship and sympathy amongst members. The elders are to hold themselves in readiness at any time to serve any member with prayer and sympathy and spiritual counsel. They are to be men who can offer the *prayer of faith* and who will respond when called upon to visit cases of sickness and trouble. The instructions as to how the elders shall act in the presence of the sick are stated. They are to pray over him, *anointing him with oil in the name of the Lord* (14). There is no place here for the Romish rite of Extreme Unction, which is administered only when a person is dying.

When the twelve apostles were sent forth they 'anointed with oil many that were sick, and healed them' (Mk. vi. 13). This seems to be the only other instance mentioned in the New Testament where it is recorded that this method was employed. The oil in itself may have had healing properties and God may have blessed the means used in connection with those who were ill. But James says that *the prayer of faith shall save the sick, and the Lord shall raise him up.* There is no indication that James forbade the use of means. The fact that God can and sometimes does heal without the use of means should not lead us to think that the employment of medicine is dishonouring to Him. The non-Christian will use medicine without prayer; the Christian may use prayer without medicine; but both are ultimately dependent upon God. *And if he have committed sins, they shall be forgiven him* (15). The root cause of sickness and suffering is sin; here the suggestion seems to be that the illness is part of the divine chastening for sins committed. The summoning of the elders (Gk. *presbyteroi*), who, being raised up and equipped by the Holy Spirit and having, as their name indicates, spiritual maturity, were appointed to exercise spiritual care and oversight of the Church along with the bishops or overseers (Gk. *episkopoi*), would in itself imply, in some measure, an acknowledgment of failure.

James now moves on to the subject of mutual prayer. *Confess your faults one to another, and pray one for another, that ye may be healed* (16). There is no justification here for the vicious practice of auricular confession. The directions have reference to what has gone before. When the elders anointed the sick man with oil he would probably be encouraged to confess his faults in prayer to God that they might be sure of the patient's penitence or, perhaps, so that they might have some explanation of the causes leading to his malady. Or, James may be referring to sins which have injured both parties and not to sins which have no bearing on the life of another. Confession would then be the means of seeking mutual forgiveness in the spirit of our Lord's command in Mt. v. 23, 24. Indiscriminate confession is not to be entertained: it is like sowing germs of disease in the minds and lives of others. The greatest thing we can do for another is set forth in the words, *pray one for another* (16). 'The writer urges the habit of mutual prayer and intercession, that when sickness comes there may be a quicker work of healing in the absence of spiritual impediments to the exercise of supernatural powers working through natural media' (Cam. Bible).

For an illustration of the prayer that prevails James turns to the Old Testament. He reminds his readers that Elijah was *a man subject to like passions as we are* (17) and yet he prayed earnestly, first that it might not rain, and then that it might rain; and both prayers were answered (1 Ki. xvii, xviii). Elijah knew how to use the mighty instrument of prevailing prayer. Through prayer he became what he was and wielded the power he did. *The effectual fervent prayer of a righteous man availeth much* (16); RV 'the supplication of a righteous man availeth much in its working', i.e. works so effectively as to bring about great and blessed results. The man who prays must be righteous, i.e. in right relationship with God and man. The words *effectual fervent* are used to translate the Greek *energoumenē. Energeō* means to work effectually and here has no reference to energy in prayer. To the righteous man prayer is dynamic: it avails and prevails.

The Epistle closes abruptly, not with any word of farewell, but with a word of exhortation. *If any of you do err from the truth* (19), i.e. from the faith and obedience of the truth, it is the duty and privilege of a Christian to seek to bring him back. Let the one who brings him back understand that *he which converteth the sinner from the error of his way shall save a soul from death, and shall hide a multitude of sins* (20). Though James does not specifically mention it, the whole context implies that the particular method in the mind of the author for bringing back the erring one is that of prayer. By prayer the erring are restored, souls are saved from death and cleansed from sin. One who wanders from Christ is in danger of death. James would have him drawn back into the true fellowship and the experience of Christ's forgiveness. 'He who wins back a wanderer from truth wins his soul as well as his person, and spreads the veil of love over the multitude of sins' (Williams, *Students' Commentary*). The faith that works is evidenced, not only by a life of devotion to the Lord, but also by a concern for the welfare of others, particularly of those who are brethren in Christ.

ANDREW McNAB.

THE GENERAL EPISTLES OF PETER
I PETER: INTRODUCTION

I. AUTHORSHIP

Although from time to time the authorship of this Epistle has been in question it is generally accepted that the letter is a genuine document, the work of the apostle Peter known to us from the Gospels and the Acts of the Apostles. Difficulties have been expressed in regard to the acceptance of the Petrine authorship on the ground that the language and style are correct and the form too idiomatic to be the work of an 'unlettered and ignorant' Galilean fisherman to whom Greek was a foreign language. A further objection is based on the striking resemblance which the letter bears in parts to some of the Epistles of Paul. Both those difficulties are answered if 1 Pet. v. 12 is taken into account. The part played by Silvanus in the production of the letter cannot be ignored. Silvanus is mentioned in 1· Thes. i. 1 and 2 Thes. i. 1 as being associated with Paul and Timothy in the authorship of these two Epistles. The Silvanus of the Epistles is the Silas of the Acts of the Apostles (see Acts xv—xviii). The employment of a scribe or an amanuensis was a common custom in the first century and the duties and privileges of such seem to have been considerable. Acting in this capacity Silvanus would be responsible for the literary quality, arrangement and style of the Epistle. The thought was still the thought of Peter; the language and style were the contribution of Silvanus.

The association of Silvanus with Paul, combined with his responsibilities as an amanuensis, meets any objection to the Petrine authorship based on similarity in thought and expression to some of Paul's writings.

A more serious objection has to be met in the argument that if Peter was the author of the Epistle bearing his name we should expect to find many more references to the events of the earthly life of our Lord in view of the fact that the author enjoyed privileged intimacy with his Master. (This contention is strongly supported by Beare in his commentary.) But after the ascension and Pentecost the apostles were more disposed to look forward to the fulfilment of the glorious hope of their Lord's second coming than backward to the events of His earthly life up to the crucifixion.

We are safe in concluding that the Epistle we are considering is the work of Peter and bears his apostolic authority and witness, while the literary mould in which it is cast is the work of Silvanus. For a full and satisfactory treatment of the subject see Selwyn's *First Epistle of St. Peter* (Macmillan, 1946), Introduction, pp. 9–16, 27ff., and Essay II, pp. 363–466.

II. THE PLACE OF WRITING

According to v. 13 the Epistle was written in 'Babylon'. Two cities having this name were known in apostolic times. One was in Egypt, probably a military post of the Roman Empire on the site of the present Cairo. The Coptic Church still holds the view that this is the Babylon referred to in the Epistle; but there seem no good grounds for supporting it. Babylon of the Euphrates is regarded by many as the place here designated. Jews in considerable numbers still dwelt at Babylon and much has been written for and against the acceptance of this view. A strong objection to the claim comes from the fact that there is neither record nor tradition to indicate that any apostle save Thomas had any association with Mesopotamia.

A third view is that the term 'Babylon' is used here symbolically of Rome. Tradition which runs back into the second century favours this. Rome is called Babylon in Rev. xvii and xviii just as in Rev. xi. 8 Jerusalem is referred to as 'Sodom', the thought being that Jerusalem then bore the marks of wickedness associated with the Sodom of Gn. xviii and xix. So in the mind of Peter the Rome of his day resembled ancient Babylon in its wealth, luxury and licentiousness. It may well be that he used the term 'Babylon' instead of Rome for reasons of prudence lest the letter should inadvertently fall into the hands of some Roman official who, reading the postscript, would take offence, a possibility which could not be ruled out and which might lead to dire consequences as far as the Christians were concerned. The view that the term 'Babylon' is here used for Rome was universally accepted in the early Christian era and commends itself today.

III. DATE

Persecution of the Christians was so common in the second half of the first century that Peter's words could be applied with equal relevance to any decade in that period. Little help, then, is to be derived from a consideration of the terms and message of the Epistle in fixing the date of writing with any degree of accuracy. But in i. 1 Peter describes his readers as 'the elect who are sojourners of the Dispersion' (RV) in the regions named. The use of the term 'Dispersion' indicates that the Christians to whom Peter was writing valued their Jewish nationality and enjoyed many of the privileges extended to the Jews by officials of the Roman Empire. The martyrdom of James, our Lord's brother, took place, according to Josephus, in A.D. 62, and it was this which made the separation between Christianity and Judaism inevitable and opened the way for the storm of persecution which was so soon to threaten the Christians. Within two years of the death of James privileges hitherto enjoyed were withdrawn from the Christians and Christianity came to be regarded as an illegal order. Roman historians, e.g. Tacitus and Suetonius, give clear indication of the growth of anti-Christian feeling in Rome in A.D. 64. It was easy for Nero to find support for his trumped-up charges against the Christians, especially the charge of incendiarism. Now Peter clearly teaches the duty of Christians to be subject to every ordinance of man for the Lord's sake and to regard civil rulers as being divinely appointed to bear rule over them (ii. 13–17). Such an exhortation would be given not after but before the Neronian persecution overtook them. That being so, the letter must have been written earlier than the summer of A.D. 64. Again, it seems more than probable that such references as those to the resurrection (i. 3, iii. 21) and to the death of Christ as a lamb without blemish (i. 19) point to the intention that the letter be read at the Paschal celebrations associated with the observance of Easter in Asia in those days. In such case the Epistle would be written in the second half of A.D. 63 in time to be received by the readers by Easter A.D. 64 just before the storm of persecution by Nero burst over them.

IV. SPECIAL CHARACTERISTICS

This is essentially the Epistle of hope, a living hope founded on the resurrection of Jesus Christ from the dead. It carries with it the assurance of a glorious inheritance which is described as incorruptible, undefiled and unfading. Peter puts these thoughts of the living hope and glorious inheritance at the opening of his letter to encourage his fellow-believers with the consolations of the gospel that they may stand fast in the day of fiery ordeal and bear patiently their sufferings and triumph over persecution, affliction and temptation.

I PETER: OUTLINE OF CONTENTS

I. SALUTATION. i. 1, 2

II. THE GREAT SALVATION. i. 3–12

III. THE CALL TO HOLINESS. i. 13—ii. 10

IV. CHRISTIAN DUTY. ii. 11—iii. 12

V. SUFFERINGS AND GLORY. iii. 13—iv. 19

VI. VICTORY AND SERVICE. v. 1–11

VII. CONCLUSION. v. 12–14

I PETER: COMMENTARY

I. SALUTATION. i. 1, 2

Calling himself by the new name Christ had given him (cf. Mt. xvi. 18), Peter greets his readers by declaring his office and authority as *an apostle of Jesus Christ* (1). As Selwyn points out, Peter wrote as an apostle with that apostolic authority which those to whom he wrote so greatly needed in their time of ordeal, the fiery trial which was to come (it had not yet come) upon them. The term 'apostle' means one commissioned, or a delegate, and thus combines the ideas of authority, ability and warrant. But his authority is not his own. Peter received it from Christ to whom he owed his appointment and to whom he was ultimately answerable. His letter is addressed to the *elect* (2), i.e. those called of God. The term is used in the LXX of God's chosen people, and the fact of election was characteristic of Israel as a whole (cf. Dt. iv. 37, vii. 6, xiv. 2). The same thought is carried over into the New Testament. In ii. 9 Christians are declared to be an 'elect race' (RV). Election is all of God, not on the grounds of any special fitness or achievement on the part of the elect. In this case the elect were very ordinary people belonging for the most part to the slave class.

The source of election is said to be *the foreknowledge of God the Father* (2). The thought embodies the idea of divine plan and purpose with a view to choice and calling. *Through sanctification of the Spirit* (2). Election is always through an agent and with a purpose. Sanctification means a separating or setting apart from common use to the service of God. This is the work of the Holy Spirit. The election of the Father in eternity is made effectual through the work of the Holy Spirit in time, working in the soul and setting it apart for God. The purpose of election is declared to be *unto obedience* (2). Election involves duty and obligation as well as privilege. Obedience is a divine requirement and an inevitable consequence of election. The *sprinkling of the blood of Jesus Christ* (2) refers to the establishment of the new covenant between God and His people by the death of Christ and the ratification thereof by His blood. The allusion is to the covenant sacrifice of Ex. xxiv.

But not only were they elect, they were *strangers scattered throughout* (1; RV 'sojourners of the Dispersion in') the whole of Asia Minor north of the Taurus range. 'The Dispersion' had come to be a technical term used to denote Jews who were scattered abroad throughout the world outside Palestine. But here it is given a much wider application and refers to Christians generally in the provinces named. In all likelihood the persons addressed were for the most part Gentiles and slaves. They are described as 'sojourners', a term which indicates the temporariness of their abode. *Grace unto you, and peace, be multiplied* (2). The ordinary Greek salutation was *charein*, 'greeting' (see Acts xv. 23, xxiii. 26; Jas. i. 1). *Charis*, which is derived from the same root, was substituted and became a technical term of the gospel and is translated 'grace', meaning God's free, unmerited favour, His love in action in Jesus Christ on behalf of sinners. The Hebrew salutation both on meeting and on parting was *shalom* ('peace'). It is the result of grace and includes both reconciliation and rest, although these are secondary to the basic meaning.

II. THE GREAT SALVATION. i. 3–12

The apostle begins his letter of consolation with an ascription of praise. *Blessed be the God and Father of our Lord Jesus Christ* (3). It was the Jewish custom in prayer to begin with an ascription of praise to God for His crowning mercies. Here Peter ascribes praise to the God who has revealed Himself in the Person of His Son Jesus Christ. See also 2 Cor. i. 3 and Eph. i. 3. *According to his abundant mercy* (3). The apostle would remind his readers that every blessing, and especially the blessing of new life in Christ, comes not because they deserve it, but solely on the ground of the abundant mercy of God (cf. Eph. ii. 4–6; see also La. iii. 22). The new birth (Jn. iii. 3–8) is the title which may be given to all the blessings which accompany and flow from the great salvation. We are begotten again *unto a lively* (RV 'living') *hope* (3), i.e. a hope that can never be extinguished. Note that it is *the resurrection of Jesus Christ* (3) that gives the hope birth, even as it did in the case of Peter himself, when he was lifted from the despair which swept over him at the trial and crucifixion of Jesus and which found expression in his threefold denial of his Lord, and was given a living hope because he knew that Christ had risen again. The resurrection is an indispensable essential of the gospel. Its importance is emphasized in 1 Cor. xv, where it is seen to be an integral part of God's mighty saving work whereby alone we can be born again.

Those who are born again enter into three great blessings in addition to the 'living hope' which has already been noted. These are an *inheritance* (4), a safe keeping (5), and a perfected salvation (5–9). The inheritance was a very real factor of blessing in the experience of a Jew in Old Testament times (cf. Dt. xv. 4, xix. 10, xxxiv). In verse 4 Peter contrasts that old inheritance with the inheritance of the Christian. The old was subject to destruction by invading armies who robbed them of their land. The Christian inheritance is *incorruptible*. The apostle makes frequent use of this word (i. 18, 23, iii. 4, v. 4). See also Lk. xii. 33. It is *undefiled*. The earthly inheritance of the Jew had often been defiled by Israel's sin. The Christian's is *reserved in heaven* where nothing that defileth can ever enter in (Rev. xxi. 27). It *fadeth not away*. Canaan had often been subject to blasting by mildew and by the hot east winds which frequently brought plagues of locusts as well as drought (2 Ch. vi. 28; Dt. xxviii. 22–24; 1 Ki. viii. 37; Am. iv. 9; Hg. ii. 17). The inheritance of the Christian is beyond the blight of change. The Greek word translated *reserved* is a military term (from Gk. *tēreō*, 'to guard') and suggests constant watchfulness. No harm can come to the inheritance because it is safely guarded or kept in heaven, beyond the reach of earthly powers to touch or harm. But not only is the inheritance guarded for the heirs, the heirs are likewise guarded for the inheritance. They are guarded by *the power of God* (5), which is stronger far than the might of the persecutor. This divine guarding becomes operative in the believer's experience through faith.

Salvation ready to be revealed in the last time (5). Salvation is not only a present blessing through which we receive forgiveness, justification, sanctification and other divine gifts; it will be realized in its fulness only when we are presented faultless before the throne, made like Him, perfected and lacking nothing. This salvation in its fullest sense is ready now and is waiting to be manifested *in the last time* (cf. 1 Jn. ii. 18; Jude 18; Jn. vi. 40). In the light of the eschatological nature of this Epistle this phrase may be taken as equivalent to 'the end of all things' (iv. 7).

The apostle now makes reference to the trials which were besetting them. Even in the midst of these trials and persecutions they could rejoice greatly in the assured possession of salvation. This seems to be the force of *wherein* (6). A better rendering is perhaps 'wherefore', i.e. in view of the foregoing considerations. It is because they have this living hope, inheritance, safe guarding and perfected salvation that they are able to rejoice greatly now, even though *for a season* (RV 'for a little while') they are *in heaviness through manifold temptations* (6). Their sufferings were only temporary and were not to be compared with the glory that was theirs in Christ. They were *in heaviness* (Gk. *lypēthentes*, 'to be distressed', 'grieved' or 'put to grief') because of the variety, intensity and frequency of their trials. But they are to remember that there is purpose in trial, and faith is not proved genuine until it has been tested by suffering. *The trial* (RV 'the proof') *of your faith* (7). The Greek word *dokimion* is translated by Hort as 'that which is approved as genuine' in your faith. The reference is to that which is left after what is false has been refined away. As gold is tried and purified by fire, so faith is tested. Only that which stands the test is of full quality. But even gold, so purified, still belongs to the world of perishable things. Faith, on the other hand, purified by suffering, takes its place among those things that are imperishable. Hence it is *much more precious* than gold which, even when it is purified, perisheth. *At the appearing* (RV 'revelation') *of Jesus Christ* (7). All the testing and suffering needed for the refining will seem as nothing compared with the *praise and honour and glory* which will be the reward. *Whom having not seen, ye love* (8). Although they had not had the privilege of seeing and knowing Christ in the flesh as Peter himself had done, nevertheless faith triumphed over this lack of actual vision and so they were able to rejoice. Their joy was *unspeakable*, i.e. too deep for words, and already marked with the splendour of heaven where they shall see Him face to face (cf. 1 Cor. xiii. 12). Through the trials that pressed upon them they clung believingly to Christ and were thus enabled to rejoice in His care and deliverance. *Receiving* (9) implies obtaining and appropriating, or making their own now. *The end of your faith* (9) refers to the completion and crown of their trust. Already they were receiving a foretaste of that perfect salvation which they would enjoy in its fulness hereafter. The greatness and glory of this salvation are supported by two facts. First, the Old Testament writers pointed forward to it; secondly, angels would fain look into it.

The prophets (10). The men of the Old Testament looked forward to the time when the promises of God which they had received regarding the salvation of His people would be fulfilled. They looked for the Messiah to come and redeem His people Israel. *Who prophesied of the grace that should come unto you* (10). Hort cites Acts xi. 23 and refers the words to the grace shown in the admission of the Gentiles to the Christian Church. But there seems no good reason why it should be thus limited and not rather made applicable to the whole outpouring of grace in their Christian life and experience of which their admission to the Christian Church was but an example. *Searching what, or what manner of time the Spirit of Christ which was in them did signify* (11). That the prophets spoke under the inspiration of the Spirit was recognized in Old Testament times (cf. 2 Sa. xxiii. 2; Is. lxi. 1), as well as in the Christian era (2 Pet. i. 21). Note that the Holy Spirit is here called 'the Spirit of Christ' (cf. Acts xvi. 7, RV; Rom. viii. 9; Gal. iv. 6; Phil. i. 19). These passages indicate that the New Testament writers were moved by the Spirit of Christ and it is interesting that the same designation is applied to the Spirit who inspired Old Testament prophets (cf. Heb. iii. 7, ix. 8, x. 15). He came to glorify Christ and to speak of Him. He was in the prophets as the Spirit of revelation communicating truths which they could not have foreseen or discovered, and as the Spirit of inspiration affording spiritual aid in setting forth and declaring the truth. The prophets are said to have *inquired and searched diligently*, i.e. in their own Scriptures, to find when and under what conditions the Messiah would come. It was revealed to them that He would come as the Suffering Servant (cf. Is. liii), but that after His sufferings would come His *glory*, or 'triumphs' (Gk. *doxas*). The plural form corresponds to the plural *sufferings*. The singular form *doxan* is used in 1 Pet. i. 21, where the reference is to the resurrection, and in 2 Pet. i. 17 where it is the glory of the transfiguration to which allusion is made. The result of their intense search was a further revelation that in their work as prophets of the Messiah they were serving not their own generation but the generation to which Peter now addressed himself. Note that those who *preached the gospel* (12) to them were inspired and enabled to proclaim the good news by the same Holy Spirit as that by whom the prophets were inspired to write.

Which things the angels desire to look into (12). Not only the prophets but the angels as well are eager to understand the mystery. 'The word translated "look", though it can mean simply "to stoop down to look" (cf. Lk. xxiv. 12; Jn. xx. 11), often suggests a stolen glimpse and it is probable that the meaning here is that the angels would fain peep into the blessedness of our salvation, but actually cannot do that because it is beyond their apprehension' (*First Epistle of Peter*, by C. E. B. Cranfield).

III. THE CALL TO HOLINESS. i. 13—ii. 10

a. The redeemed are called to obedience (i. 13–21)

Peter now passes to the practical implications of what he has been setting before them. In view of the foregoing considerations (*wherefore*), he appeals to them to live holy lives. This is the responsibility that rests upon them now as Christians. The supreme purpose of redemption is to make men holy.

Gird up the loins of your mind (13). The reference is to the binding up of the loose-flowing robes of the Oriental which hamper freedom of movement. It is a call to the pilgrim attitude. Note that it is the loins of the *mind* to which the apostle refers. He would summon them to strenuous thinking so that they might understand the things he is writing to them and be able to exercise an intelligent faith (cf. 1 Cor. xiv. 20 and Eph. i. 18). The pilgrim temper is sobriety (cf. also iv. 7, v. 8). Although actual intemperance was a pressing temptation to them, the exhortation *be sober* (13) means more than avoidance of drunkenness. It means seriousness and alertness in thought and conduct. They are to exercise a becoming self-control and live a balanced, steadfast life. Confronted by the difficulties of the way the pilgrim's strength is *hope* (13). Peter has already reminded them what this living hope is (3). He now encourages them to look forward to and anticipate the grace that will be brought to them at the appearing of Jesus Christ (see verse 10).

As obedient children (14). The call to holiness is necessarily a call to obedience. Obedience is a favourite word with Peter in this Epistle (cf. i. 2, 22, iii. 1, 6, iv. 17). The first duty of man has ever been to obey God, keeping His commandments and doing His will (Lv. xviii. 4, 5). The need for this was continually stressed in the teaching of Christ. Obedience manifests itself in *not fashioning yourselves according to the former lusts in* (RV 'in the time of') *your ignorance* (14). Lust is natural inclination run wild, overleaping all restraint and asserting its own imperious will. The old pagan lusts of the past ('the time of your ignorance', suggesting that the recipients of the letter were mostly Gentiles) continued to have an insidious attraction. Their obedience to Christ would deliver them from the snare of these if they were prepared to leave them behind and refrain from fashioning themselves according to them.

As he which hath called you is holy, so be ye holy (15). The exhortation is enforced by a quotation from Leviticus (xi. 44), a book whose key-word is 'holiness' (cf. Lv. xix. 2, xx. 7, 26). In the Old Testament the root meaning of the word 'holy' is separated, withdrawn from ordinary use and set apart for a sacred use. The underlying thought would seem to be that the holy God had chosen them to be His people, therefore they too must be holy if they are to enjoy fellowship with Him (cf. the New Testament phrase, 'called to be saints'). *Conversation* (15); RV 'living'. Such holiness will express itself in outward conduct. *If ye call on the Father, who . . . judgeth* (17). The argument is that since they claim God as their Father, and pray to Him as such, they must respect His authority. He is Father; He is also Judge and His judgment is impartial, *without respect of persons* (17). Hence the apostle's exhortation to *pass the time of your sojourning here in fear*—not merely fear of punishment from the Judge, but fear of grieving the Father. The word translated *pass* is the Greek *anastrephō*, meaning 'to conduct oneself'.

But the truest and strongest motive of all for fear is in the fact of redemption. *Redeemed* (18); Gk. *elytrōthēte*, meaning released on payment of the ransom price. The noun, *lytron*, signifies the price paid; here it is not money, but the *blood of Christ* (19) who 'came to give His life a ransom for many' (Mt. xx. 28; Mk. x. 45; see also 1 Tim. ii. 6). Israel's deliverance from bondage was probably in the apostle's mind as he thought of the deliverance of the Christians from the bondage of sin. That being so it would be the Paschal Lamb that he had in mind when he used the phrase *as of a lamb without blemish*

and without spot (19; see Ex. xii. 5). The reference to *silver and gold* may be an allusion to the manumission of slaves. A slave could save the money he earned with a view to buying his freedom. Some of those to whom this letter was addressed had probably hoped to do so. But while silver and gold could purchase that freedom it was powerless to effect freedom from the dominion of sin. Nothing less than the blood of Christ the Lamb of God could suffice for that. *Vain conversation* (18); i.e. an empty traditional manner of life, a life without purpose or direction.

Foreordained (RV 'foreknown') *before the foundation of the world* (20). Redemption was part of God's eternal purpose. In the fulness of time Christ was manifested to put away sin by the sacrifice of Himself. Note the RV rendering 'was manifested at the end of the times for your sake'. 'With these words "for your sake" the writer focuses the whole divine counsel of redemption upon his readers' (Selwyn). The gospel is essentially personal. *Who by him do believe in God* (21). See RV. As Cranfield points out, the word translated 'believers' in the RV is not the participle but the verbal adjective which usually has the meaning 'loyal'. The double meaning may be intended. Through Christ we believe and through Him also we are kept loyal to God.

As a sign that He was satisfied with Christ's finished work and that it was adequate for our redemption God *raised him up from the dead, and gave him glory* (21). Hort sees in these words a correspondence with Is. lii. 13. God is the divine author of the resurrection (cf. Acts iii. 15, iv. 10, v. 30, x. 40). *That your faith and hope might be in God* (21); i.e. this is God's purpose in making manifest the Christ (20). Notice how faith and hope are closely entwined in this Epistle.

b. The need for spiritual growth (i. 22—ii. 3)

Purified your souls in obeying the truth (22). Some commentators see here a reference to baptism. The new converts have submitted to the truth of the gospel and have been baptized and thereby cleansed. If, as has been suggested, this Epistle was of the nature of a baptismal homily intended to be read at Easter there may be such an allusion here (cf. iii. 21). But the words *the truth* may be equivalent here to the whole gospel which, when believed and obeyed, brings cleansing to the soul. (Note that the words *through the Spirit* (22) are not found in the best MSS and are omitted by the RV and RSV.) This cleansing will manifest itself in *unfeigned love of the brethren* (22). Any mere show of love would be a denial of the truth. The practical test of holiness of life and obedience to the truth is love for others (cf. 1 Jn. iv. 7, 11, 20). Such love must be fervent. The Greek is *ektenōs*, meaning 'on the stretch', extended to the full. It must also be the product of a *pure heart*, for only when the heart is pure can the motives be pure.

In verse 23 Peter returns to the fact of their

having been 'begotten again' (see verse 3). The supernatural origin or source from which believers have been *born again* is here the Word of God, which is no mere perishing instrument or sacramental symbol, lost in the using, and hence corruptible, but something which lives by the divine principle of the life which it conveys, and hence incorruptible.

In i. 24, 25 we have a quotation from Is. xl. 6, 8 which serves to set in contrast the transiency of human life and all human things, however glorious, with the ever-living and everlasting Word of God. *All flesh is as grass* and cannot resist the ravages of time. On the other hand, there stands the eternal truth of God which is both living and life-giving. This is the good tidings of Jesus Christ and His redemptive work which has been declared to them by His heralds.

The apostle now proceeds to give further marks of the holy life and, in doing so, describes Christians under four figures. They are *newborn babes* (2) who must now grow in grace by feeding on the Word of God. They are *lively* (RV 'living') *stones* (5) in the heavenly temple of which Christ is the *chief corner stone* (6). They are a *holy priesthood* (5; cf. verse 9) to offer up spiritual sacrifices. They are *the people of God* (10), the true Israel who now bear the honoured titles applied in the Old Testament to Israel after the flesh.

Wherefore (1); this carries the thought back to what the author has already said regarding the privileges and possessions of those who are 'begotten again'. It introduces some practical aspects of their position in Christ and of the life they are to live. They are to put away all *malice* (RV 'wickedness'), which is a comprehensive word for all evil of the pagan world (Selwyn), *and all guile*, or deceitfulness, *and hypocrisies*, e.g. the temptation to join the Church from false motives, *and envies*, the bane of religious work which was evident even among the Twelve (Lk. xxii. 24ff.), *and all evil speakings*, the fruit of envy. All these are sins of the spirit and consequently hinder growth in holiness. The word translated 'evil speakings' (Gk. *katalaliai*) means detractions (Bengel). Here the habit of disparagement rather than of open slander is denounced. These things are to be laid aside as a garment is laid aside (cf. Eph. iv. 22; Col. iii. 9; 2 Cor. iv. 2). Renunciation had a large place in the life and teaching of primitive Christianity.

The hindrances having been removed it was reasonable to expect growth. They were as yet but babes in Christ, so Peter exhorts them to be like newborn babes in their desire for spiritual food necessary for spiritual growth. They are to *desire* (Gk. *epipothēsate*, expressive of intense longing) spiritual nourishment, i.e. *the sincere milk of the word*; RV 'spiritual milk which is without guile'. The interpretation depends on the translation of *logikon*, which the RV renders 'spiritual'. Some commentators, adhering to the meaning of *logos* and following the AV transla-

tion, render it 'flowing out of the Word of God'. Hort and others give the translation as 'rational', 'reasonable', as in Rom. xii. 1. While *logos* denotes a 'word', the adjective *logikos* is never used with the meaning assigned to it here in the AV. It is, of course, true that the Word of God nourishes the soul as milk nourishes the body, and from the closing verses of chapter i we may infer that this is really the analogy which is being used by Peter. *If so be ye have tasted that the Lord is gracious* (3), then you will naturally desire the spiritual nourishment referred to and at the same time put away all the hindering things mentioned. This verse is based on Ps. xxxiv. 8.

c. The Church as a spiritual temple (ii. 4-10)

The apostle now changes the subject, and goes on to deal with the Church, the people of God, the new Israel. Christ is *a living stone* (4), both because He is alive for evermore (Rev. i. 18) and because He is life-giving (see Jn. i. 4, xi. 25, xiv. 6, xx. 31). Those who come to Him themselves become living stones and are built together upon Him into *a spiritual house* (5) or temple. The word 'house' has often this specific meaning (e.g. Jn. ii. 17). For a full discussion on this point see Selwyn's note (*First Epistle of St. Peter*, pp. 286ff.).

Disallowed (RV 'rejected') *indeed of men* (4). The phrase is a reference to Ps. cxviii. 22 which is quoted in verse 7. Peter has in mind the rejection of our Lord by the elders and people of Israel which led to His crucifixion. *Precious* (4); RV mg. 'honourable'. The Greek *entimos* is the regular word for 'esteemed, held in honour'. Though dishonoured by man He is honoured by God (cf. Phil. ii. 9ff.).

The adjective *zōntos, lively* or 'living', is used in verse 5 probably to point the contrast between the Christian who is born again and has received new life and the pagan who is still dead in trespasses and sins, as well as between the Christian Church and the pagan temple. The living stones are built together into a spiritual temple, Jesus Christ Himself being the chief corner stone. The idea of the temple leads on naturally to the priesthood and sacrifices (5). There is a priesthood of all believers and the sacrifice they offer is not one of animals or birds, but of themselves (cf. Rom. xii. 1). But such sacrifices are not acceptable because of anything in the offerer or in the offering. They are *acceptable to God* only when offered *by* (RV 'through') *Jesus Christ*, joined to His perfect sacrifice of Himself and offered in His name (cf. Heb. xiii. 15).

Verses 6-8 contain a series of quotations from the Old Testament emphasizing or elucidating what has already been said about Christ as the stone. The first is from Is. xxviii. 16 with a note added on the word 'precious' (7a). Note Paul's use of the same quotation in Rom. ix. 33, x. 11. The second reference (7) is to Ps. cxviii. 22, another favourite messianic prophecy of the early Church and one used by our Lord Himself (Mt. xxi. 42; Acts iv. 11; Eph. ii. 20). The third quotation (8) is from Is. viii. 14 and is also used by Paul (Rom. ix. 33). Notice how unbelief (7) and disobedience (8) are linked and result in stumbling. It is by their attitude to the stone that men are judged. To the unbeliever who rejects the Stone it becomes a rock of offence and a stumblingblock (cf. 1 Cor. i. 18–25). *Whereunto also they were appointed* (8). This too is part of the divine purpose in that it was foreseen as inevitable. Both the redemptive mission and work of Christ and its rejection and rejectors were within the counsel and purpose of God (Hort). Cf. Rom. ix. 22–24.

In verse 9 the titles applied to Christians are taken direct from the description of the people of God in the Old Testament (see, e.g., Ex. xix. 5; Is. xliii. 21; see also Rev. i. 5, 6). These are taken over by Christian believers as the new Israel, an elect race, entitled to all the privileges and called to accept the responsibilities of God's chosen people. They are to be *a royal priesthood* (cf. Rev. i. 6). The two offices of king and priest were jealously kept apart in Israel (cf. 2 Ch. xxvi. 16–21), but in Christ they blend. He is a priest upon His throne (Zc. vi. 13) and all His followers are kings and priests unto God. All that the priest was in Old Testament times in his relation to God and in his relation to men the Christian in his corporate and in his individual life must be. *A holy nation* is a term expressive of the covenant relationship existing between God and Israel (Ex. xix. 6). Israel failed in keeping that relationship and was temporarily set aside; but those who, Jew or Gentile, have accepted Christ are constituted another nation with the obligation to holiness. Further, God had chosen Israel to be peculiarly His own, hence they were *a peculiar people* (RV 'a people for God's own possession'). This figure is also carried over and made applicable to believers in Christ. They are God's special people. The Greek word translated 'people' is *laos* which in the LXX is a technical term for Israel as distinguished from all other peoples. But Christian privilege is always for service. To *show forth* is to advertise or to proclaim as a herald (cf. 1 Cor. xi. 26). For *praises* RV reads 'excellencies'. The reference is not only to God's character but also to His mighty and noble acts (cf. Ps. xl. 2). Here the apostle has particularly in mind the redemption wrought in Christ for us by His death and resurrection. We are called out of the darkness of nature, sin, ignorance and unbelief and brought into the light and liberty of the gospel. *Which in time past were not a people, but are now the people of God* (10). The reference is to the children of Gomer, Lo-ruhamah (Ho. i. 6) and Lo-ammi (Ho. i. 8, 9), apt descriptions of Israel alienated from God but later reconciled to God. The terms 'in time past' and 'now' correspond to the terms 'darkness' and 'light' above. Ho. ii. 23, which speaks of the reversal of God's disowning of unfaithful Israel, has been fulfilled in

Christ. Not only on Israel but also on the Gentiles has this blessing been bestowed.

IV. CHRISTIAN DUTY. ii. 11—iii. 12

a. The Christian citizen (ii. 11–17)

Having dealt with the special privileges which were theirs as the new Israel, the apostle proceeds to outline some of the principles which ought to govern their lives as members of, and in relation to, the community of which they are now a part. His form of address is significant. *Beloved* is a common vocative in the New Testament but it is especially opportune here since the need for brotherly love has been emphasized in i. 22 as one of the manifestations of the holy life to which they were called. *Strangers* (11); RV 'sojourners'; Gk. *paroikos*, meaning a person living in a foreign country where he has no citizenship rights. *Pilgrims;* Gk. *parepidēmos*, a person staying temporarily in a place which is not his home. If, as is implied, life in the foreign country is on a lower level than that in the sojourners' native land, they must not adopt its customs but must behave honourably and in such a way as to uphold the good name of their land. Negatively, they are to abstain from fleshly lusts, i.e. the desires that originate in man's corrupt nature as well as those connected with the appetites of the body (cf. Gal. v. 19–21). *Fleshly* describes man in his alienation from God, and includes the whole of human nature in its fallen state. These are forces which *war against the soul* (Gk. *psychē*). The term occurs also in i. 9, 22, ii. 25, iv. 19 and denotes the higher element in man's nature (cf. Rom. vii. 23; Jas. iv. 1). Positively, they are to have their *conversation honest* (RV 'behaviour seemly') *among the Gentiles* (12), commending themselves to men's moral judgment, so that even if non-Christians should slander them their slanderers will be compelled by the evidence of their consistently Christian lives to acknowledge the God of the Christians and to glorify Him by believing on Him while He is still visiting His people. The exact significance of *the day of visitation* (12) is difficult to determine. In Is. x. 3 it denotes the day when Jehovah shall appear to right the oppressed and punish the oppressors. Here it may simply mean the day when God will visit His people in order to deliver them from their persecutors or when He will visit the oppressor in judgment. See also Lk. xix. 44 where the day of visitation is identified with Christ's offer of salvation to Israel. They are to manifest this seemly behaviour by submitting to civil authority, by being loyal subjects of the emperor and by obeying his representatives. The key-note of the whole section is submission, or subordination (cf. ii. 18, iii. 1). Peter seems to prefer the aorist imperative to the present in commands, pointing rather to the definite decision to submit than to the continual act of submission. The phrase *every ordinance of man* (13) is difficult. The Greek *anthrōpinē(i) ktisei* is lit. 'human creature' or creation. The meaning may be, therefore, 'Be subject to every man for the Lord's sake', introducing the whole section dealing with the duty of a Christian in the various relationships of life. The subjection is to be a voluntary act remembering our Lord's example and done for the honour of His name. For His sake they are to recognize and accept their responsibilities and obligations of citizenship in submission to the lawful claims of the State. They are to be subject to *the king, as supreme*, in their case the Roman emperor, Nero, and to his deputies. Christian obligation is not dependent on the personal goodness of the ruler but rather on the office represented and the duties they are called upon to perform (cf. Rom. xiii. 1-7). It is God's will that by acting uprightly and obediently in this way they should *put to silence* (lit. 'muzzle'; cf. Mk. i. 25, iv. 39; Mt. xxii. 34) their slanderers (15). The charge of rebellion against Caesar, levelled at our Lord, seems already to have been levelled at His followers, and probably arose out of a misinterpretation of the Christian liberty which they claimed. They were free, but their freedom was limited by, and conditioned upon, their being servants or bondslaves of Christ. The true Christian still finds his perfect freedom in the service of his Master, an idea which is repugnant to totalitarian ideology. The question arises how far a Christian is under obligation to obey the commands of civil rulers. In so far as obedience to civil law does not involve disobedience to God we are to submit for the Lord's sake. It is conceivable that a Christian can show greater loyalty to the State by disobeying its commands, e.g. when these commands are plainly unlawful and contrary to the teaching of Holy Scripture. Acts iv. 19, v. 29 afford clear guidance in the matter. The section concludes with a fourfold command. *Honour all men* (see verse 13n. above). *Love the brotherhood* (cf. i. 22). *Fear God. Honour the king* (17). This twofold command is an adaptation of Pr. xxiv. 21, 'My son, fear thou the Lord and the king'.

b. Servants and masters (ii. 18-25)

The underlying thought is still that of submission. *Servants*, Gk. *oiketai*, i.e. household servants or slaves, as contrasted with *douloi*, used to denote bondslaves such as those employed, e.g., in labour gangs. *With all fear* (18); not the fear of reprisals from their masters but reverential fear of God which ought to lead them as Christians to render faithful service. The phrase *for conscience toward God* in the next verse would seem to support this interpretation. Submission is not to be dependent upon the worthiness or unworthiness of the master. They are to serve faithfully not only those who are *good and gentle* but also *the froward*, Gk. *skolios*, curved or crooked, used here metaphorically of what is morally crooked or perverse. *For this is thankworthy* (RV 'acceptable') ... (19). There is no merit attached to enduring punishment which is deserved as the result of

wrongdoing; but to endure punishment which is undeserved is worthy of commendation, for thereby God is glorified (cf. Mt. v. 46-48; Lk. vi. 27-35). Commentators are somewhat divided on the interpretation of the phrase *for conscience toward God* (19). Calvin, Alford and Westcott, for example, take it as meaning 'on account of the consciousness of the presence and will of God'. On the other hand Bengel interprets it as meaning 'on account of the consciousness of a mind which does things good and pleasing to God, even though they please no man'. This latter seems preferable as being more in keeping with the New Testament use of the term 'conscience'. *For what glory is it?* (20); Gk. *kleos*, meaning credit, good report, fame or renown. *Buffeted;* Gk. *kolaphizō*, to strike with the fists. The same word is used of the buffeting of our Lord in Mk. xiv. 65.

For even hereunto were ye called (21). The meek, submissive, patient bearing of undeserved suffering is part of their high calling in Christ. *Christ also suffered for us* (21). Peter is careful to emphasize the substitutionary aspect of Christ's suffering. It was 'on our behalf' (cf. verse 24 below). Because of that there is an obligation of gratitude to act in a Christlike way even in the midst of suffering. *An example;* Gk. *hypogrammos*, under-writing or tracing; the idea is one of reproducing the letters traced in the headline of a child's copy-book. *Who did no sin, neither was guile found in his mouth* (22; cf. Is. liii. 9). The sinlessness of Christ is essential to His sufficiency as a Saviour in His sacrificial work for sinners, and is a point of emphasis not only here but throughout the whole account of the divine plan of redemption. See also Heb. vii. 26. It recalls the lamb without blemish and without spot mentioned in i. 19 above. *Who, when he was reviled, reviled not again* (23), a reference undoubtedly to what He endured during His trial. For the silence of Christ cf. Mk. xiv. 61, xv. 5, and cf. Is. liii. 7. The evil accusations of His enemies brought no answer from His holy lips. He left it to the Father to vindicate Him, for His judgment is just and His verdict unassailable (cf. i. 17 above).

In verse 24 the apostle again lays stress upon the substitutionary work of Christ on the cross (cf. Is. liii. 12). Note the phrase *our sins*. Peter has already made it clear that He did no sin (22). This aspect of the atonement is essential to a saving faith in Christ. 'The bearing of our sins means suffering the punishment of them in our place' (Cranfield, *ad loc.*). The purpose of the sufferings of Christ is clearly stated. Christ identified Himself with us sinners, bearing our sin on to the cross. We now identify ourselves with Him in His death, and henceforth are to *live unto righteousness*, i.e. our lives are to be rightly related to God and to man. *Stripes;* Gk. *mōlōpi*, meaning bruises, or wounds from stripes. The word is used figuratively of the stroke of divine judgment administered vicariously to Christ on the cross. *For ye were as sheep going astray* (25; cf. Is. liii. 6). In their past lives they had wandered and strayed like lost sheep. Selwyn finds a parallel to this in Ezk. xxxiv which would apply both to the lapsed Jews of the Dispersion and to the pagans who had now been brought into the Christian communities in Asia Minor. But now the lost sheep had been brought back to the fold, and have *returned unto the Shepherd and Bishop of your souls* (25). The Shepherd feeds and sustains, seeks, gathers into the fold, tends, guards from enemies and leads into green pastures (cf. Jn. x. 10; Ps. xxiii. 1–4; Is. xl. 11). The Bishop (Gk. *episkopos*, 'overseer') guides and directs. The word came to be used as the title for officers sent by the Athenians to manage the affairs of subject states. It is not used here in any technical or ecclesiastical sense but merely in the sense of an overseer. Later it came to be used as one of the titles of the Christian ministry.

c. Husbands and wives (iii. 1–7)

The apostle now deals with the duty of the Christian in the marriage relationship. It is probable that he had particularly in mind Christian wives of pagan husbands and Christian husbands of pagan wives, although his counsel is not necessarily confined to these. In the nature of things the former group would be more numerous as a class than the latter owing to the greater authority exerted by the husband. When a pagan wife became a Christian she could not reckon on her husband following her in that faith. On the other hand, if the husband became a Christian, it was quite likely that his wife would join him in this. *Likewise* (1). Just as the spirit of Christ was to be manifested in the social relationships already mentioned so it must be manifested in the everyday life of the home. Note that it is the marriage relation which Peter has in mind and not that between men and women generally. There is no ground here for an argument in favour of the inferiority of women to men. The attitude which the apostle enjoins is not merely the conventional, submissive attitude of his day but the expression of the Christian readiness to subordinate self to others. It is by this manifestation of the Christlike spirit on the part of the wife that husbands who *obey not the word* are *without the word* won by the behaviour of their wives (1). Here 'the word' is used in two different senses. The first occurrence has a reference to the Word of God or the gospel, whereas the second refers simply to ordinary speech or use of words. The husbands who refuse to obey the Word of God may be won by the seemly Christian behaviour of their wives without the latter having to speak a word, which might serve only to harden the husband's heart against the gospel. *Coupled with fear* (2); i.e. that reverence which is an essential ingredient of the Christian life. The Christian wife's submission to her husband has an evangelistic purpose—to win him to faith in Christ. Her real beauty is not dependent on outward adornment, finery or

display, but *the ornament of a meek and quiet spirit* (4; cf. 1 Tim. ii. 9f.). 'Not the ostentation of outward ornament but the inward beauty of the heart' (Selwyn).

The gold and apparel are corruptible and will perish, but the meek and quiet spirit is in the sight of God very precious. Bengel distinguishes between meekness and quietness by regarding the former as giving no cause for disturbance while the latter bears calmly the disturbance caused by others. *The hidden man of the heart* (4). 'Scripture regards the heart as the sphere of divine influence (Rom. ii. 15; Acts xv. 9) . . . . The heart as lying deep within, contains the hidden man (1 Pet. iii. 4), the real man. It represents the true character but conceals it' (J. Laidlaw in H.D.B.). *The holy women* (5). The reference is to 'women who pre-eminently represented the holiness of Israel's calling, i.e. its "saints"; cf. Mt. xxvii. 52' (Selwyn). They trusted or hoped in God that to them might be given the honour of being the mother of the Messiah. *Calling him lord* (6); see Gn. xviii. 1–15. *Whose daughters ye are* (6). Christian wives would become true daughters of Sarah through spiritual likeness. Gk. *tekna* is used metaphorically to denote spiritual affinity. The significance of the phrase 'not put in fear by any terror' (6, RV) seems obscure. The Greek word *phobos* is always used in the Epistle in a good sense of reverence or respect except here and in iii. 14. The grounds of fear may have been that of persecution by their pagan husbands who would attempt to compel them to leave their faith, or a display of bad temper on the part of the husband. Perhaps, as Cranfield suggests, fear or terror should be taken in a general sense so that 'fearing God they are to be free from other fears'.

Peter now exhorts the husbands to fulfil their duty to their wives. They are to dwell with their wives *according to knowledge* (7), i.e. showing practical understanding and tact in all the relationships of married life. *Giving honour unto the wife* (7). If we compare ii. 13 and 17 with this verse it will be seen that the term *honour* has in it some sense of subjection. So the husband is to exercise a measure of Christian subordination to self in regard to his wife. The woman is described as *the weaker vessel* because she is physically weaker in some respects than the man. There is no question here of intellectual or moral inferiority although, in the ancient world, this was taken for granted. The man is held to be the stronger vessel in the sense of being more muscular and of carrying heavier responsibilities in the home as bread-winner and support of the family (cf. 1 Thes. iv. 4). The ground for the husband's thus honouring the wife is stated in the phrase *as being heirs together of the grace of life* (7). This may mean that, since they are both Christians, they share equally in that eternal life which acceptance of the gospel brings. Others feel that, because Peter is probably addressing here husbands of pagan wives, the reference is to the power to transmit natural life by bringing other human beings into the world. A final word is added. Lack of understanding between husband and wife, selfishness on the part of either, or anything that would tend to domestic friction, will surely have its effect upon the spiritual life and will be a hindrance to the prayer life of those concerned.

d. Living together in the Christian community (iii. 8–12)

These verses summarize the whole section by introducing a last consideration. The *finally* (8) serves to mark the transition from the detailed duties already outlined in the relationships mentioned to a general statement of the essentials in Christian character. They must be 'likeminded' (RV). Divisions in Church or family life are not glorifying to God (cf. Jn. xvii. 21ff.; Rom. xv. 5f.; 1 Cor. i. 10; Phil. ii. 2). *Having compassion one of another*; lit. 'be sympathetic'. The word means suffering together with others. We belong to one body in Christ, hence the application of 1 Cor. xii. 26. *Love as brethren*. Note the AV mg., 'loving to the brethren'. Brotherly love is the badge of the Christian (Jn. xiii. 35) and the sign that we have passed from death to life (1 Jn. iii. 14, iv. 20). *Be pitiful* (RV 'tenderhearted'). There is a danger of becoming hardened to hearing of other people's suffering. *Be courteous;* RV 'humbleminded'. Gk. *tapeinophrōn*, 'of lowly mind'. Humility is an essential of true Christian character, and is a thought often in the mind of the apostles (cf. v. 5; Rom. xii. 16; Jas. iv. 10). Verse 9 is the application to the believer of our Lord's example given in ii. 23. The word translated 'reviled' there is the same as the word rendered 'railing' here (see RV). Here the apostle is passing on the teaching he himself received from Christ. See, e.g., Mt. v. 44; Lk. vi. 27f. The author closes this section of the Epistle with a paraphrase of Ps. xxiv in the LXX. In all likelihood the freer translation and emendation of the text was the work of Silvanus. *He that will love life* (10); not length of life but quality of it. *And see good days* probably refers to the good things (e.g. the inheritance of verse 9) reserved for them (cf. i. 4). Such a one must refrain from evil-speaking and from evil of every description and do that which is right and true. He must be unremitting in his endeavour after peace (cf. Mt. v. 9), remembering that God's eye is ever upon him for his guidance or to mark the divine approval or displeasure, and that His ear is attentive to his prayer for direction or help. On the other hand *the face of the Lord is against them that do evil* (12). The face of the Lord stands for the manifestation of the divine presence, here set in opposition to the way of the wicked.

V. SUFFERINGS AND GLORY. iii. 13—iv. 19

a. Christ our example in meeting hostility and suffering (iii. 13–22)

The mention of evil-doers leads to the apostle's next thought expressed in a rhetorical question.

Followers of (13); RV 'zealous of'; Gk. *zēlōtai*. A 'zealot' is an uncompromising partisan, and was the name applied to the extreme section of the Pharisees in their bitter antagonism to the Romans. It has in it the idea of wholeheartedness and singleness of purpose, and the application is obvious here. But God's protection does not mean that they are immune from persecution. *But and if ye suffer* (14). The Greek optative mood is used here and in verse 17 would envisage a contingency not pressing but remote for some of them. When the suffering is *for righteousness' sake* they may claim the fulfilment of Mt. v. 10. They are not to give themselves up to the *terror* which their enemies would seek to instil (cf. Is. viii. 12 in LXX), but contrariwise are to have a reverential fear of Christ which will enable them to enthrone Him as Lord in their hearts (15). *An answer* (15); Gk. *apologia*, originally a speech made by a prisoner in his defence and later applied to the treatises written in defence of the Christian faith. Peter implies that the persecutors would be hostile and slanderous in their criticism of the faith, and it was necessary that as converts they should be well grounded in the fundamental truths (cf. i. 13) so as to give *a reason of* (Gk. *logon peri*, 'a rational account') *the hope* unto which they had been begotten again (i. 3). *Meekness* represents their attitude to their questioners; *fear* (AV mg. 'reverence') their attitude to God. By behaving thus they will have, or will maintain, *a good conscience* (16) and will put to shame their false accusers. Peter returns here to the thought of ii. 12. *Conversation* (16); better, as in RV, 'manner of life'. For verse 17 cf. ii. 20. *Also* (18) links our Lord with those who, with a good conscience, suffer for righteousness' sake. He stands beside them, having been Himself falsely accused and having *suffered for sins* not His own. But He is not just an example. His cross is primarily an atonement. Reference has already been made to the sufferings of Christ (ii. 21ff.), but the emphasis there was on His meekness; here it is on His triumph. Here, too, His passion is thought of as vicarious—*the just for the unjust* (cf. Is. liii. 5)—and as atoning in its efficacy—*for sins*. The completeness of the sacrifice is noted in the word *once* (cf. Rom. vi. 9f.; Heb. vii. 27, ix. 12, 26, 28, x. 10). The purpose of Christ's death is simply stated. We are alienated from God through sin, but Christ, through His atonement, has made possible our return to God. Our access to God depends solely on the merits of Christ's work on the cross. *Being put to death in the flesh* has probably a reference to the violence of Christ's death as well as to the reality of it. But He was *quickened by* (RV 'in') *the Spirit*. The reference is not to the Holy Spirit, but to Christ's human spirit as distinct from His body. Verses 19–22 present numerous difficulties and there have been many explanations offered by commentators. Selwyn quotes here an excellent note by Alford (*q.v.*).

By which (RV 'in which', i.e. in which state of

spirit quickened after physical death) *also he went and preached unto the spirits in prison* (19). The first three words are in the Greek *en hō(i) kai*. Moffatt, following Rendel Harris and supported by Schultz, seeks to circumvent the difficulty by rendering this verse, 'It was in the Spirit that Enoch also went and preached to imprisoned spirits'; but there are textual and other difficulties which disallow this explanation. It seems quite clear that it was Christ Himself, not Enoch, who went and preached. From the context, *the spirits in prison* denote the generation who were disobedient in Noah's day, while the words 'spirits' and 'prison' refer to their present disembodied condition in a place of judgment in the unseen world (cf. 2 Pet. ii. 4–9). The crucial point in the passage lies in what is said of Christ's preaching to them. Although the Greek *ekēryxen*, meaning 'preached', is usually followed by its object in the New Testament, it is sometimes used absolutely, and there seems no good reason why the interpretation which strikes one most naturally should not be accepted, viz. that Christ, put to death in the flesh and made alive again in the spirit, went in this spiritual state and preached to those spirits who had once been disobedient, but are viewed as now possibly receptive of His message. (Selwyn favours the interpretation, not that Christ preached the gospel to them but that He made proclamation to them of the approaching end of their power as a result of His victory.) For the descent of Christ into Hades see Acts ii. 27, 31; Rom. x. 6–8; Eph. iv. 8–10.

The longsuffering of God waited in the days of Noah (20); i.e. to give man time for repentance. But man ignored God's claims and the stroke of judgment fell (Gn. vi; see also 2 Pet. iii. 5–9). Noah, his wife, three sons and their wives (*eight souls*) obeyed God, entered the ark and *were saved by* (RV 'through') *water*. The Greek *dia* may be regarded as both local and instrumental. As Noah passed safely through the waters of the flood in the ark, so the baptized pass through the water of baptism safely into the Church, in which sense *dia* is used locally. Or (as Alford, Plumptre) the allusion to baptism in verse 21 requires *dia* to be taken as instrumental, i.e. as the waters of the flood carried the ark to safety so baptism carries the Christian. The figure of baptism means *not the putting away of the filth of the flesh*, i.e. not the mere cleansing of the body, *but the answer of a good conscience toward God;* better, 'a pledge' to God proceeding from 'a clear conscience' given in the promise, made at baptism, to renounce the world, the flesh and the devil. (See Cranfield *in loc.*) On the manward side baptism is a confession of Christian discipleship; on the Godward side it is a pledge so to live as to maintain a 'conscience void of offence toward God, and toward men' (Acts xxiv. 16). This is possible *by the resurrection of Jesus Christ* (21) which is at once the ground of righteousness and the guarantee of victory. Christ has ascended *into heaven* and is in the place of honour at God's right hand, where all the hierarchy of heaven

submit to Him (22). Cf. 1 Cor. xv. 27; Eph. i. 22; Phil. iii. 21.

b. A further call to holy living (iv. 1–6)

Peter now returns to the main theme of iii. 14–18, the passage iii. 19–22 being parenthetical. *Forasmuch* in iv. 1 connects with iii. 18 and brings the sufferings of Christ to the attention of the readers once more. *Arm yourselves likewise with the same mind* (1). This is not the same exhortation as Paul gave to the Philippians (Phil. ii. 5). The Greek word *ennoia* means 'consideration', 'knowledge', 'thought' or 'idea'. The phrase means, therefore, 'put on as a coat of armour this knowledge'. Note the RV rendering which makes verse 2 the reason for the exhortation. It is so that 'ye no longer should live . . . to the lusts of men, but to the will of God'. Paul uses the same thought in his Epistles where it is developed more fully. See especially Rom. vi where 'reckon ye also yourselves to be dead indeed unto sin, but alive unto God' (verse 11) conveys the same meaning as Peter's exhortation here. *He that hath suffered in the flesh hath ceased from sin* (1) has been variously interpreted. Some commentators see only a general reference to the purifying effects of suffering (cf. i. 6, 7), which, having regard to the context, seems somewhat inadequate. Others, pointing out that the reference to Christ's suffering in the flesh is clearly a reference to His death, interpret the phrase in this sense here, and make it mean 'strengthen yourselves with this thought as you face martyrdom, that death brings cessation of the struggle against sin'. The context, however, with its strong call to cease from sin now (i.e. during 'the rest of your time in the flesh'), suggests that the thought of identification now with our Lord's death is in Peter's mind, with perhaps the added thought that their present or future sufferings are a sign of that identification. Their past life (i.e. before their conversion) had been a sufficiently long time to devote to indulging these appetites, 'doing what the Gentiles like to do' (RSV) as opposed to doing the will of God. A catalogue of these wrong desires follows (3). *Lasciviousness;* Gk. *aselgeia*, i.e. excess, licentiousness, absence of restraint; *lusts;* Gk. *epithymias*, i.e. strong desire of any kind (see note on ii. 11); *excess of wine;* RV 'winebibbers', i.e. habitual drunkards; *revellings;* Gk. *kōmos*, probably social drinking parties; *banquetings;* RV 'carousings', Gk. *potos*. In classical Greek the word is used of drink, as distinct from food, and carried no moral connotation (see Selwyn *in loc.*). It is used for a 'feast' in Gn. xix. 3, LXX. Such feasts might easily become occasions of drinking to excess. *Abominable idolatries;* Gk. *athemitos*, abominable, unrighteous; translated 'unlawful' in Acts x. 28. Bengel gives the meaning as actions 'by which the most sacred law of God is violated'. The three perfect tenses in the Greek (*past, to have wrought*, and *when we walked*) emphasize the thought that these things are now behind them. If these words were addressed to the newly baptized their appropriateness would be self-evident, for baptism in the early Church represented a crisis in the life of the Christian and signified a clean break with the old life. Their former pagan associates could not understand the transformation in their lives and abused them, perhaps in an effort to quieten their own consciences. Peter has already indicated that such will be put to shame (see iii. 16); now he warns that they *shall give account to him that is ready to judge the quick* (i.e. the living) *and the dead* (5). His judgment is impartial and from it there is no appeal.

Verse 6 has been variously interpreted. Very divergent views are held and it would be unwise to build any important doctrine on the basis of this verse only. Apart from the apparent connection with the statement in iii. 19 there seems little justification for arguing from it that the gospel was offered to the dead as dead, i.e. after they had died. Probably the truer meaning of the apostle's words is that those who are now dead had the gospel preached to them while they were alive. Selwyn suggests that in verse 5 the apostle had in mind past and present members of the Church and their persecutors and, in verse 6, the first of these only. Because of their confession of Christ in the flesh they had been judged and condemned by men's judgment. The Greek *kata anthrōpous* means 'according to the standards of men'. He does not mean that they had been judged as men are judged, which would have required *kata anthrōpōn*. But they were to live *according to God* (Gk. *kata theon*) *in the spirit*. To live in the spirit is to live as God lives, i.e. eternally.

c. Using God's gifts for the benefit of others (iv. 7-11)

Lest some should think that the judgment to which the apostle refers is very remote he proceeds to warn them and to exhort them. *But* (7); better, 'moreover', as if to emphasize the importance of the subject. *The end of all things is at hand* (cf. Jas. v. 8). In the New Testament the coming of the Lord which would mark the close of the age was believed to be imminent and there was much counsel as to how men should live with that end in view. Peter gives four lines of conduct to be observed. First, *be ye therefore sober, and watch* (RV 'of sound mind, and be sober') *unto prayer* (7). The Greek *sōphronein* denotes the cool head and balanced mind in contrast to *mania*, which is undue excitement. Prayer is the great corrective of a shallow, limited view of life and enables us to look beyond the circumstances of the present and to keep the end in view (cf. Mk. xiii. 33). Secondly, *have fervent charity* (RV 'being fervent in your love') *among yourselves* (8). See notes on i. 22 and iii. 8. The clause *for charity shall cover the multitude of sins* is somewhat obscure. Note the RV. It may mean that if you love the brethren fervently you will be ready to forgive them again and again; or, God's love covers the multitude

of your sins, so out of gratitude to Him you must love fervently (strenuously). The former seems preferable as an interpretation here. For 'cover' see Ps. xxxii. 1. Thirdly, Peter's readers are to *use hospitality one to another without grudging* (RV 'murmuring') (9). This may be regarded either as an exhortation in view of the approach of the end, or as a way in which fervent love is to be shown (cf. Mt. xxv. 31–46; Rom. xii. 13; 1 Tim. iii. 2; Heb. xiii. 1f.). In the early Church the ministry was peripatetic and it was necessary that the Christian messengers should be welcomed and entertained. But even here there were difficulties. Some of the preachers might presume upon their privileges. Hence the admonition 'without murmuring'. In the fourth place there must be generous stewardship of every Christian gift (10). Each has been endowed with some particular gift from God and they are to use that gift as those who shall give account of their stewardship. The exercise of any special aptness for any piece of work for the Church in the name of the Lord was to be regarded as ministering unto Him. Several gifts are mentioned specially. There is the gift of preaching. *Let him speak as the oracles of God* (11); i.e. as one who utters the word which God has given him. Likewise, *if any man minister*, i.e. renders any service, *let him do it as of the ability which God giveth*. Note the RV rendering, 'ministering as of the strength which God supplieth.' The word translated 'supplieth' originally meant 'to lead a chorus' in the theatre, then 'to defray the expenses of bringing out a chorus at a public festival'. Hence to supply or equip as of an army or a fleet and usually with the sense of abundance. See Cranfield *in loc.* God's supplies are unstinted and unlimited. But all is to be done to the glory of God. This is the true motive for all activity in the life of the Christian. The section closes with a doxology. Cf. v. 11, 14.

d. A call to patient endurance (iv. 12-19)

The letter now reverts to its original and fundamental theme of the time of suffering which was to come or had already come upon the Christian community in Asia Minor. The apostle has uttered a doxology and it may be taken for granted that his original intention was to close the Epistle at this point. But now, on second thoughts, he feels he has not said enough on the great and urgent matter on which he is writing. He begins again with the same vocative as he used in ii. 11: *Beloved* (12). They were not to be amazed that trials and persecutions should come, but rather were they to *rejoice* (13). Trials are to be expected by the very nature of the Christian witness, which is a rebuke to the worldly spirit. The trial they are to undergo is described as *fiery* (Gk. *pyrōsei*). *Pyrōsis* means a burning, an exposure to the action of fire or a testing by fire. Peter has already made reference to such testing (i. 6, 7), and this fits in with the meaning here. It is by trial and persecution that the reality of faith is tested. But chiefly were they to take comfort and courage from the fact that they were *partakers of Christ's sufferings* (cf. Col. i. 24). The word translated *inasmuch* is the Greek *katho*, meaning 'in the measure in which'. To rejoice in such suffering now will mean that, when Christ shall appear in the glory of His Father, then will they rejoice with great exultation. If it is for the name of Christ that they are persecuted they are truly blessed (Mt. v. 11). *The spirit of glory and of God* (14); Gk. *to tēs doxēs kai to tou theou pneuma*. Cf. the RV rendering. Selwyn thinks that the expression *to tēs doxēs* represents the Shekinah, the visible brightness of the glory of God's presence. The AV translation meets the case satisfactorily. 'God's Holy Spirit who is Himself glorious and the source of glory and whose presence is the pledge of future glory rests upon His persecuted Church' (see Cranfield *in loc.*).

Naturally, the man who by his own wickedness or folly brings suffering upon himself has no right to claim these consolations. Hence, let no one bring dishonour upon Christ by suffering for wrongs wilfully committed. The fact that such a warning was necessary is a reminder of the low standard of morals of the people with whom the first Christian messengers had to deal. The term *evildoer* (15) is wide and includes all evil. *A busybody* (RV 'meddler') *in other men's matters* (15). The zeal of converts is proverbial and is not always mixed with tact. It is possible to draw persecution upon oneself through needless interference in the affairs of others. *If*, however, *any man suffer as a Christian* he should keep in mind the fact that there is no shame attached to such suffering and that one who bears the name of Christ has the responsibility of glorifying God in and through the suffering. The word *Christian* is found only three times in the New Testament, here and in Acts xi. 26 and xxvi. 28. It would still be a term of abuse when Peter used it. *The time is come that judgment must begin at the house of God* (17). The stormy times already breaking upon the Church were a beginning of the testing and sifting process; but the end is not yet. The thought that divine judgment begins with the Church is derived from the Old Testament (cf. Je. xxv. 29; Ezk. ix. 6). *The house of God* stands here for the people of God, not merely the temple. If judgment is so severe for the people of God, its severity is beyond description for the unbeliever (17b, 18; cf. Lk. xxiii. 31). But the Christian has a secret which the unbeliever has not. He can commit himself into God's hand with perfect confidence, knowing that God cannot fail.

VI. VICTORY AND SERVICE. v. 1–11

a. The pastoral office (v. 1–4)

Peter now addresses specifically those who have special responsibilities in the Church. The fiery trial coming upon the Church will make faithfulness in the pastoral office all the more needful. The term *elders* (1) here refers to official position

in the Church and not to age as in verse 5. It includes those who have some sort of authorized pastoral function and responsibility. The word is really 'presbyter' and gives us a glimpse of the simple organization of the primitive Church borrowed from village life and the customs of the Jewish synagogue. A peripatetic ministry has already been noted and here we have further evidence of the beginning at least of local organization. The term 'elder' or 'presbyter' was interchangeable with 'bishop' or 'overseer'. Note that Peter assumes no ecclesiastical superiority but with profound humility puts himself on a level with those whom he exhorts. He was an actual *witness of the sufferings of Christ* (1) and might have stood apart as an apostle. He has already spoken of the *glory that shall be revealed* (1; see iv. 13 and cf. Mt. xix. 28). As in i. 5, he thinks of himself as experiencing now blessings which in their fulness are still future. The work of the elder is to *feed* (RV 'tend') *the flock of God* (2), i.e. do the whole work of the shepherd (cf. Jn. xxi. 15–17; see also ii. 25 above). Note that it is God's flock, not the elders', and He is not indifferent as to the manner in which His sheep are treated. The duties must be undertaken willingly, even eagerly, but not for financial gain. Peter is not objecting here to a paid ministry or to the labourer receiving his hire. What he is warning against is the sin of covetousness, eager catching at emoluments. With verse 3 cf. Mk. x. 41–45. They must avoid all seeking of power or position through which they might fall into the snare of showing a ·haughty or overbearing manner towards the members of the Church. Instead, by their holy lives, they are to be *ensamples to the flock* (3). All their service is to be inspired by the prospect of the Lord's coming and of the servant's reward. Those who faithfully fulfil the office of under-shepherd will receive the prize from the hands of the chief Shepherd Himself when He comes in glory. The reward is described as *a crown of glory that fadeth not away* (4), another example of Peter's dislike for all that is fading and corruptible. This crown is not the emblem of royalty but rather the garland or wreath which was the reward of victory in the Greek athletic festivals (cf. 1 Cor. ix. 25; 2 Tim. iv. 8; Jas. i. 12; Rev. ii. 10, iii. 11). When Christ shall come His glory will be revealed (see verse 1 above). The reward of the faithful and humble under-shepherd is that he will be given a share in the glory and joy of his Lord.

b. A call to humility and trustfulness (v. 5–7)

Peter now addresses the *younger*, Gk. *neōteroi*. The term probably refers here not only to their being more youthful in age but also younger in the faith and in Christian experience. As such they may have been tempted to become restive under the authority of the elders mentioned in verse 1. They are therefore enjoined to be subject to their seniors from whom the official elders of the Church would normally be drawn. Whether the apostle is enjoining upon younger men respect for age or exhorting the younger pastors to submit to the authority of the presbyters is not clear. The writer does not propound the theory that youth must be suppressed; he is simply saying that the young ought to show deference to age and experience.

He now passes to a general application of the duty of humility which is incumbent on all members of the Church without exception. They are to 'gird' themselves with it (see RV). The reference is to the *lention*, the linen cloth or towel used by slaves and with which our Lord girded Himself before washing the disciples' feet, an act which was itself expressive of what the apostle here enjoins (see Jn. xiii. 4). God sets His face against the proud (cf. Pr. xvi. 5). The humble, on the other hand, are rewarded by increasingly richer supplies of grace. *Humble yourselves therefore* (6; Gk. *tapeinōthēte*); the word means not simply 'humble yourselves' but also 'allow yourselves to be humbled', accept your humiliations (so Selwyn). *The mighty hand of God* (6) is a common figure in the Old Testament to describe God's intervention in human affairs (cf. Ex. iii. 20, vii. 5, xv. 6; Dt. iv. 34, ix. 29). *In due time* (6); Gk. *en kairō(i)*. In classical Greek the phrase means 'at the propitious time'; here it signifies 'in His own good time', i.e. at the revelation of Jesus Christ. Meantime they are exhorted to manifest the spirit of true humility toward God by casting all their anxieties upon Him, knowing assuredly that He cares for them (7; cf. Mt. vi. 26–32; Lk. xii. 23–31; see also Ps. lv. 22).

c. An exhortation to be watchful and steadfast (v. 8–11)

Be sober (cf. i. 13, iv. 7), *be vigilant* (8; RV 'watchful'; cf. Mk. xiii. 33–37, xiv. 37f.). The duty and necessity of watching in obedience to our Lord's command must have been indelibly imprinted on Peter's heart. Here sobriety and watchfulness are enjoined because of the *adversary*, Gk. *antidikos*, in a legal sense an accuser in a trial before a judge. *The devil*; Gk. *diabolos*, a calumniator, false accuser. He is referred to under various figures, e.g. as the adversary of God's purpose (Jn. xii. 31; 2 Thes. ii. 8f.; Rev. xii. 9f.), as the father of lies (Jn. viii. 44; Acts v. 3; 2 Thes. ii. 10; Rev. xii. 9), and as the great accuser or slanderer (Rev. xii. 10). The titles which Peter here uses express the hostility of the devil to the Christian and his life in Christ as well as the methods of false accusation and slander which he employs. *As a roaring lion*. This graphic simile of the devil as a lion depicts the strength and destructiveness of the adversary; the fact that he is described as walking about denotes his ubiquity (cf. Jb. i. 7). Peter in all likelihood had in mind the persecution and the temptation to falter which would accompany it. There was only one way in which to meet the adversary in this guise (cf. Jas. iv. 7). Such opposition calls for strong determination, hence *stedfast* (9), i.e. unshaken (by his attempts to terrorize) 'in your faith' (RV), i.e. in Him who is mighty to deliver. They must

not imagine that the church in Asia Minor is alone in suffering persecution. There are others who are in the same worldly surroundings as they and in whom the same sufferings are taking their course. So resisting and so remembering they will prove the sufficiency of God's grace. The parallels between 1 Pet. v. 10f. and 1 Thes. v. 23ff., 2 Thes. ii. 13ff. and Heb. xiii. 21f. would seem to indicate a common authorship, or the perusal of common material, or both. The influence and work of Silvanus could account for this. *The God of all grace;* He is the Author and Source of grace sufficient for every circumstance of need; *who hath called us unto* (i.e. 'to share in') *his eternal glory* (already referred to in verses 1 and 4) *by Christ Jesus* (10). See RV; both the calling and the glory are 'in Christ'. Note how Peter contrasts with the eternal glory the transient nature of the suffering (cf. 2 Cor. iv. 17). *Make you perfect;* RV 'shall himself perfect'. The Greek *katartizō* means to render fit or complete; it is used of mending nets in Mt. iv. 21 and Mk. i. 19 and is translated 'restore' in Gal. vi. 1. It does not necessarily mean that the thing to which it is applied has been damaged, though it may do so; it signifies rather right ordering and arrangement. Cf. Jas. i. 4. *Stablish;* Gk. *stērizō*, meaning to make stable. Cf. verse 9 above where the adjectival form *stereos*, meaning 'firm', is rendered 'stedfast'. *Strengthen;* Gk. *thenoō* is not found in classical Greek but *sthenein*, to be strong, is. Here it probably has reference to the strength needed to resist the devil, which strength God alone can give. Note that the word *settle*, which conveys the idea of laying a foundation, does not occur in the RV. It is not found in the best MSS but seems to have been added probably under the influence of Col. i. 23. Peter closes his exhortations here with another doxology (cf. iv. 11 and v. 14). He, as it were, raises his voice in blessing the God of all grace, the faithful Creator, who is able to do all that has been outlined in the exhortations.

VII. CONCLUSION. v. 12–14

For note on *Silvanus* and on *Babylon* see *Introduction*. Peter here states his purpose in writing the Epistle. He has exhorted and testified to *the true grace of God wherein ye stand*. RV renders the last three words as a further exhortation, 'stand fast therein'. 'The grace which they had experienced in conversion and in the blessedness and progress of the Christian life was no delusion, as they were tempted to suppose by their troubles, but the genuine grace of God' (Bennett). In this they are to stand fast (cf. 'stedfast in the faith' in verse 9 above). *Marcus my son* (13). There seems no doubt that this was Mark, the evangelist, whose indebtedness to Peter for much of the material in the Gospel bearing his name is recognized. From the time that Paul asked Timothy to bring Mark back with him to Rome (2 Tim. iv. 11) tradition associates him with Peter. Papias says that he became Peter's 'interpreter', and as such composed the second Gospel from what he remembered of the apostle's teaching. *Greet ye* (RV 'salute') *one another with a kiss of charity* (RV 'love') (14). See also Rom. xvi. 16; 1 Cor. xvi. 20; 2 Cor. xiii. 12; 1 Thes. v. 26. The kiss was a regular feature of the Eucharist and if, as some think, this letter was to be read at the Easter A.D. 64 observance of the Lord's Supper, the exhortation here can be readily understood. It was the sign and pledge of unity and love between brethren. Great importance was attached to the necessity of reconciliation between those who had quarrelled ere they sat down at the table of the Lord. The kiss was the token of such reconciliation being effected. Judas the traitor chose a kiss as the sign of identification of our Lord (Mk. xiv. 44) and this implies that it was in common use among the disciples of Jesus. It was used as a token of affection as well as of reconciliation (cf. Lk. xv. 20; see also Lk. vii. 45). *Peace be with you all that are in Christ Jesus* (14); cf. i. 2. Only those who are in Christ know this peace, but all who are in Him may know it. The salutation of the risen Lord was 'Peace' (Lk. xxiv. 36; Jn. xx. 19f., 26).

II PETER: INTRODUCTION

I. AUTHORSHIP

The question of the authorship of 2 Peter is one of the difficult problems of New Testament criticism. On the grounds of the delay in its final acceptance as canonical and of certain features in phraseology and style it is alleged that the Epistle was not written by Peter. External evidence in support of the Petrine authorship is meagre. The first writer to mention its name is Origen (*c.* A.D. 240) who speaks of the two Epistles of Peter and in one place quotes 2 Pet. i. 4 and gives it the name of Scripture. The Epistle was not acknowledged as canonical until the Council of Carthage in 397. Eusebius, Bishop of Samaria, regarded it with some degree of suspicion and placed it among the disputed books. Jerome, on the other hand, included the Epistle in his Vulgate Version although he had some hesitancy in so doing on account of difference of style from 1 Peter. This difficulty he overcame by supposing that the apostle employed two different amanuenses or interpreters. Other scholars like Augustine, Epiphanius, Rufinus and Cyril received it as genuine. At the Reformation Erasmus rejected it, but Luther entertained no doubt as to its genuineness. Calvin felt some hesitancy in accepting it because of apparent discrepancies between it and 1 Peter.

The opinion of modern scholars is strongly divided. Salmon, Zahn, Plummer and Bigg argue for the Petrine authorship, while Chase and Mayor, arguing from ancient literature and the internal evidence of the Epistle itself, arrive at the conclusion that 2 Peter is not an apostolic document. In their judgment it was certainly not written in the first century of our Lord but probably about the middle of the second century; therefore, they conclude, it was not written by Peter. It would seem that a good case could thus be made out against the Petrine authorship, but too much stress cannot be laid on the argument from ancient literature. For, as Salmon and his school point out, Irenaeus, Justin Martyr, the 'Shepherd of Hermas', the 'Didache' and Clement of Rome were all acquainted with the Epistle and made allusions to it in their writings. Such evidence in favour of the Petrine authorship is as valid as that produced by Chase and his followers against it. The general acceptance of the Epistle, after full discussion and weighing of the evidence, by the Council of Carthage is a further strong point which must be taken into account.

When we turn to an examination of the internal evidence regarding authorship we have to meet, first of all, the direct claim of i. 1. The author calls himself Simon Peter and declares that he is an apostle of Jesus Christ. Then in iii. 1 he states that he has already written an Epistle to those whom he is now addressing. Again, in i. 16–18 he claims that he saw Christ on the mount of transfiguration. He is also conversant with the Epistles of Paul (iii. 15f.). From his references to and use of the Old Testament Scriptures we gather that he was a Jew. He was an old man and was expecting death soon (i. 13ff.). The spiritual condition of his readers is well known to him (i. 4, 12, iii. 14, 17) and he is on intimate terms with them, addressing them as 'beloved' (iii. 1, 8, 14, 17).

Further, while it was on the ground of dissimilarity between the two Epistles in their style, diction and, to some extent, contents that John Calvin and others hesitated to accept it, we cannot ignore the fact that there is a strong similarity between the two writings in these matters. For instance, words and phrases rarely found in other writings are common to both Epistles, e.g. 'precious' (1 Pet. i. 7, 19; 2 Pet. i. 1); 'virtue' (1 Pet. ii. 9; 2 Pet. i. 3; found elsewhere only in Phil. iv. 8); 'supply' (1 Pet. iv. 11; 2 Pet. i. 5); 'love of brethren' (1 Pet. i. 22; 2 Pet. i. 7); 'behold' (1 Pet. ii. 12, iii. 2; 2 Pet. i. 16; in 1 Peter it is in verbal form and in 2 Peter in substantival form, 'eyewitnesses'); 'without blemish' . . . 'without spot' (1 Pet. i. 19; 2 Pet. iii. 14). In addition there is a similarity in teaching which must be recognized. Notice, for example, the references to 'the end of the age' (1 Pet. i. 5, iv. 7; 2 Pet. iii. 3, 10); 'prophecy' (1 Pet. i. 10–12; 2 Pet. i. 19f., iii. 2); the flood (1 Pet. iii. 20; 2 Pet. ii. 5, iii. 6); and Christian liberty (1 Pet. ii. 16; 2 Pet. ii. 19).

Again, words are used by the writer of this Epistle which are used almost exclusively by Peter in the Acts of the Apostles. Examples are 'obtained' (i. 1; Acts i. 17); 'godliness' (i. 7;

Acts iii. 12); 'unlawful' (ii. 8; Acts ii. 23); 'day of the Lord' (iii. 10; Acts ii. 20); 'wages of iniquity' (ii. 13, 15; Acts i. 18). These would seem to indicate that the speaker in the Acts is the man who wrote this letter.

Still further, the writer appeals to certain facts in the life of Peter that are almost biographical. For instance, in addition to his claim in i. 16–18, he speaks of 'putting off of my tabernacle . . . even as our Lord Jesus Christ signified unto me' (i. 14, RV). The reference is undoubtedly to Jn. xiii. 36, xxi. 18f. He indirectly claims the inspiration without which true prophecy is impossible (i. 19–21). His testimony throughout is personal, emphatic and direct, and the letter reads much like Peter's plain way of speaking of himself at the Council of Jerusalem (Acts xv).

Much has been made of the similarity between this Epistle and that of Jude, who appears to quote from 2 Peter. It would be too strong to say that the priority of the two Epistles has now been finally settled. Many recent writers still give the priority to Jude while others give it to Peter. For example, Zahn argues with great force in favour of the view that 2 Peter is the older and that Jude cites from it. The real difference between the two is that between prediction and fulfilment. Peter predicts the advent of the false teachers (ii. 1) and his principal verbs are in the future tense (cf. ii. 1, 2, 3, 12, 13). He employs the present tense in describing the character and conduct of the libertines (ii. 17f.), but their presence and disastrous teaching he puts in the future (ii. 13, 14). Jude, on the other hand, refers to these same corrupters as being already present in the midst of God's people and doing their deadly work. Jude urges his readers to remember the words which the apostles of Christ had before spoken and then proceeds to cite 2 Pet. iii. 3 in almost the exact terms. Peter writes of what is approaching, Jude of what has actually arrived and in so doing expands what Peter has written. Chronology too gives priority to Peter. Peter died before the fall of Jerusalem (A.D. 70) while the Epistle of Jude is generally accepted as having been written after that event, probably A.D. 75–80. This is of some importance in that it is evident that Jude endorses 2 Peter as being apostolic and likewise canonical, for he recognizes Peter as an apostle and gifted with the prophetic spirit.

II. OCCASION AND DATE

We gather (i. 14) that the Epistle was written not long before the apostle's martyrdom and the date would therefore be about A.D. 66 or 67. News had reached him regarding the work of false teachers in the Church and he exhorts the Christians to perseverance in truth in the midst of error and infidelity. He warns the false teachers of their guilt and danger and points to the second coming of the Lord as being for them not an occasion for rejoicing but for judgment. The Christians, on the other hand, should live in the light of that coming, and he urges upon them holiness and diligence coupled with humility as befitting those who watch for His appearing.

II PETER: OUTLINE OF CONTENTS

I. SALUTATION. i. 1, 2

II. THE CHRISTIAN'S GROWTH. i. 3–21

III. FALSE TEACHERS. ii. 1–22

IV. THE CHRISTIAN'S HOPE. iii. 1–18

II PETER: COMMENTARY

I. SALUTATION. i. 1, 2

The apostle greets his fellow-Christians giving first his old name *Simon*, followed by the name *Peter*, given him by the Lord. He designates himself as *a servant* (RV mg. 'bondservant'), or slave, implying absolute ownership and obedience, and *an apostle of Jesus Christ*. An apostle was literally one bearing a commission (see 1 Pet. i. 1n.). He addresses his readers not, as in 1 Peter, as strangers and elect, but as those who *have obtained like precious faith with us*. Their faith is of equal standing, hence 'equally precious' (RV mg.). Gk. *isotimon* means of equal value, held in equal honour (cf. Acts xv. 7–11). The common possession of a precious faith is the bond between them. This faith is received apart from the merit of the recipient and only on the basis of the *righteousness of God*. See Rom. iii. 20–26 where this term is fully explained. The RV and RSV readings suggest that the reference here is to God the Son only. In verse 2 there is no such ambiguity and it seems best to follow the AV and to see in verse 1 also a reference to God the Father, as well as to *our Saviour Jesus Christ*. The greeting *Grace and peace be multiplied* (2) is in a form which is confined to Peter and Jude. In 1 Peter the believers can rely on God multiplying grace and peace to them in their sufferings. So in 2 Peter they could be equally sure of adequate grace for, and abundant peace in, the apostasy that was rearing its head (see 1 Pet. i. 2n.). But such blessings would come through their knowing *God* and *Jesus our Lord*.

II. THE CHRISTIAN'S GROWTH. i. 3–21

All things that pertain unto life and godliness (3). God is the source of all spiritual growth. The life referred to is the new life in Christ, and godliness is the expression of that spiritual life. The *divine power* is the source of the divine gifts which come through the same channel as the grace and peace of i. 2, viz. *through the knowledge of him that hath called us to glory and virtue* (RV 'by his own glory and virtue'; for *virtue* RSV reads 'excellence'). Cf. 1 Pet. ii. 9. The 'glory' of Christ was the glory of His revelation of the Father (Jn. i. 14). Some think that the 'virtue' of Christ does not here mean His moral excellence (to assert that would be unnecessary), but rather His supreme energy and power. On the whole it seems preferable to accept the interpretation that it does refer to His supreme purity and holiness and to regard the 'glory and virtue' as corresponding to the 'life and godliness' of the previous clause and as expressing together His 'divine power'. The word for *promises* (4) is peculiar to 2 Peter, occurring here and in iii. 13 where it has to do with 'new heavens and a new earth, wherein dwelleth righteousness'. One of the prevalent errors was a sceptical attitude to the second coming of our Lord and the refutation of that error is one of the main purposes of the Epistle. Here Peter refers to the matter in a preliminary way by a declaration that the gifts of Christ relate to the future as well as to the present. His promises are *precious* because they are not mere empty words; they are *exceeding great* because they point to the perfection and completion to which our present life is leading. *Partakers of the divine nature* (4). The object of the promises is to bring men back to God, to have the lost image of God restored. For *the corruption that is in the world through lust* see Jas. i. 14 and 1 Pet. ii. 11.

God has done all that is necessary in implanting the divine nature, but the culture of the new life thereby received must be taken care of by the recipient in dependence upon the power of the Holy Spirit. Hence the apostolic exhortation to exercise *all diligence* and *add* (Gk. *epichorēgein*), i.e. to supply or minister in addition. The sense conveyed by the word is that of rendering the service expected of one in virtue of one's position. *To your faith virtue; and to virtue knowledge* (5). Note the RV rendering which translates the preposition as 'in' throughout. Each quality is regarded as a kind of soil or atmosphere in which its successor is nourished. The word used for knowledge here is *gnōsis*, meaning knowledge which admits of expansion, not *epignōsis*, as in verses 2 and 3, which conveys the sense of full knowledge. *Temperance* (6); i.e. self-control (Gk. *engkrateia*, the power of holding oneself in). *Patience;* i.e. endurance. *Godliness* denotes true reverence for God (cf. i. 3, iii. 11). *Brotherly*

kindness (7). See 1 Pet. i. 22n. The true badge of Christian discipleship is love one to another (Jn. xiii. 35). It is the presence in abundance of *these things*, the seven graces mentioned, that produces in the believer fruitful activity in Christ. *Barren* (8); RV 'idle'. When they do abound Christ is known more and more fully. On the other hand, the absence of these things is an indication of spiritual blindness (9). The RV mg. suggests a deliberate closing of the eyes. *Cannot see afar off;* RV 'seeing only what is near'; i.e. short-sighted in respect to heavenly things through having the eyes fixed on the things of time and sense (cf. 2 Cor. iv. 18). A sign of being in this state is that such a person forgets *that he was purged from his old sins,* i.e. the pardon and purifying with which the Christian life began.

In verse 10 the apostle renews his exhortation to diligence because of the solemn possibilities indicated in verses 8 and 9. *Make your calling and election sure;* cf. 1 Pet. i. 2 where the divine side is emphasized. Here the human response to the divine call is stressed. The divine election is realized through man's response to God's revelation. The outcome of this diligence is then set forth. *Ye shall never fall* (10); RV 'stumble'; cf. Jude 24. *Ministered unto you abundantly* (11); RV 'richly supplied'. In verse 5 the apostle has told them what they are to 'supply'. Here he tells them what, if they do so, will be richly supplied to them. God will spare no expense to perfect their lives and crown them with blessing.

The exhortations of verses 3–11 are now confirmed in verses 12–18 by a personal appeal and by a consideration of the great certainties as supported by the apostolic witness of the transfiguration and by the word of prophecy. It is clear that one of the leading ideas in this passage is remembrance. His readers know the truth but, lest they take it for granted and so lose the force of it in their lives, the apostle declares his intention to keep it fresh in their memories, to put them *always in remembrance of these things* (12), as long as he is *in this tabernacle* (13). The Greek word is *skēnōma*, 'tent', used metaphorically of the body as the habitation of the soul (cf. 2 Cor. v. 1). The word is a reminder of the frailty and temporary nature of the earthly body. The comparison of the body with a tent suits the general conception of life as a pilgrimage. He speaks of his departure as putting off *this my tabernacle* (14) and declares that Christ had shown him 'by what death he should glorify God'. The allusion is to our Lord's prediction in Jn. xxi. 18. Note the RV rendering, 'knowing that the putting off of my tabernacle cometh swiftly', i.e. suddenly, without warning. He is solicitous that after he has gone they should have these truths in remembrance. *Decease* (15); Gk. *exodos*, 'a way out', the same word as is used in the account of the transfiguration (Lk. ix. 30f.).

The apostle strengthens his position by a

reference to his own personal witness of the transfiguration of Christ. He, as well as the other apostles, did not follow *cunningly devised fables* (16); Gk. *mythoi*, 'myths' (cf. 1 Tim. i. 4, iv. 7; 2 Tim. iv. 4; Tit. i. 14). The reference is to the false charges preferred against them by their persecutors of deliberately inventing stories as a means of obtaining money and influence. Peter asserts that they were not dealing with fictions of the human imagination but with historical facts when they preached *the power* (cf. i. 3) *and coming of our Lord Jesus Christ* (16), a reference to the second advent. His mind goes back to what he had witnessed on the mount of transfiguration. He and the other two disciples were *eyewitnesses of his majesty* (16). The transfiguration is regarded here as an anticipation, earnest, or pledge of the glory to be revealed 'when the Son of man shall come in his glory'. Peter with James and John had witnessed the Father's testimony to the Son, the proof of the power and authority of the gospel message. The voice came from *the excellent glory* (17); Gk. *megaloprepēs*, from *megas*, great, and *prepō*, to be fitting or becoming; hence majestic, that which is becoming a great man. (Cf. John's testimony in Jn. i. 14, 'we beheld his glory'.) The prophetic confirmation follows. The argument is that the Old Testament prophecy concerning the Messiah had been made *more sure* (19) by being confirmed by the transfiguration, together with the facts of the earthly life and ministry of Jesus. These prophetic Scriptures are as 'a lamp shining in a dark place' (19, RV). The darkness shows the need of divine light. In Greek the word *dark* is *auchmēros*, from *auchmos*, meaning drought produced by excessive heat; hence it signifies dry, murky, dark, and is translated 'squalid' in the RV mg. The light of Scripture shows up the filth of sin. *Until the day dawn, and the day star arise* (19); another reference to the second coming of the Lord (cf. verse 16). The day star comes as the harbinger of the dawn and is followed by the glorious appearing of the full light of the sun. In this connection Dr. W. Griffith Thomas (*The Apostle Peter*) suggests that the phrase *in your hearts* should be separated from the words *until . . . the day star arise*, and linked with the words *take heed*; otherwise the implication would be that the Christians were at that time in darkness, which gives an erroneous idea to the whole meaning of the apostle.

Verse 20 has reference to the wresting of Scripture by the false teachers who are considered in chapter ii. *Interpretation;* Gk. *epilyseōs*, meaning unloosing, unfolding, disclosing. *Private;* Gk. *idios*, lit. 'one's own'. This may be interpreted in two ways. The thought may be similar to that of 1 Pet. i. 10–12; i.e. the writers of Scripture did not give their own explanation of God-breathed words but had the true meaning revealed to them. Or it may refer to those who have received the prophecies and have in mind the false teachers Peter is about to describe who propagate their own 'private' and untrue inter-

pretations of the Old Testament Scriptures. No man could produce a prophecy whenever he wished to do so. Prophecy comes by the illumination of the Holy Spirit and men cannot understand or interpret it apart from the aid of the same Holy Spirit. This is the only direct reference in the Epistle to the Holy Spirit. Peter is very clear regarding the origin of Scripture. The prophecy was brought to him as it is brought to us. Note the importance of the Greek *pheromenoi*, being 'borne' or 'carried along' by the Holy Spirit. Paul makes the great declaration (2 Tim. iii. 16) that all Scripture is 'given by inspiration of God' and so asserts the inspiration of the writings. Here Peter declares that holy men of God were borne along by the Holy Spirit, thus asserting the inspiration of the writers. The figure he uses is a very vivid one. They are carried along by the Holy Spirit as a vessel is borne along by the wind. This does not involve any conclusion that they were unconscious instruments or mere machines; but it does most emphatically involve a control and a 'carrying' power which are quite beyond anything that the human will or imagination can claim for itself. Here is a basis not only for the doctrine of the inspiration of the Scriptures but also for the doctrine of the entire trustworthiness or 'infallibility' thereof (see also 1 Pet. i. 11f.).

III. FALSE TEACHERS. ii. 1–22

It is round this chapter that the Peter-Jude controversy has been waged (see *Introduction*). The similarity between the two is most striking, cf. especially 2 Pet. ii. 2, 4, 6, 11, 17; Jude 4–18. The I.C.C. suggests that the errors denounced by both writers took their origin from Corinth, that the disorder was spreading, that Peter took alarm and wrote his second Epistle, sending a copy to Jude with the warning that the danger was urgent, and that Jude at once issued a similar letter to the churches in which he was personally interested. Compare the notes given here with the commentary on Jude.

a. Marks of the false teachers (ii. 1–3)

This chapter opens with a reminder that in the history of Israel many false prophets arose; cf. 1 Ki. xxii; Je. xxiii; Ezk. xiii; Zc. xiii. 4, etc. Our Lord had also warned against false teachers; cf. Mt. vii. 15, xxiv. 11f. These warnings Peter now confirms. From the latter part of the chapter it may be gathered that the false teachers had already appeared and were at work in the Church (see verses 9–19). The word *privily* conveys the suggestion of the presence of a spy or traitor. Cf. Gal. ii. 4 where Greek *pareisaktos* is translated in RV as 'privily brought in'. In the same verse Greek *pareiserchomai* is translated 'came in privily'. In both instances the reference is to Judaizers brought in by the circumcision party to accomplish the overthrow of the faith. Cf. also Jude 4 where Greek *pareisduō* is translated 'crept in privily'. The characteristic mark of these false teachers is that they introduce *damnable* (RV 'destructive') *heresies* (1); RV mg. 'sects of perdition'. The Greek *hairesis* denotes primarily 'choice' or 'choosing'; then that which is chosen and hence an opinion, especially a self-willed opinion, which leads to division and the formation of sects (cf. Acts xxiv. 5). The term 'heresy' in the New Testament implies not erroneous opinion only but accompanying false standards of conduct. A heresy is always a denial of Christ's work and authority. *The Lord that bought them* (Gk. *despotēs*) implies absolute lordship and dominion, a thought which is carried further by the apostle by bringing in the idea of 'buying', as a master buys a slave (cf. 1 Pet. i. 18; 1 Cor. vi. 20, vii. 23). Note that Peter is in no doubt as to what the result of such conduct will be.

From the remainder of the Epistle it is evident that the heresy was that of antinomianism, i.e. the doctrine that under the gospel dispensation the moral law is not binding since faith alone is sufficient for salvation. *Pernicious ways* (2) is better rendered as in RV, 'lascivious doings'. *The way of truth* will be discredited in the eyes of the world because of the laxity of morals permitted, preached and practised by the false teachers and those who were drawn into their net through their use of *feigned* (or 'fabricated') *words* (3), Gk. *plastois*, 'moulded' (cf. Eng. 'plastic'), and through their *covetousness*, or greed of gain, by which they exploited the unwary. But their doom was certain. Judgment *lingereth not* (3); i.e. is not idle in working itself out; nor does *damnation* (RV 'destruction') slumber, but is watchful, waiting for the appointed hour.

b. The certainty of judgment (ii. 4–9)

This is confirmed by three illustrations from the Old Testament.

i. The fall of the angels (ii. 4). *If God spared not the angels that sinned.* See notes on Jude 6–8. There is no specific reference in the Old Testament to a fall of angels unless Gn. vi. 1–4 be interpreted in this way. There are, however, frequent references in the book of Enoch to such a fall and descriptions of its nature. These may themselves be derived from an interpretation of the Genesis passage which regards the 'sons of God' as angels. Plummer, in Ellicott's Commentary, suggests that the false teachers may have used this book in their corrupt teaching and that Peter introduces the reference here as a kind of *argumentum ad hominem* against them. Then Jude, recognizing the allusion, adopted it and made it more plain. *But cast them down to hell;* Gk. *tartarōsas.* 'Tartarus' was the name given to the deepest abyss of the lower world and was regarded as being far below Hades, although sometimes the term was used as being synonymous with it. *And delivered them into chains of darkness.* Authorities are divided between this translation and that of the RV, 'pits of darkness'; i.e. between the Greek *seirais* and

seirois. Probably the term 'pits' is more in keeping with the thought of Tartarus immediately preceding. In either case the meaning is clear. *To be reserved unto judgment.* In the apocalyptic book of Enoch vi—xix (*Translations of Early Documents Series*) an account is given of the fallen angels and Enoch's relation to them. Enoch is shown the darkness and there he saw 'the prisoners (the angels) suspended, reserved for and awaiting the eternal judgment'.

ii. The deluge (ii. 5). *Noah* is described as *a preacher of righteousness.* It is explicitly stated in Genesis that 'Noah was a just man and perfect in his generations, and Noah walked with God' (Gn. vi. 9). *Noah the eighth person.* According to Greek idiom this is equivalent to 'Noah and seven others' (cf. RV).

iii. The overthrow of Sodom and Gomorrah (ii. 6–9). Note the parallelism with Lk. xvii. 26–29; see Jude 7n. No mention is made by Jude of the deliverance of Lot. The description of Lot as given by Peter is significant. So righteous was he that his soul was grieved every day by the lascivious life of the lawless men around him (7; see RV). Verse 9 is the apodosis, or second half, of the conditional sentence of which verses 4–8 are the protasis, or first half. The sentence therefore reads 'For if God spared not the angels . . . and spared not the ancient world but preserved Noah . . . and turned the cities of Sodom and Gomorrah into ashes . . . but delivered righteous Lot . . . (then) *the Lord knoweth how to deliver the godly out of temptations*' (Gk. *peirasmos*, used here in the sense of trial rather than solicitation to evil). He knows also how to 'keep the unrighteous under punishment' (RV) now; the reference is not merely to their being punished at some future date. The verb is used in the passive voice, lit. 'being punished'. *Unto the day of judgment;* cf. the Old Testament term 'day of Jehovah', the time when God manifests Himself to vindicate righteousness. In the New Testament it is associated with the second coming of Christ to judge the world. 'The wicked already suffer for sin but the full measure of their punishment will be inflicted hereafter' (Cent. Bible).

c. The false teachers further described (ii. 10–16)

There is no break in the Greek between verses 9 and 10 although the apostle seems to proceed to give a further and fuller description of the false teachers. The evil is regarded as existing among those who made profession of Christianity. Their character is described first as licentious and wilful. They are libertines, carnal, gratifying defiling lusts; they also defy the authority of civil powers, i.e. they practise their abominations so as to keep out of the reach of the letter of the law. The term *government*, or dominion (Gk. *kyriotēs*), is used twice by Paul (Eph. i. 21; Col. i. 16) and is translated 'lordship'. So also Jude 8. It may refer to our Lord, for the false teachers despised the Lordship of Christ which was the central theme of apostolic preaching. 'Daring, self-willed, they tremble not to rail at dignities' (10, RV). *Dignities;* Gk. *doxa,* i.e. an appearance commanding respect or manifestation of glory; it is used of angelic powers in respect of their state as commanding recognition. Verse 11 is obscure and difficult. The audacious conduct of the false teachers is contrasted with the more becoming demeanour of the angels who, when withstanding evil, do not abuse their opponents. The interpretation is made more clear by reference to Jude 9.

Peter now deals with more of their characteristics. They are *natural brute beasts* (RV 'creatures without reason'); i.e. he regards them as being born mere animals, *made to be taken and destroyed* (12). As animals are trapped through their eagerness to satisfy their appetite so self-indulgence betrays these false teachers to their ruin (see Cent. Bible). The whole context implies an unspeakable depth of degradation and infamy. No language can be too strong in which to express the apostle's scornful condemnation. He next points out their recklessness. They are qualified neither by spiritual nor intellectual power for the office of teacher which they have assumed and so they *speak evil of the things that they understand not.* But their doom is certain. They shall *utterly perish in their own corruption* (12). The Greek idiom, showing the emphasis from the repetition of the same root both in the noun and the verb, is preserved in the RV. Having done wrong to others, they will incur the retribution of being similarly wronged themselves.

Peter now deals with their sensuality. They *count it pleasure to riot in the day time* (13). This was considered the height of self-indulgence and sin (cf. Acts ii. 15; Rom. xiii. 13, 14; 1 Thes. v. 7). The Greek *tryphē,* translated by the RV here 'to revel', is cognate to the word *etryphēsate* of Jas. v. 5 which RV translates 'lived delicately'. It is possible therefore that 'in the day time', Gk. *en hēmera(i),* may mean 'in a day of judgment', i.e. in a great crisis in the history of the Church and the world. These men are also hypocrites. *Spots they are and blemishes, sporting themselves with their own deceivings* (RV 'revelling in their love-feasts') *while they feast with you* (13). The MSS both here and in Jude 12 vary between Greek *apatais,* 'deceivings', and *agapais,* 'feasts of love'. The latter is more generally favoured. The love-feasts were at first connected with the observance of the Lord's Supper, but afterwards separated from it. They were a witness of the new brotherhood in which rich and poor met together (see 1 Cor. xi. 17–22). The meaning of the passage seems to be that even while these false teachers were living in sin they did not hesitate to associate themselves with the Christian love-feasts, making even these an occasion for revelling. Their sensuality was reflected in their eyes and they were quite unable to restrain themselves from the sin of self-indulgence. The depth of their sin is sounded in the phrase *beguiling unstable souls* (14); RV 'enticing unstedfast souls'. Not only do they themselves

indulge in awful iniquity but they also allure weak and young Christians to their way of life. And so to their greed of gain already mentioned is added this wantonness. Their whole character is summed up in the apostle's next word, *cursed children* (cf. 'son of perdition', 2 Thes. ii. 3; 'children of wrath', Eph. ii. 3): *which have forsaken the right way, and are gone astray, following the way of Balaam* (14, 15; cf. Nu. xxii. 23, xxxi. 8, 16). Balaam is depicted in the Old Testament narrative as one who had the true prophetic impulse, being commissioned of God to utter the message from Him. But he allowed the greed of gain to triumph over that prophetic impulse to his own ultimate undoing. No comparison could have better shown the particular sin of the false teachers and the doom to which it led. Balaam stands out in the sacred record as an instance of one who knew what was right and deliberately did what was wrong, thus exhibiting the awful danger of trifling with conscience or trying, as it were, to bargain with God in such a way that the profits of disobedience may be reaped without formally disobeying Him. His attempt to twist God's will into conformity with his own plans and aims wrought disaster for Israel and brought him to a disastrous and dishonoured end. In his footsteps and towards his doom the false teachers were taking their daring self-willed way. Note the repetition from verse 13, *loved the wages of unrighteousness,* to emphasize the parallelism between the false teachers of the Old Testament and those of the New.

d. The influence of the false teachers (ii. 17–19)

They are *wells without water* (17); i.e. empty and having no real vitality. Like clouds in a storm they are unstable and unreliable (cf. Eph. iv. 14, 'carried about with every wind of doctrine'), i.e. they have no settled principles. Their ruin is again foretold. *The mist of darkness* (17); RV more graphically describes it as 'blackness of darkness'. The apostle declares that the teaching of these heretics is both pretentious and demoralizing. It consists of *great swelling words of vanity* (18; Moff. 'arrogant futilities'), an expression which carries the ideas of exaggeration, boastfulness, unreality and emptiness. It is demoralizing in that it finds easy victims in those who are *clean escaped from them who live in error* (18), and, appealing to their latent passions, seduces them into the way of sensual self-indulgence. The tragedy is seen in the fact that, though these teachers are proclaiming freedom in the realms of thought and life, the abolition of moral restrictions and the gratification of natural desires, they are actually forging fetters for those who are their dupes. They are mastered by their own evil desires and are therefore themselves in grievous bondage.

e. Falling from grace (ii. 20–22)

Whether these verses refer to the false teachers themselves or to those who are led astray by them has been for long a matter of controversy.

On the whole it seems best to regard the particulars of judgment here set forth as applicable to the false teachers. If the reference is to converts who have been deceived and betrayed through weakness and inexperience, the hopelessness of their ruin seems almost incredible. On the other hand, the punishment reserved for teachers who have done such despite to truth and purity does seem appropriate. These men had not been hypocrites and pretenders all the time. Through Jesus Christ they had once *known the way of righteousness* (21) and had even followed it with the result that they had escaped from the 'defilements of the world' (20, RV). But now they had again become entangled and ensnared. For the thought of verse 21 see Heb. vi. 4–6, x. 26–31, 39, and the Appendix III to Hebrews dealing with the warning passages in that Epistle. There is something not only disappointing but, in a sense, disgusting in such a fall from the heights of Christian experience to the depths of degradation. This finds expression in two proverbs, the first of which is taken from Pr. xxvi. 11 and the second from an unknown source. The point of the proverbs is that the sins to which the false teachers had returned were utterly loathsome and the fact that they had fallen into them showed that, at heart, they were still evil. Their nature, in which sin was so deeply ingrained, was unchanged.

IV. THE CHRISTIAN'S HOPE. iii. 1–18

a. The promise of our Lord's coming (iii. 1–7)

The closing chapter of the Epistle opens with a reference to the apostle's purpose in writing, namely, to *stir up your pure minds by way of remembrance* (cf. i. 12), to remind them of the teaching of the prophets and the apostles and especially of the warnings that in the last days men would arise who would laugh at the idea of any second coming of the Lord from heaven. Some have mistaken iii. 1 for the opening of another Epistle which was combined with the first and second Epistles by unknown editors. The verse is, in reality, a resumption of i. 12, 13 and is intended to lay special stress on the explanation of the appearance of the false teachers.

In all their pernicious doctrine there was one point which was specially disastrous, namely, their scoffing scepticism with reference to the second coming. The questioning of this not only struck at the very root of apostolic teaching but inevitably had an adverse effect on the moral life of the Christian community, encouraging a loosening of moral ties and a sinful self-indulgence. Peter now brings the question to the forefront, exposes the weakness of the arguments put forth by the false teachers on the question of our Lord's delaying His coming, and, setting before his readers the truer point of view, exhorts to a manner of life befitting those who look for the Lord from heaven. He stirs up their 'sincere minds' (so RV; cf. 1 Cor. v. 8; 2 Cor. i. 12, ii. 17; Phil. i. 10). The apostle bears testimony to the reality of their spiritual life. An effective antidote to false doctrine is to recall and dwell on the teaching already received. The apostle appeals to the same witnesses as those already invoked in i. 16–21. He unites a reference to Old Testament prophecy and apostolic teaching, which is described as the *commandment* (2), and exhorts them to give particular heed to this teaching in the light of the dangers surrounding them. These dangers are threefold: scoffing, evil living and scepticism (3, 4). This scepticism struck at a most deeply cherished expectation, namely, the imminent return of the Lord. The realization of that hope was not yet and there seemed no ready answer to the question of the sceptics who argued that *since the fathers fell asleep* there had been a continuity of the natural order. The reference may be either to the progenitors of Israel or to the first generation of the disciples of Christ who had died without seeing the advent for which they had looked (cf. 1 Thes. iv. 15). Lest their hope should fade into doubt or into complete despair Peter proposes a corrective. He shows the unreality and deliberate sin of such scepticism. They have wilfully ignored the plain teaching of Gn. i, the record of creation. The earth, the heavens, the water were made by the divine fiat, *by the word of God* (5). Besides, *the world that then was, being overflowed with water, perished* (6). Therefore it is not true to say that all things have continued as they were from the beginning. He proceeds to warn scoffers that, as formerly water was God's instrument for destruction, so now fire waits only God's time to do the same work. Though God may delay, His judgments are certain and His instrument ready at hand (cf. ii. 3n.).

b. An explanation of the delay (iii. 8–10)

This is found in the character and purpose of God. God is not limited by time. There is a difference between the divine and human methods of computation. *One day is with the Lord as a thousand years* (8), a deduction from Ps. xc. 4 (LXX), 'A thousand years in thy sight are but as the day'. In the eternity of God a thousand years count for less than a day in the short life of man. Man's life belongs to the temporal order and is marked by time divisions. The eternal order is other than that of time. The delay therefore is no indication of divine heedlessness. Any seeming delay is rather to be interpreted as dictated by merciful compassion. His purpose is one of love and mercy (9). His delay is an increased opportunity for salvation. It is not because God has forgotten but because He loves that the coming is delayed. *The day of the Lord will come*, however; that is absolutely certain (10). His longsuffering is balanced by justice. It will come suddenly, *as a thief in the night*, when men are not looking for it (cf. Mt. xxiv. 43; 1 Thes. v. 2). Hence the need for unceasing vigilance and preparedness. On that day *the heavens shall pass away* (cf. Mk. xiii. 24; Is. xxxiv. 4) *with a great noise* (Gk. *rhoizēdon*). The noun *rhoizos* is used of the whizzing of the arrow or the rustling of wings; here, however, it seems to refer to the roaring of a fire, or probably to the rolling of the heavens together as a scroll (cf. Is. xxxiv. 4). *Elements* (10); Gk. *stoicheia*. The RV mg. 'heavenly bodies' (i.e. the sun, moon and stars) supplies the interpretation on which there is fairly general agreement.

c. Practical issue (iii. 11-13)

So terrible a prospect bringing to a close the present dispensation ought to have a powerful effect on life and conduct. The mind of man can picture nothing more awful than to be caught unready and unprepared by such a divine visitation. On the other hand it ought to be to the believer an incentive to holy living. In Greek the words *holy conversation* and *godliness* (11) are in the plural, signifying 'all kinds of'. Holy living will have the effect of causing them to look for and desire earnestly (RV mg. 'hastening') *the coming of the day of God* (12). This expression is unusual; it is spoken of as the time 'by reason of which' (RV) these physical convulsions are to take place and as ushering in the *new heavens and a new earth, wherein dwelleth righteousness* (13); i.e. righteousness has her permanent home there. *According to his promise* (13); cf. Is. lxv. 17, and for the fulfilment see Rev. xxi. 1.

d. Closing exhortations (iii. 14-18)

The apostle argues that the logical outcome of these warnings and promises should be an earnest endeavour after a holy life. The attitude that befits a man who is looking for the coming is one neither of idle anticipation nor of feverish dread, but of confident watchfulness and preparation. He gives diligence that he *may be found of him in peace* (14), not the peace of quietude and stillness but of harmony and absence of discord; i.e. co-operation without friction or hindering disturbance between man's will and God's. *Without spot, and blameless* (14); Gk. *aspiloi kai amōmētoi* in contrast to the false teachers who are described as *spiloi kai mōmoi* in ii. 13. As under the old covenant the offering made to God must be whole and sound, so the consecration of the Christian to God must be free from any taint of self. *The longsuffering of our Lord is salvation* (15); Peter reaffirms what he has already said in verse 9. Instead of complaining about the seeming delay in the Lord's return and describing it as slackness, they should regard it as a graciously bestowed

opportunity for repentance and for working out that salvation which God had wrought in them. *Even as our beloved brother Paul also . . . hath written*. It is impossible to say with certainty to which of the Pauline letters Peter refers, but a reference to the Epistle to the Romans seems most probable. Peter refers to Paul as being not only a fellow-Christian but a colleague and brother apostle, and he freely acknowledges Paul's inspiration and authority, *the wisdom given unto him*. In this way he disabuses the minds of his readers of any difference between the Pauline and Petrine teaching and attitude towards the second coming. The estimate already given to Paul's Epistles is also indicated. They were associated with the Old Testament Scriptures as the Word of God. Even at this early date the *unlearned and unstable* had begun to *wrest* (16), i.e. twist or stretch as on the rack, the teaching of the apostle in the same way as they did the other Scriptures. 'Unlearned' here really means untrained in the study of the Scriptures.

Peter's last warning is *Beware lest ye . . . fall from your own stedfastness* (17). They have been faithfully warned of the dangers besetting them and of the possibility of their own failure in face of them. The false teachers were able and influential. There was all the more need therefore for constant watchfulness on the part of the Christians lest they should be carried away by them. It was very natural that the apostle's last injunction should be *grow in grace, and in the knowledge of our Lord and Saviour Jesus Christ* (18). The grace is that of which Christ is the Giver. It surrounds and upholds them and is the very atmosphere of their life. As they abide in it they are to keep on growing, for it is only by continuous growth that the possibility of falling can be effectually overcome (cf. 1 Pet. ii. 2). But they are also to grow in knowledge of their Lord. Knowledge of God implies personal experience and continuous fellowship, the secret of Christian steadfastness and progress.

To him be glory both now and for ever. Amen (18), a form of doxology of which Jude 25 is an expansion and adaptation. The expression translated *for ever* is unique. It is rendered by RV mg. as 'unto the day of eternity'. In spite of all the perplexities, oppositions and failures, the Christians are exhorted to praise God and to ascribe to Him glory both now and unto that eternal day, the dawning of which will be heralded by the coming of the Lord.

ANDREW MCNAB.

THE EPISTLES OF JOHN

I JOHN : INTRODUCTION

The Epistles which bear the name of John are anonymous. The first Epistle has neither address nor signature. But there are such close affinities with the fourth Gospel in style and subject-matter that most scholars agree that all four writings are from the same hand. Even those few who think otherwise are constrained to admit that the writer of the first Epistle must have been someone strongly influenced by the Gospel writer. There is no good reason for rejecting the tradition that the writer of all four documents was the apostle John, the son of Zebedee.

There is a close connection between the Gospel and the first Epistle; indeed, the Epistle is in effect a sequel to the Gospel. The Gospel is specifically said to have been written 'that ye might believe that Jesus is the Christ, the Son of God; and that believing ye might have life through his name' (Jn. xx. 31). The Epistle was written 'unto you that believe on the name of the Son of God; that ye may know that ye have eternal life' (1 Jn. v. 13). The Gospel was written to awaken life-giving faith in Jesus Christ; the Epistle to justify assurance of the possession of it and to give instruction in the truths of the faith.

The Epistle was written at a time when false teaching of a Gnostic type had made its appearance and had even caused some to secede from the church (ii. 19). Gnosticism took on many forms, but its basic assumptions seem always to have been that matter is evil, and only spirit is good, but that by knowledge (Gk. *gnōsis*) of a kind known only to the initiates the spirit of man might be released from its material prison and rise upward to God. Where such a system was combined with Christianity serious results followed. In the first place it denied the possibility of a real incarnation, for God, being good, could not be thought of as coming into contact with evil matter; and this in turn ruled out the possibility of an atonement, for the Son of God could not have suffered on the cross. Then again, if salvation came by knowledge it could be held that right living was completely unimportant, and the worst forms of Gnosticism cast their cloak of knowledge over rank licentiousness. The Epistle is steadily addressed to the exposure and refutation of such erroneous claims. 'John in this Epistle sets forth three marks of a real knowledge of and fellowship with God, lacking which all claims to possess these high privileges were false. These marks are, first, righteousness of life, second, brotherly love, and third, faith in Jesus as God incarnate' (*Search the Scriptures*, I.V.F., p. 284). These three themes will be found continually reappearing throughout the letter.

The Epistle is dominated by two great thoughts of God—God is light (i. 5) and God is love (iv. 8, 16). God is the sun in the spiritual sky, the source of light to the minds and of warmth to the hearts of His children. From this comes the responsibility that the children should live up to the highest moral standards and, as we have noted already, this is stressed again and again (see, e.g., ii. 1–6, iii. 3, 6, 9, v. 1–3). But we do not find anything like a harsh or distant admonition; rather the author addresses his readers with intimate knowledge, fatherly solicitude and tender concern—'Little children'; 'Beloved'; 'My little children, let no man deceive you'; 'Little children, keep yourselves from idols'.

I JOHN : OUTLINE OF CONTENTS

I. PROLOGUE. i. 1–4

II. THE CONDITIONS OF FELLOWSHIP WITH GOD. i. 5—ii. 6

III. RIVAL LOVES. ii. 7–17

IV. THE CHRISTIAN AND THE ANTICHRIST. ii. 18–28

V. CHILDREN OF GOD. ii. 29—iii. 3

VI. CHILDREN OF GOD AND CHILDREN OF THE DEVIL. iii. 4–10

VII. BROTHERLY LOVE A CRUCIAL TEST OF RIGHTEOUSNESS. iii. 11–24

VIII. THE SPIRIT OF TRUTH AND THE SPIRIT OF ERROR. iv. 1-6

IX. THE LOVE OF GOD. iv. 7-21

X. LOVE, FAITH AND VICTORY. v. 1-5

XI. WITNESSES TO THE DIVINITY OF JESUS CHRIST. v. 6-12

XII. CONCLUSION. v. 13-21

I JOHN : COMMENTARY

I. PROLOGUE. i. 1-4

These verses form one highly compressed and complicated sentence in the Greek, and it is not without difficulties. But the following seem to be the important points.

The gospel message is being summed up in the pregnant phrase *the Word of life* (1), where *Word* recalls Him who was in the beginning 'with God' and 'was God' (Jn. i. 1), who was 'made flesh' and took up His dwelling among men (Jn. i. 14), and *life* reminds us that 'in him was life; and the life was the light of men' (Jn. i. 4). This gospel was no novelty or afterthought (it was from the beginning), nor was it concerned with some mythical figure like the shadowy forms of the Greek mysteries, but with a genuine historical Person, who had been *heard* and *seen* and even *handled* (1; cf. Lk. xxiv. 39; Jn. xx. 20, 24ff.). The gospel message is not a theory or fancy tale, but the record of the life and presence among men in tangible form of the living God in the person of His Son.

In the sudden parenthesis which breaks in abruptly in verse 2 John sets forth his justification for thus speaking of Jesus Christ, namely, that he speaks from personal experience. What he told was not only no 'cunningly devised fable' (2 Pet. i. 16), nor even a carried tale, but a first-hand record of blessed privileges enjoyed by himself and many more in familiar intercourse with Jesus Christ during the days of His flesh. It was news too good to keep to themselves; they must *bear witness*.

The gospel message was proclaimed to the recipients of the Epistle in order that they might enjoy fellowship with those who proclaimed it. But the clause *that ye also may have fellowship with us* (3) does not only mean 'that there may be friendly relations between us', but 'that you may share with us our relationship with the Father and the Son'. The basic idea in fellowship (Gk. *koinōnia*) is that of having things in common, of partnership or sharing, and it is often used of business affairs (cf. Lk. v. 10). Specifically Christian fellowship is a sharing in the common life in Christ through the Holy Spirit, and it points us to the gift of God. It is fellowship *with the Father, and with his Son Jesus Christ* (3). In verse 4 both *write* and *we* are emphatic in the Greek, stressing both that the message is in a precise and abiding form, and that it was

written 'by those who had full authority to write' (Westcott). In the second clause it is not certain whether we should read *your joy* or 'our joy' (RV), the manuscript evidence being slightly in favour of 'our'. But it does not greatly matter which we read for, as Brooke reminds us, 'In the spiritual harvest, sower and reaper rejoice together.' The essential point is that true joy comes only from fellowship with God.

II. THE CONDITIONS OF FELLOWSHIP WITH GOD. i. 5—ii. 6

Having made it clear that the purpose of his writing is that his readers may enter into fellowship, John now proceeds to deduce from the nature of God the conditions of fellowship. *God is light*, he says, *and in him is no darkness at all* (5; cf. Ps. xxvii. 1; Jn. i. 4-9), the symbolism directing our minds to the splendour and purity of God and to the illumination to which our lives are exposed. Nothing can be hid from Him (cf. Ps. xc. 8), and because He is light He will demand that His people *walk in the light* (7).

The writer now deals with three obstacles to fellowship. First, there is the allegation that we have fellowship with Him while we walk in darkness (6). This is a lie, for since God is light it is not possible to be in fellowship with Him and at the same time to be in darkness. Light and darkness are incompatible. We are reminded that Christianity is essentially practical. In the case of such men as those John is describing the life gives the lie to the lip. The phrase *walk in the light* (7) probably looks back to our Lord's words in Jn. xi. 9, 10. In view of verse 5 we may interpret *as he is in the light* as expressing the completeness of the fellowship of the Son with the Father. It is only when we are living rightly that we can be said to be in fellowship with each other (see verse 3), and John proceeds to stress that cleansing from sin comes only from *the blood of Jesus Christ* (7). This last expression means 'the life given up in death' and not simply 'the life' as some commentators allege. *Cleanseth* is in the continuous present and signifies 'goes on cleansing'.

The second false teaching which is opposed is that of maintaining that *we have no sin* (8). 'To have sin' means more than 'to sin', and includes the idea of 'the principle of which the sinful acts are the several manifestations' (Brooke). It expresses the idea of responsibility for sins committed which was apparently denied by the Gnostic teachers. We might compare the man today who says that sin is just a disease, or weakness, due to heredity, environment, necessity or the like, so that it is his fate and not his fault. Such a man does but deceive himself. By contrast, *if we confess our sins* we receive a forgiveness which is rooted in the nature of our God who is *faithful and just* (9).

The third error is to say *we have not sinned* (10). In effect, this claim to sinlessness calls God a liar for, quite apart from specific passages in God's Word, the whole of God's dealings with men implies that man is a sinner requiring salvation. To deny this is to reject *his word*.

In contrast with all this John sets the truth. He faces the fact that Christians are not faultless; yet he does not regard this as something which may be viewed complacently, for the purpose of his writing is *that ye sin not* (ii. 1). But sin does occur, and he goes on to speak of God's provision whereby *we have an advocate with the Father, Jesus Christ the righteous: and he is the propitiation for our sins* (1, 2). The word translated *advocate* is *paraklētos*, used elsewhere in the New Testament only of the Holy Spirit (who is referred to as another 'Paraclete' in Jn. xiv. 16). Its essential meaning is 'one called to the side of' another in order to render assistance. It was used frequently in the law courts of the counsel for defence or of others called to assist, as, for example, by giving evidence. The thought here is that Jesus pleads for sinners. We have two indications of the manner of His activity on our behalf: the first in that He is called *the righteous*, which shows us that our deliverance is not in defiance of but in accordance with right; and the second in that He is *the propitiation for our sins*. This expression reminds us of the process of making atonement by the offering of sacrifice in the Old Testament, and also of the wrath of God towards everything that is evil, which wrath is to be reckoned with in any process of salvation. By His death on the cross Christ has made a full atonement, and we need fear the wrath no more. The very Son of God, at once the plea and the Pleader, sacrifice and Priest, must prevail in the counsels of a God who is 'faithful and just' (i. 9), i.e. true to His promises and consistent with Himself.

Next comes a test by which men can know whether, in spite of failures, they are in the right relationship with God, walking in fellowship with Him. This test is whether they keep His commandments or not, for it is impossible that those who really know God should be unaffected in their daily living by this knowledge. As Paul put it: 'if any man be in Christ, he is a new creature: old things are passed away; behold, all things are become new' (2 Cor. v. 17). So inevitable is this that the man who claims to know God, but does not keep His commandments, is

called *a liar* (4). By contrast, God's love is *perfected*, i.e. is achieving its object and end, in the man that *keepeth his word* (5). *Abideth in him* (6). This is a clear reference to our Lord's teaching which John had recorded in his Gospel (see Jn. xv. 4–11). The description of life as a 'walk' was a favourite expression with Paul. Here the thought links up with i. 6, 7, above. The Christian's life should be marked by that unbroken, consistent fellowship with God which so characterized the life of our Lord.

III. RIVAL LOVES. ii. 7–17

The commandment spoken of in verses 7, 8 is not defined, but there can be no doubt that it is the commandment of Christian love. This is not a novelty, but *an old commandment which ye had from the beginning* (7), where *the beginning* has been understood either of the beginning of Christian faith, or of the giving of the law under Moses, or even earlier. It is not easy to decide, but probably the definition of the old commandment as 'the word which ye heard' (RV) points us to the first (cf. Jn. xiii. 34). Also, if we are right in linking verse 6 with Jn. xv, this may have led John to recall the way in which our Lord repeated the commandment in that discourse (see Jn. xv. 12). The commandment is *new* (8) in the sense that it must continually be related to the changing situation of the recipients. Progress is made and circumstances change and so the commandment is always new. There is always a new urgency about the old command for those for whom Christ died.

This commandment, as Moffatt puts it, is 'realized in him and also in yourselves, because the darkness is passing away and the true light is already shining' (8). Christ has Himself fulfilled the command to love, and He infuses a like love into His followers, so that a man's attitude to his brother reveals whether he is walking in the light or in the darkness. If he displays love, he walks with a sure foot, for love rids his heart of everything that would cause him to stumble. If he displays hatred, let him say what he will, he is on the wrong track and it will lead him to ruin, for hate blinds the eyes (9–11).

John has an appeal to make, but before making it he recognizes the Christian experience of his readers. Verses 12–14 consist of two sequences each with a threefold address, to *children, fathers* and *young men*. Considerable ingenuity has been expended upon the definition of these classes, and on the change of tense from 'I write' to 'I wrote' (RV mg.). It is true that there is a certain appropriateness in the allocation of qualities, as knowledge to fathers (those old in the faith) and strength to young men; but, inasmuch as all the qualities mentioned are the possession of all believers, it is probably best to regard the division as a stylistic device adding emphasis, for as Dodd says, 'all Christians are (by grace, not nature) children in innocence and dependence on the heavenly Father, young men in strength, and fathers in experience.'

Having thus made it clear that he writes to those whose *sins are forgiven* (12), who know God (13) and who have experience of victory over evil (14), John now comes to the great rival love and makes his appeal to *love not the world* (15). By the *world* John means human society apart from Christ and opposed to God, for he is concerned with those lower, earthly passions which are incompatible with *the love of the Father. The lust of the flesh* (16) stands for the gratification of the flesh in all its forms; *the lust of the eyes* for those things which appeal to the eyes particularly (perhaps we are not wrong in applying the term to anything superficial); 'the vainglory of life' (RV) for the empty self-glorification of the worldling (cf. the three factors which led Eve to disobey God, Gn. iii. 6). Such things show us the monstrosity which the world, left to itself, has made of itself. It is a passing show on its way to ruin. *But he that doeth the will of God abideth for ever* (17).

IV. THE CHRISTIAN AND THE ANTICHRIST. ii. 18–28

Little children, it is the last time (18); lit. 'a last hour'. It is possible that 'last hour' means the last period before the end of the world, or the passing of the old régime and the dawning of the Christian era. But there is no article in the Greek; we should therefore translate 'a last hour' with the emphasis on the general character of the times rather than the relation to the end point. Human history proceeds by periods of slow unfolding until a crisis is reached, an age is ended, a new age begins, and men say 'it can never be the same again'. John is saying that there has come such a last hour. Evidence for this is the appearance of not only one but *many antichrists* (18), where antichrist may be thought of as representing a temper, a spirit prevalent in many forms and persons. Westcott seems to be right in thinking of antichrist as one who 'assails Christ by proposing to do or to preserve what He did while he denies Him'.

Verse 19 is an important one for the doctrine of the Church. It is clear that these people had been members of the visible Church, they had fulfilled the outward requirements for church membership; but although it was *from us* they went out, yet it can be said of them *they were not of us*. This reminds us that more than outward membership of the visible Church is required if we are to be members of the Body of Christ, and also that we must not expect that the visible Church will always be composed entirely of true believers. It may even number anti-christs among its professed adherents.

Ye have an unction (20). For the notes on this verse see the next paragraph. The cardinal error of the heretics, as we noted in the *Introduction*, was their denial that *Jesus is the Christ* (22), i.e. their refusal to recognize that in the man Jesus of Nazareth we see the eternal Son of God taking upon Himself our nature. A common Gnostic position was that the divine Christ came down upon Jesus at His baptism and left Him before the crucifixion, and it is some such denial that Jesus *was* the Christ that John is attacking. He regards it as the fundamental lie, subversive of all truth. The man who deliberately goes wrong here is not to be depended upon anywhere. That is a tremendous thing to say, but it means that the evidence that in Jesus of Nazareth God and man are indissolubly united is so strong that the man who will not accept it is not to be trusted at any point. He is guilty of the radical lie (cf. Mk. xi. 27–33). Moreover this denial of the Son has consequences with regard to the Father (23), for if Jesus is not the very Son of God then it is not the love of God that we see revealed in His life and death. It is only as we receive Him that we become sons of God (cf. Jn. i. 12); thus, if we reject Him, we are not members of the heavenly family and have no right to call God our Father.

John sees two safeguards: the gift of the Holy Spirit (20, 27) and the simple, original gospel message (24). The gift of the Spirit is called an *unction from the Holy One* (20), i.e. from the Lord Jesus Christ (Jn. xvi. 7). If we follow the reading of the oldest manuscripts the result of this is that 'ye all know' (rather than *ye know all things*). A characteristic of the Gnostics was the claim to a secret knowledge known only to a select group. John points out that there is no such select group in Christianity, for God gives His Holy Spirit to all believers, and they all have knowledge. Therefore, while there is a very real place for Christian teachers (as the very writing of the Epistle shows), it is nevertheless true that ultimately the Christian is independent of man and owes his illumination directly to God (27).

The other safeguard is the simple gospel message, *that which ye have heard from the beginning* (24). This gospel does not pander to intellectual or spiritual dilettantism, but is a simple message calling to strenuous living by faith. Perhaps because it is so simple, men like the heretical teachers are always tempted to elaborate and make it other than it is, and thus John solemnly urges his readers to let this message *abide* in them (24) or, what amounts to the same thing, to abide in Christ (28). It is only this abiding that can give us confidence before Him.

V. CHILDREN OF GOD. ii. 29—iii. 3

The division of chapters is unfortunate here as it separates the expression of wonder in iii. 1 from that which evoked it, the being born of God. In ii. 29 we are reminded that *he is righteous*, and this gives us a test whereby we may distinguish the true Christian, for 'know ye', says John (the verb should probably be taken as imperative as mg. of both AV and RV), 'that everyone who practises righteousness has been begotten of Him.' Those who show qualities of character like His give evidence of their heavenly birth. Having said this, the wonder and the grace of it arrest John. 'Look!', he says, 'look at such love! Children of God! Is there any-thing like it?' He uses the Greek word *tekna* which draws attention to community of nature rather than to rights and privileges, in other words to our being born again rather than to adoption. Notice the addition in RV 'and such we are'. Not only are we called God's children, but we really are such in actual fact. All this springs from the amazing love which God has lavished upon us, a love which vitalizes, which generates new life, bestowing upon men something of God's own nature and installing them as members of His family. A love like this, and the life it engenders, is something the world does not understand in the recipient any more than it understood the Saviour Himself (cf. Jn. i. 10, 11).

All this is very wonderful, but from iii. 2 we see that there is more to follow. The exact interpretation of this verse is difficult, but the general thought is clear. It is probable that we should translate 'if he shall be manifested' (RV) and not 'if it shall be manifested' (RV mg.); but the second part of the verse can be understood in two ways. We may be thought of as like Him because only those who are like Him can see Him; or perhaps the thought is that the vision of God makes men like Him. Again, it is not quite clear whether the verse refers to the Father or the Son, but this does not greatly matter since he that sees the Son sees also the Father (Jn. xii. 45, xiv. 9). But what is quite clear is that great things are in store for the Christian when he sees Him and is made like Him. This prospect is a present stimulus to get rid of every-thing in heart and life that does not tally with the perfect purity of the Son of God (3), so that as He is not ashamed to call them brethren they may not shame Him nor be ashamed at His coming (see ii. 28).

VI. CHILDREN OF GOD AND CHILDREN OF THE DEVIL. iii. 4–10

John knew that the reaction of the heretical teachers (see *Introduction*) to his 'purify' (3) would be to inculcate their pernicious doctrine of the sufficiency of knowledge and its superiority to mere righteous living. Hence he goes straight on to demonstrate that those who sin are children, not of God, but *of the devil* (8), and he begins by pointing out that 'sin is lawlessness' (4, RV), the Greek construction implying that the two are identical. Lawlessness here does not mean a state of being without law, but the assertion of the individual will against and in defiance of the law of God, the refusal to live in accordance with the revealed standards of right and wrong.

How alien such an attitude as this is to that of the child of God is at once apparent when we remember the purpose for which the Son of God came into the world, namely, *to take away our sins* (5), to *destroy the works of the devil* (8). Sin in all its forms is the very antithesis of the kingdom of God, and there is an irreconcilable opposition between Christ and everything that is evil. It is against this background that we must understand the very strong statements of verses 6 and 9: *whosoever abideth in him sinneth not; he cannot sin, because he is born of God.* These statements should not be watered down. There is an incompatibility between sinfulness and Christian profession, and we must never grow complacent in our attitude towards sin, even occasional sin. At the same time we must notice that the force of the Greek continuous present in these verses is to stress the habitual attitude. Thus verse 6 might be paraphrased 'Whoever abides continually in Him does not keep on sinning; whoever keeps on sinning has not seen Him and does not know Him'; and similarly in verse 9, 'Whoever has been begotten of God does not commit sin habitually, because His seed remains continually in him; and he cannot keep on sinning because he has been begotten of God.' John is not thinking in terms of individual acts of sin (which would require the aorist tense in the Greek) but of habitual attitudes, and he is saying in strong terms that the life a man lives reveals the source from which he draws his life. If he is born again from above he will habitually lead the life of a born-again person, in spite of stumbles; if he continually sins he is of the devil, so that the false teachers were wrong in saying that sin does not matter. As righteous living characterized the Master, so it must characterize the servant (7). This verse does not mean, of course, that the Christian is as righteous as his Lord, any more than the statement that man is made in the image of God means that he is equal with Christ, who is also said to be the image of God (2 Cor. iv. 4; Col. i. 15), as Augustine long ago pointed out. It simply is an emphatic way of saying that life is the test; if we are Christ's we shall be Christlike.

VII. BROTHERLY LOVE A CRUCIAL TEST OF RIGHTEOUSNESS. iii. 11–24

The closing words of verse 10 suggest a close connection between righteousness and brotherly love, and this is reinforced in the section which follows, where the Christian's whole duty is summed up in the obligation to exercise love (11; cf. Rom. xiii. 8). There is acute psychological insight in verse 12 where we see the motive for Cain's murder of Abel springing from the con-trast between his own evil life and the good life of his brother. Wickedness always hates the goodness that shows it what it ought to be, and Christians accordingly ought not to be surprised when they find the world hating them (13). But if it is characteristic of the world to hate, it is just as characteristic of the Christian to love, and, indeed, it is *because we love the brethren*

(14) that we know we are really Christ's. The man who lacks such love is still in the death of sin, being in fact a murderer, for the essential part of being a murderer, at least from the divine point of view, is the inward attitude of which the outward deed is but the expression (15; cf. Mt. v. 21ff.).

In verse 16 we should omit *of God* which occurs only in late MSS; the sense of the verse is well brought out by Moffatt: 'We know what love is by this, that He laid down His life for us.' But when we have come to realize something of the greatness of God's love we realize also that it imposes obligations upon us, and we must be ready to give our lives for others. But John is practical. Dying for others may never actually be demanded, but there will often be the need for ready help, when not words but deeds (18) reveal the existence of brotherly love.

In the verses which follow there is reassurance for sensitive consciences. The Greek of verses 19, 20 is difficult, and several translations have been suggested, but the most probable interpretation seems to be as follows. *Hereby* refers to what has gone before: we know that we are of the truth because love is being manifested in our living. But if we have doubts about this, *if our heart condemn us* (20), then we shall obtain reassurance by reflecting that God is the Judge, not our hearts, and that He has perfect knowledge. Men in all humility may see only their shortcomings and therefore experience misgiving. But God, who gives the love, takes account of a host of brotherly acts for which men dare not take credit (cf. Mt. xxv. 37–40). When he goes on to say *if our heart condemn us not* (21), John is not thinking of people who make a claim to sinlessness or who are insensitive to sin, but 'the action of a lively faith which retains a real sense of fellowship with God' (Westcott). If we have such a sense of peace then we have *confidence towards God*. The Greek word *parrhēsia*, translated *confidence* (RV 'boldness'), derives from two words meaning 'all speech' and thus denotes first a freedom, fluency of speaking, and then the attitude of boldness which gives rise to such speaking.

This word, with its associations of bold speaking, leads on naturally to the thought of prayer, and we learn that keeping the commandments is indispensable for answered prayer (22). This does not mean that God never answers the prayer of a sinner, for clearly He does at times; but we are among continuous present tenses again. As we continue to pray God continues to answer as we continue to keep the commandment, this latter being immediately defined as believing *on the name* of Jesus Christ (23). For prayers to be continually answered we must exercise faith, a truth often insisted upon in Scripture. The chapter concludes with a further ground for assurance, namely, in the Holy Spirit given to us (24). Our assurance depends upon what God has done for us, and not on our puny efforts.

VIII. THE SPIRIT OF TRUTH AND THE SPIRIT OF ERROR. iv. 1–6

The reference to the Spirit in the preceding verse leads on to the important question of how to distinguish truth from error when there were many claiming to be inspired. The problem was not a new one, for we read of false prophets in the Old Testament, and again Paul had found it necessary to give a ruling on when a man is speaking by 'the Spirit of God' (1 Cor. xii. 3). John now warns his readers that *many false prophets are gone out into the world* (1), from which we see that the problem had become an urgent one for them. The fact that they are said to have *gone out* seems to imply that they were the seceders mentioned in ii. 19, and the perfect tense of the Greek verb points to their continuing activity. They had evidently left the church and claimed inspiration for their heretical utterances, so that it became incumbent on believers not to accept unquestioningly everything that was told them by men in the position of teachers, but to *try* (RV 'prove') *the spirits*. The touchstone, as we see from verses 2, 3, is their attitude to Jesus Christ. The false teachers denied a real incarnation (see *Introduction*), but every God-inspired man *confesseth that Jesus Christ is come in the flesh* (2). The Greek construction puts the stress on the Person rather than on a proposition; that is to say, it is confession of Jesus Christ and Him come in the flesh, rather than confession that He is come in the flesh, that is meant. So, conversely, the false teacher is one who 'confesseth not Jesus' (3, RV). This is the distinctive note of the antichrist (see ii. 18n.).

Such make an appeal to the *world* (5), the word not being used in a neutral sense, but of the world as opposed to the things of God (cf. ii. 15n.). The false prophets really belong to the world, so it is not to be wondered at that they are accepted by the world, or that the true teachers are not so accepted (6). This fact gives John another test whereby truth and error may be discerned. Notice the *ye are of God* (4, 6), and the assurance of victory in both these verses. Falsehood may be powerful and pretentious, but truth will prevail.

IX. THE LOVE OF GOD. iv. 7–21

Once more the writer returns to the thought that the Christian must display love, and he reinforces it by another of his characteristic double statements, putting the truth first in its positive form, *every one that loveth is born of God, and knoweth God* (7), and then in its negative form, *he that loveth not knoweth not God* (8). There can be no doubt that love is of the very essence of Christian character, for *God is love* (8). This is a profound statement (reiterated in verse 16) of the essential nature of God, for it means far more than 'God loves', true and important though this is. It implies that the essential nature of God is love, and that, accordingly, everything that He does is done in love. This love *was manifested* (9), the Greek aorist focusing attention on the single decisive manifestation rather than the continual evidence of His care for His children. John is making it clear that the love of God is something that is revealed in its fulness only in the cross, and accordingly he emphatically disclaims the idea that our puny love for God gives us any real idea of love (10). Real love is to be seen only in God's love for us, i.e. in His sending His Son as *the propitiation for our sins*. Note the resounding paradox of this verse, that God is at once loving and wrathful, and His love provides the propitiation which averts the wrath from us. 'So far from finding any kind of contrast between love and propitiation, the apostle can convey no idea of love to anyone except by pointing to the propitiation' (James Denney, *The Death of Christ*, Tyndale Press, p. 152).

But if God is love, His children should be like Him, and John presses home the practical point that they should show, not, as one might suppose, love to God, but brotherly love (11), which love is the evidence of God's presence in us and of the fact that His love *is perfected in us*, i.e. has attained its end and aim in us (12; cf. ii. 5). The indwelling of the Spirit is closely connected with this (13), for, as Paul reminds us, love is the first of the fruits of the Spirit (Gal. v. 22). The statement that *no man hath seen God* (12) is quoted from John's Gospel (i. 18). The thought is taken up and expanded in verse 20 below.

In verse 14 the readers are reminded of the personal experience and testimony of the apostles, the *we* being emphatic in the Greek. But from here he moves inevitably to the *whosoever* of verse 15, for all Christians know the blessed experience of the indwelling of God. God is love, and to abide in love is to abide in God. This, of course, must be understood in its context, for John is far from asserting the sentimental notion that any man who has affection for another is thereby dwelling in God. Rather he is concerned with that love which flows from an appreciation of the love of Calvary. It is this love which is perfected in us (17). Follow the RV reading here; AV is almost certainly wrong. It is not our love but His that is in question, His love that operates within us and produces love to others. The result of this is a fearless outlook on the coming judgment (18). Here the *parrhēsia* is viewed from an angle different from that in chapter iii (see note on iii. 20). There it came from obedience; here it is from a wholehearted acceptance of the love of God which produces in us Christlike qualities. *Perfect* (Gk. *teleia*) *love*, love that has attained its end (*telos*), casts out fear. It views the world as God does. So *we love* (*him* should be omitted as in RV; it is love in general that is meant), *because he first loved us* (19). The initiative in love is always with God. This brings John, in the last two verses of the chapter, back to the thought that the Christian is a man who is displaying love to others. If he claims to love God but hates his fellow-man *he is a liar* (20). Love of God and hate of man are incompatibles.

X. LOVE, FAITH AND VICTORY. v. 1–5

In this brief paragraph thoughts of love, faith and obedience are crowded in, and we have an interesting commentary on Paul's conception of 'faith which worketh by love' (Gal. v. 6). Notice again the insistence on the incarnation, *Jesus is the Christ* (1); it is only the man whose faith is grounded on this certainty who can be said to be begotten of God. Here, too, we have a reiteration of the close connection between love of God and love of the brethren. But whereas, before, love of the brethren was regarded as the evidence that love of God exists, here it is the fact that we love God that shows us we really have love for the brethren (2). The love of God is defined as keeping His commandments, for real love to Him is always attended by obedience. When it is said that these commandments *are not grievous* (3), the thought is not that the service of God is an easy thing, but that His commandments are not an irksome burden. The standard He sets before His children is the highest, but He gives to them His Holy Spirit and transforms them through His love, so that the keeping of the commandments, though still difficult, is not an oppressive task. The world and its attractions continually tempt God's children, but *whatsoever is born of God overcometh the world* (4). The statement is made in its most abstract form, 'whatsoever' rather than 'whosoever', and this puts the emphasis on the power from God and not on the believer. But this power is victoriously operative only in believers, so there immediately follows *this is the victory that overcometh the world, even our faith*, and this is repeated in a different form in verse 5. This does not mean that faith is a human merit which overcomes in its own right. Faith is necessarily faith in God and, as Dodd says, 'It means committing ourselves to the love of God as it is expressed in all that Jesus Christ was and all that He did.'

XI. WITNESSES TO THE DIVINITY OF JESUS CHRIST. v. 6–12

The whole of verse 7 of AV is omitted in RV because it was not written by John. It first appeared in a Latin version three hundred years after John was dead, and not in any Greek manuscript till a thousand years later. What is stated in it is quite true, but it does not require attention in any endeavour to understand John's thought.

The victor in the war against the world of falsehood, hostility and godlessness has just been said to be the man who believes that Jesus is the Son of God. Here there follows a concise statement of the complete identification of Godhead and manhood in Jesus of Nazareth. It possibly has in view those who taught that the divine Christ came in the Spirit upon Jesus at the baptism, but left Him before the crucifixion. They would accept a coming *by water* but not a coming *by blood*. But John will not have it that the spectacle of an ideal life brings victory. For that an atoning death was essential, hence the emphatic addition *not by water only, but by water and blood* (6). The Spirit is then cited as bearing witness; the Greek construction pointing to the meaning, 'He continually bears witness', rather than to some such event as Pentecost. With *the Spirit is truth* cf. Jn. xvi. 13.

The threefold witness mentioned in verse 8 has been the subject of much discussion, but there seems no good reason for giving *the water* and *the blood* here a meaning different from that in the immediately preceding section. The thought then is that the sending of the Spirit and the historical facts of the baptism and crucifixion of the Lord form a threefold witness to the Person of Christ impressive in their unity. Others see a reference to the two sacraments, but, while this is possible, it should yet be noted that the Lord's Supper is not elsewhere referred to as 'the blood', and this, taken with verse 6, indicates that the interpretation given above is preferable. Since each of the three is from God the witness may be said to be *the witness of God* (9), which is to be preferred to what men say. But those who believe on the Son have the testimony within themselves (10); they put their trust in the Son and from their own experience find evidence of His divinity. By contrast, those who do not believe God make of Him a liar, for, by their attitude in the face of the evidence afforded by God's actions in history and by the experience of the Church, they are rejecting 'the witness which God has witnessed concerning His Son' (10, translating literally).

In verse 11 *the record* should be 'the witness' (as RV) to bring out the continuity of the thought. The writer then brings this section to an impressive close by summing up the witness, characteristically giving both the positive and negative aspects. Life eternal is God's gift to men, and this is closely associated with the Son, being indeed *in his Son* (11). Consequently to have the Son is to have the life, while not to have the Son inevitably means not to have the life (12).

XII. CONCLUSION. v. 13–21

The purpose of the Epistle is now summed up in a single sentence (13; see RV) from which we see the importance of assurance. The Epistle is written 'that ye may know that ye have eternal life' and to them 'that believe on the name of the Son of God'. As they approach God in prayer such believers have a freedom in speaking which is well expressed in the Greek *parrhēsia* (see iii. 21n.), a *confidence* (14), a certainty that they will be heard. God hears, and we know, says John, that *we have* (note the present tense) *the petitions that we desired of him* (15). Like other great promises of answers to prayer this one is attended by a condition, *if we ask any thing according to his will* (14). In Mk. xi. 24 believing prayer is insisted on; in Jn. xiv. 14 prayer must be in the name of Jesus; in Jn. xv. 7 abiding in Christ is thought of as the condition; while in 1 Jn. iii. 22 obedience is the prerequisite. There are

various ways of putting it but always the thought is that prayer is not an attempt to persuade God to do our will; rather it is an activity in which believing children approach their heavenly Father in a sincere endeavour to place themselves in the line of His will. Prayer is a means of setting forth God's righteous purposes, not a way whereby we may gratify our selfish and personal desires.

Having established that prayer must be in accordance with God's will and that such prayer is heard and answered, the writer goes on to indicate this principle in action. Prayer should be made for a sinning brother who sins a sin *not unto death*, this being distinguished from *sin unto death*. In this last expression we should follow the RV mg. and omit the article, for it seems to denote a state rather than a specific action. At the same time we must bear in mind that John does not define this sin. It is strange, therefore, that most interest in the passage is not in the duty to which it calls, namely, prayer for the erring brother, but inquisitiveness as to the sin unto death, as if, should we know that and avoid it, other sins would not much matter. As if to meet just that position John goes on to say, *All unrighteousness is sin* (17); indeed it is just because all unrighteousness is to be avoided that he is urging the necessity for prayer against it. He does not say what is sin unto death, but he most likely has in mind our Lord's warning concerning blasphemy against the Holy Spirit (see, e.g., Lk. xii. 10). The New Testament clearly teaches that it is possible to go so far in rebellion against God and in rejection of His Son that the power to repent is irrevocably lost (cf. Heb. x. 26–31, xii. 17 and see Appendix III to the commentary on Hebrews, p. 1116).

The Epistle is now rounded off with a threefold *we know*, drawing attention to three glorious certainties of the believing soul. In verse 18 we have another strong reminder that *whosoever is born of God sinneth not*, i.e. he does not remain in sin (see note on iii. 6, 9), and this is emphasized by the second half of the verse, 'he that was begotten of God keepeth him, and the evil one toucheth him not', accepting the rendering of the RV, for the evidence of the MSS and of the Greek constructions employed seems to show that John was thinking of the way Jesus Christ looks after His own and protects them from the assaults of the devil.

The second member of the trilogy must be understood in the light of what has gone before. There is a cleavage between the world and the people of God, and the two are not to be confused, as the heretical teachers confused them, by saying that the Christian may live in accordance with worldly standards. *We know that we are of God* (19), and this means the sharpest of breaks with all that is worldly, for 'the whole world lieth in the evil one' (RV).

The third *we know* introduces the grounds for our assurance, namely, *that the Son of God is come, and hath given us an understanding* (20).

Again we notice the stress on the fact of the incarnation which is so characteristic of this Epistle. So it is that 'we know him that is true, and we are in him that is true, even in his Son Jesus Christ' (RV). The word translated 'true' (*alēthinos*) is not the usual word for true (*alēthēs*), but a word signifying 'genuine', 'reliable', a word whose opposite is not 'false' so much as 'shadowy', 'unreal'. This word is used again in the expression *This is the true God*, where we get the thought of God as genuinely existing, as real, in contrast with the *idols* mentioned in the next verse. It is possible to understand this of Jesus Christ, who has just been mentioned, but probably it signifies 'This Being whom we have described, who is love, who sent forth His Son to be the propitiation for our sins, who gives us the gift of everlasting life'. This God, and this God alone, is real.

So we come to the final word, *Little children, keep yourselves from idols*. There is no reason for thinking that John's readers were in danger of bowing down to figures of wood and stone, and we must understand idols as signifying those things which men substitute for the true God. The false teachers of that day set before men a conception of God which was distorted and unreal, and this could justly be termed an 'idol'. This exhortation is always in season, for there is a perpetual tendency to substitute man-made conceptions of God for the revelation of the God and Father of our Lord Jesus Christ. In the twentieth century, no less than in the first, God's children must keep themselves from every idol.

II AND III JOHN: INTRODUCTION

These Epistles, like 1 John, bear the name of no author, the writer simply designating himself 'the elder'. In style and contents there are many resemblances to the first Epistle, so that most scholars are convinced that all three letters are from the same hand. The second Epistle seems to be addressed to a church (see the notes), but exactly which church we have no means of knowing. The third Epistle is a purely private letter to the presbyter's friend Gaius. Both have in mind those teachers wandering from church to church which were such a feature of the life of the early Church, the second Epistle urging the readers not to receive those teachers who were heretical, and the third complaining that a certain Diotrephes had not received the brethren. For the rest there are few indications as to the occasions which brought them forth, and all that we can say is that the second Epistle seems to envisage much the same situation as the first, though possibly in a different church. Probably we should think of all three Epistles as having been written at about the same time (toward the end of the first century) from Ephesus, where John lived, to various destinations in Asia Minor.

II JOHN: COMMENTARY

The writer of the Epistle styles himself the Presbyter (or Elder), and assumes that the recipients will know who he is. He calls the recipients *the elect lady and her children* (1). The weight of evidence in the terms of the letter itself (e.g. the use of the plural *ye* in later verses, and the salutation from *thy elect sister* in verse 13) suggests that this is not an individual and her household but is a cryptic designation for a church and its members. The salutation, in which the writer associates with himself all who have *known the truth* (1), begins with, revolves round, and ends in love and truth. It has given him great satisfaction to find some of the elect lady's children *walking in truth* (4) according to the commandment, and he proceeds, much as in the first Epistle, to emphasize the place of the commandment of love (5, 6; see 1 Jn. ii. 7–11), the close connection between obedience and love being brought out. In verse 7 the deceivers 'went out into the world' (translating literally), so we have the same sort of situation as that indicated in 1 Jn. ii. 19, and here again antichrist is linked with a refusal to acknowledge a real incarnation. The false teachers evidently spoke proudly of themselves as 'advanced' (see RV; *whosoever transgresseth* of verse 9 is, according to a better reading, 'everyone advancing'), and John points out that it is possible to advance right out of Christianity. The safeguard is to abide in the *doctrine of Christ* (9). The true Christian must not receive those who bring not this doctrine (10), for to encourage them is to share the responsibility for their evil deeds (11). But there the writer stays his hand and defers all else for an early personal visit and talk.

III JOHN: COMMENTARY

This is a personal letter from the Elder to his well-loved friend Gaius, whom he greets warmly (1, 2) and congratulates for his well-known hospitality (5, 6), after referring to his spiritual progress (3, 4).

Verses 5–8 give us a glimpse of early Church practice. Not only apostles, but ordinary brethren as well, travelled from church to church, receiving hospitality as they went from their fellow-Christians (cf. Heb. xiii. 2; 1 Pet. iv. 9).

Gaius is commended for the faithful way in which he offered hospitality to such visitors even when the brethren were strangers to him (5). These brethren appear to be on the move again, and Gaius is urged to help them when they come to him (6) for they are refusing to receive help from pagans (7). There is therefore an obligation on Christians to give them necessary aid, by which the givers become *fellowhelpers to the truth* (8).

But all men do not respect this Christian duty, and Diotrephes, who would seem to have held a position of some authority, is singled out for mention. This man had resisted John, perhaps suppressing one of his letters (9), certainly ignoring its injunctions and refusing to have anything to do with the brethren (10). It is not said that he held heretical views, but simply that he was ambitious for power. John urges Gaius not to follow such bad examples (11). He follows this with a doctrinal statement which is strongly reminiscent of the first Epistle (see, e.g., 1 Jn. iii. 6). He then commends a certain Demetrius (12) and, as in the second Epistle, brings the letter to a close with kindly messages in the hope of an early meeting.

R. J. DRUMMOND.
LEON MORRIS.

THE GENERAL EPISTLE OF JUDE

INTRODUCTION

The writer of this short Epistle describes himself as 'Jude, the servant of Jesus Christ, and brother of James'. Several men bearing this name are mentioned in the New Testament. Among the apostles there were two, Judas Iscariot, the traitor, and Judas (Lk. vi. 16; Acts i. 13) who is described in the AV as 'the brother of James'. The writer of this Epistle has been identified by some with this Judas who was one of the Twelve. But the designation 'brother of James' found in the lists of the apostles is a mistake; it should be 'the son of James' as in RV. Moreover the reference to the apostles made by the writer of the Epistle (verse 17) conveys the impression that he was not himself one of them.

Another interpretation which identifies the author with the Judas who is mentioned as one of the brothers of Jesus (Mt. xiii. 55; Mk. vi. 3) has received much greater support. While, during His earthly life, the brethren of Jesus did not believe in Him (Mt. xii. 46ff.; Mk. iii. 31ff.; Lk. viii. 19ff.; Jn. vii. 3–9), they are found among the disciples in the beginning of Acts (Acts i. 14), and James became a foremost leader of the church in Jerusalem (Acts xv. 13, xxi. 18ff.; Gal. ii. 9). This short letter preserved in the New Testament has been widely regarded as a genuine writing of the less well-known brother, Jude.

Nothing in the Epistle itself rules out the possibility of its having been written at a date that could fall within the lifetime of Jude, presumably a younger son in the earthly home of Jesus. The condition of things in the Church with which the letter deals, while it could correspond with the situation brought about by the Gnosticism of the second century, was not unknown in the end of the first century. The first Epistle to the Corinthians gives evidence of conditions similar to those reflected in the Epistle, and the way in which the author writes conveys the impression that he is stirred by something that has newly emerged and that has just begun to show itself. Such considerations have led even some who do not regard Jude, the brother of Jesus, as the author of the Epistle to assign it nevertheless to the end of the first century. If the author is not Jude the brother of Jesus nothing is known about him except his name.

The Epistle was called forth by the situation which had shown itself within the Church. Men under the profession of Christianity were indulging in open immorality, 'turning the grace of God into lasciviousness'. Along with this, they showed low moral standards in other directions. In theory and in practice they were perverting the gospel doctrine of grace. Though the letter bears no particular address, it seems to have been written to some special community of Christians, a Gentile church susceptible to pagan contacts, known to the writer, among whom the false view of the Christian religion was being disseminated. The author sends this vigorous letter to counteract the baneful influence that presses upon his readers, rallying them to a true stand. For a discussion of the probable relationship between this letter and the second Epistle of Peter see *Introduction* to the commentary on that Epistle and the introductory note to 2 Pet. ii.

OUTLINE OF CONTENTS

I. OPENING GREETING. Verses 1, 2

II. THE OCCASION AND PURPOSE OF THE LETTER. Verses 3, 4

III. THREE WARNING EXAMPLES. Verses 5–7

IV. THE FALSE BRETHREN. Verses 8–16

V. CHARGE TO TRUE CHRISTIANS. Verses 17–23

VI. CLOSING DOXOLOGY. Verses 24, 25

COMMENTARY

I. OPENING GREETING. Verses 1, 2

Jude is a form of the Jewish name Judah. *The servant;* i.e. 'bondslave'; 'one who is at the disposal of Jesus Christ for service in His cause' (Moffatt). The word is used also by Paul (Phil. i. 1), James (Jas. i. 1) and Peter (2 Pet. i. 1) to describe their relationship to Christ. It is a particularly suggestive word in the case of Jude and James if they were the Lord's 'brothers'. *Brother of James;* see *Introduction.*

To them that are sanctified; rather, as RV, 'beloved'. A better rendering of the whole clause is 'To those who are called, beloved in God the Father and kept for Jesus Christ' (RSV). 'Called' means that they have been invited and have responded. 'Kept for Jesus Christ'; i.e. kept safe against the day of His coming that they may share His glory. Cf. Rom. i. 7; 2 Thes. i. 10. The three phrases 'called', 'beloved', 'kept' describe the true Christian life, setting it in marked contrast to the kind of life lived by the false brethren about which Jude must write so much as he proceeds. *Mercy* (2; Gk. *eleos*) denotes the undeserved pity of God, corresponding to Paul's 'grace' in his greetings. Both words express the unmerited goodness of God which is at the root of His fellowship with men. *Peace* is the Hebrew word of salutation which, with an added fulness of Christian meaning, is frequently used in the Epistles of the New Testament. *Love;* i.e. the love of God. Jude's greeting desires for his readers a continually increasing experience of the mercy, peace and love of God.

II. THE OCCASION AND PURPOSE OF THE LETTER. Verses 3, 4

Jude had been planning to write a tract or treatise about the Christian salvation, but the appearance in the Church of false brethren made him take up his pen to write a letter of earnest summons to uphold the true standard of Christianity. See the introductory note to 2 Pet. ii and compare the commentary on that chapter with the notes given here.

When I gave (3); RV 'while I was giving'; he had been giving thought to the writing of a letter or treatise which was to be about *the common salvation,* or rather, as in RV, 'our common salvation'. He means the salvation that was extended to him and to them, Jew and Gentile together, or the salvation in which they were alike deeply interested. But the situation that had arisen in the Church compelled him to write immediately to deal with it. The AV *it was needful* hardly brings out the sense of urgency. Better 'I was constrained' (RV) or 'I found it necessary' (RSV). *Ye should earnestly contend* (3). This gives the positive and practical challenge of the letter. Frequently it is quoted as a summons to uphold orthodox doctrine, 'the faith which was once for all delivered unto the saints' (RV) being interpreted as the body of Christian dogma, to be contended for in creed and theological argument. But orthodox faith, when rightly held, must issue in godly living, and the aspect of the Christian religion ('the faith') with which Jude is chiefly concerned in the Epistle is the moral life which is the expression of it. The attack to be met is an attack against fundamental principles of Christian behaviour. *The faith,* Christian religion as a whole, is committed to Christians to be defended not only by sound doctrine but also by the life they live. Notice the force of *once,* RV 'once for all' (Gk. *hapax*). Jude follows Paul in regarding the gospel as something which, in its unchangeable entirety, has been handed by God to men for them to hand on to others. Cf. Gal. i. 8, 9, 11, 12; 2 Tim. i. 13, ii. 2.

Verse 4 describes the false brethren whose presence and influence in the Church have roused Jude to write. Three charges are brought against them which are to be found repeated again and again throughout the letter. First, they were *ungodly men* (cf. verses 15, 18). Secondly, they were immoral. To turn *the grace of our God into lasciviousness* means that they maintained that God's grace, His free and abundant pardon of sin, allowed them to do evil, allowed them in this instance to discard morality, and to do it in the name of the Christian gospel. This misrepresentation of the doctrine of grace is dealt with by Paul in Rom. vi. Thirdly, they are full of a spirit of rebellion against authority (cf. verses 8f., 18). Note the RV rendering 'denying our only Master and Lord, Jesus Christ'. 'God' does not occur in the oldest MSS, so that the whole clause refers to Christ. The RV brings out further that there are two different Greek words behind the twice used 'Lord' of the AV. The Greek words are *despotēs,* a sovereign master, a master of slaves, and *kyrios,* Lord. The former word occurs only ten times in the New Testament; the latter, of very frequent occurrence, is the usual designation given to Jesus Christ as 'Lord' (see 2 Pet. ii. 1n.). *Crept in unawares* (4); RSV renders 'admission has been secretly gained'. *Who were before of old ordained to this condemnation.* The word is used by Paul in Rom. xv. 4 with reference to things written in the Old Testament, and is to be understood here as having a similar reference. In this instance Jude is thinking of the condemnation pronounced against men who live as the false brethren lived. The meaning is not that these men were 'foreordained' or 'elected' to condemnation, but that the condemnation which such men would bring on themselves had been ordained and even written down long before. It was written down in exemplary events as much as in formal declarations.

III. THREE WARNING EXAMPLES. Verses 5-7

These particular examples are chosen because of some correspondence between the conduct of those involved and the behaviour of the false brethren in the Church.

a. The judgment of the unfaithful Israelites (verse 5)

I will therefore. 'I will' does not denote the future tense, but translates a particular Greek word, *boulomai*, I wish, I desire. Jude is saying 'I want, therefore, to remind you'. *Though ye once knew this.* Moffatt, following certain versions, transfers *once* from this phrase and puts it with *having saved*; it then stands in a natural antithesis to 'afterward' in the phrase *afterward destroyed them that believed not. This*; lit. 'all things'; Jude's readers knew all these things of which he was to remind them. If we retain the order as given in the AV and RV, then 'ye know all things once for all' seems to be parallel to the phrase 'the faith which was once for all delivered' in verse 3. The way in which God works in the Old Testament is part of the gospel revealed to them. The parallel between the faithless Israelites and the false brethren lay in the fact that both had identified themselves with God's people and then apostatized.

b. The judgment of the fallen angels (verse 6)

This is one of the difficult verses of the Epistle. The main idea of a judgment on fallen angels is plain and is appropriate to Jude's purpose. The apostasy of the false brethren from their Christian standing is presented as parallel to the fall of angels, and it is shown that not even the highest position of privilege once occupied shields from judgment. The difficulties of the verse emerge in the explanation of the statements about the angels, and in determining whether this warning example is taken, like the others, from the Old Testament or from another source.

It is said of the angels, first, that they *kept not their first estate.* The Greek word *archē* has the meaning 'beginning', from which the AV rendering *first estate* is doubtless derived. But it also means 'rule', which seems the preferable sense here. Therefore follow AV mg. and RV and read 'principality'. Moffatt renders it 'rank', and Brook 'the sphere allotted to them by God'. There is the idea not merely of their position, but of a position assigned by God as their orbit in which they are to move according to God's rule. Secondly, Jude says that they *left their own habitation.* This does not describe the expulsion of the angels from their 'proper habitation' (RV), but their action in leaving it. One interpretation of the phrase is that it describes the angels coming down to the earth (see below). Moffatt paraphrases the two clauses, 'who abandoned their own domain, instead of preserving their proper rank', which conveys the idea of disobedience and revolt against the rule of God, without hinting at the form the revolt took.

Is Jude's allusion to a fall of angels taken from the Old Testament or from another source? Its source is traced by some to Gn. vi. 1-4. That passage has been interpreted variously. It has been taken as describing a fall of angels who came down from heaven to earth and fell a prey to lust. On the other hand, the passage is interpreted as having no reference to angels at all, but as describing an intermarrying between two races of men. If the latter interpretation is accepted, the passage would not afford any real basis for Jude's allusion. The idea of a fall of angels by their coming down to earth and succumbing to lust is, however, found in the book of Enoch, and it is to this that Jude seems to be referring. It is thought by some that the Enoch doctrine is developed from the Genesis passage. A possible reason why Peter and then Jude should refer to such a work is suggested in the note on 2 Pet. ii. 4.

c. The overthrow of Sodom and Gomorrha (verse 7)

The sin of these cities was fornication (see Gn. xviii, xix), to which the false brethren were likewise a prey. The doom of the cities was an example of the judgment to which they were exposed. *In like manner.* Follow the RV reading which takes *in like manner* along with *giving themselves over to fornication* and also inserts 'with these'. The force of the phrase 'in like manner with these' would seem to be a reference to the fallen angels and their sin, to which the sin of Sodom and Gomorrha corresponded. The doom of the cities was an example; their destruction in fire might serve as a type of 'eternal fire' (see RV mg.).

IV. THE FALSE BRETHREN. Verses 8-16

Jude turns now to the men with whose presence in the Church he is concerned and who, in spite of such warning examples, sin after the same pattern. *Likewise also* (8); lit. 'likewise nevertheless also'; RV 'yet in like manner'. Despite these examples the false brethren act in the same way. The evil characteristics underlined throughout are sensual indulgence and a spirit of self-willed rebelliousness. *These filthy dreamers defile the flesh* (8). The word 'filthy' has been supplied by the translators; there is no corresponding word in the Greek. Calling the men 'dreamers' may point to the way in which they conjure up wayward fancies and imaginations which, in their case, are of an impure kind. Their evil imaginations, moreover, do not remain imaginations but are translated into actions. They *defile the flesh.* The phrase implies that the flesh itself, in its true life, is not impure; it is defiled only by misuse. *Despise dominion* (8). The Greek *kyriotēs* occurs only four times in the New Testament (see Eph. i. 21; Col. i. 16; and the parallel passage, 2 Pet. ii. 10). The word means 'lordship' in the abstract sense; in the concrete sense it means divine or angelic lordship, usually with reference to a celestial hierarchy. Some commentators take the word to refer here to divine lordship; e.g. by Brook who writes 'render "the Lordship", i.e. Christ or God'. Others interpret it as angelic lordship; cf. Moffatt 'the Powers celestial'. Or the meaning may be to despise authority, lordship in the abstract sense, so denoting the spirit of revolt. *And speak evil of dignities* (8). Gk. *doxas*, plural from *doxa*, glory; so 'the glories' (RV mg.), 'angelic Glories' (Moff.). Many take this to be another term referring to angelic beings of a celestial hierarchy. If this is the correct interpretation of 'dominion' and 'dignities', the actual sin of the false brethren to which Jude refers is something that we cannot explain. It is unlikely that such terms would be used in reference to rulers in the Church, although such an interpretation would yield good sense (see below on verse 11). But whatever its precise meaning, the verse suggests the spirit of self-assertiveness and revolt, expressing itself in violent words.

Their behaviour stands in marked contrast to that of Michael, the archangel guardian of Israel, who did not use violent speech even to the devil. Michael is mentioned in Dn. x. 13, xii. 1 and in Rev. xii. 7. But there is no mention in the Old Testament of that to which Jude alludes here. In the account of the death of Moses, the AV suggests that God buried him, but the RV mg. says simply 'he was buried'. The locality of his death is given, in the neighbourhood of Pisgah in the land of Moab, but the spot of the sepulchre was unknown. Jude's reference is drawn from an account in a piece of Jewish literature, *The Assumption of Moses*, written possibly at the beginning of the first century. An appendix to this work gives the story of the dispute of Michael and Satan over the body of Moses after his death, resulting in his triumphal 'assumption' to heaven. The devil had claimed the body of Moses on the ground that he was a murderer (Ex. ii. 11). This was blasphemy which Michael could not tolerate, yet he did not charge the devil with blasphemy, but said simply *The Lord rebuke thee* (9).

Repeating that the false brethren are guilty of abusive speech, Jude weaves in with that charge the other thread of condemnation that runs through his letter, their perverted morals. They act wrongly both in respect of things beyond their understanding and in respect of things well within it. *But these speak evil of those things which they know not* (10). The charge may be general in its scope, asserting that they 'scoff at anything they do not understand' (Moff.), so charging them with lack of spiritual understanding. Or the railing in which they indulge may be what has already been declared, 'they speak evil of dignities' (8), and Jude means then that all that belongs to that realm of 'the glorious ones' is beyond their understanding. They speak against what, in their spiritual ignorance or blindness, they do not understand. But if they are without spiritual understanding they at least have instinctive knowledge of the physical life, but here they betray a moral perversion. *Naturally* (10); i.e. by instinct. *As brute beasts;* i.e. like the lower creatures which are without reason. This phrase should be taken with *know naturally*, not with *corrupt themselves*. They have a natural instinctive knowledge, such as animals have, on the level of animal life; but even this knowledge is in their case perverted and ruins them.

Jude now compares the false brethren with traditional representatives of evil mentioned in the Old Testament—Cain (Gn. iv), Balaam (Nu. xxii—xxiv) and Korah (Nu. xvi)—comparisons which afford examples of wrongdoing like theirs. *They have gone in the way of Cain* (11). This does not mean that, like Cain, they were guilty of murder; there is no suggestion that that was one of their sins. Cain had come to be regarded as a typically unrighteous man and the false brethren are classed with him. *The error of Balaam for reward* (11). See 2 Pet. ii. 15n. The nation of Israel, when in proximity to the people of Moab in the wilderness, became involved in the idolatrous worship of Moab with its immorality (see Nu. xxv). This was attributed to Balaam and may be the particular *error of Balaam* to which Jude is referring. It is then another allusion to the immorality allowed by the false brethren. The thought covers, however, any disobedience to the known will of God for the sake of gain. *Perished in the gainsaying of Core* (11). The other sin of the false brethren, their spiritual rebelliousness, is in the line of the rebellion of Korah who revolted against the authority of Moses. This comparison might favour interpreting verse 8 as pointing to a revolt against the authority of apostolic rulers in the Church.

Having classified the false brethren with these typical representatives of wrongdoing, Jude now describes them in a series of vivid metaphors.

There is considerable variety in the punctuation of verse 12 in the Greek texts and translations, resulting in different groupings of its phrases. For example, the AV and RV punctuate the first two phrases differently although both suggest that they are closely linked. In the Greek the word translated *without fear* stands immediately after *when they feast with you*, and is linked with that phrase by the punctuation. The AV and the RV, however, connect the word with what follows in the Greek and so render *feeding themselves without fear. These are spots in your feasts of charity. Feasts of charity* is better rendered 'love-feasts'. The Greek word is *agapai*, plural of *agapē*, 'love'. As well as being used for 'love', the word was used in the early Church for 'the love-feast'—'an evening meal partaken of by Christians, either accompanied or followed by the Eucharist. Such common meals were sacred, and intended to be expressive of the union of Christians in their Head' (Souter, *A Pocket Lexicon to the Greek New Testament*). The false brethren joined in the love-feast. *They feast with you* may express simply that they sat down to share in the love-feast, while they were not real members of the fellowship; or the word (one word in the Greek) may have the force Moffatt gives it, 'carousing in your midst' (see also RV). The love-feast was sometimes the occasion of disorder (cf. 1 Cor. xi. 21f.) and men of the stamp Jude is referring to would quite possibly be among those guilty of such conduct. *Spots*; Gk. *spilades*. It is possible that the word means a spot of disfigurement. RV has 'hidden rocks', from Gk. *spilas*, a rock over which the sea dashes, a reef. Either meaning gives a good sense; the false brethren were disfigurements to the Christian fellowship, or they were like treacherous reefs, a comparison bringing out their deceitful character and the danger they were to others. *Feeding themselves without fear*. The last two words, as noted above, should perhaps be connected with *when they feast with you*. The Greek word rendered 'feeding' means properly 'to shepherd'; hence the RV translation 'shepherds that . . . feed themselves'. The phrase is a quotation or echo of Ezk. xxxiv. 8, 'the shepherds fed themselves'. The false brethren were false shepherds or false leaders, setting themselves up as guides in the Church.

Clouds they are without water (12). Follow RV and omit 'they are'; the words are not in the Greek and the catalogue of comparisons reads more forcibly without them. The comparison describes the deceitful and useless character of the men; they bring no benefit to anyone, like clouds that give no rain—whether dark scudding clouds that cause gloom or light clouds that mock those who are looking for rain. *Carried about of winds* may suggest either the weak character of the false brethren (cf. Eph. iv. 14), or their being swept away in judgment. *Trees whose fruit withereth, without fruit*. Better, as in RV, 'autumn trees without fruit', i.e. trees which are found without fruit in autumn when fruit is expected—the sure evidence of their unfruitful nature. *Twice dead* applied to trees would emphasize that there was no hope of new life in the spring; used of the false brethren it may express Jude's judgment on them, that they are doubly dead spiritually; first in their pre-Christian life and again even in their nominally Christian life. If the gospel has not brought life to them they are doubly dead. *Plucked up by the roots* describes the doom of the unfruitful trees and implies judgment on the false teachers.

Raging waves of the sea, foaming out their own shame (13). The false brethren, like the tossing sea, are never at rest, and as the waves of the stormy sea throw up foam and seaweed and refuse on its surface, so these men cover themselves with shame (cf. Is. lvii. 20). The phrase *wandering stars* points to disobedience in departing from the true course. These men have violated the law of their being and are out of their proper orbit (cf. verse 6). In consequence they are changed from being lights, as stars, to being themselves in darkness.

To the parallels between the false brethren and outstanding representatives of evil-doing drawn from the Old Testament and to his own vivid figurative descriptions, Jude adds the quotation of a 'prophecy' ascribed to *Enoch* (14),

who is mentioned in the genealogy given in Gn. v. This, however, is not a quotation from the Old Testament. The words are to be found in a work called *The Book of Enoch*, written in the second and first centuries B.C. and well known to the writers and readers of the New Testament. (See the General Article, 'The Apocryphal and Apocalyptic Literature', p. 53.) It belongs to the apocalyptic literature of that period and contains messianic teaching, including a description of the judgment the Messiah would eventually execute. The passage which Jude quotes might be considered by him to have direct reference to these false brethren about whom he was writing, for they were living 'in the last time' (18) when the messianic judgment described in the book was imminent. At the same time, the description of the *ungodly* (15) in the passage quoted fitted in with the very things charged against the false brethren, their ungodly deeds and their arrogant words, so that the passage could be quoted about them on that ground. *To execute judgment* (15) does not mean to inflict the penalty of condemnation, but to carry through the general assize in which all men, godly and ungodly alike, are concerned. What follows refers to the ungodly. *To convince;* better, as in RV, 'to convict'. The word means to show to be guilty. Note the repetition of *ungodly* and compare the description of the false brethren given in verse 4.

In verse 16 Jude adds yet more lines to the description he has already given of these men. They are *murmurers*; i.e. grumblers with the spirit of smouldering discontent. *Complainers*; i.e. such as blame their lot and destiny and are discontented. *Walking after their own lusts*. Here, perhaps, the word has the more general meaning of 'desires'; but it may be another reference to their sensual passions. In this description of the false brethren Jude may be grouping them with the murmurers among the Israelites in the wilderness, in line with all he has written above (see verse 11). *Their mouth speaketh great swelling words*. This is another reference to the arrogant speech of the false brethren, which has been emphasized all through the Epistle. *Having men's persons in admiration because of advantage*. A final addition to the long series of epithets by which the false brethren have been portrayed; they show admiration for and pay attention to the people they think will bring them some advantage.

V. CHARGE TO TRUE CHRISTIANS.
Verses 17–23

From describing the false brethren, Jude now turns to give guidance to the true members of the Church as to how they are to bear themselves in view of the presence of these men. The fact that such men are to be found within the Church is not to confuse them, for it had been declared by the apostles that this situation would develop (17–19). They must, on their part, maintain their faith and purity (20, 21). And, if they can, let them help the moral and spiritual recovery of any (22, 23).

The words *mockers . . . who should walk after their own ungodly lusts* (18) are in close line with what Jude has already said about the false brethren. The emphasis is still on contemptuous speech and immorality. *These be they who separate themselves* (19); RV 'These are they who make separations'. The Greek verb *apodiorizō* means 'I make an (invidious) distinction' (Souter). The reference is not to ecclesiastical divisions but to social distinctions (cf. verse 16). *Sensual*. Gk. *psychikos*, an adjective from the noun *psychē*, 'the principle of life and the basis of its emotional aspect, animating the present body of flesh, in contrast to the higher life' (Souter). It denotes the natural life of man without the Spirit of God. The last phrase of the verse expresses the same thing from the opposite aspect.

The way in which the true members of the Church are to safeguard their Christian life is now presented. By *your most holy faith* (20), indicated as the foundation on which they are to build, may be meant either the personal faith in their heart, or, and perhaps more probably here, the Christian religion they have professed, 'the faith once delivered unto the saints' (see verse 3). This *holy faith* requires a life in keeping with its holiness to be reared up upon it. The call to 'build' suggests the strong and stable character which should mark their Christian life; contrast the type of life seen in the false brethren and described in the metaphors of verses 12, 13. *Praying in the Holy Ghost*. Prayer is an essential exercise in the Christian life, one of the means of carrying on the building to which the readers are summoned. The suggestion in the call, *keep yourselves* (21), is keep yourselves safe as in a fortress, so that you are not carried away by the forces of evil like the false brethren. The sphere of safety is *in the love of God*, i.e. they are so to live that He can act towards them in love and not in judgment. The expectation of *eternal life* (21) is to be cherished. This expectation will be a contribution to the maintaining of a Christian life in this world. *Mercy* is the basis of Christian hope to the end. The final acceptance, like the initial acceptance, rests not on merit or achievement, but on mercy. The phrase *unto eternal life* connects with *mercy*, declaring its outcome or results; 'the mercy . . . that ends in life eternal' (Moff.). Note the fourfold activity of the spiritual life—building, praying, keeping, looking.

Verses 22 and 23 describe the attitude to be adopted toward the false brethren. Though he has written sternly about the character and conduct of the false brethren, Jude charges the true members of the Church to aid the spiritual recovery of any whom it may be possible to win back. *And of some have compassion, making a difference* (22). The meaning of the first phrase is plain; it calls for the attitude of compassion and pity. Various constructions, however, are put on the second phrase, which in the Greek is one word, a participle from the verb *diakrinō*, to

'separate', 'distinguish'. In the Received Text the participle is in the nominative case, so the 'distinguishing' is something to characterize the readers addressed by Jude. This is the force of the AV rendering; they are to distinguish between individuals and so adjust their attitude toward them, having mercy and compassion on some. In other Greek texts, the participle is in the accusative case and so refers to something in those to whom pity is to be shown. Moreover another meaning of the Greek verb is 'I doubt', 'I waver'. This construction and meaning give the RV rendering 'on some have mercy who are in doubt'; cf. 'have mercy on the waverers' (Moff.). Those described as 'in doubt' or 'waverers' may be people shaken in their faith by the false teachers, though not yet carried away by their teaching; or they may be some of the false teachers themselves, who are hesitating and beginning to doubt. Another meaning suggested for the participle is 'when they argue' or 'while they dispute' (see RV mg. and Weymouth). The true members of the Church are to show a spirit of compassion toward the false teachers while they are arguing with them. The Greek text is ambiguous and all these interpretations are possible. Perhaps the RV rendering gives the best sense since it may be presumed that those who are still 'in doubt' are those most likely to be won back. In verse 23 the Greek texts vary, as may be seen by comparing the AV and RV renderings. *With fear*. Not by fear, i.e. by striking fear into the heart of the wrongdoers, but rather 'save *in* fear', the phrase describing the attitude of those who are to act as helpers. The fear intended is possibly the fear lest they themselves be contaminated. Moffatt translates 'trembling as you touch them'. *Pulling them out of the fire*. The thought is probably derived from Am. iv. 11 or Zc. iii. 2 and depicts something snatched into safety at the last moment. *Hating even the garment spotted by the flesh*. In Zc. iii. 2 Joshua, the High Priest, who, as representative of the nation, is described as 'a brand plucked out of the fire', is depicted as 'clothed in filthy garments', which however are taken away, so that he may be arrayed in new raiment. This has suggested Jude's reference to the garment stained by the flesh, which symbolizes the sin by which the false brethren have corrupted themselves. With compassion for the sinner must go abhorrence of the sin.

VI. CLOSING DOXOLOGY. Verses 24, 25

Surrounded as they are with false brethren, whose presence and influence may constitute a danger to their spiritual life and suggest the possibility of lapsing from a true faith, the true members of the Church are left with the thought of God's power to keep them *from falling* (24). The Greek word *aptaistous* is unusual in the New Testament, and means 'not stumbling'. *To present you*; lit. to set you, to make you stand. It is the positive aspect corresponding to the negative 'not stumbling'. *Faultless;* Gk. *amōmos*, without blemish, umblemished; it is the word used of sacrificial animals. 'To keep you not stumbling' covers the course of Christian life in this world; 'to present you faultless' refers to their sure position in the world to come, in the *presence of his glory. With exceeding joy.* The word denotes wild joy, exultation; the joy of victory, triumph and relief. The text of verse 25 is uncertain and variations occur. The word *wise* is omitted from some MSS and is dropped from the RV. Some Greek texts, which are followed by the RV, introduce after *Saviour* the words 'through Jesus Christ our Lord'. This phrase may be linked with 'Saviour'—'God our Saviour through Jesus Christ our Lord' (Moff.); or it may be taken with the ascription of praise that follows—'through Jesus Christ our Lord be glory, and majesty, dominion and power' (Wey.). Some texts read merely *both now and ever* as in AV. But notice the RV 'before all time, and now, and for evermore' which has good MS authority. Jude is asserting the supremacy, past, present and future, of the one and only God and Saviour in words which are coloured by some of the *exceeding joy* which all will experience when they come at last into His glorious presence.

ROBERT ROBERTSON.

THE REVELATION

INTRODUCTION

I. AUTHORSHIP

The author of the Revelation designates himself simply as John. Though a resident of Asia Minor (or rather, proconsular Asia) he was clearly a Hebrew Christian, as the language and style of the book reveal, and held a position of influence among the churches of that area. It was natural, in view of the strong tradition that John the son of Zebedee migrated to Ephesus, for early Christian writers to identify John the apostle with the Seer who wrote the Revelation. The weightiest factor in support of such a conclusion is, perhaps, the manner in which the prophet simply calls himself 'John', as though there were no other Christian leader in that area with whom he could be confused. The many remarkable affinities of thought and diction between the Gospel and Apocalypse in matters of detail similarly demand the recognition of some sort of connection in the authorship of the two books.

On the other hand, the general presentation of thought and, still more, of style and diction in the Revelation differs so widely from the Gospel as to make a common authorship of the two books problematic. The matter would be considered settled from this consideration alone were it not complicated by the view, vigorously championed by C. C. Torrey, that the Revelation was written in Aramaic; on this assumption the extraordinary Greek of the book would be accounted for by its being translated with minute literalness. If another writer made this translation, the argument as to the difference of style in the Revelation and Gospel would fall to the ground, or at least lose its main force, for no one can maintain that the fourth evangelist wrote polished Greek.

Rather than make an arbitrary decision on so complicated a question it is wiser to admit that at present we are not in a position to affirm or deny that the prophet was the apostle of the same name (see *The New Bible Handbook*, I.V.F., pp. 408ff.). However, the authorship of this book is the least important question to be considered in regard to it; it does not in the least affect the interpretation of the text. In any case, the title 'The Revelation of St. John the Theologian' (AV, 'the Divine'; Gk. *Theologos*) is a misnomer; the book claims to be 'The Revelation of Jesus Christ which God gave unto him . . . and he sent and signified it by his angel unto his servant John' (i. 1). The book gains its value from its origin, not from the identity of its human author. The contents of the book are consistent with such an origin.

II. DATE

Recent writers on the Revelation have tended to support the earliest Christian tradition that it was written towards the close of Domitian's reign, i.e. about A.D. 96. The book reflects the beginnings of a storm of persecution soon to burst in full fury on the Christians of Asia and ultimately on the Church everywhere. John, a prominent Christian leader, has already been exiled, a fact which seems to point to official determination to eradicate the Church, root and branch. Compulsion in respect of Emperor-worship appears imminent. This accords perfectly with conditions existing in Asia Minor during the persecution instigated in Domitian's reign.

On the other hand it should be mentioned that several notable scholars prefer an earlier date, either in Nero's reign (so Lightfoot, Westcott, Hort) or in Galba's short rule, A.D. 68 (so Torrey). The view is based on a literal interpretation of Rev. xi. 1, 2 and xvii. 9–11. The balance of probability seems to favour the Domitianic date, but we cannot be certain.

III. INTERPRETATION

In the main the various types of exposition of the Revelation reduce themselves to four. The Preterist view regards the prophecies as wholly concerned with the circumstances of John's day, having no reference whatever to future ages. The Historicist interpretation construes the visions as a preview of history from the time of the writer to the end of the world. The Futurist explanation places the relevance of the visions entirely at the end of the age, largely divorcing them from the prophet's time. The Poetic view considers all hard and fast canons of interpretation to be illegitimate; the prophet simply describes, by means of his powers of artistry, the sure triumph of God over all evil powers.

Liberal scholars largely endorse the Preterist view and repudiate the predictive elements of the book; many, however, accept as valid the principles of God's moral government which lie at the root of the prophet's teaching. The Reformers generally adopted the Historicist view. They identified the persecuting power with papal Rome. Rigidly interpreted, however, this view seems to be contrary to the analogy of all other prophecy in the Bible. The Futurist view was that of the earliest centuries of the Church and is widely held by evangelical Christians today. In its popular form, however, it is open to serious criticism, in that the historical setting of the book is almost wholly ignored. Indeed, it is often said that John wrote the Revelation not for his own age but for the Church of the end time. Hence the book is made to yield information and ideas such as the prophet had never dreamed of. Vagaries of this sort drive many readers to value the book solely from an aesthetic viewpoint, denying that it ever had a specific occasion in view.

The symbols, nevertheless, do mean something. John was more than a poet setting forth in vague images the triumph of God over all evil. He wrote for the churches under his care with a practical situation in view, viz. the prospect of the popular Caesar worship of his day being enforced on all Christians. No man who said 'Jesus is Lord' could also confess 'Caesar is Lord'; the latter demand threatened the existence of the whole Church of God. Grasping the principles involved, John was given to see the logical consummation of the tendencies at work, mankind divided to the obedience of Christ or Antichrist. On the canvas of John's age, therefore, and in the colours of his environment, he pictured the last great crisis of the world, not merely because, from a psychological viewpoint, he could do no other, but because of the real correspondence between his crisis and that of the last days. As the Church was then faced with a devastating persecution by Rome, so will the Church of the last days find itself violently opposed by the prevailing world power. The outcome of that great struggle will be the advent of Christ in glory, and with Him the establishment of the kingdom of God in power. John clearly regarded the end as at hand (i. 1–3), but this 'foreshortened perspective' no more invalidates his utterances than it does those of the Old Testament prophets and of our Lord Himself, for it is characteristic of all prophecy.

The following exposition, then, seeks to interpret the visions of this book as the readers must have done to whom they were first addressed, recognizing, nevertheless, that their proper fulfilment awaits the day known neither to man nor angel, but which is yet within the authority of God (Acts i. 6).

OUTLINE OF CONTENTS

I. PROLOGUE. i. 1–8

II. VISION OF THE SON OF MAN. i. 9–20

III. THE LETTERS TO THE SEVEN CHURCHES. ii. 1—iii. 22

IV. THE VISION OF HEAVEN. iv. 1—v. 14

V. THE SEVEN SEALS. vi. 1—viii. 5

VI. THE SEVEN TRUMPETS. viii. 6—xi. 19

VII. THE BACKGROUND OF THE EARTHLY CONFLICT. xii. 1—xiv. 20

VIII. THE SEVEN BOWLS. xv. 1—xvi. 21

IX. THE FALL OF BABYLON. xvii. 1—xix. 21

X. THE CONSUMMATED KINGDOM. xx. 1—xxii. 5

XI. EPILOGUE. xxii. 6–21

COMMENTARY

I. PROLOGUE. i. 1–8

a. Superscription (i. 1–3)

Here are set forth the source of the book (1), the nature of its contents (2) and the blessed results of taking it to heart (3).

A *Revelation* (1) is an uncovering of something hidden, used here in the sense of a 'vision and its interpretation' (Charles). The ultimate source of this revelation is God Himself; He gave it to Jesus Christ for the benefit of the Church (*his servants*); it was therefore sent through the mediation of an angel to John who, in turn, passed it on to the 'seven churches' (4), and so to the whole Church of God. It tells of *things which must shortly come to pass* (1); 'shortly' expresses the normal prophetic attitude and is emphasized throughout the New Testament (see, e.g., Lk. xviii. 8; Rom. xvi. 20; 1 Cor. vii. 29–31; Jas. v. 8; 1 Pet. iv. 7; Rev. i. 3, xxii. 20).

The revelation is further defined as *the word of God, the testimony of* (borne by) *Jesus Christ, all things that he* (the seer) *saw.* In i. 9 and xx. 4 the first two phrases are linked to stand for the whole truth of God; here it means the *words of this prophecy* (3).

The blessing is invoked on the one reading aloud to the assembled congregation and on those hearing and observing that which is enjoined. There are two classes here, not three; the last two participles are governed by one subject. Cf. Lk. xi. 28.

b. Greeting (i. 4, 5a)

The seven churches which are in Asia (4), i.e. the Roman province of that name, are enumerated in verse 11. It is hardly to be doubted that they also represent the Church in its completeness, as is seen in the conclusion to each of the seven letters, 'He that hath an ear, let him hear what the Spirit saith unto the churches'. (*He*) *which is, and which was, and which is to come* (4) is a title for God, stressing both His eternity and vital relation to history. The last clause (*which is to come*, instead of the expected 'which will be') is not only a conscious allusion to the second coming of Christ, but implies that the most important event of the future is that appearing which will also be the coming of God.

The seven Spirits which are before his throne (4) is probably a designation of the Holy Spirit. It may have originated in the seer's mind through the popular interpretation of Is. xi. 2, 3 as being a sevenfold spiritual endowment of the Messiah (the 'seven eyes of the Lord that run through the whole earth' of Zc. iv. 10; see Rev. iv. 5 and v. 6) and his representation of the Church by the seven churches to whom he particularly writes. Modern expositors (and some ancients, e.g. Andreas and Arethas) frequently interpret the seven Spirits as angelic beings, perhaps the seven archangels of Jewish angelology, and regard the conception as going back, through the Persian religion, to the Babylonian worship of the sun, moon and five planets. Charles adheres to this view (though regarding their presence here as due to interpolation) because in iii. 1 the seven Spirits of God appear to be similar to the seven 'stars' (which represent the angels of the churches). But nowhere is it said that these Spirits worship God, though all other classes of angelic beings are mentioned as so doing. Concerning iii. 1 Kiddle writes, 'When we acknowledge that the seven in each instance conveys the idea of unity and completeness, rather than diversity, so that we are to think of the Spirit and the Church rather than seven Spirits and seven churches, then we are in sight of a possible solution. . . . The seven Spirits and the seven stars . . . are the prophetic Spirit and the celestial character of the Church, in whom the Spirit gives life' (Revelation, Moff. Comm., p. 87).

Jesus is *the faithful witness* (5) not alone in respect of this revelation but as concerning the whole truth of God. Cf. Jn. xviii. 37. He is *the first begotten of the dead* (5) in the sense of being the first to rise from the dead, and so the 'firstfruits of them that sleep' (see Col. i. 18 and 1 Cor. xv. 20). But John may also be quoting Ps. lxxxix. 27, 28. In this passage 'the firstborn' was interpreted by the Jews of the Messiah in the sense of 'sovereign' (even God was sometimes called 'first begotten' or 'firstborn'). If this thought predominates in John's mind, then Jesus is here said to be 'sovereign of the dead', a fitting parallel to *prince of the kings of the earth* (5), both titles being true of Him in virtue of His resurrection.

c. Benediction (i. 5b, 6)

Translate, 'Unto him that loveth us, and loosed us from our sins by his blood, and made us to be a kingdom, priests unto his God . . .'. The reading followed by the AV *washed us* (instead of 'loosed us') is almost certainly mistaken, being due perhaps to the influence of vii. 14. The difference in tenses is significant, the love being constant, the redemption once for all. Loosing from sins by blood sets forth redemption in terms of ransom. The whole benediction harks back to the exodus from Egypt, verse 6 being quoted from Ex. xix. 6. Through the deliverance wrought by His death and resurrection, Christ has brought His people out of the bondage of sin and made them a kingdom in which all are priests. Some regard the 'kingdom' as signifying a nation under a king, but in view of such passages as Rev. v. 10, xx. 6, xxii. 5, it seems likely that it here means a nation of kings.

d. The second advent (i. 7, 8)

Verse 7 reproduces Mt. xxiv. 30, except that the clauses are transposed: 'Then shall appear the sign of the Son of man in heaven: and then shall all the tribes of the earth mourn, and they shall see the Son of man coming in the clouds of heaven with power and great glory'. The declaration links together two Old Testament Scriptures, Dn. vii. 13 and Zc. xii. 10. The corresponding point in the vision of this book is xix. 11–21. As at the close of the book, so here, the prophet utters a hearty assent to this promise, 'It is so, Amen'.

Alpha and *Omega* (8) are the first and last letters of the Greek alphabet. It is probable that the phrase translates for Greek readers the Hebrew idiom whereby the first and last letters of the Hebrew alphabet were used to express the entirety of a thing. It was said, e.g., that Adam transgressed the law 'from aleph to tau'; Abraham, on the contrary, kept the law 'from aleph to tau'. Here the meaning is that God is the Lord of all history, its beginning, its end and the whole course between. Such an affirmation is needed by Christians in a day when the powers that be are opposed to the Church. We may note that this saying is attributed to Christ in xxii. 13; older expositors sometimes thought that He is the speaker here also, but clearly the view is mistaken; it is spoken by 'the Lord God' (RV) . . . *the Almighty*, a title which John frequently uses and which, in the LXX of Ho. xii. 6 and Am. ix. 5, translates the Hebrew 'Lord God of hosts'.

II. VISION OF THE SON OF MAN. i. 9–20

The tribulation and kingdom in which John and his readers share as Christians are a present experience and possession, as also the patient endurance which Jesus supplies. All three elements are gained in union with Him, but the first and third lead to a fuller appropriation of the second at its consummation. Cf. Jn. xvi. 33; Rom. v. 3; 2 Tim. ii. 12. John's share of tribulation is alluded to in the mention of his being in Patmos *for the word of God, and for the testimony of Jesus Christ* (9); he was there in consequence of his faithfulness to the gospel, not in voluntary exile to receive more revelations. Cf. Rev. vi. 9. Does the fact that he says he *was* (or 'found himself') in Patmos imply that he wrote the book after leaving the island?

I was in the Spirit (10) means that John fell into a state of ecstasy (lit. 'became' in Spirit), so occasioning the vision that follows. It happened *on the Lord's day* (10), not, as some take it, 'on the day of the Lord', as though John was transported to live in that day, but 'on the day consecrated to the Lord', a phrase which became technical in the second century for Sunday. The term 'the Lord's day', as Deissmann has shown, is probably the defiant Christian replacement of 'Emperor's day', which was celebrated at least monthly in Asia Minor, if not weekly. This originally indicated the day of the Pharaoh's accession to the throne of Egypt, or his birthday (E.B. iii. 2815); the idea was taken over by the Roman Emperors. As a memorial of the day of Christ's resurrection, and so of His exaltation to sovereignty, 'the Lord's day' is thus a peculiarly fitting title. The *great voice, as of a trumpet* (10) was presumably that of the Son of man. It is difficult not to feel that *seven churches* (11) are chosen because of the sacred nature of that number. The seven which were singled out, however, had a special claim to be recipients of these letters, as they lay on a route forming a sort of inner circle round the province of Asia. Moreover, according to Ramsay, these cities were centres of the seven postal districts of this area, and so would be the best centres for circulating the letters to the other churches in the province.

The voice (12) here represents the speaker. The *seven golden candlesticks* (12) (RV mg. 'lampstands') remind us of the seven-branched candlestick in the holy place of the temple (Ex. xxv. 31; cf. Zc. iv. 2). That temple, however, had been destroyed and the candlestick transported to a heathen temple in Rome. Wherein the Jews had failed, the Christian churches were now called to succeed—to be lights in a dark world. The phrase *one like unto the Son of man* (13), or 'one like unto a son of man' (RV), recalls Dn. vii. 13; it implies that this Person is not just a man, and doubtless is used with the remembrance of our Lord's use of this title (it does not occur in the Epistles). The description that follows draws freely from Dn. x. 5, 6. The significance of this presence *in the midst of the seven candlesticks* (13), i.e. the churches, scarcely requires mention. The word for the *garment* (13) worn by Christ was used of the High Priest's robe; but it is doubtful whether any such association is in mind here for this robe was worn also by men of high rank generally. The description of the white hair is a deliberate reminiscence of Dn. vii. 9, where it belongs to the 'Ancient of days'. The application to Christ of the attributes of God is a constant phenomenon in this book. Compare the 'feet like unto burnished brass' (15, RV) with Dn. ii. 33–35. Swete thinks the *many waters* (15) are the Aegean Sea roaring about Patmos.

A symbolic picture is given in verse 16 that was never meant to be painted! The *stars* are in the power of Christ, the *sword* symbolizes His judicial authority and might. *The sun* shining *in his strength* goes back to Jdg. v. 31 but also recalls the transfiguration (Mt. xvii. 2).

For verse 17 cf. Dn. x. 9; see also Jos. v. 14; Is. vi. 5; Ezk. i. 28. *I am the first and the last* (17; also in ii. 8 and xxii. 13) is spoken of Jehovah in Is. xliv. 6 and xlviii. 12. Its meaning is the same as verse 8. *I am he that liveth, and was dead* (18) is a preferable translation to the RV 'the Living one', for the contrast is between the eternal life inherent in the Son and the abject death that He suffered. That life triumphed over death, consequently *I am alive for evermore*; this latter predicate is applied to the Father in iv. 9, 10 and x. 6. The possession of 'the keys of death and of Hades' (18, RV) was won by His resurrection and signifies the conquest of death.

A rough division of the Revelation given to John is furnished in verse 19. *The things which thou hast seen* are the vision just given; *the things which are* relate to the existing state of the churches and the letters about to be given; *the things which shall be hereafter* are the subsequent visions of the book. This should not be pressed to imply that everything without exception in chapters iv—xxii refers to the time future to John, let alone to the time of the end of all things. The seven stars and seven lampstands of the vision are now interpreted for John (20). The latter represent the churches, the former are more obscure. It seems strange to interpret the seven stars as being seven *angels* in the ordinary meaning of the term, even if they are guardian angels; for it would be superfluous to write to them by the agency of John (see, e.g., ii. 1) and, in any case, the contents of the letters are wholly concerned with the churches themselves. Many expositors, therefore, hold that the angels represent officials of some kind in the churches, whether delegates or overseers. This is possible, although it is wholly exceptional in apocalyptic for angels to symbolize men. It is perhaps better to regard them as personifying the heavenly or supernatural life of the churches as they are seen in Christ, and so the character which they are called to realize, just as the candlesticks represent the earthly life of the churches as men see them outwardly.

III. THE LETTERS TO THE SEVEN CHURCHES. ii. 1—iii. 22

It has been suggested that these letters were written earlier than the main part of the book and were sent separately to the churches addressed; later they were amplified and joined together so that all the churches might benefit from them. The theory is not objectionable but it is doubtful, for the letters are closely connected with the beginning and the end of the book; excise the passages involved and what is left constitutes very abrupt messages. Each letter is addressed to the 'angel' of the church and opens with a description of Christ drawn from the introductory vision, the particulars mentioned having special relevance to the church in question. The designation of Christ in the letter to the Laodiceans forms an exception, being a reminiscence of the greeting with which the Revelation commences. Similarly a promise concerning rewards to be bestowed at the second advent concludes each letter; these promises usually have a special fitness for the individual churches and are given a visionary embodiment in the closing chapters of the book.

a. The letter to the church in Ephesus (ii. 1–7)

Ephesus was the largest city of Asia and the centre of Roman administration in that province. It took the title of 'Temple Warden', originally in reference to the famous temple of Artemis, but later extending to the two or three temples devoted to the cult of the Emperors. Here Paul founded the church which became the centre for evangelizing the rest of the province, and here resided the apostle John. The Ephesian church, accordingly, must have become by this time the foremost one in the East, with the possible exception of Antioch. Kiddle suggests that this letter was placed first, not so much because of the importance of the church as of the warning delivered to it. (For a similar reason the letter to the Laodiceans was placed last.)

The designation of Christ in verse 1 is both an encouragement and a warning. The seven stars are in His grasp (i.e. He maintains their spiritual life), and His presence is coextensive with all the churches. But the power that sustains is also capable of judicial removal; the title thus prepares the hearer for verse 5. *I know* (1) is a truth of similar dual import. It heads every one of the seven letters, sometimes imparting comfort (e.g. ii. 9, ii. 13, etc.), sometimes causing shame (e.g. iii. 1, 15). Here it precedes a commendation. The *works* of the Ephesians are *labour* and *patience* (2); the former manifests itself in efforts to overcome false teachers (2), the latter in patient endurance in the face of opposition, whether from false prophets or from other sources (3). The evil men are those who call themselves prophets, and they are not. Cf. Paul's predictions in Acts xx. 29, 30; 1 Tim. iv. 1–3. It is possible that the chief offenders are the Nicolaitans mentioned in verse 6.

The failure of the Ephesians is perhaps the perversion of their chief virtue; opposition to false brethren led to censoriousness and divisiveness in the church, so causing them to leave their first love. This would interpret the 'love' referred to as brotherly love. It may, however, relate to love towards God; cf. Je. ii. 2, 5. Since the one manifestation of love is impossible without the other, we may perhaps include both in our text (cf. Mk. xii. 30, 31 with 1 Jn. iv. 20). *I will come unto thee quickly* (5) means that the Lord will 'come' in a special visitation of judgment. See also ii. 16. An instance of His 'coming' in blessing is to be found in iii. 20. Such statements in no wise conflict with the truth of the final appearing, a fact which theologians have not always remembered when speaking of the 'coming' of Christ to the believer and of His 'advents' in history, as though the recognition of these lesser appearings in any way invalidated the truth of the great appearing.

The Nicolaitans were reputed from early times to have been the followers of Nicolaos of Antioch, one of the seven (Acts vi. 5). We gather from ii. 14, 15 that they held the same error as the Balaamites, viz., teaching to eat things sacrificed to idols and to commit fornication. These were the chief matters condemned by the decree of the apostolic council (Acts xv. 29). It is noteworthy that Balaam and Nicolaos have more or less the same etymology (Balaam—'he has consumed the people'; Nicolaos—'he overcomes the people'). If this is the teaching so strenuously resisted by the Ephesians (see verse 2), then it must have been widespread indeed.

The injunction *He that hath an ear . . .* (7) is repeated in connection with the promises to the overcomer in all the seven letters. It is frequently on the lips of our Lord in the Gospel records (Mt. xiii. 9, 43, etc.). *The Spirit* is the Holy Spirit, yet the speaker is Christ. For a similar phenomenon cf. Rom. viii. 9–11 and 2 Cor. iii. 17. The 'overcomer' depicts the Christian as a faithful warrior for Christ, 'the victorious member of the Church, as such, apart from all consideration of the circumstances' (Swete). There seems little justification for limiting the term, as some would wish, to the martyrs only, though it is true that the overcomer can finally demonstrate the completeness of his victory only by remaining faithful until death. Cf. 2 Esd. vii. 57, 58: 'Here is the intent of the battle to be fought by man born upon earth; if he be overcome, he shall suffer . . . if he conquer he shall receive what I have said' (i.e. paradise).

To eat of the tree of life (7) is to partake of the fulness of eternal life; the tree is situated *in the midst of the paradise of God*, the heavenly Jerusalem that is to be manifested on earth for redeemed man (see xxi. 10, xxii. 2). The blessings of the first creation, lost by man, are restored in yet fuller measure at the 'regeneration' (Mt. xix. 28).

b. The letter to the church in Smyrna (ii. 8–11)

This city was one of the most prosperous in Asia Minor and took the name of 'metropolis'.

Here the Jews were unusually numerous and powerful; their bitter antagonism to the Christian Church appears not only in this letter but in that of Ignatius to the Smyrnaeans. The title of Christ (8) appears in i. 17. This church, shortly to be severely tested, needed to be reminded that their Saviour was Lord of history and conqueror of death (cf. verse 10). Contrast the condition of the Christians in Smyrna with the material wealth and spiritual poverty of the Laodiceans (iii. 17). The *blasphemy* of the Jews (9) would be against Jesus primarily, but they were capable of blaspheming even the God they confessed. The Smyrnaean Christians later reported that the Jews joined the pagans in clamouring for the death of Polycarp, Bishop of Smyrna, on the ground of his opposition to the state religion! Hence, instead of their constituting an assembly of God, they had become *the synagogue of Satan* (9; see also iii. 9). Since it is denied that the Jews had a right to retain their national name, it is evident that Christians are regarded as the true heirs of Abraham, as in Rom. ii. 28. The things which the believers here are about to suffer may be connected with the opposition of the Jews. Such distress is to extend for *ten days* (10), i.e. a short period. It is sometimes held to be identical with the 'great distress' of vii. 14, but it seems more likely that a local persecution is in mind. The *devil* ('slanderer') will then be a means of testing the Christians; such testing by persecution is to be distinguished from that mentioned in iii. 10, the hour of testing which is to come upon the whole world, for from the latter the Christians are to be preserved (cf. vii. 2f., xii. 6).

The *crown of life* (10) alludes to the wreath bestowed on the winner in the games, 'the crown which consists of life'. Swete points out that the crown is not a diadem, but an emblem of festivity; in which case the wreath is a fitting symbol of life, for the latter has to be understood in the light of the closing descriptions of the book, a life of holy privilege, enjoyment, and of distinctions of awards (cf. 1 Cor. ix. 25, 27). *The second death* (11). In xxi. 8 this is defined as *the lake which burneth with fire and brimstone*. It is a rabbinic phrase; cf. the oft-quoted Jerusalem Targum on Dt. xxxiii. 6, 'Let Reuben live in this age and not die the second death whereof the wicked die in the next world'. Charles aptly compares 1 Enoch xcix. 11, 'woe to you who spread evil to your neighbours, for you shall be slain in Sheol', a conception which did not imply annihilation, as 1 Enoch cix. 3 makes clear.

c. The letter to the church in Pergamum (ii. 12-17)

Pergamum (RV) was described by Arethas as 'given to idolatry more than all Asia'. Behind the city stood a hill, a thousand feet high, covered with heathen temples. Foremost of all was the huge altar of Zeus on a platform cut out of the rock, dominating the city. Emperor worship was established there earlier than at Ephesus or Smyrna so that in due course Pergamum became the recognized centre of the cult in Asia. Hence it was said of this church that it dwelt *where Satan's seat* (RV 'throne') *is* (13). Herein lay the cause of the peculiar difficulties of the Christians of Pergamum.

The title in verse 12 echoes i. 16 and anticipates ii. 16. *My faith* (13) abbreviates 'faith in me'. The information as to Balaam's teaching is gained through combining Nu. xxv. 1, 2 with xxxi. 16. The Christian counterpart of Balaam probably despised the flesh, and so discounted the importance of physical purity, justifying his actions, perhaps, by the perversion of Paul's teaching (repudiated by him in Rom. iii. 8 and vi. 1), 'Let us continue in sin, that grace may abound'. The meaning of verse 15 is either, 'You also have in your midst Nicolaitans, who teach as Balaam taught Israel', or 'You also, as well as the Ephesians (6), have the Nicolaitans with you', the comparison with Balaam being implicit. The former meaning seems preferable. Verse 16 presents a preliminary 'second advent' to judgment if the Pergamenes do not repent. See note on ii. 5. The promise to the conqueror (17) alludes to the current Jewish expectation that manna would descend from heaven again when Messiah is manifested. See 2 Baruch xxix. 8. Here, of course, the manna typifies spiritual life, just as 'water of life' and 'fruit of the tree of life' (xxii. 17, 19). The promise is particularly fitting for those tempted to join in festivities in which food sacrificed to idols was eaten. Denying themselves those dainties, the Christians were to look forward to richer fare in the kingdom of God.

The *white stone* (17) is difficult of interpretation owing to the many uses to which pebbles were put by the world of antiquity, each use yielding an excellent symbolic sense. Thus a white stone given by a jury to one on trial signified acquittal, a black one guilt. The victor's pebble gave him entrance to all public festivals. The *tessera hospitalis* was in two parts, inscribed with two names and exchanged, so that each person had an open invitation to the house of the other. The High Priest had twelve stones on his breastplate inscribed with the names of the twelve tribes. This by no means exhausts the possibilities. Our interpretation will be partly conditioned by our understanding of the *new name* which is engraved on the stone. If the name is of Christ or of God (cf. iii. 12 and xix. 12), then there may be an allusion to the conception of the power inherent in the name of God; the Christian shares God's might and appropriates for himself, in a manner none other can, the character of God. If the name is a new one bestowed on the Christian, then the allusion is to the habit of bestowing new names on persons who have attained to a new status, as Abram and Jacob became Abraham and Israel; the white stone then signifies the overcomer's right to enter the kingdom of God in a character all of his own, moulded by the grace of God in him.

d. The letter to the church in Thyatira (ii. 18-29)

Thyatira was the smallest of the seven cities. It had no temple devoted to the worship of the Emperors, so that Christians here were not so troubled by the cult as those in the preceding churches. The problem of this church centred in the compromising situations created by commercial interests. Thyatira was an industrial city, renowned for its many trade guilds. To these societies it was as necessary to belong as it is for the modern artisan to be a member of his appropriate trade union; otherwise it involved an ostracism that would make business all but impossible. The difficulty in the path of the Christian linking up with such guilds was the necessity of joining in the periodical common meals when meat was eaten that had been dedicated to a pagan deity (perhaps the patron god of the guild). One can well see that certain broadminded Christians would not hesitate to participate in such festivities, holding that 'an idol is nothing' (1 Cor. viii. 4). Excuse might soon be found for the licentiousness in which these meals so often culminated; and the next step would be to join in the general debauchery. This was openly advocated by the Nicolaitans, and one can understand how it found such a ready acceptance in Thyatira where 'business is business' would be the common sentiment.

The title is taken from i. 14, 15, *Son of God* (18) perhaps being suggested by Ps. ii. 7, as the Psalm is later extensively quoted. Note that the *eyes like unto a flame of fire* anticipate verse 23, and the glowing feet verse 27. Charles holds that *thy works* (19) are defined by the qualities that follow, thy love and service and faith and patience; if this is a correct reading, it is important for the interpretation of what the writer means by being 'judged according to works' (xx. 12-14). The prophetess who imparts the teaching of the Nicolaitans is symbolically named Jezebel, for the queen of that name tried to establish an idolatrous cult in place of the worship of Jehovah and was herself accused of whoredom and witchcraft (2 Ki. ix. 22). Note the curious insertion in some MSS of 'thy wife Jezebel' which implies that the 'angel' of the church was its overseer. From verse 21 we infer that 'Jezebel' had been earlier warned, without avail, either by John or by some other Christian leader. The *bed* into which Jezebel is to be cast is paralleled by *great tribulation* (22), so that it is a bed of suffering which is here meant. The idiom is a Hebrew one and occurs in 1 Macc. i. 5 and Judith viii. 3. It is possible that they *that commit adultery with her* (22) are to be distinguished from *her children* (23) in the sense that the former were sufficiently influenced by Jezebel as to compromise their Christian loyalties, the latter wholly embraced her doctrine; the former are to be chastised, the latter exterminated. By such judgments the churches will realize that Christ *searcheth the reins* (kidneys) *and hearts* (23). In Hebrew usage, reins are the seat of the emotions while the heart is the seat of the intellect. The 'deep things of Satan' (24, RV) may be a satirical allusion to the Gnostic claim exclusively to know the deep things of God; such wisdom is satanically inspired, not divine. Otherwise it reflects Nicolaitan teaching that the Christian should boldly participate in the excesses of heathenism and demonstrate that he is immune from their pollution. Christians who acted in this fashion boasted of their knowledge of the deep things of Satan and so scorned their more scrupulous brethren. For *none other burden* (24) cf. Acts xv. 28, 29; the two chief precepts of the apostolic council were abstention from food sacrificed to idols and from immorality. The overcomer is here defined as *he that keepeth my works unto the end* (26). He is to receive a delegation of Christ's authority *over the nations* (26), and share in His triumph over the rebellious peoples (27); the latter function is part of the former and anticipates the coming of Christ to judgment (xix. 11f.) rather than the millennial rule proper (xx. 4-6). The verb translated 'rule' in verse 27 should be rendered by 'destroy'. *The morning star* (28) appears to be Christ Himself (as in xxii. 16); greater than the privilege of ruling for Christ will be the unhindered enjoyment of His fellowship.

e. The letter to the church in Sardis (iii. 1-6)

Sardis was a city of bygone glory. Once the capital of the ancient kingdom of Lydia, it sank into oblivion after the Persian conquest until Tiberius rebuilt it after an earthquake. The city was well known for two things: its dyeing and woollen industries, and its profligacy. The church in Sardis appears to reflect the history of the city; once it had a name for spiritual achievement, now it was lifeless (1); licentiousness marked the Christians as well as the pagans, so that only a few had *not defiled their garments* (4), i.e. besmirched their Christian profession. Accordingly it was censured with a stringency surpassed only in the letter to the Laodiceans. The title reflects i. 4 and i. 16. Christ is spoken of as the possessor of *the seven Spirits*, possibly to represent His complete knowledge of the deeds of the churches (see v. 6), though it may also hint at the spiritual gifts He is ready to impart in contrast to the lifelessness of the church. For *the seven stars* (1) see i. 4n., i. 20n. Note that, although some Christians remain faithful to their Lord (4), the church as a whole is characterized as dead; for that condition all are held responsible. For the first half of verse 2 cf. Mt. xxiv. 42; for the latter half cf. Dn. v. 27. The tenses of verse 3 are unusually varied: 'Keep in mind (present) how you received and still hold on to the gift of God (perfect) and how you gave a hearing (aorist) to the gospel; continue to hold it fast (present) and bring yourself to repentance (aorist)'. *If therefore thou shalt not watch* (3) echoes Mt. xxiv. 43, 44 and refers to the final advent. Some scholars consider that Rev. xvi. 15 has been displaced and should immediately precede this statement. Certainly

xvi. 15 reads strangely in its present position and accords well here, but admittedly the suggestion is pure conjecture.

His name (5). Names, according to a contemporary usage, are synonymous with 'persons'. The Christians who soiled their garments presumably did so by accommodating themselves to the heathen customs of their neighbours. He that maintained in purity his character and testimony was to accompany the Christ in a robe of greater glory. For the walking with Christ Swete compares the companying of the Twelve with Him in the days of His ministry. The conqueror is doubly assured of this privilege. Contemporary apocalyptic literature viewed the resurrection body as a garment of glory. The idea is used by Paul (e.g. 2 Cor. v. 4), and seems to appear in this book also (e.g. iv. 4). But vii. 13, 14, xix. 8 seem to have moral purity chiefly in mind in the use of this symbol, while, as Swete points out, the wearing of white sometimes expresses festivity (Ec. ix. 8) and victory (2 Macc. xi. 8). It would appear that a complexity of ideas attaches to this picture; it is wiser to accept the whole yet to recognize that the ethical element is especially in mind.

The blotting out from *the book of life* (5) recalls Ex. xxxii. 32, where the book is a register of the citizens of the theocratic kingdom; here it is the register of the eternal kingdom, as in Dn xii. 1 and many New Testament passages (see Lk. x. 20; Phil. iv. 3; Heb. xii. 23). See Rev. xx. 12 and 15 where this is explained. For the confession of the victor cf. Mt. x. 32.

f. The letter to the church in Philadelphia (iii. 7–13)

Philadelphia, owing to its frequent earthquakes, had a small population; the church appears to have been correspondingly feeble (see verse 8, *thou hast a little strength*). There is no hint of persecution from pagan authorities, nor of heresies within the church; as at Smyrna, the Jews created the trouble here (9). In impressive contrast to the letter that precedes and that which follows, there is neither rebuke nor warning from the Lord for this church, but simply commendation and exhortation. The predicates *holy* and *true* (7), here applied to Christ, are in vi. 10 referred to God, one of the many indications in this book that the attributes of God are shared by Christ. Jesus is *true* in the sense of 'true to His word', i.e. faithful. This is spoken in connection with His possessing *the key of David* (7), a phrase that recalls i. 18 but actually quotes Is. xxii. 22; it claims for Christ the power of admitting individuals or shutting them out from the city of David, the new Jerusalem, the messianic kingdom. The relevance of this appears in the parenthesis of the next verse and again in verse 9. The Jews of the city were no more worthy to be called Jews than their compatriots in Smyrna, and like them are designated a *synagogue of Satan* (9). This verse declares that one day, presumably at the establishment of the messianic kingdom, they will be forced to recognize that these despised Christians are in truth the companions of the Son of man, the heirs of the kingdom of God. This latter claim the Jews had evidently so far denied. 'You Christians', said they, 'are excluded from the kingdom; it is for us Jews.' 'Not so', declares the Lord; 'I am true to my promise. I alone have the key of admission to the kingdom. I have set before my people a door of entrance into it which no one can shut. They shall enter the kingdom, and the homage which you Jews expect the Gentiles to pay you (Is. lx. 14) you will have to render to them.' This interpretation gives coherence to apparently disconnected statements and accords with the promise of verse 12. The faithfulness of this struggling community (8) is to have its fitting compensation. *The hour of temptation* (RV 'trial') from which the Lord is to preserve these Christians (10) is not the 'time' during which the judgments of God are on the earth, but the trials themselves. Cf. Mk. xiv. 35, where 'hour' represents the horrors of the cross and its attendant circumstances. The tribulation spoken of is directed towards *them that dwell upon the earth* (10), a phrase technical in this book for the unbelievers of the world (cf. xi. 10). For a pictorial representation of this promise see vii. 1–4.

The conqueror is to be *a pillar in the temple* (12) of the new age; xxi. 22 makes it clear that there is to be no temple other than God and the Lamb in the heavenly Jerusalem. The promise here given is thus an assurance of inseparable unity with God in the eternity that is to be. If *I will write upon him the name of my God* (12) continues the metaphor of the pillar, so that the inscription is thought to be on the pillar and not on the victor's forehead, we may perhaps refer to 1 Macc. xiv. 26–48, which relates how the deeds of Simon Maccabaeus were inscribed on tablets of brass; these tablets were fixed 'upon pillars in mount Zion', 'within the precinct of the sanctuary in a conspicuous place'. A permanent record of Simon's greatness was thus ensured. The boast of the overcomer, however, is not to be in his deeds but that he bears the name of God, and of the city of God, and Christ's new name; i.e. he belongs to God and to Christ manifested in glory (xix. 12), and is a citizen of the new Jerusalem, the eternal kingdom of God (xxi. 2).

g. The letter to the church in Laodicea (iii. 14–22)

Laodicea was situated on the bank of a river and stood at the junction of three great roads traversing Asia Minor. Naturally enough it became a large commercial and administrative centre. Three facts known about the city throw light on this letter: it was a banking centre and extremely wealthy; it manufactured clothing and woollen carpets; it had a medical school. The church was not accused of immorality, nor of idolatry, nor of open apostasy (persecution was unknown in Laodicea). The terrible condemnation pronounced over it was due to the pride and self-satisfaction of the pagan element within the church, so that it was all but entirely devoid of fellowship with Christ. The stern characterization of its spiritual condition (17) and the admonition to repentance (18) are both couched in terms of the three activities of the city.

As *the Amen* (14) Jesus is the embodiment of the truthfulness and faithfulness of God (see Is. lxv. 16, RV mg.); the Christian use of 'Amen' adds the thought that He is also the Guarantor and Executor of the declared purposes of God. Such a designation stands in vivid contrast to the faithlessness of the Laodiceans. Similarly the title *the beginning of the creation of God* (14) (better translated 'the principle' or 'source' of creation) exalts Christ as Creator above the proud but puny creatures that boast in their self-sufficiency. In verse 16 is written a condemnation unequalled in the New Testament as an expression of the abhorrence of Christ. The reference is to the last judgment (cf. Lk. xiii. 25–28). Verses 17 and 18 form one statement: *Because thou sayest . . . I counsel thee to buy . . .* The claim of the Laodiceans is not merely that they need nothing but that their wealth, moral as well as material, is entirely due to their own efforts. Their real condition is shown to be one of poverty, in spite of their money; nakedness, despite their abundance of cloth; blindness, though they have many physicians. This church, therefore, alone of all the seven, is called 'the pitiable one'. Their only recourse is to 'buy' (cf. Is. lv. 1) from Christ the tested gold of a regenerate spirit, purity of heart that may issue in resurrection glory (Rev. vii. 13, 14) and grace to enable them to perceive spiritual realities (cf. 1 Cor. iii and 2 Cor. iv). The nauseating condition of the Laodiceans has not quenched the love of Christ for them; His scathing judgments are but the expression of a deep affection that would lead them to repentance. The gracious invitation that follows is given, not to the church collectively (which would demand, 'if *you* hear my voice . . .'), but to each individual within it, an offer of Christ to be a partner even in the commonest activities of life. Commensurate with the high privilege offered to these all but apostate Christians is a promise transcending the six that have preceded. Just as the believer asks Christ to share his domain in this transitory life, so the Lord will invite him, if he endures to the end, to share the throne given Him by the Father in the ages that are to be. The fulfilment of the promise is portrayed in Rev. xx. 4–6, the millennial rule, and xxii. 5, the eternal reign in the new Jerusalem.

IV. THE VISION OF HEAVEN. iv. 1—v. 14

The scene of John's vision changes from earth to heaven and remains there until chapter x, after which the point of view continually alternates. It is noticeable that, whereas the description of the throne of God in chapter iv contains no reference to Christ, in the following chapter

He dominates the picture as the slain Lamb of God. Concerning this Kiddle writes, 'In iv, the theme is that of the omnipotent Creator, reigning majestic and remote in a heaven from which man is excluded. The God whom John sees is the heaven of the old dispensation. In v, the focus of the seer's eyes changes, and with incomparable dramatic force he describes his vision of the Redeemer in whom lies every hope of man's salvation, every hope of a future kingdom of justice' (Moff. Comm., p. 67).

The first voice which I heard (1) is that of Christ. As the Lord revealed the true condition of His churches and His position in relation to them, so He now opens heaven to John's view, and His position in relation to that. The former was a revelation of 'things which are'; this begins the unveiling of *things which must be hereafter* (1; cf. i. 19).

The fact that John saw a door opened in heaven implies that he was already in an ecstatic condition; the statement *immediately I was in the spirit* (2), accordingly, may well indicate a yet higher degree of spiritual exaltation. The first object to catch John's eye was *a throne* (2). That is important; it hints that the first thing to be known about heaven is that the God who dwells therein possesses absolute authority over the universe. The prophet does not describe God; he simply speaks of various colours seen through the light of a many-hued cloud, colours such as can emanate only from precious stones (3). Doubt attaches to the stones enumerated by John, but the most treasured type of *jasper* was green, the *sardine* was red, while the word translated *emerald* is thought to be the rock crystal which shows a rainbow of prismatic colours. The object of the *rainbow* is primarily to conceal the form of God; yet it is significant that a rainbow performs this service and not an ordinary cloud, for the bow is a perpetual reminder of God's covenant to restrain His wrath from man on earth (Gn. ix. 13); the memorial of the covenant in heaven is thus nothing less than the glory of God which hides Him from angelic view. The *four and twenty elders* (4), though subordinate to the four living creatures (see verse 6, RV), are mentioned before them, perhaps so as not to interrupt the description of the latter's activities. From the characteristics of the elders, as they appear in the subsequent visions, it is manifest that they are angelic beings; it is nevertheless not impossible to conceive of them as also the heavenly representatives of the people of God in their twofold aspect as priests and kings, in which case the number twenty-four, with its reminiscence of twelve tribes and twelve apostles, fittingly symbolizes the messianic people of both dispensations, as the Church has delighted to recognize. This view, however, is to be distinguished from that which regards the elders as a symbol for the people of God removed from earth and present in heaven. For *the seven Spirits of God* (5) see v. 6. It is not said that the *sea of glass* (6) is a literal sea but that it looks like one, 'as it were a glassy sea' (RV). It is an adaptation of the conception of waters above the firmament (Gn. i. 7; see 2 Enoch iii. 3), but is here introduced to emphasize the remoteness of the majesty of God. *Four beasts* (RV 'four living creatures') stand *about the throne* (6). Their description is drawn from Ezekiel's vision of the cherubim (Ezk. i), but considerably modified (7). The chief differences are that the cherubim in Ezekiel each have four faces, here they have only one. The former possess 'wheels full of eyes round about', here the creatures themselves possess the eyes. The ceaseless worship rendered to God by them may well represent the subjection of all nature to God. The Jews themselves interpreted Ezekiel's vision in this way, regarding the man as chief representative of creatures, the eagle of birds, the lion of beasts, and the ox of cattle. The ancient symbolizing of the four winds and the four chief constellations of the Zodiac by these four figures, if known to John, would but serve to strengthen this view. The song of the cherubim implies that the certainty of the future triumph of God is rooted in His very nature; the Lord, who is holy and almighty, *is to come* (8). The thanksgiving of the living creatures (9), inspiring the renunciation by the twenty-four elders of their crowns (10, 11), is not the continual worship of verse 8 but adoration given in special crises. See, e.g., v. 8 and 14, xi. 15–18, xix. 4. The elders recognize that only one is worthy to take pre-eminence in creation, and He the Creator (11). He willed the existence of all things. He has the right to deal with them in sovereign freedom. All creation should acknowledge its subjection to Him and ascribe the *glory* and the *honour* and the *power* to His name.

The seer continues to describe what he saw: Concerning the book *sealed with seven seals* (v. 1) Zahn writes, 'The word *biblion* itself permits of many interpretations, but for the readers of that time it was designated by the seven seals on its back beyond possibility of a mistake. Just as in Germany before the introduction of money orders everyone knew that a letter sealed with five seals contained money, so the most simple member of the Asiatic churches knew that a *biblion* made fast with seven seals was a testament. When a testator died the testament was brought forward, and, when possible, opened in the presence of the seven witnesses who sealed it; i.e. it was unsealed, read aloud and executed. . . . The document with seven seals is a symbol of the promise of a future kingdom. The disposition long ago occurred and was documented and sealed, but it was not yet carried out. . . . As to the opening of the seals, the point of comparison is not so much that no one knows the contents of God's will as that they still await realization. No one is authorized to open the will except the Lamb; the returning Christ will open the testament of God and execute it' (*Introduction to the New Testament*, Vol. III, pp. 393f.). The angel needs to be *strong* (2) since his voice has to

carry throughout heaven, earth and the realm of the dead (3). *Under the earth* signifies Hades (cf. Eph. iv. 9; Phil. ii. 10). *The Lion of the tribe of Juda* (Gn. xlix. 9), *the Root of David* (Is. xi. 1, 10), won the victory for all time by virtue of His death and resurrection, so as *to open the book, and to loose the seven seals thereof* (5). The redemption wrought by Christ had in view the establishment of God's kingdom in power. The description of the *Lamb* (6) combines two very different uses of this figure in Hebrew thought. It stands *as it had been slain* and so reminds us of the slaughtered lamb of Is. liii. 7; Jesus is the Servant of Jehovah, suffering in innocence for the sake of men. On the other hand, the lamb has *seven horns*; a horn in the Old Testament symbolizes power (Ps. lxxv. 4–7) and royal dignity (Zc. i. 18); Jesus has kingly power in a complete measure (the significance of *seven*); by His victory He fulfils the hope of Judaism that a Warrior-Lamb should arise and redeem Israel from her enemies (see, e.g., Test. Simeon xix. 8). The nature of Christ's redemptive victory, however, was far removed from the current expectations of the Jews. Observe that the once-slain Lamb possesses *the seven Spirits of God sent forth into all the earth* (6). Cf. Jn. xvi. 7f. In the Old Testament the *seven eyes* (signifying omniscience) belong to Jehovah (cf. Zc. iv. 10). Though the four creatures fall down in worship with the twenty-four elders, it seems that only the latter have the harps and bowls of incense (8). The angelic nature of the elders is confirmed by the description of their offering up of the *prayers of the saints*; in Judaism this task is performed by the archangels (see Tobit xii. 15; Test. Levi iii. 7). The creatures and the elders sing *a new song* (9), because Christ has opened a new era by His redemptive work and is shortly to consummate His victory in the triumphant kingdom of God. Cf. Is. xlii. 9, 10, which speaks of the new song in a similar context. The redemption is viewed as a purchase, at the price of Christ's life, a ransoming from the enslaving and hostile power of sin. The figure must not be pressed so as to answer, or even posit, the query 'To whom was the price paid?' That question was never meant to be asked. Note that in verses 9 and 10 the AV follows a wrong reading in making the angelic beings the objects of Christ's redemption. Read as in RV 'Thou . . . didst purchase . . . men of every tribe . . . and madest them to be a kingdom and priests'. To be 'a kingdom and priests' was Israel's vocation (Ex. xix. 6), a privilege given also to the Church (1 Pet. ii. 9). The RV follows the harder, and therefore more likely, reading in the second half of verse 10, 'they reign (not *shall reign*) upon the earth'. Possibly this conveys the notion that Christians, not imperial dignitaries, are the true sovereigns of earth even in this dispensation. More probably it is a proleptic reference to the millennial rule of the saints (see xx. 4–6), in which case it is erroneous to regard the millennium as the reign of the risen martyrs only, for this reference includes the whole Church. The angelic multitudes now take up the song of praise to the Lamb (11-14; cf. Dn. vii. 10). The doxology has reference to the power and blessings received by Christ on the commencement of His messianic reign (see xi. 17). All creation in heaven, earth, sea and Hades (13) joins the host of angels and archangels. They sing the praise, not of the Lamb alone, nor of God alone, but of God and the Lamb jointly. The exalted position of Christ in relation to God and the universe could not be more clearly set forth.

V. THE SEVEN SEALS. vi. 1—viii. 5

Many complex elements flow together to form the panorama which the prophet now describes. The division of the messianic woes into seven may ultimately go back to the doom prophecy of Lv. xxvi where four times it is stated 'I will chastise you seven times for your sins' (verses 18, 21, 24, 28). If that be so, the appropriateness of the testament with its seven seals to portray these judgments is a secondary factor and not the cause of the sevenfold division. Moreover, Charles has pointed out that our Lord's eschatological discourse contains the seven judgments enumerated by John; in Luke's Gospel (see chapter xxi) they are in the same order, except that John places the earthquakes last, owing to his consistent portrayal of earthquakes as the immediate precursor of the consummation; see viii. 5, xi. 13, xvi. 18. Thus, in respect of the content of the seals, the prophet has apparently followed our Lord's discourse; but for the form of the opening four judgments he has used a vision of Zechariah (the vision of four chariots and horses that go to the four quarters of the earth, Zc. vi), adapting the symbolism to suit his purpose.

a. The first seal (vi. 1, 2)

The reading Come and see (1) interprets the call of the living creatures as addressed to the seer. But the words 'and see' are a later addition; the command is directed to the rider who appears on the opening of the seal. The same is true of verses 3, 5, 7.

Many interpreters regard the conquering horseman as Christ and compare the vision of the returning Lord in xix. 11f. It must be admitted, however, that the only thing in common with the two pictures is the white horse, which is a symbol of victory. Others hold that the rider represents the triumph of the gospel, and cite Mk. xiii. 10. This latter suggestion is more plausible, but in view of the similarity of the four riders it seems more natural to interpret all as portraying the last judgments. This horseman signifies invasion, or warfare generally.

b. The second seal (vi. 3, 4)

The strife created by the rider on the horse that was red (4) appears to denote both international and civil warfare. The doubling of the first woe in this manner has caused some to feel that the first rider represents a specific victorious Empire

(especially the Parthian) while the second has a general reference. This is possible, but it should be noted that the same repetition occurs in each report of the eschatological discourse (Mt. xxiv. 6, 7; Mk. xiii. 7, 8; Lk. xxi. 9, 10).

c. The third seal (vi. 5, 6)

The rider on a black horse denotes famine. The balance in his hand suggests scarcity of food. The prices quoted are prohibitive. A penny (Gk. dēnarion) was a labourer's day wages (Mt. xx. 3f.); a measure of wheat (Gk. choinix, about two pints) would suffice for one man's daily ration, but not for his family. Wheat would therefore be unprocurable by the poor. Three measures of barley would go further, but even so it would still remain a bare subsistence allowance with the possibility of starvation in some instances. On the other hand, see thou hurt not the oil and the wine presupposes ample supplies of less needed goods. A few years before the writing of this book (A.D. 92), an acute shortage of cereals, together with an abundance of wine in the Empire, caused Domitian to order the restriction of vine cultivation and an increase of corn growing; the order created such a furore it had to be abandoned. The text may have such a situation in mind.

d. The fourth seal (vi. 7, 8)

Hades followed, accompanied by Death, a reminder that not even physical death would give respite to sinners; the nether world and the judgment awaited them. For the four plagues—sword, and famine, and pestilence (translated 'death' in the LXX), and beasts—see Ezk. xiv. 12-21.

e. The fifth seal (vi. 9-11)

The souls of the martyrs were said to be under the altar (9) because they had been 'sacrificed'; cf. Phil. ii. 17; 2 Tim. iv. 6. This position was one of honour, not humiliation. Charles quotes Akiba as saying, 'Whoever was buried in the land of Israel was just as if he were buried under the altar, and whoever was buried under the altar was just as if he were buried under the throne of glory' (Aboth R.M. 26). The martyrs were slain for the word of God, and for the testimony (given by Jesus; see xii. 17) which they held (9). The testimony was that which they had received, not given. The white robe given to the martyrs (11) signifies a pledge of the glorious immortality to be bestowed at the 'first resurrection' (xx. 4-6), with perhaps a hint that the victory was already theirs. Observe that this incident forms an integral part of the last judgments on earth, for the prayer for vengeance (10) is answered and the end thereby hastened; see viii. 1-5. For the thought that the coming of the day of God tarries for the last martyr cf. 2 Esd. iv. 33-36.

f. The sixth seal (vi. 12-17)

The description of the effects of the sixth seal draws from numerous Scriptures, including the

Gospels. The underlying thought of these cosmic disturbances is, perhaps, the impossibility that life should continue under such circumstances; the end is at hand, *the great day of his wrath is come* (17). For the earthquake as a sign of the end cf. Ezk. xxxviii. 19f.; for the sun and moon, Joel ii. 31; for the falling of stars and the rolling up of heaven, Is. xxxiv. 4; for the hiding in the rocks, Is. ii. 10; for the prayer to the mountains, Ho. x. 8; for the great and unbearable day of wrath, Joel ii. 11. These signs of the consummation are too regular in eschatological writings for them to be regarded as wholly figurative. Yet that they are not to be taken too literally appears from the picture of heaven being removed as a scroll at the close of the millennial age (xx. 11), and the imploring by men that the mountains, which have already moved out of their place, should fall on them. Note the sevenfold classification of men here (15). *The wrath of the Lamb* (16) shows the Christ in the character hinted at in His possession of seven horns (v. 6), i.e. complete power to establish righteousness and execute justice (cf. vi. 10).

g. An interlude between the sixth and seventh seals (vii. 1–17)

An interlude in the progress of the visions is given in chapter vii. It explains the position of Christians during the execution of the judgments that have been described. First a backward look is taken, to show how the Church is secured from the evils experienced by the godless world, then a forward look enables the seer to relate the fulfilment of God's act of protection; he sees the triumphant people of God at the close of the great distress, arrayed in splendour and ascribing their salvation to the grace of God and the Lamb (11). There seems little doubt that the two companies here in view are essentially the same. The one hundred and forty-four thousand out of every tribe of the children of Israel (vii. 4) symbolize the entire Church of the end time; this is implied by vii. 3, for *the servants of our God* in the Christian dispensation can only be the Church. Further, since the distresses of the last days are world-wide, the whole company of God's people need His protection, not simply one section of it (the Jews).

After, these things (1) marks a new vision; it is not a note of time in relation to the events of the previous vision but introduces a fresh comprehension of truth by the prophet. For the purpose of this vision the earth is regarded as rectangular, an angel standing at each corner governing the destructive wind that blows from his quarter. No further description is supplied to relate what happens when the four angels let loose their winds. Possibly John here recounts an earlier vision that portrayed the sealing of God's people against destruction caused by the four winds in the last days; the fury of the winds would represent the whole manifestation of judgment symbolized by the seals, trumpets and bowls. For the thought of sealing the saints in a

time of peril cf. Ezk. ix. 144,000 symbolizes 'fixedness and full completion, 12 x 12 taken a thousandfold' (Alford). Israel was often referred to as 'the twelve tribes' to denote the whole nation without any thought of its constituent parts (Acts xxvi. 7). The enumeration of the tribes one by one here serves to emphasize the completeness of the number of God's saints for whom He cares during the coming ordeal. For the Church as the true Israel cf. Rom. ii. 28, 29; Gal. iii. 29, vi. 16; Phil. iii. 3; Jas. i. 1; 1 Pet. i. 1 with ii. 9. The order of the tribes is curious in a number of ways. Judah heads the list, an unusual procedure amongst the Jews; here it is due to its being the tribe of the Messiah. Dan is omitted whereas Manasseh appears, although the latter is included in Joseph. Irenaeus explained this as being due to the ancient belief that Antichrist was to spring from Dan. The half tribe of Manasseh was then inserted to make up the number twelve. Buchanan Gray discovered that if vii. 5c, 6 (i.e. Gad to Manasseh) were placed after verse 8, the list would conform to the usual enumeration of the Jewish tribes by which they are arranged according to descent from their mothers: the sons of Leah are Judah to Zebulun; the sons of Rachel, Joseph and Benjamin; the sons of Leah's handmaid, Gad and Asher; the sons of Rachel's handmaid, Naphtali and Dan (here replaced by Manasseh). It is possible, therefore, that our text originally maintained this order but suffered a dislocation by a copyist in early days.

After this (9) again marks a logical rather than a chronological sequence. The result of the sealing of Christ's faithful followers is their ultimate vindication in glory. A great multitude (9); the Church is seen triumphant in heaven. *White robes* signify resurrection glory, and *palms* victory and gladness after war (cf. Mk. xi. 8; 1 Macc. xiii. 51). *Salvation to our God . . . and unto the Lamb* (10) echoes Ps. iii. 8, 'Salvation belongeth unto the Lord'; see also Rev. xix. 1. The victors here ascribe their redemption to God and the Lamb; they are not desiring 'salvation' to be given to God and the Redeemer. The *Amen* (12) of the angelic orders endorses the praise of the redeemed multitude, while they, too, add their thanksgiving.

John's answer to the elder's question (13) implies 'I also would like to know'. The *great tribulation* (14) out of which the multitude has come is not intended as a general designation of tribulation, which is the Christian's normal lot, but has specific reference to the trial at the close of this age. On the other hand, there is no warrant for the common assumption that the multitude consists of martyrs only. The vision depicts the scene after the cessation of trials (the present tense 'come' (14, RV) is to be understood in the light of the statement 'they *washed* their robes and *made* them white . . .'); it thus has in mind one generation only of Christians, the last. Yet the latter part of the passage seems to refer to the whole Church. The difficulty is relieved if we remember that the seer prophesies of a day that to him is almost on the horizon; he has no thought of intervening ages. The last persecution may come at any moment. The Church was still in its second generation and John had no reason to anticipate a third. The glorification of the Bride with her Lord was at hand. To his mind, therefore, to speak of Christians who came through the great distress was to denominate the major part of the Church. Those who had gone before, having witnessed a good confession, would doubtless be included in this throng, but it was superfluous to mention them. The Church of the present was the subject in view and it fills John's canvas. For us, nearly two millenniums later, the Church is mainly the Church triumphant in heaven; it is therefore possible to recognize that the AV is spiritually true, *These are they which came out of great tribulation . . .* and read therein our own names. They *have washed their robes, and made them white in the blood of the Lamb* is a symbolic expression, not to be taken literally, of the forgiveness of sins through faith in the Christ who died for men. It is possible to translate, as some do in xii. 11, 'in the blood of the Lamb' as 'through the blood of the Lamb'; the washing and making white of robes then signifies the overcoming of sin in life by virtue of the power of Christ's atonement, a retrospect on the whole struggle of life rather than on the moment of conversion. Charles translates the last part of verse 15 'He that sitteth upon the throne shall cause his Shekinah to abide upon them'. The phrase is unique. The Shekinah was the manifestation of God's presence amongst men, especially in the tabernacle and the temple at Jerusalem. After the pilgrimage through the wilderness it was of very rare occurrence in Israel; to the Christian it is promised as a constant privilege. Verses 16 and 17 are a statement drawn from Is. xlix. 10 and xxix. 8: Christ assuages the thirst of man by providing in Himself the antidote to his restlessness, the complete counterpart to man's unsatisfied desires.

h. The seventh seal (viii. 1–5)

A *silence in heaven* (1) occurred in order to hear the prayers of the saints. There is a Jewish tradition that 'in the fifth heaven are companies of angels of service who sing praises by night but are silent by day because of the glory of Israel', i.e. that Israel's praises may be heard. In our text, however, the thanksgiving of heaven is quieted to hear not praises but cries for deliverance from the suffering Christians on earth. The appearance at this juncture of the seven archangels with seven trumpets (2) interrupts the sequence of the vision and, in thought at least, is to be considered after verse 5. *Incense* offered with *the prayers of all saints* (3) serves to make them acceptable before God. If human prayers are to be effective they must be cleansed from all taint of selfishness and sinfulness. It is doubtful that two altars appear in this verse. The one

altar in heaven seems to partake of the character both of the altar for burnt offerings and of the altar of incense that stood in the most holy place. The prayers of the saints are answered. The fire that burned the incense is thrown to earth and becomes a means of judgment. There follow *voices, and thunderings, and lightnings, and an earthquake* (5). These phenomena reveal that the end has come and the kingdom of God established; see xi. 19 (consequent on the seventh trumpet) and xvi. 18 (following the seventh bowl).

VI. THE SEVEN TRUMPETS. viii. 6—xi. 19

As the seven seals fall into two groups of four and three, so the seven trumpets divide themselves, the first four having distinct reminiscences of the Egyptian plagues at the exodus. In xv. 3 the second coming is tacitly compared to the exodus (the redeemed sing the song of Moses and of the Lamb); so here that redemption is heralded by like plagues on the ungodly. Note further that the eschatological use of the trumpet goes back to the sounding of a trumpet at the theophany of Sinai (Ex. xix. 13–20). For examples of the use of the trumpet at the last day see Joel ii. 1; 1 Cor. xv. 52; 1 Thes. iv. 16.

a. The first trumpet (viii. 7)

The first trumpet affects one third of earth; cf. the plague of hail and fire in Ex. ix. 24. *All green grass* was burned up, that is, in the third part of the earth which was affected; the locusts of ix. 4 are forbidden to hurt the grass of the earth, which would not exist if this were a universal judgment.

b. The second trumpet (viii. 8, 9)

The second trumpet affects one third of the sea. As the Nile was turned into blood in the first Egyptian plague (Ex. vii. 20, 21), so the third part of the sea here.

c. The third trumpet (viii. 10, 11)

The third trumpet causes one third of fresh waters to become poisonous, and so continues the thought of the previous plague; cf. xvi. 3–7. Since the star that falls at the sounding of the fifth trumpet (ix. 1) is an angelic being, it is possible that *Wormwood* (11) is also an angel. For the bitter waters cf. Je. ix. 15, xxiii. 15.

d. The fourth trumpet (viii. 12)

The fourth trumpet darkens a third part of the heavens. Instead of 'the day should not shine for the third part of it, and the night in like manner' (RV) read with the Bohairic version, 'the third part of them should not shine during the day and during the night in like manner'. This corresponds in a measure to the Egyptian plague of darkness (Ex. x. 21–23).

Woe (13) is now thrice repeated by the angel because the three last plagues are particularly grievous and are entitled the first, second and third woes. They are directed *to the inhabiters of the earth*, i.e. the non-Christian world in distinction from the Church.

e. The fifth trumpet (ix. 1–12)

The fifth trumpet introduces a plague of demonic locusts. The fact that the star seen by John lies 'fallen unto the earth' (1, RV) does not necessitate its being a 'fallen' angel. The movement is narrated merely to show that the 'star' came down from heaven to earth to open the abyss, wherein dwelt the demonic hordes. Clouds *as the smoke of a great furnace* (2) would remind John's readers of the volcanoes they had seen, but they are intended rather to convey the impression of an advancing cloud of locusts (see Joel ii. 10). The comparison of these demon hosts to locusts goes back to the vision of Joel alluded to, where it is said that the locust armies look like war horses running to battle, rattle like chariots, charge like mighty men, darken the heavens (Joel ii. 4–10) and have fangs like lions (Joel i. 6). In addition to these features, John declares the locusts have power to inflict pain like *scorpions* (3); see also ix. 10. Verse 4 indicates the reason for the scorpion sting; the locusts are sent not to harm vegetation but only such men as *have not the seal of God in their foreheads. Five months* (5) is the normal length of a locust's life (spring and summer). Scorpions inflict agony but rarely kill men. The likeness between the head of a locust and that of a horse (7) was often mentioned by ancient writers. The *hair as the hair of women* (8) refers to their long antennae, lion-like teeth to their destructiveness, *breastplates of iron* (9) to their scales. The crowns of gold and human faces (7), however, emphasize that they are no ordinary locusts but demons. Hence their king is *Abaddon* (11), a name that in the Old Testament denotes the depths of Sheol and means 'destruction' (cf. Jb. xxviii. 22).

Whether this plague is intended to symbolize the pangs of men's stricken conscience (as Swete believes), or is intended to be taken more literally, it is hard to say. It is possible that both in this and the following woe John depicts the troubling of humanity by actual demonic powers; such a view would accord with the New Testament teaching on demons generally.

f. The sixth trumpet (ix. 13–21)

The sixth trumpet brings a demonic army from the Euphrates. A voice from *the golden altar* initiates the plague (13), thus connecting it with the cries of the martyrs in heaven and the prayers of the saints on earth (cf. viii. 4, 5). *The four angels* (14) are ministers of wrath. The river Euphrates formed 'the ideal limit' of the land of Israel (Driver; see Gn. xv. 18); beyond it used to lie the great Empires of Babylon and Assyria. As armies came from these unknown territories to ravage disobedient Israel of old, so would more terrifying horses arise to punish the godless world. Nothing in the programme of God is accidental. The precise moment of this invasion is fixed 'in a definite hour of a definite day, in a definite month of a definite year' (Charles). The unimaginable figure of two hundred million (see Ps. lxviii. 17) hints that this

whole description in verses 16–19 is not intended to be taken too literally. The horsemen seem to be of little account; it is the horses that terrify and destroy. Corresponding to the deadly *fire and smoke and brimstone* (17) which proceed from the horses' mouths, the riders have breastplates of fiery red, smoky blue and sulphurous yellow. Monsters of this sort were not unknown to heathen mythology; possibly John deliberately uses such terms to declare that the devices of this hellish multitude beggar the most terrifying imaginations of pagan superstition, even including the brutes of primeval chaos. The plague fails to produce a salutary effect on the God-opposing world; men yet persist in idolatry, with its attendant evils, and find no place of repentance (20, 21).

g. Interlude between the sixth and seventh trumpets (x. 1—xi. 14)

Just as John inserted a parenthesis between the sixth and seventh seals, so he does between the sixth and seventh trumpets. His purpose in this interlude is to emphasize the certain proximity of the end (x. 1–7), the validity of his prophetic ministry (x. 8–11), the security of the Church (xi. 1, 2) and the power of its witness in the era of Antichrist (xi. 3–13). Throughout this section the seer lays prophetic writings much under contribution, both canonical and otherwise, and re-applies them with great freedom; particularly is it necessary to bear this in mind when interpreting chapter xi.

i. The proximity of the end (x. 1–7). The *mighty angel* (1) is sometimes identified with Christ, but it is unlikely that He would be referred to as an angel; see Dn. xii. 7. The rainbow about his head may be due to the radiance of his face gleaming through the cloud that surrounded him. Since the Hebrew word for foot (*regel*) can also mean leg, we ought perhaps to read 'his legs as pillars of fire'. In view of verse 11, the *little book* (2) seems to include the rest of the visions of this book. The *seven thunders* (3) were not uttered by the angel, for they followed his cry, but probably came from God or Christ (as also the command of verse 4). For a reason not made known to us John is forbidden to reveal the message of the thunders. Some compare 2 Cor. xii. 4, but not aptly, for the revelation could hardly be greater than that of chapters iv and v. Kiddle suggests it was a revelation given for John's own illumination but which he must not digress to record in view of the importance of the rest of this vision, a view which is as plausible as any yet propounded. For x. 5–7 cf. Dn. xii. 7. The angel stands on earth and sea because his message is of world-wide importance. The burden of his declaration is that there shall be *time no longer* (6), i.e. no more delay. God's purpose for mankind, revealed to the prophets, is now to be accomplished; the *seventh angel* (7) is on the point of sounding his trumpet and then will the end come.

ii. John's commission as a prophet reaffirmed

(x. 8–11). This part of the vision recalls Ezk. ii. 9—iii. 3. As in Ezekiel's case, eating the book caused both sweetness and bitterness, a phenomenon due, however, to the mixture of blessings and woes to be announced rather than to the sweetness of obediently proclaiming what is bitter. The import of the passage seems to be a reaffirmation of John's prophetic commission.

iii. **The security of the Church (xi. 1, 2).** In this short oracle the temple at Jerusalem is measured off, together with its worshippers, for protection in a period of trial (cf. Ezk. xl. 3f.; Am. vii. 7–9). The outer court of the Gentiles and the city itself are left to the domination of a heathen oppressor for three and a half years. Some expositors have interpreted this to mean that the prophecy was written before A.D. 70 while the temple was still standing. But it is difficult to harmonize this standpoint with the book as a whole, which is concerned with the welfare of the Christian Church, not the Jewish nation. John's vision is intended to portray the spiritual security of the Church during the era of Antichrist's sway. It follows that we should not expect to be able to allegorize every detail of the picture but be content with grasping its general meaning. *The temple of God, and the altar, and them that worship therein* (1) convey one idea, the Church (cf. 1 Cor. iii. 16). Similarly *the court which is without the temple* and *the holy city* (2) together represent the world outside the Church. It is a bold transformation, but verse 8 implies that the one-time 'holy city' has now become one with sinful Sodom, Egypt the oppressor, and the tyrannous Empire that wars against the Messiah. For the *forty and two months* (2) cf. xii. 6 ('a thousand two hundred and threescore days') and xii. 14 ('time, and times, and half a time'), all equivalent expressions for the three and a half years of Antichrist's rule. The same reckoning appears in Dn. vii. 25, xii. 7, but its precise significance is still obscure.

iv. **The prophecy of the two witnesses (xi. 3–14).** This involves similar principles as verses 1, 2. The two witnesses originally were Moses and Elijah. For the latter's expected appearance before the Messiah's coming, see Mal. iv. 5. Moses also was thought by some to have been translated to heaven and to be returning with Elijah; Johanan ben Zakkai declared that God said to Moses 'If I send the prophet Elijah, ye must both come together'. It could be argued that John intended the prophecy to be understood literally, but certain indications in the text suggest that the vision refers to the missionary activity of the whole Church. The beast is said to *make war* on the two witnesses (7), a curious phrase in reference to two individuals, but it is applied to the Church in xiii. 7; men from the whole world view their martyred forms and rejoice in their subjugation (9), an impossible thought if two individuals in Jerusalem were meant; and the witnesses are represented by lampstands (4), a figure applied to the Church in chapter i. The passage, accordingly, illustrates

the Church's powerful witness in the era under review by means of a well-known Jewish expectation. Verse 4 shows why there are two witnesses rather than only one (Elijah): John has in mind Zechariah's vision of the two olive trees standing on either side of the golden lampstand (Zc. iv). There the two trees probably represented Joshua and Zerubbabel, the lampstand Israel. John makes the one lampstand become two to conform to the two trees, and declares that both the olive trees and the lampstands mean the same thing, the Church in its prophetic capacity. The lampstand had already become seven to represent the seven churches (i. 12, ii. 1); it is an easy transition to make them become two to correspond to the two prophets, though here the whole Church is typified by the lampstands, not a part of it. *Sackcloth* (3) is worn by the witnesses because of the grave character of their message. The extraordinary power of the Church is set forth in verses 5 and 6 in terms reminiscent of Elijah and Moses. The destroying fire recalls 2 Ki. i. 10f.; the ability to prevent rain, 1 Ki. xvii. 1; the turning of waters to blood and the smiting of earth with plagues, Ex. viif. In verse 7 we have the first mention of the beast, *that ascendeth out of the bottomless pit*, i.e., as RV, 'that cometh up out of the abyss'. He is spoken of as if well known, but fuller descriptions of him occur in chapters xiii and xvii. Note the similarity of words used in xiii. 7 to describe the warfare of the beast against the Church.

The great city (8) means what Bunyan represented as 'Vanity Fair' (Kiddle). Throughout the rest of the book the phrase is used of the harlot city Rome (xvi. 19, xvii. 18, xviii. 10f.), so that in one remarkable stroke of the pen John identifies Jerusalem with Sodom, Egypt and Rome, and all together with the world that rejected and killed the Son of God. Jew and Gentile combine in seeking to crush the testimony of the faithful witnesses of Christ, just as they sought to destroy the Lord Himself (9). Refusal to allow a corpse to be buried signifies the greatest depth of ignominy to which a man could be subjected; see Ps. lxxix. 3 and the book of Tobit. The Church is crushed by its enemies *for three days and an half* (11) corresponding to the years of its testimony, 'a short triumph in point of fact, but long enough to bear the semblance of being complete and final' (Swete). At the conclusion of the three and a half days *the Spirit* (RV 'breath') *of life from God entered into them, and they stood upon their feet*. This is a quotation from Ezk. xxxvii. 10, which referred to the spiritual quickening of the nation Israel. Possibly, therefore, this resurrection is to be taken figuratively, signifying a revival so tremendous as to awe the world; but it may describe the rapture of the saints (cf. 1 Thes. iv. 16, 17) and so be equivalent to the first resurrection (xx. 4–6). Cf. the earthquake here (xi. 13) with that recorded in vi. 12. The number *seven thousand* (13) would suitably indicate a tenth of the population of Jerusalem. In making the city represent the world-city of Vanity Fair, John had no need to alter the figure, for seven thousand could be interpreted to mean any considerable number. Note that these events at last evoked some sort of repentance from the hitherto unrepentant race (13).

h. The seventh trumpet (xi. 15–19)

The seventh trumpet, as the seventh seal, is followed by the advent of the kingdom of God. Since the sounding of the seventh trumpet is intended to bring the third woe (14) but no calamity is described, it is evident that we are to expect a further elucidation of the matter later on. Such an expansion is provided in xiv. 19, 20 and chaper xviii. Meanwhile, great voices proclaim, 'The kingdom of the world is become the kingdom of our Lord, and of his Christ' (15, RV), a joint rule which is to know no end; it signifies the millennial reign merging into the eternal bliss of the new creation (xx—xxii). The customary attribute of God is significantly shortened (see RV); no longer is it said that He 'is to come', for He 'has come'! *Thou hast taken to thee thy great power, and hast reigned* (17); the eternal reign has 'begun' in that there has commenced a new exercise of the sovereignty of God over man, a sovereignty which at no time in history had been abandoned but which, in His wisdom, had been voluntarily limited. The song of thanksgiving (17, 18) marks an ordered progress of thought which is observed later in the book: God has begun His eternal rule, i.e. the millennial kingdom (xx. 4–6); the nations were angry, rising in rebellion (xx. 8, 9); God's wrath manifested itself in judgment (xx. 9); the dead were judged (xx. 11–15); the saints rewarded in the city of God (xxi) and the sinners destroyed in the lake of fire (xx. 15, xxi. 8).

The temple in heaven is opened to reveal the ark of the covenant (19). The manifestation of the ark to men at this point implies that the goal of the covenant, which is the promise of the kingdom, is now in the act of coming to pass. Lightnings, earthquake and hail, etc., testify that the consummation has arrived (cf. viii. 5, xvi. 17–21).

VII. THE BACKGROUND OF THE EARTHLY CONFLICT. xii. 1—xiv. 20

Since the seven trumpets followed on the seven seals, it is a natural expectation that the seven bowls will immediately be poured out, so that the story of the birth pangs of the kingdom may be completed. Instead, however, a lengthy parenthesis intervenes. It is necessary to reveal the true nature of the conflict which the Messiah ends at His appearing before the débâcle itself can be appreciated and understood. The struggle in which the saints are involved is not simply the efforts of a minor religious community to resist the persecutions of an Empire; this but forms the platform of a more terrifying content wherein the age-old adversary of God and man strives by every subterfuge of politics and heathenism to thwart the purpose of God centred in His Church. The 'parenthesis' is thus seen to be the core of the book. It covers the whole messianic period, from the birth of Christ to the consummation.

a. The woman and her child (xii. 1–17)

The Greeks told a story of the birth of Apollo remarkably parallel to that in verses 1–6. The Egyptians similarly related the birth of Horus; in fact the story, in modified forms, seems to have been universally told. Clearly John has employed a well-known narrative (first adapted, apparently, by a Jew) both to illustrate his own theme and tacitly to exclude all heroes of other faiths from the position of World-Redeemer. Such treatment of pagan sources is similar to his use of Jewish narratives, such as those in chapters vii and xi; the message they are made to yield is in both cases neither pagan nor Jewish, but Christian through and through. To the heathen nations of the ancient world the travailing woman (xii. 1, 2) would have been a goddess crowned with the twelve stars of the Zodiac. The Jew would have seen in her his own people, headed by the twelve patriarchs. John shows that she represents neither of these, but the true believing people of God of both old and new dispensations, the messianic community.

The dragon is identified in verse 9 with Satan. His *seven heads and ten horns* (3) show him to be the Antichrist of the spiritual world, just as his agent, 'the beast' (xiii. 1), is the earthly Antichrist sharing his characteristics. The figure was used in Daniel to describe the nature of four successive world powers of history. In Daniel the seven heads were divided among the four beasts, while here they are retained in one horrible concentration of evil. The ten horns are similarly traditional and in the earthly anti-Christian power are applied to ten kings (Dn. vii. 24; Rev. xvii. 12). *His tail drew the third part of the stars of heaven* (4) echoes a victory of the devil over angelic powers, but whether John intended by this feature anything more than an allusion to the dragon's great power is hard to say. The statement of the child's destiny (5; see Ps. ii. 9) explains the dragon's desire to devour him, for the nations he regarded as his legitimate prey. In its original reference the meaning would be that the child was snatched to the throne of God for safety while yet an infant; but the 'catching up' is sufficiently similar to the victorious ascension of Jesus to make plain its real meaning in this context.

The people of God are safe from the devil's wiles during the period of Antichrist's reign of terror (6). This accords with the teaching of vii. 1–8, xi. 1, 2; it anticipates the downfall of Satan described in verses 7–12 and is enlarged in 13–17. The *war in heaven* (xii. 7–12) may signify an attempt to storm the refuge of the Child-Redeemer. Hence the heavenly protagonist is an archangel leading the hosts of God; he it is that wins the victory over the devil and his demonic followers. His conquest brings in *the kingdom of our God* (10; cf. Dn. xii. 1–3). But the addition of verse 11 by our prophet transforms the whole scene. The real means of the dragon's overthrow was the atoning work of Christ; His people share that victory by their testimony to His saving power in their lives. The angelic conquest becomes a mere figure for the victory of Christ and His saints. The initiation of the kingdom of God through the redemption on the cross is a close parallel to the Johannine and Pauline teaching that our Lord's death and resurrection were the occasion of Satan's downfall and the establishment of the kingdom age with all its attendant blessings. The Revelation, accordingly, cannot be said to be wholly devoid of 'realized' eschatology. Charles has successfully solved a long-standing linguistic difficulty by translating verse 7 'Michael and his angels had to fight with the dragon'. See I.C.C., pp. 321, 322.

That old serpent (9) is that which tempted Eve in Eden. *Devil* (*diabolos*) is the Greek equivalent of the Hebrew *Satan*, both meaning 'slanderer'. The text implies that Satan can no longer fulfil his function of falsely accusing the saints before God (see Jb. i and Zc. iii) for Christ has secured their acquittal and reconciled them to God through His atonement. Accordingly, the devil concentrates on his abilities as dragon, serpent and deceiver.

Kingdom (10) is perhaps better rendered here 'sovereignty'; but cf. Col. i. 13, 14, where the thought is very similar; for the casting down of Satan cf. Jn. xii. 31–33. The redemption of Christ is the prime cause of the saints' victory (11); their testimony confirms its efficacy in their lives. In verse 12 read with RV, 'Woe for the earth and for the sea'. The expression corresponds to John's frequent designation of the unbelieving world as 'the inhabiters of the earth' (xi. 10, xiii. 8, etc.); it is here used in distinction from the heavenly sphere where Satan formerly dwelt. The *short time* (12) is defined in verse 14; the period of Antichrist's reign is here seen to be an administration of the devil through him.

The dragon now turns his attention to the woman, i.e. the Church, having failed in the case of its Lord: cf. Jn. xv. 20. For xii. 14 see note on verse 6 above. The woman is nourished 'because of' rather than *from the face of* the serpent. In the symbolism setting forth its attack on the woman the serpent is regarded as a water monster, indeed the personification of the sea. Hence the woman flees for refuge into *the wilderness* (14), where a sea monster can have no place. Not to be outdone, the serpent sends a flood of water after her, but the earth swallows it up, so that nothing more can be done by him (15, 16). The picture well illustrates the spiritual security of believers against all that the devil can do in his attempts to destroy them.

b. Antichrist and his prophet (xiii. 1–18)

In verse 1 both the MS evidence and the context favour the reading of RV 'he stood upon the sand of the sea', rather than the AV *I stood*. The dragon, having failed alone to crush the Christ and His people, calls to his aid a helper. The beast comes *out of the sea* (1), thereby showing its character as a sea monster (like the dragon; see notes on xii. 3, 15, 16 and cf. Dn. vii. 3) and as demonic (according to xi. 7 the sea is equivalent to the abyss). The second beast, on the other hand, comes *out of the earth* (11). This difference corresponds to that between *behemoth*, the land monster (Jb. xl. 15f.) and *leviathan*, the sea monster (Jb. xli), creatures which, in the prophetic books, served to typify the God-opposing powers (see, e.g., Is. xxvii. 1, li. 9; Ezk. xxxii. 2f., etc.).

The details of the sea monster are drawn from Dn. vii. We learn from Rev. xvii. 5, 9 that it represents the power of Rome, the *seven heads* being a succession of Emperors and the *ten horns* ten allied kings (xvii. 12); the names *of blasphemy* are the divine titles claimed by Roman sovereigns. The characteristics of leopard, bear and lion in Dn. vii. 4–6 were shared out among three prior Empires. Here they combine in one terrifying unity of power and wickedness, the leopard signifying cruelty and cunning, the bear strength, the lion ferocity. One of the heads was 'smitten unto death; and his death-stroke was healed' (3, RV). Clearly the reference is to the death of one of the Emperors. But of whom is it said that the death-stroke was healed, the Emperor in question or the Empire of which he was a part? Gunkel believed the latter, for a monster suffering from the loss of one of its heads has itself received a mortal blow; the historical reference could then be to the murder of Julius Caesar, whose death endangered the security of the Empire (*one of his heads* in John's Hebraic Greek could mean 'the first of his heads'). Most expositors are inclined to interpret the healing of the death-stroke as of the head (Emperor) in question, who is then identified with the beast itself (as in verses 12, 14 and 17). That could only mean that one of the Emperors was to rise from the dead and sum up in himself the character of the devil-inspired Empire. Precisely that was being asserted of Nero at the time of the writing of this book; for though he committed suicide in A.D. 68, it was widely believed he would return to lead the eastern powers against Rome. See further on xvii. 8, 11, and note IXd on the anti-Christian Empire.

The world worships both the devil and the false Christ who sums up in himself the characteristics of the Empire (4). The *mouth speaking great things* (5) is asserted of the anti-God power in Dn. vii. 8, 20. For the *forty and two months* cf. xi. 2, 3, xii. 14. During this time the beast is said to be given authority *to continue*, i.e. to act wickedly; cf. Dn. viii. 12, xi. 36. Note that, although the dragon gave the beast his authority over the earth, the real permission for his blasphemous utterances and deeds, and even the duration of his reign, comes from God; see also verses 7, 10, 14, 15. The sovereignty of God is never more apparent than during the rule of Antichrist. Cf. verse 6 with 2 Thes. ii. 4, and verse 7 with Dn. vii. 21. The reference of the words *from the foundation of the world* (8) is uncertain; they can be linked with the slaying of the Lamb, as in AV and RV, or with the writing of the saints' names in the book of life, as in RV mg. Both meanings are equally true; for the former cf. 1 Pet. i. 19, 20, for the latter Eph. i. 4. The difficulty is settled for most by an appeal to xvii. 8, where almost identical language is used, connecting the phrase with the writing in the book. Nevertheless the word order is decidedly against this interpretation, unless it were true that the book as we have it is a translation from John's original writing. The AV rendering is preferable to the RV in verse 10; the Church is assured that justice will be meted out to the oppressors and murderers of earth. There is, however, a third reading current, differing from both the AV and RV, viz., 'If any man is for captivity, into captivity he goeth: if any man must be killed with the sword, with the sword must he be killed.' The sense is thereby wholly changed, expressing the resignation that Christians are to adopt in face of possible incarceration or martyrdom. This accords closely with Je. xv. 2, xliii. 11, and is perhaps to be preferred. If the AV is followed, the statement is made up by a combination of the utterances of Jeremiah referred to and Mt. xxvi. 52.

A second beast comes to the aid of the first as his prophet. *He had two horns like a lamb* (11), simulating the character of Christ, but his words were devilish; cf. Mt. vii. 15. That the second beast *causeth the earth . . . to worship the first beast* (12) seems to indicate that this figure represents the priesthood of the cult of the Emperor. It is later called 'the false prophet' (xv. 13, xix. 20, xx. 10). Yet as the seven-headed, ten-horned beast signifies the anti-Christian Empire embodied in a personal Antichrist, it is likely that this heathen priesthood is also represented in a supreme head that directs its devilish work. Such an interpretation agrees with the later statements that the false prophet and Antichrist are thrown 'alive' into the lake of fire (xix. 20, xx. 10), for it is doubtful that in such contexts one beast represents an individual and the other a corporate body. Those passages, in fact, may imply that the false prophet is a demonic being like the Antichrist. Heathen priests had little compunction in resorting to tricks, such as the production of fire, apparently from heaven (13), and by ventriloquism to make an idol talk (15). It is possible, however, that John means that the miracles wrought by the false prophet will be genuine. It is a recognized feature of Christian prophecy of the Antichrist; cf. Mk. xiii. 22; 2 Thes. ii. 9. The mark of the beast (16) on non-Christian people is a counterpart of the seal of God on Christians (vii. 1–8); they both serve to show one's allegiance, whether to God or the devil. If the two designations are intended to denote spiritual qualities as well as a means of external identification, they hint that character tends to exclude influences not in accord with it— in the case of believers, Satanic influences, in the case of unbelievers, the gracious operations of the Holy Spirit. A man becomes increasingly in the image of his master. The immediate effect of receiving the mark of the beast consists in the social ostracism of those who refuse it. It involves nothing less than the proclamation by the State of economic warfare against the Church (17).

The mark of the beast reproduced either his name or the number formed by adding together the numerical values represented by the letters of his name (in Greek and Hebrew there are no separate numerals, the letters of the alphabet have to serve this purpose also). Six hundred and sixty-six is his number. The solutions of this riddle amount to almost as many. Gunkel and many others insist that it does not represent the name of an individual; the phrase *it is the number of a man* (18) simply means 'it is a human computation' in distinction from a supernatural reckoning (cf. xxi. 17). Such interpreters frequently regard the number as a symbol for the constant falling short of perfection by Antichrist, since each digit is one less than seven; it is pointed out that the Sibylline Oracles (i. 328) remarks that the number of the name of Jesus is 888, one better than perfection. Gunkel himself does not accept this suggestion, but thinks the number serves to identify the Roman Empire with the chaos monster, from which the portrait of the dragon and the beast is drawn in this book ('Primal Chaos' in Hebrew equals 666). The idea has been unduly minimized on the ground that John's readers could hardly have stumbled on such a remote solution, since they knew only Greek. Accordingly the modern exegete favours instead the solution 'Nero Caesar', written defectively in Hebrew! But if the former would be unintelligible to Greek-speaking people, so would the latter, even though 'Nero Caesar' transcribed in Hebrew from a Latin spelling gives the alternative number 616 which is found in some MSS. Clement's suggestion 'The Latin kingdom', written in Greek, is attractive; not only does it give the required 666, but 'The Italian kingdom' gives the alternative 616.

Strange as it may appear, it is not impossible that all the above solutions may be right. It is likely that since John used a Hebrew source in this chapter, the original name was a Hebrew one and the number was not invented by him. As he knew the chaos myth and was a Hebrew, the name *Tehom Qadmonah*, 'Primal Chaos', would not be beyond him. Further it is suggested in our interpretation of xvii. 8, 11 that the prophet fused the myths of the chaos monster and Nero Redivivus to form his picture of the Antichrist; the adversaries of the Church so perfectly embodied the ancient power of evil that they could both be described under the same historical summary, viz. they were and are not, and are about to come up out of the abyss, and go into perdition. A number, therefore, which could denote that evil principle as well as the Empire and individual in which it should be incarnated was more than heart could wish for, a perfect representation of devilry.

c. The 144,000 on Mount Zion (xiv. 1–5)

The purpose of this, and the following visions of this chapter, is to strengthen Christians for the trials implied in the preceding account of Antichrist's reign. The identity of the 144,000 seems determined by vii. 1–8 and v. 9, 10. John would hardly represent two different groups by such an extraordinary and obviously symbolical number, especially when he adds that both companies bear the mark of God in their foreheads (vii. 3, 4, xiv. 1). The multitude is defined as they *which were redeemed from the earth* (3), an echo of the description of the Church in v. 9. Further, they are said to be standing on Mount Zion (1), i.e. the heavenly Jerusalem of the millennial age (xxi. 9f.); this also conforms to the song of thanksgiving in v. 10, but it represents an advance on the previous picture of the 144,000 where this multitude is still on earth (vii. 1–8) and afterwards viewed in heaven, though not yet entered upon their kingly privileges (vii. 9–17). We therefore take this vision to portray the Church possessing the advent glory of Christ in the millennial age.

The theme of the Lamb and the heavenly Jerusalem found in this chapter is expanded in xxi. 9f. The name written on the foreheads of the Christians (1) explains the nature of the 'seal' spoken of in vii. 1–8. The angelic hosts sang 'a new song' (v. 9) but only the 144,000 could learn this one (3); evidently it deals with the experience of redemption, which only saved sinners could know. Our interpretation of this verse is conditioned by our identification of this company with that in chapter vii; it is impossible, therefore, to regard it as numbering unmarried men only. It seems best to interpret the language of verse 4 as symbolic, denoting the spiritual purity of men and women who form the bride of Christ (cf. 2 Cor. xi. 2). Such terms are not inapt in a vision portraying the glorified Church with her Lord in the heavenly Jerusalem; see xxi. 9f. If *aparchē* is to be rendered here *firstfruits*, the latter part of the verse connects with such Scriptures as Jas. i. 18; 2 Thes. ii. 13, RV mg.; but it could be translated by its usual LXX meaning 'sacrifice', for such a thought is peculiarly apt in this prophecy of the testimony, suffering and martyrdom of Christ's chosen ones.

d. The day of wrath (xiv. 6–20)

The succession of short oracles in this section is unified by the use of six angels, who announce the judgment and carry it out. Equally with the former vision it is intended to strengthen the Christian's nerve, the one vision being a requital of good, the other a requital of evil works.

i. **The first angel (xiv. 6, 7).** A last warning is given to unbelieving men. All the nations are summoned to repentance and the worship of God. The message is called an 'eternal gospel',

for the eternal blessings of the good news still remain for those who will respond. This oracle seems to record the final fulfilment of Mk. xiii. 10.

ii. **The second angel (xiv. 8).** The fall of *Babylon* is recounted at greater length in chapter xviii. This symbolic name for Rome appears in 1 Pet. v. 13, the Sibylline Oracles v. 143, 159 and 2 Baruch xi. 1.

iii. **The third angel (xiv. 9–13).** This is a warning that forms a complement to the preaching of the eternal gospel in verses 6, 7. For the unmixed cup (not 'watered down') cf. Ps. lxxv. 8. For the fire and brimstone cf. Is. xxxiv. 8–10, which itself is reminiscent of Gn. xix. 24, 25. *The patience of the saints* (12) finds an additional spur in the contemplation of the awful doom of the worshippers of the beast, just as the knowledge that some of them will be called to suffer incarceration and death gives a like stimulus (xiii. 10). The benediction on *the dead which die in the Lord* (13) serves the same purpose; Christians who face the prospect of suffering for the sake of the name know that they shall rest in the company of their Lord and receive a recompense for their faithfulness.

iv. **The fourth angel (xiv. 14–16).** It is common to regard these verses as depicting the gathering of the Church by Christ at His coming and verses 18–20 as the gathering of the unbelieving world for judgment; it is possible that this is the true reading of the passage, especially in view of the use of the phrase *one like unto the* (RV 'a') *son of man* in verse 14 (cf. i. 13). Yet it seems strange that Christ should be commanded by an angel to perform His saving work. His description, too, lacks the splendour of the visions of the Lord in i. 12f. and xix. 11f. It seems better, accordingly, to regard the humanlike form as an angel, sharing something of the glory of Christ like the 'strong angel' of x. 1. The reaping of the wheat and gathering of grapes then represent one all-inclusive act of judgment as in Joel iii. 13, on which these two visions are based. For the reaping of earth by angelic instrumentality cf. Mt. xiii. 41, 42.

v. **The fifth angel (xiv. 17).** Observe that the angel here who also had a sharp sickle *came out of the temple* as did the fourth angel.

vi. **The sixth angel (xiv. 18–20).** This angel who commands the vine-gatherer to reap the ripe grapes of the earth *came out from the altar*, and is named, he that hath *power over fire*. This links up with vi. 9–11, viii. 1–5, ix. 13, xvi. 7, and exemplifies once more the connection between the sacrifice of God's saints and the advent of the kingdom. The symbolism of the messianic judgment (19, 20) as a treading of grapes goes back to Is. lxiii. 3. The city outside which the treading of the winepress takes place is presumably the world-city, 'Babylon the great' (see xi. 8, xviii. 2).

VIII. THE SEVEN BOWLS. xv. 1—xvi. 21

The bowls are said to initiate 'plagues, which are the last, for in them is finished the wrath of God'

(1, RV). This is often linked with the fact that no description was given of the seventh trumpet, although it brought the end (xi. 15); it is then suggested that the contents of the bowls consist of events consequent upon the sounding of the last trumpet. This is possible. It should be noticed, however, that the contents of the seven bowls are very similar to those of the seven trumpets; in most cases the difference appears to lie in the amplification of the earlier plagues by the later. The second and third bowls, for example, seem simply to reveal that the second and third trumpet plagues have increased in extent. The fourth trumpet affects the sun in one way, the fourth bowl in another (viii. 12, xvi. 8). The fifth and sixth trumpets have an extraordinary correspondence with the fifth and sixth bowls (ix. 1–21, xvi. 10–16). The earthquake after the seventh trumpet seems to be that consequent on the seventh bowl, only more fully described (xi. 19, xvi. 17f.). Thus the bowls give a fuller revelation of what had already been shown under the trumpet judgments, together with certain new features. As to the conquerors by the glassy sea (2), their song celebrates the approaching conversion of the nations consequent on the completion of the 'righteous acts' of God (4, RV); the vision therefore exults in the effects of the last plagues rather than heralds their coming; it is proleptic and serves to underline the statement of verse 1, 'in them is finished the wrath of God' (RV).

a. Visions introductory to the bowls (xv. 1–8)

This chapter consists of two separate visions, the former portraying the Christian confessors who had emerged triumphantly from the great distress (2–4), the latter telling of the appearance from the heavenly temple of seven angels bearing the bowls of plagues (5–8). Verse 1 serves as a superscription for chapters xv—xvi. It supplies a pictorial equivalent of the more formal prophetic utterance, 'The vision (or burden) of the last plagues'. The judgments are the *last* inasmuch as they culminate what has gone before and include the final blows against the wickedness of a devil-inspired generation.

i. The first vision (xv. 2–4). The glassy sea is *mingled with fire* because of impending judgment. The confessors have defied *the beast*, refused to adore *his image* and abjured the mark which is *the number of his name* (2). *The song of Moses . . . and the song of the Lamb* is one, recalling the triumph song of the Israelites on the shore of the Red Sea (Ex. xv). The name of Moses is conjoined with that of Christ because a similar, though greater, deliverance has been wrought from a similar, though greater, foe. The comparison of final redemption with the exodus is common in the prophets (cf. Is. li. 9–11). Every line of the song is reminiscent of the prophets and psalmists: *Great and marvellous are thy works* (cf. Ps. cxi. 2, xcviii. 1, cxxxix. 14); *just and true are thy ways* (cf. Ps. cxlv. 17; Dt. xxxii. 4); *King of Saints* (RV mg., 'of nations'). *Who shall not fear thee . . . ?* (3, 4; cf. Je. x. 7); *all nations shall come . . .* (4; cf. Ps. lxxxvi. 9); 'thy righteous acts have been made manifest' (RV; cf. Is. xxvi. 9; Ps. xcviii. 2). The approach and worship of the nations seem to anticipate their conversion in the millennium.

ii. The second vision (xv. 5–8). The tabernacle was called 'the tent of the testimony' (Nu. ix. 15) as the ark containing the tablets of the covenant was kept therein. Since the ark was later housed in the temple, the temple itself was sometimes called a tabernacle (Ps. lxxxiv. 1, 2; Ezk. xli. 1). Here, accordingly, the second clause is to be rendered 'the temple, namely the tabernacle of the testimony in heaven, was opened'. It emphasizes that the judgments about to be executed are the expression of God's righteousness. RV says the angels were 'arrayed with precious stone, pure and bright', instead of *pure and white linen* as AV. But the Greek words for 'stone' (*lithon*) and 'linen' (*linon*) are very similar, so that it is hard to tell which is right. See, however, Ezk. xxviii. 13. The golden bowls, as containers of the wrath of God, may have been prompted by the frequent Old Testament use of 'cup' to denote God's measure of judgment on sinners (cf. xiv. 9, 10). *The temple was filled with smoke from the glory of God* (8). For similar occasions of this phenomenon in the Old Testament see Ex. xl. 35; 2 Ch. vii. 2, 3; Is. vi. 4; Ezk. x. 4, xliv. 4.

b. The seven bowls described (xvi. 1–21)

i. The first bowl (xvi. 2). The plague of the first bowl has no counterpart in those of the trumpets, but like several of the latter it recalls the Egyptian plagues (cf. Ex. ix. 10, 11).

ii. The second bowl (xvi. 3). Cf. the first Egyptian plague (Ex. vii. 17f.). Whereas the second trumpet affected a third of the sea (viii. 8), this spreads through all seas.

iii. The third bowl (xvi. 4–7). The same Egyptian plague is in mind. Cf. the third trumpet (viii. 10, 11). Note in verse 5 the divergence of texts followed by AV and RV. There may be a double thrust here (6). To be drunk with blood in the Old Testament signifies slaughter by the sword; cf. Is. xlix. 26. The altar concurs in this judgment; cf. vi. 10 and xiv. 15–18n.

iv. The fourth bowl (xvi. 8, 9). The fourth bowl stands in contrast to the fourth trumpet (viii. 12); but see verses 10 and 11.

v. The fifth bowl (xvi. 10, 11). The fifth bowl sends darkness on Antichrist's Empire; cf. Ex. x. 21 and the darkness over a third part of earth after the fourth trumpet. Charles suggests that the excessive pain of this plague is due to the demon locusts of the fifth trumpet, whose appearance, coinciding with smoke from the abyss, darkened the sky, and which caused torments to the adherents of the beast (ix. 1–6); such an interpretation would accord with the relation of the trumpets and bowls outlined in the introduction to chapters xv—xvi.

vi. The sixth bowl (xvi. 12–16). The sixth trumpet also affects the Euphrates (cf. ix. 13f.), a matter that can hardly be coincident. But while the sixth trumpet brings forth demonic hosts, the sixth bowl prepares for the invasion of the Empire by *the kings of the east* (12; RV 'from the sunrising'). These latter are further described in xvii. 12, 13; they put themselves at Antichrist's behest (xvii. 17), ravage the harlot city and war with the Lamb (xvii. 14). Cf. verse 15 with iii. 3. If this is the original position of this verse, the warning is not without point (cf. Mt. xxiv. 43f.; 1 Thes. v. 2, 4). There are seven benedictions in this book: cf. i. 3, xiv. 13, xix. 9, xx. 6, xxii. 7, 14. The signification of *Armageddon* (16) is unknown. The usual translation 'Mountain of Megiddo' can hardly be correct for there is no mountain at Megiddo. Conjectural derivations from Hebrew (such as *har migdo*, 'his fruitful mountain', i.e. Jerusalem) are hardly to the point, since John's readers knew no Hebrew. It is possible that neither John nor his friends attempted any explanation of the name; it was used not so much to designate a place as an occasion, viz. the last well-known uprising of the wicked that issues in the establishment of the kingdom of God.

vii. The seventh bowl (xvi. 17–21). The seventh bowl is poured on *the air* (17), conveying the notion of something even more portentous than the havoc wrought on the 'earth' (2) or 'sea' (3) or 'waters' (4) or 'sun' (8); it signifies the final blow against the forces of evil, both human and satanic (Eph. ii. 2). Hence the voice (of God?) proclaims *It is done* (17). Cf. 'It is finished' (Jn. xix. 30) and see Rev. xxi. 6. In verses 18 and 19 is given at last the meaning of the lightnings, etc., that followed the seventh trumpet (xi. 19) and seventh seal (viii. 5); they accomplish the destruction of the anti-Christian civilization. Through the earthquake (cf. vi. 12) the great city was rent into three parts. A hyperbolic description of the magnitude of the earthquake is given in verse 20. The size of the hailstones (21) befits the terrifying proportions of this last shaking of the heavens and earth (Hg. ii. 21); a talent weighs about a hundredweight. The Egyptians endured a plague of great hailstones (Ex. ix. 24), an alliance of armies pursued by Joshua was routed by them in Beth-horon (Jos. x. 11), while the hosts of Gog were to expect a like fate (Ezk. xxxviii. 22); this event eclipses all such descriptions. It subdues men, but it does not lead them to repentance. The ultimate issues of these happenings are given in greater detail in chapters xvii—xix.

IX. THE FALL OF BABYLON. xvii. 1—xix. 21

These three chapters expand the visions of the sixth and seventh bowls (xvi. 12–21). xvii. 1—xix. 10 are largely concerned with the fate of the Empire (i.e. the seventh bowl); xix. 11–21 recounts in fuller measure the destruction of Antichrist and his followers (the sixth bowl). Chapter xvii explains the situation that leads up to the doom of God's enemies, with especial reference to the anti-Christian kingdom (xviii) and at the same time sheds light on certain obscurities in chapter xiii.

a. A vision of Babylon in her glory (xvii. 1–6)

The angel's words to John could form a fitting title to chapters xvii and xviii: *The judgment of the great whore that sitteth upon many waters.* As chapter xvii describes the circumstances of her downfall, the promise in the title is not actually fulfilled until chapter xviii. The city of Tyre is called a harlot by Isaiah (xxiii. 16, 17), as also is Nineveh by Nahum (iii. 4f.), while the latter part of verse 2 quotes Jeremiah's description of Babylon (li. 7), just as that latter city was addressed by the prophet as 'thou that dwellest upon many waters' (Je. li. 13). From verse 9 it is clear that Rome is in John's mind. In this description, therefore, as in the apocalyptic figure of verse 3, he teaches that this Empire includes in itself the wickedness of all its predecessors. The beast that represents the Empire is similarly portrayed as the dragon (cf. xii. 3), thereby showing its affinity with it. The symbol of a woman sitting on *a scarlet coloured beast* (3) originally denoted a unity, the beast being an earlier, the woman a later, representation of one and the same chaos monster. For John, however, it forms a suitable picture to illustrate the relationship between the capital city and the Empire. At first sight it appears strange that in verse 1 the harlot *sitteth upon many waters*, whereas in verse 3 she dwells in a *wilderness*. The explanation may be that John is recalling Isaiah's prophecy against Babylon, the title of which is 'the oracle of the wilderness of the sea' (Is. xxi. 1); it is noteworthy that the LXX omits the last three words. The luxury and moral filth of the city are here vividly set forth, again with the aid of Jeremiah's characterization of Babylon. The exhibition of the name on the harlot's forehead (5) probably alludes to the custom of Roman harlots who similarly displayed their names on their brows. The prefix *MYSTERY* could be a part of the inscription; but it is more likely that it shows the name is not to be taken literally (cf. xi. 8, 'the great city which spiritually is called Sodom and Egypt'). Moffatt translates 'by way of symbol'. The title serves to characterize the tyrant city as of the same nature as that against which the old prophets so vehemently prophesied; it is the 'MOTHER OF THE HARLOTS (or HARLOTRIES, Vulg. and Primasius) AND OF THE ABOMINATIONS (i.e. IDOLATRIES) OF THE EARTH' (5, RV). Rome brought about the moral ruin of the whole Empire. The allusion in verse 6 includes not only the Neronic persecution, but also the general custom of taking martyrs to Rome to die in the amphitheatre.

b. The vision explained: Babylon's doom (xvii. 7–18)

The interpretation of this section is rendered difficult by a fluctuation in the symbolism. In verses 10 and 11 the beast is said to incarnate itself in a king who once lived and reappears as the last Emperor of an unholy succession; i.e. he is an individual. Yet it is clear that verses 1–6 speak of a city and Empire, not an individual or even a line of rulers (Emperors are only heads, not the whole beast). With this agree verses 9, 10, the seven hills denoting the city of Rome, the head-quarters of the anti-Christian Empire. Since the use of the beast with seven heads and ten horns to represent the godless persecuting world-power is traditional, it is almost certain that John is drawing on prior sources rather than composing something wholly original (cf. chapter xii); this may account for some of the ambiguity. Most expositors interpret verse 8 with the aid of verse 11 and consider that the entire passage describes an individual Antichrist; the expression *was, and is not, and yet is* (i.e. about to come) in verse 8 is felt to be wholly explicable by the myth of the resuscitated Nero, whose return from the dead to fight against Rome was widely expected when this book was written. With this expectation verses 16 and 17 fit in admirably.

There is, however, another possible line of interpretation. It is admitted by all that verses 1–6 portray the Empire, not an individual. If John used an earlier writing in compiling verses 7–18 that source also referred to the beast as the Empire. It is thus not improbable that the Christian prophet also had the Empire particularly in view. If so verse 8a is to be explained primarily not of Nero resurrected but of the Empire. From such Scriptures as Is. xxvii. 1, xxx. 7, li. 9, 10 it is clear that the Old Testament prophets deliberately applied the symbol of the 'chaos monster' to the nations hostile to Israel, especially to Egypt, but not alone to that power. God had conquered that monster in the beginning. It is lying dormant for the time being (cf. Is. xxx. 7, rv), but it is about to strike again. At such a time God would destroy it once and for all. 'The beast that was, and is not, and is about to come up out of the abyss, and to go into perdition' (cf. Is. xxvii. 1) thus describes this monster by outlining its history. A reasonable solution appears to be that John here fused two symbols to convey his message, that of the chaos monster and that of Nero Redivivus. The beast is the power of evil, manifesting itself throughout history in the godless Empires, but now in the Roman Empire. Thus far it has lain more or less dormant; shortly it will rise from its recumbency and reveal itself in a fury of wickedness, incarnating itself in the resurrected Nero. With this key to the passage in mind, we may attend to its details.

The explanation given by the angel (7) is a direct continuation of the preceding vision; it tells whom the woman and the beast represent. It is to be expected, therefore, that the interpretation will involve more than one member of the beast. The beast *was, and is not* (8); i.e. it had an existence as an evil and anti-God power before, but has been silenced. Isaiah calls Egypt 'Rahab that sitteth still' (Is. xxx. 7), i.e. the chaos monster, rendered helpless by God. Rome is given a similar name here, it *was, and is not*, but *yet is*, i.e. shortly it is about to come up out of the abyss and achieve a work of horror like the Pharaohs, the Assyrian kings and Antiochus Epiphanes of old. Nevertheless it is to go into perdition—the chaos monster cannot triumph over God, neither can Rome. As verse 11 relates this to Nero about to come again to earth, we may take it that the full possession by Rome of the characteristics of the chaos monster can be only when it incarnates itself in the returned Nero. This demonic king so fully shares the nature of the power of evil that their history can be delineated in the same terms. He is the beast incarnate. Such a fearful manifestation of supernatural power causes all on earth to wonder, except those whose names are written in the book of life. A dual interpretation of the seven heads is given so as to identify the beast beyond doubt. Rome was familiarly known as 'the city of the seven hills'. The beast is thus located in Rome. But the heads represent kings. Whatever the number *seven* may have meant to earlier writers, to John it was a symbol of completeness; *five are fallen* (10) means the majority have passed; the *one is* refers to the contemporary sovereign; another Emperor will reign but *when he cometh he must continue a* 'little while' (10); the short duration of his rule is enforced by the consideration that 'the time is at hand' (i. 3).

After the last human Emperor the beast will reveal itself in all its bestiality. *The beast that was, and is not* (8) is the age-long power of evil; he will show himself as the eighth king, yet not in reality an eighth, for he will manifest himself in the form of one of the seven, i.e. Nero. In the context of verses 9 and 10 it seems that the statement 'the beast . . . is himself also an eighth' (11, rv) must mean that the whole Empire, or rather the evil genius that characterizes the Empire, incarnates itself in the eighth king. The emphasis is on the Empire in its entirety. It must not be read as 'The beast Nero is an eighth king, as well as one of the seven'; the descriptive clause *was, and is not* denotes the chaos monster Empire in the first instance, and only secondarily Nero. When, however, the beast is said to 'come up out of the abyss', the emphasis is on the person who is its embodiment.

The ten kings confederate with Antichrist (12) may be rulers of satellite states or governors of provinces. Bousset suggests, with less probability, they may be demonic powers of a like nature to their leader. The ultimate fate of the ten kings is immediately recounted so as to complete their description (14). Logically this verse should follow 17 after the narration of their part in the destruction of the Empire. Some commentators, accordingly, transfer it to that place. But apocalyptists do not always keep to a strictly logical sequence. This verse really anticipates xix. 19f.; if from one point of view it is superfluous in this vision, from another its position here is fully intelligible. Its meaning is either that they that are with Him, called and chosen and faithful (14), will share in this conquest of Antichrist and his helpers, or that they, as well as the Lamb, will conquer Antichrist in their moral life (cf. xii. 11).

While the waters of Babylon were literally meant in Jeremiah's prophecy (see note on verse 1) the prophet regards them as aptly symbolizing the peoples over which Rome rules (15). Antichrist, with his confederates, will help in the destruction of Rome, which is otherwise accomplished by the great earthquake (xvi. 19). Both modes of destruction are due to the active providence of God. The language of verse 16 is drawn from Ezekiel's description of the chastisement of Israel (Ezk. xxiii. 25–29). No explanation is given why the anti-Christian ruler turns against the anti-Christian city. The popular Nero story expected him to arise solely to overwhelm the Empire; yet this whole chapter, and xiii, 5 explicitly, assumes that he will first rule over the Empire and with its aid rage against the works of God for three and a half years. This procedure well illustrates John's method of freely adapting his sources in order to convey the message God has given him for the instruction of His saints. The woman is Rome (18), the mistress of the world of John's day.

c. A dirge upon Babylon (xviii. 1–24)

This chapter is modelled on the doom songs of the Old Testament prophets over the hostile nations of their times. So reminiscent is it of these that it may be said to summarize all prophetic oracles on the doom of unrighteous peoples. The prophecies against Babylon (Is. xiii, xxi, xlvii; Je. 1, li) and Tyre (Ezk. xxvi, xxvii) appear to have been especially in John's mind. The glory of this angel (1) is described in words used by Ezekiel of the Shekinah returning to the restored temple (Ezk. xliii. 2). For similar portrayals of angelic splendour cf. x. 1f. and xiv. 14. *Babylon the great is fallen, is fallen* (2) is a quotation of Is. xxi. 9. For the rest of the verse cf. Is. xiii. 21, 22. Strictly speaking this picture is inconsistent with xix. 3; it is not impossible that John deliberately mixes his symbolism, expecting his readers to exercise caution in interpreting it. Cf. both verses with Is. xiii. 19–22. In verse 3 some expositors prefer an alternative reading to the word 'fallen' (RV), reading *pepōtiken* (caused to drink; cf. AV) instead of *peptōkan* (have fallen). The first clause then becomes 'For she made all the nations to drink of the wine of the wrath of her fornication'; it lays to Rome's charge the responsibility for the corruption of the whole earth. Cf. verse 4 with Je. li. 6, 45; Is. lii. 11; also verse 5 with Je. li. 9; and verse 6 with Je. xvi. 18, l. 29; Is. xl. 2. Is the cry of verse 6 directed to the avenging armies of Antichrist and his allies? See xvii. 12, 13, 16, 17. Rome's judgment is to be proportionate to her self-glorification, wantonness and pride; cf. Is. xlvii. 7–9. It is possible that in verse 8, as in vi. 8, *thanatos* should be translated

by 'pestilence' rather than by *death*. We may also translate *penthos* by 'calamity' instead of *mourning*, so making the three plagues 'pestilence and calamity and famine'. The destruction by fire is performed by the invading hosts under Antichrist; cf. xvii. 16.

The lamentation over Babylon is uttered by the kings of the earth (9, 10), the merchants of the earth (11–17a) and the shipowners and sailors (17b–19). John is here particularly indebted to Ezekiel's doom song upon Tyre (Ezk. xxvi, xxvii). Note that the *kings of the earth* (9) are those mentioned in xvii. 18, not those in alliance with the beast (xvii. 16, 17). Cf. Ezk. xxvi. 16, 17. The substance of each lamentation is the same, viz., *in one hour is thy judgment come* (10; see verses 17, 19).

With verse 11 cf. the list of merchant nations that traded with Tyre (Ezk. xxvii. 12–24) and their astonishment and fear (Ezk. xxvii. 35, 36). Verses 12 and 13 furnish a list of goods sold by the merchants to Rome. Cf. the imports of Tyre (Ezk. xxvii. 12–24). *Thyine wood* (12) came from North Africa and was especially used for making expensive tables. *Ivory* was popular among Romans both for decorating furniture and ornaments. *Cinnamon* is an aromatic spice, *amōmon*, translated *odours* (13) or 'spice' (RV), was a fragrant plant from India, used for making costly hair unguent. *Chariots* here are of a special kind (Gk. *rhedai*), having four wheels, often expensively decorated. Two words are used here for slaves: *sōmata*, 'bodies', and *psychai anthrōpōn*, 'souls of men', the latter phrase occurring in Ezk. xxvii. 13. Perhaps John employed both terms to express his abhorrence at so brutal a system that crushed men's bodies and souls alike.

Swete observes that while the kings lament over Babylon for the strength that has departed (10), the merchants think mainly of the wealth that has vanished; so also the mariners in verse 19.

The appeal to heaven and the Church to rejoice over the judgment of Babylon (20), forming a strong contrast to the foregoing lamentations, appears to come from the prophet himself. Whether it is meant as such or no, xix. 1–7 forms a fitting response to the cry. The symbolic action of the angel (21–24) is suggested by a like one performed over Babylon by Jeremiah (li. 63, 64). *Mousikōn*, translated *musicians* (22), RV 'minstrels', should be rendered 'singers' as in Test. Judah xxiii. 2. The sentence recalls Ezk. xxvi. 13. The clauses that follow, describing the cessation of crafts, industry, the joys of marriage, and all means of illumination, reproduce Je. xxv. 10 but in a different order. *Thy merchants were the great men of the earth* (23) was first spoken by Isaiah concerning Tyre (xxiii. 8). It is adduced as a reason for Rome's judgment because, to judge from verse 3, its merchants fostered the 'wantonness' of the city, and that out of sheer greed, and so were themselves bound up with the luxurious vice of Rome. Isaiah had already commented on the sorceries of the original Babylon (xlvii. 12), and Nahum brought a similar charge against Nineveh (iii. 4). The *sorceries* (23) here inveighed against may be taken in the literal sense of witchcraft, but more likely it represents 'the witchery of gay and luxurious vice and its attendant idolatries, by which the world was fascinated and led astray' (Swete). Cf. verse 24 with Mt. xxiii. 35, wherein our Lord so accuses Jerusalem. John's statement is justified not only by the ferocious persecutions which he anticipated to arise in the great distress but also by his conception of Rome as the incarnation of the spirit of evil that has ever assaulted God's people (see notes on xvii. 7–18).

d. Notes on the anti-Christian Empire

One main question calls for consideration from the reading of chapters xiii, xvii and xviii. If Rome is the Empire of John's visions, are they not discredited, seeing that Rome subsequently was not destroyed but became a world centre of Christianity? There is, of course, no doubt at all that Rome was, indeed, the harlot city of John's visions. The prophet all but names it in xvii. 9, 18 and by his use of the mystic name Babylon (see notes on xiv. 8). Rome was, to John, the quintessence of the anti-God spirit manifested in earlier ages but now come to the full. As such it was the last Empire over which the devil should hold sway. The impending appearance of a personal Antichrist, who would embody its wickedness, was to be but a short-lived phenomenon. John seems to suggest that the messianic judgments would soon fall and the sway of Rome give place to the millennial reign.

Before passing judgment on this matter, it is necessary to recall that John's viewpoint in no way differs from that of his predecessors in the prophetic office. All the prophets looked for the overthrow of the oppressor nation of their day, followed by the establishment of the kingdom of God. Isaiah looked for the messianic deliverance to follow on God's judgment of Assyria (see, e.g., Is. x, xi), Habakkuk on the destruction of Babylon (Hab. ii. 2, 3). Jeremiah, Isaiah and Ezekiel all prophesied of the setting up of the kingdom after the return of the Jews under Cyrus (e.g. Je. xxix—xxxi; Is. xlix, li; Ezk. xxvi). Haggai, writing after that return, foretold the advent of the kingdom following the completion of the temple that was then in course of rebuilding (Hg. ii), while every vision of Daniel placed the end after the overthrow of Antiochus Epiphanes. Similarly in the New Testament the second coming of Christ appears to be expected in the not distant future (e.g. Rom. xiii. 11f.; 1 Cor. vii. 29f.; Heb. x. 37; Jas. v. 8; 1 Pet. iv. 7; 1 Jn. ii. 18; Rev. i. 3). Even our Lord places His teaching regarding His second advent side by side with His prophecies concerning the fall of Jerusalem (see Mk. xiii).

John was no exception to this rule. Revelations of the consummation of the age were given to him. They were not novel; they accorded with the faith of the rest of the Church, though they

formed an advance on it. The whole Church looked for a last rebellion under an Antichrist as the precursor of the end, and had no doubt as to the issue of the conflict. John saw that Rome was already playing the part of Antichrist. As the outcome of these tendencies was precisely that which the former prophets had spoken of, he applied his visions to his situation. Rome was the harlot city, a demonic Emperor was to be the personal Antichrist, and the priesthood of the Emperor's cult would supply the false prophet. The stage was set for the end and John described the drama. That the end did not come then does not invalidate the essence of his prophecy, any more than in the other prophets of whom we have spoken. The many Antichrists since John's day have increasingly approximated to his portrait and will culminate in one who will suit it perfectly.

What of John's picture of Antichrist himself? Many expositors understand his apparent reproduction of the Nero legend in a literal sense. It should be noted, however, that John has not employed this idea in isolation but has fused it with the Tiamat saga. The latter is used in a purely allegorical sense, as is apparent from the fact that the monster represents the devil, the Empire and the personal Antichrist in turn. That John gave the slightest credence to the original myth of the slaying of Tiamat by Marduk is out of the question, although he would almost certainly have known it. His ability to transform popular stories as a means for proclaiming the gospel is seen in his application of the World-Redeemer myth in chapter xii. In similar fashion he took over the legend of Nero's return from the dead as an excellent picture of Antichrist, but with no thought of declaring his belief in it; he simply says that Antichrist will be a devilish agent of a like order to the Nero of current expectation.

A consideration that clinches this point, for the present writer at least, is John's knowledge of a far earlier prophecy concerning one returning from death to take an active part in the End-time: Malachi had said that Elijah would come before the day of the Lord (Mal. iv. 5). John must have known how our Lord applied this prophecy to John the Baptist; he himself put it to an even wider use in applying it to the Church (chapter xi). It was therefore both simple and natural for him to represent Antichrist as working 'in the spirit and power of Nero' (cf. Lk. i. 17) by employing the story of 'Nero Redivivus' without further explanation; in view of the teaching about 'Elijah Redivivus', none further was necessary.

e. Thanksgiving for the judgment of Babylon (xix. 1–10)

The paeans of praise that thunder from heaven are inspired by the manifest justice of God in destroying the anti-Christian Empire, but they may also incidentally form a response to the exultant cry of the prophet in xviii. 20. This finds confirmation if we may regard the first thanksgiving as coming from the angelic host (cf. v. 11, 12); the responsive *Amen; Alleluia* (4) is then given by the twenty-four elders and four cherubim, followed by the pealing forth of the praises of the Church (6, 7); this corresponds to the sequence in John's call for rejoicing on the part of 'heaven, and ye saints, and ye apostles, and ye prophets' (xviii. 20, RV). It is a constant phenomenon of this book to set over against the revelation of God's righteous judgments on the wicked the worship of heaven and redeemed humanity, the theme of such worship usually being the judgments referred to: see, e.g., vii. 9f. after the seals; xi. 15f. after the trumpets; xiv. 1f. after the ravaging of Antichrist; xv. 2ff. in anticipation of the bowls. The statement that *salvation, and glory, and honour, and power* belong to our God (1), coming at this point, implies that God has manifested these attributes. The song therefore expands vii. 10 and has a similar meaning to xii. 10. *True and righteous are his judgments* (2) was said by the altar after the outpouring of the third bowl (xvi. 7, RV); cf. also xv. 3. The two great crimes of the harlot civilization were its corrupting of earth and murder of Christians.

If the new heaven and earth of xxi. 1f. is to be regarded as a completely new creation, the expression *for ever and ever* (3) must here be limited to the thousand years of the millennium; the ashes of the ruined city presumably disappear with the old earth. The employment of this and kindred phrases in biblical literature is often very loose (cf. especially the Psalms), but in such passages as iv. 9, v. 13, xi. 15, xxii. 5 it clearly means eternity; presumably it has this meaning in xiv. 11. The twenty-four elders and four living creatures endorse the thanksgiving of the angelic host (4; cf. v. 14). A voice *out of the throne* calls on the Church to join in this service of thanksgiving (5). As the four living creatures are closest to the throne, it is likely to be one of their number who so cries, certainly not Christ, who would never say *praise our God* (cf. iii. 12). The description of those called upon as *all ye his servants, and ye that fear him, both small and great* (5) excludes the possibility that a select body from the Church, such as the martyrs, is alone in view. The 'wife of the Lamb' (7) is the whole Church, not a section of it. The first line of the Church's thanksgiving should be rendered 'Hallelujah: for the Lord God the Almighty has begun to reign' (6; cf. xi. 17). The marriage symbol applied to Christ and the Church expresses the close and indissoluble union of Christ and His redeemed people. The marriage is said to have *come* (7) at this point in the same sense in which Babylon was said to have 'fallen' in xiv. 8; i.e. it is on the point of coming to pass. The Church is prepared. As soon as the beast and his armies are slain, the 'wedding' takes place and the bride begins her consummated life in the new age (xx. 4f., xxi. 9ff.). For the symbol of the Church as the Bride of Christ cf. Mt. xxii. 2f., xxv. 1f.; 2 Cor. xi. 2; Eph. v. 23f. Observe in verse 8, which is prob-

ably a comment of John rather than a part of the song, the delicate balance between the grace of God and human response: 'it was given to her that she should array herself in fine linen, bright and pure' (RV); i.e. the raiment comes from God; but the fine linen is the righteous acts of the saints. Cf. Phil. ii. 12, 13. For the varying shades of meaning conveyed by the symbolism of the vesture of the saints, cf. iii. 5, vi. 11 and notes.

They which are called (9), RV 'bidden', are conceived to have accepted the invitation, unlike those mentioned in Mt. xxii. 14. The guests and the bride are one; cf. xxii. 9, 10 where the bride is also the holy city. The angel's declaration *These are the true sayings of God* may relate particularly to the visions from xvii. 1 to this point, including the assurance of the coming of the marriage supper just alluded to. Cf. xxi. 6, which takes in the whole book. The angel refuses John's worship by numbering himself with the rest of God's servants (10). See note on xxii. 8, 9. The angelic hosts and the Church alike hold fast to *the testimony of* (i.e. borne by) *Jesus*. That testimony includes both the historic witness of the Lord, preserved by the Gospels, and that which He continues to impart by His Spirit, such as the revelations of this book. The explanatory clause that follows means either that the teaching of Christ made known in past and present is the *spirit* or essence (Moff. 'breath') of prophecy, or that the Holy Spirit who inspires prophecy interprets to the prophet Christ's testimony, both revealed and unrevealed. The former interpretation seems to fit the context better; the latter accords with Jn. xv. 26, 27.

f. The messianic judgment of Armageddon (xix. 11–21)

The name *Faithful and True* (11) recalls iii. 14. The rest of the verse appears to have Is. xi. 3–5 in view. Christ has *many crowns* (12; RV 'diadems') because He is KING OF KINGS, AND LORD OF LORDS (16): cf. 1 Macc. xi. 13. His unknown name (12) brings to mind the secret name He will bestow on His own after this event (ii. 17, and especially iii. 12). In view of these last two references it is unlikely that all created beings are excluded from knowing His name (as Swete believes). Bousset suggests that the fact of its secrecy may be bound up with the popular belief that power attaches to the knowledge of a name. If Christ's name carries with it power over all creation, then at present He is sole possessor of that power, He alone knows His name; but when He has vanquished His enemies at His coming He will share His authority with His faithful ones and therefore His name too. The background of this conception is admittedly non-Christian, as John would fully recognize; but the spiritual meaning it is made to yield by this interpretation does find acknowledgment throughout the New Testament. It is possible, therefore, that this is the meaning. The blood-spattered garment of the Lord is intended to remind the reader of Is. lxiii. 1–6. Christ is the heavenly vintager. If Bousset's interpretation of verse 12 is correct, the identification of the Messiah with *the Word of God* (13) does not reveal the secret of the unknown name. Its mention here alludes, perhaps, to the creative power of the Lord, conjuring up for us the Old Testament associations of 'the Word' (cf. also Wisdom xviii. 15).

The armies which were in heaven (14) certainly include angelic companies (cf. xii. 7, xiv. 14–20) and probably risen saints too (see xvii. 14 and note on ii. 27), though the saints' conquest referred to in xvii. 14 may only be their spiritual victory over the beast. On either view, the conquest is achieved primarily not by the following hosts but by the Lamb (cf. verses 15, 21). In view of xv. 4, xx. 3, which imply the existence of nations at the beginning of the millennium, it seems that only those peoples hostile to Christ are in mind in verses 15 and 19–21. For the imagery employed cf. i. 16; Is. xi. 4; Ps. ii. 9; Is. lxiii. 1–6.

Swete thinks that Christ's third name (16) is 'displayed on His habit where it falls over the thigh'. Since, however, some MSS omit the phrase *on his vesture and* while others simply omit *and*, it is possible that these words are a marginal note inserted to explain the text, and to show how the name could be observable on the Lord's thigh. Charles elucidates thus: 'The Seer sees in the vision the divine warrior and his heavenly horsemen—not halting but sweeping downwards from heaven and onwards against the serried armies of the beast, false prophet and the kings of the earth, and, as they thunder along, their garments stream behind them, and so on the thigh of the leader is disclosed the name: "King of Kings and Lord of Lords".' The angel's summons to the birds of prey (17) is drawn from Ezekiel's vision of the overthrow of Gog and Magog (xxix. 17–20). It is to be observed, however, that the actual assault of Gog and Magog does not take place till the end of the millennium (xx. 7–9); this accords with Ezekiel's vision, which places the last evil attack after the establishment of the messianic kingdom. The picture of a feast for birds of prey at the dawn of the kingdom may be a satirical allusion to the well-known comparison of the kingdom of God with the spreading of a banquet; see Is. xxv. 6; Lk. xiv. 15f., xxii. 30. No description in verses 19–21 is given of the battle, only the array of the contending hosts. There is evidently no real struggle; the Antichrist and his prophet are *cast alive into a lake of fire* (20) that burneth with brimstone and their armies slain with a sword of Christ (21). The *lake of fire*, while having ultimately a similar meaning to Gehenna (Valley of Hinnom, see Je. vii. 31), is a representation of hell developed from the conception of the abyss. In 1 Enoch xviii. 4f. it is said, 'I saw there something like an invisible cloud; for by reason of its depth I could not look over, and I saw a flame of fire blazing brightly. . . . And I

asked one of the holy angels who was with me and said unto him, "What is this shining thing? for it is not a heaven but only the flame of a blazing fire, and the voice of weeping and crying and lamentation and strong pain." And he said unto me, "This place which thou seest, here are cast the spirits of sinners and blasphemers, and of those who work wickedness".' If John uses symbols drawn from this circle of ideas, it is clear that he cannot imply the annihilation of those cast into the lake; cf. also Rev. xx. 10. The slaying of Antichrist's armies is the sword that came out of Christ's mouth is to be interpreted by xiv. 14–20, i.e. it is wholly judicial; cf. Is. xi. 4. Accordingly, such an interpretation as that of Swete, which makes the 'slaying' to be the annihilation of enmity against God in man (Eph. ii. 16) and the 'sword' to be the word of God that saves man (cf. Heb. iv. 12), so that Armageddon is in reality the conversion of the nations, is hardly to be received. The judgment here described appears to entail the physical destruction of those involved, their spirits presumably being despatched to Hades.

X. THE CONSUMMATED KINGDOM.
xx. 1—xxii. 5

Now that the judgments of God, described under the figures of seals, bowls and trumpets, have been completed (xv. 1) and the anti-Christian city, Empire ruler and false prophet have been destroyed (xvii—xix), and God has begun His rule (xix. 6), and the marriage of the Lamb has come (xix. 7), we expect that at last the long-awaited and constantly heralded kingdom will be manifested. Our expectation is not disappointed: the establishment and nature of this kingdom form the theme of the closing chapters of the book.

We see that it is a kingdom in time (xx. 4–6) and eternity (xxi. 1–5). Such was the usual interpretation of xx. 1—xxii. 5 by the early Church and such is the generally accepted opinion of modern scholarship. It has been challenged afresh in recent years by expositors who prefer the line of interpretation popularized by Augustine, that the millennium is the present Church age and the first resurrection the spiritual quickening of Christians by the Holy Spirit. Hendriksen, in his book *More Than Conquerors*, identifies the binding of Satan (xx. 1–3) with his ejection from heaven (xii. 9), the thousand years of the Church's power (xx. 4–6) with its time of triumphant witness (xi. 2–6, xii. 14f.), the onset of Gog and Magog (xx. 7–9) with the persecution of the Church by Antichrist (xi. 7f., xiii. 7f.), the ensuing destruction of those armies (xx. 9) with Armageddon (xvi. 14, xix. 19–21), and the last judgment (xx. 11–15) with the messianic judgment (xiv. 14f.).

This is a plausible and interesting reconstruction of John's visions, but the present writer feels that it can scarcely be maintained on close investigation. In xii. 9 Satan is cast out from heaven, where he may no longer exercise his function of accusing the saints before God, to earth, which is thenceforward his permitted sphere of operations; xx. 1–3 reveals an advance on this situation, for there he is taken from earth, which he may no longer corrupt, to the abyss, the abode of evil spirits and the penal section of Hades (ix. 1, xi. 7); on no account is it permissible to confuse the earth with the abyss. Satan's expulsion from heaven to earth is followed by a more intense activity on his part among the nations (xii. 12f., xiii. 1f.), but his imprisonment in the abyss renders him helpless with regard to them (xx. 3); while the former period is characterized as 'a short time' (xii. 12) the latter lasts a thousand years. The messianic judgment of xiv. 14f., coming as it does at the close of the parenthesis of chapters xii–xiv, may have no specific counterpart among the other visions of the book, but may simply picture the fact of Christ's judgment of earth at the end of the age. If a corresponding vision be sought for it, we should probably identify it with Armageddon (cf. xiv. 19, 20 with xix. 11–15, 21); in any case it is a judgment of the end-time, whereas xx. 11f. describes the judgment of all generations of history. Furthermore, it appears to be overlooked that xx. 1–3 is vitally linked with xix. 20, 21; the latter tells of the fate of the Antichrist and false prophet, the former continues without a break to narrate what happens to the one who inspires them; it is coincidence, and an unfortunate one, that the chapter division occurs at xix. 21. For the unity of this evil trinity in the events described in xix. 19—xx. 3 see xvi. 13–16. As xix. 11f. expands the earlier account of Armageddon, so it completes the picture by outlining the fate of each instigator of the battle. We conclude, therefore, that an impartial reading of these visions compels the recognition of a doctrine of the millennium in chapter xx.

To decide what are the limits of the description of the millennium is a much more difficult task. With Kelly, Zahn and Charles (writers of very different modes of thought), the present writer inclines to add xxi. 9—xxii. 5, 14, 15 to xx. 1–10 as relating to the millennial kingdom, and that for the following reasons. First, xxi. 24–27 describes the heavenly Jerusalem in terms that presuppose a continuation of earthly existence; nations receive blessing from the city, kings bring their glory to it, the unclean are denied access to it. This may be an employment of earthly figures to describe heavenly realities, but it seems more natural to read it as portraying the earthly kingdom of God, particularly if it be granted that that kingdom is expounded in chapter xx. Secondly, the leaves of the tree of life heal the nations (xxii. 2). This is comprehensible when applied to the millennium but strangely asserted of risen humanity existing in heavenly conditions. Thirdly, in connection with the imminence of Christ's return in glory (xxii. 10–13), a blessing is pronounced on those who have the right to come to the tree of life and enter the

city (xxii. 14), and a warning given that evil-doers will be kept outside the city (xxii. 15). Admittedly this could describe the good and evil in the eternal state, but it seems more probable that the wicked have no part in the new heaven and earth but are confined to 'the lake of fire'; the statement is much more feasible if it represents conditions in the millennium, and the confusion of symbols created by the former view is thereby avoided.

On the whole, therefore, it seems best to regard xxi. 1–5 as descriptive of the city of God in the new heaven and earth, but xxi. 9—xxii. 5 as portraying the city after its descent to earth in the millennial age. In that case, xx. 1—xxii. 5 forms a condensed and uninterrupted narrative of events from the coming of the Lord to the dawn of the timeless age, while xxi. 9ff. is a retrospect of the kingdom of God on earth. This view is not free from difficulties but it seems to do justice to the text better than the usual interpretation, which regards xxi. 1—xxii. 5 as wholly relating to the eternal state.

a. The binding of Satan (xx. 1–3)

For the *bottomless pit* (1), RV 'abyss', cf. ix. 1f., xi. 7. The conception of binding spirits and imprisoning them is adumbrated in Is. xxiv. 21–23. The idea played a great part in later Jewish literature: see especially Tobit viii. 3; 1 Enoch x. 4, 11, 12, lxxxviii. 1–3; Jubilees xxiii. 29; Test. Levi xviii. 12. In these books there is no question of this figure being used to denote the restricting of one from certain activities in the world while leaving him free in other respects; it signifies a complete removal as to a prison, usually in the depths of the underworld. Verse 7, accordingly, speaks of Satan's release at the end of the thousand years as a loosing *out of his prison*. The duration of the earthly kingdom of God for a thousand years appears elsewhere only in 2 Enoch xxxiii, a book of very uncertain date. There the history of the world is given as comprising seven thousand years, the first six thousand corresponding to the six days of creation, the last thousand forming a counterpart to the Sabbath. It is possible that John adopted the figure of a thousand years for the kingdom of God on earth rather to show its character as God's 'rest' for mankind than as determining its duration in time (cf. 2 Thes. i. 7; Heb. iv. 1f.; Acts iii. 19–21). It is one of the many instances in this portion of the book of the 'last' things being made like the 'first' (Ep. Barnabas vi. 13).

b. The millennium (xx. 4–6)

It will be observed that no description is here given of the conditions of life in the millennium, only a bare statement as to what sort of persons exercise rule in it. A characterization of the life of this era is provided in xxi. 9—xxii. 5. The *thrones* (4) seen by John recall Dn. vii. 9. But of whom is it said that *they sat upon them*? Most exegetes interpret them as the company immediately named, viz. *the souls of them that were beheaded*; it is then assumed that the further succeeding phrases also denominate this body, so that 'such as worshipped not the beast, neither his image, and received not the mark upon their forehead and upon their hand' (RV) denotes the martyrs only. This exposition is only partly correct, for we have already seen that participation in the kingdom is promised to every Christian that overcomes (see ii. 26–28, iii. 12, 21), while v. 9, 10 declares that the whole Church is to reign on earth, and xix. 7 rejoices that 'the marriage of the Lamb is come, and his wife hath made herself ready'. It is curious exegesis that makes the wife of the Lamb in xix. 5–9 the martyrs only but in xxi. 2f. the whole Church. Accordingly, it seems best to interpret the clause *I saw thrones, and they sat upon them* of 'Christ and His assessors, the apostles (Mt. xix. 28) and saints (1 Cor. vi. 3)'. The especial mention of the martyrs, in view of their place in this book, is only to be expected (cf. their position in vi. 9–11, viii. 3–5; cf. ix. 13n., xvi. 7n.) and is a deserved piece of encouragement. Since the statement *they lived* (4) evidently means 'they came to life', a figurative term for resurrection from the dead, it is likely that such as *had not worshipped the beast . . .* further denotes the martyrs. It is not impossible, however, that this latter half of the verse has in mind overcomers who had escaped martyrdom and thus that the phrase *they lived* includes both a resurrection from the dead and the transformation of living saints (cf. 1 Cor. xv. 51, 52). The opening statement of verse 5 shows with all the clarity desired that *the first resurrection* is a literal resurrection from the dead, not a synonym for the new birth. An apocalyptist is at liberty to change his imagery freely so long as he makes his meaning clear, and in this John succeeds to a remarkable extent. It is a mistake to identify apocalyptic with chaotic thinking, as some writers imply; every line of this book refutes such a notion. One is reluctant, therefore, to believe that the prophet could speak so confusedly of two such different conceptions of resurrection without any indication of his change of reference. Since *the second death hath no power* (6) over the participants in the first resurrection, we may infer that they have been finally acquitted and do not appear at the last judgment; cf. Jn. v. 24. It is to be admitted, however, that the last-named inference is by no means a necessary one. That Christians are to be *priests* as well as kings in the millennium hints that there is a ministry for them to perform in that age amongst earth's inhabitants, perhaps with especial reference to evangelism.

c. The last insurrection of evil (xx. 7–10)

It has already been pointed out (in the note on xix. 17, 19) that John is no innovator in placing the final assault of evil after the establishment of the kingdom of God on earth. In doing this he but follows faithfully Ezekiel's prophecy of the invasion of the Holy Land by Gog and Magog after the commencement of the messianic king-

dom (Ezk. xxxviii, xxxix). (A similar sequence of events is given in the Sibylline Oracles (Bk. III, 663–674), 2 Baruch lxx. 7 and the third-century Apocalypse of Elijah; 2 Esd. xiii. 30–36 should also be compared.) The loosing of Satan (7) is according to God's command; the abyss is 'unlocked' by an angel (cf. verse 1). By this means the prophet parallels the divine oracle to Gog. 'I will bring thee against my land, that the nations may know thee, when I shall be sanctified in thee, O Gog, before their eyes' (Ezk. xxxviii. 16, RV). In Ezekiel's prophecy Magog appears to be both the land from which Gog came (xxxviii. 2) and a nation (xxxix. 6); it is therefore possible that Gog is to be viewed as the leader and Magog his people, with whom are associated the peoples of Meshech and Tubal (xxxviii. 2). These nations were probably situated about the south-eastern parts of the Black Sea, a vague and unknown area as far as the knowledge of the Hebrews went. Other allies north of the Black Sea are enumerated in Ezk. xxxviii. 6, but Persians, Ethiopians and East Africans are mentioned in xxxviii. 5, so that John feels himself justified in using the terms *Gog and Magog* (8) to denote all the members of the hostile alliance, coming from the four corners of the earth. Their number is said to be *as the sand of the sea*, but we may take it that John bore in mind the passage already quoted from Ezk. xxxviii. 16, which makes it clear that a strictly limited proportion of the earth's populace is involved in this last insurrection. *The camp of the saints* (9) presumably is the heavenly Jerusalem. An extraordinary parallel to this picture of the destruction by fire of Gog and Magog occurs in 2 Esd. xiii. 1–11. John, however, is still following Ezekiel (xxxviii. 22). The devil shares the fate of the beast and false prophet. It suggests that the false prophet is regarded as truly an individual, and perhaps as demonic, as his two companions; see xiii. 11f., xvi. 13f., xix. 20. But there is a contrary possibility; see xx. 14.

d. The last judgment (xx. 11–15)

If the departing of heaven and earth from the face of God is to be taken in any literal sense as a precursor of the new heavens and earth (cf. 2 Pet. iii. 10–13), then the solitary spectacle of the great white throne as the one reality upon which men may gaze is indeed an awesome sight; cf. 2 Esd. vii. 30–43. But the description may be purely poetic, to enhance the terrifying grandeur of the scene. The Judge is God Himself; but cf. xxii. 12. The second resurrection is taken for granted in verse 12 and only indirectly described in verse 13. The sea as a receptacle of the dead may be singled out for mention in view of the horror felt by the ancients at burial at sea. It is emphasized that all will be raised for judgment, whatever their mode of death and wherever their grave. The trial of men *according to their works* as *written in the books* (12) stresses the complete justice of the procedure. The picture is taken from Dn. vii. 10, which may reflect both current court procedure and the habit of Persian kings to record every detail of their provinces through an elaborate spy system. It is to be noted that *the book of life* (12, 15) has a testimony to give separate from that of the other books. Concerning this Alford writes: 'Those books and the book of life bore independent witness to the fact of men being or not being among the saved: the one by inference from the works recorded: the other in inscription or non-inscription of the name in the list. So the books could be as vouchers for the book of life.'

Death and hell (RV 'Hades') (14) represent the fact of dying and the condition entered upon after death, i.e. the unresurrected life. Both phenomena are symbolically represented as having ceased by their being cast into the lake of fire. For *the lake of fire* (15) as the equivalent of Gehenna see note on xix. 20. The thought is the same as 'the eternal fire' of Mt. xxv. 41, the complete reverse of 'eternal life' (Mt. xxv. 46). It may consequently be described as *the second death* (14). For an excellent parallel cf. 2 Baruch lxxxvi. 4: 'Go now . . . and instruct the people so far as thou art able, that they may learn so as not to die at the last time, but may learn in order that they may live at the last times.'

e. The new creation (xxi. 1–8)

The creation of *a new heaven and a new earth* (1) is taught in Is. lxv. 17, lxvi. 22, and is implied in Ps. cii. 25, 26; cf. Mt. v. 18; Mk. xiii. 31; Lk. xvi. 17; 2 Pet. iii. 12. It finds frequent mention in the apocalyptists who, however, push to an extreme a thought undoubtedly latent in this doctrine, that the present creation (or at least its present form) is insufficient to be the scene of the perfected, eternal kingdom of God. (For an excellent statement of this view, see 2 Baruch xliv. 8–12, lxxiii. 1—lxxiv. 3.) The assertion that the sea is *no more* has in mind the current personification of the sea as the quintessence of evil; whatever else is meant here, therefore, the main sentiment is the exclusion of evil from the new order of life. *The holy city* (2) is further described in xxi. 9ff., though there its manifestation in the millennial age is probably in view, while here it is shown as the final goal of redeemed humanity in the eternal state. The city is in reality the Church, *prepared as a bride adorned for her husband*; this aspect of the Church's relation to Christ has already been set forth in xix. 7–9 (see notes). A voice from the throne proclaims God's unity with man henceforth. *The tabernacle of God* (3) may here relate not to the 'tabernacle in the wilderness' but the Shekinah glory; the Greek equivalent *skēnē* has a similar sound to the Hebrew Shekinah, and the latter came to be regularly used as one of the alternative terms for the name of God; cf. Pirke Aboth iii. 3, 'When two sit and there are between them words of Torah, the Shekinah rests between them'. Observe the textual variants in the last clause of this verse as seen in RV mg. Cf. verse 4 and vii. 17; 1 Cor. xv. 54; Is. xxxv. 10. The

thought of verses 4 and 5 is applied in 2 Cor. v. 17 to the present experience of the Christian, who has already been translated into the kingdom of God (Col. i. 13) and tastes the powers of the age to come (Heb. vi. 5). The RV 'They are come to pass' (6) is less preferable than the AV *It is done*; see note on xvi. 17. Observe that God is *Omega* as well as *Alpha, the end* as well as *the beginning*; His character guarantees the truth of this revelation and the certainty of the consummation it heralds. The gracious promise added (6) echoes Is. lv. 1. A final encouraging promise to the Christian who endures is given in verse 7; *all things*, the blessings of the holy city in the millennium and in the new creation, will be his inheritance.

In contrast to the overcomer who inherits the kingdom stand those who preclude themselves from it. Foremost are *the fearful* (8) or rather cowardly, who for fear of man deny Christ and worship Antichrist (contrast 2 Tim. i. 7, 'God has not given us a spirit of cowardice'). With these are conjoined the *unbelieving* or, perhaps, 'faithless', including both renegade Christians and pagans; cf. Tit. i. 15, 16. *The abominable* have become so through their worship of the beast; see xvii. 4, 5. The sentiment of this verse echoes New Testament teaching as a whole; cf., e.g., Mt. xxv. 41–43; Lk. xiii. 28; Jn. iii. 36; 1 Cor. vi. 9, 10; Jas. v. 1f.; 1 Pet. iv. 17, 18; etc.

f. The heavenly Jerusalem (xxi. 9—xxii. 5)

For reasons that suggest that this section relates to the city of God in the millennial age, rather than in the eternal state, see introduction to chapters xx—xxii. The revelation of the bride has been anticipated in xix. 7–9, where it is said that she has made herself ready for her Husband. Here the promise is fulfilled, not, however, in terms of the bridal metaphor but under the figure of a city. (For a strangely close parallel to this procedure, cf. 2 Esd. x. 25–27.) Verse 10 is so similar to Ezk. xl. 2 that we must suppose John had it in mind. It would seem, accordingly, that the prophet saw the city descend out of heaven on to the mountain whereon he stood. Heaven comes to earth in the kingdom of God. The city's light is compared to that of *a jasper stone, clear as crystal* (11); i.e. it has a glory like that of the Creator, whose appearance is also stated to be like a jasper (iv. 3).

The *wall great and high* (12) serves the dual purpose of keeping out those who have no part in the blessings of the city (xxi. 27, xxii. 14, 15) and of stressing the eternal security of its inhabitants. The *twelve gates* are inscribed with *the names of the twelve tribes of the children of Israel* (12), i.e. the 'Israel of God', the Church; see notes on vii. 1–8, xi. 1, 2. By this feature John claims that 'through the churches, in every part of the world (here twelvefold but one, as in chapters i—iii they were sevenfold but one), lies the entrance to the city of God' (Kiddle). The *twelve foundations* (14) seem to be not superimposed on each other but to form a continuous chain of varied kinds of stone right round the city wall, divided up by its twelve gates. *The twelve apostles* correspond to *the twelve tribes* of verse 12 and, like the latter, connote the collective whole of the body rather than the individual members; there is, therefore, no need to speculate as to whether or not Paul's name is included in the 'twelve' and if so whose name was omitted; the question does not arise.

The city lieth foursquare (16); it is hardly to the point to cite that the Greeks regarded the square as a symbol for perfection; it is more likely that this shape is mentioned to recall the holy of holies in the ancient temple, which also was a cube (1 Ki. vi. 20); the whole city is a sanctuary for God and partakes of the holiness of the ancient inner shrine. *Twelve thousand furlongs* (16) (Gk. *stadioi*) represents 1,500 miles, though to translate it into modern mileage equivalents is to rob the measurement of its obvious symbolism—an infinite multiple of twelve (note the prominence of the number twelve in this vision of the Church's glory). The meaning of this huge figure is illuminated by the rabbinical saying that Jerusalem would be enlarged till it reached the gates of Damascus and exalted 'till it reached the throne of God'. The heavenly Jerusalem stretches from earth to heaven and unites them into one. *An hundred and forty and four cubits* (17) (seventy-two yards) again derives its significance from being a perfect multiple of twelve. If the preceding explanation of the great height of the city be acceptable, there is no need to stress the apparently absurd disparity between the height of the city and that of the wall; the wall is stout enough to serve its purpose, but the city has the extraordinary function of uniting earth and heaven. There is little doubt that, as in the case of its measurements, so with the enumeration of the city's materials, John deliberately uses the language of symbol; he is not simply describing fantastic wealth. He has already said that the sheen of the city is like jasper, the appearance of God (see verse 11n.); he now declares that the city wall is entirely built of it. The pure gold may allude to such a thought as that in iii. 18. The twelve foundation stones of the wall, despite certain dissimilarities in our translations, appear to be identical with those of the High Priest's breastplate (Ex. xxviii. 17–20). With regard to these it has been established through evidence drawn from Philo, Josephus, and Egyptian and Arabian monuments, that each of these jewels represented one of the twelve signs of the Zodiac. An examination of the order of the precious stones in our text yields the astonishing result that they portray the progress of the sun through the twelve signs but in the reverse order. Such a phenomenon could not be accidental. From it Charles deduces that John hereby shows that the holy city of his visions has nothing to do with the current pagan speculations about the city of the gods. That thought is accentuated by the inscription of the names of the twelve tribes on the city gates and those of the apostles on the city's foundations. In a city

modelled on the holy of holies there is no need of a *temple* (22); all is holy and God is everywhere adored. Cf. Jn. iv. 21. With verse 23 cf. verse 11n.; see also Is. lx. 19, 20. As in the latter passage, earthly conditions are clearly in view. The thought is enriched by recalling that the original readers would have been familiar with the heathen conception of the sun and moon as themselves deities; far from being gods, their native glory pales into dimness by reason of the splendour of the Lord God and the Lamb.

Verses 24–26 reproduce the substance of Is. lx. 3–11. They depict the intercourse between the city of God and the nations of earth during the millennium. For all who will have it, fellowship between heaven and earth is unbroken in that age.

There still exist on earth, even when Satan no longer exercises his influence, the 'unclean' and 'he that maketh an abomination and a lie' (27, RV). For such there is, as it were, 'a flaming sword which turned every way, to keep the way of the tree of life' (Gn. iii. 24). With this and the following verses cf. xxii. 14, 15.

The *river of water of life* (xxii. 1), in view of vii. 17, xxi. 6, xxii. 17, denotes a purely spiritual conception, 'the fountains of the waters of life' perhaps being viewed, as it were, as the source of this pure river. We remember that the Garden of Eden had a river (Gn. ii. 10) and in Ezekiel's vision a river flowed from the temple, possessed of natural healing properties (Ezk. xlvii. 8–11). The punctuation of RV at the close of the verse is preferable to AV: the river proceeds from the throne 'in the midst of the street thereof'. *The tree of life* (2), unlike in Gn. ii. 9, iii. 22, is here treated collectively; there are trees on either side of the river, bearing a different fruit for every month of the year and leaves with healing properties. The picture is taken from Ezk. xlvii. 7, 12 but, as in the case of water of life, the healing powers of the leaves are taken in a purely spiritual sense. Through the Church men will quench their spiritual thirst in the kingdom of God and receive spiritual sustenance, thus gaining healing for the wounds of sin. This supplies a pictorial counterpart to the prophetic song of xv. 4.

There shall be no more curse (3) may simply mean that nothing unclean or abominable shall find entrance into the holy city (xxi. 27). But it is more likely that we have here a deliberate contrast to the curse pronounced in the original paradise that brought woe on all creation (Gn. iii. 14–19). The effects of that curse have been completely overcome in the new Jerusalem. The goal of redeemed humanity is *they shall see his face* (4). Such a vision will involve the transformation of the beholders into the same likeness (1 Jn. iii. 2). For the name on their foreheads see notes on iii. 12, xix. 12. In verse 5 the absolute statement of the RV is the better reading, 'there shall be night no more'; but the AV is essentially correct, *there shall be no night there*, for as in xxi. 23 the city of God is in mind (see note on xxi. 23). It is sometimes felt that the statement *they shall reign for ever and ever* is set over against 'they lived and reigned with Christ a thousand years' (xx. 4), the latter being temporal, the former eternal. This may be correct, but certainly not in the sense that the larger reference excludes the smaller, as though the millennium must have ended at this time; cf. the parallel assertion in regard to the rule of God in xi. 15, where 'he shall reign for ever and ever' includes the millennial reign.

XI. EPILOGUE. xxii. 6–21

In this conclusion three themes find prominent expression: the authenticity of the visions narrated (verses 6, 7, 16, 18, 19), the imminence of Christ's coming (verses 6, 7, 10–12, 20), and the necessity for holiness in view of the impending consummation (verses 10–15). It is impossible to be sure as to the identity of the speakers in the various paragraphs. Verses 6, 7, 16 look like utterances of Christ, verses 10–15 words of the angel, verses 8, 9, 17–19, 20b, 21 additions of John. But a great deal of variation is possible, especially if, as some think, there have been dislocations in the text subsequent to its publication. In the last resort it matters little; the speaker is ultimately Christ, whose messenger the angel is (9), and whose utterances John records as a prophet (10).

The speaker (6, 7) seems to be our Lord. His *sayings* (RV 'words'), as His character, *are faithful and true* (iii. 14, xix. 11). He comes *quickly* (7): there is no warrant for translating Gk. *tachy* as 'suddenly'; such an interpretation would make strange sense of verse 6, 'things which must suddenly (*en tachei*) come to pass', an impossible rendering in view of the teaching of the book. See further the note on i. 1. The inclusion of verses 8 and 9 by John does not necessarily mean that some of his earliest readers engaged in angel worship, though it is true that the practice had a place among the Jews (e.g. Test. Dan. vi. 2; Test. Levi v. 5) and even among Christians (Col. ii. 18). John's experience is natural enough and its narration here needs no other explanation than its actual occurrence and intrinsic interest. It is not so much a polemic against angel worship as a correction of the over-exaltation of all instruments of revelation; angels and prophets and ordinary Christians are all on one plane before God.

The injunction in verse 10 is the reverse of that in Dn. viii. 26, xii. 4, 9, and of what we see in Jewish apocalypses generally. Whereas the latter prophesied of (ostensibly) remote times, John's message was of immediate importance (*the time is at hand*) and was issued in his own name. There is irony in the utterance of verse 11 in so far as it relates to the wicked. Daniel had said (Dn. xii. 10) that in the last days many would be purified by their experience of trial, but the wicked would act wickedly; i.e. in the last crisis men will come out in their true colours and range themselves either on God's side or with the devil.

That teaching is continually stressed in this book (vii. 1–8, xi. 1, 2, xii. 6, xiii. 1—xiv. 5, etc.). Here it receives its final exposition. Since *the time is at hand*, let the man who insists on clinging to evil continue therein; he shall soon meet his judgment. As for the righteous and holy, let them guard themselves, lest they fall away with the error of the wicked; their Lord will soon come for their redemption and reward. To make of this statement a doctrine of the irremediable fixity of men in the last times, which to John had all but dawned, is unwarrantable, both from the context and the general teaching of the book (e.g. xxii. 17, xiv. 6, 7, xv. 4, xxi. 6–8). Cf. verse 12 and xi. 18; Is. xl. 10; Rom. ii. 6. Also for verse 13 see note on i. 8.

In verse 14 we have the last benediction of this kind in the book: *they that do his commandments* or, as in RV, 'they that wash their robes' virtually means 'they that overcome'; see vi. 11n. The conjunction of verse 15 with this verse seems to demand that the *right* (to come) *to the tree of life* and to *enter in through the gates into the city* relate to privileges of the millennial kingdom; cf. xxi. 24—xxii. 2.

Verse 15 almost repeats xxi. 8. See note on xxi. 27. Elsewhere in Scripture *dogs* denote adherents of heathenish worship; cf. Dt. xxiii. 18 (where 'dog' means a male prostitute), Mt. xv. 26; Phil. iii. 2 (where 'dogs' means the mischievous Judaizers). Swete, accordingly, inclines to identify them here with the abominable of xxi. 8 (see note). Verse 16 is a further attestation by the Lord of the authenticity of the prophecy; cf. i. 1, xxii. 6. Christ as *the root and the offspring of David* fulfils Is. xi. 1. As *the bright and morning star* He is Himself the fulfilment of His promise to the overcomer in ii. 28 (see note).

Read naturally, verse 17 appears to teach that the Holy Spirit, especially as active in the prophets (xix. 10), joins the Church in calling upon Christ to come to earth, according to His promise (7, 12). The hearer of the prophecy of this book, as it is read in the churches, is bidden to do likewise. The repentant sinner is invited to partake with the saints in the gift of eternal life from Christ. Some, however, interpret all the entreaties to 'come' as addressed to the sinner.

John has been harshly judged by many for concluding his prophecy with the statement contained in verses 18 and 19, which almost amounts to a curse. Certainly it was a customary precaution for ancient writers to protect their works against mutilation and interpolation by adding such an anathema (cf. 1 Enoch civ. 10, 11; 2 Enoch xlviii. 7, 8; Letter of Aristeas ccx—ccxi). Swete, however, objects to such an interpretation of John's meaning: 'If the solemn warning of the present verse was intended in this sense, it has signally failed; for in no other book of the New Testament is the text so uncertain as in the Apocalypse. But, like its archetype in Deuteronomy (iv. 2, xii. 32), it has a deeper reference; it is no mere *lapsus calami*, no error of judgment or merely intellectual fault which is condemned, but the deliberate falsification or misinterpretation of a divine message. It is not the letter of the Apocalypse, but its spirit which is thus jealously guarded.' We may thus not inaptly compare Paul's conclusion of 1 Cor. xvi. 22.

John's response to the promise of Christ (20) corresponds to the Aramaic watchword already referred to in 1 Cor. xvi. 22, 'Maranatha', 'Our Lord come'. The benediction (21) reminds us that the prophecy is in reality a letter, its lessons to be personally appropriated. Only by the grace of the Lord Jesus can that victory be gained which shall receive the recompense portrayed in this book. Let us not receive it in vain.

G. R. BEASLEY-MURRAY.